The Dictionary of Art · volume thirty-three

The Dictionary of Art

33

Wax

TO

Zyvele

✳

Appendices

GROVE

The Dictionary of Art

edited by JANE TURNER, in thirty-four volumes, 1996

This edition is distributed within the United Kingdom and Europe
by Macmillan Publishers Limited, London, and within the United States and Canada by
Grove's Dictionaries Inc., New York.

Text keyboarded by Wearset Limited, Sunderland, England
Database management by Pindar plc, York, England
Imagesetting by William Clowes Limited, Suffolk, England
Printed in the United States of America by RR Donnelley & Sons Company, Willard, Ohio

British Library Cataloguing in Publication Data

The dictionary of art
  1. Art - Dictionaries 2. Art - History -
    Dictionaries
  I. Turner, Jane
  703

ISBN 1-884446-00-0

Library of Congress Cataloging in Publication Data

The dictionary of art / editor, Jane Turner.
  p. cm.
  Includes bibliographical references and index.
  Contents: 1. A to Anckerman
  ISBN 1-884446-00-0 (alk. paper)
  1. Art—Encyclopedias.
  I. Turner, Jane, 1956–
N31.D5 1996   96–13628
703—dc20   CIP

Contents

List of Colour Illustrations

PLATE I. **Wood**

1. Karelian birch secrétaire–à–abattant, w. 958 mm, Russian, *c.* 1800 (Luton Hoo, Beds/Photo: Werhner Collection/Bridgeman Art Library, London)

2. Boxwood Royal Gittern, l. 760 mm, English, *c.* 1290–1330 (London, British Museum/Photo: Trustees of the British Museum)

PLATE II. **Wood**

1. Pear–wood sculpture by Hans Daucher: *Cupids Playing,* 420×760×162 mm, from Augsburg, *c.* 1530 (Vienna, Kunsthistorisches Museum/Photo: Kunsthistorisches Museum)

2. Mahogany tambour desk, inlaid with light wood, white pine and elm, 1054×959×501 mm, made by John Seymour and Son, Boston, Massachusetts, 1794–1804 (Winterthur, DE, H. F. Du Pont Winterthur Museum/Photo: Winterthur Museum)

PLATE III. **Wood**

1. Cedar-wood cabinet with gilded ebony decoration, h. 696 mm, Egyptian, from the tomb of Tutankhamun (*reg c.* 1332–*c.* 1323 BC), New Kingdom, 18th Dynasty (Cairo, Egyptian Museum/Photo: Robert Harding Picture Library, London)

2. Iroko-wood chest, carved to imitate basketwork, 2.12×0.67×0.50 m, from Benin City, Nigeria, 19th century (London, British Museum/Photo: Trustees of the British Museum)

PLATE IV. **Wood**

1. Zelkova and amboyna mirror-box, with brass plates, 115×178×212 mm, Korean, Chosŏn dynasty, 19th century (London, Victoria and Albert Museum/Photo: Board of Trustees of the Victoria and Albert Museum)

2. Oak cabinet, veneered with olive-wood, acacia and other woods, 2125×1785×620 mm, from the Northern Netherlands, *c.* 1690 (Amsterdam, Rijksmuseum/Photo: Rijksmuseum)

General Abbreviations

The abbreviations employed throughout this dictionary, most of which are listed below, do not vary, except for capitalization, regardless of the context in which they are used, including bibliographical citations and for locations of works of art. The principle used to arrive at these abbreviations is that their full form should be easily deducible, and for this reason acronyms have generally been avoided (e.g. Los Angeles Co. Mus. A. instead of LACMA). The same abbreviation is adopted for cognate forms in foreign languages and in most cases for plural and adjectival forms (e.g. A.= Art, Arts, Arte, Arti etc). Not all related forms are listed below. Occasionally, if a name, for instance of an artists' group or exhibiting society, is repeated within the text of one article, it is cited in an abbreviated form after its first mention in full (e.g. The Pre-Raphaelite Brotherhood (PRB) was founded...); the same is true of archaeological periods and eras, which are abbreviated to initial letters in small capitals (e.g. In the Early Minoan (EM) period...). Such abbreviations do not appear in this list. For the reader's convenience, separate full lists of abbreviations for locations, periodical titles and standard reference books and series are included as Appendices A–C at the end of this volume.

A.	Art, Arts	Anthropol.	Anthropology	Azerbaij.	Azerbaijani
A.C.	Arts Council	Antiqua.	Antiquarian, Antiquaries	B.	Bartsch [catalogue of Old Master prints]
Acad.	Academy	app.	appendix		
AD	Anno Domini	approx.	approximately	b	born
Add.	Additional, Addendum	AR	Arkansas (USA)	BA	Bachelor of Arts
addn	addition	ARA	Associate of the Royal Academy	Balt.	Baltic
Admin.	Administration			bapt	baptized
Adv.	Advances, Advanced	Arab.	Arabic	BArch	Bachelor of Architecture
Aesth.	Aesthetic(s)	Archaeol.	Archaeology	Bart	Baronet
Afr.	African	Archit.	Architecture, Architectural	Bask.	Basketry
Afrik.	Afrikaans, Afrikaner	Archv, Archvs	Archive(s)	BBC	British Broadcasting Corporation
A.G.	Art Gallery				
Agrar.	Agrarian	Arg.	Argentine	BC	Before Christ
Agric.	Agriculture	ARHA	Associate of the Royal Hibernian Academy	BC	British Columbia (Canada)
Agron.	Agronomy			BE	Buddhist era
Agy	Agency	ARIBA	Associate of the Royal Institute of British Architects	Beds	Bedfordshire (GB)
AH	Anno Hegirae			Behav.	Behavioural
A. Inst.	Art Institute	Armen.	Armenian	Belarus.	Belarusian
AK	Alaska (USA)	ARSA	Associate of the Royal Scottish Academy	Belg.	Belgian
AL	Alabama (USA)			Berks	Berkshire (GB)
Alb.	Albanian	Asiat.	Asiatic	Berwicks	Berwickshire (GB; old)
Alg.	Algerian	Assist.	Assistance	BFA	Bachelor of Fine Arts
Alta	Alberta (Canada)	Assoc.	Association	Bibl.	Bible, Biblical
Altern.	Alternative	Astron.	Astronomy	Bibliog.	Bibliography, Bibliographical
a.m.	ante meridiem [before noon]	AT&T	American Telephone & Telegraph Company	Biblioph.	Bibliophile
Amat.	Amateur	attrib.	attribution, attributed to	Biog.	Biography, Biographical
Amer.	American	Aug	August	Biol.	Biology, Biological
An.	Annals	Aust.	Austrian	bk, bks	book(s)
Anatol.	Anatolian	Austral.	Australian	Bkbinder	Bookbinder
Anc.	Ancient	Auth.	Author(s)	Bklore	Booklore
Annu.	Annual	Auton.	Autonomous	Bkshop	Bookshop
Anon.	Anonymous(ly)	Aux.	Auxiliary	BL	British Library
Ant.	Antique	Ave.	Avenue	Bld	Build
Anthol.	Anthology	AZ	Arizona (USA)	Bldg	Building

Bldr	Builder	Chin.	Chinese	Cur.	Curator, Curatorial, Curatorship
BLitt	Bachelor of Letters/Literature	Christ.	Christian, Christianity	Curr.	Current(s)
BM	British Museum	Chron.	Chronicle	CVO	Commander of the [Royal] Victorian Order
Boh.	Bohemian	Cie	Compagnie [French]		
Boliv.	Bolivian	Cinema.	Cinematography	Cyclad.	Cycladic
Botan.	Botany, Botanical	Circ.	Circle	Cyp.	Cypriot
BP	Before present (1950)	Civ.	Civil, Civic	Czech.	Czechoslovak
Braz.	Brazilian	Civiliz.	Civilization(s)	$	dollars
BRD	Bundesrepublik Deutschland [Federal Republic of Germany (West Germany)]	Class.	Classic, Classical	d	died
		Clin.	Clinical	d.	denarius, denarii [penny, pence]
Brecons	Breconshire (GB; old)	CO	Colorado (USA)		
Brez.	Brezonek [lang. of Brittany]	Co.	Company; County	Dalmat.	Dalmatian
Brit.	British	Cod.	Codex, Codices	Dan.	Danish
Bros	Brothers	Col., Cols	Collection(s); Column(s)	DBE	Dame Commander of the Order of the British Empire
BSc	Bachelor of Science	Coll.	College		
Bucks	Buckinghamshire (GB)	collab.	in collaboration with, collaborated, collaborative	DC	District of Columbia (USA)
Bulg.	Bulgarian			DDR	Deutsche Demokratische Republik [German Democratic Republic (East Germany)]
Bull.	Bulletin	Collct.	Collecting		
bur	buried	Colloq.	Colloquies		
Burm.	Burmese	Colomb.	Colombian	DE	Delaware (USA)
Byz.	Byzantine	Colon.	Colonies, Colonial	Dec	December
C	Celsius	Colr	Collector	Dec.	Decorative
C.	Century	Comm.	Commission; Community	ded.	dedication, dedicated to
c.	circa [about]	Commerc.	Commercial	Democ.	Democracy, Democratic
CA	California	Communic.	Communications	Demog.	Demography, Demographic
Cab.	Cabinet	Comp.	Comparative; compiled by, compiler	Denbs	Denbighshire (GB; old)
Caerns	Caernarvonshire (GB; old)			dep.	deposited at
C.A.G.	City Art Gallery	Concent.	Concentration	Dept	Department
Cal.	Calendar	Concr.	Concrete	Dept.	Departmental, Departments
Callig.	Calligraphy	Confed.	Confederation	Derbys	Derbyshire (GB)
Cam.	Camera	Confer.	Conference	Des.	Design
Cambs	Cambridgeshire (GB)	Congol.	Congolese	destr.	destroyed
can	canonized	Congr.	Congress	Dev.	Development
Can.	Canadian	Conserv.	Conservation; Conservatory	Devon	Devonshire (GB)
Cant.	Canton(s), Cantonal	Constr.	Construction(al)	Dial.	Dialogue
Capt.	Captain	cont.	continued	diam.	diameter
Cards	Cardiganshire (GB; old)	Contemp.	Contemporary	Diff.	Diffusion
Carib.	Caribbean	Contrib.	Contributions, Contributor(s)	Dig.	Digest
Carms	Carmarthenshire (GB; old)	Convalesc.	Convalescence	Dip. Eng.	Diploma in Engineering
Cartog.	Cartography	Convent.	Convention	Dir.	Direction, Directed
Cat.	Catalan	Coop.	Cooperation	Directrt	Directorate
cat.	catalogue	Coord.	Coordination	Disc.	Discussion
Cath.	Catholic	Copt.	Coptic	diss.	dissertation
CBE	Commander of the Order of the British Empire	Corp.	Corporation, Corpus	Distr.	District
		Corr.	Correspondence	Div.	Division
Celeb.	Celebration	Cors.	Corsican	DLitt	Doctor of Letters/Literature
Celt.	Celtic	Cost.	Costume	DM	Deutsche Mark
Cent.	Centre, Central	Cret.	Cretan	Doc.	Document(s)
Centen.	Centennial	Crim.	Criminal	Doss.	Dossier
Cer.	Ceramic	Crit.	Critical, Criticism	DPhil	Doctor of Philosophy
cf.	confer [compare]	Croat.	Croatian	Dr	Doctor
Chap., Chaps	Chapter(s)	CT	Connecticut (USA)	Drg, Drgs	Drawing(s)
		Cttee	Committee	DSc	Doctor of Science/Historical Sciences
Chem.	Chemistry	Cub.	Cuban		
Ches	Cheshire (GB)	Cult.	Cultural, Culture	Dut.	Dutch
Chil.	Chilean	Cumb.	Cumberland (GB; old)	Dwell.	Dwelling
				E.	East(ern)

EC	European (Economic) Community	figs	figures	Heb.	Hebrew
Eccles.	Ecclesiastical	Filip.	Filipina(s), Filipino(s)	Hell.	Hellenic
Econ.	Economic, Economies	Fin.	Finnish	Her.	Heritage
Ecuad.	Ecuadorean	FL	Florida (USA)	Herald.	Heraldry, Heraldic
ed.	editor, edited (by)	*fl*	*floruit* [he/she flourished]	Hereford & Worcs	Hereford & Worcester (GB)
edn	edition	Flem.	Flemish	Herts	Hertfordshire (GB)
eds	editors	Flints	Flintshire (GB; old)	HI	Hawaii (USA)
Educ.	Education	Flk	Folk	Hib.	Hibernia
e.g.	*exempli gratia* [for example]	Flklore	Folklore	Hisp.	Hispanic
Egyp.	Egyptian	fol., fols	folio(s)	Hist.	History, Historical
Elem.	Element(s), Elementary	Found.	Foundation	HMS	His/Her Majesty's Ship
Emp.	Empirical	Fr.	French	Hon.	Honorary, Honourable
Emul.	Emulation	frag.	fragment	Horiz.	Horizon
Enc.	Encyclopedia	Fri.	Friday	Hort.	Horticulture
Encour.	Encouragement	FRIBA	Fellow of the Royal Institute of British Architects	Hosp.	Hospital(s)
Eng.	English	FRS	Fellow of the Royal Society, London	HRH	His/Her Royal Highness
Engin.	Engineer, Engineering			Human.	Humanities, Humanism
Engr., Engrs	Engraving(s)	ft	foot, feet	Hung.	Hungarian
Envmt	Environment	Furn.	Furniture	Hunts	Huntingdonshire (GB; old)
Epig.	Epigraphy	Futur.	Futurist, Futurism	IA	Iowa
Episc.	Episcopal	g	gram(s)	ibid.	*ibidem* [in the same place]
Esp.	Especially	GA	Georgia (USA)	ICA	Institute of Contemporary Arts
Ess.	Essays	Gael.	Gaelic		
est.	established	Gal., Gals	Gallery, Galleries	Ice.	Icelandic
etc	*etcetera* [and so on]	Gaz.	Gazette	Iconog.	Iconography
Ethnog.	Ethnography	GB	Great Britain	Iconol.	Iconology
Ethnol.	Ethnology	Gdn, Gdns	Garden(s)	ID	Idaho (USA)
Etrus.	Etruscan	Gdnr(s)	Gardener(s)	i.e.	*id est* [that is]
Eur.	European	Gen.	General	IL	Illinois (USA)
Evangel.	Evangelical	Geneal.	Genealogy, Genealogist	Illum.	Illumination
Exam.	Examination	Gent.	Gentleman, Gentlemen	illus.	illustrated, illustration
Excav.	Excavation, Excavated	Geog.	Geography	Imp.	Imperial
Exch.	Exchange	Geol.	Geology	IN	Indiana (USA)
Excurs.	Excursion	Geom.	Geometry	in., ins	inch(es)
exh.	exhibition	Georg.	Georgian	Inc.	Incorporated
Exp.	Exposition	Geosci.	Geoscience	inc.	incomplete
Expermntl	Experimental	Ger.	German, Germanic	incl.	includes, including, inclusive
Explor.	Exploration	G.I.	Government/General Issue (USA)	Incorp.	Incorporation
Expn	Expansion			Ind.	Indian
Ext.	External	Glams	Glamorganshire (GB; old)	Indep.	Independent
Extn	Extension	Glos	Gloucestershire (GB)	Indig.	Indigenous
f, ff	following page, following pages	Govt	Government	Indol.	Indology
		Gr.	Greek	Indon.	Indonesian
F.A.	Fine Art(s)	Grad.	Graduate	Indust.	Industrial
Fac.	Faculty	Graph.	Graphic	Inf.	Information
facs.	facsimile	Green.	Greenlandic	Inq.	Inquiry
Fam.	Family	Gr.-Roman	Greco-Roman	Inscr.	Inscribed, Inscription
fasc.	fascicle	Gt	Great	Inst.	Institute(s)
fd	feastday (of a saint)	Gtr	Greater	Inst. A.	Institute of Art
Feb	February	Guat.	Guatemalan	Instr.	Instrument, Instrumental
Fed.	Federation, Federal	Gym.	Gymnasium	Int.	International
Fem.	Feminist	h.	height	Intell.	Intelligence
Fest.	Festival	ha	hectare	Inter.	Interior(s), Internal
fig.	figure (illustration)	Hait.	Haitian	Interdiscip.	Interdisciplinary
Fig.	Figurative	Hants	Hampshire (GB)	intro.	introduced by, introduction
		Hb.	Handbook	inv.	inventory

Inven.	Invention	m	metre(s)	Moldov.	Moldovan
Invest.	Investigation(s)	m.	married	MOMA	Museum of Modern Art
Iran.	Iranian	M.	Monsieur	Mon.	Monday
irreg.	irregular(ly)	MA	Master of Arts; Massachusetts (USA)	Mongol.	Mongolian
Islam.	Islamic	Mag.	Magazine	Mons	Monmouthshire (GB; old)
Isr.	Israeli	Maint.	Maintenance	Montgoms	Montgomeryshire (GB; old)
It.	Italian	Malay.	Malaysian	Mor.	Moral
J.	Journal	Man.	Manitoba (Canada); Manual	Morav.	Moravian
Jam.	Jamaican	Manuf.	Manufactures	Moroc.	Moroccan
Jan	January	Mar.	Marine, Maritime	Movt	Movement
Jap.	Japanese	Mason.	Masonic	MP	Member of Parliament
Jav.	Javanese	Mat.	Material(s)	MPhil	Master of Philosophy
Jew.	Jewish	Math.	Mathematic	MS	Mississippi (USA)
Jewel.	Jewellery	MBE	Member of the Order of the British Empire	MS., MSS	manuscript(s)
Jord.	Jordanian	MD	Doctor of Medicine; Maryland (USA)	MSc	Master of Science
jr	junior	ME	Maine (USA)	MT	Montana (USA)
Juris.	Jurisdiction	Mech.	Mechanical	Mt	Mount
KBE	Knight Commander of the Order of the British Empire	Med.	Medieval; Medium, Media	Mthly	Monthly
KCVO	Knight Commander of the Royal Victorian Order	Medic.	Medical, Medicine	Mun.	Municipal
kg	kilogram(s)	Medit.	Mediterranean	Mus.	Museum(s)
kHz	kilohertz	Mem.	Memorial(s); Memoir(s)	Mus. A.	Museum of Art
km	kilometre(s)	Merions	Merionethshire (GB; old)	Mus. F.A.	Museum of Fine Art(s)
Knowl.	Knowledge	Meso-Amer.	Meso-American	Music.	Musicology
Kor.	Korean	Mesop.	Mesopotamian	N.	North(ern); National
KS	Kansas (USA)	Met.	Metropolitan	n	refractive index of a medium
KY	Kentucky (USA)	Metal.	Metallurgy	n.	note
Kyrgyz.	Kyrgyzstani	Mex.	Mexican	N.A.G.	National Art Gallery
£	libra, librae [pound, pounds sterling]	MFA	Master of Fine Arts	Nat.	Natural, Nature
l.	length	mg	milligram(s)	Naut.	Nautical
LA	Louisiana (USA)	Mgmt	Management	NB	New Brunswick (Canada)
Lab.	Laboratory	Mgr	Monsignor	NC	North Carolina (USA)
Lancs	Lancashire (GB)	MI	Michigan	ND	North Dakota (USA)
Lang.	Language(s)	Micrones.	Micronesian	n.d.	no date
Lat.	Latin	Mid. Amer.	Middle American	NE	Nebraska; Northeast(ern)
Latv.	Latvian	Middx	Middlesex (GB; old)	Neth.	Netherlandish
lb, lbs	pound(s) weight	Mid. E.	Middle Eastern	Newslett.	Newsletter
Leb.	Lebanese	Mid. Eng.	Middle English	Nfld	Newfoundland (Canada)
Lect.	Lecture	Mid Glam.	Mid Glamorgan (GB)	N.G.	National Gallery
Legis.	Legislative	Mil.	Military	N.G.A.	National Gallery of Art
Leics	Leicestershire (GB)	Mill.	Millennium	NH	New Hampshire (USA)
Lex.	Lexicon	Min.	Ministry; Minutes	Niger.	Nigerian
Lg.	Large	Misc.	Miscellaneous	NJ	New Jersey (USA)
Lib., Libs	Library, Libraries	Miss.	Mission(s)	NM	New Mexico (USA)
Liber.	Liberian	Mlle	Mademoiselle	nm	nanometre (10^{-9} metre)
Libsp	Librarianship	mm	millimetre(s)	nn.	notes
Lincs	Lincolnshire (GB)	Mme	Madame	no., nos	number(s)
Lit.	Literature	MN	Minnesota	Nord.	Nordic
Lith.	Lithuanian	Mnmt, Mnmts	Monument(s)	Norm.	Normal
Liturg.	Liturgical	Mnmtl	Monumental	Northants	Northamptonshire (GB)
LLB	Bachelor of Laws	MO	Missouri (USA)	Northumb.	Northumberland (GB)
LLD	Doctor of Laws	Mod.	Modern, Modernist	Norw.	Norwegian
Lt	Lieutenant	Moldav.	Moldavian	Notts	Nottinghamshire (GB)
Lt-Col.	Lieutenant-Colonel			Nov	November
Ltd	Limited			n.p.	no place (of publication)
				N.P.G.	National Portrait Gallery
				nr	near

Nr E.	Near Eastern	Per.	Period	Ptg(s)	Painting(s)
NS	New Style; Nova Scotia (Canada)	Percep.	Perceptions	Pub.	Public
		Perf.	Performance, Performing, Performed	pubd	published
n. s.	new series			Publ.	Publicity
NSW	New South Wales (Australia)	Period.	Periodical(s)	pubn(s)	publication(s)
NT	National Trust	Pers.	Persian	PVA	polyvinyl acetate
Ntbk	Notebook	Persp.	Perspectives	PVC	polyvinyl chloride
Numi.	Numismatic(s)	Peru.	Peruvian	Q.	quarterly
NV	Nevada (USA)	PhD	Doctor of Philosophy	4to	quarto
NW	Northwest(ern)	Philol.	Philology	Qué.	Québec (Canada)
NWT	Northwest Territories (Canada)	Philos.	Philosophy	R	reprint
		Phoen.	Phoenician	r	recto
NY	New York (USA)	Phot.	Photograph, Photography, Photographic	RA	Royal Academician
NZ	New Zealand			Radnors	Radnorshire (GB; old)
OBE	Officer of the Order of the British Empire	Phys.	Physician(s), Physics, Physique, Physical	RAF	Royal Air Force
				Rec.	Record(s)
Obj.	Object(s), Objective	Physiog.	Physiognomy	red.	reduction, reduced for
Occas.	Occasional	Physiol.	Physiology	Ref.	Reference
Occident.	Occidental	Pict.	Picture(s), Pictorial	Refurb.	Refurbishment
Ocean.	Oceania	pl.	plate; plural	reg	regit [ruled]
Oct	October	Plan.	Planning	Reg.	Regional
8vo	octavo	Planet.	Planetarium	Relig.	Religion, Religious
OFM	Order of Friars Minor	Plast.	Plastic	remod.	remodelled
OH	Ohio (USA)	pls	plates	Ren.	Renaissance
OK	Oklahoma (USA)	p.m.	post meridiem [after noon]	Rep.	Report(s)
Olymp.	Olympic	Polit.	Political	repr.	reprint(ed); reproduced, reproduction
OM	Order of Merit	Poly.	Polytechnic		
Ont.	Ontario (Canada)	Polynes.	Polynesian	Represent.	Representation, Representative
op.	opus	Pop.	Popular	Res.	Research
opp.	opposite; opera [pl. of opus]	Port.	Portuguese	rest.	restored, restoration
OR	Oregon (USA)	Port.	Portfolio	Retro.	Retrospective
Org.	Organization	Posth.	Posthumous(ly)	rev.	revision, revised (by/for)
Orient.	Oriental	Pott.	Pottery	Rev.	Reverend; Review
Orthdx	Orthodox	POW	prisoner of war	RHA	Royal Hibernian Academician
OSB	Order of St Benedict	PRA	President of the Royal Academy	RI	Rhode Island (USA)
Ott.	Ottoman			RIBA	Royal Institute of British Architects
Oxon	Oxfordshire (GB)	Pract.	Practical		
oz.	ounce(s)	Prefect.	Prefecture, Prefectural	RJ	Rio de Janeiro State
p	pence	Preserv.	Preservation	Rlwy	Railway
p., pp.	page(s)	prev.	previous(ly)	RSA	Royal Scottish Academy
PA	Pennsylvania (USA)	priv.	private	RSFSR	Russian Soviet Federated Socialist Republic
p.a.	per annum	PRO	Public Record Office		
Pak.	Pakistani	Prob.	Problem(s)	Rt Hon.	Right Honourable
Palaeontol.	Palaeontology, Palaeontological	Proc.	Proceedings	Rur.	Rural
		Prod.	Production	Rus.	Russian
Palest.	Palestinian	Prog.	Progress	S	San, Santa, Santo, Sant', São [Saint]
Pap.	Paper(s)	Proj.	Project(s)		
para.	paragraph	Promot.	Promotion	S.	South(ern)
Parag.	Paraguayan	Prop.	Property, Properties	s.	solidus, solidi [shilling(s)]
Parl.	Parliament	Prov.	Province(s), Provincial	Sask.	Saskatchewan (Canada)
Paroch.	Parochial	Proven.	Provenance	Sat.	Saturday
Patriarch.	Patriarchate	Prt, Prts	Print(s)	SC	South Carolina (USA)
Patriot.	Patriotic	Prtg	Printing	Scand.	Scandinavian
Patrm.	Patrimony	pseud.	pseudonym	Sch.	School
Pav.	Pavilion	Psych.	Psychiatry, Psychiatric	Sci.	Science(s), Scientific
PEI	Prince Edward Island (Canada)	Psychol.	Psychology, Psychological	Scot.	Scottish
Pembs	Pembrokeshire (GB; old)	pt	part	Sculp.	Sculpture

SD	South Dakota (USA)	suppl., suppls	supplement(s), supplementary	Urb.	Urban
SE	Southeast(ern)	Surv.	Survey	Urug.	Uruguayan
Sect.	Section	SW	Southwest(ern)	US	United States
Sel.	Selected	Swed.	Swedish	USA	United States of America
Semin.	Seminar(s), Seminary	Swi.	Swiss	USSR	Union of Soviet Socialist Republics
Semiot.	Semiotic	Symp.	Symposium		
Semit.	Semitic	Syr.	Syrian	UT	Utah
Sept	September	Tap.	Tapestry	*v*	*verso*
Ser.	Series	Tas.	Tasmanian	VA	Virginia (USA)
Serb.	Serbian	Tech.	Technical, Technique	V&A	Victoria and Albert Museum
Serv.	Service(s)	Technol.	Technology	Var.	Various
Sess.	Session, Sessional	Territ.	Territory	Venez.	Venezuelan
Settmt(s)	Settlement(s)	Theat.	Theatre	Vern.	Vernacular
S. Glam.	South Glamorgan (GB)	Theol.	Theology, Theological	Vict.	Victorian
Siber.	Siberian	Theor.	Theory, Theoretical	Vid.	Video
Sig.	Signature	Thurs.	Thursday	Viet.	Vietnamese
Sil.	Silesian	Tib.	Tibetan	viz.	*videlicet* [namely]
Sin.	Singhala	TN	Tennessee (USA)	vol., vols	volume(s)
sing.	singular	Top.	Topography	vs.	versus
SJ	Societas Jesu [Society of Jesus]	Trad.	Tradition(s), Traditional	VT	Vermont (USA)
Skt	Sanskrit	trans.	translation, translated by; transactions	Vulg.	Vulgarisation
Slav.	Slavic, Slavonic			W.	West(ern)
Slov.	Slovene, Slovenian	Transafr.	Transafrican	w.	width
Soc.	Society	Transatlant.	Transatlantic	WA	Washington (USA)
Social.	Socialism, Socialist	Transcarpath.	Transcarpathian	Warwicks	Warwickshire (GB)
Sociol.	Sociology	transcr.	transcribed by/for	Wed.	Wednesday
Sov.	Soviet	Triq.	Triquarterly	W. Glam.	West Glamorgan (GB)
SP	São Paulo State	Tropic.	Tropical	WI	Wisconsin (USA)
Sp.	Spanish	Tues.	Tuesday	Wilts	Wiltshire (GB)
sq.	square	Turk.	Turkish	Wkly	Weekly
sr	senior	Turkmen.	Turkmenistani	W. Midlands	West Midlands (GB)
Sri L.	Sri Lankan	TV	Television		
SS	Saints, Santi, Santissima, Santissimo, Santissimi; Steam ship	TX	Texas (USA)	Worcs	Worcestershire (GB; old)
		U.	University	Wtrcol.	Watercolour
SSR	Soviet Socialist Republic	UK	United Kingdom of Great Britain and Northern Ireland	WV	West Virginia (USA)
St	Saint, Sankt, Sint, Szent			WY	Wyoming (USA)
Staffs	Staffordshire (GB)	Ukrain.	Ukrainian	Yb., Y.-b.	Yearbook, Year-book
Ste	Sainte	Un.	Union	Yem.	Yemeni
Stud.	Study, Studies	Underwtr	Underwater	Yorks	Yorkshire (GB; old)
Subalp.	Subalpine	UNESCO	United Nations Educational, Scientific and Cultural Organization	Yug.	Yugoslavian
Sum.	Sumerian			Zamb.	Zambian
Sun.	Sunday	Univl	Universal	Zimb.	Zimbabwean
Sup.	Superior	unpubd	unpublished		

A Note on the Use of the Dictionary

This note is intended as a short guide to the basic editorial conventions adopted in this dictionary. For a fuller explanation, please refer to the Introduction, vol. 1, pp. xiii–xx.

Abbreviations in general use in the dictionary are listed on pp. vii–xii; those used in bibliographies and for locations of works of art or exhibition venues are listed in the Appendices.

Alphabetization of headings, which are distinguished in bold typeface, is letter by letter up to the first comma (ignoring spaces, hyphens, accents and any parenthesized or bracketed matter); the same principle applies thereafter. Abbreviations of 'Saint' and its foreign equivalents are alphabetized as if spelt out, and headings with the prefix 'Mc' appear under 'Mac'.

Authors' signatures appear at the end of the article or sequence of articles that the authors have contributed; in multipartite articles, any section that is unsigned is by the author of the next signed section. Where the article was compiled by the editors or in the few cases where an author has wished to remain anonymous, this is indicated by a square box (□) instead of a signature.

Bibliographies are arranged chronologically (within a section, where divided) by order of year of first publication and, within years, alphabetically by authors' names. Abbreviations have been used for some standard reference books; these are cited in full in Appendix C. Abbreviations of periodical titles are in Appendix B. Abbreviated references to alphabetically arranged dictionaries and encyclopedias appear at the beginning of the bibliography (or section).

Biographical dates when cited in parentheses in running text at the first mention of a personal name indicate that the individual does not have an entry in the dictionary. The presence of parenthesized regnal dates for rulers and popes, however, does not necessarily indicate the lack of a biography of that person. Where no dates are provided for an artist or patron, the reader may assume that there is a biography of that individual in the dictionary (or, more rarely, that the person is so obscure that dates are not readily available).

Cross-references are distinguished by the use of small capital letters, with a large capital to indicate the initial letter of the entry to which the reader is directed; for example, 'He commissioned LEONARDO DA VINCI . . .' means that the entry is alphabetized under 'L'.

W

[continued]

Wax. Substance composed of varying proportions of esters, acids, alcohols and hydrocarbons and similar in composition to fats. Waxes are relatively stable compounds and have a low toxicity and mild odour. Most natural waxes are solid at room temperature but soften or liquefy at higher temperatures. They are insoluble but emulsify easily in water and are soluble in some organic solvents (e.g. turpentine). Waxes range in colour from white through yellow to brown and black, although they can discolour when exposed to natural light or due to the action of additives or solvents.

I. Types and properties. II. Techniques and uses. III. Conservation.

I. Types and properties.

Natural waxes are obtained from animal, vegetable and mineral sources. Beeswax is the most common of natural waxes. It is a secretion of the glands on the abdomen of the 'worker' bee, primarily of the domestic species (*Apis mellifica*), and is made ductile through chewing and impregnation of saliva by the insect. The colour of beeswax can vary, depending on the original source of the pollen. Heather, which has white pollen, produces a wax that has little colour, but sainfoin pollen, being yellow, produces an ochre-yellow wax. African beeswax is dark in colour, and Turkish beeswax is bright red.

Beeswax is refined by immersing canvas bags filled with the honeycomb in boiling water, although it is also possible to use organic solvents to extract the wax from the honeycomb. Beeswax that has been refined in this way retains some colour but can be bleached by exposure to ultraviolet light or by the use of chemical agents, for example chlorine, potassium bichromate, potassium permanganate or hydrogen peroxide. Bleached and refined beeswax is usually more dense and brittle than unrefined wax. Beeswax melts at 63–66°C and is used for many different purposes, for example the making of candles and sculpture, pharmaceutical products and in the food industry. Beeswax is also the major component of the wax used in encaustic painting.

Chinese insect wax or cochineal wax is produced from the secretion of the *Coccus ceriferus*, deposited on ash trees. The wax is relatively hard, melting between 79 and 83°C, and is white and odourless. It is used for making candles and polishes and as a protective layer on paper and textiles.

Suint, first produced in the 19th century, is extracted from water in which sheep's fleece has been washed. When dried it is pale yellow in colour, with a faint but agreeable odour. When added to water it creates stable emulsions. As lanolin (with the addition of 25% water) it is used in the pharmaceutical industry and in the production of paint.

Spermaceti wax comes from the oil on the head of the sperm-whale. It is a white, translucent powder with a crystalline structure and contains some glycerides. It melts between 41 and 44°C. It was first used in the 18th century and is employed in pharmaceutical products and to soften beeswax and occasionally in the restoration of works of art.

Carnauba wax is derived from the exudate of the leaves of the *Copernicia cerifera*, the Brazilian carnauba palm. After it has been extracted through beating the leaves, it changes in colour from light yellow to dark grey. It is the hardest of natural waxes, melting between 83 and 86°C, and is used for making candles, polishes, as a protective layer on rope, and for glazing paper. It is also one of the components of printers' ink, lubricants, varnishes, lacquers and enamels. Phonograph cylinders were formerly made out of this type of wax, and it can be combined with other components to make precision moulds. It can also be used in the restoration of works of art.

Candelilla wax is made from the *Euphorbia cerifera* plant that grows mainly in northern Mexico and Texas. It is yellow-brown in colour and is hard and brittle. It is used in the manufacture of plasters, polishes, ebonite varnishes, gummed paper and sealing wax, and as a water and insect repellant and to harden softer waxes.

Japan wax is a by-product of lacquer from the *Rhus succedanea*, originally from China and Japan. It contains 10% glycerine and is rather soft, melting between 50 and 52°C. It is used for polishes, cosmetics, in the production of pastels and crayon and in treating leather.

Mineral waxes are obtained from fossil sources; ozokerite is the most common and is extracted from bituminous deposits. It is dark yellow, with a greenish tone, and has a characteristic aromatic odour. Refined ozokerite is known as ceresin, which is white. Both ozokerite and ceresin are used in the production of cosmetics, paints, varnishes and printers' ink. They can occasionally be found in the composition of wax overlaid on sculpture. Montan wax, brown or blackish in colour, is obtained from coal or lignite and is used as a substitute for carnauba wax when sufficiently pale in colour. Waxes extracted from petroleum, which are not true waxes, have been widely used since 1830. Paraffin wax is produced in a number of grades of purity and melts between 50 and 60°C. Microcrystalline waxes are often used as a plasticiser, as they contain more residual oil.

Synthetic waxes are produced by chemical processes. Stearine is the commercial name given to the ester of glycerine. It is an opaque, white substance produced by the hydrolysis of fat. It has been used as a substitute for beeswax since 1821 to make candles and subsequently for sculpture, bonded with such pigments as zinc white.

BIBLIOGRAPHY
T. W. Cowan: *La Cire: Histoire, production, fabrication* (Paris, 1911)
N. Margival: *Cires et encaustiques* (Paris, 1937)
H. Kuhn: 'Detection and Identification of Waxes, Including Punic Waxes, by Infra-red Spectrography', *Stud. Conserv.*, ii (1960), pp. 71–80
H. Bennet: *Industrial Waxes* (New York, 1975)
P. E. Kdattukudy, ed.: *Chemistry and Biochemistry of Natural Waxes* (Amsterdam, 1976)
J. S. Mills and R. White: 'Natural Resins of Art and Archaeology: Their Sources, Chemistry and Identification', *Stud. Conserv.*, xxiii (1977), pp. 12–31
R. White: 'The Application of Gas Chromatography to the Identification of Waxes', *Stud. Conserv.*, xxiii (1978), pp. 57–68
D. Besnainou: *Cire et cires: Etude sur la composition, l'altération, la restauration, la conservation des oeuvres céroplastiques* (diss., Paris, Inst. Francais Rest. Oeuvres A., 1984)

II. Techniques and uses.

1. Sculpture. 2. Painting. 3. Seals.

1. SCULPTURE.

(i) Techniques. There are two main techniques for producing wax sculpture: modelling and casting. The plasticity of wax for modelling can be improved by the addition of grease and oils; animal fat, Venice turpentine, turpentine and pitch also act as solvents or plasticizers. It can be made harder by the addition of resins. In time, these additives darken the composition, because of the processes of oxidation and polymerization on drying. By lowering the melting point, some compositions can remain adhesive for a long time. As the volatile elements evaporate, however, shrinkage can occur, and cracks form (*see also* §III below).

The composition of wax used for cast objects differs only slightly from that of wax used in modelling. The composition is made harder, and consequently has a higher melting point, by the addition of natural resins, for example rosin or dammar. Cast wax pieces are also more durable, although the colour also tends to darken. Synthetic resins are used in preference to wax for the hyper-realism of modern waxworks (*see* §1(ii)(b) below).

Bleached wax can be coloured by the addition of pigments, either mixed directly with molten wax or in a dilute turpentine solution. Care must be taken to ensure that the grains of pigment are fine and evenly sized, otherwise the largest will colour the wax in proportion to their density. This will alter the appearance of the surface by darkening the areas in relief. Flesh tints should be lightly coloured in order to appear translucent. The appearance of clothing on wax figures can be achieved with the addition of kaolin, aluminium or plaster, which produces more opaque areas. Some wax is also coloured by applying liquid coloured wax or oil paint to the surface.

Modelling in wax involves the same technique as modelling in clay. The model is built up by the addition of small balls of wax, sometimes on to an armature, depending on the desired form, then worked with a cold or warmed spatula. This technique is particularly suitable for making studies and models.

Casting is the most common technique of producing wax sculpture. A rough model in clay, wax or plastilina is made, and a plaster mould is taken of it. Molten wax is then poured into the mould and can be coloured with pigments at this stage if necessary. Once the wax has solidified the mould is removed and the piece finished by hand with a spatula.

Certain precautions are necessary with this technique. The plaster mould should be made of several, well-oiled layers of between 10 and 30 mm thick, in order to avoid damaging the wax on its removal. It is important that the plaster mould be saturated with water at a temperature of 80°C, in order that, when pouring, the wax remains molten and thus avoids trapping air bubbles. The wet mould also prevents the wax from sticking to the plaster, making the object easier to remove.

Cast wax objects can be strengthened by placing cloth or fibre that has been impregnated with wax inside the mould. For larger models and those that might have areas of weakness, it is advisable to use a framework or armature made out of metal, wood, bone or plaster.

The molten wax must be poured at a temperature just above its melting point. If the temperature is too high there is a risk of changing the properties of the wax and a darkening in colour. When the molten wax begins to harden, any excess must be removed to ensure an even distribution and to avoid cracking once the wax has solidified completely.

Low-relief wax sculpture is always attached to a base, made of slate, glass (with a coat of coloured wax on the reverse), marble or wood covered with fabric, paper or paint. The wax is attached to the base by metal strips or with adhesives, for example hide glue with or without litharge, natural resin or a mixture of wax and resin.

For information on the lost-wax casting process *see* METAL, §III.

(ii) History.

(a) Small-scale works. Wax has been widely used for sculptures on a small scale, due to its malleability, ease of preparation and ability to harden without cracking. The use of wax for artificial flowers, as well as figurines for funeral ceremonies, from which the tradition of naturalistic life-size figures developed (*see* §(b) below), was known in the ancient world. Wax was most widely employed, however, for the production of sketches or modelli (*see* MODELLO, §II) that were often built up on wire armatures and used for casting works in metal by the lost-wax method; many wax objects of this type have therefore not survived. In the 15th and 16th centuries wax modelling and casting emerged as an art in its own right (see fig. 1), particularly in Italy (*see* ITALY, §X, 3), where such sculptors as Jacopo Sansovino produced finished wax models. In

1. Wax sculpture by an unknown artist: *Leda and the Swan*, 250×200 mm, late 16th century or early 17th (Écouen, Musée de la Renaissance, Château)

the second half of the 16th century such medallists as Antonio Abondio (*see* ABONDIO, (1)) began to make portrait medallions in coloured wax, often embellished with textiles, gems and pearls. In the 17th century GAETANO ZUMBO exploited the realism afforded by the use of coloured waxes to produce illusionistic, macabre tableaux, as well as anatomical models.

Small wax sculptures continued to be produced in the 18th century and early 19th by such sculptors as John Flaxman in England and Edme Bouchardon and Clodion in France. Classicizing profile heads or busts in light-coloured wax against a background of darker wax also came into fashion. The malleability of wax, and consequently its ability to convey movement, also made the material widely popular among late 19th-century French sculptors, such as Antoine-Louis Barye and PIERRE-JULES MÈNE, known for their figurative sculpture, particularly of animal subjects. This quality was also exploited by the sculptor MEDARDO ROSSO in his impressionistic works. With the development in the 20th century of patent modelling materials, such as Plasticine, and more durable synthetic resins, the use of wax for small sculptures declined.

BIBLIOGRAPHY

E. Dubois: *La Statuaire: Modelage-moulage et terre cuite* (Paris, n.d.)
S. Blondel: 'Les modeleurs en cire', *Gaz. B.-A.* (1882)
G. Le Breton: 'Histoire de la sculpture en cire', *Ami Mnmts & A.*, vii (1893), pp. 269–78
——: *Essai historique sur la sculpture en cire* (Rouen, 1894)
F. A. A. Goupil: *Manuel général du modelage en bas relief et ronde-bosse, du moulage et de la sculpture* (Paris, 1949)
R. Reilly: *Portrait Waxes* (London, 1953)
J. K. W. Badien: *Technique du moulage* (Paris, 1967)
E. J. Pyke: *A Biographical Dictionary of Wax Modellers* (Oxford, 1973)
E. Bolton Stanwood: *Wax Portraits and Silhouettes* (Boston, 1974, Detroit, 2/1974)
C. D. Clarke: 'Modelling and Casting for Wax Reproductions', *Tech. Stud.*, iv (1975)
La ceroplastica nella scienza e nell'arte: Atti del I congresso internazionale della biblioteca della rivista di storia delle scienze mediche e naturali: Firenze, 1977, xx
B. Lanza and others: *Le cere anatomiche della Specola* (Florence, 1979)
A. Parenti: *La ceroplastica* (Florence, 1980)

DIDIER BESNAINOU

(b) Life-size figures. Displays of life-size wax figures, usually known as waxworks, derive from the tradition in antiquity of bearing funeral effigies of deceased leaders. This practice was revived at the English and French courts in the 14th century and was maintained by some English nobles into the 18th century. In France, Michel Bourdin modelled a life-size wax funerary portrait bust of *Henry IV* in 1611; illicit wax replicas of this work toured provincial fairs, and one was exhibited in Amsterdam in the 1630s at one of the first recorded commercial displays of life-size wax portraits. In 1668 Louis XIV granted the sculptor ANTOINE BENOIST a monopoly to show effigies (untraced) of the French royal family and court, which were often dressed in clothes provided by the subject. Benoist also modelled figures (untraced) at the English court in 1684, and in 1688, at the renewal of his privilege, toured his wax 'puppets' around fairs in France.

Waxworks were recorded in England at the Bartholomew Fair in 1647, and a tableau of the *Last Supper* was noted by John Evelyn at the French Ambassador's lodgings in 1672. The figures in Westminster Abbey, London, are the most important surviving group of early English waxworks, dating from 1686 to 1806. These figures were displayed as a fund-raising tourist attraction from the early 18th century until 1839, by which date they had much deteriorated. After further damage in 1941, they were fully restored and put on exhibit again. In the late 17th century the German Johann Schalch (1623–*c.*1704) travelled throughout northern Europe with his wax models of court figures, visiting London in 1685. A rival modeller was Mrs Goldsmith (*fl* 1695–1703), who made the effigies in Westminster Abbey, London, of *Frances, Duchess of Richmond*, which cost £260 in 1703, *William III* and *Mary II*. The most celebrated English waxworks of the late 17th century and early 18th was that of Mrs Salmon (1650–1740), established in 1693, whose 140 figures included diverse tableaux and a booby-trapped mechanical figure of *Old Mother Shipton*. The exhibition continued under Mrs Salmon's name until 1831. Her closest rival was Benjamin Rackstrow (*d* 1772), whose 'Museum of Anatomy and Curiosities' contained similar subject groups and a large number of anatomical pieces verging on the titillating. Serious anatomical waxwork collections had appeared in Europe in the late 17th century, of which the most renowned was 'La Specola' in Florence, founded in 1675 on the Medici collections.

2. Wax tableau of *Louis XVI and his Family* by Mme Tussaud, life-size, 1790 (London, Madame Tussaud's Ltd)

Popular late 18th-century waxworks included the Sylvesters' 'Cabinet of Royal Figures', and that of Patience Wright (1725–86), who had come to London in 1772 after the destruction of her waxworks in New York, the first in America. More celebrated are the waxworks of Dr Philippe Curtius (1737–94). As a physician in Berne, he had made wax anatomical models, and portraits for friends; these so impressed Louis-François de Bourbon, Prince de Conti, that he brought Curtius to Paris in 1761. In 1767 he was joined by his niece, Marie Grosholtz (1761–1850), later Mme Tussaud, whom he taught wax modelling. Curtius moved his 'Salon de Cire', with tableaux of the French royal family, to the Palais Royal in 1770 and in 1783 opened on the Boulevard du Temple the infamous 'Caverne des Grands Voleurs', the basis of the later 'Chamber of Horrors', which, during the Revolution, was filled with wax casts of the heads of guillotined nobility. After Curtius's death, Mme Tussaud brought most of the collection to England, touring Britain between 1802 and 1835 before settling in London. The exhibition moved to its present site on the Marylebone Road in 1884, and the recumbent figure of Mme du Barry, the *Sleeping Beauty* (1765), by Curtius and the tableau of *Louis XVI and his Family* (see fig. 2) by Mme Tussaud are still among the most celebrated exhibits, although severe losses were incurred in a disastrous fire in 1925 and during World War II. Other celebrated waxworks collections are in the Panoptikum in Hamburg (1879) and the Musée Grévin, Paris (1882).

By 1900 waxworks, often featuring tableaux reminiscent of Victorian genre painting, were to be found in some 190 British and 200 American towns and resorts, but they rapidly became unfashionable after 1918. With the arrival of Pop art in the 1960s, however, the super-realism of waxworks again became acceptable. Their enduring popularity can be explained by the potential for verisimilitude offered by the medium and the popular fascination with the appearance of the famous and infamous. While Curtius and Mme Tussaud ensured accuracy by taking life or death masks of their subjects, present likenesses are established by modelled clay portrait heads, achieved with the assistance of numerous photographs and measurements; from these, the casting moulds are created. Synthetic resins are often used instead of wax. The illusion is enhanced by the use of human hair and original or closely copied clothes.

BIBLIOGRAPHY

E. J. Pyke: *A Biographical Dictionary of Wax Modellers* (Oxford, 1973)

E. V. Gatacre and L. Dru: 'Portraiture in the Cabinet de Cire de Curtius and its Successor, Madame Tussaud's Exhibition', *La ceroplastica nella scienza e nell'arte: Atti del I congresso internazionale della biblioteca della rivista di storia delle scienze mediche e naturali: Firenze, 1977*, xx, pp. 639–48

J. Adhémar: 'Les Musées de cire en France, Curtius, le "Banquet Royal", les têtes coupées', *Gaz. B.-A.*, xcii (1978), pp. 203–14

R. D. Altick: *The Shows of London* (Cambridge, MA, and London, 1978)

ROBERT WENLEY

2. PAINTING. Wax has been widely used as a binder in the manufacture of paint and as a stabilizer in commercially produced oil paints (*see* PAINT, §I), as well as a matting agent in varnishes and oil paint. A warmed mixture of beeswax and resin has traditionally been employed in fresco painting to provide decorative areas in relief to which metal leaf is applied. In the late 19th century Thomas Gambier-Parry developed the technique of 'spirit fresco painting', involving heating a mixture of resin, wax, oil of spike lavender and copal, with pigments; this was applied to plaster that had been coated with whiting and lead white mixed with turpentine.

The main use of wax in painting, however, has been in the technique of ENCAUSTIC PAINTING, in which dry pigments are mixed with molten wax on a heated metal palette, then applied to a support; a heat source is then passed close to the surface to 'burn in' the colours by fusing them to the support. Encaustic painting was widely used in the ancient world and described by Pliny the elder, Vitruvius and Plutarch; attempts were made to revive the technique in Europe in the 18th century. There is, however, considerable debate concerning the media and processes originally used and whether a number of painting methods involving wax can be described as encaustic: wax can be dissolved in turpentine and is made water-soluble by the addition of alkali and thus can be combined with a wide variety of paints; several emulsions of waxes, oils and resins have also been patented as artists' media (*see also* PAINT MEDIUM).

BIBLIOGRAPHY
F. Pratt and B. Fizel: *Encaustic Materials and Methods* (New York, 1949)
J. Ayres: *The Artist's Craft: A History of Tools, Techniques and Materials* (Oxford, 1985)
L. Masschelein-Kleiner: *Ancient Binding Media, Varnishes and Adhesives* (Rome, 1985)

For further bibliography *see* ENCAUSTIC PAINTING.

HILTON BROWN

3. SEALS. Small pieces of wax stamped with a device or emblem have been widely used for the purposes of authentication, most commonly of letters or documents; the word 'seal' applies both to the matrix or die that stamps the impression and to the impressed material. Although wax seals were occasionally employed in the Islamic world (*see* ISLAMIC ART, §VIII, 14), their use was mainly confined to the Byzantine empire and Western Europe, where their importance greatly increased during the Middle Ages.

The substance employed for medieval wax seals was a mixture of beeswax, Venice turpentine and pigment, usually vermilion, although yellow, off-white and green seals are also extant. Shellac (*see* LACQUER, §I, 2) was introduced in the 17th century and eventually replaced beeswax.

A stick of sealing wax was held under a flame in order to melt a drop of wax, which was then impressed with a seal matrix. These usually took the form of a stamp or signet ring and were commonly made from brass, occasionally silver or carved hardstones or marble. In Byzantium sealing cones were also used. These are small cones of hardstone or bronze (used from the 10th century) with an intaglio sealing device carved into the bezel-like base, with a tiny loop at the apex for suspension. Until the early 11th century in Western Europe a wax seal was affixed *en placard* (directly to the parchment) and pressed partially through a slit to prevent it falling off. In the late 11th century and throughout the 12th a second, counter-seal was usually added and appended to fastenings of silk cord, hemp, leather or parchment.

In Western Europe wax seals were initially used only by royalty, nobility or by high-ranking ecclesiastics, and as they were the only means of validating official documents or private correspondence constituted a symbol of power and legality. By the late 12th century, however, seals had been adopted to represent towns (*see* LONDON, fig. 13), guilds, colleges, marine companies and similar bodies, and objects as varied as caskets of relics and bundles of wool were sealed. Medieval wax seals could be up to 100 mm in diameter and were typically either round or in pointed ovals; they are linked iconographically to medals and coins, usually with a central device surrounded by an abbreviated inscription within plain or beaded borders. Many seals are among the finest expressions of the art of miniature relief work (e.g. seal of the City of Bruges, 1281; Rouen, Bib. Mun.). Imagery and lettering, generally in Latin, alluded to the owner or owning body. On the death of the owner of a personal seal the matrix was often defaced to render it invalid.

3. Wax seal of the Augustinian priory of St Mary, Merton, Surrey, showing the *Virgin and Child Enthroned* (obverse), 90×55 mm, 1241 (London, British Museum)

Motifs common to royal seals were kings and queens enthroned, portraits, princes on caparisoned horses, coats of arms, lions, falcons, castles and barbicans. Ecclesiastical subjects included the *Virgin and Child*, saints, views of cathedrals and abbeys and full-length portraits of church dignitaries. Thirteenth-century designs of elaborate Gothic architectural canopies frequently dominate the figure beneath (e.g. seal of Augustinian priory of St Mary, Merton, Surrey, 1241; London, BM; see fig. 3). Other motifs included animals, birds, fishes, flowers and plants, monograms, emblems of office, shields, mottoes, rebuses and occasionally satirical characters. Backgrounds were frequently enlivened by pin-pricked or diaper patterns. Renaissance designs introduced a fashion for private seals of engraved hardstones set into gold finger rings or fobs.

Between the 13th and 17th centuries English seal cutters were renowned for their skill and the rich complexity of their designs (e.g. seal of Elizabeth I, 1563; London, BM); one of the finest later engravers was Thomas SIMON, who worked for Charles II. From the 17th century to the early 20th wax seals remained an emblem of authority for documents of state and law. Personal seals, which constituted the largest group, became simply an adornment and gradually went out of use.

BIBLIOGRAPHY

A. B. Tonnochy: *Catalogue of British Seal-dies in the British Museum* (London, 1952)
J. Favier: *La Vie au moyen âge illustrée par les sceaux* (Paris, 1985)
R. H. Ellis: *Catalogue of Seals in the Public Record Office* (London, 1986)
T. A. Heslop: 'English Seals in the Thirteenth and Fourteenth Centuries', *Age of Chivalry: Art in Plantagenet England, 1200–1400* (exh. cat., ed. J. Alexander and P. Binski; London, RA, 1987)

III. Conservation.

The type of wax, additives and colorants can contribute to the state of preservation of a wax artefact; most forms of deterioration, however, result from environmental factors. A temperature of just 30°C can cause slumping, while excessive cold can lead to embrittlement and cracking. Shrinkage and eventual cracking may also occur when important plasticizers are leached out of some waxes as a result of fluctuations in temperature; these plasticizers may be seen as white crystals on the surface. In relative humidities over 65%, wax may grow mould, which also attacks important structural elements. Oxidation, catalyzed by light, causes darkening in wax and can lead to structural changes and hardening.

Such additives as fats can migrate out of the wax to form sticky droplets on the surface. Pigments may discolour or even move around in the wax. Discolouration can also result from solvent cleaning: turpentine appears to leave brown residues on the surface, while ammonia causes blanching. Methods of manufacture can also contribute to poor preservation. For example, wax built around an armature may crack due to restricted movement, and a wax artefact built up in layers can delaminate due to different drying rates in the layers.

Wax has a tendency to attract and embed dust, which can only be effectively removed using solvents. Solvent cleaning, however, partially removes the surface and may affect surface paint or pigmentation. If the risk to the artefact is too great, it is advisable not to clean. Coating the artefact is also not recommended, as varnish often yellows with time and becomes difficult to remove without damaging the surface. Regular dusting should overcome the need for either coating or solvent cleaning.

If solvent cleaning is necessary, water containing a small amount of detergent should be used initially. Heavily embedded dirt may require such a solvent as alcohol, iso-propyl alcohol or petroleum spirit to soften the surface enough to lift the dirt. Cleaning should be carried out over a small area at a time, applying the solvent with a brush and then drawing it off the surface with a dry brush. Rinsing in water is essential to remove residual solvent or detergent. White crystals on the surface may be removed effectively by using iso-propyl alcohol.

Dowelling a broken wax artefact is generally not recommended, as it involves too much structural interference. Instead, wax can be joined with adhesive, although it is difficult to achieve a strong bond. Three of the more effective adhesives for this purpose are Hxtal NYL1 epoxy resin, PVA emulsion and Paraloid B72 acrylic resin. Filling losses in a wax artefact is necessary only for structural and, sometimes, aesthetic reasons. The wax used for filling should be softer than that of the artefact to facilitate removal if necessary. Wax fills can be pigmented and can be cast or built up and carved back.

Despite the relative chemical stability of wax, its sensitivity to temperature fluctuations means that, ideally, wax artefacts should be stored in stable conditions with a temperature of around 20–22°C and with a relative humidity of 50±5%. Covered display is recommended to prevent dust accumulation. Alternatively, artefacts should be dusted daily with a soft brush. Lighting is also an important consideration, due to potential oxidation, discolouring and slumping. Wax objects should be stored covered in a box and not left in contact with such materials as tissue that may fuse with the surface. Most basic conservation treatments are in fact quite delicate operations that should best be undertaken by a qualified conservator in order to prevent damage to the object.

BIBLIOGRAPHY

V. J. Murrell: *The Care of Wax Objects* (London, 1970)
D. Reid of Robertland and A. Ross: 'The Conservation of Non-metallic Seals', *Stud. Conserv.*, xv/1 (1970), pp. 51–62
V. J. Murrell: 'Some Aspects of the Conservation of Wax Models', *Stud. Conserv.*, xvi/3 (1971), pp. 95–109
——: 'A Discussion of Some Methods of Wax Conservation and their Application to Recent Conservation Problems', *Papers of the First International Congress on Wax Modelling: Florence, 1975*, ed. L. S. Olschki
H. Kuhn: *Conservation and Restoration of Works of Art and Antiquities*, i (London, 1986)
E. Pearlstein: 'Fatty Bloom on Wood Sculpture from Mali', *Stud. Conserv.*, xxxi/2 (1986), pp. 83–91
J. S. Mills and R. White: *The Organic Chemistry of Museum Objects* (London, 1987)
V. Kaufmann: 'Restoration of an 18th Century Half Life-size Anatomical Figure Modelled in Beeswax', *The Conservator*, xii (1988), pp. 25–30
CATE HARLEY

Waxed paper negative. *See under* PHOTOGRAPHY, §I.

Wayne, June (Claire) (*b* Chicago, 7 March 1918). American painter, printmaker, tapestry designer, writer and lecturer. She left school at 15 to become a painter, using her given names, June Claire, but her reputation was made after her marriage, when she became June Wayne. Her first exhibition, in 1935, of watercolours based on Ben Day dots, took place a quarter of a century before the birth of Pop art and won her an official invitation to Mexico. Pursuing a rich diversity of ideas, fashionable and unfashionable, she often anticipated aesthetic developments. For example, her spatial constructions of 1950—ink drawings on glass slotted into a framework—predated Rauschenberg's by 14 years, while the imagery of her lithograph *Strange Moon* (1951; see Gilmour, no. 12)—an expanded chequer-board traversed by floating discs—preceded Op art by a decade. Her lithographic illumination (1958) of John Donne's *Songs and Sonets* was among the first books in the French *livre de peintre* tradition to be published in the USA.

Hired by the Federal Art Project in 1938, Wayne painted mills, factories and the Chicago River. Her wartime training in production illustration sparked an interest in optics and perspective, which she explored after World War II as a Los Angeles modernist. In 1948 she fell in love with lithography as a primary means of expression, and her painted allegories of invented characters in situations inspired by Kafka, were often derived from prints, rather than vice-versa.

Wayne's international reputation depends not only on her work as an artist but also on the flair with which she helped to transform the ecology for artists' prints as founding director of the Tamarind Lithography Workshop in Los Angeles, which she ran from 1960 to 1970 with the financial backing of the Ford Foundation (*see* LITHOGRAPHY, §II, 2(ii)(c)). During the Tamarind years Wayne often had to set her own work aside, as the delay in completing her magnificent self-portrait *Wave 1920* (1968–70; see Gilmour, no. 91/II) attests. From 1970, however, she explored many new themes, and between 1971 and 1973 she realized 11 magisterial tapestries in France, using such powerful lithographs as *At Last a Thousand* (1965; see Gilmour, no. 82/II), *Verdict* (1970; see Gilmour, no. 101) and *Wave 1970* (1970; see Gilmour, no. 108) as cartoons.

In the late 1970s Wayne devised a figurative suite of 20 lithographs (1975–9; e.g. Gilmour, no. 141) as an affectionate tribute to her mother, Dorothy; its importance as a feminist statement was recognized during its extensive American exhibition tour. But the drama of space travel had gripped her imagination, and in collaboration with Edward Hamilton, her personal printer, she began to imagine 'the ineffably beautiful but hostile wilderness of astrophysical space', harnessing sophisticated oxidation patterns on zinc to provide metaphors for its invisible forces. The exquisite minimalist striations of *Dawn Wind*, *Silent Wind* and *Night Wind* (1975; see Gilmour, nos 134–6) reveal her subtle mastery of monochrome, but she also conceived several radiant colour portfolios, among them *Stellar Winds* (1979), *Solar Flares* (1983) and *My Palomar* (1984), in which a square, ambiguously alternating as detail or field, voyages through interstellar space. Wayne's later prints (1989–92; see Gilmour, nos 274–7) faced mortality in a skittish series that continued the theme of energy and matter and were inspired by James Ensor's skeletal self-portrait.

WRITINGS
'The Male Artist as a Stereotypical Female', *A. J.*, xxxii/4 (1973), pp. 414–16
'The Tradition of Narrative Tapestry', *Craft Horizons*, xxxiv/4 (1974), pp. 26–9, 49
'The Creative Process: Artists, Carpenters and the Flat Earth Society', *Craft Horizons*, xxxvi/35 (1976), pp. 30–31, 64, 67
'Broken Stones and Whooping Cranes: Thoughts of a Wilful Artist', *Tamarind Pap.*, xiii (1990), pp. 16–27, 94
'Avant-Garde Mindset in the Artist's Studio' and 'Obscenity Reconsidered', *Mutiny and the Mainstream: Talk that Changed Art, 1975–1900*, ed. J. Seigel (New York, 1992), pp. 238–40, 309–10
'Walking backwards into the Twenty-first Century: Redesigning the Ecology of the Arts', *Amer. A.*, vi/1 (1992), pp. 2–5

BIBLIOGRAPHY
M. Baskett: *The Art of June Wayne* (Berlin and New York, 1969) [monograph with cat. rais. of prts, ptgs and drgs to 1968]
M. Jarry: 'The Tapestries of June Wayne', *Cimaise*, xxi/117–18 (1974), pp. 56–65
B. Kester: 'The Tapestries of June Wayne', *Craft Horizons*, xxxiv/6 (1974), pp. 36–9, 80–81
K. Smith: 'June Wayne: Breaking the Stereotype', *Currânt*, ii/1 (1976), pp. 15–25
R. M. Fitzgibbons: 'Artist in Residence: June Wayne', *Amer. Artist*, xciii/442 (1979), pp. 46–9, 100
S. Stowens: 'June Wayne: The *Dorothy Series*', *Amer. Artist*, xciii/442 (1979), pp. 50–55, 97–100
C. Adams: *American Lithographers: The Artists and their Printers* (Albuquerque, 1983), pp. 173, 181–4, 196–203
A. Raven: 'Cognitos: June Wayne's New Paintings', *A. Mag.*, cix (1984), pp. 119–21
J. Watrous: *A Century of American Printmaking 1880–1980* (Madison, WI, 1984)
L. Lewis: 'June Wayne's Investigations of Time', *Print News*, vii/2 (1985), pp. 10–12
June Wayne: The 'Djuna' Set (exh. cat. by A. Raven, B. Kester and P. Gilmour, Fresno, CA, A. Mus., 1988) [ptgs, prts, taps]
June Wayne: Lithographs from the 'Djuna' Set, 1950–88: A Thematic Retrospective (exh. cat. by R. Conway and R. Weisberg, New York, Assoc. Amer. Artists, 1988)
Turning the Tide: Early Los Angeles Modernists 1920–1956 (exh. cat. by P. J. Karlstrom and S. Ehrlich, Santa Barbara, CA, Mus. A., 1990), pp. 136, 157–60
R. Weisberg: 'June Wayne's Quantum Aesthetics', *Woman's A. J.*, xi/1 (1990), pp. 3–8
P. Gilmour: 'A Love Affair with Lithography: The Prints of June Wayne', *Prt Q.*, ix/2 (1992), pp. 142–76 [with cat. rais. of the prts 1948–91]
——: *The Prints of June Wayne: A Catalogue Raisonné* [in preparation]
PAT GILMOUR

Waywike, Maynard. *See* VEWICKE, MAYNARD.

Weale, W(illiam) H(enry) J(ames) (*b* London, 8 March 1832; *d* London, 26 April 1917). English art historian. He was educated at King's College, London, from 1842 to 1848. From an early age he was interested in medieval Christianity, and in February 1849 he converted to Roman Catholicism. He had a lifelong interest in Christian symbolism and iconography and, above all, liturgy. Another early interest was in Belgian churches (he had visited every parish church by the age of 19) and memorial tablets. In 1855 he moved to Bruges, where his antiquarian interests led him to undertake work in the restoration and preservation of ancient monuments. In 1863 he launched *Le Beffroi*, a periodical concerned with the conservation of monuments and historic buildings, the study of medieval art and the promotion of the Neo-Gothic style. In this, and in *La Flandre* (a magazine published on Weale's initiative in 1867), he published much of the information he discovered while researching the city's archives. He also established the Guild of St Thomas and St Luke, which lasted until 1914 and was responsible for much of the interest in the Neo-Gothic in Belgium. In 1865 he founded the Société Archéologique in Bruges, which collected objects for a museum collection, which subsequently became the core of the present Gruuthusemuseum in Bruges.

Weale drew up an inventory of the art collection in Bruges. His *Catalogue…de l'Académie de Bruges* (1861) provided the first scholarly description of the city's collection of Old Masters, and his catalogue *Objets d'art religieux à Malines* (1864) was the first survey of its kind in Belgium. From 1860 onwards, in the course of researching the Bruges archives, he discovered remarkable documents relating to Flemish Primitive artists and was able to discredit various apocryphal stories concerning Hans Memling and Jan van Eyck. He discovered such artists as Gerard David and Aelbrecht Cornelis and identified many of their works, giving masterly descriptions of these in his monographs. In 1867 he organized the first Old Masters exhibition in Belgium and composed a catalogue called *L'Ancienne Ecole néerlandaise.*

In 1876 Weale tried unsuccessfully to become keeper of the Bruges city archives, and two years later he returned to London, where he used his specialist knowledge on behalf of public institutions and private collectors. He organized various exhibitions of Old Masters, miniatures and manuscripts and compiled works on liturgies such as *Bibliographia Liturgica* (1886) and *Analecta Liturgica* (1888–1902). He also dealt in Neo-Gothic devotional prints and sculpture from Flanders. From 1890 to 1897 he was Keeper of the National Art Library, South Kensington, London, a post from which he was dismissed because of the drastic reforms he had introduced. In 1902 he published the catalogue *Les Primitifs flamands à Bruges*, which, with his other writings on art, demonstrates the value of his documentary research and his regard for accuracy and completeness, although several of the attributions he made in this book were rejected by other art historians, notably Georges Hulin de Loo.

WRITINGS

Catalogue du Musée de l'Académie de Bruges (Bruges, 1861)
Bruges et ses environs (Bruges, 1862, rev. 4/1884)
Catalogue des objets d'art religieux du moyen âge, de la renaissance et des temps modernes… à Malines (Brussels, 1864)
Gerard David, Painter and Illuminator (London, 1895)
Hans Memling (London, 1901)
Exposition des Primitifs flamands et d'art ancien (Bruges, 1902)
The van Eycks and their Art (London, 1912)

BIBLIOGRAPHY

BNB; NBW
Obituary, *The Tablet* (5 May 1917)
M. W. Brockwell: 'W. H. J. Weale, the Pioneer', *The Library*, n.s. 5, vi (1951), pp. 200–11
L. van Biervliet: 'Leven en werk van W. H. James Weale, een Engels kunsthistoricus in Vlaanderen in de 19de eeuw', *Acad. Anlct.: Kl. S. Kst.*, 53 (1991) [with Eng. summary]
——: *De brieven van W. H. James Weale aan Jozef A. Alberdingk Thijm 1858–1884* (Bruges, 1991)
——: 'Archief van W. H. James Weale in de provinciale bibliotheek en cultuurarchief van West-Vlaanderen', *Handelingen Gen. Geschied., Soc. Em.*, 129 (Bruges, 1992), pp. 189–212

LORI VAN BIERVLIET

Weathervane [weathercock]. Item for indicating wind direction, usually made by blacksmiths of wrought iron or copper and placed on public buildings, churches and private dwellings. The weathervane was invented by the Greeks, and in 48 BC a vane, in the form of 'Triton', was installed on the Horologion of Andronikos Kyrrhos (the so-called Tower of Winds), a weather observatory in Athens. The Romans created weathervanes because of their belief that wind direction could foretell the future. Marcus Terentius Varro described a weathervane located on his villa in which the wind direction was indicated on the inside by a shaft through the ceiling, which was connected to the vane. The Vikings had quadrant-shaped weathervanes, which influenced the design of weathervanes until the 10th century. An early Viking example is in the Statens Historiska Museum, Stockholm. During the medieval period a papal decree stated that a rooster (often in the form of a weathervane) should be placed on each church in order to serve as a reminder of the betrayal of Jesus. Early recorded weathervanes illustrated in medieval art include those in the manuscript of the poet Caedmon's *Ark* (c. AD 1000), the drawings in the *Benedictional of St Aethelwold* (1024) and the Bayeaux Tapestry, illustrated with an 11th-century vane being set on Westminster Abbey, London. Wulfstan's *Life of St Swithin* describes a vane of the 10th century. Birds and fantastic animals were popular subjects depicted on vanes: a large gilt eagle vane was placed at Aachen by Charlemagne; a dragon weathervane (c. 1202), thought to be of Norse origin, was set on the church in Ghent; a large weathercock was placed on Old St Paul's Cathedral in London by 1240. In Spain a 4.2 m-high bronze figure vane of Faith was placed on Seville Cathedral in 1568, and in Granada a vane in the form of an armed Moor was set on the Casa del Gallo. In Italy a banner-shaped vane was installed in the 11th century on S Marco, Venice, and an angel vane was installed at an early date on the cathedral in Milan. In England a grasshopper vane was installed at the first Royal Exchange in London in 1570. Christopher Wren used vanes in his architecture, such as the one in the form of an emblazoned key at St Peter-upon-Cornhill, London. Inigo Jones preferred pointer-type vanes, although the swan at the church of St Paul's, Covent Garden, London, is ascribed to him. During the 18th century vanes were of such diverse shapes as barques or fish. In the USA, banner-shaped vanes and weathercocks were used in the 17th century; there exists a 1656 Dutch imported vane at the First Church, Albany, NY. The most famous American vane is the grasshopper on Faneuil Hall, Boston, MA, made in 1749 by Shem Drowne (1683–?1750), which was modelled after the Royal Exchange vane (*see* UNITED STATES OF AMERICA, fig. 52). An important 19th-century weathervane in the form of Diana by Augustus Saint-Gaudens was 3.9 m high, made of hammered copper and designed for Madison Square Garden, New York. During the second half of the 19th century weathervanes were usually mass produced in factories and became widely available.

BIBLIOGRAPHY

R. Plantagenet: 'La Girouatte', *A. Déc.*, xxii (Dec 1909), pp. 185–92
J. Gardner: *English Ironwork of the XVIIth & XVIIIth Centuries* (London, 1911)
A. Needham: *English Weather Vanes* (Haywards Heath, 1953)
K. Fitzgerald: *Weather Vanes and Whirligigs* (New York, 1967)
C. Klamkin: *Weathervanes: The History, Design and Manufacture of an American Folk Art* (New York, 1973)

CHARLES J. SEMOWICH

Webb, Sir **Aston** (*b* Clapham, London, 22 May 1849; *d* London, 21 Aug 1930). English architect. After attending school in Brighton, he was articled for five years from 1866 with Banks & Barry, London, while also attending classes at the Architectural Association. He established his own practice in 1873 and was soon joined by Edward Ingress Bell (1836–1914), whose precise role in the partnership has always been a slight mystery. Their first large venture came with their successful competition design of 1885 for the Victoria Law Courts in Birmingham: a structure clad in terracotta, with rich detailing, completed in 1891. There followed a number of smaller works in London: 23 Austin Friars; 13–15 Moorgate (1890–93), in a Franco-Flemish style; the French Protestant Church, Soho Square (1891–3); and the Royal United Services Institution, Whitehall (1893–5), with its cherubic figures by William Silver Frith (1850–1924). In 1890 Webb began a major restoration of the church of St Bartholomew-the-Great, Smithfield, and built one of his few residential works, referred to by Nikolaus Pevsner as the 'astonishing Jacobean fantasy', Yeaton-Peverey House (1890–92), near Shrewsbury, Salop. Webb also contributed three major buildings in South Kensington, London. The first, won in an invited competition (1891), was for a major addition to the Victoria and Albert Museum with a façade to Cromwell Road. With this design, Webb stretched his talent for mixing Renaissance styles to its limit, creating a skyline broken by pavilion domes, campaniles and, at the centre of the principal façade, a column-tiered tower supporting an open crown. Webb's other two buildings in South Kensington, the Chemistry and Physics Building (1898–1906; destr.) for the Royal College of Science and Technology and the Royal School of Mines (1908–13), Prince Consort Road, were very much in the restrained French classicism of the late 18th century admired in the Edwardian period.

Major works outside London included the school community of Christ's Hospital (1893–1902), created in the countryside near Horsham, W. Sussex. Built in red brick in the Jacobean style, the school has an immense central quadrangle enclosed by the chapel, dining and school halls, with colonnades on the east and west sides. In contrast, Webb's Britannia Royal Naval College (1897–1905) is prominently sited above the town of Dartmouth, Devon, like a palatial English Baroque country house. In 1901 Webb & Bell embarked upon a grand Beaux-Arts scheme for Birmingham University, where long, red-brick buildings of a distinctly Moorish silhouette were intended to radiate in a semicircular formation from the central axis of a tall minaret clock tower. By 1909 the first stage of development was complete; the second phase began after World War I but the Beaux-Arts plan was then abandoned.

One of Webb's most prominent urban-planning schemes in London was the Queen Victoria Memorial Scheme, won in limited competition in 1901, in which he widened and replanted the Mall in the fashion of a Parisian boulevard. At one end Webb erected Admiralty Arch (1903–9), with curving wings, which cleverly hides the bend into Charing Cross. At the other end of the Mall stands Buckingham Palace; there in 1912–13 Webb refaced Edward Blore's weakly designed frontage of 1847–50 in the French classical style of Louis XVI, an appropriate backdrop to the *rond-point* that swirls about Thomas Brock's great memorial sculpture to *Queen Victoria*. Webb was reputed to have had the largest architectural practice in Britain during the Edwardian period. He also received commissions abroad; his Law Courts (1903) in Hong Kong, for example, exemplify the ideals of Empire that were embodied in much of his architecture. Webb was President of the RIBA (1902–4) and of the Royal Academy (1919–24), and he was knighted in 1904; he received the Royal Gold Medal for Architecture in 1905 and the American Gold Medal in 1907.

BIBLIOGRAPHY

DNB

W. Lucas: 'The Architecture of Sir Aston Webb PRA', *Bldg News*, cxviii (1920), pp. 63–4

Obituary, *Architect & Bldg News*, cxxiv (1930), p. 261; *RIBA J.*, xxxvii (1930), pp. 710–11, 744

N. Pevsner: *Shropshire*, Bldgs Eng. (Harmondsworth, 1958), p. 331

A. Service: *Edwardian Architecture* (London, 1977)

A. S. Gray: *Edwardian Architecture: A Biographical Dictionary* (London, 1985)

NEIL R. BINGHAM

Webb, Boyd (*b* Christchurch, 3 July 1947). New Zealand photographer. He studied at the Ilam School of Art in Christchurch (1968–71) and from 1972 to 1975 at the Royal College of Art in London, where he settled. Though trained as a sculptor, he chose to work with photography, concentrating at first on realistic scenes with curious details and odd juxtapositions of objects. He developed his mature style in the 1980s, creating purely theatrical and artificial images from constructed sets and actors, without resorting to trick photographic techniques. Works such as *Renounce* (1984; Sydney, A.G. NSW), with their incongruous objects and bizarre setting, are designed to puzzle the viewer, so demanding further reflection.

BIBLIOGRAPHY

Boyd Webb (exh. cat., essay S. Morgan, London, Whitechapel A.G., 1987)

Webb, Charles (*b* Sudbury, Suffolk, 26 Nov 1821; *d* Melbourne, 9 Aug 1898). Australian architect of English birth. He worked in London for the English architect and illustrator Thomas Allom (1804–72). In 1849 he emigrated to Melbourne and entered a partnership as architect and surveyor with his brother James, who was already established in business as a local builder. Their first prominent commission was St Paul's church in the centre of Melbourne (1850), subsequently replaced by Butterfield's Cathedral. The partnership ended in 1854, when James went to England, and Webb practised for four years in partnership with Thomas Taylor. His design for St Andrew's church, Brighton, Melbourne (1856–7), shows unmistakable characteristics of buildings that he had sketched before leaving England. Melbourne Grammar School (1856) is the most important building of this phase, designed in the dark local bluestone, but Tudor in character. Webb's work is difficult to characterize. It includes two important terrace rows of houses, Burlington Terrace (1866–71) and Parliament Place (1878–87; now Tasma), both in Brighton, and Mandeville Hall, Toorak (1877), which is fully decorated and furnished by Gillows of London. His municipal buildings include the Royal Arcade (1869) and Grand Hotel (1883–8; now Windsor Hotel).

His churches were mainly Gothic Revival, his schools and institutions were usually mock-Tudor, and his houses, hotels, warehouses and shops were Italianate or otherwise Renaissance-derived.

AUDB

BIBLIOGRAPHY

J. Denton and B. Marshall: *Charles Webb: Early Melbourne Architect* (diss., U. Melbourne, 1967)

C. Bridges-Webb: 'Charles Webb (1821–98)', *Vict. Hist. Mag.*, xli (1970), pp. 396–423

MILES LEWIS

Webb, John (i) (*b* Little Britain, London, 1611; *d* Butleigh, Somerset, 30 Oct 1672). English architect. The son of a gentleman, he was sent to Merchant Taylors' school in the City of London and while still in his teens he became a pupil of Inigo Jones (whose relative—the daughter of a first cousin, it seems—he subsequently married). Throughout the 1630s he gained wide experience in mechanics, the fine arts and architectural design by assisting with Jones's most ambitious masques and in his remodelling of St Paul's Cathedral. In effect, Webb was Jones's clerk and draughtsman for jobs outside the scope of the Office of Works; his first independent designs, most notably a projected villa-like lodge at Hale, Hants, date from 1638. Webb's preoccupation during the Civil War was architectural design: numerous annotated drawings of the orders, of house plans, of designs for churches, and of details for windows and doorways constitute a thorough survey of classical architectural vocabulary, even if they do not amount to the full illustrated text of a projected treatise. The reconstruction drawings (probably under Jones's guidance) that he made during this time of the various types of ancient house give a particularly impressive indication of his study of Renaissance treatises.

The Civil War badly disrupted the development of Webb's career. He was active on the royalist side and in contact with the imprisoned Charles I, presenting him in 1647 with a design (Chatsworth, Derbys) for a new Whitehall Palace in London. In 1649, however, Philip Herbert, 4th Earl of Pembroke (a convinced Parliamentarian), employed Webb to design a palatial London mansion (unexecuted; Oxford, Worcester Coll.), as well as to re-create his fire-damaged state rooms at Wilton House in Wiltshire (*see* WILTON, §1). Like Pembroke, Webb also may have transferred his political allegiance. His patrons in the 1650s included the Parliamentary general, Thomas, Lord Fairfax (1612–71), and Colonel Edmund Ludlow (?1617–92) of Maiden Bradley, Wilts, as well as others active in Parliament during that decade, notably Chaloner Chute (*c.* 1630–1659) of the Vyne, Hants, and Sir John Maynard of Gunnersbury, Middx (1602–90; *see* VILLA, fig. 7). This did not prevent Webb working for royalists too: he rebuilt the seat of John Manners, 8th Earl of Rutland (1604–79), Belvoir Castle, Leics, following damage sustained in the war, and added to Lamport Hall, Northants, for Sir Justinian Isham (1610–74). But Webb's apparent pragmatism may have contributed to his greatest disappointment when, following the Restoration, he was not appointed Jones's successor as Surveyor of the Works. His two most important buildings of the 1650s have both been destroyed: Gunnersbury House, Middx (*c.* 1658), his most strongly Palladian house, and his only public building,

the block for the College of Physicians in the City. This was destroyed in the Great Fire of 1666 and is known only from Webb's preliminary designs of 1651 (Oxford, Worcester Coll.). It included a library, which, in its spaciousness and diffused lighting, may have influenced Christopher Wren's great library at Trinity College, Cambridge.

In 1660 Webb was passed over for the Surveyorship in favour of the amateur Sir John Denham (1615–69), a poet and royalist with no practical experience of building. On Denham's death in 1669 the place eluded him again, this time because Charles II chose to recognize Wren's promising talent. Webb had to be content with whatever royal employment came his way; this was to include the fortifications at Woolwich, the staging of plays and, more particularly, a new royal palace at Greenwich. Webb had been involved with palace design since 1638, when Charles I is recorded as having first pursued seriously the idea of rebuilding the Tudor palace of Whitehall to a new design that would incorporate Jones's Banqueting House. At this stage Jones must have been the designer, but at least five different schemes (Oxford, Worcester Coll., and Chatsworth, Derbys), all drawn by Webb, figure in the numerous surviving designs. Finally, in 1661 Webb made a group of designs (unexecuted; Chatsworth, Derbys) for a much more compact palace; here the Banqueting House was balanced by a chapel and together they flanked an entrance carrying a monumental portico.

At Greenwich Palace (*see* GREENWICH, §1) from *c.* 1661 Webb developed this last idea. His scheme was for a palace in three ranges around an open-ended courtyard facing the Thames. The centre range was to have had a giant central portico with a dome over it. Such a Baroque ensemble was without precedent in England; its closest parallel was Louis Le Vau's contemporary Collège des Quatre Nations in Paris. However, at Greenwich only the shell of the west range (the surviving King Charles block) was built. This employs a giant order, with smooth shafts set against boldly rusticated walling, and windows crowned by dramatically emphasized voussoirs. Webb had already added a giant portico, the first in England, to the Vyne in 1654–5, and rustication was a feature of his most tautly composed house, Amesbury, Wilts (*c.* 1661); but the large-scale elements and strongly textured walls of the King Charles block show a decisive break with Jones's style.

Webb's contribution to interior decoration is also important. His state rooms at Wilton are by far the best surviving indication of Jones's idiom, but his unrealized drawings for the interiors at Greenwich (London, RIBA Lib.) show interesting developments. The ceiling designs are not beam patterns after Jones, but free-flowing scrolls of flowers and foliage, clearly foreshadowing the virtuoso plasterwork typical of the 1670s and 1680s. Similarly, naturalistic wood-carving is indicated in his designs for the friezes and swags, a foretaste of the later style of work by Grinling Gibbons and others.

One of the most characteristic features of Webb's architecture, doubtless inspired by Jones, is his use of composed capitals. Only at Greenwich did he use a conventional order. The fluted capitals on the portico at the Vyne and for the College of Physicians derive from an antique marble then in the 2nd Earl of Arundel's collection; but most of the fanciful capitals on the overmantels at Wilton are from heraldic sources. Webb went so far as to prepare a 'Book of Capitals' (Chatsworth, Derbys), probably intended for publication, in which he recorded all the capitals for the buildings designed by him between 1649 and *c.* 1658.

In 1655 Webb edited and published Jones's theories on Stonehenge in *The Most Notable Antiquity Called Stone-Heng*. Jones's hypothesis that it was a Roman temple of the Tuscan order was subsequently challenged by Dr William Charleton in *Chorea gigantum* (1663), and Webb returned to the fray two years later with *A Vindication of Stone-Heng Restored*. Webb's efforts to preserve Jones's books and drawings helped to preserve his own, for until the present century no clear distinction between their work was made. (In 18th-century publications many of his drawings appear as by Jones.) Thus, despite the destruction of many of his buildings, Webb's architectural achievements can still be ascertained, revealing him to have been a creative link between Inigo Jones and the broad and varied tradition of subsequent English classical architecture.

WRITINGS
ed.: *The Most Notable Antiquity Called Stone-Heng* (London, 1655)
A Vindication of Stone-Heng Restored (London, 1665)

BIBLIOGRAPHY
Colvin
W. Kent: *Designs of Inigo Jones*, 2 vols (London, 1727, 2/1770/*R* 1965) [all designs attrib. to Jones are either by Webb or drawn by him]
H. A. Tipping: 'The Vyne, Hampshire, II', *Country Life*, xlix (21 May 1921), pp. 612–19
M. D. Whinney: 'Some Church Designs by John Webb', *J. Warb. & Court. Inst.*, vi (1943), pp. 142–50
——: 'John Webb's Drawings for Whitehall Palace', *Walpole Soc.*, xxxi (1946), pp. 45–107
O. Hill and J. Cornforth: *English Country Houses: Caroline* (London, 1966), pp. 75–87 [Wilton]
C. E. Newman: 'The First Library of the Royal College of Physicians', *J. Royal Coll. Phys.*, iii/3 (1969), pp. 209–307
J. Harris: *Catalogue of the Drawings Collection in the RIBA: Inigo Jones and John Webb* (Farnborough, 1973)
J. Harris and A. A. Tait: *Catalogue of the Drawings by Inigo Jones, John Webb & Isaac de Caus at Worcester College, Oxford* (Oxford, 1979)
A. Pritchard: 'A Source for the Lives of Inigo Jones and John Webb', *Archit. Hist.*, xxiii (1980), pp. 138–40
J. Bold: 'John Webb: Composite Capitals and the Chinese Language', *Oxford A. J.*, iv/1 (1981), pp. 9–17
E. Eisenthal: 'John Webb's Reconstruction of the Ancient House', *Archit. Hist.*, xxviii (1985), pp. 7–31
J. Bold: *John Webb's Architectural Theory and Practice in the Seventeenth Century* (Oxford, 1989)

JOHN NEWMAN

Webb, John (ii) (*b* Odstock, Wilts, 28 March 1776; *d* Hay-on-Wye, 18 Feb 1869). English priest and historian. He was educated at St Paul's School, London, and Wadham College, Oxford. He studied both Latin and Norman French and became one of the leading palaeographers of his time, much in demand to read and interpret early documents in courts of law. He had been a friend since boyhood of Sir Henry Ellis, Librarian of the British Museum, and was one of a group of scholars associated with the Camden Society and the Society of Antiquaries of London, to which he was elected in 1819. His various historical studies included works on Gloucester, including an essay on the Cathedral, published in 1829. Many of his shorter papers were published in *Archaeologia*; he also edited a number of manuscripts, especially on antiquities in Gloucestershire and Herefordshire, which were published by the Camden Society. He was responsible in 1856 for the rebuilding of St Mary's, Tretire, near Ross-on-Wye, of which he was rector. The family papers, noted in the early 20th century as being in the family home at Odstock, are no longer traceable, but some of Webb's notes are preserved in the City Library, Hereford.

WRITINGS
'An Essay on the Abbey of Gloucester', *History and Antiquities of Gloucester Cathedral*, ed. J. Britton (Chiswick, Middx, 1829)

BIBLIOGRAPHY
DNB
Obituary, *The Athenaeum* (6 March 1869), pp. 344–5

DAVID CAST

Webb, Philip [Phillippe] **(Speakman)** (*b* Oxford, 12 Jan 1831; *d* Worth, W. Sussex, 17 April 1915). English architect and designer. He was articled from 1849 to 1852 to the architect John Billing (1818–63) of Reading. Billing retained him as assistant until 1854 when Webb joined the firm of Bidlake & Lovatt in Wolverhampton. Appalled by the effects of heavy industry in that city, he left after four weeks, returning to Oxford to work for G. E. Street. In 1856, while working as Street's chief clerk, he was made responsible for a new pupil, William Morris, with whom he formed a close friendship. (It was to be Webb who, when Morris died in 1896, designed his tomb (Kelmscott, Oxon, St George) after a Viking ridged tomb-house.) Later that year Webb and Morris moved with Street to London, where both became closely involved with the Pre-Raphaelite circle. This group and its patrons provided Webb with a steady supply of clients after 1859 when he set up his own practice, his first commission being the design for Morris's new home, Red House (1859), Bexleyheath, Kent. Webb's output was small because, following Street's example but lacking his speed, he designed every detail himself. He lived and worked in Gray's Inn, London, and employed only a couple of assistants.

In 1861 Webb was a founding partner of Morris, Marshall, Faulkner & Co., whose formation was largely the result of Morris and his friends collaborating on the decoration of Red House; Webb was chiefly responsible for its success until reorganization in 1875. He helped with its management, secured clients, designed fireplaces and panelling for domestic interiors, most of the firm's furniture (*see* MORRIS, WILLIAM) and several other products including stained glass. His sideboards and tables of the late 1860s and 1870s were to have a strong influence on Arts and Crafts furniture.

Webb rejected Greek Revival architecture as unsuited to England's climate and light, and he saw no prospect of good building developing from a Gothic revival, convinced as he was by John Ruskin's view that commercialism had degraded architecture by suppressing the individual craftsman's creative spirit, the very quality that was perceived to have made medieval buildings great. Webb developed a philosophy of design that excluded historicism, yet was in tune with tradition. Common sense decreed a convenient plan, suitable orientation, well-lit rooms with spatial variety, modern amenities, the use of technological improvements such as sash windows and iron beams, first-class craftsmanship and the avoidance of fashionable or

Philip Webb: south front of Standen, East Grinstead, W. Sussex, 1891

symbolic features. Believing that ideas come from experience, and that it was his duty to give buildings an English character and to fit them unobtrusively into the landscape, he sought inspiration in vernacular architecture, which, aristocractic and humble alike, pre-dated the introduction of the Palladian style. As a basis for his major projects, Webb used ancient building types in place of specific styles. Three of his finest houses are all examples of this: a quadrangular castle with corner towers (1872; destr. 1954) at Rounton Grange, East Rounton, N. Yorks; a Border peel-tower (1876) at Four Gables, Brampton, Cumbria, and a fortified house (1891) at Standen, East Grinstead, W. Sussex. Fitting each building into its site, using local materials (where he paid great attention to colour) and traditional forms, giving all elevations equal importance and relating all details to one another, created what Webb termed a consistent whole, harmonious with its surroundings. In 19 Lincoln's Inn Fields (1868), London, and Smeaton Manor (1876), Great Smeaton, N. Yorks, he proved that, in both town and country, great individuality was possible within this approach.

Webb's first three houses, Red House, Sandroyd (now Benfleet) Hall (1860), Cobham, Surrey, and Arisaig House (1863; rebuilt), Highland—of which the first was later cited as a source for that antithesis of his philosophy, the modern movement—reflect the designs of schools and parsonages by Street and William Butterfield. Red House, so-named for its red bricks and tiles, is an accomplished

essay in this manner, with an L-plan similar to that of Butterfield's Alvechurch rectory (1855), Hereford & Worcs. The north wing included a dining-room and accommodation for bachelor friends on the ground-floor, and on the first floor a studio and drawing-room; services and bedrooms were in the west range. Gothic in spirit rather than to the letter, Red House was given deep porches, steep roofs, sash windows set into pointed arches and, within, red-brick fireplaces and arches, and some exposed roof timbers. By 1868 Webb's approach had matured: Red Barns, Redcar, Cleveland, and West House, Chelsea, London, demonstrate this with their simply modelled wall-planes and sophisticated interior finishes. Some early buildings were, like Red House, studio houses for artists, a new type for a new class of owner. One of these, 1 Palace Green (1868), Kensington, London, was to be used as a source for the Queen Anne style—a style dismissed by Webb as a dilettante fashion. Others, notably Oast House (1872), Hayes Common, Middx, and Coneyhurst (1883), Ewhurst, Surrey, were prototypes for another new category, the smaller country house for middle-class clients. All but the first of his large country houses have Webb's three-division arrangement (family block to the west, major offices in the centre, and single-storey minor offices round a kitchen yard at the east end), such as his largest house, Clouds (1880), East Knoyle, Wilts, and Standen (see fig.). Both Standen and Smeaton Manor, with their greater emphasis on axes, and their north entrance courts and north-facing service rooms separated from major rooms to the south by a cross-passage, reveal Webb's interest in John Vanbrugh's planning: Castle Howard, N. Yorks, for example, where Webb did some minor work in 1872. Philip Webb's most important non-domestic buildings were St Martin's Church (1874), Brampton, Cumbria, and Bell Brothers' Offices (designed 1883; executed 1889–91), Middlesbrough.

In 1883, believing that a revival of art would follow social change, Webb became a socialist; his political activities were to help Morris give art a place in socialist theory. Webb never published his views on architecture or illustrations of his buildings, nor were any pupils articled to him, but his work became widely known to architects in London and, in the 1890s, to students. For many young architects the Society for the Protection of Ancient Buildings (SPAB), founded by Morris in 1877, became a school of building with Webb as its tutor. The methods of repair Webb developed for the SPAB and his private preservation of buildings such as Forthampton Court (1889), Tewkesbury, made him one of the most important of early conservationists. His views on architecture spread to the London County Council architects' department and to practices throughout the country, as well as to the garden city and suburb developments that influenced most council housing schemes. In January 1901 Webb retired to a rented cottage at Worth, Sussex, but his disciples, who included Edwin Lutyens, continued to reap the benefit of his national vernacular approach in their inventive English houses (built between 1880 and 1914), which were so admired and influential in Germany and the USA.

DNB

BIBLIOGRAPHY

G. L. Morris: 'On Philip Webb's Town Work', *Archit. Rev.* [London], ii (1897), pp. 198–208

G. Jack: 'An Appreciation of Philip Webb', *Archit. Rev.* [London], xxxviii (1915), pp. 1–6

W. R. Lethaby: *Philip Webb and his Work* (London, 1935/*R* 1979)

J. Brandon-Jones: 'The Work of Philip Webb and Norman Shaw', *Archit. Assoc. J.*, lxxi (1955), pp. 9–21, 40–47

——: 'Philip Webb', *Victorian Architecture*, ed. P. Ferriday (London, 1963), pp. 247–64

A. C. Sewter: *The Stained Glass of William Morris and his Circle*, 2 vols (London, 1974–5)

J. Brandon-Jones: 'The Importance of Philip Webb', *William Morris & Kelmscott* (London, 1981), pp. 87–92

H. Smith: 'Philip Webb's Restoration of Forthampton Court Gloucestershire', *Archit. Hist.*, xxiv (1981), pp. 92–102, pl. 35

R. Spence: 'Theory and Practice in the Early Work of the Society for the Protection of Ancient Buildings', *A School for Rational Builders* (London, 1982), pp. 5–9

J. Brandon-Jones: 'Arts and Crafts', *Archit. J.* (Dec 1984) [supplement]

R. Curry and S. Kirk: *Philip Webb in the North* (Middlesbrough, 1984)

RIBA Drawings Collection: T–Z (Amersham, 1984)

Philip Webb in the North (exh. cat. by R. Curry and S. Kirk, RIBA N. Reg., Teesside Branch)

S. Kirk: 'Webb's Wonder', *Bldg Des.* (18 Aug 1986), pp. 12–13

M. McEvoy: 'Webb at Brampton', *Archit. J.*, cxc (25 Oct 1989), pp. 40–51, 56–63

E. Hollamby: *Red House, Bexleyheath, 1859, Philip Webb* (London, 1991)

C. Dakers: *Clouds: The Biography of a House* (New Haven and London, 1993)

O. Garnett, ed.: *Standen*, National Trust (London, 1993)

S. Kirk: *Philip Webb: Domestic Architecture*, (diss., U. Newcastle upon Tyne, 1990)

——: *Philip Webb: Life and Work* (in preparation)

SHEILA KIRK

Webb, Thomas, & Sons. English glass company, near Stourbridge, W. Midlands. In 1835 Thomas Webb (1802–69) inherited the White House glassworks from his father, John Webb (1774–1835). The following year he withdrew from the partnership of Webb & Richardson, which operated the Wordsley Flint glassworks near Stourbridge, to devote his attention to the White House glassworks. He then withdrew from Thomas Webb & Co., which operated the White House glassworks, to set up his own firm Thomas Webb & Sons, which operated the Platts glasshouse from 1837 to 1856 and then the Dennis glassworks, built in 1855 at Dennis Hall, Amblecote, near Stourbridge. In 1863 Thomas Webb retired and was succeeded by his sons Thomas Wilkes Webb (1837–91) and Charles Webb. During the 1860s the firm played an important role in the development of English glass. Their Artistic Director James O'Fallon was an engraver who excelled in Celtic-style ornament. The most distinguished engraver at the Dennis glassworks was the Bohemian Frederick Kny who engraved the Elgin jug (1879; London, V&A) and in the 1880s pioneered rock-crystal engraving with his fellow-countryman William Fritsche (1853–1924).

In the mid-1870s Thomas Wilkes Webb commissioned the glassmaker John Northwood (1836–1902) to decorate a cameo glass called the 'Pegasus' vase. It was completed in 1882 and is decorated with a frieze depicting Neptune and Amphitrite and a winged-horse finial (Washington, DC, N. Mus. Amer. A., Gallately Col., on permanent loan to Washington, DC, N. Mus. Amer. Hist.). The cameo workshops expanded rapidly under Thomas Woodall (1849–1926) and George Woodall (1850–1925), who had been trained at the firm of J. & J. Northwood. Wares were wheel-engraved, and the technique of acid-etching was increasingly used. The classical-figure style was superseded by floral decoration. However, the quality of cameo work declined, and the department closed *c.* 1906. During the 1880s the range of glassware expanded and came to include the production of such art glass as 'Queen's Burmese' glass, which was based on the 'Burmese' glass developed by the Mount Washington Glass Works in the USA, 'Peach' glass and 'Bronze' glass, which was the company's patented iridescent glass. In 1919 the Dennis glassworks were acquired by the newly formed company called Webb's Crystal Glass Co. Ltd, and in 1964 it became part of Crown House Ltd, producing utilitarian household wares.

BIBLIOGRAPHY

H. W. Woodward: *Art, Feat and Mystery: The Story of Thomas Webb & Sons, Glassmakers* (Stourbridge, 1978)

R. J. Charleston: *English Glass and the Glass Used in England, c. 400–1940* (London, 1984)

K. SOMERVELL

Webber, John (*b* London, 6 Oct 1751; *d* London, 29 April 1793). English painter of Swiss descent. He was the son of the Swiss sculptor Abraham Wäber, who had moved to London in the early 1740s. In 1757 Webber was sent to Berne for his education: from 1767 to 1770 he was apprenticed to the landscape painter and printmaker Johann Ludwig Aberli, who specialized in mountain and lake views, executed in delicate watercolour and grey wash. From 1770 Webber studied at the Académie Royale in Paris, where he learnt to paint in oil (e.g. *Portrait of a*

Sculptor, early 1770s; Berne, Kstmus.). In 1773 and 1774 he toured the countryside around Paris with the engraver Jean Georges Wille, making chalk sketches of picturesque hovels in a hatched, fussy style. Webber's rural landscapes of this period frequently include a genre element, as can be seen in the pen, brush and watercolour drawing of *An Amorous Encounter at a Well* (1773; Frankfurt am Main, Städel. Kstinst.); this awareness of human incident was to be an important element of his subsequent work.

In 1775 Webber returned to London and entered the Royal Academy Schools. His oil *Portrait of an Artist* (1776) impressed Daniel Carl Solander, an associate of Captain James Cook; as a result, from 1776 to 1780 Webber was the official artist on Cook's third voyage in the *Resolution*, which aimed to find a passage around the north of America. Webber was charged with recording 'everything that was curious' and made drawings on all stages of the voyage. The *Resolution* visited the Cape of Good Hope, Tasmania and New Zealand; Cook's expedition spent a year in the South Pacific before sailing west and discovering the Sandwich Islands (now Hawaii). The voyage continued up the west coast of America as far north as Icy Cape before returning to the Sandwich Islands, where Cook was killed by natives, and thence back to London. Webber made detailed sketches and drawings, using either pencil or pen and black wash; he provided accurate coastal profiles for navigation and portrayed the landscape, weather conditions and vegetation that he encountered, as well as recording the customs, houses, artefacts and appearance of native peoples (North American and Pacific) long since extinct or changed beyond recognition (e.g. *Nootka Sound on the Pacific Coast of North America*, London, BM; see fig.). He witnessed Cook's murder, and his painting of the event was engraved by William Byrne (1743–1805) and Francesco Bartolozzi in 1784.

Following his return to England in 1780, Webber made finished drawings and oversaw their engraving for the official account of Cook's expedition. Until its publication in 1784 Webber's material was classified, but afterwards he made full use of subjects from Cook's voyage in his oils and other media. In finished watercolours, such as *A View in Vaitepiha Valley* (London, BL), he emphasized the lush and peaceful beauty of the Pacific. His watercolour palette—light yellow, green, pink and blue, underpinned by grey wash shadow—gives his tropical scenes a Rococo delicacy. A judicious collection of Pacific artefacts gathered on the voyage, for example the feather cloak that appears in the *Death of Captain Cook*, was an aid to his inspiration; his ethnographic collection was bequeathed to the library of Berne.

In 1785, the year that he was elected ARA, Webber collaborated with Philippe Jacques de Loutherbourg on costumes and stage scenery for *Omai*, a Covent Garden pantomime based on Cook's voyage. In 1786–7 he made etchings of South Seas views that were more atmospheric and aimed at a less specialized audience than the illustrations to Cook's *Voyage*; these were aquatinted by Marie Katharina Prestel. Between 1788 and 1792 he produced more South Seas views, this time using the new technique of softground etching (proofs at New Haven, CT, Yale Cent. Brit. A.). These were aquatinted, hand-coloured and

John Webber: *Nootka Sound on the Pacific Coast of North America* (London, British Museum)

published by John Boydell (with an accompanying text) as *Views in the South Seas*.

In 1786 Webber toured the west of England and the following year journeyed through France, Switzerland and Italy. In 1788 he was in south Wales and the year after in Derbyshire with William Day (1764–1807), an amateur artist and geologist whose work Webber greatly influenced. *Landscape with Rocks in Derbyshire* (New Haven, CT, Yale Cent. Brit. A.) shows the habits of minute observation that Webber had developed on Cook's voyages applied to rock forms. The subdued palette of grey and blue washes typical of Webber nevertheless conveys the romantic, unpeopled grandeur of the subject. Webber was again in Wales in 1790 and 1791; from the evidence of drawings, he also visited the Lake District and the Isle of Wight. Throughout his career he painted occasional portraits in oils, including a sensitive portrait of *Capt. James Cook* (1782; Australian priv. col.; another at Hull, Trinity House) and *An African Boy* (1792; Berne, Hist. Mus.). He first exhibited British views at the Royal Academy in 1790; the following year he was elected RA. His wide circle of artistic friends included the watercolour painters Thomas Hearne and Joseph Farington. The contents of his estate were auctioned at Christie's, London, on 14–16 June 1793.

PRINTS
J. Cook: *A Voyage to the Pacific Ocean* (London, 1784)
Views in the South Seas (London, 1808)

BIBLIOGRAPHY
O. Warner: 'John Webber', *Apollo*, lvi (1952), pp. 84–6
B. Smith: *European Vision and the South Pacific, 1768–1850* (Oxford, 1960)

M. Hardie: *The Eighteenth Century* (1966), i of *Water-colour Painting in Britain* (London, 1966–8), pp. 235–6
A. Murray-Oliver: *Captain Cook's Artists in the Pacific, 1769–1779* (Christchurch, 1969)
B. Smith: 'Captain Cook's Artists and the Portrayal of Pacific People', *Art History*, vii (1984), pp. 295–312
R. Joppien and B. Smith: *The Voyage of the Resolution and the Discovery* (1988), iii of *The Art of Captain Cook's Voyages* (New Haven and London, 1987–)

SUSAN MORRIS

Weber, Antal (*b* Pest [now Budapest], 9 Oct 1823; *d* Budapest, 4 Aug 1889). Hungarian architect. He studied at the Akademie der Bildenden Künste, Vienna. His early works include the remodelling (*c.* 1860) of the country house of the Esterházy family at Galánta (now Galanta, Slovakia) and a country house (completed 1862) for Count István Erdődy at Vörösvár (now Rotenturm, Austria), which displays oriental and Venetian motifs and has a massive tower as at Galánta. After the late 1860s Weber was active in Budapest and designed buildings in an eclectic style combining Hellenistic and Italian Renaissance themes. The dominant feature of both the headquarters (1874) of the Serbian church and the town house (1875) of Gedeon Halász, both in Budapest, is a colonnaded façade reminiscent of Jacopo Sansovino's Libreria Vecchia di S Marco (1537–54), Venice. Weber's largest public building, the Institute of Biology and Mineralogy (1882–5), Budapest, has a façade with a central row of arches supported by double columns, with pedimented projections on either side.

BIBLIOGRAPHY
E. Ybl: 'Weber Antal', *Épités-és közlekedéstudományi közlemények*, i (1957), pp. 417–42

JÓZSEF SISA

Weber, Bruce (*b* Greenburg, PA, 29 March 1946). American photographer. He studied under Lisette Model and later became a major figure in international fashion photography. His best-known work derives from advertising assignments for the fashion designers Calvin Klein, Ralph Lauren and Karl Lagerfeld, presenting the unique synthesis of an uncompromising personal vision with an interpretation of varied historical influences. His low-angle shots of men in heroic poses recall the images of Aryan youths made in the 1930s, while some of his studio portraits evoke the spirit of classic Hollywood portraiture. His work contains a highly charged eroticism and plays on sexual ambiguity, as for example in his photographic journal *O Rio de Janiero* (New York, 1986).

PHOTOGRAPHIC PUBLICATIONS
Per lui (Milan 1985)

BIBLIOGRAPHY
Bruce Weber Photographs (Pasadena)
J. Cheim, ed.: *Bruce Weber* (New York, 1989)

ALEXANDRA NOBLE

Weber, Lorenzo Maria (*b* Florence, 1697; *d* Florence, ?1765). Italian medallist. One of the most characteristic exponents of Florentine Baroque medallic art, he was apprenticed to Jacopo Mariani and Giovanni Bottari, then studied sculpture under Giovanni Battista Foggini. In 1720 he became a pupil of Massimiliano Soldani, medallist and die-engraver at the Florentine Mint. Grand Duke Cosimo III de' Medici appointed Weber as Soldani's successor (1722), a position he held until late in life. From 1743 to 1749 he made plaquettes, snuff boxes, medals and similar items for the Doccia porcelain manufactory. According to his autobiography (1753) he engraved over 250 coin dies for the mints of Florence and Lucca but, while no coins with his signature have been recorded, most portraits on these 1722–65 coinages are probably by him. In an inventory (1753; Vannel and Toderi) of his medals he records 23 pieces. Others, originating after 1753, can probably be added, such as *Francesco dal Poggio* (1725), *Accession of Francis III of Lorraine* (1739), *Gian Gastone de' Medici* (1732), *Maria Theresa* (1743) and *Peter Leopold, Grand-Duke of Tuscany* (1765). All these pieces are signed, either on obverse or reverse: LMV, occasionally also LAVR.M.VEBERIVS F, or L. M. WEBER. Diameters range up to *c.* 93 mm.

BIBLIOGRAPHY
Forrer; Thieme–Becker
K. Lankheit: *Florentinische Barockplastik* (Munich, 1962), pp. 193–5, 243–4 [Weber's autobiography of 1753]
E. J. Pyke: *A Biographical Dictionary of Wax Modellers* (Oxford, 1973), p. 155, fig. 297
The Twilight of the Medici: Late Baroque Art in Florence, 1670–1743 (exh. cat. by S. F. Rossen, Detroit, MI, Inst. A.; Florence, Pitti; 1974), pp. 150–53
A. S. Norris and I. Weber: *Medals and Plaquettes from the Molinari Collection at Bowdoin College* (Brunswick, ME, 1976), pp. 48–50
V. Johnson: *Dieci anni di studi di medaglistica* (Milan, 1979), p. 129
F. Vannel and G. Toderi: *La medaglia barocca in Toscana* (Florence, 1987), pp. 237–50

MARK M. SALTON

Weber, Max (*b* Belostok, Russia [now Białystok, Poland], 18 April 1881; *d* Great Neck, NY, 4 Oct 1961). American painter, printmaker, sculptor and writer. He was born of Orthodox Jewish parents and in 1891 emigrated with his family to America. After settling in Brooklyn, NY, Weber attended the Pratt Institute (1898–1900), where he studied art theory and design under Arthur Wesley Dow (1857–1922). Dow's extensive knowledge of European and Far Eastern art history, together with his theories of composition, made a lasting impression on Weber. Weber was in Paris from 1905 to 1908 and studied briefly at the Académie Julian. He developed a close friendship with Henri Rousseau and helped to organize a class with Henri Matisse as its instructor. Visits to the ethnographic collections in the Trocadéro and other Parisian museums extended his sensitivity to non-Western art, while travels through Spain, Italy and the Netherlands broadened his knowledge of the Old Masters.

For several years following his return to America in January 1909, Weber's art consisted largely of still-lifes and nudes in the landscape which gave strong evidence of his assimilation of Matisse's theories of decorative harmony and the primitivism evident in the work of Pablo Picasso. By 1910 Weber was contributing articles on art and colour theory to Alfred Stieglitz's pioneering journal, *Camera Work*, and in that year arranged the first one-man show of the work of Henri Rousseau in the USA at Stieglitz's 291 Gallery. Stieglitz was one of the first to recognize Weber's talent and in 1911 gave him his second one-man exhibition. In 1914 Weber published his first volume of poetry, *Cubist Poems*, which confirmed his interest in Picasso and primitive art. From 1914 to 1918 Weber taught art history and appreciation at Clarence

White's School of Photography, New York, and in 1916 published *Essays on Art*, one of the few theoretical tracts produced by an American modernist. In its emphasis on the importance of instinct in the creation of a work of art and its stress on the spiritual over the material, it reveals Weber's great sympathy for the mystical interpretations of the nature of abstract art advanced by Wassily Kandinsky. Weber's art during these years explored the sights, sounds, rhythms and intensity of the urban environment by using a combination of bold colours, intersecting planes and a kaleidoscopic array of observed and remembered fragments from the urban scene. Such paintings as *Chinese Restaurant* (1915; New York, Whitney) and *Rush Hour, New York* (1915; Washington, DC, N.G.A.; *see* UNITED STATES OF AMERICA, fig. 16) were among the most exciting and advanced work done by an American artist following the Armory Show. During these years Weber also began to explore the possibilities of abstract form in a series of small sculptures that earned him a reputation as a sculptural innovator in the USA. He also turned more towards printmaking and the graphic arts and demonstrated his sympathy for various radical political causes by contributing drawings to such leftist journals as *Revolt* and *Modern School*. His second volume of poetry, *Primitives: Poems and Woodcuts* of 1926, featured a number of woodcuts done during the late 1910s.

In the decade following World War I Weber developed a more expressionistic approach and an interest in narrative themes derived from his Jewish heritage. During the 1920s and 1930s his art became more introspective and conservative, and he turned towards genre subjects, which revealed his renewed interest in the human figure. In the 1940s and 1950s his work became more lyrical, and he turned once again to sculpture.

WRITINGS

'Chinese Dolls and Modern Colorists', *Cam. Work*, 31 (1910), p. 51
'The Fourth Dimension from a Plastic Point of View', *Cam. Work*, 31 (1910), p. 25
'To Xochimilli, Lord of Flowers', *Cam. Work*, 33 (1911), p. 34
Cubist Poems (London, 1914)
Essays on Art (New York, 1916)
Primitives: Poems and Woodcuts (New York, 1926)

BIBLIOGRAPHY

Max Weber Retrospective Exhibition, 1907–1930 (exh. cat., ed. A. H. Barr jr; New York, MOMA, 1930)
Max Weber (exh. cat., ed. L. Goodrich; New York, Whitney, 1949)
S. Leonard: *Henri Rousseau and Max Weber* (New York, 1970)
P. B. North: *Max Weber: The Early Paintings (1905–1920)* (diss., Wilmington, U. DE, 1974)
A. Werner: *Max Weber* (New York, 1975)
D. R. Rubenstein: *Max Weber: A Catalogue Raisonné of his Graphic Work* (Chicago, 1980)
Max Weber: American Modern (exh. cat., ed. P. North; New York, Jew. Mus., 1982)
L. D. Henderson: *The Fourth Dimension and Non-Euclidean Geometry in Modern Art* (Princeton, 1983), pp. 164–82

RUTH L. BOHAN

Webster, Thomas (*b* Pimlico, London, 20 March 1800; *d* Cranbrook, Kent, 23 Sept 1886). English painter. His father, a member of George III's household, had him educated in the Chapel Royal, St James's, as a chorister. However, he showed a strong inclination for painting and in 1820 entered the Royal Academy Schools, London. In 1825 he won the first medal for painting. He became ARA in 1840 and RA in 1846, moving in 1856 to Cranbrook, Kent, where he became the leading figure in the CRANBROOK COLONY of artists.

Webster began as a portrait painter, but, when asked to design a subject picture, he devised a scene of boys attacking a toy doll with a toy cannon that pleased him enough to paint it as *Rebels Shooting a Prisoner* (untraced) and exhibit it at the Society of British Artists in 1825. He produced similar small-scale subject pictures in oil and watercolour with an apparently untroubled consistency and little stylistic development for the rest of his long career.

Webster's *The Boy with many Friends* (exh. RA 1841; Bury, A.G. & Mus.) centres on an apprehensive schoolboy whose receipt of a package of provender and gifts has attracted crowds of his fellows eager to help him rifle through the parcel. It is an interior scene, distinguished, like many of his pictures, for the effects of light streaming in from both the left and the right. Charles Dickens thought Webster so excellent a painter of children that *Squeers School—Dotheboys Hall* (untraced) was painted expressly for the novelist. Webster apparently perceived no brutality in the subject (Mrs Squeers administering brimstone and treacle to the hapless boys), although he preferred gentler themes, and his work tends to an amiable sweetness. *Sickness and Health* (exh. RA 1843; London, V&A) is reminiscent of the pictures of C. R. Leslie, particularly in its bright colour and liquid handling. It shows a young female invalid, seated outside by a cottage door on a sunny day, while her sisters cavort to the sounds of an organ grinder. Although our sympathies are engaged by the poignant contrast, there is no serious moral intended. Instead Webster used the painting to display his skill in rendering expression and in characterizing the features of people of different ages, class and gender. The popular success of such pictures was furthered by engravings made after them.

Webster's best-known picture, *The Village Choir* (1847; London, V&A), was commissioned by the collector John Sheepshanks and illustrates a passage from Washington Irving. Webster represented the confined interior of a church and the varied expressions on the faces of the instrumentalists and choristers in such a way as to elicit a sympathetic and amused response. Unlike such genre painters as David Wilkie or William Mulready, who imbued their subjects with moral complexity, Webster's tales were told directly. To look at Webster's pictures is to observe one of the ways in which the picture-buying public in the 19th century liked to see children, rustics or the poor represented; his work presents a mythic ideal of an England where each person is content in his/her station, and a general benignity appears to reign. The contents of his studio were auctioned at Christie's on 21 May 1887.

DNB

BIBLIOGRAPHY

The Cranbrook Colony (exh. cat. by A. Greg, Wolverhampton, A.G., 1977)
L. Lambourne: *An Introduction to 'Victorian' Genre Painting* (London, 1982)

MICHAEL ROSENTHAL

Wechselburg, Schlosskirche. Former abbey church, *c.* 20 km north-west of Chemnitz, Germany. Count Dedo von Groitzsch (*d* 1190) had the church built for the

Augustinian abbey of Heiligen Kreuz at Zschillen between 1160 and 1180. There was a consecration in 1168, probably only of the east part. From 1278 to 1543 the church belonged to the Teutonic Order and was rededicated to SS Maria und Johannes Evangelista. It is clear from the structure that the church was built in stages from east to west. The five-bay basilica originally had a flat ceiling supported on squat piers. The crossing arches are supported on cruciform piers and the transepts, almost square, have eastern apses; of the south apse only the arch survives. The chancel is slightly rectangular and is closed by a semicircular apse. The northern side apse is incorporated in a two-storey annexe to the chancel, presumably intended as the sacristy. The hall crypt below the chancel, which extended as far as the crossing, was demolished in 1683; the blind arcade in the apse relates to this raised level. The chancel bay was intended from the first to be vaulted.

The westwork survives only as a narrow, two-storey transverse transom with very thick walls projecting at the side. It formerly supported octagonal towers connected by a transverse structure as high as the top free-standing floor, on the Lower Saxon model. The outside of the building is articulated by moulded pilasters and arcade friezes in two tiers around the apse. The crocket capitals both inside and outside the apse are more advanced stylistically than seems possible from the early consecration date. On the north side is a double portal with a two-bay porch, its vault supported on richly decorated columns.

The interior is dominated by the rood screen in the east bay of the nave. Demolished in 1683, its fragments were reassembled in 1972 in its former position. Conceived as a screen incorporating the pulpit, it has a projecting middle section that also forms a ciborium for the altar of the Cross. Above it a large trilobe arch supports the rood *Crucifixion* group, which rises to the apex of the crossing arch. The two-storey chancel-screen wall, the pulpit balustrade and the spandrels of the ciborium have various large relief figures below blind arcades and high-quality architectural decoration. At the centre of the pulpit balustrade *Christ* is shown in a mandorla, surrounded by *Symbols of the Evangelists* and accompanied by the *Virgin* and *St John the Baptist*. To the left of the pulpit is the *Brazen Serpent*, on the right the *Sacrifice of Isaac*. *Cain and Abel* appear in the spandrels of the arch. In the upper row of the rood-screen wall are four Old Testament figures: *Daniel*, *David*, *Solomon* and a prophet (*Isaiah*). In the bottom row *Abraham* and *Melchizedek*, almost life-size, stand directly beside the altar of the Cross and at the same level, being thus related to the sacrifice of the Eucharist. As well as a Crucifix of the three-nail type, the wooden *Crucifixion* group (see fig.) shows the *Virgin* and *St John the Baptist* standing above two crouching kings (representing the subjugation of paganism and Judaism); *God the Father* is shown with the dove in the trefoil above the cross, while the trefoils flanking the latter have two flying angels, and the reawakened *Adam* appears below.

The sculptures of Wechselburg, produced in 1230–35, are closely related to those of the west portal of Freiburg Cathedral and are among the finest in this specifically Saxon/Lower Saxon style. They combine French influences with elements of an indigenous tradition. Byzantine motifs might possibly have been introduced through

Wechselburg, Schlosskirche, view of the rood screen showing the *Crucifixion* group at the centre, *c.* 1230–35

pattern books. Also important is the tomb of *Dedo and Mechthild von Groitzsch* (after 1190), whose reclining figures should be seen in the context of 13th-century Saxon sculpture.

BIBLIOGRAPHY

H. Küas and H.-J. Krause: *Die Stiftskirche zu Wechselburg*, 2 vols, Corpus der romanischen Kunst im sächsisch-thüringischen Gebiet, A/ii (Berlin, 1968)

E. Hütter and H. Magirius: *Der Wechselburger Lettner* (Weimar, 1983)

DETHARD VON WINTERFELD

Wechter, Georg, I (*b* Nuremberg, 1526; *d* Nuremberg, 28 March 1586). German painter, engraver and designer. Although he described himself as a painter, he is best known for his designs for gold and silver. In 1571 he produced a design for the Akeley Cup (Nuremberg, Ger. Nmus.; see fig.), named after and shaped like the bell-flower, which subsequently became a masterpiece for the Nuremberg goldsmiths' guild. His most influential contribution to goldsmithing was his pattern book *30 Stück zum verzachnen für die Goldschmied verfertigt Geörg Wechter 15 Maller 79 Nürnberg* (Nuremberg, 1579; e.g. Berlin, Kupferstichkab.), which offered 30 designs of various types of vessels in forms that came readily within the scope of the competent goldsmith who could not create designs himself. Wechter introduced a new version of low-relief strapwork ornament that contrasted with the popular high-relief strapwork style created in the 1530s at Fontainebleau (*see* STRAPWORK). His designs are characterized by low-relief strapwork composed of interlacing C- and S-curves covering the whole surface of the vessel. His

Georg Wechter I: design for the Akeley Cup, etching, 292×131 mm, 1571 (Nuremberg, Germanisches Nationalmuseum)

followers Bernhard Zan, Jonas Silber and Paul Flindt II used and developed flat, chased strapwork in their work.

BIBLIOGRAPHY
A. Winkler: 'Die Gefuss und Punzenstecher der deutschen Hochrenaiss- ance', *Jb. Kön.-Preuss. Kstsamml.*, xiii (1892), pp. 93–107
J. F. Hayward: *Virtuoso Goldsmiths and the Triumph of Mannerism, 1540– 1620* (London, 1976), pp. 237–8
Renaissance Ornament Prints and Drawings (exh. cat., ed. J. S. Byrne; New York, Met., 1981), pp. 19, 38–9
Wenzel Jamnitzer und die Nürnberger Goldschmiedekunst, 1500–1700 (exh. cat., Nuremberg, Ger. Nmus., 1985)

☐

Wechtlin, Hans [Master of the Crossed Staffs; Pilgrim, Johann Ulrich; Vuechtelin, Johannes] (*b* Strasbourg, *c.* 1480–85; *d* after 1526). German woodcut designer. Documentary evidence about him is sparse. Both his father and grandfather were citizens of Strasbourg. He was recorded in 1505 in Nancy, and in 1506–7 in Witten- berg, where he must have met Lucas Cranach the elder. He was registered as a citizen of Strasbourg on 16 November 1514, being still active there in 1526. A few drawings were formerly attributed to Wechtlin, but these attributions are often contested. Wechtlin's emblem, two crossed pilgrim's staffs, was identified in 1777 by von Murr. Bartsch (1808) considered Wechtlin as the inventor of chiaroscuro print, but this is no longer accepted. Whether Wechtlin cut his own prints is unknown.

The dating of Wechtlin's woodcuts is very hypothetical. Like his Strasbourg contemporary Hans Baldung, he was clearly familiar with the Burgkmair–de Negker chiaroscuro technique. Of the prints generally accepted as Wechtlin's, the majority are religious in theme. Strauss (1973) cata- logues 12 works, all executed between 1510 and 1516, but the Cabinet des Estampes of the Bibliothèque Nationale, Paris, has a further four specimens, the *Adoration of the Magi*, the *Resurrection*, *Christ Appearing to his Mother* and *Christ before Caiaphas*, which were also used by the Strasbourg publisher Johann Knoblouch in illustrated Passion publications of 1506 and 1508. Several of Wecht- lin's religious works, such as *St Christopher*, the *Virgin on a Grassy Bank* and the *Virgin and Child Surrounded by a Renaissance Frame*, have compositions deriving from Dü- rer. The last of these is also known in a version in the Cabinet des Estampes without its frame, and indeed Wechtlin's Renaissance frames could be used in detach- ment: a block appearing in the *Ottonis Phrisigensis rerum ab origine mundi* of 1515 was reused as a book illustration in 1545 by Cammerlander. Likewise, the frame of the *Skull in a Renaissance Frame* was copied by Jacob Köbel of Oppenheim, who used it for a title-page decoration. *Christ on the Cross with the Virgin, St Mary Magdalene and St John* (Paris, Fond. Custodia, Inst. Néer.; see fig.), another woodcut with an ornamental frame, was printed from four separate blocks.

Besides the religious works, there are four Classical pieces: *Orpheus Enchanting the Animals* and *Pyramus and Thisbe* illustrating Ovid, *Alcon of Crete Freeing his Son* taken from Valerius Flaccus' *Argonautica*, and a picture of *Pyrgoteles*, the celebrated cameo-carver of the reign of Alexander the Great. A *Knight and Lansquenet* is another adaptation of Dürer. A woodcut by Wechtlin of *Physicians Attending to a Leper* illustrates Hans von Gersdorf's *Feldbuch der Wandarznei* (pubd Schott, Strasbourg, 1517), but the attribution of other illustrations in this anatomical text is disputed. A design of a pilgrim holding Jean Gerson's coat of arms on the title-page of Gerson's *Prima pars opera* (pubd Knoblouch, Strasbourg, 1514) is attrib- uted to Wechtlin by Passavant. A portrait drawing of *Philip Melanchthon* (see Lödel, 1863, no. 13) is accepted as Wechtlin's by Passavant, but its authenticity was dis- puted by Röttinger in Thieme–Becker.

BIBLIOGRAPHY
Thieme–Becker
A. von Bartsch: *Le Peintre-graveur*, vii (1808), p. 449 [under 'Pilgrim']
H. Lödel: *Des Strassburger Malers und Formschneiders Johannes Wechtlin Holzschnitte in Clairobscur* (Leipzig, 1863)

Hans Wechtlin: *Christ on the Cross with the Virgin, St Mary Magdalene and St John*, chiaroscuro woodcut, 272×186 mm, 1510–16 (Paris, Fondation Custodia, Institut Néerlandais)

J. D. Passavant: *Le Peintre-graveur*, iii (Leipzig, 1863), pp. 327–35 [under 'Pilgrim']

R. Muther: *Die deutsche Buchillustration . . ., 1460–1530* (Munich, Leipzig, 1884; Eng. trans., 1972), nos 1382 4

M. Geisberg: *Deutsche Einblatt-Holzschnitt in der ersten Hälfte des XVI. Jahrhunderts*, xxxv (Munich, 1924–9), nos 1481–98

——: *Bilder-Katalog zu Max Geisberg der deutsche Einblatt-Holzschnitt in der ersten Hälfte des XVI. Jahrhunderts* (Munich, 1930), pp. 256–7, nos. 1481–98

W. Strauss: *Chiaroscuro. The Clair-obscur Woodcuts by German and Netherlandish Masters of the XVIth and XVIIth Centuries* (New York, 1973), pp. 38–60, nos 19–30 [selective bibliog. of older publications and chiaroscuro]

M. Geisberg: *The German Single-leaf Woodcut, 1500–1550* (New York, 1974), nos 1485, 1486, 1491–5, 1497

M. Hébert: *Inventaire des gravures des écoles du Nord* (Paris, 1982), pp. 344–8, nos 1404–17

HANS J. VAN MIEGROET

Weckmann [Weckman], Niklaus [Claus] (*b* 1450/55; *d* after 1526). German sculptor. His name appears several times in the roll book of burghers of Ulm between 1481 and 1526. In 1490 he was commissioned to produce a high altarpiece for St Martin's church, Biberach, similar in construction and appearance to those at Sterzingen and Blaubeuren. This, his major work, was destroyed during the iconoclasm of 1531. Its eight painted Passion scenes were once thought to be by Martin Schongauer.

The Ulmer Museum, Ulm, has three relief panels by Weckmann: *St Catherine of Alexandria* (*c.* 1510) may have formerly belonged to the cloister of Heggbach, while two other high reliefs, a *Nativity* and an *Adoration of the Magi*, were once wing panels of the high altar (*c.* 1515) at Attenhofen parish church, where the predella showing the *Twelve Apostles* and additional paintings can still be seen. The altars at Biberach and Attenhofen were carved in limewood and originally polychromed. The two Nativity scenes have retained some of their former colour, while the *St Catherine* panel has had its colours removed. Weckmann was familiar with Flemish scenes of the Adoration of the Magi, and his Virgin embodies the ideal of the period.

Weckmann's work was formerly attributed to the workshop of Jörg Syrlin (ii) until the restoration of the statue of *St Stephen of Gundelfingen* revealed his full signature and the date 1528. It is presumed that Weckmann's workshop was one of the biggest of its kind in Ulm, if not in southern Germany, and that Weckmann was one of Ulm's leading sculptors. In style his work belongs to the Late Gothic tradition, yet his workshop produced its own characteristics—elongated ear-lobes, bushy hair strands and highly modelled drapery folds, which already suggest the fashion of the Northern Renaissance. His two sons, Claus Weckmann and Hieronymus Weckmann, worked as painters.

BIBLIOGRAPHY
Thieme–Becker

J. Baum: *Ulmer Plastik um 1500* (Stuttgart, 1911)

H. Rott: *Quellen und Forschungen zur süddeutschen und schweizerischen Kunstgeschichte im XV. und XVI. Jahrhundert: II. Alt Schwaben und die Reichsstädte* (Stuttgart, 1934)

G. Jasbar: *Ulmer Museum* (Ulm, 1987)

HANNELORE HÄGELE

Weddell, William (*b* 13 May 1736; *d* London, 30 April 1792). English collector, patron and politician. In 1762 he inherited Newby Hall, N. Yorks, and a considerable fortune. The following year he embarked on a Grand Tour that was to be the formation of his advanced Neo-classical taste. In Paris he viewed the collections of Louis-Philippe, Duc d'Orléans, and Jean de Jullienne; while there he also ordered a set of Gobelins tapestries incorporating medallions of the 'Loves of the Gods' after designs by François Boucher (Newby Hall, N. Yorks). Furnished with introductions to Cardinal Alessandro Albani and other connoisseurs, as well as to the painter–dealers Gavin Hamilton and Thomas Jenkins, with whom he dealt most, Weddell arrived in Rome in December of that year. During his time in the city he concentrated on acquiring a collection of antique marbles. His best-known and most expensive purchase was the much restored Barberini *Venus*, which he is said to have paid for in annual instalments, made over many years. Jenkins supplied Weddell with an expensive statue of *Minerva* and, through Bartolomeo Cavaceppi, Weddell acquired a hermaphrodite term similar to one owned by Johann Joachim Winckelmann. Other purchases from Cavaceppi included a *Priapus*, a *Seated Muse* and various pedestals, as well as a Roman tripod and cauldron at one time owned by Albani. From Giovanni Battista Piranesi, Weddell bought a tripod with a cauldron and omphalos; these, together with his later portrait bust by the sculptor Joseph Nollekens (1789; Newby Hall, N. Yorks), were reproduced by Nollekens in his design for Weddell's marble monument (Ripon Minster, N. Yorks).

Altogether the sculptures Weddell purchased cost him over £8000.

Weddell also bought pictures. He commissioned a pair of exceptional works from Hamilton, the Miltonic *Il Penseroso* and *L'Allegro* (both untraced), which were engraved by Domenico Cunego in 1768; other purchases included Annibale Carracci's *St Catherine*, a large landscape by Philipp Peter Roos, two portraits by Pompeo Batoni (all Newby Hall, N. Yorks) and a conversation piece by Nathaniel Dance-Holland, *William Weddell, His Servant Janson and the Rev. William Palgrave*, now in the Bearsted collection (Upton House, Warwicks, NT). Further commissions and purchases of this period include Weddell family portraits by Prince Hoare (ii) the younger, Hugh Douglas Hamilton and Joshua Reynolds, and Diego Velázquez's *Boy with a Falcon* (all now Muncaster Castle, Cumbria).

Following his return to England Weddell became a member of the Roman Club and the Society of Dilettanti; he was also made an MP. In 1771 he married Elizabeth Ramsden, sister-in-law of his political patron, Charles Watson-Wentworth, 2nd Marquess of Rockingham. His energies were chiefly directed, however, towards transforming Newby Hall into a fit setting for his collection. After brief essays with John Carr and William Chambers, Weddell employed Robert Adam (i) from 1767 to realize his own ideas. The remodelled interiors include a magnificent library and a room specially designed to display the Gobelins tapestries (*in situ*). Their greatest achievement is the stunning sculpture gallery, unique for its time, consisting of a central rotunda and a pair of flanking rectangular rooms. The ceiling decoration and a number of pedestals were devised by Adam, and the gallery still contains Weddell's collection.

The minor York architect William Belwood (1738–90) also contributed to the improvements to the house and its outbuildings. The park was landscaped in 1766 by Thomas White the elder (1736–1811), and a flower garden was laid out by Weddell's friend William Mason (i) during the same period.

BIBLIOGRAPHY

A. Michaelis: *Ancient Marbles in Great Britain* (London, 1882)
S. R. Peirce: 'Thomas Jenkins in Rome', *Antiqua. J.*, xlv (1965), pp. 200–29
J. Low: 'French Taste in London: William Weddell's Town House', *Country Life*, clxvi (27 Dec 1979), pp. 2470–72
——: *The Art and Architectural Patronage of William Weddell (1736–1792) of Newby Hall and his Circle* (diss., U. Leeds, 1981)
——: 'Newby Hall: Two Late Eighteenth-century Inventories', *Furn. Hist.*, xxii (1986), pp. 135–75
R. Middleton: 'The Sculpture Gallery at Newby Hall', *AA Files*, xiii (1986), pp. 48–60

JILL LOW

Wedgwood. English firm of ceramic manufacturers. It was founded in 1759 by Josiah Wedgwood (i) (*bapt* Burslem, Staffs, 12 July 1730; *d* Burslem, 3 Jan 1795; *see* §1 below) and was to become one of the most successful and influential English ceramic factories. Although during the early 19th century the factory's fortunes declined, during the 1840s it regained its former prestige. In the late 20th century the factory was best known for its extensive production of table and ornamental wares.

1. The founder. 2. Subsequent history of the factory.

1. THE FOUNDER. Josiah Wedgwood (i) was the 12th and youngest child of Thomas Wedgwood (1685–1739) and Mary Wedgwood of the Churchyard Pottery, Burslem. He received a basic education in Newcastle-under-Lyme, but his studies were cut short by the death of his father. He immediately went to work for his eldest brother, Thomas Wedgwood (1717–73), who had inherited the family pottery, and on 11 November 1744 he was apprenticed to him for five years.

In 1754 Wedgwood entered into partnership with the established potter Thomas Whieldon of Fenton Vivian. It was there that he began a long series of carefully recorded experiments that were to dominate his working life. His first major achievement is precisely recorded for 23 March 1759, when he made a successful formula for 'Green Glaze'. This new, brilliant colour was particularly suitable for use on moulded, naturalistic wares in such fruit and vegetable shapes as cauliflowers, cabbages and pineapples. The block moulds were made by such block-cutters as William Greatbatch (1735–1813).

On 1 May 1759 Wedgwood started work on his own account at the Ivy House Works, Burslem, which he rented from his cousins John Wedgwood (1705–80) and Thomas Wedgwood (1703–76) of the Big House, Burslem. There he continued with his experiments to create 'a species of earthenware for the table, quite new in its appearance, covered with a rich and brilliant glaze, bearing sudden alterations of heat and cold'. This fine, cream-coloured earthenware (creamware) could be used for both functional and ornamental items, and its success enabled Wedgwood to move to the larger premises of the Brick House Works in 1762. At this stage large quantities of wares were sent to Liverpool for transfer-printed decoration by the firm of Sadler & Green. During a visit to Liverpool in the spring of 1762 Wedgwood met the merchant Thomas Bentley (1730–80) for the first time. It was not, however, until the end of 1768 that Wedgwood and Bentley entered into an informal partnership to make 'ornamental Earthenware or Porcelain Viz Vases, Figures, Flowerpots, Toilet Furniture, & such other Articles as they shall from Time to Time agree upon'. From 1769 most ornamental wares were impressed with the special stamp WEDGWOOD & BENTLEY. By August 1769 the partnership was consolidated and Bentley had moved to London to run the Wedgwood showroom (est. 1765) and to supervise the enamelling workshop. The ceramic artists employed there included David Rhodes, who managed the workshop from 1770.

After the successful completion of a teaset with a pattern of raised green flowers on a gold ground, ordered for Queen Charlotte in 1765, Wedgwood was given permission to style himself 'Potter to Her Majesty' and to call his cream-coloured earthenware 'Queen's Ware'. This enormously popular ware gave him a vast, profitable export trade with Europe, America and the Indies, and was given extra impetus by comprehensive illustrated catalogues, produced from 1774 (*see* INDUSTRIAL DESIGN, fig. 1). Among the most notable special commissions were two services made for Catherine II, Empress of Russia: the 'Husk' pattern service (1770); and the larger and more prestigious 'Frog' service (1773–4; *see* ENGLAND, fig. 61), which comprised 952 pieces each hand-painted in enamels in 'mulberry' monochrome with a topographical scene of the English countryside based on contemporary engravings, and the frog emblem. Queen's Ware could also be manufactured to imitate such hardstones as agate, porphyry, granite and Blue John. The effects were produced by three methods: by mixing or 'wedging' different stained clays; by dusting metallic oxides on to the surface; or by trailing or painting the surface with coloured slips.

In 1767 Wedgwood had purchased the Ridgehouse Estate, a property of some 350 acres near Burslem, where he constructed a purpose-built factory. The site was situated beside the Trent & Mersey Canal (completed 1771), the use of which dramatically reduced the cost of transport of such raw materials as clay and coal, as well as the finished wares, in particular to the ports of Liverpool and Hull. The Etruria works (named after the area in Italy in which some Greek pottery, thought to be Etruscan, was excavated) was formally opened on 13 June 1769 and rapidly became a model for the pottery industry. In celebration of the opening, Wedgwood and Bentley made six Black Basalte 'First Day's Vases' (see fig.). Black

Basalte, a refined stoneware stained with cobalt and manganese oxides, was perfected by Wedgwood in 1768. It proved to be an ideal medium for the reproduction of cameo and intaglio gems, small bronzes and busts. Items included such large ornamental wares as vases, plaques, medallions and busts. In 1769 Wedgwood took out a patent for the method of hand-painting in encaustic colours on to Black Basalte, in imitation of Greek Red-figure vases and probably inspired by the Comte de Caylus's seven-volume work *Recueil d'antiquités égyptiennes, étrusques, grecques, romaines et gauloises* (Paris, 1752–67) and P.-F. H. d'Hancarville's four-volume *Collection of Etruscan, Greek and Roman Antiquities from the Cabinet of the Honble Wm Hamilton* (Naples, 1766–76).

Wedgwood produced several more bodies, such as Rosso Antico (a red stoneware), Cane (a yellow stoneware), Terracotta (a white stoneware) for ornamental wares, but none was as successful or as popular as his creation in 1771 (perfected 1774-5, after a total of more than 5000 recorded experiments) of what he called Jasper, 'a species of white porcelaine'. This dense, white stoneware could be thinly potted and either stained throughout with metal oxides or coloured with a thin wash; bas-relief

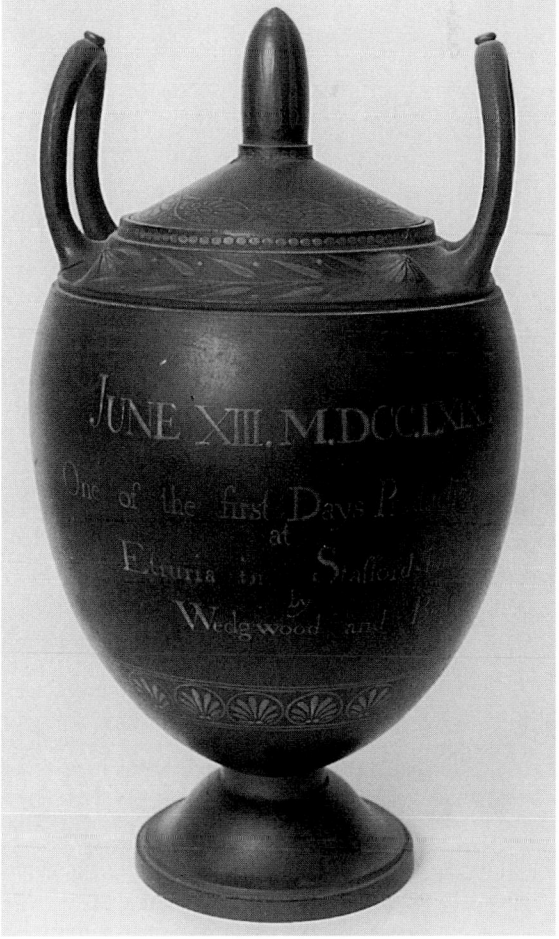

Josiah Wedgwood and Thomas Bentley: 'First Day's Vase', Black Basalte with encaustic Red-figure decoration, h. 254 mm, 1769 (private collection); front and back views

ornament was then applied to the ground of either blue, green, yellow, lilac, grey or brown. Wares included cameos that could be mounted on clocks, rings, buckles (*see* METAL, colour pl. II, fig. 3), brooches, hat pins and boxes (e.g. satinwood box with five jasper cameos, late 18th century; Nottingham, Castle Mus.); tablets, medallions, intaglios, busts, figures and vases, all produced in the Neoclassical taste popularized by the Adam brothers. The rapid success of Jasper led to a number of such eminent artists as John Flaxman, George Stubbs and Henry Webber (1754–1826) being employed to provide designs for low-reliefs. Plaques and medallions were also provided by Lady Diana Beauclerk (1734–1808), Emma Crewe (*fl* 1787–1818) and Lady Elizabeth Templetown (1747–1823). Wedgwood considered his copy of the Portland Vase (London, BM) to be his finest ceramic achievement. The first successful Jasper copy was produced around September 1789 and was intended for named subscribers.

Wedgwood was not only an eminent potter but also a great pioneer, especially with the development of the use of such factory equipment as the engine-turning lathe, introduced to the pottery industry in 1763. His scientific work, for which he was elected a Fellow of the Royal Society in January 1783, included the construction of a colorimetric thermoscope that measured the heat inside the kiln. Later he developed and perfected a graded thermometer or pyrometer. In 1789 he was requested by Sir Joseph Banks to carry out trials on samples of clay sent back from Australia by Captain Arthur Philip following the arrival of the First Fleet in Sydney Cove on 26 January 1788. Using this clay he produced a series of medallions designed by Henry Webber showing *Hope Encouraging Art and Labour, with Peace* (1789; London, BM). Wedgwood was a philanthropist and an ardent supporter of the French Revolution (1789) and the American War of Independence (1776); he also actively campaigned for the abolition of slavery.

WRITINGS

K. E. Farrer, ed.: *Wedgwood Letters*, 3 vols (Manchester, 1903–6/*R* 1974)
A. Finer and G. Savage, eds: *The Selected Letters of Josiah Wedgwood* (London, 1965)

BIBLIOGRAPHY

E. Meteyard: *The Life of Josiah Wedgwood*, 2 vols (London, 1865–6/*R* Ilkley, 1980)
R. Reilly: *Josiah Wedgwood, 1730–1795* (London, 1992)

GAYE BLAKE ROBERTS

2. SUBSEQUENT HISTORY OF THE FACTORY. After the death of Josiah Wedgwood (i) in 1795, the Etruria factory was inherited by his second son, Josiah Wedgwood (ii) (*b* Burslem, 1769; *d* Staffs, 1843). He was, however, a reluctant potter and lived in Dorset, leaving the management of the firm to his cousin Tom Byerley. In 1805 the decline in factory discipline and standards of production obliged Josiah Wedgwood (ii) to return to Staffordshire to take over active control of the business. He continued to fulfil this duty for 36 years.

Although this was not a prosperous period for the firm, improvements were made to the factory, and the range of wares produced was expanded. A steam engine was bought in 1802 from Boulton & Watt to drive flint-grinding machines and throwers' wheels. New ceramic wares included whiteware (a white earthenware intended to compete with porcelain), underglaze blue printed decoration and lustre (introduced 1805), a remarkable 'variegated lustre' decoration (*c.* 1809), bone china (1812) and Stone china (1821). The 'Egyptian' style, which Josiah Wedgwood (i) had pioneered as ornament for his Black Basaltes, was revived and augmented for use with the Rosso Antico and Cane bodies. Except for the blue-printed decoration, none of these new wares was a commercial success or achieved lasting popularity. Bone china was withdrawn *c.* 1828 and was not reintroduced for 50 years. The technique for making large objects in Jasper was lost and production of all Jasper was discontinued.

Francis Wedgwood (1800–88) was no more enthusiastic a manufacturer than his father, Josiah Wedgwood (ii), whom he succeeded at Etruria in 1841, but he too was obliged by financial circumstances to become one. In 1843 he accepted John Boyle (*d* 1845), who had previously been in partnership with Herbert Minton of the Minton Ceramic Factory, as an equal partner; less than a year later, however, the factory and the whole estate, including 111 houses 'chiefly occupied by persons employed at the Etruria Works', were put up for auction. The factory failed to find a buyer. After Boyle's death, Robert Brown (*d* 1859) took his place as a partner in the firm. This new partnership was a success. Wedgwood's Carrara—a version of the white statuary porcelain known as Parian—was introduced *c.* 1848, and Jasper returned to production after an absence of 15 years. Wedgwood exhibited in London at the Great Exhibition of 1851, and it was noted with approval that 'this eminent house [was] again prepared to assert its position among the principal art manufactures of the present day'. After Brown's death, Francis Wedgwood was able to buy Brown's share of the firm, and he took his sons, Godfrey Wedgwood (1833–1905), Clement Francis Wedgwood (1840–89) and Laurence Wedgwood (1844–1913), into partnership. Numbers employed at the factory rose from 380 in 1847 to 530 in 1862. Under the direction of this generation the firm made progress towards regaining lost prestige, especially by the production of majolica, the reintroduction of large Jasper vases and bone china, and in the employment of artists, notably Emile Lessore (1805–76) and Thomas Allen (1831–1915), the first art director.

In 1895 three cousins of the fifth generation, Cecil Wedgwood (1863–1916), Francis Hamilton Wedgwood (1867–1930) and Kennard Laurence Wedgwood (1873–1950), registered the firm as a private limited company. In 1902 the company received an order for a large bone-china service for the White House, Washington, DC, its most prestigious tableware order since the 'Frog' service made for Catherine II.

During the first quarter of the 20th century trade was slow and the business unprofitable. The Wedgwoods could do little more than keep the factory going. The best of Wedgwood's design at this period came from the art director John Goodwin, Alfred Hoare Powell (1865–1960) and Ada Louise Powell (1882–1956), but the most startling addition to production was the range of 'Fairyland Lustre' designs by Susannah Margaretta (Daisy) Makeig-Jones (1881–1945), many examples of which can be seen in the

Wedgwood museum at Barlaston, Staffs. Meanwhile, subsidence had caused parts of the Etruria factory to sink some 50 feet below their original level.

Josiah Wedgwood (v) (1899–1968), a great-great-great-grandson of Josiah Wedgwood (i), became managing director of the company in 1930. Together with three cousins—Clement Tom Wedgwood (1907–60), John Hamilton Wedgwood (b 1907) and Hensleigh Cecil Wedgwood (b 1908)—he decided to move the factory to a site at Barlaston, bought in 1935, where they built the most up-to-date ceramics factory in Europe. Electrically fired tunnel ovens were installed for the firing of all types of ware. During the next 30 years the company's reputation was rapidly restored, aided by designs from the art director Victor Skellern (1909–66) and such distinguished artists as Keith Day Pearce Murray (1892–1981), John Rattenbury Skeaping (1901–80), Eric Ravilious, Edward Bawden and Arnold Machin (b 1911). In 1967 Wedgwood became a public company, and Arthur Bryan (b 1923) was appointed the first Chairman and Managing Director from outside the family. After 19 years of almost continuous expansion, largely by acquisition, the company was taken over by Waterford Glass, and the two companies were consolidated as Waterford Wedgwood.

BIBLIOGRAPHY
J. C. Wedgwood: *History of the Wedgwood Family* (London, 1908)
A. Kelly: *Decorative Wedgwood in Architecture and Furniture* (New York, 1965)
B. Wedgwood and H. Wedgwood: *The Wedgwood Circle, 1730–1897* (London, 1980)
G. Wills: *Wedgwood* (London, 1980)
M. Batkin: *Wedgwood Ceramics, 1846–1959* (London, 1982)
R. Reilly: *Wedgwood*, 2 vols (London, 1989)
——: *Wedgwood Jasper* (London, 1994)
——: *Wedgwood: The New Illustrated Dictionary* (Woodbridge, 1995)
The Genius of Wedgwood (exh. cat., ed. H. Young; London, V&A, 1995)
ROBIN REILLY

Weegee [Fellig, Usher; Fellig, Arthur] (b Złoczew, Austria [now Poland], 12 June 1899; d New York, 26 Dec 1968). American photographer of Austrian birth. He emigrated to the USA in 1910 and took numerous odd jobs, including working as an itinerant photographer and as an assistant to a commercial photographer. In 1924 he was hired as a dark-room technician by Acme Newspictures (later United Press International Photos). He left, however, in 1935 to become a freelance photographer. He worked at night and competed with the police to be first at the scene of a crime, selling his photographs to tabloids and photographic agencies. It was at this time that he earned the name Weegee (appropriated from the Ouija board) for his uncanny ability to make such early appearances at scenes of violence and catastrophe.

Weegee made only a meagre existence from his photographs, mostly shots of bloody murders, fires, the seedy Bowery district and sympathic views of people who lived on the streets of New York at night. Weegee became a master of the sensational. Despite this fact, one of his most famous images is *The Critic* (see *Naked City*, pp. 130–31), a photograph of high society. It captures the tiara-crowned heads and diamond-laden necks of the wealthy Mrs George Washington Kavanaugh and Lady Peel, who are both scorned by the sneering silhouette of a middle-aged street woman. *The Critic* was very different from Weegee's many bloody street scenes from the time, for example the image of a murdered racketeer (see *Naked City*, p. 87).

In 1945 Weegee published his first book, *Naked City*, followed in 1946 by *Weegee's People*. The success of *Naked City* was tremendous and ensured his financial security. Having suddenly achieved this fame, Weegee went to Hollywood where he maintained his nocturnal schedule but made portraits of film stars and fashionable night spots, which he published in 1953 in *Naked Hollywood*. In 1945 Weegee also received the professional approbation of Edward Steichen, then Director of Photography at MOMA, New York, who included Weegee's work in the exhibition *50 Photographs by 50 Photographers*. Having gained recognition after the mid-1940s as a photographer in circles outside the tabloid press, he turned to more self-consciously artistic photo-caricatures of celebrities using distorting trick lenses, for example *Marilyn Monroe* (see *Naked Hollywood*, cover).

Weegee usually used a standard press camera, a Speed Graphic with a 4×5 inch format and automatic flash. He had little knowledge of, and little interest in, purely artistic photography, and neither his compositions nor his prints were made with particular care in the early part of his career. Weegee's artistic ingenuousness is demonstrated by the one term he adapted from art, 'Rembrandt lighting': by this he referred to the use of a dark background with the subject in bright light; he accomplished tonal selection automatically by the use of flash. This lighting was the key to the striking effect of his photographs: with it, he claimed, he could render a gruesome scene less distasteful, while still providing enough high-contrast detail to help the publisher to sell newspapers, even when reproduced in the dots of newspaper half-tones.

Weegee also made many night photographs using an infra-red flash, allowing him to photograph voyeuristically such scenes as lovers at a film or on a park bench (see *Weegee's People*, part 1, no. 10). With infra-red film and flash he also captured high society at night. This lighting made women's make-up garish, emphasized their facial veins and deleted dental caps in the smiles of New York's privileged classes; *After the Opera . . . At Sammy's Night Club on the Bowery* (see *Weegee's People*, part 2, no. 19) illustrates this well. Weegee can be seen as the American counterpart to Brassaï, who photographed Paris street scenes at night. Weegee's themes of nudists, circus performers, freaks and street people were later taken up and developed by Diane Arbus in the early 1960s.

WRITINGS
Weegee by Weegee: An Autobiography (New York, 1961)

PHOTOGRAPHIC PUBLICATIONS
Naked City (New York, 1945)
Weegee's People (New York, 1946/R 1975)
Naked Hollywood (New York, 1953)
with R. Ald: *Weegee's Creative Camera* (Garden City, 1959)

BIBLIOGRAPHY
C. Westerbeck: 'Night Light: Brassaï and Weegee', *Artforum*, xv/4 (1976), pp. 34–45
A. Talmey: *Weegee* (Millerton, 1978)
J. Coplans: *Weegee's New York* (New York, 1982)
MARY CHRISTIAN

Weekes, Henry (*b* Canterbury, 1807; *d* Ramsgate, Kent, 28 June 1877). English sculptor. He was apprenticed to William Behnes in 1822 and studied at the Royal Academy (1823–6), winning a silver medal for sculpture in 1826. In 1827 he became an assistant to Francis Chantrey, with whom he remained until the latter's death in 1841; he then took over Chantrey's studio and completed his unfinished works, including the bronze equestrian statue of *Arthur Wellesley, 1st Duke of Wellington* (1841–4; London, Royal Exch.). In 1852 Weekes was elected an ARA and a full member of the Royal Academy in 1860; from 1869 until his death he was Professor of Sculpture there. He was the most successful establishment sculptor of the mid-Victorian period. His sculpture and writings, more than any other contemporary sculptor's, embodied current beliefs in fusing classicism and realism. Although he essentially maintained Chantrey's outlook, he was more intellectual than his mentor and had a wider imaginative range. Like Chantrey, he varied the format of his many portrait busts according to the subject; they ranged from the classical herm type in *Henry William Whitbread* (marble, 1864; Southill Park, Beds) to historical realism in *Sir Joshua Reynolds* (marble, 1874; London, Leicester Square).

Two of Weekes's greatest works are church monuments that combine accurate, boldly modelled portraiture with emotional effectiveness. His high-relief funerary monument to *Samuel and Elizabeth Whitbread* (marble, 1846; Cardington, Beds, St Mary) portrays Elizabeth Whitbread kneeling on a cushion, a pose borrowed from Chantrey's monument to *Reginald Heber* (1835; London, St Paul's Cathedral); here, however, she leans affectionately on her husband's shoulder. Weekes's monument to *Percy Bysshe Shelley* (marble, 1854; Dorset, Christchurch Priory) takes realism a stage further: the drowned poet, supported by the idealized figure of his wife, still seems to glisten with water and appears as a bloodless corpse, rather than a heroic Neo-classical nude. Similar interplay between idealism and realism is evident in the statue of the *Young Naturalist* (marble, 1870; Leeds, C.A.G.). Weekes contributed the marble group *Manufactures* to the series of sculptures dealing with 'industrial arts' on the Albert Memorial (1864–70; London, Kensington Gdns) and executed lively historical portrait statues of *Dr John Hunter* (marble, 1864; London, Royal Coll. Surgeons England) and *Charles II* (marble, 1870; London, Cent. Crim. Court, Old Bailey).

Weekes's Royal Academy lectures, which were published posthumously as *Lectures on Art*, cover such topics as taste, style, idealism and realism in sculpture, colour in sculpture and education. He ruefully recognised that sculpture 'as an art is limited and can never be popular'. Well aware of the ossified Neo-classical tradition and its increasing irrelevance in the face of the advance of science, Weekes nevertheless believed in avoiding excessive realism and distanced himself from the flamboyance of Carlo Marochetti. This standpoint made him oppose the application of colour to sculpture, although he believed that devices such as deep undercutting were necessary to convey the identity of the figure and the theme. Echoing Chantrey, he acknowledged the limitations of theorizing, asserting that 'practical instruction can be carried on in the schools only, with the modelling tool in hand, and the clay to operate upon'. Yet sculpture was not merely manual labour; Weekes held out John Flaxman as an exemplar to students when he told them: 'I wish you to be thinking men.' Weekes's very moderation led his reputation to be eclipsed soon after his death by the New Sculpture, but his lectures confirm Read's point that 'they are the most consistent and intelligent exposition of sculptural thinking in the Victorian era and, as far as published material goes, exceptional if not unique'.

WRITINGS
Lectures on Art (London, 1880) [with a short sketch of the author's life]

BIBLIOGRAPHY
Gunnis
N. Penny: *Church Monuments in Romantic England* (New Haven and London, 1977)
B. Read: *Victorian Sculpture* (New Haven and London, 1982)

MARK STOCKER

Weeks, John (*b* Townlake, Sydenham, 16 July 1886; *d* Auckland, 14 Sept 1965). New Zealand painter and teacher. He studied at the Elam School of Art, Auckland, from 1908 to 1910 under Archibald Nicoll (1886–1953). He travelled extensively in Europe and Australia as well as visiting Morocco, Tunisia and Algiers in 1927–8. In 1926 and 1928 he studied at the André Lhôte Academy in Paris. As a lecturer in painting at the Elam School of Art from 1930 to 1954, he had a considerable influence on a generation of Auckland artists. Weeks was an eclectic artist who painted landscapes, still-lifes and figurative compositions. His style was heavily influenced by the decorative and colouristic aspects of the Ecole de Paris painters. Some of his painting shows a belated response to Synthetic Cubism, for example *Limestone Gorge, King Country* (*c.* 1943; Auckland, C.A.G.). In his later years Weeks is credited with painting some of the first abstract works by a New Zealand artist. *Composition with Figures* (*c.* 1940; Wellington, Mus. NZ, Te Papa Tongarewa) is a decorative arrangement of nude female figures painted with the rich colour and feeling for the textural qualities of paint for which Weeks was renowned. Much of his work was destroyed when the Elam School burnt down in 1948.

BIBLIOGRAPHY
M. Day: *The Works of John Weeks in the National Collection* (Wellington, 1970)
G. Docking: *Two Hundred Years of New Zealand Painting* (Wellington, 1970), pp. 130–34

MICHAEL DUNN

Weenix [Weenincks; Weenincx; Weeninx]. Dutch family of artists. The architect Johannes Weenix had four children: a son (1) Jan Baptist Weenix, who became a painter, and three daughters, the youngest of whom, Lijsbeth, married the painter Barent Micker (1615–87), whose brother Jan Christiaensz. Micker (*c.* 1598–1664) was probably Jan Baptist's first teacher in Amsterdam. In 1639 Jan Baptist, who specialized in painting Dutch Italianate landscapes and harbour views, married Justina d'Hondecoeter, daughter of the landscape painter Gillis d'Hondecoeter, sister of Gysbert (1604–53) and Niclaes (1607/8–42), both also landscape painters, and aunt of Melchior d'Hondecoeter. They had two children: (2) Jan Weenix, who became a still-life, landscape and portrait painter, and Gillis Weenix, about whom little is known.

(1) Jan Baptist [Giovanni Battista] **Weenix** (*b* Amsterdam, 1621; *d* Huis ter Mey, nr Utrecht, ?1660–61). Painter, draughtsman and etcher. After possibly training with Micker, Weenix is said by Houbraken to have studied with Abraham Bloemaert in Utrecht and then with Claes Cornelisz. Moeyaert for about two years in Amsterdam. Weenix's earliest known work is a signed and dated drawing of an Italianate landscape with goats and sheep, a shepherd resting near a Classical pillar and a large group of trees (1644; Vienna, Albertina). His early painting *Sleeping Tobias* (1642; Rotterdam, Boymans–van Beuningen) is related thematically to works by Moeyaert and Rembrandt. Weenix's supple contours, liquid brushwork and rich colour, however, already reveal the qualities that were prized by later artists and collectors.

In 1642, shortly after the birth of his son (2) Jan, Jan Baptist made his will in Amsterdam before setting out for Italy. He arrived late in 1642 or in 1643 and stayed in Rome for four years. There he became a member of the Schildersbent, the Netherlandish artists' society founded in 1623, and was given the nickname 'Ratel' (Dut.: rattle) on account of a speech defect. By 1645 the artist was in the service of a 'Kardinaal Pamfilio', often assumed to be Cardinal Giovanni Battista Pamphili, who, however, had already become Pope Innocent X in 1644. By 1647 Weenix had adopted what became his standard signature: *Gio*[vanni] *Batt*[ist]*a Weenix*, presumably in the Pope's honour. Schloss (*Essays in Northern European Art*, 1983) suggested that the cardinal referred to in 1645 may have

been Innocent X's nephew, the art-loving Prince Camillo Pamphili, and Houbraken's assertion that Weenix was introduced into the Pope's service by Camillo seems to be confirmed by records of payment to the artist (in 1645 and 1646) found among Camillo's papers in the Pamphili archives.

By June 1647 Weenix was once again in Amsterdam, at which time his portrait was painted by Bartholomeus van der Helst (untraced, engraved by Jacobus Houbraken). Weenix's *Landscape with Ford and Rider* (1647; St Petersburg, Hermitage) shows all the characteristics of his mature, painterly and fluid style. The subject of sunlit ruins may have been inspired by similar works of Viviano Codazzi.

Weenix often employed architectural motifs, thus inspiring many other artists, notably Nicolaes Berchem. Sometimes the ruins are identifiable, such as the temple of Jupiter Tonans in *A Hunting Party near Ruins* (1648; Cleveland, OH, S. A. Millikin priv. col., see 1965 exh. cat., no. 97). He also inserted depictions of sculpture, such as the Medici vase and Giambologna's *Rape of the Sabine Women*, into his fantasy landscapes. The *Dioscuri* from the Capitol in Rome found their way into the background of Weenix's *Port Scene* (1649; Utrecht, Cent. Mus.; see fig.). The scene is painted in warm colours: yellow, green and blue for the foreground, where the figure of the horseman is painted in shades of orange, red and grey, while his female companion's clothing is in a sumptuous blue-grey. The brushwork is refined and supple. From this date

Jan Baptist Weenix: *Port Scene*, oil on canvas, 1.06×1.58 m, 1649 (Utrecht, Centraal Museum, on loan from The Hague, Dienst Rijksverspreide Kunstvoorwerpen)

Weenix began to produce the Italian harbour views for which he is best known, combining fanciful or real Classical ruins, colonnades, tombs, pyramids or obelisks with picturesque figures in a conscious fusion of past and present.

Weenix also painted a few still-lifes and some portraits, including one possibly of the French philosopher *René Descartes* (Utrecht, Cent. Mus.), which is signed and can be dated *c.* 1647–9, between the philosopher's arrival in Holland and his death in 1650. He also painted an impressive family portrait, *Aernhout van Wyckersloot and Christina Wessels with their Children Angelina, Petronella and Jan Aernout* (Utrecht, Cent. Mus.), in which he depicted himself at the left holding a palette and mahlstick.

The artist had moved to Utrecht by the time he was elected an officer of the painters' college there in 1649, along with the Dutch Italianate landscape painters Cornelis van Poelenburch and Jan Both. By 1653 Weenix was acting as painter and agent for the wealthy art collector from Utrecht Willem Vincent, Baron van Wittenhorst (*d* 1674). Weenix's figures are increasingly monumental from this time; the architectural elements are more forcefully expressed, and he paints in the slightly nervous, agitated style practised by such contemporaries as Adam Pynacker, Nicolaes Berchem and Jan Asselijn (e.g. *Sleeping Woman*, 165?; Munich, Alte Pin.).

By 1657 he was living in the Huis ter May, a mansion (destr.) near de Haar, not far from Utrecht. His last known painting, which enjoyed a great reputation in the 18th century, *Italian Peasants in Front of an Inn* (1658; The Hague, Mauritshuis), is related in theme to earlier works. At the left a seated woman holds a child in her lap; nearby two dogs play, while a small herd of sheep and a goat rest at the right. The fleeces of the sheep are meticulously rendered, and the contrast of light and shade is stronger than in his previous work.

Some confusion as to when and where the artist died has arisen, due to the suggestion that he may have been a certain Jan Wenincx who died at Doetinchem, Gelderland, sometime before 1663. However, since it cannot be proved that this Jan Wenincx was a painter, there seems little reason to dispute Houbraken's statement that Weenix moved to the Huis ter May three years before his premature death in 1660 or 1661. In his sister's will of November 1663 Weenix was mentioned as deceased.

According to Houbraken, Weenix's pupils included his son (2) Jan, his nephew Melchior d'Hondecoeter and his cousin Nicolaes Berchem. The family link with Berchem has yet to be verified, and Houbraken's statement that Berchem studied with Weenix is also problematic. The two artists are said to have travelled together to Italy; however, no firm evidence exists to substantiate a trip by Berchem, who was two years older than Weenix and already had pupils of his own by 1642. Nevertheless significant stylistic affinities exist between the two artists, perhaps because they were both apprenticed to Claes Cornelisz. Moeyaert at approximately the same time. Berchem's fantasy Italian harbour scenes painted after 1654 reveal his debt to Weenix. The two artists collaborated on the *Calling of St Matthew* (*c.* 1665; The Hague, Mauritshuis), which is signed by both. The various parts of the painting have yet to be attributed to separate hands. The sheep and other animals in the foreground, as well as some of the figures, were probably painted by Weenix, while the woman riding a donkey is probably by Berchem. Jan Baptist also collaborated with other artists: he signed a *Landscape with Figures and Animals* (untraced, see *Gaz. B.-A.*, ix (1861), p. 305) with Bartholomeus van der Helst, and a *Seaport* (*c.* 1648–9; Vienna, Gemäldegal. Akad. Bild. Kst.) with Jan Asselijn.

Drawings by Weenix range from topographical studies of both Italian and Dutch subjects, such as the red chalk drawing of the *Colosseum* in Rome (Leiden, Rijksuniv., Prentenkab.) and the signed view of *Nijenrode*, a castle in Breukeleen (Amsterdam, Rijksmus.), to landscapes and scenes of rustic farm buildings. He also made a number of sensitive figure studies, some of them on blue paper, for example the *Man Playing 'Koten'* (Amsterdam, Rijksmus.). His drawings are sometimes confused with those of his son as well as those of Maerten Stoop (1620–47) and Emanuel Murant (1622–1700). Only a few etchings can be securely attributed to Jan Baptist Weenix. They show bulls and cows and are reminiscent of similar subjects by Berchem.

(2) Jan Weenix (*b* Amsterdam, ?June 1642; *bur* Amsterdam, 19 Sept 1719). Painter and draughtsman, son of (1) Jan Baptist Weenix. Jan probably received his first instruction as a painter from his father, and it is possible that he helped finish certain of his father's works. He probably remained in Utrecht after his father's death. By 1664 he had become a member of the Guild of St Luke in Utrecht without, however, having submitted the required entrance painting, which he provided by 1668. There are several documented references to Jan in the late 1660s. He inherited a legacy along with his uncle, the painter Barent Micker, and other family members in 1667, at which time Gillis, his younger brother, apparently still required a guardian. He received another legacy in 1668, the year of his marriage, and in 1669 served as a witness for the inventory of the painter Jacob de Hennin (1629–*c.* 1688) in The Hague. In 1675 he and his wife were living in Amsterdam, of which Jan became a citizen.

He most likely began to paint in his own right after his father's death; at the age of 18 he signed and dated *Shepherds in an Italian Landscape* (1660; untraced, see Schloss, *Oud-Holland*, 1983, fig. 1). His first works are Italianate genre scenes set in landscapes or exotic ports modelled on his father's successful compositions, with which they are sometimes confused. However, Jan's execution is more precise than his father's and his colouring subtler, while his contrasts of light and dark are stronger. The two artists also used different figure types. Typically Jan Baptist Weenix's figures are hearty and round-faced while Jan's are more elegant and refined. This difference also corresponds to a general shift in taste after mid-century, when many artists adopted a more slender, attenuated figure type accompanied by a corresponding interest in elegant, aristocratic clothing. Jan generally signed his paintings: *J. Weenix*, most often including a date. Jan's mature genre style is evident in a *Landscape with Figures* (1664; London, Dulwich Pict. Gal.) representing a shepherd with his herd and his dogs resting in an Italianate landscape. Like his father, Jan often included architectural ruins and antique statues in his paintings, including a sculpture of a man about to strike another, identified as either *Cain and Abel* or *Samson Killing a Philistine*, which was also used in paintings by other 17th-century Dutch artists such as Gerrit Dou, Pieter Codde and Jan van der Heyden.

In the course of the 1670s Jan adapted the harbour compositions of his father, introducing explicitly amorous figures in contrast to his father's more generally demure figure groups. In the same period other artists began to modify the cast of characters to include scenes of debauchery and merrymaking in an exotic setting. Whereas the earlier Italianate harbour scenes by Nicolaes Berchem were dependent on works by the elder Weenix, the later ones reveal his interest in depicting amorous couples, to the extent that some are called the *Prodigal Son*. This kind of imagery has rightly been interpreted within a moralizing context; however, the mood of enjoyment and gaiety somewhat undermines the admonitory intent.

After 1680 Jan abandoned harbour scenes in favour of the numerous still-lifes of dead game and birds, flower pieces and statuary for which he is best known, such as *Still-life with Dead Hare* (1682; Karlsruhe, Staatl. Ksthalle), which shows a meticulously rendered hare with small birds and hunting gear. Exquisitely painted and observed, this scene and others like it are set against an elegant, park-like background with sculpture, urns, putti and palatial houses, flooded with warm, romantic lighting. These hunting or trophy still-lifes, while not always appreciated in the 20th century, were highly valued in the 17th century. Hunting was a royal sport and a favourite aristocratic activity; it was strictly regulated and illegal for even the rising bourgeoisie. It has been suggested, therefore, that these still-lifes were purchased by wealthy burghers in order to lend themselves a degree of social prestige (Sullivan, 1984). Although they could not hunt, they could buy art. Jan and his cousin Melchior d'Hondecoeter, who painted similar hunting still-lifes, emphasized the textural and colouristic beauty of their subjects. Among the artist's few floral still-lifes are the lovely bouquets with exotic flowers such as a passion flower (1692; Lyon, Mus. B.-A.) and another stunning signed and dated example (1696; London, Wallace; see fig.).

At the beginning of the 18th century the hunting still-life became increasingly popular for stately wall decorations. From *c.* 1702 to 1714 Jan served as court painter to the Elector Palatine John William of Düsseldorf, for whom he painted 12 large hunting scenes designed as wall panels (*c.* 1710–14) for the Elector's lodge, Schloss Bensberg, near Cologne, fragments of which survive (Munich, Alte Pin.). These paintings have been interpreted as an allegory of abundance placed before the feet of the Elector. Goethe saw these impressive works *in situ* in 1774 and claimed that Weenix had surpassed nature in visually rendering every tactile value of his subject.

Jan also painted portraits set in classicizing surroundings, for example *Abraham van Bronckhorst* (1688; Amsterdam, Rijksmus.), which shows the sitter full-length and wearing an elegant robe over his everyday clothing, accompanied by a slender dog. Among his distinguished sitters were Sybrand de Flines and his wife Agnes Block, who was a well-known horticulturist and patron of the arts in Amsterdam.

Jan Weenix: *Flowers and Fruit*, oil on mahogany panel, 799×595 mm, 1696 (London, Wallace Collection)

Jan's drawings include a series of birds drawn in oiled black chalk with coloured wash (e.g. Amsterdam, Rijksmus.) and several botanical studies. Among his figure drawings is a compositional study in brush and grey wash (Amsterdam, Rijksmus.) for an unidentified painting showing either the finding of Moses or the recognition of Achilles.

Jan's only known pupil, Dirk Valkenburg (1675–1721), imitated his master so closely that it is sometimes difficult to tell works by the two artists apart.

BIBLIOGRAPHY

A. Houbraken: *De groote schouburgh* (1718–21)

G. J. Hoogewerff: 'Het spokend ruiterstandbeeld' [The haunting equestrian statue], *Mdbl. Beeld. Kst.*, xviii (1941), pp. 257–66

W. Stechow: 'Jan Baptist Weenix', *A. Q.* [Detroit], xi (1948), pp. 181–98

Nederlandse 17e-eeuwse Italianiserende landschapschilders (exh. cat., ed. A. Blankert, Utrecht, Cent. Mus., 1965; rev. and trans. as *Dutch 17th-century Italianate Landscape Painters*, Soest, 1978), pp. 174–84

A. Cludzikowski: 'Jan-Baptist Weenix, peintre d'histoire', *Bull. Mus. N. Varsovie/Biul. Muz. N. Warsaw.*, vii/1 (1966), pp. 1–10

W. Stechow: 'A Wall Paneling by Jan Weenix', *Allen Mem. A. Mus. Bull.*, 27 (Fall 1969), pp. 13–25

R. Ginnings: *The Art of Jan Baptist Weenix and Jan Weenix* (diss., Wilmington, U. DE, 1970)

P. Eikemeier: 'Der Jagdzyklus des Jan Weenix aus Schloss Bensberg', *Die Weltkunst*, xlviii (1978), pp. 296–8

S. A. Sullivan: 'Jan Baptist Weenix: *Still-life with a Dead Swan*', *Bull. Detroit Inst. A.*, lvii (1979), pp. 64–71

C. Schloss: *Travel, Trade and Temptation: The Dutch Italianate Harbor Scene, 1640–1680* (Ann Arbor, MI, 1982)

——: 'The Early Italianate Genre Paintings by Jan Weenix (ca. 1642–1719)', *Oud-Holland*, xcvii (1983), pp. 69–97

——: 'A Note on Jan Baptist Weenix's Patronage in Rome', *Essays in Northern European Art Presented to Egbert Haverkamp Begemann on his Sixtieth Birthday* (Doornspijk, 1983), pp. 237–8

S. A. Sullivan: *The Dutch Gamepiece* (Totowa, NJ, 1984)

J. M. Kilian: 'Jan Baptist Weenix—1643 bis 1647: Zur Datierung des zeichnerischen Frühwerks anhand von Signaturänderungen', *Niederdt. Beitr. Kstgesch.*, xxxiii (1994)

JENNIFER M. KILIAN

Weeper [mourner; Fr. *pleurant*]. Figure, most often sculptured, associated with a tomb or burial-place; more specifically a group of tomb figures popular in the late 14th century and early 15th. The use of mourning figures on the sides of tomb-chests or cenotaphs seems to have started in the court circles of France during the 13th century. The tomb of *Philippe Dagobert* (*d c.* 1235; Saint-Denis Abbey), for example, has a series of simple niches containing robed clerics in relief. Although each figure shows a slightly different gesture, they are all frontally posed. Early weepers might represent angels, clerics or the family of the deceased, and they were often garbed in clerical or liturgical robes. Throughout the 13th century and most of the 14th this appears to have been the most popular type of mourner figure, with examples throughout Europe, such as the tomb of *Edmund Crouchback, Earl of Lancaster* (*d* 1296; London, Westminster Abbey; *see* LONDON, §V, 2(ii)(a)) or the tomb of *Otto III of Ravensberg* (*d* 1305; Bielefeld, Neustädter Marienkirche).

The second stage of development of weepers occurred from the late 14th century with the series of tombs created for the Valois family of France. Jean de Marville was hired by Philip the Bold, Duke of Burgundy, to create his tomb (Dijon, Mus. B.-A.), which was completed by CLAUS SLUTER and Claus de Werve by 1411. The tomb had 41 individual figures set in a deep and elaborate arcade. Sluter endowed each figure with a unique personality that is reflected in the pose and manner of grief (see fig.). The

tomb of *John the Fearless, Duke of Burgundy, and Margaret of Bavaria* (Dijon, Mus. B.-A.), which was made from 1443 by Juan de la Huerta and Antoine Le Moiturier, follows the pattern created by Sluter, as does that of *Jean, Duc de Berry* by JEAN DE CAMBRAI (weepers in Bourges, Mus. Berry). The Hours of Louis de Laval-Chatillon (Paris, Bib. N., MS. lat. 920, fol. 334*v*), attributed to Jean Colombe, shows this type of tomb in a church setting.

Most weepers reflect contemporary liturgical, processional and burial customs, which became increasingly elaborate from the second half of the 14th century as the Black Death and numerous wars contributed to ideas of the precarious nature of life. Interest grew in tombs, tomb architecture, chantry chapels, state funeral processions and liturgy, especially the Office of the Dead. Memorial masses were endowed for perpetual prayer for the soul of the deceased, to which mourner figures on tombs could contribute visually. The figures on the tomb of *Philip the Bold* were influenced by the funeral procession from Hal in Brabant, where the Duke died, to his burial-place in the Charterhouse of Champmol in Dijon. The cortège included horses, the coffin, the family of the Duke, the court, clerics and—once at Dijon—townspeople, all arrayed in mourning clothes specially ordered by the Duke. Around the tomb Sluter arranged liturgical figures, Carthusians and court figures. Each costume is slightly different, each individual being appropriately garbed. This type of funeral procession is depicted in the Chronicles of Charles VII (Paris, Bib. N., MS. fr. 2691, fol. 11r).

The last stage of development of weepers can be seen in the tombs of *Philippe Pot* (*d* 1493; *see* GOTHIC, fig. 30), *Isabella of Bourbon* (*d* 1465; Amsterdam, Rijksmus.) and *Maximilian I, Holy Roman Emperor* (Innsbruck, Hofkirche; *see* INNSBRUCK, §3(i)). Philippe Pot's armour-clad body is carried on a slab by six black-robed mourning figures derived from Sluter's type of mourner. The tomb figures of Isabella and Maximilian wear contemporary court dress rather than clerical garb. They act as dynastic witnesses as much as mourning figures.

With the change of tomb design in the 16th century, the use of mourning figures decreased, but as late as the 19th century, in Antonio Canova's tomb of Empress Maria-Theresa's daughter *Maria Christina* (*c.* 1798–1805; Vienna, Augustinerkirche) or Augustus Saint-Gaudens's Adams Memorial (1894; Washington, DC, Rock Creek Cemetery), the concept and figure of a mourner is used.

BIBLIOGRAPHY

A. Kleinclausz: 'L'Art funéraire de la Bourgogne au Moyen Age', *Gaz. B.-A.*, n. s. 3, xxvi (1901), pp. 441–58; xxvii (1902), pp. 299–320
H. s'Jacob: *Idealism and Realism: A Study of Spiritual Symbolism* (Leiden, 1954)
E. Panofsky: *Tomb Sculpture: Four Lectures on its Changing Aspects from Ancient Egypt to Bernini* (New York, 1964)
Les Pleurants dans l'art du Moyen Age en Europe (exh. cat., ed. P. Quarré; Dijon, Mus. B.-A., 1971)
K. Bauch: *Das mittelalterliche Grabbild* (Berlin, 1976)
P. Ariès: *Images of Man and Death* (Cambridge, MA, 1985)
K. Morand: *Claus Sluter: Artist at the Court of Burgundy* (Austin, 1991)

SARA JANE PEARMAN

Weepers from the tomb of *Philip the Bold, Duke of Burgundy* (*d* 1404) by Claus Sluter and Claus de Werve, alabaster, h. 413 mm, completed by 1411 (Cleveland, OH, Cleveland Museum of Art)

Weerdt [Weert], **Adriaen de** (*b* Brussels, *c.* 1510; *d* Cologne, *c.* 1590). Flemish painter, draughtsman and engraver. He studied in Antwerp with Christiaen van de

Queborn (*c.* 1515–78) and painted landscapes in the manner of Frans Mostaert. De Weerdt went to Italy *c.* 1560, probably visiting Rome and Venice. After his return to the Netherlands he moved to Brussels where he soon became a successful painter. His style reflected the influence of such Italian artists as Parmigianino, whose work he had studied during his stay in Italy. Bénézit referred to a series of paintings showing the *Life of the Virgin.* Thieme–Becker mentioned only two paintings attributable to the artist (a *Madonna*, Kassel, Schloss Wilhelmshöhe, and a grisaille representing the *Life of the Virgin*, Warsaw, N. Mus.) and a few drawings: a *Landscape* (Amsterdam, Rijksmus.) and four sheets with scenes from the *Story of Ruth* (Vienna, Albertina). In 1566, de Weerdt moved to Cologne, where he probably met the sculptor Willem Danielsz. van Tetrode, as de Weerdt published a print of a now lost sculpture group by van Tetrode (*Venus, Jupiter and Mercury*; *c.* 1574).

BIBLIOGRAPHY

Bénézit; Thieme–Becker

Kunst voor de beeldenstorm [Art before iconoclasm] (exh. cat., ed. V. Heijn; Amsterdam, Rijksmus., 1986), i, pp. 165

I. M. Veldmann: *De wereld tussen goed en kwaad: Late prenten van Coornhert* (The Hague, 1990)

——: 'Keulen als toevluchtsoord voor Nederlandse kunstenaars (1567–1612)', *Oud Holland*, cvii (1993), pp. 34–57

JETTY E. VAN DER STERRE

Weese, Harry (Mohr) (*b* Evanston, IL, 30 June 1915). American architect. He received his architectural training at Massachusetts Institute of Technology, Cambridge, MA (1934–8), with one year at Yale University, New Haven, CT. He then studied at Cranbrook Academy, Bloomfield Hills, MI (1938–9), with Eliel Saarinen. In 1940–41 he worked briefly for Skidmore, Owings & Merrill and then formed a short-lived partnership with Benjamin Baldwin (*b* 1913). During World War II he served as a naval engineering officer (1942–6). Following the war he again worked briefly for Skidmore, Owings & Merrill (1946–7) before reopening his office in Chicago, first as Baldwin and Weese, and after 1947 as Harry Weese and Associates.

Although a firm believer in a Functionalist approach to architecture, Weese acknowledged being strongly influenced by the Saarinens and especially by Alvar Aalto; this is evident in his use of brick and wood and his careful retention of human scale. He was also among the first architects of his generation to refer directly to Chicago building traditions, incorporating bay windows in his Walton Apartments (1956), 277 East Walton Street, Chicago, which recall those of the Reliance Building by Burnham & Root. His American Embassy (1959), Accra, Ghana, demonstrated a sensitive adjustment to climatic conditions, and the Old Town Apartment Building (1960), 235 West Eugenie Street, Chicago, has an intimate scale in the midst of the city. Other important works by Weese include the Arena State Theater (1961), Washington, DC; the Time–Life Building (1970), Chicago; and the stations (1977) of the Washington Metro, Washington, DC. Weese was also among the first architects of this generation to focus on the need to restore and refurbish important historic artefacts, as indicated in his sensitive restorations of Adler & Sullivan's Auditorium; the Field Museum of

Natural History, Chicago; and Daniel H. Burnham's Orchestra Hall, Chicago, all 1967. In his late work Weese continued to advise on and build transit systems and to expand the restoration and adaptive reuse of older buildings, as well as designing office buildings and housing complexes.

BIBLIOGRAPHY

Contemp. Architects

'Harry Weese and Associates of Chicago', *Space Des.*, 138 (Feb 1976), pp. 5–36

A. O. Dean: 'Harry Weese of Chicago', *AIA J.*, lxvii/5 (1978), pp. 56–65

'Harry Weese: Humanism and Tradition', *Process: Archit.*, 11 (1979) [whole issue]

L. Doumato: *Harry Mohr Weese* (Monticello, IL, 1981) [bibliog.]

LELAND M. ROTH

Wegman, William (*b* Holyoke, MA, 12 Feb 1943). American photographer, video artist, conceptual artist, sculptor, draughtsman and painter. He studied painting at the Massachusetts College of Art, Boston, MA (BFA, 1965), and at the University of Illinois at Urbana-Champaign, IL (MFA. 1967). During these years he produced Minimalist sculptures and paintings. In the early 1970s he used video and photography, primarily as a means of documenting such conceptual works as *Untied On Tied Off* (1972), a photograph of the artist's feet with one shoe on, untied, the other with the shoe tied to his ankle. These documents gave way to photographs that took on greater artistic qualities in terms of composition and technique, while he continued to use concepts and approaches seen in the earlier pieces (particularly irony, humour and satire on both popular culture and the high culture of contemporary art). He was most well known in the 1970s for his photographic and video works featuring his Weimaraner dog, Man Ray. By 1979 Wegman was working with large-format Polaroid film, a hyper-realistic medium highly paradoxical to the contrived situations in which Man Ray was placed, for example *Frog/Frog II* (1982; Col. Helen Lewis Meyer), for which Wegman attached green fins and artificial frog's eyes to Man Ray. He started making drawings *c.* 1973, many of which were executed in pencil on typing paper. They combine a Minimalist aesthetic with humour and often cynical satire, and in many an inscribed text is an integral part (e.g. *Ol' Blue Nose*, 1976). He continued with colour photography into the late 1980s, with his new dog Fay Ray, but in 1985 he also turned to painting. In a Post-modernist vein, these works possess a translucent tonality and linear decoration reminiscent of the work of Raoul Dufy. These works, such as *Migratory Architecture* (1988; New York, Holly Solomon Gal.), were bereft of humour but contained a juxtaposition of imagery from various cultural contexts.

BIBLIOGRAPHY

M. Lavin: 'Notes on William Wegman', *Artforum*, xiii/7 (1975), pp. 44–7

Wegman's World (exh. cat. by L. Lyons and K. Levin, Washington, DC, Corcoran Gal. A., and elsewhere, 1983)

M. Kunz, ed.: *William Wegman: Paintings, Drawings, Photographs, Videotapes* (New York, 1990)

□

Wegmann, Gustav Albert (*b* Steckborn, 9 July 1812, *d* Zurich, 12 Feb 1858). Swiss architect. He studied at the

Technische Hochschule, Karlsruhe (1832–3), under Heinrich Hübsch and Friedrich Eisenlohr. In 1833 he directed work on the buildings in the botanic garden at Heidelberg, and in 1835 he studied in Munich under Friedrich von Gärtner. From 1836 he worked in Zurich. His reputation rests on his public buildings in Zurich, which were compact structures that made sparing use of classical and historical ornamentation. They include the Kantonsspital (1836–8), built jointly with Leonhard Zeugheer, and the main railway station (1846–8). Wegmann's great interest in technical matters included advanced heating systems, sanitary arrangements and the solution of constructional problems, as in a greenhouse (1836–8) for the botanic garden in Zurich. Between 1839 and 1842 he built the Kantonsschule on the Rämibollwerk, closely modelled on Karl Friedrich Schinkel's Bauakademie in Berlin. The round-arched windows and sparse ornamentation of the heavy cube of the Mädchenschule (1850–51) at Grossmünster, near Zurich, harmonize with the neighbouring historic minster. In his only Gothic Revival building, the freemasons' temple at Lindenhof (1852), Wegmann incorporated the remnants of a Gothic cloister, and the stylistic unity extended into such details as the ritual objects. After 1850 he produced various residential buildings, notably those erected on the Tiefenhöfe in collaboration with Anselm Stadler and M. Koch, which had residential accommodation over glazed ground floors for commercial use. Wegmann's work, which embraced practically every type of building, including the Calvinist church (1842–3) at Nettenbach, indicates that he was stylistically a pluralist, but always concerned to achieve the utmost practicality.

SKL

BIBLIOGRAPHY
G.-W. Vonesch: *Der Architekt Gustav Albert Wegmann* (Zurich, 1981)
CORNELIA BAUER

Wegmann, Jakob. *See* WÄGMANN, JAKOB.

Weidemann [Opdahl; Johansen], **Jakob** (*b* Steinkjer, Nord-Trøndelag, 14 June 1923). Norwegian painter. After training with local artists at the Kunsthåndverksskole in Bergen (1939–40) and at the Kunstakademi in Oslo (1941–2), he took part in the resistance movement during the occupation of Norway in World War II and was forced to flee to Sweden in 1944; soon after this he lost the sight in his right eye. At the Kunsthögskola in Stockholm in 1944–5 he met several internationally oriented fellow students and was inspired by his teacher Sven Erixon's unconventional understanding of art and by the imagination and vital colours displayed in Erixon's paintings. Weidemann had a one-man exhibition after his return to Norway in 1946 (Oslo, Blomqvist Ksthandel), which was a critical and popular success. The colouristic virtuosity of his pre-war paintings of nudes and light-filled interiors was succeeded by formal abstractions, interpreted with a naive surreal quality and expressive colour contrasts, such as *Partisan* (1946; Oslo, Kommunes Kstsaml.). Until 1950 Weidemann combined inspiration from the Cobra Group's bold handling of colour and materials and Cubism's manipulation of form and space. The painting *Three Sculptures* (1950–51; Oslo, Mus. Samtidskst), with its shift to more muted colour contrasts and rhythmically placed block-like forms, refers back to a visit to the Galerie

Denise René in Paris. In the following six to seven years Weidemann's compositions were taken to formal extremes using few, contrasting colours and impersonal brushstrokes, as in *Black-and-yellow Composition* (1957; Oslo, Akersaml.).

The exhibition in 1961 at Kunstnernes Hus (The Artists' House), where Weidemann presented his first nature-inspired, tactile and expressive works, resulted in a breakthrough for abstract art in Norway and at the same time secured his place as a pioneer of Norwegian non-figurative painting. His *Forest Ground* pictures from this period, for example *Forest Ground III* (1961; Høvikodden, Henies-Onstads Kstsent.), reveal his debts to Serge Poliakoff, Antoni Tàpies and *Art informel*. Within a geometric structure, the dark and mysterious nature of the forest is presented through its leaves, bark, wild birds and stones. The colours, applied with thick impasto and worked with the palette knife, glow in a tangible and material way. Weidemann's transition from oil to tempera alone, for a period of about three years, reflected a poetic sense of colour that is also apparent in watercolours from the same period, for example *From the Peak* (1964; Oslo, N.G.).

From 1950 onwards Weidemann regularly executed decorative commissions. His first ecclesiastical project (1965), which involved a mural and stained-glass windows for the church of his home town, Steinkjer, led to a new range of religious subject-matter. His monumental paintings from this period, for example the *Road to Jerusalem* (1964–5; Høvikodden, Henies-Onstads Kstsent.), are considered to be among his most important works. In this painting his skilled use of colour is apparent: vibrating strokes in shades of pink, green and red break out from a lively dark blue background with passionate and explosive force. Such power gives an emotive impression of ascension in the wall and ceiling painting (1971) at Alfaset Cemetery Chapel. From the late 1960s Weidemann lived in an old farm house at Ringsveen in Lillehammer where he painted lyrical interpretations of the transitory beauty of light and its cosmic forces. From a central point of broad and spontaneous strokes, his vision of a Nordic nature emerged, transformed into a poetic and shimmering mist of rainbow colours (e.g. *Aurora Borealis I–II*, 1984–5; Høvikodden, Henies-Onstads Kstsent.). Weidemann represented Norway at the São Paulo Biennale in 1959 and at the Venice Biennale in 1966.

NKL

BIBLIOGRAPHY
Jakob Weidemann (exh. cat., foreword O. H. Moe; Høvikodden, Henies-Onstads Kstsent., 1975)
E. Egeland: *Jakob Weidemann* (Oslo, 1978)
K. Hellandsjø: *Jakob Weidemann og det abstrakte maleris gjennombrudd i Norge, 1945–65* [Jakob Weidemann and the emergence of abstract painting in Norway, 1945–65] (Oslo, 1978)
E. Egeland: *Weidemann: Portrett av en norsk modernist* (Oslo, 1986) [with Eng. summary]
SUSANNE RAJKA

Weidensdorfer, Claus (*b* Coswig, nr Dresden, 19 Aug 1931). German printmaker and draughtsman. He studied at the Hochschule für Bildende Künste in Dresden (1951–6) under Erich Fraass (1893–1974), Max Schwimmer (1895–1960) and Hans Theo Richter. He worked as an art teacher until 1957, and from 1957 to 1966 he was an assistant in graphic art in the art education department of the Hochschule für Bildende Künste in Dresden. His early works were indebted to the purist concept of printmaking as a black-and-white art of which Richter was a proponent. The fluency of Schwimmer's draughtsmanship influenced Weidensdorfer's work, as did the art of Chagall. In the 1960s there were some parallels between Weidensdorfer's work and that of Dieter Goltzsche. The main strands of his work are a mildly ironic cheerfulness in treating everyday life and the wisdom of proverbs and animal fables, sometimes with an altered meaning, for example the *Cat and the Chimney-sweep* (etching, 1964) and *Crow in the Yard* (etching, 1965; see 1990 exh. cat., no. 60). The theme of music consistently interested Weidensdorfer. He employed the motif of rhythm, of sweeping movements and of facial contortion lying between rapture and ecstasy, for example in *Harlequin with a Trombone* (drypoint, 1964; see 1990 exh. cat., p. 11) and *Woman Pop Singer* (lithograph, 1973; see 1990 exh. cat., p. 26).

From the mid-1970s the intensity of Weidensdorfer's work increased. In lithographs such as *Couple in the Tram* (1975) and *Old Couple* (1975; see 1990 exh. cat., p. 30), his portraiture achieves a new psychological acuteness. The internal tensions of relationships in all their ambivalence can be clearly felt. Thereafter he was interested in the use of colour in printmaking. His prints are often large in format and the modelling exaggerated. In the 1980s the themes of urbanization and alienation, of loss of individuality and isolation in modern civilization, were expressed in the motifs of the town, the station (e.g. *Station Exit*, etching overdrawn in ink, 1983; Berlin, Altes Mus.) and the street. Spaces, the link between inside and outside,

became images of confinement and longed-for expanse, a symbol of location.

BIBLIOGRAPHY

Claus Weidensdorfer (exh. cat., text by G. Barthel; Karl-Marx-Stadt, Gal. Oben, 1981)

Claus Weidensdorfer: Das graphische Werk (exh. cat. by G. Muschter and A. Muschter, Leipzig, Mus. Bild. Kst., 1990) [with detailed bibliog.]

Claus Weidensdorfer: Aus einem isolierten Land. Fünf Zeichner und eine Zeichnerin aus der ehemaligen DDR (exh. cat. Basle, Kstmus., 1992)

ANITA KÜHNEL

Weiditz [Weyditz; Widitz; Wyditz; Wydytz; Wydyz]. German family of artists, active in the Upper Rhine region from the mid-15th century to the mid-16th. The sculptor Bartholomäus Wyditz (*d* after 1477) from Meissen in Saxony married the daughter of the painter Marx Doiger (*d* 1477) in Strasbourg in 1469 and took up residence there. His son (1) Hans Weiditz (i) was probably the father of (2) Hans Weiditz (ii) and was also the father of (3) Christof Weiditz (i). (4) Christof Weiditz (ii) was the son of the latter.

BIBLIOGRAPHY

Thieme-Becker; *LK*

(1) Hans Weiditz (i) (*b* ?Strasbourg, ?*c*. 1475; *d* Strasbourg, ?1516). Sculptor. He was probably trained in his father's workshop but he worked as a master in Freiburg im Breisgau between 1497 and 1514. Until 1508 he is described as a *Bildhower* (sculptor) in the lists of the painters' guild. The parish account books for 1510 record a payment for carved wooden rosettes for keystones in the chancel of Freiburg Cathedral (originals now Freiburg im Breisgau, Augustinmus.). Between 1512 and 1516 he

Hans Weiditz (i): altar of the *Adoration of the Magi*, painted limewood, h. 920 mm, 1505 (Freiburg im Breisgau, Cathedral); reconstructed 1823

probably worked on the carved sections (vinescroll decoration and predella) of both the high altarpiece and the Schnewlin altarpiece (*c.* 1514–15) in the cathedral, in collaboration with the painter HANS BALDUNG. After 1515 he probably returned to Strasbourg.

In addition to commissions for altarpieces in the cathedral and monasteries of Freiburg (executed in an accomplished, delicate Late Gothic style), Hans produced small sculpture groups for private patrons, such as the signed boxwood *Adam and Eve* (Basle, Hist. Mus.). His altar of the *Adoration of the Magi* (*Three Kings* altar; see fig.), produced for the private chapel of Dr Konrad Stürtzel of Buchheim, is signed and dated 1505. In 1808 it was transferred from the Baslerhof in Freiburg to the cathedral; in 1823, enlarged by Joseph Dominikus Glänz (1778–1841), it was erected in the chancel, preserving Hans's figures and decorations. Other authenticated works include the figures of the *Virgin* and *St Agnes* from a small altarpiece, probably made *c.* 1500 (formerly Adelhausen monastery; now Freiburg im Breisgau, Augustinmus.). The figure of *St Agnes* bears the monogram HW. He probably made the *Adam and Eve* group at the same time. The carved sections of the high altarpiece and the Schnewlin altarpiece can be attributed to him both on grounds of style and because of the significance of his work for the paintings of Hans Baldung. Other attributions are sometimes disputed: an *Annunciation* group from Heilbronn (Berlin, Bodemus.); an *Annunciation* relief (Florence, Bargello); a *St Roch* from Altsimonswald and a *St John* of 1503 from Kenzingen (both Freiburg im Breisgau, Augustinmus.); a relief of *St Anne with the Virgin and Child* in St Pierre-le-Vieux, Strasbourg (*c.* 1520); a relief with the *Flight into Egypt* (Freiburg im Breisgau, Augustinmus.); a *Crucifixion* relief (New York, Cloisters); a *Crucifixion* relief (Berlin, Bodemus.); a figure of an old wife (Frankfurt am Main, Liebieghaus); and a *Grieving Job* (Cologne, Schnütgen-Mus.).

Hans Weiditz's outstanding skill as a sculptor found many followers and imitators both in Freiburg and its vicinity and in Strasbourg and the northern Upper Rhineland. He seems to have had a large workshop, first in Freiburg, then in Strasbourg. His early works reflect the graceful, delicate Gothic carving of Strasbourg around 1480, but in the large, sweeping forms of the late works he developed forms and motifs from the drawings of Albrecht Dürer.

BIBLIOGRAPHY

Thieme–Becker

G. Münzel: 'Der Dreikönigsaltar von Hans Wydytz im Freiburger Münster', *Freiburg. Münsterbl.*, vi (1910), pp. 1–22
C. Sommer: 'Beiträge zum Werk des Bildschnitzers Hans Wydytz', *Oberrhein. Kst*, iii (1928), pp. 94–104
I. Schroth: 'Zum Werk des Schnitzers Hans Wydyz', *Z. Schweiz. Archäol. & Kstgesch.*, xxii (1962), pp. 87–109
Kunstepochen der Stadt Freiburg (exh. cat. Freiburg im Breisgau, Augustinermus., 1970), pp. 187–97
Spätgotik am Oberrhein, 1450–1530 (exh. cat., ed. E. Zimmermann and others; Karlsruhe, Bad. Landesmus., 1970), pp. 182–96
M. Baxandall: *The Limewood Sculptors of Southern Germany* (New Haven and London, 1980), pp. 281–2
G. van der Osten: 'Zur Kleinplastik von Hans Wydyz dem Älteren und seiner Werkstatt', *Anz. Ger. Nmus.* (1981), pp. 44–55
U. Krentel: *Der Dreikönigsaltar d. Hans Wydyz im Freiburger Münster* (diss., U. Bonn, 1987)
U. Heinrichs: 'Ein Kreuzigungsrelief von Hans Wydyz in der Skulpturengalerie Berlin Dahlem', *Aufsätze zur süddeutschen Skulptur des 15. und 16. Jahrhunderts*, ed. R. Schneider (in preparation)

INGEBORG KRUMMER-SCHROTH

(2) Hans Weiditz (ii) (*b* ?Freiburg im Breisgau, before 1500; *d* Strasbourg, *c.* 1536). Woodcut designer, probably

Hans Weiditz (ii): *Cardamine pratensis* (lady's smock), watercolour drawing (Berne, Botanisches Institut und Botanischer Garten, Lib III 1-3, fol. 60); preparatory to his woodcut for *Herbarum vivae eicones* by Otto Brunfels (Strasbourg, 1530–36)

the son of (1) Hans Weiditz (i). Between 1530 and 1534 he is documented as a member of the Strasbourg guild 'zur Stelze', which included metalworkers, glaziers, painters and printers. The only works that can be certainly attributed to him are the woodcuts to the *Herbarum vivae eicones* (pubd Schott, Strasbourg, 1530–36; Ger. edn as *Contrafaytes Kräuterbuch*, 1532) by Otto Brunfels (1488–1534). Some preparatory watercolour drawings for these woodcuts, surviving in the *Platter-Herbarium* (Berne, Botan. Inst. & Gtn; see fig.), are astonishing in their precision and fidelity to nature, including such details as wilted leaves and damage by insects. Together with the woodcuts they were an important step in the foundation of botany as a scientific discipline.

In Brunfels's herbal Weiditz is described as 'very famous', and later Johann Fischart (1550–90) in *Accuratae effigies pontificum maximorum* (Strasbourg, 1573) named him among Strasbourg artists, along with Heinrich Vogtherr and Hans Baldung. The discrepancy between Weiditz's fame and the paucity of his extant works led Röttinger (1904) to assign to him the work of the illustrator of a German edition of Petrarch's *De remediis utriusque fortunae* entitled *Von der Artzney bayder Glück* (pubd Steyner, Augsburg, 1532; see MASTERS, ANONYMOUS, & MONOGRAMMISTS, §I: MASTER OF PETRARCH; see AUGSBURG, fig. 5). Some of the Petrarch woodcuts, which were completed in 1520, were also used in a German edition of Cicero's *Officia* (pubd Steyner, Augsburg, 1531): on two cuts in this Röttinger discovered the initials H.W. In the late 16th century the Basle collector Basilius Amerbach listed works by the Master of Petrarch as by 'H. Widitz'. In the light of this proposal Weiditz's slender output was enlarged by an impressive group of the most original woodcuts in 16th-century Germany; it was suggested that he had spent years in the Augsburg workshop of Hans Burgkmair I, with whom the Master of Petrarch shows close stylistic affinities.

This thesis found general acceptance (Dodgson, Friedländer, Fraenger) until Musper, followed by Buchner, distinguished two hands in the vast oeuvre thus ascribed to Weiditz, contrasting works from Augsburg with those from Strasbourg. In the lack of further evidence, opinion remains divided on the issue.

BIBLIOGRAPHY
Thieme–Becker
H. Röttinger: *Hans Weiditz, der Petrarkameister*, Studien zur Kunst, *50* (Strasbourg, 1904)
C. Dodgson: *Catalogue of Early German and Flemish Woodcuts Preserved in the Department of Prints and Drawings in the British Museum*, ii (London, 1911), pp. 139–86
M. J. Friedländer: *Holzschnitte von Hans Weiditz* (Berlin, 1922)
T. Musper: *Die Holzschnitte des Petrarkameisters: Ein kritisches Verzeichnis* (Munich, 1927)
E. Buchner: 'Der Petrarkameister als Maler, Miniator und Zeichner', *Festschrift Heinrich Wölfflin* (Munich, 1924), pp. 209–31
H. Koegler: 'Die Überlieferung vom Namen des Hans Weiditz', *Oberrhein. Kst*, i (1925–6), pp. 78–82
W. Fraenger: *Altdeutsches Bilderbuch: Hans Weiditz und Sebastian Brant*, Denkmale der Volkskunst, 2 (Leipzig, 1930)
W. Rytz: *Faksimileausgabe der Pflanzenaquarelle des Hans Weiditz aus dem Jahre 1529* (Berne, 1936)
W. Scheidig: *Die Holzschnitte des Petrarca-Meister: Zu Petrarcas Werk 'Von der Artzney bayder Glück'* (Berlin, 1955)
Welt im Umbruch: Augsburg zwischen Renaissance und Barock, i (exh. cat., Augsburg, Rathaus, 1980–81), pp. 115–16
From a Mighty Fortress: Prints, Drawings and Books in the Age of Luther, 1483–1546 (exh. cat. by C. D. Andersson and C. Talbot, Detroit, MI, Inst. A.; Ottawa, N.G.; Coburg, Veste Coburg; 1981–82), pp. 158–66, 382
J. Wirth: 'Hans Weiditz, illustrateur de la réforme à Strasbourg', in *Von der Macht der Bilder, Beiträge des C. I. H. A. Kolloquiums 'Kunst und Reformation'*, ed. E. Ullmann (Leipzig, 1983), pp. 299–318
German Drawings from a Private Collection (exh. cat. by J. Rowlands, London, BM; Washington, DC, N.G.A.; Nuremberg, Ger. Nmus.; 1984), pp. 39–40
Die Renaissance im deutschen Südwesten zwischen Reformation und Dreissigjährigen Krieg (exh. cat. by H. Appuhn and others, Heidelberg, Schloss, 1986), i, pp. 303, 323–6
The Age of Dürer and Holbein: German Drawings, 1400–1550 (exh. cat. by J. Rowlands, London, BM, 1988), pp. 208–10

KRISTIN LOHSE BELKIN

(3) Christof Weiditz (i) (*b* Freiburg im Breisgau, *c.* 1500; *d* Augsburg, 1559). Medallist, sculptor and goldsmith, son of (1) Hanz Weiditz (i). From 1523 to 1525 he worked in Strasbourg, from 1525 to 1526 in Swabia (Ulm, Öttingen), and from 1526 to 1529 in Augsburg. In 1529 he travelled to Spain in the retinue of Emperor Charles V, then to the Imperial Diet in Augsburg. In 1530–1 he accompanied the Imperial court to the Rhineland and Low Countries. In 1532 he returned through Nuremberg and Regensburg to Augsburg, where he stayed for a time. After an initial refusal he was admitted to the sculptors' guild, although his work as a goldsmith provoked guild protests. He probably journeyed to Saxony in 1537 and 1539, and, if the English costumes in his *Trachtenbuch* (Nuremberg, Ger. Nmus., MS. Hs. Nr. 22474) are his work, he may also have spent some time in England.

More than a hundred commemorative medals and models dated between 1523 and 1544 are authenticated works of Christof and others are attributed. In addition to modelling many German burghers and princes, in 1529 he modelled *Charles V*, *Johann Dantikus*, Bishop of Ermland, *Hernán Cortes* (*d* 1547), the conqueror of Mexico, the Genoese admiral *Andrea Doria* and other famous people. Christof also produced small sculptures, such as the wooden *Fortune* (Florence, Bargello), and goldsmith's work, including a dagger with *Fortune* and the signature 'Christof Weyditz in Augusta Vindelica faciebat' (ex-Hist. Mus., Dresden). A life-size clay bust in the Victoria & Albert Museum, London, is generally considered to be a self-portrait. Christof began work on his *Trachtenbuch* in 1529 on his journey to Spain, recording folk scenes and costumes, with later additions from other countries. (4) Christof Weiditz (ii) is sometimes attributed with the *Trachtenbuch*, working after (3) Christof Weiditz (i)'s designs.

BIBLIOGRAPHY
Forrer; *LK*; Thieme–Becker
G. Habich: *Die deutschen Medailleurs des 16. Jahrhunderts* (Halle, 1916)
T. Hampe: *Das Trachtenbuch des Ch. Weiditz von seinen Reisen nach Spanien und der Niederlanden* (Berlin and Leipzig, 1927)
G. Habich: *Die deutschen Schaumutzen des 16. Jahrhunderts*, 2 vols (Munich, 1929–34)
P. Grotemeyer: *'Da ich het die gestalt': Deutsche Bildnismedaillen des 16. Jahrhunderts* (Munich, 1957)
P. Arnold: *Medaillenbildnisse der Reformationszeit* (Berlin, 1967)
J. Roubier and J. Babelon: *Das Menschenbild auf Münzen und Medaillen von der Antike bis zur Renaissance* (Leipzig, 1967)
Die Renaissance im deutschen Südwesten zwischen Reformation und Dreissigjahrigem Krieg (exh. cat., by H. Appuhn and others, Heidelberg, Schloss, 1986), ii, pp. 577, 589, 593, 600, 602

(4) Christof Weiditz (ii) (*b* ?Strasbourg, ?*c.* 1517; *d* ?Strasbourg, before 1572). Painter and woodcut designer, son of (3) Hans Weiditz (ii). He took over a printing business with David Kannel in 1537, which he sold in 1539. In 1562 a demand was made for a work produced for Paulus Hector Mair, a councillor of Augsburg, for which Christof Weiditz had received advance payments. In 1565 Christof bought two houses. Authenticated works are his designs for woodcuts (two of which are signed) of 92 knights for Mair's treatise *Bericht und anzeigen aller Herren Geschlecht der lobl. Stadt Augspurg*, whose first edition was printed by Weiditz and Kannel in Strasbourg in 1538. A second, expanded edition was printed by M. Kriegstein in Augsburg in 1550.

BIBLIOGRAPHY
Thieme–Becker
H. Röttinger: *Hans Weiditz: Der Petrarkameister* (Strasbourg, 1904)
F. Ritter: *Histoire de l'imprimerie alsacienne aux XVe et XVIe siècles* (Strasbourg and Paris, 1955)
E. Nienholdt and G. Wagner-Neumann, eds: *Katalog der Lipperheidischen Kostümbibliothek* (Berlin, 1965), ii, p. 620

INGEBORG KRUMMER-SCHROTH

Weidmann, Leonhard (*fl* 1568–96). German mason and master builder. In 1568, when he became a citizen of Rothenburg ob der Tauber, Bavaria, he was paid for a plan to rebuild the Renaissance wing of the town hall, on which work began in 1570. Opinions vary concerning the extent to which Weidmann's scheme was followed, as he did not qualify as a master craftsman until 1575. The town hall, one of the finest in Franconia, reconciles the traditional high gabled façade with the heavily stressed horizontals of the long side elevation, exposed to the market square, by locating a three-storey oriel at the angle. Weidmann's work is seen in the Gothic wing, too, where he carved the bar in the courtroom.

In 1574–8 Weidmann worked on the reconstruction of the hospital and was responsible for its Renaissance doorway. He is credited also with the Hagemeisterhaus in the courtyard of the hospital, an effective composition built up from a two-storey cube with a tent-shaped roof, set off by a higher stair tower crowned by an open lantern. The old Grammar School (Gymnasium, 1589–91) is assigned to Weidmann on stylistic grounds: horizontal bands of moulding separate the three floors, the windows are arranged in pairs, as at the town hall, and an obliquely fenestrated octagonal stair tower crowned by a bulbous cupola is introduced in front of the façade. The house known as the Baumeisterhaus, which was built by Weidmann in 1596 for a town councillor, is the most important Renaissance building in Rothenburg, notable for the particularly rich figurative decoration on its façade.

BIBLIOGRAPHY
W. Döderlein: 'Zur Vorgeschichte des "Neuen Baues" am Rathaus zu Rothenburg o. Tb', *Hist. Jb. Görres-Ges.*, lxi (1941), pp. 256–81
W. Tunk: 'Der Stilwandel um 1600 im Spiegel der Entstehungsgeschichte des Nürnberger Pellerhauses', *Kunstgeschichtliche Studien*, ed. H. von Tintelnot (Breslau [Wrocław], 1943), pp. 291–314
V. Mayr: *Rothenburg ob der Tauber* (Berlin, 1978)
H. W. Lübbeke: *Mittelfranken* (1986), v of *Denkmäler in Bayern* (Munich)

WERNER BRODA

Wei dynasty. Northern Chinese dynasty founded by the Tuoba or Toba people, dating to AD 386–556. After the collapse of the unifying Western Jin dynasty (265–316), the Chinese court fled south to Nanjing and left the north to various alien invaders. Northern China was then ruled by a series of Sixteen Kingdoms (310–439). Eventually the Tuoba branch of the Xianbei people came to power as the Northern Wei dynasty (386–534), and by the mid-5th century they succeeded in reunifying all the north. After a period of peace the Xianbei generals on the frontiers revolted in 534, and the Northern Wei was succeeded by two overlapping states, the Eastern (534–50) and Western (535–56) Wei.

During the Wei period Buddhism was widely adopted and became the chief inspiration for figurative art (*see* BUDDHISM, §III, 8(ii)). As a salvationist religion, it particularly appealed to Chinese affected by the chaos after the collapse of the Han empire (206 BC–AD 220), who had lost faith in traditional Chinese ways. The non-Chinese origin of Buddhism also attracted the Wei rulers, most of whom became ardent believers and great patrons of Buddhist art. They commissioned vast rock-cut temples adorned with paintings and sculpture at Yungang, Longmen, Mt Maiji and Dunhuang. Many Buddhist bronze sculptures were made in the Wei, though few survive, since they were often melted down at times when Buddhists were persecuted (*see also* CHINA, §III, 1(ii)(b)). Landscape painting also became increasingly important, as is evident in wall paintings (*see* CHINA, §V, 3(i)(a)) and on carved stone sarcophagi.

Although the Wei was a time of geographical division, China benefited greatly during the period from foreign influences; Buddhism, for example, brought knowledge pertaining to financial institutions and bridge and road engineering. Many Wei institutions such as taxation, land reform and militia systems were inherited and developed by later Chinese dynasties.

1. NORTHERN. The Northern Wei (AD 386–534) capital was initially at Pingcheng, near modern Datong in Shanxi Province. Then in 493–4 Emperor Xiaowendi (*reg* 471–99) moved the capital south to Luoyang, Henan Province. Here, a large-scale, magnificent new city was built on the ruins of the old Chinese capital (for city plan *see* LUOYANG), and by 534 the population exceeded half a million.

Apart from a brief period when the emperor Taiwudi (*reg* 424–51) favoured the Daoist church and heavily persecuted Buddhists, Buddhism was fostered and Buddhist art and architecture flourished under state and private patronage. To compensate for earlier iconoclasm and to commemorate ancestors, a series of cave temples was instigated at YUNGANG, close to the capital at Pingcheng, reportedly in 460. Thousands of craftsmen, many from Central Asia, worked for about 35 years to create the cave temples (originally an Indian concept), adorning them with Buddhist sculpture and paintings. When Xiaowendi moved the capital to Luoyang he ordered more Buddhist cave temples to be carved at nearby LONGMEN. A Chinese style gradually evolved: the colossal Yungang static icons reflect Gandharan influence (from an area in modern Afghanistan and Pakistan) but the Longmen sculpture is more linear in style. The earliest paintings and stucco Buddha and *bodhisattva* images at Dunhuang, Gansu

Province, also date from the Northern Wei period. Buddhism also inspired pagoda architecture (*see* CHINA, §II, 4(i)(c) and fig. 17); in the first third of the 6th century the Northern Wei competed with the Liang (502–57) kingdom in Buddhist good works. Burial pottery, probably dating from after the move of the capital, is quite different from that of the Han period (206 BC–AD 220), with an emphasis on frontality and symmetry that suggests an interaction with Buddhist art.

As the nomadic Tuoba became accustomed to a sedentary existence and recognized the need for bureaucracy to control an increased population and enlarged state, their reliance on Chinese institutions grew. The wealthy also developed a taste for Chinese luxuries and culture. Sinicization was an important factor in the decision to move the capital to Luoyang. Under Xiaowendi Chinese became the official language, intermarriage with Chinese was actively promoted and the use of Tuoba language, names and clothing was forbidden. The emperor took the Chinese name Yuan, dropping the name Tuoba. The contrast between the former 'barbarian' north and the 'civilized' south grew less marked. The speed and compulsory nature of assimilation, however, annoyed the northern frontiersmen, who felt neglected by the remote, sinicized court and were materially less well-off than their southern clansmen. Mutinies by garrison soldiers led to the fall of the Northern Wei, and in 534 northern China was divided into Eastern and Western Wei kingdoms.

2. EASTERN. The Eastern Wei (AD 534–50) had a capital at Ye (modern Anyang) in southern Hebei Province and controlled an area east of Luoyang. The dynasty was established by a Chinese former Northern Wei garrison commander, Gao Huan (496–547), and his sons. Under the Eastern Wei, Buddhism continued to be the chief artistic inspiration. The oldest stone pagoda chapel extant in China, at Shentong si at Mt Tai in Shandong Province, probably dates to this period. An inscription dating it to 544 is questionable, but the unrestored sculpture is Eastern Wei in style. Sculpture at the limestone hill shrines of AD 537 in Licheng County, Shandong Province, though derivative of Northern Wei models, possesses the greater rotundity typical of Eastern Wei style. In 550 Gao Huan's son, Gao Yang, became emperor. Although he kept the capital at Ye and ruled over the same territory, he established the NORTHERN QI DYNASTY.

3. WESTERN. The Western Wei (AD 535–56) was established by Yuwen Tai (*reg* 535–51), a member of the Yuwen clan of the Xianbei people. He ruled with the help of survivors of the sinicized aristocracy of Luoyang and was dependent largely on ethnic Chinese in the civil administration and the army. The dynasty had a capital at Chang'an (modern Xi'an) in Shaanxi Province, and controlled the land west of Luoyang. The area of modern Sichuan Province became part of the territory in 553. As a state, the Western Wei was considerably smaller than the Eastern Wei and so at a disadvantage in terms of population. However, the efficient bureaucracy, recruited for ability rather than birth, and well-organized army, based on a system later inherited by the Sui (581–618) and Tang (618–907) dynasties, proved effective. Wall paintings and stucco images of Buddhist subjects of the Western Wei period occur in the DUNHUANG caves, Gansu Province. Mortuary figures, many made in moulds and glazed, began to be less stiff and have more facial expression than in earlier periods; the many different ethnic types portrayed reflect the cross-cultural influences of the time (*see* CHINA, §VII, 3(iii)(b)). In 557 Yuwen Tai's son, retaining a capital at Chang'an, inaugurated the NORTHERN ZHOU DYNASTY (557–81).

BIBLIOGRAPHY

Les grottes de Touen-Houang: Peintures et sculptures bouddhiques des époques des Wei, des Tang et des Song (Paris, 1914–21), R as *Grottes de Touen-Houang: Carnet de notes de Paul Pelliot: Inscriptions et peintures rurales*, ed. N. Vandier-Nicholas, 6 vols (Paris, 1981–92)
A. Soper: 'Life Motion and the Sense of Space in Early Chinese Representational Art', *A. Bull.*, xxx/3 (1948), pp. 167–86
——: 'The Northern Liang and Northern Wei in Kansu', *Artibus Asiae*, xxi (1958), pp. 131–64
——: 'Two Stelae and a Pagoda on the Central Peak, Mt. Sung'; *Archvs Asian A.*, xvi (1962), pp. 41–8
——: 'The Cave-chapels of the Northern Dynasties: Donors, Beneficiaries, Dates', *Artibus Asiae*, xxvii (1966), pp. 241–70
Chūgoku bijutsu [Arts of China], 3 vols (Tokyo, 1964–5); vol. ii (1969) trans. as *Buddhist Cave Temples, New Researches* (Tokyo and Palo Alto, 1968–70)
'Shanxi Datong Shijiazhai Bei Wei Sima Jinlong mu' [The Northern Wei Tomb of Sima Jinlong at Shijiazhai, Datong, Shanxi], *Wenwu* (1972), no. 3, pp. 20–33
A. Juliano: *Art of the Six Dynasties: Centuries of Change and Innovation* (New York, 1975)
'Hebei Ci xian Dongchen cun Dong Wei mu' [Excavation of an Eastern Wei tomb at Dongchen cun, Ci xian, Hebei], *Kaogu* (1977), no. 6, pp. 391–400
'Hebei Zanhuang Dong Wei Li Xizong mu' [Excavation of the Eastern Wei tomb of Li Xizong in Zanhuang, Hebei], *Kaogu* (1977), no. 6, pp. 382–90
A. Juliano: *Teng-Hsien: An Important Six Dynasties Tomb* (Ascona, 1980)
'Hanzhong shi Cuijiaying Xi Wei mu qingli ji' [Record of the inspection of the Western Wei tomb at Cuijiaying, Hanzhong], *Kaogu Yu Wenwu* (1981), no. 2, pp. 21–4
W. F. J. Jenner: *Memories of Loyang: Yang Hsuan-chih and the Lost Capital (493–534)* (Oxford, 1981)
R. Whitfield: *The Art of Central Asia*, 3 vols (Tokyo, 1982)
R. Whitfield and A. Farrer: *Caves of the Thousand Buddhas: Chinese Art from the Silk Route* (London, 1990)

CAROL MICHAELSON

Weie, (Viggo Thorvald) Edvard (*b* Christianshavn, 18 Nov 1879; *d* Copenhagen, 9 April 1943). Danish painter. He was self-taught, except for a short period of study under Kristian Zahrtmann at the Kunstnernes Studieskoler, Copenhagen (1906–7). On his first journey abroad to Italy in 1907 he was impressed by the Mediterranean light, which influenced his later desire to introduce lighter colours into his painting. His maturation as an artist, however, took place in Denmark. His first paintings were naturalistic, with a colour scale close to grey. He described this early work as realistic–impressionistic, with a rhythmical weighing out of form and colouring, the chief emphasis being laid on the colouring, as in the *Painter's Mother* (1908; Copenhagen, Stat. Mus. Kst). In 1912 Weie visited Paris for the first time, and later in the same year he stayed on the island of Christiansø. Both of these experiences led to a new stage in his development. The colour surface gained a broader and more Cubist character. He began a series of freely-imaginative figurative compositions, in which sea, rocks and figures were woven into a turbulent drama. Among these are different depictions of Poseidon, such as *Poseidon Rushing over the Sea Surrounded* *by Nereids and Tritons* (1917; Copenhagen, Stat. Mus. Kst), in which the brushstrokes are violent and the colour tones restrained. He continued to execute heroic compositions into the 1920s. At the same time he produced paintings lacking in spatial depth, in which the brushstrokes are scarcely evident. The pictures appear to be charged with mystic dreams and nervous impressions. The last 20 years of Weie's life were characterized by a long series of compositions that show a more intense and free abstraction, together with a continuing experimentation with colours and a lighter and more obvious brush control. He became absorbed in the abstract qualities of colours that were rich and glowing, as in *Interior with Figure* (1923; Århus, Kstmus.) and *Dante and Virgil after Delacroix* (*c.* 1925; Oslo, N.G.). Weie expressed his views on art in his book *Poesi og kultur* (Poetry and culture).

For illustration *see* DENMARK, fig. 10.

WRITINGS
A. Weie, ed.: *Poesi og kultur* (Copenhagen, 1951)

BIBLIOGRAPHY
Akvareller og tegninger af Edvard Weie [Watercolours and drawings by Edvard Weie] (exh. cat. by E. Poulsen, Copenhagen, Stat. Mus. Kst, 1982)
E. Klange: *Edvard Weie: Form og symbol* (Århus, 1984)
Edvard Weie (exh. cat. by H. Bramsen, E. Poulsen and L. Gottlieb, Copenhagen, Stat. Mus. Kst, 1987)

RIGMOR LOVRING

Weikersheim, Schloss. German castle on the River Tauber in the province of Baden-Württemberg; the seat of the Counts (later Princes) of Hohenlohe. In 1586 Wolfgang II, Count of Hohenlohe (1546–1610), began the conversion of the medieval moated castle into a prestigious residence. The design by Georg Robin (*d* 1590) probably envisaged a building on the ground-plan of an equilateral triangle, but only the south wing (1595–1603), built by Wolf Beringer, was completed. Its exterior was adorned with six scrollwork gables (1598). The large Rittersaal, one of the most elaborate of the period, has a coffered wooden ceiling by Elias Gunzenhäuser (*fl* 1583–1606), the coffering filled with realistic hunting scenes (1600–01) by Balthasar Katzenberger (*fl* 1600–13). The Renaissance garden (*c.* 1600) beyond the moat was replaced in 1708 by a Baroque garden designed by Daniel Mathieu. Garden sculptures (1708–25) by members of the Sommer family include the figure of *Hercules Fighting the Hydra*, the Olympian gods, the four elements, the four seasons and the four winds. A series of 16 dwarf figures caricaturing contemporary courtiers is the only gallery of garden sculptures inspired by Jacques Callot that has survived in its entirety. An orangery (1719–23), with two wings designed by Johann Christian Lüttich (*b c.* 1685), was built at the south end of the garden, its open section on the main axis of the garden, giving a free view of the surrounding countryside. Lüttich also erected two low arcaded and curved buildings (1729) linking the Schloss with the market square of the town of Weikersheim.

BIBLIOGRAPHY
W.-G. Fleck: *Schloss Weikersheim und die hohenlohischen Schlösser der Renaissance* (Tübingen, 1954)
H. R. Hitchcock: *German Renaissance Architecture* (Princeton, 1981)
K. Merten: *Schloss Weikersheim* (Munich, 1981)

REINHARD ZIMMERMANN

Weill, Berthe (*b* 1865; *d* 1951). French art dealer. She entered the art trade in the 1890s, at about the same time as Ambroise Vollard, but did not prosper as dramatically as he did, which may partly explain the acidic portrait she painted of him in her memoirs. The policy she pursued through the Galerie Berthe Weill, founded in Paris in 1901, was based on offering exhibitions to a wide range of relatively little-known artists. She was the first Parisian dealer to show the work of Pablo Picasso, and most of the artists associated with both Fauvism and Cubism exhibited at her gallery. However, she did not concentrate on particular individuals or stylistic tendencies, nor did she build up a large stock of paintings. Consequently artists tended to move to other galleries if they became successful. In 1917 she gave Amedeo Modigliani his only one-man exhibition in his lifetime, and in the 1920s she regularly exhibited the work of Jules Pascin, the French painter Emilie Charmy (1878–1974) and Per Krohg, and she had partial contracts with Raoul Dufy and the French painter Edouard-Joseph Goerg (1893–1969). She was critical of the atmosphere of speculation that developed in the late 1920s and particularly of the role of auction sales in promoting it. The gallery suffered in the Depression of the 1930s but survived the decade. After World War II Weill was awarded the Légion d'honneur for her services to French art.

WRITINGS
Pan! Dans l'oeil! ou trente ans dans les coulisses de la peinture contemporaine 1900-1930 (Paris, 1933)

BIBLIOGRAPHY
Bénézit
'Portraits de marchands: Mme Berthe Weill', *Beaux-A.* (22 Dec 1935)

MALCOLM GEE

Weimar. German city on the River Ilm in Thuringia with a population of *c.* 63,500. It was the residence of the dukes (grand dukes from 1815) of Saxe-Weimar until 1918. A castle was first mentioned in 975, and the city was founded *c.* 1245; both became the property of the Wettin electors of Saxony *c.* 1373. The dukes and their families were the most important patrons, and building activity was centred on the Schloss (1438). SS Peter and Paul, a hall church incorporating an earlier church, was built between 1498 and 1500 and contains a triptych by Lucas Cranach the younger (1555). The Schloss has a 16th-century gatehouse, which was remodelled (1545) by Nikolaus Gromann (*fl* 1537–74), who also built the Grünes Schloss (1562) and the Cranach Haus (1549) on the market. Weimar became the capital of the Saxe-Weimar duchy in 1547. After a fire (1618) destroyed much of the Schloss, a new building was begun in 1619 by Giovanni Bomalino (*fl.* 1614–33). The original design was altered *c.* 1650 by Johann Moritz Richter (1620–67) to create an open *cour d'honneur*. Work on the unfinished building stopped in 1664. Extensive building during the first half of the 18th century included the Jakobskirche (1713) by Christian Richter II, the Baroque remodelling (1735–45) of SS Peter and Paul by Johann Adolf Richter (1682–1768), the Gelbes Schloss (1704), a school (1715) and a riding school (1715). Near Weimar several *maisons de plaisance* were put up, for example the Lustschloss (1736–41) at Dornburg by GOTT-FRIED HEINRICH KROHNE.

The present appearance of Weimar is largely due to Anna Amalia, Duchess of Saxe-Weimar, and her son, Charles Augustus, Duke of Saxe-Weimar (*see* WETTIN, (10) and (11)). The population rose from *c.* 6,000 in 1750 to 10,000 in 1825, which necessitated the construction of new city walls. The Grünes Schloss was rebuilt by August Strassburger as a library (1761–6), later named the Herzogin Anna Amalie Bibliothek, after the duchess: it is a late Rococo room with semicircular ends and a gallery, and it contributed to Weimar's rise as a centre of learning. This was reinforced by the presence of Christoph Martin Wieland (1733–1813), Johann Gottfried Herder, Friedrich Schiller and Johann Wolfgang von Goethe.

The Schloss burnt down again in 1774, but lack of a resident architect and funds prevented rebuilding until 1789; Goethe served on the building commission and three architects were involved in short succession. From 1789 to 1790 Goethe's protégé Johann August Arens reused the shell of the ruin (see fig.), remodelling a wide passageway and staircase in the east wing, which included an elegant, raised colonnade facing the river. Nikolaus Friedrich von Thouret designed some of the interior decoration (1798–1800). The north and east wings were not completed until Heinrich Gentz took control (1800–03). The Schloss later became a museum and art gallery. Gentz also remodelled such ducal and municipal buildings as the riding school, the new wing of the library and the assembly rooms.

From 1776 Charles Augustus and Goethe created a landscaped park along the river to the south-east of the Schloss and city. Garden buildings included both a Gothic Revival folly (1786–7; replaced in 1811 by a folly of similar style that was later named the Tempelherrerhaus) and the Neo-classical Römisches Haus (1792–7) designed by Arens, a summer-house for the duke; it is a small Ionic temple with sturdy Doric substructures. Charles Augustus also supported such artists as Louise Seidler. There were few notable building projects in the town at this time, apart from Goethe's remodelling (1792) of his own house (now Goethe-Nationalmuseum) on Frauenplan and the large mansion (from 1780) of the councillor, entrepreneur and publisher Friedrich Justin Bertuch (1747–1822), which was built in five phases (now a museum tracing the history of Weimar). In 1816 CLEMENS WENZESLAUS COUDRAY was appointed Oberbandirektor and built the west wing (1822–34) of the Schloss. During *c.* 30 years in office, Coudray executed ducal, municipal and private commissions and created an atmosphere of understated Neo-classicism in the town centre. The end of his influence was heralded when his plans for the new town hall were rejected in favour of a Gothic Revival design (after 1837) by Heinrich Hess (1794–1865). Meanwhile, at the Freie Zeichenschule, which was founded in 1776 with G. M. Kraus as the director, HEINRICH MEYER taught such students as Friedrich Preller.

To accommodate the growing population, which rose from 16,000 in 1871 to 35,000 in 1919, the city expanded to the north, with a railway station (1843) and the Ducal Museum (1861–8; destr.), designed by Josef Zítek and executed by Karl Martin von Stegmann, as focal points.

Weimar, view from the north-east, showing the Schloss (centre left) and the River Ilm in the foreground, engraving by Johann Müller after Georg Kraus, 420×561 mm, *c.* 1800 (Weimar, Graphische Sammlung)

Stanislaus Graf von Kalckreuth (1820–94) became founding director in 1859 of the Kunstschule and inaugurated the Weimarer Malerschule, which had a special interest in landscape painting. Among those to teach and study in Weimar were Arnold Böcklin, Charles Verlat, Franz von Lenbach, Max Liebermann and CHRISTIAN ROHLFS. Henry Van de Velde lived in Weimar from 1902 to 1917 and built the new Kunstschule (1904) and the Kunstgewerbeschule (from 1905). The two amalgamated in 1919 under the directorate of WALTER GROPIUS to form the Staatliches Bauhaus (see BAUHAUS, §1). Harry Graf Kessler (1868–1937) started the Cranach-Presse in 1913 and produced some beautiful, hand-printed, illustrated books. In 1936, in the area between the station and the inner city, Hitler began building the Gauforum, a large square surrounded by office buildings and a hall for festivities by Hermann Giesler. It was left unfinished in 1942. Weimar was heavily damaged by bombing on 9 February 1945, but the historic centre was subsequently restored.

BIBLIOGRAPHY

W. Huschke: *Die Geschichte des Parkes von Weimar* (Weimar, 1951)
E. Schmidt, ed.: *Die Stadtpfarrkirche zu St. Peter und Paul in Weimar* (Berlin, 1955)
W. Scheidig: *Das Schloss zu Weimar* (Weimar, 1962)
A. Jericke and D. Dolgner: *Der Klassizismus in der Baugeschichte Weimars* (Weimar, 1974)
G. Günther and L. Wallraff: *Geschichte der Stadt Weimar* (Weimar, 1975)
C. Schädlich: *Die Hochschule für Architektur und Bauwesen Weimar: Ein geschichtlicher Abriss*, Weimarer Schriften, xv (Weimar, 1985)
W. Scheidig: *Die Geschichte der Weimarer Malerschule, 1860–1900* (Weimar, 1991)
Genius huius loci, Weimar: Kulturelle Entwürfe aus fünf Jahrunderten (exh. cat., Weimar, Ksthalle, 1992)
G. Günther and others, eds: *Weimar: Lexikon zur Stadtgeschichte* (Weimar, 1993)
J. Seifert, ed.: *Die Weimarer Klassikerstätten: Geschichte und Denkmalpflege* (Weimar, 1993)

JARL KREMEIER

Weinbrenner, (Johann Jakob) Friedrich (*b* Karlsruhe, 29 Nov 1766; *d* Karlsruhe, 1 March 1826). German architect, urban planner, writer and teacher. He was one of the most important architects consistently to employ strict Neo-classical tenets in the context of urban planning. As city architect of KARLSRUHE, Weinbrenner shaped the architectural image of the enlarged city, and his ideas came to influence all public architecture in the district of Baden. However, the persistence with which he clung to the architectural idiom he had introduced earned him the harsh criticism of the younger generation.

1. Education and early influences. 2. Urban plans for Karlsruhe. 3. Public and religious buildings. 4. Teaching and writings.

1. EDUCATION AND EARLY INFLUENCES. Weinbrenner learnt carpentry in his father's workshop and also attended craft school and drawing classes. Due to the lack of an adequate teacher in Baden, he studied in Switzerland (1788–90), Vienna and Dresden. He was also influenced and greatly inspired by a visit to Berlin (1791–2), especially by the work of Carl Gotthard Langhans and Hans Christian Genelli. While in Berlin he also produced a design for a Protestant church for Karlsruhe, his first piece of independent work in the Neo-classical style. A five-year stay in Rome (1792–7), however, influenced the development of his style decisively. There he studied ancient architecture, met the art historian, writer and teacher Aloys Hirt and encountered the ideas of the young avant-garde assembled in the city, including several former pupils of the Académie Royale d'Architecture in Paris who had been awarded the Prix de Rome. These contacts and the publications he read played a determining role in his work at this time and influenced his first concrete plans for Karlsruhe.

Cubic structures, unified wall surfaces, large rectangular rooms with coffered barrel vaulting, Doric columns and thermal windows are the salient features of Weinbrenner's plans for the reconstruction of ancient buildings and of his ideal designs for a city gate, an armoury and a royal burial vault. His first concrete designs for Karlsruhe, including the first Rathaus design (1794) and the synagogue (1798), are in a similar style, and his work of this period has affinities with French Revolutionary architecture. His subsequent designs, however, lost some of their uncompromising harshness in execution. Nevertheless, it was these early stylistic characteristics that determined Weinbrenner's whole architectural work up to his last building, the Mint in Karlsruhe (1826).

2. URBAN PLANS FOR KARLSRUHE. In 1797, after his return from Rome, Weinbrenner entered the administration of Baden as a building inspector. After brief visits to Strasbourg and Hannover, he was made head of the Baden Bauverwaltung (building administration) in 1800, at a time when the debate on the remodelling of the centre of Karlsruhe was in urgent need of resolution. In 1809 he became Chief Director of the department. Through his involvement in urban planning he had a significant influence on building activity in the region and soon took over all the important projects, while also being responsible for the systematic creation of an effective decentralized administration, to supervise building activities throughout Baden.

Weinbrenner's first 'general architectural plan' for Karlsruhe (1797) and a revised version of 1803 formed the basis not only of the design of the town's market square but also of the arrangement of the main axis leading south from the palace (in the centre of the original radial layout), the so-called Via Triumphalis, with the market square, the Rondellplatz and the Ettlinger Tor (destr.). Although Weinbrenner took the idea for this axis and the squares on it from earlier plans and from some existing buildings, he persistently strove to give it its own coherent identity. The market square is divided into two across its breadth; on its narrower, south section Weinbrenner's Evangelische Stadtkirche (1807–16; see fig.1) to the east faces his Rathaus (1815–25) to the west, while the broader north section is flanked by three-storey commercial buildings, in front of which massive free-standing, single-storey market buildings were to form U-shapes facing opposite each other. In this way the walls of the square are staggered in depth and height. A bridge leads southwards across an open navigational canal, and the centres of the two halves of the square contain monuments, as does the Rondellplatz, a circular area lying further south at the intersection of the north–south axis with two roads, derived from the Baroque urban plan of the later 19th century. Still further

1. Friedrich Weinbrenner: Evangelische Stadtkirche, Marktplatz, Karlsruhe, 1807–16

south, the Ettlinger Tor, on the north side of which the street again widens to form a square, continues the north–south axis towards the open countryside.

This north–south axis also facilitated the ordered development of the southern part of the city, whereas the Baroque street plan of 1715 had only allowed expansion along the Lange Strasse to the east and the west. Weinbrenner himself took up this idea of expansion to the south in his ambitious so-called Tulla Plan (1812), but neither the necessary approval of the sovereign nor the funds were available to realize this design, which anticipated urban developments of the 19th century. However, the basic character of both plans, for the Via Triumphalis and for the expansion to the south, with their elements of axiality, serial development and sequence of squares, still owes much to 18th-century ideas. In developing model houses for the northern half of the market square, in the layout of new roads and in the expansion to the south, Weinbrenner took up the Baroque idea of the town as *Gesamtkunstwerk*. The clearest evidence of this idea of an integrated city design is his plan (1808) for remodelling the Lange Strasse with tall, uniform, three-storey arcades placed in front of the irregular façades of the civic houses and commercial buildings. The design once again reflected the ideas Weinbrenner had developed in the 1790s in Rome: a series of semicircular arches on slender, sharp-edged piers, closely spaced openings that seem cut out of the walls, bear witness in their austere language to the

sublimity of the city's urban space. Although this plan of 1808 was never realized, Weinbrenner's corner buildings, on the acute- and obtuse-angled corner plots resulting from the peculiarities of the Baroque urban plan, determined the appearance of Karlsruhe in the 19th century. Round corner towers between the two street frontages and towering roofs were the trained carpenter's response to irregular ridgelines.

3. PUBLIC AND RELIGIOUS BUILDINGS. Weinbrenner's early synagogue (1798; destr. 1871) has an exterior which combines the restraint of the typical town house, several storeys high, with a Gothic-arched portal suggestive of the building's religious function and with Egyptian-style pylons surmounted by scotia-moulded cornices that point towards the Near Eastern origins of Judaic religious architecture. Internally, however, the forecourt is dominated by the regular spacing of squat Doric columns, while the prayer hall takes its character from the massive, semicircular, coffered barrel vaulting (see fig. 2), all elements of an architectural language Weinbrenner had formulated in Rome. Weinbrenner's Stadtkirche and Rathaus, standing opposite each other in the market square, are basically similar in shape, although the similarity has been blurred by alterations to the Rathaus plans. In each case a dominant main building is flanked by low, self-contained structures and joined to them by communicating arms—an arrangement that is entirely Palladian in its

2. Friedrich Weinbrenner: prayer hall of his early synagogue, Karlsruhe, 1798 (destr. 1871); pen and ink drawing by Weinbrenner's pupil Christoph Arnold, 525×449mm (private collection)

grouping of elements into a single, cohesive whole. This arrangement occurs in many of Weinbrenner's later designs and buildings, such as the Mint (1826), as well as his town palaces and garden houses which were modelled on Palladio's Villa Rotonda, near Vicenza. The Pantheon motif incorporated in the Roman Catholic church of St Stephan (1808–14; rest. 1951–4) had preoccupied Weinbrenner since his first designs (1791–2) for the Evangelische Stadtkirche. Like many architects of the late 18th and early 19th century, he considered the Pantheon in Rome an exemplary union of the perfection of the centralized structure with the dignity of an ancient columned portico. In a series of variations on his original plan Weinbrenner tried to produce a similar synthesis that would also have its own identity, but this idea could not be realized in the setting of the market square, which demanded a unified style. It was only achieved away from the town centre at St Stephan, built on an isolated plot.

Although Weinbrenner's work was limited mainly to Karlsruhe and Baden, his reputation as a theatre architect extended far beyond the state borders. The construction of the Residenztheater (from 1804) in Karlsruhe was followed by plans for Schaffhausen, Baden-Baden, Gotha, Leipzig, Dresden and Düsseldorf. However, the designs were only implemented in Leipzig (1817) and Baden-Baden (1821), while his theatre plans for Düsseldorf (1820) could not withstand criticism from Karl Friedrich Schinkel in Berlin.

The use of the architectural orders is a persistent stylistic feature of Weinbrenner's oeuvre. However, while he used the Ionic and Corinthian orders to illustrate a hierarchy of building values, they were not applied consistently. Decorative friezes and other decoration are only found on a few buildings. Contemporaries described his architecture as 'sober' and 'dry', or even 'clumsy' (Schinkel). Gothic architecture had little influence on Weinbrenner's designs, although it is given some attention in his writings. Apart from the synagogue in Karlsruhe, he used Gothic elements in garden buildings, botanical buildings and the Gothischer Turm (1802) in the garden for Margravine Amalie Friederike in Karlsruhe.

4. TEACHING AND WRITINGS. Weinbrenner also played an important role as a teacher of architecture in Karlsruhe, founding a private institute there in 1800. After years of state support and planning (from 1808) for a technical school, the Polytechnische Schule, incorporating Weinbrenner's school of architecture, was finally founded in Karlsruhe in 1825; the city's present university developed from it. The most important of Weinbrenner's pupils were Christoph Arnold (1779–1844) and Friedrich Arnold (1786–1854), Georg Moller, Friedrich Dyckerhoff (1774–1845), Alexis de Chateauneuf (1799–1853), Heinrich Hübsch, Joseph Berckmüller (1800–79), Friedrich Eisenlohr and Melchior Berri. Pupils sometimes worked for years at Weinbrenner's school, and sometimes only for a few months, as in the case of Friedrich von Gärtner. While the older pupils (such as the Arnolds and Dyckerhoff) later continued to work in Weinbrenner's manner and in some cases (e.g. Moller) took up responsible posts, the younger ones (such as Hübsch, Berckmüller and Eisenlohr) rejected his classical doctrines, a course that Hübsch defended in his essay *In welchem Style sollen wir bauen?* (Karlsruhe, 1828).

Weinbrenner also published several works on architecture, notably *Über Theater in architektonischer Hinsicht*, which reflected his experiences in building the theatre in Karlsruhe. His *Ausgeführte und projektierte Gebäude* remained incomplete, as did his ambitious *Architektonisches Lehrbuch*, a work addressed primarily to younger pupils to whom he sought to give both practical and aesthetic guidance. Its dissemination was intended to lead to an improvement in architectural standards. In 1817 Weinbrenner began his autobiographical writings, the *Denkwürdigkeiten*, which covered only the period from his birth to his return from Rome in 1797. Towards the end of his career Weinbrenner withdrew from architectural debate, preoccupied by practical business concerns.

WRITINGS

Über die wesentlichen Theile der Säulen-Ordnungen (Tübingen, 1809)
Über Theater in architektonischer Hinsicht mit Beziehung auf Plan und Ausführung des neuen Hoftheaters zu Carlsruhe (Tübingen, 1809)
Architektonisches Lehrbuch, 3 vols (Tübingen and Stuttgart, 1810–25)
Entwürfe und Ergänzungen antiker Gebäude, 2 vols (Karlsruhe and Baden, 1822, 1834) [contains Weinbrenner's reconstruction designs from his period in Rome]
A. Schreiber, ed.: *Friedrich Weinbrenner: Denkwürdigkeiten aus seinem Leben* (Heidelberg, 1829)
K. K. Eberlein, ed.: *Friedrich Weinbrenner: Denkwürdigkeiten aus seinem Leben, von ihm selbst geschrieben* (Potsdam, 1920)
Ausgeführte und projektierte Gebäude, 3 vols (Karlruhe and Baden, 1822, 1830, 1835; 2 edn W. Schirmer, 1978)

BIBLIOGRAPHY

A. Valdenaire: *Friedrich Weinbrenner: Sein Leben und seine Bauten* (Karlsruhe, 1919, 4/1985)
F. Hirsch: *100 Jahre Bauen und Schauen*, 2 vols (Karlsruhe, 1928, 1932)

E. Lacroix: 'Zur Baugeschichte des Karlsruher Marktplatzes: Ein Beitrag zur Geschichte des Städtebaus im 19. Jahrhundert', *Z. Gesch. Oberrheins,* xlvii (1934), pp. 24–57

——: 'Die Entwürfe für einen neuen Marktplatz in Karlsruhe: Eine städtebauliche Konkurrenz um 1800', *Oberrhein. Kst* (1940)

A. Valdenaire: 'Der Karlsruher Marktplatz', *Z. Gesch. Oberrheins,* lvii (1948), pp. 415–49

W. Huber: *Die Stephanienstrasse: Ein Stück Bau- und Kulturgeschichte aus Karlsruhe* (Karlsruhe, 1954)

A. von Schneider, ed.: *Denkwürdigkeiten* (Karlsruhe, 1958)

A. Tschira: 'Der sogenannte Tulla-Plan zur Vergrösserung der Stadt Karlsruhe', *Werke und Wege: Eine Festschrift für Dr. Eberhard Knittel zum 60. Geburtstag* (Karlsruhe, 1959)

S. Sinos: 'Entwurfsgrundlagen im Werk Friedrich Weinbrenners', *Jb. Staatl. Kstsamml. Baden-Württemberg,* viii (1971), pp. 195–216

K. Lankheit: 'Friedrich Weinbrenner: Beiträge zu seinem Werk', *Fridericiana, Z. U. Karlsruhe,* no. 19 (1976)

W. Schirmer: *Friedrich Weinbrenner, 1766–1826* (exh. cat., Karlsruhe, Staatl. Ksthalle, 1977)

K. Lankheit: *Friedrich Weinbrenner und der Denkmalskult um 1800* (Basle and Stuttgart, 1979)

Friedrich Weinbrenner, Architect of Karlsruhe (exh. cat., ed. D. B. Brownlee; Philadelphia, U. PA, Architectural Archives, 1986/7)

C. Elbert: *Die Theater Friedrich Weinbrenners, Bauten und Entwürfe* (Karlsruhe, 1988)

W. Schirmer: 'Grosse kassettierte Tonnengewölbe: Römische Entwürfe und ihre Bedeutung im Werk des Autodidakten Friedrich Weinbrenner', *Revolutionsarchitektur: Ein Aspekt der europäischen Architektur um 1800* (exh. cat., Frankfurt am Main, Dt. Architmus.; Munich, Neue Pin.; 1990)

WULF SCHIRMER

Weiner, Tibor (*b* Budapest, 29 Oct 1906; *d* Budapest, 8 July 1965). Hungarian architect, critic, urban planner and furniture designer. After graduating in 1929 from the Hungarian Palatine Joseph Technical University, Budapest, he joined the Bauhaus in Dessau, where he worked under Hannes Meyer. Weiner attended the CIAM II Congress (1929), Frankfurt, and, convinced that the architect's mission was to serve and transform society, he followed Meyer and his group to the USSR in 1931. There, as assistant professor at the Technical University, Moscow, he contributed, with HANS SCHMIDT and Konrad Püschel, to urban planning projects, in particular the underground railway system, Moscow, and the development of the city of Orsk. Weiner left the USSR in 1933, and, after working in Basle from 1934 to 1936, in 1937–8 he was employed by Grete Schütte-Lihotzky (*b* 1897) in Paris, designing furniture for children. In 1939 he moved to Chile, where he became a professor of architecture (1946–8) at the University of Santiago. In 1948 he returned to Hungary and was appointed chief architect of the urban development project at Sztálinváros (now Dunaújváros), a new industrial town begun in 1949, which was built entirely in the Socialist Realist style. From 1952 to 1957 Weiner was editor of the architectural journal *Magyar Épitőmüvészet.*

BIBLIOGRAPHY

Z. Farkasdy: 'Tibor Weiner, 1906–65', *Magyar Épitőmüvészet,* 3 (1965), p. 57

Wechselwirkungen (exh. cat., ed. H. Gassner; Kassel, Neue Gal., 1986), p. 587

ÁKOS MORAVÁNSZKY,
KATALIN MORAVÁNSZKY-GYÖNGY

Weingarten Abbey. Benedictine monastery at Weingarten, a small town 6 km north of Ravensburg in Baden-Württemberg, Germany, noted for its Baroque church. The Benedictines established themselves on the site in 1056; their huge church was consecrated in 1182, and, despite damage by several fires, it survived until replaced by the Baroque building (begun 1715; consecrated 1724). When secularized in 1802, the monastery had jurisdiction over a territory of 306 sq. km with a population of 11,000 and received a yearly income of 120,000 guilders. In 1922 the Benedictines reoccupied part of the monastic complex.

In 1684 Caspar Moosbrugger, at the invitation of Abbot Willibald Koboldt, established the basic design: a domed crossing set between a long nave with wall-piers and a similar choir of almost equal length. In 1715, during the abbacy of Sebastian Hyller, Franz Beer prepared a new version of this scheme, but he left the project early in 1716 after arguments about costs. Plans by Johann Jakob Herkommer in 1715 and his nephew Johann Georg Fischer in 1717 fixed the configuration of the vaults. Initially, Hyller entrusted the construction to Andreas Schreck, a lay brother in the monastery, but by late 1717 Donato Giuseppe Frisoni had assumed supervisory control. He built the dome, façade and top sections of the towers. The elegant white stucco of the interior was begun in 1718 by Franz Xaver Schmuzer. That year Cosmas Damian Asam (*see* ASAM, §I(2)) was contracted to paint the vault frescoes, his largest commission (over 1000 sq. m) and one that in content, sensibility and perception inflated the significance of fresco in relation to the architecture.

The two towers of the façade frame a convex centre topped by an elaborate gable. A livelier version of this façade animates the church in an ideal project of 1723 for the monastery (drawings in Weingarten Abbey), prepared as part of an unsuccessful campaign to obtain sovereign status: the church stands as the centrepiece within a gigantic, rectangular monastic complex, enriched on the flanks with curved wings and pavilions.

The church is both longitudinal and centralized. Nave and choir together are 102 m long but remain dominated by the voluminous drum and dome of the crossing, which rise almost 60 m above, while the vestibule, choir and transept arms all end in semicircles that bring the eye back to the crossing. Sail vaults are supported by wall-piers that stand in the space like free-standing shafts, with pilasters clustered around their front ends. Between the chapels they are carved away above and below by tall, broad-arched openings, and concave balconies are pushed back towards the wall. The outer wall is extensively glazed by two tiers of arched windows topped by Diocletian windows, so that the expansive white interior is flooded with light. Among the *c.* 60 monasteries built within the southern territories of the Holy Roman Empire between the late 17th century and the late 18th, the church at Weingarten Abbey, which influenced the design of those at Einsiedeln and Ottobeuren, remains a distinctive example.

BIBLIOGRAPHY

N. Lieb: *Barockkirchen zwischen Donau und Alpen* (Munich, 1953)

A. Raichle and P. Schneider: *Weingarten* (Munich, 1953)

Festschrift zur 900-Jahr-Feier des Klosters, 1056–1956 (Weingarten, 1956)

N. Lieb: *Die Vorarlberger Barockbaumeister* (Munich, 1960)

G. Spahr: *Die Basilika Weingarten* (Sigmaringen, 1974)

CHRISTIAN F. OTTO

Weinman, Adolph Alexander (*b* Karlsruhe, 1870; *d* New York, 1952). American sculptor and medallist of German birth. He was brought up in New York from the age of ten. He was apprenticed as a carver of wood and ivory under F. R. Kaldenberg, also studying at the Cooper Union School and later for five years at the studio of the sculptor Philip Martiny. From 1895 he served as assistant to Olin L. Warner and from Warner's death in 1896 until 1898 he worked under Augustus Saint-Gaudens. There then followed five years in the studio of Charles H. Niehaus (1855–1935) and two years under Daniel C. French, with whom he worked on the figures of *The Continents* (1907) for the New York Customs House. In 1906 he set up his own studio. Saint-Gaudens was without doubt the major influence on his work, and most of Weinman's work was, like that of Saint-Gaudens, modelled to be cast in bronze. He belonged to the generation of sculptors working in the USA who continued the French tradition of naturalistic, Romantic bronzes well into the 20th century. His statue of *Major General Alexander Macomb* (1906–8; Detroit, MI, Public Square) is a fine example. Besides free-standing works, he produced sculpture as architectural decoration (e.g. Pennsylvania Station, New York) and like Saint-Gaudens worked in relief.

Weinman's interest in medals stemmed from his visit to the World's Columbian Exposition in Chicago (1893), at which a room was devoted to the work of European medallists. In 1896 he modelled a portrait medal of his mother, which was followed by two portraits of children. One of his earliest commissions for a struck medal came with the Louisiana Purchase Exposition of 1904, and in the following year he collaborated with Saint-Gaudens on Theodore Roosevelt's inauguration medal. For over 40 years he was one of America's foremost medallists. One of his last medals, the Society of Medallists' 39th medal, *Genesis*, which he modelled in 1949, demonstrates his unchanging style. He designed and modelled the half-dollar and ten-cent coins of 1916. His son Robert A. Weinman followed his profession.

BIBLIOGRAPHY

Forrer: vi, pp. 427–8, viii, pp. 266–70; Thieme–Becker
Catalogue of the International Exhibition of Contemporary Medals, 1910 (New York, 1911), p. 357
S. P. Noe: *The Medallic Work of A. A. Weinman* (New York, 1921)
Exhibition of American Sculpture (exh. cat., New York, 1923), pp. 246–7
The Beaux-Arts Medal in America (exh. cat. by B. A. Baxter, New York, Amer. Numi. Soc., 1988)

PHILIP ATTWOOD

Weir. American family of artists and teachers.

(1) Robert Walter Weir (*b* New York, 18 June 1803; *d* New York, 1 May 1889). Painter and teacher. By his own account he was self-taught, with the exception of a few lessons from an unknown heraldic painter named Robert Cooke. However, after exhibiting a few works that were praised by the local press, he was sent to Italy by a group of New York and Philadelphia businessmen for further studies. There he trained with Florentine history painter Pietro Benvenuti. After three years in Europe (1824–7), he returned to New York, where he quickly became a mainstay of the artistic community. In 1831 he was elected to membership in the National Academy of Design in New York, and three years later he was made instructor of drawing at the US Military Academy in West Point, New York, a post he held for the next 42 years. Most scholars agree that he was more important as a

teacher than as a painter. His best-known work is the *Embarkation of the Pilgrims* (1837–43), which hangs in the Rotunda of the US Capitol Building in Washington, DC.

BIBLIOGRAPHY

K. Ahrens: *Robert Walter Weir* (diss., Newark, U. DE, 1972)
Robert Weir: Artist and Teacher of West Point (exh. cat., ed. W. Gerdts and J. Callow; West Point, US Mil. Acad., 1976)

MARK W. SULLIVAN

(2) John Ferguson Weir (*b* West Point, NY, 28 Aug 1841; *d* Providence, RI, 8 April 1926). Painter, teacher and sculptor, son of (1) Robert Walter Weir. He grew up at the US Military Academy at West Point, where he was taught by his father. His earliest paintings record the handsome landscape of the surrounding countryside, including *View of the Highlands from West Point* (1862; New York, NY Hist. Soc.). By November 1862 Weir had settled in New York, occupying quarters in the Studio Building on West Tenth Street where he became friendly with many of the well-known artists residing there. He also made important contacts through the Century and Athenaeum Clubs and the Artists' Fund Society. He made his début at the National Academy of Design with an *Artist's Studio* (1864; Los Angeles, CA, Co. Mus. A.), a detailed view of his father's painting room at West Point. The picture's favourable reception led to his election as an Associate of the National Academy of Design. However, it was the *Gun Foundry* (1866; Cold Spring, NY, Putnam County Hist. Soc.), set in the West Point Iron and Cannon Foundry, that established Weir as one of the most important 19th-century American painters of industrial themes. The foundry also inspired his *Forging the Shaft* (1867–8, destr. 1869; replica 1877; New York, Met.). Other themes undertaken by Weir included several variants of *Christmas Eve* (1864; New York, C. Assoc.).

From December 1868 until August 1869 Weir made his first trip to Europe; then he moved to New Haven, CT, as the first Director of the recently founded Yale School of the Fine Arts, the first professional art school to be established on a American campus. During his 44-year tenure there, Weir organized an ambitious programme of artistic training, modelled on that of the Ecole des Beaux-Arts in Paris. During this period he lectured widely at institutions along the East Coast and wrote extensively on art topics for such periodicals as the *New Englander, Princeton Review, Harper's New Monthly Magazine, North American Review* and *Scribner's Magazine*. He also acted as commissioner for the art section of the 1876 Centennial Exposition in Philadelphia. His duties at Yale made it difficult for him to maintain his national reputation as a painter, but Yale provided him with regular portrait commissions, which included several sculptures, the most important being those of *Benjamin Silliman* (1884; Sterling Chemistry Laboratory) and *Theodore Dwight Woolsey* (1895–6; opposite the College Street entrance to the Old Campus). During his years in New Haven, his palette gradually lightened, in part due to the influence of his half-brother, (3) Julian Alden Weir. Still-life themes began to interest him, and paintings inspired by the local landscape also became more prominent in his work, for example *East Rock* (*c.* 1900; New Haven, CT, Colony Hist. Soc. Mus.).

UNPUBLISHED SOURCES

New Haven, CT, Yale U. Lib. [John Ferguson Weir papers, mss and archvs]

Washington, DC, Smithsonian Inst., Archvs Amer. A. [John Ferguson Weir papers]

BIBLIOGRAPHY

T. Sizer, ed.: *The Recollections of John Ferguson Weir* (New York, 1957)

——: 'Memories of a Yale Professor', *Yale U. Lib. Gaz.*, xxxii (1958), pp. 93–8

L. Dinnerstein: 'The Iron Worker and King Solomon: Some Images of Labor in American Art', *A. Mag.*, liii (1979), p. 112–17

B. Fahlman: 'John Ferguson Weir: Painter of Romantic and Industrial Icons', *Archvs Amer. A. J.*, xx (1980), pp. 2–9

D. B. Burke: 'John Ferguson Weir (1841–1926)', *American Paintings in the Metropolitan Museum of Art*, ii (New York, 1985), pp. 566–74

BETSY FAHLMAN

(3) Julian Alden Weir (*b* West Point, NY, 30 Aug 1852; *d* New York, 8 Dec 1919). Painter, printmaker and teacher, son of (1) Robert Walter Weir. His art education began in the studio of his father. There he and his half-brother (2) John Ferguson Weir acquired an appreciation for the Old Masters, particularly of the Italian Renaissance and of the 17th-century Dutch schools. While Weir pursued in his art a course very different from that of his father and half-brother, his personality as well as his artistic attitudes were shaped by them. In the winters of 1870–71 and 1871–2, he continued his studies at the National Academy of Design in New York, where his instructor was Lemuel Wilmarth (1835–1918).

Weir arrived in Paris in the autumn of 1873 and remained there for almost four years. He enrolled in the studio of Jean-Léon Gérôme and on 27 October 1874 became a matriculant at the Ecole des Beaux-Arts, where he drew such studies as *Male Nude Leaning on a Staff* (1876; New Haven, CT, Yale U. A.G.). He also studied at the Ecole Gratuite de Dessin, often called the Petite Ecole, and in independent classes taught by Gustave Boulanger and Louis-Marie-François Jacquesson de la Chevreuse (1839–1903). He also travelled to Belgium, the Netherlands and Spain. During the summers he worked in the French villages of Portrieux and Pont-Aven, where he painted landscapes and peasant subjects including *Interior—House in Brittany* (1875; priv. col., see Burke, 1983, p. 53) and the *Oldest Inhabitant* (1875–6; Youngstown, OH, Butler Inst. Amer. A.). He first exhibited at the Paris Salon in 1876. Weir developed close friendships with Jules Bastien-Lepage and Pascal-Adolphe-Jean Dagnan-Bouveret, who drew him into an international circle of naturalists, under whose influence he painted *Children Burying a Dead Bird* (1878; Washington, DC, N. Mus. Amer. A.).

When Weir returned to New York in 1877, he was quickly established in the vanguard of an internationally trained generation of painters that transformed American art around 1880. He joined many organizations founded or supported by these young painters including the Tile Club, the Art Club, the American Watercolor Society, the Society of Painters in Pastel and the Society of American Artists. He began a long and active career as a teacher at the Cooper Union and the Art Students League. He had first exhibited at the National Academy in 1875 and was elected an Associate in 1885 and an Academician the following year.

From the early 1880s Weir chose a wide variety of subjects and worked in styles that reveal his continuing contact with European art and artists. His still-life paintings range from ambitious arrangements of flowers and elaborate decorative objects, such as *Roses* (1883–4; Washington, DC, Phillips Col.), to smaller, more intimate compositions of kitchen items and a few flowers or pieces of fruit. Some of his figure paintings, among them *In the Park* (*c.* 1879; later cut into three separate canvases, see Burke, 1983, pp. 92, 99), a scene of modern urban life, reveal the influence of Edouard Manet, whom Weir met in 1881, but others, such as *Idle Hours* (1888; New York, Met.), show the enduring effect of his academic training. He also acted as an agent for Erwin Davis in purchasing works by Manet (e.g. *Woman with a Parrot*, 1866; New York, Met.).

During the 1880s and 1890s Weir began to experiment with pastel and watercolour and achieved daring effects that do not appear in his oil paintings until a later date. Many of his small and informal pastels seem to have been done for his own satisfaction. He often combined watercolour and pastel, achieving richly textured surfaces with high-keyed colours, applied with free, broad strokes. From about 1887 to 1893 he also made prints, mainly etchings and drypoints, characterized by the seemingly fragmentary nature of their compositions and the artist's use of broken lines to suggest the qualities of light and air.

For the final three decades of his life Weir was most strongly affected by Impressionism. Around 1890, influenced by the work of his friends Theodore Robinson and John H. Twachtman, he turned more often to landscape subjects, producing small, freshly brushed views of the Connecticut countryside, for example the *Farmer's Lawn*, (*c.* 1890; priv. col., see Burke, 1983, p. 192), and informal figure studies, mainly of his wife and children posed out-of-doors. He worked on mural decorations for the Columbian Exposition in Chicago (1893). Among his most important Impressionist works are those inspired by Japanese prints, of which he was an avid collector. These include such landscapes as the *Red Bridge* (*c.* 1895; New York, Met.) and a series of life-size figure studies (e.g. *Baby Cora*, 1894; priv. col., see Burke, 1983, pl. 25), in which he used Oriental devices, most notably asymmetrical compositions brought close to the picture plane and unconventionally cropped. By about 1897 the academic character of Weir's earlier work reasserted itself in more representational views of Connecticut, as in two versions of the *Factory Village* (1897; New York, Met., and Witton, CT, The Weir Farm Her. Trust), and in less adventurous figure studies. From 1902 until his death he painted idealized, somewhat sentimental portraits of women and pleasant landscapes, typically with soft, regularized brushstrokes and a silvery palette of pale blue and green.

Weir achieved tremendous recognition during his lifetime: he exhibited widely in one-man shows, annuals and international expositions; he won awards and medals; he was among the founder-members of the popular Ten American Painters in 1897; and from 1915 to 1917 he served as President of the National Academy. An important collection of his work can be found at Brigham Young University, Provo, UT.

WRITINGS

'Jules Bastien-Lepage', *Modern French Masters: A Series of Biographical and Critical Reviews*, ed. J. C. Van Dyke (New York, 1896/*R* 1976), pp. 227–35

'What Is Art?', *A. & Dec.*, vii (1917), pp. 316–17, 324, 327

BIBLIOGRAPHY

J. B. Millet, ed.: *Julian Alden Weir: An Appreciation of his Life and Works* (New York, 1921)

A. Zimmerman: 'An Essay towards a Catalogue Raisonné of the Etchings, Dry-points and Lithographs of Julian Alden Weir', *Met. Papers*, i/2 (New York, 1923), pp. 1–50

D. W. Young: *The Life and Letters of J. Alden Weir* (New Haven, 1960) [incl. extensive quotations from the artist's corr.]

J. Alden Weir: American Impressionist, 1852–1919 (exh. cat. by J. A. Flint, Washington, DC, N. Mus. Amer. A., 1972)

J. Alden Weir and the National Academy of Design (exh. cat. by D. B. Burke, New York, N. Acad. Des., 1981)

D. B. Burke: *J. Alden Weir: An American Impressionist* (Newark, DE, 1983) [extensive bibliog.]

DOREEN BOLGER

Weir, R. W. S. *See* SCHULTZ, ROBERT WEIR.

Weirotter [Weyrotter], **Franz Edmund** (*b* Innsbruck, *bapt* 29 May 1733; *d* Vienna, 11 May 1771). Austrian painter, draughtsman and etcher. After training in Innsbruck and Vienna, he worked for Elector Johann Friedrich of Mainz, producing ten overdoors for his palace in Mainz, besides landscapes, architectural views and naval and maritime scenes. Joining the pupils of Jean-Georges Wille in Paris in 1759–63, he transferred his ambitions to drawing and printed graphics, practised copying Dutch and Flemish works and developed a masterly etching technique, which he applied to his own drawings. His landscape series, mostly comprising six or twelve small-format etchings, in only a few cases dated or signed on the plate, were published by Wille, François Joullain, Gabriel Huquier, Prevost, François Chéreau I and Basan & Poignant, sometimes in several editions. Visiting Rome in 1763–4, Weirotter met Johann Joachim Winckelmann (1717–68) and Henry Fuseli; he then returned to Paris. In 1767 he was appointed professor of landscape drawing at the Vienna Akademie, through the mediation of his friend Jacob Mathias Schmutzer (1733–1811). He published etchings of ruins from his Italian journey in editions with lavish dedication sheets. After Weirotter's death Basan & Poignant published a large folio volume, the *Oeuvres de F.-E. Weirotter*, with 215 graphic works. Of equal importance are *c.* 250 drawings in silver point, red chalk or charcoal, many with a sepia or bistre wash, sometimes giving virtually a watercolour effect. Few works can be documented as belonging to his small output of oil paintings.

BIBLIOGRAPHY

Oeuvres de F.-E. Weirotter, peintre allemand, contenant 215 paysages et ruines, dessinés d'après nature, tant en France qu'en Italie, gravés à l'eau forte avec beaucoup de goût par lui-même (Paris, 1771)

H. Quintern: 'Franz Edmund Weirotter (1733–1771)', *Tirol. Heimatbl.*, liii (1978), pp. 50–60

SONJA WEIH-KRÜGER

Weis, Johann Martin (*b* ?Strasbourg, 1711; *d* Strasbourg, 24 Oct 1751). French draughtsman and engraver. He was a resident of Strasbourg, whose work has received little attention from the Paris-orientated historians of 18th-century French engraving. However, he trained in Paris under Jean-Baptiste de Poilly and his most important work, the *Représentation des fêtes données par la ville de Strasbourg pour la convalescence du Roi* (IFF, xiii, nos 29–39), was in large part executed by the celebrated Paris engraver Jacques-Philippe Lebas. This commemorative volume, 'invented, drawn and directed' by Weis, records the elaborate celebrations on the occasion of Louis XV's visit to the city in 1744. It consists of 11 double-spread folio prints, which combine a minutely detailed description of the buildings of the city with a strong pictorial sense. Weis's name also appears on the *Good Mother* (1744), one of a series of prints made in Paris with false attributions to Jean-Siméon Chardin, but the bulk of his work, produced in Strasbourg, consists of prints of topographical subjects and contemporary events. His son, also called Johann Martin Weis (1738–1807), followed a similar career.

BIBLIOGRAPHY

Thieme–Becker

E. Bocher: *Les Gravures françaises du XVIIIe siècle*, iii (Paris, 1876), p. 54

Y. Sjöberg: *Inventaire du fonds français après 1800*, Paris, Bib. N., Dépt. Est. cat., xiii (Paris, 1974), pp. 104–7 [IFF]

EMMA BARKER

Weisgerber, Albert (*b* St Ingbert, 21 April 1878; *d* Fromelles, nr Ypres, Belgium, 10 May 1915). German painter and printmaker. He studied decoration at the Kreisbaugewerksschule in Kaiserlautern (1891–3) and began work in a decorator's studio in Frankfurt am Main. However, in 1894 he moved to Munich to resume his studies, first at the Kunstgewerbeschule and later under Franz von Stuck at the Akademie der Bildenden Künste (1897–1901). For some years he concentrated on poster design and book illustration, contributing a total of 500 drawings to *Jungend: Illustrierte Wochenschrift für Kunst und Leben* from 1899. His early paintings such as the portrait of *Ludwig Scharf II* (*c.* 1905; Munich, Staatsgal. Mod. Kst) were executed in dark-toned academic style, but an exhibition of French Impressionism in Berlin in 1905 so impressed him that he went to Paris for nearly a year (until May 1906). Despite his association with the circle of artists around Matisse, he was more influenced by the work of Cézanne. In 1907 he made a second visit to Paris and joined Phalanx in 1909. In the latter year he was visited by Hans Purrmann and Matisse. By 1911 with a third visit to Paris and travels to Rome and Naples, he had established himself as one of the foremost German Impressionists. As well as such lyrical scenes as *Munich Hofgarten* (1911; Munich, Lenbachhaus), in common with many of his German contemporaries, Weisgerber reconceived classical scenes in an energetic style, for example in *Amazon Camp* (1910; Stuttgart, Staatsgal.). In 1912 he had a one-man show in the Kunsthaus, Zurich, and a year later participated in the annual Kunstausstellung in Munich. Although using an Impressionist style, he was equally at home in Expressionist circles, and this undoubtedly influenced his election to the presidency of the Neuen Münchner Sezession (1913). In the last four years of his career he was obsessed with sacrificial subject-matter from the Old and New Testaments, which he had originated in the theme of St Sebastian (e.g. *St Sebastian Felled by Arrows*, 1910; Munich, Staatsgal. Mod. Kst). While not exclusively tragic (e.g. *David and Goliath*, 1914; Saarbrücken, Saarland-Mus.), these final works strip away historical references to concentrate upon the fate of the isolated individual, as in *Absalom* (1914; Hamburg, Ksthalle).

BIBLIOGRAPHY
Albert Weisgerber (exh. cat. by W. Weber, Heidelberg, Mus. Stadt., 1962)
S. Ishikawa-Franke: *Albert Weisgerber: Leben und Werk* (Saarbrücken, 1978)
Albert Weisgerber, 1878–1915 (exh. cat. by T. Heuss and W. Weber, Mainz, Landesmus., 1979)

Weisman. American collectors. Frederick R. Weisman (*b* Minneapolis, MN, 27 April 1912) and his wife, Marcia Weisman [née Simon] (*b* Portland, OR, 22 Aug 1918), sister of Norton Simon, were married in 1938 and began collecting art in the late 1940s, but their first major purchase, a sculpture by Arp, *Ombre de Nuage* (1960) and a painting by Alexei Jawlenski, *Still-life with Citrus* (Pasadena, CA, Norton Simon Mus.), was made in the early 1960s. Their interest in American Abstract Expressionists was encouraged by the New York art collector and dealer, Ben Heller, and this led to the purchase of works by Arshile Gorky, Willem de Kooning, Barnett Newman, Jackson Pollock, Mark Rothko and Clyfford Still. They continued to collect American artists as they came to prominence, such as Sam Francis, Jasper Johns, Ellsworth Kelly, Roy Lichtenstein, Robert Rauschenberg and Andy Warhol. They also supported artists working in California, including Larry Bell, Joe Goode (*b* 1937), Robert Irwin, Edward Kienholz, Ed Moses (*b* 1936) and Edward Ruscha.

The Weismans were the subject of a double portrait by David Hockney, *American Collectors (Fred and Marcia Weisman)* (1968; see M. Livingstone, *David Hockney*, 1981, pp. 122–3), which features works by Henry Moore and William Turnbull in their collection. They were also among the subjects of paintings screenprinted by Andy Warhol, *Frederick Weisman* (1974) and *Marcia Weisman* (1975; see D. Whitney, *Andy Warhol: Portraits of the 70s*, 1979, pp. 130–31, 132–3). They divorced in 1981. The collection was split and each continued to collect. Frederick Weisman collected younger, international artists and established the Frederick R. Weisman Art Foundation in 1982. Marcia Weisman collected 20th-century works on paper and continued to support artists based in California. She founded the Cedars-Sinai Hospital art programme in Beverley Hills, CA, placing thousands of works in hospital rooms, and was one of the founders of the Museum of Contemporary Art, which opened in Los Angeles in 1986. The Frederick R. Weisman Museum of Art, designed by Frank Gehry, opened at the University of Minnesota, Minneapolis, in 1993.

BIBLIOGRAPHY
The Marcia Simon Weisman Collection (exh. cat., Los Angeles, CA, Mus. Contemp. A.)

HENRY T. HOPKINS

Weiss, Wojciech (*b* Leorda, nr Zakopane, 4 May 1875; *d* Kraków, 6 Dec 1950). Polish painter, draughtsman and printmaker. He gave up his music training to study painting at the School of Fine Arts in Kraków (1892–9) under Leon Wyczółkowski. His career began with mythological and historic paintings, but, influenced by the writer and theorist Stanisław Przybyszewski (1868–1927) and his satanic 'ideology', he moved to Expressionism. He created dynamic compositions with figures clasped in diabolic dance, depicted with aggressive colours, as in *Possession* (1899–1900; Warsaw, Mus. Literature), which shows Przybyszewski in a somnambulistic trance. This character appears also in *Demon (at the Café)* (1904; Kraków, N. Mus.), one of Weiss's best-known paintings. His landscapes from the turn of the century are masterpieces of sensual expression of colours (e.g. *Radiant Sunset*, 1900–02; Poznań, N. Mus.). He was one of the first Polish poster designers, in his case in an Art Nouveau style. In 1898 he joined the society 'Sztuka' ('Art'); later he became a member of the Vienna Secession (1906–8). In 1910 he was appointed professor at the Academy of Fine Arts in Kraków (a post he held until his death), but the most inventive period of his career was over. He moved to Post-Impressionism and painted joyful portraits, still-lifes and landscapes. *The Manifesto* (1950; Warsaw, N. Mus.), a portrait of a group of workers with a red banner, documents Weiss's brief encounter with Socialist Realism but still shows his particular sensitivity to colours and his talent for depicting emotions.

BIBLIOGRAPHY
Wojciech Weiss, 1875–1950 (exh. cat., ed. A. Ławniczakowa, Poznań, N. Mus., 1977)
Pejzaże Wojciecha Weissa [Landscapes of Wojciech Weiss] (exh. cat., ed. Ł. Kossowski; Kielce, N. Mus., 1985)

ANNA BENTKOWSKA

Weissenbruch. Dutch family of artists. The first generation of the family included the amateur painter and collector Johannes Weissenbruch (1787–1834) and his brother, the engraver Johan Daniël Weissenbruch (1789–1858), three of whose sons were also artists: (1) Jan Weissenbruch, who was widely known for his sun-drenched townscapes, the lithographer Frederick Hendrik Weissenbruch (1828–87) and the engraver Isaac Weissenbruch (1826–1912). Johannes's son (2) Jan Hendrik Weissenbruch was a watercolour painter of landscapes and beach views and is regarded as one of the masters of the HAGUE SCHOOL; a younger son, Frederik Adrianus Weissenbruch (1826–82), was an engraver. The third generation included Jan Hendrik's son Willem Johannes Weissenbruch (1864–1941), who was also a painter.

BIBLIOGRAPHY
Jan en Johann Hendrik Weissenbruch: Schilderijen, aquarellen en grafiek (exh. cat., Laren, Singer Mus., 1960)
Jan en Johan Hendrik Weissenbruch (exh. cat., Breda, De Beyerd, 1961)

(1) Jan [Johannes] Weissenbruch (*b* The Hague, 18 March 1822; *d* The Hague, 15 Feb 1880). Painter and printmaker. He studied at the Koninklijke Academie van Beelden de Kunsten in The Hague and was also a pupil of Salomon Leonardus Verveer. Like Verveer, he chiefly painted town views, favouring the small towns along the Rhine and the Lek. His earliest works, such as the *Oude Kerk at Scheveningen* (1843; priv. col., see Laanstra, no. 43-2), show the influence of the currently fashionable Romantic style, with its brown tone, rather viscous touch, rounded shapes and contrasts between light and shade

Jan Weissenbruch: *View of the Rotterdam Fish Market*, lithograph, 134×199 mm, 1849 (Amsterdam, Rijksmuseum)

strongly recalling the work of Wijnand Nuyen. Weissenbruch's watercolours of this period, such as *View of the Bant Windmills on the River Senne at Brussels* (Amsterdam, Hist. Mus.), are also Romantic in feeling. However, the *Dunne Bierkade in The Hague* (ex-William II col., The Hague, see Laanstra, no. 47-4) shows increased attention to the treatment of surfaces and an intimate, calm atmosphere that is characteristic of Weissenbruch. With *View of the St Catharine-Gasthaus in Arnhem* (*c.* 1850; St Petersburg, Hermitage) he completely abandoned Romantic colouring, choosing a light, bright palette that would distinguish him for the rest of his career: clear blue sky, white plasterwork, beaming sunlight, warm red roofs and red accents in the figures' clothing are all typical of his later works.

Weissenbruch made lithographs of many of his paintings for the periodical *Kunstkronijk*. His first lithographs date from 1841 and show his admiration for English and French lithographers very clearly. The fine, five-colour lithograph *Suburb* (1859; e.g. Amsterdam, Rijksmus.) shows the influence of J. D. Harding's coloured lithographs. Weissenbruch also adopted Samuel Prout's strictly linear compositions, as in *View of the Rotterdam Fish Market* (1849; see fig.); the cross shape also dominates many of his paintings and watercolours. His etchings are generally less rigidly composed. Weissenbruch began etching around 1846, and in 1848 he founded the Haagse Ets club with a few colleagues. Forty-nine of his etchings have been recorded: they include such townscapes as *View of the Schenkweg in The Hague* (1849; e.g. The Hague,

Gemeentemus.), some figure subjects and portraits. Weissenbruch had a large collection of old prints, and borrowings are evident in some etchings, for example *Rembrandt's Studio* (n.d.; e.g. The Hague, Gemeentemus.).

Weissenbruch's painting technique changed little after 1850, although it is difficult to determine precisely when his works were produced, as they are seldom dated. Detailing gradually made way for a flatter treatment of surfaces, as in *View of the Korte Voorhout in The Hague* (*c.* 1860; Enschede, Rijksmus. Twenthe). The composition also becomes more daring, with an increasingly abrupt treatment of space in such works as *Town Gate at Leerdam* (Amsterdam, Rijksmus.) and the *Prinsengracht in The Hague* (The Hague, Gemeentemus.).

BIBLIOGRAPHY
W. Laanstra: *Johannes (Jan) Weissenbruch: Schilder-graficus, 1822–1880* (Amsterdam, 1986)

ANNEMIEKE HOOGENBOOM

(2) Jan Hendrik [Hendrik Johannes] **Weissenbruch** (*b* The Hague, 19 June 1824; *d* The Hague, 24 March 1903). Painter, cousin of (1) Jan Weissenbruch. He referred to himself and signed his work as Jan Hendrik Weissenbruch. From 1840 he attended drawing lessons with the Norwegian painter Johannes Löw, and from 1846 he was taught by Bartholomeus J. van Hove at the Koninklijke Academie van Beeldende Kunsten in The Hague. His early paintings clearly show the influence of van Hove and Andreas Schelfhout, although it is uncertain whether he was actually taught by the latter. His father, an avid collector, owned works by both artists.

In 1847 Weissenbruch entered his first work in the Exhibition of Living Masters in Amsterdam, and two years later he sold one of his paintings to the Teylers Museum in Haarlem. Around 1850 he often painted with Johannes Destrée (1827–88) in the Dekkersduin in The Hague and made working visits to Arnhem and Haarlem. The detailed panoramic drawings (e.g. *Rhine Panorama near Oosterbeek*, 1847; Amerongen, priv. col., see 1983 exh. cat., p. 276) and watercolours Weissenbruch made during these visits clearly reveal his relationship with such Dutch Romantics as Schelfhout and Wijnand Nuyen (1813–39). *View of Haarlem* (*c*. 1845–50; The Hague, Gemeentemus.) is reminiscent of Schelfhout while differing from the work of the previous generation in its cooler tones and less idealized conception. The influence of Jacob van Ruisdael's *View of Haarlem* (*c*. 1660; The Hague, Mauritshuis) is noteworthy; Weissenbruch was undoubtedly familiar with it, for he made numerous copies of paintings by Ruisdael, Paulus Potter and Johannes Vermeer in the Mauritshuis. Weissenbruch looked to these three masters for inspiration, unlike other Hague school painters, such as Jozef Israëls and Johannes Bosboom, who were influenced by Rembrandt and Hals. Vermeer's influence can be seen in, for example, *The Kitchen* (watercolour; The Hague, Gemeentemus.).

In 1866 Weissenbruch joined the Société Belge des Aquarellistes in Brussels. In 1870 the Gemeentemuseum in The Hague bought his *View of the Trekvliet* (1870) from the Exhibition of Living Masters; two years earlier he had painted a smaller version of this view (Amsterdam, Rijksmus.). In 1873 the Museum Boymans–van Beuningen in Rotterdam acquired his *Landscape with Windmill near Schiedam* (1873). During these years Weissenbruch taught Victor Bauffe (1849–1921), Théophile de Bock and Johannes Heppener (1826–98). From 1875 he regularly went to stay near the villages of Noorden and Nieuwkoop in South Holland, where he painted some of his finest waterside scenes. Because Weissenbruch and Willem Roelofs were determined not to make these villages, especially Noorden, into an artists' colony like that of Laren, they corresponded about it in a secret code. In 1882 Weissenbruch resumed contact with Vincent van Gogh, whom he had first met in 1873. Towards the end of the 1880s Weissenbruch began to use a lighter colour scheme. In 1899 the Amsterdam art dealer Frans Buffa & Zn organized a large exhibition that was a financial success and also contributed to the spread of Weissenbruch's fame.

In 1900 Weissenbruch undertook his only journey to Fontainebleau and Barbizon; the artists' resort had become a place of pilgrimage, far removed from the working colony it had been. Weissenbruch's place as a Hague school painter emerges particularly from his use of certain light effects. His landscape watercolours are among the finest works produced by the group. He also painted a number of Hague street scenes; the views of his house and studio (The Hague, Gemeentemus.) in the Kazernestraat and those of the fish stalls around the Grote Kerk in The Hague are among the best-known examples of this genre. In these paintings he altered the scene slightly for the sake of the composition, reducing the proportions and making the roofs taller. With light and sky as their main motifs, Weissenbruch's beach views differ from those of Anton Mauve and Hendrik Willem Mesdag, expressing the stillness of the beach rather than seaside activity. Weissenbruch often made more than one version of a particular scene; at least six variants are known, for example, of his *Beach View* (e.g. 1887; The Hague, Gemeentemus.), while there are four versions of the *Woman by a Farmstead in Noorden* (e.g. Wassenaar, priv. col., see 1983 exh. cat., p. 284) and five of the *View of Haarlem (Souvenir de Haarlem)* (e.g. The Hague, Gemeentemus.).

Like Paulus Gabriël, Weissenbruch constructed his compositions according to mathematical rules, although his sometimes extremely free handling of the brush seems to suggest a less rigorous approach. He used a number of standard formulae (the division of light and dark, the arrangement of the various elements etc), which, applied differently in each case, created a tight structure. He managed to achieve a harmonious spread of light and well-balanced division of the picture plane even in his smaller paintings, as can be seen in the *Shell Wagons* (200×270 mm; The Hague, Gemeentemus.), in which the contrast between light and shadow makes the shell wagons stand out sharply against the sky. He produced his best work when he was in his seventies; his final landscapes— among them the *Beach View* of 1901 (The Hague, Gemeentemus.)—seem almost abstract in nature. He used his subjects merely as a vehicle to render tonalities, touches of the brush and a variety of surfaces. Mondrian was especially interested in these landscape paintings. Weissenbruch was recognized internationally after 1900, when American and Canadian collectors especially began to express an interest in his work.

FRANSJE KUYVENHOVEN

BIBLIOGRAPHY

Scheen
C. Vosmaer: *Hendrik Johannes Weissenbruch* (Amsterdam, 1885)
M. Rooses, ed.: *Het schildersboek: Nederlandsche schilders der negentiende eeuw, in monraphieën door tijdgenoten* [The book about painters: Dutch painters of the 19th century, in monographs by contemporaries], i (Amsterdam, 1898), pp. 122–38
Schilderijen en aquarellen door J. H. Weissenbruch (exh. cat., Amsterdam, Frans Buffa & Zn, 1899)
Catalogus der schilderijen en aquarellen uit de nalatenschap van J. H. Weissenbruch [Catalogue of paintings and watercolours from the estate of J. H. Weissenbruch] (sale cat., The Hague, Pulchri Studio, 1904)
E. B. Greenshields: *The Subjective View of Landscape Painting: With Special Reference to J. H. Weissenbruch and Illustrations from Works of his in Canada* (Montreal, 1904)
H. de Boer: 'Weissenbruch als aquarellist', *Elsevier's Geïllus. Mdschr.*, xxxiv/68 (1924), pp. 66–70
Tentoonstelling van werken door J. H. Weissenbruch uit de verzameling Hidde Nijland [Exhibition of works by J. H. Weissenbruch in the Hidde Nijland Collection] (exh. cat., Utrecht, Ver. 'Voor de kunst', 1925–6)
H. E. van Gelder: *J. H. Weissenbruch* (Amsterdam, 1940)
J. de Gruyter: *De Haagse school*, i (Rotterdam, 1969), pp. 60–75 [with Eng. summary]
The Hague School: Dutch Masters of the 19th Century (exh. cat., ed. R. de Leeuw, J. Sillevis and C. Dumas; Paris, Grand Pal.; London, RA; The Hague, Gemeentemus.; 1983), pp. 274–92
De Haagse school: De collectie van het Haags Gemeentemuseum (exh. cat., The Hague, Gemeentemus., 1988)
W. Laanstra and S. Ooms: *Johan Hendrik Weissenbruch, 1824–1903* (Amsterdam, 1992)

GEERT JAN KOOT

Weissenkircher [Weissenkirchner], **Hans Adam** (*b* Laufen, *bapt* 10 Feb 1646; *d* Graz, *bur* 16 Jan 1695). Austrian painter. Born into a Salzburg family of artists, he trained in Italy, mainly with Johann Carl Loth in Venice. Like most of Loth's many pupils, he took on much of the master's forceful, Caravaggesque style. He also travelled to Rome, Florence and Bologna, where he encountered the ideas of the classically minded Bolognese academy, which were better suited to his rather conservative talent. His entire future output was thus suspended between this idealism and Venetian naturalism.

Engaged by Prince Johann Seyfried von Eggenberg as court painter, Weissenkircher returned to Austria in 1678 and settled in Graz. His major achievement, the 'Planeten-saal' (1678–85) at Schloss Eggenberg in Graz, contains an allegorical cycle bringing together the planets, signs of the zodiac, elements and constellations to create a remarkable programme glorifying the house of Eggenberg. Weissenkircher was the first Austrian awarded such an important decorative commission, thus heading the Austrian Baroque artists who brought the long Italian and Dutch primacy in Austrian art to an end. Other work for the Eggenberg family includes many mythological or religious paintings, besides large-scale altarpieces (e.g. in the churches of Strass, St Veit am Aigen, Übelbach, Wildon, Weikendorf), mainly influenced by the work of Guido Reni and Pietro da Cortona; Weissenkircher's work was in turn to have a decisive impact on Styrian painting. His graphic work is limited to a few surviving sketches and designs for allegorical prints, generally engraved in Augsburg (e.g. Graz, Alte Gal.; Graz, Schloss Eggenberg).

BIBLIOGRAPHY
A. Rosenberg-Gutmann: *H. A. Weissenkirchner: Sein Leben und seine Kunst* (Graz, Vienna and Leipzig, 1925)
B. Ruck: *H. A. Weissenkircher: Fürstlich Eggenbergischer Hofmaler* (diss., Graz, Karl-Franzens-U., 1982)
H. A. Weissenkircher (exh. cat., ed. by B. Ruck; Graz, Schloss Eggenberg, 1985)

BARBARA RUCK

Weissman, A(driaan) W(illem) (*b* Amsterdam, 1858; *d* Haarlem, 13 Sept 1923). Dutch architect, architectural historian and critic. He was trained by the city architect of Amsterdam, Bastiaan de Greef (1818–99), and his assistant, Willem Springer, and from 1891 to 1894 he himself served in this capacity, building the Oosterbegraafplaats (East Cemetery; 1892–3) and the Stedelijk Museum (1893–5). The eclecticism that dominated late 19th-century Dutch architecture came naturally to Weissman, who favoured the use of local brick with stone trim to achieve a lively, permanent polychromy. The Stedelijk Museum was in the popular Dutch Renaissance style, but early designs for the East Cemetery show an acquaintance with the buildings of H. H. Richardson, whose work was influential in the Netherlands. Differences of opinion over the construction of the Museum led to Weissman's resignation shortly before its completion. His other major buildings include the concert hall De Vereeniging in Nijmegen; some houses in Amsterdam; and in the new extensions to Amsterdam under the Woningwet (Housing Act) of 1901, he designed hundreds of dwellings for Eigen Woning, a housing society whose architect he became in 1911; these included 408 dwellings (1923–5) in Amsterdam South. With the new century and these commissions for workers' housing, Weissman's work became more utilitarian. He became a proponent of *Zakelijkheid* and was fiercely resistant to the picturesque innovations of the Amsterdam school, whose productions he criticized in witty verses penned under the name 'Candidus'. Originally these appeared in *Architectura*; when the supporters of the Amsterdam school took over this journal, he published his biting poems in *De Bouwwereld*, which he edited from 1921 until his death.

WRITINGS
Het Gemeente Museum te Amsterdam (Amsterdam, 1895)
De gebakken steen (Amsterdam, 1905)
Geschiedenis der Nederlandsche bouwkunst [History of architecture in the Netherlands] (Amsterdam, 1912)

BIBLIOGRAPHY
Thieme–Becker
Nederland bouwt en baksteen, 1800–1940 (exh. cat., Rotterdam, Mus. Boymans, 1941)
A. W. Reinink: *Amsterdam en de Beurs van Berlage: Reacties van tijdgenoten* [Amsterdam and the exchange by Berlage: reactions from contemporaries] (The Hague, 1975)
H. Searing: 'Amsterdam South: Social Democracy's Elusive Housing Ideal', *VIA IV: Culture and Social Vision* (1980), pp. 67–8
M. Beek: *Drie eeuwen Amsterdamse bouwkunst* (Amsterdam, 1984) [cat. of archit. drgs in the A. A. Kok col.; Amsterdam, Sticht. Ned. Inst. Archit. & Stedebouw]

HELEN SEARING

Weisweiler, Adam (*b* Korschenbroich or Neuwied, 1744; *d* Paris, 15 June 1820). French cabinetmaker of German birth. Traditionally believed to have been apprenticed to David Roentgen in Neuwied, by 1777 he was established in the Rue du Faubourg Saint Antoine, in Paris, and on 26 March 1778 he was elected Maître Ebéniste. Specializing in the production of luxury pieces, Weisweiler executed consoles, break-front commodes, secrétaires, work-tables and *guéridons* of great delicacy and high quality. His furniture was often set with plaques of Sèvres porcelain, panels of pietra dura, Oriental lacquer or gilt-bronze, and occasionally Wedgwood medallions. Most of these materials were provided by the marchand-merciers for whom he worked, especially Dominique Daguerre, who supplied Marie-Antoinette with such pieces as Weisweiler's elegant work-table (1784; Paris, Louvre). Through Daguerre he also provided furniture for the English Prince Regent (later George IV) for Carlton House, London.

Weisweiler's furniture is characterized by its clear lines, interlaced stretchers and fluted and tapering supports often ending in short peg-top feet. Also typical is the use of plain veneers, especially mahogany and ebony, rather than pictorial marquetry, and of exquisite gilt-bronze ornaments, some of which have been attributed to Pierre Gouthière. Undulating ribbon and leaf mouldings, friezes depicting a combination of trumpeting fauns, goats, cornucopias, birds and *rinceaux* motifs, as well as vertical supports in the form of caryatids holding baskets on their heads, are frequently found on his pieces.

Weisweiler's business survived the French Revolution and prospered during the Directoire and Empire periods. He received commissions from the Bonaparte family and collaborated with the bronzeworker Pierre-Philippe Thomire and the firm headed by Lucien-François Feuchère. Notable among his pieces from this period is a pair of jewel-cabinets (1806; one in Arenenberg, Napoleonmus.) made for Queen Hortense of Holland. Weisweiler retired in 1809.

BIBLIOGRAPHY
G. de Bellaigue: *The James A. de Rothschild Collection at Waddesdon Manor: Furniture, Clocks and Gilt Bronzes*, ii (London, 1974), pp. 883–4
P. Lemonnier: *Weisweiler* (Paris, 1983)
D. Ledoux-Lebard: *Les Ebénistes du XIXe siècle, 1795–1889* (Paris, rev. 2/1984), pp. 623–6
A. Pradère: *French Furniture Makers: The Art of the Ebéniste from Louis XIV to the Revolution* (Malibu, 1989), pp. 388–403
DANIËLLE GROSHEIDE

Weisz, László. *See* MOHOLY-NAGY, LÁSZLÓ.

Weitsch, Johann Friedrich [Pascha] (*b* Hessendamm, nr Wolfenbüttel, 16 Oct 1723; *d* Salzdahlum, 6 Aug 1803). German painter, engraver, sculptor and administrator. He began his career as a pattern writer, then became a professional soldier. During this time he trained as a draughtsman, painter and copyist. From 1756 he was employed at the Fürstenberg porcelain factory as a painter and model draughtsman. He continued his artistic training on trips to other German cities (e.g. Nuremberg, Ansbach, Düsseldorf) and to the Netherlands, where he was also occasionally active as an art dealer. He was engaged by Charles I, Duke of Brunswick, and he took up residence in Salzdahlum; he was appointed gallery inspector of the Duke's collection in Salzdahlum in 1789. With his wide variety of functions—as an artistic adviser, a modeller of porcelain works and miniature busts and as a painter—he played an important role in artistic life in Brunswick. In 1795 he became a member of the Preussische Kunstakademie in Berlin.

Weitsch's principal talent was as a landscape painter. He painted mostly landscapes with ruins and animals in the Dutch style. His contemporaries praised his truth to nature in the depiction of local scenes: he produced a series of landscapes for Bishop of Hildesheim Fredrick Wilhelm von Westphalen, of views of the Harz Mountains based on studies from nature (Brunswick, Herzog Anton Ulrich-Mus.). He also produced a series of engravings with his favourite motifs of rocks, waterfalls and forests, and painted idyllic landscapes with allegorical meanings in the classical style, such as *Allegory on the Death of Anton Raphael Mengs* (*c.* 1780–82; Düsseldorf, Kstmus.). A table service painted with views of the Brunswick countryside after a model by Weitsch was produced for Charles I (*c.* 1765–8; Brunswick, Herzog Anton Ulrich-Mus.).

His two sons, Friedrich Georg Weitsch (1758–1828) and Anton Weitsch (1764–1841), were both painters.

BIBLIOGRAPHY
Thieme–Becker
A. Müller Hofstede: *Der Landschaftsmaler Pascha Johann Friedrich Weitsch, 1723–1803* (Brunswick, 1973)
KLÁRA GARAS

Weitzen. *See* VÁC.

Weitzmann, Kurt (*b* Klein Almerode, Germany, 7 March 1904). American art historian of German birth. He studied at the universities of Münster, Würzburg and Vienna and gained his doctorate from Berlin University. A grant from the German Archaeological Institute enabled him to study in Greece in 1931, and he remained an associate of the Institute until 1934. He joined the Princeton Institute for Advanced Studies in 1935 and taught at the university, becoming professor of art history and archaeology in 1950, a post he held until his retirement in 1972. Between 1956 and 1965 he made five trips to the monastery of St Catherine on Mt Sinai as part of a project to make a complete photographic record of the monastery's artistic monuments. Weitzmann supervised the cataloguing of the representational arts, including the detailed study of manuscript illumination in the library, and the study and restoration of the apse mosaic in the monastic church, but he was particularly concerned with the cataloguing of the large but little-known collection of icons held by the monastery. The results of his study are presented in his most important work, *The Monastery of Saint Catherine at Mount Sinai* (1976), which increased understanding of Byzantine icon production from the 6th century, with far-reaching implications for the history of art in general. He also produced numerous publications on Byzantine manuscript illumination and contributed studies on the influence of the Classical heritage on Byzantine art and the relationship between the art of the Latin West and that of the Byzantine empire.

WRITINGS
Illustrated Manuscripts at St Catherine's Monastery on Mount Sinai (Collegeville, 1973)
The Icons: From the Sixth to the Tenth Century, i of *The Monastery of Saint Catherine at Mount Sinai* (Princeton, 1976)
The Icon (London, 1978)
Classical Heritage in Byzantine and Near Eastern Art (London, 1981)
Art in the Medieval West and its Contacts with Byzantium (London, 1982)
Studies in the Arts at Sinai (Princeton, 1982)
A. N. PALMER, J. VAN GINKEL

Wejchert [née Adamczewska], **Hanna** (*b* Radom, Poland, 29 July 1920). Polish architect, urban planner and teacher. She received a Diploma in Architecture from Warsaw Technical University in 1946 and a PhD in 1959. In 1946 she joined the faculty of the Warsaw School of Architecture, where she was appointed professor in 1975. Her architectural partnership with her husband, Kazimierz Wejchert (1912–93), began in 1947. They worked principally in urban planning and design, and their major project was the new town of Tychy, just south of the industrial centre of Katowice. The master plan was completed in 1951, and building continued into the mid-1980s. The town is organized around two intersecting axes—a railway line running east-west and a north-to-south green belt leading to a lake and wooded area—and was designed to have four districts, each with about 25,000 people. The Wejcherts were interested in integrating the town with its natural surroundings, and in maintaining references to its history. Their main inspiration came from medieval towns that gradually expanded around a central unit (e.g. town hall, church or square). They attempted to avoid urban sprawl and resisted the use of high-rise structures, keeping most buildings to between four and eleven storeys. Regarding architects as servants to society, the Wejcherts extended this function into architectural education and theory as well.

WRITINGS
Wpływ realizacji na przemian miasta [The influence of realization on the changing image of a town] (Warsaw, 1968)
with K. Wejchert: 'New Towns in Poland', *New Towns* (University Park, PA, 1976)

BIBLIOGRAPHY
Contemp. Architects
H. Skibniewska: 'L'Urbanisme pologne', *Archit. Aujourd'hui*, 118 (1964–5), pp. 76–9

WALTER SMITH

Welch, Robert (*b* Hereford, 21 May 1929). English industrial designer and silversmith. He trained as a silversmith at the Birmingham School of Art. In the summer of 1953, while a student at the Royal College of Art (1952–5), he won a travelling scholarship to Sweden where he participated in a design course organized by the Swedish Council of Industrial Design. In the following year he went to Norway and worked with the silversmith Theodor Olsen. It was in Scandinavia that the potential of stainless steel as a material was brought to Welch's attention, and in his final year at the Royal College the topic of his thesis was stainless-steel tableware. In 1955 he was appointed design consultant to J. & J. Wiggin, a small manufacturer of stainless-steel hollow-ware who marketed their products under the name Old Hall, a position he held for the next 25 years. Among Welch's designs for Old Hall is the 'Alveston' cutlery range (1962), which won a Design Council award in 1965. In the same year that Welch joined Old Hall, he established a silversmithing workshop and design practice in an 18th-century mill at Chipping Campden, Glos. Welch's work in silver, at the heart of the revival of silversmithing, includes a collection of silver for Heal's and a number of commissions for the Goldsmiths' Company, both of London. His designs for industry include cast-iron and enamel cookware for Carl Prinz of Solingen (1966), the 'Serica' range of glass goblets for the Bridge Crystal Glass Co. and lamps for Lumitron Ltd. In 1965 he became the Royal Designer to Industry.

BIBLIOGRAPHY
G. Hughes: 'Robert Welch: Goldsmith and Silversmith', *Connoisseur*, cliii (1963), pp. 190–95
——: *Modern Silver throughout the World* (New York, 1967)
C. Forbes, ed.: *Robert Welch: Design in a Cotswold Workshop* (London, 1973)

DONNA CORBIN

Welf [Guelph; Guelf; Brunswick], House of. German dynasty of rulers, patrons and collectors. The first notable patron of the Welf dynasty was (1) Henry the Lion, Duke of Saxony and Bavaria (*reg* 1142–80), who initiated an extensive building programme in Brunswick in the mid-12th century. Although deprived of his duchies in 1180 (due to conflict with the Holy Roman Emperor), he retained control of the Welf family lands of Brunswick and Lüneburg. In 1209 his second son became Holy Roman Emperor as Otto IV (*c.* 1174–1218), the only member of the Welf family to take this title. Under the Emperor's patronage work was begun *c.* 1216 on the construction of the Cistercian monastery of Riddagshausen near Brunswick. The Emperor's nephew Otto the Child, Duke of Brunswick and Lüneburg (*d* 1252), finished building the Stiftskirche (now the cathedral) at Brunswick, which Henry the Lion had begun in 1173. During Otto's reign the church was richly decorated with wall paintings, and a double tomb was built (*c.* 1230) for the remains of Henry the Lion and his consort, Matilda of England (1156–89), which is one of the finest works of 13th-century Saxon sculpture. United under Otto the Child, Brunswick and Lüneburg were repartitioned after his death by his sons and further partitioned in 1409.

From 1547 Henry II, Duke of Brunswick-Wolfenbüttel (*reg* 1514–68), restored the town of Wolfenbüttel (in the family's possession since 1255), which had suffered greatly in the Schmalkaldic War. There he created the Neustadt (now the Heinrichstadt) and developed the ducal Schloss (1556–9) on a grand scale. The chief contributor to this work was Francesco Chiaramella (*fl* 1552–78), who created the imposing chapel (destr. 1796), a tower-like building with a majestic dome and four corner towers (see fig.).

Wolfenbüttel, Schlossplatz, with the chapel and Schloss (left) and Zeughaus (right) of the Dukes of Brunswick-Wolfenbüttel; engraving by Caspar Merian, 201×395 mm, 1654 (Brunswick, Herzog Anton Ulrich-Museum)

Henry II's son and successor, Julius, Duke of Brunswick-Wolfenbüttel (*reg* 1568–89), who embraced the Protestant faith, made further alterations to the Schloss and began to construct an elaborate system of bastions. He is regarded as '*ingenior et inventor*' of probably the first Renaissance city in Germany to be laid out according to a plan. His son (2) Henry Julius, Duke of Brunswick-Wolfenbüttel (*reg* 1589–1613), who continued the urban development of Wolfenbüttel, was one of the first German princes of the Baroque era whose court was distinguished by a brilliant intellectual and artistic life.

At the death of Henry Julius's son Frederick Ulrich, Duke of Brunswick-Wolfenbüttel (*reg* 1613–34), the dukedom passed by agreement to (3) Augustus, Duke of Brunswick-Wolfenbüttel (*reg* 1635–66), of the collateral line of Dannenberg, a scholar and collector who founded the Bibliotheca Augusta (now the Herzog August Bibliothek) in Wolfenbüttel. His cultural interests were inherited by his sons, (5) Anton Ulrich, Duke of Brunswick-Wolfenbüttel (*reg* 1685–1714), one of the most outstanding German Baroque princes, and Ferdinand Albert, Duke of Brunswick-Bevern (1636–87), whose taste as a Baroque collector is evidenced by a substantial library and *Kunstkammer* in Schloss Bevern. Anton Ulrich's son, Augustus William, Duke of Brunswick-Wolfenbüttel (*reg* 1714–31), sought to emulate the brilliance of his father's household. From 1718 he had a palace constructed in Brunswick by the architect Hermann Korb. In Wolfenbüttel he adorned the Schloss with a Baroque façade (1715) and rebuilt the Trinitatiskirche (1716–22), which had been destroyed by fire in 1705.

A kinsman of the house of Brunswick-Wolfenbüttel, (4) George William, Duke of Calenberg and Celle (1624–1705), travelled extensively, bringing foreign influences (notably those of France and Italy) to the architecture of his residence at Celle. He was the elder brother of Ernest Augustus, Elector of Hannover (1622–98), whose son became George I, King of Great Britain (*see* HANOVER, House of), in 1714.

In 1735 the duchy devolved on the Bevern branch of the dynasty. (6) Charles I, Duke of Brunswick-Wolfenbüttel (*reg* 1735–80), opened the family art collection to the public. His son (7) Charles II, Duke of Brunswick (*reg* 1780–1806), brought up in the spirit of the Enlightenment, travelled in Britain, France and Italy, where he came under the influence of Johann Joachim Winckelmann. This led him to lose his taste for the late Baroque style, and he began to favour the antique forms of early Neo-classicism, soon reflected in building activity in Brunswick, which was marked by severity, economy and practicality rather than by a desire for splendour. The dukedom was in abeyance in 1806–13 and from 1884 until, in 1913, William II, Emperor of Germany, acknowledged the claim of his son-in-law, Ernest Augustus III, Prince of Hannover (1887–1953), who became Duke of Brunswick but who, like other German rulers, was deposed in 1918.

See also BRUNSWICK, §1 and WOLFENBÜTTEL.

NDB

BIBLIOGRAPHY
F. Thöne: 'Wolfenbüttel unter Herzog Julius, 1568–1589', *Braunschweig. Jb.*, 3rd ser., xxxiii (1952), pp. 1–74
J.-C. Klamt: *Die mittelalterlichen Monumentalmalereien im Dom zu Braunschweig* (diss., Berlin, Freie U., 1968)
C. Rauterberg: *Bauwesen und Bauten im Herzogtum Braunschweig zur Zeit Carl Wilhelm Ferdinands, 1780–1806*, i of series B of *Braunschweiger Werkstücke* (Brunswick, 1971)
F. N. Steigerwald: *Das Grabmal Heinrichs des Löwen und Mathildes im Dom zu Braunschweig*, ix of series A of *Braunschweiger Werkstücke* (Brunswick, 1972)
R. Moderhack, ed.: *Braunschweigische Landesgeschichte im Überblick* (Brunswick, 1976, rev. 3/1979)
Barocke Sammellust: Die Bibliothek und Kunstkammer des Herzogs Ferdinand Albrecht zu Braunschweig-Lüneburg (1636–1687) (exh. cat., Wolfenbüttel, Herzog August Bib., 1988)
S. Brenske: *Der Hl. Kreuz-Kyklus in der ehemaligen Braunschweiger Stiftskirche St Blasius*, xxv of series B of *Braunschweiger Werkstücke* (Brunswick, 1988)

JOHANNES ZAHLTEN

(1) Henry the Lion, Duke of Saxony and Bavaria (*b c.* 1129; *reg* 1142–80; *d* Brunswick, 6 Aug 1195). The son of Henry the Proud (*reg* 1137–8), he inherited conflict with Conrad III (*reg* 1138–52), Holy Roman Emperor, who had confiscated Saxony and Bavaria from the Welfs in 1138. Henry regained the duchies in 1142 and 1156, respectively, ruling them until he was placed under imperial ban in 1180, and was forced to live in exile in England until 1185.

Henry's wealth afforded him widespread patronage in the fields of science, literature, architecture and art. He encouraged the growth of cities and commerce, founding Munich in 1158 and restoring Lübeck in 1159, two years after much of the town had been destroyed by fire (*see* LÜBECK, §1). He developed Brunswick into a fortified ducal residence, using nearby Goslar as a model for his palace, and rebuilding St Blasius as a cruciform basilica (now the cathedral; *see* BRUNSWICK, §1). This building, begun in 1173, was the first in Lower Saxony to have its nave and aisles vaulted and served as a model for other churches in the area. In the same year the foundation stone of Lübeck Cathedral was laid in Henry's presence, and he made annual grants towards construction there and at Ratzeburg Cathedral (from 1170).

The most widely known work of art associated with Henry is the bronze lion erected in 1166 outside Dankwarderode Schloss, Brunswick (*see* ROMANESQUE, fig. 74). It was originally gilded, and metallographic analysis indicates that it was cast in the Brunswick area, using ore from the Harz Mountains. It is the earliest large, free-standing sculpture north of the Alps and is an appropriate symbol of the Duke's power at its peak. Under Henry, the promotion of trade with the Baltic advanced the reception of Byzantine art into Northern Europe. He also visited Emperor Manuel I (*reg* 1143–80) in Constantinople while on a pilgrimage to Jerusalem in 1172–3. He established a goldsmiths' workshop in or near Brunswick to produce receptacles to house the many relics and gifts he returned with, such as the Apostles arm reliquary (Cleveland, OH, Mus. A.). These and a variety of furnishings, including the altar of the Virgin and a seven-branched bronze candelabrum (both *in situ*), he bequeathed to Brunswick Cathedral, thereby increasing the so-called Welf Treasure (dispersed; mainly in Berlin, Tiergarten, Kstgewmus.).

Among these benefactions was the Gospels of Henry the Lion (Wolfenbüttel, Herzog August Bib., Cod. Guelf. 105 noviss. 2°; Munich, Bayer. Staatsbib., Clm. 30055), the most important extant manuscript associated with

Henry (for illustration and further discussion *see* CHRYSOGRAPHY and WOLFENBÜTTEL). Commissioned from Helmarshausen Abbey and painted (*c.* 1185–8) by the monk Herimann, it contains 41 full-page miniatures, including 2 depictions of Henry and his second wife Matilda (1156–89), whom he married in 1168. Another manuscript from Helmarshausen, a fragmentary Psalter (London, BL, Lansdowne MS. 381), also portrays the ducal couple. Matilda was the daughter of Henry II, King of England, and Eleanor of Aquitaine (1122–1204), and, through her connection with the Angevin court, introduced courtly poetry, based on French models, to Henry's circle.

Henry's life became the subject of myth in the 12th-century *Heinrich-Sage*; illustrations of heroic episodes from this saga can be found throughout Europe, for instance in the carvings (*c.* 1230; Copenhagen, Nmus.) originally on the church tower of Valthjofsstadhur, Iceland. A specific Welf style, distinct from that of the Hohenstaufen, cannot be ascribed to the products of Henry's patronage; in terms of scale and quality, however, the works associated with him rival those of the imperial court and represent a high point in Romanesque artistic achievement.

BIBLIOGRAPHY

O. von Falke, R. Schmidt and G. Swarzenski: *Der Welfenschatz* (Frankfurt am Main, 1930)
P. Barz: *Heinrich der Löwe* (Bonn, 1977)
Die Zeit der Staufer, 2 vols (exh. cat., Stuttgart, Württemberg. Landesmus., 1977)
The Gospels of Henry the Lion, by C. de Hamel (sale cat., London, Sotheby's, 6 Dec 1983)
K. Jordan: *Henry the Lion* (Oxford, 1986)

S. A. WOODCOCK

(2) Henry [Heinrich] **Julius**, Duke of Brunswick-Wolfenbüttel (*b* Schloss Hessen, 15 Oct 1564; *reg* 1589–1613; *d* Prague, 30 July 1613). A many-talented personality, he was one of the most outstanding rulers of Lower Saxony. Although his palace at Wolfenbüttel was acknowledged as a model of its kind, the expense of his establishment, his disregard of corporate interests, the increased taxes that he imposed and his claim to the city of Brunswick made him unpopular with his subjects. He managed to secure an imperial ban against Brunswick but could not bring about the subjection of the city. From 1607 until his death he lived at the imperial court at Prague and, as director of the Privy Council and a close confidant of the Holy Roman Emperor Rudolf II, played a significant role in European politics. Like the Emperor he was a patron of literature, science and the arts. He wrote dramas and was the first German prince to maintain professional actors permanently at his court in Wolfenbüttel, introducing a new era of German drama, in which the 'theatre of action' replaced the humanistic theatre of the Reformation.

Henry Julius not only was a collector of works of art but also produced paintings, some of which are extant (e.g. *Italian Landscape*, *c.* 1590; Brunswick, Landesmus.), and is said to have executed the designs for his own palaces at Halberstadt (destr.) and Gröningen (1568–94; destr. 1817). Through his commissions for buildings he exercised a decisive influence on the Duchy's architecture, for example the Juleum (1592–7) at Helmstedt, erected by Paul Francke, Schloss Erichsburg, Schloss Hessen and the barracks at Halberstadt. His main building activity took place in Wolfenbüttel, where he continued the development of the fortifications, joining the fortress on the embankment (the location of the ducal Schloss) with the Heinrichstadt to form a single, fortified residential area. The richly ornamented imperial gateway at the eastern approach was the work of Hans Vredeman de Vries. Paul Francke, the architect responsible for developing the Schloss from 1569, added the high Hausmannsturm (1614), with ornamental gables, and also transformed the Schlossplatz by building the large, rectangular Zeughaus (1613) with its row of massive dormer windows (see fig. above). Paul Francke's principal late work executed for the Duke, the Kirche Beatae Mariae Virginis (1608–*c.* 1626) in Wolfenbüttel, was one of the first monumental Protestant church buildings in Germany; it served as the parish church and as the court church and, until 1750, as the burial-place of the ducal family.

BIBLIOGRAPHY

K. Seelecke: 'Paul Francke: Ein fürstlicher Baumeister zu Wolfenbüttel', *Braunschweig. Jb.*, 3rd ser., xxvi (1940), pp. 29–57
F. Thöne: 'Wolfenbüttel in der Spätrenaissance: Topographie und Baugeschichte unter den Herzögen Heinrich Julius und Friedrich Ulrich (1589–1634)', *Braunschweig. Jb.*, 3rd ser., xxxv (1954), pp. 5–116
——: 'Hans Vredeman de Vries in Wolfenbüttel', *Braunschweig. Jb.*, 3rd ser., xli (1960), pp. 47–68
H. Lietzmann: *Herzog Heinrich Julius zu Braunschweig und Lüneburg (1564–1613): Persönlichkeit und Wirken für Kaiser und Reich*, Quellen und Forschungen zur Braunschweigischen Geschichte, xxx (Brunswick, 1993)

(3) Augustus, Duke of Brunswick-Lüneburg-Wolfenbüttel (*b* Dannenberg, 10 April 1579; *reg* 1635–66; *d* Wolfenbüttel, 17 Sept 1666). After studying at the universities of Rostock, Tübingen and Strasbourg, he completed his education at Padua and with a Grand Tour to Italy, Malta, the Netherlands and France. In 1604 he settled at Hitzacker, Lower Saxony, where he began to collect books and objects of vertu and maintained an extensive correspondence with learned friends, including the theologian Johann Valentin Andreae (1586–1654) and the collector and dealer Philipp Hainhofer. He also visited the imperial courts at Prague and Vienna and attended the coronation (1612) of the Holy Roman Emperor Matthias at Frankfurt am Main.

From 1635, when the reunited duchy of Brunswick-Wolfenbüttel was assigned to him, Augustus resided at Brunswick; he returned to Wolfenbüttel in 1642, when the city was liberated from imperial occupation. Thereafter he set about rebuilding his desolate country and developing Wolfenbüttel into a Baroque capital. Encouraged by works on architectural theory in his library, he embarked on a systematic course of planning, although retaining the city's historic buildings. He modernized and extended the fortifications, transformed the embankment fortification into an imposing palace complex (see fig. above), promoted the completion of the Kirche Beatae Mariae Virginis and laid out the Auguststadt as a planned residential district for craftsmen, in the centre of which was the half-timbered Johanniskirche (1661–4).

Augustus's main concern, however, was the enlargement of his library. With remarkable industry and in a systematic manner, he assembled 135,000 publications in 31,000 volumes. During his lifetime the Bibliotheca Augusta (now Herzog August Bibliothek) was housed in two long rooms above the ducal stables; subsequently it was moved to the library rotunda (1706–13; destr.) built by Hermann Korb. The contents of the library represented all disciplines; the arrangement of the books reveals that the Duke regarded it as an intellectual cosmos. The same intention is apparent in his collection of clocks (Brunswick, Herzog Anton Ulrich-Mus.), his chief interest next to books: his perception of the clock as a representation of the universe, as well as his fascination with its mechanism, can be discerned. The Duke was regarded by his contemporaries as an outstanding collector and scholar: numerous poems and verses were addressed to him, probably more than to any other prince of the Baroque period.

BIBLIOGRAPHY

Sammler, Fürst, Gelehrter: Herzog August zu Braunschweig und Lüneburg, 1579–1666 (exh. cat., Wolfenbüttel, Herzog August Bib., 1979)

(4) George William [Georg Wilhelm], Duke of Calenberg and Celle (*b* Schloss Herzberg, Harz, 16/26 Jan 1624; *d* Wienhausen, nr Celle, 1705). As ruler of Calenberg (1648–79) and Celle (1665–1705), he was initially frequently absent, travelling extensively throughout Europe, especially to Italy and the Netherlands, much to the annoyance of his provincial diet. In 1676 he married his mistress, Eléonore d'Olbreuse (1639–1722), under whose austere influence he settled down to rule his people and preside over a cultured court at Celle. The present appearance of Schloss Celle (*see* CELLE, §2) is due largely to the Baroque alterations (1665–*c*. 1700) undertaken by the Italian architects Lorenzo Bedogni (*d* 1670) and Giuseppe Arighini (*fl* 1670–1700). The interior decoration (1670–77) was the work of Giovanni Battista Tornielli (*fl* 1670–83). Precious tapestries from Flanders and Brabant, damask wall-coverings from Venice and furniture from Paris completed the furnishings.

The Schloss also contains a theatre designed by Giuseppe Arighini in 1674. Although Baroque alterations, with Italian influences, were undertaken at the same time in the parish church by the same artists, the town itself reveals the taste of the French-born Duchess (*see* CELLE, §1). The Duke's plan to extend Celle in the Baroque style, influenced by both French and Dutch ideas, never came to fruition. Through the children of his daughter Sophia Dorothea (1666–1726), who married his nephew George, Elector of Hannover (1660–1727), subsequently George I, King of Great Britain (*reg* 1714–27), the Duke became an ancestor of the monarchs of Great Britain and Prussia.

BIBLIOGRAPHY

O. Weltzien: *Celler Geschichte* (Celle, 1926)

H. Siebern, ed.: *Die Kunstdenkmäler der Provinz Hannover*, III/v (Hannover, 1937)

S. Busch: *Hannover, Wolfenbüttel und Celle: Stadtgründungen und Stadterweiterungen in drei Welfischen Residenzen vom 16. bis zum 18. Jahrhundert* (Hildesheim, 1969)

Celle: Das Schloss, ii of *Dokumentation der Stadtsparkasse* (Celle, 1980)

Sophie, Kurfürstin von Hannover (1630–1714) (exh. cat., Hannover, Hist. Mus. Hohen Ufer, 1980)

(5) Anton Ulrich, Duke of Brunswick Wolfenbüttel (*b* Hitzacker, 4 Oct 1633; *reg* 1685–1714; *d* Schloss Salzdahlum, nr Brunswick, 27 March 1714). Son of (3) Augustus, Duke of Brunswick-Wolfenbüttel. His tastes were moulded by his father, at whose court his literary inclinations were stimulated and his love of the theatre encouraged. His education was mainly in the hands of the distinguished scholar Justus Georg Schottelius (1612–76). Anton Ulrich's Grand Tour (1655–6) included visits to the courts at Darmstadt, Stuttgart and Durlach and to Strasbourg and the court of Louis XIV, King of France, in Paris. His visit there strengthened his resolve to combine courtly life on the French model and nurture of the arts with a stately exercise of sovereignty.

Anton Ulrich's elder brother, Rudolf Augustus, Duke of Brunswick-Wolfenbüttel (1627–1704), appointed him governor in 1667 and joint ruler in 1685. At this time Anton Ulrich initiated the construction of the opera houses at Wolfenbüttel (1688; destr.) and Brunswick (1689–90; destr. 1943–5) and the first Trinitatiskirche (1693–1700; destr. 1705) and the new library building (1706–13; destr. 1887) for the Bibliotheca Augusta in Wolfenbüttel. He appointed Gottfried Wilhelm Leibniz (1646–1716), the polymath and philosopher (who had also been employed by Augustus), as director of the Bibliotheca Augusta at Wolfenbüttel and consulted him on scholarly, political and artistic matters.

Anton Ulrich's most important building enterprise was Schloss Salzdahlum (destr. 1812; see fig.), which was conceived as a 'rival residence' to his brother's official seat of government and to the electoral palace at Hannover-Herrenhausen. Work began in 1688, and it was virtually complete when the architect, Johann Balthasar Lauterbach, died. Under his successor, Hermann Korb, the orangery and more wings to house the art collections were added after 1700. It was a timber-frame building clad with plaster; set amid large gardens, it had the appearance of a huge stone building. Although the inspiration of Versailles was evident, the Duke knew the latter only from engravings and descriptions, but elements from castles in France, the Netherlands and northern Italy that he had seen on later journeys were also incorporated in the design. Schloss Salzdahlum was influential in the development of castle construction in Germany in the 18th century, notably in its central staircase and adjoining banqueting room, the *sala terrena* overlooking the garden and the buildings housing the ducal collections. The Grosse Galerie (1701) at Salzdahlum was the first independent gallery built for the express purpose of housing paintings and sculptures in Germany.

In his own lifetime the Duke's collections were widely known, attracting many visitors. His gallery contained important works (now in Brunswick, Herzog Anton Ulrich-Mus.) by Italian, Netherlandish and Dutch masters, in particular Rembrandt and his circle, and he also collected sculptures, Italian maiolica, French enamel paintings, porcelain, ivory, East Asian arts and crafts, textiles, natural history exhibits, wax reliefs, an extensive number of engravings and clocks and scientific instruments. His collection thus mirrored his aim of reproducing the order of an ideal world.

Anton Ulrich became sole ruler of the Duchy in 1704 but failed to achieve the status of Elector. He raised the status of his family, however, by marrying his granddaughters to Charles of Spain, subsequently the Holy Roman Emperor Charles VI, and Alexis, Tsarevitch of Russia (1690–1718). Anton Ulrich's conversion to the Catholic faith in 1710, which created a great stir, inspired him to

Schloss Salzdahlum, near Wolfenbüttel, built for Anton Ulrich, Duke of Brunswick-Wolfenbüttel, by Johann Balthasar Lauterbach, begun 1688 (destr. 1813); engraving by Petrus Schenk the younger, 500×600 mm, after 1715 (Brunswick, Herzog Anton Ulrich-Museum)

build the Catholic parish church of St Nicholas (1710–12; destr. 1943–5) in Brunswick.

BIBLIOGRAPHY
G. Gerkens: *Das fürstliche Lustschloss Salzdahlum und sein Erbauer Herzog Anton Ulrich von Braunschweig-Wolfenbüttel*, xxii of *Quellen und Forschungen zur Braunschweigischen Geschichte* (Brunswick, 1974)
Herzog Anton Ulrich von Braunschweig: Leben und Regieren mit der Kunst (exh. cat., Brunswick, Herzog Anton Ulrich-Mus., 1983)
J. Zählten: '"Ein Schema von einer bessern Invention...": Giovanni Antonio Pellegrinis Ölskizze für die barocke Bibliotheksrotunde in Wolfenbüttel', *Festschrift für Bruno Bushart* (Munich, 1994)

(6) Charles [Karl] **I**, Duke of Brunswick-Wolfenbüttel (*b* Brunswick, 1 Aug 1713; *reg* 1735–80; *d* Brunswick, 26 March 1780). Great-grandson of (3) Augustus, Duke of Brunswick-Wolfenbüttel. He was receptive to the principles of the Enlightenment and mercantilism and, when he succeeded to the dukedom, promoted trade and industry through the state enterprises he founded, which included the mirror-glass factory in Grünenplan (1740) and the FÜRSTENBERG PORCELAIN FACTORY (1747); he also supported the establishment (1763) of a lacquerware factory, owned by Georg Siegmund Stobwasser (*b* 1740), in Brunswick. Among his other achievements were the foundation (1745) of the Collegium Carolinum in Brunswick, the forerunner of the Technische Universität, his school reforms and the establishment of teacher-training colleges.

In 1754 he opened the ducal art collections to the public and in 1770 entrusted management of the ducal library in Wolfenbüttel to Gotthold Ephraim Lessing. During his reign several late Baroque buildings were constructed in Brunswick, including the Kammergebäude (1764) and Schlösschen Richmond (1768–9), and the Rathaus in the Neustadt was renovated (1773–85).

BIBLIOGRAPHY
S. Ducret: *Geschichte der Fabrik*, i of *Fürstenberger Porzellan* (Brunswick, 1965)
Weisses Gold aus Fürstenburg: Kulturgeschichte im Spiegel des Porzellans, 1747–1830 (exh. cat., Brunswick, 1988)
F. A. Christiani and S. Baumann: *Braunschweiger Lackkunst: Führer durch die Schausammlung, Veröffentlichungen aus dem Städtischen Museum Braunschweig*, lxiv (Brunswick, 1993)
JOHANNES ZAHLTEN

(7) Charles [Karl] **II**, Duke of Brunswick-Wolfenbüttel (*b* Brunswick, 30 Oct 1804; *reg* 1815–30; *d* Geneva, 18 Aug 1873). Great-grandson of (6) Charles I. An orphan, in 1815 he became the ward of George, Prince Regent, later George IV, King of Great Britain. Differences of opinion regarding the age at which the Duke reached his majority (18 or 21) led to strife between them, and the Brunswick political authorities lodged a complaint against the Duke with the Assembly of the German Diet. In 1830 he was forced to leave Brunswick in a popular uprising believed to have been directed by influential circles. Thereafter he lived in London, Paris and Geneva. His extravagant lifestyle and exploits, including crossing and re-crossing the Channel in a balloon, made him a popular figure with the press. He succeeded in increasing his large fortune immeasurably by skilful investments and speculations. His famous diamond collection of over 1200 items resulted in his being known as 'the diamond duke'. As a result of the Franco-Prussian War (1870) Charles went into exile in Geneva. He made that city heir to his immense fortune; in return the city was required to erect a monument to him in the style of the tomb of Cansignorio della Scala in S Maria Antica, Verona (see SCALA, DELLA and fig.). The monument in the Place des Alpes (in situ) was completed in 1879, though the equestrian statue of the donor by Charles-François-Marie Iguel (1827–97) had to be removed and placed alongside it a few years later for structural reasons.

BIBLIOGRAPHY
O. Böse: *Karl II., Herzog zu Braunschweig und Lüneburg: Ein Beitrag zur Metternich-Forschung* (Brunswick, 1956)
T. Dénes: *Charles II, Duc de Brunswick, et Genève* (Geneva, 1973)
E.-H. Grefe: *Gefährdung monarchischer Autorität im Zeitalter der Restauration: Der braunschweigische Umsturz von 1830 und die zeitgenössische Publizistik* (Brunswick, 1987)

GEORG RUPPELT

Wellcome, Sir Henry S(olomon) (*b* Almond, WI, 21 Aug 1853; *d* London, 25 July 1936). British pharmaceutical manufacturer and collector (naturalized 1910), of American birth. Around 1897 he began to form the collection that became in 1913 the Wellcome Historical Medical Museum in Wigmore Street, London. Its purpose was to illustrate the history of medicine, which Wellcome interpreted anthropologically as the evolution of manifestations of the instinct for self-preservation. Wellcome collected avidly, both in person and through agents in many countries. By 1936 the collection contained *c.* 900,000 items, including paintings, prints and photographs; sculpture; medical and pharmaceutical antiques; prehistoric flints; trephined skulls; amulets; ethnographic objects; and manuscripts and printed books. Interest in the development of such documentary techniques as photography and typography influenced many of Wellcome's acquisitions (e.g. incunabula from William Morris's library, 1898). After Wellcome's death the collection passed by bequest to the trustees of the Wellcome Trust. Much of it was sold at auction, and much was also dispersed by gift or loan to 144 museums, mainly in Britain. Yet vast amounts still remain together in two London institutions active in research and education: books and prints etc in the Library of the Wellcome Institute; and museum objects (e.g. ceramics, instruments, sculpture and medical ethnography) in the Wellcome Museum of the History of Medicine, a department of the Science Museum.

WRITINGS
'Graeco-Roman Surgical Instruments Represented in Egyptian Sculpture', *History of Medicine*, xxiii of *XVIIth International Congress of Medicine: London, 1913*, pp. 207–10
BIBLIOGRAPHY
H. Turner: *Henry Wellcome: The Man, his Collection and his Legacy* (London, 1980)
G. Russell: 'The Wellcome Non-medical Material', *Mus. J.: Organ Mus. Assoc.*, lxxxvi (1986), pp. S1–S36

G. M. Skinner: 'Sir Henry Wellcome's Museum for the Science of History', *Medic. Hist.*, xxx (1986), pp. 383–418

WILLIAM SCHUPBACH

Wellesley. Anglo-Irish family of patrons and collectors.

(1) Arthur Wellesley, 1st Duke of Wellington (*b* Dublin, ?1 May 1769; *d* Walmer Castle, Kent, 14 Sept 1852). Soldier, statesman, patron and collector. His collecting activities owed more to military skill than aesthetic judgement. After the Battle of Vitoria in June 1813 he captured paintings, prints and drawings that had been taken by Joseph Bonaparte from the Spanish royal collections; among these were such masterpieces as Correggio's *Agony in the Garden* (mid-1520s) and Velázquez's *Waterseller of Seville* (*c.* 1620; both London, Apsley House). Wellington shared aristocratic British taste for 17th-century Dutch genre painting, and in Paris after 1815, through the French dealer FERRÉOL DE BONNEMAISON, he acquired several important examples, including Jan Steen's *A Wedding Party* (1667; London, Apsley House). He also commissioned contemporary pictures in the same vein, most notably David Wilkie's *Chelsea Pensioners Reading the Waterloo Despatch* (1822; London, Apsley House), which cost him £1260.

In 1816 Wellington bought Apsley House (*c.* 1772–8), London, designed by Robert Adam (i). In 1828–9 he had his architect, Benjamin Dean Wyatt, reface the exterior in Bath stone, add the portico and remodel the interior in his preferred Louis XIV style, to include a gallery for the annual Waterloo banquets. He continued to collect mainly in order to record the chief protagonists (on both sides) of the Napoleonic Wars: hence the portraits of his generals in the Striped Drawing-room and Antonio Canova's over-life-size nude sculpture of Napoleon (marble, 1806) in the stairwell of Apsley House. His collection was also enriched by grateful allies with gifts, including the Sèvres Egyptian service and the Portuguese service known as the 'Wellington Plate' (see PORTUGAL, fig. 18). Apsley House and most of its contents were given to the nation by Gerald Wellesley, 7th Duke of Wellington, in 1947.

In 1817 Wellington received Stratfield Saye, Hants, as a gift from Parliament, and plans for a vast new Neoclassical palace on the site were drawn up by B. D. Wyatt and several other architects, including Charles Robert Cockerell and Charles Heathcote Tatham. However, Wellington preferred to impress his powerful personality on the more modest fabric of the original house, and nothing was done apart from minor additions by Wyatt in 1822 and 1838.

The Duke's chief importance to art was as a subject for artists. Despite his well-known dislike of sitting, his likeness was endlessly recorded—a head and shoulders by Goya (London, N.G.) and works by the humblest of engravers—on canvas, tin-plate and on ceramics. His aquiline nose and political setbacks were a fertile target for the caricaturist, and his death provoked a rash of monuments, the most ambitious being a project (1857–1912) for St Paul's Cathedral, London, by Alfred Stevens (ii) (see LONDON, fig. 26).

BIBLIOGRAPHY
E. Wellesley: *A Descriptive and Historical Catalogue of the Collection of Pictures and Sculpture at Apsley House*, 2 vols (London, 1901)

Lord Gerald Wellesley and J. Steegman: *The Iconography of the First Duke of Wellington* (London, 1935), suppl. by R. Walker: *National Portrait Gallery: Regency Portraits*, i (London, 1985), pp. 533–42
Apollo, xcviii (Sept 1973) [issue dedicated to Apsley House]
Apollo, cii (July 1975) [issue dedicated to Stratfield Saye]
C. M. Kauffmann: *Catalogue of Paintings in the Wellington Museum* (London, 1982)
C. Truman: *The Sèvres Egyptian Service, 1810–12* (London, 1982)

OLIVER GARNETT

(2) Henry Wellesley (*b* 1791–4; *d* Oxford, 11 Jan 1866). Clergyman, curator, writer and collector, nephew of (1) Arthur Wellesley, 1st Duke of Wellington. The son of Richard Colley Wellesley, Marquis Wellesley, he entered Christ Church, Oxford, to study Classics in 1811, graduating with a BA in 1816 and an MA in 1818. He was ordained and in 1816 started to study law at Lincoln's Inn in London. He was appointed vicar of Flitton-with-Silsoe, Beds, in 1827, rector of Dunsfold, Surrey, in 1833, and rector of Woodmancote, Sussex, in 1838, resigning the last post in 1860. At the time of his death he was rector of Herstmonceux, Sussex. From 1842 to 1847 he was Vice-Principal of New Inn Hall, Oxford, and was made Principal in 1847 by his uncle, the Duke of Wellington, who was at that time Chancellor of the university. While at Oxford he became curator of the Bodleian Library, the university galleries and the Taylorian Institution, where he made particular efforts to expand the library. He was a member of the Sussex Archaeological Society from its foundation in 1846 and contributed three papers to *Collections of the Sussex Archaeological Society*. Wellesley was the author of several books, including *Stray Notes on the Text of Shakespeare* (London, 1865), and was editor of *Anthologia Polyglotta* (London, 1849), a collection of verses each of which was in Latin, Greek and English, and in some cases in French, German and Italian as well. During his lifetime he accumulated a large collection of Old Master drawings and engravings. This was sold after his death in June and July 1866 over a period of 14 days. The catalogue lists 2454 items in all, most of them drawings. A great many of the Old Masters were represented, including Michelangelo, Raphael, Leonardo, Dürer, Titian, van Dyck, Rubens and Rembrandt. Of particular note were the numerous drawings and etchings by Claude and a complete set of the etched works of Giulio di Antonio Bonasone.

BIBLIOGRAPHY
DNB
Catalogue of the Memorable Cabinet of Drawings by the Old Masters and Collection of Engravings Formed by the late Rev. Dr. Wellesley (London, 1866)
Obituary, *Gent. Mag.*, i (1866), p. 440

Well-head [puteal]. In its most essential form, a screen-wall or parapet, analogous to a precinct wall, surrounding a taboo place in the Greek and Roman world; also a means of enclosing a well or pit (Lat. *puteus*) in the earth. One type, a *bidental*, signified a place struck by lightning, consecrated and enclosed by the priests, where propitiatory offerings were made to the lightning. The puteal Libonis (untraced) was a *bidental* in the Forum Romanum: it appears on coins as a parapet, circular in plan, adorned with garlands, lyres and the hammer of Vulcan. It is typical of the architectural type commonly employed by both Greeks and Romans as well-heads. Larger well-heads, such as the one found at the Sanctuary of Fortuna Primigenia at Praeneste, sometimes took the form of a circular parapet supporting a monopteros. Alternatively, the well-head or parapet itself was sometimes surrounded by a monopteros or tholos (circular columnar buildings), as in the well (perhaps a *bidental*) of Numerius Trebius in the Triangular Forum at Pompeii.

Prominent religious monuments such as these undoubtedly inspired a multitude of smaller well-heads intended for both public and private use. Excavations in Sicily and Pompeii have unearthed cylindrical well-heads of terracotta, decorated on their exterior surface as altars. Well-heads sculpted in limestone and marble have been found in Delos and Pompeii. In the typical Pompeian house rainwater from the roofs collected in the *impluvium*, whence it was drained off into a cistern beneath the floor. A well-head was sometimes placed above such a cistern, located along the border of the *impluvium*. Pernice attempted to establish an evolutionary sequence for the Pompeian types, beginning with a simple fluted kind that he believed represented the Hellenistic or pre-Roman style in Pompeii. By contrast, magnificent sculpted marble well-heads were sought out by wealthy Romans of the late Republic and early Empire. Athens seems to have been the source of these, as testified by Cicero's request to Atticus (*ad Att.*, I.x) to send him two figured well-heads (*putealia sigillata*) from there. The type is represented in numerous examples taken from the luxurious villas of the Roman campagna and the Bay of Naples and now to be found in the museums of Rome and Naples (where they have traditionally been employed as statue bases). They have circular bases reminiscent of Ionic columns. Leaf patterns and cyma reversa were the mouldings most often applied. (One example [Naples, Mus. Archeol. N., 6675] has a fascia with crossed meander crowned by cyma reversa and bead and reel.) Above the base rises a sculpted frieze. The effect of an elegant sculpted altar is completed by a cyma recta moulding that answers the base moulding, but is somewhat lighter.

The sculpted friezes of such *putealia sigillata* may consist simply of garlands suspended from bucrania (bulls' skulls), emphasizing the sacred origins of the type even if employed in the decorative context of a private portico. Two examples (Naples, Mus. Archeol. N., 6676 and 120 175) show garlands of ivy and olive respectively suspended from filleted bucrania. A third example from Capreae (Naples, Mus. Archeol. N., 120 129) has branches of oak suspended from nails by means of fillets which also hold attributes of Hercules. The most elaborate plant decoration may be found in another well-head from Capreae (Naples, Mus. Archeol. N., 6671) with grapevines reminiscent of the miraculous plant depicted on the Ara Pacis (see ROME, ANCIENT, fig. 23). Certainly the most important *puteal sigillatum* is the Madrid Puteal (see fig.) which was seen by Schneider as a reflection of the central group of the east pediment of the Parthenon (see ATHENS, §II, 1(ii)). Although Schneider's argument has lost much of its force through subsequent studies of the Parthenon, the connection of a NEO-ATTIC decorative sculpture with a famous Athenian model remains plausible. Rather similar to the Madrid Puteal is another in Naples (Mus. Archeol. N., 6670), apparently an assembly of seven male deities

(Dionysus, Hercules, Mercury, Jupiter, Mars, Apollo and Aesculapius), but in reality nothing more than a simple array. The composition, if it can be called that, suggests that of contemporary Pompeian wall paintings that depict the seven planetary divinities, in which the dramatic unity characteristic of Classical prototypes gave way to a new syntax of symbols. The same obstacles to interpretation are present in another Neo-Attic puteal (Rome, Mus. Capitolino, 1019), on which 12 Olympians are depicted in archaizing style. They seem to form two processions that converge, and have been variously interpreted as the return of Hephaistos to Olympos, the birth of Athena or the apotheosis of Herakles. None of these interpretations works: the frieze is simply a Roman expression of the sacred, an array of symbols.

When interpreting the friezes on marble well-heads, whether bucrania and garlands or assemblies of the gods, the original meaning of the type must be kept in mind. Since the well-head is the wall of a sacred enclosure, it is adorned with the powerful symbols of religion. As a part of the decoration of a peristyle garden in a Roman luxury villa, the sacred well-head forms an ensemble with the CANDELABRUM and the *oscillum* (mask hung from a tree), which were also decorative forms taken from religious cult.

BIBLIOGRAPHY
Enc. A. Ant.: 'Puteale'; *Pauly–Wissowa*: 'Puteal'
R. Schneider: *Die Geburt der Athena* (Vienna, 1880) [Madrid Puteal]
J. Rada y Delgado: *Catalogo del Museo arqueológico nacional. . .Madrid*, I/i (Madrid, 1883), no. 2691
J.-A. Hild: 'Puteal', *Dictionnaire des antiquités grecques et romaines*, iv, ed. E. Saglio, E. Pottier and C. Daremberg (Paris, 1903), pp. 778–9
W. Helbig: *Führer durch die öffentlichen Sammlungen klassischer Altertümer in Rom*, ii (Leipzig, 1912–13, rev. Tübingen, 4/1966), no. 1244 [Capitoline puteal]
E. Pernice: *Hellenistische Tische* (Berlin and Leipzig, 1932), pp. 14, 36
E. Nash: *Pictorial Dictionary of Ancient Rome*, ii (London, 1962, rev. 2/1968), pp. 259–61 [puteal Libonis]

EUGENE DWYER

Well-head, known as the Madrid Puteal, with frieze of Hephaistos and Zeus, marble, *c.* 2nd century BC–1st century AD (Madrid, Museo Arqueológico Nacional)

Wellington. Capital city of New Zealand. It is situated at the southern tip of the North Island on Port Nicholson, an inlet of the Cook Strait. The city (population *c.* 345,000) has a fine, almost landlocked harbour surrounded by steep hills (see fig.); it is one of the country's most important ports as well as the centre of government. Maori settlement in the district began around AD 1200. Organized European settlement began in 1840, when the New Zealand Company purchased land from the Maori Ngati Toa and Te Atiawa tribes. A grid layout of the new town was heavily distorted by the city's harbour and hilly setting. Major earthquakes in 1848 and 1855 led to the use of timber for virtually all buildings until the 1880s; consequently fire became a problem in the first decades of settlement. Rangiatea Church (1851) at Otaki, built by local Maori under Chief Te Rauparaha and Octavius Hadfield of the Church Missionary Society, is a rare synthesis of two cultures, with Maori structural and decorative schemes integrated in a building of European form. The pro-cathedral of Old St Paul's, begun in 1866 to the Gothic Revival design of FREDERICK THATCHER, is dramatic in its interior use of native timbers. Two later timber churches are St Peter's (1879) and St John's, both by THOMAS TURNBULL.

Wellington, New Zealand, view of harbour and houses at Mt Victoria

In 1865 Wellington succeeded Auckland as the seat of government, leading to much new public architecture. WILLIAM HENRY CLAYTON designed a new Government House (1868–71; destr.), Parliament Buildings (1873; destr.) and Government Buildings (1876) all in timber. Land was reclaimed from the harbour in order to build the latter, and most of the commercial heart of the city was subsequently built on reclaimed land. Near by, in an area later known as the Residential E zone, narrow and steep streets were built up in the 1870s, with timber cottages one room wide and occasionally as high as five storeys because of the city's unusual topography. Masonry construction was introduced in the Supreme Court Building (1879) by P. F. M. Burrows (1842–1920), and then in Thomas Turnbull's commercial buildings. The best surviving example of these was built for the National Mutual Assurance Company (1884).

In the early 20th century steel-framed buildings appeared: the Public Trust Building (1905–9) by JOHN CAMPBELL is a notable example. Contemporary with this building, and in a strongly functional maritime tradition, is Shed 21 on the waterfront, one of a series of brick cargo-handling buildings that reflect the city's importance as a port. A new Parliament Building, also by John Campbell, was begun in 1912. Designed in an Edwardian Baroque style, its completion was interrupted by World War I; the Legislative Department was later moved to the 'Beehive', a dramatic circular building designed in 1964 by the English architect BASIL SPENCE. During the economic Depression of the 1930s, the Dominion (later National) Museum and the National Art Gallery were completed in a stripped classical style by WILLIAM HENRY GUMMER (with C. R. Ford), providing a home for the national art collection and for the New Zealand Academy of Fine Arts; the museum and gallery were amalgamated in 1992 to form the Museum of New Zealand Te Papa Tongarewa. In 1940 Gummer's second State Insurance Building marked the arrival of European Modernism, but the influence of the Modern Movement is best marked by Massey House (1952), by the Austrian-born architect ERNST PLISCHKE. In the subsequent three decades the city was transformed by curtain-walled tower buildings and the heavy loss of buildings built before 1930, partly as a result of the need for greater protection from earthquakes. Futuna Chapel (1958–61; see NEW ZEALAND, fig. 4), Karori, by the architect JOHN SCOTT (with sculpture by James Allen) and buildings such as those by IAN ATHFIELD and ROGER WALKER have a distinctive character well suited to the harbour capital.

In the fine arts European influences were not marked until the end of the 19th century. The Fine Arts Association, which was established in 1882 and which became the New Zealand Academy of Fine Arts seven years later, sought to represent traditional European standards, but more innovative were those European artists influenced by Impressionism who arrived around the same time. The most important of these was the Scottish painter JAMES NAIRN, who settled in Wellington in 1890 and helped found the Wellington Art Club in 1892. Nairn's bright *plein-air* landscapes include such works as *Wharf at Kaikoura with the SS Wakatu* (1903; Auckland, C.A.G.). After a period of stagnation in the early 20th century,

interest in the fine arts was revived in the 1930s by the establishment of the National Gallery and by the arrival of a new wave of European artists, including CHRISTOPHER PERKINS and Roland Hipkins, who introduced a combination of romanticism and Surrealism that later influenced such artists as RITA ANGUS. In the 1950s and 1960s abstract works were produced by Don Peebles (*b* 1922) and GORDON WALTERS, but notable among the following generation of artists was Brent Wong (*b* 1945), who executed realistic local landscapes.

See also NEW ZEALAND, especially §§II, III, XI and XII.

BIBLIOGRAPHY
L. Ward: *Early Wellington* (Wellington, 1929)
A. Mulgan: *The City of the Strait* (Wellington, 1939)
F. L. Irvine-Smith: *The Streets of my City* (Wellington, 1948)
G. L. Adkin: *The Great Harbour of Tara* (Wellington, 1959)
C. Fearnley: *Vintage Wellington* (Dunedin, 1970)
W. Main: *Wellington through a Victorian Lens* (Wellington, 1972)
G. Anderson: *Fresh about Cook Strait* (Auckland, 1984)
J. Cattell, ed.: *Historic Buildings of Wellington* (Wellington, 1986)
CHRIS COCHRAN

Wellington, 1st Duke of. *See* WELLESLEY, (1).

Wellington, John B(ooker) B(lakemore) (*b* Lansdown, nr Bath, *c*. 1860; *d* Elstree, 1939). English photographer and scientist. He studied architecture but took up photography before completing his studies. John Wellington collaborated with George Eastman of the Kodak Company, Rochester, NY, in the 1880s and became the first manager of the Kodak works in Harrow, Middx (1891–3). He then moved to Elliot and Sons, Barnet, Greater London, and later, with his brother-in-law H. H. Ward, he founded the company of Wellington and Ward, manufacturers of photographic plates, films and papers, of which he was scientific and technical Director. As a photographer he made all his own cameras, printing frames and emulsions, and coated his own plates. Wellington cannot be identified with any particular school of aesthetics, since his work varied greatly from pictorial landscapes to the period between *c*. 1912 and 1929 when he produced sensitive studies of his young family (e.g. *Mother's Jewels*) and pictorial photographs of domestic scenes of family and friends. Some of his later works could have been photographs taken for publicity purposes.

BIBLIOGRAPHY
F. C. Lambert: 'The Pictorial Work of J. B. B. Wellington', *Pract. Photographer*, 14 (1904), pp. 1–5
M. F. Harker: *The Linked Ring: The Secession in Photography, 1892–1910* (1979), p. 163
MARGARET HARKER

Wells. Cathedral city in Somerset, England, named from several springs that attracted habitation from the Neolithic period. Excavated finds indicate a Roman settlement, but the history of the city begins with the establishment of Christianity, traditionally *c*. AD 705. A collegiate church existed in the 8th century, and the episcopal see was founded in 909. In 1088 the see was moved to Bath (*see* BATH (i), §2), to be restored only in 1244 when the sees were combined.

Wells is dominated by the cathedral and Bishop's palace (*see* §1(i) and 2 below). North of the precinct is the Liberty of St Andrew, an extra-parochial township independent of the ancient parishes of SS Thomas and Cuthbert, an area of c. 16 ha used from the 14th century for canons' houses. It includes the Vicars' Close, a street of planned houses built in 1348 with a chapel and a hall linked to the cathedral by the Chain Gate (1459). On Cathedral Green the Dean's house partly dates from the 15th century. The market-place contains the *nova opera*, a terrace of houses built c. 1456 by Bishop Bekynton (d 1465), with his Penniless Porch leading to Cathedral Green.

St Cuthbert's church has a fine Perpendicular tower built c. 1410, and the town has a group of 15th-century almshouses. The rusticated town hall was built in 1779. The museum, in a canonical house of the 16th and 17th centuries, exhibits mainly Iron Age artefacts from Somerset. Wells has a population of c. 9000 and some light industry, but is still centred on its medieval core.

BIBLIOGRAPHY

J. H. Parker: *Architectural Antiquities of Wells* (Oxford and London, 1866)

C. M. Church: *Chapters in the Early History of the Church of Wells* (Taunton, 1894)

D. S. Bailey: 'The Liberty, Wells', *British Archaeological Association Conference Transactions: Medieval Art and Architecture at Wells and Glastonbury: Wells, 1978*, pp. 54–61

For further bibliography *see* §1(i) below.

1. Cathedral. 2. Bishop's palace.

1. CATHEDRAL. The present cathedral, dedicated to St Andrew, was built in two major periods: c. 1185–1240 and c. 1275–1350. It contains fine sculpture, monuments and stained glass.

(i) Architecture. (ii) Sculpture. (iii) Stained glass.

(i) Architecture. Traditionally founded in AD 705 next to a sacred spring, the original cathedral lay south of the present church. An apsidal foundation beneath the cloister may represent the enlargement of a primitive church following the elevation of Wells to cathedral rank in 909. An undated, detached Lady chapel further east created an axial group between the minster and the sacred pool, a string of churches similar to that of St Augustine's Abbey, Canterbury. The Lady chapel was later joined to the apse, and eventually to a new square-ended church, possibly built by Bishop Giso (*reg* 1060–88), who instituted a quasi-monastic canonical foundation perhaps based on the Rule of St Chrodegang (d 766). The early Lady chapel survived much altered until it was replaced in the 15th century.

(a) c. 1185–1240. The present cathedral, built of local Doulting limestone, was begun c. 1185 by Bishop Reginald de Bohun (*reg* 1174–91), and there was a consecration in 1239. The original plan had a three-bay aisled presbytery with a square ambulatory, an aisled transept projecting three bays each side of a crossing tower, an aisled ten-bay nave and a spreading west front with bases for twin towers outside the aisles. A rectangular cloister south of the nave formed part of this scheme. The principal entry to the church was a two-bay, two-storey north porch halfway along the nave. The square plan, the presbytery wrapped within three lean-to roofs recalling Romsey Abbey (c. 1110), Hants, is very English. The aisled transept, after those of Winchester and Ely cathedrals, appears proportionately large, especially as the total length of Wells (c. 91 m) barely exceeded the nave of Anglo-Norman

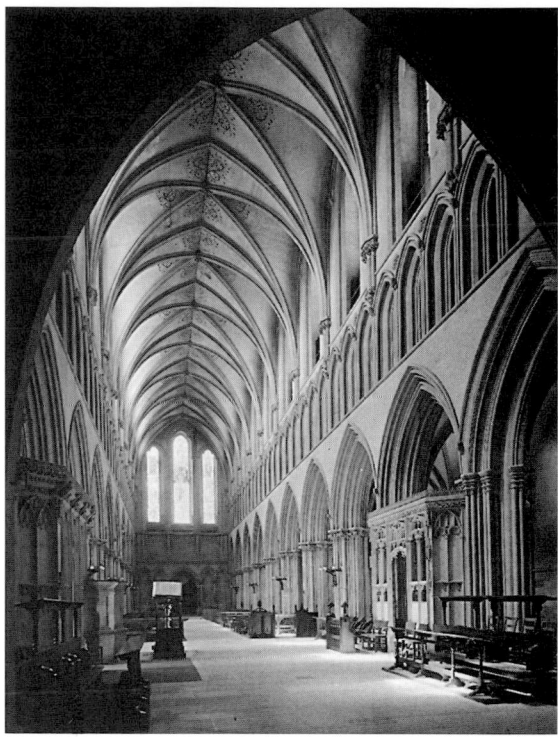

1. Wells Cathedral, nave interior looking west, begun c. 1185

Winchester. The extramural west towers belong to another English tradition found at Rochester Cathedral (c. 1145) and, more locally, Malmesbury Abbey (c. 1150). The 12th-century east end and choir elevations were later remodelled and extended, only the arcades and aisle elevations surviving, but the transept and nave are remarkably intact.

The whole church was rib-vaulted. The three-storey elevation is in the Anglo-Norman thick-wall tradition (*see* THICK-WALL STRUCTURE), and Wells thus follows the tradition of pointed Late Romanesque buildings (e.g. the west bays of Worcester Cathedral, c. 1170). The vault was sprung low enough to receive buttressing below the level of the aisle roof, and the clerestory, already set back within a deep mural passage, is minimized as an interior feature. The interior is dominated by the elevation wall, which is rooted to the floor by massive, bundled piers.

Visually, however, nave and transept are all pointed, monochrome and free of any lingering Romanesque treatment. Subtle changes occurred between choir, transept and nave. The choir elevation, traced against the central tower, had a broad bay design with piers of tightly clustered colonnettes, thick, densely moulded pointed arches with plain spandrels, a 'triforium' with twin pointed arches with continuous mouldings and a single-light, pointed clerestory window. The clerestory design exploits the double thickness of the wall, with a tall, arched interior opening framing a window in the outer skin, the sill elevated to avoid the aisle roof. This gives a tall clerestory almost as high as the main arcade, yet the glazed area is small, deeply recessed and hardly visible from below. The corbelled vault-support shafts spring immediately above the main arcade spandrels, the vault springing being just above the floor level of the clerestory passage.

The transept bays are narrower and the arcades more acutely pointed. The middle storey openings are similarly constricted and have fewer mouldings, while the clerestory unit fits more snugly within the vault. The clerestory windows are actually smaller. The aisleless terminal walls have a mid-zone with five linked arches, a motif continued in the nave.

The nave, long, low and horizontal, best illustrates the early work (see fig. 1). Tight bundles of colonnettes with individual foliate capitals support deeply incised multiple arcade mouldings. The 'triforium' openings, now trebled and continuously linked, further stress the horizontal emphasis. The vault-support shafts are pushed almost to the clerestory floor level. The height of the quadripartite vault is slightly over 20 m; the ribs have twin roll mouldings, and the wall arches are deeply stilted round the clerestory.

Between the fifth and sixth bays there occurred a building break of uncertain date, perhaps associated with the Interdict of 1208–13; but it may be comparable to a similar break at Westminster Abbey (c. 1272), which denotes the completion of the monks' choir. The Wells canonical choir may have occupied the three eastern bays of the nave, which would also account for the placing of the porch. The principal changes in the new work were vertical masonry tooling, the use of larger blocks and more elaborate foliate capitals. The internal sculpture of Wells (see §(ii) below) represents perhaps the best Early English collection, predominantly foliate and becoming less stiff as the work proceeds.

The exterior of the late 12th-century building was very simple, with strong, unbroken horizontals of aisle, lean-to roof, clerestory and high roof. The unadorned windows, and the virtual absorption of the aisle buttressing within the depth of the wall, gave a more Romanesque than Gothic profile. The great west façade (see §(ii) below), probably started by Adam Lock (d 1229) and continued by Thomas Norreys (fl 1229–49), is many-layered and dominated by niches, which flank the minuscule doors, frame the triple lancets of the west wall and wrap around every angle and buttress. The colonnettes, emphasized by blue lias shafts (rest.), resemble some permanent scaffolding. The effect, however, remains horizontal, emphasized by the strong basement plinth, unbroken string courses and the abrupt, flat top of the original sculpture screen. The Perpendicular west towers were added c. 1370 (south, by William Wynford) and c. 1410.

(b) c. *1275–1547*. By the mid-13th century the cathedral, now organized with a Dean and Chapter, had an establishment of 53, and the adoption of the Use of Sarum apparently prompted the building of a chapter house. A document of 1307 mentions the great cost involved, and another surviving manuscript was signed within the building in 1319. Sculptural links with Exeter Cathedral would confirm a terminus of c. 1307. The typically English, polygonal chapter house stands upon an undercroft perhaps begun much earlier and leads from the north choir aisle by a twisting stair that also serves the Chain Gate. The exterior has large, four-light traceried windows filled with various cusped and foiled shapes, the slight ogees of which suggest a date after 1291. The interior (*see* CHAPTER HOUSE, fig. 3), dominated by the central clustered vault support, demonstrates the two principal interests of the Decorated style at Wells: spatial manipulation and vaulting effects. The repeated rib-vault cones give an intensely linear effect, enhanced by the triangular gabled wall arcades with miniature buttresses, clustered vault shafts and repeating jamb decoration.

From c. 1320 the 12th-century presbytery was remodelled and extended, beginning at the east with the new Lady chapel and retrochoir (see fig. 2). The plan provided both extra processional space and a possible shrine for the prospective (uncanonized) saint, Bishop William of March (*reg* 1293–1302; *see* §(ii) below). The new work on the Lady chapel was referred to in 1325, and in 1326 the chapel was 'newly built'. The Lady chapel is an irregular octagon, the three western sides penetrating the retrochoir, which is two bays deep, with projecting north and south chapels. The north–south row of piers from the re-entrant angles of the chapels is split into an elongated hexagon. The vault patterns form a central square surrounded by triangles and trapezoids. The three canted western walls of the Lady chapel rest on the eastern piers of the cross-axial hexagon, which are bigger than the western pair. The erratic plan and absence of parallel walls were original in concept and not imitated elsewhere. The diagonal sight-lines present near-frontal views of the large windows, with identical patterns of reticulated tracery, and the eastward

2. Wells Cathedral, retrochoir interior looking north-east into Lady chapel, c. 1320

distortion makes the space seem larger, resembling a chapter house with no central support, but instead an eight-point, domed stellar vault of unusual shape and richness. The interplay of spatial volumes is a hallmark of early 14th-century English architecture, but the east end of Wells is also an exercise in vaulting, the low cones of the retrochoir swirling unpredictably with seemingly endless ribs creating a rich linear effect. So numerous are the ribs that some have literally nowhere to go and terminate in carved bosses.

In contrast to the Early English work, the east end is richly polychrome, with dark polished shafts, huge areas of stained glass and, formerly, painted sculpture and bosses. The capitals are seaweed, and the tracery throughout is based upon repeated units—lozenges in the retrochoir, fishscale reticulations in the Lady chapel, both proto-Perpendicular and reflecting current London designs. The many links with contemporary work at Exeter Cathedral suggest that the architect was THOMAS OF WITNEY.

The rectangular choir (see fig. 3) was rebuilt and extended (perhaps by WILLIAM JOY) after c. 1330, the new eastern bays displaying the full scheme, amended somewhat for the earlier western section. There are three storeys with a large clerestory containing intersecting tracery or lozenges. The mullions extend down to the arcade level, although the line is broken by the revealed depth of the elevational wall. Rectilinear panels frame gabled niches gouged from the wall. While the concept is Perpendicular, the execution is more typical of the Decorated style, with undulating walls and foliate sculpture. In an attempt to unite the wall planes into a unified façade like that of the choir of Gloucester Abbey (now Cathedral), two-tier

angled gables cover the clerestory jambs; they may have been imitated at Prague Cathedral (see PRAGUE, §IV, 2(i)). The east window shows the clearest tendency towards the Perpendicular style, with dominant verticals and stacked lozenges. The pointed barrel vault of the choir is embellished by a mesh rib vault, with cusped panels and sculpted bosses.

The central tower had been raised by a single, large storey between 1315 and 1322. The inverted strainer arches inserted c. 1350 to support the crossing constitute the most dramatic late medieval addition to the interior. Continuous mouldings and giant circles create an impact that is both theatrical and technically sound. The crossing fan vault dates from 1475–90. Other additions include the heavily buttressed, flat-topped west towers (see §(a) above), the rebuilt cloister (c. 1420–1508), two stone-cage chantry chapels in the nave (1424–1489) and an early Renaissance pulpit of 1547.

BIBLIOGRAPHY
J. Bilson: 'Notes on the History of Wells Cathedral', Archaeol. J., lxxxv (1928), pp. 23–68
J. A. Robinson: 'Documentary Evidence Relating to the Building of the Cathedral Church of Wells', Archaeol. J., lxxxv (1928), pp. 1–22
L. S. Colchester and J. Harvey: 'Wells Cathedral', Archaeol. J., cxxxi (1974), pp. 200–14
British Archaeological Association Conference Transactions: Medieval Art and Architecture at Wells and Glastonbury: Wells, 1978 [articles by P. Crossley, P. Draper and A. Klukas]
J. Bony: The English Decorated Style (Oxford, 1979)
R. Morris: Cathedrals and Abbeys of England and Wales (London, 1979)
W. Rodwell: Wells Cathedral: Excavations and Discoveries (Wells, 1979, rev. 1980)
L. S. Colchester, ed.: Wells Cathedral: A History (Shepton Mallet, 1982)
N. Pevsner and P. Metcalf: Southern England (1985), ii of The Cathedrals of England (Harmondsworth, 1985)
L. S. Colchester: Wells Cathedral (London, 1987)

FRANCIS WOODMAN

(ii) Sculpture. The cathedral incorporates the largest body of early Gothic sculpture in England, all of it carved between the episcopates of Reginald de Bohun (1174–91) and William Bytton I (1247–67). It falls into three main groups: the figurative and foliage carving adorning the capitals and corbels of transepts and nave, the tympana of the nave triforium and the north porch; the series of retrospect effigies of the pre-Conquest bishops in the choir aisles; and the statuary on the west front.

The architectural decoration of the cathedral (see fig. 1 above), carried out between c. 1185 and 1229, is the culmination of the approach to ornament found in a group of buildings of that time, stretching from St David's Cathedral to Glastonbury Abbey and anticipated at Malmesbury Abbey. Characteristics include the continuation of mouldings round the lancet window without the interruption of capitals, the omission of neckings dividing shaft and capital, and the application of bosses to the wall surface. This last feature can be traced at Cluny Abbey, where surviving fragments and others recorded by Jean-Claude Barat (Nevers, Bib. Mun., MS. 110 [2N. 382]) in the early 1850s bear striking resemblances to the earliest nave tympana of the triforium at Wells.

The proliferation of narrative detail in the south transept and of grotesque incidents in the nave spandrels draw upon other media. Similarities between the Wells transept foliage, from which the nave foliage developed, and surviving metalwork such as the Trivulzio candlestick in

3. Wells Cathedral, choir interior looking east, 1330s

4. Wells Cathedral, west front (before restoration), begun *c.* 1230

Milan Cathedral suggest the study of altar furnishings. The sophisticated pierced foliage spandrels of the earlier Lady chapel of the cloister and the north porch suggest a metalwork technique. The dragon corbel in the north transept east aisle can be compared with the dragon crozier in the cathedral library, almost certainly from the tomb of Bishop Jocelyn (*reg* 1206–42), probably brought by him from Limoges in 1213 after the Interdict.

The remains of the Anglo-Saxon bishops were translated from the earlier cathedral site to the choir aisles during the rebuilding. The decision to give them full-size recumbent effigies may have been part of the campaign to establish the episcopal primacy of Wells over Bath. Bishop Jocelyn probably commissioned the effigies of *Sigar*, *Eilwin*, *Burwold*, *Levericus* and one unidentified, soon after his accession. Their stiff poses and chunky forms may be deliberately archaic, but can be compared to the figures of *c.* 1200 from the chapter house of St Mary's Abbey, York (York, Yorks Mus.). The tombs of *Giso* and *Dudoc*, the last bishops before the Norman Conquest, flanked the high altar of the earlier cathedral, and their effigies occupy similar positions again, but they do not match the sequence

and were probably carved about 15 years later than the rest.

Jocelyn also resumed work on the west front, almost certainly on the appointment in 1229 of Thomas Norreys to succeed Adam Lock as Master Mason. The first design had probably included a succession of tall, blind lancets, such as dominated the north and south transept elevations before alteration, but above the stringcourse a new design (see fig. 4) is apparent, showing the influence of Lincoln Cathedral, whose architect, Geoffrey de Noiers, may have been related to Thomas Norreys. At Wells aedicules, composed of marble shafts with crockets behind them (as in the Lincoln east transept), and gablets house a vast array of sculptured figures. The south tower return niches may never have been filled, but the main façade and the northern return accommodated 176 statues, life-size on the 2 lower tiers, larger above; 127 survive. There were 49 quatrefoils of biblical narrative (35 of them still filled). Of 30 demi-angels in quatrefoils, 21 survive. The frieze of 85 panels representing the *Resurrection* is almost complete. Moreover only the lowest range and the central vertical tier of sculptures suffered damage as a result of iconoclasm.

The *Virgin and Child* in the tympanum of the west door and the *Coronation of the Virgin* above have lost their heads. The *Christ* in the gable was originally carved on two stones, of which the upper is lost. Where sheltered, the figures are in remarkable condition with some surviving paint. Cleaning and conservation in the 1970s revealed their superb quality.

The overall theme of the west front is the Church Triumphant. The lowest tier of standing figures south of the central door are *Prophets* and *Patriarchs* with Old Testament scenes from the *Creation* to the *Blessing of Jacob* in the quatrefoils above them; the corresponding spaces on the north were occupied by contemporaries of Christ, of which the *Four Marys*, *Joseph of Arimathea* and *Nicodemus* are identified, above them the New Testament quatrefoils from the *Annunciation* to the *Ascension*. The two upper tiers of standing figures represented, to the south, *Confessors*, including perhaps St Edward the Confessor, and to the north, *Martyrs*, including many English saints. The central bay shows the meeting of *Solomon and the Queen of Sheba*, with *Virgins*, one probably St Etheldreda of Ely, above them. The figures of the resurrected dead are distinguished only by headgear and sexual attributes. The gable was to be crowned by the Nine Orders of the angels with four trumpeters, the Twelve Apostles, and, reigning over all, the blessing Christ. The gable figures, with the exception of the *Christ*, were apparently empty until the 15th century. The topmost niches were filled by David Wynne in 1985, the lower part of his *Christ* copying the surviving knees of the original.

The whole scheme represented the Heavenly Jerusalem as described in Books 20 and 22 of St Augustine's *City of God*, a text certainly consulted both here and at Salisbury Cathedral. The programme was particularly appropriate to the Palm Sunday procession according to the Sarum Rite, when part of the ceremony included singing anthems in front of the cathedral, with the choirboys singing through the apertures concealed behind the demi-angels in the west front. Thus the sculptures themselves seemed to take part in a remarkable liturgy that fused Palm Sunday, commemorating Christ's entry into earthly Jerusalem, with his final triumphant entry into the heavenly Jerusalem.

The *Virgin and Child* in the tympanum, with its censing angels and voussoir attendants, is typical of Transitional sculpture c. 1215, and probably the only part carved before the design was altered. Stylistically, the other sculptures compare with the figures on the west front of Amiens Cathedral of the 1220s (*see* AMIENS, §1(ii)). The only comparative material in England besides the female figure at Lanercost Priory (Cumbria) and the *Christ* in the refectory of Worcester Cathedral is the range of early 13th-century effigial sculpture, including *William Longespée, Earl of Salisbury* (d 1226), in Salisbury Cathedral. Other sculpture by the Wells workshop includes a *Virgin and Child* at St Bartholomew's Hospital in Bristol.

As the workshop showed no acquaintance with developments at Reims Cathedral in the 1230s and 1240s, or of the innovations at the Sainte-Chapelle in Paris (1240s), the Wells campaign probably dates between 1230 and 1250. Several hands can still be discerned, none obviously from France. A division of labour between drapery specialists and head carvers can be deduced as distinctive head types do not match distinctive drapery forms.

In the south transept the conjunction of the relic chamber with the grand tomb of *Bishop William of March*, with two great relief heads and an array of lesser sculptures, suggests a focus for canonization. There are punning hares on the tomb of *Bishop Harewell* (d 1386), and an alabaster effigy of *Bishop Ralph of Shrewsbury* (d 1363). A panelled tomb of the mid-15th century in the chapel of St Calixtus has a fine alabaster *Annunciation*. Misericords from the choir-stalls of c. 1325–40 include the *Flight of Alexander*.

BIBLIOGRAPHY

M. Roberts: 'Noah's Ark', *Friends Wells Cathedral Rep.* (1973), pp. 10–14

L. S. Colchester: 'The West Front Seen through Visitors' Eyes', *Friends Wells Cathedral Rep.* (1977), pp. 22–5

P. Tudor-Craig: '13th-century Corbels from the Former Cloister Walk Reused c. 1425 in Bubwith's Library', *Friends Wells Cathedral Rep.* (1980), pp. 14–15

L. S. Colchester: 'Corbels of the Sugar Chantry', *Friends Wells Cathedral Rep.* (1982), pp. 16–19

T. Hoving: 'A Present from Bishop Reginald', *Friends Wells Cathedral Rep.* (1983), pp. 16–17

L. S. Colchester: 'Dragons, Serpents and St Michael', *Friends Wells Cathedral Rep.* (1984), pp. 18–23

P. Blum: 'Liturgical Influences on the Design of the West Front at Wells and Salisbury', *Gesta*, xxv/1 (1986), pp. 145–50

Age of Chivalry: Art in Plantagenet England, 1200–1400 (exh. cat., ed. J. Alexander and P. Binski; London, RA, 1987), pp. 99–101, nos 102, 243–4, 257, 470, 526–7, 530

N. Ramsey: 'Imagine my Surprise (Tomb in St Calixtus' Chapel)', *Friends Wells Cathedral Rep.* (1988), pp. 12–14

For further bibliography *see* §(i) above.

PAMELA TUDOR-CRAIG

(iii) Stained glass. None of the original glazing of the Early English parts of the building survives; one window of the chapter house staircase contains naturalistic foliage, perhaps dated c. 1286. Much more remains in the later parts of the building, although glazing sequences have been disturbed. The suggested relationship of the glass at Wells with glass in the chapel of Merton College, Oxford, and the Lady chapel of the cathedral, or with the glass of the Minster and St Denys in York, remains unproven.

The glazing of the chapter house, recorded in the 17th century as being of biblical stories, is now fragmentary; foliage survives in the tracery lights, and there are roundels of the *Resurrection*. Inscriptions scattered in the five windows of the Lady chapel commemorate canons and indicate a date in the 1320s. Each window was originally filled with two tiers of canopied niches containing figures or scenes. In the north window are kings from an *Adoration of the Magi*, and in the tracery lights are bold large heads of patriarchs and saints (see fig. 5), and symbols of the Evangelists. The east window was reconstructed in 1845 by William Willement. The Lady chapel workshop seems to have provided glass of comparable high quality for the retrochoir and eastern bays of the choir aisles, but there they used silver stain. The canopy-work is slightly more complex, and there are more busts of saints in the tracery lights. Other subjects in the tracery lights are representations of the Virgin and Child with angels, the *Crucifixion*, SS Michael and John the Baptist.

The scheme for the upper windows of the choir must be slightly later, perhaps 1340–45. In the clerestory windows there are standing saints under canopies that develop

5. Wells Cathedral, Lady chapel, *St Dunstan* stained glass, *c.* 1325

into three-dimensional pinnacle-work. In the tracery lights are figures from the Resurrection of the Dead that link up with more in the upper parts of the great east window. This may be by a different workshop, and from its colour scheme of red, green and yellow (and a little blue), it has been named 'the Golden Window'. The main lights are filled with a *Tree of Jesse* in which the vine wreathes its way through the architecture but in front of the standing figures. The effect is almost as sculptural as the west front. There is some important early Renaissance glass dispersed about the building, one panel dated 1507, others of *c.* 1520, from the workshop of Arnoult de Nimègue, and parts of a cycle from St Jean Rouen (acquired 1813; other scenes in Glasgow, Burrell Col.). The west window includes curious glass of 1660–70.

BIBLIOGRAPHY
L. S. Colchester: *Stained Glass in Wells* (Wells, 1952)

For further bibliography *see* §(i) above.

M. Q. SMITH

2. BISHOP'S PALACE. The Bishop's palace offers a rare example of a medieval episcopal residence, subsequently moated, fortified and landscaped. The earliest phase, partly 'ruined' to suit the 18th-century taste for the Picturesque, dates from the 13th century. The straggly layout runs north–south, west, then south–west. The north–south core is a two-storey, early 13th-century block containing undercrofts, a hall, solar and garderobe tower. The plate-tracery windows form part of Benjamin Ferrey's restorations (1846), which gave the building its look of a Victorian school-house. The block-house southern chapel (see fig. 6), by Bishop Robert Burnell, has hard-edged geometric tracery, although some ogees, Purbeck marble shafts, a tierceron vault and plentiful depressed arches suggest stylistic links with the chapter house entry. The ruined Great Hall running south-west has tracery connections with the chapter house itself, although the exact sequence of Burnell's palace remains obscure. The huge transomed windows of the (then) unfortified palace are notable, and the hall retains evidence of an early arrangement of kitchens and screens passage. The walls and gate-house surrounding the palace complex followed a licence to crenellate of 1341. Later additions include two 16th-century oriels over the moat. There is a fine 15th-century barn.

BIBLIOGRAPHY
J. Cherry and P. Draper: 'Excavations in the Bishop's Palace, Wells', *British Archaeological Association Conference Transactions: Medieval Art and Architecture at Wells and Glastonbury: Wells, 1978*, pp. 52–3

For further bibliography *see* §1(i) above.

FRANCIS WOODMAN

Wells [née Boyce], **Joanna Mary** (*b* 1831; *d* London, 15 July 1861). English painter. She admired and was influenced by the Venetian masters and by John Everett Millais, and from an early age she drew with concentration and dedication. She was encouraged by her elder brother, the landscape painter GEORGE PRICE BOYCE, who was part of the Pre-Raphaelite circle. She studied with J. M. Leigh from 1852, and in 1855 she enrolled at Thomas Couture's studio in Paris. Her painting *Elgiva* (priv. col.) was accepted at the Royal Academy, London, in 1855 and received attention, including a mention in John Ruskin's *Academy Notes*. She continued to exhibit works such as *Homestead on the Surrey Hills* at the Royal Academy and the Society of British Artists between 1853 and 1857. She also wrote occasionally for *Saturday Review*. In Rome, in 1857, she married her long-standing suitor, the miniature painter Henry Tanworth Wells (1828–1903). She died in childbirth a few years later.

BIBLIOGRAPHY
D. G. Bachmann and S. Piland: *Women Artists: An Historical, Contemporary and Feminist Biography* (Metuchen, NJ, 1978)
P. Gerrish Nunn: *Victorian Women Artists* (London, 1987), pp. 146–58

6. Wells, Bishop's palace, the chapel from the west, with Bishop Burnell's Great Hall, from *c.* 1280

Wells, William (*b* 1768; *d* Penshurst, Kent, 11 Aug 1847). English patron and collector. He came from a rich family of shipbuilders. Wells preferred the work of early Victorian artists such as Edwin Landseer and Frederick Lee, whose low-toned canvases harmoniously blended with his 17th-century Dutch and Flemish pictures, and chose subjects that reflected his interests in hunting, shooting and the countryside. Landseer painted many such sporting pictures for Wells, including *The Sanctuary* (by 1842; Brit. Royal Col.), and from the early 1830s was a frequent visitor at Redleaf, Wells's estate in Kent. Wells entertained many other artists there, who obliged him by contributing sketches to his two Redleaf albums (priv. col.).

Wells was generous towards artists who conformed to his standards and ruthlessly critical of those who did not. While visiting John Constable's studio, he told the artist that his vivid landscapes were too extreme and accused him of having lost his way. Constable attributed Wells's 'wicked conduct' to 'the vanity of connoisseurship'. Like other patrons of his class, Wells believed it was his role to steer artists along the correct path.

Wells was a trustee of the National Gallery, London, to which he bequeathed Guido Reni's *Coronation of the Virgin*. He left the remainder of his collection to his nephew, William Wells, who gradually disposed of it through Christie's (e.g. 27 April 1860).

BIBLIOGRAPHY

J. D. Passavant: *Tour of a German Artist in England* (London, 1836), i, p. 227; ii, pp. 71–2

G. Waagen: *Works of Art and Artists in England*, ii (London, 1838), p. 404

John Constable's Correspondence, ed. R. B. Beckett (Ipswich, 1962–8), vii, pp. 97–8

E. Bond: 'Mr. Wells and Joseph Wells', *Country Life*, clx (23 Dec 1976), pp. 1923–4

DIANNE SACHKO MACLEOD

Welsch, Maximilian von (*b* Kronach, 1671; *d* Mainz, 1745). German architect and engineer. He was educated in the Jesuit Academia Ottoniana in Bamberg, and in 1692 began a military career that took him, as an officer in the corps of engineers, on campaigns through much of Europe. Lothar Franz von Schönborn, Prince Bishop and Elector of Mainz, engaged him in 1704, appointing him Director of Military Construction *c.* 1712 and entrusting him with the design, rebuilding and construction of fortifications in Mainz and forts at Philippsburg, Drusenheim, Forchheim, Kronach, Rosenberg, Kehl and Erfurt. Welsch's advice was also sought for other fortifications, such as those at Würzburg and Königshofen. In these many projects he offered unusual but effective solutions.

The clever use of site conditions that Welsch showed in his fortifications probably paved the way for his architectural career, and the six months he spent during 1714 working with Johann Lukas von Hildebrandt in Vienna must have heightened his sense of architectural design. His first large-scale work, the Schloss (designed 1707; built 1708–21) in Biebrich, was rigid and reserved, but a few years later, for Schloss Favorite (designed after 1708; begun *c.* 1716; destr. 1793) near Mainz, Welsch produced an animated composition of gardens, orangery and six pavilions, loosely inspired by Louis XIV's château of Marly. From 1714 onwards he created the extensive gardens (destr. early 19th century) and massive stables that provided the grandiose setting for Lothar Franz's huge palace at Pommersfelden. About 1720 he established the layout of the C-shaped, multi-court plan of the Residenz in Würzburg (*see* WÜRZBURG, §2), begun by Lothar Franz's nephew, Prince Bishop Johann Philipp Franz von Schönborn. For the orangery (1722–4) at Fulda he produced a sparse, elegant building in which the walls were reduced to supporting elements and decoration minimized. Welsch later managed to transpose this architectural language to the arsenal (1738–41) in Mainz, creating a restrained, decorous structure.

Throughout his career Welsch also designed religious buildings, but his work in this area remained conventional. This is true not only of such early projects as the unexecuted design (1718–19) for the new façade for the Romanesque cathedral in Würzburg or the centralized Schönborn Chapel (1720–21; unexecuted; *see* NEUMANN, BALTHASAR) attached to the cathedral transept, but also of his later designs, including the monastery church (begun 1741) at Amorbach and the pilgrimage church (1744; unexecuted) of Vierzehnheiligen. These designs were more indebted to the 16th-century church of Il Gesù in Rome than to the challenging ecclesiastic work of Welsch's contemporaries and competitors, in this case above all Balthasar Neumann. He also designed numerous altars, ranging from the monumental main altar (1710) in the pilgrimage church of Schönenberg, near Ellwangen, to the airy elegance of the main altar (1739) in St Quintin, Mainz. Welsch's drawings, finely rendered and finished with colour washes, are detailed and precise, clear and striking. His extensive collection of specialized drawing instruments survives (Mainz, Landesmus.) and includes rare examples of what once were more common tools of the profession among architects and engineers.

BIBLIOGRAPHY

J. Meintzschel: *Studien zu Maximilian von Welsch*, Quellen & Darstell. Fränk. Kstgesch., viii/2 (Würzburg, 1963)

W. Einsingbach: 'Zum Leben des Mainzer Barockarchitekten Maximilian von Welsch zwischen 1693 und 1704 und der Bericht über seine Reise in die Niederlande, nach Frankreich und England in den Jahren 1699–1700', *Mainz. Z.*, lxvii/lxviii (1972/3), pp. 214–29

F. Arens: *Maximilian von Welsch* (Munich, 1986)

CHRISTIAN F. OTTO

Welser. German family of merchants and patrons. From the early 13th century the Welsers were members of the patrician class of Augsburg. There are records of their merchant company from 1420, and with the foundation of another company by the brothers Bartholomäus Welser (*d* 1484), Jakob Welser (*d* 1483), Lukas Welser (*d* 1494) and Ulrich Welser (*d* 1497/8) the merchant activities of the family became especially prominent. The company was at its most prosperous under the management of Bartholomäus Welser V (1484–1561). Markus Welser (1558–1614) was one of the most significant figures in the intellectual history of late humanism in Augsburg and the leading spirit behind many cultural initiatives in his native town. He had an influence on such works of art as the showpiece *Augustus*, *Mercury* and *Hercules* fountains in the Maximilianstrasse and the Goldener Saal in the Rathaus (1615–20); he also had some say in the iconographic programme of the latter, thus sustaining and employing many artists and craftsmen from Augsburg and elsewhere. Ill-advised business and political decisions by Matthäus Welser (1584–c. 1614) overstretched the company's financial resources, eventually leading to its bankruptcy in 1614.

BIBLIOGRAPHY

W. Baer, ed.: *Augsburger Stadtlexikon: Geschichte, Gesellschaft, Kultur, Recht, Wirtschaft* (Augsburg, 1985), pp. 407–8

B. Roeck: *Elias Holl: Architekt einer europäischen Stadt* (Regensburg, 1985), pp. 174–5

Elias Holl und das Augsburger Rathaus (exh. cat., ed. W. Baer; Augsburg, Rathaus, 1985)

K. Sieh-Burens: *Oligarchie, Konfession und Politik im 16. Jahrhundert: Zur sozialen Verflechtung der Augsburger Bürgermeister und Stadtpfleger, 1518–1618*, Schriften der Philosophischen Fakultäten der Universität Augsburg: Historisch-sozialwissenschaftliche Reihe, xxix (Munich, 1986), pp. 75–90

WOLFRAM BAER

Weltausstellung. *See* INTERNATIONAL EXHIBITION.

Welti, Albert (*b* Zurich, 18 Feb 1862; *d* Berne, 7 June 1912). Swiss painter and etcher. He studied at the Akademie der Bildenden Künste in Munich from 1881 to 1885. He returned to Zurich, where he studied under Arnold Böcklin, with whose intellectual approach to painting he identified. Although he broke off this apprenticeship in 1890, his work thereafter continued to reflect Böcklin's influence, in both its choice of subject-matter and strong sense of colour, as in *Nessus and Deianeira* (1895; Zurich, Ksthaus). In 1895 Welti moved back to Munich, where he stayed until 1908.

Instead of exploring subject-matter taken from Classical mythology, Welti began to take a strong interest in traditional German subjects, for example *Walpurgis Night* (1897; Zurich, Ksthaus). Many of his paintings owed a great deal to early German art, and he was also inspired by German Romantic painters, as in *German Landscape* (1901; Basle, Kstmus.), which reveals the influence of Joseph Anton Koch. The great wealth of narrative detail in Welti's pictures helped him achieve considerable popularity at an early date, and his works were acquired directly by Swiss museums (e.g. *Removal of the Penates* (1905; Winterthur, Kstmus.)).

Welti nevertheless became increasingly isolated in the art world during the 1900s: his work was out of step with that of more modernist painters then experiencing considerable success throughout the German-speaking regions of Europe. Towards the end of his life, in order to reassert his reputation as a painter, he undertook a commission to decorate the Ständeratssaal in the Bundeshaus in Berne, a project which was beyond him both artistically and technically. He had already contributed to its decoration in 1904, when he produced a glass painting, the *Textile Industry*. Welti moved to Berne to work on the Bundeshaus mural, which depicted a *Landsgemeinde*, one of the earliest forms of constitutional democracy still surviving in contemporary Switzerland. Here, and in other parts of central Switzerland, he subsequently made countless studies and, collaborating with the painter Wilhelm Balmer (1865–1922), incorporated these into the mural, which is still *in situ*. Welti's sudden death left Balmer to complete the project.   After a major memorial exhibition held by the Kunsthaus in Zurich in 1912, Welti's work fell into relative neglect, after a change in contemporary artistic taste. Welti achieved lasting recognition, however, through his prints, which he produced from 1885. The medium he chose almost exclusively was etching; his work reveals a delight in narrative detail comparable to that in his paintings, but his prints often deal with subjects with symbolic meaning, such as *Journey into the 20th Century* (1899) and the *Haven of Marital Bliss* (1906) (see Gloor, pls 29, 30).

WRITINGS

A. Frey, ed.: *Briefe*, 2 vols (Zurich, 1916–20)

BIBLIOGRAPHY

Albert Welti, 1862–1912 (exh. cat. by A. Frey, Zurich, Ksthaus, 1912)

W. Wartmann: *Albert Welti, 1862–1912: Vollständiges Verzeichnis des graphischen Werkes* (Zurich, 1913)

B. Curiger: *Albert Welti im Kunsthaus Zürich* (Zurich, 1984)

L. Gloor: *Albert Welti, 1862–1912* (Stäfa, 1987)

LUKAS GLOOR

Welzenbacher, Lois (*b* Munich, 20 Jan 1889; *d* Absam, Tyrol, 13 Aug 1955). German architect and teacher. He trained as a bricklayer and after graduating from the Technische Hochschule, Vienna, he gained practical experience in various architectural studios in Munich. He also studied architecture (1912–14) at the Technische Hochschule, Munich, under Friedrich von Thiersch and Theodor Fischer. After World War I he set up his own architectural practice in Innsbruck. Together with Erich Mendelsohn, Hans Scharoun, Hugo Häring and Alvar Aalto, Welzenbacher was one of the leading exponents of organic architecture in Europe. His career began with the Settari House (1922–3) at Bad Dreikirchen, South Tyrol, a romantic country house whose design responds to the context of the Alpine landscape with a rather dramatic baroque form. He then developed a more dynamic, free-form approach that was influenced by Mendelsohn, also a student of Fischer, and he built the Buchroithner House, Zell am See, and the Rosenbauer House (1929–30) at Pöstlinberg, Linz, with slightly rounded volumes accented by semicircular balconies. This approach culminated in the Heyerovsky House (1932) at Zell am See, whose helical, organic form echoes the topography of the site; the building is an architectural gesture inspired by the lake and mountain scenery towards which it is orientated, and it creates a remarkable synthesis between modern architecture and landscape. Welzenbacher moved to Munich between 1931 and 1943. After 1933, when Hitler came to power, he returned to earlier ideas by combining his sculptural approach with the folk tradition of the South Tyrol; this is best demonstrated in the Schmucker country house (1938–9) at Ruhpolding, Oberbayern. In the late 1930s and early 1940s he also completed the Siebel factory in Halle an der Saale, a large-scale work of modern architecture. In 1947 he became a professor at the Akademie der Bildenden Künste, Vienna.

BIBLIOGRAPHY

Q. Harbers: *Lois Welzenbacher: Arbeiten der Jahre 1919–1931* (Munich, 1931)

F. Achleitner and O. Uhl: *Lois Welzenbacher, 1889–1955* (Salzburg, 1968)

V. Šlapeta: 'Organic Architecture in Central Europe and Alvar Aalto', *Abacus*, ii (1980), pp. 114–39

R. Gieselman and S. Hauser, eds: 'Lois Welzenbacher, 1889–1955: Bauten und Projekte', *Prologomena*, xiii/1 (1984) [special issue]

VLADIMÍR ŠLAPETA

Wen. Chinese family of artists. The Wen family formed the core of the Wu school artists active in Suzhou, Jiangsu Province, during the 16th century. They were descended from a prominent family, which since the Song period (960–1279) had produced distinguished scholars and officials. The most talented among them was (1) Wen Zhengming, who personally tutored his two sons, Wen Peng (1498–1573) and (2) Wen Jia, and his nephew (3) Wen Boren. Wen Peng (1489–1573) was a calligrapher and advisor to the collector Xiang Yuanbian. He also collaborated with his younger brother Jia on painting, poetry and calligraphy projects.

(1) Wen Zhengming [Wen Cheng-ming; *ming* Bi; *hao* Hengshan] (*b* Suzhou, Jiangsu Province, 1470; *d* Suzhou, 1559). Painter and calligrapher. He was considered one of the Four Masters of the Ming period (1368–1644), along with Shen Zhou, Tang Yin and Qiu Ying. The most famous member of the second generation of WU SCHOOL artists, he profoundly influenced later painters. He was remarkable for his individuality as well as for the variety and range of his creativity. Although he was a thorough and diligent student, Wen Zhengming repeatedly failed the national examinations, the third level of civil service examinations. Finally, a local governor recommended him to a post in Beijing, where he lived from 1523 to 1527, working in the Hanlin Academy (*see* CHINA, §V, 4(i)(d)) on the history of the Zhengde period (1506–21). Disillusioned by life in politics, he returned to Suzhou to become the focus of its artistic community.

Wen was deeply immersed in the study of the past. In common with his teacher, Shen Zhou, he drew on the works of the Yuan period (1279–1368) scholar-painters for inspiration, including the Four Masters of the Yuan: HUANG GONGWANG, WU ZHEN, NI ZAN and WANG MENG. The Yuan master Zhao Mengfu (*see* ZHAO, (1)) exercised the most pervasive influence on Wen, and he also studied earlier styles of the Tang (AD 618–906) and Song (960–1279) periods. The wealth of material available in Suzhou collections made all this feasible. Once he was totally familiar with these earlier styles, Wen reworked them to incorporate his own distinctive style, frequently expressing his awareness of history through inscriptions on his paintings. He specialized in garden scenes, which were often depictions of particular places in Suzhou; trees, especially pine, cypress and juniper; mountainscapes with an emphasis on rocks; commemorations of scholarly events such as journeys or departures; and illustrations of literature. He typically worked with refined, precise brushstrokes combined to form a complex surface pattern. As a literati painter (*see* CHINA, §V, 4(ii)), he sought to express his own personality in his work, and his highly controlled intellect is always apparent behind the painting.

In *Summer Retreat in the Eastern Grove* (handscroll, ink on paper, *c.* 1512; New York, Met.; *see* CHINA, fig. 101), Wen combined the three traditional arts of a scholar: poetry, calligraphy and painting. At the end of the painting he wrote one poem in running script (*xingshu*) in the style of HUANG TINGJIAN, a second poem in cursive script (*caoshu*) in the style of HUAISU as transmitted by Huang Tingjian, and a third poem in running script in the style of SU SHI. His selection reveals his good taste and skill in the styles of these earlier masters. The cool, precise painting is in the mode of Ni Zan. The composition is orderly and clear; the forms do not touch the lower edge of the scroll and are thus set back from the viewer. Clusters of rocks are placed along a subtle diagonal, leading the viewer from the lower right to upper left, and are topped by a few sparsely foliated trees. These motifs, along with the empty pavilion, are reminiscent of Ni Zan's work. The austerity of the composition is reiterated by the economy of brushwork: there is nothing superfluous. Wen succeeded in capturing a fresh, cool garden scene through his keen comprehension of artistic antecedents.

Master's Liu's Garden (hanging scroll, ink and colour on paper, 1543; New York, Marie Hélène and Guy Weill priv. col.) exemplifies a later treatment of the garden theme. This extraordinarily finely painted image was done for a friend, Liu Lin (1474–1561), who had just retired from government service. Wen painted a garden retreat based on ones already existing in Suzhou in anticipation of what his friend would probably construct. Two crossed willows invite the viewer across the water to enter the thatched gate and then back through the V-shaped arrangement of trees towards the lofty pavilion, where a scholar entertains a visitor. At the upper left Wen brushed a poem and dedication in standard script (*kaishu*), referring to the delightful view and peaceful atmosphere. The brushwork is soft and lyrical, with delicate pastel colouring: warm brown washes describe earth forms and tree trunks; pale blue and ink dots define the foliage.

By contrast, in *A Thousand Cliffs Vying in Splendour* (see fig.) there is a palpable sense of movement created by tilting, twisting forms. Within the constricted limits of the scroll, Wen piled rock on rock to build up a richly patterned mountainscape inspired by considerations of formal design rather than verisimilitude. The composition is densely packed, and the drawing is firm and incisive rather than soft and feathery. In the foreground two scholars sit enjoying the nearby pool and waterfall. Several trees connect this with the overwhelming mountain in the background; there is no view into the distance to offer relief. The mountain itself is constructed of rock masses topped by small pines in the mode of Huang Gongwang. The tightly controlled composition and strong brushwork make this commanding work one of Wen's masterpieces.

Wen made repeated use of the motifs of pine, cypress and juniper, which have particular connotations of the perpetual struggle of the human will. In *Old Cypress and Rock* (*Gubo tu*; handscroll, ink on paper, *c.* 1550; Kansas City, MO, Nelson–Atkins Mus. A.) Wen exploited the complex design of the cypress in its echoing of the shape of the rock. The range of ink tones from soft, wet grey to dense, dry black is astonishing; the virtuoso brushwork, based on calligraphic technique, alludes to Zhao Mengfu. As in *A Thousand Cliffs Vying for Splendour*, there is little three-dimensional space. Wen emphasized the flat, decorative pattern of the forms. The painting and its ten accompanying poems express wishes for a quick recovery from illness of the poet, playwright and calligrapher Zhang Fengy (1527–1613). The cypress symbolizes perseverance, the promise of youth and the healing powers inherent in the plant.

Wen Zhengming: *A Thousand Cliffs Vying in Splendour*, hanging scroll, ink and light colours on paper, 1326×340 mm, 1550 (Taipei, National Palace Museum)

Typical of classical scholars of the 16th century, Wen was a prolific poet. Much of his output reflects the formal grace of poetry masters of the Tang and Song dynasties, and it is rich in the visual imagery of landscapes and the changing seasons. Renowned also as a connoisseur, Wen was frequently called on to authenticate new additions to Suzhou collections, and he conducted careful research into the history of painting. Although his writing was refined and meticulous, it never attained the same stature as his painting and calligraphy. His collected writings were published in 1543 in *Futian ji* ('Extensive fields collection').

As a youth Wen Zhengming was a poor calligrapher, but he practised diligently and eventually he and his life-long friend Zhu Yunming were recognized as the two greatest calligraphers of the Ming period. Not only did Wen write in the modern script types of regular (*kaishu*), running (*xingshu*) and cursive (*caoshu*), but as part of his exploration of the past he also wrote in the archaic seal (*zhuanshu*) and clerical (*lishu*) scripts. During his years as an official in Beijing, Wen brushed poems on a suitably impressive imperial scale. In *Waiting upon the Emperor's Return from the Southern Suburbs* (*Gonghou dajia huan zi nanjiao*; hanging scroll, ink on paper; New York, Met.) Wen used formal imagery and large, blocky standard script characters to please the emperor. The style is derived from the great Song-period calligrapher Huang Tingjian, with the emphatic use of the diagonal 'oar stroke'. During his own lifetime Wen was best known for his small regular script (*xiao kaishu*) based on that of Wang Xizhi (*see* WANG (i), (1)); *Lu Ji's The Art of Letters* (*Lu Ji Wenfu*; handscroll, ink on paper, 1544–7; New York, Met.) offers a neat and precise example of this. It is marked by a stable, systematic composition and well-balanced proportions. The full-bodied characters are accentuated by sharp points, and the thinning and thickening strokes impart a lithe rhythm.

Wen's free and spontaneous running script is represented in a series of letters to his family (1523; Lyme, NH, Mr and Mrs Wan-go H. C. Weng priv. col.) and a letter to Hua Yun (1549; New York, Met). Both are imbued with informal natural rhythms and written with an exposed brush tip (*lufeng*; *see* CHINA, §IV, 1). Wen had two styles of cursive script: one was lean and firm, based on Wang Xizhi, to which Wen contributed angularity and tapering finishing strokes; the other, freer style combined elements from Huaisu and Huang Tingjian. The *Huangting jing* (handscroll, ink on paper, 1558; Lyme, NH, Mr and Mrs Wan-go H. C. Weng priv. col.), a Daoist scripture that discusses the nourishment of the human body, is a rare example of Wen's seal script, in which he re-created the style of the late 8th-century AD calligrapher Li Yangbing.

See also CHINA, §§IV, 2(vi)(b) and V, 4(ii) and figs 101 and 134.

(2) Wen Jia [Wen Chia; *zi* Xiuzheng, *hao* Wenshui] (*b* Suzhou, Jiangsu Province, 1501; *d* Suzhou, 1583). Painter and calligrapher, son of (1) Wen Zhengming. He received a formal classical education and benefited from contact with the learned associates of his father. He succeeded in passing the local *xiucai* (first degree) examinations and was appointed *gongsheng* (tribute student). He did not pass the provincial *juren* (second degree) examinations and had an undistinguished government career. A highly cultured gentleman, Wen Jia was a member of the third generation of the WU SCHOOL, and his early works show the profound influence of his father. His activity as a calligrapher was overshadowed by the greater reputation of his older brother Wen Peng (1498–1573), who practised the full range of script types: seal (*zhuanshu*), clerical (*lishu*), regular (*kaishu*) and cursive (*caoshu*). The two brothers were lively participants in Suzhou literati life, often collaborating on projects that combined painting, poetry and calligraphy. Together they compiled the *Tingyun guan tie*, an anthology of calligraphy published in 1560 (*see also* CHINA, §IV, 2(vi)(b)).

Highly regarded as a connoisseur, Wen Jia was frequently asked to authenticate masterpieces, especially after the death of his father. He wrote colophons on paintings by Chen Huang (*fl* AD 725–56), Guo Xi, Ma Yuan, Zhao Mengfu, Shen Zhou, Wen Zhengming, Zhou Chen, Tang Yin, Qiu Ying and Chen Shun. After the painting and calligraphy belonging to the powerful official Yan Song (1480–1565) were confiscated, Wen Jia was invited to write the catalogue *Qianshan tang shuhua ji*, dated 1569.

Wen Jia's paintings are modest and refined, with numerous allusions to the past. His unpretentious brushwork epitomizes the literati ideal of *pingdan* (plainness). Most of them illustrate poetry or document scholarly activities. From 1525 to 1559 he explored a variety of different themes and styles. After the death of Wen Zhengming in 1559, Wen Jia focused on consolidating his own artistic personality. He worked in the mode of masters of the Yuan period (1279–1368): NI ZAN was a particular favourite, since his paintings embodied the elegant refinement that most appealed to Wen Jia. Wen's paintings from the 1560s include illustrations of a poem by Bai Juyi (AD 772–846), *Pipa Xing* ('Lute song'; hanging scroll, ink and light colour on paper, 1569; Osaka, Mun. Mus.), and another by Su Shi, *Chibi fu* ('Ode on the red cliff'; handscroll, ink on paper, 1563; Nanjing, Jiangsu Prov. Mus.). His integral involvement with the Suzhou literati is affirmed by *Parting by the River Bank* (handscroll, ink and colour on paper, *c.* 1563; San Francisco, CA, Asian A. Mus.). It was painted to commemorate the departure of the official Yuan Zunni (1523–74) to Beijing to take the *jinshi* examinations and has farewell poems by six of his friends following the painting.

The last 13 years of Wen Jia's life were prolific. He wrote a large number of colophons and continued to work in the mode of Ni Zan, as well as to illustrate poetry such as *Landscape in the Spirit of Verses by Du Fu* (album leaf, 1576; Taipei, N. Pal. Mus.). His repertory expanded to include mythical Daoist scenic spots, for example *Daoist Landscapes* (handscroll, 1573; Tokyo, N. Mus.) and *On the Isles of the Immortals* (hanging scroll, n.d.; Taipei, N. Pal. Mus.). *Landscape Dedicated to Xiang Yuanbian* (see fig.) celebrated the Suzhou collector's 54th birthday. Huangfu Fang (1503–82) composed a birthday song that Wen Jia wrote on the scroll. The painting depicts a scholarly gathering with blunt brushstrokes reminiscent of SHEN ZHOU. It incorporates a deliberate creation of spatial ambiguity through a slanted horizon to the left of the background mountain mass. This device represents a new

Wen Jia: *Landscape Dedicated to Xiang Yuanbian*, hanging scroll, ink and colour on paper, 1175×400 mm, 1578 (New York, Metropolitan Museum of Art)

direction in painting and anticipates the distortions employed by Dong Qichang and Wang Yuanqi. Although the Wu school tradition declined during the late 16th century, there were certain innovations that were continued by later artists, particularly those active in the area of Songjiang. Wen Jia epitomized the typical scholar–artist active within his circle as a poet, calligrapher, painter and connoisseur.

See also CHINA, §V, 4(ii).

(3) Wen Boren [Wen Po-jen; *zi* Dezheng; *hao* Wufeng] (*b* Suzhou, Jiangsu Province, 1502; *d* Suzhou, 1575). Painter, nephew of (1) Wen Zhengming and cousin of (2) Wen Jia. He was renowned for his mean personality: as a youth he lost a legal dispute with his uncle and teacher, Wen Zhengming, and was imprisoned. Like Wen Jia, he failed the provincial *juren* (second degree) civil service examinations. Perhaps because of his cantankerous character, he did not often participate in Suzhou scholarly gatherings, nor was he as actively involved in WU SCHOOL activities as were his cousins Wen Peng (1498–1573) and Wen Jia; his paintings do not usually bear inscriptions by his contemporaries, and colophons by him are rare. The critic Wang Shizhen (1526–90) marvelled at how such a vile person could produce such fine landscapes.

Apart from *Miniature Portrait of Yang Jijing* (handscroll, ink and light colours on paper, 1526; Taipei, N. Pal. Mus.), Wen Boren's paintings are landscapes. He followed the Wen family style, using meticulous brushstrokes and an elongated format for hanging scrolls. The few times he painted in the mode of a master of the Yuan period (1279–1368) he chose WANG MENG, whose complex, interweaving rock forms and twisting trees suited Wen Boren's personality. *Dwellings of the Immortals Amid Streams and Mountains* (hanging scroll, ink and colour on paper, 1531; Cambridge, priv. col.) represents this style. A serpentine mountain mass is richly textured with numerous trees, rocks, buildings and figures. The deep pastel colours and the use of the archaic fishnet pattern to represent water also refer to Wang Meng's style. The luxuriant elegance of the painting is, however, derived from Wen Zhengming. The *Four Myriads* (*Siwan tu*; four hanging scrolls, ink and colour on paper, 1551; Tokyo, N. Mus.) is considered his masterpiece. The scrolls are extremely dense, full compositions that portray the four seasons with repeated use of bamboo for spring, pines for summer, sunlit waves for autumn and snowy peaks for winter. At other times Wen Boren worked in a sparse style, as in *Lute Song: Saying Farewell at Xunyang* (short handscroll, ink and light colour on paper; Cleveland, OH, Mus. A.), an illustration of the 'Pipa Xing' ('Lute song'; n.d.) by the poet Bai Juyi (AD 772–846). Water reeds, moon, maple tree and boats on the watery expanse are motifs from the prose poem. A poignant mood is evoked by the spacious composition, precise brushstrokes and soft, pale colours. The water is portrayed with the archaic fishnet pattern that originated in the Tang period (AD 618–907), when the poem was written.

River Landscape with Towering Mountains (see fig.) depicts scholars enjoying nature. The tall, narrow proportions and light, feathery brushwork reflect the influence

Wen Boren: *River Landscape with Towering Mountains*, hanging scroll, ink and colours on paper, 1270×381 mm, 1561 (Seattle, WA, Seattle Art Museum)

of Wen Zhengming. The composition is divided horizontally into two halves, with a separate spatial system for each half. In the foreground are riverside pavilions, trees and figures viewed from an elevated perspective. In the background, the mountains recede along a zigzag axis. They are treated in a volumetric fashion and topped with pines reminiscent of the Yuan master Huang Gongwang. The branches and foliage of the foreground trees weave together to create an intricate surface design. The contrast and tension between the upper and lower sections bring new life to this traditional theme.

The ruler under whom Wen Boren lived, the Jiajing emperor (*reg* 1522–66), was an avid patron of Daoism and contributed to its increased influence and practice during the 16th century. Like Wen Jia, Wen Boren painted Daoist themes, for example *Fanghu* (hanging scroll, ink and colour on paper, 1563; Taipei, N. Pal. Mus.), a portrayal of one of the Daoist islands of the immortals, and *Spring Dawn at Dantai* (handscroll, ink and colour on paper, n.d.; Taipei, N. Pal. Mus.).

See also CHINA, §V, 3(iii).

BIBLIOGRAPHY

Chinese Calligraphy (exh. cat. by Tseng Yu-ho Ecke, Philadelphia, PA Mus. A., 1971)
Friends of Wen Cheng-ming: A View from the Crawford Collection (exh. cat. by M. F. Wilson and K. S. Wong, New York, China House Gal., 1974)
A. D. Clapp: *Wen Cheng-ming: The Ming Artist and Antiquity* (Ascona, 1975)
Wu pai hua jiushi nian [Ninety years of Wu school painting] (exh. cat., Taipei, N. Pal. Mus., 1975)
The Art of Wen Cheng-ming (exh. cat. by R. Edwards, Ann Arbor, U. MI, Mus. A., 1976)
Traces of the Brush: Studies in Chinese Calligraphy (exh. cat. by Shen Fu and others, New Haven, CT, Yale U. A.G.; Berkeley, U. CA, A. Mus.; 1977)
J. Cahill: *Parting at the Shore: Chinese Painting of the Early and Middle Ming Dynasty, 1368–1580* (New York, 1978)
Eight Dynasties of Chinese Painting: The Collections of the Nelson Gallery–Atkins Museum, Kansas City, and the Cleveland Museum of Art (exh. cat. by Wai-Kam Ho and others, Kansas City, MO, Nelson–Atkins Mus. A.; Cleveland, OH, Mus. A.; 1980)
The Literati Vision: Sixteenth Century Wu School Painting and Calligraphy (exh. cat. by A. R. M. Hyland, Memphis, TN, Brooks Mus. A., 1984)

ALICE R. M. HYLAND

Wen Boren. *See* WEN, (3).

Wenceslas, King of Germany. *See* LUXEMBOURG, (4).

Wenceslas [Wenzel], Prince of Liechtenstein. *See* LIECHTENSTEIN, House of (4).

Wenceslas Bible. A sumptuous six-volume Bible in German (530×565 mm; Vienna, Österreich. Nbib., Cods 2759–64), made *c.* 1390–95 for Wenceslas IV, King of Bohemia (*see* LUXEMBOURG, House of, (4)). It is one of the most fully illustrated medieval Bibles even though the decoration extends only as far as the book of Nehemiah, just over halfway through the Old Testament. In contrast to the more usual scheme of a single illustration at the beginning of each book, found in most Gothic Bibles, the Wenceslas Bible has miniatures for almost every chapter, and occasionally more than one in a chapter. The total number of completed illustrations is almost 600, and would have been over 1000 had it been finished. Framed

miniatures, often with scenes in two registers, are placed within the columns of text (see fig.; *see also* BIBLE, fig. 5). The same illustrative system is used in the Antwerp Bible (1401–3; Antwerp, Mus. Plantin–Moretus, M15.1–2), probably made for Konrad of Vechta, controller of the Royal Mint (1401–3) and later the King's Chancellor. Border bars with foliage and figure scenes unrelated to the text are also used in the Wenceslas Bible. Many of these border scenes are of secular subjects and evoke the world of courtly society. They include scenes of scantily clad women and wild men attending the King in various situations of his dressing and bathing. The exact meaning of these scenes is unclear but some sort of erotic symbolism seems to be intended. Such an apparently incongruous juxtaposition of the sacred and secular is reminiscent of border decoration in England and France earlier in the 14th century.

Several illuminators worked on the Bible: the Genesis, Exodus, Balaam, Solomon, Ezra, Ruth and Samson Masters are named after the books or subjects that they illustrated. The Genesis and Balaam Masters were from an older generation whose work originated in Bohemian painting of the third quarter of the century. Their painting shows strong Italianate elements derived from north Italian artists, particularly Giusto de' Menabuoi and Altichiero. The work of the Exodus and Ezra Masters shows the influence of the new style introduced into Bohemia in the 1380s in the work of the panel painter, the Master of Třeboň. Their work in the Bible has elegantly posed,

Wenceslas Bible, *The Discovery of the Cup in Benjamin's Sack*; miniature by the Balaam Master, 530×565 mm, *c.* 1390–95 (Vienna, Österreichische Nationalbibliothek, Cod. 2759, fol. 46*r*)

somewhat elongated, figures with softly modelled faces and draperies with cascades of flowing folds; some of the artists show an interest in strong contrasts of light and shade. This so-called Soft Style occurs in both painting and sculpture in Bohemian art. While the Wenceslas Bible shows the style in an early form, its fullest expression is found in the Bible of Konrad of Vechta and other works of the early 15th century.

BIBLIOGRAPHY
M.-L. Vermeiren: 'La Bible de Wenceslas du Musée Plantin-Moretus à Anvers', *Gulden Passer*, xxxi (1953), pp. 191–229
J. Krasa: *Die Handschriften König Wenzels IV* (Prague, 1971)
E. Bachmann: *Gothic Art in Bohemia* (Oxford, 1977), pp. 56–60
Der Wenzelsbibel: Codices Vindobonenses 2759–2764, 9 vols (Graz, 1981–90) [facs. and commentary]
F. Unterkircher: *König Wenzels Bibelbilder: Die Miniaturen aus Genesis der Wenzelsbibel* (Graz, 1983)
A. Erlande-Brandenburg, J. Grosjean and M. Thomas: *La Bible de Prague* (Paris, 1989)

NIGEL J. MORGAN

Wen Cheng-ming. *See* WEN, (1).

Wen Chia. *See* WEN, (2).

Wenck, Ernst (Gustav Alexander) (*b* Reppen [now Rzepin, Poland], 18 March 1865; *d* Berlin, 23 Jan 1929). German sculptor. He began his apprenticeship at the age of 14 as a woodcarver in Berlin, continuing his studies from 1881 to 1885 at the Kunstgewerbemuseum and from 1885 to 1890 at the Hochschule der Künste, under Fritz Schaper. From there he won a Rome scholarship and travelled to Paris.

As a regular contributor to exhibitions from 1891, in his first works Wenck worked under the influence of a neo-Baroque style, notably in *Group of Atlants* for the Postmuseum in Berlin (*c.* 1895; destr., copies *in situ*). From 1897 to 1905 several bronze statues of Kaiser Wilhelm I (Berlin, Spandau, Zitadelle) were made in a traditional style. Wenck won a prize for the neo-classical *Girl Drinking* (marble, 1901; ex-N.G., Berlin), which enjoyed tremendous popularity and was widely reproduced. His search for greater simplicity in form and content had led him at this time towards a version of neo-classicism, although he also assimilated the influence of Rodin and Jugendstil, leading to such works of powerful plasticity and inner tension as *Fountain of the Money-counter* (shell-lime, 1912; Berlin, Pappelplatz). He moved increasingly towards a stylization and archaic simplification of form, as in *Linos* (1914; Berlin, N.G.), a highly expressive depiction of a falling figure.

After World War I Wenck adopted more Expressionist tendencies, for example in the expressively elongated figures of *Baptismal Group with Font* (1919; Berlin, Steglitz, Lukaskirche). While he favoured a formulaic severity in portraits such as the tomb sculpture *Herm Bust of Eugen Richter* (after 1919; Hagen-Delstern cemetery, nr Wuppertal), his tomb of *Max Sering* (shell-lime, 1922; Berlin, Dahlem, St-Annen-Kirche cemetery), representing a dying soldier chiselled from a narrow block, marked the extreme of blatant expressiveness in his work. Wenck joined the Berlin Secession in 1915 and was a committee member from 1921; in 1922 he became a member of the Akademie der Künste.

BIBLIOGRAPHY
P. Springer: 'Ein Kaiser-Wilhelm-Denkmal von E. Wenck', *Berlin. Mus.: Ber. Staatl. Mus. Preuss. Kulthes.*, iii/5 (1975), pp. 7–11
P. Bloch and W. Grzimek: *Das klassische Berlin* (Frankfurt am Main, 1978)
E. Müller-Lauter: 'Grabmäler in Berlin IV—Exempel: Die Friedhöfe im Bezirk Zehlendorf', *Berliner Forum*, ix (1985), pp. 50ff
G. Hoppen: *Ernst Wenck (1865–1929): Ein Berliner Bildhauer zwischen Neubarock und Expressionismus* (diss., in preparation)

GISELA HOPPEN

Wenckebach, (Ludwig) Willem (Reijmert) (*b* The Hague, 12 Jan 1860; *d* Santpoort, 25 June 1937). Dutch painter, draughtsman and illustrator. He first trained as a landscape gardener in Amsterdam. In 1878–9, however, he received lessons in painting from the cattle painter Dirk van Lokhorst (1818–93) and he was working in Drenthe, Gelderland and North Brabant. During that time he also received tuition from the marine painter Jacob Eduard van Heemskerck van Beest (1828–94). Wenckebach lived and worked in Utrecht from 1880 to 1886, in Amsterdam until 1898 and thereafter in Santpoort.

Wenckebach's preference was for traditional genres such as land-, river- and townscapes; in the latter, his drawings of views of old Amsterdam in particular are well known. In his style of painting and choice of subject-matter, he showed himself to be a late follower of the HAGUE SCHOOL. Through a number of publishers he received many commissions as an illustrator and designer of books. In this field he collaborated on, among other things, the Verkade albums, a large series devoted to the history and nature of the Netherlands, and various children's books. He is, however, particularly well known for his work for the *Nieuws van de Dag*.

BIBLIOGRAPHY
Scheen
J. F. Gebhard, ed.: *Oud Amsterdam* (Amsterdam, 1907)
A. A. Kok: 'De prenten van L. W. R. Wenckebach', *Mdbl. Bond Heemschut*, ii (1938)
H. Rowaan, ed.: *Wenckebach's Amsterdam* (Amsterdam, 1970)
E. Braches: *Het boek als nieuwe kunst, 1892–1903* (Utrecht, 1973)
A. M. van de Waal and H. de Vries, eds: *Amsterdam omstreeks 1900* (Amsterdam, 1974)

G. JANSEN

Wendelstam [Stam; Wendel; Wendelinus; Wendell; Wendelstamm; Wendel Stamm]**, Johan** [Jan] (*b* Giessen, Hessen; *fl* Sweden, 1641; *d* Stockholm, 1669/70). German sculptor, active in Sweden. He arrived in Sweden in 1641, at the invitation of Maria Eleonora of Brandenburg, Dowager Queen of Sweden (1599–1655), and was first a member of Jost Henne's workshop (1642–5). From 1646 he worked for the city of Stockholm, and from 1648 he was court sculptor. Among his surviving works are: the portal and decorative gable of the house at Stortorget 20 (1650) and the portal of Själagårdsgatan 2 (1659–60) in Stockholm; the fine Ionic columns with entablatures in the main portico (*c.* 1655–6) of Skokloster Slott, Uppland; the portals (*c.* 1654) of the parish church of Vadsbro, Södermanland; and the sculptural work of the mortuary chapels of Eric Ryning (1592–1654), with his burial monument (1656) at Vadsbro, and of Nils Ryning (*d* 1631), with a tomb monument (1656), in the church of Sköldinge, Södermanland. Wendelstam may also have been the architect of both chapels. They are small, towerlike, polygonal structures crowned by wooden lanterns and spires, similar to the more elaborate chapel (*c.* 1637) of Herman Wrangel (1584–1644) attached to the former monastery church at Skokloster, which was in turn influenced by the memorial chapel (1632–3) of Gustav II Adolf, King of Sweden (*reg* 1611–32), at Riddarholm Church in Stockholm. Wendelstam's chapel vault in Sköldinge is of a basically Gothic design, but the rib consoles are shaped as characteristic snub-nosed cherubs' heads, a rather cheerful treatment in an otherwise solemn environment.

Wendelstam also made portrait busts, such as that of *Count Per Brahe the Younger* (*c.* 1665; Visingsö, Brahe church). He was an exponent both of the older post-Gothic and later German-Netherlandish Renaissance styles (as shown at Stortorget 20, Stockholm, and the mortuary chapel in Sköldinge) and of a stricter classicism (as shown in the portico columns in the main portico of Skokloster Slott).

BIBLIOGRAPHY
SVKL; Thieme–Becker
E. Andren: *Skokloster* (Stockholm, 1948)
G. Axel-Nilsson: *Dekorativ stenhuggarkonst i yngre vasastil* [Ornamental sculpture of the later Vasa style] (Stockholm, 1950)
TORBJÖRN FULTON

Wendelstein. German term for a tower housing a spiral staircase, both of a sumptuous nature.

Wendland, Winfried (*b* Gröben, nr Teltow, 17 March 1903). German architect and administrator. After studying at the Baugewerbeschule, Berlin, he worked in various architectural offices in 1926–7, and independently from 1928, building churches, chapels and parish halls in the new housing estates in and around Berlin during the 1930s. These buildings, usually without towers, are of brick, cruciform in plan and with façades formed of a peaked gable and round window. The main interior spaces serve both for church services and parish meetings. The saddleback roofs have open wooden roof trusses. Traditional in style and materials, they reflect the ideas both of the Heimatschutzbewegung, a movement concerned with preserving the German regional heritage, and of the National Socialist cultural organizations to which Wendland belonged. During this period Wendland also worked as a curator in the state art schools, as an official in the Prussian Ministry of Culture, as a member of the governing board of the Deutscher Werkbund and as co-editor of the periodical *Kunst und Kirche*. Through these activities he actively promoted the artistic ideas of NAZISM. For instance, on the occasion of the political realignment of the Deutscher Werkbund with the Nazi state in 1933, he wrote against Neues Bauen, Rationalism and foreign influences on German architecture, and in favour of an indigenous, regional and patriotic style. From 1949 Wendland held various positions in connection with Protestant church building in Potsdam. From 1962 to 1975 he was also the commissioner in charge of artistic matters for the Protestant Church in East Berlin.

Important extant examples of his work include the cemetery chapel in Tetlow (1934) and the parish hall in Berlin-Staaker (1936).

WRITINGS
Kunst und Nation: Ziel und Wege der Kunst im Neuen Deutschland (Berlin, 1934)
Kirchenbau in dieser Zeit: Bilder, Berichte und Gedanken zum Neubau und Wiederaufbau (Berlin, 1957)
BIBLIOGRAPHY
E. Kiel, ed.: *Kirchenbau heute: Dokumentation, Diskussion, Kritik* (Munich, 1969)
J. Campbell: *The German Werkbund* (Princeton, 1978), pp. 249–52
ROLAND WOLFF

Wendt, Jochim Matthias (*b* Dageling, ?June 1830; *d* Adelaide, 7 Sept 1917). Australian silversmith and jeweller of Danish birth. He served his apprenticeship in Dageling, Denmark, before moving in 1854 to Adelaide, where he established a business that within a decade became one of the city's two main retail outlets for silver and jewellery. Branches were subsequently opened at Mount Gambier in South Australia and Broken Hill in New South Wales. From 1862 the firm regularly exhibited at intercolonial and international exhibitions, receiving awards, for example at the Australian Intercolonial Exhibition of 1866–7 in Melbourne, Victoria, the Centennial International Exhibition of 1876 in Philadelphia and the Exposition Universelle of 1878 in Paris. In 1867 Wendt was granted a royal warrant by Prince Alfred, Duke of Edinburgh (1844–1900), during his visit to the colonies. He appears to have specialized in presentation pieces, ranging from standing cups and epergnes to mounted emu eggs. Many incorporate such local motifs as cast figures of aborigines, kangaroos and emus. The best of these pieces (e.g. the Schomburgk Cup, *c.* 1865; Adelaide, Botan. Gdns) are attributed to Julius Schomburgk (?1818–93), who is believed to have been Wendt's principal designer and maker between 1863 and 1870. After Wendt's death the business continued under the same name as a family concern.

BIBLIOGRAPHY
J. B. Hawkins: *Nineteenth Century Australian Silver*, ii (Woodbridge, 1990)
JUDITH O'CALLAGHAN

Wendt, Lionel (George Henricus) (*b* Colombo, 3 Dec 1900; *d* Colombo, 20 Dec 1944). Ceylonese photographer and musician. He was introduced to photography at a very early age during visits to A. W. Andree's home and studio. It was only in the last ten years before his death that he returned to the medium with greater dedication and seriousness. Between 1919 and 1924 he qualified as a barrister in England and also became an accomplished pianist after studying at the Royal Academy of Music. Four years after his return from England he abandoned his legal career and became a pianist, often accompanying renowned foreign musicians at recitals in Colombo.

By 1930 Wendt's involvement in the arts had earned him a pivotal place in the development of the modern movement in Ceylon. Alborada, his new residence in Colombo, which he designed and decorated in a contemporary style with prints and his own photographs, became a centre for intellectuals such as the painter George Keyt (*b* 1901), the poet and future Nobel laureate Pablo Neruda and the architect Andrew Boyd (*fl* 1929–58). Although not a painter himself, Wendt became one of the founder-members and the most influential patron of the avant-garde 43 Group, which he set up in Colombo in 1943 with Harry Pieris (1904–1988), George Keyt, Geoffrey Beling (*b* 1907) and Justin Pieris Deraniyagala. The Group's first exhibitions were held in Wendt's residence in Colombo, and later many of the artists were invited to exhibit as a group in London and at the Venice Biennale. Wendt was also a founder-member of the newly-formed Photographic Society of Ceylon.

By 1932 Wendt had become more concerned with photography, experimenting with new techniques and renewing old processes, including solarization, photomontages and bromide prints (*see* PHOTOGRAPHY, §I). His lively experiments in still photography led to work with film. In the next two years Wendt made two visits to England in order to work with Basil Wright (1907–87) and John Grierson (1898–1972) on the *Song of Ceylon* (1934), recognized as an outstanding documentary film, for which he chose the locations and served as both photographer and narrator.

Wendt's approach to photography represents a radical departure from many of his contemporaries and makes him the first truly modern photographer in Ceylon (now Sri Lanka) and the first to use the medium in an artistic and contemporary manner. Moreover, his involvement with other arts, especially film, music and painting, combined with a sensitive appreciation of the artistic heritage of both the East and West, enabled him to mix modern and traditional images in his work.

In 1963 the Lionel Wendt Centre, a special arts centre, housing also the headquarters of the Photographic Society of Ceylon, was completed on a site at Guildford Crescent, Colombo, which included Alborada.

BIBLIOGRAPHY

'Death of Mr Lionel Wendt, Gifted Pianist and Photographer', *Ceylon Daily News* (21 Dec 1944)
Lionel Wendt's Ceylon (London, 1950)
Rediscovering Lionel Wendt (exh. cat. by M. Fonseka, Colombo, 1994)

ISMETH RAHEEM

Weng Tonghe [Weng T'ung-ho; *zi* Shengjie, Renfu, Shengfu; *hao* Shuping, Songchan, Pingsheng, Yunzhai] (*b* Changshu, Jiangsu Province, 19 May 1830; *d* 3 July 1904). Chinese calligrapher, writer and official. He came first in the national examinations, the third stage in the civil service examinations, to receive his *jinshi* degree in 1856. He was tutor to the Tongzhi emperor (*reg* 1862–74) and then to the Guangxu emperor (*reg* 1875–1908); at the same time he held various other positions in the Qing (1644–1911) government. Because of his involvement in the short-lived reform movement of 1898, Weng was stripped of his ranks and sent home that same year.

As a calligrapher, Weng Tonghe was regarded as the only successor to LIU YONG: he was the only famous calligrapher of the late Qing period to write in the copybook style, following the traditional copybook models at a time when it had become the fashion to use ancient models such as bronzes and stelae (*see* CHINA, §IV, 2(vii)). As a youth, he studied typical copybook sources: OUYANG XUN, CHU SUILIANG, ZHAO MENGFU and DONG QICHANG, who were great practitioners of regular (*kaishu*)

and running (*xingshu*) scripts. Later, Weng was influenced by the strong and stable writing of YAN ZHENQING, who was also popular among the calligraphers who took stelae as their models, and from about the age of 50 he studied the cursive scripts (*caoshu*) of SU SHI and MI FU. Weng also investigated stelae inscribed in clerical script (*lishu*), such as the *Liqi bei* (AD 156), *Yiying bei* (AD 153; both Confucius Temple, Qufu, Shandong Province) and *Zhangqian bei* (AD 186; Dongping, Shandong Province). His most successful scripts continued to be large regular (*da kaishu*), running and small running (*xiao xingshu*) and cursive scripts. His small running cursive (*xingcaoshu*) calligraphy may be seen on a fan dated 1889 (Shimonaka, xxiv, pl. 77); to accommodate the arc of the fan, full-length columns alternate with shorter ones. The rhythmic differences of the columns combine with strokes that vary from soft thickness to wavering fineness, and the quaver of Weng's hand and the unexpected jerks lend a natural asymmetry. Completely unpretentious, it is similar in style to the calligraphy of Su Shi, who was the author of the text. The plain naturalness, balance and ease of his writing are also evident in a large-scale pair of hanging scrolls, *Couplet on Confucian and Daoist Virtues* (undated; New Haven, CT, Shen C. Y. Fu priv. col.). Working with a brush full of ink, Weng made thick, rounded, solid strokes. The well-spaced characters are firm and organized and illustrate what Yang Shoujing said of his work: 'it was full of the fragrance of old pines, without a trace of the unskilled.'

BIBLIOGRAPHY

Hummel: 'Weng T'ung-ho'
K. Shimonaka, ed.: *Shodō zenshū* [Complete collection of calligraphy], xxiv (Tokyo, 2/1961)
Y. Uno: *Chūgoku shodōshi* [A history of Chinese calligraphy] (Tokyo, 1962), pp. 367–78
Traces of the Brush: Studies in Chinese Calligraphy (exh. cat. by Shen Fu and others; New Haven, CT, Yale U. A. G., Berkeley, U. CA, A. Mus.; 1977)
Yu Jianhua: *Zhongguo huajia da zidian* [Dictionary of Chinese painters] (Shanghai, 1981), p. 750

ELIZABETH F. BENNETT

Weng T'ung-ho. *See* WENG TONGHE.

Wen Jia. *See* WEN, (2).

Wen Lou. *See* VAN LAU.

Wenning, Pieter (Willem Frederick) (*b* The Hague, 9 Sept 1873; *d* Pretoria, 24 Jan 1921). South African painter and printmaker of Dutch birth. He was a self-taught artist and left Holland in 1905 to take up employment in the Pretoria branch of a Dutch bookselling firm. He painted and etched landscapes and still-lifes during weekends only until 1916, when a group of patrons made it possible for him to spend three months painting full-time in Cape Town. He found the misty winter climate of the Cape peninsula, being closer to the atmosphere of his homeland than the harsh, sunlit expanses of the Transvaal, suited to his temperament and style. During that and later visits he produced enough saleable work to repay his benefactors and to continue painting full-time. Unfortunately his practice of working incessantly outdoors, regardless of inclement weather, also undermined the fragile health that had originally driven him from Holland.

Although Wenning revelled in the wooded landscapes of the Cape, he eschewed the picture-postcard sentimentality typical of the work of most of his contemporaries. His formats are small, but the flat colour planes and decorative, rhythmical contours—both especially pronounced in his still-life studies—are brisk and confident, as in *Landscape at Mowbray* (Pretoria, A. Mus.) and *Hibiscus* (Johannesburg, A.G.; both undated).

Wenning's style, which gave rise to a school known as Cape Impressionism, derived initially from the atmospheric landscapes of the Dutch Hague school and was influenced later by his study of Oriental art. Although he never taught nor associated himself with any group, Wenning was a pioneering figure in South African art, breaking away from the academic realism that prevailed during the first quarter of the 20th century.

BIBLIOGRAPHY
Berman
G. Boonzaier and L. Lipshitz: *Wenning* (Cape Town, 1949)
J. du P. Scholtz: *D. C. Boonzaier en Pieter Wenning* (Cape Town, 1973)
H. Wenning: *My Father* (Cape Town, 1976)
E. Berman: *Painting in South Africa* (Halfway House, 1993)
ESMÉ BERMAN

Wen Po-jen. *See* WEN, (3).

Wen Tong [Wen T'ung; *zi* Yuke; *hao* Xiaoxiao Xiansheng, Jinjiang Daoren, Shishi Xiansheng] (*b* Zitong, Sichuan Province, 1018; *d* Wanqiu, Chenzhou [modern Huaiyang], Henan Province, 1079). Chinese scholar and painter. He is associated with the establishment of ink-bamboo painting as a major genre of literati painting.

From an educated Confucian family in Sichuan Province in the south-west, Wen was a diligent student of the classics and on attaining the title of *jinshi* in the national-level civil-service examination of 1049 ranked fifth out of 500. Despite his erudition and talent, however, he never served in high government positions, spending much of his career as a civil functionary in Sichuan and Shaanxi provinces, away from the fast-paced manoeuvrings of party politics in the capital, Bianliang (modern Kaifeng, Henan Province). Wen's gentle and unassuming character was most comfortable in the solitude of nature, where he found the embodiment of his personal ideals in nature's 'gentleman' (*junzi*), bamboo (*see* CHINA, §V, 3(vi)). As a painter of bamboo, which he claims to have painted as a means of self-cultivation in his pursuit of the Dao ('way'), Wen earned lasting fame.

Wen's close friend and cousin, SU SHI, the eminent statesman, poet and art theorist of the late 11th century, was instrumental in bringing attention to Wen. The narrative accounts of Wen's paintings of bamboo by Su Shi and his brother Su Che (1039–1112) are among the most compelling descriptions of the creative act in Chinese literature. Following clearly prescribed models from an early philosophical work, the *Zhuangzi*, they liken Wen to Cook Ding and Wheelwright Bian, craftsmen who attained the Dao through absolute mastery of their métier. However, the personal identification of Wen with his subject—bamboo—is a new twist and a key element in the developing literati theory of the arts, which sought to establish painting's potential for revealing the personality of the artist (*see* CHINA, §V, 4(ii)).

Two large and related hanging scrolls in ink on silk (Taipei, N. Pal. Mus. and Guangzhou, A.G.) best exemplify Wen Tong's ink-bamboo. Both represent a large and weathered branch of bamboo dipping and rising in an inverted S-curve and recall Su Shi's descriptions of Wen's bent bamboo, the strange shapes of which are caused by the constrictions of the gulley where it grows, a fitting image of the ideal Confucian gentleman who bends without yielding. Nearer and further leaves are distinguished by gradations in ink tone, in keeping with a detailed account of Wen's technique by the contemporary critic Mi Fu, and the marvellous sense of organic development accords well with Su Shi's descriptions of Wen engaged in the creative act. Wen is credited with being the founder of the ink-bamboo tradition. His followers were numerous; they are collectively designated the Huzhou school of bamboo painting, after Wen's final assignment as governor of Huzhou in Zhejiang Province.

BIBLIOGRAPHY
Franke: 'Wen T'ung'
Su Shi: *Jing jin Dongpo wen ji shi lue* [Collected prose of Su Shi] (11th century); *R* in Sibu congkan (Shanghai, 1919–37)
Su Che: *Luancheng ji* [Collected works of Su Che] (11th century to early 12th); *R* in Sibu congkan (Shanghai, 1919–37)
Mi Fu: *Hua shi* [History of painting] (preface *c.* 1103); *R* in Meishu congshu (Shanghai, 1911–18)
O. Sirén: *Chinese Painting: Leading Masters and Principles* (London and New York, 1956–8), ii, pp. 11–18, 87; iii, pls 182–4
Yu Fengbian: *Su Shi Wen Tong* [Su Shi and Wen Tong]; *R* in Zhongguo huajia congshu (Shanghai, 1957)
T. Toda: 'Koshu chikuha ni tsuite: Sōdai bunjinga kenkyū' [Regarding the Huzhou school of bamboo painting: a study in Song literati painting], *Bijutsu Kenkyū*, 236 (1964), pp. 15–30
Xia Yuchen: 'Ji Su Shi *Gumu zhu shi* Wen Tong *Mozhu* he juan' [Notes on the combined scroll of Su Shi's *Old Tree, Bamboo and Rock* and Wen Tong's *Ink-bamboo*], *Wenwu* (1965), no. 8, pp. 24–30
S. Bush: *The Chinese Literati on Painting: Su Shih (1037–1101) to Tung Ch'i-ch'ang (1555–1636)* (Cambridge, MA, 1971), pp. 12, 29–43
PETER C. STURMAN

Wen T'ung. *See* WEN TONG.

Wentworth, Charles Watson-, 2nd Marquess of Rockingham. *See* WATSON-WENTWORTH, CHARLES.

Wentworth, Richard (*b* Western Samoa, 1947). English sculptor. He studied at Hornsey College of Art, London, from 1965, and worked with Henry Moore in 1967. He also studied at the Royal College of Art, London (1968–70). With artists such as Bill Woodrow and Tony Cragg, Wentworth shared an interest in the unexpected correlation of found objects and industrial materials. He was drawn to imaginative displacements of common objects presented within a high art context (e.g. lightbulbs cased in wire baskets, garden implements slotted in office furniture). In *Mercator* (1985) and *Between 8 and 9* (1989; both exh. London, Lisson Gal.), large galvanized-metal sheets bend in rhythmic waves, and dexian (office) frames soar skywards in a light-hearted parody of industrial interiors. The titles of Wentworth's works, sometimes drawn from children's tales, are as enigmatic as his constructions. During 1993–4 he participated in the Berliner Künstlerprogramme at the daad galerie.

BIBLIOGRAPHY
Richard Wentworth (exh. cat. by L. Cooke and S. Morgan, London, Lisson Gal., 1984)

Richard Wentworth: 'Making Do and Getting By' (exh. cat., London, Tate, 1984)

M. Warner: *Richard Wentworth* (London, 1993)

□

Wentzel, (Nils) Gustav (*b* Christiania [now Oslo], 7 Oct 1859; *d* Lillehammer, 10 Feb 1927). Norwegian painter. He was descended from a Bohemian family of glassmakers who settled in Norway *c.* 1750. He studied at Knud Bergslien's art school (1879–81) and at the same time at the Royal School of Design in Christiania, and in 1883 he was a pupil of Frits Thaulow, who introduced him to *plein-air* painting. Wentzel paid a short visit to Paris that same year and stayed there again in 1884 as a pupil of William-Adolphe Bouguereau at the Académie Julian. In 1888–9 he studied with Alfred Roll and Léon Bonnat at the Académie Colarossi. During this period he painted mainly interiors with figures, the urban middle-class and artisans in their homes, and also artists' studios. His earliest paintings, for example *Breakfast I* (1882; Oslo, N.G.), render detail with a meticulousness unsurpassed in Norwegian Naturalism. Wentzel's work gradually adopted an influence from contemporary French painting, including a more subtle observation of the effects of light and atmosphere on local colour, as in the *Day After* (1883; Trondheim, Trøndelag Kstgal.) and *Breakfast II* (1885; Oslo, N.G.). Scenes from the Norwegian countryside became more frequent, such as *Old Folks* (1888; Oslo, N.G.). The *Dance in Setesdal* (1891; Oslo, N.G.) represents a more romantic note in his work, which predominated in the early 1890s. Later he preferred landscapes, especially snowscapes, rural scenes etc, as subjects, although he did not maintain the standard of his earlier work.

NKL   BIBLIOGRAPHY

J. Thiis: *Norske malere og billedhuggere* [Norwegian painters and sculptors], ii (Bergen, 1907), pp. 136, 332, 335–40

L. Østby: *Fra naturalisme til nyromantikk* [From Naturalism to neo-Romanticism] (Oslo, 1934), pp. 56–7, 63–4, 88–91, 117, 119–20

K. Wentzel: 'Gustav Wentzel', *Kst & Kult.*, xxviii (1942), pp. 1–18 [by his wife]

——: *Gustav Wentzel* (Oslo, 1956)

K. Nilsen: *Blant kunstnere i det gamle Asker* [Among artists in old Asker] (Bærum, 1979), pp. 78–83

                                        LEIF ØSTBY

Wentzinger, Johann Christian (*b* Ehrenstetten, 10 Dec 1710; *d* Freiburg, 1 Aug 1797). German sculptor, painter, stuccoist and architect. He went to Italy as a journeyman and spent two years (1729–31) in Rome, then six months in Strasbourg. His earliest surviving work is the font at the monastery of St Peter in the Black Forest. From 1735 to 1737 he was in Paris, where he attended and won prizes at the Académie de St Luc. In 1737 he carved the large figures for the high altar of Oberried Monastery, and in 1740 he made eight huge stone figures for the portal (destr. 1768) of the monastery of St Blasien in the Black Forest, and also made models for the stairwell figures. Wentzinger signed the contract for the magnificent tomb of *General von Rodt* in Freiburg im Breisgau Cathedral in 1743. In 1745 he made a model of the *Mount of Olives* for the church of St Martin in Staufen (now in Frankfurt am Main, Liebieghaus). For the new building at Schloss Ebnet, near Freiburg, he created the stone relief on the gable, figures representing the seasons in the park and stucco sculptures for the salon, modifying the original plans for the building by decorative embellishments. He also painted the double portrait (1748–50; Heidelberg, priv. col.) of the owner of Schloss Ebnet, *Baron von Sickingen*, and his wife. His *Self-portrait with a Portfolio* must also have been painted *c.* 1750; an earlier *Self-portrait* dates from *c.* 1740. There is a signed and dated overdoor with a still-life breakfast scene from 1753 and other unsigned overdoors belong with it. Five overdoors were mentioned in Wentzinger's estate. In 1752 he made models of figures for the library at the monastery of St Peter.

In 1757 Wentzinger was awarded his largest commission and worked on it until the summer of 1760. He prepared designs for the interior decoration of St Gall Abbey in Switzerland, including stucco decorations, ceiling paintings, stucco reliefs and putti, and the stone figures on the façades. The stucco and stone figures were his own work, while Hans Georg Gigl (*d* 1765) and Matthias II Gigl (*fl* 1761) executed the decorative stuccowork, and the Swabian painter Josef Wannenmacher (1722–80) executed the paintings to Wentzinger's designs and under his direction. Three-dimensional models, drawings and oil sketches of these works survive. Wentzinger had already acquired citizenship of Freiburg and bought a house there in 1755, and on his return from St Gall he bought another plot on the Münsterplatz, where he built a fine town house, the Haus zum schönen Eck, with a frescoed ceiling over the stairwell, seven sculpted heads over the windows and a bronze *Self-portrait* on the balcony.

Wentzinger was able to live without financial worries, and in his later years he mainly produced only the designs for large commissions, which were then realized by other sculptors. Thus, in 1763 he was engaged as a consultant for the high altar at Kirchhofen, and in 1768 he designed the font for Freiburg im Breisgau Cathedral and supervised its execution and installation by the Freiburg craftsmen Josef Hörr (1732–85) and Anton Xaver Hauser (1716–72). In 1769 he made clay models for Ettenheim parish church, which were executed by A. Fuchs. In 1770 he was commissioned to design and erect a triumphal arch for the entry into the town of Archduchess Maria Antonia (later Marie-Antoinette, Queen of France). From 1776 Wentzinger was again at work in St Blasien. He designed the choir stalls and altars and painted the ceiling pictures (destr. 1870) with Simon Göser in 1779–80. At the same time he produced architectural designs for the Freiburg poorhouse, for which, among other undertakings, he executed the ceiling paintings.

As well as the works for which there is documentary evidence and those that are signed, many sculptures in clay, wood and stone have been attributed to Wentzinger (see Krummer-Schroth). His style had a great impact on artists in Breisgau and south-west Germany. He was apparently not a master in a craft guild but a sculptor with an academic training, so he did not have any direct apprentices or pupils. His assistants were always artists qualified in their own right, who nevertheless adopted his late Rococo style.

Thieme–Becker   BIBLIOGRAPHY

H.-R. Hitchcock: *Rococo Architecture in Southern Germany* (London, 1968)

I. Krummer-Schroth: *Johann Christian Wentzinger: Bildhauer, Maler und Architect, 1710–97* (Freiburg im Breisgau, 1987)

INGEBORG KRUMMER-SCHROTH

Wenzel, King of Germany. *See* LUXEMBOURG, (4).

Wen Zhengming. *See* WEN, (1).

Werefkin, Marianne (von) (*b* Tula, nr Moscow, 11 Sept 1860; *d* Ascona, 6 Feb 1938). Russian painter, active in Switzerland. Her father was a commander-general in the Russian army and her mother a trained artist who encouraged Werefkin to draw from an early age. In 1883 Werefkin attended the Moscow Art School, receiving tuition from Illarion Pryanishnikov (1840–94), a member of the Wanderers group. In St Petersburg this Realist direction was reinforced from 1886 by her private tutor Il'ya Repin, with whom she studied for ten years. A hunting accident in 1888 crippled the thumb and index finger of her right hand, but Werefkin persevered with her career, contributing to the first exhibition of the St Petersburg Artists' Association in 1891. At this time she concentrated on large oil paintings, predominantly character portraits, in dark colours (*Russian Peasant in Fur*; 1890, priv. col., see 1980 exh. cat.). At Repin's studio in 1891 she met Alexei Jawlenski, who became her constant companion.

After the death of her father in 1895, Werefkin and Jawlenski settled in Munich. They acquired a house in the bohemian Schwabing district, which became a popular venue for gatherings of artists of which Werefkin was the undisputed leader. At first she dedicated herself to promoting Jawlenski's career and only herself resumed painting in 1902. However, her partially published theoretical excerpts, *Lettres à un inconnu*, published as *Briefe an einen Unbekannten* (1901–5), reveal a thorough knowledge of Russian and French Symbolist aesthetics and a formulation of Expressionist concepts. A trip to Paris in 1905 provided her with first-hand knowledge of the works of the Fauves, the Nabis and Odilon Redon.

In 1908 Jawlenski and Werefkin worked alongside Vasily Kandinsky and Gabriele Münter in Murnau and, in 1909, were instrumental in the formation of the Neue Künstlervereinigung München. Werefkin participated in the association's three exhibitions before her resignation in 1912. Apart from contributing to the Blaue Reiter exhibition at Herwarth Walden's Sturm-Galerie in Berlin, Werefkin's works also featured in a German Expressionist exhibition there in 1912. Her paintings produced in Munich were executed in tempera and were unsigned and undated. They included landscapes, which occasionally depicted the impact of industrialization on rural scenes, for example *Roof-Tile Factory* (*c.* 1910; Wiesbaden, Mus. Wiesbaden), and paintings with social subject-matter such as peasants and washerwomen. These works displayed rigorous simplification of contours, flattening of space and non-naturalistic use of colour.

At the outbreak of World War I in 1914, Werefkin and Jawlenski emigrated to Switzerland. In Zurich in 1917 they came into contact with the Dadaists and attended sessions of the Cabaret Voltaire. By 1918 they had settled in Ascona and, after their final separation in 1920, Werefkin remained there. She entered into the spirit of the international artistic community in the town and, with six other artists, formed the group, the *Grossen Bären* (Great Bears), who exhibited in the Kunsthalle, Berne, in 1925. The group received widespread recognition while exhibiting with Christian Rohlfs and Karl Schmidt-Rottluf at the Galerie Nierendorf, Berlin, in 1928. On the whole her later work accentuated her earlier stylistic tendencies through the attenuation of motifs and increasingly gestural application of paint. Mystical and religious associations also became prevalent in her work and titles, for example *Ave Maria* (*c.* 1927; Ascona, Mus. Com. A. Mod.). Werefkin's theoretical writing and oeuvre made a valuable contribution towards the Expressionist movement.

WRITINGS

Briefe an einen Unbekannten, 1901–5, ed. C. Weiler (Cologne, 1960)

BIBLIOGRAPHY
O. Fischer: *Das neue Bild* (Munich, 1912)
G. Pauli: *Erinnerungen aus 7 Jahrzehnten* (Tübingen, 1936)
L. Buchheim: *Der Blaue Reiter und die Neue Künstlervereinigung München* (Feldafing, 1959)
J. Hahl-Koch: 'Marianne Werefkin und der russische Symbolismus', *Slav. Beitr.*, xxiv (1967)
R. Gollek: *Der Blaue Reiter im Lenbachhaus München* (Munich, 1974)
Marianne Werefkin, Gemälde und Skizzen (exh. cat., ed. S. Russ, B. Fäthke and H. Hahl-Koch; Wiesbaden, Mus. Wiesbaden, 1980)
S. Behr: *Women Expressionists* (Oxford, 1988)
B. Fäthke: *Marianne Werefkin* (Munich, 1988)
M. Witzling: *Voicing our Visions: Writings by Women Artists* (London, 1992)

SHULAMITH BEHR

Werenskiold, Erik (Theodor) (*b* Vinger, 11 Feb 1885; *d* Oslo, 23 Nov 1938). Norwegian painter, draughtsman and printmaker. He studied in Christiania (later Kristiania, now Oslo) in 1873–5 under Julius Middelthun, who discovered his unusual gift for drawing, and then at the Akademie der Bildenden Künste in Munich (1876–9). Among his early paintings, *Female Half-nude* (1877; Bergen, Billedgal.) is typical in revealing an interest in individual personality and psychology even in a traditional academic subject. In 1878, while on a visit to Kristiania, Werenskiold met the collector and editor Peter Christien Asbjørnsen (1812–85) and was engaged as an illustrator for his new edition of Norwegian fairy tales (Kristiania, 1879). Together with Theodor Kittelsen, he continued to contribute illustrations to Absjørnsen's publications. In his drawings for tales such as *De Kongsdøtre i berget det blå* ('The three princesses in the mountain-in-the-blue'; Kristiania, 1887), he achieved a striking combination of realistic observation, fantasy and humour, his imaginary creatures being especially successful. During the 1880s Werenskiold was also active as a painter. He left Munich early in 1881 and settled in Paris where he came to know the work of contemporary French artists. He was initially intrigued by both Naturalism and Impressionism, but eventually found it impossible to abandon the feeling for form and line that he sensed as lacking in these styles. In 1883 he returned to Norway and soon became the chief promotor of a strictly national art, based on the study of Norwegian landscape and folk life. *Girls of Telemark* (1883; Oslo, N.G., see fig.) and *Peasant Burial* (1885; Oslo, N.G.) are naturalistically detailed studies of Norwegian daily life. At this time Werenskiold began his long series of portraits representing outstanding compatriots that eventually included *Edvard Grieg* (1892; Stockholm, Nmus.) and *Henrik Ibsen* (1895; Oslo, N.G.).

Erik Werenskiold: *Girls of Telemark*, oil on canvas, 800×980 mm, 1883 (Oslo, Nasjonalgalleri)

Towards the end of the decade, after a second stay in Paris as the pupil of Léon Bonnat, Werenskiold's style changed, the colour becoming richer, the brushwork more expansive and less explicit. Some portraits from the 1890s, for example that of the musician *Erika Nissen* (1892; Oslo, N.G.), seek to evoke the creative world of the sitter, in this case, her absorption in music marked by the inevitable loneliness of the creative personality. The landscapes from this period are also distinct from earlier ones: nature is rendered in a much more lyrical manner, as in *Autumn* (1891; Göteborg, Kstmus.) and in the paintings from Werenskiold's beloved Telemark such as *Summer Evening at Kviteseid* (1893; Oslo, N.G.), which are painted with blurred contours and delicate, subdued tones to express with a certain intimacy the sense of peace to be found in the Nordic summer landscape at sunset. As always, children are favourite subjects, both in some of the Telemark landscapes and in such works as *Sister and Brothers* (1897; Oslo, N.G.), a painting especially notable for its emotive use of colour. In the 1890s Werenskiold worked again as an illustrator. He became artistic editor and the main contributor for the illustrated edition of *Snorri Sturlasons Kongesagaer* ('Snorre Sturlasons's sagas of the Norse Kings'; Kristiania, 1896–9). His swift and forceful line in the drawings for this work is well matched to Snorre's emphatic prose. It is in strong contrast to his style in the drawings (Oslo, N.G.) made to illustrate Jonas Lie's novel *The family at Gilje* (Kristiania, 1893–1903), which are executed in a soft, finely nuanced and detailed manner, often using a chiaroscuro that reflects Werenskiold's deep admiration for Rembrandt's drawings and etchings. Werenskiold's interest in Norwegian medieval ballads also led to a commission to decorate Fridtjof Nansen's dining room at Polhøgda with friezes in a simplified decorative style showing scenes from the story of *Liti Kjersti* (1904–7).

Werenskiold confronted contemporary developments abroad in visits to Berlin in 1905 and to Paris in 1908, seeing much of van Gogh's work and also that of Cézanne, who especially impressed him and remained a strong influence for the rest of his life. From 1907 he adopted Cézanne's method of building mass and space by contrasting pure colour; this may be seen in *Lomen Churchyard* (1908; Skien, Billedgal.). It was at this stage also that Werenskiold embarked on printmaking, producing over the next 30 years a total of about 80 etchings and, from 1917, 150 lithographs. He found his major inspiration in the etchings of Goya, but his subjects generally reflected those of his paintings, such as portraits (etchings of *H. B. Kinck*, 1914 and 1920), scenes with children (etchings of *Boys Skiing*, 1916), folk legends (lithograph of the giant *Askeladden*, 1929) and landscape (lithograph view of the hill *Falketind*, 1935). During the last two decades of his life Werenskiold's pictorial style changed very little, but several new subjects emerged, most notably pictures on social themes such as *The Dinner* (1928–30; Oslo, N.G.). Throughout his career Werenskiold wrote frequently in the Norwegian press on art both in Norway and abroad.

WRITINGS

Kunst, kamp, kultur [Art, struggle, culture] (Kristiania, 1917) [collected articles, 1881–1910]

BIBLIOGRAPHY

Bénézit; *NBL*; *NKL*

Erik Werenskiold (Kristiania, 1913) [illus.]

T. Svedfelt: *Erik Werenskiolds konst* [Erik Werenskiold's art] (Stockholm, 1938/R 1947)

E. Blomberg: 'Werenskiold som tecknare' [Werenskiold as a draughtsman], *Konstrevy*, xvi (1940), pp. 46–57

E. Ingebretsen: *Erik Werenskiolds tegninger* [Erik Werenskiold's drawings] (Oslo, 1941)

L. Østby: 'Erik Werenskiold', *Amer. Scand. Rev.*, xliv (1956), pp. 38–49

Erik Werenskiold: Drawings (exh. cat., Oslo, Kstforen., 1965) [text in Norw. and Eng.]

L. Østby: *Erik Werenskiold* (Oslo, 1966)

A. Elvin: 'Werenskiolds bokillustrationer', *Biblis* (Stockholm, 1973), pp. 8–75

L. Østby: *Erik Werenskiold: Tegninger og akvareller* [Erik Werenskiold: drawings and watercolours] (Oslo, 1977) [with Eng. summary]

A. Elvin: 'Erik Werenskiold och två folkvisor' [Erik Werenskiold and two folktales], *Kst & Kult.* [Oslo], xi (1978), pp. 221–38

Northern Light: Realism and Symbolism in Scandinavian Painting, 1880–1910 (exh. cat., New York, Brooklyn Mus., 1982)

1880-årene i nordisk maleri [The 1880s in Nordic painting] (exh. cat., Oslo, N.G.; Stockholm, Nmus.; Helsinki, Anderson Mus. A.; Copenhagen; Stat. Mus. Kst; 1985), pp. 264–71

Maleren og tegneren Erik Werenskiold [The painter and draughtsman Erik Werenskiold] (exh. cat., Modum, Blaafarveværk, 1985)

Dreams of a Summer Night: Scandinavian Painting at the Turn of the Century (exh. cat., ACGB, 1986)

LEIF ØSTBY

Werff, Adriaen van der (*b* Kralinger-Ambacht, nr Rotterdam, 21 Jan 1659; *d* Rotterdam, 12 Nov 1722). Dutch painter and draughtsman. He was apprenticed to the portrait painter Cornelis Picolet (1626–79) from 1668 to 1670 and then from *c*.1671 to 1676 to Eglon van der Neer in Rotterdam. From 1676 van der Werff produced small portraits and genre paintings as an independent master; the *Cook and Hunter at a Window* (1678; New York, priv. col.; see Gaethgens, no. 2) and *Man and Woman Seated at a Table* (1678; St Petersburg, Hermitage) perpetuate the thematic and stylistic traditions of Gerrit Dou, Gabriel Metsu, Frans van Mieris and Gerard ter Borch (ii) but are distinguished by their greater elegance and richness of costume and interior. Van der Werff's portraits date mainly from the years 1680–95 (e.g. *Two Children with a Guinea-pig and a Kitten* (1681; London, Buckingham Pal., Royal Col.)). The motif of children with animals recalls van der Neer, while the careful depiction of fabrics recalls the Leiden school of 'Fine' painters. His *Portrait of a Man in a Quilted Gown* (1685; London, N.G.) resembles compositions by Caspar Netscher and Nicolaes Maes: a figure leaning against a balustrade, before a landscape. Van der Werff's work is, however, more elegant, in part because of the depiction of fabrics, but also because of

the inclusion for the first time of Classical sculpture, in this case the Farnese *Flora* (Naples, Mus. N.), copied from Jan de Bisschop's engraved *Signorum veterum icones* (The Hague, 1668–9).

Children Playing before a Statue of Hercules (1687; Munich, Alte Pin.) is a genre piece enhanced by a moralizing theme (exhorting young artists to persevere on the path of science and art). In this work the 'Fine' painting technique is united with Classical and classicizing elements. Van der Werff took his subject from Cesare Ripa's *Iconologia* (Dut. edn, 1644); the children were based on van der Neer's *Children at Play* and *Two Boys with a Birdcage* (both Brunswick, Herzog Anton Ulrich-Mus.); and the Classical sculpture group of *Hercules and the Hydra* was inspired by Artus Quellinus the elder's sculpture in the Amsterdam Stadhuis (now Royal Palace), François Perrier's engraved *Segmenta nobilium signorum et statuarium* (Rome, 1638) and the print after Domenichino's *Scourging of St Andrew* (Rome, Oratory of S Andrea Apostolo presso S Gregorio al Celio) reproduced in Jan de Bisschop's *Paradigmata graphices variorum artificium* (The Hague, 1671). This, van der Werff's multi-figured composition set in a large space, is the first incidence of the deliberate use of Classical art as a source.

In 1687 van der Werff, by then a successful artist, married the wealthy Margaretha Rees (1669–1731), whose guardian, Nicolaes Anthonis Flinck, owned a collection of prints and paintings through which van der Werff became further acquainted with Classical and Renaissance art, as well as the French and Italian Baroque styles. In Amsterdam Flinck also introduced van der Werff to Jan Six, a collector of Italian drawings and Classical sculpture, and to Philip de Flines, the head of the literary classicizing society Nil Volentibus Arduum, founded together with Gérard de Lairesse in 1669. Van der Werff's *Architectura and Pictura* (1692; mostly destr.; the middle part depicting *Fame* was discovered in 1994 and is now in Rotterdam, Hist. Mus., see Gaethgens, no. 37) is a *trompe l'oeil* ceiling piece in the manner of Lairesse's allegorical wall and ceiling paintings for de Fines. The *Amorous Couple* (1694; Amsterdam, Rijksmus.) typifies van der Werff's sensual, mythologically inspired works produced from 1685 to 1695. It contrasts with the severely classicizing style, with exaggeratedly slender, idealized nude figures, that he later adopted.

In 1691 and 1695 van der Werff was head of the Rotterdam Guild of St Luke. In 1696 his *Children Playing before a Statue of Hercules* was acquired by Johan Wilhelm, Elector Palatine, who also ordered a *Judgement of Solomon* and a *Self-portrait* (both Florence, Uffizi). The following year van der Werff received a contract that made him the highest-paid court painter, with the stipulation that he should work exclusively for the Elector for six months of every year at an annual salary of 4000 guilders. From this time on, van der Werff's work consisted primarily of religious subjects, in which he perfected his much-admired smooth style. Compared with an early version of *Hagar Brought before Abraham* (1696; St Petersburg, Hermitage), that painted for the Elector (1699; Munich, Alte Pin.) exhibits a complete transition to classicism in its ordered composition, monumental and classicizing draperies and idealized figure of Abraham (derived from prints after

Roman sculptures of the Tiber and the Nile). This painting is one of the erotically tinged Old Testament scenes that van der Werff had been painting since 1693, a group that also included *Lot and his Daughters* (1694; Dresden, Gemäldegal., destr.; see Gaethgens, no. 43).

For the *Entombment* (1703; versions Munich, Alte Pin., and St Petersburg, Hermitage), van der Werff received a hereditary title of nobility (invariably reflected in his signature after 1703) as well as a commission for 15 paintings depicting the *Mysteries of the Rosary* (Schleissheim, Staatsgal.), including the *Presentation of Christ* (1705) and the *Annunciation* (1706). The *Rosary* series was completed in 1716 with the allegory of the *Homage of the Arts to their Patrons* (sketches Munich, Graph. Samml.). In this painting (see fig.), figures representing Painting, who holds the artist's own self-portrait, and the Free Arts venerate a double portrait of the Elector and his wife which surmounts a pyramid with an inscription praising the Elector as a patron. A recurring feature of van der Werff's work is the repeated use of motifs, as in the *Judgement of Paris* (1712; Dresden, Gemäldegal., destr.; see Gaethgens, no.31) in which Paris is a repetition of the figure of Adam in *Adam and Eve* (1711; Brunswick, Herzog Anton Ulrich-Mus.). The figure of Venus in *Venus and Cupid* (1716; London, Wallace) recalls that of Diana in *Diana and Callisto* (1704; Rotterdam, Boymans–van Beuningen), which, in turn, was derived from Cornelis

Adriaen van der Werff: *Homage of the Arts to their Patrons*, oil on panel, 813×573 mm, 1716 (Schleissheim, Staatsgalerie im Neuen Schloss Schleissheim)

Cort's print after a painting by Titian (Vienna, Ksthist. Mus.).

After the death of the Elector in 1716, van der Werff depended on the open market, where his work fetched high prices. In 1722 he sold ten paintings, including the *Venus and Cupid*, one of six known paintings of *Mary Magdalene* (1719; destr.; see Gaethgens, no. 100) and the *Finding of Moses* (1722; Rennes, Mus. B.-A. & Archéol.), to Gregory Page of Greenwich for 34,600 guilders.

Van der Werff was internationally admired as the most important Dutch painter during his lifetime, but late 18th-century art critics denigrated his 'ivory' flesh tones and slick technique as 'lifeless' (even while collectors still paid high prices for his work). The 19th century stigmatized him as a betrayer of the 'true' Dutch realistic style. He was, in fact, the last great 'Fine' painter, who succeeded in adapting this popular style to history subjects with classically inspired figures. His students included Philip van Dijk, Hendrik van Limborch (1681–1759), Bartholomeus Douven (1688–after 1726), Johann Christian Sperling (1690–1746) and his brother and collaborator, Pieter van der Werff (1661–1722), a painter of portraits and genre pieces in Adriaen's early style.

BIBLIOGRAPHY
Adriaen van der Werff (1659–1722): Hofmaler des Kurfürsten Johann Wilhelm von der Pfalz (exh. cat. by P. Eikemeier, Munich, Alte Pin., 1972)
Adriaen van der Werff (Kralingen 1659–1722 Rotterdam) (exh. cat. by D. P. Snoep and C. Tiels, Rotterdam, Hist. Mus., 1973)
B. Gaethgens: *Adriaen van der Werff, 1659–1722* (Munich, 1987); reviews by M. Royalton–Kisch: *Burl. Mag.*, mxxx (1989), pp. 41–2, and J. Becker: *Oud-Holland*, cv (1991), pp. 74–81
De Hollandse fijnschilders: Van Gerard Dou tot Adriaen van der Werff (exh. cat. by P. Hecht, Amsterdam, Rijksmus., 1989), pp. 248–79
C. Thiels: 'Adriaen van der Werff, schilder van kamerstukken', *Rotterdamse meesters uit de Gouden Eeuw* [Rotterdam masters of the Golden Age], (exh. cat., ed. N. Schadee; Rotterdam, Hist. Mus., 1994), pp. 153–64, cat. nos 70–78
J. E. P. LEISTRA

Wergant, Fortunat. *See* BERGANT, FORTUNAT.

Werkman, Hendrik Nicolaas (*b* Leens, 29 April 1882; *d* Bakkeveen, 10 April 1945). Dutch painter and printmaker. In 1896 he saw an exhibition of Vincent van Gogh's work, and when he started to paint in 1917, it was initially in an Expressionistic style, akin to that of van Gogh, but later in a manner which was close to the expressionism of De Ploeg (The Plough), the Groningen artists' society that he joined in 1920. In 1922 he saw an exhibition in Groningen of the art of De Stijl artists. His printing business, which he had run from 1907, went bankrupt in 1923; after this he continued to print but at a smaller business. In addition to commercial print he produced posters, programmes for De Ploeg and the magazine the *Next Call*, through which he reached the European avant-garde.

Werkman's *vrije werken-druksels* (free work-prints), as he called them, were, until 1929, abstract compositions with geometric shapes, letters and figures, which betray the influence of De Stijl and of Constructivism. In 1929 he travelled to Cologne and Paris. After 1929 he also used a stamp-technique; in his work figurative and abstract elements alternate. From 1934 he applied stencils, usually in combination with other printing techniques. In 1939 he met Willem Sandberg who organized an exhibition of his work at the Stedelijk Museum in Amsterdam. During World War II he printed and published a large number of illegal publications under the name of the Blauwe Schuit (Blue Barge). An important publication was the Hassidic Legends. Shortly before the liberation he was captured and executed without trial by the Sicherheitsdienst.

BIBLIOGRAPHY
J. Martinet and W. Sandberg: *Hot Printing: Catalogus van druksels en voorlopige catalogus van gebruiksdrukwerk, litho's etsen, noutsneden tiksels en schilderijen van Hendrik Nicolaas Werkmaan* (Amsterdam, 1963); Eng. trans. by J. Brockway as *Hot Printing: Catalogue of the 'Drukselprints', General Printed Matter, Lithographs, Etchings, Woodcuts, Typewriter Compositions and Paintings by Hendrik Nicolaas Werkman* (Amsterdam, 1963)
Hendrik Nicolaas Werkman, 1882–1945: Een Kenze uit 'druksels' en gebruiksdrukwerk/A Selection of 'Druksel' Prints and General Printed Matter (exh. cat. by J. Martinet, Amsterdam, Stedel. Mus., 1977)

JOHN STEEN

Werl [Wörl], Hans (*b* Munich, *c.* 1570; *d* Munich, 1608). German painter and draughtsman. In 1588–9 he was working as a journeyman for Alexander Paduano at the court in Munich and in 1594 he became court painter to William V, Duke of Bavaria. The high regard that he enjoyed was reflected in his salary, which was almost as high as Peter Candid's. His carefully worked miniatures and his subtle though hardly original altarpieces and devotional pictures, such as the *Auxiliary Saints* (*c.* 1590; Munich, Frauenkirche), fulfilled the requirements of the Counter-Reformation, and he constantly received important commissions. In 1600 he painted the altarpiece of the *Virgin in Glory with Female Saints* for the newly built chapel of the Residenz. In 1601 he collaborated with Candid in painting scenes from Bavarian history, for example the *Battle at Mühldorf* (Burghausen, Staatsgal. Hauptburg) in the Herkulessaal of the Residenz, and in 1602 he painted the ceiling of the Schwarzer Saal (destr. 1944), created as an architectural perspective. He was consulted as a specialist and on occasion even described as an architect. His portraits (1593–1608; seven, Berchtesgaden, Schlossmus.; five, Schleissheim, Neues Schloss; one, Munich, Bayer. Nmus.) of the ducal family, even the miniatures, are notable for their precision and factual accuracy.

Thieme–Becker   BIBLIOGRAPHY
B. Knüttel: 'Zur Geschichte der Münchner Residenz, 1600–1610', *Münchn. Jb. Bild. Kst.*, n. s. 2, xviii (1967), pp. 187–210
Zeichnung in Deutschland: Deutsche Zeichner, 1540–1640, i (exh. cat. by H. Geissler, Stuttgart, Staatsgal., 1979–80), pp. 150–51

HEINRICH GEISSLER

Wermuth, Christian (*b* Altenburg, 16 Dec 1661; *d* Gotha, 3 Dec 1739). German medallist. He trained in Dresden as a die-cutter with Ernst Caspar Dürr (*fl* 1683–92) and as an engraver with a man named Pieler. In 1686 he became a die-cutter at the Mint of the House of Schwarzburg in Sondershausen, becoming Court Medallist to the House of Saxe-Gotha in 1688. He refused the post of die-cutter in Berlin offered to him in 1703. Although he remained in Gotha, he received the title of Royal Prussian Court Medallist. In 1699 he received an Imperial privilege that permitted him to strike medals in his own house and was intended to protect his work against unauthorized imitation. In his workshop he trained numerous apprentices, including his three sons and his eldest daughter, as expert die-cutters. More than 1300 medals were produced in this workshop, among them a series of 214 portraits of Roman and Holy Roman Emperors, about 100 satirical medals, numerous pieces for members of the European royal families (e.g. *King James II*; London, BM), as well as others commemorating contemporary events. His medals were available in gold, silver, copper and pewter and were offered for sale in printed catalogues entitled *Specificatio derer Medaillen oder Schau-Stücke*, of which several editions appeared between 1698 and 1713.

BIBLIOGRAPHY
ADB; Forrer; Thieme–Becker
J. H. Lochner: *Sammlung merkwürdiger Medaillen*, vi (Nuremberg, 1742)
C. Wohlfahrt: *Christian Wermuth: Ein deutscher Medailleur der Barockzeit* (diss., Halle, Martin Luther-U., 1979)
H. Hennrich and W. Steguweit: 'Sammlung Christian Wermuth', *Alte Taler des Münzkabinetts Gotha* (Gotha, 1983), pp. 11–13

HERMANN MAUÉ

Werner. German family of artists, active in Sweden. Johan Werner the elder (*b* Jägerndorf, *c.* 1600; *d* Vadstena, 10 March 1656) was working in Sweden, probably by 1619, as a decorator, possibly in the castle at Vadstena, Östergötland. From 1637 he was employed as court painter by Count Per Brahe the younger (1602–80). His main work was the sculptured and painted decoration (1637–1660s) of the Brahe Church on the island of Visingsö in Lake Vättern. He was also asked to execute paintings and sculptures (1650s) in the castle at Läckö, but much of this work probably remained unfinished. In addition, he executed a rather naive panoramic equestrian portrait of the Count (1649; Bålsta, Skoklosters Slott), depicting him in a vast landscape in which three of his residences can be seen. Johan Werner the younger (*b c.* 1630; *bur* Gränna, 10 Nov 1691), the son of Johan Werner the elder, also worked for the Count as a portrait painter, sculptor and master builder. He designed the small town hall (*c.* 1675) of Gränna in Småland, a town founded by Brahe. As a sculptor in wood and as a painter, he cooperated with his father in the long-term project of interior decorations in the Brahe Church and in Läckö Castle for Magnus Gabriel De la Gardie. As figure sculptors, the Werners can best be judged from their *Apostles* and *Angels* made for the Brahe Church. Although awkward in stature, the figures now and then show surprisingly vivid and energetic faces on the verge of humorous caricature. As wall painters, the Werners were naively expressive, as evidenced in the rendering of the family tree in the Brahe Church. Finally, they seem to have been much occupied as copyists of Brahe family portraits and of portraits of Swedish kings and queens, most of which are lost. Possibly they painted original portraits from life too, but this is harder to prove. Johan Werner II may have been responsible for a rather large oil portrait of the governor of the province of Småland, *Johan Björnsson Printz (1592–1663)*, in the parish church of Bottnaryd near Jönköping. It depicts an immensely obese man, seemingly in his late 50s or 60s, dressed in black and wearing armour: one hand is on the ivory knob of his stick while the other holds a plumaged hat. Body and dress are summarily, almost plainly, executed, but the broad, massive face conveys a calm, if watchful authority. It is a straightforward likeness without any trace of idealization. If this portrait really is an original by Werner, he was a skilful if somewhat crude portraitist, but Werner's authorship is by no means secure. Although neither was a great artist, the two Werners were remarkable representatives of Swedish provincial art.

BIBLIOGRAPHY

SVKL; Thieme–Becker

A. Hahr: *Konst och konstnärer vid M. G. De la Gardies hof* [Art and artists at the court of M. G. De la Gardie] (Uppsala, 1905)

W. Nisser: *Per Brahe d y:s, 'hofkonterfeijare'* [Per Brahe the younger's 'court painter'], ix of *Meddelanden fran Norra Smålands Fornminnesförening* [Reports from the antiquarian association of northern Sweden] (Jönköping, 1929), pp. 25–90

A. L. Romdahl: 'Johan Werner d a:s, förlagebok, Röhsska konstslöjdmuseet' [Johan Werner the elder, inventory, Röhss art museum], *Arstryck* (Gothenburg, 1949)

G. Axel-Nilsson: *Dekorativ stenhuggarkonst i yngre vasastil* [Ornamental sculpture of the later Vasa style] (Stockholm, 1950)

F. Eltving: *Kring Johan Björnsson Printz, II: Om familjeporträtten* [About Johan Björnsson Printz, II: on his family portraits] (Gothenburg, 1988)

TORBJÖRN FULTON

Werner, Anton (Alexander) von (*b* Frankfurt an der Oder, 9 May 1843; *d* Berlin, 4 Jan 1915). German painter and illustrator. He studied at the Akademie der Künste in Berlin from 1859 and in 1862 moved to Karlsruhe, where he studied with Johann Wilhelm Schirmer, Ludwig Des Coudres (1820–78) and Adolf Schrödter. Under the influence of Karl Friedrich Lessing he became interested in history painting. He was a friend of the poet Victor von Scheffel and illustrated his works (e.g. *Gaudeamus*, 1867). In 1867 he was in Paris and in 1868–9 in Italy. On returning to Germany in 1870 he received his first important commissions. He specialized in detailed scenes of contemporary events, particularly those involving soldiers. His best-known work, *William of Prussia Proclaimed Emperor of Germany, 18th January 1870* (1877, destr.; version, Friedrichsruh, Bismarck-Mus.), depicts the event he had witnessed at Versailles; it is a typical example of his sober, Naturalistic style and his taste for patriotic subjects. In 1874 he became a member of the Akademie der Künste in Berlin and a year later was appointed director. In 1909 he succeeded Hugo von Tschudi as director of the Nationalgalerie in Berlin. Werner was a favourite of William II, who appears in many of his paintings. Both their meticulous detail and military subjects appealed to the Emperor and his circle but were much criticized and ridiculed by progressive circles, as was Werner's reactionary attitude towards politics and culture. His work, immensely popular during his lifetime, fell out of favour with the rise of modernism, which he had implacably opposed.

BIBLIOGRAPHY

P. Paret: 'The Tschudi Affair', *J. Mod. Hist.*, liii (1981)

D. Bartmann: *Anton von Werner* (Berlin, 1985)

SEPP KERN

Werner, Joseph, II (*b* Berne, *bapt* 22 June 1637; *d* Berne, 1710). Swiss painter, active in France and Germany. His work is diverse in form—ranging from portrait miniatures to ceiling paintings—and eclectic in manner, drawing on a wide range of 17th-century influences. Like his biography, it is marked by restlessness and inner division. The surviving oeuvre securely attributed to him comprises only 56 oil paintings, 47 miniatures, 60 drawings and 2 etchings (Glaesemer). The quality is uneven, and a clear line of development is difficult to discern. A decline in Werner's creative powers set in long before his death.

Werner was the son of a painter of the same name (*fl*1637; *d* after 1675). He left the Calvinist milieu of Berne in 1649 to train in Basle and from 1650 learnt oil painting in Frankfurt am Main under Matthäus Merian (ii), a cosmopolitan and versatile painter. He went on to Italy between 1652 and 1654. In the tradition of Hans Rottenhammer II, Friedrich Brentel I and Johann Wilhelm Baur, Werner treated the subject-matter of the large-format panel painting with great delicacy. In a *Self-portrait* produced in Rome (1662; London, V&A; see fig.), the only known work from his Italian stay, the 25-year-old artist is seen in full possession of his technical powers, exhibiting the self-confidence of an academically trained painter. In Rome he was in contact, either as pupil or friend, with such artists as Nicolas Poussin, Carlo Maratti and Andrea Sacchi, whose influence is seen in a sometimes contradictory way in his work. The gloomy solemnity of Salvator Rosa was also an important stimulus.

Werner gained a reputation in Italy that led Louis XIV to summon him in 1662 to Paris, where he was successful primarily as a painter of portrait miniatures in mythological guise—for example *Louis XIV as Apollo in his Chariot*

Joseph Werner: *Self-portrait*, watercolour on parchment, 221× 154 mm, 1662 (London, Victoria and Albert Museum)

(*c.* 1663–4; Versailles, Château). He now gave a precious, Manneristic quality to the treatment of figures, especially to the facial expression, creating a courtly effect. Even in his earlier work, for example *St Hubert* (1664; Berne, Kstmus.), we find a highly detailed depiction of landscape, reminiscent of Elsheimer, that can be regarded as a German element in his painting. This was accompanied by a taste for sumptuous architecture, parks, fountains and other examples of nature constrained and controlled. Werner was fond of emphasizing the conceptual, philosophical character of his art in such elaborate allegories as *Allegory of Justice* (1662; Berne, Kstmus.).

Werner left Paris in 1667, settling for 13 years in Augsburg, at that time the leading centre for bourgeois art in southern Germany. There, the following year, he married Susanna Mayr, a sister of the painter Johann Ulrich Mayr. He was in contact with Joachim von Sandrart, who worked in Augsburg in 1670–74, and with other artists who had formed a private academy. From Augsburg Werner undertook a number of short journeys to such places as Zurich, Innsbruck and Munich, where he executed a ceiling painting (1672/3; *in situ*) in Schloss Nymphenburg. Earlier, in 1669/70, he had painted eight miniatures with scenes from the *Life of the Virgin* (Munich, Residenzmus.) for Electress Henrietta Adelaide of Bavaria. A number of oil paintings in a harsh chiaroscuro style are known from the Augsburg period. Their composition is strongly influenced by Poussin, as in *Perseus with the Nymphs* (Augsburg, Schaezlerpal.) and a *Last Supper* (1676) in the Protestant Heilig-Kreuz-Kirche. He also produced a number of drawings (five examples in Hamburg, Ksthalle), mainly ghostly scenes with magicians, witches, treasure-diggers and demons, like sketches from the circle of Johann Heinrich Schönfeld, also then working in Augsburg. Displaying agitated brushwork, they form a curious contrast to his academic pieces with their stress on the rational. Finally, a few delicately drawn ideal portraits of girls in profile (example, 1677; Vienna, Albertina) have survived from the Augsburg period.

Werner left Augsburg in 1680 for unknown reasons, returning to his native Berne. Between 1680 and 1682 he must also have gone to Vienna to paint seven miniature portraits (Munich, Residenzmus.) of the imperial family. In their joyless formality they are no match for the portraits of his Paris period. In Berne, Werner's talent was focused on his preferred field of miniature painting. The citizens required of him mainly conventional portraits painted in oils (e.g. *Maria Steiger as a Child*, 1696; Schloss Toffen, nr Berne), a task that he performed with technical skill but little psychological insight. He also produced decorative works for interiors, sometimes with allegorical statements, for example an overdoor at Schloss Toffen. In keeping with his pedagogical convictions he formed a private academy on Sandrart's model. It laid the foundation for a modest flowering of Bernese art in the 18th century and ensured him a lasting reputation in his homeland.

Werner's prestige as an exponent of the academic idea was such that in 1696 he was appointed director of the academy founded by Elector Frederick III of Brandenburg, although he was hardly known as an artist in Berlin. However, he proved to have neither the authority as an artist nor the organizational abilities to head the institute,

and after the fall of the minister responsible for his appointment, Eberhard von Dankelmann, in 1699, Werner too was relieved of his post and kept on merely as rector. He left Berlin in 1707, without having given any significant proof of artistic merit. He spent his last years in Berne; here too he was no longer productive.

BIBLIOGRAPHY

J. von Sandrart: *Teutsche Academie* (1675–9); ed. A. R. Peltzer (1925)

J. C. Füssli: *Geschichte der besten Künstler in der Schweiz*, ii (Zurich, 1769)

I. Kunze: 'Joseph Werner', *Pantheon*, xxx (1942), pp. 163–7

Augsburger Barock (exh. cat., Augsburg, Rathaus and Holbeinhaus, 1968), pp. 153–5, 275–8

J. Glaesemer: *Joseph Werner, 1637–1710* (Zurich and Munich, 1974)

HELMUT BÖRSCH-SUPAN

Werner, Theodor (*b* Jettenburg, Württemberg, 14 Feb 1886; *d* Munich, 15 Jan 1969). German painter. He trained at the Staatliche Akademie der Bildenden Künste, Stuttgart (1908–9), before travelling in Europe (1909–14). Having served during World War I, he returned to Stuttgart, moving to Paris in 1930. There he began for the first time to escape the various European artistic influences of the age, particularly those of Paul Cézanne and Juan Gris, towards whose work he had been vaguely orientating his paintings. He joined the group Abstraction–Création. Without abandoning his figurative means of representation, the basic elements of his work circled around his central artistic concern, the complementary function of figure and ground, line and surface.

Werner took part in the first *Documenta* exhibition in Kassel (1955), exhibiting *Creatio ex Nihilo* (mixed media on canvas, 1.17×1.27 m, 1942–4; Munich, Staatsgal. Mod. Kst), a work from the first mature phase of Werner's work, which ended *c.* 1949. As a member of the Zen group (1950–55), he was already one of the most important representatives of the German *Art informel*. During the 1950s he experimented with the now autonomous components of colour, line, structure and facture. Calligraphic signs and cubical, geometrical forms fill his paintings, whose early expressive colourfulness was replaced towards the end of the decade by subdued, monochromatic tonalities. Experiments with new ways of doing things extended from spray techniques via monochromatic printing to the use of sand or large particles of paint to create an enriched, thickened and cracked paint surface. These various media are all carried by the rhythmic nature of the composition, which also shapes one of Werner's major works, the mural (1954) for the foyer of the concert hall at the Hochschule für Musik, Berlin. Keeping the emphasis on compositional rhythm, in his late work of the 1960s he concentrated on the representation of ideograms, undeciphered and undecipherable signs, which are brought out by the spatula from a monochrome surface. Condemned as 'degenerate' during World War II (*see* ENTARTETE KUNST), he lived in Berlin from 1946 until 1959, when he moved to Munich.

BIBLIOGRAPHY

Theodor Werner: Werke aus den Jahren 1901–1961 (exh. cat., W. Berlin, Akad. Kst., 1962)

B. Lohkamp: *Theodor Werner: Ein Beitrag zur Geschichte der deutschen Malerei und Kunstästhetik* (diss., U. Munich, 1975)

Theodor Werner (exh. cat., Munich, Staatsgal. Mod. Kst, 1979)

BEATRICE V. BISMARCK

Wernher, Sir **Julius** (*b* Darmstadt, 9 April 1850; *d* London, 21 May 1912). British industrialist, collector and philanthropist of German birth. He was educated in Frankfurt and in 1871 he went to South Africa, where he worked in the diamond mining industry. With Alfred Beit, elder brother of Sir Otto Beit, he founded what became the Central Mining and Investment Corporation, and he became a British citizen in 1898. Wernher was a generous benefactor of hospitals and educational institutions. He was created baronet in 1905.

In addition to his London home, Bath House (destr. *c.* 1960) in Piccadilly, Wernher acquired in 1903 Luton Hoo in Bedfordshire, rebuilt in the 1760s by Robert Adam for John Stuart, 3rd Earl of Bute. He commissioned alterations to both houses in the then fashionable French 18th-century style of interior decoration, creating an ornate background for the display of his collection of European art. Of his acquisitions, the pictures alone numbered 250; they included Joshua Reynolds's portrait of *Lady Caroline Price*, acquired in 1893; Titian's portrait of *Giacomo Doria*, purchased *c.* 1902; *Christ Taking Leave of his Mother* by Albrecht Altdorfer, purchased *c.* 1904 (all Luton Hoo, Beds); and Antoine Watteau's *La Gamme d'amour* (London, N.G.). Such pictures as these reflect the considerable breadth of Wernher's taste in art, as do his extensive collections of sculpture, medieval ivories, Renaissance metalware, Limoges enamels, maiolica, jewels and tapestries. His wife, Lady Wernher, born Alice Sedgwick Mankiewicz (m. 1888, *d* 1945), formed a unique collection of English porcelain. Their son, Sir Harold Augustus Wernher (1893–1973), and his wife, Lady Anastasia (Zia) Wernher, also added to the family collections, which remained the property of their descendants at Luton Hoo until the 1990s, when financial difficulties led to the sale of some items.

BIBLIOGRAPHY
A. A. Longden, J. Natanson and H. A. Wernher: *The Wernher Collection* (Luton Hoo, 1950)
R. Trevelyan: *Grand Dukes and Diamonds* (London, 1991)

JANET SOUTHORN

Wersin, Wolfgang von (*b* Prague, 3 Dec 1882; *d* Bad Ischl, 13 June 1976). German designer and painter of Czech birth. He studied architecture at the Czech Technical University in Prague (1900–01) and the Technische Hochschule in Munich (1901–4), where he gained his preliminary diploma in architecture in 1904. From 1902 to 1905 he also studied drawing and painting at the Lehr- und Versuch-Atelier für Angewandte und Freie Kunst in Munich. After military service he became a tutor there from 1906 onwards; his future wife and constant collaborator in later years, the German printmaker and draughtswoman Herthe Schöpp (1888–1971), was one of his pupils. In 1909 he began working as a designer for numerous firms, including the Behr furniture factory and the Meissen porcelain manufacturers. East-Asian forms characterized many of his furniture designs, but eventually he detached himself from any kind of influence, including rural folk art, and achieved a timelessly classical style of great objectivity, revealed above all in articles for everyday use,

such as porcelain, glass and tableware (examples in Munich, Bayer. Nmus., Neue Samml., and Berlin, Tiergarten, Kstgewmus.).

Through his experience in planning exhibitions for the Neue Sammlung des Bayerischen Nationalmuseum between 1925 and 1929, Wersin was commissioned as its chief curator in 1929. The exhibitions he held there, such as *Der billige Gegenstand* or *Ewige Formen*, brought well-made, functional, reasonably priced objects within reach of wider sections of the public. Unjustly deprived of his post by the National Socialists in 1934, von Wersin left Munich in 1944 after further years as a designer and adviser for various firms, and moved to Upper Austria. From 1948 to 1963 he ran a master-class in interior design at the Kunstschule der Stadt Linz. Until late in life he was President of the Österreichische Werkbund and participated in its exhibitions.

WRITINGS
Das elementare Ornament und seine Gesetzlichkeit (Ravensburg, 1941)
Das Buch vom Rechteck—Gesetz und Gestik des Räumlichen (Ravensburg, 1956)

BIBLIOGRAPHY
Vom Adel der Form zum reinen Raum: Wolfgang von Wersin zum 80. Geburtstag (Linz, 1962)
Wolfgang von Wersin (1882–1976): Gestaltung und Produktentwicklung (exh. cat., Linz, Stadtmus., 1983)
B. Mundt: *Produkt-design, 1900–1990: Eine Auswahl*, Berlin, Tiergarten, Kstgewmus. cat., 43 (Berlin, 1991), pp. 88–9

ELKE OSTLÄNDER

Wertinger, Hans (*b* Landshut, *c.* 1465–70; *d* Landshut, 1533). German painter and woodcutter. An artist as ambitious as Lucas Cranach I, he became one of Germany's first accredited court painters, working for the Dukes of Landshut in the triangular area defined by Ingolstadt, Straubing and Munich. The son of a functionary working for the Dukes, he was probably first taught by a certain Sigmund Gleismüller (*c.* 1449–1511). Hans Mair (Mair von Landshut), who had come from Augsburg and had settled in Landshut, seems to have prompted him to work as a journeyman in Augsburg. His acquisition of citizen's rights in Landshut in 1491 suggests he was a master by that date. Mair seemingly procured him a series of commissions between 1497 and 1499 from Prince Bishop Philipp of Freising (1480–1541). The only work to survive from this period, however, is the large panel of the *Life of St Sigismund* (1498) in Freising Cathedral. It retains the deep tones associated with Augsburg painting, and its shape, with a pointed arch at the top, must also have been developed in Augsburg. As in Mair's work, several scenes are assembled in the arch and the side sections, creating a cramped Late Gothic framing architecture, but Wertinger divests this of fantastical elements. The large heads and bulky angular bodies are also typically Late Gothic, yet the scenes of Sigismund's martyrdom are set out in a peaceful way.

Wertinger could already here employ journeymen. In the following period, however, he would have received no commissions from the court at Landshut as the deaths of George the Rich in 1503 and of his successor Albert III in 1508 brought court life to a temporary standstill. At this time Wertinger received commissions (untraced) from Elector Frederick III of Saxony. Glass paintings in the

Hans Wertinger: *Alexander and his Doctor Philip*, oil on panel, 1.08×1.25 m, 1517 (Prague, National Museum)

north choir window of St Jakob in Straubing, relating to the guild of braziers, and possibly also that church's badly preserved *Three Kings* window, likewise belong before 1511, the year of Wertinger's first surviving dated work. This is a glass pane in the Heiliggeistkirche at Landshut painted with the Bavarian coat of arms. His teacher Gleismüller is documented as the designer; it is Gleismüller's only known work.

Of Wertinger's paintings, it is only those dating from 1515 onwards that have been preserved in considerable numbers. This was also the year of his first woodcuts, made for Johann Weyssenburger, who had moved to Landshut from Nuremberg in 1513: first, a single sheet known as the *Opening of the Abyss* and the Classical *Calumny of Apelles*; then the title woodcuts for a translation of Sallust by the Landshut humorist Dietrich von Pleningen (1450–1520), addressed to Emperor Maximilian; and later, *c.* 1517, a *Raising of Lazarus*, quite different from an earlier window on the same theme in Neuötting. Wertinger's output as a painter from 1515, showing his fully developed style, includes many portraits and glass paintings, but also altar wings, frescoes and easel paintings.

The portraits include one of his old patron *Prince-Bishop Philipp of Freising* (1515; Munich, Alte Pin.) and a series of six of the Prince-Bishop's close relatives (1515; four, Munich, Bayer. Nmus.). Other official commissions from 1515 include the portrait of *Degenhart Pfäffinger* (1471–1519) (priv. col., see V. Liedtke: 'Hans Wertinger und Sigmund Gleismüller: Zwei Hauptvertreter der Altlandshuter Malschule', *A. Bavar.*, i (1973), pp. 50–83, pl. 10), his agent at the court of Saxony, and the strange portrait of the Freising court dwarf *'Ritter Christoph'* (Madrid, Mus. Thyssen-Bornemisza), one of the earliest German full-length portraits. In 1516 he portrayed *Duke Ludwig X* (Munich, Bayer. Nmus.) in a white robe with slit sleeves under a dark fur-trimmed cloak, sitting on a bench with open countryside in the background. In 1517, under the guise of a history picture, *Alexander and his Doctor Philip* (Prague, N. Mus.; see fig.), Wertinger painted portraits of the two brothers and reigning dukes, Ludwig X and William IV, and of his sisters Sabine and Susanne; possibly the picture also contains a self-portrait. This painting indicates the high status he enjoyed at Landshut, which led to his installation as court painter in 1518, when he was presented with a court robe.

In the portraits, no doubt strongly influenced by the Danube school and Albrecht Altdorfer, Wertinger from the very first showed a liking for luxuriant golden festoons as decorative framing features. These were later replaced by shorter garlands with side tassels and finally, in works of the mid-1520s such as the diptych of *Duke William IV* and his wife (1526; Munich, Bayer. Nmus.), by twining bands of tendrils. At the same time the landscape in the background gained in importance. The facial features of the richly clad princes and court officials were represented only as a record of their outer appearance, with no attempt at conveying any depth of expression, and the hands were always depicted in the same way. The crucial thing is the rich decorative nature of the overall impression. The colouring becomes ever lighter and softer. This is particularly true of the glass paintings, which include the *St Anne* window and the splendid *Annunciation* (both 1527) in the Liebfrauenkirche at Ingolstadt. It also applies to the two early altar wings in the sacristy of Gündelkofen Pfarrkirche, near Landshut. On the front of the panels the *Freeing and Crucifixion of Peter* are shown in crowded groups set on a gold ground in a highly vertical format. The outer sides with the *Transfiguration of Christ* and *Agony in the Garden* have rich landscapes as backgrounds. In his late work at Freising Cathedral, the *Entombment*, the scene is likewise incorporated into the landscape. Wertinger's frescoes for the castle chapel and ducal suite at Burg Trausnitz in Landshut and the prince-bishop's Residenz in Freising have virtually vanished: only the *Seven Sorrows of Mary* in the church at Elsenbach bei Neumarkt gives some idea of his work in this field.

Wertinger was popularized mainly by two series of pictures of the months and the seasons; these are convincingly ascribed to him, and can be regarded as the finest product of his travels in the Tyrol in 1523. Eight pictures of the months have been preserved in the Germanisches Nationalmuseum in Nuremberg; apart from one small panel (St Petersburg, Hermitage), a second series, which on the basis of the five known paintings might also be of months rather than of seasons, is scattered in private collections. Their dimensions—c. 320×404 mm or 220×400 mm—indicate that they were used as wall panelling in a room. The scenes are set out in horizontal bands using bright local colours and encircled by golden festoons, and show typical activities such as countryfolk picnicking in *June* or nobles riding out to hunt with their falcons in *July*. There are no levels of allegorical meaning, nor any signs of the zodiac; the people go about their business in a carefree way. In the second series Wertinger expands the composition of Dürer's woodcut *Men Bathing* widthwise, with a loss of tension. Even so, some pictures from this series are more convincing than the Nuremberg ones, like *Deerhunting and Hayharvesting* (Bologna, priv. col., see Ehret, pl. 15). Knightly and peasant pastimes are strictly segregated by a fence with nets on it. The small Nuremberg panels are overladen with details, but there is a greater sense of depth in the landscape. In the other series, which must be later, the eye is drawn more to the foreground so that the naively depicted scenes unfold in all their immediacy.

Works from Wertinger's final years include a table-top with a map of Bavaria (1531; Munich, Bayer. Nmus.), hunting, bathing and dining scenes reminiscent of the months and seasons series, and lastly a 1532 epitaph panel for the chaplain Georg Widmann with the *Lamentation* (Freising, Diözmus.), a convincing recent attribution.

BIBLIOGRAPHY

G. Ehret: *Hans Wertinger: Ein Landshuter Maler an der Wende der Spätgotik zur Renaissance* (diss., U. Munich, 1976)

HANS GEORG GMELIN

Wertmüller, Adolf Ulric [Ulrik] (*b* Stockholm, 19 Feb 1751; *d* Chester, DE, 5 Oct 1811). Swedish painter. He was trained in sculpture and painting at the Stockholm Academy and was a student of Joseph-Marie Vien in Paris (1772–5) and Rome (1775–9). In 1781 he settled in Paris, painting *Ariadne on the Shore of Naxos* (1783; Stockholm, Nmus.), a meticulously executed Neo-classical work. He became a member of the French Academy in 1784 and First Painter to Gustavus III of Sweden. The latter commissioned him in 1784 to paint the massive *Marie Antoinette and her two Children Walking in the Trianon Gardens* (Stockholm, Nmus.). Wertmüller's most interesting work, *Danaë and the Shower of Gold* (1787; Stockholm, Nmus.), a masterpiece of mythological portrayal, is the foremost example of Swedish Neo-classical painting. A lack of portrait commissions in Paris prompted Wertmüller in 1788 to go and work for wealthy merchants in Bordeaux, Madrid and Cadiz. His career as a portrait painter proceeded successfully; his portraits display an unsentimental and cool, smooth style. In 1794 he went to Philadelphia where he painted *George Washington* in an intimate, realistic manner (1794; New York, Met.). During the following two years he produced portraits in Philadelphia, Annapolis and New York. Wertmüller went back to Sweden from 1797 to 1799, mostly painting family and friends. In 1800 he returned to the USA. His *Danaë*, which was shown to the public in Philadelphia in 1806, led to some commissions in 1806–8, but from 1802, due to failing sight, Wertmüller almost wholly abandoned painting for farming in Delaware.

BIBLIOGRAPHY

SKVL

M. N. Benisovich: 'Wertmüller et son livre de raison intitulé la Notte', *Gaz. B.-A.*, xlviii (1956), p. 51

——: 'Further Notes on A. U. Wertmüller in the United States and France', *A. Q.* [Detroit], xxvi (1963), pp. 7–30

F. D. Scott: *Wertmüller: Artist and Immigrant Farmer* (Chicago, 1963)

G. W. Lundberg: *Le Peintre suédois de Marie-Antoinette: Adolf Ulrik Wertmüller à Bordeaux, 1788–1790* (Bordeaux, 1970)

——: *Le Peintre suédois: Adolf Ulrik Wertmüller à Lyon, 1779–1781* (Lyon, 1973)

MARIANNE UGGLA

Werve, Claus de. *See* CLAUS DE WERVE.

Wéry, Emile-Auguste (*b* Reims, 3 Sept 1868; *d* ?June 1935). French painter. He trained in Paris at the Ecole des Beaux-Arts and started exhibiting at the Salon des Artistes Français, winning medals in 1897, 1898 and 1900. As a young man he introduced his friend and neighbour, Matisse, to an Impressionist style. Wéry, however, courted official success despite working in an Impressionist manner in such works as *Ferrymen of Amsterdam* (Paris, Mus. A. Mod. Ville Paris). In 1906 he exhibited a decorative frieze (untitled, repr. in *The Studio*, xxxvi, 1906, p. 368) at the Exposition Universelle in Liège and later that year was made Chevalier de la Légion d'honneur. He continued working in a decorative mode and received a diplôme d'honneur from the French government in 1925.

BIBLIOGRAPHY

P. Desjardins: 'Les Salons de 1899', *Gaz. B.-A.*, xxii (1899), pp. 132–56
L. Houticq: 'A travers les Salons', *A. & Déc.*, xxxvi (1914), pp. 1–14
J. D. Flam: *Matisse: The Man and his Art* (London, 1986), p. 42

TOM PARSONS

Wesel, Adriaen van (*b c.* 1417; *fl* Utrecht, 1447–89). North Netherlandish wood-carver. His name first appears in 1447 when he became a warden of the saddlers' guild in Utrecht, an office that he held nine times and for which a minimum age of 30 was specified, suggesting a birth date of about 1417. The first record of his work dates from 1475, when, at the age of at least 58, he received a commission for a carved altarpiece from the Confraternity of Our Lady, 's Hertogenbosch. The altarpiece was completed within the two years allocated, and van Wesel was paid an additional 36 Rhenish guilders above the 350 specified in the commission. Two small carved oak shutters representing the *Emperor Augustus and the Tiburtine Sibyl* and *St John on Patmos* survive in the possession of the confraternity and form a basis for the identification of other fragments from the carved wooden altarpiece. The shutters would have served a raised central section about 1.25 m wide, while large carved wings would presumably have been attached to the main body of the altarpiece, which alone must have been about 3.5 m wide. A reference to images beneath the altarpiece in 1477/8 suggests that there was also a predella. The altarpiece was polychromed in 1508/9, and two further shutters, added in 1488/9, were painted on the exterior by Hieronymus Bosch at an unspecified date and on the interior by Gielis van Panhedel in 1522/3.

Other carvings originally belonging to the lost altarpiece are: *Joseph with Music-making Angels*, a *Kneeling Virgin* from a *Nativity*, the *Meeting of the Magi*, the *Visitation* and the *Death of the Virgin* (all Amsterdam, Rijksmus.); a *Group of Shepherds* (Utrecht, Catharijneconvent); a *Virgin Reading*, probably from an *Annunciation* (Bruges, Gruuthusemus.); and a fragment of the *Adoration of the Magi* (untraced). A *St Barbara* and a small *Virgin and Child* from a *Tree of Jesse* may also have formed part of the altarpiece. The arrangement of scenes within the altarpiece is unclear, but the greater width of the *Meeting of the Magi* fragment suggests that it might have formed part of the central scene.

All other works by van Wesel are lost. The commission he received in 1484 for an altarpiece costing 1000 guilders for the high altar of the Nieuwe Kerk, Delft, specified that it should resemble the one in the church of St Mary, Utrecht, for which he was also responsible. He carved three groups for the high altar of the Buurkerk, Utrecht, in 1487 and began a carved altarpiece for the St Agnietenberg Convent, commissioned by Bishop David of Burgundy and costing 325 guilders. Seven carvings made in 1489 for the predella of the high altarpiece of Utrecht Cathedral are his last documented work.

The quality of van Wesel's carving lies in its expressive simplicity and economy of detail. Youthful facial types such as the angel musicians have a distinctive naivety, the hair tends to be arranged in zigzag curls and the drapery falls in angular and uncomplicated folds. The complex composition of the *Meeting of the Magi*, for example, demonstrates the carver's virtuosity, while gestures such as that of the angel gently supporting the head of *St John on Patmos* illustrate his unaffected and homely narrative style.

Among the important attributed wood-carvings are a *Group of Horsemen*, a *Virgin and Child* and a *St Agnes* (Amsterdam, Rijksmus.); a *Descent from the Cross* (Berlin, Bodemus.) and a *Holy Family* (Utrecht, Catharijneconvent). The stone angels decorating the spandrels of the arches in the Chapel of Rudolf van Diepholt in Utrecht Cathedral are sometimes attributed to van Wesel.

BIBLIOGRAPHY

D. P. R. A. Bouvy: *Middeleeuwsche beeldhouwkunst in de noordelijke Nederlanden* (Amsterdam, 1947), pp. 72–81, *passim*
J. Leeuwenberg: 'Het werk van den Meester der Musiceerende Engelen en het vraagstuk van Jacob van der Borch opnieuw beschouwd', *Oud-Holland*, lxiii (1948), pp. 164–79
P. T. A. Swillens: 'De Utrechtsche beeldhouwer Adriaen van Wesel, ±1420–na1489', *Oud-Holland*, lxiii (1948), pp. 149–63
Middeleeuwse kunst der noordelijke Nederlanden (exh. cat., Amsterdam, Rijksmus., 1958), nos 295–303
T. Muller: *Sculpture in the Netherlands, Germany, France and Spain, 1400–1500*, Pelican Hist. A. (Harmondsworth, 1966), pp. 89–90
J. Leeuwenberg and W. Halsema-Kubes: *Beeldhouwkunst in het Rijksmuseum* (Amsterdam, 1973), pp. 48–54, nos 16–18
W. Halsema-Kubes: 'Twee onbekende retabelfragmenten van Adriaen van Wesel', *Bull. Rijksmus.*, xxviii (1980), pp. 155–66
Adriaen van Wesel (exh. cat. by W. Halsema-Kubes, G. Lemmens and G. de Werd, Amsterdam, Rijksmus., 1980–81) [good Eng. summaries, pls and bibliog.]

KIM W. WOODS

Wesel, Andries van. *See* VESALIUS, ANDREAS.

Weser Renaissance. Term given to the art, and in particular the architecture, created in the region along the River Weser and adjacent areas in Germany between *c.* 1520 and *c.* 1620. Money earned by noblemen fighting as mercenaries in foreign wars—especially in the Netherlands—and an expansion in agricultural trade were two of the main contributory factors to the spate of new building that occurred in the region during this period. The most important architectural undertakings were castles, as well as town halls and town houses, although churches were also built in this style (for illustration *see* BÜCKEBURG); some of these buildings were decorated with reliefs, statues or ornamental stonework. One of the most important architects active in the earliest phase of the Weser Renaissance was Jörg Unkair (*d* 1552), who probably came from Württemberg. He was followed by Cord Tönnis and Hermann Wulff, both from the Weser region; they had a decisive influence on local architectural style between *c.* 1550 and *c.* 1575. In that period its distinguishing characteristics were strict proportioning and, in some cases, drastically reduced decoration, as, for example, in the Haus Rike (1568–9) in Hameln and the Hexenbürgermeisterhaus (1568–71), which was built by Wulff in Lemgo. After 1570 local building was dominated by the influence of such Netherlandish architects as Cornelis Floris and Hans Vredeman de Vries; at this period, existing links between the Netherlands and the Weser region were being reinforced by trade, and other transactions related to building: sandstone from Obernkirchen in the Weser hills was supplied for the construction of Antwerp Town Hall (1561–3), and such Netherlandish artists as Arend Robin (memorial plaques and showpiece fireplaces in Stadthagen) and Jan Robijn II (sculptural work at Stadthagen Town Hall) were active in that part of Germany.

During the Weser Renaissance, castles were typically constructed on a regular plan with several wings. Existing buildings were often united in one scheme, as, for example, at Schloss Neuhaus (from 1524) near Paderborn, on which Unkair collaborated and where the following characteristics of the Weser Renaissance are visible: *Zwerchhäuser*—dormer-type structures, often several storeys high, placed at right angles to saddle roofs that are sometimes nearly equal in height to the main roof; *Utluchten*—bays, rectangular on plan, that rise supported from the ground floor; and polygonal staircase towers—inserted at Schloss Neuhaus into the corners of the courtyard. The semicircular *welsche Giebel* or Italian gables, characteristic of the early Weser Renaissance, are also present at Schloss Neuhaus. They resemble those gables, ranged according to height and size, that were used in north Italy and Venice from *c.* 1475, and attest to the influence of Italian Renaissance architecture in the Weser area. These new forms were employed alongside the existing repertory of Late Gothic secular building, which included the mouldings used on windows and doorframes, the window members, highly decorated spiral staircases and other elements, all of which were part of an indigenous tradition (e.g. castles at Schulenburg, Stadthagen and Detmold). Buildings erected from 1560 to 1570 show a strong Netherlandish influence in their curved gables, high windows with stone mullions and transoms, and strapwork decoration, as well as rustication suggesting chip-carving (*Kerbschnitt*). The Late Gothic forms began to disappear about this time. Buildings such as Celle Town Hall (begun *c.* 1570) or the castles at Varenholz and Hämelschenburg (both *c.* 1590) are among the finest built in this style. The most widely used building material in the area was red sandstone from Obernkirchen an der Weser, in addition to locally quarried stone and bricks. Timber was rarely introduced on exteriors, but much employed, in the traditional way, in the interiors. Slight traces of colour remain, indicating that the buildings may have been painted to some extent, and at Schloss Varenholz, lozenge-shaped sgraffito decoration in the inner court is still partly preserved. Most castles in the Weser region were constructed over a lengthy period; as a result, important monuments of the Weser Renaissance show different stylistic influences. After the hiatus caused by the Thirty Years War (1618–48), no further building activity of any distinction took place in the area for a considerable period; thus the works created during the Weser Renaissance remain an outstanding feature of that part of Germany.

BIBLIOGRAPHY
M. Sonnen: *Die Weserrenaissance: Die Bauentwicklung um die Wende des 16. und 17. Jahrhunderts an der oberen und mittleren Weser und in den angrenzenden Gebieten* (Münster, 1918)
H. Kreft and J. Soenke: *Die Weserrenaissance* (Hameln, 1964, 6/1986)
Kunst und Kultur im Weserraum von 800–1600: Ausstellung des Landes Nordrhein-Westfalen (exh. cat., ed. H. Eichler; Corvey, Benediktinerabtei, 1966), i, pp. 272–95; ii, pp. 683–94
H.-R. Hitchcock: *German Renaissance Architecture* (Princeton, 1981)
H.-J. Kadatz: *Deutsche Renaissancebauten: Von der frühbürgerlichen Revolution bis zum Ausgang des Dreissigjährigen Krieges* (Berlin, 1983)
G. U. Grossmann: *Renaissance entlang der Weser: Kunst und Kultur in Nordwestdeutschland zwischen Reformation und Dreissigjährigem Krieg* (Köln, 1989)
GUNTER SCHWEIKHART

Wespin(, de) [Tabachetti; Tabaguet; Vespinis]. Flemish family of artists. The most extensively documented member is the sculptor Jean [Giovanni] de Wespin (*b* Dinant, *c.* 1569; *d* ?Varallo, Valsesia, 1615), whose father was a marble merchant. Having received some training at either Namur or Dinant, Jean travelled in 1587 to Italy to work at the court of Vincenzo I Gonzaga, Duke of Mantua. Except for a visit to Dinant in 1588, he remained in Italy for the rest of his life. He is principally remembered for his statues at the SACROMONTE at Varallo in the Valsesia. These life-size terracotta figures are grouped together within chapels in *tableaux* representing scenes from sacred history. He probably became associated with the Varallo sacromonte in 1587, at the beginning of the second phase of works at this sanctuary. A contract of 1590 states that he was to be responsible for the chapel of St Orso (destr.), the Paradise Chapel and the Calvary Chapel; of Jean de Wespin's work there, some forty human figures and nine horses now remain. The *Calvary*, on which he worked from 1599 to 1602, represents the summit of his achievement. Each statue is unsentimentally conceived as a highly realistic individual rather than as a character type. There is a slightly harsh emphasis on anatomical structure: skinny legs and arms, chests that show the bones under the skin, high-cheekboned faces, hard mouths and staring eyes. The style is simple, and religious feeling is expressed with restraint. Jean de Wespin also worked on the sacromonte at Crea in Piedmont between 1590 and 1616.

Of Jean de Wespin's two brothers, Guillaume de Wespin (*b* Dinant, *c.* 1570; *d* Dinant, *c.* 1643) was active wholly in Flanders, both as architect and as sculptor. As an architect he worked on the church of St Omer at Dinant. He also sculpted funerary monuments, including that of *Guido Salmier, Canon of Ciney* (1603) and in 1614 that of *Mme de Bassompierre* at the church of St Michel at Dinant (both destr.). Together with Adam Lottman (?1583–1660) he made the rood screen (after 1619; destr.) for the abbey of St Bertin. The youngest brother, Nicolas de Wespin (*b* Dinant, 1578), left Dinant for Antwerp in 1594, to train for a short time with the sculptor Servaes van den Blocke (*fl* 1582–1601). In 1597 he travelled to Italy, joining Jean in 1598 to work on the Crea sacromonte. He created the chapel of St Charles at the Graglia sacromonte.

BIBLIOGRAPHY
Thieme–Becker
S. Butler: *Ex voto: An Account of the Sacro Monte or New Jerusalem at Varallo-Sesia with Some Notice of Tabachetti's Remaining Work at the Sanctuary of Crea* (London, 1888)
F. Negri: 'Il santuario di Crea in Monferrato', *Riv. Stor., A., Archeol. Prov. Alessandria*, vi (1902)
A. Oger: 'Les Frères Jean et Nicolas de Wespin dits Tabaguet, sculpteurs dinantois (XVIe et XVIIe siècles): Leurs oeuvres en Italie', *An. Féd. Archéol. & Hist. Belgique*, ii (1903), pp. 899–908

M. Devigne: 'Les Frères Jean, Guillaume et Nicolas de Wespin', *An. Soc. Royale Archéol. Bruxelles*, xxix (1921), pp. 97–135; xxxi (1923), pp. 5–22

IRIS KOCKELBERGH

Wesselmann [incorrectly Wesselman], **Tom** (*b* Cincinnati, OH, 23 Feb 1931). American painter, sculptor and printmaker. He planned to become a cartoonist until his final year at the Cooper Union in New York, where he studied from 1956 to 1959 and was encouraged to become a painter. The powerful work of Willem de Kooning provided both inspiration and inhibition as he attempted to find a new direction centred around a tangible subject. Choosing the figure he began to make small collages of torn paper and found materials, as in the *Little Great American Nudes* of 1961–2; these culminated in large, aggressive compositions such as *Great American Nude #3* (1961; Washington, DC, Hirshhorn). These and giant still-lifes composed of common household objects and collage elements culled from popular advertising images, such as *Still Life #20* (1962; Buffalo, NY, Albright-Knox A.G.), brought him fame and notoriety as a founder of American POP ART. In the late 1960s an increasingly dominant eroticism emerged in works such as *Bedroom Painting #13* (1969; Berlin, Neue N.G.), with its more literal but still intense colours and tight, formal composition. The pictorial elements, exaggerated in their arabesque forms and arbitrary colouring, became significantly larger in scale in his works of the 1970s, such as a series of *Smoker* mouths; enormous, partially free-standing still-lifes moved into sculptural space, and finally became discrete sculptures of sheet metal. In the 1980s he returned to works for the wall with cut-out steel or aluminium drawings such as *Vivienne Doodle (3D)* (1986; see 1987 exh. cat., no. 1), which replicate his familiar, graceful line in enamel on cut-out metal. He was also an innovative printmaker, adapting his imagery to lithographs, screenprints, aquatints and multiples in relief. An important retrospective of his work was held in Japan in 1993–4.

WRITINGS
S. Stealingworth [T. Wesselmann]: *Tom Wesselmann* (New York, 1980) [the only substantial monograph; many colour pls, exh. list, bibliog.]

BIBLIOGRAPHY
Tom Wesselmann: The Early Years: Collages, 1959–1962 (exh. cat. by C. Glenn, Long Beach, CA State U., A. Gals, 1974)
Wesselmann (exh. cat., New York, Sidney Janis Gal., 1987)
Tom Wesselmann: Paintings, 1962–1986 (exh. cat., intro. J. McEwen; London, Mayor Gal. and Mayor Rowan Gal., 1988)
Wesselmann (Prints and Multiples) (exh. cat., Tokyo, Hara Mus. Contemp. A., 1990)
Tom Wesselmann: Recent Still Lifes and Landscapes (exh. cat., intro. S. Hunter; Tokyo, Gal. Tokoro, 1991)
Tom Wesselmann: A Retrospective Survey 1959–1992 (exh. cat. by M. Livingstone, Tokyo; Sapporo; Shiga; Osaka; 1993–4)

CONSTANCE W. GLENN

Wessén, Natanael. Swedish collector and physician. Wessén formed his collection and undertook research into Chinese art at the same time as pursuing his medical profession. His collection, which concentrated on early Chinese art with an emphasis on bronzes of the Shang (*c.* 1600–*c.* 1050 BC) and Zhou (*c.* 1050 256 BC) periods, became the most outstanding private collection of its nature in Sweden, equalled only by that of King Gustav VI Adolf. Formed in the 1930s and 1940s, with the help of such scholars and connoisseurs as Orvar Karlbeck, Bernhard Karlgren and Osvald Sirén, Wessén's collection was also one of great refinement. Karlgren used examples from the collection for his articles in the *Bulletin of the Museum of Far Eastern Antiquities* (Stockholm) and in 1969, together with Jan Wirgin, wrote a monograph on the collection that contained illustrations of nearly all the objects. Prominent pieces from Wessén's collection were exhibited at the Östasiatiska Museum, Stockholm, in 1969.

BIBLIOGRAPHY
B. Karlgren and J. Wirgin: *Chinese Bronzes: The Natanael Wessén Collection* (Stockholm, 1969)
Ancient Chinese Bronzes from the Stoclet and Wessén Collections (exh. cat. by G. Eskenazi; London, Eskenazi Ltd, 1975)
Ancient Chinese Bronzes and Gilt Bronzes from the Wessén and Other Collections (exh. cat. by G. Eskenazi; London, Eskenazi Ltd, 1980)

S. J. VERNOIT

Wessex, Kings of. Anglo-Saxon family of rulers and patrons.

(1) Alfred [the Great], King of Wessex (*b* Wantage, Oxon, AD 849; *reg* 871–99; *bur* Winchester, 28 Oct 901). In 871 he became king of a country suffering from long internal strife with the immigrant Scandinavians. He recorded that the Anglo-Saxon people were uneducated: churches had been full of books during his childhood, but no one could understand them, and they had consequently been destroyed. Surviving evidence suggests that little new fine art had been produced for decades. In 878, in order to solve these problems, he nominally converted the Scandinavians, and a lasting settlement was negotiated, with both parties swearing on a common God. He imported foreign scholars and founded a court school. After 884 he introduced a legible script, established the Anglo-Saxon Chronicle and sponsored the production of books. He was a notable and productive scholar and translated several works by Bede Orosius, Boethius and the *Liber regulae pastoralis* by Gregory I, of which a copy with minor decoration, made in his lifetime, survives (Oxford, Bodleian Lib., MS. Hatton 60).

Alfred's artistic heritage was mixed. Travels to Rome had made him familiar with Italian, Byzantine and Carolingian art, yet surviving English manuscripts display a recognizably Hiberno-Saxon style, while stonework and metalwork have strong Scandinavian elements. Little fine art survives from Alfred's reign. His biographer, Asser, states that Alfred commissioned 'treasures incomparably fashioned in gold and silver', and that he had 'wonderful and precious new treasures' made to his own design; surviving examples of metalwork may illustrate this aspect of his patronage. The Alfred Jewel (Oxford, Ashmolean; see JEWELLERY, colour pl. IV, fig. 1), a gold and enamel reading pointer, certainly dates from Alfred's reign. The enamel is possibly continental, but the gold setting is a traditional Anglo-Saxon beast head decorated with the long-practised techniques of granulation and chasing. The Fuller Brooch (London, BM; see ANGLO-SAXON ART, fig. 12) is executed in the traditional materials of silver and niello, but its style is continental, and its imagery of the Five Senses was quite new. Such other objects as the Abingdon Sword (Oxford, Ashmolean) show a similar combination of established techniques and new designs.

Other than metalwork, Asser only mentions buildings in wood and stone constructed in Alfred's reign. A painted building block from Alfred's reign was reused by his son, Edward the Elder (*reg* 899–925), for the New Minster at Winchester. It shows the head of a saint, linear and unmodelled, with thickened eyebrows extended to define the bridge of the nose, and there is a fragment of axe-pattern. These features are paralleled in the native tradition (e.g. the Canterbury Codex Aureus; Stockholm, Kun. Bib. MS. A. 135) but may also have been influenced by contemporary Roman mosaics, for example those at S Prassede, S Cecilia in Trastevere and S Marco.

Although attempts have been made to find in Alfred's patronage the impetus for the Winchester style (typified by luxuriant foliage) of Anglo-Saxon painting, manuscripts from Alfred's reign are barely decorated, and what foliage there is derives from the Hiberno-Saxon tradition; the same is true of metalwork, and the wall fragment lacks foliage completely. Something approaching Winchester-style foliage is found on St Cuthbert's stole (Durham, Cathedral Treasury), but this was made during Edward the Elder's reign. In his cultural activities Alfred was primarily a reformer, utilizing existing skills but infusing them with new ideas.

BIBLIOGRAPHY

Alfred, King of England, Called the Great (London, 1858)

M. Rickert: *Painting in Britain in the Middle Ages* (London, 1954), pp. 33–6

C. R. Dodwell: *Anglo-Saxon Art: A New Perspective* (Manchester, 1982)

S. Keynes and M. Lapidge: *Alfred the Great: Asser's Life of Alfred and Other Contemporary Sources* (London, 1983)

L. Webster: 'The Legacy of Alfred', *The Golden Age of Anglo-Saxon Art* (exh. cat., ed. J. Backhouse, D. H. Turner and L. Webster; London, BM, 1984)

PIPPIN MICHELLI

(2) Athelstan, King of Wessex (*b* AD 895; *reg* 924/5-939; *d* Gloucester, 27 Oct 939). Grandson of (1) Alfred, King of Wessex. He was the first West Saxon king to rule over all England. He pursued and extended the policy of unification of his father, Edward the Elder (*reg* 899–925), and his grandfather, bringing Northumbria under his rule and pushing boundaries forward to the south and southwest. The numerous contacts with the royal houses of continental Europe established during his reign, formalized through the marriages of his four half-sisters, confirm his standing as one of the great medieval English kings. He was instrumental in founding and endowing churches and monasteries, particularly in the kingdom of Wessex, which resulted in a slow but steady increase in the production of books. A number of continental manuscripts were brought to England as gifts from the German and French royal houses and undoubtedly influenced the 10th-century flowering of Anglo-Saxon painting. Such manuscripts as the late 9th-century Coronation Gospels (London, BL, Cotton MS. Tib. A. II) from Lobbes, near Liège, presented by Athelstan to Christ Church, Canterbury, and originally a gift to Athelstan from his brother-in-law, Otto I, and the so-called Athelstan Psalter (London, BL, Cotton MS. Galba A. XVIII), a 9th-century Carolingian manuscript with Anglo-Saxon insertions, probably a present from Athelstan to the Old Minster (Cathedral) at Winchester, provided models for English artists. Bede's *Lives of St Cuthbert* (Cambridge, Corpus Christi Coll.,

MS. 183), one of the books given by Athelstan to the shrine of St Cuthbert at Chester-le-Street in 934 (along with the Durham embroideries; *see* ANGLO-SAXON ART, fig. 15), contains the earliest surviving presentation miniature in English art (fol. 1*v*) and shows significant borrowings from Carolingian manuscript illumination.

BIBLIOGRAPHY

DNB

J. A. Robinson: *The Times of Saint Dunstan* (Oxford, 1923)

F. M. Stenton: *Anglo-Saxon England* (Oxford, 1943, 3/1971)

R. Deshman: 'Anglo-Saxon Art after Alfred', *A. Bull.*, lvi (1974), pp. 176–200

The Golden Age of Anglo-Saxon Art, 966–1066 (exh. cat., ed. J. Backhouse, D. H. Turner and L. Webster; London, BM, 1984)

□

Wessing, Koen (*b* Amsterdam, 26 Jan 1942). Dutch photographer. He studied at the Rietveld Academy in Amsterdam and then with the Dutch photographer Ata Kando, also working as a freelance press photographer in Amsterdam. From the end of the 1960s he worked as a documentary photographer in the tradition of politically engaged, concerned photography. His early work showed the influence of Ed van der Elsken with its interest in human drama, its use of a direct, lively approach and a dark printing technique; but he soon evolved a personal style, combining these elements with a strong formal approach.

Wessing made his first major photo-reportage in Paris during the student revolts in 1968, publishing it as *Parijs, 1968* (Amsterdam, 1968). From the 1970s he became deeply involved with the political situation of South America, later publishing collections of these images, such as *Chile, September 1973* (Amsterdam, 1974) and *Van Chili tot Guatemala: Tien jaar Latijns-America* ('From Chile to Guatemala: ten years in Latin America') (Amsterdam, 1983; Ger. trans., 1983). The most striking aspect of his photography is a sense of danger and aggression achieved through strong pictorial contrasts and symbolic details, seen in *Chile* (1973; see 1978 exh. cat., no. 78), where a man walks down a street apparently oblivious to the phalanx of armed policemen to his right. In the Netherlands Wessing received various documentary commissions from the Amsterdam Fund for the Arts and in 1976 made a series entitled *Andere culturen in onze cultuur* ('Other cultures within our culture') for the Historical Department of the Rijksmuseum.

BIBLIOGRAPHY

Fotografie in Nederland, 1940–75 (exh. cat., ed. E. Barents; Amsterdam, Stedel. Mus., 1978)

P. Tereehorst: 'Koen Wessing', *Dut. A. & Archit. Today*, xx (1986)

HRIPSIMÉ VISSER

West, Benjamin (*b* Springfield [now Swarthmore], PA, 10 Oct 1738; *d* London, 11 March 1820). American painter and draughtsman, active in England. He was the first American artist to achieve an international reputation and to influence artistic trends in Europe. He taught three generations of his aspiring countrymen. His son Raphael Lamar West (1769–1850) was a history painter.

1. Life and work. 2. Reputation.

1. LIFE AND WORK.

(i) Early career, 1738–60. (ii) Italy and early years in England, 1760–92. (iii) President of the Royal Academy, 1792–1805. (iv) Later career.

(i) Early career, 1738–60. He was one of ten children of a rural innkeeper whose Quaker family had moved in 1699 from Long Crendon, Bucks. In romantic legends perpetuated by the artist himself, he is pictured as an untutored Wunderkind. However, it has become clear that West received considerable support from talented and generous benefactors. West's earliest known portraits, *Robert Morris* and *Jane Morris* (both West Chester, PA, Chester Co. Hist. Soc. Mus.), date from about 1752. He spent a year (probably 1755–6) painting portraits in Lancaster, PA, where one of his subjects, William Henry (Philadelphia, PA, Hist. Soc.), a master gunsmith, told him of a nobler art than painting faces—that of depicting morally uplifting historical and biblical episodes. West obliged him by painting the *Death of Socrates* (*c.* 1756; priv. col., see von Erffa and Staley, no. 4), which, notwithstanding its crude style and frieze-like composition, anticipated European Neo-classical painting by several decades. Rev. William Smith (1727–1803), principal of the College of Philadelphia, was so impressed by the work that he gave West informal instruction in Classical art, literature and history.

In 1756, West moved to Philadelphia, PA, where he was taught by, among others, William Williams and John Valentine Heidt (*c.* 1700–1780), a Moravian lay preacher who had been trained as a painter and metal-engraver. Williams lent West his landscapes to copy, as well as editions of Charles Alphonse Du Fresnoy's *De arte graphica* and Jonathan Richardson's *An Essay on the Theory of Painting*. West spent almost a year painting portraits in New York, hoping to earn enough to study in Italy. In 1760 two leading Philadelphia families, the Allens and the Shippens, gave him free passage to Italy and later advanced him £300 as payment for copies of Old Master paintings he was to make for them.

(ii) Italy and early years in England, 1760–92. West embarked for Livorno in April 1760. E. P. Richardson described his journey as an act of profound importance to American art; West was the first American painter to transcend the boundaries of the colonial portrait tradition, to enlarge the field of subjects that painting could deal with and eventually to take part in the great movements of Neo-classical and Romantic idealism that were to dominate European culture for the next 75 years.

West arrived in Rome in July. Personal charm, good looks, excellent letters of introduction and his unique position as an American (and a presumed Quaker) studying art in Italy endeared him at once 'in a constant state of high excitement' to artistic society. Anton Raphael Mengs taught him at the Capitoline Academy and sent him to study art collections in northern Italy. He was made a member of the academies at Bologna, Florence and Parma. Gavin Hamilton, who in the early 1760s was painting the first works in the Neo-classical style, spent time with West, no doubt conveying to him his enthusiasm for antiquity.

West arrived in England in August 1763, intending to make a short visit before he returned to America. He showed two Neo-classical works that he had painted in Rome, the *Continence of Scipio* (*c.* 1766; Cambridge, Fitzwilliam) and *Pylades and Orestes* (1766; London, Tate), at the Society of Arts exhibition of 1766, where they caused an artistic furore. 'He is really a wonder of a man', his patron, William Allen, wrote to Philadelphia, 'and has so far outstripped all the painters of his time [in getting] into high esteem at once. . . . If he keeps his health he will make money very fast' (see Kimball and Quin). On the advice of his American patrons he decided to stay in England. He married Elizabeth Shewell, the daughter of a Philadelphia merchant, in London in 1764. One of West's admirers, Dr Robert Hay Drummond, Archbishop of York, asked him to paint an episode famous in Roman history, *Agrippina Landing at Brundisium with the Ashes of Germanicus* (1768; New Haven, CT, Yale U., A.G.). West drew on his sketches and drawings of Classical dress, sculpture and architecture to depict a moment frozen in history with a haunting sense of time, place and actuality. He combined a cool palette with a severe composition and calculated gestures. The work created a sensation when it was exhibited in 1768. With this picture of Roman courage, grief and conjugal virtue, West became at once the foremost history painter in England and the most advanced proponent of the Neo-classical style in Europe.

George III, who admired the picture, asked West to paint for him another episode from Roman history, the *Departure of Regulus from Rome* (1769; Brit. Royal Col.), and thereafter made him historical painter to the King with an annual stipend of £1000, which freed West from the need to support himself by painting portraits. The King commissioned West to paint 36 scenes depicting the *History of Revealed Religion* for the Royal Chapel at Windsor Castle. Although saints and the Virgin were excluded as subjects, they broke the Protestant barrier in English churches against 'Popish pictures'. West completed 18 large canvases, including the *Last Supper* (1784; London, Tate). However, they were never installed, and remained in the artist's studio until after his death. Between 1787 and 1789 he also painted for the King's Audience Room at Windsor a series of vast canvases celebrating British victories during the Hundred Years War and the Foundation of the Order of the Garter (Brit. Royal Col.). West's concern for accurate detail reflects the antiquarian research of Joseph Strutt and marks a considerable advance on earlier 18th-century history painting in England.

In 1771 West exhibited the *Death of General Wolfe* (see fig. 1), the painting for which he is best known. Despite the advice of his peers and of the King, he painted Wolfe and his men as they were dressed at Quebec in 1759 rather than in Greek or Roman attire, although by including an Indian guide in the foreground he was able to display a more conventional talent for painting the nude. The work was an immediate popular and critical success; four replicas were commissioned, including one for the King. West's achievement in bringing a new realism to history painting by his care in recording the exact details of the participants and their costume was widely recognized. Reynolds predicted that it would 'occasion a revolution in the art'. At the same time the composition made a ready appeal to the emotions of the spectator by recalling the long tradition of the Christian Pietà. He followed a year

1. Benjamin West: *Death of General Wolfe*, oil on canvas, 1.52×2.14 m, 1770 (Ottawa, National Gallery of Canada)

later with another historical painting, *William Penn's Treaty with the Indians* (1771–2; Philadelphia, PA, Acad. F.A.). West was one of the first artists to realize the commercial and publicity value of mechanical reproduction of his works: engravings of these paintings (by John Hall, 1775, and William Woollet, 1776) were sold by the tens of thousands in Europe and America.

(iii) President of the Royal Academy, 1792–1805. In 1768 West and three other dissident officers of the Society of Artists, at the King's suggestion and with his financial support, had drawn up an 'Instrument of Foundation' for a new association of 40 artists to be called the Royal Academy of Arts. Joshua Reynolds was the first president, and when he died in 1792, West was elected to succeed him. As President of the Royal Academy, the major recipient of the King's patronage and the leading artist in Neo-classical and realistic history painting, West held a position of commanding authority in English art. His influence was further extended by what came to be known as 'the American school'. Almost from the time of his arrival in London, West's home and studio became a haven for American artists seeking advice, employment or instruction. Matthew Pratt, who stayed for two and a half years, was followed by a succession of other students remarkable both for their number and their talent. The first generation included Gilbert Stuart (his paid assistant for some four years), Charles Willson Peale, Ralph Earl, Joseph Wright, William Dunlap, John Trumbull, Robert

Fulton (1765–1815), Henry Benbridge and Abraham Delanoy (1742–95). Even West's severest critics have allowed that he was an unfailingly kind and generous mentor, not only to Americans but also to English pupils. He made known his admiration for the early work of William Blake and Turner, and he gave Constable encouragement that was gratefully acknowledged. John Singleton Copley, though never his student, sought West's advice on taking up a career in London.

West's influence was extended as a discreet seller, trader and collector of works of art. He was known to be the King's buyer at auctions, was often consulted on appraisals, attributions and prices of paintings and testified in some notable lawsuits involving artists' fees and the quality of engravings. In 1779 he and a colleague were commissioned to place a valuation on 174 Old Master paintings in the collection of Robert Walpole at Houghton Hall in Norfolk (Walpole had urged Parliament to buy his entire collection, but Catherine II, Empress of Russia, acquired it at West's price of £40,555). West engaged in a costly and unsuccessful speculative venture with his pupil John Trumbull in attempting to import Old Master works from France. His great triumph came in 1785, when he bought for 20 guineas at auction, amid general laughter, a dirty, waxencrusted landscape, having identified it as Titian's *Death of Actaeon* (London, N.G.).

West was able to keep George III's favour throughout the American War of Independence (1775–83), despite his unconcealed sympathy for his rebellious countrymen. He was, indeed, almost a member of the royal household, with working rooms in Buckingham House and Windsor Castle. In the 1790s, however, he was criticized at the court for holding 'French principles' and for praising Napoleon Bonaparte. He incurred the dislike of Queen Charlotte, and George, intermittently ill after 1788, wavered in his friendship and support. In 1802, during the lull in the war with France, West made a five-week visit to Paris, where Napoleon met with him, and French artists, including David, paid him homage. Thereafter West's stipend as history painter to the King and his *History of Revealed Religion* commission were cancelled. His troubles were further compounded by two improvident sons, the death of his ailing wife in 1814, heavy debts, a bad investment in American land, a decline in public favour and a group of hostile Royal Academicians, including Copley, who in 1805 forced him to resign as President.

(iv) Later career. At 66 West accomplished a remarkable recovery. He found a new wealthy patron in William Beckford of Fonthill Abbey, Wilts. He scored a stunning popular success with the *Death of Lord Nelson* (1806; Liverpool, Walker A.G.). He surpassed that triumph with two huge religious paintings: *Christ Healing the Sick in the Temple* (2.74×4.27 m, 1811; London, Tate), which he painted over a ten-year period for the Pennsylvania Hospital in Philadelphia, was sold to the British Institution for the unheard-of price of 3000 guineas (four years later an 'improved version' was sent to the hospital; *in situ*); *Our Saviour Brought from the Judgement Hall by Pilate to Caiaphas the High Priest*, commonly known as *Christ Rejected* (5.08×6.60 m, 1814; Philadelphia, PA, Acad. F.A.), is still more ambitious in scale than *Christ Healing the Sick* (it includes more than 60 faces) and was greeted with great popular and critical acclaim. West introduced still another new direction in painting with his huge *Death on the Pale Horse* (see fig. 2). Drawing on contemporary conceptions of the Sublime, it combines Christian imagery of the Apocalypse with pagan myth in a frenzy of movement that foreshadows Delacroix and the Romantic movement in European art. West introduced the Romantic style into portrait painting with his small *General Kosciuszko in London* (1797; Oberlin Coll., OH, Allen Mem. A. Mus.) and *Robert Fulton* (1806; Cooperstown, NY, Mus. State Hist. Assoc.). In 1806 he accepted the pleas of the Royal Academicians to resume the presidency and to restore harmony to the Academy.

West's last years were productive and relatively peaceful. He testified before a government commission on the value of 'those sublime sculptures', the Parthenon Marbles. He played a role in the founding of the British Academy, which became the National Gallery. He continued pioneering work he had undertaken in the new medium of lithography, having contributed to *Specimens of Polyantography* (1803). He achieved a new celebrity in 1816 with the publication of the first volume of his biography by John Galt. He welcomed, taught and sometimes housed members of another generation of talented young American students, among them Washington Allston, Rembrandt Peale, Samuel Morse, Charles Bird King, Charles Robert Leslie and Thomas Sully.

2. REPUTATION. West's reputation as an artist and teacher began to decline with his death. For more than a century, because of the weakness of his technique and lack of imagination in much of his work, his paintings were ignored or were cited as examples of all that was meretricious in art. Critical opinion began to change with a

2. Benjamin West: *Death on the Pale Horse*, oil on canvas, 4.47×7.65 mm, 1817 (Philadelphia, PA, Pennsylvania Academy of the Fine Arts)

bicentennial exhibition of his work at the Philadelphia Museum of Art in 1938. He is generally recognized as 'a stylistic innovator of immense influence' and as the artist who first attempted to bring American art into contiguity with European art.

BIBLIOGRAPHY

J. Galt: *The Life, Studies, and Works of Benjamin West. Composed from Materials Furnished by Himself*, 2 vols (London, 1816–20)

W. Dunlap: *A History of the Rise and Progress of the Arts of Design in the United States*, 3 vols (New York, 1834/*R* 1969)

W. Sawitzky: 'The American Work of Benjamin West', *PA Mag. Hist. & Biog.*, lxii (1938), pp. 433–62

J. T. Flexner: *America's Old Masters: First Artists of the New World* (New York, 1939, rev. 2/1967), pp. 19–97

——: 'The American School in London', *Bull. Met. Mus. A.*, n. s., vii (1948), pp. 64–72

E. P. Richardson: *Painting in America: The Story of 450 Years* (New York, 1956)

D.A. Kimball and M. Quinn: 'William Allen–Benjamin Chew Correspondence, 1763–1764', *PA Mag. Hist. & Biog.*, xc (1966)

G. Evans: *Benjamin West and the Taste of his Times* (Carbondale, 1959)

Drawings by Benjamin West and his Son Raphael Lamar West (exh. cat. by R. S. Kraemer, New York, Pierpont Morgan Lib., 1975)

J. Dillenberger: *Benjamin West: The Context of his Life's Work, with Particular Attention to Paintings with Religious Subject Matter* (San Antonio, 1977)

R. C. Alberts: *Benjamin West: A Biography* (Boston, 1978)

K. Garlick, A. Macintyre and K. Cave, eds: *The Diary of Joseph Farington, 1793–1821*, 16 vols (New Haven, 1978)

E. P. Richardson: 'West's Voyage to Italy, 1760, and William Allen', *PA Mag. Hist. & Biog.*, cii (1978), pp. 3–26

D. Evans: *Benjamin West and his American Students* (Washington, DC, 1980)

A. U. Abrams: *The Valiant Hero: Benjamin West and Grand-style Historical Painting* (Washington, DC, 1985)

W. Greenhouse: 'Benjamin West and Edward III: A Neoclassical Painter and Medieval History', *A. Hist.*, viii (1985), pp. 178–91

H. von Erffa and A. Staley: *The Paintings of Benjamin West* (New Haven, 1986)

ROBERT C. ALBERTS

West, James (*b* Prior's Marston, Warwicks, ?1704; *d* Preston on Stour, Glos, 2 July 1772). English lawyer, politician, antiquary, collector and patron. He began collecting when young; on 4 January 1736, a fire in his rooms in the Inner Temple, London, where he practised as a barrister, destroyed his collection of 'curiosities', valued at £3000. West pursued a successful career in law and politics, but his personal interests were antiquarian. He was a fellow of the Society of Antiquaries from 1728 and President of the Royal Society, to which he was elected in 1726, from 1768 until his death. He collected prints and drawings, largely of famous men, and assisted James Granger (1723–76) with the prints for his *Biographical History of England* (1769). He also purchased coins, medals, curiosities and plate and, above all, books and manuscripts. He specialized in incunabula and the works of early English printers, including William Caxton and Wynkyn de Worde (*d c.* 1534). West's library, much of which came from that of the antiquary Bishop White Kennett (1660–1728), was sold over 24 days in March and April 1773 at The Piazza, Covent Garden, London, by the auctioneer Abraham Langford (1711–74); it raised £2927. Many of the manuscripts are now included in the Lansdowne Collection (London, BL). West's antiquarian interests were reflected in a large collection of early English histories and romances, and he was among the pioneer patrons of 'Gothick' architecture; in 1750 he commissioned John Phillips (*c.* 1709–75) to rebuild his country seat, Alscot House, near Preston on Stour, in a Rococo–Gothick style derived from the pattern-books of Batty Langley.

BIBLIOGRAPHY

Colvin; *DNB*

T. F. Dibdin: *Bibliomania or Book-madness* (London, 1876)

M. Girouard: 'Alscot Park, Warwickshire', *Country Life*, cxxiii (15 May 1958), pp. 1064–7; (22 May 1958), pp. 1124–7; (29 May 1958), pp. 1184–7

DAVID RODGERS

West [née Dods; known as Jasulaitis, 1960–82], **Margaret** (*b* Melbourne, 31 Aug 1936). Australian jeweller and teacher. In 1976 she graduated from the Royal Melbourne Institute of Technology with a Diploma of Art in gold- and silversmithing. From 1979 she lived in Sydney, where she taught jewellery and design at Sydney College of the Arts. Her early work is predominantly made in stainless steel, generally in sheet form using rivet construction. In the late 1970s she began to experiment with surface textures: hammering, abrading and painting the metal. The origins and symbolism of body adornment became a dominant and continuing concern in her work, and her jewellery was reduced to such basic formal elements as bibs (e.g. *Bib for an Ostrich, c. 1982 (Protection Factor 5.6)*, 1982; Canberra, N.G.) and discs using not only steel but also lead, stone, wood and feathers. From the mid-1980s she began to produce work that questions 'the contextual qualification of meaning', as described in her 'Work Statements' (1987). This includes such non-wearable examples as the 'Casket' series (1985–7; e.g. *Casket: Grey Matter*, 1987; Melbourne, N.G. Victoria), where sand, feathers and groups of assorted objects are given context through their containment in wooden and metal boxes. Her exhibitions became installations, sometimes incorporating photographic images. Both as teacher and practitioner, West was pre-eminent in Australia in promoting a theoretical approach to jewellery production.

BIBLIOGRAPHY

Four Australian Jewellers (exh. cat. by J. O'Callaghan, Melbourne, N.G. Victoria, 1987)

JUDITH O'CALLAGHAN

West, (Walter) Richard [Dick] [Wah-Pah-Nah-Yah: 'Lightfoot Runner'] (*b* Darlington, OK, 8 Sept 1912). Native American Cheyenne painter and sculptor. He studied at the Haskell Institute, Lawrence, KS, from 1931 until 1936, then at the Bacone Junior College, Muskogee, OK, from 1936 until 1938. He received a BA degree at the University of Oklahoma, Norman, in 1941. Between 1941 and 1942 he taught as an art instructor at the Phoenix Indian School, AZ, and, after a period in the US Navy, again from 1946 until 1948. In 1947 he was appointed director of the Art Department at Bacone Junior College, a position he held until 1970. His paintings depict the traditional Plains Indian life and ancient ceremonies in a strong linear style and bold colours. He also worked as a muralist, providing murals for the U.S. Post Office, Okemah, OK (1941), the Bacone College (1963) and the North Campus of the University of Oklahoma, Norman, OK. His *Southern Cheyenne Sun Dance, the Great Medicine Lodge Ceremony* (1973; priv. col.) and *Cheyenne Winter Games* (n.d.; Tulsa, OK, Philbrook A. Cent.) illustrate his skill and understanding of the watercolour medium, while his *Wolf Dance* (1940; Norman, OK, U. OK Mus. A.) is a dramatic portrayal of a Cheyenne ceremony. In 1977 he retired from his position as chairman of the Division of Humanities at the Haskell Indian Junior College, Lawrence, KS, to devote himself full time to painting and sculpture. In 1980 he maintained an office and studio at Bacone Junior College and continued to lecture and teach on a part-time basis as Professor Emeritus of Art. In May 1986 he moved to Tijeras, NM, where he maintained a studio.

BIBLIOGRAPHY
J. O. Snodgrass: *American Indian Painters: A Biographical Directory* (New York, 1968)
M. Libhart, ed.: *Contemporary Plains Indian Painting* (Anadarko, OK, 1972)
Who's Who in American Art (New York and London, 1973)
M. Archuleta and R. Strickland: *Shared Visions: Native American Painters and Sculptors in the Twentieth Century* (New York, 1991)
IMRE NAGY

West, Robert (*fl* 1752–61; *d* Dublin, 1790). Irish stuccoist. He is a typical example of the many plasterers working in Dublin during the mid-18th century whose work remains largely unidentified. In 1752 he was described as a plasterer when admitted as a freeman of the City of Dublin. In 1756 he was paid £534 for 'plaistering and stucco' in the city's Rotunda Hospital, where it is thought he decorated the staircase ceiling. In 1761 he worked at 9 Cavendish Row and at 4 and 5 Parnell Square, three houses built by Bartholomew Mosse (1712–59), Master Builder of the Rotunda.

West is variously described in legal documents as plasterer, Master Builder and merchant, and it is known that he developed property in Lower Dominick Street, Granby Row, Great Denmark Street and City Quay. He built 20 Lower Dominick Street before 1758, and the ceilings there can be attributed to him. Various motifs in the hall—serrated acanthus in high relief and birds holding flowers—are also to be found in the staircase hall of 56 St Stephen's Green. This latter work is crowded and crudely modelled, though the ceiling of Lower Dominick Street's hall is one of the most daringly conceived and freely modelled Rococo ceilings in Dublin. Here, trophies of musical instruments, caryatids and birds standing on pedestals are close in treatment to those in the Rotunda Chapel. At Florence Court, Co. Fermanagh, the dining-room ceiling is similar to that in the back drawing-room of 9 Cavendish Row, with its flat acanthus set within robust rectangular mouldings. Although West is popularly associated with the bird motifs found in Dublin Rococo plasterwork, few are actually to be found in the houses where he is known to have worked. Nothing by West can be dated later than 1761, a fact that may be explained by his increasing interest in property development.

BIBLIOGRAPHY
C. P. Curran: *The Rotunda Hospital, Dublin* (Dublin, 1946)
——: *Dublin Decorative Plasterwork* (London, 1967)
WILLIAM GARNER

Westall. English family of painters and illustrators. Richard Westall (*b* Hertford, 1765; *d* London, 4 Dec 1836) was apprenticed in 1799 to John Thompson, a heraldic engraver in London. The miniaturist John Alefounder (*d* 1795) advised Westall to take up painting, and in 1784 he exhibited a portrait drawing (untraced) at the Royal Academy. He became a student at the Royal Academy Schools in 1785, an ARA in 1792 and an RA in 1794. He exhibited over 300 works at the Royal Academy and 70 at the British Institution, including such large watercolours as *Cassandra Prophesying the Fall of Troy* (exh. London, RA 1796; London, V&A), which are painted in violent and sometimes excessive colours. Others, such as *The Rosebud* (1791; New Haven, CT, Yale Cent. Brit. A.), tend towards a Rococo prettiness. His principal expertise was book illustration. He was employed by John Boydell, Thomas Macklin and Robert Bowyer, and he illustrated Milton's poetical works (3 vols; London, 1794–7). He painted five pictures for Boydell's Shakespeare Gallery, including a *Scene from Henry VIII* (1790s; Washington, DC, Folger Shakespeare Lib.). In 1814 he held a solo exhibition at his house in Upper Charlotte Street, London. His output was prolific, but unfortunate picture dealings led to poverty.

Richard's brother William Westall (*b* Hertford, 12 Oct 1781; *d* London, 22 Jan 1850) became a probationer at the Royal Academy Schools in 1801. His ability led Benjamin West to propose him as the artist to accompany Captain Matthew Flinders's voyage to Australia in the same year. Westall joined Flinders for two years, after which he visited China and India. His records of these voyages include a sketch of *Port Jackson* (1804; London, V&A) and his later painting, a *View in a Mandarin's Garden* (exh. London, RA 1814; untraced); they were also used to illustrate Flinders's *A Voyage to Terra Australis* (London, 1814). After a brief stay in England in 1805 he went to Madeira and Jamaica. He returned to London in 1808 and held an exhibition of works based on these travels. Although the exhibition was unsuccessful, he became a member of the Old Water-Colour Society in 1811 and an ARA in 1812. His skill at topographical illustration led to the production of aquatints and lithographs for such publications as *Views of the Lakes and the Vale of Keswick* (London, 1820) and *A Picturesque Tour of the River Thames* (London, 1828).

BIBLIOGRAPHY
DNB; Redgrave
Obituary, 'Memoir of William Westall, ARA', *A. J.* [London], xii (1850), pp. 104–5
B. Smith: *European Vision and the South Pacific, 1768–1850* (Oxford, 1960/R 1969), pp. 141–6
SHEARER WEST

Westerholm, Victor (Axel) (*b* Turku, 4 Jan 1860; *d* Turku, 19 Nov 1919). Finnish painter. He studied at the School of Drawing in Turku from 1869 to 1878. In 1878 he travelled to Düsseldorf and enrolled at the Kunstakademie, where he attended classes on landscape painting by Eugen Dücker until 1886. He spent his summers in Finland, on the Åland Islands, preparing sketches that provided the groundwork for many of the paintings he produced in Düsseldorf. Although Westerholm began working according to the principles of studio painting, his vivid studies are often imbued with the crispness of the *plein-air* style. In the early 1880s he concentrated on painting autumnal scenes and rapidly became the leading landscape artist of the younger generation with such works as the *Mail-packet Jetty at Eckerö* (1885; Hämeenlinna, A. Mus.).

After leaving Düsseldorf Westerholm shifted completely to *plein-air* painting. At first he worked at his summer residence in the Åland Islands, where he became the central figure in a colony of Finnish and Swedish *plein-air* painters known as the Önningeby group. Between 1888 and 1890 he made several journeys to Paris, where he studied at the Académie Julian. He became preoccupied with the creation of light and, more than any Finnish artist before him, took his inspiration from the Impressionists; his large-scale *Birch-felling* (1888; priv. col., see Reitala, pl. 55), as well as several other smaller landscapes painted in Paris, are among the first examples of Finnish Impressionism.

During the 1890s Westerholm's work was also influenced by neo-Romanticism. His winter scenes of the river Kymi and the Åland Islands depict the rushing waters of the river and snow-covered shores. These broad panoramas, filled with a nationalistic love of the local landscape, represent his major Finnish themes. Towards the turn of the century he began to introduce Symbolist features into his winter landscapes. The most important works from his Åland collection are *View over Åland* (1896; Helsinki, Athenaeum A. Mus.) and *The Åland Islands* (1899–1909; Turku, A. Mus.). After 1910 he once again returned to a lighter, more picturesque idiom. From 1887 to 1898 and from 1904 to 1915 Westerholm was the principal instructor at the Turku School of Drawing and from 1891 held the post of custodian of the Turku Arts Association. He was one of the most influential teachers of his day, and his expertise was a valuable asset to the development of the permanent collection at the Turku Art Museum. Among his pupils were Wäinö Aaltonen and Juho Rissanen.

BIBLIOGRAPHY
A. Reitala: *Victor Westerholm* (Porvoo, 1967)

AIMO REITALA

Westerik, Co [Jacobus] (*b* The Hague, 2 March 1924). Dutch painter and printmaker. He trained at the Koninklijke Akademie van Beeldende Kunsten (1942–7) in The Hague. He made his debut in 1945, achieving fame with the painting *Fishwife* (1951; The Hague, Rijkdienst Beeld. Kst, on loan to Groningen, Groninger Mus.), for which he won the Jacob Maris prize in 1951. From 1955 until 1958 he taught at the Vrije Academie and between 1958 and 1971 at the Koninklijke Academie voor Beeldende Kunsten, both in The Hague. In 1964 his first one-man exhibition was held at the Gemeentemuseum in The Hague. From 1969 until 1970 he taught at the Ateliers '63 in Haarlem.

Westerik's subjects included mainly figures, interiors, landscapes and self-portraits. He also depicted scenes from everyday urban life with disproportionate objects, which gave the images a surrealistic quality. He represented human sensory experiences in nature, including the very painful, with an expressive realism. In terms of erotic tension his work is closely linked to that of Balthus. The viewpoints that he adopts as a painter are particularly notable: many close-ups, often from a frog's or a bird's perspective. Reality is represented in a systematic manner with little depth. The painter's attention was geared towards the expression of flesh, metal, cloth, wood and other material. To achieve this he used a variety of techniques and media. His paintings are in oil and tempera on rather small canvases; for his prints he used lithography, serigraphy, etching, drypoint, as well as working in watercolour, ink, pen and crayon.

BIBLIOGRAPHY
Co Westerik (exh. cat., Rotterdam, Mus. Boymans–van Beuningen, 1981)
W. A. L. Beeren: *Co Westerik: Schilder, Peintre, Maler, Painter* (Venlo, 1982)
Co Westerik (exh. cat., W. Berlin, Staatl. Ksthalle; Saarbrücken, Saarland-Mus.; The Hague, Gemeentemus.; 1983)

JOHN STEEN

Westermann, H(orace) C(lifford) (*b* Los Angeles, CA, 11 Dec 1922; *d* Danbury, CT, 3 Nov 1981). American sculptor. After working in logging camps in the Pacific Northwest, he joined the US Marine Corps in 1942 and served as a gunner for three years. The psychological terror that he experienced during World War II became an underlying theme in his later work, in particular in the *Death Ships*, for example *Death Ship USS Franklin Arising from an Oil Slick Sea* (pine, ebony and enamel, 1976; London, Charles and Doris Saatchi priv. col, see 1981 exh. cat., no. 33), as did the war-generated code of honour in which machismo, self-reliance and fitness figured prominently. After touring the Far East as an acrobat with the U.S.O. (United Services Organization), he enrolled in 1947 at the School of the Art Institute of Chicago. In 1954, after a year in Korea with the Marine Corps, he left the Art Institute and began to make sculpture.

Westermann's sculptures, made of varnished or painted wood and *objets trouvés*, conjoin Expressionism, the unexpected juxtapositions of Dada and Surrealism, and a craft approach to composition that he had developed while working as a carpenter to support himself, exemplified by *Mad House* (see fig.) and *Antimobile* (laminated Douglas fir, plywood and metal, 1966; New York, Whitney). Underlying them is his conviction that individuals are powerless to control the events of their lives or to affect the impending and unpredictable destruction around them. His depiction of the anxiety of living in a threatening world is mitigated by the refinement and beauty of his craftsmanship, and by humour, which he most often elicits through visually paradoxical combinations of contradictory or opposing characteristics and verbal and visual puns. In the *Big Change* (laminated pine plywood, 1963; New York, William Copley priv. col., see 1978 exh. cat., p. 23), for example, the materiality of wood is contradicted by the impression that it is a soft, pliable substance; the title of *Walnut Box* (walnut wood, walnuts and plate glass, 1964; Chicago, Mr and Mrs E. A. Bergman priv. col., see 1978 exh. cat., p. 19) refers both to the type of wood from which it is made and to the real walnuts with which it is filled. In 1961 Westermann moved to Brookfield Center, CT, and settled with the painter Joanna Beall (*b* 1935), whom he had married in 1959, in the caretaker's cottage attached to her family home. During the 1960s Westermann's predilection for punning, autobiographical themes and use of discredited, vernacular materials exerted a strong influence on artists in Chicago and San Francisco who responded to his non-formalist attitude towards art.

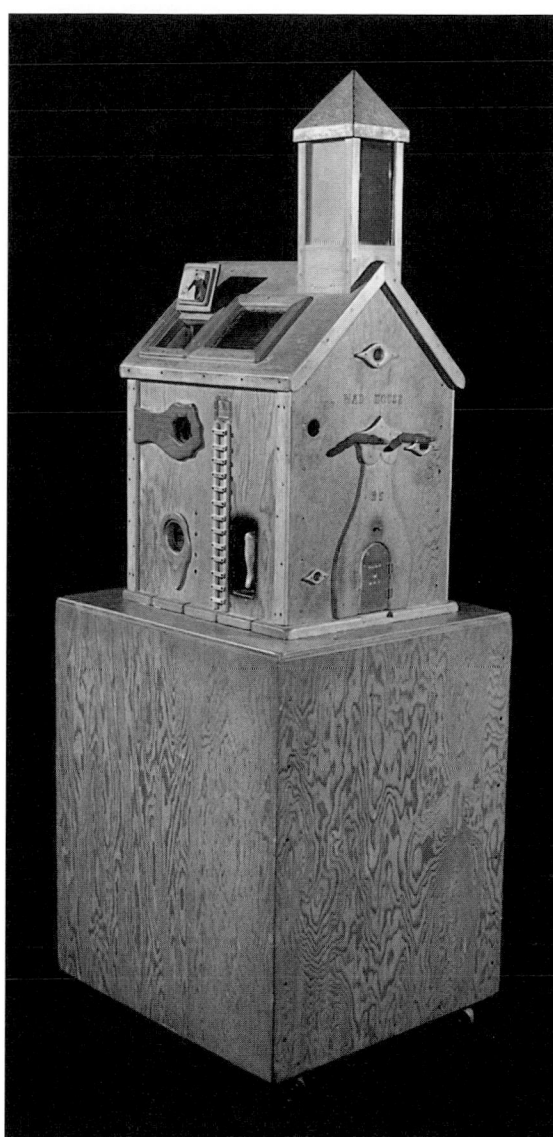

H. C. Westermann. *Mad House*, Douglas fir, metal, glass and enamel, 996×457×463 mm, 1958 (Chicago, IL, Museum of Contemporary Art)

BIBLIOGRAPHY
H. C. Westermann (exh. cat. by M. Kozloff, Los Angeles, CA, Co. Mus. A., 1968)
H. C. Westermann (exh. cat. by B. Haskell, New York, Whitney, 1978)
H. C. Westermann (exh. cat. by D. Adrian, ACGB, 1981)
B. Barrett, ed.: *Letters from H. C. Westermann* (New York, 1988)
                                                    BARBARA HASKELL

Western Chalukyas. *See* CHALUKYA, §2.

Western Ganga [Gaṅga]. Indian dynasty that ruled parts of south India from the 4th to 11th centuries AD. (There was no relationship with the Eastern Gangas, who ruled parts of eastern India from the 5th to 15th centuries.) The Western Gangas, though at times subordinate to the Kadambas, the CHALUKYAS OF BADAMI and the RASHTRAKUTA dynasty, maintained their prominence longer than many dynastic families. From their capital at Talkad (Talakāḍu), the Western Gangas ruled the area called Gangavadi, comprising southern Karnataka and part of Tamil Nadu, a position that often forced them to participate in the power struggles between the PALLAVA, PANDYA and CHOLA dynasties; in the 11th century the Cholas annexed most of Gangavadi. The Western Gangas were active supporters of the Digambara sect of Jainism in south India, and a number of Ganga period monuments survive at the sacred Jaina site of SRAVANA BELGOLA. The most notable of these, a colossal monolithic granite image of the Jaina saint Bahubali, known locally as 'Gommateshvara', was sponsored by Chamundaraya, general and minister to the Western Ganga king Racamalla IV (*reg c.* 974–99). Dedicated in 983, it stands *c.* 18 m high, which makes it among the world's tallest free-standing sculptures (*see* INDIAN SUBCONTINENT, fig. 220). Another major late 10th-century site with Jaina temples is Kambadahalli (*see* INDIAN SUBCONTINENT, §V, 7(vi)(c)). The Western Gangas also supported Brahmanical temples; the best surviving examples are in Karnataka, at Narasamangala and Begur.

BIBLIOGRAPHY
M. A. Dhaky: 'Ganga Jaina Sculpture', *Aspects of Jaina Art and Architecture*, ed. U. P. Shah and M. A. Dhaky (Ahmadabad, 1973), pp. 195–203
K. R. Srinivasan: 'Jaina Art and Architecture under the Gangas of Talakad', *Aspects of Jaina Art and Architecture*, ed. U. P. Shah and M. A. Dhaky (Ahmadabad, 1973), pp. 161–84
                                            ANDREW L. COHEN

Western Sahara [Arab. Sahara' al-Gharbiyah; formerly Spanish Sahara]. Desert region on the north-west coast of Africa. It is bordered by Morocco to the north, by Algeria to the north-east and by Mauritania to the east and south. Comprising a geographical area of *c.* 226,000 sq. km, Western Sahara consists of two regions: Saguia al-Hamra in the north and Wadi al-Dhahab (Rio de Oro) in the south. There is little agriculture, and most of the population (*c.* 75,000) is nomadic. In the late 1980s about a quarter of the population were employed in the extraction of phosphate. Hassaniyya, an Arabic dialect, is the language of the majority, although the national languages are Arabic and Spanish.

The Neolithic rock art found at, for example, Saguia al-Hamra suggests that hunting and pastoral groups once lived in this area. By the 4th century BC trading links with the Mediterranean region had been established. In medieval times the area was occupied by Sanhadja Berber tribes. A rich intellectual and economic life developed around Sijilmasa (est. AD 757; now in modern Morocco), but the town fell into ruin in the 14th century, and the area was dominated thereafter by Arabic-speaking Muslim bedouin. Later religious and intellectual centres included Rissani (now in Morocco) and Tamgrout near Zagora (now in Morocco), which is famous for its 18th-century *zawiya* library. In the mid-1880s the Spanish government claimed a protectorate over the coastal region, and by 1934 Spanish Sahara was established, first as a colony (until 1958) and then as a province of Spain. In 1976 the Spanish left, and since then the Algerian-backed independence movement, the Polisario Front, has been at war with Moroccan forces.

In the early 1990s Western Sahara's political status and future remained unclear. This entry covers art in Western Sahara since colonial times. (For the arts of the area in earlier times, including rock art, *see* AFRICA, §VII, 1; *see also* BERBER.)

The traditional arts of Western Sahara are those of nomadic desert life, still followed by most of the population in the 1990s. These include the manufacture of carved wooden beams and poles for tents, the weaving of camel- and goat-wool, and the use of brightly painted camel- and goat-skins to produce blankets, carpets, tent panels, cushions, bags, camel saddles, harnesses and women's palanquins. There is also a metalworking tradition, in which copper and iron are used to make cooking utensils and weapons, while jewellery is made mostly from silver with some use of gold, shells and glass beads. Decorations on these items consist of simple geometric designs, with a few floral motifs, and the limited use of Arabic or Libyco-Berber calligraphy. Traditionally, wood-, leather- and metalworking were practised by a tribe of ambulant artisans, the Ma'almin Hadadi.

The traditional building material of the Saharan area is pisé (rammed earth or clay). In 1899 Ma al-'Aynayn, a religious leader and writer who played an important part in the resistance movement against the French, built the city of Smara at an oasis to the south of Saguia al-Hamra. He used urban techniques and materials, including stone, transported the 300 km from Tarfaya by hundreds of camels. The ruins of the kasba and mosque of Shaykh Ma al-'Aynayn in Smara are the major Muslim monuments in Western Sahara.

Further developments of traditional architectural forms include an infusion of colonial styles, as seen in the town built by the Spaniards alongside old Smara, and a more modernist style evident in such buildings as the Instituto de Villa Cosneros and the Instituto de Enseñanza Media in the capital Aaiun (Laayoun), a city that expanded in the 1970s and 1980s. Art patronage and education are scarce although, in an attempt to counteract the decline of traditional crafts, the Spanish colonial government established the Escuela de Artes y Oficios, Villa Cisneros (now Dakhla). It continues to cater primarily for an expatriate European and tourist market.

BIBLIOGRAPHY

A. de Porras Zavala: 'Artifices del desierto', *Africa* [Madrid], vi/92–3 (Aug–Sept 1949), pp. 14–16
H. Nowak: 'Smara: Die heilige Stadt des Ma El Ainin', *Almogaren*, iii (1972), pp. 235–48
R. Santamaría: 'La ciudad santa de Smara y la belleza de Guelta Zemmur', *Africa* [Madrid], xxv/377 (May 1973), pp. 23–4
M. Sijelmassi: *Les Arts traditionelles au Maroc* (Paris and Casablanca, 1986), pp. 29–33, 65–79
Saharauis: Vida y cultura tradicional del Sahára Occidental (exh. cat., Madrid, Mus. N. Ethnol., 1990)

☐

Western Samoa. *See under* SAMOA.

Westervoorde, W. J. van. *See under* WITSEN, WILLEM.

Westfalen, Arnold von. *See* ARNOLD VON WESTFALEN.

Westin, Fredric (*b* Stockholm, 22 Sept 1782; *d* Stockholm, 13 May 1862). Swedish painter and draughtsman. From 1792 to 1807 he studied at the Kungliga Akademi för de Fria Konsterna under Lorens Pasch and Louis Adrien Masreliez. While there he excelled in the classes of the Ornamentskola and in 1806–7 he received gold medals for the Akademi's prize subject. Although he was awarded a travel scholarship by the Akademi, it is thought that he never left Sweden. In 1815 he became Professor at the Akademi, a position he held for 41 years, and was its Director from 1828 to 1840. Inspired by the examples of Jacques-Louis David and Anne-Louis Girodet, his paintings, combining as they do aspects of classicism and Romanticism, reflect the spirit of the time, in which there was a highly subjective approach to the Antique. He painted several altarpieces for churches in Stockholm and other Swedish towns: among them are the *Resurrection* (1825; Stockholm, Kungsholms Church) and the *Transfiguration* (1828; Stockholm, Jakobs Church), done in a sentimental manner.

In addition to paintings of religious and historical themes, Westin executed several scenes of mythological subjects, among them *Cupid and Psyche* (Stockholm, Nmus.), *Hebe and the Eagle* (1832; Stockholm, Rosendals Slott) and *Phaëthon Asking to Drive the Chariot of Apollo* (1810). These paintings were compared to the work of Raphael and Correggio and were at that time called 'painted poetry'. His many portrait commissions included *King Karl XIV on Horseback* (1838; Närke, Skjernsunds Slott), *Coronation of Queen Desideria* (1856; Stockholm, Kun. Slottet) and the *Wachtmeister Family* (1823; Johannishus Slott). The arrangements of these portraits are conventional and unimaginative and lack depictions of character. These deficiencies should not be blamed on Westin, however; he was constantly praised for painting as his sitters requested, to flatter their appearance. His drawings (e.g. *Alexis Wellenbugh*, 1861; *Princess Eugenie*, 1906; both Stockholm, Nmus.), however, are artistically and technically superior.

SVKL   BIBLIOGRAPHY
                        A.-G. WAHLBERG

Westlake, Nathaniel. *See under* LAVERS, BARRAUD & WESTLAKE.

Westmacott. English family of sculptors. They were leading sculptors of funerary monuments in the 18th and 19th centuries and also specialized in chimney-pieces and other forms of architectural sculpture. The first member of the family, (1) Richard Westmacott (i), married Sarah Vardy, daughter of the furniture-carver Thomas Vardy. They had a large family, including three sons who became sculptors: the eminent (2) Richard Westmacott (ii) and his younger brothers, (3) Henry Westmacott and George Westmacott (*fl* 1799–1827). Richard (ii)'s son (4) Richard Westmacott (iii) was also well known, as was his cousin James Sherwood Westmacott (1823–1900), son of (3) Henry Westmacott.

(1) Richard Westmacott (i) [the elder] (*b* ?Stockport, Cheshire; *bapt* 15 March 1747; *d* London, 27 March 1808). He received a gentleman's education, but then took up sculpture, working principally as a monumental sculptor in marble, but also carving marble chimney-pieces. One of the most remarkable of these is that carved in 1778 for the music-room at Cobham Hall, Kent (*in situ*), which has life-size figures of a shepherd boy and a dancing girl and a frieze relief of *Aurora* after Guido Reni, the whole demonstrating his sympathy with the Baroque. He also designed some chimney-piece tablets for reproduction in biscuit porcelain by Josiah Wedgwood.

Westmacott's best-known monument is that to *James Lenox Dutton* (marble, 1791; Sherborne, Glos, St Mary Magdalene), in a mixed style: the angel, sheltering medallion portraits of the deceased and his wife Jane and trampling on a skeleton representing Death, is a classical female figure with the wings of an angel as shown in Christian iconography. The modelling is highly skilled, but the excellent design of this piece is not paralleled in Westmacott's many other monumental works. Some of these were made to designs by the architect James Wyatt; they worked together, for example, on the monuments to *William, 2nd Viscount Barrington* (marble, 1793; Shrivenham, Oxon, St Andrew), and to *Henry Herbert, 10th Earl of Pembroke* (marble, 1794; Wilton, Wilts, St Mary and St Nicholas).

In 1796 Westmacott obtained the royal appointment of Mason for Kensington Palace, London, but, despite this recognition of his work and many commissions for monuments, he was declared bankrupt in 1803. He was able, however, to continue monumental work until 1805.

□

(2) Sir Richard Westmacott (ii) (*b* London, 15 July 1775; *d* London, 2 Sept 1856). Son of (1) Richard Westmacott (i). He was apprenticed at 14 to his maternal grandfather Thomas Vardy. He travelled to the Continent in 1792 and studied at the Accademia di S Luca in Rome (1793–6). He won first prize for his terracotta relief *Joseph Confiding Benjamin to Judah* (Rome, Accad. N. S Luca) in the student competition of 1795. While in Rome, he made the acquaintance of Antonio Canova and purchased antiquities for the architect Henry Holland. On returning to London in 1796, Westmacott established himself in Mayfair. He made his debut at the Royal Academy exhibition of 1797 with two marble portrait busts, including one of *Sir William Chambers* (London, Soane Mus.). He was elected an ARA in 1805 and became a full RA six years later.

Westmacott was the leading sculptor of civic and national monuments of his generation, winning many prestigious government and private commissions. He obtained eight of the thirty-six commissions for national monuments ordered by the Committee of Taste from 1803 to 1823. The first and most important of these is the monument to *Gen. Sir Ralph Abercromby* (1803–9; London, St Paul's Cathedral; see fig.), a dramatic, narrative marble group that established his reputation. Beginning with the monument to *Francis Russell, 5th Duke of Bedford* (1809; London, Russell Square), he gained fame for his skill in monumental bronze casting, a craft he helped to revive in early 19th-century England. Several of his most important outdoor public memorials are in bronze, including those erected to *Horatio, Admiral Viscount Nelson* (1806–9, Birmingham, Bull Ring; 1810–13, Bridgetown, Barbados); *Arthur Wellesley, 1st Duke of Wellington* ('*Achilles*', 1822; London, Hyde Park); *Frederick Augustus,*

Duke of York (1830–34; London, Carlton House Terrace); and *George III* (a colossal equestrian statue, h. 10 m, 1824–30, Windsor Great Park, Berks; another equestrian statue, 1818–22, Liverpool, Monument Place). He also produced the colossal bronze group designed by Matthew Cotes Wyatt as a memorial to *Viscount Nelson* (1813) in Liverpool.

Westmacott's works display considerable stylistic diversity, but can broadly be described as Neo-classical. His high esteem for Greco-Roman art led him on occasion to produce works such as the *Achilles* (London, Hyde Park) that represent little more than variations on famous antique sculptures. Typically for the period, his public monuments fluctuate between the presentation of classicizing allegorical themes (e.g. monument to *Charles James Fox*, marble, 1809–16; London, Westminster Abbey) and relatively lifelike portraiture in contemporary dress (e.g. monument to *Major Generals Sir Edward Pakenham and Samuel Gibbs*, marble, *c.* 1816; London, St Paul's Cathedral). One of his most unusual commissions was for a series of eight figures in stone (*c.* 1813–18) for the staircase of Ashridge Park, Herts. Representing the founders and benefactors of the destroyed monastery that once stood on the site, these figures from medieval history effectively contribute to the neo-Gothic ambience of the recently built estate. In addition, Westmacott created marble figures and reliefs for the galleries of some of the most distinguished collectors of the era. Several of these, notably *Cupid Made Prisoner* (1827; Petworth House, W. Sussex, NT), reveal a lyrical side to his work and bear Rococo flourishes, as well as showing Canova's influence.

Most of Westmacott's work was funerary sculpture. At least 60 of the 240 memorials attributed to him are inscribed, plain or simply decorated tablets that were largely executed by studio assistants. The finest of his commemorative sculpture includes several masterpieces. The marble relief erected to the *Hon. John Yorke* (*d* 1801; Wimpole, Cambs, St Andrew) epitomizes the sculptor's early, short-lived austere style. In the church monuments of his mature years abstract tendencies are softened. The monument to *John William Egerton, 7th Earl of Bridgewater* (marble, 1825; Little Gaddesden, Herts, SS Peter and Paul) evokes the warm intimacy of an Italian Renaissance Holy Family group.

Several works demonstrate a preference for gracefully delicate, if not sensual, female figures, such as the entwined marble angels of the monument to *Mrs Elizabeth Eardley-Wilmot* (*d* 1818; Berkswell, Warwicks, St John Baptist), or the peasant girl on the monument to *Lord and Lady Penrhyn* (marble, 1819; Llandegai, Gwynedd, St Tegai), who is paired with a stalwart quarryman wearing a leather apron and carrying tools. Such attention to naturalistic detail also characterizes the *Houseless Traveller* (marble, 1822; Bowood, Wilts), created as a memorial to Mrs Elizabeth Warren, a great benefactor of migrant workers. The pathetic figure of a destitute young mother, cradling her infant, so captivated Henry Petty-Fitzmaurice, 3rd Marquis of Lansdowne, that he arranged to purchase it. A replica was installed in Westminster Abbey in 1824. The sentimental interpretation of the doleful subject appealed to the public and critics alike, and the figure was immor-

Richard Westmacott (ii): monument to *Gen. Sir Ralph Abercromby*, marble, 1803–9 (London, St Paul's Cathedral)

talized in engravings, poetry and Parian ware reproductions.

Westmacott succeeded John Flaxman as Professor of Sculpture at the Royal Academy and held the post from 1827 until he died nearly 30 years later. His numerous honours culminated in a knighthood conferred by Queen Victoria in 1837. He exhibited at the Royal Academy for the last time in 1839, and his last public work was the pediment group for the British Museum, the *Progress of Civilization* (stone, installed 1851; *in situ*).

MARIE F. BUSCO

(3) Henry Westmacott (*b* 1784; *d* 1861). Son of (1) Richard Westmacott (i). He began work at a young age, producing a marble monument to *Henry Roberts* at Swanscombe, Kent, in 1796. Thereafter he produced nearly 50 church monuments. Between 1806 and 1810 he did work in connection with John Flaxman's marble monument to *Horatio, Admiral Viscount Nelson* at St Paul's Cathedral, London. In 1816 he carried out repairs to the mausoleum at Cobham Hall, Kent, where his father had produced an outstanding chimney-piece.

Like his father, Henry was noted for his chimney-pieces. Extensive work done by him at Kensington Palace, London, the residence of the Princess of Wales, included in 1808 four chimney-pieces of statuary marble, one of spar marble and one of bardiglio marble. Later he executed several more chimney-pieces for the same palace. One was executed by him, together with a marble plinth, at Brighton Pavilion (1822–3). In 1825 he worked at Buckingham Palace in London.

Henry Westmacott and his brother George Westmacott produced the base for the *Achilles* statue (London, Hyde Park) by their elder brother Richard. Henry's work also included decorative sculpture for Dodington Park (1809–12), Glos, and Fonthill Abbey (1807–22; destr.), Wilts. He exhibited at the Royal Scottish Academy (1830–36), having moved to Scotland about 1830, and at the Royal Academy, London (1833–5).

James Sherwood Westmacott, Henry Westmacott's son by his first wife, Eliza (née Stewart), is known for his historical statues and sculptures for church interiors; he exhibited at the Royal Academy and the Great Exhibition (1851), among other places.

(4) Richard Westmacott (iii) [the younger] (*b* London, 14 April 1799; *d* London, 19 April 1872). Son of (2) Richard Westmacott (ii). He wanted at first to become a barrister, but at his father's urging joined his studio to train as a sculptor. After going to the Royal Academy schools and spending the years 1820–26 in Italy, he worked initially with his father in Mayfair, London. Later, in the 1830s and 1840s, he appears to have taken over most of his father's practice. *Richard Westmacott, Jnr*, as he signed himself, produced about 40 church monuments and several busts and gallery portraits. Like the rest of his family, he carried out many commissions for marble chimney-pieces. About 1840 he and Robert Sievier executed two chimney-pieces at Chatsworth House, Derbys. He also produced many marble and stone reliefs, notably the monumental pedimental relief of the Royal Exchange, London (stone, 1842–4; *in situ*), the smaller-scale *Go and Sin No More* (marble, 1849; London, RA) and the *Cymbal Player* at Chatsworth (marble, 1832). He exhibited at the Royal Academy from 1827 to 1855, becoming RA in 1849, and succeeded his father as Professor of Sculpture in 1857. His marble busts include those of *Sir Sidney Smith* (exh. RA 1829; untraced), *Lord John Russell* (1843; Woburn Abbey, Beds) and *Cardinal John Henry Newman* (exh. RA 1841; untraced). He produced many funerary monuments, an example of high quality being that in marble to *Charlotte Egerton* (*d* 1845; Tatton Park, Ches, NT).

□

BIBLIOGRAPHY

Gunnis

M. Whinney: *Sculpture in Britain, 1530–1830*, Pelican Hist. A. (Harmondsworth, 1964); rev. by J. Physick (Harmondsworth, 1988), pp. 366–97

N. B. Penny: 'The Sculpture of Sir Richard Westmacott', *Apollo*, cii (1975), pp. 120–27

——: *Church Monuments in Romantic England* (London and New Haven, 1977)

A. Yarrington: *The Commemoration of the Hero 1800–1864: Monuments to the British Victors of the Napoleonic Wars* (New York and London, 1988)

M. Busco: 'The *Achilles* in Hyde Park', *Burl. Mag.*, cxxx (1988), pp. 920–24

MARIE F. BUSCO

West Mexican art, Pre-Columbian. Art produced in the period before European contact in the 16th century in the culture area of West Mexico, which comprises the modern Mexican states of Jalisco, Colima, Nayarit and Michoacán.

1. Introduction. 2. Architecture. 3. Pottery and clay figurines. 4. Other arts.

1. INTRODUCTION. West Mexican art is characterized by some of the most distinctive styles of PRE-COLUMBIAN MESOAMERICA. There has, however, been little systematic research into or study of West Mexican material in its archaeological context; most examples have been obtained through the looting of sites and the consequent destruction of all information regarding archaeological context and provenance. The unique qualities of West Mexican art, pertaining particularly to the shaft-tomb tradition, lacked monumentality. Few Mesoamerican deities were represented, and there was an emphasis on the portrayal of realistic anthropomorphic and zoomorphic ceramic figures. This aspect may have had a symbolic connection with shamanism and relates primarily to tomb offerings. West Mexican art seems to have functioned on the level of village-centred or domestic cults, rather than in the state-level civic or religious ceremonies of nuclear Mesoamerica.

Among the earliest ceramic complexes are Capacha in Colima (*c.* 1450 BC) and El Opeño in Michoacán (*c.* 1500 BC), followed by Chupícuaro (Guanajuato; *c.* 500–*c.* 1 BC) and later by the famous shaft-tomb figures of Jalisco, Colima and Nayarit (*c.* 200 BC–*c.* AD 600; *see* MESOAMERICA, PRE-COLUMBIAN, §III, 2(iii)(a)). By the Post-Classic period (*c.* AD 900–1521) the cultures of West Mexico had become increasingly Mesoamericanized, and most major art styles bear a strong resemblance to those of the Mesoamerican Central Highlands (*see* MESOAMERICA, PRE-COLUMBIAN, §II, 3(ii) and (v); and 4(ii) and (v)).

In general, the relationship between West Mexican art and that of other Mesoamerican cultures and artistic traditions seems to have been complex and is not yet fully understood. During the Early to Middle Pre-Classic periods (*c.* 2000–*c.* 300 BC), although OLMEC styles appear to have been ancestral to some of the most fundamental forms of Mesoamerican art, Olmec materials were virtually unknown north-west of the Balsas River. This has led some scholars to suggest that, during this formative period, West Mexican culture had a parallel development and was not really part of the Mesoamerican tradition. In fact, some artistic styles of this period in West Mexico bear closer resemblance to styles of Central and South American art than to anything in Mesoamerica, which might suggest the existence of a 'cultural corridor' along the Pacific Ocean coast from Sinaloa in the north to Ecuador–Colombia in the south.

From *c.* AD 1 to *c.* 700, during the end of the Late Pre-Classic period (*c.* 300 BC–*c.* AD 250) and the Classic period (*c.* AD 250–*c.* 900), the most widespread style in Mesoamerica was that of TEOTIHUACÁN (*see* MESOAMERICA, PRE-COLUMBIAN, §II, 3(ii)), also rare in West Mexico except for a few isolated finds. This seems to confirm the notion that the peoples of West Mexico, while following a typically Mesoamerican mode of life, were able to do so without too much outside interference from the Central Highlands states. By the Post-Classic period, however, the situation had changed radically. The Sinaloa–Nayarit–Jalisco region came into the Mesoamerican cultural sphere, exemplified best by changes in architecture, by MIXTEC motifs on the ceramics of the AZTATLÁN complex and by the late appearance of stelae in domestic or ceremonial contexts. From this time on, West Mexico became part of the mainstream of Mesoamerican artistic traditions.

The northern frontier of Mesoamerica fluctuated through time, alternately contracting and expanding. Up until the period of maximum expansion (*c.* AD 900) the Chalchihuites culture flourished in what are now the arid steppes of north-western Mexico. Several truly Mesoamerican traits featured in this region, among them the mound–plaza complex and the ball-game. At Cerro del Huistle, northern Jalisco, there was a TZOMPANTLI, *chacmool* sculpture (*see* MESOAMERICA, PRE-COLUMBIAN, §IV, 4(ii)(c)) and hall of columns at least two centuries before such features appeared in central Mesoamerica, suggesting that they originated in the north and diffused southward to nuclear Mesoamerica before they came to characterize Post-Classic Mesoamerican art and architecture.

In Michoacán the TARASCAN state consolidated its territorial expansion about AD 1350, and its well-defined artistic style serves to identify the region that came under the aegis of this polity. Tarascan architecture, metallurgy and stone sculpture contrast markedly with the more village-centred and smaller-scale art and iconography of the West Mexican shaft-tomb cultures. Tarascan artisans excelled in the manufacture of ceramics (including miniature vessels and clay pipes) and lapidary works combining obsidian, turquoise and other fine stones. Historical sources attest to the excellent quality of Tarascan featherwork, of which nothing survives.

2. ARCHITECTURE. Pre-Columbian architecture in West Mexico during the Classic period (c. AD 250–c. 900) was characterized by the Teuchitlán tradition (see MESOAMERICA, PRE-COLUMBIAN, §III, 2(iii)(b)), comprising circular civic–ceremonial complexes, primarily in the lake district of Jalisco and usually associated with shaft tombs, ballcourts (see BALLCOURT, §1), obsidian workshops and large irrigated agricultural fields. Other forms of architecture, particularly domestic, are largely unknown because of poor preservation and a lack of intensive archaeological research. By Early Post-Classic times (c. AD 900–c. 1200) civic–ceremonial architects in West Mexico imitated Mesoamerican Central Highland forms: circular complexes were replaced by more typically Mesoamerican pyramids–platforms set around square or quadrangular plazas.

3. POTTERY AND CLAY FIGURINES. Because of poor preservation of organic remains, most archaeological material from the earliest periods in West Mexico consists of ceramics or other non-perishable materials. The widespread distribution and stylistic changes according to time and area of production of ceramics have made them the most studied material by archaeologists and art historians. In fact, West Mexico seems to have been one of the areas where ceramics were first used in Mesoamerica—a type known as 'pox pottery' (i.e. poorly fired and thus pockmarked), dated c. 2300 BC, from sites in coastal Guerrero.

The Capacha ceramic tradition, one of the earliest following 'pox pottery', comprises vessels that bear a strong resemblance to material from Early and Middle Pre-Classic or Formative (c. 2000 BC–c. 300 BC) central Mesoamerica, and also to ceramics from coastal Ecuador, including stirrup-spout pots and gourd-shaped vessels, with incised and punctate decoration. But besides its ceramics, little else is known of the Capacha tradition, except that it was distributed in Colima, Jalisco, Michoacán and probably Nayarit (see also CAPACHA-OPEÑO). The El Opeño tradition of Michoacán offers a more complete view of Formative Western Mexico. The El Opeño site itself is famous for its shaft tombs (the earliest yet found) and for the offerings found inside them. These include negative-painted vessels, anthropomorphic figurines depicting ball-players, miniature stone *yugos* (yokes), probably related with the ball-game, and small votive objects of shell and green stone. El Opeño ceramics were stylistically linked with the TLATILCO and Tlapacoya pottery from the Pre-Classic Central Highlands.

From c. 500 BC a new artistic tradition developed in West Mexico. Named after the site where it was first

1. West Mexican anthropomorphic figurine, clay with white geometric decoration on red slip, from Chupícuaro, c. 6th–1st centuries BC (Morelia, Museo del Estado de Michoacán)

identified, the CHUPÍCUARO tradition was one of the richest and most varied ceramic styles in Mesoamerica. Its geometric, polychrome decoration on vessels and figurines (see fig. 1) influenced later styles not only in the west but also in central Mexico and other areas of Mesoamerica, particularly towards the northern frontier.

The best-known artistic manifestation of Pre-Columbian West Mexico began c. 200 BC: the shaft-tomb art of Jalisco, Colima and Nayarit. Anthropomorphic and zoomorphic hollow clay figurines of remarkable craftsmanship and complex symbolism were made in large numbers. Depicting warriors, shamans, dogs, fish, birds and other forms of wildlife, as well as scenes of everyday village life, these figurines have been found mostly by looters in the tombs of what were probably chieftains. It has been argued that many of these figurines depict scenes or objects best interpreted within the context of shamanistic beliefs, such as curing activities, divinatory practices or use of psycho-active substances.

Three major styles have been identified for shaft-tomb clay figures, each style to some extent corresponding to the geographic boundaries of the three modern states. The Colima style is characterized by representations of humans (hunchbacks, burden and water-carriers, horned beings, possibly shamans), flora (pumpkins, gourds, fruits etc) and fauna (mammals, insects, reptiles, crabs, molluscs, fish, turtles, armadillos etc; the most widely represented are dogs, ducks and parrots). Most of these figures are modelled in red clay, with other colours appearing rarely; occasionally negative decoration is used. Most of these figures served as containers, being provided with a spout integrated into the design of the vessel. The Nayarit style has an abundance of colour (red, black, orange, buff and negative) but a less developed modelling technique. Forms include vessels (ollas, dishes and bowls) and figures, which represent mainly human beings (warriors, musicians, women with vessels, sick people and couples). Pots are decorated with symmetrical geometric designs. The Jalisco style combines modelling with painting; normally only two colours were used: red on cream or buff and white on red. Anthropomorphic figures appear to be static and hieratical, including representations of warriors and women with breasts covered by tattoos.

4. OTHER ARTS. The mortuary offerings from the shaft tombs consist, aside from human and animal skeletal remains, pottery and figurines, of a range of non-ceramic objects. These include ornaments and other objects of shell and, occasionally, bone, for example trumpets, neck-laces, armlets and bracelets, nose-rings and earrings, pec-torals and *atlatl* (spear thrower) finger loops, and stone artefacts, such as *metates* (quern stones) and *manos* (rub-bing stones), axes, obsidian cores, flakes, scrapers, blades, points and polished pieces called 'mirrors', slate 'mirrors', encrusted pyrites, necklaces, pectorals and small anthropomorphic and zoomorphic images. Objects of other materials (cloth, feathers, wood, basketwork and matting) as well as foodstuffs and liquids were also undoubtedly placed in the tomb chambers, but these have not survived.

The non-ceramic artefacts of Pre-Columbian West Mexico have been studied less than the pottery. Neverthe-less, shellwork was abundant—not surprisingly, in view of the fact that West Mexico includes an extensive coastal stretch along the Pacific Ocean—and included the use of both Pacific and Atlantic species. Shell artefacts include beads, earrings, necklaces, bracelets, discs and other or-naments, sometimes with zoomorphic, anthropomorphic or other shapes, including such deities as Tláloc (the god of rain). It seems likely that both freshwater and seashell species were regarded as ritually important in ancient West Mexico. Lapidary work was also important, and some West Mexican chiefdoms seem to have controlled both the turquoise mines in the northern frontier of Mesoam-erica and the trade routes that brought this prized material to the Central Highlands, Southern Highlands and beyond.

The most important technological and artistic innova-tion in West Mexico after ceramics was metallurgy, which appeared in this area *c.* AD 800, long before it did so in the rest of Mesoamerica (*see* MESOAMERICA, PRE-COLUM-BIAN, §IX, 5). Objects of many forms and functions were made in copper, bronze, silver and gold, both decorative artefacts (bells, rings, lip plugs and other jewellery) and functional ones (tweezers, needles, adzes, axes, hoes and projectile points). Techniques included the lost-wax proc-ess, casting, annealing and hammering.

Stone sculpture was abundant in West Mexico, although its scale and level of craftsmanship are somewhat inferior to that of sculpture in nuclear Mesoamerica. There are many styles, and the subject-matter includes primarily anthropomorphic, zoomorphic and anthropo-zoomor-phic figures (see fig. 2). Several iconographic themes have been identified, most of them dealing with concepts of fertility. Petroglyphs are also abundant throughout western

2. West Mexican anthropo-zoomorphic figure with the head of a coyote, basalt, h. 619 mm, from Michoacán (Los Angeles, CA, County Museum of Natural History)

Mexico. Fieldwork in Jalisco and Nayarit in the 1980s and early 1990s discovered a vast corpus, including many styles and designs, both painted on and pecked out of rocks. Some of the symbols, such as concentric circles, have been interpreted as markers where shamans would station themselves during ritual ceremonies, probably linked with bringing rain.

Important collections of ceramics and other materials pertaining to the shaft tombs are held by the Los Angeles County Museum of Natural History; the Natalie Wood Collection of Pre-Columbian Ceramics at the University of California, Los Angeles (mostly Chuícuaro, i.e. pre-shaft tombs); and the Museo Nacional de Antropología, Mexico City.

BIBLIOGRAPHY

J. D. Frierman, ed.: *The Natalie Wood Collection of Pre-Columbian Ceramics from Chupícuaro, Guanajuato, Mexico, at UCLA* (Los Angeles, 1969)
Sculpture of Ancient West Mexico: Nayarit, Jalisco, Colima (exh. cat. by M. Kan, C. W. Meighan and H. B. Nicholson, Los Angeles, CA, Co. Mus. A., 1970)
H. von Winning and O. Hammer: *Anecdotal Sculpture of Ancient West Mexico* (Los Angeles, 1972)
B. Bell, ed.: *The Archaeology of West Mexico* (Ajijíc, Mexico, 1974)
C. W. Meighan, ed.: *The Archaeology of Amapa, Nayarit* (Los Angeles, 1976)
I. Kelly: *Ceramic Sequence in Colima: Capacha, an Early Phase* (Tucson, 1980)
O. Schöndube: 'La tradición de las tumbas de tiro', *Historia de Jalisco*, ed. J. M. Muriá, i (Guadalajara, 1981), pp. 173–214
J. Gallagher: *Companions of the Dead: Ceramic Tomb Sculpture from Ancient West Mexico* (Los Angeles, 1983)
M. Foster and P. Weigand, eds: *The Archaeology of West and Northwest Mesoamerica* (New York, 1985)
J. B. Mountjoy: *Proyecto Tomatlán de salvamento arqueológico: El arte rupestre*, Colección Scientífica, INAH, clxiii (Mexico City, 1987)
D. Hosler: 'The Metallurgy of Ancient West Mexico', *The Beginning of the Use of Metals and Alloys*, ed. R. Maddin (Cambridge, MA, 1988), pp. 328–43
M. A. Hers: *Los Toltecas en tierras chichimecas*, Cuad. Hist. A., xxxv (Mexico City, 1989)
L. J. Galván: *Las tumbas de tiro del Valle de Atemajac, Jalisco*, Colección Scientífica, INAH, ccxxx (Mexico City, 1991)
J. B. Mountjoy: 'West Mexican Stelae from Jalisco and Nayarit', *Anc. Mesoamerica*, ii (1991), pp. 21–34
A. Oliveros: 'El valle Zamora–Jacona: Un proyecto arqueológico en Michoacán', *Origen y desarrolo en el occidente de México*, ed. B. Boehm de Lameiras and P. C. Weigand (Zamora, Mexico, 1991), pp. 239–50
E. Williams: 'The Stone Sculpture of Ancient West Mexico', *Anc. Mesoamerica*, ii (1991), pp. 181–92
——: *Las piedras sagradas: Escultura prehispánica del occidente de México* (Zamora, Mexico, 1992)

EDUARDO WILLIAMS

Westminster, 1st Duke of. *See* GROSVENOR, (3).

Westminster, 1st Marquess of. *See* GROSVENOR, (2).

Weston, Edward (Henry) (*b* Highland Park, IL, 24 March 1886; *d* Carmel, CA, 1 Jan 1958). American photographer. He was the quintessential 20th-century American photographer, enduring a lifetime of financial insecurity and emotional anxiety for the singular pursuit of his craft and aesthetic ideals. His intricately detailed journals, which he called his 'daybooks' and which date from 1923 to 1943, convey an intimate sense of his creative life.

1. 1902–22. Weston took his first photographs in 1902 with a Bullseye camera, a gift from his father. He migrated to Los Angeles in 1906, by then an accomplished amateur photographer. He returned to Chicago *c.* 1908 to study commercial photography at the Illinois College of Photography and then returned to Los Angeles, where he worked for the Mojonier Studio, a commercial portrait studio, between *c.* 1909 and 1911. In 1909 he married Flora Chandler, with whom he had four sons. They moved to Tropico (now Glendale), Los Angeles, where Weston had established his own portrait studio by 1911–12.

Weston exhibited his fine Pictorial platinum prints in numerous international photographic salons and was often singled out in reviews as an original, artistic and perceptive talent. His portraits became known for their individuality and precise characterization, and his studio was popular and successful. To keep up with the demand, he invited Margrethe Mather (*c.* 1885–1952), another talented photographer, to become a partner in the business. Weston later claimed that Mather was the first important person in his life. They sometimes worked together and signed prints accordingly. Mather's esoteric interests in Oriental imagery largely influenced Weston's creative portraiture of *c.* 1917–21, which was characterized by simplified asymmetrical designs and exaggerated shadows, as in *Epilogue* (1919; Tucson, U. AZ, Cent. Creative Phot.). Mather frequently became his model and set up many of his fine images. Another early influence was the Dutch photographer Johan Hagemeyer (1884–1962), whom Weston first met *c.* 1917. Hagemeyer's cosmopolitan sophistication and intellectual pursuits in music and literature attracted and inspired Weston. Hagemeyer had also visited Alfred Stieglitz at his Gallery 291 in New York in 1916 and was well versed in the aesthetics of modern art and photography. He became Weston's principal sounding-board for discussions about Weston's artistic development in the early 1920s.

In 1922 Weston's work underwent an important transition during a trip east to visit his sister in Ohio and Stieglitz in New York. For the first time he decided to photograph an industrial form when he visited the Armco steel mill in Middletown, OH. The alien shapes of smoke-stacks and their complexity of arrangement and design led him to use the capabilities of the camera to the maximum and to delineate as much detail as possible, as in *Armco Steel, Ohio* (1922; Tucson, U. AZ, Cent. Creative Phot.). Although Hagemeyer and another mutual friend and photographer, Imogen Cunningham, had already discovered industrial imagery on the West Coast, Weston appropriated it and became the primary advocate for a new sharp-focused photography suited to the description of modern architecture and machinery.

2. 1923–7. In 1923 Weston left his studio in the care of Mather and sailed to Mexico with Tina Modotti, his favourite model. His three years in Mexico, interrupted by a six-month return to California, were a time of intense self-evaluation and growth. He became part of the revitalized Mexican artistic movement and was a friend of Diego Rivera and José Clemente Orozco. Weston developed a refreshingly new form of candid portraiture in his heroic heads taken with a Graflex camera against the clear Mexican sky, creating portraits such as that of *Manuel Hernández Galván* (1924; Tucson, U. AZ, Cent. Creative Phot.). His stark realism in diverse studies of nudes, such

as *Tina Modotti on the Roof* (1924; Mexico City, Mus. N. A.) and toilet bowls, for example *'Excusado' from Above* (1925; Mexico City, Mus. A. Mod.), reflected a growing concern for formal perfection and enigmatic, subliminal eroticism.

Weston left Modotti and returned to California permanently in 1926, moving into his old Glendale studio. In 1927 he met Henrietta Shore (1880–1963), a Canadian-born artist, who had studied in Europe and New York and travelled extensively before settling in California in the mid-1920s. Shore painted in an abstracted organic precisionist style and often depicted botanical and shell imagery of an erotically suggestive nature within an amorphous framework. Her paintings elicited in Weston an immediate and ecstatic response. They reinforced his own ideas of nature studies freed from non-essential details, which captured the life-force within the form. He asked to borrow her unusual shell collection with which he created a remarkable series of nautilus studies.

In his still-lifes of 1927–30, Weston used the simplest elements such as fruits, cheeses, vegetables and kitchen utensils to create photographic archetypes that record the quintessence of the object. Perhaps his most famous image, *Pepper No. 30* (1930; see fig.), which he described as 'a pepper so dynamic it becomes terrific with implied esoteric force' (*Daybooks, ii*, p. 182), clearly illustrates his attempt to present objectively the texture, rhythm and form of an element of nature, and also to reveal the essence of the object, thus creating an image more 'real' and 'comprehensible' than the object itself. Concurrently, his working technique became fastidious and dogmatic, concentrating on contact prints on glossy paper from large-format negatives (8×10 or 4×5 inches) on which no retouching was allowed. He often enlarged smaller negatives or used an internegative to create an 8×10-inch print.

3. 1928–50. With his son Brett (*b* Los Angeles, CA, 1911), Weston moved first to San Francisco in 1928 and then to Carmel, CA, in 1929, where he discovered an aesthetic and spiritual sanctuary in the terrain of Point Lobos, a coastal area that he found stimulating for the rest of his life (*see* PHOTOGRAPHY, colour pl. X). In 1929, with Edward Steichen, he organized the American section of the landmark exhibition *Film und Foto*, held at the Deutscher Werkbund, Stuttgart. He was also a founder-member of the San Francisco Bay Area's GROUP f.64 in 1932. Weston was the first photographer to receive a Guggenheim Fellowship in 1937 to document the American West. He and the writer Charis Wilson (*b* San Francisco, CA, 1914), to whom he was married from 1938 to 1945, travelled extensively through California, Arizona, New Mexico, Nevada, Oregon and Washington, and he took about 1500 negatives, many of which were published in Charis Wilson's *California and the West* (New York, 1940, rev. 2/1978). In 1941 he undertook another travel project and photographed the American South and East Coast for an illustrated edition of Walt Whitman's *Leaves of Grass* (New York, 1942).

The Museum of Modern Art in New York presented a major retrospective exhibition of Weston's work in 1946. Weston photographed on Point Lobos until 1948 when he was stricken with Parkinson's disease, which prevented him from taking any further photographs. His last photographs were published as *My Camera on Point Lobos* (ed. A. Adams, Boston, 1950/*R* New York, 1968).

WRITINGS

N. Newhall, ed.: *The Daybooks of Edward Weston*, 2 vols (New York, 1961–6/*R* 1971)
P. Bunnell, ed.: *Edward Weston on Photography* (Salt Lake City, 1983)

BIBLIOGRAPHY

M. Armitage, ed.: *The Art of Edward Weston* (New York, 1932)
The Photographs of Edward Weston (exh. cat. by N. Newhall, New York, MOMA, 1946)
M. Armitage, ed.: *Fifty Photographs: Edward Weston* (New York, 1947)
D. W. Thompson: 'Edward Weston', *Untitled #1* (1972) [phot. quarterly of the Friends of Photography, whole issue]
B. Maddow: *Edward Weston: Fifty Years* (New York, 1973/*R* 1978)
H. Jones, ed.: 'Weston to Hagemeyer: New York Notes', *Cent. Creative Phot.*, 3 (1976)
C. Wilson: *Edward Weston: Nudes* (New York, 1977)
Edward Weston's Gifts to his Sister (exh. cat. by K. K. Foley, Dayton, OH, A. Inst., 1978)
Edward Weston: Photographs and Papers, Tucson, U. AZ, Cent. Creative Phot. Guide series, 3 (Tucson, 1980)
Edward Weston and Clarence John Laughlin: An Introduction to the Third World of Photography (exh. cat., New Orleans, LA, Mus. A., 1982)
A. Conger: *Edward Weston in Mexico, 1923–1926* (Albuquerque, 1983)
J. L. Enyeart: *Edward Weston's California Landscapes* (Boston, 1984)
B. Newhall and A. Conger, eds: *Edward Weston Omnibus* (Salt Lake City, 1984)
P. C. Bunnell and D. Featherstone, eds: 'EW 100: Centennial Essays in Honor of Edward Weston', *Untitled #41* (1986) [phot. quarterly of the Friends of Photography, whole issue]
H. Jones, ed.: *Edward Weston: Color Photography* (Tucson, 1986)
B. Newhall: *Supreme Instants: The Photography of Edward Weston* (Boston, 1986)
A. Stark: 'The Letters from Tina Modotti to Edward Weston', *The Archive*, Tucson, U. AZ, Cent. Creative Phot. Research series, 22 (Tucson, 1986), pp. 4–81

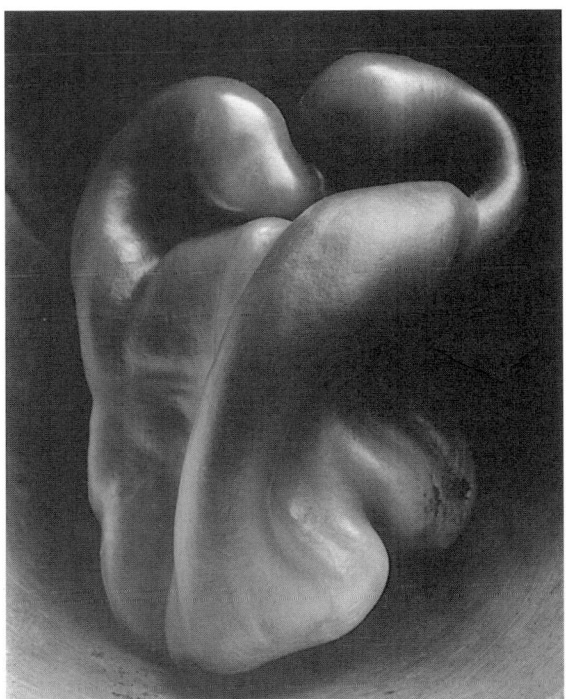

Edward Weston: *Pepper No. 30*, photograph, 1930 (Tucson, University of Arizona, Center for Creative Photography)

Edward Weston in Los Angeles (exh. cat. by W. Naef and S. Danly, San Marino, CA, Huntington A.G., 1986)

The Monterey Photographic Tradition: The Weston Years (exh. cat. by A. Conger and I. Latour, Monterey, CA, Peninsula Mus. A., 1986)

RICHARD LORENZ

Westra, Ans (*b* Leiden, 28 April 1936). New Zealand photographer of Dutch birth. She emigrated to New Zealand in 1957. She was best known for extensively documenting the lives of the Maori during the 1960s, 1970s and early 1980s. Much of her work was produced for *Te Ao Hou*, the magazine of the Department of Maori Affairs, and for the School Publications Branch of the New Zealand Education Department. Her humanist approach was heavily influenced by the photographic exhibition *The Family of Man*, which she saw in Amsterdam in 1957. In 1964 the publication of Westra's *Washday at the Pa* by the Education Department showed the difference between Maori and European attitudes to photography. Recounting a day in the life of a poor Maori family, this semi-fictional photo-essay was alternately attacked as untruthful and insulting, and defended as an accurate and noble portrayal.

PHOTOGRAPHIC PUBLICATIONS

Maori (Wellington, 1967)

Notes on the Country I Live in (Wellington, 1972)

Whaiora: The Pursuit of Life (Wellington, 1985)

BIBLIOGRAPHY

J. Bayly: 'Ans Westra: Finding a "Place" in New Zealand', *Witness to Change. Life in New Zealand: Photographs, 1940–1965* (exh. cat., Wellington, NZ, City Art Gallery, 1985), pp. 66–83

ROBERT LEONARD

Westreenen van Tiellandt, Baron **Willem Hendrik Jacob van** (*b* The Hague, 2 Oct 1783; *d* The Hague, 22 Nov 1848). Dutch collector. The only child of very rich parents, he was able to devote his whole life to a few honorary sinecures and to his hobbies, in particular to the accumulation of his collections. Under the influence of his cousin Johan Meerman (*see* MEERMAN, (2)), he began to collect old and new books, antiques and coins at an early age, and between 1796 and his death van Westreenen amassed important collections through purchases made both at home and abroad. He developed a particular interest in medieval manuscripts and the early history of the printed book. At the auction of Johan Meerman's estate in 1824, van Westreenen was the principal buyer after the English collector Sir Thomas Phillips, and he acquired numerous manuscripts and incunabula. At his death, he bequeathed his house on the Prinsessegracht in The Hague, with his collections, including several hundred medieval manuscripts and more than 1450 incunabula, Egyptian, Greek and Roman antiquities, as well as Classical and older coins, to the Dutch State, and it now forms part of the Rijksmuseum Meermanno–Westreenianum.

BIBLIOGRAPHY

J. H. Kernkamp: *Inventaris der familiepapieren Meerman, van Westreenen, Dierkens en van Damme aanwezig in het Museum Meermanno–Westreenianum* (The Hague, 1948)

P. J. H. Vermeeren: 'W. H. J. baron van Westreenen van Tiellandt als handschriftenverzamelaar', *Bibliotheekleven*, xlvii (1962), pp. 603–9

D. van Velden: *Journaal van W. H. J. baron van Westreenen van zijn reizen naar Londen, Cambridge en Oxford in de jaren 1834 en 1835* (The Hague, 1972)

R. Ekkart: 'The Dutch Museum of the Book', *A. Lib. J.*, xii (1987), pp. 25–8

RUDOLF EKKART

Westwork [Ger. *Westwerk*]. Ecclesiastical, semi-independent western forebuilding, containing certain distinct elements: a multi-storey internal space, commonly raised upon a crypt vestibule and culminating in a tower structure, surrounded by aisles with surmounting galleries, and with subsidiary stair-turrets expressed as external features, the whole ensemble having some specific liturgical use. The westwork occurred in western Europe between *c.* AD 800 and *c.* 1200, with several variants. The concept of the *Westwerk* is Germanic and problematic. The word applies only in German. To the French, several types of west block can be styled *Westwerk*, with little distinction made between the strictly defined *Westwerk*, a *clocher-porche* ('tower-porch') or a *massif occidental* ('western block'). In English the word is used with similar flexibility. It appears that in the Middle Ages the general term *turris* was used.

The first true westwork may have been that at Centula (790–99; now SAINT-RIQUIER ABBEY), known only through documents and illustrations, the precise reconstruction remaining a matter of debate. The abbey church built by Abbot Angilbert may have included an oblong transverse west block of at least two storeys, carrying a drum tower and flanked by circular turrets. The main entrance was through a basement crypt vestibule, with a low vault carried upon rows of columns. The two-part entrance contained the font and an altar and was later the site of Angilbert's tomb. The basement vault supported the main upper Saviour's Chapel, which was reached by the stair-turrets. The central space of the Saviour's Chapel was enclosed on three sides by aisles, while a screen wall divorced the chapel from the nave of the abbey church to the east. The chapel was sufficiently large to permit the whole community to attend mass on certain feast days. The surmounting drum tower was possibly wooden rather than stone and may have been a lantern tower. Centula contains the basic elements of most later westworks, in particular a cult altar, here to the Saviour, and the surrounding galleries for the boys' choir. Additionally, it provided a founder's mausoleum.

Charlemagne's own palace chapel at Aachen (*c.* 800; *see* AACHEN, §2(ii)(a)) immediately introduced a variant on this theme. The surviving rectangular western block has several levels but is more closely integrated with the main church interior. The vaulted vestibule leads straight into the aisle of the polygonal church. It is flanked by stair-turrets giving access to an upper tribune, containing the Emperor's throne, which also forms part of the gallery level of the main church. A third storey within the west block provided a relic chamber and was possibly topped by an inset, rectangular lantern tower. In addition, the intermediate throne-tribune may have had an external 'appearance' balcony, and it also provided direct access to Charlemagne's palace. The western block did not contain a major altar space, nor did it fulfil any specific liturgical function. Charlemagne heard mass from the high altar down below, and thus Aachen stands somewhat apart from the mainstream of westwork development. Nevertheless, the status of the building led to lasting imitation, and it is probably the source of such 11th-century small-scale west blocks as Jumièges Abbey (Seine-Maritime, France).

A number of other early westworks are known only imperfectly. They include a documented example at Fécamp Abbey (Seine-Maritime, France, *c.* 825 or perhaps *c.* 980; destr.), Reims Cathedral (850–60; destr., but illustrated on the tomb (destr.) of its founder *Archbishop Hincmar, d* 882) and at Hildesheim Cathedral (Lower Saxony, Germany, *c.* 870), which survives in part. Corvey an der Weser (Westphalia, Germany, *c.* 885; see fig. 1), however, still conveys a good impression of a substantial Carolingian westwork on the model of Saint-Riquier. Constructed between 873 and 885, it was added to the abbey church founded in 822 as a daughter house of Corbie (Picardy, France). Few alterations have been made to the massive westwork: the central tower was destroyed by the raising of the whole structure in the Romanesque period, and an arcaded gallery was inserted between the western stair-turrets, thus changing the external profile. The original arrangement consisted of the surviving square block extending the full width of the church, a central multi-storey porch projecting from the middle of the west façade, and twin stair-turrets rising from the western angles. A square tower rose above the centre of the block, forming a striking group with, and possibly touching, the forward turrets. The interior follows Saint-Riquier: a vaulted basement entry, access stairs to a tall upper chapel (dedicated to St Vitus), with aisles and galleries on three

sides and an eastern screen wall. Special architectural emphasis was applied to the central western bay at gallery level—perhaps a reference to the throne-tribune of Aachen. The first-floor interior was possibly intended as an Imperial presence-chamber.

St Ursmer, Lobbes (Hainault, Belgium), preserves sections of a 9th-century Carolingian westwork of a far smaller and slightly different type. Originally the exterior was two bays deep, with a two-storey west porch with attached turrets designed to touch the western angles of a central lantern. The interior had a raised platform space above the vaulted basement entry, but with a single-storey side aisle to the north, south and west, and possibly an eastern screen wall. The design, which might be considered an embryonic western transept, was more open than Corvey, with a greater internal integration of the main nave and westwork spaces.

In the Ottonian period (10th–11th centuries) the westwork developed in a number of ways, some blurring the strict definition of a semi-independent tower structure. St Cyriakus at Gernrode (Lower Saxony, Germany), founded by Otto I (*reg* 936–73) in 961, had a west block with flanking towers forming a cliff-like west façade. The present west apse was built later. The three western bays of the nave penetrate the west block, where they are covered by a raised platform, while the extension of the lateral galleries of the nave embraces the west block in the form of first-floor vestibules. At St Pantaleon, Cologne (see fig. 2, and *see also* COLOGNE, fig. 11), founded by

1. Westwork, Corvey an der Weser Abbey, Germany, interior looking north-west, *c.* AD 885

2. Westwork, St Pantaleon, Cologne, Germany, interior looking west, dedicated AD 980

Archbishop Bruno, brother of Otto I, the westwork (dedicated 980) consists of a square space beneath a tower, forming a terminal western bay to the nave, with two-storey projecting wings entered through twin arches north and south, and a larger, double-storey porch-vestibule (rebuilt) with flanking rectangular stair-turrets. It is debatable whether the main space was open to the tower interior in the form of a lantern or ceiled at nave height as at present, though the tower would seem somewhat pointless if it did not function as a light source. The original ensemble may have resembled the external Carolingian design of Lobbes, but the interior differed radically, being open to the nave floor level throughout and abandoning the elevated independent chapel, which formerly had been the prerequisite for a westwork. With St Pantaleon, the distinction between a westwork and a west block or *massif occidental* becomes very blurred. Similarly at St Peter, Werden (North Rhine, Germany), where the westwork was dedicated in honour of the Saviour in 943, the crypt vestibule is eliminated and the main space is brought level with the nave floor. Again, there is doubt concerning the original internal height, but while the spatial flow proceeds uninterrupted from westwork to nave, the specific dedication suggests the reservation of the main westwork floor space by means of internal fittings.

At Winchester (Hants, England), a substantial westwork (*see* WINCHESTER, figs 3e and 3f) appears to have been added to the Anglo-Saxon cathedral between 971 and 994 by bishops Aethelwold and Aelfeah (984–1005). It stood over the tomb of Winchester's main saint, Swithun, and excavation suggests the presence of a large rectangular central structure with apses north and south, the main western entry incorporating an earlier free-standing tower, which was connected with an inner vestibule, while a further eastern vestibule linked the main space with the cathedral nave. A contemporary observer described the building as having 'many chapels . . . , which keep the entry of the threshold doubtful . . . since open doors are seen on every hand' (Wulfstan the Cantor: *Life of St Swithun* (before 1005); London, BL, MS. Royal 15.C.VII). The exact reconstruction of the westwork remains problematic, but its addition at Winchester was doubtless connected with the reforming Council held there in 973. Continental monastic reforms based on the abbeys of Fleury, Ghent and Gorze were adapted and codified for English use in the *Regularis Concordia*, which specified three main liturgical areas within any church, the *oratorium*, *ecclesia* and *chorus*. Assuming that the three sanctuaries were placed axially, the Winchester westwork would correspond with the required *oratorium*, although, like most medieval terms, the word had a variety of meanings.

Many continental and English churches before *c.* 1050 have western tower structures of unusual complexity, more than a simple tower but less than a full westwork. St Hadelin, Celles-le-Dinant (Hainault, Belgium; *c.* 1040) has a western tower the width of the central nave alone, with flanking circular stair-turrets within the angles of the tower and nave aisles. The tower had no western entry, aisles or galleries, merely an enclosed rectangular space open to the nave and raised slightly above the main floor level. Beneath is a low vaulted crypt. Stairs lead to a high upper chamber with an eastern opening almost at nave clerestory level. The upper chamber was possibly open the full height of the tower and presumably contained a major altar. The whole ensemble might be seen as a westwork within a regular tower. Deerhurst Priory (Glos, England) preserves an even smaller version of a 'tower-westwork', with a narrow oblong multi-storey structure divided into at least four levels. The ground floor has a two-part entry vestibule, probably built after *c.* 1000, above an earlier porch. The low first-floor level, with unknown access, has an off-centre door leading east, presumably to allow for an altar space. The door must have led on to a wooden gallery against the west end of the nave. The taller, second-floor chamber has viewing arches down into the nave, plus an external western door that once led to a balcony. The top storey has a doorway leading east into the original roof-space above a flat ceiling over the nave. The internal spaces are small (*c.* 5.5×3.0 m) compared with a clear space in Corvey, even without the aisles, of more than 9 m square. The compression of so many potential liturgical areas into so small a space at Deerhurst shows clearly the extreme desire for altar space and the richness and complexity of the contemporary reformed liturgy.

The western tower block at JUMIÈGES ABBEY (*c.* 1040) is larger, though less complex. A bold, salient entry porch supports a tall, vaulted first-floor chamber, open to the nave below and reached by twin stairs contained within turrets flanking the porch. These are extended as polygonal towers, taller than the main western vessel. The integration of the block recalls Aachen, for the raised vaulted chamber forms an essential part of the processional route around the nave at tribune level, and, while it would have been possible to place an altar space within the eastern opening, the positioning of the access doors to the nave tribunes would have been inconvenient. Like much of Jumièges, the west block echoes Ottonian forms without slavishly copying their function.

The combination of liturgical and potentially secular spaces within Imperial westworks became more complex during the 11th and 12th centuries. ST GERTRUDE, NIVELLES (Brabant, Belgium), had a 10th- or 11th-century central western tower block with an apse, flanked by lower wings containing stairs, all set in front of a west transept. By the 12th century the westwork had grown to contain a large apse open to the main nave, flanking entrance vestibules, raised upper chapels in galleries above the west choir and further chambers above; the whole block was surmounted by a three-domed imperial chamber, which was used as a local law court until modern times. The massive exterior profile included twin turrets and a large central tower. St Servatius, Maastricht (Limburg, Netherlands; see fig. 3), has a similar 12th century westwork, with a massive rectangular profile and twin towers emerging through the roof. Apart from major and lateral altar spaces and chambers, the interior is memorable for the giant domed hall at the highest level, reached by broad spiral stairs. The impression given is more one of a palace than a church. This shift of emphasis, at least within Imperial westworks, may have originated in the 11th-century cathedral at Speyer (see SPEYER, §1), where,

although the exact form of the original westwork is lost, the evidence suggests that the secular function was pre-eminent.

The development of paired western towers the size of an aisle bay or larger, as opposed to mere access stair-turrets, further complicates the history of the development of the westwork. Many westworks built before c. 1050 were surmounted by a single rectangular tower, often grouped with minor flanking turrets. Their presence is purely practical, the main tower for lantern-light, the turrets for stair access. However, the external grouping must have been pleasing, and soon after 1000 tower groups appeared that were clearly arranged more for ornament than function. The twin-towered façade appeared c. 1015 at both Strasbourg Cathedral (see STRASBOURG, §III, 1) and Cluny Abbey (see CLUNIAC ORDER, §III, 1). Here the towers rose directly above the western terminal bays of the aisles, albeit of an aisled narthex at Cluny. The intervening western façade acts as the terminal wall of the nave interior rather than being the central element of a semi-independent westwork structure. While such developments ultimately led to such Gothic twin-towered façades as the cathedrals of Reims and Cologne, they also had an immediate and complicating effect on the whole concept of the westwork. In structures such as ST PHILIBERT, TOURNUS (c. 1020–30), the independent multi-storey westwork was combined with the twin-towered aisled narthex of Cluny II, creating one of the richest and most puzzling early Romanesque buildings. It is vaulted throughout and is entered through a crypt vestibule of 9 m square, as in many westworks, but the access stair-turrets to the main upper level are placed over the western corner bays and continue upwards as low towers flanking a gable end. The main first-floor chapel, here dedicated not to the Saviour but to St Michael, as at Cluny, abandoned the centralized plan beneath a lantern tower, adopting instead the three-bay, basilican plan of the Cluny narthex.

From the late 12th century the westwork was superseded by the Gothic west front, essentially a screen façade with paired towers, although in Germany the single west tower emerged as the most popular form, perhaps an echo of the westwork. The last true westwork is probably that of St Patrokli, Soest (c. 1200), which has aisles with galleries surrounding a great central tower, with stair-turrets rising behind. The disappearance of the westwork was due largely to the emergence of the secular cathedral as the mainspring of architectural fashion. Monastic churches had their own complex liturgical requirements, especially in those areas influenced by early Germanic reforms, but the different liturgical emphasis of Cluniac reform, plus the overwhelming success of French Gothic, quickly rendered the westwork unfashionable and unnecessary.

See also CHURCH, §II, 3(i).

EARLY SOURCES
Regularis concordia (10th century); ed. T. Symons, Nelson's Medieval Texts (London, 1953)

BIBLIOGRAPHY
H. Claussen: *Karolingische und ottonische Kunst* (Wiesbaden, 1957)
L. Grodecki: *L'Architecture ottonienne* (Paris, 1958)
K. J. Conant: *Carolingian and Romanesque Architecture, 800–1200*, Pelican Hist. A. (Harmondsworth, 1959, rev. 2/1978)
C. Heitz: *L'Architecture religieuse carolingienne* (Paris, 1963)

3. Westwork, St Servatius, Maastricht, Netherlands, view from the south, 12th century

——: *Recherches sur les rapports entre architecture et liturgie* (Paris, 1963)

F. Oswald: *Vorromanische Kirchenbauten* (Munich, 1966)

A. Verbeek: *Kölner Kirchen* (Cologne, 1969)

J. Hubert: *Carolingian Art* (London, 1970)

H. Kubach and A. Verbeek: *Romanische Kirchen am Rhein und Maas* (Neuss, 1971)

J.-L. Genicot: *Les Eglises mosanes du XIe siècle* (Leuven, 1972)

H. Kubach: *Romanesque Architecture* (New York, 1975)

D. Parsons: 'The Pre-Romanesque Church of St-Riquier: The Documentary Evidence', *J. Brit. Archaeol. Assoc.*, cxxx (1977), pp. 21–51

G. Binding and B. Lohr: *Kleine Kölner Baugeschichte* (Cologne, 1978)

E. Fernie: *The Architecture of the Anglo-Saxons* (London, 1983)

FRANCIS WOODMAN

Wet [Wett], Jacob Willemsz. de, I (*b* Haarlem, *c.* 1610; *d* ?Haarlem, after 5 Sept 1675). Dutch painter and draughtsman. It seems unlikely that he is the same as the Jacobus de Wit who was a member of the Alkmaar Guild of St Luke in 1637 or as the Jan de Wet (*b* Hamburg, *c.* 1617) who was a pupil of Rembrandt. Sumowski has disentangled his work from that of Gerrit de Wet (*d* 1674), Daniel Thievaert (1613–57) and of his own son, Jacob de Wet the younger (*b* Haarlem, *c.* 1640; *d* Amsterdam, 11 Nov 1697). De Wet's works are predominantly of biblical and mythological subjects, and his early painting, the *Raising of Lazarus* (1633; Darmstadt, Hess. Landesmus.), is close to the work of Jan Pynas and Pieter Lastman. Another painting of the same subject, executed in 1634, is much closer to Rembrandt's work of the early 1630s, and the pronounced emotional content and strong chiaroscuro in much of his work may indicate that he was a pupil of Rembrandt. His later work places a greater emphasis on the landscape backgrounds, often relegating the figures to an almost incidental role, with a use of colour closer to Cuyp's idyllic scenes (e.g. *Landscape with a Ferry*, London, N.G.). A number of drawings by de Wet exist, including his sketchbook (*c.* 1636; Haarlem, Gemeentearchf, MS. Hs 230), which is predominantly pre-Rembrandtesque in style. The sketchbook also notes his pupils, who included Paulus Potter (1642) and his own son. Jacob de Wet the younger worked in Edinburgh and copied a series of paintings depicting the Kings of Scotland (Edinburgh, Pal. Holyroodhouse, Royal Col.), as well as executing some of the decorative work in Holyroodhouse.

BIBLIOGRAPHY

A. Bredius: 'Het schetsboek van Jacob de Wet', *Oud-Holland*, xxxvii (1919), pp. 215–22

A. Chudzikowski: 'Les Eléments rembrandtesques dans l'oeuvre de Jacob de Wet', *Biul. Hist. Sztuki*, xiii (1956), pp. 428–42

W. Sumowski: *Gemälde der Rembrandt-Schüler*, iv (Landau/Pfalz, 1983–90)

B. Haak: *The Golden Age: Dutch Painters of the Seventeenth Century* (New York, 1984), pp. 256, 273

W. Sumowski: *Drawings of the Rembrandt School*, x (New York, 1990), pp. 5321–5409

Wettin, House of. German family of rulers, collectors and patrons (see fig.). Different branches ruled as dukes and electors of Saxony, kings of Poland and, from the early 19th to the early 20th century, as kings of Saxony. Frederick, Margrave of Meissen, was awarded the Duchy of Saxe-Wittenberg in 1423, which he ruled (1423–8) as Frederick I, Elector of Saxony. His son Frederick II (*reg* 1428–64) succeeded him and was succeeded in turn by his sons (1) Ernest, Elector of Saxony, and (2) Albert,

Duke of Saxony, who, at his command, ruled jointly until 1485, when they divided the House of Wettin and its lands into the Ernestine and Albertine branches. Ernest's son (3) Frederick III, Elector of Saxony, was a notable patron of the arts, commissioning a new palace and church and filling the latter with reliquaries and paintings by such artists as Lucas Cranach the elder. Albert's son (4) Henry, Duke of Saxony, instituted the conversion of the duchy to Protestantism, but limited financial means restricted his activities as a patron. Henry's son (5) Augustus I, Elector of Saxony, established the Dresden *Kunstkammer* and promoted the architectural expansion of Dresden, the capital of the Albertine line. The patronage of Augustus's grandson (6) John-George I, Elector of Saxony, was constrained by the Thirty Years War. However, John-George's great-grandson (7) Frederick-Augustus I, Elector of Saxony, and from 1697 Augustus II, King of Poland, used royal building and town architecture to illustrate his absolute power. During his reign Saxon Baroque architecture and the visual arts reached an unprecedented peak and the decorative arts also flourished, notably the production of Meissen porcelain of which he had a vast collection. His son (8) Frederick-Augustus II, Elector of Saxony, was, like his father, a comparatively unsuccessful politician yet a notable patron and collector who contributed to the development of the arts in Saxony and Poland, where he reigned as Augustus III. His son (9) Albert, Duke of Saxe-Teschen, shared his father's and grandfather's passion for collecting and built up the Albertina, a unique collection of drawings and copper-engravings. (10) Anna Amalia, Duchess of Saxe-Weimar, was a member of the Ernestine branch of the family, and under her cultured patronage Weimar became the focal point of Germany's intellectual life. Her son (11) Charles Augustus, Duke of Saxe-Weimar, shared her active enthusiasm for the arts, pursuing a highly developed cultural policy and building up a large collection. The Ernestine territories were divided into small duchies, and members of these lines both founded and married into royal dynasties (see fig.). Members of the Albertine line reigned as kings of Saxony from 1806 until 1918 when the kingdom was abolished.

□

(1) Ernest [Ernst], Elector of Saxony (*b* Meissen, 24 March 1441; *reg* 1464–86; *d* Colditz, 26 Aug 1486). Elder son of Frederick II, Elector of Saxony (*reg* 1428–64).

(2) Albert [Albrecht] [the Brave], Duke of Saxony (*b* Grimma, 31 July 1443; *reg* 1464–1500; *d* Emden, 12 Sept 1500). Brother of (1) Ernest, Elector of Saxony. At their father's command, the brothers initially ruled Saxony jointly until 1485 when Ernest insisted that it be divided into electorate and duchy. This action temporarily weakened Saxony's political power and resulted in the division of the Wettin family into the Ernestine and Albertine branches. While Ernest, Elector of Saxony, expanded the realm by annexations, Albert, Duke of Saxony, worked to centralize the state's finances and developed regional mining from which both branches of the family subsequently benefited. Between 1488 and 1493 Albert was the representative of emperors Frederick III and Maximilian

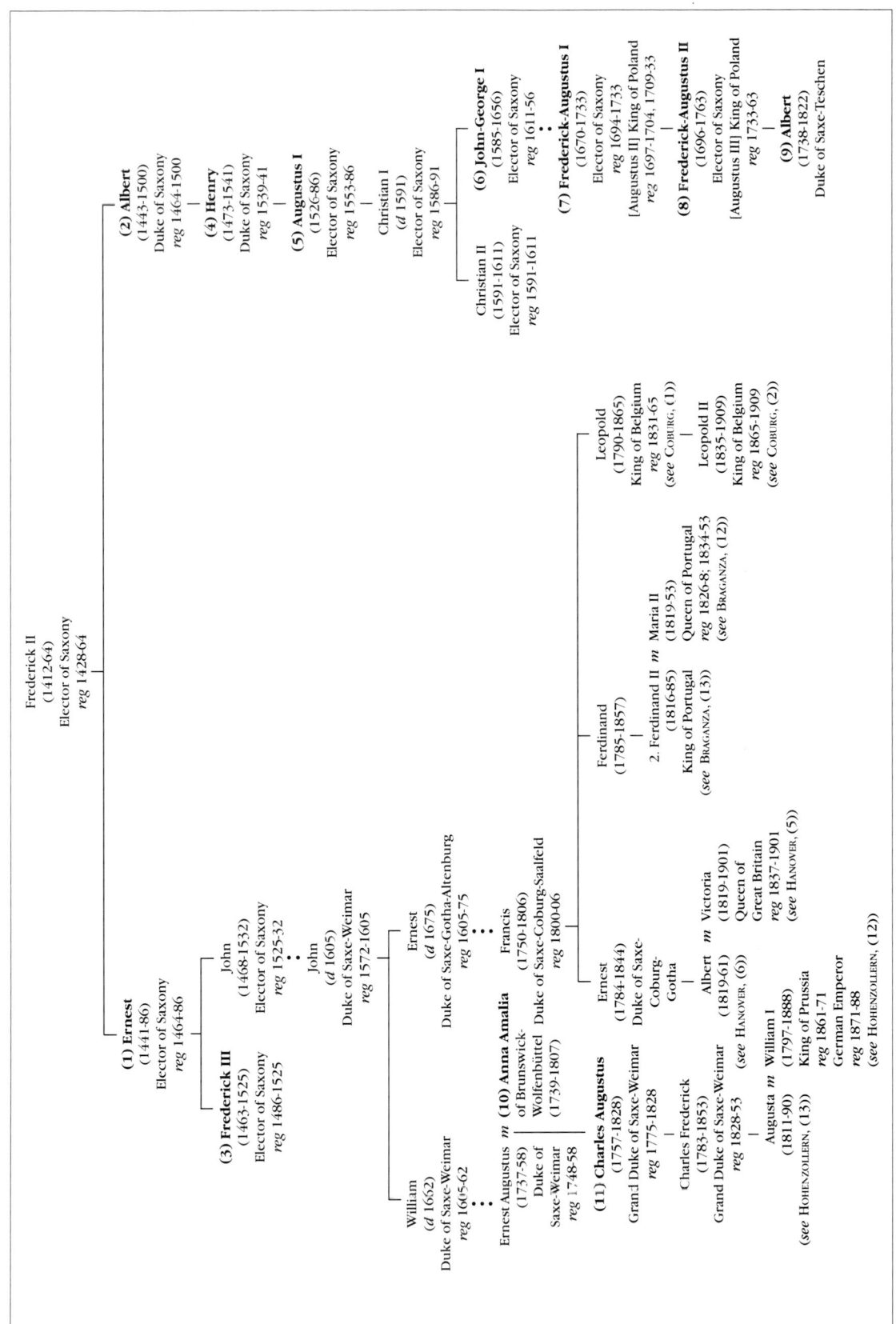

Family tree of the Wettin dynasty

in the Netherlands and from 1493 served as governor of Friesland.

The brothers are primarily known for their architectural projects, jointly sponsored, most significantly the building and renovation of the palaces at Meissen, Dresden and Torgau. Work began in Meissen in 1471, under the direction of ARNOLD VON WESTFALEN, and was largely completed by 1525. Albrechtsburg, as the palace was named from 1676, is noted for its elaborate and varied vaulting patterns, grand staircase and sizeable rooms. Despite its grandeur, the palace was rarely lived in since the brothers preferred Dresden, and Frederick III, Elector of Saxony (see (3) below), moved the electoral court to Wittenberg in 1486. From 1710 to 1864, however, Albrechtsburg was the centre of the Meissen porcelain industry (see MEISSEN, §3).

The full-length brass funerary plaques, located in the Fürstenkapelle in Meissen Cathedral, were produced in memory of Ernest, Elector of Saxony, in 1495 by Peter Vischer the elder and probably by his workshop c. 1500 for Albert, Duke of Saxony. Arnold von Westfalen also added a new west wing (from 1471) to the main courtyard of the palace in Dresden; it included a chapel with elaborate star vaults and grand staircase, little of which survived the radical alteration and rebuilding between 1548 and 1556. Albert commissioned Conrad Pflüger to supervise work on the hall in the western wing (1480–82) of Schloss Hartenfels at Torgau.

NDB   BIBLIOGRAPHY

R. Bruck: *Friedrich der Weise als Förderer der Kunst* (Strasbourg, 1903; *R* Nendeln, 1979), pp. 87–8

H.-J. Mrusek, ed.: *Die Albrechtsburg zu Meissen* (Leipzig, 1972)

P. Findeisen and H. Magirius: *Die Denkmale im Bezirk Leipzig: Die Denkmale der Stadt Torgau* (Leipzig, 1976), pp. 125–37

H.-J. Mrusek: *Drei sächsische Kathedralen: Merseburg, Naumburg, Meissen* (Dresden, 1976), pp. 275–6, 368, 375

B. Gonschor: 'Bauforschung am Dresdener Schloss', *Denkmale in Sachsen*, ed. H. Müller and H. Magirius (Weimar, 1978), pp. 225–33

(3) Frederick [Friedrich] **III** [the Wise], Elector of Saxony (*b* Torgau 17 Jan 1463; *reg* 1486–1525; *d* Lochau bei Torgau, 5 May 1525). Son of (1) Ernest, Elector of Saxony. On becoming Elector, he selected Wittenberg as his capital and transformed the town into a fitting capital, commissioning a new palace (1490–1525), possibly from Conrad Pflüger, who later built the Schlosskirche (1496–1503). The saintly relics he collected for display in the church were inventoried in Lucas Cranach I's *Das Wittenberger Heiltumsbuch* (Wittenberg, 1509): 5005 relics were stored in 168 reliquaries fashioned in gold and silver by Paul Müllner (*fl* 1502–46) and other leading goldsmiths. Cranach's 117 woodcuts show their diversity of design. Most of the reliquaries were later melted down or disappeared. By the early 1520s the Elector had amassed 18,970 relics, last shown in 1523.

The best account of the church's artistic riches is provided in Christoph Scheurl's *Oratio* (Leipzig, 1509), which lists Dürer's *Adoration of the Magi* (1504; Florence, Uffizi), Cranach's *St Catherine* altarpiece (1506; Dresden, Gemäldegal. Alte Meister) and Hans Burgkmair I's *St Sebastian* (1505; Nuremberg, Ger. Nmus.) among the paintings that decorated the church's 20 altars. Cranach's *Trinity* (c. 1515–20) for the high altar, Conrat Meit's *Virgin*

and Child with Forty Angels (1507–9) and the wooden Crucifix (1505–6) by Tilman Riemenschneider were destroyed by fire in 1760. In c. 1520 two life-size alabaster statues of the *Elector* and his brother *John of Saxony* (1468–1532), kneeling in prayer, were placed in the choir. The brass epitaph (1527; *in situ*) of the Elector by Peter Vischer (ii), which includes a full-length portrait depicting him holding the electoral sword, was approved as Vischer's official masterpiece (*see* VISCHER, (4)).

Lucas Cranach the elder, court painter from c. 1505, produced for the Elector dozens of altarpieces, portraits, hunting scenes, murals, prints and miscellaneous designs for other craftsmen (*see* CRANACH, (1)). Jacopo de' Barbari and Conrat Meit were among several talented masters who worked briefly for him, as was Adriano Fiorentino, who created a bronze bust of *Frederick the Wise of Saxony* (1498; Dresden, Grünes Gewölbe). Significantly, he was the first noble patron of Albrecht Dürer, who produced at least seven paintings for him, the earliest a portrait (1496; Berlin, Staatl. Ksthalle), the last the *Martyrdom of the Ten Thousand* (1508; Vienna, Ksthist. Mus.), and at his request trained a young Saxon artist in Nuremberg (1501–3). In 1524 Dürer created his famous portrait engraving of the Elector (B. 104), who was also among the first German princes to commission and collect portrait medals.

The Elector's artistic patronage was extensive, allegedly including building projects in Torgau, Belzig, Lochau, Eilenburg, Altenburg, Neu Lochau, Grimma, Colditz, Weimar, Hirtzberg, Eisenach, Wartburg and Liebenswerd. In 1502 he founded the University of Wittenberg, at which, in 1512, Martin Luther became professor of theology. As the Protestant Reformation waxed, the Elector protected Luther, though he himself remained a Catholic. He surrounded himself with capable scholars and administrators and corresponded with such scholars as Conrad Celtis (1459–1508), Erasmus and Johannes Thurmayn (Aventinus; 1477–1534), as well as Dürer.

NDB   BIBLIOGRAPHY

L. Cranach: *Das Wittenberger Heiltumsbuch* (Wittenberg, 1509; facs., Unterschneidheim, 1969)

R. Bruck: *Friedrich der Weise als Förderer der Kunst* (Strasbourg, 1903; *R* Nendeln, 1979) [excellent on his patronage]

P. Kalkoff: *Ablass und Reliquienverehrung an der Schlosskirche zu Wittenberg unter Friedrich dem Weisen* (Gotha, 1907)

P. Grotemeyer: 'Die Statthaltermedaillen des Kurfürsten Friedrich des Weisen von Sachsen', *Münchn. Jb. Bild. Kst*, n. s. 2, xxi (1970), pp. 143–66

F. Anzelewsky: *Albrecht Dürer: Das malerische Werk* (Berlin, 1971), pp. 19–40, 72–5, 82, 105

Lukas Cranach, 2 vols (exh. cat. by D. Koepplin and T. Falk, Basle, Kstmus., 1974–6), pp. 185–252

F. Bellmann, M.-L. Harksen and R. Werner: *Die Denkmale im Bezirk Halle: Die Denkmale der Lutherstadt Wittenberg* (Weimar, 1979), pp. 90–107, 235–67

W. L. Strauss: *Sixteenth-century German Artists*, 10 [VII/i] of *The Illustrated Bartsch*, ed. W. Strauss (New York, 1980) [B.]

B. Stephan: 'Kulturpolitische Massnahmen des Kurfürsten Friedrich III., des Weisen, von Sachsen', *Lutherjb.*, xlix (1982), pp. 50–95

I. Ludolphy: *Friedrich der Weise: Kurfürst von Sachsen, 1463–1525* (Göttingen, 1984)

C. C. Christensen: *Princes and Propaganda: Electoral Saxon Art of the Reformation* (Kirksville, MO, 1992)

J. C. Smith: *German Sculpture of the Later Renaissance, c. 1520–1580: Art in an Age of Uncertainty* (Princeton, 1994), pp. 16, 36, 128, 134, 136, 138–9, 167, 178, 319–20, 322, 338, 350, 387, 404, 449, 481

(4) Henry [Heinrich] [the Pious], Duke of Saxony (*b* Dresden, 16 March 1473; *reg* 1539–41; *d* Dresden, 18 Aug 1541). Son of (2) Albert, Duke of Saxony. After a pilgrimage to the Holy Land in 1498, he served briefly as governor of Friesland and from 1505 ruled in Freiberg and Wolkenstein before becoming Duke of Saxony in 1539. His short reign was especially significant since he instituted the conversion of the duchy to Lutheranism. Although his financial means never allowed him to match the patronage of Frederick III, Elector of Saxony (*see* (3) above), he did commission numerous paintings and sculptures for his palaces in Freiberg and Wolkenstein. Lucas Cranach I executed several portraits of Henry and his family, including the full-length portraits of *Henry, Duke of Saxony* and his wife *Katharine of Mecklenburg* (1514; Dresden, Gemäldegal. Alte Meister), which are among the most famous of German Renaissance paintings. Cranach produced at least three other portraits of the Duke (1528, New York, priv. col.; 1528, Kassel, Schloss Wilhelmshöhe; 1537, Dresden, Gemäldegal. Alte Meister) and a drawing (1526; untraced) for a commissioned portrait of the Duchess.

Between 1528 and 1533 the Duke employed Peter Dell (i), who carved four limewood reliefs of the *Crucifixion, Resurrection, Holy Teaching* (all Dresden, Grünes Gewölbe) and the *Fall of the Rebel Angels* (untraced). The *Resurrection* and the *Holy Teaching* exhibit specifically Lutheran iconographies and thus reveal the Duke's gradual conversion to Lutheranism. His financial support for artistic embellishments to Freiberg Cathedral included his donation of the stone baptismal font (1531) and erection of the princes' gallery (1537) over the entrance to the choir. In contrast to his Catholic predecessors, who were buried in Meissen Cathedral, he chose Freiberg as his funerary site. His simple slab was placed originally beneath the gallery before being moved into the choir. His sons followed his lead, and during the second half of the 16th century Freiberg Cathedral was transformed by Giovanni Maria Nosseni into one of Europe's grandest family mausolea. CARLO DI CESARI DEL PALAGIO executed the life-size bronze figures (1590–93) for the tombs (1586–95).

NDB

BIBLIOGRAPHY

S. Issleib: 'Herzog Heinrich als evangelischer Fürst, 1537–1541', *Beitr. Sächs. Kirchgesch.*, xx (1906), pp. 143–215
L. Bruhns: *Würzburger Bildhauer der Renaissance und des werdenden Barock, 1540–1650* (Munich, 1923), pp. 41–3
M. J. Friedländer and J. Rosenberg: *Die Gemälde von Lucas Cranach* (Berlin, 1932); rev. as *The Paintings of Lucas Cranach* (Ithaca, 1978), nos 60–61, 306–7, 318, 319–319A, 352, fig. 9
J. L. Sponsel: *Das Grüne Gewölbe zu Dresden*, iv (Dresden, 1932), p. 120
H. M. Kühn: *Die Einziehung des geistlichen Gutes im Albertinischen Sachsen, 1539–1553* (Cologne and Graz, 1966), pp. 17–71
Lukas Cranach, 2 vols (exh. cat. by D. Koepplin and T. Falk, Basle, Kstmus., 1974–6), i, p. 408; ii, p. 696
S. Baumgartner: *Reise zum Heiligen Grab 1498 mit Herzog Heinrich dem Frommen von Sachsen*, ed. T. Kraus (Göppingen, 1986)
J. C. Smith: '"Verbum domini manet in aeternum": Medal Designs by Sebald Beham and the Reformation in the Duchy of Saxony', *Anz. Ger. Nmus.* (1987), pp. 205–26
——: *German Sculpture of the Later Renaissance, c. 1520–1580: Art in an Age of Uncertainty* (Princeton, 1994), pp. 62–4, 68–71, 98, 128, 167, 175, 181, 183, 367, 425

JEFFREY CHIPPS SMITH

(5) Augustus [August] **I**, Elector of Saxony (*b* Freiberg, 31 July 1526; *reg* 1553–86; *d* Dresden, 12 Feb 1586). Son of (4) Henry, Duke of Saxony. He established a *Kunstkammer c.* 1560 in the Residenz at Dresden, containing pictures of the emperors, copies of paintings by Titian, an alabaster copy of Michelangelo's *Times of Day* from the tomb of *Lorenzo de' Medici* in S Lorenzo, Florence, and technical and scientific instruments. His main claim to fame, however, is his promotion of the architectural expansion of Dresden through his issue of regulations enabling the town to be developed as Saxony's capital (*see* DRESDEN, §I). In 1559–63 a new customs house was built by Melchior Trost (*fl* 1527/8; *d* 1559) and Paul Buchner; in 1568 the Jägerhof was constructed in Altendresden, and in 1586 building work started on the Stallhof (1586–91; now the Johanneum), which was probably designed by Hans Irmisch (1526–93). Of particular architectural merit was the Lusthaus (1590, destr. 1747) built by Giovanni Maria Nosseni. In 1555 Augustus commissioned a statue depicting him receiving the electoral sword from his late brother, Maurice, Elector of Saxony (*reg* 1547–53), from the sculptor Hans Walther (1526–1600); since 1896 it has been kept beneath the Jungfernbastei, Dresden. Another monument (1563; *in situ*) to *Maurice, Elector of Saxony* by Antonius von Zerun was erected in the funerary chapel of the Albertine line of the House of Wettin in Freiberg Cathedral. The Elector extended Schloss Moritzburg (1582–4) and built Schloss Augustusburg (1568–73; designed by Hieronymus Lotter (1497–1580), mayor of Leipzig), Schloss Annaburg (1571–3) and Schloss Lichtenburg (1573–81).

BIBLIOGRAPHY

ADB; *NDB*; Thieme–Becker
C. Gurlitt: *Die Kunstdenkmäler Dresdens*, xxi–xxiii of *Beschreibende Darstellung der älteren Bau- u. Kunstdenkmäler des Königreichs Sachsen* (Dresden, 1903)
R. Kötzsche and H. Kretzschmar: *Sächsische Geschichte* (Frankfurt am Main, 1965), pp. 219–35
F. Löffler: *Das alte Dresden* (Frankfurt am Main, 1966)

(6) John-George [Johann Georg] **I**, Elector of Saxony (*b* Dresden, 15 March 1585; *reg* 1611–56; *d* Dresden, 18 Oct 1656). Grandson of (5) Augustus I, Elector of Saxony. He ruled during the period of the Thirty Years War (1618–48) when few resources were available for the promotion of art and architecture. In 1617, however, he completed the Jägerhof in Dresden and had alterations made to the pleasure palace at the Jungfernbastei. Other commissions included sandstone statues of the Holy Roman Emperors from Charles V to Ferdinand II and of the Saxon electors since Maurice (*reg* 1547–53), which were erected on a second floor added to the building. In 1632 he extended the fortifications of the Neustadt quarter of Dresden, adding four gates. After 1650 he built Schloss Hoflössnitz, north of Dresden. He donated two guild masterpieces (1614, 1619) to the Dresden council silver collection.

For bibliography *see* (5) above.

WERNER ARNOLD

(7) Frederick-Augustus [Friedrich August] **I**, Elector of Saxony [Augustus II [Augustus the Strong], King of Poland] (*b* Dresden, 12 May 1670; *reg* Saxony, 1694–1733, Poland, 1697–1704, 1709–33; *d* Warsaw, 1 Feb 1733). Great-grandson of (6) John-George I, Elector of Saxony. Although his domestic and foreign policies were only partially realized, he brought Saxon Baroque architecture (particularly in Dresden) and the visual arts to an unprecedented peak, while his religious tolerance enabled the spirit of enlightenment to develop, raising Leipzig to the first rank of German scholarship. Even during his own lifetime he was known as 'the Strong' because of his physical stature and exceptional strength. From the early days of his reign court ceremonies and processions were carefully stage-managed and served to underline his role as absolute monarch.

Frederick-Augustus received a thorough scientific and artistic education. Among his teachers was the architect Wolf Caspar von Klengel, who taught him military architecture, mathematics and drawing. He was also influenced by his upbringing at the court in Dresden, which at the time of his father, John-George III, Elector of Saxony (*reg* 1680–91), was distinguished by its many splendid festivities. In 1686 he travelled to Denmark, and in 1687–9 he made the Grand Tour through Germany, France, the Netherlands, England, Spain, Portugal and the Habsburg countries; this journey had an important influence on his later activities as a builder, organizer of festivities and collector. In 1697 he obtained the elective throne of Poland (reigning as Augustus II, also known as Augustus the Strong) by giving huge sums of money to the Polish aristocracy and by agreeing to become a Catholic. Saxony was the heartland of Protestantism, and the now King of Poland showed himself highly tolerant in allowing his subjects to continue to practise their existing beliefs; this led to fruitful competition in church building between the Protestant bourgeoisie and the Catholic court in Saxony, and at Dresden in particular. He was dethroned in 1704, following military defeat by Sweden, but regained control of Poland in 1709.

Frederick-Augustus used not only royal building but also town architecture to illustrate his absolute power in both Saxony and Poland (*see* POLAND, §XI, 2). Until Dresden was destroyed in 1945, it was a monument to his taste and patronage (*see* DRESDEN, §I, 2). To his credit, he accepted the suggestion of the architects Johann Freidrich Karcher (1650–1726) and Andreas Gärtner (1654–1727) that the height of the roofs of the houses be standardized. Royal architects advised the civilian builders and suggested types of buildings and improved designs; the building regulations of 1720 laid down the height limit for every street. The most important building was the Zwinger (1711–28; rest. after 1945), designed by Matthäus Daniel Pöppelmann and BALTHASAR PERMOSER. It is ephemeral festival architecture translated into solid stone, framing a festival square and intended as the forecourt of a castle that was never built (for illustration *see* PÖPPELMANN, MATTHÄUS DANIEL; *see also* DRESDEN, §IV, 2 and fig. 2). The King created a residential landscape around Dresden which was intended to serve his pleasure and project his image; he rebuilt Schloss Moritzburg (1723–36), Schloss Pillnitz (1720/1–30) and the Japanisches Palais (originally the Holländisches Palais, begun 1715; converted and renamed 1727–30; destr. 1945; rebuilt 1952). He was artistically talented, and among the surviving 135 of his own drawings (Dresden, Staatsarchv, LOC. 2097), which are mainly of military subjects, are designs for civilian buildings, plans for gardens and decorations for festivals; there are also a few alterations

made by him to plans drawn up by his architects. He showed no preference for any single architect but instead would ask several to submit designs so that many of his castles are collaborations by several architects; for example the Japanisches Palais incorporated plans by ZACHARIAS LONGUELUNE, Pöppelmann and Jean de Bodt. In addition, the architects represented different styles, including the southern German High Baroque and the cool, classical Baroque of France; all were given complete freedom to develop their ideas.

Among Saxony's efficient and very traditional craft industries, the production of Meissen porcelain was particularly encouraged by Frederick-Augustus, not only for economic reasons but for its artistic prestige and his passion for collecting (*see* MEISSEN, §3(i)); his own vast collections of East Asian and Meissen porcelain (*c.* 57,000 pieces) were kept in the Japanisches Palais, which he had built specially to house the collection. The court jeweller JOHANN MELCHIOR DINGLINGER created numerous pieces for him (see fig.), notably the table centrepiece depicting the *Court of Aurangzeb* (1701–7; Dresden, Grünes Gewölbe), conceived by the King himself, and

Frederick-Augustus I, enamel, portrait medallion with gold surround by Johann Melchior Dinglinger, enamel, 100×80 mm, 1712 (Dresden, Grünes Gewölbe)

remarkable swords (e.g. *c.* 1720; Dresden, Hist. Mus.; *see* ARMS AND ARMOUR, §II, 1).

One of the King's most important tasks as patron was the systematic reorganization and considerable extension of the family collections, which were also opened to the public, albeit on a restricted basis. They included the print rooms (1720), the Grünes Gewölbe (1721), the collection of antiquities (1728) and above all the picture gallery, created in 1722 when the Stallhof, dating from the 16th century, was converted into a gallery by Raymond Leplat (1644–1742). An inventory was drawn up of all the paintings in the royal palaces and 535 works were assembled to form a prestigious collection that included the *Sleeping Venus* (*c.* 1509; Dresden, Gemäldegal. Alte Meister) by Giorgione and Titian. His artistic advisers were KARL HEINRICH VON HEINECKEN and FRANCESCO ALGAROTTI and his preferred periods for collection the High Renaissance and Baroque. Among the most important acquisitions were tapestries of scenes from the *Life of SS Peter and Paul* (Rome, Pin. Vaticana) based on the cartoons by Raphael and *Leda and the Swan* by Peter Paul Rubens.

BIBLIOGRAPHY

P. Haake: *König August der Starke: Eine Charakterstudie* (Munich and Berlin, 1902)

C. Gurlitt: *August der Starke: Ein Fürstenleben aus der Zeit des deutschen Barock* (Dresden, 1924)

H. Poenicke: *August der Starke* (Göttingen, 1972)

D. Schaal: 'Barocke Hoffeste in Dresden', *Barock und Klassik* (exh. cat., Vienna, 1984)

K. Czok: *August der Starke und Kursachsen* (Leipzig, 1987)

VOLKER HELAS

(8) Frederick-Augustus [Friedrich August] **II**, Elector of Saxony [Augustus III, King of Poland] (*b* Dresden, 17 Oct 1696; *reg* 1733–63; *d* Hubertsburg, 5 Oct 1763). Son of (7) Frederick-Augustus I, Elector of Saxony. He converted from Protestantism to Catholicism in 1712 to ensure his succession to the Polish throne and was educated through travels in Germany, Italy and France (1711–14). In many ways he continued his father's policies, leading Poland and Saxony into wars that were economically and socially disastrous, and, as a patron, contributing greatly to the development of the arts (*see also* POLAND, §XI, 2). In both politics and the arts he was advised by Prince Aleksander Józef Sułkowski (1695–1762) and after 1738 HEINRICH BRÜHL, who masterminded most of his projects. He resided mainly in Dresden, moving with his court to Warsaw only in 1756. In both cities he continued urban and architectural projects undertaken by his father and commissioned many of the same artists.

In Dresden Frederick-Augustus completed the Japanisches Palais (from 1727), designed by Matthäus Daniel Pöppelmann, Zacharias Longuelune, Johann Christoph Knöffel and Jean de Bodt, the Frauenkirche (1726–43; destr. 1945; under reconstruction late 1990s) designed by Georg Bähr (*see* BÄHR, GEORG, and fig.) and the Dreikönigskirche (1732–9) by Pöppelmann and Bähr. In 1738 the King commissioned GAETANO CHIAVERI to build the Roman Catholic Hofkirche (completed 1755; damaged 1945; rest.), an elegant Rococo church crowned with statues and an open belfry. Although during his reign the late Baroque and Rococo styles predominated, there were also the beginnings of Neo-classicism, and the Blockhaus

(1732–49) by Longuelune and his pupil Knöffel, influenced by French classicism, exemplifies the trend towards greater severity. An avid collector, the King enlarged the Dresden art collections established by his predecessors, paying particular attention to paintings and prints (*see* GERMANY, §XIII), and in 1744–6 Knöffel remodelled the Stallhof gallery to house new acquisitions. In 1746 a group of important paintings, including Titian's *Tribute Money* (*c.* 1568; London, N.G.) and *Portrait of a Lady in White* (Florence, Pitti), was acquired from the ducal gallery at Modena. Raphael's Sistine *Madonna* (ex-S Sisto, Piacenza; Dresden, Gemäldegal. Alte Meister) was acquired in 1754 through KARL HEINRICH VON HEINECKEN, who in 1746 had been appointed director of the Kupferstichkabinett and through his systematic programme of acquisitions as well as through his writings had laid the foundations of modern museology. The circle of court artists was international: Louis de Silvestre (*see* SILVESTRE (i), (2)), Adám Mányoki and briefly Anton Raphael Mengs all executed portraits for the King; Bernardo Bellotto was commissioned to supply views of Dresden and Pirna (1747–55; *see* BELLOTTO, BERNARDO, and fig. 1) which display the architectural development of both towns in that period; Johann Alexander Thiele (1685–1752) contributed *vedute* and landscapes; Ismael Israel Mengs (1688–1764) was the court miniaturist; court ceremonies and military parades were depicted by the painter and theatrical designer Johann Samuel Mock; and Marcello Bacciarelli's task was to copy the masterpieces in the Royal Gallery and execute portraits. The King continued his father's patronage of other arts and crafts. The porcelain factory in Meissen flourished during his reign, with Johann Joachim Kändler as one of the chief artists. The wide range of Meissen products included animal figures and large commissions for the Japanisches Palais as well as sumptuous services for the dowries of the King's three daughters, who were known as the 'Porcelain Princesses' (*see* MEISSEN, §3(i) and fig. 2).

In Poland the King developed the French Rococo style introduced by his father and continued his projects, though in some instances with less élan. The Warsaw buildings designed by the court architects (destr. World War II; some designs, Dresden, Staatsarchv) were well documented in engravings by Pierre Ricaud de Tirregaille (*fl* 1723–62) in *Plan de la ville de Varsovie* (1762). The King completed the remodelling of the Saxon Palace in Warsaw, which was designed to close the vista of the Saxon Axis, his father's chief project. Joachim Daniel Jauch, director of the Royal Office of Works from 1736 to 1754, designed the wings and stables that enclosed the large court. The gardens were decorated with an amphitheatre, theatre, riding-school and other pavilions, most of which were designed by Carl Friedrich Pöppelmann (1697–1750). Jauch was succeeded by Johann Friedrich Knöbel (1724–92), who was active in Poland from 1753 to 1765, and he is believed to have remodelled the royal residence in Grodno (Lithuania) with a fashionable U-shaped ground-plan and designed the chapel. The remodelling of the Royal Castle in Warsaw (destr. 1944; rebuilt 1971–84), carried out in the 1740s at the initiative of the Polish parliament, was the greatest contribution to the architecture of Warsaw during his reign. The initial designs supplied by Chiaveri were altered by other architects, and the works were supervised by Antonio Solari (1700–73). The emphasis was placed on the new eastern Saxon wing (completed 1746) with a façade (*c.* 1740) facing the Vistula; it was a late Baroque structure with three projections and Rococo architectural decoration (1741–52; destr. 1944; reconstr. 1971–84) by Jan Jerzy Plersz. The interiors were rearranged and redesigned (by Longuelune and Jauch), the parliamentary rooms were separated from the King's apartment, and new state and private rooms were built, including the Senatorial Hall, New Deputies' Hall and Queen's Suite.

BIBLIOGRAPHY

F. Löffler: *Das alte Dresden: Geschichte seiner Bauten* (Dresden, 1956, rev. 4/1962)
W. Hentschel: *Die sächsische Baukunst des 18. Jahrhunderts in Polen* (Berlin, 1967)
The Splendor of Dresden: Five Centuries of Art Collecting (exh. cat. by J. Menzhausen and others, Washington, DC, N.G.A.; New York, Met.; San Francisco, CA, F.A. Museums; 1978–9)

ANNA BENTKOWSKA

(9) Albert (Casimir) [Albrecht (Kasimir)], Duke of Saxe-Teschen (*b* Moritzburg, 11 July 1738; *d* Vienna, 10 Feb 1822). Son of (8) Frederick-Augustus II, Elector of Saxony. As the son of one of the most important collectors and connoisseurs of his day, he was exposed to artistic stimulation at an early age. He entered Austrian service in 1759, during the Seven Years War, and in 1766 married Marie Christine of Austria, daughter of Empress Maria-Theresa, who created him Duke of (Saxe) Teschen. While Governor of Hungary (1765–80) in Pressburg (Bratislava, Slovakia) and Governor General of the Netherlands (1780–92) in Brussels, he built up a unique collection of drawings and copper-engravings, acquiring many works from the collection of one of his art agents Jacopo Durazzo, and, at auction in 1794, from the collection of CHARLES-JOSEPH-EMMANUEL DE LIGNE. To these were added the prints by Albrecht Dürer from the Hofbibliothek that he had been given in 1796 by the Holy Roman Emperor Francis II (1768–1835). The Albertina, as the collection was known, had to be kept temporarily in Dresden before being housed in the palace at the Hofburg in Vienna from 1801. The collection (230 folders containing some 13,000 prints) includes many masterpieces by famous artists and is notable for its systematic method of arrangement. The Duke allowed access to it during his lifetime; after his death the collection became a fideicommissum and now forms the basis of the Graphische Sammlung Albertina (*see* AUSTRIA, §XIV).

ADB   BIBLIOGRAPHY

A. Bettelheim and O. Redlich: *Österreichisches biographisches Lexikon, 1815–1950*, i (Graz and Cologne, 1954), p. 13
W. Koschatzky: *Die Albertina und ihr Gründer Herzog Albert von Sachsen Teschen. Die Albertina und das Dresdener Kupferstichkabinett* (Dresden, 1978), pp. 11–18

GERALD HERES

(10) Anna Amalia, Duchess of Saxe-Weimar (*b* Wolfenbüttel, 24 Oct 1739; *d* Weimar, 10 April 1807). Descendant of (3) Frederick III, Elector of Saxony. The daughter of Charles I, Duke of Brunswick-Wolfenbüttel, and Philippine Charlotte of Prussia (1716–1801), she inherited a strong inclination to science and the arts. In 1756 she married Ernest Augustus II, Duke of Saxe-Weimar (1737–58), and at his death she became regent during the minority of her son (11) Charles Augustus, Duke of Saxe-Weimar. During the regency her patronage was crucial to Weimar's development as the focal point of German intellectual life (*see* WEIMAR). She constantly extended the library established by William Ernest, Duke of Saxe-Weimar (1662–1728), which housed many rare books and manuscripts, attracting scholars and poets. She enjoyed drawing, playing music and composing and showed great interest in a German national theatre; in 1771 she inaugurated the Seyler Theatre Society, with the best actors in Germany. In 1772 she appointed as her son's tutor Christoph Martin Wieland (1733–1813), who as editor (from 1773) of the *Teutsche Mercur*, a monthly journal devoted to the arts and science, further increased the momentum of Weimar's development into the centre of German classicism.

After her son's majority (1775), the Duchess applied herself entirely to her active artistic and scientific interests. Her close connection with the cultural epoch between Rococo and classicism can be seen at her residence, the Wittumspalais, designed by Johann Gottfried Schlegel, the ceiling paintings (1775–85; *in situ*) of which were by Adam Friedrich Oeser. She held soirées in the Tafelrunde room where she gathered representatives of science, literature and art, including Wieland, Johann Wolfgang von Goethe and Johann Gottfried Herder. Georg Melchior Kraus (1737–1806), the first director of the Freie Zeichenschule (est. 1777), depicted one such gathering (1795; Weimar, Wittumspal. & Wielandmus.). From 1788 to 1790 the Duchess was in Italy, where she purchased works for the Weimar art collections by artists such as Angelica Kauffman, Maximilian Joseph von Verschaffelt, Friedrich Bury, Johann Georg Schütz (1755–1813), Heinrich Lips (1758–1817), Philipp Hackert, Georg Hackert (1755–1805), Wilhelm Tischbein, Peter Birmann and Heinrich Meyer.

NDB   BIBLIOGRAPHY

W. Bode: *Anna Amalia, Herzogin von Weimar*, 3 vols (Berlin, 1899/*R* 1909)
H. Wahl: *Das Wittumspalais der Herzogin Anna Amalia* (Leipzig, 1927)
C. E. Vehse: *Der Hof zu Weimar* (Leipzig and Weimar, 1951)
A. Jericke and D. Dolgner: *Der Klassizismus in der Baugeschichte Weimars* (Weimar, 1975)
F. Kühnlenz: *Weimarer Porträts: Männer und Frauen um Goethe und Schiller* (Rudolstadt, 1975)
A. Schwarz: *Weimar* (Leipzig, 1993)

(11) Charles Augustus [Carl August; Karl August], Duke (from 1815 Grand Duke) of Saxe-Weimar (*b* Weimar, 3 Sept 1757; *reg* 1775–1828; *d* Schloss Graditz, nr Torgau, 14 June 1828). Son of (10) Anna Amalia, Duchess of Saxe-Weimar. From 1772 he studied under the philosopher and poet Christoph Martin Wieland, who, together with Anna Amalia, influenced his enthusiasm for the arts, which resulted in his subsequent active cultural policy. During the last year of his minority he toured Europe, meeting Goethe, whom he invited to Weimar and who subsequently became his mentor and influenced most of his political and cultural decisions. After attaining his majority (1775), from 1776 the Duke embarked on important reforms in Saxe-Weimar. The presence of Wieland, Goethe, Johann Gottfried Herder and later Friedrich Schiller enticed many other poets and scholars to Weimar. In 1777 the Freie Zeichenschule was founded, at which many famous artists subsequently taught. Goethe lectured on anatomy at the school and, with Heinrich Meyer, from 1799 to 1805 edited the art periodical *Propyläen*. The ducal Schloss in Weimar, rebuilt under Goethe's direction, housed a large art collection, including sculpture by Jean-Antoine Houdon, which the Duke opened to the public in 1809.

Having led his subjects against the armies of the French Revolution (1792–3) and in the Napoleonic Wars, at the Congress of Vienna (1815) he achieved elevation to Grand Duke. In 1816 he was the first German ruler to give his country a constitution.

NDB
BIBLIOGRAPHY
W. Bode: *Karl August von Weimar: Jugendjahre* (Berlin, 1913)
——: *Der Weimarische Musenhof* (Berlin, 1920)
H. Wahl: *Die Bildnisse Carl Augusts von Weimar* (Weimar, 1925)
F. Kühnlenz: *Persönlichkeiten, Begegnungen, Ereignisse aus drei Jahrhunderten Weimarer Kulturgeschichte* (Rudolstadt, 1970)
A. Jericke and D. Dolger: *Der Klassizismus in der Baugeschichte Weimars* (Weimar, 1975)
A. Pretsch and W. Hecht: *Das alte Weimar* (Weimar, 1975)
A. Schwarz: *Weimar* (Leipzig, 1993)
INGRID SATTEL BERNARDINI

Wewoke, Maynerd. *See* VEWICKE, MAYNARD.

Weyden, van der. South Netherlandish family of painters. Active in both Tournai and Brussels, (1) Rogier van der Weyden was one of the most renowned painters of the 15th century, though his reputation declined after the loss of important works in the 17th century and is only now being reinstated. He was probably trained by the Master of Flémalle and he also clearly knew the work of Jan van Eyck; his interests differed from theirs, however, and he became increasingly concerned with developing the emotional impact of his religious paintings. He was also an innovative and influential portrait painter. Rogier apparently established a large workshop and had many imitators, but none achieved the subtlety and expressive power of his paintings. His son Pieter van der Weyden is usually identified with the anonymous MASTER OF THE LEGEND OF ST CATHERINE (*see* MASTERS, ANONYMOUS, AND MONOGRAMMISTS, §I), a painter active in Brussels *c.* 1470–1500. Pieter's son (2) Goswijn van der Weyden presumably trained with his father and grew up in Brussels in an artistic circle deeply imbued with the stylistic influence of his famous grandfather.

(1) Rogier [Roger] **van der Weyden** (*b* Tournai, *c.* 1399; *d* Brussels, 18 June 1464).

I. Life and work. II. Working methods and technique. III. Critical reception and posthumous reputation.

I. Life and work.

1. Documentary evidence. 2. Authenticated works. 3. Stylistic development.

1. DOCUMENTARY EVIDENCE. Rogier van der Weyden was the son of Henri de le Pasture, a cutler in Tournai, and Agnès de Watreloz. His birthdate is estimated from the facts that he was stated to be 35 in April 1435 and 43 in September 1441. Before or in 1427 he married Elisabeth Goffaert (*c.* 1405–77), whose father was a prosperous shoemaker in Brussels. Rogier may have lived for a time

in Brussels: his eldest child Cornelis (*b* 1427) was sometimes referred to as 'de Bruxella' but was not necessarily a native of Brussels. On 5 March 1427 'Rogelet de le Pasture, natif de Tournai' was apprenticed to the Tournai painter Robert Campin. This Rogelet duly completed his apprenticeship in 1431 and on 1 August 1432 became a master of the Tournai guild. Despite much debate, it would appear that Rogelet was Rogier van der Weyden, though it has also been argued that in 1427 Rogier was a married man well past the normal age of apprenticeship and that Rogelet must have been a second Tournai painter of the same name. JACQUES DARET, however, was in his twenties when in 1428 he was apprenticed to Campin, and other instances can be cited of married apprentices. The political situation at Tournai in 1427–8 was unusual, and the guild system was not functioning normally. Van der Weyden maintained connections with Tournai and the Tournai guild of painters, which in 1464 held a funeral service in his honour. It would seem that Rogier and Rogelet were indeed the same person.

By April 1435 van der Weyden was living in Brussels; and in May 1436 he was the town painter of Brussels. Apparently in 1443–4 he acquired from an alderman's heirs properties near the Cantersteen, and he lived there until his death, when he was buried in the church of St Gudule. Undoubtedly prosperous, he made substantial investments in Tournai securities in April 1435 and September 1441 and in Brussels securities in June 1436 and April 1459: from his investments, he and his family derived a handsome annual income. He made generous gifts of money and pictures to the charterhouses of Scheut, outside Brussels, and Hérinnes, near Enghien, where his son Cornelis was an inmate. By 1462 he was a member of the Confraternity of the Holy Cross established at the church of St Jacques sur Coudenberg, Brussels, and between 1455 and 1457 he was one of the administrators of the infirmary and the charitable foundation 'Ter Kisten' of the Brussels Béguinage. Though no copy of his will has been found, he is known to have made bequests for the support of the poor in two Brussels parishes and to the Charterhouse of Hérinnes.

Unlike Jan van Eyck, Rogier never held a salaried position at the Burgundian court, but he worked on several occasions for Philip the Good. His fame quickly spread beyond Tournai and Brussels. In 1445 John II, King of Castile, gave a triptych by 'Magistro Rogel, magno, & famoso Flandresco' to the Charterhouse of Miraflores near Burgos, which he had founded in 1442. In July 1449 Leonello d'Este, Marquis of Ferrara, showed to Cyriac of Ancona a triptych of the *Lamentation* by 'Rugiero in Bursella', and in 1450–51 a payment was made on Leonello's behalf to the 'excelenti et claro pictori M. Rogerio' for 'paintings' and on account for other pictures commissioned by Leonello, two of them apparently for his studio at Belfiore. Nicholas of Cusa, cardinal and theologian, mentioned 'Roger the greatest of painters' in a text of 1453. According to the humanist Bartolomeo Fazio, writing in 1456, Rogier was said to have visited Rome during the Jubilee of 1450 and to have admired a fresco by Gentile da Fabriano in S Giovanni in Laterano. Fazio also described several paintings by Rogier, including the triptych at Ferrara mentioned by Cyriac of Ancona;

paintings on cloth of the *Passion of Christ*, then in the possession of Alfonso V of Aragon at Naples and apparently bought by him from a Florentine merchant at Rome in 1455; and a picture in an unidentified Genoese collection showing a woman sweating in her bath. In December 1460 Bianca Maria Sforza, Duchess of Milan, wrote to Philip the Good and to the Dauphin of France—the future Louis XI, then residing near Brussels—that she was sending her painter Zanetto Bugatto to be instructed by Rogier (whom the Milanese secretary mistakenly called 'Gulielmus'). In March 1461 the Milanese ambassador in Brussels reported that Zanetto had quarrelled with 'Magistro Rogero, pictore nobilissimo' but that, after the intercession of the Dauphin, Rogier had agreed to take Zanetto back into his household on condition that he paid for his keep and promised not to drink wine for a year. On 7 May 1463 the Duchess wrote to 'Nobili viro dilecto Magistro Rugerio de Tornay, pictori in Burseles', dwelling on his fame and thanking him in fulsome terms for instructing Zanetto.

Contemporary documents give pitifully little information on Rogier's artistic activity. The only recorded commission for a major painting is for a triptych ordered in 1455 by the Abbot of St Aubert at Cambrai and delivered in 1459 by Rogier's wife and assistants. The subject is not mentioned in the Abbot's accounts, but payments are entered for placing the large triptych on trestles in different parts of the abbey church in order to determine where it could be seen to best advantage. Other major undertakings included the colouring of two funerary monuments for Philip the Good, but Rogier also accepted minor commissions and in 1441 was paid for having painted a dragon for a procession at Nivelles. The most ambitious task he is known to have completed was the decoration of one wall of a court room, then known as the Golden Chamber and now as the Salle des Mariages, in Brussels Town Hall. There he painted four *Scenes of Justice* representing episodes in legends associated with Emperor Trajan and with Herkinbald, a mythical Duke of Brabant. Each of the vast panels, calculated to have been *c.* 3.5 m high, with approximately life-size figures, was subdivided into two sections, and one of the eight sections contained a self-portrait, mentioned by Cardinal Nicholas of Cusa, who visited Brussels in 1452. The panels were admired by generations of visitors to Brussels, before being destroyed during the bombardment of the town by the French in 1695. Some idea of their appearance can be gained from descriptions and from a free, compressed version in tapestry (Berne, Hist. Mus.), woven before 1461. The first panel is stated to have been dated 1439, and it is likely that all four were completed well before 1450.

2. AUTHENTICATED WORKS. Three surviving paintings may be considered securely authenticated works by Rogier van der Weyden: the Miraflores Triptych, representing scenes from the *Life of the Virgin* (Berlin, Gemäldegal.; see fig. 1); the *Descent from the Cross* (Madrid, Prado; see fig. 2 below); and the *Crucifixion* (Madrid, Escorial; see fig. 4 below). The first was given in 1445 to the Charterhouse of Miraflores by John II of Castile, as is known from an entry in the *Libro del Becerro* of the monastery (now lost but copied by the 18th-century

traveller Ponz). There is no reason to question the authority of this record. It was long thought that the triptych in Berlin was a copy of another, bequeathed by John II's daughter Isabella, Queen of Spain (*d* 1504), to the Capilla Real at Granada (two mutilated panels, the *Nativity* and the *Pietà*, remain in the Capilla Real; the third panel, the *Resurrected Christ Appearing to the Virgin*, is in New York, Met.), but scientific examination (Grosshans, 1981) has established that the Berlin triptych is certainly the original and that the Granada triptych is a later copy, painted in Spain probably for Isabella and possibly by one of her court painters trained in the Netherlands.

The *Descent from the Cross* was first recorded in 1549 in the collection of Mary of Hungary at the château of Binche, Hainaut. It passed to her nephew Philip II of Spain, who gave it to the Escorial in 1574; in the inventory of that year, it is stated to have been painted by 'Maestre Rogier'. It was engraved in 1565 with the legend 'M. Rogerij Belgae inuentum' and mentioned as the work of Rogier by Molanus, Opmeer and van Mander. According to several 16th-century texts, it came from the chapel of Our Lady Without the Walls at Leuven, built in 1364 by the Great Archers' Guild and later the meeting-place of the Confraternity of Our Lady of the Sorrows. The small crossbows included on the tracery at the corners of the picture indicate that it was painted for the Great Archers' Guild; and indeed, according to Molanus, it was from the Archers that Mary of Hungary acquired it. The picture was probably painted shortly before 1443, the date of a copy that forms the centre part of the Edelheer Triptych (Leuven, St Pieterskerk). In 1574 Rogier's original had wing panels (untraced), the exteriors of which were painted by El Mudo; the paintings on the interior surfaces may also have been executed for Philip II (Steppe). Though it is likely that the *Descent* was protected by shutters from the start, it is not certain that it ever had wing panels painted by Rogier.

The great *Crucifixion* was also given to the Escorial in 1574 by Philip II of Spain. The inventory of that year states that it was painted by 'Masse Rugier' and came from the Charterhouse of Brussels (i.e. the Charterhouse of Scheut). It is now known that in 1555 a *Crucifixion*, 'donata a magistro Rogero pictore', was sold from Scheut (Soenen, 1979). An obituary of the monastery, written in 1556 but presumably compiled from earlier and reliable sources, states that Rogier van der Weyden gave money and pictures to the charterhouse (Soenen, 1972); the *Crucifixion* must have formed part of this gift and was apparently painted for the charterhouse, which was founded in 1455–6.

3. STYLISTIC DEVELOPMENT. The fact that van der Weyden probably ran a large and busy workshop (*see* §II, 3 below) makes the attribution of further works to him and his assistants extremely complicated. The three authenticated pictures set superbly high standards of design and execution, and it is against these standards that further attributions to Rogier must be judged. Few of the attributed paintings can be securely dated, and there is little agreement among art historians over the chronology of Rogier's work. Since questions of attribution, dating and workshop practice cannot be fully resolved, any attempt

to give a chronological survey of Rogier's output must inevitably be speculative.

(i) Early period, *c.* 1432–*c.* 1442. (ii) Middle period, *c.* 1442–*c.* 1450. (iii) Late period, 1450s and 1460s.

(i) Early period, c. *1432*–c. *1442.* It is generally agreed that Rogier was a pupil or follower of the MASTER OF FLÉMALLE (*see* MASTERS, ANONYMOUS, AND MONOGRAMMISTS, §I), and consequently it would seem likely that Rogier's earliest independent works would show a strong reliance on the Flémalle style. If the Master of Flémalle is to be identified as Robert Campin and Rogier as his apprentice Rogelet de le Pasture, these pictures would have been executed in or shortly after 1432, when Rogelet became a master of the Tournai guild and when Rogier was a man in his early thirties.

Many art historians have proposed that the small *Virgin and Child* (Madrid, Mus. Thyssen-Bornemisza), the diptych of the *Virgin and Child* and *St Catherine* (Vienna, Ksthist. Mus.) and the *Visitation* (Leipzig, Mus. Bild. Kst) should be classified as early works by Rogier, painted shortly after he left Campin's workshop. This group, however, is not particularly coherent in style, especially if it is recalled that the Thyssen *Virgin* and the small *St George and the Dragon* (Washington, DC, N.G.A.) are apparently from the same series (Hand and Wolff). None of these paintings shows the feeling for geometric harmony found in Rogier's authenticated pictures, and the same may be said of the *Annunciation* (Paris, Louvre; *see* NETHERLANDS, THE, fig. 33), which, with its wing panels representing a *Donor* (the figure is entirely overpainted and the head a later insertion) and the *Visitation* (both Turin, Gal. Sabauda), has also been claimed to be an early work by Rogier (but see Périer-d'Ieteren). All of these pictures should perhaps be reclassified as by assistants or imitators, even if they may have been executed within van der Weyden's workshop, which, at least in the early stages of his career, appears to have been rather loosely organized.

The fragment of the *Magdalene Reading* (London, N.G.) provides a better basis for defining Rogier's early style, since it is clearly by the same hand as the Miraflores Triptych and the *Descent from the Cross*; it is also clearly similar to the *Virgin and Child* allegedly from Flémalle (now Frankfurt am Main, Städel. Kstinst. & Städt. Gal.), from which the Master of Flémalle takes his name. The *Magdalene* must have come from a large painting of the *Virgin and Child with Saints*; at least one other fragment, a *Head of ? St Joseph* (Lisbon, Fund. Gulbenkian), is from the same panel; and a drawing (Stockholm, Nmus.) is evidently a copy, probably from the late 15th century, after part or parts of the same composition. The *Virgin and Child in a Niche* (Madrid, Prado) is similar in style to the *Magdalene* fragment and yet more successfully composed. The systems of parallel diagonals intersect more or less at right angles and are in almost perfect accord with the principal diagonals of the panel. Van der Weyden may have found it easier to deal with this relatively simple composition of three figures, placed in a highly abstracted setting, than with the more complex compositional problems of the *Virgin and Child with Saints*, in which the figures are arranged in a domestic interior; although each individual figure maintains a geometric balance, the composition as a whole, as far as can be judged from the fragments and the copy, may have lacked the rhythm and changeless perfection of Rogier's later work.

In the Miraflores Triptych (see fig. 1) the figures are seen behind arches and within totally improbable architectural structures. The iconography is here rather complex, with subsidiary scenes in grisaille simulating carvings on the archivolts and embrasures, but the interactions of pattern, colour and emotion between the three panels have been most carefully considered. The enclosed space and

1. Rogier van der Weyden: Miraflores Triptych, oil on panel, each section 770×480 mm, *c.* ?1435 (Berlin, Gemäldegalerie)

diffused light of the interior in the *Nativity* on the left, where the Virgin, dressed in white, peacefully contemplates her Child, is contrasted with the open structure in the central *Pietà*, in which the Virgin, dressed in red and crushed by grief, embraces the corpse of Christ, who is stretched in a dramatic, stiff and quite unlikely pose across her knee. The landscape, where the lines curve oppressively downwards, weighs on the stooping figures; whereas in the third panel, the *Resurrected Christ Appearing to the Virgin* on the right, the stresses are vertical, the landscape is open and spacious, and fields and interior are flooded with a joyous light as the Virgin, dressed in blue, turns from tearful contemplation to recognize the miracle of the Resurrection.

In all these paintings Rogier is using Flémallesque conventions in his idealization of the heads, in his stylization of the gestures, in his methods of composition and in his concern for balance of narrative, decorative and emotional interest. In a stylistically related picture, *St Luke Drawing a Portrait of the Virgin* (Boston, MA, Mus. F.A.; versions at Bruges, Groeningemus.; St Petersburg, Hermitage; and Munich, Alte Pin.), he offered homage to Jan van Eyck by adapting his composition from that of Jan's *Virgin and Child with Chancellor Rolin* (Paris, Louvre). The resemblance was even more marked before Rogier painted out the underdrawn angel hovering above the Virgin's head (Faries). A comparison between the two pictures shows how different were Jan's and Rogier's interests, for Rogier has closed the composition at the top and related its forms more closely to the shape of the panel by introducing more marked diagonal emphases, which once again echo the principal diagonals of the support. Less concerned than van Eyck with complex symbolism and with creating an illusion of spatial depth, he was more anxious to achieve a decorative perfection of abstract pattern and to convey the emotional reactions of his figures. Here this is especially evident in the awkward curling movements of the fingers and toes of the Child, who wriggles in delight as he looks at his mother.

In the triptych of the *Crucifixion* (Vienna, Ksthist. Mus.) the figures are once again sharply observed, but the arabesques of the floating loincloth of Christ, beautiful in themselves and balancing the diagonals of the composition, show a disregard for the laws of gravity and for the accurate depiction of reality, a feature that became increasingly obvious in later paintings. The unidentified donors of the *Crucifixion* are dressed in the fashions of *c.* 1440. Perhaps only slightly later is the triptych of the *Nativity* (Berlin, Gemäldegal.), in which the donor is usually identified as Pieter Bladelin (*d* 1472), an immensely rich and eminent official of the Burgundian court (Dhanens). The centre panel depends on the Master of Flémalle's *Nativity* (Dijon, Mus. B.-A.), and the resemblance was still closer before Rogier decided against including the floating scrolls, present in the underdrawings of all three panels of the triptych (Grosshans, 1982).

These few paintings appear to form a coherent group. The stylistic dependence on the Master of Flémalle is quite marked; some attention is still being paid to the logic of spatial recession and to proper relationships of scale; the figures are often arranged in little circles across the foregrounds; their heads are frequently rather too large;

and in the more complex compositions, where many figures are arranged in elaborate settings, the design of the parts is sometimes more successful than the composition of the whole. This applies most strikingly to the *Virgin and Child with Saints* and the triptych of the *Nativity*, where the whole triptych lacks the commanding coherence of design found in the less elaborate compositions and in the later pictures, even though each individual figure is a masterpiece of design (the Tiburtine Sibyl in the left wing being particularly beautiful) and the decorative relationships between forms are carefully thought out (e.g. the contours of the donor's face are 'rhymed' with those of the broken wall immediately behind). A case may therefore be made for dating this group relatively early in Rogier's career, though it would be foolhardy to attempt to construct an exact chronology. Commissions would undoubtedly have overlapped, and for much of this period Rogier and his assistants must have been mainly occupied with the lost *Scenes of Justice*.

(ii) Middle period, c. *1442–c. 1450.* In the *Descent from the Cross* (see fig. 2), probably painted very shortly before 1443, Rogier broke more decisively with the Flémallesque tradition and abandoned any pretence of obeying the laws of spatial recession. The picture resembles those carved altarpieces in which wooden figures are set in gilded and painted boxes; indeed the spectator cannot be entirely sure whether the *Descent* is a representation of an event or an image of an image. The cross is much too small ever to have supported the body of Christ and the figures are cramped into the gilded box, which cannot actually contain them. The servant on the ladder at the back even appears to have caught his sleeve in the tracery at the front of the box. The spatial inconsistencies are not immediately obvious, for the principal junctions of the structure are carefully obscured, but they induce a calculated feeling of unease in the beholder. The figures, their tears and their clothes seem to be observed with extreme care, and Christ's wounds, where the blood clots and separates, are rendered with clinical exactitude; yet several of the figures are wilfully distorted for compositional effect. Because of the immutable harmonies of the design, the figures give a first impression of changeless stability; yet all of them are precariously posed, and some are falling. The bystanders have similar expressions of pious grief, and there are few passages of extreme agitation; yet the picture is immensely moving and disturbing, not because Rogier has attempted accurately to reconstruct what happened when Christ's body was taken from the cross but because the image works on the emotions of the beholder by indirect and often abstract means.

Rogier's disdain of accurate representation and spatial logic and his confidence in his ability to produce startlingly memorable images of immense dramatic power became very apparent in the great altarpieces of the late 1440s: the polyptych of the *Last Judgement* (Beaune, Mus. Hôtel-Dieu), datable between 1443 and 1451 and painted for Nicolas Rolin, Chancellor of Burgundy, and the triptych of the *Seven Sacraments* (Antwerp, Kon. Mus. S. Kst.), painted for JEAN CHEVROT, Bishop of Tournai, also a man of great influence at the Burgundian court. The *Last Judgement* (for illustration *see* ROLIN, (1)) was painted for

2. Rogier van der Weyden: *Descent from the Cross*, oil on panel, 2.2×2.62 m, *c.* 1442 (Madrid, Museo del Prado)

the altar of a chapel adjoining the principal hospital ward of the Hôtel-Dieu and was visible to the sick and dying as they lay in their beds. Fortunately, perhaps, it would normally have been kept closed, so that the invalids would have seen only the portraits of Rolin and his wife and the grisailles of the *Annunciation, St Anthony* and *St Sebastian*; only occasionally would they have seen the magnificent but terrifying *Last Judgement*. The central figure of St Michael weighs souls in his balance with improbable delicacy and complete impassivity as he appears to step forward from the surface of the panel. In the figures of the damned, compelled by invisible forces to enter Hell, Rogier showed how powerfully he could depict the extremes of human emotion.

In the *Seven Sacraments* the figures are once again drawn to several different scales according to their importance in the Church's hierarchy. The problem of uniting the three distinct fields of the triptych was effortlessly solved by representing the aisles in the wings, and the nave of a great church in the centre panel, all seen in accurate perspective. Christ hangs on an extravagantly high cross; he and the mourners could be either polychromed sculptures or human flesh. Little is explained, unless in the Latin inscriptions on the scrolls held by the seven angels; but the image, superficially highly artificial, is convincing and

acceptable, largely because of its perfect and balanced beauty. Some of the heads are portraits: the bishop administering the sacrament of confirmation is Chevrot himself. Other heads are painted on separate supports and glued on to the panels, apparently indicating that they are portraits of people who could not be brought to pose in Rogier's studio. An assistant, or assistants, would have been sent to take their likenesses. The triptych may have been painted for Chevrot's foundation at his birthplace, Poligny in Franche-Comté, rather than for his cathedral at Tournai: the stuck-on portrait heads are possibly likenesses of his associates at Poligny. Some of the figures were copied by illuminators who worked on the *Roman de Girart de Roussillon* for Philip the Good (Vienna, Österreich. Nbib., Cod. 2549). Since their miniatures may be dated shortly after 1448, when payment was authorized for the transcription of the text, the *Seven Sacraments* may be placed in the 1440s.

The Braque Triptych (Paris, Louvre), depicting half-length figures of *St John the Baptist, Christ between the Virgin and St John the Evangelist* and the *Magdalene*, was owned by, and was perhaps commissioned for, a Tournai couple, Jehan Braque (*d* 1452) and Catherine de Brabant; it may be dated towards 1452 and shows that Rogier maintained connections with his birthplace long after his move to Brussels. It is rather closely related in style to the Beaune polyptych but, being much smaller in scale, is more exquisitely detailed and finished.

Two paintings have often been associated with Rogier's supposed visit to Italy in 1450: the *Virgin and Child with Saints* (Frankfurt am Main, Städel. Kstinst. & Städt. Gal.) and the *Lamentation* (Florence, Uffizi). Neither is of sufficient quality for an attribution to van der Weyden himself to be sustained; both, moreover, are on oak panels and therefore unlikely to have been painted in Italy. They should be classed as workshop pieces, and their Italianate iconographies may be explained by supposing that they were Italian commissions and that the patrons sent elaborate instructions, or even specimen drawings, to the Brussels studio. This was, of course, the procedure followed when Italian patrons commissioned tapestries in the Low Countries. There is consequently no reason to date the two pictures to 1450 or to see them as landmarks in the chronology of Rogier's paintings.

(iii) Late period, 1450s and 1460s. Few pictures other than portraits can be assigned to van der Weyden's later years. The Escorial *Crucifixion*, evidently painted after 1454, sets a superbly high standard of design, which is matched perhaps only in the Columba Triptych (Munich, Alte Pin.), representing the *Annunciation*, the *Adoration of the Magi* (see fig. 3) and the *Presentation in the Temple*. At this stage in his career Rogier seems to have become so successful that he rarely had the opportunity to give much attention to religious commissions, most of which he would have delegated to assistants. The Columba Triptych itself, though undoubtedly designed by Rogier, was clearly executed in collaboration with several assistants, one of whom seems even to have painted the portrait of the donor. The triptych comes from the church of St Columba at Cologne, where in 1801 it was in a chapel founded by Goddert von dem Wasservas, a prominent citizen of Cologne. The chapel, however, may have been founded after Rogier's death and there is no absolutely conclusive

3. Rogier van der Weyden: *Adoration of the Magi*, central panel from the Columba Triptych, oil on panel, 1.38×1.53 m (central panel), *c.* 1455 (Munich, Alte Pinakothek)

4. Rogier van der Weyden: *Crucifixion*, oil on panel, 3.25×1.92 m, *c.* 1455–6 (Madrid, Escorial)

evidence that the donor was Goddert. On the other hand, certain iconographic peculiarities and the number of early copies and versions produced by local artists suggest that the triptych was commissioned for Cologne; the assistant who delivered it to Cologne may then have inserted the donor's portrait. Difficult to date precisely, the triptych is normally assigned to the 1450s.

The Escorial *Crucifixion* (see fig. 4) may be seen as the culmination of van der Weyden's achievement. Like the *Descent from the Cross*, it is staged in a completely unlikely setting which concentrates attention on the figures. The red hanging forming the background has been neatly folded into squares which provide a grid controlling the composition and relating the three figures in an extraordinarily subtle way. Much of the interest in the painting lies in the contrast between the trembling, unstable Virgin, whose contour expresses a graceful shudder and whose draperies fall in broken diagonals, and the steadfast St John the Evangelist, where the principal accents are long, unbroken verticals. Such use of abstract means to convey emotional effect and such disdain for a straightforward narrative approach seem typical of van der Weyden, who

was here working, without interference from a patron, on a huge picture, which he was to give to a local monastery.

The donor portraits of the *Crucifixion* and *Nativity* triptychs and of the Beaune polyptych provide a basis for attributing independent portraits to Rogier, and these can be dated according to the sitters' dress or, occasionally, according to biographical evidence. (Only one portrait should be classed with the earlier group of religious paintings: the beautiful *Portrait of a Young Woman* (Berlin, Gemäldegal.), which is close in style to portraits by the Master of Flémalle and in which the sitter retains a degree of individuality unusual in Rogier's work.) The later portraits are: the *Portrait of a Man* (Madrid, Mus. Thyssen-Bornemisza); *Antoine, Grand Bâtard de Bourgogne* (Brussels, Mus. A. Anc.), datable after 1456; *Francesco d'Este* (New York, Met.); and the *Portrait of a Young Woman* (Washington, DC, N.G.A.; see fig. 5). A separate group is formed by the half-length diptychs, in which a donor worships the Virgin and Child. Only one such diptych by Rogier survives: the much damaged *Virgin and Child* (Tournai, Mus. B.-A.) belongs with the portrait of *Jean de Gros* (Chicago, IL, A. Inst.). Two other diptych portraits exist: the damaged and neglected *John I, Duke of Cleves* (Paris, Louvre), datable after 1451, and *Philippe de Croÿ* (Antwerp, Kon. Mus. S. Kst.), which is datable before 1461 and which is possibly, but not certainly, to be paired with another *Virgin and Child* (San Marino, CA, Huntington Lib. & A.G.). Rogier did not invent the half-length diptych form, which was known at the beginning of the 15th century, but he may have done much to revive its popularity. The portrait of *Jean de Gros* is painted on a panel of normal proportions for a portrait and may be earlier than the *Philippe de Croÿ*, which is on a taller panel: the elongated format made both panels of a diptych easier to compose. Other portraits by van der Weyden are known only from early versions and copies: his portraits of *Philip the Good*, wearing a chaperon (versions at Dijon, Mus. B.-A.; Windsor Castle, Berks, Royal Col.; and elsewhere) and bareheaded (versions in Madrid, Pal. Real; and elsewhere); a portrait of Philip's wife *Isabella of Portugal* (version at Malibu, CA, Getty Mus.); and a portrait of their son *Charles the Bold* (best version at Berlin, Gemäldegal.).

All these portraits are similarly composed. The heads, fairly evenly lit, are turned in pure three-quarters view, the contours of the noses being tangential to the corners of the far eyes. The compositions are pyramidal, and the hands, if they are included, are usually compressed into secondary pyramids and appear to rest on the frames. This method of composition, evidently evolved by Rogier, solves the problem of explaining the cutting of the sitter by the lower edge of the frame, which becomes a window opening; in the later examples, such as the *Portrait of a Young Woman* (Washington, DC, N.G.A.; see fig. 5), the sitters are resolved into patterns of diagonals in harmony with the principal diagonals of the panels. As in the religious paintings, contour lines tend to be simplified into geometric shapes, and the sitters are idealized according to Rogier's usual conventions of beauty, even when this necessitates a small amount of distortion: the ear of the *Young Woman* is raised to make her neck look longer and to take its place within the pattern of curves and lines created by her head. All Rogier's sitters have the same

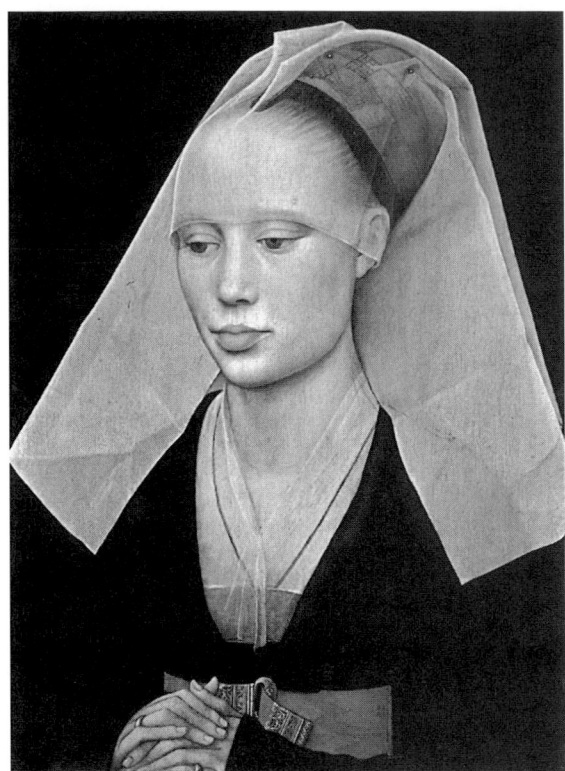

5. Rogier van der Weyden: *Portrait of a Young Woman*, oil on panel, 340×255 mm, *c.* 1460 (Washington, DC, National Gallery of Art)

expression of pious nobility, achieved by raising the eyebrows, lengthening the noses, concentrating attention on the eyes and lower lips and giving the contours of the faces an exaggerated linear interest. As Rogier painted many of the most eminent persons of the Burgundian court, he was assuredly a fashionable and successful portrait painter, and the degree of stylization that he imposed on his sitters must have been acceptable to them if not desired by them. This highly subjective attitude to his sitters, in which he imposes his own ideals on them, makes his portraits similar in conception to his religious paintings, where narrative interest is subordinated to Rogier's own highly individual vision of his subject.

No other paintings by van der Weyden of secular subjects have survived, but the lost *Scenes of Justice* must not be forgotten, nor the picture described by Fazio as a woman sweating in her bath. The latter may have resembled the picture by a German artist known as the *Liebeszauber* (Leipzig, Mus. Bild. Kst.)

II. Working methods and technique.

1. DRAWINGS. The most cursory examination of van der Weyden's paintings reveals that he was a draughtsman of awesome accomplishment. Using studies from nature, he would have made preliminary drawings for paintings; finished contract designs, which would have been shown to patrons who were placing important commissions and who, before reaching final agreements, would have wanted to have accurate ideas of what they would be getting; and

pattern drawings for use within the workshop. They would have been of heads, hands, animals, plants, textiles or interiors; single figures and groups of Christ, the Virgin and saints. They formed a body of reference material that was being constantly added to and recycled. Some of the pattern drawings may have been shown to clients or assembled on a pastiche basis to create standard religious subjects. Such drawings were highly valued, copied and recopied and were an important part of any artist's equipment. Rogier's would have been inherited by his painter son Pieter, and at least some passed into the possession of Pieter's son (2) Goswijn van der Weyden (Campbell, 1979).

In the Low Countries drawings were not collected and preserved in any systematic way; consequently, relatively few have survived. Among the few extant drawings attributed to Rogier, only one, the *Portrait of a Lady* (London, BM), can be classified as a life drawing, while three can be claimed as pattern drawings created for use in his workshop: the heads of *St Joseph* (Oxford, Ashmolean) and the *Virgin* (Paris, Louvre) and the *Virgin and Child* (Rotterdam, Mus. Boymans–van Beuningen). Almost certainly executed by an assistant in van der Weyden's workshop was the drawing known as *The 'Scupstoel'* (New York, Met.), a design datable to the 1440s for one of the capitals on the façade of Brussels Town Hall. As painter to the town of Brussels, van der Weyden would have been responsible for designing decorations for municipal buildings, but the inferior quality of the drawing suggests that he delegated this unimportant task to an assistant.

The surviving drawings give a most inadequate idea of the range of material used in Rogier's workshop, but the existence of many more drawings can be deduced from the paintings. Infra-red reflectograms reveal that in the *Nativity* triptych floating scrolls were underdrawn in all three panels; but they were never painted. They appear, however, in a version of the triptych by a follower (New York, Cloisters). It seems that Rogier made a finished design for his triptych in which scrolls were included; that the underdrawing of the triptych followed this design; but that, subsequently, Rogier or his patron, or both in association, decided against the scrolls. The contract design, with the scrolls, would have remained in the workshop, to be used like other reference drawings and to be reproduced by the follower. It is, in fact, fairly usual to discover that a version of a well-known composition is closer to the underdrawn than to the finished original: both are copied from a common source, the contract design.

The same pattern drawings were used, for example, for the dogs in the *Seven Sacraments* and the Columba Triptych; for the faces of *? St Joseph* (Lisbon, Fund. Gulbenkian) and the oldest king in the Columba Triptych; and for the patterned textiles worn by the woman supporting the Virgin in the Prado *Descent from the Cross*, hung on the altar in the *Exhumation of St Hubert* (London, N.G.; see fig. 6) and draped over the floor beneath the Virgin Annunciate in the Columba Triptych.

Infra-red photographs and reflectograms demonstrate that, although Rogier approached different commissions in different ways, major alterations occur only rarely—for example in the right wing of the Miraflores Triptych,

6. Rogier van der Weyden and assistants: *Exhumation of St Hubert*, oil on panel, 880×805 mm, *c.* 1440 (London, National Gallery)

where the background was completely changed after the underdrawing was finished. It seems that compositions were normally worked out with care in preliminary drawings and contract designs, before work was started on the underdrawings. Rogier on occasion executed the underdrawing himself, as in the Prado *Descent from the Cross*, where the drawing is of wonderful boldness and assurance; but in other cases, for example the Columba Triptych, he apparently delegated to assistants the routine task of transferring the finished designs to the panels. In the Beaune *Last Judgement* several styles of underdrawing have

been discerned, which may correspond to the contributions of Rogier himself and several assistants (Veronée-Verhaegen).

In the Prado *Descent from the Cross* some of the minor alterations give interesting insights into Rogier's creative process: the Virgin's right hand was drawn hanging in a pose that directly echoed that of Christ's right hand but has been painted with the fingers curled, to reinforce the circular rhythms of the composition; and the head of the servant behind the Magdalene was revised but painted on the same axis as the underdrawn head. This axis is a radius of the circle formed by Christ's left forearm and the Magdalene's back and falling mantle, so that Rogier's feeling for simple geometric accords is made very apparent.

2. PAINTING TECHNIQUE. The paint samples taken from the Prado *Descent from the Cross* show that Rogier used the same limited range of pigments as the other Netherlandish painters of the time and that, whereas van Eyck and Dieric Bouts isolated the chalk ground from the paint by applying a thin layer of oil, Rogier here used a pinkish–greyish priming for the same purpose (van Asperen de Boer and others, 1983). As X-ray photographs of Rogier's paintings seem to indicate that he used white a little more liberally than van Eyck, presumably these two factors explain why Rogier's pictures appear slightly less translucent and jewel-like in colour than van Eyck's; it may have been a taste for less intense colour that led him to evolve such painting methods.

It would appear that Rogier and his assistants used drying oils as painting media but that, at least on occasion, they worked over underpaintings in egg tempera. Seen under the microscope, Rogier's panels are revealed to be miracles of painterly skill; his love of detail was even more developed than van Eyck's. In some of his pictures Rogier included minutiae that can never have been noticed by his contemporaries. In the *Magdalene Reading* (London, N.G.), the red ruling lines in the book are invisible to the naked eye and the tiny bookmarks are only just discernibly of different colours: two green, one blue and one red. The fur of her dress is striped wet in wet into a first application of grey and then dragged with a dry brush to produce a feathered effect. In her cloth of gold underdress Rogier has used impasted paint with admirable sureness of touch: here he has clearly painted in oil without a thinner, which makes his skill seem all the more remarkable. More interested than van Eyck in linear detail, he has used different, perhaps less surprising and less economical but equally startling, methods to achieve an impression of infinite detail.

3. WORKSHOP PRACTICE. No serious study has yet been made of van der Weyden's workshop or of the parts played by his assistants in its collaborative production. There is little historical evidence to indicate how many apprentices, journeymen and other assistants he employed at any given time. His 'ouvriers' were mentioned in a document of 1459; Zanetto Bugatto 'studied' with Rogier between 1460 and 1463; and Hans Memling may have been Rogier's pupil. But large numbers of other artists could very well have passed longer or shorter periods in the van der Weyden studio. It is relatively easy to distinguish, in works designed by Rogier, the clumsy contributions of incompetent assistants, for example the dove in the *Annunciation* of the Beaune polyptych; but it is more difficult to detect the contributions of highly trained collaborators.

The *Dream of Pope Sergius* (Malibu, CA, Getty Mus.) and the *Exhumation of St Hubert* (London, N.G.; see fig. 6 above) were seen during the 1620s at Ste Gudule in Brussels by the French traveller Dubuisson-Aubenay, who stated that they were by Rogier. They were then displayed as a diptych in a chapel dedicated to St Hubert, and it

seems reasonable to assume that the two panels were commissioned for the chapel at the time of its foundation in 1437. It is possible that originally there were more than two panels in the series. Though the principal heads—those of Sergius in the *Dream*, and the bishop on the left and St Hubert in the *Exhumation*—are comparable to the heads in the Miraflores Triptych and may therefore have been painted by Rogier, the two panels appear to have been designed and executed by several other painters. One of them was apparently the artist who was responsible for *The 'Scupstoel'* drawing, to which the petitioners in the middleground of the *Dream* are stylistically similar. It may be that the two panels were produced by teams of assistants in Rogier's workshop shortly after his establishment in Brussels, when he himself would have been fully occupied with the *Scenes of Justice*. For the execution of the *Scenes of Justice*, he would have required numerous assistants, and at that stage in his career he would not have had the opportunity to train them all thoroughly. The *Dream* and the *Exhumation* could be seen as an important, if unsympathetic, commission for the principal church in Brussels. Rogier might have delegated both the design and the execution of the panels to his ablest assistants and himself painted only the principal heads.

On other occasions commissions seem to have been entrusted to one assistant who was made largely responsible for design and execution. The Sforza Triptych of *Christ on the Cross* (Brussels, Mus. A. Anc.), evidently painted in the mid-1440s for Alessandro Sforza of Pesaro and probably to be identified with the *Crucifixion* listed as by Rogier in a Pesaro inventory of 1500, is uniform in style, apart from the head of Alessandro himself, which is painted on a separate support and glued on to the centre panel. The rest of the triptych appears to have been designed and painted by one artist, presumably one of Rogier's assistants, who adapted his master's compositions and patterns, borrowed from the Vienna *Crucifixion* and the triptych of the *Nativity*, but maintained a recognizably personal style. Not a good draughtsman or designer, he was nervous of flamboyant effects, tended to favour unbroken vertical contour lines and compositional accents, and was not consistently careful in his study of nature. His facial types are readily distinguishable and the expressions always vacuous. The *Virgin and Child with Saints* (Frankfurt am Main, Städel. Kstinst. & Städt. Gal.), apparently a Florentine commission, may be by the same hand and is thoughtlessly composed and drawn. The saints' legs and feet are poorly articulated and the angels' wings are carelessly forced into the curved space at the top of the panel. Even if it is assumed that these were uninteresting commissions and that Rogier thought that Italian patrons would have little sense of artistic quality, it seems surprising that he should have delegated both design and execution to a relatively incompetent assistant.

Other problematic pictures may similarly have been painted by assistants working within the studio on a relatively independent basis. The *Annunciation* (New York, Met.), the *St John the Baptist* triptych (Berlin, Gemäldegal.), the *Lamentation* (Florence, Uffizi) and the diptych of the *Virgin and Child* (Caen, Mus. B.-A.) and *'Laurent Froimont'* (Brussels, Mus. A. Anc.) are among many paintings that are close in style to van der Weyden but fall below the standard of quality set by his authenticated pictures. They are probably workshop pieces, and it is perhaps feasible to assign them to stylistic groups as the work of identifiable assistants. It is less easy to detect the hands of these assistants in altarpieces such as the Beaune *Last Judgement* or the Columba Triptych, where assistants were working on Rogier's designs, in collaboration with him and under his direct supervision. It may never prove possible to make a neat distinction between workshop pieces and paintings by highly trained assistants who had left the studio to set up their own businesses or indeed between the work of former assistants and that of painters simply influenced by Rogier and closely imitating his style.

III. Critical reception and posthumous reputation.

Van der Weyden may be seen as having developed the example of the Master of Flémalle, but in an increasingly personal, if not idiosyncratic, direction. Like the Master, Rogier was a superb draughtsman and designer and much concerned with the emotional impact of his work. Unlike the Master, he was not interested in straightforward narrative painting, and he was more ready than his mentor to distort or to depict what may seem, to an objective and soulless viewer, logically absurd. Though Rogier clearly knew the work of Jan van Eyck, which on occasion he directly imitated, van Eyck's interests differed so much from his own that Jan's influence on him could be only very superficial. Rogier's superior command of line, movement and facial expression is well demonstrated if the youngest king in his Columba Triptych is compared with van Eyck's figure of St George in his *Virgin and Child with Canon van der Paele* (1436; Bruges, Groeningemus.).

Success came to van der Weyden early in his career, and after van Eyck's death in 1441 there was no-one to challenge his ascendancy. His influence on all branches of the visual arts became so strong that artists and patrons seem to have come to visualize the standard religious subjects and their protagonists much as Rogier saw them. Because his workshop was evidently large, his compositions were efficiently repeated, varied and distributed, so that many of his inventions quickly gained a wide currency. The figures of the Virgin and Child in his *St Luke Drawing a Portrait of the Virgin* were constantly copied in half-length versions produced both inside and outside his workshop. His conception of the Pietà, which he may first have brought to perfection in the Miraflores Triptych, was striking and novel: the dramatic diagonals formed by the stiff and emaciated corpse of Christ, with the parallel diagonals of the Virgin embracing him, made for a highly expressive and memorable image, which had the additional advantage of avoiding difficult foreshortenings in the nude body of Christ. This composition could be readily adapted for different purposes and patrons, both within the workshop (cf. the versions in Brussels, Mus. A. Anc., London, N.G., and Madrid, Prado) and by imitators outside. Rogier's depiction became the standard way of representing the subject until well into the 16th century. Similarly, Rogier's portrait formula was widely followed over a long period and his half-length diptychs were also very influential. It was perhaps Rogier who, in his much repeated half-length compositions of the *Descent from the Cross*, evolved the half-length narrative picture. As the originals do not survive, it is difficult to judge whether workshop patterns or paintings by Rogier himself were the sources from which the numerous extant versions were taken.

While some of van der Weyden's most fanciful ideas, for instance his Pietà composition, the framing arches of the Miraflores Triptych and the floating loincloth of Christ in the Vienna *Crucifixion*, were often adapted by his imitators, his more radically abstract conceptions were seldom borrowed, and then only tentatively. Copyists were inclined to rationalize the artificial setting of the Prado *Descent from the Cross*, and painters who executed versions of the Beaune *Last Judgement*, the Escorial *Crucifixion* and the Columba Triptych usually tried to revise or eliminate some of the less logical passages or imitated individual figures rather than whole compositions. In so doing, they naturally lost much of the expressive force that Rogier had achieved by irrational and abstract means, and their works seem prosaic and dull by comparison. None of his followers had his command of drawing, line and pattern, and so their compositions lack the harmony of design that Rogier consistently achieved. Not surprisingly, his extreme subtlety of invention and his contempt for mere representation were quite beyond his pupils and imitators.

That van der Weyden was famous in his own lifetime is demonstrated by several contemporary texts and by the importance of the commissions he secured. Though his fame endured into the 16th and 17th centuries, confusions began to arise concerning the 'Roger of Bruges' whom Italian writers had highly praised. He was, of course, van der Weyden; but van Mander, failing to realize this, wrote biographies of two apparently distinct painters, Roger of Bruges and Rogier van der Weyden, the latter confounded with Rogier's great-grandson of the same name, an Antwerp painter. In the 16th century the *Descent from the Cross* and the great *Crucifixion* were removed from the Low Countries to the relative obscurity of the Escorial; in 1695 the *Scenes of Justice*, Rogier's most accessible paintings and perhaps his most impressive, were destroyed. This makes more understandable the fact that Rogier's name was more or less totally forgotten during the 18th century and that 19th-century art historians had the greatest difficulty in discovering a secure basis for reconstructing his achievement. Many quite unworthy pictures were placed under his name, and consequently his reputation was re-established very slowly. Only with the discovery that the Miraflores Triptych is unquestionably by Rogier and that the Escorial *Crucifixion* is an exceptionally well-authenticated work has it become possible to take a more critical view of Rogier's output. As mistaken attributions are rejected, so van der Weyden's artistic stature increases, and he is coming to be acknowledged as one of the supreme masters of 15th-century art.

BIBLIOGRAPHY

EARLY SOURCES

B. Fazio: *De viris illustribus* (MS., 1456; Florence, 1745); Eng. trans. by M. Baxandall: 'Bartholomaeus Facius on Painting: A 15th-century Manuscript of *De viris illustribus*', *J. Warb. & Court. Inst.*, xxvii (1964), pp. 90–107

J. Molanus: *Historiae Lovaniensium libri XIV* (MS., *c.* 1575); ed. P. F. X. de Ram (Brussels, 1861), p. 609

K. van Mander: *Schilder-boek* ([1603]–1604), fols 206*v*-7
A. Ponz: *Viaje* (1772–94); ed. C. M. de Rivero (1947), p. 1045

GENERAL

BNB; Thieme–Becker
M. J. Friedländer: *Die altniederländische Malerei* (Berlin and Leiden, 1924–37), ii (1924), pp. 11–54; Eng. trans. as *Early Netherlandish Painting* (Leiden, 1967–76)
J. Destrée: *Roger de la Pasture–van der Weyden*, 2 vols (Paris and Brussels, 1930)
E. Renders: *La Solution du problème van der Weyden–Flémalle–Campin*, 2 vols (Bruges, 1931)
E. Lamalle: *Chronique de la chartreuse de la chapelle à Hérinnes-lez-Enghien* (Leuven, 1932)
P. Rolland: *Les Primitifs tournaisiens: Peintres et sculpteurs* (Brussels and Paris, 1932)
E. Panofsky: *Early Netherlandish Painting: Its Origins and Character* (Cambridge, MA, 1953)
M. Davies: *The National Gallery, London* (1954), iii/2 of *Les Primitifs flamands: I. Corpus de la peinture des anciens Pays-Bas méridionaux au quinzième siècle* (Antwerp, 1954)
S. Ringbom: *Icon to Narrative* (Åbo, 1965)
M. Sonkes: *Dessins du XVè siècle: Groupe van der Weyden* (1969), v of *Les Primitifs flamands: III. Contributions à l'étude des primitifs flamands* (Brussels, 1969)
P. M. Kendall and V. Ilardi: *Dispatches with Related Documents of Milanese Ambassadors in France and Burgundy, 1450–1483*, ii (Athens, OH, 1971)
N. Veronée-Verhaegen: *L'Hôtel-Dieu de Beaune* (1973), xiii of *Les Primitifs flamands: I. Corpus de la peinture des anciens Pays-Bas méridionaux au quinzième siècle* (Antwerp, 1951–)
M. Comblen-Sonkes: *Guide bibliographique de la peinture flamande du XVè siècle* (Brussels, 1984)
J. O. Hand and M. Wolff: *Early Netherlandish Painting*, Washington, DC, N.G.A. cat. (Washington, DC, 1986)
Le muse e il principe: Arte di corte nel Rinascimento padano, 2 vols (exh. cat., Milan, Mus. Poldi Pezzoli, 1991)

MONOGRAPHIC WORKS

H. Beenken: *Rogier van der Weyden* (Munich, 1951)
M. Davies: *Rogier van der Weyden* (London, 1972)
L. Campbell: *Van der Weyden* (London, 1979)
Rogier van der Weyden (exh. cat., Brussels, Mus. Com., 1979) [with bibliog.]
O. Delenda: *Rogier van der Weyden* (Paris, 1987)

SPECIALIST STUDIES

A. Wauters: 'Roger Vanderweyden, ses oeuvres, ses élèves et ses descendants', *Rev. Univl. A.*, i (1855), pp. 421–33; ii (1855), pp. 5–36, 85–99, 165–76; (1856), pp. 245–65, 326–38
J. D. Passavant: 'Der Maler Roger van der Weyden', *Z. Christ. Archäol. Kst.*, ii (1858), pp. 1–20, 120–30, 178–80
A. Pinchart: 'Roger de le Pasture', *Bull. Comm. Royales A. & Archéol.*, vi (1867), pp. 408–94
A. Vernarecci: 'La libreria di Giovanni Sforza signore di Pesaro', *Archv Stor. Marche & Umbria*, iii (1886), pp. 501–23
F. Malaguzzi Valeri: *Pittori lombardi del quattrocento* (Milan, 1902), pp. 126–7 [contains corr. relating to Zanetto Bugatto and Rogier]
A. Hocquet: 'Roger de la Pasture, peintre tournaisien', *Rev. Tournais.*, ix/5 (1913), pp. 113–21
——: 'Roger de la Pasture: La Profession du père de l'artiste', *Rev. Tournais.*, ix/7 (1913), pp. 153–6
F. Winkler: 'Der Meister von Flémalle und Rogier van der Weyden', *Kstgesch. Auslandes*, ciii (1913) [whole issue]
C. W. Pierce: 'The Sforza Triptych', *A. Stud. Med., Ren. & Mod.*, vi (1928), pp. 39–45
E. Frankignoulle: 'Notes pour servir à l'histoire de l'art en Brabant', *An. Soc. Royale Archéol. Bruxelles*, xxxix (1935), pp. 13–204
E. Kantorowicz: 'The Este Portrait by Roger van der Weyden', *J. Warb. & Court. Inst.*, iii (1939–40), pp. 165–80
A. M. Cetto: 'Der Berner Traian und Herkinbald-Teppich', *Jb. Bern. Hist. Mus.*, xlii/xliv (1963–4), pp. 5–230
D. De Vos: 'De Madonna-en-Kindtypologie bij Rogier van der Weyden', *Jb. Berlin. Mus.*, xiii (1971), pp. 60–161
M. Soenen: 'Chartreuse de Scheut à Anderlecht', *Monasticon Belge* (Liège, 1972), iv/6 of *Province de Brabant*, pp. 1385–1427
L. Campbell: 'The Early Netherlandish Painters and their Workshops', *Le Dessin sous-jacent dans la peinture, Colloque III: Le Problème Maître de Flémalle–van der Weyden: Louvain-la-Neuve, 1979*, pp. 43–61

M. Faries: 'The Underdrawn Composition of Rogier van der Weyden's *St Luke Drawing a Portrait of the Virgin*', ibid., pp. 93–9
N. Reynaud and J. De Coo: 'Origen del retablo de San Juan Bautista atribuido a Juan de Flandes', *Archv Esp. A.*, xli (1979), pp. 128–44
M. Soenen: 'Un Renseignement inédit sur la destinée d'une oeuvre bruxelloise de van der Weyden', *Rogier van der Weyden* (exh. cat., Brussels, Mus. Com., 1979), pp. 126–8
E. Dhanens: 'Nieuwe gegevens betreffende het Bladelin-Retabel', *Bijdragen tot de geschiedenis van de kunst der Nederlanden opgedragen aan Prof. Em. Dr. J. K. Steppe*, ed. M. Smeyers (Leuven, 1981), pp. 45–52
R. Grosshans: 'Rogier van der Weyden: Der Marienaltar aus der Kartause Miraflores', *Jb. Berlin, Mus.*, xxiii (1981), pp. 49–112
——: 'Infrarotuntersuchungen zum Studium der Unterzeichnung auf den Berliner Altären von Rogier van der Weyden', *Jb. Preuss. Kultbes.*, xix (1982), pp. 137–77
C. Périer-d'Ieteren: '*L'Annonciation* du Louvre, Université Libre de Bruxelles', *An. Hist. A. & Archéol.*, iv (1982), pp. 7–26
J. R. J. van Asperen de Boer and others: 'Algunas cuestiones técnicas del *Descendimiento de la Cruz* de Roger van der Weyden', *Bol. Mus. Prado*, iv (1983), pp. 39–50
R. H. Marijnissen and G. van de Voorde: 'Een onverklaarde werkwijze van de Vlaamse primitieven', *Acad. Anlct.: Kl. S. Kst.*, xliv/2 (1983), pp. 43–51
J. K. Steppe: 'Mécénat espagnol et art flamand au XVIe siècle', *Splendeurs d'Espagne*, 2 vols (exh. cat., ed. J.-M. Duvosquel and I. Vandevivere; Brussels, Pal. B.-A., 1985), i, pp. 247–82
M. W. Ainsworth and M. Faries: 'Northern Renaissance Paintings: The Discovery of Invention', *Bull. St Louis A. Mus.*, n. s., xviii/1 (1986)[whole issue]
L. Campbell: 'The Tomb of Joanna, Duchess of Brabant', *Ren. Stud.*, ii (1988), pp. 163–72
J. R. J. van Asperen de Boer, J. Dijkstra and R. van Schoute: 'Underdrawing in Paintings of Rogier van der Weyden and Master of Flémalle Groups', *Ned. Ksthist. Jb.*, xli (1990)[whole issue]
J. Dijkstra: *Origineel en kopie: Een onderzoek naar de navolging van de Meester van Flémalle en Rogier van der Weyden* (diss., U. Amsterdam, 1990)
C. Ishikawa: 'Rogier van der Weyden's *St Luke Drawing the Virgin* Re-examined', *Boston Mus. Bull.*, ii (1990), pp. 49–64
A. Kulenkampff: 'Der Dreikönigsaltar (Colomba-Altar) des Rogier van der Weyden', *An. Hist. Ver. Niederrhein, Alte Erzbistum Köln*, cxcii/cxciii (1990), pp. 9–46
A. Smolar-Meynart: 'Des origines à Charles Quint', *Le Palais de Bruxelles: Huit siècles d'art et d'histoire* (Brussels, 1991), pp. 15–90
J. Dumoulin: 'Les Eglises paroissiales de Tournai au 15e siècle: Art et histoire', *Les Grands Siècles de Tournai (12e–15e siècles): Recueil d'études publié à l'occasion du 20e anniversaire des Guides de Tournai* (Tournai and Louvain-la-Neuve, 1993), pp. 257–78
J. Dumoulin and J. Pycke: 'Comptes de la paroisse Sainte-Marguerite de Tournai au 15e siècle: Documents inédits relatifs à Roger de la Pasture, Robert Campin et d'autres artistes tournaisiens', ibid., pp. 279–320
L. Campbell: 'Rogier van der Weyden and his Workshop', *Proc. Brit. Acad.* (1994)

LORNE CAMPBELL

(2) Goswijn van der Weyden (*b* Brussels, *c.* 1465; *d* Antwerp, after 1538). Grandson of (1) Rogier van der Weyden. He became a burgher of the town of Lier in 1497 and from 1499 executed various works for the abbey of Tongerloo. Around 1500 he settled in Antwerp, where he directed a flourishing workshop employing several apprentices. That year he also joined the Guild of St Luke, of which he was made Dean in 1514 and 1530. Georges Hulin de Loo attributed to Goswijn a cycle of eight panels (of which seven have survived) on the *Life of St Dimpna* (Geneva, priv. col.), part of a large altarpiece executed *c.* 1505 for the abbey church of Tongerloo. He also ascribed to Goswijn the altarpiece of the *Marriage of the Virgin* (known as the 'Colibrant Triptych'), painted *c.* 1515–17 for the church of Sint Gommarus in Lier, and a *Virgin and Child with a Donor Couple* (also known as the 'Kalmthout Donation' *c.* 1511–15; see fig.), which shows stylistic analogies with the *Life of St Dimpna*. The

Goswijn van der Weyden: *Virgin and Child with a Donor Couple* (the 'Kalmthout Donation'), oil on panel, 1.53×1.53 m, *c.* 1511–15 (Berlin, Bodemuseum)

early date of the latter makes it contemporaneous with the ANTWERP MANNERISM of such artists as Jan Gossart, Jan de Beer and Jan Wellens de Cock, but although these panels and the *Marriage of the Virgin* have some of the formal characteristics of Mannerism, Goswijn cannot be described as a representative of that movement. Rather, he should be seen as a painter of the Brussels school, somewhat limited in his horizons, but susceptible to the influence of contemporary artistic fashion. In comparison with the *Life of St Dimpna*, the *Marriage of the Virgin* is more monumental in its composition and more crowded with figures, which are arranged symmetrically within a richly sculptured architectural interior. The figures, wrapped in flowing draperies, are sturdy and somewhat stiff.

The other works generally attributed to Goswijn do not seem to form a homogeneous ensemble. They comprise a number of poor-quality altarpieces: the *Legend of St Catherine*, the *Virgin and Child* (both untraced), the *Virgin and Child* in Burgos Cathedral, an *Adoration of the Magi*, another *Virgin and Child* (both London, Buckingham Pal.), which is related to the 'Kalmthout Donation' and was recently attributed to Goswijn (Campbell), and the triptych of the *Bearing to the Temple* (Lisbon). The lack of stylistic unity, which makes the attribution of these works problematic, may be explained by the collaboration of assistants in the artist's workshop. The style of the paintings attributed to Goswijn, most of which are narrative in character, is clearly that of the Brussels school. The facial types, the treatment of hands, hair and headgear, particularly in the *Life of St Dimpna*, as well as the chromatic range, show clear similarities with the works of the Master of the Joseph Sequence, although the handling is looser. An echo of this style can also be seen in Brussels tapestries of the period. Finally, the influence of Antwerp painters, especially of Quinten Metsys, can be discerned in some of the female figures, while the realism of the landscapes is similar to those of Gerard David. Technically, Goswijn's work is fairly perfunctory, and overall his artistic personality remains extremely ill-defined.

BIBLIOGRAPHY

Thieme–Becker

G. Hulin de Loo: 'Ein authentisches Werk von Goosen van der Weyden im Kaiser-Friedrich-Museum: Die gleichzeitigen Gemälde aus Tongerloo und Lier und die Ursprünge der Antwerpener Schule um 1500', *Jb. Kön.-Preuss. Kstsamml.*, xxxiv (1913), pp. 59–88

M. J. Friedländer: 'Die Antwerpener Manieristen von 1520', *Jb. Kön-Preuss. Kstsamml.*, xxxvi (1915), pp. 65–91

——: *Die altniederländische Malerei* (Berlin, 1924–37), xi (1933), pp. 31–4; Eng. trans. as *Early Netherlandish Painting*, xi (Leiden, 1974), pp. 22–3, 107

J. Roosval: 'Les Peintures des retables néerlandais en Suède', *Rev. Belge Archéol. & Hist. A.*, iv (1934), pp. 311–20

L. Campbell: 'The Pictures in the Collection of Her Majesty the Queen', *The Early Flemish Pictures* (Cambridge, 1985), pp. 121–3

G. Passemiers: *Goossen van der Weyden, 1465–1538/45: Peintre de l'école anversoise* (Brussels, 1987)

M.-L. Lievens-de Waegh: *Le Musée national d'art ancien et le Musée national des carreaux de faïence de Lisbonne*, i (Brussels, 1991), pp. 196–231

C. PÉRIER-D'IETEREN

Weyer, Gabriel (*b* Nuremberg, 5 Nov 1576; *d* Nuremberg, 17 Sept 1632). German painter and draughtsman. His earliest signed drawings are dated 1597 (Munich, Staatl. Graph. Samml.) and 1598. They show him as one of the first Nuremberg artists to adopt the Mannerist style of such Dutch artists as Hendrick Goltzius and Abraham Bloemaert. He acquired this, initially at least, through their prints, including those by Jacob Mathem after their designs. In his drawing of the *Noli me tangere* (1598; Nuremberg, Ger. Nmus.; see fig.), Weyer's Magdalene closely resembles a common Bloemaert female type, while the figure of Christ reveals a probable familiarity with the designs of Bartholomäus Spranger, then in Prague. This Netherlandish influence can also be seen in an undated *Allegory of Painting* drawing and in a sketchbook dated 1601 (both Nuremberg, Ger. Nmus.). A couple of years after his marriage in 1600, Weyer may have travelled as a journeyman to the Netherlands, since several signed and dated (1602, 1603 and 1604) drawings are bound with older Antwerp school drawings in a sketchbook (Berlin, Kupferstichkab.) perhaps bought on such a journey (see Held); but he could easily have purchased the book somewhere in Germany.

Between 30 August 1604 (when he became a master painter in Nuremberg) and 1613, little is known about Weyer's activities. A *Fall of Phaethon* drawing of 1613 (Vienna, Albertina) is probably a preparatory design for an illusionistic ceiling painting. In the same year the city council of Nuremberg decided to restore and redecorate the great hall of the Rathaus, the extensive painted cycles

Gabriel Weyer: *Noli me tangere*, pen and ink with purple wash, heightened with white, on rose-tinted paper, 200×144 mm, 1598 (Nuremberg, Germanisches Nationalmuseum)

designed by Dürer and executed (1520–22) by his followers having grown too faint. Initially Weyer assisted Paul Juvenel I, Georg Gärtner the younger and Jobst Harrich (*fl* 1580–1617), but was soon ordered to paint new scenes on the gables of the east and west, or short, walls of the great hall. On the east wall, on either side of the central window and directly above existing allegories of *Strength* and *Clemency*, both shown as male warriors, Weyer painted *Charity* and *Justice and Peace* (removed 1904; replaced with copies by Hans Kogl, destr. World War II; fragments of original mounted on panel, Nuremberg, Stadtmus. Fembohaus). His three female Virtues and accompanying putti are not too different from earlier figures like *Mary Magdalene*, though they are somewhat heavier and more calmly posed. The west wall was demolished soon afterwards to make way for Jakob Wolff the younger's Palladian-style façade. Weyer's paintings here, commissioned in 1621, may have simply repeated his 1613 design. His signed and dated sketch for this wall (1621; Bremen, Ksthalle) shows *Fame* on the left opposite *Victory*, with a Turkish captive. As Mende has observed, the style of this drawing is very close to Weyer's *Judgement of Paris* (1614; Basle, Kstmus.), *Diana* (1614; Berlin, Kupferstichkab.) and *Andromeda* (1615; Dresden, Kupferstichkab.). As well as these paintings (copied 1904, destr. World War II), which differed somewhat from the drawing, Weyer also contributed figures of *Wisdom* and *Vainglory*, among others, on the lower register of the western wall.

Weyer's success in this project undoubtedly prompted his selection in 1615 as city painter, a post he retained until his death. Unfortunately, with the exception of the city hall cycles, only one surviving painting, the portrait of *Gustavus Adolphus* (1623; Augsburg, Staats- & Stadtbib.), has been identified. Numerous later drawings by the artist still exist. Among the most attractive are *Perseus and Andromeda* (1620; Cambridge, MA, Fogg), *Angelica and Medoro* (1623) and the *Presentation in the Temple* (1631; both Nuremberg, Ger. Nmus.). His designs were occasionally copied by printmakers such as Heinrich Ulrich (*fl* 1595; *d* 1621), Peter Isselburg and Dietrich Krüger. The last made at least 16 engravings after Weyer's drawings, including *Mary with the Dead Christ* (1613), the *Seven Virtues* and the *Holy Family* (both 1614). Weyer may also have created a few of his own prints. After his death in 1632, Weyer's fame waned rapidly and he was not even mentioned in Joachim von Sandrart's *Teutsche Academie* (Nuremberg, 1675–9).

BIBLIOGRAPHY

Thieme–Becker
J. Held: 'Notizen zu einem niederländischen Skizzenbuch in Berlin', *Oud-Holland*, 50 (1933), pp. 273–88
Barock in Nürnberg, 1600–1750 (exh. cat., Nuremberg, Ger. Nmus., 1962), pp. 41–2
C. von Heusinger: 'Eine Zeichnung Gabriel Weyers in der Kunsthalle Bremen', *Niederdt. Beitr. Kstgesch.*, ix (1970), pp. 161–8
M. Mende: *Das alte Nürnberger Rathaus*, i (Nuremberg, 1979), esp. pp. 298–332 [excellent disc. of Weyer's activities for the city council]
H. Geissler, ed.: *Zeichnung in Deutschland: Deutsche Zeichner, 1540–1640*, i (exh. cat., Stuttgart, Staatsgal., 1979), pp. 210–11
Drawings from the Holy Roman Empire, 1540–1680 (exh. cat. by T. D. Kaufmann, Princeton U., NJ, A. Mus., 1982), pp. 92–3

JEFFREY CHIPPS SMITH

Weyerman, Jacob Campo (*b* Charleroi, 9 Aug 1677; *d* The Hague, 9 March 1747). Dutch writer and painter. He trained as a flower painter in Breda and studied at Utrecht University. He travelled extensively through western Europe and executed paintings for the English gentry. Although most famous for his numerous critical and satirical writings, he published *De leevensbeschryvingen der Nederlandsche konstschilders en konstschilderessen* in three volumes in 1729; a fourth volume appeared posthumously in 1769. The work covers more than 700 Dutch painters of the 17th and 18th centuries and follows the biographical tradition of Vasari, Karel van Mander I and Arnold Houbraken. Written in an entertaining style, Weyerman's comments on painters and their works are more practical than theoretical, and his opinions of collectors, art dealers and the art market give a unique inside view of the seamier side of the early 18th-century art world.

WRITINGS

Den ontleeder der gebreeken [The analyst of deficiencies] (Amsterdam, 1723)
Den echo des Herelds (Amsterdam, 1725)
De leevensbeschryvingen der Nederlandsche konstschilders en konstschilderessen [Lives of the Dutch painters], i–iii (The Hague, 1729); iv (Dordrecht, 1769)
Den vrolyke tuchtheer [The merry disciplinarian] (Amsterdam, 1729)

BIBLIOGRAPHY

Medel. Sticht. Jacob Campo Weyerman (1977–)
P. Altena and W. Hendrikx: *Het verlokkend ooft: Proeven over Jacob Campo Weyerman* [Enticing fruit: essays on Jacob Campo Weyerman] (Amsterdam, 1985)

T. J. Broos: *Tussen zwart en ultramarijn: De levens van schilders beschreven door Jacob Campo Weyerman, 1677–1747* [Between black and ultramarine: the lives of artists written by Jacob Campo Weyerman, 1677–1747] (Amsterdam, 1990)

TON J. BROOS

Weyr, Rudolf (von) (*b* Vienna, 22 March 1847; *d* Vienna, 30 Oct 1914). Austrian sculptor. He at first wavered between the study of architecture and that of sculpture, but the success of his sculptural sketches while a student at the Vienna Akademie determined his choice of career. His mentor, Josef Cesar (1814–76), provided contacts with the architects Gottfried Semper and Carl Hasenauer, who in 1875 contracted Weyr, in advance of all others, to execute sculptural decorations for the Naturhistorisches Museum and Kunsthistorisches Museum, Vienna, on which they were at that time engaged. Among Weyr's contributions were many of the spandrel figures, the major part of the cupola decorations and several polychromed caryatids. He afterwards became one of the main artists at work on the new Ringstrasse buildings (e.g. the *Justice* and *Medicine* groups for the university). Weyr, like the sculptor V. O. Tilgner, was influenced by French models and was attracted to the neo-Baroque, contributing with his relief compositions and silhouette effects to the very climax of the style. His preference for refinement and rich compositions meant that he was at his best in scenic works and designs for such small-scale objects as medals or table centrepieces in precious metals. When, on the occasion of the Imperial Silver Wedding in 1879, Hans Makart designed and directed the main part of the legendary pageant—the cultural climax of the Ringstrasse era—Weyr made a celebrated contribution, executing the *Railway* float, in which the theme was symbolized by the fire god's triumphal wedding with a water nymph. The influence of the Rococo revival can be seen in Weyr's figures, which are more formally and decoratively inventive than involved with sentiment or action. His virtuosity in architectural sculpture may be seen especially in the *Bacchus* frieze (1881–2) on the main façade of the Burgtheater, Vienna, in which sublime sensuality and a dissolution of the composition in light and shadow are held in check by an unobtrusive compositional balance. For the Hofburg he produced one of the multi-figured fountains of the Michaelertrakt, showing *Austria's Power at Sea* (1895). In collaboration with Hasenauer and Carl Kundmann, Weyr executed a monument, largely after his own design, to the poet and dramatist *Franz Grillparzer* (1876–89; Vienna, Volksgarten), in which the large illusionistic reliefs depict the most famous scenes from Grillparzer's plays. The Art Nouveau influence, already visible in his oeuvre before 1900, developed after that date, although the French element remained important. The partly unresolved conflict between tradition and renewal, however, characterizes his later public monuments in Vienna (e.g. *Hans Canon*, 1905, Stadtpark; *Brahms*, 1902–8, Resselpark). More successful in this respect are the tensely watching lions for Otto Wagner's Nussdorfer Wehr (1898) and the numerous memorials, such as that to the victims of the Ringtheater fire (1886; Vienna, Zentralfriedhof) executed in collaboration with Otto Hofer (1847–1901). Weyr's style is highly typical of the Viennese fin-de-siècle milieu, combining historicism's exquisitely furnished dreams with a concise realism and modernist features.

BIBLIOGRAPHY

R. Feuchtmüller and W. Mrazek: *Kunst in Österreich, 1860–1918* (Vienna, 1964)

R. Rieger-Wagner, ed.: *Die Wiener Ringstrasse*: IX/i: *Die Denkmäler der Wiener Ringstrasse* (Wiesbaden, 1973); IX/ii: *Die Plastik der Ringstrasse, 1890–1918* (Wiesbaden, 1976); IX/iii: *Die Plastik der Wiener Ringstrasse von der Spätromantik bis zur Wende um 1900* (Wiesbaden, 1980)

Burgtheater und Historismus (exh. cat., Schloss Grafenegg, 1976)

W. Kitlitschka: *Grabkult und Grabskulptur in Wien und Niederösterreich* (St Pölten, 1987)

WALTER KRAUSE

Weyrotter, Franz Edmund. *See* WEIROTTER, FRANZ EDMUND.

Whall, Christopher (Whitworth) (*b* Thurning, Northants, 16 April 1849; *d* London, 23 Dec 1924). English stained-glass artist and teacher. He received his artistic education at the Royal Academy Schools, London (1868–74), and later in Italy, where he made copies of 15th-century paintings. Returning to London in 1879 he was commissioned to design some stained-glass windows, but it was not until the late 1880s that he devoted himself almost exclusively to the craft. He worked for a time for the glass manufacturers James Powell & Sons as a freelance designer while teaching himself the technical processes of stained glass and in 1887 set up his own studio–workshop near Dorking, Surrey. In 1890 the architect J. D. Sedding asked Whall to design and make a window for St Mary's, Stamford, Lincs. It was the first of many collaborations with leading architects who, like Whall, were active in the Art Workers' Guild and the Arts and Crafts Exhibition Society. In 1896 Whall was appointed the first teacher of stained glass at the newly founded Central School of Arts and Crafts, London, and later taught at the Royal College of Art, London. His teaching methods and aesthetic philosophy are contained in his influential book *Stained Glass Work* (1905). The Lady Chapel and Chapter House windows (1898–1913) at Gloucester Cathedral, which Whall made with his pupils and apprentices, are his most important work. In creating a style sympathetic to the architectural context he developed a distinctive vocabulary of forms derived from nature and from the study of medieval glass and combined these with superlative materials and craftsmanship. Whall's many pupils included his daughter Veronica Whall (1887–1967), Karl Parsons (1884–1934) and Paul Woodroffe (1875–1954). In the USA his influence was transmitted through the work of the Boston artist–craftsman Charles Connick (1875–1945).

WRITINGS

Stained Glass Work (London, 1905)

BIBLIOGRAPHY

Christopher Whall, 1849–1924: Arts & Crafts Stained Glass Worker (exh. cat. by P. Cormack, London, William Morris Gal., 1979)

P. D. Cormack: 'Re-creating a Tradition: Christopher Whall and the Arts & Crafts Renascence of English Stained Glass', *Art and the National Dream*, ed. N.G. Bowe (Blackrock, 1993), pp. 15–42

PETER CORMACK

Wharf. *See* DOCK.

Wharton [née Newbold Jones], **Edith** (*b* New York, 24 Jan 1862; *d* Pavillon Colombe, nr Paris, 11 Aug 1937). American writer. She was born into a wealthy New York family and was educated privately; she travelled widely, settling in France in 1907. Her first book was *The Decoration of Houses* (1898), written in collaboration with the Boston architect Ogden Codman (who had remodelled her home at Newport, RI, in 1893). Their aim was to raise the standard of decoration in modern houses to that of the past through a return to 'architectural proportion' and an avoidance of the 'superficial application of ornament'. Each room should be furnished for comfort and according to its use and should be organically related to the rest of the house and the quality of life to be expressed. The work was successful and influential among both the public and such decorators as Elsie De Wolfe and William Odom. Wharton's house in Lenox, MA, the Mount, built to her design from 1901 by Francis L. V. Hoppin (after Codman's early dismissal), displayed many of the classical features of symmetry, decorum and restraint found in her book.

Wharton's second art-historical work, *Italian Villas and their Gardens* (1904), provides a competent survey of Renaissance garden planning and villa architecture, with a reading list (as in *The Decoration of Houses*) in four languages and short biographies of the designers cited. She draws a modern lesson from the 'harmony of design' of the Italian garden, its logical divisions and the relation of its architectural lines to those of the villa and the landscape. The accompanying illustrations from original watercolours by Maxfield Parrish are fanciful and vague, inappropriate to the rigorous accuracy of the text, as reviewers (and Wharton herself) were quick to note. Her most serious travel book, *Italian Backgrounds* (1905), with more suitable line drawings by E. C. Peixotto (1869–1940), contends that a study of Italy is like the paintings of Vittore Carpaccio or Carlo Crivelli, the formal foreground being the property of the guidebook that must be known before the background, which is the province of the 'dreamer' and the 'student'. Descriptions of Italian towns and buildings are thus interspersed with speculations about the dating and provenance of obscure works of art. Although Wharton produced no other art-historical writings, her fiction shows a continuing interest in the effect of taste, setting and décor as a gauge for character and situation.

WRITINGS

with O. Codman: *The Decoration of Houses* (New York, 1898); repr. with critical essays by J. B. Bayley and W. A. Coles (New York, 1978)

Italian Villas and their Gardens (New York, 1904/*R* 1976)

Italian Backgrounds (New York, 1905)

A Backward Glance (New York, 1934) [autobiography]

BIBLIOGRAPHY

'Pen and Pencil in Italy' [review of *Italian Villas and their Gardens*], *The Critic*, xlvi/2 (1905), pp. 167–8

R. W. B. Lewis: *Edith Wharton: A Biography* (London, 1975)

J. Fryer: *Felicitous Spaces* (Chapel Hill and London, 1986), pp. 53–199

EDWINA BURNESS

Whately [Whateley], **Thomas** (*d* London, 26 May 1772). English writer, garden designer and politician. An MP from 1761 until his death, he served as a Treasury Secretary in 1764–5, helping to draft the Stamp Act (1765), a key document in events that led to the American Revolution in 1775. Whately's writings include his *Observations on*

Modern Gardening, for which he is perhaps best remembered. This work describes a large number of English landscape gardens, some in great detail, and attempts to analyse and categorize them. It was considered by his contemporary Horace Walpole to be 'a system of rules pushed to a great degree of refinement' ('On Modern Gardening', *Anecdotes of Painting in England*, ed. R. N. Wornum, 1849, iii, p. 807). Whately described gardens as such (e.g. Stowe, Bucks), as well as in relation to farms (e.g. The Leasowes, W. Midlands), parks (e.g. Painshill Park, Surrey) and ridings (e.g. Piercefield, Gwent). He examined specific features, such as buildings, rocks, trees and the form of the land, and this led him to reject overtly emblematic uses of temples, statues or inscriptions—all of which featured in early 18th-century English gardens—in favour of less contrived effects. Visitors to gardens would often use the *Observations* as a guidebook, and Whately's Romantic sensibility and attention to seasonal and atmospheric effects helped to popularize it in Europe. Whately's modest practical contribution to garden design comprised the small garden that he laid out in an abandoned chalkpit at Nonsuch Mansion, Cheam, Surrey, the home he shared with his brother, and the garden of his friend William Gilpin (both destr.).

WRITINGS
Observations on Modern Gardening (London, 1770, 6/1801)

BIBLIOGRAPHY
DNB
C. P. Barbier: *William Gilpin: His Drawings, Teaching and Theory of the Picturesque* (Oxford, 1963), p. 161
J. D. Hunt: 'Emblem and Expression in the 18th-century Landscape Garden', *18th C. Stud.*, iii (1971), pp. 294–317
J. Archer: 'Character in English Architectural Design', *18th C. Stud.*, xii (1979), pp. 339–71

MICHAEL SYMES

Wheatley, Francis (*b* London, 1747; *d* London, 28 June 1801). English painter. He trained at William Shipley's Academy in London. In 1762, 1763 and 1765 he won prizes for drawing from the Society of Artists, and in 1769 he enrolled in the newly established Royal Academy Schools. He is recorded as having studied under a Mr Wilson in 1762 (Royal Society of Arts, *Minutes of Committees*, 1763, p. 17); this may have been the portrait painter Benjamin Wilson or, less likely, the landscape painter Richard Wilson. Wheatley was abroad in 1763, probably in the Low Countries and France, and in 1766 he made his first trip to Ireland. He was elected a Fellow of the Society of Artists in 1770 and became a director in 1774.

Wheatley's early work consists mainly of small-scale, full-length portraits (e.g. *Portrait of a Gentleman*, traditionally called '*George Basil Wood*', *c*. 1778–9; ex-Mellon col., sold London, Christie's, 17 Nov 1989, lot 21) and conversation pieces (e.g. *Family Group with a Black Servant*, *c*. 1774–5; London, Tate) in the manner of Benjamin Wilson and Johan Zoffany, as well as a few landscapes. His friend John Hamilton Mortimer, with whom he collaborated on a number of works, including the ceiling of the saloon (1771–3) at Brocket Hall, Herts, was also an influence on him; it was probably from Mortimer that he derived the luscious application of paint in his rendering of fabrics. Wheatley's small portraits and conversation pieces in outdoor settings display an appreciation of nature (his

backgrounds are, however, rarely topographical) and reveal an eye for the placement of figures in landscape.

In 1779 Wheatley, with the wife of a fellow artist, fled to Dublin to escape his creditors. He continued his portrait practice there and made a name for himself by painting two large-scale subject pictures, each depicting a contemporary event: *View of College Green with a Meeting of the Volunteers* (Dublin, N.G.) and the *Irish House of Commons* (1780; Lotherton Hall, W. Yorks). Both are enlivened by the inclusion of innumerable portraits. In 1783 he returned to London where, having completed another large contemporary narrative picture, the *Riot on Broad Street* (destr. by fire at the engravers), he began working for the print publisher John Boydell. Although Wheatley continued to produce portraits, landscapes and even some history paintings (e.g. *Theseus and Hippolyta Find the Lovers*, New York, priv. col., see Webster, fig. 118) and pictures for Boydell's Shakespeare Gallery, it was those works that Boydell had engraved—illustrations for novels, other forms of literature and various genre subjects—that won for Wheatley his lasting reputation.

Many of the themes in engravings made after Wheatley are in the sentimental and moralizing vein popularized by Jean-Baptiste Greuze, but touched with a more refined sense of decorative prettiness (e.g. *Love in a Mill*, engr. 1787). The best-known series of engravings is the *Cries of London* (14 paintings exh. RA, 1792–5; e.g. Upton House, Warwicks, NT), which illustrate itinerant, usually female, merchants selling their wares (see fig.). Published between 1793 and 1797, with captions in French and English (an indication of the strength of the market for them on the

Francis Wheatley: *Milk Below!*, from his engraved series *Cries of London*, after his own paintings, 1792–5 (London, Guildhall Library, Print Room)

Continent), these engravings have never lost their popularity. Wheatley was elected RA in 1791, but his last years were plagued by gout and debts.

For an illustration of a painting by Wheatley *see* GENRE, fig. 3.

BIBLIOGRAPHY
E. K. Waterhouse: *Painting in Britain, 1530–1790*, Pelican Hist. A. (Harmondsworth, 1953, rev. 4/1978), pp. 319–20
M. Webster: *Francis Wheatley* (London, 1970)

JOHN WILSON

Wheatstone, Sir Charles (*b* Gloucester, 6 Feb 1802; *d* Paris, 19 Oct 1875). English physicist and photographic inventor. He began his career as a musical instrument maker and was professor of Experimental Physics at King's College, London, by 1834. He was elected a Fellow of the Royal Society in 1838 and was knighted in 1868. He is usually remembered for contributions to acoustics and electric telegraphy, but his interests also included optics and photography. From 1832 he established the principle of stereoscopy and constructed the first stereoscopes. In 1838 Wheatstone presented a long paper on the subject, which discussed his discovery that an illusion of a three-dimensional object could be produced from two slightly different flat pictures viewed simultaneously, one by each eye. He called the instrument that he devised to view the pictures the stereoscope. Although it was received enthusiastically, interest in the stereoscope was purely scientific until the invention of photography. Wheatstone then persuaded his close associate William Henry Fox Talbot, and later Henry Collen (1800–75) and Antoine Claudet, to produce stereoscopic pairs of photographs. The stereoscope eventually became one of the most popular scientific toys of the 19th century, although in a form devised *c.* 1849 by Sir David Brewster (1781–1868), which was rather different to Wheatstone's instrument. Brewster and Wheatstone subsequently engaged in a celebrated dispute over priority of invention of the stereoscope.

In 1834 Wheatstone also demonstrated the freezing of moving objects when illuminated by a sudden spark in a darkened room, which later enabled flash photography to be developed.

See also PHOTOGRAPHY, §I.

WRITINGS
'Contributions to the Physiology of Vision—Part the First: On Some Remarkable, and Hitherto Unobserved, Phenomena of Binocular Vision', *Philos. Trans.*, xi (1838), pp. 371–94

BIBLIOGRAPHY
H. Collen: 'Earliest Stereoscopic Portraits', *J. Phot. Soc.*, i/16 (1854), p. 200
Obituary, *Proc. Inst. Civ. Engin.*, xlvii (1877), pp. 283–90
A. T. Gill: 'Early Stereoscopes', *Phot. J.*, lix (1969), pp. 546–59, 606–14, 641–51
B. Bowers: *Sir Charles Wheatstone* (London, 1975)
S. F. Joseph: 'Wheatstone's Double Vision', *Hist. Phot.*, viii/4 (1984), pp. 329–32

J. P. WARD

Wheeler, Candace (Thurber) (*b* Delhi, Delaware Co., New York, 1827; *d* 5 Aug 1923). American designer. She came from a prosperous and artistic background. She saw the Royal School of Needlework's exhibition at the Centennial International Exhibition of 1876 in Philadelphia, which inspired her to found, in 1877, the Society of Decorative Arts of New York City, the aim of which was to restore the status of crafts traditionally associated with women and provide them with the opportunity to produce high-quality, handmade work which could be profit-making. The Society, which generated sister branches in major American cities, taught many design and craft techniques, but art needlework remained the focus. In 1879 Wheeler entered into partnership with Louis Comfort Tiffany (*see* TIFFANY, §2) to form Louis C. Tiffany & Associated Artists, which, by the early 1880s, was the most successful decorating firm in New York. She designed embroideries, textiles and wallpaper for the company, but in 1883 the partnership was dissolved. Wheeler retained the Associated Artists name and continued to practise (portière, *c.* 1884; New York, Met.). While still handling private commissions, she was asked by textile manufacturers to produce designs for such mass-produced fabrics as printed cotton. In addition to working in the Japanese idiom she was instrumental in initiating designs inspired by traditional American patchwork, indigenous flora and fauna and events from American history and literature. In 1893 she was appointed Director for the Women's Building at the World's Columbian Exposition in Chicago. At the end of 1899 she retired from Associated Artists but continued to contribute to Arts and Crafts literature.

WRITINGS
The Development of Embroidery in America (New York and London, 1921)

BIBLIOGRAPHY
A. I. Prather-Moses: *Women Workers in the Decorative Arts* (Metuchen, NJ, 1981)

JOHN MAWER

Wheeler, Gervase (*b* ?London, *c.* 1815; *d* London, *c.* 1872). English architect and writer. He was the son of a jeweller and trained under R. C. Carpenter. In the 1840s he emigrated to the USA and established a practice first in Hartford, CT, later moving to Philadelphia. From 1851 to 1860 he worked in New York. In 1860 his address was listed as the Brooklyn Post Office (destr.), a building that he had designed. Apparently Wheeler returned to London in the same year, for his name no longer appeared in New York city directories after that date. In London he continued to practise architecture and in 1867 became a FRIBA.

Most of Wheeler's known commissions were for houses. His designs, which appeared in architectural periodicals and in his own books, contributed to the growing body of literature in the USA that concentrated on the detached middle-class dwelling as a building type. A champion of affordable housing, Wheeler attracted the attention of A. J. Downing, who published designs for houses by Wheeler in his book *The Architecture of Country Houses* (New York, 1850), as well as in *The Horticulturist*, the journal that he edited. The large house that Wheeler built in 1849 for Henry Boody in Brunswick, ME, was praised by Downing for its well-conceived plan and its economical construction. He also admired its board-and-batten exterior as it expressed the internal frame. The house was one of the early and best examples of this form of construction that, largely because of Downing's proselytizing, became a popular feature of American Gothic Revival houses. The brick Patrick Barry house (1855) in Rochester, NY, was built in an Italianate style, which

Wheeler regarded as particularly suited to suburban residences. Sited on grounds laid out by the nurseryman who commissioned the building, the Barry house is a splendid example of the mid-Victorian ideal of the union of picturesque architecture with cultivated nature.

Downing's endorsement of Wheeler's work must have encouraged Wheeler to think that a successful career lay before him in the USA, but with the publication of Wheeler's *Rural Homes* in 1851, Downing abruptly withdrew his support. In a review of the book—which, with Downing's works, was one of the earliest American pattern books of house design—Downing called Wheeler a 'pseudo-architect from abroad' who 'borrowed from the works of native authors who have trodden the same ground more earnestly and truthfully before him'. Downing was particularly incensed over Wheeler's inadequate verandahs. Wheeler's Henry Olmsted house (1849; destr.) in East Hartford, CT, was criticized by Downing for its excessively tall roof, which would make the bedrooms hot in summer.

Downing's rejection must have hurt Wheeler's chances of attracting clients. The number of works Wheeler is known to have designed is small, although he managed to secure commissions from Bowdoin College, Brunswick, ME, and Williams College, Williamstown, MA, and for New York University. Rockwood (begun 1849; destr.), the estate near Tarrytown, NY, which he designed for Edwin Bartlett, was one of the finest country seats in the USA. In 1855 Wheeler published another book on domestic architecture, *Homes for the People*, which illustrated a number of wooden houses with decorative external framing reflecting the influence of medieval half-timbering as well as contemporary continental picturesque architecture. When he returned to England, he published a third volume on house architecture, *The Choice of a Dwelling* (1871). In it he discussed certain American practices and suggested that they might be adapted for British usage. He also praised American houses for the way reception rooms could be thrown together by means of sliding doors to form larger spaces to accommodate the 'party-giving spirit of the Americans', and illustrated plans of houses he had designed during his time in the USA.

WRITINGS
Rural Homes: Or Sketches of Houses Suited to American Country Life (New York, 1851)
Homes for the People, in Suburb and Country (New York, 1855/R 1972)
The Choice of a Dwelling (London, 1871)

BIBLIOGRAPHY
Macmillan Enc. Architects
V. J. Scully jr: 'Romantic Rationalism and the Expression of Structure in Wood: Downing, Wheeler, Gardner and the "Stick Style", 1840–1876', *The Shingle Style and the Stick Style* (New Haven, CT, rev. 1971), pp. xxiii–lix [this introductory essay is not in first edn of 1955]
M. Tomlin: 'The Domestic Architectural Styles of Henry Hudson Holly', *Country Seats and Modern Dwellings* (Watkins Glen, NY, 1977), pp. 3–12
FRANCIS R. KOWSKY

Wheeler, John. *See under* ARCHITECTS' CO-PARTNERSHIP.

Wheeler, (Robert Eric) Mortimer (*b* Glasgow, 10 Sept 1890; *d* London, 22 July 1976). English archaeologist. Educated at Bradford Grammar School and University College, London, he was made Director of the National Museum of Wales, Cardiff, in 1924, before moving to London as Keeper and Secretary of the London Museum (now the Museum of London) in 1926, where he also established the post-graduate Institute of Archaeology (1937) within the University of London. After active military service during World War II he reorganized archaeology in India as Director General of Archaeology (1944–8). On his return to London he began to reform and reshape the British Academy as Honorary Secretary. Meanwhile, he was a tireless excavator of some of the most notable sites in Britain, including the Roman temple complex at Lydney Park, Glos (1928–9; pubd 1933), the Roman city of Verulamium (now St Albans; 1930–33; pubd 1936), Maiden Castle (1934–6; pubd 1943) and Stanwick (pubd 1951–2; pubd 1954). By his actions, writings, lectures and excavations, Wheeler exercised a profound influence on the discipline of archaeology. He conceived archaeology as a synthesis of art and science, and increasingly dependent on the methodology of the natural sciences. His frequently quoted maxim was that the proper aim of the archaeologist was to 'dig up people'. Through his early grasp of the importance of the media, in particular, from the 1950s, the power of emerging television, Wheeler was to the public the most famous British archaeologist of the 20th century. This popular acclaim was matched by recognition in both academic and official circles, in Britain and abroad, of his administrative successes as well as his contribution to the study of Iron Age and Roman Britain and the archaeology of the Indian subcontinent, by his application of rigorous standards in the practice of field excavation and insistence on the importance of stratification (*see* ARCHAEOLOGY, fig. 3).

WRITINGS
Archaeology from the Earth (Oxford, 1954)
Still Digging (London, 1955)
Alms for Oblivion: An Antiquary's Notebook (London, 1966)
The British Academy, 1949–1968 (London, 1970)

BIBLIOGRAPHY
J. Hawkes: *Mortimer Wheeler: Adventurer in Archaeology* (London, 1982)
HUGH CHAPMAN

Wheelwright, Edmund M(arch) (*b* Roxbury, MA, 14 Sept 1854; *d* Thompsonville, CT, 14 Aug 1912). American architect and writer. He studied architecture at Massachusetts Institute of Technology and worked for Peabody & Stearns in Boston, McKim, Mead & Bigelow in New York and E. P. Treadwell in Albany, NY, before establishing his own practice in 1883. He took Parkman B. Haven (1858–1943) as his partner in 1888, the firm becoming Wheelwright & Haven, and added Edward H. Hoyt (1868–1936) to the firm in 1912 (Wheelwright, Haven & Hoyt). He was strongly influenced by developments in England and the Continent, as a result of an extended sketching tour abroad in 1881–2.

As City Architect of Boston (1891–5), Wheelwright designed about a hundred municipal buildings—hospitals, fire and police stations, park facilities and especially schools—as well as reforming his own department. He also had a large and varied independent practice and served as consulting architect for several major museums, including the Boston Museum of Fine Arts.

Combining historical precedents with his rich imagination, Wheelwright used a broad range of styles, as in the stone and shingle picturesque summer seaside cottage (1883, destr.) for E. C. Stedman at Newcastle, NH; the sedate half-timbered, multi-gabled Islesboro Inn (1890, destr.), Islesboro, ME; the redbrick Choate Burnham School (1894), South Boston, with features derived from the northern Italian Renaissance; the Georgian Revival façade, in red brick with limestone dressings, of the Horticultural Hall (1900), Boston, which has a sequence of pilasters to an ornamental entablature; and the Lampoon Building (1909), Harvard University, Cambridge, MA, with its Gothic-inspired treatment of the red brick. Wheelwright was noted for his practice of freely combining diverse stylistic elements within a single design. He was the author of many scholarly articles as well as a book, *School Architecture*, and his municipal designs were also published.

UNPUBLISHED SOURCES
Boston, MA, Hist. Soc. [Wheelwright family papers]
Boston, MA, Pub. Lib. [Haven & Hoyt Col.]

WRITINGS
F. W. Chandler, ed.: *Municipal Architecture in Boston from Designs by Edmund M. Wheelwright, City Architect, 1891 to 1895*, 2 vols (Boston, 1898)
School Architecture (Boston, 1901)

BIBLIOGRAPHY
G. W. Sheldon, ed.: *Artistic Country-seats: Types of Recent American Villa and Cottage Architecture with Instances of Country Club-houses*, 2 vols (New York, 1886)
'Annual Reports of the Architect Department', *Documents of the City of Boston* (Boston, 1891–4)

CAROLE A. JENSEN

Wheler, Sir George (*b* Breda, Holland, 1650; *d* Durham, 15 Jan 1723). English traveller and collector. He was born into a royalist family exiled in Holland and educated at Oxford. His significance derives from his travels in Greece and the Near East in 1675–6, accompanied by Jacob Spon, a French physician. In 1682 he published *A Journey into Greece* and was knighted. Shortly after this he took orders, became a canon of Durham Cathedral and spent the latter part of his life as a rector in Co. Durham. In Greece he collected coins (which he bequeathed to Durham Cathedral) and marbles and inscriptions, which he gave to Oxford University in 1683. He was also an assiduous botanist. The chief importance of Wheler and Spon (who published his own account of their journeys) is as the originators of Greek travel literature: they provided the best reports of Greece and its antiquities available before James Stuart and Nicholas Revett's *The Antiquities of Athens* (1762–); they were also the last Western travellers to see the Parthenon before it was severely damaged by a gunpowder explosion. Compared to Spon, Wheler was less wholeheartedly enthusiastic about Classical Greece and more interested in Greece's Christian heritage. He has sometimes been censured for sententiousness, but his narrative has some charm and is also responsive to the landscape. His account was more widely read than Spon's *Voyage d'Italie, de Dalmatie, de Grèce et du Levant* (Lyon, 1678); it was translated into French and thus became known on the Continent as well as in Britain.

WRITINGS
A Journey into Greece (London, 1682)

DNB
T. Spencer: *Fair Greece Sad Relic* (London, 1954)
D. Constantine: *Early Greek Travellers and the Hellenic Ideal* (Cambridge, 1984)

RICHARD JENKYNS

Whidden & Lewis. American architectural partnership formed in 1889 in Portland, OR, by William M(arcy) Whidden (*b* Boston, MA, 10 Feb 1857; *d* Portland, OR, 27 July 1929) and Ion Lewis (*b* Lynn, MA, 26 March 1858; *d* Portland, OR, 27 Aug 1933) and active until Lewis's death. Both Whidden and Lewis attended the Massachusetts Institute of Technology (MIT), Cambridge, during the mid-1870s. After MIT, Whidden spent four years at the Ecole des Beaux-Arts in Paris. He returned to New York in 1882 and joined McKim, Mead & White. Under McKim, Whidden worked on the Portland Hotel design and supervised construction until work was halted late that year. Whidden returned east to work in Boston. In 1888 he was commissioned to oversee completion of the hotel. After graduation from MIT Lewis was employed by Peabody & Stearns in Boston. He left the firm in 1882 and formed a partnership with Henry Paston Clark. A few years later he moved west, working for a time in Chicago before his arrival in Portland in 1889, when he visited Whidden and stayed to join him in partnership. The arrival of Whidden & Lewis marked the coming-of-age of architecture in Portland. They introduced the latest East Coast styles, particularly the Colonial Revival in residential designs, and the neo-classic revivals in commercial and institutional projects. Whidden & Lewis was Portland's pre-eminent architectural firm for two decades. Notable examples of their work include Portland Public Library (1891; destr. 1914) (inspired by McKim, Mead & White's Boston Library), the Hamilton Building (1893), the Renaissance-Revival Portland City Hall (1895), the Arlington Club (1909) and Multnomah County Courthouse (1909).

BIBLIOGRAPHY
T. Vaughan and G. McMath: *A Century of Portland Architecture* (Portland, 1967)
T. Vaughan and V. Ferriday, eds: *Space, Style and Structure: Building in Northwest America*, 2 vols (Portland, 1974)
R. Marlitt: *Matters of Proportion: The Portland Residential Architecture of Whidden & Lewis* (Portland, 1989)

GEORGE A. McMATH

Whieldon, Thomas (*b* nr Stoke-on-Trent, 1719; *d* 1786). English potter. He was presumably apprenticed near Stoke-on-Trent and by 1740 had become a master potter at Fenton Low. In 1747 he leased new premises at Fenton Vivian, bought this property in 1748 and the following year acquired Fenton Hall. By this time he is known to have had 19 employees and to have taken Josiah Spode (i) (*see* SPODE CERAMIC WORKS) as an apprentice, possibly with William Greatbatch (1735–1813). Spode left in 1754 when Whieldon took Josiah Wedgwood as partner (*see* WEDGWOOD, §1). Whieldon retired *c.* 1780, when the pottery was demolished. He is noteworthy for having launched the careers of Wedgwood, Spode, Greatbatch, Robert Garner (1733–89) and J. Barker. He also gave his name to a type of cream-coloured earthenware sponged with such coloured oxides as copper and manganese, covered in a clear, lead glaze, called 'Whieldon' or 'Tortoiseshell' ware. The forms were sometimes modelled by such eminent contemporary blockcutters as Aaron Wood (*see* WOOD (iii)) and Greatbatch. Whieldon's account and memorandum book for 1749–53 mentions 'creamcolr' and 'Glazd Images' (figures), while Wedgwood's experiment book of 1759 lists white, salt-glazed wares as 'the principle article of our manufacture' as well as 'an imitation of tortoiseshell'. Production at Fenton Vivian also included solid agate wares, red and black stoneware, green-glazed creamwares in vegetable forms and scratch-blue stoneware.

UNPUBLISHED SOURCES

Stoke-on-Trent, City Mus. & A.G. [account and memorandum book, 1749–53]

BIBLIOGRAPHY

S. Shaw: *History of the Staffordshire Potteries* (Hanley, 1829/*R* London, 1900)

A. Mountford: 'Thomas Whieldon's Manufactory at Fenton Vivian', *Trans. Eng. Cer. Circ.*, viii/2 (1972), pp. 164–82

R. Reilly: *Wedgwood*, 2 vols (London, 1989)

ROBIN HILDYARD

Whistler, James (Abbott) McNeill (*b* Lowell, MA, 11 July 1834; *d* London, 17 July 1903). American painter, printmaker, designer and collector, active in England and France. He developed from the Realism of Courbet and Manet to become, in the 1860s, one of the leading members of the AESTHETIC MOVEMENT and an important exponent of JAPONISME. From the 1860s he increasingly adopted non-specific and often musical titles for his work, which emphasized his interest in the manipulation of colour and mood for their own sake rather than for the conventional depiction of subject. He acted as an important link between the avant-garde artistic worlds of Europe, Britain and the USA and has always been acknowledged as one of the masters of etching (*see* ETCHING, §V).

From his monogram JW, Whistler evolved a butterfly signature, which he used after 1869. After his mother's death in 1881, he added her maiden name, McNeill, and signed letters *J. A. McN. Whistler*. Finally he dropped 'Abbott' entirely.

1. Life and work. 2. Working methods and technique. 3. Personality and influence.

1. LIFE AND WORK.

(i) Early life, 1834–59. (ii) 1859–66. (iii) 1866–77. (iv) 1877–94. (v) Later life, 1894–1903.

(i) Early life, 1834–59. The son of Major George Washington Whistler, a railway engineer, and his second wife, Anna Matilda McNeill, James moved with his family in 1843 from the USA to St Petersburg in Russia, where he had art lessons from a student, Alexander O. Karitzky, and at the Imperial Academy of Science. In 1847 he was given a volume of William Hogarth's engravings, which made a great impact on him. In 1848 he settled in England, attending school near Bristol and spending holidays with his step-sister Deborah and her husband, the collector (Francis) Seymour Haden, who sent Whistler to Charles Robert Leslie's lectures at the Royal Academy, London, and showed him his Rembrandt etchings. William Boxall painted Whistler's portrait (exh. RA 1849; U. Glasgow, Hunterian A.G.), showed him the Raphael cartoons at Hampton Court Palace and gave him a copy of Mrs Jameson's *Italian Painters* (1845).

After Major Whistler's death in 1849, James returned to America and entered West Point Military Academy, NY, in 1851. At Robert W. Weir's classes he copied European prints. He also produced caricatures and illustrations to Walter Scott and Dickens, influenced by Paul Gavarni and George Cruikshank. Whistler's first published work was the title-page of a song sheet, *Song of the Graduates* (1852). Although he received top marks for art and French, he had to leave West Point in 1854 for failing chemistry. He joined the drawing division of the US Coast and Geodetic Survey in Washington, DC, where he learnt to etch (e.g. the *Coast Survey Plate*, 1855; Kennedy, no. 1). In 1855 he left, took a studio in Washington and painted a portrait of his first patron, *Thomas Winans* (untraced; see Young and others, no. 3). He made his first lithograph, the *Standard Bearer* (Levy, no. 3) with the help of Frank B. Mayer (1827–99) in Baltimore.

At 21 Whistler sailed for Europe, determined to make a career as an artist. He joined the Ecole Impériale et Spéciale de Dessin in Paris, where Degas was also a student, and in 1856 entered Charles Gleyre's studio. His copies in the Louvre included Ingres's *Roger Freeing Angelica* (copy; U. Glasgow, Hunterian A.G.; Y 11). With Henri Martin he saw Dutch etchings and Velázquez's paintings at the Manchester Art Treasures Exhibition in 1857. In Paris he met the English painters Edward Poynter, T. R. Lamont (1826–98), George Du Maurier and Thomas Armstrong, and in 1857 he asked them to etch illustrations to accompany his studio scene *Au sixième* (K 3) in an ultimately abortive joint venture known as 'PLAWD'. Whistler was encouraged to etch from nature by Haden. In 1858, while touring the Rhineland with an artist–friend Ernest Delannoy, he etched five or six plates and traced others from sketches. *Douze eaux-fortes d'après nature* (known as the 'French Set') has seven Rhineland plates, dramatic compositions with finely modelled figures drawn with confident and varied line. Dedicated to Haden, 20 sets were printed in 1858 at Auguste Delâtre's shop, and a further 50 sets were later printed in London. Also in 1858 Whistler met Henri Fantin-Latour and Alphonse Legros, who shared his interest in printmaking and respect for Courbet and Dutch 17th-century and Spanish art. Together they formed the informal Société des Trois. Whistler went with Fantin-Latour to the Café Molière and showed the 'French Set' to Courbet and Félix Bracquemond.

In November 1858 Whistler painted his first major oil, *At the Piano* (Cincinnati, OH, Taft Mus.; Y 24), which features Deborah Haden and her daughter. The predominantly sombre tonality and broad brushwork reflect his study of Courbet and Velázquez. The figures have a convincing solidity set against the rectangles formed by the dado and pictures on the wall behind a formula Whistler often applied in later works. Rejected at the Salon in 1859, it hung with works by Legros and Fantin-Latour (with which it had obvious affinities) at François Bonvin's studio, where Courbet admired it.

(ii) 1859–66. The failure of *At the Piano* in Paris and the favourable reception given the 'French Set' in Britain

encouraged Whistler to move in 1859 to London, where he remained for most of his life. That same year he took rooms in Wapping on the River Thames and began the series of etchings known as the 'Thames Set' (*Sixteen Etchings of the Thames*). He completed most of the etchings that year, taking just three weeks to capture the fine detail of rickety warehouses and barges in *Black Lion Wharf* (K 42). The success of this series established Whistler's reputation as an etcher.

In 1860 *At the Piano* was accepted by the Royal Academy and bought by John Phillip. *The Times* critic wrote 'it reminds me irresistibly of Velasquez' (17 May 1860). The same year Whistler began to paint *Wapping* (Washington, DC, N.G.A.; Y 35) from the balcony of The Angel, an inn at Cherry Gardens, Rotherhithe. He reworked the picture completely over four years: at first Joanna Heffernan, the coppery red-haired Irish model who became his mistress, was posed looking out over the Thames; later she was seated with two men at a table, a sailor from the Greaves boatyard and an old man, for whom Legros was later substituted. This colourful and atmospheric picture was bought by Winans and shown in New York in 1866 and at the Exposition Universelle in Paris in 1867.

Joanna posed in Paris in December 1861 for *Symphony in White, No. 1: The White Girl* (Washington, DC, N.G.A.; Y 38), the first of Whistler's four *Symphonies in White*. It was rejected by the Royal Academy and hung at a small London gallery. Whistler claimed that the subject was not the heroine of Wilkie Collins's novel *The Woman in White*, first published serially in 1859–60, 'it simply represents a girl dressed in white standing in front of a white curtain' (*The Athenaeum*, 5 July 1862). In 1863 it shared a *succès de scandale* with Edouard Manet's *Déjeuner sur l'herbe* at the Salon des Refusés. It was Paul Mantz, in the *Gazette des Beaux Arts*, who called it a 'Symphonie du blanc'; he was the first to associate Whistler's paintings with music. Later Whistler blamed Courbet for the painting's realism, and between 1867 and 1872 he reworked it to make it more spiritual.

Whistler's first contact with the Pre-Raphaelites was in 1862, when he met Dante Gabriel Rossetti and Algernon Swinburne. In 1863 he moved to Chelsea, near Rossetti's home and the boatyard of the Greaves family, two of whose members, Walter and Henry (1850–1900), became his followers. In 1863 he met the architect E. W. Godwin and went to Amsterdam with Legros to see Rembrandt's prints. Neither Paris nor London suited Whistler's health and he had to convalesce by the sea, where he painted his first great seascape, the *Coast of Brittany* (1861; Hartford, CT, Wadsworth Atheneum; Y 37), and the powerful *Blue and Silver: Blue Wave, Biarritz* (1862; Farmington, CT, Hill-Stead Mus.; Y 41). In 1865 he painted Courbet in *Harmony in Blue and Silver: Trouville* (Boston, MA, Isabella Stewart Gardner Mus.; Y 64). The two artists found much in common, including Jo, and Courbet painted her as *La Belle Irlandaise* (1865; New York, Met.; versions, Kansas City, MO, Nelson–Atkins Mus. A., priv. cols).

From 1863 Whistler began to introduce oriental blue-and-white porcelain, fans and other *objets d'art* from his own extensive collection into his paintings, signalling his increasing interest in Japonisme. Initially, these objects formed little more than props to what remained in both composition and finish essentially traditional Western genre subjects. Important examples include *Purple and Rose: The Lange Leizen of the Six Marks* (1863–4; Philadelphia, PA, Mus. A.; Y 47), which was given a specially designed frame with related oriental motifs, and *La Princesse du pays de la porcelaine* (1863–4; Washington, DC, Freer; Y 50; see fig. 1). However, in February 1864 Whistler painted an oriental group, *Variations in Flesh Colour and Green: The Balcony* (Washington, DC, Freer; Y 56), which also incorporates compositional elements from the Japanese woodcuts of Suzuki Harunobu and Torii Kiyonaga's *Autumn Moon on the Sumida*. Although signed in 1865, it was reworked, even after exhibition at the Royal Academy in 1870. Whistler planned to enlarge it, but in his preliminary sketch, possibly started in 1867 (U. Glasgow, Hunterian A.G.; Y 57), the figures became more Greek than oriental, as his interests began to shift. He liked the collection of Tanagra statuettes owned by his Greek patrons, the Ionides family. In 1865 he had met

1. James McNeill Whistler: *La Princesse du pays de la porcelaine*, oil on canvas, 2.00×1.16 m, 1863–4 (Washington, DC, Freer Gallery of Art)

Albert Moore and both artists painted women in semi-Classical robes. By 1868 Whistler was at work on the '*Six Projects*' (Y 82–7), decorative paintings of women with flowers, but, fearing that one of his studies, *Symphony in Blue and Pink* (Washington, DC, Freer; Y 86), was too similar to Moore's work, he abandoned the project. He blamed Courbet for his failures and felt he lacked the basic draughtsmanship of an artist such as Ingres.

(iii) 1866–77. During the mid-1860s Whistler went through a time of artistic and emotional crisis. He fell out with Legros, who was replaced by Moore in the Société des Trois, and he quarrelled finally with Haden in 1867. When his mother had moved in with him in late 1863, Jo had had to move out. To escape from family pressures, Whistler left for Valparaíso in 1866 to help the Chileans in the war of liberation against Spain. He saw little fighting but painted his first night scenes, including *Nocturne in Blue and Gold: Valparaíso Bay* (Washington, DC, Freer; Y 76). On his return to London he left Jo, but she looked after his illegitimate son, Charles, born to the parlour-maid, Louisa Hanson, in 1870.

Without Jo, Whistler lacked a regular model, and in 1871 he asked his mother to pose. He struggled to perfect a simple composition with her sitting in profile before rectangular areas of dado, wall, curtain and picture, using thin broad brushstrokes for the wall, narrow expressive strokes for hands, flesh and curtain. The finished painting was exhibited at the Royal Academy in 1872 as *Arrangement in Grey and Black No. 1: Portrait of the Artist's Mother* (Paris, Mus. d'Orsay; Y 101). Whistler wrote in *The World* on 22 May 1878, 'To me it is interesting as a picture of my mother; but what can or ought the public to care about the identity of the portrait?' He went on to explain, 'As music is the poetry of sound, so is painting the poetry of sight, and subject matter has nothing to do with harmony of sound or colour.'

In 1869 Whistler started to paint the Liverpool ship-owner F. R. Leyland at Speke Hall, near Liverpool. The *Arrangement in Black: Portrait of F. R. Leyland* (1870–73; Washington, DC, Freer; Y 97) hung in Whistler's first one-man exhibition at the Flemish Gallery, London, in 1874, which Rossetti, who introduced them, claimed had been financed by Leyland. A superb portrait of Leyland's wife, *Symphony in Flesh Colour and Pink* (1871–3; New York, Frick; Y 106), was shown in the same exhibition. Whistler also made lovely drypoints and drawings of the Leyland daughters, Elinor and Florence (1873; U. Glasgow, Hunterian A.G.; see 1984 Glasgow exh. cat., nos 83–90), but did not finish their portraits. Pennell believed that the '*Six Projects*' were intended for Leyland's house at 49 Prince's Gate, London. Leyland let Whistler paint the dining-room (designed by Thomas Jeckyll) to harmonize with *La Princesse du pays de la porcelaine* (see fig. 1 above), which he had bought in 1872. *Harmony in Blue and Gold: The Peacock Room* (Washington, DC, Freer; Y 178) became a major decorative scheme and one of the finest achievements of the Aesthetic Movement, but it so exceeded the original commission that artist and patron eventually fell out over the cost (*see* §2(v) below).

It was Leyland who in 1872 suggested that Whistler call his night pictures 'Nocturnes'. At the Dudley Gallery

2. James McNeill Whistler: *Harmony in Grey and Green: Miss Cicely Alexander*, oil on canvas, 1.90×0.98 m, 1872 (London, Tate Gallery)

Harmony in Blue-Green—Moonlight was bought in 1871 by the banker W. C. Alexander, but it was re-named *Nocturne: Blue and Silver—Chelsea* (London, Tate; Y 103). Alexander so liked the portrait of Whistler's mother that in 1872 he ordered portraits of his daughters. Cicely suffered 70 sittings for *Harmony in Grey and Green: Miss Cicely Alexander* (Y 129; see fig. 2). Thomas Carlyle was the subject of *Arrangement in Grey and Black, No. 2* (1872–3; Glasgow, City Mus. & A.G.; Y 137), which shares the severely restricted and sombre palette, solemn mood and economical composition of Whistler's portrait of his mother. It was the first of Whistler's oils to enter a British public collection, in 1891.

A red-headed English girl, Maud Franklin, took Jo's place as Whistler's mistress and principal model. Although she looks lovely in *Arrangement in White and Black* (c. 1876; Washington, DC, Freer; Y 185) and subtle in

Arrangement in Black and Brown: The Fur Jacket (1876; Worcester, MA, A. Mus.; Y 181), she is depicted as a sombre figure in *Arrangement in Yellow and Grey: Effie Deans* (1876; Amsterdam, Rijksmus.; Y 183). Effie Deans, the heroine of Scott's *Heart of Midlothian*, was an odd subject for Whistler, but perhaps appropriate because Maud, like Effie, bore an illegitimate child (by Whistler in 1878).

(iv) 1877–94. By the late 1870s the artistic uncertainties of the 1860s had been resolved, but Whistler was in severe financial difficulties. In 1877 he sent *Nocturne in Black and Gold: The Falling Rocket* (1875; Detroit, MI, Inst. A.; Y 170), one of a series on Cremorne Gardens, to the first Grosvenor Gallery exhibition. John Ruskin wrote that he 'never expected to hear a coxcomb ask 200 guineas for flinging a pot of paint in the public's face' (*Fors Clavigera*, 2 July 1877). Whistler sued him for libel. At the Old Bailey in November 1878, asked if he charged 200 guineas for two days' work, Whistler said, 'No, I ask it for the knowledge which I have gained in the work of a lifetime.' He won damages of a farthing and faced huge costs. His account of the trial, *Art and Art Critics*, was published in December the same year.

On 8 May 1879 Whistler was declared bankrupt. He destroyed work to keep it from creditors, and the White House in Chelsea (destr.), which had been designed for him by E. W. Godwin and completed only the previous year, had to be auctioned. In 1880 he left for Venice with a commission from the Fine Art Society for a set of 12 etchings. In fact he made 50 etchings, including *Nocturnes* (K 184, see fig. 3; K202, 213) and *Doorways* (K 188, 193, 196), of unsurpassed delicacy. He drew 100 pastels, including the glowing *Sunrise on the Rialto* and *Bead Stringers*, with the figures set in a close hung with washing, brought alive by touches of colour (both Washington, DC, Freer; 1984 Freer exh. cat., nos 246, 255). The Society showed the first 12 *Etchings of Venice* in December 1880. Whistler had to print 25 sets, but he kept trying to perfect them, and Frederick Goulding completed the editions after Whistler's death. A second set, *Twenty-six Etchings of Venice*, exhibited in 1883 and published by Dowdeswell's in 1887 in an edition of 30, was printed by Whistler with rare efficiency within a year.

The brewer Sir Henry Meux commissioned Whistler to paint portraits of his wife. The result, a luscious *Arrangement in Black* (1881–2; Honolulu, HI, Acad. A.; Y 228), delighted Degas at the Salon of 1882, while *Harmony in Pink and Grey* (1881–2; New York, Frick; Y 229) was exhibited at the Grosvenor Gallery the same year. In 1883 Théodore Duret discussed with Whistler the problem of painting men in evening dress and posed, a domino over his arm to add a note of colour, for *Arrangement en couleur chair et noir* (New York, Met.; Y 252; see fig. 4). To keep a unified surface, the whole canvas was repainted ten times before the Salon of 1885. Whistler sent work to the Impressionist exhibitions at the Galerie Georges Petit in

3. James McNeill Whistler: *Nocturne*, etching and drypoint, 202×298 mm, *c.* 1879–80 (Glasgow, University of Glasgow, Hunterian Art Gallery)

4. James McNeill Whistler: *Arrangement en couleur chair et noir: Portrait of Théodore Duret*, oil on canvas, 1.93×0.91 m, 1883 (New York, Metropolitan Museum of Art)

1883 and 1887 and to Les XX in Brussels in 1884. His own exhibition *Notes—Harmonies—Nocturnes*, including the painting *Angry Sea* (Washington, DC, Freer; Y 282) and the watercolour *Nocturne: Amsterdam in Winter* (Washington, DC, Freer; 1984 Freer exh. cat., no. 117), hung at Dowdeswell's in 1884. A second show in 1886 had pastels of models in iridescent robes and such watercolours as *Gold and Grey—The Sunny Shower, Dordrecht* (U. Glasgow, Hunterian A.G.).

On 20 February 1885 Whistler gave his 'Ten o'clock lecture'. 'Nature', he said, 'contains the elements, in colour and form, of all pictures, as the keyboard contains the notes of all music. But the artist is born to pick, and choose, and group with science, these elements, that the result may be beautiful.' Whistler believed that art could not be made nor understood by the masses; a Rembrandt or a Velázquez was born, not made, and if no more masters arose, 'the story of the beautiful is already complete—hewn in the marbles of the Parthenon—and broidered, with the birds, upon the fan of Hokusai—at the foot of Fusiyama.'

Whistler's followers included Walter Sickert and Mortimer Menpes, who helped him print the Venice etchings, and in January 1884 they joined him at St Ives in Cornwall. In 1885 Whistler joined Sickert in Dieppe and went with William Merritt Chase to Antwerp, Haarlem and Amsterdam. In the same year he showed a portrait of the violinist *Pablo de Sarasate* (Pittsburgh, PA, Carnegie; Y 315) at the Society of British Artists, to which he had been elected the previous year. In 1886 he became President of the Society. He reorganized the exhibitions and brought in such young artists as Menpes, William Stott of Oldham (1857–1900), Waldo Story (1855–1915) and the Belgian Alfred Stevens as members and invited Monet to exhibit. When he was forced to resign in 1888 after objections to his exhibiting policy, his friends left too: 'the "Artists" have come out, and the "British" remain', he told the *Pall Mall Gazette* (11 June 1888).

Whistler started to paint Beatrice Godwin (1857–96), the wife of E. W. Godwin and daughter of the sculptor John Birnie Philip, in 1884: her portrait, *Harmony in Red: Lamplight* (U. Glasgow, Hunterian A.G.; Y 253), hung at the Society of British Artists exhibition of 1886–7. Beatrice and Maud Franklin both exhibited as Whistler's pupils at the Society. They fought over Whistler and Maud lost. Beatrice's husband died in 1886, and Whistler married her in August 1888. They had a working honeymoon in France, where he taught her to etch. In his 'Renaissance Set' he isolated architectural details, little figures and hens, in such etchings as *Hôtel Lallement, Bruges* (K 399), and painted such elegant watercolours as *Green and Blue: The Fields, Loches* (Ithaca, NY, Cornell U., Johnson Mus. A.).

A set of six lithographs, *Notes*, was published by Boussod, Valadon & Cie. in 1887. With Beatrice's encouragement Whistler made lithographs, including stylish portraits of her sister Ethel. The *Winged Hat* and *Gants de suède* (W 25–6) appeared in the *Whirlwind* and *Studio* in 1890. Whistler hoped to popularize the medium but found the clientele limited. Experiments in Paris with colour lithography, as in *Draped Figure Reclining* (W 156), were halted by problems with printers.

In 1889 Whistler made a set of ambitious etchings, including the *Embroidered Curtain* (K 410), in Amsterdam, which he felt combined 'a minuteness of detail, always referred to with sadness by the critics who hark back to the Thames etchings, . . . with greater freedom and more beauty of execution than even the Venice set or the last Renaissance lot can pretend to'. Among the eager American purchasers of these etchings was Charles Lang Freer, who met Whistler in 1890 and amassed a huge collection of his work (now in the Freer Gallery of Art, Washington, DC). In 1891 Mallarmé led a successful campaign for the French State to acquire Whistler's portrait of his mother. The following year Whistler drew for *Vers et prose* a sympathetic portrait of Mallarmé (W 66), who became one of his closest friends, and Whistler was himself drawn into the Symbolist circle. In 1892 the Whistlers moved to Paris.

Whistler remained a combative public figure. In June 1890 William Heinemann had published Whistler's *Gentle Art of Making Enemies*—letters and pamphlets on art, designed by Whistler to the last jubilant butterfly. A second edition included the catalogue of his Goupil Gallery retrospective in 1892, *Nocturnes, Marines & Chevalet Pieces*, incorporating early reviews of his work. In 1894 George Du Maurier's *Trilby* appeared in *Harper's* with the character of 'the Idle Apprentice' based on the student Whistler, but he forced Du Maurier to make it less explicit. Sir William Eden commissioned a small full-length portrait of his wife in 1894 (U. Glasgow, Hunterian A.G.; Y 408). No price was set, and the amount and manner of payment upset Whistler. He kept the panel and changed the figure. Eden sued him, but Whistler won on appeal. Whistler later published his own account in *Eden v. Whistler: The Baronet and the Butterfly*.

(v) Later life, 1894–1903. In December 1894 Whistler's wife became ill with cancer. They visited doctors in Paris and London and went in September 1895 to Lyme Regis in Dorset. Beatrice returned to London, but Whistler stayed to confront an artistic crisis, which echoed his emotional one. Samuel Govier posed for lithographs (e.g. the *Blacksmith*; W 90) and the masterly oil, the *Master Smith of Lyme Regis* (Boston, MA, Mus. F.A.; Y 450). Whistler felt he had fulfilled his *Proposition No. 2*: 'A picture is finished when all trace of the means used to bring about the end has disappeared.' Back in London, he held an exhibition of lithographs at the Fine Art Society. In 1896 he drew poignant portraits of his dying wife, *By the Balcony* and *The Siesta* (W 122, 124), and made his last nocturne, a superb lithotint, *The Thames* (W 125). Beatrice died on 10 May 1896.

The same year Whistler took a studio at 8 Fitzroy Street and in 1897 set up the Company of the Butterfly to sell his work, but it was not effective. In Paris his favourite model was Carmen Rossi (Y 505–7). Whistler, together with Alphonse Mucha, helped her set up an art school (the Académie Carmen) in 1898, where he and the sculptor Frederick MacMonnies taught. Carl Frieseke (1874–1942) and Gwen John were among the pupils, the most dutiful of whom, Inez Bate and Clifford Addams (1876–1932), became Whistler's apprentices. The school closed in 1901.

In April 1898 Whistler was elected President of the International Society of Sculptors, Painters and Gravers. Aided by Albert Ludovici jr (1852–1932), John Lavery and Joseph Pennell, he supervised exhibitors and exhibitions, designing a monogram and catalogues. His friends Rodin and Monet sent work; other contributors included such Frenchmen as Toulouse-Lautrec, Bonnard, Vuillard and (under protest from Whistler) Cézanne; northern Europeans Gustav Klimt, Max Klinger, Max Liebermann, Jacob Maris, Franz von Stuck, Hans Thoma and Fritz Thaulow; and many Scots, led by George Henry, James Guthrie and E. A. Walton. The Society's exhibitions were outstanding for their quality and unity.

In 1899 Whistler went to Italy and visited the Uffizi in Florence and the Vatican, where he liked Raphael's *Loggie*

but little else. He spent summers by the sea: at Pourville-sur-Mer in 1899 he painted panels of the sea (e.g. *Green and Silver: The Great Sea*), whose strength belies their size, and of shops, simple and geometrical (e.g. *La Blanchisseuse, Dieppe*; both U. Glasgow, Hunterian A.G.; Y 517, 527). In poor health he spent the winter of 1900–01 in Algiers and Ajaccio, Corsica, painting, etching and filling sketch-books with drawings of robed Arabs, donkeys and busy streets (U. Glasgow, Hunterian A.G.). In October 1901 he sold his Paris house and studio and moved to Cheyne Walk, London. Freer took him on holiday in July 1902, but he fell ill at the Hôtel des Indes in The Hague. The *Morning Post* published an obituary, which revived him, and he went on to visit Scheveningen, the Mauritshuis and the galleries in Haarlem.

Whistler was cared for after the death of his wife by her young sister, Rosalind Philip, who became his ward and executrix. After Whistler's death in 1903, she bequeathed a large collection of his work to the University of Glasgow, including two introspective self-portraits (*c.* 1896; Y 460–61).

2. WORKING METHODS AND TECHNIQUE. Whistler's oeuvre is considerable and of particular technical interest: about 550 oils, 1700 watercolours, pastels and drawings, over 450 etchings and 170 lithographs are known.

(i) Paintings. Whistler's early oil paintings vary in technique as he bowed to conflicting influences, Dutch art above all. Usually he painted thickly and broadly with brush and palette knife. His first over-emphatic use of colour soon modified, and he became sensitive to small variations in colour and tone. In the 1860s he used longer strokes, varying their shape and direction to describe details, with creamy ribbon-like strokes for draperies or water. In the 1870s his brushwork became bold, sweeping and expressive. He liked the texture of coarse canvas. The paint was thin and allowed to drip freely. Some of his *Nocturnes*, painted on a grey ground, have darkened badly. In the 1880s he began to work direct from nature, on panels only 125×200 mm. He painted freely, with creamy paint, making few alterations, whereas his later works were painted thinly, the brushwork softer and often showing signs of repeated reworking. His taste was refined and brushwork and colour schemes elegant. Not easily satisfied, he left many works incomplete and destroyed others.

Whistler perfected his use of watercolour when illustrating the catalogue of Sir Henry Thompson's collection of Nanjing china in 1878. In the 1880s he worked on white paper laid down on card of the same size as his small panels of the period. In the late 1880s he tried linen and in the late 1890s used brown paper. He painted thinly, leaving areas blank to suggest light or texture. He outlined a subject in pencil or brush, then added washes quickly with small brushes, altering, but rarely rubbing out.

(ii) Etchings and drypoints. Whistler usually worked on the plate directly from nature, and he proofed and printed most plates himself. He brushed acid on the plate with a feather to get the strength of line required. He used various colours of ink, mainly black at first and brown later. In 1886 his first *Proposition* stated that etchings should be small because the needle was small; and no margin should

be left outside the plate-mark. After 1880 he trimmed etchings to the plate-mark, leaving a tab for his butterfly signature. He liked Dutch paper, torn from old ledgers, and fine Japanese paper. Apart from published sets, most were printed in small editions.

In Whistler's earliest etchings, influenced by Dutch art, intricately cross-hatched shadows blur outlines. The Thames etchings were drawn with a fine needle in fine detail, the foreground bolder, with lines scrawled across the plate. The plates were then bitten and altered little. The drypoints of the 1870s were drawn more freely, with longer lines and looser shading, giving silky, misty effects. They went through several states, because the lines wore down or because Whistler changed his mind, and were printed with a lustrous burr. The '*Venice Set*' was more elaborate. The design was drawn with short, delicate lines, etched quite deeply. Mistakes were burnished out and re-etched, and areas touched up with drypoint. In printing, a thin film of ink was smoothed across the plate to provide surface colour. Some plates went through a dozen states. The plates of the 1880s often had only a single state. They were smaller and simpler, with less surface tone, subjects vignetted and drawn with a minimum of short, expressive lines. Usually only one area was drawn in detail, shaded like velvet. The Dutch etchings of 1889 were larger and had many states. In the first he outlined the design, enriching it later with a variety of shading and cross-hatching softened with rubbing down, drypoint and some surface tone. His last etchings achieved amazing richness and variety in a single state, showing Whistler in total command of the medium.

(iii) Lithographs. Whistler's earliest lithographs and litho-tints were drawn on stone and printed by Thomas Way & Son. Most later ones were drawn on transfer paper and transferred to stone and printed by Way's press. The transfer paper obtained from Way was mechanically grained, but later Whistler used a smooth paper, which he preferred. He sometimes worked on textured board or paper to add to the variety of line. The grain affected the appearance of the drawing and the success of the transfer. Whistler used the whole range of chalks in his first lithographs (e.g. *The Toilet*; w 6), hard and medium chalk, and some so soft it was applied with a stump of paper, and dark areas scraped down again. In the 1890s he usually drew with a hard crayon and used stumping for soft, velvety effects. For lithotints, Way mixed a wash to his own prescription, prepared stones for the artist and proofed and printed the result. Whistler made alterations in Way's printing office. He experimented, but destroyed his failures. His first colour lithograph in 1890 (w 99) was to have had five colours, but two sheets did not transfer. Later experiments were more successful (w 100–01).

Whistler's lithographs were published in small editions, of six plus two or three proofs in 1878, up to twenty-five by 1895. There were exceptions: *Old Battersea Bridge* (w 12), for instance, had over 100 pulled by 1896. Some drawings were transferred to several stones and printed in large numbers for journals, such as 3000 of *The Doctor* (w 78) for *Pageant* in 1894. Whistler's style was similar to that in chalk drawings of the same period, with firm, expressive lines, broken outlines and simple diagonal

shading. He usually vignetted his subject and built up the details with flickering, curving lines, with cross-hatching enriching the shadows.

(iv) Pastels and other drawings. Most of Whistler's pastels were small (125×200 mm) and drawn on brown paper. The earliest, in black and white, were indecisive, a maze of circling lines. Around 1870 his line became more angular and economical. In Venice he gained confidence, outlining a view with lively and expressive strokes of black chalk and illuminating it with rich colours, shading or scumbling large areas for variety in texture. His later pastels were mostly of models, draped or nude, in his studio. Delicate and rainbow-coloured, his pastels became freer, more loosely drawn and increasingly expressive in his last years.

The early St Petersburg sketchbook (U. Glasgow, Hunterian A.G.) includes careful drawings of figures, immature and weak in line. Whistler's juvenile drawings were small vignettes, drawn jerkily with repeated angular, broken outlines, neatly cross-hatched and accented so that faces look like masks. His teenage drawings are a scrawl of zig-zag cross-hatching, with vague outlines. In his sketchbooks of 1858 (Washington, DC, Freer; see 1984 Freer exh. cat., pls 152–92), pencil studies from nature combine angular outlines and stylized shapes with softer, more varied shading. The few sketches surviving from the 1860s have simple shapes and curving outlines. Working drawings from the 1870s, mostly in pen, were straightforward. Shading replaced cross-hatchings. Caricatures were stylized, with jagged, pot-hooked lines. His sketchbooks were small (100×150 mm) and in constant use through the 1880s and 1890s (U. Glasgow, Hunterian A.G.). Lively, broken lines, punctuated with dots, were used expressively. About 1900 his work became tentative, with silvery shading and very free, loose outlines.

(v) Designs and interior decoration. Whistler designed floor-matting (Cambridge, MA, Fogg; Cambridge, Fitzwilliam), dresses for his sitters, such as Mrs Leyland (Washington, DC, Freer; 1984 Freer exh. cat., pls 229–34), book covers for E. R. Pennell and Charles Whibley (Washington, DC, Lib. Congr.) and his own pamphlets and books (Washington, DC, Freer; see 1984 Freer exh. cat., pls 283–93). He also designed furniture and painted *Harmony in Yellow and Gold: The Butterfly Cabinet* (U. Glasgow, Hunterian A.G.; y 195), originally for a fireplace designed by E. W. Godwin for William Watts's stand at the Exposition Universelle, Paris, in 1878. Whistler paid considerable attention to the framing of his own pictures, in the 1860s choosing chequered, basket-weave or bamboo patterns, and in the 1870s painting fish-scale patterns on the frame itself to accord with the tone or subject of his painting. In the 1880s he used a flat, beaded frame, in shades of gold to complement the picture. In the 1890s he developed a standard gilt frame with deep moulding and decorated with narrow beading for his paintings and pastels.

Whistler made gouache studies of colour schemes for interiors for W. C. Alexander (U. Glasgow, Hunterian A.G.; see 1960 exh. cat., cover), Ernest Brown of the Fine Art Society (Glasgow, U. Lib.), ships for the walls of his Lindsey Row houses (U. Glasgow, Hunterian A.G.; see 1984 Glasgow exh. cat., nos 106–7) and others, but the schemes themselves have not survived. His major decorative projects were carried out for F. R. Leyland: besides the 'Peacock Room' he decorated the staircase at 49 Prince's Gate (Washington, DC, Freer; Y 175). Although Whistler claimed he painted the 'Peacock Room' without a preliminary sketch, a large cartoon, pricked for transfer, for the panel of rich and poor peacocks at the south end of the room survives (U. Glasgow, Hunterian A.G.). Whistler, aided by the Greaves brothers, did the designs in gold leaf and painted in cream and verdigris blue over the ceiling, leather-covered walls, wood panelling and window shutters.

3. PERSONALITY AND INFLUENCE. Whistler's personality was central to his art and career. While in Paris, he read Henri Murger's *Scènes de la vie de bohème* (1848) and was captivated by the bohemian world it portrayed, in which artists lived slightly apart from the rest of society and by a more relaxed moral code. In dress and manner Whistler presented the image of the immaculate dandy. In his work this attitude was reflected in a relentless perfectionism. He combined wit with a truculent aggressiveness towards critics and criticism. He shared with the other great dandy of the period, Oscar Wilde, a certain recklessness about the demands of money and social decorum. He survived bankruptcy in 1879 with dignity and became widely accepted in his later years as a great artist, but he remained by choice an outsider.

The ideas Whistler expounded so fluently have perhaps been as influential in the long term as his own work. He encouraged artists to recognize the pictorial possibilities of the urban landscape, notably the Thameside area of London, both in daylight and darkness. In this respect Sickert (his most important pupil) was his direct heir. Whistler's emphasis on evocative colour and mood helped to undermine the position that literal naturalism had occupied as the dominant style in Victorian painting in Britain and the USA. In the USA Whistler was an important influence on such exponents of Tonalism as Thomas Wilmer Dewing and Dwight William Tryon.

Through his own work and the exhibitions he organized, Whistler helped to introduce avant-garde artistic ideas from the Continent to Britain, where they were particularly well-received in Scotland. His technical mastery and imaginative exploration of etching did much to inspire the etching revival in Britain and France in the late 19th century and the early 20th, and his decorative work anticipated the achievements of Art Nouveau.

UNPUBLISHED SOURCES
Centre for Whistler Studies, Glasgow, U. Lib. [correspondence, ledgers, photographs and press-cuttings bequeathed by his sister-in-law]
Washington, DC, Lib. Congr. [correspondence, photographs, press-cuttings and contemporary letters about him accumulated by his biographers E. R. Pennell and J. Pennell]

WRITINGS
The Gentle Art of Making Enemies (London, 1890, rev. 2/1892)
Eden v. Whistler: The Baronet and the Butterfly, a Valentine with a Verdict (Paris and New York, 1899)
C. Barbier: *Correspondance Mallarmé—Whistler* (Paris, 1964)
J. A. Mahey: 'The Letters of James McNeill Whistler to George A. Lucas', *A. Bull.*, xlix (1967), pp. 247–57
N. Thorp, ed.: *Whistler—MacColl—Wright: Art History Papers* (Glasgow, 1979)

J. Newton: 'La Chauve-souris et la papillon: Correspondance Montesquiou—Whistler', *Nottingham Fr. Stud.*, xx/1 (May 1981), pp. 30–41; xxi/1 (May 1982), pp. 9–25
M. F. MacDonald and J. Newton: 'Letters from the Whistler Collection (University of Glasgow): Correspondence with French Painters', *Gaz. B.-A.*, n. s. 6, cviii (1986), pp. 201–14
M. F. MacDonald and J. Newton: 'Correspondence Duret—Whistler', *Gaz. B.-A.* (Nov 1987), pp. 150–64
N. Thorp, ed.: *Whistler on Art: Selected Letters and Writings, 1849–1903* (Manchester, 1994)

BIBLIOGRAPHY

CATALOGUES RAISONNÉS
E. G. Kennedy: *The Etched Work of Whistler* (New York, 1910) [K]
——: *The Lithographs by Whistler: Arranged According to the Catalogue by Thomas R. Way* (New York, 1914)
M. Levy: *Whistler Lithographs: A Catalogue Raisonné* (London, 1975) [L]
A. M. Young, M. F. MacDonald, R. Spencer and H. Miles: *The Paintings of James McNeill Whistler*, 2 vols (New Haven, 1980) [Y]
M. F. MacDonald: *James McNeill Whistler: Drawings, Pastels and Watercolours* (London and New Haven, 1995)

MONOGRAPHS AND EXHIBITION CATALOGUES
T. Duret: *Histoire de J. McN. Whistler et de son oeuvre* (Paris, 1904, rev. 2/1914); Eng. trans. as *Whistler* (London, 1917)
M. Menpes: *Whistler as I Knew him* (London, 1904)
O. H. Bacher: *With Whistler in Venice* (New York, 1908)
E. R. Pennell and J. Pennell: *The Life of James McNeill Whistler*, 2 vols (London and Philadelphia, 1908, rev. 6/1920)
T. R. Way: *Memories of James McNeill Whistler* (London, 1912)
E. R. Pennell and J. Pennell: *The Whistler Journal* (Philadelphia, 1921)
James McNeill Whistler (exh. cat., ed. A. M. Young; London, ACGB, 1960)
D. Sutton: *James McNeill Whistler: Paintings, Etchings, Pastels and Watercolours* (London, 1966)
D. Holden: *Whistler Landscapes and Seascapes* (New York, 1969)
From Realism to Symbolism: Whistler and his World (exh. cat., New York, Wildenstein's; Philadelphia, Mus. A.; 1971)
G. Fleming: *The Young Whistler, 1834–66* (London, 1978)
H. Taylor: *James McNeill Whistler* (New York, 1978)
Whistler: Themes and Variations (exh. cat., ed. B. Fryberger; Palo Alto, Stanford U., Mus. & A.G.; Claremont Colls, CA, Gals; 1978)
Whistlers and Further Family (exh. cat., ed. N. Thorp and K. Donnelly; Glasgow, U. Lib., 1980)
James McNeill Whistler at the Freer Gallery (exh. cat., ed. D. P. Curry; Washington, DC, Freer, 1984)
Notes, Harmonies and Nocturnes (exh. cat., ed. M. F. MacDonald; New York, Knoedler's, 1984)
Whistler Pastels (exh. cat., ed. M. F. MacDonald; U. Glasgow, Hunterian A.G., 1984)
James McNeill Whistler (exh. cat., ed. D. Sutton; text M. Hopkinson; essay N. Senzoku; Tokyo, Isetan Mus. A; Sapporo, Hokkaido Mus. Mod. A.; Shizuoka, Prefect. Mus.; Osaka, Daimaru Mus.; 1987–8)
R. Getscher: *James Abbott McNeill Whistler Pastels* (London, 1991)
H. Honour and J. Fleming: *The Venetian Hours of Henry James, Whistler and Sargent* (London, 1991)
L. Merrill: *A Pot of Paint: Aesthetics on Trial in Whistler v. Ruskin* (Washington, 1992)
R. Anderson and A. Koval: *James McNeill Whistler: Beyond the Myth* (London, 1994)
James McNeill Whistler (exh. cat., text R. Dorment and M. F. MacDonald; London, Tate; Paris, Mus. d'Orsay; Washington, DC, N.G.A.; 1994–5)

PRINTMAKING
J. Pennell: 'Whistler as Etcher and Lithographer', *Burl. Mag.* (Nov 1903), pp. 160–8
E. G. Kennedy: *The Etched Work of Whistler* (New York, 1910/R San Francisco, 1978)
R. H. Getscher: *Whistler and Venice* (diss., Cleveland, Case W. Reserve U., 1970)
Whistler, the Graphic Work: Amsterdam, Liverpool, London, Venice (exh. cat., ed. M. F. MacDonald; London, Agnew's; Liverpool, Walker A.G.; Glasgow, A.G. & Mus.; 1976)
The Stamp of Whistler (exh. cat., ed. R. H. Getscher; Oberlin Coll., OH, Allen Mem. A. Mus.; Boston, Mus. F.A.; Philadelphia, Mus. A.; 1977–8)

Lithographs of James McNeill Whistler: From the Collection of Steven Louis Block (exh. cat., ed. N. Spink; Washington, DC, Int. Exh. Found., 1982–5)

K. Lochnan: *The Etchings of James McNeill Whistler* (New Haven, 1984)

N. Smale: 'Whistler and Transfer Lithography', *Tamarind Pap.*, vii (Fall 1984), pp. 72–83

Drawing near: Whistler Etchings from the Zelman Collection (exh. cat., ed. R. Day; Los Angeles, Co. Mus. A., 1984–5)

M. F. MacDonald: 'Whistler's Lithographs', *Prt Q.*, v (1988), pp 20–58

SPECIALIST STUDIES

P. Ferriday: 'Peacock Room', *Archit. Rev.* [London], cxxv (1959), pp. 407–14

M. F. MacDonald: 'Whistler's Last Years: Spring 1901—Algiers and Corsica', *Gaz. B.-A.*, n. s. 6, lxxiii (1969), pp. 323–42

A. Grieve: 'Whistler and the Pre-Raphaelites', *A. Q.*, xxxiv (1971), pp. 219–28

N. Pressley: 'Whistler in America: An Album of Early Drawings', *Met. Mus. J.*, v (1972), pp. 125–54

M. F. MacDonald: 'Whistler's Designs for a Catalogue of Blue and White Nankin Porcelain', *Connoisseur*, cxcviii (1975), pp. 290–91

——: 'Whistler: The Painting of the *Mother*', *Gaz. B.-A.*, n. s. 6, lxxxv (1975), pp. 73–88

J. Newton and M. F. MacDonald: 'Whistler: Search for a European Reputation', *Z. Kstgesch.*, xli (1978), pp. 148–59

M. F. MacDonald and J. Newton: 'The Selling of Whistler's "*Mother*"', *Amer. Soc. Legion Honor Mag.*, xlix/2 (1978), pp. 97–120

I. M. Horowitz: 'Whistler's Frames', *A. J.* [New York], xxxix (Winter 1979–80), pp. 124–31

R. Spencer: 'Whistler's Subject Matter: *Wapping*, 1860–64', *Gaz. B.-A.*, n. s. 6, c (1982), pp. 131–41

D. P. Curry: 'Whistler and Decoration', *Antiques*, cxxvi (1984), pp. 1186–99

M. F. MacDonald and J. Newton: 'Rodin, Whistler, and the International', *Gaz. B.-A.*, n. s. 6, ciii (1984), pp. 115–23

R. Spencer: 'Whistler and James Clarke Hook', *Gaz. B.-A.*, n. s. 6, civ (1984), pp. 45–8

Venice: The American View (exh. cat. by M. M. Lovell, San Francisco, CA, F. A. Museums; 1984–5), pp. 134–67

R. Anderson: 'Whistler in Dublin, 1884' *Irish A. Rev.*, iii/3 (1985), pp. 45–51

J. Winter and E. W. Fitzhugh: 'Some Technical Notes on Whistler's Peacock Room', *Stud. Conserv.*, xxx (1985), pp. 149–53

T. Watanabe: 'Eishi Prints in Whistler's Studio? Eighteenth-century Japanese Prints in the West before 1870', *Burl. Mag.*, cxviii (1986), pp. 874–81

R. Spencer: 'Whistler's First One-man Exhibition Reconstructed', *The Documented Image*, ed. G. P. Weisberg and L. S. Dixon (Syracuse, NY, 1987), pp. 27–50

J. F. Heijbroek: 'Holland vanaf het water: De bezoeken van James Abbott McNeill Whistler aan Nederland', *Bull. Rijksmus.*, xxxvi/3 (1988), pp. 225–56

R. Spencer: *Whistler: A Retrospective* (New York, 1989)

S. Bliss: 'Conservators Use New Approach to Restore Freer Gallery Icon', *Smithsonian Inst. Research Reports*, lx (Spring 1990), pp. 3, 6

For further bibliography see R. H. Getscher and P. G. Marks: *James McNeill Whistler and John Singer Sargent* (New York, 1986).

MARGARET F. MacDONALD

Whistler, Rex [Reginald] **(John)** (*b* London, 24 June 1905; *d* Normandy, 18 July 1944). English painter, illustrator and designer. He demonstrated a talent for drawing, particularly humorous illustration, while at school. Encouraged by his parents, he entered the Royal Academy of Arts Schools in London under Charles Sims. He did not, however, enjoy the atmosphere of the Academy and transferred to the Slade School of Fine Art, London, where he was considered to be one of the best young artists of his generation. Whistler embarked on an academic study of art history and architecture. He had no real relationship with avant-garde contemporaries, but an affinity with such classical and romantic painters as Poussin, Claude, Watteau, Boucher and Canaletto. He also showed a strong interest in Georgian architecture. After leaving the Slade, he was commissioned to paint a mural for the Tate Gallery restaurant in London: he depicted a pastoral scene that encircled the room, the *Pursuit of Rare Meats* (1926–7). Whistler was a prolific illustrator, creating hand-coloured pen drawings for Jonathan Swift's *Gulliver's Travels* (London, 1931); one of his best-known publications was *OHO* (London, 1946), a children's book with text by Laurence Whistler featuring reversible faces. He painted murals in private houses, for example at Plas Newydd, Gwynedd (*see* CAPRICCIO, fig. 2), as well as a triptych at the Brompton Oratory, London (*see* ORATORIANS), and many portraits of members of London society, including *Edith Sitwell* and *Cecil Beaton* (both priv. cols). He also designed furniture, buildings, theatre sets (*see* THEATRE, §III, 4(ii)(b)) and costumes for national productions. He died on his first day of action during service in World War II.

BIBLIOGRAPHY

L. Whistler: *Rex Whistler, his Life and his Drawings* (London, 1948)

L. Whistler and R. Fuller: *The Work of Rex Whistler* (London, 1960)

Whitaker, Henry (*fl* London, 1825–50). English designer. His influential pattern books reflect styles from the late Regency period to the early Victorian. His designs were executed for a number of important clients, including Queen Victoria (at Osborne House, Isle of Wight), Brownlow Cecil, 2nd Marquess of Exeter, William Spencer Cavendish, 6th Duke of Devonshire, and Hugh Percy, 3rd Duke of Northumberland. Whitaker's *Designs of Cabinet and Upholstery Furniture in the Most Modern Style* (London, 1825) contains 50 plates of designs for furniture and curtains. The designs are chiefly in the then current late Grecian manner, with a tendency towards rich ornament. In 1826 he published *Practical Carpentry*, which cites Thomas Hope as the major furniture reformer of the day, and includes a few Grecian designs. *Five Etchings from the Antique* (London, 1827) is a book of Classical vase designs. Whitaker's most important work is the *House Furnishing, Decorating and Embellishing Assistant* (London, 1847). Also published in the same year as the *Practical Cabinet Maker and Upholsterer's Treasury of Designs*, it contains 111 plates of furniture and fitments (including metalwork and porcelain) in the 'Grecian, Italian, Renaissance, Louis-Quatorze, Gothic, Tudor and Elizabethan styles. Interspersed with Designs Executed for the Royal Palaces, and for some of the Principal Mansions of the Nobility and Gentry, and Club Houses'. The majority of the designs are in the Italian Renaissance and Elizabethan styles, and the cabinetmakers Hollands and Bantings are mentioned as having made some of the pieces. In 1849 Whitaker published a book of formal botanical designs, *Materials for a New Style of Ornament*.

BIBLIOGRAPHY

E. Joy: *English Furniture, 1800–1851* (London, 1977)

Pictorial Dictionary of British 19th Century Furniture Design, intro. E. Joy (Woodbridge, 1977)

ROSAMOND ALLWOOD

Whitby. English coastal town in the county of North Yorkshire, known as a centre of jet production in the 19th century (*see* JET, §2).

White, Clarence H(udson) (*b* West Carlisle, OH, 8 April 1871; *d* Mexico City, 8 July 1925). American photographer and teacher. A self-taught photographer, he began taking photographs in 1893 and soon developed a style that showed the influence of Whistler, Sargent and Japanese prints. He was elected to the LINKED RING group of Pictorial photographers in 1900 and was a leading member of the PHOTO-SECESSION from 1902. His evocative photographs of rural landscapes and of his family celebrate the joys and virtues of the simple, middle-class way of life that existed in the USA before World War I (e.g. *Ring Toss*, 1899; Washington, DC, Lib. Congr.).

By 1906 White was already a major figure in American photography and moved to New York, where he began a close professional and artistic relationship with Alfred Stieglitz that lasted until 1912. His work was published in *Camera Work* in July 1903, Jan 1905, July 1908, July 1909 and Oct 1910. In 1908 he began teaching photography, founding in 1910 his own Summer School of Photography in Seguineland, Maine, with F. Holland Day, Max Weber and Gertrude Käsebier, and the highly successful and influential Clarence White School of Photography in New York in 1914. Although his own photography went into decline during the last decade of his life, his students included Laura Gilpin, Karl Struss (*b* 1886), Dorothea Lange, Paul Outerbridge, Ralph Steiner (*b* 1899) and Anton Bruehl.

BIBLIOGRAPHY
Symbolism of Light: The Photographs of Clarence H. White (exh. cat., Wilmington, DE, A. Mus., 1977)
W. Naef: *The Collection of Alfred Stieglitz* (New York, 1978)
TERENCE PITTS

White, Howard Judson. *See under* GRAHAM, ANDERSON, PROBST & WHITE.

White, John (*fl* 1585–93). English watercolourist. His drawings are among the earliest known images of the North American continent by an English artist. He is thought to have accompanied an exploratory expedition to the New World led by Sir Martin Frobisher (?1535–94) in 1577 and another sponsored by Sir Walter Ralegh (1552–1618) in 1584. In 1585 White served as official artist on a venture sponsored by Ralegh to establish the first English settlement in North America, on the Island of Roanoke, Virginia. Although this venture failed, Ralegh sponsored a second settlement expedition in 1587, naming White governor of the colony.

On the 1585 expedition, White collaborated with the scientist Thomas Harriot (1560–1621) in charting the North American coastline and recording the New World's native inhabitants, flora and fauna (*see* NATIVE NORTH AMERICAN ART, fig. 5). In producing his finished watercolours, White consulted works by the Huguenot artist Jacques Le Moyne de Morgues, who had visited Florida from 1563 to 1565. Many of White's images were issued as engravings by Theodor de Bry in Harriot's *A Briefe and True Report of the New Found Land of Virginia*, published in 1590 by de Bry as the first part of his series *America*. White also produced copies of his watercolours for the naturalists John Gerard (1545–1612) and Thomas Penny (*c.* 1530–88). His surviving drawings are in the British Museum and the British Library, London.

White's images rendered the unfamiliar landscape and native flora and fauna of the New World accessible to English viewers. His diagrammatic pictures of larger scenes, particularly Indian settlements, portray the New World as a fruitful, well-ordered environment in which settlers might thrive. He represented individual animals and plants in the conventional terms of the specimen drawing, allowing previously unknown organisms to be named and ordered according to traditional systems of classification.

BIBLIOGRAPHY
L. Binyon: 'The Drawings of John White', *Walpole Soc.*, xiii (1924–5), pp. 19–24
P. Hulton and D. Beers Quinn, eds: *The American Drawings of John White, 1577–1590*, 2 vols (London, 1964)
W. Sturtevant: 'First Visual Images of Native America', *First Images of America*, ed. F. Chiappelli (Berkeley, 1976), pp. 417–54
P. Hulton: 'Jacques Le Moyne de Morgues and John White', *The Westward Enterprise*, ed. K. Andrews, N. Canny and P. Hair (Liverpool, 1978), pp. 195–214
——: *America, 1585: The Complete Drawings of John White* (London, 1984)
AMY MEYERS

White, Joseph (*b* Bristol, 28 Dec 1799; *d* Saint John, NB, 15 Jan 1870). Canadian potter of English birth. In 1814 he was apprenticed to the Bristol potter J. D. Pountney. Later, with his brother James White, he carried on a successful business in Bristol making Rockingham, black teapots and stoneware jugs (1828–55). The brothers' leadless liquid glaze for stoneware was of such quality that London potteries, including Doulton, purchased supplies of it. They retired in 1855 and Joseph White jr (1829–75) took over the pottery. In 1864 Joseph White's son Frederick J. White (1838–1919) persuaded him to buy the Courtenay Bay Pottery, Crouchville, New Brunswick. There he quickly introduced the 'latest English designs' in moulded earthenware and 'superior' stoneware with his Bristol glaze. Though the Crouchville pottery failed under his sons, his grandson James W. Foley (1857–1904), whom he had trained, set up his own pottery in Saint John. White's Foley descendants potted there until 1964, when fire destroyed the premises. The works then transferred to Labelle, Quebec, and, as the Canuck Pottery Ltd, made ornamental earthenware, including moulded jugs.

DCB
BIBLIOGRAPHY
W. J. Pountney: *Old Bristol Potteries* (Bristol, 1920), pp. 268–70
E. Collard: *Nineteenth-century Pottery and Porcelain in Canada* (Montreal, 1947, rev. 2/1984)
ELIZABETH COLLARD

White, (Anna) Lois (*b* Auckland, 2 Nov 1903; *d* Auckland, 19 Sept 1984). New Zealand painter and teacher. A student at the Elam School of Fine Arts, Auckland, from 1923, she later taught there between 1934 and 1963. Her predilection for figure compositions was encouraged by Archibald Fisher (1896–1959), whose meticulous attention to draughtsmanship and tonal modulation of form left their distinctive mark on her work. White drew on three main areas for her subject-matter: the Bible, allegory and contemporary social issues. *War Makers* (1937; Auckland, C.A.G.), an animated multi-figure composition satirizing war profiteers, is typical of her output. Her mural *Controversy* was destroyed when the Elam School burnt down in 1948.

BIBLIOGRAPHY
A. Kirker: *New Zealand Women Artists* (Auckland, 1986), pp. 121–4
ANNE KIRKER

White, Minor (Martin) (*b* Minneapolis, MN, 9 July 1908; *d* Boston, MA, 24 June 1976). American photographer and writer. He took his first photographs as a child with a Kodak Box Brownie camera and later learnt darkroom procedures as a student at the University of Minnesota. After graduating in 1933 with a degree in botany and English, he wrote poetry for five years while supporting himself with odd jobs. He moved to Portland, OR, in 1938 and became increasingly interested in photography. During 1938–9 he worked for the Works Progress Administration Federal Arts Project as a creative photographer documenting the early architecture and waterfront of Portland. In 1941 MOMA in New York exhibited several of his images. His first one-man show, photographs of the Grande Ronde-Wallowa Mountain area of north-eastern Oregon, opened at the Portland Art Museum in 1942.

White served in the Army Intelligence Corps from 1942 to 1945, during which time he wrote about photography but took few photographs. He visited Alfred Stieglitz in New York at his gallery, An American Place, in 1946 and was profoundly affected by the meeting. Stieglitz's discourse on the photograph as an 'equivalent', a metaphor for an internal state, provided White with the theoretical motif around which his future work crystallized. White eventually formed a classification system for all photographs: documentary, pictorial, informational and Equivalent. To him, a photograph became an Equivalent when it transcended its original and customary purposes, such as the other categories, and more specifically when it evoked a heightened emotion. He compared the significance of an Equivalent to the 'intimations of immortality' of William Wordsworth (1770–1850) and suggested that curiosity and courage were prerequisites for the discovery of such images. His equivalence concept was a form of spiritual discipline for the photographer as well as for the active viewer, and the process of photographing and interpreting photographs became a search for a cosmic essence. He wrote:

'Not equal to   equivalent to
Not metaphor   equivalence
Not standing for   but being also
Not sign   but direct connection
                        to invisible Resonance'
(*Mirrors Messages Manifestations*, p. 41).

During the 1940s White began to present his work in titled sequences, arranging the images to create associations, moods and complementary statements. The configuration of his photographs and words, inspired by his interest in Gestalt theory, allowed viewers to read his work while sustaining what he called a 'feeling state'. Another method in which White translated physical materials and technique into symbolic manifestation was his use of infrared film in the mid–1950s. The film created interesting visual contrasts but, more importantly for White, it penetrated beyond the range of visible light and theoretically revealed things that cannot ordinarily be seen.

In 1952 White was a founder of the influential quarterly publication *Aperture* and served as its publisher and editor until 1975. He joined the staff of George Eastman House in Rochester, NY, in 1953 and taught at Rochester Institute of Technology. In his continual search for a spiritual source, White adopted various aspects of Zen philosophy and was especially devoted to the philosophy of Georgii Invanovich Gurdjieff (?1877–1949). He taught at Massachusetts Institute of Technology from 1965 until his retirement in 1974.

For illustration of his work *see* PHOTOGRAPHY, fig. 28.

PHOTOGRAPHIC PUBLICATIONS
Mirrors Messages Manifestations (New York, 1969)
Being without Clothes (New York, 1970) [incl. photographs by White and others]
Octave of Prayer (New York, 1972) [incl. photographs by White and others]

WRITINGS
ed.: *Aperture* (1952–75)
with P. Lorenz and R. Zakia: *The New Zone System Manual* (New York, 1968); rev. version, with P. Lorenz and R. Zakia (New York, 1976)

BIBLIOGRAPHY
J. Baker Hall: *Minor White: Rites & Passages* (New York, 1978)
P. C. Bunnell with M. B. Pellerano and J. B. Rauch: *Minor White: The Eye that Shapes* (Princeton, 1989)
RICHARD LORENZ

White, Robert (*b* London, 1645; *d* London, 1703). English engraver and draughtsman. He was trained by David Loggan as a line-engraver and portrait draughtsman. Although he drew a self-portrait when he was 16 and his first print (before 1666) was a portrait, much of White's early work was topographical. In 1671 he drew and engraved a bird's-eye view of the London Royal Exchange. In his notebooks George Vertue claimed that White also drew 'many buildings' for Loggan, perhaps for his views of Oxford and Cambridge, *Oxonia illustrata* (1675) and *Cantabrigia illustrata* (1688), and for John Slezer's *Theatrum Scotiae* (1693), to which Loggan also contributed.

White established himself as one of London's leading line-engravers of portraits, working after contemporary artists including Lely, Kneller, John Riley, Mary Beale and Michael Dahl. He also worked from his own drawings, taken from life; these were drawn in Loggan's manner, using black lead on vellum, sometimes with the face lightly tinted in brown wash. Between 1666 and 1702 he produced some 400 engraved plates, mainly of public and literary figures, the best known being his portraits of John Bunyan and Samuel Pepys, prefixed to editions of their writings. His prints were skilful but uninspired and did little to perpetuate line-engraving against the rising popularity of mezzotint.

Besides portraits, White engraved numerous book illustrations and frontispieces, including plates after A. D. Hennin in Anthony à Wood's *Historia et antiquitates Universitatis Oxoniensis* (1674) and the headpiece to the first Oxford Almanack, probably from a design by Robert Streeter. Despite his prolific practice and large fees, White died in penury. His son, George White (*c.* 1671–1732), was a mezzotint engraver.

BIBLIOGRAPHY
DNB
H. Walpole: *Anecdotes of Painting in England, with Some Account of the Principal Artists*, ed. R. N. Wornum, iii (London, 1862), pp. 947–53
C. F. Bell and R. L. Poole: 'English Seventeenth Century Portrait Drawings in Oxford Collections', *Walpole Soc.*, xiv (1926), pp. 64–71
G. Vertue: 'Note-books', *Walpole Soc.*, xviii (1929–30), p. 131

E. Croft-Murray and P. Hulton: *British Drawings: 16th and 17th Centuries*, London, BM cat., i (1960), pp. 539–40

DAVID BLAYNEY BROWN

White, Robin (*b* Te Puke, NZ, 12 July 1946). New Zealand painter and printmaker. In 1967 she graduated in fine arts from the University of Auckland and trained as a teacher. The following year she moved to Paremata near Wellington, and in 1971 moved south to Dunedin to work full-time as an artist. The relationship between her painting and printmaking was always important to her development. In both she presented flat, simplified frontal images, as in *Jerry at the Paekak Pub* (1971; Lower Hutt, Dowse Mus.). The legacy of Rita Angus was central to her work, and she was frequently grouped with the New Zealand painter Don Binney (*b* 1940) and Michael Smither as an artist exploring realist concerns in a regional context. She was keen to make her images widely accessible through her silk-screen prints; in these she often simplified further the architectural and landscape forms of her environment. The birth of her son led to the inclusion of family imagery in works such as the screenprint *Buzzy Bee for Siulolovao* (1977). In 1982 she moved with her family to the republic of Kiribati, formerly the Gilbert Islands, to work with the Baha'i community. There she produced artists' books, prints and watercolours, largely concentrating on her immediate island environment.

BIBLIOGRAPHY

A. Taylor and D. Coddington, eds: *Robin White, New Zealand Painter* (Martinborough, 1981)
C. P. Eyley: 'Robin White in Kiribati', *A. NZ*, 31 (1984), pp. 30–33

JIM BARR, MARY BARR

White, Stanford. *See under* McKIM, MEAD & WHITE.

White, William (*b* Blakesley, Northants, 1825; *d* London, 22 Jan 1900). English architect, designer and writer. After training in the provinces and in the London office of George Gilbert Scott I, where friendship with G. E. Street reinforced his enthusiasm for medieval Gothic, he started in independent practice in Truro, Cornwall, in 1847. The schools and vicarages White designed at this period, especially the ambitious rectory of St Columb Major (1849–50), show a stylistically advanced liking for asymmetry and simplified forms and a feeling for vernacular materials. From 1851, when White returned to London, he wrote extensively, his contributions to *The Ecclesiologist* helping to create the theoretical basis for High Victorian Gothic. Advocating Gothic principles rather than medieval precedents, he argued for an architectural aesthetic derived from the geometry of plane and mass, asymmetrically composed, functionally expressive and employing colour to denote the structure. His own buildings developed these features into a markedly personal idiom. Particularly important are vicarages at Halstead (1854) and Little Baddow (1858), both in Essex; shops and houses (1855) at Audley, Cheshire; the Bank House (1856) at St Columb Major, Cornwall; the churches of All Saints (begun 1852; interior destr. World War II), Notting Hill, London, Christ Church (1856), Hatherden, and Christ Church (1857), Smannel, both Hants, and the elaborately decorated Holy Trinity (1859–66), Islington, London. In his finest church, St Michael (1859–70), Lyndhurst, Hants, bold massing is set against concentrated carved detailing. White's most important domestic works are the remodelling of Bishops Court (1860–64), Devon, a masterpiece of subtle polychromy, and Humewood (1866–70), Co. Wicklow, Ireland, a major exercise in geometrical composition. Church restoration occupied much of his later career, although he also designed a number of new churches in Battersea, London, the most interesting being the concrete and brick St Mark's (1873–4).

WRITINGS

'Upon Some of the Causes and Points of Failure in Modern Design', *The Ecclesiologist*, n. s., ix (1851), pp. 305–13
'Modern Design', *The Ecclesiologist*, n.s., xi (1853), pp. 313–30
'On Windows', *The Ecclesiologist*, n.s., xiv (1856), pp. 319–32
'A Plea for Polychromy', *Builder*, xix (1861), pp. 33–4
'Ironwork: Its Legitimate Uses and Proper Treatment', *Trans. RIBA*, xvi (1865–6), pp. 15–30
'Descriptive Sketch of a Mansion at Humewood, Co. Wicklow', *Trans. RIBA*, xix (1868–9), pp. 78–88

BIBLIOGRAPHY

T. H. Watson: 'The Late William White, FSA', *RIBA J.*, n. s. 3, vii (1900), pp. 145–6
P. Thompson: 'The Writings of William White', *Concerning Architecture*, ed. J. Summerson (London, 1968), pp. 226–37
S. Muthesius: *The High Victorian Movement in Architecture, 1850–1870* (London, 1972)

CHRIS BROOKS

White, Bishop **William Charles** (*b* Devonshire, 22 Aug 1873; *d* Toronto, 24 Jan 1960). Canadian priest, archaeologist and museum curator of British birth. He went to Canada with his parents as a child and was educated at Wycliffe College, Toronto. After his ordination into the Anglican Church, he went to China in 1897 as a missionary and in 1909 was consecrated as the first bishop of Henan Province. During his time in Henan he also pursued research into Chinese art and archaeology, including a study of the tombs at Jincun (5th–2nd centuries BC), near Luoyang. He returned to Toronto in 1934 to become Keeper of the East Asiatic Collection, Assistant Director of the Royal Ontario Museum and Professor of Chinese Archaeology at the University of Toronto. From 1941 to 1948 he was also Director of the School of Chinese Studies there; he retired from all of these posts in 1948. In the field of Chinese art and archaeology his writings embraced a broad range of subjects from ancient tomb-tile pictures, bronzes and temple frescoes to ink-bamboo drawings by the 18th-century artist Chen Lin. About 3000 fragments of oracle bones that he collected in China entered the Royal Ontario Museum, Toronto, in 1931. The museum also houses his collection of bronzes, sculpture, jades and glass.

WRITINGS

Tombs of Old Lo-yang: A Record of the Construction and Contents of a Group of Royal Tombs at Chin-ts'un, Honan, Probably Dating 550 BC (Shanghai, 1934)
An Album of Chinese Bamboos: A Study of a Set of Ink-bamboo Drawings AD 1785 (Toronto, 1939)
Tomb Tile Pictures of Ancient China: An Archaeological Study of Pottery Tiles from Tombs of Western Honan, Dating about the Third Century BC (Toronto, 1939)
Chinese Temple Frescoes: A Study of Three Wall-Paintings of the Thirteenth Century (Toronto, 1940)
Bone Culture of Ancient China: An Archaeological Study of Bone Material from Northern Honan, Dating about the Twelfth Century BC (Toronto, 1945)

Bronze Culture of Ancient China: An Archaeological Study of Bronze Objects from Northern Honan, Dating from about 1400 BC–771 BC (Toronto, 1956)

BIBLIOGRAPHY

Obituary, *Globe and Mail* (25 Jan 1960)

H. Chin-hsiung: *Oracle Bones from the White and Other Collections* (Toronto, 1979)

S. J. VERNOIT

White Birch Society [Shirakabaha]. Japanese society of literary figures and artists formed in Tokyo in 1910 by, among others, the novelists Saneatsu Mushanokōji (1885–1976) and Naoya Shiga (1883–1971), and the painter and critic Muneyoshi Yanagi. The society produced an eponymous monthly journal, the first issue of which appeared in April 1910. The aim of the journal was to discuss ideas on Western literature and art and to introduce to Japan the work of such major Western artists as Cézanne, van Gogh and Rodin. The society greatly influenced young Japanese artists, such as Ryūsei Kishida, whose early work was inspired by late Impressionism, and who was a founder of the Grass and Earth Society of Western-style painters. The society also held exhibitions of Western art (principally reproductions), including a show of Western prints (Tokyo, 1911) and another showing the work of Rodin, Renoir and Bernard Leach. The society's journal ran for 160 issues, until August 1923.

WRITINGS

Shirakaba, 1–160 (1910–23)

BIBLIOGRAPHY

Shirakaba to Taishōki no bijutsu [Art of the Shirakaba and Taishō period] (exh. cat. by T. Mushanokōji, Tokyo, Met. A. Mus., 1977)

S. Sasaki and T. Sakai, eds: *Kindai Nihon bijutsushi* [History of modern Japanese art] (Tokyo, 1977)

YASUYOSHI SAITO

White bole. *See under* BOLE.

White Canons. *See* PREMONSTRATENSIAN CANONS.

Whitefriars Glass Works. *See under* POWELL, JAMES & Sons.

Whitehead, John (*b* Ashton-under-Lyne, Lancs, 1726; *d* Oporto, 15 Dec 1802). English architect, diplomat and mathematician. He was largely responsible for the British influence in 18th-century Oporto, both in its planning and in its culture and social life. Several important buildings can be attributed to him. In 1756 he was appointed British Consul in Oporto by the Merchants of the Factory and held the post until his death. In 1774 he produced plans in the Palladian style for rebuilding houses in Praça da Ribeira, a square facing the River Douro in Oporto, and for adjacent streets. Many houses built to his designs still exist, most notably the Factory House. This was completed in 1790 and has been used ever since as the headquarters of the British Port shippers. The house has three floors and a mezzanine. The sombre façade is in marked contrast to the elegance of the principal reception-rooms decorated in Adam style. A Palladian loggia with seven arched openings leads to the entrance hall, which is divided into three aisles by six columns supporting shallow vaults.

On Whitehead's recommendation, the local authorities accepted plans from John Carr of York for a general hospital, S António, begun in 1770. Whitehead's pupil and assistant Joaquim da Costa Lima Sampaio designed the Royal Palace (subsequently Museu Nacional Soares dos Reis) in a style inspired by Carr's hospital and also the British Chapel completed in 1818.

Whitehead also invented a system of water measurement adopted by the authorities in Lisbon and Oporto. As Consul, he obtained permission for the first official Anglican cemetery in Oporto (inaugurated 1788), where a monument to him has been erected. His portrait, painted posthumously by an unknown artist, hangs in the Factory House.

BIBLIOGRAPHY

J. Pinto Ferreira: *A praça da Ribeira* (Oporto, 1953)

R. Taylor: 'The Architecture of Port Wine', *Archit. Rev.* [London], cxxix (1961), pp. 388–98

J. de F. Delaforce: *The Factory House at Oporto* (London, 1979, rev. 2/1983)

—: *Anglicans Abroad: The History of the Chaplaincy and Church of St. James at Oporto* (London, 1982)

JOHN DE F. DELAFORCE

Whiteley, Brett (*b* Sydney, 7 April 1939; *d* Thirroul, nr Wollongong, 15 June 1992). Australian painter, sculptor and printmaker. He was already preoccupied with art while at Scots School in Bathurst, for which he painted several murals *c.* 1955–6 on sporting themes; he later studied intermittently at the Julian Ashton School in Sydney (1957–9). He was awarded the Italian Travelling Scholarship in 1959 and spent some time in Italy before arriving in London in mid-1961, where he achieved fame when the exhibition *Recent Australian Art*, at the Whitechapel Art Gallery, included some of his latest works. His earlier work had shown the effects of sources such as Rembrandt, Honoré Daumier and William Dobell, but by this time he was painting in a boldly sensuous style of his own, emphasizing formal qualities and replete with erotic allusion. These elements were subsequently developed in his art, though becoming increasingly figurative, deployed to symbolize human estrangement and aspects of alternative lifestyle, while owing something to the work of Francis Bacon and the French *intimistes*. Simultaneously, Whiteley created animal imagery as an analogy to human depravity. On returning to Sydney in 1965 he began depicting Australia, especially its beach life, as a similar dichotomy, even incorporating items of detritus into his paintings as sardonic collage. Such 'Pop art' elements reappeared in numerous mixed-media sculptures embodying even more acerbic violations of convention. From 1961 he began producing prints on similar themes in various traditional media, as well as screenprinted posters and prints. A year spent in the USA (1967) on a Harkness Fellowship increased his sense of alienation and accentuated an interest in non-European cultures. A plan to settle permanently in Fiji with his family miscarried, and they returned to Australia in 1969. Thereafter Whiteley made the transition from virtual cult figure to visionary artist of extremely personal sensibilities and preoccupations.

BIBLIOGRAPHY

S. McGrath: *Brett Whiteley* (Sydney, 1979)

Brett Whiteley: Graphics 1961–1982 (exh. cat. by R. Mandy, Perth, A.G. W. Australia, 1983)

J. McKenzie: Obituary, *The Guardian* (18 June 1992)

ROBERT SMITH

White Mountain. *See* BÍLÁ HORA.

Whiting, Cliff (*b* Te Kaha, NZ, 6 May 1936). Maori wood-carver, painter and teacher. As a member of the Whanau-a-Apanui tribe he was educated in the rural community of Te Kaha until he began teacher training in 1955 at Wellington Teachers College. He was quickly selected as an art specialist as a result of the Department of Education's determination to develop Maori and Western European culture in schools. Whiting and other young Maori artists, supported by Gordon Tovey, the national arts and crafts adviser, were able to explore traditional and contemporary Maori art. In the late 1960s, encouraged by Pine Taiapa, he began working on *marae* (communal centres), carving and restoring buildings. Whiting's innovative use of themes and materials placed art at the centre of the revitalization of Maori communities. From the 1970s Whiting was the leading authority on the restoration of Maori buildings, as well as working with local communities on new buildings like those at the Takahanga *marae*, Kaikoura. He also undertook significant national commissions such as the carved and painted mural *Te wehenga o Rangi Raua Ko Papa* ('The separation of Rangi and Papa', 1969–76; Wellington, NZ, N. Lib.). His work was included in many national and international exhibitions, including *Te ao marama* ('To the world of light') at the Sydney Opera House (1986) and *Headlands* (1992). He was appointed to the Council for Maori and Pacific Arts in 1979 and became Chairman in 1988. In 1993 he took up the position of Director of Maori and Bicultural Studies at the Museum of New Zealand, Te Papa Tongarewa.

WRITINGS

'Te Po, te whaiao, te ao marama: From out of the Darkness, the World of Being, to the World of Light', *Headlands: Thinking through New Zealand Art* (exh. cat., Sydney, Mus. Contemp. A., 1992), pp. 112–22

BIBLIOGRAPHY

D. Nicholas and K. Kaa: *Seven Maori Artists* (Wellington, 1986), pp. 8–15

JIM BARR, MARY BARR

Whitney. American family.

(1) Gertrude Vanderbilt Whitney [née Vanderbilt] (*b* New York, NY, 9 Jan 1875; *d* New York, 18 April 1942). Sculptor, patron, collector and museum founder. She studied sculpture under the Norwegian Hendrick Christian Andersen (*b* 1872), under James Earle Fraser (1876–1953) at the Art Students League, New York, and before 1914 under Andrew O'Connor (*b* 1874) in Paris, where she also received private critiques from Auguste Rodin. Gertrude's experiences in a hospital that she established at the beginning of World War I, in Juilly, France, inspired sketches of soldiers, their wives and nurses. She developed these into sculptures for her war memorials in New York, which were conspicuous for their dramatic realism. They included two reliefs on the Victory Arch (1918–19; destr.), Madison Square; the war memorial on Washington Heights (1921), for which she was awarded a medal by the New York Society of Architects; *Soldiers and Sailors* (bronze, 1922; New York, Mitchel Square); and the monument (1924) erected in Providence, RI, to commemorate US Army troops who landed at Saint-Nazaire. Other commissions included the Titanic Memorial (1914), Washington, DC, the equestrian monument to *William F. Cody*

(Buffalo Bill) (h. 2.44 m, 1924), Public Square, Cody, WY, and the memorial to *Columbus* (h. 2.34 m, 1929), Palos de la Frontera, Spain. She was also noted for her architectural and fountain sculptures, including her Pan Fountain (1908), which was awarded a prize by the Architectural League of New York. In 1915 her El Dorado Fountain won the bronze medal at the Panama Pacific International Exposition in San Francisco, CA. In 1939 her last sculpture, *To the Morrow* (or the *Spirit of Flight*), (h. 21.34 m, incl. base) was installed at the World's Fair in New York. In 1934 she was elected an honorary member of the American Institute of Architects. By birth and by her marriage to Harry Payne Whitney, Gertrude was sufficiently wealthy to act as a generous supporter of other artists and as a collector on a substantial scale.

From 1907 she maintained a studio in MacDougal Alley, Greenwich Village, New York, in which she exhibited work by promising young artists. A friend of Arthur B. Davies and Robert Henri, leading members of the Eight (i), Gertrude bought four of the seven paintings sold from the group's exhibition at the Macbeth Galleries in New York in 1908. She also supported the Madison Gallery in New York, where a liberal group of artists, including Walt Kuhn (1877–1949) and Jerome Myers (1867–1940), developed the idea for an Independents exhibition, which was to become the famous Armory Show (1913; 69th Regiment Armory). In 1915 she established the Friends of the Young Artists, and in 1918 the Whitney Studio Club, with a membership of several hundred and the most active programme in the USA for presenting the work of the new generation of North American artists. In 1930 she founded the Whitney Museum of American Art in New York, donating to it a collection of 700 works of art. The museum opened to the public on 18 November 1931 and has since become a major force in American art through its collections, publishing programme and exhibitions, including the influential Whitney Annuals.

BIBLIOGRAPHY

Memorial Exhibition: Gertrude Vanderbilt Whitney (exh. cat., preface J. Force; New York, Whitney, 1943)
E. P. Hoyt: *The Whitneys: An Informal Portrait, 1635–1975* (New York, 1976)
D. Robbins: 'Statues to Sculpture, 1890–1930', *200 Years of American Sculpture*, ed. T. Armstrong and others (New York, 1976), pp. 113–59, 320–21
B. H. Friedman: *Gertrude Vanderbilt Whitney* (New York, 1978)

(2) John [Jock] **Hay Whitney** (*b* Ellsworth, ME, 17 Aug 1904; *d* 1982). Publisher, diplomat and collector, nephew of (1) Gertrude Vanderbilt Whitney. He was the son of the philanthropists Payne Whitney and Helen Hay Whitney. He studied at Yale University, New Haven, CT, and at the University of Oxford, England. He was introduced to the fine arts by his mother, a poet and a collector of French Impressionist paintings. His first purchases, made while at Yale, included American portraits, sporting prints, etchings by Whistler and paintings by George Stubbs and Ben Marshall. From the 1920s he built up a major collection of European paintings, including works by Balthus, Cézanne, Chardin, Corot, Courbet, Degas, Gauguin, Monet, Picasso, Odilon Redon, Auguste Renoir, Georges Rouault, Henri Rousseau, Seurat, Toulouse-Lautrec, van Gogh and Vuillard; and by the North

American artists George Bellows, Thomas Eakins, Winslow Homer, Edward Hopper, Sargent, Gilbert Stuart, Whistler and Andrew Wyeth. The John Hay Whitney Collection was exhibited from December 1960 to January 1961 at the Tate Gallery, London. From 1930 John was a trustee and from 1946 to 1956 the Chairman of MOMA in New York. His career included financial interests in theatre and film, including *Gone with the Wind* and *Rebecca*. During World War II he served as a colonel in the US Eighth Air Force, and from 1956 to 1960 he was Ambassador to Great Britain.

BIBLIOGRAPHY

The John Hay Whitney Collection (exh. cat., intro. J. Rothenstein; London, Tate, 1960–61)

J. Lipman, ed.: *The Collector in America* (New York, 1961/*R* London, 1971), pp. 62–73

E. P. Hoyt: *The Whitneys: An Informal Portrait, 1635–1975* (New York, 1976)

J. Russell: 'John Hay Whitney, 1904–1982', *A. America*, lxx (1982), p. 5

EDWARD BRYANT

Whitney, Anne (*b* Watertown, MA, 2 Sept 1821; *d* Boston, MA, 23 Jan 1915). American sculptor and writer. She achieved eminence not only as a sculptor but also as a campaigner for social justice, pressing for the abolition of slavery and equality for women. From 1846 to 1848 she ran a small school in Salem, MA. She also wrote and became well known in New England literary circles. In 1855 Whitney turned to sculpture, studying at the Pennsylvania Academy of Fine Arts (1860) and in Boston (1862–4) with William Rimmer. Her sculptures often carried social messages: *Africa* (1864) depicts a woman awakening from the sleep of slavery. Between 1867 and 1876 she visited Munich, Paris and Rome. The most celebrated work of this period, *Roma* (1869), a seated figure of a decrepit beggar woman, wearing medallions of monuments, symbolizes the decay of the city. Scandalized, the authorities prevented its public display, but several versions were later exhibited in Rome, in London, and at the World Columbian Exposition (1893), Chicago. In 1876 Whitney moved to Boston. Her subjects included such women as *Harriet Beecher Stowe* (1892; Hartford, CT, Stowe House). In 1902 she cast a statue of the abolitionist *Charles Sumner*, but it was set up publicly in Harvard Square, Cambridge, MA, only in 1929, after its initial rejection by the Boston Arts Committee on the grounds of Whitney's gender.

BIBLIOGRAPHY

The White Marmorean Flock: 19th-century American Neo-classical Sculpture (exh. cat., ed. W. H. Gerdts jr; Poughkeepsie, NY, Vassar Coll. A.G., 1972)

P. Dunfold: *A Biographical Dictionary of Women Artists in Europe and America since 1850* (Philadelphia, 1989, rev. Hemel Hempstead, 2/1990)

C. S. Rubinstein: *American Women Sculptors* (Boston, MA, 1990)

Whittemore, Thomas (*b* Cambridge, MA, 2 Jan 1871; *d* Washington, DC, 8 June 1950). American archaeologist and Byzantinist. He graduated at Tufts College (Medford, MA) in 1894 and taught there until 1911, switching from English to art history in 1906; in the late 1890s he studied in the Harvard graduate school programme. Early in 1911 he went to Egypt to work with the Egypt Exploration Society, for which he excavated at Abydos and Balabish until early in 1915. Important to his subsequent career was his establishment in 1915 of a relief programme in the Balkans and Russia for Russian refugees; in 1916 he organized a distinguished committee that supported his work until 1931. His post-war activities focused on the education of young Russian exiles, whose clandestine departures from their homeland and establishment in Western countries he oversaw. From 1927 to 1930 he taught art history at New York University.

In 1930 Whittemore founded a Byzantine Institute, later incorporated in Boston. He envisaged a tripartite operation—a research institute in Paris, fieldwork in Istanbul and a managing and publications office in Boston—and he quickly gave substance to this plan. During his extensive travels he gave lectures and raised money while also contributing his own inheritance; his Russian protégés were in time often able to help. He tirelessly expounded the values and significance of east Christian art according to his own sometimes poetic but convincing views, at the root of which lay deep religious conviction and a genuine, if personal, aesthetic creed.

From 1930 to 1933 he worked in Coptic monuments and began the research library that was later established as his institute's centre in Paris (4, Rue de Lille). Although not a scholar in the grand tradition, he nevertheless had an excellent sense of what had to be done in the field, and by the early 1930s he had conceived a plan of uncovering the Hagia Sophia mosaics recorded by Gaspare Trajano and Giuseppe Fossati in the previous century, a plan that would lead to a major change in the study of Byzantine art. On 19 July 1932 Kemal Attatürk finally allowed him to work in the building. There and in other Byzantine churches in Istanbul, Whittemore continued to work for his remaining 18 years. By 1933 the first instalment of his *Mosaics of Hagia Sophia in Istanbul* had appeared; the fourth and last was published two years after his death. Much of the writing was done in Paris by others, but as with fieldwork, the plan and directive force were Whittemore's.

After the narthex the crew, led by E. J. W. Hawkins, cleaned the gallery mosaics of the *Deësis* and the imperial portraits, the apse mosaic and its attendant archangel, and the saints of the north tympanum wall of the nave. No restoration was done: Each tessera or each mosaic was revealed and cleaned using simple tools: dental picks, brushes of various rigidities, and the like; chemicals were forbidden. In 1935 the church was turned into a museum.

Meanwhile the Paris library grew, under the care of its librarian Boris Ermoloff and his assistant Vladimir Rayevsky; both had come out of Russia in the 1920s. Publications included not only the mosaics reports but numerous articles of varying scholarly significance, some of them still essential reading, all of them part of Whittemore's plan to publicize his work. The institute was joined to Dumbarton Oaks and the library conveyed to the French government after Whittemore's death.

WRITINGS

Whittemore's papers and correspondence are largely in his Paris library, now part of the Ecole des Langues Orientales Vivantes. Much archaeological material, in particular photographs, is at Dumbarton Oaks, Washington, DC.

The Mosaics of Hagia Sophia at Istanbul: Preliminary Reports, 4 vols (Oxford, 1933–52)

'Mosaics of Aya Sophia', *Actes du IVe congrès international des études byzantines* (Sofia, 1936), pp. 202–6

'The Mosaics of S. Sophia at Istanbul', *Amer. J. Archaeol.*, xlii (1938), pp. 219–26

DAB

BIBLIOGRAPHY

Obituary, *New York Times* (9 June 1950); *Life* (25 Dec 1950)

P. Lemerle: Obituary, *Byzantion*, xxi (1951), pp. 281–3

W. L. MacDonald: 'The Uncovering of Byzantine Mosaics in Hagia Sophia', *Archaeology*, iv (1951), pp. 89–93

G. Constable: 'Dumbarton Oaks and Byzantine Field Work', *Dumbarton Oaks Pap.*, xxxvii (1987), pp. 171–6

WILLIAM L. MacDONALD

Whittingham. English family of printers and publishers. Charles Whittingham (i) (*b* nr Coventry, 16 June 1767; *d* 5 Jan 1840) was apprenticed to a bookseller and printer, Richard Bird, from 1779 to 1786. In the late 1780s Whittingham set up as a printer in Fetter Lane, London. The earliest piece of printing associated with him is Edward Young's *Night Thoughts* (1792). His association from 1803 with the bookseller John Sharpe resulted in several series, including the *British Classics* (1803), *Sharpe's British Theatre* (1804) and *British Poets* (1805); Whittingham issued his own *British Poets* series in 100 volumes in 1822. From 1803 he used some of the earliest Stanhope presses and traded as the Stanhope Press until 1811, when, having moved part of his business to Chiswick, he adopted the Chiswick Press imprint. By then he was also working for almanac and book publishers and publishing books himself. In 1827 he went into partnership with his nephew Charles Whittingham (ii) (*b* Mitcham, Surrey, 30 Oct 1795; *d* 21 April 1876), who had trained with him since 1810, but the collaboration was not successful, and in 1828 Whittingham the younger moved to London. His uncle retained control of the press until his death.

During his early years of independence Whittingham the younger printed mainly for members of the book trade, notably William Pickering (1796–1854), with whom he worked on a refined Antique style of production that was fully developed from the 1840s in the Chiswick Press books. Whittingham was also interested in the possibilities of colour relief printing. His Book of Common Prayer (1844) included facsimiles of 16th- and 17th-century editions, and a Prayer Book of 1864 used 16 decorative borders copied from a Book of Hours (Paris, 1525) by Geofroy Tory. In 1892 the nature of the business was considerably altered by the introduction of steam-powered presses.

BIBLIOGRAPHY

A. Warren: *The Charles Whittinghams, Printers* (New York, 1896)

G. Keynes: *William Pickering, Publisher: A Memoir and a Check-list of his Publications* (London, 1969)

J. Thompson Ing: *Charles Whittingham the Younger and the Chiswick Press 1852–59* (diss., U. Berkeley, California, CA, 1985)

LAURA SUFFIELD

Whittredge, (Thomas) Worthington (*b* nr Springfield, OH, 22 May 1820; *d* Summit, NJ, 25 Feb 1910). American painter. With little education but with a longing to be an artist, he went at the age of 17 to Cincinnati, OH, where he served an apprenticeship as a sign painter to his brother-in-law Almon Baldwin (1800–70). In the summer of 1842 Whittredge opened a daguerreotype studio in Indianapolis, IN, but left the following summer when it proved an unsuccessful venture. He then joined B. Jenks to work as a portrait painter in Charleston, WV, but dissolved the arrangement because of his partner's alcoholism. Thereafter Whittredge decided to concentrate on landscapes, though he is documented as having painted some earlier. His first surviving landscape, *Scene near Hawk's Nest* (1845; Cincinnati, OH, A. Mus.), is in the picturesque manner of the Hudson River school painter Thomas Doughty. A year later he adopted the style of Thomas Cole, as did William Lewis Sonntag, with whom he defined a distinctive regional style. Around the same time Whittredge began painting directly from nature. *Rolling Hills* (Atlanta, GA, High Mus. A.) has a light-filled palette that suggests contact with the Philadelphia artist Russell Smith (1812–96).

Despite his growing success, Whittredge decided to go to Europe for further training. After securing sufficient commissions from Cincinnati patrons, he left in May 1849, accompanied by Benjamin McConkey. They settled in Düsseldorf, and, like other American painters, Whittredge enjoyed the benefits of the Düsseldorf Akademie without formally enrolling in it, thanks to the protection of Emanuel Gottlieb Leutze. He lived for a year in the attic of the landscape painter Andreas Achenbach (1815–1910), then became a member of the circle around Karl Friedrich Lessing, whom he accompanied on a tour of the Harz Mountains in 1852. From 1853 his paintings, such as *Summer Pastorale* (Indianapolis, IN, Mus. A.), follow the naturalistic vein of Lessing's follower Johann Wilhelm Schirmer. Whittredge spent the summer of 1856 sketching in Switzerland with Albert Bierstadt; in September they moved to Rome, where they were joined later by Sanford Robinson Gifford and William Stanley Haseltine. Whittredge remained in Italy for three years painting scenic landscapes as souvenirs for tourists; like *Landscape near Rome* (1858; Youngstown, OH, Butler Inst. Amer. A.), these are in the prevailing Düsseldorf style.

Whittredge seems to have returned to America in 1859. After visiting Newport, RI, and Cincinnati, he moved to New York, where he rented quarters in the recently completed Tenth Street Studio Building and gained almost immediate recognition. In 1860 he was elected an associate of the National Academy of Design, New York, becoming a full member two years later. *View of West Point* (Boston, MA, Mus. F.A.), the first work he painted after returning from Europe, shows that initially he experienced great difficulty adjusting to the differences in topography and style between American and European landscapes. However, his membership of the Century Club put him in contact with the mainstream of American art and thought. Through his friendships with the painter Asher B. Durand and the poet William Cullen Bryant, Whittredge developed a mature style that is seen in his great forest landscape, *Old Hunting Ground* (1864; Winston-Salem, NC, Reynolda House).

In summer 1866 Whittredge joined General John Pope's inspection tour of the Missouri Territory, which consolidated his vision of the United States. He travelled to Colorado in 1870 with John Frederick Kensett and Gifford, and again in 1871 with John Smillie. Such Western scenes as *Crossing the Ford* (1867–70; New York, C.

Assoc.) are unusual in treating the frontier not as mountainous vistas but as a pastoral Eden. The height of his career came in the mid-1870s: he served two terms as President of the National Academy of Design (1874–7) and was a prominent member of the paintings committees for the Centennial Exhibition in Philadelphia, responsibilities that kept him from painting.

By the late 1870s there was an evident change in Whittredge's style, inspired by the Barbizon school. Such scenes of Newport of the early 1880s as *Second Beach* (Minneapolis, MN, Walker A. Cent.) show the heightened *plein-air* style of Charles-François Daubigny. In 1880 Whittredge moved to Summit, NJ, and his work from the mid-1880s, notably *Dry Brook, Arkville* (Manchester, NH, Currier Gal. A.), is marked by a new introspection under the influence of George Inness, who lived near by. By 1890 Whittredge had reverted to his earlier Hudson River school style, but he continued to experiment with the latest tendencies, including a modified Impressionism in *Artist at his Easel* (New York, Kennedy Gals). In 1893 he visited Mexico with Frederic Edwin Church, and he continued to paint with some regularity to the age of 83.

UNPUBLISHED SOURCES
Washington, DC, Smithsonian Inst., Archvs Amer. A. [account bk; sketchbooks]

WRITINGS
The Autobiography of Worthington Whittredge (MS; c. 1905; Washington, DC, Smithsonian Inst., Archvs Amer. A.); ed. J. I. H. Baur (Brooklyn, 1942/R 1972)

BIBLIOGRAPHY
S. Omoto: 'Berkeley and Whittredge at Newport', *A. Q.* [Detroit], xxvii/1 (1964), pp. 43–56
Worthington Whittredge Retrospective (exh. cat. by E. H. Dwight, Utica, NY, Munson–Williams–Proctor Inst., 1969)
A. F. Janson: 'Worthington Whittredge: Two Early Landscapes', *Detroit Inst. A. Bull.*, lv/4 (1977), pp. 199–208
——: 'Worthington Whittredge: The Development of a Hudson River Painter, 1860–1868', *Amer. A. J.*, xi/2 (1979), pp. 71–84

ANTHONY F. JANSON

Wibald of Stavelot (*b* 1098; *d* Monastir [now Bitolj], 1158). South Netherlandish abbot and patron. He was professed as a Benedictine monk on 19 March 1117 and rose to become Abbot of Stavelot and Malmédy (1130), Montecassino (1137) and Corvey (1146). A zealous supporter of monastic reform, he participated in a number of councils (Pisa, 1137, and Reims, 1148) and was adviser to the bishops of Liège. Politically he played an influential role as adviser and envoy to three Holy Roman Emperors: Lothair II (*reg* 1125–37), Conrad III (*reg* 1138–52) and Frederick I Barbarossa (*reg* 1152–90). He was sent to Italy and elsewhere, took part in the Second Crusade and twice travelled to the court of Manuel I (*reg* 1143–80) in Constantinople for Frederick I Barbarossa. The purpose of his first journey there—during the winter of 1155–6—was to negotiate Frederick's marriage to Manuel I's cousin. On the way back from his second journey (1157–8), which was an attempt to restore deteriorating relations between the German and Byzantine empires, Wibald died in Monastir. A year later his body was taken home and buried in front of the high altar of the abbey church of Stavelot.

Wibald enjoyed great political influence and contributed significantly to the growth of artistic activity in the Meuse area in the middle of the 12th century. Over 400 of his letters have survived, but they contain little information about his patronage. In a famous letter of 1148 he corresponded with a certain *aurifaber G* about an unfinished work, but this Master 'G' cannot be identified with Godefroid of Huy, as some scholars have suggested. Wibald had a head reliquary made for the relics of Pope Alexander I (*c.* 105–*c.* 115 AD), which were placed inside on Good Friday (13 April) 1145; it consisted of a silver gilt repoussé bust on a portable altar (Brussels, Musées Royaux A. & Hist.; *see* RELIQUARY, fig. 3). Wibald also commissioned three costly retables for the abbey church of Stavelot. One (untraced) had gold reliefs with scenes of the *Passion* paid for in part by Frederick I Barbarossa and Manuel I. The other two were of silver. One was dedicated to St Remaclus (*d* 670–76) and contained his reliquary, as can be seen from a drawing of 1661 (Liège, Archvs Etat). All that remains of it are two round champlevé enamel plaques (Frankfurt am Main, Mus. Ksthandwk; Berlin, Tiergarten, Kstgewmus.) and two inscriptions (Stavelot, Trésor). The other, a triptych (New York, Pierpont Morgan Lib.; *see* ROMANESQUE, fig. 78) with illustrations from the legend of the True Cross, was probably made by order of Wibald to house two small Byzantine Triptychs with relics of the True Cross and Holy Nails, presumably gifts from Manuel I Komnenos to Wibald in 1155–6. The Maasland Triptych (New York, Pierpont Morgan Lib.), which Wibald most likely had made, was clearly based on Byzantine prototypes and later served as an example for several other reliquaries of the True Cross (*c.* 1160, New York priv. col.; *c.* 1160, Liège, Sainte-Croix, Trésor).

BIBLIOGRAPHY
J. J. M. Timmers: *De kunst van het Maasland*, i (Asscn and Maastricht, 1971), pp. 318–20, 335, 352
Rhein und Maas: Kunst und Kultur, 800–1400 (exh. cat., ed. A. Legner; Cologne, Josef-Haubrich-Ksthalle; Brussels, Musées Royaux A. & Hist.; 1972–3)
F.-J. Jakobi: *Wibald von Stablo und Corvey (1098–1158): Benediktinischer Abt in der frühen Stauferzeit* (Münster in Westfalen, 1979)
The Stavelot Triptych: Mosan Art and the Legend of the True Cross (exh. cat., ed. W. Voelkle; New York, Pierpont Morgan Lib., 1980)
R. Kroos: *Der Schrein des heiligen Servatius in Maastricht und die vier zugehörigen Reliquiare in Brüssel* (Munich, 1985), pp. 49–50, 94, 98–9

A. M. KOLDEWEIJ

Wicar, Jean-Baptiste(-Joseph) (*b* Lille, 22 Jan 1762; *d* Rome, 27 Feb 1834). French painter, draughtsman and collector. He was the son of a cabinetmaker and from 1772 studied drawing at the Ecole de Dessin in Lille with the painters Louis-Jean Guéret (*fl* 1767–77) and Louis Watteau. Initially he was supported in his studies by César d'Hespel, Bishop of Lille; subsequently he obtained a stipend from the city of Lille, to study for two years in Paris with the engraver Jacques-Philippe Lebas. In 1781 Wicar entered the studio of Jacques-Louis David, whom he accompanied to Rome in 1784, returning to Paris the following year; in 1787 he began to make designs for a catalogue of the Florentine grand-ducal collection, *Tableaux, statues, bas-reliefs et camées de la Galerie de Florence et du Palais Pitti*; the four-volume work was published between 1789 and 1807.

Wicar spent the early years of the French Revolution in Florence and Rome. Returning to Paris in 1793, he was appointed a member and then Secretary of the Société

Populaire et Républicaine des Arts; he participated in the official commissions of the National Convention and was named a member of the Conservatoire du Muséum. With the fall of Robespierre, Wicar lost his position and was briefly imprisoned; he returned to Italy in 1797, having been appointed by the French authorities to select works of art to be removed to France. He spent the rest of his life in Italy, chiefly in Rome and Naples, where Joseph Bonaparte made him Director of the academy of fine arts. A popular painter of portraits and history paintings in the style of David, he was elected to the Accademia di S Luca, Rome, and to academies in Milan and Bologna, and was appointed Chevalier de l'Ordre des Deux Siciles.

Beginning around 1795, Wicar made three successive collections of high-quality, mostly Italian drawings. His first collection, which included a number of important drawings by Raphael, was left for safe-keeping in Florence, where Antonio Fédi (1771–1843) sold them to the English collector William Young Ottley. In 1823 the collection was sold through the dealer Samuel Woodburn to Thomas Lawrence.

In 1801 Wicar began a second collection of Italian drawings, which in 1823 he sold to Woodburn, who resold it to Thomas Dimsdale; after the latter's death the best Italian drawings entered Lawrence's collection, and many of them, including a large collection of drawings by Raphael, eventually passed to Oxford University and the British Museum. Through Woodburn, other drawings were bought by William II of the Netherlands (1792–1849), the Louvre, the British Museum and various private collectors. Wicar's third and final collection included many of the drawings from his first, which he had reclaimed from Fédi. He bequeathed around 1300 drawings and some other works of art to the Société des Sciences et des Arts de Lille, to which he had been elected in 1805; this collection became the core of the cabinet de dessins at the Musée des Beaux-Arts in Lille.

Wicar's Italian drawings represented virtually all subjects and periods from the early Quattrocento to his own time; there were also German, French and Netherlandish drawings and over 3000 engravings by Albrecht Dürer, Lucas van Leyden, Giovanni Battista Piranesi and others. Wicar also owned bas-reliefs and paintings, including a number of copies of Italian Renaissance paintings, as well as a portrait of *Philip IV* by Velázquez and a *Deposition* by Fra Angelico (both Lille, Mus. B.-A.). Several inventories of his collections were made: when he left Naples in 1807; at the request of Pius VII in 1826; and after Wicar's death.

UNPUBLISHED SOURCES
Rome, Archv Cent. Stato, Camerale II, Busta 7, f. 200, no. 99 [inventory of Wicar's collection made at the order of Pius VII; copy of provenance index, Santa Monica, CA. Getty Cent.]
Santa Monica, CA, Getty Cent. [letter from J.-B. Wicar to Francesco Giangiacomo, 27 May 1807; includes list of 50 paintings in his collection]

BIBLIOGRAPHY
Ville de Lille, Musée Wicar: Catalogue des dessins et objets d'art légués par J.-B. Wicar (Lille, 1856)
L. Gonse: 'Le Musée Wicar', *Gaz. B.-A.*, n. s. 1, xiv (1876), pp. 406–13; xv (1877), pp. 80–95, 386–401; xvi (1877), pp. 393–409, 551–60; xvii (1878), pp. 44–70, 193–205
B. F. Beaucamp: *Le Peintre lillois Jean-Baptiste Wicar (1762–1834): Son oeuvre et son temps* (doctoral thesis, Lille, U., 1939)
Collection J. B. Wicar du Musée de Lille: Dessins de Raphaël (exh. cat., Lille, Mus. B.-A., 1961)
M. V. Cresti: 'Disegni di J. B. Wicar all'Accademia di Belle Arti di Perugia: Una galleria di ritratti napoleonici', *Florence et la France: Rapports sous la Révolution et l'Empire, Actes du colloque, Florence, 1971,* pp. 387–97
F. Mazzocca: 'Canova e Wicar', *Florence et la France: Rapports sous la Révolution et l'Empire, Actes du colloque, Florence, 1971,* pp. 399–436
R. W. Scheller: 'The Case of the Stolen Raphael Drawings', *Master Drgs*, xi (1973), pp. 119–37
Le Chevalier Wicar: Peintre, dessinateur et collectionneur lillois (Lille, 1984)
M. Gordon and M. Aldega: *Jean-Baptiste-Joseph Wicar: Drawings* (in preparation)   □

Wichman, Erich (*b* Utrecht, 11 Aug 1890; *d* Amsterdam, 1 Jan 1929). Dutch painter and printmaker. He studied in Germany (1904–7) and from 1909 read chemistry and history of art at the University of Utrecht. He also took painting lessons with A. van Krefeld. Between 1914 and 1921 he worked in Amsterdam as a painter, writer and critic. In 1913 he exhibited his first abstract paintings, in which Futurist and Expressionist influences, and in particular that of Vasily Kandinsky, can be seen. As well as paintings, murals, watercolours and drawings he produced etchings, engravings and lithographs. He also made jewellery boxes in silver and enamel and masks in bronze and silver, all in an Expressionist style. At the same time he published in *Der Sturm* magazine. He contributed to the Erste Deutsche Herbstsalon in Berlin (1913) and to the Salon des Indépendants in Paris (1914). From 1915 he made caricatures. With Theo van Doesburg in 1916 he was a founder-member of De Anderen. The magazine *De Stijl* invited him to contribute in 1917, but later, in 1919, he dissociated himself from it. Between 1921 and 1924 he travelled to Paris, Vienna, Berlin, Munich and Italy. He returned an admirer of Benito Mussolini and set up an anarcho-fascist party. From 1927 he worked for the fascist publication *De Bezem*. In 1925 he made some stained-glass windows for the Dutch pavilion at the *Exposition internationale des arts décoratifs et industriels modernes* in Paris.

BIBLIOGRAPHY
Erich Wichman, 1890–1929: Tussen idealisme en rancune [Erich Wichman, 1890–1929: between idealism and rancour] (exh. cat., Utrecht, Cent. Mus., 1983)

JOHN STEEN

Wichmann, Ludwig (Wilhelm) (*b* Potsdam, 10 Oct 1788; *d* Berlin, 29 June 1859). German sculptor. He entered Johann Gottfried Schadow's studio at the age of 12. One of his first independent works was the *Figure of a Sleeping Girl* (1806; Berlin, Alte N.G.), which was for a long time considered to be Schadow's work. After a period (1809–13) in the Paris studios of François-Joseph Bosio and Jacques-Louis David, in which sculptors and engravers also worked, Wichmann returned to Schadow's studio in Berlin. In 1818 he succeeded Emanuel Bardou (1744–1818) as sculpture tutor at the Kunst- und Gewerbeschule, and he became a member of the Akademie der Künste and tutor in ornamentation the following year.

After a trip to Italy (1819–21) with his brother Karl (1775–1836), also a sculptor, Wichmann established a studio with him in Berlin. They primarily undertook portrait commissions and made a name for themselves in this genre; the best portrait busts of this period include *Tobias Feilner* and *Prince Radziwill*. Wichmann was enlisted by Christian Daniel Rauch as a collaborator on the memorial monument to the *Wars of Liberation*, on the Kreuzberg, and from 1820 onwards he executed eight large statues representing allegories of battle, after his own designs, and from those of Rauch and Friedrich Tieck.

Wichmann also received commissions from Karl Friedrich Schinkel, which included *St Michael and Two Angels* (1828) over the portal of the Friedrich Werderscher Kirche, executed in terracotta, and four female figures, in sandstone, as acroteria for the Altes Museum, Berlin (*in situ*). For the Berlin Schlossbrücke he produced one of the eight marble groups, *Nike Raises the Wounded Man*, in 1853. His late works include two monumental statues of *Johann Joachim Winckelmann*: in bronze for the *Monument to the Scholar as Writer* in Stendal (1846–59); and in marble for that of the *Working Archaeologist* (Berlin, Altes Mus.).

BIBLIOGRAPHY

Thieme–Becker

J. G. Schadow: *Kunst-Werke und Kunst-Ansichten*, (Berlin, 1849, rev., ed. G. Eckardt, 1987)

'G. Schadow und sein Schülerkreis', *Johann Gottfried Schadow* (exh. cat., E. Berlin, N.G., 1964–5), pp. 246–52

P. Bloch and W. Grzimek: *Das klassische Berlin: Die Berliner Bildhauerschule im 19. Jahrhundert* (Vienna, 1978), pp. 55–8

Ethos und Pathos: Die Berliner Bildhauerschule, 1786–1914 (exh. cat., ed. P. Bloch, S. Einholz and J. von Simson; Berlin, Hamburg. Bahnhof, 1990)

JUTTA VON SIMSON

Wicker. Term that describes both natural and man-made materials used for BASKETWORK; in the late 20th century it became almost exclusively associated with furniture. The natural materials, which are still worked mainly by hand, are obtained from the willow family (*Salix*) and from the trailing, vinelike rattan palm (*Calamus* and *Daemonorops*); the hard outer skin of the rattan provides 'cane', which is split and used for weaving, while the hard inner core is properly known as 'reed', but also called cane. The artificial fibres are made mainly from machine-woven, twisted paper, often stiffened with glue sizing and reinforced with fine metal wire.

Wickerwork is as old as basketmaking, itself one of the oldest known crafts. The materials are inexpensive, pliant and easy to work when wet, and robust structures can be made by interweaving a stout framework of rods or stakes with cane or fresh osier withies. Evidence from Mesopotamia, Egypt, Greece and Rome suggests that in ancient times a wide range of products was made, including seat furniture, footstools, headrests, cradles, coffins, mats, hats, shoes and tea-strainers, as well as an enormous variety of boxes and baskets. In fact, until the 19th century the vast majority of wicker items produced all over the world were non-furniture objects. These have been mainly appreciated by anthropologists and ethnographers: art and design historians, generally speaking, have considered them unworthy of attention because of their humble materials and association with everyday utilities and work. By contrast, the study of wicker furniture is validated because, at the very end of the 19th century and at the beginning of the 20th, it became a central concern of avant-garde architects and designers. At that period European design reformers became fascinated by what they considered ethnic craftwork, uncorrupted by the effects of industrialization and supposedly offering pure examples of function determining form. Through their efforts, exhibitions of such work, including a great deal of basketry, regularly toured around art and design institutions in Britain, Austria and Germany in order that designers and manufacturers might better understand the relationship of function and material to form and decoration.

1. Before 1900. 2. 1900 and after.

1. BEFORE 1900. The earliest surviving wicker furniture was made in ancient Egypt, where it was preserved by the extremely dry atmosphere of the tombs. The pieces indicate a similarity of construction, particularly in the wrapping of the joints, to techniques used in the late 20th century, as do those illustrated in ancient Greek and Roman stone carvings. Wicker furniture was described by such Roman authors as Pliny (*see* ROME, ANCIENT, §X, 3), who said that soft, pliant willow provided great comfort, especially when used for reclining chairs; but there is no evidence that its use by the wealthier classes continued after the collapse of the Roman empire.

The making of wicker furniture was an extension of basketmaking and therefore took place in willow-growing/basketmaking areas. Little is known about it during the Middle Ages, but it appears to have been a relatively cheap product used by the poorer classes right up to the 19th century. By the 16th century references to 'twiggen', 'wanded', wicker, willow, 'rodd', withy and osier chairs (to name the commoner regional terms) abound in household inventories from all levels of society. Wicker was also widely used to make cradles and birdcages, sometimes for firescreens, and occasionally for the side panels of food cupboards. Where timber was scarce, it was used for beds, hanging shelves, window shutters and coffins. Basketwork chairs were used by nursing mothers, the old and the infirm; they were also considered particularly suitable for infants.

Cane was introduced into European furniture-making in the second half of the 17th century, when it was imported from the Malay Peninsula by the East India Company. It became fashionable in England and France for weaving the backs and seats of chairs. These caned chairs, as they are known to distinguish them from later cane ones, were light and pleasantly exotic, and they remained in favour with the upper classes throughout the 18th century. It was only in the second half of the 19th century, when the tough, fibrous core of Malaysian and Indonesian rattan palm began to be used in China, Europe and the USA, that cane furniture and wickerwork became widespread, the peak of their popularity lasting from *c.* 1870 to 1920.

Wickerwork appealed to the general mood of Orientalism, and its handcrafted nature attracted adherents of the Arts and Crafts Movement, as did its aesthetic qualities, which also found admirers in the Aesthetic Movement. 'Artistic, Odd and Inexpensive', it was the perfect way for the newly rich middle classes of the USA and Europe to add touches of beauty and exoticism to their homes and gardens without financial ruination. Although wickerwork had never been very expensive, the large-scale production and mail-order distribution of the larger American companies of the second half of the 19th century made this furniture more widely available to the American domestic market and to foreign consumers than ever before.

Wicker furniture had been made in the USA in colonial times, but not a great deal was produced. In the early 19th century, however, caned seat furniture became popular, and in the 1870s the machine-weaving of sheets of cane was introduced, together with machines for boring holes in seat furniture in order to accelerate the production of caned seats. Imported wicker furniture, mainly from East Asia, was gaining in popularity around the middle of the century, but a dramatic development in wicker furniture production within the USA meant that by 1860 the vast bulk of it was manufactured internally. This was due, in part, to the entrepreneurial activities of one man, a Massachusetts grocer named Cyrus Wakefield, who in 1844 began experimenting with the rattan ballast discarded on the dockside after it had been used to protect cargoes from the East. By 1855 he had founded what was to become a highly successful business importing rattan and producing furniture. At first, he combined cane (usually wrapped around a wooden frame) with locally grown willow; later, he utilized the strong inner core of the cane. In 1897 the Wakefield Rattan Co. merged with Heywood Bros of Gardner, MA (the largest chair manufacturer in the USA, which specialized in bentwood, Windsor and wicker chairs), to become the world's largest producer of wicker furniture.

The pieces, which became increasingly ornate as the century progressed, were enormously popular as porch and garden furniture and also began to be accepted as indoor furniture. The range of products was vast: the 1885 Wakefield catalogue illustrated 71 different designs for rocking-chairs alone (priced at £2–17); it also showed suites of indoor furniture, together with a host of individual pieces, including baby-carriages, work-baskets, lampstands, bookcases and music stands. The use of lacquer introduced colour into the furniture from 1883. Although

some pieces continued to be imported from East Asia, notably the well-known 'Peacock throne' and 'Hour-glass' chair popularized at the Philadelphia Centennial Exhibition of 1876, the American wicker industry grew from strength to strength until, at the beginning of the 20th century, it met with unexpected competition from abroad. This time the threat of imports came not from Asia but from well-designed and well-made cane furniture from Austria, Germany and Britain.

2. 1900 AND AFTER. Willow work had been carried out in parts of the Austro-Hungarian empire since the late 1820s, when the government sponsored basketmaking as a winter occupation in agricultural areas. State subsidies assisted the development of new and better types of willow, and the craft was taught by teachers trained at the Imperial School, Vienna. By c. 1900 the curriculum of the school reflected the new ideas about art and design prevalent in the Austrian capital. The outburst of creative activity in Vienna in the late 1890s gave birth to cooperative ventures between artists, architects and designers and local crafts or trades in order to produce relatively cheap items of everyday use. Leading members of the Vienna Secession, in a desire to democratize art and design, concerned themselves with designing furniture in willow, cane and bentwood (e.g. chairs designed by Hans Vollmer, 1904; see fig. 1).

In Germany the number of firms producing cane and willow furniture in the years before World War I was extensive. Just as in Austro-Hungary, avant-garde architects and designers believed design should be applied to everyday items produced in bulk, and not simply to expensive one-off products. Many of them, most notably Henry Van de Velde, Peter Behrens and Richard Riemerschmid, believed that there should be closer links between educational institutions and the manufacturing sector, and all three men produced designs for cane or willow furniture. Many German firms decided to employ a professional designer, often an architect or academic, or

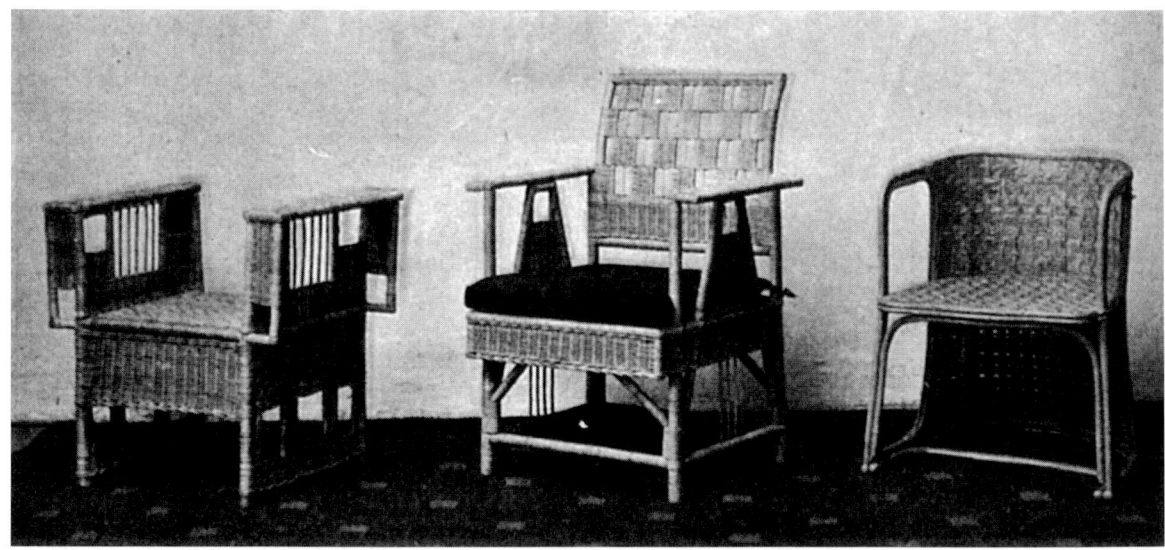

1. Wicker chairs designed by Hans Vollmer and made by Prag-Rudniker, Austria; from an illustration in *The Studio* (Jan 1904)

2. Wicker furniture made by Dryad of Leicester on display at the Franco-British Exhibition, Brussels, 1908

a combination of both, in order to raise the design standards of their goods so that the German economy might better compete in international markets. The most notable partnership between designer and cane manufacturer in Germany was that between the firm of Theodor Reimann of Dresden and Richard Riemerschmid.

Cane and willow furniture was produced in other European countries, including the Netherlands (where the leading architect P. J. H. Cuypers designed cane furniture), Switzerland, Belgium and France, but it was England that was to provide the strongest competition to the German and Austrian firms that were exporting well-designed and soundly made goods all over the world, including Britain itself.

When *The Studio* published an article on Austrian wicker furniture in 1904, the British market was swamped with imports while the native trade languished. Determined to redress the situation, Benjamin Fletcher, headmaster of Leicester School of Art, decided to emulate the Continental initiatives and to make links between his institution and local crafts and trades (Leicester was situated near a traditional willow-growing area and already had an established labour force). He visited Austria and Germany in 1906 and brought back some cane furniture to Leicester, where, with the assistance of Charles Crampton, one of the most skilled basketmakers in the area, he began to experiment in the design and construction of cane furniture.

In 1907 the firm of Dryad was founded in Leicester by Fletcher's close friend Harry Hardy Peach (1874–1936), with Fletcher as designer and Crampton one of the four

workers. Dryad aimed at producing well-made, well-designed furniture that was light, comfortable and appropriate to modern living. Both Fletcher and Peach considered the rigid geometric shapes favoured by the Vienna Secession inappropriate to such a pliant material as cane. In the manner of certain German designs, Dryad pieces show a greater sensitivity to the material and reflect Arts and Crafts notions of honesty in materials. Furthermore, the originators of Dryad considered that harsh geometric forms did not 'commend themselves to British notions of comfort or fit the homely reserve of English houses'. In Dryad furniture (see fig. 2) the comfort came mainly from the shaping of the basic form, which, when woven with the slightly springy cane, rendered virtually unnecessary the use of upholstery or cushions. In general, Fletcher's designs adapted the sense of movement found in Art Nouveau to the malleability of the cane, restricting the stylistic vocabulary of the Vienna Secession to detailing and an emphasis on the linear. Dryad was immensely successful, employing nearly 200 people by 1914, by which date it was exporting its goods all over the world, including the British colonies and South America. It even broke into the massive American market, obtaining retail outlets in New York and Chicago.

Other new firms were established in the area, but after World War I the trade became increasingly competitive. The war seriously affected production, and some firms never fully recovered; those that did found that they faced even stiffer competition as firms sought to keep down costs. Some did it by using less skilled labour, but this showed in loose and uneven weaving, some by adopting more openweave styles, which took less labour and materials. Others abandoned willow and cane in favour of the new 'artificial fibers' marketed in the USA from 1904, but it was not until Marshall B. Lloyd (1858–1927), of Menominee, MI, invented a machine in 1917 to weave wicker from twisted paper that the price of wicker furniture was dramatically reduced. The machine-woven wicker (reinforced by thin wire) offered a close weave at cheap costs and soon put many cane and willow furniture-makers out of business. No firm recognized the new threat more than Heywood-Wakefield, which took over the Lloyd Manufacturing Co. in 1921. A franchise was established in Britain in 1922, and W. Lusty & Sons Ltd of London produced its famous 'Lloyd Loom' pieces from 1922 to 1962. In 1912 fibre furniture had accounted for only 15% of wicker furniture production in the USA, but by 1920 it had risen to almost 50% and by the end of the decade to 80%. The situation was similar in Britain, as wicker firms either abandoned cane and willow or produced artificial fibres in an effort to stay in business.

The rapid demise of the wicker furniture trade in the 1930s should not obscure its immense popularity in the early 1920s, when wicker graced some of the world's finest ocean liners, hotels, restaurants and cinemas, as well as country clubs, sports clubs and vehicles, from aeroplanes to motor-buses. It has been argued that once wicker furniture was made by machine it lost some of its charm, but this can hardly account for its downfall in the 1930s in the face of Modernism. Customers who wanted light and modern-looking furniture appropriate for the new machine age then chose tubular steel instead of wicker. There was some copying in cane of the popular styles in tubular steel, particularly in Britain, Germany and the USA, but the days of wicker were numbered. Both natural and artificial wicker seemed quaint by comparison with the hard, shiny steel. Some use was made of cane in the 1950s, when sculptural forms were sought after, but by then there were a whole new range of plastics available, which were just as light, colourful and malleable but spoke more of a machine age. In the 1980s, however, wicker returned to favour, precisely because of its nostalgic references to a pre-machine age.

See also BAMBOO.

BIBLIOGRAPHY

A Completed Century: The Story of the Heywood-Wakefield Company, 1826–1926 (Boston, 1926)
R. Saunders: *Collecting and Restoring Wicker Furniture* (New York, 1976)
P. Corbin: *All About Wicker* (New York, 1978)
F. Thompson: *The Complete Wicker Book* (New York, 1979)
Cane Furniture Hand Made by the Angraves [cat. pubd by Angraves Invincible Registered Cane Furniture Ltd] (Leicester, [1980])
G. Dale: 'Lloyd Loom Furniture', *Ant. Colr*, li/2 (1980), pp. 52–4
A. Heseltine: *Baskets and Basket Making* (Aylesbury, 1982)
Heywood Brothers and Wakefield Company: *Classic Wicker Furniture: The Complete 1898–1899 Illustrated Catalog*, intro. R. Saunders (London, 1982)
R. Saunders: *Collectors Guide to American Wicker Furniture* (New York, 1983)
P. Kirkham: 'Willow and Cane Furniture in Austria, Germany and England, *c.* 1900–14', *Furn. Hist.*, xxi (1985), pp. 128–31
——: 'Dryad Cane Furniture', *Ant. Collct.*, xix/9 (1985), pp. 11–15
——: *Harry Peach, Dryad and the DIA* (London, 1986)
E. B. Ottilinger: *Korbmöbel* (Salzburg, 1990)
C. G. Gilbert: *English Vernacular Furniture, 1750–1900* (London, 1991)
J. Lee Curtis: *Lloyd Loom: Woven Fibre Furniture* (London, 1991)

PAT KIRKHAM

Wickes, George (*bapt* Bury St Edmunds, 7 July 1698; *d* Thurston, Suffolk, 31 Aug 1761). English goldsmith. In 1712 he was apprenticed to the goldsmith Samuel Wastell, and in 1720 he gained the freedom of the Goldsmiths' Company, London. He registered his first marks in 1721–2, giving his address as Threadneedle Street; his earliest known extant works, two silver mugs (priv. col., see Barr, fig. 5), date from this time. In 1730 he moved to Norris Street and entered into a partnership with John Craig, which continued until 1735, when Wickes moved to the King's Arms, Panton Street, and began working independently. In that year he was appointed goldsmith to Frederick, Prince of Wales, and the ledgers of his business (London, Garrard & Co.; V&A) record the numerous commissions from royalty, aristocracy and gentry, and are the only surviving examples from the 18th century, indicating that Wickes built up a large and successful enterprise. Such members of the Prince's circle as Francis, Lord North (later Earl of Guilford), who ordered tureens from Wickes in 1735 (priv. col., see exh. cat., no. 2), may have been influential in his appointment. The Pelham Gold Cup (1736; priv. col., see exh. cat., no. 5), designed by William Kent and made for Colonel James Pelham, Private Secretary to the Prince of Wales, is one of Wickes's most important works; the design was reproduced by John Vardy in his book *Some Designs of Mr Inigo Jones and Mr William Kent* (1744) and was widely copied by later London goldsmiths. The elaborate silver-gilt centrepiece (1745; Brit. Royal Col.) made for the Prince by Wickes was also based on a design by Kent. Most of Wickes's work is in the exuberant Rococo style popularized by the Prince, for example the 170-piece dinner service (1745–7; priv. col., see Barr, app. II) made for James Fitzgerald, 20th Earl of Kildare (later Duke of Leinster; 1722–73). Such features as castwork in Wickes's pieces are of equal quality to that made by contemporary Huguenot goldsmiths, for example Paul de Lamerie; in fact, the attribution of a number of works to either Wickes or de Lamerie has been disputed. The ledgers of Wickes's business indicate that he employed a number of subcontractors, the most important of whom was Edward Wakelin, who had virtually taken control of the manufacturing side of the firm by 1747. He supplied Wickes with tableware in the Rococo style, for example a set of silver-gilt vases (1753; Burghley House, Cambs) and an unusual pair of tureens with wave-patterned and ribbed bodies (1755; Al Tajir priv. col.; see exh. cat., no. 15). In 1750 Wickes took his former apprentice Samuel Netherton (1723–1803), and not Wakelin, into partnership. In 1760, however, on the retirement of both Wickes and Netherton, Wakelin and John Parker (who had been apprenticed to Wickes in 1751) took over the business.

BIBLIOGRAPHY

A. G. Grimwade: *Rococo Silver, 1727–1765* (London, 1974)
——: *London Goldsmiths, 1697–1837: Their Marks and Lives* (London, 1976, rev. 3/1990)
E. Barr: *George Wickes, 1698–1761: Royal Goldsmith* (New York, 1980)
Royal Goldsmiths: The Garrard Heritage (exh. cat., London, Garrard & Co., 1991)

SARAH YATES

Wickhoff, Franz (*b* Steyr, 7 May 1853; *d* Venice, 6 April 1909). Austrian art historian. He came from a respected burgher family from Upper Austria. After studying art history at Vienna University under Rudolf von Eitelberger (1817–85) and Moriz Thausing (1838–84), he attended the Institut für österreichische Geschichtsforschung (1877–9), where he was trained in philological techniques of documentary research. Classical archaeology also made a lasting impression on him. In 1880 he successfully submitted a dissertation, *Eine Zeichnung Dürers nach der Antike*. From 1879 to 1885 he was curator of the textiles collection at the Österreichisches Museum für Kunst und Industrie. In 1882 he became a private scholar; in 1885 he was appointed an associate professor and in 1891 a full professor of art history at the University of Vienna.

Wickhoff opposed dilettantism and undisciplined enthusiasm in aesthetic matters and was keen to put art history on an exact scientific foundation. He took as his model the self-styled scientific 'experimental' method of Giovanni Morelli, which he developed into a comparative analysis of styles.

Apart from the strict, methodical study of the work of art itself, it was no less important to Wickhoff to take account of its position within the context of intellectual and cultural history. He expressed this idea in numerous essays, above all on Renaissance art, that also reflected his preference for Italian landscapes. His fundamental concern was to present all artistic creation within a global historical context, setting out his programme in 'Über die historische Einheitlichkeit der gesamten Kunstentwicklung' (1898). This epoch-spanning perspective gave rise to his main work on the 6th-century manuscript known as the 'Vienna Genesis' (Vienna, Österreich. Nbib., Cod. theol. gr. 31), which he published in 1895 in collaboration with Wilhelm von Hartel (1839–1907). This work, like the contemporary studies of Alois Riegl, helped initiate a reassessment of the art of late antiquity, formerly regarded as a symptom of decadence. It is also notable for Wickhoff's coinage of the term 'illusionistic' to describe the style of the manuscript's illuminations, which he upheld as a creative achievement.

Wickhoff showed a profound understanding of contemporary art in his public support for Gustav Klimt, moreover showing himself to be a talented landscape painter in a number of small works. He also had strong literary inclinations. His uncompromising method made Wickhoff the real founder of the Vienna school of art history. His institute produced numerous prominent scholars, including Max Dvořák, Hans Tietze and Julius von Schlosser. His scholarly approach is documented in the review *Kunstgeschichtliche Anzeigen*, founded in 1904. In 1891–2 he produced a catalogue of the Italian drawings in the Graphische Sammlung Albertina, the most important outcome of his practical work. The *Beschreibendes Verzeichnis der illuminierten Handschriften in Österreich*, the first two volumes of which he published in 1905, was another of his initiatives, as was an unrealized project for a catalogue raisonné of Raphael's drawings.

UNPUBLISHED SOURCES
U. Vienna, Institut für Kunstgeschichte [letters, mss, notes, three ptgs]

WRITINGS
'Die italienischen Handzeichnungen der Albertina', *Jb. Ksthist. Samml. Allhöch. Ksrhaus.*, xii (1891), pp. ccv–cccxiv; xiii (1892), pp. clxxv–cclxxxiii

W. von Hartel and F. Wickhoff, eds: 'Die Wiener Genesis', *Jb. Ksthist. Samml. Allhöch. Ksrhaus.*, xv/xvi (1895), supplement; *R* Graz (1970)
'Über die historische Einheitlichkeit der gesamten Kunstentwicklung', *Festgaben für Büdinger* (Innsbruck, 1898), pp. 3–11
Kunstgeschichtliche Anzeigen (Innsbruck, 1904–9)
Beschreibendes Verzeichnis der illuminierten Handschriften in Österreich, 2 vols (Leipzig, 1905)
M. Dvořák, ed.: *Die Schriften Franz Wickhoffs*, 2 vols (Berlin, 1912–13)

BIBLIOGRAPHY
NÖB
M. Dvořák: 'Franz Wickhoff', *Biog. Jb. & Dt. Nekrol.*, xiv (1909), pp. 317–26
G. Glück: 'Franz Wickhoff', *Repert. Kstwiss.*, xxxii (1909), pp. 386–90
J. von Schlosser: 'Nekrolog: Franz Wickhoff', *Mitt. Österreich. Inst. Geschforsch.*, xxx (1909), pp. 554–60 [bibliog.]
H. Tietze: 'Franz Wickhoff', *Kunstchronik*, xx (1909), pp. 369–72
M. Dvořák: 'Franz Wickhoffs letzte literarische Projekte', *Offizieller Bericht über die Verhandlungen des IX. internationalen kunsthistorischen Kongresses in München 1909* (Leipzig, 1911), pp. 63–72
J. von Schlosser: 'Die Wiener Schule der Kunstgeschichte: Rückblick auf ein Säkulum deutscher Gelehrtenarbeit in Österreich', *Mitt. Österreich. Inst. Geschforsch.*, xiii (1934), pp. 161–81
G. Glück: 'Franz Wickhoff', *Alte & Neue Kst*, ii (1953), pp. 41–5
F. Glück: 'Briefe von Franz Wickhoff und Max Dvořák an Gustav Glück', *Festschrift Karl M. Swoboda* (Vienna, 1959), pp. 103–32
I. Kalavrezou-Maxeiner: 'Franz Wickhoff: Kunstgeschichte als Wissenschaft', *Akten des XXV. internationalen Kongresses für Kunstgeschichte. Wien und die Entwicklung der kunsthistorischen Methode* (Vienna, 1983), pp. 17–22
E. Lachnit: 'Hermann Dollmayr, ein frühvollendeter Repräsentant der Wiener kunsthistorischen Schule und sein Wirken im Kamptal; mit einem Anhang: Ein Brief von Franz Wickhoff zur Veröffentlichung seiner Dollmayr-Biographie', *Kamptal-Studien*, v (Gars am Kamp, 1985), pp. 149–62
——: 'Neuentdeckte Dokumente zum Professorenstreit um Klimts "Philosophie"', *Wien. Jb. Kstgesch.*, xxxix (1986), pp. 205–20

EDWIN LACHNIT

Widener, Joseph E. (*b* Philadelphia, PA, 19 Aug 1872; *d* Elkins Park, nr Philadelphia, 26 Oct 1943). American collector and museum patron. Sharing his passion he developed the extensive art collection formed by his father, P. A. B. Widener (1834–1915), with continued help from their friend John G. Johnson. Among additions he made were the painting by Raphael known as the Small Cowper *Madonna* (*c*. 1505), two paintings by Rembrandt (the *Portrait of a Lady with an Ostrich-feather Fan*, and the *Portrait of a Gentleman with Tall Hat*, both *c*. 1667) and Donatello's *David* of the Casa Martelli. His father had left him the disposition, but not the ownership, of the collection, which was to go to a public institution. In 1941 Joseph E. Widener chose the National Gallery of Art in Washington, DC. The 76 important paintings and thousands of decorative objects (valued at £30–50 million), comprise one of the gallery's five founding donations. The collection was dismantled and the objects removed from Lynnewood Hall, Widener's home near Philadelphia, and he helped plan its installation in the museum built by his friend Andrew Mellon. From 1919 to 1924 Widener served as trustee of the Philadelphia Museum of Art.

BIBLIOGRAPHY
Works of Art from the Widener Collection, National Gallery of Art (Washington, 1942)
J. Walker: *The National Gallery of Art* (New York, 1975, 2/1984)

GRETCHEN G. FOX

Widitz. *See* WEIDITZ.

Widman, Lazar (*b* Plzeň, 13 Dec 1697; *d* Jan 1769). Bohemian sculptor. His father, Kristián Widman (*d* 1725), was the sculptor of the Marian column (1681) in Plzeň and another (1713–14) in Písek. The sculptures of the latter, which is the more refined of the two, were probably the work of Lazar Widman, who was his father's apprentice but considerably surpassed him as an artist. In the 1730s he probably worked on statues for the bridge in Plzeň, and certainly on the Marian column (1740) in Stříbro. His oeuvre is extensive: in 1727 he made decorations for the palace chapel in Dolní Lukavice and worked for the counts of Vrtba. In 1735–8 he decorated their church in Žinkovy; around 1740, the palace chapel in Křimice; and in 1745, the *cour d'honneur*, the park and village green. The statues there represent the highest point of his early work: their form is clear, the movement graceful and the drapery cut into dramatic folds. Their subjects—Amazons and exotic slaves—are as unusual as the materials: alabaster, bone and marble. Of these there remain some small carvings of Bacchanalian scenes, the figures of *Cronos* and *Niobe*, nude wrestlers and large groups of Antique subjects with a background of ruins: the movement is mostly skilfully rendered. At the same location is Widman's remarkable large sculptural group of *St George and the Dragon* (1746). Around the same time he decorated the church in nearby Vejprnice: the statues there are more emphatic in their movement, while their drapery is more classicizing. His most interesting work is that for yet another church of the Vrtba counts, the Romanesque St Gall in Poříčí nad Sázavou (1745–51), where he worked jointly with the cabinetmaker Daniel Pilát on its furnishings, made in the historical mode of the Baroque Gothic. The statues from this church have flowing gestures, simple drapery and well-defined facial expressions. Even more classicizing are his statues (*c.* 1747) for the altar in the Konopiště palace chapel, the statue of *St Joseph* (after 1750) situated at the corner of the Servite priory in the Old Town Square in Prague and the garden statues in Smilkov. In his last works, the side altars (1762) for Vejprnice and the statues (1768) on the wall surrounding the church in Žinkovy, Widman anticipated the changes to come and explored to the utmost limits the potential of his style.

BIBLIOGRAPHY
Thieme–Becker
P. Toman: *Nový slovník československých výtvarných umělců* [New dictionary of Czechoslovak artists], ii (Prague, 1950), p. 698
O. J. Blažíček: *Sochařství baroku v Čechách* [Baroque sculpture in Bohemia] (Prague, 1958), pp. 114, 221–7
                                    IVO KOŘÁN

Widnmann, Ritter Max von (*b* Eichstätt, 16 Oct 1812; *d* Munich, 6 March 1895). German sculptor. He entered the Munich Akademie der Bildenden Künste as a pupil of Konrad Eberhard and Ludwig von Schwanthaler as early as 1825. He continued his studies under Bertel Thorvaldsen during a period from 1836 to 1839 spent in Rome, and under his influence he completely adopted the Neoclassical style. On his return to Munich he attracted the attention of Ludwig I, King of Bavaria, who commissioned many sculptures from him. After Schwanthaler's death in 1848 Widnmann inherited his position at the Munich Akademie, where he taught sculpture students until his retirement in 1887.

On his appointment Widnmann was described by the Akademie as belonging to the 'purely classical trend' and manifesting 'at the same time his skill in treating Romantic subjects'; the official commissions allocated by Ludwig I, such as the conventional busts for the Ruhmeshalle or the colossal statues of outstanding Bavarian historical personalities, epitomize the conflict of aspirations in sculpture in Munich at this period. The final impression made by Widnmann's 1862 statue of *Ludwig I* on the Odeonsplatz in Munich (based on a design by Schwanthaler) has been described as unfortunate, especially because of the unharmonious grouping of the horseman and the accompanying standing figures. He was more successful with the statue of *Schiller*, made for Munich in 1863 and now displayed on the Maximiliansplatz; this is one of Widnmann's most notable works, distinguished from his other Munich portrait commissions such as *Leo von Klenze* and *Goethe* by a certain spontaneity which enlivens the conventional gestures and attributes.

BIBLIOGRAPHY
ADB; Thieme–Becker
A. Heilmeyer: *Die Plastik des 19. Jahrhunderts in München* (Munich, 1931)
J. Gamer: 'Goethe-Denkmäler—Schiller-Denkmäler', *Denkmäler im 19. Jahrhundert: Deutung und Kritik*, ed. H.-E. Mittig and V. Plagemann (Munich, 1972), pp. 149–50
G. Finckh: '"Plastisch, das heisst antik, zu denken . . ." Die Bildhauerei an der Münchner Akademie und der Klassizismus von Roman Anton Boos (1733–1810) bis Adolf von Hildebrand (1849–1921)', *Tradition und Widerspruch: 175 Jahre Kunstakademie München*, ed. T. Zacharias (Munich, 1985)
          CLEMENTINE SCHACK VON WITTENAU

Więcek, Magdalena (*b* Katovice, Silesia, 23 July 1924). Polish sculptor. She studied at the Higher School of Plastic Arts, Sopot (1946–9), and at the Academy of Fine Arts, Warsaw (1949–51). She made her début in the early 1950s with several award-winning monumental Socialist Realist sculptures, such as *Miners* (versions of 1952 and 1954) and *Friendship* (1952; Warsaw, Pal. Cult. & Sci.). She contributed two works, *Mother* and *Protest*, to the famous exhibition of 1955 at the Arsenal Gallery in Warsaw that marked the end of Socialist Realism in the visual arts. These compositions, along with *Time of the Atom* and *Two* from the second half of the 1950s, are mutilated, expressive forms, representing distant reminders of once-living human bodies that have undergone a catastrophe and wasted away. She progressed in the 1960s to abstract sculptures (e.g. *Flame*, 1966), forms composed from plaster of Paris or concrete on a metal skeleton. After the mid-1960s her works were based on the principle of dualism and dialogue, which extended to both forms and materials (the plasticity of metal juxtaposed to the rigidity of stone). During the late 1960s and 1970s the cycles *Lotne*, *Oderwania* and *Sacra* appeared. These are dynamic, monumental compositions, often produced in a townscape of concrete housing estates. After 1977 she produced the *Dialogues with Time* cycles as well as drawings composed of alternating black-and-white areas intersected by black-and-white lines.

BIBLIOGRAPHY
Magdalena Więcek, rzeźby i rysunki [Magdalena Więcek, sculptures and drawings] (exh. cat., ed. L. Wilkowa; Poznań, N. Mus., 1974)
A. Kępińska: *Nowa sztuka polska w latach 1945–1978* [New Polish art 1945–1978] (Warsaw, 1981)
                                    EWA MIKINA

Wiedemann, Guillermo (*b* Munich, 1905; *d* Key Biscayne, FL, 1969). Colombian painter of German birth. He studied at the Kunstakademie in Munich under the German painter Hugo von Habermann (*b* 1899) and the German painter and printmaker Adolf Schinnerer (1876–1949). He lived in Berlin in 1931–2, coming into contact with Max Liebermann, and in 1933 he exhibited with the Neue Sezession in Munich. He decided to leave Germany for political reasons, particularly after Hitler's persecution of 'degenerate' art, and in 1939 he travelled to Colombia; he acquired Colombian nationality seven years later. He was immediately dazzled by the local population and by tropical plant life, which he began to interpret with an extremely expressive line and bold use of colour.

All vestiges of representation later disappeared from Wiedemann's work, and he devoted himself, particularly in his watercolours, to a lyrical use of colour that led him to pure abstraction. These paintings, in spite of their freedom of expression and colour, were characterized by strong lines and an underlying geometrical emphasis. Afterwards he made collages using humble materials such as wire, string, plaster, cloth and paper, which he transformed into aesthetically unified compositions notable for their rhythmic sequences. Wiedemann's work, particularly because of its poetic, spontaneous and experimental nature, influenced both abstract and figurative art in Colombia.

BIBLIOGRAPHY
M. E. Iriarte: *El arte descubre un mundo: Guillermo Wiedemann* (Bogotá, 1985)
Cien años de arte colombiano (exh. cat. by E. Serrano, Bogotá, Mus. A. Mod., 1985)

EDUARDO SERRANO

Wiedewelt, Johannes (*b* Copenhagen, 1 Sept 1731; *d* Copenhagen, 14 Dec 1802). Danish sculptor, writer and designer. He was the son of the sculptor Just Wiedewelt (1677–1757) and trained in the shop belonging to his father and godfather, the sculptor Didrik Gercken (1692–1778). In 1750 Wiedewelt travelled to Paris, where he worked under the sculptor Guillaume Coustou (ii), and studied contemporary French sculpture. Despite his subsequent admiration for Classical antiquity, he continued to work in this style throughout his career. In 1753 he won the silver medal from the Académie Royale de Peinture et Sculpture in Paris. The following year he went to Rome, where he came into contact with such leading cultural figures as Anton Raphael Mengs and Johann Joachim Winckelmann, whose knowledge of Classical art and judgement of contemporary works greatly influenced Wiedewelt. He kept all the studies made in Italy for later use as a source of inspiration.

Wiedewelt had returned to Copenhagen by 1758 and was soon elected a member of the Kongelige Danske Kunstakademi there. Among his first commissions were the marble sarcophagus of *Christian VI* (1760–68; Roskilde Cathedral, chapel of Frederick V) and the sculptural decoration in Italian and Norwegian marble and sandstone for the gardens of Fredensborg Palace, begun in 1760. After the death of Frederick V in 1766, Wiedewelt was commissioned to carve the marble monument (1769–77) to the king for his chapel in Roskilde Cathedral. The grandiose monument consists of a column representing the apotheosis, together with a portrait medallion of the king. Below is a sarcophagus with a relief representing

Peace, Prudence, Fortitude and the Felicity of the Century, virtues appropriate to the dead king's administration. On each side, personifications of Denmark and Norway mourn the monarch. In the following years Wiedewelt produced a substantial number of sculptures and decorations for the royal family, the nobility and the bourgeoisie. These included monuments, such as the memorial to *J. H. E. Bernstorff* (marble, 1783; Lyngbyvejen); sepulchral monuments, such as that to *Walter Titley*, an English minister (marble, 1769; Copenhagen, St Petri Kirke); and interior decoration, such as that for the banqueting hall of Christiansborg Palace (1765; destr. 1792).

In 1768–9 Wiedewelt travelled with Nicolas-Henri Jardin to France and England. On this trip he made careful notes of what he saw. His visits to Stonehenge and Stowe, Bucks, in England influenced his designs for Julianhøj (1776), an old barrow tumulus, and for the memorial grove (1779–89), both at JAEGERSPRIS. During the 1780s he was affected by illness but nevertheless continued to work steadily. His last years were troubled by financial difficulties, though he produced some of his most important works at this time, including the tombs of *Morten Wærn* (1797) and *Georg Nielsen* (1798; both Copenhagen, Assistens Cemetery) and the marble figure of Fidelity and a relief representing Justice on the Column of Liberty on Vesterbrogade, Copenhagen (1792–7). His last work was the granite monument to the sailors killed during Nelson's assault on Copenhagen in 1801 (1802; Copenhagen, Holmens Cemetery).

Wiedewelt also published a number of books, including *Tanker om smagen udi konsterne* [Thoughts on taste in the arts] (1762) in which he stated his views and opinions on art. This was of great importance for Danish art history, although the book demonstrates his dependence on the ideas of Winckelmann, and large parts of the book are taken directly from his writings. Wiedewelt also published an explanation of the drawings for the sculptures in Fredensborg gardens, under the title *Til Kongen* [To the King] (1762) and *Aegyptiske og Romerske oldsager* [Egyptian and Roman antiquities] (1786). He also made designs for coins and medals, such as those commemorating the death of Frederick V (1766) and the law of naturalization (1776; both Copenhagen, N. Mus.); furniture, such as the coin cabinets in the Royal Coin Collection of the Nationalmuseet, Copenhagen; festive decorations; and book illustrations and caricatures. Many of his drawings are in the library of the Kongelige Danske Kunstakademi in Copenhagen. Wiedewelt was a professor at the Kongelige Danske Kunstakademi in 1761 and was elected Director eight times. He drowned in circumstances that might suggest suicide. Wiedewelt was the first Danish artist to practise Neo-classicism using theoretical knowledge of Classical antiquity. The iconographic content of his work was of great importance to him, and he was painstakingly correct in his allegorical compositions, but his great dramatic sense, coupled with his technical brilliance, prevented a dry academicism.

WRITINGS
Tanker om smagen udi konsterne [Thoughts on taste in the arts] (Copenhagen, 1762)
Til Kongen [To the King] (Copenhagen, 1762)

Aegyptiske og Romerske oldsager [Egyptian and Roman antiquities] (Copenhagen, 1786)

BIBLIOGRAPHY

DBL

F. J. Meier: *Efterretninger om billedhuggeren Johannes Wiedewelt* [Information on the sculptor Johannes Wiedewelt] (Copenhagen, 1877)

K. W. Tesdorff: *Johann Wiedewelt: Dänemarks erster klassizistischer Bildhauer* (Copenhagen, 1933)

T. Holck-Colding: 'Johannes Wiedewelt, 1731–1802', *Dansk Kunst Historie*, ed. V. Poinlsen, E. Lassen and J. Danielsen, iii (Copenhagen, 1972), pp. 86–95

H. Lund: *Mindelunden i Jægerspris* (Copenhagen, 1976)

——: *De kongelige lysthaver* (Copenhagen, 1977)

——: 'Wiedewelts Dydens og Ærens Tempel', *Enten Eller* (exh. cat., ed. S. Brøgger; Copenhagen, Sophienholm, 1980), pp. 35–44

E. Brodersen: 'Wiedewelts møde med den engelske have' [Wiedewelt's encounter with the English garden], *Cras*, xxxv (1983), pp. 23–30

K. Kryger: 'Der Philosoph: Ein Raffaelisches Motiv in Wiedewelts Werk', *Hafnia*, ix (1983), pp. 9–24

——: *Allegori og borgerdyd: Studier i det nyklassicistiske gravmæle i Danmark, 1760–1820* [Allegory and civic virtue: studies in the Neo-classical sepulchral monuments in Denmark, 1760–1820] (Copenhagen, 1985)

Johannes Wiedewelt (exh. cat., ed. S. Brøgger; Copenhagen, Sophienholm, 1985–6)

KARIN KRYGER

Wiegele, Franz (*b* Nötsch, Kärnten, 23 Feb 1887; *d* Nötsch, 17 Dec 1944). Austrian painter. After training as a smith he studied at the Akademie der Bildenden Künste in Vienna from 1907 to 1911 and, as a member of the Neukunstgruppe, he was involved in the 1911 exhibition in Hagenbund. With the help of Klimt and Carl Moll he was able to travel to Paris, the Netherlands and Algiers in the following years. He was interned by the French in Algiers at the start of World War I and handed over to the Swiss in 1917 in an exchange of prisoners. From 1925 onwards he lived in Nötsch, where he was one of the founders of the Nötsch School with his brother-in-law Anton Kolig. He declined a professorship at the Akademie der Bildenden Künste in Vienna in 1936. He was killed during a bombing raid on Nötsch.

The main subject of Wiegele's oil paintings and drawings was the male form, in portraits, groups or nudes, although he preferred female models. Particularly in his early works the figures seem like painted sculptures, as in *Nudes in the Forest* (1911; Vienna, Belvedere). After 1920 he adopted a more open style of painting; the plasticity, emphasized in the main parts of the painting, is contrasted with a cursory application of paint at the edges, as in *Isepp Family Portrait* (1927–8; Vienna, Belvedere).

BIBLIOGRAPHY

R. Milesi: *Franz Wiegele* (Klagenfurt, 1957)

Franz Wiegele: Gemälde (exh. cat., ed. A. Rohsmann; Klagenfurt, Kärntner Landesgal., 1987)

EDWIN LACHNIT

Wiegers, Jan (*b* Kommerzijl, 31 July 1893; *d* Amsterdam, 30 Nov 1959). Dutch painter, sculptor and printmaker. He trained as a sculptor with Dirk de Vries Lam (1896–1937) at the Academie Minerva in Groningen, and he was taught painting at the Koninklijke Academie van Beeldende Kunsten in The Hague by Frederik Jansen (1856–1928) and at the Academie van Beeldende Kunsten in Rotterdam by the Belgian A. H. R. Van Maasdijk (1856–1931). In 1912 he visited the Sonderbund Exhibition in Cologne. With introductions from Van Maasdijk he travelled as 'churchpainter' through Germany and Switzerland.

In addition to painting and sculpture he produced woodcarvings and church furniture. In June 1918 he became one of the co-founders of De Ploeg, a society that aimed to bring Groningen artists together. During World War II the society was closed because the work of its members was considered degenerate. At this time Wiegers's work, much of which depicted landscapes and interiors, was influenced by the Bergen school and artists such as Henri Le Fauconnier and Leo Gestel. For reasons of health he stayed in Davos, Switzerland (1920–21), where he had close contacts with Ernst Ludwig Kirchner. He introduced Kirchner's Expressionism to his Dutch painter friends Jan Altink (1885–1971) and Johan Dijkstra (1896–1978), and his own paintings, drawings and woodcuts of this period show his influence. He also adopted Kirchner's painting technique of dissolving the oils in petrol with beeswax and then applying them on to an unprimed, absorbent coarse canvas (e.g. *Landscape with Red Trees*, c. 1924; Amsterdam, Stedel. Mus.). This gives his paintings a very matt appearance. Wiegers's etchings include a portrait of *Kirchner* (1925) and among his sculptures is a bust of *Hendrik Nicolaas Werkman* (1926; both Groningen, Groninger Mus.). In 1934 he moved to Amsterdam, where he co-founded the magazine *De kroniek van kunst en kultuur*.

BIBLIOGRAPHY

Jan Wiegers (exh. cat., Amsterdam, Stedel. Mus., 1960–61)

A. Venema: *De Ploeg, 1918–1930* (Baarn, 1978)

JOHN STEEN

Wiehl, Antonín (*b* Plasy, 26 April 1846; *d* Prague, 4 Nov 1910). Bohemian architect. He studied at the Czech Polytechnic (1863–8) with Josef Zítek. After completing his studies he worked with František Schmoranz in Slatiňany, where he was schooled in good craftsmanship. This was followed by a period as assistant to Josef Niklas (1817–77), after which he became an independent designer and builder, while still occasionally collaborating with others. Wiehl principally designed town houses in the Renaissance Revival style, and his first buildings were directly influenced by the Italian Renaissance. After 1882 his buildings showed the influence of the Czech Renaissance, the chief characteristics of which were the use of graffiti and fresco with ornamental and figural decoration, on which he collaborated with some of the best-known contemporary Bohemian painters and sculptors. Particularly notable is the so-called Wiehl house (1895), 792/II, Wenceslas Square, Prague. Other important buildings, all in Prague, include the Prague Waterworks (1883; now the Bedřich Smetana Museum), in the Staré Město (Old Town) district, where he worked with Osvald Polívka; the Municipal Savings Bank (1892–4); the parsonage of St Petr (1893–4) and the Slavín or Pantheon (1889–93) in the Vyšehrad cemetery. Wiehl also planned the overall design and a number of individual pavilions at the National Jubilee exhibition in 1891 in Prague, and he took part in the competition (1908) for the National Museum and the Old Town Hall. He held several positions in societies concerned with historic buildings, and he contributed articles to Viennese and Bohemian architectural journals. During his last years he became deaf and gave up social life, becoming a recluse and producing numerous sketches, unexecuted designs and paintings. He is perhaps the most characteristic representative of the Czech Renaissance Revival, the major historicist style in 19th-century Bohemia.

BIBLIOGRAPHY

Z. Wirth: *Antonín Wiehl a česká renesance* [Antonín Wiehl and the Czech renaissance] (Prague, 1921)
Y. Janková: *Motivy z českých dějin na novorenesančních fasádách 19. století* [Motifs from Czech history in 19th-century neo-Renaissance façades] (Prague, 1986), pp. 257–73

YVONNE JANKOVÁ

Wieland, Johann Georg (*b* Worblingen, ?21 Sept 1742; *d* Mimmenhausen, 8 Feb 1802). German sculptor. He was probably first trained by Joseph Anton Feuchtmayer at Mimmenhausen and his early figures, with their sharp contrapposto, were clearly influenced by Feuchtmayer's sculpture. He is recorded as a journeyman in Salem in 1770 and from 1778 he was back in Mimmenhausen. He worked under Johann Georg Dirr (whose daughter he married in 1780) on the redecoration of the monastery church at Salem, and after Dirr's death he completed the work himself in 1799. The interior of the Late Gothic church contains some of the most important Neo-classical decorations in south Germany. The grey austerity of the original architecture and Dirr's and Wieland's new alabaster sculpture complement each other impressively. The clearly visible tectonic system of the old church finds its natural counterpart in Wieland's severely cubic, classicizing altars, which were in part inspired by the published designs of François de Neufforge. Wieland also worked in the monastery buildings at Salem: in 1780 he executed a panelled room with complete alabaster facing, in 1786–91 he worked on the library, and from 1788 he redecorated the Fürstenzimmer. Among his other works are the monument to *Hermann von Königsegg-Rotenfels* (*d* 1799) in the parish church at Aulendorf, where he also collaborated on the Marmorsaal at the castle, an altar in the monastery church (1783) at Weissenau and the high altar (1786) in the parish church at Salem (now in the parish church in Herdwangen).

BIBLIOGRAPHY

O. Aufleger: *Altäre und Skulpturen des Münsters zu Salem* (Munich, 1892)
L. Schnorr von Carolsfeld: *Der plastische Schmuck im Inneren des Münsters zu Salem aus den Jahren 1774–84 von Johann Georg Dürr und Johann Georg Wieland* (diss., U. Berlin, 1906)
Barock in Baden-Württemberg vom Ende des Dreissigjährigen Krieges bis zur französischen Revolution (exh. cat., Karlsruhe, Bad. Landesmus.; Bruchsal, Schloss; 1981), i, pp. 254–6
U. Knapp: *Johann Georg Wielands Tätigkeit für die Freie Reichsabtei Salem* (Friedrichshafen, 1984)
——: *Salem: Die Gebäude des ehemaligen Zisterzienserabtei und ihre Ausstattungen* (in preparation)

ULRICH KNAPP

Wieland, Joyce (*b* Toronto, Ont., 30 June 1931). Canadian painter and film maker. She studied at the Central Technical School, Toronto. Passionately committed to the exploration of the aesthetic perspective of the woman artist, Wieland was a role model to several generations of younger artists. Her major canvases of the 1960s, Abstract Expressionist in nature, were often based on female sexual imagery. Early work in animation led her to explore serial imagery in her paintings and mixed media constructions of this period. From 1962 to 1970 she and her husband, artist Michael Snow, lived in New York where she established her reputation as an experimental film maker, creating such award-winning films as *Rat Life and Diet in North America* and *Reason over Passion* (both 1968). In 1971 the National Gallery of Canada mounted *True Patriot Love/Véritable amour patriotique*, the first exhibition dedicated to the work of a living Canadian woman artist. In this exhibition she collaborated with craftswomen in a variety of media, including quilting, embroidery and knitting, to create art that addressed the issues of nationalism, ecology and the traditional role of the woman artist. In 1976 she made a feature-length film, *The Far Shore*. Returning to painting in the late 1970s, she created a series of delicate pastels. Her later work is marked by a visionary quality, seen for example in *Artist on Fire* (1983; Oshawa, McLaughlin Gal.).

BIBLIOGRAPHY

True Patriot Love/Véritable amour patriotique (exh. cat., Ottawa, N.G., 1971) [incl. interview with the artist]
M. Fleming, L. Lippard and L. Rabinovitz: *Joyce Wieland* (Toronto, 1987)

JOYCE ZEMANS

Wielant, Guillaume. *See* VRELANT, WILLEM.

Wienecke, Johann Cornelius (*b* Heiligenstadt, Eichsfeld, 24 March 1872; *d* Apeldoorn, 1945). Dutch medallist. He studied applied arts in Amsterdam and fine arts at the academies of Antwerp and Brussels, going on to the Académie Colarossi and the Académie Julian in Paris; he also trained with the sculptor Denys Puech. In 1898 he won a competition with a gold, silver and bronze plaquette in low relief, which was presented by the City of Amsterdam to Queen Wilhelmina in commemoration of her coronation. This encouraged him to undertake more small-scale work, and he trained in Paris under the medallist Henri Auguste Jules Patey (1855–1930) before joining the Royal Mint, Utrecht. His early medal designs, such as those for the Java Syndicate of Sugar Refiners (gold) or the commemoration of the birth of the Princess Juliana in 1909 (silver), are usually symmetrical and of an extreme intricacy, with trees and flowers playing an important part. They won him international fame in the early 20th century; he was knighted in 1907 and became Chief Engraver at the Dutch Royal Mint. He engraved many dies for the coinage of the Netherlands and in 1923 executed a silver jubilee medal for Queen Wilhelmina. Many of his medals and plaquettes were produced by the Utrecht firm founded by Carel Joseph Begeer.

BIBLIOGRAPHY

Forrer; Thieme–Becker

PHILIP ATTWOOD

Wiener Neustadt. Town in southern Lower Austria. It was the most important new town founded in Austria in the Middle Ages, and parts of its fortified medieval centre survive. Duke Leopold VI (*reg* 1198–1230) founded Wiener Neustadt shortly after the Babenberg dynasty inherited the duchy of Styria in 1192. The town was intended to guard the road between Vienna and Graz and the border of the Babenberg territory facing Hungary. A rectangle 680×600 m on a flat site was enclosed within walls with 12 towers and a gate in the middle of each side. The town plan, which was clearly based on that of a Roman *castrum*, was defined by two streets, one running north–south and the other east–west. At the intersection the rectangular main square was laid out with the Nikolauskapelle in the centre. The streets divided the town into four quarters: the Frauenviertel to the north-west, named after the parish church, the Liebfrauenkirche; the Deutschherrenviertel to the north-east; the Dreifaltigkeitsviertel to the south-east; and the Brüderviertel to the south-west. Part of the ransom (20,000 marks of silver in Cologne weight, i.e. 5000 kg of silver) that Duke Leopold V (*reg* 1177–94) had received for the release of King Richard I of England (*reg* 1189–99) was used for the construction of the fortifications. While Gerhartl (1979) stated that Italian architects were responsible for the plan, Wagner-Rieger (1988) saw the return to Classical models as a typical phenomenon of the proto-Renaissance.

The Liebfrauenkirche was built next to the first town castle, which was abandoned *c.* 1250. The church is mentioned in a legal document of 1207, and the first parish priest is named in 1209. In 1238 the church was used for a royal wedding, and in 1246 Frederick II the Quarrelsome (*reg* 1230–46), the last Babenberg duke, lay in state there. The building was first consecrated before 1259, with a provisional final consecration in 1279. The Late Romanesque–Early Gothic aisled basilica had a pair of west towers 60 m high (taken down in 1886–99 and rebuilt with some details altered). The nave dates from the late Babenberg period and is rib-vaulted in continuous bays (see fig.). This earliest building phase has significant

Wiener Neustadt, Liebfrauenkirche, interior of nave looking west, consecrated before 1259

stylistic connections with late Hohenstaufen Romanesque, such as Bamberg Cathedral; the church marks the transition to 'Babenberg SONDERGOTIK', as seen in the Stephansdom, Vienna (*see* VIENNA, §V, 1(i)), and LILIENFELD ABBEY. The Brauttor on the south side, built *c.* 1238, is an example of the 'Norman' style of the reign of Emperor Frederick II (*reg* 1212–50), which was also used by Frederick the Quarrelsome. About 1300 a transept and a long choir flanked by two rectangular side chapels were built to replace the Late Romanesque choir. This gave the Liebfrauenkirche a total length of 65 m and a width of *c.* 25 m. In 1449 Emperor Frederick III (*reg* 1440–93) had rulers' galleries built in the side chapels. From 1468 Frederick III made the Liebfrauenkirche the seat of a bishopric (transferred to St Pölten in 1785). In this period the wooden figures of the *Twelve Apostles* attributed to LORENZ LUCHSPERGER were placed on the nave piers. North of the parish church directly on the town wall is the former Dominican convent, St Peter an der Sperr, built as part of the town fortifications. It was altered between 1450 and 1475 by PETER VON PUSICA. There are no surviving medieval remains of the headquarters of the Teutonic Knights, who were summoned to protect Wiener Neustadt in 1245.

The Dreifaltigkeitsviertel contained the Landesfürstliche Burg, which is mentioned in 1260 as a quadrangular building with four corner towers. In 1379 Leopold II, Duke of Styria (*reg* 1358–86) extended the castle and had the Gottesleichnamskapelle built in it. The castle underwent further alteration during the reign of the Habsburg Emperor Frederick III, who used it as an imperial residence from 1452. Jakob Kaschauer's statue of *Frederick III* (after 1453) is located on the heraldic wall of the castle. The façade of the Georgskapelle, built by Pusica from 1449 to 1460, projecting from the exterior of the castle, has been compared by Wagner-Rieger (1972) to Italian Renaissance palaces. The Neukloster, founded in 1227 as a Dominican friary, was also in the Dreifaltigkeitsviertel; when it was transferred to the Cistercians in 1444 Pusica converted the original basilican nave into a hall church. The Neukloster contains the tomb slab of *Empress Eleonore* (*d* 1467) with relief-carving attributed to Nicolaus Gerhaert. The Brüderviertel is named after the Franciscans, who were established there before 1240 (perhaps in 1224). The nave of the Minoritenkirche was demolished in the 16th century, but the surviving four-bay choir probably dates back to the endowments (1304 and 1328 respectively) of Blanche Capet, Duchess of Austria (*d* 1305) and Elizabeth (*d* 1330), wife of Frederick, King of Germany (*reg* 1314–30). In 1362 the monastery was given to the Capuchins.

The town was severely damaged by fire in 1834, but Late Gothic houses with loggias have survived on the north side of the main square. A 13th-century Romanesque town house was one of the many buildings destroyed in 1945. Outside the town is the Spinnerin am Kreuz, the richly articulated tabernacle pillar built in 1382–4 by Michael Chnab (*see* MICHAEL OF WIENER NEUSTADT).

BIBLIOGRAPHY

W. Boeheim: 'Beiträge zur Geschichte der Liebfrauenkirche in Wiener Neustadt', *Mitt. Ksr.-Kön. Zent.-Comm. Erforsch. & Erhaltung Kst- & Hist. Dkml.*, n.s., xii (1886), p. 141

F. Staub: 'Notizen zur Baugeschichte der Liebfrauenkirche in Wiener Neustadt', *Ber. & Mitt. Altert.-Ver. Wien*, xxvi (1890), pp. 130–36; xxvii (1891), pp. 157–74

J. Mayer: *Geschichte von Wiener Neustadt*, 4 vols (Wiener Neustadt, 1924–8)

R. K. Donin: *Die Bettelordenskirchen in Österreich*, Zur Entwicklungsgeschichte der Gotik (Baden bei Wien, 1935)

R. Feuchtmüller: 'Die kirchliche Baukunst am Hof des Kaisers und ihre Auswirkungen', *Friedrich III: Kaiserresidenz Wiener Neustadt* (exh. cat., Wiener Neustadt, St Peter an der Sperr, 1966), pp. 199–208

F. Halmer: *Burgen und Schlösser zwischen Baden-Gutenstein-Wiener Neustadt* (Vienna, 1968), pp. 122–36

R. Wagner-Rieger: 'Die Bautätigkeit Kaiser Friedrichs III', *Wien. Jb. Kstgesch.*, xxv (1972), pp. 140–42

G. Gerhartl: *Der Dom zu Wiener Neustadt, 1279–1979* (Vienna, Cologne and Graz, 1979)

R. Wagner-Rieger: 'Bildende Kunst: Architektur', *Zeit der frühen Habsburger: Dome und Klöster, 1279–1379* (exh. cat., Wiener Neustadt, Stadtmus., 1979), pp. 117–18

——: *Mittelalterliche Architektur in Österreich* (St Pölten and Vienna, 1988)

MARIO SCHWARZ

Wiener Schmidt. *See* SCHMIDT, JOHANN GEORG.

Wiener Werkstätte [Ger.: 'Viennese workshop']. Viennese cooperative group of painters, sculptors, architects and decorative artists founded by Josef Hoffmann and Kolo Moser in 1903 and active until 1932.

1. INFLUENCES AND AIMS. The group was modelled upon C. R. Ashbee's Guild of Handicraft. Under the artistic direction of Hoffmann and Moser and with the financial patronage of the industrialist Fritz Warndorfer (*b* 1868), they sought to rescue the applied arts and artistic craftwork from aesthetic devaluation brought on by mass production. Their aim was to re-establish the aesthetic aspect of the everyday object. As a long-term goal they strove to promote the cultivation of general public taste by bringing the potential purchaser in close contact with the designer and craftsworker. The offices, studios and workshops at Neustiftgasse 32 were designed by Moser with that purpose in mind.

The Wiener Werkstätte believed that artistic endeavour should permeate all aspects of everyday life; no object was so menial that it could not be enhanced by beauty of form and execution. It was postulated that this maxim, rooted in the work of William Morris and the Arts and Crafts Movement, gave direction to cultural progress. The moral and social aspect of the workshops was also influenced by the credo derived from John Ruskin and Morris, and adopted by Ashbee, that the craftsworker should work under humane conditions and in an artistic atmosphere. The profits of the cooperative were shared by not only the financier but also the designer and executor. Charles Rennie Mackintosh also influenced the group, which is evident in the puristic simplicity and geometric austerity of their early objects, for example a brass vase by Moser (1903–4; Vienna, Mus. Angewandte Kst; see fig.). Mackintosh and Margaret Macdonald had exhibited work to the Viennese public in the eighth exhibition held at the Secession (1900). Hoffmann and Moser were intrigued with the elegance and sensibility of their creations.

The Japanese-inspired components of the workshops' products were also important. The Secession had dedicated their sixth exhibition (1900) to Japanese art, and in Vienna in 1901 the Österreichisches Museum für Kunst und

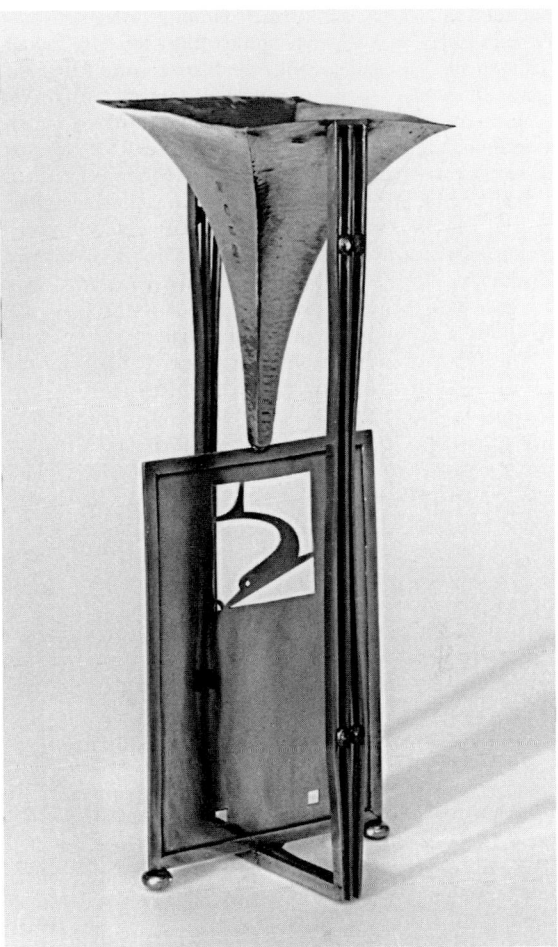

Wiener Werkstätte vase by Kolo Moser, brass, h. 300 mm, 1903–4 (Vienna, Österreichisches Museum für Angewandte Kunst)

Industrie (now Österreichisches Museum für Angewandte Kunst) exhibited the woodcuts of Katsushika Hokusai. The textile patterns (*see* AUSTRIA, §XI, 2) and inlay designs of Hoffmann and Moser share strong similarities with Japanese stencils and prints. The distinctive trademark of the Wiener Werkstätte included the initials of both the designer and the executing craftsworker. The fine arts and the applied arts were awarded the same level of importance. The primary concern of the group was to respect the inherent decorative and functional qualities of the material used and to work within its natural properties.

2. MAJOR DESIGNS AND COMMISSIONS. The works of the Wiener Werkstätte were made known to the public through various local and international exhibitions: the exhibition at the Hohenzollern-Kunstgewerbehaus in Berlin (1904), the show at the Galerie Miethke in Vienna (1905), the Imperial Royal Austria exhibition at Earl's Court, London (1906), and the *Kunstschau* in Vienna (1908) were the most celebrated. Early articles published in *Deutsche Kunst und Dekoration* (1904) and *The Studio* (1906) furthered their popularity. The projects of the group in which all aspects of their art came into play

provided the foundation of their fame: the sanatorium at Purkersdorf (1903–5), the Modesalon Flöge in Vienna (1904; destr.), the Palais Stoclet in Brussels (1905–11) and the Fledermaus Cabaret in Vienna (1908; destr.). These projects were important for the development of the modern interior. In the sanatorium the clear, simple lines of Hoffmann's cubistic architecture set the tone for the hygienic austerity of the interior rooms, which were designed by Moser. Comfort and luxury, practicality and functionality formed an aesthetic whole. In the case of the Modesalon Flöge, the rooms and their furnishings were designed by Hoffmann and Moser so cooperatively that individual ascriptions do not hold.

The Wiener Werkstätte were given complete financial freedom by Baron Adolphe Stoclet for the decorations (*in situ*) for his house in Brussels, which was designed as a GESAMTKUNSTWERK; every detail was designed with great care and with its integral relationship to the aesthetic whole in mind. The ceramic tiles and maiolica were executed by Bertold Löffler and Michael Powolny, who had founded the Wiener Keramik workshop in 1906; their distribution was taken over by the Wiener Werkstätte in 1907. Ludwig Heinrich Jungnickel painted an animal frieze for the nursery, and Carl Otto Czeschka furnished the breakfast room. Gustav Klimt designed a mosaic frieze for the dining-room, for which he used unconventional materials, placing precious metals and stones, inexpensive materials and ordinary objects side by side. As part of the Fledermaus commission, over 1000 postcards representing witty themes were printed. Artists including Oskar Kokoschka, Czeschka, Rudolf Kalvach and Egon Schiele were responsible for their exceptional artistic quality. Powolny and Löffler were responsible for the wall and floor tiles.

The Wiener Werkstätte gained new artistic stimulus under the influence of Dagobert Peche. He was appointed manager of the artists' workshops in 1915, and in 1917 he became the director of the branch in Zurich. In 1919 he became artistic director. The sale-rooms were furnished according to his designs. His extremely delicate and elegant ornamental forms, his sense of noble colour contrasts of white with gold and his feeling for an original, wilful use of floral motifs brought a new spontaneity into the workshop. Early designs for useful household utensils had been made of simple, inexpensive white-lacquered and perforated sheet metal with glass inserts. Fruit baskets, flower-holders, sugar and jam containers took on different variations of basic geometric shapes well suited for everyday use. However, despite functionalism being one of the foremost objectives of the group, some of the designs seemed so bizarre to the purchasing public that it was decided to have the finished products photographed in use for didactic purposes. Hoffmann eventually came to the conclusion that it was impossible to convert the masses aesthetically and recognized that inevitably they were catering to an élitist few.

3. FINANCIAL DIFFICULTIES AND DISSOLUTION. The Wiener Werkstätte were constantly faced with irresolvable financial problems. The idealistic programme, which called for the costly production of handmade, unique objects, was unprofitable. In addition, commissioners often refused payment because of technicalities or deadline difficulties. Moser left the group in 1907 because Wärndorfer had approached Moser's wealthy wife, Editha Mautner-Markhof, for financial assistance without prior consultation with him. Although the circle of customers included such affluent and influential names as the Wittgenstein family, Broncia and Hugo Koller, Hans Böhler (?1884–1961) and Carl Moll, the enterprise was liquidated for the first time in 1914. Wärndorfer was forced to leave the cooperative under pressure of debts. In 1915 the banker and industrialist Otto Primavesi became the new business manager. Under his direction and with his international connections, the Wiener Werkstätte opened up branches in Berlin (1916), Marienbad (1916–17), Zürich (1917), New York (1922) and Velden at Wörthersee (1923). In 1913 the Wiener Keramik was taken over by Gmundner Keramik. However, the branch in Karlsbad, founded in 1909, had to close down its women's fashion department due to unprofitability. Eduard Josef Wimmer-Wisgrill (1882–1961), then the Director, suggested that women's accessories be sold. Wimmer-Wisgrill had succeeded Czeschka as Director, who in turn had accepted a professorship at the Kunstgewerbeschule in Hamburg but still submitted designs to the group. The deeply rooted misunderstanding of its cause was partly responsible for economic failure and ultimate liquidation of the Wiener Werkstätte in 1932. A public brought up on the historicist style created by Hans Makart and steeped in the opulent interiors of the palaces and public buildings on the Ringstrasse could not easily condition itself to the new functional purism of the Wiener Werkstätte, which did not fulfil the public's need for self-representation and display.

BIBLIOGRAPHY

L. Hevesi: *Acht Jahre Secession* (Vienna, 1906)
W. Müller-Wulckow: *Wiener Werkstätte, 1903–1928* (Vienna, 1928)
Die Wiener Werkstätte: Modernes Kunsthandwerk von 1903 bis 1932 (exh. cat. by W. Mrazek, Vienna, Mus. Angewandte Kst, 1967)
D. Baroni and A. d'Auria: *Josef Hoffmann e la Wiener Werkstätte* (Milan, 1981; Ger. trans., Stuttgart, 1984)
W. Neuwirth: *Die Keramik der Wiener Werkstätte*, i (Vienna, 1981)
W. J. Schweiger: *Wiener Werkstätte: Kunst und Handwerk, 1903–1932* (Vienna, 1982; Eng. trans., London, 1984)
Wiener Mode und Modefotografie: Die Modeabteilung der Wiener Werkstätte (exh. cat. by A. Volker, Vienna, Mus. Angewandte Kst, 1984)
Traum und Wirklichkeit: Wien, 1870–1930 (exh. cat., Vienna, Kstlerhaus, 1985)
J. Kallir: *Viennese Design and the Wiener Werkstätte* (New York, 1986)

CYNTHIA PROSSINGER

Wierandt, Caspar Vogt von. *See* VOGT VON WIERANDT, CASPAR.

Wierda, Sytze Wopkes (*b* Wynjeterp, Friesland, 28 Feb 1839; *d* Sea Point, Cape Province, 10 Dec 1911). South African architect and engineer of Dutch birth. He trained as a carpenter but became an architect and chief inspector to the Netherlands Railways, the service of which he entered in 1866. He gained wide architectural experience and supervised the construction of the Centraal Station, Amsterdam. In November 1887 he became a member of the Dutch Royal Institute of Engineers and was appointed Government Architect and Engineer of the Transvaal Republic in South Africa. The name of the post was changed in 1895 to Chief of Public Works. Under Wierda's guidance the department built up a considerable band of architects and draughtsmen who were responsible for many public buildings, mostly in developing urban areas and bearing the characteristic stamp of the Republican style. Wierda became a member of the South African Association of Engineers and Architects in 1894. He left Pretoria in 1901/2 when the British forces took over the Public Works Department during the Boer War (1899–1902), and he opened a practice in Johannesburg. There he was joined by Obermeyer in partnership. In 1908 he settled at Sea Point in Cape Town.

Wierda is best known for his work as Chief of Public Works. After the discovery of payable gold on the Witwatersrand in 1886 the Transvaal experienced a period of rapid urban growth, and many court buildings, post offices and government buildings had to be built. To facilitate efficient design Wierda standardized building elements, as he had done in his training at the Dutch railways. He adapted much of his Dutch experience for South African work. The Public Works Department (PWD) designs are characterized by sober, simple general shapes with a symmetrical subdivision highlighting a central portion (gable, tower or portico). In the detailing a much richer and freer hand is visible through varying types of roof-windows, doors, windows and colourful materials. Unlike the European prototypes with their strong vertical emphasis, the PWD buildings in the Transvaal were more horizontal in form, as were most buildings in the region. Buildings of more than one storey could only be found in the central areas of Pretoria and Johannesburg. The horizontality of design reflected the predominantly agrarian lifestyle and relative isolation of the republic at the time. It is specifically in the ornamentation of the PWD buildings that Wierda tried to proclaim Western civilization. For most of the detailing he borrowed from the treasures of the Dutch Renaissance and in that respect followed the taste of his countrymen in the Netherlands.

Wierda's first design, the Raadsaal (1888–92; for illustration *see* PRETORIA), Pretoria, came to be his most famous. It has a commanding position on Church Square and, through strong massing and details such as a double-height portico and pavilions with mansard roofs, it dominates its surroundings despite neighbouring tower blocks. His Palace of Justice (1896–1902) across the square lacks cohesion but complements this historical row of buildings on the western side of the square. In Johannesburg he designed the Rissik Street Post Office (1895–7) on Market Square, which also became a landmark. Official buildings were erected in most of the bigger Transvaal towns, and they often determined the character of the towns for decades. Notable examples exist in Krugersdorp, Boksburg and Potchefstroom, and they are recognizable by their red brick façades and neo-Renaissance ornamentation in white sandstone.

BIBLIOGRAPHY
D. E. Greig: *A Guide to Architecture in South Africa* (Cape Town, 1971)
H. M. Rex: *Die lewe en werk van Sytze Wopkes Wierda in Nederland, met verwysing na sy betekenis vir die Zuid-Afrikaansche Republiek* [The life and work of Sytze Wopkes Wierda in the Netherlands, with reference to his importance to the South African Republic] (diss., U. Pretoria, 1974)
D. Picton-Seymour: *Victorian Architecture in South Africa* (Cape Town, 1977)
G-M. VAN DER WAAL

Wieringen, Cornelis Claesz. van (*b* Haarlem, *c.* 1580; *d* Haarlem, 29 Dec 1633). Dutch draughtsman, painter, etcher and navigator. His name first appears in the Haarlem records in 1597. It is generally assumed that he was a pupil of Hendrick Vroom, whose work strongly influenced his own. Documentary sources confirm that he maintained close friendships with both Hendrick Goltzius, who made woodcuts after his drawings (see fig.), and Cornelis Cornelisz. van Haarlem. Van Wieringen was more than once governor of the Haarlem Guild of St Luke, a position in which he was responsible for updating the guild's outmoded organization. He specialized in seascapes and received commissions from the city of Haarlem, the Dutch Admiralty in Amsterdam and others. His interest lies primarily in his influence on Dutch marine painters of the 17th century. His son Claes Cornelisz. van Wieringen (*fl* 1636), also a painter, died young.

1. DRAWINGS. The preliminary catalogue by Keyes contains sixty-five examples of drawings by Cornelis van Wieringen, only one of which has a reliable signature (Paris, Fond. Custodia, Inst. Néer.). Accurate attributions are often difficult since van Wieringen followed closely not only drawings with sea subjects by Vroom but also landscapes by Goltzius and Jacques de Gheyn II. In 1613 the Amsterdam publisher Jan Claesz. Visscher published 14 landscape etchings after van Wieringen. These etchings—made by Visscher himself—are partly in the tradition of Pieter Bruegel the elder and were important for the development of realistic Dutch landscape painting. Furthermore, they form a starting-point for the attribution of van Wieringen's drawings. Van Wieringen also executed tapestry designs, including, in 1629, that for the *Capture of Damiatta* for the city of Haarlem; the huge tapestry, woven by Joseph Thienpont, can still be seen in its original place in the town hall in Haarlem. The tapestry's patriotic theme—a heroic moment in the history of Haarlem's fleet at the time of the Crusades—recurs in drawings and paintings by the artist.

2. PAINTINGS. In his paintings, too, van Wieringen shows himself strongly dependent on the example of Vroom, using even the same deep greenish-blue tones. The paintings are easier to identify than the drawings, since quite a few are either signed and dated or documented. What is considered his most important work is the large, fully documented *Battle of Gibraltar* (1.8×4.9 m, 1622; Amsterdam, Ned. Hist. Scheepvaartsmus.). Interestingly, the ships in this picture also appear in engravings after Pieter Bruegel. The subject is again patriotic and has political implications: the triumph of the Dutch navy, led by Admiral Jacob van Heemskerck, over the Spanish fleet at Gibraltar in 1607. The *Battle of Gibraltar* was commissioned by the Amsterdam Admiralty as a gift to Prince Maurice, Commander-in-Chief over the united forces of the Dutch Republic. Van Wieringen also made a number of smaller scenes with ships at sea; these are mostly on wood and have no political bearing. The colours are reminiscent of Flemish painting.

BIBLIOGRAPHY
H. van de Waal: *Drie eeuwen vaderlandsche geschieduitbeelding* [Three centuries of national history in images], 2 vols (Amsterdam, 1952), pp. 200, 247, 251–2

Cornelis Claesz. van Wieringen (after): *Seascape with Sailing Vessels*; woodcut by Hendrick Goltzius, 93×142 mm, *c.* 1610 (London, British Museum)

L. J. Bol: *Die holländische Marinemalerei des 17. Jahrhunderts* (Brunswick, 1969, rev. 1973), pp. 29–35
G. S. Keyes: 'Cornelis Claesz. van Wieringen', *Oud-Holland*, xciii (1979), pp. 1–46

E. K. J. REZNICEK

Wierix. Flemish family of artists. They were active mainly in Antwerp in the last quarter of the 16th century and the first quarter of the 17th. Anton Wierix I (*c.* 1520/25– *c.* 1572) was registered as a painter in 1545–6, after an apprenticeship of seven years with the otherwise unknown painter Jan Verkelen. Anton I is sometimes also referred to as a cabinetmaker. Given his professions, it is unlikely that he taught any of his three sons, (1) Jan Wierix, (2) Jerome Wierix and (3) Anton Wierix II, all of whom have left large numbers of engravings. Both Jan and Jerome probably trained with a goldsmith, and Anton II presumably studied with one of his older brothers, probably Jan. Although listed as Lutherans in 1585, it seems likely that the Wierix brothers returned to Catholicism soon afterwards, because much of their engraved work was commissioned by the Jesuits and other militant Counter-Reformation sects; their prints played an important role in the recapturing of the southern Netherlands for the Catholic Church. Despite this, all three brothers were famous for their disorderly conduct, and, in a letter of 1587 to the Jesuit priest Ferdinand Ximenes, the Antwerp publisher Christoph Plantin complained that whoever wanted to employ the Wierix brothers had to go and look for them in the taverns, pay their debts and fines and recover their tools, which they had pawned; having worked for a few days, they would then return to the tavern. There

is enough archival evidence to corroborate Plantin's story, but, on the other hand, the sheer mass of engravings produced by Jan and Jerome and their excellent quality indicates a certain amount of hard work on their part. Anton II's son, Anton Wierix III (1596–before 21 Sept 1624), who was probably trained by his uncle Jerome, joined the guild in 1621–2 but died too young to have had a significant oeuvre. In 1620 Christine, one of the daughters of Jerome, married the engraver Jan-Baptist Barbé (*c.* 1578–after 1649).

(1) Jan [Hans; Johannes] **Wierix** (*b* Antwerp, 1549; *d* Brussels, *c.* 1618 or shortly afterwards). Engraver, draughtsman and publisher. Presumably as part of his early training, in 1563 and 1565 he made copies of engravings after Dürer and other artists. His first dated prints were published as early as 1568. By the following year he was employed by Christoph Plantin, to whom he introduced his brother (2) Jerome Wierix in 1570. At the time Jan was living in the Lombaardevest, amid many other booksellers and engravers. He worked for Plantin's publishing house, the Officina Plantiniana, more often than Jerome, and already in 1570 and 1571 Plantin paid Jan's drinking debts. From then onwards Jan's name appears regularly in Plantin's accounts and letters.

In 1572–3 Jan was listed as a master engraver in Antwerp. He married Elisabeth, the daughter of the glass painter Nicolaas Bloemsteen (*fl* 1540–1610), in 1576, but left her soon afterwards, and from 1577 to 1579 was recorded in Delft. There he witnessed and engraved the stranding of dead whales on the beach of Ter Heyde in

1577 (M-H, no. 1736), and over the next year executed small oval portraits of prominent Delft citizens. These were probably engraved on silver rather than copper plates, as was the portrait of *Philip Marnix de Sainte-Aldegonde* (1581; Amsterdam, Rijksmus.). In 1581 Jan was prosecuted by Count Günther von Schwarzburg for failing to execute a commission for a two-sided silver medallion bearing portraits of the count and his wife.

After his return to Antwerp in 1579, Jan resumed his work for Plantin (see fig. 1), while also working for such publishers as Hans Liefrinck, Jan-Baptist Vrients, Phillip Galle, Gérard de Jode and Willem and Godevaard van Haecht (1546–*c.* 1599), as well as occasionally publishing his engravings himself. Besides inventing his own compositions, Jan engraved the designs of Frans Floris, Gillis Mostaert, Crispin van den Broeck and, most frequently, Marten de Vos. The latter seems regularly to have provided Jan with drawings specially designed to be engraved.

Apart from his engravings, Jan made a considerable number of miniature pen drawings, possibly beginning in the 1590s, although signed and dated examples occur mostly *c.* 1607–8; these are executed in a meticulous engraver-like technique, using dots and minute crosshatching (see fig. 2). By the time he made these drawings Jan had left Antwerp, where he is last documented in 1594, the same year he was already drawing miniatures at the Brussels court of Archduke Ernst of Austria. He was probably already living in Brussels in 1601, for on 28 July he was absent from Antwerp at the conclusion of a deal involving family property. He is explicitly recorded as resident there in 1612. In an engraving done at the age of 67, of *Orpheus with the Animals* (1615, M-H, no. 1603), Jan proudly proclaimed that, in spite of his old age, he had not forgotten his skills. His last dated work is a drawing of the *Pietà* (1618; New York, priv. col.).

(2) Jerome [Hieronymous] **Wierix** (*b* Antwerp, 1553; *d* Antwerp, 1 Nov 1619). Engraver, brother of (1) Jan Wierix. At his father's death, one of the guardians to whom he was entrusted was Jerome Manacker, who was probably a close relative of the goldsmith of the same name (*fl* Antwerp, 1520–56). Jerome also began his training by making engravings after Dürer, an activity in which he showed himself to be more precocious than his older brother. He joined Christoph Plantin in 1570 and, like his brother, became a master in 1572–3. In 1574 Plantin paid a fine for Jerome, who had been arrested drunk at night. The publisher was even more exasperated by Jerome's lifestyle than by Jan's, and after he had rescued Jerome from prison the next year, he decided not to continue to employ him. From 1577, the date of his first independent engraving, Jerome worked for several other publishers. Between 1577 and 1580 he made many prints for Willem van Haecht and his nephew Godevaard van Haecht (1546–99). These were mostly allegorical and political in theme and demonstrate a sympathy for those rebelling against the Spanish.

Jerome's dissolute lifestyle got him into serious trouble in October 1578: in a state of inebriation, he threw a beer jug at the wife of an innkeeper and hit her on the head. When she died six weeks later, he was arrested. His friends and family paid large sums of money to the victim's family

1. Jan Wierix: *Christoph Plantin*, engraving, 115×97 mm, 1588 (Brussels, Bibliothèque Royale Albert 1er, Cabinet des Estampes)

and Jerome appealed to Archduke Matthias of Austria for pardon, as a result of which after a year of imprisonment he was released. (The few engravings dated 1579 were probably done before the accident.) In the first years after his pardon he obviously worked hard, for there are many engravings dated between 1580 and 1588. These were mainly published by Jan-Baptist Vrients (*fl c.* 1575–1610), Hans Liefrinck, Hans van Luyck (*fl c.* 1580), Johann Sadeler (i) and Adriaan Huybrechts (*fl* 1573–1614). Occasionally, Jerome again worked for Plantin, for whom he executed, for instance, many of the illustrations in Geronimo Nadal's Counter-Reformatory books, the *Evangelicae historiae imagines* and the *Adnotationes et meditationes in Evangelia* (M-H, nos 1989–2141). Jerome had two pupils from 1588 to 1589, Samuel van Hoogstraten and Jacob de Weert (1569–after 1600), and in 1614 he took Jan van de Sande (1600–1664/5) as an apprentice. In 1587 he had married Dymphna de Backer [Beckers] (*d* before 1601), but the marriage was not a success: within the first three years his wife ran away from him six or seven times. They nonetheless had five children, one son and four daughters. Jerome's later years were less wild than his youth, and by the time he died he was wealthy enough for his estate to be the subject of a fierce struggle among his children.

(3) Anton Wierix II (*b* Antwerp, *c.* 1555–9; *bur* Antwerp, 11 March 1604). Engraver, brother of (1) Jan Wierix. He was probably taught by Jan. By 1579 he had engraved two plates for a series of four satirical prints, published by Willem van Haecht (M-H, nos 1663, 1666); the other two were by (2) Jerome Wierix (M-H, nos 1664–5). This is the earliest of many examples of collaboration between the two brothers. In 1587 Anton went into a short-lived partnership (of only three months) with Hans Liefrinck, and in 1590–91 he became a master. This

2. Jan Wierix: *Studio of Apelles*, pen and brown ink on parchment, 251×316 mm, 1600 (Antwerp, Museum Mayer van den Bergh)

coincided with his marriage (4 Oct 1590) to Catharina, daughter of the glass painter Gummarus van den Driessche; like Jerome's, this marriage produced one son and four daughters. Anton II was also frequently in difficulties over debts, sometimes pawning his copperplates. His work includes a great number of religious scenes, some designed by himself, others after work by such artists as Marten de Vos and Crispin van den Broeck. After Anton's early death, Jerome took over his copperplates and published several of Anton's engravings under his own name. The work of his son, Anton Wierix III, has often been confused with that of the father.

BIBLIOGRAPHY

M. Mauquoy-Hendrickx: *Les Estampes des Wierix conservées au Cabinet des Estampes de la Bibliothèque royale Albert Ier: Catalogue raisonné*, 3 vols (Brussels, 1978–83) [with 'Notices biographiques et documents d'archives' by C. van de Velde, iii/2, pp. 513–74; M–H]
C. Van de Velde: *Jan Wierix: The Creation and the Early History of Man, 1607–1608* (London, 1990)

CARL VAN DE VELDE

Wiertz, Antoine (Joseph) (*b* Dinant, 22 Feb 1806; *d* Brussels, 18 June 1865). Belgian painter and sculptor. He was from very humble origins, but his talent for drawing was detected at an early age. He was sent to the Antwerp Academie, where he attended classes given by W. J. Herreyns (1743–1827) and Mathieu Ignace Van Brée.

During a stay in Paris from 1829 to 1832 he came into contact with the Romantic painters, in particular Théodore Géricault, who fostered his admiration for Rubens. In 1832 he won the Belgian Prix de Rome and in 1834 left for Italy where the works of Raphael and, above all, Michelangelo made an overwhelming impression on him. In Rome he abandoned the landscapes and scenes from Roman life, for which he showed a certain talent, and embarked on a much more ambitious work, the *Greeks and the Trojans Contesting the Body of Patroclus* (1835; Brussels, Mus. Wiertz; see fig.). The painting proved the turning-point in Wiertz's career. Its frenzied composition and violently contorted figures excited considerable interest in Rome. Children fled from it with cries of horror, a fact that delighted the painter. Bertel Thorvaldsen commented, 'This young man is a giant'—a somewhat hasty judgement, constantly repeated by later biographers, which nevertheless determined his subsequent development. In Antwerp and Liège Wiertz was at once acclaimed. He then sent the picture to Paris, expecting final consecration of his genius. However, it was badly hung in the Salon, went unnoticed by the public and was criticized by the press. Wiertz's bitter disappointment was expressed in an undying hatred of Paris, which he never ceased to attack for its dissipation, stupidity and artistic incompetence. In 1839 he settled in Liège with his mother, painting grandiose mythological and historical subjects, which he believed would immortalize him, and portraits to earn a living. The latter, such as the *Artist's Mother* (1838; Brussels, Mus. A. Anc.), were passable, while the former were merely superficial pastiches of Rubens and Michelangelo. However, the new Belgian State was keen to discover 'geniuses of the national art' and admired his weakly Raphaelesque *Education of the Virgin* (1843, Brussels, Mus. Wiertz) and in particular the *Revolt of the Rebel Angels* (1842; Brussels, Mus. Wiertz), a huge picture that Wiertz painted in a few weeks, in an effort to match the panache of Rubens's brushwork.

Wiertz believed himself to be the equal of his idol, Rubens. In an open letter to the Minister of the Interior he asked permission to be allowed to paint his *Revolt of the Rebel Angels* opposite Rubens's *Descent from the Cross* in Antwerp Cathedral. Having painted his *Triumph of Christ* (1848; Brussels, Mus. Wiertz), he wished to have Rubens's *Road to Calvary* moved to his studio in the Rue des Renards. Although none of his demands were met, many believed in Wiertz's genius: his *Flight into Egypt* was commissioned for the main altar of the church of St Joseph, and *Christ at the Tomb* and a second version of *Patroclus* (1845; Brussels, Mus. Wiertz) were well received by the public and local press. After the death of his mother in 1846 Wiertz moved to Brussels, and in 1850 he negotiated successfully with the Belgian government to have a studio, based on the temple of Paestum, built for his use. He moved in within a year and, relieved of most of his material worries, he was at last able to devote himself fully to his art. In fierce monastic isolation he worked there until his death, happily adopting the lifestyle of a painter-philosopher.

Uneducated and with naive delusions of grandeur, Wiertz dubbed himself a 'painter of the mind'. However, he was unable to discover a sufficiently vigorous pictorial language in which to express his barely digested humanitarian, pacifist, egalitarian and Christian ideas. The result was simplistic and hollow allegories on a vast scale such as the *Beacon of Golgotha* (1859; Brussels, Mus. Wiertz). The sensationalism of his major canvases was tinged by voyeurism in such works as the *Young Witch* (1857) and the *Two Young Girls or the Beautiful Rosine* (1847; both Brussels, Mus. Wiertz), in which a beautiful young woman confronts a skeleton in a manner anticipatory of the Belgian Symbolists. He also produced crude *trompe l'oeil* paintings and sculptures of agonized conflict such as *Second Epoch—Strife* (Brussels, Mus. Wiertz). For the large pictures intended for posterity he invented a 'matt painting' technique, which he believed would supersede oil painting and which he tried unsuccessfully to copyright. The technique proved impermanent, the colours draining into the canvas. At his death in 1865 he bequeathed his work to the State in its entirety and his studio was soon turned into a museum. The contents of the Musée Wiertz cruelly reveal the artist's limitations. Yet he remains a fascinating phenomenon, an artist with sufficient arrogance (bordering almost on madness) to convince not only his contemporaries but also himself of his own genius.

BIBLIOGRAPHY
E. Fierlants: *Oeuvre complète d'Antoine Wiertz*, 2 vols (Brussels, 1868)
I. Wybo-Wehrli: 'Le Séjour d'Antoine Wiertz à Rome', *Bull. Mus. Royaux B.-A. Belgique*, xxii/1–4 (1973), pp. 85–146

Antoine Wiertz: *Greeks and the Trojans Contesting the Body of Patroclus*, oil on canvas, 5.20×8.52 m, 1835 (Brussels, Musée Wiertz)

A. Moerman and F. C. Legrand: *Antoine Wiertz, 1806–1865* (Paris, 1974)

M. Beks: *Antoine Wiertz: Genie of charlatan* (Oosterbeek, 1981)

DOMINIQUE VAUTIER

Wies Church. Pilgrimage church situated 3 km south-east of Steingaden in Upper Bavaria, Germany. An outstanding work of Bavarian Rococo, it stands in a forest meadow against a background of the Trauchgau Mountains. It is the last collaborative work of the brothers Johann Baptist Zimmermann and Dominikus Zimmermann. About 1743 Abbot Hyazinth Gassner (*d* 1745) of the Premonstratensian monastery of Steingaden commissioned Dominikus Zimmermann to design a church to house a miraculous image of the *Flagellation*; Wies Church was executed in 1745–57. The nave, an elongated oval surrounded by eight pairs of supports in an alternately wide and narrow spacing, opens on to an ambulatory. On the west side a vestibule with organ gallery was added, to the east a long choir with an apsidal end, flanked at ground-floor level by an ambulatory and on the upper floor by galleries. On the east side a tower and the priest's house adjoin the building.

The transformation of traditional architectural articulation, a process that is already visible in Dominikus Zimmermann's earlier churches at Steinhausen and Günzburg, is manifested more strongly in Wies Church. The supports in the main hall are hybrid forms that combine the profile of pillar and column, the capitals dissolving in rocaille ornamentation, the arcades set in oscillation by volutes (for an illustration of the interior *see* ROCOCO, fig. 4). Instead of a cornice or frame, a swirling stucco zone with vase niches and balconies surrounds and cuts into the ceiling fresco. In the choir the entablature and arcades are transformed into rocaille cartouches, with the ceiling paintings of the ambulatory made visible through the openings pierced in them. This ornamental transformation of the internal framework is matched on the exterior by the swirling lines of the windows. The wide spacing of the slender supports, the breaking up of wall surfaces with fenestration, and the ornamental openings at the base of the choir vaulting flood the interior of the church with light from all sides. In order to achieve this effect, lath and plaster construction was used instead of solid masonry for the vaulting. These areas were transformed by Johann Baptist Zimmermann's frescoes into bright celestial spaces, with the ceiling over the nave depicting the parousia and that of the choir, *God the Father Accepting the Arma Christi*. The small ceiling frescoes in the ambulatory of the nave represent *Christ's Act of Grace and Remission of Sins* and in the choir galleries, *Miraculous Healings*. The designer of the pictorial programme was probably Father Magnus Straub from Steingaden. The altars, pulpit, abbot's box and statuary are integrated with the whole building in iconography, colour and decorative treatment. The interior and exterior of the church was completely restored from 1985 to 1991.

BIBLIOGRAPHY

T. Muchall-Viebrook: *Dominikus Zimmermann* (Leipzig, 1912), pp. 49–58

A. Feulner: *Die Wies* (Augsburg, 1931)

H. Schnell: *Die Wies* (Munich, 1934, rev. 10/1960)

C. Lamb: *Die Wies* (Berlin, 1937, rev. Munich, 3/1964)

H. Schnell: 'Kaspar Moosbrugger und der Grundriss der Wies', *Das Münster*, iii (1950), pp. 183–6

B. Rupprecht: *Die bayerische Rokoko-Kirche* (Kallmünz, 1959), pp. 37–42

H. Bauer: *Il Rococo tedesco nella cattedrale di Wies*, L'arte racconta, xl (Milan, 1965)

H.-R. Hitchcock: *German Rococo: The Zimmermann Brothers* (London, 1968), pp. 68–79

H. Bauer and B. Rupprecht, eds: *Corpus der barocken Deckenmalerei in Deutschland*, i (Munich, 1976), pp. 600–23

H. Schnell: *Die Wies, Wallfahrtskirche zum gegeisselten Heiland: Ihr Baumeister Dominikus Zimmermann, Leben und Werk* (Munich and Zurich, 1979)

T. Finkenstaedt: 'Zur Baugeschichte der Wieskirche', *Jb. Ver. Christ. Kst München*, xi (1980), pp. 109–15

H. Bauer and A. Bauer: *Johann Baptist und Dominikus Zimmermann: Entstehung und Vollendung des bayerischen Rokoko* (Regensburg, 1985), pp. 58–63, 230–46, 303, 324

Die Wies, Geschichte und Restaurierung, Arbeitsheft, Bayerisches Landesamt für Denkmalpflege, lv (Munich, 1992)

CHRISTINA THON

Wieser, Ferenc (*b* Pest [now Budapest], Dec 1812; *d* county of Moson, Hungary, 30 Aug 1869). Hungarian architect. He was trained at the Polytechnikum and the Akademie der Bildenden Künste, Vienna. From 1837 he worked briefly in József Hild's office, then travelled extensively in Europe. He made frequent visits to England and married an Englishwoman. Wieser's work is notable for the variety of styles he employed. For example, the János Weber villa (1845–8; destr., see *Magyar Épitőmüvészet*, lxxix/1 (1988), p. 145, no. 8) in Buda (now Budapest) was a symmetrical block with English Gothic Revival features; the Pietsch House (1850–51; destr.) in Pest displayed some characteristics of the Italian Renaissance style; the Pichler House (1855–7) in Pest is a rare example in Hungary of the Venetian Gothic style favoured by John Ruskin; and the spire (1859–63) of the Franciscan church, Pest, shows influences of English Baroque. His competition design (1861; unexecuted, see *Magyar Épitőmüvészet*, lxxix/1 (1988), pp. 150–51, nos 18–19; original designs Budapest, Hung. N. Archvs) for the provisional parliament building, Budapest, was for a Renaissance Revival edifice with a cast-iron structure for its central hall.

BIBLIOGRAPHY

D. Komárik: 'Wieser Ferenc, 1812–1869', *Művészttörténeti Értesítő*, xxxvi/1–4 (1987), pp. 142–54

JÓZSEF SISA

Wieser, Wolfgang. *See* WISER, WOLFGANG.

Wiesner, Arnošt (*b* Malacky, Slovakia, 21 Jan 1890; *d* Liverpool, 15 July 1971). Slovak architect. He studied architecture at the Akademie der Bildenden Künste, Vienna, under Friedrich Ohmann. He later became Ohmann's assistant, although his architectural philosophy was at that time much more influenced by Adolf Loos. Between 1919 and 1939 he worked in Brno where he carried out much of his work, which, in the spirit of Loos, anticipated the principles of modern traditionalism. His most important building was the municipal crematorium (1925–30), Brno, a modern interpretation of the Mesopotamian ziggurat. He also built several houses in Brno, the Morava building (1927), the post office (1934–6) in Šumperk, northern Moravia, and the Moravian Bank (1929–31; with Bohuslav Fuchs), Brno; all exhibit a bold but traditional approach with fine detailing in natural materials. In 1939, after the political disintegration of Czechoslovakia, he went to England where he worked in architectural schools in Oxford and Liverpool.

BIBLIOGRAPHY

F. Achleitner: 'Ernest Wiesner +', *Bauforum*, v/29 (1972), pp. 13–15

Arnost Wiesner, 1890–1971 (exh. cat. by V. Šlapeta, Olomouc, 1981) [with list of works]

V. Šlapeta: 'Brno: Una capitale dell'architettura moderna', *Parametro*, 114 (1983), pp. 12–64

VLADIMÍR ŠLAPETA

Wiet, Gaston (Louis Marie Joseph) (*b* Paris, 18 Dec 1887; *d* Neuilly-sur-Seine, 20 April 1971). French historian of Islamic art. Son of Maxime Wiet and Berthe Rousseau and descendant of the English poet Sir Thomas Wyatt, from 1905 to 1908 Wiet studied Arabic, Persian and Turkish and Islamic history at the Ecole Nationale des Langues Vivantes, Paris, as well as acquiring a degree in law. In 1909 he joined the French Institut d'Archéologie Orientale in Cairo, where he met the orientalists Louis Massignon, Jean Maspéro, MAX VAN BERCHEM, Henri Massé, René Basset, René Dussaud, Maurice Gaudefroy-Demombynes and William Marçais. In 1911 he was appointed professor of Arabic at the University of Lyon. He continued there until 1926, interrupted when he lectured on Arabic literature at the Egyptian University of Cairo and fought in World War I, receiving the croix de guerre for bravery. A member of the Académie des Inscriptions et Belles-Lettres since 1925, Wiet continued the publication of van Berchem's corpus of Arabic inscriptions. In 1926 King Fu'ad I of Egypt appointed Wiet director of the Museum of Arab Art (later Islamic Art) in Cairo, and he began to publish catalogues of the museum collections. With Etienne Combe and JEAN SAUVAGET he edited the *Répertoire chronologique d'épigraphie arabe* and was a member of the Committee for the Preservation of Arab Monuments (Cairo). Inspired by the exhibition of Persian art held at the Royal Academy, London, in 1931 he organized an exhibition (1935) of Persian art in Cairo. From 1936 to 1938 he lectured on the history of Islamic art at the Ecole du Louvre, Paris. Otherwise he remained in Cairo until he was appointed professor of Arabic language and literature at the Collège de France in 1951. Wiet also published editions and translations of many Arabic texts, including the history of Cairo by the 15th-century Egyptian historian al-Maqrizi, and works about many aspects of Islamic art and Egyptian history as well as translations of contemporary Egyptian authors.

WRITINGS

ed. of Aḥmad ibn 'Alī al-Maqrīzī: *al-Mawā'iẓ wa'l-i'tibār bi-dhikr al-khiṭaṭ wa'l-āthār* [Exhortations and consideration for the mention of districts and monuments], *Mém.: Inst. Fr. Archéol. Caire*, xxx, xxxiii, il, liii, lxvi (1911–27)

Lampes et bouteilles en verre émaillé, Cairo, Mus. Islam. A. cat. (Cairo, 1929/*R* 1982)

Matériaux pour un corpus inscriptionum arabicarum: Première partie: Egypte, 2, *Mém.: Inst. Fr. Archéol. Caire*, lii (1929–30)

Album du Musée Arabe du Caire (Cairo, 1930)

ed. with E. Combe and J. Sauvaget: *Répertoire chronologique d'épigraphie arabe*, 16 vols (Cairo, 1931–)

Objets en cuivre, Cairo, Mus. Islam. A. cat. (Cairo, 1932)

with L. Hautecoeur: *Les Mosquées du Caire*, 2 vols (Paris, 1932)

L'Exposition persane de 1931 (Cairo, 1933)

Exposition d'art persan (Cairo, 1935)

Les Stèles funéraires, Cairo, Mus. Islam. A. cat., ii, iv–x (Cairo, 1936–42)

Miniatures persanes, turques et indiennes: Collection de son excellence Chérif Sabry Pacha (Cairo, 1943)

Soieries persanes (Cairo, 1947)

Mohammed Ali et les beaux-arts (Cairo, 1949), pp. 265–88

with A. Raymond: *Les Marchés du Caire: Traduction annotée du texte de Maqrīzī* (Cairo, 1979)

with H. M. el-Hawary: *Matériaux pour un corpus inscriptionum arabicarum: Quatrième partie: Arabie*, *Mém. Inst. Fr. Archéol. Caire*, cix/1 (1985)

BIBLIOGRAPHY

N. Elisséeff: Obituary, *J. Asiat.*, cclix (1971), pp. 1–9

An. Islam., xi (1972) [issue devoted to Wiet]

Studies in Memory of Gaston Wiet, ed. M. Rosen-Ayalon (Jerusalem, 1977), pp. 345–56

S. J. VERNOIT

Wiethase, Heinrich Johann (*b* Kassel, 9 Aug 1833; *d* Cologne, 9 Dec 1893). German architect. He attended school in Kassel and then learnt the craft of bricklaying before studying at the Gewerbeschule (until 1851) with Georg Gottlob Ungewitter. Ungewitter then sent him to Cologne to learn the mason's trade under Vincenz Statz. Wiethase subsequently joined (1855) the offices of Julius Raschdorff to work on the reconstruction (1855–7; destr. 1944; rebuilt) of the Gürzenich, the medieval Cologne festival hall, and then joined those of Friedrich von Schmidt. When Schmidt later went to Milan to teach, he handed his office in Cologne and all unfinished projects over to Wiethase, who went to Berlin (1860–62) to qualify as a private architect. In 1862 he won the Schinkelpreis with a Gothic Revival design. After his return to Cologne he was actively employed as an architect and restorer until his death. He was involved in the debate regarding the preservation of Cologne's historic buildings, and restored the city walls and gates (after 1881). He co-founded the Architekten- und Ingenieurvereins für den Niederrhein und Westfalen and became director (1899) of the register of Rhineland historic monuments. Although he was a prolific architect of town halls, schools and private houses, he designed a particularly large number of churches, mostly Roman Catholic. His excellent draughtsmanship enabled him to develop his own ornamental vocabulary, which in his early churches employed the 'Hohenstaufen' style. These included St Alphons (1864–5) in Aachen and the nearby church (1864–9) at Eilendorf. Most of his churches, however, were in the Gothic style, which he used with elegance. Few survived World War II undamaged but his larger churches include those at Hüls (1865–70), near Krefeld, Dülken (1871–5), Waldniel (1878–83) on the Lower Rhine and St Johann Baptist (1879–86; rest.) in Bonn. For the Jakobskirche (1877–86) at Aachen, the tower of which is a city symbol, Wiethase returned to the 'Hohenstaufen' style.

BIBLIOGRAPHY

A. Verbeek: *Rheinischer Kirchenbau im 19. Jahrhundert* (Cologne, 1954)

H. Kisky: 'Die katholische Pfarrkirche St Michael in Waldniel und ihr Baumeister Heinrich Wiethase', *Niederrhein*, xxv (1958)

——: *Waldniel: Rheinische Kunststätten* (Neuss, 1959)

E. Coester: 'Heinrich Wiethase: Sein Werk im Kreis Düren und die dazu erhaltenen Zeichnungen', *Dürener Geschbl.*, xlvii (1968)

W. Weyres and A. Mann: *Handbuch zur rheinischen Baukunst des 19. Jahrhunderts* (Cologne, 1968)

W. Weyres: 'Rheinischer Sakralbau im 19. Jahrhundert', *Die deutsche Stadt im 19. Jahrhundert*, ed. L. Grote (Munich, 1974), pp. 175–88

W. Bertz-Neuerburg: 'Kurzbiographien der Architekten und Baumeister', *Kunst des 19. Jahrhunderts im Rheinland: Architektur, II*, ed. E. Trier and W. Weyres (Düsseldorf, 1980), p. 555

W. Marquass: *Heinrich Johann Wiethase: Privatbaumeister in Köln* (diss., Aachen, Rhein.–Westfäl. Tech. Hochsch., 1980)

W. Weyres: 'Katholische Kirchen im alten Erzbistum Köln und im rheinischen Teil des Bistums Münster', *Kunst des 19. Jahrhunderts im Rheinland: Architektur, I*, ed. E. Trier and W. Weyres (Düsseldorf, 1980), pp. 75–193

WILLY WEYRES

Wigand, Albert (*b* Ziegehaid on Hessen, 24 Aug 1890; *d* Leipzig, 17 May 1978). German painter, draughtsman and collagist. He took his teaching diploma in art as a pupil of Lothar von Kunowski (*b* 1866) in Düsseldorf in 1913. During World War I he served as a soldier and then continued his studies with Otto Ubbelohde in Grossfelden at Marburg on the Lahn (1920–22). From 1923 to 1924 he studied at the Kunstgewerbeschule in Berlin with Igor von Jakimow. For most of his life he earned a living by manual labour rather than through his art. In 1925 he took a post as a window-dresser in Dresden, which he kept until 1943. Thereafter he was employed as an unskilled worker in the Dresden-Reick gasworks until 1945. After World War II he worked as a street-light keeper in Plauen, Dresden (until 1956).

Most of Wigand's work comprises drawings made with a soft pencil in a style that barely changed throughout his life. His earliest-known works are drawings and woodcuts (1917–19): while those of 1917 are realist in style, by 1919 an Expressionist approach is visible. In the 1920s he also produced lavishly coloured watercolours. He was a painter of subtle moods and loved the quiet brightness of everyday themes. His interest, therefore, lay not in the Baroque metropolis of Dresden, but rather in the little-noticed squares of the suburbs and the workers' quarters. Street scenes and interiors are the main subjects of his work. He worked in black chalk, casually, during short breaks at work, and also in pencil, drawing ink and quills. Occasionally he used coloured pencils and tempera.

In autumn 1946 Wigand exhibited at the first Allgemeine Kunstausstellung in Dresden, a show that was a sign of a new cultural beginning, held in a city that had been badly destroyed by bombing. He was not, however, a well-known artist by this date. From the mid-1950s paintings and collages predominated in his work, and the new theme of the still-life came to the fore. The simple, quiet compositions are reminiscent of the works of Chardin. The French influence in Wigand's work is recognizable, in particular his love of Bonnard, Braque and Utrillo. Most of his later work comprised collages, which demonstrate clearly his development from a sensitive realism towards abstraction. It was not until old age that he was able to devote himself to his art.

BIBLIOGRAPHY

L. Lang: *Begegnungen im Atelier* (Berlin, 1975)

Albert Wigand (exh. cat., Dresden, Gal. Nord, 1979)

CHRISTOPH TANNERT

Wigand, Ede Thoroczkai. *See* THOROCZKAI WIGAND, EDE

Wight, Peter B(onnett) (*b* New York, 1 Aug 1838; *d* Pasadena, CA, 8 Sept 1925). American architect and writer. In 1855 he graduated from the Free Academy in New York, and from 1859 to 1871 he practised in New York. He is best known for his National Academy of Design (1863–5; mostly destr. 1901), which was on Fourth Avenue and 23rd Street, New York, and which he won in competition (1861), with a design heavily influenced by John Ruskin's theories and reminiscent of the Doge's Palace in Venice. With Russell Sturgis, his partner during 1863–8, he helped found a society dedicated to the ideals of Ruskin and the Pre-Raphaelites, the Association for the Advancement of Truth in Art. Wight's articles in the society's journal *The New Path* (1863–5) advocated honest construction and the Gothic style. Wight's Yale School of Fine Arts Building (1864–6, now Street Hall), New Haven, housed the first college art school in America. The decoration and furnishings he designed for his Brooklyn Mercantile Library (1865, 1867–9; destr.) and his furniture and wallpaper produced in the 1870s anticipated the American Arts and Crafts Movement.

Following the great Chicago fire of 1871, Wight moved to Chicago where, in partnership with Asher Carter (1805–77) and William H. Drake (*b* 1837), he designed commercial buildings and houses. Daniel H. Burnham and John Wellborn Root were draughtsmen in the office. In 1874 Drake and Wight patented a fireproof iron column that was subsequently much used. From 1881 to 1891 Wight operated his own fireproofing company. He was responsible for the innovative fireproof construction of many important Chicago buildings, for example Jenney's Home Insurance Building (1883–5). He also wrote widely on architecture and fireproofing technology and frequently reviewed Chicago school work.

WRITINGS

National Academy of Design: Photographs of the New Building with an Introductory Essay and Description (New York, 1866)

'Remarks on Fireproof Construction', *Archit. Rev. & Amer. Builders' J.*, ii (1869), pp. 99–108

'The Origin and History of Hollow Tile Fire-proof Floor Construction', *Brickbuilder*, vi (1897), pp. 53–5, 73–5, 98–9, 149–50

'Reminiscences of Russell Sturgis', *Archit. Rec.*, xxvi (1909), pp. 123–31

BIBLIOGRAPHY

S. B. Landau: *P. B. Wight: Architect, Contractor, and Critic, 1838–1925* (Chicago, 1981)

SARAH BRADFORD LANDAU

Wiig Hansen, Svend (*b* Møgeltønder, Sønderjylland, 20 Dec 1922). Danish sculptor, painter and printmaker. He studied sculpture at the Kunstakademi, Copenhagen, between 1946 and 1950, and he later taught there (1971–6). Although he began his career as a sculptor, he soon began painting. In his sculpture he was largely concerned with expanding the boundaries of classical forms and techniques. His sculptures are also a reaction against academicism. Choosing such pliant materials as clay, plaster, lead and cement and also using bronze, Wiig Hansen preferred to alter the conception of the sculpture as he worked, concerned to manifest his forms' expressive potential. The resulting unity of tension and balance is revealed in *Mother Earth* (1953; Herning, Kstmus.), which is typically voluminous, with dramatically swelling contours, and *Torso* (1954, Copenhagen, Stat. Mus. Kst). For Wiig Hansen the human body became a symbol of worldly angst, and the image of the deformed, crippled or grotesque human form is central to his sculptural and two-dimensional work.

Wiig Hansen was self-taught as a painter. The human figures in his paintings have the projection of sculptural forms, and his experience as a sculptor is detectable in their plastic conception. His preferred motifs are the simplified, realistic figures of lonely people with poignant, averted faces, for example *Figure in a Room* (1959; Humlebæk, Louisiana Mus.). He also often turned to the self-portrait to expose his personality in grotesque representation. He did not work with a consistent palette, however. In the 1960s his use of colour was influenced by the Cobra group, especially in powerful strokes of red, yellow, green and blue, as in *Movement* (1962; Herning, Kstmus.). His handling of paint was at first reticent, but it became more fluid and expressionist. In his printmaking he explored contrasts between black and white to great effect. He worked primarily with linocuts (e.g. *Mankind*, 1959; Herning, Kstmus.) and etchings (e.g. *Seeking*, 1958; Copenhagen, Stat. Mus. Kst).

BIBLIOGRAPHY
B. Irve: *Svend Wiig Hansen* (Copenhagen, 1971)
Svend Wiig Hansen (Copenhagen, 1975); Eng. trans. by D. Holmes
G. Jespersen: 'Svend Wiig Hansen', *Kunstnere omkring os* [Artists around us] (Copenhagen, 1976), pp. 50–57
Wiig Hansen: Tegninger/Drawings (exh. cat., Oslo, Munch-Mus., 1981)
RIGMOR LOVRING

Wiik, Maria (Catharina) [(Katarina)] (*b* Helsinki, 2 Aug 1853; *d* Helsinki, 19 June 1928). Finnish painter. She studied in Paris at the Académie Julian from 1875 to 1876 under Tony Robert-Fleury and continued her studies with him in the same studio between 1877 and 1880. Her paintings appeared at the Salon for the first time in 1880 (e.g. *Marietta*, 1880; Helsinki, priv. col., see Katerma, p. 31). The realist techniques Wiik absorbed in Paris came to form the basis of her work, tranquil in composition and restrained in colour. Her favourite subjects were relatively small-scale portraits such as *Hilda Wiik* (1881; Helsinki, Athenaeum A. Mus.) and still-lifes (e.g. *Still-life*, *c.* 1880; Helsinki, Athenaeum A. Mus.). Like many other foreign painters Wiik went to Brittany to paint. In 1883 4 she worked in Concarneau and Pont-Aven, where her enthusiasm for *plein-air* painting brought immediacy to her work and greater brightness to her colours (e.g. *Breton Farm*, 1883; Naantali, Föreningen Hedvigsminne). She preferred to record her impressions in portraits, although she also painted small, light-filled landscapes. In 1889 Wiik worked under the direction of Puvis de Chavannes in Henri Bouvet's studio in Paris, and in the same year she visited St Ives where she painted, among others, two major works: *Out in the World* (Helsinki, Athenaeum A. Mus.) and the *St Ives Girl* (Helsinki, priv. col., see Katerma, p. 93). Both works show Wiik moving towards an ever more internalized and minimal mode of expression, thereby taking part in the process that led, in the 1890s, to a general abandonment of realism in favour of a greater emphasis on emotion. *Out in the World*, which shows an old woman's sad parting from a young girl who is leaving home to begin work, shows a change in technique with the use of more united colour surfaces and of tone painting. (This work was awarded a bronze medal at the Exposition Universelle in Paris in 1900.) During the 1890s and the early 20th century Wiik's travels were concentrated in Scandinavia, although she visited Paris in 1905. After 1900 she turned from a realist approach to one influenced by Symbolism, taking up sombre and emotional themes, for

instance in *The Story* (1903; Turku, A. Mus.). She also tried to apply Impressionist ideas on colour but failed to recapture the sensitivity and spontaneity of early works painted in Paris. The deterioration of her eyesight made it more difficult for her to work.

BIBLIOGRAPHY
H. Westermarck: *Tre konstnärinnor* [Three women artists] (Helsinki, 1937)
P. Katerma: *Maria Wiik* (diss., U. Helsinki, 1954)
Sieben finnische Malerinnen (exh. cat., ed. S. Sarajas-Korte, S. Sinisalo and L. Ahtola-Moorhouse; Helsinki, Acad. F.A.; Hamburg, Ksthalle; 1983)
S. Sarajas-Korte: 'Maria Wiik', *A. Suom. Taide*, iv (1989), pp. 225–7
R. Konttinen: *Tutuus enemmän kuin kauneus: Nai staiteilija, realismi ja naturalismi 1880–luvulla* [Maria Wiik, truth before beauty: a woman artist, realism and naturalism in the 1880s] (Helsinki, 1991), pp. 30–33
SOILI SINISALO

Wiiralt, Eduard. *See* VIIRALT, EDUARD.

Wijck [Wyck]. Dutch family of painters and draughtsmen. (1) Thomas Wijck was active for a short time in Italy and is best known for his scenes of popular life set in Roman squares and courtyards, themes he continued to paint even after his return to the northern Netherlands. He travelled to England shortly after the Restoration and was followed there by his son and pupil (2) Jan Wyck, who remained in Britain for the rest of his career and played an important role in the development of English sporting painting.

(1) Thomas Wijck (*b* Beverwijck, nr Haarlem, ?1616; *bur* Haarlem, 19 Aug 1677). His date of birth, reported by Houbraken, cannot be confirmed in documents. His training probably took place in Haarlem. He journeyed to Italy, presumably by 1640, the year in which a 'Tommaso fiammingo, pittore' (Thomas the Fleming, painter) is documented as residing in Rome in the Via della Fontanella. In 1642 Wijck was once again in the northern Netherlands, enrolled in Haarlem's Guild of St Luke. It is unlikely that the artist was again in Rome in the spring of 1644 (as Busiri Vici maintained), given the fact that on 22 May of that year he was married in Haarlem. His presence in his native city is further documented in 1658, 1659, 1669 and 1676.

Given the lack of dated works by Wijck, it is difficult to establish which paintings he executed in Rome, since even after his return to the Netherlands he painted Dutch Italianate themes, using black chalk and wash drawings done from life in Rome, a large number of which have survived. It is likely that the paintings most directly reflecting the work of northern artists active in Rome *c.* 1640 and those depicting the city's landscape with the greatest sense of immediacy and realism date from his Roman period and the years shortly thereafter. Works that can be dated to the 1640s include the *View of the Aracoeli* (Munich, Alte Pin.), the *Market Place at the Portico d'Octavia* (priv. col., see Trezzani, fig. 7.8), the *Roman Courtyard with a Blacksmith* (priv. col., see Trezzani, fig. 7.4) and the *Washerwomen in a Courtyard* (Warsaw, N. Mus.; see fig.), for which there is a preparatory drawing of a deserted courtyard (Amsterdam, Rijksmus.). Whatever Wijck's training, these paintings show that during his stay in Rome, Wijck was aware of the late works of Andries Both, such as Both's *Musicians in a Courtyard* (Munich, Alte Pin.). Wijck also harked back to the works of Pieter van Laer (Il Bamboccio), whose paintings were despatched

Thomas Wijck: *Washerwomen in a Courtyard*, oil on canvas, 410×354 mm, before 1642 (Warsaw, National Museum)

regularly to Haarlem from Rome, so Wijck may have seen examples even before travelling to Italy. Through examples of van Laer's work, such as *Travellers in a Courtyard* (Florence, Uffizi) and *Flagellants* (Munich, Alte Pin.), Wijck learnt to structure his characteristic views of courtyards and small squares framed, in the foreground, by archways and enclosed, in the background, by rooftops and loggias.

Wijck presented a 'backstreet' view of Rome, bereft of the great Classical and Renaissance monuments that were the main focus of attention for other Dutch Italianates and, more especially, for their northern clientele. It is rarely possible to identify specific locations in his works, but despite or perhaps because of this, Wijck's views of the city, undoubtedly composed in the studio according to specific structural principles, seem more convincing and more realistic than those created by the Italianate artists of the second half of the 17th century. Scenes of Roman popular life crowded with small figures, so typical of the Bamboccianti (followers of van Laer), are of relatively little importance when compared with Wijck's overwhelming interest in the urban setting. Yet some of Wijck's paintings, for example the *Morra Players* (Vienna, Gemäldegal. Akad. Bild. Kst.) and the *Peasants in a Courtyard* (Philadelphia, PA, Mus. A.), show strong connections with the *bambocciata* paintings (low-life scenes) of the early 1640s and in particular with the work of the so-called Master of the Small Trades, who may perhaps be identifiable with the young Jan Lingelbach.

There is a much greater concentration on landscape elements in paintings such as *Washerwomen* (Hannover, Niedersächs. Landesmus.) and *View of the Ponte Molle* (Brunswick, Herzog Anton Ulrich-Mus.), which is partly based on an engraving of the same subject by Jan Both. A

vital part of Thomas Wijck's development as a landscape artist was undoubtedly the example set by Jan Asselijn, who was probably active in Rome between 1639 and 1643, and perhaps also that set by the much older artist Filippo Napoletano, who, in works such as the *Mill* (Florence, Pitti), had earlier displayed the same propensity for realism and the same method of structuring his compositions.

In the course of his travels in Italy Wijck probably also visited Naples. Though unconfirmed by documents, there are a number of views by his hand relating to the Gulf of Naples, for example the small and highly realistic *View of the Bay of Naples* (Naples, Causa priv. col., see Trezzani, fig. 7.15) and the imaginary views of harbours showing Mt Vesuvius and the Torre di S Vicenzo in the background with figures of travellers and exotic Orientals in the foreground (e.g. *Imaginary View of a Port*, Munich, Alte Pin.). These imaginary harbour and shore scenes enriched with picturesque figures were highly prized by 18th-century collectors and connoisseurs. Wijck's example may have inspired other northern Italianates to enrich their thematic repertory with Neapolitan subjects.

In his last years Wijck produced works closely linked in style and subject-matter to Dutch genre painting. They are completely independent of his Italianate works, while still preserving some of the artist's earlier compositional devices. For instance, an arch frames the scene of a mother and child in the *Dutch Interior* (Copenhagen, Stat. Mus. Kst). Interior scenes with alchemists (e.g. Brunswick, Herzog Anton Ulrich-Mus.; Munich, Alte Pin., 856) were typical of the artist according to Horace Walpole. Walpole also recalled the artist's visit to London, during which he is said to have painted views of the city before the Great Fire of 1666 (e.g. Badminton House, Glos) and also depicted the fire itself (e.g. Chatsworth, Derbys). This journey probably took place between 1660 and 1668, a period during which Wijck is not recorded in his homeland. Walpole's statement that the artist died in London in 1682 is incorrect.

BIBLIOGRAPHY

Thieme–Becker
A. Houbraken: *De groote schouburgh* (1718–21), ii, pp. 16–17
H. Walpole: *Anecdotes of Painting in England, 1762–80*, ii (London, 1869, rev. 2/1876), p. 234
Nederlandse 17e-eeuwse Italianiserende landschapschilders (exh. cat. by A. Blankert, Utrecht, Centraal Mus., 1965); rev. and trans. as *Dutch 17th-century Italianate Landscape Painters* (Soest, 1978), pp. 144–6
M. Roethlisberger: 'Around Filippo Napoletano', *Master Drgs*, xiii/1 (1975), pp. 23–6
L. Salerno: *Pittori di paesaggio del seicento a Roma*, i (Rome, 1977), pp. 342–7
A. Busiri Vici: 'Porti, piazzette, casolari di Roma e dintorni di Tomaso Fiammingo', *L'Urbe*, xli/4 (1978), pp. 9–14
C. S. Schloss: *Travel, Trade, and Temptation: The Dutch Italianate Harbour Scene, 1640–1680* (Ann Arbor, 1982)
L. Trezzani: 'Thomas Wijk', *The Bamboccianti: Painters of Everyday Life in 17th-century Rome*, ed. G. Briganti, L. Trezzani and L. Laureati (Rome, 1983), pp. 223–37, figs 7.1–7.16
Die Niederländer in Italien (exh. cat. by R. Trnek, Vienna, Bib. Akad. Bild. Kst., 1986), pp. 212–22
A. C. Steland: 'Thomas Wijck als italienisierender Zeichner: Beobachtungen zu Herkunft, Stil und Arbeitsweise', *Wallraf-Richartz-Jb*, xlviii–xlix (1988), pp. 215–47, figs. 1–35

LUDOVICA TREZZANI

(2) Jan Wyck (*b* Haarlem, 29 Oct 1652; *d* Mortlake, nr London, 17 May 1700). Son of (1) Thomas Wijck. A marriage certificate issued on 22 November 1676 describes the artist as 'Jan Wick of St Paul's Covent Garden, gent., widower, about 31 ...', suggesting that he was born *c.* 1645, but his correct birthdate is known from the inscription on a mezzotint portrait of him by John Faber II (1684–1756) after a painting by Sir Godfrey Kneller. Jan is first documented on 17 June 1674, when he appeared before the court of the Painter-Stainers' Company in London and vowed to pay both his own and his father's quarterly fees. The certificate of 1676 relates to his second marriage, to Ann Skinner (*d* 1687), who between 1678 and 1683 bore him four children, all of whom died young. After Ann's death in 1687, he married Elizabeth Holomberg (*d* 1693) in 1688 and moved to Mortlake. Between 1689 and 1693 they had two sons and a daughter.

During his lifetime Wyck travelled throughout the British Isles: among his surviving works are landscape paintings of Scotland and Jersey and drawings of subjects around London, Oxford and Bristol. Vertue called him a 'Dutch Battel-Painter of grate note', a description justified by his early *Cavalry Skirmish* (Ham House, Surrey, NT), painted for the Duke of Lauderdale in a style reminiscent of Philips Wouwerman and Jacques Courtois (il Borgognone). The *Battle of Bothwell Brig* (1679; Duke of Buccleuch, priv. col.) was probably painted for John Scott, Duke of Monmouth and Buccleuch (1649–85). Wyck also recorded several military expeditions of King William III, for example the Battle of the Boyne and the Siege at Namur. He also specialized in portraits of military officers

on horseback and, especially, in hunting scenes, a genre in which he achieved great fame. Vertue (ii, p. 141) wrote: 'His Hunting Pieces are also in grate Esteem among our Country-Gentry, for whom he often drew Horses and Dogs by the Life.' His hunting scenes are usually set in wide, hilly landscapes, rendered with a strong sense of colour. Wyck was also an accomplished marine painter, as can be seen from his signed *Whitehaven Harbour from the Sea* (1686; Holker Hall, Cumbria), a painting made for Sir John Lowther, who was one of the artist's patrons. Wyck occasionally collaborated with Kneller, adding horses and landscape to his equestrian portraits.

Wyck was active as a draughtsman. He was commissioned to draw a series of hunting scenes for Richard Blome's two-volume encyclopedia *Gentleman's Recreation* (London, 1686), which includes the *Death of the Hart*, for which the drawing survives (London, BM; see fig.)

John Wootton, the first important English painter of hunting scenes, was a pupil of Wyck in the late 1690s, and several of his compositions reflect those of his master. Wyck's equestrian portraits were influential, in particular among artists of the early 18th century, such as Wootton and David Morier (*c.* 1705–70).

BIBLIOGRAPHY
'The Note-books of George Vertue', *Walpole Soc.*, xx (1932), pp. 1–158
M. H. Grant: *The Old English Landscape Painters* (Leigh-on-Sea, 1958), pp. 46–7, pls 16, 17
E. Croft-Murray and P. Hulton: *XVI and XVII Centuries*, i of *Catalogue of British Drawings*, London, BM (London, 1960), pp. 551–5, pls 290b, 295, 296
O. Millar: 'Jan Wyck and John Wooton at Antony', *NT Yb.* (1975–6), pp. 38–41
J. Harris: *The Artist and the Country House: A History of Country House and Garden View Painting in Britain, 1540–1870* (London, 1979), pp. 43, 44, 60, 109, pls 53, 100
K. J. Müllenmeister: *Meer und Land im Licht des 17. Jahrhunderts*, iii (Bremen, 1981), pp. 111–12, pls 580–81
Drawing in England from Hilliard to Hogarth (exh. cat., ed. L. Stainton and C. White; London, BM, 1987), pp. 204–6, cat. nos 162–3

L. J. WASSINK

Wijdan Ali. *See* ALI, WIJDAN.

Wijdeveld, Hendrik [Hendricus] **T(heodorus)** (*b* The Hague, 4 Oct 1885; *d* Amsterdam, 1989). Dutch architect, writer, furniture designer and teacher. He trained in the offices of J. van Straaten (1897–9) and P. J. H. Cuypers (1900–04), and he became acquainted with K. P. C. de Bazel and J. L. Mathieu Lauweriks, the leaders of the Nieuwe Kunst movement. From 1905 to 1908 he worked in England in J. Groll's office and attended evening classes at the Lambeth School of Art. He worked with L. M. Cordonnier first on the Vredespalais in The Hague and then from 1911 to 1914 in Lille. He returned to the Netherlands during World War I, entering architectural competitions and designing furniture and toys. He also wrote articles for architectural periodicals and in 1918 began directing *Wendingen*, the periodical of the AMSTERDAM SCHOOL. In that year he visited Berlin, where he met the Expressionist architect Erich Mendelsohn and the critic Alfred Behne. He began to concentrate on producing utopian plans, such as the reorganization of Vondelpark (1919–20; unexecuted), Amsterdam, with a Volkstheater as its central element. His most important executed plans

Jan Wyck: *Death of the Hart*, pen and brown ink and wash, 298×210 mm, 1686 (London, British Museum)

date from 1920–24: housing blocks in Amsterdam on the Hoofdweg, on the corner of the Insulindeweg and the Celebesstraat, and on the corner of the Amstelkade and Vechtstraat. In 1925 he was responsible for designing the Dutch section of the Exposition Internationale des Arts Décoratifs et Industriels Modernes in Paris, which represented the last manifestation of the Amsterdam school. From the 1920s he concentrated on theatre costume and became increasingly interested in international art and architecture, devoting seven issues of *Wendingen* in 1925 to Frank Lloyd Wright. In 1947–50 and 1962 he lectured in the USA.

WRITINGS

Regular contributions to *Architectura* [Amsterdam], *Bouwknd. Wkbld Archit.* and *Wendingen* (1918–25)

BIBLIOGRAPHY

G. Fanelli: *Architettura moderna* (Florence, 1968)
W. de Wit, ed.: *The Amsterdam School: Dutch Expressionist Architecture, 1915–1930* (Cambridge, MA, 1983)

MARTY TH. BAX

Wijnants [Wynants], **Jan** [Johannes] (*b* ?Haarlem, *c.* 1635; *d* Amsterdam, *bur* 23 Jan 1684). Dutch painter. Suggested dates for his birth range from 1605 (Bode) to 1635 (Brown); Bredius's proposed birthdate of *c.* 1630–35 (rejected by Hofstede de Groot and MacLaren) is almost certainly correct, with the later part of this period being the most acceptable. Wijnants's father was probably the art dealer Jan Wijnants, who was recorded as a member of the Haarlem Guild of St Luke in 1642. Jan the younger is documented in Haarlem several times until his departure for Amsterdam around 1660. A document pertaining to his father (see Bredius, p. 180) implies, however, that in 1653 Wijnants the younger was in Rotterdam, where the painters Ludolf de Jongh and Adam Pynacker were active. Perhaps the most important early influence on Wijnants was de Jongh's brother-in-law, Dirck Wijntrack (before 1625–78), noted for his paintings of wildfowl. There is much evidence to suggest that the two artists often worked together during the 1650s.

Although Hofstede de Groot dated 12 of Wijnant's pictures to an early period from 1643 to 1652, most of these can be assigned to a later period either on stylistic grounds or by a correct reading of the dates, or else reattributed to other artists (Stechow, 1965). Wijnants probably began to paint shortly after 1650. Among his earliest certain dated works is the *Cottage* (1654; untraced; see Stechow, 1965, fig. 6). The painting is signed by both Wijnants and Wijntrack, and the chickens, ducks and other birds in the foreground are clearly by Wijntrack's hand. Wijntrack may also have been responsible for the wildfowl in the slightly later *Peasant Cottage* (Amsterdam, Rijksmus.). In both of these characteristic early paintings brick farm buildings and cottages occupy a major portion of the composition.

In 1659 Wijnants is again documented in Haarlem, and in the paintings of this period, such as *Landscape with a Dead Tree and a Peasant Driving a Sheep along a Road* (1659; London, N.G.), the buildings, considerably smaller, have been relegated to the middle distance. The stark tree-trunk, a motif derived from Jacob van Ruisdael, was to re-emerge as a kind of leitmotif in Wijnant's paintings of the second half of his career. By December 1660 Wijnants

had moved to Amsterdam, where he married Catharina van der Veer. He remained there for the rest of his life, keeping an inn to supplement his income (he was constantly falling into debt). He was buried in the graveyard of the Leidsekerk.

Almost all of Wijnants's later paintings, such as *Landscape with a Sandy Slope* (St Petersburg, Hermitage), are landscapes, particularly dunescapes based on the broad ridge of sand dunes near Haarlem. Wijnants followed in the tradition of dune painting established by Pieter de Molijn, Philips Wouwerman, van Ruisdael and others. Typical of his early work of the 1660s is *Landscape with Cattle* (1661; London, Wallace; see fig.). A sense of space is created in the left half of the picture by the pattern of the trees and meandering, ribbon-like paths that diminish as they recede into the distance. Sunlight appears to fall naturally on fields and dunes, highlighting at strategic points the blond tones of the sand. By contrast, the right half of the picture builds up to a dense clump of trees reminiscent of those in van Ruisdael's forest pictures of the mid-1650s. The staffage, almost certainly not by Wijnants, has been attributed to Adriaen van de Velde, who according to Houbraken was Wijnants's pupil. This remains conjectural given Wijnants's presumed birthdate, but there is no doubt that the two artists occasionally worked together. Johannes Lingelbach also added figures to some of Wijnants's paintings, including *Landscape with a Sandy Slope* and *Landscape with Huntsmen* (1661; Bonn, Rhein. Landesmus.).

There is no reason to doubt Wijnants's authorship of *View of the Herengracht, Amsterdam* (Cleveland, OH, Mus. A.), although as a topographical urban scene it is apparently unique in terms of subject-matter. It must have been painted between 1660 and 1662 since the trees are reminiscent of those in Wijnants's dated works of 1661 (Stechow, 1965); the figures in the painting are in the style of Lingelbach, although not by him. During the mid-1660s Wijnants also painted the best of his Italianate landscapes, for example the *Angler* (1665; untraced; see Stechow, 1966, fig. 331), which find their closest parallel in the work of Jan Hackaert from the 1660s. Wijnants never travelled to Italy, however, and it is difficult to judge the date of his first and last Italianate works.

Wijnants's later paintings are characterized by the frequent inclusion of a blasted elm or oak tree dominating the foreground. Two examples are the *Hawking Party with a Falconer* (1666; Buckingham, priv. col., see *Apollo*, viii/45 (1928), p. 118), of which there is a signed replica (London, Kenwood House), and the somewhat later *Landscape with Two Dead Trees* (London, N.G.). Highly stylized foliage and fallen tree-trunks are also common motifs in these later works, which suggest, in addition to the influence of van Ruisdael, that of such artists as Pynacker and Otto Marseus van Schrieck, both of whom were working in Amsterdam from around 1660.

Wijnants's pictures appealed strongly to the 18th-century English collectors' enthusiasm for Dutch landscapes. His paintings also influenced 18th- and 19th-century artists, including François Boucher, Thomas Gainsborough and John Crome; the latter is said to have had a painting by Wijnants in his collection. Perhaps it was the decorative, blue tonality of Wijnants's works of

Jan Wijnants: *Landscape with Cattle*, oil on canvas, 635×905 mm, 1661 (London, Wallace Collection)

the 1660s and 1670s that was preferred by artists and collectors alike to the restricted palette of earth tones used by landscape artists in the 1620s and 1630s during the so-called 'tonal phase' of 17th-century Dutch painting.

BIBLIOGRAPHY
A. Houbraken: *De groote schouburgh* (1718–21), iii, p. 90
J. Smith: *A Catalogue Raisonné of Works of the Most Eminent Dutch, Flemish and French Painters*, vi (London, 1835), pp. 225–82
——: *Supplement to the Catalogue Raisonné of Works of the Most Eminent Dutch, Flemish and French Painters* (London, 1842)
W. Bode: *Great Masters of Dutch and Flemish Painting* (London, 1909), p. 211
A. Bredius: 'Een en ander over Jan Wijnants' [A few things about Jan Wijnants], *Oud-Holland*, xxix (1911), pp. 179–84
C. Hofstede de Groot: *Verzeichnis*, viii (1923), pp. 463–639
N. Maclaren: *The Dutch School*, London, N.G. cat. (London, 1960)
W. Stechow: 'Jan Wijnants: *View of the Heerengracht, Amsterdam*', *Bull. Cleveland Mus. A.*, lii/10 (Dec 1965), pp. 164–73
——: *Dutch Landscape Painting of the Seventeenth Century* (London, 1966/R 1981)
Dutch Landscape: The Early Years (exh. cat., ed. C. Brown; London, N.G., 1986)
L. B. L. HARWOOD

Wilars dehonecort. *See* VILLARD DE HONNECOURT

Wilcop, de. *See* VULCOP, DE.

Wilde, Bernard de (*b* Ghent, 31 July 1691; *d* Ghent, 24 March 1772). Flemish architect. His earliest known work was the Pakhuys (warehouse; 1719; destr. 1897), Ghent, in which the main emphasis was on the wide, projecting, central range, pierced by round-headed apertures set off by rusticated joints, the whole surmounted by a triangular pediment. The horizontals of the building were accentuated by projecting cornices and the balcony balustrades. The Tuscan and Corinthian pilasters and the large urns above the attic confirmed the influence of the French style of elevation. De Wilde's concern to distinguish his work from traditional Ghent architecture by turning to French models is also to be seen in his designs (1738; Ghent, Rijksarchief te Gent) for the Guard House (now the Handelsbeurs commercial exchange) and the headquarters of the Guild of St Sebastian, both situated on the Kouter, a large square in southern Ghent. The Guard House, executed by DAVID 'T KINDT, comprises a ground-floor, attic and a mansard roof; with its projecting central range pierced with round-headed apertures, Tuscan pilasters, a triangular pediment and rustication, the building recalls the Pakhuys built 20 years earlier. The rocaille decoration and the cartouche set at an angle, the first examples of Ghent Rococo, are taken up again in his design for the headquarters of the Guild of St Sebastian. De Wilde is also attributed with the Hôtel Falligan (1755), Ghent: the triangular pediment, rocaille ornamentation, central range, round-headed apertures and sculpted decoration all recall his earlier work. The façade of the hôtel, however, with its multiplicity of apertures and greater degree of animation, is more firmly an example of Ghent Rococo, a variant of French rocaille that has its roots in Flemish Baroque.

BNB   BIBLIOGRAPHY
H. Pauwels: *Aspecten van de burgerlijke architectuur te Gent tijdens de Rococo-periode* [Aspects of the civil architecture of Ghent during the Rococo period] (diss., Ghent U., 1948)
——: *De Bouwmeester van de Corps de Garde op de Kouter* [The architect of the Guard House on the Kouter], *Hand. Maatsch. Gesch. & Oudhdknd. Gent*, iv/1 (1949), pp. 112–19
——: *De ontwikkeling van de burgerlijke gevelarchitectuur te Gent, van de 16de tot het einde van de 18de eeuw* [The evolution of façades in civil architecture in Ghent from the 16th century to the end of the 18th] (diss., Ghent U., 1950)
M. Fredericq-Lilar: 'Bernard de Wilde et les caractères de l'architecture gantois du XVIIIe siècle', *Etud. 18ème Siècle*, ii (1975), pp. 15–21
——: *L'Hôtel Falligan, chef d'oeuvre du Rococo gantois* (Brussels, 1977)
——: *Franse franje naar Gentse maat* [French décor in the Ghent style] (exh. cat., Ghent, 1984), p. 46

MARIE FREDERICQ-LILAR

Wilde, Johannes [János] (*b* Budapest, 2 June 1891; *d* London, 15 Sept 1970). British art historian and teacher. He studied with Max Dvořák at Vienna University, where he gained his PhD. In 1923 he joined the Vienna Kunsthistorisches Museum, becoming an Austrian citizen in 1928. In 1939 he fled to England where, in 1941, he started teaching at London University. In 1947 he became a British subject; and in 1948 he was appointed Reader in the History of Art at London University and, until his retirement in 1958, Deputy Director of the Courtauld Institute.

Wilde's work on Italian (and particularly Venetian) paintings in the Kunsthistorisches Museum earned him an international reputation: he made original use of evidence from X-rays of paintings, analysing the creative processes they revealed. His approach to art history emphasized the relationship of a work to the circumstances and original location of its commission, and his teaching was always directed towards this end. Two important series of Courtauld lectures, on Michelangelo and on 16th-century Venetian painting, were subsequently published. A distinguished Michelangelo scholar, his catalogue of the British Museum's collection of Michelangelo drawings was a major achievement.

WRITINGS
M. Hirst: Obituary, *Burl. Mag.*, cxiii (1971), pp. 155–7 (157) [incl. complete list of writings]
Venetian Art from Bellini to Titian (Oxford, 1974)
Michelangelo (Oxford, 1978)

BIBLIOGRAPHY
Burl. Mag., ciii (June, 1961) [issue ded. Wilde]
Burl. Mag., cxiii (March, 1971) [issue ded. Wilde]

WARREN HEARNDEN

Wilde, Oscar (Fingal O'Flahertie Wills) (*b* Dublin, 16 Oct 1854; *d* Paris, 30 Nov 1900). Irish writer and patron. He was educated at Portora Royal School, Trinity College, Dublin, and Magdalen College, Oxford, where he established himself as a leading figure in the AESTHETIC MOVEMENT. Wilde espoused the doctrine of Art for Art's Sake, formulated by Théophile Gautier in the 1830s, and the rarefied hedonism recommended by Walter Pater, who encouraged his literary career. He also adopted the romantic socialism of William Morris, sharing his belief in the artistry of the unfettered craftsman and the importance of beauty in everyday life. He spread his aesthetic philosophy in a series of lectures given in North America in 1882 and later in England. His early writing reveals the influence of the French Decadents; in particular *The Picture of Dorian Gray* (1890) was largely inspired by Joris-Karl Huysmans's *A rebours* (Paris, 1884).

In April 1877, while still at Oxford, Wilde reviewed the opening exhibition of the Grosvenor Gallery, London, for the *Dublin University Magazine*, praising work by Edward Burne-Jones and G. F. Watts; he also approved of James Abbott McNeill Whistler's *Arrangement in Grey and Black, No. 2: Thomas Carlyle* (Glasgow, A.G. & Mus.) while adversely criticizing his *Nocturne in Black and Gold: The Falling Rocket* (Detroit, MI, Inst. A.). He met both Burne-Jones, who remained a lifelong favourite, and Whistler in 1879 when he shared the London lodgings of the portrait painter Frank Miles (1852–91). Wilde and Whistler were seen as the leading exponents of Aestheticism during the 1880s; both courted publicity and were rewarded by frequent caricatures and parodies, the most famous of which, the comic opera *Patience* (1881) by W. S. Gilbert and Arthur Sullivan, caricatured Whistler in English performances and Wilde in American ones. Their personal relationship, although outwardly friendly, was uneasy, for Whistler resented the younger man's growing fame. They were undoubtedly close during the early 1880s following a review in a Dublin newspaper of 5 May 1879 in which Wilde referred to Whistler as the greatest painter in London. Their friendship expanded Wilde's appreciation of art from the anecdotal to include the paintings of Claude Monet and Camille Pissarro and even Whistler's *Nocturnes* to which Wilde paid tribute in at least two poems, *Harmony: Impression du Matin* (1881) and *A Symphony in Yellow* (1889). The increasingly acerbic relationship with Whistler ceased after Wilde published in 1890 *The Critic as Artist*, which extols the merits of the critic at the expense of the artist.

Wilde's adherence to Aesthetic principles of design had begun at Oxford with the purchase of blue-and-white porcelain and culminated in a commission to E. W. Godwin to design a house at 16 Tite Street, Chelsea, London, in 1884. The drawing-room ceiling was designed by Whistler, and the house contained drawings by Burne-Jones, lithographs of Venice by Whistler and works by his disciple Mortimer Menpes, who was a godfather to Wilde's younger son, Vyvyan, born in 1886. Later additions included paintings by Charles Ricketts and Adolphe Monticelli, a drawing of *Mrs Patrick Campbell* by Aubrey Beardsley, and *Love among the Schoolboys* (1865; priv. col.) and *Sacramentum amoris* (1868) by Simeon Solomon.

Wilde took a keen and intelligent interest in the appearance of his books. *The Happy Prince* (1888) has a cover designed by Walter Crane and illustrations by George Percy Jacomb-Hood (1857–1929). Henceforth, with the exception of *Salomé* (1894), which was illustrated by Beardsley (who incorporated caricatures of the author in his drawings), Wilde entrusted all his books to Ricketts and Charles Shannon. Ricketts designed *A House of Pomegranates* (1891) with Shannon, *Poems* (1892) and the *Sphinx* (1894), and Shannon designed *Lady Windermere's Fan* (1893). Wilde suggested Fernand Khnopff as a suitable artist for *The Ballad of Reading Gaol* (1897), but nothing came of it.

Wilde sat for many portraits and was the subject of innumerable caricatures, being lampooned by Carlo Pellegrini, Whistler and Max Beerbohm. He is a prominent figure in William Powell Frith's *The Private View of the Academy* (1881; priv. col, see V. Holland: *Oscar Wilde*, London, 1960, rev. 1966/*R* 1988, p. 57) and was active as a patron during his American and Canadian tour of 1882.

In February 1885, at the height of his success, Wilde was accused of sodomy by Archibald William Douglas, 8th Marquess of Queensberry, father of Lord Alfred Douglas, with whom Wilde was infatuated. After two trials Wilde was sentenced to two years hard labour on 25 May 1895; on his release he fled to France. While in Paris, Wilde became friendly with William Rothenstein, from whom he bought a pastel portrait of himself and commissioned a drawing of Douglas; Rothenstein introduced him to Charles Conder, whose painted fans he greatly admired. During his exile Wilde was portrayed several times by Henri de Toulouse-Lautrec. A splendid and massive memorial to Wilde's connection with the visual arts is Jacob Epstein's monument (1909–12) to him in Père-Lachaise cemetery in Paris.

WRITINGS

Complete Works, 4 vols (London, 1908/*R* 1969)
R. Hart-Davis, ed.: *The Letters of Oscar Wilde* (London, 1962)
R. Ellmann, ed.: *Oscar Wilde: A Collection of Critical Essays* (London, 1969)
R. Hart-Davis, ed.: *More Letters of Oscar Wilde* (London, 1985)

BIBLIOGRAPHY

H. Pearson: *Oscar Wilde: His Life and Wit* (London, 1946)
H. Montgomery Hyde: *Oscar Wilde: A Biography* (London, 1963)
R. Ellmann: *Oscar Wilde* (London, 1987)

DAVID RODGERS

Wilde, Samuel De. *See* DE WILDE, SAMUEL.

Wildens, Jan (*b* Antwerp, 1585–6; *d* Antwerp, 16 Oct 1653). Flemish painter and draughtsman, active also in Italy. He was an important and proficient landscape painter who worked with Rubens and other masters in Antwerp.

1. TO 1614. Jan's father, Hendrik Wildens, died young, and his mother, Magdalena Vosbergen, married Cornelis Cock (*fl* 1629–37); his stepsister married the painter Cornelis de Vos. In 1596 he was apprenticed to Pieter Verhulst (*d* 1628), none of whose work has survived, and in 1604 he became a master in the Antwerp Guild of St Luke. On 22 May 1613, shortly before departing for Italy, Wildens made a will, in which he stated his age as 27. The few works that belong to the period before Wildens left Antwerp for Italy are clearly influenced by Jan Breughel II, Adriaen van Stalbemt, Josse de Momper and Gillis van Coninxloo. These include the series of drawings of the *Twelve Months*, of which prints were made by Hendrik I Hondius (ii) (Hollstein, ix, nos 31–4, as Hendrik 'II' Hondius (i)), Jacob Matham (Hollstein, xi, nos 361–4) and Andries Stock (1580–1648) (Hollstein, xxviii, nos 11–14); the print of *January* is dated 1614, not 1644 (as in Hollstein). The same stylistic influences are also evident in some of Wildens's paintings: the *Mountainous Landscape with a Village and a Pond* (sold London, Sotheby's, 8 May 1946, lot 81; see Adler, fig. 17) is similar in composition to de Momper's *Mountainous Landscape with a Bay* (Detroit, MI, Inst. A.), while Wildens's *River Landscape*

with a Castle and Farmhouse in the Foreground (ex-F. Mont priv. col., New York, see Adler, fig. 18) could almost be described as a compilation of van Stalbemt's *Landscape with a Farmhouse* (Cologne, Wallraf-Richartz-Mus.) and his *Castle by a Pond* (Berlin, Bodemus.).

2. AFTER 1614. Once in Italy, Wildens's style underwent a change, precipitated particularly by the work of Paul Bril, evident in *The Seasons* (*c.* 1615–16; Genoa, Pal. Bianco), a series of paintings corresponding to the prints published by Hondius, Matham and Stock. *January* and *April* retain the schematic rigidity of the prints, whereas *August* and *September (Autumnal Hunt)* (see fig.) have a surprising degree of realism and spontaneity of detail. Presumably he was back in Antwerp by August 1616. In a letter to John Gage dated 14 March 1617, Dudley Carleton laments that on Gage's visit to Antwerp the previous September he could not introduce him to an exceptional landscape painter who had previously been living in Italy; this almost certainly refers to Wildens.

Between 1616 and 1620 much of Wildens's work was for Rubens, though he was never formally employed by him. Wildens produced the landscape backgrounds for various scenes in the designs for the *Decius Mus* tapestry series and for other history paintings, including the *Rape of the Daughters of Leucippus* (*c.* 1618; Munich, Alte Pin.), *Samson and the Lion* (*c.* 1618; Madrid, Duque de Hernani priv. col., see Held, pl. 458), *Cimon and Iphigenia* (*c.* 1617–18; Vienna, Ksthist. Mus.) and *Diana and her Nymphs Departing for the Chase* (*c.* 1616; Cleveland, OH, Mus. A.). In 1619 Rubens acted as a witness to Wildens's marriage to Maria Stappaert. She died in 1624 after producing two sons, who both became painters: Jan Baptist Wildens (1620–37) and Jeremias Wildens (1621–53). Maria's niece Hélène Fourment became Rubens's second wife. Also in 1624 Wildens opened a picture gallery—which was later successfully run by Jeremias, by whose death it boasted 700 paintings—and produced the outstanding *Winter Landscape with Hunter* (Dresden, Gemäldegal. Alte Meister). His works from these years employ decorative forms, loose compositions and a broad technique reminiscent of Rubens, though the earlier influences of Breughel, van Stalbemt and Bril still continue to play a significant role. Wildens never adopted the tempestuous element of Rubens's style, preferring a calm and gentle approach expressed in marked symmetry of composition and soft, subtle colours. The contrast is evident in Wildens's serene *Landscape with a Shepherd* (Antwerp, Kon. Mus. S. Kst.), which was partly inspired by Rubens's more dynamic *Landscape with a Shepherd and his Flock* (London, N.G.).

After Rubens's death in 1640, Wildens (who was one of his executors) concentrated on producing landscapes, such as the *Wooded Landscape with Diana and her Nymphs* (Brunswick, Herzog Anton Ulrich-Mus.), that use the same vibrant light found in Rubens's late landscapes or the same sketchy character (e.g. *Wooded Landscape with Soldiers and a Battle in the Distance*, Kettwig an der Ruhr, Germany, H. Girardet priv. col., see Adler, fig. 121). Wildens also painted landscape backgrounds for Jacob Jordaens, Frans Snyders, Paul de Vos, Abraham Janssen,

Jan Wildens: *September (Autumnal Hunt)*, oil on canvas, 1.23×1.92 m, *c.* 1615–16 (Genoa, Galleria di Palazzo Bianco)

Jan Boeckhorst, Gerard Segers, Cornelis Schut and Theodoor Rombouts. His pupils were Abraham and Philip Lees and Hans Rymaker.

BIBLIOGRAPHY

Hollstein: *Dut. & Flem.*

M. Rooses and C. Ruelens: *Correspondance de Rubens et documents épistolaires concernant sa vie et ses oeuvres*, ii (Antwerp, 1894), p. 104

J. Denucé: *De antwerpsche 'konstkamers': Inventarissen van kunstverzamelingen te Antwerpen in de 16de en 17de eeuwen* (Antwerp, 1932), pp. 157, 309

Y. Thiéry: *Le Paysage flamand au XVIIe siècle* (Paris and Brussels, 1953), pp. 113–16

W. Adler: *Jan Wildens: Der Landschaftsmitarbeiter des Rubens* (Fridingen, 1980)

J. S. Held: *The Oil Studies of Peter Paul Rubens: A Critical Catalogue*, 2 vols (Princeton, 1980)

The Age of Rubens (exh. cat., ed. P. C. Sutton; Boston, MA, Mus. F.A.; Toledo, OH, Mus. A.; 1993–4), pp. 559–66

Flemish Drawings in the Age of Rubens (exh. cat. by A.-M. Logan, Wellesley Coll., MA, Davis Mus. & Cult. Cent., 1993–4), pp. 224–5

HANS DEVISSCHER

Wildenstein. French family of dealers and writers. In 1875 the first branch of the Wildenstein Gallery was opened in Paris. In 1902 a branch of the gallery was opened in New York, and subsequently branches were opened in London and Buenos Aires. By 1905 the status of the gallery was synonymous with the most highly prized Old Masters.

(1) Nathan Wildenstein (*b* Fekersheim, Alsace, 8 Nov 1851; *d* Paris, 24 April 1934). He was the first member of the family to become a dealer. In 1870 he left Alsace for France, where he initially dealt in textiles, before accidentally becoming involved in dealing when he was asked to sell a painting. Two years later he made his first sales coup when he bought and sold a François Boucher painting for a tenfold profit (Clay, p. 80). Nathan was one of the first to realize the possible potential of selling art works as luxury goods to a new wealthy bourgeois clientele. Dealers such as Paul Durand-Ruel sponsored contemporary artists, whereas Nathan was significant for his success in fostering a taste for Old Masters and 18th-century French painting and sculpture, first among European collectors such as Baron Edmond de Rothschild and later among American collectors such as J. Pierpont Morgan. Under Nathan, a policy of building up large stocks of works by the most prestigious artists was formulated. Purchases, sometimes acquired at relatively high prices, were—though sometimes sold quite quickly to contemporary collectors—more often hoarded in gallery stockrooms to maximize profit.

(2) Georges Wildenstein (*b* Paris, 16 March 1892; *d* Paris, 13 June 1963). Son of (1) Nathan Wildenstein. He became involved in the running of the Wildenstein establishments in 1910 and took over control on the death of his father. Under Georges, although the galleries continued to be known for their stocks of Old Masters, significant holdings of Impressionist and Post-Impressionist painters, among them several paintings by Paul Gauguin (e.g. *Breasts with Red Flowers*, 1899; New York, Met.), were also built up. The wealth and eminence of the Wildenstein Galleries by the late 1950s was such that in its New York gallery alone it was estimated that there were *c.* 2000 paintings in store, including 2 by Sandro Botticelli, 8 by Rembrandt and 12 by Nicolas Poussin among the Old Masters; while the gallery aimed always to have at least 20 by Auguste

Renoir and 10 works each by Paul Cézanne, Paul Gauguin and Vincent van Gogh. During Georges Wildenstein's life Wildenstein Galleries presented *c.* 600 exhibitions. Though generally eschewing 20th-century art, Georges published the Surrealist magazine *Documents* and in 1930 lent his Paris gallery for the International Surrealist exhibition. He was an art historian in his own right with numerous articles and books to his credit; in 1924 he founded the weekly *Arts*; in the 1930s he became director of the *Gazette des Beaux-Arts*; and in New York between 1941 and 1946 he ran *La République française*.

WRITINGS

Ingres (New York, 1954)
Fragonard, aquafortiste (Paris, 1956)
Le Goût pour la peinture dans la bourgeoisie parisienne entre 1550 et 1610 (Paris, 1962)
Chardin (Zurich, 1963)
Gauguin (Paris, 1964)

(3) Daniel Wildenstein (*b* Verrières-le-Buisson, 11 Sept 1917). Son of (2) Georges Wildenstein. He was the third family member to have overall control of the Wildenstein empire. Initially he was a museum director before taking over the running of the Paris and New York branches in 1959, those in London and Buenos Aires in 1963, and founding the American Institute of France in New York. He wrote a number of scholarly articles and other publications.

WRITINGS

Inventaires après décès d'artistes et de collectionnaires français du XVIIIe siècle (Paris, 1967)
Claude Monet: Biographie et catalogue raisonné (Paris, 1974)
Gauguin (New York, 1974)

BIBLIOGRAPHY

J. Clay: 'L'Epopée des Wildenstein', *Réalités* (March 1959), pp. 76–83, 102
P. Cabanne: *The Great Collectors* (London, 1963)
R. Moulin: *Le Marché de la peinture en France* (Paris, 1967)

A. DEIRDRE ROBSON

Wilding, Alison (*b* Blackburn, Lancs, 1948). English sculptor and draughtswoman. She trained in London at Ravensbourne College of Art (1967–70) and the Royal College of Art (1970–73), where she specialized in sculpture. An interest in perceptual and philosophical questions concerning the nature of art underlay the preoccupation with light, territories, boundaries and their embodiment in matter that was evident in such works as *Without Casting Light on the Subject* (1975; destr.), an installation comprising a chair, table, lights, sheets of slate and glass, and other objects. The arrangement of the work suggested a quasi-scientific investigation of the properties, status and relation of things. From 1978 she was occupied more with the purely material and physical. *Untitled* (1980; AC Eng), two brass bags placed in a roughly circular wall of zinc, was a pivotal work and mapped out elemental sculptural concerns that she later consolidated, especially an interest in the sensual and textural properties of materials and their location in space and light. Another recurrent feature of her work in this period was a preoccupation with dual forms, as in *Nature: Blue and Gold* (brass, ash, oil and pigment, 1984; London, Brit. Council). Here, and in later works, Wilding's discerning feel for material qualities combined with her use of traditional sculptural processes such as modelling, carving and casting to explore contrast and similarity and to develop a highly sensitive and unique

visual language. Wilding has drawn regularly since 1988. Her *Angry Drawings* series (charcoal and oil crayon on paper, 410×590 mm, 1988; e.g. London, Tate) are unrestrained graphic scrawls across the paper surface.

BIBLIOGRAPHY

Alison Wilding (exh. cat., London, Serpentine Gal., 1985) [incl. an informative essay by L. Cooke]
Alison Wilding: Sculptures, 1987–88 (exh. cat., London, Karsten Schubert, 1988–9)
Base: Alison Wilding, Sculptures 1982 93 (exh. cat., Newlyn, A.G., 1993)
Alison Wilding: New Works at Tate Gallery St Ives (exh. cat., St Ives, Tate, 1994)

Wildt, Adolfo (*b* Milan, 1 March 1868; *d* Milan, 12 March 1931). Italian sculptor. He was born into a poor family and in 1880 entered the studio of the sculptor Giuseppe Grandi (1843–1894). Between 1882 and 1887 Wildt learnt to work marble in the studio of Federico Villa and from 1885 to 1886 frequented the Accademia di Belle Arti di Brera, Milan, where he made studies after the Antique and Michelangelo. In 1894 he met the German collector Franz Rose (1854–1912) and agreed that in return for an annual stipend he would assure Rose exclusive rights on the first exemplar of each of his works. Protected and isolated by this arrangement, Wildt immersed himself in his work. He became increasingly interested in symbolism and experimented with marble to produce effects of opalescent transparency such as the self-portrait *Mask of Pain* (1908; Florence, Uffizi). Rose's death in 1912 forced Wildt to confront the art market. He was awarded the Principe Umberto prize in 1913, and this marked the beginning of his good fortune with the Italian critics. He was backed by the journalist and critic Margherita Sarfatti and in 1925 joined the steering committee of the NOVECENTO ITALIANO, participating in its major exhibitions of 1926 and 1929, as well as abroad.

Wildt's mature work such as *St Francis* (1926; Milan, priv. col., see 1983 exh. cat., no. 155) was characterized by a profound psychological content and a Gothic elegance. Stylistically it owed little to the monumentalism of the Novecento, but Wildt's choice of themes such as religion, nationalism and the family corresponded closely to the Novecento ideology. He ran an art school in Milan from 1921 to 1922 which was organized like a medieval workshop and specialized in marble-carving. In 1921 his book *L'arte del marmo* was published, and in 1923 he was appointed head of the sculpture department at the Brera academy. Fausto Melotti and Lucio Fontana were among his pupils.

WRITINGS

L'arte del marmo (Milan, 1921)

BIBLIOGRAPHY

G. Anziani and L. Caramel: *Scultura moderna in Lombardia* (Milan, 1981)
P. Mola: *Adolfo Wildt, 1894–1912* (diss., Milan, U. Cattolica, 1981)
Il 'Novecento italiano' (1923–1933) (exh. cat., ed. R. Bossaglia; Milan, Pal. Permanente, 1983)

SIMONETTA FRAQUELLI

Wild West and frontier art. Genre of art inspired by the land and the peoples of the American West, particularly in the period during and shortly after white settlement of the area. It was practised first by explorer–artists and later by permanent settlers of the area. Incorporating the media of painting, drawing and sculpture, such art records the

Henry F. Farny: *Song of the Talking Wire*, oil on canvas, 562×1012 mm, 1904 (Cincinnati, OH, Taft Museum)

dramatic topography west of the Mississippi River extending to the Pacific Ocean and often deals with the frequently violent events that helped to shape its settlement. The first major depictions of the area occurred in the years prior to the American Civil War (1861–5), but the heyday of Wild West and frontier art was between 1880 and 1910, when such artists as CHARLES M. RUSSELL and FREDERIC REMINGTON lived and worked there, depicting the cowboys and Native Americans of the region. It was this type of art that gave rise to the romantic notion of the West as an area of danger, excitement and dramatic confrontation, stirring the imagination of many easterners. Aspects of the life and culture of the West continued to be treated into the first half of the 20th century. However, by this time both white settlers and their culture had long been dominant, and consequently the fascination that the region had formerly exercised over white artists dwindled.

In 1819–20 the topographer Stephen Long (1784–1864) followed the Platte River to the present site of Denver and then south-east to the present Fort Smith, AR. On his return east he prepared a map, which did much to draw attention to the existence of the desert regions in the USA. In the 1830s and 1840s a few early artist–explorers journeyed to the West to depict scenes of aboriginal cultures and wilderness, displaying their results to those in search of vicarious adventure. The most accomplished of the artists prior to the Civil War was the Swiss KARL BODMER. He travelled up the Missouri River with Prince Maximilian of Wied–Neuwied in 1833–4, a journey that provided the source for such exquisite watercolours as *Two Ravens* (1834; Omaha, NE, Joslyn A. Mus.). In 1837 ALFRED JACOB MILLER journeyed to the Rocky Mountains and recorded the American West in a series of watercolours (e.g. the *Trapper's Bride*, Omaha, NE, Joslyn A. Mus.) depicting the life of the Indians and fur traders. At this

time such Indian tribes as the Assiniboine, the Arapahoe and the Comanche moved relatively freely across the plains on horses, while major westward migration by white settlers did not really begin until the birth of a viable cattle industry after the Civil War. Russell was one of the first eastern artists to settle in the West, and from 1880 he lived as a trapper and cowboy. His illustrations, often for *Harper's Weekly*, and his paintings (e.g. *Wagon Boss*, 1909; Tulsa, OK, Gilcrease Inst. Amer. Hist. & A.) depict the exciting and dangerous aspects of frontier life. Remington, although living in New York, made frequent visits to the West to document the displacement of the Indians and buffalo by white men and longhorn cattle. The handling of paint in his later works (e.g. *Pony Herder*, 1909; for illustration *see* REMINGTON, FREDERIC) often approaches Impressionism. Both Russell and Remington had an intimate knowledge and love of the West that is often revealed in their works. These two artists also produced bronze sculptures of cowboys, Indians and horses (e.g. Russell's *Smoking Up*, *c.*1903; St Petersburg, FL, Mus. F.A., and Remington's *Mountain Man*, 1903; Cody, WY, Buffalo Bill Hist. Cent.). Other sculptors who continued these themes were Cyrus Dallin (1861–1944), who often worked on a large scale (e.g. *Appeal of the Great Spirit*, 1908; Boston, MA. Mus. F.A.), and Hermon Atkins MacNeil (1866–1947), who produced such works as *Chief of the Multnomah Tribe* (bronze, 1907; Tulsa, OK, Gilcrease Inst. Amer. Hist. & A.).

Henry F. Farny (1847–1916) was also an easterner who was lured by the subject-matter of the West. Before moving to New York in 1867, he worked in Cincinnati for engravers and lithographers and was an illustrator for *Harper's Weekly*. He painted in the tight, precise manner of the Düsseldorf school and studied in Munich in 1875–6. He first visited Sioux Indian Territory in 1881 and by

1890 had turned exclusively to painting, recording the quieter aspects of Indian life and their vanishing culture. He is best known for *Song of the Talking Wire* (see fig.), a painting that shows the Indians' attempts to come to terms with the white man's technology. Such artists as Joseph Henry Sharp (1859–1953), WILLIAM TYLEE RANNEY and ARTHUR FITZWILLIAM TAIT depicted the hardships encountered by those who settled in rugged and unexplored terrain. Sharp rendered many Indian portraits (e.g. *Yellow Tail, Crow Indian Chief, Montana*, *c.* 1901–16; St Petersburg, FL, Mus. F.A.), while Ranney painted large-scale genre pictures of pioneer families, hunters and trappers (e.g. *Advice on the Prairie*, 1853; Malvern, PA, Claude J. Ranney priv. col.). Tait, although working mostly in the Adirondack Mountains, dramatically captured the dangers of mountain life in such paintings as *A Tight Fix: Bearhunting in Early Winter* (1856; Detroit, Manoogian priv. col., see 1983–4 exh. cat., p. 124). He was also skilled at painting scenes of hunters, trappers and dead game. JOHN MIX STANLEY was another artist who emphasized the romantic melodrama of pioneer and Indian life, though in a quieter, less dramatic, if no less stereotypical, way, as in *Prairie Indian Encampment* (*c.* 1870; Detroit, MI, Inst. A.). He used his daguerrotypes, taken on expeditions to New Mexico, California and the Oregon Territory, as aids for his painting. The works of these men were widely disseminated through illustrations in various weekly and monthly magazines.

Many of the artists who painted the western landscape were trained in Europe. ALBERT BIERSTADT and WORTHINGTON WHITTREDGE both studied in Düsseldorf and THOMAS MORAN in England. Bierstadt first went to the West with the explorer and soldier Frederick W. Lander (1821–62) in 1859, and in the 1860s he produced his most celebrated works, a series of large paintings of the majestic Rocky Mountains (e.g. *Storm in the Rocky Mountains, Mount Rosalie*, 2.1×3.6 m, 1866; New York, Brooklyn Mus.). Whittredge's scenes of the West, such as *Crossing the Ford* (1867–70; New York, C. Assoc.), are unusual in treating the frontier not as a series of mountainous vistas but as a pastoral Eden. Moran's vivid watercolours (e.g. *Mammoth Hot Springs*, 1872; Washington, DC, N. Mus. Amer. A.), reminiscent of Turner's work, interpret the beauty of the Yellowstone area of Wyoming and are said to have convinced Congress to make the area the first national park in the world. His oils depict the same subject-matter: the canyons, cliffs, buttes and geysers of the American West (e.g. *Grand Canyon of the Yellowstone*, 1872; Washington, DC, US Dept Inter., on loan to Washington, DC, N. Mus. Amer. A.). Both of these artists painted their canvases to be shown primarily in eastern galleries and to be seen by the eastern public. The Taos Ten, a colony of artists that included Joseph Henry Sharp, Bert Greer Philips (1868–1956) and Oscar Edmund Berninghaus (1874–1952), was organized in 1897 in the Taos region of northern New Mexico and was one of the last groups to make almost exclusive use of the subject-matter of the West. Nevertheless, the styles of group members were influenced by Manet and his followers and by the works of Duchamp, Picasso, Matisse and Braque exhibited in the Armory Show in New York in 1913. The principal painting from the colony is *Jury for Trial of a Sheepherder*

(1936; Denver, CO, Mus. W.A.), by Ernest Blumenschein (1874–1960), who incorporated elements of Mexican–American and Indian folklore into his expressionistic and often socially conscious works.

BIBLIOGRAPHY
Joseph Henry Sharp and the Lure of the West (exh. cat. by C. S. Dentzel, Great Falls, MT, C. M. Russell Mus., n.d.)
H. Inman: *The Old Santa Fe Trail* (New York, 1897)
R. F. Adams and H. E. Britzman: *Charles M. Russell: The Cowboy Artist* (Pasadena, 1948)
R. Taft: *Artists and Illustrators of the Old West, 1850–1900* (New York, 1953)
L. M. Bickerstaff: *Pioneer Artists of Taos* (Denver, 1955)
M. H. Brown and W. R. Felton: *Before Barbed Wire* (New York, 1956)
Albert Bierstadt: Painter of the American West (exh. cat. by G. Hendricks, Fort Worth, TX, Amon Carter Mus., 1973)
R. B. Hassrick: *Cowboys and Indians: An Illustrated History* (New York, 1976)
P. H. Hassrick: *The Way West: Art of Frontier America* (New York, 1977)
Henry Farny (exh. cat. by D. Carter, Cincinnati, OH, A. Mus., 1978)
Thomas Moran: Watercolours of the American West (exh. cat. by C. Clark, Fort Worth, TX, Amon Carter Mus.; Cleveland, OH, Mus. A.; New Haven, CT, Yale U.A.G.; 1980–1)
A New World: Masterpieces of American Painting, 1760–1910 (exh. cat., ed. T. E. Stebbins jr; Boston, MA, Mus. F.A; Washington, DC, Gal. A.; Paris, Grand Pal.; 1983–4)

W. C. FOXLEY

Wilford, Michael. *See under* STIRLING, JAMES.

Wilheim, Jorge (*b* Trieste, 23 April 1928). Brazilian architect and urban planner. He graduated as an architect-planner from Mackenzie University, São Paulo, in 1952 and his early works included the general hospital (1954), Santa Casa, Jaú, a typical International Style design of intercommunicating, long, low blocks, and the urban plan for the new town of Angelica (1956). In 1957 he led a team that took part in the national competition to develop a master-plan (unexecuted) for the new capital, Brasília, and in 1965 he produced a preliminary urban plan for Curitiba; this was based on his theory of urbanization as a continuous process that made elaboration of a plan in itself less important than the creation of organizations able to implement appropriate measures. This theory was used in all the plans financed by the Ministry of the Interior in the 1960s and 1970s. Other urban plans in which Wilheim was involved include those for Joinville, Santa Catarina, (1965; unexecuted); Osasco, São Paulo (1966); Goiânia (1968); São José dos Campos (1969); and Campinas (1969). Wilheim also designed a large number of public buildings in collaboration with other architects, for example Anhembi Park (1967–73), São Paulo's main exhibition and convention hall, on 44 ha of land on the banks of the River Tiête; and the Museu de Arte Contemporânea (1975; with Paulo Mendes da Rocha) at the University of São Paulo, a square building with sharply angled walls, raised on columns. In 1981 he won an important competition for the replanning of Vale do Anhangabaú (1991), São Paulo, redesigning the traffic systems beneath an 8-ha pedestrian park incorporating a plaza for cultural events and an open exhibition space, together with bus and metro stations. He played an active role in public life as head of three government offices in São Paulo: the State Secretariat of Economy and Planning (1975–9); the Municipal Secretariat of Planning (1983–5) and, from 1986, the Secretariat of the Environment. He also led EMPLASA (the state agency for metropolitan planning) in the formulation of a new development plan for São Paulo (1992–2000). In 1992 work began on the construction of his new Opera House and Cultural Centre for the Performing Arts, São Paulo.

WRITINGS

São Paulo Metropole 65 (São Paulo, 1965)
O Substantivo e o adjetivo (São Paulo, 1976)
Espaços e palavras (São Paulo, 1985)

BIBLIOGRAPHY

H. E. Mindlin: *Modern Architecture in Brazil* (Amsterdam and Rio de Janeiro, 1956)
'Museu de Arte Contemporânea, Universidade de São Paulo', *Módulo*, 42 (1976), pp. 60–67

REGINA MARIA PROSPERI MEYER

Wilhelm, Heinrich (*b c.* 1585; *d* Stockholm, 3 April 1652). German sculptor and architect, also active in Sweden. From *c.* 1620 he lived in Hamburg, where he executed works in marble and alabaster. He was a so-called Free Master, which makes it certain that he was highly valued by his patrons. Although he was probably very productive during his Hamburg period, no traces of his work are left there; nor does the single, documented work by him in Germany survive, a large altarpiece in the Nicolaikirche in Elmshorn, executed *c.* 1640 but destroyed already in 1657 and now known from a contemproary description. One other German work has been attributed to Wilhelm on stylistic grounds: a big wall epitaph (1637) for *Johan Schönbach* in Schleswig Cathedral.

In 1635 the Swedish Lord High Chancellor Axel Oxenstierna (1583–1654), invited him to Sweden to work on the Palace of the Nobility in Stockholm. After the death of its architect, Simon de la Vallée, in 1642, Wilhelm made new designs for the Palace, but they were never executed. Settling in Sweden, he chiefly executed burial monuments in black marble and white alabaster in a style midway between North German Mannerism and Baroque. His main works include the monument (1640–45) to *Gabriel Gustafsson Oxenstierna* (1587–1640) in Tyresö Church, Södermanland, and wall epitaphs of members of the Oxenstierna family in the cathedral and Riddarholm Church in Stockholm and in the parish church of Jäder in Södermanland and members of the Sture family in their chapel in Uppsala Cathedral. Though richly ornamented with scrolls, decorative and allegorical figures and vivid outlines, Wilhelm's monuments appear measured and dignified and are technically of a very high standard. Despite the partly corresponding ornamental elements used, his works contrast sharply with the more bulky, ostentatious and over-decorated monument (1643) of *Herman Wrangel* (1584–1644) in Skokloster Church and the monument (1649–52) to *Carl Carlsson Gyllenhielm* (1574–1650) in Strängnäs Cathedral, their more discreet style reflecting the quiet confidence of the well-established Oxenstierna family. In the epitaph (1650–52) of *Johan Adler Salvius* (1590–1652) in Stockholm Cathedral, Wilhelm developed a still more strict and classically severe style.

BIBLIOGRAPHY

SVKL; Thieme–Becker
G. Axel-Nilsson: *Dekorativ stenhuggarkonst i yngre vasastil* [Ornamental sculpture of the later Vasa style] (Stockholm, 1950)

TORBJÖRN FULTON

Wilhelmina, Margräfin of Bayreuth. *See* HOHENZOLLERN, (6).

Wilhelm of Cologne, Master [?Wilhelm von Herle] (*fl* 1358–72; *d* before 1378). German painter. In 1380 the chronicler of Limburg extolled the ability of Master Wilhelm of Cologne, 'the best painter in the German lands', who was much admired for depicting the human figure 'as if it were alive'. If, as is frequently asserted, the author did refer to the prosperous Wilhelm von Herle, the only painter named Wilhelm documented in Cologne during the preceding decades, the news of Wilhelm's death had not reached him at the time of writing.

Wilhelm von Herle was first mentioned in the town records in 1358, when he purchased a residence in the painters' quarter. In 1368 he was admitted into the Wine Confraternity; recorded property purchases of 1370, 1371 and 1372 suggest that he presided over a thriving workshop. A document settling a dispute over his will shows that by 1378 he had died, and suggests that his widow had agreed to marry his pupil, Herman Wynrich van Wesel (*fl* Cologne, 1378–1413).

There is no plausible hypothesis to connect Master Wilhelm with any surviving work. The only documentary evidence shows that he was paid for a frontispiece for the lost *Eidbuch der Stadt Koeln* (1370), and the attribution of frescoes from the town hall remains speculative. The date of his death militates against any identification as the Master of St Veronica or the Master of St Lawrence (*fl c.* 1415–30).

BIBLIOGRAPHY

J. J. Merlo: *Kölnische Künstler in alter und neuer Zeit* (Cologne, 1850), rev., ed. E. Firmenich-Richartz and H. Keussen (Düsseldorf, 1895) [for documentary sources]
C. Aldenhoven: *Geschichte der Kölner Malerschule* (Lübeck, 1902)

BRIGITTE CORLEY

Wilhelmshöhe. *See* KASSEL, §3.

Wilhelmson, Carl (Wilhelm) (*b* Fiskebäckskil, Bohuslän, 12 Nov 1866; *d* Göteborg, 24 Sept 1928). Swedish painter and lithographer. Wilhelmson trained first as a commercial lithographer in Göteborg. In 1886 he enrolled as a student of decorative painting at Valand College of Art where his teacher was Carl (Olof) Larsson. In 1888, having obtained a travel grant, he went to Leipzig to study lithographic technique. From 1890 to 1896 he lived in Paris, where he worked as a lithographer and commercial artist and studied at the Académie Julian. Wilhelmson's preferred subject-matter was the coastal landscape of Bohuslän and the people of its little fishing villages with their huddles of wooden houses. There is no trace of ethnography in his depictions of local life; they are full of serious realism and display a sensitive insight into the perilous life of the fishermen, with which he had been familiar since childhood. *In the Village Shop* (1896; Stockholm, Nmus.) depicts his mother with customers in the shop she kept after her husband's death. *Resignation* (1895) and the *Sick Child* (1896; both Stockholm, Nmus.) are reminiscent of the work of Christian Krohg in the 1880s.

Towards the turn of the century Wilhelmson concentrated more on figured landscapes and his paintings became more monumental. In *Fishwives on the Way Home from Church* (1899; Stockholm, Nmus.) his earlier Illusionism began to yield to a more expressive and decorative style, with emphasis on the flatness of the surface and on local colours. He spent the summers of 1900 and 1902 at Utterbyn near Torsby in Värmland as the guest of his pupil, the painter and wood-engraver Anna Sahlström (1876–1956), at her parents' farm. There he painted the monumental and Romantic twilight pictures *Saturday Evening* (1900; Stockholm, Thielska Gal.) and *June Evening* (1902; Göteborg, Kstmus.). The latter shows a group of young people listening entranced to a peasant playing the violin after the day's work. Also at Utterbyn he created his finest portrait, *Daughter of the Farm* (1902; Göteborg, Kstmus.), which depicts Anna Sahlström, dressed in her Sunday best black silk, seated in a serene, meditative pose, in the polished drawing-room of the farmhouse, while the evening sunlight falls on the field of newly mown hay outside the window. In 1901 the Utterbyn landscape also provided the background for the painting commissioned by Pontus Fürstenberg for Göteborg City Library (oil on canvas, 1901; now Göteborg, Polhemsgym.), in which female figures personifying Poetry and Art meet a group of people eager for enlightenment.

In such paintings as *On the Mountain* (1905; Göteborg, Kstmus.) there may be a symbolic element; this shows old fishermen gazing westwards into the sunset to gauge the next day's weather: the sinking sun foreshadows the ending not only of the day, but also of life. Wilhelmson painted several depictions of popular piety in Bohuslän; in such works as *Churchgoers in a Boat* (1909; Stockholm, Nmus.) the bright colours of the clothing combine to splendid effect with the overall solemnity of the scene.

His monumental painting (cloth, 1906–8; *in situ*) for the Stockholm Central Post Office shows the Skeppsbro wharf in Stockholm crowded with dockers and travellers. Wilhelmson's final great work was his only fresco painting, commissioned for the courtroom in the County Governor's official residence in Göteborg (1927; *in situ*). It is divided into three parts, *Fishing, Stonecutting* and *Agriculture*, depicting the most important sources of livelihood in Bohuslän.

Wilhelmson was outstanding among his Swedish contemporaries for his genuine interest in the rural population of his native region of Bohuslän and also of other Swedish provinces at a time of National Romanticism. He was a realistic illustrator of the life of the people and captured his models' individuality and dignity without undue sentimentality or over-emphasis of the picturesque. He avoided the more Synthetist form of his contemporaries chiefly through his faceted style of colour application, frequently leaving patches of white background visible: this contributes to the light-filled atmosphere, particularly in his late works. Although he did not attempt the process of optical colour blending he came close at times to a Pointillist style. From 1897 to 1910 he was principal of Valand College of Art, and from 1912 until his death he ran a private art school in Stockholm. In 1925 he was appointed professor of figure painting at the Stockholm Academy of Art.

SVKL

BIBLIOGRAPHY

S. Rönnow: *Carl Wilhelmsons folklivsmålningar* [Carl Wilhelmson's paintings of peasant life] (Stockholm, 1928)

A. Romdahl: *Carl Wilhelmson* (Stockholm, 1938)

A. Hedvall: *Bohuslän i konsten* [Bohuslän in art] (Stockholm, 1957), pp. 223–40

H.-O. Bostrom: 'Carl Wilhelmson som kvinnoskildrare' [Carl Wilhelmson as a depictor of women], *I Sekelskiftets Ljus*, ed. B. Rapp (Stockholm, 1990), pp. 158–79

HANS-OLOF BOSTRÖM

Wiligelmo [Wiligelmus; Guglielmo da Modena; Gulielmo da Modena] (*fl c.* 1099–*c.* 1120). Italian sculptor. He is considered to be the first great artistic personality in Italian sculpture, although he is known only from the epigraph on the façade of Modena Cathedral, which reads: 'Your sculpture, Wiligelmo, now shows how much honour you are worthy of among sculptors'. The flanking figures of the prophets *Enoch* and *Elijah* are carved from the same block and have, therefore, been considered to be signed works, enabling other attributions to Wiligelmo to be made, both at Modena Cathedral and elsewhere in the immediate region.

Wiligelmo must have worked at Modena Cathedral from *c.* 1099 to *c.* 1110. Some of his sculptures were reassembled in the later 12th century by the Campionesi, and there is some dispute as to their original use, some scholars considering them to have formed part of liturgical furnishings and others insisting that they were always intended for a position on the façade (*see* MODENA, §1(ii)). Wiligelmo was responsible for the four Genesis reliefs, the dedication plaque, the two torch-bearing putti and the decorative programme of the central portal, all on the west façade; for the many figured capitals of the exterior; and probably also for the series of large single figures from the metopes (Modena, Mus. Lapidario), which originally served as demarcations of the bays at the top of the nave walls. Other works by his hand are the four large prophets from the jambs of the portal of the old cathedral at Cremona, dating from before the earthquake of 1117, and the fragments of three *Labours of the Months* from a lost portal at the nearby Cluniac abbey church of San Benedetto Po (San Benedetto Po, Civ. Mus. Polironiano; Romanore, priv. col.).

These works, which are all carved in marble, are characterized by the use of large, stocky figures in profile with big heads and feet, solemn expressions and angular yet dramatic movements in the narrative scenes (*see* MODENA, fig. 2). The figures are usually set under decorative arches. In the past scholars have seen connections to the early schools of Romanesque sculpture in Aquitaine and Aragon, but opinion now tends to consider these all as simultaneous and independent developments of monumental sculpture. Inspiration seems to be drawn more from ivory-carving, metalwork and Roman sculpture. Provincial Roman works (e.g. Modena, Mus. Stor. & A. Med. & Mod.) served as direct models for several of Wiligelmo's works, as did Carolingian and Ottonian ivory-carvings and local manuscript illumination. From such varied sources Wiligelmo created a monumental figure-style emerging from the plane of the relief. The doleful figures of the atlantids and that of the dying Cain in the Genesis reliefs can be compared to the large single metope figures, which are of an even more monumental nature. Most of Wiligelmo's sculptures bear inscriptions that identify the figures or include more elaborate texts of a biblical, secular or liturgical character.

Other works at Modena Cathedral and on neighbouring monuments, which are carved in a slightly different figure style but date from approximately the same period, have been attributed to masters in Wiligelmo's workshop. The sculptures of the side portals at Modena, the Porta dei Principi and the Porta della Pescheria, are the work of sculptors designated the Master of San Geminiano and the Master of the Artù respectively (Salvini, 1956). They follow the arrangement of Wiligelmo's main portal, but the figures are smaller and more agile, full of expressive intensity, forming a new, more energetic narrative style. The Porta dei Principi is the first known example of a two-storey porch-portal supported by column-bearing lions or atlantids: a distinctive north Italian form, the creation of which has been associated with Wiligelmo. The fragments of the Evangelists' symbols now set above the rose window on the main façade at Modena share features with sculpture (a pulpit bearing Evangelist symbols) at S Maria della Neve, Quarántoli, at Cremona (fragments of Genesis reliefs and some atlantids bearing columns from the old façade, now in Cremona Cathedral and Milan, Mus. Civ. Milano) and at the nearby Benedictine abbey of Nonantola. The jambs of the main portal at Nonantola have been attributed to the 'Master of Astolfo', a pupil of Wiligelmo, and the fragments reassembled in the tympanum after an earthquake in 1117 have been thought to come from a pulpit. The same master also probably carved the north portal of Piacenza Cathedral. All these sculptors clearly belonged to a large workshop under the direction of Wiligelmo, which also included the young NICHOLAUS.

BIBLIOGRAPHY

A. K. Porter: *Romanesque Sculpture of the Pilgrimage Roads* (Boston, 1923/R New York, 1966)

G. de Francovich: 'Wiligelmo da Modena e gli inizi della scultura romanica europea', *Riv. Reale Ist. Archeol. & Stor. A.*, vii (1940), pp. 225–94

R. Salvini: *Wiligelmo e le origini della scultura romanica* (Milan, 1956)

——: *La scultura romanica in Europa* (Milan, 1963)

A. C. Quintavalle: *Da Wiligelmo a Nicolò* (Parma, 1966)

——: *Wiligelmo e la sua scuola* (Florence, 1967)

——: *Romanico padano, civiltà d'occidente* (Florence, 1969)

——: 'Piacenza Cathedral, Lanfranco and the School of Wiligelmo', *A. Bull.*, lv (1973), pp. 40–57

P. Piva: 'I mesi di Polirone', *Commentari*, n.s., xxv (1974), pp. 271–4

Atti del convegno internazionale degli studi. Romanico padano, romanico europeo: Parma, 1977 [includes articles by F. Gandolfo and C. Verzar]

P. Piva: *Da Cluny a Polirone: Un recupero essenziale del romanico europeo* (San Benedetto Po, 1980)

A. C. Quintavalle and others: *Romanico mediopadano: Strada, città, ecclesia* (Parma, 1983) [cat. of exh. held in 1977]

Lanfranco e Wiligelmo. Il duomo di Modena: Quando le cattedrali erano bianche (exh. cat., Modena, 1984), 3 vols

S. Stocchi: *Emilie Romane*, Nuit Temps (La Pierre-qui-vire, 1984)

Atti del convegno internazionale degli studi. Wiligelmo e Lanfranco nell'Europa romanica: Modena, 1985

For further bibliography *see* MODENA, §1(ii) and ROMANESQUE, §III, 1(vi)(c).

CHRISTINE B. VERZAR

Wilkie, Sir David (*b* Cults, Fife, 18 Nov 1785; *d* off Malta, 1 June 1841, *bur* off Gibraltar). Scottish painter.

1. Life and painted works. 2. Drawings.

1. LIFE AND PAINTED WORKS.

(i) Scotland, 1785–1805. Wilkie may have inherited his rectitude and tenacity, even his nervous inhibitions, from his father, the minister of his native parish. Though little responsive to schooling, he showed an early inclination towards mimicry that expressed itself in drawings, chiefly of human activity. In these he was influenced by a copy of Allan Ramsay's pastoral comedy in verse, the *Gentle Shepherd* (1725), illustrated by David Allan in 1788. One of the few surviving examples of his early drawings represents a scene from it (*c.* 1797; Kirkcaldy, Fife, Mus. & A.G.). Wilkie cherished the demotic spirit of this book and its illustrations throughout his life.

By 1799 Wilkie had determined to become a painter, and in that year, despite parental misgivings, he entered the Trustees' Academy in Edinburgh. The curriculum devised by the Academy's Master, John Graham (1754/5–1817), included exercises in history painting. Wilkie's two suriving essays in this genre, *Diana and Callisto* (1803–4; Norfolk, VA, Chrysler Mus.) and *Patie Disbelieves Sir William's Prophecy* (1803; Duke of Buccleuch priv. col.), both show his unwillingness to subordinate his gift for the vivid observation of everyday life to the academic conventions of history painting. He left the Academy in 1804.

In 1803 Wilkie began to produce pot-boiler portraits of middle-class men and women from his own part of Fife. Most were painted in the manner of Henry Raeburn; in the finest, *William Bethune-Morrison with his Wife and Daughter* (1804; Edinburgh, N.G.), observation again prevailed over stylistic convention. Although he was obliged to continue painting portraits to support himself, he recognized that neither history nor portrait painting was his true vocation. In 1804–5 he painted his first genre piece, *Pitlessie Fair* (Edinburgh, N.G.), a human panorama set in his native parish. This assemblage of commonplace incident was based on 17th-century Dutch and Flemish prints and on a shrewd study of his social surroundings. The picture was the key to Wilkie's subsequent development. While it contains the germ of many later compositions, it also brought home to the artist his lack of training. In search of the competitive stimulus of other painters and a wider market for his work he travelled to London in 1805.

(ii) London, 1805–25. Wilkie enrolled as a student at the Royal Academy and in 1806 exhibited the *Village Politicians* (Scone Pal., Tayside), which brought him instant fame. Further success came with the exhibition of the *Blind Fiddler* (1806; London, Tate) in 1807 and the *Rent Day* (1807–8; priv. col.; engraved by Abraham Raimbach, 1817) in 1809, which were bought by Sir George Beaumont and Henry Phipps, 1st Earl of Mulgrave (1755–1831), respectively. Although these paintings were still, albeit decreasingly, dependent on David Teniers (ii) and 17th-century genre painting, they were perceived as marking a new artistic era. Wilkie's originality lay less in his opposition to current academic values than in his artful individualizations of character and manipulation of detail, and in his ability to relate figures together with a psychological realism which went beyond the 18th-century tradition of sentimental genre represented by Thomas Gainsborough and George Morland. His penetration of human expression, which extended to the subtlety of mixed emotions, was helped by his knowledge of acting and of Charles Bell's *Essay on the Anatomy of Expression in Painting*

(1806). Although a penetrating and persistent student of nature (as witnessed by drawings which rank among the highest in British draughtsmanship), Wilkie also sometimes used small clay models, set as if on a stage, in composing and lighting his groups.

The evolution of Wilkie's style was always unsteady and at times reversionary. In *Village Festival* (1809–11; London, Tate) and *Blind Man's Buff* (1812; Brit. Royal Col.) he paid a new attention to the plasticity of form, binding figures together in groups and introducing more colour and fluidity of paint. In this the modulating lights of Adriaen van Ostade and Rembrandt played a part. From 1809 he employed John Burnet and Abraham Raimbach among others to produce line-engravings after his paintings. As he justly calculated, these prints both popularized his work and gave it a surer economic footing. In 1809 he was elected an ARA and in 1811 an RA.

Wilkie's art reached maturity around 1813, beginning with pictures of a relative emotional quietude, softer modelling and a yellowy overall tone, for instance *Letter of Introduction* (1813; Edinburgh, N.G.) and *Distraining for Rent* (*see* SCOTLAND, fig. 11). Later, emotions became more sharply expressed, shadows deeper, colour stronger, the paint more unctuous and the touch more broken, for example *Duncan Gray* (1819; Edinburgh, N.G.) and the *Penny Wedding* (see fig. 1). He acknowledged his debt to Rembrandt more directly in *Bathsheba* (1817; Liverpool, Walker A.G.). During this time Wilkie had visited Paris (in 1814 and 1821) and the Low Countries (in 1816), where his study of Rembrandt was complemented by that of Titian and Rubens. His search for a freer and less exhausting technique was imposed in part by the need to keep abreast of his undiminishing but sometimes burdensome success.

The culmination of this period was *Chelsea Pensioners Reading the Gazette of the Battle of Waterloo* (1818–22; London, Apsley House), commissioned by the Duke of Wellington. To the public it was his triumph, a summary of his anecdotal power, expressive of patriotic sentiment in a classless pictorial language. At the 1822 Royal Academy it received the unprecedented honour of a protective railing. In the same year George IV made a state visit to Edinburgh, the first by a sovereign of the United Kingdom. As ever ambitious, and urged by an unbroken attachment to his native country, Wilkie went to Edinburgh to observe this piece of pageantry. The result was the long-laboured *Entrance of George IV into Holyrood House* (1823–30; Edinburgh, Pal. Holyroodhouse, Royal Col.), a painting of contemporary history which he preferred to describe as one of his 'portraits in action'. On the death of Raeburn in 1823 Wilkie was appointed King's Limner for Scotland, an office that involved the execution of ceremonial portraits.

To the professional anxieties of a naturally anxious man were added, late in 1824, two personal tragedies: the deaths of his mother, the centre of his domestic life in Kensington (he never married), and of two brothers with dependent children. He suffered a nervous breakdown and was advised to recuperate by travelling.

1. David Wilkie: *Penny Wedding*, oil on panel, 644×956 mm, 1818 (British Royal Collection)

(iii) Travels and later life, 1825–41. Wilkie left London in July 1825, arriving in Rome in November, where he stayed until February 1826, discovering, notably, the frescoes of Raphael. In 1826 he travelled widely, making prolonged stays in Naples, Parma, Venice, Munich, Dresden, Vienna and Florence. In Parma and Dresden he made a study of Correggio.

He was in Rome from December until April 1827 and cautiously began to paint again. In May 1827 he left for Genoa to buy portraits by Anthony van Dyck for Sir Robert Peel, before spending the summer in Geneva. He then undertook the uncommon venture of visiting Spain and was in Madrid from October until March 1828, studying Velázquez and Titian. In April he went to Seville to study Murillo and returned to London in June.

Back in England, Wilkie began what seemed a new career. He had been away for three years and felt that it should not be seen that he had, in his own words, visited 'Italy and Spain for nothing'. His experience abroad had deepened his understanding of the grand tradition, although he remained faithful to his earliest models, combining his appreciation of Correggio with that of van Ostade, and of Velázquez with that of Teniers (ii).

In 1829 he exhibited eight pictures at the Royal Academy, an unprecedented number for him. Four of these represented aspects of popular religious life observed in Rome during the Holy Year, including *Cardinal Washing Pilgrims' Feet* (1826–7; Glasgow, A.G. & Mus.); three celebrated the recent Spanish struggle for independence, for example the exceptionally bold *Siege of Saragossa* (1828; Brit. Royal Col.); and one was his first full-scale public portrait, *Thomas Erskine, Ninth Earl of Kellie* (1824–5 and 1828; Cupar, Fife, County Hall), which had been commissioned by his native county of Fife. George IV bought five of these pictures, a deliberate act of generosity which confirmed Wilkie's popularity among the highest ranks of aristocratic patrons. In 1830 Wilkie succeeded Thomas Lawrence as Painter in Ordinary to the King, a post he retained under William IV (by whom he was knighted in 1836) and Queen Victoria. Although he painted a few striking portraits of royalty, for example *William IV* (1832–3; London, Apsley House), and of men of rank and position, he remained apprehensive about portraiture. Some of his best portraits of this later period were private commissions, for instance *William Esdaile* (1836; priv. col., see *Burl. Mag.*, civ (1962), p. 116).

Wilkie's other works of the period tended towards historical anecdote. Generally larger than before, fluent, and ambitiously rich in painterly effect, they contain a relatively restricted number of figures, presented with a new amplitude. A few display his interest in the *tableaux-vivants* he had seen on his Continental travels, which had become fashionable in London. Typical are *Columbus at La Rabida* (1834–5; Raleigh, NC, Mus. A.), *Napoleon and the Pope* (1835–6; Dublin, N.G.) and *Josephine and the Fortune Teller* (1836–7; Edinburgh, N.G.). The supreme example is *Sir David Baird Discovering the Body of Sultan Tippoo Sahib* (see fig. 2). Closer in style to his earlier work, but with added sweetness of feeling, are such pictures as *First Ear-ring* (1834–5; London, Tate) and *Peep-o'-day Boys' Cabin* (1834–5; London, Tate), the product of a foray after topical picturesque novelty in the west of

2. David Wilkie: *Sir David Baird Discovering the Body of Sultan Tippoo Sahib*, oil on canvas, 3.49×2.68 m, 1839 (Edinburgh, National Gallery of Scotland)

Ireland in 1835. (The Lowland Wilkie had sought similar novelty in the Scottish Highlands in 1817 and in Spain in 1827.) '*The Cotter's Saturday Night*' (1836–7; Glasgow, A.G. & Mus.), a subject from Robert Burns, and *John Knox Dispensing the Sacrament* (two versions, the first begun 1838, both left unfinished 1840; Edinburgh, N.G.) reveal Wilkie's renewed faith in his cultural roots.

Wilkie's work from 1828 had a mixed reception. Many admirers of his earlier more domestic manner, which they had likened to the poetry of George Crabbe and novels of Walter Scott, were disconcerted by his homage to the Old Masters studied on his travels in southern Europe. Like Joshua Reynolds, whom he admired, Wilkie was always curious about the technical mysteries of painting. Much of his later work, particularly where he used bitumen to create an impression of Old-Masterly richness, has now altered in appearance and is difficult to judge.

Wilkie's admiration for Italian art reached back to Giotto, and his tendency to find virtue in both the life and art of the past had a bearing on the last journey of his life. In 1840 he left to study the people of the Holy Land. Travelling overland via the Danube and Constantinople, he arrived in Syria in early 1841 and remained in Palestine until April, with five weeks in Jerusalem. Although no finished paintings survive from this period, he made oil sketches, which included a *Christ before Pilate* (1841; priv. col., see 1958 exh. cat., p. 39), conceived in terms of contemporary life. He returned through Alexandria, where he painted a small portrait, *Mehmed Ali* (1841; London, Tate). He died on his way back to London and was buried at sea. Turner paid tribute to his friend and rival in *Peace: Burial at Sea* (London, Tate).

2. DRAWINGS. Wilkie was a prolific and assured draughtsman in the great European tradition of figure drawing. He was particularly influenced by the *trois crayons* manner of Rubens, which he applied to highly finished portraits and such figure drawings as *Study of a Female Nude* (*c.* 1815; Oxford, Ashmolean). The bulk of his drawings relate directly to his paintings. For major early works like *Pitlessie Fair* he produced chalk or pencil sketches characterized by an uncertain line and absence of contrasting tone, through which he sought to establish elements of the composition (e.g. Edinburgh, N.G.). He was rarely a simple recorder of nature or the specifics of contemporary life, preferring to use drawings to capture a fleeting expression or a compelling pose, for example in *A Woman Tiring her Hair* (Oxford, Ashmolean), which developed out of a sketch for *Chelsea Pensioners* (Oxford, Ashmolean). Increasingly, he explored the dramatic possibilities of chiaroscuro in Rembrandtesque pen, ink and wash drawings such as *The Burial of the Scottish Regalia* (*c.* 1835; U. Glasgow, Hunterian A.G.).

Wilkie's drawings grew larger and more elaborate as his style developed. Mature works such as *A Lantern-bearer and Figures* (*c.* 1835; London, V&A) combine softly modelled chalk and freely washed watercolour backgrounds. The many intensely coloured drawings produced on his final trip to the Middle East—studies of both local costume and character (e.g. *Portrait of Sotiri, Dragoman of Mr Colquhoun*; Oxford, Ashmolean)—are among his finest graphic achievements.

BIBLIOGRAPHY

A. Cunningham: *Life of Sir David Wilkie*, 3 vols (London, 1843) [letters and journals, incl. 'Remarks on Painting'; the fundamental source of inf.]
M. T. S. Raimbach, ed.: *Memoirs and Recollections of the late Abraham Raimbach* (London, 1843)
J. Burnet: *Practical Essays on the Fine Arts* (London, 1848)
T. Taylor: *Life of Haydon from his Autobiography*, 3 vols (London, 1853)
J. Burnet: *The Progress of a Painter* (London, 1854) [novel]
——: 'Recollections of my Contemporaries: The Early Days of Wilkie', *A.J.* [London], n.s., vi (1860), pp. 236ff
B. R. Haydon: *Correspondence*, ed. F. W. Haydon, 2 vols (London, 1876)
R. S. Gower: *Sir David Wilkie* (London, 1902)
W. Bayne: *Sir David Wilkie* (London, 1903) [like Gower, this is a usable, if old-fashioned, popular biography with illustrations]
Paintings and Drawings by Sir David Wilkie (exh. cat. by J. Woodward, London, RA; Edinburgh, N.G.; 1958)
B. R. Haydon: *Diary*, ed. W. B. Pope, 5 vols (Cambridge, MA, 1960–63)
Sir David Wilkie: Drawings into Paintings (exh. cat. by L. Errington, Edinburgh, N.G., 1975)
J. Farington: *Diary*, ed. K. Garlick, A. Macintyre and K. Cave, 16 vols (London, 1978–84)
Fourteen Small Pictures by Wilkie (exh. cat. by H. Miles, London, F.A. Soc., 1981)
Sir David Wilkie: Drawings and Sketches in the Ashmolean Museum (exh. cat. by D. Blayney Brown, London, Morton Morris, 1985)
Tribute to Wilkie (exh. cat. by L. Errington, Edinburgh, N.G., 1985)
Painting in Scotland (exh. cat. by D. Macmillan, U. Edinburgh, Old Coll., Upper Lib.; London, Tate; 1986)
Sir David Wilkie of Scotland (exh. cat., ed. W. Chiego; New Haven, CT, Yale Cent. Brit. A.; Raleigh, NC Mus. A.; 1987)

HAMISH MILES

Wilkin, Charles (*b c.* 1750; *d* London, 28 May 1814). English miniature painter and engraver. He exhibited portraits (1783–1808) at the Royal Academy, London, but is best remembered for his stipple engravings, notably the large *Cornelia* (1792), after Joshua Reynolds's portrait of *Lady Cockburn and her Children* (exh. RA 1774; London, N.G.), and *Mrs Parkyns* (1795) after John Hoppner. Wilkin also published a delightful series of *Portraits of Ladies of Rank and Fashion* (1797–1803) in five parts of two prints each, 'executed in a manner to unite the Higher Finishing of Painting with the Spirit and Freedom of Drawing'; these were after Hoppner but 'the Difficulty that attends getting Mr Hoppner's Pictures' delayed the work and obliged Wilkin to use three paintings of his own. His sons Frank Wilkin (1800–42) and Henry Wilkin (1801–52) were portrait painters who also exhibited at the Royal Academy.

BIBLIOGRAPHY

O'Donoghue; Thieme–Becker
Gent. Mag., lxxiv (July 1814), p. 35
A. Graves: *The Royal Academy of Arts*, viii (1906), p. 274
Reynolds (exh. cat., ed. N. Penny; London, RA, 1986), pp. 259–60

DAVID ALEXANDER

Wilkins, Ricardo. *See* KAYIGA, KOFI.

Wilkins, William (*b* Norwich, 31 Aug 1778; *d* Cambridge, 31 Aug 1839). English architect, writer and collector. A 'profound knowledge of the principles both of Grecian and Gothic architecture' generated the career of Wilkins, who was also remembered as 'a most amiable and honourable man'. He promoted the archaeological Greek Revival in Britain and a Tudor Gothic style. More intellectual than imaginative, his architecture was distinguished by a deft and disciplined manipulation of select historical motifs, a refined sense of scale and intelligent planning, outmoded by the time of his death. Besides his architecture and extensive antiquarian writings, Wilkins assembled an eclectic art collection and owned, or had a financial interest in, several theatres in East Anglia.

The theatres and Wilkins's architectural bent were inherited from his father, a Norwich architect also called William Wilkins (1751–1815), who assisted Humphry Repton from 1785 to 1796 and established a successful domestic practice, mainly in the Gothick style. His eldest son was educated at Norwich School, then at Gonville and Caius College, Cambridge, from which he graduated Sixth Wrangler in 1800 and won the Worts Travelling Bachelorship in 1801. Before beginning his two-year tour of Italy, Sicily, Greece and Asia Minor, Wilkins had exhibited at the Royal Academy and been elected to the Society of Antiquaries. These travels established his enthusiasm for Greek design, reinforced his architectural ambition and provided material for his first book, *The Antiquities of Magna Graecia*. Publication was delayed by several significant commissions. To Osberton House, Notts (*c.* 1805–6), he added the earliest full-size Greek Doric portico in Britain, while at Downing College, Cambridge (1804/5–22; completed 1875 by E. M. Barry), notably at the Master's Lodge (1807–8; see fig.), and for the East India College at Haileybury, Herts (1805–9), he accurately imitated sections of Athenian monuments, chiefly the Erechtheion. At Downing College and Haileybury the educational and residential facilities were arranged on pioneering campus plans. His reputation was boosted by his design for the Nelson Pillar in Sackville Street (later

William Wilkins: Master's Lodge, Downing College, Cambridge, 1807–8

O'Connell Street), Dublin (1807–9; destr. 1966), and the sensational transformation of the Grange, Northington, Hants (*c.* 1808–9; altered; *see* GREEK REVIVAL, fig. 2). Here he reordered the floor levels of the 17th-century house to accord with a hexastyle Theseion Doric portico attached on the east front and carried its monumentality to the flanks with deep tetrastyle porticos modelled on the Choregic Monument of Thrasyllus in Athens but providing adequate internal lighting.

In 1809 Wilkins and his Cambridge friend, George Gordon, 4th Earl of Aberdeen, prepared a translation of books three to six of Vitruvius' *On Architecture*, printed in 1813–17 as *The Civil Architecture of Vitruvius* (dated 1812) and valuable for the clarification of the passages on optical refinements in Greek design. It contributed to Wilkins's appointment in 1814 as editor of the publications financed by the Society of Dilettanti, to which he had been elected in 1809. He also evolved a less academic Gothic idiom, starting with Pentillie Castle, Cornwall (1810–11; destr. 1968). Inspired by East Anglian 16th-century manors, he created a carefully detailed but regularly ordered Tudor style for Dalmeny House, Lothian (1814–19), notable for having ornamental Coade stone. The pattern was progressively matured at Tregothnan, Cornwall (1815–18), and Dunmore Park (1820–22; destr. 1972), Stirlingshire (now Central Region), and influenced William Burn and Charles Barry. Wilkins's pupils Benjamin Ferrey, G. F. Jones and J. H. Stevens were to work predominantly in the Gothic style.

In 1815 Wilkins designed the Nelson Column at Great Yarmouth, Norfolk (1814–17), capping a Doric shaft with a caryatid peristyle supporting a figure of Britannia, the latter two in Coade stone. In 1816 he recommended the acquisition of the Elgin Marbles by the British government, despite reservations about their quality, and published *Atheniensia, or Remarks on the Topography and Buildings in Athens.* The following year he won the prestigious competition for a Waterloo monument in Portland Place, London, a project that was aborted due to government retrenchment. He continued evolving a flexible Greek Revival style, as in the effective marriage of propylaea

portico with octagonal steeple for St Paul's Church, Nottingham (1821–2), or the blend of Greek and Renaissance elements on the fashionable United University Club, London (1822–3; with J. P. Gandy-Deering, 1787–1850). No pedant, he also incorporated progressive utilitarian ideas in the radial layout of cell blocks for the New Norfolk County Gaol, Norwich (1820–24), echoed in the smaller Huntingdon County Gaol (1826–8).

Wilkins was thus well qualified to undertake important institutional commissions at Cambridge and London. In 1821, invited to design the New Court at Trinity College, Cambridge (completed 1827), he finally settled on a plain Gothic scheme, continuing the main tradition of collegiate architecture. His respectful attitude paid greater dividends in the New Quadrangle of Corpus Christi College (1822–6) and the New Buildings and screen of King's College (1823–8). The halls and libraries at Corpus and King's in particular combine medieval structure and ornamental forms, being convincingly historical yet functional. He also designed the first non-denominational English university, University College, London (1826–30). A magnificent single E-plan complex provided facilities for teaching, in a non-residential plan centred on an elevated decastyle Corinthian portico crowned by a Renaissance-style dome and originally intended to be fronted by a propylaea screen. Although only the main block was completed, the College was lauded as 'a chaste and truly classic specimen of Grecian Architecture' (*The Times*, 6 Aug 1838). Equally advanced in plan and use of cast iron was St George's Hospital, London (1826–30), which accommodated 400 patients in hygienic conditions.

In 1832 Wilkins won the competition for a combined National Gallery and Royal Academy in Trafalgar Square, London; the Gallery later occupied the Academy wing (when the Academy moved to Piccadilly). He wanted to erect a Temple of the Arts, nurturing contemporary art through historical example, as described in his *Letter to Lord Viscount Goderich*. Official parsimony and awkward requirements such as the reuse of columns from the portico of Carlton House compromised his architectural invention so that the façade is excessively long, staccato in composition and meagre in scale. Unwarranted public censure on its opening in 1838—which overlooked the remarkable iron and glass toplighting—speeded the decline of his health. Unplaced in the Houses of Parliament competition (1835), he had returned to Cambridge in 1837. In the same year he was elected Professor of Architecture at the Royal Academy, and although he did not live to deliver any lectures, some perhaps appear in his last book, *Prolusiones architectonicae (1837)*. He was buried in the crypt of the chapel he designed for Corpus Christi College.

WRITINGS

The Antiquities of Magna Graecia (Cambridge, 1807)

The Civil Architecture of Vitruvius: Comprising those Books of the Author which Relate to the Public and Private Edifices of the Ancients (London, 1813–17, dated 1812) [trans. of Vitruvius: *De architectura*, intro. written anon. by George Gordon, 4th Earl of Aberdeen, entitled 'An Historical View of the Rise and Progress of Architecture amongst the Greeks']

Atheniensia, or Remarks on the Topography and Buildings in Athens (London, 1816)

Report on the State of Repair of Sherborne Church (Sherborne, 1828)

An Appeal to the Senate on the Subject of the Plans for the University Library (Cambridge, 1831)

Letter to the Members of the Senate of the University (Cambridge, 1831)
An Apology for the Designs of the Houses of Parliament Marked Phil-Archimedes (London, 1836)
A Letter to Lord Viscount Goderich on the Patronage of the Arts by the English Government (London, 1836)
Prolusiones architectonicae or Essays on Subjects Connected with Greek and Roman Architecture (London, 1837)

BIBLIOGRAPHY

Colvin
Gent. Mag., lix (1839), pp. 426–7 [main obituary]
G. Martin: 'Wilkins and the National Gallery', *Burl. Mag.*, cxiii (1971), pp. 318–29
R. W. Liscombe: *William Wilkins, 1778–1839* (Cambridge, 1980) [standard study, fully illus.]
J. Geddes: 'The Grange, Northington', *Archit. Hist.*, xxvi (1983), pp. 35–48
C. M. Sicca: *Committed to Classicism: The Building of Downing College, Cambridge* (Cambridge, 1986)

R. WINDSOR LISCOMBE

Wilkinson, Charles (Kyrle) (*b* London, 13 Oct 1897; *d* Sharon, CT, 18 April 1986). American archaeologist, curator and collector. Trained as an artist at the Slade School, University College, London, in 1920 he joined the graphic section of the Egyptian Expedition to Thebes, organized by the Metropolitan Museum of Art. During the 1920s and 1930s Wilkinson painted facsimiles of Egyptian tomb paintings in the museum collection, and he joined museum excavations in the Kharga Oasis (Egypt) and Qasr-i Abu Nasr and Nishapur (Iran). Transferred to the curatorial staff of the museum in 1947, he became curator in 1956 of the new Department of Ancient Near Eastern Art, which merged with the Department of Islamic Art in 1957. Through his energetic collaboration on major excavations at Hasanlu, Nimrud and Nippur, Wilkinson greatly expanded the Ancient Near Eastern collections at the Metropolitan Museum. After his retirement from the museum in 1963, he taught Islamic art at Columbia University and was Hagop Kevorkian Curator of Middle Eastern Art and Archaeology at the Brooklyn Museum, New York (1970–74). Wilkinson's numerous publications include exhibition catalogues and monographs. He collected Iranian ceramics, metalwork and Qajar works of art, many of which he and his wife donated to the Metropolitan and Brooklyn museums.

WRITINGS

Iranian Ceramics (exh. cat., New York, Asia House Gals, 1963)
Two Ram-headed Vessels from Iran (Berne, 1967)
Chess: East and West, Past and Present (exh. cat., New York, Met, 1968)
Nishapur: Pottery of the Early Islamic Period (New York, 1973)
Ivories from Ziwiye and Items of Ceramic and Gold (Berne, 1975)
Nishapur: Some Early Islamic Buildings and their Decoration (New York, 1986)

SHEILA R. CANBY

Wilkinson, Leslie (*b* London, 12 Oct 1882; *d* Sydney, 20 Sept 1973). English architect and teacher, active in Australia. He was apprenticed in 1900 to C. E. Kempe, a stained-glass designer, and later that year to the architect J. S. Gibson. Wilkinson studied architecture at the Royal Academy, London, from 1902 to 1906, winning the Academy's Silver and Gold Medals and subsequently travelling in England, France, Italy and Spain. He joined the staff of the School of Architecture, University College, London, serving as an assistant professor from 1910 to 1918. He held a commission from 1914 to 1918 in the London University Officer Training Corps, and in 1918 he was appointed as Australia's first Professor of Architecture, at the University of Sydney. Dean of the Faculty of Architecture there from 1920 to 1947, he was a witty, erudite and influential teacher, discouraging 'fads' and stressing the importance of correct orientation for buildings and rooms. He designed various buildings on the university campus, the Physics Building (1926) being the largest, as well as many private residences. In his work, particularly for houses, he favoured a free 'Mediterranean' idiom, using simple, pitched roofs, lime-washed brickwork, shuttered 12-pane windows and restrained classical details: an early example is 'Greenway' (1923), his own house at 24 Wentworth Road, Vaucluse, Sydney. The timeless, flexible style of Wilkinson's houses remained unchanged during 50 years of practice. Through his architecture, teaching and stimulating personality, Wilkinson influenced a generation of Australian architects in the 1920s and 1930s.

BIBLIOGRAPHY

R. E. Apperly: *Sydney Houses, 1914–1939* (MArch thesis, Sydney, U. NSW, 1972), pp. 163–72
R. N. Johnson: 'Leslie Wilkinson and his Architecture', *A. & Australia*, xii/1 (1974), pp. 58–71
M. Dupain and others: *Leslie Wilkinson: A Practical Idealist* (Sydney, 1982)

RICHARD APPERLY

Will, Philip, jr. *See under* PERKINS & WILL.

Willaerts. Dutch family of painters. The marine painter (1) Adam Willaerts was one of the many Protestants who emigrated from Flanders to the northern Netherlands at the end of the 16th century. He had three sons who became painters, at least two of whom, (2) Abraham Willaerts and (3) Isaac Willaerts, studied with him and painted marine subjects as well as portraits. Unlike his father and younger brothers, the eldest son Cornelis Willaerts (1600–66) was a history painter who also painted portraits and landscapes, including Arcadian scenes in the manner of Cornelis van Poelenburch. He remains a shadowy figure, by whom only one signed work is known, *Husband and Wife with Little Daughter before a Landscape* (Mersham, Kent, Mrs Irby priv. col.).

(1) Adam Willaerts (*b* Antwerp, 1577; *d* Utrecht, 4 April 1664). During his early years in Antwerp he was impressed with the colourful paintings of the Fleming Jan Breughel the elder, but the subject and style of his earliest known picture, *Dutch East Indiamen off the West African Coast* (1608; Amsterdam, Hist. Mus.), presumably painted after the artist's arrival in Holland, shows the influence of the Dutch marine painter Hendrick Cornelisz. Vroom. In this painting Willaerts adopted Vroom's austere compositional scheme of an uninterrupted horizontal expanse of water with no framing devices, but he lacked Vroom's skill in depicting ships.

In 1611 Willaerts became one of the founder-members of the Utrecht Guild of St Luke, serving as Dean during the periods 1620–22, 1624–31 and 1636–7. Utrecht had a strong religious life, in which a tradition of Catholicism survived, and this affected Willaerts's subject-matter. He painted several seascapes with biblical themes, such as *Christ Preaching from a Boat* (1621; sold London, Sotheby's, 10 Dec 1975), which recalls Breughel's *Sea Harbour*

Adam Willaerts: *Chamois Hunt on the Coast*, oil on wood, 0.68×1.55 m, 1620 (Hamburg, Hamburger Kunsthalle)

with *Christ Preaching* (Munich, Alte Pin.) with its assembly of figures in colourful costumes. In this painting, however, Willaerts devoted more space to water and placed Christ in a Vroom-like Dutch ship, thus associating the Christian scene unhesitatingly with Dutch shipping. In Willaerts's *Miraculous Draught of Fishes* (Ripon, Earl of Swinton priv. col.) the Disciples have disembarked from a Dutch flagship. Most of Willaerts's marine paintings are beach scenes with many figures in the foreground and decorative lateral framing devices, such as trees, rocks and castles. Pure seascapes without such additional motifs are rare and mainly confined to the early period. In later works, such as the *Dutch Beach Scene* (1613; Amsterdam, P. de Boer priv. col.) and the dramatic *Storm at Sea* (1614; Amsterdam, Rijksmus.), he tried to emulate Vroom's compositional formulae, but in the *Sea Battle off Gibraltar* (1617; Amsterdam, Rijksmus.) he introduced decorative parallel bands of tiny wave crests and used a three-zone colour scheme (brown foreground, green middle distance, pale blue sky) derived from Breughel and Mannerist painting. Willaerts retained these attractive but artificial colours long after they had become outdated by the naturalistic palette of Dutch 17th-century marine painting.

In 1619 the landscape painter Roelandt Savery, another native of Flanders, settled in Utrecht. His wild rocky and wooded scenes, which often included animals, inspired Willaerts, who began to incorporate animals as coastal motifs in his marine paintings, as in the *Chamois Hunt on the Coast* (1620; Hamburg, Ksthalle; see fig.), in which a chamois hunt set in alpine rocks is featured next to an expanse of sea with Dutch ships in full sail. In 1623 Willaerts painted the *Arrival of Frederick V, Elector Palatine, with his Wife Elizabeth Stuart, at Flushing, 1613* (sold London, Sotheby's, 27 Nov 1968, lot 128) to coincide with Vroom's painting of the same subject (Haarlem, Frans Halsmus.). In an earlier painting by Willaerts the splendid ship the *Prince Royal*, which carried Frederick and Elizabeth on their festive voyage, appears surrounded by other shipping (1619; Amsterdam, Ned. Hist. Scheepvaartsmus.). High on the rocky coast on the right is the

castle of Prague, where Frederick became the 'Winter King'. Willaerts used the motif of this castle in other related marine paintings, forsaking geographic accuracy for the sake of symbolic allusion to Frederick's kingdom (Luttervelt). Later paintings, for instance *Mouth of the Maas at Den Briel* (1633; Rotterdam, Mus. Boymans–van Beuningen), combine a view of a harbour with, in the foreground, a portrait group, which has been attributed to Adam's son (2) Abraham Willaerts.

Like Vroom, Adam Willaerts painted harbour views of Dutch cities. The huge decorative *View of Dordrecht* (1629; Dordrecht, Dordrechts Mus.), in a long horizontal format typical of Vroom, is one of Willaerts's masterpieces. The artist painted his self-portrait in a boat prominently placed in the centre foreground.

After 1650 Willaerts sometimes collaborated with Willem Ormea (*d* 1673), a painter of still-lifes of fish, adding the background of sea, coast and shipping to Ormea's catch of fish displayed on a beach. Some of these scenes are biblical, featuring the *Miraculous Draught of Fishes* (Bruges, Comm. Openb. Onderstand).

(2) Abraham Willaerts (*b* Utrecht, *c.* 1603; *d* Utrecht, 18 Oct 1669). Son of (1) Adam Willaerts. After training with his father he later studied with Jan van Bijlert in Utrecht and with Simon Vouet in Paris. In 1624 he became a master of the Utrecht Guild of St Luke; from 1637 to 1644 he was in Brazil in the entourage of Count John Maurice of Nassau-Siegen, and in 1659 he visited Naples and Rome. His marine paintings closely follow those of his father, for example *Coast Scene* (1647; Haarlem, Frans Halsmus.), but often have an atmospheric softness, as in *Beach Scene with Ruin* (1662; Brunswick, Herzog Anton Ulrich-Mus.). Abraham's foreign travels had little effect on his style but resulted in Mediterranean harbour views (real and imaginary), such as *Harbour of Naples* (London, N. Mar. Mus.). He painted a series of portraits, both single figures (several were admirals) and family groups (e.g. Cambridge, Fitzwilliam; Schleissheim, Neues Schloss). He also contributed portraits in the foreground of some of his father's harbour scenes.

(3) Isaac Willaerts (*b* Utrecht, *c*. 1620; *d* Utrecht, 24 June 1693). Son of (1) Adam Willaerts. In 1637 he was a master, and in 1666 the dean, of the Utrecht Guild. His mediocre coastal scenes are derived from his father's but are more loosely painted (e.g. *Marine Scene with Rocky Coast and Ruin*, Utrecht, Cent. Mus.). He also followed his father in contributing marine backgrounds to Ormea's still-lifes of fish. His paintings of southern ports resemble those of his brother (2) Abraham Willaerts.

BIBLIOGRAPHY
R. van Luttervelt: 'Een zeegezicht met een historische voorstelling van Adam Willaerts', *Historia*, xii (1947), pp. 225–8
L. J. Bol: *Die holländische Marinemalerei des 17. Jahrhunderts* (Bunswick, 1973), pp. 63–80
M. Russell: *Visions of the Sea: Hendrick C. Vroom and the Origins of Dutch Marine Painting* (Leiden, 1983), pp. 179, 182
                                                    MARGARITA RUSSELL

Willard, Daniel Wheelock. *See under* BABB, COOK & WILLARD.

Willard, Solomon (*b* Petersham, MA, 26 June 1783; *d* Quincy, MA, 27 Feb 1861). American architect. He trained in Petersham, MA, and moved in 1804 to Boston, where he distinguished himself as a carpenter and wood-carver working for the architects Charles Bulfinch, Asher Benjamin, Alexander Parris and Peter Banner (*fl* 1795–1828). Between 1810 and 1818 Willard made trips to the mid-Atlantic states where he worked with the artists and architects Benjamin Rush, Maximilian Godefroy, Robert Mills and Benjamin Latrobe. Bulfinch commissioned a wooden model of the United States Capitol from Willard in 1817 and installed versions of Willard's hot air furnace in the Capitol and the President's house. Willard assisted Alexander Parris in the design of Boston's first Greek Revival buildings, the Sears mansion (1816) and St Paul's Cathedral (1820). As an independent architect Willard worked in Grecian, Gothic and Egyptian styles, but his buildings are uniformly heavy in appearance owing to his preference for local Quincy granite. Willard designed less than ten major buildings in his career; most of his energy between 1825 and 1843 went into the design and supervision of the Bunker Hill Monument, a 68 metre-high granite obelisk in Charlestown, MA. He moved to Quincy to supervise the extraction of granite from quarries for this monument and for buildings by other architects, such as the Merchant's Exchange (1836) in New York by Isaiah Rogers.

WRITINGS
Plans and Sections of the Obelisk on Bunker's Hill (Boston, 1843)

BIBLIOGRAPHY
W. Wheildon: *Memoir of Solomon Willard* (Boston, 1865)
J. Winsor: *The Memorial History of Boston*, iv (Boston, 1880–81)
T. Hamlin: *Greek Revival Architecture in America* (New York, 1944/R 1964)
W. Edwards: *Historic Quincy, Massachusetts* (Quincy, MA, 1946, rev. 1954)
                                                    JACK QUINAN

Willaume, David (*b* Metz, 7 June 1658; *d c*. 1740). English goldsmith of French origin. The son of a goldsmith, Adam Willaume, he arrived in London from France *c*. 1685 and became a freeman of the Goldsmiths' Company by 1694. His first known mark was registered in 1697, but it is likely that he had been manufacturing articles for several years. He became one of the most successful Huguenot goldsmiths. By 1698 he had made a pair of single bottle wine-coolers (Chatsworth, Derbys) for William Cavendish, 4th Earl and 1st Duke of Devonshire. This is the earliest known pair of English wine-coolers, and they illustrate French influence. Willaume's output was prolific, and his patrons included many of the nobility. Although he never achieved the office of Royal Goldsmith, a number of pieces made by him during the reigns of Queen Anne and George I are engraved with the royal arms, for example a large ewer and basin (1705) supplied to Thomas Wentworth, 3rd Earl of Strafford, on his appointment as ambassador to Berlin. Willaume's business, which included a banking department, was highly profitable, and in 1728 he retired to his newly acquired estate at Tingrith, Beds. His son David Willaume II (1692–1761) then registered his first mark and took control of his father's business. David Willaume's daughter Anne (1691–1733) married the Huguenot goldsmith DAVID TANQUERAY.

BIBLIOGRAPHY
J. F. Hayward: *Huguenot Silver in England, 1688–1727* (London, 1959)
A. G. Grimwade: *London Goldsmiths, 1697–1837: Their Marks & Lives* (London, 1976, rev. 3/1990)
                                                    STEPHEN T. CLARKE

Wille. French family of artists of German origin. Having moved to Paris at the outset of his career, (1) Jean-Georges Wille gradually established himself as a leading engraver, initially of portraits after fashionable artists, but later turning to genre scenes. His *Journal* is an important source for Parisian art life in the later 18th century. Wille's son (2) Pierre-Alexandre Wille was a painter of sentimental genre scenes in the manner of his teacher Jean-Baptiste Greuze.

(1) Jean-Georges [Johann Georg] **Wille** (*b* Königsberg, Hessen, 5 Nov 1715; *d* Paris, 15 April 1808). Engraver, collector, dealer and patron. Apprenticed to an alcoholic painter and then to a gunsmith, he moved to Paris in 1736. Penniless, and with only rudimentary training as a draughtsman and engraver, he first found employment engraving metalwork for gunsmiths. He was then commissioned by a printseller, Michel Odieuvre (1687–1756), to do some (badly paid) plates for the *Recueil des portraits des rois de France* (1738; Portalis and Beraldi, no. 87). An introduction to Hyacinthe Rigaud from the German engraver Georg Friedrich Schmidt (1712–75) led Rigaud to offer Wille the opportunity to engrave his portrait of *Charles Fouquet, Maréchal de Belle-Isle* (1743; PB 35). This, and an engraving of Rigaud's wife, *Elisabeth de Gouy* (1743), made Wille's reputation. For the next ten years he concentrated on portraits, notably after Rigaud (e.g. *Jean de Boullongne*, 1748, PB 38) and after Louis Tocqué (e.g. *Charles Edward Stuart*, 1748, PB 42; *Comte de Saint-Florentin*, 1751, PB 78; and *Jean-Baptiste Massé*, 1755, PB 70).

Wille's studio became one of the most important printmaking centres in Paris, and a meeting-place for artists, collectors, dealers and, above all, young German engravers who wanted to train in Paris, including Balthazar

Anton Dunker and Franz Edmund Weirotter. As a result he had considerable influence on engraving in Germany. However, unlike Jacques-Philippe Lebas, who ran the other great Paris studio, Wille worked alone on the plates he signed. After obtaining French citizenship he was approved (*agréé*) by the Académie Royale in 1755; for six years he worked on his *morceau de réception*, a portrait of the *Marquis de Marigny* (PB 69) after Tocqué, completing it in 1761. This was the last portrait he engraved, since his deteriorating eyesight no longer allowed him to engrave with the precision he demanded for his portraits. During the 1750s, however, he had also begun to engrave genre scenes and pictures from the northern schools. In 1754 he engraved a *Death of Cleopatra* (PB 13) after Caspar Netscher, which he followed with several plates after Gerrit Dou, including *Woman Winding Wool* (1755; PB 7) and *Woman Reading* (1762; PB 18) as well as the *Cook* (1764) after Peter Adolf Hall. Wille made full use of the free access he had to the best collections in France of Dutch paintings, including those of the Comte de Vence, Jean de Jullienne, Louis Simon Lempereur and Johann Anton Peters.

An avid collector himself, Wille bought paintings, drawings, engravings, medals and curios at public sales and he also commissioned paintings. The collection he sold in December 1784 was only a small proportion of the number of works that had passed through his hands, even though the catalogue lists 100 paintings and over 4000 drawings: Wille kept the best works while frequently re-selling others he had bought or commissioned. In this way he was able to help German and Swiss artists, including Weirotter and Johann Balthazar Bullinger I, to become known in Paris, often acting as a middle-man for French collectors and such foreigners as Charles-Frederick, Grand Duke of Baden (*d* 1811), and for Frederick V of Denmark (1723–76). His success as a cultural intermediary between the French and German worlds resulted in Wille's election to membership of several foreign academies, including Augsburg (1756), Vienna (1768), Copenhagen (1770) and Berlin (1771). Wille owned drawings by Rigaud, Adam Frans van der Meulen, François Boucher, Jean-Baptiste Greuze and many others. Of the 17th-century Dutch paintings in his collection he made engravings after Godfried Schalcken's *Family Concert* (1767–9; PB 16) and Isaack van Ostade's *Good Friends* (1776; PB 15); he also made engravings after some of the paintings by his contemporaries that he owned, including Christian Wilhelm Ernst Dietrich's *Wandering Musicians* (1764; PB 4) and *Hagar Introduced to Abraham by Sarah* (1775; PB 2), and Pompeo Batoni's *Death of Mark Antony* (1778; PB 1). His love of genre painting brought him close to Greuze, to whom he entrusted as a pupil his son (2) Pierre-Alexandre Wille. From the 1770s his son's work constituted the essence of his purchases and provided the subject-matter for his last engravings. By the 1780s he had virtually retired from engraving but continued to augment his stock of plates by ordering more from Weirotter, Robert Daudet, Joseph de Longueil and other former pupils. Having sold his collection of paintings and drawings in 1784 he sold his prints in December 1786. By the time of the French Revolution, an event he greeted with satisfaction, he had become blind and lived out his final years in straitened circumstances. His way of using the burin to engrave most of each plate in very precise and regular strokes was universally acclaimed by contemporaries, and it was his best pupil, Charles-Clément Bervic, who under the Empire became the leading French engraver.

Between May 1759 and October 1793 Wille kept a *Journal*. Its almost daily entries record not only his own social and working life but also the art life of Paris and the activities of its principal figures, providing an unusually detailed source for the last decades of the *ancien régime*. Wille's own formative years are covered in the *Mémoires* he compiled in his eighties.

UNPUBLISHED SOURCES

Paris, Archvs N., 219AP [personal papers and MSS]

WRITINGS

Mémoires (1715–43) and *Journal* (1759–93); ed. G. Duplessis as *Mémoires et Journal de Jean-Georges Wille, Graveur du Roi*, 2 vols (Paris, 1857)

BIBLIOGRAPHY

Portalis–Beraldi [PB]

C. Leblanc: *Catalogue de l'oeuvre de Jean Georges Wille, Graveur du Roi* (Paris, 1847)

W. E. Kellner: 'Neues aus dem schriftlichen Nachlass des Jean-Georges Wille', *Mitt. Oberhess. Geschver.*, xlix (1965), pp. 144–89

H.-T. Schulze Altcappenberg: '*Le Voltaire de l'art*': Johann Georg Wille (1715–1808) und seine Schule in Paris (Munich, 1987)

(2) Pierre-Alexandre Wille (*b* Paris, 19 July 1748; *d* Paris, after 1821). Painter, son of (1) Jean-Georges Wille. Between 1761 and 1763 he trained under Jean-Baptiste Greuze, who was a friend of his father, and later under Joseph-Marie Vien. Approved (*agréé*) by the Académie Royale in 1774, he devoted himself to painting sentimental genre scenes, such as the *Last Moments of a Beloved Wife* (1784; Cambrai, Mus. Mun.), in Greuze's manner. He also executed paintings for his father to engrave, including *French Patriotism* (1781) and the *Double Reward of Merit* (1785; both Blérancourt, Château, Mus. N. Coop. Fr.–Amér.). Having played an active role in the French Revolution, he is barely documented thereafter. A drawing of *Danton Led to the Scaffold* (Paris, Carnavalet) was attributed to him by Maison.

BIBLIOGRAPHY

L. Hautecoeur: 'Pierre-Alexandre Wille le fils, 1748–?1821', *Archvs A. Fr.*, n. s., vii (1913), pp. 440–66

K. E. Maison: 'Pierre-Alexandre Wille and the French Revolution', *Master Drgs*, x (1972), pp. 34–5

De David à Delacroix: La Peinture française de 1774 à 1830 (exh. cat., Paris, Grand Pal.; Detroit, MI, Inst. A.; New York, Met.; 1974–5), pp. 672–4

CHRISTIAN MICHEL

Willems, Florent (*b* Liège, 8 Jan 1823; *d* Neuilly-sur-Seine, Oct 1905). Belgian painter, active in France. He trained at the Academie in Mechelen. He first exhibited in Paris at the Salon of 1840, and in 1844 he settled there, working as both a restorer and a painter. He modelled his work on that of Dutch genre painters of the 17th and 18th centuries. Willems emulated their meticulous technique, as seen especially in his depiction of silks and brocades in *The Bride's Toilette* (Brussels, Mus. A. Mod.). He also adopted their subject-matter: the majority of his works are genre scenes set in the 16th and 17th centuries, such as *The Widow* (1850; Brussels, Mus. A. Mod.). Willems also painted scenes of contemporary life, for example *A Party at the Duchess's House* (Brussels, Mus. A. Mod.), in which the furniture and clothing are portrayed with considerable realistic detail. In all Willems's work the anecdotal element was dominant, and his paintings thus appealed easily to a wide audience. He influenced the work of his pupil and compatriot Alfred Stevens. His son Charles-Henri Willems (*fl* 1901–13) was a portrait painter in Paris.

BIBLIOGRAPHY

Bénézit; Thieme–Becker

P. B. Gheusi: *Florent Willems* (Paris, 1905)

J. F. Buyck and A. A. Moerman: *Schilderkunst in België ten tijde van H. Leys, 1815–1869* [Painting in Belgium at the time of H. Leys, 1815–1869] (Antwerp, 1969)

Catalogus schilderijen 19de en 20ste eeuw, Antwerp, Kon. Mus. S. Kst. cat. (Antwerp, 1977), p. 493

RICHARD KERREMANS

Willemsens, Abraham. *See under* MASTERS, ANONYMOUS, & MONOGRAMMISTS, §I: MASTER OF THE BÉGUINS.

Willemssens, Louis [Ludovicus] (*bapt* Antwerp, 7 Oct 1630; *bur* Antwerp, 12 Oct 1702). Flemish sculptor. He probably trained with Artus Quellinus (i), with whom he may have collaborated on the marble reliefs of the Stadhuis (built 1648–65), now the Royal Palace, Amsterdam. He became a master in the Guild of St Luke in Antwerp relatively late, in 1661 or 1662. He may have held the post of sculptor to William III, Prince of Orange. His high contemporary reputation is attested by the remarks on the excellent quality of his work in the travel diary for 1687 of the Swedish architect Nicodemus Tessin (ii).

Many of Willemssens's works, both religious and secular, are untraced. Among those that survive is a pulpit (1673–5; *in situ*) supported by four allegorical statues for the St Jacobskerk in Antwerp. The statue of *Theology* is imbued with a refined elegance of a late Baroque character, while the figure of *Truth* recalls the classicizing style of François Du Quesnoy's *St Susanna* in S Maria di Loreto, Rome. Also for the St Jacobskerk, Willemssens produced marble statues of *St John Preaching in the Wilderness*, *God the Father* (above the altar in the chapel of the Holy Sacrament) and *St Paul* (1686) as well as two confessionals (*c.* 1692). For Antwerp Cathedral he made the communion bench (1680) in the chapel of St Anthony and contributed to the altar of the Coopers (1678), of which only some marble reliefs remain (now behind the main altar), one of them by Willemssens. He also worked for more modest churches, such as that at Bazel, near Antwerp.

Among Willemssens's other works were the stalls for the Cistercian abbey of St Bernard at Hemiksem, near Antwerp, in collaboration with Artus Quellinus (ii) and Henricus Franciscus Verbrugghen. The somewhat ascetic oak figures of saints from this ensemble were moved to the church of St Lambert at Wouw, north Brabant (Netherlands), in 1827. Several terracotta *bozzetti* by Willemssens are in the Musées Royaux des Beaux-Arts de Belgique, Brussels, including *St Martin of Tours*, a modello for a funerary monument in the Begijnhofkerk, Lier, near Antwerp. An imposing marble bust in armour of *Don Juan Domingo de Zúñiga y Fonseca, Governor of the Spanish Netherlands* (Antwerp, Kon. Mus. S. Kst.) has been attributed to him. He may have sculpted three altars, of which only a few figures remain, for the cathedral at Paderborn, Westphalia. Willemssens's sculpture, elegant

and slightly mannered, marks the transition from the Baroque to the Rococo style in Flanders.

BIBLIOGRAPHY

G. H. W. Upmark: 'Ein Besuch in Holland 1687 aus den Reisenschilderungen des schwedischen Architekten Nicodemus Tessin d.J.', *Oud-Holland*, xviii (1900), pp. 117–28, 144–52, 199–210

A. E. Brinckmann: *Barock-Bozzetti*, iii (Frankfurt am Main, 1925), pp. 44–7, pls 21–2

J. L. Broeckx: 'Ludovicus Willemssens, 1630–1702: Antwerpsch beeldhouwer', *Gent. Bijdr. Kstgesch.*, vii (1941), pp. 137–71

M. Coppens: *Koorbanken in Nederland: Barok* (Amsterdam and Brussels, 1943)

Europäische Barockplastik am Niederrhein: Grupello und seine Zeit (exh. cat., Düsseldorf, Kstmus., 1971), pp. 329–31, pls 161, 181a

La Sculpture au siècle de Rubens dans les Pays-Bas méridionaux et la principauté de Liège (exh. cat., Brussels, Mus. A. Anc., 1977), pp. 286–94

G. V. van Hemeldonck and I. Kockelbergh: *Kunst en Kunstenaars in de notariële akten van de 18de eeuw* [Art and artists in the notarial documents of the 18th century] (Antwerp, 1985–6), pp. 64–5

HELENA BUSSERS

Willendorf. Group of eight sites in Wachau, Austria. These sites have yielded important remains of Upper Palaeolithic date (*c.* 40,000–*c.* 10,000 BP), including a famous figurine of a woman known as the Willendorf Venus (see fig.; *see also* PREHISTORIC EUROPE, §II, 3(i)). The sites have been known since the mid-19th century, when collectors started to search them for bones and archaeological objects, but it was the construction of a railway between Mauthausen and Krems that prompted the official excavations, which started in 1908 under Josef Bayer and Hugo Obermaier and continued until 1955, when Fritz Felgenhauer was director. The material recovered from the excavations is held by the Naturhistorisches Museum, Vienna. The best-explored area, Site II, had the longest stratigraphic sequence. The lower levels (1–4) were Aurignacian (*c.* 40,000–*c.* 25,000 BP), while the upper levels (5–9) belonged to the Gravettian culture (*c.* 30,000–*c.* 18,000 BP) and displayed an evolution from level 5, which had many gravette stone points, via three levels with many-pointed stone blades, to level 9, which had Kostyonki-type shouldered points (*see* PREHISTORIC EUROPE, §II, 4); Willendorf represents the westernmost point of distribution of this special type of stone tools. Level 9 was one of the richest of Willendorf II. The fauna was typical of the steppe, but with some forest elements, and included reindeer, ibex, bison, red deer, horses, mammoths, wolves, red foxes, arctic foxes, wolverines, bears and lions.

The Willendorf Venus was found in 1908 in level 9, near a large hearth but 250 mm deeper than it, in pure loess (wind-laid sand, silt and clay); no pit was observed, so it is not possible to make a direct association with the cultural level. It is made from oolitic limestone, deeply coloured with red ochre, and measures 110 mm high. Except for the faceless head, which has a complicated hairstyle of curls arranged in rows, it is a highly realistic rendering of an obese woman with broad hips, pronounced buttocks, large breasts, short legs and slender arms, bent to rest on the breasts. A less detailed ivory figurine of a woman was found, placed on a mammoth's jawbone, in a pit *c.* 10 m from the spot where the first figure was found; ivory fragments point to nearby on-site production. It is one of the largest-known Palaeolithic figurines, measuring

Willendorf, female figurine, known as the Willendorf Venus, limestone, h. 110 mm, Gravettian culture, *c.* 30,000–*c.* 18,000 BP (Vienna, Naturhistorisches Museum)

230 mm high, although the head and the feet are broken off. The breasts and buttocks are not separated, and the legs are closed; the arms are in different positions. A third, apparently unfinished, ivory female figurine (h. 90 mm) is oval in outline with similar proportions to the first piece.

BIBLIOGRAPHY
J. Bayer: 'Die Venus II von Willendorf', *Eiszeit & Urgesch.*, vii (1930), pp. 48–54
F. Felgenhauer: 'Willendorf in der Wachau: Monographie der Paläolithifundstellen I–VII', *Mitt. Prähist. Komm. Österreich. Akad. Wiss.*, viii–ix (1956–9), pt 1, pp. 1–217; pt 2, pp. 1–79; pt 3, figs 1–124
W. Angeli: *Die Venus von Willendorf* (Vienna, 1989)

JOACHIM HAHN

Willette, (Léon-)Adolphe (*b* Châlons-sur-Marne, 31 July 1857; *d* Paris, 4 Feb 1926). French illustrator, printmaker and painter. After studying at the Ecole des Beaux-Arts, Paris, Willette entered the studio of Alexandre Cabanel where he encountered Rodolphe Salis, the future founder in Montmartre of the Chat Noir cabaret (1881) and journal (1882). As a member of the Club des Hydropathes (1874–81), a group of writers, actors and artists who met regularly at a café in the Quartier Latin and from 1881 at the Chat

Noir, Adolphe Willette became associated with the anti-establishment, humorous and satirical spirit of the avant-garde artistic community in Montmartre.

Willette was an early and regular illustrator of the *Chat Noir* and *Courrier français* (founded in 1885), the two principal (albeit tongue-in-cheek) chronicles of Montmartre. For two years from 1888 Willette and the poet Emile Goudeau published the satirical journal *Le Pierrot*: in 1896 and 1897 they collaborated on the sporadically issued journal *Vache enragée* which served as a forum for the artists of Montmartre. Willette is best known for his numerous sympathetic depictions of a pierrot (e.g. *Pierrot pendu*, lithograph, in A. Marty: *L'Estampe originale*, vi, 1894), who resembles the artist himself and serves as a metaphor for the alienation of artists from society.

Willette's philosophical and political views were a strange combination of anarchism, socialism, nationalism, militarism, anti-Catholicism and anti-Semitism, all of which he promoted in his prints and illustrations. In 1889 he created a lithographic poster announcing his candidacy on an anti-Semitic platform for the local legislative election. His illustrations during the 1890s for Edouard Drumont's journal *Libre parole* graphically put forth the fanatical anti-Semitic rhetoric of the writer-politician. Together Willette's images and Drumont's essays helped to establish the virulently anti-Semitic environment in France at the end of the century. Other prominent satirical journals for which Willette worked were *Le Rire*, *Assiette au beurre* and *Canard sauvage*. Although less prolific as a printmaker, he created three lithographs for André Marty's *L'Estampe originale* (1893–5).

Willette executed numerous decorative schemes for cabarets, dance halls and cafés. He also decorated the waiting-room of the Hôtel de Ville, Paris (1904).

WRITINGS
Feu Pierrot: 1857–19? (Paris, 1919) [autobiography]
BIBLIOGRAPHY
The Circle of Toulouse-Lautrec (exh. cat. by P. D. Cate and P. Boyer, New Brunswick, Rutgers U., Zimmerli A. Mus., 1985), pp. 186–91

PHILLIP DENNIS CATE

William I [William the Conqueror], King of England and Duke of Normandy (*b c.* 1027; *reg* 1066–87; *d* 9 Sept 1087). Ruler and patron of Norman birth. Duke of Normandy from 1035, he married a blood relation, Matilda of Flanders, in 1053. As penance, William founded an abbey for men (St Etienne) and Matilda a convent for women (La Trinité), both in Caen, in the 1060s (*see* CAEN, §§1 and 2). He conquered England in 1066 and immediately began a campaign of castle building to subjugate his kingdom. They were wooden castles, motte and bailey designs, as illustrated on the BAYEUX TAPESTRY (Bayeux, Mus. Tap.). William also founded Battle Abbey (E. Sussex; destr.) on the site of the Battle of Hastings. The Romanesque church had an apse and ambulatory plan.

Later, some important royal castles were rebuilt in stone. Three stone keeps, surviving in varying condition, date from William's reign: London (begun *c.* 1080), Colchester, Essex (*c.* 1085), and Canterbury (mentioned in 1086). They remain the biggest keeps ever constructed in England. Colchester, the largest at some 50×45 m, stands on the podium of a Claudian temple. Like the Tower of

London it is rectangular, but its three-storey elevation was not as tall. Canterbury was three-storey and almost square but only half the size of Colchester. All stood within Roman walls. William also built the unusual gatehouse-keep (*c.* 1070) at Exeter, and a square keep (*c.* 1080) at Pevensey, E. Sussex. In 1070 he built a palace hall at Winchester, which was subsequently destroyed.

BIBLIOGRAPHY

A. L. Poole: *From Domesday Book to Magna Carta, 1087–1216*, Oxford History of England (Oxford, 1951, rev. 1955)
S. Toy: *The Castles of Great Britain* (London, 1953, rev. 3/1963)
C. Brooke: *The Saxon and Norman Kings* (London, 1963, rev. 3/1972)
H. M. Colvin, ed.: *The History of the King's Works*, i, ii (London, 1963)
F. Barlow: *William the Conqueror* (London, 1964)
——: *Edward the Confessor* (London, 1970)

FRANCIS WOODMAN

William I, King of Prussia and Emperor of Germany. *See* HOHENZOLLERN, (12).

William I, King of the Netherlands. *See* ORANGE NASSAU, (9).

William I, Stadholder and Prince of Orange. *See* ORANGE NASSAU, (1).

William II, King of Prussia and Emperor of Germany. *See* HOHENZOLLERN, (16).

William II, King of Sicily. *See* HAUTEVILLE, (2).

William II, King of the Netherlands. *See* ORANGE NASSAU, (10).

William III, Stadholder, Prince of Orange and King of England and Scotland. *See* ORANGE NASSAU, (5).

William [Wilhelm] **IV**, Duke of Bavaria. *See* WITTELSBACH, §I(2).

William IV, King of Great Britain. *See* HANOVER, (5).

William IV, Stadholder and Prince of Orange. *See* ORANGE NASSAU, (7).

William [Wilhelm] **V**, Duke of Bavaria. *See* WITTELSBACH, §I(4).

William V, Stadholder and Prince of Orange. *See* ORANGE NASSAU, (8).

William [Wilhelm] **VIII**, Landgrave of Hesse-Kassel. *See* HESSE-KASSEL, (2).

William and Mary style. Term applied primarily to decorative arts produced in The Netherlands and England during the reign (1689–1702) of William III and Mary II (*see* ORANGE NASSAU, (5) and (6)) and that spread also to North America at the end of the century. It covers a vocabulary of visual forms rather than a movement, and is represented by richly ornamented furniture, displays of wares from the Far East, embossed and engraved silver, ceramics, luxurious textiles, architectural ornament and garden design. The decorative arts of the 1690s reflect the blending of French, Dutch and English ornamental styles as well as an increased taste for exotica. Although at war with France, William III admired the sophistication of

French culture and encouraged the immigration of Huguenot refugees, the French Protestants who fled from France after 1685 when Louis XIV revoked the Edict of Nantes, which had guaranteed them freedom of worship (*see* HUGUENOTS). William's leading designer was the Huguenot architect and etcher Daniel Marot, a versatile artist trained at the court of Louis XIV (*see* MAROT, (2)). Marot's stylistic idiom is best exemplified in the Dutch palace of HET LOO, in Gelderland (for illustration *see* MAROT, (2)), and its gardens (*see* GARDEN, §VIII, 4(v) and fig. 53) renovated by William and Mary in the 1680s, and in the many designs commissioned and often executed for the monarchs' English palaces of Hampton Court and Kensington, London. The continuing influence of designs by Marot (*see* DISPLAY OF ART, fig. 10) and William's recurring requests for the latest in French furniture and textiles (obtainable only by open violation of the laws against trade with France), attest to the French accent in international taste. Over 100 of Marot's designs for objects large and small in various media were published in his *Oeuvres* (The Hague, 1703; republished, with *c.* 126 plates, Amsterdam, *c.* 1712); the resemblance of the prints to surviving objects is remarkable, proving his pervasive influence.

Queen Mary was an avid collector of oriental luxury goods (*see* ENGLAND, fig. 86), inspired a craze for Japanese, Chinese and Dutch ceramics, and supervised the architectural renovations and gardens at Kensington Palace and HAMPTON COURT PALACE. Such English artists as the architect Sir Christopher Wren and the artist and sculptor Grinling Gibbons, both of whom had been employed by earlier Stuart monarchs, continued in favour. Gibbons's delicate wood-carvings of flowers, fruit, birds, game and foliage (for illustration *see* GIBBONS, GRINLING) were aesthetically related to Dutch still-life painting. Appointed Master Sculptor and Master Carver in 1693, he executed wash drawings (London, Soane Mus.) for prospective interiors in the new apartments at Hampton Court, which demonstrate an intimacy of ornamentation well suited to his Anglo-Dutch patrons and include architectural assemblages of Mary's Oriental porcelain and Delftware.

The Dutch taste for such domestic features as black-and-white tiled floors and blue-and-white Delftware became part of an eclectic, international vocabulary. The extraordinary success of English and Dutch commercial shipping (notably the East India Company), brought Chinese porcelain, Indian fabrics and Indonesian and Malaysian sea-shells as well as botanical specimens and woods (e.g. ebony) to Europe. The result was a decorative style that was not only eclectic, but distinctively exotic—as in japanned furniture, lacquerwork, elaborately inlaid ornamental cabinets for collections of curiosities, Delftware combining Western and Eastern motifs (*see* DISPLAY OF ART, §VI), Chinese silks and damasks, gilded wall-coverings and intricately wrought Huguenot metalwork. A similar confluence of styles is seen in English gardens of the 1690s, for example at Chatsworth, Derbys, Hampton Court, and Westbury Court, Wilts (*see* GARDEN, §VIII, 4).

Following the royal example, expensive, elaborate objects of virtuoso craftsmanship became the fashion among the wealthy in the growing number of refurbished or new country houses (*see* ENGLAND, fig. 38). Huguenot craftsmen who had been trained in France under the administration of Jean-Baptiste Colbert and Charles Le Brun dramatically improved the quality of English manufactures. A Dutchman, Gerrit Jensen, was appointed Cabinet Maker to the royal household of William and Mary in 1689, and through the products of his shop in St Martin's Lane, London, sold furniture in the style of Marot. Meanwhile, wealthy merchants began to display their status by incorporating mirrors and chimney-glasses in their houses; and caned seats replaced old 'turkey-work' chairs. Although English craftsmen tried to copy the continental techniques their methods were inferior; nevertheless, they supplied a market unable to afford the Huguenot pieces or those that were imported illegally.

For further information on the William and Mary style in Europe and America *see* ENGLAND, §§V, 3, VI, 3, VII, 2, VIII, 2, IX, 1(iii); NETHERLANDS, THE, §§V, 2; VI, 2; VII, 2; IX, 1(ii); and UNITED STATES OF AMERICA, §VI, 1.

BIBLIOGRAPHY
P. Thornton: *Seventeenth-century Interior Decoration in England, France and Holland* (New Haven, 1978)
The Quiet Conquest: The Huguenots, 1685–1985 (exh. cat. by T. Murdoch, London, Mus. London, 1985)
The Anglo-Dutch Garden in the Age of William and Mary (exh. cat., ed. J. Dixon Hunt and E. de Jong; Apeldoorn, Pal. Het Loo; London, Christie's; 1988–9); also in *J. Gdn Hist.*, viii/2–3 (1988) [whole issue]
Courts and Colonies: The William and Mary Style in Holland, England and America (exh. cat., New York, Cooper-Hewitt Mus.; Pittsburgh, PA, Carnegie Mus. A.; Washington, DC, Smithsonian Inst.; 1988)
The Age of William III and Mary II: Power, Politics and Patronage, 1688–1702 (exh. cat., ed. R. Maccubbin and M. Hamilton-Phillips; New York, Grolier Club; Washington, DC, Folger Shakespeare Lib.; 1988–9)
The Dutch Garden in the Seventeenth Century: Dumbarton Oaks Colloquium on the History of Landscape Architecture, XII: Washington, DC, 1990
M. HAMILTON-PHILLIPS, R. P. MACCUBBIN

William Augustus, Duke of Cumberland. *See* HANOVER, (2).

William de Brailes (*fl c.* 1230–60). English illuminator. A William de Brailes (variously spelt) is cited in six documents (*c.* 1230–60) relating to Oxford. These establish that he lived with his wife Celena in Catte Street among other professionals engaged in book production. None of these documents, however, mentions his trade. It seems most probable that the documented William de Brailes may be identified with the illuminator W. de Brailes, whose name appears in two manuscripts associated with Oxford. The name occurs twice in a Book of Hours (*c.* 1240; London, BL, Add. MS. 49999; *see* GOTHIC, fig. 64), beside historiated initials that open the final prayers. Both initials contain the bust of a tonsured figure, one of which (fol. 43*r*) is identified by a caption in French that clearly identifies his profession: *w. de brail' qui me depeint*. In the *Last Judgement* miniature of the six leaves from a Psalter in the Fitzwilliam Museum, Cambridge (*c.* 1240; MS. 330, leaf 3), the artist is shown being rescued from hell by the avenging angel, and is identified by the scroll he holds, inscribed *w. de brail' me fecit* (see fig.).

The development of the university, already dominating Oxford in the 13th century, created a demand for both scholarly and religious books. The quantity of surviving manuscripts with an Oxford origin suggests a lively book

William de Brailes: *Last Judgement*; illumination from a Psalter, 255×175 mm, *c.* 1240 (Cambridge, Fitzwilliam Museum, MS. 330, leaf 3); the artist is identified by inscription in the bottom right semicircle

trade, and this is confirmed by the documented presence of numerous scribes, parchment-makers and illuminators, many of whom lived in and around Catte Street. To judge from his two signed manuscripts and the group that can therefore be ascribed to his hand, de Brailes's contribution was to the luxury trade, continuing the tradition of illumination already established in Oxford by such works as the Huntingfield Psalter (*c.* 1210–20; New York, Pierpont Morgan Lib., MS. M. 43) and the Lothian Bible (*c.* 1220; New York, Pierpont Morgan Lib., MS. M. 791). This tradition was based on professional collaboration between a variety of scribes, decorators and illuminators working simultaneously.

William de Brailes is known also to have collaborated, although his two signed manuscripts are substantially, if not wholly, his own work. For certain projects he was evidently the chief artist and designer, as in a Psalter (*c.* 1240–50; Oxford, New College, MS. 322), in which he painted most of the historiated initials (some on separate pieces of parchment, stuck in place) and certain complete folios, but left much of the minor decoration to others. Elsewhere his hand can be identified only as a casual contribution to the work of another designer, for example in the Stockholm Psalter (*c.* 1230–40; Stockholm, Nmus., B. 2010).

Characteristically, de Brailes created small manuscripts, following the early 13th-century trend, derived from Paris, towards portable books. They are richly embellished with penwork decoration, crisply painted single-line initials and line-fillers, and the text is usually illustrated with numerous narrative historiated initials. He tended to design small spaces to enclose the narrative, dividing full pages into a pattern of variously shaped medallions. Two sets of now detached leaves (six leaves in Cambridge, Fitzwilliam, MS. 330, and one in New York, Pierpont Morgan Lib., MS. 913; Baltimore, MD, Walters A.G., MS. 106 and Paris, Mus. Marmottan, 24 and 7 leaves respectively) demonstrate his use of pictorial prefaces, commonly found in illustrated Psalters in the 13th century, but also incorporated into Bibles and Books of Hours. Both groups of single leaves are small in scale, and the Fitzwilliam pages are divided into medallions surrounded by foliate decoration. De Brailes was a master story-teller. His small squat figures fill the frames of both initials and medallions, sometimes spilling into the margins. Their elongated and expressive arms, emphatic forefingers and twisting poses are the keys to 'reading' de Brailes. Often stylistically wayward, his work lacks elegance and grandeur, but is always clear in conveying meaning and humour.

BIBLIOGRAPHY
G. F. Warner: *Descriptive Catalogue of the Illuminated Manuscripts in the Library of C. W. Dyson Perrins* (Oxford, 1920), nos 4–5
S. C. Cockerell: *The Work of W. de Brailes: An English Illuminator of the Thirteenth Century*, Roxburghe Club (Cambridge, 1930)
H. Swarzenski: 'Unknown Bible Pictures by W. de Brailes and Some Notes on Early English Bible Illustration', *J. Walters A.G.*, i (1938), pp. 55–69
E. G. Millar: 'Additional Miniatures by W. de Brailes', *J. Walters A.G.*, ii (1939), pp. 106–9
G. Pollard: 'William de Brailes', *Bodleian Lib. Rec.*, v/4 (1955), pp. 202–9
——: 'The Construction of English Twelfth-century Bindings', *The Library*, xviii (1962), pp. 13–14
N. J. Morgan: *Early Gothic Manuscripts (I) 1190–1250* (1982), iv of *A Survey of Manuscripts Illuminated in the British Isles*, ed. J. J. G. Alexander (London, 1975–), pp. 30, 113–23
Duke Humfrey's Library and the Divinity School, 1488–1988 (exh. cat., ed. A. C. de la Mare and S. Gillam; Oxford, Bodleian Lib., 1988)
C. Donovan: *The de Brailes Hours: Shaping the Book of Hours in Thirteenth-century Oxford* (London, 1991)

CLAIRE DONOVAN

William of Orange, Stadholder, Prince of Orange and King of England and Scotland. *See* ORANGE NASSAU, (5).

William of Prene (*fl* 1284–92). English craftsman, active in Ireland. He is the only medieval craftsman active in Ireland whose career can be traced in any detail in documentary sources. During the 1280s he was much involved in a programme of royal castle building, part of a strategy of fortification to quell the more rebellious areas of the country. Although his specific achievements as an architect and builder are a matter of conjecture, his activities provide an insight into the organization of royal building in the 13th century.

William apparently came from the village of Preen in Shropshire. By Easter 1284 he was being paid as a master carpenter in Dublin, and on 30 August of the same year Edward I appointed him Carpenter of the King's Houses and Castles in Ireland 'with one shilling a day for his sustenance and forty shillings a year for his robes'. As there was no master mason with equivalent status, and as William was subsequently described as 'Keeper of the King's Works in Ireland', it appears that he exercised general control over all royal building in the country. This included matters of finance, materials and employment of workmen, as well as design. Such an appointment was unusual both in England and in Ireland at this time.

William's name is associated with work at the castles of Newcastle MacKinegan (Co. Wicklow), Athlone, Rindown and Roscommon (all Co. Roscommon). He was also responsible for the construction of a timber bridge over the River Shannon at Limerick. Roscommon is one of the most imposing castles in Ireland, and its characteristically Edwardian plan, with a symmetrical disposition of towers, has led to comparisons with Harlech in Wales. Much of the building was carried out between 1284 and 1292 during William's tenure of office and probably under his supervision, though the design was evidently established before his appointment.

During this period William lived in some style in a house at Chapelizod on the outskirts of Dublin, and by 1292 he had become a wealthy man, possessing property and privileges in various parts of the country. Not all his wealth, however, was honestly acquired. Between 1286 and 1288 he was fined £20 for illicitly selling timber from royal forests and for not conducting himself 'properly and loyally' at Rindown and Roscommon. Far more serious charges followed in 1292, when he was brought before the justices in Dublin. Most of the charges concerned embezzlement of various sorts, such as selling off iron and nails from royal stocks for his own profit or exaggerating the number of workmen he employed to his own financial advantage. He was also accused of 'faulty work' on the bridge at Limerick, which had evidently collapsed, drowning 80 men in the process. This charge is a relatively rare example of a medieval craftsman being held legally responsible for the quality of his work. William was found guilty on several of the charges, fined £200 and dismissed from royal service. William subsequently appealed to Edward I against his sentence and disputed the conduct and legality of his trial. Although he received some redress, he was not reinstated in office, and he was described as a felon in subsequent records. Although William's behaviour was unscrupulous, it should be seen against a background of fraud and corruption that was rife in the Dublin administration at the time. The scale of his embezzlement underlines the financial as well as the architectural responsibilities that could devolve to a master craftsman in the Middle Ages.

BIBLIOGRAPHY
R. A. Stalley: 'William of Prene and the Royal Works in Ireland', *J. Brit. Archaeol. Assoc.*, cxxxi (1978), pp. 30–49

ROGER STALLEY

William of Sens (*fl* 1174–8). French architect. He is known only from the account by the monk Gervase of the rebuilding of Canterbury Cathedral (*see* CANTERBURY, §III, 1) after the fire of 1174, which records that William was chosen from among many masters from France and

England 'on account of his lively genius and good reputation'. He directed the rebuilding until a fall from the scaffolding in 1178 forced him to retire to France. He is described as a 'craftsman most skilled in wood and stone' who devised ingenious machines for lifting stone and provided the assembled sculptors with moulds (templates) for shaping stones. William seems to have brought sculptors and glaziers with him, as the style of the capital sculpture and of the stained glass executed under his direction has very close parallels in France. Despite his patronym, his architecture shows only general connections with Sens Cathedral, but specific features—such as the proportions of the three-storey elevation, the forms of the piers and capitals, especially the use of marble shafts *en délit*, the sexpartite vaults and the buttressing systems—show William's close acquaintance with contemporary building in Flanders and north-east France, particularly the cathedrals of Cambrai, Arras, Valenciennes and Laon, and with buildings in and around Paris, such as Saint-Denis Abbey, Notre-Dame (Paris), Saint Leu d'Esserent Priory and Champeaux Abbey. At the behest of the monks, William retained where possible the fabric of their destroyed church and preserved something of its character by incorporating traditional Anglo-Norman features such as the clerestory passage.

BIBLIOGRAPHY
Harvey
Gervase of Canterbury: *Tractatus de combustione et reparatione Cantuariensis ecclesiae* [*c.* 1200]; Eng. trans. in F. Woodman: *The Architectural History of Canterbury Cathedral* (London, 1981), pp. 91–3
J. Bony: 'French Influences on the Origins of English Gothic Architecture', *J. Warb. & Court. Inst.*, xii (1949), pp. 1–15

PETER DRAPER

William of Wykeham, Bishop of Winchester (*b* Wickham, Hants, 1324; *d* Bishop's Waltham, Hants, 1404). English ecclesiastic, statesman and patron. William used to be thought of as an architect, even as the inventor of the Perpendicular style, and it is no doubt because of this misapprehension that there are statues of him on the façades of the Royal Academy and the Victoria and Albert Museum, London. He was born into a peasant family in Hampshire and educated in Winchester. By 1350 he was in the employment of the Bishop of Winchester, and by 1356 in that of Edward III. That year he became clerk of works at Windsor Castle, and there he came in contact with William Wynford, Master of the King's Works at Windsor; Wynford was later employed on all William of Wykeham's major building projects.

William's success at Windsor established him in his career. By 1363 he was Lord Privy Seal and the King's factotum, and in 1366 he became Bishop of Winchester and thus one of the richest men in England. Edward III then made him his Chancellor, a position he held until 1371. In 1373 he was impeached and disgraced, but in 1377 he was pardoned and his revenues were restored. Under Richard II he was Chancellor again from 1389 to 1391, but from 1377 his main interest was clearly in his educational foundations and in rebuilding his cathedral. The three major architectural complexes that he initiated, New College, Oxford, Winchester College and the nave of Winchester Cathedral, were all designed by William Wynford.

Work began on New College in 1379. Though it was not the earliest college foundation in Oxford, it was the first, there or at Cambridge, to be built complete to one design, with all its appurtenances, and its scale and provision vastly exceeded those of its predecessors. Grouped round one quadrangle were the warden's lodgings, quarters for the Fellows, the library and muniment tower, and, the main feature, a chapel and hall placed end to end (as in Wynford's design for Windsor). The chapel became the model for every subsequent chapel in Oxford colleges of medieval foundation. Outside the quadrangle stood cloisters, a bell-tower, a tithe-barn, a huge kitchen and a lavatory that is almost as large. The buildings are in the early Perpendicular style, solid, massive and well proportioned.

Winchester College, intended to supply scholars to New College, was built between 1387 and 1394 and is similar in style to New College. Its plan closely follows that of New College, on a smaller scale and with some modifications; there is no structural antechapel, the position of chapel and hall are reversed and there seems originally to have been no library. Work on rebuilding the Norman nave of Winchester Cathedral began in 1394, again under Wynford's direction. It was completed after William of Wykeham's death, with funds provided in his will. The new work encased the Norman structure.

To adorn these works of architecture, William commissioned sculpture (some of which remains at New College and Winchester College); woodwork (fine misericords at both colleges); and stained glass by Thomas of Oxford (a substantial amount remains at New College and a few fragments in Winchester College Chapel). He also acquired some resplendent personal possessions, most notably his crozier, mitre and jewel, all preserved at New College.

See also OXFORD, §3(i); WINCHESTER, §III, 1(ii); WINDSOR CASTLE, §1; and WYNFORD, WILLIAM.

BIBLIOGRAPHY
Bishop Lowth: *Life of William of Wykeham* (London, 1758; suppl. 1759)
G. H. Moberly: *Life of William of Wykeham* (Winchester, 1887)
W. Hayter: *William of Wykeham: Patron of the Arts* (London, 1970)
R. L. Storey: 'The Foundation and the Medieval College, 1379–1530', *New College, Oxford, 1379–1979*, ed. J. Buxton and P. Williams (1979), pp. 3–43
J. Harvey: 'The Buildings of Winchester College', *Winchester College: Sixth-centenary Essays*, ed. R. Custance (Oxford, 1982), pp. 77–127

WILLIAM HAYTER

Williams, Amancio (*b* Buenos Aires, 19 Feb 1913; *d* Buenos Aires, 14 Oct 1989). Argentine architect and urban planner. He was the son of the composer Alberto Williams. He first studied engineering and aviation and became a leading member of the Rationalist Grupo Austral, before graduating as an architect from the University of Buenos Aires in 1941; he then went into practice in Buenos Aires. Williams became well known for his daring design experiments, manipulating space and utilizing technology to the full; they include such projects as 'Dwellings in Space' (1942), International Airport (1945) and 'Hanging Office Building' (1946), all in Buenos Aires; the latter was conceived as four huge concrete columns with beams and upper arcades from which the floors were hung. His built works include the Concert Hall (1942–53), Buenos Aires, and the House over the Brook (1943–5; see fig.), constructed for his father in Mar del Plata; with the aim of raising the building off the ground but eliminating columns, the structure was designed like a bridge, supported on a parabolic curve.

In 1947 he travelled to Europe and met Le Corbusier whose work he greatly admired; he published the Charte d'Athènes of CIAM in Buenos Aires and in 1948 he founded the Architectural Studies Centre there on the French model. He also supervised the building (1949–54) in La Plata of the only house in Latin America designed by Le Corbusier, using ramped first-floor access as a solution to the restricted frontage. Between 1943 and 1958 Williams also prepared regional plans for Patagonia, Buenos Aires, Corrientes and El Tigre; he designed three hospitals in Corrientes (1948–53) and the shell-form Bunge y Born Pavilion (1966), Sociedad Rural Annual Exposition, Buenos Aires. Later, unexecuted projects included some reinforced-concrete, vaulted and shell-roof buildings, the West German Embassy (1968; with Walter Gropius), Buenos Aires and Antarctic City (1985). Although most of Williams's work remained unexecuted, it achieved great impact both locally and internationally where it was often exhibited, receiving many honours and awards, and it played an important role in the development of modern architecture in Argentina.

See also under ARGENTINA, §II.

BIBLIOGRAPHY

R. Gonzáles Capdevila: *Amancio Williams* (Buenos Aires, 1955)

M. Waisman: *Documentos para una historia de la arquitectura argentina* (Buenos Aires, 1978)

J. Silvetti, ed.: *Amancio Williams* (Cambridge, MA, 1987)

LUDOVICO C. KOPPMANN

Williams, Fred(erick) (*b* Melbourne, 23 Jan 1927; *d* Melbourne, 22 April 1982). Australian painter. He studied at the National Gallery Art School in Melbourne, attending private classes at the George Bell Art School (1943–7). His earliest paintings and drawings were nearly all studio-based compositions, including portraits, nudes and figure compositions, often reflecting an early and lasting enthusiasm for Daumier. He also studied the art of Australian artists such as Hugh Ramsay, whose influence can be seen in *Head of a Boy* (*c.* 1945; see McCaughey, 1980, p. 10).

From 1952 to 1957 Williams studied part-time at the Chelsea School of Art and the Central School of Arts and Crafts in London. He painted, drew and etched the street-life of London and was particularly attracted to music halls, which he also painted, for example *The Metropolitan* (gouache, 1952–4; see McCaughey, 1980, p. 70). In London, Williams became very familiar with modern and contemporary art through frequent visits to museums and also through handling the works that passed through the picture framing shop where he worked. When Williams returned to Australia in 1957 landscape became his main subject.

In the period from 1957 to 1962 Williams concentrated on the Australian bush and the dense eucalyptus forest of the coastal plains and hills. His view of these landscapes was first influenced by the work of French artists, most notably Paul Cézanne but also Georges Braque and Henri Matisse, applying their sense of the simplification of form.

Amancio Williams: House over the Brook, Mar del Plata, 1943–5

Williams largely shed his Parisian influence in series of works on the forest theme, such as *Sherbrooke* (1961; Sydney, A.G. NSW), pursuing a dense and monumental image of the bush through a variety of media. In 1962 he began to visit the You Yangs, a group of rocky hills near Melbourne, producing the *You Yangs* series (1963–4; e.g. *You Yangs II*, Canberra, N.G.), which established his reputation in Australia. In these paintings Williams applied his own form of pointillism, reducing the landscape to abstract geometric motifs. This was the first of a number of landscape series painted in the 1960s; most were of subjects near to Melbourne, such as the *Upwey Landscape* series (1965–6; e.g. *Upwey Landscape II*, 1965; Canberra, N.G.), the *Lysterfield* series (1965–8; e.g. *Hillside Landscape, Lysterfield*, 1966–7; Rupert Murdoch priv. col., see McCaughey, 1980, p. 190) and the *Fire* series (1968; e.g. *Fire Approaching*, see McCaughey, 1980, p. 201). He produced gouache sketches working directly from nature, then worked these up in oil in the studio through series of oil studies, frequently also producing etchings.

In the 1970s Williams both painted further afield and enlarged his range of subject-matter, becoming particularly interested in marine subjects. The *Walkerville* paintings (oil on canvas, 1971; see McCaughey, 1980, p. 232) are notable examples. His working method and palette also changed: he often made his first sketch in oil rather than gouache and painted in a greater variety of brighter colours. He chose to paint dramatic landscapes instead of the bleak landscapes of the bush. In 1972 he accepted his first public commission, murals for the Adelaide Festival Theatre (*in situ*; see McCaughey, 1980, p. 228), for which the main sketching was done on the Murray River in Loxton, South Australia.

In the last eight years of his career, Williams produced more landscape series with strong themes, his last being the *Pilbara* series (1979–81), which remained intact as a series as it was acquired by Con-Zinc Rio Tinto Australia, the Melbourne mining company that had invited him to explore the north-west region of Australia.

BIBLIOGRAPHY

J. Mollison: *Fred Williams: Etchings* (Sydney, 1968)

P. McCaughey: 'Fred Williams', *A. Int.*, xvi/9 (1972), pp. 23–9

——: *Fred Williams* (Sydney, 1980)

PATRICK MCCAUGHEY

Williams, Hugh William [Grecian] (*b* 1773; *d* Edinburgh, 23 June 1829). Scottish painter of Welsh descent. Born aboard his father's ship during a voyage to the West Indies, he was orphaned when quite young and raised by his grandmother in Edinburgh, where he studied at Alexander Nasmyth's private drawing-school, together with David Wilkie and John Thomson of Duddingston. He became a well-known topographical painter, noted initially for such romantic watercolour views of Scotland as *Cottage of the Ploughlands near Edinburgh* (1814; Glasgow A.G. & Mus.). Between 1816 and 1818 he made an extensive tour of Italy, Greece and the Greek islands, returning to Scotland to publish a two-volume book of his travels (1820). His exhibition of views of Greece held in Edinburgh in 1822 was received with enthusiasm and earned him the nickname 'Grecian' Williams. His practice was to work up his watercolour sketches in the studio, adding opaque watercolour, oil paint and varnish, as in *Temple of Poseidon, Cape Sunion* (1828; Edinburgh, N.G.). His Arcadian settings reveal his admiration for the work of Poussin and Claude, and his increasingly broad handling of paint his knowledge of Turner. Two further volumes of engravings were published in 1829.

PRINTS

Travels in Italy, Greece and the Ionian Islands, 2 vols (Edinburgh, 1820)
Select Views in Greece, with Classical Illustrations, 2 vols (London, 1829)

BIBLIOGRAPHY

D. Irwin and F. Irwin: *Scottish Painters: At Home and Abroad, 1700–1900* (London, 1975), pp. 228–31
F.-M. Tsigakou: *The Rediscovery of Greece: Travellers and Painters of the Romantic Era* (London, 1981)
D. Macmillan: *Scottish Art, 1460–1990* (Edinburgh, 1990)

□

Williams [née Terry], **Jane** (*b c.* 1770s; *d* Cork, 17 April 1845). Irish silversmith. The daughter of CARDEN TERRY, she had the distinction of being the only female silversmith in Cork during the late 18th century and the early 19th. She was married on 6 August 1791 in St Peter's Church, Cork, to her father's apprentice, John Williams (1771–1806), who entered into partnership as a silversmith with Carden Terry in 1795. Jane Williams, who lived at Grand Parade, Cork, continued business as a silversmith after her husband's death and sent many silver pieces to be assayed in Dublin, where she registered a mark in 1806. She worked with her father from 1807. Their joint mark appears on a marrow scoop (Washington, DC, N. Mus. Women A.) made in 1810 and on a freedom box (Washington, DC, N. Mus. Women A.; *see* IRELAND, fig. 23) made in 1814. The business was closed shortly after Carden Terry's death in 1821.

BIBLIOGRAPHY

D. Bennett: *Collecting Irish Silver* (London, 1984)
P. Glanville and J. Faulds Goldsborough: *Women Silversmiths, 1685–1845*, Washington, DC, N. Mus. Women A. cat. (Washington, DC, 1990)

For further bibliography *see* IRELAND, §V, 5.

DOUGLAS BENNETT

Williams, Sir (Evan) Owen (*b* London, 20 March 1890; *d* Berkhamsted, Herts, 23 May 1969). English engineer and architect. He began his career as an apprentice engineer to the Metropolitan Electric Tramway Company in London in 1906. Through part-time study he gained a first-class honours degree in civil engineering from the University of London (1911) and became an associate member of the Institution of Civil Engineers in the same year. His life-long interest in reinforced-concrete design began in 1912 when he became an assistant engineer with the British subsidiary of the American concrete specialist firm, the Indented Bar and Concrete Engineering Company. Two years later he joined the Trussed Concrete Steel Company of England, another design firm with American origins. As Chief Estimator and Designer with this firm Williams was involved in the design of many standard concrete-framed factory buildings, including the Gramophone Company Factory (now the EMI Building), Hayes, Middx, which was designed in collaboration with the architect Arthur C. Blomfield (1863–1935). During World War I, between 1916 and 1919, he designed aircraft for the Wells Aviation Company and concrete ships for the Admiralty at Poole, where he headed a design and research team.

In 1920 Williams established his own practice as a consulting engineer, one of only a few in Britain at that time specializing in reinforced-concrete design. His most important breakthrough came in 1921 when he was appointed consulting engineer for the design of the principal buildings to the British Empire Exhibition (1924), Wembley, London, working with the architect John Simpson. This was the first major non-industrial building project in Britain to make extensive use of reinforced concrete, and most of the neo-classical style concrete buildings were completed to Williams's structural designs. Although the majority were demolished after the exhibition, the larger structures remained: the Wembley Stadium, designed with twin towers capped with thin concrete domes, the Palace of Arts, Palace of Industry and Palace of Engineering (destr. *c.* 1976). Williams's contribution to this project established his reputation as Britain's leading expert in concrete design, a reputation confirmed by the award of a knighthood in 1924 at the early age of 34.

Williams's project architect at Wembley was Maxwell Ayrton (1874–1960), with whom he shared a commitment to the evolution of modern forms of concrete construction through effective architect–engineer collaboration, and their joint work continued during the 1920s. Many of their schemes were bridge structures, including the Lea Valley Viaduct (1924), Hackney, London; the principal bridges (1924–8) along the A9 road from Perth to Inverness; and a mass-concrete arched bridge (1925–30) at Wansford, Cambs. In each of these schemes they successfully exploited the visual and technical possibilities of reinforced concrete. Their joint building projects, however, were less successful, failing to capitalize on the formal potential of the material largely because of Ayrton's unwillingness to discard his traditional stylistic approach to architectural design. It was undoubtedly this failure that ultimately persuaded Williams to establish himself as an architect and pursue an independent design career based on a Functionalist philosophy best expressed by his well-known catch-phrase 'The law of least action'.

Owen Williams: Boots Wets Factory, Beeston, Nottinghamshire, 1930–32

Williams's first project as an architect–engineer came in 1929 with his appointment to design the new Dorchester Hotel in London. The reinforced-concrete structure of his building was not only highly advanced for its time but also architecturally accomplished, possessing restrained Modernist elevations with concrete walls that were cast behind permanent formwork of terrazzo panels. Early in the construction programme, however, a dispute arose between Williams and his client, Malcolm McAlpine, on the issue of decoration. This was combined with disquiet in architectural circles that an engineer had been given such a prestigious job, and it provoked Williams's resignation and his replacement by William Curtis Green. Green radically altered the interior decoration but effected only a modest restyling of Williams's elevations.

In the next two years Williams completed two buildings that firmly established his reputation as one of Britain's leading Modernist architects: the *Daily Express* Building (1931; with Ellis and Clarke), London, a glass-fronted concrete structure, and the Boots Wets Factory (1930–32; see fig.), Beeston, Notts. The latter, a flat-slab structure enclosed with glass walls and containing vast atrium-style production spaces, received widespread acclaim; for many contemporary commentators it established Britain's long-awaited acceptance of the International Style, and comparisons were made with work in Europe, despite the building's connection with the early work of the Trussed Concrete Steel Company in the USA. Other successful projects followed: the Empire Pool (1934) at Wembley, with vast concrete portal spans of nearly 80 m; the Pioneer Health Centre (1935), Peckham, London; the Boots Drys Factory (1935–8), Beeston; and two more buildings for the *Daily Express* at Manchester and Glasgow (1938 and 1939). Although Williams's work in the early 1930s was revered by many Modernists, he had no direct involvement

in the British Modern Movement and on two occasions declined to join its main organization, the MARS Group. This self-imposed isolation was partly responsible for the decline in his influence as the decade proceeded. Moreover, some of his later buildings lacked the structural clarity of the early work; his smaller projects in particular were often criticized as clumsy by those who argued that his abilities as an architect were restricted to the large scale.

During World War II Williams resumed his work on concrete ship design, developed plans for a prefabricated concrete house, 'Wilvan', and undertook speculative design work on aircraft hangar design. The latter bore fruit in 1950 when his firm was appointed to design a new maintenance headquarters building for the British Overseas Airways Corporation (BOAC) at Heathrow Airport, London. The daring reinforced-concrete design for this complex project was completed in 1955. With the exception of this building and the *Daily Mirror* Building (1961; with Anderson, Forster and Wilcox), London, most of Williams's post-war career was connected with Britain's motorway programme. Of all his motorway projects from the 1950s and 1960s, the most memorable are the much criticized bridges (1959) on the M1 from Luton to Dunchurch and the Spaghetti Junction (1967–72), Birmingham. Throughout his career Williams wrote articles about his work and, particularly in the 1930s, about the philosophy of concrete design that he did so much to establish in Britain.

WRITINGS
'The Construction of the British Empire Exhibition', *Concr. & Constr. Engin.*, xix/7 (1924), pp. 420–27
'Factories', *RIBA J.* (1927), pp. 54–5
'Bridges', *RIBA J.* (1928), pp. 296–304
'The Portent of Concrete', *Architects' J.*, lxxiv (1931), p. 829
'Architecture: Trade, Profession or Calling', *Archit. Assoc. J.*, lxviii/768 (1952), pp. 98–105

with O. T. Williams: 'The London to Birmingham Motorway: Luton–Dunchurch: Design and Execution', *Proc. Inst. Civ. Engin.*, xv (1959–60), pp. 353–86

BIBLIOGRAPHY

D. Cottam: 'Engineered Architecture', *Architects' J.*, clxxxiii/17 (1986), pp. 12–15

——: *Architectural Principles in an Age of Functionalism* (diss., U. Liverpool, 1986)

D. Sharp: 'Owen Williams', *Bldg Des.*, 783 (1986), pp. 24–9; 784 (1986), pp. 22ff

G. Stamp: 'Owen Williams as Architect', *The Architect*, xciii/4 (1986), pp. 48–53

Sir Owen Williams, 1890–1969 (exh. cat. by D. Cottam and G. Stamp, London, Archit. Assoc., 1986)

DAVID COTTAM

Williams, Pyotr. *See* VIL'YAMS, PYOTR.

Williams, William (*b* Bristol, *bapt* 14 June 1727; *d* Bristol, 1791). American painter of English birth. An unwilling apprenticed seaman, he jumped ship in North America (1747) and for 30 years in Philadelphia, PA, and New York pursued a variety of occupations: painter of stage scenery, ship decoration, portraits and landscapes, and teacher of drawing, lettering and gilding. He is most famous for having given the young Benjamin West his first training in painting in the late 1740s in Philadelphia. In 1776 he returned penniless to England, where West made him welcome in his home and studio, occasionally using him as a model.

Despite confusion with works by several other American artists of the same name, up to 12 paintings have been identified as American works by Williams. These include a *Self-portrait* that shows the artist, in a dark green dressing-gown and a puce-coloured velvet cap, looking out from working at his easel, and a full-length portrait of a *Gentleman and his Wife* (1775), which shows Mr and Mrs William Denning standing against a fanciful romantic landscape containing a thatched mill, a ruined castle and a Norman church tower (both Winterthur, DE, du Pont Mus.). Uneven in execution and primitive in style, his group portraits were among the first 'conversation pieces' painted in North America.

BIBLIOGRAPHY

W. Sawitzky: 'William Williams: The First Instructor of Benjamin West', *Antiques*, xxxi (1937), pp. 240–42

J. T. Flexner: 'The Amazing William Williams: Painter, Author, Musician, Stage Designer, Castaway', *Mag. A.*, xxxvii (1944), pp. 243–6, 276–8

——: *American Painting: First Flowers of our Wilderness* (Boston, 1947), pp. 179–85

W. H. Gerdts: 'William Williams: New American Discoveries', *Winterthur Port.*, 4 (1968), pp. 159–68

D. H. Dickason: 'Benjamin West on William Williams: A Previously Unpublished Letter', *Winterthur Port.*, 6 (1970), pp. 128–33

——: *William Williams: Novelist and Painter of Colonial America* (Bloomington, 1970)

E. P. Richardson: 'William Williams: A Dissenting Opinion', *Amer. A. J.*, iv/1 (1972), pp. 3, 23

ROBERT C. ALBERTS

Williamsburg. North American town in the state of Virginia, USA. It has a population of *c.* 10,000 and is notable for its 18th-century buildings, many of which were restored (from 1927) or reconstructed through the patronage of John D. Rockefeller jr (*see* ROCKEFELLER, (1)). It was formally founded and laid out in 1699 as Virginia's new capital, superseding the settlement of Middle Plantation (founded 1633), which had served as temporary capital during the rebuilding of Jamestown (1698), following a fire. Williamsburg was the first American city to embody effectively the full range of Classical and Baroque principles of design; the interiors of its early 18th-century buildings were typically decorated in the WILLIAM AND MARY STYLE.

Williamsburg was probably designed by the state's governor, Francis Nicholson, who supported the Bishop of London's Commissary in Virginia, Rev. James Blair, in his successful effort to obtain a Royal Charter for the College of William and Mary (built 1693–1700) as the temporary seat of Virginia's government. The College was probably designed by the Office of the King's Works (headed by Sir Christopher Wren) as a three-storey quadrangular building; unfinished when it burnt down, it was rebuilt in 1705–15 as a two-storey block facing east, with projecting hall and chapel (1732) to the west. The siting of the College strongly influenced the layout of the rest of the city.

The original survey of the site exists, but other plans have been lost; of those made in the early 1780s during the Yorktown campaign of the American Revolution (1775–83), the most detailed is the so-called Frenchman's Map (*c.* 1782). Similarly, the only 18th-century print of the city's buildings is a single engraving (*c.* 1740) called the Bodleian Plate (see fig.). The survey shows a town of 200 acres, with an additional 63 reserved for access roads to the York and James rivers to north and south, major routes of arrival and departure. The town is bisected by Duke of Gloucester Street, which, at 30 m, was of a width unprecedented in the colonies; it provided the axial link between the College and the Capitol (1699–1705). The spacious Market Square is at the centre, crossed east–west by Duke of Gloucester Street and north–south by England Street. There is evidence that 'W' and 'M' ciphers honouring William III and Queen Mary (possibly conceived by Nicholson) were originally incorporated to give diagonal access and emphasis to buildings planned for Market Square and the area around the Capitol; the octagonal, brick Powder Magazine (1714–15) may have been located at the centre of the angle of the Market Square cipher; the Courthouse of 1771, however, was not aligned with the Magazine but with the centre of the Square, which had probably been altered by that date.

The unusual, but peculiarly American, feature of the arrangement of buildings on the main street is that a college and legislative structure terminate vistas that in Europe would usually by occupied by a palace and church. The Capitol was the first legislative building in North America to be so called. Its nominative allusion to the Roman civil basilica is enhanced by its form, with two-storey rectangular piles with semicircular apses on the south façade, linked by an open loggia supporting a conference room above. Its lofty, Dutch-inspired cupola probably responds to that on the first college building. In 1701 Nicholson was authorized to purchase 63 acres, on which the Governor's house would be built (1705–20). The house's novel style, excessive cost and sumptuousness—previously unknown in the colony—caused it to be called derisively the Governor's Palace. Its site, surrounded on three sides by ravines, adjoined Williamsburg's northern boundary; topography and the existence of the first Bruton

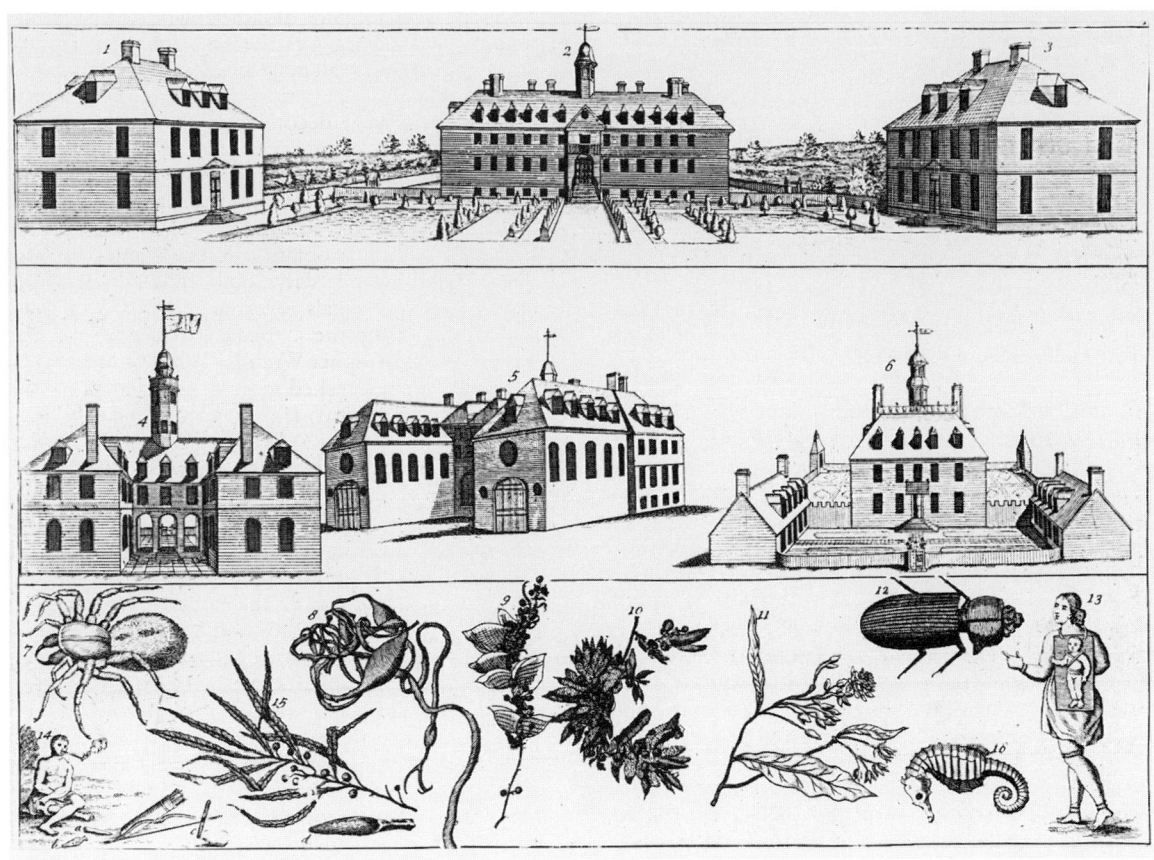

Williamsburg, engraving known as the Bodleian Plate, *c.* 1740 (Colonial Williamsburg, VA)

parish church (1683; rebuilt 1711–15 by James Morris to a plan by Governor Alexander Spotswood) were probably factors in the site's selection. The creation of Palace Green to the south, an allée of 65×330 m, provided a vista to the Palace from Duke of Gloucester Street, linking the church and Palace visually. The Palace was indebted stylistically to Dutch architecture, with flanking symmetrical forecourt dependencies, and proved influential (if controversial) with lavish formal gardens, vistas to north and south and descending terraces, which led to what Governor Spotswood called his 'fish-pond', a dammed creek that made a 'fine canal' by 1720. An early response to the arrangement of buildings at the Palace came when the College built Brafferton Hall (1723) and the President's House (1732) as forecourt dependencies of the main building. A departure from the English medieval tradition of quadrangular buildings, this domestic model was the precedent for many American campuses, where a single dominant building is flanked by a series of less imposing structures.

Spotswood also designed the Magazine and Bruton parish church. While the dimensions of the church are determined by a play of proportions derived from the equilateral triangle, symbolic of the Holy Trinity, those of the Magazine follow a Classical ratio of one to two, first seen in Virginia with the original design of the College in 1693. The location of the Magazine and Courthouse in the square also provides an allusion to the Roman forum,

as do the former's octagonal form and the Roman portico intended for the Courthouse. A fire in the Capitol (1747) necessitated its reconstruction and redesign, also motivating construction of the Secretary's Office near by. By 1772, when the Courthouse and Public Hospital (1769–72) were complete, Williamsburg possessed a full array of carefully arranged public buildings unmatched by any other North American city by that date; these last two structures also show the move away from the Wren-like style of earlier buildings towards a more Palladian style, anticipating forthcoming classical revivals.

The important new urban and architectural relationships of Williamsburg seem to have had a marked influence on THOMAS JEFFERSON during his years as a student, legislator and governor in the city, despite his criticism of the workmanship of construction. When he wrote much later that the success of the republic hung on 'two hooks' (strong education and local government), Williamsburg's plan stood to exemplify this view. The city is also the clearest American precedent for Pierre-Charles L'Enfant's plan for Washington, DC (1791; *see* WASHINGTON, DC, §I, 2 and fig. 1), with the Capitol linked to the President's House (now White House) by Pennsylvania Avenue. Williamsburg's initial status soon declined, however, when it ceased to function as Virginia's capital; RICHMOND, with its more central location, was chosen instead in 1779.

BIBLIOGRAPHY

M. Whiffen: *The Public Buildings of Williamsburg* (Williamsburg, 1958)
——: *The Eighteenth-century Houses of Williamsburg* (Williamsburg, 1960, rev. 1984)
N. H. Schless: 'Dutch Influence on the Governor's Palace, Williamsburg', *J. Soc. Archit. Historians*, xxviii (Dec 1969), pp. 254–70
G. Patton: 'The College of William and Mary, Williamsburg, and the Enlightenment', *J. Soc. Archit. Historians*, xxix (March 1970), pp. 24–32
Colon. Williamsburg (1977–)
C. Hosmer: *Preservation Comes of Age*, 2 vols (Charlottesville, 1981)
Official Guide to Colonial Williamsburg, Colonial Williamsburg Foundation (Williamsburg, 1985)
P. Kopper: *Colonial Williamsburg* (New York, 1986)
J. D. Kornwolf: *'So Good a Design': Anglo-Dutch Sources for the Architecture of the College of William and Mary and Williamsburg, 1693–1732* (Williamsburg, 1989)

JAMES D. KORNWOLF

Williams-Ellis, Sir **(Bertram) Clough** (*b* Gayton, Northants, 28 May 1883; *d* Plas Brondanw, Gwynedd, 8 April 1978). English architect. The son of a clergyman and Cambridge don, he was brought up in North Wales and studied at Trinity College, University of Cambridge, proceeding without a degree to spend a short time at the Architectural Association School in London. He was in private practice in London and Wales from 1905 and designed many small, mostly residential buildings before 1914, completing the enlargement of Llangoed Castle, Powys, and embarking on the creation of a formal garden at Plas Brondanw, the 17th-century house he had inherited and restored. In the 1920s, after war service in the Welsh Guards and the Royal Tank Corps, he became a fashionable architect and decorator, adopting a light classical style with an imaginative use of colour. As well as many house designs, his work at this time included Bishop's Stortford School Memorial Hall (1922), the First Church of Christ Scientist (1927), Belfast, and the Lloyd George Memorial (1948), Llanystumdwy, Gwynedd. He also designed schools, hospitals, hotel buildings and new village centres including Cushendun (1910–25), Co. Antrim, and Cornwell (1939), Oxon; but perhaps his best-known work was the creation of the village of Portmeirion in Gwynedd

Clough Williams-Ellis: Portmeirion, Gwynedd, from 1926

(from 1926), based on an extension to an existing hotel. This project enabled him to combine his interests as architect and propagandist for sensitive development of the environment (see fig.). The colour-washed buildings are grouped in a picturesque manner with great respect for the wooded site, which borders a tidal estuary; the buildings also reveal an interest in Mediterranean building and traditional construction, and many incorporate items salvaged from demolished buildings.

Williams-Ellis wrote extensively about architecture and planning; he was particularly concerned for the protection of the countryside and the national heritage, and he campaigned for the National Trust and for the formation of national parks. A few of his buildings glancingly acknowledge the Modern Movement (notably Laughing Water Restaurant (1933), Cobham, Kent) but he remained true to his earlier style throughout his later (mostly domestic) work such as the remodelling of Nantclwyd Hall (*c.* 1955–70), Clwyd, and Dalton Hall (1971), Cumbria. He was briefly the first Chairman of Stevenage New Town Development Corporation (1946–7), but was better known after World War II as a conspicuous and unashamed exponent of architectural delight. His colourful personality and wit helped to popularize architecture, and Portmeirion was admired by Lewis Mumford and Frank Lloyd Wright, among others. He was created CBE in 1958 and knighted in 1972.

WRITINGS

with J. Eastwick-Field and E. Eastwick-Field: *Building in Cob, Pisé, and Stabilized Earth* (London, 1919, rev. 1947)
with A. Williams-Ellis: *The Pleasures of Architecture* (London, 1924, rev. 3/1954)
England and the Octopus (London, 1928, rev. Penrhyndeudraeth, 1975)
Portmeirion: The Place and its Meaning (London, 1963, rev. Penrhyndeudraeth, 1973)
Architect Errant (London, 1971)

BIBLIOGRAPHY

Obituary, *Architects' J.*, clxvii/15 (1978), p. 688

ALAN POWERS

Williams-Wynn, Sir **Watkin**, 4th Baronet of Wynnstay (*b* Wynnstay, Denbigh [now Clwyd], 19 April 1749; *d* Wynnstay, 29 July 1789). Welsh landowner and patron. He began his Grand Tour in June 1768. In Rome he commissioned Pompeo Batoni to paint a portrait of himself with his travelling companions (1768–72; Cardiff, N. Mus.), as well as a picture of *Bacchus and Ariadne* (1774; Italy, priv. col., see 1982 exh. cat., p. 19, fig. 10). In Naples he visited the excavations at Herculaneum and Pompeii and purchased the Baron d'Hancarville's two volumes illustrating the vase collection from William Hamilton (i). Returning through Rome, Sir Watkin commissioned a terracotta bust of himself from Christopher Hewetson (1769; Dublin, N.G.). He reached London in February 1769. Reynolds's portrait of Sir Watkin with his mother (London, N.G.), begun in 1768, was completed about this time. Another portrait by Reynolds (Sir W. Williams-Wynn priv. col.) was commissioned after Sir Watkin's marriage to Lady Henrietta Somerset in April 1769 and shows the couple in van Dyck costume. For his bride, Sir Watkin ordered a silver-gilt toilet service from the London goldsmith Thomas Heming (Cardiff, N. Mus.); exuberantly Rococo, its design recalls a service of

1766 made for George III's sister, Caroline Mathilda. When Lady Williams-Wynn died in July 1769, Sir Watkin ordered from Joseph Nollekens (ii) a Neo-classical monument to her (St Mary, Ruabon, Clwyd).

In 1770 Sir Watkin extended his patronage to two landscape painters, Richard Wilson and Paul Sandby. He commissioned a pair of landscapes from Wilson, a *View near Wynnstay* and the *Castle of Dinas Bran from Llangollen* (1770–71; New Haven, CT, Yale Cent. Brit. A.), both showing views in the Valley of the Dee. During the summer of 1770 Sandby spent nearly six weeks at Wynnstay, giving drawing lessons, and from 21 August to 4 September 1771 he accompanied Sir Watkin on a tour through the wildest scenery of north Wales; it provided Sandby with twelve subjects for his *Views in North Wales* of 1776, as well as five subjects for *Views in Wales* of 1777. A second tour to Italy, also with Sandby, was cancelled because of Sir Watkin's second marriage, to Lady Charlotte Grenville, in December 1771. In the same year work began on 20 St James's Square, Sir Watkin's London house, designed by Robert Adam.

In the 1770s Sir Watkin purchased a number of paintings, both contemporary and Old Master, including Nathaniel Dance's *Garrick as Richard III* (1771; Stratford-on-Avon, Town Hall) and Poussin's *Landscape with a Snake* (1648; London, N.G.). *Perseus and Andromeda* by Anton Raphael Mengs (St Petersburg, Hermitage) was completed in Rome for Sir Watkin in 1778 but was never delivered. Reynolds painted Sir Watkin's son as the *Infant St John the Baptist c.* 1774, as well as a group portrait, *Lady Williams-Wynn with her Children* (c. 1784; both Sir W. Williams-Wynn priv. col.), while Sir Watkin was depicted by the same artist presiding over a meeting of the Society of Dilettanti in 1777 (Soc. Dilettanti, on loan to London, Brooks's Club).

At the end of the 1770s Sir Watkin turned his attention to Wynnstay, where several small buildings were erected in the park to designs by Capability Brown, whose plans for the park were carried out by an assistant. James Wyatt also executed work there in the 1780s; an elegant gateway by him survives. After Sir Watkin's death his mother commissioned Wyatt to design a fluted column, 35.35 m high, to his memory.

BIBLIOGRAPHY

P. Howell and T. W. Pritchard: 'Wynnstay, Denbighshire', *Country Life*, cli (23 March, 30 March and 6 April 1972), pp. 686–9, 782–6, 850–53
P. Hughes: 'Paul Sandby and Sir Watkin Williams Wynn', *Burl. Mag.*, cxiv (1972), pp. 459–66
——: 'The Williams Wynn Silver in the National Museum of Wales', *Connoisseur*, clxxxiv (1973), pp. 33–7
B. Ford: 'Sir Watkin Williams Wynn: A Welsh Maecenas', *Apollo*, xcix (1974), pp. 435–9
Pompeo Batoni and his British Patrons (exh. cat. by F. Russell, London, Kenwood House, 1982), p. 19

PETER HUGHES

William the Englishman (*fl* 1178–86). English architect. In the account by the monk Gervase he is recorded as directing the works at Canterbury Cathedral (*see* CANTERBURY, §III, 1(i)) from 1178 to 1184 and is succinctly characterized as 'William by name, English by nation, small in body, but in workmanship of many kinds acute and honest'. This is all that is known of him, unless he is to be identified with a William the Englishman, a chaplain,

who built a church at St Jean d'Acre (now 'Akko) in the Latin Kingdom of Jerusalem in 1192, or with the William 'Anglicanus' who was a carpenter in the service of King John (*reg* 1199–1216) in 1214. Gervase gives no indication that William had previously worked at Canterbury under his predecessor, William of Sens, but the continuity of building makes it difficult to disentangle their respective contributions to the design of the east end of the cathedral. The Trinity Chapel and Corona were built under his direction and the transepts remodelled, but the conception and design may have been by William of Sens. The new features introduced under English William indicate that, although English, he was conversant with the latest developments in north-east France, and changes in the style of the stained glass show that a new team of glaziers was brought over from France. The significant innovations include the arrangement of the middle storey of the elevation like a triforium, the introduction of rose windows and of circular column bases and abaci, and the use of some of the earliest datable flying buttresses. These and the skeletal construction of the aisle walls (comparable to the eastern chapel at St Rémi, Reims, and the upper transept chapels at Laon Cathedral) may indicate the area in which William was trained.

BIBLIOGRAPHY

Harvey
Gervase of Canterbury: *Tractatus de combustione et reparatione Cantuariensis ecclesiae* [*c.* 1200]; Eng. trans. in F. Woodman: *The Architectural History of Canterbury Cathedral* (London, 1981), pp. 93–8
J. Bony: 'French Influences on the Origins of English Gothic Architecture', *J. Warb. & Court. Inst.*, xii (1949), pp. 1–15

PETER DRAPER

William the Silent, Stadholder and Prince of Orange. *See* ORANGE NASSAU, (1).

Willinges, Johann (*b* Oldenburg, *c.* 1560; *d* Lübeck, 24 [?14] Aug 1625). German painter and draughtsman. From 1590, through his marriage to a painter's widow, he was a master in the Lübeck painters' guild, which he headed in 1594 and 1605. He received numerous commissions, usually from private donors, for church furnishings, epitaphs and portraits. His training in Venice is clearly apparent in his works; Tintoretto in particular had a lasting influence. A leading representative of north German Mannerism, he was regarded in Lübeck as an inventive painter, but in fact his paintings derived not only from works by Tintoretto but, above all, from engravings by Johann Sadeler I, Crispijn van de Passe I and Adrian Collaert (*c.* 1560–1618), which reappear, for example, in his paintings of Old Testament scenes and allegories (1597) on the panelling of the Lübeck Rathaus (now St Annen-Kloster). Following the destruction of his main works, a rood screen (1591–5; Lübeck, Marienkirche) and a *Crucifixion* (Lübeck, Petrikirche), evaluation of his paintings is difficult. More accessible are his few drawings, according to Geissler (1979–80 exh. cat.) derived from Christoph Schwarz and his Munich school: they have a looser line and show a freer and more independent treatment of mainly mythological motifs.

BIBLIOGRAPHY

Thieme–Becker
T. Riewerts: 'Der Maler Johann Willinges in Lübeck', *Z. Dt. Ver. Kstwiss.*, iii (1936), pp. 275–302

——: 'Johann Willinges in Lübeck: Die Umwelt eines norddeutschen Malers um 1600', *Nordelbingen*, xiv (1938), pp. 207–71
Zeichnung in Deutschland: Deutsche Zeichner, 1540–1640, ii (exh. cat. by H. Geissler, Stuttgart, Staatsgal., 1979–80), pp. 126–7
A. Zimmermann: 'Ein "Frauenraub" von Johann Willinges', *Nordelbingen*, lii (1983), pp. 53–7
R. Jürgens: 'Ein Lübecker Bild Kaiser Karls IV.—gemalt von Johann Willinges?', *Nordelbingen*, lv (1986), pp. 73–8

ANDREAS BLÜHM

Willink, Albert Carel (*b* Amsterdam, 7 March 1900; *d* Amsterdam, 19 Oct 1983). Dutch painter. After studying architecture at the Technische Hogeschool in Delft (1918–20), he decided to become a painter. In 1920 he went to Berlin where he had lessons from Hans Baluschek (1870–1935). He followed the activities of the artists associated with Der Sturm and in 1922 joined the Novembergruppe, with whom he exhibited some abstract work at *Die grosse Berliner Kunstausstellung* in the Glaspalast. He was also in touch with avant-garde groups and publications, such as *Zenith* in Belgrade and *Het Overzicht* ('The survey'), later called *De Driehoek* ('The triangle') in Antwerp.

In addition to graphic work Willink published literary texts. Through Jozef Peeters he became acquainted with Eddy du Perron (1899–1940), whose work he illustrated. From 1924 he reincorporated figurative elements in his work, partly under the influence of Fernand Léger. In the same year he was given his first one-man exhibition in the Heystee building in Amsterdam. From 1925 until 1928 he was given yearly exhibitions at De Onafhankelijken (The Independents) in Amsterdam. He submitted work to the *Architectuur, schilderwerk, beeldhouwwerk* exhibition at the Stedelijk Museum in Amsterdam in 1929.

Willink began to study academic painting techniques and developed an expressive use of the paint. He painted primarily figurative works and landscapes. He often placed figures in a historic setting, as in *Last Visitors to Pompeii* (1931; Rotterdam, Mus. Boymans–van Beuningen), which also includes a self-portrait. His preference for the late 19th-century architecture of Amsterdam is evident in the portrait of his wife *Wilma* (1932; The Hague, Gemeentemus.) and that of his artist friend *Charles Roelofsz* (1932; Amsterdam, Stedel. Mus.). In addition he painted scenes of gardens and parks with Neo-classical sculpture; he also painted self-portraits in a historic setting, for example *The Preacher* (1937; The Hague, Dienst Rijksverspr. Kstvoorwerpen, on loan to Utrecht, Cent. Mus.). The paintings of the late 1930s give a pessimistic outlook on life. Many critics saw in his work a reflection of the socio-economic and political crises of the time. The unreal, sometimes threatening atmosphere is created by contrasting light effects and by burning cities and ruins. The painting *Simeon the Stylite* (1939; The Hague, Gemeentemus.) has been interpreted as a precursor of the approaching disaster of World War II. The landscape was based on a photograph from an American magazine; the figure of Simeon is a self-portrait. His work was often partly based on photography and partly on reality. The unusual combination of figures and objects (or in some cases their absence) lent a surreal character to some of his works. With Pyke Koch, with whom he had joint exhibitions during the early 1930s, he is considered a magic realist. Willink himself preferred the term 'fantastic realist'. In 1939 he was given his first retrospective exhibition at the Museum Boymans–van Beuningen in Rotterdam.

From 1941 until his death Willink painted a large number of commissioned portraits. During World War II he refused to join the Kulturkammer and to sell his work to the Nazis. In 1950 he published *De schilderkunst in een kritiek stadium*, in which he complained about the government's exclusive preference for abstract, non-figurative art. From 1950 he also painted exotic animals, such as anteaters, zebras, giraffes, turtles and marabous in classical landscapes. From 1962 he produced five paintings of sculptures in the Parco dei Mostri in Bomarzo, Italy, set against a background of satellite launchers (e.g. *Balance of Powers*, 1963; Ghent, Mus. S. Kst.), followed in 1969 by Martian landscapes. In the 1970s he and his wife Mathilde (1938–78) were important figures in Amsterdam's alternative scene.

WRITINGS
De schilderkunst in een kritiek stadium [Painting at a critical stage] (Amsterdam, 1950, rev. 1981)

BIBLIOGRAPHY
W. Kramer and M. Roscam Abbing: *Willink* (The Hague, 1973)
H. F. C. Jaffé: *Willink* (Amsterdam, 1988)

JOHN STEEN

Willis, Beverly (*b* Tulsa, OK, 17 Feb 1928). American architect. She studied at the University of Hawaii, Honolulu, training for two years as an engineer but later switching to studio art (BFA, 1954). During the 1950s she worked in Honolulu, designing sculptures and furniture. In 1960 she moved to San Francisco, where she began working on small-scale housing and theatre renovation, and in 1966 she established her own architectural practice there. Her work is aimed at a balance between the traditional and new, an attitude nurtured through several renovation projects in San Francisco (e.g. three 19th-century buildings on Union Street, 1963), which anticipated a nation-wide trend towards the restoration of old buildings in large cities. She also specialized in private residences and buildings for the visual and performing arts. In the Pool House (1985) at Yountville, CA, she imposed a Modernist geometry on classical proportions and layout. The house takes the form of a propylaeum-like gate, with the central pedimented opening flanked by square cubicles. A more playful geometry—also with classical references—is seen in the earlier Margaret S. Hayward Playground Building (1979), San Francisco. Of all her structures for the performing arts, the building for the San Francisco Ballet (completed 1984) is the best known. It has the grand proportions of the surrounding Beaux-Arts buildings of the San Francisco Civic Center, but displays a Modernist clarity in its smooth wall surfaces and sweeping window spaces, the latter revealing the interior functions. The four-storey structure is the first to house all aspects of a major professional dance institution, from administrative areas to rehearsal halls.

BIBLIOGRAPHY
S. Woodbridge: 'Old and New Buildings House Dance Companies', *Prog. Archit.*, lxiii/9 (1982), pp. 30–31
C. Lorenz: *Women in Architecture: A Contemporary Perspective* (New York, 1990), pp. 134–7
D. C. Davidson: 'Beverly Willis', *Inland Architect & News Rec.*, xxxv/1 (1991), p. 48

WALTER SMITH

Willis, Browne (*b* Blandford St Mary, Bucks, 1682; *d* Whaddon Hall, Bucks, 5 Sept 1760). English antiquary and architectural historian. Educated at Westminster School and Christchurch, Oxford, he took an active part in the revival of the Society of Antiquaries of London in 1717. Of substantial private means, he was among the earliest scholars to base their information on the evidence of records and registers. His surveys of the cathedrals of England and Wales started with St David's, published in 1716, and was completed in 1730. His history of Buckingham was published in 1755. In his field Browne was a pioneer, nothing on such a comprehensive scale having been attempted before; his descriptions of some cathedrals remain unchallenged. The great value of his architectural descriptions and the plans and drawings lies in the information they give of the fabric and ornaments as they existed more than 200 years ago. Much that he observed and commented on has disappeared or been drastically altered.

UNPUBLISHED SOURCES
London, BL, MSS Cole 5821–5861
Oxford, Bodleian Lib., MSS Bodl. 16294–403

WRITINGS
A Survey of the Cathedral Church of St Davids and the Edifices Belonging to it as they Stood in the Year 1715 (London, 1716)
A Survey of the Cathedral Church of Llandaff (London, 1718)
An History of the Mitred Parliamentary Abbies and Conventual Cathedral Churches, 2 vols (London, 1718–19)
Survey of St Asaph (London, 1720); *R* with biographical note, as 2 vols (Wrexham, 1801)
A Survey of the Cathedrals of York, Durham, Carlisle, Chester, Man, Lichfield, Hereford, Worcester, Gloucester and Bristol, 2 vols (n.p., 1727)
A Survey of the Cathedrals of Lincoln, Ely, Oxford and Peterborough (London, 1730)
The History and Antiquities of the Town, Hundred and Deanry of Buckingham (London, 1755)

BIBLIOGRAPHY
DNB
J. Nichols: *Literary Anecdotes of the 18th Century*, 9 vols (London, 1812–15), ii, p. 186
J. G. Jenkins: *The Dragon of Whaddon: Life and Work of Browne Willis, 1682–1760* (High Wycombe, 1953)

JOHN HOPKINS

Willis, Robert (*b* London, 27 Feb 1800; *d* Cambridge, 28 Feb 1875). English writer, teacher and archaeologist. After receiving his degree in mathematics at Cambridge in 1826 he was ordained priest the following year. In 1829 he was awarded a fellowship for the study of mechanics, and in 1837 he was elected Jacksonian Professor of applied mechanics at Cambridge, a position he held with distinction until his death, publishing a major book in 1841. Willis was also interested in the practical world, and in 1851 he was a juror for the Great Exhibition, at the Crystal Palace, London, reporting on manufacturing tools and lecturing on this subject, the following year, to the Royal Society of Arts.

Throughout this period Willis also studied architecture and archaeology. In 1835, after a tour of Gothic buildings in France, Germany and Italy, he published a study that was a considerable advance in its rigour and clarity on the work of earlier scholars such as THOMAS RICKMAN. His paper on Gothic vaults, published in 1841, was a remarkably thorough and sympathetic examination of a complicated problem. A year later he published his invention of the cymagraph, a machine for making exact copies of

mouldings. In 1844 he published *Architectural Nomenclature of the Middle Ages*, a work that is still of value, on the vocabulary of architecture in the Middle Ages. After the foundation of the Archaeological Institute in London in 1844, Willis was one of its most popular and energetic members. His well-attended lectures in London and Cambridge were the forum in which he worked out a series of studies of English ecclesiastical buildings, including the cathedrals of Canterbury (1844), Winchester (1845), York (1846), Norwich (1847), Salisbury (1849), Oxford (1850), Wells (1851), Chichester (1853), Gloucester (1860), Peterborough (1861), Worcester (1862), Lichfield (1864) and the abbeys of Sherborne and Glastonbury (1865). His method was 'to bring together all the recorded evidence that belongs to the building; to examine the building itself for the purpose of investigating the mode of its construction, and the successive changes and additions that have been made to it; and lastly, to compare the recorded evidence with the structural evidence as much as possible' ('The Architectural History of Winchester Cathedral', *Proc. Royal Archaeol. Inst. GB & Ireland*, ii (1846), p. 1). Through his example and work he had a considerable influence on medieval studies in England and, to a lesser extent, in other parts of Europe. He also published an edition of Villard de Honnecourt; his study of the architecture of Cambridge University was published posthumously by his nephew, John Willis Clark (1833–1910).

WRITINGS
Remarks on the Architecture of the Middle Ages, Especially of Italy (Cambridge, 1835)
Principles of Mechanism (London, 1841, 2/1870)
Architectural Nomenclature of the Middle Ages (Cambridge, 1844)
The Architectural History of Canterbury Cathedral (London, 1845)
Fac-simile of the Sketch Book of Willars de Honecourt, with Commentaries and Descriptions by M. J. B. A. de Lassus (London, 1859)
The Architectural History of Chichester Cathedral (Chichester, 1861)
The Architectural History of the Cathedral and Monastery at Worcester (London, 1865)
The Architectural History of Glastonbury Abbey (Cambridge, 1866)
The Architectural History of the Conventual Buildings of the Monastery of Christ Church in Canterbury (London, 1869)
J. W. Clark, ed.: *The Architectural History of the University of Cambridge, and of the Colleges of Cambridge and Eton*, 3 vols (Cambridge, 1886/*R* 1976, intro. D. Watkin)
Architectural History of Some English Cathedrals: A Collection in Two Parts of Papers Delivered during the Years 1842–63, 2 vols (Chicheley, 1972–3)
His papers are in Cambridge University Library

BIBLIOGRAPHY
DNB
A. E. Shipley: *A Memoir of John Willis Clark* (London, 1913)
P. Frankl: *The Gothic: Literary Sources and Interpretations through Eight Centuries* (Princeton, 1960), pp. 529–31
N. Pevsner: *Some Architectural Writers of the Nineteenth Century* (Oxford, 1972), pp. 52–61
R. Mark: *Robert Willis, Viollet-le-Duc and the Structural Approach to Gothic Architecture* (Princeton, 1976)
J. Crook, ed.: *Winchester Cathedral: Nine Hundred Years, 1093–1993* (Guildford, 1993), pp. 185–8

DAVID CAST

Willmann, Michael (Lukas Leopold) (*b* Kaliningrad [Königsberg], *bapt* 27 Sept 1630; *d* Lubiąż [Leubus], 26 Aug 1706). German painter. The son of the painter Peter Willmann (*fl* 1627; *d* 1665), he trained in the Netherlands in the early 1650s, making contact with Rembrandt and his circle. However, the element of characteristically Counter-Reformation pathos in Willmann's work seems to derive from studying Rubens and van Dyck. Willmann's skill as a landscape painter also derives from Dutch models. Around 1653 (or even later) Willmann tried to establish himself as an artist in Prague. However, the artistic dominance of Karel Škréta prevented him from making his mark, so he moved to Berlin, where he found employment at the court of Frederick William, Elector of Brandenburg, in 1657–8. He may have returned briefly to Prague, but following his conversion to Catholicism in 1660–61, he settled finally at Lubiaż Monastery near Wrocław, where he married in 1662. From here he had a wide field of work open to him in the service of the Cistercian monasteries and the nobility of Silesia, Bohemia and Moravia over a period of four decades. He also worked for other religious orders, painting for instance an altarpiece for the Premonstratensians at Strahov Monastery in Prague.

The early painting of the *Adoration of the Shepherds* (*c.* 1660; Prague, church of the Assumption) may date from Willmann's temporary stay in Prague, but was apparently delivered from Lubiaż. In this work Willmann was already harmonizing Flemish influences and his more personal use of the paintbrush into a homogeneous unity. This was achieved by a sketchlike approach and emphatic chiaroscuro effects produced by quick light-coloured brushstrokes on a dark ground. This flickering light becomes a major factor in Willmann's representations of the saints, illuminating their usually painful martyrdoms. To an artist who had lived through the horrors of the Thirty Years War such visions of utter brutality may have seemed none too remote. A comparison between the two altarpieces the *Murder of St Wenceslas* (1702–3; Kutná Hora, church of the Assumption) and the *Flaying of St Bartholomew* (1705; Pardubice, St Bartholomew; see fig.) even reveals a heightening of the horror. Dark night, a wan light and spilt blood are the ingredients of Willmann's unprecedentedly direct vision of torture and slaughter. The strength of feeling in his paintings has been attributed to the status of Lubiaż as a bastion of the Counter-Reformation in Protestant-ruled Silesia. As official painter for the Cistercian Order in the province, Willmann often slipped into the role of Catholic apologist. In contrast to Škréta with his theatrically discursive unfolding of the action, Willmann emphasized the critical climax of the event.

In contrast to the unremitting brutality of the altarpieces, Willmann's pure devotional pictures, frescoes (1692–5; Břevnov, church of St Joseph) and landscapes achieve a tender intimacy. In landscape painting he was the only German painter in the later 17th century to assimilate outside influences (such as that of Flanders) into a powerful view of nature that was independent of his models (e.g. *Landscape with Cistercian Monks*, 1667; Nuremberg, Ger. Nmus.). Like many great artists Willmann had very few direct imitators. Only Jan Liška (*c.* 1650–1712), Willmann's stepson, followed in the footsteps of this leading representative of High Baroque art in Bohemia. Willmann's highly emotional concept of a picture remained a model even in the late Baroque period, attracting the profound interest of, for example, Franz Anton Maulbertsch.

Michael Willmann: *Flaying of St Bartholomew*, oil on canvas, 3.0×1.5 m, 1705 (Pardubice, St Bartholomew)

BIBLIOGRAPHY
E. Kloss: *Michael Willmann* (Breslau [Wrocław], 1934)
E. Hubala: 'Malerei', *Barock in Böhmen* (exh. cat., ed. K. M. Swoboda; Munich, 1964), pp. 203–4
B. Bushart: *Deutsche Malerei des 17. und 18. Jahrhunderts* (Königstein im Taunus, 1967), p. 17
P. Preiss: 'Malerei', *Kunst des Barock in Böhmen*, ed. O. J. Blàžiiček, P. Preiss and D. Hejdova (Recklinghausen, 1977), p. 170ff, nos 37, 37a
HANNES ETZLSTORFER

Wills, Frank (*bapt* Exeter, 25 Dec 1822; *d* Montreal, 23 April 1857). English architect active in North America. He was employed as a young man in Exeter by the architect John Hayward (1808–91), during which time he worked for the Anglican priest John Medley (1804–92), designing a Gothic canopied tomb in St Thomas's, Exeter, and the chapel of St Andrew (1841–2), Exwick. He also illustrated Medley's essay on Exeter Cathedral in *Transactions of the Exeter Diocesan Architectural Society* (1843) with his office colleague, Henry Dudley (1813–94). In 1845 Medley was appointed Anglican Bishop of Fredericton, New Brunswick, and commissioned Wills to design a cathedral for the city. Wills moved to Canada that year.

His initial design for Christ Church Cathedral was modelled on St Mary's, Snettisham, Norfolk, where Wells had done some restoration work. This exemplar did not satisfy the influential British periodical, *The Ecclesiologist* (1846), which criticized the design for being more appropriate to a parish church than a cathedral: 'No cathedral would have a choir and transept lower than the nave. Nor is the singular clerestory, in which the alternate windows are circular, at all suited for a cathedral.' Unusually, construction started at the west end with the nave and aisles (1845–9), where many details, such as the central section of the façade and the quadrant arches at the east end of each aisle, were borrowed from Snettisham. However, alternating round and octagonal nave arcade piers and pointed clerestory windows replaced the complex Snettisham examples. A shortage of funds prevented completion of the cathedral in a single campaign and Wills's design for the east end was later superseded by a new design for the crossing tower and a choir with a roof as high as the nave that was supplied by William Butterfield through the Ecclesiological Society. This design was essentially that constructed by Bishop Medley in 1849–53, probably in consultation with Wills, although the choir was lengthened, which pleased the editors of *The Ecclesiologist*.

While progress on the cathedral was delayed, Wills designed St Anne's Chapel (1846–7), Fredericton, again for Bishop Medley, drawing in part on a design published by A. W. N. Pugin in 1843. The chapel is an aisleless two-cell plan with a south porch and a sacristy to the north of the chancel. Demonstrating the principles of ecclesiology, it is fitted correctly with a font immediately west of the south doorway, a pulpit and lectern flanking the chancel arch, a rood screen, carved seating, Minton tiles for the nave and chancel floors and the reredos, stained glass and altar plate copied from *Instrumenta ecclesiastica*, containing designs by Butterfield for ecclesiastical furnishings, published by the Ecclesiological Society (1844–7). The architectural details of the chapel are Early English, but the attenuated proportions of the overall design are Victorian rather than medieval. Elsewhere in New Brunswick, Wills designed the Anglican churches at Burton, Maugerville and Newcastle.

The delays on Fredericton Cathedral precipitated Wills's move to New York before 1848. In 1849 he became the official architect of the New York Ecclesiological Society, for whom he designed a model church based on St James the Less (1846–50), Philadelphia, PA, and its 13th-century source, St Michael's, Long Stanton, Cambs, which was published in the *New York Ecclesiologist* (1849), a journal that exerted a strong influence on the design of Protestant Episcopal churches in North America. In 1850 Wills published his *Ancient Ecclesiastical Architecture*, in which he repeated the arguments put forward by Pugin in *True Principles* (1841) but adapted Pugin's polemics to suit local conditions. Wills's book was therefore a landmark in the history of the Gothic Revival in North America. Wills developed a thriving practice and in 1851 established a partnership with Dudley, who moved to New York in that year. Works of this period include St Peter's (1850–51), Milford, CT, with Early English details and a two-cell plan with a south-west tower-porch; the smaller Episcopal

Christ Church (*c.* 1850), Napoleonville, Assumption Parish, LA; the Chapel of the Cross (1855), Annandale, MS; Christ Church, Oberlin, OH; and the more monumental projects for the Episcopalian Trinity Church (1850), San Francisco, and St Peter's, Philadelphia.

By 1856 Wills's partnership with Dudley had been dissolved, and he was again in Canada. Here his most important extant work from this period is Christ Church, the Anglican cathedral in Montreal, which was designed in 1857 and built after his death by Thomas Seaton Scott (1826–95). The design was based on the completed Fredericton Cathedral but includes more elaborate Decorated detailing and an octagonal chapter house to the south of the choir. Wills also designed the Anglican churches at Barton, Glanford and St Mary's, near Brantford, Ontario. His work continued to influence architects in the Maritime Provinces for some years, and he played a significant role in spreading the ideas of the Gothic Revival and ecclesiology in North America.

UNPUBLISHED SOURCES
Fredericton, Dioc. Archvs, on dep. Prov. Archvs NB [drgs of Fredericton Cathedral]

WRITINGS
Ancient English Ecclesiastical Architecture and its Principles Applied to the Wants of the Church at the Present Day (New York, 1850)

BIBLIOGRAPHY
DCB
A. W. N. Pugin: *The True Principles of Pointed or Christian Architecture* (New York, 1841/*R* 1973)
The Ecclesiologist, v (1846), p. 81
Instrumenta ecclesiastica (London, 1847–56)
NY Eccles., ii (1849)
D. S. Richardson: *Christ Church Cathedral, Fredericton, New Brunswick* (MA thesis, New Haven, CT, Yale U., 1966)
P. Stanton: *The Gothic Revival and American Church Architecture: An Episode in Taste, 1840–1856* (Baltimore, 1968)

MALCOLM THURLBY

Willumsen, Jens Ferdinand (*b* Copenhagen, 7 Sept 1863; *d* Cannes, 4 April 1958). Danish painter, printmaker, sculptor, ceramicist, architect and collector. He studied from 1881 at the Kunstakademi in Copenhagen and in 1886 at Peder Severin Krøyer's Frie Skole there. His style changed radically during his travels in France and Spain (1888–9) and during a stay in France, where he met and exhibited with French artists, including Paul Gauguin. In Brittany he painted several scenes of local people, similar to Gauguin's work of this period, for example *Two Women Walking, Brittany* (1890; Frederikssund, Willumsens Mus.). In such works Willumsen emphasized the element of vigorous movement. From the start of his career Willumsen also made prints (etchings from 1885, lithographs from 1910 and woodcuts from 1920): early, more realistic works, such as the Copenhagen townscape of *Woman Out for a Walk* (1889) soon gave way to a bolder, more Symbolist approach, as in *Fertility* (1891), which showed his wife Juliette in an advanced stage of pregnancy and raised a storm of protest when exhibited at the Copenhagen Frie Udstilling (Free Exhibition), which Willumsen and others had founded. His major work from this period is *Jotunheim* (1892–3; Frederikssund, Willumsens Mus.; see fig.), which he began during a trip to Norway in 1892 and completed in Paris the following year. Its combination of mountain landscape and human figures conveys Willumsen's faith in the spiritual unity of man

Jens Ferdinand Willumsen: *Jotunheim*, oil on canvas, painted zinc and enamel on copper, 1.5×2.7 m, 1892–3 (Frederikssund, J. F. Willumsens Museum)

and his environment. Willumsen's interest in the production of ceramics led, in 1897, to his appointment as artistic director at Bing & Grøndahl's porcelain factory. Although Willumsen worked with ceramics only in the 1890s, he produced about a hundred pieces during this period: portraits, figures, vases and cremation urns (*see* COPENHAGEN, fig. 3). His works often combine the functional, decorative and symbolic, for example the vessel-shaped *Father, Mother and their New-born Child* (1891; Copenhagen, Kstindustmus.). Through Willumsen's efforts, the factory won first prize at the Exposition Universelle in Paris in 1900.

From about 1900 Willumsen embarked on a series of compositions on the theme of the relationship between man and nature. *Mountain Climber* (1904; Copenhagen, Hagemanns Koll.; 1912; Copenhagen, Stat. Mus. Kst) presents the figure of an emancipated woman who derives strength and energy from nature. In *After the Storm* (1905; Oslo, N.G.; 1916; Frederikssund, Willumsens Mus.) nature is a brutal force seeking to crush humanity. The large painting *Sun and Youth: Children on the Beach* (1910; Göteborg, Kstmus.) depicts the next generation struggling with the force of the sea. In contrast to the more restrained style of his Symbolist work of the 1890s, Willumsen's nature paintings were created in an Expressionist style, with bold colours, sharp tonal contrasts and vigorous line. In the 1910s Willumsen settled permanently in the south of France and also travelled to Spain. Under the influence of El Greco's colouring, he painted a series of brilliant townscapes and landscapes, for example *Beside the Fountain at Toledo* (1915; priv. col., see Mentze, p. 211). Willumsen also continued printmaking, producing such notable portrait lithographs as *Mother Kissing her Baby* (1910) and a powerful series of etchings on the brutality of war, for example the *Belgian Prisoner* (1918). The following decade was mainly devoted to the completion of the coloured marble *Great Relief* (4.40×6.40 m, 1893–1928; Frederikssund, Willumsens Mus.) in which Willumsen attempted to convey his view of the necessary mixture of positive and negative aspects in man's existence. The relief, begun during Willumsen's Symbolist period in Paris, was completed in a style that combined naturalistic and decorative form. While the *Great Relief* is Willumsen's most ambitious work, it was executed long after its conception and so lacks freshness and spirit.

Willumsen's major work from the 1930s was the series *Trilogy of the Dying Titian* (Frederikssund, Willumsens Mus.), in which he showed his own death and his resurrection as half-man, half-tiger. While in Venice during this period Willumsen painted a number of colourful city views incorporating special light effects, water reflections and a dramatic atmosphere of decline and decay. Willumsen also designed bold and effective posters, including posters for exhibitions. He designed and built two studio villas for his own use, the first in 1896 at Hellerupvej, Copenhagen, and the second in 1907 at Strandagervej, Copenhagen. The second villa, with its unusually formed doors and windows, resembled a monumental sculpture. After the 1890s Willumsen generally lived apart from other Danish artists, spending most of his later life in the south of France. In 1957, however, a museum dedicated to Willumsen was established in Frederikssund, outside Copenhagen. This now houses many of his major works as well as items from his own collection, which numbers over 2000 works including painting, graphic and decorative art and sculpture.

BIBLIOGRAPHY

J. F. Willumsen: Maleri, skulptur, tegninger og grafik (exh. cat., Oslo, N.G., 1947)

E. Mentze: *J. F. Willumsen* (Copenhagen, 1957)
S. Schultz: *J. F. Willumsen* (Copenhagen, 1967) [prints]
R. Nasgaard: *Willumsen and Symbolist Art, 1888–1910* (diss., New York U., 1973)
J. F. Willumsen og Den Frie Udstillings første år [J. F. Willumsen and the Free Exhibition's first year] (exh. cat., Frederikssund, Willumsens Mus., 1982)
L. Krogh: *J. F. Willumsens Museum: Katalogbog* (Frederikssund, 1986)

LEILA KROGH

Wilpert, Joseph (*b* Eiglau, Silesia, 21 Aug 1857; *d* Rome, 13 Feb 1944). German archaeologist and priest. He studied philosophy and theology at the Jesuit academy in Innsbruck, where he was ordained in 1883. Through the mediation of Cardinal Friedrich Egon von Fürstenberg (1853–92) of Olmütz he made a study trip to Rome in 1884 and became curate at the seminary at the Campo Santo. There he began the independent research into Early Christian art that was to be his life's work. In 1892 he was awarded an honorary doctorate by the theological faculty of Münster University, Westphalia; he was appointed Protonotary Apostolic in 1903 and Dean of Münster University in 1924. From 1926 he taught at the Pontificio Istituto di Archeologia Cristiana and published frequently in the *Römische Quartalschrift* edited by A. de Waal. His many other writings include several standard works on Early Christian wall paintings and mosaics in Rome and on Early Christian sarcophagi. Of a more autobiographical nature was his *Erlebnisse und Ergebnisse im Dienst der christlichen Archäologie.*

The lasting value of Wilpert's art-historical work is reflected in the publication of a new edition of his *Die römischen Mosaiken* in 1976, which also contains the results of more recent research. Although some of his interpretations, topographical information and chronology of Christian monuments have been superseded, his thorough and extraordinarily extensive research on the iconography relating to St Peter and the early Church laid the foundations for further detailed study of Early Christian art. His interest in current theological controversies, however, tended to bias his otherwise masterly reconstructions of Early Christian paintings and mosaics in order to stress the primacy of Rome over the Eastern Church, whose pre-iconoclastic art was at the time poorly understood. His somewhat antiquarian approach led to the discovery of much historical documentation, which stimulated theological and art-historical enquiry but tended to neglect artistic considerations. Of undiminished value, however, are Wilpert's collections of source material and large colour photographs of building interiors: before being photographed, the wall mosaics were cleaned and any subsequent painted or stucco additions removed. In many cases these photographs constitute a unique record of interiors that have subsequently undergone structural alteration.

WRITINGS
Die Malereien der Katakomben Roms (Freiburg, 1903)
Die römischen Mosaiken und Malereien der kirchlichen Bauten vom 4. bis zum 13. Jahrhundert, ed. W. N. Schumacher, 4 vols (Freiburg, 1916, rev. 2/1976)
I sarcofagi cristiani antichi, 5 vols (Rome, 1929–36)
Erlebnisse und Ergebnisse im Dienst der christlichen Archäologie (Freiburg, 1930)

BIBLIOGRAPHY
Riv. Archeol. Crist., xv (1938), pp. 6–16 [bibliog. list of his works]
E. Dassmann: 'Joseph Wilpert und die Erforschung der römischen Katakomben', *Röm. Qschr.*, suppl. vol. xxv (1977), pp. 160–73
P. J. Nordhagen: 'Working with Wilpert', *Acta Archeol. & A. Hist. Pertinentia*, n. s., v (1985), pp. 247–57

GREGOR M. LECHNER

Wils, Jan (*b* Alkmaar, 22 Feb 1891; *d* 1972). Dutch architect. He studied architecture at the Technische Hogeschool, Delft, and worked as a draughtsman for H. P. Berlage in The Hague from 1914 to 1916 when he opened his own office in Voorburg. Shortly afterwards, he met Vilmos Huszár and Theo van Doesburg, cofounders of the radical periodical DE STIJL, which gave its name to a distinctive movement from the 1920s. One of the goals of De Stijl was the working collaboration of painters and architects, and Wils consistently put this ideal into practice; for example, van Doesburg acted as colour consultant for his De Lange house (1917), Alkmaar, and his Hotel De Dubbele Sleutel (1918; destr. *c.* 1975, see Ex and Hoek, 1986, p. 191), Woerden. He also became a newspaper critic and writer at this time, writing both for *De Stijl* and for *Wendingen*, the publication of the expressionist Amsterdam School, and was a prominent member of the Hague Art Circle. Wils's best works were realized after his resignation from De Stijl in 1919; his town houses (1919) in Alkmaar, on which Huszár acted as colour consultant, were his first buildings to incorporate flat roofs and were designed in accordance with De Stijl principles. He became known as 'Frank Lloyd Wils' because of his admiration for the work of Frank Lloyd Wright, although Wils's designs were too original to be judged as derivative. For example, he used an unconventional housing type and construction methods for his housing development Daal en Berg (1920), Papaverhof, The Hague, although the plan echoed work by Wright. Wils was unable to build much in the early 1920s because of financial difficulties, but he developed several designs of horizontal, flat-roofed buildings of brick and concrete, with small but strongly defined vertical elements, large, steel-framed windows and very detailed ornament. His later works of 1925–35 showed the influence of Functionalism, for example the Olympic Stadium (1928), Amsterdam, which had a heavily walled appearance, the Citroen building (1929) and the Cinema City theatre (1935), both in Amsterdam; the latter used a steel frame and was hailed as a prime example of functionalist building. Wils continued to design after World War II; works included the Hotel Bouwes (1952–61), Zandvoort, and the Chamber of Commerce (1956–9), The Hague.

BIBLIOGRAPHY
E. Godoli: *Jan Wils, Frank Lloyd Wright e De Stijl* (Florence, 1980)
S. Ex and E. Hoek: 'Jan Wils', *De beginjaren van De Stijl, 1917–1922* (Utrecht, 1982; Eng. trans., Cambridge, MA, 1986), pp. 184–203

SJAREL EX

Wilson, Alexander (*b* Paisley, Strathclyde, 6 July 1766; *d* Philadelphia, PA, 23 Aug 1813). American draughtsman of Scottish birth. After an unsuccessful attempt to establish himself in the Paisley weaving trade and a failed start as a poet, he moved in 1794 to the USA. For about ten years he was a school teacher in New Jersey and eastern

Pennsylvania, finally, in 1802, taking a post at a school at Gray's Ferry, PA, where he came to know William Bartram. Bartram encouraged Wilson's nascent interest in ornithology, which soon developed into an ambition to create a comprehensive illustrated book on North American birds, resulting in the *American Ornithology* (1808–14). Bartram also helped Wilson to learn to draw birds, offering him the use of his library so he could study illustrations of American birds by such 18th-century naturalists as Mark Catesby and George Edwards (1694–1773). Wilson also came to know Charles Willson Peale, in whose museum, an important research centre for Philadelphia naturalists, he drew many of the birds included in the *American Ornithology* from mounted specimens. He travelled extensively in search of new birds, encountering other naturalist-artists, including John Abbot (1751–*c*. 1840) and JOHN JAMES AUDUBON, along the way.

Wilson's drawings for the *American Ornithology* are remarkably fine for an artist who learnt to draw so late in life, but they are far simpler in composition than Audubon's works; indeed, they are even less complex than the 18th-century prototypes that he had studied in Bartram's library. His images remain essentially specimen drawings, stressing anatomical features over behaviour or habitat as the defining characteristics of a species. Alexander Lawson (1772–1846), the primary engraver of the plates for *American Ornithology*, composed larger, more integrated scenes from Wilson's material by creating collages with the individual drawings and filling in background details before engraving the plates. The engravings become particularly elaborate in the final volume of the *Ornithology*, which was completed the year after Wilson's death. This suggests that while Wilson was able to oversee the publication of his work, he preferred to adhere to the straightforward anatomical clarity that suited the needs of systematic science, rather than attempting to explore the complicated network of physical and behavioural relationships that had become the focus of more revolutionary scientific research.

PRINTS

American Ornithology, 9 vols (Philadelphia, 1808–14, rev. 1824–5); suppl. by C. L. Bonaparte, 4 vols (Philadelphia, 1825–33)

BIBLIOGRAPHY

G. Ord: *Sketch of the Life of Alexander Wilson* (Philadelphia, 1828)
R. Cantwell: *Alexander Wilson: Naturalist and Pioneer* (Philadelphia, 1961)
C. Hunter, ed.: *The Life and Letters of Alexander Wilson* (Philadelphia, 1983)

AMY R. W. MEYERS

Wilson, Andrew (*b* Edinburgh, 1780; *d* Edinburgh, 27 Nov 1848). Scottish dealer, painter and teacher. He trained in the Edinburgh studio of the painter Alexander Nasmyth, followed by a short period of study at the Royal Academy in London, and he practised intermittently as a landscape painter throughout his career. In 1799 he left England to tour Italy. During two years there he became familiar with many of the great art collections in Genoa, Naples and Rome, and it was his knowledge of these collections that he later turned to profit as an adviser and picture agent for various collectors. Wilson returned to Genoa in 1803, by which time many of these same collections were being hastily put up for sale, a direct result of Napoleon's penal

tax on the Italian nobility. By 1806 he had sent 54 Old Master pictures back to London, including paintings by Titian, Bartolomé Esteban Murillo and Claude Lorrain. However, London was flooded with works of art from European collections broken up as a result of the Napoleonic Wars, and Wilson had difficulty in selling important pictures, such as Peter Paul Rubens's the *Brazen Serpent* (*c*. 1630s; London, N.G.). He attempted, without success, to arrange a subscription lottery for it, and William Buchanan eventually bought the painting for £1260.

Leaving the picture dealing business for a time, Wilson resumed landscape painting. He became a member of the Associated Society of Artists in 1808, exhibiting at the Royal Academy and later at the British Institution. He also held the post of drawing-master at Sandhurst Military Academy from 1808 until his return to Edinburgh in 1818 to take up the post of Master of the Trustees' Academy (later the Royal Institution). He also became personal art agent to John Hope, 4th Earl of Hopetoun, and John Hope, 5th Earl of Hopetoun. Between 1817 and 1827 Wilson obtained for Hopetoun House in Lothian a conservative collection of Old Master paintings, ranging from Aelbert Cuyp's *Landscape with Cattle* to Anthony van Dyck's the *Marquis of Spindle* (both Hopetoun House, Lothian). He regularly exhibited his own landscape paintings in Edinburgh during the 1820s, for example *View of Tivoli* (1825; Edinburgh, N.G.).

In 1826 Wilson moved to Italy, where he remained until just before his death. He lived mainly in Genoa and scoured the city's remaining collections, searching out paintings suitable for export. Wilson's main buyer was the Royal Institution, which relied on him to form its collection. In one case, it liberally authorized him to offer a minimum of £1500 for one of his major finds, van Dyck's *Lomellini Family* (*c*. 1623–7; Edinburgh, N.G.). A painting wrongly attributed to Rubens (now thought to be from his studio), the *Adoration of the Shepherds* (Hopetoun House, Lothian), was sold to Lord Hopetoun for £1000, Wilson taking 5% commission. He also supplied paintings to other buyers, sometimes through the Scottish painter David Wilkie; several van Dyck portraits were sold to Sir Robert Peel in this way. Wilson continued to paint the Italian landscape and was successful in selling a number of his own paintings, mainly to buyers in Italy.

UNPUBLISHED SOURCES

Hopetoun, Hopetoun Papers Trust [MSS 620, 816]
Edinburgh, N. Lib. [Wilkie MSS 3812, 6363; Wilson discharge]
Edinburgh, Royal Inst. [Minute and letter books, Scottish Record Office]

BIBLIOGRAPHY

DNB
Obituary, *A. J.* [London] (1851), p. 85
B. Skinner: 'Andrew Wilson and the Hopetoun Collection', *Country Life*, cxliv (1968), pp. 370–72
D. Irwin: *Scottish Painters at Home and Abroad, 1700–1900* (London, 1975)
F. Haskell: *Rediscoveries in Art* (London, 1976)
H. Brigstocke: *William Buchanan and the Nineteenth Century Art Trade: 100 Letters to his Agents in London and Italy* (London, 1982)

A. M. LINK

Wilson, Arnold Manaaki (*b* Ruatoki, Bay of Plenty, NZ, 1928). Maori sculptor. His tribal affiliation is Tuhoe/Takimoana, Te Arawa/Tarawhai. He was the first Maori to graduate with honours in sculpture at the Elam School of Fine Arts, University of Auckland (1953). Like many other Maori artists, he pursued a career in art education, enrolling at Auckland Teachers' College in 1954. Between 1975 and his retirement in 1989 he worked as an education officer for the Department of Education in Auckland and as Director of Te Mauri Pakeaka Cross Community Arts Programme. Wilson was widely acknowledged as one of the most influential artists of the Maori art movement that emerged in the 1950s. Working first in realistic figurative forms made from clay, wood, stone and metal, he moved increasingly towards a stylized multi-media form incorporating aspects of traditional Maori symbolism: he considered that 'myths and legends have a store of inspiration for us ... the more we look the more is revealed'. After 1989 he worked on a number of commissioned works.

MEGAN TAMATI-QUENNELL

Wilson, Benjamin (*b* Leeds, 21 June 1721; *d* London, 6 June 1788). English painter, etcher and scientist. He was the 14th child of Major Wilson, a wealthy York clothier whose house was decorated by a French artist, Jacques Parmentier (*d* 1730). His father's business failed and Wilson moved to London, where he became a clerk and began to study painting, possibly with Thomas Hudson. In 1746 and 1748–50 he was in Dublin, where he practised successfully as a portrait painter. On his return to London he settled into Godfrey Kneller's old house in Great Queen Street and built up a lucrative portrait practice, which was probably patronized chiefly by Yorkshiremen in London. One of these, Sir John Savile, later Earl of Mexborough, may have introduced him to Edward Augustus, Duke of York (1739–67), who in 1773 appointed Wilson painter to the Board of Ordnance, though he painted little after 1769.

Wilson was one of the leading portrait painters in England during the 1750s. Like Reynolds, he made dramatic use of Rembrandtesque chiaroscuro, although his intention may have been to hide the weakness in his drawing rather than to emphasize the mystery of his sitters. He exhibited little: four portraits at the Society of Artists (1760–61) and a history painting at the Royal Academy in 1783.

In 1766 the Duke of York engaged Wilson to organize the preparation and scenery painting for his private theatre in James Street. He was then appointed manager and painted a large picture of one of the amateur actresses, *Lady Stanhope as Calista in 'The Fair Penitent'* (*c.* 1767; ex-Agnew's, London, 1984). Wilson was also connected with the professional stage and developed a stormy relationship with David Garrick, who roused the artist's professional jealousy when he enticed away Wilson's most gifted and useful assistant, Johan Zoffany, in 1762. The nursing of Zoffany's style through the transition from German decorative to English conversational was Wilson's greatest contribution to the art of the 18th century.

In 1753 Wilson painted one of the earliest theatrical conversation pieces, *David Garrick and Mrs Bellamy in 'Romeo and Juliet'* (versions in New Haven, CT, Yale Cent., and London, Theat. Mus.). Unlike many later paintings in this genre, which are sometimes wrongly thought to represent actual performances, there is every reason to suppose that Wilson's depiction of the tomb scene is an accurate reproduction of the scene as it was performed. Wilson's use of paint is often disappointingly thin and flat and his palette morbid, but he was capable of a sensuous freedom that adds to the purely documentary significance of such scenes as that from *Romeo and Juliet.* Dramatic lighting was another essential component of his theatrical work. He produced other portraits of Garrick—as *Hamlet* and *King Lear* (both untraced; mezzotints by McArdell, 1754 and 1761)—as well as the principal paintings for Garrick's great Shakespeare Jubilee at Stratford-upon-Avon (1769), including a full-length portrait of *Shakespeare* for Stratford Town Hall (destr. 1946). Wilson's portraits of Garrick were engraved several times, and he was himself a fine etcher; he is thought to have deceived Hudson with a convincing Rembrandt pastiche, *Companion to the Coach*, in 1751. An example of his etching is the popular caricature made on the theme of the repeal of the American Stamp Act, *The Repeal; or, the Funeral of Miss Ame-Stamp* (1766).

To contemporaries Wilson was best known as a scientist. From 1746 he published occasional treatises on electricity, and he corresponded with Benjamin Franklin about lightning conductors. He became a Fellow of the Royal Society in 1751.

BIBLIOGRAPHY

H. Randolph: *Life of General Sir Robert Wilson* (London, 1862) [biography of Wilson's son]

K. A. Burnim: *David Garrick, Director* (Pittsburgh, 1961)

GEOFFREY ASHTON

Wilson, Charles (*b* ?Glasgow, 19 June 1810; *d* Glasgow, 6 Feb 1863). Scottish architect. He trained initially with his father John Wilson, a builder, before entering the office of David Hamilton in Glasgow in 1827, becoming his principal assistant by 1833. There he worked on the later stages of Hamilton Palace (from 1822; destr.), Strathclyde, and may have become familiar with the unexecuted schemes, including some by Charles Percier and Pierre-François Fontaine, commissioned by the 10th Duke of Hamilton for the building. David Hamilton's Romanesque Revival designs for Lennox Castle (1837–41), Lennoxtown, Strathclyde, probably influenced several of his early church designs, notably Strathbungo (1839; rebuilt), Glasgow, and West Church (1845), Rothesay, Strathclyde.

When only 31 Wilson secured the commission for the mental hospital (1841) at Gartnavel, Glasgow. This huge double quadrangle design was in the Tudor Gothic idiom favoured in the 1820s by William Wilkins and William Burn. It established his position as the leading architect in Glasgow following Hamilton's death, but more importantly it led him to visit mental institutions in Britain and France, which enabled him to see Paris and, if only briefly, become familiar with the architecture of Félix-Jacques Duban and Pierre François Henri Labrouste.

Throughout the 1840s the influence of French and German round-arched classicism became increasingly marked in Wilson's work. Gryffe (1841; altered), Strathclyde, still followed the asymmetrical Italianate villa models of Hamilton's late work, as did the boldly detailed astylar classical Breadalbane Terrace (1845; now Hill Street) and Windsor (now Kirklee) Terrace (1845), both in Glasgow.

The beginning of his mature style was marked by his Glasgow Academy (1846; now Strathclyde Regional Headquarters), a design related to Leo von Klenze's War Office (1826–30) in Munich. It developed into a large-scale High Renaissance manner, which reached a climax with two buildings of 1856 in Glasgow: the temple-like Queen's Rooms (now Christian Science Church), La Belle Place, derived from Alberti, and the Free Church College, crowning Woodlands Hill with a soaring Lombardic campanile balanced by a smaller pair of towers flanking the Corinthian façade of the church.

Wilson also laid out the crest of Woodlands Hill with Park Terrace (1854) and Park Circus (1855), their curving terraces providing townscapes of great drama. Although the French roofs of the large houses of Park Terrace were the first such in Glasgow, his smaller Italianate designs had more individuality. A favourite motif, also used by his friend Alexander Thomson and perhaps derived from Karl Friedrich Schinkel, was the triplets of recessed arches alternating with single arches, which he used at 144–52 Buchanan Street (1847; destr.), Glasgow, and Hazel Hall (1854; destr.), Dundee. His use of classical details in city architecture had a lasting influence on Glasgow architects such as his pupil James Boucher (d 1906) and John Burnet. He built only one major country house, the castellated Neo-Tudor Lewis Castle (1848), Stornoway, Western Isles, but he designed a number of medium-sized mansions in a Scottish version of Jacobean architecture, with refined detail, such as St Helen's (1850), Dundee. He was not greatly interested in Gothic, although the Early English detailing of St Paul's (1852), Dundee, the sole survivor of a group of Greek-cross plan churches, shows—like the refinement of his drawings—his fastidious approach to everything he built.

BIBLIOGRAPHY

Papworth

D. Thomson: 'The Works of the Late Charles Wilson', *Proceed. Philos. Soc. Glasgow*, xiii (1880–82), pp. 552–69

A. Gomme and D. Walker: *The Architecture of Glasgow* (London, 1969, 2/1987), pp. 88–102, 303–4

DAVID WALKER

Wilson, Colin (Alexander) St John (*b* Cheltenham, 14 March 1922). English architect, teacher and writer. He was educated at Corpus Christi College, University of Cambridge (MA 1942), and then, after service in World War II, he studied at the Bartlett School of Architecture, University of London (1946–9). In 1950 he joined the London County Council Architects' Department, where he worked in the Housing Division, first under Robert Matthew and then under Leslie Martin; at this time the LCC was among the pioneers of responsible, modernist public authority housing under the impetus of post-war enthusiasm for the Welfare State. Wilson left the LCC in 1955 to take up a lectureship at the School of Architecture, University of Cambridge, and he set up in private practice there. He designed the influential exhibition *This is Tomorrow* (1956), staged at the Whitechapel Art Gallery, London, the other participants including Alison and Peter Smithson, members of the Independent Group at the Institute of Contemporary Arts, London, of which Wilson was also a member. He also designed several distinguished small houses in and around Cambridge, for example two houses (1961–4) in Grantchester Road and the Cornford House (1965–9), Madingley Road, the brick and timber construction of which is a variation of the vernacular.

From 1956–70 Wilson worked in partnership with Leslie Martin, who had left the LCC to become Professor of Architecture at Cambridge and had begun to practise locally. Wilson worked on several of the buildings in Cambridge that, in the 1960s, brought Martin the reputation of one of the most geometrically inventive and rigorously disciplined of British architects. These included the Harvey Court residential building (from 1958) for Gonville and Caius College; a new building for the School of Architecture (1960) at Scroope Terrace; and another residential building (from 1960) for Peterhouse. He also worked with Martin on the group of specialist libraries (from 1959) at the University of Oxford and on the project (from 1962) for rehousing the British Library in a new building south of the British Museum, London; this proposal caused prolonged controversy because it would have involved demolishing large parts of well-established Bloomsbury townscape, and it was eventually abandoned, leading to the decision to build the new library on a site at St Pancras for which Wilson was appointed architect in 1975.

Wilson became Professor of Architecture at Cambridge in 1975 after Martin's retirement (1972) and the death of his successor, William Gough Howell (1922–74). He designed a small extension (1979) to the British Museum and from an office in London continued as architect of the new British Library on Euston Road, London (see fig.), a long-term project (construction started in 1982) of unusual planning and structural complexity. Designed in close collaboration with the client and users of the building, it includes two major wings: one whose long, low-rise and

Colin St John Wilson: British Library, Euston Road, London, begun 1982

flat-roofed form follows the angled street frontage adjacent to St Pancras Station, and another that is composed of pavilion-like sections with sloping roofs that once again recall the vernacular.

During this period Wilson also worked on housing (1977) for the London borough of Haringey; a new library building (1984) and a catering and commercial development (1985) for Queen Mary College, University of London; and a memorial library (1985) for Bishop Wilson School, Springfield, Essex. His experience as an architectural teacher extended also to the USA: he was a visiting critic at Yale University School of Architecture, New Haven, CT (1960, 1964 and 1983), and was Bemis Visiting Professor of Architecture at Massachusetts Institute of Technology, Cambridge (1970–72). He had a special interest in scientific method and in architectural and aesthetic theory as well as in other forms of contemporary art, and his approach to architectural philosophy had a stabilizing influence on a generation of younger architects. He became a trustee of the Tate Gallery, London (1973–80), and of the National Gallery, London (1977–80).

WRITINGS
'Architecture: Public Good and Private Necessity', *J. RIBA*, lxxxvi/3 (1979), pp. 107–15
'The Historical Sense', *Archit. Rev.* [London], clxxvi/1052 (1984), pp. 68–70
Architectural Reflections: Studies in the Philosophy and Practice of Architecture (Oxford, 1992)

BIBLIOGRAPHY
P. McGuire: 'Echoes of Aalto: The Architecture of Colin St John Wilson', *Bldg Des.*, 417 (1978), p. 15
'New Building for the British Library', *Archit. Rev.* [London], clxiv/982 (1978), pp. 339–44
'Portrait of the Artist: Colin St John Wilson', *Architects' J.*, clxviii/41 (1978), pp. 658–9
J. Glancey: 'British Museum Extension, Bloomsbury, London', *Archit. Rev.* [London], clxix/1007 (1981), pp. 46–52
J. M. RICHARDS

Wilson, George Washington (*b* Banffshire [now Grampian], 7 Feb 1823; *d* Aberdeen, 9 March 1893). Scottish photographer and painter. He served an apprenticeship as a carpenter but decided to become a painter and trained at art schools in Edinburgh and London. After several years as a drawing-master in Aberdeen, he joined the photographic business of John Hay jr in 1853. In 1855 Wilson opened his own photographic studio in Aberdeen. By the 1860s it was one of the most prolific and successful photographic businesses in Scotland. He won international acclaim as a landscape photographer and was particularly famed for his instantaneous photographs such as *View in Leith Docks* (undated albumen print; Edinburgh, N.P.G.), which makes telling use of *contre-jour* effects in the silhouetting of ships' masts against the sky. He received royal patronage, becoming photographer to Queen Victoria in Scotland. At the International Exhibition of 1862, Wilson was awarded a medal for 'the beauty of his small pictures of clouds, shipping, waves etc. from nature'. From 1876 he relied on assistant photographers to provide new negatives, employing a large staff of photographers and studio assistants, and by the 1880s Wilson was running the world's largest photographic printing establishment at St Swithin, Aberdeen. The initials 'GWW' appear on all of the photographs produced by the Wilson firm, which was taken over by his sons after his death, but do not indicate that Wilson was himself the photographer in every case. The firm's output of albumen prints from wet collodion negatives was generally of a technically high standard. Mass-produced, picturesque views such as *Tighnalechan, Aberfeldy* (albumen print; Edinburgh, N.P.G.) were the precursors of the picture postcard and served much the same purpose.

BIBLIOGRAPHY
R. Taylor: *George Washington Wilson: Artist and Photographer* (Aberdeen, 1981)
J. R. Hume and T. Jackson: *George Washington Wilson and Victorian Glasgow* (Aberdeen, 1983)
J. S. Smith: *George Washington Wilson and Royal Deeside* (Aberdeen, 1984)
JULIE LAWSON

Wilson, Henry (*b* Liverpool, 1864; *d* Menton, France, 7 March 1934). English architect and designer. He studied at the Kidderminster School of Art before being articled to the architect Edward James Shrewsbury (*d* 1924) in Maidenhead, Berks. He then worked in the offices of John Oldrid Scott, John Belcher and J. D. Sedding. After Sedding's death Wilson succeeded to the practice and completed many of Sedding's schemes, notably the Church of the Holy Redeemer, Exmouth Street, London; St Peter's, Mount Park Road, Ealing; and Holy Trinity, Sloane Street, London (1889–1900). Wilson followed Sedding's ideals in uniting crafts with building. His designs, however, were more original and grander in scale. Particularly outstanding are his Byzantine schemes for the redecoration of St Bartholomew's, Brighton (*c*. 1898; only partly executed), and his completion of the chapel and library (1890–96) at Welbeck Abbey, Notts. Two of Wilson's designs were especially influential: the Public Library (1890–91), Ladbroke Grove, London, and the tower of St Clement's (1895), Boscombe, Hants. From about 1895 Wilson turned increasingly to designing metalwork, church plate and furnishings, jewellery and sculpture, becoming a gifted artist-craftsman of the Arts and Crafts Movement. From 1901 he taught metalwork at the Royal College of Art and at the Central School of Arts and Crafts, both in London. He was Master of the Art Workers Guild in 1917 and President of the Arts and Crafts Exhibition Society (1915–22). He was the first editor of the *Architectural Review* (1896–1901).

WRITINGS
A Memorial to the Late J. D. Sedding (London, 1892)
'Art and Religion', *Archit. Rev.* [London], vi (1899), pp. 276–8
Silverwork and Jewellery (London, 1903)

BIBLIOGRAPHY
A. B. Pite: Obituary, *The Times* (12 March 1934)
F. W. Troup: Obituary, *RIBA J.* (24 March 1934), pp. 539, 588–9
N. Taylor: 'Byzantium in Brighton', *Archit. Rev.* [London], cxxxix (1966), pp. 274–7
J. Browning: 'Arts and Crafts Loyalist', *Country Life*, clvi (12 Sept 1974), pp. 700–02
MARGARET RICHARDSON

Wilson, Richard (i) (*b* Penegoes, Montgoms [now in Powys], 1713 or 1714; *d* Colomendy, Denbs [now in Clwyd], 11 May 1782). Welsh painter, active in Italy and England. He began his career as a portraitist who also painted landscapes but committed himself to the latter genre in the early 1750s while in Italy. He painted and drew Italian scenery and idealized classical landscapes not only in Italy but after his return to England, only later developing this manner to include British scenery too. He was also influenced by Dutch landscape painting, particularly the work of Aelbert Cuyp. Wilson was a founder-member of the Royal Academy and enjoyed considerable success until the early 1770s, but his last years were penurious and his reputation in decline. Through William Hodges, a former pupil who published a short essay on Richard Wilson in 1790, and through other ex-pupils (notably Joseph Farington and Thomas Jones), the status of Wilson's work improved; gradually it began to influence the artists of J. M. W. Turner's generation.

1. London and Italy, to c. 1757. 2. England and Wales, c. 1757–82.

1. LONDON AND ITALY, TO c. 1757. Wilson's father, a clergyman, provided him with so thorough a Classical education that, according to Benjamin Booth, in later life he could quote Horace *extempore* 'on any subject mentioned'. His mother was related to the Wynnes of Leeswood, Denbs (now in Clwyd)—Sir George Wynne was probably her brother, possibly her nephew—and thus she had distant connections with such great Welsh families as the Williams-Wynns of Wynnstay in the same county. From 1729 Sir George Wynne (who owed his wealth to lead-mining) financed Wilson's training under Thomas Wright (*fl* 1728–37), a portrait painter in London. The death of Wilson's father in 1728 may explain this sponsorship and the unusual phenomenon of a young gentleman such as Wilson professing a taste for art yet with a view to earning his living by it.

From 1735 Wilson painted portraits independently and, after 1737, landscapes as well. Initially, Wynne's assistance apparently obviated any need for Wilson to depend on art for his living, but by the 1740s he was painting portraits seriously, patronized chiefly by the Lyttelton family of Hagley Hall (now in Hereford & Worcs). He also made connections with other useful people such as Dr Francis Ayscough (1700–63); through him Wilson gained access to the circle of Frederick, Prince of Wales, although any hope of preferment from that quarter was scotched with Frederick's death in 1751. Wilson's full-length portrait of Sir Thomas Lyttelton's natural son *Commodore Thomas Smith* (1744; Hagley Hall, Hereford & Worcs) is an extremely competent early example: Smith stands in the newly fashionable cross-legged pose, telescope in hand, with a seascape background to indicate the success of his maritime career. In 1746 Wilson donated a pair of landscape roundels depicting *St George's Hospital* and the *Foundling Hospital* to the Foundling Hospital, London (both *in situ*), a charitable institution for which William Hogarth strongly campaigned. The date of these roundels suggests that Wilson associated from early on with Hogarth and the painters who frequented the St Martin's Lane Academy; it may have been through them, as well as through his own experience, that Wilson came to realize that artists could no longer rely on traditional forms of aristocratic support (of the kind that Richard Boyle, 3rd Earl of Burlington, had extended to William Kent a few years earlier, for example). Hogarth and his circle were painting for a market; from now on Wilson would follow suit.

In the autumn of 1750 Wilson arrived in Venice. According to Farington, he left England 'more with a view to improvement in that branch of art which he had hitherto professed [i.e. portraiture] than with any intention of devoting himself to another'. Wilson would have seen those young aristocrats, from whom he expected patronage, setting off on the Grand Tour and, like Joshua Reynolds, must have understood what benefits would accrue through visiting Italy himself. This would give him not only the opportunity to study Italian painting and the remains of antiquity at first hand, but also a means to meet other artists and, more importantly, potential patrons. Wilson stayed a year in Venice; he studied the works of Titian but also painted landscapes in the contemporary Venetian Rococo manner, a style probably partly derived from his friendship with Francesco Zuccarelli. Late in 1751 Wilson travelled to Rome with William Locke of Norbury. There, alert to the work of such artists as Salvator Rosa, Nicolas Poussin, Claude Lorrain and Jan Frans van Bloemen (whose work particularly impressed him), he soon developed an eclectic landscape manner. Taken to Wilson's apartments by Joseph Wilton, Joseph Vernet (who was friendly with members of the British artistic colony there) 'expressed surprise that a landscape painter of such ability should have wasted time in painting portraits'. Wilton told this to Wilson 'who then became decided, and from that time confined himself to landscape only'. This was probably in 1752.

In 1754 Wilson was sketching the ruined antique Villa of Maecenas at Tivoli, where, according to Booth, he was 'in company with the Earls of Pembroke, Thanet, Essex and Ld Viscount Bolingbroke who [all] dined and spent the day together on the spot under a large tree'. Not only does Wilson appear to have been thought gentleman enough to socialize thus with aristocrats, he was also making useful connections: *Tivoli: Villa of Maecenas* (*c.* 1756–7; London, Tate) was probably a commission from Sackville Tufton, 8th Earl of Thanet; and for Henry Herbert, 9th Earl of Pembroke, Wilson later painted several views of his country house, Wilton, in Wiltshire. By now he was enjoying some success: he took pupils and he was patronized well by British visitors. In 1753 he painted views of *Rome from the Villa Madama* (New Haven, CT, Yale Cent. Brit. A.) and *Rome: St Peter's and the Vatican from the Janiculum* (London, Tate) for William Legge, 2nd Earl of Dartmouth, (1731–1801), for whom he produced 68 drawings (dispersed; see Ford) of Roman scenes in 1754. *Rome: St Peter's and the Vatican* is colder in hue and less atmospheric than many paintings of this period, but otherwise both of these views in oil are representative of Wilson's Roman work. They include extensive vistas with topographical content, foreground repoussoirs, tonal banding to indicate distance (reminiscent of the scheme deployed by Claude), and figures and ruined masonry or sculpture placed in the foreground.

This was an art in and with which Wilson showed himself to be as learned as his patrons. His representations of Italy allude to a fictive Arcadia in a manner associated with Claude, and to a lesser extent with Dughet. The ruins they and Wilson introduced into such pictures induced the beholder to contemplate a past that seemed peculiarly real to the Classically educated British aristocrat (see fig. 1).

1. Richard Wilson: *Tivoli: the Cascatelli Grandi and the Villa of Maecenas*, oil on canvas, 500×660 mm, 1752 (Dublin, National Gallery of Ireland)

As John Dyer wrote in *The Ruins of Rome* (1740), a poem typical of many on this theme, to perceive the remains of ancient grandeur against the fallen condition of modern Rome was to emphasize the necessity of exercising firm moral and social regulation. Otherwise, modern Britain risked being dragged down by luxury from what was widely agreed to have been a state of virtually unprecedented power and wealth. Wilson addressed those who were undertaking that programme of education which would fit them, as public figures, to exercise political power; his success in selling landscapes to them demonstrates how this learned vision was entirely in sympathy with the attitudes of those selected by him for his clientele.

2. ENGLAND AND WALES, *c.* 1757–82. Wilson probably left Italy in 1757, Farington recording that he said 'for what he had seen and what he had learned, as to expense he stood indemnified. He took from England eighty pounds, and brought back one hundred'. Wilson then established himself in London, taking pretentious apartments in the artists' quarter of Covent Garden, where he had a studio and exhibition room as well as rooms for his pupils; they paid 50 guineas for two years' tuition. With these trappings went real success: Hodges wrote that soon after returning Wilson 'attained the highest reputation'; he was among those who founded the Incorporated Society of Artists (1759), with which he exhibited some 36 pictures between 1760 and 1768. He gained a reputation for 'the classical turn of thinking in his works, and the broad, bold and manly execution of them; which, added to the classical figures he introduced into his landscapes, gave them an air more agreeable to the taste of the true connoisseurs and men of learning'.

In support of this is the fact that the *Destruction of the Children of Niobe* (*c.* 1759–60; New Haven, CT, Yale Cent. Brit. A.) was bought directly from exhibition at the Society of Artists in 1760 by William Augustus, Duke of Cumberland, brother of the late Frederick, Prince of Wales, and therefore a purchaser of the most exalted caste. A second version was bought by Francis Egerton, 3rd Duke of Bridgewater, a third by Joseph Wilton, and in 1761 William Woollett made a fine and very popular engraving after the composition. The *Niobe* is a learned, 'grand style' landscape. Similar examples include the *White Monk* (many versions, e.g. Toledo, OH, Mus. A.), *Solitude* (three versions, e.g. 1762; Swansea, Vivian A.G. & Mus.), which is based on a passage from James Thomson's poem *The Seasons* (1730), and *Celadon and Amelia* (*c.* 1765; untraced; see Constable, p. 165), also from Thomson, and which Woollett subsequently engraved. These were all subjects that Wilson would repeat on demand. Obviously popular, they successfully attempted to imbue landscape with elevated philosophic content. *Niobe*, set in a storm scene similar to those by Vernet, constitutes a lesson on the consequences of hubris; the attitudes of Wilson's figures are based on the *Niobe* group that he had seen in the gardens of the Villa Medici, Rome (Florence, Uffizi). In the *White Monk*, a 'classical' landscape, he concerned himself with the relation between harmony and disharmony in the natural world. Besides these, Wilson was replicating his Italian landscapes and painting British ones as well. Both types found a ready market. With their suggestive associationist imagery the former functioned as souvenirs; the latter catered more to the taste for topography. *Tabley House, Cheshire* (*c.* 1764–6; priv. col., see 1982 exh. cat., p. 231) was commissioned by Sir John

Fleming Leicester. The house is shown in the distance of a broad panorama, in the foreground of which stretches the lake, calm in the declining light, with a group of indolent figures, one angling, on its near bank. This format 'naturalizes' the house within its park, which had been landscaped in the style of Lancelot Brown and was thus largely non-productive, for the hallmark of the Brownian park was conspicuous wastage of land.

Wilson chose also to paint places in Wales and England notable for their historical associations: *Pembroke Town and Castle* (*c.* 1765–6; Cardiff, N. Mus.) is an elevated species of antiquarian illustration, while *Holt Bridge on the River Dee* (*c.* 1761–2; London, N.G.; see fig. 2) is composed in the manner of a classical landscape in which elevating qualities of the Claudean type are transferred to depictions of native British scenery. In 1769 Sir Watkin Williams-Wynn, the enormously rich Denbighshire magnate, commissioned two paintings from Wilson, the *View near Wynnstay* and *Castle of Dinas Bran from Llangollen* (both 1770–71; New Haven, CT, Yale Cent. Brit. A.). These pictures not only display the vast extent of Williams Wynn's land (he also owned the ancient Welsh fortress) but show members of the labouring poor (at rest in one, at work in the other); by referring to Claude and Dughet through his composition and handling of paint, Wilson further enforced certain perceptions in a particular way.

The beholder was encouraged to contemplate Williams Wynn's paternalistic benevolence (transmitted via the employed and contented figures) and understand the particular historical and cultural identity of Wales as a place of timeless Arcadian simplicity, maintained under his aegis.

Wilson's fortunes began declining soon after these pictures were completed, possibly because what he could provide was less in demand from his clientele but possibly also because of the rise of a new class of patrons unsympathetic to so socially exclusive an ideology. He moved to a series of increasingly mean apartments from 1772. As he was known to be impatient with connoisseurs and had, furthermore, become alcoholic his social attractiveness was not enhanced. The penury of his later years was eased by the Royal Academy, which made him its librarian, but by the time of his death his art was no longer the success it once had been. Possibly Reynolds, who in his 14th *Discourse* (1788) denigrated Wilson's landscapes, may have been instrumental in inculcating a taste less genuinely learned than Wilson's own had been. Yet Wilson's formal achievements in attaining effects of lustre and luminosity remain striking, as do also the grandeur and originality of his compositions. He was painting in a period of profound instability within British society, and his art was the result of an individual attempting to cater

2. Richard Wilson: *Holt Bridge on the River Dee*, oil on canvas, 1.48×1.93 m, *c.* 1761–2 (London, National Gallery)

for a particular market, which came no longer to share his aspirations.

UNPUBLISHED SOURCES

London, B. Ford priv. col. [Benjamin Booth papers]

BIBLIOGRAPHY

W. Hodges: 'An Account of Richard Wilson, Esquire, Landscape Painter, F.R.A.', *Eur. Mag. & London Rev.*, xvii (June 1790), pp. 402–5

J. Farington: *Diaries* (1793–1821); ed. K. Garlick and A. Mackintyre (i–vi) and K. Cave (vii–xvi) as *The Diaries of Joseph Farington*, 16 vols (New Haven and London, 1978–84)

B. Ford: *The Drawings of Richard Wilson* (London, 1951)

W. G. Constable: *Richard Wilson* (Cambridge, MA, 1953)

D. Sutton, ed.: *An Italian Sketchbook by Richard Wilson*, 2 vols (London, 1968)

D. H. Solkin: 'Some Variations by Richard Wilson on a Theme by Gaspard Dughet', *Burl. Mag.*, cxxiii (1981), pp. 410–14

Richard Wilson: The Landscape of Reaction (exh. cat. by D. H. Solkin, London, Tate, 1982)

D. H. Solkin: 'The Battle of the Ciceros: Richard Wilson and the Politics of Landscape in the Age of John Wilkes', *A. Hist.*, vi (1983), pp. 406–22

MICHAEL ROSENTHAL

Wilson, Richard (ii) (*b* London, 24 May 1953). English sculptor. He studied at the London College of Printing (1970–71) and the Hornsey College of Art (1971–4) and at Reading University (MFA, 1974–6). In 1983 Wilson joined with Paul Burwell and Anne Bean to form Bow Gamelan, an ensemble that staged sound and sculpture events in the UK and Europe. The use of free-form and percussion and spontaneous assemblage of found-objects influenced Wilson's later ambitious projects. These included *One Piece at a Time* (1987), a Television South West arts project, in which 1200 car parts were suspended by cords in the north tower of the Tyne Bridge at Newcastle upon Tyne, which fell in sequence over five weeks as the cords were cut mechanically; the noise of the crashing pieces was recorded and played back cumulatively each day. In 1987 Wilson created *20:50* (installed Matt's Gal., London, 1987; Saatchi Col., London, 1991): a field of sump oil filled the space, with a path at waist-height running through it; the space underwent perspective disjunction when reflected in the oil. For *Watertable* (installed Matt's Gal., 1994) Wilson excavated a hole large enough to take a billiard table down to floor level and bored a well through table and floor to reveal the water level that runs beneath the City of London.

BIBLIOGRAPHY

Richard Wilson: Sheer Fluke (exh. cat., text by W. T. Stearn; London, Matt's Gal., 1985)

Richard Wilson (exh. cat., London, Matt's Gal., 1989)

Richard Wilson (exh. cat., ed. F. Meschede; Berlin, daad gal., 1993) [Eng./Ger. text]

Wilson, Robert (*b* Waco, TX, 4 Oct 1941). American performance artist, writer, draughtsman, printmaker and stage designer. He studied painting in Paris under the American painter George McNeil (*b* 1908) in 1962, before completing a degree in interior design at the Pratt Institute in New York from 1962 to 1965. After serving an apprenticeship in architecture to Paolo Soleri in Phoenix, AZ, from 1965 to 1966, he returned to New York and began to work as a performance artist, creating a range of theatrical productions that combine music, text, dance and design. He earned his reputation with productions such as *Deafman Glance* (first staged in 1970 at the University Theater in Iowa City, IA) and *A Letter to Queen Victoria* (première at the Teatro Caio Melisso in Spoleto, Italy, and extensively toured in 1974); many of these were large-scale, marathon extravaganzas in which a series of images, formed from the conjunction of actors, dancers and set designs, unfolded to the accompaniment of music. Abandoning traditional theatrical elements such as ordered narrative content and the compression of real time, he favoured an avant-garde approach influenced by composers, choreographers and artists active in New York from the early 1960s.

Wilson drew from a wide range of influences and relied heavily on the collaboration of other individuals. The visual sophistication of his productions owed much to his training as a painter and interior designer; moreover, the charcoal drawings and lithographs that he produced in relation to his stage designs, which helped him finance his elaborate productions, were convincing as works of art in their own right, and the stylized furniture and other objects designed by him for the stage became increasingly sculptural in form. In Waco, he had studied under Byrd Hoffman, a ballet teacher who emphasized body awareness techniques. After moving to New York, Wilson taught Hoffman's methods to handicapped children, and his interest in working with brain-damaged and physically disabled children evolved into collaborative relationships later in his career, notably in *Deafman Glance*.

One of Wilson's most admired works, *Einstein on the Beach* (première at the Festival d'Avignon in July 1976 and subsequently performed throughout Europe and at the Metropolitan Opera House in New York), was a collaboration with the composer Philip Glass, and was structured as an opera in four acts. It is regarded as a culmination of Minimalism in music and as an important event in the evolution of American theatre. While it referred to the physicist Albert Einstein as a point of departure, it made use of his biography only as an inspiration for recurrent images such as a train, a trial scene and a spaceship. There was no logical narrative content, only images, music and texts divided into segments ordered by a simple mathematical scheme. Some of the text and the organizing language of numbers was provided by Christopher Knowles, a brain-damaged young man once diagnosed as autistic, with whom Wilson often collaborated.

The CIVIL warS, conceived by Wilson as his most ambitious project, was originally intended for presentation at the 1984 Olympic Arts Festival in Los Angeles. It was conceived as a 12-hour-long opera that would draw its performers from all over the world, echoing the structure of the Olympic Games and creating a communal atmosphere more generally associated with festivals of rock music. While drawing much of his source material from 19th-century American cultural history (particularly pertaining to the American Civil War of 1861–5), he also included anachronistic references to Henry IV, submarines and spaceships. Various segments of the opera were performed in European cities, but the work as a whole was not produced in Los Angeles as planned because sufficient funding could not be raised. The grandeur of Wilson's visions and the extravagance of his productions were consistently better received in Europe than in the USA.

BIBLIOGRAPHY
F. Quadri: *Il teatro di Robert Wilson* (Venice, 1976)
Civil Wars, Drawings, Models and Representations (exh. cat. by A. Bellol, Los Angeles, CA, Parsons School Des., 1984)
S. Brecht: *The Theatre of Visions: Robert Wilson* (Frankfurt am Main, 1978)
J. Rockwell and others: *Robert Wilson: The Theater of Images* (New York, 1984)
Parkett, 16 (1988), pp. 28–131 [special issue]
L. Shyer: *Robert Wilson and his Collaborators* (New York, 1989)
Robert Wilson's Vision (exh. cat., Boston, MA, Mus. F.A., 1991)
PATTI STUCKLER

Wilson, W(illiam) Hardy (*b* South Creek, NSW, 14 Feb 1881; *d* Richmond, Victoria, 16 Dec 1955). Australian architect and writer. He was articled (1899–1904) to Sydney architects Kent & Buden and attended evening classes at Syndey Technical College, where he was President of the Architectural Students Society, graduating in 1904; his student exercises favoured Art Nouveau. He then undertook further study and travel in England, Europe and North America (1905–10) that introduced him to the Georgian Revival, led by Edwin Lutyens in England, and the Colonial and Roman Revivals, promoted by McKim, Mead & White in the USA. Seeking a new architecture free of all Victorian trappings, Wilson was convinced by his overseas studies of the relevance to the Australian climate of Mediterranean arcades, shuttered openings and garden schemes. On his return to Sydney in 1910, he spent some months drawing the surviving examples of late Georgian architecture in Australia; these studies, which were published in 1924 as *Old Colonial Architecture in New South Wales and Tasmania*, revealed his skills as a draughtsman and colourist, and influenced much of his architectural work thereafter when he became the acknowledged leader of the Colonial Revival in Australia. In 1911 he went into practice in Sydney with his friend Stacey Arthur Neave (1883–1941) and designed a series of relatively modest neo-Georgian cottages, whose highly ordered façades stood out strongly in streets of houses heavily decorated with curvaceous Federation style fretwork. His finest early commission was Eryldene (1913–

14) at Gordon, Sydney; its colonnaded north-facing verandah flanked by pavilions was derived in general form from the colonial bungalow Horsley (*c.* 1832) at Horsley Park, Sydney. His own house, Purulia (1916) at Wahroonga, Sydney, is very simple: Georgian sash windows flanked by shutters are set in plain rendered walls topped by a hipped roof of irregular clay shingles. The plan, designed for a family without servants, has a simple arrangement of rooms about the kitchen, a novel concept for its time. Another similar work is Macquarie Cottage (1921) at Pymble, Sydney. Whenever possible Wilson also designed the garden, using simple axes and pergolas in conjunction with plants favoured in the early 19th century. His major urban work, Peapes Department Store (1922–3) in central Sydney, is a grander version of a Georgian shop, originally with interiors featuring handsome timber panelling and circular top-lit galleries. Wilson was interested in developing new forms of colonial architecture and a trip to China in 1922 made him aware of the potential of a fusion of classical and oriental styles, seen, for instance, in his tennis pavilion (1924) at Eryldene with Chinese style vermilion and gold columns and curved roof. In 1927 Wilson retired from practice but his partners, S. A. Neave and John L. Berry (*fl c.* 1918–*c.* 1931), continued to build excellent neo-Georgian buildings into the 1930s.

WRITINGS
Old Colonial Architecture in New South Wales and Tasmania (Sydney, 1924)
BIBLIOGRAPHY
C. Pearl: *Hardy Wilson and his Old Colonial Architecture* (Sydney, 1970)
C. Simpson, H. Tanner and others: *William Hardy Wilson: A 20th Century Colonial, 1881–1955* (Sydney, 1980)
HOWARD TANNER

Wilton. English town in Wiltshire. It was the capital of ancient Wessex and the residence and burial place of Saxon kings. A nuns' church was founded there in the 8th century; later destroyed by Danish invaders and rebuilt by Alfred, King of Wessex, it became particularly famous in the 12th and 13th centuries. Little remains of the many medieval parish churches: the town declined in the 14th

1. Wilton House, south front, begun by Isaac de Caus, 1636; altered and completed by John Webb (i), *c.* 1648–51

century with the increasing importance of nearby Salisbury. At the Dissolution of the Monasteries, Wilton Abbey became a country mansion (*see* §1 below). The Wilton Royal Carpet Factory was established in the 18th century and became famous for the production of Axminster and Wilton carpets (*see* §2 below). The parish church of SS Mary and Nicholas was built in 1841–5 by Thomas Henry Wyatt in an Italianate Romanesque style. The building incorporates pieces of genuine Cosmati mosaic work, including parts of the Shrine of Capoccio (1256), acquired in 1768 by Sir William Hamilton (i) from S Maria Maggiore in Rome.

1. WILTON HOUSE. The former Wilton Abbey buildings were granted after the Dissolution of the Monasteries to Sir William Herbert, later 1st Earl of Pembroke (*d* 1570). Work on this quadrangular house and its associated garden was begun by Isaac de Caus for Philip Herbert, 4th Earl of Pembroke, in the 1630s and continued, after a fire in 1647, into the early 1650s, with contributions from Inigo Jones and John Webb (i).

(i) House. The genesis of the 1630s design is well known. John Aubrey related that Charles I 'did put Philip. . .Earle of Pembroke upon making this magnificent garden and grotto, and to new build that side of the house that fronts the garden with two stately pavilions at each end, all *al Italiano*'. The King had recommended Jones, his Surveyor of the Works, as architect, but Jones's involvement appears to have been confined to overseeing at a distance, nominating and then advising the executant architect Isaac de Caus (*see* CAUS, DE, (2)), and approving the designs for ceilings and doors, which were made by Webb. Following the 1647 fire, which gutted the new south side staterooms, Webb was in sole charge of their reinstatement. It is this south front (see fig. 1) and these staterooms that have come to be regarded as pre-eminent examples of English Palladianism.

De Caus's work on the house began in 1636 with the taking down of the old south range, before a new grand front, nearly 130 m long, was begun in alignment with the central avenue of the garden (see below). After it had been started, this scheme (drawing in Oxford, Worcester Coll. Lib.) was drastically reduced, perhaps as a result of the 4th Earl's financial difficulties, its place being taken by the curtailed version that substantially survives. In effect the revision involved taking half of the grand design, omitting the central portico and adding the two stately pavilion towers, perhaps derived from Vincenzo Scamozzi's *Idea dell'architettura universale* (1615). These, Wilton's most distinctive and emulated features, were an afterthought dictated not only by the need to provide vertical emphasis to the façade but also by the need to harmonize with the older Tudor towers on the north side of the house.

The 1630s plan was maintained by Webb in his post-fire redecoration of the staterooms. The most complete survivals from this period, the Double Cube (see fig. 2) and Single Cube Rooms, are distinguished by deeply coved, painted ceilings, richly carved swags and garlands set on to the wall panelling and Francophile chimney-pieces, designed by Webb after the engravings of Jean Barbet (*fl* 1635–53). Other rooms in this wing retain their Webb

2. Wilton House, the Double Cube room by John Webb (i), *c.* 1647, maintaining the original plan of Isaac de Caus

chimney-pieces, but redecoration in 1735–9 by Andien de Clermont (*d* 1783) and remodelling by James Wyatt in the early 19th century have altered their original appearance and arrangement.

A fire in the north range in 1705 prompted the rebuilding that was recorded by Colen Campbell, but all traces of this work, and the later 18th-century work in the west range by William Chambers, were obliterated during Wyatt's building campaign. His provision of corridors ('cloisters') around all four sides of the internal courtyard made necessary improvements to the convenience of Wilton, providing independent internal access to all rooms on the ground and principal floors; but his other alterations, prompted by a romantic pursuit of the house's monastic origins, were less defensible.

Wyatt's failure to plan in advance and to supervise the works caused innumerable problems and unnecessary expense. The losses of the older work, in the north and west ranges especially, appear to have been considerable. Yet, although the original house has not survived intact, enough remains to demonstrate how it came to be the archetype of many of the great houses of the 18th century. The two greatest neo-Palladian houses, Holkham Hall (1734–65, by Kent, Burlington and Brettingham) and Houghton Hall (1722–35, by Campbell), both Norfolk, were indebted to it for their massing, and it continued to provide a rich source of Palladian details until beyond the mid-18th century.

(ii) Garden. The laying out of the formal gardens at Wilton was begun by Isaac de Caus in 1632. The original scheme

is recorded in two elevated prospect drawings (Oxford, Worcester Coll. Lib.), which show it aligned with the proposed new south front. The gardens were commented upon first by Lt. Hammond, who was given a guided tour in 1635 by the architect himself. Along with statues and other features Hammond was shown a 'rare Water-worke now making, and contriuing by this outlandish Engineer, for the Singing, and Chirping of Birdes, and other strange rarities, onely by that Element'. The de Caus grotto and gardens survived to be seen by Celia Fiennes c. 1685, but replanting and rearrangement were in progress soon after.

The gardens were landscaped in the later 1730s by Henry Herbert, 9th Earl of Pembroke, who dammed the River Nadder to create a lake. This 'natural' landscape, ornamented by the Palladian Bridge (1737), which was designed by the Earl himself in collaboration with Roger Morris, is recorded in the views (1758–60; Wilton House, Wilts) painted by Richard Wilson (i) for Henry Herbert, 10th Earl of Pembroke (1734–94).

BIBLIOGRAPHY

Lt. Hammond: *A Relation of a Short Survey of the Western Counties: Made by a Lieutenant of the Military Company in Norwich in 1635* (MS. 1635); ed. L. G. Wickham Legg, Camden Miscellany, 3rd ser., xvi (London, 1936)
I. de Caus: *Wilton Garden* ([London, 1654]/R London, 1982)
J. Aubrey: *The Natural History of Wiltshire* (MS. c. 1685); ed. J. Britton (London, 1847), p. 83
C. Campbell: *Vitruvius Britannicus*, ii (1717), pls 61–2
C. Morris, ed.: *The Journeys of Celia Fiennes* (London, 1947, rev. 1949), pp. 9–10
A. A. Tait: 'Isaac de Caus and the South Front of Wilton House', *Burl. Mag.*, cvi (1964), p. 74
Sidney [Herbert], 16th Earl of Pembroke: *A Catalogue of the Paintings and Drawings in the Collection at Wilton House* (London, 1968)
J. Harris and A. A. Tait: *Catalogue of the Drawings by Inigo Jones, John Webb and Isaac de Caus at Worcester College, Oxford* (Oxford, 1979)
R. Strong: *The Renaissance Garden in England* (London, 1979)
G. Popper and J. Reeves: 'The South Front of Wilton House', *Burl. Mag.*, cxxiv (1982), pp. 358–61
J. Bold with J. Reeves: *Wilton House and English Palladianism* (London, 1988)
J. Bold: *John Webb* (Oxford, 1989), pp. 57–69, 174
J. Heward: 'The Restoration of the South Front of Wilton House: The Development of the House Reconsidered', *Archit. Hist.*, xxxv (1992), pp. 78–117

JOHN BOLD

2. CENTRE OF CARPET PRODUCTION. Pile strip carpets were available in England before their manufacture at Wilton, but the patent taken out on 18 July 1741 for the weaving of Brussels carpets was in the names of two Wilton men, John Barford, an upholsterer, and William Moody, a clothier, and a London merchant, Ignatius Couran. Within a few years the Brussels carpet technique had been refined so that it was possible to produce a second type of carpet, known as a Wilton carpet, that had a velvet-like pile made by cutting the loops of the Brussels carpet (see CARPET, fig. 4). It was not long before both techniques were adopted by weavers in KIDDERMINSTER, and for the rest of the century the two towns were in close competition. Carpet production at Wilton was dependent on outwork weavers working in their own homes, a system that continued into the 19th century. In 1836 a Mr Blackmore, owner of the main Wilton factory, bought and transferred to Wilton the looms and stock of the factory at AXMINSTER and so introduced the production of hand-knotted carpets at Wilton. His enterprise was extremely

successful, winning acclaim at the Great Exhibition of 1851 in London and receiving many royal commissions. Wilton became the manufacturing centre of fine-quality floor coverings, producing both hand-knotted and machine-woven carpets. Its reputation continued into the 20th century with the Wilton Royal Carpet Factory having the foresight and enterprise to extend its production to include designs suited to modern interiors. The manufacture of hand-knotted carpets, however, ceased in 1957.

BIBLIOGRAPHY

A. F. Kendrick and C. E. C. Tattersall: *Handwoven Carpets: Oriental and European* (London, 1926)
C. E. C. Tattersall and S. Reed: *British Carpets* (London, 1966)
B. Jacobs: *Axminster Carpets* (Leigh-on-Sea, 1969)
C. Gilbert, J. Lomax and A. Wells-Cole: *Country House Floors, 1660–1850*, Temple Newsam Country House Stud., iii (Leeds, 1987)

JENNIFER WEARDEN

Wilton, Joseph (*b* London, 16 July 1722; *d* London, 25 Nov 1803). English sculptor. He was the son of William Wilton (*d* 1768), a plasterer who ran an extremely profitable factory making papier-mâché ornaments. He trained with Laurent Delvaux at Nivelles in Flanders and from 1744 under Jean-Baptiste Pigalle in Paris. In 1747 he travelled to Italy; three years later in Rome he was awarded the Jubilee gold medal by Benedict XIV. By 1751 he was in Florence, where he began to gain a considerable reputation for his copies of antique sculpture. The bald, undraped marble portrait of *Dr Antonio Cocchi* (1755; London, V&A) is the only surviving bust from life produced by Wilton during this Italian period. In 1755 he returned to England accompanied by the architect William Chambers, the sculptor G. B. Capezzuoli (*fl* 1755–82) and the painter Giovanni Battista Cipriani. Initially he set up his workshop at his father's house in Charing Cross, London. His bust of *Philip Stanhope, 4th Earl of Chesterfield* (1757; London, BM) reveals the continuing influence of antique sculpture and the bold yet sensitive modelling of the features, which he probably learnt from Pigalle. In 1757 he married Frances Lucas, and within a year their first child was born. In 1758 he and Cipriani were appointed directors of the Richmond House Gallery, a collection of antique casts at Richmond House, London, owned by Charles Lennox, 3rd Duke of Richmond and Lennox (see LENNOX, (2)). The casts had been chosen by Wilton during his stay in Italy, and the collection included at least two marble copies by him, the *Apollo Belvedere* and the Medici *Faun* (both untraced).

Wilton worked in close association with Chambers and Robert Adam, producing chimney-pieces and decorative sculpture. A portrait of Wilton with his wife and daughter (*c.* 1760; London, V&A), attributed to Francis Hayman, shows him working on a modello for one of a pair of telamonic chimney-pieces for Northumberland House (now London, V&A, and Syon House). These were derived from the Farnese *Captives* (Naples, Mus. Archeol. N.), then in the Palazzo Farnese, Rome. Although the execution of this work was undertaken by Benjamin Carter (*d* 1766), Wilton probably supplied the marble, for he had considerable dealings with Carrara marble merchants.

In 1760 Wilton was appointed Carver of State Coaches to George III; he immediately began collaboration with Chambers, Capezzuoli and Cipriani on a new state coach

(London, Buckingham Pal., Royal Col.). Completed in 1762, it was built in the large workshops that Wilton set up opposite London's Marylebone Fields. In 1761 he was appointed Statuary to His Majesty; as a result he obtained commissions for a statue of *George III* (1764; untraced) for the Royal Exchange and an equestrian statue of that monarch for Berkeley Square, London. This was executed in lead under Wilton's supervision, but by 1812 it was collapsing under its own weight and had to be dismantled.

In 1760 Wilton had also won the commission for a monument to *General James Wolfe* (1772; London, Westminster Abbey; see fig.) in competition with Adam, Chambers, Louis-François Roubiliac, John Michael Rysbrack and Henry Cheere. By 1765 the finished model was in Wilton's workshop, and the monument was set up seven years later. It was largely the work of assistants, with Nathaniel Smith (*c.* 1741–1800) sculpting some of the figures and Capezzuoli making the bronze relief that depicts the taking of Quebec in 1759. The nude figure of Wolfe displays Wilton's mastery of anatomy, and the surrounding soldiers are represented in contemporary dress, as Benjamin West was also to show them in his

Joseph Wilton: *General James Wolfe*, marble, 1772 (London, Westminster Abbey)

painting of the *Death of General Wolfe* (1771; Ottawa, N.G.). However, Wilton's statue of Wolfe was later unfavourably compared in the *Gentleman's Magazine* (1783) with Roubiliac's unexecuted model: 'the one tells the story like a genius, the other like a newswriter'. Wilton's later monuments include that to *Wriothesley Russell, 2nd Duke of Bedford* (Chenies Manor, Bucks), erected in 1769 to Chambers's designs. This work, in which the Apollo-like Wriothesley is attended by his kneeling duchess, is Neo-classical in style and strongly contrasts with the monument to *Archbishop Tillotson* (Sowerby, W. Yorks), commissioned by George Stanfield and completed in 1796. The full-length figure of Tillotson stands in a niche with one hand outstretched, and deeply undercut draperies display a Baroque vitality rare in Wilton's work. As Whinney noted, despite receiving better training than any other English sculptor working in the 18th century, Wilton seemed unable to resolve the conflicting choices of style available to him, his work hesitating between a progressive Neo-classicism and the late Baroque style of the previous age.

Wilton was a competent draughtsman, and a number of drawings from his Italian period and designs for his later monuments survive, such as that (London, priv. col.) of the figure of Charity from Bernini's tomb of *Alexander VII* (1671–8) in St Peter's, Rome. He usually worked up his initial ideas into a model and then translated the result into marble. The preparatory terracotta and finished marble bust of *Oliver Cromwell* (both 1762; London, V&A) provide an instructive example of the skill with which Wilton could carry through an initial design. Much of the execution of his larger works was carried out by assistants.

In 1768 Wilton had inherited a considerable fortune from his father, and, although he became a founder-member of the Royal Academy that year, this new-found wealth resulted in his increasing lack of interest in continuing to work as a sculptor. Instead he cultivated social success. J. T. Smith recorded Wilton's extravagant way of life in the 1780s, but by 1786 his extensive properties had to be auctioned. His continued excesses resulted in bankruptcy in 1793. Three years after he was appointed Keeper of the Royal Academy, a position he retained until his death.

BIBLIOGRAPHY

Gunnis

J. T. Smith: *Nollekens and his Times*, ii (London, 1829)

A. Cunningham: *The Lives of the Most Eminent British Painters, Sculptors and Architects*, iii (London, 1830)

J. Pye: *The Patronage of British Art* (London, 1845)

H. Honour: 'English Patrons and Italian Sculptors', *Connoisseur*, cxli (1958), pp. 224–6

M. Whinney: *Sculpture in Britain, 1530–1830*, Pelican Hist. A. (Harmondsworth, 1963, rev. 2/1988)

T. Hodgkinson: 'Joseph Wilton and Doctor Cocchi', *V&A Mus. Bull.*, iii (1967), pp. 73–80

J. Physick: *Designs for English Sculpture, 1680–1860* (London, 1969)

M. Whinney: *English Sculpture, 1720–1830* (London, 1971)

B. Allen: 'Joseph Wilton, Francis Hayman and the Chimneypieces from Northumberland House', *Burl. Mag.*, cxxv (1983), pp. 195–202

TESSA MURDOCH

Wimar, Charles [Carl; Karl] **(Ferdinand)** (*b* Siegburg, nr Bonn, 19 Feb 1828; *d* St Louis, MO, 28 Nov 1862). American painter and photographer of German birth. He arrived in St Louis in 1843. From 1846 to 1850 he studied painting under the St Louis artist Leon de Pomarede (1807–92). In 1852 he continued his studies at the Kunst-akademie in Düsseldorf, where he worked with Josef Fay (1813–75) and Emanuel Gottlieb Leutze until about 1856. In 1858, having once more based himself in St Louis, he travelled up the Mississippi in order to draw and photograph Indians. Wimar joined a party of the American Fur Trading Company and made several journeys between 1858 and 1860 up the Mississippi, Missouri and Yellowstone rivers in search of Indian subjects. His painting, the *Buffalo Hunt* (1860; St Louis, MO, Washington U., Gal. A.), became one of the original works in the collection of the Western Academy of Art. In 1861 Wimar was commissioned to decorate the rotunda of the St Louis Courthouse with scenes of the settlement of the West (mostly destr.).

Among Wimar's favourite subjects, even while working in Germany, were scenes of Indians at war and hunting buffalo. He depicted them with vigour and energy, adapting the linear Düsseldorf figural style to active poses (e.g. *Indians Pursued by American Dragoons*, 1853; St Louis, MO, Mon. Club). In later works he softened his technique yet continued his scrupulous concern for accurate details of costume and gesture (e.g. *Indians Approaching Fort Benton*, 1859; St Louis, MO, Washington U., Gal. A.).

BIBLIOGRAPHY

Charles Wimar: Painter of the Indian Frontier, 1828–1862 (exh. cat. by P. T. Rathbone, St Louis, MO, A. Mus., 1946)

A. Englaender: 'Karl Friedrich Wimar, der Indianermaler aus Siegburg', *Heimatbl. Siegkreises*, xxi/67 (1953), pp. 62–4

——: 'Der Indianermaler Wimar in Heidelberg', *Heidelberg. Fremdenbl.* (1960–61), pp. 2–4

America through the Eyes of German Immigrant Painters (exh. cat., ed. A. Harding; Boston, MA, Goethe Inst., 1975)

The Hudson and the Rhine: Die amerikanische Malerkolonie in Düsseldorf im 19. Jahrhundert (exh. cat. by W. von Kalnein, R. Andree and U. Ricke-Immel, Düsseldorf, Kstmus.; Bielefeld, Städt. Ksthalle; 1976)

LESLIE HEINER

Wimmel, Carl Ludwig (*b* Berlin, 12 Jan 1786; *d* Hamburg, 16 Feb 1845). Prussian architect. He was the son of the master mason Johann Heinrich Wimmel (1749–1818), who worked with such architects as Carl Gotthard Langhans and David Gilly. Wimmel first trained as a carpenter (1802–5) but then went on to study architecture under Langhans. Around 1807 he left Berlin for Hamburg, studying there under Christian Friedrich Lange (1768–1833) until 1809. With the help of Lange and a charitable trust, the Hamburgische Gesellschaft zur Beförderung der Künste und Nützlichen Gewerbe, Wimmel spent four years travelling, studying in Karlsruhe under Friedrich Weinbrenner and then visiting Paris and Italy. Wimmel returned to Hamburg in 1814 and joined the city building department. He prepared his first city plan in 1816 and became Director of Building in 1818. His early designs in Hamburg include the modest St Paulikirche (1819–20) and the English Reformed Church (1825–6; destr.); his municipal theatre (1826–7; destr.) and the terraced houses on the Esplanade (1827–30) were in a simple, late Neoclassical style. With Franz Forsmann (1795–1878) he designed the Johanneum (1836–9; destr.), a large educational complex (for illustration *see* RUNDBOGENSTIL), and the Börse (1837–41), both in Hamburg and both using the *Rundbogenstil*. In 1841 he toured extensively in Great Britain as a member of a Prussian delegation studying model prisons and asylums. His subsequent design for a prison in Hamburg (1841–2; unexecuted), in a castellated style, had a cruciform plan, a radical departure from conventional German prison lay-outs.

BIBLIOGRAPHY

Thieme–Becker

E. Hannmann: *Carl Ludwig Wimmel, 1786–1845*, Studien zur Kunst des 19. Jahrhunderts, xxxiii (Munich, 1975)

D. Watkin and T. Mellinghoff: *German Architecture and the Classical Ideal, 1740–1840* (London, 1987)

☐

Wimmer, Dezső. *See* CZIGÁNY, DEZSŐ.

Wimmer, Hans (*b* Pfarrkirchen, Lower Bavaria, 19 March 1907). German sculptor. When he was 17 he made ten illustrations for the ninth canto of Homer's *Odyssey*, which demonstrated his early artistic ability; he developed his talent after school in Hermann Kroeber's drawing class. His interest in ancient Greece, its art and its myths, which appeared first in the illustrations, remained in his later work. From 1928 to 1936 he studied intermittently with the sculptor Bernhard Bleeker (*b* 1881) at the Akademie der Bildenden Künste in Munich. The style of his early work can be seen as a Baroque-inclined deviation from Adolf von Hildebrand's traditional classical realism.

On travels through Europe, which Wimmer undertook after his studies, Aristide Maillol, Charles Despiau, Ernst Barlach and Wilhelm Lehmbruck became major stimuli for his work. In 1939, during a stay in Rome at the Villa Massimo, he was introduced to Western archaeology by his friend Ludwig Curtius. It was not, however, until after World War II that Wimmer was able to bring together these diverse influences. Modesty, humility and suffering, which characterized the expression of his portraits, figures and depictions of animals after 1945, can be understood as a translation of his psychological experiences of the war. The earliest post-war portrait *Ernst Buschor* (bronze, h. 340 mm, 1946; Munich, Staatsgal. Mod. Kst) no longer shows the expansive life-force of the earlier works but rather embodies the physiognomy of the current spirit of the age in Germany. Despite the many portraits that Wimmer made *Buschor* remained his favourite. By his own account, it was the beauty rather than the specific character of an object that he sought to represent. In accordance with this his sculptures are formed more strictly in terms of architectural and stereometrical principles of construction after 1945, following a basic symmetrical pattern. The archaic simplicity of the form, seen, for example, in the life-size *Kneeling Boy* (bronze, 1953–4) at the Platz vor der eidgenössischen Zentralbibliothek, Berne, goes hand in hand with the expression of an ascetic inner attitude. For Wimmer, this understanding of the relation between outer appearance and inner being was programmatic. In his book *Über die Bildhauerei* (1961) he asked, 'Does not the outer form express the spirit?' The book also reveals to what extent Wimmer was concerned with the balance between timeless stylization and lifelike naturalism, while he characterizes the simplicity of a work of art not as childlike naivety but rather the result of an awareness of the variety and richness of detail. The connection between reticently sensory experiences on the one hand with classical sources of sculpture on the other represents a declaration of the artist's dedication to the regularity and meaningfulness of nature. It is also, therefore, a protest against the deforming tendencies of contemporary art. In this respect one can also understand the process, begun in the mid-1960s, of abandoning the increasingly formal simplicity, which had been present up until then. This makes figures such as *Aglaia* (bronze, h. 1.7 m, 1969; Bielefeld, Städt. Ksthalle) more rounded, open and lively. The *Four Elements* (1976), the bronze doors of the Lampe banking-house in Bielefeld, combine this stylistic development with the artist's favourite subjects including horses or reclining figures in exemplary form.

BIBLIOGRAPHY

H. K. Röthel: *Der Bildhauer Hans Wimmer* (Munich, 1964)

Hans Wimmer: Das grosse Pferd: Bildwerke und Handzeichnungen (exh. cat., Bremen, Ksthalle, 1967)

Hans Wimmer: Zeichnungen und kleine Plastiken (exh. cat., Mannheim, Städt. Ksthalle, 1969)

U. Weisner: *'Die vier Elemente': Die Bronzetür von Hans Wimmer an der Lampe Bank am Alten Markt in Bielefeld: Herrn Rudolf August Oetker zum 60. Geburtstag, 20. September 1976* (Bielefeld, 1976)

BEATRICE V. BISMARCK

Winchester [Lat. Venta Belgarum; Old Eng. Wintanceaster]. English cathedral city and county town of Hampshire. It was the principal royal city ('capital') of Late Saxon and Early Norman England (late 9th century–early 12th).

I. History and urban development. II. Centre of manuscript production. III. Cathedral.

I. History and urban development.

1. Before 1066. 2. 1066–1538. 3. After 1538.

1. BEFORE 1066. Winchester lies on the west bank of the River Itchen, 20 km from Southampton Water, at its intersection with an ancient east–west downland route. The region was settled before 1000 BC. A settlement now known as Oram's Arbour was established to control the river crossing and surrounded by a bank and ditch *c.* 100 BC; there is no evidence of settlement beyond the end of the 1st century BC. The defences of the Roman town, founded between AD 70 and AD 80, overlapped the eastern half of Oram's Arbour and the position of the gateways established the city's framework for the next two millennia. By at least AD 100 there was a regular grid plan, laid out to follow islands of relatively higher ground in the valley floor, and sophisticated side-street drainage systems. A large stone building (*c.* AD 100) in the central *insula* may have been the forum and basilica. The earliest houses were of timber, with glazed windows, painted walls and tessellated floors, including black-and-white mosaics; most were rebuilt from the mid-2nd century AD in flint, or on flint ground walls. The defences were remodelled *c.* AD 200 to enclose an area of 58.2 ha, making it the fifth largest city in Roman Britain. The whole circuit was given a stone wall in the early 3rd century; this remained the core of the city wall throughout the Middle Ages. There was increased industrial activity, including weaving, during the second half of the 4th century and external bastions were added to the walls, suggesting that it was a defended administrative base and supply centre.

The population declined rapidly after *c.* AD 400, and there is little evidence for any activity during the next 250 years, although Germanic pottery in the latest Roman layers shows the presence of Anglo-Saxon elements by the 5th century AD. It would appear, however, that it continued to act as a centre of authority, with a royal residence for the kings of Wessex perhaps dating from the immediate post-Roman period and located next to the forum. The church founded *c.* 648 by Cenwalh, King of Wessex (*reg* 643–72), was probably intended as a 'palace chapel' (later Old Minster; *see* §III, 1(i) below). Whereas trade and industry in Middle Saxon Wessex were concentrated downstream on the Solent at Hamwic (founded 8th century; now Southampton), Winchester became the ceremonial and administrative centre, with a postulated royal residence, a cathedral church (from 660) and its community, and an unknown number of smaller, enclosed, private estates (one of which has been excavated at Lower Brook Street) belonging to those of high social rank. The south gate was blocked (and probably the north gate as well) and all traffic diverted between the Roman west and east gates. Here a hollow-way, up to 50 m in width, was worn into the hill on a line later to become High Street, probably so that tolls could be collected on goods entering and leaving the walled area. Although there seems to have been little commercial activity within the walls, some service trades probably operated towards the east in the area known by 902–3 as 'Cæpstræt' ('market street'; now Broadway), where evidence for intensive iron-working has been found; this street may also have served for periodic markets and fairs. The rest of the former city seems to have lain open. The Roman streets were lost: buildings were constructed over them and an early route from the cathedral meandered east across the Roman pattern to pass through the walls at a possible gate at the north east angle of the enclosure later known as Wolvesey (see below). Large areas were given over to meadows and cultivation.

During the mid-9th century this open structure changed decisively. Occupation seems to have begun on some scale outside the walls in the area of the later western suburb, with burials made in a new cemetery just inside the walls to the west of the later Staple Gardens. In 859, according to a poem (*c.* 970–80; London, BL, MS. Reg. 15, C.vii) by Wulfstan the Cantor, Bishop Swithun (*reg c.* 852–62) built a bridge over the Itchen outside Eastgate, on the line of the main thoroughfare. The Roman defences were refurbished in the second half of the 9th century, perhaps as early as the reign of Ethelbald, King of Wessex (*reg* 855–60), and possibly at the same time as Swithun's work on the bridge, as an account of the Viking attack on the city in 860 suggests that there were walls to be breached.

The extent of the damage caused by the Vikings is not known, but during the next two decades a rectilinear network of streets was laid out within the walls using a module of 4 rods or poles (20.12 m). These streets ran for 8.63 km and required 8000 tonnes of flint cobbles. They were laid out on either side of High Street, parallel to which back streets provided rear access. A regular system of parallel north–south streets lay at right angles to High Street, and their outer ends were linked by a wall-street running right round the city inside the defences. This plan allowed rapid deployment of defensive forces to any threatened part of the perimeter. A force capable of manning defences more than 3 km in length could be secured only by organizing and apportioning the land inside the walls for permanent settlement on a secure economic basis. This was achieved by the *insulae* of the new street system, which filled the whole available space of 58.2 ha within the walls, a clear indication of its creators' urban expectations. In its newly planned form Winchester was the largest urban centre in England at this date, but whether it was created by Alfred the Great in the 880s or by one of his elder brothers remains unclear. It provided the model for Alfred's other urban *burhs* in Wessex and for the newly founded defensive towns on which the unity of the English state was based during the reconquest of the Danelaw by Edward the Elder (*reg* 899–925) and Athelstan (*reg* 924/5–939). In Winchester the Anglo-Saxon street layout survives almost unchanged, framed by defences and the sites of gates inherited from the Roman period.

During the 10th and 11th centuries the street frontages were gradually built up, especially along High Street, where the first survey in the Winton Domesday (*c.* 1110; London, Soc. Antiqua., MS. 154) reveals a pattern of property ownership and occupation already ancient and complex. Extensive suburbs grew up along all the approach roads, especially to the west and north, until the city far exceeded its Roman size. Inside the walls the principal changes took place in the south-east quarter. From *c.* 900, and especially after *c.* 964, the 9th-century street network was obscured by the foundation of religious houses and the later expansion of their precincts. By 1000 the three monasteries (Old Minster, New Minster and Nunnaminster) and two palaces covered a quarter of the walled city. Together they formed the principal royal and ecclesiastical centre of the Late Saxon kingdom, the forerunner of Westminster and the basis for the later, anachronistic claim that Winchester was once the 'capital' of England. These buildings and their precincts have left their mark in the open spaces and large enclosed gardens, for example Abbey Gardens, that still characterize the area to the exclusion of all commercial activity.

Old Minster survived, much rebuilt and extended (*see* §III, 1(i) below). New Minster (901–3) was built immediately to the north of Old Minster; its vast basilican plan, the largest in England at the time, suggests that its prime purpose was to serve as the borough church of the refounded town, although it was also to be the burial-church of Alfred and his family. The proximity of New Minster and Old Minster was a constant source of friction for nearly two centuries, as the sound of their bells and singers clashed. Nunnaminster was a house for women, founded before 902–3 by Alfred's widow Ealhswith (*d* ?905) on her estate on the south side of Cæpstræt, just inside Eastgate. It survived as St Mary's Abbey until its dissolution in 1539. Like Nunnaminster, the bishop's palace at Wolvesey probably began as a private enclosure ('Wulf's island') on higher ground on the valley floor. However, sometime before 975–9 Bishop Aethelwold appears to have acquired the property to create a private residence for the bishop removed from the seclusion of the monasteries, all three of which he had reformed during the previous decade. By 1000 the residence included a hall, the bishop's chamber and perhaps a prison.

The buildings of this quarter were the setting for a great outburst of artistic and intellectual activity. The artists of the Winchester school (*see* §II below) drew and painted manuscripts and walls, cast bells, carved stone and ivory, worked glass and clay, for the adornment of churches and shrines, the person and the home. Masons, sculptors and carpenters built on a scale, and with an eclectic inspiration, never before attained in England. Music sounded throughout these buildings, while Latin and English prose and verse was written that could be elaborate, artistic and full of Classical allusion, or simple and unadorned.

2. 1066–1538. Winchester surrendered to the Normans in November 1066 without a struggle. Early in 1067 an earthwork castle was built on the highest point within the walls, occupying the existing salient at the south-west angle of the Roman defences. Four years later the royal palace in the centre of the city was extended north to High Street, and on the enlarged site William I built his hall and palace (destr.). The new cathedral was begun in 1079 (*see* §III, 1(ii) below); a first dedication in 1093 was followed immediately by the demolition of Old Minster. The building of the bishop's palace at Wolvesey (ruined) began *c.* 1100, the reconstructed Nunnaminster (St Mary's Abbey; destr.) was dedicated in 1108, and New Minster was demolished and its community moved to new buildings at Hyde, outside Northgate, *c.* 1110. Within 50 years all the great buildings had been rebuilt on a vastly larger scale, in a new style and using new masonry techniques. The basic pattern of the Anglo-Saxon city survived, however, and there is no evidence at this time of the rebuilding of ordinary domestic houses, the introduction of new building methods or new types of domestic equipment. Yet the legacy of the Norman Conquest is still evident: although the castle has gone, its mass is a dominant feature of the city plan, and the administration of justice and of the county stem from institutions established within it. Similarly, the bishop still resides at Wolvesey in a Baroque house (1684) beside the ruins of the Norman episcopal palace.

Early Norman Winchester was second in size to London, but in some ways it was the principal city of England. The treasure was kept in the castle until the late 12th century. Whenever William I and William II (*reg* 1087–1100) were in England at Easter, they wore their crown at Winchester in a great ceremony that linked palace and cathedral. The custom was maintained until 1104 by Henry I (*reg* 1100–35) but was then gradually abandoned, weakening the bonds between the city and the Crown. The recently enlarged royal palace seems to have been abandoned in the early 12th century in favour of a new palace in the castle. Passing to the bishop, the old palace was apparently fortified and played an important role in the siege of Winchester (1141) before being demolished. The castle palace was greatly embellished under Henry II and Henry III, notably by the Great Hall (1222–36; *see* HALL, fig. 2), but in 1304 the royal apartments were burnt and the castle was never again used as a royal residence. Thereafter the king usually stayed at Wolvesey.

From the time of the episcopate of HENRY OF BLOIS (*reg* 1129–71) the bishop was the principal power in the city, a position first seen in his survey of all the properties in the city in 1148, which forms the second part of the Winton Domesday (see above). His creation at Wolvesey of one of the greatest Romanesque houses in England, his benefactions to the cathedral and the other city churches, and his foundation (*c.* 1136) of the hospital of St Cross reflect the immense wealth derived from the richest see in England. Bishop William of Wykeham (*reg* 1367–1404) remodelled the private apartments at Wolvesey in 1372–7, and in 1382 founded the College of St Mary (later Winchester College) in the southern suburb, much of it built by William Wynford between 1387 and 1404.

3. AFTER 1538. The fortunes of the major institutions within the city walls were partly independent of the long economic decline that began at this time and continued beyond the dissolution of the religious houses in 1538–9. Although the cathedral body was reformed under a dean and chapter in 1541, and the college survived unimpaired, the city reached its lowest ebb after the dissolution and did not begin to revive until the second half of the 17th century. The occupied area within the walls gradually contracted. Gardens and orchards replaced houses, starting in the higher streets to the west and those parts of the north–south streets furthest from High Street. The decline is seen most clearly in the loss of the city's churches. In the 12th century there were at least 57 parish churches, but only 33 remained by *c.* 1400, 26 by *c.* 1500 and 12 by 1600; by 1800 9 medieval parish churches survived, only 4 of which stood within the walls. This shift in population towards the valley floor reflected the need for water in Winchester's cloth-finishing industries, but at the same time the western and, to some extent, the northern and southern suburbs were abandoned in favour of the growth of the eastern suburb. This pattern is clearly visible in the first map of Winchester (see fig. 1).

In 1631 the castle was granted to Sir Richard Weston (1577–1635) and converted into a private mansion. Besieged by Parliament in 1642 and 1645, and slighted in 1651, its ruins were demolished in 1683 to make way for Wren's palace for Charles II (*see* WREN, CHRISTOPHER, §I, 5). Although the King's House, as it became known, was abandoned unfinished in 1685, the city's fortunes began to recover, no longer based on the cloth-finishing trades and the annual fair on St Giles' Hill, but increasingly on its popularity as a gentry town. This trend was confirmed by the use of the King's House during the wars of the 18th century as a military prison, a refuge for clergy from revolutionary France and finally as a barracks, and by its reconstruction in 1809–11 as one of the principal depots of the British Army.

William Godson's map of 1750 shows that throughout the 18th century the occupied area within the walls remained limited to High Street, the north–south route of

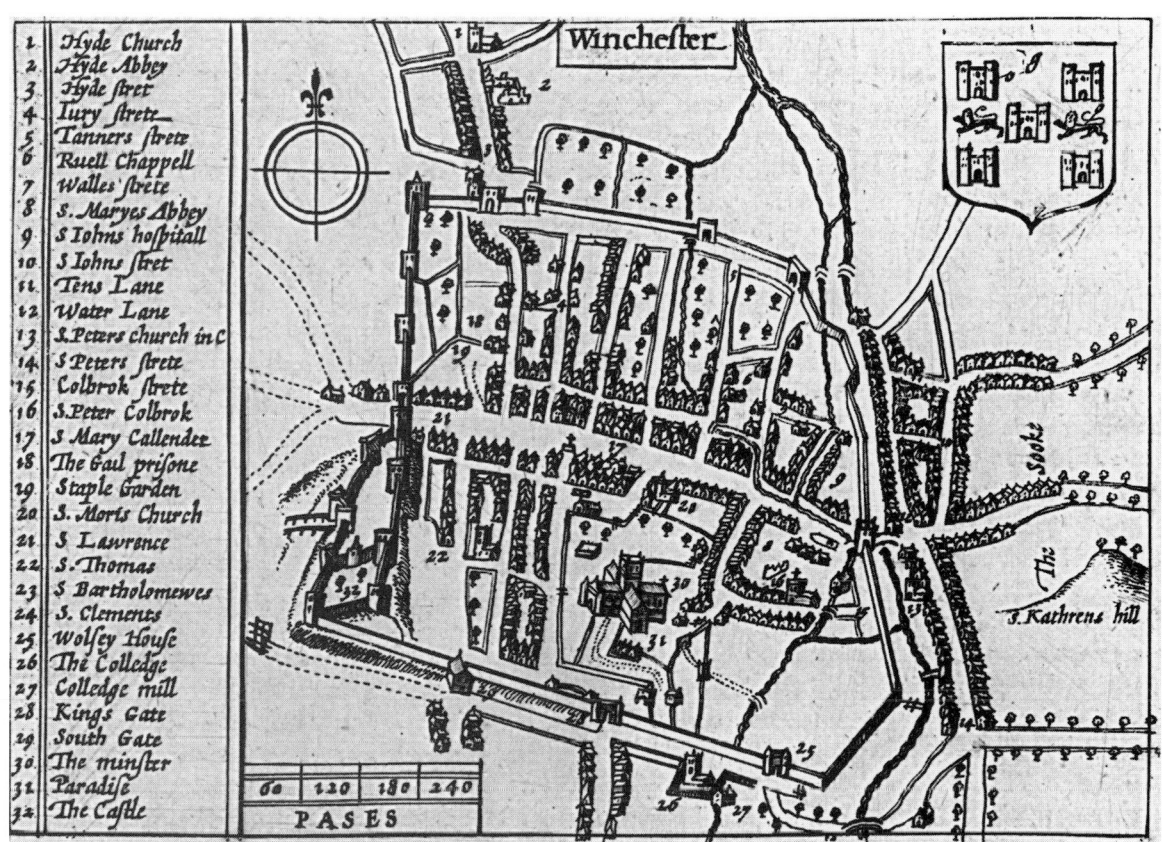

1. Winchester, aerial view, early 17th century; engraving from J. Speed: *The Theatre of the Empire of Great Britain* (London, 1611–12)

Southgate and Jewry Streets, the fringes of the cathedral close, and the eastern suburbs. Gradual recolonization of the open areas began *c*. 1800, and by 1836, as Richard C. Gale's map shows, this process was well advanced. With the arrival of the railway in 1839, first the western and then the southern suburbs were rapidly developed.

The foundations of Winchester's prosperity in the 19th century rested on the Church, the courts, the army and the county. A correspondingly important commercial element grew up to service these markets. These trends were well established before the arrival of the railway, but in the second half of the 19th century the walled area became fully built up, and the suburbs expanded on all sides, far exceeding the furthest medieval limits of the early 12th century. Changes to the topography of the walled area were few until the mid-20th century, but major public buildings permanently changed the city's skyline. These buildings include the County Hospital (1758; destr.) in Parchment Street, the County Gaol (1805), by George Moneypenny (*b* 1768), in Jewry Street, the new Guildhall (1871–3, by Jeffery & Skiller) in Broadway, the County Offices at the north end of the former site of the castle (which emerged with the creation of Castle Avenue in 1895–6), and the rebuilding of the barracks (1899–1904) after the King's House was destroyed by fire in 1894. St George's Street and the south end of Jewry Street were widened in the 1950s. The line of the city's ancient defences was not seriously breached until the construction of a new County Hall (1959–60, 1965–7), north of Westgate, although much of the wall and four of the gates had been demolished in the later 18th century (Eastgate, Northgate and Southgate, destr. 1791). Nevertheless, the city's street pattern still remains that of the 9th century, framed by the lines of defences and the sites of gates laid down in the later 1st century AD.

BIBLIOGRAPHY

B. Cunliffe and J. Collis: *Winchester Excavations, 1949–1960*, 2 vols (Winchester, 1964–78)
N. Pevsner and D. Lloyd: *Hampshire and the Isle of Wight*, Bldgs England (Harmondsworth, 1967)
M. Biddle, ed.: *Winchester in the Early Middle Ages: An Edition and Discussion of the Winton Domesday*, Winchester Studies, 1 (Oxford, 1976)
B. Carpenter Turner: *Winchester* (Southampton, 1980)
A. Rosen: 'Winchester in Transition, 1580–1700', *Country Towns in Pre-industrial England*, ed. P. Clark (Leicester, 1981), pp. 144–95
R. Cunstance, ed.: *Winchester College: Sixth-centenary Essays* (Oxford, 1982)
M. Biddle: 'The Study of Winchester: Archaeology and History in a British Town', *Proc. Brit. Acad.*, lxix (1983), pp. 93–135 [biblig. of archaeol. res., 1949–81]
M. Biddle and B. Clayre: *Winchester Castle and the Great Hall* (Winchester, 1983)
D. Keene: *Survey of Medieval Winchester*, Winchester Studies, 2 (Oxford, 1985) [bibliog. of hist. writing on Winchester]
M. Biddle: 'Seasonal Festivals and Residence: Winchester, Westminster and Gloucester in the Tenth to Twelfth Centuries', *Anglo-Norman Stud.*, viii (1986), pp. 51–72
——: *Wolvesey: The Old Bishop's Palace, Winchester* (London, 1986)
——: 'Early Norman Winchester', *Domesday Studies*, ed. J. C. Holt (Woodbridge, 1987), pp. 311–31
——: 'Winchester: The Rise of an Early Capital', *Prehistoric, Roman and Early Medieval* (1988), i of *The Cambridge Guide to the Arts in Britain*, ed. B. Ford (Cambridge, 1988–91); rev. as *The Cambridge Cultural History* (Cambridge, 1992), pp. 194–205
——: *Object and Economy in Medieval Winchester*, Winchester Studies, 7/ii (Oxford, 1990)
G. D. Scobie and others: *The Brooks, Winchester: A Preliminary Report on the Excavations, 1987–88*, Winchester Museums Service, Archaeology Report, 1 (Winchester, 1991)
B. Kjølbye-Biddle: 'Dispersal or Concentration: The Disposal of the Winchester Dead over 2000 Years', *Death in Towns: Urban Responses to the Dying and the Dead, 100–1600*, ed. S. Bassett (Leicester, 1992), pp. 210–47

MARTIN BIDDLE

II. *Centre of manuscript production.*

An Orosius manuscript (early 10th century; London, BL, Add. MS. 47967) and a copy of Gregory the Great's *Pastoral Letters* (*c*. 890–7; Oxford, Bodleian Lib., MS. Hatton 20) are two rare survivals of six major works translated by or under the direction of Alfred himself, and both may have originated at Winchester. From the surviving evidence, the great period of the Winchester school was, however, between 966 and 1066, after the reform of the Old and New Minsters by St Aethelwold, Bishop of Winchester (*see also* ANGLO-SAXON ART, §IV, 2). The New Minster Charter (966; London, BL, Cotton MS. Vesp. A. VIII), with its presentation scene depicting King Edgar (*reg* 959–75), is generally held to be the earliest example of the Winchester style in painting. The Benedictional of St Aethelwold (*c*. 980; London, BL, Add. MS. 49598) with 28 extant full-page miniatures (*see* ANGLO-SAXON ART, fig. 9) and careful Caroline script by the scribe Godeman, including a dedication in gold letters, is the best example of late 10th-century Winchester illumination. The work is characterized by the use of large acanthus leaves ('Winchester acanthus') in the framing devices, calm figures and agitated drapery lines (particularly the hems). Techniques range from line drawing, to painted figures set against a plain parchment background, to fully painted miniatures. The iconography is partly derived from continental sources both in ivory (e.g. the Metz Casket, Brunswick, Herzog Anton Ulrich-Mus.) and in manuscripts (e.g. the Drogo Sacramentary, Paris, Bib. N, MS. lat. 9428; *see* MISSAL, fig. 1), and there are clear stylistic affinities with Franco-Saxon manuscripts; such contacts were apparent as early as the period of King Athelstan (*reg* 924/5–39).

Godeman was also the scribe of two Gospel fragments (London, Coll. Arms, Arundel MS. 22) and possibly of the Ramsey Benedictional (Paris, Bib. N., MS. lat. 987). A second scribe working on this latter manuscript after 1023 can also be linked with a number of manuscripts that show similar characteristics of decoration and script, although they were made for various patrons and there is no firm evidence to localize them. These include the Missal of Robert of Jumièges (before 1023; Rouen, Bib. Mun., MS. Y.6; *see* ANGLO-SAXON ART, fig. 11), the later parts of the Copenhagen Gospels (late 10th century and *c*. 1020; Copenhagen, Kon. Bib., MS. G.1), the Trinity Gospels (*c*. 1015–25; Cambridge, Trinity Coll., MS. B.10.4) and the Kederminster Gospels (*c*. 1020; Langley Marsh, St Mary's, Kederminster Lib., no. 267, on loan to London, BL, Loan MS. 11).

Other manuscripts that can be associated with Winchester suggest that the scribes and artists trained there may have been peripatetic. The Benedictional (more properly Pontifical) of Archbishop Robert (perhaps Robert of Jumièges or Robert of Rouen; last quarter of the

10th century; Rouen, Bib. Mun., MS. Y.7) is textually linked with Winchester as is the Ramsey Psalter (late 10th century; London, BL, Harley MS. 2904), although it may have been written for use at Ramsey or for a person associated with both places. The fine line drawing of the *Crucifixion* (fol. 3*v*) in the latter is the work of an artist who worked at Fleury on a copy of Cicero's *Aratea* (late 10th century; London, BL, Harley MS. 2506). This artist also collaborated on a number of manuscripts made with north French scribes and illuminators, for example two late 10th-century Gospels (Boulogne, Bib. Mun., MS. 11 and New York, Pierpont Morgan Lib., MS. M. 827, respectively). A single drawing in another Fleury book (Orléans, Bib. Mun., MS. 175) has also been attributed to this artist.

More securely dated is the later prayerbook of Aelfwine, Dean of the New Minster (before 1032–5; London, BL, Cotton MSS Titus D. XXVI–XXVII) and the New Minster *Liber vitae* (*c.* 1031; London, BL, Stowe MS. 944), both partly written by the scribe Aelsinus and containing line drawings by the same hands. This type of tinted line drawing reached its apogee in the Tiberius Psalter (mid-11th century; London, BL, Cotton MS. Tib. C. VI; see fig. 2). The scribe of this glossed Psalter also worked on the Cantatorium and Herbal of the Old Minster (Oxford,

2. Winchester school, *Descent into Limbo*; tinted line drawing from the Tiberius Psalter, 248×146 mm, mid-11th century (London, British Library, Cotton MS. Tib. C. VI, fol. 14*r*)

Bodleian Lib., MS. Bodley 775 and London, BL, Cotton MS. Vitell. C. III, respectively). Another Psalter from this period (London, BL, Arundel MS. 60) may have been made for any one of the Winchester foundations; it shows a hardening of drapery style that looks forward to post-Conquest developments. A Gospels (Oxford, Wadham Coll., MS. A. 18. 3), although written in a post-Conquest script, must have derived its iconography and framing devices from such a manuscript as the Benedictional of St Aethelwold.

It is not until the mid-12th century that manuscripts comparable in quality to those produced in the Anglo-Saxon period were made in Winchester (*see* ROMANESQUE, §IV, 2). These are the Winchester Psalter or Psalter of Henry of Blois (*c.* 1150; London, BL, Cotton MS. Nero C. IV) and the two Bibles (*c.* 1160 and *c.* 1170–80; Oxford, Bodleian Lib., Auct. MSS E. inf. I-2; *see* INITIAL, MANU-SCRIPT, fig. 2) and the WINCHESTER BIBLE (*c.* 1160 and *c.* 1170–90; Winchester, Cathedral Lib.; *see* MANUSCRIPT, colour pl. V, fig. 1). The script of the latter is probably by a single scribe, although some leaves were supplied by the scribe of the Bodleian Bible, the text of which is thought to have been used to correct that of the Winchester Bible. Professional artists of diverse origins, who were familiar with the latest trends in painting, both in England and in Europe, appear to have worked on the Winchester Bible from time to time and it remains unfinished.

BIBLIOGRAPHY

English Romanesque Art, 1066–1200 (exh. cat., ed. G. Zarnecki, J. Holt and T. Holland; London, Hayward Gal., 1984)
The Golden Age of Anglo-Saxon Art, 966–1066 (exh. cat., ed. J. Backhouse, D. H. Turner and L. Webster; London, BM, 1984)

M. A. MICHAEL

III. Cathedral.

The first Bishop of Winchester, Wini, was consecrated in AD 660 in the church of SS Peter and Paul (later Old Minster; *see* §1(i) below). The cathedral was rebuilt several times and the see was moved to an adjacent and partly overlapping site in 1093 (*see* §1(ii) below).

1. Architecture. 2. Painting. 3. Sculpture. 4. Stained glass.

1. ARCHITECTURE.

(i) Anglo-Saxon. (ii) From 1079.

(i) Anglo-Saxon. The first church (*c.* 648) was apparently intended as the chapel of an adjacent royal residence. It became the principal royal burial-place of Wessex and the late Anglo-Saxon kingdom; from the early 10th century it was known as Old Minster. After 971, when the relics of St Swithun were translated from his original grave outside the west door of the first church, Old Minster became an important place of pilgrimage. St Aethelwold reformed the community of secular canons as a regular Benedictine house in 964. The *Regularis concordia*, the rule under which the monks and nuns of England were henceforth to live, was probably promulgated at Old Minster *c.* 971, and the community, now St Swithun's Priory, played a leading role in monastic reform at several refounded or newly founded houses. During the latter part of the 10th century Old Minster was one of the principal centres of English intellectual, literary and artistic achievement (*see* §II above).

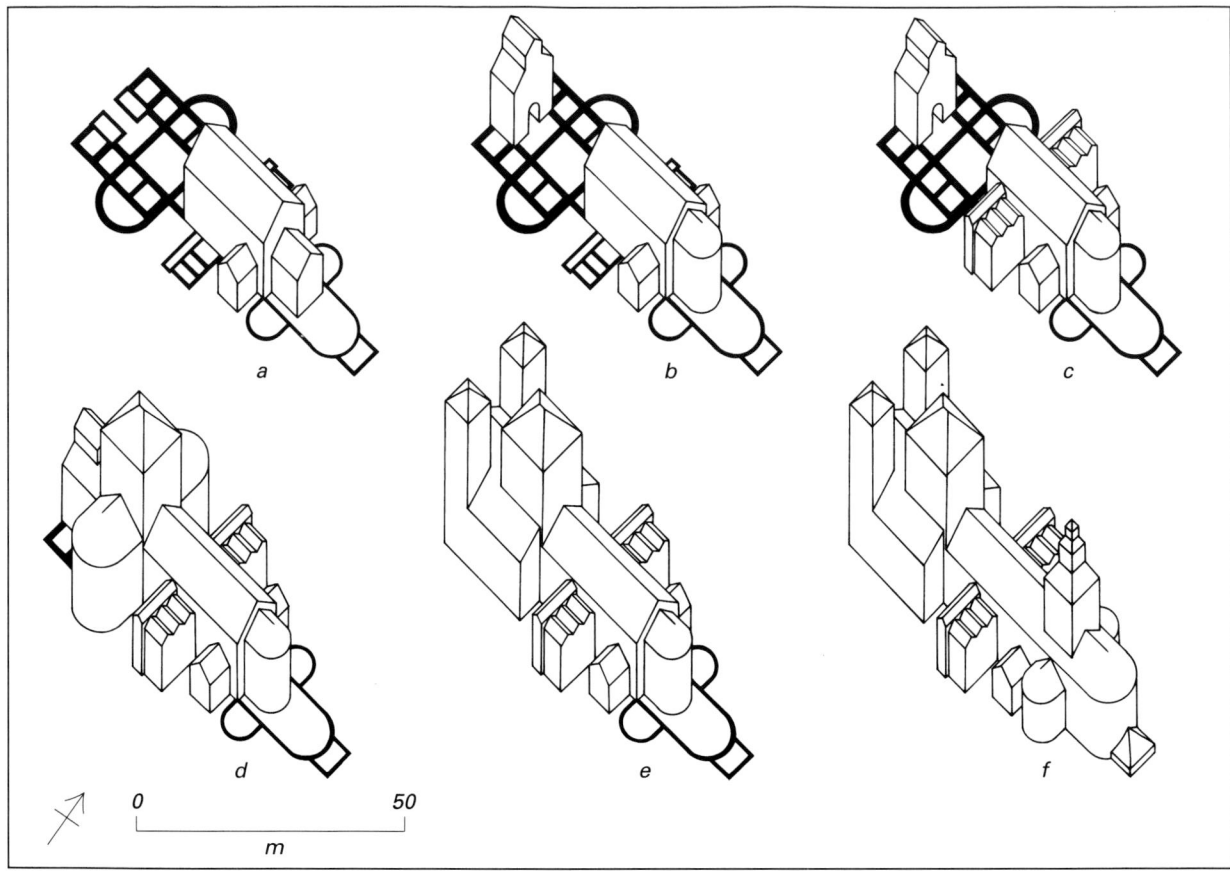

3. Winchester, Old Minster; reconstruction drawings: (a) *c.* AD 648; (b) mid-8th century; (c) early 10th century; (d) after 971; (e) 980; (f) *c.* 993–4

The site of Old Minster beyond the immediate exterior of the present cathedral's nave was excavated in 1964–9. The first church, built over a street along the south side of the forum (*see* §I, 1 above), was cruciform with rectangular north and south porticus and a square east end (see fig. 3a). From the later 7th century, burials were made around the church. St Martin's tower (early to mid-8th century), a detached axial structure probably intended as the gate-house to the cemetery and cathedral complex, was built to the west (3b). The east porticus was then remodelled to provide an enlarged triumphal arch and a lengthened apsidal termination.

Soon after the foundation of the rival New Minster in 901–3, a massive west façade was added to Old Minster, with chapels to the rear (3c). A double-apsed building was erected after 971 around the site of St Swithun's original tomb, between the west end of the original church and St Martin's tower (3d). Within a few years, however, the church was almost entirely reconstructed on a monumental scale by Aethelwold and Bishop Aelfeah (*reg* 984–1006). The 7th-century nave was heightened and the double-apsed martyrium was rebuilt as a huge, rectangular west-work (dedicated 980; 3e) of ultimately Carolingian inspiration (*see* WESTWORK). The east end was then vastly extended to provide a new apse with an outer crypt (3f). The high altar was raised over a second crypt, with a lateral apse to the north (and probably the south). These works were dedicated *c.* 993–4.

Old Minster was a vast church, more than 76 m in length; reconstructions suggest that the westwork was 50–60 m high. Its rich decorations included wall paintings, coloured and probably painted window glass (*see* ANGLO-SAXON ART, §§IV, 1 and VII), glazed floor tiles with relief decoration and architectural sculpture in the style of the Benedictional of St Aethelwold (*c.* 980; London, BL, Add. MS. 49598; *see* §II above; *see also* ANGLO-SAXON ART, fig. 9). After the dedication of the east end of the Norman cathedral in 1093 (*see* §(ii) below), Old Minster was demolished and its stone was reused. The area of the former westwork was surfaced to provide a memorial court around a free-standing monument over St Swithun's original tomb.

BIBLIOGRAPHY

M. Biddle and R. N. Quirk: 'Excavations near Winchester Cathedral, 1961', *Archaeol. J.*, cxix (1962), pp. 150–94

Antiqua. J., xliv–l (1964–70), lii (1972), lv (1975) [excav. rep. by M. Biddle]

D. J. Sheerin: 'The Dedication of the Old Minster, Winchester, in 980', *Rev. Bénédictine*, lxxxviii (1978), pp. 261–72

The Golden Age of Anglo-Saxon Art, 966–1066 (exh. cat., ed. J. Backhouse, D. H. Turner and L. Webster; London, BM, 1984), pp. 133–8 [sculp., window glass, tiles and bell-mould frag.]

L. A. S. Butler and R. K. Morris, eds: *The Anglo-Saxon Church: Papers on History, Architecture and Archaeology in Honour of Dr H. M. Taylor* (London, 1986), pp. 1–31 [18–25], 196–209 [articles by M. Biddle and B. Kjølbye-Biddle]

M. Biddle and B. Kjølbye-Biddle: *The Anglo-Saxon Minsters at Winchester*, Winchester Studies, 4/i (Oxford, in preparation)

M. Lapidge: *The Cult of St Swithun*, Winchester Studies, 4/ii (Oxford, in preparation)

M. Biddle and B. Kjølbye-Biddle: 'Winchester: The Old and New Minsters', *South-east England* (in preparation), iv of *Corpus of Anglo-Saxon Stone Sculpture*, ed. R. Cramp (Oxford, 1984–)

MARTIN BIDDLE, BIRTHE KJØLBYE-BIDDLE

(ii) From 1079.

(a) 1079–c. 1200. The Anglo-Norman cathedral was begun in 1079 by Bishop Walkelin (*reg* 1070–98), on a site immediately south of Old Minster. The church was built mainly of Quarr limestone from the Isle of Wight, supplemented with oolitic limestone from the Bath area. An anecdote in the priory's 12th-century annals (London, BL, Cotton. Domit. A.xiii) suggests that a supply of building timber was assured by William I. By 1093 the entire east arm of the church was complete, together with the transepts and perhaps three bays of the nave. The monks of St Swithun's Priory moved from Old Minster into the new cathedral on 8 April, when a first dedication took place, and the demolition of Old Minster allowed the rest of the nave to be completed, probably by *c.* 1105.

Most of the architectural features of Bishop Walkelin's cathedral were derived from orthodox prototypes in Upper Normandy, although no one church can be identified as the exemplar (*see also* ROMANESQUE, §II, 6). The Romanesque work has mostly been obliterated by successive remodellings: except for the crypt, the original east arm was replaced after 1200. The eastern termination had an apse and ambulatory, but Winchester differed from such continental examples as Rouen Cathedral and the abbey churches at Jumièges and Saint-Wandrille in its prolonged eastern chapel flanked by square-ended chapels in line with the presbytery aisles (see fig. 4). The high altar was on the chord of the apse, its position now represented by the Great Screen.

The Romanesque transepts survive (*see* ENGLAND, fig. 2), and their elevations are broadly typical of the rest of the Anglo-Norman cathedral. There are three storeys of equal height, as at St-Etienne, Caen and Cerisy-la-Forêt: a main arcade in two plain orders; a gallery, with paired sub-arches; and a clerestory with tall, stilted arches in front of the windows, flanked by short, narrow arches. The clerestory design in the terminal bays is the anomalous consequence of an abortive scheme to provide towers at the corners of the transepts. Unusually, the transepts have aisles both to east and west and at the ends, giving a full processional circuit at ground floor and gallery levels; this arrangement was later adopted at Ely Cathedral. There is evidence for up to 12 side-altars against the east walls at both levels. Decoration is restrained: the capitals are plain cushion types, and there is no evidence of 11th-century polychromy.

The nave is notable for its length (12 surviving bays); until the mid-14th century it terminated in a western structure projecting north and south beyond the aisle walls. The most likely interpretation is that the west front comprised twin towers, possibly flanking a central balcony for royal ceremonial; this would have echoed the final westwork of Old Minster, while being similar in its broad

conception (although not in the design of its lowest stage) to the original west front at La Trinité, Caen.

The central tower collapsed in 1107 and was rebuilt almost immediately with exaggeratedly massive piers and improved masonry techniques. The capitals of the rebuilt tower and adjacent transept bays show stylistic advances, with the introduction of scallops and stylized foliage; the vaulting in the bays was rebuilt with ribs instead of the groin vaults seen in some of the original bays (in others ribs were added under the groins to match those of the 12th-century rebuild).

In the mid-12th century there was renewed interest in the cult of St Swithun. Henry of Blois elevated the saint's reliquary behind the high altar and created a feretory

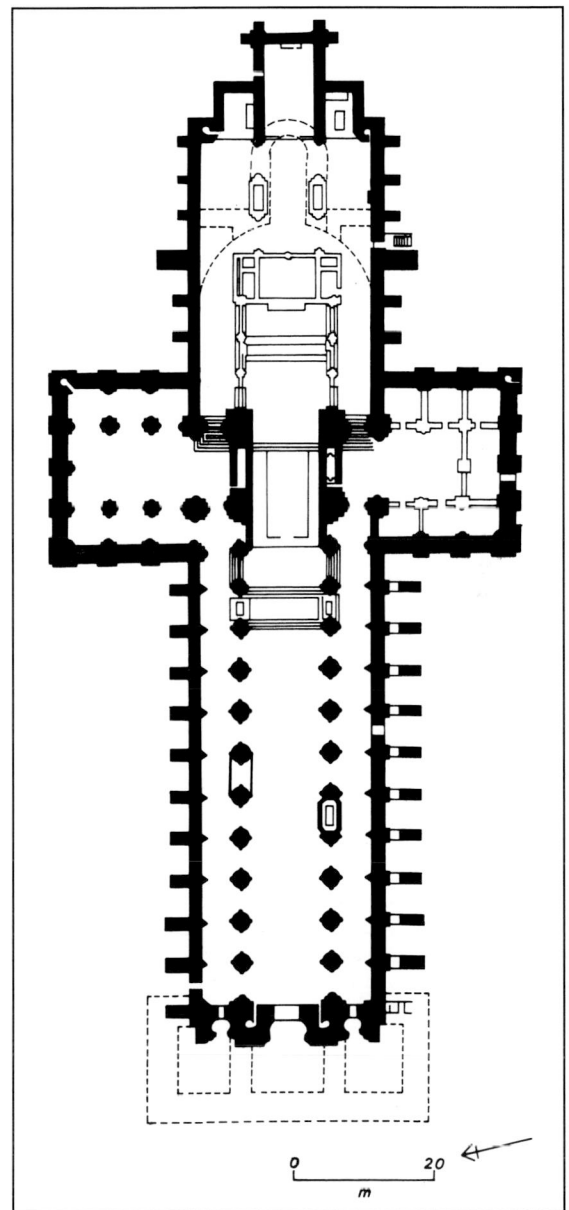

4. Winchester Cathedral, begun 1079, plan

platform, around which the bones of pre-Conquest monarchs and bishops were displayed in lead coffers. (Previously they had been buried around Swithun's original grave (*see* §(i) above).) A tunnel under the feretory platform, the 'Holy Hole', allowed pilgrims limited proximity to the relics. A chapel over the site of Swithun's empty grave, just north of the west end of the new cathedral, formed a second focus of veneration. Henry of Blois was also responsible for the creation of a Treasury (*c.* 1160) in the south transept, with fluted pilasters that seem inspired by Burgundian architecture.

(b) After c. 1200. The construction of a huge retrochoir from *c.* 1200 more than doubled the area of the eastern arm. Problems with the foundations resulted in some changes of design during what appears to have been a protracted campaign. As eventually built, the retrochoir was a spacious, three-bay, aisled hall, with a central vessel only slightly higher than the aisles (see fig. 5). To the east the Lady chapel, flanked by two shorter chapels, reproduced the Romanesque scheme in squared-up form. The retrochoir, which has stylistic affinities with contemporary work at Lincoln Cathedral, is notable for its elegant use of contrasting materials (light-coloured Caen stone and dark Purbeck marble piers, wall-shafts and string courses) and for its extensive spreads of floor tiles (from 1260; *in situ*).

Around 1310 the east arm was further remodelled. The Romanesque apse was demolished and the retrochoir arcade was continued westwards, initially by just one bay, in a high, two-storey elevation. The east gable of the choir was supported on a two-bay transverse arcade, above an elaborately decorated feretory screen. Niches in this screen

5. Winchester Cathedral, interior of the retrochoir looking northeast, *c.* 1200–25

contained statuettes relating to the remains of saints and bishops preserved in mortuary chests above. The feretory platform remained *in situ*, and the entrance to the Holy Hole was incorporated within the new screen. Thomas of Witney seems to have been responsible for the start of this work (*c.* 1310–15), but his successor, possibly William Joy, continued the remodelling of the presbytery arcades and the entire arcade was rapidly completed, up to the crossing tower.

Under Bishop Edington (*reg* 1345–66) the Romanesque west front was replaced by the present façade with a deep triple porch that shares features with the south transept (*c.* 1331–6) of Gloucester Cathedral; the remainder of the west front, including a great west window (*see* §4 below), was possibly built in a second phase (see fig. 6). He also began to remodel the west end of the nave aisles—two bays on the north side and one on the south—introducing high aisle windows cutting across the level of the Romanesque gallery. This implies an intention eventually to replace the three storeys of the Norman nave by a two-storey elevation. The work was eventually resumed in 1394 by his successor, William of Wykeham, whose architect, William Wynford, devised a scheme to replace the Norman main arcade with one more than half as high again; the rest of the gallery storey and the clerestory were united to form tall clerestory windows over a vestigial, balcony-like triforium stage. Both Edington and Wykeham were buried in chantry chapels on the south side of the nave. The star vault of the nave was probably completed by 1420.

A substantial bequest from Cardinal Henry Beaufort (*reg* 1404–47) led to sweeping changes in the high-altar area after 1450. The Great Screen was completed by 1476, although its statuary, which shows strong Netherlandish influence, may have been added slightly later (*see* §3 below). In that year Swithun's relics were moved to a huge shrine (destr. 1538) in the middle of the retrochoir. To the south of the shrine Beaufort's chantry chapel had been erected, followed, almost immediately, by the chantry of William Waynflete (*reg* 1447–86; see fig. 5 above) to the north.

About 1500 the easternmost bay of the Lady chapel, already rebuilt in the 14th century, was again remodelled. Bishop Richard Fox (*reg* 1501–28) rebuilt the east gable of the presbytery (1503–5), inserting wooden vaulting that echoes Wykeham's nave vault of a century earlier. The work continued in 1506–9 with the reconstruction of the presbytery aisle vaults, and in 1513–18 Fox's chantry chapel was built. Early Renaissance elements appear in the final phase of Fox's building works: the stone screens inserted into the presbytery arcades of 1525 and the mortuary chests (1525–30) above them. Also strongly Renaissance in character is Bishop Gardiner's chantry chapel (*c.* 1556–8), which shows affinities with contemporary work at Henry VIII's palace of Nonsuch, notably that of craftsmen associated with Nicholas Bellin of Modena.

Since the Reformation, building work in the cathedral has been small-scale and mostly decorative. In 1634 a timber vault was inserted into the central tower, above the choir, and four years later the rood-screen, which stood three bays west of the crossing, was taken down and replaced by a new choir-screen designed by Inigo Jones.

6. Winchester Cathedral, west front, second half of the 14th century

The latter was first replaced in 1820 by a stone Gothic Revival screen by William Garbett (*c.* 1770–1834), and then by a wooden openwork screen (1875, by the elder George Gilbert Scott) that mirrors the 14th-century return stalls. As the water-table lies just below ground level, the cathedral was completely underpinned with concrete in 1905–12 to preserve it from collapse. The Cathedral Close contains a few vestiges of its monastic past, notably the chapter house (late 11th century) and the Deanery porch (early 13th century). The priory guest-house, known as the Pilgrims' Hall, has an early hammerbeam roof (*c.* 1308).

BIBLIOGRAPHY

R. Willis: 'The Architectural History of Winchester Cathedral', *Proc. Royal Archaeol. Inst. GB & Ireland*, 11 (1846); as booklet (1846/*R* Winchester, 1980)
P. Draper: 'The Retrochoir of Winchester Cathedral', *Archit. Hist.*, xxi (1978), pp. 1–17
——: 'Winchester Cathedral Deanery', *Proc. Hants Field Club & Archaeol. Soc.*, xxxxiii (1987), pp. 125–73
British Archaeological Association Conference Transactions: Medieval Art and Architecture at Winchester Cathedral: Winchester, 1980
J. Crook: 'The Romanesque East Arm and Crypt of Winchester Cathedral', *J. Brit. Archaeol. Assoc.*, cxlii (1989), pp. 1–36
——: 'The Pilgrims' Hall, Winchester: Hammerbeams, Base Crucks and Aisle-derivative Roof Structures', *Archaeologia*, cviiii (1991), pp. 129–59
J. Crook and Y. Kusaba: 'The Transepts of Winchester Cathedral: Archaeological Evidence, Problems of Design, and Sequence of Construction', *J. Soc. Archit. Historians*, l (1991), pp. 293–310
J. Crook, ed.: *Winchester Cathedral: Nine Hundred Years, 1093–1993* (Chichester, 1993)

JOHN CROOK

2. PAINTING. The most notable surviving wall paintings are in the Holy Sepulchre chapel in the north transept. The removal of the 13th-century paintings for conservation in the 1960s revealed sections of an earlier phase. It is evident that alterations in the early 13th century made it necessary to repaint the chapel *c.* 1220. The surviving parts of the 12th-century scheme, all in fresco, include a *Deposition*, the *Entombment* (*see* ROMANESQUE, fig. 54), the *Three Marys at the Tomb* and the *Descent into Limbo* on the east wall, and on the south wall a *Resurrection of the Dead* and a badly damaged sinopia drawing that may have shown scenes of Christ before the high priest and Pilate. The 13th-century scheme, which includes *Christ Pantokrator* and scenes from the *Infancy of Christ* in roundels in the vaults, largely follows that of the earlier scheme. The 12th-century paintings are finer and are very close stylistically to the later illumination of the roughly contemporary WINCHESTER BIBLE. Much of the iconography is of

Byzantine derivation, in keeping with the general trend of late 12th-century English painting (*see* ROMANESQUE, §IV, 1). The vault of the late 12th-century Guardian Angels chapel in the retrochoir is painted with angels in roundels (*c.* 1225–30); the decorative background was probably added some 40 years later. In the Lady chapel, beyond the retrochoir, there are wall paintings, now very faint, representing the *Miracles of the Virgin* (*c.* 1510–20).

BIBLIOGRAPHY

D. Park: 'The Wall Paintings of the Holy Sepulchre Chapel', *British Archaeological Association Conference Transactions: Medieval Art and Architecture at Winchester Cathedral: Winchester, 1980*, pp. 38–62
D. Park and P. Welford: 'The Medieval Polychromy of Winchester Cathedral', *Winchester Cathedral: Nine Hundred Years, 1093–1993*, ed. J. Crook (Chichester, 1993), pp. 123–38

3. SCULPTURE. Next to Westminster Abbey, Winchester Cathedral contains the largest and finest range of surviving medieval figure sculpture in England, although little remains *in situ*. The main survivals are the late 14th- and 15th-century vault bosses and corbel tables of the nave, the bosses (*c.* 1500) of the Lady chapel and Bishop Langton's chantry chapel, and those of the choir vaults. The wooden bosses of the choir high vault show the Instruments of the Passion, royal arms and emblems, and arms connected with Bishop Fox and his successive sees, which date the bosses to 1503–9. The stone aisle bosses may have been carved between 1513 and 1528; the lateral screens of the choir are dated 1525 and ornamented with Renaissance-style designs. The choir-stalls (*c.* 1308) are attributed to the Norfolk carpenter William Lyngwode. The panels in the spandrels over the rear seats show lively human and animal carving. Further east, additional stalls (dated 1541) have decorative panels with developed Renaissance influence. The tomb effigies of the bishops include the mid-13th-century Purbeck marble heart tomb of *Aymer de Valence*, the alabaster effigies of *William Edington* (*d* 1366) and *William of Wykeham* (*d* 1404), the freestone one of *William Waynflete* (*d* 1486) and the *transis* of *Richard Fox* (*d* 1528) and *Stephen Gardiner* (*reg* 1531–55).

Much of the sculpture now displayed in the Triforium Gallery, although defaced by iconoclasts, is even more impressive. The rich decorative detail of the Romanesque material is well illustrated by a capital (*c.* 1150–55) with fighting monsters, commissioned by Henry of Blois who also imported the Tournai marble font (*c.* 1150), with scenes from the *Life of St Nicholas*, and a statue sometimes identified as *Ecclesia* (*c.* 1230–35), now in the retrochoir and formerly in the Deanery porch. Purbeck marble spandrels (*c.* 1260) come from the shrine of St Swithun. The decorative wood sculpture of the choir-stalls (*c.* 1308) is rivalled by a fine head stop (*c.* 1310) and by excellent corbels (*c.* 1320–30) in the central chapel of the north transept. Three heads may have belonged to large figures from Wykeham's chantry chapel (before 1404), although stylistically they are characteristic of the second quarter of the 14th century. It is more likely that some headless figures, strongly influenced by alabaster sculpture, came from the reredos of the Guardian Angels Chapel. The sculptures (mid-1470s) from the Great Screen include a *Virgin and Child*, *God the Father*, large bodiless heads, and

figures, mostly headless, from the smaller niches. These may be divided into two groups, one strongly Netherlandish in character and the other more easily related to native sculpture. An early 16th-century fragment of an *Angel Annunciate* retains much of its complex polychromy.

For illustration of later sculpture *see* FLAXMAN, JOHN, fig. 1.

BIBLIOGRAPHY

J. Vaughan: *Winchester Cathedral: Its Monuments and Memorials* (London, 1919)
C. J. P. Cave: *The Roof Bosses of Winchester Cathedral* (Winchester, 1955)
J. Crook: 'The Thirteenth Century Shrine and Screen of St Swithun at Winchester', *J. Brit. Archaeol. Assoc.*, cxxxviii (1985), pp. 125–31
A. J. Smith: *The Life and Building Activity of Richard Fox, c. 1448–1528* (diss., U. London, 1988)
J. A. Hardacre: *Winchester Cathedral Triforium Gallery* (Winchester, 1989)
P. G. Lindley: 'The Great Screen of Winchester Cathedral: I', *Burl. Mag.*, cxxxi (1989), pp. 603–15
——: 'The Medieval Sculpture of Winchester Cathedral', *Winchester Cathedral: Nine Hundred Years, 1093–1993*, ed. J. Crook (Chichester, 1993), pp. 97–122

PHILLIP LINDLEY

4. STAINED GLASS. Apart from panels of grisaille brought from Salisbury Cathedral, all the original glazing is contemporary with the campaigns of remodelling the cathedral (*see* §1(ii) above). Although often fragmentary, the glass indicates the changes that took place between the mid-14th century and the early 16th.

Angel musicians under canopies of a design transitional between Decorated and Perpendicular survive in the tracery of the west window of the south nave aisle and form part of Bishop Edington's scheme of *c.* 1365. Much more survives of the glazing documented in the will of William of Wykeham of *c.* 1380. The glass seems to be by Thomas of Oxford and his colleagues, who were responsible for the glazing of Wykeham's twin foundations, New College, Oxford (*see* OXFORD, §3(ii)) and Winchester College.

The great west window of the nave, in design a successor to the great east window at Gloucester Abbey (now cathedral), was vandalized by Cromwellian troops in 1642 and later filled with debris from other windows. The original programme comprised a triptych with the *Life of Christ* flanked by Apostles and Prophets with scrolls. Scenes and figures were set under canopies with orange stain, set against backgrounds alternately ruby and blue. Of Wykeham's glazing of the nave clerestory, only one of the single figures beneath canopies remains *in situ*; others have been moved into the north clerestory of the choir. The deacons and a female saint, and the design of their canopies, are directly comparable with Thomas of Oxford's work in the ante-chapel of New College, *c.* 1380, but the Winchester glass may be as late as 1420. Canopy tops, perhaps of *c.* 1440, survive in the nave aisles.

The quality of Bishop Waynflete's scheme of *c.* 1460 can still be recognized in the choir clerestory, especially in the second window from the east on the north side: there are angels in the tracery and four Prophets (two of them composite figures) in the upper main lights, set in elegant three-dimensional niches. This work has been attributed to John Glazier, who also worked at All Souls College, Oxford. The choir glazing was completed between 1501 and 1528 for Bishop Fox, who was responsible for the first set of instructions to the glaziers at King's College

Chapel, Cambridge (*see* CAMBRIDGE (i), §2(ii)). The great east window was damaged by ill-judged restoration in 1852, but the north-east clerestory window still has original glass in the tracery, and canopy-tops that follow designs used half a century earlier. Scenes from the *Life of the Virgin* and female saints survive in the tracery of the choir aisles.

Small fragments of original glazing survive in the Lady chapel. A *Tree of Jesse* window is recorded but the present one by C. E. Kempe commemorates Queen Victoria's Diamond Jubilee in 1897. In the north transept is a set of windows by William Morris, and in the south transept a popular memorial window to Izaak Walton (1593–1683), author of the *Compleat Angler* (1653).

BIBLIOGRAPHY

J. D. Le Couteur: *Ancient Glass in Winchester* (Winchester, 1920, 2/1928)

M. Q. SMITH

Winchester Bible. Large two-volume Bible (now bound in four volumes, *c.* 580×396 mm; Winchester Cathedral Lib.), perhaps originally from the former Benedictine cathedral priory of St Swithun (now Winchester Cathedral). It may be identifiable with the Bible that was given to the charterhouse of Witham in Somerset, although it has been argued that this is probably another Bible (Oxford, Bodleian Lib., MS. Auct. E. inf. 1; *see* INITIAL, MANUSCRIPT, fig. 2). The gift to Witham was the result of pressure from King Henry II on the monks of St Swithun, and on hearing this the prior of Witham, St Hugh of Lincoln, returned the book to Winchester. If the Bible now in Winchester was that given to Witham, its text, if not all its illumination, must have been completed before 1186, the year St Hugh became Bishop of Lincoln.

Although the script of the Winchester Bible was mainly the work of one scribe, it was decorated by several artists working in widely different styles, both figural and decorative, which could span the period *c.* 1160–90. This raises the issue as to whether the Bible was illuminated over a long period or was executed in two campaigns, one of *c.* 1160 and the other of *c.* 1170–90. It is difficult to imagine that artists of such widely differing attitudes could be contemporaries, although it is possible that some worked in conservative styles concurrently with others who were introducing new ideas. An understanding of the artists involved is complicated by the fact that some of them painted over drawings by others with the consequent interaction between the various styles. The differences between the artists suggest that they were lay professionals of diverse origins and artistic backgrounds, who were employed to decorate a Bible produced within the monastic scriptorium. Blank spaces in the book and illustrations left in a drawn stage reveal that its decoration was never completed. The biblical books are introduced by large historiated initials, while a few (I Samuel, Judith and Maccabees) have full-page frontispieces, but others just ornamental initials. The leaf for I Samuel seems to have been an afterthought and was never incorporated in the Bible, but has, by chance, survived (575×388 mm; New York, Pierpont Morgan Lib., MS. M. 619), and has scenes from the *Life of David*. The other two leaves with full-page illustrations were never painted but their underdrawings are complete.

The nomenclature for the various artists proposed by Oakeshott (1945) has been widely accepted. Of the early artists, the Apocrypha Drawings Master and the Master of the Leaping Figures (*see* MANUSCRIPT, colour pl. V, fig. 1), the former's style seems to originate from St Albans, and he may be the same artist who illustrated a copy *c.* 1150 of Terence for St Albans Abbey (Oxford, Bodleian Lib., MS. Auct. F. 2. 13; *see* ROMANESQUE, fig. 62). He may have been trained in western France or Normandy, where there are closer parallels to his work than in England. His figures are characterized by energetic, mannered poses and gestures. The other artist working *c.* 1160, the Master of the Leaping Figures, is of English origin and his style was perhaps formulated in Winchester itself since it resembles that of the Winchester Psalter (London, BL, Cotton MS. Nero C. IV). The figures of this artist show the Byzantinizing dampfold style that had been introduced into England in the 1130s, probably first at Bury St Edmunds. The Winchester version of the style is characterized by dramatic poses and leaping movements, which give this Master his name. He painted over some of his own drawings, maintaining the essentially linear character of this style, but much of his work was overpainted by the later artists working *c.* 1170–90.

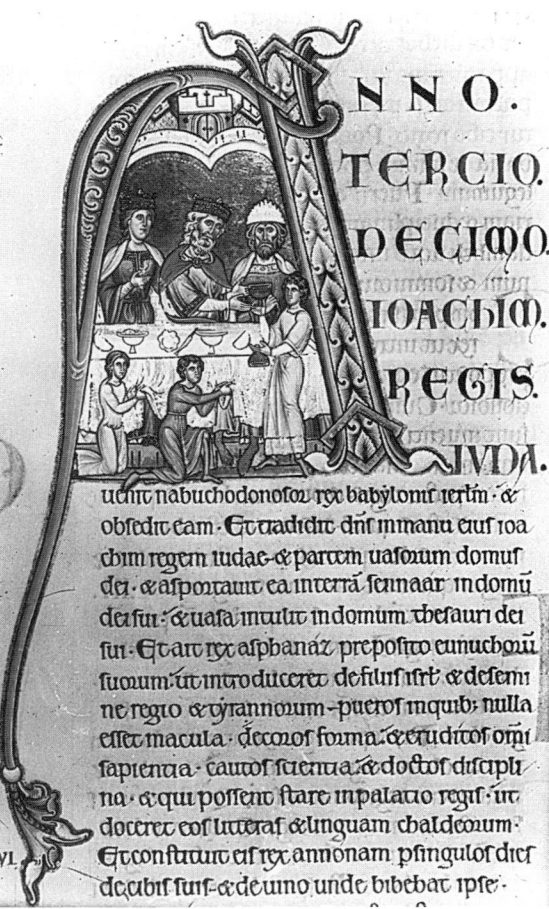

Winchester Bible, *Nebuchadnezzar and the Three Hebrew Children*, historiated initial by the Master of the Morgan Leaf, *c.* 1170–90 (Winchester, Cathedral Library, vol. ii, fol. 190r)

The second group of artists working on the Bible have been named the Master of the Morgan Leaf (after the leaf in New York; see fig.), the Amalekite Master, the Master of the Genesis Initial and the Master of the Gothic Majesty. These all worked in various interpretations of contemporary Byzantine style, whether derived from Italian intermediaries or directly from Byzantine sources: the same artists worked on wall paintings in the Holy Sepulchre Chapel in Winchester Cathedral (*see* WINCHESTER, §III, 2) and at the chapter house at Sigena Monastery in Spain (*see* SIGENA MONASTERY, §1). They transformed the Byzantine models of figures and head types into versions with more naturalistic facial expressions and drapery types. This is particularly true of the Master of the Gothic Majesty, whose work parallels the Transitional or Early Gothic style of the 1180s and 1190s found, for example, in the work of Nicholas of Verdun and the sculptors of Sens and Laon (*see* TRANSITIONAL STYLE). His style is very close to that of the artist who illuminated *c.* 1200 a Psalter for Westminster Abbey (London, BL, Royal MS. 2. A. XXII), which is a fully developed example of the Early Gothic style in England.

See also ROMANESQUE, §IV, 2(vi)(d) and (g).

BIBLIOGRAPHY

W. Oakeshott: *The Artists of the Winchester Bible* (London, 1945)
L. M. Ayres: 'The Work of the Morgan Master at Winchester and English Painting of the Early Gothic Period', *A. Bull.*, lvi (1974), pp. 201–23
——: 'The Role of the Angevin Style in English Romanesque Painting', *Z. Kstgesch.*, xxxvi (1974), pp. 193–223
C. M. Kauffmann: *Romanesque Manuscripts, 1066–1100* (1975), iii of *A Survey of Manuscripts Illuminated in the British Isles*, ed. J. J. G. Alexander (London, 1975–), no. 83
L. M. Ayres: 'English Painting and the Continent during the Reign of Henry II and Eleanor', *Eleanor of Aquitaine: Patron and Politician*, ed. W. W. Kibler (Austin, 1976), pp. 116–45
——: 'Collaborative Enterprise in Romanesque Manuscript Illuminations and the Artists of the Winchester Bible', *Medieval Art and Architecture at Winchester Cathedral: British Archaeological Association Conference Transactions: Leeds, 1980*, pp. 20–27
W. Oakeshott: *The Two Winchester Bibles* (Oxford, 1981); review by T. A. Heslop in *A. Hist.*, v (1982), pp. 94–100
——: 'Some New Initials by the Entangled Figures Master', *Burl. Mag.*, cxxvi (1984), pp. 230–32
——: 'The Origin of the "Auct." Bible', *Bodleian Lib. Rec.*, xi (1985), pp. 401–6

NIGEL J. MORGAN

Winck [Wink], **Johann Christian Thomas** (*b* Eichstätt, 19 Dec 1738; *d* Munich, 2 Feb 1797). German painter and etcher. After a five-year apprenticeship to the painter of sculptures Anton Scheidler (*fl* 1745–after 1775) in Eggenfelden and short stays in Augsburg and Freising, he returned to Eichstätt and trained for a further year with the sculpture painter Jacob Feichtmayr (*fl* 1735–67). From 1759–60 he was in Munich, first as assistant to Johann Michael Kaufmann (1713–?86), then as theatre painter at the electoral court, working to the designs of Lorenzo Quaglio, among others. His designs for the Elector's Gobelins factory were recorded in a series of large-format oil paintings. In 1769 he became court painter.

Winck is regarded as the most heavily employed fresco painter in Munich in the later 18th century. His first major fresco (Starnberg, St Joseph) was completed in 1766; in the same year he worked at St Remigius, Raisting (nr Weilheim), and from 1767 in St Johann Baptist, Inning, but none of these early works have survived intact. His most important early work (1768) is in the Wallfahrtskirche zum Heilige Kreuz in Loh (nr Deggendorf). In 1769 he painted the Wallfahrtskirche St Leonhard (*see* GERMANY, fig. 21) near Dietramszell (nr Wolfratshausen), employing a popular narrative style that inserted rustic genre figures into a broad landscape frame using soft, broken colour tones. The unified, warm dark-brown colouring comes from his study of Dutch painting. While Winck retained the formal pattern of the Rococo fresco, he mingled illusionism with naturalistic types that destroy the visionary quality and treated the fresco as a panel painting.

Winck's next major frescoes (1770) were for SS Peter and Paul, Eching (nr Landsberg) and for Schloss Zell an der Pram, Schärding, Upper Austria (1771–2). Apart from the frescoes at Zell and the decoration of the two halls in Schloss Schleissheim (1774–5), he always treated religious subjects in his frescoes. Among the frescoes (1773) at St Vitus, Egling (nr Landsberg), the large cupola painting of the *Martyrdom of St Vitus* is outstanding for its sureness of drawing and mastery of perspective. A further high point in Winck's maturity is marked by the works (1777) in the Wallfahrtskirche St Salvator in Bettbrunn (nr Riedenberg). Here Neo-classical motifs intrude. The architecture is executed more strictly to ancient models, and the structure of the work is clear and readily grasped, each figure being shown separately in a simple, natural pose. In his decoration (1782–4) of the Pfarrkirche of Maria Himmelfahrt, Schwindkirchen (nr Mühldorf), he produced an exemplary work of late Bavarian Rococo art: the *Coronation of the Virgin*, his most crowded work, is one of his main achievements.

Winck led illusionist ceiling painting forward to Neo-classicism and forms a counterpart in the history of style to Martin Knoller and Januarius Zick. He was also a productive painter of altarpieces. In his devotional paintings, oil sketches and small-format paintings his sketching style of painting, developed from his drawing technique, is seen to advantage. His chiaroscuro manner betrays an indebtedness to Rembrandt's successors.

BIBLIOGRAPHY

A. Feulner: 'Christian Wink (1738–1797): Der Ausgang der kirchlichen Rokokomalerei in Südbayern', *Altbayer. Mschr.*, xi (1912), pp. 1–62
H. Clementschitsch: *Christian Wink, 1738–1797* (diss., U. Vienna, 1968)
G. P. Woeckel: 'Ölskizzen von Thomas Christian Winck in Mainz', *Mainz. Z.*, lxiii/iv (1968/9), pp. 119–22
W. Neu: *Katholische Pfarrkirche St. Remigius, Raisting* (Munich and Zurich, 1979)
B. Ulm: *Schloss Zell an der Pram. Freskenzyklus von Christian Wink* (Ried and Innkreis, 1980)
K. Kraft: *Katholische Pfarrkirche St. Johann Baptist in Inning* (Munich and Zurich, 1983)
F. X. Schlagberger: 'Der Maler für das Volk: Thomas Christian Winck, Münchner Hofmaler im Ausgang des Rokoko', *Unser Bayern*, xxxii (1983), pp. 62–4

Winck [Winckh; Wink; Winkh], **Joseph Gregor** (*b* Deggendorf, 8 May 1710; *d* Hildesheim, 11 April 1781). German painter and sculptor. Formerly thought to be the brother of Johann Christian Thomas Winck, he in fact acquired his surname from a stepfather. Nor was he the grandfather of the sculptor Friedrich Carl Franz Winck

(1796–1859). He probably started his training in Augsburg—his antecedents lie in south German late Baroque—and may have served his apprenticeship and journeyman years in Holland. He was in Mannheim in 1743 and then worked in Hildesheim, providing an allegorical ceiling painting (1743–4, 1752–3; destr.) for the renovated Rittersaal in the cathedral, and in Brunswick, where he executed a stucco relief for the main gable of the opera house (1747–8; destr. 1864).

Winck married in 1753 in Hildesheim and executed commissions for its prince-bishop during the following years. The *Legend of St Clement* (*c.* 1755–8) on the ceiling of the chapel of Schloss Liebenburg (Goslar) is one of his most mature works. Although it is painted on a flat ceiling, perspective is used to give the illusion of a vault, with standing figures from scenes relating to the saint's life encircling his apotheosis in the centre of the picture and forming the edge of the apparent vault. The apse is painted with illusionistic architectural features, and the altarpiece shows the *Immaculate Virgin with the Fall of Man*. The frescoes (1760–65) in the Immakulata-Kirche in Büren (Paderborn), among the most important works of his later years, constitute the only large project that has been preserved and completely documented.

BIBLIOGRAPHY
H. Dreyer: *Joseph Gregor Winck, 1710–1781: Ein Beitrag zur Geschichte der Barockmalerei in Norddeutschland* (Hildesheim and Leipzig, 1925)
H. Braun: *Joseph Gregor Winck, Deggendorf 1710–Hildesheim 1781: Leben und Werk eines Barockmalers in Norddeutschland*, ii of *Forschungen der Denkmalpflege in Niedersachsen*, ed. H.-H. Möller (Hameln, 1983)
SONJA WEIH-KRÜGER

Winckelmann, Johann Joachim (*b* Stendal, 9 Dec 1717; *d* Trieste, 8 June 1768). German art historian. His writings on the sculpture of ancient Greece and Rome redefined the history of art and provided a theoretical apologia for Neo-classicism. *Geschichte der Kunst des Alterthums* (1764) was a standard reference on the art of the ancient world until well into the 19th century. Winckelmann revolutionized archaeological studies by providing a framework for stylistic classification of antiquities by period of origin, whereas previous antiquarian scholars had concerned themselves almost exclusively with questions of subject-matter. His analysis of the aesthetics of Greek art and his account of the conditions that encouraged its flowering, which highlighted the importance of climate and the political freedom of the ancient Greek city states, had a major impact in the art world of his time. His scholarly celebrations of masterpieces of ancient sculpture were particularly popular and were widely quoted in travel books and artistic treatises.

1. LIFE AND WRITINGS. The son of a cobbler, Winckelmann studied Greek and Latin, as well as theology, mathematics and medicine, at the universities of Halle and Jena. After five years as a Classics teacher in Seehausen, he was employed in 1748 in Count Heinrich von Bünau's library at Nöthnitz in Saxony, researching the latter's history of the early Holy Roman Empire. He moved to Dresden in 1754 and became involved with artistic circles at the court of Augustus III, Elector of Saxony, and became friends with the painter Adam Friedrich Oeser. The publication of his polemical essay *Gedanken über die*

Nachahmung der griechischen Werke in der Malerey und Bildhauerkunst (1755) established his reputation. Winckelmann's intensely argued case for the pre-eminence of the ancient Greeks, his call for a return to the pure forms of a Greek art that he knew only from verbal descriptions and from engravings and casts after Greco-Roman copies and his attack on the corruption of modern art, if not entirely original, struck a strong chord among contemporaries, and it was soon translated into French, English and Italian. His phrase 'eine edle Einfalt und eine stille Grösse', characterizing the essence of the Greek ideal, became a slogan of the 18th-century classical revival.

Winckelmann moved to Rome in 1755 after a controversial religious conversion that opened the way to patronage by the Catholic Church. In 1758 he entered the service of Cardinal Alessandro Albani, well known as a collector of antiques. On arriving in Rome, he worked on a treatise on Greek taste in collaboration with the painter Anton Raphael Mengs, who painted his portrait (1756–61; New York, Met.) and whom he later hailed as 'a phoenix arisen from the ashes of the first Raphael'. Although unfinished, the treatise provided the basis for lyrical descriptions of Greco-Roman statuary, such as the *Apollo Belvedere*, the *Laokoon* (see ROME, ANCIENT, fig. 59), the Belvedere *Antinous* and the Belvedere *Torso* (all Rome, Vatican, Mus. Pio-Clementino), later incorporated in *Geschichte der Kunst des Alterthums*. A version of his description of the *Torso* was published separately in 1759. Essays on connoisseurship (1759), on grace (1759) and on beauty (1763) continued Winckelmann's polemic for a classical taste in the visual arts. He achieved public recognition as an antiquarian scholar with *Description des pierres gravées du feu Baron de Stosch* (1760), a treatise on antique engraved gems, then highly prized as exemplars of artistic taste, and the subject of learned dissertations by other connoisseurs and antiquarians such as Pierre-Joseph Mariette and the Comte de Caylus.

Winckelmann's central achievement was his *Geschichte der Kunst des Alterthums* (1764), which was supplemented by *Anmerkungen über die Geschichte der Kunst des Alterthums* (1767). The earliest plan for the book dates from August 1756, and the manuscript was sent to the publisher in December 1761. The book's core is an analysis of the art of ancient Greece and Rome, complemented by discussions of ancient Egyptian, Etruscan and Near Eastern art. Although Winckelmann's visual evidence was almost exclusively Greco-Roman, he was instrumental in initiating the modern view, current since the discovery of 'original' Greek sculpture such as the Parthenon marbles in the 19th century, that later Hellenistic and Roman art was an inferior imitation of earlier Classic Greek art.

Winckelmann's subsequent publications, a study of ancient allegories and emblems, *Versuch einer Allegorie, besonders für die Kunst* (1766), and an illustrated catalogue of previously unpublished or little known antiquities, *Monumenti antichi inediti* (1767), were less innovative. They remained largely within the bounds of conventional antiquarian erudition, elucidating the meanings of visual motifs through citations from ancient Greek and Roman literature. Winckelmann did, however, establish an important principle of iconographic interpretation, namely that almost all Greek and Roman art, with the exception of a few Roman public monuments, was 'ideal' in content, and featured mythological subjects, rather than representations from history. His work as an antiquarian scholar also included studies on architecture, notably his *Anmerkungen über die Baukunst der Alten* (1762), and reports on the excavations at Herculaneum (1762 and 1764).

Winckelmann's international reputation as an expert on Greek and Roman antiquities brought him official recognition as Commissioner of Antiquities to Pope Clement XIII in 1763, and he received honorary membership of various learned societies, including the Society of Antiquaries in London. His first visit to Germany since his departure for Rome, undertaken in the spring of 1768 in the company of the sculptor Bartolomeo Cavaceppi, ended in disaster. He inexplicably cut short his itinerary after attending an audience with the Empress Maria-Theresa in Vienna and on his way back to Rome was murdered in a hotel room in Trieste.

2. INFLUENCE. Winckelmann has been called the father of modern art history because *Geschichte der Kunst des Alterthums* established an important new paradigm for defining the history of an artistic tradition. The idea of elaborating a pattern of development through a logical sequence of period styles became hugely influential for the new scholarly study of the history of art that emerged in the 19th century. He set out a comprehensive history of ancient Greek art where previously there had only been vague speculation about rise and decline, or compilations of details about famous artists culled from such literary sources as Pliny. Building on the new stylistic analysis of antiquities pioneered by the Comte de Caylus in *Recueil d'antiquités égyptiennes, étrusques, grecques, romaines et gauloises* (1752–67), and drawing on the exegesis of texts on the history of Greek art of earlier Classical scholars such as Francis Junius's *De pictura veterum* (1694), Winckelmann forged a highly effective synthesis of the available visual and verbal evidence that continues to inform accounts of ancient Greek art to this day. It was the first comprehensive attempt to rethink the larger patterning of the history of art since Giorgio Vasari's *Le vite de' piu eccelenti architetti, pittori et scultori* (1550, rev. 2/1568).

Later art historians echo the models of stylistic development Winckelmann pioneered when they trace a systematic pattern of rise and decline, or, like Heinrich Wölfflin, adumbrate a less qualitative structural change in modes of visual representation, as Winckelmann did when he distinguished between an early high style and a late beautiful style in Classic Greek art. However, partly because he had almost no concrete remains of early Greek sculpture, Winckelmann was untypically selfconscious about the speculative nature of his history. He insisted that it was a conceptual 'system', not to be confused with a chronological compilation of historical detail. A disparity between the fragmentary material facts and the schema used to endow history with a coherent pattern was not disguised, as often happens in later, seemingly more objective, histories of art. Winckelmann could even countenance that his elaborate reconstruction of the Antique from its surviving traces was no more than an illusion produced by an impossible desire to recover a totality that had been irretrievably lost.

Winckelmann's account of ancient statuary is striking for its vivid evocation of the homoerotic charge of the male body in Greek art. It is this and his insistence on the darker symbolic resonances of the still marble forms of the Greek ideal that link him with such writers as Friedrich Nietzsche and Walter Pater, both of whom brought to the fore the contradictions sustaining modern interest in the art of antiquity. At the same time, Winckelmann's involvement with the minutiae of scholarly erudition and commitment to a systematic ordering of history place him at the beginning of a tradition of modern art-historical scholarship now institutionalized in museums and universities.

See also CASANOVA, (2).

UNPUBLISHED SOURCES

Paris, Bib. N. [notebooks; for listing see A. Tibal: *Inventaires des manuscrits de Winckelmann déposés à la Bibliothèque nationale* (Paris, 1911)]

WRITINGS

Gedanken über die Nachahmung der griechischen Werke in der Malerey und Bildhauerkunst (Dresden, 1755; repr. in R, rev. 2/1756); Eng. trans. by H. Fuseli (London, 1765/R 1972)
'Beschreibung des Torso Belvedere zu Rom', *Bib. S. Wiss. & Frejen Kst.*, i (1759), pp. 23–41; repr. in R
'Von der Grazie in der Kunst', *Bib. S. Wiss. & Frejen Kst.*, i (1759), pp. 13–23; repr. in R; Eng. trans. by H. Fuseli (London, 1765/R 1972)
Description des pierres gravées du feu Baron de Stosch (Florence, 1760/R 1970)
Anmerkungen über die Baukunst der Alten (Leipzig, 1762/R 1964)
Geschichte der Kunst des Alterthums (Dresden, 1764/R 1966, rev. in 2 vols, Vienna, 2/1776); Eng. trans., ed. G. H. Lodge, 4 vols (London, 1849–72, rev. in 2 vols, 1881)
Versuch einer Allegorie, besonders für die Kunst (Dresden, 1766/R 1964)
Anmerkungen über die Geschichte der Kunst des Alterthums (Dresden, 1767/R 1966)
Monumenti antichi inediti, 2 vols (Rome, 1767/R 1967)
J. Eiselein, ed.: *Sämtliche Werke* (Donaueschingen, 1825–9)
W. Rehm, ed.: *Briefe*, 4 vols (Berlin, 1952–7)
——: *Kleine Schriften, Vorreden, Entwürfe* (Berlin, 1968) [R]
D. Irwin, ed.: *Winckelmann: Writings on Art* (London, 1972)

BIBLIOGRAPHY

K. Justi: *Winckelmann und seine Zeitgenossen*, 2 vols (Leipzig, 1866–72, rev. 4/1956)
W. Pater: 'Winckelmann', *Studies in the History of the Renaissance* (London, 1873), rev. as *The Renaissance: Studies in Art and Poetry* (London, 1877; rev. 4/1893; ed. D. L. Hill, Berkeley, 1980), pp. 141–85
H. R. Jauss: 'Geschichte der Kunst und Historie', *Geschichte Ereignis und Erzählung*, ed. R. Koselleck and W. D. Stempel (Munich, 1973), pp. 175–209; Eng. trans. as *Toward an Aesthetic of Reception* (Minneapolis, 1982)
H. Dilly: *Kunstgeschichte als Institution* (Frankfurt am Main, 1979)
M. Fried: 'Antiquity Now', *October*, 37 (Summer 1986), pp. 87–97
T. W. Gaehtgens, ed.: *Johann Joachim Winckelmann, 1717–1768* (Hamburg, 1986)
E. Pommier, ed.: *Winckelmann: La Naissance de l'histoire de l'art à l'époque des Lumières* (Paris, 1991)
A. Potts: *Flesh and the Ideal: Winckelmann and the Origins of Art History* (New Haven and London, 1994)

ALEX POTTS

Wind, Edgar (*b* Berlin, 14 May 1900; *d* London, 12 Sept 1971). German art historian active in Germany, the USA and England. His work transcends the conventional categories of academic specialization, combining philosophical and aesthetic insight with a sensitive eye and an exceptional range of historical and literary learning. He studied Classics, philosophy and art history in Berlin, Freiburg and Vienna, obtaining his D.Phil. in 1922 in Hamburg under Erwin Panofsky with a thesis on the relation between aesthetic appreciation and historical scholarship. The neo-Kantian influence of Ernst Cassirer in Hamburg was superseded by the pragmatism of Charles S. Pierce, which he encountered while teaching philosophy at North Carolina (1925–7). On his return to Hamburg as research assistant at the Bibliothek Warburg, this pragmatism was infused with Aby Warburg's concept of cultural history, interest in the psychological potency of images and fascination with significant detail. The close relationship between the two men is documented in Warburg's diaries. After submitting his anti-Kantian treatise, *Das Experiment und die Metaphysik*, Wind became Privatdozent in philosophy at Hamburg University (1930–33). A masterly essay on 18th-century portraiture (1932), the first application of his insight and learning to the concrete analysis of particular works, marked a wholly new approach to English art.

He played a decisive role in the transfer of the Warburg Library from Nazi Germany to London (Buschendorf, 1993), becoming Deputy Director of the Warburg Institute (1934–42) and founding editor, with Rudolf Wittkower, of the *Journal of the Warburg Institute* (1937), to which he contributed his first articles on Renaissance iconography. He lectured on the typological programme of the Sistine ceiling and on the conciliation of Platonic with Aristotelian philosophy in Raphael's *School of Athens*. Finding himself in the USA at the outbreak of World War II, he lectured and taught widely there: at the Pierpont Morgan Library and the Museum of Modern Art, New York; the Institute of Fine Arts, New York University (1940–42); the University of Chicago (Professor of Art, 1942–4); and Smith College, Northampton, MA (Neilson Research Professor, then Professor of Philosophy and of Art, 1944–55). With subtlety and wit, Wind applied his formidable learning to the recovery of lost modes of perception. He explored the revival of the ancient mysteries in the Neo-Platonic art and philosophy of the Renaissance, elucidating poetic metaphor and visual conceit (studies later published in *Pagan Mysteries in the Renaissance*, 1958). His works were seminal even when controversial, as when he pointed to the Ovidian source of Giovanni Bellini's *Feast of the Gods* (1948). Shortly after his Chichele Lectures at All Souls College, Oxford, 'Art and Scholarship under Julius II', Wind became the first Professor of the History of Art at Oxford (assigned to the faculty of Modern History), and Fellow of Trinity College (1955–67). His university lectures made a powerful impression on their vast audiences and were long remembered; he reached a wider public through the broadcast of his Reith Lectures in 1960, which affirmed with deep commitment the dual nature of art in a tract for the times, *Art and Anarchy*. For the meaning of Giorgione's *Tempesta* he offered a solution of surprising simplicity (1969), while his late paper on the Prophets and Sibyls (1965) reflected a lifelong preoccupation with Michelangelo's theological sources and the confluence of paganism and Christianity in Renaissance Rome.

UNPUBLISHED SOURCES
Oxford, Bodleian Lib. [scholarly papers and drafts; biog. mat.]

WRITINGS
Hume and the Heroic Portrait: Studies in Eighteenth-century Imagery (Hamburg, 1932; Eng. trans., Oxford, 1986)
Das Experiment und die Metaphysik (Tübingen, 1934)
Bellini's Feast of the Gods: A Study in Venetian Humanism (Cambridge, MA, 1948)
Pagan Mysteries in the Renaissance (London, 1958, rev. Oxford, 3/1980)

Art and Anarchy (London, 1963, rev. with intro. by J. Bayley, 3/1985)
'Michelangelo's Prophets and Sibyls', *Proc. Brit. Acad.*, li (1965), pp. 47–84
Giorgione's 'Tempesta': With Comments on Giorgione's Poetic Allegories (Oxford, 1969; rev. It. trans., Milan, 2/1992)
The Eloquence of Symbols: Studies in Humanist Art (Oxford, 1983, rev. 1993) [with bibliog. of Wind's pubd writings, and a biog. mem. by H. Lloyd-Jones, pp. xiii–xxxvi]

BIBLIOGRAPHY
H. Schlaffer: 'Gelehrsamkeit: Über Edgar Wind', *Akzente*, 2 (1982), pp. 158–67
B. Buschendorf: '"War ein sehr tüchtiges gegenseitiges Fördern": Edgar Wind und Aby Warburg', *Idea: Jb. Hamburg. Ksthalle*, iv (1985), pp. 165–209
S. Ferretti: 'Edgar Wind: Dalla filosofia alla storia', *La Cultura*, xxix (1991), pp. 346–57
P. Hadot: 'Métaphysique et Images', *Préfaces* (1992), pp. 33–37 [disc.]
R. Klibansky: 'Edgar Wind: Itinéraire d'un philosophe historien d'art', *Préfaces* (1992), pp. 28–32 [disc.]
B. Buschendorf: 'Auf dem Weg nach England: Edgar Wind und die Emigration der Bibliothek Warburg', *Porträt aus Büchern: Bibliothek Warburg und Warburg Institute*, ed. M. Diers (Hamburg, 1993), pp. 85–128

JAYNIE ANDERSON

Wind catcher [Arab. *bādahanj*, *malqaf*; Pers. *bādgīr*]. Traditional form of natural ventilation and air-conditioning built on houses throughout the Middle East from North Africa to Pakistan. Constructed at least since the 2nd millennium BC in Egypt, wind catchers have also been used to cool caravanserais, water cisterns and mosques. Consisting of an open vent built on the roof facing into or away from the prevailing wind, wind catchers have shafts carrying the air down through the roof into the living area below, thereby ventilating and cooling the spaces. Wind catchers are generally placed above the summer rooms of courtyard houses. On the Iranian plateau, where the finest wind catchers are built, the vents are in the tops of brick towers which capture the faster airstreams above the general roof level. When there is little air movement, as on summer afternoons, the wind catcher acts as a chimney, drawing warm air up the shaft and through the living areas from the courtyard. In coastal settlements, towers generally face onshore winds. Most inland towers also face prevailing winds but in some desert settlements in the Yazd region of central Iran, where the prevailing wind is hot and dusty, vents similarly face away from the wind, and the preferred air from the courtyard is drawn through the summer rooms. In Iraq and central Iran, wind catchers are important in moderating the climate of the deep basements used as summer living rooms. In the Gulf and in Sind (the lower Indus region) wind catchers serve ground- and first-floor summer rooms.

BIBLIOGRAPHY
Enc. Iran.: 'Bādgīr' [Wind catcher]; *Enc. Islam/2*: 'Bādgīr' [Wind catcher]
A. Badawy: 'Architectural Provision against the Heat in the Orient', *J. Nr E. Stud.*, xvii (1958), pp. 122–8
S. Roaf: 'Wind-catchers', *Living with the Desert*, ed. E. Beazley and M. Harverson (London, 1982), pp. 57–72

SUSAN ROAF

Winde, William (*d* Westminster, London, 28 April 1722). English architect and soldier. His ancestors were Norfolk gentry and his grandfather, Sir Robert Winde, was a Gentleman of the Privy Chamber to Charles I. His father, Henry Winde, was a royalist who died in exile in the Netherlands in 1658. By that time William was a junior officer in command of English troops at Bergen-op-Zoom. At the Restoration he left for England to claim his patrimony. He enjoyed the patronage of William, 1st Lord Craven (1606–97), who was his godfather, and it was doubtless through the latter's influence that in 1661 he was made gentleman usher to Elizabeth, the exiled Queen of Bohemia (daughter of James I). In 1667 he obtained a commission in the King's Troop of the Royal Regiment of Horse and for the next ten years served as a cavalry officer, attaining the rank of captain in 1678. There is evidence, however, that he was already concerning himself with military architecture and had expectations, which were not realized, of obtaining an appointment in the Office of Ordnance. Despite gallant service at the Battle of Sedgemoor in 1685, promotion eluded him, and after the Revolution of 1688 he gave up further hope of a military career and concentrated on architecture.

From the 1660s Winde practised as a gentleman architect. There is reason to think that he received instruction in architecture from Sir Balthazar Gerbier, whom he succeeded as the architect of Lord Craven's country house at Hampstead Marshall (c. 1663–c. 1688; destr. 1718), Berks. He also rebuilt Combe Abbey (1682–5), Warwicks, for Lord Craven. Other important commissions were Powis (later Newcastle) House (1684–9; rebuilt 1930–31), Lincoln's Inn Fields, London, and Buckingham House (1702–5; now incorporated in Buckingham Palace), Westminster, where, however, he may have taken over a design already made by William Talman. Although conclusive evidence is lacking, Winde was almost certainly the architect of Belton House (1685–8), Lincs, and very likely of Dingley Hall (c. 1685), Northants.

Winde ranks as one of the principal English country-house architects of the late 17th century. Although not as innovative as Roger Pratt or Talman, he was responsible for some very handsome houses of a type that derived from Pratt's Clarendon House (1664–7; destr. 1683), Piccadilly, London. Though generally astylar, the houses were distinguished externally by enriched cornices and pediments, prominent hipped roofs crowned by cupolas and end bays brought forward as shallow wings. Their plan was a fairly simple variant of the 'double pile', but the principal rooms were embellished with carving and plasterwork of great accomplishment, carried out by a team of craftsmen regularly employed by Winde which included the sculptor Edward Pierce (ii), the plasterer Edward Goudge and the carpenters Jonathan and Edward Wilcox. These men generally submitted their own designs for workmanship to be executed in accordance with a general scheme laid down by Winde; his responsibilities as a serving officer meant that his visits to a building site were necessarily only intermittent. Nevertheless, he retained control by correspondence and personally examined all the accounts before authorizing payment.

Winde also acted as a landscape gardener, though no surviving layout can be attributed to him. Drawings by Winde are in the Bodleian Library, Oxford, and in the British Library there is an unpublished treatise on mathematics (1688), which includes sections on military architecture and cartography.

Colvin

BIBLIOGRAPHY

G. Beard: 'William Winde and Interior Design', *Archit. Hist.*, xxvii (1984), pp. 150–62

H. Colvin, ed.: 'Letters and Papers Relating to the Rebuilding of Combe Abbey, Warwickshire, 1681–1688', *Walpole Soc.*, l (1984), pp. 248–309

HOWARD COLVIN

Winders. Belgian family of architects.

(1) Jean-Jacques Winders (*b* Antwerp, 14 May 1849; *d* Antwerp, 20 Feb 1936). His father was one of the most important building contractors in Antwerp and he was introduced to the art of building at an early age by helping to supervise his father's construction projects. His rapid success as an architect was helped by participation in various competitions, particularly the national competition (1873) for a monument to the liberation of the Scheldt; his winning design was completed and unveiled in Antwerp in 1883. During this period Winders also built the Pauwels Factory (1875), the Steenackers Warehouses (1879) and several upper-class residences in Antwerp. These were all Flemish Renaissance Revival designs, and Winders became known as one of the leading exponents of this style in Antwerp. His principal buildings are located in the southern district of Antwerp, where new urban development was taking place. His most important public building was the Koninklijk Museum voor Schone Kunsten (1877–90), which he won with a national competition entry co-designed with Frans Van Dyck. An equally significant work was his own house, 'Den Passer' (The Pair of Compasses; 1883), at Tolstraat, Antwerp. In this highly articulated design he achieved a full synthesis of his ideas concerning the revitalization of the Flemish Renaissance style, and it earned him an international reputation. Following this period of intense architectural activity, during which he also built the town hall (1875) in Gilly, Winders was appointed to a teaching post at the Academie voor Schone Kunsten, Antwerp, and became a member of various academic institutions. He built little after 1900.

BIBLIOGRAPHY

H. Stynen: 'Kunst brengt gunst: Jean-Jacques Winders, 1849–1936, en de neo-Vlaamse renaissance', *Mnmt & Landschappen*, 6 (1986), pp. 6–26

Musée des archives d'architecture moderne: Collections, Brussels, Mus. Archvs Archit. Mod. cat. (Brussels, 1986), pp. 372–5

(2) Maxime Winders (*b* Antwerp, 23 April 1882; *d* Brussels, 10 Sept 1982). Son of (1) Jean-Jacques Winders. From 1892 to 1907 he completed a full course of study, including architecture, painting and sculpture, at the Koninklijke Academie voor Schone Kunsten, Antwerp, and worked in the studio of his father. Helped by family ties with the Banque Nationale de Belgique, he received commissions to design numerous bank buildings in Antwerp after 1909, as well as the city's main diamond exchange (1910), which were in an eclectic, classicist style. However, he owed his reputation principally to his reconstruction (1916–27) for the bank of the Tafelronde, a 15th-century guild house in the Grote Markt, Leuven, where he removed the Neo-classical structure that had been substituted at the beginning of the 19th century and restored the Gothic style of the original. This project demonstrated both his attachment to Belgium's architectural past and a virtuosity in handling different styles. He was also in charge of the excavations (1938) that brought to light the burial place of Margaret of York, wife of Charles the Bold, Duke of Burgundy, in the church of the Récollets, Mechelen. During both world wars he was in charge of official missions for the protection of Belgium's artistic heritage, particularly the safety and repatriation of such works as Jan van Eyck's *Adoration of the Mystic Lamb* altarpiece (*c.* 1423–32; Ghent, St Bavo). Maxime Winders was a prolific architect and he continued to produce private mansions, industrial buildings and monuments in Brussels and Antwerp until the 1960s.

BIBLIOGRAPHY
Musée des archives d'architecture moderne: Collections, Brussels, Mus. Archvs Archit. Mod. cat. (Brussels, 1986), pp. 376–83

ANNETTE NÈVE

Windhoek. Capital of Namibia. It is situated in the geographic centre of the country at an altitude of 1700 m and has a population of 120,000 (1991 estimate). German colonial troops founded the town in 1890, building a fort (Alte Feste) along a row of water springs on high ground to the east, parallel to the historic transportation route. The main street was known until 1990 as the Kaiserstrasse and afterwards as Independence Avenue. The early buildings were of masonry, with pitched corrugated iron roofs and encircling verandahs, the details of which were derived from German Neo-classicism. The apogee of this colonial verandah-style is the Parliamentary Building of the Government of Namibia (1910–13), by State Architect Gottlieb Redecker (1871–1945), which is known colloquially as the Tintenpalast. In the last years of German stewardship over Namibia, which ended in 1915, Windhoek was subjected to an urban restructuring that included remodelling the Ausspannplatz at the southern end of Kaiserstrasse to become fan-shaped and the reshaping of the intersection leading up to the military buildings at the northern end as a minor Place de l'Etoile; and the termination of the cross-axis—midway, at the Troop Garden—at its upper/eastern end by the building of the Christuskirche (1907–10; also by Redecker) on a traffic island. The most striking private buildings remaining from this period are three Rhenish castles on the crests of hills to the south by Wilhelm Sander (1861–1930); the Wilhelmine villas to the north; and the groups of commercial buildings along Independence Avenue. During South African rule over Namibia (1915–90), the town expanded with suburbs, townships such as Katatura, and high-rise buildings with a network of cool arcades in the central business district. The outstanding library, museum and archives complex (1954–6) was designed by Hellmut Stauch. Zoo Park (originally the Troop Garden) was opened to Independence Avenue at the time of Namibian Independence in 1990, when the street was transformed into a boulevard and Post Street into a pedestrian mall, providing the basis for a major westward expansion to the CBD, the first since the German era. Despite a post-Independence boom, vestiges of German planning and building still determine the character of the town.

Windhoek has a high number of art galleries for its size and is a prominent arts centre in southern Africa. The National Art Gallery was established in 1947 as the South West African Arts Association. The Association presents the Stanswa Biennale and was instrumental in an upsurge of artistic activity in Namibia in the second half of the 20th century. Earlier the city was a base for European artists inspired by Namibia's landscape and wildlife (e.g. Thomas Baines, Axel Eriksson, Carl Ossmann, Johannes Blatt, Adolph Jensch, Otto Schröder and Fritz Krampe), while John Muafangejo (1943–87) was the first black Namibian artist to be admired both in Windhoek's art galleries and internationally (*see* NAMIBIA). Other artists connected with the city are Joseph Madisia (*b* 1954), a painter, draughtsman and graphic artist; Joachim Voigts (1907–94), a book illustrator; Heinz Pullon (*b* 1930), a versatile etcher and engraver; the sculptor Dörte Berner (*b* 1942), whose works are often in steatite soapstone; and the highly regarded English-born photographer Amy Schocman (*b* 1942). A speciality of farms surrounding Windhoek is the weaving of carpets and tapestries with organic and geometric patterns or narrative scenes executed in Karakul wool.

BIBLIOGRAPHY
Berman
W. Peters: *Baukunst in Südwestafrika, 1884–1914* (Windhoek, 1981)
M. Meaker: 'Adolph Jensch: Prayers in Paint', *Rössing* (Dec 1984), pp. 12–16
J. Phillips: 'Old Namibia, through the Eyes of Thomas Baines', *Rössing* (Dec 1984), pp. 1–7
A. Lillienthal: 'Südwester Künstler: Eine Auswahl', *1884–1984: Vom Schutzgebiet bis Namibia*, ed. K. Becker and J. Hecker (Windhoek, 1985)
A. Schoeman: 'Four Namibian Artists', *Rössing* (April 1988), pp. 6–11
W. Peters: 'An Outline of the Architecture in South West Africa/Namibia, 1914–1989', *Lantern* (Aug 1989), pp. 63–72

WALTER PETERS

Windisch, Jörg [Georg] (*d* Passau, 8 Aug 1466). ?Bohemian architect, active in Germany. Shortly after 1450 Prince-Bishop Ulrich III appointed him successor to Hans Hesse in the building of Passau Cathedral. He directed the design and construction of the transept; the date 1462 is inscribed between the two upper windows of the south transept. The rich decoration of the transept suggests Bohemian influence. He is also generally credited with the planning of the crossing dome, which was not built until 1524. He is supposed to have prepared the plan for the nave of the parish church at Eferding, Austria, the foundation stone of which was laid two days before his death. Until 1811 his tomb was in the cloister of Passau Cathedral.

BIBLIOGRAPHY
Thieme–Becker
E. Ullmann: *Deutsche Architektur und Plastik, 1470–1550* (Gütersloh, 1984)

VERENA BEAUCAMP

Window. Opening in a wall to admit light and air, mostly covered with glass, but also with paper or wood. The term derives from the Old Norse word *vindauge*, meaning 'eye of the wind'. Historically, windows have taken on numerous diverse forms and functions. In cases where defensive considerations were paramount, windows were small, inconspicuous and confined to the upper levels of buildings (e.g. Catal Hüyük, Turkey, *c.* 6000 BC; Himeji Castle, Japan, AD 1568–1600). To reduce light and heat, stone buildings in ancient Egypt often had no windows on the outside walls at all; instead, narrow slits were carved into the ceiling (e.g. Temple of Hathor, Dendara, begun 80 BC). The function of a window can be almost completely aesthetic or symbolic, as when serving as a frame for the presentation of royalty to an audience. One example was the Egyptian 'window of appearance', which first appeared in the Amarna period (e.g. Tomb of *Meryre II*, el-Amarna, Egypt). It was a tall, vertical window, raised from ground level and closed with a double door. This usage continued late into Egyptian history (e.g. palace of Rameses III at Medinet Habu). Another example was the *jharoka-i-darshan* ('window of viewing'), placed high on the exterior wall of forts and palaces in Mughal India, where the emperor appeared to his subjects every morning at dawn. In religious architecture, where light is often symbolic of the divine, windows serve an obviously important function, as in the clerestories and apses of such churches as S Apollinare in Classe (consecrated 549), Ravenna. This reached its fullest development in the stained-glass windows of such Gothic churches as Notre-Dame at Chartres (*see* CHARTRES, §I, 3). At Sainte-Chapelle, Paris, walls give way to a surface that is almost entirely composed of lancet windows, held together by a skeletal stone framework (*see* PARIS, §V, 2(iii)).

From ancient Roman times windows were framed by pillars or pilasters and capped with pediments. The practice continued through the Renaissance and into the 20th century, within various classical revival styles. Windows could be rectangular, square, curved or pointed, receding into, or projecting from, the wall. Balconies or an elaborate sill could also be placed below them. Window pediments became very ornate in the 18th century throughout western Europe, particularly in Spain and Portugal. The tradition of arranging windows of uniform size in horizontal rows on multi-storey buildings was established in the Renaissance (e.g. Alberti's Palazzo Rucellai, Florence, from *c.* 1453). An experiment with this form occurred in the International-style Cité Moderne (1922–5), Brussels, by Victor Bourgeois, where rows were broken up in favour of an asymmetrical arrangement. The so-called 'French window', with double casements opening as doors and reaching to the floor, has been popular in Western domestic architecture since the late Renaissance. This fashion was made use of in the context of the fine arts by Marcel Duchamp in his punningly titled *Fresh Widow* (1920), a set of French windows, with the eight panes of glass covered with black leather. Large networks of windows have been used extensively in skyscraper design, and one of the first skyscraper façades to consist almost entirely of a grid of windows was Louis Sullivan's Carson Pirie Scott Store (1898–1904), Chicago, IL (*see* SULLIVAN, LOUIS, fig. 2). The use of a load-bearing metal frame for the outer walls allowed for multi-storey stretches of windows. The Seagram Building (1954–8), Park Avenue, New York, by Ludwig Mies van der Rohe and Philip Johnson, could be seen as the culmination of this trend, a building that, from the outside at least, appears to be almost all windows.

In eastern Asia, paper is a traditional medium for covering windows, although grids of bamboo or wood are also used. In the Islamic countries of northern Africa, and of western and southern Asia, windows often frame elaborate networks of geometric or vegetal motifs, carved of stone or wood, which reduce heat by filtering the intense light, while admitting cooling breezes. In the West, glass is the usual covering for windows. Although clear glass is the norm, stained glass continues to be used for a variety of expressive ends. Early 20th-century examples include *View of Oyster Bay* (1905; New York, Met.) by Tiffany & Co., which presents a landscape view of stained glass while blocking the view to the 'real' landscape beyond it. The almost contemporary *Tree of Life* (1904) window from the Darwin D. Martin House, Buffalo, NY, designed by Frank Lloyd Wright, uses stained and clear glass much more abstractly, geometricizing the landscape motif and using it as a symbol of the bond between mankind and nature, a bond that is stated much more literally in traditional Chinese and Japanese architecture, as in Katsura Detached Palace, Kyoto (17th century; *see* KYOTO, §IV, 10). Here, sliding panels open up wall-size windows, breaking down the distinction between interior and exterior space, while also often deliberately framing a specific landscape or garden view.

See also LIGHTING; and GLASS, §IV, 2.

BIBLIOGRAPHY
C. F. Ansley, ed.: *The Columbia Encyclopedia* (New York, 1946)
A. Badamy: *A History of Egyptian Architecture: The Empire (The New Kingdom)* (Berkeley and Los Angeles, 1968)
J. J. Norwich, ed.: *Great Architecture of the World* (New York, 1975)
N. Menocal: 'Form and Content in Frank Lloyd Wright's *Tree of Life* Window', *Elvehjem Mus. A. Bull.* (1984), pp. 18–32
B. Fletcher: *A History of Architecture* (London, rev. 19/1987)
J. Masheck: 'Alberti's *Window*', *A.J.* [New York], l/1 (1991), pp. 34–41

WALTER SMITH

Windrim, James Hamilton (*b* Philadelphia, PA, 4 Jan 1840; *d* Philadelphia, 26 April 1919). American architect. He was in the first class to graduate from Girard College, Philadelphia, in 1856 and trained as a draughtsman with Archibald Catanach, the mason who built John Notman's Holy Trinity Episcopal Church (1856–9) in Philadelphia. Early in the 1860s Windrim was sent to Pittsburgh to supervise construction of the Union Depot that was being built by the Pennsylvania Railroad. When he returned to Philadelphia (1867) he won the competition for the Masonic Temple (1868–73), built on the north side of Penn Square. An extravaganza of Romanesque ornamentation, it has equally rich interiors by George Herzog (1845–1913). His other major works in Philadelphia included the Academy of Natural Sciences (1872), the US Centennial Agricultural Hall (1876) in Fairmount Park, and the Italianate Kemble House (mid-1880s), which resembles McKim, Mead & White's Villard House complex (1882–6) in New York City. He served (1889–91) as Supervising Architect of the United States in Washington but returned to Philadelphia to take up the post of Director of Public Works, in which capacity he built the classical Richard Smith Memorial Gateway (1897) in Fairmount Park. After 1909 he practised in conjunction with his son John T. Windrim; one of their most important works was a planned residential complex of 800 houses and service buildings designed for the Girard Estate adjacent to the original Stephen Girard House of 1798.

BIBLIOGRAPHY
MEA
'James H. Windrim', *National Cyclopedia of American Biography*, iii (New York, 1893), p. 422
'James H. Windrim', *Steel and Garnet*, i (1911), pp. 7–8
G. B. Tatum: *Penn's Great Town: 250 Years of Philadelphia Architecture Illustrated in Prints and Drawings* (Philadelphia, 1961)

J. Poppliers: *James Hamilton Windrim* (M.A. thesis, U. PA, 1962)
——: 'The 1867 Philadelphia Masonic Temple Competition', *J. Soc. Archit. Historians*, xxvi (1967), pp. 278–84
E. Teitelman and R. W. Longstreth: *Architecture in Philadelphia: A Guide* (Cambridge, MA, 1974)

LELAND M. ROTH

Windsor Castle. English castle and royal residence in Berkshire.

1. Before *c.* 1516. 2. Later history.

1. BEFORE *c.* 1516. One of a series of castles that William I (*reg* 1066–87) established around London, Windsor occupied the nearest strong point in the Thames Valley to the west of the city. From William's reign date the motte and also the distinctive elongated arrangement of lower, middle and upper baileys (see fig. 1) that exploits the lie of the land at the top of a great chalk cliff south of the river. By the reign of Henry I (*reg* 1100–35) the creation of a large hunting forest, together with the proximity of London, made this a favoured royal residence as well as a fortress. The Round Tower, the stone shell-keep on the motte, may date from this time. The systematic replacement of timber defences by stone walls with rectangular interval towers was begun by Henry II in 1165, but work on the lower bailey was unfinished at his death in 1189. The completion and partial refashioning from 1221 to 1230 of the south and west parts of the lower bailey were both a reparation of damage sustained during the French siege of 1216 and a political gesture substantiating the young Henry III's authority. The interval towers, among the earlier English examples of the standard 13th-century type, are half-cylindrical to the outside and larger and more massive than Henry II's towers.

After Henry III's marriage in 1236, the modernization began of his grandfather's residential buildings, that is, the more accessible and ceremonially important apartments on the north side of the lower bailey and the more private ones (the 'King's Houses') against the north wall of the upper bailey. The building accounts suggest that the upper bailey works were as uncoordinated in their layout and as luxurious in their decoration as Henry III's other major houses at Clarendon (Wilts) and Havering (Essex). The most important work of his reign was a new set of apartments built in 1240–48 east of the hall and lodgings in the lower bailey: chambers for the King and Queen north of a cloister and a large chapel of St Edward to the south. The arcading on the north side of the wall separating chapel and cloister preserves a number of French Gothic features new to England; and the lost windows of the chapel may well have incorporated bar tracery some five years before the architect of the chapel, Henry of Reyns (*d* 1253), employed it at Westminster Abbey. In overall design the chapel was not French, for its plan was rectangular and it had a timber vault, which the King had ordered should imitate masonry and resemble the vault over the 'new work' (presumably the transepts; *c.* 1230–40) at Lichfield Cathedral (Staffs). The small west portal is closed by doors with splendid scrolled ironwork signed *Gilebertvs*. Two heads from wall paintings of kings (*in situ*) in the cloister and west porch and a fragment of a richly carved Purbeck marble font in the chapel are the only other surviving decorative elements.

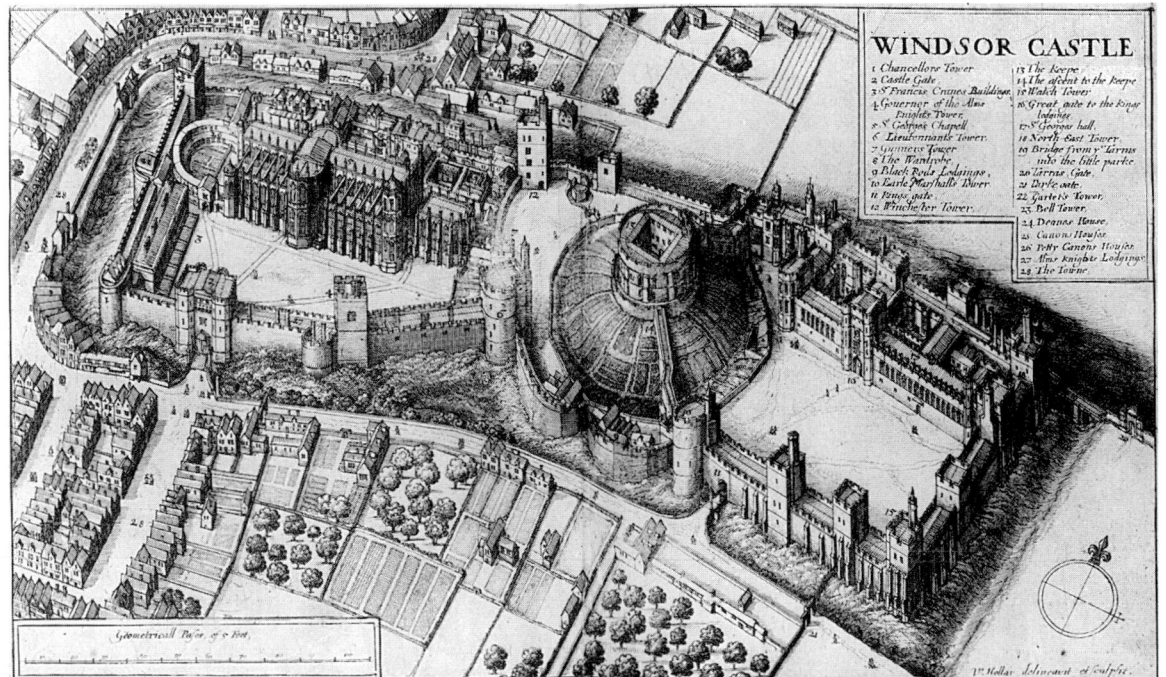

1. Windsor Castle, from the south-east, begun 11th century; engraving by Wenceslaus Hollar, from E. Ashmole: *The Institution, Laws and Ceremonies of the Most Noble Order of the Garter* (Oxford, 1672)

Edward III built more of Windsor than any other medieval king. From 1350 Henry III's chapel was refitted as the collegiate chapel of the Order of the Garter (founded in 1348) and dedicated to St George. The adjoining cloister and chambers were rebuilt to accommodate the canons. The entrance porch (completed by 1352) to this complex has a traceried vault of an ashlar-shell construction that comes closer to the classic form of fan vault than any other example of this date. The cloister tracery combines elements derived from the two earliest Perpendicular buildings, the cloister and chapter house (finished *c.* 1349) of Old St Paul's Cathedral and the south transept (*c.* 1331–6) of Gloucester Abbey Church (now Cathedral). The transferral of the lower bailey lodgings to the college of St George suggests the intention to rebuild the 'King's Houses' on the upper bailey as a self-contained palace, although this was not actually carried out until 1357–68 (*see* WYNFORD, WILLIAM).

Edward III's new upper bailey lodgings were the most costly work of domestic architecture undertaken by the English crown before the reign of Henry VII. The aim was to create a fixed base for the royal household equal in capacity to the Privy Palace at Westminster. As most of Edward's work was rebuilt in the late 17th century and the early 19th (*see* §3 below), the disposition and functions of all but a few of the rooms are unknown, as is the appearance of all the main first-floor rooms save one. Also unknown is the extent to which the retention of 12th- and 13th-century masonry affected the layout round three courtyards, which, from east to west, were given over to services, major public rooms and the private apartments of the royal family. Along with a degree of coherent planning and consistent execution virtually unprecedented in English palace architecture, the most important innovation was the extent to which the main south front was treated as a unified and regular façade despite the disparate functions of the spaces behind. This near-regularity was of hierarchical significance, for the rooms behind the façade—the great hall, household chapel and king's great chamber—were the most important in the ensemble. Other advanced features were the two-storey cloister-cum-corridor round the central courtyard and the architecture of the hall roof (destr.), where the pierced Perpendicular screenwork above the principals anticipated the great roof of Westminster Hall (from 1394; *see* LONDON, §V, 3(i)(a)). Against the east and south sides of the upper bailey were built long ranges of standardized lodgings for household officers. These and the end-to-end arrangement of the hall and chapel in the palace block influenced New College, Oxford (*see* OXFORD, §3), the founder of which, William of Wykeham, had been Clerk of Works at Windsor from 1356 to 1361. The master mason in 1350–68 was John Sponlee (*fl* 1350–?86), and the carpentry was directed by the King's Chief Carpenter, William Herland (*d* 1375).

In June 1475 work began on clearing a site for a new St George's Chapel immediately west of the old one. Integral to this scheme were lodgings and a cloister for the vicars opposite the site of the future west front of the chapel. The horseshoe plan alludes to Edward IV's Yorkist fetterlock badge. The curvilinear trusses anticipate 16th-century timber-framing. Edward's concern that the Order of the Garter be as splendid as the Order of the Golden Fleece (*see* CHIVALRY, ORDERS OF), headed by his brother-in-law Philip the Good, 3rd Duke of Burgundy, clearly influenced his decision to embark on this project, and his new chapel was the most ambitious work of church architecture undertaken by any western European monarch in the late 15th century. The aim was evidently to build a chapel in the guise of a minster, like that which some Arthurian romances place at Camelot, seat of the prototypical chivalric society. Hence the basilican format, the consistent use of stone vaulting, the long choir and nave, the square ambulatory linking up with the old chapel, the transepts and (unexecuted) lantern-tower over the crossing, and the basing of the internal elevations (*see* ENGLAND, fig. 3) on the two grandest works of Perpendicular cathedral architecture of the previous century, the choir of Gloucester Abbey (now Cathedral) and the nave of Canterbury Cathedral (*see* CANTERBURY, fig. 9). In its extreme flatness, the lierne vault prepared for but not executed by the original architect Henry Janyns (*see* JANYNS, (2); *see also* VERTUE, (2)) is comparable only to that planned at Eton College Chapel, where Janyns had been apprenticed *c.* 1453–4. The fan vaulting in the aisles has the flattened profile and refined decoration characteristic of the many fan vaults built in Janyns's native Oxfordshire from the 1440s.

The chaste, polished architecture of Janyns's choir was offset by the exuberant yet controlled architectural fantasy of the choir-stalls (1478–83). Although made by English craftsmen and conceived within the distinctive English traditions of stall design, the detailing of the tall, spired canopies is so heavily influenced by Netherlandish architecture and church furnishings that Edward IV, who was in Holland and Flanders in 1471, may well have been involved. The King's two-storey chantry-cum-oratory, integrated into the north side of the chancel, seems to have no exact counterpart elsewhere. Henry VII's contributions include most of the choir aisle vaulting, the apsidal Lady chapel (*c.* 1494–1501) intended to house his tomb and the shrine of Henry VI, and perhaps the apsidal and distinctly bay window-like transepts (see fig. 2). The bulk of the nave was built *c.* 1503–6 with money bequeathed by Henry VII's confidant, Sir Reginald Bray (*d* 1503). The design conforms closely to that of the choir, and although one bay longer than first intended, the nave does not detract from the precocious near-symmetry that the south front of the chapel displays towards the lower bailey.

The only important later medieval alteration to the palace block was the addition at its north-west corner of a short range containing well-lit rooms on both first and second floors ('Henry VII's Tower'; *see* JANYNS, (3)). Work was complete by 1501, but since the starting date is not documented it cannot be known whether its fantastic star-plan bay windows (partly destr. *c.* 1800) could have influenced those of Henry VII's Richmond Palace (*see* TUDOR, (1)). Either Richmond or Windsor was the source of the similar bays on Henry VII's chapel (1503–9) in Westminster Abbey. In the lower bailey Henry III's gatehouse was replaced *c.* 1510–16. The broad proportioning of its towers was no doubt a piece of contextually inspired conservatism.

2. Windsor Castle, St George's Chapel, begun 1475

BIBLIOGRAPHY

W. H. St J. Hope: *Windsor Castle: An Architectural History*, 2 vols (London, 1913)

L. G. Wickham Legg: 'Windsor Castle, New College, Oxford, and Winchester College: A Study of the Development of Planning by William of Wykeham', *J. Brit. Archaeol. Assoc.*, 3rd ser., iii (1938), pp. 83–95

C. J. P. Cave and H. S. London: 'The Roof-bosses in St George's Chapel, Windsor', *Archaeologia*, xcv (1953), pp. 107–22

J. H. Harvey: 'The Architects of St George's Chapel', *Rep. Soc. Friends St George's*, iv/2 (1961), pp. 48–55; iv/3 (1962), pp. 85–95

H. M. Colvin, ed.: *The History of the King's Works* (London, 1963–82), ii, pp. 864–88; iii, pp. 302–33; v, pp. 313–41; vi, pp. 373–402

P. E. Curnow: 'Royal Lodgings of the 13th Century in the Lower Ward of Windsor Castle: Some Recent Archaeological Discoveries', *Rep. Soc. Friends St George's*, iv/6 (1965), pp. 218–28

P. Kidson: 'The Architecture of St George's Chapel', *The Saint George's Chapel Quincentenary Handbook*, ed. M. Bond (Windsor, 1975), pp. 29–39

W. C. Leedy: *Fan Vaulting: A Study of Form, Technology and Meaning* (London, 1980), pp. 220–24

C. Tracy: *English Gothic Choir-stalls, 1400–1540* (Woodbridge, 1990), pp. 47–57

C. Wilson: *The Gothic Cathedral: The Architecture of the Great Church, 1130–1530* (London, 1990), pp. 217–21

CHRISTOPHER WILSON

2. LATER HISTORY. After the completion of St George's Chapel, few major changes or additions were made to Windsor Castle until 1675. The Restoration of the monarchy (1660) may be linked to the restoration of Windsor Castle itself. Glorification of monarchy as well as the influence of the château of Versailles explain the major rebuilding (1675–83) undertaken for Charles II by Hugh May (1622–84). Edward III's buildings in upper ward (formerly upper bailey), including St George's Hall, were demolished, and a new palace was created. Little survives of May's austere façades, which represented a

stylistic compromise between contemporary classicism and the surviving medieval structure (see fig. 3 below). The Baroque interiors were far richer than the exteriors suggested. The chief artists involved were ANTONIO VERRIO, GRINLING GIBBONS and the gilder René Cousin. Only three of Verrio's twenty ceilings, the King's Dining Room, the Queen's Audience Chamber and the Queen's Presence Chamber, survive. Their iconography, glorifying Charles II and Queen Catherine of Braganza (1638–1705), has been described as 'fulsomely and unrealistically propagandist in the manner accepted throughout Europe in the seventeenth century' (Colvin, v, p. 322). By contrast, Gibbons's carvings have always been admired, and many were recycled during the next major rebuilding of 1824. Another important addition that directly emulated Versailles is the Long Walk (1685), a 5 km avenue, originally of elms, forming a southern approach from Windsor Great Park. Few further changes were made until the late 18th century. It was a reflection of burgeoning Gothic Revivalism that James Wyatt (see WYATT, (2)) 'gothicized' several of the state apartments. He removed many of May's round-topped windows and reconstructed the apartments, providing a new state staircase (1800–04; destr.) and the surviving grand vestibule. The latter's attenuated proportions and fan vaulting resemble Wyatt's work at Fonthill Abbey (1796–1813; part destr.), Wilts. George III's insanity from 1811 and Wyatt's death in 1813 delayed progress until, in 1824, Parliament voted £150,000 for Jeffry Wyatville's rebuilding programme (see WYATT, (3)), a sum eventually exceeded seven times over.

George IV, like Charles II, saw the reconstruction of Windsor Castle in symbolic terms—as an affirmation of

3. Windsor Castle, east front of the upper ward before alteration (top) and after alteration (bottom) by Jeffry Wyatville, from 1824, watercolours (Windsor, Windsor Castle, Royal Library); from W. M. St John Hope: *Windsor Castle: An Architectural History*, i (London, 1913), pl. 47

the continuity of the monarchy. In accordance with fashionable, picturesque Gothic Revivalism the intention was to revive the spirit of Edward III without neglecting the comfort or elegance of a royal residence. Wyatville's rebuilding (see fig. 3) won Walter Scott's admiration for evoking 'much Gothic feeling'. Important in this respect was the raising of the Round Tower by 10 m to give stronger central emphasis and to offset the enlarged state and private apartments. Rebuilding necessitated the destruction of much 17th-century work including May's Royal Chapel (1684–6), possibly the finest Baroque interior in England. St George's Hall, with Verrio's paintings of the *Black Prince* and the *Apotheosis of Charles II*, was replaced by an arid Gothic hall (destr. 1992) lacking scale and grandeur. Nevertheless, Wyatville's stylistic consistency in the progression from the great staircase (destr.), through the guard chamber to St George's Hall itself must be recognized. An open courtyard was transformed into the Waterloo Chamber, a picture gallery. The Grand Reception Room (destr. 1992), furnished and decorated in French Rococo style, reflected George IV's Gallomania. The castle's furnishings by Morel & Seddon (*see* SEDDON) fuse effectively with the architecture and are comfortably eclectic in their Rococo, Louis XVI, Empire and Gothic

Revival styles. The last is apparent in the State Dining Room furniture (part destr. 1992), probably made in 1827 from the designs of the 15-year-old A. W. N. Pugin (*see* PUGIN, (2)). While Wyatville's Gothic soon became outmoded, his asymmetrical skyline influenced Charles Barry in the Houses of Parliament (*see* LONDON, §V, 3(ii)). But Wyatville's Windsor was not merely picturesque; it reconciled ceremony with ease of circulation, comfort and privacy. The only important Victorian addition was Anthony Salvin's anticlimactic grand staircase (1866). In the 1980s restoration began on the Round Tower, and in 1992 the north-east corner of the castle, including St George's Hall, the private chapel and the State Dining Room, were badly damaged by fire.

BIBLIOGRAPHY
The Official Guide to Windsor Castle (London, 1949, rev. 26/1986)
O. Morshead: *Windsor Castle* (London, 1951, rev. 2/1957)
N. Pevsner: *Berkshire*, Bldgs England (London, 1966/R 1988)
G. de Bellaigue and P. Kirkham: 'George IV and the Furnishing of Windsor Castle', *Furn. Hist.*, viii (1972), pp. 1–34
D. Linstrum: *Sir Jeffry Wyatville: Architect to the King* (Oxford, 1972)
R. Mackworth-Young: *The History & Treasures of Windsor Castle* (Andover, 1982, rev. 2/1988)
D. Watkin, ed.: *The Royal Interiors of England from Watercolours First Published by W. H. Pyne in 1817–20* (London, 1984)

G. Worsley: 'Windsor Castle, Berkshire', *Country Life*, clxxxvii (1993), pp. 30–33
M. Girouard: *Windsor: The Most Romantic Castle* (London, 1995)
For further bibliography *see* §1 above.

MARK STOCKER

Windus, B(enjamin) G(odfrey) (*b* ?London, 1790; *d* ?London, 1867). English patron. He belonged to a long-established family firm of coachmakers; he was also a director of Globe Insurance and patented a medicine for children called 'Godfrey's Cordial'. He began to collect watercolours by J. M. W. Turner about 1820 and by the late 1830s had amassed some two hundred, including the largest single group of the *Picturesque Views in England and Wales* series. John Ruskin knew the collection well, describing it as 'for me, the means of writing *Modern Painters*'; and it was at Windus's house on Tottenham Green, London, that Turner first thanked Ruskin for his defence. Windus's library, lined with elaborately framed Turner watercolours, was painted by John Scarlett Davis (1835; London, BM).

Windus's large and miscellaneous collection of English paintings and drawings also included works by Henry Fuseli, William Etty, Richard Parkes Bonington, Thomas Girtin, Daniel Maclise and John Frederick Lewis, important groups of drawings by David Wilkie and Thomas Stothard, and (from the 1850s) numerous works by the Pre-Raphaelites. Among these were John Everett Millais's *Isabella* (1848–9; Liverpool, Walker A.G.) and *Ophelia* (1851–2; London, Tate); William Holman Hunt's *The Scapegoat* (1854–5; Port Sunlight, Lady Lever A.G.; for illustration *see* HUNT, WILLIAM HOLMAN); Dante Gabriel Rossetti's *Lucretia Borgia* (1860–61; London, Tate); John Brett's *The Hedger* (1859–60; priv. col.); Charles Allston Collins's *Berengaria* (1850; Manchester, C.A.G.); and a number of works by Ford Madox Brown, notably *The Last of England* (1852–5; Birmingham, Mus. & A.G.), *Wycliffe* (1847–8; Bradford, C.A.G.) and *Carrying Corn* (1854–5; London, Tate). Many of Windus's purchases were made through the dealer D. T. White, and he was known for the generosity with which he opened his collection to the public. His collection was auctioned at Christie's on 14–17 February 1868.

BIBLIOGRAPHY
'The Collection of B. G. Windus, Esq., at Tottenham Green', *Art-Union*, iii (1839), p. 49
W. Robinson: *History and Antiquities of . . . Tottenham* (London, 2/1840), i, pp. 83–90 [description of house and col.]
V. Surtees, ed.: *The Diaries of George Price Boyce* (Norwich, 1980), p. 68, note 3
S. Whittingham: 'The Turner Collector: B. G. Windus', *Turner Stud.*, vii/2 (1987), pp. 29–35
S. Whittingham, ed.: 'Windus, Turner & Ruskin', *J. M. W. Turner, R. A.*, ii (1993), pp. 69–116 [doc.]

JOHN CHRISTIAN

Windus, William Lindsay (*b* Liverpool, 8 July 1822; *d* London, 9 Oct 1907). English painter. He trained in Liverpool, chiefly under a local portrait painter, William Daniels (1813–80), and at the Liverpool Academy, where he exhibited from 1845 and was an active member from 1848. He first painted figure compositions of historical themes and subjects taken from Shakespeare and Scott, modelled stylistically on William Etty and using bitumen

for romantic light effects. An example is the compelling *Anne Askew in Prison* (1849; Liverpool, Walker A.G.). At the suggestion of his patron John Miller, in 1850 Windus visited London, where he saw Millais's controversial *Christ in the Carpenter's Shop* (London, Tate) at the Royal Academy. He became the leader of a small group of sympathetic artists at the Liverpool Academy, including William Davis, who emulated the style of the Pre-Raphaelites. During the 1850s they awarded a £50 prize almost annually to Pre-Raphaelite painters, including Holman Hunt, Millais and Madox Brown, and associated and exhibited with them at the Hogarth Club, London, between 1858 and 1861. Added to his concern for moral seriousness of subject, this Pre-Raphaelite influence led Windus to an exploration of natural lighting in outdoor settings and to fine brushwork, but in a tentative, muted colour range. These characteristics first appeared in *Burd Helen* (Liverpool, Walker A.G.; *see* LIVERPOOL, fig. 2), an illustration of a Scottish ballad and his first work to be exhibited at the Royal Academy in 1856. There Rossetti brought it to the attention of Ruskin, whose enthusiastic review appeared in his *Academy Notes*. Ruskin called it the second picture of the year after Millais's and 'thoughtful and intense in the highest degree', although this appraisal was totally reversed in his later dismissal of the modern subject of *Too Late* (exh. RA 1859; London, Tate), which Windus nevertheless considered his best work. Apart from these works, only two later small landscapes can be called Pre-Raphaelite: *The Outlaw* (1861–2; Manchester, C.A.G.) and the *Stray Lamb* (Liverpool, Walker A.G.).

Windus's easily undermined self-confidence, financial instability, and melancholia resulting from his wife's death in 1862 all served to reduce his creative output. Subsequent compositions remained as sketches, and many trials were destroyed. In those that survive the style has a lively fluidity, and such works as the *Second Duchess* (London, Tate) show Rossetti's influence. Windus moved to Walton-le-Dale, near Preston, after his wife's death and to London around 1879–80. He showed sketches twice at the New English Art Club (1886 and 1899), but he painted little in later life.

BIBLIOGRAPHY
F. M. Brown: 'The Progress of Art as *Not* Shown at the Manchester Exhibition', *Mag. A.*, xi (1888), p. 122
E. R. Dibdin: 'William Lindsay Windus', *Mag. A.*, xxiii (1900), pp. 49–56
H. C. Marillier: *The Liverpool School of Painters* (London, 1904), pp. 241–54
A. Staley: *The Pre-Raphaelite Landscape* (Oxford, 1973), pp. 138–9
M. Bennett: *Merseyside Painters, People and Places: Catalogue of Oils in the Walker Art Gallery, Liverpool* (Liverpool, 1978), i, pp. 227–32
The Pre-Raphaelites (exh. cat., ed. L. Parris; London, Tate, 1984) [section on Windus by M. Bennett]

MARY BENNETT

Windward Islands. *See under* ANTILLES, LESSER.

Wines, James. *See under* SITE.

Winged Victory of Samothrace. *See* NIKE OF SAMOTHRACE.

Wingfield, Percy. *See* BULLOCK, WYNN.

Winghe [Winghen], van. Flemish family of painters and draughtsmen.

(1) Joos [Jodocus; Jost] **van** [a] **Winghe** (*b* Brussels, *c.* 1544; *d* Frankfurt am Main, 11 Dec 1603). Van Mander tells us that van Winghe showed great artistic talent at an early age and was sent to Rome, where he stayed in the household of a cardinal for four years. He returned to Brussels in 1568 and began painting for ecclesiastical and private patrons. Van Mander mentions as important early works an altarpiece of the *Last Supper* for St Gaugericus' Church (destr. 1793) and privately owned pictures of the *Conversion of Paul* and *Samson and Delilah* (probably the painting now in Düsseldorf, Kstmus.). Van Winghe attained the honoured position of painter to Alessandro Farnese after the latter became Governor of the Netherlands in 1578, but he forfeited this post to Otto van Veen when he moved to Frankfurt in 1584, probably, like many others, escaping the intolerant Spanish rule.

The earliest Frankfurt documents identify van Winghe as a portrait painter, but the evidence of his work there concerns only history paintings, such as two allegories, *Belgium and Religion Freed from Tyranny by Time* and *Justice Shielding Innocence from Tyranny* (both untraced), and two versions of *Apelles and Campaspe* (both Vienna, Ksthist. Mus.), which, together with the *Samson and Delilah*, are his only surviving paintings. His main activity in Frankfurt seems to have been the preparation of drawings for reproductive prints in a grisaille manner of pen-and-wash with white heightening. A dozen drawings and a larger number of engravings after his designs by Jan Sadeler I, Raphael Sadeler I, Crispijn de Passe (i), Theodor de Bry and others are the most important record of his accomplishments. These include multiple versions of a select range of subjects and display van Winghe's interest in rearranging figure groups within architecturally defined spaces to develop rhythms of pose and gesture. In the two preparatory drawings (Brunswick, Herzog Anton Ulrich–Mus. and Dresden, Kupferstichkab.; see fig.) for his most famous composition, the *Night Banquet with Masqueraders* (engraving by Jan Sadeler I, Hollstein, no. 559), dancing figures, props and passages of flickering light are readjusted to create the most animated effect.

Van Winghe's approach to figure drawing and composition reveals a thorough knowledge of Venetian painting and central Italian Mannerism, and a probable acquaintance with the second school of Fontainebleau (Ambroise Dubois, Toussaint Dubreuil), which has led scholars to suggest he stayed in Paris on his return from Italy.

Joos van Winghe: *Night Banquet with Masqueraders*, pen and brown ink, brown wash, white heightening over black chalk, 362×457 mm, *c.* 1588 (Dresden, Staatliche Kunstsammlungen, Kupferstichkabinett)

Both French and Venetian influences, for example of Tintoretto, are seen in the extravagant, theatrical figures and architecture of the *Samson and Delilah*, which is also the subject of an engraving by Raphael Sadeler I (1589; Hollstein, no. 180). On the other hand, the paintings of *Apelles and Campaspe*, which may date a decade apart, show in the earlier version direct borrowings from Federico Zuccaro's *Vera Intelligenza* (engraved by Cornelis Cort; Hollstein, no. 21), and in the later work (*c.* 1600–03) the influence of the more static compositions of the Mannerists from the court of Rudolf II. In this painting, Apelles has the features of the Rudolfine painter Bartholomeus Spranger, whom van Winghe met in Frankfurt in the 1590s. Van Winghe's colour schemes show a typically late Mannerist balance of brilliant, jewel-like hues against a dark, neutral background.

(2) Jeremias van Winghe (*b* Brussels, 1578; *d* Frankfurt, 1645). Son of (1) Joos van Winghe. Jeremias made pen-and-wash drawings in the manner of his father, although his full share of the extant drawings has not been determined. On his father's death, he studied with Frans Badens in Amsterdam and spent several years in Italy before re-establishing himself as a portrait painter in Frankfurt. On marrying the daughter of a jeweller in 1616, he became a merchant in his stepfather's trade but returned to painting again in 1640. Three portraits are known to be by him: *Johann Maximilian zum Jungen* and *Salome von Stallburg* (both Frankfurt am Main, Städel. Kstinst.), and *Portrait of a Jeweller* (Darmstadt, Hess. Landesmus.). He also painted kitchen scenes and still-lifes (e.g. *Kitchen Scene*, Frankfurt am Main, Hist. Mus.).

BIBLIOGRAPHY
Thieme–Becker
K. van Mander: *Schilder-boeck* ([1603]–1604), fol. 264
W. K. Zülch: *Frankfurter Künstler, 1223–1700* (Frankfurt am Main, 1935), pp. 378–9, 481–2
G. Poensgen: 'Das Werk des Jodocus a Winghe', *Pantheon*, xxviii/6 (1970), pp. 504–15
J. R. Judson: 'A New Joos van Winghe Drawing', *Ned. Ksthist. Jb.*, xxiii (1972), pp. 37–40
G. Poensgen: 'Zu den Zeichnungen des Jodocus a Winghe', *Pantheon*, xxx/1 (1972), pp. 39–47
K. Renger: 'Joos van Winghes *Nachtbancket met een Mascarade* und verwandte Darstellungen', *Jb. Berlin. Mus.*, xiv (1972), pp. 161–93
The Age of Bruegel: Netherlandish Drawings in the Sixteenth Century (exh. cat. by J. O. Hand and others, Washington, DC, N.G.A.; New York, Pierpont Morgan Lib.; 1986–7), pp. 306–10
W. W. Robinson: 'Two Drawings by Joos van Winghe', *Master Drgs*, xxvii (1989), pp. 314–21
DOROTHY LIMOUZE

Winkler, Franz K. *See* SCHUYLER, MONTGOMERY.

Winkler, Ralf. *See* PENCK, A. R.

Winogrand, Garry (*b* New York, 14 Jan 1928; *d* Tijuana, 19 March 1984). American photographer and teacher. He studied painting at City College, City University of New York, under the GI Bill (1947–8), transferring to Columbia University, New York (1948–51), where he joined the students' camera club. He abandoned painting and took up photography, studying under Alexey Brodovitch at the New School for Social Research, New York (1951). In 1952 he joined the Pix photographic agency, working with a 35-mm camera and flash. Aside from commercial assignments, his interest in the human body in movement led him to create a series of photographs at Stillman's Gymnasium, Manhattan. His 'snapshot' aesthetic extended to photographing ballet dancers, showgirls, boxers, and bathers on the beach. From 1954 he was represented by Brackman Associates and his work began appearing in *Collier's*, *Sports Illustrated* and *Pageant*. Influenced by Walker Evans and Robert Frank, he aimed for instinctive, narrative pictures that required little or no caption. In 1955 Winogrand's work was included in the *Family of Man* photographic exhibition at MOMA, New York. From 1957, when the readership for illustrated magazines waned, he found a new market for his work in advertising. He began *c.* 1960 to document New York street life in such photographs as *Coney Island* (1960; Rochester, NY, Int. Mus. Phot.). His first photographic publication *The Animals* (1969) looked with irony at city dwellers' attitudes to the impotence of caged animals displayed in a zoo (e.g. *Untitled (European Brown Bear)*, 1962; New York, MOMA). From 1969 he taught photography at the School of the Art Institute of Chicago and from 1973 at the University of Texas at Austin, while continuing his commitment to photojournalism. He was best known for his anecdotal, often comic photographs of street parades, awards ceremonies, art gallery openings and city night-life, most of which were taken during the 1970s.

PHOTOGRAPHIC PUBLICATIONS
The Animals, text by J. Szarkowski (New York, 1969)
Public Relations, text by T. Papageorge and J. Szarkowski (New York, 1977)
BIBLIOGRAPHY
B. Diamonstein, ed.: *Visions and Images: Photographers on Photography* (New York, 1981/*R* 1982), pp. 179–91
J. Szarkowski: *Winogrand: Figments from the Real World* (New York, 1988)

Winsor, Jacqueline [Jackie; Jacque] (*b* St John's, Nfld, 20 Oct 1941). American sculptor and draughtswoman of Canadian birth. She studied at the Yale Summer School of Art and Music, New Haven, CT (1964) and at the Massachusetts College of Art, Boston (1965), before attending Rutgers State University of New Jersey (MFA 1967). Winsor emerged in the late 1960s and early 1970s as part of an informal group of sculptors (including Eva Hesse and Bruce Nauman), whose work went under such labels as process art, 'anti-form', and 'eccentric abstraction'. The unifying aspect of these individuals' works lay in their development from the specific, object-based and non-referential works of Minimalist sculptors such as Donald Judd to include such reference sources as metaphor, allegory or simile. Winsor consistently used such geometric forms as the cube and sphere, and she interrelated process with appearance: *Chunk Piece* (1970; priv. col.), for example, consists of a rope (d. 915 mm) with frayed ends, wound from a linear form into a solid mass by the process of its making. In such works as *Laminated Plywood* (plywood, 0.19×1.22×1.22 m, 1973; New York, MOMA) the sculptural process is extended to other human activities, from nailing to piercing/puncturing, and from carving to digging/scooping. Although not directly initiated by personal events, Winsor believed that these and later works correspond to specific occurrences in her life. Between 1977 and 1982 Winsor concentrated on three major process-orientated works whose final appearances were determined by chance: *Burnt Piece* (1977–8), *Painted Piece* (1979–80) and *Exploded Piece* (1980–82).

BIBLIOGRAPHY

Jackie Winsor (exh. cat., essay by P. Schjeldahl; Kerguehennec, Cent. A. Contemp., 1988) [Fr. and Eng. text]

Jackie Winsor (exh. cat., essays by P. Schjeldahl and J. Yau; Milwaukee, WI, A. Mus.; Newport Beach, CA, Harbor A. Mus.; Raleigh, NC Mus. A.; Akron, OH, A. Mus.; 1991–3)

CECILE JOHNSON

Winston. American collectors. Lydia Winston [née Kahn] (*b* Detroit, MI, 13 Nov 1897; *d* New York, 14 Oct 1989), ceramicist and daughter of Albert Kahn, and her husband Harry Lewis Winston (*d* 1965) became the major collectors of Italian Futurist art outside Italy. Lydia Winston studied ceramics at the Cranbrook Academy of Art and for a short while designed ceramics for the Saarinen partnership. She began collecting in the late 1930s, supported enthusiastically by Harry Winston. In addition to the Futurists, she acquired (sometimes directly from the artists) major works by Léger (*Seated Woman*, 1912), Miró (the *Brothers Fratellini*, 1927), Brancusi (the *Blonde Negress*, 1933), Jackson Pollock (*Moon Vessel*, 1945) and Mondrian (*Composition in Black and White with Blue Square*, 1935), and a large body of work by Karel Appel and other Cobra artists. Several dealers and specialists guided her. Alfred Stieglitz instilled in her the concept of responsibility; she never sold or traded in art. Rose Fried, who ran the Pinacoteca Gallery in New York, first suggested in 1945 that she try representing every significant art movement of the century, then encouraged her to look specifically for Futurist works. Gino Severini sold her the *Dancer of the Sea* (1913), and descendants of Umberto Boccioni, Giacomo Balla and Filippo Tommaso Marinetti made available to her essential examples of Futurism, such as Balla's *Labour* and the *Stairway of Farewells* (1908), and shared their direct memories. Following the death of Harry Winston, her second husband Barnett Malbin (*d* 1985) gave her equally strong support. She made generous bequests to several museums, and when her avant-garde collection was auctioned in 1990 it set new records, fetching £74 million. It is now held by Yale University, New Haven, CT.

BIBLIOGRAPHY

G. Baro: 'Futurism Preserved: Lydia Winston Malbin', *The Collector in America* (New York, 1970), pp. 180–89

Futurism, a Modern Focus: The Lydia and Harry Lewis Winston Collection (exh. cat. by L. Shearer and M. W. Martin, New York, Guggenheim, 1973)

Cobra and Contrasts: The Lydia and Harry Lewis Winston Collection (exh. cat. by E. Sharp and W. Sandberg, Detroit, MI, Inst. A., 1974)

The Collection of Lydia Winston Malbin, Futurist and Modern Paintings and Sculpture (sale cat., New York, Sotheby's, 12–16 May 1990)

DIANE TEPFER

Winter, Fritz (*b* Altenbögge, Westphalia, 22 Sept 1905; *d* Herrsching, nr Munich, 1 Oct 1976). German painter. A self-taught artist, he began to paint *c.* 1924. Before becoming a student at the Dessau Bauhaus, he worked as a miner and as an electrician. He began by studying theatre but turned to painting in 1929, studying under Oskar Schlemmer, and also Kandinsky and Klee, who were both influential on his artistic ambitions and theory. His abstract pictures of this time reveal a debt to these artists, as well as the influence of Arp and Naum Gabo.

Between 1929 and 1931 Winter frequently went to Davos to visit Kirchner with whom he had a vigorous exchange of ideas. He worked with Gabo in Berlin in 1930. He taught for a short time at the Pädagogische Akademie in Halle. In 1933 he moved to Munich, and in 1935 he retreated to Diessen am Ammersee. From 1935 he created representations of dynamic areas of light, fantastic landscapes with crystalline geometric forms and translucent compositions that are partly reminiscent of the work of Lyonel Feininger, for example *Light* (1935; priv. col., see Lohberg, pl. 623). His main technique lay in the linear structure of the composition, which he described as a *grille*. The combination of the colour and the structure created a graduated picture space as in *Linear Composition* (1935; Munich, Staatsgal. Mod. Kst). Classified by the Nazis as a 'degenerate' artist, he was banned from painting or exhibiting. Nevertheless, the climax of Winter's work was the series *Driving Forces of the Earth*, painted in 1944 during a period of convalescence: the glowingly depicted energy present in dark spaces was the subject for over 40 small oil paintings.

After military service and a period as a Russian prisoner of war, Winter returned to Germany in 1949 and was a co-founder of ZEN 49. In Paris in 1950 he became familiar with the work of Pierre Soulages and other French abstract artists. At this time he strove in his work for a synthesis between a clearly defined form (rectangle, circle or a tachistic mark) and colour, which together suggested space. In 1953 he was invited as a guest lecturer to the Landeshochschule in Hamburg, and from 1955 until 1976 he taught at the Kunsthochschule in Kassel, applying Bauhaus teaching techniques. In the last six years of his creative life he returned to compositions with a purely linear orientation, which he enhanced with bold colours.

WRITINGS

'Gestaltungselemente in der Malerei', *Abstrakte Maler lehren*, ed. G. Hassenpflug (Munich, 1959), pp. 27–51

BIBLIOGRAPHY

K. Gabler: *Das graphische Werk von Fritz Winter* (Frankfurt am Main, 1968)

H. Keller: *Fritz Winter* (Munich, 1976)

Fritz Winter: Triebkrafte der Erde, 1932–1944 (exh. cat., ed. E. Herzog; Münster, Westfäl. Landesmus., 1981)

G. Lohberg: *Fritz Winter: Leben und Werk* (Munich, 1987)

SEPP KERN

Winter, Janus [Adrianus; Johannes; Jacobus] de (*b* Utrecht, 28 May 1882; *d* Den Helder, 5 Aug 1951). Dutch painter and printmaker. He began painting *c.* 1907 in the style of the Hague school. After 1912 his work was influenced by that of Vasily Kandinsky and the Theosophist theory of the thought form, as expounded by C. W. Leadbeater and Annie Besant. He also experimented with psychic automatism. His Expressionist landscapes depict certain moods, partly through their colour symbolism. His vegetation and animal scenes are representations of emotional sensations; the visionary portraits are often depicted in the shape of flowers, such as the orchid. Like Theo van Doesburg, Louis Saalborn (1891–1957) and Laurens van Kuik (1889–1963), he also painted aesthetic colour sensations influenced by music. His work after 1914 was influenced by Chinese painting. In 1918 he became associated with the idealistic journal *Das Wort*. From 1923 he lived alternately in Utrecht and Paris.

BIBLIOGRAPHY
J. Gevers: *Janus de Winter* (Amsterdam, 1985)

JOHN STEEN

Winter garden. See CONSERVATORY.

Wintergerst, Joseph (*b* Wallerstein, 3 Oct 1783; *d* Düsseldorf, 25 Jan 1867). German painter. He studied from 1804 at the Akademie der Bildenden Künste in Munich and the Akademie der Bildenden Künste, Vienna, where he joined the group of artists around Friedrich Overbeck and in 1809 co-founded the Lukasbund (*see* NAZARENES). In the spring of 1811, Wintergerst joined this group in Rome, where he remained until 1813, painting subjects from the Old Testament and from history. His work was close in style to that of his friend, the painter Franz Pforr, and was characterized by its planar shapes and patterns as well as bright and flat colours in tapestry-like compositions. After leaving Rome in 1813, Wintergerst held posts as a teacher of drawing in Aarau, Switzerland, and in Ellwangen and Heidelberg, before settling in Düsseldorf in 1822. Two years later he became inspector at the Düsseldorf Kunstakademie.

Wintergerst's most notable work comes from this period: the chivalric scene, *Count of Habsburg and the Priest* (1822; Heidelberg, Kurpfälz. Mus.), a subject taken from the ballad by the German poet Friedrich Schiller, also treated by Pforr in a celebrated painting of 1810 (Frankfurt am Main, Städel. Kstinst.). Wintergerst showed the Count with his retinue in a forest clearing, giving his horse to a priest so that the latter can cross a river in comfort on his way to perform the last rites for a dying man. Although analogous with Pforr's neo-primitive and descriptive style, Wintergerst's picture does not attain the charm or ingenuity of Pforr's work, largely because of its selfconscious naivety, dryness and predictability. By the mid-1820s Wintergerst's creative powers began to wane and in the later 1830s he abandoned painting altogether.

BIBLIOGRAPHY
J. Jensen: 'Das Werk des Malers Josef Wintergerst', *Z. Dt. Ver. Kstwiss.* (1967)
Die Düsseldorfer Malerschule (exh. cat., Düsseldorf, Kstmus., 1979)

RUDOLF M. BISANZ

Winterhalder [Winterhalter]. German family of artists active chiefly in Moravia. Adam Winterhalder (*d* 1737) was a sculptor in Vöhrenbach in the Black Forest; of his three sons, all sculptors, the eldest, Anton [Antonín] Winterhalder (1699–1758), worked mostly in Olomouc, Moravia, sometimes in collaboration with his next brother, (1) Josef Winterhalder (i); the latter, working in the tradition of Baldasarre Fontana and Balthasar Permoser, influenced by Georg Raphael Donner, executed much sculpture in Moravia. The youngest brother, Johann [Jan] Michael Winterhalder (1706–59), worked mostly in Germany. His son, (2) Josef Winterhalder (ii), was a painter whose Baroque style was influenced by Mannerism: he was particularly noted for his frescoes and decorative schemes for churches in Moravia, and also in Hungary and Austria.

(1) Josef Winterhalder (i) (*b* Vöhrenbach, Black Forest, 10 Jan 1702; *d* Vienna, 1769). Sculptor. He came to Bohemia by way of Munich and Vienna, where he studied (1726–8) at the Academy. His artistic mentor in matters of composition, self-expression and economy of detail was Georg Raphael Donner, whose sure touch in understanding the internal structure of a figure is to be felt in all Winterhalder's work. The earliest example of this is the figural decoration of the stairway at the prelature of the Premonstratensian monastery at Hradisko near Olomouc; it dates from *c.* 1730, when Winterhalder joined the workshop at Olomouc, which had previously been run by Johann Sturmer (*c.* 1675–1729). In 1731, in collaboration with his brother Johann Michael, Winterhalder completed the pulpit in the church of the Assumption of the Virgin at Svatý Kopeček, Olomouc. Thereafter he was entrusted with an extensive project at the Hradisko prelature. His scenes in relief from the Old and New Testaments in the window reveals testify to the influence of Baldassare Fontana.

Having executed (1737) the sculptural group of *St John of Nepomuk* in front of the façade of Hradisko monastery, Winterhalder was employed on decorating the Cathedral of St Wenceslas, Olomouc. At Brno he created the figures of *St Cyril* and *St Methodius*, *St Wenceslas* and *St Ludmilla* on the plinth in front of the Dominican church of St Michael. Taking Balthasar Permoser as his stylistic exemplar, he executed a monumental commission at Náměšt nad Oslavou, where, as well as the interior decoration of the parish church of St John the Baptist, the hospital chapel of St Anne and sculptures on the bridge leading to the castle, he carried out the greater part of a secular group on the bridge across the River Oslava; his collaborator was Alexander Jelínek. Next, in collaboration with Dominik Kirchner (*fl c.* 1743) and Damascen Schwarz (*b* 1721; *fl c.* 1743), Winterhalder decorated the high altar (1743) at the Dominican church in Brno in a style resembling his work at Náměšt; his attractive and delicate Rococo figures are suffused with emotion.

Throughout the 1740s Winterhalder received commissions from the Dominicans, both at Brno (pulpit, 1745) and at Uherský Brod, where he created side altars for the church of the Assumption of the Virgin, and a statue of *St Vincent* in front of the church. He subsequently also executed the St Florian Fountain and side altars for the church of the Immaculate Conception. The St Norbert group (1753) in the courtyard of Svatý Kopeček, the joint work of Winterhalder and his brother Anton, displays profound pathos and a deeply felt understanding of the subject. His reliefs at the prelature chapel of the Cistercian monastery at Velehrad exhibit the influence of the painter Paul Troger, but the altars (1760) at St Martin in Třebíč once again display a resemblance to Permoser's work. Winterhalder's last work in Moravia was the pulpit (1760) for St Nicholas at Znojmo. Even though he worked in Moravia for many years, often in collaboration with Moravian sculptors, his focus of inspiration was elsewhere, in Vienna, where he moved in the 1760s.

(2) Josef Winterhalder (ii) (*b* Vöhrenbach, Black Forest, 25 Jan 1743; *d* Znojmo, Moravia, 1807). Painter, nephew of (1) Josef Winterhalder (i). He first trained with his uncle; between *c.* 1763 and 1768 he was a member of the workshop of the Austrian painter Franz Anton Maulbertsch, whose views on style, colour and light exerted on him a powerful influence that was continued in his subsequent work. After his first stay in Moravia, collaborating with Vincenz Fischer and Josef Hauzinger (1728–86) in Bratislava, Winterhalder parted company (*c.* 1768) with Maulbertsch. In 1773 he returned to Moravia and settled at Znojmo, working mainly in the south. Apart from easel paintings he produced tapestry cartoons, altarpieces and decorative schemes, such as the *Apparition of SS Augustine and Norbert* (1778; Brno, Morav. Gal.). From 1773 to 1782 he was mainly occupied on church commissions, including the altarpiece of the *Death of St Joseph* at the church of the Scourged Christ at Dyje. He also worked (1776) at St Vitus in Jemnice and painted a ceiling fresco (1776) for the Benedictines in the presbytery of the monastery church of SS Peter and Paul at Rajhrad near Brno. He was the author of frescoes (1781–2) in the Premonstratensian church of the Assumption of the Virgin at Brno-Zábrdovice.

It was probably his earlier connection with Maulbertsch that secured for Winterhalder in 1798 a commission to execute frescoes at the cathedral of Szombathely in Hungary. In 1805 he painted ceiling frescoes in the library of the monastery at Geras in Austria. The dissolution of several Moravian monasteries by the Emperor Joseph II brought Winterhalder's work there to an end; but he continued to work on secular buildings, including castles at Zdislavice (1789), Jinošov, Tavíkovice, Dukovany (1791) and Uherčice, and at Brno in the hall of the Estates House (1777) and the old town hall (1790). His sometimes idiosyncratic approach to decorative painting is apparent, for instance, in St Lawrence, Dačice, where the high altar (1787) consists exclusively of a fresco. Winterhalder was a more lyrical painter than Maulbertsch, and his use of light and colour was more muted. His style tended towards Mannerism rather than Neo-classicism, though he evidently strove to be in tune with the Enlightenment. Although Winterhalder's powers of expression were not as strong as that of Maulbertsch, his art was an important element in late Baroque painting in Moravia.

UNPUBLISHED SOURCES

O. Schweigl: *Abhandlung von den bildenden Künsten in Mähren* (?1784; Brno, State Archvs, MS. G11/196)
J. Winterhalder *mladší* [the younger]: *Mährische Künstler in Znaim und Gegent* (?1796; Brno, State Archvs, MS. F.M.60)
J. P. Cerroni: *Skitze einer Geschichte der bildenden Künste in Mähren und Ost-Schlesien* (1807; Brno, State Archvs, MS. G12, Cerr I), pp. 32–4

BIBLIOGRAPHY

A. Königová: *Život a dílo moravského barokního umělce Josefa Winterhaldera staršího* [The life and work of the Moravian Baroque artist, Josef Winterhalder the elder] (diss., Brno, Masaryk U., 1949)
M. Hanavská: *Dílo Josefa Winterhaldera mladšího na Moravě* [The work of Josef Winterhalder the younger in Moravia] (diss., Brno, Masaryk U., 1952)
K. Garas: 'Josef Winterhalder (1743–1807)', *Bull. Mus. Hong. B.-A.*, xiv (1959), pp. 75–90
M. Stehlík: 'Nástin dějin sochařství 17. a 18. věku na Moravě' [Outline of the history of sculpture in the 17th and 18th centuries in Moravia], *Sborník prací filozofické fakulty brněnské univerzity 1976* [Symposium of the faculty of philosophy, university of Brno, 1976], pp. 23–40
Barock in Mähren (exh. cat. by V. Kratinová, Vienna, Belvedere, 1988)
I. Krsek: 'Malířství pozdního baroka na Moravě' [Late Baroque painting in Moravia], *Dějiny českého výtvarného umění* [History of Czech art], ii (Prague, 1989), pp. 790–817
M. Stehlík: 'Sochařství vrcholného baroka na Moravě' [High Baroque sculpture in Moravia], *Dějiny českého výtvarného umění* [History of Czech art], ii (Prague, 1989), pp. 510–39

MILOŠ STEHLÍK

Winterhalter, Franz Xaver (*b* Menzenschwand, Baden Württemberg, 20 April 1805; *d* Frankfurt am Main, 8 July 1873). German painter and lithographer. He trained as a draughtsman and lithographer in the workshop of Karl Ludwig Schüler (1785–1852) in Freiburg im Breisgau and went to Munich in 1823, sponsored by the industrialist Baron Eichtal. In 1825 he began a course of study at the Akademie and was granted a stipend by Ludwig I, Grand Duke of Baden. The theoretical approach to art of the Akademie under the direction of Peter Cornelius was unfamiliar to him, as in Freiburg he had been required to paint in a popular style. He found the stimulus for his future development in the studio of Joseph Stieler, a portrait painter who was much in demand and who derived inspiration from French painting. Winterhalter became his collaborator in 1825. From Stieler he learnt to make the heads of figures emerge from shadow and to use light in the modelling of faces. He moved to Karlsruhe in 1830 with his brother Hermann Winterhalter (1808–92), who had also trained with Schüler and had followed him to Munich.

In 1832–4 Winterhalter travelled to Italy, financed by Leopold, Grand Duke of Baden. In Rome in 1834 he joined the circle of French painters around Horace Vernet. He was appointed court painter at Baden in that same year and moved to Paris. With *Il dolce farniente* (1835; Christie's 17 June 1994, lot 87, see 1987 exh. cat., no. 9), exhibited at the Salon of 1836, Winterhalter achieved his first major success. The painting, which is on a large scale, depicts a genre scene set in Naples, its composition inspired by Raphael's *Parnassus* (1509–11; Rome, Vatican, Cappelle, Sale & Gal. Affrescate). The sugary mood brought about by his treatment of light sets it apart from the work of the contemporary Nazarene painters. In 1838 the French king Louis-Philippe gave Winterhalter a commission for a portrait (for illustration *see* ORLÉANS, House of, (7)), thereby establishing his position as the most sought-after portrait painter among the higher echelons of the nobility in Europe. His oeuvre includes state portraits of the Belgian, English and French royal families. His brother Hermann moved to Paris in 1840, and from then on they worked together. In 1842 Winterhalter received his first commission from the British court. For some time afterwards he went to England for several weeks each year to carry out portrait commissions. The combination of formality and intimacy that so pleased his patrons is expressed in the many single and group portraits of members of the British royal family. The *Royal Family* and *Albert Edward, Prince of Wales (When Two Years Old)* (both 1846; Osborne House, Isle of Wight, Royal Col.; see fig.) demonstrate Winterhalter's ability to unite the traditional iconography of authority with the representation of a bourgeois family.

Winterhalter and his brother left Paris in 1848 and stayed in Switzerland and Brussels. They returned to Paris in 1849. *Florinda* (1852; London, Buckingham Pal., Royal

Franz Xaver Winterhalter: *Albert Edward, Prince of Wales (When Two Years Old)*, oil on canvas, 1.27×0.88 m, 1846 (Osborne House, Isle of Wight, Royal Collection)

Col., see 1987 exh. cat., no. 38) is inspired by a 16th-century Spanish ballad that was rediscovered in the Romantic period. He used the same composition three years later for the *Empress Eugénie Surrounded by her Ladies-in-waiting* (Compiègne, Château), a group portrait in the manner of a *fête champêtre* that brought him fame in Second Empire France. The composition, the corporeality of the depiction and the characterization of the women create a sense of idealization that relates the work to the art of the Louis XVI period admired by the emperor and empress. The picture was shown in a special room at the Exposition Universelle, Paris, in 1855, and Winterhalter was awarded a first-class medal for his contribution to the exhibition. He followed this work with single portraits that record the French empress at various stages in her life. After the Franco-Prussian War of 1870–71 Winterhalter settled in Karlsruhe. All his portraits dating from 1834 onwards were commissioned by the court at Baden, to which he was officially credited.

Concerning Winterhalter's method of working, it is thought that, practised as he was at drawing and representing figures, he painted directly on to the canvas without making preliminary studies. He himself decided on the dress and pose of his sitters. He painted in a smooth style, using quick but impersonal brushstrokes. Many of the portraits were copied in his workshop or reproduced as lithographs.

BIBLIOGRAPHY

F. Wild: *Nekrologe und Verzeichnisse der Gemälde von Franz Xaver Winterhalter* (Zurich, 1894)

Franz Xaver Winterhalter and the Courts of Europe, 1830–70 (exh. cat. by R. Ormond and C. Blackett-Ord, London, N.P.G., 1987)

BARBARA LANGE

Wiriot, Pierre. *See* WOEIRIOT, PIERRE.

Wise, Henry (*b* 1653; *d* Warwick, 15 Dec 1738). English garden designer. About 1687 he joined the group venture of GEORGE LONDON at Brompton Park, a nursery fast becoming the largest and best-stocked in London. By 1694 he was London's sole business partner, and was subsequently co-translator of their two gardening directories. London's influential position in the royal gardens helped provide a ready market for Brompton's stock, and Wise too became increasingly involved in work for the Crown. Between 1689 and 1692 he improved the gardens at Hampton Court Palace: the ground was re-levelled, avenues of timber planted in neighbouring Bushey Park, and a basin dug to receive the Diana Fountain. During the 1690s he and London developed a useful working partnership, with Wise managing Brompton while London scoured England's country seats for commissions.

At Anne's succession in 1702 Wise was appointed Royal Gardener, and numerous alterations and additions on Crown property were made by him over the next few years. At the palaces of Hampton Court and Kensington parterres were remodelled, mazes and wildernesses planted, and new avenues struck out across the adjacent deer-parks. In 1704 he was made Deputy Ranger of St James's Park, London; there he planted new avenues of lime and widened the canal. The following year he began work at Blenheim Palace, Oxon, then under construction by John Vanbrugh. Wise established new timber plantations and avenues in its massive park, quincunx and flower gardens at the south front of the palace, and a kitchen garden of 3.24 ha within walls 4.2 m high. He also assisted in constructing the initial causeway in front of the palace for Vanbrugh's bridge over the diminutive River Glyme, but, after Vanbrugh's sudden dismissal in 1716, Wise also withdrew. During his time at Blenheim he maintained numerous Crown projects; for example, his Thames-side 'Maastricht' garden at Windsor Castle, where from 1708 he struggled unsuccessfully to drain the frequently flooded grounds.

A skilled horticulturalist, Wise retained his post of Royal Gardener after George I's succession in 1714. He continued to maintain and further embellish the gardens of the royal palaces with conventional Franco-Dutch embroidered parterres, basins, canals and mazes; he still planted out their hunting parks in a geometry of stars, rides and avenues of profitable hardwood timber. Only in the year following the King's death in 1727 was Wise, in his seventies, ousted by Charles Bridgeman, his former pupil at Blenheim. However, shrewd property investments over the years had made Wise a wealthy man; retiring to Warwick Priory, Warwicks, bought years before, he spent his last years refashioning the gardens there.

WRITINGS

ed., with G. London: *The Compleat Gard'ner* (London, 1699); trans. of J. de la Quintinie: *Instructions pour les jardins fruitiers et potages* (Paris, 1690) [abridged edn of J. Evelyn's trans., 1693] ed., with G. London: *The Retir'd Gard'ner*, 2 vols (London, 1706); i, trans. of F. Gentil: *Le Jardinier solitaire* (Paris, 1704); ii, trans. of L. Liger: *Le Jardinier fleuriste et historiographe* (Paris, 1704)

BIBLIOGRAPHY

D. Green: *Gardener to Queen Anne: Henry Wise (1653–1738) and the Formal Garden* (London, 1956)
J. Harvey: *Early Nurserymen* (London, 1974)

ROBERT WILLIAMS

Wiser [Wieser; Wisinger], **Wolfgang** (*d* after 1501). German architect. He is first mentioned in the records of Wasserburg in 1470 as a resident master with citizen status, mainly involved with church building, fortifications and domestic architecture. His first works would have been executed under Stefan Krumenauer (*see* KRUMENAUER, (2)), the builder of St James' Church at Wasserburg. There he completed the side chapels and built spiral stairs in the corner piers; his master's mark is set above the spiral stairs. The chapel vaults have four S-shaped ribs and a ring in the place of a boss. Between 1470 and 1478 he continued work on the tower, building the three upper storeys (the spire was never built) and enlivening them with thin shafts, pinnacles set above corners, twisted colonnettes and a large ogee-arched window in the centre. In 1483–5 he built the small church of St Achatz on the right bank of the River Inn. The vaults and capitals are similar to those of the outer castle chapel at Burghausen, begun in 1479. He may also have been involved in work on the nearby church at Kircheiselfing, which was begun slightly later. As at Wasserburg and Burghausen, but here for no compelling reason, the piers of the north side are shifted half a bay's width, so that the transverse axes between the piers are oblique. Between 1501 and 1502 he built his last work, the two-storey cemetery chapel of St Michael at Wasserburg.

BIBLIOGRAPHY

S. Graf Pückler-Limburg: *Die Spätgotik im Inn- und Alztal* (Hirschenhausen, 1932), pp. 37–42
E. Egg: *Kunst in Tirol* (Innsbruck, 1970), p. 90
E. Ullmann: *Deutsche Architektur und Plastik, 1470–1550* (Gütersloh, 1984), p. 113

VERENA BEAUCAMP

Wiślica. Town in southern Poland, on two islands in the marshy valley of the River Nida. In the early Middle Ages it was the site of one of the main princely residences and commercial settlements along the route from Bohemia to Kraków via Sandomierz to Russia. At the tip of one of the islands stood an early 11th-century stronghold and a group of residential buildings; the settlement below included the church of St Nicholas (11th century; foundations exposed) and the collegiate church of St Mary.

1. ST MARY. The present collegiate church was founded *c.* 1350 by King Kasimir III (the Great) of Poland and is the outstanding example of the type of axial-pillar church built by masons associated with the court at Kraków during his reign. There were two previous buildings on the site. The first church, also a royal foundation, with a small congregation of canons, was built about the mid-12th century. Its remains were discovered beneath the floor of the Gothic church in excavations between 1958 and 1963. Built of limestone, it had a single nave with an apsed presbytery and a gallery at the west end. Under the

presbytery was a three-aisled, four-pier crypt, with groin vaults and a west entrance. A tomb was situated on the axis of the building under the crypt stairs. About 1170 the floor of the centre aisle was laid with pale pink plaster decorated with a figurative engraving: two square panels, corresponding to the bays, are separated and edged with border strips filled with motifs of twining palms and four medallions featuring fabulous beasts, probably symbolizing the four sins of the General Confession. Between the eastern pair of piers, in front of the altar steps, is a Tree of Life, flanked by confronted lions. Each of the panels contains three praying figures (orants): a man accompanied by a woman and a youth in the west panel, and the figures of a priest, an old man and a boy in the east. These are surmounted by a partly preserved inscription engraved in Latin hexameters. The orants probably represent Prince Kazimierz Sprawiedliwy (later Kasimir II the Just, *reg* 1177–94), who ruled in Wiślica from 1166, and members of his family. While the technique is linked to the engraved plaster floors of Saxony, such as at St Liudger, Helmstedt, and Hildesheim Cathedral, the iconography has no close parallels in central Europe.

The building of the second church was connected with the reform of the canons' congregations and the foundation of new prelacies at the end of the 12th century or the beginning of the 13th, probably on the initiative of the Bishop of Kraków. The new building was a three-aisled basilica with a two-tower west façade and a gallery between the towers. The presbytery ended in a plain wall with rectangular side chapels. The interior had a glazed ceramic tile floor, and the style in general was clearly influenced by Cistercian architecture in southern Poland. Except for the towers, which collapsed in 1923, most of this church was demolished in the 14th century to make way for the Gothic collegiate church.

St Mary's church is one of a number of churches founded after 1350 by Kasimir III. In the late Middle Ages Wiślica was a royal borough within Lesser Poland, which was the political centre of the Polish monarchy. Kasimir's ecclesiastical foundations were particularly important here: they are stylistically related to the buildings erected in central Europe in the second half of the 14th century under the patronage of Emperor Charles IV and Louis d'Anjou, King of Hungary (*reg* 1340–82). Features these buildings had in common included reduced architectural detail and a double-nave plan with axial pillars that accentuated the sense of centrality within.

The present church at Wiślica is of limestone ashlar. It has a narrow, three-bay presbytery with an apse of five sides of an octagon and quadripartite vaulting. The nave is a rectangular hall, wider than the choir, its smooth walls pierced with narrow lancet windows. The vault is supported on wall brackets and three polygonal axial piers, from which rise the vault ribs, all of equal thickness, to form a series of interlinked star patterns (see fig.). The vault design helps to mask the division into bays and reinforces the feeling of centrality and indivisibility of the interior. The vault bosses (many of which were destroyed in World War I) had heraldic designs, and genre and religious scenes.

The church has three entrance doors. Over the south door is an inscribed low relief made in 1464, more than a

Wiślica, collegiate church, interior of the nave looking east, third quarter of the 14th century

century after the consecration, depicting Kasimir III presenting a model of the building to an enthroned Virgin and Child. The frescoes in the presbytery, produced between 1397 and 1400 by Byzantine–Russian painters, were commissioned by King Vladislav V Jagiellon (*reg* 1386–1434), who had been Grand Duke of Lithuania from 1377. A Gothic canon's house, which was built near the collegiate church *c*. 1460 by Canon Jan Długosz of Kraków, is a red-brick single-storey building with fine sandstone detailing. Długosz also erected a large belfry of brick and stone west of the church.

Wiślica church suffered severe damage in World War I and was partly rebuilt by Adolf Szyszko-Bohusz (*b* 1883). After the excavations of 1958–63, the floor of the Gothic church was supported on a steel truss to protect the remains of the earlier churches below.

BIBLIOGRAPHY

A. Tomaszewski: 'La Collégiale de Wiślica', *Cah. Civilis. Méd.*, v (1962), pp. 67–74

P. Crossley: *Gothic Architecture in the Reign of Kasimir the Great: Church Architecture in Lesser Poland, 1320–1380* (Kraków, 1985), pp. 188–90

A. Tomaszewski: 'L'Archéologie, la conservation et la présentation d'un monument historique: La Collégiale de Wiślica en Pologne', *ICOMOS Information*, i/2 (1985), pp. 24–30

P. Crossley: 'Kasimir the Great at Wiślica', *Romanesque and Gothic: Essays for George Zarnecki* (Woodbridge, 1987), pp. 39–48

ROBERT M. KUNKEL

Wiśnicz. Group of settlements in Lesser Poland (Małopolska) on the River Leksandrówka, on the Hungary-

Kraków trade route. It consisted of the settlements of Wiśnicz Magna (or Maior; now Wiśnicz Stary: 'Old Wiśnicz') founded in the 13th century and Wiśnicz Parva (or Minor; Wiśnicz Mały: 'Lesser Wiśnicz') founded in the 14th century. It was originally the property of the Gryfita family. From the 14th century to the mid-16th Wiśnicz belonged to the Kmita family, who built a castle with a tower in the first half of the 14th century, which served as a watch-tower for knights. The Grand Marshal, Piotr Kmita (1477–1553), rebuilt the castle between 1515 and 1553 as a Renaissance residence and also built a church in Wiśnicz Stary in honour of St Adalbert. The castle was unusual in that it was built in a regular plane with three towers in the corners.

The most significant period for Wiśnicz came in the first half of the 17th century, when it was owned by the Lubomirski family. From around 1615 Stanisław Lubomirski began to extend the old Kmita castle into a magnificent 'palazzo in fortezza' residence. The Baroque castle-residence, enhanced by a new chapel, loggia, apartments and staircase, was surrounded by five-sided bastion fortifications with a magnificent gate. In 1616 Stanisław Lubomirski founded the town of Wiśnicz Nowy ('New Wiśnicz') and built the Town Hall (1620; rebuilt 19th century), situated in the market place, the parish church of the Assumption (1620–47), and the fortified monastery of the Discalced Carmelites (1622–35). The architect of these works was Mattia Trapola (*fl* 1616–23). It is also possible that Andrea Spezza worked here in 1615–21. The stuccowork in the castle chapel and in the church of the Discalced Carmelites was the work of Giovanni Battista Falconi in 1633–5.

The Swedish invasion of the mid-17th century destroyed the Carmelite church, and its works of art, library and collections were stolen. In the 18th century Wiśnicz was owned in turn by the Sanguszko, Lubomirski, Potocki and Zamoyski families; during this period the interiors of the castle were converted, including the Knights' Hall and Gallery. From the end of the 18th century Wiśnicz's major buildings were in decline: in 1783 the monastery of the Discalced Carmelites was dissolved (the cloister became a prison, and the church was partly demolished), while fires destroyed the castle in 1831 and the town's wooden buildings in 1863. During World War II the town was badly damaged again, and the synagogue (built 1863), among many other buildings, was demolished. In 1949 conservation work began, with the intention of converting the castle into a museum.

BIBLIOGRAPHY

A. Majewski: 'Zamek w Wiśniczu' [The castle in Wiśnicz], *Teka Konserwatorska*, iii (1956), pp. 33–102

M. Ksiażek: 'Zarys rozwuju przestrzennego Starego i Nowego Wiśnicza' [Outline of the development of Old and New Wiśnicz], *Teka Kom. Urb. & Archit.*, xiii (1979), pp. 47–55

M. Wjcikiewicz: 'Studia nad zabudowa Wiśnicza Nowego' [Studies on the development of Wiśnicz Nowy], *Teka Kom. Urb. & Archit. Pol. Acad. Nauk*, xiv (1980), pp. 43–9

P. S. Szlezynger: 'Fortyfikacje klasztoru karmelitow bosych w Wiśniczu Nowym' [The fortifications of the Discalced Carmelites Monastery in Wiśnicz Nowy], *Kwart. Archit. & Urb.*, xxviii (1983), pp. 275–83

——: 'Kościół karmelitw bosych w Wiśniczu Nowym' [The church of the Discalced Carmelites in Wiśnicz Nowy], *Kwart. Archit. & Urb.*, xxxiii (1988), pp. 113–39

MARIA BRYKOWSKA

Wisselingh, van, & Co. Interior design workshop established in Amsterdam in 1898 by E. J. van Wisselingh & Co., a firm of art dealers. The Kunstwerkplaats manufactured designs for furniture, batik and metalwork by GERRIT WILLEM DIJSSELHOF (e.g. chair, c. 1900; Amsterdam, Stedel. Mus.), C. A. LION CACHET (e.g. rosewood chair with batik decoration, c. 1900; The Hague, Gemeentemus.) and T. W. NIEUWENHUIS; the production of matching soft furnishings was contracted out to other firms. These luxurious interiors were part of the decorative element in the Nieuwe Kunst. They were by far the most expensive available in the Netherlands, and despite initial large commissions, the business was subsequently less prosperous, as the circle of clients who could afford such interiors was too small to finance such costly production. Dijsselhof and Lion Cachet left the workshop in 1903 and 1906 respectively; Nieuwenhuis stayed until 1924, when the workshop went into liquidation.

BIBLIOGRAPHY

L. Gans: *Nieuwe Kunst: De Nederlandse bijdrage tot de Art Nouveau: Dekoratieve kunst, kunstnijverheid en architektuur, omstreeks 1900* [Nieuwe Kunst: the Dutch contribution to Art Nouveau: the decorative arts, the applied arts and architecture, c. 1900] (Utrecht, 1966)

H. Olyslager and M. Wardenaar: 'Van Wisselingh & Co.: Een meubelwerkplaats in Amsterdam, 1898–1924', *Kunstlicht*, viii (1982–23), pp. 34–7

F. Leidelmeijer and D. van der Cingel: *Art Nouveau en Art Deco in Nederland* (Amsterdam, 1983)

PETRA DUPUITS

Wissing, Willem (*b* Amsterdam, 1656; *d* Stamford, Lincs, 10 Sept 1687). Dutch painter, active in England. After training in The Hague under Willem Doudijns (1630–97) and Arnoldus van Ravestyn (1615–90), he worked in England from 1676, when he was admitted to the Dutch Reform Church in London. As a pupil and assistant in the studio of Peter Lely, Wissing readily found patronage at court and inherited some of Lely's large and fashionable practice after his master's death in 1680. Wissing rapidly emerged as the principal rival to Godfrey Kneller and was commissioned to paint *Charles II* (c. 1683; Windsor Castle, Berks, Royal Col.) and other members of the royal family, including Queen Catharine of Braganza (1638–1705), Prince George of Denmark (1653–1708) and James, Duke of Monmouth (1649–85). Wissing found particular favour with James II, who in 1685 sent him to the Netherlands to paint portraits of his Dutch son-in-law, *Prince William III of Orange Nassau*, and his daughter, the *Princess Mary*, the future William III and Mary II (many versions of the original portraits in the Brit. Royal Col. survive, e.g. London, N.P.G.).

The polished elegance of Wissing's style, the luxuriant profusion of details he often crowded round his sitters and the lustrous rendering of drapery and ornament may derive from a period of study in France; these traits recall the work of French portrait painters such as Nicolas de Largillierre, who had also worked in Lely's London studio. Wissing collaborated with other artists, notably the Dutch painter–engraver Jan van der Vaardt, with whom he painted the portrait of *Frances Theresa Stuart, Duchess of Richmond and Lennox* (1687; London, N.P.G.; *see* DRESS, fig. 42), as well as those of the *Princess of Denmark* (later Queen Anne), *William III*, and *Lady*

Mary Radcliffe in a sumptuous full-length that was engraved in mezzotint by Bernard Lens II. Of the other printmakers who reproduced much of Wissing's oeuvre, the most important and prolific was John Smith. Although there is no evidence of a formal contract, Wissing may have employed the native British artist Francis Barlow to paint birds, animals and landscape elements in some of his work. Towards the end of his life Wissing enjoyed patronage from the Brownlow family in Lincolnshire and John, 5th Earl of Exeter at Burghley House; the latter installed a tablet to the painter's memory at St Martin's, Stamford.

BIBLIOGRAPHY

E. Waterhouse: *Painting in Britain, 1530–1790*, Pelican Hist. A. (Harmondsworth, 1953, rev. 3/1978), pp. 112–13

M. Whinney and O. Millar: *English Art, 1625–1714* (Oxford, 1957), pp. 177–8

O. Millar: *The Tudor, Stuart and Early Georgian Pictures in the Collection of Her Majesty the Queen* (London, 1963), pp. 21–2

D. Piper: *Seventeenth-century Portraits, 1625–1714*, London, N.P.G. cat. (Cambridge, 1963), pp. 223–5

R. Simon: *The Portrait in Britain and America* (Oxford, 1987), pp. 13, 86, 100

MARTHA HAMILTON-PHILLIPS

Wistar, Caspar (*b* Hilspach [now Hilsbach], Germany, Feb 1696; *d* Philadelphia, PA, ?April 1752). American glass manufacturer of German birth. He moved to Philadelphia in 1717 and learnt to make brass buttons, for which he quickly became famous and from which he earned an ample income. Wistar was the first person to make glass profitably in America. He bought 2000 acres of land on Alloways Creek in Salem Co., NJ, and brought four German glass blowers to his 'Wistarburgh' factory, which opened in 1739.

The major products of the factory were window glass, a wide variety of bottles and vials, and such scientific equipment as electrical tubes and globes used to generate static electricity in experiments in the 1740s and 1750s. Table wares in colourless, bottle-green and pale blue glass were produced regularly, though sparingly. Free-blown covered bowls, small buckets or baskets, tapersticks, candlesticks, mugs and tumblers, some made with part-size moulds, have been attributed to Wistar through historical association and through laboratory analysis. Decoration, using certain *Waldglas* motifs, was generally restrained.

The operation grew and prospered under Wistar. In addition to the glasshouse, his business included button-making, real estate and the importation of English window and table glass for stores in Philadelphia and Alloway. After his death, his son Richard Wistar (1727–81) ran the operation until the hostilities and volatile markets during the American Revolution made production impossible. When Wistarburgh closed in 1780, the village included two furnaces with annealing ovens, two separate houses with flatting ovens for making window glass by the cylinder method, a pottery, a cutting house, stamping mills, a rolling mill for clay, ten dwelling houses, a mansion house and a store, with 250 acres cleared, 1500 acres of woodland, stables for sixty cattle, a barn, a granary and a wagon house. Both before and after Wistarburgh closed, glass craftsmen from the factory founded their own furnaces or worked for other glass manufacturers.

BIBLIOGRAPHY

A. Palmer: 'Glass Production in Eighteenth-century America: The Wistarburgh Enterprise', *Winterthur Port.*, xi (1976), pp. 75–101

The Wistars and their Glass 1739–1777 (exh. cat. by A. Palmer, Millville, NJ, Wheaton Village, Amer. Glass Mus.), 1989)

ELLEN PAUL DENKER

Wit, Jacob de (*bapt* Amsterdam, 19 Dec 1695; *d* Amsterdam, 12 Nov 1754). Dutch painter, draughtsman, etcher and writer. He was the leading 18th-century Dutch decorative painter, specializing in Rococo ceiling and room decorations and groups of putti painted naturalistically in colour or as imitation reliefs in grisaille. His preparatory drawings for ceiling decorations were collected during his own lifetime, but he also executed independent finished drawings specifically for collectors (e.g. *Three Hovering Putti*; Leiden, Rijksuniv., Prentenkab.).

At the age of nine de Wit was apprenticed to Albert van Spiers (1666–1718), a painter of ceiling pictures and overmantels who had studied with Gérard de Lairesse and in Rome. From 1708 de Wit studied at the Koninklijke Academie in Antwerp and, from 1709 to 1712, with the history painter Jacob van Hal (1672–1718). In 1711–12 de Wit made drawn copies of the 36 ceiling pictures designed by Rubens in the Jesuit church in Antwerp (now St Carlo Borromeo). When these were destroyed by fire in 1718, de Wit worked up his drawings into several series in different media, including watercolour (e.g. Antwerp, Stedel. Prentenkab., and U. London, Courtauld Inst.) and red chalk (London, BM). The series in red chalk follows Rubens's originals most closely and may have served as the model for a book of engravings by Jan Punt produced between 1751 and 1763. Earlier, de Wit had himself prepared 11 etchings after Rubens's ceiling. His own sizeable art collection included paintings by Rubens, among them the original oil sketch of *St Eugenia* (untraced) of which de Wit made a watercolour copy (Antwerp, Stedel. Prentenkab.), and the older Flemish master remained the single greatest source of inspiration throughout de Wit's career. De Wit also copied works by van Dyck, as in his chalk drawing of the *Blessed Herman Joseph before the Virgin* (U. London, Courtauld Inst.) after van Dyck's painting (Vienna, Ksthist. Mus.) at that time also in the Jesuit church.

In 1713 de Wit became a member of the Antwerp Guild of St Luke. He then moved to Amsterdam where, as a Catholic, he was commissioned by Father Aegidius de Glabbais, the priest of the Roman Catholic conventicle church of Moses and Aaron (destr.) on the Oude Houtgracht, to execute several paintings: a wall decoration (1716; Amsterdam, Waterlooplein, church of Moses and Aaron); five friezes with saints' heads (1716; Antwerp, St Jacobskerk; preliminary drawing, Amsterdam, Rijksmus.); a ceiling picture representing *Sacred Music* (1721; Wilmette, IL, Thomas Flannery priv. col., see Staring, 1969, ill. 8); and a large altarpiece with an *Annunciation* (1722; Amsterdam, Waterlooplein, church of Moses and Aaron). De Wit's only known portraits are of *Father Aegidius de Glabbais with Attendants* (1718; Utrecht, Catharijneconvent), a grisaille profile of *Sir Isaac Newton* (Karlsruhe, Staatl. Ksthalle) and several portrait and self-portrait drawings (versions, Haarlem, Teylers Mus., and Amsterdam, Rijksmus.). In 1722 de Wit painted a *Descent of the*

Holy Ghost for Roermond Cathedral (*in situ*), and four years later he executed *Guiding Mankind from the Old to the New Testament* (1726; Utrecht, Catharijneconvent; preparatory drawing, Frankfurt am Main, Städel. Kstinst. & Städt. Gal.) for a private patron. In his altarpieces, which he painted throughout his life, van Dyck's influence remained strong.

De Wit produced ceiling paintings on canvas for Catholic as well as Reformed and Baptist patrons both in and outside Amsterdam. Besides the example of de Lairesse, de Wit was probably influenced by the decorative work of Giovanni Antonio Pellegrini, whom he perhaps knew, since Pellegrini worked in The Hague in 1718 and in Antwerp. De Wit copied Pellegrini's small ceiling picture of *Aurora* (The Hague, Mauritshuis) in a pen-and-wash drawing (Amsterdam, Rijksmus.). De Wit's ceiling paintings are always conceived from a single viewpoint and suggest a glimpse into the sky. Initially strongly influenced by Rubens's figure types and compositions, de Wit later developed a more slender type of woman and child, set in more colourful, charming, airy and informally composed ceiling pictures. In these the decorative effect was sometimes achieved at the expense of correctly rendered drapery, foreshortening and anatomy (he often gave his figures exaggeratedly long, thick necks), as in *Gods and Signs of the Zodiac* for Herengracht 366, Amsterdam (1718; Amsterdam, Bijbels Mus.), *Apollo, Minerva and the Nine Muses* (1730; Amsterdam, Rijksmus.) and *Dawn Driving away the Darkness* (1735; Sarasota, FL, Ringling Mus.; preparatory oil sketch, Brussels, Mus. A. Anc.). For the Raadhuis in The Hague de Wit painted a ceiling decoration in 1738, of which only the grisaille corner pieces of putti with attributes of *Temperance, Freedom, Fortitude* and *Industry* are preserved (*in situ*); the modello for the central panel is possibly the *Allegory of Government* (New York, Met.). Many of de Wit's oil sketches were subsequently sold as the work of French artists François Lemoyne or François Boucher. A false signature and date, *f. Boucher 1753*, was even added to de Wit's oil sketch (Paris, Mus. Jacquemart-André) for his ceiling picture *Hercules at the Crossroads* (1725; Rotterdam, Mus. Boymans–van Beuningen).

Apart from his ceiling decorations, de Wit was renowned for smoothly painted grisailles imitating stucco reliefs, which were called 'witjes' (a play on his name, *Wit* [Dut.: 'white']). These are mostly of groups of putti. The earliest known example forms the corners to an oil sketch of *Zephyr and Flora* (1723; Toledo, OH, Mus. A.) for an untraced ceiling decoration. In 1743, he painted grisaille corner-pieces to *Apollo Surrounded by the Nine Muses* representing putti as *Pastoral Song, Epic, Comedy* and *Elegy* (The Hague, Mauritshuis). Among his best imitation reliefs is the overdoor *Joseph Gathering Corn during the Seven Years of Plenty* for the Amsterdam Stadhuis (now Royal Palace; see fig.). There, in 1737, he also completed his best-known work: *Moses Choosing the Seventy Elders* (*in situ*). For this large canvas (5.20×12.55 m) he received 8500 guilders. Although this moderately Baroque room decoration is successful overall, the individual figures, apart from Moses, are not convincingly rendered, partly because of their weakly painted drapery. De Wit's most important private commission in this genre is the series of

Jacob de Wit: *Joseph Gathering Corn during the Seven Years of Plenty*, oil on canvas, 3.39×1.60 m, *c.* 1737 (Amsterdam, Stichting Koninklijk Paleis)

BIBLIOGRAPHY

J. Punt: *De plafons, of gallerystukken uit de kerk der eerw P. P. Jesuiten te Antwerpen, geschildert door P. P. Rubens: Naer deszelfs echte schilderyen geteekent door Jacob de Wit, en in 't koper gebragt door Jan Punt* [The ceiling or gallery pictures from the Jesuit church in Antwerp, painted by P. P. Rubens: drawings after these paintings by Jacob de Wit engraved by Jan Punt] (Amsterdam, 1751)

A. Staring: *Jacob de Wit, 1695–1754* (Amsterdam, 1958)

J. R. Martin: *The Ceiling Paintings for the Jesuit Church in Antwerp* (1968), i of *Corpus Rubenianum Ludwig Burchardt* (Brussels, 1968), chap. iii

A. Staring: 'Verspreid werk van Jacob de Wit uit de Mozes en Aäronkerk' [Dispersed work by Jacob de Wit from the Moses and Aaron church], *Miscellanea I. Q. van Regteren Altena* (Amsterdam, 1969), pp. 164–5

Dutch Masterpieces from the Eighteenth Century: Paintings and Drawings, 1700–1800 (exh. cat. by E. R. Mandle, Minneapolis, MN, Inst. A.; Toledo, OH, Mus. A.; Philadelphia, PA, Mus. A.; 1971–2), pp. 113–18

C. W. Fock: 'Een kamer van Jacob de Wit thuisgebracht' [An interior by Jacob de Wit brought home], *Ned. Ksthist. Jb.*, xxi (1980); Eng. trans. as 'A Lost Ceiling Decoration by Jacob de Wit', *Bull. Allen Mem. A. Mus.*, xxxix (1982), pp. 19–30

Jacob de Wit: De Amsteltitiaan/The Titian of the Amstel (exh. cat., Amsterdam, Sticht. Kon. Pal., 1986)

J. van Tatenhove: 'Tekeningen door Jacob de Wit voor de Ovidius van Picart' [Drawings by Jacob de Wit for Picart's Ovid], *Leids Ksthist. Jb.*, (1987), pp. 211–34 [Eng. summary]

——: 'Jacob de Wit', *Delineavit & Sculp.*, 1 (1989), pp. 31–2

——: 'Jan Stolker (1724–1785)', *Delineavit & Sculp.*, 3 (1990), pp. 35–6

J. E. P. LEISTRA

Witdoeck, Hans [Jan] (*b* Antwerp, *bapt* 8 Dec 1615; *d* ?Antwerp, after 24 June 1642). Flemish engraver, draughtsman and dealer. He was a pupil of the engraver Lucas Vorsterman (i) in 1630–31 and a year later was registered as engraver and dealer in Antwerp's Guild of St Luke. He worked with the painter Cornelis Schut I until 1635 and made many engravings after Schut's work. From 1635 Witdoeck worked for Rubens, the last of the reproductive engravers to work for the great master. After Rubens's death in 1640, Witdoeck probably devoted most of his time to dealing. He married in 1642.

Witdoeck's early work, the engravings after Schut, follow the traditional style used by such artists as Phillip Galle and his workshop: dry lines with many curves and an emphasis on plasticity. Witdoeck's best work, however, is a series of eight scenes after Rubens, carefully executed under the master's supervision. Witdoeck captured the movement and variety of colour in Rubens's work with virtuosity, fully exploiting the use of black, grey and white tones. One fine example is *Abraham and Melchizedek* from 1616 (*NedKL*, no. 1). The engravings after Rubens are large in format, for example the *Raising of the Cross* (1638; *NedKL*, no. 8), a monumental print on three sheets. There are a number of preliminary drawings for prints by Witdoeck, some retouched by Rubens. Several prints by Witdoeck after Cornelis Schut were published by Johannes Meyssens (1612–70) as late as the 1640s.

BIBLIOGRAPHY

Thieme–Becker; Wurzbach

W. Kloek: *Beknopte catalogus van de Nederlandse tekeningen in het Prentenkabinet van de Uffizi te Florence* (Utrecht, 1975), nos 624–6

I. Pohlen: *Untersuchungen zur Reproduktionsgraphik der Rubenswerkstatt* (Munich, 1985), pp. 130–40, 283–301

MANFRED SELLINK

Witéz, Johannes. *See* VITÉZ, JOHANNES.

With, Pieter de (*fl* Amsterdam, 1650–60). Dutch draughtsman and etcher. The signature *P DE With* occurs

---

five paintings depicting the *Story of Jephthah*, painted for Herengracht 168 (now Amsterdam, Ned. Theat. Inst.), Amsterdam (1734; *in situ*), for which Isaac de Moucheron painted the landscapes. One of de Wit's last works is another ceiling decoration, depicting *Zephyr and Flora* (1751, untraced; preliminary study, Oberlin Coll., OH, Allen Mem. A. Mus.), for Rapenburg 65 in Leiden. After his death it was de Wit's grisailles rather than his ceiling or room paintings and altarpieces that attracted such followers as Elias van Nijmegen and Dionys van Nijmegen, Aert Schouman, Dirk van der Aa (1731–1809) and Abraham van Strij I.

WRITINGS

Teekenboek der proportien van 't menschelyke lighaam [Sketchbook of proportions for the human figure] (Amsterdam, 1747, 2/1790) [with engravings by Jan Punt after de Wit's drawings]

on two pen-and-ink drawings, an *Arcadian Landscape with Shepherd* (Amsterdam, Rijksmus.) and a *Landscape with Fishermen* (Paris, Fond. Custodia, Inst. Néer.). Characteristic of both is the use of parallel lines of varying density to describe undulating forms. In the same style is a similar landscape drawing (Besançon, Mus. B.-A. & Archéol.) signed *de with* and a sheet in the British Museum, London, with the (later?) inscription *Pieter de wit[h]* on the verso. This use of line derives from Italian landscape drawings by Titian or Domenico Campagnola that are known to have been studied or copied by Rembrandt. De With was probably Rembrandt's pupil in the first half of the 1650s, and his drawings seem to confirm the Italian biographer Filippo Baldinucci's claim that Rembrandt willingly lent his studio material to other artists. De With must have borrowed the Italian drawings before 1658, when Rembrandt's collection of drawings was sold.

A dozen etchings can be attributed to de With on the basis of these four drawings, including some previously attributed to Rembrandt. These are mainly Dutch landscapes with farms, which are closely related to Rembrandt's etchings of 1640–50. The monogram *PDW* can be distinguished on some of the prints (e.g. B. 245 and 254): one also bears the date 1659 (B. 255). As well as these signed works there are a number of drawings attributed to him that show he was strongly influenced by Jacob Koninck (Rotterdam, Mus. Boymans–van Beuningen). A few watercolour landscapes, formerly ascribed to Adam Elsheimer, can be given to de With on the basis of a sheet inscribed *P D With* in the *album amicorum* of Jacobus Heyblocq (The Hague, Kon. Bib.). The style of these drawings differs considerably from the calligraphic sheets in his earlier Italianate manner.

BIBLIOGRAPHY

A. von Bartsch: *Le Peintre-graveur* (1803–21) [B.]
Landschapstekeningen van Hollandse meesters uit de XVIIe eeuw (exh. cat., Brussels, Mus. A. Anc., 1968), pp. 182–3
W. Sumowski: *Drawings of the Rembrandt School*, x (New York, 1990)

B. P. J. BROOS

Withers, Frederick Clarke (*b* Shepton Mallet, Somerset, 4 Feb 1828; *d* New York, 1 Jan 1901). English architect, active in the USA. Following architectural training in Dorchester and London (where he worked with Thomas Henry Wyatt and David Brandon), he emigrated to the USA in 1852 at the invitation of the landscape architect A. J. Downing. At Downing's office in Newburgh, NY, Withers worked with Calvert Vaux, another English immigrant architect. Downing died soon after, but Withers stayed in Newburgh, first in partnership with Vaux and then working on his own. There he designed a number of Gothic Revival houses and churches, including the David Clarkson house (1856), the Frederick Deming house (1859; gutted; library installed New York, Met.) and First Presbyterian Church (1859; now Calvary Presbyterian Church). A number of houses on which Withers had assisted Downing and Vaux appeared in Vaux's book *Villas and Cottages* (New York, 1857).

After brief service as an engineer in the Union army during the Civil War, Withers moved to New York in 1863. There he joined Vaux in a partnership that lasted until 1872. During this period, Withers enlarged his reputation as a designer of churches, typical of which are St Paul's Episcopal Church (1864; unfinished) in Newburgh and St Luke's Episcopal Church (1869) in Beacon, NY. These buildings conformed to rules for church design laid down by the Ecclesiologists, unlike Withers's more adventurous, polychromatic brick Dutch Reformed Church (1859) in Beacon, which was an early instance of the influence of the teachings of John Ruskin among a small group of progressive American architects. The publication in 1873 of his book *Church Architecture*, a collection of many of his church plans, confirmed Withers as a designer of archaeologically correct Gothic churches. Notable among his later ecclesiastical commissions are the Astor Memorial Reredos (1876) in Trinity Episcopal Church, New York, and his largest church, the chapel of the Good Shepherd (1888), Roosevelt Island, New York.

In the years immediately following the Civil War, Withers became one of the leading practitioners of the High Victorian Gothic style in the USA. He reserved this modern expression of Gothic for secular structures, to create such buildings as the Jefferson Market Courthouse and Prison (1874; possibly with the assistance of Vaux), now the Greenwich Village branch of the New York Public Library, a design strongly reminiscent of William Burges's entry for the Law Courts competition of 1866. The Hudson River State Hospital, Poughkeepsie, NY (1866), and College Hall (1875) at Gallaudet College, Washington, DC, are two of several collaborative ventures of the 1860s and 1870s with Vaux and Frederick Law Olmsted who, as the nation's leading landscape architects, designed the grounds around the buildings.

Although architectural thought in America changed greatly in the 1880s and 1890s, Withers remained committed to Gothic Revival principles of design. He maintained an active practice until the time of his death, albeit with diminishing success: his last building, the New York City Prison (begun 1896; destr.), designed jointly with Walter Dickson (1834–1903), was unfinished when he died. He enjoyed a career that spanned the entire second half of the 19th century and is best remembered for his association with the mid-century revolution in domestic architecture fostered by Downing.

WRITINGS

Church Architecture (New York, 1873)

BIBLIOGRAPHY

F. R. Kowsky: 'The Architecture of Frederick Clarke Withers (1828–1901)', *J. Soc. Archit. Hist.*, xxxv (1976), pp. 83–109
——: *The Architecture of Frederick Clarke Withers and the Progress of the Gothic Revival in America after 1850* (Middletown, CT, 1980)

FRANCIS R. KOWSKY

Withers, Walter (Herbert) (*b* Aston, Warwicks, 22 Oct 1854; *d* Eltham, Victoria, 13 Oct 1914). Australian painter of English birth. He studied at the Royal Academy and South Kensington Schools (1870–82) in London and arrived in Melbourne on 1 January 1883 to work on the land for 18 months. He joined the life classes at the National Gallery of Victoria (1884–7), while employed as a lithographic draughtsman, and returned to Europe in 1887–8 to attend the Académie Julian in Paris. Back in Australia, he exhibited with the Victorian Artists' Society and painted with the HEIDELBERG SCHOOL artists, based at Eaglemont from October 1889 to June 1890. He was nicknamed 'the orderly colonel' for his organized habits. He leased the south end of the Heidelberg mansion 'Charterisville' from September 1890, painting prolifically, teaching and accommodating numerous fellow artists. The critic Sidney Dickinson named him, with Arthur Streeton, as a leader of 'the "Heidelberg School" . . . for out-of-door painting' ('Two exhibitions of paintings', *Australasian Critic*, 1 July 1891, p. 240). Withers remained mainly in Heidelberg until 1903, painting lyrical, essentially Barbizon-inspired, landscapes.

Withers was fascinated by the elements, his modest themes and muted tones dramatized by effects of changing weather and times of day. Two atmospheric studies of settled farming country, *A Bright Winter's Morning* (1894) and *Tranquil Winter* (1895), were among the first 'Australian Impressionist' paintings purchased by the National Gallery of Victoria, Melbourne. Withers's exceptional Art Nouveau decorative mural scheme of 1902 in the entrance hall of 'Purumbete', Camperdown, Victoria, depicted the development of the property by the Manifold family. He continued to teach and in 1903 settled in Eltham. In his later years he painted breezy seascapes, many in watercolour, as well as scenes of the bush. He was a founder-member of the Australian Art Association (1912) and a trustee of the National Gallery of Victoria (1912–14).

BIBLIOGRAPHY

A. McCubbin: *The Art and Life of Walter Withers* (Melbourne, 1919)
A. Humffray: 'Tranquility and Tempest: The Paintings of Walter Withers', *The Gallery on Eastern Hill*, ed. C. B. Christesen (Melbourne, 1970), pp. 37–52
Walter Withers: A Survey (exh. cat. by M. Rich, Geelong, A.G., 1975)
Golden Summers: Heidelberg and beyond (exh. cat. by J. Clark and B. Whitelaw, Melbourne, N.G. Victoria, 1985, rev. 1986)
A. MacKenzie: *Walter Withers: The Forgotten Manuscripts* (Melbourne, 1987)

JANE CLARK

Withoos [Calzetti; Galzetta Bianca], **Matthias** [Matteo] (*b* Amersfoort, 1627; *d* Hoorn, 1703). Dutch painter, active also in Italy. He was the pupil of Jacob van Campen and Otto Marseus van Schrieck. In 1648 Withoos went to Italy with van Schrieck and Willem van Aelst. He became a member of the Schildersbent in Rome. While in Italy his patrons included Cardinal Leopoldo de' Medici. By 1653 Withoos had returned to Amersfoort, but, when the French occupied the town in 1672, he moved to Hoorn.

Withoos is best known for his still-lifes. These often depict the base of a tree trunk with a longer view of a sand-dune or hilly landscape and show small animals, reptiles and insects among thistles and other plants. The plants and wildlife are painstakingly depicted, often in strongly differentiated areas of light and shade. Some of his works, such as the *Vanitas in a Graveyard* (Stockholm, Eric Vaaeur priv. col.), which shows a ruined graveyard with a pyramid and Classical urns, have *vanitas* connotations. In the foreground is an arrangement of *vanitas* symbols such as skulls, a globe, a book and an hour-glass. Withoos used cool colours, which contributes to the mysterious atmosphere and recalls the *sfumato* technique of 16th-century Venetians. The painting is probably indebted to Salvator Rosa's *Democritus* (Copenhagen, Stat. Mus. Kst), which was exhibited in the Pantheon in Rome in 1651 and known either directly, or through a print, by

Withoos (see Bergström). Withoos also painted views of Dutch ports (e.g. *Grashaven near Hoorn*, 1675; Amsterdam, Rijksmus.).

Five of Matthias Withoos's children were also painters: Johannes Withoos (*b* Amersfoort, 1648; *d* Hoorn, 1685) painted landscapes; Pieter Withoos (*b* Amersfoort, 1654; *d* Amsterdam, 1693) and Frans Withoos (*b* Amersfoort, 1657; *d* Hoorn, 1705) specialized in watercolours of insects and flowers; Alida Withoos (*b* Amersfoort, 1659 or 1660; *d* Hoorn, after 1715) painted still-lifes and landscapes; Maria Withoos was principally a watercolour painter.

BIBLIOGRAPHY

Thieme–Becker
A. Houbraken: *De groote schouburgh* (1718–21)
I. Bergström: *Dutch Still-life Painting in the Seventeenth Century* (London and New York, 1956), pp. 182, 184–6
L. J. Bol: *Holländischen Mahler des 17. Jahrhunderts nahe den grossen Meister* (Brunswick, 1969), pp. 338, 340, 379–80
W. Bernt: *Die niederländische Malerei und Zeichner des 17. Jahrhunderts* (Munich, 1979–80), iii, pp. 1491–2

H. G. DIJK-KOEKOEK

Witkiewicz [Witkacy], **Stanisław Ignacy** (*b* Warsaw, 24 Feb 1885; *d* Jeziory, Polesie, 17 Sept 1939). Polish writer, art theorist, painter and photographer. He was the son of the architect, painter and critic Stanisław Witkiewicz (1851–1915), creator of the 'Zakopane style' (*see* POLAND, §§II, 3; V and fig. 5). He spent his childhood in Zakopane in the Tatra Mountains and was educated at his family home, a place frequented by artists and intellectuals, and also through his many travels to Eastern and Western Europe. From his wide acquaintance with contemporary art, he was particularly impressed by the paintings of Arnold Böcklin. Witkiewicz's often interrupted studies (1904–10) under Józef Mehoffer at the Academy of Fine Arts in Kraków had less influence than his lessons in Zakopane and Brittany with Władysław Slewiński, who introduced him to the principles of Gauguin's Synthetism. Witkiewicz abandoned the naturalism of his first landscapes, executed under the influence of his father, rejected linear perspective and modelling and began to use flat, well-contoured forms and vivid colours, as in *Self-portrait with Flowers and Fruit* (1913; Warsaw, N. Mus.). But his art escapes all classification, and any similarities to contemporary trends are only superficial. In the so-called 'period of the monsters' (1908–14) he created Expressionist-like compositions with fantastic creatures and deformed, ugly human figures. He exploited the 'perverse harmony' of complementary colours and turbulent forms.

In 1914 Witkiewicz travelled to Ceylon and Australia accompanying, as photographer and draughtsman, the anthropologist Bronisław Malinowski (1884–1942). He went from Australia to Petrograd (St Petersburg) and was an officer in the Tsarist army during World War I. His reaction to the intensity of light, colours and emotions in the tropics, and to the experience of war and revolution, as well as contacts with Russian artists, was of major importance. He continued to paint and to take photographs, looking for similar effects in both disciplines. Full-frame images, close-ups, a focus on eyes and multiplication became typical of his portraiture, as in the photographic *Multiple Self-portrait in Mirrors* (1915–17; see Jakimowicz, p. 24, fig. xiii). He returned from Russia in 1918 with the manuscript of his most important philosophical treatise, on Pure Form (Warsaw, 1919). The same year he joined the Formists and, along with Leon Chwistek, became the leading theorist of the group. He contended that the metaphysical essence was fundamental to all kinds of art aiming to represent the mystery of existence. Works executed in Pure Form expressed, in artistic or literary terms, his concept of Being as based on Unity in Multiplicity (e.g. 1921–2; *Felling the Forest. Fight.*; Łódź, Mus. A.). Witkiewicz also stressed the importance of 'dynamics of directional tensions', an idea of inner movements alien to the Futurist fascination for speed, energy and machines. He viewed the future in catastrophic terms, foreseeing the inevitability of cultural decline and the suppression of individuality by the interests of the community and by technology. In 1925 he organized in Zakopane an experimental Formist Theatre that presented several of his plays, staged and designed by himself.

Very consciously, Witkiewicz gave up practising Pure Form (he did not renounce its theory) and, by establishing his own one-man 'Portrait Painting Firm', with published rules for customers, he moved towards more 'commercialized' art. He created hundreds of pastel portraits, some under the influence of alcohol and drugs, for example *Michał Choromański* (1930; Wrocław, N. Mus.). Witkiewicz committed suicide on hearing the news of the invasion of Poland by the Soviet army. He was barely comprehended by his contemporaries and it was many years after his death before his art and philosophy were understood and valued; it was to influence work such as the theatre productions of Tadeusz Kantor.

WRITINGS

Nowe formy w malarstwie i wynikające stąd nieporozumienia [New forms in painting and the misunderstandings arising therefrom] (Warsaw, 1919, rev. 3/1974)
Cahier Witkiewicz, I (Lausanne, 1976)

BIBLIOGRAPHY

I. Jakimowicz: *Witkacy: Malarz* [Witkacy: the painter] (Warsaw, 1985)
S. I. Witkiewicz: *Photographs, 1899–1939* (exh. cat., ed. J. Lingwood; Glasgow, Third Eye Centre, 1989)
I. Jakimowicz: *Stanisław Ignacy Witkiewicz, 1885–1939: Katalog dzieł malarskich* [A catalogue of paintings] (Warsaw, 1990)
A. Micińska: *Witkacy: Życie i twórczość* [Witkacy: life and art] (Warsaw, 1991)

ANNA BENTKOWSKA

Witkiewicz-Koszczyc, Jan (*b* Urdomin, 16 March 1881; *d* Warsaw, 26 Oct 1958). Polish architect and building restorer. He began his studies in Warsaw (1899) continuing them in L'vov (now L'viv, Ukraine) in 1900–01 and Munich (1901–4), and he was active in socialist politics until 1919. His friendship with the eminent writer Stefan Żeromski (1864–1925) was an important inspiration in his work. His early buildings reflected the neo-vernacular Zakopane style created by his uncle, Stanisław Witkiewicz (1851–1915), for example the Villa Na Antałówce (1904), Zakopane, and a house and study for Żeromski (1905), Nałęczów, near Puławy. Between 1906 and 1925 Witkiewicz-Koszczyc lived in Nałęczów and Kazimierz Dolny, with a period (1916–18) in Moscow and Mińsk Litewski (now Minsk, Belarus). During this time he designed and built a variety of different provincial buildings, using an original combination of forms well suited to the landscape of the Lublin hills. He used natural, undressed stone or brick, roofs with broken gables and eaves sometimes reaching the ground (influenced by his German studies), with dormer windows and small columns with exaggerated entasis. Examples include a nursery school in Nałęczów (1906–7), a 'House of Art' for an exhibition in Częstochowa (1909), a bath-house (1920–22) and a building trades school (begun 1922), both in Kazimierz Dolny. After 1925 he lived in Warsaw to supervise the construction of his Higher School of Commerce (now the Central School of Planning and Statistics), which he began to design in 1919. The approved third version, built in stages from 1925 to 1955, comprised a group of reinforced-concrete and glass buildings, urban in character, horizontally accentuated by a cornice or an attic storey and with carefully designed construction details. In another design (1930; unexecuted), for the church of Divine Providence, Warsaw, he proposed an expressive architecture free from the influence of Functionalism. He built more than 30 buildings during his career and restored *c.* 15 architectural monuments.

UNPUBLISHED SOURCES

Wrocław, Mus. Archit. [architectural designs]

WRITINGS

Gmach biblioteczny WSH w Warszawie [Library building of the Academy of Business and Commerce in Warsaw] (Warsaw, 1933)
Budowa gmachów bibliotecznych [Construction of library buildings] (Warsaw, 1939)

BIBLIOGRAPHY

J. Zachwatowicz: 'Jan Witkiewicz-Koszczyc, 1881–1958', *Ochrona Zabytków*, 3–5 (1958), pp. 285–7
Mieczysław Kurzątkowski: *Jan Witkiewicz-Koszczyc: Lata Nałęczowskie i Kazimierzowskie* [Jan Witkiewicz-Koszczyc: Years in Nałęczow and Kazimierz] (exh. cat., Kazimierz Dolny, Reg. Mus., 1981) [index of works]
M. Leśniakowska: 'Jan Koszczyc Witkiewicz, projekty', *Arché*, 4/5 (1993), pp. 14–19, 44
——: 'Jan Koszczyc Witkiewicz, projekty i rysunki obiektów sakralnych' [Jan Witkiewicz-Koszczyc, projects and drawings of sacral objects], *Arché*, 6 (1994), pp. 25-33

OLGIERD CZERNER

Witkin, Joel Peter (*b* Brooklyn, New York, 1939). American photographer. His first recorded photographs were of freaks on Coney Island made during the 1950s, giving an early indication of his ambition to challenge the boundaries of acceptable taste. His subject-matter included death, blasphemy, sado-masochism, homoeroticism and physical deformities. He presented an extreme, Gothic, nightmare world, which could be said to border on the pornographic. Balancing this taste for the grotesque was a tendency to mysticism and an aestheticism expressed in ironic reworkings of art-historical and literary themes drawn from Rembrandt, Goya, Rubens and the late 19th-century Symbolists.

Witkin studied sculpture at the Cooper Union School, New York, and in 1974 completed an MA in photography at the University of New Mexico. From the early 1970s he worked in series: *Contemporary Images of Christ, Images of Women* and the *Rooftop* series are a bizarre testament to his perverse preoccupations. The juxtaposition of Christ with comic-strip heroes, bound and gagged women surrounded by phallic fetishes and the use of masks on subjects of both sexes, withdrawing all individual identity, were central motifs of his work in the 1970s and 1980s. Witkin's printing technique was complex and meticulous.

He frequently scratched his negatives and placed thin tissue on his photographic paper to increase light refraction and soften the image, punching holes in it to emphasize chosen areas of sharpness. On warm toned papers and using a variety of toners, his prints often have a yellowish-brown Old Master look, thereby lessening the shock of such explicit imagery.

BIBLIOGRAPHY

G. Badger: 'Beyond Arbus and Bacon—the Photographs of Joel Peter Witkin', *Zien 5* (1983), p. 20
O. Edwards: 'Dancing with Death', *Amer. Photographer* (Aug 1983), pp. 29–30
M. Kozloff: 'Contention between Two Critics about a Disagreeable Beauty', *Artforum* (Feb 1984), pp. 45–53
O. Edwards: 'Joel Peter Witkin', *Amer. Photographer* (Nov 1985), pp. 40–53
Joel Peter Witkin: Forty Photographs (exh. cat. by Van Deren Coke, San Francisco, MOMA, 1985)
J. Woody: *Joel Peter Witkin* (Pasadena, 1986)

ALEXANDRA NOBLE

Witney, Thomas of. *See* THOMAS OF WITNEY.

Witsen, Willem (Arnold) (*b* Amsterdam, 13 Aug 1860; *d* Amsterdam, 13 April 1923). Dutch painter, printmaker, photographer and critic. He came from an old Amsterdam family of wealthy aristocrats with strong cultural ties. From 1876 to 1884 he was a pupil of August Allebé at the Rijksakademie van Beeldende Kunsten in Amsterdam. J. W. Kaiser (1813–1900) and Rudolf Stang (1831–1927) instructed him in graphic arts. In 1880 he co-founded St Luke's Society of Artists with Jacobus van Looy and Antoon Derkinderen. In 1882 he visited Paris with van Looy. Between 1883 and 1888 he worked regularly at his family estate, Ewijkshoeve, south of Baarn, often staying there in the company of artistic friends—writers and musicians, as well as painters. With Jan Veth he founded the Nederlandsche Etsclub (Dutch Etching Club), which from 1885 made a strong contribution to the revival of etching in the Netherlands. Witsen was the first among his circle of friends to have his own etching press and also a camera.

Witsen had a wide range of interests and talents. Using pseudonyms such as 'Verberchem' and 'W. J. van Westervoorde' (W. J. v. W.), he wrote a number of art reviews in *De nieuwe gids*, an avant-garde magazine founded in Amsterdam in 1885. He wrote, for example, about the great Jean-François Millet exhibition held in Paris in 1887. From 1888 to 1890 he worked in London. On his return to Amsterdam he moved to Oosterparkstraat 82 (now known as the Witsenhuis), which became a meeting-place for the Tachtigers ('Eighties movements'), a group of painters and writers whose portraits he recorded in numerous photographs. As a wealthy and benevolent man, Witsen offered financial support to *De Nieuwe Gids* and to his artist friends in need. From 1893 to 1902 Witsen lived in the village of Ede before moving back to Amsterdam. He travelled extensively, in 1920–21 visiting the Dutch East Indies with Isaac Israels.

Witsen is best known for his sombre-toned and quite smoothly painted townscapes of Amsterdam, London and Dordrecht, such as the *Old Schans* (*c.* 1889; Amsterdam, Stedel. Mus.), but he also produced paintings, watercolours and etchings of landscapes (e.g. *Winter Landscape*; Amsterdam, Rijksmus.). He was inspired by Millet to paint the labourer at work in the fields, for example in *Woman Gathering Potatoes* (Amsterdam, Witsenhuis), which also owes much in its handling of light and its broad brushwork to Anton Mauve, a close associate of Witsen in the 1880s and fellow admirer of Millet. Witsen's early etchings were equally indebted to Millet and Mauve in subject-matter and mood. He used photography as an independent medium, sometimes as a mnemonic device for his paintings but never in place of a preliminary sketch.

BIBLIOGRAPHY

A. W. Timmerman: *Willem Witsen* (Amsterdam, 1912)
N. van Harpen: *Willem Witsen* (Amsterdam, 1924)
A. M. Hammacher: *Amsterdamse impressionisten en hun kring* [Amsterdam Impressionists and their circle] (Amsterdam, 1941), pp. 57–8, 65–9
R. W. P. de Vries jr: *Nederlandsche grafische kunstenaars* (The Hague, 1943), pp. 65–79
Witsen en zijn vriendenkring [Witsen and his circle] (exh. cat. by K. G. Boon, Amsterdam, Stedel. Mus., 1948)
C. Vergeer: *Willem Witsen en zijn vriendenring/De Amsterdamse bohème van de jaren negentig* (Amsterdam and Brussels, 1985)
R. van der Wiel: *Ewijkshoeve, tuin van tachtig* [Ewijkshoeve, garden of the eighties] (Amsterdam, 1988)
The Age of van Gogh: Dutch Painting 1880–1895 (exh. cat., Glasgow, Burrell Col., 1990–91); Dut. edn as *De schilders van Tachtig* (Amsterdam, Van Gogh Mus. 1991)

CHR. WILL

Witte, Emanuel de (*b* Alkmaar, *c.* 1617; *d* Amsterdam, 1691–2). Dutch painter. He was one of the last and, with Pieter Saenredam, one of the most accomplished 17th-century artists who specialized in representing church interiors. He trained with Evert van Aelst (1602–57) in Delft and in 1636 joined the Guild of St Luke at Alkmaar, but he was recorded in Rotterdam in the summers of 1639 and 1640. In October 1641 his daughter was baptized in Delft, where he entered the Guild of St Luke in June 1642 and lived for a decade, moving to Amsterdam *c.* 1652. He began his long career as an unpromising figure painter, as can be seen in the *Vertumnus and Pomona* (1644) and two small pendant portraits (1648; all Rotterdam, Mus. Boymans–van Beuningen). *Jupiter and Mercury in the House of Philemon and Baucis* (1647) and a Rembrandtesque *Holy Family* (1650; both Delft, Stedel. Mus. Prinsenhof) presage de Witte's interpretation of architectural interiors predominantly in terms of light and shade, and—in their casual drawing, comparatively broad brushwork and uncertain articulation of space—are stylistically consistent with the unsigned *Nieuwe Kerk, Delft* (*c.* 1651; Winterthur, Stift. Briner), showing the tomb of William the Silent. The latter picture is based directly on Gerrit Houckgeest's church interiors of the same years, as is de Witte's version of the *Nieuwe Kerk, Delft* (1650–51; Hamburg, Ksthalle), with the tomb seen from the rear. Like Hendrick van Vliet, de Witte turned from figure painting to a subject that had always been a perspectivist's speciality. It can be assumed, and there is evidence in inventories, that a mostly local demand in traditionally royalist Delft encouraged de Witte and Hendrick van Vliet to concentrate on national monuments and the churches that enshrined them.

However, de Witte was less interested than van Vliet in fidelity to the actual site or in the architecture itself than his initial debt to Houckgeest might indicate. From the beginning, de Witte's imagination seems to have responded more to the great spaces than to the forms of Dutch Gothic churches, to the evocative contrasts of sunlight and shadow and to the people who visited and worshipped in these communal and spiritual environments. The *Oude Kerk in Delft with Pulpit* (1651; London, Wallace; see fig.), de Witte's first dated church interior, suggests in its descending daylight some communication between the heavens and the quiet congregation; the preacher in the pulpit, unlike van Vliet's gravediggers and some of Houckgeest's tourists, plays a comparatively inconspicuous part.

In style and technique, too, de Witte soon became independent of Houckgeest's influence, producing unprecedented examples of the genre. He adopted Houckgeest's 'two-point' perspective scheme and placement of columns in the immediate foreground, but in de Witte's approach, archways and windows are as assertively shapes in the compositional pattern as a solid architectural element or a piece of furniture. In the *Oude Kerk, Delft* (Ottawa, N.G.) and other views with pulpits (e.g. *Sermon in the Oude Kerk, Delft*, c. 1653–5; Brussels, Mus. A. Anc.; the *Oude Kerk in Amsterdam during a Service*, 1654; The Hague, Mauritshuis), de Witte de-emphasized diagonal and direct recessions into depth in favour of forms spaced at rhythmic intervals from side to side. Zones of space are thus layered and interrelated by a continuous interplay of solid and void, as well as by rich harmonies of light and shade. Although this effect, seen close up, appears more painterly and less illusionistic than the more conventional cues to depth used by Houckgeest and van Vliet, at a

normal distance de Witte's paintings are persuasive representations of actual views. A somewhat similar quality is found in contemporary works by Vermeer.

De Witte's use of linear perspective was creative both because he felt free to ignore its stringent requirements and because he was able to make pictorial assets out of perspective difficulties, a practice probably learnt in part from paintings by Pieter Saenredam, whose design ideas and even subject-matter he borrowed in a number of church interiors dating from the mid-1650s to c. 1670, such as the *St Janskerk, Utrecht* (1654; Paris, Fond. Custodia, Inst. Néer.) and the *Protestant Gothic Church* (1668; Rotterdam, Mus. Boymans–van Beuningen). But de Witte's preference for orthogonal recessions along or perpendicularly through elevations probably derived from other architectural painters, such as Anthonie de Lorme (d 1673) and even Houckgeest, who had used these arrangements both before and after the early 1650s. In any event, Saenredam's paintings provided only broad ideas and compositional patterns; his more exploratory on-site drawings may have greater relevance to de Witte's paintings in that they appear to describe space as an infinite continuum made comprehensible but not measurable by architecture.

As might be expected of an artist with such an intuitive grasp of the subject, who would confidently dismiss an intrusive elevation or render capital carvings with a twist of the brush, de Witte passed without hesitation from 'portraits' of actual churches to paintings of imaginary buildings, many of which incorporate elements of Amsterdam's main churches and Stadhuis (now Royal Palace). These structures, which can be only loosely categorized, as, for example, a *Protestant Gothic Church* (1669; Amsterdam, Rijksmus.), are the ultimate examples of the 'realistic imaginary church', a theme merely intimated by such earlier architectural painters as Houckgeest and Bartholomeus van Bassen. In subject and style, then, de Witte worked rather like a landscape painter, employing plausible and sometimes actual elements to create largely invented views.

No essential change of technique was necessary when de Witte painted outdoor market scenes, such as the *Fish Stall* (1672; Rotterdam, Mus. Boymans–van Beuningen) with three figures, the more extensive townscape in the *Small Fish Market, Amsterdam* (1678; Hartford, CT, Wadsworth Atheneum) or even the *Harbour at Sunset* (Amsterdam, Rijksmus.). A few landscapes and a still-life are also recorded: a *Kitchen Interior* (Boston, MA, Mus. F.A.) and an impressive *Interior with a Woman at a Clavichord* (c. 1665; The Hague, Dienst Verspr. Rijkscol., on dep. Rotterdam, Mus. Boymans–van Beuningen; autograph version, c. 1667; Montreal, Mus. F.A.) are original contributions to Dutch genre painting. The quality of de Witte's work varied considerably, due partly to his unstable temperament, which provoked domestic and financial difficulties to which Houbraken referred. But most of his surviving works are exceptionally good and even the minor ones are distinguishable from closely related Delft views by van Vliet or views of Amsterdam churches by de Witte's only pupil, Hendrick van Streek (1659–after 1719).

Emanuel de Witte: *Oude Kerk in Delft with Pulpit*, oil on panel, 606×438 mm, 1651 (London, Wallace Collection)

BIBLIOGRAPHY

A. Houbraken: *De groote schouburgh* (1718–21), i, pp. 223, 282–7; ii, p. 292

I. Manke: *Emanuel de Witte, 1617–1692* (Amsterdam, 1963)

W. A. Liedtke: *Architectural Painting in Delft: Gerard Houckgeest, Hendrick van Vliet, Emanuel de Witte* (Doornspijk, 1982)

WALTER LIEDTKE

Witte, Jacob Eduard (*fl* 1764–*c*. 1777). Dutch architect. He began his career in the army, attaining the rank of engineer-lieutenant in 1764. In 1772 he was appointed director of public works in Amsterdam. His most famous work is the theatre (1773; destr. 1890) on the Leidseplein, Amsterdam, built of timber on stone foundations to replace the old theatre (1637) by Jacob van Campen on the Keizersgracht, which had been destroyed by fire. Although the replacement, nicknamed the 'Wooden Cabinet', was regarded as a temporary solution, it was built with considerable care and attention to detail. The block-shaped theatre had a flat façade, enlivened only by angle pilasters and a slight central projection, capped by a pediment. The façades were crowned all round by a balustrade. Anthonie Ziesenis was responsible for the pediment sculpture and the internal décor. Among the more remarkable features of the building were the double outer walls, which were filled with sawdust to keep out street noise. A stone façade based on the classical Viennese design of Bastiaan de Greef and Willem Springer was erected to cover the wooden structure in 1872 before the theatre was completely destroyed in a fire. In 1773 Witte built the Reformed Church in Oudekerk aan de Amstel, near Amsterdam, presumably to a design by Cornelis Rauws. In 1774 Witte's design for a new town hall in Groningen won second prize in a competition. Very little else is known about his life; he is said to have left for Russia in 1777, having been discharged with dishonour as director of public works.

BIBLIOGRAPHY

J. A. Worp: *Geschiedenis van de Amsterdamschen schouwburg, 1496–1772* [History of the Amsterdam theatre, 1496–1772] (Amsterdam, 1920)

PAUL H. REM

Witte, Lieven de (*b* Ghent, *c*. 1503; *d* Ghent, after 4 Feb 1578). Flemish painter and designer of stained glass and book illustrations. His dates can be deduced from several amendments to his will. Archives reveal that he was fined during the heretics' trial of 1528 because of his Reformist sympathies. In 1538–9 he was paid for painting the blazon of the Ghent rhetoricians' chamber 'De Fonteyne' for the rhetoricians' festival of 1539. Van Mander called him a good painter, particularly skilled in the depiction of architecture and perspective, and he mentioned a painting of the *Woman Taken in Adultery* (untraced) and designs for windows in St Bavo's, Ghent. De Witte's work is now known only through his designs for book illustrations. The most important publication is Willem van Branteghem's *Iesu Christi vita* (Antwerp, 1537) published by Matthias Crom, also in a Dutch and French version. The book contains a Latin acrostic on LEVINUS DE VVITTE GANDENSIS, written by Joris Cassander, which awards special praise to de Witte. It includes 186 woodcuts and numerous vignettes, in a highly characteristic style, full of picturesque and narrative detail. The woodcuts were reprinted and copied many times as illustrations to the Bible, and they also influenced the work of other artists such as Maarten van Heemskerck. De Witte also designed book illustrations for the Ghent printer Joos Lambrecht (*fl c*. 1536–56), for instance for Andries van der Meulen's *Een zuverlic boucxkin vander ketyvigheyt der menschelicker naturen* ('A fine tract on the misery of the condition of man'; 1543) and Cornelis van der Heyden's *Corte instruccye ende onderwijs* ('Brief instruction and education'; 1545).

BIBLIOGRAPHY

K. van Mander: *Schilder-boeck* ([1603]–1604), fol. 204*v*

E. de Busscher: *Recherches sur les peintres et sculpteurs à Gand aux XVIe, XVIIe, et XVIIIe siècle* (Ghent, 1866), pp. 44–5, 312–16

A. J. J. Delen: *Histoire de la gravure dans les anciens Pays-Bas et dans les provinces belges des origines jusqu'à la fin du XVIIIe siècle*, ii (Paris, 1934), pp. 55–7

I. M. Veldman: 'De boekillustratie als inspiratiebron voor de Nederlandse prentkunst van de zestiende eeuw', *Eer is het lof des deuchts: Opstellen over renaissance en classicisme aangeboden aan dr. Fokke Veenstra* [Honour is the praise of virtue: essays on the Renaissance and classicism, dedicated to Dr. Fokke Veenstra] (Amsterdam, 1986), pp. 263–5

I. M. Veldman and K. van Schaik: *Verbeelde boodschap: De illustraties van Lieven de Witte bij 'Dat leven ons Heeren' (1537)* [Edification in pictures: Lieven de Witte's illustrations for *Dat leven ons Heeren* (1537)] (Haarlem and Brussels, 1989)

ILJA M. VELDMAN

Witte, Pieter de. *See* CANDID, PETER.

Wittel, Gaspar [Caspar] **(Adriaansz.) van** [Vanvitelli, Gaspare or Gasparo] (*b* Amersfoort, 1652–3; *d* Rome, 13 Sept 1736). Dutch painter and draughtsman, active in Italy. After early training in Amersfoort in the workshop of Matthias Withoos, he went to Rome, where he is first recorded in 1675; known as Vanvitelli, he spent the rest of his life there apart from a few trips to northern Italy during the early 1690s, a stay in Naples from 1700 to 1701 and possibly other, undocumented, trips before *c*. 1730. He became one of the principal painters of topographical views known in Italy as *vedute* (*see* VEDUTA). His first recorded work in Rome comprises 50 drawings executed in 1675–6 (Rome, Bib. Accad. N. Lincei & Corsiniana, Cod. Corsiniana 1227), illustrating the plans by the hydraulic engineer Cornelis Meyer (1629–1701) to restore navigability to the River Tiber between Rome and Perugia. (Though generally accepted, the attribution of these drawings has been disputed by Zwollo.) Van Wittel's first *vedute* were also collaborations with Meyer, who illustrated one of his tracts with a series of engraved Roman views (pubd 1683 and 1685), of which those depicting the Piazza del Popolo, the Piazza S Giovanni in Laterano and the Piazza S Pietro are taken from designs by van Wittel, probably executed in 1678 and repeatedly used by the artist from the early 1680s in tempera and oil paintings. Van Wittel's first painted *vedute* date from 1680, and his style was established by the beginning of the 1690s. Even before 1690, in fact, he had elaborated his chosen compositional and perspectival principles: subsequently only the subject-matter changed.

The type of *veduta* van Wittel created has certain precedents in the work of Viviano Codazzi and Johann Wilhelm Baur, who was active in Rome during the 1640s. Anticipating the 18th-century style, van Wittel's *vedute* are, both in aim and method, realistic views structured according to rational principles of vision: they combine careful description of the subject with strict adherence to its panoramic perspective, while their point of view, which often coincides with ground-level in the view itself, corresponds exactly to that of the spectator. His choice of subject was also innovative when compared with that of his 17th-century predecessors, as can be seen particularly in his views of Rome. Since the 16th century painters had concentrated on scenes of ruined architecture overrun by vegetation, giving expression to poetic and literary themes associated with the past and with the contrast between ancient splendour and modern decay. The output of northern landscape artists active in Rome during the late 17th century tended to convey a generic Italianate atmosphere rather than showing the city and its surrounding countryside as it then appeared. Van Wittel, on the other hand, documented the most up-to-date and least familiar aspects of the modern city, remaining immune to the conventional lure of the ruins. With the exception of the Colosseum, portrayed from various points of view (e.g. 1703; Paris, priv. col., see Briganti, no. 30, 38–9), he rarely depicted the ancient monuments and religious sites of Rome. When he did, his treatment was novel, as can be seen in the *View of the Arch of Titus from the Colosseum* (e.g. 1685; Rome, priv. col.), which for the first time shows the arch from its most complete side. His *vedute* depict places not yet hallowed by tradition or different angles on well-known ones, as in the paired views of *Trinità dei Monti* and the *Villa Medici* (earliest examples 1681; Rome, Gal. Colonna) and his *View of the Campo Vaccino from the Side Stairway of Aracoeli* (1683; Rome, Gal. Colonna). There were no precedents for his *View of Campo Marzio from the Prati* (e.g. *c.* 1682; Rome, Pin. Capitolina; see fig.) or the fine series of *Views of the Tiber* between the Porto della Legna and the Ripa Grande (begun 1683), employing 15 different vantage points (e.g. 1683, Rome, Gal. Colonna; 1685, Florence, Pitti).

Van Wittel's drawings made in Lombardy resulted in the signed and dated *View of the Borromeo Islands on Lake Maggiore* (1690; Rome, Gal. Colonna) and views of the town of Vaprio d'Adda (e.g. 1719; Rome, priv. col., see Briganti, no. 187). A trip to Venice is documented by a series of *vedute*, the earliest dated 1697 (Madrid, Prado). Some of these, most notably the *View of the Piazzetta from St Mark's Basin* (Rome, Gal. Doria-Pamphili), the *St Mark's Basin towards the Grand Canal* (priv. col., see Briganti, no. 173) and the *Punta della Dogana with S Maria della Salute* (Rome, Gal. Colonna), anticipate Canaletto in their perspective layout and in the angle of the views.

Beginning in 1700 van Wittel painted views of Naples, where he went at the invitation of the Viceroy, Luis de la Cerda, Duque de Medinaceli. The most notable are his versions of the *View of Darsena* (e.g. 1702, Naples, Mus. N. S Martino; 1703, London, N. Mar. Mus.) and his *View of the Largo di Palazzo,* which was also replicated (e.g. 1701; Rome, priv. col., see Briganti, no. 199; 1700–02, Rome, Banca Commerc. It.).

Throughout his career van Wittel used drawings, made in Rome during the early 1680s and during his various travels, to create several painted versions of a single view. Many of these sheets, which were drawn from life and completed in the studio, have survived: the most interesting are in Naples (Mus. N. S Martino) and Rome (Bib. N. Cent.). The format of these studio drawings matches that of the paintings, and many of them, divided into squares, served as the artist's aide-mémoire when creating a painting, at which point they were probably used together with more rapid sketches that had been made on the spot.

Van Wittel was nicknamed 'Gasparo dagli Occhiali' (Gaspare with the spectacles) and his Bent-name (given him by colleagues in the Schildersbent, the association of Dutch and Flemish artists in Rome) was 'Piktoorts' (or

Gaspar van Wittel: *View of Campo Marzio from the Prati*, tempera on vellum, 230×430 mm, *c.* 1682 (Rome, Pinacoteca Capitolina)

Pitch-torch). His son, LUIGI VANVITELLI, became a leading architect in Naples.

BIBLIOGRAPHY
C. Lorenzetti: *Gaspare Vanvitelli* (Milan, 1934)
G. Doria: *Il 'Largo di Palazzo' a Napoli e Gaspare dagli Occhiali* (Milan, 1964)
G. Briganti: *Gaspar van Wittel e l'origine della veduta settecentesca* (Rome, 1966) [rev. edn, ed. L. Louresti and L. Trezzani, in preparation]
H. Wagner: 'Ein unbekanntes Frühwerk Gaspar van Wittels', *Berlin. Mus.: Ber. Staatl. Mus. Preuss. Kultbes.*, xviii (1968), pp. 24–9
G. Morelli: 'Appunti bio-bibliografici su Gaspar e Luigi Vanvitelli', *Archv Soc. Romana Stor. Patria*, xcii (1969–70), pp. 117–36
J. Michalkowa: 'Ancora un Vanvitelli', *Bull. Mus. N. Varsovie/Biul. Muz. N. Warszaw.*, xii/3 (1971), pp. 59–65
W. Vitzthum: 'Gaspar van Wittel e Filippo Juvarra', *A. Illus.*, iv/41–2 (1971), pp. 5–9
A. Zwollo: *Hollandse en Vlaamse veduteschilders te Rome (1675–1725)* (Assen, 1973)
Drawings by Gaspar van Wittel from Neapolitan Collections (exh. cat. by W. Vitzthum, intro. by G. Briganti; Ottawa, N.G., 1977)
Gaspare Vanvitelli (1652/53–1736): Zeichnungen und Acquarelle (exh. cat. by R. Harprath, Munich, Staatl. Graph. Samml., 1983)
All'ombra del Vesuvio: Napoli nelle veduta europea dal quattrocento all'ottocento (exh. cat., Naples, Castel S Elmo, 1990)

LUDOVICA TREZZANI

Wittelsbach, House of. Dynasty of German rulers, patrons and collectors (see fig.). The Bavarian branch of the family (*see* §I below) was helped in its rise to power by an alliance with the House of Hohenstaufen. The acquisition by marriage of the Rhineland Palatinate in the early 13th century brought division of the inheritance (*see* §II below). However, the division gave rise to cultural diversity by scattering a number of residences throughout the country. In 1329 the dynastic treaty of Pavia with the Palatinate branch provided for reciprocal inheritance and (until 1356) the alternation of the electorship between the lines. Following a decree on primogeniture (1506) by Albert IV, Duke of Bavaria (*reg* 1463–1508), Bavaria remained undivided. The Zweibrücken-Birkenfeld branch (*see* §III below) was a collateral line. On the extinction of the Bavarian and Palatinate branches in the 18th century, however, the Zweibrücken house provided the last kings of Bavaria.

BIBLIOGRAPHY
C. Haeutle: *Genealogie des erlauchten Stammhauses Wittelsbach* (Munich, 1870)
S. von Riezler: *Die Kunstpflege der Wittelsbacher* (Munich, 1911)
F. Tyroller: *Die Ahnen der Wittelsbacher* (Munich, 1951)
Biographisches Wörterbuch zur Deutschen Geschichte, iii (Munich, 1975), pp. 3204–26
Prince Adalbert of Bavaria: *Die Wittelsbacher: Geschichte einer Familie* (Munich, 1979)

DIETER J. WEISS

I. Bavarian branch. II. Palatinate branch. III. Zweibrücken-Birkenfeld branch.

I. Bavarian branch.

(1) Ludwig IV [Ludwig the Bavarian], Holy Roman Emperor and Duke of Bavaria (*b* Munich, *c.* 1282; *reg* 1294–1347; *d* Puch bei Fürstenfeld, 11 Oct 1347). He was Duke of Upper Bavaria from 1294, Count Palatine of the Rhine (until 1329) and Duke of Lower Bavaria from 1340. In 1314 he was elected King of Germany, in opposition to his cousin Frederick, Duke of Austria (1286–1330), whom he subsequently defeated and captured at the Battle of Mühldorf (1322). After defying Pope John XXII, Ludwig was excommunicated but was crowned Holy Roman Emperor in Rome in 1328. He then proclaimed a judgement of nullity on Pope John XXII and enthroned the anti-pope Nicholas V but was subsequently forced to leave Rome and in 1330 abandoned his Italian campaign. Nevertheless, in Germany the Emperor proved his fidelity to the Church, notably through foundations such as that of the Benedictine monastery of Ettal (1330), near Oberammergau, to which, according to legend, he donated the miraculous statue in marble of an enthroned *Virgin* (*c.* 1328–30), recorded in frescoes by Johann Jakob Zeiller (1752) and Franz Seraph Zwinck (*c.* 1780; both *in situ*). During Ludwig's reign the fortifications of Munich were also completed (1337); the only extant features are the Isartor and the Sendlinger Tor (*see* MUNICH, §I, 1). Later images of the Emperor can often be traced back to documents and seals produced during his reign, for example the seal of the Imperial Gold Bull (1327–8; Munich, Bayer. Hauptstaatsarchv), depicting him seated on the Lion Throne, and in an initial on the licence of freedom of Dortmund, dated 25 August 1332, which depicts him with the mayor of Dortmund and a priest (destr. 1945). A painted sandstone relief of members of the Wittelsbach family (1324; Munich, Bayer. Nmus.) from the former Lorenzkirche (destr. 1816) inspired later portraits of the Emperor, including those by Johann Jakob Dorner I (*c.* 1766–70; Munich, Bayer. Staatsgemäldesammlungen), Pieter Candid (1611–19; Munich, Residenz) and Jacopo Amigoni (*c.* 1726–8; Munich, Residenz), and the portrait medallion (*c.* 1765–9; Munich, Staatl. Münzsamml.) by Franz Andreas Schega, which served as a model for an ivory miniature (*c.* 1775; Munich, Bayer. Nmus.). Ludwig IV was able to retain power in Germany, despite interventions, until 1346, when Charles, Count of Luxembourg, secured election as the Holy Roman Emperor Charles IV. Ludwig IV died, unreconciled with the Church, from a heart attack during a bear hunt.

BIBLIOGRAPHY
C. Höfler: 'Urkundliche Beiträge zur Geschichte Kaiser Ludwigs IV.', *Oberbayer. Archv Vaterländ. Gesch.*, i (1839), pp. 45–118
J. F. Böhmer, ed.: *Albertinus Mussatus, Ludovicus Bavarus, 1327–1329*, i of *Fontes rerum Germanicarum*, ed. W. Friedensburg (Stuttgart, 1843)
G. Benker: *Ludwig der Bayer (1282–1347): Ein Wittelsbacher auf dem Kaiserthron* (Munich, 1980)
J. Wetzel: *Die Urkunden aus den Archiven und Bibliotheken Württembergs* (1991), i of *Regesten Kaiser Ludwigs des Bayern (1314–47): Nach Archiven und Bibliotheken geordnet* (Cologne, Weimar and Vienna, 1991–)
R. Suckale: *Die Höfkunst Kaiser Ludwigs des Bayern* (Munich, 1993)
H. Thomas: *Ludwig der Bayer (1282–1347): Kaiser und Ketzer* (Regensburg, Graz, Vienna and Cologne, 1993)

GREGOR M. LECHNER

(2) William [Wilhelm] **IV**, Duke of Bavaria (*b* Munich, 13 Nov 1493; *reg* 1508–50; *d* Munich, 17 March 1550). Descendant of (1) Ludwig IV, Holy Roman Emperor and Duke of Bavaria. After a regency lasting until 1511, his entitlement to the duchy of Bavaria was disputed by his brother Ludwig (1495–1545), who did not accept the law of primogeniture passed in 1506, and from 1514 to 1545 they ruled jointly, William in Upper Bavaria, Ludwig (as Ludwig X) in Lower Bavaria. The period was marked by religious conflict (after the Diet of Worms in 1521, the brothers took a firm stance against the Reformation) and by disputes with the provincial diets and the Habsburgs, although in the Schmalkaldic War (1546–7) William IV sided emphatically with the Holy Roman Emperor and the Pope, earning the sobriquet 'the Steadfast'.

William IV appointed his former tutor, Johannes Thurmayr (Aventinus; 1477–1534), as historiographer and commissioned him to write the *Bayerische Chronik* (1521–3), which marked the beginning of the scholarly historiography of Bavaria. Although delighting in tournaments and hunting and drawn to medieval chivalrous ideals, the Duke also took pleasure in Renaissance splendour and the cultivation of art. The sculptor FRIEDRICH HAGENAUER introduced the portrait medal as a new art form to the Munich court. William IV was the first duke of Bavaria to make his permanent residence in Munich in the Neuveste, to the east of which the first court garden was laid out. From 1528 he commissioned a series of sixteen history paintings, eight depicting the lives of great men and eight showing those of virtuous women. These were executed by the court painter Barthel Beham, Hans Burgkmair I, Jörg Breu (i), Melchior Feselen, Ludwig Refinger, Hans Schöpfer I, Abraham Schöpfer (*fl* 1533–before 1572) and Albrecht Altdorfer, whose *Battle of Alexander* (1529; Munich, Alte Pin.; *see* GERMANY, fig. 18) is the most notable of the works. The theme of the series, in which heroes of antiquity are related to the ruler as 'spiritual ancestors', is based on the new approach to history adopted in the Renaissance. The Duke's collection, including this series of paintings, eventually formed the basis of the Bayerischen Staatsgemäldesammlungen in Munich.

BIBLIOGRAPHY
O. Hartig: 'Die Kunsttätigkeit in München unter Wilhelm IV und Albrecht V, 1520–1579', *Münchn. Jb. Bild. Kst*, n. s., x (1933), pp. 147–225
H. Lutz: 'Das konfessionelle Zeitalter, Erster Teil: Die Herzöge Wilhelm IV und Albrecht V', *Handbuch der bayerischen Geschichte*, ed. M. Spindler (Munich, 1969), ii, pp. 297–350

DORIS KUTSCHBACH

(3) Albert [Albrecht] **V**, Duke of Bavaria (*b* Munich, 29 Feb 1528; *reg* 1550–79; *d* 24 Oct 1579). Son of (2) William IV, Duke of Bavaria. At the outset of his reign Bavaria's finances were exhausted, its administration inadequate and the Church in need of reform. Despite some of his subjects' leaning towards Protestantism, the Duke promoted Catholicism and with the support of the Jesuits preserved Bavaria for the Roman Catholic Church, although he pursued a policy of state control of the Church. By crushing opposition from nobles with Protestant sympathies in 1564, the Duke strengthened his position as ruler in relation both to the estates and to the Catholic Church. He also extended the administration and acquired new domains, leaving his successor, (4) William V, a country consolidated both politically and ecclesiastically but heavily burdened with debts as a result of the poor financial organization of the early modern state.

During this period the court of Bavaria was one of the first to promote secular art in Germany. This is clearly seen in the Duke's enlargement and rebuilding of the Munich Residenz, which he made the centre of a magnificent court (*see* MUNICH, §IV, 2). From 1559 to 1562 he had the Georgssaal (destr.), with its rich, coffered ceiling, incorporated in the late medieval Neuveste by the court architect WILHELM EGCKL, who also constructed the Marstall (1563–7; later the State Mint; now the Bavarian Department of Historic Building Conservation), thereby

bringing the Renaissance style to Munich. The latter was intended to house the ducal collections of art works and curiosities, on a plan representing a microcosm of the universe developed by the Flemish court physician Samuel van Quiccheberg. The idea for the Antiquarium (1569; *see* MUNICH, fig. 5), built in front of the Neuveste, to display the collection of antiquities was supplied by the Mantuan antiquary Jacopo Strada. The first floor of the building housed the ducal library, which Hans Fugger had built up by transferring to it his own collection and acquiring other libraries, thus providing the basis of the Bayerische Staatsbibliothek. The Duke also had the four-winged structure of his castle at Dachau (*see* DACHAU COLONY) completed (1570–73) by Egckl, one of the most notable interior features being a gilded, coffered ceiling by Hans Wisreutter (*fl* 1548–72).

The Duke took great interest in goldsmithing and even produced designs for goldsmiths' work. He employed numerous goldsmiths from Munich and others from Augsburg and Nuremberg, notably Isaak Melper (*fl* 1559; *d* 1592), Hans Reimer (*fl* 1555; *d* 1604), Georg Zeggin (*fl* 1555; *d* 1581), Heinrich Wagner (*d* 1607) and Wenzel Jamnitzer (*see* MUNICH, §III, 1). In 1571 Albert V acquired Hans Fugger's coin collection, the basis of the present Staatliche Münzsammlung, and had numerous memorial coins minted. The sculpture of the period served mainly as decoration: Hans Wörner (*fl* 1568; *d* 1573), Jordan Brechfeld (*d* 1575/6), Hans Aesslinger and Hans Aernhofer (*d* 1621) were commissioned to provide decorative sculptures for state ceremonies and for display.

The leading court painter was HANS MIELICH. In 1545 he painted a portrait (Munich, Alte Pin.) of Albert, who commissioned him in 1546 to paint miniatures (Munich, Bayer. Nmus.) of his jewellery. In 1555 Mielich painted a life-size portrait of the Duke in Spanish court costume (1555; Munich, Bayer. Nmus.) and, later, matching portraits of the Duke and the Duchess (1556; Vienna, Ksthist. Mus.). Albert V also had the scores (1560–61) of the penitential psalms of Orlando di Lasso (1563–94) and the motets (1557–9; both Munich, Bayer. Staatsbib.) of Cyprian de Rore (1516–65) inscribed in large parchment folios that Mielich decorated with miniature paintings. Mielich's last major work was for the Renaissance high altar of the Frauenkirche at Ingolstadt: when open, the winged altarpiece shows the *Virgin as Queen of Heaven with the Ducal Family* (1572).

Other painters in the Duke's service included Johann Melchior Bocksberger, who executed the ceiling painting in the pleasure-house of the Munich Residenz; Sigmund Hebenstreit (*fl* 1556; *d* 1612) and Hans Donauer I, who worked on the furnishings of the art cabinet; Hans Schöpfer I; Hans Schöpfer II (*fl* 1569; *d* 1610); and Christoph Schwarz. Hanns Lautensack was commissioned to execute woodcuts to decorate the *Annales Ducum Boiariae* (Ingolstadt, 1554) and the *Bayerische Chronik* (Frankfurt am Main, 1566) of Johannes Thurmayr (Aventinus; 1477–1534) and the *Heiligenleben* (Munich, 1574–80) by Laurentius Surius (1522–78). The Duke also had the maps of Bavaria by Philip Apian (1531–89) published in a woodcut edition (Ingolstadt, 1568) with Jost Amman and in an engraved edition (1575) by the mint warden Peter Weiner (*d* 1583). With his collections and buildings

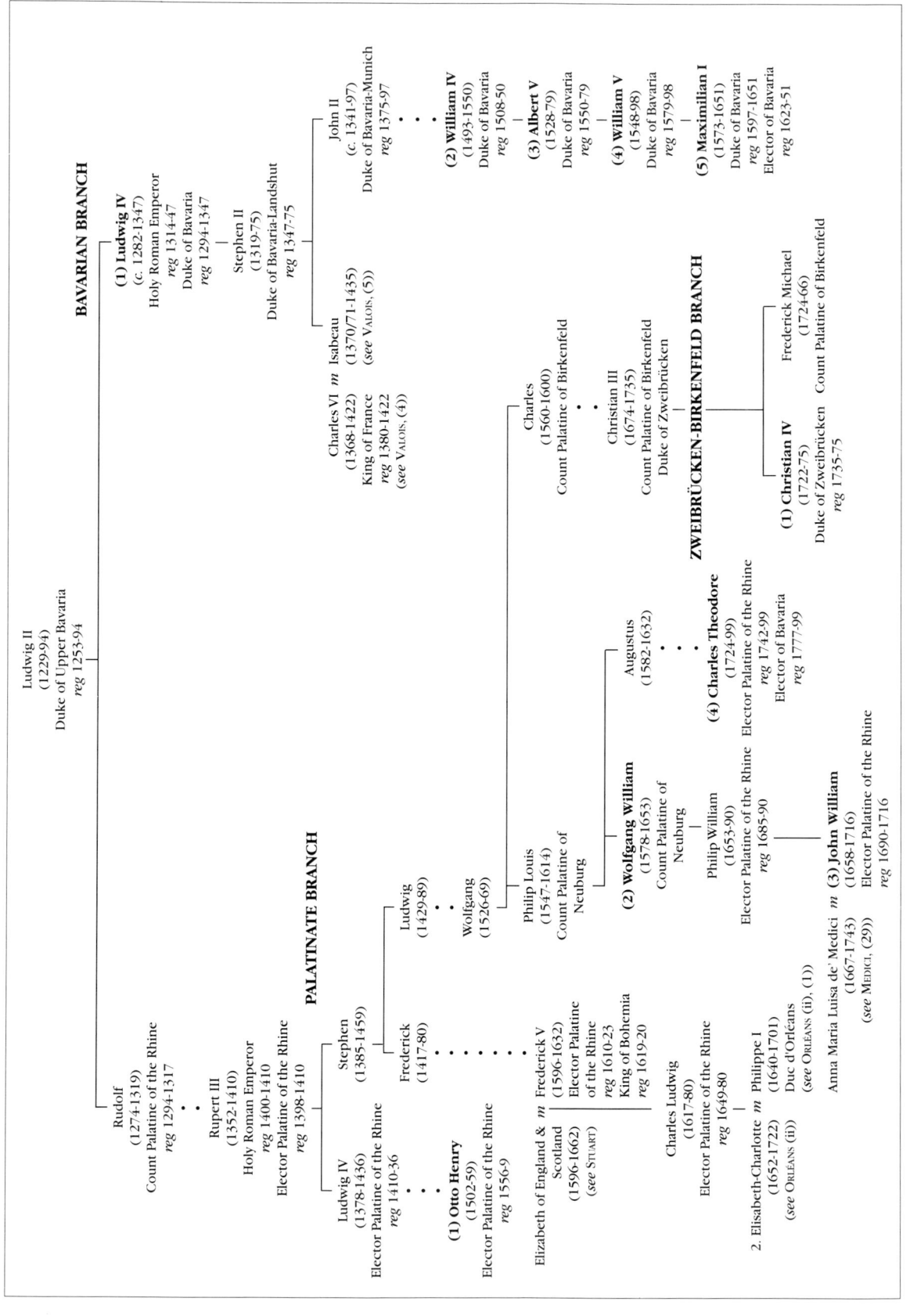

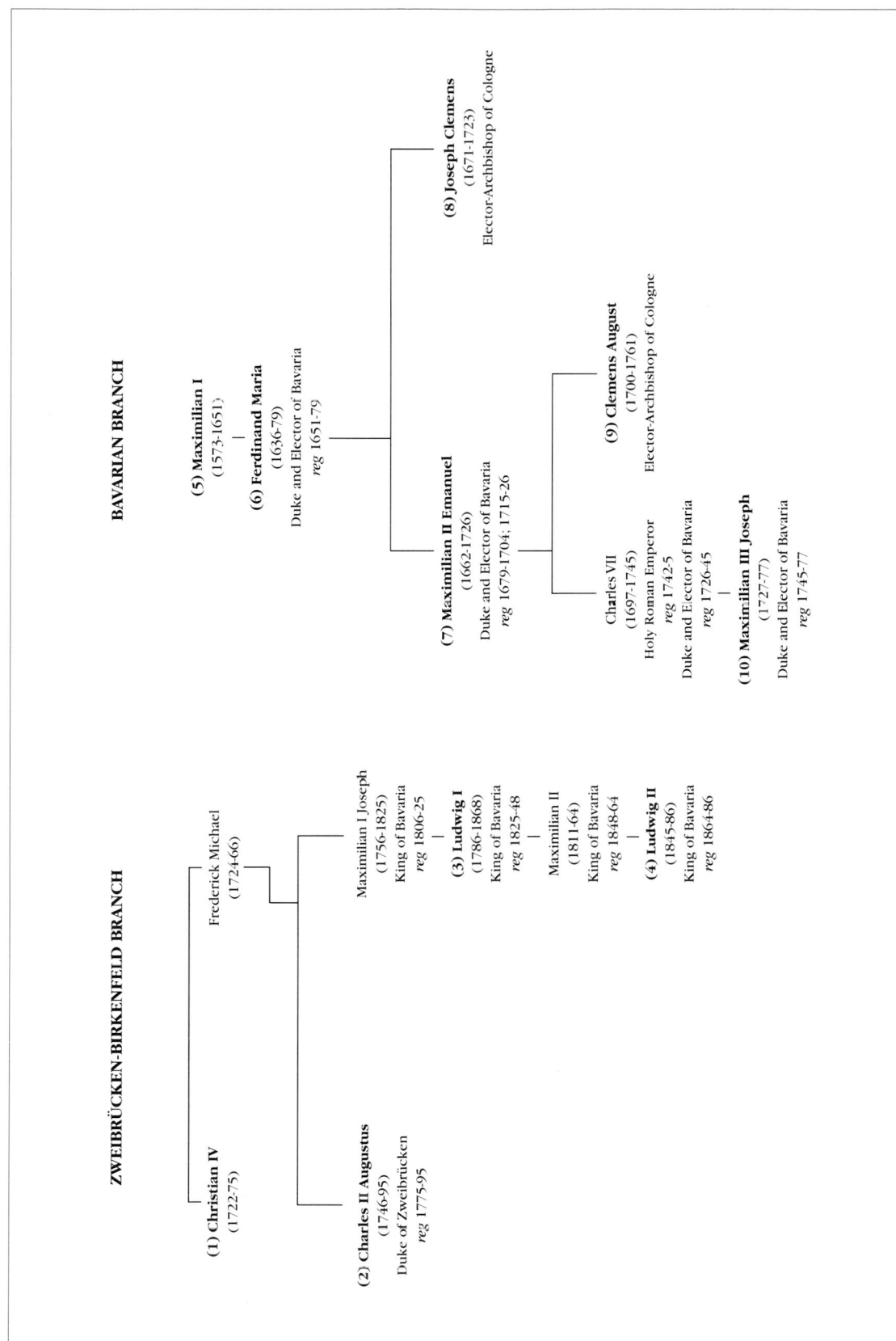

ZWEIBRÜCKEN-BIRKENFELD BRANCH

BAVARIAN BRANCH

Frederick Michael
(1724-66)

(5) Maximilian I
(1573-1651)

|

(6) Ferdinand Maria
(1636-79)
Duke and Elector of Bavaria
reg 1651-79

Maximilian I Joseph
(1756-1825)
King of Bavaria
reg 1806-25

(1) Christian IV
(1722-75)

(7) Maximilian II Emanuel
(1662-1726)
Duke and Elector of Bavaria
reg 1679-1704; 1715-26

(8) Joseph Clemens
(1671-1723)
Elector-Archbishop of Cologne

(3) Ludwig I
(1786-1868)
King of Bavaria
reg 1825-48

Charles VII
(1697-1745)
Holy Roman Emperor
reg 1742-5
Duke and Elector of Bavaria
reg 1726-45

(9) Clemens August
(1700-1761)
Elector-Archbishop of Cologne

Maximilian II
(1811-64)
King of Bavaria
reg 1848-64

(2) Charles II Augustus
(1746-95)
Duke of Zweibrücken
reg 1775-95

(10) Maximilian III Joseph
(1727-77)
Duke and Elector of Bavaria
reg 1745-77

(4) Ludwig II
(1845-86)
King of Bavaria
reg 1864-86

Family tree of the Wittelsbach dynasty

the Duke founded Munich's reputation as a city of art, and the Antiquarium and art cabinet were the first important museums north of the Alps.

BIBLIOGRAPHY

NDB

M. G. Zimmermann: *Die bildenden Künste am Hof Herzog Albrecht's V. von Bayern*, v of *Studien zur deutschen Kunstgeschichte* (Strasbourg, 1895)

O. Hartig: 'Die Kunsttätigkeit in München unter Wilhelm IV. und Albrecht V., 1520–1579', *Münchn. Jb. Bild. Kst*, n. s., x (1933), pp. 147–225

A. Kraus, ed.: *Handbuch der bayerischen Geschichte II, begründet von Max Spindler* (Munich, 1969, rev. 2/1988), pp. 52–4, 149

DIETER J. WEISS

(4) William [Wilhelm] **V**, Duke of Bavaria (*b* Landshut, 29 Sept 1548; *reg* 1579–98; *d* Schleissheim, 7 Feb 1626). Son of (3) Albert V, Duke of Bavaria. He was more artistic than intellectual and, an extravagant patron, generous far beyond his means, was incapable of controlling his financial affairs, thus diminishing his reputation and paralysing several political projects. The period of peace from 1555 to 1618, however, allowed the development of a new style of courtly Late Mannerism.

William's building activities began in 1573 with the reconstruction of Burg Trausnitz above Landshut, which had served as his residence from 1568. Friedrich Sustris presided over the construction of the Musenhof in Landshut and was also in charge of planning and determining the overall style of the interiors. The Narrentreppe ('Fool's Staircase') in Trausnitz, with its life-size figures from the *commedia dell'arte*, attributed to Sustris and his followers, was completed in 1578, but the main work was still in progress in 1579, when the Duke, at his accession, moved to Munich. Georg Stern had overall responsibility for other work at Landshut (*see* LANDSHUT, §1), building a brewery and the Rokettenhaus, the Italian extension (1575), an aviary (1577) and the link building (1578) at Trausnitz. He collaborated with Sustris on the design of the gardens at Landshut (1572–6), aided by Wilhelm Egckl, Martin Schwarz and Mathurin Morin (*fl* 1559; *d* 1589). From 1581 at the Neuveste of the Munich Residenz, Sustris built the Grottenhof wing, Gartensaal and Schwarzer Saal along the chapel courtyard (*see* MUNICH, §IV, 2).

Educated by the Jesuits in Ingolstadt, the Duke was pious from his youth and revered by the people. He took strong action against Anabaptists and witches (1584–7) and in religious matters was allied with the Habsburgs and the Papacy. Evidence of his support for the Jesuits lies in his establishment of a Jesuit college in Altötting (1593) and in his most important building scheme, the construction from 1583 of the Jesuits' Michaelskirche in Munich, under Wolfgang Miller (*b* 1537). In 1598 the sculptor HUBERT GERHARD made plaster models of all the Duke's important commissions: the terracotta sculptures by his workshop on the façade of the Michaelskirche, with the crowned figure of *Christ* (destr. 1945–6) above the statues of *Albert IV*, *Albert V* and *William V* and the bronze *St Michael and Lucifer* (1588; *in situ*; *see* GERHARD, HUBERT, fig. 1) between the two west portals. This façade, on the first large ecclesiastical building project of the Counter-Reformation, was a pioneering venture. The series of statues acclaimed the reigning dynasty, to which the Jesuits and the Counter-Reformation in Germany were bound. The Duke's tomb (begun 1592) was to have been set under the central cupola, but the latter was not carried out, and the tomb was not completed. The only items from the reign of William V that remain in the church are the figure of the angel from the holy water stoup (1593–6), the crucifix by Giambologna, the kneeling figure of *St Mary Magdalene* (1595) and the crypt plaque (*c.* 1595), both by Hans Reichle, and four reliefs of the *Awakening* and *Resurrection* (1595).

Under the Duke's guidance, Munich, like Landshut, developed into an important artistic centre. Hans Krumpper first appeared at court in 1584, as a protégé of Friedrich Sustris; in 1587 the Duke sent him to Italy, as an apprentice to Hubert Gerhard, and he later became the court sculptor (1594–5). The Fuggers of Augsburg sent numerous Italian and Dutch artists to the court in Munich, and several who had come to work on the grotto, Gartensaal and Antiquarium produced further works; in 1580–81, for example, Hans Muelich the younger (*d* 1613) delivered the altar (Munich, Alte Pinakothek) for the first Jesuit grammar school in Munich. From 1586 Christoph Schwarz worked in the Antiquarium, and in 1587 he and his colleagues Pieter Candid and Antonio Maria Viani took over the execution of nine altar pictures (1587–9); in 1591 Schwarz delivered his *Fall of Lucifer* for the Michaelskirche.

From 1589 Hans von Aachen was one of the most important portrait painters in Munich, although he did not have any firm links with the court. He painted large-scale, full-length portraits of the Duke (1590) and Duchess (1595; both Munich, Bayer. Staatsgemäldesammlungen) that became prototypes for other portraits of Bavarian dukes in the ancestral gallery in the Residenz. His interpretations far surpassed those of other artists, for example the portrait of *William V* (1605; Munich, Alte Pin.) by Hans Werl that recurs as an engraving in the *Fortitudo Leonina* (Munich, 1715).

Engravers, draughtsmen and miniature painters also contributed greatly to the propaganda generated at William's court, especially Joris Hoefnagel and Jan Sadeler I, whose engraving of the *Holy Family* (1589; Munich, Staatl. Graph. Samml.) in front of the Michaelskirche depicts the south tower before it fell down in 1590. Other engravers patronized by the Duke included Raphael Sadeler I, Augustin Braun (1590–1639), Matthäus Merian (i) and Wolfgang Kilian, who engraved a portrait of the Duke (1605) based on that by Hans Werl. The court goldsmiths were Giovanni Baptista di Scolari (*fl* 1567–82) and Hans Reimer (*fl* 1555; *d* 1604). The most spectacular piece of goldsmiths' work produced in William's reign was a jewelled sculpture of *St George* (Munich, Residenz) by Friedrich Sustris, completed *c.* 1590 by Hans Schleich (*fl* 1582; *d* 1616). Other goldsmiths at court included Andree Hueber (*fl* 1554–*c.* 1589) and Andreas Adamstett (*fl* 1502–91). Gem-engravings were made for the Duke in Milan by the brothers Jacopo da Trezzo I and Francesco da Trezzo. Other gem-engravings were produced by Giovanni Ambrogio Saracho, Simone Saracho and Stefano Saracho, while Christoph Angermair was the Duke's ivory-carver (1621–31).

Among the final building projects of the reign of William V were the Wilhelminische Veste (1593–6), the Hofbräuhaus and the chapel of the Holy Cross (1592), all in Munich. The design of the Altes Schloss at Schleissheim (*see* SCHLEISSHEIM, SCHLOSS), near Munich, incorporates Palladian motifs, based on the treatises (1590–1615) of Vincenzo Scamozzi.

After the Duke's abdication in 1598, in favour of his son (5) Maximilian I, and his withdrawal into religious seclusion (also in order to escape from his huge debts), he lived partly at Schloss Schleissheim, at Schloss Neudeck in der Au and in several forest hermitages. He had the distant, affected piety of the solitary 'Baroque ascetic', which overcame his tendency to magnificence and extravagance.

BIBLIOGRAPHY

F. A. W. Schreiber: *Geschichte des bayrischen Herzogs Wilhelm V des Frommen nach Quellen und Urkunden dargestellt* (Munich, 1860)

J. Stockbauer: *Die Kunstbestrebungen am bayerischen Hofe unter Herzog Albrecht V und seinem Nachfolger Wilhelm V*, viii of *Quellenschriften für Kunstgeschichte und Kunsttechnik des Mittelalters und der Renaissance* (Vienna, 1874)

K. Trautmann: 'Herzog Wilhelm V und die altbayerische Gartenkunst der Renaissance', *Mschr. Hist. Ver. Oberbayern*, iii (1894), pp. 2–8

J. Schweizer: 'Römische Beiträge zur Korrespondenz des Herzogs Wilhelm V von Bayern aus den Jahren 1588–1592', *Röm. Qschr. Christ. Altertkd. & Kirchgesch.*, xxiv (1910), pp. 141–200

B. Hubensteiner: 'Wilhelm V', *Bilder aus der bayerischen Geschichte* (Munich, 1953), pp. 163–70

——: 'Herzog Wilhelm V: Ein Fürst der Gegenreformation', *Unbekanntes Bayern*, ed. A. Fink, viii (Munich, 1964), pp. 147–54

L. Altmann: 'St Michael in München, Mausoleum-, Monumentum-, Castellum: Versuch einer Interpretation', *Beitr. Altbayer. Kirchgesch.*, xxx (1976), pp. 11–114

R. Raffalt: *Grosse Gestalten der Geschichte* (Munich, 1979), pp. 161–73

H. Glaser, ed.: *Quellen und Studien zur Kulturpolitik der Wittelsbacher vom 16. bis zum 18. Jahrhundert* (Munich and Zurich, 1980), pp. 7–82

GREGOR M. LECHNER

(5) Maximilian I, Duke and Elector of Bavaria (*b* Munich, 17 April 1573; *reg* 1597–1651; *d* Ingolstadt, 27 Sept 1651). Son of (4) William V, Duke of Bavaria. As the head of the Catholic League, which he helped found in 1609, he embroiled Bavaria in the long confessional struggle that ravaged Central Europe. He was at the height of his power following his victory over the Protestants at the Battle of the White Mountain outside Prague in 1620. The Holy Roman Emperor Ferdinand II rewarded him with the title of Elector in 1623 and territorial rights to the Upper Palatinate in 1628. Most of Maximilian's artistic patronage pre-dated 1630; continued fighting, including the Swedish occupation of Munich in 1632, devastated Bavaria and preoccupied him during the last decades of his reign.

Maximilian's artistic patronage centred on the Residenz in Munich, which he transformed into one of Europe's most elaborate palaces (*see* MUNICH, §IV, 2). He constructed a new Hofkapelle (1601–03), for which stuccoists, including Michael Castello (*fl* 1614–18) prepared elaborate ceiling scenes illustrating the *Litany of Loreto* (1616–18; *in situ*). The Reiche Kapelle, Maximilian's smaller private chapel, was consecrated in 1607. HANS KRUMPPER, the sculptor and architect who served (1609–34) as Maximilian's artistic supervisor, may have designed the chamber whose name derives from its sumptuous marble surfaces, silver altar (*c.* 1620–23) by Jakob Anthoni (1585–1623) and numerous silver reliquaries. In 1632 Maximilian commissioned Wilhelm Pfeiffer to produce scagliola panelling for the chapel (*in situ*), with scenes after Albrecht Dürer's *Life of the Virgin* woodcuts (*c.* 1511). The Kaiserhof,

which contained Maximilian's major private and audience rooms, as well as the grand staircase, the Kaisertreppe (1616), was erected between 1611 and 1617. Krumpper's bronze *Patrona Boiariae* (1614–16) highlights its unified, two-storey façade. Maximilian further extended the Residenz by adding the Brunnenhof (1612–15), with its Wittelsbach Fountain (*c.* 1610) with bronzes (*c.* 1611) by Krumpper and reused statues by HUBERT GERHARD, and, between 1613 and 1617, the new court garden. The identity of Maximilian's master architect is still debated. It seems, however, that a team of artists led by Krumpper, Heinrich Schön the elder and the painter Pieter Candid collaborated on its design, construction and decoration. Candid's workshop painted most of the Kaiserhof rooms, and he also provided cartoons for the tapestries (*in situ*) depicting *Otto von Wittelsbach* (1604–11) and *The Months* (1612–14), which were woven at the court. At Schleissheim, just north of Munich, Schön constructed an impressive retreat (1616–23), the design of which was inspired by Italian country villas (*see* SCHLEISSHEIM, SCHLOSS).

The Residenz housed Maximilian's diverse art collection. He expanded the ducal library, which contained about 18,300 volumes before the Swedish occupation, and by 1607 had constructed a special painting gallery adjacent to his bedroom. He particularly favoured pictures by earlier German masters, including Albrecht Altdorfer, Hans Burgkmair, Lucas Cranach I, Hans Holbein (i), Hans Holbein (ii), Hans Mielich and Georg Pencz. His favourite was Albrecht Dürer, by whom he possessed at least 20 works, including the Paumgartner Altarpiece (1498) and *Four Apostles* (1526; both Munich, Alte Pin.). He also commissioned Georg Vischer to copy Dürer's works and to paint in his style.

Under Maximilian, Bavaria became a bulwark of the Counter-Reformation. He provided funds for Jesuit schools and churches in Altötting (1600), Mindelheim (1616), Burghausen (1629) and Amberg (1638) and underwrote some of the construction costs of the Capuchin churches in Munich (1600), Landshut (1610) and Straubing (1614). He was especially devoted to the Virgin Mary, to whom he credited his victory at White Mountain (1620) and the withdrawal of Swedish forces from Munich in 1634 after over two years of intermittent occupation. In her honour he erected the Column of Mary (completed 1641) in the Marienplatz. Hubert Gerhard's over life-size gilt-bronze *Virgin and Child* stands atop a Tegernsee red marble column, 11.6 m high; the statue was originally executed in the early 1590s for the planned tomb of *William V* in the Michaelskirche and from 1613 to 1620 adorned the high altar of the Frauenkirche. On the base of the column, the four bronze putti vanquishing plague, war, heresy and famine were probably designed by Ferdinand Murmann (*fl* 1618–38) of Augsburg and cast in Munich *c.* 1638 by Bernhard Ernst (*fl* 1616–38). This celebratory monument provided the model for those in Vienna, Prague and many other towns.

BIBLIOGRAPHY

F. von Reber: *Kurfürst Maximilian I. von Bayern als Gemäldesammler* (Munich, 1892)

M. Schattenhofer: *Die Mariensäule in München* (Munich, 1971)

H. Homa, H. Brunner and G. Hojer: *Residenz München* (Munich, 1979)

B. Volk-Knüttel: *Peter Candid: Zeichnungen* (Munich, 1979)

G. Goldberg: 'Zur Ausprägung der Dürer-Renaissance in München', *Münchn. Jb. Bild. Kst*, xxxi (1980), pp. 129–75

S. J. Klingensmith: *The Utility of Splendor: Program and Plan in the Palaces of the Court of Bavaria, 1600–1800* (diss., Cornell U., 1986) [esp. pp. 36–61, 124–8]

A. von Buttlar and T. Bierler-Rolly, eds: *Der Münchner Hofgarten* (Munich, 1988) [esp. pp. 41–4, 53–4, 63–7]

JEFFREY CHIPPS SMITH

(6) Ferdinand Maria, Elector of Bavaria (*b* Munich, 31 Oct 1636; *reg* 1651–79; *d* Schleissheim, 26 May 1679). Son of (5) Maximilian I, Duke and Elector of Bavaria. Even after he came of age in 1654, his rule was heavily dependent on his council; through its neutral stance and circumspect politics, Bavaria recovered from the Thirty Years War. Initially the Elector sided with the Holy Roman Empire against France and Sweden but later increasingly inclined towards France. He introduced absolutism on the French pattern: in the course of centralization and the spread of state influence, the privileges of the estates and nobility were abolished; a mercantilist economic system was developed.

In 1652 the Elector married Henrietta Adelaide of Savoy (1636–76), who subsequently played an important part in the flowering of High Baroque in Bavaria. The previous Spanish influences were ousted, and the ceremonial of the Munich court was modelled on that of the French court. The Italian Baroque style was also introduced into Bavaria, and a large Italian colony formed in Munich (*see* MUNICH, §II, 1). From 1655 to 1657 the Kurfürstliche Opernhaus on the Salvatorplatz was renovated and enlarged by Francesco Santurini (1627–82), and Italian opera and Baroque ballet were performed there. The Turnierhaus (1660–61) on the modern Odeonsplatz was used for festival performances, riding displays and tournaments. The architects Marx Schinnagel (1612–81) and Martin Gunetzrhainer (*d* 1699), the painters Joachim von Sandrart and Johann Heinrich Schönfeld and the sculptors Balthasar Ableithner (1618–1705) and Andreas Faistenberger II (1647–1736) were employed in Munich, alongside the Italians Antonio Domenico Triva (1626–99) and Agostino Barelli. Johann Caspar Zuccalli and Enrico Zuccalli (*see* ZUCCALLI), master builders from the Grisons, also came to the Munich court.

In thanksgiving for the birth in 1662 of an heir, the future (7) Maximilian II Emanuel, the Elector and Electress had the Theatine monastery built in Munich, with the church of St Kajetan (consecrated 1675; for illustration *see* BARELLI, AGOSTINO) modelled on S Andrea della Valle (1591–1621) in Rome. The church of St Kajetan, begun by Barelli, was the first large Baroque church in Germany and became the model for Bavarian Baroque churches. Enrico Zuccalli erected its dome (1674–6); stucco decoration by Carlo Brentano Moretti, Giovanni Brenni and Giovanni Nicolo Petri (*d* 1692) was completed in 1688.

To celebrate the same event, the Elector commissioned the building of the Borgo delle Ninfe (begun 1664), the present central part of Schloss Nymphenburg (*see* MUNICH, §IV, 3). It took the form of a five-storey block with an external staircase composed of opposite flights. During its construction Agostino Barelli was again replaced (1674) by Enrico Zuccalli. The concept for the mythological decorative programme was supplied by the scholar Emanuele Tesauro of Turin; the ceiling paintings were by

Antonio Domenico Triva (1626–99) and Antonio Zanchi. After the Elector had formed a political alliance with France in 1670, the Italian influence was joined by a French one: for example, the painters Jean-Baptiste Delamonce (1635–1708) and Paul Mignard (1639–91) were employed.

BIBLIOGRAPHY

A. Kraus: 'Bayern im Zeitalter des Absolutismus (1651–1745): Die Kurfürsten Ferdinand Maria, Max II. Emanuel und Karl Albrecht', *Handbuch der bayerischen Geschichte*, ed. M. Spindler (Munich, 1969), ii, pp. 411–75

A. von Schuckmann: 'The Wittelsbachs as Patrons of the Arts, 1650–1730', *Apollo*, xc (1969), pp. 368–75

DORIS KUTSCHBACH

(7) Maximilian II Emanuel, Elector of Bavaria (*b* Munich, 11 July 1662; *reg* 1679–1704, 1715–26; *d* Munich, 26 Feb 1726). Son of (6) Ferdinand Maria, Elector of Bavaria. After a short minority he took control of the government of Bavaria in 1680 and initially concentrated on reorganizing the army. In foreign affairs he broke with the traditional policy of neutrality, forming a defensive alliance (1683) against France and Turkey with the Holy Roman Emperor Leopold I. In 1683 he took part in liberating Vienna from the Turks and in 1688 captured Belgrade, which resulted in his sobriquet the 'Blue King'. Throughout his reign the Elector's political ambitions were reflected in huge expenditure on maintaining his court. His first major project was the building of Schloss Lustheim (1684–8), for which he summoned from Italy the foremost architects, stuccoworkers and, above all, painters of the period.

From 1688 until 1697 Maximilian II Emanuel engaged in the War of the Palatinate Succession, and from 1691 he was Governor of the Spanish Netherlands. During this period the combination of traditional Netherlandish styles and the latest French taste made a deep impression both on him and on his architect, Enrico Zuccalli, whom he sent to study in the Netherlands in 1693. The result of this interlude was the 'Dutch Cabinet' (destr. 1729) at the Residenz in Munich, the earliest creation of its type in Germany and an important example of the fashion for chinoiserie. The Elector also took a keen interest in other items from East Asia, mainly porcelain, and later he had the Pagodenburg (1716–19) at the Schloss Nymphenburg in Munich (*see* MUNICH, §IV, 3) decorated and furnished in the 'Chinese' style. In the Netherlands he bought furniture, wall hangings and many paintings, his most important purchase being the collection in Antwerp of Gisbert van Colen in 1698, much of which is now in the Alte Pinakothek, Munich. Towards the end of his time in Brussels he was more strongly guided by artistic developments in Paris, owing to his employment of Joseph Vivien.

In 1701 Maximilian II Emanuel returned to Munich, where he expressed his political aspirations in terms of architecture by extending the Schloss Nymphenburg (*see* MUNICH, §IV, 3) and building the Neue Schloss at Schleissheim (*see* SCHLEISSHEIM, SCHLOSS). His alliance with France in the War of the Spanish Succession (on the promise of becoming king and emperor), however, resulted in the loss of his army and country after defeat at Schellenberg and Höchstädt (1704). Placed under the ban of the empire, he went into exile, initially in Brussels, where the life of the court soon resumed in the same splendour, but in 1706 he was forced to flee, subsequently settling in Mons, then Compiègne. Thereafter the influence of the court of Versailles determined his patronage. From 1711 artists were again commissioned, and there were large-scale purchases from Paris art dealers and jewellers. In 1713 the Elector bought a palace at St Cloud (destr. 1871), employing Germain Boffrand to undertake building alterations. In Paris he planned the refurbishment of his Bavarian residences, employing Robert de Cotte and Claude Desgots (*fl* 1679; *d* 1732) among his advisers.

In 1715, when he was restored to the electorship of Bavaria on condition that he renounce the Netherlands, Maximilian II Emanuel returned to Munich. Although he played no further role in European politics, he initiated a flowering of artistic activity at court, with such supreme achievements as the garden at Schloss Nymphenburg, with statuary and three pavilions in the park. Through his efforts the French style was introduced in Germany through developments in Munich. JOSEF EFFNER, who had trained in Paris and who was responsible for the renovation of Schloss Dachau (1715), for building Schloss Fürstenried (1715–17) and for completing Schloss Schleissheim (1719–26), was foremost among a host of court artists, of whom the Parisian landscape architect Dominique Girard and the sculptor Guillielmus de Grof were also outstanding. Nevertheless, in painting (other than portraiture) native talent gradually began to assert itself: apart from the Venetian Jacopo Amigoni, the Elector employed the decorative painters Johann Anton Gumpp, Cosmas Damian Asam, Balthasar Augustin Albrecht and Nikolaus Gottfried Stuber. The refurbishment (1725) of the electoral apartments in the Residenz at Munich, by Joseph Effner and François de Cuvilliés I, marked a final peak of artistic achievement in the Elector's reign.

BIBLIOGRAPHY
H. Lipp: *Kurfürst Max Emanuel und die Künstler* (diss., U. Munich, 1944)
L. Hüttl: *Max Emanuel: Der Blaue Kurfürst* (Munich, 1976)
Kurfürst Max Emanuel: Bayern und Europa um 1700, 2 vols (exh. cat., ed. H. Glaser; Schleissheim, Altes Schloss and Neues Schloss, 1976)
H. Rall and G. Hojer: *Kurfürst Max Emanuel, der 'Blaue König'* (Munich, 1979)
JOSEF STRASSER

(8) Joseph Clemens, Elector–Archbishop of Cologne (*b* Munich, 5 Dec 1671; *d* Bonn, 12 Nov 1723). Brother of (7) Maximilian II Emanuel, Elector of Bavaria. In 1685 he was elected Prince–Bishop of Freising (exchanged for Lüttich in 1694) and Regensburg and in 1688 Elector–Archbishop of Cologne. As far as his finances allowed, he was a generous patron, promoting music and the theatre and collecting works of art and objects of vertu, which he purchased mainly in Paris. He also initiated a number of important building projects: from 1689 Enrico Zuccalli redesigned the electoral Residenz (1697–1725) in Bonn, which had been destroyed early in the War of the Palatinate Succession (1688–97). As an ally of France in the War of the Spanish Succession (1701–13), the Elector–Archbishop was expelled from Cologne in 1706 and placed under the ban of the Holy Roman Empire. While in exile in France, he became interested in French art. He returned to Cologne in 1715, after the Peace of Baden, and in 1716 also became Prince–Bishop of Hildesheim. From 1715 building work on the electoral Residenz in Bonn continued

in the early Rococo style, based on designs by Robert de Cotte, who was also responsible for the plans for Schloss Clemensruhe in Poppelsdorf, begun in 1715. These buildings and the country house known as Vinea Domini (begun 1721–2) on the banks of the Rhine near Bonn were unfinished when the Elector–Archbishop died; work was completed by his successor, (9) Clemens August. The Elector-Archbishop's introduction of the French style in the Rhineland made a decisive impact, as did his employment there of many French artists.

BIBLIOGRAPHY
E. Renard: 'Die Bauten der Kurfürsten Joseph Clemens und Clemens August von Köln', *Bonn. Jb.*, xcix/c (1896/7), pp. 164–240
M. Braubach: *Die vier letzten Kurfürsten von Köln: Ein Bild rheinischer Kultur im 18. Jahrhundert* (Bonn, 1931)
——: 'Von den Schlossbauten und Sammlungen der kölnischen Kurfürsten des 18. Jahrhunderts', *An. Hist. Ver. Niederrhein, Alte Erzbistum Köln*, cliii–cliv (1953), pp. 98–147
E. Hegel: *Das Erzbistum Köln zwischen Barock und Aufklärung: Vom Pfälzischen Krieg bis zum Ende der französischen Zeit, 1688–1844*, iv of *Geschichte des Erzbistums Köln* (Cologne, 1979)

(9) Clemens August, Elector–Archbishop of Cologne (*b* Brussels, 17 Aug 1700; *d* Ehrenbreitstein, 6 Feb 1761). Son of (7) Maximilian II Emanuel, Elector of Bavaria. After serving as bishop of Regensburg (1716), Münster (1719) and Paderborn (1719), in 1723 he became the last Wittelsbach Elector–Archbishop of Cologne. As he also became bishop of Hildesheim (1724) and Osnabrück (1728) and Grand and German Master of the Teutonic Order (1732), he was for a time one of the wealthiest and most powerful ecclesiastical princes in Germany, albeit one of the politically less successful. Nicknamed 'Monsieur des Cinq Eglises', he maintained an artistically creative court modelled on that of Louis XV, King of France. Among his building projects in the late Baroque style were the completion (1744–56) of Schloss Clemensruhe in Poppelsdorf, near Bonn; the completion (1725) of the electoral Residenz in Bonn; Schloss Augustusburg (1725–48, 1754–70) in Brühl (see BRÜHL, SCHLOSS); numerous hunting-lodges, for example the Falkenlust (1729–37) in Brühl and Schloss Clemenswerth (1736–49), near Münster; and the church of St Michael (1735–67) in Berg am Laim, Munich. He also made a decisive contribution to the planning of Bonn. Among the artists who made his court a model of early 18th-century culture, the most important came from France and southern Germany and in particular from the court in Munich. They included the architects FRANÇOIS DE CUVILLIÉS I, who brought the French-Bavarian Rococo style to the Rhineland, and Balthasar Neumann and the portrait painters George Desmarées and Joseph Vivien. Only JOHANN CONRAD SCHLAUN, the most important architect in north-west Germany during this period, was trained at the instigation of the Elector–Archbishop. Clemens August was also an avid collector of paintings, silver and porcelain (particularly East Asian and Meissen). As one of the most important patrons of his time, he exerted a formative influence on Rococo culture in Germany.

BIBLIOGRAPHY
Kurfürst Clemens August: Landesherr und Mäzen des 18. Jahrhunderts (exh. cat., Brühl, Schloss Augustusburg, 1961)
M. Niessen: *Hoch- und Deutschmeister Clemens August, Kurfürst von Köln* (diss, U. Vienna, 1973)

Clemens August: Fürstbischof, Jagdherr, Mäzen (exh. cat., Sögel, Schloss Clemenswerth, Emslandmus., 1987)

ANDREA M. KLUXEN

(10) Maximilian III Joseph, Elector of Bavaria (*b* Munich, 28 March 1727; *reg* 1745–77; *d* Nymphenburg, 30 Dec 1777). Grandson of (7) Maximilian II Emanuel, Elector of Bavaria. At the Peace of Füssen (1745), he renounced all hereditary claims to the electorate, thereby removing Bavaria from the power-struggles of his predecessors. In the subsequent era of peace and prosperity the absolutist government was increasingly influenced by the Enlightenment, exemplified by the foundation (1759) of the Bayerische Akademie der Wissenschaften. Court life was characterized by late Rococo fashions, and the Elector, himself a composer of recognized talent, patronized musicians in particular, though he turned down an application for a post by Wolfgang Amadeus Mozart (1756–91) in 1777. From 1751 a new opera house (now the Cuvilliés-Theater) was built by François de Cuvilliés I at the Residenz in Munich. Its frescoes and stuccowork were by Johann Baptist Zimmermann and the figures and main decoration by Johann Baptist Straub. In the Residenz, Schloss Nymphenburg and Schloss Schleissheim, rooms were renovated in the late Rococo style. In the Schloss Nymphenburg (*see* MUNICH, §IV, 3), for example, the Steinerner Saal was remodelled with stuccowork by Franz Xaver Feichtmayer (i) to a design by Cuvilliés and with a ceiling painting (1755–7) by Zimmermann. Georges Desmarées was court painter from 1730. Masterpieces of Rococo sculpture produced in the reign included works by Ignaz Günther and porcelain sculpture by Franz Anton Bustelli, who worked at the newly established porcelain factory (first at Neudeck, then at Nymphenburg) from 1754 to 1763 (*see* NYMPHENBURG PORCELAIN FACTORY). At the death of Maximilian III Joseph the Bavarian line of the Wittelsbachs became extinct, and the electorate of Bavaria passed to Charles Theodore, Elector Palatine of the Rhine (*see* §II(4) below).

BIBLIOGRAPHY
A. von Schuckmann: 'The Wittelsbachs as Patrons of the Arts, 1730–80', *Apollo*, xc (1969), pp. 404–13
H. Vriesen: 'The Munich Stage in the Age of the Rococo', *Apollo*, xc (1969), pp. 376–83

DORIS KUTSCHBACH

II. Palatinate branch.

In 1214 the Wittelsbachs acquired by marriage the Rhineland Palatinate and thereby the most prestigious secular electorship. Many members of the Palatinate and numerous subsidiary lines (Simmern, Neuburg and Sulzbach) were patrons. (1) Otto Henry, Elector Palatine of the Rhine and Count Palatine of Neuberg, had the Renaissance palace named after him built in the Heidelberg Residenz. (2) Wolfgang William, Count Palatine of Neuburg, rebuilt Neuburg an der Donau and also left his mark on Düsseldorf. (3) John William, Elector Palatine of the Rhine, maintained a magnificent court at Düsseldorf, with extensive art collections. His brother Charles Philip, Elector Palatine of the Rhine (*reg* 1716–42), enlarged Mannheim into a Baroque planned town. From 1654 to 1720 members of the house were monarchs of Sweden. When the Munich line died out in 1777, Bavaria and the Palatinate were united under (4) Charles Theodore, Elector Palatine of the Rhine (Neuburg) and Elector of Bavaria, who brought the extensive art collections of the Electors Palatine to Munich.

DIETER J. WEISS

(1) Otto Henry [Ottheinrich], Elector Palatine of the Rhine and Count Palatine of Neuburg (*b* Amberg, 10 April 1502; *reg* Neuburg 1522–44, 1552–9, Palatinate 1556–9; *d* Heidelberg, 12 Feb 1559). Orphaned in 1504, Otto Henry and his younger brother Philipp (1503–48) ruled jointly in Neuburg from 1522. From 1530 Schloss Neuburg (*see* NEUBURG AN DER DONAU) was rebuilt in the Renaissance style under the direction of Hans Knotz (*fl* 1527–38). The chapel was completed in 1541 and decorated in 1543 by Hans Bocksberger I. The pictorial programme, probably influenced by works of the Nuremberg preacher Andreas Osiander (1498–1552), is one of the earliest examples of biblical decoration in a Protestant church. Knotz also built the Jagdschloss, a hunting-lodge at Grünau (begun 1530), in which the murals by Jörg Breu (ii) and Hans Windberger (*fl* 1555; *d* 1571), with mainly hunting and erotic themes, are among the few examples of secular wall painting surviving from that time.

Although initially a staunch opponent of the new religion, in 1542 Otto Henry was converted to Protestantism and thereafter established the Lutheran Church in Neuburg an der Donau. Through his extravagance and financial ineptitude, however, in 1544, on the verge of bankruptcy, he was forced to cede the administration of Neuburg to the estates and went into exile in Heidelberg and Weinheim. He was reinstated in 1552 and in 1556 succeeded Frederick II, Elector Palatine of the Rhine (*reg* 1544–56), and thereafter introduced Protestantism in the Palatinate.

The Ottheinrichsbau in HEIDELBERG, begun by the Elector in 1556, was one of the most prestigious residences in Germany (*see* GERMANY, fig. 5). The balanced façade shows the influence of the architectural theories of Sebastiano Serlio and contemporary editions of Vitruvius, and the Elector's humanist interests are illustrated by the allegorical and symbolic features of the façade programme, with figural ornamentation by ALEXANDER COLIN. As previously in Neuburg an der Donau, a pleasure garden was laid out in Heidelberg with a variety of Mediterranean and exotic plants and fountains.

The Elector owned an extensive gallery of paintings and collected medals, engravings, astronomical instruments and armour; from *c.* 1544–6 he concentrated on acquiring printed works and illustrated books. His library, later the Bibliotheca Palatina in Heidelberg, contained both earlier and contemporary works, devoted mainly to architectural theory but also to astronomy, occult sciences, religion, history and geography. He made his library available to scholars and also enlarged that of the Heiliggeist foundation, which became an important centre of learning. The collegiate church of Heiliggeist was also the university church.

BIBLIOGRAPHY
G. Poensgen, ed.: *Ottheinrich: Gedenkschrift zur vierhundertjährigen Wiederkehr seiner Kurfürstenzeit in der Pfalz (1556-1559)* (Heidelberg, 1956)

DORIS KUTSCHBACH

(2) Wolfgang William [Wolfgang Wilhelm], Count Palatine of Neuberg (*b* Neuberg an der Donau, 29 Oct 1578; *d* Düsseldorf, 20 March 1653). Although he was hardly an 'artistically' motivated patron or collector in the modern sense, he commissioned first-rate works of architecture and painting, showing unerring taste in the art of his period. Architecture formed part of his education, initially the building of fortifications. He studied the work of Daniel Speckle, one of the most important military architects of the period, and Alexander Pasqualini (ii) acted as his adviser on fortifications.

The Count was appointed 'Bauherr' (sponsor of building projects) by his father, Philipp Ludwig, Count Palatine of Neuburg (*d* 1614), for the renovation of the town centre of NEUBURG AN DER DONAU. Joseph Heintz (i) produced designs for a town hall, church, chancellery, administrative centre, granary and 'forum'. The Count overcame objections to the modern forms and size of the new Rathaus (1609) and former court church of St Maria and for the latter commissioned Rubens to paint the high altarpiece of the *Last Judgement* (1617; Munich, Alte Pin.), an indication that the Count regarded art primarily as a means of diplomacy and propaganda and of proclaiming princely splendour. The two side altarpieces, the *Adoration of the Shepherds* and *Miracle of Pentecost* (both Munich, Alte Pin.), are obviously based on Rubens' designs but were executed entirely by his studio assistants. In 1623 Rubens delivered an altarpiece, largely executed by himself, depicting the *Fall of the Angels* (Munich, Alte Pin.) for the church of St Peter in Neuburg an der Donau (now Munich, Bayer. Staatsgemäldesammlungen).

The buildings in Neuburg were in the vanguard of style and, therefore, unusually costly. These works, however, fell victim to some extent to political developments that caused the transference of Wolfgang William's centre of administration to DÜSSELDORF, where he commissioned, possibly from Deodaat del Monte, the building of the Jesuit church of St Andreas (1622–9). Antonio Serro (*fl c.* 1620–30) also worked for the Count in Düsseldorf, as well as in Neuburg an der Donau.

Portraits were important elements in the art produced for Wolfgang William, in accordance with his overriding concern for display, and works on Counter-Reformation themes reflected his conversion to Catholicism. Although his court artists were relatively mediocre, when allocating commissions he chose, apart from Rubens, such masters as Rubens's pupil Deodaat del Monte (who also worked as an architect), Johann Spilberg II, Mang Kilian (*fl* 1604–11), Philipp Kilian (1628–93) and Michiel van Mierevelt. A portrait of *Wolfgang William* (*c.* 1620–30; Munich, Alte Pin.) is attributed to Anthony van Dyck. Hans Caspar Kammerschreiber (*fl c.* 1605–17) painted a pulpit (1617) in the church of Our Lady in Neuburg an der Donau and also worked as a draughtsman, producing, for example, the album illustration of *Judith with the Head of Holofernes* (1605; Stuttgart, Württemberg. Landesbib., Cod. Hist. Q 299, fol. 204*r*). Paul Müller (*fl c.* 1615) and Hans Irrer (*fl* 1619) featured among the sculptors employed at court, and the brothers Michele Castelli (*fl* 1616) and Antonio Castelli and Johannes Kuhn (*c.* 1592–*c.* 1632) executed stuccowork.

BIBLIOGRAPHY

T. Levin: 'Beiträge zur Geschichte der Kunstbestrebungen in dem Hause Pfalz-Neuburg, 1: Wolfgang Wilhelm', *Beitr. Gesch. Niederrheins*, xix (1910), pp. 97–144

B. Fries-Kurze: 'Pfalzgraf Wolfgang Wilhelm von Neuburg', *Lebensbild. Bayer. Schwaben*, viii (1961), pp. 198–227

J. Zimmer: 'Hofkirche und Rathaus in Neuburg/Donau: Die Bauplanungen von 1591 bis 1630', *Neuburg. Kollktbl.*, cxxiv (1971)

A. Fuchs: 'Ein Stadtprojekt für pfalz-neuburgische Emigranten aus dem Nordgau von 1619', *Neuburg. Kollktbl.*, cxxxiii (1980), pp. 250–54

475 Jahre Fürstentum Pfalz-Neuburg (exh. cat., Neuburg, Schlossmus., 1980), pp. 94–6

W. Hauser: 'Die Festlichkeiten anlässlich der "Kirchweih" der Neuburger Jesuitenkirche im Oktober 1618', *Neuburg. Kollktbl.*, cxxxiv (1981), pp. 42–50

R. Schulte: *Die Pfalzgräflichen Schwestern Unsere Liebe Frau zu Neuburg an der Donau und St. Andreas zu Düsseldorf* (Munich, 1981)

R. H. Seitz and A. Lidel: *Die Hofkirche Unserer Lieben Frau zu Neuburg an der Donau: Ein Kirchenbau zwischen Reformation und Gegenreformation* (Weissenhorn, 1983)

R. H. Seitz and F. Kaess: 'Der Turm der Hofkirche zu Neuburg a.d. Donau als architektonisches und architekturgeschichtliches Problem: Der ursprüngliche Bauzustand (1618) und seine Abänderung (1624/30)', *Neuburg. Kollktbl.*, cxxxvi (1984), pp. 60–97

J. Zimmer: 'Die Fassade der Kirche U. L. Frau in Neuburg an der Donau: Plan und Bauwerk, 1603–1630', *Jb. Zentinst. Kstgesch.*, ii (1986), pp. 179–229

——: 'Bibliographisches um das Neuburger Kolloquium von 1615', *Z. Bayer. Kirchgesch.*, lvi (1987), pp. 133–51

Peter Paul Rubens: Altäre für Bayern (exh. cat. by K. Renger, Munich, Alte Pin., 1990–91)

J. Zimmer: 'Die Neuburger Medaille von 1607', *Z. Hist. Ver. Schwaben*, lxxxv (1993), pp. 49–100

JÜRGEN ZIMMER

(3) John William [Johan Wilhelm; Jan Wellem], Elector Palatine of the Rhine and Count Palatine of Neuberg (*b* 19 April 1658; *reg* 1690–1716; *d* 8 June 1716). Son of Philip William of Neuburg, Elector Palatine of the Rhine (*reg* 1685–90). Between 1674 and 1677 he visited all the great courts and art centres of Europe, and in 1778 he established his residence in DÜSSELDORF. His first marriage, in 1678, to the Archduchess Maria Anna Josepha (1654–89) strengthened his alliance with the Austrian imperial house. The Archduchess, the daughter of the Holy Roman Emperor Ferdinand III, was greatly interested in music, as was John William, who played the lira da gamba and several other instruments and supported a court orchestra of international rank. After the death of his father he became Elector Palatine in 1690. Widowed at an early age, he went to Florence and in 1691 married Princess Anna Maria Luisa de' Medici (*see* MEDICI, DE', (29)).

John William's role in international politics was less important than were his cultural policies. In them he combined historical awareness and care for the past with the curiosity of an avid collector but he was also concerned with efficiency. He first collected medals and coins and commissioned the director of his coin cabinet, Matthias de Roy, to produce a history of the Holy Roman Empire through its coins, a pioneering work both analytically and politically. John William also attempted to exploit his knowledge commercially by setting up a coin-stamping machine and by engaging designers and stamp cutters. His collection of casts of the most important ancient sculptures, assembled between 1707 and 1710, was acquired with the assistance of international mediators and agents. Among his artistic advisers were GABRIEL GRUPELLO, appointed court sculptor in 1695, and, from 1682, Jan

Frans van Douven, later to become director of the collection and who (according to Nicolas de Pigage, 1778) enlarged the Elector's collection to 348 works. From 1710 these were housed in a gallery designed by the architect Jacob Du Bois. The collection was of high quality, and the work of Rubens and other Flemish and Netherlandish painters predominated. Works by artists brought to the court, such as ANTONIO BELLUCCI, GIOVANNI ANTONIO PELLEGRINI, Domenico Zanetti (*d* 1712), Adriana Spilberg (*c.* 1652–1697) and Eglon van der Neer, were conspicuously represented, as were those of artists contractually engaged and supported outside the court, such as Adriaen van der Werff (Rotterdam), Rachel Ruysch (The Hague), Jan van Nickelen (Haarlem) and Jan Weenix (*see* WEENIX, (2)) (many of whom also executed decorative work for John William's country house Schloss Bensberg).

The Elector also encouraged the conservation of the local cultural heritage; an edict of 1707 helped to promote the art of his native region. His social omnipresence was underlined not only by numerous portraits, especially miniatures and statues, the most famous being the marble equestrian statue by Grupello for the Marktplatz in Düsseldorf (1711; *in situ*), but also by his intervention in all areas of his subjects' lives. The Düsseldorf Police and Tax Ordinance of 1710 regulated guilds and wages as well as the treatment of public spaces (façade modernization, street paving and lighting from 1705). He founded the Order of St Hubert in 1708, was made Protector of the Electorate of Bavaria (until 1714) and Lord High Steward, a post requiring him to be Governor of the Empire during an interregnum. He was chaplain of the Empire from 1710 and directed the electoral negotiations of the College of Electors in Frankfurt in 1711. After that date his continual illnesses and paralytic symptoms precluded further political activity. State finances were increasingly precarious after 1700. The Elector had no children, and after his death his collection was gradually transferred to Mannheim by his successor, Charles Philip (*reg* 1716–42).

UNPUBLISHED SOURCES

Düsseldorf, Heinrich Heine-Inst., MS. G 82–HH 159 [Giorgio Maria Rapparini: *Le Portrait du vrai mérite dans la personne sérénissime de Monseigneur l'Electeur Palatin*, 1709]
Düsseldorf, Nordrhein-Westfäl. Hauptstaatarchv [H. Kuhn-Steinhausen: *Die Hofhaltungsrechnungen der Kurfürstin Anna Maria Luisa von der Pfalz, 1691–1717*, 1960]

BIBLIOGRAPHY

F. Exter: *Versuch einer Sammlung von pfälzischen Medaillen: Schaugedachtnis- und allerley anderen Müntzen* (Zweibrücken, 1764)
F. Kuch: 'Die Bautätigkeit des Kurfürsten Johann Wilhelm', *Beitr. Gesch. Niederrheins*, xi (1897), p. 7
T. Levin: 'Beiträge zur Geschichte der Kunstbestrebungen in dem Hause Pfalz-Neuburg', *Beitr. Gesch. Niederrheins*, xix (1905); xx (1906); xxiii (1911)
H. Kuhn-Steinhausen: 'Die Bildnisse des Kurfürsten Johann Wilhelm und seiner Gemahlin Anna Maria Luisa Medici', *Düsseldorf. Jb.*, xli (1939), p. 125
K. Lankheit: 'Florentiner Bronze-Arbeiten für Kurfürst Johann Wilhelm von der Pfalz: Zu den künstlerischen Beziehungen der Häuser Medici und Pfalz-Neuburg im Spätbarock', *Münch. Jb. Bild. Kst*, n. s. 2, vii (1956), pp. 185–210
G. Adriani, ed.: *Die Rapparini-Handschrift der Landes- und Stadtbibliothek Düsseldorf* (Düsseldorf, 1958) [facs.]
H. Kuhn-Steinhausen: *Johann Wilhelm, Kurfürst von der Pfalz, Herzog von Julich-Berg (1658–1716)* (Düsseldorf, 1958) [with detailed bibliog.]
Die Gestalt des Kurfürsten Johann Wilhelm von der Pfalz (exh. cat., Heidelberg, 1958)
Johann Wilhelm, Kurfürst von der Pfalz als Mäzen (exh. cat., Düsseldorf, 1958)
Europäische Barockplastik am Niederrhein: Grupello und seine Zeit (exh. cat., Düsseldorf, 1971)
Johann Wilhelm und das Haus Pfalz-Neuburg (exh. cat., Düsseldorf, 1980) [suppl. to exh. cat. *475 Jahre Fürstentum Pfalz-Neuburg*]

MARTINA SITT

(4) Charles Theodore [Carl Theodor; Karl Theodor], Elector Palatine of the Rhine and Elector of Bavaria (*b* Droogenbosch, Brussels, 11 Dec 1724; *reg* Palatinate 1742–99, Bavaria 1777–99; *d* Munich, 16 Feb 1799). Greatgreat-nephew of (2) Wolfgang William, Count Palatine of Neuberg. He studied at the universities of Leyden and Leuven and became Elector Palatine in 1742 on the death of his guardian, Charles Philip, Elector Palatine of the Rhine (*reg* 1716–42). On the death of Maximilian III Joseph, Elector of Bavaria (*see* §I(10) above), in 1777 he also assumed control of Bavaria. In the spirit of enlightened despotism he initiated internal reforms in the government of the Palatinate but left major decisions of foreign policy to his ministers. His chief interests were the arts and sciences, and in his portrait by Johann Georg Ziesenis (1757; Munich, Bayer. Nmus.) he is depicted without any insignia of power, with a flute in one hand, the other lying on a book, in front of a cello, chessboard, notes and books and with a dog at his feet.

Charles Theodore was patron of numerous cultural institutions that attracted to MANNHEIM scholars, scientists, poets, musicians and artists. Under the influence of Voltaire, who visited him in 1753 and 1758, he established the Academia Theodoro Palatina in 1763 and also promoted the foundation of the German Society (1775), the National Theatre (1779) and the Mannheim School of Music (1777). His FRANKENTHAL PORCELAIN FACTORY, founded in 1755, achieved an importance extending far beyond the Palatinate, due to the work of such artists as Franz Konrad Linck (1730–93), Johann Friedrich Lück II (1727–97), Karl Gottlieb Lücke (1730/40–75) and Johann Peter Melchior (1742–1825).

Charles Theodore also established an academy of drawing in Mannheim (1758) and an academy of art in DÜSSELDORF in 1762; he created (1767) a gallery of antiquities in Mannheim to enable artists to study plaster casts of celebrated Classical sculptures and a collection of graphic art that was considered the most important in Europe and that was also accessible to young artists. He twice visited Rome (1774, 1783) and instituted scholarships for young artists to enable them to complete their training, especially in Italy.

Among Charles Theodore's building projects were the completion of the Schloss (1760) in Mannheim, Schloss Benrath (1755–73) near Düsseldorf, Schloss Schwetzinger (1748–62) and the Opera House (1795) in Mannheim. Among the most important artists working for him were Nicolas de Pigage, Johann Matthäus van den Branden (1716–88), Friedrich Ludwig von Sckell, Alessandro Galli-Bibiena, Giuseppe Quaglio, Peter Anton von Verschaffelt, Wilhelm Lambert Krahe, Carl Heinrich Brandt (1724–87), Franz Anton Leydensdorff (1721–95), Johann Franz van der Schlichten (1725–95), Ferdinand Kobell, Wilhelm von Kobell and Franz Innocenz Josef Kobell (1749–1822). On the death of Charles Theodore control of Bavaria and the

Palatinate passed to Maximilian IV Joseph, Duke of Zweibrücken (later Maximilian I Joseph, King of Bavaria), younger brother of Charles II Augustus, Duke of Zweibrücken (*see* §III(2) below).

NDB

BIBLIOGRAPHY

J. A. Beringer: *Kurpfälzische Kunst und Kultur im 18. Jahrhundert* (Freiburg im Breisgau, 1907)
H. Tenner: *Mannheimer Kunstsammler und Kunsthändler bis zur Mitte des 19. Jahrhunderts* (Heidelberg, 1966)
F. Schnabel: 'Die kulturelle Bedeutung der Carl-Theodor-Zeit (1924)', *Abhandlungen und Vorträge, 1914–1965* (Freiburg im Breisgau, Basle and Vienna, 1970)
S. Pflicht: *Kurfürst Carl Theodor und seine Bedeutung für die Entwicklung des deutschen Theaters* (Reichling/Oberbayern, 1976)
J. Bahns: *Kurfürst Carl Theodor zu Pfalz: Der Erbauer von Schloss Benrath* (Düsseldorf, 1979)
Krone und Verfassung: König Max I Joseph und der neue Staat: Beiträge zur Bayerischen Geschichte und Kunst, 1799–1825, iii/1–2 of *Wittelsbach und Bayern* (exh. cat., ed. H. Glaser; Munich, Staatl. Mus. Vlkerknd, 1980)

INGRID SATTEL BERNARDINI

III. Zweibrücken-Birkenfeld branch.

The Dukes of Zweibrücken (Deux Ponts), a collateral line of the Wittelsbach family, held lands in the Palatinate, on the Saar, in Lorraine and in Alsace, so that they owed allegiance to both the Holy Roman Emperor and the king of France. The dynasty was founded by Stephan, Count of Zweibrücken (1385–1459). In the 16th and 17th centuries the Simmern-Sponheim, Zweibrücken-Veldenz and Birkenfeld-Bischweiler lines existed concurrently. After the older lines died out, their possessions fell to Christian III of Birkenfeld-Bischweiler (1674–1735), who from 1733 was known as Duke of Zweibrücken. He was succeeded by (1) Christian IV, Duke of Zweibrücken, whose political leanings were towards France and who was the patron of early Classicist architects. From his accession in 1775 (2) Charles II Augustus, Duke of Zweibrücken, was formally regarded as heir to the Palatinate and Bavaria. However, he did not live to succeed to the Palatinate and Bavaria, which therefore fell to his brother, who became Elector of the Palatinate-Bavaria in 1799 as Maximilian IV Joseph, then King of Bavaria as Maximilian I Joseph (1756–1825; *reg* 1806–25), so founding the dynasty of Bavarian kings descended from the house of Zweibrücken. His son (3) Ludwig I, King of Bavaria, made Bavaria an artistic centre and gave Munich buildings in the style of Greek Antiquity and Romantic historicism. He opened his collections in the Pinakothek and Glyptothek in Munich to the public and established art galleries throughout the country. His son Otto of Bavaria (1815–67) was the first Greek king (*reg* 1832–62) of modern times. The introvert (4) Ludwig II, King of Bavaria, erected the palaces of Neuschwanstein, Herrenchiemsee and Linderhof as expressions of his dream of past absolutist glories. In 1918 Ludwig III, King of Bavaria (1845–1921; *reg* 1913–18), was expelled by the November Revolution without having abdicated. Crown Prince Rupert (1869–1955), through his mother Maria Teresa of Austria-Modena (1849–1919) the legitimate Stuart heir, was an important art connoisseur who made family art treasures available to the Bavarian state galleries in accordance with the terms of the Wittelsbach compensation fund. In the late 20th century, the head of the house was Albert, Duke of Bavaria (*b* 3 May 1905).

(1) Christian IV, Duke of Zweibrücken (*b* Bischweiler, 6 Sept 1722; *d* Herschweiler-Petersheim, 5 Nov 1775). He was a close friend of Louis XV and the Marquise de Pompadour. From 1767 he owned the former Hôtel des Lorges in Paris, renamed the Hôtel des Deux-Ponts, and had the use of an apartment at Versailles. He employed architects working in the early Neo-classical style, including Jacques Hardouin Mansart de Sagonne, who designed the hunting-lodge of Jägersburg, which was completed (1752) by Pierre Patte, as was the Duke's Paris residence, and furnished in the *goût grec* in 1756–7. He also founded a porcelain factory, a book-printing works and a weapon factory at Zweibrücken. His court painter from 1772 was JOHANN CHRISTIAN VON MANNLICH.

(2) Charles II Augustus [Karl II August], Duke of Zweibrücken (*b* Düsseldorf, 29 Oct 1746; *d* Mannheim, 1 April 1795). Nephew of (1) Christian IV, Duke of Zweibrücken. As Christian IV had made a morganatic marriage, the titles and estates of the Dukes of Zweibrücken passed to his nephew, who was regarded as the heir to the Palatinate and Bavaria. He consequently received generous financial subsidies from France and used these to furnish his new Schloss Karlsberg (1776–90). Johann Christian von Mannlich was responsible for assembling and maintaining the painting collection at the Schloss, which contained 2000 17th- and 18th-century paintings, including works from Zweibrücken's own school of painting (mostly genre subjects). There was also a print room, a collection of antiquities, a library, a collection of natural objects and an armoury. The Duke commissioned suites of chairs from the Parisian cabinetmaker Georges Jacob and acquired French gilt bronzes, silver and silk hangings. In 1793 Schloss Karlsberg was confiscated by French Revolutionary troops, but Mannlich succeeded in concealing the contents and eventually taking them to Munich. In 1794 the castle was burnt down during a Revolutionary celebration. Surviving items from the furnishings and collections (*c.* 1785; Munich, Residenz and Schloss Nymphenburg; Berchtesgaden, Schlossmus.) are of exceptionally high-quality workmanship and display a naturalistic repertory of motifs.

BIBLIOGRAPHY

J. G. Lehmann: *Geschichte des Herzogtums Zweibrücken* (Munich, 1867)
L. Réau: *L'Art français sur le Rhin au XVIII siècle* (Paris, 1922)
S. A. von Reitzenstein: 'Die Gewehrkammer von Pfalz Zweibrücken', *Zweibrücken 600 Jahre Stadt* (exh. cat., Zweibrücken, 1952)
J. Dahl and K. Lohmayer: *Das barocke Zweibrücken und seine Meister* (Zweibrücken, 1955, 2/Waldfischbach, 1957)
Prince Adalbert of Bavaria: *Der Herzog und die Tänzerin* (Neustadt, 1966)
H. Ottomeyer: '*Amor und Psyche* von Martin-Claude Monot: Fundberichte zur Geschichte eines ungewöhnlichen Ensembles (1781/2)', *Pantheon*, xxviii (1980), pp. 265–9
——: 'Die Herzöge von Zweibrücken', *Wittelsbach und Bayern*, iii/2 (exh. cat., ed. H. Glaser; Munich, Staatl. Mus. Vlkerknd, 1980), pp. 66–110
W. Weber: *Schloss Karlsberg: Die vergessene Residenz des Herzogs Karl II August* (Munich, 1984)
E. Kessler-Slotta: *Zweibrückener Porzellan, 1767–1775* (Saarbrücken, 1990)

HANS OTTOMEYER

(3) Ludwig I, King of Bavaria (*b* Strasbourg, 25 Aug 1786; *reg* 1825–48; *d* Nice, 29 Feb 1868). Nephew of (2) Charles II Augustus, Duke of Zweibrücken. He sponsored building work on a grand scale, played a decisive role in reshaping Munich and created many important art galleries there. The French Revolution in 1789 forced Ludwig's father, Maximilian IV Joseph, Duke of Zweibrücken, to flee with his family from Alsace, where Ludwig had been born. In 1799 Maximilian became Elector of Bavaria on the death of Charles Theodore, Elector Palatine of the Rhine and Elector of Bavaria (*see* §II(4) above), and the family moved to Munich. After Bavaria had been transformed into a kingdom by Napoleon in 1806, Crown Prince Ludwig was obliged to serve in the French army, which offended his markedly nationalistic feelings and dampened his idealism.

From 1805 Ludwig's enthusiasm for art took him repeatedly to Rome. In 1818 he moved into the Villa Malta on Monte Pincio in Rome and soon gathered a circle of important contemporary artists around him, including such members of the Lukasbrüder as Peter Cornelius, Julius Schnorr von Carolsfeld (*see* SCHNORR VON CAROLSFELD, (2)), Heinrich Maria von Hess, Ferdinand Olivier and Friedrich Olivier, the sculptor Bertel Thorvaldsen and the architect KARL VON FISCHER. Many of them he summoned to his court in Munich when he ascended the throne in 1825. He regarded his position as ruler as a God-given task that he endeavoured to fulfil in a dutiful and autocratic manner. Of the enterprises that he promoted in the fields of economics, finance, politics, science and the arts, he regarded the last two as a private royal obligation for the good of his subjects: he funded not only artists but also museum buildings from his own resources, then immediately gave the public access to them.

Ludwig worked effectively for the university of Bavaria (now Ludwig-Maximilians-Universität), moving it from Landshut to Munich in 1826 and attracting outstanding scholars to it. His achievements as an art collector, urban planner and sponsor of building work were, however, more far-reaching (*see* MUNICH, §I, 3). He had started to collect works of art while Crown Prince and continued to do so until the end of his life. At first he was mainly interested in antique sculpture, then Italian Renaissance painting and eventually the art of his day.

Ludwig embellished his capital simultaneously with extensive landscaped parks, for example the Englischer Garten, such well-planned squares as the Königsplatz and the Odeonsplatz and such grand avenues as the Ludwig-strasse, true to his stated intention: 'I want to turn Munich into a town which will be such a credit to Germany that no one who has not seen Munich can claim to know Germany'. As an adherent of historicism, he favoured an eclectic assortment of antique, Byzantine Revival, pseudo-Romanesque and Gothic Revival stylistic elements, to which his choice of architects conformed. LEO VON KLENZE was a representative of the Neo-classical style and Friedrich von Gärtner an adherent of the Gothic Revival style (*see* GÄRTNER, (2) and fig.). Klenze started work on the Ludwigstrasse in 1816 and continued to work on it until 1830; Gärtner completed it after Ludwig's abdication. Ludwig's role in bringing it into being was so crucial that the royal thoroughfare could almost be considered his own work. Gärtner's Feldherrnhalle, built in 1840 in the style of the Loggia dei Lanzi in Florence, stands at its southern end, and his Siegestor (1843–52), built in imitation of a Roman triumphal arch, limits it to the north. There are also grand town houses on either side, for

example Klenze's Leuchtenberg Palais (1818–21), and such public buildings as the Bayerische Staatsbibliothek (1832–43) and the university (1835–40), both by Gärtner. The church buildings commissioned by Ludwig also display the characteristic co-existence of historical styles: Byzantine late classical at Klenze's Allerheiligen-Hofkirche (1826–37), a form of Romanesque at Georg Friedrich Ziebland's Bonifaziusbasilika (1835–40), Italian Early Gothic in Gärtner's Ludwigskirche (1829–44), for which Cornelius painted frescoes (e.g. the *Last Judgement*, 1839; *in situ*), and High Gothic Revival at Daniel Ohlmüller's Maria-Hilf-Kirche (1831–9) in Au near Munich.

Of the museums commissioned by Ludwig, two were by Klenze: the Glyptothek (1816–30) for Greek and Roman sculpture and the Alte Pinakothek (1826–36 for Old Master paintings) (*see* KLENZE, LEO VON, figs 1 and 2, and MUSEUM, fig. 5). The Kunstausstellungsgebäude (1838–45; now the Staatliche Antikensammlungen) on the Königsplatz, which was intended to cater for artistic events, was designed by Ziebland. The Neue Pinakothek (1846–53; destr. World War II, rebuilt 1975–81), last in the series of museum buildings, was built by August von Voit; it was dedicated to 19th-century painting and sculpture and later became the largest and most important collection of works of art from this period in Germany.

Ludwig's involvement in building palaces was limited essentially to extending the Residenz in Munich (*see* MUNICH, §IV, 2) by adding the Königsbau (1826–35), for which Schnorr von Carolsfeld produced frescoes (destr.) based on the Nibelungen legend, and the Festsaal (1832–42) overlooking the Hofgarten, both by Klenze. Ludwig devoted himself with greater enthusiasm to the architecture of monuments and memorials. The first of these was Klenze's Walhalla (1830–42) near Regensburg, built in the style of an antique temple and housing busts of eminent Germans. Johann Gottfried Schadow, Friedrich Tieck and Christian Daniel Rauch were among the sculptors commissioned to produce busts for the Walhalla.

The Befreiungshalle on the Michelsberg, near Kelheim, built to commemorate the Wars of Liberation (1813–15), was started in 1842 with Gärtner as the architect and continued from 1847 by Klenze. The interior contains 34 monumental statues of victories, while the exterior is decorated with 18 colossal figures of Germanic maidens with tablets inscribed with the names of the nations that contributed to Napoleon's overthrow.

Klenze's Ruhmeshalle (1843–53) above the Theresienwiese in Munich is a variant of the Walhalla, containing 80 busts of distinguished Bavarians, some by Max von Widumann. In front of the Ruhmeshalle is a gigantic statue symbolizing *Bavaria* by Ludwig von Schwanthaler. A 'Hall of Fame' in the Neue Pinakothek contained plaster busts, mainly of artists. The series of paintings (1827–42; Munich, Schloss Nymphenburg) by Joseph Karl Stieler for the Schönheitsgalerie in the Neue Pinakothek was intended as a tribute to female charms. The revolution in France in 1848, as well as Ludwig's affair with the Spanish dancer Lola Montez, which increasingly interfered with his role in government, resulted in public pressure for reform. Ludwig abdicated on 20 March 1848, although he continued to work on his artistic projects until his death.

BIBLIOGRAPHY

F. Noack: *Das Deutsche Rom* (Rome, 1912), pp. 118–29

R. Oldenbourg: *Die Epoche Max Josephs und Ludwigs I*, i of *Die Münchener Malerei im 19. Jahrhundert*, ed. E. Ruhmer (Munich, 1922, rev. 1983)

F. Noack: *Das Deutschtum in Rom*, i (Stuttgart, 1927)

A. von Reitzenstein and H. Brunner: *Bayern*, i of *Reclams Kunstreiseführer Deutschland* (Stuttgart, 1956, rev. 7/1964)

W. Mittlmeier: *Die Neue Pinakothek in München, 1843–1854* (Munich, 1977)

R. Bauer: 'König Ludwig von Bayern: Eine Lebenskizze', *Glyptothek München, 1830–1980* (exh. cat., Munich, 1980), pp. 18–22

(4) Ludwig II, King of Bavaria (*b* Munich, 25 Aug 1845; *reg* 1864–86; *d* Schloss Berg, nr Starnberg, 13 June 1886). Grandson of (3) Ludwig I, King of Bavaria. As the son of Maximilian II, his childhood was Spartan, bleak and isolated. The intellectual education that was forced upon him never took deep root; his natural bent was towards intense, romantic enthusiasm and aristocratic idealism. He was interested primarily in architecture and from 1867 devoted himself to it with exorbitant financial outlay and no sense of stylistic direction. While sculptors, painters and craftsmen of ephemeral value decorated his late Romantic castles, Ludwig neglected the progressive artists of his day. Everything that he regarded as great and exalted seemed to him to be embodied in the person and work of the composer Richard Wagner, whom he patronized from 1864.

Ludwig's passion for building was equally extravagant and served mainly to satisfy his narcissistic sense of majesty. He built several castles in picturesque sites that are among Bavaria's main tourist attractions. The villa at Schloss Linderhof in its alpine setting at Graswangtal is still relatively intimate in character; it was designed in 1869 and built between 1870 and 1874 by Georg von Dollmann and decorated and furnished by Franz von Seitz (1817–83) and Eugen Drollinger until 1878, with more magnificence than taste. Julius Hofmann (1840–96) succeeded Dollmann as director of the building work. The extensive gardens were laid out by Carl von Effner as a combination of the French and English concepts of a park. A grotto dedicated to Venus and a Moorish pavilion bought by Ludwig in 1867 at the Exposition Universelle in Paris invoked an exotic atmosphere reminiscent of the work of Wagner. Linderhof was the only one of Ludwig's castles that he lived to see completed (1884).

In contrast to Linderhof, Schloss Herrenchiemsee (*see* PALACE, fig. 4), based on Versailles, has an official, stately character; building was begun by Dollmann in 1878 and was continued after 1883 by Hofmann and others. Philipp Perron (1840–1907), F. Brochier and Michael Wagmüller were among those employed on decorating the interior and Rudolf Maison, Wilhelm von Rümann and Johann Hauttmann (1820–1903) among those responsible for the garden statuary. The design was intended to radiate the dignity of the monarchy, and the castle was conceived as a tribute to Louis XIV, King of France—Ludwig regarded him as the secret master of the house. Both castle and park remained unfinished, in a genuinely romantic state: in 1885 work had to be stopped because of the collapse of Ludwig's finances.

Schloss Neuschwanstein (*see* CASTLE, fig. 12) near Füssen embodies a third type of building, conceived as a second Wartburg transposed to the Bavarian Alps. Work on the Romanesque Revival castle began in 1868 under the architect Eduard Riedel (1813–85). Of the many state rooms that are in the residential part of the building, the Sängersaal was intended as a tribute by Ludwig to Wagner. Neuschwanstein was also unfinished when the mentally unstable King drowned in Lake Starnberg in 1886.

BIBLIOGRAPHY

A. von Reitzenstein and H. Brunner: *Bayern*, i of *Reclams Kunstreiseführer Deutschland* (Stuttgart, 1956, rev. 7/1964)

E. Hanfstaengl: *Bayerische Königsschlösser* (Munich, 1958)

G. Dehio and E. Gall: *Handbuch der Deutschen Kunstdenkmäler: Oberbayern* (Munich, rev. 3/1960)

A. Sailer: *Bayerns Märchenkönig* (Munich, 1961)

EBERHARD RUHMER

Witten, Hans. *See under* MASTERS, ANONYMOUS, AND MONOGRAMMISTS, §III: MASTER H W.

Wittet, George (*b* Scotland, 1880; *d* 11 Oct 1926). Scottish architect, active in India. After completing his articles in Perth, he worked with Sir George Washington Browne in Edinburgh and later in York. In 1904 he went to Bombay as assistant to John Begg, and three years later he succeeded him as Consulting Architect to the Government of Bombay. He was most active between 1905 and 1919, after which he gave up government service for more lucrative local private commissions. The Prince of Wales Museum of Western India, Bombay, dominated by a huge tiled concrete dome and comprising a whole series of ranges based on a scholarly interpretation of the Muslim architecture of the Deccan, was commenced to his designs in 1904 (*see* MUSEUM, fig. 7, and BOMBAY, §1).

Wittet's bold and inventive use of local building stone was carried through on his most notable work, the famous Gateway of India (1927) at Apollo Bunder, Bombay. This triumphal arch was raised to commemorate the landing of King George V and Queen Mary *en route* to the Delhi Durbar of 1911. Symbolically it was also the point of departure of the last British troops to leave India in 1948. Other important compositions by Wittet include the Institute of Science (completed 1916) and the Custom House in Bombay, and the Agricultural College (1911) and Central Government Offices (1915) at Pune, in collaboration with John Begg. Wittet was gifted with a fine compositional sense and an intuitive grasp of local detail. He developed the eclectic Indo-Saracenic style that had evolved within Bombay from the Gothic Revival designs, adapted to the tropics, of Frederick William Stevens and the great military engineers, such as General Sir Henry St Clair Wilkins (1828–96) and General John Augustus Fuller (1828–1902).

See also INDIA, REPUBLIC OF, §III, 8(i).

BIBLIOGRAPHY

Obituary, *RIBA J.*, n.s. 3, xxxiii (1926), p. 618

G. Stamp: 'British Architecture in India, 1857–1947', *J. Royal Soc. A.*, cxxix (1981), pp. 358–79

P. Davies: *Splendours of the Raj: British Architecture in India, 1660–1947* (London, 1985)

PHILIP DAVIES

Wittgenstein. Austrian family.

(1) Karl Wittgenstein (*b* 8 April 1847; *d* Vienna, 20 Jan 1913). Industrialist, collector and patron. He selfconsciously represented a new type of Austrian businessman—dynamic, entrepreneurial, forward-looking and politically liberal. Through a mixture of personal inclination, community influence and family connections, he translated these values into admiration and support for artistic modernism. He backed the Vienna Secession from the outset, providing the necessary financial guarantee to allow the construction of the exhibition building on Karlsplatz by Joseph Maria Olbrich (*see* AUSTRIA, fig. 9) in 1898 and acquiring work from many members of the association. In particular, he was an admirer and patron of Klimt and continued to support him after the split in the group in 1905. Wittgenstein fully concurred with the goal of the Secession to open up the Austrian art scene to international influence, and he was an enthusiastic collector of French Impressionist paintings. He and his wife, Leopoldine, who was an accomplished musician, passed on their passionate interest in the arts to their children, including their son (2) Ludwig Wittgenstein.

BIBLIOGRAPHY
'Karl Wittgenstein als Kunstfreund', *Neue Freie Presse* (20 Jan 1913), pp. 10–11
J. Wiegenstein: *Artists in a Changing Environment: The Viennese Art World, 1860–1918* (diss., Bloomington, IN U., 1978), chap. 4
J. K. Bramann and J. Moran: 'Karl Wittgenstein: Business Tycoon and Art Patron', *Austral. Hist. Yb.*, 15–16 (1979–80), pp. 107–27
B. Michel: 'Les Mécènes de la Sécession', *Vienne, 1880–1936: L'Apocalypse joyeuse* (exh. cat., ed. N. Ouvrard and J. Bouniort; Paris, Pompidou, 1986), pp. 180–89

MALCOLM GEE

(2) Ludwig (Josef Johann) Wittgenstein (*b* Vienna, 26 April 1889; *d* Cambridge, 29 April 1951). Philosopher and architect, son of (1) Karl Wittgenstein. Although initially interested in engineering, he went to Cambridge in 1911 to study philosophy with Bertrand Russell (1872–1970). Wittgenstein fought with distinction as a volunteer for the Austrian Army in World War I, during which he completed the 'Logisch-philosophische Abhandlung', the definitive expression of his early philosophy, after which he abandoned the subject, believing he had solved all its problems. After a revival of his interest, however, he returned to Cambridge in 1929, where he became Professor of Mental Philosophy and Logic in 1939, resigning in 1947. He adopted British citizenship in 1938. His second major work, *Philosophical Investigations*, which overturns the results of his early thought, was published posthumously in 1953; also significant is the extensive *Nachlass*.

Wittgenstein had a deep interest in the arts, and he confessed that only aesthetic questions gripped him as deeply as the conceptual questions of philosophy. He modelled a bust in the workshop of the sculptor Michael Drobil, and in collaboration with another friend, Paul Engelmann (1891–1965), a pupil of Adolf Loos, he designed for his sister the house at Kundmanngasse 19, Vienna, whose lack of ornament perfectly reflects Wittgenstein's aesthetic ideal. Wittgenstein thought, however, that he possessed only artistic understanding and taste, not creative ability, and he considered his architectural work to be merely 'reproductive', a translation of an old style into a language appropriate to the modern world.

Wittgenstein's philosophical work focuses on the nature of language and its relationship with the world. Whereas his early philosophy represents language as being fundamentally uniform and pictorial in character, mirroring the structure of the world, the later philosophy conceives it as a collection of instruments with radically diverse functions. According to the early philosophy, one must be silent about art, since what is of value in art does not possess a structure isomorphic with that of language, which therefore cannot mirror it. The later philosophy, however, ties language no more firmly to the domain of science than to that of art, and it places a welcome emphasis on the variety of the aesthetic and the ways in which forms of artistic appreciation are responses embedded in and inseparable from styles of living and entire cultures.

Two main concerns permeate Wittgenstein's later thought about art. The first is a determination to preserve the autonomy of works of art against the view of Lev Tolstoy that represents them as mere vehicles for conveying the artist's experience to the spectator, thus failing to do justice to the medium of art. The second is an opposition to any attempt to settle the most vital problems in aesthetics by means of psychological experiments determining the causes of our responses to works of art, which would fail (so Wittgenstein argued) to do justice to their directed character, and an insistence that these problems can be resolved only by certain kinds of comparison or groupings of objects. Neither the negative nor the positive aspect of the latter concern, however, is worked out in sufficient detail to carry conviction.

WRITINGS
'Logisch-philosophische Abhandlung', *An. Natphilos.*, 14 (1921), pp. 185–262; as book (London, 1922); Eng. trans. as *Tractatus Logico-philosophicus* (London, 1961, rev. 1975)
Philosophische Untersuchungen/Philosophical Investigations (Oxford, 1953, 3/1967)
Lectures and Conversations on Aesthetics, Psychology and Religious Belief (Oxford, 1966)
Vermischte Bemerkungen (Frankfurt am Main, 1977, rev. 2/1980; Eng. trans. as *Culture and Value*, Oxford, 1980)

BIBLIOGRAPHY
N. Malcolm: *Ludwig Wittgenstein: A Memoir* (London, 1958, 2/1984)
R. Monk: *Ludwig Wittgenstein: The Duty of Genius* (London, 1990)

MALCOLM BUDD

Wittig, August (*b* Meissen, 23 March 1823; *d* Düsseldorf, 20 Feb 1893). German sculptor. From 1843 to 1849 he studied under Ernst Friedrich August Rietschel at the Kunstakademie in Dresden. From 1849 to 1864 he was in Rome, where he developed his classical style. He produced reliefs and sculpted groups, preferring themes from Classical mythology and the Bible, though much of his work has been lost. The remaining examples include the romantic *Siegfried's Farewell from Kriemhild* (bronze, 1850; Dresden, Skulpsamml.) and the bronze relief of the *Entombment* for the tomb of the *Schoeller Family* (1850; Düren, Evangel. Cemetery). Contemporary critics received his works favourably, particularly because of their emotional expression, and with their support he became Professor of Sculpture at the Königliche Preussische Kunstakademie in Düsseldorf in 1864. There he created a museum of casts of Classical and other sculptures as a teaching aid and primarily used the works of Pheidias, Michelangelo and Peter Vischer (ii) as examples for his pupils. His love of Classical sculpture was reflected in his suggestion to his students that a version of the *Venus de Milo* (Paris, Louvre) should be reconstructed with Venus holding the shield of Mars before her like a mirror, though the project was never carried out. In 1869 he created a life-size bronze bust of the Director of the Kunstakademie, *Wilhelm Schadow* (Düsseldorf, Schadow-Platz), to mark the fiftieth anniversary of the institution's refounding. Wittig's last work was the model (1892) for his own grave (Düsseldorf, North Cemetery), which is decorated with a bronze Pietà.

BIBLIOGRAPHY

Thieme–Becker
P. Bloch: 'Der Bildhauer August Wittig', *Zweihundert Jahre Kunstakademie Düsseldorf*, ed. E. Trier (Düsseldorf, 1973), pp. 121–6
——: *Skulpturen des 19. Jahrhunderts im Rheinland* (Düsseldorf, 1975), pp. 56–8

INGE ZACHER

Wittig, Edward (*b* Warsaw, 21 Sept 1879; *d* Warsaw, 3 March 1941). Polish sculptor. He studied at the medal workshop of Josef Tautenhayn (*b* 1868) at the Akademie der Bildenden Künste in Vienna (1897–1900), in the workshop of the medallist Hubert Ponscarme at the Ecole des Beaux-Arts, Paris (1900–02), and also with Alexandre Charpentier. From 1903 onwards he exhibited at the Salon and at the Salon des Indépendants. In 1914 he returned to Poland, where he was appointed Professor of Sculpture at the School of Fine Arts, Warsaw (1915–20), and spent the next two years at the Faculty of Architecture of Warsaw Polytechnic. He was a member of the RHYTHM GROUP.

In Wittig's first phase (up to *c.* 1907), his work was inspired by Symbolism and the ideas of Rodin, and it already shows the disciplined Maillol-like forms that started to predominate before World War I and reached their fullest expression in the stone sculpture *Ewa* (1913–14; Paris, Jard. Trocadéro). Most of Wittig's portraits come from this period. On his return to Poland he concentrated on monuments and as a result of classicist inspirations imbued even his smallest works with a monumental character (e.g. the *Dying Knight*, bronze, 1926; Warsaw, Powązki Cemetery, enlarged 1933 as the monument to *POW Soldiers*). In his largest composition, *Airman's Monument* (bronze, 1923–31; Warsaw, destr. 1944; rebuilt 1967), he employed simplified, almost geometrical forms while maintaining the monumental expression.

WRITINGS
'Rzeźba' [Sculpture], *Sfinks* (1915), nos 7–8

BIBLIOGRAPHY
S. Rutkowski: *Edward Wittig* (Warsaw, 1925)
W. Kozicki: *Edward Wittig: Rozwój twórczości* [Edward Wittig: development of his work] (Warsaw, 1932)

WOJCIECH WŁODARCZYK

Wittkower, Rudolf (*b* Berlin, 22 June 1901; *d* New York, 11 Oct 1971). British art historian and writer of German birth. The son of Henry Wittkower and Gertrude Ansbach, he had British citizenship through his British-born father. He studied at the universities of Munich and Berlin, where under the supervision of Adolf Goldschmidt he obtained his doctorate with a dissertation on the 15th-century Veronese artist Domenico Morone. In 1923 he went to Rome, where for the next ten years he worked first as an assistant (1923–7) and then as a research fellow at the Biblioteca Hertziana, for which he began the compilation of bibliographies organized by artist and place. In 1931 he published *Die Zeichnungen des Gianlorenzo Bernini*, which he wrote in collaboration with Heinrich Brauer. After a brief period as lecturer at the Universität Köln (1933), Wittkower came to London. From 1934 to 1956 he was a member of staff at the Warburg Institute and in 1937 was a founding co-editor of the Institute's journal. From 1949 to 1956 he combined these duties with those of Durning-Lawrence Professor of the History of Art at the University of London. He was visiting professor at Harvard University in 1954 and, in 1955, at Columbia University, New York, where from 1956 he was Professor of Fine Art. On his retirement in 1969 he became Avalon Foundation Professor Emeritus of Art History at Columbia, Kress Professor at the National Gallery of Art, Washington, and Slade Professor at Cambridge.

Wittkower's interests ranged from the interpretation of symbols to problems of proportion in Renaissance architecture and every facet of Baroque art, in which fields his approach was pioneering. In his review of Wittkower's influential book *Architectural Principles in the Age of Humanism* (1949), the art historian Kenneth Clark wrote that Wittkower wished 'to dispose, once and for all, of the hedonist, or purely aesthetic, theory of Renaissance architecture', an observation endorsed by Wittkower himself in his preface to the revised edition of 1962. Through this and other studies Wittkower radically altered prevailing attitudes towards Renaissance architecture from the period of Leon Battista Alberti to that of Palladio and Palladianism. It was, however, as a scholar of 17th-century Italian art and architecture that he made his most significant contribution. In 1955 he followed up his earlier work on Bernini with a monograph *Gian Lorenzo Bernini: The Sculptor of the Roman Baroque*. These books, together with his work on the architect Francesco Borromini and on the draughtsmanship of the Carracci family, *The Drawings of the Carracci in the Royal Collection at Windsor Castle* (1952), laid the foundation for subsequent studies of the Italian Baroque. His contribution to the Pelican History of Art series, *Art and Architecture in Italy, 1600 to 1750* (1958), which he revised for the third time in June 1971, shortly before his death, quickly became the classic textbook for the period and was awarded the Bannister Fletcher Prize. His study of the artistic temperament, *Born under Saturn: The Character and Conduct of Artists* (1963), was written in collaboration with his wife Margot (née Holzman), whom he had married in 1923.

WRITINGS
with H. Brauer: *Die Zeichnungen des Gianlorenzo Bernini* (Berlin, 1931)
Architectural Principles in the Age of Humanism (London, 1949, rev. 2/1962)
The Drawings of the Carracci in the Royal Collection at Windsor Castle (London, 1952)
Gian Lorenzo Bernini: The Sculptor of the Roman Baroque (London, 1955, rev. 1966)
Art and Architecture in Italy, 1600 to 1750, Pelican Hist. A. (London, 1958, rev. 4/1973)
with M. Holzman: *Born under Saturn: The Character and Conduct of Artists* (London, 1963)

BIBLIOGRAPHY

D. Fraser, H. Hibbard and M. J. Lewine, eds: *Essays Presented to Rudolf Wittkower on his 65th Birthday*, 2 vols (London, 1967): i, *Essays in the History of Architecture* [incl. writings list up to June 1966]; ii, *Essays in the History of Art*

H. Hibbard: Obituary, *Burl. Mag.*, cxiv (1972), pp. 173–6 [incl. writings list from 1965]

JANET SOUTHORN

Wittwer, Martin (*b* Imst, Tyrol, 24 Oct 1667; *d* Pacov, Bohemia, 12 May 1732). Austrian architect. In 1695 he entered the Carmelite Order as a lay brother and was known as Brother Athanasius. He subsequently joined his compatriot Johann Martin Rass (1640–94) in Prague. Rass, who was also a lay brother, had directed (1679–96) the construction in Prague of the church of St Joseph, to the designs of Jean Baptiste Mathey. From Prague, Rass took Wittwer to Linz, where they began building a church for the Carmelites, completed by Wittwer after Rass's sudden death. The building contractor was Johann Michael Prunner, who was also responsible for building Wittwer's centralized church for the Carmelite nuns of Linz and to whom many of Wittwer's works were later attributed. At Linz, Wittwer closely followed the domed construction of the Order's church in Vienna and derived its undulating west façade from the work of Borromini. At Győr, Wittwer modelled his Carmelite church on the longitudinal oval structure of Donato-Felice Allio's church for the Salesian nuns in Vienna. The plans (1714; executed, with some modifications, 1722–5) bear his signature and are still kept in the sacristy. Wittwer's Pauline abbey church at Pápa also follows this plan. Later work included assisting in the large-scale reconstruction at the Benedictine monastery of Pannonhalma, contributing in particular to the rebuilding of the abbot's lodgings and the enormous refectory; the west façade, with twin spires, of the abbey of Tihany on Lake Balaton; the church (1714–36) with twin spires at Spital am Pyhrn, near Linz; and an almost identical church for the Premonstratensians at Zirc, Hungary. In Győr he completed the Hungarian Hospital Church and the chapel of the Calvary, and he designed the ornaments of the finely appointed façade of the former Jesuit church. His highly original motifs, found on windows and door frames, recur in practically all his works. His last work was the oval domed church of the Carmelites at Pacov, Bohemia.

BIBLIOGRAPHY

B. Grimschitz: *Johann Michael Prunner* (Vienna and Munich, 1960)

J. Schmidt: 'Die Linzer Kirchen', *Österreich. Ksttop.*, xxxvi (1964)

P. Voit: 'Martin Wittwer, Architekt der Karmelitenkirche in Győr: Beiträge zu den Beziehungen in Ungarn und der Donau-Bauschule des Barocks', *Magyar Műemlékvédelem* (1969)

PÁL VOIT

Witz, Konrad (*b* Rottweil, Württemberg, *c.* 1400–10; *d* Geneva or Basle, 1445–6). German painter. One of the great innovators in northern European painting, he turned away from the lyricism of the preceding generation of German painters. His sturdy, monumental figures give a strong impression of their physical presence, gestures are dignified and the colours strong and simple. Even scenes with several figures are strangely undramatic and static. The surface appearance of materials, especially metals and stone, is intensely observed and recorded with an almost naive precision. Powerful cast shadows help to define the spatial relationships between objects. His fresh approach to the natural world reflects that of the Netherlandish painters: the Master of Flémalle and the van Eycks. He need not, however, have trained in the Netherlands or in Burgundy as knowledge of their style could have been gained in Basle. He remained, however, untouched by the anecdotal quality present in their art, while Witz's pure tempera technique differs emphatically from the refined use of oil glazes that endows Netherlandish pictures with their jewel-like brilliance.

1. LIFE. On 21 June 1434 'Meister Konrad von Rotwil' was received into the Basle painters' guild and on 10 January 1435 he acquired Basle citizenship. His marriage to Ursula Treyger of Wangen, niece of the painter Nikolaus Ruesch (*d* 1453–4) who had emigrated from Tübingen, may soon have followed. In 1437 he was named among those seeking to revive the confraternity of St Luke; in 1441 and 1442 he was paid for paintings (untraced) in the Kornhaus and in 1443 he bought a house on the Freiestrasse in Basle. One of the wings (Geneva, Mus. A. & Hist.) from the high altarpiece for the cathedral of St Pierre, Geneva, is inscribed *hoc opus pinxit magister conradus sapientis de basilea MCCCCXLIIII* (1444). In 1446 the painter is recorded as dead. He left a widow (*d* 1448) and five young children for whom his father Hans assumed guardianship. A daughter, Katharina, entered the convent of the Magdalenes in 1454; it was said of her dowry that her father had acquired it 'with his craft'.

2. DOCUMENTED AND ACCEPTED WORK. The Heilspiegel Altarpiece (dispersed) is attributed to Witz on the basis of stylistic similarities to the signed wings in Geneva. It was painted *c.* 1435 for the choir of the Leonhardskirche in Basle and was dismantled during the iconoclasm of 1529. The central section and the predella are lost but the surviving 12 scenes from the wings allow a partial reconstruction.

The programme depends upon the *Speculum humanae salvationis* ('The mirror of human salvation'), a text attributed to the Dominican Ludolf of Saxony before 1324, in which biblical and historical events from the pre-Christian era are matched with events from the story of man's salvation. Originally the inner sides of the wings contained eight scenes. Seven of these survive: *Antipater Showing Caesar his Wounds*, *King Ahasuerus Choosing Esther as his Wife* (both Basle, Kstmus.), the *Queen of Sheba before King Solomon* (Berlin, Gemäldegal.), *Melchisedek Offering Abraham Bread and Wine* (Basle, Kstmus.), *Augustus and the Tiburtine Sibyl* (Dijon, Mus. B.-A.) and two panels for *Abishai, Sibbechai and Benaiah Bringing Water to King David* (Basle, Kstmus.; see fig.). Each scene is painted on an oak panel and shows two figures standing before a gold, patterned ground. The lost central section of the altarpiece presumably illustrated the fulfilment of these prefigurations, possibly a carved Christ in Majesty or Adoration of the Magi. When the altarpiece was closed, the outer sides showed single figures confined within narrow box-like spaces: in the upper row were *Ecclesia*, the *Angel of the Annunciation* (both Basle, Kstmus.), the *Virgin* (lost) and *Synagogue* (Basle, Kstmus.); below there were originally four saints of which only two survive, *St*

Konrad Witz: *Abishai, Sibbechai and Benaiah Bringing Water to King David* (detail), tempera on panel, 975×700 mm, *c*. 1435 (Basle, Kunstmuseum)

Augustine (Dijon, Mus. B.-A.) and *St Bartholomew* (Basle, Kstmus.). The figures are strongly modelled and have a sculptural quality reminiscent of the statues of Claus Sluter in Dijon. This characteristic feature is absent from a *St Christopher* of similar dimensions (Basle, Kstmus.) so it is not usually thought to be from the Heilspiegel altarpiece and is dated to another period.

Of the surviving altarpieces that include scenes prefiguring the Advent of Christ, such as Rogier van der Weyden's Bladelin altarpiece (Berlin, Gemäldegal.) and Dieric Bouts's *St Peter* (1464–8; Leuven, St Pieterskerk), Witz's Basle Altarpiece is both the earliest and most extensive. The Council of the Church, which had been sitting in Basle since 1431, may have influenced its iconography to express the attempt to reconcile the Roman Catholic Church with the churches of the East and to unite the Christian world (Barrucand). The presence of the Council and the commissions it was expected to generate probably provided the incentive for Witz to settle in Basle.

In spite of the signature and the date 1444, which may be a transcription of a lost inscription, it is possible that Witz's other major work, the *St Peter* altarpiece (Geneva, Mus. A. & Hist.), was never completed. Here too the central section and the predella are missing, and it is questionable whether the wings correspond to the original arrangement. At present the *Adoration of the Magi* is on the inner side of the left wing with the *Donor Presented to the Virgin Mary by St Peter* on the right. On the outer sides the scene on the left is generally referred to as the *Miraculous Draught of Fishes* with the *Liberation of St Peter*

from Prison on the right. The cathedral of St Pierre in Geneva is almost unanimously accepted as the original site of the altarpiece. It may have been dismantled and partially destroyed in the iconoclasm of 1535, and although overall the state of preservation is good, nearly all the heads are spoilt through restoration.

It has been proposed that, rather than Cardinal François de Mez (or Mies) whose arms are on the frame, the commission was placed by Amadeus VIII, Count of Savoy. He was elected antipope in 1439 in Basle and took the name Felix V (Deuchler). This theory would explain some peculiarities of the iconography and give a political significance to the *Miraculous Draught of Fishes* (*see* SWITZERLAND, fig. 5), which is set on a shore recognizable as that of Lake Geneva. This topographically accurate view, the 'first portrayal of landscape' in northern European art as it has been called, stretches across the Savoy Alps as far as the Mont Blanc Massif, encapsulating the new Patrimonium Petri, the Count's dominion, shown here as secure and peaceful; his soldiers, their banner ahead of them, ride towards the city of Geneva, washerwomen work on the bank, farmers tend the fields and a shepherdess watches over her flock. In the foreground of Christ walking on the lake, the disciples' boat and St Peter sinking into the water are intended to illustrate the special relationship of St Peter to Christ. Quite unusually several texts from the Gospels referring to the works of Christ before and after his resurrection (Matthew 14, 24–33; Luke 5, 4–11; John 21, 1–14) are incorporated into the picture. Peter is called to be a fisher of men and Christ's successor, although he remains a doubter like Amadeus as Felix V, who only took on his office with reservations, relinquishing it in 1449.

A journey to the Council of Ferrara (moved to Florence) has been claimed for Witz in connection with this commission but neither the composition, the spatial organization nor the figure-style of the Geneva Altarpiece or Witz's later works show any evidence of contact with Florentine painting. Only three other paintings are unanimously accepted as being by Witz. These are the *Annunciation* (Nuremberg, Ger. Nmus.), once the other side of the pine panel with the *Meeting at the Golden Gate* (Basle, Kstmus.) and *SS Catharine and Mary Magdalene in a Church* (Strasbourg, Mus. Oeuvre Notre Dame). There is no evidence for dating these works but they seem likely to be later than the Geneva Altarpiece. Strange inconsistencies in spatial perspective, ignoring Netherlandish and Italian developments, characterize all three scenes.

3. ATTRIBUTIONS, WORKSHOP AND INFLUENCE. Only a few overpainted fragments survive of the murals of the *Dance of Death* from the Basle Dominican cemetery. The paintings, once attributed to Holbein and engraved by Matthäus Merian the younger were, according to the latter, commissioned in 1439 to commemorate the plague. Although their condition precludes a definite conclusion the relationship with Witz's style is so close that his authorship should be considered.

Other paintings that are dependent on Witz's pictorial inventions or are close to his style, and probably produced by his immediate followers or his workshop, include the

Holy Family and Saints in a Church (Naples, Capodi-monte), the fragment of a *Virgin and Child* from Olsberg near Basle (Basle, Kstmus.), the so-called *Decision on the Redemption of Man* (Berlin, Gemäldegal.) and a panel with the *Nativity* on the outside and a votive scene on the inside (Basle, Kstmus.), which are parts of an altarpiece. The *Crucifixion* (Berlin, Gemäldegal.) with its atmospheric lakeside landscape, which was long claimed as an auto-graph work by Witz, may have been painted by a Savoyard follower (Feldges-Henning, Sterling). The painter's draw-ing style can best be discerned from his spontaneous underdrawings (Aulmann). Witz appears to have been left-handed. The *Ambraser Hofjagdspiel*, a card game with 56 pictures of the court riding to the hunt and their quarry (Vienna, Ksthist. Mus.), has the most important drawings from Witz's workshop.

In spite of his outstanding quality as a painter, Witz had remarkably little influence on the development of German art, and his achievements were only recognized at the turn of the 20th century by Burckhardt. The far-reaching change of taste that resulted from the impact of Rogier van der Weyden made Witz's style seem archaic and outmoded. No greater contrast is conceivable than the slender, mobile, emotion-laden figures of the Netherland-ish painter and the block-like immobile forms of Witz.

Thieme–Becker

BIBLIOGRAPHY

D. Burckhardt: 'Das Werk des Konrad Witz', *Festschrift der Stadt Basel zum 400. Jahrestage des ewigen Bundes zwischen Basel und den Eidgenossen* (Basle, 1901)
M. Escherich: *Konrad Witz* (Strasbourg, 1916)
H. Wendland: *Konrad Witz: Gemäldestudien* (Basle, 1924) [good illus.]
H. Rott: *Quellen und Forschungen zur südwestdeutschen und schweizerischen Kunstgeschichte im XV. und XVI. Jahrhundert: III, Der Oberrhein*, ii (Stuttgart, 1936), pp. 20–25
W. Ueberwasser: *Konrad Witz* (Basle, 1938)
J. Gantner: *Konrad Witz* (Vienna, 1942)
P. L. Ganz: *Konrad Witz: Meister von Rottweil* (Berne, 1947)
M. Meng-Köhler: *Die Bilder des Konrad Witz und ihre Quellen* (Basle, 1947)
A. Stange: *Deutsche Malerei der Gotik*, iv (Munich, 1951), pp. 127–55
H. Aulmann: *Gemäldeuntersuchungen mit Röntgen-, Ultraviolett- und Infra-rotstrahlen zum Werk des Konrad Witz* (Basle, 1958)
E. Maurer: 'Konrad Witz und die niederländische Malerei', *Z. Schweiz. Archäol. & Kstgesch.*, 18 (1958), pp. 158–66; also in *15 Aufsätze zur Geschichte der Malerei* (Basle, 1982)
H. Röttgen: *Konrad Witz: Analyse und Geschichte seiner Farbgebung* (diss., U. Marburg, 1958)
J. Gantner: *Konrad Witz: Der Heilspiegelaltar* (Stuttgart, 1962)
U. Feldges-Henning: *Werkstatt und Nachfolge des Konrad Witz* (Basle, 1968)
A. Stange: *Kritisches Verzeichnis der deutschen Tafelbilder vor Dürer*, ii (Munich, 1970), pp. 21–5
M. Teasdale-Smith: 'Conrad Witz's *Miraculous Draught of Fishes* and the Council of Basel', *A. Bull.*, 52 (1970), pp. 150–57
M. Barrucand: *Le Retable du miroir du salut dans l'oeuvre de Konrad Witz* (Geneva, 1972) [complete bibliog.]
F. Deuchler: 'Konrad Witz, la Savoie et l'Italie: Nouvelles hypothèses à propos du retable de Genève', *Rev. A.*, 71 (1986), pp. 7–16
C. Sterling: 'L'Influence de Konrad Witz en Savoie', *Rev. A.*, 71 (1986), pp. 17–32

DETLEF ZINKE

Wladislav II, King of Bohemia and Hungary. *See* JAGIEL-LON, (1).

Władysław IV, King of Poland. *See* VASA, (3).

Wleughels, Nicolas. *see* VLEUGHELS, NICOLAS.

Włodarski, Marek [Streng, Henryk] (*b* Lwów [now L'viv, Ukraine], 17 April 1903; *d* Warsaw, 23 May 1960). Polish painter. He trained at the Free Academy of Fine Arts in Lwów (now L'viv) (1920–24) and at the Académie Mo-derne in Paris (1925–6) as a student of Léger, who greatly influenced his first works, such as *The Hairdresser* (1925; Łódź, Mus. A.). He became friends with André Masson and André Breton and turned to Surrealism, as in *Floating in the Sky* (1931; Warsaw, N. Mus.). In Lwów he joined the ARTES group (1930). His left-wing sympathies mani-fested themselves in proletarian and revolutionary themes; he depicted barricades, demonstrations and workers, as in *Demonstration of Pictures* (1933; Łódź, Mus. A.). While in hiding during World War II he painted still-lifes and interiors. Imprisoned in Stutthof he drew and thus docu-mented the horrors of the concentration camp. After the war he took a teaching post at the Higher School of Art in Warsaw. He retired from official art life during the period of Socialist Realism, and in 1948 he renounced all figuration in the series of abstract seascapes executed in oil, pencil and gouache. In his abstract compositions he used pure, unrestrained colours.

BIBLIOGRAPHY
Marek Włodarski (Henryk Streng), 1903–1960 (exh. cat. by H. Piprek, Warsaw, N. Mus., 1982)

Wobeser, Hilla. *See* BECHER.

Wodiczko, Krzysztof (*b* Warsaw, 14 April 1943). Polish designer and installation artist. He trained as an industrial designer at the Academy of Fine Arts in Warsaw (1962–8). His first works, all precisely designed and executed, but functionless, were an ironic response to the invasion of modern technology (e.g. *Personal Instrument*, 1969; Łódź, Mus. A.). In 1973 he constructed the *Vehicle* (Łódź, Mus. A.). Built of wood and bicycle wheels, it can be set in motion by someone walking up and down on it or by other non-productive action, such as gesticulation. In the 1970s he also examined the relationship between the real object and its visual perception. *Drawing of a Stool* (1974; Warsaw, Gal. Foksal), flat projections of stools drawn directly on the walls, produced a three-dimensional illu-sion. These were followed by similar but more sophisti-cated experiments with line, space and perspective. After 1975 Wodiczko worked and taught in Australia and Canada. He finally settled in the USA, where he started to use a slide projection method to explore the idea of cultural and socio-political contexts of works of art. His *Public Projections*, large-scale projections on public buildings, often conveyed ironic allusions to the institutional function of the architectural structure, as in *Documenta 8*, in which a praying figure with a gas-mask and a Geiger counter was projected on to the façade of the Lutherkirche in Kassel, Germany (1987). Together with a group of the New York homeless Wodiczko constructed the *Homeless Vehicle* (1987–8) 'an instrument of survival for urban nomads'. The aim of this project was not only to supply a multi-purpose shelter and means of transport for the homeless, but also to draw attention to the problem of homelessness in modern society.

BIBLIOGRAPHY
Vision and Unity. Strzemiński 1893–1952 and 9 Contemporary Polish Artists (exh. cat., ed. F. Bless; Łódź, Mus. A.; Apeldoorn, Van Reekum Mus.; 1989), pp. 253–70
Art in Theory 1900–1990: An Anthology of Changing Ideas, ed. C. Harrison and P. Wood (Oxford, 1993), pp. 1094–7

ANNA BENTKOWSKA

Woeiriot [Wiriot], Pierre (*b* Neufchâteau, Vosges, 1532; *d* Damblain, Haute-Marne, 1599). French goldsmith, painter, sculptor, medallist and engraver. He followed his father and grandfather in working as a goldsmith until *c.* 1555, after which he was primarily active as an engraver. In that year he received two privileges for the *Pinax iconicus* (Adhémar, 6), published in 1556, and the *Livre d'anneaux d'orfèvrerie* (Adhémar, 19), published in 1561 with a dedication to the poet Barthélemy Aneau. Around 1556 he executed three engravings with historical or mythological subject-matter, the *Bull of Phalaris, Hasdrubal's Wife Throwing Herself on the Pyre* and *Phocas Led Captive before Heraclius* (Adhémar, 21–3). It was previously thought that Woeiriot went to Italy after 1550 and settled in Lyon on his return in 1554, but it now seems that he did not leave for Rome until *c.* 1559–60. At the end of 1561 he was in Nancy; he continued to make frequent visits to Lyon until 1571. On 1 December 1561 he made a contract with the dealer Antoine God to engrave 36 plates illustrating the Old Testament (Adhémar, 58), which appeared in 1580. He became a Protestant under the influence of the poet Louis Desmasures and between 1566 and 1571 illustrated the *Emblèmes ou devises chrestiennes* (Adhémar, 7) by Georgette de Montenay, lady-in-waiting to Joanna d'Albret, mother of Henry IV. He moved to Damblain in 1572.

Woeiriot engraved 431 copper plates and produced a smaller number of woodblocks, executing religious pictures, ornaments and portraits. He signed his work with his full name or, after 1562, with the monogram P.W.D.B. (Pierre Woeiriot de Bouzey, from his mother's name), together with the Cross of Lorraine. Influenced first by Bernard Salomon and Giorgio Ghisi, he also took inspiration from Maarten van Heemskerck.

BIBLIOGRAPHY
A. P. F. Robert-Dumesnil: *Le Peintre-graveur français*, vii (Paris, 1844), pp. 43–140
G. Duplessis: *Le Peintre-graveur français*, xi (Paris, 1871), pp. 324–52
A. Jacquot: *Pierre Woeiriot: Les Wiriot–Woeiriot, orfèvres-graveurs lorrains* (Paris, 1892)
J. Adhémar: *Inventaire du fonds français: Graveurs du seizième siècle*, Paris, Bib. N., Dept Est. cat., ii (Paris, 1938), pp. 158–75
M. Iwai: *L'Oeuvre de Pierre Woeiriot (1532–1599)* (Paris, 1985)

MARIANNE GRIVEL

Woensam [Wonsam; of Worms], Anton (*b* probably Worms, 1493/6–1500; *d* Cologne, in or before 1541). German woodcutter and painter. His family settled in Cologne *c.* 1510, and he was probably trained by his father, Jaspar Woensam the elder, who became the banneret of the painters' guild in 1546. There is evidence that Anton Woensam worked as a woodcutter for book printers in 1517–18. His style was at first influenced by Cologne painting and Antwerp Mannerism, and he may also have been inspired by the Master of St Severin. Later he was influenced by Bartolomäus Bruyn the elder, Joos van Cleve and Albrecht Dürer.

Woensam's extensive oeuvre, in which painting plays only a small part, can be divided into four creative periods. The earliest period (*c.* 1520) is characterized by a mixture of Late Gothic ornamental forms and Mannerist influences from the Netherlands; it was followed by a period of study (1521–6), during which his use of colour and composition became more sober and cool, and the mature period (*c.* 1527–35), during which he ripened as an independent artist, though still using models, such as the frescoes (early 16th century) by the Master of the Aachen Altar in the Hardenrath chapel in St Maria im Kapitol, Cologne. The late period, after 1535, was characterized by an emphasis on the figural, a newly acquired knowledge of perspective and the renewed influence of Antwerp Mannerism, in particular familiarity with the works of the Master of the Antwerp Crucifixion. Although there is still no definitive list of works known to be by Woensam or attributable to him, he has been attributed with 549 woodcuts (Merlo), produced primarily for Cologne printers and the Carthusian monastery in Cologne, and 45 paintings (Kisky).

In spite of adopting stylistic mannerisms and motifs, as a painter Woensam always preserved his own individuality. In *Mount Calvary* (*c.* 1540; Budapest, Mus. F.A.) he probably portrayed himself as the man between the thief on the left-hand side and the man on horseback with the lance. Especially noteworthy are his *Martyrdom of the Saints* (*Execution of the Theban Legion*) (*c.* 1520; Munich, Alte Pin.), his masterpiece *Death and Coronation of the Virgin, SS Cecilia and Valerian* (*c.* 1526/7), the *Holy Kinship* (?1530–35), perhaps made for the altar to the Holy Kinship in Worms, *Christ on the Cross with Saints from the Carthusian Order* (1530s), two altar wings of *St John the Evangelist* and *St Margaret* (1527–35; all Cologne, Wallraf Richartz-Mus.). His three-part altarpiece of the *Holy Kinship* (before 1540; Worms, Ksthaus Heylshof) is a textbook example of his stylistic combination of Old Cologne painting and Dutch Mannerism from Antwerp. Whether these three panels and the closely associated *Holy Kinship* panel in Cologne originally formed one altar or were put together only in the 19th century must remain an open question, but they are very close in both style and iconography. A few works by other artists show the influence of Woensam's painting (e.g. *Annunciation of the Birth of the Virgin to Anna*, 1524/5; Cologne, Wallraf-Richartz-Mus.) but it is not really possible to talk of a school of followers where his painting is concerned. Various designs for glass painting have also been attributed to him, but only the panel depicting *St Catherine with Donors* (*c.* 1534; Cologne, Kstgewmus.) can be regarded as authenticated.

Woensam produced many woodcut illustrations for printed books, including work for Johann Gymnicus (*c.* 1480–1544) from 1518 and for Eucharius Cervicornus (Eucharius Hirschhorn; *d c.* 1547) from 1527. The well-known *View of Cologne* (1531; Cologne, Stadtmus.; *see* COLOGNE, fig. 3) presented to the Holy Roman Emperor Charles V when he entered the town in January 1531 was made for the book printer Quentel. In 1538 Woensam produced a woodcut portrait of the *Holy Roman Emperor Charles V Seated on his Throne* (see fig.) for a title-page.

Anton Woensam: *Holy Roman Emperor Charles V Seated on his Throne*, woodcut, 246×209 mm (Stuttgart, Staatsgalerie); from *Concilia omnia, tam generalia, quam particularia, ab apostolorum temporibus in huc usque diem a sanctissimis patribus celebrata . . .*, i (Cologne, 1538)

In his subject-matter Woensam was in the Christian tradition of the Middle Ages, and there is also some satirical material. He signed the woodcuts with his initials AW combined in a monogram. Eighteen are included in *The Illustrated Bartsch* (Strauss, 1981): *Adam and Eve* (B. 1 [489]), *Samson and Delilah* (B. 2 [489]), *David and Goliath* (1529; B. 3 [489]), the *Adoration of the Magi* (1529; B. 4 [489]), the *Rest on the Flight into Egypt* (1529; B. 5 [490]), *Christ and the Children* (B. 6 [490]) and from the *Passion of Christ* (1530): the *Agony in the Garden*, the *Betrayal of Christ*, *Christ before Caiaphas*, *Christ before Pilate*, *Christ before Herod*, *Christ Tormented by his Captors*, the *Flagellation*, the *Crown of Thorns* and the *Ecce homo* (B. 7A-I [490]), *SS John the Evangelist and James the Greater* (B. 8 [490]), *St Bartholomew Standing and St Philip Drinking from a Fountain* (B. 9 [491]) and *Two Soldiers Playing Cards, Another Soldier and a Woman Drinking a Glass of Wine* (1529; B. 10 [491]). The print collection in the Staatsgalerie, Stuttgart, also has a series of woodcuts from books by Woensam. His real importance as an artist lay in his woodcuts and for about 50 years his works, which were often imitated and copied, had a decisive impact on book decoration in Cologne.

BIBLIOGRAPHY

Thieme–Becker

J. J. Merlo: *Anton Woensam von Worms, Maler und Xylograph zu Köln. Sein Leben und seine Werke: Eine kunstgeschichtliche Monographie* (Leipzig, 1864)

J. J. Merlo and E. Firmenich Richartz: *Kölnische Künstler in alter und neuer Zeit* (Cologne, 1895/R Nieeuwkoop, 1966), pp. 971–1099

H. Kisky: *Anton Woensam von Worms als Maler* (diss., Cologne, 1945)

W. L. Strauss: *Sixteenth-century German artists*, 13 [VII/iv] of *The Illustrated Bartsch*, ed. W. L. Strauss (New York, 1981), pp. 189–206 [B.]

F. G. Zehnder: *Katalog der Altkölner Malerei* (Cologne, 1990), pp. 550–63

W. Schenkluhm and others: *Stiftung Kunsthaus Heylshof [Worms]: Kritischer Katalog der Gemäldesammlung* (Worms, 1992), pp. 81–7, nos 3–5

ANDREAS STOLZENBURG

Woestyne, Gustave van de. *See* VAN DE WOESTYNE, GUSTAVE.

Wohlert, Vilhelm. *See under* BO & WOHLERT.

Wohlmut, Bonifaz. *See* WOLMUT, BONIFAZ.

Wojniakowski, Kazimierz (*b* Kraków, 1772; *d* Warsaw, 20 Jan 1812). Polish painter. He began to study painting in Kraków under one of the local guild master craftsmen. From about 1790, thanks to the protection of Father Sebastian Sierakowski, a Kraków canon and amateur architect, he studied in the studio of Marcello Bacciarelli in Warsaw. In 1794 he took part in the Kościuszko Uprising, whose purpose was to gain Poland's independence from the partitioning powers; after it was crushed he stayed in Puławy for about two years as a court painter of the Czartoryski princes. In 1797–8 Wojniakowski lived in the province of Wołyń, and thereafter in Warsaw. During the last years of his life he worked for the Polish painter Józef Kosiński (1753–1821). As a result of his unsteady character and bohemian existence, Wojniakowski never attained the rewards and social status commensurate with his talents and he died in poverty. He painted genre scenes with landscaped backgrounds in the early Neo-classicist manner, influenced to some extent by the Rococo tradition. He also painted religious pictures, as well as scenes connected with the political life of Warsaw and the Kościuszko Uprising (e.g. the *Constitution of 3 May 1791*; 1806; Warsaw, N. Mus.). However, he specialized in portraits, in which he displayed great skill in conveying the physiognomical and psychological characteristics of the model, as in the portraits of *General Józef Kossakowski* (1794; Kraków, N. Mus.) and *Izabela Czartoryska* (1796; Kraków, Czartoryski Col.). The classicism of these portraits is not based on the attributes they derived from antiquity, but rather on their exquisite, clear line drawing and their restrained and subtle use of colour, which was often reminiscent of the paintings of David. The best collection of Wojniakowski's work is at the National Museum in Warsaw.

BIBLIOGRAPHY

E. Rastawiecki: *Słownik malarzów polskich* [Dictionary of Polish painters], iii (Warsaw, 1857), pp. 61–6

T. Dobrowolski: *Nowoczesne Malarstwo polskie, I* (Wroclaw, 1957), pp. 110–16

K. Sroczyńska, ed.: *La Peinture polonaise du XVIe au début du XXe siècle*, Warsaw, N. Mus. (Warsaw, 1979), pp. 400–404

JAN K. OSTROWSKI

Wojtkiewicz, Witold (*b* Warsaw, 29 Dec 1879; *d* Warsaw, 14 June 1909). Polish painter. His unsystematic training began in 1898 at the Warsaw Drawing School and continued at the Academy of Fine Arts in Kraków (1903–6). He anticipated Polish Expressionism and was one of the most intriguing and inventive artists of the period. An ironic sense and the grotesque motifs in his works bear a similarity to James Ensor's art. The roots of Wojtkiewicz's art, however, are local. He admired the modernist paintings of Stanisław Wyspiański and Jacek Malczewski, and he held aesthetic ideas similar to those of the Romantic poet and painter Cyprian Kamil Norwid (1821–83) and of Stanisław Przybyszewski (1868–1927) and Edward Abramowski, the authors of Expressionist manifestos. He began his short career as an illustrator and postcard designer. His first known work, a watercolour entitled *Spring Is Approaching* (1900; Warsaw, N. Mus.), already shows tragic irony, depicting dead birds on snow-covered ground. After 1905 he exhibited with the 'Group of Five', also known as 'Norwid's Group'. During their exhibition at the Galerie Schulte in Berlin (1907) Wojtkiewicz's 'strange harmony of tones, painful fantasy of drawing, pathetic and moving game of colours' caught the eye of André Gide, who invited him to Paris and organized his one-man show at the Galerie Druet. Wojtkiewicz's later works (series entitled *Monomanias*, *Circuses* and *Ceremonies*) include oil and distemper paintings, watercolours, drawings and lithographs that explore the world of madness (e.g. *Circus of Madmen*, 1906) and the melancholic poetry of fairy tales (e.g. the *Rape of a Princess*, 1908; both Warsaw, N. Mus.).

BIBLIOGRAPHY

W. Juszczak: *Wojtkiewicz i nowa sztuka* [Wojtkiewicz and the new art] (Warsaw, 1965)

Witold Wojtkiewicz, 1879–1909 (exh. cat., ed. Z. Gołubiewowa; Kraków, N. Mus., 1976)

ANNA BENTKOWSKA

Wolf, Caspar (*b* Muri im Aargau, *bapt* 3 May 1735; *d* Heidelberg, 6 Oct 1783). Swiss painter and draughtsman. His Alpine canvases and studies are the most important achievements of 18th-century Swiss landscape painting. Coming from a family of cabinet makers in the village of Muri, he went to Konstanz in 1749 to study under Johann Jakob Anton von Lenz (1701–64), the episcopal court painter. From this period date four figure studies in a sketchbook (1751; Basle, priv. col., see 1980 exh. cat., no. 1). Wolf then worked as an itinerant painter in South Germany (?1753–9), being recorded in Augsburg, Munich and Passau. In 1760 he was back in Muri, painting landscapes, altarpieces and decorations on wallpaper and stoves, notably the *Landscapes with Biblical Stories and Parables*, the *Episodes from the History of the Habsburgs*, and the *Legend of St Benedict* (1762–3) on the wallpaper and panels of two rooms of the Schloss Horben near Muri. Predominant among the paintings and drawings of the 1760s were landscapes with wild rock formations, clearly showing his training in South German Rococo.

Wolf painted landscapes and overdoors in Basle in 1768–9, and then went to Paris with a letter of introduction to Philippe Jacques de Loutherbourg. During his two years in Loutherbourg's studio, moving in French landscape painting circles, Wolf became familiar with the new value placed on mountain landscapes and with the expression of the forces of nature in pictures of sea-storms. He probably also developed the practice of making oil sketches from nature. The *Landscape with Towering Rocks, Waterfall and Women Bathing* (1770; Montpellier, Mus. Fabre) dates

from this period. In 1772, back in Muri, Wolf supplied the Lucerne collector Joseph Anton Felix Balthasar (1737–1810) with paintings of sea-storms and landscapes with rocks and trees. He made a first sketching tour of the Alps in 1773. This was followed by an order from the Berne publisher Abraham Wagner (1734–82) for a series of probably 200 paintings of Alpine landscapes. Based from 1774 in Berne, Wolf made regular excursions to the mountains until 1778, producing sketches from nature in pencil and oils on card as studies for later studio canvases such as *Snow Bridge and Rainbow on the Gadmental* (1778; Basle, Kstmus.; see fig.). These paintings were publicly exhibited by Wagner in his gallery in Berne but were not for sale; they provided the originals for the series of prints *Merkwürdigen Prospekte aus den Schweizer Gebürgen* (Berne, 1776), followed by the *Alpes Helveticae* (Berne, 1777–8). Wolf appears also, however, to have prepared replicas on his own account of the gallery pictures to order in oils, gouache or watercolour. In April 1777 Wolf went to Solothurn, where he produced fantasy landscapes, paintings of the Juras and Lake Geneva, and two series of prints, *Schlösserfolge* ('castles series'; Raeber, pp. 345–6) and *Trachtenfolge* ('costume series'; Raeber, pp. 347–8).

In late November 1779 Wagner moved the Alpine collection to Paris, and there brought out a French edition of the *Merkwürdigen Prospekte* (*Vues remarquables des montagnes de la Suisse*, Paris, 1780–81) with coloured

Caspar Wolf: *Snow Bridge and Rainbow on the Gadmental*, oil on canvas, 820×540 mm, 1778 (Basle, Kunstmuseum)

aquatints by Jean-François Janinet under the direction of Joseph Vernet. Wolf exhibited the paintings themselves in a one-man show in Paris from March to May 1780. From Paris he went to Spa in Belgium, where he hoped to find clients, then spent the autumn and winter of 1780–81 in Aachen, evidently occupied with landscapes for local landowners such as the drawing *Panorama of the Landscape of Aachen* (Aachen, Stadtarchv). From early summer to autumn 1781 he was working in Cologne, Düsseldorf and Bensberg. The *View over Bensberg with the Neues Schloss* (pencil and watercolour, 1781; Basle, Kstmus.) was perhaps intended for never-completed illustrations to the *Architecture Palatinale* of Nicolas de Pigage. Besides these late pictures of lowlands and castles, both evoking Dutch models and revealing incipient Romanticism, Wolf still painted, even in the Rhineland, watercolours of Swiss Alpine landscapes. Eighty such views were exhibited in the Kurfürstliche Galerie in Düsseldorf in 1781. The period 1781–2, during which dated drawings stopped, is linked by the type of production with a third stay in Paris. Wolf's last extant works are drawings (1782–3; Basle, Kstmus.) of the castle grounds of Schwetzingen, laid out by Nicolas de Pigage.

Wolf in his Alpine work, at once topographically authentic and keenly appreciative of the forces of nature, produced highly convincing pre-Romantic landscapes without departing from the thinly stretched paintwork typical of his century. He loved painting water, in all its forms from the gushing waterfall to the blue-green ice-fall of the glacier; the green mantle of vegetation; and above all rocks, which would sometimes fill the whole picture. They are rendered with a deep insight into geological form that is already Romantic in effect, while his sense of space retains a Rococo instability. A key to Wolf's sense of the world lies in the remarkably frequent pictures of caves, such as the *Interior of the Bear Cave near Welschenrohr* (1778; Solothurn, Kstmus.). Many of the Alpine works are in Swiss private collections and museums (e.g. Aarau, Aargau. Ksthaus; Basle, Kstmus.; Winterthur, Stift. Oskar Reinhart; Zurich, Ksthaus and Schweiz. Landesmus.; etc).

PRINTS

Merkwürdigen Prospekte aus den Schweizer Gebürgen (Berne, 1776/R 1777); 1st Fr. edn as *Vues remarquables des montagnes de la Suisse* (Paris, 1780–81); 2nd Fr. edn R. S. Henzi (Amsterdam, 1785) [partly reworked by Charles Melchior Descourtis (1753–1820), also incl. works by other artists]

Alpes Helveticae (Berne, 1777–8)

BIBLIOGRAPHY

E. Spohr: *Düsseldorf: Stadt und Festung* (Düsseldorf, 1978), pp. 298, 306, 561, nos 194, 196

W. Raeber: *Caspar Wolf, 1735–1783: Sein Leben und sein Werk*, 7 of *Schweizerisches Institut für Kunstwissenschaft, Oeuvrekataloge Schweizer Künstler* (Aarau, Frankfurt am Main, Salzburg and Munich, 1979); review by B. Weber in *Kunstchronik*, xxxiii (1980), pp. 259–69

Caspar Wolf (1735–1783): Landschaft im Vorfeld der Romantik (exh. cat., ed. Y. Boerlin-Brodbeck; Basle, Kstmus., 1980)

Y. Boerlin-Brodbeck: 'Caspar Wolfs Solothurner Jahre', *Jurablätter*, xliii (1981), pp. 53–60

U. Haldi: 'Caspar Wolf (1735–1783)', *Gal. Stuker Bl.*, v (1981), pp. 2–7

Y. Boerlin-Brodbeck: 'Zur Präsenz der Schweiz in Pariser Ausstellungen des 18. und frühen 19. Jahrhunderts', *Z. Schweiz. Archäol. & Kstgesch.*, xliii (1986), pp. 353–61

Y. BOERLIN-BRODBECK

Wolf, Reinhart (*b* Berlin, 1 Aug 1930). German photographer. He studied art history and literature in Paris, Hamburg and the USA. Influenced by his encounter with American photography, he studied at the Bayerische Staatslehranstalt für Lichtbildwesen (until 1956). He then became an independent photographer in Hamburg, teaching at the Staatliche Meisterschule für Mode Photographie and setting up a studio-house in 1969. During this period he became interested in architectural photography and developed an unusual and independent way of taking 'portraits' of houses (exhibited as *Gesichter von Gebäuden*, at Photokina, Cologne, 1976), which made his reputation.

PHOTOGRAPHIC PUBLICATIONS

Sensitivity for Sale (Hannover, 1973)

Gesichter von Gebäuden (Bremen, 1980)

New York (Hamburg, 1980)

Castillos: Burgen in Spanien (Munich, 1983)

BIBLIOGRAPHY

8 deutsche Photographen (exh. cat., Cologne, Josef-Haubrich-Ksthalle, 1976), pp. 112–5, 125

Zeitprofile (Cologne, Mus. Ludwig, 1988), pp. 168–73

REINHOLD MISSELBECK

Wolfe, Ivor de. *See* HASTINGS, HUBERT DE CRONIN.

Wolfenbüttel. German town in Lower Saxony, with a population of 55,000. From 1432 to 1754 it was the sole residence and seat of government of the dukes of Brunswick–Lüneburg–Wolfenbüttel, during which time it was the cultural centre of Lower Saxony, chiefly significant for its ducal library, originally founded in 1572 by Julius, Duke of Brunswick-Wolfenbüttel (*reg* 1568–89). Wolfenbüttel was the first planned Renaissance town in Germany, and its design was influenced by the theories of HANS VREDEMAN DE VRIES. It included a castle complex, princely administrative buildings, the houses of court officials and bourgeois residential districts. A rare, unified series of half-timbered buildings of the 16th and 17th centuries can also be seen here.

A castle was first documented in Wolfenbüttel in 1188; this was destroyed in 1255, and in 1283 the Wasserburg was built as a residence for the dukes of Brunswick and Lüneburg. Destruction in 1542 caused by the Schmalkaldic War prompted the restoration of the town from 1547 by Henry II, Duke of Brunswick–Wolfenbüttel (*reg* 1514–68) (for discussion and illustration *see* WELF, House of). Out of the Wasserburg developed the ducal Schloss (1556–9) by Francesco Chiarimalla (*fl* 1552–78) and, from 1569, PAUL FRANCKE, who added the tower (1614); a south wing and new façades were later (1714–16) built by Hermann Korb. The Kirche Beatae Mariae Virginis (or Marienkirche), which towers impressively over the old town, was one of the first important church buildings of the Protestant period. Planned by Francke from 1604 and built 1608–*c.* 1626, it is an eclectic mixture of Late Gothic, Renaissance and Baroque, with a richly furnished interior influenced by Gothic hall churches. Members of the ducal house were interred here from the 16th century until 1750; Michael Praetorius (1571–1621) is also buried here. The Trinitatiskirche (1716–22) by HERMANN KORB is on the site of an earlier church (1693–1700; destr. 1705) by JOHANN BALTHASAR LAUTERBACH. It is one of the few Baroque churches in the area and has a galleried interior and a long façade of five bays plus corner towers.

Augustus, Duke of Brunswick–Lüneburg–Wolfenbüttel, played a decisive role in the town's development during the Baroque period. He was an avid collector of books (for further discussion see WELF, (3)); at his death his collection, the Bibliotheca Augusta (now Herzog August Bibliothek), held 135,000 items and was the largest contemporary library in Europe. From 1690 until his death the philosopher and mathematician Gottfried Wilhelm von Leibniz (1646–1716) was director of the library. He produced its first alphabetical catalogue, compiled from Duke Augustus's own manuscript catalogues, which were categorized according to subject. Leibniz also persuaded Anton Ulrich, Duke of Brunswick–Wolfenbüttel (see WELF, (5)), to erect a new library building (1706–13). Built by Korb, it had a galleried oval of four storeys set in a rectangular building, providing the model for a number of later library buildings. It was dismantled in 1887 after a new library (1882–6) had been built.

In 1754 the ducal residence was permanently established in Brunswick. The library, however, remained in Wolfenbüttel and, in 1770, entered a significant phase with the appointment of Gotthold Ephraim Lessing as librarian. Lessing remained in Wolfenbüttel until his death in 1781. Lack of funds prevented him from adding significantly to the library's holdings, but he was able through his publications to bring its valuable contents to wider recognition. The library currently holds 415,000 books printed before 1850 and 12,000 manuscripts (see fig.), 3000 of which date from between the early Middle Ages and the Renaissance. It is an important research institute for all aspects of Baroque culture. It also holds an important collection of 20th-century artists' books. Nearby are the Lessinghaus (1735; now a museum) and the Zeughaus (1613; see WELF, fig. 1), possibly by Francke.

Other important cultural institutions in Wolfenbüttel are the Niedersächsisches Staatsarchiv, the Braunschweigisches Landesmuseum and the Bundesakademie für Kulturelle Bildung.

Near Wolfenbüttel was Salzdahlum, an ambitious country estate with a large Schloss, erected in 1688–94 by JOHANN BALTHASAR LAUTERBACH and completed (1714) by Korb. It was built as a summer residence for Duke Anton Ulrich (for further discussion and illustration see WELF, (5)) but was demolished in 1812–13.

BIBLIOGRAPHY

G. E. Lessing: Zur Geschichte der Literatur aus den Schätzen des herzöglichen Bibliothek zu Wolfenbüttel, 6 vols (Brunswick, 1773–81)

F. Thöne: Wolfenbüttel: Geist und Glanz einer alten Residenz (Munich, 1963)

I. Recker-Kotulla: 'Zur Baugeschichte der Herzog August Bibliothek in Wolfenbüttel', Wolfenbüttel. Beitr., vi (1983), pp. 1–73

H. Möller, ed.: Die Hauptkirche Beatae Mariae Virginis in Wolfenbüttel (Hannover, 1987)

G. Ruppelt and S. Solf, eds: Lexicon zur Geschichte und Gegenwart der Herzog August Bibliothek Wolfenbüttel (Wolfenbüttel, 1992)

GEORG RUPPELT

Wolfers, Philippe (b Brussels, 16 April 1858; d Brussels, 13 Dec 1929). Belgian jeweller, designer and sculptor. The son of the master goldsmith Louis Wolfers (1820–92), he graduated from the Académie des Beaux-Arts in Brussels in 1875 and entered his father's workshop as an apprentice, where he acquired a comprehensive technical training.

Coronation of Henry the Lion and his Wife with the Crown of Eternal Life; miniature from the Gospels of Henry the Lion, c. 1185–8 (Wolfenbüttel, Herzog August Bibliothek, Cod. Guelf. 105 noviss. 2°, fol. 171v)

Influenced by the Rococo Revival and Japanese art, in the 1880s he created sensitively curved pieces in gold and silver decorated with asymmetrically distributed floral motifs, which heralded the Art Nouveau style (e.g. ewer, Le Maraudeur, c. 1880; Brussels, Musées Royaux A. & Hist.). After 1890 he produced two kinds of work: goldsmithing and jewellery designs for production by Wolfers Frères and one-off pieces that were produced to his own designs in the workshop that he had established c. 1890–92. Typical of the latter are Art Nouveau goldsmiths' work and jewellery (e.g. orchid hair ornament, 1902; London, V&A), crystal vases carved into cameos and ivory pieces. Ivory was then in plentiful supply from the Congo, and from 1893 Wolfers used it to make unusual pieces with such evocative titles as Stroking a Swan (an ivory and bronze vase with marble base, 1897; Musées Royaux A. & Hist.) and Civilisation and Barbarism (a work combining ivory, silver and marble, 1897; untraced). His creations were well received at the Exposition Internationale in Antwerp (1894) and at the Exposition Internationale in Brussels (1897). Encouraged by this success he committed Wolfers Frères to the Art Nouveau style. He exhibited at the Munich Secession (1898, 1899) and in 1900 showed an important collection of his jewellery at the Paris Salon. In 1902 he exhibited one of his most astonishing creations at the Esposizione Internazionale d'Arte Decorativa in Turin: Fairy with Peacock (untraced;

drawing, priv. col.), an electric lamp in the form of a nude ivory figure surrounded by enamelled metal peacock feathers set with precious stones.

As the fashion for Art Nouveau waned, he became less interested in jewellery and devoted himself to sculpture in precious materials, enriched with enamel, hardstones and precious stones (e.g. *Young Girl with Peacock*, 1904). In the 1920s Wolfers tried to give a new direction to goldsmithing by using austere, geometrical functional forms that could be adapted to machine production. He also created a distinctive style of interior decoration with the *Gioconda* ensemble for the Palais de la Belgique in the Exposition Universelle des Arts Décoratifs et Industriels Modernes in Paris (1925): the décor, furniture, carpets, table linen, silver and glass were all based on the theme of contrasting polygons, resulting in a series of stepped triangles (*see* BELGIUM, fig. 43).

See also BELGIUM, §IX, 1(iii).

BIBLIOGRAPHY

S. T. Madsen: *Sources of Art Nouveau* (New York and Oslo, 1956), pp. 336–42

M. Wolfers: *Philippe Wolfers: Précurseur de l'Art Nouveau*, Monographies de l'art belge (Brussels, 1965)

H. Meurrens: *Philippe Wolfers (1858–1929): Précurseur de l'Art Nouveau statuaire* (Brussels, 1972)

Philippe Wolfers juwelen, zilver, ivoor, kristal (1858–1929) (exh. cat., ed. L. Daenens; Ghent, Mus. Sierkst, 1979)

S. Henrion-Giele and J. Schotsmans-Wolfers: 'Wolfers, Phillippe', *La Sculpture belge au 19e siècle* (exh. cat., ed. J. van Lennep; Brussels, Gén. de Banque, 1990), pp. 616–18

Philippe et Marcel Wolfers: De l'Art Nouveau à l'Art Déco (exh. cat., Brussels, Musées Royaux A. & Hist., 1992)

RICHARD KERREMANS

Wolff (i). German family of architect-masons. (1) Jakob Wolff I and his eldest son, (2) Jakob Wolff II, both helped to develop the late Renaissance style, particularly in Nuremberg, where their most important projects were undertaken for the city authorities. Jakob Wolff I's younger son (3) Hans Wolff was also active in Nuremberg, where he worked mainly with his brother.

(1) Jakob Wolff I (*b* Bamberg, 1546; *d* Nuremberg, before 17 July 1612). He is first mentioned in written sources after his marriage in 1571, and in 1572–95 he is listed as a mason in the accounts of the works office of Bamberg Cathedral, carrying out repair work for a fixed annual sum; new buildings cannot be attributed to him during this period. In 1596 Wolff signed plans for the upper school in Bamberg, founded in 1586, although it was not until 1611 that they were carried out by Thomas Müllauer. Also in 1596 he became municipal architect in Nuremberg, where he was immediately entrusted with rebuilding the Fleischbrücke, modelled on the Rialto Bridge, Venice, with his son (2) Jakob Wolff II and the carpenter Peter Carl. This was followed in 1599 by a commission for the 'Portal with the Ox' at Nuremberg's covered meat market. In 1601–5 Wolff was several times granted leave by Nuremberg Council to concentrate on rebuilding the north wing of the fortress of Marienberg, Würzburg, which had been destroyed by fire. Here the barracks, the Marienturm, the Kiliansturm, the Echtersche Vorburg and possibly certain parts of the Fürstenbau can be attributed to him. In 1602–7 the house of Martin Peller

Jakob Wolff I: Pellerhaus, Nuremberg, 1602–7; from a pre-World War II photograph (subsequently reconstructed with alterations)

in Nuremberg (see fig.) was built under his direction; it is the only building by Wolff to survive (partially rebuilt after damage in World War II). The plan, with a central hall, off which open symmetrically disposed rooms, reveals his desire to introduce order into a traditional type of structure. The multi-storey façade also shows a concern to achieve a clear articulation in bays and storeys by means of cornice strips and a correct use of the orders (Tuscan, Ionic, Corinthian and Composite above a plinth storey). The decorative gable in particular, untypical of Nuremberg, points with its rich embellishment to the influence of the Netherlandish Renaissance.

In 1604 Wolff received a commission to design the new residence, the Neue Hofhaltung (1608; both wings remodelled 1695), Bamberg, for Prince-Bishop Johann Philip von Gebsattel. In 1605 Wolff was granted the freedom of Nuremberg and in 1607, with his son Jakob II, he worked as a consultant on the rebuilding of Schloss Schwarzenberg in Franconia, where the municipal architect of Augsburg, Elias Holl I, was in charge of the work. Wolff's contribution to the plan cannot, however, be exactly determined (there were changes after the alterations of 1655–69). His last work was the ground floor of a private chapel, which projects on three sides from No. 1, Josephsplatz, Nuremberg.

(2) Jakob Wolff II (*b* Bamberg, ?1571; *d* Nuremberg, 25 Feb 1620). Son of (1) Jakob Wolff I. His first project, which he worked on with his father, was the Fleischbrücke (1596–8), Nuremberg; he later collaborated with his father on other projects, including the Neue Hofhaltung, Bamberg, and Schloss Schwarzenberg. In 1600 the city of Nuremberg paid him an allowance in order to ensure his exclusive services, even though he was not then a master. It also financed a study tour of one or two years through Germany and Italy. In 1605 he became an official in the city works department alongside his father. In 1609–13 he was involved in planning and building the palace and fountain near Sulzbürg (Upper Palatinate) and between 1610 and 1612 he worked on several occasions as a building inspector, at Eichstätt (1610 and 1611) and at Heidelberg (1612). He was then put in charge of the stonemasonry (1613–14) for the Wöhrdener Tor in Nuremberg, to plans by the engineer Meinhard von Schönberg. Among the few new buildings wholly designed by Wolff in Nuremberg is the Baumeisterhaus auf der Peunt (1614–15). The manner in which its articulation is restricted to a few elements such as bays, storeys, cornice strips and rustication in a single plane is striking, especially in comparison to his father's Pellerhaus, to which he added a chapel in 1616.

Also in 1616 Wolff began his main work, the remodelling of the Rathaus in Nuremberg (*see* NUREMBERG, §IV, 3 and fig. 9). The executed design retains the medieval hall, all parts of which are concealed behind a unified, three-storey façade above a plinth storey with three portal openings. There is a simple row of windows at first-floor level and another at the second, their importance emphasized by alternating segmental and triangular pediments. The layout, with four regular blocks arranged round an arcaded court, is based on Italian palace architecture. The upper-floor corridors, giving unrestricted access to the individual rooms, are a result of this influence. The tower-like pavilions rising above the cornice at the angles and in the middle of the façade, however, recall local palace architecture, for example Aschaffenburg. In 1619, after the neighbouring Schallerhaus had been demolished, the building was extended to the north. In 1622, two years after Wolff's death, work on the town hall ceased for financial reasons, with only two wings completed. A commemorative medallion (Nuremberg, Ger. Nmus.) and an engraving by Matthäus Merian (i) give an idea of the whole structure as planned.

(3) Hans Wolff (*fl* Nuremberg, 1612–22). Son of (1) Jakob Wolff I. After his father's death in 1612 he became a municipal master builder in Nuremberg, together with his brother, working not as a designing architect but as a mason. In this capacity he was responsible for the buildings of the Electors of Mainz in Aschaffenburg in 1612, and for the site workshop of the town hall in Nuremberg, on which he worked with his brother until 1620 and with the support of the mason Nicolaus Teufel (*fl* 1620–26) in 1620–22.

BIBLIOGRAPHY
E. Mummenhoff: *Das Rathaus in Nürnberg* (Nuremberg, 1891)
T. Hampe: *Nürnberger Ratsverlässe über Kunst und Künstler im Zeitalter der Gotik und der Renaissance* (Leipzig, 1904)
R. Schatter: *Das Pellerhaus in Nürnberg* (Nuremberg, 1932)
W. Tunk: 'Der Stilwandel um 1600 im Spiegel der Entstehungsgeschichte des Nürnberger Pellerhauses', *Kunstgeschichtliche Studien* (Breslau, 1940), pp. 291–314
——: 'Der Nürnberger Rathausbau des Jakob Wolff d.J.', *Z. Dt. Ver. Kstwiss.*, 9 (1942), pp. 53–90
M. Mende: *Das alte Nürnberger Rathaus* (Nuremberg, 1979)

STEPHAN ALBRECHT

Wolff [Wolf] **(ii).** *See* WULFF.

Wolff, (Carl Konrad) Albert (*b* Neustrelitz, 14 Nov 1814; *d* Berlin, 20 June 1892). German sculptor. The son of the Neustrelitz sculptor and master builder Christian Philipp Wolff (*b* 1772), he went to Berlin in 1831 to study at the Akademie and subsequently gained acceptance in the studio of the sculptor Christian Daniel Rauch, a friend of his father's. He worked in Rauch's studio for 15 years, helping with the execution of the bronze figure group of *Polish Princes* (1828–41; Poznań, Cathedral), the statues of *Victories* for Leo von Klenze's Valhalla in Munich (e.g. *Victory Throwing a Garland*, marble, 1841; Berlin, Staatl. Museen, N.G.), and the marble sarcophagus for *Queen Frederica of Hannover* (1841–7; *in situ*) in the Herrenhausen, Hannover. Among Wolff's first independent works was a bronze figure of a girl with a lamb, known as *Innocence* (1836; Berlin, Berlin Mus.). On commission from Count Edward Raczyński, Wolff produced the over life-size seated figure of Countess Constantia Potocka Raczyński as *Hygieia* (bronze, 1840–41; *in situ*, Plac Wolność) for the Priessnitz Fountain in Poznań. In 1844–5, Wolff was in Italy (mainly Rome and Carrara), where he executed the charming Children's Fountain, intended for Sanssouci (marble replica, 1844–9; Neustrelitz, Stadtpark).

Wolff's principal works, produced mostly in his own studio after his return from Italy, included the classicizing marble group for the Schlossbrücke in Berlin, *Pallas Leads the Warrior into Battle* (1842–53; Berlin, Bodemus.), and the monumental *Man Fighting a Lion* (zinc, 1849–61) for the entrance staircase of the Altes Museum (*in situ*), Berlin, as a pendant to the bronze *Mounted Amazon Fighting a Panther* (1837–41) by August Karl Eduard Kiss. Large-scale dynastic monuments brought Wolff fame, among them the large bronze equestrian monument to *King Ernst August* (bronze, 1860; Hannover, Bahnhofsvorplatz) and the equestrian monument to *Frederick William III* in the former Berlin Lustgarten, with ten over life-size figures on the base (bronze, 1862–70; destr., see von Simson, pls 67–9). Wolff also produced monumental bronze figure sculptures, for example of *Frederick-Franz I of Mecklenburg-Schwerin* (1865–9; Ludwigslust Schloss, forecourt), and numerous busts and portrait reliefs, for example of members of the Strelitz ruling family, such as *Empress Augusta* (marble, 1873; untraced, see von Simson, pl. 113), and eminent scholars, such as *Karl Ritter* (marble, 1862; Berlin, Humboldt U. Geog. Inst.). He also sculpted individual figures and groups in marble, including *Dionysus with Eros and a Panther* (1876–84; destr., see von Simson, pls 146–9 and 152–5) for the Berlin Nationalgalerie, and a relief in bronze of the *Triumphal Entry of the Troops after the Franco-Prussian War* (1871–3; Paris, Mus. Armée) for the base of the Berlin Siegessäule (Victory column). The monumental bronze group of a *Lion Defending its Young against a Giant Snake* was erected in front of the criminal court in the Moabit district of Berlin in 1895, after Wolff's death.

Wolff contributed sculptures for several important architectural schemes, his designs being fired in sandstone-coloured terracotta at Ernst March's ceramics factory, opened in 1836. Wolff provided figures (1862; *in situ*) for the façade of the main building of the Academy of Sciences, Budapest, and a figure group of Greek gods (1878–82; *in situ*), reminiscent of Classical sculptures, for the pediment of the Schwerin Staatliches Museum. From 1866 until almost the end of his life, Wolff was Professor of Sculpture at the Berlin Akademie. His pupils included Erdmann Encke, Otto Lessing and Ernst Herter.

BIBLIOGRAPHY

Thieme–Becker

P. Bloch and W. Grzimek: *Das klassische Berlin: Die Berliner Bildhauerschule im 19. Jahrhundert* (Frankfurt am Main, Berlin and Vienna, 1978)

J. von Simson: *Der Bildhauer Albert Wolff, 1814–1892* (Berlin, 1982)

Ethos und Pathos: Die Berliner Bildhauerschule, 1786–1914 (exh. cat., ed. P. Bloch, S. Einholz and J. von Simson; Berlin, Hamburg. Bahnhof, 1990), p. 349ff

Wolff, Emil (*b* Berlin, 2 March 1802; *d* Rome, 29 Sept 1879). German sculptor. A nephew of Johann Gottfried Schadow (*see* SCHADOW, (1)), from 1815 he studied at the Akademie in Berlin and from 1818 in Schadow's studio there. In 1822 he went to Rome, where he was based for the rest of his life, and took over the studio that Christian Daniel Rauch had passed on to Ridolfo Schadow. In collaboration with Bertel Thorvaldsen and under his influence, Wolff completed the marble group of *Achilles and Penthesilea* (Berlin, Staatl. Museen, Neue N.G.) which had been left unfinished by Schadow, for whom he also produced a funerary monument (1823; Rome, S Andrea delle Fratte). Through his contact with German archaeologists and with Rauch in Berlin, Wolff was able to arrange purchases of antiquities for the Prussian royal collections. In 1836, at his own expense, he provided the terracotta pediment of the newly built Archaeologisches Institut in Rome, for which he also produced numerous portrait busts, including those of *Johann Joachim Winckelmann*, *Carlo Fea* and *Carl Niebuhr*. On commission from Ludwig I of Bavaria, he sculpted the colossal marble bust of *Winckelmann* for the Villa Albani (*in situ*).

From the late 1820s, following in the tradition established by Ridolfo Schadow, Wolff produced a series of more lyrical works, marked by sentimentality but proving popular with collectors in Berlin and Potsdam. These include figures of children as allegories of the seasons, for example *Winter* (marble, *c.* 1840; priv. col., see Bloch and Grzimek), and mythological figures (e.g. *Eros*, marble, 1836; Berlin, Staatl. Museen, Neue N.G.). For Karl Friedrich Schinkel's Schlossbrücke (1822–4) in Berlin, Wolff produced the marble group *Nike Telling Boys Tales of Heroes* (1847; *in situ*). After Thorvaldsen's death, Wolff became the busiest sculptor in Rome after Pietro Tenerani. From 1871 he was President of the Accademia di San Luca in Rome.

BIBLIOGRAPHY

Thieme–Becker

J. G. Schadow: *Kunst-Werke und Kunst-Ansichten* (Berlin, 1849, rev. ed. G. Eckardt, 1987)

Johann Gottfried Schadow (exh. cat., E. Berlin, N.G., 1964–5)

P. Springer: 'Thorvaldsen und die Bildhauer der Berliner Schule in Rom', *Bertel Thorvaldsen: Untersuchungen zu seinem Werk und zur Kunst seiner Zeit*, ed. G. Bott (Cologne, 1977), pp. 256–8

P. Bloch and W. Grzimek: *Das klassische Berlin: Die Berliner Bildhauerschule im 19. Jahrhundert* (Frankfurt am Main, Berlin and Vienna, 1978), pp. 62–5

Ethos und Pathos: Die Berliner Bildhauerschule, 1786–1914 (exh. cat., ed. P. Bloch, S. Einholz and J. von Simson; Berlin, Hamburg. Bahnhof, 1990)

D. Vogel: *Emil Wolff* (diss., U. Berlin, 1994)

JUTTA VON SIMSON

Wolff, Gustav H(einrich) (*b* Zittau, 24 May 1886; *d* Berlin, 22 March 1934). German sculptor and printmaker. After experimenting with painting, from 1920 he worked as a sculptor. His severely simplified, compact, archaistic sculptures stand alone in the artistic development of the period. He applied himself intensively, working with a variety of sculpting materials, including bronze, wood and stone (e.g. the monumental *Chimneypiece Figures*, limestone, h. 2.12 m, 1925; Hamburg, Ksthalle). His woodcuts are closely linked to his wooden sculptures; as well as figurative works, there are some woodcuts of script. Several of Wolff's works were seized by the Nazis as degenerate. Wolff's main champion was Max Sauerlandt, the director of the Museum für Kunst und Gewerbe in Hamburg, where an important selection of his works is housed, including the succinct portrait of the poet *Gottfried Benn* (1927).

BIBLIOGRAPHY

G. H. Wolff (exh. cat., foreword M. Sauerlandt; Berlin, Gal. Flechtheim, 1930)

A. Holthusen: *Gustav H. Wolff: Das plastische und graphische Werk* (Hamburg, 1964)

Gustav H. Wolff (exh. cat., Bielefeld, Städt. Ksthalle, 1971)

Gustav Heinrich Wolff (exh. cat., Friedrichshafen, Städt. Bodensee-Mus., 1984)

URSEL BERGER

Wolff [Wolf], Johann Andreas (*b* Munich, 11 Dec 1652; *d* Munich, 9 April 1716). German painter. Apprenticed to his father, the painter Jonas Wolff (*fl* 1651–80), and to Balthasar Ableither (1613–1705), he was initially influenced by Johann Heinrich Schönfeld and Johann Carl Loth. He then turned towards Italian High Baroque painting, although he is not known to have travelled to Italy. In 1680 he was appointed court painter to Maximilian II Emanuel, Elector of Bavaria in Munich, and to the Bishop of Freising. He painted mainly altarpieces, all over Bavaria and Upper Austria, but also accepted commissions for decorative work (triumphal arches etc.) and designs for sculptures. The work of this earlier period is exemplified by the *Assumption of the Virgin* (1691; Indersdorf, Klosterkirche St Maria), much in the style of Federico Barocci.

By 1693 Wolff had almost freed himself of the 'foreign manner'. In his 'high period', 1693–1708 (Waagen), his works are balanced: the figures have a markedly three-dimensional quality, for instance in the ceiling pictures (1693; mostly destr.) in the Munich Residenz. The signed drawing *Alexander the Great Donning Persian Garb* (Augsburg, Städt. Kstsamml.), shows the preparation that went into this manner. This period contained works in a dramatic mode, notably the *Assumption of Mary Magdalene* (1702; Diessen, Klosterkirche), chosen by Wolff himself as his masterpiece, as well as formal and sentimental productions. The major work of the succeeding 'picturesque style', with its gentler quality, flatter modelling and smaller groupings, is the monumental *Transfiguration* altarpiece (1712; Kremsmünster, Stiftskirche) which refers back to Raphael's treatment of the theme.

Wolff's late period (1709–16) is marked by mellow calm and the replacement of bright local colours by gentle tones. He maintained his role as court painter, working with the architect Giovanni Antonio Viscardi on the Bürgersaalkirche, Munich (1709–11; destr. 1944 but rest.). Bartholomäus Kilian II and Georg Christoph Kilian made engravings based on Wolff's works.

BIBLIOGRAPHY

Hollstein: *Ger.*; Thieme–Becker
A. Feulner: *Die Sammlung S. Röhrer im Besitz der Stadt Augsburg* (Augsburg, 1926), no. 316
L. Waagen: *Johann Andreas Wolff, 1652–1716* (Günzburg, 1932) [comprehensive inv.]
K. Schlichtenmaier: *Studien zum Münchener Hofmaler Johann Andrea Wolff (1652–1716) unter besonderer Berücksichtigung seiner Handzeichnungen* (diss., Tübingen, Eberhard-Karls-U., 1983) [incl. cat.]
Meisterzeichnungen des deutschen Barock (exh. cat. by R. Biedermann, Augsburg, Zeughaus, 1987), nos 87–9

BERNT VON HAGEN

Wolff, Johann Caspar (*b* Zurich, 28 Sept 1818; *d* Zurich, 27 April 1891). Swiss architect and writer. He trained (1833–6) with Hans Rychner in Neuenburg and then attended the Akademie der Bildenden Künste (1836–40), Munich. In 1841 he published an extensive guidebook to architecture for both specialist and lay readers, entitled *Der Baufreund*. He worked as a building administrator in Zofingen (1843–50) and as state building inspector to the Canton of Zurich (1851–65). The majority of Wolff's works were functional public buildings of block form and classical style, such as a school (1851–4) at Wohlen, the prison (1852–4) at Winterthur and the Burghölzli sanatorium (1864–70) at Zurich. His few religious buildings were Neo-classical, such as the Calvinist church (1851–4) at Wohlen, or were in historicist styles, such as the Gothic Revival Calvinist church (1854–5) at Töss, or the In Rein parish church (1863–4) at Rüfenach, which combines various historical styles. After the fire at Glarus in 1861, Wolff and Bernhard Simon drew up a plan for rebuilding the town, one of the most important new urban plans conceived in Switzerland in the 19th century. Wolff's major works had a functional emphasis and simple details, evident, for example, in alterations to the Rathaus (1867–8) at Rapperswil and in his churches. He also designed fortifications, for example at Bellinzona (1853–4).

WRITINGS

Der Baufreund (n.p., 1841)

BIBLIOGRAPHY

SKL
A. Meyer: *Neugotik und Neuromanik in der Schweiz* (Zurich, 1973)

CORNELIA BAUER

Wölfflin, Heinrich (*b* Winterthur, 24 June 1864; *d* Zurich, 19 July 1945). Swiss art historian. Starting as a student of philosophy he turned to art history under the influence of Jakob Burckhardt's teaching at Basle. However, unlike Burckhardt, he was concerned not with detailed historical inquiry but with discovering general principles for interpreting the visual character of works. What he saw as requiring interpretation was, first, how the subject-matter of painting and sculpture took its particular forms in works of art and how building materials and structures took on meaningful forms in architecture, and, second, the way such modes or formulation changed through history. He wrote almost exclusively on Renaissance and Baroque art.

Wölfflin's doctoral dissertation (1886) was on the psychological basis of our response to architectural forms. It sets out to account for the way in which what he conceives as literally present, the material of the building, can take on human significance or expressive force, employing a theory of empathy. He expanded on this approach in *Renaissance und Barock* (1888), which uses empathy theory to show how architecture could be interpreted as having expressive force without simply referring it to the spirit of the age: at the same time empathy theory is regarded as the means by which the age or race expressed itself in architecture. This provides Wölfflin with an explanation of the transformation of style through history. The force of the book, however, lies not in the theory of empathy but in the way he characterizes the metaphorical aspects of architectural forms.

A central difficulty of *Renaissance und Barock* was that empathy was conceived as a mechanism of emotional response, whereas its analyses presuppose a spectator who can read and relate architectural members and see them as drawing on a tradition. Wölfflin seems to have become aware of this, for he revised his approach in 'Die antiken Triumphbogen in Italien' (1893). Here he traces how the genre of the Roman triumphal arch, starting with that at Aosta, underwent a series of alterations in proportion and articulation that overcame early clumsiness to produce an optimally elegant solution, as in the Arch of Titus, followed by a process of decay through over-elaboration. The theory is teleological in that it assumes there is a classical solution to the problem of combining the elements that define the triumphal arch.

Klassische Kunst (1898) describes the transition from early to High Renaissance painting and sculpture in Italy, the first half of the book being a narrative and the second an exposition of theory to account for the transformation. Wölfflin initially offers three causes: a change in social ethos from bourgeois to aristocratic; a sense of human beauty in nature rather than adolescent physique; and an enhanced sophistication of visual formulation, which becomes more complex and economical. The relations between these are never clarified, and the new ethos and the new sense of beauty become elided to form one root of style, while the development of visual complexity forms a second apparently independent root.

Kunstgeschichtliche Grundbegriffe (1915) turns to the visual root of style considered in isolation, tracing the development in visual complexity from Renaissance to Baroque in both Italy and northern Europe as part of one overall phenomenon. Wölfflin does this by setting up five pairs of polarized categories to chart the differences in painting and drawing procedures between the two periods, irrespective of subject-matter: linear and painterly, plane and depth, closed form and open form, multiplicity and unity, and clearness and unclearness. The categories are loosely extended to sculpture and architecture. Linear art relies on contour delimiting discrete bodies and their internal modelling, with shadow used to enforce the distinction of forms, while the painterly (*malerisch*) mode allows shadows to pass across and diminish attention to the boundaries of forms. The second contrast is between planimetric, relief-like composition, in which forms present a revealing and lucid aspect in a plane parallel to the picture surface and the compositional organization is dominantly from side to side, and recessional composition, where the 'nerve of the painting' runs from foreground to background. The third polarity defines closed form (or 'the tectonic') such as that in which the picture's edge can be related to its internal features, making the space of the picture apparently self-contained, and open form ('a-tectonic') such as an indeterminate relation of the picture surface to the represented space. By multiplicity Wölfflin denotes an art in which the parts of the whole, the represented objects, are treated as 'free members' to be coordinated, whereas in an art of unity these parts lose their independence, subordinated to the total effect. Lastly, *Klarheit* and *Unklarheit* are applied, on the one hand, to art that purports to give entire, explicit representations and, on the other, to art that allows for certain elements to be implicit, obscure, a matter of suggestion. In effect the shift in each case is from an intuitively simpler relation between the medium and the subject to a more elusive and suggestive one. Wölfflin's later writings largely repeated these distinctions, while altering his theoretical position on the relation of artistic performance to the surrounding culture. He concentrated on what he saw as the difference between the Italian and German sense of form.

WRITINGS

Prologomena zu einer Psychologie der Architektur (diss., U. Munich, 1886); also in *Kleine Schriften* (Basle, 1946)
Renaissance und Barock (Munich, 1888; Eng. trans., London, 1964)
'Die antiken Triumphbogen in Italien', *Repert. Kstwiss.*, xvi (1893), pp. 11–27
Klassische Kunst (Munich, 1899; Eng. trans., Oxford, 1953)
Die Kunst Albrecht Dürers (Munich, 1909; Eng. trans., London, 1971)
Kunstgeschichtliche Grundbegriffe (Munich, 1915); Eng. trans. as *Principles of Art History* (London, 1932)
Kleine Schriften (Basle, 1946) [with bibliog.]
Gedanken zur Kunstgeschichte (Basle, 1947)

BIBLIOGRAPHY

E. Panofsky: 'Das Problem des Stils in der bildenden Kunst', *Z. Ästh. & Allg. Kstwiss.*, x (1915), pp. 460–67; also in *Aufsätze zu Grundfragen der Kunstwissenschaft* (Berlin, 1964)
E. Heidrich: *Beiträge zur Geschichte und Methode der Kunstgeschichte* (Basle, 1917)
B. Croce: 'Un tentativo eclettico nella storia delle arti figurative', *Nuovi saggi di estetica* (Bari, 1920), pp. 251–7
A. Hauser: *The Philosophy of Art History* (London, 1959), pp. 199–276
E. H. Gombrich: 'Norm and Form', *Norm and Form: Studies in the Art of the Renaissance* (London, 1966), pp. 89–98
L. Dittman: *Stil, Symbol, Struktur* (Munich, 1967), pp. 50–83
M. Brown: 'The Classic Is Baroque: On Wölfflin's Art History', *Crit. Inq.*, viii (1982), pp. 379–404
M. Podro: *Critical Historians of Art* (New Haven, 1982), pp. 98–151

MICHAEL PODRO

Wolff Metternich, Franz(iskus), Graf von (*b* Feldhausen, 31 Dec 1893; *d* Cologne, 25 May 1978). German art historian and conservator. He wrote his dissertation in Bonn on Early Renaissance art on the Lower Rhine, and from 1928 to 1951 he was in charge of conservation for the Rhineland. In 1933 he began teaching the care of monuments and Rhenish art at the Universität Bonn, where he was appointed honorary professor in 1939. During World War II Metternich was responsible for the protection of movable works of art in the Rhineland and in France, where he did extremely valuable work pursuant to the Hague Convention. After 1950 he worked for the West German Foreign Office to recover art works that had been taken abroad, and from 1952 to 1962 he was Director of the Bibliotheca Hertziana in Rome. Metternich's scholarly work was dedicated to the art of the Rhineland. His special interests included Romanesque architecture and murals, such as Bonn Minster, Schwarzrheindorf, St Georg and St Aposteln in Cologne; Gothic churches such as Cologne Cathedral; Renaissance buildings (for example Schloss Rheydt) and such Baroque estates as Schloss Brühl. At the Bibliotheca Hertziana he devoted himself to architecture in Rome from the 15th to the 18th century and especially to problems concerning Bramante and the building of St Peter's, Rome.

WRITINGS

Schloss Brühl. Die Kurkölnische Sommerresidenz Augustusburg (Berlin, 1934)
Bramante und St. Peter (Munich, 1975)

BIBLIOGRAPHY

Festschrift für Franz Graf Wolff Metternich mit Beiträgen von H. Adenauer (Neuss, 1973)
Festschrift für Graf Wolff Metternich zum 80. Geburtstag (Neuss, 1974)

DAGMAR PREISING

Wolffort [Wolffordt], **Artus** (*b* Antwerp, 1581; *d* Antwerp, 1641). Flemish painter. The year he was born his parents left Antwerp for Dordrecht, where Artus became a master in 1603. He returned to Antwerp *c.* 1615, initially as an assistant of Otto van Veen in whose house he was living. He executed a number of commissioned altarpieces, such as the *Ascension* and the *Assumption of the Virgin* (both *c.* 1617; Antwerp, St Paul). Most of his oeuvre, however, consists of compositions, usually with life-size figures, intended for the open market or private individuals. These are mainly scenes from the *Life of Christ* and other religious subjects, as well as mythological themes. Among his most characteristic works also are his serial representations of the *Twelve Apostles*, the *Four Evangelists* and *Four Fathers of the Church*, shown half life-size. That there are various versions, of differing quality, of most of these scenes suggests that Wolffort must have had a workshop. Among his assistants were such painters as Pieter van Lint and Pieter van Mol, whose work was clearly influenced by Wolffort and who made replicas of his compositions. Wolffort's work was virtually unknown until the late 1970s; some paintings were even thought to be early works by Rubens. The starting-point for the reconstruction of Wolffort's oeuvre is the fully signed *Women Bathing* (untraced; replica, London, V&A), together with several pictures bearing a monogram. His early work, to *c.* 1630, is stylistically close to that of van Veen. Not only is it painted in the same classicizing manner, it also uses identical motifs and compositions. The same proto-Baroque style characterizes such pieces as the *Feast in the House of Simon* (best version, Bergues, Mus. B.-A.). A more dramatically Baroque form in the Rubensian sense did not emerge in Wolffort's oeuvre until later, as in the *Adoration of the Magi* (Berlin, Schloss Charlottenburg).

BIBLIOGRAPHY
H. Vlieghe: 'Zwischen van Veen und Rubens: Artus Wolffort (1581–1641), ein vergessener Antwerpener Maler', *Wallraf-Richartz-Jb.*, xxxix (1977), pp. 93–136
J. S. Held: 'Noch einmal Artus Wolffort', *Wallraf-Richartz-Jb.*, xlii (1981), pp. 143–56

HANS VLIEGHE

Wolfgang William [Wolfgang Wilhelm], Count Palatine of Neuburg. *See* WITTELSBACH, §II(2).

Wölfli, Adolf (*b* Nüchtern, nr Bowyl, 29 Feb 1864; *d* Berne, 6 Nov 1930). Swiss artist, writer and musician. He was the youngest of eight children of an alcoholic stonebreaker whose desertion of the family precipitated the death of Wölfli's mother in 1873. After a series of sexual offences Wölfli was institutionalized with schizophrenia in 1895 in Waldau Mental Asylum, Berne, where he remained until his death from cancer. Although he drew his first pictures in 1899, his earliest surviving works date from 1904–6. His work is instantly identifiable; like Blake's it expresses a strongly personal language, as in the *High and Low Nobility of the English and British Canada Union* (1911; Berne, Kstmus.; for illustration *see* PSYCHOTIC ART). He was a prolific producer of pictorial and narrative work in folios (*Hefte*) of newspaper format (1000×750 mm). The pencil and coloured crayon drawings depict his fantasized biographical journey, portraying him either as Doufi, 'the child of poor and depraved parents', or as 'St Adolf II'. The borders are emphatic, and there are symmetrical arrangements, oval forms, circles, crosshatching and musical notation. The use of colour is original and idiosyncratic. In the accompanying narrative Wölfli's alter ego is pitched towards his own death; he assaults his victims, his crimes are punished by illness and incarceration, he is struck by lightning and destroyed by attack or by natural forces. Illustrations from the popular magazine *Über Land und Meer* (1870–80) are often collaged; and this technique was still being used in the *Campbell's Tomato Soup* collage of 1929 (Berne, Kstmus.). The abstract features, which largely replace naturalistic representation, are unified and harmonious, forming a stylized, often geometric design, recognizable sometimes as *maṇḍala*s, always as outside normality, but immensely convincing and authoritative.

In his narrative and pictorial *Funeral March* (1929–30; Berne, Kstmus.) Wölfli described himself characteristically as 'St Adolf II, Master of Algebra, Military Commander-in-Chief and Chief Music-Director, Giant Theatre-Director, Captain of the Almighty-Giant-Steamship and Doctor of Arts and Sciences, Director of the Algebra-and-Geography-Textbook-Production Company and Fusilier General, Inventor of 160 original and highly valued inventions patented for all times by the Russian Tsar and hallelujah the glorious victor of many violent battles against Giants'. The monograph on Wölfli written in 1921 by his psychiatrist, Dr Walter Morgenthaler, enthralled Rilke, who saw in Wölfli the antithesis between creativity and 'the total collapse within a human being'. Wölfli's visual art, autobiographical writing and musical composition also attracted the interest of such other artists as JEAN DUBUFFET, who was responsible for the inclusion of five of his works in the exhibition *L'Art brut préféré aux arts culturels* (1949) at the Galerie René Drouin in Paris (*see also* ART BRUT). Wölfli's 44 *Hefte*, comprising 20,000 pages, 1400 drawings and 1500 collages, are maintained by the Adolf Wölfli Foundation at the Kunstmuseum, Berne.

BIBLIOGRAPHY
W. Morgenthaler: *Ein Geisteskranker als Künstler* (Berne and Leipzig, 1921)
L'Art brut préféré aux arts culturels (exh. cat. by J. Dubuffet, Paris, Gal. René Drouin, 1949), pls 169–73
Adolf Wölfli (exh. cat., ed. E. Spoerri and J. Glaesemer; Berne, Kstmus.; Hannover, Kestner-Mus.; 1976)
The Other Side of the Moon: The World of Adolf Wölfli (exh. cat. by E. Longhauser and others, Philadelphia, PA, Moore Coll. A. & Des.; New York U., Grey A.G.; Regina, Pub. Lib., Dunlop A.G.; Berkeley, U. CA, A. Mus.; 1988–9)

HENRY WALTON

Wolgemut, Michael (*b* Nuremberg, 1434–7; *d* Nuremberg, 30 Nov 1519). German painter and woodcutter. The head of a large workshop which produced altarpieces, memorial pictures, portraits and designs for glass paintings in late 15th-century Nuremberg, he also provided notable innovations in the art of the woodcut. He is famed as the teacher of ALBRECHT DÜRER; after Wolgemut's death in 1519, Dürer added that date to a portrait of his former master done in 1516, but the 82 years mentioned in the inscription could either be Wolgemut's lifespan or his age when painted.

1. Life. 2. Work. 3. Style and workshop organization.

1. LIFE. He was the son of the painter Valentin Wolgemut (*fl* 1433/6; *d* 1469–70), who may have been the MASTER OF THE WOLFGANG ALTARPIECE (*see* MASTERS, ANONYMOUS, AND MONOGRAMMISTS, §I), though the latter's work does not begin until after mid-century. He was probably first trained in his father's workshop. Michael Wolgemut is first mentioned as a painter when instituting legal proceedings in Nuremberg in 1471 against the daughter of the Munich painter Gabriel Mälesskircher, to enforce an alleged promise of marriage. Wolgemut's testimony claims that he had worked in this artist's workshop until Lent 1471. The *Mass of Pope Leo IX* (Andechs, Klosterkirche) has been considered (Buchner) a product of this collaboration with Mälesskircher. No convincing stylistic evidence supports the hypothesis that Wolgemut contributed to a winged altarpiece (1465; Munich, Alte Pin.) produced in Hans Pleydenwurff's workshop for the St Michaels-Kirche at Hof. However, towards the end of 1472 Wolgemut married Barbara, the widow of Pleydenwurff, who had died in January. Her son Wilhelm Pleydenwurff is recorded as an assistant to his stepfather in 1493 but died a year later.

In 1479 Wolgemut repurchased Pleydenwurff's former house, 'Haus unter der Veste an der Schildröhre' (today Burgstrasse 21) and in 1493 he bought the properties adjacent to it, but sold them in 1495. Documentary information about Wolgemut's social standing is sparse. He is mentioned as examining a work by the sculptor Adam Kraft in 1503, along with Peter Vischer, Hans Behaim and Veit Stoss, and was implicated the same year, through his connection with Christoph Scheurl the elder, in the currency counterfeit affair concerning Veit Stoss, being questioned by the council. After his wife died in 1500 he married again.

2. Work.

(i) Altarpieces. An altarpiece (1479; Zwickau, St Marien) is the first work firmly documented as Wolgemut's. It is recorded in a lost inscription as the work of 'Master Michael Wolgemut, painter of Nuremberg'. The retable exploits all the possibilities of the polyptych. As well as the shrine with figures of the Virgin and saints, it has a predella and a high, tower-like superstructure, a double pair of wings and fixed wings. The insides of the inner wings are distinguished by gilded reliefs of standing saints. The painted sections of the first view show scenes from the *Life of the Virgin*; the closed wings show scenes from the *Passion*, painted by assistants. The figures in the action of the picture dominate Wolgemut's compositions. Architectonic details often have symbolic value, serving less to illustrate a local situation than to interpret the picture's subject-matter. The influence of models from the Netherlands is evident, yet Wolgemut's lack of consistency in depicting space makes it improbable that his knowledge was based on an extended stay there.

Wolgemut's style is recognizable in an altarpiece (*c.* 1485–6; Nuremberg, St Lorenz), in scenes showing the *Discovery of the True Cross* and the *Virgin Surrounded by Saints* on the insides of the wings. Their outsides, showing the *Martyrdoms of SS Catherine* and *Livinus*, were entrusted to an assistant, known as the Master of the Feuchtwanger Altar, who had already worked on the Zwickau altarpiece. A contemporary portrait by Wolgemut of the wealthy *Levinus Memminger* (see fig. 1), bearing a monogram and the subject's coat of arms, helps identify the patron here: the face matches that given to St Vitus on the wing of auxiliary saints.

Another surviving altarpiece (1486; Nuremberg, Friedenskirche), donated by Sebald Peringsdörfer of Nuremberg and his wife Katharina to the church of the Augustinian hermits, is authenticated as Wolgemut's by Johann Neudörfer's *Nachrichten von Künstlern und Werkleuten* (Nuremberg, 1547). As well as the shrine, which contains a *Lamentation*, this altarpiece has a double, movable pair of wings and fixed wings with scenes from the *Passion* and the *Life of the Virgin*. Only *Christ Carrying the Cross* and the *Resurrection* (see fig. 2) were designed and painted by Wolgemut himself; these flank the shrine with its carved figures when the altarpiece is fully opened. With the large number of figures in the turbulent *Christ Carrying the Cross* crowding, intersecting and overlapping each other, there is no space for the creation of an illusion of physical volume. The *Resurrection* is close to a treatment of the theme by Dieric Bouts, who lived in Leuven; but as the attitude of both artists to the picture space is fundamentally different, the similarity should be seen as simply a borrowed motif, probably taken from a copy of Bouts's work.

Wolgemut's monumental style of composition reached a high point with a further commission for the church of the Augustinian hermits. The altarpiece (before 1495; wings, Straubing, Jakobikirche) with paintings dedicated to the theme of the Virgin, includes a section of the Nuremberg castle buildings in the background of *Christ*

1. Michael Wolgemut: *Levinus Memminger*, panel, 337×229 mm, *c.* 1485 (Madrid, Museo Thyssen–Bornemisza)

in the Temple. Later altarpieces from Wolgemut's workshop include that preserved at the church at Windelsbach, painted by assistants *c.* 1513, for which Wolgemut's widow was still suing for payment in 1530.

(ii) Memorial pictures. Besides the large altarpieces a whole series of memorial pictures for the dead, popular in Nuremberg, was produced in Wolgemut's workshop, with his greater or lesser participation: a *Mass of St Gregory* with the coat of arms of the Heholl family; a *Lamentation* for Georg Keipper (*d* 1484; both Nuremberg, St Lorenz); the epitaph for *Michael Raphael*, Küchenmeister to King Maximilian I (*d* 1489; Nuremberg, Frauenkirche); and a *St Anne with Virgin and Child* for Anna Gross (*d* 1509; Nuremberg, Ger. Nmus.) in which the figure of the Virgin is prime evidence of the influence on Wolgemut of his former pupil Dürer.

(iii) Portraits and glass paintings. In Nuremberg Wolgemut was a leader in producing independent portraits, a genre only recently adopted by German painters: *Ursula Tucher* (1478; Kassel, Schloss Wilhelmshöhe); *Hans Tucher* (1481; Nuremberg, Tucher-Schlösschen); *Young Man* (1486; Detroit, MI, Inst. A.); *Hans Perckmeister* (1496; Nuremberg, Ger. Nmus.). In a glass painting of *Lorenz Tucher* before a prie-dieu (1485; Nuremberg, Ger. Nmus.) Wolgemut progressed from merely presenting a likeness

2. Michael Wolgemut: *Resurrection*, wing of the Peringsdörfer Altarpiece, panel, *c.* 1486 (Nuremberg, Friedenskirche)

within a predominant style to evoking the subject's personality. As a designer of glass paintings he is also attributed with the preparatory studies for windows in the chancel of St Lorenz donated by the priest Dr Petrus Knorr (1476) and Emperor Frederick III (1477) and for a posthumous donation by the priest Dr Konrad Konhofer (*d* 1452) in the same church.

(iv) Woodcuts. Both the full-page illustrations for the Franciscan Stephan Fridolin's *Schatzbehalter oder schrein der waren reichtuemer des hails vnnd ewyger seligkeit* (Nuremberg, 1491) by Wolgemut and Wilhelm Pleydenwurff and the pictures (printed with 645 blocks; *see* SALZBURG, fig. 1) of the *Weltchronik* (Nuremberg, 1493) by Hartmann Schedel are of great significance for the development of a new woodcut style.

3. STYLE AND WORKSHOP ORGANIZATION.

(i) Paintings. The characteristic Nuremberg style, with its long-lasting preference for line over colour, was decisive in Wolgemut's development. The austere features of his figures are emphasized by the avoidance of plain expanses of colour in the garments, where the fall of the folds is often developed into strong ornamental designs. Only in the landscape views, composed with particular care, does colour become important. The influence of Rogier van der Weyden, Dieric Bouts and Aelbert Ouwater is distinct, but disguised by Wolgemut through the interruption of depth by figures or landscape elements. Martin Schongauer's engravings are a further influence, becoming more significant in the Straubing altarpiece as reminiscences of Netherlandish work declined.

(ii) Woodcuts. Wolgemut decisively influenced the development of the woodcut. The preliminary drawings produced in his workshop were composed according to the laws of panel painting. Hatching of varying density allowed for a gradation of light tones and for a solidity in depicted objects. The necessary refinement of the cutting technique was only possible with close cooperation between designer and block cutter. The text of a contract for the *Weltchronik*, dated 29 December 1491, designates the partners Wolgemut and Wilhelm Pleydenwurff as responsible not only for the faultless execution of the printing blocks but also for any defects in the printing, which shows that the blocks were produced in Wolgemut's workshop itself.

(iii) Workshop. During his career Wolgemut built up a large workshop, similar to those emerging elsewhere when protective regulations were revoked or relaxed. Different sorts of artists were brought together to produce polyptychs: among the painters, the master's personal artistic achievement was submerged within his assistants' productions. Only recently have art historians been able to demonstrate the extent and significance of Wolgemut's own work. On Assumption Day 1484 'maister michel möler von Nurenberg' is documented as receiving three measures of wine and 110 gulden for an altarpiece delivered to the Stiftskirche at Feuchtwangen. The painting of this was fully entrusted to two journeymen, one being the Master of the Feuchtwanger Altar. More detailed information about the workshop business comes from a deed of guarantee from 1507, in which the Nuremberger Wilhelm Derrer stood surety for prepayments of 400 gulden (from the agreed price of 600 gulden) paid by the trustees of the Pfarrkirche of Schwabach for a new

altarpiece (Schwabach, Stadtkirche), also guaranteeing that this would be installed before the church's consecration in 1508. The text of this contract reveals that the altarpiece as a whole was entrusted to Wolgemut, who also had to gild the figures in the shrine and the reliefs inside the inner pair of wings; but only the pictures on the wings of the predella were painted by the master himself.

BIBLIOGRAPHY

Thieme–Becker

H. Thode: *Die Malerschule von Nürnberg im 14. und 15. Jahrhundert* (Frankfurt am Main, 1891), pp. 122–87

C. Dodgson: *Catalogue of Early German and Flemish Woodcuts Preserved in the Department of Prints and Drawings in the British Museum*, i (London, 1903), pp. 240–48

F. J. Stadler: *Michael Wolgemut und der Nürnberger Holzschnitt im letzten Drittel des 15. Jahrhunderts* (Strasbourg, 1913)

Albrecht Dürer (exh. cat., Nuremberg, Ger. Nmus., 1928), nos 1, 2, 13, 18, 19, 26, 27, 31, 32, 39

E. Lutze: 'Michael Wolgemut', *Pantheon*, xiv (1934), pp. 262–8 [good illustrations]

A. Schramm: *Der Bilderschmuck der Frühdrucke*, xvii/xviii (Munich, 1934/5) [illustrated with all Wolgemut's signed woodcuts]

J. Staber: 'Michael Wolgemut in München', *Z. Dt. Ver. Kstwiss.*, viii (1941), pp. 195–6

E. Buchner: 'Michael Wolgemut in Andechs', *Die Weltkunst*, xxi (1951), pp. 3–4

G. Betz: *Der Nürnberger Maler Michael Wolgemut und seine Werkstatt: Text und Katalog* (diss., U. Freiburg im Breisgau, 1955)

A. Stange: *Deutsche Malerei der Gotik*, ix (Munich and Berlin, 1958), pp. 51–64

R. Bellm: *Wolgemuts Skizzenbuch im Berliner Kupferstichkabinett: Ein Beitrag zur Erforschung des graphischen Werkes von Michael Wolgemut und Wilhelm Pleydenwurff* (Strasbourg, 1959)

P. S. Fridolin, with text and captions by R. Bellm: *Der Schatzbehalter: Ein Andachts- und Erbauungsbuch aus dem Jahr 1491*, 2 vols (Wiesbaden, 1962) [all woodcuts in their original size]

1471 Albrecht Dürer 1971 (exh. cat., Nuremberg, Ger. Nmus., 1971), nos 25, 94–5, 97–102, 104, 106–9, 114–18, 177, 227, 231, 536, 712

E. Rücker: *Die Schedelsche Weltchronik: Das grösste Buchunternehmen der Dürer-Zeit* (Munich, 1973, rev. 1985) [with copy of contract]

Die Schedelsche Weltchronik: Nach der Ausgabe von 1493, foreword by R. Pörtner (Dortmund, 1978) [reduced reproductions of the complete work]

A. Stange, rev. P. Strieder and H. Härtle, ed. N. Lieb: *Kritisches Verzeichnis der deutschen Tafelbilder vor Dürer*, iii (Munich, 1978), nos 127–42 [with full bibliog.]

Der Schwabacher Hochaltar, 11 of *Bayerischen Landesamtes für Denkmalpflege* (Munich, 1982) [rep. on a colloq. on the occasion of the altar's restoration]

G. Bauer, ed.: *Der Hochaltar der Schwabacher Stadtkirche* (Schwabach, 1983) [good illustrations]

E. Ulrich: *Studien zur Nürnberger Glasmalerei des ausgehenden 15. Jahrhunderts: Die drei mittleren Chorfenster von St Lorenz und die Werkstatt des Michael Wolgemut* (Erlangen, 1979)

H. May: *Die Entwicklung der fränkisch-nürnbergischen Malerei von 1495 bis 1525 unter besonderer Berücksichtigung des Schwabacher Hochaltars* (diss., Tübingen, 1989)

H. Scholz: *Entwurf und Ausführung: Werkstattpraxis in der Nürnberger Glasmalerei der Dürerzeit* (Berlin, 1991)

P. Strieder: *Tafelmalerei in Nürnberg, 1350 bis 1550* (Königstein im Taunus, 1993)

PETER STRIEDER

Wolgemut, Valentin. *See under* MASTERS, ANONYMOUS, AND MONOGRAMMISTS, §I: MASTER OF THE WOLFGANG ALTARPIECE.

Wollaston, John (*b* ?London; *fl* 1734–67). English painter, active in the USA. Horace Walpole mentioned in his *Anecdotes of Painting in England* (1765) that a London portrait painter, John Woolston, had a son who also became a portrait painter. From works that this son painted in London in 1744, it appears that he changed the spelling of his last name to Wollaston. The American painter Charles Willson Peale in a letter of 1812 to his son referred to Wollaston's training with a London drapery painter, but the portraits he was producing by the time he reached New York reflect abilities beyond those of a drapery painter. They are three-quarter-lengths showing little else than the subject, sombrely dressed. This style continued throughout his stay in New York (1749–51), with a growing concentration on fine apparel. The elegant dress of the females and subdued refinements of male attire advertise wealth and status. Despite a heavy reliance on engravings for pose and composition, his best portraits possess an animation about the mouth and eyes. His peculiar treatments of the eyes, slanted almond shapes, and rich fabrics in a range of colours that were touched with subtle highlights, identify even his unsigned portraits, for example *John Dies* (c. 1750; Amherst Coll., MA, Mead A. Mus.; see Craven, p. 29). Appearing in some late New York portraits is the suggestion of landscape. Judging from the number of such works that survive, at least 75, he was eagerly sought after.

In the spring of 1753 Wollaston moved to Annapolis, MD. Recorded as living there from around March 1753 until August 1754, he completed at least 55 individual portraits. Such prolific activity and the larger size of the paintings might suggest that these clients enjoyed greater wealth than their New York neighbours. Theirs now commonly included objects in the hands of his sitters, such as books for the men and flowers for the women. There are also *c.* 100 paintings of similar size featuring colonists in Virginia, where Wollaston seems to have painted from *c.* 1755 until October 1757. It appears from records that in late 1757 he accepted a position with the British East India Company and moved to Philadelphia, perhaps in search of transportation. While there he completed at least a dozen portraits before March 1759. Indications are that Wollaston's work in India, primarily legal in nature, made him wealthy. He reappeared in America briefly in late 1766 or very early 1767, painting portraits in Charleston, SC. In these, the expressionless stare that confronts the viewer is of much less importance than how closely the sitters' costumes imitates those of their wealthy English cousins. The *South Carolina Gazette* announced Wollaston's departure for England in late May 1767. His popularity in the colonies led to many copies of his work and imitation by several artists. Among his admirers were Benjamin West, who was impressed with Wollaston's New York portraits, and John Hesselius, who for a period borrowed elements of his style. Even Charles Willson Peale, while working in Annapolis as a saddler's apprentice (1754–61), found inspiration in his paintings.

BIBLIOGRAPHY

G. Groce: 'John Wollaston: A Cosmopolitan Painter in the British Colonies', *A. Q.* [Detroit], xv (1952), pp. 133–48

W. Craven: 'John Wollaston in England and New York', *Amer. A. J.*, viii/2 (1975), pp. 19–31

C. J. Weekley: *John Wollaston, Portrait Painter: His Career in Virginia, 1754–1758* (MA thesis, Newark, U. DE, 1976)

DARRYL PATRICK

Wolmut [Wohlmut; Wolmuet], **Bonifaz** (*b* Überlingen, Lake Constance; *fl* 1522; *d* Prague, before 28 April 1579). German architect. During his apprenticeship he travelled in Germany and Hungary, and from 1522 he worked at the Stephansdom, Vienna. After 1530 he was involved in fortification works and the construction of the Vienna Hofburg (Schweizer Hof). In 1534, after the death of Benedikt Ried, he applied unsuccessfully for the post of court architect in Prague. From 1539 he was in the service of King (later Emperor) Ferdinand I. In 1547, as a guild-master, he was granted the freedom of the city of Vienna, and with Augustin Hirschvogel he drew up the town plan, one of the most important sources for the history of Vienna. In 1548 Wolmut worked for private patrons in Vienna, and in 1559 he was appointed imperial architect. He stayed in Prague after leaving the imperial service in 1566, but was later readmitted to it. After his definitive retirement in 1570 Wolmut settled in Prague, where he was granted citizenship in 1571.

As early as 1554 Wolmut submitted plans, with Pietro Ferrabosco (1512–96), for alterations to Prague Castle (Hradčany); and from 1556 to 1563 he added an upper storey and roof to the Villa Belvedere in the castle complex. This distinctive building, a long pavilion with a peristyle, had been begun in 1538 in a pure Italian 15th-century style, after a model by the Genoese architect Paolo Stella. Wolmut built a banqueting hall, with an ogival roof, as an upper floor. The façade, with a Doric frieze, was articulated with an exciting rhythm of windows and niches, the solid modelling of which reflects the development of Italian 16th-century architecture.

Wolmut's design for the organ loft of Prague Cathedral, finished in 1561, combined a design based on the super-imposed orders of the Theatre of Marcellus in Rome with Gothic vaulting. Other works of these years included supervising the building of the Hvězda ('Star') summer house in Prague, designed by the amateur architect Arch-duke Ferdinand II, and a Ballcourt added in 1558. Wolmut was also busy with alterations to Lysá nad Labem Castle until 1564. From 1559 to 1563 he built the Diet hall in Prague Castle. Here he was able to hold his own in competition with Italian designers, who proposed a Ren-aissance hall with windows framed by half-columns and a coved vault. Although this type of design had been used by Wolmut in the Villa Belvedere, here he designed a Gothicizing rib vault compatible with the adjacent Vladi-slav Hall. In contrast, the lodge for the Secretary of State, which Wolmut put into the hall in 1559–63, is purely classicizing in style.

Wolmut's work in the 1560s included a new spire (1560–63) for the unfinished south tower of Prague Cathedral; a model for the Archbishop's Palace (1562); and town palaces, one for the Graf von Thurn in 1560 and a palace in Karmelitská Street, built as a speculation from 1560 to 1571. In 1563 he submitted a model for the so-called Löwenhof in Prague, and in 1567 he worked on the Small and Great Ballcourts in the royal garden at Hradčany. In 1568/9 he built the lower door in the Black Tower of Hradčany Castle, and among his later works was the new vault of the Gothic church of Our Lady and Charlemagne at Karlov, Prague.

The Great Ballcourt (see fig.) was designed as a hall structure, secured on the north side by powerful support-ing piers. The main façade had a columnar arcade of six arches flanked by two rows of niches, and the north and

Bonifaz Wolmut: Great Ballcourt (1567–9), royal garden, Hradčany, Prague

west sides were articulated with half-columns. The rich sgraffito decoration on the solid walls helped to lighten the appearance of the building and related it visually to a porticoed villa or triumphal arch.

Wolmut was one of the last architects to be trained in medieval building traditions. His complete mastery of vaulting techniques and deep understanding of the logic of Gothic design enabled him not only to hold his own with the achievements of Benedikt Ried but also to keep pace with the 'modern' developments of Italian Renais-sance architecture.

BIBLIOGRAPHY

O. Frejková: *Palladianismus v české renesanci* (Prague, 1941)
E. Bachmann: 'Ein unbekanntes Alterswerk der B. Wolmuets', *Ostdt. Wiss.*, iii/iv (1958), pp. 9ff
E. Šamánková: *Architektura české renesance* (Prague, 1961)
J. Krčálová: 'Kostel sv. Petra a Pavla v Kralovicích a B. Wolmut' [The church of SS Peter and Paul at Kralovice by B. Wolmut], *Umění*, xx (1972), pp. 297–315
J. Białostocki: *Art of the Renaissance in Northern Europe* (Oxford, 1976), pp. 74–7
J. Krčálová: *Die Kunst der Renaissance und des Manierismus in Böhmen* (Hanau, 1979), pp. 52–7, 68–73
E. Hubala: 'Palast- u. Schlossbau', *Renaissance in Böhmen* (Munich, 1985), pp. 105ff

PETER FIDLER

Wolpe, Berthold (Ludwig) (*b* Offenbach am Main, 29 Oct 1905; *d* London, 5 July 1989). German typographic designer and teacher active in England. Following an early apprenticeship with a firm of metalworkers, from 1924 to 1928 he studied with the typographical designer Rudolf Koch (1876–1934) at the Kunstgewerbeschule in Offen-bach, and later in Pforzheim, where he trained as a goldsmith. In 1929–33 he taught lettering at the Staatliche Hochschule für Bildenden Künste in Frankfurt and at the Kunstgewerbeschule in Offenbach. He designed book jackets, posters, trademarks and jewellery, as well as tapestries and metalwork (Offenbach am Main, Klingspor Mus.) in a manner rooted in medieval styles. He designed his first new typeface, Hyperion, in 1932. On a trip to London in that year he met Stanley Morison, who commissioned from him a new typeface for the Monotype Corporation (Albertus, 1935–7; bold and light versions, 1940). His other type designs include Tempest (1936), Pegasus Roman (1938) and Decorata (1955).

In 1935 Wolpe left Germany to settle in England, where he worked first for the Fanfare Press. He joined Faber & Faber Ltd in 1941, beginning an association with them that lasted until 1975; it is estimated that he designed 1500 book jackets in that time. As writer, lecturer and teacher, with a passion for alphabets, he inspired a recognition of the beauty and value of old letter forms and printers' devices. Among his books, *Renaissance Handwriting*, published by Faber & Faber in 1959, remains a standard work on the subject. He taught in London at the Camberwell School of Art and Crafts, the Royal College of Art and at the City and Guilds of London Art School.

WRITINGS
with A. Fairbank: *Renaissance Handwriting* (London, 1959)

BIBLIOGRAPHY
N. Drew: 'The Work of Berthold Wolpe', *A. & Indust.*, xxviii (1940), no. 167
Berthold Wolpe: A Retrospective Survey (exh. cat. by A. S. Osley, London, V&A, 1980)

Wols [Schulze, Alfred Otto Wolfgang] (*b* Berlin, 27 May 1913; *d* Champigny-sur-Marne, nr Paris, 1 Sept 1951). German painter, draughtsman, photographer and illustrator. In 1919, when his father was appointed head of the Saxon State Chancellery, the family moved from Berlin to Dresden. The following year Wols started taking violin lessons, showing a precocious musical talent. Having finished his studies at a grammar school in Dresden in 1931 he was too young to take the Abitur examination and so decided to abandon it. Fritz Busch, the conductor of the Dresden Opera, then offered to get him a post as a first violinist with an orchestra. Instead he worked for a few months in the studio of the photographer Gena Jonas in Dresden while also spending time as a garage mechanic.

In 1932 Wols travelled to Frankfurt am Main to study anthropology under the German ethnologist Leo Frobenius, a friend of the family, at the Afrika-Institut, though without his Abitur the plan was short-lived. He then moved to Berlin and entered the Bauhaus, recently transferred from Dessau, where he met Mies van der Rohe and László Moholy-Nagy. After only a few weeks Moholy-Nagy advised him to move to Paris; there, through Moholy-Nagy, he was introduced to Amédée Ozenfant, Fernand Léger, Hans Arp and César Domela. He soon also met many artists associated with the Surrealist movement, such as Max Ernst and Joan Miró as well as members of the group Le Grand Jeu such as the French writers René Daumel (1908–44), Roger Gilbert-Lecomte (1907–43), Georges Ribemont-Dessaignes and others; influenced by Surrealism, the group was condemned by André Breton

in 1929. Wols spent the remainder of 1932 in Paris, producing his first paintings but also working as a photographer; some of his photographs appeared in the Dutch paper *Film liga*. After returning briefly to Germany he settled in Paris in 1933, meeting Gréty Dabija, a Romanian woman previously married to the French Surrealist poet Jacques Baron (*b* 1905); he later married her himself. His photographic work of this period showed the clear influence of Surrealism. His portrait of *Roger Gilbert-Lecomte* (*c.* 1935; see 1978 exh. cat., fig. 103) with eyes closed, for example, suggests the sleeping state so beloved by the Surrealists. Other images, such as *Gréty's Mouth* (1933; see 1978 exh. cat., fig. 129), resemble works by the French photographer Jacques-André Boiffard (1902–61) in their dislocated, disturbing presentation of close-ups of the human anatomy.

At the end of 1933 Wols travelled to Barcelona and then to Ibiza, where he worked as a photographer and chauffeur in early 1934; he returned to Barcelona in the autumn, staying there for a year. Having lived without a permit in France and ignoring the summons of the German Labour Service, he was imprisoned in Barcelona in 1935 for three months before being deported back to France, where he continued his photographic work. In 1937, the year in which he adopted his pseudonym, he had an exhibition at the Librairie–Galerie de la Pléiade in Paris and became official photographer for the Pavillon de l'Elégance at the Exposition Internationale des Arts et Techniques dans la Vie Moderne held that year in Paris. Charting the period from its construction to eventual opening, his photographs appeared in fashion magazines such as *Harper's Bazaar*, *Vogue*, *Femina*, *Jardin des modes* as well as *Revue de l'art*. Those showing the pavilion during its construction allowed Wols wide scope for Surreal juxtapositions of objects, especially using the dismembered mannequins, as in *Pavillon de l'Elégance during Construction: International Exhibition* (1937; see 1978 exh. cat., p. 46). Many of these anticipate the displays at the Exposition Internationale du Surréalisme held in Paris in the following year, in which much use was made of mannequins.

At the outbreak of World War II Wols, as a German citizen, was interned for 14 months. He was not released until late 1940. During this period he concentrated on ink drawings of the sort he had been producing since 1932. His earlier works in this media, such as the *Singer and the Lovers* (gouache and ink, 1932; see 1961 exh. cat., pl. 5), showed the influence of child art and depicted fantastic creatures and curious metamorphoses. While this hallucinatory quality again links them to Surrealism, their childlike naivety bears comparison with the work of Paul Klee. His later ink drawings, such as *Large Head* (1943; Amsterdam, Stedel. Mus.), are both more fluid and detailed in style; in this case he used the visual ambiguity of the amorphous forms to suggest a head in a manner reminiscent of Salvador Dalí.

After his release from prison camp Wols moved for two years to Cassis, near Marseille, where he struggled to earn a living. The occupation of France by the Germans in 1942 forced him to flee to Dieulefit, near Montélimar, where he met the writer Henri-Pierre Roché, one of his earliest collectors. In 1945 an exhibition of Wols's drawings was held in Paris at the Galerie Drouin, but it proved a failure commercially. The following year he returned to Paris where he met Alberto Giacometti, Georges Mathieu and the writers Jean-Paul Sartre, Tristan Tzara and Jean Paulhan. He started to paint in oils in 1946 at the suggestion of the dealer René Drouin, who showed 40 of the paintings at his gallery in 1947. These pictures, such as *Yellow Composition* (1946–7; Berlin, Neue N.G.; see fig.), were executed in an informal, gestural style, with the paint applied in layers, often by means of dripping and with scratches made into the surface. The resulting works have a tremendously expressive, if disturbing, power. This new development in his art proved enormously influential, earning him the praise of artists such as Mathieu and critics such as Michel Tapié, who coined the term ART AUTRE to describe their post-war work.

In 1947 Wols began to work on a number of illustrations for books by Paulhan, Sartre, Franz Kafka, René de Solier and Antonin Artaud, such as Paulhan's *Le Berger d'Ecosse, suivi des passagers: La Pierre philosophique* (Paris, 1948). He fell ill in the same year but lacked the money to go to hospital, and throughout 1948 he worked largely in bed on these illustrations. In 1949 he took part in the exhibition *Huit oeuvres nouvelles* at the Galerie Drouin, along with Jean Dubuffet, Jean Fautrier, Roberto Matta, Mathieu, Henri Michaux and other artists with whom he had a stylistic affinity. In the last few years of his life he continued to produce fantastic ink and wash drawings, such as the *Phantom Town* (c. 1951; Hannover, Sprengel Mus.). He also developed his oil painting in such works as *The Windmill* (c. 1951; Münster, Westfäl. Landesmus.), using a thick impasto here overlaid with the explosive lines of a windmill. He applied a similar technique to watercolour to create fused and blotted areas of colour, as in *Untitled* (c. 1950; priv. col., see London 1985 exh. cat., pl. 48). Undergoing treatment for alcoholism, he moved to the country at Champigny-sur-Marne, south-east of Paris, in June 1951. His early death later that year from food poisoning helped foster the legendary reputation that grew up around him soon afterwards. His paintings helped pioneer ART INFORMEL and TACHISM, which dominated European art during and after the 1950s as a European counterpart to American Abstract Expressionism. Influenced by the writings of the Chinese Daoist philosopher Laozi throughout his life, Wols also wrote poems and aphorisms that expressed his aesthetic and philosophical ideas.

Wols: *Yellow Composition*, oil on canvas, 730×920 mm, 1946–7 (Berlin, Neue Nationalgalerie)

WRITINGS

Aphorisms and Pictures (Gillingham, 1971)
Aphorismes (Amiens, 1989)

BIBLIOGRAPHY

R. Guilly: *Wols* (Paris, 1947)
H.-P. Roché: *Wols* (Paris, 1958)
Wols (exh. cat. by W. Grohmann, Paris, Gal. Europe, 1959)
Wols: Peintures et gouaches 1932–1942 (exh. cat. by W. Haftmann, Paris, Gal. Europe, 1961)
Wols 1913–1951: Gemälde, Aquarelle, Zeichnungen (exh. cat. by W. Haftmann, W. Berlin, N.G., 1973)
Wols: Photograph (exh. cat. by L. Glozer, Hannover, Kestner-Ges., 1978)
Wols 1913–1951: Aquarelle, Druckgraphik (exh. cat. by K. Weber, Kassel, Staatl. Kstsammlungen, 1985)
Wols: Drawings and Watercolours (exh. cat. by E. Rathke, London, Goethe-Inst., 1985)
Wols: Bilder, Aquarelle, Zeichnungen, Photographien, Druckgraphik (exh. cat. by E. Rathke and others, Zurich, Ksthaus; Düsseldorf, Kstsamml. Nordrhein–Westfalen; 1989–90)

For further bibliography *see* ART AUTRE; ART INFORMEL; TACHISM.

PHILIP COOPER

Wolsey, Cardinal Thomas (*b* Ipswich, *c.* 1473; *d* Leicester, 29 Nov 1530). English prelate, statesman, patron and collector. Said to have been the son of a butcher, in 1497 he was a Fellow of Magdalen College, Oxford. By 1507 he was chaplain to Henry VII and by 1511 Privy Councillor to Henry VIII. In 1514 he became Archbishop of York and in 1515 he was created a cardinal. From this time until his fall from favour in 1529 he was the most powerful man in England. The outward manifestation of that power through buildings and their contents was the constant wonder and scandal of his political enemies; attacks upon him included those by the poet John Skelton (especially in 'Why come ye not to Court?', 1522) and Polydore Vergil (in *Historiae Anglicae*, 1534–55, xxvi).

Wolsey's three major domestic buildings all later became royal properties; thus he helped set the pattern for the scale and ambition of Henry VIII's palaces. In 1514 he leased the manor of Hampton Court from the Knights Hospitaller and built the surviving base court (completed by 1522), chapel and kitchens, as well as lodgings for himself and the King and Queen (*see* HAMPTON COURT PALACE). At York Place (later known as Whitehall Palace, destr.), his London house, major works were completed by 1519, but building continued until 1529. In 1527, when the French ambassador Joachim Du Bellay visited The More, Wolsey's Hertfordshire manor house (destr.), he considered it to be even more splendid than Hampton Court (Colvin, p. 165). (Archaeological investigation has established that there was a base court beyond the moat surrounding the courtyard house.) Wolsey's buildings were 'Tudor-Gothic' in appearance, built mainly of brick with stone dressings. Visitors noted the internal splendour and ostentation: an account of 1519 records that eight rooms, all hung with tapestry that was changed each week, needed to be crossed in order to reach Wolsey's audience chamber at York Place (Colvin, p. 305); and a mention of the 'goodly galleries, all gilt above' at The More (Colvin, p. 165) is but one indication of the crucial role Wolsey is believed to have played in the development of the gallery in English domestic architecture.

Like many late medieval churchmen, Wolsey initiated educational establishments with ambitious building plans. His foundation in 1525 of Cardinal College (later Christ Church), Oxford, involved him in an expenditure of some £25,000 over four years. The King's master masons John Lebons (*fl* 1506–29) and Henry Redman completed parts of the great quadrangle by 1529. Of his college at Ipswich, Suffolk, founded in 1527, little was completed by the time of his fall two years later, but it is known that the main buildings were to be constructed of imported Caen stone. Only a small brick gateway survives.

Wolsey's collection of Flemish pictures later became part of the royal collection. His inventory records triptychs, and in 1515 'a table for an awter, which was made by the best master of all this land' was sent to him from Antwerp. Great numbers of tapestries were noted among his possessions, largely of chivalric and Old Testament themes, common as subjects for hangings in Tudor England, but of the highest quality. In 1523 he bought a set of tapestries, the *Triumphs of Petrarch*, four of which remain at Hampton Court Palace; these have been attributed for their design to the van Orley (i) workshop in Brussels. Wolsey's favour for the species of ornament known as 'antique' (or, more accurately, 'antick') is best recorded through architectural embellishment and valuable small objects, identifying him as a patron of the latest contemporary European fashions. In 1521 the Italian Giovanni da Maiano (ii) was paid for works in terracotta for Hampton Court, including the surviving (though now resited) roundels of Roman emperors and Wolsey's coat of arms, as well as two 'histories' of Hercules. Wolsey may have been responsible for the appointment of the goldsmith Robert Amadas (*d* 1532) to the King's Jewel House; the plate later incorporated into the royal collection, largely made for Wolsey by Amadas, shows a marked preference for 'antick' decoration. The frieze and ceiling of the Wolsey closet at Hampton Court, though in large part a 19th-century reconstruction, shows the kind of lavish, gilded ornament that Wolsey, and later Henry VIII, favoured.

BIBLIOGRAPHY

J. H. Harvey: 'The Building Works and Architects of Cardinal Wolsey', *J. Brit. Archaeol. Assoc.*, 3rd ser., viii (1943), pp. 50–59
J. H. Harvey and J. G. Milne: 'The Building of Cardinal College, Oxford', *Oxoniensia*, viii–ix (1943–4), pp. 137–53
G. Cavendish: *The Life and Death of Cardinal Wolsey*, ed. R. Sylvester (London, 1959) [Cavendish was a member of Wolsey's household]
H. M. Colvin, ed.: *The History of The King's Works*, iv (London, 1982)
L. Campbell: *The Early Flemish Pictures in the Collection of Her Majesty the Queen* (Cambridge, 1985), pp. xi–l
S. J. Gunn and P. G. Lindley, eds: *Cardinal Wolsey: Church, State and Art* (Cambridge, 1991)
T. Campbell: 'Of Silk and Gold', *Country Life*, clxxxv (10 Oct 1991), pp. 92–5

MAURICE HOWARD

Wolsong. *See* CH'OE PUK.

Wolters, Mathias-Joseph (*b* Roermond, the Netherlands, 17 March 1793; *d* Ghent, 21 April 1859). Belgian engineer and architect. A member of an aristocratic family from Limburg, he started his career in tax administration under French rule and, during a stay in Paris *c.* 1810, attended classes at the Ecole Polytechnique. During a period in the service of the Dutch government he was among those who worked on the fortifications from 's Hertogenbosch to Maastricht in 1820–21 and on the Ghent–Terneuzen canal in 1825–8. After 1830 he joined the Belgian government department responsible for bridges and roads and in 1837 was appointed Chief Engineer for Eastern Flanders. A recognized authority on hydrography, he was responsible for many important hydraulic works in Flanders.

As an architect Wolters is especially interesting for his contribution to the early Gothic Revival in Belgium. The episcopal palace in Ghent, built by him in 1841–5, was among the first monumental buildings in that style in the country; it combines a symmetrical exterior with details copied from the adjacent cathedral, with an interior decoration with rich Gothic Revival stuccowork apparently inspired by English models. Mostly in the same free Gothic Revival manner, which was often characterized by the use of stucco and cast iron, he designed churches at Viane (1843–7), Heusden (1844), Sint Denijs-Westrem (1845–6), Sint Amandsberg (1846; rebuilt 1932–40), Terneuzen and De Klinge (1848–50). As an amateur historian, from 1845 he published numerous studies of the villages and abbeys in his native Limburg.

BNB   BIBLIOGRAPHY
B. De Saint-Genois: Obituary, *Messager des sciences historiques, ou archives des arts et de la bibliographie de Belgique* (Ghent, 1859), pp. 388–94
Obituary, *VI. Sch.*, v (1859), p. 72
C. F. A. Piron: *Algemeene levensbeschrijving der mannen en vrouwen van België* (Mechelen, 1860), p. 469
J. van Cleven: '19th Century: Architecture', *Flemish Art*, ed. H. Liebaers (Antwerp, 1985), p. 504
——: 'Tussen burgerlijke romantiek en grootstedelijke realiteit', *Gent en architectuur*, ed. N. Poulain (Bruges, 1985), pp. 99–100
                                   JEAN VAN CLEVEN

Women and art history. There is no lack of evidence of women's participation in the history of arts of all forms, cultures and periods, from ancient traditions, such as pottery and carving or silk-weaving and painting in China (*c.* 3000 BC), to the present and numerous forms of artistic expression. Yet traditional art history has kept us in systematic ignorance of the fact that women have always made art. It took the emergence of feminism in the late 20th century to redress the almost complete neglect of women artists by art history and to undermine the stereotyped views of art made by women.

I. Introduction. II. Western world. III. South and Central America. IV. East Asia.

I. Introduction.

When discussed, art by women was derogatively categorized as 'women's art' in order to distinguish it from 'art', which, despite its lack of adjectival qualification, had come to be exclusively identified with a canon of white men. Since the 1960s many books have been published on the history of women in all areas of the visual arts in all periods and many cultures. The evidence for women as artists is overwhelming, but the project of restoring women to the history of art has raised major historiographical, political and theoretical issues. It has been shown that it is only in the 20th century, when art history was fully consolidated as an academic discipline, that women artists were systematically effaced from the record of the history of art. This raises the question of why this has happened and produces the second problem of whether art history as established can accommodate the different histories of art that alone would account for women's experiences as

artists and make legible what they produced. It is necessary, therefore, to distinguish between the history of art as the field of historical artistic practice, and art history as the organized discipline that has studied this field in selective ways. Art history tells a story of art incompatible with understanding the histories of women in the visual arts. It is a gendered discourse that participates in the sexual divisions of society by celebrating the most highly valued creativity as the exclusive property of a select masculinity. Thus, questioning of why art by women has been neglected or, if mentioned, has been stereotyped as 'women's art', that is, as 'feminine' and other, and placed always as the negative cipher to (masculine) art, has focused attention on the ideological bases of the discourses of art history in this century. The redress of the neglect of women by art history cannot be accomplished without a major reframing of the art-historical project, shifting attention away from the idealization of the autonomous creative artist and the exclusively formal properties of art objects. Feminist critiques of art history have been developed from new theoretical positions on theories of history (challenging typical periodizations and notions of stylistic development), theories of ideology (the social investment in cultural meanings), theories of the image and text (semiotics, authorship), theories of society (the role of gender as well as class and race in social formations) and theories of the subject (challenging notions of individual agency through attention to the role of the unconscious, fantasy and psychically installed sexual difference; *see* §II, 4 below). New ways of 'reading' visual representation have been produced, while art is reconceived as a social practice, shaped by historically specific institutions, which is productive of images that are both determined within social relations of class, race, gender and sexuality and are effective in shaping social meanings and sexual identities.

II. Western world.

1. The historical record. 2. Women and the writing of art history. 3. Historical recovery. 4. Feminist critiques.

1. THE HISTORICAL RECORD. It has been possible to reclaim the history of women in the arts through surviving historical records and works, as well as from the documentation of women artists' work in the literature on Western art until the 19th century, when it was interrupted, to a virtual erasure of such knowledge by some art historians in the 20th century.

(i) Ancient to medieval. The Roman historian Pliny (AD 23/24–79) included in Book XXXV of his *Natural History* six women artists of antiquity: Timarete, Astarte and Olympia, Helen of Egypt, Kalypso and Iaia or Lala of Cyzicus. Some of these names are also listed in *De claris mulieribus* (1370) by the Italian poet Boccaccio; with Thamyris (see fig. 1), Eirene and Marcia (who is probably Iaia), they reappeared in most Renaissance commentaries as exemplars, however, of exceptional women. Women are recorded in medieval art production in both religious and secular institutions. Women's names are attached to manuscripts from AD 800 onwards. A Spanish Romanesque manuscript known as the *Beatus Apocalypse* of Girona (Girona, Mus. Catedralicio) was illustrated in part

1. *Thamyris Painting*, tempera on vellum, 75×65 mm; miniature from Boccaccio: *Des cleres et nobles femmes*, 1404 (Paris, Bibliothèque Nationale, MS. fr. 598, fol. 86)

and signed by Ende (*c.* AD 975). Forty-five books by the hand of Diemud of the cloister of Wessobrun are known, while Guda of Westphalia, another 12th-century nun, wrote and painted a *Homiliary of St Bartholomew*. Herrad of Hohenbourg (*d* 1195) produced a massive folio called the *Hortus deliciarum* (*see* ALLEGORY, fig. 2), and Hildegard of Bingen (1098–1179), who was a composer as well as an illuminator and writer on natural history, created an illuminated volume of her mystical visions, *Scivias* (1142–52; Wiesbaden, Hessische Landesbibliothek, fol. 1*r*); a volume of the official *Patrologia Latina* is devoted entirely to her works. Women's contribution to other areas of medieval art, such as secular and ecclesiastical embroidery, is widely documented (Parker, 1984), and women are recorded as being active in many medieval crafts, some of which were female monopolies. Sabina von Steinbach's stone sculptures (14th century) on Strasbourg Cathedral are signed, and legend, recounted by Vachon (1893), suggests that she was given the task of completion of the façade sculptures on the cathedral on the death of the master builder.

(ii) Renaissance to early modern. Giorgio Vasari, the Renaissance artist whose *Vite* (1550; rev. 1568) became a model for later art-historical writing, referred in this text to the women Pliny noted and in the edition of 1568 mentioned five Flemish women artists and added some contemporaries of the Italian school: Suor Plautilla Nelli; Lucretia Quistelli della Mirandola; Irene di Spilimbergo, a pupil of Titian; Barbara Longhi; Sofonisba Anguissola and her

three sisters; and the Bolognese artists Properzia de' Rossi, who was also renowned as a sculptor, and Lavinia Fontana. During the 17th and 18th centuries the works and careers of women artists were publicly discussed and celebrated. Carlo Cesare Malvasia wrote an adulatory biography of Elisabetta Sirani titled *Felsina pittrice* (1678), in which he also mentioned Fontana, Sofonisba Anguissola and Fede Galicia (1578–1630). Arnold Houbraken's book on the lives of Dutch painters *De groote schouburgh der Nederlandtsche konstschilders en schilderessen* (1718–21) included women artists in his title and named 11 of them within the book. Women had been active in Flemish art since the late 15th century (e.g. Levinia Teerlinc, 1510/20–76, and Caterina van Hermessen, after 1528–after 1587), and they were well represented in genre and still-life painting in 17th-century Holland (Judith Leyster, Clara Peeters, Rachel Ruysch).

Women were court artists, for example the Spanish sculptor Luisa Roldán, who worked for Charles II of Spain. The international reputation achieved by the Venetian pastellist Rosalba Carriera was indicated by her admission to the Accademia di S Luca in Rome (1705) and the Académie Royale de Peinture et de Sculpture in Paris (1720). Women artists were among founder-members of the Royal Academy in London in 1768: Angelica Kauffman and Mary Moser; while there were several women members of the Académie Royale in the late 18th century, including Anne Vallayer-Coster, the Berlin artist Anna Dorothea Therbusch, Elisabeth-Louise Vigée Le Brun and Adélaïde Labille-Guiard. Records of women sculptors are more intermittent for this period but include Anne Seymour Damer and Marie-Anne Collot, who worked with Falconet on the equestrian statue of *Peter the Great* (1766) in St Petersburg, modelling the Tsar's head and making portrait busts for members of the court of Catherine the Great (Opperman, 1965).

(iii) Modern. The historical record from antiquity to the 18th century was considerably expanded by the 19th century, when many women, professional and amateur, were active in the visual arts, exhibiting at salons and academies, as well as participating in new, independent art groups and taking up new media such as photography. Artists in this field include Clementina, Viscountess Hawarden (*see* fig. 2), Julia Margaret Cameron, Frances Benjamin Johnson, Mary E. Flenoy and Elise Harleston. By the end of the 19th century, when the discipline of ART HISTORY was becoming a recognized area of research and publication, a constant but fluctuating record of women in the arts was consolidated into a series of major surveys of women's participation in all branches of the visual arts: Guhl (1858), Ellet (1859), Clayton (1876), Fidière (1885), Vachon (1893), Sparrow (1905), Hirsch (1905), Ragg (1907) and Scheffler (1908). In 1904 Clara Clement produced a massive compilation of over 1000 entries, and Lü Märten produced her study *Die Künstlerin*. The *Künstlerlexikon* begun by Thieme and Becker in 1907 lists over 6000 women in the areas of painting, sculpture and printmaking.

By the mid-20th century, however, standard textbooks in use throughout university and college art history courses mentioned either very few women artists or, more often,

2. Clementina, Viscountess Hawarden: *Photographic Study of the Artist's Daughter*, albumen print from wet collodion negative, *c.* 119×92 mm, early 1860s (London, Victoria and Albert Museum)

none at all (e.g. H. W. Janson's *The History of Art*; E. S. Gombrich's *The Story of Art*); women photographers were never as completely erased as painters and sculptors. It is this fact that led women radically to reappraise modern art history and its hierarchies, which have ensured that the more highly valued the activity, the less women will be associated with it. This reflects a widespread cultural phenomenon studied by social anthropologists that reveals that social acknowledgement of the performer of social actions relates more to social status than to the nature or extent of activity performed (Ortner, 1974). In the few modern texts that do refer to women, comments are typically dismissive, revealing the use of the feminine stereotype: Rudolf Wittkower in *Art and Architecture in Italy, 1600–1750* (1965) described Rosalba Carriera's work as 'mellow, fragrant and sweet, typically feminine'; in referring to Vigée Le Brun, the most highly paid portrait painter of her time, Michael Levey in *Rococo to Revolution* (1966) wrote: 'By removing any suggestions of intelligence (naturally) as if it had been rouge, she created the limpid, fashionably artless portrait'. Drawing on a tendency that can be traced to Boccaccio and Vasari to represent any woman artist as an exception to her natural sex, who would nonetheless always betray signs of her femininity in her art, Victorian commentators on the arts erected a rigid division between the abilities, tastes and sensibilities of the sexes to create separate spheres for art by men and by women. The American critic John Jackson Jarves writing in 1871 of the group of neo-classical sculptors settled in Rome, named by Henry James 'a white marmorean flock', which included Harriet Hosmer, Emma Stebbins and Edmonia Lewis, said: 'Women are by nature likewise prompted in the treatment of sculpture to motives of fancy and sentiment rather than realistic portraiture or absolute creative imagination' (*A. J.*, x, 1871, p. 7); Léon Legrange wrote: 'Male genius has nothing to fear from female taste' (*Gaz. B.-A.*, viii, 1860, pp. 30–43). The doctrine of separate spheres functioned paradoxically. In the era of high bourgeois culture, women artists were granted a degree of recognition for their special sensibilities, which was reinforced by the formation of such women's art organizations as the Society of Female Artists (later Lady Artists) in Britain (founded 1856) and the Union des Femmes Peintres et Sculpteurs in France (founded 1881; see Garb, 1994), and the many art circles for women, such as the Verein der Berliner Künstlerinnen (founded 1867). In the different cultural regime of early 20th-century modernism, separation could and did easily become segregation, and in the atmosphere of a modernist culture that reacted against the oversexualization of 19th-century ideology by a complete denial of any value for gender difference, the very discourses that had at least acknowledged women as artists, however belittlingly, became the justification for their total exclusion, so that Janson, author of one of the most widely read textbooks, *The History of Art* (1962), could state in 1979 that no women were included in his book because no woman 'had been important enough to go into a one-volume history of art' (Salomon, 1991).

2. WOMEN AND THE WRITING OF ART HISTORY. Women have participated in the development of the discipline of art history since its emergence in the late 18th century. Their interests reflected aspects of women's circumstances in the privileged classes, and although they were never exclusively concerned with women artists, many of the first professional women art historians accommodated women artists in their historical surveys and guides to museums and collections. Johanna Schopenhauer (1766–1838) wrote *Johann van Eyck und seine Nachfolge* (1822), one of the first books on the artist and his school. Maria Dundas Graham, Lady Callcott, published the first monograph on Poussin in 1820 and in 1835 produced a *Description of the Chapel of the Annunziata dell' Arena*. A biography of Salvatore Rosa was written by Lady Morgan in 1824, while Anna Brownell Jameson, considered the first professional woman art historian, initiated work on religious and secular iconography with her *Sacred and Legendary Art* (1848). French Gothic sculpture was researched by Félicie d'Ayzac; her *Histoire de Saint-Denis* appeared in 1860–61. Mary Philadelphia Merrifield is still noted for her research and publication of treatises on painting and other art forms from the 12th and 13th centuries. She translated Cennino Cennini's treatise on painting in 1844 and in 1846 wrote *The Art of Fresco Painting*. Elizabeth Ellet, Ellen Clayton and Clara Clement wrote books on women artists, while Anna Jameson devoted part of her *Visits and Sketches* (1834) to an appraisal of women artists, while she planned a three-volume memoir on 'celebrated female Artists'.

In *Women as Interpreters of the Visual Arts, 1820–1970* (1981) Claire Richter Sherman and Adele Holcomb provided detailed studies of major women art historians and critics, including critics Margaret Fuller and Mariana Griswold Van Rensselaer, Emilia Frances Pattison, Lady

Dilke (17th- to 18th-century French art), Georgiana Goddard King (medieval Spanish art), Gisela Richter (Greek art), Erica Tietze-Conrat (Renaissance and Baroque art) and Agnes Mongan (drawings). This research shows the relations between women's work in the emergent discipline of art history and changing social and cultural attitudes towards women. While the field was still relatively undefined in the 19th century, women made major contributions to the study of art in an atmosphere in which independent travel and freelance research and writing were respectable activities for middle-class women. With greater professionalization the distinction between trained academics or curators and amateur intellectuals widened, and, although in the USA women constituted almost 50% of the initial membership of the College Art Association (founded 1917), there was growing inequality of status between men and women, as art history was firmly located in museums and universities and cultural attitudes began to dictate to women a rigid choice between work and family. The contribution of women to the formation and development of the study of the history of art has been neglected in the histories of art history; Sherman and Holcomb made an important start in this necessary area of research and reassessment of major women scholars in the field.

3. HISTORICAL RECOVERY. The re-emergence of the women's movement in the late 1960s and early 1970s precipitated a reassessment of all branches of organized knowledge. Initial recoveries of women artists made women art historians and artists begin to critique the silences and stereotypes of art history with regard to women artists, producing a series of interventions that have since challenged the authority of the discipline and questioned its practices: for instance its focus on the great, individual artist; its isolation of art from other social practices as exemplified in its typical forms; the monograph and the catalogue raisonné; its preoccupation with stylistic evolution; its separation of iconography from social meaning and ideology; its selectivity in preserving a white male canon.

(i) Redressing the neglect. From the early 1970s a steady flow of exhibitions and publications began the retrieval of knowledge about women artists that had been effaced in the 20th century, expanding that knowledge with both new research and a differently orientated analysis of the culture produced by women. The most significant were the exhibitions Old Mistresses (1972), Künstlerinnen international, 1877–1977 (1977) and Das verborgene Museum (1987), the last of which documented the art by women in Berlin's public collections, and the book Women Artists, 1550–1950 by Ann Sutherland Harris and Linda Nochlin (1976). In 1975–6 a travelling exhibition Women of Photography: An Historical Survey provided a basic historical record of women in this field, which has been supplemented by a growing number of studies on selected photographers, such as Lady Hawarden, Julia Margaret Cameron, Frances Benjamin Johnson, Imogen Cunningham, Dorothea Lange and many others active in the 20th century (Fisher, 1987). Jeanne Moutoussamy-Ashe has documented the history of African-American women photographers (1986, rev. 1993). Surveys of women in the arts published in English during the 1970s and 1980s (including Tufts, 1974; Peterson and Wilson, 1976; Honig Fine, 1978; Greer, 1979; Rubinstein, 1982; Slatkin, 1985; Heller, 1987) mainly concentrated on white European and American artists, although there was detailed study of women artists of China published as an appendix to Peterson and Wilson as early as 1976 (see §IV below). Ora Williams produced American Black Women in the Arts and Social Sciences: A Bibliographic Survey in 1973, and in the same year many women were detailed in Afro-American Artists: A Bio-Bibliographical Directory by T. Cedar Holm. Women in Germany have published on women in art (Nabakowski, Sander and Gorsen, 1980; Berger, 1982; Krull, 1984).

By the 1980s white feminist art historians responded to critique of the racism in art history and joined with women from all nations in research on women outside the West (see also §§III–IV below), particularly Lyle, Moore and Navaretta's Women Artists of the World (1984), on those working in traditions derived from African, Asian, Amerindian, Australian or Canadian traditions, and those who were part of the post-colonial diasporas (Rubinstein, 1982; Gouma-Peterson and Mathews, 1987, Sulter, 1990). A special exhibition was devoted to Japanese Women Artists, 1600–1900 (1988; see §IV below), and the National Museum of Women in the Arts, in Washington, DC, has produced exhibitions on women artists from Poland (Voices of Freedom: Polish Women Artists and the Avant-garde, 1880–1990, 1991) and from the Arab nations (Forces of Change: Artists from the Arab World, 1994). In the late 1990s work was in progress on women artists in South Africa, Korea, Japan (Shalala, 1994), India and Pakistan (1994 exh. cat. by Hashmi and Poomaya-Smith). Since it has been argued that the hierarchical division between arts and crafts echoed and reinforced a gender hierarchy, renewed attention was paid to women in design and textiles (Callen, 1979; Anscombe, 1984; Parker, 1984). Less attention has been paid to the specific history of women sculptors, although Mitchell (1989) began to work on women sculptors in France, particularly Camille Claudel and Jeanne Poupelet, and Rubenstein (1990) documented an American history. There are special case studies on Victorian women artists (Gerrish Nunn, 1986; Cherry, 1993) as well as a few major monographs (e.g. Garrard on Gentileschi, 1989, and many more on women of the 19th and 20th centuries). Research into women artists is assisted by museums intending to collect and conserve women's art, such as the National Museum of Women's Art in Washington, DC, the Verborgene Museum project in Berlin and the Frauen Museum in Bonn.

(ii) Facing theoretical issues. While it has been important to turn back the tide of ignorance by publishing surveys and monographs on women artists to ensure their inclusion in academic syllabi and culture's general knowledge (the most complete of which by the late 20th century was Chadwick's Women, Art and Society, 1990), the study of women artists is not well served by a focus on the artist in biographical isolation or by a mere replication of the standard formats and interests of mainstream art histories.

The feminist intervention in art history immediately confronts problems about text, author and sexual difference that transcend the field, to be considered also in such other areas of cultural production as film and literature: does gender make a difference? If so, is it social, cultural, psychological, biological? Is it a transhistorical fact about men or women, or is it historically and culturally variable? The position that attributes to women a given quality shared by all of the sex led certain artists and art historians to examine art made by women for a female iconography, for example the work of Judy Chicago (*see also* FEMINISM AND ART). Others argued that women's artistic production was shaped historically by social forces resulting from such facts as women's limited access to formal training in the period of the academies and their official exclusion from study from the nude model, and the general cultural ideologies about women's nature and sensibility (see fig. 3; Nochlin, 1971). Another position is that psychological factors arising from the general position of women in social and personal life affected their art, which was made in conditions that repressed their sexualities and broke their energies against a series of obstacles, such as family, illusion of success, love and so forth (Greer, 1979). The anthology *Significant Others* (1993) by Chadwick and de Courtivron has re-examined women artists in relationships with men artists, while Rogoff (1992) has provided a more theorized analysis of how to examine women artists in relation to both male culture and women's networks.

A different approach that can be loosely defined as post-structuralist located the issue in language, and the discourses of culture that institutionalized masculinity as the norm and defined femininity as deviance and insufficiency. In a world ordered by sexual imbalance, such oppositions as high/low, serious/trivial, art/craft would always echo the sexual hierarchy. Thus women art historians could not begin to discuss the cultural practices of women without deconstructing the very premises of the systemic sexism written into and performed by language and reproduced in art history's own special forms and particular discourses. A major example of the radical

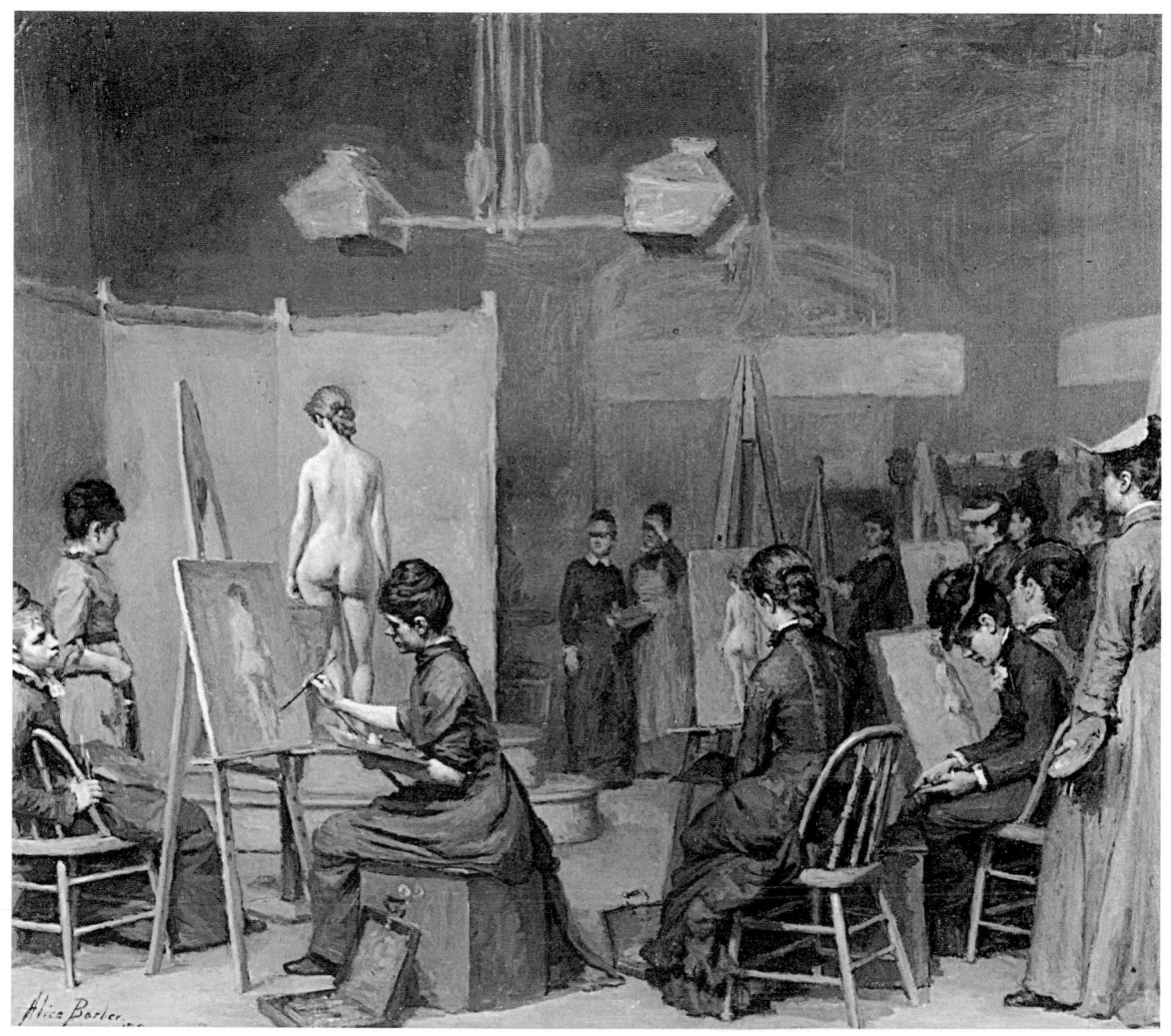

3. Alice Barber Stevens: *Women's Life Class*, grisaille, oil on board, 309×356 mm, *c.* 1879 (Philadelphia, PA, Pennsylvania Academy of the Fine Arts)

transformation is Tickner's *The Spectacle of Women* (1987), which analysed the visual history of the campaigns for women's suffrage, identifying the suffragists' use of visual spectacle, banners, postcards, posters, mass demonstrations in order to develop a visual rhetoric that challenged, while using the existing terms of, Edwardian femininity. The analysis of the war of images unleashed when women took on the bourgeois state to demand civil status was a contest about definitions of sexual difference as much as civil rights. Tickner's work revealed the importance of visual representation in society defined as a battlefield of representations. This book necessarily abolished the curatorial and art-historical distinctions between painting and posters, between performance and politics in order to establish the importance of this moment in the history of women, society and representation. Feminist art historians have, therefore, stressed the need for a social-structural analysis of the conditions of both artistic production and gender relations in order not only to situate and comprehend the forces that shaped women's lives, actions and cultural productions but also to undermine the false claims to suprasocial universality that is made for canonized white male art (*see* FEMINISM AND ART). Thus the issue of sexual difference is introduced to change the whole history of art, and not merely to reconfirm women's abnormal status within it.

4. FEMINIST CRITIQUES.

(i) Interventions. (ii) The nude. (iii) Questioning the canon. (iv) New art-historical parameters.

(i) Interventions. When Linda Nochlin published the article: 'Why Are There No Great Women Artists?' (1971), her object was not to answer the question but to expose its dangers, since it took for granted the idea of 'greatness' that is central to the canon (see also Duncan, 1975). She revealed the social and cultural pressures that determine who can and cannot make art and be acknowledged as a 'great' artist by showing the importance of extra-aesthetic factors, such as education, art institutions and prevailing cultural ideologies. Nochlin posed feminism as a catalyst for re-evaluating the discipline as a whole, because it raised such fundamental questions about the way art history obscures the social character of artistic practice and value systems. In 1981 Parker and Pollock published *Old Mistresses: Women, Art and Ideology*, borrowing the title from Gabhart and Broun's exhibition of 1972. They took up the question posed by the exhibition's authors of why there is no female equivalent for the reverential term old master. Pointing out a consistent pattern in the language used of women by art historians and critics since the 18th century, which they named 'the feminine stereotype', they argued that art history was not indifferent to women but had actively produced the terms of women's exclusion by creating a negative category against which a selective creativity, unacknowledged as masculine, was erected as the sole representative of Western culture. Furthermore, they examined the ideological bases of the division between the arts and crafts, analysed the varying history of the identity of the artist, and defined the historical moment of the revolutionary emergence of bourgeois society as that at which the terms 'woman' and 'artist' became socially and ideologically antagonistic. They argued that women

were positioned differentially in relation to dominant structures of artistic practice and definitions of artistic identity, but that they produced art as much because of as despite these conditions. Refuting a merely negative explanation, they stressed the ways in which women artists negotiated both institutions and representational traditions to produce works that require readings attuned to recognition of specificity rather than absolute difference. Finally, they explored the production relations between women artists and certain modernist movements—Surrealism (see also Vergine, 1980; Chadwick, 1985), Abstract Expressionism and conceptual art—leading up to the decisive challenge to modernism posed by the emergence of feminist practices in the visual arts in the 1970s. They established the necessity to erase the boundary between historical and contemporary art. Two anthologies edited by Norma Broude and Mary Garrard (1982 and 1992) bring together representative samples of the interventions women have made using these models and others into all periods from ancient Greece to the present. In 1987 Gouma-Peterson and Mathews provided a historical overview of the varying positions and debates produced by 'The Feminist Critique of Art and Art History' (responded to by Pollock, 1993). Lisa Tickner (1988) systematically evaluated the challenge of feminism to art history through analysis of several theorizations of the meaning of sexual difference.

(ii) The nude. One of the key areas of feminist intervention has been the portrayal of the female nude in Western art, which poses directly the question of sexuality and representation and reveals that there has been a politics of vision in the privileged field of art. Nochlin co-edited a series of papers on the theme of *Woman as Sex Object* in 1972. Duncan (1993) wrote extensively on the function of the modernist nude both in its early 20th-century context and then as a major element of the narratives of the modernist museum. Tickner's study of how contemporary artists negotiated the historical legacy of the art's appropriation of the female body in 'The Body Politic' appeared in the first volume of the Association of Art Historians' journal *Art History* (1972), creating considerable debate as the first major article to present feminist challenges to the field of representation of sexuality and the female body. Nead's *The Female Nude* (1992) explores the ambivalent status of the 'nude', which has become synonymous with 'art' in so far as the representation of the female body can be managed to figure containment and aesthetic conquest of the potentially unruly and obscene. Thus she breached the boundaries between high art and pornography, traditional culture and contemporary feminist practice in order to trace the complex web of relations around the female body, sexuality, obscenity and the discourses of aesthetics. Pollock (1993) provided a case-study of the relations between sex and race, between colonialism and modernism in the analysis of a single painting of the nude by Gauguin. Abigail Solomon-Godeau's study of the 19th-century photographic archive (1986) of images of the Countess of Castiglione produced a searching analysis of the representation of the female nude in particular and the female body in general in the

formation of photographic practices within commodity culture, with its dual fetishization of goods and sexuality.

(iii) Questioning the canon. In 1982 Nochlin posed another key question, 'Why Have There Been Great Male Ones [Artists]?', in an article analysing the social and political construction of Gustave Courbet's reputation as the 'father' of modern art. She showed that questions about the absence of women artists from art history required a complementary analysis of the ways in which the reputations of those artists who are canonized are secured. Pollock (1980) similarly identified the process by which van Gogh became the paradigmatic modern artist, articulating ancient myths about creativity, madness and genius, one key aspect of which is masculinity (see also Lipton on Picasso, and Zemel on van Gogh). Rogoff (in Broude and Garrard, 1992) applied a complementary analysis to the visual construction of artistic identity in German Expressionist self-portraiture. Salomon (1991) provided a thorough analysis of the formation of a masculinized canon by discerning in the genealogy of art-historical writing (from Vasari to 20th-century keepers of the canon such as Janson) a structure of masculine identification with heroic male creators. This idea is also proposed in Kofman's study of Freud's aesthetics (1988). Feminist work on the canon itself has led to re-readings of the works of van Gogh and Toulouse-Lautrec (Pollock, 1995); Degas (Lipton, 1986; Kendall and Pollock, 1992; Callen, 1995); Courbet (Nochlin, 1988 exh. cat.); and Rembrandt (Bal, 1991). Bringing semiotics, psychoanalysis and literary theory to break down the word/image opposition, Bal provided critical readings of the representation of gender in the work of Rembrandt and also produced a model of reading against the grain, 'reading for the woman', bringing to visibility overlooked and repressed possibilities in the figurative and narrative texts of a Baroque painter. Similar kinds of revisioning of canonical moments occur in the work of Simons on the representation of women in early Renaissance profile portraits ('Women in Frames', 1988) which elaborate issues of the gaze and its politics in representation based in the social exchange of women by men in contemporary marriage and property rituals. If the identity of the artist as masculine was increasingly established from the 19th century, women artists have had to negotiate a way to represent to themselves and to society their own creative identity. This has generated a series of studies of women's self-representation using diary materials, such as those by Mariga Bashkirtseva (Marie Bashkirtseff), Käthe Kollwitz, Paula Modersohn-Becker, or by looking at self-portraiture and photographic representation, as in the case of American Abstract Expressionist Lee Krasner (Wagner, 1988).

(iv) New art-historical parameters. Women artists and the issues raised by feminist studies cannot be accommodated within existing narratives of art history, particularly periodizations defined exclusively through stylistic change or epochal shifts that reflect unequally historical changes in the field of gender relations of importance for women. 'Did women have a Renaissance?' was a question posed and answered in the negative by the feminist historian Kelly (1984), provoking a related reconsideration of the major benchmarks in the history of art: such questions as

'Was the French Revolution a historical defeat for women?' and 'How did women—both bourgeois and working class—experience modernity and metropolitan life?' were also posed (see fig. 4; Pollock, 1988). If social relations are taken to be more determinant than simply stylistic shifts, the history of women in the arts will produce a different pattern of significant moments (as demonstrated by Tickner).

In an unpublished Masters degree thesis of 1980 Shirley Moreno focused her research on the emergence of the visual rhetoric of the erotic nude in 16th-century Venetian art, in relation to the redefinitions of concupiscence and temptation ordained by the Council of Trent and the Counter-Reformation, as well as to practices around prostitution and anxieties raised by venereal diseases, the emergence of illicit erotica and pornography, as well as traditional imagery for celebrations of marriage, and the regulation of marital alliances in changing class formations in both Venice (where such paintings were made by Titian) and Spain (by whose king they had been commissioned). Moreno concluded that the representation of woman in this form as a central category of western European painting should be understood in terms of a major shift in the organization and official definitions of sexuality represented by the cross-related institutions of the militant Roman Catholic Church and the Spanish monarchy. She utilized the concept of 'woman as sign' developed by Cowie (1978) to argue against perceiving the visual image as mere reflection of social processes. Drawing on structuralist analysis of society as a language system, Cowie

4. Margaret Bernadine Hall: *Fantine*, oil on canvas, 1.56×1.16 m, 1886 (Liverpool, Walker Art Gallery)

argued that practices of visual representation are constitutive of meanings, and that in patriarchal cultures woman becomes the sign of the exchange by which men are constituted as the key representatives of society itself. Visual systems, such as film and painting, use woman as a sign, not of womanhood or any social aspect of actual women, but to signify relations between men within a patriarchal structure. Thus feminist art historians would argue that there are no images of women, but rather that the history of art, as a privileged site of producing meaning for culture, should be analysed in terms of the varying formations of sexual difference and social power in which representation is a semiotic field, that is where signs produce meanings in relation to each other for specific and positioned users (Pollock in Kendall and Pollock, 1992).

Using the concept of 'woman as sign', Cherry and Pollock (1984) focused on British culture during the 19th century, another key moment of change in the regimes of representation around sexual difference. Studying the construction of working-class model and artist Elizabeth Siddal as Rossetti's muse, 'Siddal', in both Rossetti's drawings and the contemporary literature that manufactured the artist as a great master, they argued that the object of feminist analysis should be the discursive construction of meanings for the term 'woman' and 'artist', thus showing that they are historical and variable, while also revealing the intertextuality between verbal and visual discourses as part of a complex social totality. Not only social structures have to be considered. Visual images appeal to the viewer by offering visual pleasure, luring the spectator's gaze and arousing desire, itself the trace of formative memories. Feminists have begun to use psychoanalytical theory in the analysis of visual representation. Reconsidering Freud's essay on Leonardo da Vinci in the light of late 20th-century Lacanian revisions of psychoanalysis, Kristeva proposed an analysis of the representation of the Virgin in the work of Giovanni Bellini (1980), that used a single case study to explain the attraction and the variations of treatment of a topic of Renaissance art whose recurrence is not solely due to Christian theology but rather overdetermined by infantile memories of and psychic investment in the image of the mother. Kristeva's work on abjection (*Pouvoirs de l'horreur*, 1980) has been widely used in the analysis of representations of the maternal feminine in art and photography.

Although feminism has the potential to challenge and rewrite the entire history of art, not only to restore women's cultural contributions to the historical record, but also to allow us to read visual representations and artistic practices as distinct but necessary parts of the complex of social practices that collectively constitute society, its class, gender, sexual and race relations, the process has only just begun. There are areas more thoroughly investigated than others; modernism and Post-modernism have received considerable feminist analysis, whereas feminist interventions into Renaissance and Baroque periods are less numerous. Seventeenth-century Dutch art is a growing field, as is Classical antiquity. The study of women as painters has predominated over research into sculpture and printmaking, although areas such as embroidery and other textile forms have been reclaimed as 'women's true cultural heritage' (Mainardi, 1973). Western art is more consistently documented and researched than art by women in the rest of the world. A possible danger exists of constituting a new feminist canon, which privileges white women artists and neglects both women of colour in the West and women artists across the world. Feminist art histories of the 1970s were criticized for an unacknowledged racism; in the 1990s this challenge was being faced, stimulated by the activities of black women artists and art historians equally recovering a doubly repressed heritage of creativity. In terms of American art history, the token reference to the sculptor Edmonia Lewis is being amplified by research on sculptors Augusta Savage and Meta Vaux Fuller, while painters Alma Thomas (*b* 1895) and Georgia Jessup and multi-media artist Faith Ringgold are represented in the National Museum of Women's Art, which has also devoted a retrospective to photographer Carrie Mae Weems (1994). Hagewara (1990) has published a book in Japanese on black women artists in Britain in order to challenge the hegemony of Western ideas of art, which not only refuses acknowledgement of creativity to its own women but equally denies it to women of colour. Issues of racism in representation have been debated in contemporary art by women (Phillippi, 1987) and feminist analyses of orientalism (Nochlin, 1982, and Pollock, 1992) have pointed the way for feminism to be the catalyst by means of which issues not only of gender and sexual difference but also of social and cultural difference are consistently considered in the analysis of the history of art. In this way the interventions of women into art history can radically expand the perspectives, theories, methods and concerns of art history to produce more comprehensive and critical histories of art.

BIBLIOGRAPHY

EARLY SOURCES

C. C. Malvasia: *Felsina pittrice* (1678); ed. G. Zattori (1841)
A. Houbraken: *De groote schouburgh* (1718–21)
E. Guhl: *Die Frauen in der Kunstgeschichte* (Berlin, 1858)
E. Ellet: *Women Artists in All Ages and Countries* (New York, 1859)
E. C. Clayton: *English Female Artists* (London, 1876)
O. Fidière: *Les Femmes artistes à l'Académie royale de peinture et de sculpture* (Paris, 1885)
M. Vachon: *La Femme dans l'art* (Paris, 1893)
C. Clement: *Women in the Fine Arts from the Seventh Century B.C. to the Twentieth Century A.D.* (Boston, 1904/R New York, 1974)
A. Hirsch: *Die bildenden Künstlerinnen der Neuzeit* (Stuttgart, 1905)
——: *Die Frauen in der bildenden Kunst* (Stuttgart, 1905)
W. Shaw Sparrow: *Women Painters of the World* (London, 1905)
L. M. Ragg: *Women Artists of Bologna* (London, 1907)
K. Scheffler: *Die Frau in der Kunstgeschichte* (Berlin, 1908)
L. Märten: *Die Künstlerin* (Munich, 1914)

GENERAL

L. Nochlin: 'Why Are There No Great Women Artists?' (1971); repr. in *Art & Sexual Politics*, ed. E. Baker and T. Hess (New York and London, 1973)
Old Mistresses: Women Artists from the Past (exh. cat. by Gabhart and E. Broun, Baltimore, MD, Walters A.G., 1972)
D. Miner: *Anastasie and her Sisters: Women Artists of the Middle Ages* (Baltimore, 1974)
S. B. Ortner: 'Is Female to Male as Nature Is to Culture?', *Women, Culture and Society*, ed. M. Z. Rosaldo and L. Lamphere (Stamford, 1974)
E. Tufts: *Our Hidden Heritage: Five Centuries of Women Artists* (New York and London, 1974)
C. Duncan: 'When Greatness Is a Box of Wheaties', *Artforum* (Oct 1975), pp. 60–64; repr. in *Aesthetics and Power: Essays in Critical Art History* (Cambridge, 1993), pp. 121–32

Women of Photography: An Historical Survey (exh. cat. by M. Mann and A. Noggle, San Francisco, CA, MOMA; Santa Fé, Mus. NM; New York, Sidney Janis Gal.; Milwaukee, U. WI; and elsewhere; 1975–6)

L. Nochlin and A. Sutherland Harris: *Women Artists, 1550–1950* (Los Angeles and New York, 1976)

K. Peterson and J. J. Wilson: *Women Artists: Recognition and Reappraisal from the Early Middle Ages to the Twentieth Century* (New York, 1976)

E. Honig Fine: *Women and Art: A History of Women Painters and Sculptors from the Renaissance to the 20th Century* (London and Montclair, 1978)

G. Greer: *The Obstacle Race: The Fortunes of Women Painters and their Work* (London, 1979)

J. Collins and G. B. Optiz, eds: *Women Artists in America: 18th Century to the Present, 1790–1980* (New York, 1980)

G. Nabokowski, G. Sander and P. Gorsen: *Frauen in der Kunst* (Frankfurt am Main, 1980)

R. Parker and G. Pollock: *Old Mistresses: Women, Art and Ideology* (London and New York, 1981)

C. Richter Sherman with A. M. Holcomb: *Women as Interpreters of the Visual Arts, 1820–1970* (Westport, CT, and London, 1981)

R. Berger: *Malerinnen auf dem Weg in 20. Jahrhundert: Kunstgeschichte als Sozialgeschichte* (Cologne, 1982)

C. S. Rubinstein: *American Women Artists: From Early Indian Times to the Present* (New York, 1982)

I. Anscombe: *A Woman's Touch: Women in Design from 1860 to the Present Day* (London, 1984)

C. Lyle, S. Moore and C. Navaretta: *Women Artists of the World* (New York, 1984)

W. Chadwick: *Women Artists and the Surrealist Movement* (London and Boston, 1985)

C. Petteys: *Dictionary of Women Artists Born before 1900* (Boston, 1985)

W. Slatkin: *Women Artists in History: From Antiquity to the 20th Century* (Englewood Cliffs, 1985)

E. Krull: *Frauen in der Kunst* (Leipzig, 1986; Eng. trans., London, 1989)

J. Moutoussamy-Ashe: *Viewfinders: Black Women Photographers* (New York, 1986, rev. 1993)

P. Gerrish Nunn: *Canvassing: Recollections by Six Victorian Women Artists* (London, 1986)

N. Heller: *Women Artists: An Illustrated History* (London, 1987)

P. Gerrish Nunn: *Victorian Women Artists* (London, 1987)

R. Parker and G. Pollock: *Framing Feminism: Art and the Women's Movement, 1970–1985* (London, 1987)

D. Phillippi: 'The Conjuncture of Race and Gender in Anthropology and Art History: A Critical Study of Nancy Spero's Work', *Third Text*, i (1987), pp. 34–54

Das verborgene Museum: Dokumentation der Kunst von Frauen in Berliner öffentlichen Sammlungen (exh. cat., ed. G. Breitling and others, Berlin, 1987)

S. Kofman: *The Childhood of Art: An Interpretation of Freud's Aesthetics* (New York, 1988)

G. Pollock: *Vision and Difference: Feminism, Femininity and Histories of Art* (London, 1988)

P. Simons: 'Women in Frames: The Eye, the Gaze and the Profile in Renaissance Portraiture', *Hist. Workshop J.*, xxv (1988), pp. 4–30; repr. in N. Broude and M. Garrard: *The Expanding Discourse: Feminism and Art History* (New York, 1992)

L. Tickner: 'Feminism, Art History and Sexual Difference', *Genders*, 3 (1988); repr. in *Generations and Geographies*, ed. G. Pollock (London, 1995)

P. Gerrish Nunn and J. Marsh: *Women Artists and the Pre-Raphaelite Movement* (London, 1989)

A. Wagner: 'Lee Krasner as L. K.', *Representations*, xxv (1989); repr. in N. Broude and M. Garrard: *The Expanding Discourse: Feminism and Art History* (New York, 1992), pp. 425–35

W. Chadwick: *Women, Art and Society* (London, 1990)

P. Dunford: *A Biographical Dictionary of Women Artists in Europe and America since 1850* (London and New York, 1990)

H. Hagewara: *Kone mune no arashi* [This storm raging in my heart] (Tokyo, 1990) [Black women artists in Britain]

C. S. Rubinstein: *American Women Sculptors: A History of Women Working in Three Dimensions* (New York, 1990)

N. Broude and M. Garrard: *The Expanding Discourse: Feminism and Art History* (New York, 1992)

D. Cherry: *Painting Women: Victorian Women Artists* (London and New York, 1993)

C. Duncan: *Aesthetics and Power: Essays in Critical Art History* (Cambridge, 1993)

G. Pollock: 'The Politics of Theory: Generations and Geographies: Feminist Histories and the Histories of Art Histories', *Genders*, 17 (1993), pp. 97–120

N. Shalala: 'Creating towards Recognition: Japanese Women Artists', *Asian Art News*, iv/4 (1994), pp. 16–18

Forces of Change: Artists of the Arab World (exh. cat. by S. Mikdadi Nashashibi, Washington, DC, N. Mus. Women A., 1994)

An Intelligent Rebellion: Women Artists of Pakisthan (exh. cat. by S. Hashmi and N. Poomaya-Smith, Bradford, Cartwright Hall, 1994)

G. Pollock: *Differencing the Canon: Feminist Desire and the Writing of Art's History* (London, 1995)

SPECIALIST STUDIES

H. Opperman: 'Marie-Anne Collot in Russia: Two Portraits', *Burl. Mag.*, cvii (1965), pp. 408–10

L. Nochlin and T. B. Hess, eds: 'Woman as Sex Object: Studies in Erotic Art, 1730–1970', *Art News Annu.*, xxxviii (1972)

C. Duncan: 'Virility and Male Domination in Early Twentieth Century Vanguard Art', *Artforum* (Dec 1973); repr. in *Feminism and Art History: Questioning the Litany*, ed. N. Broude and M. D. Garrard (New York, 1982)

P. Mainardi: 'Quilts: The Great American Art', *Feminist A.J.*, ii/1 (1973); repr. in *Feminism and Art History: Questioning the Litany*, ed. N. Broude and M. D. Garrard (New York, 1982), pp. 331–46

L. Nochlin and T. B. Hess, eds: *Woman as Sex Object* (London, 1973)

E. Lipton: *Picasso Criticism, 1901–1939: The Making of an Artist Hero* (New York and London, 1976)

Künstlerinnen international, 1877–1977 (exh. cat., W. Berlin, Schloss Charlottenburg, 1977)

E. Cowie: 'Woman as Sign', *M/f*, 1 (1978); repr. in *M/f Reader*, ed. P. Adams and E. Cowie (London, 1992)

L. Tickner: 'The Body Politic: Female Sexuality and Women Artists since 1970', *A. Hist*, i/2 (1978), pp. 239–49, 263–76; repr. in R. Parker and G. Pollock: *Framing Feminism: Art and the Women's Movement, 1970–1985* (London, 1987), pp. 263–76, 336–9

A. Callen: *The Angel in the Studio: Women in the Arts and Crafts Movement, 1870–1914* (London, 1979)

C. M. Zemel: *The Formation of a Legend: Van Gogh Criticism, 1890–1920* (Ann Arbor, 1979, 2/1980)

P. Gorson: *Kunst und Krankheit: Metamorphosen der aesthetischen Einbildungskraft* (Frankfurt am Main, 1980)

J. Kristeva: 'Motherhood according to Bellini', *Desire in Language* (New York, 1980), pp. 237–70

——: *Pouvoirs de l'horreur* (Paris, 1980); Eng. trans. by L. S. Roudiez as *Powers of Horror: An Essay on Abjection* (New York, 1982)

G. Pollock: 'Artists, Media and Mythologies: Genius, Madness and Art History', *Screen*, xxi/2 (1980), pp. 57–96

L. Vergine: *L'altra metà dell'avanguardia, 1910–1940* (Milan, 1980, Fr. trans., 1982)

R. Berger: *Malerinnen auf dem Weg im 20. Jahrhundert: Kunstgeschichte als Sozialgeschichte* (Cologne, 1982, 2/1987)

N. Broude and M. D. Garrard, eds: *Feminism and Art History: Questioning the Litany* (New York, 1982)

L. Nochlin: 'The De-politicization of Gustave Courbet: Transformation and Rehabilitation under the Third Republic', *October*, 22 (1982), pp. 65–78

D. Cherry and G. Pollock: 'Woman as Sign in Pre-Raphaelite Literature: A Study of the Representation of Elizabeth Siddall', *A. Hist*, vii/2 (1984), pp. 206–27; repr. in G. Pollock: *Vision and Difference: Feminism, Femininity and Histories of Art* (London, 1988)

M. Kelly: 'Reviewing Modernist Criticism', *Art after Modernism: Rethinking Representation*, ed. B. Wallis (New York, 1984), pp. 87–103

L. Nead: 'The Magdalen in Modern Time: The Mythology of the Fallen Women in Pre-Raphaelite Painting', *Oxford A. J.*, vii/1 (1984), pp. 26–37

R. Parker: *The Subversive Stitch: Embroidery and the Making of the Feminine* (London, 1984)

M. Blind: *The Journals of Marie Bashkirtseff*, intro. by R. Parker and G. Pollock (London, 1985)

E. Lipton: *Looking into Degas: Uneasy Images of Women and Modern Life* (Berkeley and London, 1986)

A. Solomon-Godeau: 'The Legs of the Countess', *October*, 39 (Winter 1986), pp. 65–108

H. Dawkins: 'The Diaries and Photographs of Hannah Cullwick', *A. Hist*, x/2 (1987), pp. 154–87

T. Gouma-Peterson: 'Faith Ringgold's Narrative Quilts', *Faith Ringgold, Change: Painter Story Quilts* (New York, 1987), pp. 9–16

T. Gouma-Peterson and P. Mathews: 'The Feminist Critique of Art History', *A. Bull.*, lxix/3 (1987), pp. 326–57

L. Tickner: *The Spectacle of Women: Imagery of the Suffrage Campaign, 1907–14* (London, 1987)

P. Simons: *Gender and Sexuality in Renaissance and Baroque Italy* (Sydney, 1988)

L. Nochlin: 'Courbet's Real Allegory: Rereading *The Painter's Studio*', *Courbet Reconsidered* (exh. cat., ed. S. Faunce and L. Nochlin; New York, Brooklyn Mus., 1988)

M. Garrard: *Artemisia Gentileschi: The Female Hero in Italian Baroque Art* (Princeton, 1989)

C. Mitchell: 'Intellectuality and Sexuality: Camille Claudel, the Fin de Siècle Sculptress', *A. Hist.*, xxii/4 (1989), pp. 419–47

M. Sulter: *Passion: Discourses of Black Women's Creativity* (London, 1990)

M. Bal: *Reading Rembrandt* (New York and Cambridge, 1991)

S. Godeau: *Photography in the Dock* (Minneapolis, 1991)

N. Salomon: 'The Art Historical Canon: Sins of Omission', *(En)gendering Knowledge*, ed. J. Hartmann and E. Messer-Davidow (Knoxville, 1991)

R. Kendall and G. Pollock: *Dealing with Degas: Representations of Women and the Politics of Vision* (London, 1992)

L. Nead: *The Female Nude* (London and New York, 1992)

G. Pollock: *Avant-garde Gambits: Gender and the Colour of Art History* (London, 1992)

I. Rogoff: 'Tiny Anguishes: Reflections on Nagging, Scholastic Embarrassment, and Feminist Art History', *Differences*, iv/3 (1992)

W. Chadwick and I. de Courtivron: *Significant Others: Creativity and Intimate Partnership* (London, 1993)

T. Garb: *Sisters of the Brush: Women's Artistic Culture in Late Nineteenth-century Paris* (London and New Haven, 1994)

A. Callen: *The Spectacular Body: Science, Method and Meaning in the Work of Degas* (New Haven and London, 1995)

BIBLIOGRAPHIES

T. Cedar Holm: *Afro-American Artists: A Bio-bibliographical Directory* (Boston, 1973)

O. Williams: *American Black Women in the Arts and Social Sciences: A Bibliographic Survey* (New Jersey and London, 1973)

D. Bachmann and S. Piland: *Women Artists: An Historical, Contemporary and Feminist Bibliography* (Metuchen, NJ, and London, 1978)

E. Tufts: *American Women Artists, Past and Present: A Selected Bibliographical Guide* (New York, 1984)

GRISELDA POLLOCK

III. South and Central America.

Little mainstream South and Central American art history has dealt specifically with the role of the woman artist. Individual artists such as the Colombian Beatriz Gonzalez (*b* 1936) or Marisol in Venezuela are dominant figures in their respective contexts. Certain artists, such as the Colombian Débora Arango (*b* 1910) or the Cuban Amelia Peláez (1897–1968), have been re-appraised in light of feminist writings, but the problematic relationship of 'Latin American art' to that of 'international' art (see Richard) has in general taken precedence over discussions of gender divisions. The two issues have merged, however, in one instance. Late 20th-century perceptions of the art of South and Central America have been dominated by the enormous popularity of a woman artist, the Mexican Frida Kahlo. Kahlo has become not only the most famous and highly priced 'woman' artist but has also come to represent the perceived characteristics of an art produced outside the mainstream of European and North American culture (Baddeley, 1991).

The elision of these two strands of marginality within contemporary art history, the non-European and the 'feminine', has served to highlight rather than hide the role of the woman artist within Latin America. To some extent the work of the women artists of South and Central America has found a wider international audience than that of many of their male compatriots. In this sense the categorization 'woman artist', despite its intrinsic claims to represent a marginalized culture, is a more empowering category than 'Latin American', which denies an international relevance to the art it describes. Many of the stereotypes of Latin American art—decorative, naive, emotional, exotic—relate to the international stereotypes of femininity so attacked by late 20th-century feminism. Kahlo's reputation by the 1980s had grown from a recognition of these shared characteristics (see 1982 exh. cat.; Herrera, 1983). In addition to this, the traditional divisions between the arts, the high art–low art debate (which assigns a hierarchical value to particular forms of creativity) has great relevance within the context of South and Central America (Baddeley and Fraser, 1989). The culture of this region has been recognized abroad primarily via its popular art, usually anonymously produced manifestations of Latin America's complex racial and cultural mix. As with many popular craft traditions, women have played a key role in initiating and perpetuating these forms of creativity. Within the area of fine art many of the more renowned female practitioners have manifested an awareness of such popular traditions.

In Mexico, Kahlo is an archetype for such a position, but this is also found in the work of her contemporaries María Izquierdo, Olga Costa, Rocio Maldonado (*b* 1951) and Amalia Mesa-Bains (*b* 1943). The formal languages of all these artists draw heavily on the traditions of popular religious imagery and lay claim to an art of highly charged emotion. The scale and materials of Kahlo's works (e.g. *My Grandparents, My Parents and I, 1936*, New York, MOMA) echo the small votive images on tin found in many Mexican churches. Izquierdo's brightly coloured Virgins of Sorrows (e.g. *Altar of Sorrows*, 1943; Mexico City, Gal. A. Mex.) show the same mix of the aesthetic and the violent intrinsic to the Catholic tradition. These same references are found in the work of Costa (e.g. *The Fruitseller*, 1951; Mexico City, Mus. A. Mod.), with the added claim to the carefree beauty of the Mexican marketplace, with its riot of colour and carefully composed objects and produce. Maldonado and Mesa-Bains have added to this appropriation of the languages of popular art, with its evocation of the 'woman's world' of church and marketplace, a more knowing feminist aesthetic that transfers the traditions of earlier women artists to the large canvases and installations of the late 20th century; this is exemplified by, for example Maldonado's *The Virgin* (1985; Mexico City, Cent. Cult. A. Contemp.) and Mesa-Bains's installation *Queen of the Waters* (1992) for the *Arte América* exhibition (Bogotá, Bib. Luis-Angel Arango).

However, the Latin American artist's fascination with the traditions of the popular have not been the only strand of practice to produce important women artists. In Brazil the beginnings of modernist experimentation were dominated by the work of Tarsila and Anita Malfatti (1889–1964). The negative critical response to an exhibition in 1917 of Malfatti's 'fauvist' style paintings (e.g. the *Yellow Man*, 1915–16; São Paulo, Mus. A. Contemp. U. São Paulo) made her a figurehead for the Brazilian avant-garde. In 1922 both women participated in the groundbreaking 'Semana de Arte Moderna' (modern art week), which was to be instrumental in introducing the Brazilian art world to the debates of European modernism. In conjunction with the poet Oswald de Andrade, Tarsila transformed the modernist aesthetic into a more specifically Latin American and anti-colonialist movement, outlined in Andrade's 'Anthropophagite manifesto' (1928) and made visual in Tarsila's *Anthropophagy* (1929; Fund. José e Paulina Nemirovsky).

The naturalization and re-working of the prevailing international avant-garde aesthetic, initiated by Tarsila, was continued by a younger generation of artists including Iona Saldanha (*b* 1921). In her minimalist sculptures, such as *Bamboo Installation* (1969; artist's col.), she used traditional materials and ritualized compositions to create an art that links the concerns of colour field painting of the 1960s with anthropology. In Bolivia, María Luisa Pacheco and in Peru, Tilsa Tsuchiya also created a visual language that synthesized the specifics of their cultures, as both women and Latin Americans, with the demands of modernity. In both these women's works the purity of painterly abstraction is undermined: in Pacheco's subtle canvases, by the fleeting glimmer of an Andean landscape, and more obviously in Tsuchiya's references to Quechua mythology, as in *Machu Picchu* (1974; Lima, priv. col., see Baddeley and Fraser, p. 114).

A harder edged abstraction has been manifested in the work of some women artists, such as Gego and Mercedes Pardo in Venezuela but probably most notably in the work of the Brazilian Lygia Clark. In 1959 Clark (along with Lygia Pape, *b* 1929) was one of the founder-members of the Brazilian Neo-Concrete group and through her articulated sculptures (e.g. *Machine Animal* (*Bicho*), 1962; São Paulo, Fulvio and Adolpho Leirner, priv. col., see 1989 exh. cat., p. 265) gained an international reputation. Clark's highly cerebral work subverts traditional expectations of the 'irrational' nature of Latin American culture and denies expectations of a greater physicality and emotion in the work of women artists. The changing expectations of the 1980s and 1990s, in the wake of the Post-modernist rejection of a single monolithic culture, have led to the international recognition of contemporary Latin American art. Within this category the role of the woman artist has been central, an intrinsic part of a wider exploration of cultural identity.

BIBLIOGRAPHY
J. Franco: *Modern Culture of Latin America: Society & the Artist* (Harmondsworth, 1970)
Frida Kahlo & Tina Modotti (exh. cat., London, Whitechapel A.G., 1982)
H. Herrera: *Frida: A Biography of Frida Kahlo* (New York, 1983)
N. Richard: 'Post-Modernism and Perifery', *Third Text*, ii (Winter 1987–8)
J. Franco: *Plotting Women: Gender & Representation in Mexico* (London, 1989)
O. Baddeley and V. Fraser: *Drawing the Line: Art & Cultural Identity in Contemporary Latin America* (London, 1989)
Art in Latin America: The Modern Era, 1820–1980 (exh. cat. by D. Ades and others, London, Hayward Gal., 1989)
O. Baddeley: 'Her Dress Hangs Here: De-Frocking the Kahlo Cult', *Oxford A. J.*, xiv/1 (1991)
E. Lucie-Smith: *Latin American Art of the Twentieth Century* (London, 1993)

ORIANA BADDELEY

IV. East Asia.

The visual arts in which Chinese and Japanese women engaged were primarily painting, calligraphy and textile decoration. Needlework was the premier feminine art in China, where the invention of silk is credited to a legendary empress of remote antiquity, and silk production was traditionally regarded as women's work. Among the Chinese women celebrated for their textile decoration are Zhu Kerou, a 12th-century specialist in the tapestry technique known as *kesi* (slit silk), and Han Ximeng, an embroiderer active in the early 17th century. This article, however, focuses on women's contributions to the history of painting and calligraphy, the most highly esteemed and critically evaluated visual arts in China and Japan. Brief references are also made to the allied arts of print design and pottery decoration.

1. Role of women and professional artists. 2. Women as patrons. 3. Influence of women on subject and style. 4. 'Amateur' artists. 5. Records of activity.

1. ROLE OF WOMEN AND PROFESSIONAL ARTISTS. In early times the societies of China and Japan were very different, and, despite Japan's subsequent adoption of many aspects of Chinese culture, they remained distinct into the modern period. The status of women in the two countries became similar, but it was never entirely the same. Unlike Chinese women, Japanese women did not bind their feet and at certain times, such as the Heian period (794–1185), they played active roles in the formation of élite culture. Before the Heian, many women held religious and political authority in Japan: between AD 592 and 770 the country had six female rulers. As Japan embraced Confucian ideals in an attempt to re-create itself in China's image, however, the power and position of women steadily declined. In the Confucian view, an orderly society is based on hierarchical relationships, including the subordination of women to men. This social system excluded women from the halls of power and defined their proper sphere of activity as the family. Some women managed to subvert this system and take the reins of government, but most followed Confucian dictates and cultivated their various talents at home.

Socially restricted, women in both countries had few points of entry into the public art arena where professional artists, often organized in workshops, produced functional and decorative images for the Court, religious establishments and the general market. By the 1990s evidence had yet to be found that women were employed in the painting, printing or sculpture workshops of China. The few recorded Chinese women painters from the professional class belonged to its more élite ranks. They were usually the daughters of leading professional artists and probably worked at home. Daughters of Dai Jin and Qiu Ying, for instance, were known as painters. 'Miss' Qiu (personal name ?Zhu) treated figurative subjects, especially beautiful women, in a style based on her father's. She accepted commissions similar to those he received and succeeded as he did, by catering to the taste of the gentry for refined images in antique manners.

Opportunities for women to paint professionally seem to have been greater, or at least more diverse, in Japan. Some court ladies of the Heian period, notably Lady Tosa and Lady Kii, served as semi-professional painters at court, carrying out public commissions. A small number of women were affiliated with the Kanō school, the premier painting academy in Japan from the 16th to the 19th century. Kanō Yukinobu was the daughter of a pupil of Kanō Tan'yū and may also have studied with this master. Yukinobu employed a range of traditional styles, Chinese and Japanese, in depicting figures, birds and flowers, and landscapes for portable formats, usually hanging scrolls. Apparently she did not join the teams of Kanō artists who carried out large-scale decorations of castle and temple interiors. The majority of women active as professional artists in the Edo period (1600–1868) produced *ukiyoe*, pictures of the 'floating world' of the theatre and brothels. Best known in the 18th century were Yamazaki Ryū-jo and Inagaki Tsuru-jo, both of whom painted courtesans. In the 19th century women contributed to *ukiyoe* not only as painters, but also as print designers. The daughter of Katsushika Hokusai, who called herself Ōi, assisted her father in his workshop; her own works included paintings and book illustrations. The eldest daughter of Utagawa Kuniyoshi, Acho (who used the signature Yoshitori), collaborated with her father on a famous series of 70 or more prints, under the general title *Sankai medetai zue* ('Excellencies of mountain and sea illustrated'; 1852; U. Manchester, Whitworth A.G.), for which she designed the background scenes and he did the main figures.

2. WOMEN AS PATRONS. The achievements of such female artists notwithstanding, women mainly contributed to the public art arena as patrons. Religious establishments especially benefited from their support. Many women were drawn to Buddhism, which entered China around the time of Christ, and which was officially introduced into Japan in AD 552. Although originally no less patriarchal than Confucianism, Buddhism was more flexible and capable of adapting itself to different audiences, male and female. To Chinese and Japanese women it offered a socially acceptable sphere of activity and venue for personal expression outside of the family. The women in the best position to leave impressive legacies of Buddhist art were members of imperial families. Empress Wu (*reg* 690–705), the only female to rule China in her own right, used Buddhism to sanction her highly unorthodox assumption of the throne, and sponsored Buddhist art and architecture on a grand scale. She repaired the famous White Horse Monastery at Luoyang at great expense, had a five-storey pagoda housing a huge wooden image of the Buddha built on the palace grounds, and commissioned the colossal figures of the Vairochana Buddha assembly at the rock-cut Buddhist sanctuary at Longmen. The much later Empress-dowager Cisheng (1546–1614), a more representative imperial woman, provided funds for the celebrated monk–architect Fudeng to erect a bronze hall and gilt statue of the bodhisattva Guanyin at the Longchang Monastery, south-east of Nanjing, and also commissioned him to build the main hall of the Xiantong Monastery on Mt Wutai in Shanxi Province. In Japan two empresses of the Nara period (710–94), Kōmyō and Shōtoku, both sponsored colossal temples in the ancient capital of Nara. The former had built the Shinyakushiji, dedicated to the Buddha of medicine, when her husband, Emperor Shōmu, fell ill in 747. In 765 Empress Shōtoku ordered the construction of the Saidaiji ('western great temple') to rival her father's Tōdaiji ('eastern great temple') located in the eastern part of the city.

3. INFLUENCE OF WOMEN ON SUBJECT AND STYLE. As audiences as well as patrons, women popularized certain subjects and sometimes influenced the manner in which they were represented. Chinese women, for instance, embraced the bodhisattva of compassion, Guanyin, to whom they prayed for children, usually for males essential to the continuation of the patriarchal family line. Guanyin became a patron deity of women and acquired various feminine or female guises. Images of Guanyin holding a child, reminiscent of Western portrayals of the Madonna and Child, were produced in a variety of media, including painting, embroidery and porcelain, in late imperial China.

A telling example of a narrative tailored to a Japanese female audience is found in the *Tales of Gishō and Gangyō* (or *Biographies of the Six Patriarchs of the Kegon Sect*; Jap. *Kegonshū sōshi eden* or *Kegon engi*), a set of handscrolls given to the Kōzanji in Kyoto *c.* 1219–25. In the scrolls illustrating the tale of the monk Gishō, the role of the female protagonist Zenmyō is enlarged to appeal more directly to the scrolls' probable patron, Lady Sanmi, and to other women associated with the Kōzanji in the first half of the 13th century.

Within the corpus of secular literary themes shared by China and Japan were some created specifically for the education of upper-class women. Opinions on female education were always mixed, with conservatives maintaining that it was at best a waste of time. Given the Confucian emphasis on learning from history, however, it was more widely held that women could benefit from studying such edifying texts as the *Lie nü zhuan* ('Biographies of eminent women') by Liu Xiang (77–76 CE) and the *Nü xiaojing* ('Ladies' classic of filial piety') credited to a certain Madam Zheng of the Tang period (618–907). Illustrations of these and similar books served the same purpose. Early designs based on the biographies are preserved in the *Lie nü tu* ('Pictures of eminent women'), a handscroll attributed to the old master Gu Kaizhi in the Palace Museum in Beijing . Gu's name is also associated with the most famous extant Chinese didactic painting for women, the handscroll *Admonitions of the Court Instructress to the Ladies Palace*, (for illustration *see* GU KAIZHI). Illustrated scrolls of the *Nü xiaojing* were popular in the Song dynasty, and several versions datable to the Southern Song period (1127–1279) survive (see fig. 5). Although the paintings in these scrolls are ascribed to famous male artists, they were directed to female viewers, and the accompanying textual passages may have been transcribed by palace women skilled in calligraphy.

4. 'AMATEUR' ARTISTS. While restrictions on women's activities outside the home kept most Chinese and Japanese women from becoming professional artists, the private sphere of 'amateur' art provided an alternative. Many women took up the brush at home and painted as amateurs, or at least within a tradition defined as amateur even if some participants were compensated for their works. In both China and Japan painting came to be accepted as a suitable leisure pursuit for cultivated individuals, men and women. As one of the polite arts, it was closely allied with calligraphy and literature, especially

5. Ma Hezhi (attrib.): *Starting Point and Basic Principles*, handscroll, ink and colour on silk, h. 264 mm, Southern Song period, 1127–1279; illustration to chapter one of *Nü xiaojing* ('Ladies' classic of filial piety') (Taipei, National Palace Museum)

poetry. This alliance fostered the development of distinctive painting styles and preferences for certain categories of subject-matter.

In Heian-period Japan, aristocratic women and ladies-in-waiting at the court were expected to compose poetry, write an elegant hand, paint and appreciate all of these arts. They were closely involved with the distinctively Japanese pictorial genres developed at this time in connection with the vernacular literature in which women excelled. The well-known 12th-century handscroll illustrations of the *Tale of Genji* (*Genji monogatari*, *c.* 1005), the great novel by Lady Murasaki Shikibu, represent the type of small-scale pictures created to amuse Heian aristocrats, particularly women. Women also painted pictures of this type, and they are thought to have developed the highly stylized, static, colourful style they display. This style was also employed by male professional painters but, because of its close association with the Heian women's quarters, some scholars refer to it as *onnae*, or 'women's painting'.

In China, where painting was a relative latecomer to the constellation of arts known as the 'three perfections' (painting, poetry and calligraphy), the earliest known great female artist was a calligrapher known as Wei Furen (Madam Wei) or Wei Shuo (272–349 CE). She is remembered as the teacher of Wang Xizhi, the most celebrated and influential of all Chinese calligraphers. Although Wei Furen's works have been lost, a glimpse of her art may perhaps be caught in the fluid grace of her famous pupil's hand. Later men, apparently perceiving the feminine elegance underlying this classical tradition, promoted more masculine styles of writing to compete with that of Wang Xizhi.

The theoretical foundations for the Chinese tradition of scholarly 'amateur' painting, known as litcrati (*wenren*) painting, were laid in the Northern Song dynasty (960–1127) by the famous scholar–official Su Shi (1036–1101) and members of his circle. Scholarly stylistic traditions associated with certain genres, notably landscape and plant subjects, such as bamboo and flowering plum, developed through the Yuan (1279–1368) and Ming (1368–1644) periods. In the late Ming, stylistic lineages were defined, and a literati canon was established, engendering an orthodox tradition handed down to the modern period. Works produced within this tradition were held to reveal the character of their makers, but more importantly their subjects and styles signified literati values and thus class identity. The most influential critics held this type of art to be inherently superior to the work of professionals, denigrated as mere craftsmen.

During the Song period women in some of the leading literati families joined their fathers, brothers and husbands in sketching subjects such as plum blossoms and bamboo. At the Song courts women emulated officials and male members of the imperial family in practising calligraphy and painting for pleasure. Unfortunately, no paintings securely attributable to women of this time seem to have survived; our knowledge of their achievements comes wholly from such textual sources as those cited in the *Yutai huashi* compiled by Tang Souyu.

The earliest Chinese female painter whose artistic personality can be defined on the basis of both written records and cxtant works is Guan Daosheng (1262–1319). Wife of the renowned scholar–official and artist Zhao Mengfu, Guan Daosheng is also the most famous female painter in Chinese history. She is said to have depicted a range of subjects, including Buddhist figures, but to have excelled in monochrome ink-bamboo (*mozhu*). She reportedly created a distinctive type of bamboo painting featuring new-growth bamboo groves after rain. A composition of this type dated 1308, now mounted with other Yuan paintings in a handscroll belonging to the National Palace Museum in Taipei, may best represent her work. Guan Daosheng was also admired for her calligraphy. According to her epitaph, Emperor Renzong (*reg* 1312–21) collected an example of her writing, along with pieces by her husband and their son Zhao Yong, for the imperial archives, and remarked: '[This] will let later generations know that my reign not only had an expert female calligrapher, but a whole family capable in calligraphy, which is an extraordinary circumstance!' (Weidner and others).

A few other female artists are known from the Yuan, but only in the late years of the Ming dynasty (1368–1644); toward the end of the 16th century, do women begin to appear on the Chinese art-historical stage in significant numbers. This increase in the number and prominence of female artists is usually explained in terms of broader changes taking place in Chinese society in the late Ming: the growth of the market economy and merchant class, resulting in a wider dissemination of the material and intellectual aspects of élite culture. With the expansion of printing and popular literature, general literacy increased, and by the 16th century female literacy was widespread. In open-minded, affluent families of the later imperial period, literary and artistic talent could increase a young woman's chances for a good marriage to an educated gentleman. Meanwhile, in the thriving pleasure districts of Nanjing, Hangzhou and elsewhere, the number of courtesans increased. These women used the arts to entertain, as they had for centuries, but now increasingly included painting in their repertories.

Representative of the social range of female painters active in the late Ming are 'Miss' Qiu (*fl* mid–late 16th century), who was discussed above as a professional painter, the gentry woman Wen Shu (1595–1634) and the courtesan Ma Shouzhen (1548–1604). Wen Shu was born into a distinguished and artistic family in the south-eastern city of Suzhou. She was related to the painter Wen Zhengming, one of the 'Four Masters of the Ming' and the very model of the scholarly artist. Her husband was a son of another old Suzhou family, a gentleman who lived, in Ellen Laing's words, 'a life of unhurried scholarship' (see Weidner and others). The couple's straitened financial circumstances apparently led Wen Shu to sell her paintings. She was one of many well-educated women and men who, despite their allegiance to the amateur ideal, relied on their writing and painting skills as sources of income. Wen Shu specialized in finely drawn, delicately coloured depictions of plants, flowers and butterflies. A typical composition offers a close-up view of flowers, often lilies, growing by an eroded garden rock (see fig. 6). Wen Shu's art became so well known that it inspired forgery. She was also sought out by upper-class women as a painting tutor, and like Wei Furen and Guan Daosheng, became a model for later women painters of the gentry. Her immediate followers include her daughter, Zhao Zhao, and the sisters Zhou Xi and Zhou Hu (*fl* later 17th century).

So many courtesans took up the brush in the late Ming that the period might be regarded as the age of the courtesan in the history of Chinese women painters. Ma Shouzhen shared the stage with such other painting courtesans as Xue Susu (*fl* late 16th–mid-17th century), Lin Xue (*fl* first half 17th century), Gu Mei (1619–64), Dong Bai (1625–51) and Liu Shi (1618–64). All are known because of their alliances with leading literati. To win upper-class admirers, these women cultivated skills in poetry, calligraphy, painting and music, the same pastimes enjoyed by their clients. With some exceptions, such as Lin Xue, who specialized in landscape, the courtesans generally painted simple floral and plant subjects that could be easily mastered and spontaneously executed for

6. Wen Shu: *Tiger Lily and Garden Rock*, hanging scroll, ink and colours on paper, 1.14×0.40 m, Ming period, 1630 (Washington, DC, Freer Gallery of Art)

the amusement of a gentleman caller. The orchid, a metaphor for a beauty living in pure seclusion, was a favourite subject. Ma Shouzhen painted orchids in ink, or in ink and light colours, with a delicate touch and calculated refinement.

If the late Ming was the age of the courtesans, then the Qing dynasty (1644–1912) belonged to the daughters of the gentry, such as Chen Shu (1660–1736), Yun Bing (*fl* 18th century) and Ma Quan (*fl* first half 18th century). As was often the case with gentry women painters, Yun Bing and Ma Quan were born into artistic families. Yun Bing was a descendant of Yun Shouping, one of the so-called Six Masters of the Early Qing. Yun Bing took up her illustrious forebear's methods of flower painting and, of his many descendants who painted, was the most successful. People of the southern region called Yun Bing and Ma Quan 'a pair of incomparables', with the former acclaimed for her 'boneless' (unoutlined wash) method of painting flowers and the latter known for her outline technique. This conventional observation notwithstanding, the two women belonged to the same stream of Qing flower painting. Ma Quan's father, Ma Yuanyu (1669–1722), reportedly studied 'sketching from life' with Yun Shouping. Like Yun Shouping and Yun Bing, Ma Quan observed her floral and insect subjects closely, favoured a light touch and fresh colours, and made frequent reference to the art of the old masters, a standard practice in the scholarly painting tradition. Ma Quan's biography resembles Wen Shu's in several respects: she painted to help support her family, was in demand as a painting teacher, and became so famous that many forgeries passed under her name.

Chen Shu was born into a once-distinguished gentry family, but was not heir to a family painting tradition. She, however, established one. An ambitious artist, she tackled the full range of traditional Chinese painting subjects: figures, landscapes, birds, flowers and plants. Most of her surviving works are landscapes in orthodox manners or studies of birds and flowers. Most appealing are her flower sketches inspired by the work of the Ming master Chen Chun (1483–1544). Her eldest son, Qian Chenqun, a high-ranking official, presented many of his mother's paintings to the throne. Consequently, she is the female painter best represented in the former Qing imperial collection (Taipei, N. Pal. Mus.).

While the continuous and self-referential scholarly 'amateur' tradition came to dominate later Chinese painting, at least in the eyes of learned critics, in Japan 'amateur' painting enjoyed only moments of success and never dominated the field. Moreover, its two major moments in the Heian and Edo periods bear little resemblance to one another. Whereas Heian 'amateur' painting was primarily an indigenous development in which women and female society played leading roles, the amateur ideal of the Edo period was borrowed from the literati tradition of China and was cultivated mainly by men, although women also found it congenial. Several schools and styles were prominent in the Edo period, yet most respected Japanese women painters emerged from the ranks of the literati painters (*Bunjinga* or *Nanga*; *see* JAPAN, §VI, 4(vi)(c)).

Since Japanese literati painters of the Edo period took their cues from the scholarly artists of China, female artists associated with Japanese literati circles had much in common with the Chinese women painters discussed above. They likewise excelled in the 'three perfections', painted the same range of subjects, and made stylistic references to critically sanctioned old masters. Prominent among the female *bunjin* active in the 18th century was Ike Gyokuran. Along with her mother and grandmother

she operated a popular tea house in Kyoto and was a talented poet in the *waka* (classical) tradition. She was tutored in literati painting by one of its greatest Japanese exponents, her husband, Ike Taiga, and painted the

7. Ike Gyokuran: *Spring Landscape*, hanging scroll, ink and colours on silk, 1.12×0.48 m, 18th century (San Francisco, CA, Asian Art Museum of San Francisco)

standard scholarly plant subjects—bamboo, plum blossoms, orchids and chrysanthemums—and landscapes in a manner closely related to his, yet distinctive (see fig. 7).

Ema Saikō (1787–1861) and Chō Kōran (1804–79) are representative of the accomplished female literati of the 19th century. A child prodigy, initially taught by her father, Ema Saikō began studying painting at the age of 13 with a monk, Gyokurin (1751–1814). He specialized in bamboo, and this became her preferred subject. Saikō never married but became a close friend and pupil of the distinguished scholar and poet Rai San'yō. He tutored her in poetry and calligraphy and introduced her to leading literati in Kyoto, including Uragami Shunkin, with whom she continued her painting studies. Chō Kōran lived a bohemian life with her husband, travelling, writing poetry and playing the Chinese zither. She studied painting in Chinese manners with the master Nakabayashi Chikuto, and her works include ink orchids and bamboo, decorative ink-and-colour depictions of birds, flowers and butterflies, and landscapes in Chinese styles.

One of the most striking female personalities in the élite art world of 19th-century Japan was Ōtagaki Rengetsu (1791–1895), a Buddhist nun gifted in the composition of poetry in the *waka* form. She was also a calligrapher, painter and potter specializing in vessels for use in the Chinese-style of tea drinking known as *sencha* (infused tea). Her hand-modelled pots, incised or inscribed with her own poems, were widely collected in her lifetime and still enjoy great popularity. Rengetsu was also a patron of the celebrated artist Tomioka Tessai, whom she treated like a son and took into her home as her assistant. They collaborated on works in which he executed the paintings and she wrote the poetic inscriptions.

5. RECORDS OF ACTIVITY. The study of Chinese women painters is facilitated by their own awareness of their heritage. Qing women looked back to earlier female artists such as Wei Furen, Guan Daosheng, and Wen Shu, and during this period histories devoted to female calligraphers and painters appeared. The Hangzhou scholar Li E (1692–1752) compiled the *Yutai shushi* ('The Jade Terrace History of Calligraphy'), which inspired the *Yutai huashi* ('The Jade Terrace History of Painting'), a collection of notes on women painters from early times until the beginning of the 19th century. The latter was compiled by Tang Souyu, the wife of Wang Yuansun (1794–1836), a member of a distinguished scholarly family of Hangzhou and heir to a fine library. With this library at her disposal, Tang recovered information on female painters from over a hundred sources, ranging from early painting histories to the writings of Ming and Qing authors. In her book she grouped these artists according to their social status, with imperial ladies first, followed by wives and daughters, concubines, and, finally, courtesans. Within each group, the women are organized by dynasty. The largest category is the second, wives and daughters, flatteringly if condescendingly designated 'famous beauties'. These two books remain the most useful place to begin research on the female painters and calligraphers of China. Regrettably, comparable early sources about women artists in Japan do not seem to exist, although in the 18th and 19th centuries women artists were listed alongside men in biographical compilations such as *Koto shoga jinmei roku* ('Record of calligraphers and painters in the imperial capital') published in 1847.

BIBLIOGRAPHY

EARLY SOURCES

Li E: *Yutai shushi* [The Jade Terrace history of calligraphy]; repr. in *Meishu congshu* [Collected works on art] (1912–36)

Tang Souyu: *Yutai huashi* [The Jade Terrace history of painting]; repr. in *Huashi congshu* [Collected works on the history of painting] (Shanghai, 1963)

Koto shoga jinmei roku (1847)

GENERAL

F. Ayscough: *Chinese Women: Yesterday and Today* (Boston, 1937)

A. W. Hummel, ed.: *Eminent Chinese of the Ch'ing Period* (Washington, 1943)

(Ecke) Tseng Yu-ho: 'Hsueh Wu and her Orchids in the Collection of the Honolulu Academy of the Arts', *A. Asiatiques*, ii/3 (1955), pp. 197–208

Xu Bangda: 'Women Painters' Works in the Palace Museum', *Chin. Lit.*, 7 (1959), pp. 165–67

J. F. Handlin: 'Lu K'un's New Audience: The Influence of Women's Literacy in Sixteenth-Century Thought', *Women and Chinese Society*, eds M. Wolf and R. Witke (Stanford, 1975), pp. 13–38

T. Akiyama: *Heian jidai sezokuga no kenkyū* [Research on the secular painting of the Heian period] (Tokyo, 1964)

Chiang Chao-shen: 'The Identity of Yang Mei-tzu and the Paintings of Ma Yüan', *N. Pal. Mus. Bull.*, ii/2 (May 1967), pp. 1–14; ii/3, pp. 9–14

Ch'en Pao-chen: 'Kuan Tao-sheng and the National Palace Museum "Bamboo Rock"', *Gugong Jikan*, 11/4 (1977), pp. 51–84 [Eng. summary, p. 39]

Chen Yinke: *Liu Rushi biezhuan* [Suppl. biog. of Liu Rushi], 3 vols (Shanghai, 1980) [new edn of early biog.]

M. Weidner and others: *Views from Jade Terrace: Chinese Women Artists, 1300–1912* (Indianapolis, 1988), pp. 31, 67

Japanese Women Artists, 1600–1900 (exh. cat. by P. Fister, Lawrence, U. KS, Spencer Mus. A., 1988)

M. Weidner, ed.: *Flowering in the Shadows: Women in the History of Chinese and Japanese Painting* (Honolulu, 1990)

MARSHA WEIDNER

Wŏnchŏng. *See* MIN YŎNG-IK.

Wonder, Pieter Christoffel (*b* Utrecht, 10 Jan 1780; *d* Amsterdam, 12 July 1852). Dutch painter, active in England. He was largely self-taught, although between 1802 and 1804 he attended classes at the academy in Düsseldorf. In 1807 he established the Kunstliefde (Love of Art) Society in Utrecht together with other artists including Jan Kobell II. During this period he painted *Time* (1810; Amsterdam, Rijksmus.), a symbolical representation of a naked and winged old man in a strongly Neo-classical style. Wonder also painted interior scenes in imitation of the Dutch 17th-century masters.

In 1823 Gen. Sir John Murray, Bart, the Scottish collector (?1768–1827), invited Wonder to come and live in London. Murray had a strong admiration for Wonder's work and was convinced Wonder would obtain numerous portrait commissions in England. While in London, Wonder painted many portraits of the Murray family as well as of their friends and relatives. His masterpiece is *Sir John Murray's Art Gallery*, which he completed in 1830, three years after his patron's death (England, priv. col.; four oil sketches in London, N.P.G.; copy in pen and watercolour in Amsterdam, Rijksmus.; *see* DISPLAY OF ART, fig. 5). The painting depicts an imaginary gallery in which were assembled many leading British collectors of the day, including

Sir Abraham Hume, George Leveson-Gower, the Marquess of Stafford (later 1st Duke of Sutherland) and Sir Robert Peel, as well as recognizable copies of such famous Old Master paintings as Raphael's *Madonna and Child with St John* (Washington, DC, N.G.A.). It was probably painted to match a similar scene by Gonzalez Coques in Murray's collection (untraced). The *Staircase in Wonder's House in London* (1828; Utrecht, Cent. Mus.) is a similar, if less elaborate interior, remarkable for its fine rendering of surfaces and the striking fall of light. Wonder returned to the Netherlands in 1831.

BIBLIOGRAPHY
J. W. Niemeijer: 'P. C. Wonder in Engeland', *Bull. Rijksmus.*, xiii (1965), pp. 115–23
R. Walker: *National Portrait Gallery: Regency Portraits*, i (London, 1985), pp. 615–18

FRANS GRIJZENHOUT

Wong, Wucius [Wang Wuxie; Wang Wu-hsieh] (*b* Taiping, Dongguan County, Guangdong Province, 25 Oct 1936). Chinese painter, poet, critic, curator and art educator, active in Hong Kong and the USA. Wong settled in Hong Kong in 1946, becoming a pioneer in the avant-garde literary movements of the late 1950s. At the same time, he studied Chinese painting with LUI SHOU-KWAN who inspired in him a life-long search for a means to synthesize the art of the East and West, as well as to resolve the challenges of the traditional and the modern. Wong received formal training in Western art between 1961 and 1965 at the Columbus College of Art and Design, OH, and the Maryland Institute, Baltimore. On his return to Hong Kong, as staff member of the Hong Kong Museum of Art and the Swire School of Design, Hong Kong Polytechnic Institute, he became an influential advocate for Hong Kong art and design. Primarily a landscape artist, Wong captured the majesty of nature in some paintings and celebrated the sensuous and poetic moods of nature in others. Both styles reflect his intellectual approach to art and his introduction of new concepts in spatial organization and technical execution.

WRITINGS
W. Wuxie: 'Wode yishu daolu' [My artistic path], *Meishujia* (1979), no. 9, pp. 30–33
——: 'Wang Wuxie shuimohua xuan' [Selection of ink and wash paintings by Wucius Wong], *Meishujia* (1979), no. 9, pp. 33–7

BIBLIOGRAPHY
Wucius Wong (exh. cat., intro. L. Tam; Hong Kong, Mus. A., 1979)

MAYCHING KAO

Woning, De. Furniture workshop established in Amsterdam in 1902 by WILLEM PENAAT, JAN EISENLÖFFEL and the architect H. W. Mol. All three had left 'T BINNENHUIS to set up a venture that would produce good, affordable, mass-produced furniture based on the rationalist design principles of the Nieuwe Kunst style. Penaat concentrated on developing simple, aesthetic basic models for each type of furniture by improving traditional homemade furniture. Around 1908 a more decorative style was introduced that made use of more hardwoods and ornament. The 'improved' country chair was particularly successful, but the disadvantage was that Penaat's designs were copied and sold as cheaper versions. This led Penaat to trademark the models, one of his many organizational initiatives. In 1916

the workshop was taken over and renamed Nusink & Co., and it later ceased trading.

BIBLIOGRAPHY
L. Gans: *Nieuwe Kunst: De Nederlandse bijdrage tot de Art Nouveau: Dekoratieve kunst, kunstusnijverheid en architektuur, omstreeks 1900* [Nieuwe Kunst: the Dutch contribution to Art Nouveau: the decorative arts, the applied arts and architecture, c. 1900] (Utrecht, 1966)
F. Leidelmeijer and D. van der Cingel: *Art Nouveau en Art Deco in Nederland* (Amsterdam, 1983)
C. van Adrichem: *Willem Penaat: Meubelontwerper en organisator* [Willem Penaat: furniture designer and organizer] (Rotterdam, 1988)

PETRA DUPUITS

Wonsam, Anton. *See* WOENSAM, ANTON.

Wood (i). Material derived from the trunks, boughs and other hard parts of trees and shrubs and serving a wide range of artistic purposes. It has been used as a raw material for millennia, first to construct houses and make tools and weapons, and later to build temples, palaces and boats and to carve sculptures and furniture. As an organic raw material, wood is subject to destruction by fire, insects, fungi and bacteria, and even by light and water: thus the preservation and study of the relatively few wooden artefacts that have survived from early civilizations are of crucial importance.

I. Introduction. II. Varieties and uses. III. Techniques. IV. Conservation.

I. Introduction.

1. BIOLOGY. Wood represents the secondary permanent tissue of ligneous plants (trees and shrubs) that consist of trunks, branches and roots. It is produced from a formative layer known as cambium (see fig. 1a), which is between the bark and the wood. As it constantly increases in girth, cambium sheds wood cells (xylem; 1b) inwardly

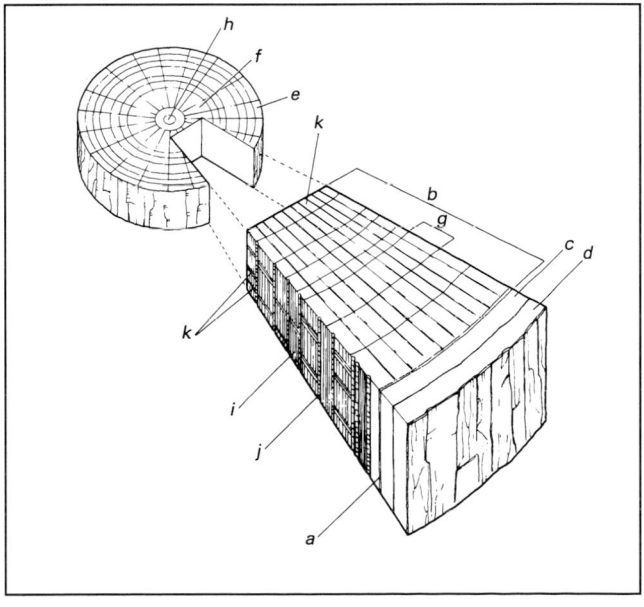

1. Cross-section through a tree trunk showing (a) cambium; (b) xylem; (c) phloem or inner bark (bast); (d) outer bark; (e) sapwood; (f) heartwood; (g) annual rings; (h) pith; (i) fibre or tracheids; (j) vessels or tracheids; (k) wood rays

and bark cells (phloem; 1c) outwardly. In this process the growth of bark is much less than the growth of wood. In older trees bark represents 10–15% of the whole and wood 85–90%. On the cross-section of a trunk with bark the following can be seen, varying according to the type of wood: the bark composed of a combination of inner bark (bast) and outer bark (1d); the wood part with sapwood (1e) and heartwood (1f), the annual or growth rings (1g) and various complexes of cell and tissue; and the central pith (1h). As wood ages, it is separated into sapwood and heartwood by processes aimed at producing a heart or core. The sapwood that lies on the outside as the living part of the trunk serves to conduct water and to hold nutrients. The heartwood—the inner core of the wood—is formed when the living cells die off; this process begins sooner or later in different species, but generally between the 20th and 40th year of a tree's life. In Europe the species of trees are divided according to the way in which the heartwood is formed. Trees that invariably form coloured heartwood are known as heartwood trees; examples include pine, larch, Douglas fir, oak, elm, walnut and cherry. Trees that may form coloured heartwood are not true heartwoods but are known as false heartwoods. These form heartwood only in certain conditions. False heartwood typically is of irregular shape in cross-section with cloud-like curving projections; examples include red heart in beech, brown heart in ash. Some trees form light-coloured heartwood; here the heartwood differs from the surrounding sapwood only in containing less water, but not in colour, for example spruce, fir, red beech, lime and pear. Such trees as birch, alder, aspen, sycamore, Norway maple and hornbeam (previously known as sapwood trees) have delayed heartwood formation. There are no differences between the sapwood and the heartwood as regards colour or moisture. The signs indicating heartwood formation can only be detected microscopically.

The tissue of wood is constructed of cells of various kinds, most of which extend lengthwise in the direction of the trunk (along the 'grain'; 1i and 1j). In the living tree these lignified cells take over the functions of conducting water and nutrients from the root to the crown and of supporting the trunk. Accordingly when the wood comes to be worked, it is fairly penetrable in the direction of the grain as well as being very rigid and strong. Across the grain—thus in a horizontal direction in relation to the standing tree—there are several ribbon-like bundles of cells that, because of their radiating pattern running from the centre of the trunk to the outer edge, are known as wood rays (1k). They take care of the transport and storage of nutrients. As a result of a secondary form of growth involving the thickening of the trunk, the tree periodically forms growth layers, known in temperate climates as annual rings. Thus the body of the wood shows three vertically superimposed main axes: the direction of the grain, the radial direction (in line with the wood rays) and the tangential direction (in line with the growth rings).

Just as coniferous and broad-leaf trees are very different in their outward structure, there are also clear distinctions in the anatomical structure of their woods (softwoods and hardwoods). In evolutionary terms conifers are very much older than broad-leaf trees. The origins of the modern coniferous families can be traced back to the Jurassic/

Cretaceous period (starting 185 or 140 million years ago), and woods with a typically coniferous structure are known from as early as the period of the mineral coal forest (Carboniferous), starting 330 million years ago. Broad-leaf trees, on the other hand, evolved mainly in the Tertiary period (65 million years ago). The wood of conifers is made up principally of tracheids, which take over both the functions of support and conduction; within an annual ring, which consists of porous early wood and denser late wood, the tracheids differ in the size of their cell cavities and the wall thickness. Wood rays represent a relatively small proportion of the volume of coniferous wood. The wood of broad-leaf trees is more evolved in terms of phylogenesis and is composed of cells that are more varied than those in coniferous wood, each being specially adapted to its particular function. This can be clearly seen in beech-wood with the division into vessels for providing water and wood fibres for support. Tracheids capable of taking over both functions and storage cells running parallel to the fibres and along the rays complete the structure.

In the different varieties of wood the substance of the wood is generally very similar in composition. Of the weight, 40 to 50% consists of cellulose, which is present in long chain molecules with a high degree of orientation. The cellulose, which is crystalline in structure, is embedded in amorphous lignin (25–30%) and hemicellulose (20–25%), which is in short chains. Thus within the individual cells wood displays a compound system in which the cellulose accounts for its great tensile strength and the lignin for its high resistance to pressure.

2. PROPERTIES. The great range of varieties of wood available means that it is always possible to choose one that meets the special requirements for any given use. On the other hand, this diversity makes it difficult to give a comprehensive review of the varieties and their specific properties. The first guide to selecting woods is the basic density, that is the relationship of the mass of a body of wood to its volume, including any cavities. Theoretically this can range from 0 (consisting only of cavities and pores) to 1.5 g/cm^3 (consisting only of cell walls); in practice the basic densities of woods lie between the very light balsa (*Ochroma lacopus*, 0.16 g/cm^3) and the very heavy lignum vitae (*Guiacum officinale*, 1.2 g/cm^3). When basic density is used as a measure, the range found among tropical woods is much wider than among native European wood varieties. Although the density of the substance forming the cell walls of all varieties of wood is the same, the differences in basic density are explained by the fact that the number of lignified cells and the thickness of their walls vary widely in test pieces of wood of the same size. Thus the basic density provides indications about the properties of the wood on which the specific amount of space occupied by the cell wall substance has a determining effect. As the basic density increases, the following also tend to increase: elasticity, hardness and resistance to wear, heat conductivity, degrees of swelling and shrinkage and the consumption of energy when machining.

Many types of wood contain extractable substances; these are highly varied in their chemical composition and have a considerable effect in determining the particular character of each variety of wood. Such substances are responsible for the colour, smell, resistance to pest infestation and chemical reactivity of the variety of wood in question. Tropical varieties of wood in particular have a countless number of these extracts and come in every colour of the palette, from the pale antiaris (*Antiaris africana*), through the lemon-yellow movingui (*Distemonanthus benthamianus*), the greenish greenheart (*Ocotea rodiei*), the brilliant red padauk (*Pterocarpus macrocarpus*), the purple amaranth or purpleheart (*Peltogyne venosa*) to black ebony (*Diospyros crassiflora*). There are also many other varieties that are popular because of decorative veins (see colour pl. IV, fig. 1), differentiated areas of colour or marked colour contrasts, such as Indian rosewood (*Dalbergia latifolia*), wenge (*Milettia laurentii*) and zebrano (*Microberlinia brazzavillensis*). The gamut of scents ranges from the highly aromatic sandalwood (*Santalum album*) to some varieties of ocotea that are aptly named 'stinkwood'. However, the reactivity of the substances contained within the wood can also be a disadvantage when the timber is being used. Among possible consequences are the corrosion of metals in contact with damp wood, interference with the setting of cement and the failure of lacquers and glues to harden. When machining some varieties of woods, workers may even experience allergic reactions.

II. Varieties and uses.

There is a vast number of types of wood throughout the world, with well over 10,000 varieties of tree having been identified and described. There are, for example, more than 500 varieties of conifer worldwide and more than 3000 different varieties of broadleaved trees in the Amazon tropical forest alone. About 80% of the Earth's forest cover is located in two large areas, one in the north of the northern hemisphere and the other in the Tropics. As regards their importance, the various types of forest tree must be judged on different criteria. Not only the properties of the wood but also the speed at which the tree grows and its size are important considerations. Thus in Germany oaks and even the yew grow slowly, while in Italy the trunks of poplars can reach a diameter of 300 mm in just six years. Different genera of tree vary markedly in their size. While in Europe conifers reach a maximum height of 50 m, some species of eucalyptus in the Australian savannah (e.g. *Eucalyptus regnans*) can grow as tall as 120 m. The tallest recorded tree, however, was a conifer (*Sequoia sempervirens*) that grew in North America.

The diversity of trees is reflected in the variety of woods, as can be seen in the way their names are listed for commercial use. These are not the botanical names of the species but those used in the timber trade and among users of wood. False names are often used particularly for imported timbers and result in confusion and the use of the wrong timber. Thus, for example, African walnut (*Masonia altissima*) is not walnut (*Juglans regia*), parana pine, or Brazilian pine, is not pine but a type of araucaria (*Araucaria angustifolia*), Western red cedar is not cedar but wood from the Cupressaceae family (*Thuja plicata*), and Philippine mahogany is not mahogany. Moreover, one false name can be used to cover several types of timber:

for example, African walnut is also used for dibétou (*Lovoa klaineana*). These false names developed when settlers applied the names of familiar woods from their native countries to different woods in the countries where they settled. They used such familiar-sounding names as oak, elm, ash, walnut, cherry and pear, as well as mahogany, cypress, cedar and teak. Besides false names there are also a large number of fanciful names, such as zebra-wood, red-wood, tiger-wood, violet-wood, rose-wood, coral-wood, iron-wood and satin-wood; while they do not suggest a different variety of wood, they can be misleading when applied to several varieties of timber.

Throughout history wood has been used in a wide variety of art forms, including architecture, sculpture, PANEL PAINTING, altarpieces (*see* ALTARPIECE), MUSICAL INSTRUMENTS, WOODCUT and WOOD-ENGRAVING, to name but a few examples. For wood sculpture and wood-carving it is the general practice to use indigenous woods as the basic material. In Japan (*see* JAPAN, §V, 1(ii)(b)) wood was a popular medium for sculptors and artist craftsmen. The main variety of wood used in the 7th century AD was camphor-wood or kusu (*Laurus camphora*). In the 8th century mainly hinoki, Japanese cypress (*Chamaecyparis obtusa*), was used alongside several other indigenous varieties. In India too (*see* INDIAN SUBCONTINENT, §§V and VIII, 8 and 19) different varieties of wood were available for sculpting and carving, and a rigorous selection was made according to the quality of the wood. Among the most important woods for carving were teak (*Tectona grandis*; see fig. 2k), shisham (*Dalbergia sissoo*; 2g), Indian rose-wood (*Dalbergia latifolia*; 2a), cedar-wood or deodar (*Cedrus deodara*), sandal-wood (*Santalum album*; 2f) and Himalayan ash (*Fraxinus floribunda*).

Wood sculpting was enormously important in Oceania (*see* PACIFIC ISLANDS, §§I, 2, and II, 6). Early carved works of art in wood were made using stone and shell tools, scrapers made out of teeth and various finishing implements (including skate bones and blades). The load-bearing posts of the houses of ancestors were often carved and painted. Identification of the wood has been carried out in a very few cases. In Africa (*see* AFRICA, §§V, 4, and VI, 2(i), 8 and 12) indigenous varieties of wood were always worked (see colour pl. III, fig. 2). These ranged from not very resistant woods that were easy to work to very durable species that were hard to work. The wood was mainly worked with adzes and knives made of iron. In the various countries of Africa it was mainly ancestral or cult figures that were worked in wood, but only very few pieces of carving more than 100 years old have survived. In Central America very few works in wood have been preserved. These include the carved wooden door supports of the Maya, which were made from sapotilla (*Achras zapota* or *Manilkara zapota*). In North America, on the other hand, there are huge totem poles mainly made from Western red cedar-wood (*Thuja plicata*), or the various masks of the different native peoples mostly made from alder-wood, maple and birch (*see* NATIVE NORTH AMERICAN ART, §III and SHELL, colour pl. II, fig. 1).

In Europe, wood sculpture particularly flourished during the Middle Ages. Until the end of the 18th century lime-wood was preferred to other varieties of wood for carving in almost every region of Europe, though on the

2. Timber samples from the Economic Botany Collections, Royal Botanic Gardens, from left to right (top row): (a) Indian rose-wood (*Dalbergia latifolia*); (b) ebony (*Diospyros ebenum*); (c) Scots pine (*Pinus sylvestris*); (d) crack willow (*Salix fragilis*); (e) lime (*Tilia vulgaris*); (f) sandal-wood (*santalum album*); (bottom row): (g) Indian shisham (*Dalbergia sissoo*); (h) oak (*Quercus robur*); (i) parasol pine (*Sciadopitys verticillata*); (j) Japanese camphor-wood (*Cinnamomum camphorum*); (k) teak (*Tectona grandis*) (London, Kew Gardens)

Upper Rhine poplar and willow-wood (2d) were also used in the 14th century, and artists from Lower Germany, Flanders, Brabant and the Rhine region worked mainly in oak (2h) and walnut. In south Germany the Siberian yellow pine also occurred more frequently. Hard, dense box-wood (*Buxus sempervirens*) was mainly used for plaquettes and small sculptures. In Italy and Spain the most popular woods were poplar, parasol pine (2i) and walnut; in France, lime (2e), poplar and walnut. Thus altogether about 20 European woods were used for wood-carving. Towards the end of the Middle Ages cedar and such imported woods as ebony (2b) were added to the list. In the 20th century a wide range of tropical and indigenous woods were used according to the preference of the craftsman, although in the 1980s and 1990s rain-forest timbers were increasingly avoided for ecological reasons.

BIBLIOGRAPHY

A. Seidensticker: *Waldgeschichte des Altertums* (Frankfurt an der Oder, 1886)

W. M. Harlow and E. S. Harrar: *Textbook of Dendrology* (New York, 1937, rev. 6/1979)

H. E. Desch: *Timber: Its Structure and Properties* (London, 1938, rev. 4/1968)

A. J. Panshin, H. P. Brown and C. C. Forsaith: *Textbook of Wood Technology* (New York, 1949); 4th edn by A. J. Panshin and C. de Zeeuw (New York, 1980)

C. P. Metcalfe, C. R. Chalk and L. Chalk: *Anatomy of the Dicotyledons*, 2 vols (Oxford, 1950)

H. Gottwald: *Handelshölzer* (Hamburg, 1958)

J. Marette: *Connaissance des primitifs par l'étude du bois du XII au XVI siècle* (Paris, 1961)

W. Sandermann: 'Holzfunde aus alten Kulturen', *Bild der Wissenschaft* (1967), pp. 207–17

B. J. Rendle: *World Timbers*, 3 vols (London, 1969–70)

M. Bramwell, ed.: *The International Book of Wood* (London, 1976)

D. Grosser: *Die Hölzer Mitteleuropas* (Berlin, 1977)

R. B. Hoadley: *Understanding Wood: A Craftsman's Guide to Wood Technology* (Newton, CT, 1980)

'Natural Variations of Wood Properties', *Proceedings of IUFRO Working Party: Oxford, 1980*

H. Willeitner and E. Schwab: *Holz: Aussenverwendung im Hochbau* (Stuttgart, 1981)

Nomenclature générale des bois tropicaux, Association Technique Internationale des Bois Tropicaux (Nogent-sur-Marne, 1982)

R. Wagenführ and G. Schreiber: *Holzatlas* (Leipzig, 1985)

H. J. Richter: *Holz als Rohstoff für den Musikinstrumentenbau* (Celle, 1988)

Holz-Lexikon (Stuttgart, 1988)

PETER KLEIN

III. Techniques.

1. Preparation. 2. Construction. 3. Decorative techniques. 4. Carving. 5. Surface finish.

1. PREPARATION. Wood requires controlled drying, called seasoning, before use to minimize shrinkage and distortion caused by loss of water. Because shrinkage is unequal in the three structural dimensions, timber tends to distort or warp as it dries. Normally, the outside of the wood, in intimate contact with the air, begins to dry before the inside; if this occurs too quickly, surface rupture, splitting and distortion will occur. Shrinkage cannot be avoided, but careful regulation of the extent and rate of drying helps to ensure that shrinkage will take place without undue distortion or damage before the wood is put to use. Before seasoning, logs are converted into square-edged pieces of timber suitable for use. Timber cut so that growth rings meet the surface at right angles (described as quarter sawn, radially or rift cut) reveals figure due to rays and tends to season slowly but retain its shape well. Timber cut so that the width of the boards is tangential to the growth rings exhibits growth ring figure. This is produced by back sawing (also described as tangential, flat or slash cutting). It seasons quickly but does not retain its shape well.

Seasoning may be carried out by the traditional method of natural air drying or by accelerated drying in kilns. Air drying is achieved by stacking boards with strips between them to allow circulation of air. The stack is raised clear of the ground and covered to keep out rain and sun. The timber dries according to the prevailing weather conditions at a rate determined by the gaps between boards and by the species and method of conversion of the timber in the stack. A rule of thumb is to allow a year for each inch of thickness. Using this method, moisture contents of 15–20% are achieved. Further drying takes place indoors in the environment where the wood is to be used. In kiln drying the timber is stacked as for air drying and placed in special kilns where the temperature, relative humidity and circulation of air can be controlled (see fig. 3). Starting with low temperature and high relative humidity, the temperature is gradually raised and the relative humidity lowered until the moisture content of the timber has been brought down to the desired level. Kiln drying is much quicker than air drying (5–30 days per inch of board thickness) and can result in moisture contents as low as 6–8% to suit applications in centrally heated environments. Kiln drying also kills eggs, larvae and adult stages of wood-boring insects.

It is difficult to season large baulks of wood (over 4 inches) without defects. Several different chemical treatments have therefore been developed to stabilize wood and prevent moisture-induced dimensional changes. Using polyethylene glycol (PEG), up to 90% reduction in shrinkage of green wood can be achieved. This is particularly appropriate for large pieces required for turning or

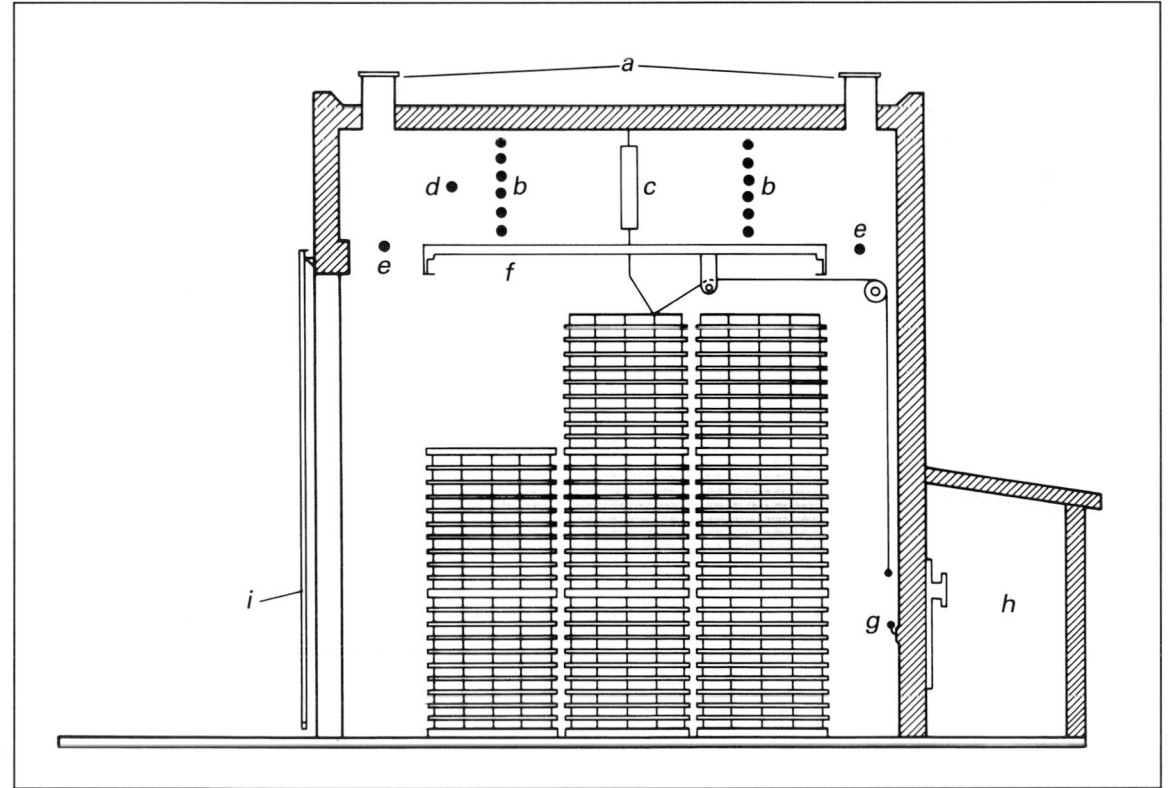

3. Timber-drying kiln, diagram: (a) automatic ventilators; (b) heating coils; (c) fan; (d) steam sprayline; (e) controller dry bulb; (f) false ceiling; (g) wet bulb; (h) control room; (i) door

carving where pieces of green timber can be worked close to the required size and shape before treatment. Chemical treatments are also used to increase resistance to fungi, wood-boring insects and fire. Several types of manmade timber products are available, including blockboard and laminboard, plywood, particle boards and fibreboards; these have the advantages of uniform strength and dimensional stability achieved by cancelling the effect of the pronounced grain direction of solid timber.

Newly converted and seasoned solid timber must be further prepared for most construction uses. The face side is selected and planed perfectly flat. One edge is selected to be the face edge and planed perfectly straight, flat and at right angles to the face side. The board is cut and planed to the correct width with edges parallel. The required thickness is then prepared by cutting and planing to gauge lines previously marked around both edges using a gauge held against the face side. One end is then marked, sawn and planed square to the face edge. The required length is measured from the prepared end and the remaining end cut and planed square to the face and edge. The process of planing an edge or end straight and square is called 'shooting'. When shaped members are required, only a modified form of preparation may be required.

Solid wood required for bending is carefully selected to be free of defects and with straight grain. Tangentially cut, air-dried timbers of species with good bending properties are most likely to be successful. Timbers with poor bending properties may be first glued to a good compressible bending wood that is later removed. Before bending solid wood it is plasticized, normally with heat and steam, to enable it to yield to compressive forces during bending.

It is not always practicable to use wood in solid form. Logs may be converted into thin sheets, called veneers, which are subsequently fixed to a stable support. Veneers are cut by one of three basic methods: sawing, slicing or rotary peeling. Wood to be veneered is prepared as for use in contruction. If a liquid glue is to be used in laying veneer, planing diagonally across the grain with a toothing plane will promote a uniform, thin glue line. A 'cross-band' veneer may be applied under the face veneer at right angles to the grain of the ground. Face veneers are cut to size and jointed for matching into patterns if required (see MARQUETRY). When cauls or presses are to be used, the pieces for built-up patterns are marked, cut and taped together before laying.

Wood surfaces should be smooth and perfectly clean before any form of finishing material is applied. Nails and pins are punched below the surface. Bruises may be removed by local application of steam. Small defects, setting-out marks and excess adhesive are removed using a smoothing plane followed by cabinet-scrapers and abrasive papers. The grain may then be raised by damping with water followed by light sanding and thorough dusting off when dry. Small holes, cracks and minor imperfections may be filled with a suitable stopping compound. Where a transparent finish is to be used, bleaching and/or staining followed by grain filling may be carried out beforehand.

BIBLIOGRAPHY

A. J. Panshin, H. P. Brown and C. C. Forsaith: *Textbook of Wood Technology* (New York, 1949, rev. 4/1980)

E. Joyce: *The Technique of Furniture Making* (London, 1970)

J. A. Walton: *Woodwork in Theory and Practice* (Sydney, 1979)

R. B. Hoadley: *Understanding Wood: A Craftsman's Guide to Wood Technology* (Newtown, CT, 1980)

R. Rowell: *The Chemistry of Solid Wood* (1984)

A. P. Schniewind: *Concise Encyclopaedia of Wood and Wood-based Materials* (Oxford, 1989)

N. D. UMNEY

2. CONSTRUCTION. For centuries wood has been an important material in architectural construction. However, as its use in this context is discussed in detail elsewhere (e.g. *see* VERNACULAR ARCHITECTURE, TIMBER STRUCTURE and ROOF), this section will concentrate on furniture construction.

Woodworking construction techniques are primarily determined by two major factors: the anatomical nature of wood and the availability of necessary tools. The nature of wood establishes the requirements for processing, preparation and joining, and tools were developed to satisfy those requirements in an efficient manner. The greatest strength of wood, in compression, tension and bending, lies in the direction of the grain; the weakest orientation is across the grain. Therefore, techniques of construction must overcome the unidirectional character of wood in order to make three-dimensional objects. This is accomplished either by carving the desired object from the solid or by joining smaller pieces of wood into a larger whole, with each piece orientated in the most advantageous way.

The full range of woodworking tools had appeared by the time of transition from the Stone Age to the Bronze Age: axe, adze, chisel, saw, piercer (drill), hammer and various scraping tools. For the most part, subsequent historical developments were less invention than refinement, as in the case of iron and steel replacing copper or bronze for cutting tools. The rotary motion lathe apparently first appeared c. 700 BC on the island of Samos. However, turned Celtic articles indicate that independent development also took place in other parts of the world. Although anticipated by the Egyptian scraper-adze, the plane was probably introduced by the Greeks and in wide use by the time of the Romans. Iron planes from the Roman period have been found at Pompeii and throughout Europe. The tools, the related woodworking techniques and all of the basic construction techniques were developed or at least anticipated by c. 500 BC. It is therefore misleading to suggest a chronological development of wood construction. In the 19th and 20th centuries improved ADHESIVES and power tools began to influence construction, as a result of individual craftsmen experimenting with new technologies in order to create inventive designs. This was most apparent in such design movements as Art Nouveau and Art Deco, as well as in the work of the Austrian Secessionists and part of the American Prairie School.

The simplest wood forms are those that are carved from the solid. This would include a felled tree trunk, perhaps crudely worked on one side with stone tools, as well as 20th-century machine-sculpted examples. Hollowing can also be accomplished with adze and scraper, in some cases assisted by fire, as in the dugout canoe. There has been periodic use of this technique in the 20th century by such craftsmen as the Americans Wharton Esherick (1887–1970) and Wendel Castle (*b* 1932). Wood that has been processed into large flat planks, either by sawing or riving (splitting), may be stacked, lashed, nailed or otherwise assembled together in what is termed 'plank' construction. Prehistorical lashing techniques survived in the earliest Egyptian furniture, for which fibre or skin thongs were used to join boards together and even to fasten legs to some pieces. Owing to the unidirectional strength of wood, it is difficult to design an adequate joint for fastening two boards together with the grain of one parallel to the other, as when fastening the bottom board of a chest to the sides. This was usually accomplished by driving a metal nail or trunnel (literally, 'tree-nail') through one board into the other. Often the wood was pre-pierced with a drill or awl to minimize the possibility of splitting. Even when the orientation of the boards allowed for the cutting of structural joints, as in the case where the ends of two boards meet at right angles, butting together and nailing persisted throughout history. Examples range from simple ancient objects to the elaborately carved and decorated Italian Renaissance cassoni and modern, inexpensive production furniture.

In the ancient world the slip-tenon developed as an alternative to some nailed plank construction (see fig. 4a). Where two boards were to be edge-fastened to create a wider panel, a number of slots (mortices), a few centimetres deep and long, were chiselled into the edges of each. When assembled, a small matching slip of wood (tenon) was inserted (4b), bridging the interface between the boards. Each mortice and enclosed tenon was then pierced and a wooden peg driven through to lock the assembly together. Although pegs have been replaced by modern adhesives, this type of construction enjoys a widespread revival in the form of 'biscuit' joinery. Here, mass-produced wafers of wood are glued into uniform, machine-produced mortices to effect the quick joining up of pieces of wood. The simplest form of construction that relies on integral joinery consists of a primary slab or slab-type element in which squared or rounded mortices are cut or bored. Into these mortices are fastened secondary elements on which corresponding tenons have been cut. Most slab-type furniture is made with either round or square mortice-and-tenon joinery, reflecting a natural distinction between joint types that are cut with processes based on axial rotation on the one hand, and 'square' or linear wood-working processes on the other. The former utilizes drill and lathe, and the latter chisel and saw. This division was institutionalized by the separate medieval guilds for craftsmen who made 'turned' objects and for those who made 'joined' objects.

The simplest example of slab construction is the split log bench into which three or four legs are socketed. A more complex slab construction is the Windsor chair, in which legs and back elements are joined to a plank seat with round mortice-and-tenon joints (4c). A less well-known example is the typical chair of ancient Egypt, in which legs and back were attached to the seat with square or rectangular mortice-and-tenon joints (see EGYPT, ANCIENT, §XVI, 6). Enormous bending stress can be applied to individual mortice-and-tenon joints, and chairs, benches and tables constructed in this fashion usually require the added support of back braces or stretchers, which are socketed into the legs. If mortices are cut completely

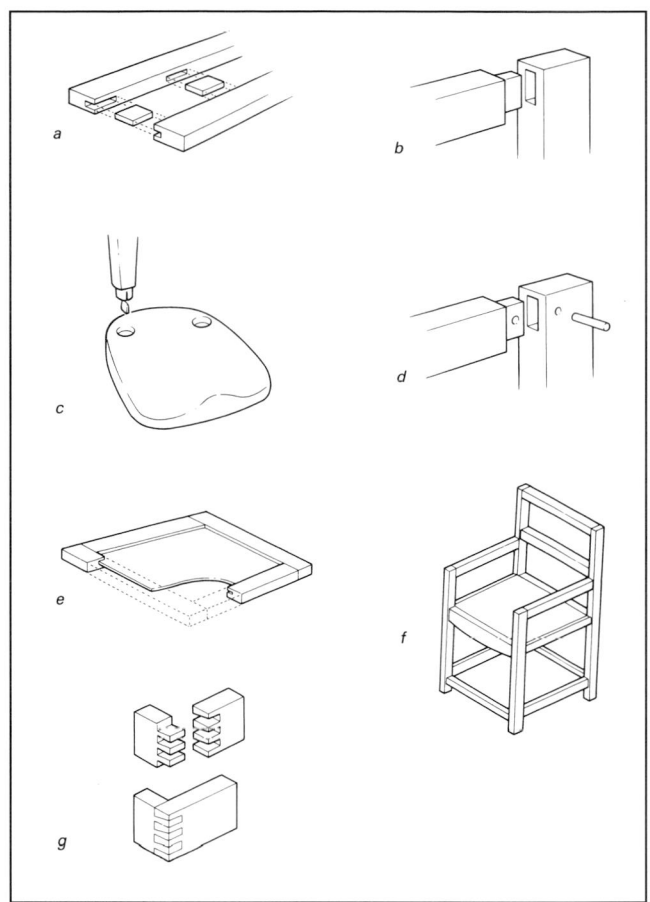

4. Types of wood joint: (a) slip-tenon; (b) mortice-and-tenon; (c) slab construction, as used in a Windsor chair; (d) pinned mortice-and-tenon; (e) frame and panel; (f) box-frame construction, as used in a chair; (g) dovetail

through the slab, structural integrity can be increased by driving a wedge into the end grain of a tenon where it emerges from the opposite side. If the mortices are 'blind' (i.e. not completely penetrating the slab but close enough to an edge), small pegs can be driven sideways through the joint to prevent the tenon from being withdrawn from the mortice (4d).

Square mortice-and-tenon joints, also pinned, are used to join up boards into a square, structural frame. Tenons are cut on the ends of one pair of 'rails', and corresponding mortices are cut into the perpendicularly orientated 'stiles'. A pair of these frames hinged in the middle of the rails to move in scissor-like fashion with fabric mounted between corresponding stiles is one of the earliest types of seating furniture: a 'camp'-type folding stool. Virtually identical examples of this construction appeared in ancient Nordic, Chinese and Egyptian cultures; the seat and legs of the modern 'director's' chair constitute another example. Open mortice-and-tenon frames may also be incorporated into other construction designs. Egyptian craftsmen often used this type of frame covered with fabric instead of a solid board in the slab construction of beds and chairs. Other examples can be seen throughout history in caned seating furniture or as applied doorframes to the open face of cupboards or other box-type objects.

In frame-and-panel construction (4e), a thinner solid board or panel is housed in a groove cut around the inside edge of the frame. With the longitudinal axis of the individual frame elements orientated around the perimeter of the assembly and the engaged board 'floating' freely within the groove, the problems of environmentally induced dimensional change in a solid piece of wood are avoided. Constructed with multiple stiles (as in a raised-panel door), rails and panels greatly expand the area that can be covered or filled with a thin, stable slab of wood. Frame-and-panel slabs (sometimes referred to as made-up panels) can also be used in plank construction, where they are simply edge joined to each other with wooden pegs or metal nails to form a box. Frame-and-panel elements were used in the plank construction of an Egyptian coffin from Tarkhan (c. 2850–c. 2600 BC; New York, Met.).

Morticed frame or frame-and-panel assemblies can be incorporated into more complex, three-dimensional box-frames. For example, four vertical stiles can be joined together with eight rails into a square or rectangular structure. If five of the openings are filled with panels, an open box is the result. Box-frame construction is also used in chair-making (4f), where the top of the box is covered with an applied wood or fabric seat and two of the vertical stiles extend above the seat to become part of the back-frame. The front stiles may also extend to become supports for arms. Solid wood panels may be fitted to some of the frame openings, but only the seat and back need be filled and even these not necessarily with wood. This method differs fundamentally from slab construction and is most recognizable in European joined chairs where many, and in some examples all, frame openings are filled with panels. The use of panels and the position of rails varied, but this type of box-frame construction has been in widespread use throughout history. Demonstrating a fundamental break with slab-type Egyptian chair construction, the Greeks used a minimalist form of box-frame construction to create the klismos chair (see GREECE, ANCIENT, §X, 4(i)(c)). In this case there are no panels and only one set of horizontal seat rails that mortice into the front and rear legs. The back, formed by continuous rear legs and a

5. 'Palmio' armchair by Alvar Aalto, laminated birch, birch plywood and solid birch, painted seat, 610×635×890 mm, 1930–33 (London, Victoria and Albert Museum)

horizontal top or crest rail, no longer required cumbersome additional support where it meets the seat.

An alternative to the mortice-and-tenon socket-type joint is the interlocking dovetail (4g). A series of dovetails is generally used to join full-width boards end to end, into a box-type structure. To this box additional elements can be added to produce various primary and secondary furniture forms. Examples of dovetail construction include drawers and the chest in which they reside.

Construction techniques that involve lamination can also be used to overcome the transverse weakness of wood, to produce curved shapes, or both. Medieval slab-built doors were constructed by bolting or riveting together multiple layers of boards with the grain of each layer orientated perpendicularly to the next. Banded together with iron straps, chests and coffers made of composite slabs of this type are very strong. With improvements in adhesive technology, glue-laminated furniture parts were introduced in the 19th century. Curved elements were made from multiple layers of thin wood, bent to shape and glued together. Thin but rigid curved shells were also produced by laminating many layers of thin veneer, usually with alternating grain direction, over a curved mould. This shell could be part of an otherwise traditionally constructed piece of furniture, or, as in the 20th century, it could become the primary structural element. Laminated and carved chair backs constructed by this method were introduced by John Henry Belter in his New York factory in the mid-19th century. Such craftsmen as Charles Eames and Alvar Aalto (see fig. 5) further refined this technology in the 20th century.

BIBLIOGRAPHY

W. L. Goodman: *The History of Woodworking Tools* (London, 1964)
H. S. Baker: *Furniture in the Ancient World: Origins and Evolution, 3100–475 BC* (London, 1966)
L. Feduchi: *A History of World Furniture* (Barcelona, 1975)
K. Seike: *The Art of Japanese Joinery* (New York, 1977)
V. Chinnery: *Oak Furniture: The British Tradition* (Woodbridge, 1979)
W. L. Goodman: 'Classical Greek Joinery', *Working Wood*, i/3 (Autumn 1979), pp. 20–24
C. A. Hewett: *English Historic Carpentry* (London, 1980)
R. B. Hoadley: *Understanding Wood: A Craftsman's Guide to Wood Technology* (Newtown, CT, 1980)
E. Klatt: *Die Konstruktion alter Möbel* (Stuttgart, 1982)
L. Chanson: *Traité d'ébénisterie* (Dourdan, 1986)
B. Forman: *American Seating Furniture, 1630–1730* (New York, 1988)

MICHAEL SÁNDOR VON PODMANICZKY

3. DECORATIVE TECHNIQUES. Many techniques used to decorate furniture and woodwork throughout history have their roots in ancient Egypt (*see* EGYPT, ANCIENT, §VII, 3). Several hundred pieces of furniture, often of great elaboration (see colour pl. III, fig. 1), survive from tombs as early as 3000 BC. In Mesopotamia, as later in Classical Greece and Rome and the Byzantine empire, very little survives apart from fragments, and decorative techniques are difficult to ascertain from such secondary sources as contemporary paintings and sculpture. As the design of much early furniture, whether fixed or movable, grew from architectural form, decorative motifs and techniques evolved in a similar manner. It is therefore important to consider the subject in relation to the surroundings for which pieces were conceived. Sometimes the same craftsmen would have worked on both. Until the 17th century almost all surviving furniture and interiors in the Western world were those of the Church and the wealthiest classes; fashion was generally driven by the desire of rulers and their courts to find sumptuous and innovative styles to rival their neighbours. Thus many techniques became widespread, with different countries developing their own specializations depending on particular traditions and influences, or the woods and other materials that were available.

Paint has been used on furniture and woodwork in a variety of ways: to represent images in the tradition of painting on canvas or panel; to create decorative coloured or patterned surfaces; or to simulate a more valuable wood or some other material such as marble or ivory (*see* §5 below and PAINTED EFFECTS). Each of these techniques executed in tempera paint can be found on ancient Egyptian furniture as well as on Greek and Roman examples. Pictorial decoration was common at various periods, sometimes with commemorative or symbolic

6. Decoration in oil paint on satinwood veneer, top of pier table, w. 952 mm, English, *c.* 1790 (London, Norman Adams Ltd)

significance. Examples include elaborately painted scenes on Florentine 16th-century marriage chests (*see* CASSONE, §1(i)), mythological or biblical scenes painted on copper panels on drawer fronts of 17th-century Flemish cabinets (*see* BELGIUM, fig. 32), portraits of deities in the decorative borders of Neo-classical painted furniture at the end of the 18th century (see fig. 6) and scenes from medieval legends painted on furniture by William Morris at the end of the 19th century. There is also a widespread tradition of simpler regional furniture in which paint generally covered the entire surface, often with vigorous and uninhibited colours and patterns. In southern Germany and France, northern Italy, Russia and Scandinavia, where even the wealthiest homes had painted furniture and painted floors, this tradition is particularly notable. In these areas most of the available wood was inferior softwood. By contrast, very few vernacular chairs in Britain were painted, apart from those used outdoors and painted, generally in green, for protection. The USA has a strong folk tradition of painted furniture, and most early pieces seem to have been painted or stained. Pennsylvanian Quakers carried on the European custom of painted dower chests, taking decorative motifs from Bible stories and medieval myths and legends. American Windsor chairs were generally painted, and in the early 19th century the Hitchcock factory (*see* HITCHCOCK, LAMBERT) popularized stencilled gilt decoration on painted chairs of inexpensive birch or maple (*see* VERNACULAR FURNITURE).

7. Marquetry of rosewood, with tortoiseshell and mother-of-pearl, on a *mueble enconchado*, h. 2.82 m, Peruvian, 18th century (New York, Christie's Manson and Woods International)

Many techniques use wood merely as a carcase to be covered up with decoration (*see* GILDING, §II, 3, and LACQUER). Where they were readily available or could be acquired through trade or conquest, fine hardwoods were also used for their own qualities, whether in the solid or veneer. These might include a striking colour or grain pattern or a burr that could be enhanced by the way it was cut and polished (see colour pl. I, fig. 1). Varnishes and oils were used for this purpose from Egyptian times onwards. Different woods were juxtaposed to create an effective contrast or laid, particularly in veneer, so that dramatic figuring might be matched in reverse or in quarters. The practice of veneering an inferior wood with a more valuable or attractive wood cut into thin sheets has been known since the Egyptian 1st Dynasty. Bandings with the grain running in different directions were also used to frame panels of figured wood and applied mouldings; these could be of great complexity or textured, such as the rippled ebony mouldings made in the Netherlands in the 17th century (*see* FRAME, fig. 57d, e and g). At the same time in northern Italy there was a fashion for pyrographic decoration or pokerwork. In the 18th century oriental influence in the West is shown in applied or pierced fretwork (*see* CHINOISERIE, fig. 2), while at all periods, except those of particular restraint, richness and texture were added with carving (*see* §4 below).

Inlay is the decoration of wood with a pattern or motif composed of pieces of wood or other materials in contrasting colours cut out and set into the solid (see colour pl. II, fig. 2). In MARQUETRY the carcase is completely covered with veneers of different colours, cut into a design and fitted together (see colour pl. IV, fig. 2). Pictorial marquetry was a comparatively late development, but geometric inlay (parquetry) is known from early Egyptian times, when thin pieces of glazed faience, such stones as lapis lazuli, painted glass and stained ivory were sometimes used. Complex inlaid furniture of the 1st century AD has been reconstructed from fragments found at Pompeii. In the 15th century walnut panels in Italian churches and palazzi were decorated with inlay of various coloured woods, known as intarsia (a term widely used on the Continent to denote both inlay and marquetry). Architectural perspectives and still-life groups of great skill survive (*see* STUDIOLO, fig. 1). In the 16th and 17th centuries the German states were famous for their exuberant inlay, and Nuremberg and Augsburg had long traditions of making fine ebony cabinets inlaid with ivory, tortoiseshell, amber, metals and hardstones (*see* GERMANY, fig. 44); these were exported all over Europe.

In 16th-century Spain and Portugal, another type of decoration with small-scale geometric patterns inlaid in precious woods, ivory and even metal derived from the long Islamic tradition of exquisite woodwork in the region (*see* ISLAMIC ART, §VII, 2(i) and MARQUETRY, colour pl. VIII, fig. 3). It is linked to similar *certosina* work carried out in Italy, particularly around Lombardy and Venice. The intricate interlaced foliage patterns known as arabesques were also derived from Islamic art, probably by way of Syrian and Egyptian metalwork of the 15th century (*see* VENETO-SARACENIC). Silver and gold from South American colonies as well as exotic woods, mother-of-pearl and tortoiseshell were much used throughout the colonial period, especially on prestigious Spanish *vargueños* and cabinets (see fig. 7). In Italy ebony cabinets were also inlaid with iron damascened with silver and gold, while in the Germanic countries and northern Italy engraved ivory, arabesque and figured (grotesque) inlay was fashionable on cabinets. The boxes and larger pieces inlaid and veneered in ivory that were imported from India in the 18th century were similarly popular (*see* INDIAN SUBCON-TINENT, §VIII, 8 and 10 and fig. 334).

The idea of marquetry of contrasting brass, pewter and tortoiseshell is thought to have been an Italian one, but it gained popularity in 17th-century France at the hands of a Dutch master craftsman, Pierre Gole. The technique was perfected, however, by the Frenchman ANDRÉ CHARLES BOULLE, from whom it took its name of boulle-work. Each material was cut into patterns and glued together to form fanciful scenes with elaborate foliate or grotesque borders (*see* MARQUETRY, colour pl. VII). Boulle used these panels in reversed pairs, known as *premier partie* and *contre partie*, to decorate either the same or matching pieces of furniture. Often the brass would be finely engraved and set in ebony with splendid gilded mounts. Further refinements were made with the addition of pewter, mother-of-pearl or stained horn. Boulle marquetry was also produced in southern Germany and continued in France through the 18th century. During the first half of the 18th century some English or Germanic furniture featured inlay of finely engraved brass panels or mother-of-pearl with decorative stringing of brass, sometimes in padouk or other hardwoods (*see* MARQUETRY, colour pl. VIII, fig. 1). The collecting of earlier French furniture by the English in the post-Revolutionary dispersals led to a revival of boullework and brass inlay in the early 19th century.

BIBLIOGRAPHY
R. Dossie: *Handmaid to the Arts* (London, 1758)
T. Sheraton: *The Cabinet Dictionary* (London, 1803)
R. Bitmead: *The London Cabinetmaker's Guide to. . .the Art of Laying Veneers of All Kinds. . .and Marqueterie, Buhl-work, Mosaic, Inlaying etc.* (London, 1873)
J. M. Ritz: *Alte bemalte Bauernmöbeln* (Munich, 1938)
F. Arcangeli: *Tarsie* (Rome, 1943)
H. S. Baker: *Furniture in the Ancient World* (London, 1966)
E. Mercer: *Furniture, 700–1700* (London, 1969)
H. Huth: *Lacquer in the West* (Chicago and London, 1971)
W. A. Lincoln: *The Art and Practice of Marquetry* (London, 1971)
I. O'Neil: *The Art of Painted Finish for Furniture and Decoration* (New York, 1971)
D. A. Fales jr: *American Painted Furniture, 1668–1880* (New York, 1972)
P. Eames: *Furniture in England, France and the Netherlands from the 12th to 15th Century* (Leeds, 1977)
D. Hawkins: *The Technique of Wood Surface Decoration* (London, 1986)
G. Manni: *Mobili in Emilia, con una indagine sulla civiltà dell'arredo alla corte degli estense* (Modena, 1986)
F. de Dampierre: *The Best of Painted Furniture* (London, 1987)
S. Digby: *The Mother-of-pearl Overlay Furniture of Gujarat* (Oxford, 1987)
CHRISTOPHER CLAXTON STEVENS

4. CARVING. Besides the knife, the basic tools of woodcarving—the technique of cutting ornament and sculpture in wood—are those used by any woodworker (see fig. 8). The type and size of tool affect the size and intricacy of the work achieved. Wood makes particular demands on the carver: as it is mainly composed of long, parallel fibres, most of its strength lies along the grain. A sharp edge running between the fibres prizes them apart,

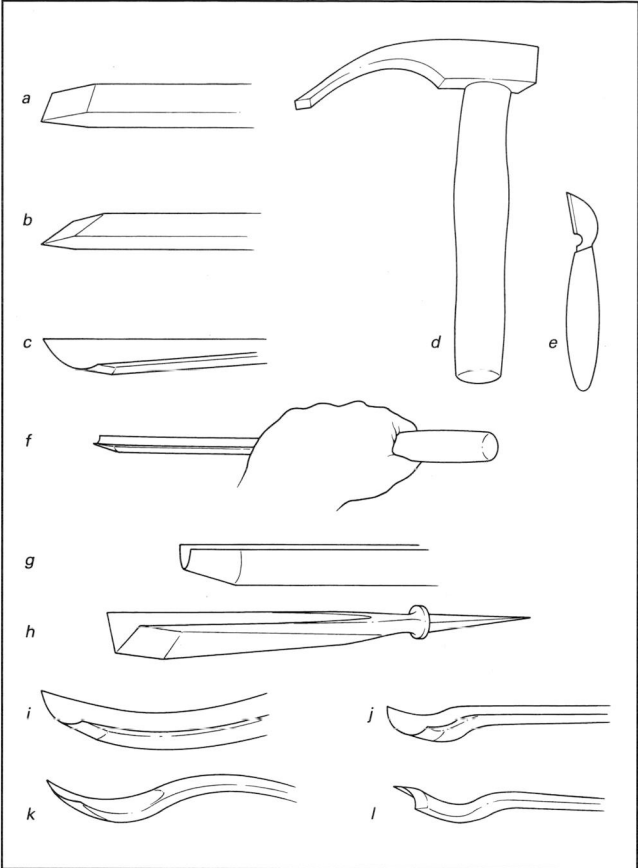

8. Woodcarving tools: (a) straight-edged chisel; (b) straight-edged skew or corner chisel; (c) straight carving gouge (shallow); (d) adze; (e) whittling knife; (f) straight gouge, showing position of hand; (g) U-shaped gouge or veiner; (h) V-shaped chisel or parting tool, showing typical tang for fixing into a handle; (i) long or salmon bent gouge; (j) short bent (spoon bit) gouge; (k) short bent (grounder) 'flat' gouge; (l) backbent gouge

causing various degrees of tearing or splitting; a blunt or rough edge will tear the fibres. This peculiarity of wood has caused the development of most shapes of tool, especially the many types of chisel, known as gouges, that have a hollow or 'flute' on one side. Tools run from a straight-edged chisel (8a) and a straight-edged 'skew' or corner chisel (8b), acutely angled at one corner and obtuse at the other, to the deepest gouge. The depth of the flute, known as the sweep, progresses from nearly flat (8c) in narrow gouges to a 'U' shape. If a gouge enters the wood with its corners above the surface, the risk of splitting when carving straight or diagonally across the grain is reduced. The flatter the gouge the more even the surface produced. Superior quality steel is essential to maintain sharpness.

Chip-carving, the simplest form of carving, involves two or more short cuts aimed at the same place in the wood from different angles and is generally used for surface decoration. Much totem pole-carving, for example, is chip-carved with an adze (8d) or axe. Many types of cut are variations of chip carving, even in such sophisticated work as the curling ringlets of hair on the head of a late

15th-century German lime-wood figure. To create this, a shallow gouge is driven into the wood, usually perpendicular to the surface, and is then pushed in from a steep angle at the side until a crescent-shaped piece of wood chips out. By repeatedly reversing the direction of the chisel for succeeding pairs of cuts, a wavy pattern will develop (see colour pl. II, fig. 1). When forming an eyeball, a berry or a small boss in the centre of a flower, for example, the same technique is used, but with the flute facing downwards. The other main type of cut, made with a knife or a chisel, is a long stroke that creates a groove on the surface of the wood or slices off an edge. Whittling is a form of carving carried out with a knife (8e). The object to be carved is usually held in one hand, and the knife is used to chip pieces out and create patterns, or to pare away larger pieces and create small sculptures. The knife can be moved with a sawing or a slicing action. As considerable pressure is needed in this process, the knife has to be used with care. Larger items can be reduced by sawing or by hewing with an axe or adze before whittling. Carving with a chisel is a faster method, as more power can be used. A particular shape of chisel can be selected to create a distinct impression in the wood that may be impossible or extremely difficult to make using only a knife. A chisel needs to be held and guided by one hand while the other hand wields a mallet to strike the end of the handle of the chisel, strikes the chisel with the base of the palm, or grips the handle of the chisel to push it. Right-handed people would usually hold the chisel in the left hand, the hand normally gripping part of the blade and handle, but experienced carvers, especially those carving decorative mouldings, work ambidextrously. As both hands are thus occupied, the object to be carved has to be held firmly. Large objects are held steady by their own weight. In some cultures, the object to be carved is held between the legs, and in the Western tradition is held by mechanical means.

Relief-carving may involve simply creating an outline of the design with shallow cuts made with a U-shaped gouge (8f), which in widths of approximately less than 5 mm is known as a 'veiner' (8g). Many carving chisels are sold unhandled. The V-shaped chisel or parting tool illustrated here (8h) has a typical tang, which is used to ream a conical hole in the handle before being driven in the last few millimetres. Extremely sharp tools are essential when carving relief work, as cuts that are diagonal to the grain are inevitably rough on one side. On one side of the cut the fibres are stroked together and cut cleanly, but on the other side are pulled apart and torn. The solution to this problem is to make a preliminary cut all around, then achieve the required depth and width by using the same or a smaller tool to cut along the rough side of the channel in the direction of the grain. At corners, where the angle of grain changes sharply, a cut in from the side across the grain is usually necessary. The surface may then be finely carved using various gouges. Deeper relief-carving involves setting down around the object using the above method or using stabbing cuts made all around and at least 2 mm outside the outline of the design. A deep gouge can then carve away the waste wood across the grain. As the required depth is reached, flatter gouges can level off the ground. The outline of the design is then cleared until

it appears to have been fretted out and fastened down. Experienced carvers, however, may establish high and low reliefs prior to cutting in the details of the design. To reach those areas of the ground that are inaccessible to straight gouges, bent gouges have been developed. These are bent in a long curve from the handle and are known as long, or 'salmon', bent gouges (8i), or are short bent and known as 'spoon bit' gouges (8j). The flatter types, known as 'grounders' (8k), are used to smooth the ground in difficult areas. Deeper spoon bit gouges are used to hollow out inside curves. To create convex inside curves, a backbent gouge (8l) is used. Once the ground is established, high- and low-relief features are roughed (bosted) out and the fine detail carved (see colour pl. I, fig. 2).

Work in the round is first roughed out with an axe or saw. Some carvers tend to start by cutting closely to profiles, but sculptors usually work in from further away, carving around the forms with deep gouges across the grain, or chopping, sawing or rasping the planes before attempting any detailed carving. Machines, for example the chainsaw and various rotary cutters, save time and can create unique textures.

Cutting letters is a specialized form of carving, achieved by a mixture of stabbing and chasing. V-shaped tools and veiners do not usually produce good letters. Carving decoy ducks and other animal forms can combine whittling and burning in the details with a pyrograph. Wire, adhesives and resins are also used in creating these types of object, as they are overpainted later.

Particularly fine stones and strops are used to sharpen chisels. Specially shaped slip stones can grind a short bevel on the inside surface of gouges. This makes a lower cutting angle on the under bevel possible, which is essential for long, sweeping cuts, and enables gouges to be used with the hollow face downwards. A steep under-bevel without another bevel inside is best for the short, scooping cuts that are used in Japanese and other traditions of carving.

Any type of wood can be carved. The ideal timber for carving is even-textured and hard enough to take fine detail. Lime is a good timber, but lacks figure, while walnut can be too dark or have too much pattern in the figure for detailing to show. The liveliest carving is created by finishing with only a chisel, then waxed or oiled. Sandpapering wood to a very fine finish can blur detail. Gilded or polychromed sculpture can be smoothed with abrasives, as detail can later be recut in the gesso.

BIBLIOGRAPHY

G. Jack: *Woodcarving: Design and Workmanship* (London, 1903/R 1978)
P. N. Hasluck, ed.: *Manual of Traditional Woodcarving* (London, 1911/R New York, 1978)
E. J. Tangerman: *Whittling and Woodcarving* (New York, 1936); rev. as *Big Book of Whittling and Woodcarving* (New York, 1990)
W. Wheeler and C. Hayward: *Practical Woodcarving and Gilding* (London, 1963/R 1973) [the most authoritative modern work]
J. C. Rich: *Sculpture in Wood* (New York, 1970/R 1992)
F. Oughton: *The History and Practice of Woodcarving* (London, 1976)
M. Baxandall: *The Limewood Sculptors of Renaissance Germany* (New Haven, CT, 1980/R 1985)
A. Bridgewater and G. Bridgewater: *The Craft of Woodcarving* (Newton Abbot, 1981)
I. Norbury: *The Technique of Creative Woodcarving* (London, 1984/R 1990)
J. Ayers: *The Artist's Craft* (Oxford, 1985)
A. T. Jackson: *Collins Complete Woodworker's Manual* (London, 1989/R 1990), pp. 272–82

Woodcarving (Lewes, 1992–)
C. Pye: *Woodcarving: Tools, Materials and Equipment* (Lewes, 1994)

DICK ONIANS

5. SURFACE FINISH. Surface coatings on wood have been found on objects dating from as early as the 1st millennium BC. Microscopic analysis of samples taken from furniture of the 8th century BC found in Gordion, Turkey, has revealed the presence of a resinous coating. THEOPHILUS, a German monk, wrote of oil-resin varnishes in the 12th century, and similar Italian recipes are known from the 15th century. In the 20th century coatings have been manufactured from a wide range of materials to achieve many appearances, from high gloss transparent natural resin finishes to opaque, synthetic painted or lacquered surfaces. Coatings on wood serve two important functions: they protect the wooden substrate from damage due to abrasion and exposure to excessive moisture, and manipulation of the finished surface can achieve a wide range of visual effects. Colour, texture and the gloss level can all be adjusted through various finishing procedures.

The surface treatment of wooden objects falls into the two general categories: transparent coatings and such decorative opaque coverings as PAINT, GILDING or LACQUER. In addition, painted surfaces were sometimes coated with a protective transparent coating. The category of decorative surfaces also includes those to which DYE or stain has been applied. Dyes and stains are used selectively to exaggerate the grain of the wood, to diminish variations in the wood and to provide contrast between various parts of an object. Before 1850 the dyes used in wood finishing were generally naturally occurring organic materials that could be dissolved in alcohol or water. Alkanet root, cochineal, madder and logwood were among the most frequently used dye materials during the 18th century. After this date, aniline dyes began to be more commonly used. Stains, which are thinly dispersed pigments suspended in a medium such as a drying oil, have also been used extensively to colour wood. Ebonizing is a method of dyeing such light woods as maple to imitate the more expensive ebony. Fuming is a method of colouring wood with chemicals in the place of dyes or stains. Woods with a high tannin content will darken when exposed to ammonia gas. This technique was used to colour much of the oak furniture of the Arts and Crafts Movement.

Pigments in an oil binder have been the preferred paint for decorating furniture; among the most notable exceptions are the tempera found on Italian cassoni (*see* CASSONE, §1) of the 15th and 16th centuries and the use of resinous binders by japanners to imitate Eastern lacquerwork in the 18th century. The methods for preparing the surface for painting are as varied as the decorative schemes. Often the wood was coated with a GESSO layer to fill the grain and provide a smooth opaque surface on which to paint, although on vernacular objects painting was frequently done directly on bare wood. Beginning as early as the 17th century, a technique known as graining was used to decorate common woods to look like the more prized varieties; marble was often imitated as well (*see* PAINTED EFFECTS). Both graining and marbling were carried out in a similar manner: the application of a base coat, a

transparent glaze coat to simulate the grain, followed by a protective varnish layer.

While painted surfaces were not always coated with additional transparent protective varnish layers, those that had been dyed, stained or left uncoloured almost always were. Drying oils, waxes and varnishes made from natural resins were the most common materials used to coat wooden objects prior to the 20th century. Natural resins, including such soft resins as the sap of living trees and insect exudate, as well as the harder fossilized tree resins, have all been used in traditional varnish-making. There are three general types of VARNISH made from natural resins: spirit varnish, essential oil varnish and fixed oil varnish. Each is applied in liquid form and dries to a hard transparent surface.

Spirit varnishes are made by dissolving one of the soft resins, such as shellac or sandarac, in alcohol. Recipes for spirit varnishes exist from as early as the 16th century, and they were the most frequently mentioned varnishes in the European cabinet making guidebooks of the 17th and 18th centuries. These varnishes were usually applied with a brush, although the French developed a technique for wiping on thin layers with a cloth around the turn of the 19th century (French polish). Essential oil varnishes consist of a RESIN dissolved in a petroleum distillate or a SOLVENT derived from the distillation of a plant sap, such as spirits of turpentine. Petroleum distillates (often referred to as naphtha in early documents) were probably in most common use until the 16th century, when the distillation of turpentine became better known. Mastic varnish was a familiar essential oil varnish, although it tended to be soft and was more appropriate as a picture varnish. An essential oil varnish made of colophony (pine sap) dissolved in spirits of turpentine was frequently used as an inexpensive furniture varnish in 18th- and 19th-century America. The most durable of the varnishes, fixed oil varnish, is made from one of the harder fossil resins such as copal or amber. As these resins are not easily dissolved in alcohol or other distillates, they can be incorporated into a varnish, needing only to be heated and ground before combination with a drying oil such as linseed oil. Fixed oil varnishes are also referred to as 'rubbing varnishes' because on hardening they can be polished with such fine abrasives as pumice and rottenstone to produce a brilliant shine.

While varnish-making has a lengthy history, it was not until the late 17th century that varnishes became the primary material for finishing furniture and other wood surfaces. Oak, which had been the predominant cabinet wood to this point, was not well suited for a varnished surface because of its coarse texture. As such fine-grained woods as walnut and mahogany became more prevalent in cabinetmaking, the use of varnish became more common. Before this time, the two most common treatments for wooden surfaces were drying oils (*see* OILS, DRYING) and WAX. Linseed oil was the most frequently used drying oil, but others such as poppy, nut and hempseed oil were also popular. Techniques involving the use of oil vary from simply soaking the wood to more elaborate polishing steps, often with the addition of PIGMENT to the oil. Wax was particularly favoured for turned work as it could simply be held against the work while it was turned on the lathe (see fig. 9). Beeswax was also combined with spirits

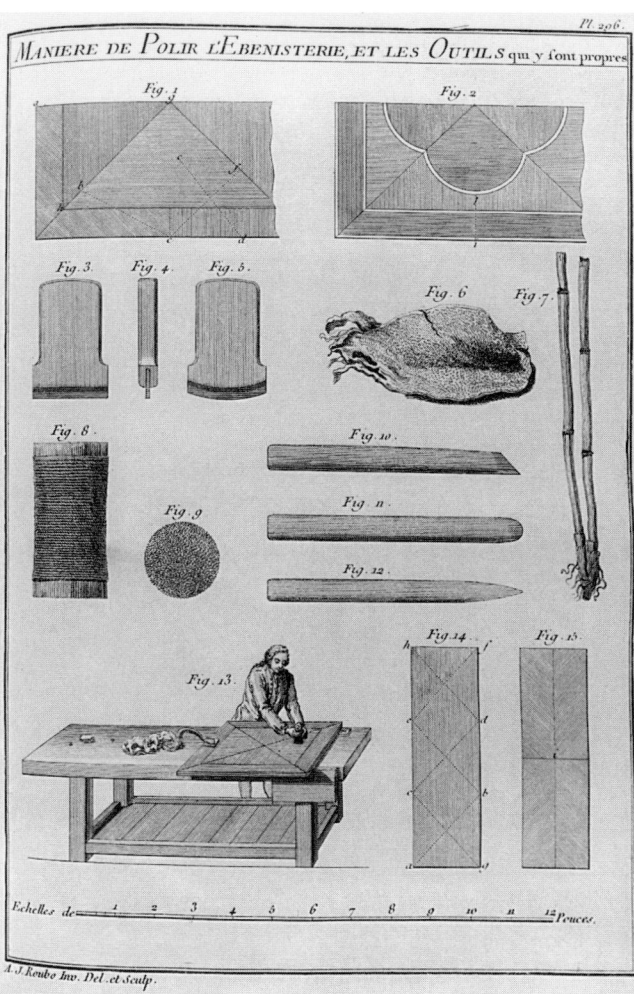

9. Diagram illustrating a method of finishing wooden surfaces, in which molten wax is applied with a cylindrical bundle of marsh grass and absorbed; the excess is removed with scrapers or shaped, wooden sticks, and the surface is buffed with a soft cloth; from André Jacob Roubo: *L'Art du menuisier* (Paris, 1774), pl. 296 (Philadelphia, PA, American Philosophical Society)

of turpentine to form a paste that could easily be applied to furniture. Both oil and wax continued to be used, primarily on more common goods, throughout the 18th century despite the increased use of spirit varnishes.

Towards the end of the 18th century varnish-making became more of a commercial endeavour with the large-scale production of fixed oil varnishes. While high-gloss spirit varnishes continued to be used for the Neo-classical and Empire furniture of the early 19th century, fixed oil varnish eventually supplanted it as the most common finish treatment; it maintained this position until well into the 20th century. In the 20th century many synthetic resins and sophisticated application techniques such as pressurized spray guns were introduced. Nitrocellulose lacquer, polyurethane and alkyd resins have been widely used in furniture finishing. These new synthetic materials vastly expand the variety of visual surface effects that can be achieved and greatly reduce application time.

BIBLIOGRAPHY

J. Stalker and G. Parker: *A Treatise of Japanning and Varnishing* (Oxford, 1688/*R* London, 1960)
J. Moxon: *Mechanick Exercises or the Doctrine of Handy-works* (London, 1703/*R* Morristown, NJ, 1989)
R. Dossie: *The Handmaid to the Arts* (London, 1758)
A. J. Roubo: *L'Art du menuisier* (Paris, 1774)
J. F. Watin: *L'Art du peinture, doreut, vernisseur* (Paris, 3/1776)
E. Middleton: *The New Complete Dictionary of Arts and Sciences* (London, 1778)
The Golden Cabinet: Being the Laboratory, or Handmaid of the Arts (Philadelphia, PA, 1793)
T. Sheraton: *The Cabinet Dictionary*, 2 vols (London, 1803/*R* New York, 1970)
P. F. Tingry: *The Painter and Varnisher's Guide* (London, 2/1816)
The Cabinet-makers Guide (Concord, MA, 1827/*R* New York, 1987)
The Painter, Gilder and Varnisher's Companion (Philadelphia, PA, 2/1854)
P. N. Hasluck: *Wood Finishing* (New York, 1906)
R. J. Gettens and G. L. Stout: *Painting Materials* (New York, 1942/*R* New York, 1966)
T. Brachert: 'Historische Klarlacke und Möbelpolituren', *Maltechnik, Rest.* (1978–9), nos 1–5
T. Z. Penn: 'Decorative and Protective Finishes, 1750–1850', *Bull. Assoc. Preserv. Technol.*, xiv/1 (1984), pp. 3–46
L. Masschelein-Klieiner: *Ancient Binding Media* (Rome, 1985)
R. Mussey: 'Transparent Furniture Finishes in New England, 1700–1825', *Old-Time New England*, lxxii (1987), pp. 287–311

JOSEPH J. GODLA

IV. Conservation.

The goal of conservation is to minimize future deterioration, to stabilize current deterioration and to repair or replace past deterioration.

1. Causes of deterioration. 2. Repair. 3. Treatment for infestation and decay. 4. Cleaning.

1. CAUSES OF DETERIORATION. Although wood is a durable material its deterioration can be brought about by agents present in the environment, by chemical decomposition and through mechanical wear in use. Outdoors, above ground, a complex combination of light, energy, and chemical and mechanical factors contribute to discoloration and disintegration, a phenomenon known as weathering. Wood kept in permanently wet conditions is susceptible to fungal decay or rot and can deteriorate rapidly. Indoors, wood is susceptible to the factors that cause weathering, but the effects are less severe.

Wood absorbs sufficient ultraviolet (UV) and visible light to undergo photochemical reactions leading to discoloration and degradation of surfaces. The initial colour change is yellowing or browning due to photo-oxidation. Woods rich in extractives (non-structural organic materials that influence colour, odour and other non-mechanical properties) may become bleached before the browning becomes observable. Wherever possible, light sources should be filtered to remove UV. The duration and intensity of exposure to visible light should be kept to the minimum. The change in dimensions of wood due to change in temperature alone is slight. However, heating is associated with drying and corresponding dimensional changes.

Changes in the moisture content of wood below the fibre saturation point (about 30%) are associated with dimensional changes. Moisture contents above about 20% are associated with fungal decay. A principal cause of weathering is frequent changes in moisture content. Stresses are set up in the wood as it swells and shrinks due to moisture gradients between the surface and the interior. Stresses are greater near the surface of the wood and may result in warping and surface rupture along the grain. Movement (the dimensional changes of wood after seasoning) is unequal in the three structural dimensions, and if not allowed for in construction damage will result (*see* §1 above). Differences in response times and grain directions between components of wooden structures lead to movement in different directions and at different rates, resulting in warping, dislocation of parts, splitting and breaking of fibres. Similar problems exist in the interaction of different materials in mixed-media objects containing wood. If wood is prevented from moving in response to changes in relative humidity, plastic compression can take place leading to permanent reduction in the maximum dimensions of the piece. Relative humidity should be kept as near constant as possible. A level of 50% (+ or −10%) is suggested for internal woodwork and often requires control of heating.

Wood-destroying fungi and soft rots cause decay in wood by disintegrating cell walls to obtain food for growth and reproduction. Based on physical and chemical changes and the resulting alterations in colour of decaying wood, wood-destroying fungi are classified as brown rots, white rots and soft rots. Fungi require temperatures in the range 24° to 38°C, oxygen, a suitable food source and adequate moisture. The critical average moisture content is 20%, below which fungi will not grow. Since absence of any of these requirements will prevent or greatly inhibit growth, methods for control are based on eliminating or modifying one or more of these conditions. Alternatively, poisoning wood with preservatives offers an effective and reliable means of protecting wood against attack by fungi.

Various insects also attack wood, and those that attack seasoned timber present the greatest hazard. Some of the most destructive pests are beetles (*Coleoptera*), damage being caused by the larvae feeding in the wood. Infestation by wood-boring insects may be distinguished by the presence of tunnels containing bore-dust (frass) within the wood and by circular flight holes on the surface. Fresh dust and clean holes with sharp edges are signs of active workings, though the larval stage may last up to five years before adults emerge. Common furniture beetle or woodworm (*Anobium punctatum*) is widespread in most temperate countries and is often present in buildings and furniture. In countries with warm temperate or tropical climates the most destructive pests of structural timber are termites (*Isoptera*). Low levels of moisture and temperature and clean, secure environments reduce the likelihood of insect damage.

2. REPAIR. Wood conservation cannot be reduced to a formula, but certain processes and procedures are in common use. Initial examination and documentation provide reference for materials, geometry, methods of construction, age and condition. Methods of examination that minimize disruption and loss are preferred (*see* TECHNICAL EXAMINATION). These include visual examination with low-power magnifiers and photography. Surface fluorescence seen under ultraviolet illumination can indicate the nature of coatings and retouches. Wood identification usually requires removal of a small sample from an inconspicuous or broken area. Samples are prepared as thin sections and examined microscopically under transmitted light. Suitably prepared cross-sections of samples of surface decoration may also be microscopically examined to establish a history of decoration and materials used. Other specialized microscopy techniques may supplement and extend these techniques. The presence of nails and screws may be detected using small hand-held metal detectors. For more complex or difficult objects X-radiography may be required to determine the nature of construction and reveal concealed metal parts. Soft X-rays can reveal the presence of live wood-boring beetle larvae. Moisture content can be measured using a variety of commercially available meters of various types. Dendrochronology or radiocarbon dating can sometimes be used to establish the age of a piece of wood and may help to confirm authenticity. Wood defects have also been detected using ultrasonic techniques. A range of specialized instrumental techniques is used for identification and examination of media adhesives and coatings.

Disassembly should only be carried out when necessary and then with the utmost care and patience. The materials and nature of construction should first be determined. All dimensions and angles should be carefully recorded and photographs taken. All parts of the object should be protected and labelled and registration marks applied to aid reassembly. Such fastenings as nails, wooden pegs and screws should be identified, labelled and removed before attempting to separate components. Animal glues can be softened by prolonged contact with water or steam, and old glue joints can sometimes be broken with pure alcohol. Wedges and cramps are used to apply force in a progressive and controlled manner to ease joints apart. Structures must be carefully supported as their centre of gravity is likely to change suddenly as they come apart. Regluing loose joints without disassembly is less satisfactory but can be done by infiltrating or injecting such a slow curing adhesive as cold-setting animal glue and 'working' the joint. Very loose joints can sometimes be stiffened by thin fillets of wood inserted into the joint, by replacing loose pegs or by attention to external reinforcements, where these already exist. False tenons are used to repair broken or badly damaged mortice-and-tenon joints, and the principle can be extended to other joint types. A mortice is cut in the end of the member from which the tenon has broken and a piece of new wood inserted to act as a new tenon.

The first stage in repairing existing components or replacing structural losses is to select material having appropriate strength, appearance, dimensional stability and working properties. Replacements are normally made in the original material unless this would cause damage or distortion or the original material is unavailable or unidentifiable. Wood is matched according to species, density, pattern and direction of growth rings, and direction of rays. Creating a surface to which replacements or detached pieces can be securely attached may involve building up or slightly cutting down original material to provide the best possible mechanical and aesthetic integration of the old and new. Consolidation of friable and degraded objects may also be required beforehand.

Repairs must provide accurately prepared shapes and sound, clean gluing surfaces. For damaged corners and carvings, a freshly prepared plane surface is adhesive bonded to an excess of suitable repair material and the excess later shaped and finished as required. Where new wood has to be inlaid into the surface of the solid, tracings or measurements of the outline of the damage are first transferred on to a suitable piece of repair material. The repair material is then cut out very slightly larger than the area of damage before being fitted in one of two ways. Where the shape of the replacement is defined by an area of flat design it can be shaped to fit precisely into the space available. Alternatively, the repair can be laid over the damage and marked round so that a very small amount of original material is then removed for a perfect fit. In this case, the shape of the repair is chosen to give the best possible aesthetic integration while restricting removal of extra original material to the minimum.

Surfaces to be bonded should be thoroughly cleaned and modified to a suitable condition before joining. Surface preparation is most important and is best done immediately before gluing. Planed surfaces on wood are preferred to sawn surfaces and finely sanded ones to those coarsely sanded. Intentionally roughening a surface does not directly improve adhesive bond quality, though it may help to create channels for the removal of excess glue and thereby promote a more nearly ideal glue line thickness. Solvent cleaning of oily or resinous timbers is beneficial. Surface preparation is critical for the durability of adhesive bonds even though initial joint strengths with untreated surfaces appear satisfactory.

Assembly of components into a complete structure follows the pattern of the original. This is normally accomplished with adhesive bonding (see ADHESIVES), though some structures are assembled without adhesive. These rely on mechanically interlocking components, either joints or such fastenings as wooden pegs, nails or screws. Repairs to part of a component are normally attached with adhesive. Animal glues are still widely used for furniture. Although they have limited resistance to moisture and are readily biodegradable, animal glues have some significant advantages for inside use. They have stood the test of time and are compatible with old material. They possess adequate strength, yet joints made with them remain reversible throughout their effective life. They are non-staining, non-toxic and non-flammable. Excess glue is easily removed, and reactivation of glue under veneers is possible. Polyvinyl acetate emulsions and epoxy resins are among other materials used for special purposes. Where setting involves loss of solvent, joints must be held together under pressure while the adhesive sets. When adhesive has been applied, assembly of components must be completed within the 'open' working time limit imposed by the adhesive. The right amount of pressure must be applied in the right places to bring all parts of the assembly into correct alignment without damage or distortion. This is normally done using various kinds of cramp. 'Softening' of wood or card is used to prevent cramps causing surface damage. Also a glue-resistant layer of silicone paper or similar material must be interposed between the softening

and the object to prevent the softening sticking to the surface. Excess adhesive should be removed before it sets. Cramping must be complete within the time limit imposed by the adhesive and must be left undisturbed while the adhesive sets. If required, shaping of repairs after attachment is done in a way that reduces the risk of damaging original material. Wood must be dry before shaping begins. When replacing substantial losses, evidence beyond reasonable doubt is required. This may include recent photographs of the object, symmetry, interpolation or evidence from other members of a set.

Careful selection of repair material makes the integration and finishing of old and new work much easier, though some colouring is usually needed. Retouching should take account of the natural colour changes that occur on aging. The light source and viewing angle can profoundly affect appearance and should be carefully chosen. Daylight is preferred because retouches made under it are less likely to show up under other light sources. Each stage of the finishing process should be tested on waste repair material before being applied to the object. The first stage of finishing is surface preparation. The general tone of the area to be coloured must not be darker than the area to be matched. If necessary a bleach such as hydrogen peroxide may be used to lighten some or all new wood before staining to the correct hue. Once the hue of the new wood is correct, a toning stain can be applied to get the desired final effect. This will be modified by surface coatings.

Several types of stain are available, each with advantages and disadvantages regarding quality of effect, permanence, grain raising, penetration and ease of use. Such chemical stains as potassium bichromate and ammonia cause colour changes by reacting with chemical components of wood. Other stains are classified according to the solubility of the dyes used. Coatings provide protection against dirt, atmospheric gases, water vapour, wear and light. They also enhance appearance by bringing out surface colours. Where a coating exists this should be matched in repairs. Where there is no coating the intended effect must be balanced against the risk to the object of leaving it uncoated. Coatings must wet the surface, be sufficiently tough to resist movement of the wood and dry at an appropriate rate. A variety of traditional materials is available including paint, VARNISH, shellac (French polish), oils and waxes. The range is extended by modern conservation materials that attempt to combine superior protection and appearance with ease of removal.

3. TREATMENT FOR INFESTATION AND DECAY. Treatment for structures damaged by wood-boring insects includes isolation of affected objects, killing all insect life present, strengthening and repairing structural damage, disguising disfigurement caused by flight holes and reducing the likelihood of reinfestation. Objects with signs of active infestation should be treated immediately. Methods vary according to their efficacy, hazards, toxicity, equipment required, cost and likelihood of damage to the object itself. Such gases as methyl bromide, ethylene oxide and hydrogen cyanide are highly effective, act quickly and have good penetration but are highly toxic to other organisms and require special apparatus to apply. The risk of staining

PLATE I

1. Karelian birch
secrétaire-à-abattant,
w. 958 mm, from
Russia, *c.* 1800
(Luton Hoo, Beds)

2. Boxwood Royal Gittern,
l. 760 mm, from England,
c. 1290–1330 (London,
British Museum)

1. Pear-wood sculpture by Hans Daucher: *Cupids Playing*, 420×162×760 mm, from Augsburg, *c.* 1530 (Vienna, Kunsthistorisches Museum)

2. Mahogany tambour desk, inlaid with light wood, white pine and elm, 1054×959×501 mm, made by John Seymour & Son, Boston, Massachussetts, 1794–1804 (Winterthur, DE, H.F. Du Pont Winterthur Museum)

PLATE III   Wood

1. Cedar-wood cabinet with gilded ebony decoration, h. 696 mm, from the tomb of Tutankhamun (*reg c.* 1332– *c.* 1323 BC), Egypt, New Kingdom, 18th Dynasty (Cairo, Egyptian Museum)

2. Iroko-wood chest, carved to imitate basketwork, 2.12×0.67×0.50 m, from Benin City, Nigeria, 19th century (London, British Museum)

1. Zelkova and amboyna mirror-box, with
brass plates, 115×178×212 mm, Korean,
Chosŏn dynasty, 19th century (London,
Victoria and Albert Museum)

2. Oak cabinet, veneered with olive-wood, acacia and other woods, 2125×1785×620 mm, from the northern
Netherlands, c. 1690 (Amsterdam, Rijksmuseum)

or damage to the object is low if the correct procedures are adopted. However, the effect is not persistent, and prevention of future reinfestation is not guaranteed. Long-term protection is afforded by applying insecticides in solution in organic solvents, and various formulations are available commercially. Permethrin is a frequently used insecticide that has replaced pentachlorophenol. Insecticidal fluids are initially slower than gas, and penetration is comparatively poor by normal means of application. Their persistence prevents reinfestation, but their continued presence in and on the object could be hazardous to those handling and working with treated surfaces. Other methods include freezing, prolonged exposure to low-oxygen environments (usually of nitrogen) and vapour phase deposition of inorganic boron.

Consolidation of seriously weakened or damaged wooden objects is used to impart strength sufficient for handling, load bearing and further conservation treatments. This ranges from consolidation of friable surface decoration to the restoration of structural strength in load-bearing members of buildings. Consolidation (see CONSOLIDANT) is accomplished by introducing a liquid (or vapour) that is converted in situ to the solid state. Consolidants should possess good adhesion, impart strength to the surface and to the structure if required and be flexible but hard. Solutions should combine high concentration with low viscosity, solvents used should be non-toxic and non-damaging to the object, and application should be simple. Ideally, conversion to the solid state should occur at a controlled rate, at room temperature and without shrinkage. Treatments should maintain their mechanical and optical characteristics for long periods but should also be reversible at least in the short term. Classes of material that have been used include epoxies, acrylics, wax and resin mixtures, poly(vinyl butyral) and Parylene. Reinforcement with new wood or other material is sometimes required to provide adequate strength while preserving original surfaces. This is normally incorporated into the structure so that it is not visible. The extent of disguise of flight holes depends on the extent to which damage interferes with normal viewing of the object. This in turn depends on the age and nature of the object and, to some extent, personal taste. A small amount of damage in old furniture may be expected and therefore acceptable. Major damage to a modern wood sculpture with smooth surfaces and flowing curves would probably require attention. Consolidant can be allowed to act as filler, but more usually surface damage is filled independently, for example with pigmented wax and resin mixtures or proprietary fillers based on synthetic thermoplastic resins.

For simple shrinkage without splitting or warping, there are three treatment options. The shrinkage may be left uncompensated, the more shrunken part may be enlarged or the less shrunken part reduced. The course of action that results in least damage to original material and provides the most easily reversible change is considered the most acceptable. Shrinkage, in the width of drawer fronts for example, may leave vertically aligned moulding extending beyond the margin of the drawer and at constant risk of being broken off during use. In such cases it is generally advisable to slightly reduce the length of the moulding to prevent further damage. Gaps may be aesthetically unacceptable or a potential source of further damage. Where separation of components without breakage has occurred it may be possible to close the gap and make up the shrinkage loss by adding an extra piece of wood. However, the symmetry of any overlying design must be preserved.

More serious failure may occur internally—within the width and thickness of the timber itself—leaving an irregularly shaped crack that may be difficult to close. Treatment depends on the nature of construction, on the nature and position of the gap or split, on the physical resistance of the components to be brought back together and on the type of surface decoration. An important step is to remedy, so far as is practicable, the causes of the problem so that a repetition does not occur. Treatment options include closing the crack and making up loss of thickness on one side or filling the gap with a fillet of wood or a softer type of adhesive-based filler. Dovetail keys may be used to hold parts together and prevent further splitting. Warping can be difficult to remedy, because most of the methods used to correct it involve serious disruption and none is entirely satisfactory. Sometimes the construction of a piece may allow the support or restraint of thin weak members by stronger ones. Soaking of the piece in water followed by drying in a position directly opposing the warp can sometimes produce the desired result. Often, however, the piece reverts to its warped state, and the application of this technique is restricted to plain wooden objects. Another alternative is to groove out the back of a solid board or the core of a veneered construction and insert strips of wood to help keep the panel flat. This, however, is a last resort, scarcely less disruptive than complete removal and remounting of a thin section of the surface on a more stable support.

4. CLEANING. Although wood may be encountered in its raw or unfinished state it has usually been coated. Cleaning may be required to prevent or reduce deterioration, to remove an aesthetic obstruction or to allow essential conservation. The ideal of cleaning is to remove all the dirt without removing or damaging any part of the object and without leaving behind any of the cleaning materials. In practice even the mildest cleaning treatments cause some damage. The need for cleaning can be reduced by proper storage and handling. The decision to clean is based on the state of the object, the estimated rate of deterioration with and without dirt, the available cleaning methods, the presence of historical or other evidence associated with the dirt, the estimated extent of damage likely to be caused by cleaning and the likelihood of the need to repeat the treatment in future. Loose dirt can be removed using a vacuum cleaner with the aid of cloths and soft brushes. Harder, more brittle dirt that is more strongly attached to the surface may, with care, be chipped off. Where dirt is more resistant it may be necessary to use abrasive methods. Mechanical cleaning methods are more suited to flat or evenly curved surfaces with no sharp re-entrants or three dimensional decoration. For removal of more elastic, rubbery or greasy kinds of dirt and for the treatment of intricate surfaces with a thin and fragile decoration SOLVENT cleaning is used.

Wax, especially the softer sorts such as beeswax, which is commonly applied at intervals to furniture, may have been allowed to build up, incorporating layers of dirt, until a rather ugly semi-hard black grease covers much of the surface. A mixture frequently used to remove this accumulated grime is known as furniture reviver. Such materials are commercially available or may be prepared by shaking thoroughly together two parts pure gum turpentine, two parts industrial methylated spirits, two parts malt vinegar and one part raw linseed oil. After application the mixture is left to act for a short time before removing loosened wax and dirt on cotton wool or cloth, followed by vigorous burnishing to remove excess oil. It is preferable, where further finishing is anticipated, to clean with white spirit to remove excess oil. A light coat of a paste wax based on carnauba wax is often applied to provide some protection and to enhance the surface. Wood surfaces that have been decorated with paint, gilding, japanning or lacquer are cleaned using methods appropriate to the form of decoration present.

BIBLIOGRAPHY

A. J. Panshin, H. P. Brown and C. C. Forsaith: *Textbook of Wood Technology* (New York, 1949); 4th edn by A. J. Panshin and C. de Zeeuw (New York, 1980)

C. H. Hayward: *Furniture Repairs* (London, 1969)

F. Oughton: *The Finishing and Re-finishing of Wood* (London, 1969)

E. Joyce: *The Technique of Furniture Making* (London, 1970)

N.-S. Bromelle, J. A. D. Darrah and A. J. Moncrieff: *Papers on the Conservation and Technology of Wood*, International Council of Museums: Subcommittee-Furniture (Madrid, 1972)

R. M. Rowell: 'Non-conventional Wood Preservation Methods', *Wood Technology: Chemical Aspects*, American Chemical Society, xxxxiii (1977), pp. 47–56

C. H. Hayward: *Staining and Polishing* (London, 1978)

Conservation of Wood in Painting and the Decorative Arts: Proceedings of the International Institute for the Conservation of Historic and Artistic Works: Oxford, 1978

D. W. Grattan: 'Consolidants for Degraded and Damaged Wood', *Proceedings of Furniture and Wooden Objects Symposium: Ottawa, 1980*

R. B. Hoadley: *Understanding Woods: A Craftsman's Guide to Wood Technology* (Newton, CT, 1980)

A. Barefoot and F. Hawkins: *Identification of Modern and Tertiary Wood* (Oxford, 1982)

B. M. Fielden: *The Conservation of Historic Buildings* (London, 1982)

P. Cunnington: *Care for Old Houses* (London, 1984, 2/1991)

D. Eckstein, M. G. L. Baillie and H. Egger: *Dendrochronological Dating*, Handbooks for Archaeologists, 2 (Strasbourg, 1984)

I. A. Melville and I. A. Gordon: *The Repair and Maintenance of Houses* (London, 1984)

R. Rowell: *The Chemistry of Solid Wood*, American Chemical Society (1984)

Proceedings of the Symposium: Adhesives and Consolidants: Paris, 1984

Proceedings of the Symposium of the Scottish Society for Conservation and Restoration: Decorative Wood: Glasgow, 1984

G. Buchanan: *The Illustrated Handbook of Furniture Restoration* (London, 1985)

Y. Wang and A. P. Schniewind: 'Consolidation of Deteriorated Wood with Soluble Resins', *J. Amer. Inst. Conserv.*, xxiv/2 (1985), pp. 77–91

Proceedings of CETBGE and the International Council of Museums: Waterlogged Wood: Study and Conservation: Grenoble, 1985

D. Hawkins: *The Technique of Wood Surface Decoration* (London, 1986)

A. F. Bravery and others: *Recognizing Wood Rot and Insect Damage in Buildings* (London, 1987)

C. V. Horie: *Materials for Conservation* (London, 1987)

D. W. Grattan and R. L. Barclay: 'A Study of Gap Fillers for Wooden Objects', *Stud. Conserv.*, xxxiii/2 (1988), pp. 71–86

M. A. Williams: *Keeping it All Together: The Preservation and Care of Historic Furniture* (Worthington, 1988)

D. Pinniger: *Insect Pests in Museums* (London, 1989)

A. P. Schniewind: *Concise Encyclopaedia of Wood and Wood-based Materials* (Oxford, 1989)

S. Bowman: *Radiocarbon Dating* (London, 1990)

R. M. Rowell: *Archaeological Wood* (Washington, 1990)

H. Munn: *Joinery for Repair and Restoration Contracts* (Builth Wells, 3/1991)

N. D. UMNEY

Wood (ii). English family of architects and writers.

(1) John Wood I (*b* Bath, *bapt* 26 Aug 1704; *d* Bath, 23 May 1754). The son of a Bath builder, he probably received a tradesman's education. In the 1720s he acquired practical experience outside Bath while working on and near grand projects of a scale that would affect his own later ambitions. These included the gardens of Robert Benson, 1st Baron Bingley (1676–1731), at Bramham Park, N. Yorks, where Wood very likely began work in 1722, and the imperfect attempt of the architect Edward Shepherd (*d* 1747)—another Bingley protégé and a Wood associate—to treat the fronts of a row of houses in Grosvenor Square, London, as a single Anglo-Palladian palace (*c.* 1728–30). Optimistic about Bath's prospects as a spa, in 1725 Wood proposed adorning this inelegant country town with such architectural features as a Grand Circus 'for the exhibition of sports', and a 'Royal Forum'. His proposals, which were intended to revive the splendour of the town's Roman past, are known only from a few lines in his book on Bath, and it is difficult to picture precisely what Wood had in mind. His realized work there began with an irregular group of lodgings (1727–30) for James Brydges, 1st Duke of Chandos, and the canalization of the River Avon between Bath and Bristol (1727).

Having found it impossible to collaborate with either Bath's landlords or its Corporation, Wood financed his own first great undertaking, Queen Square and its vicinity (1728–36). Here, in his own words, Wood gave a series of town houses 'the appearance of a palace'. His inspiration, in part, was Inigo Jones's Covent Garden Piazza (1631–7), London, and probably also his own reconstruction of the Roman camp at Bath. Wood's antiquarian aspirations likewise surfaced in his partial renovation (1734–52) of the cathedral at Llandaff, S. Glamorgan. This he believed to have been originally a Roman building laden with later, medieval additions. Stevenson (1983) persuasively argued that when Wood built his Roman vaulted hall inside part of the old nave he attempted to restore the original 2nd-century Roman church, which he believed imitated Solomon's Temple in Jerusalem.

By the mid-1730s Wood seems to have become closely associated with the magnate and philanthropist Ralph Allen (1693–1764), another moulder of Bath's fortunes. To demonstrate the merits of the golden Bath limestone, which, with Wood's advice, Allen quarried, he commissioned from Wood a splendid seat, Prior Park, to be built outside Bath. Others altered the house extensively during and after construction (begun *c.* 1734), but Wood's intentions are evident. He designed this winged Anglo-Palladian mansion as a larger and 'juster' version of Colen Campbell's Wanstead House (*c.* 1714–20), Essex. Wood saw the hillside site as resembling a Roman theatre; he therefore laid out the Prior Park ensemble on a plan derived from Vitruvius' proportional system for the Roman theatre. The degree to which he thereby united the house with its magnificent hillside setting makes Prior Park one of his finest works. Other major projects, such as the Bath General Hospital (1738–42), the Bristol Exchange and

Market (1741–3; *see* BRISTOL, fig. 2), and the Liverpool Exchange and Town Hall (1749–54), as well as further Bath terraces, rested on domestic models from the Palladian tradition. So did a key unexecuted project, a 1740 proposal for assembly rooms at Bath (engraving in Bristol Rec. Office; Bb 827.55b 10530). Competitive to the bone, Wood conceived it in rivalry with the recreation of Vitruvius' Egyptian Hall at the Assembly Rooms (*c.* 1731–2) in York by Richard Boyle, 3rd Earl of Burlington and 4th Earl of Cork.

Writing in a moribund literary tradition, Wood developed his architectural theory in the 1730s and 1740s. This was that God had revealed the laws of architectural proportion and symbolism to the Jews, and that the Greeks and Romans subsequently plagiarized from them; but, even earlier, British Druids had applied these same laws to their own megalithic architecture, such as the 'crescent' (the trilithon horseshoe) and circles at Stonehenge. Indeed, Wood believed the Druids had created one of the great antique civilizations, supposedly centred on Bath. Wood's manuscripts (London, BL, Harley MSS 7354–5) provide the key to this theory, for no straightforward statement of it reached print in either the *Origin of Building* (1741) or his *Description of Bath* (1742–3). As his theory evolved, Wood's loyalty shifted wholly to the Druids and away from their enemies, the Romans.

In his last years Wood began to fulfil his long-standing desire to build a grand circular edifice at Bath when he started the terrace that he named the King's Circus (1754–*c.* 1766). This, his masterpiece, rests on his theory. By recreating a Druid ring of houses, a subject about which he had written, Wood renewed the supposed glory of pre-Roman Bath. He united this Druid theme with others taken from the classical traditions of palace and theatre architecture, on the grounds that all were forms of the one true architecture revealed by God. It is likely that he meant the Circus as his ultimate exercise in perfect architectural principles, and as a critique on his Druid and classical predecessors, who had fallen short of those principles.

WRITINGS

The Origin of Building, or, the Plagiarism of the Heathens Detected (Bath, 1741/*R* Farnborough, 1968)

An Essay towards a Description of the City of Bath, 2 vols (Bath, 1742–3, rev. London, 1749/*R* Bath, 1969, and Farnborough, 1970)

(2) John Wood II (*b* Bath, *bapt* 25 Feb 1728; *d* Bath, 16 June 1781). Son of (1) John Wood I. He probably matriculated at University College, Oxford, but did not graduate. He directed work on the Liverpool Exchange and built virtually all the King's Circus in Bath. After lesser works, he embarked on the Royal Crescent, Bath's greatest terrace (1767–*c.* 1775). Like the Circus, this building represents the fusion of classical palace and theatre themes with a supposed Druidical architectural form, in this case the 'crescent'. A 'theatrical' curve—half the elliptical plan of the Roman Colosseum—weds this monumental building to its majestic hillside. Whatever the younger Wood's role in the invention of the Royal Crescent was, the synthesis from which the building grew was assuredly his father's doing. Even more than the Circus, the Royal Crescent became the precedent for much of the most ambitious British urban design for nearly a century afterwards. Wood produced two other notable works. Owing much to his father's assembly house project, but also deviating significantly from his father's known preferences, his New or Upper Assembly Rooms (1769–71) at last gave Bath the stately assembly house it hitherto had lacked. In 1781, the year he died, Wood capped a practical-minded literary career by publishing his humanitarian *Plans for Cottages*, a distinguished work in the Anglo-Palladian tradition.

WRITINGS

A Series of Plans for Cottages or Habitations of the Labourer, Adapted as well to Towns as to the Country (?Bath, 1781, 3/1806/*R* Farnborough, 1972)

BIBLIOGRAPHY

Colvin

W. Ison: *The Georgian Buildings of Bath from 1700 to 1830* (Bath, 1948, rev. 2/1980)

W. Bertram: *The Origins and Building of Queen Square, Bath* (diss., London, Archit. Assoc., n.d.)

C. Brownell: *John Wood the Elder and John Wood the Younger: Architects of Bath* (diss., New York, Columbia U., 1976)

A. Gomme, M. Jenner and B. Little: *Bristol: An Architectural History* (London, 1979)

C. Stevenson: 'Solomon "Engothicked": The Elder John Wood's Restoration of Llandaff Cathedral', *A. Hist.*, vi (1983), pp. 301–14

T. Mowl and B. Earnshaw: *John Wood: Architect of Obsession* (Bath, 1988) [life and work of John Wood the elder]

E. Harris, with N. Savage: *British Architectural Books and Writers, 1556–1785* (Cambridge, 1990)

CHARLES E. BROWNELL

Wood (iii). English family of potters. After working for John Astbury and Thomas Whieldon, Ralph Wood the elder (*b* Burslem, 29 Jan 1715; *d* Burslem, 12 Dec 1772) started up on his own account at the Hilltop Factory in Burslem *c.* 1754, producing plain, salt-glazed figures. He developed a technique of staining lead glazes with metallic oxides, which, combined with his fine modelling, resulted in the creation of some fine, useful and decorative items (e.g. 'Vicar and Moses' figure, *c.* 1789–1801; Stoke-on-Trent, City Mus. & A.G.) and 'Toby' jugs. Ralph's brother, Aaron Wood (*b* Burslem, 14 April 1717; *d* Burslem, 12 May 1785) was the most renowned block-cutter in Staffordshire and was reputed to have been a modeller for all the potteries in the county. His superb interpretation and skilled block-cutting gave enormous character to his figures. He was probably responsible for modelling the first, true 'Toby' jug—also known as a Twyford Jug or Step Toby—which his brother Ralph made famous. Ralph's son Ralph Wood the younger (*b* Burslem, 22 May 1748; *d* Burslem, 5 Aug 1795) inherited his father's factory and continued the established tradition. He also introduced the use of brighter enamels, which displaced the more beautiful coloured glazes and hence initiated the general degeneration in the quality of decoration. Fine modelling, graceful poses and touches of humour are the main features of his figurative work. Aaron's son Enoch Wood (*b* Burslem, 31 Jan 1759; *d* Burslem, 17 Aug 1840) ranks among the greatest of the Staffordshire potters. Not only was he a talented modeller and an artist of considerable merit, producing relief plaques and fine, portrait busts (e.g. *George Washington*, 1818; Stoke-on-Trent, City Mus. & A.G.), but he also ran a highly successful business manufacturing wares of all types with a large American export trade. He produced more than 500 designs of mostly English, French and American scenes for transfer-printed wares. At the time of his death he was generally referred to as the 'Father of the Potteries'.

BIBLIOGRAPHY
F. Falkner: *The Wood Family of Burslem* (London, 1912)
P. Halfpenny: *English Earthenware Figures, 1740–1840* (Woodbridge, 1991)
JOHN MAWER

Wood, Cecil Walter (*b* Christchurch, 6 June 1878; *d* Christchurch, 28 Nov 1947). New Zealand architect. Articled to the Christchurch architect Frederick Strouts (1834–1919) in 1893, he went to England in 1901, working for the Housing Division of the London County Council and subsequently for R. W. Schultz and Leonard Stokes. Returning to New Zealand in 1906 he entered partnership with Samuel Hurst Seager. In 1909 he began independent practice in Christchurch, establishing his reputation with large Arts and Crafts style houses. After 1920 he increasingly favoured a Colonial Georgian style for houses, most notably at Bishopscourt (1926), Christchurch. A confirmed traditionalist, Wood was an accomplished designer in Gothic Revival and classical styles. Christ's College Dining Hall (1922–5), Christchurch, a confident exercise in English collegiate Gothic, exemplifies his commitment to European traditions. St Barnabas (1925), Fendalton, St Paul's (1930), Tai Tapu, and St Barnabas (1932), Woodend, reveal his feeling for authentic Gothic forms and sensitivity to materials, whether traditional or modern. His commercial buildings show a progression from the stripped classicism of the Public Trust Building (1922), to the restrained modernism of his Post Office Savings Bank (1937), both in Christchurch. Art Deco elements combined with motifs from Maori art appear in the State Insurance Building (1933), Christchurch. The high quality of Wood's designs and his commitment to craftsmanship had an important influence on Christchurch architects of the 1950s and 1960s, including Paul Pascoe and Miles Warren.

BIBLIOGRAPHY
L. S. J. Maingay: *Cecil Walter Wood: Architect of the Free Tradition* (diss., U. Auckland, 1964)
I. J. Lochhead: 'New Zealand Architecture in the Thirties: The Impact of Modernism', *Landfall*, clii/4 (1984), pp. 466–81
R. Helms: *The Architecture of Cecil Walker Wood* (diss., Christchurch, U. Canterbury) (in preparation)
IAN J. LOCHHEAD

Wood, (John) Christopher (*b* Knowsley, nr Liverpool, 7 April 1901; *d* Salisbury, 21 Aug 1930). English painter. He studied architecture at Liverpool University; there he met Augustus John, who encouraged him to take up painting seriously. On moving to London in 1920, he met Alphonse Kahn, a wealthy Jewish art collector who took him to Paris in 1921, where he enrolled at the Académie Julian and later at the Grande Chaumière. In Paris he met the Chilean diplomat, Antonio de Gandarillas, who introduced him to a number of painters, among them Picasso. In this period Wood's contacts with artists in Paris were soon unrivalled among British artists.

Wood travelled widely with Gandarillas between 1922 and 1924 in Europe and north Africa and met Jean Cocteau in Villefranche. Wood's paintings of this period display all the awkwardness of a self-taught artist experimenting with the styles he observed in the works of friends such as Picasso, Jules Pascin and Moïse Kisling. It was through Picasso that he met Serge Diaghilev, who commissioned him to design sets for the ballet of *Romeo and Juliet*. The commission fell through.

The turning-point in Wood's brief career was his meeting with Ben and Winifred Nicholson in London in 1926. He visited them in Cumberland in spring 1928 and spent the summer and early autumn in Cornwall with them. The Nicholsons' ascetic lifestyle contrasted with the bohemian life Wood had been leading in Paris, and he was impressed by their dedication to painting. Under their influence, Wood began to paint more experimentally and to evolve a more personal style. Wood's late paintings depict scenes from the lives of fishing communities and are characterized by a *fausse naïveté* and directness fashionable in the 7 & 5 Society, of which he was a member. In this rejection of Parisian and Edwardian sophistication Wood was encouraged by the example of Alfred Wallis, whom he 'discovered' with Ben Nicholson in 1928. In 1929 and 1930 he visited Brittany, where he produced his most impressive paintings, among them *Building the Boat, Tréboul* (1928; U. Cambridge, Kettle's Yard), in which he combined technical mastery with a vision of pathos and grandeur to produce a painting of symbolic and psychological depth.

Wood died when he fell under a train at Salisbury station. He may have been delirious at the time since he was addicted to opium.

BIBLIOGRAPHY
E. Newton: *Christopher Wood, 1901–1930* (London, 1938)
Christopher Wood (exh. cat., ed. W. Mason; ACGB, 1979)
C. Harrison: *English Art and Modernism, 1900–1939* (London, 1981)
Christopher Wood: The Last Years (exh. cat., ed. H. Gresty; Newlyn, Orion Gals)
R. Ingleby: *Christopher Wood: An English Painter* (London, 1995)
JEREMY LEWISON

Wood, Edgar (*b* Middleton, Lancs, 17 May 1860; *d* Porto Maurizio, Italy, 12 Oct 1935). English architect and draughtsman. He was perhaps the most conspicuously flamboyant among the English architects of the Arts and Crafts Movement. He practised, principally from Manchester, from 1885 to *c.* 1922 and, in particular, served the textile communities of the Lancashire and Yorkshire border. He was the mainstay of the Northern Art Workers' Guild (1896–*c.* 1914), an outstanding architectural draughtsman and a master of the architectural sketch. He exhibited frequently at the Royal Academy, and examples of his work are held at the RIBA Drawings Collection in London and at numerous galleries in the north of England. From the 1880s Wood was attracted by avant-garde ideas, then represented by Aestheticism and the emerging Arts and Crafts Movement. He developed a vocabulary from vernacular styles developed in the Pennine Hills region and gradually adapted these in an extraordinary way to produce a form of proto-Expressionism. Sensitive interpretations of appropriate vernacular character are seen at Banney Royd (*c.* 1900–01), Edgerton, Huddersfield, and Holly Cottage (1904), Holly Road, Bramhall, while the most extreme examples of his expressionistic works are Lindley Clock Tower (1899–1902), Huddersfield, and the

First Church of Christ, Scientist, (1903–8; now the Edgar Wood Centre), Victoria Park, Manchester. From 1904 he worked in association with J. Henry Sellers (1861–1954), who shared similar aspirations, but each practised independently. Partly through Sellers's example, Wood's work began to show more classical influences. He also adopted concrete flat-roof construction and, from 1908, Arabic decorative motifs. Upmeads (1908), a house at Stafford, boldly demonstrates the former tendencies, and to these Wood's own house (1914–16) at 224 Hale Road, Hale, Cheshire, adds the latter's exotic richness.

BIBLIOGRAPHY

H. Muthesius: *Das englische Haus*, 3 vols (Berlin, 1904–5; Eng. trans. by J. Seligman, ed. D. Sharp, London, 1979)

M. Bunney: 'Edgar Wood', *Mod. Bauformen*, vi (1907), pp. 49–76

L. Weaver: 'Upmeads, Stafford', *Small Country Houses of Today*, i (London, 1910), pp. 202–7

J. H. G. Archer: 'Edgar Wood: A Notable Manchester Architect', *Trans. Lancs & Ches Antiqua. Soc.*, lxxiii–iv (1963–4), pp. 153–87

——: 'Edgar Wood and J. Henry Sellers: A Decade of Partnership and Experiment', *Edwardian Architecture and its Origins*, ed. A. Service (London, 1975), pp. 372–84

Partnership in Style: Edgar Wood and J. Henry Sellers (exh. cat. by J. Archer, S. Evans and J. Treuherz, Manchester, C.A.G., 1975)

J. H. G. Archer: 'Edgar Wood and Mackintosh', *Mackintosh and his Contemporaries in Europe and America*, ed. P. Nuttgens (London, 1988), pp. 58–74

JOHN H. G. ARCHER

Wood, Elizabeth Wyn (*b* Orillia, Ont., 8 Oct 1903; *d* Toronto, 27 Jan 1966). Canadian sculptor. She is best known for her modernist interpretations of the Canadian landscape in sculpture, using such unconventional materials as aluminium, tin and glass. She attended the Ontario College of Art in Toronto (1921–6), concentrating on sculpture, which had interested her since childhood. After marrying her instructor Emanuel Hahn (1881–1957) in 1926, Wood went to New York and in 1926–7 studied at the Art Students League with Robert Laurent (1890–1970) and Edward McCarten (1879–1947). In 1927 she began exploring in sculptural form the spatial relationships of landscape elements, based on personal observations recorded in many drawings made in northern Ontario. For one of these works, the marble relief *Passing Rain* (1928; London, Ont., Reg. A.G.), she was awarded the Lord Willingdon Award for sculpture in 1929. She was also occupied throughout her career with monuments and architectural sculpture, notable examples being the Welland-Crowland War Memorial (1936–9), Ont., reliefs for the Rainbow Bridge Approach Plaza (*c.* 1941) at Niagara Falls, Ont., reliefs for the Bank of Montreal in Toronto (1947–8) and the monument to *George VI* at Niagara Falls (1963).

Wood was very active in arts organizations: she was a founder-member of the Sculptors' Society of Canada in 1928 and its president from 1933 to 1935; organizing secretary of the Canadian Arts Council (1944–5), chairman of its International Relations Committee (1945–8) and vice-president (1948–9). She was the author of the brief of the Sculptors' Society of Canada to the Royal Commission on National Development in the Arts, Letters and Sciences submitted in 1949. In addition, Wood taught at the Central Technical School in Toronto from 1929 to 1958.

See also CANADA, §IV, 1 and fig. 8.

WRITINGS

'A National Program for the Arts in Canada', *Can. A.*, i/3 (1944), pp. 93–5, 127–8

BIBLIOGRAPHY

H. Voaden: 'Elizabeth Wyn Wood', *Mar. A.*, ii/5 (1942), pp. 145–9

Visions and Victories: 10 Canadian Women Artists, 1914–45 (exh. cat., London, Ont., Reg. A.G., 1983)

CHRISTINE BOYANOSKI

Wood, Francis Derwent (*b* Keswick, Cumberland, 15 Oct 1871; *d* London, 19 Feb 1926). English sculptor. He first trained at the Kunstgewerbeschule, Karlsruhe, under Heinrich Weltring (*b* 1846) and Hermann Götz (1848–1901). Returning to England in 1887, he worked as a modeller in Shropshire, first for the pottery firm Maw & Co., and then for the ironfounders Coalbrookdale Iron Co. In 1889 Wood studied sculpture under Edouard Lantéri at the National Art Training Schools in South Kensington (later Royal College of Art); he then became assistant (1890–92) to Alphonse Legros at the Slade School of Art. In 1894–5 he studied at the Royal Academy Schools, while working as Thomas Brock's assistant, and in the following year he first exhibited at the Royal Academy. In 1896 he visited Paris and exhibited at the Salon of 1897. He was Drawing Master at the Glasgow School of Art from 1897 to 1901, when he returned to London. He was elected ARA in 1910 and full Academician in 1920. Wood produced a large number of portrait busts, such as that of *Henry James* (1913), and sculptures of mythological subjects, such as *Psyche* (*c.* 1908–19; both London, Tate). During World War I he was in charge of making masks for plastic surgery at Wandsworth Hospital; in 1916–17 he was runner-up to Alfred Drury in the competition to design a statue of *Joshua Reynolds* for the Royal Academy (bronze competition models, London, Tate). After the war Wood succeeded Lantéri as Professor of Sculpture at the Royal College of Art (1918–23) and was commissioned to design various public monuments, including war memorials, such as the *Machine Gun Corps* memorial at Hyde Park Corner (1925; *in situ*).

DNB

BIBLIOGRAPHY

M. Chamot, D. Farr and M. Butlin: *The Modern British Paintings, Drawings and Sculptures*, Tate Gallery catalogues, ii (London, 1965), pp. 780–84

B. Read: *Victorian Sculpture* (New Haven and London, 1982)

S. Beattie: *The New Sculpture* (New Haven and London, 1983)

Wood, Grant (*b* nr Anamosa, IA, 13 Feb 1891; *d* Iowa City, IA, 12 Feb 1942). American painter and printmaker. He was one of the Midwestern Regionalist painters of the 1930s who, with Thomas Hart Benton and John Steuart Curry, created an art based on indigenous imagery from local surroundings. He has also been associated with American Scene painting. Wood's most famous painting, *American Gothic* (Chicago, IL, A. Inst.), features a nameless, dour farmer and his spinster daughter standing in front of a Carpenter Gothic farmhouse. Since its first appearance in 1930, cartoonists and advertisers have borrowed and parodied this staid Midwestern pair, who have come to represent an archetype of middle America.

In 1910 and 1911 Wood studied at the Minneapolis School of Design and Handicraft with Ernest Batchelder (1875–1957), a leading advocate of the English Arts and Crafts Movement. From 1912 to 1916 Wood undertook short periods of study at the University of Iowa, Iowa City, and the Art Institute of Chicago. He travelled abroad intermittently throughout the 1920s and was enrolled at the Académie Julian in Paris in the autumn of 1923. In 1932 he helped to establish the Stone City Colony and Art School, an experimental Midwestern art colony that lasted for two summers. In 1934 he was appointed Iowa State Director of the New Deal's short-lived Public Works of Art Project, and later that year he joined the University of Iowa.

Wood's early paintings were mainly landscapes and architectural views executed with a thick brush in an impressionistic style. In 1928 he travelled to Munich to supervise production of a stained-glass window he had designed for the Veterans' Memorial Building in Cedar Rapids. Ostensibly it was the 15th-century Netherlandish Masters that he saw at the Alte Pinakothek that prompted him, on his return to Iowa, to paint Midwestern themes using strong local colour and sharp contrasts. Wood was impressed by the convention of depicting universal or religious themes using settings and costumes that reflected the contemporary life of the artist. He was also attracted to the hard-edged attention to detail of the Netherlandish style (Hans Memling's in particular), visual qualities that coincided with his interest in Currier & Ives prints, American folk art and the decorative traditions of 19th-century Americana.

Wood's first Netherlandish-inspired canvas, *Woman with Plants* (1929; Cedar Rapids, IA, Mus. A.), portrays a Midwestern woman in country garb (an apron trimmed with rick-rack, a cameo brooch) holding a hardy snake plant, frequent accoutrement of the pioneer woman. The composition derives from Renaissance portraiture, with the half-length figure close to the picture plane, juxtaposed against a distant landscape, but the windmill and the shocks of corn visible over the sitter's shoulder localize Wood's painting to the American Midwest. Although Wood himself credits his trip to Munich as the catalyst for his conversion to Regionalism, other, more immediate sources for Wood's turn to Midwestern themes have been uncovered (Corn). One source is Wood's admiration for the writings of Jay Sigmund and Ruth Suckow, both of Iowa, who encouraged Midwesterners to cherish their indigenous heritage and eschew the prevalent inferiority complex regarding East Coast and European culture. *Woman with Plants* seems to be a translation into paint of the protagonist pioneer woman in Suckow's short story 'Midwestern Primitive', which appeared in *Harper's Magazine* in 1928.

From 1930 to 1932 Wood produced numerous canvases in the new style, with hard-edged detail, geometricized forms and stylized contours, often tinged with myth and wit. He enjoyed broad popularity and critical acclaim from 1930 to 1935, but by the late 1930s, as international political concerns overshadowed domestic ones, Regionalist art had come under attack for its parochialism, its Midwestern chauvinism, its narrative style and its patent refusal to keep pace with an emerging new American abstract art that would come to dominate in the post-war years.

BIBLIOGRAPHY

J. Dennis: *Grant Wood: A Study in American Art and Culture* (New York, 1975/R 1986)
J. Czestochowski, ed.: *John Steuart Curry and Grant Wood: A Portrait of Rural America* (Columbia, 1981)
W. M. Corn: *Grant Wood: The Regionalist Vision* (New Haven, 1983), p. 133
A. Nash: '*Death on the Ridge Road*: Grant Wood and Modernization in the Midwest', *Prospects*, viii (1983), pp. 281–301
S. Cole and S. Teller: *Grant Wood: The Lithographs* (New York, 1984)
K. A. Marling: 'Of Cherry Trees and Ladies' Teas: Grant Wood Looks at Colonial America', *The Colonial Revival in America*, ed. A. Axelrod (New York, 1985), pp. 294–319

M. SUE KENDALL

Wood, Robert (*b* ?Riverstown Castle, Co. Meath, *c.* 1717; *d* London, 9 Sept 1771). British traveller and antiquarian. Wood's antecedents and education are unclear, although he reputedly graduated at Oxford. However, Lord Ronald Gower despised his 'mean birth' and Robert Adam carped about his having been 'a surgeon lad in Glasgow', while Joseph Foster's *Alumni Oxonienses* does not mention his name. Even so, Horace Walpole considered him 'an excellent classic scholar' with 'taste and integrity'. According also to Walpole, Wood was 'originally a travelling tutor', a cicerone for those on the GRAND TOUR.

In Rome in 1749 he joined company with JAMES DAWKINS, a rich Jamaican plantation owner, and JOHN BOUVERIE. Together they planned to journey to Syria and there to 'rescue from oblivion the magnificence of Palmyra'. They had in mind to take views and architectural drawings of the ancient buildings such as had been done in Rome by Antoine-Baruty Desgotetz (1653–1728) and Charles-Louis Clérisseau. To make these drawings of ruined Palmyra, they retained the Piedmontese architectural draughtsman GIOVANNI BATTISTA BORRA. They sailed from Naples in May 1750 for Turkey, where Bouverie died on 8 September. In February 1751 they were at Beirut and, having proceeded to Damascus, they were amid the ruins of Palmyra in early spring. Here they spent 15 days. Borra filled his sketchbooks, two of which survive (London, Soc. Promot. Hell. Stud.), with rough views and measured details and plans, while Wood and Dawkins took measurements and copied inscriptions. On the return journey to Beirut, they stopped at Baalbek and measured the ruins there also.

Wood published *The Ruins of Palmyra* to great acclaim. Walpole wrote, 'Of all the works that distinguish this age, none perhaps excel those beautiful editions of Baalbeck and Palmyra.' In his preface Wood wrote that they had hoped the results of their labours at Palmyra might be of 'some use to the publick'. Indeed they were, for the work had an immediate and lasting influence on Neo-classical thought and taste. Wood had masterminded the operation and the publication, Borra had prepared the 57 master drawings for engravings, Bouvelie had financed the trip and Dawkins had paid all the subsequent bills (the publication of *The Ruins of Palmyra* and *The Ruins of Baalbeck* are reputed to have cost Dawkins £50,000). Most of the credit for the publications, however, has tended to go to Wood.

Immediately after the publication in 1753, Wood travelled to Rome as cicerone to the young Francis Egerton (1736–1803), Duke of Bridgewater. Here his portrait was painted by both Anton Raphael Mengs and Allan Ramsay. In 1756 he was appointed Under-Secretary of State and from 1761 to 1771 was Member of Parliament for Brackley. He was elected to the Society of Dilettanti in 1763. Despite a political career and a government appointment, he wished to be remembered as a Classicist. His magnum opus was *An Essay on the Original Genius of Homer*. He died at Putney and was buried in the 'new' burial-ground near the Upper Richmond Road. Walpole penned an epitaph for the memorial his wife raised to him.

WRITINGS
The Ruins of Palmyra, Otherwise Tedmor, in the Desert (London, 1753)
The Ruins of Balbec, Otherwise Heliopolis, in Coelosyria (London, 1757)
Comparative View of the Antient and Present State of the Troade: To which is Prefixed an Essay on the Original Genius of Homer (London, 1767)

IAIN BROWNING

Wood, Thomas Waterman (*b* Montpelier, VT, 12 Nov 1823; *d* New York, 14 April 1903). American painter. His art career dates from 1846, when he visited Boston, MA, and was either inspired or taught by the noted portrait painter Chester Harding. For the next 20 years he was an itinerant and little-known portrait painter. Then in 1867 he exhibited a set of three paintings collectively entitled a *Bit of War History* (1866; New York, Met.) at the National Academy of Design in New York. These genre paintings celebrated those freed slaves who had fought for the Union cause in the Civil War, and they touched a strong chord in the public feeling of the day. On the strength of these oils Wood was made a member of the National Academy in 1871 and in 1873 he painted what may be his best work, the *Village Post Office* (New York, NY Hist. Soc.). He eventually served as president of the Academy (1891–9) and was instrumental in the founding of a museum and several artists' organizations. He has been largely forgotten, because he tended toward sentimentalism later in his career, but his works contain a wealth of information on 19th-century life.

BIBLIOGRAPHY
Catalog of the Pictures in the Art Gallery in Montpelier, Montpelier, VT, Wood A.G. cat. (Montpelier, 1913)
Thomas Waterman Wood, PNA, 1823–1903 (exh. cat., ed. W. Lipke; Montpelier, VT, Wood A.G., 1972)

MARK W. SULLIVAN

Woodburn, Samuel (*b* 1780; *d* 1853). English dealer and collector. He was assisted at his premises at 112 St Martin's Lane, London, by his brothers Allen Woodburn, Henry Woodburn and, more actively, by William Woodburn. His reputation for expert judgement and professional integrity was universal, and he was instrumental in creating several important public and private collections in Britain and on the Continent, including those of Thomas Dimsdale, Mark Sykes and Alexander Hamilton, 10th Duke of Hamilton. Early sources state that he assisted Richard Fitzwilliam, 7th Viscount Fitzwilliam, who is said to have bequeathed him an annuity of £100. English institutions he supplied included the British Museum and the National Gallery, London, for which he made major purchases (e.g. *Cephalus Carried off by Aurora in her Chariot, c.* 1600; *Woman Borne off by a Sea God*, both by Agostino Carracci, London, N.G.); he sold some more modest paintings to John Bowes, founder of the Bowes Museum, Co. Durham. He brought to London the collections of drawings of M. Brunet, Paignon-Dijonval and Jean-Baptiste Wicar, the Marchese Antaldo Antaldi's drawings by Raphael and the superlative Rembrandt etchings that had belonged to Jan Pietersz. Zoomer and Vivant Denon. He advised Richard Seymour-Conway, 4th Marquess of Hertford, on the acquisition of paintings, but he is best known for having supplied to Thomas Lawrence drawings of supreme quality, many of which he had acquired abroad. In gratitude for Woodburn's services, Lawrence painted his portrait (*c.* 1823; Cambridge, Fitzwilliam).

In 1807 Woodburn published *Ecclesiastical Topography*, comprising etched views of 100 churches in the environs of London with accompanying text, and in 1816 *Woodburn's Gallery of Rare Portraits*, containing some 200 engravings of British historical figures from the original plates, many of them reworked, or facsimiles. Lawrence's executors commissioned from him the catalogue of Lawrence's drawings (MS., 1834; London, V&A Lib.).

After Lawrence's entire collection had been offered for sale unsuccessfully for £18,000 to King George IV, the Trustees of the British Museum, Sir Robert Peel and John William Ward, 4th Viscount Dudley and Ward, it was sold to Woodburn for £16,000. Between 1835 and 1836 he organized ten public selling exhibitions, at which William Esdaile bought works by Rembrandt and Claude and Francis Egerton, 1st Earl of Ellesmere, works by the Carracci. Some of the drawings by or attributed to Michelangelo and Raphael were sold to the Prince of Orange, later William II, King of the Netherlands, returning after the King's death to Woodburn, and, following complicated negotiations, many of these, together with others sold on the Continent, were accepted as a gift, paid for by public subscription, by the University Galleries (now Ashmolean Museum), Oxford, in 1845. The drawings retained, or re-acquired, by Woodburn for his own collection, together with paintings and works of decorative art, were sold after his death at Christie & Manson in May and June 1854, but only at sales at Christie's in June 1860 was the main body of the collection finally dispersed. The British Museum compensated in part for its earlier lack of success by making some outstanding purchases.

UNPUBLISHED SOURCES
A Catalogue of Drawings by the Old Masters . . . in the Possession of Sir Thomas Lawrence, P.R.A. at the Time of his Death Made by Messrs S & W Woodburn (1834; London, V&A Lib.)

BIBLIOGRAPHY
Obituary, *The Literary Gazette* (23 April 1853)
J. C. Robinson: *A Critical Account of the Drawings by Michel Angelo and Raffaello in the University Galleries, Oxford* (Oxford, 1870)
F. Lugt: *Marques* (1921)
D. Sutton: 'Oxford and the Lawrence Collection of Drawings', *Italian Drawings from the Ashmolean Museum, Oxford* (exh. cat., Wildenstein's, 1970), pp. vii–xxxiii

HARLEY PRESTON

Woodburytype. *See under* PHOTOGRAPHY, §I.

Woodcut [Fr. *gravure en bois, gravure sur bois*; Ger. *Holzschnitt*; It. *silografia, xilografia*; Sp. *grabado en madera, xilografía*]. Type of relief print and the process by which it is made. The term woodcut is often used loosely for any printmaking technique that employs a wooden block. Strictly speaking, however, the term applies only to cuts made on planks of wood. The precise term for the method that involves cutting the design on the end-grain of the block is WOOD-ENGRAVING. The term xylography is sometimes used to refer to both processes. This article discusses Western woodcuts, including those coloured free-hand or by stencil or printed from one or more blocks; chiaroscuro woodcuts, which are printed from at least two blocks using dark ink and white highlights on a coloured background, are discussed in a separate entry (*see* WOODCUT, CHIAROSCURO). For a discussion of woodcuts in other cultures *see* CHINA, §XIII, 19; INDIAN SUBCONTINENT, §VIII, 2; and JAPAN, §IX.

I. Materials and techniques. II. History.

I. Materials and techniques.

Woodcut is a relief-printing technique (*see* PRINTS, §III, 1), in which the printing surface is raised above other portions of the block, which are cut away so that they remain blank. The blocks are made from well-seasoned planks *c.* 25 mm thick, cut from the length of the tree and usually of fairly soft wood, such as pear; alder, beech, cherry, sycamore and walnut are also used. Because the image is reversed by printing, the design on the block must be in reverse of the intended direction. It can be drawn with pen, pencil or brush directly on the block, which may be prepared with a white ground. Alternatively, pigments brushed on to the back of a design may be transferred using a stylus. Drawings are sometimes pasted on to the surface of the block either face upwards or face down in order to reverse the design (having been oiled to make them transparent). Photographic methods of transfer became available in the 1860s, but these have been used more commonly for commercial wood-engraving than for woodcut.

Using a sharp knife, the design is cut by making two incisions along each side of the drawn lines to remove a fine shaving of wood. One incision is inclined away from the line and the other towards it, to leave a line with a conical section between two v-shaped grooves. Once the design is established, the surplus wood is removed with scoops, gouges and chisels, leaving a network of 'lines' or 'hatching' at surface level. In fact the cutter often creates graphic signs that give the impression of a cross-hatched pen drawing. During printing the summits of the lines are gradually worn down, and the blocks also often develop splits, breaks and wormholes, so that later impressions are coarser. A worn block may be copied by pasting an impression from it on to a new one and cutting a second version.

In order to withstand pressure during printing, the lines cannot be cut too thin, so woodcuts can never be as precise as engravings. Broader effects can be achieved by using gouges and chisels on their own and by exploiting the textures produced by the grain of the wood. Mistakes may be corrected by removing part of the block and inserting a plug, but the joins often open up during printing. State changes therefore usually involve removal of part of the work, not additions to the design. White-line woodcuts (*see* PRINTS, fig. 7) are created by cutting the design directly into the block, leaving large areas untouched to print as solid colour. Until the late 19th century the cutting was normally done by separate craftsmen, usually members of the carpenters' guild. Black-line woodcutting required expert training and was too laborious and time-consuming to appeal to the creative artist.

The ink used must be stiff enough to remain on the raised parts of the block and not run down into the hollows. It is applied with a dabber or, since the 19th century, with a roller. The support for the image is normally paper, preferably an absorbent type, which has been dampened before printing. Sometimes vellum or fabric is used. The first European woodcuts seem to have been stamped by hand or mallet, without a press, like early textiles. Alternatively, the back of the paper was rubbed using a burnisher, pebble or smooth wooden rubber to transfer the ink. Following the invention of movable type, known in China as early as the mid-11th century and in the West from the mid-15th century, simple screw presses came into use (*see* PRINTING); these are still used. The pressure is applied vertically and uniformly and does not need to be heavy. In the 19th century burnishing was revived as a method of taking proofs of woodcuts.

Most early woodcuts were printed in black or brownish ink, a practice that has continued; they were often coloured, either free-hand or using a stencil. Blocks may also be printed blind (without ink) to create 'seal prints' or embossed paper reliefs (*see* EMBOSSING). A single block can be printed in colours, either by selective inking of different areas of the image, or by sawing the block into sections, inking these separately and slotting them together again for printing. Colour woodcuts may also be printed from several blocks with the colours either separate or superimposed to create new shades. In Japan and, to a lesser extent, China, where woodcut has been the dominant graphic medium, complex methods of colour printing have been developed to achieve very subtle effects. A number of European artists have adopted these techniques.

BIBLIOGRAPHY

G. Petardi: *Printmaking Methods Old and New* (New York, 1959)
F. Brunner: *Handbook of Graphik Reproduction Processes/Handbuch der Druckgraphik/Manuel de la gravure* (Teufen, 1962)
K. Sotriffer: *Die Druckgraphik: Entwicklung, Technik, Eigenart* (Vienna, 1966)
P. Gilmore: *Modern Prints* (London, 1970)
F. Eichenberg: *The Art of the Print: Masterpieces, History, Techniques* (London, 1976)
E. Rhein: *The Art of Printmaking: A Comprehensive Guide to Graphic Techniques* (1976)
The Processes of Printmaking (exh. cat., ed. J. Atkinson; British Council, 1976)
W. Chamberlain: *The Thames and Hudson Manual of Woodcut Printmaking and Related Techniques* (London, 1978)
P. Gilmore: *Understanding Prints: A Contemporary Guide* (London, 1979)
A. Griffiths: *Prints and Printmaking: An Introduction to the History and Techniques* (London, 1980)
J. Dawson, ed.: *The Complete Guide to Prints and Printmaking Techniques and Materials* (London, 1981)
S. Lambert: *Printmaking* (London, 1983)

II. History.

1. Before the 15th century. 2. 15th century. 3. 16th century. 4. 17th and 18th centuries. 5. 19th century. 6. 20th century.

1. BEFORE THE 15TH CENTURY. Woodcut and stencil were probably the first printmaking processes to be

employed in Europe, although an impression on vellum of a *Crucifixion* (sold Stuttgart, H. G. Gutekunst, 13 May 1907, lot 33), described as an 'anonymous 12th-century metalcut', appears to be a rubbing, made at an unknown date, from a Romanesque metal bookcover, perhaps a damaged champlevé enamel one. The date at which woodcut printing was first used in Europe cannot be precisely determined. In China, banknotes, block-books, devotional images and landscapes had all been printed on paper from wooden blocks for centuries before the method was employed in Europe (*see* CHINA, §XIII, 19). Indian techniques of printing textiles with a mordant or resist before dyeing them may also have spread to Europe in antiquity (*see* INDIAN SUBCONTINENT, §VII, 3(i) and (ii); *see also* TEXTILE, §III, 1(ii)(b)). The surviving Late Antique fabrics found in Europe were, however, stamped directly with colour. This method was revived in the later Middle Ages, when fabrics were printed imitating expensive Asian textiles. Images of saints and biblical scenes were also printed on fabric. This may have been because paper was more expensive than cloth and often less readily available. Images on cloth could have been used in many ways unsuited to impressions on paper: sewn on to or into garments, and used as bandages, where their main purpose is likely to have been protection through the power of the saints depicted.

The invention of paper in China (*see* PAPER, §III) spread gradually through the Islamic world to reach Egypt and Morocco by AD 1100. The establishment of paper mills in Italy (1276), France (1348) and in the Holy Roman Empire (*c.* 1390) made it cheaper and more readily available. While this made it more attractive to printers, it had no great advantage over fabric as a support for religious images. The need to print playing cards on a material that could be stiffened easily may have led printers to favour paper. The growing popularity of gaming from the late 14th century soon encouraged mass production of playing cards by stencilling and/or printing. The early packs wore out and were discarded, so that only a few high-quality painted packs have survived. The printing of playing cards and pious images probably developed in parallel, for there are records of printed images of saints made around the last decade of the 14th century.

Style alone cannot provide precise dates and locations for the production of the earliest woodcuts, which are in the International Gothic style, characterized by similarities between the works produced in different geographical areas. The provenance of impressions is probably indicative of where prints were preserved rather than of where they were produced. The earliest apparent references to the technique point to its use in Italy and in Burgundy. However, only three Italian woodcuts exist that have been even tentatively dated to before 1400; the one most likely to be early is the fragmentary *Trinity with Saints* (s. 749f), which, like the majority of surviving early Italian woodcuts, is in the collection of Jacopo Rubieri (now Ravenna, Bib. Com. Classeuse). In 1393 the Duke of Burgundy paid a carpenter, Jehan Baudet, for producing '*moles et tables. . .à la devise de Beaumez*' for the Chartreuse de Champmol, near Dijon; these were probably woodblocks, after designs by the Flemish artist Jean de Beaumetz, for printing images on either fabric or paper. There is documentary evidence

for the production of images of saints in Venice (probably by means of woodblocks) from 1396, when St Catherine of Siena (1347–80) was first venerated there. However, no late 14th-century image of St Catherine of Siena has survived. During the investigation into her possible canonization, evidence was presented that a devotee had arranged that an image of her, 'easy to multiply on pieces of paper, should be shown with her attributes' and that 'several thousand of these images have been made, so that no small quantity has been distributed both in Venice itself and in the countries mentioned before [Poland, Germany, Byzantium, Dalmatia and various Italian states] and what is more this is the origin of the fact that today the images of the various saints on their feast days are multiplied on such pieces of paper'. The omission of France and Spain from the above list of countries may be significant, for printed images seem to have met with strong opposition from the guild of *imagiers* in France and to have been treated as illicit goods, which may have hampered trade in devotional woodcuts there. Playing cards, however, spread rapidly. By 1382 they were so common that at Lille card games were banned as a serious distraction from archery practice. This suggests that cards were already being mass-produced cheaply, by either woodcut or stencils.

BIBLIOGRAPHY

Hollstein: *Dut. & Flem.*; Hollstein: *Ger.*
A. von Bartsch: *Le Peintre-graveur* (1803–21)
A.-P.-F. Robert-Dumesnil: *Le Peintre-graveur français* (1835–71)
J. D. Passavant: *Le Peintre-graveur*, 6 vols (Leipzig, 1860–64/*R* New York, 1966)
A. J. J. Delen: *Histoire de la gravure dans les anciens Pays-Bas et dans les provinces belges*, 2 vols (Paris and Brussels, 1924–35)
C. Zigrosser: *The Book of Fine Prints* (London, 1937)
Prints, 1400–1800 (exh. cat., ed. H. Joachim; Minneapolis, MN, Inst. A.; Cleveland, OH, Mus. A.; Chicago, IL, A. Inst.; 1956–7)
J. Laran: *L'Estampe*, 2 vols (Paris, 1959/*R* Vaduz, 1979)
Color in Prints. . .European and American Color Prints from 1500 to the Present (exh. cat., New Haven, CT, Yale U. A.G., 1962)
H. T. Musper: *Der Holzschnitt in fünf Jahrhunderten* (Stuttgart, 1964)
A. Hyatt Mayor: *Prints and People: A Social History of Printed Pictures* (New York, 1971)
Die druckgraphischen Techniken, i: Der Holzschnitt vom 15. Jahrhundert bis zur Gegenwart (exh. cat., ed. J. Schultze and A. Winther; Bremen, Ksthalle, 1974)
The Illustrated Bartsch (New York, 1978–)
A. Gallego: *Historia del grabado en España* (Madrid, 1979)
E. Páez Ríos: *Repertorio de grabado españoles en la Biblioteca Nacional* (Madrid, 1981–5)
H. D. Saffrey: '*Imago de facili multiplicabilis in cartis*: Un document méconnu, daté de l'année 1412, sur l'origine de la gravure sur bois à Venise', *Nouv. Est.*, 74 (1984), pp. 4–7

2. 15TH CENTURY.

(i) Introduction. (ii) Holy Roman Empire. (iii) The Netherlands. (iv) France, Spain and England. (v) Italy.

(i) Introduction. Early in the century woodcut was the chief printmaking medium, although stencils were also employed. It was used almost entirely to produce playing cards and religious images, including indulgences and New-Year-greetings sheets. The earliest woodcuts were often powerful, imaginative designs, made to be coloured by hand or stencil, which gives them the effect of stained glass. As the blocks deteriorated and they were copied by lesser craftsmen, many woodcuts of mediocre quality resulted. Many early woodcuts were pinned or pasted to walls, cupboard doors, small altars and tombs, carried as

personal protection or even printed on bandages in the hope of promoting healing. They soon became torn and dirty, to be discarded and replaced by other images. Only a tiny fraction has survived, usually because they were pasted into books or used as scrap materials in book covers. Most are either unique or extremely rare.

In the second half of the century woodcut was also used for block-books (see BLOCK-BOOK) and illustrations in typographical books, alphabets, book plates and book-covers, and for portraits, maps, song-sheets, broadsheets, almanacs and other printed ephemera. The main centres of production were in the Holy Roman Empire, Italy and the Netherlands; later in the century France also played a significant role. Other countries produced few woodcuts, and these were mostly for book illustrations. The woodcuts that appear to belong to the earliest phase include the splendid large *Christ before Herod* (Schreiber, no. 265) and the fragmentary double-sided woodblock known as the *Bois Protat*, with images of the *Annunciation* and the *Crucifixion* (S 1h and 1i). It was found, together with some other, completely worm-eaten, blocks, near the abbey of La Ferté-sur-Grosne in Burgundy. This led to an attribution to the Burgundian school for the group. They are powerful images with the long, flowing lines characteristic of the International Gothic, dagged garments, large, expressive hands and angular brow-lines. However, they resemble Bohemian biblical drawings of c. 1390–1430 and may have originated there. The same is true of a small *Crucifixion* (sold London, Sotheby's, 1 Dec 1986, lot 50) and an early *Flagellation* (S 288), usually considered to be French.

(ii) Holy Roman Empire. The date and place of origin of the above works are uncertain, but various others that are broadly similar were probably made in the Salzburg region or Upper Bavaria in the early 15th century. They include *Christ Carrying the Cross* (S 336m), *St Erasmus* (S 1410d) and an important group of early 15th-century woodcuts in the Staatliche Graphische Sammlung, Munich, with scenes from the *Life of the Virgin*, Crucifixions and saints, including *St Dorothy* (S 1394; see fig. 1) and *St Sebastian* (S 1677). There are significant holdings of similar woodcuts in Nuremberg (Ger. Nmus.), Graz (Ubib.), Berlin (Altes Mus.) and Paris (Bib. N.). In these early cuts the outlines are thick and flowing, and some of the impressions have the background obscured by a brownish-black tint, leaving the graceful figures in silhouette. They wear softly draped garments with Y- and J-shaped folds, which fall in loops and hairpin bends and crumple gently at the hem. This looping soon became a mannerism, and in some cuts of c. 1420, such as *St Dorothy* (S 1395), *St Christopher* (S 1352) and *St Wolfgang* (S 1733; destr. 1942), it is quite exaggerated. The Lambach *Pietà* (S 972a) and a larger *Pietà with the Instruments of the Passion* (Stogdon, no. 1) have equally complex fold patterns. Carved wooden Pietàs were produced in southern Germany and widely exported. The woodcuts are probably based on such carvings, and other prints of figures on plinths, benches or thrones probably also reflect a copy of sculpture. Indeed woodcarving workshops may have produced woodcuts after their own statues.

1. Woodcut of *St Dorothy*, 380×195 mm, early 15th century (Munich, Staatliche Graphische Sammlung)

The existence of early copies, some unrecognized, complicates dating. Two famous Bohemian woodcuts in Vienna (Albertina), the *Holy Family* and *St Jerome* (S 637 and 1536), bear signs of being copies of important, lost, early woodcuts: the actions are carried out with the left hand, and there are areas (e.g. in the landscape behind St Jerome) where the cutter has misunderstood the image. These woodcuts are datable to c. 1410–30; the originals would have been earlier, so Bohemia may have been in the forefront of the development of woodcut. Bohemia had been relatively little affected by the Black Death, and the emperor Charles IV's patronage had led to a flowering of the arts there in the later 14th century (see LUXEMBOURG, House of, (3)). Other early Bohemian woodcuts, the *Adoration of the Magi* (S 97a), the *Throne of Mercy* (S 736; destr. 1942) and the *Virgin Enthroned* (S 1114; destr. 1942), should perhaps be dated to c. 1400–10 or even earlier. The same is true of the *Virgin of Lyon* (S 1069), often attributed to the French school but very similar to the *Virgin Enthroned*. They appear to relate to 14th-century Bohemian paintings and to Bohemian manuscripts of the late 14th century and the early 15th.

The first woodcut with a reasonably reliable date is from 1423. This is *St Christopher* (S 1349) from Buxheim Monastery. (A cut in the Bibliothèque Royale, Brussels, dated perhaps misleadingly 1418 is discussed in §(iii) below.) Five other woodcuts, believed to come from the Upper Rhine area, may be grouped together with it: an *Annunciation* (S 28) from the same source, a *Nativity* and an *Adoration of the Magi* (S 84 and 98) and a double sheet of *St Gertrude* and *St Apollonia* (S 1454a and 1234x). They have quite fully developed backgrounds, thinner lines, shading in the folds of the rather angular draperies, and inscriptions that are sometimes on banderoles. This all suggests a designer who was in touch with recent developments in the Netherlands.

The earliest woodcut signature, *ierg haspel ze Bibrach*, is on a fine image of *St Bernard Embraced by the Crucified Christ* (S 1271). Nagler quoted a death date of 1430–40 for Jerg Haspel, but his authority for this is unknown. Biberach is in Swabia, an important area for woodcut production. The style of the work is simple and direct, with curved hooks and Y-folds and without over elaborate looped draperies. A similar approach appears in the Maihingen *Pietà* (S 973) and in *St Christopher* (S 1350a). These all have the thinner line characteristic of woodcuts of *c.* 1430–40. The designs of two outstanding woodcuts of this period, an *Annunciation* and a *Visitation* (S 25b and 52b), resemble the paintings of the Master of the St Lambrecht Votive Panel. They are still almost without hatching lines but have elaborate and detailed backgrounds, a feature that became increasingly common in the middle decades of the century. Some outstanding examples are the *Agony in the Garden*, the *Last Supper*, the *Martyrdom of St Sebastian* and the *Beheading of St John the Baptist* (S 184, 166a, 1516, 1676c). A mid-century woodcut of the *Mass of St Gregory* (S 1471), signed *Bastion Ulmer* (Sebastian of Ulm, *fl* 1460), is the first signed print from this important centre of woodcut production; an 'Ulrich Formschneider' was recorded there as early as 1398, and eight blockcutters worked there in 1441–7. Woodcuts of the Virgin and Child were always in demand. Particularly striking are a half-length version (S 1023), probably of the 1440s, and another printed in white on green-tinted paper (S 1048b), to form a highly decorative devotional panel.

From the 1430s goldsmiths adapted their chasing techniques to produce copperplate-engravings printed on paper. The higher status of their craft and the finer detail achieved meant that engravings were valued more highly than woodcuts. Nevertheless, woodcuts had many advantages: they were cheap and fairly quick to produce; they could be printed in larger editions, together with type; and designers could delegate the labour of cutting. However, European woodcutters increasingly emulated the linear qualities of engravings, instead of developing woodcut's potential for printing tone, colour and texture as well as outlines.

During the late 15th century woodcut was developed into a flexible medium for reproducing hatched and cross-hatched line drawings. This took time, and some of the earlier, hatched cuts were aesthetically less pleasing than the unshaded images that had preceded them. As designers and cutters became more expert, techniques improved, and hatching lines ceased to sprout from the outlines like rigid combs. Comparison between the illustrations to the Cologne Bible of 1478–9 (e.g. London, BL, no. IB3837) and the Lübeck Bible of 1494 (e.g. London, BL, no. IC9954) indicate the advances made. The best designers of the 1480s and 1490s, such as Erhard Reuwich, Michael Wolgemut and Wilhelm Pleydenwurff, started to employ more flexible, form-following methods of shading,

preparing the way for Albrecht Dürer, who transformed the medium between 1496 and 1511. Hans Burgkmair (*see* BURGKMAIR, (2)) and MAIR VON LANDSHUT also designed some woodcuts in the new manner in the 1490s and made early experiments in printing in colour and on tinted paper.

One innovation that was only sporadically followed up in the 15th century was the use of colour-printing, for instance in initials by Johannes Fust (*c.* 1400–66) and Peter Schoeffer (*c.* 1425–1502) in the Psalter published at Mainz in 1457. They were printed, from either wood blocks or metal casts of such blocks, in red or blue and red combined (*see* BOOK ILLUSTRATION, §I, 1). In 1485 the Augsburg printer Erhard Ratdolt (*fl* 1467–1516), working in Venice, produced an edition of the *Sphaera mundi*, the astronomical treatise written by John Holywood, with diagrams printed in several colours. Venetian printers continued to use colour after Ratdolt returned to Augsburg in 1486. There he seems to have been involved in the printing of Burgkmair's work in colour and in the development of chiaroscuro woodcuts, and perhaps also of white-line woodcutting.

(iii) The Netherlands. The small number of surviving woodcuts from the Netherlands (and from France) may be due to the destruction of images by Calvinist iconoclasts, the dispersal of monastic libraries during the French Revolution (1789–95) and the Revolutionary Wars. Both were, however, important centres for illuminated manuscripts, so there may have been opposition to printed images, which would threaten the illuminators' livelihoods. Most early Netherlandish woodcuts have thin lines and are often printed in brownish ink. The much damaged *Virgin and Child in a Hortus Conclusus* (S 1160) bears the earliest date found on a woodcut—1418; a better preserved undated copy is in St Gallen (S 1161). Its similarity in linear style and shading to mid-century block-books has led many scholars to see it as a later copy with the date repeated. However, the style reflects the angular fold-structure of paintings *c.* 1420–40 by the Master of Flémalle and Jan van Eyck, so the date could be authentic. Two sensitively cut early Netherlandish woodcuts are the *Man of Sorrows* (S 864), in the manner of the Master of Flémalle, and the monumental *Prophet and Sibyl* (S 2008f). The latter has square-ended and 7-shaped pot-hooks in the drapery folds, like two further Netherlandish woodcuts, the *Last Judgement* and the *Virgin and Child in the Vine Arbour* (S 607 and 1168). This drapery style is usually dated to the mid-15th century, but again it may well be earlier.

Two woodcuts with Dutch inscriptions (and so undoubtedly from the Netherlands) are the mid-century *Mass of St Gregory* (S 1462) in pure outline and the *Virgin and Child in a Glory* (S 1108) of *c.* 1460, which has shading on some of the rays of the glory. The *Crucifixion* (830×535 mm) is a rare example of a very large-format woodcut. Stylistically it resembles the first edition of the Netherlandish *Apocalypse* block-book in Munich, as does a *St George Slaying the Dragon* (S 1448). A *Grotesque Alphabet* (S 1998) in the British Museum, London, has outlines fringed with tapered 'teeth', which are characteristic of images in Netherlandish block-books. Other Netherlandish woodcuts of the third quarter of the century have more extensive shading, for instance large images of *St John the Baptist and St Christopher* (s 1518) and a *Virgin Suckling the Child* (s 1039b).

(*iv*) *France, Spain and England.* No woodcut of before 1450 can definitely be ascribed to the French school. Some crudely cut fragments of friezes of the *Passion* (s 21c) and the *Life of St Catherine* (see 1977 exh. cat.) probably date from the mid-15th century, as does the double image of the *Trinity* and the *Adoration of the Relics of St Claude* (s 736b and 1080m). A slightly later series of the *Apostles, the Credo and the Ten Commandments* (s 1759), with French inscriptions, is akin to the Netherlandish *Apocalypse* block-book in character. However, the faces of the *Nine Heroes* (s 1945) resemble those in early French playing cards. Also characteristically French are illustrations depicting the activities of Death, such as the *Men's Dance of Death* and the *Women's Dance of Death*, published by Guy Marchant in 1485–6, and Pierre Le Rouge's *Danse macabre hystoirée* (1492). Even more powerful are Robert Gobin's *Dance of Death* woodcut illustrations in *Les Loups ravissans* (Paris, *c.* 1505), which are slashed into the block in an almost expressionistic manner. The woodcut fragment representing *The Prophet Moses and the Erithrean Sibyl* (Courboin, no. 150) is a very striking image—presumably from a series of *Prophets and Sibyls*.

The practice of selling cash-boxes and caskets with devotional images pasted into the lids as protection ensured the survival of a number of late 15th-century French woodcuts (examples, Paris, Bib. N.). These include scenes from the *Life of the Virgin* and of *Christ*, and images of saints with characteristic colouring in shades of red, green, brown and purple. Most of them resemble the precise and distinctive illustrations in the Books of Hours that became a speciality of Parisian publishers in the last decades of the century (*see* BOOK OF HOURS). A *Martyrdom of St Erasmus* (s 1410) is very similar stylistically. The fragment of an image of *King Henry VI Invoked as a Saint* (Dodgson, 1915, no. 21), perhaps the most important 15th-century woodcut issued in England, resembles Parisian work, and it was probably commissioned in France. Several late 15th-century woodcuts, including *St Bonaventura at Lyon* and the *Two Saints Roch* and the *Two Saints John* (s IX, 1282x, 1669m and 1518g), may have been cut in Savoy, or in Lyon; the latter was to become an important centre of book illustration. A few single-sheet woodcuts have survived from the south of France, including a large *Crucifixion* (s 370i), apparently influenced by Neapolitan or Spanish book illustration. In Spain and England woodcut was employed for book illustration, and Spanish books have some very fine white-line borders. Hardly any single-sheet woodcuts are known. In England (a country not otherwise to the forefront of printmaking) the so-called Schoolmaster Printer of St Albans produced the *Chroniclis of Englonde* (1485) with red initials and the *Bokys of Haukyng and Huntynge and Blasyng of Armys* (1486), with the arms printed in up to three colours.

(*v*) *Italy.* Italian imperial size paper was of larger format than papers elsewhere, so large Italian woodcuts such as the following examples could be printed without joins. The *Virgin of the Fire* (Forlì Cathedral) is revered as the wooduct saved from a fire in 1428; although it is not in the International Gothic style then current in northern Italy, scholars' doubts about its authenticity are probably unfounded, for the facial features have affinities with early Venetian devotional paintings and with the woodcut of the *Trinity with Saints*. Two other fine, large images of the *Virgin and Child* (s 1158 and 1058) are probably of mid-century date. They represent a type of devotional woodcut that provided a cheap substitute for painted images of the Virgin, and one is still pasted on to panel. A *Virgin Suckling* (s 1041) with delicate Paduan-style swags of fruit is a slightly later example.

There is more evidence of Italian woodcut production of *c.* 1430–40. In 1430 'woodblocks for playing cards and saints' were in the possession of a card-maker, Antonio da Giovanni di Ser Francesco, at Florence, while in 1440 a Paduan notary drew up a legal instrument according to which Magister Jacobus, a German dyer of skins, was to sell to Magister Cornelio de Flandria woodcuts printed and coloured, 'as was usually done', to the value of 20 golden ducats. The prices listed for individual images make it clear that *c.* 3500 impressions were involved. They were probably Italian, as the subjects correspond closely to those of the surviving Italian woodcuts in Ravenna. In 1441, however, the woodcutters and playing-card makers asked the Venetian Council for protection from foreign imports, which were ruining their trade.

Many of the woodcuts collected by Rubieri have affinities with Venetian and north Italian painting of *c.* 1430–60, notably that of Michele Giambono, Jacobello del Fiore, Antonio Vivarini and Gentile da Fabriano. A striking *Martyrdom of St Sebastian* relates closely to a Venetian miniature of 1436 attributed to Cortese. The foliated ogee arches of the frames surrounding *St Philip Benizzi* (s 1651) and *St Bartholomew* (s 1267), and the elaborate thrones on which other saints are seated, probably indicate a mid-15th century date for many of the designs, though there has been a tendency to date them later. The gentle images of female saints, especially the two versions of *St Claire of Assisi* in Ravenna (Bib. Com. Classeuse; s 1380) and Washington, DC (N.G.A.; s IX, 1756), and the *St Catherine of Siena* in Basle (s 1345), resemble early paintings of the Virgin by Jacopo Bellini.

Mendicant friars and other orders made use of woodcuts in their teaching and preaching activities. Images of Franciscan and Dominican saints and of St Augustine feature prominently among the surviving Italian woodcuts of *c.* 1450–80. Groups exist that are clearly connected in style, such as the Augustinian and Dominican saints in Ravenna (Bib. Com. Classeuse) and Washington, DC (N.G.A.); and the pairs of Lombard woodcuts of Franciscan saints in Ravenna (Bib. Com. Classeuse; s 1423 and 1987 exh. cat., no. 17) and Washington, DC (N.G.A.).

The finest 15th-century Italian single-sheet woodcuts are comparable in quality to the superb book illustrations made in Venice and Florence in the last decades of the century. One outstanding woodcut of *St Anthony of Padua* (s 1233) is clearly related to the intarsia reliquary cabinets of 1472–7 by Lorenzo Canozi and Christoforo Canozi in the basilica of S Antonio in Padua. Similar skills were required for the production of woodcuts and intarsia, and the woodcut was probably both designed by the Canozi and executed in their workshop. Though somewhat stiffly cut, a Venetian woodcut of the *Naval Battle of Zonchio* (1499) foreshadows 16th-century narrative woodcuts.

Italian woodcuts often have very decorative borders. Two fine, large late 15th-century Lombard woodcuts of *Christ Carrying the Cross* and the *Man of Sorrows* (s 919 and 855) based on designs in the manner of Andrea Solario or Gian Francesco de' Maineri have elaborate white-line scroll frames. A Florentine woodcut of the *Flagellation* (Hind, ii, pp. 449–50) of much the same period, which has a comparable border, is related stylistically to the work of Filippino Lippi. As in many Florentine book illustrations, white-line work was also used for the ground on which the figures are standing. Another high-quality Florentine devotional work, in the style of Raffaellino del Garbo, is the *Virgin and Child with St John* (s 1137).

BIBLIOGRAPHY
P. Kristeller: *Early Florentine Woodcuts* (London, 1897)
P. Heitz, ed.: *Einblattdrucke des fünfzehnten Jahrhunderts*, 100 vols (Strasbourg, 1899–1942)
K. Haebler: *Hundert Kalender-Inkunabeln* (Strasbourg, 1905)
M. Lehrs: *Holzschnitte der ersten Hälfte des XV Jahrhunderts im königlichen Kupferstichkabinett zu Berlin* (Berlin, 1908)
W. Stengel: *Holzschnitte im Kupferstichkabinett des Germanischen National-Museums zu Nürnberg.*, iii (Berlin, 1913)
C. Dodgson: *Woodcuts of the XVth Century in the John Rylands Library* (Manchester, 1915)
P. Kristeller: *Holzschnitte im Kupferstichkabinett zu Berlin, Zweite Reihe*, xxi (Berlin, 1915)
F. M. Haberditzl: *Die Einblattdrucke des XV. Jahrhunderts in der Hofbibliothek zu Wien, I. Die Holzschnitte* (Vienna, 1920)
C. Glaser: *Gotische Holzschnitte* (Berlin, 1923)
F. Courboin: *Histoire illustrée de la gravure en France*, 4 vols (Paris, 1923–8)
M. Weinberger: *Die Formschnitte des Katharinen-klosters zu Nürnberg* (Munich, 1925)
W. Schreiber: *Handbuch der Holz- und Metallschnitte des XV Jahrhunderts*, 8 vols (Leipzig, 1926–30) [s; Schreiber and others have made assignments to a planned but unpubd ninth volume, which incl. unpubd 15th-century woodcuts in the N.G.A., Washington, DC, and a woodcut block in the Louvre]
P. A. Lemoisne: *Les Xylographies du XIVe et du XVe siècle au Cabinet des Estampes de la Bibliothèque Nationale*, 2 vols (Paris and Brussels, 1927–30)
C. Dodgson: 'English Devotional Woodcuts of the Late 15th Century, with Special Reference to Those in the Bodleian Library', *Walpole Soc.*, xvii (1928–9), p. 95
Z. von Tobolka: *Die Einblattdrucke des XV Jahrhunderts auf dem Gebiete der Tschechoslowakei* (Prague, 1928–30)
C. Dodgson: *Woodcuts of the Fifteenth Century in the Ashmolean Museum* (Oxford, 1929)
——: *Woodcuts of the XV Century in the Department of Prints and Drawings*, London, BM cat. (London, 1934, 1935)
A. M. Hind: *An Introduction to a History of Woodcut, with a Detailed Survey of Work Done in the Fifteenth Century*, 2 vols (London, 1935/R New York, 1963)
E. Hodnett: *English Woodcuts, 1480–1535* (London, 1935/R Oxford, 1973)
The First Century of Printmaking (exh. cat., ed. E. Mongan and C. O. Schniewind; Chicago, IL, A. Inst., 1941)
A. Blum: *Les Primitifs de la gravure sur bois: Etude historique et catalogue des incunables xylographiques du Musée du Louvre* (Paris, 1956)
Die Kunst der Graphik: Das 15. Jahrhundert: Werke aus dem Besitz der Albertina (exh. cat., ed. E. Mitsch; Vienna, Albertina, 1963)
Fifteenth-century Woodcuts and Metalcuts from the National Gallery of Art (exh. cat., ed. R. S. Field; Washington, DC, N.G.A., 1965) [contains full details of *Einblattdrucke des fünfzehnten Jahrhunderts*]
G. Schizzerotto: *Le incisioni quattrocentesche della Classense* (Ravenna, 1971)
Les Incunables de la collection Edmond de Rothschild (exh. cat., Paris, Louvre, 1974)
Fifteenth-century Woodcuts and Other Relief Prints in the Collection of the Metropolitan Museum of Art (exh. cat., ed. R. S. Field; New York, Met., 1977)
H. Körner: *Der früheste deutsche Einblattholzschnitt* (Mittenwald, 1979)
Xilografie italiane del quattrocento da Ravenna e da altri luoghi (exh. cat., ed. E. Borea and F. Bellini; Ravenna, Bib. Com. Classeuse, 1987); review by D. Landau in *Prt Q.*, vi (1989), pp. 71–3
N. G. Stogdon: *German and Netherlandish Woodcuts of the 15th and 16th Centuries*, dealer stock cat. (Middle Chinnock, 1991)

3. 16TH CENTURY. In the 16th century woodcut was employed for a wide range of secular purposes, such as dynastic and political propaganda and polemic by various religious groups, as well as for producing religious images. The subject-matter included maps, town views, sieges, battle scenes, hunts, tournaments, portraits, comic and satirical works, popular broadsheets and genre subjects, such as banquets, peasant festivals and bathing scenes. Woodcut was also used to print wallpaper (*see* WALLPAPER, §I, 2) and other DECORATIVE PAPER. South-eastern Germany continued to be the most prolific area for woodcuts; when they were losing popularity in most other countries in the late 16th century, production there continued. The decline in the prestige of woodcut was accelerated by the use of engravings to spread knowledge of Italian Renaissance compositions. Widespread neglect of existing woodcuts also resulted, so that many are now very rare. This is especially true of the large-format friezes and other compositions for the wall.

(i) Holy Roman Empire. (ii) The Netherlands. (iii) Italy. (iv) France.

(i) Holy Roman Empire. The most influential of all 16th-century woodcut designers was the Nuremberg artist Albrecht Dürer (*see* DÜRER, (1)). He would have learnt the art of woodcut during his apprenticeship with the painter Michael Wolgemut, who designed illustrations for the publications of Dürer's godfather, Anton Koberger. Dürer was also influenced by the outstanding woodcuts for the *Dance of Death* (1489) and the Bible (1494) published in Lübeck. He demanded equally high standards from the cutter responsible for the blocks for his own early publications. These show a marked improvement in cutting over those that he designed for other publishers during his journeyman years. Dürer's woodcut production had begun *c.* 1492. His early masterpieces of *c.* 1496–8 include the *Apocalypse* series (*see* APOCALYPSE, fig. 3, and DÜRER, (1), fig. 4), *Samson and the Lion* and the *Knight and the Landsknecht* (all Hollstein: *Ger.*, nos 163–178, 107 and 265). He would have seen Venetian woodcuts on his first visit to Italy in 1494–5, but he did not adopt the Venetian outline style. The woodcuts that he published on his return have the outlines and areas of emphasis cut into the surface of the block so that they are printed under strong pressure. The shading lines, which follow and define the forms, are cut into curved planes which are carved down from the surface; they are printed under weaker pressure, giving greater variety of line. Parallel and crosshatched tonal shading is usually restricted to skies and deeply shadowed areas. Tonal shading is much more extensive in the woodcuts produced after his second visit to Italy in 1505–7, as may be seen by comparing the early blocks for the *Large Woodcut Passion* cycle (see fig. 2) and the *Life of the Virgin* (*c.* 1503–5 and 1510–11; Hollstein: *Ger.*, nos 188–207) with those added in 1510–11. The simpler, linear patterns of the later cuts created designs that were serene and less restless; what was lost in vigour of line was gained in tonal consistency and balance. The

2. Woodcut by Albrecht Dürer: *Descent into Limbo*, 284×196 mm, *c.* 1497–1500 (London, British Museum); from the *Large Woodcut Passion* cycle

influence of Venetian art undoubtedly contributed to Dürer's change from a linear to a tonal approach, but his drawings on green prepared paper, made in 1503–4 before his second visit to Venice, already indicate his interest in chiaroscuro effects.

The reign of the Holy Roman Emperor Maximilian I coincided with and encouraged a revival of German art. However, the Emperor, lacking the money to organize and build all his grandiose artistic and architectural projects, often had to be satisfied with publishing them as woodcut designs. Dürer's late woodcuts include the portrait of *Maximilian I* (1518–19; Hollstein: *Ger.*, no. 255), his *Small Triumphal Chariot* (*c.* 1518; Hollstein: *Ger.*, no. 252) and the overall design of the huge, composite *Triumphal Arch* (3409×2922 mm, 1515–17; Hollstein: *Ger.*, no. 251), for which he also produced some blocks (Hollstein: *Ger.*, nos 251–2, 255; *see* REGALIA, fig. 3). Other designers from Dürer's circle involved in work for the Emperor include Hans Schäufelein, Hans Springinklee and Wolf Traut. Schäufelein later produced a nine-sheet *Triumphal Procession of the Emperor Charles V* (1537; Dodgson, ii, pp. 49, 220). The *Triumphal Arch Erected for Charles V's Entry into Nuremberg* in 1541 was also recorded probably by Peter Flötner (Hollstein: *Ger.*, no. 27), a Swiss artist who also made fine white-line ornament woodcuts, broadsheets and designs for beds and architectural details.

Augsburg was the leading centre for the development of the colour woodcut, with the publisher Erhard Ratdolt apparently playing a major role. He had earlier published colour woodcuts in Venice. The woodcut by Lucas Cranach I (*see* CRANACH, (1)) of *St George* (1507–8; Hollstein: *Ger.*, no. 81), which was printed on blue, prepared paper in black and adhesive dusted with gold to imitate manuscript illumination, was sent from Saxony to the imperial court at Augsburg. It appears to have inspired the earliest proofs of Burgkmair's *Maximilian I on Horseback* and *St George* (both 1508; Hollstein: *Ger.*, nos 253 and 323). They were printed on tinted paper in black and in an adhesive, on to which gold, silver or a mixture of the two was dusted. Ratdolt was probably responsible for this early use of metallic pigments for prints in Augsburg and may also have cut the additional blocks that transformed them into chiaroscuro woodcuts. These were to become more popular than polychrome woodcuts. The latter technique was, however, employed by Burgkmair and Weiditz for heraldic woodcuts and also by Altdorfer.

In the 1490s Hans Burgkmair the elder had produced illustrations for the Augsburg publisher Erhard Ratdolt, including a colour-printed *Crucifixion* (Hollstein: *Ger.*, no. 46). He was much influenced by Dürer's woodcuts, and after his visit to Italy (1507), Italian motifs are evident in his work. Burgkmair and another Augsburg designer, Leonard Beck, played a very important part in Maximilian I's books and woodcut projects, including the illustrations to Melchior Pfinzing's *Der Theuerdanck* (1511–17; Hollstein: *Ger.*, nos 416–30) and to Marx Treitzsaurwein's *Der Weisskunig* (pubd 1775). Burgkmair designed the *Genealogy of the Emperor Maximilian I* (1509–12; Hollstein: *Ger.*, nos 324–415) and Beck the *Saints Connected with the House of Habsburg* (1510–22; Hollstein: *Ger.*, no. 12). Burgkmair also designed many blocks for Treitzsaurwein's *Triumphal*

Procession of Maximilian I (*c.* 1516–18, pubd 1526; Hollstein: *Ger.*, nos 552–618; *see* BURGKMAIR, (2), fig. 1), on which he collaborated with Albrecht Altdorfer, Hans Springinklee and others. Hieronymus Andreae (*d* 1556) and Jost de Negker directed the cutting of the blocks for the imperial projects, and these collaborative publications led to a rapid spread of tonal shading and of improved cutting techniques in the Holy Roman Empire. The names of some of the other cutters are known; they include Hans Frank (Lützelburger; before 1495–1526), Cornelis Liefrinck I (*c.* 1480–*c.*1545), Alexis Lindt (*fl c.* 1500–25), Wolfgang Resch (*c.* 1480–after 1537), Clause Seman, Hans Taberth and Jan de Bom (all *fl c.* 1510–17). The Emperor's death in 1519 delayed the publication of several of his woodcut projects and led to the dispersal of the teams of woodcutters to other parts of Europe.

In 1524–7 Burgkmair designed four large and dramatic woodcuts representing the *Fall of Man* (959×663 mm), the *Agony in the Garden* (970×663 mm), the *Crucifixion* (959×671 mm) and the *Mater Dolorosa* (954×670 mm; Hollstein: *Ger.*, nos 1, 40, 48 and 79). Published in the imperial city of Augsburg, they represent a powerful reaffirmation of traditional religious imagery at a time when Lutheranism was gaining ground. The woodcut by Hans Weiditz (ii) of the *Emperor Maximilian Hearing Mass* probably dates from *c.* 1519; his most striking single cut is a twelve-part *Bird's-eye View of Augsburg* (1521; Geisberg, nos 1524, 1530–41). The son of a sculptor in wood, he was a caricaturist and an illustrator of great sensitivity who worked in both Augsburg and Strasbourg.

The highly expressive woodcuts produced by Lucas Cranach I in Bavaria or Austria, before his appointment to the Saxon court in 1505, include the dramatic *Crucifixion* (1502) and a further *Crucifixion* and *Christ on the Mount of Olives* (*c.* 1502; all Hollstein: *Ger.*, nos 25–6 and 24). His *Venus and Cupid* (1506; Hollstein: *Ger.*, no 105) shows the influences of Dürer and Jacopo de' Barbari in the tectonic, three-dimensional rendering of the nude. However, in general Cranach preferred to let his figures merge into the landscape, as in the *Rest on the Flight into Egypt* (1509), *St George Slaying the Dragon* (*c.* 1512), the *Judgement of Paris* (1508) and the *Boar-hunt* (*c.* 1507; Hollstein: *Ger.*, nos 7, 82, 104 and 113). His tournament and hunting woodcuts vividly evoke the life of the Saxon court. Cranach was greatly affected by the Reformation, because the Saxon electors supported Luther, and many of his later woodcuts were illustrations to the Old Testament. With his son Lucas Cranach II and Hans Brosamer, he produced Lutheran propaganda and many portraits of Lutheran theologians, the Saxon ruling house and other supporters of the Protestant cause.

Albrecht Altdorfer was an engraver and etcher, as well as a woodcut designer. Even in woodcut he tended to work on a small scale, creating finely graduated crosshatched shadows requiring very precise cutting, notably in his tiny illustrations to the *Passion* (1515; Hollstein: *Ger.*, nos 1–40). His lyrical landscape style may be seen in two woodcuts of *St Christopher* (1513 and *c.* 1515–20), and also in *St George* (1511) and the *Judgement of Paris* (1511; Hollstein: *Ger.*, nos 56–8 and 75). Altdorfer's figures, like Cranach's, often seem to merge into their settings. The first state of his *Beautiful Virgin of Regensburg* (*c.* 1519–20;

Hollstein: *Ger.*, no. 52) was printed in colour from six blocks *c.* 1519–20. During the same period Michael Ostendorfer made woodcuts of the *Pilgrimage Church of the Beautiful Virgin of Regensburg* (1520) and of Hans Hieber's design for the proposed *New Church of the Beautiful Virgin* (*c.* 1521; Hollstein: *Ger.*, nos 6–7). He later produced the *Hunting Party in Lors Forest* (1543; Hollstein: *Ger.*, no. 10) and many fine book illustrations. The landscape of the Danube Valley featured in the woodcuts of Wolfgang Huber, Georg Lemberger and other members of the Danube school. Huber was unusual in illuminating many of his landscapes from behind with the sun's rays casting shadows towards the foreground, as in the *'Large' Crucifixion*, *St Christopher* and *St George* (all *c.* 1520; Hollstein: *Ger.*, nos 5, 9 and 10).

HANS BALDUNG spent some time in Dürer's workshop and was much influenced by the latter's early woodcuts; however, his wiry, energetic line is more abstract. He often adopted a Mannerist approach to Dürer prototypes, twisting them into something less classical and tectonic and more selfconsciously linear. When Baldung was working at Strasbourg after *c.* 1511, his style became broader and more emotive, perhaps under the influence of Grünewald, and he developed clearer, more rational shading patterns. Unlike Dürer, who in his later work reduced tonal contrasts and hatched much of the block, Baldung made more use of areas of white-line work and isolated, wiry, black outlines. Notable woodcuts of 1511–16 are the *Annunciation*, the *Nativity*, the *Lamentation*, *Christ Carried to Heaven by Angels*, *St Christopher*, *St Jerome*, *St Sebastian* and the *Fates* (Hollstein: *Ger.*, nos 6–7, 53, 56, 116, 121, 128 and 236). The Reformation affected Strasbourg profoundly; after 1520 Baldung's graphic work consisted chiefly of portraits and of secular subjects, such as the series of *Wild Horses in a Wood* (1534) and the *Bewitched Groom* (1544; Hollstein: *Ger.*, nos 238–40 and 237), which are drawn with very fine lines and tonal hatching.

The younger Nuremberg artists and engravers Barthel Beham, Hans Sebald Beham and Georg Pencz also designed woodcuts. Although Dürer's influence is clear early in their careers, it diminished following their banishment from Nuremberg for 'godlessness', the Italian journeys of Pencz and Barthel Beham, and the latter's move to work for the Wittelsbach court at Munich. There were no great patrons of woodcut there, but a series of planets and some large woodcuts of battles and banquets by Sebald Beham, Schäufelein, Jörg Breu (ii) and Heinrich Vogtherr (i) appear to have been influenced by the Wittelsbach taste for Italianate subjects and stories of Classical or Old Testament heroes and heroines. They probably reflect the subject-matter of lost secular mural decorations.

One of the most interesting woodcut designers of the mid-16th century was Matthias Gerung from Nördlingen. His anti-Catholic allegories and apocalyptic images produced mostly in the 1540s sometimes draw on the work of Dürer but usually approach the subject in new ways. Heinrich Aldegrever of Soest was primarily an engraver, but from 1528–36 he made nine woodcuts, including two in circular format, and some portraits of Anabaptist leaders. Anton Woensam's designs are mostly on a small scale and rather tightly drawn. However, his most striking woodcut is a nine-sheet panoramic *View of Cologne* (1531;

Geisberg, nos 1, 562–70; *see* COLOGNE, fig. 3), where he worked. Ambrosius Holbein and Hans Holbein the younger were accomplished and prolific designers of woodcut book illustrations for publishers in Basle and Lyon. These were mostly in a miniature format, probably inspired by Altdorfer, expertly cut by Hans Lützelburger and Veit Specklin. The Swiss painter Niklaus Manuel Deutsch designed a set of ten *Wise and Foolish Virgins* (1518, Hollstein: *Ger.*, nos 1–10), where even the wise virgins have the allure of temptresses. Urs Graf was more prolific; his most striking plates are *Two Mercenaries, a Woman and Death* (1524) and the white-line woodcuts: the series of 16 *Standard-bearers of the Swiss Confederacy* (1521; *see* PRINTS, fig. 7) and the *Satyr's Family* (1520; Hollstein: *Ger.*, nos 28, 29–44 and 47). White-line had previously been used for the borders of woodcuts and for the designs of textiles depicted in them. It had also been employed for illustrations to two works by Oswald Pelbart, including his *Pomerium de Sanctis Pelbarti ordims Santi Francisci* (Augsburg, *c.* 1502), and for the tone-blocks of chiaroscuro woodcuts.

The next generation of woodcut designers tried to refine the medium by imitating engraved lines as closely as possible. Anton Möller (i) and Melchior Lorch emulated swelling-line engravings; the latter's *Dead Father and his Three Sons* (1551; Hollstein: *Ger.*, no. 14) and the woodcuts based on his Turkish studies, such as the *Turkish Burial Ground* (1575, pubd. 1619; Hollstein: *Ger.*, no. 59), are outstanding. Virgil Solis and the Swiss artists Jost Amman and Tobias Stimmer employed a very fine and precise technique and often set their subjects within elaborate Mannerist borders. Solis's landscape and hunting scenes are among his finest prints. Amman's most striking woodcuts are the *Great Tournament in Vienna* (see fig. 3) and the eight-block *Adulterer's Bridge of King Artus* (Andresen, nos 69 and 73). His famous series of illustrations to Hans Sachs's *Eygentliche Beschreibung aller Stände auff Erden . . . aller Künsten, Handwercken und Händeln. . .* (Frankfurt am Main, 1568; Andresen, no. 231) includes depictions of various stages of woodcut production. Stimmer is known for his publications in the 1570s on the astronomical clock of Strasbourg cathedral (1984 exh. cat., no. 23), which he had decorated, and for his broadsheets and book illustrations.

(ii) The Netherlands. In the mid-15th century German woodcuts had been much influenced by Netherlandish art. The publication of Dürer's woodcuts reversed this position and inspired a generation of Netherlandish artists. The design and the line-work of Jacob Cornelisz. van Oostsanen's (*c.* 1470–1533) earliest signed woodcuts of the *Life of the Virgin* (1507; Hollstein: *Dut. & Flem.*, nos 83–9) indicate that he was already familiar with proof impressions of Dürer's *Life of the Virgin*. He liked elaborate frames, such as those for his *Round Passion* (1511–14; Hollstein: *Dut. & Flem.*, nos 67–78), which incorporated Old Testament prefigurations, and he produced a 14-block equestrian procession of the *Counts and Countesses of Holland* (1518; Hollstein: *Dut. & Flem.*, nos 146–59). His grandson Cornelis Anthonisz. was also a designer of woodcuts, including a 12-block *Bird's-eye View of Amsterdam* (1544; Hollstein: *Dut. & Flem.*, no. 46; *see* AMSTERDAM,

3. Woodcut by Jost Amman: *Great Tournament in Vienna*, 203×354 mm, 1565 (Nuremberg, Germanisches Nationalmuseum)

fig. 1). His other works were mainly biblical, satirical and allegorical scenes and portraits.

Lucas van Leyden was well established as an engraver by *c.* 1512, when he made his first six woodcut designs, of the *Power of Women* (Washington, 1983 exh. cat., nos 33–9). He was influenced by the restrained tonal range of Dürer's later woodcuts, but he lit his scenes brightly from the side. The series was clearly a success, because some years later (*c.* 1516–19) he produced a similar one with elaborate borders (Washington, 1983 exh. cat., nos 59–66). His friezes of the *Twelve Kings of Israel* and *Nine Heroes* (both 1515–17; Washington, 1983 exh. cat., nos 53 and 54) express the love of pageantry and processions characteristic of the period. Jost de Negker had cut some designs after different artists in Antwerp by 1508, before moving to Augsburg. It was, however, either Dürer's visit to the Netherlands in 1520, or the arrival of the Bavarian printmaker Nicolas Hogenberg (*c.* 1500–1539) in 1522, that led to a woodcut revival there. The artists involved were Hogenberg himself, Frans Crabbe, Jan Gossart, Jan Wellens de Cock, Jan Swart and Dirk Vellert. The subjects included biblical and mythological scenes and genre works, such as Jan Swart's *Turkish Riders* (1526; Hollstein: *Dut. & Flem.*, 8–12) and Dirk Vellert's *Protestant Schoolroom* (1526; Washington, 1983 exh. cat., no. 140). In style most of these woodcuts show a combination of influences from Dürer, Lucas van Leyden and the Antwerp Mannerists.

A large (425×366 mm) two-block woodcut of the *Deluge* published in Venice (*c.* 1524) has been attributed to Jan van Scorel; however the design of a six-block frieze of a *Lion-hunt* cut by Jan Ewoutsz. Muller and measuring 2040×276 mm is now given to Lambert Sustris (1995 exh. cat.), not to van Scorel. Van Scorel's pupil Maarten van

Heemskerck, who also went to Italy, usually had his designs engraved. However, *c.* 1548 he designed the *Story of Tobias*, the *Story of the Prodigal Son*, and *Christ and the Adulteress* for the woodcutter Dirck Volkertsz. (all Hollstein: *Dut. & Flem.*, nos 183–8, 356–9, 372). Pieter Coecke van Aelst's series of *Les Moeurs et fachons de faire de Turcs* (Antwerp, 1553; Hollstein: *Dut. & Flem.*, no. 4) has the rich elaboration of tapestry designs. He employed the regular shading patterns developed in Germany in the 1530s and 1540s. His pupil Pieter Bruegel I designed primarily for engravers. His only woodcut, *Urson and Valentin* (1566; Hollstein: *Dut. & Flem.*, no. 215), was unsympathetically cut; the line-work is too regular and the white areas hard-edged. This may explain the failure to complete the cutting of its pendant, the *Wedding of Mopsus and Nisa*, known through a nearly complete autograph drawing (1566) by Bruegel on the surviving woodblock (New York, Met). The design was published as an engraving in 1570. A number of Goltzius's small woodcut designs of landscapes and figures (Hollstein: *Dut. & Flem.*, nos 362–3, 366, 375–6, 378–81) produced in the late 1590s and later were printed in black on blue paper (for illustration *see* WIERINGEN, CORNELIS CLAESZ. VAN), and also in chiaroscuro, probably at a later date.

(iii) Italy. Venetian book illustration of the 15th century was of superb quality, but the development of the 16th-century Venetian woodcut owed more to German prototypes than to the native outline style. The city views in Hartmann Schedel's *Weltchronik* (Nuremberg, 1493) and Bernhard von Breydenbach's *Peregrinationes in Terram Sanctam* (Mainz, 1486) and Dürer's early woodcuts had a marked influence. Woodcut copies by Johannes of Frankfurt (am Main) and Jacob of Strasbourg of such Italian

engravings as Antonio Pollaiuolo's *Battle of the Ten Nudes* (*c*. 1470–75; *see* POLLAIUOLO, (1), fig. 3) and Andrea Mantegna's *Triumphs of Caesar*, which imitated their diagonal, 'broad-manner' shading, may also have played a role (*see* ENGRAVING, §II, 2(ii)). Three large woodcuts designed by Jacopo de' Barbari, the *Battle of Naked Men and Satyrs* (385×539 mm), the *Triumph of Chastity over Lust* (291×1300 mm, 1500; both Passavant) and the *Bird's-eye View of Venice* (1390×2820 mm) initiated a series of large woodcuts designed by Venetian artists. The *View of Venice* (*see* VENICE, fig. 1) was published in 1500 by the Nuremberg merchant Anton Kolb; the other two images may be slightly earlier.

The first woodcut design by TITIAN, the *Triumph of Christianity* (385×2663 mm, *c*. 1510–11; 1976–7 exh. cat., no. 1), was a monumental frieze printed from ten blocks. This was followed by the superb *Submersion of Pharaoh's Host* (see fig. 4), which he seems to have produced to further his ambition to succeed Giovanni Bellini as chief painter to the Venetian State. It was first published (*c*. 1514–15) by Bernardino Benalius, whose cutter brilliantly reproduced Titian's drawing style. The principal period for monumental woodcut in Venice was 1510–25, and apart from Titian, Giulio Campagnola and Domenico Campagnola, Pellegrino da San Daniele and Girolamo Penacchi da Treviso (*c*. 1450–*c*. 1496) all made designs. Fine early impressions of these woodcuts are extremely rare or non-existent, because their size meant they were better suited to wall decoration than to the portfolio.

Titian continued to design woodcuts, including several fine landscapes. His later works were smaller in format, more precise and less exuberant in line; they were mostly cut by Giovanni Britto. The dense mesh of black crosshatched and dotted areas in some of Domenico Campagnola's early woodcuts, such as the *Sacra conversazione*

(1517) and *Vision of St Augustine* (*c*. 1517; 1976–7 exh. cat., nos 18–19), approaches white-line work in technique. He was an engraver, so he may possibly have cut some experimental blocks himself. However, his large *Adoration of the Magi* (*c*. 1517; 1976–7 exh. cat., no. 17) was cut by Lucantonio degli Uberti, and one of his landscapes of the 1530s is signed by Niccolò Boldrini, who also worked after Pordenone and Titian. Andrea Schiavone and Giuseppe Salviati made small-scale designs in the mid-16th century, and Cesare Vecellio's eight-block *Procession of the Doge* (1976–7 exh. cat., no. 89) dates from *c*. 1555–60. Venetian woodcut book illustrations continued to be of the highest quality. They include anatomical, architectural, musical and mythological works.

The Veronese artists Paolo Farinati and Giuseppe Scolari also practised in the medium. Farinati's design for *St Roch with an Angel* (undescribed) is in black-line in a simplified version of his drawing style. Scolari used broad sweeps of black- and white-line for his powerful woodcuts, which provide the only indication of the style of his celebrated lost chiaroscuro frescoes. He cut his own blocks in an experimental fashion and did not hesitate to plug and recut large sections to improve the design. The Lombard painter and engraver Master I.B. with the Bird (Giovanni Battista Palumba; *fl* Rome, 1500–25) also designed 11 woodcuts in the first decade of the 15th century. His *Calvary* is influenced by Milanese book illustration, but *Venus, Mars and Vulcan* and *Apollo and Daphne* (Byam Shaw, nos 17, 24 and 26) are closer to Lombardo-Venetian sculpture. The *Three Graces*, the *Rape of Ganymede* and the *Kalydonian Boar Hunt* (Byam Shaw, nos 22–3, 21) combine Florentine and Roman influences. Only in his late woodcut of *St Jerome* (Byam Shaw, no. 19), however, did he employ tonal modelling. In Milan woodcut was

4. Woodcut by Titian: *Submersion of Pharaoh's Host*, 394×541 mm, *c*. 1514–15 (London, Victoria and Albert Museum)

largely confined to book illustration and records of triumphal entries. The same was true of Florence, where engraving was the dominant graphic medium. However, the Sienese painter Domenico Beccafumi was a distinguished chiaroscuro woodcutter, whose work in monochrome woodcut consists of a set of ten illustrations on the *Alchemical Properties of Metals* (1530s; Passavant, nos 10–19). Their flamelike, flickering line lends credence to Giorgio Vasari's claim that Beccafumi cut his own blocks, which was unusual. In Genoa the breaks and overlappings that give tension and energy to the outlines in Luca Cambiaso's drawings were ably reproduced by the Monogrammist G. G. N. (*fl* late 16th century–early 17th) in *Venus on a Dolphin* (Musper, pl. 209) and by an anonymous cutter in the *Rape of the Sabine Woman* (Hyatt Mayor, no. 400).

(iv) France. Relatively few French 16th-century single-sheet woodcuts have been preserved, so their history is far less well known than that of intaglio prints and book illustrations. A large woodcut of *c.* 1500, the *Passion of Christ* (*c.* 500×352 mm) after the Master of the Très Petites Heures d'Anne de Bretagne (1993–4 exh. cat.), resembles contemporary Parisian woodcuts and book illustrations in technique, though it has been coloured and gilded to give the impression of an illumination. An anonymous *Allegory of the Old and New Testaments*, tentatively dated before 1530, is Mannerist in design and more sophisticated in cutting (1994–5 exh. cat.). Three large decorative woodcuts for the wall survive: *The Cock: Good Advice, The Peacock: Bad Advice* and *The Sparrow: Bad Advice* (*c.* 1535–40; 1994–5 exh. cat.).

Gabriel Salmon (*fl c.* 1513–32), a painter who worked for the court of Lorrain at Nancy, is best known for his woodcut *Twelve Labours of Hercules* (*c.* 1528; 1994–5 exh. cat.), influenced both by German and by Italian art. His close-set, curved shading lines may be an attempt to imitate engraved lines in woodcut.

From the 1520s onwards, Venetian influence is obvious on Parisian outline book illustrations; at Lyons the miniaturist style of Hans Holbein II was more popular. Around 1550 six young woodcut artists—Germain Hoyau (*c.* 1515–83), Alain de Mathonière (*c.* 1533–75), Clément Boussy (*fl c.* 1547–50), François de Gourmont (*c.* 1537–before 1598), Bonnemère (?Marin Bonnemer, *fl c.* 1568–71), and Fauler (*fl c.* 1550)—established themselves in the Rue de Montorgueil, Paris. They and their descendants were joined by numerous other woodcutters, including Mathurin Nicolas, Nicolas Lefèvre and François Desprez, who were active in the 1560s. Publishers flourished there, producing woodcuts and engravings for the French market and for export. They made maps and genre and caricature woodcuts, such as the *Old Woman and the Young Suitor* and *When It Comes to a Merry Song* (both 1560s) and a group of woodcuts representing *Ten Musicians and an Embroideress* (*c.* 1570; 1994–5 exh. cat.), which inspired Tobias Stimmer's *Nine Muses and a Fool* (*c.* 1575; 1984 exh. cat.). They are perhaps best known for scenes from the Old and New Testaments, lives of the saints and mythological subjects after designs adapted from the school of Fontainebleau and Jean Cousin I. These were sold plain or stencil-coloured using the same hues as for late 15th-century

woodcuts; many have borders reminiscent of tapestries. French woodcuts with similar Mannerist borders include the *Histoire fort plaisante de la Vie pastorale*, a set of eight plates (Courboin, nos 223–230), and the *Twelve Months* adapted from engravings by Etienne Delaune (1985 exh. cat.).

The Wars of Religion (1562–98) led to the publication of many woodcuts. Parisian examples include the anonymous Protestant polemic *The Great Cooking-pot Overturned* (*c.* 1562), and woodcuts of the *Assassination of the Duc de Guise* and *Cardinal de Guise*, leaders of the Catholic league, and *Frère Clement's Assassination of King Henry III* (*reg* 1574–89), who had ordered their murder (*c.* 1588; see 1994–5 exh. cat.). Nicolas Castellin made 40 designs for his *Premier volume contenant quarante tableaux ou histoires diverses qui sont mémorables touchant les guerres, massacres et troubles advenus en France en ces dernières années*, published in Protestant Geneva in 1570. Jean Perrissin (before 1546–1617) and Jacques Tortorel (*fl* 1568–75)—both from Lyon—were responsible for reproducing the battles and scenes of martyrdom in woodcut and engraving, together with Jean Granthomme (*fl c.* 1570).

BIBLIOGRAPHY

Hollstein: *Dut. & Flem.*; Hollstein: *Ger.*

J. D. Passavant: *Le Peintre-graveur*, 6 vols (Leipzig, 1860–64), pp. 31, 32, 141

A. Andresen: *Der deutsche Peintre Graveur* (Leipzig, 1864)

[repr. from vol. i: *Jost Amman, 1539–1591: Graphiker und Buchillustrator der Renaissance* (Amsterdam, 1973)]

C. Dodgson: *Catalogue of Early German and Flemish Woodcuts . . . in . . . the British Museum*, 2 vols (London, 1903–11)

M. Geisberg: *Der deutsche Einblatt-Holzschnitt in der 1. Hälfte des 16. Jahrhunderts*, 43 vols (Munich, 1923–30); rev. and ed. by W. L. Strauss as *The German Single-leaf Woodcut, 1500–1550*, 4 vols (New York, 1974)

A. Lauter: *Index/Dodgson/Early German and Flemish Woodcuts: With a Concordance to Schreiber's Manual* (Munich, 1925)

M. Geisberg: *Bilder-Katalog. Der deutsche Einblatt-Holzschnitt in der ersten Hälfte des XVI Jahrhunderts* (Munich, 1930)

W. Nijhof: *Nederlandsche houtsneden, 1500–1550* (The Hague, 1931–9)

J. Byam Shaw: 'The Master I.B. with the Bird: I', *Prt Colr Q.*, xix (1932), pp. 273–97; 'The Master I.B. with the Bird: II' [includes cat.], *Prt Colr Q.*, xx (1933), pp. 9–33, 169–78

R. Mortimer and others: *Harvard College Library Dept. of Printing and Graphic Arts Catalogue: Part I, French 16th-century Books* (Cambridge, MA, 1964)

H. T. Musper: *Der Holzschnitt in fünf Jahrhunderten* (Stuttgart, 1964)

Die Kunst der Graphik. IV. Zwischen Renaissance und Barock: Das Zeitalter von Bruegel und Bellange (exh. cat., ed. K. Oberhuber; Vienna, Albertina, 1967–8)

The Danube School. Prints and Drawings (exh. cat., ed. C. Talbot and A. Schestack; New Haven, CT, Yale U. A.G., 1969–70)

L'Ecole de Fontainebleau (exh. cat., ed. M. Laclotte; Paris, Grand Pal., 1972–3)

W. L. Strauss: *Chiaroscuro. The Clair-obscur Woodcuts by the German and Netherlandish Masters of the XVI and XVII Centuries* (New York, 1973)

R. Mortimer: *Harvard College Library Dept. of Printing and Graphic Arts Catalogue: Part II, Italian 16th-century Books*, 2 vols (Cambridge, MA, 1974)

W. L. Strauss: *The German Single-leaf Woodcut, 1550–1600*, 3 vols (New York, 1975)

Titian and the Venetian Woodcut (exh. cat., ed. D. Rosand and M. Muraro; Washington, DC, N.G.A.; Dallas, TX, Mus. F.A.; Detroit, MI, Inst. A.; 1976–7)

Printmaking in the Age of Rembrandt (exh. cat. by C. S. Ackley; Boston, MA, Mus. F.A.; 1981)

J. S. Byrne: *Renaissance Ornament Prints and Drawings* (New York, 1981) [pubd in conjunction with exh., New York, Met.]

M. Hefels: *Meister um Dürer: Nürnberger Holzschnitte aus der Zeit um 1500–1540* (Ramerding, 1981)

M. Hébert: *Inventaire des gravures des Ecoles du Nord, 1440–1550*, 2 vols (Paris, 1983)

From a Mighty Forest: Prints, Drawings and Books in the Age of Luther, 1483–1546 (exh. cat., ed. C. Andersson and C. Talbot; Detroit, MI, Inst. A., 1983)

The Prints of Lucas van Leyden and his Contemporaries (exh. cat., ed. E. S. Jacobowitz and S. L. Stepanek; Washington, DC, N.G.A., 1983)

The Genius of Venice, 1500–1600 (exh. cat., ed. J. Martineau and C. Hope; London, RA, 1983) [print cat. by D. Landau]

Tobias Stimmer, 1539–1584: Spätrenaissance am Oberrhein (exh. cat., ed. D. Koepplin and P. Tanner; Basle, Kstmus., 1984)

Fontainebleau et l'estampe en France au XVIe siècle: Iconographie et contradictions (exh. cat., Nemours, Château Mus., 1985)

Gothic and Renaissance Art in Nuremberg, 1300–1500 (exh. cat., New York, Met., 1986)

Kunst voor de beeldenstorm (exh. cat., ed. J. P. Filedt Kok; Amsterdam, Rijksmus., 1986)

Chiaroscuro Woodcuts: Hendrik Goltzius and his Times (exh. cat., ed. N. Bialler; Amsterdam, Rijksmus.; Cleveland, OH, Mus. A.; 1992–3)

D. Landau and P. Parshall: *The Renaissance Print, 1470–1550* (New Haven and London, 1994)

The French Renaissance in Prints from the Bibliothèque Nationale de France (exh. cat., ed. K. Jacobsen; Los Angeles, CA, Armand Hammer Mus. A.; New York, Met.; Paris, Bib. N., 1994–5)

Fiamminghi a Roma, 1508–1608 (exh. cat., Brussels, Pal. B.-A.; Rome, Pal. Espos., 1995)

4. 17TH AND 18TH CENTURIES. For most of the 17th and 18th centuries, etching, engraving and mezzotint were the dominant printmaking media. Woodcut was considered boorish and lacking in refinement. It was used chiefly for ephemera, such as playbills and circus posters, trade cards, funeral announcements and advertisements. Numerous POPULAR PRINTS, frequently coloured by hand or stencil, were also produced and circulated widely; common subjects were religious images, including the Virgin and saints in Roman Catholic countries and Old Testament subjects in northern Europe. Other popular subjects were pictures of rulers, the *Ages of Man* and the *Seven Acts of Mercy*, as well as caricatures and satires. The same designs are found in different countries, having been either pirated or issued in different languages for different markets. The chiaroscuro woodcut process was preferred for high-quality woodcuts, but a few fine monochrome ones were made. By far the most sophisticated colour woodcuts were the overdoors, medallions, figurative panels and panoramic scenes produced for domestic use by wallpaper manufacturers in the late 18th century and the 19th.

(i) Italy and Spain. In Bologna, Giovanni Battista Coriolano made crisply cut monochrome woodcuts after Alessandro Tiarini and Guercino (B. 1–2). The Galleria Estense in Modena has a very large collection of woodblocks for popular woodcuts published by the firm of the Soliani; it includes blocks cut in the 17th and 18th centuries.

Pedro Diaz Morante's writing-book *Nuevo sistema de aprender a escribir* (Madrid, 1623–31), with blocks attributed to Andrian Boon, contains the finest 17th-century Spanish woodcuts. Publishers of popular woodcuts in the 17th and 18th centuries include the Abadal family in Moyá, Catalonia and Manresa, Guasp in Palma de Mallorca, Baltasar Talamantes in Valencia, Carreras in Girona, Pierre Porche in Reus, and Pfifferer and Estivel in Barcelona.

(ii) The Netherlands. Christoffel Jegher's large woodcuts such as *Susanna and the Elders* (for illustration *see* JEGHER, (1)), *Hercules Fighting Fury and Discord* (603×358 mm) and the *Garden of Love* (455×660 mm; Hollstein: *Dut. &*

Flem., nos 1, 15 and 17) capture more successfully than engravings the inherent energy in Rubens's designs. Jegher's use of swelling-line and of white-line in the shadows suits the scale of the prints. The technique resembles that of Giuseppe Scolari, whose woodcuts Rubens would have known. Christoffel's son Jan Christoffel Jegher (1618–67) and Peter Kints (*fl* 1610–40) made woodcuts after the tapestry designer Anthonis Sallaert. Those by Kints have extensive areas of black shadow in the elaborately looped draperies (Hollstein: *Dut. & Flem.*, nos 1–92, 201–7, 486).

Christoffel van Sichem I was the most gifted of a family of four artists of the same name who helped keep woodcut book illustration alive in the northern Netherlands in the 17th century. In his best works, a *View of Amsterdam* and some *Fantasy Portraits* after designs by Hendrick Goltzius and Jacob Matham (Hollstein: *Dut. & Flem.*, nos 137, 134–6), he employed a swelling-line technique imitating their engraved line. His son Christoffel van Sichem II also worked after Goltzius and may have cut the woodcuts after designs by Werner van den Valkert, which were normally printed in chiaroscuro; one of them, *Charon* (Strauss, 1973, no. 156), was also printed in pure line. His son Christoffel van Sichem III worked together with him, and the latter's son Christoffel van Sichem IV was a precocious woodcutter who was only 12 when he made a series of landscapes after Esaias van de Velde. Three interesting Haarlem school woodcuts were printed—like those of Goltzius—both in black on blue paper and in chiaroscuro. They are a *Marine with Merchantmen* (c. 1605–20) after Cornelis Claesz. van Wieringen, *St Paul the Hermit Fed by Ravens* (c. 1612–14), probably designed by Willem Buytewech, and an *Arcadian Landscape* (c. 1612–15), apparently after Esaias or Jan van de Velde. Of much the same date as Moses van Uyttenbroeck's *Elijah Fed by Ravens* (all 1992–3 exh. cat.). Jan Lievens's debt to Christoffel Jegher is clearly seen in *Cain and Abel* (Hollstein: *Dut. & Flem.*, no. 99). He also owed something to Goltzius, but he soon developed an entirely personal style in his rare woodcut designs. He employed both white- and black-line, including swelling-line, and used a variety of wedges and patches of wood to indicate the textures of bushes and trees in *Landscape* and the facets of garments and faces in *Venetian Nobleman* and *Man Wearing a Black Coat* (Hollstein: *Dut. & Flem.*, nos 100, 102–3). Dirk de Bray's *Christ on the Cross* (c. 1671), the portrait of *Salomon de Bray* (1664) and *The Months* (c. 1674; Hollstein: *Dut. & Flem.*, nos 25, 122 and 48–80), some after designs by his father Salomon and his brother Jan de Bray, are the most accomplished Dutch woodcuts of the end of the century. Their lines are delicate and spontaneous, quite free from cutting formulae. Woodcut was also used for the numerous children's and folk prints produced in the 17th and 18th centuries by publishers such as Jan Loots and his family. Many broadsheets were also made in the Netherlands, some of them in woodcut, including satires on the South Sea Bubble and other bubble schemes of the 1720s, for example the *Tournament of the Shareholders* (Stephens, ii, no. 1633).

(iii) Germany. After his return from Paris to Münden in 1630, Ludolph Büsinck made a number of monochrome woodcuts of figures, including peasants, beggars and

5. Woodcut by John Baptist Jackson (after Marco Ricci): *Heroic Landscape*, 417×589 mm, 1744 (London, British Museum)

swaggering cavaliers, after his own designs but in the manner of Jacques Callot and Georges Lallemand (all *c.* 1632–6; Hollstein: *Ger.*, nos 25–35). Augsburg was the main centre for popular German woodcuts, and Marx Anton Hannas' old-fashioned religious images in swelling-line technique were produced there. A similar technique was used by Abraham von Weerdt (*fl c.* 1636–*c.* 1680) working in Nuremberg for his illustrations to the Bible and Ovid and for a woodcut depicting a *Printer's Workshop*. In addition, there were secular broadsheets, such as the *Ten Ages of Life* (*c.* 1660), the *Tree of Love*, the *Conversation between Humanity and Death* (both *c.* 1700), the *Child Eater* and the *Bogeyman* (Brückner, nos 81, 89, 90, 100, 113, 114). Decorative papers with miniature designs for lining, binding and decorating were also a speciality. Some attractive small-scale work, similar to wood-engraving but still on plank wood, was done in Germany in the later 18th century by Johann Georg Unger (1715–88) and his son Johann Friedrich Gottlieb Unger (1753/5–1804).

(iv) England. Woodcut was still the medium used for popular broadsheets, ballads, chapbooks, devotional prints and playing cards. The wood-engraver Thomas Bewick recorded that in the first half of the 18th century, popular woodcuts were to be seen 'in every farmhouse, cottage and hovel'. They were produced in very large numbers, for decorating homes, taverns, barbers' shops and schoolrooms. They were sold cheaply and replaced when they

deteriorated, so few have survived. Aiming to reach this market, William Hogarth published woodcut copies cut by John Bell of two of his *Four Stages of Cruelty* (1750; Paulson, nos 189–90). They are notable for their use of black- and white-line for expressive purposes.

Woodblocks had long been used in the production of wallpaper, and in England coloured 'paper hangings' or wallpapers were being produced using woodcut and stencils by 1700 (*see* WALLPAPER, §II, 1). In 1754 John Baptist Jackson published *An Essay on the Invention of Engraving and Printing in Chiaroscuro* (London) about his method of producing multicoloured, printed wallpaper; it was illustrated with eight colour woodcuts (Kainen, nos 51–8). He also made six *Heroic Landscapes* (see fig. 5) after gouaches by Marco Ricci, printed in colour from up to five blocks (Kainen, nos 38–43). His wallpapers were notable for small framed views or scenes set within Rococo surrounds (London, V&A).

(v) France. Popular religious images, broadsheets, board-games and other ephemera continued to be made in the woodcut medium, including many of the popular, stencil-coloured 'Imagerie populaire' woodcuts, with text and image cut into the same block. The colours were typically blue, yellow, red and either pink, light grey or brown. In the 18th century bales of prints containing huge numbers of impressions (*c.* 40,000–50,000) were sent to agents around France by publishers such as Jean-Baptiste Letourmy (*fl* 1775–1854), who was based in Orléans (*see*

POPULAR PRINTS, fig. 1). However, publication of popular woodcuts at Orléans went back to 1648. Other publishing centres in the 18th century were Avignon, Cambrai, Chartres, Epinal, Montbéliard and Strasbourg. The trade was interrupted by the French Revolution, only to resume with renewed vigour in the 19th century.

Book publishers preferred to use engraved illustrations when they did not need to print image and text together. They still used woodcuts for head- and tailpieces—notably the vignettes for an edition of the *Fables* (1755–9) of La Fontaine by Jean-Baptiste Papillon, the 18th-century apologist for woodcut. Publishers found metalcuts more durable and the newly developed wood-engraving technique more precise, however, so woodcut was used less even for this purpose. Woodcut-printed wallpaper was being exported from France by the 1680s, and Jean-Baptiste Papillon and his son Jean-Michel Papillon were important manufacturers in the first half of the 18th century, while Jean-Baptiste Réveillon and other manufacturers made tremendous technical advances in the second half (*see* WALLPAPER, colour pl. IV, fig. 1).

In the 1780s and 1790s there were a growing number of figurative designs to be used as overdoors and panels on walls. These included classical and allegorical figures, architectural compositions, flower pieces and landscapes, and they paved the way for the great panoramic friezes characteristic of the early 19th century. These were the largest and most ambitious figurative woodcuts ever made, and they were, technically, the most complex woodcut images produced in Europe before Japanese techniques became known in the late 19th century. They included exotic landscapes, marines, battle scenes, hunts and scenes from classical mythology, sometimes designed by well-known painters. In 1800 woodcut was being used for many of the same purposes for which it was employed in the 16th century—for devotional and popular images, book illustrations and wall decoration. However, the complexity of prints for the wall had greatly increased, and they were now printed in a wide variety of colours.

BIBLIOGRAPHY

F. G. Stephens: *Catalogue of Prints and Drawings in the British Museum, Division I: Political and Personal Subjects*, i–iv (London, 1870–83); v–vii as *Catalogue of Personal and Political Satires Preserved in the Department of Prints and Drawings in the British Museum* by M. D. George (London, 1935–42)

J. Kainen: *John Baptist Jackson: 18th-century Master of the Colour Woodcut* (Washington, DC, 1962)

R. Paulson: *Hogarth's Graphic Works*, 2 vols (New Haven and London, 1920)

G. G. Bertelà and S. Ferrara: *Incisori bolognesi ed emiliani del '600: Catalogo generale della raccolta di stampe antiche della Pinacoteca Nazionale di Bologna, Gabinetto delle stampe, sezione iii* (Bologna, 1973)

French Popular Imagery (exh. cat., London, ACGB, 1974)

Imagerie populaire française, Quatre cents images populaires françaises, Quelques images parisiennes du XVIe siècle dites de la Rue Montorgueil (Paris, 1979)

Printmaking in the Age of Rembrandt (exh. cat., ed. C. S. Ackley; Boston, MA, Mus. F.A., 1981)

M. Martin: 'The Case of the Missing Woodcuts', *Prt Q.*, iv (1987), pp. 342–61

KATHARINA MAYER HAUNTON

5. 19TH CENTURY. At the beginning of the 19th century the woodcut in the West was in decline as a medium for independent prints but continued to be used for ephemera, such as trade cards, posters and playbills, for wallpaper designs and for illustrating cheap books, ballad sheets and broadsheets (and broadsides). However, its role as an illustrative medium was superseded by WOOD-ENGRAVING, due mainly to the influence of Thomas Bewick and contemporary practitioners of the wood-engraving technique. In Britain the finer detail produced by wood-engraving was preferred by illustrators and publishers, and woodcut continued to be used only where a cruder or more naive effect was particularly required. Most of the early 19th-century broadsheets, or 'catchpenny prints' as they were known in England, were produced by wood-engraving since it allowed printers to use simpler relief and type presses while achieving the finer tonal and linear details previously obtained only by etching or engraving. Broadsheets, with their religious, moral or topical subject-matter, flourished in Britain until the 1860s (*see* POPULAR PRINTS, fig. 2), when they were replaced by mass-circulation graphic newspapers.

The cheap, popular prints of Europe were still produced predominantly in woodcut at the beginning of the century. In France, the *imagerie populaire* emanated from the provincial towns, the subject-matter being primarily religious, although a political, topical or moral content also occurred. The style of these prints was naive, the religious prints often resembling those in medieval incunabula, for which the woodcut was ideally suited. The publication of *imagerie populaire* had ceased in most centres by 1850, except at Epinal, where the highly popular hand- or stencil-coloured images originally published by Jean-Charles Pellerin (1756–1836) were issued until the end of the century. Even here, however, the woodcut technique was superseded gradually by the introduction of wood-engraving in 1835 and lithography in the 1850s.

In Germany, as well as occurring in broadsheets and popular prints, the woodcut was used by some artists—notably Caspar David Friedrich and the comic illustrator Wilhelm Busch—for illustrative prints. The woodcut continued as the most commonly used medium for the cheap popular prints of eastern Europe and Scandinavia, especially in areas in which particular forms of folk art prevailed. In North America, although wood-engraving had become the dominant illustrative and reproductive process by the 1830s, woodcuts continued to illustrate broadsheets and also almanacs, which had begun in the early 18th century and culminated in the *Davy Crockett* series of 1830–50.

The woodcut retained its role as an important technique for the application of colour in printmaking. Earlier 18th-century innovations in the use of the colour woodcut were continued into the 19th century by GEORGE BAXTER. In 1835 he patented the Baxter process, which involved the overprinting of a print, produced by an intaglio method, with several woodblocks, each inked in a separate colour (*see* PRINTS, colour pl. VII, fig. 1). In this way be built up the appearance of a highly coloured miniature painting. In 1849 he sold the licence to, among others, J. M. Kronheim (1810–96), who also produced large quantities of highly coloured illustrative prints until the latter part of the century.

Although most of the 19th century was essentially a period of decline for the medium of woodcut, in the last decade of the century illustrative and independent artists alike began a reassessment of its artistic potential. In Britain, WILLIAM MORRIS brought new concepts to the illustration and decoration of the printed page. He began to use woodcut for the medievalist decorations in many of his own Kelmscott Press publications of the 1890s. These flowing Gothic borders and initials were often cut by Morris himself, although he still used experienced wood-engravers to provide the reproductions of the drawings he used as illustrations. His use of the woodcut was basically retrospective, and a more innovative approach stylistically was to be seen in the woodcuts produced by the illustrators of the ARTS AND CRAFTS MOVEMENT in their periodical the *Hobby Horse* (1886–92) and by Lucien Pissarro (*see* PISSARRO, (2)) for the books of his own Eragny Press, founded in 1896, where he used colour woodcut to create prints in four or five bright colours, including, unusually, gold. The use of woodblocks for colour printing had continued throughout the century with varying degrees of expertise. One of the most original and influential printers and publishers of children's books from the 1870s was Edmund Evans, who used woodblocks to produce flat tints of delicate colour over wood-engraved designs by illustrators such as Kate Greenaway.

The crude form of the popular woodcut reappeared in Britain in the 1880s, when the publisher Andrew White Tuer (1838–1900) reprinted the chapbooks of Joseph Crawhall with his archaic text and naive, hand-coloured woodcuts. However, the most creative use of the woodcut in Britain was by William Nicholson (*see* NICHOLSON, (1)) and EDWARD GORDON CRAIG. Nicholson produced colour woodcuts for *London Types* (London, 1898), *An Almanac of Twelve Sports* (London, 1895), *An Alphabet* (London, 1897) and *Twelve Portraits* (London, 1896), which included the famous portrait of *Queen Victoria* in old age, christened at the time 'the animated tea-cosy'. This image, with its large, flat areas of subdued colour, exemplified Nicholson's original, vigorous and direct cutting of the woodblock. Generally, his *de luxe* editions were printed from the original woodblocks, while other editions contained images that had been transferred into lithographs. His prints were also indicative of a new approach to the woodcut, in which imaginative designs were conceived in terms of the medium. His pupil Craig demonstrated a similar bold and direct approach to the woodcuts he produced of theatrical subject-matter.

Colour woodcut printmaking was stimulated by the great numbers of Japanese woodcuts flowing into most countries of Europe from the middle of the century (*see* JAPAN, §IX, 3). The initial influence of these prints was one of style and composition, and artists responded to these aspects with enthusiasm. However, with the general revival of interest in original printmaking at the end of the century, the technique itself was investigated. Most European 19th-century colour woodcut printmakers used an oil-based ink, but a few artists began to experiment with the subtle effects of the Japanese manner by brushing a water-based ink on to their colour blocks. John Dickson Batten (1860–1932) produced several prints in this Japanese manner in Britain in the late 1890s, as did Henri Rivière and Auguste Lepère in France.

It was in France at the end of the century that the creative potential of woodcut was exploited by artists seeking new vehicles for contemporary expression. The medium was promoted by periodicals such as *L'Ymagier*, founded by Remy de Gourmont and Alfred Jarry, which included woodcut illustrations in their issues. In 1888 Emile Bernard founded the periodical *Le Bois*, for which he provided his own roughly carved cuts in the flat, simplified style he had developed at Pont-Aven. The Swiss artist FÉLIX VALLOTTON, a member of the group of painters known as the Nabis, combined in his designs dynamic effects of large, unbroken areas of black and white with the cut-off motifs and unusual angles of Japanese prints.

It was, however, PAUL GAUGUIN who revealed the expressive strength that lay within the matrix of the woodblock. Gauguin was greatly influenced by both Japanese prints and the naivety of European popular prints. His initial essays in printmaking in 1889 were in zincograph (lithographs using zinc plates), but after his first period in Tahiti he was introduced to the woodcut, possibly by Alfred Jarry, and responded immediately to

6. Woodcut by Paul Gauguin: *Noa Noa*, 425×265 mm, 1893–4 (London, Sotheby's, 25 Oct 1990, lot 361)

the 'primitive' properties of the medium. Instead of cutting the block with traditional tools, he used coarse carpenters' gouges to carve out his designs, also filing down areas of the block with glass paper and wire brushes and incising into it with sharp points. The glyptic as well as the surface qualities of the block were thereby exploited in a new way. Gauguin's first woodcuts were produced in 1894, probably as an accompaniment to his manuscript known as *Noa Noa* (see fig. 6), although they were never issued in that form. He also experimented with colour and continued with his innovative use of the medium until the end of the century, executing further single cuts and another series for the monthly periodical *Le Sourire*.

Gauguin's woodcuts can be regarded as the precursors of the expressive 20th-century woodcut, and most certainly they also influenced the other major exponent of the medium in the late 19th century, the Norwegian artist EDVARD MUNCH. Munch was working in Paris in 1896, and it was then that he took up woodcut. He contributed to the further development of the medium by his artistic exploitation of the wood itself, scraping down the surface to reveal the grain, which he used as an integral part of the design. He also devised new ways of printing in colour by using special saws to divide his block into sections, inking them separately in different colours and then reassembling them for printing. For the rest of Europe and America, the woodcut continued in the 19th century to be utilized, for the most part, as a cruder form of wood-engraving or for colour printing. It was not until the 20th century that the work of Vallotton, Gauguin and Munch inspired the creative and expressive use of the woodcut and brought about the recognition of the medium as an independent art form.

BIBLIOGRAPHY

G. Schiefler: *Edvard Munchs graphische Kunst* (Dresden, 1923)
D. Bland: *A History of Book Illustration* (London, 1958)
C. Roger-Marx: *Graphic Art of the 19th Century* (London, 1962)
M. Vallotton and C. Goerg: *Félix Vallotton: Catalogue raisonné de l'oeuvre gravé et lithographié* (Geneva, 1972)
C. F. Ives: *The Great Wave: The Influence of Japanese Woodcuts on French Prints* (New York, 1974)
The Artistic Revival of the Woodcut in France, 1850–1900 (exh. cat. by J. Baas and R. Field, Ann Arbor, U. MI, Mus. A., 1984)
E. W. Kornfeld and E. Morgan: *Paul Gauguin: Catalogue Raisonné of his Prints* (Berne, 1988)

HILARY CHAPMAN

6. 20TH CENTURY. The history of the 20th-century woodcut cannot be entirely isolated from that of other artistic media, most notably wood-engraving and LINO-CUT. In contrast to the previous century, the woodcut flourished in the 20th century, especially in the years before World War II and in the work of the German Expressionists, although almost every leading international movement took up the medium as an important means of expression. Although it was largely neglected in the decades following the war, monumental works of the 1980s and 1990s have rediscovered the unique qualities of the woodcut.

(i) Revival: pre-World War II. (ii) Post-war developments.

(i) Revival: pre-World War II. In the first three decades of the 20th century in regional centres in Europe and the USA earlier woodcut traditions continued. Under the influence of Art Nouveau the decorative style flourished in Vienna, Munich, Dresden, Paris and elsewhere, through such artists as W. List, Carl Moll and Emil Orlik; both woodcut and linocut were media ideally suited to long sinewy contours and flat passages of colour. In the USA similar works of great quality were produced by A. W. Dow (1857–1922), Gustave Baumann (1881–1971) and others. In England the work of William Morris might be seen to be continued in that of Eric Gill, whose involvement with biblical and other book illustrations was a sign of the continuing link between the woodcut and the book since the great biblical works of the 16th century. Along with other artists, particularly in Britain, where wood-engraving enjoyed a great revival in the first decades of the century, Gill transferred freely between the woodcut and wood-engraving. In the 20th century artists who adopted the medium of woodcut still worked to the examples of Gauguin and Munch. Munch, who continued to work in the medium until his death (1944), combined a long, sinewy cutting style with a flat perspective, bold use of colour and extensive use of the wood grain to produce powerful images of *Melancholy* (see 1983 MOMA exh. cat., no. 72) and *Angst* (see 1983 MOMA exh. cat., p. iv) reinforced by the qualities of the medium itself and hence often stronger than his work on canvas or in any other medium.

In France the Fauves led the way: André Derain, Raoul Dufy, Henri Matisse and Maurice de Vlaminck all adopted the medium in the first few years of the century; working mainly in single colours (in contrast to their paintings), they began to cut with bold and irregular strokes to produce primitive-looking images in the new tradition. Matisse explored the nude, before abandoning woodcut for his greater capabilities with etching and lithography. Vlaminck's large number of woodcuts (105) include the *Head of a Woman* of c. 1906 (see 1983 MOMA exh. cat., no. 11), which exudes a mood of simplicity and contemplation similar in nature to the Pont-Aven school. Derain and Dufy developed away from the roughly hewn woodcuts of the early Fauve works to more harmonious and regular cutting. Dufy's *Fishing* (c. 1908; Castleman, no. 10) is reminiscent of the spirit of Divisionist painting, in that each stroke or cut is an object in the print. At the same time Aristide Maillol was prolific in the medium, producing woodcut illustrations for the reproduction of high-quality books, such as Longus' *Daphnis et Chloe* and Virgil's *Georgics*.

The activity of woodcut production by the leading avant-garde artists over the next decades owed a great deal to the work of leading and inspirational publishers and patrons, such as Daniel-Henry Kahnweiler, Ambroise Vollard and Tériade in France and Graf Harry Kessler (d 1937) in Germany, who actively sought out the finest contemporary artists and writers for combined projects to be produced to the highest quality to meet (and often exceed) the demand for *de luxe* editions of *livres d'artistes* from a learned and wealthy public. Such high-quality book production continued mainly until the late 1950s; after World War II they included less avant-garde works by Georges Braque, Marc Chagall, Joan Miró and others.

In Germany, under the influence of the paintings of Vincent van Gogh and the Fauves and the prints of

Munch, and inspired by the early German workshops of Lucas Cranach I, Albrecht Dürer and others, the artists of DIE BRÜCKE (first in Dresden, then in Berlin) brought about the most significant revival of the woodcut as an avant-garde expressive in the 20th century. Rejecting (and rejected by) the formal academies and Secession group (Lovis Corinth, Max Liebermann, Max Slevogt and others), whose leading artists produced sumptuous and painterly etchings and lithographs during the 19th-century printmaking revival, the artists of Die Brücke set up the Neue Secession, an exhibition group, and, while also working in other printmaking media, adopted the woodcut as their most powerful means of expression. They quickly abandoned a decorative *fin-de-siècle* style (*c.* 1906), and, combining European influences with African motifs and forms known to them from the recent discoveries of European explorers and exhibits in the ethnographic collections in Dresden, they worked aggressively on the woodblocks to produce sharp angles, broad diagonals and roughly hewn, shaded patches. Each of the four leading artists of Die Brücke (Erich Heckel, Ernst Ludwig Kirchner, Max Pechstein and Karl Schmidt-Rottluff) all created primitive nudes of haunting beauty or savagery, startling and intense portraits, and vivid and dynamic landscapes and townscapes.

Kirchner is probably best known for his psychologically intense Berlin street scenes of 1914, although his large woodcut portrait heads of 1916 and his later Swiss landscapes, among others, are also of great significance. Immediately after the tragedies of World War I, Pechstein and Schmidt-Rottluff triggered a powerful rebirth of the woodcut as a medium for religious devotion with their monumental portfolios of the *Lord's Prayer* (Pechstein, 1921; e.g. *Give Us our Daily Bread*, Gordon, pl. 11) and *Nine Woodcuts* (Rottluff; see Schiefler).

The artists of Die Brücke worked mainly in the traditional black and white but also produced startling effects with colours boldly applied in monotypal fashion to the blocks. Emil Nolde, active on the north German coast, produced numerous woodcuts, *The Prophet* (1912; see 1983 MOMA exh. cat., p. v) being one of the most dramatic examples. Ernst Barlach combined imagery from harsh German peasant life, biblical sources and mysticism to express the relationship between a higher being and Man. His series *Metamorphic Creations of God* (1920; Castleman, no. 22) and the illustrations to Goethe's *Walpurgisnacht* (Berlin, 1923) are most characteristic of this type. In Dresden, Conrad Felixmüller's woodcuts treated subjects from his immediate circle and from the working classes in the city and surrounding country, and in Berlin the work of Käthe Kollwitz (including *Death with a Woman in his Lap*, 1921, *Bread*, 1922, the *Great War* series, 1922–3, and others) championed the struggle of the proletariat and glorified the individual in the face of poverty and starvation. The stark contrast of richly inked passages of black against white, which she achieved with a restrained use of line, intensifies her provocative cry for the cause of the poor.

In southern Germany, around Munich, in the early part of the century the most progressive work was being pursued by the artists of the BLAUE REITER. Franz Marc and Heinrich Campendonck explored lyrical themes of nature and creation, intertwining multitudes of curved and flowing lines and contrasting passages of black and white, resulting in semi-abstract compositions. Vasily Kandinsky's work developed from his delicate early part-*Jugendstil*, part-Russian folk style, with such woodcuts as a *Woman with a Fan* (1903), subtly printed in colour on fine Japanese paper (he also employed the linocut to create similar works at the time), through to his finest abstractions, where the medium was ideal for contrasting colour planes. It was also used to great effect in his influential book *Klänge* (Munich, 1913) and in later works, including the most effective plates in the *Kleine Welter* portfolio (1922).

At the Bauhaus, Lyonel Feininger created some of the finest woodcuts, in which he made use of the angular and geometric elements of Cubism, which he incorporated into his city and marine subjects. Other Bauhaus artists, including Josef Albers and László Moholy-Nagy, also exploited the woodcut effectively in their geometric abstractions. Max Beckmann and Otto Dix made only a few explorations into the medium before their styles took them away from a primitive means of expression, but Dix's *Nine Woodcuts* (1919–21) present dramatic visions of German life after World War I. The woodcut flourished all over Germany until World War II in an explosion of printmaking activity that included the production of numbers of fine portfolios, such as *German Graphics of the Present* (Leipzig, 1920) and *Ganymede* (Munich, 1919–25), and the inclusion of original woodcuts in literary publications, such as *Der Zweemann* (Hannover, 1919–26) and *Genius* (Leipzig, 1919–21) and Socialist political pamphlets including *Revolution* (Munich, 1913) and *Die Aktion* (Berlin, 1911–32), in which woodcut was considered as a medium worthy of proletarian political art.

Belgian Expressionism followed lines similar to its counterpart in Germany, with the work of Jozef Cantré, Frans Masereel and others. Edgard Tytgat also produced highly individual colour woodcuts in a folk style. Of the Dada artists, Hans Arp made most extensive use of the medium for its planar qualities in representing his biomorphic forms, although the screenprint later served him well for similar reasons. Marcel Janco also made use of the medium in a limited number of works. In Britain Edward Wadsworth was responsible for some of the purest examples of Vorticist abstraction in woodcuts in 1917–19. Flat planes, cut sharply and in intricate pattern, bear striking results (e.g. *Dry Docked for Scaling and Painting*, 1918, and *Dazzle-Ship in Dry Dock*, 1918).

In Japan, the traditional home of the woodcut, there was little development in the first three decades of the century (*see* JAPAN, §IX, 3(iii)(g)). While progressive Japanese painters had become strongly influenced by Western styles, the woodcut was still firmly bound up with the complex relationship between artist and artisans in the community. K. Yamamoto and Kōshirō Onchi were among the first to look to European woodcut for inspiration. In the late 1920s U. Hiratsuka was one of the first to adopt the Western technique of cutting directly on to the block. His student Shiko Munakata is generally considered the most influential Japanese artist of the century. He became associated with the Mingei movement (a return to rural craftsmanship), and in combining Buddhist figures,

7. Woodcut by Roy Lichtenstein: *American Indian Theme II*, printed in colour, 610×725 mm, 1980 (New York, Museum of Modern Art)

Japanese legends and other traditional images in his subjects, he handcut (with a directness akin to the German Expressionists) the blocks, which when printed maintained the character of the wood.

In the 1930s and 1940s artists in Mexico and South America also made use of the woodcut as a form of proletarian expression to protest about social conditions. These artists included David Alfaro Siqueiros and Antonio Frasconi. Diego Rivera also worked to great effect with the woodblock. In the USA Leonard Baskin was also attracted to the possibilities of political expression through the medium and became a leading exponent of the woodcut.

(ii) Post-war developments. In the decades following World War II, while some of the more mature artists continued to work in the medium, either for high-quality *livres d'artistes* or, as in the case of the artists formerly of Die Brücke, to produce less dynamic work in their earlier styles, others often exploited different media (particularly the screenprint) to create their images: the mainly younger artists involved in the printmaking booms of the 1960s and 1970s in Paris and across Germany frequently made use of lithography and etching. The artists associated with

such movements as Pop, Op and kinetic art in London and New York worked extensively with the lithograph and screenprint. Those making somewhat rare use of woodcut in the 1960s included Donald Judd and Frank Stella. Helen Frankenthaler's abstract woodcut compositions from the 1970s onwards, which were printed on oriental papers, convey an impression of stained canvas. Charles Summer's compositions were imbued with the philosophy of Zen Buddhism.

In Germany, Ewald Mataré's woodcuts may be viewed as providing a transition from the work of the German Expressionists to that of such late 20th-century artists as A. R. Penck and H. A. P. Grieshaber (1909–81). The brutally cut blocks of Georg Baselitz reflect a return to the more traditional media during the 1980s. In Britain this was demonstrated in the work of Michael Rothenstein (*b* 1908). In the USA in the 1980s, after limited work in the medium in the 1970s, even such leading Pop artists as Jim Dine and Roy Lichtenstein produced major woodcut images (see fig. 7). Other artists who employed it include Susan Rothenburg and Francesco Clemente, who explored another stage of tradition by using skilled East Asian woodblock cutters to produce extremely delicate representations of his images. Friedensreich Hundertwasser used

Japanese woodcutters in Austria to produce major works alongside his screenprints.

BIBLIOGRAPHY
G. Schiefler: *Meine Graphiksammlung* (Hamburg, 1974)
R. Avermaete: *La Gravure sur bois moderne de l'occident* (Paris, 1928/R Vaduz, 1977)
R. Castleman: *Prints of the Twentieth Century: A History* (New York, 1976)
W. Chamberlain: *The Thames and Hudson Manual of Woodcut Printmaking and Related Techniques* (London, 1978)
Grafik des deutschen Expressionismus/German Expressionist Prints (exh. cat. by B. Rau, Stuttgart, Inst. Auslandsbeziehungen; Bristol, Arnolfini; 1983) [Ger. and Eng. text]
Prints from Blocks: From Gauguin to Now (exh. cat. by R. Castleman, New York, MOMA, 1983) [good pls]
F. Carey and A. Griffiths: *The Print in Germany, 1800–1933: The Age of Expressionism* (London, 1984)
D. E. Gordon: *Expressionism: Art and Idea* (New Haven, 1987)
F. Whitford and others: *Käthe Kollwitz, 1867–1945: The Graphic Works* (Cambridge, 1987)

S. R. THEOBALD

Woodcut, chiaroscuro [Fr. *clair obscur, camaïeu*; Ger. *Helldunkelschnitt*]. Early form of colour print, in which two or more woodblocks were printed one on top of the other, usually consisting of flat tonal blocks with limited chromatic range and a line block printed last. The Italian word 'chiaroscuro', which refers to contrasts of light and dark in a work of art, came to be applied from the early 16th century to drawings and woodcuts in which figures were delineated in a dark ink on a coloured background, with white strokes modelling the volumes.

1. MATERIALS AND TECHNIQUES. A chiaroscuro woodcut could be made with only two blocks: a key-block (or line-block) conveying the primary details of the design and suggesting through its hatching intermediate shading; and a tone-block of identical size creating a coloured ground interrupted by highlights, wherever cut-out lines or areas permitted the white of the paper to show through. The key-block would be cut first and printed on the tone-block itself to assist the planning of the highlights but was applied last in printing the impression. If more than two blocks were used (generally three or four but occasionally as many as ten), the key-block could be restricted to printing intermittent outlines, or dark accents, and the intermediate blocks could convey the shading and much more of the design information, with the background block still describing the highlights. For this more complex form of chiaroscuro, very careful planning of the colour separations and meticulous registration in the printing were required. Early scholars distinguished the two-block from the multi-block method by calling it *camaïeu*, that is, the 'monochrome method'.

Relatively soft fruit-wood blocks were employed, cut along the grain, not usually exceeding *c.* 500×350 mm. If a very large design was planned, it could be extended on to adjacent blocks, and, after printing, the various sheets could be pasted together to compose the whole. Andrea Andreani made several prints calling for over 40 blocks. Cutting of the design was done with knives and gouges. Inks, pounded on the surface with balls or dabbers, were oil-based and incorporated a wide range of pigments, by all appearances pure mineral colours rather than blended pigments. While neutral and closely related hues were predominant, bright colours and striking combinations also occurred. A screw-and-lever press, identical or similar to a type-press, would have been used. The pressure could be varied from one block to another to create embossed areas. A complex press especially designed for the printing of chiaroscuro woodcuts was constructed by the 17th-century Parisian painter Georges Lallemant, but it proved too expensive to operate.

Several 16th-century artists recognized that colour blocks could be combined effectively with intaglio plates. Parmigianino and Domenico Beccafumi printed tone-blocks together with etched and engraved plates respectively as early as the 1520s; Erhard Altdorfer, Crispin van den Broeck, Hendrick Goltzius and Abraham Bloemaert followed later in the century. In the 18th century the English artist Elisha Kirkall also combined woodcut with mezzotint; the most impressive revival, however, was the two-volume *Cabinet Crozat* (1729–42), which included reproductions of important French paintings and drawings in mixed-method chiaroscuros by the Le Sueur family in collaboration with the Comte de Caylus and others.

2. HISTORY. The outlines of the evolution of the chiaroscuro woodcut are preserved in correspondence of Frederick III, Elector of Saxony, in Wittenburg, and Conrad Peutinger, adviser to Emperor Maximilian I, in Augsburg. The Elector had obtained a small book, written by Peutinger, which was printed in Augsburg by Erhard Ratdolt (*fl* 1467–1516) in black, red and gold ink. This had suggested the feasibility of his court painter, Lucas Cranach the elder, designing a woodcut of *St George on Horseback* (B. 65) to be similarly printed in gold or silver. In planning the print (completed in 1507) Cranach not only kept in mind the example of ornate book printing, which in Germany had fostered a number of colour experiments, but also directly imitated the effect of the chiaroscuro drawing, a style increasingly popular since the late 15th century. He printed a key-block bearing the full design in black on a blue-tinted paper and, using a second block, printed the highlights not in white lead but in paste, to which gold and silver dust could adhere. After receiving an impression, Maximilian in turn commissioned the Augsburg painter Hans Burgkmair I to design a *St George on Horseback* (B. 23) to be printed in metallic ink on tinted paper, as well as an equestrian portrait of the *Emperor Maximilian as Christian Knight* (B. 32), reflecting his patronage of the Order of St George. However, not long after these first costly impressions in 1508, the more practical solution of printing the background colour and cutting out the highlights to allow the white of the paper to show through was developed, and the second block of each print was replaced.

Credit for this innovation is usually given to the Flemish woodcutter Jost de Negker (who began working for the Emperor in Augsburg sometime between 1508 and 1512), as his name appears in movable type in later states of these prints. While he was previously assumed to have also cut the key-blocks, this cannot be established with certainty. In 1510 Burgkmair with de Negker's involvement at some stage, produced the remarkable three-block *Lovers Surprised by Death* (B. 40), which already fully realized the pictorial potential of the chiaroscuro technique and was conceived from the outset as such. Dependence on a

Chiaroscuro woodcut by Antonio da Trento: *Martyrdom of Two Saints*, 293×481 mm, *c.* 1527 (Detroit, MI, Institute of Arts)

virtually complete key-block image had been replaced by three blocks of equal importance to the design; in a number of impressions the key-block is printed not in black but in a dark colour that modulates subtly from the lighter hues, a device repeated in the beautiful portrait of *Hans Paumgärtner* (B. 34) of 1512. In both prints the colours can be surprising: violets, pinks and indigo blues, which take the medium well beyond pure imitation of chiaroscuro drawing.

Cranach added single tone-blocks to five of his black-and-white woodcuts, including two that bear an unreliable date earlier than the *St George*, but he is now generally thought to be the imitator rather than the innovator of the true tone-block. Thereafter he took no further part in the development of the medium. Of higher quality were the chiaroscuros designed by Hans Baldung and Hans Wechtlin the elder (some eight and twelve respectively) from 1510. They likewise favoured the two-block method (sometimes called '*camaïeu*'), which became identified with the German contribution to chiaroscuro despite the brilliant three-block experiments mentioned above. Sebald Beham and other Dürer disciples produced a small body of chiaroscuros in Nuremberg, notwithstanding Dürer's lack of interest in it as a printing technique. Thereafter only sporadic interest was shown in Germany, for example by Tobias Stimmer in the 1570s, until Ludolph Büsinck produced 25 chiaroscuros after designs by Georges Lallemant from 1623 to 1629, presumably in Paris, in a style that combined French and Dutch influences.

Eight years after the Burgkmair/de Negker invention of the true chiaroscuro, the Italian woodcutter Ugo da Carpi successfully petitioned the Venetian Senate for a copyright on all his chiaroscuro designs, falsely claiming that no one had ever used the technique before. While the German influence is in fact conspicuous in his earliest, two-block chiaroscuros of *c.* 1515–17, he gradually moved away from the linear Burgkmair precedent in his three- to five-block prints towards bold, flat planes of tone and daring generalization of form, culminating in his *Aeneas Fleeing Troy* (B. 104, 12) after Raphael (1518) and *Diogenes* after Parmigianino (*c.* 1527; for illustration *see* PRINTS, colour pl. VI).

Owing to the existence of a large body of anonymous chiaroscuros closely reproducing wash or metalpoint drawings by Parmigianino, it has been assumed that the painter supervised a chiaroscuro workshop. Vasari recorded that he had instructed the cutter Antonio da Trento in this technique while in Bologna, and several excellent prints resulted, for example the *Martyrdom of Two Saints* (see fig.). However, his painting obligations and his erratic personality make unlikely the notion of an orderly system of print production on the scale of a workshop, and the survival of many of the drawings related to chiaroscuros obviates the necessity of the artist drawing directly on the block, as could otherwise have been expected. A posthumous publishing venture directed by Giuseppe Niccolò Vicentino is mentioned by Vasari and doubtless accounts for this group of prints. Outside this workshop, chiaroscuros were inspired by many sources other than wash drawings: paintings, grisailles, frescoes (including house façades), low reliefs, intarsia and engravings. In the hands of the most individual cutters, the breadth of the interpretation and the independence of the colours made reproduction a secondary concern. Certain artists, such as Beccafumi and Antonio Campi, produced fine original work as well. Several chiaroscuros resulted from the woodcut workshop centred around Titian in Venice in the mid-16th century, notably two-block cuts by Nicolò Boldrini. Antonio da Trento's and Ugo da Carpi's chiaroscuros after Parmigianino had probably been made in Bologna and, with Alessandro Ghandini, Joannes Gallus, and the monogrammist NDB resident there, the city continued to nurture the medium after the Sack of Rome (1527). In the 1580s Andrea Andreani re-established a chiaroscuro industry by reprinting and recutting earlier blocks that he had acquired, probably from Vicentino. More important, he cut a large number of new chiaroscuros of high quality in a more modern, calligraphic style, some being very ambitious multi-block projects. In the second quarter of the 17th century Bartolomeo Coriolano's somewhat insipid interpretations of designs by Guido Reni were virtually the only Italian chiaroscuros being issued. A renewed enthusiasm for Ugo da Carpi and Parmigianino in the 18th century inspired chiaroscuros in their manner by Venetian Anton Maria Zanetti (i) and the English Italophiles John Skippe, Charles Knapton and Arthur Pond. Knapton and Pond used etched plates rather than key-blocks. After perfecting the monochromatic chiaroscuro in interpretations of Veronese and other Venetian painters, John Baptist Jackson, an Englishman settled in Venice, went on to carry the woodcut into the realm of full-colour printing with his six 'heroic' landscapes after Marco Ricci (see WOODCUT, fig. 5), using perhaps as many as ten blocks, blended overlapping pigments, graded hues and selective embossing.

Netherlandish interest in chiaroscuro technique emerged in Antwerp in the mid-16th century with a body of 20 chiaroscuros attributed to Frans Floris and his circle, some employing etched plates in combination with woodcut. In Haarlem, the engraver Hendrick Goltzius produced c. 18 woodcuts in three blocks, many of these having been through prior states as one-block (on blue paper) or two-block prints. The authorship of the cutting remains uncertain. Among them are the first depictions of pure landscape using the technique. His six Classical deities in ovals display particular bravura, with dramatic key-block figures set off against white-line background detail, strong three-dimensionality replacing the flat planes of early Italian chiaroscuros (see GOLTZIUS, HENDRICK, fig. 3).

In Utrecht, a series of chiaroscuros with etched plates after Abraham Bloemaert and a pair of two-block prints by his colleague Paulus Moreelse signalled the early fading of 17th century interest in the medium in the Low Countries. Christoffel Jegher, under the supervision of Rubens, provided a splendid exception in the 1630s, with three major chiaroscuros after the master. The *Rest on the Flight into Egypt* (Hollstein, no. 4) and the *Infant Christ and St John* rely on a vigorous key-block, with tone-blocks merely as embellishment, but the *Portrait of a Bearded Man* (Hollstein, no. 20) uses subtle transitions between four blocks to achieve a painterly effect.

BIBLIOGRAPHY

Hollstein: *Dut. & Flem.*
J M Papillon: *Traité historique et practique de la gravure sur bois* (Paris, 1766)
A. von Bartsch: *Le Peintre-graveur* (Vienna, 1803–21), xii [B.]
J. D. Passavant: *Le Peintre-graveur . . . catalogue supplémentaire . . . de Bartsch*, 6 vols (Leipzig, 1860–64)
G. K. W. Seibt: 'Helldunkel iii: Chiaroscuro, Camaieu, Holzschnitte in Helldunkel', *Studien zur Kunst und Kulturgeschichte*, v (Frankfurt am Main, 1891)
A. Reichel: *Die Clair-obscur-Schnitte des XVI, XVII, und XVIII Jahrhunderts* (Zurich, 1926)
L. Servolini: *La xilografia a chiaroscuro italiana nei secoli XVI, XVII, XVIII* (Lecco, 1930)
P. Gusman: *Gravure sur bois et taille d'épargne: Historique et technique* (Paris, 1938)
Mostra di chiaroscuri italiani dei secoli XVI, XVII, XVIII (exh. cat., ed. M. Fossi; Florence, Uffizi, 1956)
Parmigianino und sein Kreis (exh. cat. by K. Oberhuber, Vienna, Albertina, 1963)
Gravures sur bois clairs-obscurs de 1500 à 1800 (exh. cat., ed. C. van Hasselt; Paris, Fond. Custodia, Inst. Néer.; Rotterdam, Mus. Boymans-van Beuningen; 1965–6)
Renaissance in Italien 16 Jahrhundert: Die Kunst der Graphik III (exh. cat., ed. K. Oberhuber; Vienna, Albertina, 1966)
A. E. Popham: 'Observations on Parmigianino's Designs for Chiaroscuro Woodcuts', *Miscellanea, I. Q. van Regteren Altena* (Amsterdam, 1969)
W. Strauss: *Chiaroscuro: The Clair-obscur Woodcuts by the German and Netherlandish Masters of the XVIIth Centuries* (New York, 1973)
Hans Burgkmair: Das graphische Werk (exh. cat., ed. T. Falk; Augsburg, Schaezlerpal., Kstsamml., 1973)
Tiziano e la silografia veneziana del cinquecento (exh. cat., ed. M. Muraro and D. Rosand; Venice, Fond. Cini, Bib., 1976)
Chiaroscuro Woodcuts: Hendrick Goltzius and his Time (exh. cat., ed. N. Bialler; Amsterdam, Rijksmus.; Cleveland, OH, Mus. A.; 1993)
D. Landau and P. Parshall: *The Renaissance Print, 1470–1550* (New Haven and London, 1994)
German Renaissance Prints (exh. cat., ed. G. Bartrum; London, BM, 1995)

JAN JOHNSON

Wood-engraving [Fr. *gravure sur bois debout*; Ger. *Holzstich*. Type of relief print related to the WOODCUT, and the process by which it is made. The two processes are, however, quite distinct (see §1 below), despite the terms 'woodcut' and 'wood-engraving' having been used synonymously to refer to any image printed from a wooden surface. Although it was probably used first in the 17th century, it was not until the 18th that wood-engraving could be identified confidently as a distinct engraving process.

1. Materials and techniques. 2. History.

1. MATERIALS AND TECHNIQUES. The wood-engraver's block is made from a hardwood, preferably boxtree (*Buxus sempervirens*). The boxwood block is made from roundels cut across the grain, so that the closely formed growth rings of the tree are clearly apparent on the surface of the prepared block. By working against this grain the wood-engraver is able to execute very fine work. The disadvantage of boxwood is its generally small girth; for a print or illustration bigger than 150–200 mm, several separate pieces of boxwood have to be joined together. Tongue-and-grooved blocks, glued and/or screwed together, were used before the invention in the mid-19th century of the bolted block, a multiple boxwood block held together by nuts and bolts located in grooves cut into the back of the individual blocks. In the late 20th century multiple blocks were once again of the glued kind. Blocks are conventionally supplied 'type high', that is at a thickness that allows them to be locked in a printing press ready for printing.

The wood-engraver uses a variety of tools closely related to those used by metal-engravers (see ENGRAVING, §I and fig. 1). These fall into two groups: those for engraving lines and textures (gravers or burins, spitstickers and tint

1. Wood-engraving by Thomas Bewick: *The Tail-less Macauco and the Moongooz* (London, British Museum); from his *General History of Quadrupeds* (Newcastle upon Tyne, 1790)

tools); and those for clearing areas of the block (scorpers and chisels). To clear large areas, a routing machine may be employed. The design to be engraved can be committed to the surface of the block in several ways: by drawing directly on to the block; by tracing a drawing; or by photographing on to the engraving surface. For much of the 19th century there was a professional divide between the designer of wood-engraved illustration and the engraver, the latter being seen as an interpreter or translator. When artist–engravers became interested in the process, conception and execution came to be the sole responsibility of the artist.

During engraving the sides of the block are gripped by hand on a leather sandbag. Coordinating with the tool held in the other hand, the engraver is then able to manipulate the block more easily and to execute curved lines. Unlike in woodcutting, where the knife is drawn towards the body, all work is done away from the body. During most of the period of its employment as a commercial reproductive process, apprentice engravers were schooled in the correct manner of working, which tended towards a standardized 'finish'. The modern artist–engraver is constrained only by the degree of experimentation he wishes to try and by the scope of his imagination.

If an inked but unengraved block is passed through the press, it produces a rectangle of unbroken black. As the engraver works on the block, lines, textures and spaces are created by the removal of wood by the tools. These appear as white on the print itself. It is argued not only that this 'white line' is the most natural way of creating a wood-engraved image but also that as a matter of principle a design should be conceived from the start in terms of white marks on a black surface. The commercial wood-engravers were required to make facsimiles of illustrators'

pen-and-ink and wash drawings and worked largely in 'black line', where the engraver imitates the pen drawing by removing all the wood from around drawn lines, thus leaving them cleanly in relief. Pure use of the 'white line' is seen by some artist–engravers as a commitment to the true principles of the process, and the use of 'black line' as a failure to understand these principles. In practice it is not uncommon to see both 'white' and 'black' line in use in any one wood-engraved image.

To secure a perfect print from the wood-engraved block demands the best inks, paper and printing technique. In general a fairly stiff, high-quality printer's ink is used, and Indian and Japanese papers are preferred. Papers that are either too hard or too soft will not take a good impression. It is possible to print from a wood-engraved block by hand and produce a reasonable print, but it is usual to pull proofs in a printing press. Both hand and machine presses are used. If carefully printed, the boxwood block can deliver thousands of good impressions before wear becomes a factor. The surface, however, is always vulnerable to accidental damage, and in the 19th century electrotype casts were made from the blocks and used in the actual printing, the blocks themselves being kept as masters from which further 'electros' could be made.

Alongside the dominant tradition of black-and-white wood-engraving runs the colour print pulled from a number of wood blocks, usually one for each colour, printed in fine register over a 'key' or outline block. Both commercial engravers and artist–engravers have used the process.

2. HISTORY. The invention of wood-engraving cannot be ascribed to any one person nor to a specific date. It was probably one of several processes developed by the general engraver from the 17th century onwards. Occasionally white-line engraving showing evidence of graver rather than knife work can be found in 17th-century printed ephemera. It is, however, only in the work of THOMAS BEWICK in Britain in the latter half of the 18th century that it is seen as a specific technique. Bewick combined the skills of drawing and engraving (see fig. 1). His use of the white line is considered exemplary by modern artist–engravers, and its legitimacy as *the* principle of engraving on wood was expressed in his own writing. Although there were contemporaries active in wood-engraving, such as Robert Branston (1778–1827) in Britain and Theophile Unger (1730–1804) in Germany, Bewick's technical brilliance combined with the novelty of his work has secured for him the misleading sobriquet of 'the father of wood-engraving'.

Another contemporary, William Blake, executed only a handful of wood-engravings, but his influence has been as great as Bewick's. The romantic spirituality of Blake's illustrations to *The Pastorals of Virgil* (London, 1821) are in direct contrast to the closely observed detail of Bewick's natural history illustrations and the anecdotal realism of his celebrated vignettes. It is, however, precisely the pastoral sublimity of Blake, together with an unrestrained use of white line, that has endeared him to later generations of artist–engravers.

The apprentices of Bewick, Branston and their contemporaries were the first generation of engravers able to make a livelihood solely from wood-engraving, and for a while Britain was a centre of excellence to which foreign publishers turned for their wood-engravings. British engravers began working abroad, and Charles Thompson (1791–1843) is widely credited with introducing the new technique into France, although native engravers (e.g. Louis Henri Brevière (1797–1869) were at work there. Whether British engravers introduced the new technique into Europe or foreign engravers learnt from the British example is a question of dissemination that is not yet resolved.

During the first three decades of the 19th century wood-engraving was only slowly adopted commercially as a process for the illustration of books. With the advent of a popular illustrated press in the 1830s and 1840s, however, the advantages of engraving on wood as a relatively cheap reproductive process secured its general use. Printed by machine presses (all Bewick's work had been printed on the traditional hand-press), the wood-engraved illustrations to *The Penny Magazine* (1832–45), *Punch* (1841–) and *The Illustrated London News* (1842–) set a trend and a standard for later developments in both wood-engraving and illustration. The *Magazin pittoresque* (1833), *L'Illustration* (1843) and *Le Monde illustré* (1857) in France and *Die Illustrierte Zeitung* (1843) in Germany were likewise founded on the process. For half a century, from the 1830s, wood-engraving was the dominant reproductive process used by publishers in Europe and North America, and not until the successful introduction of the photomechanical line-block and half-tone plate was it made obsolete. During this period much of the best illustration was reproduced by wood-engraving, and the reputations of such illustrators as John Gilbert, John Leech, Charles Keene and John Tenniel in Britain, Felix Octavius Carr Darley and John La Farge in the USA, Gustave Doré, J. J. Grandville and Ernest Meissonier in France, and Adolph Menzel, Ludwig Richter and Wilhelm Busch in Germany are largely due to the process. Engravers too gained reputations: Edward Dalziel and his brothers, John Barak Swain (*c.* 1815–38) and William James Linton in Britain, Héliodore Joseph Pisan (1822–90) and Stéphane Pannemaker (1847–1930) in France and the Vogels, Wilhelm Pfnorr (1792–1869) and Robert-François-Richard Brend'Amour (*b* 1831) in Germany, for example, were all internationally known wood-engravers.

As a result of internal development and competition with the new phototechnologies, some commercial engravers built up reproductive engraving skills in order to interpret original art work. A controversy about the legitimacy of the 'New School', polarized by William James Linton and Timothy Cole during the 1880s, was not resolved before the inevitable success of the photomechanical processes rendered all such debate academic.

At the point in the 1890s at which wood-engraving as a viable commercial process was virtually obsolete, artist-engravers adopted it as a means of original expression. In Britain early work was done by Charles Ricketts, Charles Hazelwood Shannon, Lucien Pissarro and William Nicholson, all but the latter using the process as a simple reproductive medium for their own pen-and-ink drawings,

2. Wood-engraving by Auguste Lepère: *A Side-view of Rouen Cathedral*, 1888 (London, British Museum); from *Rouen Illustré* (Paris, 1913)

which often appeared as illustrations in private-press books as well as individual prints. William Morris used wood-engraved illustration at the Kelmscott Press, and it was at that period that the tradition of employing wood-engraved illustration in private-press books began.

In France, Auguste Lepère was one of the few commercial wood-engravers of any nation to make the successful transition to the ranks of artist–engravers (see fig. 2), and in Europe generally original wood-engraving became an established part of the graphic arts. Gauguin's woodcuts have had much the same inspirational value for engravers as Blake's work. In Germany, Italy and the Netherlands there were engravers associated with the early adoption of wood-engraving as a mode of self-expression in print. During the first two decades of the 20th century the teaching of wood-engraving became centred in the art schools. In Britain, Noel Rooke (1881–1953) was an influential teacher at the Central School of Art and Crafts, London. His best-known students include John Farleigh (1900–1965), Robert Gibbings (1889–1958) and Clare Leighton (1898–1989). Between 1918 and 1939 wood-engraved prints and illustrations, for both private press and commercially produced books, enjoyed something of a vogue in Britain and Europe. The commitment of artist-engravers to the process can be followed through the number of societies and publications embracing wood-engraving. The Society of Wood Engravers was formed in Britain in 1920, and in 1923 a more experimental group formed the English Wood Engraving Society. In France, Pierre Gusman (*b* 1862), who along with Auguste Lepère had founded the Société des Gravures sur Bois Original as early as 1893, published *La Gravure sur bois en France au XIXe siècle* in 1929. In Germany the strident woodcut work of the Expressionists has proved to be the enduring tradition from the period. In eastern Europe, Russia, Poland, Hungary, the Czech Republic and Slovakia have all contributed to the appeal of the wood-engraved image, most notable being the work of the Russians Vladimir Favorsky and his pupil Andrey Goncharov (1903–79). In the latter half of the 20th century wood-engraving, if less favoured than earlier, was still being practised by artist-engravers and enjoying short, recurrent bouts of fashion for book and advertising illustration.

For John Jackson's *The Wood-engraver's Hands*, see PRINTS, fig. 6.

BIBLIOGRAPHY

J. Jackson and W. A. Chatto: *A Treatise on Wood Engraving: Historical and Practical* (London, 1839/*R* Detroit, 1969)
W. J. Linton: *Wood Engraving: A Manual of Instruction* (London, 1884)
——: *The Masters of Wood Engraving* (London, 1889)
P. Kristeller: *Kupferstich and Holzschnitt in vier Jahrhunderten* (Berlin, 1905/*R* 1922)
H. Furst: *The Modern Woodcut* (London, 1924)
N. Rooke: *Woodcuts and Wood Engravings* (London, 1926)
D. P. Bliss: *A History of Wood-engraving* (London, 1928/*R* 1964)
P. Gusman: *La Gravure sur bois en France au XIXe siècle* (Paris, 1929)
C. Leighton: *Wood Engraving and Wood Cuts* (London, 1932)
B. Sleigh: *Wood Engraving since 1890* (London, 1932)
G. E. Mackley: *Wood Engraving* (London, 1948)
K. Lindley: *The Woodblock Engravers* (Newton Abbot, 1970)
G. Wakeman: *Victorian Book Illustration: The Technical Revolution* (Newton Abbot, 1973)
A. Garrett: *A History of British Wood Engraving* (Tunbridge Wells, 1978)
E. de Mare: *The Victorian Woodblock Illustrators* (London, 1980)
R. K. Engen: *Dictionary of Victorian Wood Engravers* (Cambridge, 1985) [useful bibliographies]
Victorian Illustrated Books, 1850–1870: The Heyday of Wood-engraving (exh. cat., London, BM, 1994)

LEO. JOHN DE FREITAS

Woodhouse. Irish family of medallists. William Woodhouse (*b* Dublin, 1805; *d* Woodville, Co. Wicklow, 6 Dec 1878), son of John Woodhouse (i) (*d* 1836), a Dublin die-sinker, trained in Birmingham with the medallist Thomas Halliday (*fl* 1810–54). His medal of *George Gordon, 6th Baron Byron* (bronze and white metal; see Brown, i, no. 1222), engraved on the poet's death in 1824, won a Society of Arts prize. In 1828 he executed a medal of *Daniel O'Connell* (silver, white metal and brass; see Brown, i, nos 1325–6). Having returned to Dublin, where he set up his own business, throughout the 1830s and 1840s he produced medals for a wide range of societies and institutions. When he retired in the 1850s his son John Woodhouse (ii) (*b* Dublin, 1835; *d* Dublin, May 1892) took over the unfinished work. He had studied at the art schools of the Royal Dublin Society and cut his first die in 1853: the Irish harp on the reverse of his father's white metal medal of *William Dargan* (see Brown, ii, no. 2524) for the Great Industrial Exhibition in Dublin. He remained one of the foremost medallists in Dublin, designing and engraving many medals, including that for the Irish National Exhibition in 1882 (silver, bronze and white metal; see Brown, ii, no. 3130), until in the mid-1880s ill-health prevented him from continuing. Both William and John (ii) were skilful exponents of the Neo-classical medal, the prevailing style throughout the 19th century in Britain and Ireland.

Forrer; Strickland

BIBLIOGRAPHY

W. Frazer: 'The Medallists of Ireland and their Work', *J. Royal Hist. & Archaeol. Assoc. Ireland*, n. s. 3, vii (1885–6), pp. 608–9; viii (1886–7), pp. 189–208

A. E. Went: *Irish Coins and Medals* (Dublin, 1978)
L. Brown: *British Historical Medals*, i–ii (London, 1980–87)

PHILIP ATTWOOD

Woodrow, Bill (*b* Henley, Oxon, 1 Nov 1948). English sculptor. In 1980 he first devised his characteristic method of making sculpture, forming a new object or objects from the skin of a found domestic appliance as in *Twin-tub with Guitar* (1981; London, Tate). Woodrow worked in such a way as to leave evident the original identities of the constituent items as well as the mode of transformation. His work is distinguished by its reliance on discarded consumer durables redolent of contemporary urban experience and by a witty and skilful manipulation of this raw material into a kind of three-dimensional drawing. These juxtapositions of images and objects from ordinary life do not constitute didactic statements, but have an elliptical, poetic content. In later work Woodrow continued greatly to expand his raw material to encompass car doors and bonnets, industrial units and textiles, while also elaborating the symbolic and narrative implications of his constructions, for example *Life on Earth* (1984; Ottawa, N.G.), in which a group of vinyl chairs and a consumer durable are cunningly metamorphosed into an improvised theatre for a 'home movie', where the fish on film seem to watch the human audience with as much curiosity as that of the spectator scrutinizing the work of art. In the late 1980s, while retaining the symbolic and narrative elements characteristic of his earlier work, he began to work first in welded steel and then in cast bronze (e.g. *Listening to History*, 1995; artist's col., see 1996 exh. cat., p. 35).

BIBLIOGRAPHY

Bill Woodrow: Sculpture 1980–86 (exh. cat. by L. Cooke, Edinburgh, Fruitmarket Gal., 1986)
M. J. Jacob: 'Bill Woodrow: Objects Reincarnated', *A Quiet Revolution: British Sculpture since 1965*, ed. T. A. Neff (London, 1987), pp. 156–75
Bill Woodrow: Fools' Gold (exh. cat. by J. Roberts, London, Tate; Darmstadt, Inst. Mathildenhöhe; 1996–7)

LYNNE COOKE

Woodruff, Hale (Aspacio) (*b* Cairo, IL, 26 Aug 1900; *d* 1980). American painter, printmaker and teacher. He was a leading artist of the Harlem Renaissance (*see* AFRICAN AMERICAN ART, §2) and studied at the John Herron Institute, Indianapolis, the school of the Fogg Art Museum, Harvard University, Cambridge, MA, the Académie Scandinave and the Académie Moderne, Paris. He also worked with Henry Ossawa Tanner in Paris (1931) and studied mural painting with Diego Rivera in Mexico City (1936). From the European schools he learnt strong composition and the narrative power of Goya. He was concerned to amplify the problems of Black Americans and his murals (which are indebted to Rivera) carry sharp commentaries on the poor social conditions of his compatriots and forebears in Georgia (e.g. the Amistad Murals, Tallageda College, AL). In the South, Woodruff discovered and taught several talented artists including Frederick Flemister, Robert Neal and Albert Wells, all of whose work bore the mark of Woodruff's bold style and methods. From the 1950s his work became increasingly abstract (e.g. *Celestial Gate*, Atlanta, GA, Spelman Coll.).

Woodruff's work as a painter was equalled by his graphic productions, including many wood engravings, in which medium he relied on his knowledge of French Cubism and Expressionism to create images of protest against racial segregation. He taught at the Harlem Community Art Center, New York (1945), Atlantic University (1931–45) and New York University (1945).

BIBLIOGRAPHY
J. A. Porter: *Modern Negro Art* (New York, 1943), pp. 18–21, 123–4, 161–2
Two Centuries of Black American Art (exh. cat. by D. D. Driscoll, Los Angeles, CA, Co. Mus. A., 1976), pp. 73, 100, 153
P. Hastings Falk, ed.: *Who Was who in American Art: Compiled from the Original Thirty-four Volumes of 'American Art Annual: Who's who in Art': Biographies of American Artists Active from 1898–1947* (Madison, CT, 1985)

Woods, Shadrach. *See under* CANDILIS-JOSIC-WOODS.

Woodstock, Thomas of, Duke of Gloucester. *See* PLANTAGENET, (5).

Woodville. Family of artists of American descent.

(1) Richard Caton Woodville (*b* Baltimore, 30 April 1825; *d* London, 13 Aug 1855). Painter. Although he grew up in Baltimore and is known for his American genre paintings, he created most of his work abroad. He relied during his schooling on engravings and art books, possibly studying with the Baltimore artist Alfred Jacob Miller and copying works in the Baltimore collection of Robert Gilmor, which was strong in Dutch and Flemish paintings, and had at least two genre works by William Sidney Mount. By 1842, when Woodville enrolled briefly at medical school, he was working as a portrait painter, although he soon turned his efforts to genre scenes. He exhibited *Scene in a Bar-room* (untraced) at the National Academy of Design, New York, in 1845 and the same year went to Düsseldorf, where he studied with Carl Ferdinand Sohn. Absorbing to stunning advantage the careful draughtsmanship, use of local colour, complex figural groupings and precise finish of the Düsseldorf school, Woodville produced a small but accomplished group of genre paintings that comprise his life work.

Some of these paintings transposed traditional genre motifs into American settings. For instance, in 1851 he created the painting *Sailor's Wedding* (Baltimore, MD, Walters A.G.), in which a colourful wedding party crowds the chambers of a magistrate. In addition to the careful attention given to the furnishings, he included such character types as the cocksure sailor and demure bride, tipsy-looking father and commandeering mother of the bride. Two paintings incorporate card-playing in an American tavern setting: the *Card Players* (1846; Detroit, MI, A. Inst.) and *Waiting for the Stage* (1851; Washington, DC, Corcoran Gal. A.). However, he also painted period costume pieces such as the *Cavalier's Return* (1847; New York, NY Hist. Soc.).

Several of Woodville's paintings focus on American politics, a topic that interested the artist during at least two visits home. The best-known of these works, during his lifetime as well as today, is *News of the Mexican War* (1848; New York, N. Acad. Des.), which was exhibited at the American Art Union in 1849 and distributed as a folio

engraving by Alfred Jones (1819–1900) in 1851 to 14,000 subscribers. One reason for the painting's popularity is that it captures the unpopularity of the war and the cynical assessment that it was fought primarily for the fortunes to be made in land speculation and slavery. Another work on a political theme is *Politics in the Oyster House* (1848; Baltimore, MD, Walters A.G.), in which two American men, one considerably older than the other, discuss politics. The younger man leans forward, newspaper in hand, arguing with conviction; but his companion looks out of the space with a bored expression.

Woodville's works, which he submitted regularly to the American Art Union from 1847, were received in America with high enthusiasm. His sensitivity to American self-definition, his solid grasp of anecdote, and his clear light and colour earned him wide praise. The Baltimore collector William T. Walters bought a number of his paintings after his death, and the Walters Art Gallery is today the major repository. Woodville died accidentally of an overdose of morphine, taken medicinally, in London.

BIBLIOGRAPHY
Richard Caton Woodville, an Early American Genre Painter (exh. cat. by F. Grubar, Washington, DC, Corcoran A.G., 1967)
B. Groseclose: 'Politics and American Genre Painting of the Nineteenth Century', *Antiques*, cxx (Nov 1981), pp. 1210–17
ELIZABETH JOHNS

(2) R(ichard) Caton Woodville (*b* London, 7 Jan 1856; *d* London, 17 Aug 1927). Painter and illustrator, posthumous son of (1) Richard Caton Woodville. Like his father he studied in Düsseldorf. He arrived in London in 1876 at the time of the Russo-Turkish War, when battle painting was enjoying a temporary vogue in England; he therefore chose to make battle scenes his speciality. He exhibited regularly at the Royal Academy from 1879. The drama and violence of his pictures found particular favour with the army and the Crown, and he received several commissions to commemorate British military exploits in Egypt and the Sudan (e.g. *H.R.H. The Duke of Connaught with the Guards at Tel-el-Kebir*, 1884; British Royal Col., on loan to Camberley, Army Staff Coll.). He rarely witnessed battle himself and as an illustrator it was his practice to work up sketches by other artists sent from the site of a campaign. His best-known drawn work was for the *Illustrated London News* (his depictions of the Irish poor in 1880 in this journal were particularly admired by van Gogh), and *Boy's Own Paper*.

WRITINGS
Random Recollections (London, 1914)
BIBLIOGRAPHY
F. Villiers: *Peaceful Personalities and Warriors* (London, 1907), pp. 24–5
Obituary, *The Times* (18 Aug 1927)
PAUL USHERWOOD

Woodward, Benjamin. *See under* DEANE & WOODWARD.

Woodyer, Henry (*b* Guildford, Surrey, 1816; *d* Padworth, Berks, 10 Aug 1896). English architect. From a wealthy family, he was educated at Eton College and at Merton College, Oxford. In the 1840s he may have met A. W. N. Pugin, whose influence upon him is notable. He lived at the same address as William Butterfield at The Adelphi, near the Embankment, Westminster, and seems to have assisted him briefly in 1844, sharing his vigorous attitude to architecture. By 1845 he was designing churches in an assured 'Middle Pointed' (Decorated) style, and in 1849–51 built Holy Innocents, Highnam, Glos, for his school friend Thomas Gambier-Parry, who decorated its interior with murals. He then moved to Guildford, and in 1852 to Grafham, Surrey, where he built Grafham Grange (begun 1854; altered 1893–1906), for himself, and his most characteristic church, St Andrew's (1860–61), as a memorial to his wife. Although his style did not develop widely, his spiky, tight detailing shows ingenuity, typically in peculiar dormer-windows, traceried screens, and integrated arrangements of reredos, east window and roof. The naturalistic foliage of his corbels, capitals and reredoses foreshadows the designs of the Arts and Crafts Movement. He was never a member of any professional bodies.

UNPUBLISHED SOURCES

London, Council for the Care of Churches [MS. of G. L. Barnes: *Henry Woodyer, Architect, 1876–96*, (n.d.)]

ANTHONY QUINEY

Woollams & Co. English wallpaper manufacturing company founded in London *c.* 1835 by William Woollams (1782–1840). He was apprenticed to John Sherringham (*fl* 1780s), a master paper-stainer, and by 1837 had a factory in Marylebone, London, where he printed papers for J. G. Crace and other clients. Two of his three sons, William Woollams (*d* 1859) and Henry Woollams (*d* 1876), carried on the business, which in 1876 passed to their cousin Frederic Aumonier, who had worked as Henry's assistant since 1853.

The firm specialized in high-quality block prints and flocks for the luxury end of the market (*see* WALLPAPER, colour pl. IV, fig. 2). At the Great Exhibition in 1851 in the Crystal Palace, London, the firm showed block-printed damasks, gilded flocks and panel decorations. In the 1860s rich three-dimensional designs were printed in bright colours, often using large numbers of blocks and featuring flowers within Rococo scrolls together with Gothic motifs flocked on a diaper background ('Diaper' pattern, 1867; U. Manchester, Whitworth A.G.). Cylinder machine prints in up to eight colours were also produced from *c.* 1849, but the firm was best known for luxury products. Competition from embossed wall coverings led to the development of new ranges including stamped gold papers (1864), embossed imitation leathers (1866) and raised flocks (*c.* 1877), a technique that combined embossing and flocking.

Later collections featured the work of such freelance designers as A. F. Brophy (1846–1912), George Haité and C. F. A. Voysey. Aumonier was a close friend of Arthur Silver, and both the SILVER STUDIO and Frederic's sister Louise Aumonier (1846–1901) contributed designs to the firm. In 1895 a range of machine prints was introduced, but falling demand for papers at the top end of the market led to the takeover of the company by Arthur Sanderson & Sons in 1900.

BIBLIOGRAPHY

A. V. Sugden and J. L. Edmondson: *A History of English Wallpaper, 1509–1914* (London, 1926)
C. C. Oman and J. Hamilton: *Wallpapers: A History and Illustrated Catalogue of the Collection of the Victoria and Albert Museum* (London, 1982)
A Decorative Art: 19th Century Wallpapers in the Whitworth Art Gallery (exh. cat. by J. Banham, U. Manchester, Whitworth A.G., 1985)

CLARE TAYLOR

Woollaston, Sir M(ountford) T(osswill) (*b* Taranaki, 11 April 1911). New Zealand painter. He resolved to become a painter in the early 1930s, when the influence of early modernism was only just beginning to trickle down to colonial New Zealand. He had little formal training, but early paintings such as *Artist's Wife* (*c.* 1937; Auckland, C.A.G.) show the influence of Paul Cézanne, absorbed through reproductions. Similarly, the examples of R. N. Field, arriving from Europe, and Helen F. V. Scales (1887–1985), returning from there, were crucial. Field's paintings released him from naturalistic colour, while Scales's showed him how to deploy this released colour for spatial effects.

From the 1950s Woollaston began to increase the scale of his paintings, developing the gestural and apparently spontaneous approach that marked his mature style. Dispensing with detail, his broad handling drew greater attention to the logic by which his paintings were constructed. In works such as *Above Wellington* (1.76×2.74 m, 1986; Wellington, Mus. NZ, Te Papa Tongarewa) he continued to develop his formal means with increasing authority.

BIBLIOGRAPHY

R. O'Reilly: 'M. T. Woollaston: Art and Development', *Landfall*, ii/3 (1948), pp. 208–13
M. T. Woollaston (exh. cat. by L. Bieringa, Manawatu, A.G., 1973)
G. Barnett: 'M. T. Woollaston: The Later Works', *A. NZ*, 44 (1987), pp. 72–7

G. BARNETT

Woollett, William (*b* Maidstone, 15 Aug 1735; *d* London, 23 May 1785). English printmaker. Apprenticed to John Tinney (*fl* 1729–61) in London, he was also a member of the St Martin's Lane Academy. His earliest works are such staples of trade engraving as bill heads (Fagan, nos 4–6), watchpapers (F 8–9) and views of country houses and Oxford University. He rose to fame with his print of the *Destruction of the Children of Niobe* (1761; F 42; exh. cat., no. 36) after the painting by Richard Wilson (*c.* 1759–60; New Haven, CT, Yale Cent. Brit. A.), which was a bestseller. While he earned £150 for making the plate, the publisher John Boydell is said to have made £2000, partly from continental sales. His technique aimed at conveying a full range of tones and surfaces, and involved extensive preliminary etching to different depths, followed by engraving. His work was admired by French engravers, who had traditionally enjoyed a higher reputation than their English counterparts. He was a friend of George Stubbs and made prints of the *Spanish Pointer* (1768; priv. col., see F 59; Lennox-Boyd, no. 10) and the quartet of paintings *Shooting* (1769–71; F 67–70; LB 11–14; paintings, New Haven, CT, Yale Cent. Brit. A.). In 1769 the painter Thomas Jones was moved to call Woollett 'the first Landscape Engraver in the World'. He was involved with the Society of Artists in the period 1765–77 as variously a Fellow, a Director and Secretary. Just before the publication of another major work, the *Death of General Wolfe* (1776; F 93) after Benjamin West's painting (1770; Ottawa, N.G.) of a contemporary subject treated in the manner of a history painting, Woollett was named Engraver in Ordinary to George III. Benjamin West and John Boydell were among the contributors to the cost of erecting a marble monument by Thomas Banks in Woollett's honour in the West Cloister of Westminster Abbey.

BIBLIOGRAPHY
L. Fagan: *A Catalogue Raisonné of the Engraved Works of William Woollett* (London, 1885) [F]
Painters and Engraving: The Reproductive Print from Hogarth to Wilkie (exh. cat. by D. Alexander and R. Godfrey, New Haven, CT, Yale Cent. Brit. A., 1980)
S. Lambert: *The Image Multiplied: Five Centuries of Reproductions of Paintings and Drawings* (London, 1987)
C. Lennox-Boyd, R. Dixon and T. Clayton: *George Stubbs: The Complete Engraved Works* (London, 1989) [LB]

ELIZABETH MILLER

Woolley, Ken(neth Frank) (*b* Sydney, 29 May 1933). Australian architect. He was a trainee in the New South Wales Government Architect's Branch in 1950–54 while studying at the University of Sydney, where he graduated in 1955. He continued as a design architect for the government until 1963, except for 18 months (1956–7) spent in Europe, including a period working for Chamberlin, Powell & Bon in London. Woolley achieved early recognition as the project architect for the Fisher Library (1957–62), University of Sydney, and the NSW State Office Block (1960–64), Sydney. Both are modernist, largely glass-walled buildings that drew inspiration from the work of Mies van der Rohe, but sun-shading was incorporated in their façades by the projection of floor slabs. In 1961 Woolley began to design a series of low-cost house types for the speculative housing market, principally for the firm of Pettit & Sevitt, and these provided radically improved models for suburban housing. His own house (1961–2) at Mosman, Sydney, built of untreated brick and sawn timber with a tiled, monopitch roof, is one of the most celebrated houses of the SYDNEY SCHOOL. Designed on a square module and stepped in both plan and section to fit its steep bushland site, it paralleled contemporary Dutch structuralist ideas in its spatial richness, achieved with rigorously limited means. In 1964 Woolley became a partner in the practice of Ancher, Mortlock, Murray & Woolley (after 1975 Ancher, Mortlock & Woolley). Larger brick-and-tile buildings in the idiom of the Sydney school include the Students Union (1964–7) at the University of Newcastle, reminiscent of work by Alvar Aalto, and terraced hillside housing (1965–8) at Darling Point, Sydney. After the 1960s Woolley's architecture was characterized by a great flexibility of design approach, governed by his concern for appropriateness to place. Important later works include the orange-tile-clad Australian Embassy (1973–8), Bangkok, which responds to the local climate with an open undercroft bridging a lake; the serpentine Park Hyatt Hotel (1986–9), Sydney, which follows the curving shoreline of Campbell's Cove; and the ABC Radio and Orchestral Centre (1987–92), Sydney. In 1993 he was awarded the Gold Medal of the Royal Australian Institute of Architects.

BIBLIOGRAPHY
Contemp. Architects
J. Taylor, P. Cox and H. Guida: *Australian Architects 2: Ken Woolley* (Redhill, ACT, 1985)
H. Beck and D. Jackson: 'Ken Woolley', *Archit. Australia*, lxxxii/5 (1993), pp. 28–35 [RAIA Gold Medal issue]

RORY SPENCE

Woolley, Sir (Charles) Leonard (*b* Upper Clapton, 17 Apr 1880; *d* London, 20 Feb 1960). English archaeologist. He was educated at New College, Oxford, where he took a First in *Literae Humaniores* (1903) and a Second in Theology (1904), and he became an assistant in the Ashmolean Museum under Arthur Evans in 1905. In 1907 he joined D. Randall McIver in excavating at Karanog and Buhen in Nubia. After a brief period excavating in Italy, he was chosen in 1912 to succeed Reginald Campbell Thompson as Director of the British Museum excavations at CARCHEMISH in north Syria, working there until 1914 and also in 1920.

In 1920–21 Woolley directed the excavations at EL-AMARNA on behalf of the Egypt Exploration Society, but his most significant work began in 1922, when he was invited by the British Museum and the Museum of the University of Philadelphia to direct excavations at UR in southern Iraq. During his 12 seasons there, and at the small neighbouring temple site of TELL AL-UBAID (1922–34), he revealed the rich Sumerian Early Dynastic civilization, notably in the 'Royal Cemetery'. He was knighted in 1935. His final excavations (1936–9 and 1946–9) were at TELL ATCHANA (anc. Alalakh) and the small neighbouring coastal site of Al-Mina in the Turkish Hatay. During World War II, with the rank of Lieutenant Colonel, he had responsibility for the art and libraries of Europe, a reflection of his eminence in the art world.

Woolley's main contribution to art history was his uncovering of important monuments and artefacts. Though these included useful evidence from Tell Atchana, el-Amarna and Al-Mina, the most notable material was that of the 3rd millennium BC Sumerian city states at Ur and Tell al-Ubaid. He published his results with exemplary rapidity, describing his discoveries in clear, concise English. However his publications on art as such, *The Development of Sumerian Art* (London, 1935) and *Mesopotamia and the Middle East* (published posthumously, London, 1961), made no real contribution in terms of evaluation or synthesis.

WRITINGS
Dead Towns and Living Men (London, 1920, rev. 1954)
Ur Excavations, 10 vols (London and Philadelphia, 1927–76)
A Forgotten Kingdom (London, 1953, rev. 1959)
Spadework (London, 1953)
Excavations at Ur (London, 1954)
Alalakh: An Account of the Excavations at Tell Atchana in the Hatay, 1937–1949 (London, 1955)
As I Seem to Remember (London, 1962)
BIBLIOGRAPHY
DNB

T. C. MITCHELL

Woolner, Thomas (*b* Hadleigh, Suffolk, 17 Dec 1825; *d* London, 7 Oct 1892). English sculptor and poet. He ranks with John Henry Foley as the leading sculptor of mid-Victorian England. He trained with William Behnes and in 1842 enrolled as a student at the Royal Academy, London. In 1844 he exhibited at Westminster Hall, London, a life-size plaster group, the *Death of Boadicea* (destr.), in an unsuccessful attempt to obtain sculptural commissions for the Houses of Parliament. His earliest important surviving work is the statuette of *Puck* (plaster, 1845–7; C. G. Woolner priv. col.), which was admired by William Holman Hunt and helped to secure Woolner's admission in 1848 to the Pre-Raphaelite Brotherhood. The work's Shakespearean theme and lifelike execution, stressing Puck's humorous malice rather than traditional ideal beauty, made it highly appealing. Although eclipsed by Hunt, John Everett Millais and Dante Gabriel Rossetti, Woolner was an important figure in the Brotherhood. He contributed poetry to its journal, *The Germ* (1850), and his work was committed to truthfulness to nature more consistently than that of any other Pre-Raphaelite, except for Hunt. This is evident in Woolner's monument to *William Wordsworth* (marble, 1851; St Oswald, Grasmere, Cumbria). This relief portrait, which conveys both the poet's physiognomy and his intellect, is flanked by botanically faithful renditions of flowers, emphasizing Wordsworth's doctrine that in Woolner's words, 'common things can be made equally suggestive and instructive with the most exalted subjects'.

Like the other Pre-Raphaelites in the early 1850s, Woolner received few commissions, and in 1852 he emigrated to Australia. His move inspired Ford Madox Brown's *The Last of England* (see BROWN, FORD MADOX, fig. 2). Woolner was no more successful in gold prospecting than in sculpture, although he found some demand for his portraits. While still in Britain he had begun to model medallion portraits (e.g. *Alfred Tennyson*, 1849–50; Lincoln, Usher Gal.) that were cast in bronze, a medium not explored by any other artist working in Britain until Alphonse Legros in the 1880s. The medallions Woolner modelled in Australia included *Charles Joseph La Trobe* (1853–4; Melbourne, N.G. Victoria). Like their marble counterpart, the *Wordsworth* monument, they were executed in precise profile; their accurate, detailed modelling was unmatched by any contemporary artist. Woolner's failure to obtain the commission for a statue of *William Charles Wentworth* in Sydney prompted his return in 1854 to London, where he subsequently became much more successful, receiving commissions both for ideal sculpture (of imagined subjects) and for portraiture. The *Lord's Prayer* or *Mother and Child* (1856–7; Wallington House, Northumb., NT) portrays the triumph of Christianity, embodied in the mother and child, over savagery, represented by a relief figure derived from Hunt's *Rienzi* (1848–9). A similar emotional tenderness is found in the life-size group *Constance and Arthur* (marble, 1857–62; Barkway House, Suffolk), a fusion of portrait and ideal sculpture, which portrays a deaf-mute brother and sister, Constance and Arthur Fairbairn, seated together in close communication. Its uncompromising naturalism saves the work from sentimentality, and it drew much admiration at the 1862 London International Exhibition and inspired a poem (*Deaf and Dumb: A Group by Woolner*) by Robert Browning.

Most of Woolner's work consisted of portrait statues; the marble bust of his friend *Alfred Tennyson* (1856–7; Cambridge, Trinity Coll.) helped to establish his success in this area, leading Read (1984) to regard him as 'arguably the greatest of the Pre-Raphaelite portraitists'. The success of the bust, which shares the realistic characteristics of

Woolner's other work and shows his enjoyment in rendering the textures of contemporary costume, led to the production of several replicas and to numerous commissions for other such works. Among these were busts of *Thomas Combe* (1863) and *William Ewart Gladstone* (1866; both Oxford, Ashmolean) and of *John Henry Newman* (1866; Oxford, Keble Coll.). Several busts also served as monuments, notably those of *Richard Cobden* (1865) and *Charles Kingsley* (1876; both London, Westminster Abbey).

By the 1860s Woolner's oeuvre extended to portrait statuary. A much-praised work that was exhibited at the South Kensington Museum before being shipped to New Zealand was *John Robert Godley* (see fig.). Woolner rendered Godley with Pre-Raphaelite realism, showing him clutching his hat and shawl; but also, with a classical dignity, contemplating his task as founder of the Canterbury Settlement. The *Godley* statue's success led to the commission for *Henry Temple, 3rd Viscount Palmerston* (bronze, 1867–76; London, Parliament Square). Woolner's other major portrait statues include *Prince Albert* (marble, 1864; Oxford, U. Mus.), which shows Woolner's virtuosity in rendering drapery folds; *William Whewell* (marble, 1873; Cambridge, Trinity Coll.), the realism of which extends to conveying the moisture of the eyes; and the seated *John Stuart Mill* (bronze, 1878; London, Victoria Embankment Gdns), the intellectual intensity of which compares with that of the *Godley* statue. In addition, Woolner made

Thomas Woolner: *John Robert Godley* (detail), bronze, over life-size, 1863–7 (Christchurch, NZ, Cathedral Square)

numerous statues for British colonies, the best known being the dramatically gesturing portrait of *Captain James Cook* (bronze, 1874–8; Sydney, Hyde Park). Woolner's most important architectural sculpture comprised eleven marble statues and two reliefs for Alfred Waterhouse's Manchester Assize Courts (1863–7; destr.; some statues, Manchester, Courts of Justice). The medieval severity and simplicity of these sculptures attempted to suit both their historical subjects and their architectural Gothic Revival setting.

To some extent Woolner's style softened by the mid-1870s, although he remained consistent in his pursuit of realism. His last work, *The Housemaid* (bronze, 1892; London, Salters' Company), is a rare item in his oeuvre of contemporary genre sculpture. It shows the kneeling maid, dressed in her plain frock and cap, wringing out her cloth. The work assumes a classical grace without compromising the essential realism. *The Housemaid* may be interpreted as Woolner's corrective to what he probably regarded as the gimmickry of the New Sculpture. While by the mid-1880s this movement had largely eclipsed Woolner's style, the demand for his work remained high, as did his personal reputation. Edmund Gosse, the champion of the New Sculpture, praised Woolner in 1883 for his 'joyous and robust' qualities and his independence of Neo-classical conservatism.

Woolner was elected Associate of the Royal Academy in 1871 and a Member in 1874; in 1877 he was appointed its Professor of Sculpture, but resigned in 1879 without having delivered a lecture there. Woolner was a friend of Thomas Carlyle, Edward Lear, Gladstone, Tennyson and Robert Browning, and was thus one of very few 19th-century sculptors to associate on equal terms with eminent contemporaries. *The Times*, in his obituary, called him the 'uncompromising foe of shams, of claptrap, and of superficiality', and his poetry was widely acknowledged as sharing the truthfulness and force of his sculpture.

BIBLIOGRAPHY
DNB; Gunnis
F. T. Palgrave: *Essays on Art* (London and Cambridge, 1866)
E. Gosse: 'Living English Sculptors', *C. Monthly Mag.*, xxvi (1883), pp. 163–85
A. Woolner: *Thomas Woolner, R.A., Sculptor and Poet: His Life in Letters* (London, 1917), p. 334
R. Trevelyan: 'Thomas Woolner, Pre-Raphaelite Sculptor: The Beginnings of Success', *Apollo*, cv (1978), pp. 200–05
B. Read: *Victorian Sculpture* (New Haven and London, 1982), p. 24
——: 'Was There Pre-Raphaelite Sculpture?', *Pre-Raphaelite Papers*, ed. L. Parris (London, 1984), pp. 97–110
The Pre-Raphaelites (exh. cat., London, Tate, 1984)
M. Stocker: '"Ready to Move and Speak": Thomas Woolner's Statue of Godley', *Bull. NZ A. Hist.*, ix (1985), pp. 19–25
Pre-Raphaelite Sculpture: Nature and Imagination in British Sculpture, 1848–1914 (exh. cat., ed. B. Read and J. Barnes; London, Matthiesen F.A.; Birmingham, Mus. & A.G.; 1991–2), pp. 21–45, 141–67

MARK STOCKER

Wootton, John (*b* Snitterfield, Warwicks, *c.* 1682; *d* London, 13 Nov 1764). English painter. He probably received some instruction from Jan Wyck in the 1690s, and he was possibly patronized from an early age by the aristocratic households of Beaufort and Coventry (as was Wyck), perhaps while working as a page to Lady Anne Somerset at Snitterfield House, Warwicks. However, there seems to be no real evidence for this save his early painted view of the house and the family's later acquisition of many of his works. Joseph Farington saw a painting of *Diana and the Nymphs* (1707; untraced) at Antony House, Cornwall, but Wootton's earliest extant dated work is the horse portrait *Bonny Black* (1711; Belvoir Castle, Leics). By this time he had begun to establish himself in London, having moved there before his first marriage, to Elizabeth Walsh, in 1706. He was a subscriber to the first English Academy of Painting and Drawing in 1711 and by 1717 had been elected a steward of the Virtuosi Club of St Luke's.

Despite being known primarily as a horse painter, Wootton never specialized in sporting art alone. Partly for this reason, and partly through his patrons, he became generally well respected and evidently wealthy, moving *c.* 1727 to Cavendish Square. George Vertue wrote at this point:

> Mr J. Wotton [sic] by his assiduous application & the prudent management of his affairs rais'd his reputation & fortune to a great height being well esteemed for his skill in landskip paintings amongst the professors of art & in great vogue & favour with many persons of ye greatest quality, his often visiting of Newmarket in the seasons produced him much imployment in painting race horses, for which he had good prices, 40gns. for a horse and 20 for one of a half-leng cloth.

Wootton's prices for sporting pictures were controversial (George II was among those who doubted the value for money Wootton's work provided) but his position as England's foremost sporting artist between *c.* 1710 and *c.* 1740 was indisputable.

In his early hunting scenes he skilfully adapted the compositional and stylistic formulae provided by Wyck and his Netherlandish predecessors. For horse portraits he looked to Abraham van Diepenbeeck, Philips Wouwerman and Aelbert Cuyp, but for his views of Newmarket he developed a topographical approach essentially of his own making. In all three areas he worked prolifically (perhaps with studio assistance) and was patronized widely. In his later sporting work he attempted to 'classicize' his subject-matter through stylistic borrowings from Claude Lorrain and Gaspard Dughet, aiming to elevate sport pictorially to the high moral status claimed for it by its advocates. By *c.* 1740, however, the reality of contemporary sport was understood in wider circles to be anything but morally admirable. John Constable's later condemnation of Wootton as one who 'painted country gentlemen in their wigs and jockey caps, and placed them in Italian landscapes resembling Gaspar Poussin [Dughet] except in truth and force' was anticipated from the early 1740s by patrons who began to turn to the ultimately less ambitious art of sporting painters such as James Seymour. In the sporting sphere Wootton's swan-song was the series of large-scale paintings (*c.* 1730–40) produced for the entrance halls of Althorp House (Northants), Longleat House (Wilts) and Badminton House (Glos), all of which survive *in situ*.

As a landscape painter, Wootton is remembered both for his detailed topographical views, such as *View from Box Hill, Surrey* (1716; Lady Anne Cavendish Bentinck priv. col.), and for his pastiches of the imaginary classical landscapes of Gaspar Dughet and Claude Lorrain, such as

John Wootton: *Preparing for the Hunt*, oil on canvas, 1.20×1.25 m, *c.* 1740–50 (New Haven, CT, Yale Center for British Art)

Coastal Scene with a Rock Arch (Chillington Hall, Staffs). As a topographical artist, he competed unsuccessfully with Peter Tillemans (also his rival in sporting art). Although he seems never to have visited Italy (as was once believed), his contribution in the field of classical landscape was substantial, though Richard Wilson exploited more eloquently the taste for ideal landscape that Wootton had helped to create.

Despite his humble birth and evidently scant education, Wootton was clearly attracted to 'literary' landscape painting, encouraged by his patron Edward Harley, 2nd Earl of Oxford, a staunch Tory who patronized a famous coterie of literary figures. Through Harley, Wootton came into contact with John Gay, Alexander Pope, Matthew Prior and Jonathan Swift, though quite how seriously they took their 'horse painting' colleague is not clear. He was undoubtedly a more prominent member of the group of painters and sculptors, including Michael Dahl, Christian Friedrich Zincke and John Michael Rysbrack, who also gathered at Harley's house, Welbeck Abbey, Notts. Wootton is shown standing among such figures in Gawen Hamilton's *A Club of Artists* (1735; London, N.P.G.).

Wootton's experience in painting such scenes as *Preparing for the Hunt* (*c.* 1740–50; New Haven, CT, Yale Cent. Brit. A.; see fig.), as well as his numerous sporting and landscape paintings, brought him commissions for battle pictures. In this field he attempted some ambitious essays in a Netherlandish vein, such as the *Siege of Tournay* (1742; Royal Col.) and the *Battle of Blenheim* (*c.* 1743; London, N. Army Mus.). However, his abilities were generally better suited to small-scale works of simple composition. Wootton was usually a sound judge of his own shortcomings and frequently employed other painters, especially portrait painters, to contribute to his more important canvases. He collaborated with Dahl, Thomas Gibson, William Hogarth, Thomas Hudson, Charles Jervas, Godfrey Kneller and Jonathan Richardson. He may also have worked with the landscape painter Thomas Payne (*fl* 1762–7; possibly Wootton's pupil), though any professional cooperation with George Lambert (i), with whom he was competing for patronage by the 1750s, is unlikely. Wootton gave up painting by *c.* 1760 and sold his extensive collection of paintings, prints and drawings (both contemporary and Old Master) early in 1761. He was outlived by his son Henry, who as a child had been portrayed (with his family) by Gawen Hamilton, holding a landscape drawing in his hand; it is not known whether the younger Wootton later pursued an artistic career.

Wootton's art was little admired after the late 18th century, and only from the mid-20th century was it accorded some significance in the history of the development of English landscape painting. Wootton's artistic versatility and considerable output, allied to the affable relations he enjoyed with his patrons, were the envy of many of his contemporaries. He may have been, as one commentator wrote, both 'a cunning fellow' and 'the dirtiest painter I ever saw', but—unlike his immediate successors at the forefront of landscape and sporting art, Richard Wilson and George Stubbs—he was rarely short of employment: a testimony to his sophisticated business acumen and undoubted willingness to work in as many genres as his market required.

BIBLIOGRAPHY

W. Gilbey: *Animal Painters from the Year 1650* (London, 1900)
G. Kendall: 'Notes on the Life of John Wootton with a List of Engravings after his Pictures', *Walpole Soc.*, xxi (1932–3), pp. 23–42 [the principal biographical source for Wootton's middle and later career]
'The Note-books of George Vertue', *Walpole Soc.*, xxii (1933–4), p. 34
Noble Exercise: The Sporting Ideal in Eighteenth-century British Art (exh. cat., ed. S. Deuchar; New Haven, CT, Yale Cent. Brit. A., 1982)
John Wootton, 1682–1764: Landscapes and Sporting Art in Early Georgian England (exh. cat., ed. A. Meyer; London, Kenwood House, 1984)

STEPHEN DEUCHAR

Worcester. English centre of ceramic production. Pottery was made in and around Worcester, Hereford & Worcs, from pre-Roman times but its importance as a centre of ceramic production did not begin until the mid-18th century. In 1751 the Worcester Porcelain Co. was founded by Dr John Wall (1708–76), a physician, William Davis, an apothecary, and 13 other partners in Warmstry House on the banks of the River Severn. In the articles of agreement it was stated that the special porcelain body had been invented by Wall and Davis, but it has subsequently been proved that it had been developed from that used by Benjamin Lund in the first Bristol porcelain factory and earlier at the short-lived Limehouse porcelain factory in London. The recipe, using soapstone (steatite) from the Lizard peninsula, Cornwall, produced a fine, soft-paste porcelain that did not crack or craze in contact with hot liquids, which made it especially useful for tewares.

By August 1752 the company advertised in the *Gentleman's Magazine* a sale at the Worcester Music Meeting for a 'great variety of ware, and 'tis said at a moderate price'. Teawares, sauce and cream boats, jugs and pickle dishes were made in large quantities, mostly painted with chinoiseries in underglaze cobalt blue. A quantity of multicoloured ware was also produced, some of it imitating the styles of the Meissen porcelain factory. At first shapes were based on English silverware but by 1760 they had become more influenced by East Asian forms. Proportions were always harmonious, with handles and spouts being well balanced, which made for a high degree of practicality. By 1755 the use of transfer-printing increased production, thus widening opportunities for a larger market. The public success of wares with Robert Hancock's portrait of Frederick II, King of Prussia, in 1757 (see fig.) justified the opening of a trade warehouse in London. In the 1760s some white or partly decorated, underglazed wares were sold to James Giles (1718–80) in London for enamelling, and the factory increasingly used coloured grounds, such as the famous blue-scale ground, and elaborate decoration in the style of the Sèvres porcelain factory. Some vases and figures were also produced, but tableware remained the major product.

In the 1770s there was a rapid escalation in the field of blue-printed wares, especially after the death of Dr Wall in 1776 when the factory was continued by William Davis. In 1783 the company became Davis & Flight after the business was bought by Thomas Flight (1726–1800). For a few years the factory struggled, producing mainly poor-quality, blue-printed wares. In 1788 a visit by George III, who bought a service of a pattern called 'Royal Lily', gave the factory a much needed boost. The granting of the Royal Warrant in 1789 set the seal of approval on the rejuvenated firm.

About 1787 Robert Chamberlain, who had been a painter at Dr Wall's factory, set up a rival Worcester firm in the Diglis area of the town. At first he produced a proto, hard-paste porcelain, then a bone china and also a highly translucent frit porcelain called 'Regent China', which marked the patronage of the Prince Regent (later George IV). In 1802 the company produced a Japan-style

Worcester bell-shaped porcelain mug, transfer-printed with portrait of Frederick II, King of Prussia, from an engraving by Robert Hancock, h. 112 mm, *c.* 1757 (London, Phillips Fine Art Auctioneers)

service for Horatio, 1st Viscount Nelson (1758–1805), following his visit to the factory.

The Davis & Flight firm was called Flight & Barr from 1792 after a new partner, Martin Barr (1757–1813), was brought in. Family changes resulted in a change of name in 1804 to Barr, Flight & Barr. From 1813 to 1840 the firm was known as Flight, Barr & Barr. During these periods the quality of production reached its apogee, the emphasis still being on useful wares in the soapstone formula. Ground-laying, painting, jewelling and gilding equalled anything produced in Europe, and many of the craftsmen were trained by Thomas Baxter (1782–1821), who had a major stylistic influence on the factory. Typical of the firm's products in the early 1800s were rich Japans or Imari palettes and high Regency feather, shell and bird motifs, and landscapes set in jewelled panels within coloured grounds. In 1830 a banqueting service was made for William IV, but within a few years the cessation of the supply of soapstone and the need to produce bone china seems to have led to a gradual loss of enthusiasm.

In 1840 Flight, Barr & Barr merged with the Chamberlain factory to become Chamberlain & Co. In 1852 a partnership called Kerr & Binns took over the concern and concentrated production at the Diglis factory. Artistic qualities improved, and in 1862 a joint stock company called the Worcester Royal Porcelain Co. was formed; this title continued to be used in the late 20th century. The factory increasingly concentrated on such ornamental objects as figures and vases, modelled by James Hadley (1837–1903) and made in the popular glazed parian porcelain. In 1889 the company acquired another rival firm, Grainger & Co., which had been established c. 1806, and in 1905 it purchased James Hadley's breakaway factory, which had been formed in 1896.

In the 20th century Royal Worcester, as it is generally known, developed an international reputation, especially in the fields of porcelain ovenware and limited-edition bone china figures of birds and horses by such modellers as Dorothy Doughty (1892–1962) and Doris Lindner (d 1979). Their useful wares in bone china have also been of a consistently high standard both in the revival of traditional styles and in the introduction of modern shapes and patterns.

For further illustration see ENGLAND, fig. 63.

BIBLIOGRAPHY
H. Sandon: Worcester Porcelain, 1751–1793 (London, 1969/R 1980)
——: Royal Worcester Porcelain from 1862 (London, 1973/R 1984)
——: Flight and Barr Worcester Porcelain (Woodbridge, 1978)
L. Branyan, N. French and J. Sandon: Worcester Blue and White Porcelain (London, 1981, rev. 1989)
G. Godden: Chamberlain–Worcester Porcelain (London, 1982)
S. Spero: Worcester Porcelain (London, 1984)
HENRY SANDON

Worcestre [Botener; Worcester], **William** (b Bristol, 1415; d c. 1483). English topographer. He is the first recorded English antiquary and is particularly known for his *Itinerary*. An undergraduate at Oxford in 1432, he entered the service of Sir John Fastolf (?1378–1459) and travelled widely as an administrator of Fastolf's many estates. He spent 12 years as Fastolf's executor, and in the settlement he was awarded property in Norwich and

Southwark and a house in Bristol. Worcestre's principal antiquarian adventure was a journey from Norwich to St Michael's Mount in Cornwall. He left a daily diary of his trip (Cambridge, Corpus Christi Coll., MS. 210). The manuscript includes material for a chronicle of recent history, and Worcestre seems also to have been collecting information for a topography of England. He noted inter-town distances, courses of rivers and lists of bridges, and extracted details from chronicles and calendars. He was keenly interested in the classical revival, and to the plan of a historical guidebook he added detailed architectural descriptions with dimensions, the latter recorded either with a measure or by 'steppys meis' (Harvey, p. 28). His great achievement was his Survey of Bristol, included in MS. 210, the most painstaking and detailed piece of topographical fieldwork undertaken before the great topographers of the next century started work. A plan of medieval Bristol has been reconstructed from his notes.

UNPUBLISHED SOURCES
Cambridge, Corpus Christi Coll., MS. 210 [diary of journey from Norwich to St Michael's Mount]

WRITINGS
J. Nasmith, ed.: Itineraria Symonis Simeonis et Willelmi de Worcestre, quibus accedit Tractatus de Metro (Cambridge, 1778)
J. H. Harvey, ed.: William Worcestre: Itineraries (Oxford, 1969)

BIBLIOGRAPHY
DNB
J. Dallaway: Antiquities of Bristow in the Middle Centuries including the Topography by William Worcestre and the Life of William Canynges (Bristol, 1834)
K. B. McFarlane: 'William Worcester, a Preliminary Survey', Studies Presented to Sir Hilary Jenkinson (Oxford, 1957), pp. 196–221
JOHN HOPKINS

Work of art. See ART, WORK OF.

Workshop. See STUDIO.

Workshop for the Restoration of Unfelt Sensations [Latv. Nebijušu Sajūtu Restaurēšanas Darbnīca; NSRD]. Latvian association of artists, architects and designers, active from September 1982 until 1989. It introduced video and computer art, new music and hybridized art genres to a conservative public in Latvia towards the end of the Soviet period. Its very name implied preconditions of stricture and privation, and its multidisciplinary methods served to expand critical discourse when Latvian cultural identity and collective political consciousness were undergoing a symbiotic revival, with the restoration of independence as a goal. NSRD founders Juris Boiko (b 1954) and Hardijs Lediņš (b 1955), both self-taught artists, organized Actions that some critics considered to be subtle acts of political dissent. Their *Walk to Bolderāja*, an annual pilgrimage begun in 1982 to an off-limits Soviet submarine base (representing thwarted access to the West), took place along railroad tracks that recalled the mass deportations of Balts to Siberia during the 1940s, to which Boiko's parents fell victim. Workshop members included Aigars Sparāns (b 1955), Dace Šenberga (b 1967) and Imants Žodžiks (b 1955). Together they produced numerous video projects, music recordings and performances, and three exhibitions. Much of this work was created under the rubric Approximate Art, an admixture of Zen Buddhism and Californian high-tech philosophy originated by

Lediņš that is also associated with the artist Miervaldis Polis (*b* 1948). In keeping with its global focus NSRD pursued international contacts and collaborations, which members continued in their subsequent individual careers.

BIBLIOGRAPHY
'Werkstatt zur Restauration nie empfundener Gefühle', *Riga: Lettische avantgarde* (exh. cat., W. Berlin, Staatl. Ksthalle, 1988), pp. 68–73
'Ungefähre Kunst in Riga: Gespräch zwischen der "Werkstatt zur Restauration nie verspürter Empfindungen" und Eckhart Gillen', *Niemandsland,* 5 (1988), pp. 32–50

MARK ALLEN SVEDE

World of Art [Rus. Mir Iskusstva]. Group of Russian artists and writers active 1898–1906, revived as an exhibiting society, 1910–24. SERGE DIAGHILEV provided the motive force for the formation of the group in St Petersburg in 1898, and for the publication of its journal, *Mir Iskusstva*, from 1898 to December 1904. The Nevsky Pickwickians, grouped around Alexandre Benois, preceded the World of Art and formed its initial core. In the first issue of the journal Diaghilev, who with Benois had a wide knowledge of recent western European art, declared his commitment to a renaissance of Russian art, avoiding pale reflections of foreign trends yet also resisting a narrow nationalism. The World of Art provided a focus for Symbolist and Aesthetic tendencies in Russia, but its diversity of talents meant that it had only a limited degree of stylistic coherence.

World of Art group members stressed vigour and elegance simultaneously, a combination well illustrated in the work of Léon Bakst (see fig.). They also emphasized individualism and a sense of decoration, and they openly embraced exoticism allied to Post-Impressionist or Symbolist techniques, design and themes. The World of Art also sought an interaction of the arts. The colour experiments of the composer Aleksandr Skryabin (1872–1915) and the Symbolist work of the Lithuanian painter–composer Mikalojus Čiurlionis were much admired within the group. Ultimately this striving for a synthesis of the arts found vigorous expression in the production of Diaghilev's BALLETS RUSSES, founded in 1909. Here the designers were equal in importance to the composers, choreographers and dancers as contributors to the spectacle.

Diaghilev had begun to organize exhibitions in 1897, and he had sole responsibility for the first World of Art exhibition. This opened at the Stieglitz School of Technical Drawing in St Petersburg on 22 January 1899. Entitled *Mezhdunarodskaya vystavka kartin zhurnala 'Mir Iskusstva'* ('International Exhibition of Paintings from the "World of Art" Journal')—the only international exhibition held by the World of Art—it assembled over three hundred works from nine countries. The Russian contingent included Bakst, Benois and Konstantin Somov from St Petersburg as well as such Moscow painters as Konstantin Korovin, Isaak Levitan, Mikhail Nesterov and Mikhail Vrubel'. Foreign contributors provided a spectacular if inconsistent display, with works by Arnold Böcklin, Eugène Carrière, Degas, Akseli Gallen-Kallela, Monet, Gustave Moreau, Puvis de Chavannes and Whistler. Diaghilev also had sole responsibility for organizing the World of Art exhibition of 1900, but from 1901 there was an exhibitions committee comprising Diaghilev, Benois and Serov. Submission was by invitation, and the exhibitors

Léon Bakst: design for the cover of a souvenir programme of the Ballets Russes *L'Après-midi d'un faune* showing Nijinsky as the faun, pencil, charcoal, watercolour, gouache and gold on cardboard, 392×272 mm, 1912 (Hartford, CT, Wadsworth Atheneum)

formed the core of the World of Art: Bakst, Benois, Ivan Bilibin, Viktor Vasnetsov, Yevgeny Lansere, Isaak Levitan, Filipp Malyavin, Mikhail Nesterov, Anna Ostroumova-Lebedeva, Konstantin Somov, as well as Aleksandr Golovin, Konstantin Korovin, Sergey Malyutin and Mariya Yakunchikova.

Moscow artists increasingly dominated the exhibitions, which in 1902 included Mikhail Vrubel''s colossal *Demon Downcast* (1901: St Petersburg, Rus. Mus.). Other exhibitors included Pavel Kuznetsov, Nikolay Sapunov and Leonid Pasternak. The exhibition of 1902–3, held in Moscow, incorporated 17 works by Valentin Serov and 24 by Vrubel', and was the début of Nicholas Roerich. In 1903 Mstislav Dobuzhinsky also exhibited. A number of the artists went on to form the exhibiting society UNION OF RUSSIAN ARTISTS. After the closure of the journal a final exhibition opened in St Petersburg in 1906 incorporating a retrospective of Viktor Borisov-Musatov as well as works by the newcomers Mikhail Larionov, Alexei Jawlensky and Nikolay Milioti. The World of Art disbanded in 1906, having diversified and lost its tenuous unity. Many of the former members subsequently contributed to *Apollon*, the magazine edited by Sergey Makovsky from 1909.

In 1910 Benois revived the World of Art as an exhibition society. From then until 1924 it held 21 exhibitions in St

Petersburg (Petrograd), Moscow, Kiev and Rostov-on-Don. While it continued to exhibit work by early World of Art members, it increasingly responded to new trends and ultimately to distinctly Soviet developments. Among new members it included Natan Al'tman, Chagall, Kandinsky, El Lissitzky, Kuz'ma Petrov-Vodkin, Tatlin and Georgy Yakulov.

BIBLIOGRAPHY

C. Spencer and P. Dyer: *The World of Serge Diaghilev* (London, 1974)
N. Lapshina: *Mir Iskusstva* (Moscow, 1977)
J. E. Bowlt: *The Silver Age: Russian Art of the Early Twentieth Century and the 'World of Art' Group* (Newtonville, MA, 1979, rev. 2/1982)

JOHN MILNER

World's Fair. *See* INTERNATIONAL EXHIBITION.

Worlidge, Thomas (*b* Peterborough, Cambs, 1700; *d* Hammersmith [now in London], 22 Sept 1766). English painter and etcher. He took drawing lessons from the Genoese painter Alessandro Maria Grimaldi (1659–1732), and with Grimaldi's son Alexander (1714–1800) he went *c.* 1736 to Birmingham, where he worked as a glass painter. He married Grimaldi's daughter, Arabella, and moved to London in the mid-1730s. He lived in Covent Garden and while there became acquainted with the engraver Louis Pierre Boitard (*d* 1758). Possibly because of his proximity to the London theatres, Worlidge's early works were often theatrical portraits. He made a drawing on vellum of *Theophilus Cibber* (1735; Windsor Castle, Berks, Royal Col.), a painting of *David Garrick as Tancred* (*c.* 1745; London, V&A) and a miniature of the mimic *Samuel Foote* (London, V&A). His watercolour of the comic actress *Kitty Clive as the Fine Lady in Garrick's 'Lethe'* (untraced) was copied for a Bow porcelain figurine (*c.* 1750–52). In the 1750s and 1760s Worlidge worked in the Bath area, drawing and painting portraits in miniature, pencil, crayon and oil. His most popular works were portrait heads in pencil, which were much in demand by fashionable Bath society. He exhibited at the Society of Artists in 1761 and 1765, and at the Free Society in 1762 and 1765–6.

Worlidge's skill as an etcher increased his popularity and, like Benjamin Wilson, he became known for his pastiches of Rembrandt etchings. He began producing these etchings from 1751 (becoming known as the 'English Rembrandt'), and his works were often mistaken for originals. Sometimes he merely copied Rembrandt, as in the *Hundred Guilder Print* (1766), but more often he used Rembrandt's technique and subject-matter in inventive and unusual ways. His etching *Self-portrait in Soft Cap* (1754) alludes directly to Rembrandt's *Self-portrait Leaning on a Stone Sill* (1639; *see* REMBRANDT VAN RIJN, fig. 5), and *Sir Edward Astley as Jan Six* (etching and drypoint, 1765) depicts Astley (1729–1802)—Worlidge's patron and a collector of Rembrandt prints—in an appropriate guise. Worlidge also invented his own subjects, using aspects of Rembrandt's technique, though never quite achieving his tonal subtlety. Occasionally he contributed etchings to illustrated books: his *Mowers at Dinner* is a rare landscape etching produced for an edition (1752) of Christopher Smart's *Poems on Several Occasions*.

In 1763 Worlidge moved to a house formerly belonging to Thomas Hudson; later he retired to Hammersmith. An auction of his collection took place over 25–31 March and 8–9 December 1766; it included prints by Rembrandt, Dürer and Callot, indicative of his careful studies over the years of Old Master prints. His posthumous reputation was high, and in 1768 his last wife (he married three times and had over thirty children) completed the publication of his drypoints in *A Select Collection of Drawings from Curious Antique Gems . . . Etched after the Manner of Rembrandt* (1768), which Worlidge had begun publishing in parts from 1754. His pupils included William Grimaldi (1751–1830), possibly a relation of his former teacher, and George Powle (*fl* 1764–70). Many other etchers imitated Worlidge's Rembrandtesque style, but with less success.

UNPUBLISHED SOURCES

London, BL, Add. MS. 3394–408, Dodd MS. [memento of Worlidge]

BIBLIOGRAPHY

C. Dack: *Sketch of the Life of Thomas Worlidge* (Peterborough, 1907)
'The Note-books of George Vertue', *Walpole Soc.*, xxii (1934) [indexed in xxix (1947)]
H. A. Hammelmann: 'Etcher with a Velvet Tone: Thomas Worlidge', *Country Life*, cxlv (20 Feb 1969), pp. 414–15
D. Foskett: *A Dictionary of British Miniature Painters*, 2 vols (London, 1972)
Rembrandt in 18th-century England (exh. cat. by C. White, D. Alexander and E. D'Oench, New Haven, CT, Yale Cent. Brit. A., 1983)

SHEARER WEST

Wörlitz. Town in Saxony-Anhalt, eastern Germany, 16 km east of Dessau in the Elbe valley, and the site of Schloss Wörlitz and its extensive park, Germany's first garden of major importance in the English landscape style. This large park (112.5 ha) was created between 1764 and *c.* 1805 as part of the summer residence of Prince FRANCIS OF ANHALT-DESSAU, and it was open to the public from the very beginning. Its numerous early Neo-classical and neo-Gothic buildings, monuments and bridges in various styles are a programmatic reflection of the ideas of the Enlightenment. Thus the poplars of ERMENONVILLE were faithfully reproduced, as was Jean-Jacques Rousseau's tomb (1782), while Gotthold Ephraim Lessing's advocacy of religious tolerance was reflected in a temple (1789–90) that was equipped as a synagogue (fittings stripped by the Nazis). The garden was largely conceived by Prince Francis himself and the architect FRIEDRICH WILHELM ERDMANNSDORFF, who were both profoundly influenced by travels in England and Italy; evidence of a lasting enthusiasm for Italy is seen in the Insel Stein (1788–96), which was laid out to resemble southern Italian landscapes, culminating in a reproduction of Mt Vesuvius.

The western section of the garden, which includes a 'Romantic' part, is dominated by rapidly changing vistas, while the later, eastern section is more expansive. Erdmannsdorff's Neo-classical architecture was in part inspired by models from ancient Rome, for example his Pantheon (1795–7). The palace itself (1769–73) is Palladian, the first of its type in Germany. Its classicist interiors and their furnishing with older and contemporary works are particularly noteworthy. A Gothic House (1773; extensions until 1813) was built in the park by Georg Christoph Hesekiel (1732–1818), with Erdmannsdorff's collaboration; it proved highly influential for the development of German Gothic Revival architecture (as did Hesekiel's parish church of Wörlitz, 1805–9). The neo-Gothic rooms of the house contain an early collection of

German Renaissance art and over 200 Swiss paintings on glass. Wörlitz was a pinnacle of landscape design and garden architecture in Anhalt-Dessau and gave vital impetus to artistic developments in Germany. The grounds today have museum status.

BIBLIOGRAPHY

A. Rode: *Beschreibung des fürstlichen anhalt-dessauischen Landhauses und englischen Gartens zu Wörlitz* (Dessau, 1788, 2/1798); ed. A. Rode, H. Ross and L. Trauzettel as *Der englische Garten zu Wörlitz* (Berlin, 1987)
C. A. Boettiger: *Reise nach Wörlitz* (1797); ed. E. Hirsch (Wörlitz, 1988)
A. Rode: *Das gotische Haus zu Wörlitz . . .* (Dessau, 1818)
M.-L. Harksen: *Die Kunstdenkmale des Landes Anhalt: Stadt, Schloss und Park Wörlitz* (Burg, 1939)
E. Hirsch: *Progressive Leistungen und reaktionäre Tendenzen des Dessau-Wörlitzer Kulturkreises in der Rezeption der aufgeklärten Zeitgenossen* (diss., U. Halle, 1969)
E. Paul: *Wörlitzer Antiken* (Wörlitz, 1977)
R.-T. Speler: *Friedrich Wilhelm von Erdmannsdorff: Begründer der klassizistischen Baukunst in Deutschland* (diss., U. Halle, 1981)
E. Hirsch: *Dessau-Wörlitz: Aufklärung und Frühklassik* (Leipzig, 1985)
——: *Der Ursprung der deutschen Neugotik im aufgeklärten Dessau-Wörlitzer Reformwerk* (Dessau, 1987)
R. Alex and P. Kühn: *Schlösser und Gärten um Wörlitz* (Leipzig, 1988)
R. Alex: *Das gotische Haus* (Wörlitz, 1989)
——: *Schloss Wörlitz* (Wörlitz, 1989)

REINHARD ALEX

Wormald, Francis (*b* Dewsbury, Yorks, 1 June 1904; *d* London, 11 Jan 1972). English palaeographer, liturgist and art historian. Educated at Eton and Magdalene College, Cambridge, he worked in the department of manuscripts at the British Museum (1927–49) and was Professor of Palaeography at King's College, University of London (1950–68), and director of the Institute of Historical Research (1960–67). His early work was almost entirely on liturgical texts and included the three volumes on English calendars published for the Henry Bradshaw Society (1934–46). He continued to publish on liturgical texts throughout his life but from the late 1930s, particularly after the death of M. R. James in 1936, he became the most influential figure in the study of English illuminated manuscripts; he also helped to emphasize the need for the study and publication of medieval liturgical texts. His studies were mainly concerned with Anglo-Saxon and Romanesque material with a few devoted to later medieval illumination and iconography. In these his knowledge of palaeography, historical sources and the liturgy was always to the fore. His most important books on art history were *English Drawings of the Tenth and Eleventh Centuries* (London, 1952) and the posthumous *The Winchester Psalter* (London, 1973). He also published numerous articles.

WRITINGS
J. J. G. Alexander, T. J. Brown and J. Gibbs, eds: *Collected Works*, 2 vols (London, 1984–8)

BIBLIOGRAPHY
J. Brown: 'Francis Wormald', *Proc. Brit. Acad.*, lxi (1975), pp. 523–60

NIGEL J. MORGAN

Worms. German city in Rhineland-Palatinate with a population of *c.* 80,000. The site was first settled by the Celts (as Borbetomagus) and later became a Roman garrison town (Civitas Vangionum) and the capital of the Vangiones region; sections of the forum walls still stand. In AD 413 Worms became the capital of the Burgundian kings, and as such was the setting for the *Nibelungenlied* (*c.* 1200), but it was destroyed by the Huns in 436. When it was rebuilt by the Merovingian kings, it also became the seat of a bishopric. In 1184 it became an imperial free city. Although Worms became very powerful and played an important role in the rivalries between the crown, the pope and the dukes, very few buildings survive from the medieval period. The church of St Paul was built by Bishop Burchard (*reg* 1000–25), who was particularly influential in strengthening the bishopric. Only parts of the original 11th-century structure survive; the church was modified in the 13th century and partly rebuilt in the 18th. The cathedral (*see* §1 below) is one of the finest examples of middle and Late Romanesque architecture in Germany. A Jewish community was established in the city from about the 10th century; the early medieval synagogue, which was almost completely destroyed in 1938, was rebuilt in 1958–61. The Jewish cemetery nearby, one of the oldest and largest in Europe, was laid out around the 11th century. Many Imperial Diets were held at Worms, notably that of 1521 at which Martin Luther was outlawed. The city was greatly impoverished by the Thirty Years War (1618–48) and then virtually destroyed by the French in 1689. It declined rapidly, and began to prosper again only with the development of new industries in the 19th century. It was badly damaged in World War II, but has since been rebuilt.

□

1. CATHEDRAL.

(i) Architecture. Worms Cathedral, dedicated to St Peter, is built over remains dating back to late antiquity. The present building stands largely on the foundations of a church erected under Bishop Burchard (consecrated 1018). The building was a long, aisled basilica, which had a double chancel, a flat ceiling, an eastern transept with square arms, a straight east choir and a western apse with cylindrical towers. The bases of the west towers and an 11th-century addition have survived, as have some 10th-century tombs of ancestors of the Salian dynasty (*see* GERMANY, fig. 3).

The new building was begun with the east choir *c.* 1125–30, followed by the vault of the eastern sections (1132–7), the north nave arcade (1161–3) and the aisle walls. By the time of the consecration in 1181 the west choir, which extends west of the old ground-plan, was probably complete. The cathedral is now a fully vaulted basilica on the *gebundenes System*, with rib vaults over the main vessel and groin vaults in the aisles. The crossing is surmounted by an octagonal tower, after the precedent of Speyer Cathedral (*see* SPEYER, §1(i)), while over the west choir is another, slightly different octagonal tower between the west towers. Important features are the east façade with its rectangular casing and round towers, facing the town; the early vault with flat ribs over the east choir and transept; and the elevation of the nave and aisles, which is based on Speyer. The nave elevation changes not only from bay to bay, but also from north to south, the north side following the system actually executed at Speyer, the south following the unexecuted one. A three-storey effect is produced by the partial articulation of the wall above the arcades. The west choir (after 1171), with strongly three-dimensional articulation, is characterized by the polygonal five-eighths termination, containing a rose window and crowned by a stone roof above which the octagonal tower rises.

(ii) Sculpture. Architectural ornament is largely limited to the west choir, which has simple capitals with rough-hewn leaves, much imitated in Alsace. Early figural sculptures, however, include the lions and bears on the window sills of the eastern façade and the masks among the arch friezes of the east towers. The architect, with a mason's square and monkey on his shoulder, is mounted on a column in the eastern dwarf gallery, the base of which rests on human and animal protomes. Eagle and acanthus capitals with masks adorn the north portal, while the damaged tympanum showing *Christ with St Peter and the Virgin, Bishops and Donors* (*c.* 1160) has survived from the south portal. It represents a surprisingly advanced sculptural style, showing an understanding of organic forms and featuring rich folds of drapery. Probably part of the south portal are important fragments built into a Gothic chapel after the 13th century: *Daniel in the Lions' Den*, the prophet *Habakkuk* and fragments of lions. Since comparable precedents are lacking, a link with north Italian sculpture must be considered. Animal and human protomes are also found on the dwarf gallery of the west choir and below the tower responds, but they are inferior in quality and expressive power to the fragments from the south portal. The latter was remodelled in Gothic style *c.* 1300 in imitation of the west façade of Strasbourg Cathedral (*see* STRASBOURG, fig. 4). The programme combines a complete spectrum of subjects from the Old and New Testaments with the *Evangelists* around the *Coronation of the Virgin.* The 15th- and 16th-century epitaphs from the cloister are important documents of Upper Rhenish sculpture. The very fine 'Dreijungfernstein' in the Nikolauskapelle is an example of the Soft style *c.* 1420.

BIBLIOGRAPHY
R. Kautzsch: *Der Dom zu Worms*, 3 vols (Berlin, 1938)
D. von Winterfeld: *Der Dom zu Worms* (Königstein im Taunus, 1984)
DETHARD VON WINTERFELD

Worms, Hans von. *See* HANS VON WORMS.

Wormser, Jacobus. *See under* VORKINK & WORMSER.

Wornum, (George) Grey (*b* London, 17 April 1888; *d* New York, 11 June 1957). English architect. He studied at the Slade School of Art, London. He was then articled to his uncle Ralph Selden Wornum, and he attended classes at the Architectural Association. His first work was a studio (1910) for Hugh Goldwin Riviere (1869–1956). During service in World War I he lost his right eye (1916). He resumed his career in 1919, first with Philip D. Hepworth (1888–1963) and then from *c.* 1921 to 1930 with Louis de Soissons, their works including a water garden (1920), Hayling Island, Hants, and several of the Douglas Haig Memorial homes. In 1932 he won the competition for new headquarters for the Royal Institute of British Architects at 66 Portland Place, London. His design, which owed much to contemporary Swedish neoclassicism, was a stylish compromise between classical formalism and incipient modernism. Its symbolic sculpture

and wide range of applied decoration make it one of the most interesting surviving interiors of the 1930s.

Wornum's practice increased considerably after the RIBA building, notably with the Ladbroke Grove housing estate (1936, with E. Maxwell Fry, Robert Atkinson and C. H. James), No. 39 Weymouth Street (1936) and the highways depot for the City of Westminster (1936), Gatliff Road, all in London. In 1938 he was appointed architect for the first-class accommodation of the Cunard Line's *Queen Elizabeth.* From 1945–55 he was in partnership with Edward Playne, incorporating the practice of Aston Webb. His post-war works included municipal housing schemes for various London boroughs and a much acclaimed plan for Parliament Square (1950). In the 1940s the severe handicaps that he suffered after World War I crippled him so much that he had to move to a warmer climate, first in Bermuda and then California. He was awarded the Royal Gold Medal in 1952.

BIBLIOGRAPHY
RIBA J., xlii (Nov 1934) [whole issue on the RIBA bldg]
Obituary, *Builder*, cxcii (1957), p. 1115
M. Richardson: *66 Portland Place: The London Headquarters of the Royal Institute of British Architects* (London, 1984)
MARGARET RICHARDSON

Worpswede colony. Colony of German artists founded in 1897 in the village of Worpswede near Bremen. In 1889 the painters Fritz Mackensen, Otto Modersohn (1865–1943) and Hans am Ende (1864–1918) moved to the village where they painted in the *plein-air* tradition of the Barbizon school. From the beginning they were closely connected with Carl Vinnen (1863–1922), who lived on his farm at Ostendorf, Bremerhaven. In 1892 they were joined by Fritz Overbeck (1869–1909) and in 1894 by Heinrich Vogeler.

Mackensen, the most academic of the Worpswede painters, had his first success with large figure paintings, such as *Religious Service on the Moor* (1886–95; Hannover, Hist. Mus. Hohen Ufer; see fig.). The ideological elevation of the peasant class appears more intensely in his work than in that of the other Worpswede artists. Am Ende's importance lay in his graphic work, for example *Cottage on the Moor* (1895; Bremen, Ksthalle). He also taught Vogeler, Overbeck and Mackensen the technique of etching. Modersohn was more concerned than the other artists with an analysis of art history and modern painting. His early paintings, such as *Cloud* (1890; Fischerhude, Otto-Modersohn-Mus.), reproduce a very independent vision of form and colour. The period of collaboration with Paula Modersohn-Becker, whom he married in 1901, gave them both artistic impetus. Landscape was always Modersohn's most important subject. The large number of sketches, which were preparations for paintings, express a poetic relationship with nature within a solid pictorial structure and have a great deal of painterly value, for example *Autumn Evening on the Moor* (1904; Essen, Mus. Flkwang). In his paintings and graphic work, Overbeck sometimes emphasized the elemental forces of nature.

Vinnen, who did not live in the village, was not a member of the narrower circle of the Worpswede painters, nor was Vogeler. The latter did not seek the primeval character of nature and the plain simplicity of the peasant

Fritz Mackensen: *Religious Service on the Moor*, oil on canvas, 231×372 mm, 1886–95 (Hannover, Historisches Museum am Hohen Ufer)

population, but projected his longings into the landscape in the form of dream-like, stylized fairy-tale figures. Wholly committed to Jugendstil in his early works, he was influenced by the Pre-Raphaelites, Aubrey Beardsley and William Morris, and produced a large body of graphic work. As well as this he worked as an architect and made art and craft designs; in 1908 he founded, with his brother, the Worpsweder Werkstätten carpentry workshop.

In 1895 the Worpswede artists exhibited in the Kunsthalle, Bremen, and then in the Glaspalast, Munich, which was particularly successful. By 1897, however, when they officially founded the Künstlervereinigung Worpswede, the first tensions already existed between the friends. In 1899 Modersohn left the organization, which he found restricting, as did Overbeck and Vogeler. The differences between these artists and Mackensen and am Ende finally led in 1901 to the breaking of relations. Despite these tensions, Worpswede became an attraction for other artists: in 1899 Karl Krummacher (1867–1955) came to the village and continued the tradition of the first Worpswede artists; in 1902 Walter Bertelsmann (1877–1963) stayed in Worpswede, having been a pupil of am Ende.

Of all the Worpswede painters, Paula Modersohn-Becker was the only one who, despite her short life, won recognition far beyond Worpswede. She had moved there in 1898, full of admiration for the artists' group, and had become a pupil of Mackensen, although she was more influenced by the painting of Otto Modersohn. Once she had dealt artistically with the lyrical and escapist regional art, she found the village restricting and developed her abstract vision of the visible world through a study of

French art in Paris, resulting in works such as *Self-portrait with Hand on Chin* (1901; Hannover, Niedersächs. Landesmus.). During his years in Worpswede, Vogeler's property Barkenhoff became the centre of a circle of artists and writers, including Modersohn and Modersohn-Becker, the sculptor Clara Rilke-Westhoff (1878–1954) and the writers Rainer Maria Rilke, Carl Hauptmann, Rudolf Alexander Schröder and Alfred Walter Heymel. In 1903 Rilke was commissioned to write the *Worpswede Monographie*. Worpswede soon lost its primeval character at the edge of a large moor and became an artists' village and tourist attraction.

BIBLIOGRAPHY

R. M. Rilke: *Worpswede: Monographie einer Landschaft und ihrer Maler* (Bielefeld, 1903)
Worpswede: Aus der Frühzeit der Künstlerkolonie (exh. cat., Bremen, Ksthalle, 1970)
H. Wohltmann: *Worpswede: Die ersten Worpsweder Maler und ihre Bedeutung für die deutsche Kunst* (Worpswede, 1971)
H. W. Petzet: *Heinrich Vogeler: Von Worpswede nach Moskau* (Cologne, 1972)
O. Modersohn (exh. cat., Hannover, Kstver.; Münster, Westfäl. Landesmus.; 1978)
Worpswede: Eine deutsche Künstlerkolonie um 1900 (exh. cat., Bremen, Ksthalle, 1980)
Worpswede: Eine deutsche Künstlerkolonie um 1900 (exh. cat., Vienna, Künstlerhaus; Hannover, Niedersächs. Landesmus.; 1986)

HANS GERHARD HANNESEN

Worringer, Wilhelm (*b* Aachen, 13 Jan 1881; *d* Munich, 29 March 1965). German art historian. He studied art history at Freiburg, Berlin and Munich, before submitting his doctoral dissertation in Berne in 1907. This thesis, entitled *Abstraktion und Einfühlung: Ein Beitrag zur Stilpsychologie*, was first published in Neuwied in 1907 as a dissertation. Somewhat unusually, it was recommended to, and reviewed favourably by, the writer Paul Ernst, whose article in *Kunst and Künstler* swiftly prompted a publication in book form the following year. It is a peculiar feature of Worringer's reception that his first publication not only established his reputation as a significant art historian, but has seldom been out of print since 1908. That a doctoral thesis should have had such a profound impact, not only for art historians and theorists, but also for generations of creative writers and intellectuals, is almost unprecedented.

Abstraktion und Einfühlung takes as its starting-point Theodor Lipps's theory of empathy, the notion that the work of art maximizes our capacity for empathy, that beauty derives from our sense of being able to identify with an object. While conceding that a mimetic urge exists in man, drawing on the ideas of Alois Riegl, Worringer denies any necessary connection between mimesis and art: if Egyptian art was highly stylized, he argued, this was not because its artists were incompetent and failed to reproduce external reality accurately, but because Egyptian art answered a radically different psychological need. In mimetic works, he argued, we derive satisfaction from an 'objectified delight in the self'; the aim of the artist is to maximize our capacity for empathizing with the work. This kind of art springs from a confidence in the world as it is, a satisfaction in its forms, something embodied in Classical and Renaissance art. By contrast, the urge to abstraction, exemplified variously by Egyptian, Byzantine, Gothic or primitive art, articulates a wholly different response to the universe: it expresses man's insecurity and seeks to answer transcendental or spiritual needs. Thus in certain historical periods man is confidently assertive and finds satisfaction in 'objectified delight in the self', abandoning himself in contemplation of the external world, but in periods of anxiety and uncertainty he seeks to abstract objects from their contingency, transforming them into permanent, absolute, transcendental forms.

It is not difficult to appreciate the fascination that Worringer's theory held for the writers and intellectuals of the Expressionist generation in Germany. He supplied a theoretical justification, and an aesthetic category, for the revival of interest in Early German art and for the simultaneous discovery of primitivism. His theory also had a sociological dimension: the fear and alienation that 'primitive man' had experienced in the face of a hostile universe had, he argued, prompted an urge to create fixed, abstract, and geometric forms, while Renaissance individualism had weakened this capacity for abstraction. The modern experience of industrialization, the sense that individual identity was threatened by a hostile mass society, had rekindled the need for abstract forms to counteract a sense of what Karl Marx, among others, had defined as alienation. It seemed to many that Worringer's thesis offered a new blueprint for a modernist aesthetic. Although derived in essence from the aesthetic theories of Lipps and Riegl, it offered a justification for the formal distortion of Post-Impressionism and Expressionism. The reflections on art of Emil Nolde and Ernst Ludwig Kirchner and the aesthetic theory of Carl Einstein (1885–1940; his *Negerplastik* of 1915 was one of the most important studies of primitive art in German) are unthinkable without Worringer's influence. Nor was his impact confined to Germany: T. E. Hulme's *Speculations*, first published in book form in 1924, is, on its author's own admission, heavily dependent on Worringer's ideas.

Worringer's second major publication, *Formprobleme der Gotik* (1911), developed the closing section of his earlier thesis into a fully-fledged account of Gothic art and architecture. Once again, Worringer operates with a definition of the Gothic that is all-embracing: Gothic, for him, is all the art of the western world that was not shaped by classical Mediterranean culture, all art, in short, that did not directly reproduce nature. Starting with the latent Gothic in early Northern ornament, characterized by its repetition, geometric pattern and flowing line, Worringer moves on to examine cathedral statuary, and finally Gothic architecture, with its 'will to expression, striving towards the transcendental'. His attempts to locate his theories in specific historical contexts have come to be uncomfortably reminiscent of the misuse of such ideas by the National Socialists. Such statements as: 'the land of the pure Gothic is the Germanic North', a formulation that actually reflects Worringer's fondness for employing antithetical terms, like North/South, Gothic/Renaissance, abstraction/empathy, have acquired unfortunate ideological connotations. Perhaps this helps to explain why Worringer's work has suffered from comparative critical neglect, for despite the undeniable importance of his early writings and many passing references to his achievements, there is no full-length critical study devoted to him. Furthermore, his rehabilitation of abstraction as an aesthetic principle was so enthusiastically received and so widely disseminated as to become a commonplace of German modernism, a fact that paradoxically tended to obscure his unique contribution.

Worringer himself was aware of the fact that his two earliest works overshadowed all that he subsequently wrote. He lectured at the Universität Bern until 1914, and it was there that he completed *Die altdeutsche Buchillustration* (1912). After spending the years of World War I on active service, he subsequently taught at the Universität Bonn, before moving to Königsberg in 1928. This period saw the publication of *Ägyptische Kunst* (1927) and *Griechentum und Gotik* (1928). He remained in Königsberg until 1945, before moving to the Universität Halle in the Soviet Zone. In 1950, a year after the founding of the German Democratic Republic, Worringer left East Germany for the West, settling in Munich, where he died.

WRITINGS

Abstraktion und Einfühlung: Ein Beitrag zur Stilpsychologie (Munich, 1908/*R* Munich, 1976; Eng. trans., London, 1953) [first pubd as a diss., Neuwied, 1907]

Lukas Cranach (Munich, 1908)

Formprobleme der Gotik (Munich, 1911; Eng. trans., London, 1957)

Die altdeutsche Buchillustration (Munich, 1912)

Urs Graf: Die Holzschnitte zur Passion (Munich, 1923)

Die Kölner Bibel (Munich, 1923)

Die Anfänge der Tafelmalerei (Leipzig, 1924)

Deutsche Jugend und östlicher Geist (Bonn, 1924)

Buch und Leben des hochberühmten Fabeldichters Aesopi, Ulm 1475 (Munich, 1925)

Ägyptische Kunst: Probleme ihrer Wertung (Munich, 1927; Eng. trans., London, 1928)

Otto Pankok: 24 Kohlezeichnungen mit einer Einführung (Munich, 1927)

Griechentum und Gotik: Vom Weltreich des Hellenismus (Munich, 1928)

Über den Einfluss der angelsächsischen Buchmalerei auf die frühmittelalterliche Monumentalplastik des Kontinents (Halle, 1931)
Fragen und Gegenfragen: Schriften zum Kunstproblem (Munich, 1956)

BIBLIOGRAPHY
M. Finch: *Style in Art History: An Introduction to Theories of Style and Sequence* (New Jersey, 1974)
H. Lützeler: *Kunsterfahrung und Kunstwissenschaft: Systematische und entwicklungsgeschichtliche Darstellung und Dokumentation des Umgangs mit der bildenden Kunst*, 3 vols (Freiburg, 1975)
L. Dittmann, ed.: *Kategorien und Methoden der deutschen Kunstgeschichte, 1900–1930* (Stuttgart, 1985)
RHYS W. WILLIAMS

Worsley, Sir Richard (*b* Appuldurcombe, Isle of Wight, 17 March 1751; *d* Wroxall, Isle of Wight, 8 Aug 1805). English collector. His seat was Appuldurcombe House (partly destr.) on the Isle of Wight, and he was variously MP for Newport and Newtown. After a notorious scandal involving his wife and Charles Henry Mordaunt, 5th Earl of Peterborough, Worsley chose to dedicate himself to collecting and travel, undertaking a long journey in the Levant, including Egypt and the Crimean peninsula, accompanied by Willey Reveley (*d* 1799) as draughtsman. He left Rome in February 1785, reaching Athens in May; he was in Asia Minor in the spring of 1786, returning to Rome in April 1787. Worsley collected many original Greek sculptures, principally reliefs, and in so doing he can be distinguished from most contemporary British collectors of antiquities. In Rome he was in touch with Thomas Jenkins and purchased gems from Sir William Hamilton (i). Worsley's plan to publish a sumptuous illustrated catalogue of his collection was developed in Rome, where he employed Vincenzo Dolcibeni (*fl* 1782–1807) to make drawings to be engraved; Ennio Quirino Visconti assisted with the text. Both were currently engaged in the production of the illustrated catalogue of the Museo Pio-Clementino in Rome, founded by Pope Clement XIV, which no doubt inspired Worsley. Though dated 1794, the two volumes of the *Museum Worsleyanum* were first published in 1798 and 1802 respectively. On his return to England in 1788 Worsley became close to such antiquarians as Charles Townley and Richard Payne Knight. He was British Resident in Venice (1793–6), and there Giovanni Maria Sasso acted as his adviser. Through his niece his property and estates passed to the Earls of Yarborough; his collection of antiquities remains at Brocklesby Park, Lincs.

WRITINGS
Museum Worsleyanum or a Collection of Antique Basso Relievos, Bustos, Statues and Gems, 2 vols (London, 1794–1802, 2/1824)

BIBLIOGRAPHY
DNB
A. Michaelis: *Ancient Marbles in Great Britain* (Cambridge, 1882), pp. 115–17
GERARD VAUGHAN

Worthington, Thomas (Locke) (*b* Salford, Lancs, 11 April 1826; *d* Alderley Edge, Ches, 9 Nov 1909). English architect. His career paralleled and contributed to the development of Victorian Manchester. The design for his best-known work, the Manchester Albert Memorial with its canopied statue, was published in 1862; it was apparently earlier than George Gilbert Scott's conception for the Albert Memorial in Kensington, which nevertheless seems to have been designed independently.

Worthington was articled to the firm of Bowman & Crowther in Manchester. His subsequent career was technologically distinguished, in keeping with the dissenting, reforming zeal of the Industrial Revolution's birthplace. One socially advanced building was his Leaf Street Baths (1854), Hulme, Ches, which translated Italian Gothic to new technology. He corresponded with Florence Nightingale about hospital design, and his Chorlton Union Workhouse (1865; now part of Withington Hospital) was a pioneering example of her pavilion planning. As early as 1870 he made self-contained workmen's flats (Greengate, Salford, destr.). Merchant clients also commissioned Unitarian churches around Manchester, such as his boldly Early English Brookfield Church (1869–71), Gorton.

In the Manchester Town Hall competition of 1868, won by Alfred Waterhouse, Worthington's turreted design, with its whiff of Scott's St Pancras Hotel, was highly commended. The Venetian Gothic Memorial Hall (1865) in Albert Square and the Police Courts (1868), with their campanile, were his. He also built big, picturesque mansions such as the Towers (1868; now part of the Shirley Institute), Didsbury, for the owner-editor of the *Manchester Guardian*.

His firm practised as Worthington & Elgood, 1880–93, and later as Worthington & Son(s). Two sons were architects: Percy Scott Worthington (1864–1939), who won a Royal Gold Medal in 1930 and was knighted in 1935; and (John) Hubert Worthington (1886–1963), OBE, who was knighted in 1949.

BIBLIOGRAPHY
RIBA J., xvii (1909–10), pp. 99, 233; xlvi (1939), pp. 950, 983
J. RIBA, lxx (1963), p. 422
A. Pass: 'Thomas Worthington, Practical Idealist', *Archit. Rev.* [London], clv (1974), p. 268
——: 'Thomas Worthington', *Art and Architecture in Victorian Manchester*, ed. J. H. G. Archer (1985), Manchester, pp. 81–101
PRISCILLA METCALF

Wörtz [Wörz], Hans (*fl* 1585–1623). German cabinetmaker. The documents showing that in 1585 he was working for the Bavarian court, and that the court of Mantua wished to secure his services, indicate that he possessed unusual qualities as an artist and craftsman: this is confirmed by his principal works, which have not survived, but are recorded in illustrations. Wörtz was commissioned to execute all the carpentry for the interior of the former Dominican monastery church in Ulm, later called the Dreifaltigkeitskirche or Spitalkirche (destr. World War II). The perfectly unified furnishings included the high altar (1618), the pulpit with its superstructure, the gallery balustrade, the signed choir stalls (1623) and the pews in the nave. In 1891 the general appearance of the richly carved furnishings was severely impaired by the application of brown varnish, and in 1944 bombing destroyed them completely.

BIBLIOGRAPHY
Thieme–Becker
H. Krins: 'Instandsetzung und Imbau der Dreifaltigkeitskirche in Ulm im Rahmen des Schwerpunktprogrammes der Landesregierung', *Dkmlpf. Baden-Württemberg*, xiii (1984), pp. 60–63
ELISABETH GUROCK

Wotruba, Fritz (*b* Vienna, 23 April 1907; *d* Vienna, 28 Aug 1975). Austrian sculptor and architect. While training in an engraving and die-stamping workshop in Vienna (1921–4), he took evening classes in life-drawing at the Kunstgewerbeschule, Vienna, before in 1926 joining Anton Hanak's sculpture class where he met the metal sculptor Marian Fleck (*d* 1951), whom he married in 1929; in 1928 they both left the school after disagreements with the teacher. During his career as a die-stamper and engraver, Wotruba studied in 1927 with Professor Eugen Gustav Steinhof (*b* 1880) and carried out his first experiments in stone in 1928–9, including *Male Torso* (limestone; priv. col.). In 1930 he travelled to Düsseldorf and Essen, where he examined the works of Wilhelm Lehmbruck and Aristide Maillol and became a friend of Josef Hoffmann.

In 1933, with a group of unemployed people, Wotruba made the monument *Man, Condemn War* (see Breicha, 1967, p. 65), which was installed in the cemetery in Donawitz but later destroyed by the Nazis. At this time he was in contact with Hans Tietze, Herbert Boeckl and others. During the February disturbances in 1934 Wotruba temporarily left Vienna with his wife and moved to Zurich, returning the same year, however, with the help of Carl Moll. After the Germans marched into Austria in 1938 he fled again with his wife via Düsseldorf to Berlin, where Max Liebermann's widow put the garden-house on the Wannsee at his disposal. Wotruba spent the years between 1938 and 1945 in exile in Switzerland and made his studio in Zug a meeting-place for many emigrants, including Marino Marini and Germaine Richier. In this period he produced sculptures of archaic strictness and heavy, weighty form, which already reveal a tendency towards reduction and geometrical simplification, for example *Head* (limestone, 1941; Winterthur, Georg Reinhart priv. col., see Jaray, p. 127).

In 1945 Herbert Boeckl arranged Wotruba's employment at the Akademie der Bildenden Künste, Vienna, where he took over the running of a master class at the end of the year. In 1946 he produced the *Large Standing Woman* (also called *Female Cathedral*; Zug, Fritz Kamm priv. col., see Jaray, p. 127), which established a new style, namely a renunciation of anatomy and the accentuation of the basic structures of the human body. Many important artists, musicians and writers visited his flat at this time, including Gottfried von Einem, Josef Matthias Hauer and Leo Hochner. In 1948 Wotruba undertook the costume and stage design of the *Soldier's Tale* by Igor Stravinsky and C. F. Ramuz, which had its first performance in the Grosser Konzerthaussaal in Vienna. In the following years he travelled to Munich, Brussels and London, where he met Henry Moore. From this time his works showed increased tectonic qualities and reduction to basic geometrical structures, leading to block-like forms and freer formal rhythms (*see* AUSTRIA, fig. 23). From 1953–4 he turned to a rather pillar-like form in his figures, assembling moulded cylindrical forms into a softer, more 'female' structure. He took on many commissions for individual and grouped figures but also for reliefs, for example the frieze for the Otto Glöckel-Schule in Linz (1953; *in situ*) and the relief of human figures for the Austrian pavilion at the Exposition Universelle, Brussels (1957; now Vienna, Mus. 20. Jhts).

In 1959, commissioned by the director Gustav Rudolf Sellner, Wotruba made a Classical cycle for the stage; costumes and masks for the performance of the Sophocles dramas *Oedipus Rex*, *Oedipus at Colonus*, *Antigone* and *Elektra* at the Burgtheater, Vienna. In 1963 he also designed the costumes for Wagner's *Ring der Nibelungen* for the Festwoche performance in Berlin in 1967. In the same year Werner Hofmann organized a large exhibition of Fritz Wotruba's work in the Museum des 20. Jahrhunderts, Vienna. In 1964 Wotruba started work on a figurative relief for the Auditorium Maximum at the Philipps-Universität in Marburg an der Lahn, opened in 1965. In 1965 a committee of representatives from the Church, the regional administration and industry awarded him a commission for the design of a monastery and church for the Carmelite order, a project that collapsed due to opposition from a number of sources, and finally ended with the building of the Holy Trinity church in Mauer, Vienna, which opened a year after his death. He consistently received a large number of public commissions, including a place of worship and a sculpture for the forecourt of the church of St Michael in Lucerne in 1967, a sculpture to the memory of *Richard Wagner* in Mainz (1970) and a bronze sculpture (1974) for the Dianabad, Vienna. With great enthusiasm and creative energy he worked on many different projects until the end of his life. His pioneering artistic concept and style were imitated and continued by many Austrian and foreign artists.

See also AUSTRIA, §IV,5.

WRITINGS

M. Jaray, ed.: *La Sculpture du 20e siècle* (Neuchâtel, 1961)
Otto Breicha, ed.: *Schriften zum Werk: Europäische Perspektiven* (Vienna, Frankfurt, Zurich, 1967)

PRINTS

Wieland Schmied, ed.: *Zeichnungen, 1925–1972* (Vienna, Frankfurt, Berlin, 1973)
Druckgrafik, 1950–1975 (Vienna, 1989)

BIBLIOGRAPHY

E. Canetti: *Fritz Wotruba* (Vienna, 1955)
O. Breicha: *Wotruba: Figur als Wiederstand* (Salzburg, 1977)
G. Peichl, ed.: *Hommage à Wotruba* (Vienna, 1985)

ULRIKE GAISBAUER

Wotton, Sir Henry (*b* Boughton Malherbe, Kent, 1568; *d* Eton, Berks, Dec 1639). English diplomat, collector and writer. He spent much of his life as English ambassador in Venice, where he helped many important collectors associated with the Stuart court to buy works of art. He later published the first book devoted to the theory of architecture to be written in English.

1. DIPLOMACY AND COLLECTING. He was the fourth son of Thomas Wotton, a landed gentleman, and was educated at Winchester and at New and Queens Colleges, Oxford. In 1587 his father died, leaving him a miserly annuity that was to have adverse financial repercussions for the rest of his life. In the following year he left England and travelled abroad for seven years, latterly acting as an intelligence agent for Robert Devereux, 2nd Earl of Essex. In 1595 he returned to England, where he was admitted to the Inner Temple and became a secretary to Essex. The following year he took over responsibility for the Earl's intelligence network in Transylvania, Poland, Italy and Germany.

Following Essex's downfall in 1601, Wotton, who was closely associated with his master, went into exile in Italy, residing first in Venice and later in Florence, where he attended the court of Ferdinand I, Grand Duke of Tuscany. In 1602 he was instrumental in revealing a plot against the life of James VI of Scotland, and he returned to England on the latter's accession to the English throne as James I in 1603. He was kindly received, knighted and offered a choice of ambassadorships. Wotton, partly because of his knowledge and love of the city and partly for financial reasons, chose to become ambassador to the Republic of Venice, where he remained, though not continuously, for the next 20 years. In 1604, while staying in Augsburg, he committed the indiscretion of inscribing, in Latin, his notorious definition of an ambassador as 'an honest man, sent to lie abroad for the good of his country', which put his career in serious jeopardy when it became known to James I in 1611. By August 1614 he was sufficiently in the King's favour to serve his second term in Venice, returning to England in 1619 before his final Venetian residence from 1621 to 1624.

Throughout his ambassadorship Wotton assisted a number of English noblemen to acquire Venetian works of art. In April 1608 he received a portrait of his patron *Robert Cecil, 1st Earl of Salisbury*, by John de Critz and had it copied in mosaic (Hatfield House, Herts) as a gift for Salisbury's son. He also acquired Palma Giovane's *Prometheus and the Eagle* (untraced) for Salisbury. In 1622, during his final Venetian period, he was active on behalf of George Villiers, 1st Duke of Buckingham, to whom he sent a *Virgin and Child* by Titian (untraced), a painting by Palma Giovane, identified by Horace Walpole in the 1649 catalogue of Buckingham's collection as *King David in his Old Age Sitting on a Throne to which a Young Damsel is Brought* (untraced), and a still-life of grapes for Buckingham's sister, the Countess of Denbigh. In a letter of 2 December 1622 which records these purchases he tells the Duke, 'I have put a servant of mine, by profession a painter, to make a search in the best towns through Italy, for some principal pieces'. Wotton also advised on purchases for the royal collection and in 1631, back in England, he was summoned to Whitehall to give his opinion on some newly arrived pictures sent from The Hague.

Wotton's own collection was modest and acquired more from association than from connoisseurship. In his will he left five paintings by Odoarto Fialetti—*Doge Leonardo Donato Giving Audience to Sir Henry Wotton* and four portraits of Doges (London, Hampton Court, Royal Col.)—to Charles I; also a portrait of a Doge attributed to Titian (London, Hampton Court, Royal Col., now identified as a copy of Titian's portrait of *Doge Andrea Gritti*) and a portrait of *Elizabeth, Queen of Bohemia* by Gerrit van Honthorst (London, Hampton Court, Royal Col.). He also left the *Four Seasons* (untraced) by Jacopo Bassano to Sir Francis Windebank (1582–1646) and a number of pictures to Eton College, of which he had become Provost in July 1624.

2. WRITINGS. In 1624 Wotton published his architectural treatise *The Elements of Architecture*. In the introduction he acknowledged that it was largely borrowed from Vitruvius and Leon Battista Alberti. He rejected the historical approach to his subject, which had already been successfully essayed by Giorgio Vasari, and instead adopted a 'logicall' position. Like Alberti, he stressed fitness of purpose, taking as his principal thesis that 'the end must direct the operation' and 'the end is to build well'. He identified 'commodity, firmness and delight' as the three requirements of a good building. Although he resolved that a square is the best shape for a building, he particularly praised Andrea Palladio among contemporary architects. If *The Elements of Architecture* is self-confessedly derivative, it is written with considerable flair and humour: 'a good parler [parlour] in Egypt would perchance make a good celler in England', he noted when discussing climate; and, when defining the Orders of columns, he described the Corinthian as 'a columne lasciviously decked like a courtesan'.

Part two of the *Elements* covers decoration, with Picture and Sculpture attending on Architecture 'like two of her principal gentlewomen'. Sculpture is given pre-eminence as being a 'nearer affinity' to Architecture and, consequently, more natural. He gives a brief history of art from the ancient Greeks and adopts a standard of beauty between nature and the ideal, writing of Dürer and Michelangelo, 'the German did too much express that which was, and the Italian that which should be'. There is no evidence to suggest that the book was at all influential, but it has the merit of being the first book devoted to architecture written in English.

Wotton, who received a royal pension of £200 a year in 1627, increased to £500 in 1630, spent the last years of his life in happiness at Eton College, pursuing his passion for fishing with his great friend Izaak Walton.

WRITINGS
The Elements of Architecture (London, 1624)

BIBLIOGRAPHY
L. Pearsall Smith: *The Life and Letters of Sir Henry Wotton*, 2 vols (Oxford, 1907)

DAVID RODGERS

Wouda, Hendrik (*b* Leeuwarden, 10 May 1885; *d* Wassenaar, 25 Oct 1946). Dutch architect and furniture designer. He trained as an apprentice (*c.* 1905–14) in the offices of H. P. Berlage and of Eduard Pfeiffer (1889–1929) in Munich. From 1917 to 1934 he worked as an interior designer for the firm of H. Pander & Zonen in The Hague, also designing a shop (1932; destr.) for them in Rotterdam. He designed mass-produced furniture, lighting and interiors for homes, offices, ships and exhibitions. His first well-known commission was for the interiors of the Villa Sevensteyn (1920–21) built by W. M. Dudok in Zorgvliet Park, The Hague. They are characterized by a strongly marked simplicity, a cubic joining together of volumes, well-balanced spatial effects and a practical division of the floor-plan. He also practised independently as an architect; in his designs, such as that for the Villa De Luifel (1924) in Wassenaar, Wouda showed himself to be strongly influenced by Frank Lloyd Wright. The division of its façades is dominated by horizontal accents, and the buildings are generally low; penthouses, balustrades and built-on flower boxes, as well as large windows, provide accents on the exterior.

Although Wouda's subsequent practice included several houses, he is best known for his furniture, for which he evolved a simple rectilinear style combining elements from Wright, De Stijl and Art Deco; an example is his oak sideboard of *c.* 1924, partly painted in red and black (The Hague, Rijksdienst Beeld. Kst). The influence of Art Deco is especially evident in the bold geometric patterns applied to some of his later designs and in his personal application of colours.

WRITINGS

'Het landhuis "De Luifel" te Wassenaar', *De Fakkel*, v (1925), pp. 55–7

BIBLIOGRAPHY

A. van der Boom: 'Interieur-ontwerpen van H. Wouda', *Op de Hoogte* (1928), pp. 174–7

Winkels en winkelpuien (Rotterdam, 1933), ix of *Moderne Bouwkunst in Nederland*, ed. H. P. Berlage and others (Rotterdam, 1932-5), pp. 38-40, 51

W. Retera Wzn.: 'Bij Wouda's werk', *Elsevier's Geillus. Mdschr.* (1940), pp. 19–27

M. Teunissen and A. Veldhuisen: *Hendrik Wouda, 1885–1946* (Rotterdam, 1989)

MONIQUE D. J. M. TEUNISSEN

Wouters, Frans (*b* Lier, ?12 Oct 1612; *d* Antwerp, late 1659). Flemish painter and dealer. He was apprenticed to Pieter van Avont and then in 1634 moved to Rubens's studio, where he may have worked on the decorations for the *Pompa introitus Ferdinandi*. In 1634/5 he became a master in Antwerp's Guild of St Luke and shortly afterwards entered the service of Emperor Ferdinand II in Vienna. In spring 1637, however, he was in England, working on various commissions for Charles I, including ceiling paintings with mythological themes. At the same time he executed a number of small landscapes with figures and must also have been in contact with van Dyck. By 1641 Wouters had returned to Antwerp, where, in his capacity as a dealer, he assisted in the valuation of the

Frans Wouters: *Landscape with Diana and her Nymphs*, oil on panel, 860×910 mm, 1636 (Vienna, Kunsthistorisches Museum)

paintings from Rubens's estate. He was also involved in the sale of the Duke of Buckingham's collection by the Parliamentary Commissioners in 1648. At about the same time Wouters began to work for Archduke Leopold William.

Wouters's style and subject-matter are closely linked to the taste of his clients: the small format of his paintings, their decorative landscape compositions and largely mythological staffage are related to the fact that the work was primarily intended for aristocratic buyers and for an art trade that was international in outlook. His earliest known work is the *Landscape with Diana and her Nymphs* (1636; Vienna, Ksthistmus.; see fig.), which reflects the influence of the late Mannerist style of Josse de Momper. By that time, however, Wouters had also become aware of Rubens's personal interpretation of landscape. This is evident in such works as the *Landscape with Diana and Callisto* (Kroměříž, Castle) and the *Landscape with a Rainbow* (British Royal Col.), with the Venetian rendering of trees, the pastoral mood of the landscapes and the anatomical treatment of the figures. From *c.* 1648, after he had entered the service of Archduke Leopold William, Wouters produced work of a different character. Under the influence of van Dyck, his figures assumed an extreme elongated appearance while their emotional expression became sentimental and more emphatic. Wouters painted mythological landscapes and biblical scenes in this style, for example *Hagar in the Desert* (Vienna, Ksthistmus.).

BIBLIOGRAPHY
G. Gluck: *Rubens, van Dyck und ihr Kreis* (Vienna, 1933), pp. 222–43
M.-L. Hairs: *Dans le sillage de Rubens: Les Peintres d'historie anversois au XVIIe siècle* (Liège, 1977), pp. 48–52

HANS VLIEGHE

Wouters, Rik (*b* Mechelen, 21 Aug 1882; *d* Amsterdam, 11 July 1916). Belgian painter, sculptor, draughtsman and printmaker. From the age of 11 he worked in the studio of his father, an ornamental sculptor. After studying painting in 1899 at the Akademie van Schone Kunsten in Mechelen, he went to Brussels in 1902 to study sculpture under Charles Van der Stappen; although he did not stay there long, he continued to sculpt, taking up painting only in 1911. In 1905 he married Hélène Duerinckx, known affectionately as Nel, who first worked for him as a model earlier in the year. They were rescued from poverty only in 1911, when Wouters signed a contract with the Galerie Giroux in Brussels.

Wouters was particularly productive as a painter from 1912 to 1914, painting some of his best works, such as the portrait of his wife entitled *Woman with Yellow Necklace* (1912) and *The Flautist* (1914; both Brussels, Mus. A. Mod.), in which a man in pensive pose is set against a landscape seen through a window. An exhibition held at the Galerie Giroux at this time was highly successful. After being called up in 1914 Wouters saw action at Liège; after the fall of Antwerp he was interned in the Netherlands, first in the camp at Amersfoort, then in the camp at Zeist, where he was allowed to work. On his release in June 1915 he settled in Amsterdam with Nel and worked there intensively in spite of suffering from cancer of the jaw, which proved fatal after three operations.

Wouters was a passionate observer of life, obsessed by the image of the moment, hence his numerous drawings carried out in brush and India ink. He also worked in pastel and watercolour, often using Nel as his model. As a painter he was concerned with the play of light and reflection, as in *Woman by the Window, Amsterdam* (1915; Antwerp, Kon. Mus. S. Kst.). In his sculpture he also sought to capture life as accurately as possible, using effects of light after the manner of Rodin, for example in the bust-length portrait of Nel entitled *In the Sun* (bronze, 1911; Brussels, Mus. A. Mod.). He produced a few sculpted portraits, including a *Bust of James Ensor* (bronze, 1913; Brussels, Mus. A. Mod.), as well as monumental works such as the *Mad Virgin* (bronze, h. 1.95 m, 1912; Antwerp, Kon. Mus. S. Kst.) and *Domestic Worries* (bronze, h.2.22 m, 1913; Cologne, Mus. Ludwig).

BIBLIOGRAPHY
A.-J.-J. Delen: *Rik Wouters, zijn leven, zijn werk, zijn einde* (Antwerp, 1922)
N. Wouters: *La Vie de Rik Wouters à travers son oeuvre* (Brussels, 1944)
Rik Wouters (exh. cat., foreword W. Vanbeselaere; Antwerp, Kon. Mus. S. Kst., 1957)
R. Avermaete: *Rik Wouters* (Brussels, 1962/*R* 1986)
Rik Wouters (exh. cat., Antwerp, Kon. Mus. S. Kst., 1989)

ROGER AVERMAETE

Wouwerman [Wouwermans], **Philips** [Philippus] (*b* Haarlem, *bapt* 24 May 1619; *d* Haarlem, 19 May 1668). Dutch painter and draughtsman. He was the eldest son of the painter Paulus [Pauwels] Joostens Wouwerman of Alkmaar (*d* 28 Sept 1642), whose two other sons, Pieter Wouwerman (1623–82) and Johannes Wouwerman (1629–66), also became painters. Philips probably received his first painting lessons from his father, none of whose work has been identified. According to Cornelis de Bie, Wouwerman was next apprenticed to Frans Hals, although no trace of Hals's influence is discernible in Wouwerman's work. Wouwerman is also reputed to have spent several weeks in 1638 or 1639 working in Hamburg in the studio of the German history painter Evert Decker (*d* 1647). While in Hamburg, he married Annetje Pietersz. van Broeckhof. On 4 September 1640 Wouwerman joined the Guild of St Luke in Haarlem, in which in 1646 he held the office of *vinder* (agent or 'finder'). Given the many southern elements in his landscapes, it has repeatedly been suggested that Wouwerman must have travelled to France or Italy, but there is no documentary evidence that he left his native Haarlem for more than short periods. During his lifetime he must have attained a certain degree of prosperity, as demonstrated by the relatively large sums inherited by each of his seven children after his wife's death in 1670. However, there is no confirmation for Houbraken's statement that Wouwerman's daughter Ludovica took with her a dowry of 20,000 guilders when she married the painter Hendrik de Fromantiou (1633/4–after 1694) in 1672.

Wouwerman was undoubtedly the most accomplished and successful 17th-century Dutch painter of horses, which were included in his many small cabinet pictures depicting battle scenes, hunting scenes, army camps, smithies and stables. That he was a more versatile painter, however, is shown by his sensitively executed silvery-grey

Philips Wouwerman: *Battle Scene*, oil on canvas, 1.39×1.90 m, 1646 (London, National Gallery)

landscapes, his genre scenes and his few, original religious and mythological pictures. He was also exceptionally productive: although he lived to be only 48 years old, more than 1000 paintings bear his name, but some of these should be attributed to his brothers Pieter and Johannes. Only a small number of drawings by Philips are known.

In spite of Wouwerman's extensive oeuvre, it is difficult to establish a chronology, since only a comparatively small number of his paintings are dated. The style of his signature enables pictures to be dated only within wide limits: a monogram composed of P, H and W was used only before 1646, after which he used a monogram composed of PHILS and W. His earliest dated work, depicting a *Military Encampment* (1639; sold London, Christie's, 10 Oct 1972, lot 13), is of minor quality, but his talents developed rapidly in the 1640s. During that period the artist was strongly influenced, both in style and subject-matter, by Pieter van Lacr, who had returned to Haarlem from Italy in 1638. Houbraken claimed that Wouwerman obtained sketches and studies by van Laer after the latter's death, and van Laer's influence is clearly demonstrated in *Attack on a Coach* (1644; Vaduz, Samml. Liechtenstein), in which several figures and details are quotations from the older artist's work. During the mid-1640s most of Wouwerman's compositions are dominated by a diagonal hill or dune, with a tree as repoussoir and a few rather large figures, usually with horses. Three works dated 1646, a *Landscape with Peasants Merrymaking in front of a Cottage* (Manchester, C.A.G.), a *Battle Scene* (London, N.G.; see fig.) and a *Landscape with a Resting Horseman* (Leipzig, Mus. Bild. Kst.), show that Wouwerman gradually developed his own style, while continuing to be inspired by the work of van Laer.

By 1649 Wouwerman's sombre palette had become more colourful and his compositions increasingly horizontal. At about the same time his pictures began to reflect a growing interest in landscape, and during the first half of the 1650s the artist produced a number of paintings that demonstrate his mastery of the subject. In a *Landscape with Horsemen* (1652; GB, priv. col., see Stechow, fig. 41), painted in silvery tones, the figures and horses have been reduced to rather insignificant staffage. Genre elements continued to play an important role in most of his paintings, however, as can be seen in one of his most successful works of that period, *Festive Peasants before a Panorama* (1653; Minneapolis, MN, Inst. A.). Perhaps nowhere else in his oeuvre did the artist succeed in producing such a happy synthesis of genre and landscape elements. During the second half of the 1650s Wouwerman produced many fanciful hunting scenes, often with a vaguely Italian setting and brighter local colours; these were particularly sought after in the 18th century and the early 19th, especially in France. Although only a few dated works from the last decade of his life survive, these reveal a tendency towards a more sombre palette and show a slight decline in artistic skill. Van Laer's influence on Wouwerman's style had almost disappeared, but his work continued to influence Wouwerman's choice of subject-matter.

Wouwerman had several pupils, including Nicolaes Ficke (*b c.* 1620), Jacob Warnars and the Swedish artist Koort Witholt in 1642; Antony de Haen (1640–before 1675) studied with him in 1656. Emanuel Murant (1622–*c.* 1700), Hendrick Berckman (1629–79), Barend Gael (*c.* 1630/40–after 1681) and his own two brothers were also pupils. Wouwerman also had many followers. All the important collections created during the 18th and the early 19th century, including those that form the nucleus of the museums in St Petersburg, Dresden and The Hague, contain a large number of his works. Between 1737 and 1759 Jean Moyreau (1690–1762) published 89 engravings after paintings by Wouwerman. From the mid-19th century Wouwerman's popularity declined, but in the late 20th century there was a revival of interest in his work.

BIBLIOGRAPHY

Thieme–Becker

C. de Bie: *Het gulden cabinet* (1661), p. 281

A. Houbraken: *De groote schouburgh* (1718–21), ii, p. 71

J. Moyreau: *Oeuvres de Philippe Wouwermens gravées d'après ses meilleurs tableaux* (Paris, 1737–59)

J. Smith: *A Catalogue Raisonné of the Works of the Most Eminent Dutch, Flemish and French Painters*, i (London, 1829), pp. 199–358; ix (London, 1842), pp. 137–233

C. Hofstede de Groot: *Holländischen Maler* ii (1908), pp. 274–659

S. Kalff: 'De gebroeders Wouwerman', *Elsevier's Geïllus. Mdschr.*, xxx (1920), pp. 96–103

W. Stechow: *Dutch Landscape Painting* (London and New York, 1966), pp. 29–31

Masters of 17th-century Dutch Landscape Painting (exh. cat., ed. P. C. Sutton; Amsterdam, Rijksmus.; Boston, MA, Mus. F.A.; Philadelphia, PA, Mus. A.; 1987–8), pp. 527–34

F. J. Duparc: 'Philips Wouwerman's *Festive Peasants before a Panorama*', *Bull. Minneapolis Inst. A.* (1991)

——: 'Philips Wouwerman, 1619–1668', *Oud Holland* cvii (1993), pp. 257–86

FREDERIK J. DUPARC

Wprost. *See* STRAIGHT AHEAD.

Wredow, August (Julius) (*b* Brandenburg an der Havel, 5 June 1804; *d* Berlin, 21 Jan 1891). German sculptor. He studied under the sculptor Christian Daniel Rauch from November 1823 and at the Akademie in Berlin under Johann Gottfried Schadow. Among his early sculptures are *Anatomy* (ex-Berlin, Akad. Kst.; destr.) and the *Wounded Philoctetes*. In 1827 he moved to Rome where he was in close contact with the Danish sculptor Bertel Thorvaldsen and achieved recognition with his statue of *Ganymede as a Shepherd Boy* (marble, 1828–30; Potsdam, Schloss Charlottenhof). This nude figure combines classical austerity with the more sentimental and naturalistic approach derived from the Berlin tradition of sculpture; with its soft flesh tints and supple structure, it effectively humanized the accepted sculptural style. Wredow's approach was similar in *Paris Arming Himself for Battle* (marble, *c.* 1833–4) and in *Praying Boy* (1831–2; both Potsdam, Orangerie) and other classical figures. During the preparation of these works he spent most of his time in Italy (Carrara and Rome) and stayed there until he settled permanently in Berlin in 1841. When Wredow's design for a cycle on the theme of the wars of 1813–15 against Napoleon was rejected in 1842, he joined other sculptors of the Rauch school to work on one of the eight groups for Karl Friedrich Schinkel's Schlossbrücke. Wredow's contribution, not completed until 1857, shows *Iris Carrying the Fallen Warrior up to Olympus* (marble; *in situ*).

In 1843 Wredow became a member of the Berlin Akademie, where he was subsequently a professor and member of the Senate. Two years later he designed the statues of the *Twelve Apostles*, reminiscent of works by Thorvaldsen, for the Nikolai Church in Helsinki (*in situ*). Of these, he executed the figures of *Andrew, Bartholomew, John, Philip* and *Jude*, while the other statues were entrusted to Hermann Schievelbein, Gustav Blaeser and Heinrich Berges (1805–52). Wredow also produced a few portrait busts, including *Empress Catherine II* (1830; Donaustauf, Walhalla), but his work was essentially bound up with Neo-classicism, especially mythological and ideal themes. In his last two decades Wredow supported the Zeichen- und Kunstgewerbeschule in Brandenburg, which later took his name. He commissioned the school building, completed in 1878, and donated an extensive collection of art, ornaments and crafts, as well as his own works still in his possession (untraced).

ADB   BIBLIOGRAPHY
P. Bloch and W. Grzimek: *Das klassische Berlin: Die Berliner Bildhauer-schule im 19. Jahrhundert* (Frankfurt am Main, 1978), pp. 111, 129–31, 147, 198–200, 465–6
P. Springer: *Schinkels Schlossbrücke in Berlin: Zweckbau und Monument* (Frankfurt am Main, 1981)

                                                M. PULS

Wren, Sir **Christopher** (*b* East Knoyle, Wilts, 20 Oct 1632; *d* London, 25 Feb 1723). English architect. The leader of the English Baroque school, he was the creator of St Paul's Cathedral, London, completed in his lifetime, and remains the most famous architect in English history.

I. Life and work. II. Critical reception and influence.

I. Life and work.

1. Introduction. 2. *c.* 1660–*c.* 1670. 3. *c.* 1670–*c.* 1700. 4. After *c.* 1700.

1. INTRODUCTION. Needless confusion persists over the year of Wren's birth because a previous child called Christopher, his father's first name, had been born but immediately died in November 1631. From his father, who was the rector of East Knoyle, a rural parish, Wren acquired his interest in numbers, structures and mechanical contrivances, as well as his loyalty to the monarchy in politics and support of the episcopacy and the sacraments in religion. The Wren family remained steadfastly—and in some cases heroically—royalist and episcopalian through-out the Civil War and the Interregnum, the periods that coincided with most of Wren's teens and twenties respectively. After five years at Westminster School, London, and three of private study, in 1649 Wren went to Wadham College, Oxford (BA 1651, MA 1653). There, and subsequently while a Fellow of All Souls, he was associated with the group of mathematical and natural scientists who after the Restoration in 1660 were to form the nucleus of the Royal Society. He learnt from them the primacy of scientific enquiry over political and religious conviction (for the group embraced men of diverse persuasion) and the attitudes and methods of the new sceptical and experimental science pioneered by Galileo and popularized in England by Francis Bacon, 1st Baron Verulam and Viscount St Albans.

In 1657 Wren was appointed Professor of Astronomy at Gresham College in the City of London. In his inaugural lecture he first stressed the importance of arithmetic and geometry, the only human truths 'void of all uncertainty', as the basis not only of his own profession but of all activities and the key to all disciplines. The modern distinction made between pure and applied science was then unknown, and he went on to discuss the usefulness of astronomy in studies as divergent as seamanship and theology. Five years later navigation and the date of Easter were among the subjects of his lectures as Savilian Professor of Astronomy at Oxford, but his early academic interests also included anatomy, mechanics, optics and the design of meters and gauges of various kinds.

No-one perhaps saw Wren's citation of Vitruvius in his lecture in 1657 as an omen; nevertheless it was during the late 1650s in London and Oxford that the seeds of architecture were sown in his mind. By the end of his tenure of the Savilian Chair (1661–73) he was established as an architect and appointed to design a new St Paul's Cathedral in London, but his inaugural term (in the autumn of 1661) was marked by a long absence in the capital, in connection with the repair of Old St Paul's and a royal invitation to supervise the refortification of Tangier, a recently acquired British outpost in the Mediterranean. Wren declined this invitation, but the favours offered him on this occasion included, significantly, the reversion of the post of Surveyor of the King's Works (*see* OFFICE OF WORKS) on the death of Sir John Denham (1615–69).

If Wren had died at the age of 30, he would have had a small but secure place in the history of science, but what is notable in retrospect is the common thread, in all his scientific endeavours, of visible demonstration; it was this that led him to architecture. Both in the geometry of solids and voids, which he considered the primary basis of beauty, and in the visual impression proper to the accidents of site and function, which he considered only a little less important, architecture was for Wren the ultimate demonstration of truth as well as of social order. The distinction, which he defined in a fragmentary essay, between natural (geometrical) and customary (associative) beauty corresponds roughly to the difference between reason and intuition, and his insistence on the former was tempered by the latter in both theory and practice. Indeed he cannot have been unaware of the part played by intuition in mathematical thought itself. Initially Wren learnt architecture by looking, reading and asking questions. By 1663 he had designed a simple building, a new chapel (1663–5) for Pembroke College, Cambridge, and when in July 1665 he began a nine-month visit to Paris he was expecting to meet both François Mansart and the Italian Gianlorenzo Bernini, who was there for the summer. France offered him a far greater range of classical architecture than did the works in England of Inigo Jones, and he managed to meet a number of other architects and engineers, both French and Italian. This he evidently thought to be adequate experience, for he did not visit Italy and never again went abroad. Nevertheless, without the accident of the Great Fire of London in 1666 and the patronage of Charles II he might have remained largely a paper architect, the first of a number of Oxford amateurs.

2. *c.* 1660–*c.* 1670. The principal executed buildings designed before Wren's visit to France show both a considerable knowledge of Renaissance source-books and the vigorous disregard for received solutions that led him constantly to return to first principles. The new chapel of Pembroke College was the gift to the college of Bishop Matthew Wren (1585–1667), the architect's uncle. It was, before the addition of a chancel in 1880, a simple box whose pretty plaster ceiling and excellent woodwork probably owe more to the craftsmen involved than to Wren. But in the street front he combined, rather as Leon Battista Alberti had done before him, elements from a Classical temple front and a triumphal arch. The wiry and unripe foliage of his Corinthian order, unorthodox but not unstudied, already shows his inventiveness within the Classical vocabulary of detail.

The more ambitious Sheldonian Theatre (1664–9) in Oxford, the gift of Archbishop Gilbert Sheldon (1598–1677) to the University, is still used for its original purpose of accommodating degree ceremonies. The Sheldonian took from ancient Roman theatres its D-shaped plan and the opened canvas awning, which was depicted in paint around the edge of its illusionistic ceiling (displaying allegorical figures arrayed in the heavens), the work of the painter Robert Streeter (1668–9); every other aspect of the building was as unprecedented as its function. Wren's problem, in this stageless theatre designed for real, not illusory, events, was to shelter and seat a large audience whose focus would be on the Vice-Chancellor's chair. By the use of truss girders he was able to dispense with internal pillars so as to make the ceremonies clearly visible to all; the tiered and raked seating, the need for ample illumination and the provision of a ceremonial entrance determined the disparate outside elevations. The south front is derived from Renaissance sources: superimposed orders culminating in an applied temple front identify the gable end, frame the main door and confirm the celebratory inscription in the lower frieze. A quite different and astylar system articulates the sides and the polygonal 'theatre' end; a high rusticated basement forms the outside of the tiered seating, and the attic storey immediately above consists mostly of windows. This 'functional' elevation, seemingly lacking a principal storey, was originally crowned by a row of equally unclassical oval dormer windows, removed when the roof was reconstructed in 1801–2. The Sheldonian should not be seen as naive or picturesque but rather as a conscious attempt to reconcile, in a new type of building, Royal Society rationalism and the Vitruvian requirements of commodity, firmness and delight.

France not only made real for Wren a kind of architecture previously only imagined but specifically introduced him to the form that was henceforth to dominate his architectural thought: the dome (*see* MASONRY, §III, 3(iv)). In May 1666, only a few weeks after his return to England, he produced a report and proposals for replacing the decrepit centre and spireless tower of Old St Paul's Cathedral (*see* LONDON, §V, 1(i)) by new crossing-piers and a tall dome, which, he believed, would give London a worthy landmark; by early August he had amplified his ideas through drawings (Oxford, All Souls Coll., II.4–7). In appearance and even in levels the dome design of 1666 prefigures the one he was finally to build

40 years later, although the latter's greater complexity of design and structure reflects not only the real necessities of statics but also the architect's own development over the intervening decades. Both comprise a drum full of windows, an inner masonry shell and a higher, outer lead-covered timber cupola with a tall lantern. Wren's first design remained on paper, less because of its mixed reception than because during the first week of September 1666 the cathedral was so badly damaged in the Great Fire of London that in his view a total rebuilding was the only safe course of action.

Within about a week after the Fire, Wren produced a plan for a new city of straight streets and broad avenues. Formal though it seems, by comparison with the chequer-board plans proposed by some of his contemporaries, Wren's plan is remarkably natural and varied. But the redistribution of property it would have entailed, even in a city burnt to the ground, precluded any possibility of following what Wren probably saw, in any case, as only a draft for discussion. Apart from the City churches and a new St Paul's he did not rebuild London, although there can be no doubt that, as one of the six surveyors in charge of reconstruction, he helped establish the new legal standards for materials and construction imposed after the Fire by the London Building Acts.

The restoration of commercial and domestic life in London was more urgent than the cathedral, but by April 1668 Wren was discussing the latter, and a wooden model, today known as the First, was completed in March 1670. For three years this was the accepted design, comprising two virtually independent parts, a vaulted and galleried hall and a domed western vestibule. Wren was not yet architect to St Paul's, but he was negotiating unofficially with the Dean. During 1670–71, however, he designed and saw the commencement of 15 new parish churches. In March 1669 he had become Surveyor of the King's Works; his appointment to St Paul's on 12 November 1673 and the conferment of a knighthood at about the same time (probably the occasion for the making of his marble portrait bust, now in the Ashmolean, Oxford, by the sculptor Edward Pierce (ii)), set the seal on his architectural career.

3. *c.* 1670–*c.* 1700.

(i) London churches and Temple Bar. (ii) Trinity College and St Paul's Cathedral. (iii) Hampton Court Palace, the Royal Hospitals and other projects.

(i) London churches and Temple Bar. Wren's ability as a designer of churches appears principally in three respects: in his practical approach to the setting of Protestant worship, in the variety of plan solutions he devised and in the wealth of invention displayed in his towers and steeples. Four parish churches were quickly repaired after the Fire, probably by City surveyors, but Wren was responsible for the design and construction of 47 new buildings. Surviving drawings show the help of draughtsmen impossible to name, and the buildings are certainly not all his personal creation in the way that the Sheldonian and St Paul's are: his colleague Robert Hooke undoubtedly helped in the design of some of them.

Post-Reformation England had been generally over-provided with churches, and Wren was thus the first

1. Christopher Wren: interior of the dome of St Stephen Walbrook, London, begun 1672 (restored by 1987)

architect to face seriously the problem of designing for the Anglican liturgy. In 1711, in a paper of advice written for the benefit of another church-building programme, he succinctly identified the prime requirement as an 'auditory' in which all could see and hear, with additional seating in galleries placed over the side aisles—a formula not unlike that of his Sheldonian Theatre. He used this form, with a token chancel containing the altar table, in all the larger churches. The example he cited, St James, Piccadilly, is not in the City but in Westminster: it was built by Wren in 1676–84 to serve a new area of growth in London's West End; although virtually rebuilt after war damage in 1940, this is also in appearance the best surviving example. Some of the smaller churches are also basilican but without galleries (e.g. St Magnus, 1671–8, London Bridge).

Many of the smaller and less regularly shaped church sites stimulated Wren's invention. Although some churches comprised a single cell or had only one side aisle, he also designed domed polygonal plans (St Benet Fink, St Antholin; both destr.) and several versions of a Greek cross within a square (e.g. St Anne and St Agnes, Gresham Street; St Martin Ludgate). Some of the single cells were also domed (St Swithin, destr.; St Mary Abchurch). Many plans, relying on old foundations, were only approximately rectangular, expressing a geometry that is a matter of perceptible space rather than of angular precision. Some of the churches could only ever have been perceived as wholes from inside, since the secular buildings surrounding them precluded any coherent external view; some thus offer a single ornate façade to the street, for example the east end of St Peter-upon-Cornhill, whose undistinguished west, entrance end is hidden in the small churchyard.

Even the most ambitious of the churches, St Stephen Walbrook (1672–9), has a very plain exterior. Inside it is notable for its perfect geometrical regularity, its craftsmanship of the highest standards, and a complex and ambiguous plan which combines basilican and both Latin and Greek cruciform elements with a centralizing dome rising from eight equal arches supported on columns (see fig. 1). The exceptional character of St Stephen Walbrook may be partly due to the patronage of the Grocers' Company, but it can hardly be accidental that it was designed (the only church begun in 1672) while Wren was concerned with the new and much grander centralized design for St Paul's that led to the Great Model of 1673. Restoration work at St Stephen Walbrook, completed in 1987, included the recovery of the original fenestration by opening blocked windows, structural reinforcement and the installation of an altar designed by Henry Moore under the centre of the dome. This concept was inevitably outside the limits of 17th-century Anglican liturgy or seating arrangements; however, the entire loss of its original box pews and other permanent seating had already effectively reduced the interior to the unfurnished spaciousness shown, albeit fictitiously, in 18th-century prints, and the altar in fact complements the dome without destroying the original complexity of readings of the interior.

Wren's spirit is in fact not easy to find today in the City churches, of which about half survive of the 47 with which he was involved. He certainly thought of them as congenial, unemotional, harmonious buildings filled with clear daylight; in most cases pews have been cut down or taken out, other fittings altered, seating rearranged and clear windows replaced by inappropriate stained glass. The same is true of his other Westminster church, St Clement Danes (1680–82) in the Strand, a basilican replacement for a medieval building. St Clement is unusual both in the elaboration of its plaster barrel vault and in the rounded east end culminating in a small apse, which Wren provided in order to make the fullest use of an irregular site.

Eighteenth-century London owed to Wren not its plan or its secular buildings but its skyline. The view down the Thames from Westminster, most tellingly recorded in Canaletto's views (e.g. *The Thames and the City of London from Richmond House, c.* 1747; Goodwood House, W. Sussex), survived with little change until the early 20th century, although by then building heights had started to rise. Those in the vicinity of St Paul's are still strictly limited by law, but the loss of the historic skyline is due not only to commercial exploitation since *c.* 1960 of modern high building techniques but almost as much to a gradual and general increase in the number of storeys. In the City of Wren and Canaletto, the only buildings higher than five floors were St Paul's, the Monument to the Great Fire (1671–6; designed by Wren in collaboration with Robert Hooke) and the larger church towers and steeples. Towers and belfries were an accepted provision in the rebuilding programme, but initially most of them were simple in form. The notable exception was the 66 m Portland stone steeple of Wren's St Mary-le-Bow, Cheapside; completed in 1680, it remained for almost 20 years a sample of prospective achievement.

One other City structure of this period that may be claimed as Wren's creation survives far from its original site: Temple Bar, the western gateway to the City; totally rebuilt in 1670–72 by order of Charles II, it was removed in 1878 to Theobalds Park, Herts. Wren's son possessed the original drawings; its façades show a sophisticated approach to classical design characteristic in its disregard of received patterns of elevation and detail.

(ii) Trinity College and St Paul's Cathedral. If Wren's stylistic development from the 1660s to the 1690s may be considered an accelerated counterpart of the development of Italian architecture from Filippo Brunelleschi to Pietro da Cortona, then the 1670s correspond to his 'High Renaissance' period. The new library (1676–84) for Trinity College, Cambridge, invites comparison with Jacopo Sansovino's Libreria Marciana (built from 1536), Venice, not through any direct influence, nor merely because both are traditional long upstairs libraries above open loggias, but also because the main elevations of each depend equally on an expert, practised and sympathetic handling of superimposed storeys of arcades buttressed by half columns. Wren had first used a similar combination in the main façade of the Sheldonian Theatre; at Trinity College the unit of an arch flanked by half columns became the module for the whole building, carried through its thickness by the correspondence of solids—piers, window-sides, bookstacks and ceiling beams—in three dimensions with what appears to be complete logicality. Wren's logic, however, is illusory, since he dispensed with any correspondence in levels between the external division into two equal storeys and the spacious interior which occupies almost three-quarters of the total height. By filling in the tympana of the lower arches, he was able to support the library floor behind them, immediately above the imposts of the arcade; thus the whole height from these imposts up to the sills of the large windows above is occupied inside by the bookstacks, and the light to the interior is ample and uninterrupted. The striking disparity between the front and back elevations accords with Wren's belief, affirmed in a fragmentary essay, that things not visible together need not be alike; what holds the whole design elegantly together is the three-dimensional modular grid expressed through the orders and piers on the outside and the bookcases and ceiling beams on the inside. The thoroughness of Wren's attention to both practical and aesthetic aspects of the design is evident from the explanatory letter that accompanied his designs: flooring was specified for quietness and warmth, windows for soundness, and while the open ground-floor area under the Library was consciously modelled on the Athenian stoa, Wren at this date equally consciously eschewed the strong contrast of scale that an exterior giant order would have made.

Wren's 'High Renaissance' period also included both the Great Model for St Paul's (1672–3) and the design from which actual construction finally began in July 1675. The chief recorded criticism of the (First) 1670 model was that it was not grand enough; encouraged to raise his sights, Wren started again and designed a centralized domed church in the manner of Donato Bramante's and Michelangelo's St Peter's (*see* ROME, §V, 14(ii)(a)), but with the addition of a vestibule and giant portico at the west end. This deceptively simple design, which received royal approval in November 1673, survives in the Great Model (London, St Paul's Cathedral; see fig. 2). The whole is dominated by the dome, whose ring of supporting piers,

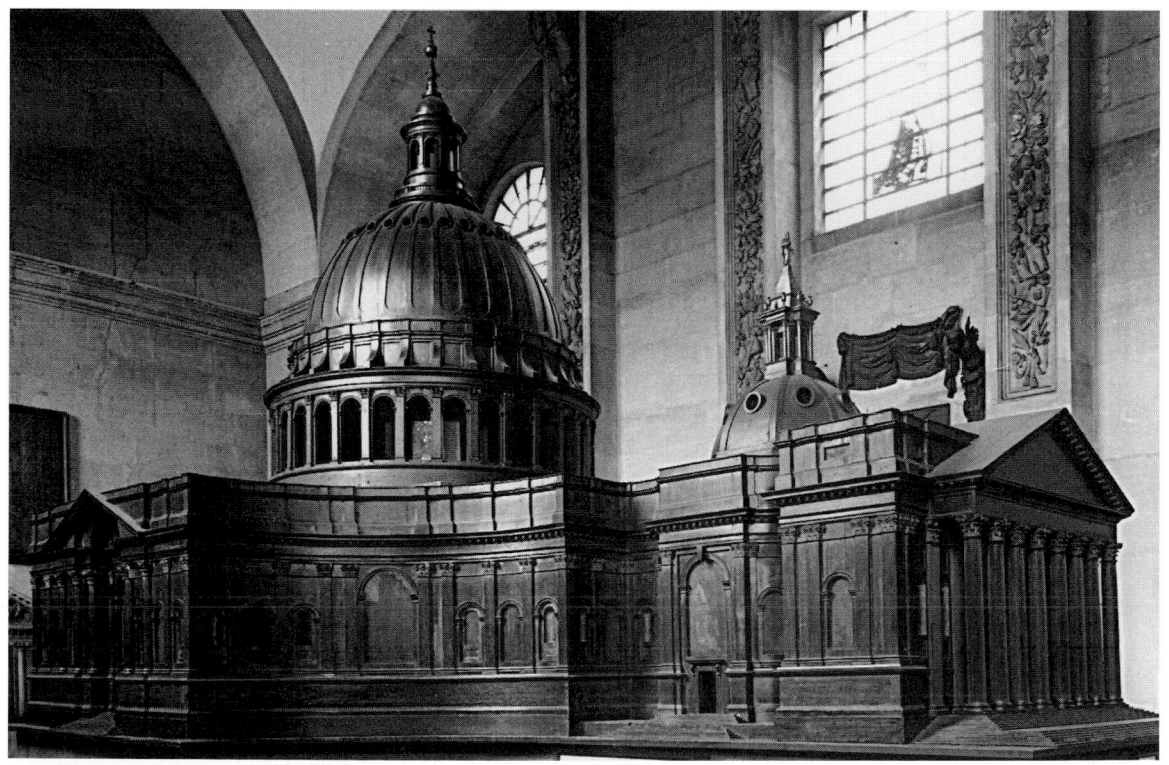

2. Christopher Wren: Great Model for St Paul's Cathedral, London, wood, l. 5.5 m, 1673 (London, St Paul's Cathedral)

if built, would have spanned 38 m, and in it Wren for the first time produced a design whose colossal scale derived—like that of the Doric temple—from internal consistency rather than from a relation to human dimensions. The centre of the dome had been marked out on site in the summer of 1673—the nearest St Paul's ever came to a foundation ceremony—but there were crucial objections both to a structure that, unlike a traditional cathedral form, could be raised only whole and not piecemeal and to a design for a Protestant church that so vividly recalled those of Counter-Reformation Rome.

However much the abandonment of this noble design may be regretted, there is no doubt that the perfection of a model completed in 18 months is imaginary, and that in the 30 years or so needed for its construction in the building economy of his time, Wren would have introduced many changes not merely in decorative details but in larger aspects of its appearance. The rejection affected him profoundly: having at last obtained a proper brief, he resolved as his son related 'to make no more Models, or publicly expose his Drawings'. In conditions of near-secrecy he designed a long Latin-cross basilican church (the 'Warrant' design; Oxford, All Souls Coll.) which received approval by a royal warrant on 14 May 1675. By that time, however, the design was already out of date, and Wren was reworking every dimension of the plan and every detail of the elevations; through the accidental survival of many drawings more is known about this period than about any other, and it is clear that Wren was using drawing as the principal means of research and development in the design process, working out design features individually before recombining them in complete plans, elevations and sections. Masons' contracts were completed on 15 July 1675, and two days later a water supply was laid to the site for the commencement of a design twice removed from the Warrant and recognizably the basis of what was built. Indeed, few changes were made to the body of the church apart from an increase in the amount of decorative carving.

Work was thus begun not on the traditional Latin-cross plan approved in May 1675 but on one in which the western part is, both inside and outside, sharply differentiated from the three-bay nave proper, equal in length to the choir. Thus the building appears to have a stretched but centralized plan with a western annexe. The elevations too were changed: the basilican aisled structure is completely encased in a continuous two-storey screen wall which gives both statical bracing and massive visual support to a dome almost as wide as that of the Great Model, a feature of every one of Wren's designs for St Paul's. The massive exterior thus created also hides the flying buttresses that strengthen the main vaults and appears virtually independent of the building within. This separation was carried on into the dome itself, from the many varied drawings of 1675 to the final structure.

The 1675 warrant had praised a design capable of completion, unlike the Great Model, 'by parts'; St Paul's was built in the traditional order from east to west, but sound statical reasons led Wren to begin all four quadrants of the crossing almost at once, by early 1676. Thereafter, as the building accounts show, work proceeded westwards and upwards in a manner that kept the contractors occupied almost continuously: contracts were made section by section, each trade from foundations to roofing moving gradually from east to west, to be followed by the workmen of the next stage. On the other hand, determination to see his work realized as a whole must account, at least in part, for the fact that even the choir was not ready for use until 1697 when most of the nave and west end were almost finished.

(iii) Hampton Court Palace, the Royal Hospitals and other projects. Wren's son and biographer counted as one of his father's major achievements the completion of St Paul's within his lifetime (at the age of 78); in domestic architecture Wren was less fortunate. While the accident of the Great Fire gave him the unique occasion for a great religious building, continued stringency in royal finances denied him equal success in secular building. Charles II, anxious to preserve as far as possible both the image and the reality of absolute monarchy, devoted to architecture more of his exchequer than he could afford; the earlier palace projects of his reign were, however, entrusted to other designers. John Webb (i), called out of early retirement, designed the new palace at Greenwich, London, begun in 1664 and abandoned five years later; the only range to be constructed would later condition the development of Wren's Greenwich Hospital. Windsor Castle, Berks, was outside the control of the King's Surveyor, and the extensive refitting there from c. 1675 onwards, together with the design of new state suites, was entrusted to Hugh May; when Wren took charge on May's death in 1684 the work was virtually complete, and his only opportunity for a full Baroque interior design was in a new Roman Catholic chapel in 1685 (destr. 1698) in Whitehall Palace for James II. This showed a sumptuous blend of illusionistic painting and carving, which delighted the diarist John Evelyn as much as the popish ceremonial he witnessed there shocked him.

In the early 1680s the Royal Hospital, Chelsea, London, and Winchester Palace, Hants, offered Wren the chance of large-scale secular work, in which he faced problems not only of complex planning and organization but of relating monumental buildings to the human scale of the user. At Winchester, begun in 1683 and roofed and abandoned on the death of Charles II two years later, planning was the more serious problem. Although finished chiefly in brick and ostensibly a hunting-lodge for the New Forest, the building was to be a full-scale palace, axially linked by a new street to the medieval cathedral. Winchester had been the ancient Saxon capital of England, and its remoteness from London and accessibility from the English Channel recommended it to a king increasingly reliant on confidential subsidies from Louis XIV of France. The disposition of the state rooms around three sides of an open court, with a central giant portico and a dome, probably derived from the project at Greenwich by Webb (i), but Winchester's progressively widening series of base-courts would unequivocally have recalled the town front of Louis's Versailles (*see* VERSAILLES, §1).

New foreign policies made Winchester unattractive to succeeding monarchs, and the main block was eventually fitted up, without its dome or state interiors, as a barracks (destr. after a fire in 1894). From 1682 to 1692 Wren's

3. Christopher Wren: south (Privy Garden) and east (park) ranges of Hampton Court Palace, London, begun 1690

Royal Hospital at Chelsea was built. Charles II's political skill in maintaining a standing army, together with philanthropic responses to the first major domestic war since the 15th century, led to the idea of pensions for retired or disabled soldiers and a home on the lines of the Hôtel des Invalides recently built in Paris for Louis XIV. Charles gave his patronage and some money, but most of the construction was financed by donations and a levy on soldiers' pay. The Royal Hospital was also modelled on Greenwich, around three sides of a court with a giant-order frontispiece in the middle of both the court and the outside elevations of each range. These features are appropriate in scale to the whole building, and the large scale is maintained throughout the centre range, housing the hall to one side of an octagonal vestibule and the chapel to the other. On the other hand, the side ranges are, apart from the frontispieces, domestic in scale, the pitched roofs and the regular fenestration on three storeys and attic dormers resembling the highest class of town housing of the time. The side ranges contain long wards flanking a central spine wall; each ward consists of a row of spacious cubicles opening on to a well-lit corridor and offering both privacy and a sense of community. In 1686 low wings were added to form side courts and provide service ranges and an infirmary. Apart from the 18th-century substitution of sash windows for casements and the modernization of furnishings and services, the hospital retains its character as well as its function, a tribute to the practicality and high standards of the original design.

Of three great projects for William and Mary, Hampton Court and Greenwich Hospital were half-built and the new palace at Whitehall was never started. The new sovereigns visited Hampton Court early in 1689; they liked the location but found the Tudor palace old-fashioned and requested new designs (*see* HAMPTON COURT

PALACE). Wren's first thoughts were for a complete rebuilding, a square court reminiscent of (though much smaller than) that of the Palais du Louvre in Paris, with open service courts to the north and west. This project, known from sketches, was too expensive and time-consuming, and within five months work had begun on the executed building which amounts to half a palace: east and south ranges, containing in the angle between them a fairly small court, 33×35 m. This solution allowed the retention of the Tudor chapel and great hall and the extensive kitchens and other offices, while providing new state apartments for the King and Queen and two main façades which offered the traveller from London, whether by road or river, the appearance of an enormous palace on a scale approaching that of Versailles (see fig. 3).

Like the two great buildings of the early 1680s and unlike French prototypes, the new Hampton Court was built not of stone but, in the interests of economy and speed, of locally made brick with stone dressings. Although construction was stopped when Queen Mary died at the end of 1694, the burning down of old Whitehall Palace on 4 January 1698 gave its completion a new urgency. The King's apartments were ready by 1700, and during the following year the parallel between William's country palace and that of the French king was demonstrated by the reception of embassies there, although no provision was made for government offices. Either from choice or at the sovereigns' wish the exteriors of Hampton Court are much richer in relief than those of the Royal Hospital or even Winchester, including trophies of arms and figurative reliefs appropriate to the status of a monarch who had led his armies to victory and who, although newly responsible to Parliament by the Revolution settlement of 1689, was far from being the mere figurehead of modern constitutional monarchy.

4. Christopher Wren: Royal Hospital (now the Royal Naval College), Greenwich, London, 1696–1716

Whitehall Palace was a rambling mass of buildings and courtyards to which successive monarchs from Henry VIII onwards had made additions without any coherent plan (*see* LONDON, §V, 5). Architecturally the most notable were Inigo Jones's Banqueting House (1619–22) and two ranges designed by Wren: James II's Catholic chapel, already mentioned, with a council chamber and gallery (1685–87), and a house for Queen Mary (1688–93) with a terrace fronting the River Thames. The 1698 fire destroyed or gutted the main palace buildings, leaving only Jones's Banqueting House (which Wren ordered extraordinary action to save), the Office of Works in Scotland Yard to the north and the mainly administrative buildings west of the street towards St James's Park. Wren immediately surveyed the site and drew out two alternative designs for a new Whitehall, but these had no more success than any of those made by various hands over the preceding 60 years. William III, who had always found the locality too damp for comfort, left the provision for rebuilding to Parliament; the latter saw no pressing need for a massive symbol of monarchy, and English bureaucracy was not yet sufficiently advanced to require another Versailles to house it. The site was gradually redeveloped, but the drawings (Oxford, All Souls Coll., V. 1–14), mostly in Wren's hand, show that in his sixties he had solved the problems of scale and massing, handling large contrasting blocks and sequences of courts. The nearest indication of this effect is at Greenwich, the definitive design for which was made at about the same time.

The Royal Hospital (now the Royal Naval College) at Greenwich was founded in 1694 by William and Mary as a maritime counterpart of Chelsea; it was to be built on the site of Greenwich Palace and to incorporate the new range designed by John Webb (i) and abandoned 25 years earlier (*see* GREENWICH, §2). Almost from the start it was conceived on a grander scale than its prototype, except

for two flaws. First, grandeur did not extend to its funding, which was even more haphazard than at Chelsea and resulted in slow and fitful progress. Secondly, the site grant excluded a central strip of land between Inigo Jones's Queen's House (1616–19 and 1630–35) and the River Thames: although Wren was able to build the matching block intended by Webb on the other side of the Queen's House axis, he could neither realize nor imitate Webb's intended central block intersecting the axis. Greenwich remains a complex in two halves on either side of a void, and Wren's solution was to build rectangular courts behind the Webb block and its counterpart, framing the axial view of the Queen's House with long colonnades and the tall domed vestibules to the hall and chapel (see fig. 4). As in a classical landscape, the sky and the distant hill occupy the centre of vision, framed by large masses; visually the effect is brilliant and dramatic, and Greenwich ought always to be approached by river rather than through the winding roads of south-east London.

4. AFTER *c.* 1700. At the death of William III in 1702 Wren was nearly 70. Although retirement was neither mandatory nor financially secured, his activity had become more selective. His practice relied increasingly on empiricism and delegation, and his staff included the capable William Dickinson and the brilliant Nicholas Hawksmoor. He seems to have given the latter a free hand in those parts of Greenwich away from the central axis, and it was Hawksmoor who fretted for the next 30 years over the administration's failure to complete the original design. On the other hand, Wren reserved some projects to himself, most notably the completion of St Paul's and the City skyline.

In 1697 Parliament renewed the tax on coal, which funded St Paul's and the City churches, specifically providing for additional steeples to already finished towers. These included the pagoda-like St Bride (1702–3), Fleet Street, the square Christ Church (1703–4), Newgate Street, and the interplay of convex and concave stages (reminiscent of the style of Francesco Borromini) at St Vedast (1709–12), Foster Lane, whose steeple had to be pre-assembled at Greenwich because the churchyard was too small for the work. These and other large structures not only put the finishing touches to Wren's vision of the City but seem also to have affected the final form of the dome and west towers of the cathedral, completed in 1710. At the last possible moment (1704) he abandoned the complex plan and profile of the dome in favour of very simple geometrical shapes, simultaneously changing the capped cylinders of the western towers to groups of columns arranged in a dramatic interplay of concave and convex shapes surely indebted, through engravings, to the style of the Roman Baroque. Thus the dome became one simple shape among many complex ones, including the cathedral's towers.

The London skyline was Wren's swan-song although, in spite of a serious illness in 1711 (revealed through handwriting), he continued to lead an active life. But in 1715 his office of Surveyor was put in the hands of a new Board of Works, and three years later his patent, having been granted not for life but at the King's pleasure, was revoked. At the age of 86 he perhaps had no more to contribute; nevertheless his dismissal was the result of personal and political intrigue, and its manner was abrupt. He moved out of the official house in Scotland Yard, Whitehall, where he had lived for almost 40 years, and retired to a house at Hampton Court; he was buried in St Paul's Cathedral which, as a brief Latin inscription above his tomb proclaims, is his true monument.

II. Critical reception and influence.

St Paul's has always attracted adverse criticism, for, having in the preliminary design process rid himself of received ideas, Wren produced a building that fits no-one's preconceptions. In architecture, as in the sciences, he returned constantly to first principles, refining and evolving his art from a tentative classicism based on Sebastiano Serlio and French models to a style that may justly take its place in the international late Baroque of Carlo Fontana (iv), Jules Hardouin Mansart and Johann Bernard Fischer von Erlach.

Although it is inaccurate to speak of a 'Wren school', many minor architects and builder-designers felt his influence. He showed little interest in private house design, and the debt to him of buildings for which he was not responsible, such as St Mary's, Ingestre, Staffs, or the first College of William and Mary in WILLIAMSBURG, VA, cannot be defined.

Anthony Ashley Cooper, 3rd Earl of Shaftesbury, attacked Wren's buildings and his supposed monopoly of English architecture in his *Letter Concerning Design* (1712), and during the 18th century Wren was commonly held to have lacked Taste. In the late 20th century he has too often been seen as an honorary Georgian, but it does him no service to gloss over the coarser vigour of much of his art: his contemporaries in literature were not the Augustans but John Bunyan, Henry Vaughan, John Dryden and Samuel Pepys. His fragmentary essays show that while his grasp of theory was sound he preferred practice; his architecture shows that while in theory geometry was the foundation of everything, in practice the eye took precedence.

Colvin

BIBLIOGRAPHY

C. Wren [the younger]: *Parentalia, or Memoirs of the Family of the Wrens* (London, 1750/*R* Farnborough, 1965) [incl. the architect's own fragmentary essays and the incomplete 'Tracts on Architecture']
The Wren Society, 20 vols (Oxford, 1924–43)
A. F. E. Poley: *St Paul's Cathedral, London* (London, 1932) [measured drgs]
G. Webb: *Wren* (London, 1937)
T. F. Reddaway: *The Rebuilding of London after the Great Fire* (London, 1940)
C. G. T. Dean: *The Royal Hospital, Chelsea* (London, 1950)
J. Summerson: *Sir Christopher Wren* (London, 1953)
E. F. Sekler: *Wren and his Place in European Architecture* (London, 1956)
J. Summerson: 'The Penultimate Design for St Paul's Cathedral', *Burl. Mag.*, ciii (1961), pp. 83–9
——: 'Drawings of London Churches in the Bute Collection', *Archit. Hist.*, xiii (1970), pp. 30–42
M. Whinney: *Wren* (London, 1971/*R* 1987)
J. A. Bennett: 'Christopher Wren: The Natural Causes of Beauty', *Archit. Hist.*, xv (1972), pp. 5–22
D. J. Watkin, ed.: *Architects*, iv of *Sale Catalogues of the Libraries of Eminent Persons*, iv (London, 1971–2), pp. 1–43
H. M. Colvin and others: *1660–1782* (1976), v of *The History of the King's Works*, ed. H. M. Colvin (London, 1963–82)
J. A. Bennett: *The Mathematical Science of Christopher Wren* (Cambridge, 1982)
K. Downes: *The Architecture of Wren* (London, 1982, rev. Reading, 1988)
Sir Christopher Wren (exh. cat., ed. K. Downes; London, Whitechapel A.G., 1982)
K. Downes: *Sir Christopher Wren: The Design of St Paul's* (London, 1988) [illus. cat. of drgs]
——: 'Sir Christopher Wren, Edward Woodroffe, J. H. Mansart, and Architectural History', *Archit. Hist.*, xxxvii (1994), pp. 37–67
KERRY DOWNES

Wrenthorpe. English centre of ceramic production. Several kilns, extensive waste deposits and documentary sources suggest large-scale production at Wrenthorpe, W. Yorks, dating to between the 15th and 18th centuries. Wares were made from local clays; they were decorated with imported white-firing clay and were fired in six-flued and bonfire kilns using both wood and coal. The principal and best-known wares were the red-bodied, chocolate-glazed Cistercian wares decorated with trailed slip and pads of white clay, often with stamped or incised decoration, including stylized floral and stag's head motifs. Forms included posset pots, chafing dishes, costrels, lids and small jugs. From the late 16th century plates were also produced.

BIBLIOGRAPHY

J. W. G. Musty: 'Medieval Pottery Kilns', *Medieval Pottery from Excavations: Studies Presented to Gerald Clough Dunning*, ed. V. Evison, H. Hodges and J. G. Hurst (London, 1974), pp. 41–65
MICHAEL R. McCARTHY

Wright. American family of architects and designers. (1) Frank Lloyd Wright (for portrait *see* ARCHITECT, fig. 3) was one of the acknowledged masters of 20th-century architecture. His sons (2) Lloyd Wright and (3) John Lloyd Wright also became architects; Lloyd Wright was in addition a landscape designer and John Lloyd Wright a designer of toys, while a third son, David Wright, became an executive with a firm manufacturing concrete blocks, which Frank Lloyd Wright used extensively in his work.

(1) Frank Lloyd (Lincoln) Wright (*b* Richland Center, WI, 8 June 1867; *d* Phoenix, AZ, 9 April 1959). He is one of the most universally acclaimed and admired of all American architects, and his name is known worldwide, to laymen as well as to architects and historians. Yet, unlike other important architects whose reputations rest at least in part on the influence of their work in shaping the architecture of their time, Wright's buildings and theories seem to have had only a slight impact on the evolution of 20th-century architecture. While the example of his buildings may have nurtured the early development of Walter Gropius, Le Corbusier and Ludwig Mies van der Rohe, the mature work of these architects seems largely unaffected by Wright. Instead, his work came to be appreciated primarily for its intrinsic artistic qualities, especially those dealing with spatial definition and surface articulation. That his architecture should be so highly regarded for its inherent values is remarkable testimony to the magnitude of his genius.

1. Training, early influences and work, before 1901. 2. Prairie houses and mature work, 1901–13. 3. Decorative years, 1914–34. 4. Late work, 1935 and after.

1. TRAINING, EARLY INFLUENCES AND WORK, BEFORE 1901. His father, William Russell Cary Wright, was a lawyer with qualifications in music and the ministry. A widower with young children, he was Superintendent of Schools in Richland County, WI, when he married Anna Lloyd Jones, a young teacher from a local Welsh Unitarian pioneer farming family. The marriage was not happy, ending in divorce in 1885. Frank Lloyd Wright was the first child and only son of Anna's family of three children. He became the special object of his mother's devotion, acquiring from her the tenacious determination of her pioneering background; to his father he owed his artistic gifts and lifelong love of music.

After leaving school Wright went to work for the engineer Allan D. Conover in Madison; he also studied engineering at the University of Wisconsin, Madison, for two quarters until 1887, when he went to Chicago to seek his fortune in architecture. There he worked first for Joseph Lyman Silsbee, an architect who had designed religious buildings for the Lloyd Jones family. From early 1888 to mid-1893 he served as chief draughtsman for Adler & Sullivan, whose designing partner, Louis Sullivan, was then gaining recognition for the unique style of architecture he was forging. In 1891 Wright began to design houses in his spare time and, as this practice was not authorized by his contract, his employment was terminated in June 1893. In 1889 Wright married Catherine Tobin and later that year they moved into a house Wright designed for them in Oak Park, a suburb of Chicago. During this ensuing decade of marital stability, during which Catherine bore him six children, Wright worked to perfect his own architectural expression. Wright absorbed the essentials of picturesque design from Silsbee, whose houses consisted of asymmetrically organized rooms of contrasting shapes opening into each other through wide doorways, the spatial flow accentuated by long diagonal views that often continued outside on to wide porches. The complex exterior massing of these houses echoed the irregularity of their interior plans and volumes. If Wright

derived his fascination for complex interior spaces from Silsbee, however, his mastery of plane and mass came from Louis Sullivan. In early 1888 he joined Adler & Sullivan, acting as their chief draughtsman from 1889 to mid-1893; during the years 1887 to 1889, Louis Sullivan designed buildings of a stark, abstract character, almost devoid of ornament. Although Wright believed that his interest in plain surfaces and simple masses resulted from play with the geometric Froebel kindergarten blocks his mother gave him when he was nine years old, it is more likely that he came to appreciate the rugged beauty of abstract masses through the influence of Sullivan.

It was Wright's destiny to integrate Sullivan's formal abstraction with Silsbee's involved spatial effects, and in working towards that end Wright evolved the system of design for which he is famous. He termed it 'organic'. Wright was also inspired by Japanese architecture, from which he derived his method of using solid and transparent rectangular planes to define space. These originated in the fixed and sliding screens and their framing members which make up the walls and interior partitions of traditional Japanese wooden houses. Another significant attribute of Wright's design process may be traced to the same source: the planning module, a rectangular grid laid over drawings to regulate the placement of walls, windows and doors, thus giving a consistent scale to a building. These reflected the simple planning grids of Japanese timber buildings—such as the Phoenix Villa that Wright saw in 1893 at the World's Columbian Exposition, Chicago—that were derived from the use of the 2×3 m tatami mat which regulated room sizes. Wright also found inspiration in the abstract aesthetics of Japanese prints, which Wright later collected, exhibited and wrote about. From the English Victorian Gothic Revival Wright borrowed the casement window which he arranged most often in horizontal bands that served both to open up and to echo the rectangular shape of the wall planes from which he constructed his houses and, at the same time, illuminated their interiors with nearly continuous horizontal bands of light.

The development of Wright's mature architecture may be traced in a series of house designs of the 1890s, beginning with the brick house for James Charnley, which he designed in 1891 while with Adler & Sullivan. Its abstract massing and formal composition was based on Sullivan's experiments with pure geometry in the late 1880s. The same theme reappeared in the William Winslow House (1894), River Forest, IL, also of brick. Not until 1900 was Wright able to design an equally abstract house of wood frame. He accomplished this by replacing traditional weather boarding with plaster in the house he built that year for B. Harley Bradley, Kankakee, IL. In doing so he was influenced by the modern plaster houses of English architects such as C. F. A. Voysey.

2. PRAIRIE HOUSES AND MATURE WORK, 1901–13. In 1901 Wright published a project for 'A Home in a Prairie Town' (*Ladies' Home J.*, xviii/3, Feb 1901, p. 17); it was characterized by continuous hip roofs of low pitch extended to cover the carriage entrance, a continuous screen or frieze of casement windows, and a wall and base course below them. Together these gave the design a horizontal character, which Wright likened to the level

character of the Midwestern prairie. It was a type of house that decades later would be called by historians 'the Prairie house', though the actual relationship between these houses and the prairie should not be taken too literally since Wright built many of them for sites distant from the Midwestern prairie. This approach culminated in 1902 in the house he designed for Ward Willits, Highland Park, IL (*see* UNITED STATES OF AMERICA, fig. 8). In that year Wright finally achieved the kind of pure design he had been seeking in the Willits House (1902–6; see fig. 1) and the Larkin Building (destr. 1950), Buffalo, NY. In each of them the two fundamental attributes that would continue to characterize Wright's architecture for the rest of his career may be discerned. One is the way his buildings are organized around interlocking spatial units defined by solid and transparent planes. The other is the simplicity of expression accorded each surface, which serves to convert the planes and masses into abstract geometric shapes and masses.

Between 1903 and 1913 Wright designed many brilliant variations on the theme of the Willits House. They included houses for Darwin Martin (1903–6), Buffalo, NY; Thomas Hardy (1905), Racine, WI; Steven Hunt (1907), La Grange, IL; Avery Coonley (1907–10), Riverside, IL; Isabel Roberts (1908), River Forest, IL; Fred Robie (1908–10), Chicago; Mrs Thomas Gale (1909), Oak Park; and Francis Little (1913–14; destr.), Lake Minnetonka, MN. The houses are usually of two storeys, set on projecting masonry platforms or podiums and built of brick, stone or wood frame, the latter clad either with horizontal weather-boarding or smooth-finished stucco. A few were designed for execution in reinforced concrete

and even concrete block, although none of these were built. In general they are characterized by horizontal wall planes, grouped casement windows and widely overhanging hipped or flat roofs. Outside walls rise from a podium to the lower edge of the first-floor (second storey) windows, which form a horizontal frieze around the house just below the eaves. The podium and lower walls connect the houses directly to the earth, thus visually eliminating the basement; in some cases, as in the Robie House, Wright was able to build the house over an above-ground basement. Living areas consist of interconnected spaces defined by wall and window screens and by ceilings of contrasting heights, most focused on a massive wood-burning fireplace, the symbolic centre of family life. Bedrooms often have ceilings that slope up to a central ridge in the manner of a tent, for example in the Robie House, then continue over the window heads to become the light-coloured plaster underside of overhanging eaves, symbolizing the protective character of the roof and also serving to reflect a soft, mellow light into the bedrooms. The interiors were integrated with the surrounding landscape by terraces, courts and wall planes extended into the gardens.

In the early years Wright had relatively few commissions for non-residential buildings. The largest and most significant executed examples were the Larkin Building, Buffalo, NY, and Unity Temple (1905–8), Oak Park. Both were similar in the way their interior volumes were expressed on the exterior. Both had a vertically orientated rectilinear space at the centre, with subsidiary volumes opening into it at various levels, and they were both originally designed to have brick walls trimmed in stone. In the Larkin Building

1. Frank Lloyd Wright: view and plans of the Willits House, Highland Park, IL, 1902

2. Frank Lloyd Wright: auditorium of Unity Temple, Oak Park, IL, 1905–8

the central work space rose through five office floors treated as galleries which looked into this central space over solid balustrades slightly set back from the faces of full-height, internal brick piers with deep, ornate capitals. The work space was naturally lit by roof lights and the galleries by continuous windows above built-in filing cabinets. The walls, floors and roof of the Larkin Building were supported by a cage of steel beams, a system also planned for Unity Temple, but in 1906 Wright decided to build the church of reinforced concrete and it became the first of his many buildings in this material. Another project of this period, the 25-storey San Francisco Call Building (1912; unexecuted), San Francisco, would have been his first tall building in reinforced concrete, conceived as a rectangular slab skyscraper with concrete load-bearing walls.

The auditorium of Unity Temple (see fig. 2) is conceived as a cube of space surrounded on three sides by two levels of balconies and on the fourth by the chancel. The central space expands horizontally into the subsidiary spaces and at the top of the auditorium it follows the underside of the ceiling through stained-glass windows, continuing outside as the soffit of the overhanging roof. At the same time the central space is transfused with a mellow light filtering down through the translucent art glass rooflights overhead. Another element of the composition is provided by corner staircases, derived from the Larkin Building, each housed in its own vertical block. The exterior (see fig. 3) consists of planes, rectangular masses, ornamental piers and projecting roof overhangs that express the interconnected spatial units of the interior. The exterior concrete surfaces, although lightly textured with an exposed pebble aggregate, are largely unadorned, except for the ornamental piers and flower boxes.

Wright recognized that his method of composing buildings—in which the traditional self-contained 'box' punctured by doors and windows was broken down into opaque planes and transparent screens merging inside and outside—was revolutionary, and he began to write about it in 1908. He asserted that he designed from the inside

outwards, meaning that he did not begin with a preconceived idea of the exterior form or its details, as he supposed most other architects did, but with the building's requirements, both material and subjective, from which he developed a suitable plan and spatial configuration. Only then did he define interior spaces with rectangular screens, both solid and transparent, and raise the elevations that gave physical reality to the spaces enclosed. That Wright actually worked in this manner is certain from the testimony of his employees, both between 1902 and 1910 and after 1931. Architecture conceived of in this way, growing like a plant 'from the ground up into the light by gradual growth' he called 'organic' (see ORGANIC ARCHITECTURE and Wright's essay (1910) of the same name (Kaufman and Raeburn)).

In Wright's mature architecture there is virtually no hint of historic styles, and he realized that to achieve integrated artistic compositions he would also have to design the furniture and furnishings for his buildings. For those residential clients who could afford both house and custom-designed fittings, Wright provided interiors of the highest quality, for example in the two houses for Francis Little (see UNITED STATES OF AMERICA, fig. 29); the Martin House, where he designed such items as complex rectilinear oak bookcases and tables, upholstered settles, and armchairs with circular seats, and coloured, geometrically patterned art glass windows (examples in Buffalo, NY, Albright-Knox A.G.); and the Robie House, where he designed settles and chairs, lamps, rugs, and a massive dining-table with lamps and flower vases at the corners and tall, rigidly rectangular slat-backed dining-chairs (U. Chicago, IL, Smart Mus. A.). For these and many of his early houses, he also designed coloured, geometrically patterned art glass windows. Wright also designed the metal office furniture and filing cabinets for the Larkin Building as well as other fittings (New York, MOMA).

In 1905 Wright made his first visit to Japan, where he studied Japanese architecture and collected *ukiyoe* prints. At this time, however, his personal life changed dramatically as a result of his liaison with Mrs Mamah Cheney, the wife of a client for whom he built a house in Oak Park in 1904. In 1909, accompanied by Mrs Cheney, he went to Europe to arrange for the first extensive publication (1911) of drawings and photographs of his architecture by Ernst Wasmuth of Berlin; much of the preparatory work was carried out with the help of his eldest son, Lloyd Wright. The Wasmuth portfolio may have influenced a number of early Modern Movement architects in Europe, including Mies van der Rohe, Le Corbusier and Walter Gropius. On his return to the USA in 1911 Wright built Taliesin, a country home for himself and Mrs Cheney in the Lloyd Jones valley near Spring Green.

In 1913 Wright designed Midway Gardens (destr. 1929), Chicago, a place for outdoor dining while listening to a symphony orchestra. It was his version of a continental outdoor pleasure garden, for which he also designed murals, decorative sculpture, interiors, furniture and other objects such as ceramics and table-lamps. The design of Midway Gardens marked an aesthetic turning-point in the direction of greater interest in decorative and ornamental surface treatment, while retaining the spatial complexity of his earlier work. In August 1914, when Midway Gardens

3. Frank Lloyd Wright: north front of Unity Temple, Oak Park, IL, 1905–8

was nearly complete, Wright's affair with Mrs Cheney ended in tragedy when a deranged servant murdered her, her children and four others at Taliesin after setting fire to the living-quarters.

3. DECORATIVE YEARS, 1914–34. Although Wright rebuilt Taliesin, for the next decade he was a wandering architect, living variously in Tokyo, Los Angeles and Arizona as well as at Taliesin. In 1913 he had made preliminary drawings for the Imperial Hotel, Tokyo, and he returned there with his drawings late in 1916, accompanied by the artist Miriam Noel, with whom he had begun a liaison. During World War I and after he spent considerable periods of time in Japan, returning permanently to the USA only in 1922 after the completion of the hotel. He was assisted in Tokyo by Antonin Raymond, who had worked for him at Taliesin, and who stayed on in Japan afterwards to develop a large practice. The greater emphasis on surface texture and colour that had been apparent in Midway Gardens was clearly evident in the Imperial Hotel (1919–21), where Wright used elaborately carved local stone to accentuate the brick structure. It was unusual in being a low building in a dense city, which spread out over its site in the form of five distinct yet related structures. A central wing provided hotel services: entry, reception and dining; guest rooms were in two outer wings separated from the service wing by courtyards; a cross-axial wing gave the public access from a side street

to private dining-rooms and to the entertainment wing at the rear, consisting of a cabaret, theatre and banquet hall, one above the other. Wright designed the interiors and furniture of the hotel, including the well-known series of hexagon-backed chairs and oak occasional tables (examples New York, Cooper-Hewitt Mus.). It is said that the building survived the great Kanto earthquake of 1923 because of its reinforced-concrete raft foundation. It was demolished in 1968.

During the time Wright travelled between the USA and Japan, he designed the vaguely Pre-Columbian Barnsdall House (1916–22), Los Angeles, and after his return he continued in the decorative vein of the Imperial Hotel with a number of designs for concrete-block houses. These are distinguished by their rich ornamentation producing a textile-like wall pattern both inside and out, achieved by casting geometric designs into outer and inner blocks, which were tied together with steel reinforcing. Among the best of the block buildings are houses for Mrs George Millard, 'La Miniatura' (1923), Pasadena, CA, for Charles Ennis (1924) and for Dr John Storer (1924), both in Los Angeles; Phi Gamma Delta Fraternity House (1924; unexecuted), Madison, WI, and San Marcos in the Desert Resort Hotel (1927–9; unexecuted), Chandler, AZ. Meanwhile Wright's relationship with Miriam Noel, whom he married in 1922, had proved disastrous because of her mental instability and they were divorced in 1927. In 1925 he had met Olgivanna Milanoff, the daughter of a Montenegrin judge, whom he took to live with him at Taliesin following a second fire there in that year, and their marriage in 1927 ushered in a period of domestic tranquillity in his life that lasted until his death.

During the years before and after the Depression, writing, teaching and the dissemination of his ideas played a major part in Wright's work at a time when commissions were scarce. In 1927 he and Olgivanna were planning to convert the abandoned Hillside Home School, near Taliesin, that he had built for his aunts in 1903, into a new educational institution. Originally intended as an art school, it became a place where aspiring architects could receive instruction from Wright. Known as the Taliesin Fellowship, the school opened in 1932 and aimed to educate the whole person: in the communal life fostered by the Fellowship, students assisted with farming, food preparation and other chores, performed as musicians and thespians, and worked as draughtsmen. In 1927–8 Wright contributed a series of theoretical articles to the *Architectural Record*, and in 1930 he was invited to give the Kahn Lectures at Princeton University, which were published in 1931 as *Modern Architecture* (also in *The Future of Architecture*, 1953). He subsequently lectured extensively in the USA, Europe and South America. In 1932 Wright's *An Autobiography* appeared, to be followed by a series of books that brought him worldwide publicity, enhancing his international reputation and providing fees, royalties and commissions that helped to ensure the financial security of the Fellowship. Among the best known are *The Disappearing City* (1932), *The Future of Architecture* (1953), *The Natural House* (1954) and *A Testament* (1957).

In *The Disappearing City* Wright published his ideas for Broadacre City, solving the problem of suburban sprawl, which Wright characterized as 'the city that is everywhere and nowhere'. He recognized that this phenomenon—the result of widespread ownership of motor cars—was not only very different from 19th-century rail- and tramway suburbs, but was also a trend that might well make existing cities redundant (*The Disappearing City*). It was the culmination of his thinking on urban planning that began in the early years of his career. Between 1895 and 1904 he made a number of plans for subdividing suburban blocks so that homes built on them might be more freely arranged than was possible on the narrow rectangular lots then in fashion. In 1914 an invitation by the Commercial Club of Chicago to provide a model subdivision caused him to consider broader planning issues. It was not, however, until the early 1930s that he began to think seriously about how an entire community might be laid out in a less rigidly urban and more expansively suburban fashion. The result he called Broadacre City. A model was made at Taliesin in 1933 to demonstrate how Wright's concept of a decentralized, low-density, self-sufficient community, based on humanistic and organic values, might work in practice. But there was little support for Wright's vision, founded as it was upon a plethora of liberal concepts that proved unacceptable to politicians and uneconomic to developers. As a result, Broadacre City was largely ignored as impractical and utopian.

4. LATE WORK, 1935 AND AFTER. An incredibly rich and varied second career began for Wright in 1935 with the commission from Edgar J. Kaufmann for a country house at Bear Run, near Pittsburgh, PA. The result was Fallingwater, a multi-level structure of rugged stone walls and smooth concrete terraces cantilevered over a waterfall (for illustration *see* CANTILEVER). Its remarkable character, which sets the house outside Wright's previous and subsequent practice, brought him immediate international acclaim. The Johnson Wax Administration Building (1936–8), Racine, WI, is no less unique: a smooth, curvilinear, streamlined building of brick, indirectly lit through rooflights and continuous bands of glass tubing, its main roof carried on elegant tapered mushroom columns (for illustration *see* OFFICE BUILDING; *see also* LIGHTING, fig. 4). Wright designed painted tubular steel office furniture in curvilinear forms that echoed those of the building. In 1938 Wright began to build a second Taliesin in the Arizona desert north-east of Phoenix, which he called Taliesin West; the activities of the Taliesin Fellowship were thereafter split seasonally between the two centres. Wright built Taliesin West with sloping walls of what he called 'desert concrete', natural desert stones laid in concrete. While echoing the colours, texture and forms of the surrounding desert, the walls also supported shed roofs framed in timber and covered with stretched canvas which served to flood the interiors with diffused desert sunlight (*see* ARTIST'S HOUSE, fig. 6). The result was a loosely integrated complex of angular structures which seemed at home in the desert even though distinct from it.

In this immensely creative period Wright also developed the Usonian house, intended as a relatively low-cost home affordable by the middle classes. Wright believed that his Usonian homes, cleansed of historic traditions and styles and organically united with the landscape, were appropriate dwellings for the free people of democratic 'Usonia' (United States of North America). The houses were long and low, emphasizing the horizontal lines in a modernized version of his early houses, and they were built without basements directly upon concrete slabs under which heating pipes were installed. Roofs were typically flat, with wide overhangs. The garage was replaced by a roofed but otherwise open car-port attached to the house. Its purpose was to provide a dramatic accent on the entrance side of the house, achieved by boldly cantilevering its roof out into space. Living and dining areas were integrated, with kitchens reduced to alcoves and bedrooms occupying a separate wing. The main living areas, defined by ceilings of contrasting heights and focused on a massive fireplace, faced on to garden terraces through glass-filled French doors. The first of these houses to be built was designed in 1936 for Herbert Jacobs at Madison. More than 100 Usonian houses were subsequently built throughout the USA, a typical example being the Pope-Leighey House (1940; see fig. 4), Falls Church, VA, later moved to Woodlawn Plantation, Mount Vernon, VA, and now owned by the National Trust for Historic Preservation.

In spite of the visual and spatial diversity of Wright's late work, it is possible to identify two common characteristics of this period: surfaces became smooth or lightly textured, with ornament virtually eliminated; and innovative geometric planning grids, incorporating triangles, hexagons and circles, were introduced as well to generate unusually shaped interior volumes as well as exterior forms. Triangular grids, for example, became the planning module for as many as 100 homes designed between 1936 and 1959 and also for such non-residential buildings as the First Unitarian Church (1947–51), Shorewood Hills, WI, which has a dramatic triangular roof of acute pitch over the sanctuary. Wright had previously used a triangular grid in a project (1929; unexecuted) for St Mark's-in-the-Bouwerie, high-rise blocks of two-storey apartments in New York. In addition to the angular walls produced by the grid, these towers also were to have floors cantilevered from a central spine of reinforced concrete, which Wright likened to a tree trunk. The same structural system was used in the Johnson Wax Laboratory Tower (1944–50), Racine, WI, the external form of which continued the streamlined character of the earlier administration building, with rounded corners and bands of brick and glass-tube cladding. The 'tree-trunk' structure was also used in the Harold Price Tower (1956), Bartlesville, OK, a combined office and apartment building clad in glass and copper; and it was envisioned for the Mile-High Skyscraper (1956; unexecuted) projected for Chicago, the faceted walls of which formed an elongated pyramid tapering to a needle-like point. In the Beth Shalom Synagogue (1954–7), Elkins Park, PA, a triangular ground-plan was developed into a hexagonal structural pyramid filled in with translucent fibreglass panels which illuminate the interior with a diffuse milky light, while the hexagon was used as a planning device in the Paul Hanna House (1936–7), Palo Alto, CA, and the Arizona State Capitol (1957; unexecuted), Phoenix.

Wright's use of the circle as a planning device can also be traced back to the 1920s, although he did not employ it regularly until the late 1930s. Examples include Olin Terraces, a civic centre for Madison later renamed Monona Terrace when the project was revived in the 1950s (1938; unexecuted but built in a revised form on the original site in 1995–6); the so-called solar hemicycle house for Herbert Jacobs (1943), Middleton, WI, laid out as a segment of a circle, its south wall of glass and its north wall an earth berm; and the Friedman House (1948), Pleasantville, NY. The spiral first appeared as a motor car ramp leading to a mountain-top planetarium overlook (1925; unexecuted) but did not appear again until the first designs for the Solomon R. Guggenheim Museum (1943), New York, resulting in the extraordinary (and functionally controversial) upwardly expanding helix of the main gallery (built 1956–9); it also appeared in the graceful ramp in the V. C. Morris Shop (1948), San Francisco; and in the house (1950; see fig. 5) built for his son David Wright at Phoenix. In the 1950s the circle, used both as a planning tool and as a formal element, occurred more and more often in Wright's work, as seen in the segmental arches and dome of the Marin County Government Center (1957–66), San Rafael, CA, and the space-age Greek Orthodox Church (1959), Wauwatosa, WI, which resembles a flying saucer.

Wright continued to work actively as an architect, teacher, lecturer and writer until his death in 1959 just two months short of his 92nd birthday. Although his work has

4. Frank Lloyd Wright: living room of Pope-Leighey House, Falls Church, VA, 1940; house now at Woodlawn Plantation, Mount Vernon, VA

5. Frank Lloyd Wright: David Wright House, Phoenix, AZ, 1950

been widely admired since the beginning of the 20th century, relatively little of a scholarly or critical nature was written about it during his lifetime, the first book about his architecture in English being published only in 1942 when Wright was 75 years old. Between then and 1976 only a handful of scholarly books about Wright appeared and most of them dealt with contextual issues, though in 1976, beginning with a study of the Usonian house, there began a steady stream of books about Wright's architecture. Once the archives at Taliesin West were fully opened for research in the mid-1980s, and copies of their correspondence, drawings and photographs deposited at the Getty Center for the History of Art and the Humanities, Santa Monica, CA, the pace of scholarly study and critical reassessment of Wright's work began to accelerate.

UNPUBLISHED SOURCES

Santa Monica, CA, Getty Cent.

Scottsdale, AZ, Frank Lloyd Wright Found.

WRITINGS

'The Art and Craft of the Machine', *Catalogue of the Fourteenth Annual Exhibition of the Chicago Architectural Club* (exh. cat., Chicago, IL, Archit. Club, 1901) [no pagination]

'In the Cause of Architecture', *Archit. Rec.*, xxiii (1908), pp. 155–221

The Japanese Print: An Interpretation (Chicago, 1912, rev. 2/New York, 1967)

'In the Cause of Architecture: Second Paper', *Archit. Rec.*, xxxv (1914), pp. 405–13

'Non-competitive Plan', *City Residential Land Development: Studies in Planning; Competitive Plans for Subdividing a Typical Quarter Section of Land in the Outskirts of Chicago*, ed. A. Yeomans (Chicago, 1916), pp. 95–102

An Autobiography (New York, 1932, rev. 4/1977)

The Disappearing City (New York, 1932); rev. 2 as *When Democracy Builds* (Chicago, 1945); rev. 3 as *The Industrial Revolution Runs Away* (New York, 1969)

'Frank Lloyd Wright', *Archit. Forum*, lxviii (1938) [whole issue devoted to Wright's buildings, mainly 1920–38]

F. Gutheim, ed.: *Frank Lloyd Wright on Architecture: Selected Writings, 1894–1940* (New York, 1941) [contains unpubd writing, but mostly abridged]

'Frank Lloyd Wright', *Archit. Forum*, lxxxviii (1948) [whole issue devoted to Wright's buildings, mainly 1938–48]

The Future of Architecture (New York, 1953) [reprints of previous writings]

The Natural House (New York, 1954) [four chaps reprint earlier writings; five new chaps]

A Testament (New York, 1957)

E. Kaufmann and B. Raeburn: *Frank Lloyd Wright: Writings and Buildings* (New York, 1960) [selections from Wright's writings]

O. Wright: *Frank Lloyd Wright: His Life, his Work, his Words* (New York, 1966) [incl. prev. unpubd writings, illus. of work by Taliesin Associated Architects and other mat.]

A. Crawford: 'Ten Letters from Frank Lloyd Wright to Charles Robert Ashbee', *Archit. Hist.*, xiii (1970), pp. 64–73

N. Smith, ed.: 'Letters (1903–1906) by Charles E. White, Jr, From the Studio of Frank Lloyd Wright', *J. Archit. Educ.*, xxv (1971), pp. 104–12

In the Cause of Architecture (New York, 1975) [reprinted articles from *Archit. Rev.* [New York], 1927–8]

B. Pfeiffer, ed.: *Frank Lloyd Wright: Letters to Apprentices* (Fresno, 1982)

——: *Frank Lloyd Wright: Letters to Architects* (Fresno, 1984)

P. Meehan, ed.: *The Master Architect: Conversations with Frank Lloyd Wright* (New York, 1984)

B. Pfeiffer, ed.: *Frank Lloyd Wright: Letters to Clients* (Fresno, 1986)

——: *Frank Lloyd Wright: The Guggenheim Correspondence* (Fresno, 1986)

——: *Frank Lloyd Wright: Collected Writings*, 6 vols (New York, 1992–)

PHOTOGRAPHIC PUBLICATIONS

Frank Lloyd Wright: Ausgeführte Bauten und Entwürfe (Berlin, 1911); *R* as *Studies and Executed Buildings by Frank Lloyd Wright* (Palos Park, 1975); *R* as *Drawings and Plans of Frank Lloyd Wright: The Early Period, 1893–1909* (New York), 1983

Frank Lloyd Wright: Ausgeführte Bauten (Berlin, 1911; *R* as *Frank Lloyd Wright: The Early Work* (New York, 1968); *R* as *The Early Work of Frank Lloyd Wright: The 'Ausgeführte Bauten' of 1911* (New York, 1982)

'Frank Lloyd Wright', *Wendingen*, vii (1925) [whole issue]

'Frank Lloyd Wright', *Archit. Forum*, lxviii (1938), pp. 1–102 [whole issue devoted to Wright's buildings, mainly 1920–38]

'Frank Lloyd Wright: A Selection of Current Work', *Archit. Rec.*, cxxiii/5 (1958), pp. 167–90

Drawings for a Living Architecture (New York, 1959)

A. Drexler: *The Drawings of Frank Lloyd Wright* (New York, 1962)

Y. Futagawa, ed.: 'Frank Lloyd Wright: Houses in Oak Park and River Forest, Illinois (1889–1913)', *Global Archit.*, xxv (Tokyo, 1973) [whole issue]

——: 'Houses by Frank Lloyd Wright: 1', *Global Interiors*, ix (1975) [whole issue]

Y. Futagawa, ed.: 'Houses by Frank Lloyd Wright: 2', *Global Interiors*, x (1976) [whole issue]

A. Izzo: *Frank Lloyd Wright: Three-quarters of a Century of Drawings* (Florence, 1976, rev. New York, 1981)

D. Hanks: *The Decorative Designs of Frank Lloyd Wright* (New York, 1979)

'Frank Lloyd Wright', *A + U* (1981) [whole issue contains photographs of Wright's archit.]

Y. Futagawa, ed.: *Frank Lloyd Wright* (Tokyo, 1984–8), 12 vols [drgs from col. at Scottsdale, AZ, Frank Lloyd Wright Found.]

P. Guerrero: *Frank Lloyd Wright: An Album from Frank Lloyd Wright's Photographer* (New York, 1994)

BIBLIOGRAPHY

GENERAL

T. Tallmadge: 'The Chicago School', *Archit. Rev.* [Boston], xv (1908), pp. 69–74; also in *Architectural Essays from the Chicago School*, ed. W. Hasbrouck (Park Forest, 1967), pp. 3–8

H. Berlage: 'Neuere amerikanische Architektur', *Schweiz. Bauztg*, lx (1912), pp. 148–50, 165–7; Eng. trans. by D. Gifford, ed. in *The Literature of Architecture* (New York, 1966), pp. 607–16

V. Scully: *The Shingle Style: Architectural Theory and Design from Richardson to the Origins of Wright* (New Haven, 1955, rev. 1971)

R. Adams: 'Architecture and the Romantic Tradition: Coleridge to Wright', *Amer. Q.*, ix (1957), pp. 46–62

P. Blake: *The Master Builders: Le Corbusier, Mies van der Rohe, Frank Lloyd Wright* (New York, 1960, rev. 1976)

M. Peisch: *The Chicago School of Architecture: Early Followers of Sullivan and Wright* (New York, 1964)

L. Eaton: *Two Chicago Architects and their Clients: Frank Lloyd Wright and Howard Van Doren Shaw* (Cambridge, 1969)

S. Sorell: 'Silsbee: The Evolution of a Personal Architectural Style', *Prairie Sch. Rev.*, vii (1970), pp. 5–21

H. Brooks: *The Prairie School: Frank Lloyd Wright and his Midwest Contemporaries* (Toronto, 1972)

MONOGRAPHS, EXHIBITION CATALOGUES AND COLLECTIONS OF ESSAYS

The Work of Frank Lloyd Wright (exh. cat., Chicago, IL, Archit. Club, 1902)

The Work of Frank Lloyd Wright (exh. cat., Chicago, IL, Archit. Club, 1914) [work between 1911 and 1914]

H. Wijdeveld, ed.: *The Life-work of the American Architect Frank Lloyd Wright* (Santpoort, 1925, rev. New York, 1965)

H. de Fries, ed.: *Frank Lloyd Wright: Aus dem Lebenswerke eines Architekten* (Berlin, 1926)

J. Badovici: *Frank Lloyd Wright: Architecte américain* (Paris, 1932) [compilation of mat. prev. pubd in *Archit. Viv.*]

H. Hitchcock: *In the Nature of Materials: 1887–1941, The Buildings of Frank Lloyd Wright* (New York, 1942)

J. Wright: *My Father Who Is on Earth* (New York, 1946)

G. Manson: *Frank Lloyd Wright to 1910: The First Golden Age* (New York, 1958)

V. Scully jr: *Frank Lloyd Wright*, Masters of World Architecture (New York, 1960)

N. K. Smith: *Frank Lloyd Wright: A Study in Architectural Content* (Englewood Cliffs, 1966)

R. Twombly: *Frank Lloyd Wright: An Interpretive Biography* (New York, 1973); rev. as *Frank Lloyd Wright: His Life and his Work* (New York, 1979)

W. Storrer: *The Architecture of Frank Lloyd Wright: A Complete Catalogue* (Cambridge, 1974) [guide to Wright's buildings]

H. Jacobs: *Building with Frank Lloyd Wright: An Illustrated Memoir* (San Francisco, 1978)

R. Sweeney: *Frank Lloyd Wright: An Annotated Bibliography* (Los Angeles, 1978)

D. Hanks: *The Decorative Designs of Frank Lloyd Wright* (New York, 1979)

E. Tafel: *Years with Frank Lloyd Wright: Apprentice to Genius* (New York, 1979)

H. Brooks, ed.: *Writings on Wright: Selected Comment on Frank Lloyd Wright* (Cambridge, 1981)

O. Graf: *Frank Lloyd Wright und Europa: Architekturelemente, Naturverhältnis, Publikationen, Einflüsse* (Stuttgart, 1983)

P. Meehan: *Frank Lloyd Wright: A Research Guide to Archival Sources* (New York, 1983)

B. Gill: *Many Masks: A Life of Frank Lloyd Wright* (New York, 1987)

C. Bolon and others, eds: *The Nature of Frank Lloyd Wright* (Chicago, 1988)

B. Pfeiffer, ed.: *Frank Lloyd Wright: In the Realm of Ideas* (Carbondale, 1988)

E. Kaufmann jr: *Nine Commentaries on Frank Lloyd Wright* (New York, 1989)

G. Hildebrand: *The Wright Space: Pattern and Meaning in Frank Lloyd Wright's Houses* (Seattle, 1991)

S. Kohmoto: *The Frank Lloyd Wright Retrospective* (exh. cat., Tokyo, Sezon Mus. A., 1991)

R. McCarter, ed.: *Frank Lloyd Wright: A Primer on Architectural Principles* (New York, 1991)

T. Marvel, ed.: *The Wright State: Frank Lloyd Wright in Wisconsin* (exh. cat., Milwaukee, WI, A. Mus., 1992)

N. Menocal, ed.: *Wright Studies: Taliesin, 1911–1914* (Carbondale, IL, 1992)

M. Secrest: *Frank Lloyd Wright* (New York, 1992)

A. Alofsin: *Frank Lloyd Wright—The Lost Years, 1910–22: A Study of Influence* (Chicago, 1993)

W. Storrer: *The Frank Lloyd Wright Companion* (Chicago, 1993)

Frank Lloyd Wright, Architect (exh. cat., ed. T. Riley; New York, MOMA, 1994)

SPECIALIST STUDIES

R. Spencer jr: 'The Work of Frank Lloyd Wright', *Archit. Rev.* [Boston], vii (1900), pp. 61–72 (*R* Park Forest, 1964)

L. Sullivan: 'Concerning the Imperial Hotel, Tokyo, Japan', *Archit. Rec.*, liii (1923), pp. 332–52

H. Hitchcock: 'Frank Lloyd Wright and the "Academic Tradition" of the Early 1890s', *J. Warb. & Court. Inst.*, vii (1944), pp. 46–63

'Frank Lloyd Wright and Architecture around 1900', *Acts of the Twentieth International Congress of the History of Art: Princeton, 1963*, iv, pp. 3–87

H. Brooks: 'Frank Lloyd Wright and the Wasmuth Drawings', *A. Bull.*, xlviii (1966), pp. 193–202

T. Hines: 'Frank Lloyd Wright—The Madison Years: Records versus Recollections', *WI Mag. Hist.* (1967), pp. 190–91, and *J. Soc. Archit. Historians*, xxvi (1967), pp. 227–33

D. Hoffmann: 'Frank Lloyd Wright and Viollet-le-Duc', *J. Soc. Archit. Historians*, xxviii (1969), pp. 173–83

J. O'Gorman: 'Henry Hobson Richardson and Frank Lloyd Wright', *A.Q.* [Detroit], xxxii (1969), pp. 292–315

'The Pope-Leighey House', *Hist. Preserv.*, xxi (1969), pp. 2–120 [whole issue]

E. Michels: 'The Early Drawings of Frank Lloyd Wright Reconsidered', *J. Soc. Archit. Historians*, xxx (1971), pp. 294–303

C. Besinger: 'Comment on "The Early Drawings of Frank Lloyd Wright Reconsidered"', *J. Soc. Archit. Historians*, xxxi/3 (1972), pp. 217–20

R. Twombly: 'Organic Living: Frank Lloyd Wright's Taliesin Fellowship and Georgi Gurdjieff's Institute for the Harmonious Development of Man', *Wisconsin Mag. Hist.*, lviii (1974–5), pp. 126–39

——: 'Saving the Family: Middle-class Attraction to Wright's Prairie House (1901–1909)', *Amer. Q.*, xxvii (1975), pp. 7–71

J. Sergeant: *Frank Lloyd Wright's Usonian Houses: The Case for Organic Architecture* (New York, 1976)

D. Hoffmann: *Frank Lloyd Wright's Fallingwater: The House and its History* (New York, 1978)

H. Brooks: 'Frank Lloyd Wright and the Destruction of the Box', *J. Soc. Archit. Historians*, xxxviii (1979), pp. 7–14

P. Hanna: *Frank Lloyd Wright's Hanna House: The Clients' Report* (Cambridge, 1982)

E. Kaufmann jr: 'Frank Lloyd Wright's Mementos of Childhood', *J. Soc. Archit. Historians*, xli (1982), pp. 232–7

——: 'Frank Lloyd Wright at the Metropolitan Museum of Art', *Bull. Met.*, xl (1982), pp. 5–47

N. Levine: 'Frank Lloyd Wright's Diagonal Planning', *In Search of Modern Architecture: A Tribute to Henry-Russell Hitchcock*, ed. H. Searing (Cambridge, 1982), pp. 245–77

J. Meech-Pekarik: 'Frank Lloyd Wright and Japanese Prints', *Bull. Met.*, xl (1982), pp. 48–64

J. Quinan: 'Frank Lloyd Wright's Reply to Russell Sturgis', *J. Soc. Archit. Historians*, xli (1982), pp. 238–44

P. Turner: 'Frank Lloyd Wright and the Young Le Corbusier', *J. Soc. Archit. Historians*, xlii (1983), pp. 350–59

D. Hoffmann: *Frank Lloyd Wright's Robie House* (New York, 1984)

K. Smith: 'Frank Lloyd Wright and the Imperial Hotel: A Postscript', *A. Bull.*, lxvii (1985), pp. 296–310

J. Quinan: *Frank Lloyd Wright's Larkin Building* (Cambridge, 1987)

N. Menocal: 'Frank Lloyd Wright as the Anti-Victor Hugo', *American Public Architecture*, ed. C. Zabel and others (University Park, PA, 1989)

S. Robinson: 'Frank Lloyd Wright and Victor Hugo', *Modern Architecture in America: Visions and Revisions*, ed. R. Wilson (Ames, IA, 1991), pp. 106–11

T. Turak: 'Mr Wright and Mrs Coonley', *Modern Architecture in America: Visions and Revisions*, ed. R. Wilson (Ames, IA, 1991), pp. 144–63

D. Hoffmann: *Frank Lloyd Wright's Hollyhock House* (Mineola, NY, 1992)

K. Smith: *Frank Lloyd Wright: Hollyhock House and Olive Hill* (New York, 1992)

K. Nute: *Frank Lloyd Wright and Japan* (New York, 1993)

R. Sweeney: *Wright in Hollywood: Visions of a New Architecture* (New York, 1994)

PAUL E. SPRAGUE

(2) (Frank) Lloyd Wright jr (*b* Oak Park, IL, 31 March 1890; *d* Los Angeles, 31 May 1978). Son of (1) Frank Lloyd Wright. He had already become a skilled draughtsman before attending the University of Wisconsin, Madison (1907–9), where he studied agronomy and engineering with the aim of becoming a landscape architect. In 1909–10 he went to Italy to help his father with the preparation of drawings for the Wasmuth portfolio (Berlin, 1910). After travelling in Europe he returned to the USA, where he worked first in the Herbarium of Harvard University, Cambridge, MA, and then joined Olmsted & Olmsted, landscape architects and planners in Boston. In 1911 he was sent to San Diego to work on the site for the Panama–California International Exposition (1915) in Balboa Park. The firm then withdrew from the project, but Wright stayed in California and entered the office of Irving Gill. There he worked on the new industrial city of Torrance (1911–13), CA, both with Gill on the construction of buildings, and with the Olmsteds on the site and planting. In 1915 he formed a brief partnership with the landscape architect Paul Thiene, producing a variety of designs including such Italian gardens as those (both 1915–16) for Ben Meyer in Beverly Hills and for John L. Severence in Pasadena.

In 1916 Wright began an independent practice as both an architect and a landscape architect, supplementing his income by designing film sets for Paramount Pictures in Hollywood. In 1917, when the USA entered World War I, he moved to New York to work as a designer in the newly formed Standard Aircraft Factory and, later, in the architectural office of Rouse & Goldstone. He returned to Los Angeles in 1919 to work for his father on the landscaping of Aline Barnsdall's Olive Hill housing (1917–20), Hollywood, and a number of other projects in the early 1920s. His first independent house, the Weber House (1921), Los Angeles, was a variation on his father's Prairie houses, but he quickly adapted the Spanish and Pre-Columbian traditions of California and Mexico in such works as the Sowden House (1926), Los Angeles; the Derby House (1926), Chevy Chase; and his own house and studio (1927), Los Angeles. Some of these designs incorporate Spanish Colonial Revival features, while others, such as the Samuel–Navarro House (1926–8), Hollywood, reflect Art Deco. A wide range of designs followed, from the Hollywood Bowl (1924–8) to Los Angeles Civic Center (1925; unexecuted), and from drive-in markets, restaurants and service stations to a structurally innovative project (1931; unexecuted) for Los Angeles Roman Catholic Cathedral. Among the most noted of his later buildings is the Wayfarer's Chapel (1946–51), Palos Verdes Peninsula, Portuguese Bend, CA, in which he realized his ideal of integrating architecture and landscape design: it is a glass building with massive timber and light steel framing in geometric forms, set within what appears to be a fragment of primeval Californian forest.

BIBLIOGRAPHY

P. Schindler: 'The Samuel House, Los Angeles', *Archit. Rec.*, lxvii/6 (June 1930), pp. 502–30

——: 'Modern California Architects', *Creative A.*, x/2 (1932), pp. 111–15

A. B. Cutts, jr: 'The Hillside Home of Ramon Navarro: A Unique Setting Created by Lloyd Wright', *CA A. & Archit.*, xliv/1 (1933), pp. 11–13, 31

H. R. Hitchcock and A. Drexler: *Built in USA* (New York, 1952), pp. 32–3, pls 124–5

E. McCoy: 'Lloyd Wright', *A. & Archit.*, lxxxiii/10 (1966), pp. 22–6

Lloyd Wright, Architect: 20th-century Architecture in an Organic Exhibition (exh. cat. by D. Gebhard and H. von Breton, Santa Barbara, 1971)

E.Wright: *Lloyd Wright Drawings* (New York, 1987)

(3) John Lloyd Wright (*b* Oak Park, IL, 12 Dec 1892; *d* San Diego, 20 Dec 1972). Son of (1) Frank Lloyd Wright. He attended the University of Wisconsin, Madison, but did not graduate; he later took studio classes at the Art Institute of Chicago, but his abilities as a designer were developed in his father's Oak Park studio. In 1912 he followed his older brother Lloyd to San Diego, where he entered the office of Harrison Albright and was responsible for the design of the Golden West Hotel (1912), San Diego, an early reinforced-concrete building. His first independent commission, the Wood House (1912), Escondido, CA, was a variation on his father's Prairie houses. From 1913 to 1919 he worked for his father and accompanied him to Japan. He returned to the Midwest in 1920, and in that year, while working in the Chicago office of Schmidt, Garden & Martin, he designed one of the USA's best-known toys, the Lincoln Logs. In 1926 he set up his own practice and produced a small body of Art-Deco/Expressionist designs, including the Dunes Arcade Hotel (1927), Dunes State Park, IN, and the Burnham House (1934), Long Beach City, IN. After World War II he moved to Del Mar in southern California. In such houses as the McPherson House (1947), Del Mar, and the Compton House (1948), La Jolla, CA, he modified his father's Usonian house schemes with frequent references to the California bungalow, then enjoying great popularity. He continued his interest in the design of toys and in 1949 introduced the first of a number of sets of Wright Blocks.

WRITINGS

My Father who is on Earth (New York, 1946)

'Del Mar Studio–Home for the Architect', *Archit. Rec.*, civ/10 (1948), pp. 100–03

'Lichenaceous Ornament', *House & Home*, i/1 (1952), pp. 136–7

BIBLIOGRAPHY

'Wright Blocks Developed by Designer of Lincoln Logs', *Archit. Rec.*, cvii/3 (1950), p. 12

W. R. Hasbrouck: 'Earliest Work of John Lloyd Wright', *Prairie Sch. Rev.*, vii/2 (1970), pp. 16–19

S. K. Chappell and A. Van Zanten: *Barry Byrne, John Lloyd Wright: Architecture and Design* (Chicago, 1982)

DAVID GEBHARD

Wright, Andrew (*fl* 1532; *d* London, March–May 1543). English decorative and heraldic painter. He was employed by the Crown at least as early as 1532, when he headed a team engaged on painting and gilding the roof and casements of a new gallery and providing decorations for Henry VIII's study at the Palace of Westminster, London. By patent dated 19 June he was granted the reversion of the office of Serjeant Painter, at the customary annuity of £10, and had succeeded to it by the end of the year, on the death of John Brown. In 1533 he was paid £5 6s. 8d. for four large banners for the funeral of the King's sister Mary, Duchess of Suffolk. Four years later he charged 40s. each for 15 trumpet-banners of sarsenet painted with the King's arms; another typical commission was to paint and gild a closed coach for the King. His office must have been profitable, for his will of 1543 shows that he had acquired property at Stratford-le-Bow and Southwark, London, and had an establishment at Cowden, Kent, for the making of the yellowish pigment 'pynck'. He described himself and his sons Christopher and Richard as Painter Stainers and mentioned a deceased relative George Wright, who in 1527 had done decorative painting for revels at Greenwich Palace. Andrew Wright was a parishioner of St Vedast, Foster Lane, off Cheapside, London, a district always popular with painters.

BIBLIOGRAPHY

E. Auerbach: *Tudor Artists* (London, 1954), pp. 13–14, 54–5, 109, 144–5, 193

MARY EDMOND

Wright, David (*b* Melbourne, 1948). Australian glass artist. He studied architecture at the University of Melbourne and graduated in 1972. Largely self-taught in the production of glass, he was active in the development of various kiln-working techniques applied to architectural glass. Following his first exhibition of autonomous glass panels in 1976, Wright was awarded numerous church and public commissions including a vast wall of glass (1976) for the Reception Centre at the Royal Zoological Gardens in Melbourne; a set of windows (1987) for the new Parliament House in Canberra; and a window cycle (1988) for the St James's Anglican church in Sydney. Wright's compositions are notable for their rhythms, juxtaposed fields of loose pattern and simple, organic imagery that often alludes to the processes of germination and growth. Many of the artist's smaller, autonomous panels are assembled from mechanically fastened sections of glass with contrasting surface treatments and textures. A series of exhibition pieces made reference to medical X-ray images and incorporated fused motifs and figures with cloudy abstract passages of chemically treated glass.

BIBLIOGRAPHY

J. Zimmer: *Stained Glass in Australia* (Melbourne, 1984)

GEOFFREY R. EDWARDS

Wright, Edmund (William) (*b* London, 1822; *d* Adelaide, 5 Aug 1886). Australian architect of English birth. In the 1830s he was articled to the Borough Surveyor's office in Bermondsey, London, later becoming government clerk of works at Yarmouth. After some years working as a civil engineer in Canada, he emigrated to South Australia, arriving in May 1849. Shortages of resources induced by the eastern colonies' gold-rush frustrated his attempts to start a practice until 1853. His best-known works came from partnerships. With E. J. Woods (1837–1913) he produced the Town Hall, Adelaide (1863–6); and with Woods and E. A. Hamilton, the General Post Office (1867–72). Facing each other in the city's centre, the massive neo-Renaissance piles that vied for prominence were broadly detailed in local stone. In a park in north Adelaide the latter partnership also built the imposing but restrained Brougham Place Congregational Church (1860–72). Reminiscent of St Philip's (1710–25), Birmingham, by Thomas Archer, it was more austerely puritan in detail.

Wright practised alone between 1872 and 1879. In 1876 he supervised construction of the vibrant, richly ornamented Bank of South Australia, King William Street, Adelaide. Although the building (now restored) has been attributed to him and is called Edmund Wright House, it was almost certainly designed by Lloyd Tayler of Melbourne. In 1879 Wright formed a partnership with Joseph H. Reed (1857–1901); in 1886 they were joined by J. A. Beaver. There was enough stylistic difference in the work of Wright's successive partnerships to suggest that he was not primarily engaged in design. As mayor of Adelaide (1859) and as co-founder of the Institute of Architects (1886) he was politically prominent in the profession's early period in the colony.

BIBLIOGRAPHY
E. Jensen and R. Jensen: *Colonial Architecture in South Australia* (Adelaide, 1980)

DONALD LANGMEAD

Wright, Edward (*fl* 1720–30; *d* 1750). English writer. A native of Stretton in Cheshire, he left England in March 1720 on the Grand Tour, as the companion of George Parker (1697–1764), the future astronomer. After journeying through France they passed most of the next two years in Italy, staying in the most popular cities—Rome, Naples, Florence, Venice—and elsewhere, before returning via Innsbruck, Augsburg and the Netherlands. In 1730 Wright published an account of his journey, and it is on this that his fame rests. Though more a personal memoir than a guidebook, it is structured so as to be useful to other travellers. He includes practical information, historical anecdotes and accounts of the Venetian Carnival and other spectacles. However, most space is given to descriptions of monuments and works of art, and the book includes a vocabulary of artistic technical terms, and a detailed index of painters and their works and of antiquities. The whole work is illustrated by some 40 large-scale, fold-out plates, engraved by Gerard Vandergucht after drawings made mainly by Wright himself. Some show interesting curiosities, such as the meridian in Bologna and Ligurian methods of viniculture, but most portray works of art, especially Classical monuments and inscriptions and such useful travel aids as a plan of the sculpture gallery in the Palazzo Vecchio in Florence. Wright's book was much consulted by Grand Tourists and was republished in 1764.

WRITINGS
Some Observations Made in Travelling through France, Italy, &c in the Years 1720, 1721 and 1722, 2 vols (London, 1730, 2/1764)

DNB

BIBLIOGRAPHY
S. Klima, ed.: *Letters from the Grand Tour* (London and Montreal, 1975), pp. 15, 91, 92, 185

JANET SOUTHORN

Wright, John Michael (*b* London, May 1617; *d* London, July 1694). English painter. He was the son of James Wright, a tailor, and from 1636 to 1641 was apprenticed to the Edinburgh portrait painter George Jamesone. In the early 1640s he left Scotland for Rome, where he painted his earliest known portrait, *Robert Bruce, 1st Earl of Ailesbury* (Tottenham House, Wilts, Marquess of Ailesbury priv. col.). He was soon sufficiently prosperous to collect books, prints, paintings, gems and medals, some of which were listed by the English amateur painter Richard

Symonds in the early 1650s, when the collection included works attributed to Mantegna, Michelangelo, Raphael, Titian and Correggio. Wright probably worked as a copyist and dealer, but his own work was sufficiently admired for him to be elected to the Accademia di S Luca in 1648. In 1653/4 he won a place in the suite of Archduke Leopold William of Austria, Governor of the Spanish Netherlands, and left Italy for Flanders.

In 1656 Wright arrived in London from Dunkirk. The entry recording his arrival in the official register of visitors noted that he had also worked in France. He soon established a thriving practice and by 1658 was referred to in William Henderson's *Art of Painting* as one of the best artists in England. This reputation was not undeserved, for his portraits of the late 1650s reveal an original and distinctive manner, combining the realism of Jamesone with a Roman taste for allegory and an elegance that may owe something to his time in France. In 1658 he painted, probably posthumously, Oliver Cromwell's favourite daughter *Elizabeth Claypole as Minerva* (London, N.P.G.), and in the following year *Col. John Russell* (Ham House, Surrey, NT), in a style that shows an awareness of the work of William Dobson, but with a French elegance to which Dobson never aspired. As a Catholic, Wright had high hopes of patronage with the return of the Stuarts in 1660: he was commissioned to paint the ceiling of Charles II's bedchamber in Whitehall and, according to John Evelyn, an overmantel of *St Catherine* for the Queen's Privy Chamber. The ceiling, *Astraea Returns to Earth* (Nottingham, Castle Mus.), owes a debt to the Baroque ceilings of Pietro da Cortona.

As further evidence of royal favour, the King granted Wright the rare privilege of holding a number of lotteries for paintings in his collection, which took place between 1662 and 1666. This suggests that Wright may have had financial difficulties in the 1660s, and there is no doubt that the court and fashionable patrons preferred the languid sensuousness of Sir Peter Lely to Wright's more realistic and individual portraits. Towards the end of the decade Wright's fortunes improved. He painted the charming double portrait of the children *Lady Catherine Cecil and James Cecil, 4th Earl of Salisbury* (*c.* 1668; Hatfield House, Herts) and in 1669 was visited by Cosimo III de' Medici, later Grand Duke of Tuscany, who commissioned a portrait of *George Monk, 1st Duke of Albemarle*. In 1670 Wright was commissioned to paint 22 full-length portraits of the judges who had arbitrated over the disputes caused by the Fire of London in 1666; the paintings were completed between 1671 and 1675 for £36 each. They were hung in the Guildhall, London, where they were admired by Evelyn as good likenesses, but were severely damaged in the 18th century. Only two survive. In 1673 Wright painted one of his finest works, the *Family of Sir Robert Vyner* (England, priv. col., see exh. cat.), in which Sir Robert, his wife and two children are posed informally in a realistic garden, probably drawn from nature. Two years later he was at Blithfield, Staffs, painting six family portraits for Sir Walter Bagot, one of which, a tender and informal double portrait of *Lady Mary Bagot and her Granddaughter*, is in Wolverhampton Art Gallery. This commission is recorded in correspondence between Sir Walter and Wright, in which the latter unsuccessfully attempted to raise the agreed price from £140 to £200. He worked in Dublin in 1679 and 1680, a visit that resulted in one of his most striking portraits, that of *Sir Neil O'Neill in Irish Dress* (London, Tate).

In February 1685 James II succeeded to the throne and, almost immediately, sent an embassy to the Vatican under Roger Palmer, Earl of Castlemaine (1634–1705), with Wright as Steward. They arrived in Rome at Easter 1686, and Wright immediately began designing the settings, carriages and costumes required and commissioning artists and craftsmen to execute them. The large portrait of *Charles II Enthroned*, which dominated the official banquet given in Rome by Castlemaine, may have been the one painted by Wright in 1676 (London, Royal Col.). Wright recorded the procession, banquet and audience in *An Account of His Excellence Roger Earl of Castlemaine's Embassy . . . to His Holiness Innocent XI*, which was published in Italian in 1687 and English the following year. The unsuccessful embassy left Rome in June 1687 and arrived in London in October. The expulsion of James II in 1688 dashed Wright's hopes of further preferment, and he lived in London in relative poverty for the rest of his life.

BIBLIOGRAPHY
C. H. Collins Baker: *Lely and the Stuart Portrait Painters*, 2 vols (London, 1912)
John Michael Wright: The King's Painter (exh. cat. by S. Stevenson and D. Thomson, Edinburgh, N.P.G., 1982)

DAVID RODGERS

Wright, Joseph (*b* Bordentown, NJ, 16 July 1756; *d* Philadelphia, PA, 13 Sept 1793). American painter, sculptor and engraver. He probably received his first art training from his mother, the modeller in wax Patience Lovell Wright (1725–86). After the death of his father in 1769, he was placed in the Academy in Philadelphia, while Patience opened a waxworks in New York. In 1772 she moved to London to open a studio and waxworks there; by the spring of 1775 Joseph joined her and was the first American-born student admitted to the Royal Academy Schools, where he won a silver medal for 'the best model of an Academy figure' in December 1778. In 1780 he exhibited publicly for the first time with *Portrait of a Man* in the annual exhibition of the Society of Artists of Great Britain. In that year he caused a scandal at the Royal Academy by exhibiting a portrait of his mother modelling a head of King Charles II, while busts of King George III and Queen Charlotte looked on (ex-artist's col.). He went to Paris in December 1781 and, while there, painted several portraits of *Benjamin Franklin* (version, *c.* 1782; London, Royal Soc. A.) from observation and from the 1778 pastel by Joseph Siffred Duplessis (1725–1802).

He sailed from Nantes in early autumn 1782; his ship was wrecked on the coast of Maine ten weeks later. He returned to Philadelphia where he painted his first known American portrait in June 1783, *Anne Shippen Livingston and her Daughter* (ex-Livingston priv. col.). Late in the summer of 1783, at the request of the federal government, Wright went to Rocky Hill, NJ, where he made a plaster cast of the face of George Washington, from which he modelled the first known sculpture of the president. He executed several other versions in different media (e.g.

wax) and also painted a small oil-on-panel portrait from life (1783; Philadelphia, PA, Hist. Soc.). In 1786 Wright moved to New York where he painted some of his most stylish and finished portraits, such as *Frederick Augustus Muhlenberg*, first Speaker of the US House of Representatives (*c.* 1786–90; Washington, DC, N.P.G.). He returned to Philadelphia, probably in the autumn of 1790.

Wright worked as an engraver for the newly founded US Mint. He is known to have cut dies for a medal honouring the Revolutionary War general Henry Lee and for an unissued quarter-dollar coin. Among the works he left unfinished is a well-known self-portrait with his wife and three children (Philadelphia, PA Acad. F.A.).

BIBLIOGRAPHY
Joseph Wright: American Artist, 1756–1793 (exh. cat. by M. H. Fabian, Washington, DC, N.P.G., 1985)

MONROE H. FABIAN

Wright, Russel (*b* Lebanon, OH, 3 April 1904; *d* New York, 21 Dec 1976). American designer. He took summer painting courses at the Cincinnati Academy of Art and in 1920 moved to New York to study sculpture at the Art Students League. He studied law at Princeton University, NJ (1921–4), but was chiefly interested in stage and prop design for college plays. He spent weekends in New York working on theatre projects with Norman Bel Geddes and in 1924 abandoned university for a career in theatre design. In 1927 he married Mary Small Einstein (*d* 1952), who became his business manager and the driving force behind his subsequent success. In 1930 he established a workshop in New York, making stage props and whimsical objects for speciality shops, including small animals hand-cut from aluminium sheet. He soon progressed to designing all manner of metal and ceramic objects for the home, influenced by Bauhaus ideas for functional design, although his simple, rounded forms were entirely his own. Similar to such contemporaries as Walter Dorwin Teague, Raymond Loewy and Henry Dreyfuss (1904–72), he championed an American approach to design, free from mannerisms and appealing to use. He created bar accessories, ice buckets, beer pitchers and bowls from spun aluminium, a metal he thought suitably democratic, and after 1932 introduced aluminium oven-to-tableware, the dishes, coffee pots and casseroles embellished with rattan frames, cork bases and wood or cane handles (e.g. coffee urn, spun aluminium and wood, *c.* 1935; Paul F. Walter priv. col., see Wilson, Pilgrim and Tashjian, p. 335). In 1934 his work was included in the landmark *Machine Art* exhibition at MOMA, New York, and the same year presented his first collection of coordinated furniture, made by the Heywood-Wakefield Co., Gardner, MA. It was followed in 1935 by his rectilinear 'American Modern' range, built from solid, naturally finished maple-wood and mass-produced by the Conant Ball Co., Gardner, for which Mary Wright coined the now-familiar term 'blonde'. In 1937 he designed his popular 'American Modern' ceramic dinnerware, with its organic, tapering forms and prominent spouts and lips to teapots and jugs (e.g. selection of 'American Modern' tableware, *c.* 1939–59; London, V&A), which was produced from 1939 by the Steubenville Pottery, East Liverpool, OH. Over the next two decades he was engaged in the design of everything from flatware to the first usable plastic tableware to textiles to interiors. In 1955, three years after the death of his wife, he abandoned his New York practice for a working retirement at Dragon Rock, his showpiece home near Garrison, NY (built 1941–61). In 1958 he travelled extensively in South-east Asia as a consultant for the US government, on a cooperative plan to aid in the export to the USA of selected East Asian crafts.

WRITINGS
Guide to Easier Living (New York, 1951)

BIBLIOGRAPHY
W. J. Hennessey: *Russel Wright: American Designer* (Cambridge, MA, and London, 1983)
A. Duncan: *American Art Deco* (London, 1986)
R. G. Wilson, D. H. Pilgrim and D. Tashjian: *The Machine Age in America, 1918–1941* (New York, 1986)

☐

Wright, von. Finnish family of painters and illustrators. They were descended from a Scottish family who moved to Sweden in the 17th century. The von Wright brothers were brought up in a remote region in central Finland and were almost entirely self-taught. They began their careers as zoological illustrators in Stockholm and were among the finest Finnish artists of the first half of the 19th century.

(1) Magnus von Wright (*b* Haminalahti, nr Kuopio, 13 June 1805; *d* Helsinki, 5 July 1868). In 1826 he moved to Stockholm, and in 1828 with his brother (2) Wilhelm von Wright he began publishing *Svenska foglar* ('Swedish birds'), the series of bird illustrations that rapidly established the brothers' reputation in Finland and Sweden. The work, completed in 1838, consists of 180 hand-tinted lithographs.

Magnus returned to Finland in 1829 and settled in Helsinki, where he played a key role in the development of Finnish art. He worked as a teacher of drawing at the University of Helsinki from 1847 until his death. His works are small-scale, intimate landscapes and scenes from city life that reveal an accurate and sensitive observation of nature; for example, *Annegatan 15: A Cold Winter Morning* (1868; Helsinki, Athenaeum A. Mus.). He toned down his palette to create a muted atmosphere. The only journey he made beyond Sweden took him in 1857 to Düsseldorf, where he studied for a short time under Hans Gude. Although Gude had a certain amount of influence on his landscape painting, Magnus's work always retained a quality of the Biedermeier style. Some of his best works were produced in the last year of his life.

JUKKA ERVAMAA

(2) Wilhelm von Wright (*b* Haminalahti, nr Kuopio, 5 April 1810; *d* Marieberg, Orust Island, 2 July 1887). Brother of (1) Magnus von Wright. In 1828 he began work with Magnus in Stockholm on the illustrations for *Svenska foglar* ('Swedish birds'), published between 1828 and 1838. Wilhelm remained in Stockholm, became a Swedish citizen and made an important contribution to zoological research and illustration in that country. Between 1835 and 1848 he was employed as the draughtsman of the Academy of Sciences, and he was a member of the Academy of Fine Art. In the 1840s he moved to the island of Orust, on the west coast of Sweden, where he was appointed fisheries inspector.

As a zoological illustrator, Wilhelm was the most productive and versatile of the three brothers. He drew, lithographed and coloured countless depictions of birds, as well as mammals, fish, butterflies, insects and sea organisms, with the utmost precision but also with a keen eye for decorative and colouristic effects. *Skandinaviens fiskar* ('The fish of Scandinavia') appeared between 1836 and 1857, and he published illustrations in various books and reviews. He executed a few oil paintings: for example *Hanging Wild Ducks: Still-life* (1851; Helsinki, Athenaeum A. Mus.). In 1856 he was struck with paralysis, and for the remainder of his life he was unable to work. His home at Marieberg has been opened as a museum; the main collections of his drawings are preserved in the library of the Academy of Sciences and the Athenaeum Art Museum, Helsinki, and the Library of Stockholm University.

PONTUS GRATE

(3) Ferdinand von Wright (*b* Haminalahti, nr Kuopio, 19 March 1822; *d* Haminalahti, 31 July 1906). Brother of (1) Magnus von Wright and (2) Wilhelm von Wright. He grew up under the influence of his brothers and became a skilled ornithological illustrator at a very young age. He remained in Sweden from 1837 until 1844 and worked as a draughtsman, helping his brother Wilhelm. After returning to Finland he set his sights on a career as a painter. During the second half of the 1840s he was still searching for his proper path, and he experimented with a number of subjects: birds, still-lifes, landscapes and portraits.

The most significant stage of Ferdinand's career began in the early 1850s, while staying with his brother Wilhelm on the west coast of Sweden. It may have been at this time that he became acquainted with early 19th-century Danish, and perhaps even Norwegian, painting. During this period he matured surprisingly quickly into a fine landscape artist. His works of the 1850s occupy a central place in the history of Finnish landscape painting. They are characterized by a romantic and lyrical conception of nature. Occasionally they display more monumental features or a sense of drama, stemming from the growing contemporary revival of Finnish nationalism; examples include *View over Haminalahti* (1853), *Garden in Haminalahti* (*c.* 1856; both Helsinki, Athenaeum A. Mus.) and *Storm in Haminalahti* (1857; Vaasa, Pohjanmaan Mus.).

In 1858 Ferdinand travelled to Dresden and studied under Siegwald Dahl (1827–1902), an animal painter and the son of the Norwegian landscape artist J. C. Dahl. Ferdinand abandoned landscape painting and concentrated once again on bird subjects; during the ten years after his visit he painted the majority of his most important depictions of birds. These include a number of finely coloured pictures of water-fowl, doves, ptarmigan, and dramatic portrayals of birds of prey (e.g. *Great Horned Owl Attacking a Hare*, 1860; Helsinki, Athenaeum A. Mus.).

In his later work Ferdinand partially returned to landscape painting and broadened his subject-matter. However, the major part of his output consisted of small, commissioned pieces on bird themes, of variable quality. In 1886 he painted the relatively large (1.24×1.89 m)

Fighting Capercaillie (Helsinki, Athenaeum A. Mus.), which is probably the most popular image in Finnish art. By the 1870s he had become a recluse at his estate in Haminalahti and was finding it difficult to keep abreast of the rapidly changing art scene.

BIBLIOGRAPHY

A. Lindström: *Taiteilijaveljekset von Wright* [The von Wright brothers and their art] (Helsinki, 1932)
J. Ervamaa: 'Käsityöläismaalareista von Wright-veljeksiin: Taiteilijan urasta ja asemasta Suomessa' [Painting from its origins in craft to the work of the von Wright brothers: a look at the profession and position of the artist in Finland], *Taidehist. Tutkimuksia/Ksthist. Stud.*, iii (1977), pp. 9–53
Taiteilijaveljekset von Wright/Konstnärsbröderna von Wright [The von Wright brothers and their art] (exh. cat., ed. T. Arkio; Helsinki, Athenaeum A. Mus.; Stockholm, Nmus.; 1982–5)
Konstnärsbröderna von Wright: Magnus von Wright 1805–1868, Wilhelm von Wright 1810–1887, Ferdinand von Wright 1822–1906 (exh. cat., ed. P. Grate; Stockholm, Nmus., 1985)
A. Leikola, J. Lokki and T. Stjernberg: *Bröderna von Wrights fåglar* [Birds of the von Wright brothers] (Höganäs, 1989)

JUKKA ERVAMAA

Wright, Willard Huntington (*b* Charlottesville, VA, 1888; *d* New York, 11 April 1939). American critic and writer. When he was 19 he became literary critic for a West Coast newspaper. In 1912 he moved to New York, first working as editor for *The Smart Set*, then as a newspaper editorial writer and art critic for *Forum* and *International Studio*. In these periodicals he wrote defences of modern art, attacking conservatives in the American art establishment. He also co-authored a book on aesthetic philosophy, *The Creative Will* (London, 1916) with his brother, the Synchromist painter STANTON MACDONALD-WRIGHT, and published a number of non-art books.

Wright's most important critical work was *Modern Painting: Its Tendency and Meaning* (New York, 1915), in which he attempted to explain modern art as an evolutionary process from Eugène Delacroix, Gustave Courbet and the Impressionists to Post-Impressionism and Cubism. The idiosyncrasy of his approach was to place Synchromism as the pinnacle of modern artistic development. In 1916 Wright organized the *Forum Exhibition of Modern American Painters* at the Anderson Galleries, New York, to display the work of American modernists whom he thought were being neglected. He returned to San Francisco in the same year, where he worked as an art critic and lectured on modern art. His last art book was *The Future of Painting* (New York, 1923).

BIBLIOGRAPHY

G. Levin: *Synchromism and American Color Abstraction, 1910–1925* (New York, 1978)
W. C. Agee: 'Willard Huntington Wright and the Synchromists: Notes on the Forum Exhibition', *Archvs Amer. A.J.*, xxiv/2 (1984), pp. 10–15
J. Loughery: 'Charles Caffin and Willard Huntington Wright, Advocates of Modern Art', *A. Mag.*, lix/5 (1985), pp. 103–9

A. DEIRDRE ROBSON

Wright, William (*fl* 1608; *bur* London, 5 April 1654). English sculptor. He was a tomb sculptor who appears to have trained as a haberdasher. He lived and worked at Charing Cross, Westminster, London, where he is first recorded in 1607–8. His artistic career began in partnership with the obscure John Key, with whom in 1608 he made the memorial to *Sir William Paston* (North Walsham, Norfolk, St Nicholas), a work that followed convention in its reliance on height and architectural display for effect. Wright continued to work in this manner, with some idiosyncrasies and refinements of detail, when commemorating *Edward Talbot, 8th Earl of Shrewsbury* (*c.* 1619; London, Westminster Abbey), *Sir Robert Gardener* (*c.* 1620; Elmswell, Suffolk, St John the Baptist) and *Edward Seymour, Earl of Hertford, and his Family* (*c.* 1621; Salisbury Cathedral). Later, however, he adopted the fashion for shrouded effigies, revealing a talent for figure sculpture in the tombs of *Anne, Lady Deane* (1634; Great Maplestead, Essex, St Giles) and *Sir John Denham* (*c.* 1639; Egham, Surrey, St John the Baptist). The weakness of his later work is in the design, which is sometimes very bizarre: columns intrude between the spectator and the effigies of *Sir Richard Scott* (1640; Ecclesfield, S. Yorks, St Mary), *Sir Lionel Tollemache, Bart* (*c.* 1640; Helmingham, Suffolk, St Mary) and *Sir Robert Wiseman* (*c.* 1641; Willingale Doe, Essex, St Christopher).

Wright's workshop found favour during the early years of the Commonwealth. The monument to *Henry Ireton* (destr. 1660) in Westminster Abbey was paid for in 1654 by order of the Council of State and the Lord Protector, Oliver Cromwell, who was the father-in-law of the deceased.

BIBLIOGRAPHY

K. A. Esdaile and E. Esdaile: 'William Wright of Charing Cross, Sculptor', *Assoc. Archit. Soc. Rep. & Pap.*, xlii (1934), pp. 221–32
M. Whinney: *Sculpture in Britain, 1530–1830*, Pelican Hist. A. (Harmondsworth, 1964, rev. 2/1988)

ADAM WHITE

Wright of Derby, Joseph [Wright, Joseph] (*b* Derby, 3 Sept 1734; *d* Derby, 29 Aug 1797). English painter. He painted portraits, landscapes and subjects from literature, but his most original and enduringly celebrated works are a few which reflect the philosophical and technological preoccupations of the later 18th century and are characterized by striking effects of artificial light. He was the first major English painter to work outside the capital all his life: apart from spells in Liverpool (1768–71), Italy (1773–5) and Bath (1775–7), he lived and worked in his native Derby, though exhibiting in London at both the Society of Artists (1765–76, 1791) and the Royal Academy (1778–82, 1789–90, 1794). Reappraisal of his achievements has followed Nicolson's monograph of 1968.

1. Early career, to 1773. 2. Voyage to Italy and later career.

1. EARLY CAREER, TO 1773. Wright was the third son of a Derby attorney. He trained as a portrait painter in the London studio of Thomas Hudson from 1751 to 1753, then returned to Derby where he painted a penetrating, detached *Self-portrait* (*c.* 1753–4; Derby, Mus. & A.G.) in van Dyck costume, as well as portraits of his relations, friends and members of prominent local families. During a further period of study with Hudson (1756–7) he became friends with John Hamilton Mortimer. In Derby, Wright continued to paint members of the rising middle classes, professional people and local landed gentry; such portraits would form his main source of income throughout his career. In 1760 he attracted a number of portrait commissions by travelling through the Midland towns of Newark, Retford, Boston, Lincoln and Doncaster. In addition to

half- and three-quarter-length single portraits, Wright began to paint more ambitious group portraits, such as *James and Mary Shuttleworth with One of their Daughters* (1764; Lord Shuttleworth priv. col., see 1990 exh. cat., p. 45). He painted without the help of studio assistants and sometimes enhanced his compositions with poses borrowed from Old Masters such as Rembrandt or Raphael; this and his excellence at rendering drapery make his portraits often attractive, despite a directness of approach that can rarely have flattered.

Alongside the portraits Wright began in the early 1760s to paint subject pictures of figures in dark interiors illumined by candles or lamps. Their dramatic contrasts of light and shade, derived from masters such as Rembrandt, Gerrit van Honthorst, Godfried Schalcken and ultimately Caravaggio, give these images great clarity of form and detail as well as powerful visual impact, as for instance in the *Three Persons Viewing the 'Gladiator' by Candlelight* of 1765 (priv. col., see 1990 exh. cat., p. 61). The largest and most unusual of these scenes are *A Philosopher Lecturing on the Orrery* (1766; Derby, Mus. & A.G.; see fig. 1) and *Experiment on a Bird in the Air Pump* (1768; London, Tate; for illustration *see* ENLIGHTENMENT, THE). The philosopher in the first shows the movements of the solar system, through a type of model named after the Earl of Orrery, to a group of laymen whose faces are lit up by the lamp that represents the sun. In the second a scientist demonstrates the nature of a vacuum by pumping the air from a glass vessel containing a bird, eliciting responses ranging from the detached concentration of male observers to the distress of two young girls concerned for the suffering bird. These works, embodying the wide contemporary enthusiasm for scientific and technological development, were unique in their combination of the scientific portrait group—recalling Rembrandt's *Anatomy Lesson of Dr Tulp* (1632; The Hague, Mauritshuis)—expressive depiction of emotion in a contemporary popular setting and striking Caravaggesque contrasts of light and shadow. The accurate depiction of scientific equipment and processes reflects Wright's personal acquaintance with Midlands figures such as the polymathic Erasmus Darwin, scientist and poet, the pottery manufacturer Josiah Wedgwood and the Derby mechanic and geologist John Whitehurst (1713–88), who, with others like Matthew Boulton and James Watt (1736–1819), formed the Lunar Society *c.* 1764–5. The group promoted theoretical discussion, but with a view to practical improvements in trade and industry.

The scientific scenes established Wright's reputation in London and, following them, many of his major pictures were engraved by William Pether, Valentine Green, John Raphael Smith and others. He was, however, based in

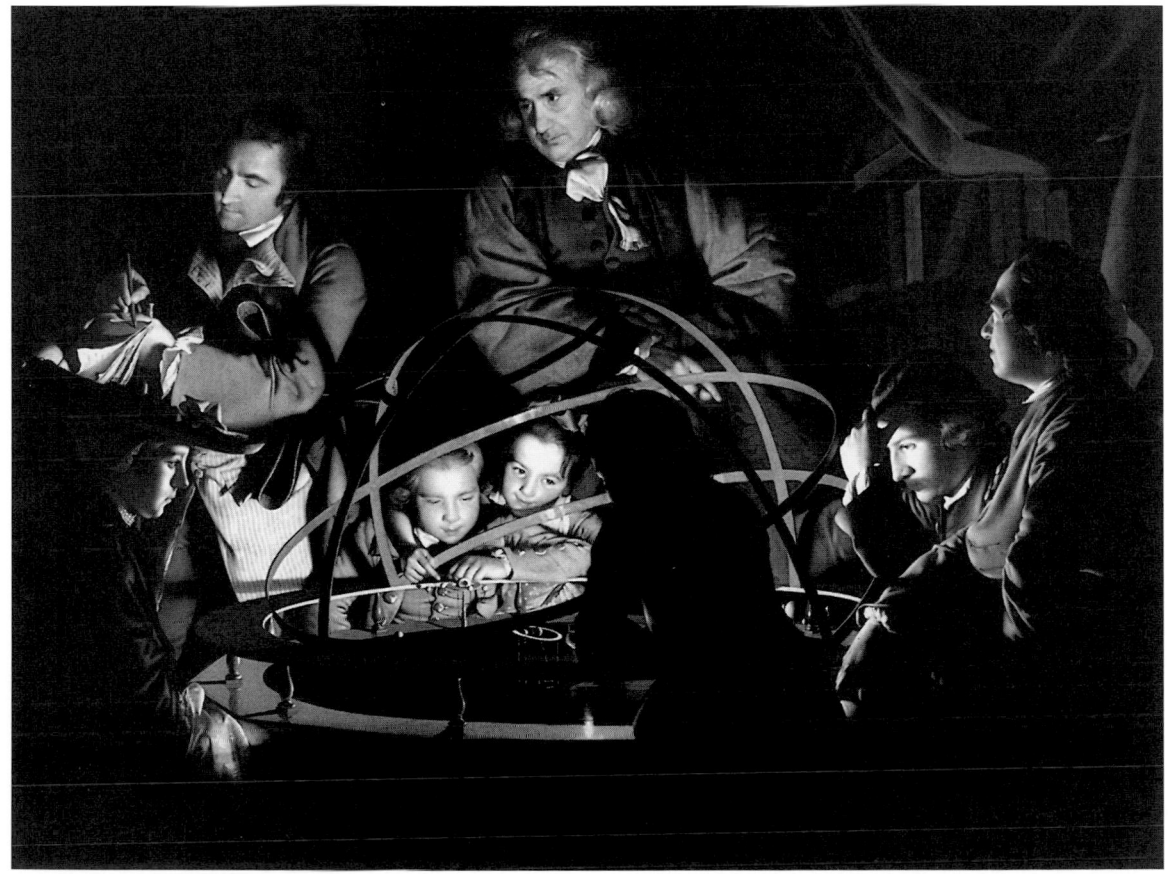

1. Joseph Wright of Derby: *A Philosopher Lecturing on the Orrery*, oil on canvas, 1.47×2.03 m, 1766 (Derby, Museum and Art Gallery)

Liverpool from 1768 to 1771, producing paintings for Radbourne Hall, Derby, in 1770 with his friend Mortimer. He continued to paint portraits of Midlands and northern sitters, the finest of which is perhaps of his friends *Mr and Mrs Coltman* (?1771; London, N.G.), who, recently wed, are shown about to set out riding in a landscape setting recalling Gainsborough's open-air portraits. Between 1771 and 1773 Wright painted several nocturnal scenes, again combining modern subjects with a historical style. The moonlit tumbledown building in *Blacksmith's Shop* (1771; two versions, New Haven, CT, Yale Cent. Brit. A. and Derby, Mus. & A.G.) recalls traditional nativity settings, while the muscular workmen illuminated by the glowing ingot, here and in *Iron Forge* (1772; London, Tate, see 1990 exh. cat., p. 102) with its introduction of modern machinery, elevate the subjects from popular genre towards the level of the modern history painting being simultaneously introduced in America by Benjamin West. Further nocturnes, *Iron Forge Viewed from Without* (1773; St Petersburg, Hermitage)—bought from Wright for Catherine the Great—and the *Earthstopper on the Banks of the Derwent* (1773; Derby, Mus. & A.G.), influenced by such Dutch landscape painters as Aert van der Neer, show, like *Mr and Mrs Coltman*, a newly developing interest in landscape.

Other paintings from the same period present melancholy scenes of man confronted by death, inspired by literary sources. *Philosopher by Lamplight* ('*Hermit Studying Anatomy*', 1769; Derby, Mus. & A.G.) recalls Salvator Rosa's *Democritus* (Copenhagen, Stat. Mus. Kst.), Dürer's *Melencolia* engraving and the hermits of 17th-century artists like Gerard Dou, but Wright was probably also influenced in his choice of imagery by the 18th-century British 'graveyard' poets—Robert Blair, Edward Young and Thomas Gray. Another nocturne, *Miravan Breaking Open the Tomb of his Ancestors* (1772; Derby, Mus. & A.G.), seems to derive from an as yet unidentified literary source; its macabre romanticism is close in spirit to the work of Mortimer and of Johann Heinrich Fuseli, and to the contemporary Gothic novel. A third subject in the same vein, the *Old Man and Death* (1773; Hartford, CT, Wadsworth Atheneum), illustrates one of Aesop's *Fables*; an alarmed old man, seated by a ruin in a daylight landscape, faces Death in the form of a skeleton standing before him.

2. VOYAGE TO ITALY AND LATER CAREER. In October 1773 Wright departed for Italy, arriving in Rome in February 1774 with his pupil Richard Hurlestone (*d* 1777), the portrait painter John Downman and the sculptor James Paine (1745–1829). Here he made friends with George Romney, Ozias Humphry and Jacob More. A common enthusiasm for Michelangelo, as advocated by Fuseli who was currently working in Rome, led Wright and Romney to make studies from the Sistine Chapel. During his two years based in Rome, Wright sketched Classical sculptures and architecture (drawings, Derby, Mus. & A.G.; London, BM; New York, Met.) and recorded the city's spectacular *Girandola* or annual firework display (1774; Derby, Mus. & A.G.). He also sketched scenes in the Campagna and in the Kingdom of Naples, including grottoes in the Gulf of Salerno and an eruption of Vesuvius witnessed in October 1774. Oil

paintings from this material were mostly produced following his return to England, via Florence and Venice, in September 1775. Vesuvius inspired over 30 paintings during the next 20 years (e.g. 1778; Moscow, Pushkin Mus. F.A.), in which Wright probably drew on the work of the French specialist in the volcano, Pierre-Jacques Volaire, but was more generally influenced by Edmund Burke's concept of the Sublime. The contemporary scientific fascination with volcanoes is also seen in William Hamilton's *Observations on Mount Vesuvius* (1772) and the work of Wright's geologist friend Whitehurst. Wright's later, sunlit Italian landscapes of the 1780s and 1790s are close in conception to the classical landscape manner of Richard Wilson, and his coastal scenes recall those of Claude-Joseph Vernet.

Wright spent the two years after his return in 1775 in Bath, in an unsuccessful attempt to replace the recently departed Gainsborough as portrait painter to fashionable society. After his permanent return to Derby, he was elected ARA in 1781; but he quarrelled with the Royal Academy in 1783, apparently over election to full RA status. In keeping with the fashion set by Gainsborough and Romney, his later portraits are more penetrating in their characterization, often more complex in their iconography and generally more subdued in colouring. The exceptional informality and melancholy pose of *Brooke Boothby* (1781; London, Tate), a philosophical Staffordshire nobleman seen reclining by a woodland stream, clutching a volume by his friend Jean-Jacques Rousseau, make for one of the most singular images in 18th-century art of man retreating into communion with nature, the theme of Rousseau's writings. The *Rev. D'Ewes Coke, his Wife Hannah and Daniel Parker Coke MP* (1782; Derby, Mus. & A.G.) and the *Rev. Thomas Gisborne and his Wife Mary* (1786; New Haven, CT, Yale Cent. Brit. A.) are seen as genteel amateur artists, on sketching trips in the countryside. Wright also painted imposing portraits of leading figures of the Industrial Revolution like the textile manufacturers *Richard Arkwright* (1789–90; priv. col., on loan to Derby, Mus. & A. G.) and *Samuel Oldknow* (*c.* 1790–92; Leeds, C.A.G.). Oldknow holds a roll of his muslin, while Arkwright is proudly seated by a model of the innovative water-powered cotton spinning frame which made his huge fortune.

Wright increasingly depicted themes from literature in his later career. He responded to the contemporary cult of sensibility in several versions of two scenes from Lawrence Sterne's *A Sentimental Journey* (1768): *The Captive* (e.g. 1774, Vancouver, A.G.; and late 1770s, Derby, Mus. & A.G.) and *Maria* (1777, priv. col., see 1990 exh. cat., p. 107; 1781, Derby, Mus. & A.G.); a prisoner languishing in his cell and a distraught village girl abandoned by her lover—both melancholy, emotive subjects. The taste for Classical themes led to *Corinthian Maid* (*c.* 1783–4; New Haven, CT, Yale Cent. Brit. A.), showing the traditional origin of painting when a potter's daughter traced the shadow of her lover on a lamplit wall. This was a commission from Wedgwood, with some of his pottery and a kiln inserted as accessories. In the later 1780s Wright contributed three paintings to John Boydell's Shakespeare Gallery in London, including a lamplit *Tomb Scene from Romeo and Juliet* (1789–90; Derby, Mus. & A.G.).

2. Joseph Wright of Derby: *Landscape with Rainbow*, oil on canvas, 0.81×1.07 m, *c.* 1794–5 (Derby, Museum and Art Gallery)

The increasingly frequent landscapes in Wright's later output—British as well as Italian—show him seeking for truthful observation of natural phenomena, such as rock formations or effects of light and atmosphere, without sacrificing aesthetic values like poetry, beauty, drama and composition. He painted several views of *Matlock High Tor* (e.g. mid-1780s; Cambridge, Fitzwilliam) and other rocky parts of Derbyshire. Another Derbyshire landscape, *Arkwright's Cotton Mills by Night* (*c.* 1782; priv. col., see 1990 exh. cat., p. 199), reveals Wright once again as an innovator, giving to one of the landmarks of the Industrial Revolution an elevated treatment previously reserved for country houses. Wright's late landscapes often show a great sensitivity to varying effects of light and weather, as in the sky suffused with pink light of the *Landscape with Figures and a Tilted Cart* (*c.* 1790; Southampton, C.A.G.) or the leaden, rain-filled sky that heightens the contrasts of the *Landscape with Rainbow* (*c.* 1794–5; Derby, Mus. & A.G.; see fig. 2). A visit to the Lake District in 1793 or 1794 inspired a series of poetic views, including *Rydal Waterfall* (1795; Derby, Mus. & A.G.) and *Derwent Water* (1795–6; New Haven, CT, Yale Cent. Brit. A.).

BIBLIOGRAPHY

W. Bemrose: *The Life and Works of Joseph Wright, A.R.A., Commonly Called Wright of Derby* (London, 1885)

F. D. Klingender: *Art and the Industrial Revolution* (London, 1947, rev. 2/1972)

E. K. Waterhouse: *Painting in Britain, 1530–1790*, Pelican Hist. A. (Harmondsworth, 1953)

R. Cummings: 'Boothby, Rousseau and the Romantic Malady', *Burl. Mag.*, cx (1968), pp. 659–66

B. Nicolson: *Joseph Wright of Derby, Painter of Light*, 2 vols (London, 1968)

R. Cummings: 'Folly and Mutability in Two Romantic Paintings: *The Alchemist* and *Democritus* by Joseph Wright', *A. Q.* [Detroit], xxxiii (1970), pp. 247–75

R. Paulson: *Emblem and Expression: Meaning in English Art of the Eighteenth Century* (London, 1975), pp. 184–203

D. Fraser: *Joseph Wright of Derby (1734–1797)* (Derby, 1979)

Joseph Wright of Derby: Mr and Mrs Coltman (exh. cat., ed. A. Braham; London, N.G., 1986)

Wright of Derby (exh. cat., ed. J. Egerton; London, Tate, 1990)

A. Bermingham: 'The Origin of Painting and the Ends of Art: Wright of Derby's Corinthian Maid', *Painting and the Politics of Culture: New Essays on British Art, 1700–1850*, ed. J. Barrell (Oxford, 1992), pp. 135–65D.

D. Solkin: 'Re Wrighting Shaftesbury: The Air Pump and the Limits of Commercial Humanism', *Painting and the Politics of Culture: New Essays on British Art, 1700–1850*, ed. J. Barrell (Oxford, 1992), pp. 73–99

S. Daniels: *Fields of Vision: Landscape Imagery and National Identity in England and the United States* (Cambridge, 1993), pp. 43–79

DAVID FRASER

Wrightsman, Charles B(ierer) (*b* 1895; *d* 1986). American collector. He acquired an impressive collection of French decorative art and Old Master and Impressionist paintings that his wife Jayne (Larkin) Wrightsman continued to expand after her husband's death. Wrightsman amassed his fortune through the Standard Oil company of Kansas, of which he was President between 1932 and 1953. With the dispersal of many European collections following World War II the Wrightsmans were able to decorate their houses in New York, Florida and London with works of the highest quality. These became the subject of a celebrated legal case in 1970, when Wrightsman attempted to have the US$8.9 million that he had spent on art declared an investment in order to qualify for tax allowances. He lost his case on the grounds that the Wrightsmans plainly took personal pleasure in their collection. Wrightsman's private enjoyment of his art did not, however, prevent him from being a particularly important patron of the Metropolitan Museum of Art, New York. As well as becoming a trustee (1956), he gave the museum the spectacular Wrightsman Galleries. These include paintings by such masters as El Greco, Johannes Vermeer, Giambattista Tiepolo, George Stubbs, Camille Pissarro and Monet as well as important sculptures such as Jean-Antoine Houdon's bust of *Denis Diderot* (1773). The rooms are also filled with exquisite 18th-century French furniture and other objects, including carpets and porcelain: comprehensive catalogues of the collection were published between 1966 and 1973.

BIBLIOGRAPHY

F. J. B. Watson: *The Wrightsman Collection*, 5 vols (New York, 1966–73)
J. Walker: *Self-portrait with Donors: Confessions of an Art Collector* (Boston, 1974), pp. 252–69
G. Barker: 'Passionate Possessors: The Cast Changers', *ARTnews* (Jan 1991), pp. 107–23

CHRISTOPHER MASTERS

Writing. *See* SCRIPT.

Writing-table. *See under* BUREAU.

Wróblewski, Andrzej (*b* Wilno [now Vilnius, Lithuania], 15 June 1927; *d* Zakopane, 23 March 1957). Polish painter and writer. He produced his first paintings under the supervision of his mother, the graphic artist Krystyna Wróblewska (*b* 1904). In 1945–52 he studied painting at the Academy of Fine Arts, Kraków, in the studios of Zygmunt Radnicki (*b* 1894), Zbigniew Pronaszko, Hanna Rudzka-Cybisowa (*b* 1897) and Jerzy Fedkowicz (*b* 1891). At the same time he studied the history of art and became involved in art criticism, publishing his exhibition reviews and polemical articles in cultural journals. From 1950, Wróblewski worked at the Academy of Fine Arts, Kraków. He exhibited from 1946 at exhibitions significant for contemporary Polish art, including the exhibition *Sztuki nowoczesnej* ('Modern art'; Kraków, Pal. A., 1948) and the *Wystawa młodej plastyki* ('Young plastic arts exhibition') at the Arsenal, Warsaw (1955). Although during the 1940s Wróblewski produced only abstract compositions, he had a strong tendency towards realism, using a simple, but often ambiguous style. In 1948, he founded the Mutual Improvement Group (Grupa Samokształceniowa) at the Academy of Fine Arts, Kraków, which called for realistic art (freed from the surrealistic use of metaphor) at the Festival of Art Schools in Poznań in 1949, thus contributing to the introduction of Socialist Realism into Poland. Also in 1949 Wróblewski produced one of his most prominent cycles of paintings, *Execution by Firing Squad* (e.g. Poznań, N. Mus.).

Wróblewski's most conformist Socialist Realist canvases were painted in the early 1950s. After 1955, however, he repeatedly returned to allusion and metaphor in compositions with well-defined colour schemes. Such paintings as *The Queue Continues* (1956; Warsaw, N. Mus.) depict human existence in simple form using figural symbols. Wróblewski's tendency to simplify his compositions and his use of an almost poster-like shorthand led to the comparison of his work with Pop art. Although he almost went unnoticed at the Arsenal exhibition, because of the influence of his paintings of 1956–7 Wróblewski began to be considered the most important of the Arsenalists. His work and his attitude to the involvement of the artist in contemporary life influenced the work of artists from the groups Wprost and Gruppa.

For bibliography *see* ARSENALISTS.

WOJCIECH WŁODARCZYK

Wrocław [Ger. Breslau]. Polish city on the River Odra (Ger. Oder) in Lower Silesia, *c.* 300 km south-west of Warsaw. Wrocław developed on several islands in the river and on its south bank, originally as a trade centre on the amber route linking the Baltic Sea with the Roman Empire. A Slav settlement on Ostrów Tumski (Cathedral Island) is associated by some scholars with the Bohemian prince Vratislav I (*reg* AD 895–921). By 990 the town was ruled by the Piast princes, and a bishopric was established in 1000. Ostrów Tumski remained independent of the town, the south part of which was walled and moated. Romanesque architecture and sculpture flourished in Wrocław from the 12th century under the patronage of the magnate Piotr Włostowic (*c.* 1080–*c.* 1153), his wife Maria and Bishop Walter of Malonne (*d* 1169). In 1134 Maria Włostowic founded the Augustinian abbey and the church of the Virgin on Piasek Island. At nearby Ołbin, Piotr Włostowic erected the Benedictine abbey and the church of St Vincent (1138; destr. 1529), and in 1149 Bishop Walter founded the second cathedral on Ostrów Tumski. Portals and tympana surviving from these churches are fine examples of Romanesque sculpture (*see* POLAND, fig. 10).

In 1241 Wrocław was ravaged by the Tatar-Mongols. Soon afterwards it received two new charters (*c.* 1242 and 1261), and in the 1270s several privileges granted to the burgesses by Henry IV, Prince of Silesia (*reg* 1266–90), speeded the rebuilding of the city with a regular street network, a rectangular market place (212×175 m) and adjoining salt market (102×92 m). An early and influential manifestation of Gothic architecture in Wrocław was the cathedral presbytery (1244–72). In 1288 Prince Henry founded the church of the Holy Cross (completed *c.* 1350), a hall church elevated on a crypt. The churches of St Mary Magdalene, St Elizabeth and St Dorothy were built in the 14th century, and some older buildings were remodelled in the new style. The rectangular ambulatory, added *c.* 1320–50 to the cathedral, became a local characteristic. The town hall, a fine example of Late Gothic, was erected before 1299, and in 1471–1504 it was extended and decorated with ornamental reliefs and gables (see fig.). Wrocław exchanged artists, works of art and ideas with

Kraków, hence the similarities in the prominent pier buttresses in their buildings and common iconographic types in sepulchral and devotional sculpture, such as the *Virgin Standing on a Lion* and the *Beautiful Madonna*.

Wrocław was a cosmopolitan city with a large German population, although it always had strong cultural links with Poland. From 1335 it was politically dependent on the king of Bohemia, to whom it was enfeoffed, and from 1526 it was ruled by the Habsburgs until Prussia took over in 1741. These developments were unfavourable to the arts and Wrocław declined into a provincial frontier town. The authorities concentrated on building fortifications, commissioning Hans Schneider von Lindau (1542–1606), who repeated the defence system he had constructed at Gdańsk; in 1634 a Dutch system was introduced by Valentin von Saebisch (1578–1657). The Protestant domination of the first half of the 17th century delayed the introduction of Baroque, but by the turn of the century there was a revival in the city's art. The Jesuit Church (1689–98) and College (1726–32; now the university) were built on the west bank of the Odra by Christoph Tausch, Johann Albrecht Siegwitz (*fl* 1724–56), Franz Joseph Mangoldt (*fl* 1725–53) and Christoph Hackner (1663–1741). Within the College is the Leopoldina Hall, which is lavishly decorated with wall paintings and stuccowork. Many buildings were remodelled in Baroque style, for example the Augustinian abbey (1709–30; now the university library) on Piasek Island. The Electoral Chapel, designed by Johann Bernhard Fischer von Erlach and decorated by Carlo Carlone and Ferdinand Maximilián Brokof, was added to the cathedral in 1716–24. Carl Gotthard Langhans, the chief representative of Neo-classicism, designed the Bishop's Palace (after 1791) with his pupil Karl Gottfried Geissler (1754–1823) and the residences of the Wallenberg-Pachalys (1785–7) and the Hatzfelds (1765–75; destr. 1945). Fortification works were undertaken again after 1741 on the orders of Frederick II and, on an even larger scale, between 1768 and 1783 under the supervision of Gerhard Cornelius von Wallrave (1692–1773). Massive earthworks and bastions encircled the town on both banks, as well as Ostrów Tumski and other islands. A romantic park laid down in 1780–84 in Szczytniki was connected to the town by an avenue in 1792 and more parks replaced the fortifications from 1807 when Wrocław was briefly under French occupation. The north arm of the Odra was drained and Ostrów Tumski ceased to be an island. At the end of Świdnicka Street in the southern part of the town the French laid out a square (140×140 m; now Kościuszko Square) for military parades.

A range of styles was adopted for public buildings constructed in the 19th century and in the 20th before World War II. Examples include the Neo-classical Börse with Empire-style sculptural ornament (1822–4), the theatre (1837–41; both by Karl Ferdinand Langhans; now the opera house) and the Renaissance/Baroque Revival museum (1883–6; by Carl Friedrich Endell, 1843–91; now the National Museum). Art Nouveau forms, influenced by the Berlin Secession, were often mixed with historicist styles. Innovative steel construction was used in 1908 in two market halls at Nanker Square and Zieliński Street, with Gothic Revival and Art Nouveau façades designed

Wrocław, town hall, before 1299; altered 1471–1504

by Richard Plüddemann (1846–1910) and Friedrich August Küster (*b* 1869). Max Berg's circular Centennial Hall (1912–13), with a dome 65 m in diameter, made use of ferro-concrete. The department store on Szewska Street, built in 1927 of steel, glass, travertine and bronze, was a pioneering project by Erich Mendelsohn. During World War II Wrocław was extensively damaged, but many historic buildings, including the cathedral and other Gothic churches, have been reconstructed. The main art collections are in the National Museum, the Archdiocesan Museum (est. 1898) and the Ossolineum (opened 1947, L'vov (now L'viv). In 1985 the *Panorama of the Racławice Battle* (1894) by Jan Styka (1858–1925), Wojciech Kossak and others, the only circular painting preserved in Poland, was opened to the public in the purpose-built Panorama Building.

BIBLIOGRAPHY

L. Burgemeister and G. Grundmann: *Die Kunstdenkmäler der Stadt Breslau*, 3 vols (Breslau, 1930–34)

K. Maleczyński, M. Morelowski and A. Ptaszycka: *Wrocław: Rozwój urbanistyczny* [Wrocław: urban development] (Warsaw, 1956)

M. Bukowski and M. Zlat: *Ratusz Wrocławski* [The Wrocław Town Hall] (Wrocław, 1958)

M. Bukowski: *Katedra Wrocławska* [Wrocław Cathedral] (Wrocław, 1962)

T. Broniewski and M. Zlat, eds: *Sztuka Wrocławia* [Art in Wrocław] (Wrocław, 1967) [with Eng. foreword]

M. Starzewska: *Die Museen in Wrocław: Führer* (Wrocław, 1974)

Rassegna, xi, 40/4 (Dec 1989) [issue dedicated to art life and architecture in Wrocklaw]

ANNA BENTKOWSKA

Wtenbrouck, Moses van. *See* UYTTENBROECK, MOSES VAN.

Wtewael [Utenwael; Uytewael; Wttewael], **Joachim (Anthonisz.)** (*b* Utrecht, 1566; *d* Utrecht, 1 Aug 1638). Dutch

Joachim Wtewael: *The Deluge*, oil on canvas, 1.48×1.83 m, 1592–5 (Nuremberg, Germanisches Nationalmuseum)

painter and draughtsman. He was one of the last exponents of MANNERISM. From *c.* 1590 until 1628, the year of his latest known dated paintings, he employed such typical Mannerist formal devices as brilliant decorative colour, contrived spatial design and contorted poses. He sometimes combined such artifice with naturalism, and this amalgam represents the two approaches Dutch 16th- and 17th-century theorists discussed as *uyt den geest* ('from the imagination') and *naer 't leven* ('after life'). Wtewael's activity reflects the transition from Mannerism to a more naturalistic style in Dutch art. Slightly over 100 of his paintings and about 80 drawings are known. Subjects from the Bible and mythology predominate; he also painted several portraits, including a *Self-portrait* (1601; Utrecht, Cent. Mus.).

According to his contemporary van Mander, the artist was trained in his father's glassworks in Utrecht. He spent four years (*c.* 1588–92) in Italy and France with his patron Charles de Bourgneuf de Cucé, Bishop of St Malo. Wtewael's large canvas of the *Apotheosis of Venus and Diana* (1590–92; priv. col., see Lowenthal, 1986, pl. 2) displays familiarity with the styles of Parmigianino and the Fontainebleau school, exalting the goddesses of love and

hunting in a suave, elegant manner, in which pink, flesh and yellow tones predominate. Wtewael had returned to Utrecht by 1592, when he was admitted to the saddlers' guild, to which painters then belonged. His earliest Utrecht works reflect an enthusiastic response to Haarlem developments of the late 1580s. Hendrick Goltzius, Cornelis Cornelisz. van Haarlem, and their mentor van Mander had formed a trio that exercised powerful influence throughout the northern Netherlands. The Haarlem late Mannerist style was indebted to the exaggerated Italianate manner of the Fleming Bartholomaeus Spranger, a friend and colleague of van Mander. In *The Deluge* (1592–5; Nuremberg, Ger. Nmus.; see fig.), Wtewael based the convoluted, muscular figures on Goltzius's engravings the *Disgracers* (1588; Hollstein, viii, nos 306–9) after designs by Cornelis van Haarlem. Other typical features are the contrasting pale and ruddy flesh tones of the figures, their upturned faces, prominent noses and splayed fingers and toes. The landscape style reflects that of Abraham Bloemaert, a fellow Utrecht artist, who had also been influenced by Haarlem Mannerism. Wtewael's earliest known signed and dated work, *Parnassus* (1594; Dresden, Gemäldegal., destr.; see Lowenthal, 1986, pl. 4), was a small painting on copper that used as a model Goltzius's drawing of the *Judgement of Midas* (1590; New York, Pierpont Morgan Lib.), which had departed from Spranger's style in its restrained, orderly grace. The classicizing style of such works initiated an important trend in Dutch art. Wtewael's *Apotheosis*, *Deluge* and *Parnassus*, with their contrasting sizes, supports and artistic styles, typify his protean abilities. Throughout his career he varied these factors, producing quite different treatments of a given subject. For example, he depicted the *Adoration of the Shepherds*, one of his favourite themes, on small coppers (e.g. 1601; Stuttgart, Staatsgal.), canvases and panels of medium size (e.g. 1598; Utrecht, Cent. Mus.; *c.* 1606; Oxford, Ashmolean) and a monumental canvas (1618; Pommersfelden, Schloss Weissenstein). His relatively meticulous painting technique is consistent for both large and small works.

Around 1600 Wtewael and the artists of the Haarlem circle began to temper the extravagance of their designs. In his *Kitchen Scene with the Parable of the Great Supper* (1605; Berlin, Bodemus.) Wtewael based the composition on gently receding diagonals, while retaining the Mannerist formula of two openings into depth. Figural poses are only moderately contorted. He treated the subject traditionally, filling the foreground with foodstuffs and figures that signify earthly temptations, which distract the viewer from the scene of salvation in the background. He used familiar Netherlandish motifs, such as a kitchen maid putting chickens on a spit, which alludes to the colloquialism *vogelen* (to bird, meaning to fornicate). Such wordplays, together with the modern Dutch costumes and furnishings, made the picture's didacticism readily accessible to his contemporaries. Many motifs in the painting have both positive and negative connotations, with the ambiguity left to the viewer to contemplate, thereby confronting him with the moral choices of everyday life. Wtewael often constructed his works on this principle, in keeping with current Dutch practice.

In his later works Wtewael developed an especially sophisticated use of Mannerist contrivance. For example in *Moses Striking the Rock* (1624; Washington, DC, N.G.A.) the procession of Israelites winds with choreographic grace into the distance, the hues of their garments ranging from dusky pink to silvery green. Yet here too he introduced realistic elements, such as the vividly depicted animals and kitchen utensils in the foreground. The influence of Venetians such as Jacopo Bassano, evident in these genre motifs, remained important to Wtewael.

Wtewael's drawings are as varied in style as his paintings. Typically he worked in ink with wash and white heightening on white or buff-coloured paper. He sometimes used chalk, as in *Christ Blessing the Children* (Detroit, MI, Inst. A.). In style, the drawings, too, developed from a boldly expressive manner, as in the *Wedding of Peleus and Thetis* from the 1590s (Berlin, Kupferstichkab.), to the refined treatment of the same subject from 1622 (Haarlem, Teylers Mus.). Sometimes the function of a drawing is difficult to determine; highly finished sheets, such as the last named, may be records that he used as models for painted replicas, which are numerous. In 1596 he made designs for two glass windows in the St Janskerk, Gouda. Several of his designs were engraved, most notably the

Thronus justitiae (1606; Amsterdam, Rijksmus., see Lowenthal, 1986, figs 58–71), 13 scenes of justice plus titlepage by Willem Swanenburgh.

Wtewael was a flax merchant and politician as well as an artist. A Calvinist sympathizer and supporter of Prince Maurice of Orange Nassau, he was elected to the Utrecht town council several times. He was among the foundermembers of the painters' own St Luke's Guild in 1611. One of his sons, Peter Wtewael (1596–1660), was also a painter, whose works until recently were confused with his father's. Peter Wtewael's oeuvre comprises five signed paintings (e.g. *Adoration of the Shepherds*, 1624; Cologne, Wallraf-Richartz Mus.; *Way to Calvary*, 1627; priv. col.) and about twenty attributed ones.

BIBLIOGRAPHY
C. M. A. A. Lindeman: *Joachim Anthonisz. Wtewael* (Utrecht, 1929)
A. W. Lowenthal: 'Some Paintings by Peter Wtewael (1596–1660)', *Burl. Mag.*, cxvi (1974), pp. 458–67
E. McGrath: 'A Netherlandish History by Joachim Wtewael', *J. Warb. & Court. Inst.*, xxxviii (1975), pp. 182–217
S. Helliesen 'Thronus justitiae: A Series of Pictures of Justice by Joachim Wtewael', *Oud-Holland*, xci (1977), pp. 232–66
A. W. Lowenthal: *Joachim Wtewael and Dutch Mannerism* (Doornspijk, 1986)
——: 'Wtewael's Netherlandish History Reconsidered', *Ned. Ksthist. Jb.*, xxxviii (1987), pp. 215–25
——: *Joachim Wtewael: Mars and Venus Surprised by Vulcan* (Malibu, 1995)
ANNE W. LOWENTHAL

Wu. *See* MOKUAN SHŌTŌ.

Wu Bin [Wu Pin; *zi* Wenzhong; *hao* Zhixian] (*b* Putian, Fujian Province; *fl c.* 1568–1626). Chinese painter. One of the most talented of a small group of mid-17th-century professional artists active in Nanjing and Beijing, whose paintings of landscapes and figural compositions presented an alternative mode to the prevailing style of the amateur scholar-painters. Under the Wanli emperor (*reg* 1573–1620), Wu was called to service at the southern Ming (1368–1644) capital of Nanjing. He served mainly as a court painter but was also employed by private patrons and Buddhist temples. In the 1620s he was overheard criticizing the notorious eunuch Wei Zhongxian (1568–1628) and subsequently imprisoned. Thereafter, records of Wu cease.

The conservative landscapes and narrative paintings that Wu executed for the court are best represented by the handscroll *Greeting the Spring* (1600; Cleveland, OH, Mus. A.) and the album *Record of the Year's Holidays* (Taipei, N. Pal. Mus.). These fine-line, colourful early paintings, characterized by incidental detail and decorative effect, represent meticulous professional variants on the late WU SCHOOL style, the amateur landscape painting tradition based in Suzhou, Jiangsu Province, in the mid-Ming period.

By the first decade of the 17th century, however, Wu was pursuing a new landscape mode based on Northern Song (960–1127) models (*see* CHINA, §V, 3(vi)(a)). Professional painters from Wu's native Fujian had begun a Song revival in the early Ming period; in addition, Wu had the opportunity while in Nanjing to study old master paintings in both the imperial and private collections and to meet other painters, notably Mi Wanzhong (1570–1628), likewise engaged in reviving Northern Song styles.

Wu Bin: *View of Tiantai Mountain* (detail), handscroll, ink and light colours on silk, 0.30×1.45 m, 1607 (Honolulu, HI, Honolulu Academy of Arts)

Wu must also have been exposed to European paintings and prints presented by Jesuit missionaries to the court (*see* CHINA, §XIII, 19(ii)). The representational and illusionistic concerns of Western art may have stimulated an interest in the native Northern Song style, which similarly aimed at naturalistic effects.

Wu's new landscape style is best represented by paintings such as *Streams and Mountains Far from the World* (1615; Takatsuki, Hashimoto priv. col.), *Landscape with Palaces* (Berkeley, U. CA, A. Mus.) and a *View of Tiantai Mountain* (1607; Honolulu, HI, Acad. A.; see fig.). Northern Song influence is readily apparent in Wu's monumental scale, monolithic vision and naturalistic rendering of surface effects. However, whereas Northern Song artists painted stable and rational landscapes representing microcosmic versions of an ideal cosmic order, Wu produced mannerist renditions of the earlier style, attenuating and distorting classical forms to create a visionary world of fantastic structures, whose undulating, unbalanced shapes often have no logical connection, and where the distinction between solid and void is no longer clear. The Song idiom is also the model for Wu's painstakingly naturalistic surface detail on cliffs, with peaks swathed in convincing mists and believable shadows cast over their sides. Wu thus sets up a constant tension between the real and the unreal and seems to suggest that the coherence of the Song world order, though he longs for it, no longer has meaning for the Ming.

Wu also played a central role in the late Ming revival of figure painting. A lay Buddhist, he received commissions from temples to paint images of Buddhist *luohan* (Skt *arhat*s; 'enlightened ones'). His best-known figure paintings include the handscroll *Five Hundred Luohan* (Cleveland, OH, Mus. A.) and the album *Deities of the Surangama Sutra* (Taipei, N. Pal. Mus.). As in his adaptation of the Song landscape mode, Wu alludes to but then distorts an earlier painting style. His *luohan* are clearly modelled after those of the Five Dynasties (AD 907–60) monk–painter

GUANXIU, but they are caricatures and figures of irony. Wu thus intimates that *luohan*, embodiments of spiritual transcendence, have no more place in the sullied world of the Ming than the harmonious landscapes of the Song.

BIBLIOGRAPHY

Putian xianzhi [Putian Gazetteer] (1758), *juan* 30, p. 26; *R* Zhongguo fangzhi congshu, lxxxi (Taipei, 1968)

J. Cahill: 'Wu Pin and his Landscape Paintings', *Proceedings of the International Symposium on Chinese Painting: Taipei, 1970*, pp. 637–722

——: *The Compelling Image: Nature and Style in Seventeenth-century Chinese Painting* (Cambridge, MA, 1982)

——: *The Distant Mountains: Chinese Painting of the Late Ming Dynasty, 1570–1644* (New York and Tokyo, 1982)

DAWN HO DELBANCO

Wu Changshi [Wu Ch'ang-shih; Wu Ch'ang-shuo; *ming* Jun, Junqing] (*b* Anji, Zhejiang Province, 1844; *d* Shanghai, 1927). Chinese painter and calligrapher. As a leading figure in the SHANGHAI SCHOOL during the early 20th century, he was largely responsible for rejuvenating the genre of bird-and-flower painting by introducing an expressive, individualistic style more generally associated with literati painting. He began his artistic career with the traditional study of literature and ancient inscriptions before moving to calligraphy (*see* CHINA, §IV, 2(vii)) and painting.

Contact with the artistic community in the cultural and commercial metropolis of Shanghai during the late 19th century opened up to Wu the possibility of a professional artist's career. He painted not only landscapes and figures but boldly expressionistic bird-and-flower paintings that found great favour in the Shanghai art market. The source of this broad appeal lay partly in the freshness and liveliness of his brushwork and use of colour, but it was also bolstered by the cultural prestige of his strong scholarly background. Wu was one of the most successful artists to adapt the élitist Chinese literati painting tradition to the demands and realities of early 20th-century bourgeois patronage. In typical scholarly fashion he considered his calligraphy to be superior to his painting and his seal-carving (*see* CHINA, fig. 338) based on ancient inscriptions to be better than his calligraphy. However, despite placing his painting in the lowest rank, it was as a painter that he made his living and gained a popular reputation.

Besides bringing scholarly prestige to the Shanghai school, Wu contributed to the evolution of its style mainly through his use of colour (especially bright reds and greens hitherto rarely employed in literati painting), his innovative and unusual compositions and the careful balance between wildness and discipline in his brushwork. These features are evident in *Green Peaches and Rock* (ink and colour on paper, 1.45×0.77 m, 1924; Hong Kong, Jackson Yu priv. col., see Mayching Kao, pl. 5). His drawings of plants and flowers show an animated brushwork derived from his study of calligraphy; his emphasis on calligraphic qualities in his painting kept him firmly within the literati tradition, while at the same time his particular circumstances allowed him to develop and popularize it. Also very much within the scholarly tradition was the integration of poetry, calligraphy and seal-carving into his work, with the emphasis always on *xieyi* ('writing the idea') or capturing the idea behind the subject rather than a literal depiction of it.

Wu's influence has remained strong in Shanghai through disciples such as Wang Geyi (*b* 1896), but his contribution to modern Chinese painting has had more than merely local significance. Neo-literati painters in other centres, notably Qi Baishi in Beijing, learnt from Wu Changshi in their efforts to keep the Chinese tradition in painting alive and relevant in the 20th century.

BIBLIOGRAPHY

Wu Changshi yi zuo [Surviving works of Wu Changshi] (Shanghai, 1928)
Zhang E and Wu Yige, eds: *Wu Changshi huaji* [Collected paintings of Wu Changshi] (Beijing, 1959)
Wu Dongbian: *Wu Changshi* (Shanghai, 1963) [a short biography]
Chang An-chih: 'Wu Chang-shuo's Flower-and-plant Painting', *Chin. Lit.*, 5 (1964), pp. 105–13
Go Shōseki, Sai Hakuseki [Wu Changshi and Qi Baishi] (1977), x of *Bunjinga Suihen: Chūgoku* [Selections of literati painting: China] (Tokyo, 1975–9/*R* 1985–6)
Wu Changshi huajian [Selected paintings of Wu Changshi] (Beijing, 1978)
Wu Changshi cai mo jingxuan/Wu Changshi: Selected Masterpieces (Taipei, 1982)
Mayching Kao, ed.: *Twentieth-century Painting* (Hong Kong, 1988)

RALPH CROIZIER

Wu Ch'ang-shih. *See* WU CHANGSHI.

Wu Changshuo. *See* WU CHANGSHI.

Wu Chen. *See* WU ZHEN.

Wu-chin. *See* WUJIN.

Wuchters, Abraham (*b* Antwerp, 1608; *d* Sorø, 1682). Dutch painter, active in Denmark. He was born of Dutch parents. In 1638 he went from Amsterdam to Copenhagen in the company of Karel van Mander III. He introduced himself at the court of Christian IV with two portraits of the Danish King (1638; Hillerød, Frederiksborg Slot), presumably both painted in Holland. After Reinholt Thim's death in 1639, Wuchters became 'drawing-master' at the Academy in Sorø, giving lessons in painting, drawing and architecture. On 26 May 1640 Christian IV granted him the privilege of having his portraits of the King

engraved, for which he went briefly to Amsterdam. From 1640 he was active mainly as a portrait painter at the Danish court. He painted elegant portraits that show above all the influence of Anthony van Dyck. In 1645 he painted the King's children, for example the portraits of *Ulrik Christian Gyldenløve* (Copenhagen, Stat. Mus. Kst) and the future *Frederick III* (Copenhagen, Amalienborg), both painted in Glückstadt. The composition of these portraits is traditional: the sitter has his right hand on his hip, there is drapery behind and in the far background a landscape. The only remarkable aspect is the unusually high light-source. In 1650 Wuchters painted the portrait of *Christence Lykke* (Århus, Overgaard); she is depicted with a sharp twist of the body, which at that time was known only from the portraits of children by van Dyck. Wuchters repeated this pose in some of his later compositions. The only paintings by Wuchters that are not portraits are the altarpieces (1654) for the church in Sorø, which were commissioned by the Academy: Wuchters painted *Christ and the Wine-press* and the *Last Supper*, a copy after Rubens's work (1635; Milan, Brera). In 1659 Wuchters went to Göteborg to paint miniature portraits (Mariefred, Gripsholm Slott, Stat. Porträttsaml.) of *Karl X Gustav*, King of Sweden (*reg* 1654–60) and his wife *Hedvig Eleonora*. The brushwork in these paintings is rougher and reveals the influence of the Haarlem school, particularly Frans Hals.

After 1660 Wuchters worked for Queen Christina of Sweden, whom he painted twice. The first portrait (1660; Uppsala U.) is innovative in its simplicity. The second (1661; Bålsta, Skoklosters Slott) shows the Queen in a

Abraham Wuchters: *Christian V*, 1671 (Hillerød, Nationalhistoriske Museum på Frederiksborg)

twisted pose, comparable to that of the portrait of *Christence Lykke*; she stands against some drapery with a landscape in the far background. In 1661 Wuchters was replaced at the Swedish court by the artist David Klöcker Ehrenstrahl and he returned to Sorø. In 1664 he moved to Copenhagen, to be succeeded by Michael von Haven as teacher at the Sorø Academy. In Copenhagen he worked in the 'heroic style' that was then popular, depicting his sitters either in mythological, Classical or theatrical costume: for example he portrayed the young *Holger Reedtz* (Copenhagen, Stat. Mus. Kst) as Cupid. In 1671 he painted the portrait of *Christian V* (see fig.), which was directly copied from van Dyck's portrait of the *Marqués Francesco de Moncada* (1635; Paris, Louvre). After the death of van Mander in 1670, Wuchters became Keeper of the Royal Paintings. When his brother-in-law Albert Haelwegh died in 1673 his salary as a copper-engraver was paid to Wuchters. In 1675 Wuchters paid for the publication of *Den Christelige Hustru* (The Christian housewife), after the original version by Jacob Cats (i). It was dedicated to Peter Griffenfeld, first Keeper of the Archives and later Chancellor, of whom Wuchters painted a portrait (Hillerød, Frederiksborg Slot). In 1679 Wuchters married Elisabeth Rømer, van Mander's widow.

BIBLIOGRAPHY

K. Madsen: 'Et og Andet om Abraham Wuchters' [A note or two about Abraham Wuchters], *Kstmus. Årsskr.* (1915), pp. 166–88

F. Becket: 'Wuchters Portraet af Rigskansler Peter Griffenfeld' [Wuchters's portrait of Chancellor Peter Griffenfeld], *Kstmus. Årsskr.* (1918), pp. 95–8

H. Gerson: *Ausbreitung und Nachwirkung der holländischen Malerei des 17. Jahrhunderts* [The spread and influence of Dutch painters of the 17th century] (Haarlem, 1942), pp. 462–5, 476, 485, 489, 490, 513

E. K. Sass: 'Bidrag til en karakteristik af Abraham Wuchters Alderdoms-vaerk' [Contribution to a characterization of Abraham Wuchters's late work], *Kstmus. Årsskr.* (1942), pp. 52–98

P. Eller: 'Abraham Wuchters', *Billedkunst og Skulptur: Rigetsmaend lader sig male, 1500–1700* [Painting and sculpture: officials who commissioned portraits, 1500–1700], Dan. Kshist., ii (Copenhagen, 1973), pp. 227–60

M. J. T. M. STOMPÉ

Wu Dacheng [Wu Ta-ch'eng; *ming* Dashun; *zi* Zhijing, Qingqing; *hao* Hengxian, Kezhai] (*b* Suzhou, Jiangsu Province, 6 June 1835; *d* 6 March 1902). Chinese calligrapher, epigrapher and collector. Born into a rich and cultured merchant family, he entered the district school at 16 and at 17 began to study seal script (*zhuanshu*) under Chen Huan (1786–1863). He received his *jinshi* degree in 1868 and became a scholar at the Hanlin Academy in Beijing, followed by two years at the Suzhou Provincial Printing Office. In succeeding years, he distinguished himself as an army officer, diplomat and civil servant. He became Governor of Guangdong Province in 1887 and of Hunan in 1892, interrupted by a period as director-general of the conservancy of the Yellow River and the Grand Canal and followed by his directorship of the Longmen Academy in Shanghai in 1898.

Wu amassed a large collection of antiquities. He became renowned as an interpreter of written characters used before the Qin period (221–206 BC) and completed a dictionary of seal characters, the *Shuowen guzhou bu* in 1883, in which calligraphy is categorized according to its provenance, e.g. from bronze and jade seal texts or from weights. By comparing these characters to those in the earliest Chinese dictionary, the *Shuowen jiezi* ('Dictionary of words and phrases'; *c.* AD 120), compiled by Xu Shen, Wu demonstrated that the characters in the *Shuowen jiezi*, accepted for centuries, were in fact based on more recent materials and not completely reliable.

Wu compiled a catalogue of his entire collection, a book transcribing and deciphering the texts on his bronzes and a catalogue of his own and important bronzes in other collections in 1886. These were followed by catalogues of his seals, jades and weights and measures. In his catalogue on seals, he imitated the Song-period (960–1279) tradition of including the imprint of each seal in his presentation, which later became normal practice.

In seal script, Wu began by studying the standard works of Li Yangbing (*fl c.* AD 759–80), but soon moved on to Jiang Sheng (?1721–99). In his 20s, Wu became familiar with older seal script models: he discovered bronze and stele rubbings and began to study the *Shuowen jiezi*. Later influences came from specific bronzes in his collection or from other rubbings, such as one from the Maogong *ding*, sent to Wu by his friend Chen Jieqi (1813–84), a great collector, archaeologist and calligrapher. The Maogong *ding* is a bronze vessel on the bottom of which is inscribed in large seal script (*da zhuanshu*) the longest Zhou-period (*c.* 1050–256 BC) text known. A pair of matched hanging scrolls (*duilian*; see Shimonaka, no. 83) reveal Wu's approach. The words are precisely spaced, the strokes stern, taut and full of power. The juxtaposition of these words in seal script, much closer to ancient pictographs than the later versions of the script, is naturally graphic. Wu adds to the complexity of the pattern through his modulation of each stroke, contrasting carefully rounded movements to the jagged, cut-off edge where the brush is more quickly lifted.

See also CHINA, §IV, 2(vii)(c).

BIBLIOGRAPHY

Hummel: 'Wu Ta-ch'eng'

K. Shimonaka, ed.: *Shodō zenshū* [Complete collection of calligraphy], xxiv (Tokyo, 1961), pp. 27–31, 162, 178; nos 82, 83

Uno Yukimura: *Chugoku shodoshi* [History of Chinese calligraphy] (Tokyo, 1962), pp. 350–52

Traces of the Brush: Studies in Chinese Calligraphy (exh. cat. by Shen Fu and others, New Haven, CT, Yale U.A.G.; Berkeley, U. CA, A. Mus.; 1977)

Yu Jianhua: *Zhongguo huajia da zidian* [Dictionary of Chinese painters] (Shanghai, 1981), p. 26

ELIZABETH F. BENNETT

Wu Daoxuan. *See* WU DAOZI.

Wu Daozi [Wu Daoxuan, Wu Tao-hsüan; Wu Tao-tzu] (*b* Yangzhe [modern Yu xian, Henan Province]; *fl c.* AD 710–60). Chinese painter. Later known as Wu Daoxuan, he is a legendary figure said to have depicted human beings, landscapes, architecture, Buddhist deities, demons, birds and animals. Reportedly, he derived his inspiration from wine and had a mercurial, responsive brushstyle, producing breathtaking vistas of natural scenery and figures across vast areas of temple wall.

Hearing of his extraordinary talents, the Emperor Xuanzong (Minghuang; *reg* 712–56) summoned Wu to his palace at Chang'an (modern Xi'an). Between 742 and 755 the emperor dispatched Wu to the Jialing River in Sichuan Province to paint the scenery. On his return, Wu stated, 'I have made no draft, but have committed all to memory.' He proceeded to paint the walls of the hall known as the Datong dian with 300 or more *li* (*c.* 150 km) of Jialing River scenery in a single day. Five dragons in the Inner Hall, painted by Wu on another occasion, supposedly had scales so lifelike that each time it was about to rain, they emitted misty vapours (the dragon symbolized imperial power over rain and irrigation). Contemporary accounts report that Wu covered 300–400 wall surfaces in Buddhist and Daoist temples in the two Tang-dynasty (618–907) capitals, Chang'an and Luoyang. Temples included the Tangxing si, Chang'an, where his masterpieces graced the Diamond Sutra Hall, and where he inscribed the *sūtra* texts himself. Also in Chang'an on the walls of the Cien si pagoda he painted Manjushri and Samanthabhadra and under the western walkway scenes of descending demons and coiling dragons; at the Jinggong si he painted the walls with scenes of hells, Indra and Brahma, and dragon spirits, and in the Yongshou si he painted the Three Central Gates with twin guardian deities.

Wu is said originally to have studied calligraphy under Zhang Xu but became dissatisfied with his achievements and turned to painting. Perhaps because of his calligraphic training, his painting is described by contemporaries largely in terms of flowing, vibrant lines, that is brushstrokes rather than areas of colour wash. In the 9th century the critic Zhu Jingxuan observed: 'Whenever I gaze at Master Wu's painting, I marvel not so much at the ornamentation, but at his brushwielding, which is peerless, always superb, exhaustively varied, driven with divine and untrammelled energy. Several walls are painted only in ink, and no-one to this day has been able to apply colours to them.' An old man told Zhu of how he witnessed Wu painting haloes on the two guardian deities of the Central Gate of the Xingshanji in Chang'an, with a large crowd gathered to watch. Wu picked up the brush and in a single stroke created a perfectly round circle entirely freehand; the brush seemed energized as if driven by celestial winds. The crowd was stunned and believed that Wu had divine help. According to another account, when the general Pei Min presented Wu with gifts of silver and gold, asking him to paint at the Tiangong si (Celestial Palace Temple) in Luoyang, Wu returned the gifts unopened, saying, 'I have long heard tell of the General's superb sword dancing. If you would but dance for me once, the energy of your sword will surely inspire my brush.' Pei Min then performed a breathtaking sword dance, after which the painter grasped his brush and in feverish inspiration, as though aided by the gods, created a painting of unmatched quality. It is said that he afterwards applied the colours himself.

These accounts indicate that Wu first executed images in ink strokes, and that the application of colour was secondary and perhaps less vital. It suggests a new approach to painting, in which ink is deployed not in a fine, even and draughtsman-like outline aiming at detailed completion, but in an expressive, descriptive and abbreviated style with strokes of undulating width. Unnamed contemporaries reported that 'the [ink] sashes on Wu's figures flutter against the wind', suggesting a swelling and shrinking in stroke width, with uneven individual segments imbued with a textural quality. This brush manner was eventually reflected, though probably subdued, in the

figure style of the Northern Song (960–1127) master LI GONGLIN, visible in the painting attributed to him, *Five Tribute Horses*.

Wu's creative, varied and spontaneous brush deployment in landscape painting was the precursor to the use

Painting in the style of Wu Daozi: detail of plectrum guard, 405×165 mm, on maple wood *biwa* lute, showing musicians on an elephant, l. 970 mm, Tang period, 8th century AD (Nara, Tōdaiji, Shōsōin)

of modelling strokes (*cunfa*) that dominated landscape painting from the Five Dynasties period (AD 907–60) onwards, effectively replacing the use of colour in texture modelling. Zhang Yanyuan (*c.* AD 815–75) noted that Wu's 'strokes and dots are not fully completed but are deliberately punctuated with spaces'. This method of rendering is used to indicate three-dimensionality and the turning of forms in space. Contemporary records indicate that Wu had a fully developed ink style with vigorous, spontaneous, 'leaflike' ink strokes describing rounded figures and imbuing them with remarkable lifelike presence and movement. He painted freehand, evidently without meticulous under-drawing or sketches, and at great speed. His brushwork must have been highly economical, with contour and modelling accomplished in reduced but enlivened brushstrokes, often combined in function, as for draperies or mountain folds. Later, ink-based painting with a sparing use of pale colours came to be known as Wu style (Wu *zhuang*).

Surviving attributions, however, do not reflect such aspects of Wu's art; paintings and rubbings feature studiously rendered figures in even, continuous and usually profuse lines. An impression of Wu's lifelike images is offered by contemporary painted sculptures of celestial guardians in the Hokkeidō and Kaidan'in (Nara, Tōdaiji). His interrupted swelling-line technique is intimated, though in a paler version and without the mastery, in the facial cartoons created by earlier craftsmen on the Hōryūji murals in Nara. A sense of his brief, descriptive brushwork in landscape is given by the mountain background of the plectrum guard on the *biwa* lute, a contemporary Tang-period piece (Nara, Tōdaiji; see fig.).

BIBLIOGRAPHY

Zhang Yanyuan: *Lidai minghua ji* [Record of famous painters of all periods] (AD 847/*R* Beijing, 1963), *juan* 2, pp. 23–5

Zhu Jingxuan: *Tang chao minghua lu* [Record of famous painters of the Tang dynasty] (9th century AD); *R* in *Meishu congshu* (Shanghai, 1936), pt 6, *juan* 1

J. Cahill: *An Index of Early Chinese Painters and Paintings* (Berkeley, 1980), pp. 21–2

K. Suzuki: *Chūgoku kaigashi* [History of Chinese painting] (Tokyo, 1981), i, pp. 61–76

Chen Gaohua: *Sui Tang huajia shiliao* [Historical material on Sui and Tang painters] (Beijing, 1987), pp. 180–220

JOAN STANLEY-BAKER

Wueluwe, Hendrik van. *See* MASTERS, ANONYMOUS, AND MONOGRAMMISTS, §I: MASTER OF FRANKFURT.

Wüest, Johann Heinrich (*b* Zurich, 1741; *d* Zurich, 1821). Swiss painter. He was a pupil of Johann Balthasar Bullinger, who introduced him to landscape painting; subsequently he studied in Amsterdam, under Jakob Maurer and then Cornelis Ploos van Amstel. His first commissions were mainly for decorative work, often on a vast scale. Before long his paintings on furniture had become comparable to the best work in the Low Countries. In 1766 he left for Paris, where he painted in more vivid colours and received sizeable commissions. In 1769 he returned on foot to Switzerland, where he helped found the Zurich Kunstgesellschaft, which retains some of his works. He worked mainly in wash, sepia and gouache; many of his works were engraved in aquatint by Franz Hegi (1774–1850). He painted a number of idyllic scenes in the style of his friend Salomon Gessner, often for foreign visitors. He also created large decorative schemes for interiors (e.g. Zurich, Hans Wollenhof).

Wüest's overall composition, carefully studied from life and distinguishing the hour of day, captures the determining characteristics of a landscape; secondary objects and foregrounds were painted freely or from imagination. Whether depicting poetic forests in the Dutch manner or alpine landscapes, Wüest responded deeply to nature (*see* SWITZERLAND, fig. 7). The influence of Caspar Wolf appears in the tonal gradations and handling of the great white masses of the glaciers. Wüest used tiny figures in repoussoir to make the imposing masses of the Alps stand out. He and his contemporaries discovered a new and more idyllic reality than their forebears in landscape, extracting subtler tonal harmonies through a mixture of compound colours. The serenity, melancholy and acute observation of his work make him one of the leading 18th-century Swiss landscape painters. His pupils include Heinrich Freudweiler and Ludwig Hess.

BIBLIOGRAPHY

From Liotard to Le Corbusier: 200 Years of Swiss Painting, 1730–1930 (exh. cat., Atlanta, GA, High Mus. A., 1988), p. 82

JEANNE-MARIE HORAT-WEBER

Wu Guanzhong [Wu Kuan-chung] (*b* Yixing, Jiangsu Province, 5 July 1919). Chinese painter and art educator. Wu trained at the Hangzhou National Academy of Art between 1936 and 1942, studying modern Western painting with Chinese artists returned from France, and Chinese painting with PAN TIANSHOU, from whom he gained a deep understanding of Chinese aesthetics. From 1947 to 1950, Wu studied oil painting in Paris at the atelier of Jean Souvérbie (1891–1981) of the Ecole Nationale Supérieure des Beaux-Arts. After his return to China in 1950 he took up a series of teaching positions, the final one at the Beijing Central Academy of Art and Design, from which he retired in 1989. The dominating influence of Socialist Realism in China after 1949 led to criticism and suppression of Wu's Western formalist approach. Nevertheless, he persisted in his search for ways to make his French experience take root in China. Travelling the country, he captured its beauty in a manner that displayed unique sensibility. By the early 1960s he had evolved a personal style fusing the rich colours of the oil medium and Western formal elements with the fluidity and spiritual vitality of traditional Chinese aesthetics. From the early 1970s he experimented with Chinese ink and colours on paper, successfully introducing new themes and stylistic innovations to a time-honoured tradition. Since the late 1970s he has exhibited and travelled widely overseas, finding new inspiration for his work. Wu enjoys critical acclaim for his vibrant synthesis of Chinese and Western art; his numerous writings shed light on his own artistic struggles, as well as his perceptions of modern Chinese art and artists.

WRITINGS

Yao yishu buyao ming [Choosing art rather than life] (Taipei, 1990)

BIBLIOGRAPHY

Wu Guanzhong: A Twentieth-century Chinese Painter (exh. cat., ed. A. Farrer; London, BM, 1992)

MAYCHING KAO

Wu-hsi. *See* WUXI.

Wujae. *See* YI (i), (2).

Wujin [Wu-chin]. County in the southern part of Jiangsu Province, China, where in 1957 a group of 13 bronze vessels was excavated at Yancheng. They were recovered from a moat of the ancient capital of the state of Yue, which occupied the area of modern Jiangsu and Zhejiang provinces in the Spring and Autumn period (722–481 BC) of the Zhon dynasty. The presence of iron tools among the bronzes indicates a date after the 6th century BC.

The vessels (Beijing, Hist. Mus.) are remarkably well preserved and virtually uncorroded, but some are executed in a rather unrefined and careless manner, for example with seams left unpolished. The decorative designs and, occasionally, the shapes of the vessels are typical of southern provincial bronze-casting. The decoration is clearly influenced by the techniques of stamping and impressing frequently employed on pottery vessels. Irregular matting designs characteristic of these bronzes were obtained by using pattern blocks made from a master mould. Typically, the vessels have a broad band of impressed ornamentation around the belly, leaving the remaining surface unadorned. One has a neck in the shape of an ox with large eyes and pointed vertical horns. The surface of the head is decorated with the small, square spirals known as *leiwen* ('thunder pattern'; *see* CHINA, §VI, 3(ii)(a)), and the neck has a decoration of feather-like scales that run in a band around the vessel. A ritual wine vessel of the *zun* type (h. 265 mm; for illustration of this and other vessel types *see* CHINA, fig. 138) has a band of close-knit decoration around the bulk of the body. This design is peculiar to southern China and it is common on pottery from the Neolithic period (*c.* 6500–*c.* 1600 BC) onwards.

Among the more conventional types and shapes, a *pan* basin (h. 158 mm, diam. 260 mm) in the exceptional shape of a three-wheeled vehicle stands out. On one side, two handles in the shape of bird- or dragon-like animals facing the basin support an axle that bears the rear wheel. Two additional wheels, which are out of alignment, are attached on either side at the front of the basin. Each wheel has six spokes and is fastened to the basin through the hub. The inside of the basin is plain, while the outside is decorated with a band of somewhat carelessly executed thunder pattern. The two animals that constitute the handles have curled-up crests, incised wings below a band of scales or feathers around their necks, and short tails.

Another site of major importance in Wujin County is Sidun, where a tomb dating to the early 3rd millennium BC was found, containing over 100 fine jades (*see* CHINA, §§I, 8(ii) and VIII, 1). Another grave (*c.* 2500 BC) of the Neolithic period contained a corpse surrounded by more than fifty ritual jades of the *zong* (square tube) type and the *bi* (circular perforated disc) type.

BIBLIOGRAPHY

Ni Zhenkui: 'Yancheng chutu de tongqi' [Bronzes unearthed in Yancheng], *Wenwu* (1959), no. 4, pp. 5–6
Xin Zhongguo de kaogu shouhuo [Archaeology in New China], Kaogu xue zhuankan, A/vi (Beijing, 1961)
M. Sullivan: *Chinese Art: Recent Discoveries* (London, 1973)
Zhongguo gu qingtongqi xuan [A selection of ancient Chinese bronzes] (Beijing, 1976)
The Great Bronze Age of China: An Exhibition from the People's Republic of China (exh. cat. ed. Wen Fong; New York, Met.; Los Angeles, CA, Co. Mus. A.; 1980–81)
Nanjing Bowuyuan: '1982 nian Jiangsu Changzhou Wujin Sidun yizhi de fajue' [The excavation in 1982 at Sidun, Wujin and Changzhou in Jiangsu Province], *Kaogu* (1984), no. 2, pp. 109–29

BENT NIELSEN

Wu Kuan-chung. *See* WU GUANZHONG.

Wulcob, de. *See* VULCOP, DE.

Wulff [Wolff; Wolf]. German family of sculptors. They were among the most talented German sculptors of the late 16th century and early 17th. Ebert Wulff (i) (*b* ?Hildesheim, *c.* 1535–40; *d* Hildesheim, 1606/7) was active in Hildesheim as early as 1568, where he carved the statue of *Hildesia* (signed and dated 1581) in the Rathaus, the roughly contemporary allegorical carvings in the Ratsapothek and the coat of arms of the Brewers' guild (1591), among other works. His double wall-tomb of *Clamor von Münchhausen* (*d* 1561) and *Elisabeth von Landsberg* (*d* 1581) of the early 1580s (Loccum, Klosterkirche) and the monument of *Canon Ernst von Wrisberg* (*d* 1590) of 1585–90 in the choir of Hildesheim Cathedral reveal his adoption of Cornelis Floris's ornamental motifs. Ebert (i), and later his sons, repeatedly used Netherlandish prints as models for decorations and figural compositional sculptures.

His son Ebert Wulff (ii) (*b* Hildesheim, *c.* 1560; *d* Hildesheim, 1609) was considerably more talented than his father, with whom he occasionally collaborated. Findel (1934) has suggested that Ebert (ii) was a journeyman in southern Germany before returning to Hildesheim some time in the early 1580s. His early work has not been identified, though several funerary monuments in the churches of Ottenstein, Suderode and Hildesheim are ascribed to him, along with seven highly naturalistic wooden reliefs of animals and birds, made in 1588 for a house (Vorder Brühl 38) in Hildesheim. In 1603 Ebert and his brother Jonas Wulff (*b* Hildesheim; *d* Hildesheim, 1619) were employed by Ernst, Graf von Schaumburg, to carve the decorations for the chapel in the Schloss Bückeburg. The better-paid Ebert was assigned the choir and Jonas the rest of the chapel. The altar table (1603–6) is Ebert's finest creation. Two kneeling angels, possibly of limewood, support the table-top with their shoulders and wings, a formula first introduced in 1544 in the Schloss at Torgau as a solution to the problem of creating a new, Protestant type of church furniture. The two angels, of which the left is superior, are powerfully monumental. Their smooth, sensuous, gold-painted flesh contrasts sharply with their flamelike hair and the animated folds of their deeply cut drapery. The resulting juxtapositions of textures and light and dark are charged with tension. In 1604 Ebert and Jonas designed and carved the Door of the Gods in the Golden Hall of the Schloss. The portal is among the most elaborate Mannerist ensembles in Germany. The architectural and decorative forms were inspired by the engravings of Wendel Dietterlin, while the nude deities, with their strong contrapposto and exaggerated poses, derive ultimately from Giambologna's statues of gods and goddesses. The rich intermingling of the heavily painted relief carvings and free-standing statues, including the life-size *Mars* and *Peace* (? *Venus*), with masks and ornamental elements, creates a dramatic and overwhelming impression. The whole is, however, a carefully conceived allegory of war and peace. In 1608 Ebert and Jonas returned to Hildesheim, where Ebert died of the plague in the following year. Jonas took over the family workshop; several epitaphs in Brunswick and Hildesheim are attributed to him. His only signed work, however, is the Diana and Actaeon Fountain in Hannover, the reliefs of which (surviving frags: Osterstrasse 38) he sculpted in 1619, the year of his own death from the plague.

The youngest brother of Ebert and Jonas, Hans (*b* c. 1570; *d* before 1641), worked at Bückeburg from 1604 until 1622. Between 1605 and 1607 he carved (and probably designed) the gateway to the Schloss with its crowning statues of *Envy* flanked by two dragons. Around 1605 he made a sandstone relief of *Mars and Venus*, after an engraving by Hendrick Goltzius of a drawing by Bartholomäus Spranger, possibly for a chimney in the palace. The two elaborate portals now at Schloss Baum were once either in the garden or part of the east wing of Schloss Bückeburg. The Ionic (or Water) portal and the Corinthian (or Music) portal are again adapted from Dietterlin's engravings. The forms and arrangements of the allegorical and mythological figures reveal Hans's debt to his brothers. Between 1611 and 1615 Hans worked on the Bückeburg Stadtkirche, and he is credited by many scholars (e.g. Hitchcock) with the architectural design of this hall church, built as a Protestant response to the St Michaelskirche (the great Jesuit church) in Munich. It is more likely, however, that Hans's contribution was limited to the pulpit, the monumental angels holding von Schaumburg's coat of arms over the principal portal and some of the architectural sculpture. Between 1620 and 1628 Hans lived in nearby Obernkirchen, the site of a vein of high-quality sandstone. After the death of his patron von Schaumburg in 1622, Hans's volume of work diminished, though he made a large stone fountain for Duke Christian of Lüneburg's Schloss in Celle between 1622 and 1626 (four of the reliefs in Hannover, Niedersächs. Landesmus.; two in Celle). Hans Wulff is documented as a citizen in Hildesheim-Neustadt in 1630; in 1641 his wife was mentioned as a widow.

BIBLIOGRAPHY

K. Findel: *Die Bildhauerfamilie Wulff in Hildesheim* (Leipzig, 1934)
S. Salzmann: 'Ein unbekanntes Grabmal von Ebert Wolff d.J. in Osterode', *Götting. Jb.*, vi (1958), pp. 117–20
J. Habich: *Die künstlerische Gestaltung der Residenz Bückeburg durch Fürst Ernst, 1601–1622* (Bückeburg, 1969)
Barockplastik in Norddeutschland (exh. cat., ed. J. Rosmussen; Hamburg and Mainz; 1977), pp. 19–22, 237–41
Zeichnung in Deutschland: Deutsche Zeichner, 1540–1640 (exh. cat. by H. Geissler, Stuttgart, Staatsgal., 1979), ii, p. 133
H.-R. Hitchcock: *German Renaissance Architecture* (Princeton, 1981), pp. 278, 338–40

JEFFREY CHIPPS SMITH

Wu Li [*zi* Yushan; *hao* Mojing Daoren] (*b* Changshu, Jiangsu Province, 1632; *d* 24 Feb 1718). Chinese painter, poet and calligrapher. He was one of the Six Orthodox Masters of the early part of the Qing period (1644–1911); the others included the Four Wangs: Wang Shimin, Wang Jian, Wang Hui and Wang Yuanqi, along with Yun Shouping (*see* ORTHODOX SCHOOL). All six were natives of southern Jiangsu Province, in the Yangzi River basin. Wu Li was a close friend of Wang Hui in his youth, and both were students of Wang Shimin and Wang Jian. Wu flirted with the philosophical tenets of Neo-Confucianism, Buddhism and Daoism but eventually converted to Christianity when he was about 50 years old and travelled to the Portuguese island of Macao with Father Philippe Couplet in 1681. He became a Jesuit priest and in 1692 headed a Jesuit mission in Jiading (in modern Shanghai Municipality). Catholicism did not inspire in Wu Li a great love of European art, and he remained a painter in the Chinese literati tradition (*see* CHINA, §V, 4(ii)). He criticized the Western emphasis on perspective, saying that, in contrast, Chinese painters did not aim for exact reproduction of form or accuarate impression of depth. Wu reiterated the Confucian precept that only eminent, cultivated men with an understanding of the essential forces of nature have the talent for ink painting, since the art was not simply a matter of technical expertise and scrupulous performance. Wu's upbringing had enabled him to become just such a cultivated man; in his youth he had studied literature under Chen Hu (1613–75) and poetry with Qian Qianyi (1582–1664), in addition to his painting studies.

Wu Li: *Landscape in the Manner of Huang Gongwang*, leaf 4 from an album of landscapes after Song and Yuan masters, ink and colours on paper, 397×268 mm, late 17th century (Taipei, National Palace Museum)

A *Lake in Spring* (hanging scroll, *c.* 1676; Shanghai Mus.), with its gradual and continuous recession and soft, naturalistic colouring, hints at a Western influence on Wu Li's style, but the great majority of his work is similar to the literati productions of the Four Wangs. He made numerous paintings in imitation of ancient masters, as can be seen in a series of landscape paintings in album format after Song (960–1279) and Yuan (1279–1368) masters. Leaf 4 (see fig.) shows a landscape in the manner of the Yuan-period master HUANG GONGWANG, duplicating Huang's use of massive ridges built up of roughly triangular configurations and interspersed with flat-topped bluffs. In his early years Huang Gongwang's style was Wu Li's main source of inspiration. Wu Li wrote that he once studied Huang's *Precipitous Ravines in Dense Forests* (destr.) when it was in the collection of Wang Shimin. Wu Li frequently combined stylistic features of each of the four great painters of the Yuan period—Wu Zhen, Ni Zan, Wang Meng and Huang Gongwang—with charming results, as in the handscroll *Passing the Summer at the Thatched Hall of Inkwell* (1679; Princeton U., NJ, A. Mus.). He adopted the sobriquet Mojing Daoren, meaning Daoist of Inkwell.

Wu Li was also a fine calligrapher. He favoured the style of Su Shi and created lively compositions with a flat, oblique brushstroke that sometimes turns, in the words of the 20th-century critic Wen Fong, like a 'twisted or folded belt'.

ECCP; *EWA*
O. Sirén: *Chinese Painting: Leading Masters and Principles*, 7 vols (London and New York, 1956–8), v, pp. 184–92; vii, pp. 446–9
R. Whitfield and Wen Fong: *In Pursuit of Antiquity: Chinese Paintings of the Ming and Ch'ing Dynasties from the Collection of Mr and Mrs Earl Morse* (Princeton, 1969), pp. 191–4, 212–16
L. C. S. Tam: *Six Masters of the Early Qing and Wu Li* (Hong Kong, 1986)
L. Xiaoping: 'Wu Li's Religious Belief and a *Lake in Spring*', *Archvs. Asian A.*, xl (1987), pp. 24–35
VYVYAN BRUNST, with JAMES CAHILL

Wultinger [Wulfinger; Wulzinger], **Stephan** (*d* before 1520). Architect probably of German origin, active in Austria. His name suggests that he may have come from Lower Bavaria (Wulzingen near Passau) or Upper Styria. He was active in Upper Austria and Styria between 1476 and 1517. The building inscriptions on the parish churches of Zell am Pettenfirst (*c.* 1490) and St Georgen in Attergau (*c.* 1496) and on the church (1513–14) in Weissenkirchen prove that they were built by him. At Whitsun 1516 Wultinger is recorded in the Admont masons' lodge book (Graz, Steiermärk. Landesarchiv), perhaps because he worked in the area controlled by that lodge; his name and his master's mark are given, and Wultinger is described as being 'from Vegklenmargk' (Vöcklamarkt), where he had built the parish church in 1512–13.

The rich adornment and twin aisles characteristic of Wultinger's churches are related to a group of Styrian double-naved hall churches built from the first half of the 15th century that depended on the Salzburg lodge, which was responsible for their elaborate decoration. Wultinger habitually placed free-standing piers within the body of the church on the axis of the windows in the side walls, so creating a sequence of opposed, triangular bays; the resulting net and star vaulting recurs like a leitmotif in almost all of his buildings. Other characteristic features of Wultinger's buildings include the use of a wide variety of free-standing pier shapes—octagonal, decagonal, smooth and cylindrical, twisted into spirals or incised with diamonds—and the rich use of sculptural decoration, particularly heads and foliage, on consoles and keystones. Wultinger's ability to manipulate space was influential, as at the parish church in Gaishorn (*c.* 1520), which has a double nave creating an effect of depth, and an inserted single-aisled choir.

W. Buchowiecki: 'Stephan Wultinger und die gotischen Kirchenbauten im oberösterreichischen Altergau', *Wien. Jb. Kstgesch.*, xi (1937), pp. 41–58
BETTINA GEORGI

Wunderkammer. *See under* KUNSTKAMMER.

Wunderlich, Paul (*b* Eberswalde, 10 March 1927). German painter. He studied at the Kunstschule in the orangery of the castle of Eutin. In 1947 he went to the Hochschule für Bildende Künste, Hamburg, and studied graphic art. He extended his training by another semester to work under Willem Gremm. In 1951 he was offered a teaching post at the school, which he held until 1961. In 1963 he became Professor for the Graphic Arts and Painting. Between 1951 and 1952, under the instruction of Emil Nolde and Oskar Kokoschka, he produced prints after their originals. In 1957 he created a series of Tachist paintings, for example *S111/57* (tempera; see Jensen, 1979, pl. 12), but he destroyed most of them later. Towards the end of the 1950s he produced his first figurative prints and paintings. In the beginning their subjects were events from more recent German history, for example the set of lithographs *20 July 1944* (1959; Berlin, Gal. Brusberg), which depicted the execution of the men who had conspired against Adolf Hitler. This subject-matter was increasingly displaced by an eroticism that is partly Surrealist, partly decorative (e.g. *Interior*, 1967; Cologne, Baukst-Gal.). In 1960 the public prosecutor of Hamburg confiscated such a cycle of prints.

During a study tour to Paris in 1961–2 Wunderlich perfected his technique in the studio of the printer Desjobert, with whom he collaborated until 1975. In 1964 he began to paint after work by the photographer Karin Székessy (*b* 1939), whom he married in 1972; from 1965 he painted exclusively using a spray gun. From 1970 to 1973 he made works after famous engravings and paintings by Dürer and Ingres. After giving up his post as professor in 1968 he made a number of study trips to New York and Switzerland. Also in 1968 he began to produce sculptural aestheticized objects of everyday use, which correspond in their fetishistic character to the highly elaborate attitude of his paintings.

D. Brusberg, ed.: *Paul Wunderlich: Werkverzeichnis der Lithographien* (Berlin, 1971)
Paul Wunderlich: Ölbilder, Gouachen, Zeichnungen, Plastiken und Druckgraphik (exh. cat., Cologne, Baukst-Gal., 1973)
J. C. Jensen: *Paul Wunderlich: Werkverzeichnis der Gemälde, Gouachen und Zeichnungen* (Offenbach, 1979)
——: *Paul Wunderlich—Werkmonographie*, 3 vols (Offenbach, 1980–)
Paul Wunderlich: Graphik und Multiples, 1948–1987 (exh. cat., Schleswig, Schleswig-Holsteinisches Landesmus., 1988)
DOMINIK BARTMANN

Wunuwun [Djiwal], **Jack** (*b* Arnhem Land, 1930; *d* Arnhem Land, 31 Dec 1990). Australian Aboriginal painter. He was the ceremonial leader of his clan, the Murrungun Djinang. He saw his art as a means to bridge the cultural gaps between Aboriginal and non-Aboriginal Australians. While he worked within the parameters of the pictorial styles of central Arnhem Land, he was also an innovator, experimenting with various techniques. Wunuwun became disenchanted with market demands for individual bark paintings: the epic dramas of Murrungun Djinang cosmology were too panoramic in scope to be captured on a single sheet of bark, and he increasingly painted in series and occasionally used canvas. His work is characterized by finely drawn naturalistic images, although it relies heavily on conventional symbolism and clan designs. His major works include *Banumbirr, the Morning Star* (natural pigment on canvas, 1987; Canberra, N.G.), a comprehensive statement on the relationships between the seasons, human and spiritual life and the individual. In 1988 Wunuwun undertook his most ambitious project, the series *Banumbirr Manikay* (Perth, W. Australia, Robert Holmes à Court Col.), comprising thirty bark paintings and one canvas relating to the Morning Star song cycle. Other later series included the diptych *In the Beginning of Time* (bark, 1990; Canberra, N.G.).

BIBLIOGRAPHY

W. Caruana, ed.: *Windows on the Dreaming: Aboriginal Paintings in the Australian National Gallery* (Canberra, 1989), pp. 94–7
A. M. Brody: *Contemporary Aboriginal Art: The Robert Holmes à Court Collection* (Perth, 1990), pp. 17–18, 84–9, 117–20
W. Caruana: *Aboriginal Art* (London, 1993), p. 54

WALLY CARUANA

Wu Pin. *See* WU BIN.

Wurmser of Strasbourg, Nicholas [Wurmser, Mikuláš] (*fl* mid-14th century). German painter. A document of 1357 refers to him as court painter to Emperor Charles IV and as a citizen of Strasbourg. In 1360 he was granted exemption for life from taxes on an estate in Mořina, but the only specific reference to his work occurs in a document of 1359, which mentions 'places and castles' in which he was to work. Work began in 1348 on Karlštejn Castle, one of the major projects of Charles IV's reign. As a painter high in Charles's esteem, Nicholas must have been involved in the first phase of decoration, including the *Luxemburg Genealogy* (begun *c*. 1356; destr. before 1597; *see* KARLŠTEJN CASTLE, §2), a wall painting in the main hall, depicting *c*. 60 figures from Noah to Charles IV; watercolour copies of the *Genealogy* (Prague, N.G., Convent of St George, Codex Heidelbergensis; Vienna, Österreich. Nbib., MS. 8330) made for Emperor Maximilian II between 1569 and 1575 show a striking similarity to the surviving figures in the *Relic* scenes in the nearby chapel of the Virgin, painted shortly after 1356. The strongly delineated features in both wall paintings have parallels in works produced for the French court, notably the portrait possibly of *King John II* (*c*. 1350–60; Paris, Louvre), attributed to Girard d'Orléans (*see* GOTHIC, fig. 66). Nicholas, trained in a French-orientated centre, probably painted both the *Genealogy* and the *Relic* scenes.

BIBLIOGRAPHY

A. Friedl: *Mikuláš Wurmser: Mistr královských portrétů na Karlštejně* [Nicholas Wurmser: master of the king's portraits at Karlštejn] (Prague, 1956) [quotes doc. in full]
Die Parler und der Schöne Stil, 1350–1400: Europäische Kunst unter den Luxemburgern (exh. cat., ed. A. Legner; Cologne, Schnütgen-Mus., 1978), ii, pp. 718–19

AMANDA SIMPSON

Würsch, Johann Melchior. *See* WYRSCH, JOHANN MELCHIOR.

Wurster, William Wilson (*b* Stockton, CA, 20 Oct 1895; *d* Berkeley, CA, 19 Sept 1973). American architect, academic administrator and teacher. After receiving his architectural degree from the University of California, Berkeley (1919), he worked in architects' offices in California and New York (1923–4). In private practice in San Francisco from 1926 to 1943, he designed over 200 houses. The Gregory farmhouse (1926–7), Santa Cruz, CA, employed with a seeming modesty the coarse wooden construction of agrarian buildings of the region. Yet it has a simplicity of planar organization and a reticence of detail that is subtly formal. From the covert complexity of this farmhouse to suburban and urban commissions, he heightened his use of local materials while enlisting aspects of international modern architecture.

In 1940 Wurster married Catherine Bauer (1905–64), an expert on social housing. After a year studying city planning at Harvard University, Cambridge, MA, he became Dean of Architecture at the Massachusetts Institute of Technology in 1944. His tenure was notable for educational innovation and the realization of campus buildings through architects associated with the school, including Baker House by Alvar Aalto. In 1950 he returned to California as Dean of the School of Architecture at Berkeley and oversaw its reorganization as the College of Environmental Design (1959).

Wurster's work was central to what came to be known as the Bay Area style, which in the post-war period posed an early regionalist challenge to American, largely East Coast, work devolving from European Modernism. From 1945 he maintained his California practice in a large group partnership with Theodore C. Bernardi (1903–90) and Donn Emmons (*b* 1910). Their numerous works include two innovative projects in San Francisco: the mixed-use Golden Gateway Redevelopment (1961–3) and the well-known adaptive reuse of a 19th-century industrial complex, Ghirardelli Square (1962–7).

BIBLIOGRAPHY

Contemp. Architects
C. K. Bauer: *Modern Housing* (Boston, 1934)
L. Mumford: 'The Skyline', *New Yorker*, xxiii/34 (1947), pp. 94–6, 99
L. Mumford and others: 'What Is Happening in Modern Architecture', *MOMA Bull.*, xv (Spring 1948), pp. 4–21
S. Woodbridge, ed.: *Bay Area Houses* (New York, 1976, rev. Salt Lake City, 1988)
R. T. Hille: *Inside the Large Small House: The Residential Legacy of William W. Wurster* (Ann Arbor, 1994)

STANFORD ANDERSON

Würtenberger, Ernst (*b* Steisslingen, 23 Oct 1868; *d* Karlsruhe, 5 Feb 1934). German painter and printmaker. After his first years of training at the Akademie der Bildenden Künste, Munich, he came into contact with Arnold Böcklin in Florence (1895–6); contrary to his usual reticence, Böcklin was very open with his interested young colleague, particularly on questions of painting technique. His final training with Ferdinand Keller (1842–1922), professor at the academy in Karlsruhe, enabled him to extend the ideas that he had formed from Böcklin's art. In 1902 Würtenberger settled in Zurich, where he specialized in portrait-painting. He was soon seen as an important figure in the city's artistic life, particularly in negotiating exhibitions and purchases of paintings by the Kunstgesellschaft in Zurich.

In his portraits Würtenberger depicted many representatives of Zurich's economic and cultural circles; in 1915 he also painted a large group portrait of the committee of the Winterthur Kunstverein. His painting of his son as *Boy with Red Cap* (1911; priv. col.) was particularly popular, as were the few figure paintings that he painted on subjects such as *Cattle-trading* (1908; Zurich, Ksthaus) and other facets of daily peasant life. He worked in an appropriately clear realism, whose sense of line and composition shows his adaptation of Ferdinand Hodler's style. In addition he painted portraits of historical personalities, particularly from German intellectual life, and worked on major woodcuts for the writings of Gottfried Keller, among others. In his own articles and publications he expressed his opinions in a sometimes pugnacious style. In 1921 he accepted a position at the Kunstschule in Karlsruhe, where he taught until the end of his life.

BIBLIOGRAPHY
F. Würtenberger: 'Das graphische Werk von Ernst Würtenberger', *Schr. Staatl. Ksthalle Karlsruhe*, i (1938) [incl. a list of Würtenberger's writings]

LUKAS GLOOR

Württemberg, House of. German dynasty of rulers and patrons. Although the family can be traced back to 1050, its extensive patronage began with Eberhard V (*reg* 1459–95), who was subsequently first Duke of Württemberg (*reg* 1495–6). He founded the university of Tübingen (1477) and donated to the Stiftskirche St Georg at Tübingen three stained-glass windows, the middle one of which shows the *Life of the Virgin* (c. 1478; *in situ*) by Peter Hemmel von Andlau and three other masters from Strasbourg, and to the Stiftskirche at Urach a richly decorated, Late Gothic prie-dieu (1472). Under Christopher, Duke of Württemberg (*reg* 1550–68), the Altes Schloss in Stuttgart was extended on a grand scale (*see* STUTTGART, §3 and fig.) and the conversion of the chancel of the Stiftskirche St Georg at Tübingen into a burial place for the ruling house, begun by Ulrich VI, Duke of Württemberg (*reg* 1504–19, 1534–50), was completed. Sem Schlör (*d* 1597–8) and Christoph Jelin (?1550–1610) were among the sculptors who created monumental tombs there and in the Stiftskirche Heiliges Kreuz at Stuttgart under Ludwig VI, Duke of Württemberg (*reg* 1568–93), who also had the Neues (or Grosses) Lusthaus (1583–93) in Stuttgart built by GEORG BEER. Eberhard VIII, Duke of Württemberg (*reg* 1628–74), enlarged the existing Kunst- und Wunderkammer thereby laying the foundation of an important art collection. (1) Eberhard-Ludwig, Duke of Württemberg, attracted Italian artists to work at the new castle he built at Ludwigsburg from 1704, and his first cousin once removed (2) Charles-Eugene, Duke of

Württemberg, invited French masters to work at Schloss Ludwigsburg and in his capital, Stuttgart.

In 1806 Württemberg became a kingdom, under the former Frederick II (1754–1816; duke 1797–1803; elector 1803–6), who became Frederick I, King of Württemberg (*reg* 1806–16.) Under his son William I, King of Württemberg (1781–1864; *reg* 1816–64), important classicist buildings were erected by NIKOLAUS FRIEDRICH VON THOURET, GIOVANNI SALUCCI and Christian Friedrich Leins (1814–92). Two generations later, in 1918, Württemberg was merged into the new German republic.

See also LUDWIGSBURG, and STUTTGART, §§1, 2 and 3.

BIBLIOGRAPHY
W. Fleischhauer: *Barock im Herzogtum Württemberg* (Stuttgart, 1958, *R* 1981)
——: *Renaissance im Herzogtum Württemberg* (Stuttgart, 1971)
R. Uhland, ed.: *900 Jahre Haus Württemberg* (Stuttgart, Berlin, Cologne and Mainz, 1984)

(1) Eberhard-Ludwig, Duke of Württemberg (*b* Stuttgart, 18 Sept 1676; *reg* 1693–1733; *d* Ludwigsburg, 31 Oct 1733). Although he faced major political and economic difficulties resulting from the Thirty Years War and the devastation wrought by the French invasion, when he attained majority his main artistic interest was the building of Schloss Ludwigsburg to the north of Stuttgart. Stimulated by travel in the Netherlands and England and by the example of Versailles, in 1704 he began the construction of what was to be Germany's largest Baroque palace. The initial plan of Philipp Jenisch (1671–1736) was taken over and redesigned by Johann Friedrich Nette (1672–1714) and finally elaborated after his death by the Italian architect Donato Giuseppe Frisoni (1683–1735). Italian artists were also employed for the interior decoration (*see* LUDWIGSBURG, §1). In 1724 Ludwigsburg became the ducal residence.

BIBLIOGRAPHY
W. Fleischhauer: *Barock im Herzogtum Württemberg* (Stuttgart, 1958, *R* 1981)
Eberhard Ludwig, Herzog von Württemberg (1676–1733). Gründer von Schloss und Stadt Ludwigsburg (exh. cat., ed. K. Merten and A. Seiter; Ludwigsburg, Schloss, 1976)
J. Zahlten: 'Ein schwäbischer Achill', *Jb. Staatl. Kstsamml. Baden-Württemberg*, xiv (1977), pp. 7–32
——: 'Hercules Wirtembergicus', *Jb. Staatl. Kstsamml. Baden-Württemberg*, xviii (1981), pp. 7–46
B. Wunder: 'Herzog Eberhard Ludwig (1677–1733)', *900 Jahre Haus Württemberg*, ed. R. Uhland (Stuttgart, Berlin, Cologne and Mainz, 1984), pp. 210–26

(2) Charles-Eugene [Karl Eugen], Duke of Württemberg (*b* Brussels, 11 Feb 1728; *reg* 1744–93; *d* Hohenheim, nr Stuttgart, 24 Oct 1793). First cousin once removed of (1) Eberhard-Ludwig. In his reign French architectural styles dominated in Württemberg, clearly reflected in the design and construction of the Baroque Neues Schloss in Stuttgart by Leopoldo Retti, begun in 1746 and completed by PHILIPPE DE LA GUÉPIÈRE. NICOLAS GUIBAL, court painter from 1755, and MATTHÄUS GÜNTHER provided interior decoration. The Duke also had other palaces built: Seeschloss Monrepos (from 1755), Grafeneck, near Münsingen (1760), Schloss Solitude (begun 1764), and Schloss Hohenheim (1781–83). In 1764 Schloss Ludwigsburg was given the largest opera house in Europe, designed by Johann Dietrich Spindler and Johann Christian Keim (1721–87). The Duke founded the Ludwigsburg porcelain factory (see LUDWIGSBURG, §2) and in Stuttgart the Academy of Arts (1761), a public library (1765) and the Hohe Karlsschule (1781–94), for children of the deserving poor, which numbered among its students Friedrich Schiller, the sculptor Johann Heinrich von Dannecker, Friedrich Distelbarth and Joseph Anton Koch.

BIBLIOGRAPHY

NDB
B. Pfeiffer: 'Die bildenden Künste unter Herzog Karl Eugen', *Herzog Karl Eugen von Württemberg und seine Zeit*, i (Esslingen, 1907), pp. 615–776
H. A. Klaiber: *Der württembergische Oberbaudirektor Philippe de La Guépière* (Stuttgart, 1959)
J. Zahlten: 'Das zerstörte Aeneas-Fresko Matthäus Günthers im Stuttgarter neuen Schloss', *Pantheon*, xxxvii/2 (1979), pp. 150–63
G. Storz: *Karl Eugen* (Stuttgart, 1981)
W. Uhlig: *Nicolas Guibal, Hofmaler des Herzogs Carl Eugen von Württemberg* (diss., U. Stuttgart, 1981)

JOHANNES ZAHLTEN

Wurzbach(-Tannenberg), Alfred von (*b* Lemberg, 22 July 1845; *d* Vienna, 12 May 1915). Austrian writer and art historian. He was the son of the poet and writer Konstant von Wurzbach-Tannenberg (1818–93). Alfred read law in Vienna but in 1876 gave up his post in the civil service to devote himself to art history and writing. He travelled extensively and from 1880 to 1883 worked as art critic for the *Wiener Allgemeine Zeitung*. His literary writings include *Zeitgenossen: Biographische Skizzen* (Vienna, 1873); the novella *Laura* (Vienna, 1873); a comedy called *Walter von Aquitanien* (Vienna, 1877); and *Lieder an eine Frau* (Stuttgart, 1881). Apart from a history of French 18th-century painting (Stuttgart, 1880), Wurzbach wrote primarily about the early German Master E.S. (whom he wrongly believed to have visited the Netherlands) and Martin Schongauer (Vienna, 1880) and about Dutch and Flemish art up to *c.* 1800 (see Writings). His most important work is the encyclopedic *Niederländisches Künstler-Lexikon* (1906–11), which is the standard dictionary of Dutch and Flemish artists.

Wurzbach also built up a large collection of drawings, engravings, etchings, books and, especially, Dutch paintings. The paintings came largely from the estate of the father of Wurzbach's wife Eugenie, née Lippmann-Lissingen. In 1954 they were bequeathed to the Akademie der Bildenden Künste in Vienna by Wurzbach's son Wolfgang (1879–1957).

WRITINGS
Die holländischen Landschafter und Thiermaler (Leipzig, 1876)
Die Meister der Niederländer und Spanier (Stuttgart, 1878)
Arnold Houbraken's Grosse Schouburgh der niederländischen Maler und Malerinnen (Vienna, 1880); trans. of A. Houbraken: *De groote schouburgh* (1718–21)
Geschichte der holländischen Malerei (Prague, 1885)
Rembrandt-Galerie (Stuttgart, 1886)
Niederländisches Künstler-Lexikon auf Grund archivalische Forschungen bearbeitet, 3 vols (Vienna and Leipzig, 1906–11/*R* Amsterdam, 1974)
Jean Gossaert de Mabeuge (Vienna, 1910)

BIBLIOGRAPHY
Meyers Konversations-Lexikon, xvii (Leipzig and Vienna, 1897), p. 905
F. Lugt: *Marques* (1921), nos 203, 2587
——: *Marques*, suppl. (1956), no. 2587a
M. Poch-Kalous: 'Das Legat Wolfgang von Wurzbach-Tannenberg an die Gemäldegalerie der Akademie der Bildenden Künste in Wien', *Jb. Ksthist. Samml. Wien*, lv (1959), pp. 159–200

CHRISTIAAN SCHUCKMAN

Würzburg. German city and capital of Lower Franconia, Bavaria. It is notable for its Baroque architecture, particularly that of Antonio Petrini in the 17th century and Balthasar Neumann in the 18th. The most notable building from this period is the Residenz, built by Neumann.

1. History and urban development. 2. Residenz.

1. HISTORY AND URBAN DEVELOPMENT. Würzburg, mentioned in a document of AD 704 as 'castellum Virteburh', is situated on the flat right bank of the River Main about halfway between Frankfurt am Main and Nuremberg. On the opposite bank rises a steep hill, the Marienberg, which takes its name from a circular church that was dedicated to the Virgin Mary in 706.

The see of Würzburg was established by St Boniface in 742, and a cathedral consecrated in Charlemagne's presence in 788. In 820 Emperor Louis the Pious granted toll privileges to the town market. As the town prospered the power of its bishops grew, and in 1030 they were granted jurisdiction over the market and the citizens' court. In the 11th century the cathedral of St Kilian was enlarged to its present external form of a Romanesque basilica with nave, aisles, transept and two west towers; two eastern towers of green sandstone, set in the angles between the transepts and the choir, modulate in section from square to octagonal.

In 1168 Emperor Frederick I, who had married Beatrice of Burgundy in Würzburg 12 years earlier, granted the city's bishops the secular title of Dukes of Franconia. By the 13th century the Prince–Bishops had taken up residence in the Marienberg fortress across the river. Built around the circular church, this complex now contains buildings from every century from the 13th to the 18th. Over the next two centuries the city evolved its own government apparatus (mayor, senators, city council), leading to tension between the city and the Prince–Bishops. The Old Town Hall dates from this period. A municipal property since 1316, it is now a conglomerate of different buildings, styles and periods: the Graf Eckartshof is Late Romanesque in its lower storeys and Late Gothic (1453) above; the two-storey Rote Bau lying behind it dates from 1660. The finest Late Gothic structure in the city is the Marienkapelle (1377–1479), a hall church with a five-bay net-vaulted nave; on its exterior were several sculptures by Tilman Riemenschneider, who was mayor of Würzburg in 1520–21 (see RIEMENSCHNEIDER, TILMAN, fig. 1), now removed to the Mainfränkisches Museum in the Marienberg and replaced with copies.

After about 1400 the economy declined and with it the authority of the city government; but under Julius Echter von Mespelbrunn, elected Prince–Bishop in 1573, Würzburg entered a new era politically, economically and culturally. Von Mespelbrunn promulgated an effective city ordinance that codified the ascendancy of the Prince–Bishops and founded important institutions, especially the Julius Hospital (1575–81; later alterations) and university (1582–91; both designed by Joris Robijn and built by WOLF BERINGER). Julius's predilection for the Gothic gave rise to the 'Julius style', with its use of older Gothic elements, such as the rose window introduced into the west front of the university church, begun in 1583 by Jan

Robijn II and completed by Antonio Petrini from 1693 to 1703.

After the devastation of the Thirty Years War (1618–48), the city prospered for a century during the 'Schönborn Age', named after three Prince–Bishops from the SCHÖN-BORN family. Large numbers of architects, painters, musicians, poets and scholars were drawn to Würzburg, among them Antonio Petrini, who spent 50 years in the city. The rebuilt city fortifications have been attributed to him, and he was also responsible for the church of Stift Haug (1670–91, rest.; for illustration *see* PETRINI, ANTONIO). In the first half of the 18th century Balthasar Neumann oversaw the design and construction of the new Residenz (*see* §2 below) and provided the city with new streets, squares and buildings (see fig. 1).

In 1803 Würzburg was secularized, and from 1807 to 1814 it was ruled by the exiled Ferdinand III, Grand Duke of Tuscany, on whose return to Italy it was incorporated into the state of Bavaria. The major architectural work of this time was the barracks (1809; converted into a women's prison in 1826–7), a Neo-classical building by Peter Speeth with ten colonnettes at attic level symbolizing the Ten Commandments. The impact of the Industrial Revolution was felt from the middle of the century onwards, and between the late 1860s and the 1890s the city's population more than doubled. In 1866 the fortifications that had restricted urban growth were taken down on the east and

south-east sides (although long stretches survive around the Marienberg and behind the Residenz); the building and rebuilding that followed involved considerable change in the old city. Würzburg was severely damaged by bombing in World War II but has since been extensively rebuilt and restored with great sensitivity.

BIBLIOGRAPHY
S. Kleiner: *Die hochfürstl. Residenz-Stadt Würzburg* (Augsburg, 1740)
T. Memminger: *Würzburgs Strassen und Bauten* (Würzburg, 1921)
F. Knapp: *Mainfranken* (Würzburg, 1928)
——: *Würzburg: 1200 Jahre deutscher Kunst* (Würzburg, n.d.)
H. Kreisel and L. Gundermann: *Würzburg* (Berlin, 1931)
M. H. von Freeden: *Balthasar Neumann als Stadtbaumeister* (Berlin, 1937)
W. Engel and M. H. von Freeden: *Würzburg* (Würzburg, 7/1963)
A. Wendehorst, ed.: *Würzburg: Geschichte in Bilddokumenten* (Munich, 1981)
R. Feurer and P. Maidt: *Gesamtansichten und Pläne der Stadt Würzburg, 15.–19. Jahrhundert: Aus der graphischen Sammlungen des mainfränkischen Museums* (Würzburg, 1988)

2. RESIDENZ. Shortly after his election as Prince–Bishop in 1719, Johann Philipp Franz von Schönborn decided to move his ceremonial and administrative headquarters from the Marienberg into the city. He discussed the undertaking with members of his family and architects including Maximilian von Welsch, Johann Dientzenhofer, and Johann Lukas von Hildebrandt. The coordinating architect, who determined most decisions concerning the design and remained in charge of the project from its

1. Würzburg, aerial view from north; engraving by J. Salver (1723), after a drawing by Balthasar Neumann, 1722 (Würzburg, Mainfrankisches Museum)

inception until his death in 1753, was BALTHASAR NEU-MANN. Of all the architects, artists and patrons who contributed to the building, only he remained throughout, from the design stage (begun 1719), construction of the shell (1720–44), to the completion of the major interiors, especially the church (Hofkirche), the stairhall and the Kaisersaal (Imperial Hall). Although the Residenz was associated with the Schönborn, and its size and splendour expressed their status, the building was not a family palace but an administrative centre for the office of Prince–Bishop: whoever served in that capacity occupied the building.

Neumann's first project of 1719 developed an existing smaller building into a U-shaped block with internal courts, the corners emphasized by slight projections, and a central pavilion. Von Welsch's elaboration of this design in 1720 established the configuration and size of the new building, with four internal courts, a larger and more elaborate *cour d'honneur*, and domed ovals centred on each flank (see fig. 2). Building began in 1720, under the direction of Neumann and Dientzenhofer. The French royal architects Robert de Cotte and Germain Boffrand were also consulted about the project in 1723, and their influence is visible in such details as the use of balconies supported on columns. Work languished after Johann Philipp Franz's death in 1724, to be resumed vigorously in 1730 after the election of Friedrich Karl von Schönborn. The site of the Hofkirche was moved from the north oval to the south-west wing, and its interior, designed in 1732, was set out

in three ovals to create a complex internal space. The eastern parts of the Residenz, begun in 1735, were roofed by 1741. With the completion of the huge vaults of the Kaisersaal and the staircase, the shell of the building was finished by December 1744. The speed of construction and quality of execution are attributable to Neumann's skilful organization of the workforce. He also assembled such first-rate artists to complete the interiors as the painter Johann Rudolf Byss, the sculptor Johann Wolfgang von der Auwera, the stuccoist Antonio Bossi, and the metalworker Johann Georg Oegg (1703–80).

Neumann carefully controlled the detail and propor-tions of the elevations, even when the design of a section was by another architect, as in Hildebrandt's central pavilion towards the garden, designed as a variation of his façade for the Upper Belvedere in Vienna but transformed by Neumann's more emphatic arrangement of engaged columns and windows. Externally, ornament was restricted to the orders and window-frames, and the elevations were enhanced with colour; architectural elements were picked out in silver against stone-coloured walls, figure sculpture was finished in porcelain white, and other sculpture was gilded; the courtyard walls were painted white to increase brightness.

Apart from the Hofkirche, the most imposing interiors are the ceremonial areas in the centre of the building. The vestibule vault, supported by four pairs of columns and four piers, is almost flat, with broad lunettes at the perimeter. The herms, by Johann Wolfgang von der

2. Würzburg, Residenz, by Balthasar Neumann, begun 1719, view from the west; from a pen drawing by Johann Christian Berndt, *c.* 1775 (Berlin, Kunstbibliothek Berlin mit Museum für Architektur, Modebild und Grafik-Design)

3. Würzburg, Residenz, by Balthasar Neumann, staircase, begun 1737; ceiling frescoes of the *Four Continents* (1752–3) by Giambattista Tiepolo

Auwera, sculpted as massive, muscular figures, seem to uphold the weight of the structure; but the spatial effect is softened by the stucco ornament and grisaille fresco. The *sala terrena*, an elongated octagon opening from the vestibule, has a shallow vault supported by free-standing columns painted to resemble marble; the ceiling fresco of 1750 by Johann Zick has bucolic scenes of the gods feasting and a procession of Diana painted in earthy tones.

The ceremonial stair, in its own hall north of the vestibule, with one flight leading to a landing from which two parallel flights return to the main floor, became standard for the 18th century, permitting the space to unfold in stages rather than putting the entire ensemble on display at a single glance (see fig. 3). The stair, supported on columns and slender piers, rises from a dark ground floor to the brilliantly lit upper levels, with uncluttered spaces, broad landings and large windows, surmounted by the grand curve of the vault with its vibrantly coloured fresco of the *Four Continents* (1752–3) by Giambattista Tiepolo (*see also* TIEPOLO, (1)). The vault, 19.0×32.6 m and rising 5.5 m from its springing point, was effectively a primitive form of reinforced concrete shell, 240 mm to 300 mm thick, made of brick and porous volcanic stone set in a bed of mortar and strengthened with iron clamps.

The walls and vault of the Weisser Saal (White Hall), a rectangular room located above the vestibule, were transformed with luxuriant, sculptural stucco by Antonio Bossi in 1744. This room leads to the Kaisersaal, an elaborate elongated octagon like the *sala terrena* below, defined by colossal engaged columns, a voluminous vault lightened by tall lunettes, and windows rising from floor to cornice. The columns are of red scagliola; mirrors, gilding and crystal chandeliers give the room brilliance and shimmer. Tiepolo's vault frescoes of 1751–2 provided a resplendent, partially mythologized vision of Würzburg history, depicting *Apollo Conducting Beatrice of Burgundy to Frederick Barbarossa*, the *Marriage of Frederick Barbarossa and Beatrice of Burgundy* and *The Investiture of Bishop Harold* as Duke of Franconia. The *cour d'honneur* was originally defined by a monumental iron grille and gate (removed 1821) by Oegg. The gardens of the Residenz were largely designed during the 1760s by Johann Michael Fischer and Johann Philipp Geigel (*fl* 1757; *d* 1800), with the participation of the gardeners Demeter and Johann Prokop Mayer (1737–1804); and sculptures (1779) by Johann Peter Wagner. They were ingeniously composed to fit the awkward spaces between building and fortification.

BIBLIOGRAPHY

G. Eckert: *Balthasar Neumann und die Würzburg Residenzpläne* (Strasbourg, 1917)
R. Sedlmaier and R. Pfister: *Die fürstbischöfliche Residenz zu Würzburg*, 2 vols (Munich, 1923)
E. Hubala and O. Mayer: *Die Residenz zu Würzburg* (Würzburg, 1984)
S. Kummer: 'Balthasar Neumann und die frühe Planungsphase der Würzburger Residenz', *Balthasar Neumann: Kunstgeschichtliche Beiträge*, ed. T. Korth and J. Poeschke (Munich, 1987), pp. 79–91

CHRISTIAN F. OTTO

Wurzelbauer, Benedikt (*b* Nuremberg, 25 Sept 1548; *d* Nuremberg, 2 Oct 1620). German metal-founder. He was among the last of Nuremberg's famous metal-founders, following the Vischer and the Labenwolf families. His mother Barbara was the daughter of Pankraz Labenwolf,

and he trained with and later worked for his uncle Georg Labenwolf. Two misconceptions exist in most literature on Wurzelbauer and the Labenwolfs. Firstly, although numerous statuettes and reliefs have been attributed to them by Bange and other scholars, these artists were metal-founders not sculptors. In virtually every case, their role was to cast the image in metal; the design and the carving of the model were tasks executed by sculptors, such as Hans Peisser and Johann Gregor van der Schardt. As their portion of the project was the last and most expensive, Wurzelbauer and the Labenwolfs were frequently mentioned in the documents. Proud of their achievements, they occasionally signed the completed work. Secondly, Wurzelbauer and the other Nuremberg metal-casters used brass, rather than bronze as has been thought by previous scholars. Recent research has demonstrated that the Nuremberg artists included a much higher percentage of zinc in their copper alloy, thus making brass, than most other German founders who blended more tin with their copper to form bronze.

Wurzelbauer began his career assisting Georg Labenwolf, who cast such major works as the great Neptune Fountain ordered by Frederick II, King of Denmark, for Kronborg Palace in 1576. Benedikt undoubtedly helped his uncle set up and test the fountain when it was temporarily erected outside Nuremberg in December 1582. In March 1583, while Labenwolf was travelling with the fountain to Denmark, the Nuremberg City Council ordered Wurzelbauer to move into the family foundry; their action was presumably to protect the family's trade secrets.

After Labenwolf's death in 1585, Wurzelbauer assumed control of the workshop and soon began to receive numerous significant commissions. Between 1585 and 1589, he cast the Fountain of the Virtues, his most famous project, for the Lorenzerplatz. Ernst von Mengersdorf, Bishop of Bamberg, ordered a large Neptune Fountain (destr.) for the garden of his residence at Geyersworth in 1590, and by 1592 Wurzelbauer had cast 14 statues for this fountain. He also produced several funerary monuments during the 1590s, including that to the Nuremberg merchant and his wife *Martin Peller* and *Maria Viatis* (1597; Nuremberg, Johannisfriedhof). In 1599 he was named a member of the greater council of the city government.

In the same year Wurzelbauer cast the Venus Fountain for Christoph Popel von Lobkowitz in Prague (Prague, N.G., Šternberk Pal.; see fig.). An important fountain (untraced) with Hercules, Athena, Venus, Diana and Ceres was made in 1603, probably for the Margrave of Baden, for the palace at Durlach. A sketch in the *Stromer Haushaltsbuch* (Nuremberg, Ger. Nmus.) is all that survives of another project, a large Mercury Fountain made for Frederick I, Duke of Württemberg (*reg* 1593–1608).

In addition to the documented projects, numerous statues and small fountains are attributed to Wurzelbauer and his workshop because of their style or their casting technique. These include a female figure ('*Pero*'; Brunswick, Herzog Anton Ulrich-Mus.) and a *Venus and Cupid* column fountain with Neptune and other figures (Vienna, Ksthist. Mus.).

Benedikt Wurzelbauer: Venus Fountain, bronze, h. 1.23 m, 1599 (Prague, National Gallery, Šternberk Palace)

As Wurzelbauer collaborated with various different sculptors, the fountains and small bronzes attributed to him vary considerably in style. For example, Wurzelbauer cast the Nuremberg Fountain of the Virtues after wooden models by Johannes Schünnemann (*fl* 1620), a little known German sculptor who 30 years later worked in the Dutch city of Bolsward. Although it is unclear whether Schünnemann or, more likely, a third, certainly local artist designed the three-tiered column fountain, it has an intricate, almost precious appearance that recalls the elaborate vessels and table ornaments of Wenzel Jamnitzer's workshop. By contrast the unknown model-carver for Wurzelbauer's Venus, Amor and Dolphin Fountain (1599–1600) in Prague was clearly influenced by the leading contemporary sculptors Johann Gregor van der Schardt and Adriaen de Vries. The soft flesh, the graciously curving forms, and the coordinated interaction of Venus and Amor represent a different, Italianate artistic tradition. Both fountains are proudly inscribed by Wurzelbauer, yet their obvious stylistic distinctions reveal Wurzelbauer's fidelity to the models he was called upon to cast.

Under the direction of his son, Johann Wurzelbauer (1595–1656), the family workshop remained the city's principal foundry throughout the earlier 17th century.

BIBLIOGRAPHY

Thieme–Becker

T. Hampe: *Nürnberger Ratsverlässe über Kunst und Künstler im Zeitalter der Spätgotik und Renaissance (1449), 1474–1618 (1633)*, ii (Vienna, 1904)

E. F. Bange: *Die deutschen Bronzestatuetten des 16. Jahrhunderts* (Berlin, 1949), pp. 108–10

H. R. Weihrauch: *Europäische Bronzestatuetten, 15.–18. Jahrhundert* (Brunswick, 1967), pp. 325–31

——: 'Beiträge zu Benedikt Wurzelbauer und Adriaen de Vries', *Umění*, xviii (1970), pp. 60–73

H. Herkommer: 'Heilsgeschichtliches Programm und Tugendlehre', *Mitt. Ver. Gesch. Stadt Nürnberg*, lxiii (1976), pp. 192–216

Europäische Kleinplastik, Brunswick, Herzog Anton Ulrich-Mus. cat. (Brunswick, 1976), p. 29

J. Riederer: 'Die Zusammensetzung deutscher Renaissancestatuetten aus Kupferlegierungen', *Z. Dt. Ver. Kstwiss.*, xxxvi (1982), pp. 42–8

Nuremberg: A Renaissance City, 1500–1618 (exh. cat. by J. C. Smith, Austin, U. TX, Huntington A.G., 1983)

——: *German Sculpture of the Later Renaissance, c. 1520–1580: Art in an Age of Uncertainty* (Princeton, 1994), pp. 217, 224, 226, 241, 289, 382–3, 460

JEFFREY CHIPPS SMITH

Wu school [Chin. Wu pai]. Term used to refer to a group of literati painters (*see* CHINA, §V, 4(ii)) active in the city of Suzhou and the surrounding area of Wu xian (Wu County) from the mid-15th century to the late 16th. Although it was not a school in the strict sense, members had similar goals: to stress the close relationship between poetry, calligraphy and painting and to communicate their own characters through the direct and spontaneous manipulation of brush and ink. In time, this latter goal superseded the mere description of external reality. Frequently these artists alluded to the past through style or theme.

Scholar–amateur painting flourished in Suzhou and elsewhere during the Yuan period (1279–1368), but the first emperor of the succeeding Ming dynasty (1368–1644), the Hongwu emperor (*reg* 1368–98), distrusted and persecuted the scholarly class. He restored the practice of summoning leading artists to court and encouraged these professional painters to revive the Southern Song (1127–1279) Academy styles of Ma Yuan and Xia Gui. These Ming court artists came to be known as the ZHE SCHOOL; as a result of their ascendancy, scholar painting virtually ceased during the early Ming period. After the capital moved from Nanjing to Beijing, during the reign of the Yonge emperor (*reg* 1403–24), artists in Suzhou were free to develop far from the influence of court. Suzhou became the most cultured city in China, with great wealth and beautiful physical surroundings, especially gardens (*see* GARDEN, fig. 24). Its large and well-educated upper class had sufficient leisure to collect books and art, plan stimulating banquets and practise calligraphy and painting; many Wu school artists came from this gentry class, and their work revived the tradition of the independent scholar–amateur.

SHEN ZHOU was the first prominent painter to emerge within the Wu school. He came from a venerable and affluent family, and his dutiful Confucian loyalty in caring for his widowed mother earned him respect and allowed him to refuse official bureaucratic appointments and live as a retired scholar. Rejecting the superficially attractive

Southern Song academic style revived by the Zhe school artists at court, he took the Yuan-period scholar-painters as his primary inspiration. He worked in the mode of each of the four masters of this group: HUANG GONGWANG, Wu Zhen, Ni Zan and WANG MENG.

Shen Zhou's *Landscape in the Style of Ni Zan* (see fig.) represents his creative reworking of an earlier style: the composition is clearly derived from Ni Zan's *Woods and Valleys of Mt Yu* (ink on paper, 943×359 mm, 1372; New York, Met.; *see* NI ZAN, fig. 2), but Shen's alterations give it a distinctly Ming flavour. Ni Zan rarely included human

Shen Zhou: *Landscape in the Style of Ni Zan*, hanging scroll, ink on paper, 1038×620 mm, 1484 (Kansas City, MO, Nelson–Atkins Museum of Art)

figures in his paintings, whereas Shen added a scholar in a lakeside pavilion awaiting the arrival of a friend's boat, which humanizes the scene. The tension created by empty space between the foreground and background in Ni Zan's painting is significantly reduced by Shen Zhou, whose trees gracefully fit the contours of the distant shore. Although the sparse, dry brushwork is based on Ni Zan, Shen made his rounder and more assertive; in addition, his forms are closer to the surface of the painting, resulting in greater visual impact. In general, Shen's treatment of Yuan styles results in clearer, more architectonic compositions, bolder and more personal brushwork and an interest in creating varying textures through the repetition of dots and lines. In addition to painting in the mode of the Yuan masters, he also portrayed the scenery of the Suzhou region and commemorated such specific occasions as a departure or a failure to pass the civil service examinations. His images are often condensed and essential.

The second great master within the Wu school was Wen Zhengming (*see* WEN, (1)), a pupil of Shen Zhou, from whom he learnt a profound appreciation of the past. Although they frequently collaborated, their artistic personalities were quite different: Shen Zhou produced abbreviated images with strong, blunt brushstrokes, while Wen Zhengming worked with complex and intricate designs that stressed dynamic motion. Wen utilized both fine and rough brushwork and worked on a miniature as well as monumental scale, sometimes depicting deep recession into space, at other times contradicting such a recession altogether (for illustrations *see also* CHINA, figs. 101 and 134). Like Shen Zhou, Wen was inspired by the scholar-painters of the Yuan period, and he too recorded the topographic features of the Suzhou area and commemorated scholarly events. He expanded the Wu school repertory to include illustrations of such famous poems as the *Lute Song* by Bai Juyi (AD 772–846) and the *Ode on the Red Cliff* by Su Shi. Themes of particular personal interest included mountainscapes and evergreen trees.

The impact of Wen Zhengming was felt directly through his creations and indirectly through his contemporaries and followers. One of these, TANG YIN, came from the merchant class, but because of his brilliant intellect became part of the literati circle; his implication in a civil service examination scandal in 1499 dashed his hopes for fame. He was a versatile and accomplished poet, calligrapher and painter, whose work includes subtle monochrome ink landscapes and bamboo paintings, elegant colourful courtesans and monumental landscapes. Qiu Ying, another Wu school practitioner, was technically the most proficient artist of his day and gained his livelihood from painting. Although he lacked scholarly training, he was highly regarded by his peers. He painted figures in the archaic plain-line (*baimiao*) style and landscapes either in pastel tones or brilliant opaque pigments.

Wen Zhengming's oldest pupil, CHEN SHUN, learnt a variety of different historical styles, of which the most influential was based on the creations of Mi Fu (*see* MI, (1)) and Mi Youren. Chen Shun defined mountains and tree foliage with colour or ink washes and rendered spectacular flower studies using the 'boneless' (*mogu*) style of washes without ink outline. His writings describe the exhilarated mood in which he painted. There is no evidence that LU ZHI ever studied with Wen Zhengming, and he was only peripherally involved with Wen's circle. Nevertheless, like Chen Shun he painted both landscapes and flowers and worked in ink monochrome as well as colour. Combining elements of both the amateur and professional traditions, he created a unique, eclectic style using crisp brushwork, bright colours and small black dots and dashes to produce scintillating landscapes.

Wen Zhengming's son, Wen Jia, and his nephew, Wen Boren (see WEN, (2) and (3)), were both talented painters who frequently employed the elongated, narrow hanging scroll proportions developed by Wen Zhengming. Wen Jia's modest paintings document scholarly activities and illustrate poetry, and he was highly respected as a connoisseur. Wen Boren was not as actively involved in Wu school activities as his cousin. His compositions have an impressive variety, ranging from the sparse to the extremely dense. Like his contemporaries, he portrayed the popular theme of scholars enjoying nature. The Wu school tradition declined during the late 16th century, when the centre of artistic activity shifted to nearby Huating (modern Songjiang), where DONG QICHANG charted new directions.

BIBLIOGRAPHY

Friends of Wen Cheng-ming: A View from the Crawford Collection (exh. cat. by M. F. Wilson and K. S. Wong, New York, China House Gal., 1974)
A. D. Clapp: *Wen Chong ming: The Ming Artist and Antiquity* (Ascona, 1975)
Wu pai hua jiushi nian [Ninety years of Wu school painting] (exh. cat., Taipei, N. Pal. Mus., 1975)
The Art of Wen Cheng-ming (exh. cat. by R. Edwards, Ann Arbor, U. MI Mus. A., 1976)
L. R. Yuhas: *The Landscape Art of Lu Chih (1496–1576)* (diss., Ann Arbor, U. MI, 1979)
L. E. McIntire: *The Landscape Paintings of the Ming Artist, Ch'en Tao-fu* (diss., Lawrence, U. KS, 1981)
A. R. Merrill: *Wen Chia (1501–1583): Derivation and Innovation* (diss., Ann Arbor, U. MI, 1981)
The Literati Vision: Sixteenth Century Wu School Painting and Calligraphy (exh. cat. by A. R. M. Hyland, Memphis, TN, Brooks Mus. A., 1984)
S. Little: 'The Demon Queller and the Art of Qiu Ying (Ch'iu Ying)', *Artibus Asiae*, xlvi (1985), pp. 5–80
A. D. Clapp: *The Painting of T'ang Yin* (Chicago, 1991)

ALICE R. M. HYLAND

Wu Ta-ch'eng. *See* WU DACHENG.

Wutai shan [Wu-t'ai shan]. *See* MT WUTAI.

Wu Tao-hsüan. *See* WU DAOZI.

Wu Tao-tzu. *See* WU DAOZI.

Wuta Wuta Tjangala. *See* UTA UTA.

Wu Tso-jen. *See* WU ZUOREN.

Wu Wei [*zi* Shiying, Ciweng; *hao* Lufu, Xiaoxian] (*b* Wuchang, Hubei Province, 1459; *d* 1508). Chinese painter. Wu was born into a family of scholar-officials. His father, who took the provincial-level civil-service degree to become a *juren*, was interested in alchemy and collected paintings and calligraphy. However, when Wu was still young, his father's dissolute life-style and then death resulted in family ruin. Wu was brought up by a provincial official; at the age of 17 he travelled to the southern capital, Nanjing, hoping to establish himself as a painter.

Early adverse circumstances meant that Wu had little hope of entering official service; instead, through the friendship and patronage of influential people, and in spite of being self-taught, he rose on the merits of his artistic abilities to a position at the court of the Chenghua emperor (*reg* 1465–87). In the Jiangnan region (south China) he met a tutor of the heir-apparent named Chu, who held the hereditary title Duke of Chengguo. Chu found work for Wu and gave him the sobriquet, or *hao*, Xiaoxian, ('Small Immortal'). Shortly before the death of the Chenghua emperor in 1488, Wu was invited to the main capital at Beijing and honoured with the title *daizhao* (painter in attendance) in the Renzhi Dian (Palace of Virtue and Knowledge), as well as a low-ranking honorary official post. He was also awarded a seal that read 'foremost among painters'. According to anecdote, Chenghua once summoned Wu to paint a scene of pine trees in a wind. Wu arrived in the imperial presence drunk, supported by two servants, but nonetheless proceeded to spill ink onto a screen on the floor and, by rubbing and smearing, to create so powerful an illusion of wind and clouds that the servants grew pale with fear; Chenghua reportedly pronounced Wu's work to be that of an immortal.

When his service ended Wu returned to Nanjing, where he gained a reputation for licentiousness and heavy drinking. Under the Hongzhi emperor (*reg* 1488–1505) he was recalled to court, but was soon granted leave to return to Wuchang to 'sweep the ancestral tombs'. The next imperial summons was accompanied by the gift of a house in a fashionable section of Beijing. However, Wu remained only two years before relocating to Nanjing. In 1508, under the Zhengde emperor (*reg* 1506–21), the painter received his final summons to the capital; he died while preparing for the journey, apparently from the effects of drink. Wu is said to have had four wives and at least four children.

Wu was an eccentric painter in the manner of Gu Kaizhi and Wu Daozi. His erratic behaviour, combined with a swift, sure technique, identifies him with the longstanding tradition in Chinese painting of the 'untrammelled' genius, whose nonconformity adds to his charm and reputation. In artistic style he was versatile (sometimes considered a defect), equally adept at disciplined, plain-line (*baimiao*) painting and at the rough 'scribbly' manner used in many paintings of Chan Buddhist or Daoist subjects. In landscape painting he was influenced by DAI JIN and is consequently classed as a ZHE SCHOOL artist. Few of Wu's surviving paintings are dated, but it is likely that his Dai Jin-flavoured landscapes are from the early part of his career. Other landscapes with figures are possibly later, featuring looser, more rapid and flowing brushwork and emphasizing a kinaesthetic dimension rather than careful delineation of form. His most impressive landscape, painted in fast-running brushwork, is *Myriad Miles of the Long River* (1505; Beijing, Pal. Mus.)

Wu's versatility is perhaps most marked in his figure paintings. The hanging scroll *Two Daoist Immortals* (Shanghai Mus.) represents what is commonly known as the artist's 'rough' style, relying for animation and intensity upon the muscular tension of the figures' poses, a nervous handling of drapery and variations in thickness of the rapid brushline. At the other extreme is the plain-line drawing (*baimiao*) manner, conveying a sense of mass and space, employed by both professional and amateur artists after the 11th-century painter Li Gonglin. *Lady Carrying a Pipa* (see fig.) represents a mixture of the two styles that possibly originated with Wu. It is not true plain-line drawing since it lacks control and precision, and there are areas of light ink wash. It does, however, retain a sense of refinement unusual in rough works. While the exact subject is uncertain, the melancholy figure, presented in profile and carrying a *pipa* (Chinese lute) in a brocade bag over her shoulder, recalls Zhao Wuniang, the heroine of the mid-14th-century play *Lute Song*, who journeyed to the capital in search of her lover. If such a reference is intended, the attempt to incorporate the energizing effect of a 'scribbly' line with the wistful dignity of plain-line style is appropriate and successful.

BIBLIOGRAPHY

O. Sirén: *Chinese Painting: Leading Masters and Principles*, 7 vols (London and New York, 1956–8), pp. 134–7
K. Suzuki: *Mindai kaigashi no kenkyū: Seppa* [A study of Ming Painting: the Zhe School] (Tokyo, 1968)
H. Holtz: *Wu Wei and the Turning Point in early Ming Painting* (MA thesis, Berkeley, U. CA, 1975)
J. Cahill: *Parting at the Shore: Chinese Painting of the Early and Middle Ming Dynasty, 1368–1580* (New York and Tokyo, 1978), pp. 98–100
R. Barnhardt and others: *Painters of the Great Ming: The Imperial Court and the Zhe School*, Dallas, TX, Mus. F.A. (Dallas, 1993)

VYVYAN BRUNST, with JAMES CAHILL

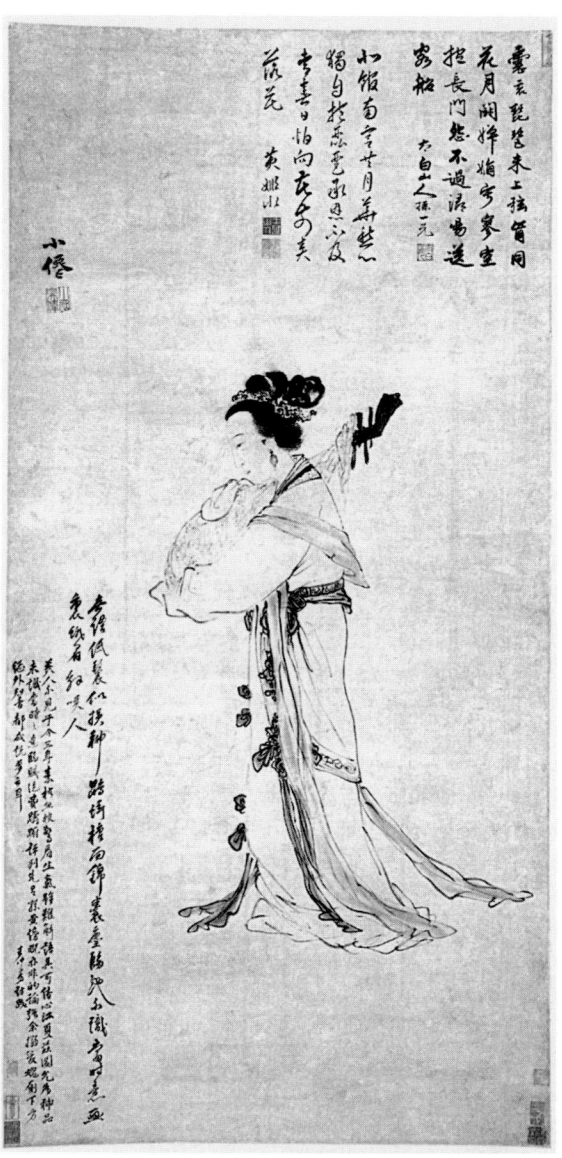

Wu Wei: *Lady Carrying a Pipa*, hanging scroll, ink on paper, 1251×613 mm, late 15th century (Indianapolis, IN, Museum of Art)

Wuwei [Wu-wei; Liangzhou]. Chinese town in central Gansu Province, historically a major communications centre and military town on the Silk Route. From the Western Han period (206 BC–AD 9), Wuwei was an important frontier post guarding a strategic part of the Great Wall in the Hexi Corridor. A large garrison was stationed at the town, manning several outlying forts and watchtowers along the Silk Route. Many Han (206 BC–AD 220) documents written on bamboo slips have been found in several of the watchtowers around Wuwei. An important Han tomb (Leitai, nr Wumei) of AD 186–219 contained bronze figurines and models of chariots and horses, including a 'flying horse' (Lanzhou, Gansu Prov. Mus.; see CHINA, §VI, 3(vi)(b) and fig. 168).

During the Northern and Southern Dynasties period (AD 310–589) Wuwei was the capital of several lesser states, including the Former Liang (313–76), the Later Liang (386–415) and the Southern Liang (397–414), and continued to play an important military role after it was occupied in AD 420 by the forces of the Northern Wei dynasty (386–534). At this period Buddhism had a pronounced influence on the area, and the sinicized foreign rulers of these rapidly succeeding dynasties were devout Buddhists. Kumarajiva (AD 344–413), the celebrated translator of Buddhist texts from Kucha, who eventually arrived in Chang'an (modern Xi'an) in AD 401, remained as a prisoner in Wuwei for over 17 years. Characteristic of Buddhist architecture of the Liang states is a type of small, octagonal, votive stupa, usually inscribed and sometimes featuring Buddhist images in relief. Caves containing Buddhist sculptures dating to the Northern Liang (AD 396–439) and Northern Wei (AD 386–534) periods are located at Mt Tianti, to the south of Wuwei; these consist of three chambers and 11 niches. A large seated Buddha displays unmistakable stylistic influence from the Buddhist sculpture of Gandhara, in modern Pakistan.

In the Tang period (AD 618–907) Wuwei was a fairly important Buddhist centre with several monasteries and temples. The pilgrim monk Xuanzang (c. AD 600–64) came through the town on his way to India and stayed for some time. At the time of Empress Wu (reg 690–705), a Dayun temple was established, as in all provincial capitals, in Wuwei; the large bronze bell (Wuwei, County Mus.) from the temple still survives. Later in the Tang period a memorial pagoda was erected by local authorities to commemorate Kumarajiva. A well-preserved, slender, octagonal brick structure of 12 storeys, it is located in the north-western part of the city. There are no signs of an earlier Buddhist temple said to have occupied the site. After the fall of the Tang dynasty in AD 907, Wuwei was under Chinese control for a brief period only. It was occupied by the Tanguts, a federation of Tibetan peoples, in 1036, becoming one of their headquarters on the Silk Route, and later came under the control of the Mongol Yuan dynasty (1279–1368). Only in the late 14th century, under the Ming (1368–1644), did the Chinese regain control of Wuwei.

The Wenchang gong is located in the south-eastern part of the city. Originally housing a Confucian academy, the temple was built in 1437–9 during the reign of the emperor Zhengtong (reg 1436–49). Structures were added and it was rebuilt and repaired in succeeding periods. The buildings, in a combination of wood and stone, have features typical of the Ming. Originally the temple consisted of three sections: Sheng gong, Wenchang gong and a Confucian school. The former two survive, but the Confucian school was destroyed during the Cultural Revolution (1966–76). The central building of the Sheng gong, the Dacheng Hall, is where worship of Confucius took place. Another important structure is the Stage Hall, standing on a raised stone platform and open in the front.

The county museum of Wuwei is housed in parts of the Wenchang gong that formerly served as memorial halls for distinguished local officials. It contains some 35,000 artefacts, including bamboo books and bronze vessels of the Han period, Buddhist stelae, stupas and sculptures of the Northern and Southern Dynasties period, Tangut inscriptions, and armour of the Yuan and Ming periods.

BIBLIOGRAPHY
The Genius of China (exh. cat. by W. Watson, London, RA, 1973), pp. 117–21
Liang Xinmin: Lishi wenhua mingcheng: Wuwei [History and culture of the famous city Wuwei] (Wuwei, 1987)
Wuwei jianshi [Brief history of Wuwei] (Wuwei, 1989)

Wuxi [Wu-hsi]. Chinese city situated at the confluence of Lake Tai and the Grand Canal, Jiangsu Province, previously an important centre of trade and the home of many merchant collectors of art.

During the Eastern Zhou period (771–256 BC) Wuxi was known for its deposits of tin, but by the time it had gained the status of a township and its present name, Wuxi ('without tin'), during the Western Han period (206 BC–AD 9), these deposits had been depleted. In the Three Kingdoms period (AD 220–80) it became a sub-prefecture. From the Sui period (AD 581–618) it was an important trade town at a junction in the network of canals and natural waterways that provided the essential means of transport in the area. The countryside around the town is highly fertile, and many kinds of crops are cultivated. From early times Wuxi was an important centre for the production of silk, although the weaving was normally done in neighbouring Suzhou.

During the Yuan period (1279–1368) Wuxi became an independent prefecture, the result of its important position as the point of transhipment of grain being sent as tax to the capital, Dadu (modern Beijing). This role greatly stimulated the economic growth of the town and laid the foundation for its flowering during the Ming period (1368–1644), when it boasted a large and wealthy merchant class. These merchants played a leading role in fostering the arts, especially painting, which became important in the area from the late Yuan period. The most famous painter from Wuxi was Ni Zan, one of China's great scholar-painters. Some of the members of the WU SCHOOL, which came to prominence early in the Ming period, hailed from the town; among them was Wang Fu, a founder-member of the group. After the decline of the Wu school Wuxi still produced good painters. One of these, Wang Wen (1497–1576), served in various lower government posts before retiring to the shores of Lake Tai. Wang Wen painted in a pleasant but very academic style and is counted among the non-conformist painters of the Ming.

During the Ming, Wuxi was also a centre for printing, and various improvements in technique were made there. The two great local families of printers, the Hua and the An, printed several editions of books with movable copper type. The famous geographer Xu Xiake (1585–1641) was a native of the village of Nanyang xian, to the north of Wuxi, where his tomb can still be seen.

Wuxi features one of the most famous classical Chinese gardens in the region south of the Yangzi River, the Jichang yuan (Ease of Mind Garden), created during the Zhengde reign period (1506–21) of the Ming dynasty (see GARDEN, fig. 21). Centred on the Lake of Embroidered Ripples (Jin huiyi), the garden extends along a north–south axis with Mt Xi in the background and contains numerous pavilions, kiosks, pathways and stone arrangements. The Jichang yuan still maintains its original layout, although the buildings are all of recent date. It served as the model for the Xiequ Garden in the Qing-period Yihe yuan (Summer Palace) in Beijing. Also in Wuxi is Xihui Park, which dates from the late Ming.

As a point of transhipment Wuxi was important in the trade in YIXING pottery. It is also famous for the small painted clay figures known as Huishan xiang ('Huishan images'), named after the place from which the clay comes. According to tradition the local peasants started to make these figures during the early Ming period as an extra source of income. Images of famous opera characters were made by the town artisans from the Qing period (1644–1911). During the Qing, Wuxi was also famous for a very extensive municipal library housing over 170,000 volumes.

BIBLIOGRAPHY
Jiangsu sheng chutu wenwu xuanji [Selection of material on archaeological finds in Jiangsu Province], Nanjing Museum (Beijing, 1963)
J. Cahill: Hills Beyond a River: Chinese Painting of the Yuan Dynasty, 1279–1368 (New York, 1976), pp. 114–20
——: Parting at the Shore: Chinese Painting of the Early and Middle Ming Dynasty, 1368–1580 (New York, 1978), pp. 58–9, 157
M. Keswick: The Chinese Garden: Art and Architecture (London, 1978)
Qian Yun, ed.: Classical Chinese Gardens (Hong Kong and Beijing, 1982), pp. 84–9
HENRIK H. SØRENSEN

Wu Zhen [Wu Chen; zi Zhonggui; hao Meihua daoren] (b Jiaxing, Zhejiang Province, 1280; d 1354). Chinese painter. Although he was well educated, especially in philosophy and swordsmanship, he never took the examinations to enter government, preferring to spend most of his life in his home town with occasional visits to such nearby towns as Hangzhou and Wuxing. A scholar of the Daoist text the *Yijing* ('Book of changes'), he practised fortune-telling to make a living. As a painter he was not as successful commercially as Sheng Mao (one of his neighbours), but he had his own circle of literati friends, including such painters as Wu Guan and Zhang Guan and such scholars as Tao Zhongyi.

As a painter, Wu is known for his landscapes and paintings of bamboo, most of which are in ink on paper, in free brushwork; his calligraphy is also noted for its cursive style (*caoshu*). His earliest known painting is *Two Junipers* (hanging scroll, ink on silk, 1328; Taipei, N. Pal. Mus.), which is strongly influenced by the 10th-century master Juran. Wu's interest in the free use of texture strokes on mountains and rocks and in the shapes of trees and branches is already apparent. *Central Mountain* (handscroll, ink on paper, 1336; Taipei, N. Pal. Mus.) shows the large, broad brushstrokes and simplified composition typical of his mature works.

In his landscapes his favourite subject is the hermit fisherman, a theme drawn from an ancient Chinese allegory, in which wise men, finding the world in turmoil, maintain their personal integrity by withdrawing from society to live like fishermen on rivers and lakes. The most famous paintings of this subject are *Fishermen*, of which two sections from an original four are extant (1336; both Beijing, Pal. Mus.), *Hermit Fisherman in Lake Dongting* (1341), *Fisherman* (1342; see fig.), *A Lonely Fisherman on an Autumn River* (all hanging scrolls, Taipei, N. Pal. Mus.) and *Fishermen, after Jing Hao* (handscroll, 1345, Shanghai Mus.; similar composition, 1342, Washington, DC, Freer). All of these display Wu's bold and free brushwork, his extremely simplified composition and his highly personal mode of expression.

Other works demonstrate Wu's facility to work in different styles. *Spring Morning on the Clear River* (Taipei, N. Pal. Mus.) is a grand landscape in the tradition of the Northern Song period (960–1127), with high mountains and deep vistas that show a strong influence of the 10th-century masters Dong Yuan and Juran. Another interesting but quite different landscape is *Eight Views of Jiahe* (1344; Taipei, Lo Chia-lun priv. col.), a topographical painting with many inscriptions indicating specific sites and locations in his home town. It is one of the rare works based on actual scenes that anticipated the development of the topographical style of landscape that flourished during the Ming period (1368–1644). However, even in this realistic portrayal of Jiaxing, his brushwork remains blunt and free. By contrast, *Poetic Feeling in a Thatched Pavilion* (1347; Cleveland, OH, Mus. A.), a landscape painted for a friend, shows a complete disregard for realistic detail, with free brushwork creating rhythmic patterns.

One of the most famous Yuan period painters of bamboo, Wu wrote long inscriptions on all his bamboo paintings, indicating his artistic lineage and expressing the symbolic significance of bamboo. These include *Bamboo and Rock* (hanging scroll, 1347), *Bamboo Studies* (album of 20 leaves, 1350; both Taipei, N. Pal. Mus.) and *Bamboo after Su Shi* (hanging scroll, 1350; Washington, DC, Freer). As indicated in his inscriptions, he followed the literati tradition of painting bamboo in monochrome black ink, first established as a literati motif by artists such as Wen

Wu Zhen: *Fisherman*, hanging scroll, ink on silk, 1.76×0.95 m, 1342 (Taipei, National Palace Museum)

Tong and Su Shi in the Northern Song period (960–1127) and Li Kan in the Yuan (1279–1368), all of whom used it to express the moral integrity and aesthetic superiority of an educated gentleman. In his album *Bamboo Studies*, painted for his son, Wu not only displayed the different manners of depicting the bamboo as used by Song and Yuan period masters but also included many other compositions of his own, portraying the bamboo growing upward, hanging downward, in a clear day, or blowing in the wind. All these bamboo paintings display a very consistent style: simple composition, bold brushwork and abstraction from nature.

Wu Zhen was not recognized as a painter until the 15th century, when a number of painters active in Suzhou, Jiangsu Province, notably Shen Zhou, the founder of the Wu school of literati painting (*see* CHINA, §V, 4(ii)), became highly interested in his style. By the late 16th century Wu was considered one of the Four Great Masters of the Yuan.

BIBLIOGRAPHY
J. Cahill: *Wu Chen: A Chinese Landscapist and Bamboo Painter of the Fourteenth Century* (diss., Ann Arbor, U. MI, 1958)
Cheng Bingshan: *Wu Zhen* (Shanghai, 1958)
The Four Great Masters of the Yuan, Taipei, N. Pal. Mus. cat. (Taipei, 1975)
J. Cahill: *Hills beyond a River: Chinese Painting of the Yuan Dynasty, 1279–1368* (New York and Tokyo, 1976), pp. 68–74, 165–6
Chen Gaohua: *Yuan dai huajia shiliao* [Historical material on Yuan-period painters] (Shanghai, 1980), pp. 403–8
Chen Chiung-kuang: *Wu Chen, Yuan Painter* (Taipei, 1983)
Sung-mu Lee Han: *Wu Chen's 'Mo-chu-p'u', Literati Painter's Manual on Ink Bamboo* (diss., Princeton U., 1983)
J. Stanley-Baker: 'Accrued Perceptions of Wu Zhen: The Fishermen Theme', *Bull. Orient. Cer. Soc. Hong Kong*, viii (1986–8), pp. 36–46
——: *Old Masters Repainted: Wu Zhen (1280–1354) Prime Objects and Accretions* (Hong Kong, 1993)

CHU-TSING LI

Wu Zuoren [Wu Tso-jen] (*b* Jiangyin County, Jiangsu Province, 3 Nov 1908). Chinese painter and arts administrator. Brought up in Suzhou, Jiangsu Province, a city known for its strong artistic tradition, he studied oil painting first at the Shanghai Academy of Fine Art (1927) and then under Xu Beihong at the Nanguo [Southern] Academy of Fine Art in Shanghai and the art department of the Central University in Nanjing. From 1930 to 1935 he was in Europe; he studied at the Ecole Nationale Supérieure des Beaux-Arts in Paris and at the Académie Royale des Beaux-Arts in Brussels, also visiting Austria, Germany, England and Italy. During this time he practised both mural and easel painting, acquiring a solid foundation in the rather conservative academic style favoured by Xu Beihong. After his return to China he was invited to teach at the art department of the National Central University, and his oil landscapes were shown at the Second National Exhibition of Fine Arts in Nanjing (1937). During the Sino-Japanese war, which began in 1937, he continued to teach at the university's art department, which had moved from Nanjing to Chongqing, Sichuan Province, and produced large oil paintings, some dealing directly with war-related themes; others, for example the *Yellow Emperor's War against Chi You*, are in the form of patriotic historical allegories.

In 1943 Wu left Chongqing to travel for two years in the remote mountains and deserts of western China, an experience that changed his art decisively. In the Qinghai and Tibetan highlands he found landscapes dramatically different from anything in central China, and he also painted the costumes and customs of the Tibetan herdsmen and their animals. In his paintings of Tibetan yaks, for example *Herding Yaks* (1963; see Hua Junwu, pl. 5), a new introduction in Chinese animal painting, he used the traditional Chinese painting tools of ink and brush, describing the animals with broad loose washes and a few dramatic brushstrokes. Although these paintings show some affinity with Xu Beihong's celebrated black ink horses, Wu's animals are even more simplified in execution and, unlike Xu's horses, are shown in their native landscapes. Wu also applied this technique to painting the camels he saw in the Gobi desert. After a visit to the ancient wall paintings in the caves at Dunhuang, Gansu Province, which further reinforced the national character of his art, he returned to Sichuan and then Shanghai, where his paintings of the west of China created a sensation.

In August 1946 Wu became head of the oil painting department and dean of studies at the newly re-established Beijing Academy of Art. In 1947 he visited London at the invitation of the British Council and again toured Europe before returning to China in 1948. After the establishment of the People's Republic of China in 1949 he was very active in the new artistic and cultural organizations, being elected vice-chairman of the National Artists' Association in 1953 and delegate to the National People's Congress in 1954. In 1955 he was appointed vice-president of the country's foremost art school, the Central Academy of Fine Arts in Beijing, of which he was president from 1958 to 1979, remaining honorary president thereafter. During these decades of heavy administrative responsibilities his artistic output declined. He continued to work mainly in black ink, although he also did oil landscapes of important national symbols, such as *Sanmen Gorge on the Yellow River* (1956; see *Selected Paintings of Wu Zuoren and Xiao Shufang*, fig. 45), and a much-acclaimed oil portrait of *Qi Baishi* (1954; see *Selected Paintings of Wu Zuoren and Xiao Shufang*, fig. 44). His best-known subject abroad is the panda (e.g. *Pandas*, ink on paper, Cheung Cho-chai priv. col., see Hua Junwu, pl. 26), which he first painted when apolitical subject-matter again became possible after the peak of the Cultural Revolution had passed and China was starting to open up to the West in the early 1970s. He painted his pandas in the same simplified black ink style that he had used to depict the yaks in Tibet almost 30 years earlier.

After his retirement in 1979 Wu became much freer to paint again, mainly in traditional Chinese ink, and to travel abroad, notably to Argentina, Australia, the USA and Canada. More cosmopolitan in his background and training than most of the leading artists of the People's Republic of China, Wu Zuoren was probably a moderating force against the extremes of politicization in the arts. However, his academic oil painting style was compatible with Soviet-inspired Socialist Realism in the 1950s, and the strong national flavour of his Chinese-style paintings fitted in with the Chinese government's nationalistic emphasis in subsequent decades. Never a Communist Party member, Wu nevertheless survived all the shifts of political policy and became one of the most consistently honoured artists of the People's Republic of China.

BIBLIOGRAPHY
Wu Zuoren huaji [Selected paintings of Wu Zuoren] (Beijing, 1962)
Tso Hai: 'The Painter Wu Tso-jen', *Chin. Lit.*, 7 (1964), pp. 94–103
Ai Zhongxin: 'The Art of Wu Zuoren', *Chin. Lit.*, 7 (1980), pp. 50–58
Selected Paintings of Wu Zuoren and Xiao Shufang/Wu Zuoren, Xiao Shufang huaxuan (1982) [bilingual text, with 50 colour illus.]
Hua Junwu, ed.: *Contemporary Chinese Painting*, intro. by Wu Zuoren (Beijing, 1983)

RALPH CROIZIER

Wyant, Alexander Helwig (*b* Evans Creek, nr Port Washington, OH, 11 Jan 1836; *d* New York, 11 Nov 1892). American painter. He began as an itinerant painter of topographical landscapes along the banks of the Ohio River *c.* 1854, influenced by such landscape artists as Worthington Whittredge and George Inness. In 1863–4 Wyant moved to New York, where he was impressed by the paintings of the Norwegian artist Hans Gude in the Düsseldorf Gallery. This led him to work with Gude in Karlsruhe, Germany, in 1865. On his way both there and back he studied paintings by Constable and used a more painterly technique especially for views of Ireland, for example *Irish Landscape* (1865; Cleveland, OH, Mus. A.). Gude's influence in Germany was very strong, when Wyant painted hard-edged but broad and expansive landscapes such as *Tennessee (formerly The Mohawk Valley)* (1866; New York, Met.). In 1873 he permanently lost the use of his right arm due to a stroke and started to paint with his left hand. *The Flume, Opalescent River, Adirondacks* (c. 1881; Washington, DC, N. Mus. Amer. A.) is typical of Wyant's later style, in which looser brushstrokes are used to paint mountain scenery. His subjects came from sketches made during summer holidays at Keene Valley, NY, in the Adirondack Mountains (1880–89) and Arkville, NY, in the Catskill Mountains (1889–92). Influenced by Constable, George Inness and the Barbizon artists, Wyant developed an introspective form of Tonalism and Tonal Impressionism. His oil and watercolour works such as *Moonlight and Frost* (1890–92; New York, Brooklyn Mus.) and *Afternoon* (1891–2; Worcester, MA, A. Mus.) influenced most of the younger Tonalists, especially Bruce Crane (1857–1934) and J. Francis Murphy.

BIBLIOGRAPHY

Alexander Helwig Wyant, 1836–1892 (exh. cat., ed. E. F. Sanguinetti; Salt Lake City, U. UT, Mus. F.A., 1968)

R. S. Olpin: *Alexander Helwig Wyant: American Landscape Painter: An Investigation of his Life and Fame and a Critical Analysis of his Work with a Catalogue Raisonné of Wyant's Paintings* (diss., Boston U., 1971)

P. Bermingham: 'Alexander H. Wyant: Some Letters from Abroad', *Archv Amer. A. J.*, xii (1972), pp. 1–8

D. O. Dawdy: 'The Wyant Diary', *Arizona & W.*, xxii (1980), pp. 255–78

ROBERT S. OLPIN

Wyatt. English family of artists. The Wyatt family is the pre-eminent example in England of an artistic dynasty. From the middle of the 18th century to the end of the 19th it produced over twenty architects and half a dozen painters, sculptors and carvers (see fig.). The family originated in Staffordshire, where earlier generations had been farmers at Weeford, near Lichfield, for several centuries. Benjamin Wyatt (1709–72), the father of (1) Samuel Wyatt and (2) James Wyatt (the best-known member of the family), branched out from farming to timber selling and building in the mid-18th century and brought up his sons to help with the business, the eldest, William Wyatt (1734–80), being trained as a surveyor and Joseph Wyatt (1739–85) as a mason. The rapid economic development of the Midlands in the 18th century and the improvement of communications with the building of canals enabled the family to extend its influence beyond Staffordshire and to become established in London and even further afield. It is possible to write a comprehensive history of English architecture from 1772, the date of James Wyatt's success at the Pantheon in Oxford Street, London, to the death of (8) Thomas Henry Wyatt in 1880 drawing only on Wyatt examples, for the family was equally prominent in the parallel fields of Neo-classicism and the Gothic Revival.

BIBLIOGRAPHY

Colvin; Gunnis

D. Linstrum: *Catalogue of the Drawings Collection of the RIBA: The Wyatt Family* (London, 1973)

J. M. Robinson: *The Wyatts: An Architectural Dynasty* (Oxford, 1979)

(1) Samuel Wyatt (*b* Weeford, Staffs, 8 Sept 1737; *d* London, 8 Feb 1807). Architect and engineer. He was brought up by his father as a carpenter to help in the family building business. In 1760 he obtained a post on his own as a carpenter at Kedleston Hall, Derbys, then being rebuilt to the design of Robert Adam for Nathaniel Curzon, 1st Baron Scarsdale. He was soon promoted by Adam to Clerk of Works with full responsibility for all the construction on site. This experience was crucial to his artistic development and enabled him to become a fashionable Neo-classical architect in his own right.

From 1768 to 1774 he collaborated with his brother (2) James Wyatt, recently returned from Italy, on a number of projects. These included several country houses such as Gunton Hall, Norfolk (c. 1770), and Heaton Hall, Lancs (c. 1772), as well as the Pantheon in Oxford Street, London (1769–72; interior destr. 1793; facade destr. 1937), where he constructed a timber dome on the model of one that he had built to Adam's design over the saloon at Kedleston. In 1774 both brothers set up independent practices in London. Samuel specialized in the design of small country houses or villas in an elegant Adam-inspired manner, notable for their idiosyncratic domed bow windows resembling tea canisters. At Doddington Hall, Cheshire (see fig.), begun in 1776 for Sir Thomas Delves Broughton, there is a central bow, while other houses, notably Belmont Park, Kent (1787–92), for Colonel John Montresor, have bow windows flanking the façade at either end. His interiors are distinguished for their ingenious geometrical plans with rooms of different shapes, and for their exquisite plaster decorations.

Samuel Wyatt was also noted as a designer of model farm buildings, the finest of which are the barns and farmhouses erected (1780–1807) for Thomas Coke, 1st Earl of Leicester, on the Holkham estate in Norfolk. Like all his buildings they are distinguished by their original and innovative use of new and patent materials including mathematical tiles, Coade stone, Penrhyn slate and cast iron. Wyatt's enthusiasm for novel materials and structural techniques reflects the influence of the Industrial Revolution, also evident in his various engineering projects. He was appointed surveyor to Trinity House (1792) and Ramsgate Harbour (1794), where he succeeded John Smeaton. He designed various buildings round the harbour at Ramsgate, including warehouses, the Pier House and a lighthouse on the pier (1794–1805; all destr.), and he designed a new headquarters building for Trinity House on Tower Hill, London (1793–6), whose elegant Portland stone façade is an accomplished piece of French-inspired classicism, among the finest of its date in London. He also built the lighthouses at Dungeness, Kent (1792), and Flamborough Head, Humberside (1806).

From the structural point of view Wyatt's most important achievement was the Albion Mill at Blackfriars, London (1783–4; destr. 1791). This project grew out of his friendship with Matthew Boulton (1728–1809) and James Watt (1736–1819) and was intended to advertise

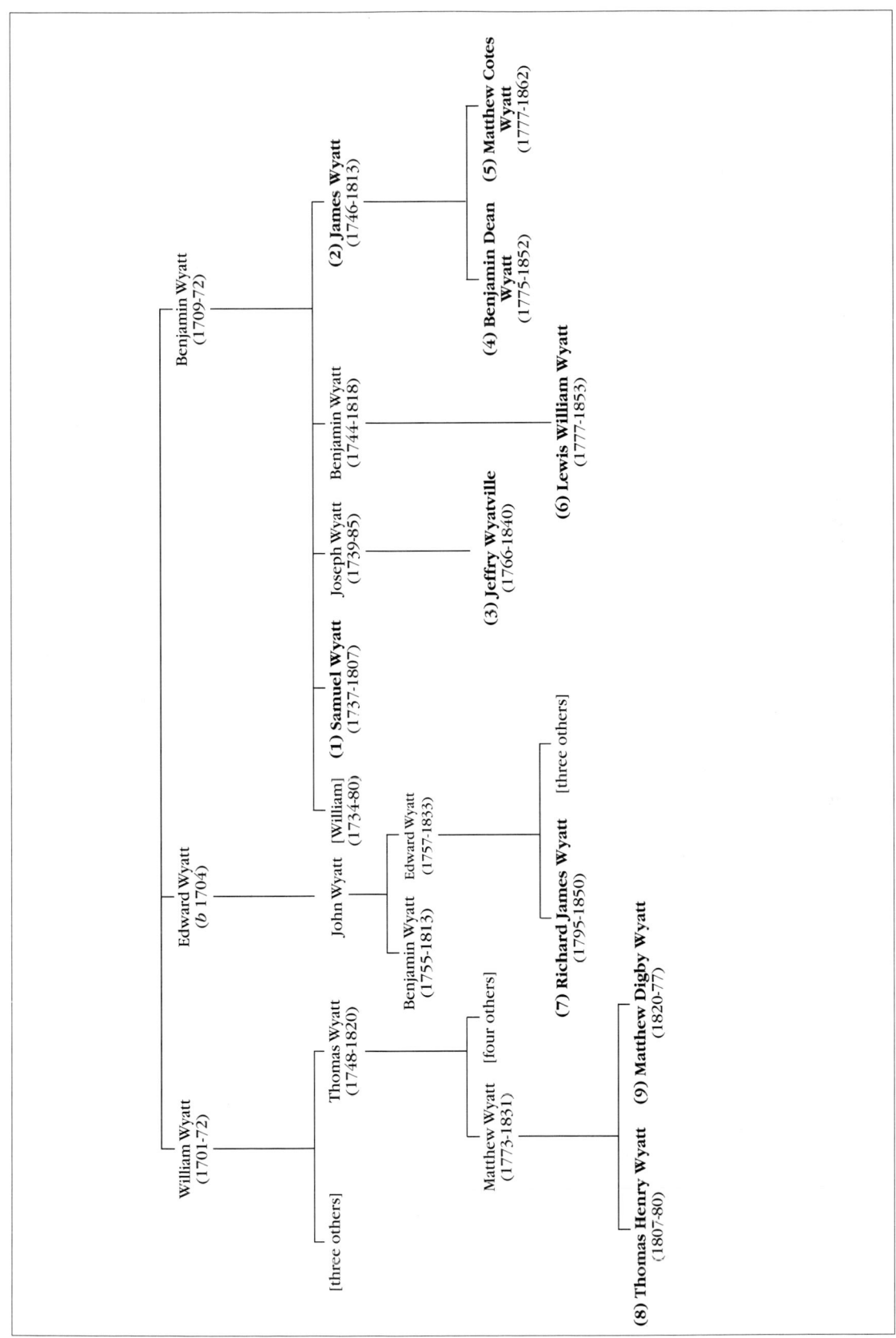

Family tree of the Wyatt family of artists

techniques reflects the influence of the Industrial Revolution, also evident in his various engineering projects. He was appointed surveyor to Trinity House (1792) and Ramsgate Harbour (1794), where he succeeded John Smeaton. He designed various buildings round the harbour at Ramsgate, including warehouses, the Pier House and a lighthouse on the pier (1794–1805; all destr.), and he designed a new headquarters building for Trinity House on Tower Hill, London (1793–6), whose elegant Portland stone façade is an accomplished piece of French-inspired classicism, among the finest of its date in London. He also built the lighthouses at Dungeness, Kent (1792), and Flamborough Head, Humberside (1806).

From the structural point of view Wyatt's most important achievement was the Albion Mill at Blackfriars, London (1783–4; destr. 1791). This project grew out of his friendship with Matthew Boulton (1728–1809) and James Watt (1736–1819) and was intended to advertise their pioneering development of the steam engine. The mill was promoted by a private company of which Wyatt was a shareholder and was the first building designed specifically to incorporate rotative steam engines. It was an ingenious piece of construction with a load-bearing timber interior, brick curtain walls, a patent slate roof and a unique floating foundation raft (48×36 m) in the form of shallow brick vaults foreshadowing the use of concrete raft foundations.

Samuel Wyatt died of a stroke while pulling on his boots to go and inspect Digswell House, Herts (1807), which he was building for the Hon. Edward Spencer Cowper. He left a number of works uncompleted, including the Headmaster's House at Rugby School, Warwicks (begun 1806), Tatton Park, Cheshire (begun 1785), Hackwood Park, Hants (begun 1805), and Panshanger, Herts (begun 1806; destr.). As an architect he was much more efficient than his brother James, and, unlike his brother, he worked in a consistently classical style. He is notable not just for the quality of his individual buildings but as a pioneering figure in a period when English building technology suddenly became dynamic after a century of stagnation.

BIBLIOGRAPHY

A. W. Skempton: 'Samuel Wyatt and the Albion Mill', *Archit. Hist.*, xiv (1971), pp. 53–73

J. M. Robinson: *Samuel Wyatt* (diss., U. Oxford, 1973)

(2) James Wyatt (*b* Weeford, Staffs, 3 Aug 1746; *d* nr Marlborough, Wilts, 4 Sept 1813). Architect, brother of (1) Samuel Wyatt.

1. STYLE AND WORKING METHODS. James Wyatt was the sixth son of Benjamin Wyatt of Weeford. He showed artistic promise at an early age and was sent by his father to Italy to study painting and architecture in the company of Richard Bagot, a Staffordshire landowner. He spent some time in Italy, training as an architectural draughtsman under Antonio Visentini in Venice and then making measured drawings of the great buildings in Rome. He returned to England in 1768 and rejoined his father and brothers, who were busy designing and building in the Midlands. He became acquainted with Robert Adam's work at Kedleston Hall, Derbys, through his brother Samuel, who was Clerk of Works there, and this had a great influence on his own architectural style. Indeed, most of his early works were elegant simplifications of Adam's designs, so much so that he was accused by the Adam brothers of plagiarism in their *Works in Architecture* (1773).

James Wyatt achieved sudden fame as the architect of the Pantheon in Oxford Street, London (1769–72; interior destr. 1792; façade destr. 1937), a place of public entertainment. It had a splendid domed interior, richly decorated with scagliola and stucco, and it immediately brought him to the notice of the fashionable world. He built up an extensive practice as a designer of country houses throughout England and Ireland, and he also became the leading public architect of his day, receiving more commissions than he could manage. His official positions included Surveyor to Westminster Abbey (1776), Architect to the Board of Ordnance (1782) and most importantly Surveyor-General and Comptroller of the Office of Works on the death of Sir William Chambers in 1796. His conduct of both public and private practice, however, was chaotic. He began his designs in a blaze of enthusiasm but then lost interest. In 1805 he was dismissed for incompetence from his post as Deputy Surveyor of the Office of Woods and Forests and only his death prevented his dismissal as Surveyor-General of the Office of Works, a position he left in such disarray that it had to be abolished.

As a designer James Wyatt was a brilliant eclectic, equally at home in the Gothic and Classical manners as well as dabbling in Jacobean, Chinese and Norman styles. His best classical work is indebted to the academic style of Chambers, as demonstrated, for example, by the beautiful domed mausoleum he built for the Pelham family at Brocklesby Park, Lincs (1787–94; see fig. 1). The more etiolated and decorative Adam-derived manner that he used in many of his interiors perhaps represents a concession to current fashion, for he later told George III that he admired Chambers and had found public taste 'corrupted by the Adams' when he returned from Italy but had been 'obliged to comply with it'. Wyatt had no consistent artistic principles and was adept at designing to please the client, a characteristic for which he has been

1. James Wyatt: mausoleum, Brocklesby Park, Lincolnshire, 1787–94

much blamed by doctrinaire critics. He was clever at adapting Classical sources, and he showed an awareness of the possibilities of the Greek Revival. The Radcliffe Observatory, Oxford (1776–94), for instance, is an ingenious variation on the Tower of the Winds at Athens, while his little domed lodge at Dodington, Avon (1798–1813), which charmingly mimics Ledoux's designs for the Parisian *barrières* (1785–9), sports the Doric order of the Temple of Apollo at Delos. The interiors of Wyatt's classical houses are particularly notable for their exquisite plasterwork, lavish use of scagliola and pretty painted decorations (*see* IRELAND, fig. 16). The rooms that he contrived within Sir Robert Taylor's shell at Heveningham Hall, Suffolk (*c*. 1780–84), are well-preserved examples and moreover retain much of their original Wyatt-designed furniture, for Wyatt, like Adam, designed many of the movable furnishings of his rooms as part of the overall scheme. He also designed items for leading Midlands manufacturers including pieces of silver for Matthew Boulton's factory at Soho, Birmingham (Quickenden, 1986).

2. GOTHIC REVIVAL AND LAST YEARS. Wyatt's greatest fame, or rather notoriety, has resided since his own day in his achievement as a Gothic architect. It was for work in this field that A. W. N. Pugin nicknamed him 'Wyatt the destroyer'. His obituary in the *Gentleman's Magazine* was more complimentary: 'His genius revived in this country the long forgotten beauties of Gothic architecture.' He played a significant role in the history of the Gothic Revival in England and fits midway between the Rococo freedom of such buildings as Strawberry Hill, Twickenham (begun 1748), and the more archaeological correctness of the 19th century. His Gothic work was distinguished for two particular qualities: accurate detail, usually adapted from well-known ecclesiastical sources, and the asymmetrical massing of the parts to create a picturesque whole. The best example of the latter was Fonthill Abbey, Wilts (1796–1813; fragment survives; see fig. 2), designed for William Beckford, with long wings radiating from a tall central tower, which collapsed (1825) after a remarkably short existence. Houses such as Norris Castle at East Cowes, Isle of Wight (1799), and Pennsylvania Castle at Portland, Dorset (1800), demonstrate his flair without relying on historicist detail, while houses like Belvoir Castle, Leics (1801–13; rest. 1816), and Ashridge Park, Herts (1808–13), parade a panoply of authentic-looking Gothic decoration.

Of his Gothic work, Wyatt's cathedral restorations were the most controversial in his lifetime and have been particularly so since. He was responsible for sweeping schemes of repair at the cathedrals of Durham, Hereford, Lichfield and Salisbury, though not for all the vandalism that has been attributed to him at these sites. Unfortunate features resulted from lack of proper supervision of the building work rather than conscious design. Nevertheless in his pursuit of what he thought were sublime effects,

2. James Wyatt: Fonthill Abbey, Wiltshire, 1796–1813 (mostly destr.); engraving by H. Winkles from a drawing by G. Cattermole for Britton's *Illustrations of England*

overall uniformity and uncluttered vistas, he showed a lack of feeling for the historical integrity of medieval buildings. At Salisbury (1789–92), for instance, he demolished two Perpendicular chantry chapels, the rood screen and a detached belfry tower in order to create a picture of the uniform 13th-century perfection that 18th-century rationalists admired. At Durham (1797–1805) he proposed reconstructing the Neville reredos to support the organ and adding a lantern and spire to the central tower, but these drastic ideas were not adopted. At Lichfield (1788–93) much of the actual work was carried out by a local architect, Joseph Potter (c. 1756–1842), but at Hereford (1788–96) the removal of the west bay of the nave in order to 'improve' the composition was Wyatt's idea. His restoration of Henry VII's chapel at Westminster Abbey (begun 1809), however, was exemplary in its careful reproduction of old masonry, but much of the work was executed by the mason Thomas Gayfere (1755–1827). Nevertheless, it marks a significant step in the development of modern restoration techniques.

The most time-consuming part of Wyatt's architectural practice was his work for the royal family. This included alterations for Queen Charlotte at Buckingham House, London (destr. 1825), and at Frogmore, near Windsor, as a classical 'Trianon' in the 1790s. His principal works for George III were the Gothic reconstruction of the upper ward at Windsor Castle with battlements, turrets and pointed windows (1803–13; completed in 1840 by (3) Jeffry Wyatville) and a huge new Gothic palace at Kew, London (1801–11). The latter remained an empty shell and was soon demolished (1827–8), though it was influential in the next generation, providing the model for Smirke's symmetrical castle designs at Lowther, Cumbria (1806–11), and Eastnor, Hereford & Worcs (1812–20).

On account of the royal favour he enjoyed, Wyatt was chosen as leader of the opposition to Benjamin West's ruling clique at the Royal Academy. In November 1805, following internal political manoeuvres, West was forced to retire and Wyatt was elected President in his place (the first architect to hold this position). Instead of resuscitating the Academy, however, as his supporters had hoped, he slept in committees, mumbled his speeches and failed to attend meetings. After only a year he resigned and West was re-elected.

The last years of Wyatt's life were overshadowed by declining health, financial problems and rows with his exasperated clients. In 1811, for example, William Beckford, in a rage at Fonthill, wrote of him: 'Where infamous Beast, where are you? What putrid inn, what stinking tavern or pox-ridden brothel hides your hoary and gluttonous limbs?' On Wyatt's death it was generally agreed that his poor circumstances had been caused by his neglect and bad management of his architectural office and his financial accounts. From 1800 onwards he suffered from a series of illnesses, and he remarked to George Dance the younger that he hoped for a sudden death. His wish was fulfilled. When driving back to London from Dodington, a new house that he was designing for Christopher Codrington in a sumptuous Neo-Roman manner influenced by Chambers, his carriage overturned and Wyatt, who was reading a newspaper at the time, hit his head on the roof and was killed instantly. He was buried in

Westminster Abbey, where his epitaph records that he was 'transcendently distinguished in his profession as an architect in this country'.

BIBLIOGRAPHY

W. Dodsworth: *A Guide to the Cathedral Church of Salisbury, with a Particular Account of the Late Great Improvements Made Therein under the Direction of James Wyatt esq.* (Salisbury, 1792)
Obituary, *Gent. Mag.*, ii (1813), pp. 296–7
J. Penn: *An Historical and Descriptive Account of Stoke Park* (London, 1813)
J. Britton: *History of the Cathedral Church of Lichfield* (London, 1820)
J. Rutter: *Delineations of Fonthill and its Abbey* (Shaftesbury, 1823)
J. Britton: *History of the Cathedral Church of Hereford* (London, 1831)
C. Hussey: 'The Universities of Oxford and Cambridge: The Radcliffe Observatory, Oxford', *Country Life*, lxvii (10 May 1930), pp. 674–81
A. Dale: *James Wyatt, Architect, 1746–1813* (Oxford, 1936)
R. A. Cordingley: 'Cathedral Innovations: James Wyatt, Architect, at Durham Cathedral, 1795–97', *Trans. Anc. Mnmt Soc.*, n. s., iii (1955), pp. 31–55
J. Summerson: 'The Classical Country House in Eighteenth Century England', *J. Royal Soc. A.*, cvii (1959), pp. 539–87
F. Fergusson: *James Wyatt* (diss., Cambridge, MA, Harvard U., 1972)
J. Harris: *Catalogue of British Drawings in American Collections* (New Jersey, 1972)
Heaton Hall: Bicentenary Exhibition (exh. cat., ed. T. Clifford and I. Hall; Manchester, Heaton Hall, 1972)
J. Frew: *James Wyatt and the Gothic Revival* (diss., U. Oxford, 1975)
E. Harris and J. M. Robinson: 'New Light on Wyatt at Fawley', *Archit. Hist.*, xxvii (1984), pp. 263–7
K. Quickenden: 'Boulton and Fothergill Silver: An Epergne Designed by James Wyatt', *Burl. Mag.*, cxxviii (June 1986), pp. 417–21

(3) Sir Jeffry Wyatville [Wyatt] (*b* Burton-on-Trent, 3 Aug 1766; *d* London, 18 Feb 1840). Architect and draughtsman, nephew of (2) James Wyatt. Wyatville is, after James Wyatt, the best-known member of the family. He was knighted, became a member of the Royal Academy, a Fellow of the Institute of British Architects, the Royal Society and the Society of Antiquaries, and also received the Grand Cross of the Ernestine Order of Saxony. He made a fortune from his profession and left £70,000 when he died. He was almost exclusively a country-house architect and was responsible for some of the most famous improvement schemes of the early 19th century. In 1835 he claimed that his 'rise in life . . . had been the effect of his own endeavours' and that by 'a straightforward course' he had arrived at riches and 'eminence beyond expectation'.

He was a son of the indolent Joseph Wyatt (1739–85) of Burton-on-Trent, one of the brothers of (1) Samuel and (2) James Wyatt. After an unhappy childhood, he tried unsuccessfully to run away to sea but then joined his uncle Samuel's architectural office in London, transferring in 1792 to his uncle James's office. He set up his own architectural and building business in London in 1799, in partnership with John Armstrong (*d* 1803). On the death of Samuel Wyatt in 1807 he took over most of his uncle's business, including several official carpentry contracts. It was only towards the end of his career that he ended his association with the building trade and conformed to current professional standards when in 1834 he was made Honorary Fellow of the newly founded Institute of British Architects (which became the Royal Institute of British Architects in 1837).

Wyatville's architectural career started well with commissions for several country houses, including the remodelling of two major Elizabethan buildings, Longleat, Wilts

(1800), for Thomas Thynne, 2nd Marquis of Bath, and Wollaton, Notts (1801), for Henry Willoughby, 6th Baron Middleton, for which he adopted a hybrid of the original Elizabethan style. Both commissions helped to establish Wyatville's reputation as an 'improver' of uncomfortable old houses. He designed a number of somewhat dreary Gothic houses, including Nonsuch, Surrey (1802–6), Rood Ashton, Wilts (1808), and Lypiatt, Glos (1809). Historically the most important of his early houses is Endsleigh Cottage, near Milton Abbot, Devon, built in 1810 for John Russell, 6th Duke of Bedford, at vast cost. Magnificently sited in a Repton landscape and ingeniously planned with a thatched roof and tree-trunk verandahs, it is one of the first fully fledged examples of a *cottage orné* and a major monument of the Picturesque. His classical work is rich yet chaste and shows to greatest advantage in the gigantic additions made to Chatsworth, Derbys (1824–46), for William Spencer Cavendish, 6th Duke of Devonshire.

Wyatville's most famous work, and the reason for his change of name from Wyatt to the more medieval-sounding Wyatville, was his reconstruction of Windsor Castle for George IV. He continued the work begun for George III by James Wyatt, and between 1824 and 1840 he created the Windsor that exists today. He raised the central keep or Round Tower by 10 m and added turrets, towers and innumerable battlements in order to improve the composition and heighten the silhouette. He also replanned the interior, adding the Grand Corridor and remodelling the staterooms, transforming the castle from an uninhabitable warren to a splendid and comfortable modern palace. However, he destroyed much of Charles II's Baroque interior and the details of his work have ugly yellow stone mouldings and harsh black mortar.

As an architect Wyatville was conscientious and capable but no more. Curiously the artistry that is lacking from many of his executed buildings can be found in his drawings. He was a great draughtsman, one of the best of the family. As a young man he produced freely drawn Neo-classical visions, in the manner of J. M. Gandy. He exhibited them at the Royal Academy with such titles as the *Palace of Alcinous* (1799), the *House of Fame* (1804) or the *Burning of Troy* (1806; all untraced). His finished architectural drawings are just as good in their different technique; several drawings are preserved in the Royal Institute of British Architects Drawings Collection. Those for the royal apartments at Windsor Castle are minor works of art in their own right.

BIBLIOGRAPHY

J. Britton: *Memoir of Sir Jeffry Wyatville* (London, 1834)
H. Ashton: *Illustrations of Windsor Castle by the Late Sir Jeffry Wyatville* (London, 1841)
D. Linstrum: *Sir Jeffry Wyatville: Architect to the King* (Oxford, 1972) [with illus. of all his principal bldgs]

(4) Benjamin Dean Wyatt (*b* London, 1775; *d* London, 1852). Architect, son of (2) James Wyatt. He was educated at Westminster and Christ Church, Oxford, but did not graduate, having shown signs of the fecklessness that was to bedevil his career. He worked in Calcutta for the East India Company from 1797 until 1803, when he returned to London claiming to be ill and entered his father's office to train as an architect. Against his father's wishes, in 1811 he entered a competition for the new theatre in Drury Lane, London, which was to replace the building destroyed by fire in 1809. His design was successful and the new theatre was built to his plans at a cost of £150,000. It was his first important commission, and it met with general acclaim. On the death of his father in 1813 Benjamin Dean took over the reins of the family business, but in an official capacity succeeded James Wyatt only as Surveyor to Westminster Abbey. The completion of several of his father's major unfinished buildings also eluded Benjamin Dean; the commission for Ashridge Park, Herts, for instance, passed to his cousin (3) Jeffry Wyatville. But within a year the most important opportunity of the period fell to him: the palace voted by a grateful parliament to the victorious Arthur Wellesley, 1st Duke of Wellington. In the event the project did not materialize and the Duke made do with the existing modest house at Stratfield Saye, Hants, to which Wyatt made additions and alterations (1822). He was also responsible for transforming Apsley House, Piccadilly, into the Duke's London palace from 1822 onwards. He made many abortive designs for other country houses, including Charlecote, Warwicks, Clumber, Notts, and Westport, Co. Mayo, Ireland, but it was for his work in London and in particular as the originator of the Louis XIV Revival style that he made his reputation. The earliest example of this Neo-Versailles type of decoration is the Elizabeth Saloon at Belvoir Castle, Leics (*c.* 1825–30), executed for Elizabeth Manners, wife of the 5th Duke of Rutland. At Belvoir, Benjamin Dean collaborated with his brothers Philip William Wyatt (*d* 1835) and (5) Matthew Cotes Wyatt, working in close association with the Duchess, herself a talented amateur architect, and the ducal chaplain, the Rev. Sir John Thoroton, on the restoration of the castle after a fire.

Benjamin Dean Wyatt first used his new French style in London in 1827 at Crockford's Club, St James's Street. It established him as the master of the Louis XIV Revival interior, which catered perfectly to the taste for grandeur in the years after the Battle of Waterloo. The finest surviving example is Lancaster House (originally called York House, later Stafford House), Cleveland Row, London, begun for Frederick, Duke of York, in 1820. It was completed for George Granville Leveson-Gower, 1st Duke of Sutherland, in 1838, though not without much quarrelling between client and architect, culminating in a lawsuit, which was decided in Wyatt's favour. The exterior is dull but dignified, while the interior contains a range of superb white and gold staterooms grouped around a full-height imperial-plan staircase embellished with Corinthian columns (copied from J. H. Mansart's chapel at Versailles, 1689–1710) and rich polychrome scagliola wall decorations simulating marble.

WRITINGS

Observations on the Principles of the Design for the Theatre now Building in Drury Lane (London, 1811, 2/1813 as *Observations on the Design for the Theatre Royal, Drury Lane*)

(5) Matthew Cotes Wyatt (*b* London, 1777; *d* London, 3 Jan 1862). Sculptor and painter, son of (2) James Wyatt. He was educated at Eton. When he was 20 he began painting portrait miniatures and, with his father's encouragement, he branched out into large-scale decorative painting. He obtained several important commissions from his father, including the ceiling of the Concert Room in Hanover Square, London (1803; destr.), allegorical panels in the dining-room at Carlton House, London (1804; destr.), for the Prince Regent (later George IV) and decorations in the state apartments at Windsor Castle (*c.* 1805–11; destr.). About 1815 he gave up painting to concentrate on sculpture. His first public commission was for the Nelson monument in Liverpool (1807–13). This was designed by Wyatt but Richard Westmacott (ii) cast the bronze statue itself. After the Battle of Waterloo, Wyatt occupied himself with megalomaniac but unexecuted proposals for a national 'Tropheum' to honour the achievements of British arms. He made his name with the memorial to Princess Charlotte (1796–1817) in St George's Chapel, Windsor (1820–24). The work unites the Baroque with the Neo-classical; the soul of the Princess floats up to heaven amid marble clouds, while her heavily shrouded corpse lies on a slab below, attended by four life-size mourners. This monument had no real precursor in English funerary art; it is likely that it was inspired by Arthur William Devis's painting of the *Apotheosis of Princess Charlotte* in Esher Church, Surrey. A few years later Wyatt repeated the formula in the monument to Elizabeth Manners, 5th Duchess of Rutland, at Belvoir Castle, Leics (completed 1828).

Wyatt received commissions for other public monuments, notably the bronze equestrian statue of *George III* at the junction of Cockspur Street and Pall Mall, London (1822–36). This was subject to long delays and when unveiled the King's prominent pigtail was the object of much derision. *The Times* of 4 August 1836 called the statue a 'burlesque effigy', and there was general disappointment that the statue had not been the subject of an open competition. The hostility so aroused reached a peak with Wyatt's last great public commission, the equestrian statue of *Arthur Wellesley, 1st Duke of Wellington* (commissioned 1839; completed 1846) placed on top of Decimus Burton's arch at Hyde Park Corner, London. This aroused a howl of public protest led by Burton, who had not been consulted, and only the direct intervention of the Duke himself prevented the statue being taken down again. It was eventually moved to Caesar's Camp, near Aldershot, in 1882.

Wyatt's private commissions were hardly less controversial than his public ones: *Bashaw* (1831; London, V&A), a marble sculpture with ruby eyes portraying Lord Dudley's Newfoundland dog, was turned down by the family trustees, who also refused to pay for it. Wyatt executed little of his own sculpture. Most of the marble carving and the bronze casting was the work of assistants. He made the designs and supervised the general execution. This explains why some of the bravura of the original conception was not always carried through into the finished work. His reputation should rest, perhaps, on his ability as a theatrical designer rather than as a sculptor.

Of Wyatt's children, his eldest son Matthew Wyatt (1805–86) was active in London as an architect early in his life and was knighted in 1848. He was responsible for Victoria Square, Pimlico, London (1837), and for houses in Paddington and Hyde Park, London, many of which were built in partnership with his brother George Wyatt (*d* 1880). Their younger brother Henry Wyatt (*d* 1899)

was also an architect. Another son, James Wyatt (1808–93), was a sculptor who exhibited at the Royal Academy (1838–44); on his father's death he completed many of the works left in his studio.

(6) Lewis William Wyatt (*b* Penrhyn, Wales, 1777; *d* Ryde, Isle of Wight, 14 Feb 1853). Architect, nephew of (2) James Wyatt. He was the son of Benjamin Wyatt (1744–1818), manager of the Penrhyn slate quarries in Wales. Lewis Wyatt joined Samuel Wyatt's office in 1795 and five years later transferred to that of James Wyatt, setting up on his own in Albany, London, in 1806. Having an independent fortune, he took time off on several occasions to travel on the Continent. In 1814, for instance, he visited France, where Napoleonic Paris made a strong impression, inspiring him to publish a *Prospectus of a Design for Various Improvements in the Metropolis* (1816) showing how the centre of London could be re-planned on similarly grand lines. In 1820 he took six months leave to study architecture and collect works of art in northern Italy and Rome, where he met Angiolo Uggeri who dedicated *Ornamenti greci antichi ed inediti* (1820) to him.

Wyatt made his name chiefly as a country-house architect, failing repeatedly to win commissions for public buildings. Though not prolific, he was a scholarly designer and as a result of his travels and his well-stocked library had an unusually wide and eclectic architectural knowledge. St Mary's, Stockport (1813–17), is a serious and substantial exercise in Perpendicular Gothic. His dining-room at Lyme Park, Cheshire (1814–17), with carvings in the manner of Grinling Gibbons, is a pioneering exercise in the late 17th-century Baroque style directly influenced by Wren's work at Hampton Court. Wyatt was one of the first architects to employ Jacobean and Tudor styles in such houses as Cranage Hall and Eaton Hall (nr Congleton, Cheshire; destr. 1963; rebuilt 1989), both designed in 1829. His eclectic historicist approach was demonstrated in his proposals for rebuilding Hawkstone Park, Salop, in 1826 for Sir Rowland Hill with rooms that were replicas of those in the old house. In the event the old house was retained and extended by Wyatt in 1832–4 in a variety of styles: early 18th-century Revival outside, Neo-classical in the dining-room and Louis XIV Revival in the drawing-room. His favourite style was rich Neo-classical, originally stimulated by interiors at Carlton House, London (1783–95; destr. 1826), where he had worked as a young man.

The most important aspect of Wyatt's designs was his handling of space. At Tatton Park, Cheshire (1807–13), he contrived an extension to the staircase hall surrounded by a series of arches and galleried landings. His principal work, Willey Park, Salop (begun 1812), develops and perfects James Wyatt's classical style. It has an octastyle Corinthian portico and brilliantly contrived processional space through the centre of the house, with an oval entrance hall, a vast central atrium lit from the top and an oval staircase hall where two sweeping flights of steps are connected to the upper galleries by a flying bridge.

Wyatt retired in 1835 to the Isle of Wight where he built a *cottage orné*, Cliff Cottage, at Puck Pool, near Ryde.

(7) Richard James Wyatt (*b* London, 3 May 1795; *d* Rome, 28 May 1850). Sculptor, second cousin of (1) Samuel Wyatt and (2) James Wyatt. He worked for his father Edward Wyatt (1757–1833), a decorative carver and picture framer in London, and was then apprenticed to the sculptor J. C. F. Rossi. In 1812 he entered the Royal Academy Schools, where he won the silver medal for the best model from life in 1815. He exhibited his first life-size classical group, a *Judgement of Paris* (untraced), at the Royal Academy in 1818. On the recommendation of Sir Thomas Lawrence, Wyatt obtained a place in Canova's studio in Rome. He left England in 1820 and spent some time in Bosio's studio in Paris, where he probably learnt the technique of finishing marble so as to give the surface a soft, warm effect.

Early in 1821 Wyatt arrived in Rome, where there was already a large community of English sculptors. On Canova's death a year later he transferred with his friend John Gibson (1790–1866) to Bertel Thorvaldsen's studio before setting up on his own. He immediately received an order from William Cavendish, 6th Duke of Devonshire, for a marble version of the plaster *Musidora* in his studio for the new sculpture gallery at Chatsworth, Derbys. Musidora is a character from James Thomson's *The Seasons* (1726–30), and Wyatt showed some originality in choosing a subject from modern poetry rather than Classical mythology for his first important work. *Musidora* was finished in 1824 and some lean years followed; by 1830, however, Wyatt was loaded with commissions from distinguished English and foreign patrons. From 1831 until his death he exhibited a new work every year at the Royal Academy in London.

Wyatt's art came to maturity in the 1830s. His statues are skilfully composed and highly finished, with a sensitive concern for detail and texture. His Neo-classical taste, well-founded on a study of the Antique, though softened by an interest in modern poetic and narrative subjects, never degenerated into sentimental naturalism or melodrama. He became best known as a virtuoso carver of life-size marble figures and groups, particularly single female figures, though he also carved some fine monuments and portrait busts. His *Nymph Going to the Bath* (exh. RA 1831; untraced) for Maximilian de Beauharnais, Duc de Leuchtenburg, was the first of a series of similar popular works, and he devised three different versions of the subject as well as many replicas. Works of this period show Canova's influence: *Flora and Zephyr* (exh. RA 1834; Nostell Priory, W. Yorks), for instance, is based on Canova's *Cupid and Psyche* (1793; Paris, Louvre). Thorvaldsen's influence is also apparent, notably in Wyatt's marble reliefs for memorials and in his statues of children.

His success and popularity reached a climax in the 1840s when he visited England. Albert, the Prince Consort, commissioned a statue of *Penelope* (c. 1841–2) from him for the Queen's apartments at Windsor Castle (*in situ*), the first of five works for Queen Victoria. The others included a *Glycera* (1848) and two versions of a *Nymph of Diana Returning from the Chase* (all Osborne House, Isle of Wight, Royal Col.).

BIBLIOGRAPHY
R. A. Martin: *Life and Work of R. J. Wyatt* (diss., U. Leeds, 1972)

(8) Thomas Henry Wyatt (*b* Lough Glin, Co. Roscommon, Ireland, 9 May 1807; *d* London, 5 Aug 1880). Architect, second cousin of (1) Samuel Wyatt and (2) James Wyatt. One of the most prolific of English architects, he trained in London at the office of Philip Hardwick before starting independent architectural practice in 1832. Through the influence of an uncle who was land agent to the extensive Beaufort estates in South Wales, he obtained most of the commissions for the large numbers of new public buildings required in the development of the Welsh valleys. With the recommendation of the Beauforts he started a country-house practice that grew to be one of the largest in England. Between 1838 and 1851 he was in partnership with David Brandon (1813–97), but he later worked on his own.

Wyatt designed over 400 buildings, many of them the work of a well-organized office of assistants. He also played an active role in public architectural affairs, sitting on committees and occupying many official positions. Though he was neither a great nor an original architect, most of his work is competent and scholarly. His early buildings are the most satisfactory, such as the simple classical Assize Court at Devizes, Wilts (1835), and the noble Italianate basilica of SS Mary and Nicholas at Wilton, Wilts (1840–45). He was responsible for numerous Gothic Revival churches and restorations, largely in the Salisbury diocese. These form a microcosm of English church building between 1830 and 1880. The great Wiltshire estate churches built in the 1860s and 1870s—Savernake, Hindon, Fonthill Gifford, Semley and Bemerton—are perhaps the best, with their well-massed exteriors, spacious interiors and the high quality of their fittings and finish. Wyatt's public buildings, by contrast, were in the classical style but the most notable have been demolished: Knightsbridge Barracks, London (1879–82), the Liverpool Exchange (1867) and the Cambridge Assize Courts (1840–43). His many country houses were mainly in a late Tudor style, but they are of little architectural merit. Orchardleigh Park, Somerset (1855–8), is typical, with its arid, gabled stone exterior and fireproof internal construction.

(9) Sir **Matthew Digby Wyatt** (*b* Rowde, Wilts, 28 July 1820; *d* Cowbridge, S. Glam., 21 May 1877). Architect, draughtsman, designer, writer and teacher, brother of (8) Thomas Henry Wyatt. He entered his brother's architectural office at the age of 16. Within a year he won a prize from the Architectural Society for the best essay on Grecian Doric, the first indication of his talent as a writer on art. In 1837 he enrolled in the Royal Academy Schools and in 1844 travelled to the Continent, where he spent two years making nearly a thousand ink and watercolour drawings of monuments. Some of these were published in facsimile as the *Specimens of Geometrical Mosaic of the Middle Ages* (1848). This led to Wyatt's introduction to Herbert Minton and the designing of tiles at Minton's; he was asked to advise directly on the floor tiles for Albert, the Prince Consort, at Osborne House, Isle of Wight.

Wyatt's writings and lectures on the applied arts brought him to the notice of an important group of members of the Royal Society of Arts, including Owen Jones, Sir Henry Cole and John Scott Russell, later nicknamed the South Kensington Group. In 1851, through this connection, he was appointed Special Commissioner and Secretary to the Great Exhibition and became the executant architect of Paxton's glass exhibition building in Hyde Park, London.

He was involved with Owen Jones in the reconstruction of the Crystal Palace at Sydenham, Kent, and the new design of the Courts of Architecture inside. He also received the commission to design decorative ironwork for Paddington Station, London, in 1852 (*see* RAILWAY STATION, fig. 2). In 1855 he was appointed Surveyor to the East India Company and designed important buildings both in England, such as Warley Barracks, Essex (1862–3), and in India, where he was responsible, with the engineer J. M. Rendel, for the bridges over the River Soane, Kent, Hullohur (*c.* 1855). Wyatt was subsequently appointed architect to the Council of India and in 1868 designed the new India Office attached to Sir George Gilbert Scott's Foreign Office in Whitehall. Wyatt cooperated closely with Scott, who later paid tribute to his tact and fair play in this difficult commission. The sumptuous courtyard of the India Office with its three tiers of arcades, inspired by the cloisters of the Certosa di Pavia, is Wyatt's finest building. The red and blue 'della Robbia' maiolica friezes were made by Minton's; they are a good example of the 'art-manufactures' promoted in the mid-19th century by the South Kensington Group.

Wyatt designed in a variety of styles, including Moorish in the smoking-room at 12 Kensington Palace Gardens, London (1865–75), Indian in the Soane Bridge and Elizabethan or Gothic for his country houses, such as the colossal Possingworth Manor, Sussex (1868). However, he preferred Classical architecture and all his best work is executed in an Italian Renaissance style: the India Office, the domed Rothschild Mausoleum at West Ham, near London (1866–8), the garden buildings at Castle Ashby, Northants (1868), and the Roman saloon at Ashridge, Herts (1864). In the lectures he gave as Slade Professor at Cambridge in 1869 he emphasized that the study of the five orders was of real practical use in training the eye to appreciate scale and design.

Architecture was only a portion of Wyatt's overall achievement. He also designed interior decoration, stained glass, tiles, carpets, metalwork, book illustration and cast-iron public lavatories; he was a talented watercolour painter and prolific author. He was among the most modern-minded designers of Victorian England, a member of the talented circle that revolved around the Prince Consort, and he was friends with Edward Lear, William Dyce and Frederic, Lord Leighton. He had an expanding architectural practice and devoted much time to organizational and committee work, and he was loaded with honours from home and abroad, including a knighthood, an honorary MA from Cambridge University and the Italian Lazzaro order. In the late 1860s Wyatt's health began to be affected by overwork and he retired to Dimlands Castle, S. Glam. He was buried at Usk in a tomb of pink granite with cast-iron railings, designed by his brother Thomas Henry Wyatt.

WRITINGS

Specimens of Geometrical Mosaic of the Middle Ages (London, 1848)
'On the Construction of the Building for the Exhibition of the Works of Industry of All Nations in 1851', *Min. Proc. Inst. Civ. Engin.*, x (1851), pp. 127–91
The Industrial Arts of the Nineteenth Century (London, 1851–3)
Paris Universal Exhibition: Report on Furniture and Decoration (London, 1856)
Illuminated Manuscripts as Illustrative of the Arts (London, 1860)

Fine Art: Its History, Theory, Practice (London, 1870) [Slade lectures at Cambridge]
An Architect's Note-book in Spain (London, 1872)

BIBLIOGRAPHY

N. Pevsner: *Matthew Digby Wyatt* (Cambridge, 1950)

JOHN MARTIN ROBINSON

Wyatville, Sir Jeffry. *See* WYATT, (3).

Wyck. *See* WIJCK.

Wyct, Boudewijn van der. *See under* MASTERS, ANONYMOUS, AND MONOGRAMMISTS, §I: MASTER OF THE GUILD OF ST GEORGE.

Wyczółkowski, Leon (*b* Huta Miastkowska, nr Siedlce, 11 April 1852; *d* Warsaw, 27 Dec 1936). Polish painter and printmaker. He studied at the Warsaw Drawing School (1869–73) under Aleksander Kamiński (1823–86), Rafal Hadziewicz (1803–86) and Wojciech Gerson; from 1875 to 1877 he studied at the Munich Kunstakademie under Alexander Wagner (1838–1918), and then at the Kraków School of Fine Arts under Jan Matejko from 1877 to 1879. Most of his early works are technically competent realistic portraits that reveal his sensitivity to colour (e.g. the *Artist's Grandmother, Mrs Falińska*, 1880; Warsaw, N. Mus.) and drawing-room scenes in the Munich tradition of anecdotal realism (e.g. *I Once Saw*, 1884; Warsaw, N. Mus.). From 1883 to 1894 he lived in the Ukraine. During his last years there he produced numerous scenes of peasant and bourgeois life. Such works as *Fishermen* (1891; Warsaw, N. Mus.) and *Croquet* (1895; Łódź, Mus. A.) were influenced in technique by the Impressionist paintings he had seen while in Paris in 1889, but were still predominantly realist in conception.

In 1895 Wyczółkowski was appointed professor at the Kraków School of Fine Arts, where he taught until 1911. In his first years in Kraków he turned towards symbolism and Polish historical themes, as in *Queen Hedwig's Crucifix* (1896; Kraków, N. Mus.); Symbolist elements endured in his later landscape paintings, notably in the series of views of the Tatra (e.g. *Mount Muich in the Tatras*, 1904; Kraków, N. Mus.). His work was also influenced at times by Art Nouveau and *Japonisme*, as seen in his still-lifes and frequent paintings of flowers (e.g. *Still-life with a Vase and Chinese Screen*, 1905; Warsaw, N. Mus.). About 1910 he abandoned oils in favour of watercolours and pastels.

Around 1900 he began exploring a variety of printmaking techniques. He searched for a medium which best suited his realistic, though spontaneous, depiction of nature (e.g. *Oaks in Białowieża*, lithograph, 1922; Warsaw, N. Mus.). He eventually concentrated on lithography, and from 1922 he dedicated most of his time to printmaking. In 1934 he was appointed professor of printmaking at the Academy of Fine Arts in Warsaw. He executed hundreds of loose sheets on subjects as varied as those of his paintings, and about twenty series of sheets devoted to particular cities, national monuments and landscapes. His most outstanding work, in printmaking as in painting, is to be found among his portraits (e.g. *Self-portrait*, fluorograph, 1904; Warsaw, N. Mus.).

BIBLIOGRAPHY
Bénézit; Thieme-Becker
M. Twarowska: *Leon Wyczółkowski: Listy i wspomnienia* [Leon Wyczół-kowski: letters and memoirs] (Wrocław, 1960)
——: *Leon Wyczółkowski* (Warsaw, 1962)
W. Juszczak: *Modernizm: Malarstwo polskie* [Modernism: Polish painting] (Warsaw, 1977) [biographical notes and catalogue by M. Liczbińska]
Polnische Malerei von 1830 bis 1918 (exh. cat., ed. J. C. Jenson; Kiel, Christian-Albrechts U., Ksthalle; Stuttgart, Württemberg. Kstver.; Wuppertal, Von der Heydt-Mus.; 1978–9)
La Peinture polonaise du XVIe au début du XXe siècle (exh. cat., Paris, Grand Pal., 1979)
Symbolism in Polish Painting, 1890–1914 (exh. cat., ed. A. Morawinska; Detroit, MI, Inst. A., 1984)

LIJA SKALSKA-MIECIK

Wydyz. *See* WEIDITZ.

Wyelant, Guillaume. *See* VRELANT, WILLEM.

Wyeth, Andrew (Newell) (*b* Chadds Ford, PA, 12 July 1917). American painter. Owing to his fragile health he was taught at home as a child by tutors and by his father Newell Convers Wyeth (1882–1945), a distinguished illustrator who gave him a rigorous training in draughtsmanship. In about 1933 he first saw the watercolours of Winslow Homer, prompting him to paint impressionistic watercolours that captured fleeting effects of light and movement, as in the *Coot Hunter* (1941; Chicago, IL, A. Inst.). He first exhibited in 1936 at the Art Alliance of Philadelphia and the following year had his first one-man show, of watercolours, at the Macbeth Gallery in New York, which sold out on the first day. In 1943 Wyeth received a lucrative offer to paint occasional covers for the *Saturday Evening Post*, as his father had done, but he refused, wishing to devote himself to more independent art.

Wyeth's earliest works were in pen and ink and watercolour but by the early 1940s he had begun to use egg tempera on gesso board, a technique he had learnt from his brother-in-law, the American painter Peter Hurd (*b* 1904). In this painstaking technique he found a good counterbalance to his natural inclination towards swift, spontaneous execution. For similar reasons he also began to use drybrush watercolour, in which a fine brush is squeezed almost dry of liquid before use. Nevertheless, watercolour remained as a means of catching observations quickly and for studies. Early examples of temperas include *Public Sale* (1943; Bryn Mawr, PA, H. W. Breyer priv. col., see 1967 exh. cat., p. 15). In 1945 Wyeth's father was killed in a railway accident and this tragedy gave greater emphasis to the introspective, melancholy strain developing in Wyeth's work. This is apparent in such temperas as *Christina's World* (1948; New York, MOMA; *see* LANDSCAPE PAINTING, fig. 12), which depicts the cripple Christina Olson in the midst of a vast expanse of grassland looking wistfully back at her house. Olson was a model for many of Wyeth's works until her death in 1969. The drybrush work *Faraway* (1952; artist's col., see Meryman, p. 51) of his son Jamie was the first Wyeth thought successful in this medium.

From the 1950s and into the 1970s Wyeth regularly painted the farm owned by Karl and Anna Kuerlner in Chadds Ford, as in *Swiss Brown* (1957; New York, Mr and Mrs A. M. Laughlin priv. col., see Meryman, p. 57), which

was named after the Swiss Brown cattle included in the scene. While continuing to paint landscapes the artist began to produce portraits in the 1960s, for example the drybrush *Up in the Studio* (1965; New York, Met.) depicting his sister Carolyn, who was also a painter. On occasions he mixed the media of drybrush and watercolour, as in *Garrett Room* (1962; artist's col., see Meryman, p. 26), which after beginning as a fluid watercolour was completed in drybrush. Between 1971 and 1985 Wyeth secretly made numerous drawings and paintings, including nudes, of Helga Testorf, a neighbour in Chadds Ford. Almost 100 of these so-called 'Helga pictures' were exhibited by the Norton Gallery and School of Art, West Palm Beach, FL, in 1996.

Wyeth's style and subject-matter changed little throughout his career, and the restrained earth colours that characterized his earlier work were continued in later paintings such as *Ring Road* (1985; priv. col., see 1987 exh. cat., p. 147). His work was enormously popular in the USA, and as a mark of this he was given a large retrospective in 1976 at the Metropolitan Museum in New York, the first time a living American artist had been accorded such an honour. With the critics, however, his reputation was less secure, largely because his style and subject-matter fell outside the avant-garde developments of American art. Travelling very little, he spent his life almost entirely in the Maine and Pennsylvania regions of the USA. To many his accessible paintings evoke some mythical rural past, striking a powerful chord in the American psyche. Like Dürer, whom he greatly admired, he placed great emphasis on observation, and his detailed style reflects this. Nevertheless, through the series of pencil and watercolour studies for a work, many details were often pared away.

BIBLIOGRAPHY
Andrew Wyeth: Temperas, Watercolours, Dry Brush, Drawings (exh. cat. by E. P. Richardson, Philadelphia, PA, Acad. F.A., 1966)
R. Meryman: *Andrew Wyeth* (Boston, 1968)
W. M. Corn and others: *The Art of Andrew Wyeth* (San Francisco, 1973)
J. Canaday: *Works by Andrew Wyeth from the Holly and Arthur Magill Collection* (Greenville, SC, 1979)
Andrew Wyeth from Public and Private Collections (exh. cat. by M. J. Albacete, Canton, OH, A. Inst., 1985)
An American Vision: Three Generations of Wyeth Art (exh. cat. by I. H. Duff and others, Chadds Ford, PA, Brandywine River Mus., 1987)

□

Wykeham, William of, Bishop of Winchester. *See* WILLIAM OF WYKEHAM.

Wyld, William (*b* London, 1806; *d* Paris, 25 Dec 1889). English painter and lithographer. The son of a businessman, Wyld worked initially in the diplomatic service, acting as secretary to the British consul in Calais. While there, he encountered Louis Francia and, through him, the work of his protégé Richard Parkes Bonington. He also met John Lewis Brown, a keen collector of Bonington watercolours, and became a lifelong friend of Horace Vernet. From 1827 to 1833 Wyld was in charge of a wine business in Epernay, where he pursued the interest in art he had conceived under the influence of these artists. He acquired a circle of patrons in the region.

Wyld made his début in the Salon in 1831 and three years later became a full-time artist. A journey to North

Africa in 1833 resulted in *Voyage pittoresque dans la régence d'Alger pendant l'année 1833* in collaboration with the lithographer Emile Lessore (1805–76). Although Wyld retained his British nationality, he worked and exhibited mainly in France. His speciality was highly worked and often brilliantly coloured views of capital cities, in watercolour or gouache (or occasionally oil), depicted from a distance in evening or early morning light (e.g. *View of Dresden by Sunset*, c. 1852; London, V&A). He travelled extensively and enjoyed considerable material success and royal patronage: in 1852 he visited Balmoral Castle, Grampian, at the invitation of Queen Victoria and executed a series of watercolour views of the area (Windsor Castle, Royal Lib.).

BIBLIOGRAPHY
P. G. Hamerton: 'W. Wyld's Sketches in Italy', *Portfolio* [London], viii (1877), pp. 126–9, 140–44, 161–4, 178–9, 193–6 [written after interviews with the artist]
M. Pointon: *The Bonington Circle: English Watercolour and Anglo-French Landscape, 1790–1855* (Brighton, 1985)
——: *Bonington, Francia and Wyld* (London, 1985)

MARCIA POINTON

Wyllie, W(illiam) L(ionel) (*b* London, 6 July 1851; *d* London, 6 April 1931). English painter and engraver. He was the son of Katherine (née Benham) Wyllie and a prosperous, minor genre painter, William Morrison Wyllie (*fl* 1852–90). He spent most of his childhood summers in France, where his parents owned houses on the coast, first at Boulogne and later at Wimereux. He began *plein-air* drawing and painting at an early age, encouraged by both his father and his stepbrother Lionel Smythe (1839–1918). After studying at Heatherley's Art School in London, (c. 1863), he entered the Royal Academy Schools in 1866 and two years later exhibited his first picture, *Dover Castle and Town* (untraced), at the summer exhibition. Though his precocious talent was again rewarded in 1869, when he won the Turner Gold Medal for Landscape with his *Dawn after a Storm* (untraced; engraved for the *Illustrated London News*, Jan 1870), the 1870s were to bring some disappointment: the Academy refused two of his pictures for exhibition in 1875, and his angry reaction was to declare the end of his artistic career and the beginning of one at sea. Though the promise was shortlived it did fulfil a lifelong ambition to sail. Several cruises in British and European waters provided the inspiration and material for his continuing career as a marine painter. His *Toil, Glitter, Grime and Wealth* (exh. RA 1883; London, Tate), a view in oils of the Thames at Greenwich, was his first major work to receive general critical acclaim. 'The Thames Mr Wyllie paints is the Thames as it is', wrote the *Magazine of Art* (May 1884, p. 314). Like so many of Wyllie's works in oil, the painting seems to be laboriously handled and lacking in both the subtlety of subject and delicacy of treatment characteristic of his more accomplished watercolours; however it was clearly well attuned to the more jingoistic currents of Victorian taste. So too, albeit at another level, were his first naval subjects—two large representations of the bombardment of Alexandria, also painted in 1883, one of which is in the National Maritime Museum, London. He was elected ARA in 1889, no doubt further assisted by the success of his exhibition of 69 watercolours at the Fine Art Society in the previous year.

In the 1890s his development as a watercolourist reached its peak: one early and fine example from this period is his *Figures on the Beach at Berck-sur-Mer* (1891; London, N. Mar. Mus.), an unpretentious and fluent work which stands in astonishing contrast with oil paintings such as the gauche and melodramatic *Leonidas* (1885; London, N. Mar. Mus.), one of his many attempted essays in the style of J. M. W. Turner. Some deterioration in the quality of his art has been detected in the years between 1905 and 1914 (notwithstanding his election as RA in 1907), which 'may well have arisen from an overconfidence in his technical abilities' (Quarm and Wyllie), but he worked with some accomplishment throughout World War I; among his several war pictures was a panel of the landings at Zeebrugge painted for the Royal Exchange, London. In his postwar years he is best remembered for his series of small and exceptionally well-crafted etchings and drypoints of London views in the 1920s and for his large and over-ambitious panorama of the *Battle of Trafalgar* (Portsmouth, Royal Naval Mus.).

Wyllie's younger brother, Charles (1859–1923), and son, Harold (1880–1973), were among the painters who followed his approach and absorbed his style, but outside the sphere of marine painting his influence was slight.

WRITINGS
Marine Painting in Water-colour (London, 1901)

BIBLIOGRAPHY
Holiday Drawings in France and Italy (exh. cat., ed. M. A. Wyllie; London, F.A. Soc., 1892)
M. A. Wyllie: *We Were One* (London, 1935)
R. Quarm and J. Wyllie: *W. L. Wyllie, Marine Artist, 1851–1931* (London, 1981)

STEPHEN DEUCHAR

Wyman, George Herbert (*b* Dayton, OH, 1860; *d* Los Angeles, CA, c. 1900). American architect. He received little formal architectural training, having had a brief apprenticeship in Dayton in the architectural office of his uncle Luthor Peters (*d* 1921), followed by a period as a draughtsman in the office of Sumner P. Hunt (1865–1938) in Los Angeles, where he moved in 1891 for health reasons. In 1893 his first and only major work was constructed. The Bradbury Building, on Third Avenue and Broadway, invokes 19th-century traditions of industrial and commercial architecture, particularly those of the early Chicago school, with its steel-frame construction and Romanesque details. Drab and undistinguished on its exterior, the interior of the five-storey building opens into a light-flooded court, surrounded by series of iron balconies, galleries, and exposed lifts and stairs, framed in masonry. The expressive potential of this open, light-filled construction is seen even in the glass letter-chutes that run parallel to the lifts. Wyman's visionary concept was probably inspired by the imagery in Edward Bellamy's utopian novel *Looking Backward* (Boston, 1888), which describes a futuristic architecture, with one building referred to as 'a vast hall of light' surrounded by windows and capped by a glass dome. The Bradbury Building stands as a precursor of the utopian tradition of later architecture in Los Angeles. After receiving several commissions in the wake of the successful reception of the Bradbury Building, Wyman enrolled in a correspondence course in architecture, after which he lost interest in the use of light as a formal element. His later office buildings, most of which have been destroyed, were characterized by their weighty solidity, as were his frame buildings, for example the National Soldiers' Home (destr.) at Sawtell, CA.

BIBLIOGRAPHY
E. McCoy: 'The Bradbury Building', *A. & Archit.*, lxx/4 (1953), pp. 20, 42–3
'Blending the Past with the Present: A Hall of Light and Life', *AIA J.*, xlviii/5 (1967), pp. 66–9
W. Jordy: *American Buildings and Their Architects* (New York, 1972)
T. Hines: 'Origins and Innovations', *Archit. Rev.* [Boston], clxxxii/1090 (1987), pp. 73–9

Wynants, Jan. *See* WIJNANTS, JAN.

Wyndham. English family of patrons and collectors.

(1) Sir **Charles Wyndham**, 2nd Earl of Egremont (*b* London, 19 Aug 1710; *d* London, 21 Aug 1763). He was the son of Sir William Wyndham, 3rd Baronet, of Orchard Wyndham, Somerset, and Catherine, daughter of Charles Seymour, 6th Duke of Somerset (1662–1748), and the stepson of Lady Elizabeth Percy, heiress to the Percy estates. In 1740 he succeeded to his father's baronetcy and in 1750 inherited estates in Cumberland and Sussex, including Petworth House, from his maternal uncle, Algernon Seymour, 7th Duke of Somerset and 1st Earl of Egremont (1684–1750). In 1761 he was appointed Secretary of State with responsibility for foreign affairs. The celebrated group of portraits by van Dyck commissioned by Algernon Percy, 10th Earl of Northumberland (e.g. *Ann Carr, Countess of Bedford*, *c.* 1635–40; Petworth House, W. Sussex, NT; *see* PERCY, (2)), passed to him by descent, together with 17th-century Old Masters collected by his grandfather, the 6th Duke of Somerset. In 1751 he invited Lancelot 'Capability' Brown to survey and redesign the grounds at Petworth, replacing the early 18th-century formal gardens with a landscaped park and pleasure ground. He also commissioned Matthew Brettingham the elder to create a new state apartment (1754–6) at Petworth, comprising the present White and Gold Room and White Library. In the 1750s he added substantially to his inheritance by forming his own collection of mainly 17th-century Italian, Dutch, Flemish and French Old Masters (e.g. Sébastien Bourdon: *Selling of Joseph*, mid-17th century; Petworth House). His collection of antique Greek and Roman sculpture, mostly bought for him by Gavin Hamilton and Matthew Brettingham the younger, acting as his agents in Rome, included the Leconfield *Aphrodite* (4th century BC; Petworth House), which has been attributed to Praxiteles.

(2) Sir **George O'Brien Wyndham**, 3rd Earl of Egremont (*b* ?Petworth, W. Sussex, 18 Dec 1751; *d* Petworth, 11 Nov 1837). Son of (1) Charles Wyndham. He attended Westminster School, London, and Eton College, Berks, and entered Christ Church College, Oxford, in 1767. He inherited from his father estates in the south, north and west of England (and later in Ireland), most notably Petworth House, W. Sussex, with its fine collections of Old Master paintings, sculpture and furniture. In 1770 he went on the Grand Tour, visiting France, Germany, Austria and the Low Countries. He had the North Gallery at Petworth enlarged in the 1780s to accommodate his father's collection of Greek and Roman sculpture and further enlarged in 1823–4 for his own acquisitions of Neo-classical sculpture, which included works by John Flaxman (e.g. *St Michael Overcoming Satan*, 1819–26; *in situ*), Joseph Francis Nollekens and John Charles Felix Rossi. In 1794 he had the Carved Room extended and rearranged the carvings by Grinling Gibbons and John Selden (*fl* 1687–97), employing the carver Jonathan Ritson (*c.* 1780–1846) to create new elements.

The Earl took a keen interest in agrarian reform, but is best remembered as a benefactor of English artists. He not only bought and commissioned works but supported artists financially, inviting a great many, often with their families, to live and work at Petworth. The most famous among these was J. M. W. Turner. Joseph Farington III, a visitor to the house in 1798, described the grand yet bohemian lifestyle of its occupants, who included the Earl's numerous mistresses and illegitimate children, with painters and sculptors at work in the corridors and park and from 10 to 30 people assembling each evening for dinner. The Earl's patronage of Turner fell into two periods: between 1802 and 1812 and from 1825 until the Earl's death. Turner was given the Old Library as a studio and in over 100 watercolour sketches (London, Tate) recorded the park, the house and daily incidents in the life of the household. He also painted a number of large oils: in 1828 the Earl commissioned from Turner four large landscapes (*in situ*) for the Carved Room (e.g. *The Lake, Petworth: Sunset, Fighting Bucks, 1827–8*).

Among other artists who enjoyed Egremont's patronage were the sculptor John Edward Carew and the painters Thomas Phillips and Charles Robert Leslie, who visited Petworth every year from 1826 until 1837 and recorded many anecdotes concerning the Earl. The Earl also acquired works by William Hogarth, William Blake, Johann Heinrich Fuseli (e.g. *Macbeth and the Witches*; Petworth House), Bartolomé Esteban Murillo, Jacob Gerritsz. Cuyp, Jean-François Millet and the Le Nain brothers. Constable was also a guest at the house in September 1834 and filled a sketch book with his impressions (e.g. *Petworth House from Petworth Park*, pencil and watercolour, 1834; London, V&A). The painting *Fête at Petworth* (1836; Petworth House) by William Frederick Witherington (1785–1865) shows the 83-year-old Earl entertaining his estate workers and villagers to a feast in 1834 that fed some 6000 people at 54 long tables set up in the park. His funeral was attended by thousands of people, and Turner was among the pall-bearers.

BIBLIOGRAPHY
The Diary of Joseph Farington III (New Haven and London, 1979)
M. Egremont: 'The Third Earl of Egremont and his Friends', *Apollo*, cxxii (1985), pp. 280–87
The Treasure Houses of Britain: Five Hundred Years of Private Patronage and Art Collecting (exh. cat., ed. G. Jackson-Stops; Washington, DC, N.G.A., 1985)
M. Butlin, M. Luther and I. Warrell: *Turner at Petworth* (London, 1989)

Wynford [Wyndeforth; Wyneforde; Wynfort], **William** (*fl* 1360; *d* 1405). English architect. He was employed as warden of masons' work at Windsor Castle in 1360, under the direction of John de Sponlee (*fl* 1350–?86). In April 1361 he was promoted to joint 'disposer of the works', and in the same year he is referred to as Master. Only in

1365–6, however, the date at which the Great Gate and the royal lodgings in the upper ward were constructed, did he receive a full year's wages. In 1365 Wynford was appointed consultant architect of Wells Cathedral (see WELLS, §1(i)), where he remained until his death and executed his most influential projects. The south-west tower, built c. 1390, set the fashion for the spireless, square-topped towers of the parish churches of Somerset. By 1372 work at Windsor Castle was nearly complete and Wynford was free to develop his private practice. From 1379 he worked for WILLIAM OF WYKEHAM, Bishop of Winchester, on Wykeham's two academic institutions: New College, Oxford (begun 1379; see OXFORD, §3(i)), and Winchester College (begun 1387). Immediately following the completion of Winchester College in 1394 he worked on the nave of Winchester Cathedral (see WINCHESTER, §III, 1(ii)), the Anglo-Norman masonry of which was being recased with Perpendicular mouldings. The cresting of narrow vertical niches with cusped heads, evident in the triforium of Winchester Cathedral and at Wells in the parapets of the towers and the internal parapet of the west window, is characteristic of Wynford's work. A depiction of Wynford survives in the glazing of the east window of Winchester College chapel.

BIBLIOGRAPHY

Harvey

L. S. Colchester, ed.: *Wells Cathedral: A History* (Shepton Mallet, 1982)

Wyngaerde, Anthonis [Anton] **van den** [Vigne, Antoine de la; Viñas, Antonio de las] (b ?Antwerp, c. 1525; d Madrid, 1571). Flemish draughtsman, etcher and painter, active also in the northern Netherlands, Italy, France, England and Spain. Although few facts about his life are known, his movements can be reconstructed from his numerous topographical drawings, most of which are preserved in Vienna (Österreich, Nbib.; 53 drawings), Oxford (Ashmolean; 47 drawings), London (V&A; 31 drawings) and Antwerp (Plantin–Moretus Mus.; 23 drawings). He was apparently also active as a townscape painter, but none of his paintings is known. His earliest dated drawing is a *View of Dordrecht* (1544; Oxford). Also assigned to the mid-1540s is a panoramic *View of London* (Oxford), a drawing so large that, although previously kept rolled, it is now mounted as 14 separate sheets. In 1552–3 he was in Italy, where he made an elaborate etched *View of Genoa*, dated January 1553 (unique impression, Stockholm, Kun. Bib.) and probably drew views of Rome (e.g. four in Oxford; one in New York, Met.; one in Amsterdam, Rijksmus.) and Naples (Oxford). By 1557 he was in the service of Philip II of Spain; that same year he accompanied Spanish troops and recorded battles in their campaign against the French. The following year he was back in the southern Netherlands, where he made a view of *Brussels* (1558; Oxford), among the last of his dated drawings of Dutch and Flemish cities. (Undated Netherlandish views, of Sluis, Damme, Bruges, Utrecht, Amsterdam and 's Hertogenbosch, among others, were probably drawn before 1558.) Later the same year he was in England, where he remained until c. 1561, when he travelled to Spain. The finished and dated drawing of *Richmond Palace from the River* (1562; Oxford) was probably executed after

he had arrived in Spain, using an earlier sketch or sketches made on the spot (for it includes, in the distance, a view of the spire of St Paul's Cathedral, London, which was destroyed by fire in 1561).

Van den Wyngaerde's task in Spain was to make topographically accurate views of the most important Spanish cities and towns, part of an ambitious plan by Philip II to document the country. A written decree from the King dated 1570 requests that all local officials give the artist their full cooperation in carrying out his commission. Over 60 of these drawings have been preserved, representing more than 50 different locations in Spain—from Cádiz to Barcelona, Burgos to Valencia, Granada to Córdoba. Also included are views of smaller, less well-known towns, such as Chinchilla and Daroca, and depictions of ancient ruins (e.g. the amphitheatre near Molvedra). The earliest dated drawing is a *View of the Palacio de Valsaín* (1562; Vienna), an important historical document since it shows the King's country house near Segovia under construction (it was destr. by fire during the reign of Charles II). The drawings also provide an interesting record of the working methods of a topographical draughtsman. For the large, finished watercolours (often more than 1.5 m in length), van den Wyngaerde generally made three types of preliminary study: a sketch of the setting and/or surroundings of the city or town (a situation study); an overall view of the whole or most of the city; and detailed studies of individual buildings or groups of structures. Drawings in the last category were invariably drawn from life, while those in the first two groups may be sketched from nature or taken from other sources.

A subsequent plan by the Antwerp publisher Christoph Plantin to publish prints after van den Wyngaerde's Spanish views was abandoned for unknown reasons. In 1587 Plantin discussed the scheme in writing with his agent in Spain, a certain Joannes Moflin, who by then had the drawings in his possession, having presumably obtained them while in the service of the King as chaplain of the royal archers. At least 15 of the large, finished drawings by van den Wyngaerde were squared for transfer, and outline drawings for the printmaker were made after them. From this, it is known that the prints would have been nearly 600 mm wide, twice as large as those in the contemporary six-volume atlas by Georg Braun and Franz Hogenberg, the *Civitates orbis terrarum* (Cologne, 1572–1618). Had Plantin's comprehensive town atlas of the Iberian Peninsula been published, it would have been the most sophisticated, monumental and accurate publication of its kind.

UNPUBLISHED SOURCES

Oxford, Ashmolean [MS. of S. Booth: *A Checklist of the Drawings of Anthonis van den Wyngaerde in the Department of Western Art, Ashmolean Museum, Oxford* (1974)]

Rijksuniv. Utrecht, Ksthist. Inst. [MS. of E. K. J. Reznicek: *Antonie van den Wyngaerde* (1957)]

BIBLIOGRAPHY

W. Ruge: 'Älteres kartographisches Material in deutschen Bibliotheken', *Nachrbl. Ges. Wiss. Göttingen, Philos. Hist. Kl.* (1906), p. 36, nos 53 and 54; (1911), p. 128, nos 74 and 76 [on van den Wyngaerde's etchings]

I. Collijn: 'Magnus Gabriel de la Gardie's samling of äldre stadsvyer och historiska planscher i Kungl. biblioteket', *Kun. Bib. Hand.*, xxxv (1912), p. 20, no. 64 [etched *View of Genoa*]

A. E. d'Ailly: 'Een tot heden onbekend gebleven plattegrond van Amsterdam uit de 16de eeuw', *Amstelodamum*, xxviii (1930), pp. 67–8; suppl., xxx (1933), pp. 79–87; both articles repr. in abbreviated form in *Gulden Passer*, n. s., xiii (1935), pp. 104–18

H. Egger: *Römische Veduten*, ii (Berlin, 1931)

B. van't Hoff: 'Une Vue panoramique inconnue de Bruxelles dessinée par Anthonis van den Wyngaerde', *An. Soc. Royale Archéol. Bruxelles*, xlviii (1948–55), pp. 146–50

——: *Het 'Stads-gezicht van Dordrecht' getekend door Anthonis van den Wyngaerde* ([The Hague], 1957)

E. Haverkamp-Begemann: 'The Spanish Views of Anton van den Wyngaerde', *Master Drgs*, vii/4 (1969), pp. 375–99

R. L. Kagan, ed.: *Ciudades del siglo de oro: Las vistas españolas de Anton van den Wyngaerde* (Madrid, 1986) [incl. rev. version of Haverkamp-Begemann, 1969]

J. Shoaf Turner: *Catalogue of the Northern Drawings in the Ashmolean Museum, Oxford* (in preparation)

JANE SHOAF TURNER

Wynnstay, 4th Baronet of. *See* WILLIAMS-WYNN, WATKIN.

Wyon. English family of medallists and sculptors. Thomas Wyon (i) (1767–1830) was Chief Engraver of His Majesty's Seals; his elder son, Thomas Wyon (ii) (1792–1817), was Chief Engraver at the Royal Mint. The latter's cousin and the most important artist of the family, William Wyon (1795–1851), expected to succeed him at the Mint in 1817, but instead the position went to Benedetto Pistrucci. However, from 1822, when Pistrucci refused to use Francis Chantrey's bust of *George IV* as a basis for the coinage, Wyon, as Second Engraver, assumed responsibility for the coinage and became *de facto* Chief Engraver.

The accurate, clear portraits, the quality of design and the technically perfect engraving of Wyon's work make him the definitive medallist of 19th-century England. His portraits of Queen Victoria were used on all British coinage until 1887 and for all postage stamps until 1902. Medallic design, however, provided Wyon with greater opportunity for artistic creativity. His lifelong admiration for John Flaxman is reflected in the *Newcastle to Carlisle Railway* medal (1840; *see* MEDAL, fig. 6), the Neo-classical reverse of which is derived from Flaxman's *Mercury and Pandora*. Designs of Wyon's own invention are the *Royal Humane Society* medal reverse (undated), in which the foreground group of two sailors comforting a dying cabin-boy exhibits Neo-classical nudity and sentiment that contrast convincingly with the Victorian melodramatics of the distant, bowler-hatted rescuers. The *St George and the Dragon* reverse for the *Prince Albert* medal (1844–5) consciously competes with Pistrucci's earlier coinage reverse of the same theme.

William Wyon's eminence was recognized by his election as ARA in 1831 and RA in 1838; he was the first medallist to be thus honoured. His stylistic fusion of Neo-classicism and realism was carried on by his son, Leonard Charles Wyon (1826–91), his cousin, the younger son of Thomas (i), Benjamin Wyon (1802–58), and Benjamin's sons Joseph Shepard Wyon (1836–73), Alfred Benjamin Wyon (1837–84) and Allan Wyon (1843–1907), all of whom were talented, if less original, medallists. Another cousin, the sculptor Edward William Wyon (1811–85), regularly exhibited at the Royal Academy between 1831 and 1876.

BIBLIOGRAPHY

Forrer

M. Jones: *The Art of the Medal* (London, 1979), pp. 105–9

——: 'The Life and Work of William Wyon', *La medaglia neoclassica in Italia e in Europa* (1981), pp. 119–40

MARK STOCKER

Wyrsch [Würsch], **Johann Melchior** (*b* Buochs, 21 Aug 1732; *d* Buochs, 9 Sept 1798). Swiss painter. After his apprenticeship (1745–8) with Johann Suter (1705–82) in Lucerne, he found employment with Franz Anton Kraus, a pupil of Piazzetta's working in Einsiedeln. In 1753 Wyrsch moved to Rome, where he studied with Gaetano Lapis and at the Académie Française, making friends with Luc-François Breton, a sculptor from Besançon. He returned to Switzerland in 1755, to paint portraits and pictures for churches. In Solothurn from 1765, he moved in 1768 to Besançon, where he founded a school of painting and sculpture with Breton. He was sought after by the Franche-Comté nobility as a portrait painter; he also wrote two publications, on the theory of portrait painting and on anatomy. He returned to Switzerland in 1784 and opened a school of drawing in Lucerne that he was obliged to give up in 1788 because of total blindness. Wyrsch went back to Buochs, where he was shot by a French soldier during the invasion of 1798; his house was set on fire, and much of his work destroyed. Among his extant paintings are *Landvogt Carl Manuel* (1785; Berne, Hist. Mus.) and *Victor Remigi Stulz* (1756; Stans, Nidwald. Mus.).

Wyrsch managed to combine the French finesse of Hyacinthe Rigaud and Nicolas de Largillierre with a Swiss matter-of-factness in his portrait painting. His sitters are less important historically than those of his contemporary, Anton Graff from Winterthur; but, like Graff, Wyrsch neither flattered nor caricatured.

WRITINGS

Folgende Anleitung zu der Proportion des menschlichen Leibs . . . (1776; Zug, Pfarrarchiv and Nidwalden, Hist. Ver.)

Gründliche auf eigene praktische Anwendung gestützte Abhandlung . . . (Rapperswil, 1834)

SKL

BIBLIOGRAPHY

P. Fischer: *Der Maler Johann Melchior Wyrsch von Buochs* (Zurich, 1938)

FRANZ ZELGER

Wyspiański, Stanisław (*b* Kraków, 15 Jan 1869; *d* Kraków, 28 Nov 1907). Polish painter, pastellist, decorative artist, illustrator, writer and theatre director. He was the son of the Kraków sculptor Franciszek Wyspiański (1836–1902) and studied at the Kraków School of Fine Arts, mostly under Władysław Łuszczkiewicz (1828–1900) and Jan Matejko. In 1889 Wyspiański and Józef Mehoffer, the school's most talented students, were appointed to complete Matejko's painted decorations for St Mary, Kraków, a task that prompted Wyspiański's interest in both decorative painting and stained glass. In 1890 he travelled in Italy, Switzerland, France and Germany, and also to Prague. In 1891 he continued his training in Paris, where he remained with intervals until 1894, studying at the Académie Colarossi under Joseph Blanc, Gustave Courtois (1852–1924) and Louis Auguste Girardot (*b* 1858). Wyspiański also worked independently in Paris, studying paintings in the museums and fascinated by

Stanisław Wyspiański: *Self-portrait*, pastel on paper, 380×380 mm, 1902 (Warsaw, National Museum)

contemporary art. Through Władysław Ślewiński, he met Paul Gauguin and members of the Nabis.

Wyspiański's talent and versatility emerged during his Paris period when he was engaged in a number of tasks linked with large-scale decoration: designs for stained-glass windows for St Mary, Kraków (with Mehoffer, 1890–91; executed later), a design for painted decoration (1891; not executed) for the Rudolfinum in Prague, and a design (1892–4; Kraków, N. Mus.; not executed) for a stained-glass window showing the *Wedding of King John Kasimir* for the cathedral in Lemberg (now L'viv, Ukraine). This last design reveals the main characteristics of Wyspiański's approach to decorative art: visionary, dramatic, expressive and formally innovative. He took up Matejko's own programme, treating aspects of Poland's past that were of significance to the present. In Paris, Wyspiański developed an allergy to oil paint and started working in pastel; he continued to work in this medium for the rest of his life. On his return from Paris, he settled in Kraków. In 1895–6, he carried out painted decoration in the presbytery of the Franciscan Church in Kraków, and he subsequently designed stained-glass windows for the same location: the *Four Elements*, the *Blessed Salomea*, *St Francis* and *God the Father* (1897–1902; *in situ*). These windows, Wyspiański's only fully realized large-scale work, are remarkable for their intensity of expression and wealth of floral ornament. In 1900–02, he created his most powerful decorative work in the cartoons for the stained-glass windows of Wawel Cathedral in Kraków representing giant skeletal figures of the historic Polish heroes *King Kasimir the Great*, *St Stanislaus* and *Henry the Pious, Prince of Kraków* (all Kraków, N. Mus.).

In his non-applied works, the most personal aspect of his work, Wyspiański's style is characterized by the use of highly expressive line, varying in thickness but always dynamic, and by flat splashes of colour to add intensity or establish nuance in atmosphere and expression. His main subjects were childhood, motherhood and the character of outstanding men and women among his contemporaries. His portraits of children (often his own) have a marked psychological intensity and a melancholy sense of transience: for example *Boy with a Flower* (1893), *Girl with Violets* (1896; both Warsaw, N. Mus.), *Sleeping Child* (1902; Poznań, N. Mus.) and *Girl with a Jug* (1902; Kraków, N. Mus.). He often presented motherhood in the image of his peasant wife Teofila and their children, for example in *Motherhood* (1902; Warsaw, N. Mus.). In his portraits of figures from the cultural life of Kraków, he concentrated on individual expression, as in his portrait of the musician *Henryk Opieński* (1898; Szczecin, N. Mus.) or that of the poet and art critic *Antoni Lange* (1899; Kraków, N. Mus.). Wyspiański's self-portraits are among his most striking works, for example that set against a background of stylized flowers (1902; Warsaw, N. Mus.; see fig.) or the *Self-portrait with Wife* (1904; Kraków, N. Mus.). His landscapes often border on Symbolism, notably in the series of *Views of the Kościuszko Mound from the Studio Window* (1904–5; Kraków and Warsaw, N. Mus., and Bytom, Mus. Upper Silesia).

Wyspiański was also active as a book illustrator. In 1896 he produced drawings for a Polish edition of the *Iliad*. He strove to bring new life to Polish book design, enriching it with elements of Art Nouveau assimilated during his stay in Paris. He put his new typographic concepts into practice in 1898–9 in the weekly magazine *Życie*, for which he acted as artistic director under the editorship of Stanisław Przybyszewski, and later in editions of his own plays and of other authors' works. Anxious to carry a concern with the visual arts beyond easel painting, he became one of the moving forces behind a programme for applied art in Poland. In 1904 he designed an exhibition room for Sztuka, the society of Polish artists founded in 1897; in 1905 he designed interiors for the Society of Physicians in Kraków (*see* POLAND, fig. 24; designs in Kraków, N. Mus.); he also designed furniture and fabrics. In 1904–5, in connection with the planned restoration of the castle and the entire Wawel complex in Kraków, he devised a plan for the reconstruction of the buildings on Wawel Hill, in which he drew on the forms of older architecture, notably that of ancient Greece. In 1902 he became professor of decorative painting at the Kraków Academy of Fine Arts.

Most of Wyspiański's output as a writer comes from the last decade of his life. For his plays, among the foremost achievements of Polish drama, he designed the sets and costumes and put his innovative staging concepts into practice, notably in his production of *Bolesław Śmiały* ('Boleslaus the Bold') in 1903. He was among the foremost European theatre reformers of the turn of the century.

BIBLIOGRAPHY

S. Przybyszewski, T. Żuk-Skarszewski and S. Świerz: *Stanisław Wyspiański: Dzieła malarskie* [Stanisław Wyspiański: paintings] (Bydgoszcz, 1925)

T. Makowiecki: *Poeta-Malarz: Studium o Stanisławie Wyspiańskim* [Poet–painter: a study of Stanisław Wyspiański] (Warsaw, 1935)

Stanisław Wyspiański: Wystawa jubileuszowa [Stanisław Wyspiański: anniversary exhibition] (exh. cat., intro. H. Blumówna; Kraków, N. Mus., 1958)

H. Blumówna: *Stanisław Wyspiański* (Warsaw, 1969)

T. Żeleński: *O Wyspiańskim* [On Wyspiański]; ed. S. W. Balicki (Kraków, 1973)

Polnische Malerei von 1830 bis 1914 (exh. cat., ed. J. C. Jensen; Kiel, Christian-Albrechts-U., Ksthalle; Stuttgart, Württemberg. Kstver.; Wuppertal, von der Heydt-Mus.; 1978–9)

Z. Kępiński: *Stanisław Wyspiański* (Warsaw, 1984)

Symbolism in Polish Painting, 1890–1914 (exh. cat., ed. A. Morawińska; Detroit, MI, Inst. A., 1984)

LIJA SKALSKA-MIECIK

X

Xanten. German town in North Rhine–Westphalia. It was the site of a Roman garrison and the town of Colonia Ulpia Traiana, and takes its name (Lat.: ad Sanctos) from the martyrs' tomb of *c.* AD 361–3, now underlying the collegiate church of St Victor (*see* §1 below); parts of the stone amphitheatre (2nd century AD) survive. The town prospered during the Middle Ages and the centre still retains its medieval plan and numerous medieval houses. Parts of the old enceinte also stand, including the twin-towered, double Klever Tor, dating from the 14th century. In the 12th century and later Xanten was culturally linked to Cologne, and objects in the treasury of St Viktor, including the reliquary shrine (1130) and the portable altar (*c.* 1175–80), are products of workshops on the Lower Rhine. A number of fine buildings in the town date from the 17th and 18th centuries. ☐

1. COLLEGIATE CHURCH. The church, dedicated to St Victor and his Companions, was traditionally founded by St Helen (*d c.* AD 330), and between the 4th and 12th centuries successive buildings arose over the martyr's tomb. The importance of Xanten, the archdeaconry for the northern part of the old archdiocese of Cologne, is testified by the cathedral-like dimensions of the present church, which has a fine treasury, furnishings, library and collegiate buildings.

The present building was founded under Provost Friedrich von Hochstaden in 1263 (see fig.). At the west end is all that remains of its Romanesque predecessor, the west choir built *c.* 1180–90 by a Master Bertholdus: a block similar to those of St Jacques, Liège, and St Servatius, Maastricht, with a two-storey interior articulated by niches and a continuous gallery, related to the west choir of St Georg, Cologne. The twin towers were heightened in the 13th century.

The Gothic church, which is 70 m long and built of tufa and trachyte, is a five-aisled, transeptless basilica of eight straight bays and a choir with a plan of angled apses in echelon, similar to those of St Yved at Braine (*c.* 1195) and the Liebfrauenkirche at Trier (from 1235). A Master Jacob is mentioned at the church in the early 14th century (*see* JACOB (i)), but his role in the building is not clear. From 1356 the building accounts are continuous until the completion of the church in 1550. The phases of construction can, however, be distinguished stylistically. The first, to 1437, comprised work as far west as the rood screen (rest. 1816 by Karl Friedrich Schinkel) at the junction of

Xanten, collegiate church, interior looking east, begun 1263

the fourth and fifth bays; the elevation and sculpture show some links with the Champagne region of France, which is close to Braine. The later phase, from 1483, more closely resembles buildings in Cologne and the Low Countries, with net vaults instead of the earlier quadripartite vaulting. The south portal was begun in 1490 by the Cologne sculptor Johann von Langenberg (*d* 1522).

Traces of grey paint lined-out with white survive on the exterior, and the interior decoration, stained glass and paintings on the nave piers were carried out as construction progressed. The choir-stalls of *c.* 1228 predate the present building, and there are Late Gothic tapestries. From 1529 to 1534 Bartholomäus Bruyn I painted for the high altar a cycle of paintings comprising the *Lives of SS Victor and Helen* and scenes from the *Life of Christ*. The general design of the Lady altar of *c.* 1530–40 goes back to Henrik Douverman, who also executed the *Tree of Jesse* on the predella. The altar was completed by Henrik van Holt and Arnt van Tricht (two reliefs). The church has been restored following its destruction by bombing in 1945.

BIBLIOGRAPHY

W. Bader, ed.: *Sechzehnhundert Jahre Xantener Dom*, Xantner Domblätter, 6 (Cologne, 1963)

G. de Werd: 'De Kalkarse beeldhouwer Arnt van Tricht', *Bull. Rijksmus.*, xxi (1973), pp. 63–90

H. E. Kubach and A. Verbeek: *Romanische Baukunst an Rhein und Maas*, ii (Berlin, 1976), pp. 1264–75 [with bibliog.]

H. P. Hilger: *Der Dom zu Xanten* (Köningstein im Taunus, 1984) [with bibliog.]

C. Bridger and F. Siegmund: 'Die Xantener Stiftsimmunität: Grabungsgeschichte und Überlegungen zur Siedlungstopographie', *Beiträge zur Archäologie des Rheinlandes*, Rheinische Ausgrabungen, 27 (Düsseldorf, 1987), pp. 63–133

G. de Werd: 'Ein Meister im Schatten Henrik Douvermans: Zum Werk des Kalkarer Bildhauers Henrik van Holt', in H. P. Hilger: *Stadtpfarrkirche St Nicolai in Kalkar* (Kleve, 1990), pp. 306–13

HANS PETER HILGER

Xanthos. Site in south-west Turkey, once the principal city of ancient Lycia. Xanthos flourished from the 7th century BC to Byzantine times, and its ruins occupy an impressive situation on a steep cliff above the River Xanthos near the modern village of Kınık. Inside the ancient city walls the two main areas are the Lycian acropolis and above this the later, Roman acropolis. Exploration of the site began in the mid-19th century after its rediscovery by the English traveller and archaeologist Sir Charles Fellows (1799–1860). Many of the important remains are in the British Museum, London.

1. ARCHITECTURE. Until the Macedonian conquest in 334 BC the architecture of Xanthos and the nearby Sanctuary of Leto (Letoön) demonstrated three main influences: Lycian or Anatolian, Persian and Greek. Though the first generally appeared before the others, they do not represent distinct chronological phases. From the end of the 4th century BC, however, the architecture of Xanthos and the Letoön conformed to the general evolution of the Hellenistic, Roman, then Byzantine Near East.

Funerary architecture was largely dependent on Lycian and Anatolian models. One form of monument consisted of tall monolithic pillars surmounted by a rectangular sarcophagus with either a stepped or a curved lid terminated by ogival gables. Such tombs include the Lion Tomb, which probably dates from the period of Lycian independence before the Persian invasion of the 540s BC, the Harpy Tomb (*c.* 480 BC) and the Inscribed Pillar ('Stele of Xanthos'; *c.* 425–*c.* 400 BC) carved on its four faces with two great inscriptions in Lycian and a twelve-line passage of Greek verse. The last supported a carved sarcophagus bearing the effigy of the dynast. Another form of monument is represented by the stone sarcophagi in a necropolis outside the walls. Some, such as the Sarcophagus of Merehi (4th century BC), imitate a type of wooden house with a flat roof resting on logs, examples of which can still be found. Others, such as the Tomb of Payava just inside the walls (4th century BC; base *in situ*, rest of tomb in London, BM) or the Sarcophagus of the Dancers (late 4th century BC), have a convex lid above a rectangular sarcophagus. Finally, there are numerous rock-cut tombs of Anatolian inspiration. The façades of the oldest tombs were copied from wooden structures, but 4th-century BC and later façades show the influence of the Ionic order.

Two buildings from the period of Persian occupation are particularly significant. The earlier, Building G (*c.* 460 BC), stood in the centre of a monumental terrace on the Lycian acropolis, with edges adorned by female

Xanthos, Nereid Monument, *c.* 425–*c.* 400 BC, reassembled in the British Museum, London

statues. It measured 6.40×4.26 m and was modelled on a flat-roofed wooden structure with two superimposed chambers, the higher of which was decorated with external and internal friezes. This building anticipated the famous Nereid Monument (*c.* 425–*c.* 400 BC; see fig.), which has been reassembled in the British Museum, London. This stood at the southern edge of a hill, again at the centre of a terrace, facing the Lycian acropolis. Its base had lower courses of limestone and upper ones of marble, crowned by two courses of ovolos. Instead of the earlier imitations of wooden houses, it was surmounted by a small Ionic temple. In the intercolumniations were female statues, possibly representing nereids (sea nymphs), which recall the figures surrounding the terrace of Building G.

Except for a theatre, which was altered in Roman times, and large sections of the rampart, few Hellenistic remains are visible at Xanthos itself. The excavation of the Letoön, however, has revealed several Hellenistic structures, notably three temples on the rocky central platform, stoas lining the sanctuary on the north and west, and a propylon. The most important temple, dedicated to Leto, was an Ionic building measuring 30.25×15.70 m with a deep pronaos and a false opisthodomos. A small 5th-century BC Lycian temple was enclosed by its cella. A second (Doric) temple of similar dimensions stood further east and again enclosed a small Lycian edifice. The monumental nymphaeum, consisting essentially of two ranges of buildings separated by a pool, is the most remarkable Roman building at the Letoön. The east range dates from the Republican period, the west from the 2nd century AD. It comprises a slightly curved portico (27×4 m) and a large rectangular chamber (12.55×10.50 m) flanked by semicircular exedrae. The most notable Early Christian and even middle Byzantine building at Xanthos is a large basilica with a monumental entrance leading into an atrium surrounded by three stoas. The eastern stoa took the place of a narthex and gave access to the aisled nave of the basilica via three doors. The nave communicated with the sanctuary via three further passages. The nave and aisles were decorated with geometric pavements.

2. SCULPTURE. The sculpture from Xanthos essentially consists of monumental funerary works, mostly associated with the main architectural tombs (*see* §1 above) and nearly all now in the British Museum, London. Archaic sculpture includes the sarcophagus that surmounted the Lion Tomb. This is decorated on its north and south faces with a couchant lion and lioness in high relief, and on its east and west faces with figures of a foot soldier, a cavalryman and a man fighting a lion, all of which are of Archaic Lycian type. The later Harpy Tomb (*see* LYCIA) bears four scenes in relief executed in East Greek style. On the north and south faces are audience scenes, each framed by bird-like creatures with women's heads. These bear small female figures representing the souls of the dead. On the east and west faces are scenes of people bearing offerings. Building G on the Lycian acropolis crowned the terrace on which it stood with a frieze of satyrs and beasts. This too is in East Greek style. The terrace itself carried a series of female figures at intervals. At the base of the building ran a frieze of cockerels and chickens and probably placed halfway up at the level of the principal room were friezes depicting a procession of dynasts on the exterior and a banqueting scene on the interior. The Nereid Monument includes four friezes. Two of these are at the top of the podium: the lower frieze represents a series of armed encounters between Greeks and Barbarians; the upper frieze depicts successive episodes from the siege of a city. On the architrave is a third frieze on which figures bearing tribute, a boar hunt and battle scenes can be identified. The fourth frieze surrounds the top of the cella walls and comprises scenes of banqueting and sacrifice. The pediment also has sculpted decoration, and the building is crowned with acroteria representing abduction scenes. The base of the Tomb of Payava carries a large battle scene on one face and an audience scene on the other. The figure of a warrior mounting or dismounting his chariot occurs twice on the convex faces of the lid. The gabled ends of the Sarcophagus of the Dancers bear figures of *kalathiskos* dancers (i.e. carrying flared baskets or crowns), a subject that often occurs in sculpture of the second half of the 5th century BC in northern and eastern Greece. The lid carries battle and hunting scenes.

At the Letoön about 14 statues (Antalya, Archaeol. Mus.), some colossal, had apparently been destroyed and buried between the faces of the rear walls of a Roman stoa. They date from the 2nd century BC and are the only Hellenistic works among the sculptures so far found in southern Anatolia, which otherwise all date from Imperial Roman times.

BIBLIOGRAPHY

F. N. Pryce: *Prehellenic and Early Greek* (1928), I/i of *Catalogue of Sculpture in the British Museum* (London, 1928–), pp. 117–48

P. Demargne: *Les Piliers funéraires* (1958), i of *Fouilles de Xanthos* (Paris, 1958–)

H. Metzger: *L'Acropole lycienne* (1963), ii of *Fouilles de Xanthos* (Paris, 1958–)

P. Coupel and P. Demargne: *Le Monument des Néréides* (1969), iii of *Fouilles de Xanthos* (Paris, 1958–)

H. Metzger: *Anatolie*, ii (Geneva, 1969), pp. 61–78, 108–48

P. Demargne and E. Laroche: *Tombes-maisons, tombes rupestres et sarcophages* (1974), v of *Fouilles de Xanthos* (Paris, 1958–)

P. Demargne and W. P. Childs: *Le Monument des Néréides: Le Décor sculpté* (1989), viii of *Fouilles de Xanthos* (Paris, 1958–)

H. Metzger and others: *La Région nord du Letôon, les sculptures, les inscriptions gréco-lyciennes* (1992), ix of *Fouilles de Xanthos* (Paris, 1958–)

HENRI METZGER

Xavery [Saveri; Savery], **Jan Baptist** (*b* Antwerp, 30 March 1697; *d* The Hague, 19 July 1742). Flemish sculptor. He was the son of the Antwerp sculptor Albertus Xavery (1664–1728), who was probably his first teacher. Xavery entered the studio of Michiel van der Voort I, where he remained until moving in 1719 to Vienna, from where he travelled to Italy. He returned in 1721 and settled in The Hague, where, in 1725, he became a member of the Confrerie Pictura, the painters' guild. In the same year he married Maria Christina Robart, and the couple had two sons: the painter Frans Xavery, who became a master in 1768, and the painter Jacob Xavery IV (1736–after 1779). In 1729 Jan Baptist Xavery became Court Sculptor to Prince William IV of Orange Nassau. In the early years of his career Xavery was strongly influenced by Jacob Marot, as may be seen in his portrait of *Prince William IV* (marble, 1733; The Hague, Mauritshuis), which is fluently sculpted and sparsely embellished. Later, Xavery's style became more elaborate, as may be seen in the *Allegory of Faith* (1735; Haarlem, Grotekerk). It would seem that Xavery also worked briefly in Kassel *c.* 1737 for Frederick I, Landgrave of Hesse-Kassel (*reg* 1730–51). It is probable that he was related to the sculptor Pieter Xavery.

See also NETHERLANDS, THE, §§IV, 3 and X, 1.

BIBLIOGRAPHY

Thieme–Becker; Wurzbach

J. Immerzeel: *De levens en werken der Hollandische en Vlaamsche kunststschilders, beeldhouwers, graveurs en bouwmeesters* [The lives and works of the Dutch and Flemish painters, sculptors, engravers and architects] (Amsterdam, 1843), iii, pp. 254–5

M. D. Ozinga: 'Jan Baptist Xavery als decoratief-architectonische ontwerper' [Jan Baptist Xavery as a decorative and architectural designer], *Miscellanea I. Q. van Regteren-Altena* (Amsterdam, 1969), pp. 166–73

L. J. Van der Klooster: 'Jan Baptist Xavery (1697–1742): Documentatie over enkele van zijn werken' [Jan Baptist Xavery (1697–1742): documents concerning some of his work], *Ned. Ksthist. Woordbk.*, xxi (1970), pp. 99–138

IRIS KOCKELBERGH

Xavery, Pieter (*b* Antwerp, *c.* 1647; *d* ?Antwerp, after 1674). Flemish sculptor. He left Antwerp in 1670 for Leiden, where he enrolled as a student of mathematics at the university. He may have been a colleague of Rombout Verhulst. However, Xavery's work shows a greater inclination towards genre and picturesque caricature than Verhulst's. This is particularly marked in his exuberant, small terracotta figures with their oversized heads and prominent facial features, such as *Two Laughing Jesters*, *Lady with a Lapdog*, *Two Madmen* and *Lady Portrayed as Flora* (all 1673; Amsterdam, Rijksmus., all signed). Small-scale works in other media include his signed and dated ivory *Adam and Eve* (1671; Amsterdam, Rijksmus.) and his bronze *Peasant Boy and Girl* (both *c.* 1675; Amsterdam, Rijksmus.). His terracotta relief of the *Flagellation of Christ* (1667; Bruges, Gruuthusemus.) is a rare example of a religious subject. Xavery also worked on some monumental works, including stone figures for the pediment and gable decoration (*c.* 1671–2) of the Gravensteen, Leiden, the pediment sculpture (1673) for the house of the 'Vergulde Turk' on the Breestraat and a group of 23 figures of lawyers and judges for the Vierschaar (all *in situ*). He remained active in Leiden until 1674, after which there is no record of his activity.

BIBLIOGRAPHY
A. Staring: 'De beeldhouwer Pieter Xavery', *Oud-Holland*, xliv (1927), pp. 1–15
E. Pelinck: 'Nieuws over den beeldhouwer Pieter Xavery', *Oud-Holland*, lix (1942), pp. 102–9
E. Neurdenberg: *De zeventiende eeuwsche beeldhouwkunst in de noordelijke Nederlanden* [17th-century sculpture in the northern Netherlands] (Amsterdam, 1948), pp. 242–5
M. Vandenven: 'Pieter Xavery', *De beeldhouwkunst in de eeuw van Rubens* [Sculpture in the century of Rubens] (Brussels, 1977), pp. 294–6

CYNTHIA LAWRENCE

Xega, Spiro (*b* Opar, Korçë, 1863; *d* Korçë, 26 March 1953). Albanian painter. In his youth he worked for several years as an apprentice in an icon workshop in Istanbul. He later returned to Korçë, where he opened his own atelier. Under the influence of contemporary progressive ideas he abandoned religious painting and embraced the patriotic subject-matter connected with the Albanian national renaissance. He was self-taught as an easel painter and concentrated on portraits and group compositions. Such paintings as the *Unit of Shahin Matraku* (1930; Tiranë, A.G.) and *Skanderbeg* (1931; Tiranë, A.G.) portray the heroism of the people from a naive and romantic viewpoint and show Xega's passion for the details of traditional costume and the influence of local colouration on his palette.

BIBLIOGRAPHY
D. Dhamo: 'Scanderbeg dans nos beaux-arts', *Studia Albanica*, 2 (1967), pp. 107–16
Artet figurative Shqiptare [Albanian figurative art] (Tiranë, 1978), pls 7, 8

SULEJMAN DASHI

Xell, Georg. *See* GSELL, GEORG.

Xenokrates (*fl* Athens, *c.* 280 BC). Greek sculptor and writer. Though none of his work has survived, three statue bases signed by a Xenokrates and dating from the early 3rd century BC are extant. According to Pliny (*Natural History* XXXIV.lvxxxiii) he was a pupil either of Euthykrates, the son of Lysippos, or of Teisikrates, the pupil of Euthykrates (thus closely associated with the Sikyonian school of sculpture headed by Lysippos; *see* GREECE, ANCIENT, §IV, 2(iv)), and he 'surpassed them both in the number of his statues, and wrote volumes about his art'. In the only other mention of Xenokrates in the text of the *Natural History* (he is also cited in the index to book XXXIV as having written a treatise on the working of sculpture in metal) Pliny named him, along with Antigonos of Karystos, as the source for the observation that the painter Parrhasios was a master draughtsman (XXXV.lxviii). In fact, Pliny's whole discussion of the

history of sculpture and painting is generally regarded as having been heavily influenced by Xenokrates. In this system, both arts gradually evolved towards perfection as each succeeding artist added something new, such as proportion or the rendering of certain details. In both cases the sequence culminated in a great master of the Sikyonian school, Lysippos in sculpture and Apelles in painting. Perhaps because he was a practising sculptor himself, Xenokrates seems to have used formal and technical criteria, rather than a work's subject-matter or moral effect, to evaluate artistic achievement. Numerous references to the history of painting and sculpture in writers other than Pliny are thought to derive from Xenokrates' accounts: he was the art critic best known to the Romans of the late Republic, whose taste he greatly influenced.

BIBLIOGRAPHY
K. Jex-Blake and E. Sellers: *The Elder Pliny's Chapters on the History of Art* (London, 1896/*R* Chicago, 1976), pp. xvi–xxxvi
B. Schweitzer: 'Xenokrates von Athen', *Schr. Königsberg. Gelehrten Ges.: Geistwiss. Klasse*, ix (1932), pp. 1–52

□

Xenophon (*b* Athens, *c.* 428/427 BC; *d* ?Athens, *c.* 354 BC). Greek general, historian and writer. From a wealthy Athenian family, he became an enthusiastic follower of Socrates. Shortly before Socrates' death, he left Athens. He served as a general under Cyrus in Asia Minor and later accepted the patronage of Sparta, where he settled and wrote most of his major works. His writings include histories (*Hellenica, Anabasis*) and narratives of Socrates' philosophical activity (*Memorabilia, Apology, Oeconomicus, Symposium*).

Xenophon's *Memorabilia*, written some time between 370 and 354 BC, includes two dialogues (III.x.1–8) between Socrates and contemporary artists. The historical status of the two conversations is unclear, but since Xenophon's aim was to show that Socrates had made new beneficial contributions to the city, it may be assumed that the ideas expressed in the dialogues would have been found both correct and novel by Xenophon's audience. In the first, Socrates asks the painter Parrhasios how he uses colour to represent (*ekmimeisthai*) visible objects and suggests that it is not by taking a single model, but by combining features from objects of many sorts. He then asks whether Parrhasios can represent the characteristics of the soul that 'most strongly inspire longing and desire'. Parrhasios is puzzled and wonders how something that has no colour or shape can be depicted. Socrates instructs him that the soul can be represented through facial expression and bodily gesture, which are signs of it. They agree that only a good soul gives pleasure to the beholder. In the other dialogue Socrates addresses the sculptor Kleiton and asks him how he makes his statues of athletes look so alive. Kleiton does not know. Socrates tells him that it is by rendering the different parts of the body as they appear under the strain of motion. He then directs Kleiton's attention to the soul, saying that the beholder's pleasure will be heightened if careful modelling of facial features reveals the inner feelings of the type of person represented.

These conversations show three important aspects of Greek popular thought about art in this period. First, artistic *mimesis* was not understood as an exact copying of individuals; its concern was with general types, the aim being to convey the general impression of the type. Second, there was a strong and apparently new interest in the depiction of inner states through the treatment of facial expression and posture. Third, the passage displays the pervasively ethical character of Greek aesthetic thought: it was quickly agreed that only the representation of good people could yield pleasure.

WRITINGS
Memorabilia, ed. E. Marchant, Loeb Class. Lib. (London and New York, 1923)

BIBLIOGRAPHY
G. Sörbom: *Mimesis and Art* (Uppsala, 1966), pp. 78–99 [trans. and analysis of *Memorabilia* III.x.1–8]

MARTHA C. NUSSBAUM

Xerography (i). *See* ELECTROGRAPHY.

Xerography (ii). *See under* PHOTOGRAPHY, §I.

Xia [Hsia] dynasty. Traditional but unverified first Chinese dynasty, supposed to date from the early 2nd millennium BC and to precede the SHANG DYNASTY (*c.* 1600–1050 BC). The Xia dynasty is said to have lasted about 439 years, beginning with the ruler Yu and ending with the degenerate Jie. Arguments about Xia culture generally stem from Zhou period (*c.* 1050–256 BC) texts, in which the Xia are described as having controlled an area in the middle Yellow River valley; some scholars contend that these texts are euhemerized histories. There are no contemporary writings corresponding to the Shang oracle bones (*see* CHINA, §IV, 2(i)), nor have discoveries identified a corresponding archaeologically defined culture. The Xia's supposed dates cover the early part of the bronze-producing ERLITOU culture that existed in Henan Province, and the site of Erlitou in Yanshi County, Henan Province, may be Xia. Erlitou ceramics seem to have evolved from LONGSHAN culture pottery; there are grey earthenwares of natural clay or sand, black wares and red, white and brownish wares, some possibly prototypes of later Shang bronze shapes. Erlitou bronze ritual vessels (*see* CHINA, fig. 146) are particularly striking and were cast in pottery moulds. In the Erlitou tombs were bronze ritual vessels, ornaments and many jades.

BIBLIOGRAPHY
H. Maspero: *La Chine antique* (Paris, 1927); Eng. trans. by F. Kierman as *China in Antiquity* (Boston, 1978)
J. Rawson: *Ancient China: Art and Archaeology* (London, 1980)
D. Keightley, ed.: *The Origins of Chinese Civilization* (Berkeley, 1983)
J. Rawson: *Chinese Bronzes: Art and Ritual* (London, 1987)

CAROL MICHAELSON

Xia Gui [Hsia Kuei; *zi* Yuyu] (*b* Lin'an [modern Hangzhou], Zhejiang Province; *fl c.* 1195–*c.* 1235). Chinese painter. Xia Gui and his close contemporary MA YUAN are considered the two greatest painters of the Southern Song (1127–1279) Academy (*see* CHINA, §V, 4(i)(c)). They established the Ma–Xia style, a term that came to describe not merely their own work but an entire aesthetic.

Early writers provide little biographical information about Xia Gui. Zhou Mi, in his account of the Southern Song capital Lin'an (*c.* 1280), included both Xia and Ma Yuan in a list of ten painters under the heading *Yuqian*

huayuan ('Art academy in the imperial presence'). Zhuang Su wrote (1298) that Xia was a *zhihou* (usher) in the Academy under Emperor Lizong (*reg* 1225–64) and that he painted landscapes and figures. This is partly corroborated by the deciphering of a seal belonging to Lizong's empress, Xie, on a handscroll of *Twelve Views of Landscape*, of which four views survive (ink on silk; Kansas City, MO, Nelson–Atkins Mus. A.). Zhuang Su further associated Xia's painting with the degenerate taste of a declining dynasty and described him as 'exceedingly common and distasteful', and 'only able to realize a name for himself in his own time'. Tang Hou included Xia in a brief list of famous Academy artists (*c.* 1320) but dismissed the importance of all except Li Tang.

The early rejection of Xia Gui can be explained by the rise of anti-Academic literati taste in the early part of the Yuan period (1279–1368). Towards the end of the Yuan, however, evaluation of Xia Gui became more positive both among those of Academic taste and among the literati. In 1365 Xia Wenyan wrote that Xia Gui was a *daizhao* (painter in attendance) under Emperor Ningzong (*reg* 1195–1224) when he received the honour of the *jindai* ('golden belt'), and that he painted human figures, distilling 'high and low'. Xia Wenyan also described Xia Gui's technique: ink tones like the laying on of powdery colours, brushwork that was venerable and time-honoured, and ink that flowed dripping and wet, 'unique'. In painting landscapes, no Academician since Li Tang was his equal. His snow scenes were entirely after FAN KUAN.

In 1344 Ni Zan, writing about a Xia Gui mountain landscape no longer extant, clearly defined the artist's place in painting history: he suggested that a tradition with roots in JING HAO and Fan Kuan and developed by LI TANG, who moved to Lin'an at the end of his life, culminated in Xia Gui and Ma Yuan. Even the late Ming scholar–painter Dong Qichang, who usually disapproved of Academy artists, commended Xia. In 1627 he wrote, with respect to the *Twelve Views* handscroll, that Xia Gui followed Li Tang but with greater cursoriness. He particularly praised Xia's handling of ink, 'now dissolving, now disappearing', such that the ink play (*moxi*) of Mi Fu and Mi Youren was at his brushtip. This was high praise indeed, for the Two Mis were considered the epitome of scholar–painter ideals. The growing acceptance of Xia Gui within a defined tradition was partly due to his strong and forceful style, especially in painting winter landscapes. In recognition of this style, the painter, calligrapher and statesman Wang Duo (1592–1652) attributed to Xia Gui an anonymous Song hanging scroll, *Landscape* (Taipei, N. Pal. Mus.), citing the Fan Kuan–Li Tang relationship and comparing the painting's stark and sombre snow and rocks to 'cold iron' (*hantie*).

Scholars are uncertain about the authenticity of paintings attributed to Xia Gui. Two important album leaves in the shape of rounded fans, *Gazing at the Waterfall* (ink and colour on silk; Taipei, N. Pal. Mus.) and *Full Sail on the Misty River* (ink on silk; Cleveland, OH, Mus. A.), appear to indicate an early Xia Gui style closely connected with 12th-century painting, especially the followers of Li Tang. Both have signatures, but that on the latter is open to interpretation and has been attributed by some to Xia

Gui's son, Xia Shen, despite being in a believable 12th-century style. Five paintings define the subtleties of Xia's mature style: *A Pure and Remote View of Streams and Mountains* (see fig.); the four surviving views in *Twelve Views of Landscape*; an album leaf in the shape of a rounded fan, *Sailboat in the Rain* (ink and slight colour on silk; Boston, MA, Mus. F.A.); a small hanging scroll, *Landscape* (ink on silk; Tokyo, N. Mus.); and a leaf from the album *Hikkōen* ('The brush-tilled garden'), *Rainy Landscape* (Tokyo, Nakamura priv. col.). Characteristic features of these are close promontories with active, leaning trees; leaves created by moist, melting ink-touches, perhaps with a 'split brush'; crisp, swordlike, bare branch-ends; sharp cliffs accented by 'axe-cut strokes' (*fupi cun*), a convention inherited from Li Tang; gentle washes for land surfaces or distant mountain ranges; probing landspits fingering open areas of water and sky; and mists fading into the distance leaving only the spare suggestion of far hill-crests or light wash melting into silent spaces. Some landscapes were wet and bending with the movement of wind and rain, others embraced by quiet mists, and yet others crystal clear with sculpted, firm mountain peaks. Small figures, including travellers, fishermen, scholars and priests, inhabit Xia Gui's landscapes, perhaps indicative of the appearance of his alleged figure paintings, none of which survive. Other abbreviated forms include a bridge, boat, gateway, rustic hamlet or temple; Xia was noted for the free-hand rendering of architectural elements (without a ruler).

Xia Gui's son, Xia Shen, continued his father's general style, partially exemplified by Wang Cuxiang's (1501–68) copy (1541) of a 14-leaf Xia Shen album (Tapei, N. Pal. Mus.). Xia Gui's influence, particularly in association with that of Ma Yuan, pervaded painting throughout East Asia. The Ma–Xia style was stressed by the painters Sun Junze (*fl* early 14th century) and Wang Li (*b* 1322) and in the 15th and 16th centuries became the foundation of the so-called ZHE SCHOOL, headed by Dai Jin. In Japan, Xia Gui's style had a major influence on ink painting of the Muromachi period (1333–1568) (*see* JAPAN, §VI, 4(ii)).

BIBLIOGRAPHY

EWA: 'Hsia Kuei'

Zhuang Su: *Hua ji buyi* [*Painting* continued: a supplement] (1298); *Hua ji, Hua ji buyi*, ed. Deng Chun and Zhuang Su (Beijing, 1963)

Xia Wenyan: *Tuhui baojian* [Precious mirror for examining painting] (1365/*R* Shanghai, 1936), chap. 4, p. 79

Ni Zan: *Qingbi ge quanji* [Pure and secret pavilion: complete collection], ed. Cao Peilian, Yuan dai zhenben wenji huikan [Collection of precious literature from the Yuan dynasty] (1713/*R* Taipei, 1970), chap. 9, p. 15b

O. Sirén: *Chinese Painting: Leading Masters and Principles* (London and New York, 1956–8), ii, pp. 119–24; iii, pls 297–307

Deng Bai and Wu Fuzhi: *Ma Yuan yu Xia Gui* (Shanghai, 1958)

Gugong shuhua lu [Record of calligraphy and painting in the Palace Museum], 4 vols (Taipei, 1965), ii, chap. 4, pp. 56–61; iii, chap. 5, p. 106; iv, chap. 6, pp. 59–61, 184–5

Xia Gui: *A Pure and Remote View of Streams and Mountains* (detail), handscroll, ink on paper, l. *c.* 8.23 m (Taipei, National Palace Museum)

J. Cahill: *An Index of Early Chinese Painters and Painting: T'ang, Sung and Yüan* (Berkeley, 1980), pp. 87–92

M. Loehr: *The Great Painters of China* (New York, 1980), pp. 208–11

Eight Dynasties of Chinese Painting: The Collections of the Nelson Gallery-Atkins Museum, Kansas City, and the Cleveland Museum of Art (Cleveland, 1980), pp. 72–8

Kuo Chi-sheng: 'Towards Understanding a "Snowscape" Attributed to Hsia Kuei', *N. Pal. Mus. Bull.*, xvi/5 (1981), pp. 3–17

Xu Bangda: *Gu shuhua wei e kaobian* [Examinations of the authenticity of ancient paintings and works of calligraphy], 4 vols ([Nanjing], 1984) ii, pp. 16–18

K. Suzuki: *Chugoku kaiga shi* [History of Chinese Painting] (Tokyo, 1985), ii, pp. 145–56; pls 41, 73–8

R. Edwards, 'Hsia Kuei or Hsia Shen?', *Bull. Cleveland Mus. A.*, cxxiii/10 (1986), pp. 390–405

RICHARD EDWARDS

Xi'an [Sian, Hsi'an; formally Chang'an, Ch'ang-an]. Capital of Shaanxi Province, China, and most significant as the nucleus of an archeologically rich area, the artefacts of which document the remarkable continuity of Chinese civilization.

Xi'an is located in the fertile loess valley of the Wei River, which was settled as early as Paleolithic times (before *c.* 6500 BC). For over 1000 years the capital of the empire was intermittently located there (see fig.). From the 2nd century AD to the 14th it marked the eastern terminus of the Silk Route and hence was especially open to new ideas introduced from Central Asia. The city was most important during the Tang period (AD 618–907; see fig. (e)), when its cosmopolitan and tolerant cultural life reflected its significance as a trading centre. With the fall of the Tang, the city was largely destroyed; although it was rebuilt in the 14th century (f), it never regained its cultural primacy.

The ongoing importance of the region around Xi'an has been manifested in the sequence of dynastic capitals in the immediate vicinity. The earliest capital was established by the Zhou dynasty (*c.* 1050–256 BC), first at Feng (see fig. (a)) and later at Hao (b). The first emperor of China, Qin Shi Huangdi (*reg* 221–210 BC), built his capital at Xianyang (c). Later, the first Han Emperor, Liu Bang (*reg* 206–195 BC), built the capital of Chang'an (d) just

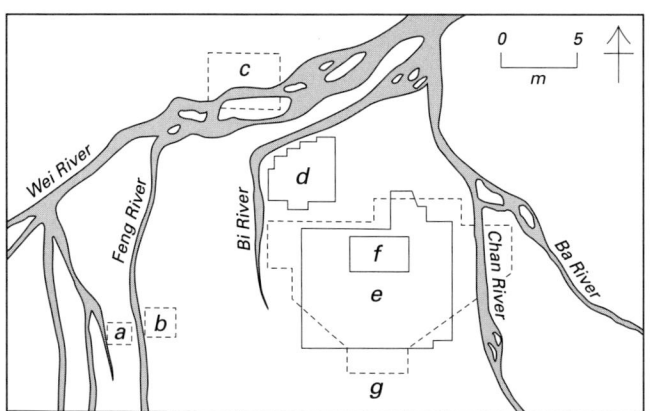

Xi'an, plan showing the locations of dynastic capitals at different periods and the later cities: (a) Feng and (b) Hao, both capitals of the Western Zhou dynasty, *c.* 1050–256 BC; (c) Xianyang, capital of the Qin dynasty, 221–206 BC; (d) Chang'an, capital of the Western Han dynasty, 206 BC–AD 9; (e) Daxing, capital of the Sui (AD 581–618) and Tang (AD 618–907) dynasties; (f) Xi'an, Ming (1368–1644) and Qing (1644–1911) periods; (g) Xi'an, 20th century

south of Xianyang. Orientated along a north–south axis, it was laid out in a grid pattern that established the prototype for the city plan of Xi'an. Both Xianyang and Chang'an have sometimes been confused as ancient names for Xi'an, but the capital site actually shifted somewhat to the south-east. When China was reunified under the Sui dynasty (AD 581–618) the capital was situated in almost exactly the same location as the modern city (g).

Early Xi'an was built within protective walls, a model of Chinese grid city planning (*see* CHINA, §II, 3 and fig. 29). The Ming-period (1368–1644) walls, built on the foundations of the Tang walls, are still visible, consisting of ramparts made of tamped earth originally encased in clay bricks. Many of the city's major architectural structures reflect its cosmopolitan nature. The first Muslims came to Xi'an from the area of modern Xinjiang and from Guangzhou (Canton). They constructed the Qingzhen si, the Great Mosque, in AD 742 with the backing of the Tang Emperor Xuanzong (*reg* 712–56). It was greatly restored and expanded in the 14th century and the present buildings probably date from no earlier than the 18th century. The mosque is an excellent example of the sinification of foreign architecture: the symmetrical plan along an east–west axis and the five courtyards are essentially Chinese in character. The minaret is a pagoda and the buildings all follow Chinese prototypes. At the same time, all the elements essential to Muslim worship, such as the plan of the Great Hall, are foreign, and all the carved calligraphic inscriptions are in Arabic (*see also* CHINA, §II, 5(iv)).

The Shaanxi Provincial Museum in Xi'an was originally a Confucian temple. It is symmetrical in plan, balancing religious structures and courtyards. In addition to representing excellent examples of Chinese architecture, the buildings house one of the richest collections of ancient artefacts in China, including a *beilin* ('forest of stelae'). This collection of 1095 stone tablets originated in AD 837 with carved inscriptions of the 12 classics of Chinese literature. Some of the inscriptions date to the Han period (206 BC–AD 220) but most are Tang or later. Many of the stones were carved by famous calligraphers and form an important record of the development of Chinese calligraphy. The collection also includes the stele of AD 781 that was inscribed in both Chinese and Syrian to mark the establishment of the Nestorian church in China (for illustration *see* NESTORIANISM).

The original Dayan ta (Great Wild Goose Pagoda) of the Da Ci'ensi (Temple of Great Goodwill) was built *c.* AD 652 to house the Buddhist *sūtra*s brought back from India by the monk Xuanzang (AD 600–64). The present structure and its symmetrically planned subsidiary buildings were constructed in Ming style and date from 1580. The earliest pagoda was probably closer to Indian prototypes, but the modern replacement is square in plan, built of stone and brick, with its original ten storeys reduced to seven. The adjacent temple contains statues of 18 *luohan* ('enlightened ones') modelled in clay supported by armatures. The features of most of the figures are more Indian than Chinese, emphasizing their Indian origin.

The bell-tower at Xi'an, which was first built in 1384, was moved several times so as always to mark the centre of the city. The existing structure consists of a brick foundation surmounted by a two-storey wooden tower. It was built without nails according to traditional Ming construction principles and is a good example of the Chinese roofing system.

For other significant archaeological finds located near Xi'an *see* BANPO, XIANYANG and LINTONG.

BIBLIOGRAPHY
D. Tokiwa and T. Sekino: *Shina bukkyō shiseki* [Buddhist monuments in China], i (Tokyo, 1926)
K. Adachi: *Chō-an shiseki no kenkyū* [Research on the historical remains of Chang'an] (Tokyo, 1933)
E. Reischauer: *Ennin's Travels in Tang China* (New York, 1955)
J. Fontein and Wu Tung: *Han and T'ang Murals Discovered in Tombs in the People's Republic and Copied by Contemporary Chinese Painters* (Boston, 1976)

MARY S. LAWTON

Xia Nai [Hsia Nai] (*b* Wenzhou, Zhejiang Province, 7 Feb 1910; *d* Beijing, 10 June 1985). Chinese archaeologist. He gained his diploma in history at Qinghua University, Beijing, in July 1937, then studied at the Institute of Archaeology, University of London, under Mortimer Wheeler. He received his doctorate in 1939, with a dissertation on Egyptian archaeology. At the beginning of World War II he spent more than a year at the Egyptian Museum in Cairo.

After his return to China in 1941, Xia directed several excavations, particularly in Gansu Province. He was able to refute Johan Gunnar Andersson's (1874–1960) early datings for the QIJIA culture, discovered by Andersson in Guanghe County, Gansu. Xia showed that the Qijia culture dates to *c.* 2000–*c.* 1600 BC, after, not before, the Yangshao culture (*see also* CHINA, §VII, 3(i)(b)). In autumn 1951 he led the excavations of the Warring States (403–221 BC) and Han-period (206 BC–AD 220) tombs near Changsha, Hunan Province. His research on the development of these tomb complexes laid the foundation for the investigation of the culture of the state of Chu.

During 1956–8 Xia directed the excavations of Ding ling, tomb of the Wanli emperor (*reg* 1573–1620) in Changping, near Beijing. Xia considered this excavation to have been unsuccessful, since some items enclosed in the tomb, such as textiles and picture scrolls, decayed when the tomb was opened, owing to inadequate means of preservation. He therefore prevented Guo Moruo (1892–1978), Director of the Academy of Social Sciences, from carrying out the excavation of Qian ling, tomb of the emperor Gaozong (*reg* AD 649–83), in Qian xian [Qian County], Shaanxi Province.

Xia helped lead the excavation of the Shang-period (*c.* 1600–*c.* 1050 BC) site at PANLONGCHENG (1963 and 1974). In 1977 he published a fundamental work, a complete chronological list of all the known Stone Age finds in China, drawn up with the aid of the most modern scientific methods. A further area of research was the Western contacts of early China. He clarified the Han-period origins of economic and other links between China and the Middle East.

Up to his death, Xia held the offices of Vice-director of the Chinese Academy of Social Sciences and Director of the Archaeological Institute at the same academy. He also enjoyed wide international recognition: he was a communicating member of the British Academy and the Deutsches Archäologisches Institut, and a foreign member of the National Academy of Sciences in the USA and the Kungliga Vitterhets Historia och Antikvitets Akademi (Royal Academy of Letters, History and Archaeology) in Sweden.

WRITINGS
Jade and Silk of Han China, trans. and ed. by Chu-tsing Li (Laurence, KA, 1983)

BIBLIOGRAPHY
Zhongguo kaoguxue yanjiu lunji: Jinian Xia Nai xiansheng kaogu wushi zhounian [Collection of research articles on archaeology in China: in memory of Xia Nai on his 50th anniversary in archaeology] (Xi'an, 1987), pp. 1–48

PETRA KLOSE

Xiang [Hsiang]. Chinese family of artists.

(1) Xiang Yuanbian [Hsiang Yüan-pien; *zi* Zijing; *hao* Molin] (*b* Jiaxing, Zhejiang Province, 1525; *d* 1590). Chinese collector. Many items from his collection of calligraphy and paintings were later incorporated into the Qing dynasty (1644–1911) imperial collection and other private and public collections; examples include the hand-scroll attributed to Gu Kaizhi, *Admonitions to the Palace Instructress* (London, BM; *see* GU KAIZHI), and Zhao Mengfu's handscroll *Autumn Colours on the Qiao and Hua Mountains* (1295; Taipei. N. Pal. Mus.; *see* ZHAO, (1)).

Xiang's birthplace, Jiaxing, is known for its painters. Xiang came from a family of high-ranking government officials; his father, Xiang Quan, seems to have accumulated a fortune from commerce, however. Xiang Yuanbian failed the provincial civil service examination and devoted himself to his business, probably including a pawnshop, and to collecting. Several books have been ascribed to him, but the authorship of *Jiaochuang jiulu* ('Nine records written before a palm-shaded window'), on antiques, has been questioned, and two other works, *Xuanlu bolun* ('Discussion of Xuande bronzes'), on Xuande reign period (1426–35) bronzes, and *Noted Porcelains of Successive Dynasties with Comments and Illustrations by Hsiang Yuan-pien* (translated by Stephen W. Bushell and first published in 1908), are spurious. Judging from a small number of his own extant paintings, Xiang also dabbled in and was quite gifted at literati-style painting.

Because Xiang did not compile a catalogue of his collection, other sources must be used to reconstruct his collecting activities. Letters from the Suzhou artist Wen Peng (1498–1573), elder son of Wen Zhengming and an accomplished calligrapher and connoisseur, indicate that Wen advised Xiang on his purchases. Wen Jia, younger brother of Wen Peng, may also have offered advice, though there is no written evidence; he certainly sold paintings to Xiang, added colophons to works in Xiang's collection and in 1578 painted a landscape as a birthday gift (for illustration *see* WEN (2)). The simple and austere style of Xiang's own painting may have been partly inspired by Wen Jia and Wen Zhengming. Xiang was also close to such other Suzhou artists as Wang Guxiang (1501–68), Peng Nian (1505–66) and Feng Fang (*fl* 16th century) and was acquainted with Zhan Jingfeng (1533–*c.* 1602) a discriminating contemporary connoisseur from Anhui Province. Another source of influence was the painter QIU YING, who lived and spent much time with the Xiang family tutoring Xiang Yuanbian and making free-hand or traced copies of paintings in the Xiang collection. In 1541 Qiu copied a painting by the 8th-century artist Zhou Fang; the next year Xiang Yuanbian copied a painting by the 10th-century artist Huang Quan, probably under the guidance of Qiu, since Huang painted in a refined academic manner. Qiu also painted the handscroll *Garden of Self-enjoyment* (Cleveland, OH, Mus. A.) while living with the Xiang family.

In the 18th century the Qianlong emperor (*reg* 1736–96) admired Xiang Yuanbian, praising him in many of his colophons inscribed on works in the imperial collection. Qianlong even called a studio in the Summer Palace in Jehol (modern Chengde, Hebei Province) the Tianlai shuwu, after Xiang's own Tianlai ge (Pavilion of Heavenly Music). However, Xiang has often been criticized for applying too many of his seals to works that he collected, thereby diminishing the aesthetic quality of the pictorial surface, a practice that Qianlong repeated. Xiang was also criticized by Zhan Jingfeng as vulgar and miserly. Indeed, he often recorded the price he paid on the work of art itself and was nervous when he felt he had spent too much. Nonetheless, the many high-quality and historically important extant works from Xiang's collection attest to his discriminating eye and taste, and his activities shaped the later study of Chinese painting.

BIBLIOGRAPHY

DMB: 'Hsiang Yuan-pien'
E. J. Laing: 'Ch'iu Ying's Three Patrons', *Ming Stud.*, 8 (Spring 1979), pp. 49–56
Kwan S. Wong: 'Hsiang Yüan-pien and Suchou Artists', *Artists and Patrons: Some Social and Economic Aspects of Chinese Painting*, ed. Chu-tsing Li, J. Cahill and Wai-kam Ho (Kansas City, 1989), pp. 155–8
Chen Zufan: 'Textual Research on Xiang Molin's Family and his Collection of Chinese Calligraphy and Paintings', *Duoyun*, xx/1 (1989), pp. 79–86

JASON C. KUO

(2) Xiang Shengmo [Hsiang Sheng-mo; *zi* Kongzhang; *hao* Yi'an, Xushanqiao] (*b* Jiaxing, Zhejiang Province, 1597; *d* 1658). Chinese painter, grandson of (1) Xiang Yuanbian. He grew up in cultured surroundings with access to Yuanbian's collection. Through family connections he knew some of the leading artistic figures of the late Ming period (1368–1664), including the painting theorist Dong Qichang, who was employed as a tutor in the household and later contributed inscriptions to some of Xiang's paintings. Referring to Zhang Yanyuan's analysis in *Lidai minghua ji* ('Record of famous painters of all periods'; completed *c.* 847) of the first law of painting put forward in the 6th century by Xie He in *Gu huapin lu* ('Classification of painters'), Dong praised Xiang's works for expressing the vital movement inherent in things (*qiyun* or *shenyun*, 'spirit resonance'), whereby an artist achieves accurate representation. Xiang also knew a number of painters from Songjiang, an art centre near Shanghai, including Chen Jiru. Xiang wrote that in his youth he was forced to paint at night because his father made him study for the official examinations by day, despite the fact that he had no enthusiasm for a career in government affairs. His love of art and his confidence in his ability are suggested by a dream he recorded: 'One night I dreamt that my brush stood up like a pillar more than ten feet tall. I climbed up and occupied the top of it, clapping my hands, laughing and talking. Since then, I have felt as if I were inspired and have often achieved fine results while

imitating the works of ancient masters.' However, he not only copied old masterworks but also drew inspiration from nature.

In 1645 the Manchus occupied Nanjing, and Xiang Shengmo and his relatives were forced to flee south. Their art collection was largely destroyed and several members of the family committed suicide. Xiang survived and expressed his anguish in poetry and in painting. *Jiaxing xian zhi*, the local history, records that in his later years he lived a life of poverty along the Fuchun River, selling his paintings to survive. Xiang's most important work is a series of six landscape handscrolls on the theme of eremetic withdrawal. Traditionally a wise ruler would summon a virtuous recluse to his government, and the recluse would demonstrate the purity of his spirit by declining the invitation or serving only briefly before retreating once more to the wilderness. The earliest of the paintings, *Calling the Hermit* (1625–6; Los Angeles, CA, Co. Mus. A.), seems strongly influenced by Dong Qichang, whom the artist visited in Songjiang (1625–6), and who had painted a picture on the same theme, *Calling the Hermit at Qingxi* (handscroll, ink on paper, 1611; Lyme, NH, priv. col., see Cahill, pl. 39). But whereas Dong took pains to play down narrative content or easily readable depictions of nature, Xiang presented the viewer with a long composition that blends fanciful, animated landscape forms with mundane activity: gentlemen fishing, crossing bridges or sitting in thatched houses. Xiang's scrolls painted after his family's ruin are shorter, smaller works that required less of his time and were probably more saleable. Chu-tsing Li suggests that the colour red, which appears more often in Xiang's works after 1645, is a visual allusion to his loyalty to the pre-Manchu Ming rulers whose family name, Zhu, means 'red'.

BIBLIOGRAPHY

DMB: 'Hsiang Sheng-mo'
O. Sirén: *Chinese Painting: Leading Masters and Principles*, v (London, 1956), pp. 38–40
Chu-tsing Li: 'Hsiang Sheng-mo's Poetry and Painting on Eremetism', *Proceedings of the Symposium on Paintings and Calligraphy by Ming I-min* (Hong Kong, 1976), pp. 531–59
J. Cahill: *The Distant Mountains: Chinese Painting of the Late Ming Dynasty, 1570–1644* (New York, 1982), pp. 130–32

VYVYAN BRUNST, JAMES CAHILL

Xianyang [Hsien-yang]. Town in Shaanxi Province, China, north-west of the city of Xi'an. Xianyang was the capital city of the state of Qin and then of the Qin dynasty (i.e. from 350 BC to 206 BC). The exact location of the old Qin capital is controversial. It has been argued convincingly that the remains are divided between Changling station, Yaodian Zhen and Dianshang cun, and that part of it is buried at the bottom of the Wei River, 15 km east of modern Xianyang.

Xianyang was set up as a capital by Prince Xiaogong (*b* 381 BC; *reg* 361–338 BC; *d* 338 BC). Qin Shi Huangdi, the 'First Emperor of Qin' (*reg* 221–210 BC), settled 120,000 wealthy families there and had extravagant palaces built for himself. When the Qin were defeated the city was burnt by the Chu rebel leader Xiang Yu. Under the Han dynasty (206 BC–AD 220) it was re-established further west and renamed first Xincheng, then Weicheng. At the end of the period the town was derecognized and became nameless. Under the Tang dynasty (AD 618–907) the name of Xianyang was restored.

In the late 1950s archaeologists began to excavate the area identified as the site of the Qin capital and found ancient pottery kilns. In 1973 an archaeological work station was established by the Institute of Archaeology of Shaanxi Province, Shaanxi Provincial Relic Committee and Xianyang City Relic Committee. Part of the ruins of the Qin palaces was uncovered in 1974–5 (now referred to as palace Complex 1). New excavations were made in 1979 (Complex 3) and again in 1980–82 (Complex 2). Palace complexes 1 and 2 are earlier than Complex 3. All show signs of conflagration. Excavation showed that the architecture was based on an overlapping design, incorporating houses, pavilions on terraces, lofts and balconies. The building materials were mud bricks and timber. Finds include wall paintings, eave tiles, potsherds with calligraphy in seal script (*zhuanshu*) or clerical script (*lishu*), money, bricks, copperware, ironware, copper ornaments and daily utensils made mainly of clay, but also of bronze, copper and iron (Xian, Shaanxi Prov. Mus.; Xianyang Mus.). The wall paintings in complexes 1 and 2 were largely destroyed, but those of Complex 3 are relatively well preserved. These are long, scroll-type paintings, extending from one room to another. Carts and horses, wheat heads, guards of honour, buildings, figures and geometric patterns are among the decorative elements. The colours of the wall paintings are principally black, red, blue and white, though some are green and yellow. Eave tiles were either round or semicircular. Most had patterns based on one of three themes: animals, such as deer, birds and insects; plants; or clouds. The cloud patterns, more common in Complex 3, represent water, which of the Five Elements of early Chinese philosophy was considered the dominant one for the Qin dynasty.

BIBLIOGRAPHY

'Qin du Xianyang diyi hao gongdian jian zhu yizhi jianbao' [Brief report on the remains of Palace Structure 1 at the Qin capital Xianyang], *Wenwu* (1976), no. 11, pp. 12–41

'Qin du Xianyang disan hao Gongdian jianzhu yizhi fajue jianbao' [Brief report on the excavation of the remains of Palace Structure 3 at the Qin capital Xianyang], *Kaogu yu wenwu* (1980), no. 2, pp. 34–41

Li Xueqin: *Eastern Zhou and Qin Civilizations* (New Haven and London, 1985), pp. 231–5

'Qin Xianyang gong dier hao jianzhu yizhi fajue jianbao' [Brief report on the excavation of the remains of Palace Structure 2 at Qin Xianyang], *Kaogu yu wenwu* (1986), no. 4, pp. 9–19

HAIYAO ZHENG

Xiao Shufang [Hsiao Shu-fang] (*b* Zhongshan County, Guangdong Province, 19 Aug 1911). Chinese painter. She studied Chinese painting in Beijing in 1925; in 1926 she enrolled in the Academy of Art in Beijing to study Western painting; she then attended the art department of the Beiping Central University in Nanjing. In 1937 she went to Europe to study sculpture. On her return to China she worked in art schools and from 1949 taught watercolour, oil and traditional Chinese painting at the Central Academy of Fine Arts in Beijing. Her work was widely exhibited in China and abroad, notably after 1979, when she travelled with her husband, Wu Zuoren, for a series of lectures and joint exhibitions in Asia, Europe and the USA. After 1972 Xiao concentrated on Chinese flower painting, for which she is best known. She worked in a style that fused watercolour techniques with the *mogu* ('boneless') manner of traditional Chinese painting, creating an elegant and graceful world of luminous colours and translucent washes.

BIBLIOGRAPHY

Selected Paintings of Wu Zuoren and Xiao Shufang/ Wu Zuoren Xiao Shufang hua xuan (Beijing, 1982) [bilingual text]

Xiao Shufang: *Rongbao Zhai huapu, 50: Huahui bufen* [Rongbao zhai painting manual, 50: Flower painting] (Beijing, 1991)

MAYCHING KAO

Xiao Yuncong [Hsiao Yün-ts'ung; *zi* Chimu; *hao* Wumen Daoren] (*b* Wuhu, Anhui Province, 1596; *d* 1673). Chinese painter and poet. He was born some 150 km north of the region inhabited by artists of the ANHUI SCHOOL, with which he became associated, and was a contemporary of its leading member, Hongren. His family hoped he would pursue an official career, but Xiao failed the civil service examinations and instead became a semi-professional painter. He joined the loyalist Fu she (Restoration Society) in 1638 and in 1645 was forced to flee Wuhu in the face of invading Qing troops. On his return two years later he found his house ruined.

Perhaps partly from a need to make money, Xiao participated in two important printing projects, the *Lisao tu* ('Illustrations to the poem *Lisao*'; *c.* 1645) and the *Taiping shanshui tu* ('Topographical illustrations of the Taiping region'; 1648). Both projects brought together some of the best artists of 17th-century China and are exceptional examples of woodblock-carving and printing, an art that flourished in Anhui Province during the Ming period (1368–1644; for further discussion of printing of this period *see* CHINA, §XIII, 19(ii)). Xiao contributed 64 illustrations for the *Lisao tu*, including the image for the title poem itself (*Lisao* or *Encountering Sorrow*; attributed to the 4th-century BC poet Qu Yuan). The motive for publication of these poems, which had been given political interpretations since the Han period (206 BC–AD 220), may have been to express bitterness over the fall of the Ming dynasty, a feeling expressed by Xiao in his own poetry. The figures and animals that Xiao painted in the *Lisao tu*, with their awkward and sometimes grotesque distortions, were perhaps similarly inspired, a reflection of Xiao's dissatisfaction with his own aborted official career as well as with political developments. Like his contemporary Chen Hongshou, he transformed the mannerisms of figure drawing by artisans and craftsmen of his period into original and engaging images. The combination of poetry, imitations of old painting styles and local topographical interest seen in the *Taiping shanshui tu*, for which Xiao provided 43 scenes of Taiping Prefecture, was a novel format.

Xiao Yuncong's best work appeared in albums and handscrolls: he seems to have been uncomfortable with the large hanging-scroll format. His early style, dependent on Song period (960–1279) models, was often fussy and crowded with detail. Although he attempted hanging scrolls in the dry, linear manner typical of Anhui school artists, such works lack the overall compositional unity of the best Anhui paintings. Albums painted by Xiao in the 1650s (e.g. album, 1653; Hefei, Anhui Prov. Mus.) contain leaves after 10th-century landscapists such as Li Cheng,

Jing Hao and others. Xiao improved considerably as a painter in the late 1660s and early 1670s. Xiao's mature paintings often included overlapping, simplified forms, red-robed figures and a combination of pale blue and red-brown washes with strokes of shaded wash. A long handscroll, *Landscape with Mountains and Rivers* (1669; Los Angeles, CA, Co. Mus. A.), demonstrates the painter's technical prowess in using a dry-brush manner to construct compositions of great formal complexity.

BIBLIOGRAPHY

O. Sirén: *Chinese Painting: Leading Masters and Principles* (London and New York, 1956–8), v, pp. 114–15
S. Chin: 'The Older Anhui Masters', *Shadows of Mt Huang: Chinese Painting and Printing of the Anhui School*, ed. J. Cahill (Berkeley, 1981), pp. 67–8
Chinesische Szenen, 1656/1992: Die 13 Meter lange Bildrolle des Malers Xiao Yuncong aus dem Jahr 1656 (exh. cat. by A. Lutz and Huang Qi, Zurich, Mus. Rietberg, 1992) [biog. by M. Kramer]

VYVYAN BRUNST, with JAMES CAHILL

Xiao Zhao [Hsiao Chao] (*b* Huce, Shanxi Province; *fl c.* 1130–62). Chinese painter. During the political disorders at the end of the Northern Song dynasty (960–1127) he found refuge in the Taihang Mountains, where he pursued a path of brigandage and captured the painter Li Tang. Startled by the discovery that his victim's baggage contained only the tools of painting, according to Zhuang Su and Xia Wenyan he decided to abandon robbery for painting. As Li Tang's pupil he went with him to the south and became a major figure at the reconstituted imperial Painting Academy in Lin'an (now Hangzhou, Zhejiang province), capital of the Southern Song dynasty (1127–1279). He was a favourite of the emperor, Gao zong (*reg* 1127–62), being appointed a *dai zhao* ('painter-in-attendance') with the honorary title *di gong lang* ('gentleman for meritorious achievement').

Xiao's early recorded achievements were a commission for wall paintings in the Xianying Temple (destr.), a Daoist shrine on the edge of West Lake, Hangzhou, dedicated to an immortal who was believed to have protected Gao zong during perilous days in the north; landscape paintings executed in a single night (aided by four flagons of wine) on the four walls of an imperial building called the Liang Hall (destr.) on the West Lake island of Gushan; and a fan painting (untraced), to which Gao zong had added a couplet, in the 13th-century collection of Zhuang Su. Xiao is also documented as having painted landscapes and figures, strange pines and odd-looking stones. One complaint, noted by Xia Wenyan, suggested he used too much ink. The 12th-century critic Li Chengsou praised his handling of space 'so that in emptiness there is substance'. He is said to have concealed his signature among the rocks and trees, a characteristic evident on the most impressive painting usually attributed to Xiao, a large hanging scroll entitled *Temple on the Mountainside* (Taipei, N. Pal. Mus.). Other paintings that may reflect his style (strongly influenced by Li Tang) are found in the Liaoning Provincial Museum and the Tianjin Art Museum.

BIBLIOGRAPHY

Li Chengsou: *Hua shan shui jue* [Secrets of landscape painting] (12th century); in Yu Jianhua: *Zhongguo hualun lei bian* [Chinese painting theory by categories] (Hong Kong, 1973), p. 622
Zhou Mi: *Wulin jiu shi* [Old matters concerning Hangzhou] (*c.* 1280); in Meng Yuanlao and others: *Dongjing menghua lu: Wai si zhong* [Five Song local histories of Kaifeng and Lin'an] (Shanghai, 1962), pp. 409, 422
Zhuang Su: *Hua ji buyi* [*Painting* continued: a supplement] (1298); *Hua ji, Hua ji buyi*, ed. Deng Chun and Zhuang Su (Beijing, 1963), pp. 8–9
Xia Wenyan: *Tuhui baojian* [Precious mirror for examining painting] (1365/*R* Shanghai, 1936)
Li E: *Nan Song yuan hua lu* [Southern Song Academy: record of painting] (1721); in Huang Binhong and Deng Shi, eds: *Meishu congshu* [Collected historical texts on art] (Shanghai, rev. 1947/*R* 1975), xvii, §2, pp. 56–60
Liaoning sheng bowuguan cang hua ji [Paintings in the Liaoning Provincial Museum], 2 vols (Beijing, 1962), i, p. 39 [includes works attributed to Xiao]
Gugong shuhua lu [Record of calligraphy and painting in the Palace Museum], 4 vols (Taipei, 1965), v, pp. 76–7
J. Cahill: *An Index of Early Chinese Painters and Painting: T'ang, Sung and Yüan* (Berkeley, 1980), p. 93
Xu Bangda: *Gu shuhua wei e kaobian* [Examinations of the authenticity of ancient paintings and works of calligraphy], 4 vols ([Nanjing], 1984), ii, pp. 8–13
J. K. Murray: 'Ts'ao Hsün and Two Southern Sung History Scrolls', *A. Orient.*, xv (1985), pp. 1–29
Suzuki Kei: *Chūgoku kaiga shi* [History of Chinese painting], ii (Tokyo, 1985), pp. 109–16, pl. 40

RICHARD EDWARDS

Xiasi [Hsia-ssu]. Chinese necropolis in Xichuan County, Henan Province, consisting of 25 tombs and 5 chariot pits dating from the late 7th century BC to the late 6th. Tomb M2, the largest tomb, has a shaft measuring 9.2×6.5 m in plan, at the bottom of which was a wooden coffin chamber measuring 7.7×4.5 m; the tomb probably belonged to an official of the southern state of Chu, Wei (or Yuan) Zifeng (*d* 548 BC), and tombs M1 and M3 to his wife and concubine. Tomb M2 yielded the set of seven tripods (*ding*) cast for a prince and chancellor of Chu, Wangzi Wu (Prince Wu), between 558 and 552 BC (all the Xiasi bronzes are in Zhengzhou, Henan Prov. Mus. and Henan Prov. Cult. Relics Res. Inst.; see CHINA, §VI, 3(iv)).

Other bronzes recovered from the tombs include a chime of 26 bells (the Wangsun Gao *zhong*), ritual vessels and weapons, testifying to the dominant role of Chu in the formation of the southern style of bronzework, the characteristics of which are articulated vessel forms bearing heavy zoomorphic appendages, elaborate openwork and relief ornaments. The Wangzi Wu *ding* display many of these characteristics: angular profiles, relief decoration and heavy, flangelike appendages topped with animal masks (*taotie*). Similar flanges occur on a bronze vessel of the *gui* type from Tomb M1 and a pair of *li* (tripods) from M2. A pair of *hu* (wine vessels) from Tomb M1 exhibit even more extreme architectonic forms, achieved through abrupt breaks in profile and the use of massive zoomorphic handles and feet in a style imitating Chu woodwork sculptures of tigers (see CHINA, §XIII, 26(ii)). Wooden prototypes also lie behind two of the most unusual of the Xiasi bronzes, a *zu* (chopping board) and a *jin* (vessel stand) from M2. Unlike its wooden prototypes, however, the *jin* and its appendages are composed entirely of complex honeycombed openwork made by the lost-wax casting process (see CHINA, §VI, 2(iii)(b)). Although the *jin* provides one of the earliest extant examples of the use of the technique in Chinese bronzework, its handling is so assured that a period of prior development must be assumed. In both the openwork decoration and the relief ornament on the vessels and bells, there is an emphasis on tightly packed, small, curling forms, which also appear on several pieces of jade. Tomb M2 contained the earliest securely datable group of Eastern Zhou (771–256 BC) inlaid bronzes, including a *guan fou* (ablutionary vessel) inlaid with copper dragons, the fluid profiles of which are reminiscent of lacquer painting, and a *ge* (halberd blade) with a gold inscription, a fashion previously associated more strongly with the south-eastern states of Wu and Yue than with Chu.

BIBLIOGRAPHY

'Henan sheng Xichuan xian Xiasi Chunqiu Chu mu' [The Spring and Autumn period Chu tombs at Xiasi in Xichuan County, Henan Province], *Wenwu* (1980), no. 10, pp. 13–20, pls 1–2

'Henan Xichuan xian Xiasi yihao mu fajue jianbao' [Brief excavation report on Xiasi Tomb 1 in Xichuan County, Henan], *Kaogu* (1981), no. 2, pp. 119–27, pl. 1

L. von Falkenhausen: 'Chu Ritual Music', *New Perspectives on Chu Culture During the Eastern Zhou Period*, ed. T. Lawton (Washington, DC, 1991), pp. 47–106

C. Mackenzie: 'Chu Bronze Work: A Unilinear Tradition, or a Synthesis of Diverse Sources?', *New Perspectives on Chu Culture During the Eastern Zhou Period*, ed. T. Lawton (Washington, DC, 1991), pp. 107–57

COLIN MACKENZIE

Xiben. *See* OUYANG XUN.

Xilokeratidi. *See under* AMORGOS.

Ximenes. *See* CISNEROS, FRANCISCO JIMÉNEZ DE.

Ximenes, Ettore (*b* Palermo, 11 April 1855; *d* Rome, 20 Dec 1926). Italian sculptor. He attended the Accademia di Belle Arti in Palermo (1868–71) under the guidance of the sculptor Vincenzo Ragusa (*b* 1841). In 1872 he moved to Naples, where he was influenced by Domenico Morelli and Stanislao Lista (1824–1908), and was also in close contact with Vincenzo Gemito. Between 1874 and 1880 he lived in Florence, supported by a grant, and became familiar with various aspects of Renaissance sculpture, which enhanced his eclectic tendency. In 1878 he travelled to Paris, where he came into close contact with the work of Rodin and Jean-Baptiste Carpeaux. On returning to Italy he began a period of extraordinary artistic productivity, and from 1885 to 1894 was Director of the Istituto Statale d'Arte in Urbino. His original training was strictly realist, and he was also influenced by the Renaissance Revival in Italian sculpture in the late 19th century. His first public works, including the monuments to *Giuseppe Garibaldi* in Pesaro (1887) and Milan (1895), are characterized by a strong realistic tendency, both in the handling of the material and in the rendering of the subject. At the Venice Biennale, Ximenes exhibited his plaster maquette for the bronze statue of *Giuseppe Zanardelli* (1905) in the Corte d'Appello, Brescia, which represents the statesman wrapped in a toga over modern clothes. The *Zanardelli* tomb (1906) in the Cimitero Vantiniano, Brescia, shows a more modernist tension in its composition with the bronze group of *The Family* set against an emphatically floral background, parts of which were in painted stucco (destr.). A similar tendency appears in the bronze group representing *The Law* for the monument to *Victor-Emanuel II* (1885–1911) in Rome. Between 1913 and 1920 Ximenes planned a large monumental group to commemorate *Giuseppe Verdi* in Parma, of which all that remains is one bronze plate in the Piazza Marconi. The plate shows a

portrait of Verdi and an *Allegory of Music and Poetry*: on the reverse is the *Battle of Legnano*, scenes depicting Verdi's *Sicilian Vespers* and *Victor-Emanuel II in Parma*. This work showed the influence of Rodin and such Art Nouveau artists as Leonardo Bistolfi, as well as the friezes created by Aristide Sartorio for the Palazzo di Montecitorio (1908–12) in Rome. From 1911 until his death Ximenes worked mostly on foreign commissions, for example in New York, Buenos Aires, Rio de Janeiro and Kiev. Between 1919 and 1926 he worked with the architect Manfredo Manfredi (1859–1927) in São Paulo, Brazil, on the *Monument to Independence*. Ximenes also worked in the fields of painting and drawing, illustrating the story *Il vino* by Edmondo de Amicis, and *Nei boschi incantati* by Pietro Petrocchi.

BIBLIOGRAPHY

A. Venturi and V. Fleres: *Ettore Ximenes* (Bergamo, 1928)

M. F. Giubilei: 'Ettore Ximenes', *Il liberty italiano e ticinese* (Lugano, Campione d'Italia and Rome, 1981), pp. 73–4

I. de Guttry, M. P. Maino and M. Quesada: *Le arti minori d'autore in Italia dal 1900 al 1930* (Bari, 1985), pp. 296–301

G. Panazza: 'La scultura', *Brescia postromantica e liberty, 1880–1915* (Brescia, 1985), pp. 170–72, 265

V. Terraroli: 'Marmi e bronzi di affeto e memoria', *Atlante Bresc.* (1987), no. 10, pp. 40, 47

——: *Il Vantiniano* (Brescia, 1990), pp. 30, 53–5, 90

M. de Micheli: *La scultura dell'ottocento* (Turin, 1992), pp. 250–55

VALERIO TERRAROLI

Ximénez [Jiménez], Miguel (*fl* Saragossa, 1462; *d* 1505). Spanish painter. He was of Castilian origin and worked in Aragon during the reign of Ferdinand and Isabella. His workshop in Saragossa was inherited by his son Juan, who was also a painter and a follower. Between 1482 and 1496 Miguel Ximénez collaborated with the painter Martín Bernart of Saragossa on a series of altarpieces, notably the high altar retable (1485; Saragossa, Mus. Prov. B.A.) from the church at Blesa (Teruel), which depicts the *Legend of the True Cross*. In his independent works, the altarpiece (Madrid, Prado) for S María, Ejea de los Caballeros (Saragossa), that of the *Virgin of Villaverde* in the church at Luna (Saragossa) and that of *St Martin of Tours* for S Pablo, Saragossa (Saragossa, Mus. Prov. B.A.), a development is noticeable from a Gothic style of Netherlandish and German origin, influenced by Rogier van der Weyden and Martin Schongauer, to the more naturalistic language of the Renaissance, with experiments in perspective and modelling.

BIBLIOGRAPHY

M. C. Lacarra Ducay: *Primitivos aragoneses en el Museo Provincial de Zaragoza* (Saragossa, 1970), pp. 101–59

——: 'Influencia de Martin Schongauer en los primitivos aragoneses', *Bol. Inst. & Mus. Camón Aznar*, xvii (1984), pp. 18–23

——: 'Miguel Jiménez (Zaragoza, 1462–1505)', *Aragón y la pintura del renacimiento* (Saragossa, 1990), pp. 37–43

M. C. LACARRA DUCAY

Ximénez de Urrea, Francisco (*b* 1589; *d* 1647). Aragonese antiquary, historian and collector. He was a learned ecclesiastic who formed a large library and museum, which held a number of antiquities formerly collected by Gaspar Galcerán de Gurrea Aragón y Pino. Like Gurrea and Vincencio Juan de Lastanosa, with both of whom he maintained close relations, he was intensely interested in numismatic studies, and his collections of Punic, Greek and Roman medals, into which he absorbed the collections of the Duque de Villahermosa (1526–81) and Gurrea, eventually numbered more than 6000. He devoted much attention to the interpretation of Iberian coins, a study that was pioneered by the circle of Aragonese 17th-century antiquaries. From 1630 he was the official chronicler of Aragón, and he compiled a number of manuscript works on the history of Aragón. He was in correspondence with François Filhol (d after 1662), a canon and antiquary of Toulouse, whose collections and library were much admired in Aragón.

BIBLIOGRAPHY

R. del Arco y Garay: *La erudición en el siglo XVII y el cronista de Aragon Andreo de Uztarroz* (Madrid, 1950)
R. W. Lightbown: 'Some Notes on Spanish Baroque Collectors', *The Origins of Museums*, ed. O. Impey and A. Macgregor (Oxford, 1985), p. 140

R. W. LIGHTBOWN

Ximeno, Matías (*fl* 1639–51). Spanish painter. He was a minor painter, active in the region of Guadalajara and in Madrid, who confined himself to religious subjects and to landscape, a relatively rare genre in Spanish Baroque painting. His works are often based on engravings of Flemish paintings; he had a conventional drawing style and a poor sense of colour, and his figures frequently lack expression.

The earliest known works by him are the paintings for the altarpiece in the collegiate church at Pastrana, near Guadalajara, of 1639. There are ten figures of female saints and a *St Francis* and a *Crucifixion* in the upper part. In these works Ximeno made strong use of chiaroscuro, but they are of modest technical quality. In 1640 he painted the *Adoration of the Shepherds*, the *Annunciation* and the *Adoration of the Magi* for the altarpiece of S María del Rey at Atienza, near Guadalajara. The paintings of *St James* (1649) and *St Bartholomew* (1651), both in Leon Cathedral, are signed but of very poor quality. Of four signed paintings of the *Immaculate Conception*, one is in the church at Pastrana, one in Sigüenza Cathedral and the others in private collections in Saragossa and Valdepeñas. Ximeno's lack of technique in landscape painting is apparent in these works. His landscapes have biblical, hagiological or mythological subjects, for example *Landscape with Pyramus and Thisbe* (Madrid, Real Acad. S Fernando, Mus.); in them he used the masses of trees to produce strong chiaroscuro effects and to mark the stages of recession in space.

BIBLIOGRAPHY

D. Angulo Iñiguez and A. E. Pérez Sánchez: *Pintura Madrileña del segundo tercio del siglo XVII* (Madrid, 1983), pp. 376–87
A. Pérez Sánchez: *Pintura barroca en España: 1600–1750* (Madrid, 1992), pp. 92–3

ENRIQUE VALDIVIESO

Ximeno y Planes, Rafael (*b* Valencia, 1759; *d* Mexico, 1825). Spanish painter, also active in Mexico. His early years in Valencia were strongly influenced by his uncle, the painter Luis Planes (1742–1821), who taught him drawing and whose work has sometimes been attributed to his nephew and pupil. Ximeno was closely involved in the academic world in which he spent his whole career. He was very young when he attended the Academia de S Carlos in Valencia, where he won prizes in painting in 1773 and in life drawing in 1775. In the same year he left to study at the Academia de S Fernando, Madrid, under Manuel Monforty Asensi, and eventually, after a failed attempt in 1778, he won a scholarship to study at the Accademia di S Luca, Rome. At these academies he received a training based on the strictest classicism, which he later implanted in Mexico.

In Madrid, Ximeno was attracted to the art of Anton Raphael Mengs, whose works he copied between 1775 and 1778, including the portrait of the *Marquesa de los Llanos* and *Self-portrait* (copies in Valencia, Mus. B.A.) and the *Annunciation* (untraced), copied from Mengs's last work of 1779. Ximeno also copied paintings in the Spanish royal collections, including *SS Peter and Paul* (*c.* 1755; Valencia, Mus. B.A.), after the painting by Guido Reni, and *St Sebastian* (*c.* 1755; Valencia, Mus. B.A.), after the painting by Titian, then in the sacristy of the Escorial. Equally classical in style is the *Meeting Between Two Commanders* (*c.* 1780; Madrid, Real Acad. S Fernando, Mus.) and the *Eternal Father Reprimanding Adam and Eve* (*c.* 1780; Valencia, Mus. B.A.) painted in Rome, where Ximeno was much influenced by the works of Raphael.

In May 1794 Ximeno went to Mexico to direct the teaching of painting at the Real Academia de S Carlos de Nueva España, founded in 1783. There he had the opportunity to guide the academy towards Neo-classicism. He introduced important reforms in teaching methods, among which was the introduction in 1795 of the study of anatomy using live models. He was appointed Director General in 1798 on the death of the engraver Jerónimo Antonio Gil.

Ximeno's religious paintings in Mexico include the great monumental groups in the *Assumption of the Virgin* (1809–10; destr. 1967) for the dome of the metropolitan cathedral, which brought him considerable fame. He depicted the same theme, including the *Coronation of the Virgin* (1812–13), in the chapel of the Palacio de Mineria, Mexico City, which is important as the only extant monumental group by Ximeno.

Ximeno's portraits are considered to be his most accomplished works, and their pictorial quality is seen in his portrait of *Jerónimo Antonio Gil* (before 1798; Mexico City, Pin. Virreinal); it is regarded as one of the most important examples of Neo-classical painting during the period of the viceroys. Ximeno's portrait of the Spanish sculptor and architect *Manuel Tolsá* (*c.* 1795; Mexico City, Iglesia de la Profesa) is also very fine. These works express the purest classical style and show the artist's concern with portraying the sitter's character.

Ximeno was an excellent draughtsman and illustrator of books. His drawings (Valencia, Mus. B.A.) include *St Andrew, St James* and *St Thomas the Apostle*. A fine group of drawings, *Cuaderno de Viaje* (Mexico City, Soc. Exalumnos Fac. Ingen.), with scenes observed on his journey from Europe to Mexico, was published in 1985.

BIBLIOGRAPHY

D. Angulo Iñiguez: *La Academia de Bellas Artes de Mexico y sus pinturas españolas* (Seville, 1936), p. 45
X. Moysssén: 'Las pinturas perdidas de la catedral de Mexico', *An. Inst. Invest. Estét.*, 39 (1970), pp. 87–112
T. A. Brown: *La Academia de San Carlos de Nueva España de 1792 à 1810* (Mexico City, 1976), p. 33
X. Moysssén: 'Una maqueta de Rafael Ximeno', *An. Inst. Invest. Estét.*, 48 (1978), pp. 67–70

A. Espinós Díaz and C. Garcia Saiz: 'Algunas obras de Rafael Ximeno y Planes anteriores a su llegada a Mexico', *Archv Esp. A.*, 202 (1979), pp. 115–35
X. Moyssén: *El pintor Rafael Ximeno y Planes su libreta de dibujos* (Mexico City, 1985)
Catalogo de la exposición Tolsa, Ximeno, Fabregat: Trayectoria artistica en España siglo XVIII (exh. cat. by A. Espinós Díaz and others, Valencia, 1989)

ADELA ESPINÓS DÍAZ

Xinyang [Hsin-yang]. City and district in southern Henan Province, China. Two large tombs, generally considered to date from the 4th century BC, were found at Changtaiguan, north of the city of Xinyang. Tomb 1 probably belonged to a dignitary of the southern state of CHU.

The two tombs, like those at Changsha in Hunan Province and at Shou xian in Anhui Province, display many features typical of Chu culture and are a testament to its widespread influence. They have wooden, compartmentalized 'outer coffins', like the tombs found in the JIANGLING region. Although pillaged before they were discovered in 1956, the tombs contained a sizeable number of personal effects in a reasonably well-preserved state, those in Tomb 1 of a higher quality than those in Tomb 2. Notable are a peal of 13 bronze bells; some zither fragments painted with hybrid animals, dragons, hunters with bows and arrows, and musicians; and two wooden lacquered sculptures of guardian animals (h. 1.52 and 1.28 m) with protruding eyes, tongues hanging down on to their chests and heads crowned with antlers. The coffins were lacquered, as were many other items, such as earthenware and wooden objects (more than 200 pieces), the backs of bronze mirrors and carved figures. In addition to the commonly used black and vermilion, gold, silver and other colours were employed for some motifs. A large drum stand, typical of Chu design, is in the form of two birds with long necks, standing back-to-back and perched over two crouching tigers (1.62×1.40 m). Next to a group of bamboo strips, some of which recorded the personal effects in Tomb 1, was a collection of utensils used to shape the bamboo prior to writing.

Some technical and stylistic elements suggest that the objects found may date to the second half of the 4th century BC. These include gold and silver inlay on iron belthooks (*see* CHINA, XIII, fig. 313); gilding on bronze rings fixed to zoomorphic masks; decoration consisting of diagonal compositions with an assortment of whorls, hooks and triangles; the use of inverted symmetry; and the play of colour opposites.

BIBLIOGRAPHY
Henan Xinyang Chu mu wenwu tulu [Archaeological remains from the Chu tombs at Xinyang, Henan] (Zhengzhou, 1959)
K. C. Chang: 'Major Aspects of Ch'u Archaeology', *Early Chinese Art and its Possible Influence in the Pacific Basin*, ed. N. Barnard, i (New York, 1972), pp. 5–52
Li Xueqin: *Eastern Zhou and Qin Civilizations* (New Haven and London, 1985)
Xinyang Chu mu [Chu tombs at Xinyang] (Beijing, 1986)

Xinzheng [Hsin-cheng]. County and small county town in Henan Province, China. In 1923 approximately 100 stylistically diverse bronzes, ranging in date from the 8th to the 6th century BC, were discovered at Lijialou during the digging of a well. The site is probably the tomb of a prince of the small state of Zheng, who reigned during the first half of the 6th century BC.

The earliest ritual vessels include *li* tripods, *gui* vessels and a square *fang yan* vessel for steaming food (for illustrations of vessel types *see* CHINA, fig. 138). Shapes and decoration, the latter composed of large-scale dragons in low relief with wide, ribbon-like bodies, connect the vessels with those dating from the first part of the Eastern Zhou period (771–256 BC) excavated at SHANGCUN LING, Henan Province.

Of three series of bells from Xinzheng, one consisting of four *bo*, one comprising nine *yong zhong* and one with ten *yong zhong* (for description of these types *see* CHINA, §VI, 1(ii)), the *bo* differ most in style from the earliest ritual vessels from the site, though their decoration, comprising interlaced dragons that stand out clearly in low relief, retains some of the same spirit. These bells were probably cast during the 7th century BC. Many of the other bronzes have a shared motif of interlaced dragons delineated within a square or a rectangle, the repetition of which gives their surface a homogeneous and refined texture. This decoration, which occurs in numerous variations from the end of the 7th century BC, sometimes on a very small scale, was named the 'Hsin Ch'eng pattern' by Ludwig Bachhofer.

Xinzheng, *fang hu* ritual vessel, one of a pair, bronze, h. 1.18 m, late 7th century to 6th century BC (Beijing, Palace Museum)

The Xinzheng bronzes are perhaps known principally for two pairs of monumental square *fang hu* vessels (see fig.) and a *lei* vessel. These demonstrate an eccentricity of taste both in their elements in the round, sometimes with openwork, and in the complexity of their surface decoration, based on birds and serpentine dragons. They were probably inspired by the artistic tradition of the state of Chu in the south, or even produced in that region; some elements also echo the Jin tradition of bronze decoration. One of the *fang hu* pairs is almost identical in style to vessels dating to *c.* 550 BC discovered at Tomb 2 at Xiasi in Xichuan (Henan Province) and to another pair dating from the beginning of the 5th century BC from the tomb of the Marquis of Cai at Shou xian (Anhui Province). The existence of a tradition of bronze sculpture is attested by a single piece. The only comparable extant examples are lacquered wood statues (4th century BC) with prominent eyes found at XINYANG.

A few bronzes from Xinzheng can be related on stylistic grounds to the tradition of the state of Jin (modern Shanxi Province). Some are undoubtedly the products of Jin workshops, notably a series of six *ding* tripods that are identical to vessels excavated in the vicinity of modern Houma, the site of the capital of Jin founded in 585 BC. These connections with Jin are further supported by the discovery at Houma of remains of clay pattern blocks and moulds having similar or identical decoration.

There are many unanswered questions associated with the Xinzheng bronzes. Of the two inscriptions on bronzes in the group, one is too badly eroded to be read and the other remains the subject of divergent interpretations.

BIBLIOGRAPHY

Sun Haibo: *Xinzheng yiqi* [Archaeological remains from Xinzheng] (Beijing, 1937)
L. Bachhofer: *A Short History of Chinese Art* (London, 1946)
M. Loehr: *Ritual Vessels of Bronze Age China* (New York, 1968)
Tan Danjiong: *Xinzheng tongqi* [Bronzes from Xinzheng] (Taipei, 1977)
The Great Bronze Age of China: An Exhibition from the People's Republic of China (exh. cat., ed. Wen Fong; New York, Met.; Los Angeles, CA, Co. Mus. A.; 1980–81)
J. So: 'Hu Vessels from Xinzheng: Toward a Definition of Chu Style', *The Great Bronze Age of China: A Symposium: Los Angeles, 1981*, pp. 64–71
Li Xueqin: *Eastern Zhou and Qin Civilizations* (New Haven and London, 1985)

ALAIN THOTE

Xizang Zizhiqu. *See* TIBET.

Xochicalco. Pre-Columbian site in western Morelos, Mexico, *c.* 40 km south-west of Cuernavaca. The site and region were occupied continuously from *c.* 900 BC, but are known especially for the Late-Classic-period (*c.* AD 600–*c.* 900) occupation, when an urban and ceremonial centre with monumental architecture was built around and on the artificially terraced hills known as Cerro Xochicalco and Cerro la Malinche and on the adjacent hills and plains.

The archaeological zone was first mentioned by Fray Bernardino de Sahagún in the 16th century. The Jesuit Antonio Alzate visited the site in 1777, conducted some primitive excavations on the Pyramid of the Feathered Serpent and wrote a report in 1791. The Jesuit Pedro Marquez also visited the site, and his report was used by Alexander von Humboldt to describe the site and publish some illustrations of it in 1810. In 1877 Antonio Peñafiel

made a study of the monumental architecture then known. Excavations were conducted by Leopoldo Batres from 1908 to 1910, when the Pyramid of the Feathered Serpent was restored, and Eduard Seler made a study of the sculpture. Further excavations were carried out by Eduardo Noguera between 1934 and 1950, and by Cesar Sáenz from 1961 to 1967. The site and its region were explored by Jaime Litvak King between 1965 and 1972 and by Kenneth Hirth between 1977 and 1984. Excavation of the site's outer wall was begun in the 1980s by Norberto González and Silvia Garza.

The earliest occupation comprised two small hamlets in the Middle Pre-Classic period (*c.* 1000–*c.* 300 BC), west of the Late Classic ceremonial precinct. During the Late Pre-Classic period (*c.* 300 BC–*c.* AD 250) these grew from *c.* 0.2 ha to *c.* 5.5 ha, and the concentration of the population shifted southwards. Population continued to increase through the Early Classic period (*c.* AD 250–*c.* 600), occupying *c.* 32 ha, but was dispersed in clusters rather than concentrated in a single urban centre. Several small temple mounds were the only public architecture at this time. During this period Xochicalco was probably a regional centre in the extensive trading empire of TEOTIHUACÁN.

Expansion took place after *c.* AD 600 and continued through the Late Classic period. Most of the major monuments of the ceremonial precinct were built during this period, and Xochicalco, with an estimated maximum population of 20,000, covered *c.* 4 sq. km. These developments coincided with the waning of Teotihuacán's power, and the concentration of Xochicalco's ceremonial centre on the prominent hilltops, together with the construction of walls and ditches, may indicate a growing rivalry between several urban centres asserting their power as Teotihuacán declined.

The summit of Cerro Xochicalco became the administrative and ceremonial core of the city. The slopes of the hill, the slopes of Cerro la Malinche and the saddle between them were artificially altered into terraces. Smaller areas of ceremonial architecture were constructed on hills to the north, south and west of the core. Between these, élite residences were concentrated on the upper terraces nearest the ceremonial centres. The site seems to have been deliberately divided into public and restricted space.

The ceremonial and élite areas of the site covered *c.* 63 ha. Surveys and excavations here have uncovered temple platforms, temples, administrative buildings, ballcourts, 'palaces', streets and causeways, military defences and caves associated with an underground observatory. Construction appears to have followed a careful urban plan. The central acropolis complex, the Ceremonial Plaza, comprises a walled plaza group containing the three most important temple platforms: the Pyramid of the Feathered Serpent, Mound 2 and Structure A. To the west of this plaza are élite residential complexes, and the vertical sighting shaft of the underground observatory is at the north-west corner. At lower elevations, other élite ceremonial zones are located to the south and west, connected by streets and pavements: the Central Plaza, containing the temple Structure E; the northern ballcourt, a multi-roomed 'palace' complex and 20 circular platforms on the saddle between the Central Plaza and Cerro la Malinche; and a partially cleared pyramid-platform on Cerro la

Malinche. On Cerro de la Bodega, to the north-east of Cerro Xochicalco, stood another, still unexcavated, élite plaza complex.

The Pyramid of the Feathered Serpent comprises a TALUD-TABLERO type of platform supporting the three sloping walls of an open-fronted chamber. The *talud–tablero* form differs from that at Teotihuacán in having a tall *talud* and relatively short *tablero*, the latter topped by a flying cornice resembling those at Gulf Coast TAJÍN. The *talud* is faced with andesite slabs carved in relief (see fig.), and the structure's name derives from the eight undulating figures of feathered serpents, forming frames for carved glyphs with both MAYA and Southern Highland ZAPOTEC calendrical figures, and seated personages wearing Maya-style headdresses. The upper part is carved with a frieze of warriors with darts and shields. The mixture of styles, influences and calendrics has led to one conclusion that the structure was erected in commemoration of the adjustment of the Mesoamerican calendrical system (*see* MESOAMERICA, PRE-COLUMBIAN, §II). Another interpretation is that the carvings represent the dynastic history of a local ruler or a list of conquests.

Temple Structure E, the Temple of Three Stelae, contained three stelae (Mexico City, Mus. N. Antropol.), each carved on all four sides with reliefs representing Tlaloc (god of water), a sun god and a fertility or moon goddess. They were erected between *c.* AD 600 and 700 and appear to be associated with major events in the agricultural cycle. In a smaller Chamber of Offerings on the south-west corner of the Structure E platform a stone *yugo* (Mexico City, Mus. N. Antropol.), associated with the Mesoamerican ball-game, was excavated (*see* MESOAMERICA, PRE-COLUMBIAN, §II, 3(i)). Other objects associated with the three stelae included a cache of Maya- and Zapotec-style greenstone figurines, Teotihuacán figurines, 'eccentric' chipped obsidian shapes, shell, jade and turquoise beads, and Late-Classic-period Teotihuacán, TOLTEC, MIXTEC and other pottery (Mexico City, Mus. N. Antropol.; Cuernavaca, Mus. Reg.). At the northern ballcourt were found the two uncarved stone marker rings (now set into the sloping side walls of the court) and a parrot-headed sculpture, presumed to be a ballcourt marker (Mexico City, Mus. N. Antropol.).

Xochicalco's importance decreased during the latter half of the Late Classic period, and the site was largely abandoned by *c.* AD 900. Construction in the core area had ceased, and the residential area had shrunk to *c.* 11.5 ha. Partial reoccupation took place in the Late Post-Classic period (*c.* AD 1200–1521), when Tlahuica peoples occupied the region. The site expanded to *c.* 92.5 ha in the late 13th century and the 14th, and a ceremonial precinct was built on Cerro Temascal, just west of the Late Classic ceremonial centre. The site was abandoned again by *c.* 1500 but remained an important religious shrine. It was not included in 16th-century Aztec tributary lists for the region, although a small Aztec garrison was established there just before the Spanish Conquest of 1519–21.

BIBLIOGRAPHY
A. Peñafiel: *Monumentos del arte mexicano antiguo* (Berlin, 1890)
E. Noguera: 'Cerámica de Xochicalco', *Mexico Ant.*, vi (1947), pp. 273–98

Xochicalco, Pyramid of the Feathered Serpent, detail showing relief carving on *talud*, *c.* AD 600–*c.* 900

I. Marquina: *Arquitectura prehispanica* (Mexico City, 1950, 2/1964/*R* 1981), pp. 129–45
A. Caso: 'Calendario y escritura de Xochicalco', *Rev. Mex. Estud. Antropol.*, xviii (1962), pp. 49–79
G. Kubler: *The Art and Architecture of Ancient America*, Pelican Hist. A. (Harmondsworth, 1962, rev. 3/1984), pp. 56–7, 68–73
J. Litvak King: 'Xochicalco en la caída del clásico: Una hipótesis', *An. Inst. N. Antropol. & Hist.*, vii (1970), pp. 131–44
M. P. Weaver: *The Aztecs, Maya and their Predecessors: Archaeology of Mesoamerica* (New York, 1972, rev. 2/1981), pp. 227–31
J. E. Hardoy: *Ciudades precolombinas* (Buenos Aires, 1964; Eng. trans. by J. Thorne, New York, 1973), pp. 89–99
C. Sáenz: 'El enigma de Xochicalco', *Hist. Mex.* (1974), pp. 159–84
C. B. Hunter: *A Guide to Ancient Mexican Ruins* (Norman, 1977), pp. 130–46
J. Kelly: *The Complete Visitor's Guide to Mesoamerican Ruins* (Norman, 1982), pp. 96–102
K. Hirth: 'Xochicalco: Urban Growth and State Formation in Central Mexico', *Science*, 225 (1984), pp. 579–86
K. Hirth and A. Cyphers Guillén: *Tiempo y asentamiento en Xochicalco* (Mexico City, 1985)

DAVID M. JONES, JAIME LITVAK KING

Xsell, Georg. *See* GSELL, GEORG.

Xuarez. *See* JUAREZ.

Xu Beihong [Hsü Pei-hung; Ju Peon] (*b* Yixing, Jiangsu Province, 19 July 1895; *d* Beijing, 26 Sept 1953). Chinese painter and art educator. The most acclaimed Western-trained artist in modern China, he influenced the development of 20th-century Chinese painting through his role as art teacher and administrator as well as his painting.

Xu's father was a village teacher and painter. Forced to support the family after his father's early death, in 1915 Xu went to Shanghai, cultural and commercial centre of

Xu Beihong: *Five Hundred Followers of Tian Heng* (detail), oil on canvas, early 1930s

modern China. There he earned a living by painting popular pictures of beautiful ladies and enrolled as a student in the French department of Zhendan University. He became acquainted with such luminaries of the art and intellectual world as Gao Jianfu, Kang Youwei and Wang Guowei (1877–1927) and gained the support of Cai Yuanpei (1868–1940), the influential chancellor of Peking [Beijing] University and a firm believer in modern art education, who arranged for Xu to go to Paris on a Chinese government scholarship.

Xu was in Europe from 1919 to 1927, with one brief trip home. In Paris he studied at the Ecole des Beaux-Arts, acquiring a solid foundation in drawing, anatomy and the Western academic tradition. He also studied in Berlin and travelled widely throughout the Continent. His extensive stay and serious study in Europe made him the first Chinese artist to have a deep understanding of Western art and culture based on direct experience.

On returning to China, Xu was immediately prominent in China's modern art circles. He started teaching at the bohemian centre of Western modernism in Shanghai, the Nanguo Academy of Fine Art, moved briefly to Beijing to administer the art department at Peking University, but held his most important post, head of the art department, at the newly formed Central University in Nanjing. Through his teaching, writing and frequent exhibitions, Xu became a powerful force for the introduction of Western art; his influence was rivalled only by Liu Haisu at the long-established Shanghai Academy of Fine Art.

However, despite his fashionable Parisian clothes and manners, Xu was not among the most radical of Western-style modernists. His formal academicism, closer to 19th-century European tradition than 20th-century avant-garde styles, was considered old-fashioned by such new groups as the Shanghai-based Juelan she ('Storm and Stress Society'), who took their inspiration from Post-Impressionism, Cubism and Surrealism (see also CHINA, §V, 3(iv)(a)). Xu's oil paintings do seem outdated by contemporary Western standards. However, the fundamentals of Western oil painting—shading and chiaroscuro, scientific anatomy, fixed-point perspective—were still relatively new in China. Xu set technical standards for a new generation of Chinese oil painters and, perhaps more important, encouraged the influence of Western realism in Chinese ink painting.

In his own work, Xu tried to transfer his Paris training to subjects relevant to the cultural and political needs of 20th-century China. He painted large historical paintings in the European academic style. Two examples from the early 1930s are the *Five Hundred Followers of Tian Heng* (see fig.) and *Waiting for our Prince*. Apparently he was not satisfied with oils for presenting Chinese subject-matter, for by the end of the decade he switched to ink, although he retained elements of Western perspective, composition and anatomy for his large work *Yu Gong Moves the Mountain*. Relying on his Paris-acquired skill in sketching from life, Xu brought a strong element of realism and solidity to his Chinese-style ink paintings. He was especially proficient at studies of animals, including the galloping horses for which he is best known in the West.

While at the top of the modern Chinese art world in Nanjing and Shanghai, Xu also did much travelling. In 1933–4 he went to Europe as China's representative at an official exhibition of modern Chinese painting and had individual exhibitions in Berlin, Milan and elsewhere. The following year he travelled and sketched in Guangxi Province and during World War II alternated trips to India and South-east Asia with residence in Chongqing, Sichuan Province, as Director of the Fine Art Research Institute, Central Research Academy. After the war, he settled in Beijing as head of the Beiping [Beijing] Academy of Art and in 1949, with the founding of the People's Republic, became Director of the new Central Academy of Fine Arts and Chairman of the National Artists' Association. Xu's influence on the organization of the arts in Communist China was great, but a stroke in 1951 ended his artistic and administrative career.

In the People's Republic, Xu has continued to be honoured both on account of his accomplishments and because his students and followers occupied important posts in the new art establishment. Xu's academic style and high technical standards in oil painting also proved to be quite compatible with the Soviet-inspired SOCIALIST REALISM of the 1950s. In the longer perspective of Chinese art history, Xu can be seen as an important early pioneer in the introduction of Western art to China and in the adaptation of it to China's national style and character.

BIBLIOGRAPHY

Beihong huaji [Collected paintings of Xu Beihong], 4 vols (Shanghai, 1932–9)

Beihong sumiao xuan [Selected sketches by Xu Beihong] (Beijing, 1955)

Xu Beihong caimo hua [Xu Beihong's ink paintings] (Beijing, 1959)

Xu Beihong youhua [Xu Beihong's oil paintings] (Beijing, 1960)

Chu Tan: 'The Painter Hsu Pei-hung', *Chin. Lit.* (1963), no. 12, pp. 96–105

'Xu Beihong', *Biographical Dictionary of Republican China*, ed. H. Boorman and R. Howard (New York, 1967–71), ii, pp. 134–6

Xu Beihong Huaji [Collected paintings of Xu Beihong], 2 vols (Beijing, 1979–84) [best collection of his ink paintings]

Ai Zhongxin: *Xu Beihong yanjiu* [Research on Xu Beihong] (Shanghai, 1981)

Liao Jingwen: *Xu Beihong yi sheng* [Xu Beihong: a life] (Beijing, 1982)

RALPH CROIZIER

Xu Daoning [Hsü Tao-ning] (*b* Chang'an [modern Xi'an], Shaanxi Province, *c.* AD 970; *d c.* 1052). Chinese painter. Originally a vendor of medicinal herbs, he initially painted landscapes to attract potential customers. After attaining fame, he 'frequented the manorial homes of princelings and officials', for whom he painted murals, hanging scrolls and handscrolls. He was a familiar guest of the rich and powerful in both Chang'an and the capital, Bianliang (modern Kaifeng), in Henan Province. Famous clients included Huang Tingjian's father, Huang Shu (1018–58). Huang Tingjian later eulogized one of Xu's paintings:

> I met Drunken Xu in Chang'an . . .
> Quite tipsy, he would wield a worn brush dripping with ink,
> With the force of an avalanche, his hand never stopping.
> In a few feet, mountains and rivers would stretch over ten thousand miles,
> And fill the hall with a bleak and chilly air.
> A rustic monk returns to his temple, followed by the boy.
> A fisherman is hailed by the traveller waiting to ford the stream.
> (trans. M. F. Wilson)

Xu Daoning (attrib.): *Fishermen's Evening Song* (*Yufu tujuan*; detail), handscroll, ink and light colours on silk, 489×2096 mm, first half of the 11th century (Kansas City, MO, Nelson–Atkins Museum of Art)

It seems that Xu was active in the capital around 1040. It is known that in 1042 he offended the prefect of Chang'an and took refuge in Huanzhou (now Huan xian), Gansu Province, but returned to Chang'an in 1043–4.

Although considered vulgar and plebeian by the irascible Mi Fu in his *Hua shi* ('History of painting'; *c.* 1103), Xu was ranked by most early critics as one of the great landscape masters after Fan Kuan and Li Cheng. It was noted that whereas in his early years Xu had a meticulous and laborious style, he eventually developed an individual, eccentric mode of brush deployment characterized by speed, animation and compelling power. A marked use of wet ink was observed in his later paintings of desolate and cold northern barren scenes. Wen Tong inscribed Xu's painting *Wintry Woods*: 'Although Master Xu studies the style of Li Yingqiu [AD 919–*c.* 967], in ink strokes he criss-crosses with abandon entirely in his own manner.' By the Xuanhe era (1119–26) of the reign of Huizong, Xu's influence had become such that the descendants of his contemporary Qu Ding were said to have taken up Xu's style and not their own family tradition in order to survive. The *Xuanhe huapu* ('Xuanhe collection of painting'; preface 1120) lists 138 works by Xu: themes include river fishing scenes, autumnal mountains, layered mountains, snow scenes, mists, woods and rocks, summer rains, vernal travels, cloudy spring mountains, wintry woods and re-turning geese.

Liu Daochun lists Xu's three areas of excellence as woods and trees, level distance (*ping yuan*) and wild waters. He admires Xu's vigorous, uninhibited compositions, which reflect the spirit of Li Cheng. Guo Ruoxu remarked on Xu's abbreviated and highly individual brushwork, with which he created sheer precipices and sinewy, firm woods and trees. Yuan-period (1279–1368) writers, noting Xu's origins as a medicine peddler, claim that his early brushwork had a touch of the common and vulgar, qualities that were shed only in his middle years, when his style became more restrained and abbreviated. They remark on his blunt and straight brush-wielding, with the entrance of the stroke exposed and the entire length a firm, straight-edged line.

A handscroll entitled *Qiushan xiaosi* ('Desolate temple amid autumn mountains'; Kyoto, Fujii Yurinkan Mus.), associated with Xu, exhibits characteristics that may correspond to descriptions of his early meticulous style. However, for such technically correct works, in which the brushwork is self-effacing and hidden, it is not easy to identify the artist. The scroll's relatively weak structure suggests that it may represent a work of the Li–Guo school (Li Cheng and GUO XI) from after the Yuan period. Its high vantage-point, close foreground, large crossed bare trees and tendency to block out the far distance all point to the perception of the early part of the Ming (1368–1644).

An unsigned handscroll in ink on silk with light colours, *Yufu tujuan* ('Fishermen's evening song'; see fig.), on the other hand, can be relatively securely identified with contemporary descriptions of Xu's late style, though it lacks an end-section and the artist's signature. The scroll possesses the hoary grandeur associated with painting of the early part of the Northern Song period (960–1127). The masterly and natural deployment of ink wash is typical of the Li Cheng school; the scale and the dwarfing of human presence, as well as the sense of a light source in the play of light and dark, all point to an early dating. The roughness and spontaneity of the masterly modelling strokes (*cun*) correspond to descriptions of Xu Daoning's late style, as does the use of wet blobs rather than ink circles to depict watery rocks.

BIBLIOGRAPHY
Franke: 'Hsü Tao-ning'
Liu Daochun: *Shengchao minghua ping* [Critique of famous paintings of the present (Song) dynasty] (1059), *juan* 2
Guo Ruoxu: *Tuhua jianwen zhi* [Experiences in painting], *juan* 6 (preface 1075), *juan* 4; *R* in Huashi congshu (Taipei, 1974); Eng. trans. in A. C. Soper: *Kuo Jo-hsü's 'Experiences in Painting' (T'u-hua chien-wen chih): An Eleventh Century History of Chinese Painting* (Washington, DC, 1951/*R* 1971)
Mi Fu: *Hua shi* [History of painting] (*c.* 1103)
Xuanhe huapu [Xuanhe collection of painting] (preface 1120), *juan* 11
Xia Wenyan: *Tuhui baojian* [Precious mirror for examining painting] (1365/*R* Shanghai, 1936)
H. Sofukawa: 'Kyō Dōnei no denke to sansui yōshiki ni kansuru hitotsu kōsatsu' [A study of the life and landscape paintings of Xu Daoning], *Tōhō Gakuhō*, lii (1980), pp. 415–500
Chen Gaohua, ed.: *Song Liao Jin huajia shiliao* [Historical material on artists of the Song, Liao and Jin dynasties] (Beijing, 1984), *juan* 279–88
JOAN STANLEY-BAKER

Xue Ji [Hsüeh Chi; *zi* Sitong; *hao* Shaobao] (*b* Fenyang, Shanxi Province, AD 649; *d* Wannian County, 713). Chinese calligrapher and scholar–official. Born into a family of high officials from north China, he rose to important positions at the courts of the usurping Empress Wu Zetian (*reg* AD 690–705) and Emperor Zhongzong (*reg* 705–10). After the second accession of Emperor Ruizong (*reg* 684–90, 710–12), he was made a scholar at the Zhaowen Academy and given various other royal appointments. When Emperor Xuanzong (*reg* 712–56) came to power, however, Xue became involved in the princess Taiping's plot to poison the new emperor and was forced to commit suicide.

As a young man Xue Ji studied calligraphic works of the early part of the Tang period (AD 618–907) in the collection of his grandfather, the minister Wei Zheng (AD 580–643), and his own style thus came to resemble that of early Tang calligraphers. He was so strongly influenced by CHU SUILIANG that his works were often mistaken for Chu's, leading to the popular saying: 'Buy a Chu, get a Xue'. Together with that of his cousin Xue Yao (*fl c.* AD 700), his orthodox and traditional style was popular and influential among court officials. In AD 699, when Empress Wu Zetian wrote in her own hand the text for a stele (*Shengxian taizi bei*, 'Stele for the crown prince who ascended to the Immortals') in commemoration of the crown prince, who had died young, Xue Ji was among the seven officials commissioned to write eulogies on the reverse of the stele (Yanshi County, Henan Province, rubbing in Beijing, Pal. Mus.). Here Xue's calligraphy displays a mixture of the styles of Yu Shinan (AD 558–638) and Chu Suiliang. The only other work that can be reliably attributed to Xue Ji is a commemorative stele for a Sui period (AD 581–618) Buddhist monk, *Xinxing chanshi bei* ('Stele for the Master of Meditation Xinxing'; AD 706; destr.), preserved as a rubbing of the Song period (960–1279; Kyoto, Ōtani U. Col.). This is executed in a rigid and austere regular script (*kaishu*), close in style to that of Chu Suiliang. Some sources report that Xue also excelled in painting, especially of cranes.

BIBLIOGRAPHY
Liu Xu and others: *Jiu Tang shu* [Former history of the Tang], *juan* 37 [compiled in later Jin period, AD 936–46]
Ouyang Xiu and others: *Xin Tang shu* [Later history of the Tang], *juan* 98 [compiled in Song period, 960–1279]
G. Sotoyama: 'Setsu Shō' [Xue Ji], *Shodō zenshū* [Complete collection of calligraphy], ed. K. Shimonaka, viii (Tokyo, 2/1957), pp. 188–9
ROGER GOEPPER

Xul Solar [Schulz Solari, Oscar Agustín Alejandro] (*b* San Fernando, 14 Dec 1888; *d* 10 May 1963). Argentine painter. He was self-taught and spent many years of his youth visiting Europe, holding his first exhibition in Milan in 1920. He returned in 1924 to Buenos Aires where, like Emilio Pettoruti and other artists who had also familiarized themselves with new trends in Europe, he became part of the first wave of the avant-garde in Argentina. Undeterred by the hostile reactions aroused by his first exhibitions, he remained resolved to pursue an unconventional approach throughout his life.

Although Xul Solar's work made use of characteristic Surrealist elements such as twinned images, fantastic perspectives and the animation of the inanimate, his forms are fundamentally abstract and mystical. He thought of his art as a way of revealing the spiritual dimensions of man, and to this end he referred to magic, occult philosophy, astrology and linguistics, bringing together descriptive and invented forms, cabalistic numbers and gestural marks, vanishing points and spatial ruptures into an extravagantly inventive poetic narrative, as in *Saint Dance* (1925; Buenos Aires, Marion and Jorge Helft priv. col., see 1989 exh. cat., p. 142).

Xul Solar's development exemplifies a creative drive towards the expression of an exalted state of awareness, beginning with works produced between 1919 and 1930, characterized by accents of colour within a rarefied light; among these pictures, in which objects appear to materialize within a spatial order that supports them and fixes them in place, are a series of monochromatic works. From 1930 he pursued the esoteric aspects of his art with greater single-mindedness, and after 1960 he gave greater prominence to colour and transformed his images into clearly legible signs on a static support. His pictures are small and are generally painted in watercolour and tempera, as in *Deep Valley* (1944; Buenos Aires, Soc. ALART). His highly original world view and philosophical preoccupations led him to devise, among other inventions indicating the subtlety and complexity of his imagination, a general American language (Neocriollo), a universal language that he called Panlengua, and a game (panjuego) based on chess.

BIBLIOGRAPHY
O. Svanascini: *Xul Solar* (Buenos Aires, 1962)
J. López Anaya: *Xul Solar* (Buenos Aires, 1980)
Art in Latin America: The Modern Era, 1820–1980 (exh. cat. by D. Ades, London, Hayward Gal., 1989), pp. 142–3
HORACIO SAFONS

Xuriguera, Josep de. *See under* CHURRIGUERA.

Xu Wei [Hsü Wei; *zi* Wenchang] (*b* Shanyin [modern Shaoxing], Zhejiang Province, 12 March 1521; *d* 1593). Chinese painter, calligrapher, essayist, poet and dramatist. He was born to the concubine of a minor official and was

Xu Wei: *Flowers and Other Plants* (detail), handscroll, ink on paper, 300×1053 mm, mid-16th century (Nanjing, Jiangsu Provincial Museum)

reared by his father's second wife after his father's death. In 1540 he passed the first test leading to higher government examinations. He was married the following year and moved with his wife's family to Guangzhou (Canton). Xu retreated to a monastery in 1550, after the deaths of his wife and stepbrothers, and attempted the higher civil service examination but failed repeatedly. While in the monastery Xu Wei turned his energies to writing and painting, producing paintings, plays, poetry and essays on opera. His literary reputation resulted in his appointment as personal secretary to Hu Zongxian, the commander-governor of the south-east coastal provinces, a post he held until 1562, when his patron was accused of treason and imprisoned. Between 1552 and 1561 Xu Wei four times attempted the provincial examinations, the second stage in the civil service examinations, with no success. From 1562 Xu became increasingly unstable: in 1565 he attempted suicide, and the following year he stabbed his third wife to death in a fit of madness and was sentenced to death. Friends interceded and he was released from prison in 1572. The last two decades of Xu's life were marred by illness and heavy drinking. He died in poverty at the age of 73.

Xu Wei's mental illness and his painting style have earned him a reputation as a 'mad painter', continuing the tradition of unorthodox ZHE SCHOOL artists such as Shi Zhong (1438–c. 1517), who worked in a rough and 'splashy' manner that recalled certain 8th- and 9th-century eccentric painters such as WU DAOZI and Sun Wei. These artists frequently painted at gatherings, often while intoxicated, splashing ink on the silk in an apparent frenzy; they would then return to the work and, with a few calculated touches, transform their indecipherable markings into a recognizable composition. The subjects of Xu's paintings are not unconventional in themselves. *Landscape with Figures* (handscroll; Tokyo, priv. col., see Cahill, figs 81–2) includes travellers and a meditative gentleman among rocks and trees. The landscape, however, is rendered rapidly with broad, wet strokes. The leaves of the trees appear to have been flung from the brush; rock forms are daubed on moist paper. Another intensely emotional work is *Bamboo* (Washington, DC, Freer; *see* CHINA, fig. 127). In Xu Wei's acknowledged masterpiece, *Flowers and Other Plants* (see fig.), a similarly dramatic and apparently random method of execution can be seen. At first glance, the ink washes and quick, scratchy lines of the melon seem to have little representational function. A moment later, the brushstrokes resolve themselves into a coherent image: a fruit, a leaf, a twisting stem. Xu Wei's mastery of ink and the dynamic movement of his brush account for the ease with which the viewer moves from the first perception to the second. He conveys the weight of the melon, its delicate shades and the springiness of the vine, and leaves the viewer with a simultaneous appreciation of the physical properties of ink monochrome painting and the artist's skill in representing form.

See also CHINA, §IV, 2(vi)(b).

DMB: 'Hsü Wei'   BIBLIOGRAPHY
Yu-ho Tseng Ecke: 'A Study of Hsu Wei', *A. Orient.*, v (1963), pp. 243–54
J. L. Faurot: *Four Cries of the Gibbon: A Tsa-chu Cycle by the Ming Dramatist Hsu Wei* (Ph.D. diss., Berkeley, U. CA, 1972)
J. Cahill: *Parting at the Shore: Chinese Painting of the Early and Middle Ming Dynasty, 1368–1580* (New York, 1978), pp. 159–63

VYVYAN BRUNST, with JAMES CAHILL

Xu Xi [Hsü Hsi] (*b* Jinling [now Nanjing], late 9th century AD; *d* ?Jinling, before 975). Chinese painter. A master of the flower-and-bird genre that became firmly established during the Five Dynasties period (AD 907–60), Xu Xi is a legendary figure in the traditions of Chinese painting (*see* CHINA, §V, 3(v) and (vi)). His work was praised during his lifetime by Taizu (*reg* 960–76), the first emperor of the Northern Song dynasty (960–1127), and by influential critics and emperors of later periods; not long after his death, however, Xu Xi was known only through literature.

Xu Xi came from a family of respected government officials, but he remained aloof from public office, preferring to wander in gardens, observing flowers, insects and birds. Descriptions of his painting suggest he applied ink freely and rapidly and added colour loosely, emphasizing ink brushwork, for, by his own accounts, he was not concerned with subtleties of colour. This contrasts sharply with the then prevailing trends of meticulously applied, solid colours in areas bounded by fine ink outline. His style was contrasted with that of HUANG QUAN, and by the 11th century the two were viewed as representing opposing traditions that have remained crucial to traditional Chinese painting. Huang's opulent style came to be known for stressing colour, lifelike appearance and the luxuriant flowers and birds of exotic gardens. Xu's style, in contrast, was known for emphasizing brushwork, lifelike vitality and wilderness habitats, as well as familiar details of the everyday.

Early accounts of Xu Xi's work do not refer to the concept of *xieyi* ('sketching the idea'; *see* CHINA, §V, 4(ii)) in reference to his impressionistic style. Errors of punctuation in early texts have probably allowed this anachronism to creep into 20th-century translations. Nevertheless, the free brush style attributed to Xu Xi was popular among later literati and amateur artists as an alternative to the meticulous traditions of the Academy and aristocracy.

Franke: 'Hsü Hsi'   BIBLIOGRAPHY
Guo Ruoxu: *Tuhua jianwen zhi* [Experiences in painting], *juan* 6 (preface 1075); *R* in Huashi congshu (Taipei, 1974); Eng. trans. in A. C. Soper: *Kuo Jo-hsü's 'Experiences in Painting' (T'u-hua chien-wen chih): An Eleventh Century History of Chinese Painting* (Washington, DC, 1951/*R* 1971)
J. Cahill: *An Index of Early Chinese Painters and Paintings: T'ang, Sung, and Yüan* (Berkeley, 1980)
Chen Gaohua, ed.: *Song Liao Jin huajia shiliao* [Historical material on artists of the Song, Liao and Jin dynasties] (Beijing, 1984)
S. Bush and Hsio-yen Shih: *Early Chinese Texts on Painting* (Cambridge, MA, 1985)

JAMES ROBINSON

Xydias Typaldos, Nikolaos (*b* Kephallinia, 1826; *d* Athens, Feb 1909). Greek painter. He studied in Italy and at the Ecole des Beaux-Arts in Paris, where he lived until his return to Greece in the late 1890s. Primarily a portrait and still-life painter, he remained faithful to academic Realism throughout his period in France, where he received numerous commissions and wide recognition. His *Still-life with Melons, Pomegranates and Bottle* (*c.* 1885; Athens, N.G.) is characteristically detailed and dramatically lit. While in Athens he concentrated on themes from popular Greek tradition and village and genre scenes (e.g. *Anafiotika*; Athens, N.G.), which, though painted in freer brushstrokes, were unlike the Impressionist works of his progressive Athenian contemporaries.

BIBLIOGRAPHY
C. Christou: *E ellenike zographike, 1832–1922* [Greek painting, 1832–1922] (Athens, 1981), pp. 36–9

EVITA ARAPOGLOU

Xylography. Term sometimes used to refer to the processes of WOODCUT and WOOD-ENGRAVING. ☐

Xyngopoulos, Andreas (*b* Athens, 1891; *d* Athens, 22 April 1979). Greek archaeologist and art historian. He graduated from the School of Philosophy at the University of Athens in 1924. From 1928 until 1930 he studied Byzantine art at the Ecole Pratique des Hautes Etudes in Paris under Charles Diehl and Gabriel Millet, gaining his doctorate in 1937. From 1920 until 1940 he also worked in the Greek archaeological service, mainly in Macedonia, as ephor of Byzantine monuments. In 1940 he was elected professor of Byzantine archaeology at the University of Thessaloniki, where he taught until he retired in 1956. In 1966 he became a member of the Academy of Athens. His work covered wide areas of Byzantine and post-Byzantine art. As an archaeologist, his two most important discoveries were the mosaics (5th century) in Hosios David at Thessaloniki and those in the church of the Holy Apostles (14th century) in the same city. He was a prolific author of books and articles.

WRITINGS
Euretirion mesaionikon mnimeion Athinon [Inventory of the medieval monuments of Athens] (Athens, 1929)
I psiphidoti diakomisis tou naou ton Agion Apostolon Thessalonikis [The mosaic decoration of the church of the Holy Apostles in Thessaloniki] (Thessaloniki, 1953)
Thessalonique et la peinture macédonienne (Athens, 1955)
Epistimoniki drasis—epistimonika dimosieumata [Scholarly activities—scholarly publications] (Athens, 1965)
The Mosaics of the Church of St. Demetrius in Thessaloniki (Thessaloniki, 1965)

BIBLIOGRAPHY
Louisa Laourdas: *Balkan Stud.*, xx (1979), pp. 518–19
P. Zepos and M. Chatzidakis: *Nea Estia*, cv (1979), pp. 749–51
Ch. Bakirtzis: *Ellinika*, xxxii (1980), pp. 393–5

DIMITRIS TSOUGARAKIS

Y

y. For compound Castilian Spanish surnames joined by this conjunction, *see under* the part of the surname that precedes it.

☐

Yablonskaya, Tat'yana (Nilovna) [Yablons'ka, Tetyana (Nilovna)] (*b* Smolensk, 24 Feb 1917). Ukrainian painter of Russian birth. She studied at the Kiev Art Institute (1935–41) under Fyodor Krichevsky (1879–1947), and in such pictures as *Bread* (1949; Moscow, Tret'yakov Gal.) she treated genre motifs in the monumental tradition established by Krichevsky. In the mid- to late 1960s she painted a cycle of canvases based on subjects drawn from Ukrainian countryside in a style derived from national artistic traditions, as in *Summer* (1967; Moscow, Tret'yakov Gal.). From the end of the 1960s she painted canvases embodying her reflections on human destiny and the meaning of life, for example *Life Goes On* (1971; Kiev, Mus. Ukrain. A.) and *Flax* (1978; Moscow, Tret'yakov Gal.). On the whole Yablonskaya's work is marked by an attempt to overcome Socialist-Realist dogma by turning to the 'eternal themes' of human life; hence her neo-Symbolism and her return to the artistic experiments of the beginning of the century and the era of Art Nouveau. In her works of the 1970s and 1980s impressionistic elements became more noticeable and her palette grew richer and more varied.

BIBLIOGRAPHY
L. Vladich: *Tat'yana Nilovna Yablonskaya* (Kiev, 1958)
L. I. Popova and V. P. Tseltner: *T. N. Yablonskaya* (Moscow, 1968)
Ye. G. Korotkevich: *Tat'yana Yablonskaya* (Moscow, 1980)

V. P. TSEL'TNER

Yadava [Yādava; Seuna]. Dynasty that ruled parts of the northern Deccan, India, from the 12th century to the 14th. The Yadavas of Devagiri were members of the last Hindu monarchy of the Deccan. They claimed descent from a mythical king, Yadu, but the first historical prince of the house was Dridhaprahara, who began as a vassal of the RASHTRAKUTA dynasty at Chandor, near Nasik, in the early 9th century. His son and successor, Seunachandra, is said to have named his dominions and subjects after himself. His fourth descendant, Billama II (*reg c.* 1000), transferred his allegiance to the Chalukyas of Kalyana (*see* CHALUKYA, §2), who subsequently supplanted the Rashtrakutas. A remote descendant, Billama V (*reg c.* 1185–93), later captured a major part of the territory of his Chalukya overlord Someshvara IV and proclaimed his independence, establishing his capital at Devagiri (*see* DAULATABAD). He also led an aggressive campaign in the north against the PARAMARA and Chalukya dynasties. However, the credit for firmly establishing Yadava dominions goes to Billama V's grandson Singhana of Simhana (*reg c.* 1200–47), who also enlarged the kingdom; the mightiest king of the house, he also assumed imperial titles. Although Singhana's successors kept the kingdom intact, and tried to expand it in 1307, while his great-grandson Ramachandra (*reg* 1271–1310) was struggling with HOYSALA forces on the southern border of the kingdom, Devagiri was captured and annexed by 'Ala al-Din Khalji, thus ending the Yadava dynasty.

BIBLIOGRAPHY
J. F. Fleet: *Dynasties of the Kanarese Districts of the Bombay Presidency, from the Earliest Historical Times to the Muhammadan Conquest of AD 1318* (Bombay, 1882)
R. G. Bhandarkar: *Early History of the Deccan* (Bombay, 1895, rev. Calcutta, 3/1928)
A. V. N. Murthy: *The Sevunas of Devagiri* (Mysore, 1971)
J. N. Singh Yadav: *Yadavas through the Ages, from Ancient Period to Date* (Delhi, 1992)

H. V. TRIVEDI

Yagi, Kazuo (*b* Kyoto, 4 July 1918; *d* Kyoto, 28 Feb 1979). Japanese ceramicist and teacher. He was the son of the ceramicist Issō Yagi (1894–1973). In 1937 he graduated from the sculpture department of the Kyoto Municipal School of Arts and Crafts. He then became an apprentice at the Ceramic Research Institute of the Ministry of Commerce and Industry, where he studied ceramic sculpture with Numata Ichiga (1873–1945). In 1948 he formed the Sōdeisha group, an avant-garde group of ceramicists and sculptors that included Osamu Suzuki (*b* 1926), Hikaru Yamada (*b* 1924), Tetsuo Kanō (*b* 1927) and Yoshisuke Matsui (*b* 1926). During this period he formulated a style using sculptural forms that disregarded utilitarian considerations. This style directly influenced contemporary artistic thought and had a great impact on Japanese avant-garde ceramics. He received the grand prize at the 2nd International Ceramic Exhibition in Ostend in 1959 and at the 3rd International Ceramic Exhibition in Prague in 1962. His unglazed works with high-temperature firing (e.g. *Cloud Remembered*, 1959; New York, MOMA) and, from 1964, his black unglazed works with low-temperature firing demonstrate the diverse types and colours of Yagi's style. He saw his work as a form of dialogue with his clay material. This was reflected in a combination of rationality and an individual poetic sense as he sought after forms that illustrated the special characteristics of the clay body. In 1971 he retired as professor from the Kyoto City University of Arts.

BIBLIOGRAPHY

Kazuo Yagi (exh. cat. by S. Kimura and T. Uchiyama, Kyoto, N. Mus. Mod. A.; Tokyo, N. Mus. Mod. A.; 1981) [in Jap. and Eng.]

Y. Inui: *Yagi Kazuo*, xiv of *Yakimono no bi gendai Nihon tōgei zenshū* [A pageant of modern Japanese ceramics], ed. A. Imaizumi (Tokyo, 1982)

MITSUHIKO HASEBE

Yagul. Site in Mexico, in the Valley of Oaxaca, inhabited as early as *c.* 400 BC; an extremely compact small city flourished there in the Late Post-Classic period (*c.* AD 700–1521). Its present name derives from the Zapotec terms for tree (*yaga*) and old (*gula*). Its centre occupies a large natural terrace on the south side of a high hill; the top was fortified, and houses covered the slopes. Since no modern community covers the Yagul remains, its temples, palace, secular public buildings, ballcourt and streets are clearly visible.

Around 400 BC ceramic sculptures with Olmec traits were placed in burials at Yagul (Oaxaca, Mus. Reg.). The site was nearly uninhabited until *c.* AD 700. When nearby LAMBITYECO was abandoned *c.* AD 700, its inhabitants apparently moved to Yagul, where they undertook the first major constructions at the site. However, the preservation of later buildings has left their work covered over. After *c.* AD 1000 invading MIXTEC lords imposed their ways on a subject population that was probably Zapotec in part, and the late architecture of Yagul is stylistically related to that of nearby MITLA (*see also* MESOAMERICA, PRE-COLUMBIAN, §III, 4); for example, in the Palace of the Six Patios the two easternmost buildings have a striking architectural similarity to the northernmost palaces at Mitla, and the geometric stone mosaic panels at Yagul in several cases show designs also used at Mitla. Since, with the exception of Tomb 7, remains of Monte Albán Period V are poorly represented at Monte Albán itself, and remains of this date at Mitla are largely inaccessible, Yagul became the first Mesoamerican site to offer materials in quantity for study of daily life shortly before the Spanish Conquest. Artefacts included many fine pottery serving bowls, of subhemispherical shape and well finished, and high-quality effigy jars (Oaxaca, Mus. Reg.). While the architecture of Yagul was less exquisitely finished than that of Mitla, the contrast is exaggerated by the fact that buildings at Yagul had been stripped of cut stone for centuries, until archaeological exploration began in 1954. The ground-plan may derive from that of the hilltop site of Santo Domingo de Oaxaca, on the border of the Mixtec and Cuicatec regions and north of the Valley of Oaxaca.

Shortly after the Conquest in 1521, the Spanish resettled Yagul's people (as they did those of many other defensible hilltop towns in Mexico) on a nearby flat area, creating the town now called Tlacolula. This move marked the end of the high motivation level evident even in ordinary workmanship at Yagul.

BIBLIOGRAPHY

I. Bernal: 'Ruinas de Santo Domingo, Oaxaca', *Bol. INAH*, xxiv (1966), pp. 8–13

——: 'The Mixtecs in the Archaeology of the Valley of Oaxaca', *Ancient Oaxaca: Discoveries in Mexican Archaeology and History*, ed. J. Paddock (Stanford, 1966), pp. 345–66

R. Chadwick: 'The Tombs of Monte Albán I Style at Yagul', *Ancient Oaxaca: Discoveries in Mexican Archaeology and History*, ed. J. Paddock (Stanford, 1966), pp. 245–55

C. Wicke: 'Tomb 30 at Yagul', *Ancient Oaxaca: Discoveries in Mexican Archaeology and History*, ed. J. Paddock (Stanford, 1966), pp. 336–44

I. Bernal and L. Gamio: *Yagul: El Palacio de los seis patios* (Mexico City, 1974)

JOHN PADDOCK

Yahudiya [Yahoudeh; Yahûdîyeh; Yahoudiyé; Yehūdīyah], **Tell el-** [Arab.: 'Mound of the Jews'; Egyp. Nay-ta-hut; Gr. Leontopolis]. Egyptian site 31 km north of Cairo near Shibin el-Qanatir in the Nile Delta. It was excavated by Heinrich Brugsch, Edouard Naville, F. Ll. Griffith and Flinders Petrie in the late 19th century and early 20th, and by Shehata Adam in the 1950s. Although occupation of the site may have commenced during the Early Dynastic Period (*c.* 2925–*c.* 2575 BC), the earliest evidence dates from the Middle Kingdom (*c.* 2008–*c.* 1630 BC) and the Second Intermediate Period (*c.* 1630–*c.* 1540 BC). Two cemeteries include graves dating from the 12th Dynasty (*c.* 1938–*c.* 1756 BC) to the Greco-Roman Period (332 BC–AD 395). The 'Hyksos Camp' is a rectangular earth enclosure with rounded ends measuring *c.* 515×490 m, with a gateway in the eastern face. This enclosure consists of an inner vertical mud-brick wall, faced on the exterior by an inclined bank, or glacis, of plastered sand with a ditch beyond; no wall surmounted the bank. One theory is that, because of its similarity to Syro-Palestinian fortifications of the period, it was built by Near Eastern immigrants for military purposes. However, a more accepted interpretation is that it had a religious function, owing to certain parallels with cultic earthworks at Heliopolis and Mendes. Inside the enclosure on the north-east, the existence of a temple of Ramesses II (*reg c.* 1279–*c.* 1213 BC) was suggested by finds of a colossal granite statue of the King and a dyad representing him with the god Re. A temple and palace of Ramesses III (*reg c.* 1187–*c.* 1156 BC) to the west yielded alabaster blocks and faience tiles with motifs of rosettes, cartouches, foreign captives and *rekhyt*-birds. A later period temple to the goddess Bast was implied by statuary remains showing this deity. North-east of the enclosure is the Jewish city and temple established in 154 BC by the exiled priest and general Onias by permission of Ptolemy VI (*reg* 180–145 BC). A rock-cut Jewish cemetery lies near by. The settlement, modelled after Jerusalem, was abandoned after the closure of the temple by Vespasian in AD 71.

LÄ

BIBLIOGRAPHY

T. Hayter Lewis: 'Tell el-Yahoudeh (The Mount of the Jew)', *Trans. Soc. Bibl. Archaeol.*, vii (1881), pp. 177–92

E. Brugsch-Bey: 'On et Onion', *Recl Trav. Relatifs Philol. & Archéol. Egyp. & Assyr.*, viii (1886), pp. 1–9

E. Naville: *Mound of the Jew and the City of Onias* (London, 1887)

F. Ll. Griffith: *The Antiquities of Tell el Yahûdîyeh* (London, 1890)

W. M. F. Petrie: *Hyksos and Israelite Cities* (London, 1906)

Comte du Mesnil du Buisson: 'Compte rendu sommaire d'une mission à Tell el-Yahoudiyé', *Bull. Inst. Fr. Archéol. Orient.*, xxix (1929), pp. 155–78

B. Porter and R. L. B. Moss, eds: *Topographical Bibliography*, iv (1934–)

Comte du Mesnil du Buisson: 'Le Temple d'Onias et le camp Hyskôs à Tell el-Yahoudiyé', *Bull. Inst. Fr. Archéol. Orient.*, xxxv (1935), pp. 59–71

S. Adam: 'Recent Discoveries in the Eastern Delta: December 1950–May 1955', *An Service Ant. Egypte*, lv (1958), pp. 301–24

G. R. H. Wright: 'Tell el-Yehūdīyah and the Glacis', *Z. Dt. Palästina-Ver.*, lxxxiv (1968), pp. 1–17

A. Badawy: *A Monumental Gateway for a Temple of Sety I* (New York, 1973)

ANN BOMANN

Yahya, Tepe [Pers. Tappa-yi Yaḥyā]. Site in the province of Kirman in south-east Iran, which has provided a sequence for the archaeology of the area from the early 5th millennium BC to the Parthian or Sasanian period in the early centuries AD (*see* IRAN, ANCIENT, §I, 2). The site is a mound 19.8 m high with an almost circular base 187 m in diameter. It was excavated by C. C. Lamberg-Karlovsky of the Peabody Museum, Harvard University, from 1967. The finds are in the Archaeological Museum in Tehran and at the Peabody Museum, Harvard University.

Neolithic (Period VII, *c.* 4900–*c.* 3900 BC) and Chalcolithic (Periods VI–V, *c.* 3800–*c.* 3300 BC) remains include numerous houses with spacious storage facilities, a large number of clay figurines of sheep or goats and some stone figurines; one female figurine of chlorite was found in a storage magazine, resting face down and associated with numerous stone and bone tools. Carved chlorite vessels (made from locally quarried stone), a miniature human head and a large alabaster ram are particularly fine examples of 5th-millennium BC sculpture from the Iranian plateau.

After a gap of 300 to 400 years, Tepe Yahya was settled by Proto-Elamites (Period IVC, *c.* 2900 BC) whose ceramics, tablets and cylinder-seal impressions are paralleled at SUSA, TALL-I MALYAN and TEPE SIALK. A large administrative building, covering over 550 sq. m, was excavated in this level. The subsequent settlement (Period IVB.2–6, *c.* 2400–*c.* 2000 BC) is characterized by individual houses and workshops devoted to the production of carved chlorite vessels decorated with complex designs based on architecture and mythology. These vessels were exported to Susa, Mesopotamia and even Syria, probably via the Gulf.

There was some later occupation of the site (Period IVA, *c.* 2000–*c.* ?1800 BC; Period III, *c.* 700–*c.* 525 BC) and massive Achaemenid and Hellenistic platforms and large houses were found in Period II (*c.* 475–*c.* 275 BC), followed by a Parthian or Sasanian settlement (Period I, *c.* 200 BC–*c.* AD 225), which is poorly preserved.

BIBLIOGRAPHY
C. C. Lamberg-Karlovsky: 'The Proto-Elamite Settlement at Tepe Yahya', *Iran*, ix (1971), pp. 87–96

——: 'Tepe Yahya, 1971: Mesopotamia and the Indo-Iranian Borderlands', *Iran*, x (1972), pp. 89–100

C. C. Lamberg-Karlovsky and M. Tosi: 'Tracks on the Earliest History of the Iranian Plateau: Shar-i Sokhta and Tepe Yahya', *E. & W.*, xxiii (1973), pp. 21–57

P. L. Kohl: 'The Balance of Trade in Southwestern Asia in the Mid-Third Millennium B.C.', *Current Anthrop.*, xix (1978), pp. 463–92

C. C. Lamberg-Karlovsky, ed.: 'Excavations at Tepe Yahya, Iran, 1967–1975: The Early Periods', *Bull. Amer. Sch. Prehist. Res.*, 29 (1986)

P. Damerow and R. Englund: 'The Proto-Elamite Tablets from Tepe Yahya', *Bull. Amer. Sch. Prehist. Res.*, 30 (1989)

C. C. LAMBERG-KARLOVSKY

Yahya al-Sufi [Pīr Yaḥyā ibn Naṣr al-Ṣūfī al-Jamālī] (*fl* 1330–51). Ottoman calligrapher. According to the Safavid chronicler Qazi Ahmad, Yahya studied calligraphy with Mubarakshah ibn Qutb Tabrizi (*fl c.* 1323), one of six pupils of YAQUT AL-MUSTA'SIMI (*see also* ISLAMIC ART, §III, 2(iii)(c)). Yahya was a mystic, hence his epithet al-Sufi, and, after working for the warlord Amir Chupan, he moved to the court of the Injuid ruler of Shiraz, Jamal al-Din Abu Ishaq (*reg* 1343–54), hence his epithet al-Jamali. He penned several manuscripts of the Koran, including small, single-volume copies (1338–9, Istanbul, Mus. Turk. & Islam. A., MS. K 430; 1339–40, Dublin, Chester Beatty Lib., MS. 1475) and a large, 30-volume copy (4 vols, 1344–6; Shiraz, Pars Mus., MS. 456). The latter manuscript was probably commissioned by Abu Ishaq's mother, Tashi-khatun, who bequeathed it to the Shah Chiragh Mosque at Shiraz. Each folio has five lines of majestic *muḥaqqaq* script, although the illumination by Hamza ibn Muhammad al-'Alawi is of poor quality, like that of many of the manuscripts produced at Shiraz under the Injuids (*see* ISLAMIC ART, §III, 4(v)(b)). Yahya also designed architectural inscriptions, including one recording Abu Ishaq's visit to Persepolis in August 1347 and another recording Abu Ishaq's repairs in 1351 to the Khudakhana, the small building for Koran manuscripts in the court of the Friday Mosque at Shiraz.

BIBLIOGRAPHY
Qāżī Aḥmad ibn Mīr Munshī: *Gulistān-i hunar* [Rose-garden of art] (*c.* 1606); Eng. trans. by V. Minorsky as *Calligraphers and Painters* (Washington, DC, 1959), p. 62

S. M. T. Mustafavi: *Iqlīm-i Pārs* (Tehran, Iran. Solar 1343/1964), pp. 59, 64, 66, 347; Eng. trans. by R. N. Sharp as *The Lands of Pārs* (1978), pp. 44, 226

D. James: *Qur'āns of the Mamlūks* (London and New York, 1988), pp. 162–73; nos 63–4, 69

SHEILA S. BLAIR

Yaka. Bantu-speaking people inhabiting Popokabaka, Kenge and Kasongo Lunda sectors of Bandundu Province, south-western Zaïre, and Uige Province of northern Angola; they number *c.* 245,000. The Yaka are bordered to the west by various groups of the Kongo ethnic complex, to the north by the Teke-Mfinu and Mbala peoples, to the east by the Suku and to the south by the Holo, Southern Suku and Chokwe. Reference to Suku art in particular is made here. Yaka ethnicity is complex. They are ruled by Luwa lords of Lunda origin and encompass enclaves of Tsaamba and Suku as well as such political splinter groups as the Pelende. European penetration of the region began in the 1880s, since when there has been a gradual decline in the demand for art objects and in standards of craftsmanship. Some traditions of masking and figure carving persisted into the late 20th century. Yaka masks function as personalized extensions of charm specialists, protecting the fertility of the young against harmful influences. The statuettes serve as supports for substances concerned with prohibitions and transgressions. Both deal with human life, its protection and continuity.

In addition to masks and statuettes, the Yaka and their neighbours are noted for their figurative carving on fly-whisks, cups, combs, headrests, pipes and musical instruments. The latter objects comprise the leadership paraphernalia associated with paramount and regional chiefs, subordinate officials, lineage headmen and ritual specialists. Examples of Yaka art are held by many museums with African collections. One of the best collections is that of the Koninklijk Museum voor Midden-Afrika, Tervuren, Belgium. Yaka arts have been quite widely illustrated (see bibliography).

1. Mask and masquerade. 2. Figure sculpture.

1. MASK AND MASQUERADE. The major use for masks among the Yaka is in association with male initiation and circumcision rites, known as Mukanda or N-khanda. In these rites adolescent males are subjected to rigid discipline and taught respect for the elders, endurance and the rules of behaviour in adult society. A variety of masks assure and protect the future fertility of the initiand and range in roles from awesome cursing/healing masks to those that ensure a generous reception for the initiates following their period of seclusion.

The performances of the largest and most powerful masks are terrorizing. These masks include a wooden one called Kakuungu (c. 850 mm high on average), characterized by inflated cheeks, massive features and a prominent chin. It is painted red and white, with the chin area generally white or the face divided vertically between the two colours. Regarded as the oldest as well as the most powerful of all masks, Kakuungu was owned and often worn by the charm specialist (yisidika) of the initiation camp. It was one of a series of instruments employed to ensure the well-being of the youths. Kakuungu customarily appeared on the day of circumcision, on the day of departure from the N-khanda camp and, occasionally, for the release from food restrictions. Its principal function was to frighten the candidates into obedience and respect for their elders and to threaten anyone who harboured evil intentions against one of the initiates. Kakuungu also appeared in the event of a crisis and, outside of the initiation context, was used to treat impotence in men and sterility in women.

Mbawa, another 'terrorizing' mask, is clearly distinct from Kakuungu in form, materials and size (being c. 1.5 m to the tip of its horns). Mbawa is constructed of bamboo splints bound into an oval or near-spherical structure covered with painted raffia cloth. Two horns are attached at the top of the mask. These are either wooden ones that extend from two armature-like basketry cones or actual animal horns directly appended to the mask. A raised border serving as a decorative headdress stretches in front of the horns and crowns the head. Frequently, a ridge divides the face vertically and serves as a nose. The raffia cloth surface is covered with a resin and, once dry, is painted in solid colours. Like Kakuungu, Mbawa appeared on the day of circumcision, on the departure from N-khanda and at the release from food restrictions. Rarely, if ever, however, did the two masks appear together. With its horns, Mbawa is associated with the buffalo, pakasa. In the far south Mbawa is carved of wood and may depict a buffalo or a horse-size variety of antelope; composite masks with a human face and animal characteristics are also found.

The most widespread mask, Mweelu, is a netted head-covering made of twined raffia fibre, to which are attached a profusion of feathers. The facial features are composed of painted gourds, sections of bamboo, or the upturned beak of a hornbill. Mweelu is considered essential for N-khanda initiation and may be represented by a single mask, a pair or several pairs. It first appears during N-khanda, worn by the camp officials in charge of food supplies. To augment the food provided by the village women, Mweelu descends upon the village to snatch groundnuts, cassava and maize from the startled villagers, or to beg for food by means of signs. All the uninitiated flee and take cover at Mweelu's approach. Mweelu also ensures safe-conduct for the boys when they emerge from the N-khanda camp. At this time Mweelu dances into the village to seek gifts of kaolin from, among others, the chief and the charm specialist.

A wooden helmet mask with a human face and coiffure, and often surmounted by an animal or human figure, has been found among some Yaka with historical links to the Suku and among their Suku neighbours to the east and south. It is generally called Mbala among the Yaka and Hemba among the Suku. In the traditional initiation of the Suku, a notable of the village treated the mask with a concoction of powerful ingredients and sprinklings of the blood of a cock. This activated the mask's power and made it dangerous to touch. Once the older initiates had been taught to dance, they were permitted to don a pair of Hemba masks and dance into the village at the N-khanda closing festivities (fig. 1). For this dance, additional charms were placed inside the mask or attached to its shaggy fringe. These would 'shoot' any witch that attempted to harm the dancer.

Dance masks of the northern Yaka perform in a series, comprising Kambaandzia and Kholuka with pairs of Tsekedi, Myondo and Ndeemba appearing between them. Kambaandzia and Kholuka are the most significant of these. Kambaandzia consists of a wooden armature in the shape of a cap with a turned-up oblong brim. In front of the projecting brim is a small oval head nearly hidden in the surrounding fibre fringe. Over this surface is stretched cotton material, or, in earlier times, raffia cloth, covered with black resin and painted in rows of triangles and cross-hatched areas set off in red, white, blue and yellow. Kambaandzia appears the evening before the appearance of the other masks. It dances briefly and receives gifts from bystanders. It is then placed on the ground before the drummers. After the festivities and the subsequent tour throughout the region, it is returned to the sculptor who made it. He places it near a termite hill, burns it and anoints himself with its ashes. Kambaandzia represents a type of gazelle (tsetsi), a slight animal that inhabits the tropical forest valleys, which is renowned among hunters and in tales as a trickster figure.

Kholuka (known also as Mbala) and the mask pairs that precede it in the series have a head and coiffure made of splints and raffia fabric, and facial features and projecting ears carved from wood. The nose on these masks is very prominent, occasionally being very long and curving upward. The conical coiffures are surmounted by puppet-like images of both humans and animals in a variety of scenes with both sexual and procreative themes.

The elements that distinguish one variety of named dance mask from another are arbitrarily chosen, the decision being left ultimately to the sculptor who names them. Wooden face masks are ranked according to their

1. Yaka masked performers, Buandi village, Kasongo Lunda zone, Bandundu, Zaïre; from a photograph by Eliot Elisofon, 1951

size, with the largest or most expressive face used for those of higher rank. Animal faces rank lowest in the series, although this may occasionally be reversed for dramatic effect or if the image is regarded as exceptionally well made. Similarly, those coiffures with the highest projections are generally associated with higher-ranking masks.

2. FIGURE SCULPTURE. Yaka statuettes and the figural imagery on such objects as combs, adzes and headrests tend to be highly expressive, particularly in the rendering of the facial features. Male and female figures are generally in an upright posture (fig. 2). The torso is treated either as a cylindrical shape or as a swelling, bulbous form that appears to fit into the spread of the upper thighs. The shoulders are either flat or almost non-existent, while the arms are attached to the body behind the neck or upper torso. The head is treated in greater detail, with projecting and often exaggerated ears, nose and mouth. The eyes are set in shallow cavities and appear to be closed or squinting. The characteristic headgear of leaders appears in a wide range of forms, often projecting both upwards and laterally or in one, two or three sweeping crests. A greater degree of naturalism, less angularity and less characterization are the dominant characteristics of Suku figure sculpture, while distinctly oval heads, rounded features and elaborate polychrome decoration are typical among the Nkanu and Zombo to the west. Antelope horns, as well as various packets, sticks, bones and feathers are inserted, suspended, wrapped or applied to carvings, and statuettes frequently bear evidence of ritual preparation. Within the corpus of Yaka free-standing imagery there are subtle transitions between what may be termed core characteristics and the carved imagery often considered distinctive of their Kongo, Teke, Mbala and Chokwe neighbours (*see* KONGO, §1; TEKE, §2; and CHOKWE AND RELATED PEOPLES, §1(ii)).

BIBLIOGRAPHY

M. Plancquaert: *Les Sociétés secrètes chez les Bayaka*, Bibliothèque Congo, xxxi (Leuven, 1930)

H. Himmelheber: 'Les Masques bayaka et leurs sculptures', *Brousse* (1939), no. 1, pp. 19–39

R. Devisch: 'Signification socio-culturelle des masques chez les Yaka', *Bol. Inst. Invest. Cient. Angola*, ix (1972), pp. 151–76

L. de Beir: *Religion et magie des Bayaka* (Saint-Augustin, 1975)

A. P. Bourgeois: 'Suku Drinking Cups', *Afr. A.*, xii/1 (1978), pp. 76–7, 108

——: 'Mbwoolo Sculpture of the Yaka', *Afr. A.*, xii/3 (1979), pp. 58–61, 96

——: *N-khanda Related Sculpture of the Yaka and Suku of Southwestern Zaire* (diss., Bloomington, U. IN, 1979; microfilm, Ann Arbor, 1979)

——: 'Kakungu among the Yaka and Suku', *Afr. A.*, xiv/1 (1980), pp. 42–6, 88

——: 'Masques Suku', *A. Afrique Noire*, 39 (1981), pp. 26–41

——: 'Yaka Masks and Sexual Imagery', *Afr. A.*, xv/2 (1982), pp. 47–50, 87

——: 'Yaka and Suku Leadership Headgear', *Afr. A.*, xv/3 (1982), pp. 30–35, 92

——: 'Mukoko Ngoombu: Yaka Divination Paraphernalia', *Afr. A.*, xvi/3 (1983), pp. 56–9, 80

——. *Art of the Yaka and Suku* (Meudon, 1984) [Eng. & Fr. text]

D. Biebuyck: *Southwestern Zaire* (1985), i of *The Arts of Zaire* (Berkeley, Los Angeles and London, 1985–)

A. P. Bourgeois: *The Yaka and Suku* (1985), vii/D/1 of *Iconography of Religions*, ed. T. P. van Baaren and others (Leiden, 1985)

——: 'Helmet-shaped Masks from the Kwango-Kwilu Region and Beyond', *Iowa Studies of African Art: Art and Initiation in Zaire, 1990*, iii, pp. 121–36

——: 'Initiation Inthronisation bei den Yaka in Zaire', *Männerbande, Männerbünde: Zur Rolle des Mannes im Kulturvergleich*, i (Cologne, 1990), pp. 301–8

2. Yaka figure sculpture, wood, 489×127×140 mm, before 1930 (Iowa City, University of Iowa Museum of Art)

R. Devisch: 'From Physical Defect towards Perfection: Mbwoolu Sculptures for Healing among the Yaka', *Iowa Studies of African Art: Art and Initiation in Zaire, 1990*, iii, pp. 63–90

A. P. BOURGEOIS

Yakchŏn. *See* NAM KU-MAN.

Yakob, Peter. *See* KLODT, PYOTR.

Yakovlev, Aleksandr (Yevgeniyevich) [Iacovleff, Alexandre; Jacovleff, Alexandre] (*b* St Petersburg, 13 June 1887; *d* Paris, May 1938). Russian painter, graphic artist and designer. His initial training in 1905–13 was at the Academy of Arts, St Petersburg, where he studied principally under Dmitry Kardovsky. From 1909 Yakovlev contributed regularly to national and international exhibitions, and he was a member of both the World of Art group and the Union of Russian Artists. He was awarded an Academy scholarship for study in Italy and Spain in 1914–15, an experience that left an indelible mark on his stylistic evolution, as is clear from his recourse to Italian Renaissance devices and motifs in paintings such as his portrait of the Mexican artist *Roberto Montenegro* and *The Violinist* (both 1915; St Petersburg, Rus. Mus.).

Just before the October Revolution of 1917 Yakovlev and his close friend Vasily Shukhayev were regarded as the representatives of a new classicism in Russian art, and, in fact, the graphic clarity and materiality of their drawings and paintings bring to mind the contemporary poetry of Anna Akhmatova and Mikhail Kuzmin, leaders of the Acmeist movement (*see* ACMEISM). Yakovlev, Shukhayev, Grigor'yev, Kuzma Petrov-Vodkin and other graduates of the Academy of Arts moved in the same circles as these literati, frequenting the cabarets in St Petersburg and contributing to Sergey Makovsky's review *Apollon*. Artistically and temperamentally, Yakovlev and Shukhayev were very close, and their red chalk and sanguine portraits and figure studies are often remarkably similar to each other. Their collaborative double portrait as *Harlequin and Pierrot* (1914; St Petersburg, Rus. Mus.) summarizes their mutual sympathy and respect.

In 1916 Yakovlev became a professor at the Institute of Art History in Petrograd (now St Petersburg), and, together with Grigor'yev and Sergey Sudeykin, he designed the interior of the Prival Komediantov (Comedians' Halt) cabaret in Petrograd. After travelling in Mongolia, China and Japan he settled in Paris in 1920. He achieved his reputation in the West as an ethnographical draughtsman: in 1925 he accompanied the Citroën Central Africa Expedition as an official artist and in 1931 did the same for the Citroën Trans-Asiatic Expedition, collaborations that resulted in superb depictions of native types, rituals and scenes. Yakovlev spent three years as Chairman of the Department of Painting at the School of the Museum of Fine Arts, Boston, MA, and returned to Paris in 1937.

BIBLIOGRAPHY
M. Birnbaum: *Jacovleff and Other Artists* (New York, 1946)
Alexandre Iacovleff (exh. cat., Cambridge, MA, Gropper A.G., 1972)
N. Yelizbarashvili, ed.: 'Pis'ma V. I. Shukhayeva A. Ye. Yakovlevu iz Italii (1912–13) i Peterburga (1914–15)' [V. I. Shukhayev's letters to A. Ye. Yakovlev from Italy (1912–13) and St Petersburg (1914–15)], *Panorama Isk.*, 8 (1985), pp. 173–90

JOHN E. BOWLT

Yakuglas. *See* JAMES, CHARLIE.

Yakulov, Georgy (Bogdanovich) (*b* Tiflis [now Tbilisi], 2 Jan 1884; *d* Erevan, 28 Dec 1928). Georgian stage designer and painter of Armenian origin, active in Russia. He studied at the Moscow School of Painting, Sculpture and Architecture (1901–3) but was expelled after a disagreement over the teaching methods. Posted to the Far East during military service, he became acquainted with Far Eastern decorative art, which inspired the works he exhibited with the Blue Rose group after his return to Moscow in 1907 (e.g. *The Races*, 1905; Moscow, Tret'yakov Gal.). His work of this time refers to traditional Chinese and medieval European art refracted through Art Nouveau, in an attempt to create a new decorative style in easel painting. In Moscow he often designed the décor for artistic soirées and balls, creating architecturally decorative compositions whose basic components were painted panels. In 1910 he travelled to Italy and in 1912–13 he worked in Paris, where he became acquainted with Sonia Delaunay and Robert Delaunay. In 1913 Yakulov took part in the first Herbstsalon at the gallery Der Sturm in Berlin. In winter 1913–14 he became involved in the debates surrounding Futurism, and together with the Futurist composer Artur Lur'ye and the poet Benedikt Lifshits he published a manifesto 'My i Zapad' ('We and the West', Petrograd, 1914). In his work Yakulov used Cubist and Futurist conventions, but he remained outside Russian artistic groups, exhibiting at the avant-garde Dobychina Gallery in Petrograd as well as with the World of Art group. His painting is characteristically light, with the transparency of watercolour. After the Revolution of 1917 he became, however, an active member of the 'leftist federation' of painters in Moscow, and he recruited Vladimir Tatlin and Aleksandr Rodchenko, among other avant-garde artists, to design the Café Pittoresque in Moscow, which turned out to be a demonstration of the decorative possibilities of abstract art.

Yakulov made his début as a stage designer in early 1918 by creating an unusual skeleton-like construction for Aleksandr Tairov's production of *Obmen* ('The exchange', by Paul Claudel) at the Kamerny Theatre, Moscow. Yakulov made his most successful designs for Tairov, including E. T. A. Hoffmann's *Princess Brambilla* (1920) and Charles Lecocq's *Giroflé-Girofla* (1922; both Moscow, Bakhrushin Cent. Theat. Mus., and Erevan, Pict. Gal. Armenia). In them he used a new type of dynamic alternating set, which combined old theatrical techniques with modern abstract forms. This kind of set created brilliant possibilities for the actors' skill in improvisation. He also designed the sets for Prokofiev's ballet *Le Pas d'acier*, which was performed by Serge Diaghilev's company at the Théâtre Sarah Bernhardt in Paris in 1927. An improvisation on the theme of mechanization and urbanism, the set was largely Constructivist and used kinetic devices. Yakulov's unrealized plans include designs for Vsevolod Meyerhold's production of Vladimir Mayakovsky's *Misteriya-Buffa*. Personally acquainted with avant-garde poets, Yakulov also sometimes illustrated books of poetry and magazines. In 1923, together with Vladimir Shchuko, he submitted a design in the competition for a monument to the *26 Commissars of Baku* (Erevan, Pict.

Gal. Armenia), which employs the asymmetrical, spiral forms he favoured and was undoubtedly influenced by Tatlin's *Monument to the Third International*.

BIBLIOGRAPHY
Notes et Documents, Société des Amis de Georges Yakoulov, 1–4 (Paris, 1967, 1969, 1972, 1975)
S. Aladzhalov: *Georgy Yakulov* (Yerevan, 1971)
E. Kostina: *Georgy Yakulov* (Moscow, 1979)
C. Amiard-Chevrel: 'Princesse Brambilla d'aprés E. T. A. Hoffmann, mise en scène de Tairov', *Les Voies de la Création Théâtrale*, vii (Paris, 1980), pp. 127–53
                                                    V. RAKITIN

Yakunchikova [Yakunchikova-Weber], **Mariya (Vasil'yevna)** (*b* Wiesbaden, 31 Jan 1870; *d* Chêne Bougerie, nr Geneva, 27 Dec 1902). Russian painter, decorative artist and designer. She was a major Symbolist artist in Russia and played a significant role in the revival of folk traditions in Russian art in the late 19th century. She grew up in Moscow and studied (1885–8) under Yelena Polenova and Vasily Polenov as an external student at the Moscow School of Painting, Sculpture and Architecture. Subsequently she joined Yelena Polenova's group for the study of the historical and archaeological monuments of Moscow and became closely associated with the ABRAMTSEVO group. From 1888 she spent winters in Paris, where she enrolled as a student at the Académie Julian. Her paintings, sometimes consisting of melancholic depictions of decaying mansions in the manner of Viktor Borisov-Musatov, were dominated by decorative landscapes. Always striving to express the synthetic inner vitality of organic life, she concentrated on forest motifs (e.g. *The Window* and *Aspen and Fir Tree* (both pokerwork and oil on panel, 1896; Moscow, Tret'yakov Gal.). In 1894 she organized an exhibition in Paris of women's applied art and from 1895 organized and participated in exhibitions of folk art, such as that of the Russian pavilion at the Exposition Universelle in Paris, for which, with Aleksandr Golovin and Natal'ya Davydova (1873–1926), she designed the interior inspired by folk craft. She also exhibited from 1899 with the WORLD OF ART and in 1901–2 with the Moscow group known as 36 Artists. In 1899 she designed the cover of issues 13–24 of *Mir iskusstva*. The asymmetrical arrangement of juniper berries, ancient orthography and a stylized depiction of a swan in a lake surrounded by fir trees culminating in a variety of Christian crosses is one of the most evocative expressions of Russian Art Nouveau. Her decorative work encompassed pokerwork, furniture design, toys, ceramics and embroidery, as in the appliqué panel *Little Girl and the Wood Spirits* (1899; Chêne Bougerie, I. S. Weber Col.).

BIBLIOGRAPHY
Mir Isk., 3 (1904) [issue dedicated to Yakunchikova]
N. Polenova: *Mariya Vasil'yevna Yakunchikova* (Moscow, 1905)
M. Voloshin: 'Tvorchestvo M. Yakunchikovoy' [The creative work of M. Yakunchikova], *Vesy* (1905), no. 1, pp. 30–38
M. Kiselev: *Mariya Vasil'yevna Yakunchikova* (Moscow, 1979)
M. Yablonskaya: *Women Artists of Russia's New Age, 1900–1935* (London, 1990), pp. 14–22
                                                    JEREMY HOWARD

Yakutia. *See under* RUSSIA, §XII, 4.

Yamachawan [Jap.: 'Mountain teabowls']. Generic term for various types of unglazed Japanese tableware produced from the late Heian period (794–1185) to the Muromachi period (1333–1568), mainly in the Tōkai region (Aichi and Gifu prefectures) and Shizuoka and Mie prefectures. The name *yamachawan* first appeared in the *Engishiki* (a 10th-century record of court regulations). Production centres that later made high-quality glazed ceramics, such as SETO, Atsumi (Aichi Prefect.) and TOKONAME, began as *yamachawan* kilns. During the late Heian period kilns such as SANAGE, which had produced ash-glazed wares (*see* JAPAN, §VIII, 2(ii)(b)), also switched to making unglazed *yamachawan*. This change was brought about by a decline in the demand for high-quality wares from aristocratic patrons in Kyoto and an increased demand for utilitarian wares by small provincial farmers. Mass production brought with it a decline in quality: clay became coarser, and precise wheel-throwing techniques were replaced by the simpler coil-and-throw method. The evolution of *yamachawan* can be divided into the following four stages.

Early *yamachawan* (mid–late 11th century) were ash-glazed and made of fine, dense clay. They were fired with high-quality ash-glazed wares. Ash-glazed ware sets consisting of a large bowl and a small dish were replaced by *yamachawan* sets, consisting of a large bowl and a small bowl. The large bowl was deep, almost hemispherical in shape, with a high triangular foot, and was *c.* 60 mm high, opening out to 160 mm in diameter. The small bowl was *c.* 40 mm high, opening out to a diameter of 120 mm. Some sets have etched lines or floral designs just below the rim.

During the early to mid-12th century almost all *yamachawan* were unglazed and made with coarse clay. *Yamachawan* kilns multiplied and a system of mass production was established, though the area of supply was restricted to the Tōkai region. The large bowl became lower and flatter in shape, 170 mm in diameter and 55 mm high, and the small bowl nearly became a plate, less than 30 mm in height. Products from this period show sand and chaff marks on the underside of the foot. These are thought to be from materials placed between the pieces to prevent adhesion during firing, an indication that not much time elapsed between the shaping and the firing of the pots. Certain kilns specialized in the production of *yamachawan* urns, four-lugged jars, *misuji* jars and roof-tiles to meet rising demand from farmers. At this stage there was also an influence from Chinese pottery and porcelain, in particular, from the four-eared urns and bowls of white porcelain of the Southern Song period (1127–1279). Notable examples are bowls with turned back or bevelled rims, which imitate thick-rimmed white porcelain wares.

From the late 12th century to the mid-13th, variety increased, with kilns in various regions having a different range of products. In particular, what are known as standardized *yamachawan*, made of fine clay and fired alongside glazed pottery, were produced in northern Tōkai, in Seto and MINO. Standardized *yamachawan* were widely exported, particularly to Kamakura (Kanagawa Prefect.). In southern Tōkai, in Tokoname and Atsumi, *yamachawan* with rough surfaces were produced. Characteristics of the third stage include the greater linearity of the body shape, the more pronounced chaff marks on the underside of the foot and the sharper edge of the rims. The bowls became smaller, with the diameter of the large bowl decreasing to

140 mm, height 50 mm; the small bowl lost its base and became like a small plate.

From the late 13th century to the early 15th, production of *yamachawan* gradually declined. During the 14th century the increased production of glazed tablewares, such as flat bowls, teabowls and small green-glazed plates, hastened the process. The large bowl further decreased in size to a diameter of 130 mm and became almost flat with no feet. The small bowl became flat with a height of only 10 mm.

MASAAKI ARAKAWA

Yamada, Mamoru (*b* 1894; *d* 1966). Japanese architect. After graduating in engineering from the School of Architecture at Tokyo Imperial University in 1920, he founded the Japan Secession Group (Bunriha Kenchikukai) with other students from the university, including Sutemi Horiguchi. This was the first movement in support of modern architecture in Japan, and its members were greatly influenced by the German Expressionists, the Vienna Secession and Art Nouveau. In 1920 they staged an exhibition of drawings and models, and, although they had little opportunity to demonstrate their ideas in actual projects, the group was important in introducing Expressionism to Japan. Yamada then became an engineer in the Communications Ministry (1920–45), and his early work for the Ministry clearly reveals an Expressionist style. For example the Central Telegraph Building (1925; destr.), Tokyo, which incorporated the parabolic curve as a motif, was the first building in Japan to break away from a strictly formalist style. In later works the Expressionist influence was replaced by a simpler modernism. The Communications Ministry Hospital (1937), Tokyo, is an important example, executed in the simple, clear forms of the International Style; its white interior tiling, floor-to-ceiling glazing, functional surfaces and unified plan indicated the course that modern Japanese architecture would take. In 1949 Yamada opened his own architectural office and worked on a number of hospital projects such as the Welfare Pension Hospital (1954), Osaka. In 1951 he also became a lecturer in construction in the engineering department at Tōkai University, Tokyo.

BIBLIOGRAPHY
S. Koike: *Contemporary Architecture of Japan* (Tokyo, 1954)
U. Kultermann: *New Architecture in Japan* (London, 1967)

EIZO INAGAKI

Yamaguchi, Katsuhiro (*b* Tokyo, 22 April 1928). Japanese sculptor and video artist. He graduated from the law school, Nihon University, in Tokyo in 1951. In the same year he formed Experimental Workshop with the poet Shūzō Takiguchi, and others, and presented a wide range of avant-garde activities, mixing fine art, music and performance. In the series *Vitrine* (1952) he created two-dimensional works with an optical effect using glass sheets. In the early 1960s he created sculpture from wire-mesh and from stretched cloth. He participated in the *New Japanese Painting and Sculpture* exhibition at MOMA, New York, in 1965. In the same year he created his first work using light, *Relation of C* (Tokyo, Met. A. Mus.), and exhibited the light sculpture *Bridge on May* at the Venice Biennale in 1968. He organized an international exhibition *Electro-magica* at the Sony Building in Tokyo in 1969 and began to be regarded as a leader in the realm of art and technology. In 1972 he organized Video Hiroba, a group of video artists based in Tokyo, and from then he worked mainly in this medium. At the São Paulo Biennale of 1975 his video work won the Premio Industria Villares, and in 1981 a retrospective exhibition was held at the Kanagawa Prefectural Gallery. He also produced projects for the Japan World Exposition of 1970 and the Kōbe Portopia Exposition of 1981.

WRITINGS
Robot Avant-garde (Tokyo, 1985)

BIBLIOGRAPHY
360° Yamaguchi Katsuhiro (Tokyo, 1981)

AKIRA TATEHATA

Yamaguchi, Takeo (*b* Seoul, 23 Nov 1902; *d* Tokyo, 27 April 1983). Japanese painter. After graduating from the Western painting (*Yōga*) department at the Tokyo Art School, he went to France, staying in Paris until 1931. There he was inspired by the work of Saeki Yūzō (1898–1928) and was also influenced by Cubism. After returning to Japan he joined the Second Division Society (Nikakai) and developed an abstract style in such works as *Garden A* (1936; Tokyo, Musashino A. U., Mus.–Lib.). After World War II he lived in Tokyo and in the 1950s produced geometric, monochromatic paintings such as *Composition* (1955; Tokyo, N. Mus. Mod. A.), using either yellow ochre or russet on a black ground. His work displayed the influence of a number of styles, however, including biomorphism. He exhibited in 1955 and 1963 at the São Paulo Biennale and represented Japan in the Venice Biennale of 1956. In the 1960s, in contrast to the earlier placement of a single block of colour on a black ground, he exhibited works in which he gradually employed a broader palette. In such paintings as *Parallel* (1968; Tokyo, N. Mus. Mod. A.) the treatment of form was less distinct, and the surfaces of his paintings became impastoed in yellow ochre and russet, embodying a distinctive fusion of Western and Asian moods.

BIBLIOGRAPHY
Yamaguchi Takeo—Horiuchi Masakazu (exh. cat., Tokyo, N. Mus. Mod. A., 1980)
Y. Inui: 'Yamaguchi Takeo no shigoto' [The work of Takeo Yamaguchi], *Yamaguchi Takeo sakuhinshū* [Collection of works by Takeo Yamaguchi] (Tokyo, 1981)
T. Asano: 'Takeo Yamaguchi: L'Art de la contemplation', *Takeo Yamaguchi/Yoshishige Saitō: Pionniers de l'art abstrait au Japon* (exh. cat., Brussels, Mus. A. Mod., 1989)

TORU ASANO

Yamalo-Nenets region. *See under* RUSSIA, §XII, 4.

Yamamoto, Riken (*b* Beijing, 15 April 1945). Japanese architect. He graduated from Nihon University, Tokyo, in 1968, received an MA from Tokyo University of Fine Arts and Music in 1971 and was a research student under Hiroshi Hara at the University of Tokyo from 1971 to 1973. He opened his own office, Riken Yamamoto & Field Shop, in 1973 in Tokyo. Yamamoto joined Hara in the latter's field surveys of villages in various countries and this experience may account for his design approach, which might be best described as 'topological'. His works, which are primarily residential, are not notable for any stylistic consistency, yet they all demonstrate a concern

Yamamoto Baiitsu: *Scholars in a Landscape*, one of a pair of six-panel folding screens, ink and light colours on paper, 1.53×3.56 m, *c.* 1850 (Washington, DC, Freer Gallery of Art)

for the way spatial arrangements symbolize family relationships, and Yamamoto used unconventional means to delineate different functional areas such as public and private. The modern Japanese city is seen as an increasingly hostile environment, and Yamamoto's urban houses depend on internal courtyards and rooftop terraces for breathing space. Examples of his work include the Yamamoto house (1978), Fujii house (1982), and Rotunda (1987), all in Yokohama, the Kubota house (1978) in Tokyo, and the Ishii house (1978) in Kawasaki. Rotunda, a mixed-use building with the owner's flat on top, has a distinctive large canopy with a delicate steel-frame structure and a cover of Teflon fibre and polyester.

BIBLIOGRAPHY
D. Morton: 'Japanese Minimalism', *Prog. Archit.*, lxi (1980), pp. 99, 114–17
M. Zardini: 'Riken Yamamoto, a Young Japanese Architect', *Casabella*, dxxxvii (1987), pp. 4–15

HIROSHI WATANABE

Yamamoto Baiitsu [Yamamoto Shinryō; Baiitsu; Baika; Gyokuzen](*b* Nagoya, 1783; *d* Nagoya, 1856). Japanese painter. He was the son of a sculptor, who worked for the Owari clan. He probably first studied with Yamamoto Ranei, a minor Kanō school artist, who later switched to painting *ukiyoe* ('pictures of the floating world'). Another possible early teacher was Yamada Kyūjō (1747–93), a prominent exponent of literati (Jap. *Nanga* or *Bunjinga*) painting in Nagoya, who died when Baiitsu was only ten years old. It is more likely that Baiitsu studied under Chō Gesshō (1770–1832), a Shijō school painter (*see* JAPAN, §VI, 4(viii)) and *haiku* poet who was a pupil of Kyūjō. Baiitsu also claimed to have been influenced by the Nagoya artist Tanaka Totsugen (1767–1823), founder of the *Yamatoe* revival (*Fukko Yamatoe*) movement. The most formative influence on Baiitsu's approach to painting was that of his mentor, the merchant and collector Kamiya Ten'yū (1710–1801), who also patronized other literati painters, including Nakabayashi Chikutō (1776–1853). Baiitsu studied and copied Ten'yū's collection of Chinese paintings of the Yuan (1279–1368) to Qing (1644–1911) periods, a practice he continued throughout his career. He was also instructed by him in Chinese painting methodology and, under his guidance, developed an interest in a variety of literati pursuits, including the collecting and connoisseurship of Chinese painting, the preparing of tea in Chinese style (*sencha*) and the writing of Japanese classical verse (*waka*) and Chinese-style poetry.

Baiitsu visited Kyoto in his youth and in 1832 moved there. In 1854 he returned to Nagoya, where he became an important leader in literati painting circles and an official painter for the Owari daimyo. He maintained an unusual position as a member of artistic and intellectual circles in three of Japan's most thriving geographical centres: Nagoya, Kansai (Kyoto–Osaka area) and Kantō (Tokyo and its extended environs).

Baiitsu was a naturally gifted painter able to assimilate Chinese painting techniques and styles while creating his own clearly identifiable style marked by graceful and meticulous brushwork. He is best known for his exquisite bird-and-flower paintings (e.g. the pair of screens *Birds and Flowers of the Four Seasons*, 1735; Nagoya, Mun. Mus.), which comprised about half his total output. His other paintings were of more orthodox literati themes, mostly landscapes (e.g. the screen *Scholars in a Landscape*, *c.* 1850; Washington, DC, Freer; see fig.) and depictions of the plants known as the 'four gentlemen' (bamboo, chrysanthemum, plum and orchid).

BIBLIOGRAPHY
R. Kanematsu: *Chikutō to Baiitsu* [Chikutō and Baiitsu] (Tokyo, 1910)
P. J. Graham: 'Japan through an Artist's Eyes: The True-view Pictures of Yamamoto Baiitsu', *Orientations* (1985), pp. 12–27
——: 'Yamamoto Baiitsu no Chūgoku e kenkyū' [Yamamoto Baiitsu's study of Chinese painting], *Kobijutsu*, lxxx (1986), pp. 62–75

PATRICIA J. GRAHAM

Yamasaki, Minoru (*b* Seattle, WA, 1 Dec 1912; *d* Detroit, MI, 6 Feb 1986). American architect. He studied architecture at the University of Washington (1930–34) and at New York University (1934–5). He worked for important firms in New York and later in Detroit, where he established his own practice in 1949. The Lambert Air Terminal (1956), St Louis, MO, reflected technical principles of mainstream modernism in its thin shell concrete vaults and brought Yamasaki professional prominence. During international travels he became impressed with Gothic and Indian styles as well as indigenous Japanese building, from which he developed a romantic, non-functionalist and very personal modernism that incorporated delicacy, symmetry and understatement in a search for elegance and repose. This synthetic style characterized the McGregor Center (1958), Detroit, with its prismatic glass skylights and reflecting pool; the Michigan Consolidated Gas building (1963), Detroit, with its precast surface tracery; and the Dhahran Air Terminal (1961), Saudi Arabia, with its references to Islamic arcuation beneath concrete canopies.

Although his work was controversial, Yamasaki was commissioned to design the World Trade Center (1974; with Emery Roth & Sons), New York, a pair of 110-storey towers isolated on a plaza (see NEW YORK, fig. 5). It received heavy criticism, which reflected the growing unpopularity of high modernism. His late international works often reinterpreted earlier solutions. Thin concrete shells at the Eastern Province Air Terminal (1985), Riyadh, Saudi Arabia, recalled the Lambert Air Terminal; and the Founder's Hall (1982), Shiga Prefecture, Japan, revised a high tentlike enclosure of reinforced concrete and steel cable used in Temple Beth El, Bloomfield Township, MI (1974).

WRITINGS
A Life in Architecture (New York, 1979)

BIBLIOGRAPHY
Contemp. Architects
P. Heyer: *Architects on Architecture: New Directions in America* (New York, 1978), pp. 184–95

ROBERT A. BENSON

Yamashita, Kazumasa (*b* Tokyo, 10 Feb 1937). Japanese architect. He graduated from the Tokyo Institute of Technology in 1959. He worked for Nikken Sekkei Ltd in Tokyo from 1959 to 1964, for various architectural offices including Paul Schneider-Esleben in Düsseldorf (1964) and the Greater London Council (1965), and again for Nikken Sekkei Ltd from 1966 to 1969, when he opened his own office in Tokyo. Yamashita belonged to a group of more orthodox and pragmatic architects that emerged after the Metabolist movement ended. His buildings are professionally executed in an abstract, modernist manner but he also produced 'Pop' designs such as the Face House (1973), Kyoto, and the police box (1982) at a busy intersection in the Ginza, Tokyo. Other works include the Kitamura House (1968) in Kawasaki; the Hirano Clinic (1973), a five-storey dental clinic in Kanagawa Prefecture; the 'From 1st' building (1975), a five-storey retail and commercial complex in Tokyo designed around an inner court, which provided an informal urban environment on a human scale and was awarded the Architectural Institute of Japan prize in 1976; and the Kubo House (1980) in Tokyo.

WRITINGS
'A New Compound Style', *Japan Architect*, 176 (1971), pp. 44–8

BIBLIOGRAPHY
I. Kurita, ed.: *Yamashita Kazumasa*, Nihon gendai kenchikuka shirizu [Modern Japanese architects series], iii (Tokyo, 1981)

HIROSHI WATANABE

Yamashita, Kikuji (*b* Tokushima Prefect., 8 Oct 1919; *d* Kanagawa Prefect., 23 Nov 1986). Japanese painter, printmaker, teacher and collagist. In 1937 he graduated from the Kagawa Prefectural Technical School, and the following year he went to Tokyo and studied at the Fukuzawa Institute for the Study of Painting, where be became fascinated by Surrealist painting. In 1939 his military service took him to China, where he served in the Sino-Japanese War (1937–45). His experiences of the atrocities of war deeply affected him, and he became vehemently anti-war. In 1946 he was involved in forming the Nihon Bijutsukai (Japan Art Society) and in 1947 he helped found the Zen'ei Bijutsukai (Avant-garde Art Society). In 1953 he took part in the first Nippon Ten (Japan exhibition), showing *Tale of Akebono Village at Dawn* (1953; priv. col., see exh. cat., p. 37), which portrayed with black humour an uprising of villagers protesting at repression.

Yamashita's commitment to Surrealism became total, and he was determined to expose social injustices through his style of painting (e.g. *Chikuhō Coal Field Region*, 1960; Tokushima, Prefect. Mus.). He exhibited in one-man and group exhibitions regularly throughout this period. Yamashita lectured at Zokei University in Tokyo from 1970 to 1974. His social concerns became increasingly prominent during the 1970s. In 1974 he participated in the formation of the Hitohito–kai (Hitohito Society) and he exhibited regularly in group shows at Tokyo Metropolitan Art Museum until 1984. In 1975 he exhibited at the first *Tōkyō ten* (Tokyo exhibition) also at Tokyo Metropolitan Art Museum. Despite failing health, Yamashita made some notable collages during the 1970s, including *War and the Sayama Discrimination Case Trials* (1976; see Ishiguro, pp. 78–9).

BIBLIOGRAPHY
Reconstructions: Avant-garde Art in Japan, 1945–1965 (exh. cat. by D. Elliot and K. Kaido, Oxford, MOMA, 1985), pp. 17–19, 36–7
H. Ishiguro: *Yamashita Kikuji gashū* [Collection of paintings of Kikuji Yamashita], (Tokyo, 1988)

YASUYOSHI SAITO

Yampolsky, Mariana (*b* Chicago, 6 Sept 1925). Mexican photographer, printmaker and writer. After studying humanities in Chicago, in 1944 she emigrated to Mexico. From 1945 to 1958 she worked as an engraver in the Taller de Gráfica Populars with Leopoldo Méndez. She was a founder-member in 1951 of the Salón de la Plástica Mexicana. As a photographer she was self-taught; her typical subject-matter was rural Mexico, in particular vernacular architecture and harmonious depictions of sites used for either daily or ceremonial functions. She also photographed Indian or mestizo peasants engaged in their domestic activities and celebrations, and she published educational and art books.

WRITINGS
La casa que canta: Arquitectura popular mexicana (Mexico City, 1982)
Estancias del olvido (Mexico City, 1987)
La raíz y el camino (Mexico City, 1988)

BIBLIOGRAPHY
S. M. Goldman: 'Six Women Artists of Mexico', *Woman's A. J.*, iii (1982–3), pp. 1–9

PATRICIA MASSE

Yanagi, Muneyoshi [Sōetsu] (*b* Tokyo, 21 March 1889; *d* Tokyo, 1961). Japanese philosopher and critic. He is best known as founder of the Nihon Mingeikan (Japan Folk Crafts Museum) and the MINGEI movement. He was the third son of Narayoshi Yanagi (1832–91), a naval officer and mathematician who contributed significantly to the maritime arts of his time. From 1895 to 1911 he was educated at the Gakushūin (Peers School), an institution initially for, but not restricted to, children of the imperial family and nobility. He majored in philosophy and psychology at Tokyo University from 1911 to 1913. At the Peers School in 1910 he joined a group of students in the founding of *Shirakaba* ('White birch'), a periodical of seminal importance in literature and the explanation of Western arts and ideas, which gave its name to the school of writers called the Shirakabaha (White Birch Society). Yanagi became art editor, and in the course of the group's activities he met BERNARD LEACH.

Before the *mingei* movement (*see also* JAPAN, §XV) put him in the public eye, Yanagi had been occupied principally with three subjects: the English poet and artist William Blake, the ceramics of the Korean Chosŏn period (1392–1911) and the work of the Edo-period (1600–1868) priest-sculptor MYŌMAN MOKUJIKI. Yanagi had an enduring admiration for Blake, whose work he came to know through Leach. In 1914 his study of Blake was published, and with Bunshō Jugaku (1900–92) he co-founded the journal *Blake and Whitman* in 1931. He shared Blake's intuitive approach to art, as well as his religiousness, and was influenced by Blake's sympathy for the popular revolutions in America and France. In 1914 he was introduced to Korean ceramics by the scholar Hakkyō [Noritaka] Asakawa (1884–1964), and he began to collect ceramics of the Chosŏn period, which profoundly impressed him and helped shape his view of *mingei* ('folk crafts'). In 1916 Yanagi made his first journey to Korea, then under Japanese colonial rule. In the face of re-education efforts by the colonial administration, he championed Korea's cultural sovereignty and denounced his government's oppressive policies. With his own collection of ceramics and other crafts as the basis, he established the Art Museum of the Korean People (Jap. Chōsen minzoku bijutsukan; Kor. Minjŏk misulgwan) in Seoul in 1924. Also in that year Yanagi encountered the wood sculpture of Myōman Mokujiki and became absorbed in study of the then unknown priest's life and a search for his surviving work.

The *mingei* movement can be dated from 1926 when Yanagi and the potters SHŌJI HAMADA, KENKICHI TOMIMOTO and KANJIRŌ KAWAI announced their plans for a museum of folk crafts and a rescue effort for surviving *mingei*. In September 1926 Yanagi published in the newspaper *Echigo Times* the article 'Getemono no bi' ('Beauty of lowly things')—later republished as 'Zakki no bi' ('Beauty of common wares')— which provided the basic credo of the movement. In 1929 he was invited to Harvard University, where he lectured on Mahayana ('Great Vehicle') Buddhist art and on aesthetics. There he also expounded his theories on *mingei* and organized the first American exhibition of *Ōtsue* ('Ōtsu pictures'; sold at roadside stands to travellers on the Tokaido during the Edo period). In 1931 he founded the journal *Kōgei* ('Crafts'), the voice of the *mingei* movement until 1951.

In 1936 the Japan Folk Crafts Museum was opened in Tokyo with Yanagi as director. The museum's collection was formed in the course of numerous trips by Yanagi, Hamada, Kawai and other movement leaders throughout Japan and to Taiwan, Okinawa, Korea, Manchuria, the USA and Europe.

After World War II Yanagi was increasingly preoccupied with religious studies and aesthetics based on Buddhist principles. He believed that 'true beauty' was created only in the absence of personal ambition, in an unfettered state of mind. In this vein he sought to explain the qualities of the folk Korean teabowls cherished by tea masters. He also wrote on the tea ceremony, which he believed to be in need of reform. From May 1952 until February 1953 Yanagi travelled with Hamada and the novelist Naoya Shiga (1883–1977) to Europe and the USA for meetings, lectures and workshops. In 1984 the Korean government posthumously awarded Yanagi the Jewelled Crown Cultural Medal (Pogwan munhwa hunjang).

WRITINGS
Folk Crafts in Japan (Tokyo, 1936)
'Kingdom of Beauty and Folk-Crafts', *Bull. E. A.*, 6 (1940), pp. 3–6
'The Nippon Mingei-Kwan' [The Museum of Japanese Folk-Craft], *Bull. E. A.*, 6 (1940), pp. 6–8
Yanagi Muneyoshi senshū [Selected writings of Muneyoshi Yanagi], 10 vols (Tokyo, 1954–73)
The Unknown Craftsman: A Japanese Insight into Beauty, adapted by B. Leach (Tokyo, 1972)
M. Yanagi, ed.: *Yanagi Muneyoshi zenshū* [The complete works of Muneyoshi Yanagi], 20 vols (Tokyo, 1980–2)

BIBLIOGRAPHY
S. Tsurumi: *Yanagi Muneyoshi* (Tokyo, 1976)
I. Kumakura: *Mingei no hakken* [The discovery of *mingei*] (Tokyo, 1978)
D. Suzuki and others: *Kaisō no Yanagi Muneyoshi* [Yanagi Muneyoshi remembered] (Tokyo, 1979)
E. Frolet: *Yanagi Soetsu ou les éléments d'une renaissance artistique au Japon* (Paris, 1986)

TAKAKO HAUGE

Yanagisawa Kien [Yanagisawa Rikyō; Ryū Rikyō; Kien; Chikukei] (*b* Edo [now Tokyo], 1706; *d* Kōriyama [now in Nara Prefect.], 1758). Japanese painter and calligrapher. With Gion Nankai and Sakaki Hyakusen, he was one of the pioneers of Japanese literati painting (*Nanga* or *Bunjinga*; see JAPAN, §VI, 4(vi)(e)). Born into the influential Yanagisawa family, who ruled the domain of Kōriyama, he received a Confucian education in Edo, one of his teachers being the famous Confucian scholar and calligrapher Ogyū Sorai (1666–1728). Kien also received painting lessons from a minor master of the KANŌ SCHOOL but soon became dissatisfied and began to study Chinese paintings and calligraphy of the Ming period (1368–1644), which were available to him in the form of woodblock-printed books and imported originals. He became directly acquainted with Chinese literati culture by studying with Chinese Zen monks of the Ōbaku (Chin. *Huang bo*) sect and was taught Chinese-style calligraphy (*karajō*) by Hosoi Kōtaku. Kien also mastered the Sixteen

Noble Accomplishments that were expected of a samurai, which included military arts, poetry and the tea ceremony, but his amateur artistic pursuits seem to have interested him more than his political and military duties. (He became head of his family in 1730.)

Kien's refined style, in which he displays a mastery of types of Chinese brushwork then unfamiliar in Japan, contrasts with the eclecticism he showed in his choice of models. His landscape paintings, such as the pair of hanging scrolls *Landscape of the West Lake at Hangzhou* (undated; Tokyo U. F.A. & Music; see fig.), are heavily indebted to Chinese woodblock-printed books and display a cultivated literati taste, but he is also well known for his finger paintings (*shitōga*) of bamboo and for his colourful and elaborate bird- and flower-paintings, such as the hanging scroll *Flowers of the First, Fifth and Ninth Months* (undated; Tokyo, Imp. Household Col.). The latter were executed in the academic style imported into Japan by the visiting Chinese artist Shen Nanpin in the mid-18th century (*see* JAPAN, §VI, 4(vi)(c)) and taught to Kien by the Nagasaki artist Ei Genshō (1731–78). Kien's calligraphy also shows his study of literati masters of the Ming period, such as Wen Zhenming and Dong Qichang, but is distinguished by inventive and eclectic touches of his own. His pupils included Ike Taiga and Taiga's wife, Ike Gyokuran, who helped to promote the literati style in Kyoto.

BIBLIOGRAPHY
S. Umezawa: *Nihon Nanga shi* [The history of Japanese literati painting] (Tokyo, 1919)
Y. Yonezawa and C. Yoshizawa: *Bunjinga* [Literati painting] (1966), xxiii of *Nihon no bijutsu* [The arts of Japan] (Tokyo, 1957–67); Eng. trans. by B. I. Monroe as *Japanese Painting in the Literati Style* (1974), Heibonsha Surv. Jap. A., xxiii (New York and Tokyo, 1972–7)
C. Nakabayashi: *Bunjin no shosha* [Illuminating the literati] (Tokyo, 1975)

Yanagisawa Kien: *Landscape of the West Lake at Hangzhou*, pair of hanging scrolls, ink and light colours on paper, each scroll 1366×578 mm (Tokyo, University of Fine Arts and Music)

S. Katō, Y. Nakada and Y. Iriya: *Gion Nankai, Yanagisawa Kien* (1975), xi of *Bunjinga suihen* [Selections of literati painting], ed. J. Ishikawa and others (Tokyo, 1974–9)

STEPHEN ADDISS

Yanbei Jushi. *See* DUAN YUCAI.

Yancheng. *See under* WUJIN.

Yan Ciping [Yen Tz'u-p'ing] (*fl* 1163–89). Chinese painter. He was the son of an Academy painter, Yan Zhong, originally from Shanxi Province; Yan Zhong served under Emperor Huizong (*reg* 1101–25) and moved south to serve under Emperor Gaozong (*reg* 1127–62). Yan Ciping served as *daizhao* ('painter in attendance') under the latter and his successor Xiaozong (*reg* 1163–90). Together with his brother, Yan Ciyu, he painted landscapes, figures and buffaloes, surpassing his father's achievement. Towards the end of his career, Emperor Xiaozong rewarded him with distinctions and official positions. Both Yan Ciping and Yan Ciyu (album leaves by whom are in the Freer Gallery of Art, Washington, DC, and the National Palace Museum, Taipei) are regarded as having made an important contribution to the transformation of landscape painting begun by LI TANG (see Edwards).

Yan Ciping's work is known from a few paintings only. One is a signed circular fan painting, *Villa by the Pine Path* (ink and light colours on silk, Taipei, N. Pal. Mus.). This has a compact foreground in the lower right corner, comprising a finely delineated complex of buildings framed on either side by giant pine trees, and a wide open space to the upper left, a forerunner of the 'one-corner' composition much favoured in the following century by Ma Yuan and Xia Gui.

A major work, *Herding Buffalo* (handscroll in four sections, each 350×894 mm, ink on silk, Nanjing, Jiangsu Prov. Mus.), though unsigned, bears an old attribution to Yan Ciping that is surely correct. Each section depicts one of the four seasons: the spring scene, which opens the sequence, shows all the luxuriance of fresh grasses and willow trees; in summer, two boys and their buffaloes cool off in a stream in the shade of some trees; in autumn, the leaves blow off the trees, and the herd-boy plays with a frog attached by a string; in the last, winter, the herd-boy crouches low on the back of his buffalo, completely hidden under his straw raincoat. The free ink style is not far removed from that of Li Tang and gains considerable effect from the use of large trees and figures, giving an intimate view that excludes any distant prospect. Another painting attributed to Yan Ciping has a similar theme (hanging scroll, Tokyo, Sumitomo Col.).

BIBLIOGRAPHY
Xia Wenyan: *Tuhui baojian* [Precious mirror for examining painting] (1365)
R. Edwards: 'The Yen Family and the Influence of Li Tang', *A. Orient.*, x (1975), pp. 79–92
Yu Jianhua, ed.: *Zhongguo meishujia renming cidian* [Dictionary of Chinese artists] (Shanghai, 1981), pp. 1439–40
Xu Bangda, ed.: *Zhongguo huihuashi tulu* [A catalogue of Chinese painting], i (Shanghai, 1984), pl. 100

RODERICK WHITFIELD

Yañez (de la Fuente), Enrique (*b* Mexico City, 17 June 1908; *d* Mexico City, 24 Nov 1990). Mexican architect, writer and theorist. He was a member of the Escuela Mexicana de Arquitectura, a group that from 1925 onwards sought to create an architecture that simultaneously expressed nationalism and modernity. Within this group, which was led by José Villagrán García, Yañez, with Juan O'Gorman and Juan Legarreta, represented the socialist tendency. In 1938, with Alberto T. Arai, Enrique Guerrero, Raúl Cacho, Carlos Leduc and Ricardo Rivas, Yañez formed the Unión de Arquitectos Socialistas, which had a significant influence on Mexican architecture. Their approach was characterized by an emphasis on the utilitarian and social aspects of architecture, for example the reduction of spaces to a bare minimum, and by a rejection of 'bourgeois' aesthetics. Nevertheless Yañez's own house (1935) and the Sindicato Mexicano de Electricistas Building (1938) have a certain rhythmic plasticity, albeit rationalist and sparse. Later, still in the context of developing a 'nationalist functionalism', Yañez became one of the foremost designers of hospitals in Mexico. He won the competition for the construction of the Instituto Mexicano del Seguro Social's first hospital and designed the most important hospital complex in Mexico, the Centro Médico Nacional (1954–8; destr. 1985), Mexico City. The participation in the latter of the painter José Chávez Morado and the sculptor Francisco Zúñiga, among others, made it a milestone in the movement for the 'plastic integration' of the fine arts in Mexico in the 1950s. Among his many completed projects, other noteworthy hospitals include the Adolfo López Mateos Hospital (1969–70). His published writings recount his professional experiences and discuss architectural theory and history.

WRITINGS
Hospitales de seguridad social (Mexico City, 1973)
Arquitectura: Teoría, diseño, contexto (Mexico City, 1983)
Del Funcionalismo al Post Racionalismo (Mexico City, 1990)

BIBLIOGRAPHY
R. López Rangel: *Enrique Yañez en la cultura arquitectónica mexicana* (Mexico City, 1989)
RAMÓN VARGAS

Yañez, Fernando. *See under* LLANOS AND YAÑEZ.

Yang, Yuyu. *See* YANG YING-FENG.

Yang Buzhi [Yang Pu-chih; *zi* Wujiu; *hao* Taochan Laoren, Qingyi Zhangzhe] (*b* Qingjiang, Jiangxi Province, 1098; *d* after 1167). Chinese painter. Although documented primarily as a painter of plum blossom, he is also reported to have specialized in the human figure and to have painted bamboo, pine trees, rocks and narcissus. Xia Wenyan, writing in 1365, noted Yang's personal integrity in refusing to serve the government of the Song dynasty (960–1279) because of its policy of appeasement towards the Jurchen, a nomadic people who conquered northern China and ruled as the Jin dynasty (1115–1234). Yang was one of the earliest exponents of the tradition of painting plum blossom in monochrome ink, subject-matter approved of by the literati painters whose ideals dominated painting of the following Yuan period (1279–1368). He was preceded by the Chan Buddhist priest Zhongren (*d* 1123), whose paintings define the shape of the blossoms solely in ink wash. In contrast, Yang created the circled petal (*quanban*) technique wherein the flexibility of the

brush hairs is employed to outline the shape of the whole flower. In placing greater emphasis on control of the brush, Yang brought the genre closer to calligraphy, the most scholarly of the Chinese arts. The only securely attributed example of Yang's painting that survives is *Four Stages of Blossoming Plum* (handscroll, ink on paper, 1165; Beijing, Pal. Mus.). Four separate scenes depict the blossom in various stages from bursting buds to full flowering with petals beginning to fall; the subtle rendering of the blossom combines with crisp, controlled strokes describing dark branches.

BIBLIOGRAPHY
Deng Chun: *Hua ji* [*Painting* continued] (preface dated 1167) and Zhuang Su: *Hua ji buyi* [*Painting* continued: a supplement] (completed 1298); in Huang Miaozi, ed.: *Hua ji* [*Painting* continued] (Beijing, 1963), p. 52
Zhao Mengjian: 'Three Poems on the Painting of Plum Blossoms and Bamboo' (1260), *Masterpieces of Sung and Yüan Dynasty Calligraphy from the John M. Crawford Jr. Collection* (exh. cat. by Kwan S. Wong, New York, China House Gal.; Lawrence, U. KS, Spencer Mus. A.; 1981–2), pp. 52–7
Tang Hou: *Gujin huajian* [Criticism of past and present painting], *Hua lun* [Discussions of painting] (*c.* 1320–30); in Ma Cai and others, eds: *Hua jian* [Mirror for painting] (Beijing, 1959), p. 53
Xia Wenyan: *Tuhui baojian* [Precious mirror for examining painting] (preface dated 1365); in Hua shi congshu (Shanghai, 1962)
O. Sirén: *Chinese Painting: Leading Masters and Principles*, (London, 1956–8), iii, pp. 154–61
J. Cahill: *An Index of Early Chinese Painters and Painting: T'ang, Sung and Yüan* (Berkeley, 1980), pp. 190–91
Wango Weng and Yang Boda: *The Palace Museum, Peking* (New York, 1982), pp. 182–3
M. Bickford: *Bones of Jade, Soul of Ice* (New Haven, 1985), pp. 60–71
RICHARD EDWARDS

Yangcai. *See under* FAMILLE ROSE.

Yangi. *See* ZHAMBYL.

Yangji (*fl c.* AD 632–46). Korean sculptor, calligrapher and priest. He was prominent during the reign of Queen Sŏndŏk (*reg* 632–46) of Silla. According to the 13th-century *Samguk yusa* ('Memorabilia of the Three Kingdoms') he was proficient in many arts. Three pieces of his work survive from the site of Yŏngmyo Temple, Kyŏngju, North Kyŏngsang Province: a Buddhist trinity, figures of guardians and tiles of halls and of a pagoda. Other works attributed to him include the eight guardian generals at the base of the pagoda at Sach'ŏnwang Temple, Kyŏngju, a Buddhist trinity and the *deva* kings to the right and left of it at Pŏmnim Temple, Kyŏngju, inscribed hanging boards at both Yŏngmyo and Pŏmnim temples, a further engraved pagoda and 3000 small Buddha figures (destr.).

Yangji's Buddhist sculptures were all made from clay, which he was adept at moulding. He lived at Sŏkchang Temple in Kyŏngju, the Silla capital. When the temple site was excavated, many clay artefacts assumed to be Yangji's work were discovered, among them heavenly spirits carved freely in unrestrained postures and sporting finely detailed muscles. A brick engraved with a Buddha and pagoda was also unearthed. All that remains of what have been described as the guardian generals of Sach'ŏnwang Temple amounts to no more than a single brick relief of a *deva*. The image (900×700 mm) is carved in semi-relief and reveals a figure of powerful build and taut muscles wearing elaborately decorated armour. The figure is sculpted in a lively way, demonstrating fine technique. The brick is the earliest ash-glazed sculpture known in Korea; the glaze is a grey-brown green. Clay *deva* fragments have, however, also been recovered from the Sach'ŏnwang site. These were probably fixed to the wooden pagoda that once stood there, and pointed outwards in all directions. The temple itself was founded in 679 by King Munmu (*reg* 661–81) of Unified Silla (668–918), to counter a threatened invasion from Tang China. The surviving fragments are kept at the National Museum in Kyŏngju and at the National Museum of Korea, Seoul.

BIBLIOGRAPHY

Kang Woo-bang: 'Syncretic Phenomena in Ancient Korean Art between Five Direction Gods and Four Guardians: Metamorphoses of Gods. In Connection with Restoration of Four Clay Guardians from the Sach'ŏnwangsa Temple Site', *Misul Charyo*, xxv (1979)
——: 'New Discoveries on Yangji: The Period of Yangji's Activity and his Art', *Misul Charyo*, xlvii (1991)

KANG WOO-BANG

Yangon. *See* RANGOON.

Yang P'aeng-son [*cha* Taech'un; *ho* Hakp'o] (*b* 1488; *d* 1545). Korean scholar and painter. Renowned not only as a painter but even more as a Confucian scholar, he passed the *sama* civil service examination in 1510 at the same time as his friend Cho Kwang-jo (1482–1519). The latter's ambitious plans for political and moral reforms set off major conflicts in the course of the 16th century. Yang went on to present himself for some of the highest examinations in the land, but in the wake of Cho's eventual banishment and execution in 1519 he was stripped of his titles and offices in 1520. Although in 1537 he was reprieved and subsequently offered several offices, he declined them all except the post of magistrate, which, however, he did not take up until a year before his death.

The only known painting by Yang P'aeng-son is a landscape (see fig.) bearing the inscription of a long poem signed *Hakp'o* in the top right-hand corner. Two high cliffs ranged one behind the other and capped by groups of pine trees occupy the left half of the picture. In the right half is a broad expanse of water on which a scholar in a boat is rowing towards the shore. The brushstrokes, in ink tones varying from soft to bright, outline round, cloud-shaped cliffs, bestowing an atmosphere of lightness, and the impression of a distant other world, an effect that is confirmed by the content of the poem. Yang's brush and ink technique derives from the style of painting developed by AN KYŎN in the 15th century (*see also* KOREA, §IV, 2(ii)). The attempt to render the structure of the landscape more complex and the division of the picture into two separate halves dominated by horizontal and vertical lines respectively is typical of 16th-century style, as is the attempt to create an impression of spaciousness in the picture through the broad expanse of water.

BIBLIOGRAPHY

Ahn Hwi-joon [An Hwi-jun]: *Korean Landscape Painting in the Early Yi Period: The Kuo Hsi Tradition* (diss., Cambridge, MA, Harvard U., 1974), pp. 165–71
Ahn Hwi-joon [An Hwi-jun]: 'Two Korean Landscape Paintings of the First Half of the 16th Century', *Korea J.*, xv/2 (1975), pp. 31–41
Yi Tong-ju: *Uri nara-ŭi yet kŭrim* [Studies in Korean painting] (Seoul, 1975), pp. 294–7

BURGLIND JUNGMANN

Yang P'aeng-son: *Landscape*, ink on paper, 882×465 mm, early 16th century (Seoul, National Museum of Korea)

Yang Pu-chih. *See* YANG BUZHI.

Yang Shou-ching. *See* YANG SHOUJING.

Yang Shoujing [Yang Shou-ching; *zi* Xingwu; *hao* Linsu Laoren] (*b* Yidu, Hubei Province, 1839; *d* 9 Jan 1915). Chinese calligrapher, epigraphist, geographer and bibliophile. The son of a wealthy merchant, he failed the local civil service examinations because of his inferior calligraphy. He then studied with Pan Cun (*d* 1892), who introduced him to epigraphy, the study of inscriptions on ancient objects such as bronzes and stelae. These were the models used by calligraphers of the stele studies movement (*beixue*), which was the prevalent style of the late Qing period (1644–1911). Yang received his *juren* degree, the second stage in the civil service, in 1862 but never succeeded in passing the national examinations.

Yang wrote his first scholarly work on calligraphy, a study of the Zhou to Tang periods (*c.* 1050 BC–AD 907), in 1867. He produced a sequel the following year and in 1877 wrote an investigation into the origins of regular script. From 1880 to 1884 Yang served as adviser to two Chinese ambassadors in Japan: to Ruzhang (1838–91) until 1882, then to Li Shuchang (1837–97). While in Tokyo, Yang bought great quantities of rare Chinese books, described in his *Riben fangshu zhi* ('Inquiry into books in Japan'). He became friendly with many Japanese sinologists and calligraphers and introduced them to models from the Six Dynasties period (AD 222–589), which were popular in China at the time. He taught the famous Japanese calligrapher MEIKAKU KUSAKABE and was a great influence on IWAYA ICHIROKU. As the first person to introduce early models in bronze and stone to Japanese calligraphers, Yang holds an important position in the history of Japanese calligraphy.

Yang Shoujing wrote in all four scripts: clerical (*lishu*), regular (*kaishu*), cursive (*caoshu*) and running (*xingshu*). His technique was apparently derived from a combination of copybook (*tie*) and stele (*bei*) influences: he studied OUYANG XUN and Zhang Zhao (1691–1795) as well as stelae of the Han to Six Dynasties period (206 BC–AD 589). His regular script (see Shimonaka, pl. 87) has the hoary, coarse quality of ancient stelae yet is entirely of his own creation. He loaded his brush with ink to produce apparently uncontrolled, thick swellings and let the brush dry so that it adhered unevenly and made rough, half-filled lines, creating an illusion of characters worn by weather in stone. A Northern Wei (AD 386–535) geographical text in combined cursive and running scripts (see Shimonaka, pl. 89) has a sense of speed, flamboyance and rough elegance, with steeply tilted and elongated characters and thick areas of ink contrasted to thin flips of the brush. Chinese critics found it difficult to accept wholeheartedly such spontaneous writing, with its marked irregularity and lack of visible roots in specific works of the past. It was, however, exactly this improvisation and imagination that made his work attractive to the Japanese, who commissioned pieces throughout his life.

BIBLIOGRAPHY
Hummel: 'Li Shu-ch'ang'
K. Shimonaka, ed.: *Shodō zenshū* [Complete collection of calligraphy], xxiv (Tokyo, 2/1961), pp. 163–4, 179
Y. Uno: *Chūgoku shodōshi* [A history of Chinese calligraphy] (Tokyo, 1962), pp. 353–6
Traces of the Brush: Studies in Chinese Calligraphy (exh. cat. by Shen Fu and others, New Haven, CT, Yale U. A.G; Berkeley, U. CA, A. Mus.; 1977), pp. 137, 243, 290, 292, 295, 301
Yu Jianhua: *Zhongguo huajia da zidian* [Dictionary of Chinese painters] (Shanghai, 1981), p. 1179

ELIZABETH F. BENNETT

Yangsongdang. *See* KIM (i), (1).

Yang Ying-feng [Yang Yingfeng; Yang Yuyu] (*b* Yilan, Taiwan, 4 Dec 1926). Chinese sculptor and painter. He studied architecture, sculpture and painting in Tokyo, Beijing, Taipei and Rome. In a long and productive career as art editor, teacher and artist, Yang won critical acclaim as the foremost sculptor and landscape architect in Taiwan, receiving numerous prestigious commissions for sculpture and environmental design in Taiwan and abroad. Yang's artistic development reflected the crystallization of his personal experience in the fast-changing modern world and his study of Chinese and Western art. His art evolved from realism in the 1950s to semi-abstraction in the early

1960s, when modern art movements emerged in Taiwan. Deeply influenced by Chinese philosophical concepts of the harmony of man and nature as well as the unity of life and art, Yang turned to abstraction in the late 1960s. His monumental works in cast bronze and stainless steel attempted to capture the life force of nature and the changing relationship of solids and voids within art and its environment.

BIBLIOGRAPHY
In Stainless Steel: Sculptures by Yuyu Yang (exh. cat., Taipei, Shin Kong Mitsukoshi Department Store, 1992)
Yang Yingfeng jingguan diaosu xuanji [Selection of the environmental sculptures of Yang Ying-feng] (Taipei, 1993)

MAYCHING KAO

Yangzhou [Yangchow; Yang-chou]. Chinese city in Jiangsu Province, located on the main route between north China and the southern Yangzi delta, between the Huaihe River system and the Yangzi River. Yangzhou is also the main focus of an extensive canal system in northern Jiangsu. In 486 BC Fucai, king of the state of Wu, organized the construction of the Han'gou Canal to connect the Huai and Yangzi rivers for grain shipping and built the first city here. The city was rebuilt in 319 BC during the Warring States period (403–221 BC) under the name of Guangling. At the beginning of the 7th century AD Emperor Yangdi of the Sui dynasty (AD 581–618) built the Grand Canal and toured the city three times in his short reign.

The combination of a mild climate, moderate rainfall and fertile soil has made Yangzhou and its surroundings a land of abundant produce, and its port on the Grand Canal made it a hub of land as well as water transport. By the Tang period (618–907) it was the most important port for domestic and overseas voyages and trade in eastern China. Through the Song (960–1279) and Yuan (1279–1368) periods the city built up wealth and strength, and under the Qing period (1644–1911) it experienced the peak of its prosperity. Trade and urban development benefited from the shipping of grain from the south Yangzi delta to Beijing, particularly in the Ming (1368–1644) and Qing periods, when the coastal route was mostly disused. The trade in salt and other commodities brought wealth to the city, and the exuberant lifestyle of its citizens was encouraged by repeated visits of inspection by several emperors, whose interest in Yangzhou art, music and literature stimulated local patronage. Yangzhou was a cosmopolitan city. In the late Song period Puhaddin came to Yangzhou to spread the Islamic faith and was buried on the banks of the Grand Canal. In the Tang period the monk Jianzhen set off from Yangzhou for his various attempts at the sea crossing to Japan. In the Yuan period Marco Polo served as a chief city administrator for three years. Tang-period poets visited Yangzhou and wrote about it. The Song-period literary leaders Ouyang Xiu and Su Shi were once mayors of the city.

Being a city between the north and the south, the art and architecture of Yangzhou developed a synthesized style. In painting, the so-called Eight Eccentrics of Yangzhou initiated the YANGZHOU SCHOOL. Housing and garden design also enjoyed a high reputation. Large-scale garden building was begun by the Sui emperor Yangdi (*reg*

AD 604–17), whose visits to Yangzhou brought about unprecedented development in the city. Northern craftsmen following the Sui court combined skills with their southern counterparts, and as trade grew, merchants imported craftsmen from Anhui and Jiangsu provinces, who continued the fusion of north and south in the art of garden design. In particular, Ji Cheng, the author of *Yuan ye* ('The fusing of gardens'), designed the Ying Yuan (Ying Garden) in the early 17th century. The flourishing of garden construction depended on the accumulation of wealth, especially in the 17th and 18th centuries. The art was taken to extremes when the Qing emperors—Qianlong (*reg* 1736–96) in particular—toured Yangzhou. The gardens were characterized by their skilful structuring of rockeries, intricate layout of manmade streams and lakes, harmonious combination of buildings and gardens, and exquisite interior and exterior decoration. Large quantities of rocks were carried back by salt vessels on their return journey from southern Jiangsu, northern Zhejiang, Anhui and Jiangxi provinces, and some were even shipped from south-west China; imported hardwood and marble were widely used. Imperial patronage gave Yangzhou gardens, mostly built in areas of the city where salt merchants lived, a certain palatial grandeur that immediately distinguished them from gardens found in southern Jiangsu cities such as Suzhou. Gardens that have been preserved in the city include Pianshi shanfang (Stone Slab Mountain Lodge), Ge yuan (Isolated Garden), Jixiao shanzhuang (Mountain Estate for Whistling; *see* GARDEN, fig. 26a) and Xiaopangu (Small Winding Valley). The rockery at Pianshi shanfang is believed to have been designed by the painter–monk Daoji. Ge yuan is the only example of a four-season rockery arrangement in Chinese garden history. Jixiao shanzhuang is a large residence–garden complex where double corridors are arranged to good effect. The largest residence complex is the Lu House in Kangshan Street, home of a Jiangxi salt merchant.

The city suffered catastrophic destructions as a result of war and dynastic change. Few edifices built before the mid-17th century exist. The very base for the city's existence, the Grand Canal, was gradually replaced by railways and coastal shipping in the late 19th century. Nevertheless, the late 20th-century landscape is dominated by the Grand Canal, which is still in limited use. Much work has been done on the preservation of the ancient gardens, including the Shou xi hu (Slender West Lake), the Daming si, Ge yuan, He yuan and Xiaopangu. Their glory is echoed by some modern designs, in particular the Jianzhen Memorial Hall (1963), a temple complex in the Tang style designed by architectural historian LIANG SICHENG. The Yangzhou Opera and various forms of storytelling are still carried on in the city. Traditional handicrafts include lacquerware, jade-carving, papercuts, velvet flowers, *penjing* (Jap. bonsai), shell-carving, plate-printing and embroidery. The local cuisine also excels in the visual form.

BIBLIOGRAPHY
Li Dou: *Yangzhou hua fang lu* [Record of the painted pleasure boats of Yangzhou] (1795)
O. Sirén: *Gardens of China* (New York, 1949)
Zhang Wanli and Hu Renmo, eds: *The Selected Painting and Calligraphy of the Eight Eccentrics of Yang-chow*, 8 vols (Hong Kong, 1970)
Chen Congzhou: *Yangzhou yuanlin* [The Yangzhou gardens] (Shanghai, 1983)
Mayching, ed.: *Painting by Yangzhou Artists of the Qing Dynasty from the Palace Museum* (Hong Kong, 1984)
Fu Chonglan: *Zhongguo yunhe chengshi fazhan shi* [History of canal cities in China] (Chengdu, 1985)
Liang Sicheng: *Liang Sicheng wenji* [Collection of works by Liang Sicheng], iv (Beijing, 1986)

JIN YING

Yangzhou school. Term usually applied to a group of artists active in Yangzhou in the 18th century, especially the so-called Eight Eccentrics of Yangzhou (*Yangzhou baguai*). A broader definition would include more conservative and traditional painters active there in the same period, and an earlier group of artists who lived and worked in the city in the late 17th century and early 18th.

Yangzhou had been a prosperous city since the Tang period (AD 618–907), located as it was near the juncture of the Grand Canal with the Yangzi River. By the late part of the Ming (1368–1644) it was the headquarters of the salt trade, which produced the greatest fortunes the Chinese economy had known. Merchant families of Huizhou, the equally prosperous region in southern Anhui Province, moved to Yangzhou to build garden estates and spend their fortunes in the city, and their patronage drew literary men and artists. Prominent among these patrons were two brothers, Ma Yueguan (1688–1755) and Ma Yuelu (1697–after 1766), cultured men with conservative tastes. Others evidently preferred paintings that did not conform to traditional standards of good taste. Increasingly, and no doubt largely in response to the desires of patrons and market conditions, Yangzhou-school painters abandoned the prestigious styles of the past and turned to subjects and styles that possessed more popular appeal. By the mid-18th century landscape gave way as the favoured subject to figure paintings, including portraits (*see* CHINA, §V, 3(vii)(d) and (viii)(b)), bird-and-flower subjects (*see* CHINA, §V, 3(v)(e)), auspicious and occasional pictures, portrayals of daily life and even low-life scenes. According to a maxim of the time, 'Portraits [bring] gold, flowers silver; if you want to be a beggar, paint landscapes!'

Painters active in Yangzhou in the Kangxi era (1662–1723) included several native professional masters who worked in conservative styles, for example Yuan Jiang (*c.* 1680–*c.* 1755; *see* GARDEN, fig. 23), his close associate Li Yin (*fl c.* 1690–1730), Xiao Chen (*fl c.* 1680–1720) and Gu Fuzhen (1634–*c.* 1716). The first two, along with Yuan Jiang's son (or nephew) Yuan Yao (*fl c.* 1740–60), painted large, technically finished landscapes with palaces and figures in styles derived from such Song-period landscapists as Guo Xi and Li Tang. Their works were considered 'artisan paintings', and literary contemporaries scarcely noticed them in their writings on art. More prestigious artists active in the same period came there from established artistic centres: Cheng Sui (1605–91) and Zha Shibiao from Anhui, Gong Xian and Daoji from Nanjing. Fang Shishu (1692–1751), the younger son of a salt-merchant family from Shexian in Anhui Province, moved to Yangzhou around 1730 and became a luminary in the Ma brothers' circle, painting Orthodox-style landscapes (*see also* ORTHODOX SCHOOL).

The principal stylistic source for the Yangzhou 'eccentrics' was the late style of DAOJI. Between his arrival in Yangzhou in 1696 and his death in 1708, he renounced the Buddhist order for secular life and began to paint more prolifically to earn his living. Typical late pictures seem more improvised and quickly executed than his earlier ones. Artists of less technical mastery who tried for the same effects of spontaneity and dash were prone to sloppiness, and Daoji's influence on the later Yangzhou masters may not have been wholly beneficial. The landscape artist Gao Xiang (1688–1754) studied directly with him, and Chen Zhuan (*fl* 1730s–40s), who painted blossoming-plum and other flower subjects, knew and was affected by him. Younger Yangzhou masters had little or no personal contact with Daoji but nonetheless revered and sometimes imitated him—ZHENG XIE, in particular, acknowledged him as his master in both calligraphy and painting.

The designation of the Eight Eccentrics of Yangzhou dates only from the late 19th century, and its usefulness has been disputed by scholars who point out that the list of masters varies, that not all the artists came from Yangzhou, that they were not all contemporaries, etc. While all this is true, it is also true that works by these masters exhibit common features of subject and style that differ from those typical of such other groups as the Nanjing, Anhui or Orthodox schools. Furthermore, there were bonds of friendship and mutual influence between most of the artists, and their paintings display a far higher incidence of what can properly be called eccentricity than we find in the output of other schools. This last feature is manifested in their choice of subjects, in the playful or formally distorted treatments of those subjects, in oddly unbalanced compositions and unorthodox manners of brushwork and in brilliant and daringly combined colours that broke the old, fastidious strictures.

While no definitive list of the Eight Eccentrics can be constructed, the following artists are most frequently included. HUA YAN was a versatile and prolific poet and painter born in Fujian and active in Hangzhou as well as Yangzhou. HUANG SHEN, also from Fujian, was a figure specialist who also did bird-and-flower subjects and occasional landscapes. LI SHAN served for a time in the Qing (1644–1911) imperial court, where he learnt bird-and-flower painting in the traditional manner. He later settled in Yangzhou, where he made his living as a professional painter with a loose, calligraphic manner based on the late style of Daoji. Wang Shishen (1686–1759) came from Shexian in Anhui Province and produced blossoming plum pictures with strange compositions and oddly wavering brushlines. Li Fangying (1695–1754) also painted plant subjects (see fig.) in loose brushwork, having turned to painting as a source of income after an unrewarding official career. The most famous member of the Eight Eccentrics was ZHENG XIE, who painted only bamboo, orchids and rocks. JIN NONG, from Hangzhou, claimed not to have painted before he was 50. He was the most eccentric of the group, with his crotchety calligraphy and playfully archaistic and amateurish paintings. LUO PING was Jin Nong's disciple. Another versatile and technically accomplished master like Hua Yan, he became most renowned for his portrayals of ghosts. Sometimes also

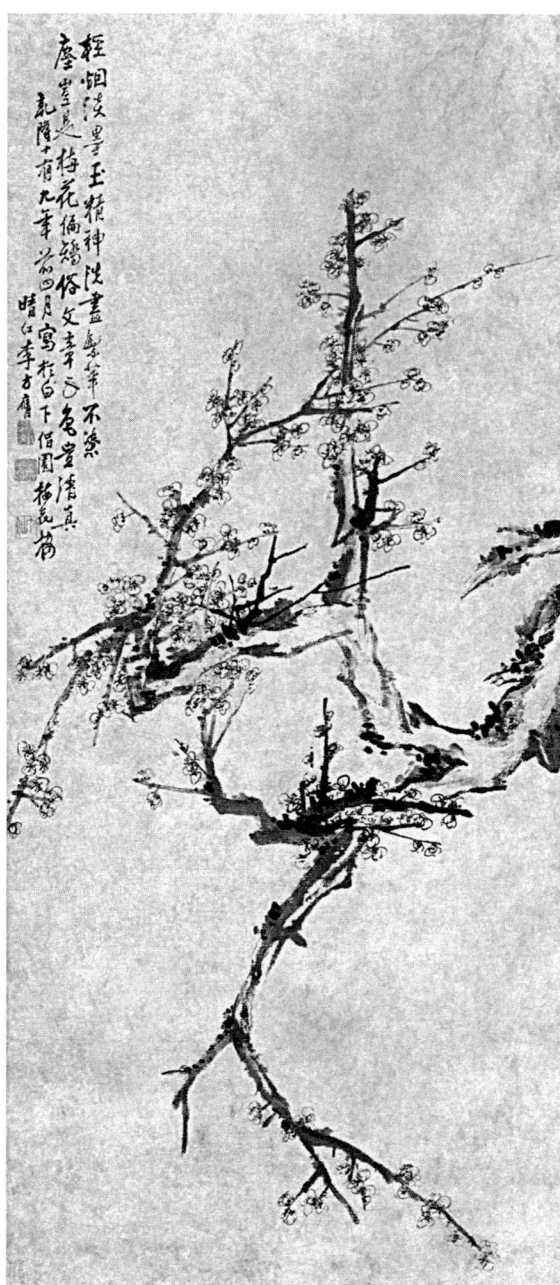

Yangzhou school painting by Li Fangying: *Branch of Blossoming Plum*, hanging scroll, ink on paper, 1061×710 mm, 1754 (Berkeley, University of California, University Art Museum)

included in the group are GAO FENGHAN, Min Zhen (1730–after 1788) and Bian Shoumin (*fl* 1725–50).

The beginnings of modern Chinese painting can be seen in the achievements of the Yangzhou masters. The artists of the 19th-century SHANGHAI SCHOOL are their direct heirs, as are such 20th-century painters as Wu Changshi and Qi Baishi. Their most important contributions included ending the dominance of landscape painting and introducing broader and less disciplined brushwork, bolder colours and ways of painting that allowed wet areas of ink and colour to suffuse and puddle. Most of all, perhaps, they moved from the time-consuming creation of individual paintings for particular patrons and clients to a faster and more repetitive production of pictures for a more popular audience. While this has been a heritage with negative as well as positive aspects, the Yangzhou school itself represents the most innovative and interesting movement in painting after the early Qing period, and paintings of this school remain popular both in China and outside.

BIBLIOGRAPHY

O. Sirén: *Chinese Painting: Leading Masters and Principles* (London and New York, 1956–8), v, pp. 235–50

W. H. Scott: 'Yangzhou and its Eight Eccentrics', *Asiat. Stud.*, i–ii (1964), pp. 1–19

Ju-hsi Chou and C. Brown: *The Elegant Brush: Chinese Painting under the Qianlong Emperor, 1735–1795* (Phoenix, 1985)

Cheng-chi (Ginger) Hsu: *Patronage in the Eighteenth Century Yangzhou School of Painting* (diss., Berkeley, CA, U. CA, 1987)

JAMES CAHILL

Yan Hui [Yen Hui; *zi* Qiuyue] (*b* Jiangshan, Zhejiang Province; *fl* late 13th century–early 14th). Chinese painter. He was a painter of Buddhist and Daoist figures, ghosts and landscapes, who was well respected as a painter by the literati by the end of the Song period (960–1279). Of some 35 paintings attributed to him, only a few can be considered to be genuine; among these, the best known are those mounted as a pair of hanging scrolls (ink and colour on silk; Kyoto, Chion'in) depicting two Daoist immortals, Li Tieguai and Liu Haichan, both of which are executed in the extremely realistic style for which Yan is known. There is special attention to physiognomy—to the point of grotesqueness—to volume and to modelling of the body, and to the strong contrast between light and dark areas. Both works also include a misty landscape that serves as a background to the figures, a feature derived from landscape painting of the Southern Song period (1127–1279). Another painting of Li Tieguai (hanging scroll, Beijing, Pal. Mus.) is done in a similar style, but using very arbitrary and eccentric lines. *Lantern Night Excursion of Zhong Kui* (handscroll, ink on silk; Cleveland, OH, Mus. A.) depicts the legendary demon-queller with a considerable entourage of demons, each with its peculiar posture or expression. An equally well-known work is *Two Monkeys on the Branch of a Pipa Tree* (Taipei, N. Pal. Mus.). In all these paintings there is a consistent style that shows Yan as a master of realism, who used eccentric brushwork to depict grotesque figures, thereby representing one early stylistic aspect of the Yuan period (1279–1368). Many of Yan's extant works are now in Japan, and only a few are in China, indicating that although Yan's style lost its appeal to later Chinese painters who were more attracted to the literati style, it found many followers in Japan.

BIBLIOGRAPHY

O. Sirén: *Chinese Paintings: Leading Masters and Principles* (London, 1956–8), iv, pp. 11–15

S. E. Lee: 'Yen Hui: The Lantern Night Excursion of Chung K'uei', *Bull. Cleveland Mus. A.*, xlix/2 (1960), pp. 36–42

J. Cahill: *Hills beyond a River: Chinese Painting of the Yuan Dynasty, 1279–1368* (New York and Tokyo, 1976), pp. 134, 151

CHU-TSING LI

Yanik Tepe. Site in north-western Iran, 32 km south-west of Tabriz. This settlement mound is 16.5 m high and extends over *c.* 8 ha. A long Chalcolithic (4th millennium BC) sequence and Early Bronze Age (3rd millennium BC) levels were excavated by Charles Burney between 1960 and 1962. Finds are in the Archaeological Museum in Tehran.

The Early Bronze Age sequence consisted of 14 Early Trans-Caucasian II levels with round houses (circles) of relatively flimsy mud-brick construction with wattle-and-daub roofing; these houses tended to become larger and more densely located in successive levels, and the bigger ones had a central post. There was often a high threshold, and the standard kitchen fittings—bin, working surface and hearth—were invariably immediately to the right of the door. Pottery with intricate incised decoration was found in enormous quantities in the circles and their surrounding courtyards. Each circle had its range of storage vessels, smaller jars, bowls and lamps. The decoration is predominantly geometric, with patterns derived from woodworking or textiles, perhaps kilims, consistent with a nomadic tradition. Animals and birds also occur in profusion but are too stylized to be readily recognizable. Parallels lie in Trans-Caucasia, and the pottery belongs to a sub-tradition of Early Trans-Caucasian culture within this zone. It may have been brought by an intrusive Indo-European element from the north. There followed five Early Trans-Caucasian III levels with rectangular buildings and undecorated pottery. The surface of the mound bore extensive traces of burning.

BIBLIOGRAPHY

C. A. Burney: 'Circular Buildings Found at Yanik Tepe in North-west Iran', *Antiquity*, xxxv (1961), pp. 237–40

Iraq, xxiii (1961), pp. 138–55; xxiv (1962), pp. 134–49; xxvi (1964), pp. 54–61 [preliminary excav. reps by C. A. Burney]

C. A. Burney and D. M. Lang: *The Peoples of the Hills* (London, 1971), pp. 43–85

A. G. Sagona: *The Caucasian Region in the Early Bronze Age*, Brit. Archaeol. Rep. Int. Ser., ccxiv (Oxford, 1984)

C. A. BURNEY

Yan Liben [Yen Li-pen] (*b* Wannian, Yongzhou [now Xi'an], Shaanxi Province, *c.* AD 600; *d* 673). Chinese painter and government official. He is the most famous painter associated with the imperial courts of the emperors TAIZONG (*reg* AD 626–49) and Gaozong (*reg* 649–83) and the most notable of the few Chinese court painters to attain exceptional official rank. He helped define the imperial taste of the Tang dynasty (618–907), depicting figures and narrative subjects in a detailed, colourful and realistic style.

Yan Liben's father, Yan Bi (563–613), born into an important aristocratic family of the Northern Wei and married to a daughter of the Northern Zhou emperor Wudi (*reg* 561–77), was himself a painter and calligrapher, who earned a place as designer, engineer and architect at the Sui-dynasty (581–618) court. Yan Liben's elder brother, Yan Lide (*d* 656), attained the important posts of Director of the Directorate for Palace Buildings and President of the Board of Works (*c.* 648). Yan Liben followed his brother in these posts and then rose to become Chief Minister of the Right in 668 and Director

Yan Liben (attrib.): *Palanquin Bearers* (detail), handscroll, ink and colours on silk, 385×1296 mm (Beijing, Palace Museum); mid-11th-century copy of 7th century original

of the Secretariat in 671, important and influential offices involved with the formulation of government policy.

Yan Liben was trained as an artist at an early age. In 626 he had the important commission of painting portraits of the 18 scholars at the court of the prince who later became Taizong. In 643 he painted portraits of 24 meritorious officials for the Lingyan Pavilion (four of these survive in the form of Northern Song (960–1127) rubbings; Beijing, Cent. Acad. A. & Des.). He also painted religious subjects, as confirmed by his inclusion in the category of painters of Buddhist and Daoist subjects in the *Xuanhe huapu* ('Xuanhe collection of painting'; preface 1120). He modelled his style on that of Zhang Sengyou (*fl c.* 500–50) and was noted for his ability to capture the true appearance of things. Thus he was ordered by Taizong to portray the foreign tribute bearers arriving at court (for an illustration of tribute bearers attributed to Yan Liben, *see* CHINA, fig. 132), as well as Prince Guo (younger brother of Taizong) heroically killing a murderous dark

tiger with a single bow shot. According to anecdote, Yan was once hurriedly called forth by Taizong to crouch by a lake and paint some unusual birds bobbing in the water that the emperor found particularly delightful. Apparently, Yan was greatly humiliated by the experience and warned his sons never to become painters. An example of Chinese historiographers' traditional bias against painters and artisans, this story, with its moral message, became indelibly linked with Yan Liben's later image.

Of the extant works attributed to Yan, *Thirteen Emperors* (handscroll, ink and colours on silk; Boston, MA, Mus. F.A.; *see* CHINA, fig. 128) is the best-known and the finest. It portrays 13 emperors ranging from the Han (206 BC– AD 220) to Sui dynasties, with identifying titles above. The latter seven are considered to be earlier and of better quality than the first six, though even the seven may represent a portion of a mid-11th-century copy of an original painted not by Yan but by another 7th-century artist, Lang Yuling. *Palanquin Bearers* (see fig.) depicts the meeting of the Tibetan envoy Lu Dongzan with Emperor Taizong (borne on a palanquin by nine maidens). It is also considered to be a mid-11th-century copy, but the attribution of the composition to Yan is slightly more secure. In both paintings, the figures are meticulously delineated with 'iron wire' lines, following an earlier tradition best exemplified by the Eastern Jin (AD 317–420) painter GU KAIZHI, but they also exhibit a concern for subtle volumetric modelling. A lively sense of design, capturing the atmosphere of court pageantry, is particularly pronounced in the portrayal of Taizong's entourage in *Palanquin Bearers*. Personality and mood are aptly expressed in individual faces and gestures, in accordance with Yan's reported talent for portraying true appearances.

BIBLIOGRAPHY
EWA: 'Yen Li-pen'
Zhang Yanyuan: *Lidai minghua ji* [Record of famous painters of all periods] (AD 847); Eng. trans. by W. Acker in *Some T'ang and Pre-T'ang Texts on Chinese Painting*, 2 vols (Leiden, 1954–74), pp. 61–398
Zhu Jingxuan: *Tang chao minghua lu* [Record of famous painters of the Tang dynasty] (9th century); Eng. trans. by A. C. Soper as 'T'ang ch'ao ming hua lu', *Archvs Chin. A. Soc. America*, iv (1950), pp. 5–25
Li Lin-ts'an: 'Yan Liben *Zhigong tu*' [*Tribute Bearers* by Yan Liben], *Dalu Zazhi*, xii/2 (1956), pp. 44–50
Chuang Yen: 'Tang Yan Liben hui *Xiao Yi zhuan Lanting tu* chuanba' [Yan Liben's *Xiao Yi Steals the Lanting*], *Dalu Zazhi*, xv/9 (1957), pp. 1–8
O. Sirén: *Chinese Painting: Leading Masters and Principles* (London and New York, 1956–8), i, pp. 96–103; ii, p. 23; iii, pls 72–8
T. Nagahiro: 'En Rittoku to En Rippon ni tsuite' [Regarding Yan Lide and Yan Liben], *Tōhō gakuhō*, xxix (1959), pp. 1–50
Tang Yan Liben Bunian tu [*Palanquin Bearers* of Yan Liben of the Tang dynasty] (Beijing, 1959)
Jin Weinuo: 'Yan Liben yu Weichi Yiseng' [Yan Liben and Weichi Yiseng], *Wenwu* (1960), no. 4, pp. 61–9
——: '*Zhigong tu* di shidai yu zuozhe' [Date and author of the *Tribute bearers* scroll], *Wenwu* (1960), no. 7, pp. 14–17
——: '*Bunian tu* yu *Lingyange gongchen tu*' [*Palanquin Bearers* and *Meritorious Officials of the Lingyan Pavilion*], *Wenwu* (1962), no. 10, pp. 13–16
Han Chuang [John Hay]: 'Hsiao I Gets the Lan-t'ing Manuscript by a Confidence Trick', *N. Pal. Mus. Bull.*, v/3 (July–Aug 1970), pp. 1–13; and v/6 (Jan–Feb 1971), pp. 1–17
Su Ying-hui: 'Du Yan Liben *Bunian tu* zhujia tiba shu suojian' [On the colophons appended to the painting *Palanquin Bearers* by Yan Liben], *Gugong Jikan*, xi/1 (1976), pp. 25–35
Jin Weinuo: '*Gu diwang tu* di shidai yu zuozhe' [Date and author of the *Emperors of Antiquity* scroll], *Meishujia*, viii (1979), pp. 38–45
J. Cahill: *An Index of Early Chinese Painters and Paintings: T'ang, Sung and Yüan* (Berkeley, 1980), pp. 23–4
Xu Bangda: *Gu shuhua weie kaobian* [Examinations of the authenticity of ancient paintings and calligraphy], 4 vols (Jiangsu, 1984), i, pp. 36–48; ii, pls 63–76
A. C. Soper: 'Yen Li-pen, Yen Li-te, Yen P'i, Yen Ch'ing: Three Generations in Three Dynasties', *Artibus Asiae*, li/3–4 (1991), pp. 199–206

PETER C. STURMAN

Yannina. *See* IOANNINA.

Yan Song [Yen Sung] (*b* Fenyi, Jiangxi Province, 1480; *d* 1565). Chinese government official, collector and poet. He came from an artisan family and passed the civil-service examination in 1505 to gain his *jinshi* degree. He subsequently held a variety of public posts before being appointed a Grand Secretary in 1542 and becoming a favourite of the Jiajing emperor (*reg* 1522–66). After intense political manoeuvring he became the chief Grand Secretary in 1548 and remained in that position until 1562, when he and his son Yan Shifan were dismissed from their posts and degraded to the status of commoner.

After his dismissal, an inventory of Yan's possessions from his various properties was compiled and published by Zhou Shilin in the *Tian shui bingshan lu* ('Record of heaven reducing the ice mountain to water'); this included estimates of the market value of the items. An abbreviated version, the *Qian shan tang shuhua ji* ('Notes on the calligraphy and paintings in the Qian Mountain Hall'), compiled by Wen Jia in 1569, listed only calligraphy and paintings; Wen claimed that it took him three months to go through them and that even then he could no more than glance at them cursorily. Wen Jia compared paintings in Yan's collection with other versions known to him and thus inadvertently acted as a check on old master paintings still extant in the mid-16th century. The catalogue remains invaluable as a record of the variety and extent to which high officials accumulated luxury goods and the prices they were prepared to pay for them. How much of his great collection was obtained legitimately is not known, but at the height of his power its size was a source of considerable public consternation and was seen as evidence of his corrupt practices. The contemporary play *Mingfeng ji* ('The cry of the phoenix'; *c.* 1565) by Wang Shizhen, in which Yan's career and downfall and the sufferings of his victims were retold, although probably largely scurrilous, was the first of its genre to portray modern society, history and manners.

BIBLIOGRAPHY
DMB: 'Yen Sung'
H. Lovell: *Annotated Bibliography of Chinese Paintings, Catalogues and Related Texts*, MI Pap. Chin. Stud., xvi (1973), pp. 14–16
C. Clunas: *Superfluous Things: Material Culture in Early Modern China* (London, 1991)

LAURA RIVKIN

Yan Wengui [Yen Wen-kuei] (*b* Wuxing [now in Zhejiang Province]; *fl* late 970s–early 11th century). Chinese painter. He probably studied with Hao Hui (*fl* 10th–11th century) of Hedong (now in eastern Shanxi Province). He served in the military until the accession of the second emperor of the Song dynasty (960–1279), Taizong (*reg* 976–97), when he set forth by boat to the capital and sold figures and landscapes on the road leading to the Celestial Gate (Tian men). He is said to have been a court official, as a result of which he was accorded the honorary title of *jiangshi lang* ('court gentleman for ceremonial service'), and to have served as the *zhubo* (recorder or archivist) in Yunying District, Yunzhou.

He rose to fame, according to one account (the *Shengchao minghua ping*, 'Critique of famous painters of the present dynasty', by the Song writer Liu Daochun), during the reign of Emperor Taizong when Gao Yi, a painter in attendance (*daizhao*) at the Hanlin Painting Academy, bought several of Yan's paintings and presented them to the Emperor, saying: 'As your servant is charged with the restoration of [flood-damaged] murals in the temple Xiangguo si, may it be submitted that for the painting of the rocks and trees in the project, only Wengui can be sure to paint them successfully.' Taizong was so impressed by the paintings and the recommendation that he appointed Yan to an unspecified position in the Academy. Another Northern Song art historian, Guo Ruoxu, wrote in the *Tuhua jianwen zhi* ('Experiences in painting'; preface 1075) that during the reign of Emperor

Zhenzong (*reg* 998–1023), Yan was a member of a team of 30,000 men who were building and painting the Daoist temple complex Yuqing zhaoying gong and that during his leisure hours he painted some landscapes. These so impressed the superintendent that Yan was recommended to the Hanlin Painting Academy for the position of usher (*zhihou*). Both accounts are uncorroborated.

In landscapes Yan Wengui did not follow the ancients but created a new style of his own, in which he represented the myriad aspects of nature with startling lifelike vividness. These landscapes came to be known as *Yan jia jingzhi* ('Yan school scenes'). Yan also excelled in depicting houses, palaces, boats and carts, usually by means of ruled lines. A characteristic peculiar to his work was the incorporation of minutely rendered architectural details within free-hand landscape passages.

Liu Daochun also reported that Yan's fan paintings pleased the Emperor and that he once painted the *Qixi* [Summer] *Night Market*, showing its bustling activities with astonishing fidelity. Yan's album *Puochuan duhai xiang* ('Pictures of boats coming back from sea'), owned by a wealthy merchant, was only about 300 mm high and depicted boats the size of small leaves and people the size of wheat grains; masts, sails, steering oars and people pointing and shouting were all rendered with amazing precision, and there were marvellous images of mighty waves, distant islands and sea monsters surging across the oceans. According to Guo Ruoxu, people kept in their homes screen paintings and hanging scrolls by Yan; and Deng Chun recorded in his *Hua ji* ('Painting continued'; *see* CHINA, §V, 5) that he owned a set of Yan's four seasons paintings (all untraced), including such evocative titles as *Waxing Moon over the Flowering Village*, *Evening Rain on the Calm River*, *Mists in the Bamboo Forest at Dusk* and *Remaining Snow at Pine Stream*. The titles, format and sequential character serve to exemplify what were later known as Yan school scenes.

The landscape painting *Towers and Pavilions amid Rivers and Mountains* (*Jiangshan louguan*; handscroll, ink on paper; Osaka, Mun. Mus. A.) bears Yan's name and is the work most consistently attributed to the artist by 20th-century art historians. In its handling of brush and ink and brush motifs, the style resembles that of his contemporary FAN KUAN, by whom Yan was much influenced. Broad, swelling strokes of thick, black ink define both the contour lines of the boulder and the horizontal plane of the mountain. The rocky surface is modelled with finer, relatively centred, short ink strokes, with slashes of horizontal accents in the area of sheer rock-faces. The work has been dated to the mid-11th century largely on the grounds of the variety of modelling strokes used; in later works attributed to the master these became more unified and stylized. The mountains are girdled in mist and the bottom is highlighted, emphasizing the vertiginous feeling and the spatial expanse between the ranges. Houses and manmade objects are unnaturally small, dwarfed by the grandeur of nature, in which men and beasts, though depicted naturalistically, serve as incidental accents. *Towers and Pavilions* accords in structure and appearance with descriptions of Yan's style by Yuan-period (1279–1368) observers. In the same period Ni Zan and Qian Weishan wrote of a painting associated with Yan called *Lonely*

Temple in Autumn Mountains (*Qiushan xiaosi*; untraced). It depicted vertiginous precipices, riders hurrying lightly on stone-paved paths, wintry winds sending off distant skiffs, in short, a hoary, autumnal panorama described in minute detail and full of antique feeling.

Another hanging scroll, called *Towers and Pavilions amid Streams and Mountains* (*Qishan louguan*) (Taipei, N. Pal. Mus.; see fig.), shows similar composition and motifs. There is an emphatic use of the small, vertical texture brushstrokes associated with Fan Kuan's modelling of rocky mountain surfaces, later called *yudian cun* ('raindrop

Yan Wengui: *Towers and Pavilions amid Streams and Mountains*, hanging scroll, ink on silk, 1039×474 mm, late 10th century (Taipei, National Palace Museum); possibly once part of a wider composition

texture strokes'). The many granite peaks rise ever higher as they recede. Overall, the painting recalls the Osaka handscroll, but the somewhat mannerized application of contour outlines and texture strokes may reveal a later interpretation of the style. Its present dimensions (1039×474 mm) and incomplete appearance suggest that it may have been part of a larger, wider composition, perhaps one of a series of six or eight panels of a screen.

BIBLIOGRAPHY

Franke: 'Yen Wen-kuei'

Liu Daochun: *Shengchao minghua ping* [Critique of famous painters of the present dynasty], 3 *juan* (Song period, 960–1279)

Guo Ruoxu: *Tuhua jianwen zhi* [Experiences in painting] (preface 1075); ed. Huan Miaozi (Shanghai, 1963); Eng. trans. by A. C. Soper as *Kuo Jo-hsü's 'Experiences in Painting' (T'u-hua chien-wen chih): An Eleventh-century History of Chinese Painting* (Washington, DC, 1951/*R* 1971)

Zhou Mi: *Yunyan guoyan lu* [Record of what was seen as clouds and mist] (Yuan period, 1279–1368)

Deng Chun: *Hua ji* [Painting continued] (preface 1167)

Yang Wangxiu: *Song Zhongxing guange chucang tuhua ji* (1199); *R* Meishu congshu

Xia Wenyan: *Tuhui baojian* [Precious mirror for examining painting] (1365/*R* Shanghai, 1963)

Zhan Jingfeng: *Dongtu xuanlan bian* (1591); *R* Meishu congshu

Sun Chengze: *Gengzi xiaoxiaji* (1660); *R* Yishu shangjian xuanshen

S. Nakamura: *Chūgoku garon no tenkai* [Development of Chinese painting theory] (Kyoto, 1965), pp. 392–400

K. Suzuki: *Chūgoku Kaigashi* [History of Chinese painting] (Tokyo, 1981), pp. 259–71

Chen Gaohua: *Song, Liao, Jin huajia shiliao* [Historical materials of Song, Liao and Jin painters] (Beijing, 1984), pp. 253–8

JOAN STANLEY-BAKER

Yanxiadu [Yen-hsia-tu]. Site in Yi xian (Yi County), Hebei Province, China. The capital of the state of Yan during the middle and later parts of the Warring States period (403–221 BC), Yanxiadu was surveyed and excavated in 1930, 1957–8, 1961–2, 1964–5, 1971 and 1973. The remains of the city are located between the Northern Yi River and Middle Yi River and cover a rough rectangle (*c.* 8 km east–west by 4 km north–south). The two rivers and two canals outside the eastern and western city walls functioned as a moat. The site is divided into an eastern and a western city, of which the eastern is the principal part. The eastern city is a rough square (*c.* 4.5 km east–west); three gates were found in its eastern, northern and western walls.

The palace area is in the northern part of the eastern city, and here four large rammed-earth foundations on earthen mounds were found: Wuyangtai, Wangjingtai, Zhanggongtai and Laomutai. Of these, Wuyangtai is the largest (*c.* 11×110×140 m). There are also three palace clusters, each of which is composed of the remains of a large structure and several small ones. A bronze *zun* vessel (see 1980 cat., no. 133; for illustration of this type *see* CHINA, fig. 138(vii)) in the shape of an elephant and inscribed with the characters *youfuyin* ('right palace manager'), suggesting its administrative function, was found at Wuyangtai. A section of clay water-pipe (see *Kaogu Xuebao*, 1, pls V, 4, 6), one end of which is shaped like a tiger's head, and a bronze animal-mask (see 1980 cat., no. 115) were found near Laomutai. Semicircular eave-tiles (see *Kaogu Xuebao*, 1, pls V, 1–3, 5) bearing various motifs, such as *taotie* animal-masks (*see* CHINA, §VI, 3(ii)(a)), double dragons or the character meaning 'mountain', were found in the area of Wuyangtai and Laomutai. Remains of

several workshops for making iron objects, weapons and bone artefacts are concentrated on the north-western part of the palace area. The residential area is in the southern part of the eastern city, and here workshops for making iron objects, weapons, coins and pottery were found. Two cemeteries with large earthen mounds are located in the north-western corner of the eastern city. Tomb 16, a square pit with two ramps running north–south, has been excavated, yielding many artefacts of pottery, stone, bone and antler, and pieces of bronzes and iron implements. The most striking discoveries from the pit are 135 painted pottery vessels (see *Kaogu Xuebao*, 2) in sets imitating ritual bronzes.

BIBLIOGRAPHY

'Hebei Yi xian Yanxiadu gucheng kancha he shijue' [Survey and excavation at Yanxiadu, Yi xian, Hebei Province], *Kaogu Xuebao* (1965), no. 1, pp. 83–106

'Hebei Yi xian Yanxiadu di shiliu hao mu fajue' [Excavation of Tomb 16 at Yanxiadu, Yi xian, Hebei Province], *Kaogu Xuebao* (1965), no. 2, pp. 79–102

Hebei Prov. Cult. Relics Res. Inst. (1980)

Li Xueqin: *Eastern Zhou and Qin Civilizations* (New Haven and London, 1985), pp. 111–18

LI LIU

Yan Zhenqing [Yen Chen-ch'ing; *zi* Qingchen; Lu Gong] (*b* Shandong Province, AD 709; *d* 785). Chinese calligrapher, scholar, writer and government official. His family, members of the gentry, moved within Shandong from the north to the south, giving him an acquaintance with the different cultural traditions of both areas. After the early death of his father he was educated by his uncle, Yan Yuansun. At the age of 28 he passed the civil service examinations to become a *jinshi*. He was prefect of Dezhou and governor of Pingyuan, both in Shandong Province, and he held high positions at the imperial library, in the Ministry of Justice and as preceptor of the crown prince. In 767 he received the title Duke of Lu (Lu Gong) for his honesty and integrity as investigation censor of the Bureau of Administration. An outstanding example of Confucian loyalty, he fought against the rebellion of An Lushan in 755 and against Li Xieli in 781; Li took him prisoner and had him strangled in 785.

Yan Zhenqing possessed a private library, compiled a dictionary and wrote prose, poetry and criticism, in particular condemning as trivial the palace style of literature. He is regarded as a revolutionary figure in Chinese calligraphy. He first studied the regular style (*kaishu*) of the early Tang-period (AD 618–907) masters, especially that of Chu Suiliang; later, when he was in his thirties, he studied cursive script (*caoshu*) with Zhang Xu at Luoyang. Extant reliably attributed works dated to between 757 and 780 clearly demonstrate the development of his calligraphy from the elegant style of the Southern Dynasties period (AD 317–589), based on that of Wang Xizhi, to a rigid structural clarity, doubtless derived from the northern tradition. His early *kaishu* script is seen in the *Pagoda Stele at the Pavilion of Many Treasures* (*Duobao ta bei*; 752) at the Qianfu si, while his mature style occurs in the *Yan Family Temple Stele* (*Yan shijia miaobei*; 780; *see* CHINA, §IV, 2(vi)). Virile strength characterizes his *Draft for a Memorial for his Nephew* (*Jizhi wengao*; Taipei, N. Pal. Mus.). Tang-period critics described his style as strong and pleasing (*qiuwan*) and those of the Song period

(AD 960–1279) as vigorous and fine (*xiongxiu*), although the painter and calligrapher Mi Fu called it vulgar (*su*). Yan's *kaishu* remains a classic model of dignity (*yan su*), a reflection of his excellence of character.

See also CHINA, §IV, 2(iii)(b).

BIBLIOGRAPHY
Liu Xu and others: *Jiu Tang shu* [Former history of the Tang] (Later Jin period, AD 936–46)
Ouyang Xiu and others: *Xin Tang shu* [Later history of the Tang] (Song period, AD 960–1279)
M. Aoki: 'Gan Shinkei no shogaku' [Study of Yan Zhenqing's calligraphy], *Shodō zenshū* [Complete collection of calligraphy], ed. Y. Shimonaka (Tokyo, 1954–68), x, pp. 10–13
The International Seminar on Chinese Calligraphy in Memory of Yen Chench'ing's 1200th Anniversary: Taipei, 1987

ROGER GOEPPER

Yapahuva [Yāpāhuva; Pali: Subha-pabbata; Sundarapabbata; Yasa-pabbata]. Sri Lankan site and capital city in the 13th century. Built around an outcrop of rock 90 m high, Yapahuva originated as a Buddhist cave monastery in the last centuries BC. The site came to prominence in the early 13th century as a defence station during the south Indian and Malay invasions. After the routing of the invaders, a well-fortified palace was built that served as the seat of Bhuvanekabahu I (*reg* 1272–84). Yapahuva was then sacked by a Pandya general, Aryachakravatti, and subsequently abandoned.

The defences exposed by excavation are roughly circular in plan and consist of two ramparts and two moats that abut the great rock on its south side. Gateways are located on the eastern and western sides. A broad flight of steps over the southern side of the outer rampart leads to the outer city. More or less in line with these steps is an ornamental stairway leading up to the remains of the king's palace. This stairway (see fig.) rises in three tiers punctuated by landings. The third flight, perhaps the grandest in Sri Lanka, is replete with lions carved in the round and mythical lion–elephants (Pali: *gaja-simha*) as wing stones. The dados round the western and eastern stylobates are ornamented with bas-reliefs of musicians, drummers, dancers and acrobats. The stairway gives access to an elaborate pillared porch with a central vestibule and two flanking guard-houses, each having a front wall of stone blocks and a window fashioned from a single, intricately carved slab of stone. The perforated slabs have rings encircling the hubs with tapering spokes, dancers, lions, swans and dwarfs (Yapahuva, Archaeol. Mus.; Colombo, N. Mus.). On either side of the porch is a parapet wall of ashlar bordering the palace terrace. Within, the remains of the brick-built palace have been excavated and conserved. The palace is of simple design, with a central hall and small side and back rooms and a lavatory. From the north-western corner of the palace terrace a series of steps gives access to the summit of the rock, where a stupa (Sinh. *dāgaba*) of modest dimensions, a large pond, a rectangular building of brick and lime mortar and several ruined buildings are located.

Outside the city to the north-east is a shrine on a stone masonry stylobate popularly known as the Temple of the Tooth Relic of the Buddha. Built partly of stone and partly of brick, the roughly rectangular building consists of a sanctum with outer and inner vestibules. Within the

Yapahuva, ornamental stairway leading to the remains of the palace of Bhuvanekabahu I, 13th century

sanctum, which is at a lower level than the vestibule, there is a circular stone plinth in two halves. The object venerated could have been a Bodhi tree, as there is no sign of a roof having been provided for the sanctum. The sanctum doorway, on the western side, is surmounted by a *makara toraṇa* (arch formed by a mythical sea creature) in stone, within which is sculpted a seated Buddha in the attitude of meditation.

BIBLIOGRAPHY
H. C. P. Bell: *Archaeol. Surv. Ceylon, Annu. Rep. 1910–11 and 1911–12*, (Colombo, 1914), pp. 52–61

RAJA DE SILVA

Yaqut al-Musta'simi [Jamāl al-Dīn ibn 'Abdallah al-Mawṣulī Yāqūt al-Musta'simī] (*d* Baghdad, 1298). Ottoman calligrapher. Yaqut served as secretary to the last Abbasid caliph, al-Musta'sim (*reg* 1242–58), and reportedly survived the sacking of Baghdad by the Mongols in 1258 by seeking refuge in a minaret. He perfected the 'proportioned script' developed by IBN MUQLA and refined by IBN AL-BAWWAB, in which letters were measured in terms of dots, circles and semicircles (see ISLAMIC ART, §III, 2(iii)). By replacing the straight-cut nib of the reed pen with an obliquely cut one, Yaqut created a more elegant hand. A master of the classical scripts known as the Six Pens (*thuluth, naskh, muhaqqaq, rayhan, tawqi'* and *riqa'*), he earned the epithets 'sultan', 'cynosure' and 'qibla' of calligraphers. He is said to have copied two manuscripts of the Koran each month, but surviving examples are rare (e.g. 1294; Istanbul, Topkapı Pal. Lib., E.H. 74). Despite their small size, a typical folio (see fig.) has 16 lines of delicate *naskh* script, with verse markers in the margin, and appears quite spacious. He had six famous pupils; their names vary in the sources but the most famous are AHMAD AL-SUHRAWARDI, YAHYA AL-SUFI and HAYDAR. Yaqut's work was prized by later collectors and calligraphers; Koran manuscripts transcribed by him (e.g. 1283–4, Istanbul, Topkapı Pal. Lib., E.H. 227; 1286–7, Tehran, Archaeol. Mus., MS. 4277) were often refurbished with

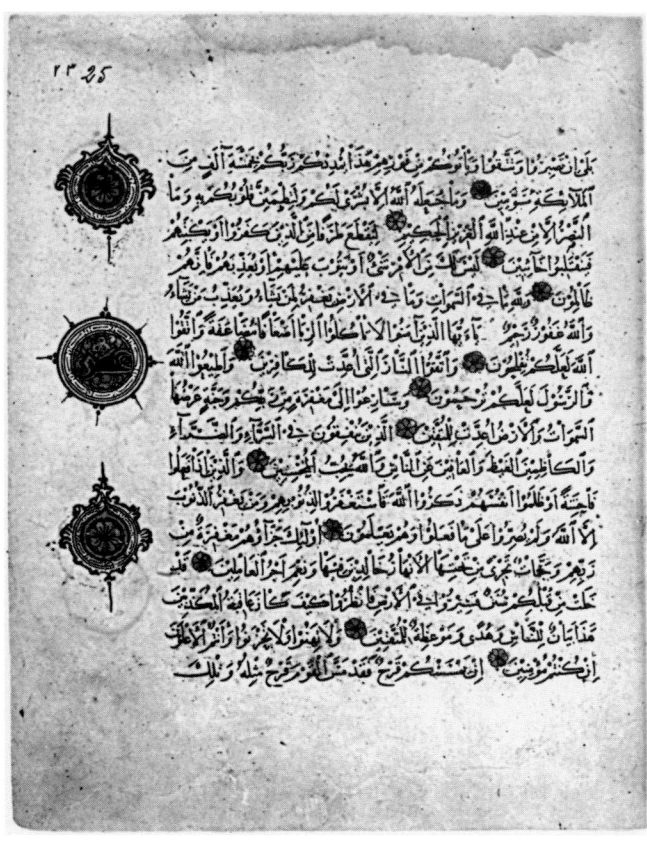

Yaqut al-Musta'simi: page from a manuscript of the Koran, 1289 (Paris, Bibliothèque Nationale, MS. arab. 6716, fol. 25*r*)

splendid illumination under the Ottomans (*reg* 1281–1924) and Safavids (*reg* 1501–1732).

BIBLIOGRAPHY

Qāżī Aḥmad ibn Mīr Munshī: *Gulistān-i hunar* [Rose-garden of art] (*c.* 1606); Eng. trans. by V. Minorsky as *Calligraphers and Painters* (Washington, DC, 1959), pp. 57–61

M. Lings: *The Quranic Art of Calligraphy and Illumination* (London, 1976), pls 23, 26–8

Y. H. Safadi: *Islamic Calligraphy* (London, 1978)

The Age of Sultan Süleyman the Magnificent (exh. cat. by E. Atıl, Washington, DC, N.G.A.; Chicago, IL, A. Inst.; New York, Met.; 1987–8), no. 13

NABIL SAIDI

Yarim Tepe (i) [Pers. Yārīm Tappa]. Site in the fertile Gurgan plain of north-eastern Iran, 125 km east of the Caspian Sea. The mound is 20 m high, but it is now reduced to little more than half its original size (diam. 180 m) by river erosion and is distinguished by its tall cliff-like southern face. It was this exposed section that indicated that Yarim Tepe could well expand what was known of the long history of settlement in north-eastern Iran, from the 6th millennium BC to the early centuries AD (see IRAN, ANCIENT, §I, 2(i) and (ii)). The site was excavated by Stronach in 1960 and 1962, and most of the finds are in the Archaeological Museum in Tehran.

The sequence begins with the establishment of an Early Chalcolithic settlement (Yarim I) in the late 6th millennium BC. The pottery is straw-tempered, slipped and painted.

After a gap of almost 1500 years (during which there is just enough evidence from the vicinity to indicate a local use of finely painted, grit-tempered Cheshmeh Ali ware), the mound was reoccupied in the Late Chalcolithic period. This Yarim II settlement has provided two distinctive, well-documented ceramics: a red ware with bold black-painted motifs and a monochrome grey burnished ware. Vessels of pattern-burnished grey ware, with motifs recalling those of the older painted pottery, predominate through much of the subsequent Yarim III or Bronze Age occupation—a time of significant international trade and urban growth.

Yarim Tepe was abandoned before 2000 BC, at a time when many other sites in north-eastern Iran appear to have met a similar fate; it was resettled in the course of the Iron Age, perhaps as late as Iron Age III (*c.* 700–*c.* 600 BC). Much of this Yarim IV pottery is either orange to brown or light grey. Finally, towards the end of the sequence, the Yarim V settlement is characterized by fine red ware bowls with black-edged flame-like patterns. Parallels for this unusual decoration point at least in part to the Parthian period (250 BC–*c.* AD 224), a time of marked prosperity throughout the Gurgan region.

BIBLIOGRAPHY

V. E. Crawford: 'Beside the Kara Su', *Bull. Met.*, xxi/8 (April 1963), pp. 263–73

D. Stronach: 'Yarim Tepe', *Excavations in Iran: The British Contribution* (Oxford, 1972), pp. 21–3

DAVID STRONACH

Yarim Tepe (ii). Group of six mounds containing remains of settlements dating from the 6th to the 1st millennium BC, situated near the town of Tall 'Afar in northern Iraq. Three of these, Yarim Tepe I, II and III, were investigated by a Soviet expedition led by R. M. Munchaev from 1969 to 1980. Finds have been distributed between the Iraq Museums in Baghdad, the Mosul Museum and the Pushkin Museum of Fine Arts, Moscow.

Yarim Tepe I, which belongs to the Hassuna culture of northern Mesopotamia (6th millennium BC), covers an area of approximately 2 ha on the banks of a stream. The mound rises 5 m above the level of the plain, and the archaeological deposits are 6.5 m deep, within which 12 levels have been identified. Architectural remains have been recorded from the earliest levels upwards. The houses are rectangles composed of a series of rooms used as living-quarters or workshops. In the larger houses there are up to 15 rooms. The walls of the houses are made up of clay slabs, and the floors were coated with clay or gypsum. Within the rooms there were round, oval and rectangular ovens as well as granaries and areas for drying grain. Kilns for firing pottery, the remains of workshops where tools were produced and round constructions possibly used as shrines were also discovered. Child burials were found under the floors of some houses.

Most of the finds from Yarim Tepe I consist of pottery, including large vessels for the storage of grain and water, pitchers, cups, bowls and pots. The vessels bear relief or incised decoration and painted designs in red and brown, using geometric motifs (zigzags, lattice patterns, lozenges, chevrons etc.). A number of typical specimens of imported Samarra wares were found. There is a group of female figurines in clay with a characteristic high coiffure. Many ornaments were found, mainly necklaces made of various kinds of stone, sea shells, bone, clay and copper. Copper objects and small lumps of ore are present at all levels. A massive lead bracelet and round and rectangular stone seals were also discovered.

Yarim Tepe II contains the remains of a settlement of the Halaf culture (5th millennium BC). The hill has been half eroded by the river, and the name Yarim Tepe (Turk.: 'half a mound') has been extended to the whole group of tells. The Yarim Tepe II settlement covers an area of 1.5–2 ha on the banks of the River Ibra. The archaeological deposit is 7 m deep, and nine levels have been identified. The settlement, with a large communal barn in the centre, consisted of more than 25 units, including multi-chambered rectangular granaries. At all levels buildings were predominantly round in plan. Houses of a tholos type with a diameter of 3–5 m had a single room, on to which rectangular annexes were built. Ovens of various kinds were excavated, among which were two-tier pottery kilns of complicated construction. The inhabitants of Yarim Tepe I and II were dependent on agriculture and stock-raising.

The pottery from Yarim Tepe II is of great interest, ranging in form from miniature cups, little bowls, plates and beakers to pots and large vessels for storing water etc. The majority bear painted decoration in a variety of colours. More than 400 designs have been counted, primarily geometric in character, but there are also representations of animals (gazelles, cheetahs, deer), birds, fish and snakes, as well as entire scenes: flocks of water fowl, birds of prey attacking gazelles etc. A popular motif is the bucranium, an image of the head of a bull. The zoomorphic and anthropomorphic vessels are of particular interest, including one in the shape of a pig, covered with intricate painting. Even more interesting is one of the outstanding works of ancient Mesopotamian art, a flask more than 200 mm high in the form of a young woman, with painted decoration representing necklaces, bracelets and long wavy hair hanging loosely down her back. A significant group of clay statuettes of women, both schematic and realistic, and a number of copper objects, among them a seal, were also found.

Buildings, pottery and figurines (including an especially varied group of animals) of exactly the same type have been recorded in the lowest, Halaf levels of the neighbouring settlement of Yarim Tepe III, which covers an area of about 4 ha. The archaeological deposits are 12 m deep, of which the lower eight belong to the Halaf culture and the upper four, with four levels, to the Ubaid period (the end of the 5th millennium BC and the first half of the 4th). The houses are rectangular, have many rooms and are divided by narrow passages. The walls are constructed of sun-dried brick. Rectangular and round ovens were found both inside the rooms and in the courtyards, while the individual graves of children and adults were discovered under the floors. Pottery types included spherical, carinated pots, bell-shaped jars and hemispherical cups. The painting is monochrome: black, brown or red paint applied to a light-brown or greenish field. The motifs are geometrical or, more rarely, representational (zoomorphic). Modelled figures include clay statuettes of goats,

sheep and dogs and individual anthropomorphic figurines. Stone tools, such as sickle blades, adzes and mattocks, are linked principally to agriculture. Ornaments are represented by beads of obsidian, marble, chalcedony and haematite.

BIBLIOGRAPHY

N. Ya. Merpert and R. M. Munchaev: 'Early Agricultural Settlements in the Sinjar Plain, Northern Iraq', *Iraq*, xxxv (1973), pp. 93–113
N. Ya. Merpert, R. M. Munchaev and N. O. Bader: 'Investigations of the Soviet Expedition in Northern Iraq (1976)', *Sumer*, xxxvii (1981), pp. 22–95
R. M. Munchaev and N. Ya. Merpert: *Rannezemledel'cheskiye poseleniya Severnoy Mesopotamii* [Early agricultural settlements of northern Mesopotamia] (Moscow, 1981)
N. Ya. Merpert and R. M. Munchaev: 'Soviet Expedition's Research at Yarim Tepe III in Northwestern Iraq (1978–1979)', *Sumer*, xliii/1–2 (1984), pp. 54–68
——: 'The Earliest Levels at Yarim Tepe I and Yarim Tepe II in Northern Iraq', *Iraq*, xlix (1987), pp. 1–36

R. M. MUNCHAEV, N. YA. MERPERT

Yarkhoto [Yarxoto; Chin. Jiaohe]. Site of an ancient city in the Turfan Oasis in the Xinjiang Uygur Autonomous Region of China. It was for a time the capital of the Uygur kingdom (9th–13th century). However, the town was mentioned earlier in the annals of the Chinese Han dynasty (206 BC–AD 220) as Jushi, the residence of the ruler of Turfan. As the name Yarkhoto ('cliff town') suggests, the town is situated on an island-like plateau surrounded by two deep river valleys. This plateau (1.5 km from northwest to south-east) is strewn with a great number of Buddhist ruins, which in the main were excavated by Aurel Stein (1900–01; 1906–7; 1914), Albert Grünwedel (1902–3; 1904–5) and Albert von LeCoq (1904–5; 1913–14). The building designated by Stein as Yar I is a monastery, the largest building—Yar II—a Buddhist sanctuary. The latter is in an architectural style widely used in Central Asia: a stupa of several storeys, with niches, and surrounded by a wall. Devotees were able to walk round the stupa in a clockwise direction and worship the cult figures—Buddhas, *bodhisattva*s etc—set in the niches. The cult objects, coloured sculptures of unfired clay and wood, bronzes, temple flags as well as a great number of painted and unpainted manuscripts found at Yarkhoto date from the 8th to 9th century AD (London, BM; New Delhi, N. Mus.). The walls of the religious buildings were probably painted, but no wall paintings have survived.

BIBLIOGRAPHY

M. A. Stein: *Serindia: Detailed Report of Explorations in Central Asia and Westernmost China*, iii (Oxford, 1921/R New Delhi, 1981), pp. 1167–8, 1175–6
——: *Innermost Asia: Detailed Report of Explorations in Central Asia, Kan-su and Eastern Iran*, ii (Oxford, 1928/R Delhi, 1980), pp. 712–18, pl. 35
A. F. D. Hulsewé: *China in Central Asia: The Early Stage, 125 B.C.–A.D. 23*, Sinica Leidensia, xiv (Leiden, 1969)
M. Yaldiz: *Archäologie und Kunstgeschichte Chinesisch-Zentralasiens (Xinjiang)* (1987), iii/2 of *Handbuch der Orientalistik*, ed. B. Spuler and others (Leiden, 1978–), pp. 123–5

M. YALDIZ

Yar [Yer] **Kurgan**. Site in Uzbekistan, on the lower Kashka River, which flourished from the 8th century BC to the 7th century AD. The site has been identified as the ancient capital of the Naksheba region in southern Sogdiana. Excavations by the Institute of Archaeology (Academy of Sciences), Uzbekistan, uncovered an area of *c.* 150 ha, bounded by an inner and outer set of fortifications. The asymmetrical inner city wall had five sides with numerous bastions, and survived to a height of 8 m. Initially constructed in the 6th century BC, it was rebuilt several times. Less of the later outer wall survives. Excavated buildings within the walls were all constructed of mud-brick and beaten clay. A large temple complex in the centre of the inner city comprised two buildings, which contained numerous traces of a fire cult. Fragments of polychrome figural wall paintings and painted clay sculpture (*see* CENTRAL ASIA, §I, 3(iii)(a)) and other objects show stylistic affiliations with artefacts from Bactria and Merv. Excavations of the largest mound revealed the remains of the upper and lower terraces of a palace. Individual workshops of a ceramic quarter were also uncovered. Remains in the excavated area of the inner city date from the 1st to the 5th century AD. The ruined Zoroastrian dakhma (tower of silence; 3rd–2nd century BC) in the outer city pre-dates the construction of the outer wall. The area also contained a later complex of monumental memorial buildings and a quarter for metalworkers. Independent structures and monumental buildings were also located outside the city.

BIBLIOGRAPHY
M. Kh. Isamiddinov and R. Kh. Suleymanov: *Yar Kurgan: Stratigrafiya i periodizatsiya* [Yar Kurgan: stratigraphy and chronology] (Tashkent, 1984)

R. SULEYMANOV

Yaroshenko, Nikolay (Aleksandrovich) (*b* Poltava, 13 Dec 1846; *d* Kislovodsk, 7 July 1898). Russian painter of Ukrainian birth. The son of an officer, he had a full military career, retiring from the army with the rank of major–general in 1892. During his military training, Yaroshenko studied drawing and painting seriously, initially on his own, then from 1864 to 1867 at evening classes at the Drawing School of the Society for the Encouragement of Artists under Ivan Kramskoy, and later as an occasional student at the St Petersburg Academy of Arts from 1867 to 1874. He became acquainted with examples of the new Russian realism of the 1860s and always remained in complete sympathy with these aesthetic ideas. From 1875 he began to participate actively in the exhibitions of the WANDERERS; he became a member from 1876 and after the departure of Kramskoy in the early 1880s he was effectively the leader. According to Il'ya Repin he was called the 'conscience of the Wanderers'. The fundamental theme of Yaroshenko's work was the life and character of figures active in the Russian liberal intelligentsia and the pro-revolutionary student body. His most successful works are devoted to this subject (e.g. *The Convict*, 1878; Moscow, Tret'yakov Gal., and the *Old and the Young*, 1881; St Petersburg, Rus. Mus.), and he also produced a large number of portraits of well-known figures in Russian arts, letters and sciences (e.g. the artists *Ivan Kramskoy*, 1876, and *Nikolay Ge*, 1890; both St Petersburg, Rus. Mus., and the poet and philosopher *V. S. Solovyov*, 1895; Moscow, Tret'yakov Gal.). The pathos inherent in the idea of social responsibility and the concern of the Russian intelligentsia for the fate of the country and people deeply impressed Yaroshenko, and is rendered with severity and restraint. He also produced pathetic renditions of subjects taken from the life of the people, for example *The Fireman* (1878), which shows the worker's life and appearance disfigured by inhuman, penitential conditions, and *Everywhere is Life* (1888; both Moscow, Tret'yakov Gal.), which demonstrates the dignity of man in extreme conditions of confinement. The latter was one of the most popular pictures among the Russian intelligentsia at the turn of the century. Yaroshenko lived primarily in St Petersburg, but he travelled widely in western Europe, the Near and Far East, the Urals, the Volga region, the Crimea and the Caucasus, producing a number of nature studies and several large paintings of the primarily mountainous landscape. From 1882 he paid annual visits to his dacha in Kislovodsk in the southern Caucasus (now the Yaroshenko A. Mus.).

BIBLIOGRAPHY
V. A. Prytkov: *Nikolay Aleksandrovich Yaroshenko: Zhizn' i tvorchestvo* [Nikolay Aleksandrovich Yaroshenko: life and work] (Moscow, 1960)
V. Porudominsky: *Nikolay Yaroshenko* (Moscow, 1979)

L. I. IOVLEVA

Yaroslavl'. City and regional centre in Russia, *c.* 280 km north-east of Moscow at the confluence of the rivers Kotorosl and Volga. It was founded *c.* 1010 by Prince Yaroslav I (*reg* 1019–54); from 1218 it served as the capital of the Yaroslavl' principality, which was subjugated to Moscow in 1463. In the 18th and 19th centuries it was a provincial capital.

In the 11th and 12th centuries Yaroslavl' consisted of a small fortress with earthen and wooden ramparts. Trade along the Volga led to its expansion, and in the 13th century a settlement grew up around the kremlin, including 17 wooden churches (destr.) and the monastery of the Saviour with its stone cathedral of the Transfiguration (1216). A stone cathedral of the Dormition (1215) was also built within the kremlin. In 1238 the town was ravaged by the Tatars and then restored. From the early 13th century to the early 14th Yaroslavl' also served as a major centre of icon production. One of the most colourful examples from this period is the *Vernicle* (first half of the 13th century; Moscow, Tret'yakov Gal.), with vermilion as the dominant colour. The head of Christ is painted with regular features and displays a great feeling of form.

During the 16th and 17th centuries Yaroslavl' became one of the largest trading centres in Russia. It was divided into three districts: the kremlin, the settlement attached to it and surrounded by ramparts, and the extensive artisans' settlements beyond (e.g. Norskaya, Tveritskaya, Yamskaya, Korovnitskaya). The oldest extant buildings are the Holy Gates (1516) and the three-domed cathedral of the Transfiguration (1516; rebuilt 17th and 18th centuries), in the monastery of the Transfiguration. In the 17th century several more churches and cell blocks were added to the ensemble, which was surrounded with towers. Elsewhere in the town are good examples of the 17th-century Yaroslavl' school of Russian architecture. A particularly common church-plan has four internal piers, supporting vaults and crowned with onion domes. The inner central space is surrounded by galleries with chapels at the eastern end and a richly decorated entrance porch. Other structures may include a refectory block abutting on to the church's west side and a bell-tower to the north-west, as well as other detached tent-shaped bell-towers. The most noteworthy churches are those of St Nicholas the Wet (1620–21), the Prophet Elijah (1647–50), St Michael the Archangel (1660s), St John Chrysostom (1649–54; see fig.), St John the Baptist (1680s), the Epiphany and the Annunciation (1690s), all of which are distinguished by the picturesque arrangement and rich decorative quality of their architectural masses, and the brilliance of their red brick walls and polychrome tiles. The use of glazed ceramics for the decoration of façades was a particular feature of Yaroslavl' architecture.

In the first half of the 16th century there was an upsurge in icon painting, although the colouring is more subdued than in earlier works, as may be seen in the icons for the iconostasis of the cathedral of the Transfiguration (c. 1516; Yaroslavl', A. Mus.). Later icon painters began to depict real historical personalities, such as *Princes Theodore, David and Constantine* (2nd half of the 16th century; Yaroslavl', A. Mus.), filling the borders with scenes of the town's history. This trend towards the authentic portrayal of events became increasingly important in the 17th century, as evidenced by the icon of *St Sergius of Radonezh* (Yaroslavl', A. Mus.) with the mass of historical scenes from his life. By the 1680s Yaroslavl' icon painters were acknowledged as among the best in Russia, one of the most renowned being SEMYON SPIRIDONOV.

Between the 1640s and 1670s Yaroslavl' also developed a school of church wall painting that unusually combined

Yaroslavl', St John Chrysostom, 1649–54

fresco and applied paint. Important works survive in the churches of St John the Baptist, the Prophet Elijah (1680–81) and St Nicholas the Wet (1640–41); among the chief artists were Stefan Yefim'yev, Sevast'yan Dmitriyev, Dmitry Grigor'yev (*fl* 1660–91) and Fyodor Ignat'yev. Many of them also worked in Moscow, Suzdal', Rostov, Vologda and Kostroma. There appear to have been two basic lines of development: one is distinguished by a monumental character, while the other is more strongly decorative and employs narrative motifs. The art of wall painting flourished in Yaroslavl' until the end of the 18th century.

During the first half of the 18th century the town's architecture continued to develop along old Russian traditions with little adoption of the Baroque style. In the 1780s the town was replanned, incorporating most of the important extant monuments but allowing for the construction of several major buildings in the Neo-classical style. These included the three interconnecting squares of Parade Square (later Demidov Square), Cathedral Square (later the Strelka) and Elijah Square (later Soviet Square), the latter surrounded by the provincial government buildings (1781–5), the gymnasium (1787–93) and the Matveyev estate (1790s).

For illustration of icons *see* ICON, colour pl. II, fig. 2; and RUSSIA, figs 20 and 21.

BIBLIOGRAPHY
N. Telyakovsky: *Starina i svyatyni goroda Yaroslavlya* [Antiquities and sacred places of Yaroslavl'] (Yaroslavl', 1913)
V. Ivanov: *Yaroslavl'* (Moscow, 1946)
A. Suslov: *Yaroslavl'* (Moscow, 1960)
E. Dobrovol'skaya and B. Gnedovsky: *Yaroslavl'* (Moscow, 1981)
V. Bryusova: *Freski Yaroslavlya XVII–nachala XVIII* [Frescoes of Yaroslav' from the 17th to the start of the 18th century] (Moscow, 1983)
S. Y. Maslenitsyn: *Yaroslavskaya ikonopis'* [Yaroslavl' icon painting] (Moscow, 1983)
P. Kozlov and V. Marcv: *Yaroslavl': Putevoditel'-spravochnik* [A guidebook to Yaroslavl'] (Yaroslavl', 1988)

D. O. SHVIDKOVSKY

Yasari. *See* ESAD YESARI.

Yasi. *See* TURKESTAN.

Yasky, Avraham (*b* Kishinev, Bessarabia [now Russian Moldova], 14 April 1927). Israeli architect of Russian birth. His family settled in Palestine in 1935 and he studied architecture at the Technion, Haifa, graduating in 1951 after the establishment of Independence (1948). After a period of three years in the office of Arieh Sharon (1900–84) and Benjamin Idelson (*b* 1911), he set up his own practice in 1954, at first in partnership (1954–7) with S. Powsner (*b* 1919), then with A. Alexandroni (1957–65); thereafter he practised as Yasky and Partners. He had a distinguished public and professional career, serving as Chairman and President of the Israel Association of Engineers and Architects, and, for five years as a Tel Aviv city councillor. In addition to numerous prizes in architectural competitions and other awards, he received the Rechter Prize for Hartzfeld Hospital (1968), Gadera, and the Rokach Prize for Bet Halohem Rehabilitation Centre (1972), Afeka. He was also awarded the prestigious Israel Prize for Architecture (1982).

Yasky's designs of the 1950s and 1960s, such as flats in Tel Aviv, an immigrants' hostel (1964) in Nazareth and dormitories (from 1969) at Tel Aviv University, show a creative and sympathetic resonance with the work of Le Corbusier. He planned the campus of Ben Gurion University in Beersheba and designed some of its major buildings (from 1969). In the 1970s he led the planning team for the Gilo neighbourhood of Jerusalem. In the following decade he produced some of the most polished and sophisticated commercial towers in Tel Aviv: the bold sweeping IBM building (1979) and Europe House (1986).

BIBLIOGRAPHY
Archit. Aujourd'hui, lxxvii (1958), pp. 69–80; cvi (1963), pp. 57, 72–73
J. Donat, ed.: *World Architecture* (New York, 1964), pp. 112–14
'Beersheba: Symbol of National Policy', *AIA Journal*, 4 (1970), pp. 27–37

GILBERT HERBERT

Yasohachi. *See* AOKI MOKUBEI.

Yassıhöyük. *See* GORDION.

Yasuda, Yukihiko (*b* Tokyo, 16 Feb 1884; *d* Kanagawa Prefect., 30 April 1978). Japanese painter. In 1898 he trained with Tomoto Kobori, and he also studied and worked with such research groups as the Kōjikai society. In 1914 he participated with Taikan Yoyokama in the revival of the Japan Art Institute. A prominent participant in the Institute's exhibitions, Yasuda displayed such sonorous works as *Solar Eclipse* (1925; Tokyo, N. Mus. Mod. A.) and *Yoshitsune and Yoritomo at Kisegawa Embankment* (1940–41; Tokyo, N. Mus. Mod. A.), which dealt with ancient Chinese history, Japanese history and legend. His style, which was based on a soft, elegant use of colour and graceful lines, was called the New Classicism (*Shinkotenshugi*), and had a great impact on the Japanese-style (*Nihonga*) painters of the time. In 1935 he became a member of the Imperial Art Institute, and in 1948 he received the Order of Cultural Merit.

BIBLIOGRAPHY
Yasuda Yukihiko gashū [Collected paintings by Yasuda Yukihiko] (Tokyo, 1965)
Jisen Yasuda Yukihiko gashū [Personally chosen collected paintings of Yasuda Yukihiko] (Tokyo, 1971)

YOSHIKAZU IWASAKI

Yasufumi Kijima. *See* KIJIMA, YASUFUMI.

Yasuhirō Ishimoto. *See* ISHIMOTO, YASUHIRŌ.

Yasui, Sōtarō (*b* Kyoto, 17 May 1888; *d* Yugawara, Kanagawa Prefect., 14 Dec 1955). Japanese painter. He studied under Asai Chū at the Shōgoin Yōga Kenkyūjo and Kansai Fine Art Academy and from 1907 to 1914 in France under Jean-Paul Laurens at the Académie Julian in Paris. At this time he painted in a style freely adapted first from the work of Camille Pissarro, seen for example in *Garden of the Thatched Cottage* (1910; Tokyo, priv. col., see Kamon, no. 10), and then from the work of Cézanne (e.g. *Red Roofs*, 1913; priv. col., see Kamon, pl. 66). In *Peacock and Woman* (1914; Kyoto, priv. col., see Kamon, pl. 17), however, affinities with classical Italian painting combined with his move towards realism are apparent. He exhibited 44 of the works he had produced in Europe, including the above, at the second exhibition of the Nikakai (Second Division Society) in 1915. These works drew great attention and he was invited to become a member of the Nikakai.

Yasui continued for some time to experiment in search of a form that would express the special characteristics of the Japanese scenery and cultural environment. At the end of the 1920s and early 1930s, however, he established a distinctive realistic style characterized by transparent colours and the formal simplification of the subject. Among the finest works of his mature period are the portrait of *Chin-Jung* (1934; Tokyo, N. Mus. Mod. A.) and the landscape *Lamaist Temple in Ch'eng-tê* (1937; Tokyo, Eisei Bunko). In 1935 he became a member of the Imperial Academy of Fine Art, and on leaving the Nikakai he helped to found the Issuikai. From 1944 to 1952 he was professor at the Tokyo Art School (now Tokyo University of Fine Arts and Music), and he received the Order of Cultural Merit in 1952.

BIBLIOGRAPHY
H. Tomiyama: *Kindai no bijutsu 42 Yasui Sōtarō* [Modern art 42: Yasui Sōtarō] (Tokyo, 1977)
Y. Kamon: *Yasui Sōtarō* (Tokyo, 1979)

TORU ASANO

Yasukazu Tabuchi. *See* TABUCHI, YASUKAZU.

Yasunobu. *See* KANŌ, (13).

Yasuo Kazuki. *See* KAZUKI, YASUO.

Yasushi Sugiyama. *See* SUGIYAMA, YASUSHI.

Yasuzō Nojima. *See* NOJIMA, YASUZŌ.

Yates, Dame **Frances (Amelia)** (*b* Southsea, 28 Nov 1899; *d* Surbiton, 19 Sept 1981). English scholar and writer. She came of a peculiarly English late Victorian family environment—Anglican, high-minded, educated without priggishness, confidently unpretentious, devoted to European travel and to Shakespeare. Her father, a naval constructor, had had to make his own way. Though he did so successfully, there was never much money. A small bequest and the combined resources of the family, however, concentrated within a small house in Claygate, Surrey, enabled Frances Yates to embark on the life of a private scholar.

Her first book, *John Florio* (Cambridge, 1934), was followed by *A Study of Love's Labours Lost* (Cambridge, 1936). Her work on Florio had introduced her to the Renaissance Italian magus-philosopher, Giordano Bruno (1548–1600), whose thought became her lifelong preoccupation. Bruno was the means of her first contact with the Warburg Institute, then recently (1933) arrived in England. She began to develop what she called a Warburgian encyclopedic approach to her work, at the same time retaining, as she did throughout her life, a marked originality and independence of thought and vision. In 1941 she joined the Institute's staff. It was her first paid job, and the association continued until her death.

Frances Yates's exciting and seminal article 'Queen Elizabeth as Astraea' (*J. Warb. & Court. Inst.*, x, pp. 27–82) was worked out during the worst days of World War II, but did not appear in print until 1947, when her great book on *The French Academies of the Sixteenth Century* was also published, in London. In both, Yates used evidence from contemporary literature, philosophy, politics, religion, ceremony, art and music. *The Valois Tapestries* (London, 1959) continued the same vein, taking the tapestries in the Uffizi as documents in the religious–political history of late 16th-century northern Europe. *Giordano Bruno and the Hermetic Tradition* (London, 1964) has been among Yates's most influential books for historians of Renaissance thought; *The Art of Memory* (London, 1966), a study of the pervasive importance of mnemonics, perhaps even more so. Her four final books were all designed ultimately to illuminate Shakespeare: *The Theatre of the World* (London, 1969) by way of the Vitruvian tradition, which she saw as important for the design of Elizabethan theatres; *The Rosicrucian Enlightenment* (London and Boston, 1972) and *Shakespeare's Last Plays* (London, 1975) by way of Protestant-imperial politics; and *The Occult Philosophy in the Elizabethan Age* (London, 1979) by way of Renaissance esoteric belief. She gathered some of her most important essays on political ceremonial and symbolism into *Astraea: The Imperial Theme in the Sixteenth Century* (London and Boston, 1975) and three other essay collections were issued posthumously (1982–4).

WRITINGS

J. N. Hillgarth and J. B. Trapp, eds: *Ideas and Ideals in the North European Renaissance* (London and Boston, 1984) [incl. full list of writings and 'autobiographical fragments']

BIBLIOGRAPHY

DNB

Frances A. Yates, 1899–1981, Warburg Institute memorial booklet (London, 1982)

J. B. TRAPP

Yatsuka, Hajime (*b* Yamagata, 10 Aug 1948). Japanese architect and critic. He was educated at the University of Tokyo, studying under Kenzō Tange and Sachio Ōtani. After graduating in 1975, he worked for Arata Isozaki from 1978 to 1983 and then established his own office in Tokyo (1984). At first he was both a designer and an architectural critic, contributing to numerous national and international journals and publications. In his architecture Yatsuka aims at an acceleration of modernism that is not only sharply critical of the reactionary, classicist and other historicist tendencies in international Post-modernism but also challenges modernist ideology and dogma. His 'deconstructionist' designs, loose assemblies of individual parts, which are influenced by contemporary French philosophy, occupy a position between Structuralism and Post-structuralism; they show affinity with the works of Rem Koolhaas (*b* 1944), Bernard Tschumi and Zaha Hadid (*b* 1950). His few completed projects include the acclaimed Angelo Tarlazzi Building (1987) in Tokyo, a 'stage set' of fragmented elements with indirect references to many avant-garde works such as the roof form of Le Corbusier's Heidi Weber Pavilion (1966) in Zurich.

WRITINGS

'Architecture in the Urban Desert: A Critical Introduction to Japanese Architecture after Modernism', *Oppositions*, 23 (Winter 1981), pp. 2–35
'Post-modernism and Beyond', *Japan Architect*, 346 (1986), pp. 59–66

BIBLIOGRAPHY

B. Bognar: *The New Japanese Architecture* (New York, 1990)
——: *The Japan Guide* (New York, 1995)

BOTOND BOGNAR

Yavan [Garav-kala]. Site in the basin of the Yavan-su River, a tributary of the Vakhsh River, 40 km south-east of Dushanbe, Tajikistan. During the Kushana or post-Kushana period (3rd century AD to early 5th), the site (*c.* 40 ha) was surrounded by a wall and a moat (now only partially preserved) and had no fewer than three city gates. The fortified citadel (h. 8 m) is clearly visible as a double hill in the centre of the site (380×200 m). The site was excavated in 1963–5 under the direction of B. A. Litvinskiy and the material housed in the Tajikistan Academy of Sciences (Dushanbe, Tajikistan Acad. Sci., Donish Inst. Hist., Archaeol. & Ethnog.).

Stratigraphic investigations on the citadel to a depth of 10 m provided a benchmark for the chronology of the whole of south Tajikistan from the late 2nd–early 1st century BC to the 4th–mid-5th century AD. This period covered six consecutive phases of construction. The stratigraphic analysis made it necessary for scholars to rethink previously accepted dates for other sites, in particular those put forward in 1953 by M. M. D'yakonov for the archaeological material from northern Bactria. Utility objects of the 4th century or early 5th were found during excavations and in shafts all over the site. These finds comprised in particular a high-quality polished tableware with a dark red engobe that was characterized by a unity of style and a great variety of form. A burial ground of the 4th-century to mid-5th outside the site contained various types of burials, including tall jars for bones. There was a special area where the corpses were cleaned of soft tissue, but seemingly according to some sort of local variant of the Zoroastrian rite, since no special ossuaries were found. Rarer finds included the first Greek inscription found in Tajikistan (the name Sochrakis inscribed on a jar from a stratigraphic layer of the 1st century BC); a set of terracotta statuettes (from different stratigraphic layers); numerous

1. Yavan, fragment of a vessel showing a pottery stamp with a representation of the Kushano-Sasanian ruler Kushanshah, Hormizd, 35×40 mm, *c.* AD 370 (Dushanbe, Tajikistan Academy of Sciences, Donish Institute of History, Archaeology and Ethnography)

2. Yavan, stone toilet tray or palette depicting a hippokampos and rider, diam. 93 mm, *c.* 1st century BC–2nd century AD (Dushanbe, Tajikistan Academy of Sciences, Donish Institute of History, Archaeology and Ethnography)

images on ceramic stamped-ware vessels (including a very important dated example of *c.* AD 370 (see fig. 1) with the portrait of a Kushano-Sasanian ruler); an imported toilet tray or palette with the image of a rider on a hippokampos (see fig. 2); and jet amulets with images of hunting scenes.

BIBLIOGRAPHY

Ye. A. Yurkevich: 'Gorodischche kushanskogo vremeni na territorii severnoy Baktrii' [A site from the Kushana period on the territory of northern Bactria], *Sovetskaya arkheologiya* (1965), no. 4, pp. 158–67

Ye. V. Zeymal': 'Pozdnekushskiye sloi v yuzhnom Tadzhikistane' [Post-Kushana layers in south Tajikistan], *Tsentral'naya Aziya v kushanskuyu epokhu* [Central Asia in the Kushana period], *Proceedings of the International Conference of the History, Archaeology and Culture of Central Asia in the Kushan Period: Dushanbe, 1968*, ii, pp. 267–9

——: *Vakhshskaya dolina v drevnosti i rannem srednevekov'ye: Arkheologicheskiye pamyatniki i dinamika irrigatsionnykh sistem levoberezh'ya doliny* [The Vakhsh valley in antiquity and the early medieval period: archaeological monuments and the dynamic of the irrigation system of the left-bank valley] (Leningrad, 1969) [summary of doctoral thesis]

Drevnosti Tadzhikistana [Antiquities of Tajikistan] (exh. cat., ed. Ye. V. Zeymal'; Leningrad, Hermitage, 1985), pp. 136–42, nos 364–85

YE. V. ZEYMAL'

Yavlensky, Aleksey. *See* JAWLENSKY, ALEXEI.

Yaxchilán. Pre-Columbian site in the modern state of Chiapas, Mexico, which flourished as an important Lowland MAYA riverine centre *c.* AD 300–800. Yaxchilán is located near the tip of a great loop in the Usumacinta River, about 48 km upstream from Piedras Negras, another important Maya city. The site attracted visitors from the early 19th century, but it only became well known following the explorations of Alfred Maudslay, Désiré Charnay and Teobert Maler, who investigated the ruins at the turn of the 20th century. Since 1975 the Instituto Nacional de Antropología e Historia has cleared much of the site and excavated and consolidated some of its most important buildings, while its sculptured monuments have been recorded by the Peabody Museum of Harvard University. These studies have provided data on 88 structures and 125 carved stone monuments. Of the latter, 18 are in the Museo Nacional de Antropología in Mexico City and 8 are in the British Museum in London; the rest remain *in situ*.

Most of the city extends as a linear chain of plazas, courts and structures for nearly 1 km along the bank of the river. Several other groups of structures occupy ridges or hilltops behind this lower section; these are somewhat isolated from one another, but some effort was made to connect them to the main groups along the river. The scheme is 'organic' in that the buildings and groups are sited to take advantage of the features of the site, rather than following the more usual Maya practice of orientating buildings towards the cardinal points.

Most of the known buildings and monuments have been dated to the Late Classic period (AD *c.* 600–*c.* 900). Many of the Late Classic structures cover earlier buildings, most of which have not been excavated. The Late Classic architecture at Yaxchilán, as in Structures 6, 19, 20, 25, 30, 33, 39 and 40, features doorways with sculptured stone lintels, heavily decorated upper façades filled with stone and stucco sculptures, and high roof-combs (ornamented stone extensions above the temple roofs) pierced by holes and covered with sculptures. These features can be seen best in Structure 33 (see fig.), which typifies the monumental architecture at Yaxchilán. This building is set on a hill that rises 50 m behind the Main Plaza and consists of a single row of vaulted stone rooms with three doorways, each with a carved stone lintel commemorating the accession of the Maya ruler Bird Jaguar IV. The heavily decorated façade above the doorways includes the remnants of three seated figures, and the great double-walled roof-comb, which rises another 6 m above the roof, included a huge figure of a man, assumed to be Bird Jaguar, seated on a throne. An almost twice life-size statue,

Yaxchilán, Structure 33, Late Classic period, *c.* AD 600–*c.* 900

one of the few known three-dimensional Maya stone sculptures, presides on a bench behind the central doorway inside the building. A stairway in front of the building had 13 carved risers, each representing a scene of the Mesoamerican ball-game.

While Yaxchilán's architecture is impressive, it is better known for its carved stone stelae, lintels and altars. These carvings, among the finest examples of Classic Maya sculpture, include hieroglyphic texts that are now known to include references to the entire dynasty of the rulers of Yaxchilán: sixteen males and one female. Many of the texts date from the reigns of two particularly powerful kings, Shield Jaguar and his son, Bird Jaguar IV.

BIBLIOGRAPHY

D. Charnay: *Les Anciennes Villes du nouveau monde: Voyages d'explorations au Mexique et dans l'Amérique Centrale* (Paris, 1885)
A. P. Maudslay: *Biologia centrali-americana: Archaeology*, 5 vols (London, 1889–1902)
T. Maler: *Researches in the Central Portion of the Usumatcintla Valley*, Mem. Peabody Mus. Archaeol. & Ethnol., ii/2 (Cambridge, MA, 1903) [whole issue]
G. F. Andrews: *Maya Cities: Placemaking and Urbanization* (Norman, OK, 1975)
I. Graham and E. Von Euw: *Yaxchilán* (1977–82), III/i–iii of *Corpus of Maya Hieroglyphic Inscriptions* (Cambridge, MA, 1977–)

GEORGE F. ANDREWS

Yayoi period. Period in Japanese archaeological and cultural chronology, c. 300 BC–c. AD 300. The Japanese have traditionally traced the origins of their social structure, native religion and aesthetics to this period (see JAPAN, §I, 2). The term Yayoi also denotes a type of unglazed pottery, typically long-necked jars and pedestalled bowls, first unearthed in the late 19th century at a site of that name near Tokyo. Yayoi pottery, with its distinctively clean lines and proportional harmony (see JAPAN, §VIII, 2(i)(b)), differs markedly from the hand-wrought, flamboyantly contoured and imaginatively conceived shapes of vessels from the preceding JŌMON PERIOD (c. 10,000–c. 300 BC), and is evidence of new and superior technology. The Yayoi period is sometimes divided into Early (c. 300–c. 100 BC), Middle (c. 100 BC–c. AD 100) and Late (c. AD 100–c. 300). Much information on the Late Yayoi period comes from Chinese contemporary histories such as the *Wei zhi* ('Wei chronicle', late 3rd century).

Of supreme significance in the Yayoi period was the introduction of wet-rice agriculture. The labour-intensive and cyclical nature of the crop required a stable and mutually cooperative labour force. The primarily nomadic way of life of the Jōmon people gave way to communal village life based on tribes or clans headed by chieftains. Wealthy landholders ruled the common people; markets thrived, and there were systems for collecting taxes and punishing wrongdoers. The earliest archaeological sites of the Yayoi period are in northern Kyushu. Dwellings had earthen floors and thatched roofs and were built over shallow, oval pits and supported by posts (see JAPAN, §III, 2). Objects excavated from burial tombs scattered between northern Kyushu and Shikoku and Honshu provide ample evidence of the rapid expansion of rice-growing, domestication of animals, bronze-casting, ironmaking, the use of the potter's wheel and formal burial practices, including secondary burials. Yayoi people wore cloth from flax and paper-mulberry fibres.

Until the late 20th century it was accepted theory that the Yayoi culture was introduced by people migrating from the mainland by way of the Korean peninsula, who absorbed the primitive native people of the Jōmon period or forced them out of the way as they settled into the fertile plains of Kyushu and Honshu. Scholars now believe that the Jōmon people may have provided the cultural base into which superior technologies were introduced, absorbed and then transmitted. Yayoi tombs have also yielded objects of Chinese origin, including swords, spears, objects made of jasper, jade and glass such as beads (*magatama*), bronze mirrors and bronze bells (*dōtaku*). Such objects accompanied early Chinese travellers to Japan—which they termed the 'land of *wa*' ('dwarf country')—from the great court of the Han dynasty (206 BC–AD 220) and as such were prized as symbols of political authority. Their size and visual impressiveness increased as they assumed greater ritualistic importance. By the late 3rd century BC and the early 4th the decorative motifs on bronze mirrors and bells were being replaced by designs of purely Japanese conception. Granaries raised off the ground, of which remains are extant, suggest further foreign influence, perhaps from South-east Asia.

BIBLIOGRAPHY

N. Egami: *The Beginnings of Japanese Art* (Tokyo, 1973)
T. Higuchi: 'Relationships between Japan and Asia in Ancient Times: Introductory Comments', *Windows on the Japanese Past: Studies in Archaeology and Prehistory*, ed. R. J. Pearson, G. L. Barnes and K. L. Hutterer (Ann Arbor, 1986), pp. 335–47

BONNIE ABIKO

Yazd [Yezd]. City in central Iran on the western edge of the central desert. Dependent on a system of underground aqueducts (Pers. *qanāt*), Yazd was an agricultural centre that flourished in the Middle Ages as an entrepôt on the trade route between Central Asia and the Gulf. The city, which was originally called Katha, dates at least from Sasanian times (AD 226–645) when it was an important centre of Zoroastrianism. In the 7th century AD it was captured by Muslim forces. Although never a capital, it had a long and important tradition of architectural patronage in the Islamic period, which is extensively reported in local chronicles. In the 10th century it had a fortified citadel and houses built of unbaked brick. The tomb known as Duvazdah Imam ('Twelve imams'; 1037–8) is notable for its early use of the trilobed squinch, a device that became a hallmark of architecture in Iran in the 11th and 12th centuries (see ISLAMIC ART, §II, 5(i)(b)). A few remains of an imposing wall (12th–14th century) also exist, but the largest building surviving from the medieval period is the Friday (congregational) Mosque near the centre of the city. Most of the building dates from the 14th century and early 15th, although the ruins of an earlier mosque (early 12th century) lie to the north-east of the present court, and the west side of the court was significantly rebuilt in the late 18th century or 19th. The main entrance portal on the east (see fig.) is crowned with a pair of attenuated minarets. The mosque has a rectangular court (104×99 m); on the south side rectangular prayer-halls flank an iwan leading to a dome. The mosque is remarkable for the extensive use of transverse vaulting and the quality of its tile revetment, including a superb mihrab (1375). In

al-Din's son, Shams al-Din, built a similar funerary ensemble (the Shamsiyya; 1328) combining a madrasa, dispensary, library and hospice for descendants of the Prophet. Surviving parts, which include a narrow arcaded forecourt flanked by rectangular halls and a monumental iwan leading to the rectangular tomb chamber, show that transverse vaulting was already in use by the 1320s.

Yazd continued to grow in the 15th century. An ensemble that included a congregational mosque and domed tomb (1418 and later) was commissioned by Pir Husayn Damghani, a local notable, in a suburb to the south, and another ensemble with a congregational mosque (1437) was built by Mir Chaqmaq, Governor of Yazd for the Timurid ruler Shah Rukh, in a suburb to the south-east. These buildings are notable for the sense of lightness achieved by piercing the walls with galleries. Interiors typically have splendid tiled minbars and dados with whitewashed walls above. At this time many of the gardens surrounding the city were also refurbished with pools, elevated arcades and summer pavilions. In 1456, however, a great flood destroyed many buildings, and the city was never again as important. Notable structures from the later period include the minarets at the entrance to the bazaar (early 19th century). Domestic architecture in Yazd and the surrounding region is characterized by tall wind catchers (*see* WIND CATCHER), which bring cooling breezes deep into interiors. The Towers of Silence, on which the Zoroastrians expose the remains of their dead, continue to be a distinctive feature of the suburban landscape. High-quality silk textiles have been made in the Yazd region for centuries and are the mainstay of an extensive network of bazaars.

BIBLIOGRAPHY

M. Siroux: 'La Masjid-e-Djum'a de Yezd', *Bull. Inst. Fr. Archéol. Orient.*, xliv (1947), pp. 119–76
D. N. Wilber: *The Architecture of Islamic Iran: The Il Khanid Period* (Princeton, 1955)
I. Afshar: *Yādgārhā-yi Yazd* [Monuments of Yazd], 3 vols (Tehran, 1969)
R. Holod-Tretiak: *The Monuments of Yazd, 1300–1450: Architecture, Patronage and Setting* (diss., Cambridge, MA, Harvard U., 1972)
R. Holod: 'The Monument of Duvāzdah Imām in Yazd and its Inscription of Foundation', *Studies in Honor of George C. Miles*, ed. D. K. Kouymjian (Beirut, 1974), pp. 285–8
J. Aubin: 'Le Patronage culturel en Iran sous les Ilkhans: Une Grande Famille de Yazd', *Monde Iran. & Islam*, iii (1975), pp. 107–18
B. O'Kane: 'The Tiled Minbars of Iran', *An. Islam.*, xxii (1986), pp. 133–54
D. Wilber and L. Golombek: *The Timurid Architecture of Iran and Turan*, 2 vols (Princeton, 1988)

□

Yazd, Friday (congregational) Mosque, main entrance portal, late 14th century; restored

the 15th century this mosque became a model for others in the Yazd region (*see* ISLAMIC ART, §II, 6(i)(b)).

Some 12 other mosques, 100 madrasas and 200 tombs were erected as Yazd prospered in the 14th century. Many were built of mud-brick and have deteriorated (e.g. madrasa of Shah Kamal; 1320) or disappeared, but the finest, such as two funerary ensembles built for members of the Nizami family, which traced its descent from the Prophet, were built of baked brick. The one for Rukn al-Din (1324–5) was erected near the Friday Mosque and included a mosque, madrasa, library, hospice and observatory, known as the Vaqt-u sa'at ('[Institute of] time and the hour') and famed for its mechanical devices. The tomb, a square chamber surmounted by a tiled dome that is elaborately painted on the interior, is the only part to survive. Rukn

Yazılıkaya (i) [Turk.: 'inscribed rock face']. Great open-air sanctuary (*c.* 1500–1200 BC) of the Hittite capital city Hattusa (*see* BOĞAZKÖY), *c.* 1.5 km north-east of the ruins of the city in central Turkey. Yazılıkaya is a rocky outcrop forming two chambers (A and B) open to the sky. These were closed off by a gradually developing series of buildings that evolved from a simple wall to more elaborate structures designed to provide the natural sanctuary with the gatehouse and entrance courtyard of the typical Hittite temple. Excavation has revealed more than one remodelling.

The main chamber A was entered through the gatehouse and courtyard with a left turn, which would have disclosed the natural gallery, its rock walls sculptured with two files of figures (on the left male figures advancing right, on the right female figures advancing left). The processions converge in a central scene at the back of the gallery, where two sets of main figures, three on the left and four on the right, confront each other. The figures of both files have been numbered consecutively from the left: the left file has 42 figures, the right 21.

The sculptures have suffered considerably from erosion, and the figures' outlines and surface details are seldom well preserved. Many figures are accompanied by groups of hieroglyphs usually placed over their outstretched hands as if they were holding them. These served to identify the figures but in general they also are poorly preserved, to the extent that it is uncertain whether all the main figures were originally so identified or not. The first sign in almost all the Hieroglyphic groups is the oval representing 'god', leaving no doubt that all the figures were deities. It has been shown that the division of gods into male and female files, and the order in which the deities occur, mostly correspond to god-lists preserved on cuneiform tablets from the Boğazköy archives. More specifically it is recognized that such lists belong to the Hurrian rather than the Hittite pantheon, and at Yazılıkaya the legible phonetically written names appear in their Hurrian forms. In most cases the accoutrements of the deities are fairly uniform. The gods normally wear a pointed, horned helmet, symbol of divinity, a belted tunic with short skirt and boots with upturned toes. Most carry maces, scimitars or other weapons over their shoulders. The goddesses wear long-sleeved dresses with full-length pleated skirts, and high straight-sided headdresses, from which fall veils.

In the central group the main pair is securely identified as the storm-god (Hurrian Teshub) and his consort Hebat, standing respectively on the shoulders of a pair of divine mountain-men and on a panther. Hebat is supported by the young god Šarruma (the only male in the female procession) standing on a panther, and two goddesses, Allanzu and the 'granddaughter of the storm-god', standing on either head of a double-headed eagle. The file of goddesses continues from there uninterrupted, and the following names have been read: Tarru-Takitu, Hutena, Hutellura, Allatu, Naparpi, ?Salusa, Tapkina, Nikkal, Sausga and ?Warsui. In the male file the storm-god is supported by a god with a name of uncertain reading, perhaps his brother, and the grain-god (Hurrian Kumarbi). Then comes Ea, the winged goddess Sausga with her two handmaidens Ninatta and Kulitta (the only females on the male side), the winged moon-god, the sun-god wearing the same garb as the Hittite kings, who were identified with him, then Astabi and three disputed gods. The regular procession is then interrupted by two bull-men standing on the hieroglyph for 'earth' supporting above their heads the hieroglyph for 'sky', and thus identified as Atlas figures. Then, after the sword-god and Mount Pisasaphi, the remaining gods' names, even where partially preserved, are uncertain. The procession ends with a mountain god and twelve closely spaced running gods, who did not have any identifying epigraphs but may be recognized as the twelve gods named in cuneiform texts as the companions of 'bloody Nergal', an underworld god.

The peculiarity of finding a pantheon identified by Hurrian names in one of the Hittite empire's holiest shrines is explained by the dynasty's strong Hurrian affinities and the increasing Hurrian cultic influence evident later in the period. The Hurrian male and female god lists, doubtless compiled for the purpose of offerings, are only one indication of such influence. The Yazılıkaya files of gods may be recognized as these lists in monumental iconographic form; indeed offerings and libations would have been made on the stone-cut bench in front of them.

A short distance from the end of the female procession, but on another rock face, is a large well-preserved relief figure of a king identified as Tudhaliya IV, one of the last known kings (*reg c.* 1260–1230 BC). He is shown in the

Yazılıkaya (i), chamber B, relief depicting a dagger god on the east wall *c.* 1230 BC

same garb as the sun-god, wearing a close-fitting cap, long draped robe and shoes with upturned toes, and holding the long, backward-curling lituus. He stands on two mountains, and is presumably represented as dead and deified. This king is intimately connected with Yazılıkaya's other gallery, chamber B, entered through a narrow cleft, to the right of chamber A, which leads to the wider end of a long narrow gallery with a stone base placed against the end wall. The gallery stretches down to the right, and on the left long wall there are three carved panels: first, a small cartouche of Tudhaliya IV, second, the representation of a colossal dagger (see fig.) with its handle made up of clustered lions and a god's head, and blade stuck deep in the ground; and third, Tudhaliya in the protecting embrace of the god Šarruma (for illustration see HITTITE). On the right wall is a panel showing 12 running gods, presumably the same underworld deities as those noted in chamber A. There are also hollowed rectangular niches on either wall. The iconography and associations of the sculpture are unmistakably funerary. It has been suggested that chamber B is the mortuary chapel of Tudhaliya IV, built by his son Suppiluliuma II, the last known Hittite king, and described in a tablet as an 'eternal peak'. A colossal statue of Tudhaliya, inscribed with his deeds, would have stood on the focal base at the end of the chamber.

If chamber B was his mortuary chapel, Tudhaliya IV was also associated with chamber A by the appearance of his relief there, and it has been supposed that the execution of the divine processions was his work, though obviously the sanctity of the site was much more ancient. It has plausibly been suggested that chamber A was the main extramural sanctuary of the storm-god, to which processions were made during the elaborate celebrations of the New Year and other festivals.

BIBLIOGRAPHY
K. Bittel: *Hattusha: The Capital of the Hittites* (New York, 1970) [with bibliog.]
K. Bittel and others: *Das hethitische Felsheiligtum Yazılıkaya* (Berlin, 1975)
H. G. Güterbock: 'Yazılıkaya: A propos a New Interpretation', *J. Nr E. Stud.*, xxxiv (1975), pp. 273–7
I. Singer: 'The *huwaši* of the Storm-God in Hattuša', *IX Türk Tarih Kongresi: Ankara, 1981*, i, pp. 245–53
H. G. Güterbock: *Les Hiéroglyphes de Yazılıkaya: A propos d'un travail récent* (Paris, 1982) [Fr. and Eng. text]
O. R. Gurney and J. D. Hawkins: [review of E. Masson: *Le Panthéon de Yazılıkaya: Nouvelles lectures* (Paris, 1981)], *Bib. Orient.*, xxxix (1982), pp. 606–15
M. Poetto: [review of E. Masson: *Le Panthéon de Yazılıkaya: Nouvelles lectures* (Paris, 1981)], *Z. Assyriol.*, lxxii (1982), pp. 154–60

J. D. HAWKINS

Yazılıkaya (ii). See under PHRYGIAN.

Ybl, Miklós (*b* Székesfehérvár, 6 April 1814; *d* Budapest, 22 Jan 1891). Hungarian architect and designer. He studied architecture at the Technische Hochschule, Vienna, where he received his diploma in 1831. On his return to Hungary he became an apprentice to Mihály Pollack. From 1836 to 1840 Ybl worked for the Viennese master builder Heinrich Koch (1781–1861), first as a draughtsman, then as a works supervisor. In this capacity he supervised the construction of the Kinský funeral chapel (1836–40) at Budenice, near Prague. He then studied (1840–42) at the Akademie der Bildenden Künste, Munich, which was dominated by Leo von Klenze and Friedrich von Gärtner. In Munich he was also influenced by the elegant buildings in the rapidly developing Ludwigstrasse. After a seven-month tour in Italy, which was equally important for his development, Ybl returned to Hungary in 1843. Having unsuccessfully applied for admission to the Builders' Guild of Pest, he entered into partnership with Ágoston Pollack (1807–72), the son of his former master. Among other projects, they refurbished the Batthyány mansion, Ikervár. Their style, influenced by Schinkel, was predominantly Neo-classical, though they also employed Renaissance Revival elements.

Ybl's first major independent commission, from Count István Károlyi, was for a Catholic parish church, with an adjoining mausoleum, parsonage and school (1845–57) at Fót. The church, modelled on von Gärtner's Romantic Ludwigskirche (1829–44), Munich, has a basilica plan with three naves linked at the end in a semicircular apse. On the west façade a pair of symmetrical towers rise above the entrance. The building is equally rich in its interior and exterior decoration, combining stone carvings in Gothic and Romanesque styles with Moorish plant motifs, which harmonize with the orders of arches at the entrance, the semicircular windows and a corbel-table with blind arcade. In the 1850s Ybl built a number of houses in the Romantic style, notably the Unger house (1852), 7 Muzeum Boulevard, Budapest, and he remodelled the Balassa house (1862), 17 Bajcsy-Zsilinszky út, Budapest. After the 1860s he worked mainly in the Renaissance Revival style, receiving a growing number of commissions in Budapest for public buildings, mansions and residential blocks. The late Renaissance-inspired headquarters of the Buda Savings Bank (1860–62; destr.), and the First National Savings Bank (1868), both Budapest, are typical of his office buildings, as is the Customs and Excise Building (1870–74; now the University of Economics), Budapest, a symmetrically arranged two-storey brick building with a central projection on the façade and three interior courtyards. Its ornamental motifs for the balustrades and window- and doorframes derive from Florentine Renaissance models, while the 'Castle Bazaar' (1875–8), Castle Hill, Buda, a structure with symmetrical descents, stairs, pergolas and a central pavilion, is reminiscent of the garden architecture of the Villa Aldobrandini (c. 1603), Frascati. His most important Renaissance Revival work is the Opera House (1875–84), Budapest, which includes neo-Baroque motifs as well as showing the influence of Sansovino and Palladio in the façade. The elegant, rich decoration of the interior with marble surfaces, mosaics, murals, statuettes and draperies among others, is counterpointed externally by the elaboration of the central mass of the building, in particular by the outward projection of the staircase of honour from the adjoining grandiose hall.

Ybl's characteristic harmony between interior and exterior design, and unity of structural and decorative aspects, such as paintings, sculptures and other objects of applied art, ensured his reputation as a leading Renaissance Revival architect.

His works in other styles, however, include Count Károlyi's manor houses at Parád (1862–72; 1885–8) and at Parádsasvár (1880–82), both near Gyöngyös, which were inspired by the architect's visit to Great Britain in 1862; a characteristically eclectic palace (1862), Pest, built for Lajos Károlyi, with Baroque motifs and caryatids; and the three-nave parish church (1866–79), Bakáts Square, Budapest, which is exceptional in its use of the Romanesque Revival style. Ybl also worked on the reconstruction (from the 1860s) of the Royal Palace, Buda, and the erection of St Stephen's Basilica (1851–1906) in Pest, following the death of the original architect, József Hild, in 1867. Both were completed after Ybl's death.

BIBLIOGRAPHY

E. Ybl: *Miklós Ybl* (Budapest, 1956)

ÁKOS MORAVÁNSZKY,
KATALIN MORAVÁNSZKY-GYŐNGY

Yeames, William Frederick (*b* Taganrog, Russia, 18 Dec 1835; *d* Teignmouth, Devon, 3 May 1918). English painter. The son of a British consul in Russia, Yeames was sent to school in Dresden after the death of his father in 1842. He also studied painting there. The collapse of the Yeames family fortune resulted in a move to London in 1848, where Yeames learnt anatomy and composition from George Scharf (1788–1860). He later took lessons from F. A. Westmacott. In 1852 he continued his artistic education in Florence under Enrico Pollastrini and Raphael Buonajuto, from whom he learnt the methods of the Old Masters. He drew from frescoes by Ghirlandaio, Gozzoli and Andrea del Sarto and painted in the Life School at the Grand Ducal Academy. He then went to Rome and made landscape studies and copied Old Masters, including Raphael's frescoes in the Vatican. His extensive study of Italian art gave him a precision and facility that assisted his artistic success upon his return to London in 1859. There he set up a studio in Park Place and became involved with the ST JOHN'S WOOD CLIQUE. He exhibited at the Royal Academy and the British Institution from 1859 and became an ARA in 1866. At first Yeames attempted large-scale decorative work, contributing the figures of Torrigiano and Holbein to the series of mosaic portraits of artists at the South Kensington Museum (1866).

Yeames gained more notoriety through historical costume paintings with a strong domestic or anecdotal flavour, such as *Amy Robsart* (exh. RA 1877; London, Tate). His *And When Did You Last See Your Father?* (exh. RA 1878; Liverpool, Walker A.G.) epitomizes this type of painting: although set during the English Civil War, the work's theme is the potentially disastrous consequences of childish honesty. In later years, he experimented with the ambiguous 'problem picture': his *Defendant and Counsel* (exh. RA 1895; Bristol, Mus. & A.G.) was so obscure in its narrative implications that *Cassell's Magazine* offered a prize for the best explanation of it. Yeames was made an RA in 1878, but increasing blindness hindered his artistic production in later life. He was a member of the Royal Academy commission sent to Paris in 1900 to oversee British artistic interests at the Exposition Universelle. He was also librarian of the Royal Academy between 1896 and 1911 and curator of the Painted Hall at the Royal Naval College, Greenwich, where he supervised the restoration of Thornhill's ceiling decoration.

BIBLIOGRAPHY

Wood

T. Taylor: 'English Painters of the Present Day: W. F. Yeames', *Portfolio [London]*, ii (1871), pp. 81–4

M. H. S. Smith: *Art and Anecdotes: Recollections of William Frederick Yeames, RA* (London, 1927) [reminiscences by Yeames's nephew]

R. Strong: *And When Did You Last See Your Father?: The Victorian Painter and British History* (London, 1978), pp. 136–44

SHEARER WEST

Yeats. Irish family of artists and writers.

(1) John Butler Yeats (*b* Tullylish, Co. Down, 12 March 1839; *d* New York, 3 Feb 1922). Painter and draughtsman. He was the father of the poet W. B. Yeats and (2) Jack B. Yeats. In 1867, after studying law in Dublin, he moved to London, where he enrolled at Heatherley's Art School. He later worked under the supervision of Edward Poynter. For the first 20 years of his career Yeats produced illustrations and genre and landscape paintings: '*Pippa Passes*' (1869–72; Dublin, N.G.), a large gouache, is distinctly Pre-Raphaelite. In the late 1880s he began to realize his gifts as a portrait painter, although his production was hampered by a lifelong inability to finish commissions on time. Over a period of 50 years he produced fewer than 100 oil paintings, his greatest output being pencil drawings. The best of these are of his family and friends. He was an admirer of George Frederick Watts and saw a similarity between Watts's approach to portrait painting and his own. In an essay on Watts written in 1906, Yeats wrote: 'the best portraits will be painted where the relationship of the sitter and the painter is one of friendship'. An example of this is his drawing of *John M. Synge* (1905; Dublin, N.G.). The portraits of his family are intimate and reflective, while those of his literary associates convey character and conviction. Yeats's interest in the modern school originated in his admiration for the tonal naturalism of James Abbott McNeill Whistler, while his understanding of Impressionism was gained through the writings of R. A. M. Stevenson (1847–1900). The drawings and oils of the turn of the century are in many ways the artist's most satisfying works.

BIBLIOGRAPHY

John Butler Yeats and the Irish Renaissance (exh. cat., ed. J. White; Dublin, N.G., 1972)

W. M. Murphy: *Prodigal Father: The Life of John Butler Yeats (1839–1922)* (Ithaca, 1978)

The Drawings of John Butler Yeats (exh. cat. by F. Cullen, Albany, NY, Inst. Hist. & A., 1987)

FINTAN CULLEN

(2) Jack B(utler) Yeats (*b* London, 29 Aug 1871; *d* Dublin, 28 March 1957). Painter, writer and graphic artist, son of (1) John Butler Yeats. He was the younger brother of the poet W. B. Yeats. He spent much of his boyhood in Co. Sligo and maintained that the landscape and light of the county inspired him to become a painter. In London he sporadically attended various art schools, including the Westminster School of Art, and worked as a black-and-white illustrator, chiefly for magazines. His early paintings were in watercolour, and he was over 30 before he began to work regularly in oils. For years his style remained essentially conservative, with some influence from Honoré Daumier, but in the mid-1920s a profound change began to take place. Yeats's handling grew much freer, his forms were defined by brushstrokes rather than by line, his hitherto dour colours grew richer and more luminous and his earlier realism gradually gave way to a moody, intimate and highly personal romanticism. These tendencies grew even more marked over the next two decades, for example in *About to Write a Letter* (1935; Dublin, N.G.), until in Yeats's final years subject-matter is sometimes buried and almost obliterated by rich impasto, bravura brushwork and flame-like areas of colour, as in *Grief* (1951; Dublin, N.G.).

Some critics have dismissed Yeats as an essentially literary artist and illustrator, but his mature work is self-contained and shows a skilful handling of paint, in spite of the whimsical folksiness of his titles. These reflected his preferred subject-matter of rural and urban Irish life: the fairs, tinkers and horse-races, as well as a special interest in the circus, music-hall and street life of Dublin. Attempts have been made to link him with European Expressionism, particularly with Oskar Kokoschka, who is known to have admired him, but Yeats seems to have guarded his own independence carefully and to have shown little obvious interest in his contemporaries. He remained an isolated figure, a modernist outside modernist movements. A friend of many writers, including the playwright John Millington Synge (whose works he illustrated and who shared his interest in west of Ireland subject-matter), John Masefield and the young Samuel Beckett, he himself wrote fantastic novels (e.g. *The Charmed Life*, London, 1938) and plays, though these are little read today. He was also an illustrator of books and ballad sheets, both in black-and-white and in pen and ink with watercolour. Yeats was a prolific artist, producing well over a thousand paintings and many thousands of drawings. Though he was given a retrospective exhibition at the Tate Gallery in 1948 and was awarded the Légion d'honneur by France in 1950, his strongest following outside Ireland was in America. He participated in the Armory Show of 1913 in New York, held important exhibitions in the USA and sold some of his finest pictures to American collectors. His reputation declined in the years immediately after his death, but the centenary show at the National Gallery in Dublin marked the start of a new wave of interest.

BIBLIOGRAPHY
Jack B. Yeats (exh. cat. by T. MacGreevy, Dublin, Waddington Gal., 1945)
T. G. Rosenthal: *Jack Yeats* (London, 1966)
H. Pyle: *Jack B. Yeats: A Biography* (London, 1970)
R. McHugh, ed.: *Jack B. Yeats: A Centenary Gathering* (Dublin, 1971)
Jack B. Yeats, 1871–1957 (exh. cat., intro. J. White; Dublin, N.G., 1971)
Irish Art: 1900–1950 (exh. cat., Cork, Crawford Mun. School A., Gal., 1975)
H. Pyle: *Jack B. Yeats in the National Gallery of Ireland* (Dublin, 1986)
BRIAN FALLON

Yefimov, Boris (Yefimovich) (*b* Kiev, 28 Sept 1900). Russian graphic artist of Ukrainian birth. He received no formal artistic training, studying in the Legal Faculty of Kiev University (1917–18). He began his professional work as a caricaturist for the Kiev newspaper *Krasnaya Armiya* in 1919. In 1920–21 he produced agitational posters for YugROSTA (the southern department of the Russian Telegraph Agency; *see* AGITPROP) in Odessa and Kiev. He moved to Moscow in 1922 and began to work regularly for the newspapers *Pravda*, *Izvestiya* and *Krasnaya zvezda* and the magazines *Ogonyok*, *Krokodil* and others.

Yefimov was principally a specialist in international affairs but in the journal *Prozhektor* (1924–34), apart from his regular political designs, he published caricatures and illustrations on local social themes. In 1924 Yefimov's album *Politicheskiye karikatury* ('Political caricatures') was published in Moscow and from 1931 such albums appeared on a regular basis.

Yefimov's early caricatures reveal the influence of the style of the satirical magazine *Novyy satirikon*, with their predominance of dialogue over action, a lightness of the use of the pen and general decorative quality. Regular work for newspapers, demanding a specific political treatment of the subject, linear simplicity and expressiveness, influenced the development of his style. He learnt much from Viktor Deni (1893–1946), who produced newspaper illustrations. By the mid-1920s Yefimov's style was fully developed, with its realistic sense of volume and weight, simplicity and expressiveness in the contours of the design, tangibility of colour and abundance of detail. Throughout his life Yefimov was one of the most productive and popular Russian caricaturists.

WRITINGS
Sorok let: Zapiski khudozhnika-satirika [Forty years: the writings of a satirical artist] (Moscow, 1961)
Rovesnik veka: vospominaniya [Recollections of one who is the same age as the century] (Moscow, 1987)

BIBLIOGRAPHY
M. Ioffe: *B. Yefimov* (Moscow, 1952)
B. Ye. Yefimov (Moscow, 1976)
B. Ye. Yefimov (exh. cat., Moscow, Cent. House of Artists; Berlin, Haus Sow.-Dt. Freundschaft; 1982)
GALINA DEMOSFENOVA

Yefimov, Nikolay (Yefimovich) (*b* 5 May 1799; *d* Moscow, 23 Sept 1851). Russian architect. After graduating from the Academy of Arts in St Petersburg in 1821, he was awarded a Gold Medal and the right to a study trip abroad. In 1826 he undertook excavations in the church of the Tithe of the Most Holy Mother of God (Desyatinnaya) in Kiev and drew up a design for a new church but the commission was passed on to Vasily Stasov. Between 1827 and 1840 he visited Greece and Constantinople but spent most of his time abroad studying architectural monuments in Italy, above all Renaissance palaces. After his return he was elected Academician and worked on the restoration of the Winter Palace after the fire of 1837. His best known works are the Ministry of State Property (1844–50; with Nikolay Benois) and the house of the Minister of State Property (1847–53; with the sculptors David Jensen (1816–1902) and Aleksandr Terebenyov; finished by Lyudvig Bonshtedt). Each building, a mirror image of the other, is in Italian Renaissance style and is an important element in the ensemble of St Isaac's Square, their façades corresponding to the façades of Andrey Shtakenshneyder's Mariinsky Palace (1839–44) on the south side. The buildings are also a paraphrase of the ensemble of the Ministry of Internal Affairs and the Ministry of Education (1827–32) on Chernyshev (now Lomonosov) Square by Karl Rossi. Yefimov's grandiose ensemble of the New Convent of the Virgin (Voskresensky Novodevich'y monastyr') on Moscow Prospect, begun in 1848, was completed by N. Sychev. The architecture of the churches in the ensemble combined Byzantine motifs similar to those used in the work of Konstantin Ton, with elements of Russian 17th-century architecture. Bonshtedt completed Yefimov's reconstruction of the City Duma (1848–52) in Renaissance Revival style.

SERGEY KUZNETSOV

Ye Gongchuo [Yeh Kung-ch'uo; *zi* Yufu, Yuhu; *hao* Xiaan, Juyuan] (*b* Panyu, Guangdong Province, 1881; *d* 1968). Chinese calligrapher, painter, archaeologist, collector, poet and government official. He was born into a wealthy, scholarly family, received a classical education and as a youth of 16 founded a school in Guangzhou (Canton) and a publishing company in Shanghai; at 17 he enrolled in law school at the Imperial University in Beijing. His studies were interrupted two years later by the Boxer Rebellion of 1900, whereupon Ye moved to Wuchang, Hubei Province, and taught history, geography and modern languages for four years. In 1906 he began his official career as a specialist in railways and communications. After 1911, Ye held various positions in the Republican government and was instrumental in the establishment of Jiaotong University in Shanghai; he also served as director of classics for several years at Peking [Beijing] University. After the Sino-Japanese War (1937–45), he gave up his government career and devoted himself to the arts and research, although he continued to serve on educational and cultural committees for the rest of his life. In particular, he became involved in the committee to organize the simplification of Chinese characters. In 1956 a definitive set of simplified characters was published, and thereafter used in mainland China.

Ye's style of calligraphy was informed by his study of ZHAO MENGFU and the stelae of the Wei period (AD 220–65) (*see* CHINA, §IV, 2(vii)). His regular script (*kaishu*) became a popular model for beginners, classically beautiful, balanced and harmonious in all its parts. It displays the five points Ye felt were most important in calligraphy: brush movement, composition, power, vital energy (*qi*) and harmony. His large running script (*da xingshu*) was written with brusque strength and a certain rough quickness; he was little concerned with detail. His small running script (*xiao xingshu*), like his regular script, shows more variety in the contrast of lines and size of words, and the overall impression, as in the preface to the *Xiaan qingmi lu* ('Record of Ye Gongchuo's collection of painting and calligraphy'), is thick and angular. In painting, Ye's favourite subject was bamboo, but he also painted orchid, plum and pine (*see also* CHINA, §V, 3(v) and (vi)). He would typically paint bamboo growing from behind a rock, as in *Xiaan Xiansheng shuhua ji* ('Collection of painting and calligraphy by Ye Gongchuo'; 1949), where the rough and heavily dotted surface of the convoluted stone provides a successful complement to the smooth, elongated patterns of the leaves and branches. His touch was consummately elegant.

BIBLIOGRAPHY
H. L. Boorman, ed.: *Dictionary of Republican China* (New York, 1971), pp. 31–3, 403–4
Ye Xiaan xiansheng shuhua xuanji [Selections of Ye Gonghuo's calligraphy and painting] (Taipei, 1975)
Yu Jianhua, ed.: *Zhongguo huajia da zidian* [Dictionary of Chinese painters] (Shanghai, 1981), p. 1218
Zhongguo shufa da zidian [Dictionary of Chinese calligraphy], i (Hong Kong, 1984), p. 989

ELIZABETH F. BENNETT

Yegotov, Ivan (Vasil'yevich) (*b* 1756; *d* Moscow, 1814). Russian architect. He initially studied sculpture and then, from 1773, he worked with Vasily Bazhenov's architectural team on Bazhenov's great though unexecuted scheme for the Kremlin Palace. He subsequently studied under Matvey Kazakov (1775–8), becoming Kazakov's main assistant, and from 1804 he was head of the Kremlin Drawing Office. He designed the Military Hospital (1798–1802) in Moscow, a somewhat unusual combination of motifs drawn both from early Neo-classicism and the nascent Empire style. The main façade features a wealth of disparate elements. Two long rows of identical apartments provided the functionally clear structure of the interior; in the centre are a vestibule, the grand staircase and the main hall (*see* MOSCOW, §IV, 1). The combination of a rational plan and artistically handled interiors also characterized his Armoury Palace (Druzheynaya Palata; 1806–12; destr.) in the Kremlin. Yegotov's experience in restoration work on the walls and towers of the Kremlin (*see* MOSCOW, §I, 1) led him to devise a historicist style that combined Gothic Revival details with features from ancient Russian architecture. He employed this mode in remodelling (before 1804) the Patriarch's Palace as the 'Commandant's House' in the Kremlin and for the service buildings (1780–90s) at the Goncharov family's country house, Yaropolets, near Moscow. The house itself remains Neo-classical, as does Lyublino (1801), the Durasov palace, originally to the south-east of Moscow and now within the municipal boundaries.

BIBLIOGRAPHY
A. P. Sedov: *Yegotov* (Moscow, 1956)

N. A. YEVSINA

Yegüih. *See under* LAMBITYECO.

Yeh Hsia-an. *See* YE GONGCHUO.

Yeh Kung-ch'uo. *See* YE GONGCHUO.

Yehūdīyah, Tell el-. *See* YAHUDIYA, TELL EL-.

Yekaterinburg [formerly Sverdlovsk]. Russian town and regional centre in the Urals, 1670 km east of Moscow. Between 1924 and 1991 it was known as Sverdlovsk. The town, named in honour of Empress Catherine I (*reg* 1725–7), was founded in 1721 on the Iset' River by the statesman and historian Vasily Tatishchev (1686–1750), together with the large Isetsky Metallurgical Factory, and was intended as an industrial, cultural and trading centre. Since the mid-18th century, Yekaterinburg has been renowned for the manufacture of stoneware, lamps and boxes made from jasper, malachite, rhodonite and porphyry, as well as for icons and carved iconostases by local artists. The Iset', which runs north–south through the town, now forms a series of interconnecting reservoirs, of which the largest is the Upper Iset' reservoir. Water from the river was formerly diverted to power the factory's engines. The regular street network, typical of an 18th-century fortified Ural factory-town, was reinforced in new general plans for the town proposed in 1804, 1829 and 1845. Numerous

18th- and 19th-century Neo-classical buildings, many by the architect Mikhail Malakhov, make up the historic part of the town. These include the Mining Office (1737–9; rebuilt by Malakhov, 1833–5), the Rastorguyev-Kharitonov Estate (1794–1824), the Malakhov House (1817–20), the Office and Hospital of the Upper Iset' Factory (1817–26) and the Aleksandr Nevsky Cathedral (first half of the 19th century). Large buildings and architectural complexes in the Constructivist style dominate the city's 20th-century architecture: the so-called House of Offices (Dom Kontor; 1930, by V. I. Smirnov), the Chekist Town Residential Complex (1931, by I. P. Antonov and V. D. Sokolov) and living-quarters for employees of the Uralmash Factory (1929–40, by P. V. Oransky and M. I. Reysher). The picture gallery (founded 1936) holds the largest collection of 'Kaslian' cast-iron sculpture, which was made in the 19th century at Kasli, c. 90 km south of Yekaterinburg.

BIBLIOGRAPHY
Sverdlovsk: Putevoditel'-spravochnik [Sverdlovsk: a guidebook] (Sverdlovsk, 1973/R 1975)
L. Kozinets: Kamennaya letopis' goroda: Arkhitektura Yekaterinburga-Sverdlovska XVIII–nachala XX veka [A chronicle in stone: the architecture of Yekaterinburg-Sverdlovsk from the 18th century to the early 20th] (Sverdlovsk, 1989)

M. I. ANDREYEV

Yela Günther, Rafael (b Guatemala City, 18 Sept 1888; d Guatemala City, 17 April 1942). Guatemalan sculptor. He was first trained by his father, Baldomero Yela Montenegro (1859–1909), who was a sculptor and marble carver. While still very young he worked with the Venezuelan sculptor Santiago González, a former student of Auguste Rodin, then resident in Guatemala, and with the Italian Antonio Doninelli, who ran a bronze foundry workshop. He was also extremely friendly with the Guatemalan painters Carlos Mérida and Carlos Valenti (1884–1912) and with the Spanish Catalan painter and sculptor Jaime Sabartés (1881–1968), who later became Picasso's secretary. His first important sculptures, both in Guatemala City, were monuments to J. F. Barrundia (1905–6) in the General Cemetery and to Isabel La Católica (1915).

Around 1921 Yela Günther went to Mexico, where he came into contact with the anthropologist Manuel Gamio, who directed his attention towards Maya and Aztec art. He also had the encouragement of Diego Rivera, who wrote enthusiastically of his work in El Demócrata (2 March 1924). One of his most important works of this period, a relief made in 1922 entitled Triptych of the Race, was demolished in the 1960s. After living in the USA from 1926 to 1930 he returned to Guatemala, settling there permanently, and produced his largest works, combining elements of sculpture and architecture. These include works in Guatemala City, notably a monument to the Leaders of the Independence (1934–5) and the mausoleum of the aviator Jacinto Rodríguez D. (1932), and in Quezaltenango a monument to the national hero Tecún Umán (a re-creation of a large Maya stele) and a monument to President Justo Rufino Barrios (1941) in the main square. His outstanding sculptures on a smaller scale include the Supreme Sadness of the Defeated Race (bronze), a bust carved in wood of the jurist Salvador Falla, and Christ from a plaster of 1936 cast in bronze in 1947 (all Guatemala City, Mus. N. B.A.). Stylistically his works combine elements

revealing the influence of Rodin and of Art Deco. He was Director of the Escuela Nacional de Bellas Artes for several years until his death.

BIBLIOGRAPHY
C. C. Haeussler Y.: Diccionario general de Guatemala (Guatemala City, 1983), iii, pp. 1660–67
L. Luján Muñoz: Carlos Mérida, Rafael Yela Günther, Carlos Valenti, Sabartés y la plástica contemporánea de Guatemala (Guatemala City, 1983)

JORGE LUJÁN MUÑOZ

Yelizarov, Viktor (Dmitriyevich) (b Pashkovo, now Tula Region, 7 Aug 1911). Ukrainian architect of Russian birth. He completed his studies at the Moscow Architectural Institute in 1937 and thereafter worked in Kiev. Under the direction of Aleksandr Vlasov he worked from 1947 to 1949 with Anatoly Dobrovol'sky, A. I. Zavarov (b 1917) and Boris Priymak (b 1909) on the design and reconstruction of the principal street in Kiev, the Kreshchatik (1947–9), which had been destroyed during World War II. The design gave the street an open structure, which provided views of picturesque hills. In 1952–7, with M. K. Shilo, he built the administrative building at Kreshchatik 29; the rhythm of its pilasters strikingly reveals the slight curve of the façade. Yelizarov was one of the first in Kiev to experiment with constructions built from large prefabricated elements, for example at Chernoarmeyskaya Street 16 (1951), and the Promstroyproyekt Design Institute (1954–5; with others), which is built from panels hung on frames. In his reconstruction with N. B. Chmutina (b 1912) of the Hotel Dnepr (1959–64) on the Kreshchatik, he reduced the former symmetrical composition reminiscent of classical design to a concise system of repeated modular elements. He also participated in the design of the Hotel Kiev (1973; with others), which is square in plan, has 18 storeys and is set on a hill above the Dnepr River; its façades are composed of cellular loggias. Yelizarov also created a number of memorial compositions, such as the monument to Lenin (1946; Boulevard Taras Shevchenko), with Vlasov and the sculptor Sergey Merkurov. The vast memorial complex of the Ukrainian State Museum of the War of 1941–5 (1981), built with the sculptor Vasily Boroday (b 1917), is set in a landscaped park and is dominated by the museum building, which is surmounted by a symbolic personification of the Motherland, executed in stainless steel.

BIBLIOGRAPHY
N. P. Bylinkin and A. V. Ryabushin, eds: Istoriya sovetskoy arkhitektury, 1917–1954 [History of Soviet architecture, 1917–1954] (Moscow, 1985), p. 182
A. V. Ryabushin: Gumanizm sovetskoy arkhitektury [Humanism in Soviet architecture] (Moscow, 1986), p. 234

A. V. IKONNIKOV

Yemen, Republic of [Arab. Al-Jumhūriyya al-Yamaniyya; formerly Yemen Arab Republic (North Yemen; Yemen) and People's Democratic Republic of Yemen (South Yemen)]. Independent republic in south-western Arabia, including Socotra and other islands, with San'a as the political capital and an estimated area of c. 636,000 sq. km. Yemen's location at the crossroads between Arabia, the Indian Ocean and Africa, and particularly on the Red Sea route, has had an impact on its cultural heritage and turbulent political history. Along the Red Sea and Gulf of

Aden stretch arid plains rising to mountains and cultivated highlands, which descend in the east to desert and the distinct region of Hadramawt. The Arab population (*c.* 11,000,000; 1990 estimate), some of African origin, is mostly Sunni and Shi'a Muslim, with small communities of Jews and Christians. The traditional tribal structure is strong, particularly in the north.

In the lst millennium BC until the first centuries AD South Arabia was the home of highly cultured city states, which owed their prosperity partly to the trade in frankincense and myrrh, native to the region. To the Greco-Roman world the land was known as 'Fortunate Arabia' (Gr. *Arabia Eudaemon*; Lat. *Arabia Felix*). When Islam arrived in Yemen *c.* AD 628, it was a province of the Sasanian empire. The RASULID dynasty (1229–1454) for a time ruled an area from Mecca in modern Saudi Arabia to Hadramawt (*see also* SULAYHID and AYYUBID). Partial occupation by the Ottomans in the 16th century was ended by the tribes led by the Zaydi Imam in 1636. The Imamate then ruled the whole of Yemen until the early 18th century, during the height of the coffee trade from the port at Mocha (*see* ZAYDI). The Ottomans returned to North Yemen from 1849 onwards, leaving in 1918. A time of isolation, poverty and war culminated in the Revolution of 1962, when the rule of the Zaydi Imams was brought to an end and the Yemen Arab Republic was founded.

In the south a revolt against the Imam in the early 18th century enabled the British to occupy Aden in 1839, with the aim of controlling the Red Sea route. Gradually they expanded their rule over the hinterland. In 1967 they ceded power to the nationalists and South Yemen became independent as a Communist State, later named the People's Democratic Republic of Yemen. After a period of armed conflict the two Yemens were united in 1990. At this time Yemen was one of the least developed countries in the world with a high illiteracy rate. Foreign aid and earnings made by Yemenis abroad were the main sources of revenue in the 1970s and 1980s. However, oil was found in the mid-1980s and there are also gas reserves. This article largely covers the art of the 19th and 20th centuries. For the earlier history of Yemen *see* ARABIA, PRE-ISLAMIC and ISLAMIC ART.

The most important art of Yemen is its religious and secular architecture (*see* ISLAMIC ART, §II, 5(ii)(d), 6(iii)(b) and 7(i)(c) and VERNACULAR ARCHITECTURE, §II, 7(vi)). Civil war, uprisings and earthquakes in the 20th century caused some destruction; modern buildings after the 1960s revolutions were made of concrete and cement blocks, particularly in the towns (e.g. Aden, al-Hudaydah, San'a, Ta'izz), and there are some high-rise buildings in Western styles. Much of the architecture, however, has not changed in style for hundreds of years and some old building techniques survive. The urgent need for restoration work is recognized and some has been undertaken. The State together with UNESCO launched a campaign in 1984 to preserve the old city of San'a; a similar campaign was introduced for the town of Shibam in Wadi Hadramawt. The styles and decoration of traditional houses vary between regions, but all use locally available material and are adapted to the climate.

The most distinctive buildings are tower houses, of between four and nine storeys, intended for one family. Built of mud-brick or stone or a combination, depending on the region, they typically contain small rooms, thick outer walls and at the top a large reception room (*mafraj*). The tower houses in the old city in SAN'A are of natural stone for the ground floor, with fired brick for the upper storeys. Walls are decorated with bands of geometric patterns formed by protruding bricks, which may be whitewashed annually. The bands surround the windows or mark the different storeys. Arched or semicircular fanlights contain coloured glass in geometric or floral patterns (*see also* ISLAMIC ART, §II, 9(v)). The former summer palace of Imam Yahya (*reg* 1904–48) at Wadi Dahr, 15 km north-west of San'a, was built in the 1930s. The multi-storey Dar al-Hajar consists of a group of palaces built on top of a rock. It has gypsum decoration in San'a style and ornate fanlights.

In Sa'da and neighbouring villages are remarkable mud houses (see fig.). The walls are made of a mixture of mud and straw, with each layer set a little inside the previous one, which gives a tapering shape. Spaces for windows are decided on as the building grows. A strip of gypsum at roof level is often elongated into points at the corners. Rada', 120 km south-east of San'a, has pale mud-brick tower houses with stone lower floors. As in Sa'da, some have alabaster window-panes, but coloured glass has generally replaced the old alabaster. The mud surfacing has to be replaced each year. The mud-brick tower houses

Mud house, Sa'da, Yemen

in Hadramawt have walls plastered with brown earth, with light lime for the upper storeys. A whiter plaster is used for decoration and the parapets on roof terraces are often whitewashed. Shibam contains over 500 tower houses, four to eight storeys high, in a compact area. Most date from the 17th century but many were rebuilt in the 19th and some have carved wooden doors with wooden locks.

On the Tihama plain along the Red Sea, however, traditional housing is low, typically either huts of reeds, sticks and palm-woods (in the north, e.g. al-Zuhra), or rubble and brick courtyard houses (in the south, e.g. Zabid, Hays). Those in ZABID are of one or two storeys and present a plain façade to the street; the wealth and taste of the family are displayed in the decoration on internal walls. Zabid also has some Ottoman architecture. A different tradition is found in Tarim in Wadi Hadramawt, where Hadrami traders who had worked in Indonesia in the 19th century followed South-east Asian styles for their houses.

The modern art movement began in Yemen in the mid-1970s. The first generation of artists had no formal training, but the Republic began to support students at art colleges abroad and exercised some patronage, believing that the arts had an important role in the new State. In the 1980s these students returned and the number of professional artists increased. Faud al-Futaih (b 1948), a painter and sculptor trained in Germany, opened the first art gallery in Yemen in 1986; Gallery Number One is in San'a and it shows works by both Yemeni and foreign artists. In 1987 the Yemeni Artists' Society was established to assist artists and arrange exhibitions of their work. Many artists depict local customs and landscapes in a realistic style.

Economic and social changes after the revolutions, including competition from imported products, caused some crafts to die out (e.g. indigo-dyeing) or decline (e.g. pottery, hand-weaving, embroidery); hand-weaving using traditional methods is rare outside Bayt al-Faqih. Many of the Yemeni Jews who emigrated to Israel in the early 1950s were craftsmen, working particularly in silver. Some silversmiths remain, however, in San'a and Sa'da. One important traditional skill is related to Yemen's distinct architectural heritage: the use of lime and gypsum to paint and decorate houses and mosques. Imported synthetic materials caused this skill to begin to die out, except in the making of stained-glass fanlights. The traditional curved dagger, jambiya, worn by Yemeni men, continues to be made (e.g. in San'a). The hilt is usually of cattle horn or, now more rarely, of rhinoceros horn; the sheaths made for the upper classes are worked in silver. A new craft that developed, due to the shortage of hardwood, was the making of metal doors ornamented with patterns and calligraphy (e.g. on the outskirts of San'a). Cultural centres that include vocational training in arts and crafts were established in North Yemen, the first being in San'a in 1975. The government also set up craft associations in 1979 to try to revive the craft industries.

Yemen was for long a difficult country to explore. CARSTEN NIEBUHR was the sole survivor of a Danish expedition in the mid-18th century. The German ethnographer Ulrich Seetzen was killed in Ta'izz in 1811, suspected of being a magician or spy. The Frenchmen Thomas Arnaud (1843–4) and Joseph Halévy (1869) and the

Austrian Eduard Glaser (1882–4) were more successful, exploring Ma'rib in particular and recording many ancient South Arabian inscriptions. The difficulties of getting to various parts of Yemen meant sporadic archaeological activity in much of the 20th century. An American team worked at Ma'rib and Timna' in the early 1950s but had to leave hurriedly. Ancient temple stones were often incorporated in new buildings; other artefacts were looted; some destruction occurred because of modern development. In 1966 the Yemen Arab Republic set up an Antiquities Department, which became the Antiquities and Libraries Board in 1973. With the help of European and American specialists it surveys and attempts to protect archaeological sites and ancient monuments, oversees excavations and develops museums.

The National Museum in San'a opened in 1971 and moved in 1987 to the Dar al-Sa'ada, a palace built in the 1930s. The museum displays archaeological finds, Islamic objects, examples of traditional culture and dress and holds foreign exhibitions. In Ta'izz the former palace of Imam Ahmad (reg 1948–62) is a museum. Built of fired mud-brick, the palace has been left as it was in 1962. The Salah Palace Museum, also in Ta'izz, contains silver jewellery, coins, costumes and Koranic manuscripts. In Aden the small Ethnographical Museum contains textiles and silverwork; the National Museum has many archaeological finds. The multi-storey Sultan's Palace in Say'un houses archaeological finds and crafts. In Tarim the al-Afqa Library (founded 1972) contains thousands of Islamic manuscripts. There are also small regional museums.

BIBLIOGRAPHY
City of Ṣanʿāʾ (exh. cat., ed. J. Kirkman; London, BM, 1976)
P. Costa and E. Vicario: Yemen: Paese di costruttori (Milan, 1977); Eng. trans. as Arabia Felix: A Land of Builders (New York, 1977)
J.-M. Bel: Le Yémen du Nord et l'architecture de la région montagneuse (Paris, 1979)
A.-R. al-Haddad: Cultural Policy in the Yemen Arab Republic (Paris, 1982)
F. Varanda: Art of Building in Yemen (Cambridge, MA, and London, 1982)
M. Hirschi and S. Hirschi: L'Architecture au Yémen du Nord (Paris, 1983)
L. Golvin and M.-C. Fromont: Thulâ: Architecture et urbanisme d'une cité de haute montagne en République Arabe du Yémen (Paris, 1984)
A. Bahnassi: Ruwwād al-fann al-ḥadīth fiʾl-bilād al-ʿarabiyya [Pioneers of modern art in the Arab countries] (Beirut, 1985)
R. B. Lewcock: 'The Conservation of the Urban Architectural Heritage of Yemen', Economy, Society & Culture in Contemporary Yemen, ed. B. R. Pridham (London, Sydney and Dover, NH, 1985), pp. 215–25
——: The Old Walled City of San'a' (Paris, 1986)
——: Wadi Ḥaḍramawt and the Walled City of Shibām (Paris, 1986)
G. Bonnenfant and P. Bonnenfant: L'Art de bois à Sanāa: Architecture domestique (Aix-en-Provence, 1987)
W. Daum, ed.: Yemen: 3000 Years of Art and Civilization in Arabia Felix (Innsbruck, 1987)
J.-M. Bel: Architecture et peuple du Yémen (Paris, 1988)
W. Ali, ed.: Contemporary Art from the Islamic World (London, 1989), pp. 287–8
S. S. Damluji: A Yemen Reality: Architecture Sculptured in Mud and Stone (Reading, 1991)
——: The Valley of Mud Brick Architecture: Shibām, Tarīm and Wādī Ḥaḍramūt (Reading, 1992)   □

Yen Chen-ch'ing. See YAN ZHENQING.

Yen-ch'eng. See under WUJIN.

Yen-hsia-tu. See YANXIADU.

Yen Hui. See YAN HUI.

Yeniseysk. Russian town in Siberia on the central course of the Yenisei River, *c.* 3400 km east of Moscow. It was founded in 1619 by Siberian Cossacks as a military fortress on the hilly left bank of the river. Until the early 19th century the town was the administrative and trading centre of an area (*kray*) and a centre for bone-carving, icon-painting and silverware. Despite the town's size, only wooden houses and churches were built until the beginning of the 18th century; brick was introduced only after devastating fires in 1702 and 1730. Churches dominate the panorama from the river. The cathedral of the Epiphany (1730–50s) in the town centre has a tall, pillar-shaped bell-tower and lavishly decorated side chapel in the Siberian Baroque style. East of this lies the church of the Resurrection (1730s–40s), decorated with ribbon brickwork. The church of the Dormition (late 18th century–early 19th), situated on a hill in the west of the town, has an elegant Baroque façade. The cathedral of the Saviour (1750s) stands within the monastery of the Transfiguration (founded 17th century), which is one of the oldest in Siberia. Its windows are framed by ceramic tiles in the form of rosettes, spirals and volutes. The gates (1780s) of the monastery have Baroque decoration. Some distance from the river lies the church of the Trinity (1770s–80s), which is decorated with finely traced brickwork. From 1778 Yeniseysk was laid out on a regular plan, mostly with two-storey brick houses in Baroque, Neo-classical and, in the early 20th century, modern styles. Many surviving 19th-century wooden houses are decorated with carved flower garlands and fern leaves. The city museum (opened 1883) contains an ethnographic collection and the works of Yenisei craftsmen.

BIBLIOGRAPHY
I. Arkhangel'sky: *Gorod Yeniseysk* [The town of Yeniseysk] (Yeniseysk, 1923)
A. I. Malyutina: *Gorod Yeniseysk* [The town of Yeniseysk] (Krasnoyarsk, 1957)
Ye. D. Dobrovol'skaya and B. V. Gnedovsky: *Vverkh po Yeniseyu* [Up along the Yenisei] (Moscow, 1980)

M. I. ANDREYEV

Yen Li-pen. *See* YAN LIBEN.

Yen Sung. *See* YAN SONG.

Yen Tz'u-p'ing. *See* YAN CIPING.

Yen Wen-kuei. *See* YAN WENGUI.

Yeo, Richard (*d* London, 3 Dec 1779). English medallist. He may have been responsible for engraving some admission tickets for the entertainments at Vauxhall Gardens, London, in the 1730s. His first known medals, and his best, are those commemorating the Battle of Culloden of 1746. Both the official medal (gold and bronze; see Hawkins, Franks and Grueber, ii, no. 283) and the larger medal portraying *William Augustus, Duke of Cumberland, as Hercules* (gold, silver and bronze; HFG, ii, 278) demonstrate Yeo's mastery as an engraver, while the imaginative allegorical reverses combine effectively with decorative Rococo flourishes. In 1749 he was appointed Assistant Engraver to the Royal Mint, London, and in 1775 he was promoted to the position of Chief Engraver, a post he retained until his death. In the 1760s and 1770s he made the dies for a number of coins of George III. His relatively small number of known medals includes the exquisite Cambridge University Chancellor's medal of 1752 (bronze; HFG, ii, 377), and among his cameo engravings is a portrait of the *Duke of Cumberland*. He was a founder-member of the Royal Academy and contributed to its exhibitions.

BIBLIOGRAPHY
DNB; Forrer; Thieme–Becker
E. Hawkins, A. W. Franks and H. A. Grueber: *Medallic Illustrations of the History of Great Britain and Ireland*, 2 vols (London, 1885) [HFG]
C. E. Challis, ed.: *A New History of the Royal Mint* (Cambridge, 1992)

PHILIP ATTWOOD

Yepes, Tomás. *See* HIEPES, TOMÁS.

Yereruyk' [Ererouk; Ereruk; Ereruyk]. Ruins of an Early Christian basilica dating from the 5th century AD to the early 6th, near the village of Ani-Pemza, Armenia, southeast of the border with Turkey and *c.* 10 km south of Ani. An Armenian inscription (probably 7th century) on the north wall of the apse identifies the church as the martyrium of the Forerunner (Karapet). A Greek inscription (6th–7th centuries) and several others in Armenian (*c.* 6th–10th centuries; 1038; and 1201–12) refer to restoration works.

The church was excavated by N. Marr in 1908; by then the vaulted roof was missing, and only the outer walls survived. Restoration work was undertaken in 1928, followed by renewed excavations in 1987. Some features resemble those of 5th-century Armenian churches, but other architectural details, such as the twin-towered west façade, gabled portals, porticos and some sculptural decorations, are similar to contemporary Syrian churches (e.g. Turmanin and Ruwayha) and indicate an early 6th-century date. Accordingly it has been suggested that the original 5th-century structure may have had additions and changes during the 6th century.

The church is a basilica constructed of tufa facing a rubble core and resting on a seven-stepped podium. A vaulted narthex was probably added to its west façade. The church has two portals on the south façade and one on the west. Its north and south porticos each terminate in a semicircular apse at the eastern end. Three pairs of pillars and three pairs of cruciform pilasters on the north and south walls originally divided the interior of the church into three aisles and four bays. There are two further pairs of pilasters on the east and west walls. The main eastern apse is flanked on each side by a two-storey rectangular chamber. The height of the three windows on the west façade indicates that the central vessel was much higher than the aisles and may have had a clerestory.

Geometric and floral motifs carved on the pediments, arches, capitals and lintels of the portals, and the semicircular window-frames with horizontal bases are similar to those on Syrian churches. The lintels also have crosses inscribed in medallions flanked either by palm trees or animals. There are traces of wall paintings on the interior walls.

BIBLIOGRAPHY
N. Marr: *Yereruiskaya bazilika* [The basilica of Yereruyk'] (Erevan, 1910, rev. 1968)

A. Khatchatrian: *L'Architecture arménienne du IVe au VIe siècle* (Paris, 1971), pp. 45–8

P. Paboudjian and A. Alpago-Novello: *Ererouk* (Milan, 1977)

L. Der Manuelian: *Armenian Architecture*, i, ed. K. Maksoudian (Zug, 1981)

F. Gandolfo: *Le basiliche armene: IV–VII secolo* (Rome, 1982), pp. 67–76

J.-M. Thierry and P. Donabedian: *Les Arts arméniens* (Paris, 1987; Eng. trans. New York, 1989)

P. Cuneo: *Architettura armena dal quarto al diciannovesimo secolo*, i (Rome, 1988–), pp. 234–6

LUCY DER MANUELIAN, ARMEN ZARIAN

Yerevan. *See* EREVAN.

Yeriho. *See* JERICO.

Yer Kurgan. *See* YAR KURGAN.

Yermenyov, Ivan (Alekseyevich) (*b* St Petersburg, 1746–9; *d* ?St Petersburg, after 1792). Russian painter and graphic artist. He studied at the St Petersburg Academy of Arts from 1761 to 1767. He won a minor award for his painting on a theme from medieval Russian history. His aptitude as a product of the Academic system is suggested by two pen-and-wash allegories: *Allegory on the Marriage of the Great Prince Pavel Petrovich and the Great Princess Natal'ya Alekseyevna* (1773; Pavlovsk, Pal. Mus.) and *Allegory on the Beneficence of Russia* (1774; St Petersburg, Rus. Mus.).

Yermenyov was one of the founders of Russian genre painting: in the early 1770s he produced a series of watercolours showing blind beggars and peasants (eight of these in St Petersburg, Rus. Mus.). Yermenyov's scenes combine an authentic record of social and physical decline with a marked severity in the treatment of motifs. Silhouettes set against a low horizon show the paupers as monumental figures. An unhurried, ritual quality and a distinctive solemnity, later characteristic of Russian genre painting, can be detected in the poses and actions shown. From 1775 to 1788 Yermenyov was in Paris under the patronage of Grand Prince Pavel Petrovich (later Emperor Paul I), and worked there under Joseph-Siffred Duplessis at the Académie Royale. Five pen-and-wash drawings, varied in both style and subject-matter, have survived from this period (Moscow, priv. col., see Savinov, pp. 131, 133, 135, 146). In Paris Yermenyov painted miniature portraits on ivory, continuing to do so on his return to St Petersburg in 1788. The only authenticated miniature by him, *Portrait of an Army Infantry Officer* (1792; St Petersburg, Rus. Mus.), is delicate and precise in execution.

BIBLIOGRAPHY

A. N. Savinov: *Ivan Alekseyevich Yermenyov* (St Petersburg, 1982)

ANDREY A. KAREV

Yermolayeva, Vera (Mikhaylovna) (*b* Petrovsk, Saratov province, 1893; *d* nr Karaganda, Kazakhstan, 1938). Russian painter, printmaker and illustrator. She studied at the school of painting, drawing and sculpture run by Mikhail Bernshteyn and Leonid Shervud in St Petersburg (1911–14), where she was influenced, through her contact with the progressive artist Mikhail Le-Dantyu (1891–1917) and the writer Il'ya Zdanevich (1894–1975), by the principles of NEO-PRIMITIVISM espoused by Mikhail Larionov. Her most productive and original contribution to Russian art started immediately after the 1917 Revolution when she founded the Today (Segodnya) collective of artists in Petrograd (St Petersburg) with the aim of producing *lubok*-style four-page children's books created from linocuts and popular prints, for example her illustrations for Walt Whitman's *O Pioneers* (*Pionery*, 1918; St Petersburg, Rus. Mus.). Although Today ceased its activities when Yermolayeva left for Vitebsk (now Viciebsk) in the autumn of 1919, she continued to illustrate children's books after 1925 for the newly created Detgiz publishing house. She drew on the formal principles of Russian signboard painting in her illustrations for Nikolay Zabolotsky's *Khoroshiye sapogi* ('Good boots'; 1928), an interest that dated from 1918 and early 1919 when she created the shop signboard collection of the Petrograd Museum of the City (now the Museum of the History of St Petersburg), as well as documenting and photographing hundreds more. These activities had been curtailed when she was sent to Vitebsk to take over the post, held by Chagall, of rector of the Vitebsk art institute. She invited Kazimir Malevich to head the painting department there in November 1919; thereafter her career and art were closely associated with his. Together they created UNOVIS in Vitebsk in early 1920, with the aim of establishing the new art as the purveyor of the new life, and to this end Yermolayeva gave lessons in Cubist principles to the public and made linocut Cubo-Futurist costume and stage designs for the 6 Feb 1920 production of Kruchenykh's 'trans rational' opera *Victory over the Sun*. In 1923 Yermolayeva and Malevich moved to Ginkhuk in Petrograd, the last training ground for the Russian avant-garde, where she was head of the colour laboratory until 1927. Her work, especially that in gouache, lost its reliance on line and became dominated by broad strokes of bright colour, although it retained its primitivist references, for example *Three Figures (Golgotha)* (1928) and *Man with a Basket* (1933; both St Petersburg, Rus. Mus.). In 1934 she was arrested because of her brother's Menshevik involvement, and she disappeared while a prison camp inmate.

WRITINGS

'Peterburgskiye vyveski' [Petersburg signboards], *Iskusstvo kommuny* (26 Jan 1919); Eng. trans. in A. Povelikhina and Ye. Kovtun: *Russian Painted Shop Signs and Avant-garde Artists* (Leningrad, 1991), pp. 191–2

'Ob izuchenii kubizma' [On the study of Cubism], *Unovis Almanakh*, 1 (1920)

BIBLIOGRAPHY

Ye. Kovtun: 'Khudozhnitsa knigi V. M. Yermolayeva' [The book artist V. M. Yermolayeva], *Iskusstvo knigi*, ed. D. Shmarinov and others (Moscow, 1975), no. 8, pp. 68–81

E. Kovtun: 'Vera Mikhailovna Ermolaeva', *Women Artists of the Russian Avant-garde, 1910–1930* (exh. cat., ed. K. Robinger; Cologne, Gal. Gmurzynska, 1979), pp. 102–10

L. Zhadova: *Malevich: Suprematism and Revolution in Russian Art, 1910–1930* (London, 1982)

Ye. Kovtun, M. Babanazarova and Ye. Gaziyeva: *Avangard, ostanovlennyy na begu* [The avant-garde stopped in its tracks] (Leningrad, 1989)

JEREMY HOWARD

Yeryomin [Yeremin], Yury (Petrovich) (*b* Kazanskaya-na-Donu, 1881; *d* Moscow, 1948). Russian photographer. He studied at the Moscow School of Painting, Sculpture and Architecture from 1901, then worked as a painter, turning to photography in the second decade of the 20th century. He experimented with complex laboratory processes but in his mature period concentrated on conventional printing. His experience as a painter was reflected in his photography, for example *Ayvazovsky's Cliff on the Black Sea* (1920), with its enigmatic light and soft transitions. In the 1920s and 1930s Yeryomin worked on several major photographic cycles including *Crimea* and *Central Asia*, and his series *Old Moscow* and *Palaces and Estates in the Moscow Area* recorded numerous architectural monuments. He exhibited in the USSR and abroad, winning awards for his work. He also illustrated books on the art of photography. In the mid-1930s he tried his hand at photojournalism, but landscape and architecture, photographed with a soft-focus lens, remained his favourite subjects.

BIBLIOGRAPHY
F. Anatoly: *Photo-artist Y. P. Yeryomin* (Moscow, 1966)
Antologiya Sovetskoy fotografii [Anthology of Soviet photography] (Moscow, 1986)
S. Morozov: *Tvorcheskaya fotografiya* [Creative photography] (Moscow, 1986)
Sowjetische Photographie der 20er und 30er Jahre (Cologne, Galerie Alex Lachmann, 1991)
D. Elliott: *Photography in Russia, 1840–1940* (Berlin, 1992)
A. N. LAVRENTIEV

Yesari. *See* ESAD YESARI.

Yevele [Evelee; Yeveley; Yivele; Yvele; Yveley; Zevele; Zhevele; Zyvele], **Henry** (*b* ?nr Yeaveley, Derbys, *c.* 1320–30; *d* London, 21 Aug 1400). English architect. He is first recorded in 1353, when he was granted the freedom of the City of London. He quickly rose to prominence and *c.* 1357 he was appointed mason to Edward, Prince of Wales (1330–76). The title of King's Deviser of Masonry, which he held from 1360 to his death, indicates that he was recognized as an architect in the modern sense, with responsibility for design, erection and maintenance of all Crown works, such as Queenborough Castle (1361–7; destr. 1650; *see also* PLANTAGENET, (4)) and Rochester Castle (repaired 1367–8). Stylistic evidence, including characteristically Perpendicular mouldings, indicates that he was responsible for the Black Prince's chantry (from 1363) in the crypt of Canterbury Cathedral. In 1371 he contracted to build the first cell and the cloister of the London Charterhouse. The Neville screen (1372–6) in Durham Cathedral has been attributed to Yevele's London workshop (*see* DURHAM, §1(ii)). He also designed John of Gaunt's chantry (1374–*c.* 1378; destr. 1666) for Old St Paul's Cathedral, London.

At Canterbury Yevele probably designed the tomb of *Edward the Black Prince* for the cathedral. Although he was not recorded as in charge of rebuilding the city walls until 1385, stylistic evidence suggests that he was responsible from the start of work in 1378, notably for the Westgate (in progress 1380). On the basis of both documentary and stylistic evidence the cathedral nave (1377–1403), which is regarded as one of the most satisfactory surviving Perpendicular interiors, has been attributed to Yevele (*see* CANTERBURY, §III, 1(v) and fig. 9). It is probable that he was consultant designer on projects for William of Wykeham, Bishop of Winchester, from 1381 (e.g. Oxford, New College). He also directed repairs at

Old St Paul's (destr.) in 1381–2 and payments were made for a new south doorway and window in 1387–8.

Yevele was appointed master mason to Westminster Abbey in 1387, although he may have been associated with work on the nave from 1375, and designed the west front and west porch (*see* LONDON, §V, 2(i)). In collaboration with Stephen Lote (*d* 1417/18) he designed the tomb-chests of *Richard II* and *Anne of Bohemia* (1394/5–7) and *Cardinal Simon Langham* (payment 1394); these resemble that made for *Edward III* (after April 1386). Yevele supervised work at the Tower of London in 1389 and directed repairs at Winchester Castle from 1390. Between 1394 and 1399 he served as architect at the new Westminster Hall and his last work was probably the vault of the north porch (1399–1400; *see* LONDON, §V, 3(i)(a)).

BIBLIOGRAPHY
Harvey
J. H. Harvey: *Henry Yevele, Architect, and his Works in Kent* (London, 1944)
——: *Henry Yevele, c. 1320–1400: The Life of an English Architect* (London, 1944)
——: *Henry Yevele Reconsidered* (London, 1952)
ANNE PUETZ

Ye Xiaan. *See* YE GONGCHUO.

Yezd. *See* YAZD.

Yi (i). Korean family of artists. (1) Sin Sa-im-dang married into the Yi family, whose ancestral home was in Tŏksu. Of her five children, (2) Yi I became an eminent Confucian philosopher, reformer and calligrapher and (3) Yi U an accomplished painter and calligrapher. Her daughter Mae-ch'ang was also an excellent painter.

(1) Sin Sa-im-dang (*b* Kangnŭng, Kangwŏn Province, 1504; *d* Seoul, 1551). Calligrapher and painter. At the age of seven she could already copy exactly the works of the 15th-century painter An Kyŏn, and from an early age she manifested further talents in poetry, writing and embroidery. Her cursive style of writing was excellent. She earned fame especially through her painting of grass insects together with ink paintings of peony and plum, flowers and birds. Her identified works all belong to one or other of the accepted categories of Korean painting. However, it is in her paintings of grass insects that her original tendencies, expressive of typical Korean sentiments, show through in the positioning of the subject-matter—bees, butterflies, dragonflies, grasshoppers, tree branches and ground cherries, also plants and animals—in a symmetrical and central upright arrangement and in her use of earthy colours. *Mice Nibbling at a Watermelon* (Seoul, N. Mus.; see fig.), attributed to Sin Sa-im-dang, is an attractive example of her style. Her son (3) Yi U and her daughter Mae-ch'ang also excelled in painting plum trees in Chinese ink.

BIBLIOGRAPHY
Yi In-sang: *Sa-im-dang-ŭi saeng'ae wa yesul* [Life and art of Sa-im-dang] (Seoul, 1978, rev. 1981)
Chŏng Yang-mo, ed.: *Hwajo, Sagunja* [Flower and bird, 'The Four Gentlemen'] (1985), xviii of *Hanguk-ŭi mi* [Beauties of Korea] (Seoul, 1977–85)
Kim Wŏn-yong and An Hwi-jun: *Hanguk misulsa* [History of Korean art] (Seoul, 1993), p. 274, pls 8–9
HONG SŎN-P'YO

Sin Sa-im-dang (attrib.): *Mice Nibbling at a Watermelon*, 380×282 mm, colour on paper, 16th century (Seoul, National Museum of Korea)

(2) Yi I [*cha* Sukhŏn; *ho* Yulgok, Sŏktam, Wujae; posthumous title Munsŏng] (*b* Kangnŭng, Kangwŏn Province, 1536; *d* 1584). Confucian scholar, statesman and calligrapher, third son of (1) Sin Sa-im-dang. His education started at home under his mother. In 1548 he passed the preliminary civil service examination. The death of his mother when he was only 15 probably prompted him to study Buddhist texts for a year in retreat in the Kumgang Mountains. In the debate on the origins of *i* (the all-pervading essence or principle in the world) and *ki* (the energizing element that gives form to *i*), his belief in the oneness of heaven and man brought him a large following among the Neo-Confucian philosophers of his time. As a state Minister of Personnel, Justice and Military Affairs, he proposed many reforming policies.

His calligraphy is valued more for the social status of the artist than for its own artistic merit. However, thanks to his mother, his training in calligraphy was quite thorough. His style shows the influence of the 4th-century Chinese master Wang Xizhi. Many specimens of his hand in the form of personal letters have survived (Kangnŭng, Yulgok Mem. Mus.). His writings have been published as *Yulgok chŏnsŏ* ('Complete works of Yulgok').

BIBLIOGRAPHY
O. Se-ch'ang: *Kŭnyŏk sŏhwa jing* [Dictionary of Korean painters and calligraphers] (Taegu, 1928/*R* 1975), p. 92
Hwang Ŭi-dong: *Yulgok ch'ŏlhak yŏngu* [The philosophy of Yulgok] (Seoul, 1975)
Yi In-sang: *Sa-im-dang-ŭi saeng'ae wa yesul* [Life and art of Sa-im-dang] (Seoul, 1978, rev. 1981), pp. 299–305
Im Ch'ang-sun, ed.: *Sŏye* [Calligraphy] (1981), vi of *Hanguk-ŭi mi* [Beauties of Korea] (Seoul, 1977–85), pl. 49

(3) Yi U [*cha* Kyehŏn; *ho* Oksan, Chukwa] (*b* 1542; *d* 1609). Painter, calligrapher and official, fourth son of (1) Sin Sa-im-dang and brother of (2) Yi I. He passed the first level of the state civil service examination in 1567 and later served as district governor of Kwesan, North Ch'ungch'ŏng Province, and Kobu, North Chŏlla Province. He was perhaps the most artistically gifted of Sin's five children. In addition to being a good painter and calligrapher he was also an accomplished poet and musician. His talents in these four fields earned him the title of 'four excellences'.

Yi U painted a wide variety of subject-matter, but like his mother and sister Maech'ang he excelled in grass-and-insect paintings and in ink-plum and ink-grape studies. According to one anecdote, his grass-and-insect paintings in ink were so realistic that when they were laid on the ground, a flock of chickens ran after them. Among his surviving paintings, *Grapes* (Nonsan, South Ch'ungch'ŏng Province, priv. col.) is perhaps the most representative of his beautiful and spirited brushwork and use of ink. His calligraphy is much more accomplished than that of his brother, Yi I. A fine example is seen in his rendering of poems by the Chinese calligrapher Huang Tingjian, written in cursive script (Seoul, Sŏnggyun'gwan U. Mus.), which display a fluent yet well-controlled movement of the brush throughout. The variation in the thickening and thinning of individual strokes also reflects the spontaneous movement of the hand tempered by considerable modulation as it continues vertically from one character to another. Yi U was also well known for his wild cursive script, a variation of cursive script executed with more freedom and verve. An example of his wild cursive calligraphy can be seen in a nine-fold screen of calligraphy (Kangnŭng, Yulgok Mem. Mus.), which was originally an album of 17 leaves of slightly varying size.

BIBLIOGRAPHY
Yu Pok-yŏl: *Hanguk hoehwa taegwan* [Pageant of Korean painting] (Seoul, 1969), pp. 169–72
Yi In-sang: *Sa-im-dang-ŭi saeng'ae wa yesul* [Life and art of Sa-im-dang] (Seoul, 1978, rev. 1981), pp. 306–18, pls 49–56
Im Ch'ang-sun, ed.: *Sŏye* [Calligraphy] (1981), vi of *Hanguk-ŭi mi* [Beauties of Korea] (Seoul, 1977–85), pl. 52
                                                          YI SŎNG-MI

Yi (ii). Korean family of scholars and painters. They were descended from Yi Kyang-gun, eighth son of King Sŏngjong (*reg* 1469–94) of the Chosŏn dynasty (the family name of this dynasty was Yi). Two of Yi Kyang-gun's great-grandsons, (1) Yi Kyŏng-yun and (2) Yi Yŏng-yun, were painters and were influenced by the Chinese ZHE SCHOOL. Yi Kyŏng-yun's son, (3) Yi Ching, a court painter, also worked in the Zhe school tradition. Two other sons, Yi Ch'uk (1566–1637) and Yi Wi-guk (*b* 1597), had the reputation of being good calligraphers.

(1) Yi Kyŏng-yun [*cha* Kagil; *ho* Nakp'a] (*b* 1545; *d* 1611). As a direct descendant of King Sŏngjong in the fourth generation, he was not allowed to sit any examinations. He did, however, achieve the title of nobility of Hangnim-su (senior fourth rank) and later gained promotion to Hangnim-jŏng (senior third rank). The artist used both titles as sobriquets. Contemporary texts reflect his reputation as a painter. Thus, Yi Myŏng-han (1595–1642) described Yi Kyŏng-yun, his son, Yi Ching, and his teacher and confidant, Kim Che (*see* KIM (i), (1)), as the most important painters of the 16th and early 17th centuries. Yi Myŏng-han also wrote that Yi Kyŏng-yun concealed his talent, so that even his son saw hardly any of his pictures.

Yi Kyŏng-yun's influence on his contemporaries can be gauged from the large number of works attributed to him. These are mostly album sheets by a number of unknown painters of the late 16th century and early 17th. They depict scholars playing chess, composing poetry or contemplating a waterfall, themes corresponding to the ideal of repose current at that time rather than to reality. The composition of these paintings shows the influence of the later period of the Chinese Zhe school. Nine album sheets (Seoul, Horim A. Mus.) might possibly be authentic (for an illustration of one of them, no. 6, see fig.). They carry handwritten poems and a lengthy colophon, dated 1598, by Ch'oe Ip (1539–1612), a leading contemporary scholar, attributing the pictures to Yi Kyŏng-yun. Ch'oe Ip identified with the painter in the latter's role as scholar and accordingly made claims for these works of the Korean Zhe school that distinguish them from those of the Chinese school and link Yi Kyŏng-yun to the tradition of Korean literati painting (see KOREA, §IV, 2(vi)). Among stylistic differences from Chinese painting are the two-dimensional treatment of landscape, which is rich in contrasts and vastly different from the delicacy of the figure painting, and the way in which the artist has given the landscape elements a geometrical, highly rhythmic character. These features are seen in two landscapes with cattle, *Riding an Ox and Blowing the Flute* and *Riding an Ox in the Shadow of Willow Trees*, dated 1604 (337×514 mm; Seoul, Cent. Stud. Kor. A., Kangsong A. Mus.; see *Kansong Munhwa*, xxvi (1984), pls 26, 27).

BIBLIOGRAPHY

Ch'oe Sun-u: 'Hangnim-jŏng-ŭi sansu inmul ch'ŏp' [An album of figure and landscape paintings by Yi Kyŏng-yun], *Kogo Misul*, vii/4 (1966), pp. 1–5

Chŏng Yang-mo, ed.: *Hwajo, sagunja* [Paintings of flowers and birds and the 'four gentlemen'] (1985), xviii of *Hanguk-ŭi mi* [Beauties of Korea] (Seoul, 1977–85), pp. 242–3, pl. 153

B. Jungmann: 'An Album of Figure and Landscape Paintings Attributed to Yi Kyŏng-yun (1545–1611)', *Festschrift for Kim Wŏn-yong* (Seoul, 1987), pp. 537–58

——: *Die koreanische Landschaftsmalerei und die chinesische Che-Schule vom späten 15. bis zum frühen 17. Jahrhundert* (Stuttgart, 1992), pp. 188–238, 256–8

(2) Yi Yŏng-yun (*b* 1561; *d* 1611). Brother of (1) Yi Kyŏng-yun. His title of nobility, Chungnim-su, is also

Yi Kyŏng-yun: *Scholar in a Landscape*, leaf 6 from an album of figure and landscape paintings, ink and colour on paper, 260×330 mm, before 1598 (Seoul, Horim Art Museum)

often used as his sobriquet. His contemporaries saw him as a less successful follower of his brother's style, like him painting landscapes, horses and small animals. His surviving paintings, however, are almost exclusively of birds and flowers. In his work Yi Yŏng-yun assimilated the influence of the Chinese Zhe school, as his brother did in his landscapes. Each developed the Zhe tradition to meet Korean sensitivities. A panel of an eight-fold screen (Seoul, N. Mus.), traditionally attributed to Yi Yŏng-yun, displays colourful bamboo and chrysanthemum bushes delightfully accentuated within a monochrome ink landscape in which two white herons stalk through a brook looking for fish. The rock formations intruding obliquely into the picture from the side and the bottom are composed of flat, contrasting layers. Like the flat mountains in the background they are dotted over with clumps of moss. The composition and style of these elements recall Yi Kyŏng-yun's landscapes, which exerted great influence on contemporary painting. The delicate effect produced by the combination of ink and colour that gives Yi Yŏng-yun's painting its charm is common in 16th-century Korean painting. However, a landscape hanging scroll (ink on paper, Seoul, N. Mus.) by Yi Yŏng-yun imitating Huang Gongwang is the earliest known Korean example after this Chinese master.

BIBLIOGRAPHY

Yu Pok-yŏl: Hanguk hoehwa taegwan [Pageant of Korean painting] (Seoul, 1969), pp. 187–9
Chŏng Yang-mo, ed.: Hwajo, sagunja [Paintings of flowers and birds and of the 'four gentlemen'] (1985), xviii of Hanguk-ŭi mi [Beauties of Korea] (Seoul, 1977–85), p. 221, pl. 48
Kim Kumja Paik: 'The Introduction of the Southern School Painting Tradition to Korea', Orient. A., xxxvi/4 (1990–91), pp. 187–8
B. Jungmann: Die koreanische Landschaftsmalerei und die chinesische Che-Schule vom späten 15. bis zum frühen 17. Jahrhundert (Stuttgart, 1992), pp. 188–238, 256–8

(3) Yi Ching [cha Chaham; ho Hŏju] (b 1581; d after 1645). Illegitimate son of (1) Yi Kyŏng-yun. As such he was not a member of the aristocracy. As a court painter he assisted in the documentation of various events at court such as the wedding ceremony in 1638 of King Injo (reg 1623–49). His paintings were so sought after that the people visiting him with rolls of cloth as payment for his work virtually blocked off the street in front of his house. Sources praise him for his mastery of various styles.

Yi Ching's works show the influence of two main sources: the Chinese Zhe school, as cultivated and transmuted by his father, and the tradition initiated by AN KYŎN. A folio from an album (Seoul, Korea U.), depicting an old man with a flying crane, is so close in style and composition to works by Yi Kyŏng-yun that it could even be plausibly attributed to him. Some ink paintings of birds and flowers indicate the strong influence of the Korean Zhe school. However, the main emphasis in his oeuvre is on monumental landscape painting. A hanging scroll painted in ink and light colours on silk (Seoul, N. Mus.) borrows from the Zhe school its style of composition based on a single angle with a broad expanse of water in the centre and distant mountains on the horizon. The rock formations created out of layers and with black moss dots recall pictures by Yi Kyŏng-yun. The more complex rendering of individual elements of the landscape, the bright ink tones and the hesitant striking technique, on the other hand, are more suggestive of the older masters, and his Landscape in Gold on Black Silk (Seoul, N. Mus.; see An Hwi-jun, ed., 1977–85, xi, pl. 108) is entirely in the tradition of An Kyŏn. Cloud-shaped ranges of mountains are stacked so that they appear to float one above the other, an impression accentuated by the general expansiveness of the picture. The surreal effect of the golden ink on a black background increases the impression of an entrancing fairytale world.

BIBLIOGRAPHY

Yi Tong-ju: Han'guk hoehwa sosa [A short history of Korean painting] (Seoul, 1972), p. 175
An Hwi-jun: 'Han'guk chŏlp'a hwap'ung-ŭi yŏn'gu' [A study of Korean painting of the Zhe school style], Misul Charyo, xx (1977), pp. 54–7
An Hwi-jun, ed.: Sansuhwa [Landscape painting], ii (1982), xii of Hanguk-ŭi mi [Beauties of Korea] (Seoul, 1977–85), pl. 108
Ch'oe Sun-u: Hanguk misul [Korean art], 3 vols (Seoul, 1983), ii, pl. 89
An Hwi-jun, ed.: P'ungsokhwa [Genre painting] (1985), xix of Hanguk-ŭi mi [Beauties of Korea] (Seoul, 1977–85), pls 39–41

BURGLIND JUNGMANN

Yi Am (i) [ho Kunhae; Koun; Ch'oja; Haengch'on] (b 1297; d 1364). Korean calligrapher. He is considered one of the last great calligraphers of the Koryŏ period (918–1392). Born into a noble family, at the age of 17 he passed his first examinations and entered the Confucian academy in Kaesŏng, where he eventually rose to prominence in the central administration. Information on his life, and in particular on his career as an official, can be found in the Koryŏsa, the history of the Koryŏ dynasty.

Yi was directly influenced by the calligraphic works of Zhao Mengfu, who at that time was considered among the greatest painters and calligraphers of Yuan-period (1279–1368) China, with which Korea had close political and cultural contacts. However, only one of Yi's calligraphic works survives, and that only as a rubbing (Seoul, priv. col.) from a stele inscription. This is the celebrated Munsu sa changgyŏng pi ('Inscription for the sūtra repository of Munsu Temple'; see Kim, Choi and Im, pl. 118), a piece written to commemorate the building of a new library for sacred texts (Skt sūtras) that provides a fine example of the master's dynamic and expressive calligraphy written in a style that had become popular in literati circles during the mid-Koryŏ (see KOREA, §V, 4). The title of the inscription, which is placed as a heading in the stele, a common feature in Koryŏ stone inscriptions, shows that Yi was also a master in writing characters in a stylized variant of large seal script (tae chŏn). He was also a writer of essays and poems, and his works can be found in the Nongsang chip sŏl ('Collected sayings of the mulberry farmer').

BIBLIOGRAPHY

O. Se-ch'ang: Kŭnyŏk sŏhwa jing [Dictionary of Korean painters and calligraphers] (Taegu, 1928/R Seoul, 1975)
Hanguk inmyŏng tae sajŏn [Encyclopedia of Korean personal names] (Seoul, 1967), p. 674b
Im Ch'ang-sun, ed.: Sŏye [Calligraphy] (1973), xi of Hanguk misul chŏnjip [The arts of Korea] (Seoul, 1973–5), pp. 62–3, 145
Kim Won-yong [Kim Wŏn-yong], Choi Sun U [Ch'oe Sun-u] and Im Chang-soon [Im Ch'ang-sun], eds: Paintings, ii of The Arts of Korea (Seoul, 1979)
Chin Hong-sŏp, ed.: Hanguk misulsa charyŏ chipsŏng [Collected references to Korean art history], ii, (Seoul, 1991), pp. 250–322

Yi Am (ii) [cha Chŏngjung; ho Tusŏngyŏng] (b 1499). Korean painter. A descendant of the royal Yi family—

founders of the Chosŏn dynasty—in the line of King Sejong and mentioned in the *Injong shillok* ('Veritable records of King Injong'), he was considered one of the most important Academy painters of his day. He was renowned for his rendering of dogs and cats and of flowers and birds, placed usually in highly formalized garden settings. His paintings exude an innocent and peaceful atmosphere. In his work he combined the 'outline' style with the 'boneless'. His paintings bear some resemblance to the type of animal paintings produced at Huizong's Northern Song Academy in the 12th century in China, although his subjects are more dynamic, if less realistic.

Only four works from his hand are thought to have survived. His most celebrated painting is *Bitch with Puppies* (see fig.). Another of his paintings, *Puppies under a Flowering Tree* (P'yŏngyang, Kor. A.G.; *see* KOREA, fig. 40), shows three puppies, two resting, one sitting up, beside a tree on which two magpies have alighted. *Cat in a Tree* (ink and colours on paper, 870×445 mm; P'yŏngyang, Kor. A.G.) shows a pair of puppies that have chased a cat up a tree bearing red flowers. One of the puppies holds a feather in its mouth, while the other is sitting on its haunches staring wistfully after the cat. The cat, relatively undisturbed, has its attention on a pair of birds flying around the tree. Although highly formalized, the painting has an air of charm and simplicity. Yi Am's works enjoyed considerable popularity in Japan during the late Muromachi period (1333–1568), to the extent that at one time he was wrongly taken for a Japanese painter. His paintings were chiefly appreciated in Japan for their decorative value in line with contemporary taste. Pyŏn Sang-byŏk (*fl* 1725–76), who is Korea's other great painter of animals, was greatly influenced by the works of Yi Am.

BIBLIOGRAPHY

Hanguk inmyŏng tae sajŏn [Encyclopedia of Korean personal names] (Seoul, 1967), p. 674b

Yi Tong-jŭ: *Ilbon sŏk-ŭi hanhwa* [Korean paintings kept in Japan] (Seoul, 1974), pp. 14–15

Korean Fine Arts: From The Works Preserved by the Korean Art Museum (P'yŏngyang, 1978), p. 28

Ch'oe Sun-u: *Hanguk misul och'ŏnhyŏn* [5000 years of Korean art] (Seoul, 1979), p. 230

An Hwi-jun: *Hanguk hoehwasa* [History of Korean painting] (Seoul, 1980, rev. 1984), pp. 146, 160

HENRIK H. SØRENSEN

Yi Bingshou [I Ping-shou; *zi* Zisi; *hao* Moqing] (*b* Ninghua, Fujian Province, 1754; *d* Yangzhou, Jiangsu Province, 1815). Chinese calligrapher, minor painter and seal-carver. He passed the civil service examination to become a *jinshi* in 1789. He then had a series of official posts, serving on the Board of Justice, as an examiner and as a prefectural magistrate first at Huizhou in Guangdong Province and then at Yangzhou in Jiangsu Province. Yi is generally recognized as a leading figure in the stele studies (*beixue*) movement in calligraphy (*see* CHINA, §IV, 2(vii)) and was designated one of the Four Great Calligraphers of the Qing period (1644–1911) by the political reformer and scholar of epigraphy Kang Youwei. He occasionally painted landscapes, few of which are extant. He was also well versed in law and philology.

In calligraphy Yi is best known for his clerical script (*lishu*) and developed his own style in running script (*xingshu*) and regular script (*kaishu*). He was a student of LIU YONG and is reported by the art historian Bao Shichen to have adopted Liu's brush technique, known as the 'dragon's pupil', which refers to the shape of the hand and fingers as they hold the brush. Yi applied this technique, however, to different calligraphic forms. A typical example of Yi's calligraphy is his *Traces* (*Xiang gu*, 1811; Princeton, NJ, J. S. Elliot priv. col.). This consists of two large characters and an inscription in Yi's usual running script style. The large characters feature circular shapes and extended horizontals, suggesting the incorporation of elements from both seal script (*zhuanshu*) and clerical script. Although this piece is impromptu and not based on a specific stele model, Yi's familiarity with Han stelae, especially those showing the transition from seal to clerical script, is clear. A possible source is one of the earliest Han stelae, *Lu Xiao Wang keshi* (56 BC; see Shimonaka, pl. 6), carved in commemoration of Prince Xiao of Lu's accession to the throne. In the small running script of this piece, there is a similar incorporation of elements from seal and clerical scripts.

Yi Am (ii): *Bitch with Puppies*, hanging scroll, ink and light colours on paper, 422×730 mm, 16th century (Seoul, National Museum of Korea)

BIBLIOGRAPHY
K. Shimonaka, ed.: *Shodō zenshū* [Complete collection of calligraphy], ii (Tokyo, 2/1958)
Traces of the Brush: Studies in Chinese Calligraphy (exh. cat. by Shen Fu and others, New Haven, CT, Yale U.A.G.; Berkeley, U. CA, A. Mus.; 1977)
Yu Jianhua: *Zhongguo meishujia renming cidian* [Dictionary of Chinese artists] (Shanghai, 1981), p. 181

ELIZABETH F. BENNETT

Yi Chae [*cha* Hŭigyŏng; *ho* Toam, Hanch'ŏn] (*b* Ubong, 1680; *d* 1746). Korean painter, calligrapher and government official. He passed the civil service examination in 1702 and served in various posts before becoming Vice-minister of the Board of Rites. He was also a Neo-Confucian philosopher (*see* CONFUCIANISM, §2(ii)). Although he is recorded as having been good at painting, none of his works has survived. On the other hand, the portrait of him by an anonymous painter (Seoul, N. Mus.; *see* KOREA, fig. 46) is one of the best-known portraits of the 18th century; in it a hint of the influence of Western painting technique, i.e. the use of chiaroscuro, can be detected. Yi Chae is portrayed in old age wearing a white scholar's robe with black trimming, called *hakch'ang'ŭi*, and a black headdress. The simplicity of the scholar's garment further enhances the penetrating expression of his eyes and the slight shading on his face. Several of his calligraphic works remain, including the stele of Kim In-hu (1510–60), but by the late 20th century none of them had yet been published.

BIBLIOGRAPHY
Kim Yŏng-yun, ed.: *Hanguk sŏhwa inmyŏng sasŏ* [Biographical dictionary of Korean painters and calligraphers] (Seoul, 1959), p. 308

YI SŎNG-MI

Yi Chae-gwan [*ho* Sodang] (*b* Yong'in, Kyŏnggi Province, 1783; *d c.* 1839). Korean painter. He was born into an impoverished noble household and was active in the later Chosŏn period (1392–1910). Because of his father's early death he became a self-taught professional painter in order to make a living. As a member of the Bureau of Painting and a royal portrait painter, he restored the portrait of King T'aejo (*reg* 1392–8), founder of the dynasty. In accordance with the practice of appointing court painters to military posts, Yi became a military official near Haeju, Hwanghae Province. Although he was a professional painter from the age of about 20, he associated closely with such middle-class literati painters as Cho Hŭi-ryong and was profoundly influenced by their literary circles. Up to his early thirties he mainly followed the Chinese Southern school but later moved towards the distinctive styles of Yi In-sang and Yun Che-hong. He established his own method of combining to excellent effect a simple structure with the tones of Chinese ink and a light colour. His later style of painting won the praise of the artist and connoisseur Kim Chŏng-hŭi, whose student he became. He enjoyed dealing with such subject-matter as landscape scenes and portraits. His portrait of Kang Yi-o (*b* 1788), grandson of Kang Se-hwang (hanging scroll, 639 mm, ink and colours on silk; Seoul, N. Mus.; *see* 1984 exh. cat., pl. 247), carries an inscription by Kim Chŏng-hŭi commending Yi's skills. Other examples of Yi's work are *Plantain and Poem* and *Figure under a Pine Tree* (both Seoul, N. Mus.; *see* 1984 exh. cat., pl. 254, for an illustration of the latter painting) and an album of scenes painted in 1837 (priv. col.).

BIBLIOGRAPHY
Kim Won-yong [Kim Wŏn-yong], Choi Sun U [Ch'oe Sun-u] and Im chang-soon [Im Ch'ang-sun], eds: *Paintings*, ii of *The Arts of Korea* (Seoul, 1979), pp. 186–7, pl. 93
5000 Years of Korean Art (exh. cat., ed. R.-Y. Lefebvre d'Argencé; San Francisco, CA, Asian A. Mus.; Seattle, WA, A. Mus.; Chicago, IL, A. Inst. and elsewhere; 1979–81), p. 188, pl. 247
An Hwi-jun, ed.: *Sansuhwa* [Landscape painting], ii (1982), xii of *Hanguk-ŭi mi* [Beauties of Korea] (Seoul, 1977–85), pl. 151
Treasures from Korea (exh. cat., intro. R. Goepper; ed. R. Whitfield; London, BM, 1984), p. 214

HONG SŎN-P'YO

Yi Che-hyŏn [*cha* Chungsa; *ho* Ikjae, Siljae, Yok'ong] (*b* Kyŏngju, 1287; *d* 1367). Korean painter, connoisseur, scholar and statesman. In 1301 he won first place in the state examination. Thereafter his official career took him steadily to the post, in 1356, of Chief Minister of the Chancellery for State Affairs. Active in the Koryŏ period (918–1392), he served five sovereigns during his years in office and made many trips to Yanjing and to Dadu, the capital of the Yuan dynasty (1279–1368), on behalf of his country. After King Ch'ungsŏn (*reg* 1308–13), who spent more time in Yanjing than in the Koryŏ capital of Songdo, had built the Man'gwŏndang (Hall of Ten Thousand Volumes) in Yanjing, Yi Che-hyŏn was called to China in 1314. There he met many eminent Chinese scholars, among them the painters Zhao Mengfu (*see* ZHAO, (1)) and ZHU DEREN. Yi Che-hyŏn is credited with having brought Zhao Mengfu's calligraphic style to Korea, where it remained popular until the 16th century (*see* KOREA, §V). In his *Ikjae nango* ('Ramblings of Ikjae') he described viewing paintings with Zhu Deren and recording their opinions on such Chinese painters as Li Kan and Ren Renfa. Yi Che-hyŏn's acquaintance with Zhao Mengfu and Zhu Deren may have served as a channel for the popularization in Korean painting of the Li–Guo school, associated with Li Cheng and Guo Xi, and the Mi school, associated with Mi Fu (all landscape painters of the Northern Song period (960–1127)).

Yi Che-hyŏn is best known for his writings, including *Ikjae chip* ('Collected works') and the dynastic annals he compiled in retirement at royal request, but several paintings are attributed to him. *Horsemen Crossing a River* (Seoul, N. Mus.) has his signature and seal (1984 exh. cat., pl. 220). Five horsemen in Mongol costume are depicted in a winter landscape. The frozen river stretches out in opposing diagonals creating an illusion of level distance. Beautifully rendered horses and the shading of the surface of the cliff in strong contrasts of light and dark are reminiscent of Zhao Mengfu and Guo Xi respectively. Yi Che-hyŏn's brushlines for the forms are thin and gentle, without drama; as a result his painting has a tremendous stillness. A portrait of Yi Che-hyŏn has survived, painted by Chen Jīanru (Seoul, N. Mus.).

BIBLIOGRAPHY
O Se-ch'ang: *Kŭnyŏk sŏhwa jing* [Dictionary of Korean painters and calligraphers] (Taegu, 1928/*R* Seoul, 1975), p. 29
S. Lee and W.-K. Ho: *Chinese Art under the Mongols: The Yuan Dynasty, 1279–1368* (Cleveland, 1968), p. 82
Yu Pok-yŏl: *Hanguk hoehwa taegwan* [Pageant of Korean painting] (Seoul, 1969), pp. 34–6

Ahn Hwi-jun: *Hanguk hoehwasa* [History of Korean painting] (Seoul, 1980), pp. 60–61
Treasures from Korea (exh. cat., intro. R. Goepper; ed. R. Whitfield; London, BM, 1984)

KIM KUMJA PAIK

Yi Chŏng (i) [*cha* Chungsŏp; *ho* T'anun] (*b* 1541; *d* after 1625). Korean painter. Active during the middle of the Chosŏn period, he was a great-great-grandson of King Sejong and bore the noble title Sŏgyang-jŏng. His work consists primarily of monochrome bamboo paintings. This genre was cultivated fairly early in Korea, mainly under the influence of the Chinese literati painters of the Northern Song period (*see* CHINA, §V, 4(ii)). From the beginning of the Chosŏn period bamboo constituted the most important examination subject for the Bureau of Painting (Tohwasŏ). Yi Chŏng's early paintings display the influence of painters of the Chinese Yuan period (1279–1368), such as Li Kan. Soon, however, elements of contemporary Ming (1368–1644) painting, especially in the style of the Zhe school, as exemplified by Zhu Duan, also appeared in his work. For instance, Yi Chŏng moved the subject in a similar way from the centre to the side of his painting and combined the bamboo motif with freely drawn sketches of boulders. In contrast to his Chinese models, he joined the bamboo leaves into bundles, which he spread out rhythmically over the entire surface of the picture. Consequently, the stems in the background with light ink tones were strongly set off from the darker ones in the foreground, making them appear as shadows and

Yi Chŏng: *Ink Bamboo*, ink on silk, 1.22×0.52 mm, early 17th century (Seoul, Ho-am Art Museum)

producing an effective expansion in depth (see fig.; *see also* KOREA, fig. 48). After Yi Chŏng, rhythm, expansiveness and the predilection for graphic patterns became characteristic traits of Korean bamboo painting, even though most of these elements had already occurred in the painting of the early Chosŏn period. Examples of Yi Chŏng's paintings of bamboo are held in the National Museum of Korea, Seoul, the Centre for the Study of Korean Arts, Kansong Art Museum, Seoul, the Ho-am Art Museum, Seoul, and private collections in Korea and Japan.

Two smaller folios of an album attributed to Yi Chŏng (Korea, priv. cols) represent Hanshan, a monk of the Tang period (AD 618–907), a popular figure in Chinese Chan (Kor. Sŏn; Jap. Zen) Buddhist painting, as he points, laughing, at the moon. These are some of the very few indications that unorthodox subjects were in fact used in painting in Confucian Korea. These expansive and striking landscapes with softly toned washes clearly indicate the extent to which Chinese painting was assimilated in late 16th-century Korea.

BIBLIOGRAPHY
Ch'oe Sun-u: 'T'anŭn-ŭi munwŏldo' [*Gazing at the moon* by T'anŭn], *Kogo Misul*, xxix (1962), pp. 323–4
An Hwi-jun: 'Hanguk chŏlp'a hwap'ung-ŭi yŏn'gu' [A study on Korean painting of the Zhe school style], *Misul Charyo*, xx (1977), pp. 24–62
5000 Years of Korean Art (exh. cat., ed. R.-Y. Lefebvre d'Argencé; San Francisco, CA, Asian A. Mus.; Seattle, WA, A. Mus.; Chicago, IL, A. Inst. and elsewhere; 1979–81), p. 176, pls 188–9
Kwon Young-pil [Kwŏn Yong-pil]: *Die Entstehung der 'koreanischen' Bambusmalerei aus der Mitte der Yi-Dynastie (1392–1910): Ihre gedankliche Begründung und Stilfragen* (diss., U. Cologne, 1985), pp. 152–68

Yi Chŏng (ii) [*cha* Konggan; *ho* Naong, among others] (*b* 1578; *d* 1607). Korean painter. Active during the middle of the Chosŏn period, he came from a family of painters extending back to his great-grandfather. His grandfather, Yi Pae-ryŏn, is nowadays commonly identified with the court painter Yi Sang-chwa, while landscape paintings survive from both his father, Yi Sung-hyo (*b* 1536), who died at an early age, and his uncle, Yi Hŭng-hyo (1537–93), who brought him up. Yi Chŏng's talent for painting manifested itself in his childhood. In 1589 he went to the Kumgang Mountains in central Korea, where he painted landscapes and heavenly kings on the walls of Changan Temple two years later. A farewell poem written by his teacher Ch'oe Ip (1539–1612) indicates that Yi Chŏng had also travelled to China. The painter died after a heavy drinking session before he had reached the age of thirty.

A small *Landscape* (album leaf, ink on paper, 345×230 mm; Seoul, N. Mus.) bears the seal '*Naong*'. In terms of composition and style this painting blends various traditions into a unified composition. While the sloping banks and the cliff in the centre are borrowed from the Chinese Southern Song and the Zhe-school tradition, the trees with their branches shaped in the form of a crab's claw, as well as the picture's division into foreground, centre and background, recall some album leaves attributed to An Kyŏn. The loose brushstrokes and the abundant application of wash hint at landscapes painted by Yi Chŏng's uncle, Yi Hŭng-hyo. An album containing twelve leaves attributed to Yi Chŏng (Seoul, N. Mus.) displays stylistic elements from the painting of the Chinese Southern school. A pair of hanging scrolls with the signature and seal of Yi Chŏng depict a dragon and a tiger (ink on paper, 1160×755 mm; Japan, priv. col.). They must have reached Japan relatively early, as the painter and connoisseur Kanō Tan'yū mentioned two pictures with the same subjects and the signature *Naong* around 1670, although he took them to be the work of a Southern Song master. Both pictures display extraordinarily forceful and generous strokes. They are important indications of an iconographic tradition emanating from Song China that had been cultivated since the Koryŏ period (918–1392) and finally entered folk painting, where it enjoyed great popularity.

BIBLIOGRAPHY

Yi Wŏn-bok: 'Yi Chŏng-ŭi tu chŏnch'ing hwach'ŏp e taehan sigo' [Two albums attributed to Yi Chŏng], *Misul Charyo*, xxxiv (June 1984), pp. 46–59; xxxv (Dec 1984), pp. 43–52

Ide Seinosuke: 'Ri Tei hitsu ryu-ko-zu ni tsuite' [On the pair of paintings of a tiger and a dragon by Yi Chŏng], *Yamato Bunka*, lxxv (March, 1986), pp. 29–38

B. Jungmann: *Die koreanische Landschaftsmalerei und die chinesische Che-Schule* (Stuttgart, 1992), pp. 105–6, 183–4, 242–4

BURGLIND JUNGMANN

Yi Chung-sŏp (*b* Pyŏngwŏn, South Pyŏng'an Province, 1916; *d* Seoul, 6 Sept 1956). Korean painter. He worked mainly in Western styles and media. He was taught by Im Yong-ryŏn (*b* 1901), who painted in the Western style, at Osan School in Chŏngju, North Chŏlla Province. In 1937 he was admitted to the Department of Western Painting in the Bunka Gakuin (Culture Academy), Tokyo, where he was introduced to new trends in Western painting. In 1940 he exhibited his work at a show sponsored by the Association of Creative Artists (Bijutsu Sōsakuka Kyōkai) in Tokyo, for which he was given a special award. In that year he and other Korean artists established the Korean Association of New Artists (Chosŏn Sin-Misulga Hyŏphoe) and continued to exhibit through that organization. He married a Japanese woman in 1945 and settled in Wŏnsan, Kangwŏn Province. During the Korean War (1950–53) his wife and two children went to Japan while he fought in the South Korean army. He died in 1956 of malnutrition and mental disorder.

Despite the fact that the last years of his life were marked by poverty and loneliness, he continued to paint and held two one-man shows, the first in T'ongyŏng, South Kyŏngsang Province, in 1953, the second in Seoul in 1955. His oil paintings, many of them executed on paper because he could not afford canvas, reflect the tormented soul of a man in a war-torn country. *White Bull* (1950; Seoul, Hongik U. Mus.; see Yun, p. 256, fig. 11) shows a strong influence of Fauvism in its vigorous brushstrokes, bold simplification and use of thick black lines. In *Couple* (1953; priv. col.; see Yun, p. 254, fig. 5) an outburst of emotion is expressed in the contortion of the two birds meeting in the air in a dramatic kiss. Other paintings display a more lyrical mood: for example, in *Peach Blossom Garden* (1953; priv. col.; see Yun, p. 249), naked babies are depicted clinging to the branches of a large peach tree in poses that recall the decoration applied to Koryŏ celadon-glazed wares (see, e.g., McKillop, p. 39). Despite the soft colours used in this painting, his strong brushstrokes and exaggerated forms come to the fore. Among his contemporaries Yi was revered as a painter

who combined modern techniques with ancient motifs in a fashion characteristic of 20th-century Korean painting.

BIBLIOGRAPHY

Yun Pŏm-mo: *Hanguk hyŏndae misul 100 nyŏn* [100 years of Korean modern art] (Seoul, 1984)

Hanguk yesul sajŏn [Dictionary of Korean Art] (Seoul, 1985)

E. McKillop: *Korean Art and Design*, London, V&A cat. (London, 1992)

Young-na Kim [Kim Yŏng-na]: 'Modern Korean Painting and Sculpture/Hanguk hyŏndae hoehwawa chogak', *Korean Art Tradition/Hanguk-ŭi yesul chŏnt-ong*, ed. Young Ick Lew [Ryu Yŏng-ik] (Seoul, 1993), pp. 151–200, pl. 14

YI SŎNG-MI

Yi dynasty. *See* CHOSŎN DYNASTY.

Yi Ha-ŭng (*b* Seoul, 1820; *d* Seoul, 1898). Korean prince regent, calligrapher and painter. When his second son acceded to the throne in 1863 as King Kojong (*reg* 1863–1907) he became Taewŏngun ('Prince regent'). He excelled in calligraphy and ink paintings of orchids. His early work shows the influence of KIM CHŎNG-HŬI, who praised Yi Ha-ŭng's ink orchid paintings as the best by a painter of his generation. In 1873 Yi Ha-ŭng retired from the regency and concentrated on calligraphy and painting. By his late fifties he had developed his own individual style of painting orchids in ink. He depicted the orchids against a plain background, making them long and thin, with razor-sharp tips. This style of representing orchids was adopted by such artists as Pang Yun-myŏng, Na Su-yŏn and Kim Ŭng-wŏn, and was very popular during the late Chosŏn period (1392–1910) and at the beginning of the Japanese colonial period (1910–45).

BIBLIOGRAPHY

Ch'oe Wan-su: *Ch'usajip* [Collected works of Kim Chŏng-hŭi] (Seoul, 1976)

——: 'Ch'usasŏp'ago' [A study of the Kim Chŏng-hŭi school of calligraphy], *Yonsongmunhwa*, xix (Seoul, 1980)

Yi In-mun [*ho* Kosong Yusu Kwandoin] (*b* 1745; *d* 1821). Korean painter. He was appointed a member of the Bureau of Painting (Tohwasŏ) and also served the court in a military position. Yi was a friend of Kim hong-do (*see* KIM (iv), (1)), the foremost artist in the Bureau at the time. Although Kim is more famous and his work is held in higher esteem, Yi's work shows an accomplished skill and refinement as well as an unusually wide range of styles. Until his sixties Yi focused on landscape painting, for example *Mountains and Rivers without End* (handscroll, ink and light colours on silk, h. 441 mm; Seoul, N. Mus.; see 1979–81 exh. cat., no. 238), which is painted in the style of the Chinese ORTHODOX SCHOOL and is regarded as one of the finest masterpieces of the end of the Chosŏn period (1392–1910). Towards the end of his life Yi painted genre scenes, for example *A Gathering of Four Friends* (see fig.), in which he used particularly expressive, bold brushstrokes contrasted with sharp, well-crafted calligraphy. The scene depicts a gathering of four scholars (one of whom is the artist), a theme popular in Chinese painting; it is perhaps for this reason that the scholars are shown in Chinese dress. Another of his representative late works is *Chatting near Pine Forest Valley* (ink and light colours on paper, 243×336 mm; Seoul, N. Mus.). Yi often used a complex *ho* that described him as a Daoist, an old pine tree and a flowing stream: Kosong Yusu Kwandoin.

Yi In-mun: *A Gathering of Four Friends*, hanging scroll, ink and light colours on paper, h. 865 mm, 1820 (Seoul, National Museum of Korea)

BIBLIOGRAPHY

5000 Years of Korean Art (exh. cat., ed. R.-Y. Lefebvre d'Argencé; San Francisco, CA, Asian A. Mus.; Seattle, WA, A. Mus.; Chicago, IL, A. Inst. and elsewhere; 1979–81)

HONG SŎN-P'YO

Yi In-no [*cha* Misu; childhood name Tŭggok] (*b* Inch-on, Kyŏnggi Province, 1152; *d* 1220). Korean literati painter, calligrapher and writer. He wrote the *P'ahanjip* (Chin. *Poxian ji*: 'Breaking the doldrums'), a collection of poems and miscellaneous stories in the *sihwa* (Chin. *shihua*) literary genre. Active in the Koryŏ period (918–1392), he was born into a well-to-do family; he became a monk but soon abandoned the religious life, passing the civil service examination in 1180. Because of his literary talent and excellence in calligraphy, he served in the Office of Compilation of History. None of his painting or calligraphy has survived, but he was supposed to have excelled in the cursive and clerical scripts and learned ink bamboo painting from An Ch'i-min, another literati painter of the Koryŏ period. According to a poem written by him on his own ink bamboo painting and recorded in the *P'ahanjip*, he considered himself an incarnation of WEN TONG, the Chinese ink bamboo painter of the Northern Song period (960–1127). In the late 12th century the literati painting

tradition had just been established in China, and through diplomatic exchanges Korean scholar–officials began to absorb the ink bamboo painting tradition of the Song period (960–1279). Yi In-no himself had been to China as secretary to an envoy. His interest in ink bamboo painting marks the early stages in the development of ink bamboo painting and, with it, literati painting theory in Korea.

WRITINGS

P'ahanjip [Breaking the doldrums] (1260), annotated Kor. trans. by Yu Chae-yŏng (Seoul, 1978)

BIBLIOGRAPHY

Kim Yŏng-yun, ed.: *Hanguk sŏhwa inmyŏng sasŏ* [Biographical dictionary of Korean painters and calligraphers] (Seoul, 1959), p. 33

YI SŎNG-MI

Yi In-sang [*ho* Nŭnghogwan] (*b* Pusan, Kyŏnggi Province, 1710; *d* Ŭmjuk, Kyŏnggi Province, 1760). Korean painter. Active in the later Chosŏn period, he was born into a noble family but as a descendant of a secondary son was barred from some social positions. From his childhood, Yi enjoyed writing and painting. He moved to Seoul and passed the primary level of the state civil service examination in 1735. Thereafter he served as a petty official for the government. He was able to secure instruction in painting, adopting a style taken from contemporary Chinese masters of the Qing period (1644–1911). From his mid-thirties he liked to paint scenes on the outskirts of the regional centres to which he was posted in his official capacity. He often also depicted the discussions of literary men.

In 1752 he resigned from his official post of county magistrate following a disagreement with his senior and spent the rest of his life in retirement at a quiet place in the vicinity of Ŭmjuk known locally as Sŏlsŏng. During this final period he completed many compositions in which solitary men formed his main material. Anxious to heighten the literary atmosphere of his work, Yi created the technique of ink painting known as *sŏnyŏm*, in which water is applied to the paper first and ink laid over it before the water has dried. His style is unique, especially in the way he depicted pine trees and rocky crags and in the clear, smooth rendering of light. His paintings influenced not just such later literary painters as Yi Yun-yŏng and Yun Che-hong but also such court painters as Kim Hong-do and Yi Chae-gwan.

Yi In-sang was greatly respected by later generations for his abilities in the 'three excellences' of painting, calligraphy and poetry. As a calligrapher he had a high reputation for his seal script (Kor. *chŏnsŏ*) and clerical script (*yesŏ*) and was also esteemed for his seal engraving (*chŏn'gak*). Representative works are *Viewing the Waterfall from under the Pine Tree* (hanging scroll, ink on paper, 1172×526 mm) and *Pine Tree in the Snow* (fan, light colour on paper, 238×632 mm), both in the National Museum of Korea, Seoul.

BIBLIOGRAPHY

M. Takaaki and Ch'oe Sun-u: 'Richō no suibokuga' [Ink paintings of the Chosŏn dynasty], *Suiboku bijutsu taikei*, suppl. ii (Tokyo, 1977)

5000 Years of Korean Art (exh. cat., ed. R.-Y. Lefebvre d'Argencé; San Francisco, CA, Asian A. Mus.; Seattle, WA, A. Mus.; Chicago, IL, A. Inst. and elsewhere; 1979–81), p. 182, pl. 225

Treasures from Korea (exh. cat., intro. R. Goepper; ed. R. Whitfield; London, BM, 1984), p. 204, pl. 240

'Yi In-sang hoehwa-ŭi hyŏngsŏnggwa pyŏnch'ŏn' [The formation and changes of Yi In-sang's painting style], *Kogo Misul*, clxi (March 1984)

HONG SŎN-P'YO

Yijae (i). *See* KONGMIN.

Yijae (ii). *See* KWŎN TON-IN.

Yi Kang-so. *See* KANG SO LEE.

Yi Ku. *See* MUNJONG.

Yi Kwang-sa (*b* Seoul, 1704; *d* Sinji Island, South Chŏlla Province, 1777). Korean painter, calligrapher and poet. Born the son of a government minister during the Chosŏn period (1392–1910), he was involved in the conspiracy of the Soron faction in 1755 and was exiled to Kilju in North Hamgyŏng Province. In 1762 he was transferred to Sinji Island, where he eventually died. He studied calligraphy with Yun Sun (1680–1741) and produced a compilation of the calligraphy of earlier Korean calligraphers, *Wŏngo chipson* ('Compilation of manuscripts'), as well as a systematic account of the theory of calligraphy. His own calligraphy, for example *Haengso sa'ŭn si* (Seoul, Korea U. Mus.), a four-line verse in running script, had a considerable influence on the calligraphy of future generations. He painted portraits in the style of the SOUTHERN SCHOOL, for example *Portrait of a High Priest* (1746; silk; 242×223 mm; Seoul, Cent. Stud. Kor. A., Kansong A. Mus.), while his landscapes reflect the influence of the WU SCHOOL. He also painted plants and insects.

BIBLIOGRAPHY

Yu Pok-yŏl: *Hanguk hoehwa taegwan* [Pageant of Korean painting] (Seoul, 1969)

Im Ch'ang-sun, ed.: *Sŏye* [Calligraphy] (1981), vi of *Hanguk-ŭi mi* [Beauties of Korea] (Seoul, 1977–85)

Yi Kye-ho [*ho* Hyuhyudang] (*b* 1574). Korean painter. Active in the middle of the Chosŏn period (1392–1910), he is said to have learnt to paint from Hong Sik (1559–1610), who served as minister to the Bureau of Painting (Tohwasŏ). Yi Kye-ho was the most celebrated painter of his time in the depiction of vines and is known to have been proud of his accomplishment. His paintings show small, round fruit on vines full of wide-open leaves arranged in fan shapes. His contrast of dark and light, entirely dependent on shades of ink, and his gentle, lively brushwork offer much natural beauty to his compositions. He developed his style under the influence of Hwang Chip-chung, also a painter of grapes and vines, and was followed by Hong Su-ju (1642–1704). His style was later taken over by Ch'oe Sŏk-hwan (*b* 1808). Representative works, all entitled *Grapevine*, are held at various museums in Seoul (N. Mus., Ehwa Women's U. Mus. and Cent. Stud. Kor. A., Kansong A. Mus.).

BIBLIOGRAPHY

An Hwi-jun: *Hanguk hoehwasa* [History of Korean painting] (Seoul, 1980)

Korean Paintings and Calligraphy of the National Museum of Korea: A Comprehensive Catalogue, ii (Seoul, 1992)

Yi Myŏng-gi (*fl c.* 1791–6). Korean painter. Active in the Chosŏn period (1392–1910), he was born into a family of *hwawŏn*, artists of the Bureau of Painting (Tohwasŏ). In 1791 he was himself appointed a court artist. For the completion of a portrait of the king he was given the rank of *ch'albang*, a post which gave him charge over a provincial office. In 1796 he collaborated with the painter Kim Hong-do to produce a portrait (colour on silk, 1480×730 mm; Seoul, N. Mus.) of the scholar Sŏ Chik-su (*b* 1735). Yi painted the face, combining realistic depiction with a lively interpretation of Sŏ's scholarly elegance. In comparison to his portraiture Yi's landscapes are not so original, merely attaining the level of picturesque. Examples are *Reading a Book under a Pine Tree* (1038×495 mm; Seoul, Ho-am A. Mus.) and *Looking at a Waterfall* (988×471 mm; Seoul, N. Mus.).

BIBLIOGRAPHY

An Hwi-jun: *Hanguk hoehwasa* [History of Korean painting] (Seoul, 1980), p. 813

Ch'oe Sun-u, ed.: *Hanguk hoehwa* [Korean painting], ii (Seoul, 1981)

An Hwi-jun, ed.: *Sansuhwa* [Landscape painting], ii (1982), xii of *Hanguk-ŭi mi* [Beauties of Korea] (Seoul, 1977–85), p. 243

HONG SŎN-P'YO

Yi'nan [I-nan]. County in south-central Shandong Province, China, where a large Han-period (206 BC–AD 220) tomb decorated with engravings, low reliefs and sculpture was found in 1953. The tomb (max. 8.70×7.55 m), in Yi'nan has attracted much interest because of its relatively naturalistic engravings.

Built of fine, dark grey limestone which, when polished, provides an excellent surface for engraving, the tomb consists of a forechamber, middle chamber and rear chamber along a roughly north–south axis, with five smaller side chambers. A post-and-lintel system is employed throughout, with cantilevered ceilings (*see* CHINA, fig. 54). This type of plan is common among late Han tombs discovered in Jiangsu and Shandong provinces. The tomb at Yi'nan is unusual, however, in that its stone columns and beams were carved to resemble the ornamented brackets and other features of wooden architecture. Since the tomb had been plundered, it yielded no artefacts of consequence.

Thin-line engraving was the most commonly used sculptural technique. Sometimes the ground was lightly chipped to enhance the contrast between figure and ground. This technique is typical of the more lavishly decorated Han tombs, as at Dahuting, in Mi xian, Henan Province, and is a sign of extraordinary expense. Because the figures at Yi'nan are more naturalistic than those at the Wu family shrines, Jiaxiang County, Shandong Province, they were once thought to date to the 3rd century AD or later (see Hsio-yen Shih). However, still more naturalistic engravings were subsequently found in other late Han tombs, for example at Dahuting. Moreover, the Yi'nan tomb has much in common with Han tombs associated with scholar-officials: structure, ground-plan, mural scheme, subject-matter drawn from the Chinese classics, and the sculptors' habit of separating different parts of the body with straight lines or contrasting patterns. Such evidence favours a late Han date for the tomb.

Lintels, columns and brackets are adorned with cloud scrolls, dragons and spirits intended to bless and protect the husband and wife who occupied the tomb. Along the walls are 73 compositions over 42 stones, which suggest something of the male occupant's life and concerns. Scenes of battle and swordplay have led some to suggest he had high-ranking military status. References to historical topics at the Yi'nan tomb, such as Zhao Dun's opposition to the tyrant Duke Ling, or Laozi's advice to Confucius regarding service under corrupt governments, also occur at other monuments erected by scholar-officials during this period. Such topics evoke the tensions between a corrupt central government and discontented provincial officials during the late Han period. Similar themes are alluded to in the representation of a variety of miraculous omens, such as the two-headed bird prominently placed on a bracket in the central chamber. Inscriptions at the Wu Liang shrine explicitly link such omens with concern over corruption in government. Both this imagery and the friezes of official carriages and lavish entertainment scenes support the supposition that the tomb belonged to a high-ranking official.

BIBLIOGRAPHY

Zeng Zhaoyu: *Yi'nan gu huaxiangshi mu fajue baogao* [Report on the excavation of the decorated tomb at Yi'nan] (Shanghai, 1956)

Hsio-yen Shih: 'I-nan and Related Tombs', *Artibus Asiae*, xxii (1959), pp. 277–312

Nagahiro Toshio: *Kandai gazō no kenkyu* [A study of Han-period pictorial art] (Tokyo, 1965), pp. 24–9

M. J. Powers: *Art and Political Expression in Early China* (New Haven, 1991), pp. 121–2, 266–8, 371–3

MARTIN J. POWERS

Ying'a. See DAI BENXIAO.

Yingcai. See under FAMILLE ROSE.

Yingchuan. See OKUDA EISEN.

Yi Nyŏng (*fl* first half of the 12th century). Korean painter. A native of Chŏnju (now in North Chŏlla Province), he was one of the first known landscape painters of the Koryŏ period (918–1392). Although he is sometimes referred to as the greatest painter of this period, very few facts are known about his life and virtually nothing definite is known about his art, as none of his highly praised paintings has survived. During the early years of the reign of King Injong (*reg* 1122–46), Yi Nyŏng accompanied the diplomat Yi Cha-dŏk to China, where he is said to have achieved great fame at the court of the Northern Song emperor Huizong (*reg* 1100–25), himself a painter and patron of the arts. The *Koryŏsa* ('History of Koryŏ') mentions that Yi Nyŏng served in the Hanlin painting academy (*see* CHINA, §V, 4(i)(b)–(c)). After his return to Korea he founded a school of painters. This produced a handful of students, who are said to have continued his style. Yi Nyŏng was repeatedly called to the Inner Palace in the Koryŏ capital of Kaesŏng to render his services as a painter to the throne. His connection with the Northern Song court doubtless helped to secure him his enduring fame. The titles of two of his paintings survive: *View of the Chesŏng River* and *Scene of the Southern Gate of Ch'ŏnsu Monastery*. It may be supposed that Yi Nyŏng painted in the mannered, formalized style characteristic of the professional landscape painters of the painting academy in Kaifeng, the Northern Song capital. Yi Nyŏng's son, Yi Kwang-p'il, was also known as a painter, but none of his works has survived.

BIBLIOGRAPHY

Yŏlchŏn [Biographies], ch. 35 of *Koryŏsa* [History of Koryŏ] (completed 1451)

Lee Ki-baik [Yi Ki-baek]: *Hanguksa sillon* (Seoul, 1961, rev. 1967 and 1976); Eng. trans. by E. W. Wagner with E. J. Schultz as *A New History of Korea* (Cambridge, MA, and London, 1984), p. 136

An Hwi-jun: *Hanguk hoehwasa* [History of Korean painting] (Seoul, 1980), pp. 82, 380

Chin Hong-sŏp, ed.; *Hanguk misulsa charyo chipsŏng* [Collected references to Korean art history], i (Seoul, 1987), pp. 284–5, 466

HENRIK H. SØRENSEN

Yinyuan Longqi. See INGEN RYŪKI.

Yi Pul-hae [*cha* T'aesu] (*b* 1529). Korean painter. The few biographical references make it difficult to decide whether he should be considered a court or a literati painter. The art historian An Hwi-jun includes him among the latter on the basis of a passage in which he is listed together with the vice-director of the Bureau of Painting (Tohwasŏ) Sin Se-rim (1521–83) as a well known follower of the scholar–painter Kang Hŭi-an. In earlier texts Yi Pul-hae is also compared to the 15th-century court painter An Kyŏn. Yi Tong-ju sees a stylistic link between his paintings and a scroll (Boston, MA, Mus. F.A.) carrying the seal Bunsei (Jap.; Kor. Munch'ŏng). These comparisons with Kang Hŭi-an and the landscape painter Munch'ŏng suggest that Yi Pul-hae may have been a follower of a 15th-century Korean tradition influenced by Chinese painting of the Southern Song period (960–1279). An album leaf bearing the seal of Yi Pul-hae (Seoul, N. Mus.; see Kim, Choi and Im, pl. 51) depicts a scholar viewing the scene from a vantage-point. Behind him looms, as if from an unfathomable depth, an immense mountain peak. The composition of the picture as well as the broad, washed-over surface of the mountain, the structure of which is suggested only by the contours, recall the style of Xia Gui, the Chinese court painter of the Southern Song Academy. The trees enveloping the small figure with their branches like 'crabs' claws' are, on the other hand, closer to the tradition of the Chinese painters Li Cheng and Guo Xi of the Northern Song period (960–1127) whose style was taken up and subsequently adapted by An Kyŏn and his followers. Two further album leaves (Seoul, priv. cols) borrow elements from the Zhe school of the Chinese Ming period (1368–1644). The Zhe school style was adopted in Korea towards the mid-16th century and came to be widely accepted through the work of such scholar–painters as Kim Che and Yi Kyŏng-yun.

BIBLIOGRAPHY

Kim Yŏng-yun, ed.: *Hanguk sŏhwa inmyŏng saso* [Biographical dictionary of Korean painters and calligraphers] (Seoul, 1959, 3/1978), p. 134

Yi Tong-ju: *Ilbon sok-ŭi hanhwa* [Korean painting in Japan] (Seoul, 1973), pp. 84–6

An Hwi-jun: 'Han'guk chŏlp'a hwap'ung-ŭi yŏn'gu' [A study on Korean painting of the Zhe school style], *Misul Charyo*, xx (1977), p. 38

Kim Won-yong [Kim Wŏn-yong], Choi Sun U [Ch'oe Sun-u] and Im Chang-soon [Im Chang-sun]: *Paintings*, ii of *The Arts of Korea* (Seoul, 1979)

An Hwi-jun, ed.: *Sansuhwa* [Landscape painting], i (1980), xi of *Hanguk-ŭi mi* [Beauties of Korea] (Seoul, 1977–85), pp. 197–8

B. Jungmann: *Die koreanische Landschaftsmalerei und die chinesische Che-Schule* (Stuttgart, 1992), pp. 181–2

BURGLIND JUNGMANN

Yiran Xingrong. See ITSUNEN SHŌYŪ.

Yiroulas. See under NAXOS, §2(i) and (ii).

Yirawala [Yirrawala; Yirwala] (*b* Liverpool River region, N. Territory, 1903; *d* 17 April 1976). Australian Aboriginal painter. He was probably the best-known exponent of the style of bark painting associated with Western Arnhem Land. His language group was Kunwinjku, and he belonged to the clan Born. In his youth he moved to Croker Island. Here his works, along with those of such artists as Jimmy Midjawmidjaw, with whom he lived for a while, were collected by the French anthropologist Karel Kupka in 1963. Subsequently, Yirawala developed a strong friendship with the art dealer Sandra Holmes, who became his primary dealer for the rest of his career. Holmes was able to establish Yirawala's reputation through a number of one-man exhibitions in Australian cities. These led to a number of art prizes, travel overseas and the award of an MBE in 1971. In the early 1970s Yirawala undertook to paint for Holmes an extensive collection of works relating to ceremonial themes. These consist of paintings of important creator figures, such as *Lumah-lumah, the Big Maraian Man* (*c.* 1971; Canberra, N.G.). The collection of 139 works was eventually bought by the Australian National Gallery in Canberra; at that stage it comprised the largest number of works by an Aboriginal artist in any public institution. The paintings reveal Yirawala's mastery of the artistic techniques used by artists from Western Arnhem Land to show the transformative potential of these creator beings. Paintings such as *Gurgurr and his Dog Mulutji* (*c.* 1971; Canberra, N.G.) vary the outline form of the figure to suggest affinities with other species or objects, in this case the shape of the full moon. Some paintings consist of purely geometric body design patterns and others combine these with figurative forms.

BIBLIOGRAPHY
S. Holmes: *Yirawala: Artist and Man* (Brisbane, 1972)
K. Kupka: *Peintres aborigènes d'Australie* (Paris, 1972), pp. xxxvii–cxi

LUKE TAYLOR

Yi Sang-bŏm [*ho* Ch'ŏngjŏn] (*b* Sŏksong, South Ch'ungch'ŏng Province, 1899; *d* 1978). Korean painter. He was born the youngest of three sons of a poor farming family. Because of his painting talent he was admitted in 1914 to the Sŏhwa misulwŏn (Academy of Calligraphy and Painting) to study under An Chung-sik and Cho Sŏk-jin. In 1923, together with other artists, including KIM ŬN-HO, PYŎN KWAN-SIK and No Su-hyŏn (1899–1978), Yi founded the Tong'yŏnsa (Association of Like-minded Students) for artists to study old and modern art together. He was also a member of the Sŏhwa hyŏphoe, an artists' organization founded in 1918, making his début as a painter at its first exhibition in 1921. In 1922 when the Japanese colonial government initiated an annual exhibition, the Chosŏn misul chŏllamhoe (Korean Art Exhibition), Yi began submitting his work, and from 1924 his submissions received the grand prize every year for ten years. He eventually became a member of the panel of judges. Because of his particularly close association with this exhibition sponsored by the Japanese colonial government he was harshly criticized after 1945 for having been pro-Japanese. However, as one of the first generation of modern Korean painters he had an enormous influence on contemporary painters in Korea.

Yi Sang-bŏm specialized in landscape painted in ink and light colours, showing ordinary Korean scenery with rice paddies, gentle hills, winding roads, thatched houses, a solitary farmer with his ox, or a lone woodcutter. He tended to prefer a long, horizontal format, but his compositions were modern in conception, owing little to the traditional handscroll despite the use of traditional media (e.g. *Morning*, ink and light colours on paper, 0.69×2.73 m; 1954; Seoul, N. MOMA; see Young-na Kim, p. 159). Unlike earlier works, in which he used meticulous brush-strokes in order accurately to portray lonely scenes of the Korean countryside, his works after 1950, such as *Landscape* (Seoul, Ho-am A. Mus.; see 1979–81 exh. cat., pl. 255), are characterized by complex, textured strokes and a strong contrast between light and dark that creates a refreshing effect.

BIBLIOGRAPHY
Yu Pok-yŏl: *Hanguk hoehwa taegwan* [Pageant of Korean painting] (Seoul, 1969), p. 1065
Yi Kyŏng-sŏng: *Hyŏndae misul* [Modern art] (1975), xv of *Hanguk misul chŏnjip* [Arts of Korea] (Seoul, 1973–5), pp. 4–9, 22–5, 136–7
O Kwang-su: *Hanguk hyŏndae hwaga ship'in* [Ten modern Korean painters] (Seoul, 1977), pp. 87–97
5000 Years of Korean Art (exh. cat., ed. R.-Y. Lefebvre d'Argencé; San Francisco, CA, Asian A. Mus.; Seattle, WA, A. Mus.; Chicago, IL, A. Inst.; and elsewhere; 1979–81)
Ch'ŏngjŏn kwa Sojŏng [Yi Sang-bŏm and Pyŏn Kwan-sik] (exh. cat., Seoul, Hyŏndae A.G.; Tongsanbang A.G.; 1985)
Young-na Kim [Kim Yŏng-na]: 'Modern Korean Painting and Sculpture/Hanguk hyŏndae hoehwawa chogak', *Korean Art Tradition/Hanguk-ŭi yesul chŏnt'ong*, ed. Young Ick Lew [Ryu Yŏng-ik] (Seoul, 1993), pp. 151–200

KIM KUMJA PAIK

Yi Sang-chwa (*fl c.* 1543–6). Korean painter. He was born into a servant family but showed great artistic skills. He was rewarded by a special royal order that appointed him to membership as a court painter (*hwawŏn*) of the Bureau of Painting (Tohwasŏ). Yi was especially famed for portraiture. In 1543 this reputation led to his nomination by the Office of Rites to take charge of illustrations for a book on virtuous women. A set of studies of Buddhist *arhat*s or disciples has been attributed to him (*see* KOREA, fig. 36). In 1546, in recognition of his portraits, he was awarded a minor honorary title. None of his compositions has been positively identified. Only a few pieces said to be by Yi survive; these reflect quite clearly the painting style of the Chinese Southern Song period (1127–1279). One such is *Walking under Pine Trees* (hanging scroll, ink and light colours on silk, 1.97×0.82 m; Seoul, N. Mus.; see Kim, Choi and Im, pl. 48).

BIBLIOGRAPHY
Kim Won-yong [Kim Wŏn-yong], Choi Sun U [Ch'oe Sun-u] and Im Chang-soon [Im Ch'ang-sun], eds: *Paintings*, ii of *The Arts of Korea* (Seoul, 1979), pp. 179–80, pl. 48
Hwi-joon Ahn [An Hwi-jun]: 'Traditional Korean Painting/Hanguk chŏnt'ong hoehwa-ŭi byŏnch'ŏn', *Korean Art Tradition/Hanguk-ŭi yesul chŏnt'ong*, ed. Young Ick Lew [Ryu Yŏng-ik] (Seoul, 1993), pp. 99–100
Koryŏ yŏngwŏnhan mi [Eternal beauty of Koryŏ] (exh. cat., Seoul, Ho-am A. Mus., 1993), pp. 104–5, 244, pls 32–6

HONG SŎN-P'YO

Yi Sŏng-min [*cha* Tŏkhu; *ho* Sojae] (*b* Chŏnju, North Chŏlla Province, 1718; *d* 1777). Korean painter. He was a member of the Bureau of Painting (Tohwasŏ). None of his works now exist, but his speciality seems to have been bird-and-animal paintings. In 1748 he accompanied the Korean envoy to Japan, where he is recorded as having executed a painting of pine and bamboo on silk. His son Chong-hyŏn was also a painter in the Bureau of Painting and excelled in landscape, and grass-and-insect and flower paintings. During the later part of the Chosŏn period (1392–1910) it was quite common for a family to be engaged in working for the Bureau of Painting for several generations.

BIBLIOGRAPHY

O. Asaoka: *Koga bikō* [Handbook of classical painting] (n.p., *c.* 1845–53); rev. K. Ota as *Zōtei Koga bikō* [Presentation of the Handbook of classical painting] (Tokyo, 1904), i, p. 2229

Kim Yŏng-yun, ed.: *Hanguk sŏhwa inmyŏng sasŏ* [Biographical dictionary of Korean painters and calligraphers] (Seoul, 1959), p. 340

Yu Pok-ryŏl: *Hanguk hoehwa taegwan* [Pageant of Korean painting] (Seoul, 1969), pp. 491, 521

YI SŎNG-MI

Yi Su-mun [Sumun; Rishūbun] (*fl* 15th century). Korean painter. He was better known in Japan, where he arrived in 1424, than in his native Korea. He is said to have been the founder of the SOGA school of painting in Japan. Certainly, together with Munch'ŏng, another painter of Korean origin active in Japan, he was an important figure in this school. His Korean style greatly influenced Japanese ink paintings and his works are preserved largely in Japan.

His typical subject-matter was landscapes, figures, flowers and birds, and ink bamboo drawings. He left several works, including the well-known *Screen of Ink Bamboo Paintings* (1424; ink on paper, 306×450 mm; priv. col.). This work is very typical of art of the early part of the Chosŏn period (1392–1910) in Korea. Its tenth or final leaf contains the signature *Sumun* along with an inscription stating that he painted it in Japan in 1424. Yi Su-mun is also remembered for several other works, including *Yo-yang Pavilion at Tung-ting Lake* (ink on paper, 1023×447 mm; priv. col.), *Doves on a Withered Tree* (destr. 1923) and a pair of six-fold screens, *Nine Elderly Scholars in Hs'ang-shan Mountain* (ink on paper, each screen 1455×316 mm; Hirata, Kinen-Kan).

BIBLIOGRAPHY

Yi Tong-ju: *Ilbon sok-ŭi hanhwa* [Korean painting in Japan] (Seoul, 1973)

An Hwi-jun: 'Sumun'gwa munch'ŏng-ŭi saengaewa jakpum' [The life and works of Sumun and Munch'ŏng], *Toksŏ Saenghwal*, xiv (1977), pp. 152–68

——: 'Chosŏn wangjo ch'ogi-ŭi hoehwawa ilbonshiljŏng shidae-ŭi sumu-khwa' [Paintings of the early Chosŏn dynasty and ink painting of the Japanese Muromachi period], *Hanguk hakpo*, iii (1978), pp. 2–21

——: *Hanguk hoehwasa* [History of Korean painting] (Seoul, 1980)

AHN HWI-JOON

Yivele, Henry. *See* YEVELE, HENRY.

Yixing. Town in Jiangsu Province, China, situated *c.* 5 km west of Lake Tai, famous during the Qing period (1644–1911) and the 20th century for its high-quality tewares made of red stoneware. Most of the kilns lie to the south of Yixing in the village of Dingshuzhen.

It has been tentatively established that the earliest purplish-red Yixing stonewares were produced as early as the Song period (960–1279); examples include two pear-shaped vessels with dark purplish stoneware body and partial olive-brown glaze, found in a disused well in Zhenjiang, Jiangsu Province, in 1961 (see Lo, p. 15).

Yixing-ware teapot in the shape of a water chestnut, h. 58 mm, *c.* 1983 (London, Victoria and Albert Museum); signed by Jiang Rong

Excavations in that area have revealed kilns as well as sherds of coarse red stoneware, including many fragments of teaware. The production of Yixing wares is first well documented for the mid-16th century (e.g. teapot from the tomb of the court official Wu Jing (*d* 1533); Nanjing, Jiangsu Prov. Mus.). It was at this time that the names of individual potters were first recorded. They adopted the practice for which Yixing became famous, that of marking their wares with their own signatures (e.g. hexagonal red stoneware teapot signed by Shi Dabin (*fl c.* 1550–1620), excavated from a Ming tomb; Yangzhou Mus.). This custom is unusual for Chinese kilns, where the potters usually remain anonymous artisans (*see* CHINA, §VII, 5). During the 18th and 19th centuries the practice continued, and in addition to the potters' names vessels were given the marks of those who commissioned the wares, with comments or poetic quotations (e.g. teapot made by Shen Xi (*fl* 1821–61) and inscribed by Zhuping, h. 76 mm; Hong Kong, Flagstaff House Mus. Teaware).

Yixing quickly gained a reputation for refined and collectable items. The kilns were patronized by scholars and gentlemen from the surrounding Jiangnan region, and items were exported to Japan and the West. This reputation has endured, and since the 1950s Yixing has turned out some of the best modern ceramics in China. Many of the older master potters, some of whom have been awarded the title Master of Arts and Crafts, learnt their skills during the 1930s, when a flourishing forgery business was run from Shanghai. In the late 20th century other younger craftsmen and women trained in a variety of techniques, from teapot-modelling to figure-carving (see 1988 exh. cat.).

Perhaps the most highly regarded type of Yixing stoneware is that commonly called *zisha* (Chin.: 'purple sand'), in reference to the deep purplish-brown colour produced when refined clay, with its high iron content, is fired under the correct conditions. When polished, this colour has a delicate bloom like that on grapeskin (e.g. teapot by Gong Chun (*fl* late 15th century–16th), h. 95 mm; Hong Kong, Flagstaff House Mus. Teaware). Yixing wares range in colour from brown, brick-red and ochre to grey, green and black tones. Almost the complete range of Yixing clay tones may be seen in some of the more elaborate pieces, such as teapots shaped as fruit and nuts (see fig.), while unusual colour combinations such as grey and yellow were used by some artisans (e.g. teapot in mango shape by Jiang Rong, h. 85 mm; 20th century; see 1988 exh. cat., pl. 7). A number of singular surface textures were achieved: quartz was sprinkled on for a 'gold dust' effect, and small pieces of rock were added for a 'pear skin' effect (e.g. cylindrical teapot, h. 85 mm; Ming period (1368–1644); Suzhou Mus.).

In addition to the unglazed ware, which is Yixing's most typical product, glazed and painted pieces were also produced. The glazes range from a high-fired mottled blue-green to a low-fired 'robin's-egg' glaze (e.g. bluish glazed cup, h. 89 mm; 17th century; London, V&A; and a 'robin's-egg' glazed teapot signed Danran Zhai (*fl* 18th century), h. 89 mm; Hong Kong, Flagstaff House Mus. Teaware). Overglaze enamel decoration was carried out in a range of bright, jazzy colours, reflecting the taste of working-class Chinese customers (e.g. enamelled wash-basin with green, black and turquoise flower scroll pattern, h. 80 mm; Nanjing, Jiangsu Prov. Mus.). Some pewter and silver encased pieces were also made (*see* CHINA, fig. 316).

Yixing wares were traditionally fired in saggars in dragon kilns (*see* CHINA, §VII, 2(ii)), though oil-fired, automated tunnel kilns are used in modern times. The reddish wares mature at 990° C while the purplish wares need at least 1100° C. The stonewares were traditionally modelled by hand from a single lump of clay and pared on the wheel when leather-hard, their handles, spouts etc. being luted on separately. This method of production is still used, although mass production with section moulds has become increasingly common.

BIBLIOGRAPHY
G. Hedley: 'I-Hsing Ware', *Trans. Orient. Cer. Soc.*, xiv (1936–7), pp. 70–86
T. Tse Bartholomew: *I-Hsing Wares* (New York, 1977)
——: 'Names Associated with I-Hsing Ware: An Index', *Bull. Orient. Cer. Soc. Hong Kong*, iv (1980), pp. 54–62
Yixing Pottery (exh. cat. by G. C. C. Tsang, Hong Kong, Mus. A., 1981)
K. S. Lo: *The Stonewares of Yi-Xing: From the Ming Period to the Present Day* (Hong Kong, 1986)
Zisha Chunhua: Innovations in Contemporary Yixing Pottery (exh. cat., Hong Kong, Flagstaff House Mus. Teaware, 1988–9)
P. N. Allen: 'Yixing Export Teawares of the 17th and 18th Centuries', *Trans. Orient. Cer. Soc.*, liii (1988–9), pp. 87–92
C. Chu and others: *The Art of the Yixing Potter: The K. S. Lo Collection, Flagstaff House Museum* (Hong Kong, 1990)

ROSE KERR

Yi Yŏng [*cha* Ch-ŏngji; *ho* Pihaedang, Maejuk-hŏn, Nang-gan-kŏsa] (*b* 1418; *d* 1453). Korean calligrapher, painter, poet and collector. Also known as Prince Anp'yŏng, he was the third son of King SEJONG. His talents in poetry, painting and calligraphy earned him the title of 'three excellences'. He sponsored many gatherings of scholars, poets and artists in his studio and became the major patron of AN KYŎN, who painted the famous *Dream Visit to the Peach Blossom Land* (1447; Tenri, Cent. Lib.) based on a dream that Yi Yŏng had related to him. Prince Anp'yŏng's collection of Korean and Chinese paintings must have served as inspiration for many contemporary painters. Its contents are known thanks to the *Hwagi* ('Notes on painting') section of the statesman Sin Suk-ju's *Pohanjae chip* ('Collected writings of Pohanjae [Sin Suk-ju]'). This is a valuable record, unique in that no other catalogue of painting collections of the Chosŏn period is known. The *Hwagi* lists 189 paintings and 33 items of calligraphy, mainly by Chinese painters and calligraphers of the Song (960–1279) and Yuan (1279–1368) periods, along with about 30 paintings by An Kyŏn. Of the Chinese paintings, 17 by Guo Xi, the 11th-century landscape painter, form the single largest group by one painter. The size of this group helps to explain the widespread vogue in Korea during the 15th and 16th centuries for works executed in the styles of Guo Xi and Li Cheng, another influential landscape painter of the 10th century. An Kyŏn's *Dream Visit to the Peach Blossom Land* is perhaps most representative of this trend in Korean painting.

In calligraphy, Yi Yŏng followed the style of the Chinese calligrapher Zhao Mengfu, known as *Songsŏlch'e* ('Song Xue's style') after Zhao's pen-name. The best example of this can be seen in Yi's colophon to the *Dream Visit* (*see* KOREA, §V). The elegance and regularity of his small regular script, as used in this instance, eventually led to its adoption for the metal printing types called *kyŏngja-ja* and *imsin-ja*, named after the designation of the cyclical years in which they were made. Yi Yŏng's strong personality is reflected in another work, *Touip'yŏn*, a small album of poems of the Tang period (618–907) now surviving only in a woodblock-printed version. The characters look so much more expansive and full of vigour that one doubts whether this work is indeed by the same person who wrote the small regular script in the colophon on An Kyŏn's work. Several stelae written by Yi also survive, one of which is the tombstone of his father.

BIBLIOGRAPHY
Kim Yŏng-yun, ed.: *Hanguk sŏhwa inmyŏng sasŏ* [Biographical dictionary of Korean painters and calligraphers] (Seoul, 1959), pp. 69–70
Kim Ki-sung: *Hanguk sŏyesa* [History of Korean calligraphy] (Seoul, 1975), pp. 396–402
An Hwi-jun: *Hanguk hoehwasa* [History of Korean painting] (Seoul, 1980), pp. 93–121
An Hwi-jun and Yi Pyŏng-han: *Mongyo towŏndo* [Dream visit to the peach blossom land] (Seoul, 1987)

YI SŎNG-MI

Ykens [Eykens; Ijkens], **Frans** (*b* Antwerp, 1601; *d* Antwerp, before 1693). Flemish painter. In 1613–14 he was apprenticed to his uncle, the flower and still-life painter Osias Beert I, and he became a Master at Antwerp in 1630. According to his own declaration (1641), Ykens travelled in Provence after his apprenticeship, staying at Aix and Marseille. He married in 1635, purchased a house in 1651 and made a will in 1666. Most of his work is signed.

Ykens's still-life and flower paintings were executed in a number of styles and formats over a long career. Under the influence of Daniel Seghers, he painted many garlands of flowers surrounding votive images by other artists, using cartouches, putti and fruits to vary the composition (versions, Oxford, Ashmolean; Paris, Louvre; Ghent, Mus. S. Kst.). He also painted bouquets of flowers in glass vases in the manner of Seghers and Jan Philip van Thielen (1618–67); these tend occasionally to sparseness and a slightly sombre effect, but variations in quality throughout

Frans Ykens: *Breakfast-piece*, 1636 (Ghent, Koninklijk Academie voor Schone Kunsten)

his work make assessment difficult. Ykens's *Breakfast-piece* of 1636 (Ghent, Kon. Acad. S. Kst.; see fig.) seems indebted to Willem Claesz. Heda; porcelain bowls of fruit to Beert and Jacob Hulsdonck (1582–1647); and larger-scale works to Frans Snyders. These last are among Ykens's most impressive works, for example the large panel 1.25 m in width combining a basket of fruit with a flower bouquet and dead birds on a wooden table-top (sold Monaco, Christie's, 7 Dec 1987). This elaborate composition is well arranged, the brushwork is characteristically lively in the Flemish manner and the bouquet fully developed. Six flower-pieces by Ykens are listed in the Rubens inventory, doubtless better examples than the weak, derivative works not uncommon in his output. During the 1640s he had at least one pupil. His niece Catharina Ykens (*b* 1659; *fl* 1688) was also a painter.

BIBLIOGRAPHY
M. L. Hairs: *Les Peintres flamands de fleurs au XVIIe siècle* (Brussels, 1955)
E. Greindl: *Les Peintres flamands de nature morte au XVIIe siècle* (Brussels, 1956)
A Prosperous Past: The Sumptuous Still-life in the Netherlands, 1600–1700 (exh. cat. by S. Segal, Delft, Stedel. Mus. Prinsenhof; Cambridge, MA, Fogg; Fort Worth, TX, Kimbell A. Mus.; 1988)

PETER MITCHELL

Yōboku. *See* KANŌ, (14).

Yogyakarta [Jogjakarta; Jokjakarta; Djogdjakarta; Djokjakarta]. Indonesian city on the River Code in southern Central Java. A few kilometres to the south are Kerta, the capital of Sultan Agung of Mataram (*reg* 1613–45), destroyed by fire in 1634, and Plered, the capital of Sultan Amangkurat I (*reg* 1645–77), abandoned in 1680. The Mataram court was re-established in Kartasura, near Surakarta to the north, but disputes over succession led in 1755 to the division of the kingdom into two and the foundation of the two sultanates of Surakarta and Yogyakarta, the latter under the rule of Sultan Hamengkubuwono I (Mangkubumi). The city can be divided into two more or less concentric parts, the sultan's palace (*kraton*), within its grounds, and the town around it. The palace was sacked by the British in 1812 and largely rebuilt from 1814 (see fig.). There remain, however, several parts from the 18th century; the most complete and the only dated one is the brick Masjid Selo (Stone Mosque), built in 1782. This small mosque (12 m long) serves as a prayer room. The interior is unadorned; externally the wall has a slightly projecting cornice, and the roof has imitation wooden tiles.

The same decorative principles can be found in the most charming part of the palace, the Taman Sari (Perfumed Garden). This was probably begun at the beginning of Sultan Mangkubumi's reign in Yogyakarta, but because of numerous restorations it cannot be precisely dated. The garden contains many enclosures and pools, some with islands, and about 50 buildings of various kinds, some very large; that on the island Kenongo has a façade 70 m long. The island could be reached only by two underwater passages lit by lantern towers rising above the surface of

Yogyakarta, palace, entrance to the main dining-room, rebuilt from 1814

the water. Halfway along one of these passages is a mosque (Sumur Gemuling) shaped like a ring, built on two levels, the lower one entirely below the water-level of the pool. In the centre of the mosque is a well, above which is a small platform formed by two arches supporting stairways; another flight of stairs leads off to the upper level of the mosque. Although most of the buildings, like the Masjid Selo, are devoid of decoration, there are some interesting exceptions: the pavilions marking the entrance and the Fountain of Youth, below the main level of the garden, have screens decorated with stucco reliefs on a brick base representing trees in which are frolicking birds; the originals were probably painted. The palace itself, consisting of juxtaposed enclosures, open pavilions and some closed buildings, is much more marked by the restoration of 1814. The buildings mostly combine forms of two different origins, traditional Javanese and 19th-century classical Western architecture. The combination is sometimes very successful, with Roman Doric or Tuscan orders juxtaposed with radiating Javanese beam-work, or long galleries with a roof supported by cast-iron European pillars and balustrades embellished with serpents (*nāga*), a traditional Javanese decorative motif.

In the city and its immediate environs are several other palaces. That at Banguntapan was immense, covering over 50 ha. All that remains is the Goa Suleiman (Suleiman's Cave), the central part of a garden below a pool. The cave was reached by passing under the pool through a subterranean passage similar to those at Taman Sari. In the interior of the cave was a bathing-place, with doors decorated with stucco trees and birds. The pools were fed by fountains in the shape of Garuda (the fabulous bird

mount of Vishnu). The palace of Warung Boto, of lesser importance, also utilizes water effects. The Belgian painter Antoine Payen (1785–1853) stayed in this palace, which was already partially ruined, during his visit to Yogyakarta in 1825. The palaces of the Pakualam and Ambarvinangun are built on the same principles as that of the sultan, with numerous enclosures, pavilions and pools. In the early 20th century the Dutch remodelled the town; for the most part the old plan was kept, but empty spaces were filled with administrative and public buildings, sometimes of some architectural note, such as the Post Office or the National Bank (the work of Eduard Cuypens and Hulwith).

Yogyakarta was in many ways the cradle of modern Javanese art. The *kraton* maintains a troupe of traditional dancers and a *gamelan* orchestra, and Sultan Hamengkubuwono IX (*reg* 1939–88) encouraged painting by ordering canvases depicting important events in Indonesian history. Numerous modern painters, including some of the most celebrated modern artists such as Affandi (1910–88), Lian Sahar (*b* 1945), Amri (*b* 1938) and the painter and ballet master Bagong (*b* 1940) lived in Yogyakarta. The city's Gadjah Mada University has a school of architecture, and the Indonesian Institute of Arts (Institut Seni Indonesia), also in Yogyakarta, has faculties of performing arts and of art and design, including crafts (*see also* INDONESIA, §IX). On the square to the north of the *kraton* is the Sono Budoyo Museum, designed in 1935 by the Dutch architect Herman Thomas Karsten (1885–1945) and partly based on a traditional Indonesian design. The museum contains some fine sculptures from the 8th and 9th centuries and from nearby temples.

BIBLIOGRAPHY
M. C. Ricklefs: *Yogyakjarta under Sultan Mangkubumi, 1749–1792* (London, 1974)
J. Dumarçay: 'Le Taman Sari: Etude architecturale', *Bull. Ecole Fr. Extrême-Orient*, lxv (1978), pp. 589–624
M. C. Ricklefs: *A History of Modern Indonesia* (London, 1981)
M. Smithies: *Yogyakarta* (Singapore, 1986)

J. DUMARÇAY

Yokohama. Japanese city and capital of Kanagawa Prefecture, on the east coast of Tokyo Bay; it is the major port serving Tokyo. The earliest record of the name Yokohama dates from 1442; however, before a foreign treaty port was created at the site in 1859, Yokohama was an insubstantial fishing village with a population of *c.* 350. While Yokohama itself has virtually no history before the Meiji period (1868–1912), its proximity to the historical city of KAMAKURA has left it with the Buddhist temples Sōjiji and Shomyōji.

Modern Yokohama was created by the Tokugawa shogunate in response to pressure applied in 1853 by the US to open several Japanese ports to foreign trade. Yokohama was chosen because it was sufficiently removed from any existing ports and yet was close enough to the capital Edo (now Tokyo) to satisfy foreign demands. The original settlement was built on land that had earlier been reclaimed from swamps, and a new road and post station were built to link it to the main road leading to Edo. The foreign community formed an extra-territorial unit under non-Japanese control until 1899. Yokohama quickly became Japan's largest port and served as Edo's window on the world, specifically on European culture. The foreign settlers in Yokohama brought Western technology and culture, including Japan's first European-style brewery, daily newspaper, architecture, gas factory and gas lights, communication services and railway. The unfamiliar customs of Western and Chinese inhabitants in Yokohama became the subject-matter for a woodblock-print genre called *Yokohamae* ('Yokohama pictures'), which was popular from 1859 to the early 1860s (see fig.; *see also* JAPAN, §IX, 3(iii)(e)). The Western military bands and flags, horse-drawn buggies and dress depicted in the *Yokohamae* by Utagawa Sadahide (1807–73) called *Sunday in Yokohama* (undated; Yokohama, Kanagawa Prefect. Mus.) were typical of the subjects that intrigued contemporary Japanese.

The first buildings in Yokohama were constructed using traditional Japanese techniques and materials. However, most of the buildings erected after a major fire in 1862 reflected 19th-century European styles and used Western materials. One such was the Kanagawa Prefectural Museum (1904; formerly the head office of the Yokohama Specie Shōkin Bank), a German Neo-Baroque building of brick and stone with a corner dome. As trade flourished and the population swelled, foreign merchants moved away from the unhealthy lowlands to higher ground behind their former settlement on the coast. They were followed in 1861 by foreign diplomatic delegations; this greatly changed the pattern of settlement in and around Yokohama.

Yokohama was designated a city in 1889, by which time it had a population of over 120,000, but it did not begin to develop as a significant industrial area until 1914. The

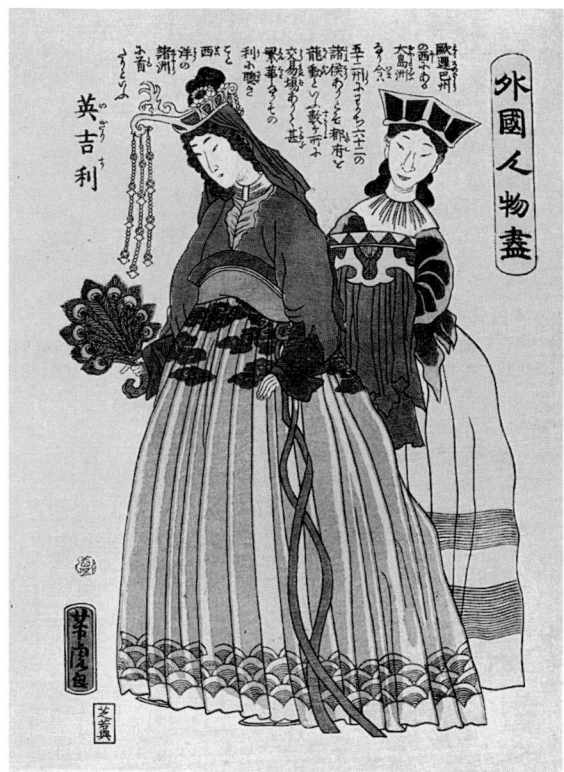

Woodblock print depicting Western customs and dress in Yokohama, 386×256 mm, 1861 (London, British Museum)

city suffered extensive damage in the Great Kantō Earthquake of 1923, and in World War II 80% of the city was destroyed by bombing and conflagration, but recovery was rapid. In 1986 Yokohama had an estimated three million inhabitants and a population density of nearly 7000 persons per sq. km. In the late 1960s, urban policies were put forward that would both preserve the city's surviving heritage and permit its development as a new international city. Parts of the foreign settlement and examples of early civic and commercial architecture remain in the old urban area.

The Shomyōji temple of the Shingon sect of Buddhism preserves a group of late Kamakura period (1185–1333) buildings, including an early 14th-century *Shakadō* (hall of Shaka, Skt Shakyamuni). The temple also houses the unique Kanazawa Library (Kanazawa Bunko), which was begun by the powerful warrior family Hōjō in the late 13th century and contains numerous Chinese and Japanese classics, *sūtra*s and Zen documents as well as sculpture, painting and calligraphy. Of particular importance are *maṇḍala*s and portraits of the Hōjō family and Shomyōji priests. Both these temple buildings were apparently rebuilt in the Edo period (1600–1868). The Zen temple of Sōjiji was originally constructed in Ishikawa Prefecture and moved to Yokohama in the late 19th century; it is one of the principal Japanese temples of the Sōtō sect. On the outskirts of the city is the Sankei'en, a park museum of traditional buildings transferred from other regions. Its existence is a telling illustration of the problem of maintaining a heritage, not only in Yokohama but in the country as a whole. The park includes such structures as the Rinshukaku (1649; moved 1915), a villa of a branch of the Tokugawa family, formerly located in the Kii Peninsula, and the Choshukaku (1634), a tea pavilion built by Tokugawa Iemitsu (1604–51).

BIBLIOGRAPHY

T. Etchū and Y. Ōto: *Nagasaki, Yokohama*, Edo jidai zushi [A pictorial history of the Edo period], xxv (Tokyo, 1976)

Kanazawa Bunko meihin zuroku [Illustrated catalogue of the famous pieces in the Kanazawa Library], Yokohama, Kanazawa Bunko cat. (Yokohama, 1981)

R. Tsuda and others: 'Kenchiku gaido Kanagawa ken' [An architectural guide: Kanagawa Prefecture], *Nihon Kenchiku Gakkai/J. Archit. & Bldg Sci.*, 1220 (1984), pp. 67–71

J. F. MORRIS

Yokoi Kinkoku [Yokoi Myōdō; Kōmori Dōjin] (*b* Kasanui, Ōmi Prov. [now Kusatsu, Shiga Prefect.], 1761; *d* Kasanui, 1832). Japanese priest and painter. The first half of his life is recorded in his autobiography. At the age of nine he became a Buddhist monk at the Jōdo (Pure Land) sect temple Sōkinji in Osaka. He left at the age of seventeen and went to Edo (now Tokyo), where he was admitted into the Jōdo temple Zōjōji in Shiba. Expelled later for frequenting the pleasure districts, he spent some years travelling. He returned to the Kyoto area and resumed his studies, later accepting a position as head priest at Gokurakuji on Mt Kinkoku, in northern Kyoto, from which he took his artist's name. In 1788 Gokurakuji was destroyed by fire, prompting Kinkoku to become an itinerant preacher and painter. He travelled as far as Nagasaki, staying at Jōdo temples and painting Buddhist deities and scenes from the life of Hōnen (1133–1212), the sect's founder. These are executed in a rather folksy version of the *Yamatoe* (traditional Japanese painting) style, using bright, opaque colours (e.g. set of four handscrolls, Shiga Prefect., Sōeji). Eventually Kinkoku settled in Nagoya where contact with a society of *haiku* poets inspired him to paint *haiga* (*haiku* paintings) in the style of Yosa Buson. He was introduced to Chō Gesshō (1772–1832), from whom he learnt to paint figures in the Maruyama–Shijō style (*see* JAPAN, §VI, 4(viii)) and landscapes strongly influenced by Goshun.

In 1804 Kinkoku became a follower of the mountain religion called Shugendō and participated in a pilgrimage to Mt Ōmine. Afterwards he received many requests for paintings depicting the sacred mountains he had climbed. He consequently turned increasingly to landscape subjects, and his style underwent a radical change. The personal style he developed was closely allied to the Chinese literati painting tradition (Jap. *Nanga* or *Bunjinga*, *see* JAPAN, §VI, 4(vi)(e)). Whereas broad applications of wash had dominated Kinkoku's earlier landscapes, after 1804, in such works as the hanging scroll *Scholar Overlooking a Rocky Promontory* (1809; New York, Mr and Mrs M. Falk priv. col.), line and texture strokes became his principal means of expression, since they better conveyed nature's powerful rhythms and internal vitality. Whereas previously Kinkoku had employed Yosa Buson's models for his figure paintings, he now found certain qualities in Buson's *Nanga* landscape style that harmonized with his own ideas. For example, he adapted Buson's system of rope-like, linear brushstrokes to describe mountain forms; however, Kinkoku used wetter and thicker brushstrokes and applied them more freely. He also simplified the rocks and trees, using fewer brushstrokes to define them. Kinkoku's dramatic compositions and frenzied brushwork evoke an intense and unsettling mood quite different from the more tranquil nature of Buson's paintings. While continuing to make pilgrimages throughout Japan to mountains revered by Shugendō followers, Kinkoku apparently remained in the Nagoya area until 1824, when he retired to his birthplace. He probably lived at a small temple, perhaps performing some priestly activities. His letters indicate that he continued to earn at least part of his income by selling or trading his paintings, which he promoted as outward expressions of his mystique, serving as amulets to repel evil spirits and bring good fortune.

WRITINGS

Kinkoku Shōnin goichidaiki [Biography of the monk Kinkoku] (n.d.); mod. Jap. trans. by S. Fujimori as *Kinkoku Shōnin gyōjōki* [Record of the monk Kinkoku's behaviour] (Tokyo, 1965)

BIBLIOGRAPHY

Kinkoku Dōjin ihō ten [Exhibition of monk Kinkoku] (exh. cat., Ōtsu, Shiga Prefect. Lake Biwa Cult. Cent., 1965)

Yokoi Kinkoku (exh. cat., Ōtsu, Shiga Prefect. Lake Biwa Cult. Cent., 1973)

S. Ishimaru: 'Yoko Kinkoku', *Kokoku & Bunka*, iv (1978), pp. 40–47

P. Fister: *Yokoi Kinkoku: The Life and Painting of a Mountain Ascetic* (diss., Lawrence, U. KS, 1983)

Yokoi Kinkoku ten (exh. cat., Ōtsu, Shiga Prefect. Lake Biwa Cult. Cent., 1984)

Kusatsu no bunjin gaka: Yokoi Kinkoku (exh. cat., Kusatsu, Shiga Prefect., Kusatsu A. and Cult. Cent., 1992)

Yokoi Kinkoku to Kurashiki (exh. cat., Kurashiki, Ōhara A. Mus., 1992)

PATRICIA FISTER

Yok'ong. *See* YI CHE-HYŎN.

Yokoo, Tadanori (*b* Nishiwaki, Hyōgo Prefect., 1936). Japanese stage designer, printmaker and painter. In 1960 he went to Tokyo and began his career as a stage designer. He was responsible for the design of such avant-garde drama as the Situation Theatre (Jōkyō Gekijō) of Jūrō Kara (*b* 1940) and the Upper Gallery (Tenjō Sajiki) of Shūji Terayama (1935–83). He also produced prints and in 1967 exhibited works in the *Word and Image* exhibition at MOMA, New York. Although he used photographs as the basis of his designs, Yokoo's prints drew upon aspects of traditional Japanese woodcuts that coincided with the style of contemporary Pop art, using in particular flat areas of colour and overtly sexual subject-matter (e.g. *X-sex IV*, screenprint, 1968; priv. col., see Yokoo, 1990, p. 13). In addition to his activity as a commercial designer, from the late 1960s he became interested in mysticism and psychedelic art, influenced in particular by travels in India in the 1970s. He produced posters with eclectic imagery similar to that of contemporary psychedelic 'underground' magazines. In 1980 he unexpectedly took up painting, prompted by a large-scale travelling exhibition of Picasso's work that he saw in New York. He painted in an expressionistic figurative style works that appeared in stage productions for Yukio Mishima (1925–70) and in productions of operas by Richard Wagner.

WRITINGS

Tadanori Yokoo: The Complete Prints (Tokyo, 1990)

BIBLIOGRAPHY
Tadanori Yokoo (exh. cat., Kyoto, Mun. Mus. A., 1966)
M. Glaser: *Tadanori Yokoo's Posters* (Kyoto, 1974)
Tadanori Yokoo (exh. cat., Amsterdam, Stedel. Mus., 1974) [broadsheet]
Exhibition of Works by Tadanori Yokoo (exh. cat., Okayama, Mus. A., 1980)
SHIN'ICHIRO OSAKI

Yokoyama, Taikan (*b* Mito, 18 Sept 1868; *d* Tokyo, 26 Feb 1958). Japanese painter. He graduated in 1893 from the painting department of the Tokyo School of Fine Arts. In 1898 Yokoyama participated in the formation of the Japan Art Institute in Tokyo and received theoretical instruction from Tenshin Okakura. He experimented resolutely and aimed to create a modern Japanese style (*Nihonga*; *see* JAPAN, §VI, 5(iii)), broadening the limits of expression in such works as *Eight Views of the Xiaoxiang* (1912; Tokyo, N. Mus.). The Japan Art Institute was closed temporarily in 1900, but Yokoyama was among its most prominent members after its revival in 1914, and he went on to produce such important works as *Lively Perpetual Motion* (1923; Tokyo, N. Mus. Mod. A.). His works range from a fluent, expressive style, in which line was subordinated to a predominant interest in colour, to a sublime style in which the use of black dominates. In 1937 he became a member of the Imperial Art Academy, and in the same year he was the first to receive the newly instigated Order of Cultural Merit.

BIBLIOGRAPHY
Yokoyama Taikan, Dai Nihon kaiga [Great Japanese paintings], 5 vols (1979–81)
YOSHIKAZU IWASAKI

Yolande of Aragon. *See* ANJOU, §II(3).

Yŏllo. *See* YUN, (3).

Yoly, Gabriel. *See* JOLY, GABRIEL.

Yŏndam. *See* KIM MYŎNG-GUK.

Yŏn'gaek. *See* HŎ P'IL.

Yŏnggok. *See* HWANG CHIP-JUNG.

Yŏnp'o. *See* YUN, (2).

York [Eboracum; Eoforwic; Jorvik]. English city, archiepiscopal see and county town of North Yorkshire, situated on the River Ouse.

I. History and urban development. II. Art life and organization. III. Buildings.

I. History and urban development.

1. AD 71–1066. 2. 1066–*c.* 1450. 3. After *c.* 1450.

1. AD 71–1066. The first surviving account of the city, written by the scholar Alcuin (*c.* 732–804), records that 'it was a Roman army built it first, to be a merchant-town of land and sea, and mighty stronghold for their governors'. York was founded by the Roman commander Q. Petillius Cerialis, who brought the Ninth Legion north from Lincoln in or shortly after AD 71. The garrison town of Eboracum remained throughout its many vicissitudes the military headquarters of imperial authority in a frontier region, retaining its ascendancy in the northern province

of Roman Britain until the collapse of imperial rule around 400. Fundamental for the future of the city was the location of Eboracum in the Vale of York, within an easily defensible triangle between the River Ouse and its little tributary, the River Foss, where the former could be bridged.

Few of the major Roman buildings (forum, amphitheatre, baths, temples and imperial palace) have been discovered. Copious archaeological finds, most notably of sepulchral inscriptions and mosaic pavements in the 19th century and of part of a Roman sewerage system in 1972, testify to the sophisticated standards of living attained by many members of the military and civilian population, the latter largely resident in the *colonia* on the south-west side of the Ouse. No clear evidence has emerged, however, to suggest that Eboracum was an especially prominent industrial or artistic centre under the Romans; and the city's best-preserved memorial to Roman military rule is the so-called Multangular Tower, a solitary but majestic survival from the early 4th-century riverside wall of the legionary fortress.

The city walls were the most enduring legacy of Eboracum, surviving the Anglian occupation of Northumbria and to be praised for their magnificence by Alcuin. They were the basis of the extended circuit erected by the Normans after 1066. The medieval walls were completed in more or less their present form by 1300 and dominate all approaches to York: narrowly escaping destruction in the early 19th century, they and the four main gates (or bars) are the best-preserved medieval urban defences in Britain.

By contrast there was to be little building in stone during the two mysterious centuries in which Roman Eboracum gradually evolved, or more probably decayed, into Anglian Eoforwic. Whether or not the city was ever completely abandoned, it seems clear that during the 5th century there was a breakdown of social order, and the early Anglian settlers migrated into the southern suburbs: here excavation in 1985 revealed that 'an Anglo-Saxon equivalent of a trading estate' existed by at least the 8th century. Of much greater consequence in ensuring York's future pre-eminence was the conversion of the Anglo-Saxons to Christianity: indeed the letter sent by Pope Gregory I to St Augustine in 601, outlining his proposals for a Christian church to be presided over by an archbishop of York as well as of London, could be considered the most influential document in the city's history. According to Bede, on Easter Day 627 the Anglian king Edwin was baptised by Paulinus in a little wooden church, which the King ordered to be built in Eoforwic; and the cathedral became the seat of one of England's only two archbishops in 735. The location of York's pre-Conquest cathedrals, however, and of most of its other churches, remains elusive. It seems most probable that the clerks of the cathedral lived in timber buildings amid the ruins of parts of the Roman *principia*, much of it standing until the 10th century. Such a modest environment did not in itself preclude the possibilities of an active scriptorium, a well-stocked library and the manufacture of metal goods (especially cross brooches) in the city; but essentially the artistic and social activity of the Anglian inhabitants of York is uncertain.

1. York, chapel to the Archbishop's Palace, *c.* 1230 (before its restoration as York Minster Library); engraving from Joseph Halfpenny: *Fragmenta Vetusta* (York, 1807), pl. 18

Thanks to recent archaeological discoveries rather than to the survival of a documentary record, the next and crucial transformation of Anglian York into the Scandinavian city of Jorvik is clearer. Despite Alcuin's earlier fears, provoked by the first onslaught of the Vikings on Lindisfarne in 793, that the foxes would come to Britain to pillage the Lord's chosen vine, evidence suggests that the Danish capture of York in 866 rapidly enhanced rather than diminished York's commercial importance. Two centuries later, after almost continuous Scandinavian or Anglo-Scandinavian rule, the Domesday Book commissioners recorded well over 1600 tenements or *mansiones* in the city, making it the largest provincial town in England. Virtually nothing is known about the details of religious life in Viking York or of the palaces and patronage of the Viking kings who ruled the city until the death of Eric Bloodaxe in 954; however, excavations conducted near Coppergate (itself an Old Norse name) during the 1970s and early 1980s have provided a vivid impression of daily life and small-scale manufacture, above all in leather, wood and bone, within the city (*see* ANGLO-SAXON ART, §II, 5). Although homes and workshops in Jorvik were cramped and squalid, even by later medieval standards, the inhabitants were often wealthy enough to own gold and silver ornaments, bone skates and jet chessmen. More significantly, it was in the Scandinavian period that York first developed certain forms of manufacture for a large market outside its walls, most durably through its important mint and well-organized workshops for the supply of sculptured crosses and grave-covers to the surrounding region.

2. 1066–*c.* 1450. The Norman Conquest of England, or more precisely William the Conqueror's own 'harrying' of Yorkshire in 1069–70, opened a new era in both the artistic and political history of York. On the evidence of the Domesday Book the city was temporarily but severely reduced by the early 1080s, one of the city's 'shires' or wards being deliberately depopulated in order to build two new Norman castles. Of these, the so-called Clifford's Tower became the headquarters of the sheriff of Yorkshire and remained the most significant symbol of royal authority over the city even after it gradually fell into disuse in the later 15th century. Equally ruthless was the decision of Thomas of Bayeux, the first Norman Archbishop of York (1070–1100), to build an exceptionally large new Romanesque cathedral on a proper east–west liturgical alignment across the area of the old Roman *principia* (*see* §III, 1(i)(a) below). This was accompanied by the reorganization and expansion of the chapter, and henceforward York Minster and its satellite buildings (see fig. 1) and institutions became the home of a powerful body of clergy, who ranked among the leading patrons of learning and art

in the medieval city. In successive building campaigns from the early 13th century onwards the archbishops and canons could afford to rebuild the whole of their Romanesque Minster to create the largest cathedral in medieval England, built over so long a period that John Ruskin allegedly and appropriately considered it to be the Acropolis of the English Gothic style. Comparable wealth was enjoyed by the Benedictine monks of St Mary's Abbey, which within a few years of its foundation immediately north of the city walls in the 1080s became, and remained, the richest monastery in northern England (*see* §III, 2 below).

By the end of the 12th century York possessed several smaller religious houses and 40 parish churches, a total surpassed among other medieval English towns only by London and Winchester. Not surprisingly, it was at this time that York became the centre of a major regional school of English sculpture, itself highly receptive to Continental influences: the life-size statues surviving from both York Minster and St Mary's Abbey (*see* §3 below) are the most spectacular pieces of stone carving produced at York in the 12th century.

The population, now used to the Norman regime, expanded during the 12th century and was further enlarged by an increasing number of immigrants, including the Jews (martyred in 1190). Owing to the navigability of the Ouse to York, the city was commercially pre-eminent in Yorkshire until the late 18th century; and the river also facilitated the use of limestone, floated down from the Tadcaster quarries, as the city's prime building material in the Middle Ages.

It was during the later Middle Ages (*c.* 1250–*c.* 1450), however, that most of the surviving monuments of medieval York were either created or completed. According to the national Poll Tax returns of 1377 (which recorded 7248 adult lay tax-payers), it was still the most populous provincial town in England; and both its political and economic affairs were now dominated by a vigorous group of merchants trading overseas, whose fraternity became a royal chartered company in 1430, several decades after they had built their own hall in Fossgate. This Merchant Adventurers' Hall, together with that of the tailors of York and the civic Common Hall or Guild Hall, remain the most striking memorials to the wealth of the richer lay citizens of York in the later Middle Ages. By contrast the greater town houses of the medieval city survive hardly at all, although there remain many examples of the less ambitious timber-framed residential accommodation with which medieval York once abounded; most noteworthy perhaps is Our Lady's Row, Goodramgate (built in 1316), and, above all, the jettied houses on either side of the Shambles.

The lay inhabitants of 14th- and 15th-century York focused their religious loyalties on their parish churches rather than the Minster, monasteries and four friaries of the city; nowhere can one more readily visualize the leading citizens of late medieval York than in the east window of All Saints' Church, North Street, where Nicholas Blackburn and his father (mayors of the city in 1412–13 and 1429–30) kneel as donors of the window they had commissioned to adorn their perpetual chantry. In no English city has late medieval stained glass survived quite so abundantly as it has in the Minster and parish churches of York.

3. AFTER *c.* 1450. By 1472, when the dean and chapter of York Minster celebrated the final completion of their cathedral, the city's remarkable late medieval prosperity had passed its apogee. Although there were to be several important additions to the architecture of York (see fig. 2) before the Reformation, notably the rebuilding of St Michael-le-Belfry by the Minster mason, John Forman (*d* 1558), as late as 1525–36, from the late 15th century the city's economy gradually deteriorated. The complaint, to use the words of the mayor and aldermen in the 1660s, that 'the shoes of our predecessors are too big for our feet, and the ornaments which they had will not serve now to cover our nakedness', continued to reverberate within the council chamber of York until recent times. Although the city continued to be an important ecclesiastical centre—and political centre too from 1540 to 1641 when the abbot's house of St Mary's Abbey was the site of the royal Council of the North—there is no doubt that the dissolution of the religious houses was the single greatest tragedy in the architectural history of York. The four mendicant convents were almost completely obliterated, St Mary's Abbey was ruined, and much of the Minster precinct became dilapidated: in 1648 the mayor and aldermen petitioned in vain that a new university might occupy the medieval buildings of St William's College (see fig. 3) and the Bedern, once the home of the cathedral's chantry priests and vicars choral. Appropriately the most celebrated building constructed in York during the century after the Reformation was the spacious mansion (destr. 1817) built on the site of the medieval archiepiscopal palace by Sir Arthur Ingram, a secretary of the King's Council of the North in the reign of James I. By the early 17th century York had ceased to be a significant manufacturing town and was adjusting to a new role as the provincial social and cultural centre of the Yorkshire nobility and gentry. Modern York owes much of its physical appearance to that long period, including not only the gentry's Georgian town houses in Micklegate and elsewhere but also the even greater splendours of Lord Burlington's Assembly Rooms (1731–2; for illustration *see* ASSEMBLY ROOMS and BOYLE, (2), fig. 4) and John Carr's Assize Courts (1773–7).

Such was the economic stagnation of 18th-century York that only after the arrival of its first railway line in 1839 did it begin to expand. The population rose from 29,000 in 1841 to 105,000 in 1981, but it was 19th-century York's inability to develop substantial industries that preserved so many of its earlier monuments. Despite the erection of the York and North Midlands Railway Station within the walls of the medieval city, the construction of new bridges and the wholesale demolition of the old timber-framed buildings that had previously given York its characteristic appearance, the fabric of the medieval and Georgian town remained substantially intact, although from the late 18th century the city had been increasingly built in locally manufactured red brick.

From the early 19th century growing numbers of visitors came to admire the city's antiquities rather than to enjoy its social amenities. In the first of many preservationist

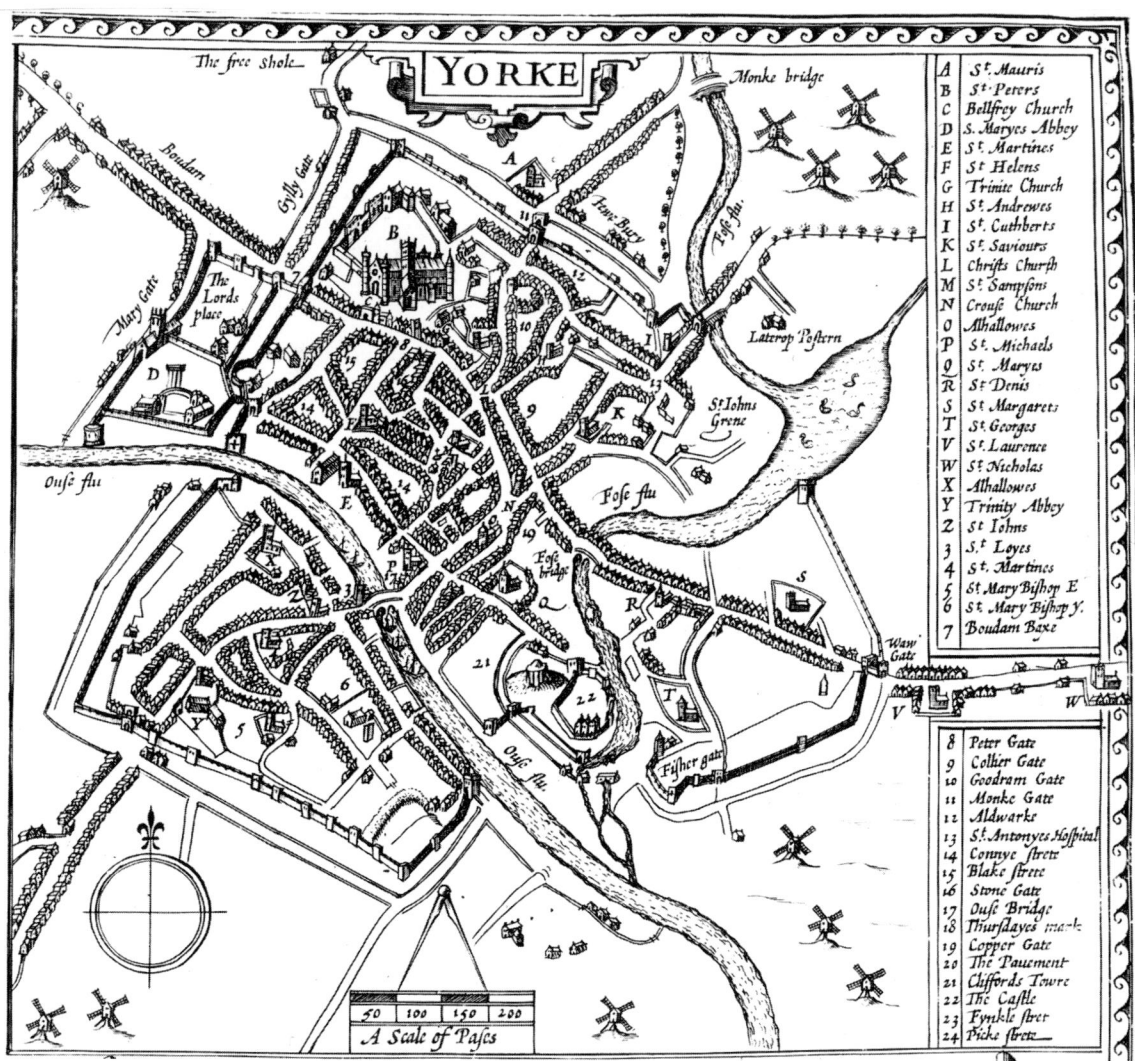

YORKE

A	St. Mauris
B	St. Peters
C	Bellfrey Church
D	S. Maryes Abbey
E	St. Martines
F	St. Helens
G	Trinite Church
H	St. Andrewes
I	St. Cuthberts
K	St. Saviours
L	Chrifts Church
M	St. Sampfons
N	Creufe Church
O	Alhallowes
P	St. Michaels
Q	St. Maryes
R	St. Denis
S	St. Margarets
T	St. Georges
V	St. Laurence
W	St. Nicholas
X	Alhallowes
Y	Trinity Abbey
Z	St. Iohns
3	S.t Loyes
4	St. Martines
5	St. Mary Bifhop E
6	St. Mary Bifhop Y.
7	Boudam Baxe

8	Peter Gate
9	Collier Gate
10	Goodram Gate
11	Monke Gate
12	Aldwarke
13	St. Antonyes Hofpital
14	Connye ftrete
15	Blake ftrete
16	Stone Gate
17	Oufe Bridge
18	Thurfdayes mal-t
19	Copper Gate
20	The Pauement
21	Cliffords Towre
22	The Caftle
23	Fynkle ftret
24	Picke ftrete

A Scale of Pafes

2. York, plan of the city in 1610; inset from John Speed's map of the West Riding of Yorkshire in *Theatre of the Empire of Great Britain*, 1611 (York Minster Library)

movements within the city, Sir Walter Scott joined the York clergy and the York-born artist William Etty to fight a successful campaign to prevent the destruction of the city's walls and bars in the 1820s. About the same time a group of local antiquaries and scholars founded the Yorkshire Philosophical Society, which established in 1829 the city's first permanent museum on the site of St Mary's Abbey. Later in the century a succession of highly successful exhibitions of paintings culminated in the building of the York Art Gallery in 1879.

Since the late 19th century York has increasingly come to depend on its artistic past rather than the present. Despite the steady decline of the railway industry, the city, by expanding its role as a cultural and tourist centre, is one of the most prosperous towns in northern England. Symbolic of this transformation was the opening of the University of York in 1963. Sited at Heslington, 3 km south of the city, the original university buildings were designed in a prefabricated 'clasp', around the largest artificial lake in Europe, by Robert Matthew, Johnson-Marshall & Partners. The university's artistic impact on the city has been considerable, if often indirect. New museums are an equally important manifestation of York's progress towards its position as England's most visited 'historic' city: the so-called Castle Museum, within the walls of the 18th-century Debtors' and Female Prisons; the National Railway Museum (established 1975, the first National Museum to be established outside London); and the York Archaeological Trust's Jorvik Viking Centre (opened 1985). York's greatest museum, however, continues to be itself.

BIBLIOGRAPHY

Alcuin: *De Pontificibus et Sanctis Ecclesiae Eboracensis Carmen* (in *Monumenta Germaniae Historica: Poetae Latini aevi Carolini*, i, ed. E. L. Duemmler, Berlin, 1881) [late 18th century]

F. Drake: *Eboracum: Or the History and Antiquities of the City of York* (London, 1736)

R. Davies: *Walks through the City of York* (London, 1880)
J. Raine: *Historic Towns: York* (London, 1893)
T. P. Cooper: *York: The Story of its Walls, Bars and Castles* (London, 1904)
P. J. Shaw: *An Old York Church: All Hallows in North Street* (York, 1908)
J. E. Morris: *Little Guide to York* (London, 1924)
F. Harrison: *The Painted Glass of York* (London, 1927)
——: *Life in a Medieval College* (London, 1952)
A. Raine: *Mediaeval York: A Topographical Survey Based on Original Sources* (London, 1955)
P. M. Tillot, ed.: *A History of Yorkshire: The City of York*, Victoria Hist. Co. England (London, 1961)
Inventory of Historical Monuments in the City of York, 5 vols, Royal Comm. Anc. & Hist. Mnmts & Constr. England (London, 1962–)
A. Stacpoole and others, eds: *The Noble City of York* (York, 1972)
R. B. Dobson: *The Jews of Medieval York and the Massacre of March 1190*, Borthwick Institute Paper, no. 45 (York, 1974)
J. Harvey: *York* (London, 1975)
D. M. Palliser: *Tudor York* (Oxford, 1979)
C. Feinstein, ed.: *York, 1831–1981: 150 Years of Social Endeavour and Social Change* (York, 1981)
Archaeological Papers from York Presented to M. W. Barley (York, 1984)
BARRIE DOBSON

II. Art life and organization.

Medieval episcopal and royal patronage of artistic production in York was ended by the Dissolution of the Monasteries in the 1530s. After the Restoration in 1660 new forms of artistic activity took root. Interest in recording the city's antiquities stirred and then developed during the 18th century. From 1670 to 1710 such gentlemen amateurs as the early topographers FRANCIS PLACE and William Lodge (1649–89) formed a group of artists and antiquaries, the Society of Virtuosi, who met at the Micklegate house of the glass painter Henry Gyles (1645–1709). Some of Place's drawings were used by Francis Drake (1696–1771) in his *Eboracum: Or, the History and Antiquities of the City of York* (1736), the first history of York (see fig. 4); but Drake had to commission London printmakers to engrave the plates. Throughout the 18th century artists visited York to record its antiquities, including Samuel Buck and Nathaniel Buck in 1719–20, and Rowlandson, Turner, Thomas Girtin and John Sell Cotman c. 1800, contributing to a solid York tradition of topographical art closely associated with the making and publishing of prints. Engravers worked in Stonegate for nearly 100 years after Robert Ledger (1717/18–1779) established the city's first printmaking business c. 1755. Joseph Halfpenny (1748–1811) and Henry Cave (1779–1836) both published etchings of York subjects. Lithography was used by William Monkhouse (1813–98) in collaboration with Francis Bedford in *Churches of York* (York, 1843).

A modest demand for portraiture developed as York became a fashionable 18th-century resort. PHILIP MERCIER painted portraits and fancy pictures for the London market from 1739 to 1751. GEORGE STUBBS painted portraits, studied anatomy and illustrated a medical book in York from c. 1745 to c. 1756. Other visiting portrait painters included Henry Pickering, John Maurice Hauck (fl 1759–67), Martin Ferdinand Quadal, Thomas Barrow (?1749–c. 1778) and Stephen Hewson (fl 1775–1805). From 1752 NATHAN DRAKE undertook a variety of painting commissions. William Peckitt (1731–95) continued the city's tradition of glass painting and the FISHER family maintained that of monumental sculpture. WILLIAM ETTY took

3. York, St William's College, c. 1460

part in a campaign that resulted in the establishment of a school of design in 1842. Among its earliest students were Albert Joseph Moore and his artist brothers.

York's first recorded art exhibition consisting of over 400 works lent by artists was held in Castlegate in 1836. Contemporary art formed part of an exhibition held at the School of Art in 1856. More ambitiously, the Yorkshire Fine Art and Industrial Exhibition of 1866 brought together contemporary works and Old Masters. It was shown in a temporary building designed by Edward Taylor, who also designed a semi-permanent building for the second exhibition (1879). When this closed the building became first the Yorkshire Fine Art and Industrial Institution, and then in 1892 the City Art Gallery; annual exhibitions were held there from 1880 to 1903. The only significant art collection in 18th-century York was a group of portraits assembled at the Mansion House. Richard Nicholson, George Townshend Andrews and John Burton (1710–71) all collected contemporary art. The City Art Gallery's collection has been enriched by various donations: the bequest of Burton's paintings in 1882; F. D. Lycett Green's collection of Old Masters (acquired mid-20th century); the collections of Eric Milner-White (Dean of York 1941–63) of late 19th- and early 20th-century paintings, and of pioneer studio pottery; and Dr W. A. Evelyn's collection of York topography.

The School of Art, City Art Gallery, university and St John's College have provided focal points for art life in York during the 20th century. Commercial galleries have flourished intermittently. The Minster continues to provide a focus for stone-carving and glass restoration, and York has become an important centre for crafts, especially pottery.

UNPUBLISHED SOURCES
York Reference Library [MS. of J. W. Knowles: *York Artists*, 2 vols]
BIBLIOGRAPHY
A Handbook to the Old York Views and Worthies Exhibition (exh. cat. by T. P. Cooper and others, York, F.A. & Ind. Exh. Bldgs, 1905)
Exhibition of Works by York Artists Since the Inauguration of the School of Arts and Science by Wm. Etty, R. A., 1842 (exh. cat., York, C.A.G., 1913)

York, *from near the confluence of the Rivers* Ouse *and* Fofs.

Thomas Lifter *of* Gifburn-park *Efqr.* Member *of Parliament for the borough of* Clithero *in the county of* Lancafter, *a great encourager of this undertaking, contributes this plate. 1736.*

4. *View of York* (1736) by C. Baron after Francis Place from Francis Drake's *Eboracum: Or, the History and Antiquities of the City of York* (London, British Library)

J. Ingamells: *City of York Art Gallery: Catalogue of Paintings* (York, 1963)
——: 'Art in 18th-century York', *Country Life*, cxlix (10 June 1971), pp. 1412–14 (17 June 1971), pp. 1530–32
——: *Catalogue of the Pictures in the Mansion House, York*, i (York, 1972)
——: 'Painting and Sculpture in York (1700–1970)', *The Noble City of York*, ed. A. Stacpoole and others (York, 1972), pp. 854–74
A Candidate for Praise: William Mason, 1725–97, Precentor of York (exh. cat. by C. B. L. Barr and J. A. S. Ingamells; York, C.A.G.; York Minster, Chapter Lib.; 1973)
J. Ingamells: 'The Elevation of the Masses', *Preview: York A.G. Bull.*, xxx (1977), pp. 1018–23
R. M. Butler: 'Views of York (1650–1845)', *York Historian*, ii (1978), pp. 31–42
The Moore Family Pictures: Paintings, Watercolours and Drawings by Albert and Henry Moore, their brothers William, John Collingham and Edwin and their Father William Moore Snr. (exh. cat., ed. J. Harnoll; York, C.A.G., 1980)
C. Myerscough: 'The Fishers of York: A Family of Sculptors', *York Historian*, vii (1986), pp. 46–59
York Through the Eyes of the Artist (exh. cat., ed. R. Green; York, C.A.G., 1990)

RICHARD GREEN

III. Buildings.

1. Minster. 2. St Mary's Abbey.

1. MINSTER.

(i) Architecture. (ii) Sculpture. (iii) Stained glass.

(i) Architecture. The cathedral church has occupied its present site since the late 11th century. No remains of the pre-Conquest buildings have been found, but the dedication to St Peter is traceable to the stone church built by King Edwin *c.* 630. Although this church was damaged by fire in 741, and Archbishop Aethelbert (766–82), assisted by Alcuin, built a church on a magnificent scale dedicated to Alma Sophia, St Peter's apparently remained the principal church of York, surviving the Danish raids of the 9th century. The cathedral complex may have included several churches, as at Canterbury, and perhaps lay to the north of the present building. St Peter's is known to have had at least one porticus and a belfry.

(a) c. *1080–c. 1225.* The Anglo–Norman cathedral was founded by Archbishop Thomas of Bayeux *c.* 1080; it was sited across the north corner of the Roman *principia*, masonry from which was reused with local limestone. The plan was partly recovered in excavation, and traces remain above ground. The building was 112 m long, cruciform in plan, with square transepts, each with an apsidal eastern chapel, and stair turrets at the crossing leading to a low tower. The eastern arm seems to have ended in an apse, and it may have had internal divisions, either walls or arcades, making very narrow 'aisles'. There is evidence of a ground-level crypt, reached by passages from the crossing. The nave was unusual in being without aisles, a plan reflected in Ripon Minster. It had a single west door flanked by buttresses.

The superstructure, which was rendered in off-white stucco lined-out in red, was articulated with pilasters and string courses, with nook shafts in the windows. Surviving composite capitals relate the building to contemporary great churches in the north of England. A pulpitum stood east of the crossing, and the liturgical arrangement may have been marked by steps.

Some time after 1100 the apse was squared off externally. A form of western building, including two towers apparently positioned closely together, was added to the nave, possibly by Archbishop Roger Pont-l'Evêque (1154–81), who was responsible for the new eastern arm, built from the 1160s. Part of the crypt survives abutting the Anglo–Norman undercroft (see fig. 5). There are remains of four bays and traces of square eastern transepts, in the form either of square chapels or running to full height. The new choir was aisled and probably rectangular, but whether it had low chapels east of the great gable is uncertain. The decoration, scallop and waterleaf capitals, pellets, chevron, decorated rolls, incised piers and detached shafts, is related to contemporary monastic architecture, placing York in the centre of architectural development in the north of England in the later 12th century.

(b) After c. *1225.* The Anglo–Norman building was entirely replaced by the present one, beginning with the south transept built by Archbishop Walter de Grey (1216–55), whose tomb is in its eastern aisle. In a building campaign lasting until the 15th century, the main patrons continued to be the archbishops and senior clergy, with specific gifts from prominent lay people such as the Percy and Vavasour families.

There is a rectangular choir of nine bays, with full-height, non-projecting eastern transepts level with the high altar at the fifth bay; main transepts of three bays with east and west aisles and a crossing tower; and an eight-bay nave with a two-tower façade. The chapter house is reached by an L-shaped vestibule leading off the north transept. The Minster, which measures 148 m externally and 70 m across the transept, is built of local limestone, and the vaulting throughout is of wood. It gives an impression of unity, bound together on the exterior by the battlemented parapet and three stylistically similar towers, and inside by the superficial resemblance of the choir to the nave. The cult of the local saint, William, was marked at his tomb in the nave and at his shrine behind the high altar, of which the remains of two successive shrine bases, in Decorated and Perpendicular styles, survive in the Yorkshire Museum.

The south transept, probably finished by 1241, and the north (rebuilt with the crossing tower *c.* 1255 by the Treasurer, John le Romeyn) differ only in detail, although the south transept was altered in the course of construction. Local building traditions, as seen, for example, in the choir of Rievaulx Abbey, continued to predominate. The three-storey elevation is embellished with shafts *en délit* and dogtooth, with stiff-leaf capitals. In the arcade, alternating with piers surrounded by detached Purbeck colonnettes (*see* PIER (ii), fig. 3), moulded piers support a gallery with a lean-to roof and twin, pointed-arched openings under a round-headed containing arch. The tympana are pierced by polylobed oculi. The clerestory passage is fronted by a row of low arches, a disposition that presupposes a wooden ceiling, despite extant vaulting shafts. A wooden barrel 'vault' was inserted during the 15th century. The south façade has a rose window, the north five huge lancets (the Five Sisters; *see* §(iii) below).

5. York Minster, pier in the north arcade of the crypt, 1160s

Next to the crossing at each side was a blind narrow bay concealing newel stairs and buttressing for the surviving Anglo-Norman work. In the early 15th century, after the nave and choir had been rebuilt, the ancient masonry of the narrow bays was cut away to allow for the aisles, and the arches were exchanged with those next to them, the upper storeys preserving the original arrangement.

With the chapter house and vestibule, built from *c.* 1280, came the first signs at the Minster of stylistic influences from southern England and the continent of Europe. Measuring 18 m across the angles, and with huge traceried windows, the chapter house is a successor to the great southern examples at Westminster Abbey and Salisbury Cathedral; but here there is no central column, and although there are signs of preparation for a stone vault, the actual vault is of wood. The stall canopies are set in a continuous undulating line, supported on Purbeck shafts and decorated with carved heads and naturalistic foliage comparable to contemporary work at Southwell Minster (Notts) and Lincoln Cathedral. The exterior is decorated with blind tracery, and on the parapet sit the remains of sculptured bears, the rebus of Treasurer FitzUrse (1335–42). The vestibule continues the theme of ornamented spaciousness, with an interior dado of framed tracery patterns and large windows, the tracery designs of which derive from London (like those of the chapter house) and from St Urbain, Troyes (France).

This awareness of work in London and France is an essential characteristic of the nave (see fig. 6). Built from 1291 to *c.* 1340, it is the only monumental English building of its day seriously to reflect French Rayonnant structural ideas, although the moulded piers and details in the aisles indicate that the architect, one Simon, was a northerner. Owing to its width (the result of siting the arcade on the footings of the Anglo-Norman outer walls), the nave looks

6. York Minster, interior of the nave looking east, 1291–*c.* 1340; vault, 1357

more Rhenish than Parisian, but the elevation shows that Simon deliberately chose to escape from the limitations imposed by an Anglo-Norman wall structure, preferring to set the clerestory passage on the exterior, and the glass on the inner wall plane. The clerestory mullions extend downwards to bind the triforium into a unified design. The flatness and verticality achieved by this solution is enhanced by the vaulting shafts, which rise uninterrupted from the floor, with small, discreet seaweed-foliage capitals. Patterns of blind tracery are deployed in the aisle dado. The sculptured figures in the triforium (four survive) and on the exterior parapet are not of French inspiration, nor is the lierne vault, built in the 1350s with a design based on intersecting groups of parallel lines; but the quadrilobe tracery in the aisles and the tabernacles for statues on the buttresses are French devices seen also at Westminster Abbey; although the straight-sided motifs in the clerestory tracery are precocious.

From *c.* 1315 the late 12th-century west block was replaced by the conventional two-tier façade, a composition of niches and housings for large sculptured groups (*see* §(ii) below), perhaps dimly reflecting the ideas of, for example, Strasbourg Cathedral. A new designer took over when work was in progress, for above ground level the ogee arch and curvilinear tracery were introduced, appearing in the niches and the great west window, glazed in 1338/9 by Archbishop Melton (1317–40). It has an eight-light composition of so-called leafstems, arranged to form a heart shape. The ogival and curvilinear work on the façade was far more influential locally than the radical design of the nave proper, which made surprisingly little impact.

The foundation-stone of the new choir was laid in 1361 by Archbishop Thoresby (1352–73), although the Zouche Chapel, built to the south from 1350, shows that the alignment must already have been decided. The eastern arm is one of the earliest monumental buildings in the emerging Perpendicular style. The four easternmost bays, built by William Hoton and Robert de Patrington, were strongly influenced by the nave design, with the same flat elevation but more rectilinear details: Perpendicular motifs in the tracery, transoms in the tall transept and eastern windows, and a more clearcut lierne design for the vault. The aisle window pattern, found also in buildings patronized by the contemporary Bishop Edington of Winchester, survives in a full-size sketch in the plaster of the masons' tracing floor above the chapter house vestibule.

After Thoresby's death work slackened, and the 12th-century choir was not demolished until the 1390s. Hugh Hedon's design for the western choir bays, while resembling the earlier work in detail, reverted to the English tradition of an internal clerestory passage and recessed glass. The east window tracery was inserted *c.* 1405, with a nine-light composition that did not yet exclude curvilinear elements; the east wall was finished with a screenlike effect of niches, pinnacles and turrets. The main crossing piers and arches were recased, and after the central tower partly fell in 1407 the new lantern was built to a modified design during the 15th century, together with the western towers, all three in Perpendicular style.

There have been more or less continuous repairs to the fabric since the 18th century. Major restorations were undertaken after fire destroyed the roofs of the choir (1829) and nave (1840). The Minster was reroofed between 1934 and 1951, and underpinned and restored in 1967–72. The south transept was reopened in 1988 after fire destroyed the roof in 1984.

(ii) Sculpture. Sculpture includes 20 decayed 12th-century statues that were reused on the 14th-century west front. They seem to consist of Old Testament precursors of Christ, Apostles and witnesses, and were probably placed on the westwork, surrounding a *Christ in Majesty*, from which the Evangelist symbols also survive. Together with the contemporary figures from St Mary's Abbey (*see* §2 below) they survive as a tantalizing portion of an extensive sculpture programme related to but distinct from Early Gothic portal programmes in France, and they indicate the importance of York as a centre for sculpture in the late 12th century.

Harvey

BIBLIOGRAPHY

R. Willis: *The Architectural History of York Cathedral* (London, 1848); as *Architectural History of Some English Cathedrals* (Chicheley, 1972)

K. Harrison: 'The Pre-Conquest Churches of York', *Yorks Archaeol. J.*, xl (1959–62), pp. 232–49

N. Coldstream: 'York Chapter House', *J. Brit. Archaeol. Assoc.*, n. s. 2, xxxv (1972), pp. 15–23

E. A. Gee: *York Minster Chapter House and Vestibule*, RCHM (London, 1974)

G. E. Aylmer and R. Cant, eds: *A History of York Minster* (Oxford, 1977)

C. Wilson: *The Shrines of St William of York* (York, 1977)

N. Coldstream: 'York Minster and the Decorated Style in Yorkshire', *Yorks Archaeol. J.*, lii (1980), pp. 89–110

D. Phillips: *Excavations at York Minster*, ii: *The Cathedral of Archbishop Thomas of Bayeux*, RCHM (London, 1985)

Age of Chivalry (exh. cat., ed. J. Alexander and P. Binski; London, RA, 1987), pp. 79, 416, 422–3

S. Oosterwijk and C. Norton: 'Figure Sculpture from the Twelfth Century Minster', *Sixty First Annual Report of the Friends of York Minster for 1989* (York, 1990), pp. 11–30

H. J. Böker: 'York Minster's Nave: The Cologne Connection', *J. Soc. Archit. Hist.*, l/ii (1991), pp. 167–80

Romanesque Stone Sculpture from Medieval England (exh. cat. by B. Heywood and others, Leeds, Henry Moore Inst., 1993)

NICOLA COLDSTREAM

(iii) Stained glass. York Minster contains the most comprehensive single collection of stained glass in Great Britain with 128 windows displaying every period of glass painting from the 12th century to the present day.

(a) 12th–15th centuries. Some late 12th-century glass is believed to have survived from Archbishop Pont L'Evêque's choir. Seven windows (rest. 1991) in the nave clerestory contain late 12th-century figurative panels, which can be compared with slightly earlier 12th-century French glass in the parish churches of Twycross (Leics), St Mary and St Nicholas, Wilton (Wilts), and St Mary and All Saints, Rivenhall (Essex). The figure of the Judean king (*c.* 1170; York Minster, Foundations), originally part of a *Jesse* window, is similar in design to figures in *Jesse* windows in Saint-Denis Abbey and Chartres Cathedral. The central lower panel of the Five Sisters window (see below) depicting *Daniel in the Lions' Den* (*c.* 1180) is probably a panel from a medallion window, of the kind that survive at Canterbury Cathedral.

Grisaille was introduced in the second half of the 13th century. The Five Sisters window (*c.* 1260) in the north wall of the north transept contains five lancets, each 16.31×1.56 m, displaying more than 100,000 individual pieces of foliate patterned greyish-white glass, with geometric designs and narrow strips of coloured glass emphasizing the pattern. (This window was reglazed 1923–5 using 13th-century lead excavated at Rievaulx Abbey.) Towards the end of the 13th century figurative panels were introduced as a centrepiece between grisaille panels, as in the windows of the chapter house and its vestibule, a design feature that was to extend into the 14th-century windows of the nave. The chapter house windows contain 20 figurative panels alternating with grisaille, nearly all dating to the late 13th century and the early 14th.

The majority of the nave windows were painted during the first half of the 14th century. Canopies, used to frame or surmount figurative panels or scenes, became more prominent than in 12th- and early 13th-century windows. In the nave windows figurative and canopy panels are alternated with grisaille. A significant technical point is that the first window from east in the north nave aisle contains what may be the first English usage of the silver-stain technique (*see* STAINED GLASS, §I, 4). Subject-matter includes the *Heraldic* window (*c.* 1310–20) and the Bell-founders window (with illustrations of bell-making). A monkeys' funeral procession is shown in the third window from the east in the north nave aisle. The *Jesse* window of *c.* 1310 in the south nave aisle was extensively reordered in 1950. The great west window (*c.* 1338), given by Archbishop Melton, has three main rows of figurative panels: in the main lights there are bishops, archbishops, apostles and Gospel scenes, with the *Coronation of the*

7. Head of *King Edward the Confessor*, stained glass panel from the Great East Window of York Minster, 1405–8, by John Thornton of Coventry

Virgin at the top of the two central lights. The nave windows can be compared to similarly dated glass in the cathedrals at Wells, Exeter and Gloucester and also to the clerestory glass of Tewkesbury Abbey (Glos).

Figure and canopy windows continued to prevail throughout the 15th century, with the canopies becoming more ornate, as is evident in the three westernmost windows of the north choir aisle and the eight westernmost windows of the choir clerestory. The choir windows display very high-quality glass painting from the first half of the century, particularly the 'giant' windows, almost 22.5 m in height, depicting *St William of York* (*c.* 1423) in the north-east transept, and *St Cuthbert* (*c.* 1440) in the south-east transept. The great east window was painted 1405–8 by John Thornton of Coventry (*fl* 1405–33) and his workshop (*see* GOTHIC, §VIII, 4). The window (23.9×9.75 m) contains 161 tracery panels, with 117 square panels in the 9 main lights. Above the upper gallery the first three rows depict Old Testament scenes from the *Creation* to the *Death of Absalom*, while below the gallery nine rows unfold the events of the *Apocalypse*. The lowest row of the window contains legendary and historical figures linked with Christianity and the see of York (see fig. 7). The characteristic style of the great east window is seen also in the *Corporal Acts of Mercy* (*see* STAINED GLASS, colour pl. II) in All Saints, North Street, York. Fragments of 14th- and 15th-century glass, including many birds and animals, survive in the Zouche Chapel.

(b) 16th century and later. In the 16th century glass painting skills declined; and the introduction in the second

half of the century of enamelled glass painting techniques meant that superficial colouring could be applied to the glass. The major 16th-century glass is in the south wall of the south transept: the early 16th-century glass of the rose window (diam. 6.81 m) is by South Netherlandish glass painters. The window (rest. since 1984) forms a dynastic symbol of the house of Tudor. The early 16th-century glass in the four lancets immediately below the rose features large figures of *St William of York*, *St Peter*, *St Paul* and *St Wilfrid*. There are close stylistic similarities between this glass and the windows of the same period and school of glass painting in Fairford Church (Glos), and in King's College Chapel, Cambridge. Additional glass by the Minster workshop is in the east window of the chapter house of the Minster. There is a small amount of 17th-century glass by Henry Gyles in the south choir aisle. The central lower panel displaying the arms of Archbishop Lamplugh (*d* 1691) shows the light yellow glass that is almost a trademark of Gyles's work. In the 18th century William Peckitt (1731–95) carried out much restoration of the Minster glass and many tracery sections of nave windows show his distinctive enamelled glass painting skills, often displaying the numerals of the year he carried out the work. His four lower lancets in the south wall of the south transept depict *Abraham*, *King Solomon*, *Moses* and *St Peter*.

In 1845 John Barnett (1786–1859) of York painted 19 figurative panels for the east window of the chapter house (removed 1959 and redeployed in the nave clerestory). The glass painting studio of C. E. Kempe & Co. worked on the five lancet windows in the east wall of the north transept between 1898 and 1903. The figures are *St Peter*, *St Paul* and *St Lawrence*, all newly painted, and *St Stephen* and *St Nicholas* (both 15th century; rest.). Twentieth-century glass in the Minster includes two medallions (1933, by Reginald Bell) in the Kings Own Yorkshire Light Infantry Chapel. Two scenes from the *Life of St Francis of Assisi* painted in 1944 by the Hungarian glass painter Ervin Bossanyi (1891–1975) were installed in the Zouche Chapel in 1975.

The Minster also contains glass brought from elsewhere, notably part of the *Jesse* window (*c*. 1380) of Thomas of Oxford (1385–1427) from New College, Oxford (*see* OXFORD, §3(ii)), installed in the south choir aisle by William Peckitt. Some French 16th-century glass is in the nave, showing the *Nativity*, the *Annunciation to the Shepherds* and the *Annunciation to the Virgin*. A *Crucifixion* (*c*. 1530) from the church of St Jean Roven, brought to England in the early 19th century, was installed in the south choir aisle in 1952. French glass of *c*. 1600 in the north choir aisle illustrates seven scenes from the legend of *St James the Great*. During the 20th century there were two long-term conservation projects on the Minster glass: the post-war restoration of the windows after their removal during World War I, and restoration of 14 nave clerestory windows in 1967–91.

BIBLIOGRAPHY

F. Harrison: *The Painted Glass of York* (London, 1927)
J. A. Knowles: *Essays on the York School of Glass Painting* (London, 1936)
D. E. O'Connor and J. Haselock: 'The Stained Glass of York', *A History of York Minster*, ed. G. E. Aylmer and R. Cant (Oxford, 1977), pp. 313–93
P. Gibson: *The Stained and Painted Glass of York Minster* (Norwich, 1979)
J. T. Brighton: 'Henry Gyles: Virtuoso and Glasspainter of York (1645–1709)', *York Historian*, iv (1984), pp. i–vi, 1–62
J. Toy: *A Guide and Index to the Windows of York Minster* (York, 1985)
T. French and D. O'Connor: *York Minster: A Catalogue of Stained Glass*, Corp. Vitrearum Med. Aevi (Oxford, 1987)
T. Brighton and B. Sprakes: 'Medieval and Georgian Stained Glass in Oxford and Yorkshire. The work of Thomas of Oxford (1385–1427) and William Peckitt of York (1731–95) in New College Chapel, York Minster and St James, High Melton', *Antiqua. J.*, lxx/2 (1990), pp. 380–415

PETER GIBSON

2. ST MARY'S ABBEY. The community that became the Benedictine abbey of St Mary was one of several to resettle the sites of ancient Northumbrian monasteries in the 1070s. Two sites proving unsatisfactory, in the mid-1080s a move was made to St Olave's Church in the western suburbs of York. In 1088 King William II (*reg* 1087–1100) assumed patronage of the abbey, granting land adjoining St Olave's and laying the foundation-stone of the new church. The eclipse of St Olave's by St Mary's was doubtless intended to demonstrate the increase in divine favour and power enjoyed by the Normans, for St Olave's had been built by the penultimate Anglo-Saxon Earl of Northumbria, and its patron, St Olaf, was a symbol of still potentially dangerous ties with Scandinavia. The relationship between this royal foundation and northern England's greatest city was probably meant to recall that between Westminster Abbey and London.

(i) The Romanesque church. (ii) 13th century and later.

(i) The Romanesque church. The plan of the Romanesque church—a Latin cross with a long aisled nave, aisled chancel and seven apses in echelon—most resembles St Alban's Abbey, and would have appeared more impressive than York Minster's singular aisleless nave. Numerous *ex situ* carved fragments, indicative of extensive remodelling after a city fire in 1137, have parallels in other products of the mid-12th-century Yorkshire school of sculpture (*see* ROMANESQUE, §III, 1(v)(b)). Close analogies between the fragmentary but high-quality stone *Virgin and Child* (*c*. 1160; York, Yorks Mus.) and the work of the principal master on the Royal Portal at Chartres Cathedral (*see* CHARTRES, §I, 2(i)) suggest direct French involvement. The ten life-size statues of *Apostles* and *Prophets*, and seven Christological voussoirs (*c*. 1180–90; York, Yorks Mus.), apparently from a single ensemble, rank as the most important extant Early Gothic sculpture in England (*see* GOTHIC, §III, 1(ii)(b)), although York Minster (*see* §1(ii) above) possesses the damaged remains of at least twenty contemporary life-size figures. The level of finish and precision of cutting of the St Mary's figures are generally lower than in the products of major Ile-de-France workshops, and the columns behind the figures merge into the shoulders instead of continuing for the full height. That the workmanship is not homogeneous is evident both in the detailed handling and in the articulation of the contrast between relaxed and weight-bearing legs (compare, for instance, *Moses* (*see* ROMANESQUE, fig. 34) with *St John* (rest.)). Analogies for the drapery design are found in the north-west portal at Sens Cathedral (from 1184; *see* SENS, fig. 3). Iconographically, the *Prophets* are dependent on the *Christophores* of the west portal at Senlis Cathedral.

The setting of the late 12th-century sculpture is unknown, but it has been suggested that it comes from the abbey's only major building of *c.* 1180, the chapter house (see fig. 8), and that it was used there in ways that were unconventional in French terms: voussoirs forming the heads of three windows in the east wall, *Apostles* and *Prophets* figures set in two tiers, both incorporated with the twelve responds of the five-bay vault. The extant west portal and windows of the chapter house (partly reconstructed) are the prime example of the northern English taste for combining Gothic foliate carving and elongated shafts with Romanesque ornament rendered with a new richness and vigour. In this they may be compared to the apparently contemporary west portal (*c.* 1180) of Selby Abbey (N. Yorks), and the portal of the upper chapel of Durham Castle. Equally, the carousels of 17 shafts, which carried the arches of the entrance from the cloister into the chapter house vestibule can be understood as outdoing earlier local examples of this motif in the crypt of York Minster and the false gallery of the nave of Selby Abbey. The capitals are apparently the first in northern England to imitate the rich crocket types used at Canterbury Cathedral by William of Sens.

(ii) 13th century and later. From *c.* 1200 until its dissolution in 1539 St Mary's Abbey was the richest monastic house in the north of England. This is attested by the remains of its 13th-, 14th- and 15th-century buildings. The eastern arm of the church (begun 1270) was a nine-bay aisled rectangle of a locally well-established type. Originally intended to be a self-contained replacement for a short Romanesque chancel, by 1279 the new east end had become the first stage of a complete rebuilding. From the standing remains and *ex situ* fragments it is clear that the original design was adhered to closely throughout. The main elevations followed the main transepts of York Minster in their general horizontality, their extremely conservative false galleries under round arches, and their low clerestories with lancets and wall passages. The detailing derived from the Angel Choir of Lincoln Cathedral. The west front was a reworking of the four-turreted south transept façade of the Minster and influenced the west front of St Peter's, Howden, and the east front of Selby Abbey. When completed in 1294 the church probably appeared old-fashioned by comparison with the Rayonnant nave of York Minster (*see* §1(i)(b) above); for the sumptuous rebuilding of the south and east claustral ranges from 1297 the style of the Minster nave (and very probably the same architect) was employed. Outstanding among extant later buildings are the defensible precinct walls, begun in response to the threat of a Scottish invasion in 1318, and the brick abbot's house (begun *c.* 1483; now part of the King's Manor), precocious in its use of terracotta architectural components.

BIBLIOGRAPHY

W. Sauerländer: 'Sens and York: An Enquiry into the Sculptures from St Mary's Abbey in the Yorkshire Museum', *J. Brit. Archaeol. Assoc.*, 3rd ser., xxii (1959), pp. 53–69

A. B. Whittingham: 'St Mary's Abbey, York: An Interpretation of its Plan', *Archaeol. J.*, cxxviii (1972), pp. 118–46

An Inventory of the Historical Monuments in the City of York, iv, Royal Comm. Anc. & Hist. Mnmts Constr. England (London, 1979), pp. xxxix–xliv, 3–24, 30–31, 37–40

C. Wilson: 'The Original Setting of the Apostle and Prophet Figures from St. Mary's Abbey, York', *Studies in Medieval Sculpture*, ed. F. H. Thompson, Society of Antiquaries, Occasional Paper, n. s. IV (London, 1983), pp. 100–121

English Romanesque Art, 1066–1200 (exh. cat., ed. G. Zarnecki; London, Hayward Gal., 1984), pp. 191, 204–8

C. Wilson and J. Burton: *St Mary's Abbey, York* (York, 1988)

CHRISTOPHER WILSON

8. York, St Mary's Abbey, chapter house entry, *c.* 1180; reconstruction

Yorke, Rosenberg & Mardall [YRM]. English architectural partnership established in 1944 by Francis Reginald Stevens Yorke (*b* Stratford-on-Avon, 3 Dec 1906; *d* London, 10 June 1962), Eugene Rosenberg (*b* Topolčany, Slovakia, 24 Feb 1907; *d* London, Nov 1990) and Cyril Mardall (*b* Helsinki, 21 Sept 1909). Yorke was the son of an architect, Francis Walter Bagnell Yorke (1880–1957), and trained at the University of Birmingham School of Architecture, before establishing a practice in London in 1930. His early work included houses at Iver (1935; destr. 1985; see *Architects' J.*, 31 Dec 1936), Bucks, Nast Hyde (1935), Herts, using reinforced concrete, and a terrace of houses (1939) at Stratford-on-Avon, all of which were flat-roofed and white-walled. A pioneer of Modernism in England, Yorke was a founder-member of the MARS group (1933) and active in CIAM, although his name became associated with the Modern Movement chiefly through his publications, which discussed work on the international scene. From 1935 to 1938 he was in partnership with Marcel Breuer, with whom he built a house (1935) at Angmering-on-Sea, Sussex, and an exhibition house (1938) at the Royal Show, Bristol.

Rosenberg qualified in 1932 after training in Bratislava, Brno and Prague; he also spent part of 1929 working for Le Corbusier in Paris. From 1934 to 1938 he was in private practice in Prague, during which time he designed a number of buildings in the International Style, for example the blocks of flats in the Štěpánská-Smečeky and the Schnirchova Street, Prague. He came to England in 1939, having already met Yorke. Mardall, whose original name was Sjöstrom, came to England in 1927 and was trained at the Polytechnic of North London and the Architectural Association School, London (1931–2), where he also taught from 1936 to 1939.

The partnership formed by Yorke, Rosenberg and Mardall in 1944 became one of the leading practices in post-war Britain, working mainly in the public sector with a breadth of experience drawn from their international origins. Among important early works were the Sigmund Pumps Factory (1948), Gateshead, a notable industrial building of its time, and schools such as the Barclay Secondary School (1950), Stevenage, and the Susan Lawrence School (1951), Poplar, London, both relaxed but highly controlled designs in brick. The practice produced buildings for education, health and industry, and developed a clean rational style that had its origins in Rosenberg's early work. The use of white tile cladding on a concrete frame was typical, as seen in the firm's own offices (1961) in Greystoke Place, London, and buildings for the University of Warwick (1966–9), Coventry, and St Thomas's Hospital (1966–75), London. Another complex, major project was Gatwick Airport, Sussex, developed according to a coherent scheme from 1957; YRM also designed housing at Stevenage and Harlow New Town, and a synagogue (1961–4) in Belfast.

The practice won several awards from the Civic Trust and the RIBA, especially in the 1960s. Yorke's involvement with it diminished in later years, although he seems to have contributed to the interest in texture of materials in the firm's immediate post-war work and to the use in buildings of work by artists such as Henry Moore, Kenneth Rowntree (*b* 1915) and Peggy Angus (*b* 1904), who were his friends. Rosenberg, also notable as a collector of modern art, retired from the partnership in 1975, as did Mardall, who subsequently entered into private practice with his wife, June Park (*b* 1920). YRM continued in operation, developing into a major multi-disciplinary organization.

WRITINGS
F. R. S. Yorke: *The Modern House* (London, 1934, rev. 1967)
——: *The Modern House in England* (London, 1937, rev. 1944)
F. R. S. Yorke and P. Whiting: *The New Small House* (London, 1954)
F. R. S. Yorke and F. Gibberd: *Modern Flats* (London, 1958, rev. 1961)

BIBLIOGRAPHY
The Architecture of York Rosenberg Mardall, 1944–1972, intro. R. Banham (London and New York, 1972)
C. Davies: 'Modern Masters', *Building*, ccxl/7182 (1981), pp. 34–6
A. Powers: *In the Line of Development: F. R. S. Yorke, E. Rosenberg & C. S. Mardall to YRM, 1930–1992* (London, 1992)
ALAN POWERS

Yorozu, Tetsugorō (*b* Tsuchisawa, Iwate Prefect., 17 Nov 1885; *d* Chigazaki, Kanagawa Prefect., 1 May 1927). Japanese painter. He went to Tokyo in 1903. At school he was fond of *suibokuga* (ink painting) and devoted himself to Zen. On leaving school (1906), he followed the Zen master Chaku Sōkatsu and joined the Zen evangelical movement in the USA. Six months later he returned to Japan and the following year he entered the *Yōga* (Western-style painting) department of the Tokyo Art School (now Tokyo University of Fine Arts and Music). At university (from 1911) he was impressed by modern art trends, particularly late Impressionism and Fauvism, and he gradually distanced himself from academic painting. His thesis painting *Nude Beauty* (1911; Tokyo, N. Mus. Mod. A.) was influenced by the work of Matisse and van Gogh and marked his start as an independent painter. In the same year he was a founder-member of the Fyūzankai with other young painters, who had gathered together to promote new artistic trends; he participated twice in the group's exhibitions.

In September 1914 Yorozu went home to concentrate on his work, remaining there until early 1916. The paintings of this period were not limited to a Fauvist style but were nearer to a Cubist form of expression, reacting sharply against contemporary movements in Europe such as Futurism and German Expressionism. After his return to Tokyo, he exhibited in the fourth exhibition of the Nikakai (Second Division Society) of 1917 with the successful painting *Leaning Woman* (1917; Tokyo, N. Mus. Mod. A.), which was the earliest Japanese work representative of this style, although the intellectual approach to form (characteristic of Cubism) did not generally take hold in Japan. In 1919, due to poverty and distress over his work, he suffered a nervous breakdown. He went to Chigazaki in Kanagawa Prefecture to recover. His style after this time became less progressive and he searched for a Japanese expression and spirit to which he added a freely-expressive brush style and form. The paintings from this time show an interest in earlier traditional painting styles, especially *Nanga* or *Bunjinga* (literati painting), combined with an individual approach. In 1922 he participated in the formation of the Shinyōkai (Spring Sun Society), founded by painters who sought a Japanese style of oil painting; the following year he became a member of the society.

BIBLIOGRAPHY

Yorozu Tetsugorō gashū [Collection of paintings of Yorozu Tetsugorō] (Tokyo, 1974)

Tetsujin garon (Zōho kaitei) [A discussion of paintings by a very robust man] (Tokyo, 1985)

ATSUSHI TANAKA

Yortan. Site near Gelembe, north-west Turkey, which flourished in the Early Bronze Age, *c.* 2700–2400 BC. Yortan was excavated in 1900–01 by Paul Gaudin, who concentrated on the extramural cemetery where he uncovered 107 burial jars each containing at least one contracted burial and associated grave goods. The finds are in the British Museum in London, the Musées Royaux d'Art et d'Histoire in Brussels and the Louvre in Paris.

The pottery from Yortan has an outstanding range of shapes, including globular jars with flaring collar-neck, globular jugs with rising spout (sometimes cut away above the handle), bird-shaped jugs, 'teapots', carinated bowls and triple jars with one over-arching basket handle. Many vessels, especially smaller ones, have three small feet. Kâmil distinguished three successive classes, of which only Class C was wheel-made. Class A, the most numerous, has a well-burnished but crumbly fabric, which is generally black or grey but sometimes red or brown. It often has incised, incised-and-white-filled, or white-painted decoration. Common designs include chevrons and horizontal bands containing zigzags, wavy lines, dashes or lozenges, while plastic ornament comprises warts, crescents, parallel bars and fluting. The fabric of Class B is harder and finer, but less burnished. The fine, hard-fired ware of Class C is light grey or light red, with no burnish and little decoration; the clay may have come from a different source.

Analogies may be made with pottery from TROY (i); but more closely related wares, sometimes more richly decorated, are known from other sites in the region bounded by Edremit and Balıkesir to the north and the River Gediz to the south. Plundered cemeteries in the Balıkesir region in particular have helped furnish many private collections and museums. In common parlance the designation 'Yortan' extends to all wares thus related to Classes A and B, but excludes Class C and related wares.

BIBLIOGRAPHY

T. Kâmil: *Yortan Cemetery in the Early Bronze Age of Western Anatolia*, BAR International Series, No. 145 (Oxford, 1982)

DONALD F. EASTON

Yoruba. Term of 19th-century European invention designating various Yoruba-speaking peoples who often claim a common origin at the city of Ife in modern Nigeria and who share, in varying degrees, language, art forms, socio-political institutions and religious beliefs and practices. Yoruba artistic traditions may be counted among the richest in Africa. Major collections of Yoruba art are preserved in Nigeria (Lagos, N. Mus.), Europe (London, BM; Paris, Mus. Homme; Berlin, Mus. Vlkerknd.; Frankfurt am Main, Mus. Vlkerknd; Munich, Staatl. Mus. Vlkerknd.; Leipzig, Mus. Vlkerknd.; and Dresden, Mus. Vlkerknd) and the USA (Los Angeles, UCLA, Fowler Mus. Cult. Hist.; New York, Amer. Mus. Nat. Hist.; Seattle, WA, A. Mus.). Smaller numbers of Yoruba art works are held by virtually every museum with a collection of African art. Yoruba art has also been widely illustrated (see bibliography).

I. Introduction. II. Art forms.

I. Introduction.

1. GEOGRAPHY AND CULTURAL HISTORY. The Yoruba people number more than 25 million in their homeland in south-western Nigeria and south-eastern Benin Republic. Their neighbours include the Borgu and Nupe to the north, the Ebira and Edo-speaking peoples to the east and the Gun, Aja and Fon to the west. Yoruba urbanism is ancient and probably dates from at least AD 800–1000, a date based on archaeological excavations at the sites of IFE and Oyo. These latter were only two of numerous complex city-states headed by sacred rulers (both women and men), councils of elders and chiefs, who, as patrons of the arts, fostered dynamic art traditions that have continued into the late 20th century.

At the end of the 18th century and during the early 19th the collapse of the Oyo–Yoruba empire ushered in a long period of widespread warfare during which millions of Yoruba-speaking peoples were dispersed to the Americas, principally Brazil (*see* BRAZIL, §III), Cuba, Haiti and Trinidad. Their late arrival and enormous numbers ensured a strong Yoruba character in the artistic, religious and social lives of their descendants in the New World. That imprint persists in many arts and in a variety of African American faiths—Lucumi, Candomblé, Sango, Santeria, Umbanda and Macumba—which continued to grow during the late 20th century, not only in South America and the Caribbean but also in urban centres across North America (Thompson, 1983). The Yoruba diaspora, scattered across West Africa in Togo, Ghana, Burkina Faso and Sierra Leone, as well as such descendants and relatives in the Americas as the Lucumi of Cuba and the Anago of Brazil, make their present numbers uncountable. More than any other African civilization, that of the Yoruba-speaking peoples has transformed art, beliefs and practices far beyond Africa's shores (*see* AFRICA, §VIII).

In addition to being shaped by long-term interactions with neighbouring cultures in Africa, Yoruba art has also, since about the mid-19th century, been influenced by Islamic, Christian and colonial traditions. Islam affected architectural and decorative art traditions, bringing about more abstracted, geometric and calligraphic designs, as well as new forms of metalwork, embroidery and leatherwork. Christianity introduced new religious icons and new architectural and liturgical forms. Colonialism and the post-colonial era brought not only European styles and forms but also new patrons for artists working in a variety of new forms and media for international markets. As in other parts of Africa, the dynamism of Yoruba artistic production has been evident in the continuing exploration of new styles and forms of art.

2. AESTHETICS AND COSMOLOGY. Yoruba aesthetic concepts are discussed in a type of philosophical discourse known as 'deep talk' (or meditations; *oro ijinle*) and provide a key to understanding the dynamics of Yoruba art as both object and process (Thompson, 1973; 1980 exh. cat.;

Abiodun, 1983; 1991 exh. cat.). Such discourse includes, but is not limited to, such ideas as: resemblance (*jijora*), balance (*idogba*), clarity (*ifarahun*), smoothness/roundness (*didon*), detail (*fifin*), completeness (*pipe*), skilful embellishment of form (*ona*), innovation/creativity (*ara*), visual playfulness or improvisation (*ere*), appropriateness (*yiye*), insight (*oju inu*), design consciousness (*oju ona*), aliveness (*idahun*) and durability (*tito*). Yoruba art might be defined summarily as 'evocative form' that is meant to be generative and transformative for both artists and viewers. At the core of Yoruba aesthetics is the saying 'character (or essence) is beauty' (*iwa l'ewa*). This refers to the essential nature of a thing or person. When art captures the essential nature of something, the work will be deemed 'beautiful'. This can, of course, include subjects that are humorous, terrifying, abhorrent or disgusting, as well as subjects that are pleasing and admirable. Beauty in art is encompassing, so long as the representation is appropriate (*yiye*) to the subject.

The Yoruba conceive of the cosmos as comprising two distinct, yet inseparable realms—the visible, tangible world of the living (*aye*) and the invisible, spiritual realm (*orun*) inhabited by the supreme creator, Olodumare, an uncountable host of deified ancestors (*orisa*), other ancestors and spirits. The Yoruba say 'the world is a market-place, the otherworld is home' (*aye l'oja, orun n'ile*). Being a transitory state, therefore, life calls for thoughtful action. Everything in the cosmos possesses a life force or performative power (*ase*), the nature of which is unique to each entity. Humans, and especially artists, are expected to use their life force, intensified through increased knowledge and wisdom that comes from reflection, interpretation and action, to create evocative forms.

Some media used by Yoruba artists tend to be gender specific. Men work metals (brass, bronze, copper and iron) and wood, while women work clay. Both men and women weave cloth, though on different kinds of looms; both dye cloth, weave mats, work with beads and paint.

II. Art forms.

1. Architecture. 2. Figurative sculpture. 3. Mask and masquerade. 4. Regalia. 5. Divination instruments. 6. Domestic arts. 7. Textiles. 8. Body arts. 9. Painting.

1. ARCHITECTURE. Since at least AD 800 Yoruba domestic architecture has consisted of clusters of small, single-storey square or rectangular buildings, joined together and disposed around impluvium courtyards. They are constructed of sun-dried clay and roofed with grass thatching and, since *c.* 1900, iron sheeting. Rooms are used primarily for sleeping and storage, with most domestic activity taking place in the courtyards or on the verandahs (*kobi*) that surround the courtyard under the overhanging eaves of the steeply pitched roofs. Such lineage compounds are generally termed 'a flock of houses' (*agbo ile*). At Ife *c.* AD 1000–1400 these courtyards were sometimes decorated with potsherd and stone pavements.

Yoruba palaces are, essentially, elaborations of this domestic model, often with many dwellings and courtyards, some devoted to specific groups and activities within the court system (Ojo, 1966; *see also* BENIN, §II; PALACE, §VIII). In royal palaces and in the compounds

of the more powerful and prosperous persons, the wooden verandah posts supporting the roofs are carved with images of women, men, children and animals. These carvings depict everyday scenes, figures of authority such as rulers, mothers, priests, warriors and diviners, along with lineage symbols and popular proverbs (see fig. 1). Entrances are often adorned with carved doors, most

1. Yoruba verandah post carved by Olowe of Ise, wood and pigment, h. 1.54 m, from the palace of the Ogoga of Ikere, Nigeria, 1910–14 (Chicago, IL, Art Institute of Chicago)

elaborate in palaces and communal shrines, but also used in the domestic compounds of prominent persons (*see* DOOR, fig. 10). Carved in low or high relief in registers, the doors are covered with genre scenes or symbols and images related to the patron or patrons who commissioned them. The composition is seriate, rather than narrative in format (Drewal and Drewal, 1987).

In the early 19th century the British introduced a style of tropical architecture comprising rectangular, wooden structures built on pilings with porches and shuttered windows. Some features were adapted by wealthy Yoruba at the coast. In the 1880s freed Yoruba artisans and architects returning from Brazil introduced a Brazilian Baroque style of architecture. This featured masonry construction, dormers, windows with multiple glass panes, heraldic sculptures, scroll lintels, balconies and balustrades. This style spread throughout much of southern Yorubaland in the late 19th century and the first half of the 20th (da Cunha, 1985).

2. FIGURATIVE SCULPTURE.

(i) General. The earliest surviving Yoruba sculpture type, at present dated to *c.* AD 1000, was created at Ife in stone and terracotta, as well as in the form of lost-wax castings in copper and leaded-brass. Its style, often characterized as idealized naturalism, occurs concurrently with other, strikingly abstract forms. The wide distribution of sculpture, in association with both the centrally located palace and the sacred groves at the perimeter of the city, suggest that this art served a variety of purposes and persons (Willett, 1967; 1989 exh. cat.). The southern Yoruba city-state of Owo, which not only maintained close artistic ties with Ife but also experienced the powerful artistic and cultural influences of Benin between the 15th and 19th centuries, created fine ivory sculpture for royalty and community leaders of both Owo and Benin (*see* BENIN) in the 17th and 18th centuries (see fig. 2). The style of this work typifies much wood and ivory Yoruba figurative sculpture produced since this period, having a large head in relation to body (generally in the proportions of 1 to 4); large, lenticular eyes; shelflike lips; and full, rounded volumes.

A special category of Yoruba sculpture consists of wooden memorial figures (*ere ibeji*), which are small standing figures of women and men (h. *c.* 150–250 mm) intended to commemorate departed twins. The Yoruba, who seem to have the highest incidence of twins (*ibeji*) in the world, regard them as sacred. Should a twin die, at whatever age, the parents may be required to commission a memorial sculpture, which they then feed, clothe, decorate, dance with and sing to, thus symbolically demonstrating their love and devotion and ensuring that the spirit remains content in the otherworld and does not call its twin to join it. Because these memorial figures have been carved in such large numbers in almost all sections of Yorubaland, scholars have been able to use them to identify regional, town, workshop and individual artists' styles (Thompson, 1971; Houlberg, 1973; Drewal, 1984; Stoll and Stoll, 1980).

Besides the early sculptural works in more permanent media and the twin figures, the Yoruba have a large repertory of wood, iron and clay sculpture that serves other sacred purposes. Religious art beautifies altars, distinguishes such religious leaders as diviners and the priests and priestesses of the gods, enhances ceremonies and serves to focus and intensify the religious experiences of devotees. Yoruba sacred art depicts worshippers, sometimes in acts of devotion, as, for example, the mother of twins depicted on a dancewand (*ose*) placed by such a woman on the shrine of Sango, known as 'the protector of twins', and carried at the god's annual festival (see fig. 3). Sometimes the devotee may be shown in a possession trance. In this case the image may be understood as showing humanity and divinity simultaneously (Drewal, 1977). The sacred aspect is foremost in Yoruba consciousness, and art is tangible proof of a worshipper's devotion, constituting a form of sacrifice (*ebo*), like all offerings, prayers and rites. Art's presence and visual power, therefore, helps to make an altar or ritual efficacious. It literally and figuratively shapes religious thought and practice.

(ii) Deities. Specific deities have specific forms associated with them.

2. Yoruba ceremonial sword (*udamalore*), carved ivory, l. 457 mm, from Owo, Nigeria, 18th century (London, British Museum)

3. Yoruba dancewand (*ose*), carved wood, h. 498 mm, from southern Egbado, Nigeria, 19th–20th centuries (Tervuren, Koninklijk Museum voor Midden-Afrika)

Eshu/Elegba. Art in honour of Eshu/Elegba, divine mediator and guardian of the crossroads between this world and the otherworld, includes paired, blackened, female and male figures enmeshed in strands of cowrie shells; figured dancehooks whose long curving coiffures are 'hooked' over priests' left shoulders during ceremonies; and conical earthen mounds with schematic facial features found in market-places, at crossroads and at entrances to domestic compounds.

Ogun. The god of iron and war, Ogun, is honoured in iron sculpture, sometimes decorated with brass. This may take the form of miniature tools, ceremonial swords, staffs, pokers, fanlike amulets and other emblems.

Osanyin. The primary art form of Osanyin, the deity of herbal medicines, is an iron staff surmounted by the commanding figure of a bird, often surrounded by other birds. This evokes the image of a tree with birds in its branches and refers both to the mystical powers of women (who transform into birds and gather in trees at night) and to the potent medicines that come from the leaves, bark and roots of forest trees. Sometimes the shaft is shaped into the form of a blade, for iron implements are required to gather such materials.

Obatala. Sculptures of men and women in a variety of media, painted white with chalk or crushed eggshells and painted blue with indigo, decorate Obatala altars. Obatala is the divine sculptor of humans and has white as his symbolic colour, for Yoruba believe that all people are born clothed in a white garment, the caul. For Yoruba white symbolizes purity, coolness, patience and morality, all of which are attributes possessed by Obatala.

Sango. Sango, thundergod and deified fourth king of Oyo, is honoured in dancewands (see fig. 3 above). These are wooden staffs carved in the form of double-bladed axes, probably in reference to Neolithic stone axes. The shafts of these wands often depict male and female devotees of Sango. The double-blade at the top, symbol of the power and presence of Sango, emerges out of the heads of the devotees and suggests the union of deity and devotee during possession trance dances. Another art form associated with Sango is a leather bag (*laba*) covered with elaborate appliquéd patterns. These bags are used to carry Sango paraphernalia, especially Sango's stone celts (*edun ara*). A third object is the Sango altar centrepiece usually in the form of either an inverted figured mortar (*odo*) or a kneeling female figure holding a large lidded bowl (*arugba*) on her head. These altarpieces enclose and elevate the primary objects associated with the deity.

Oya. Sango's deified senior wife, Oya, is the whirlwind, the powerful gust that precedes the storm. Among her sacred forms is a large circular shield with long, multi-layered strands of cowrie shells and buffalo horns filled with power substances covered with red cloth. Another is a large, figured earthen vessel, decorated with images of women, men, children, forked staffs, combs, horns and female equestrian figures.

Osun. Brass objects, especially staffs, bracelets and fans with incised designs of such aquatic and reptilian creatures as fish, lizards, crocodiles and snakes, pay tribute to another deified wife of Sango, Osun, goddess of the Osun River and patron of the Oyo–Yoruba town of Osogbo.

Yemoja. The goddess of the Ogun River and of other streams in western Yorubaland is honoured with large figured clay vessels, sometimes shaped in the form of a woman nursing a baby at the breast and darkened with deep indigo blue, as well as elaborate wood sculptures of worshipping women and children. Since Yemoja is viewed as the mother of many of the other *orisa* and of life itself, her iconography often stresses the themes of nurturing, birth and regeneration.

Orisa Oko. Massive bladelike iron staffs, made of many hoe blades with elaborate incised patterns along their lengths, an openwork cross at their midpoints and a phallic-shaped head/finial suggestive of a schematic anthropomorphic figure, are created for Orisa Oko, deity of the farm and fecundity. Placed in basins within the shrine room, the staff is usually clothed in a beaded sheath/garment with a veiled beaded crown covering the finial.

Eyinle. Earthenware vessels with lids sculpted to resemble either openwork crowns or the upper torsos of females holding small bowls are altar centrepieces for Eyinle, a hunter deity closely associated with the river goddess Osun and another hunter divinity, Osoosi. Other Eyinle art forms include figured earthen altar platforms, iron bracelets and necklaces.

3. MASK AND MASQUERADE. The Yoruba have an array of masking traditions serving multiple purposes. Here masking is a multimedia artistic mode used temporarily to materialize such normally unseen otherworldly forces as the spirits of ancestors and water spirits. The generic term for mask or masker is *eegun* ('powers concealed'). Yoruba give such concealed powers visual form, movement, sound, colour, smell and texture in spectacles (*iran*). These fleeting appearances entertain and enlighten their viewers as they confirm the omnipotence and omnipresence of sacred forces in the world and encourage their beneficence in human affairs. A few of the major Yoruba masking traditions are described here.

Egungun. These are lavish cloth ensembles, constructed in such different styles as long tubular sacks, layered lapets and rectangular forms. They may incorporate carved masks, helmet headdresses, circular sculpted trays, beaded panels and so on. They honour the spirits of ancestors and are created by the combined efforts and resources of lineage members. They may also be seen as visualizations of praise songs or *oriki* (Drewal, 1978). While the elegance and artistry of Egungun performances honour the lineage ancestors, they also serve as important status markers for the living.

Gelede. These wood masks, found among western Yoruba, consist of a hollowed head form, with or without a superstructure, that fits over the upper portion of the performer's head (*see* AFRICA, figs 84 and 15). A cloth veil attached to the lower rim of the mask partially covers the masker's face. The costume consists of a tailored bodice, a waistpiece made from either headties donated by women in the community or an embroidered/appliquéd wrapper, leggings and iron or brass ankle rattles. When the masker (who is male) represents a female, a wooden breastplate may be added. The masks and/or their superstructures depict ordinary Yoruba women and men, members of various religious, social, political or professional groups, foreigners and animals, the latter serving as metaphors for human attributes and actions. Gelede pays homage to the spiritual powers of elderly women known affectionately as 'our mothers' (Drewal and Drewal, 1983). The powers possessed by such women are comparable to those of the

gods and ancestors and may be either beneficial or harmful. Gelede imagery comments on the positive or negative impact of such individuals and groups and thus, through entertaining and enlightening performances, helps to shape society in constructive ways.

Epa/Elefon. Enormous, schematic, double-faced and pot-like headdresses, most surmounted by elaborate superstructures with single or multiple figures, are danced by young men during annual festivals among the northeastern Yoruba, the Ekiti and Igbomina (Thompson, 1971; Ojo, 1978). Such masking ceremonies honour the 'pillars' of society, that is mothers, priests/healers, warriors and rulers whose images appear in the superstructures of the headdresses. During performances, the young male maskers must leap up on a large earthen mound without faltering. The successful execution of this feat is viewed as a positive omen of communal good fortune in the coming year and is a kind of danced divination.

Agbo. Wooden cap-headdresses, depicting such water-associated creatures as fish, crocodiles, tortoises, waterfowl, snakes and the water chevrotain, honour water spirits in masking called Agbo or Ekine. The schematic or highly stylized sculptural style of many of these headdresses—bulging foreheads, tubular eyes, gaping, square mouths—clearly reveals artistic influence from Ijo-speaking peoples in the Niger River Delta from whom coastal Ijebu–Yoruba adopted and adapted this tradition. The headdresses are composed and worn horizontally as caps, evoking the way water creatures are seen when moving on the surface of the water.

Agemo. The ensembles of the Agemo (chameleon) masking society are distinguished by elaborate, circular headdresses that consist of many separately carved wooden figures of men, women and animals, especially chameleons, which crown the summit of multicoloured raffia fibre costumes. Agemo commemorates the founders of important towns and markets among the Ijebu–Yoruba and symbolically refers to the chameleon's powers to transform itself for protection and survival (Ogunba, 1985; Drewal, 1992).

4. REGALIA. Within Yoruba society, three types of leaders exist: sacred rulers, elders and chiefs/warriors. Each has a different set of regalia to signal status and power. Chiefs/warriors are awarded strands of stone, coral and glass beads as marks of their rank and privilege. Other items of their regalia are fly-whisks with carved wooden handles, appliquéd fans, bracelets and anklets. Diviners also have their own beaded regalia, consisting of elaborate, multi-stranded bead necklaces with pendant amulets and beaded bags in which they carry their paraphernalia. Rulers and council elders have even richer regalia.

(i) Rulers. Sacred rulers (*oba*) possess important art objects that distinguish their status and roles. A ruler's principal symbol is the conical beaded crown with veil (*adenla*; see fig. 4). The Yoruba say 'the ruler with beaded crown and veil is second only to the gods' (*'oba alade, ekeji orisa'*). The crown embodies the very essence of sacred rulership among the Yoruba. The awesome performative powers possessed by the ruler are intensified when the crown is

4. Yoruba beaded crown (*adenla*), h. 927 mm (New York, Brooklyn Museum)

worn. It is taboo for people to look directly at the head of the ruler because of the powers it embodies. In the past, judging from descriptions of the first audiences European visitors had with Yoruba rulers, the latter were hidden behind screens, sequestered within their palaces. Traditionally, only those able to trace direct ancestry to Oduduwa, the first ruler at Ife, can wear a beaded crown with veil.

The major elements on beaded crowns—birds, faces and the veil—have multiple associations (Thompson, 1970; Fagg, 1980; Beier, 1982). Birds surround the powerful substances embedded in the crown's summit and are often a reference to the mystical powers of women, suggesting that the ruler commands only with their support and cooperation. The face(s) that adorn conical crowns (*see* AFRICA, fig. 56) have been interpreted variously as belonging to Oduduwa, the first to wear the beaded crown; to the ever-watchful collective royal ancestors; to Olokun, the sea divinity and source of the materials used to create the crown; or to Obalufon, inventor of beads. The beaded veil masks the wearer's identity.

In addition to crowns, rulers possess a large array of other beaded objects such as coronets, staffs, fly-whisks, sandals, boots, footrests, necklaces, bracelets, anklets, fans

etc (*see* BEADWORK, colour pl. I, fig. 3). Other regalia in brass and ivory include sceptres and various costume attachments.

(ii) Elders. Paired male and female brass figures are the primary symbols of Osugbo (Ogboni), a society of male and female elders responsible for the selection, installation and removal of rulers; for burials; and for the judgement and punishment of serious crimes (1988 exh. cat.; 1989 exh. cat.). All important decisions of Osugbo are decided by debate among the titled female and male members. The paired brass-castings evoke the importance of the cooperative bond between males and females, both within Osugbo and within the larger society. Large, free-standing figures, referring to Osugbo lodge members and, by extension, to the original founding couple and all men and women in the community, are called 'owners of the house' (*onile*) and are owned jointly. Smaller, paired brass-castings (*edan*; figured as a female and male) on iron staffs and joined at the top by a chain are owned by individual Osugbo members (*see* AFRICA, fig. 33).

Osugbo society elders also own woven sashes (*itagbe* or *saki*), which they wear draped over the shoulder or wrapped around the head. They also often possess large garments, known as the 'cloth of many designs' (*olona*) and symbolic of long lives filled with many experiences.

5. DIVINATION INSTRUMENTS. Priests of the Ifa divination system possess a number of art objects that allude to a host of cosmic forces and recall valuable precedents from the past. Wooden Ifa divination trays (*opon*) are round, oval, semicircular or rectangular in shape and have a raised border, often filled with a series of images in low relief. These decorations evoke a cosmos of competing, autonomous forces (Drewal and Drewal, 1987) with the imagery in the raised borders—men, women, animals, deities, weapons, ritual regalia, genre scenes, tools etc—referring to the various forces, problems, issues, questions (and their remedies) that might be important to the clients who seek the advice and guidance of the diviner. The term *opon* means 'to flatter' (Abiodun, 1975), and thus the tray, through the artistry of its embellishments, praises the work of diviners as they seek to disclose the actions of cosmic forces.

Another divination object is the *agere* Ifa, an open or lidded cup supported by such figural compositions as nursing mothers, animals, equestrians, leaders with entourages, persons in ritual acts of prayer or offering and so on. *Agere* are used to hold the 16 palmnuts that the diviner uses to elicit verses through which various forces speak. These palmnuts symbolize the founder of Ifa divination, Orunmila, whose wife, Agere, once saved him from his enemies by hiding him inside her stomach. Since the *agere* object is understood to be a 'female' form, most examples have imagery devoted to women; yet artists and their diviner patrons are free to select other motifs (Drewal and Drewal, 1983).

A third divination object is a tapper (*iroke*) in the form of a miniature elephant's tusk most often figured with images of kneeling women, an icon connoting respect, greeting, devotion and supplication (Abiodun, 1975). The diviner strikes the pointed end of the tapper on the centre of the divination tray at the outset of divination while he invokes and praises, among others, famous ancient diviners and calls the cosmic forces to be present at the session. There is also a large bowl (*opon igede*), the lid of which has one or more faces in low relief, while the interior is often divided into four sections around a central circular compartment. Diviners store their divination equipment and other instruments in such containers, in which the divisions are symbolic of the four cardinal directions and the divining tray (*see* AFRICA, fig. 98).

6. DOMESTIC ARTS. Besides the art forms commissioned by social groups, shared communally or created to be viewed by large public audiences, numerous objects are meant for more personal, private use and appreciation. Colanut containers, often carved of wood in the form of animals or kneeling women offering bowls, are used to present colanuts to guests as a sign of peace and welcome. The image of the kneeling female recreates the gift-giving scene. Other domestic decorative arts include such objects as carved stools, some with elaborate compositions of genre scenes; intricately woven mats; bamboo platforms; polished and dyed earthen walls and floors, some with patterned pavements consisting of potsherds and stones; domestic pottery used for water storage and for cooking, mostly decorated with incised, punched and rouletted patterns; and wall paintings (*see also* §9 below). Since the second half of the 19th century Yoruba have adapted European decorative arts for their own purposes (especially in Victorian and Brazilian Baroque styles), creating new styles of furniture and elaborately carved frames for photographs, certificates and so on.

7. TEXTILES. For the Yoruba, textiles are an ancient, as well as a contemporary, mode of expressing personal beautification and enhancement. Men and women clad in wrappers that are sometimes tied with waist sashes are shown in Ife sculpture dated *c.* AD 1000. Over the centuries two woven textile traditions developed: one produced primarily by men on a movable narrow horizontal treadle loom; and the second by women on a stationary broad vertical loom with rotating warp and no treadle. Women's weave was produced for sale, for domestic use and for such special ritual garments as *olona* ('cloth of many designs') and *itagbe*, a shoulder sash used by the elders of Osugbo. The men's weave used local cotton, local silk (*sanyan*) and imported threads and is the basis for the prestige fashion ensembles worn by both men and women and known as *aso oke* (Lamb and Holmes, 1980).

Indigo-dyed cotton cloth (*adire*) is another distinctive Yoruba textile tradition, centred especially in Abeokuta and Ibadan (Barbour and Simmonds, 1971). Created and worn primarily by women since the 19th century, it is made of imported cotton cloth, which is either painted, stamped or stencilled with cassava paste (*adire eleko*) or tied and sewn and then dipped in indigo (*adire oniko*). In the late 20th century this began to be designed and worn by both men and women and sold internationally.

8. BODY ARTS. Jewellery and other body arts have a long history among the Yoruba. The earliest examples of Yoruba art show elaborate headdresses, necklaces, armlets,

bracelets and anklets of stone or glass beads. Crucibles of melted glass were found at Ife and suggest an active beadworking industry as early as AD 1000. Over the centuries, Yoruba have used beads for personal adornment, in royal and priestly regalia and as a principal symbol of the gods. Scarification, tattooing and body painting are also ancient among the Yoruba, as is evident in early Ife figural works. Some facial patterns seem to indicate special status or social role, some communicate sub-ethnic and/or lineage identity, while others such as cicatrization patterns (*kolo*) on different parts of the face and torso serve to beautify (Drewal, 1988).

9. PAINTING. While not widely known, because of its locations and transitory nature, painting has been widely practised by Yoruba women, usually priestesses, as part of ritual refurbishments of shrine walls and altars. The pigments used are produced from such local materials as camwood (red), kaolin/chalk/eggshells (white), charcoal/indigo (blue/black) and other substances to create a complex system of colour classification (*Oritameta*, 1990). Imagery is divinely inspired, for the priestess-painters create the works while in states of possession trance.

Since the turn of the 20th century, Euro-American traditions of easel painting have been introduced and practised, primarily by men. Artists have adopted and adapted this technique, sometimes incorporating such older, indigenous materials as beads to create multimedia works in a variety of styles. Some themes are drawn from Yoruba myth, history, oral tradition, literature and daily life, while others are clearly transcultural.

BIBLIOGRAPHY

G. J. A. Ojo: *Yoruba Palaces* (London, 1966)
F. Willett: *Ife in the History of West African Sculpture* (London and New York, 1967) [well-illus. with comprehensive bibliog.]
R. F. Thompson: 'The Sign of the Divine King: An Essay on Yoruba Bead-Embroidered Crowns with Veil and Bird Decorations', *Afr. A.*, iii/3 (1970), pp. 8–17, 74–80
J. Barbour and D. Simmonds, eds: *'Adire' Cloth in Nigeria* (Ibadan, 1971)
R. F. Thompson: *Black Gods and Kings: Yoruba Art at UCLA* (Los Angeles, 1971/R Bloomington and London, 1976) [well-illus. with comprehensive bibliog.]
M. H. Houlberg: '*Ibeji* Images of the Yoruba', *Afr. A.*, vii/1 (1973), pp. 20–27, 91–2
R. F. Thompson: 'Yoruba Artistic Criticism', *The Traditional Artist in African Societies*, ed. W. L. d'Azevedo (Bloomington, IN, 1973), pp. 19–61
R. Abiodun: 'Ifa Art Objects: An Interpretation Based on Oral Tradition', *Yoruba Oral Tradition*, ed. W. Abimbola (Ife, 1975), pp. 421–68
M. T. Drewal: 'Projections from the Top in Yoruba Art', *Afr. A.*, xi/1 (1977), pp. 43–9, 91–2
H. J. Drewal: 'The Arts of Egungun among Yoruba Peoples', *Afr. A.*, xi/3 (1978), pp. 18–19, 97–8
J. R. O. Ojo: 'The Symbolism and Significance of Epa-type Masquerade Headpieces', *Man*, n.s., xii/3 (1978), pp. 455–70
W. Fagg: *Yoruba Beadwork* (New York, 1980) [well-illus.]
V. Lamb and J. Holmes: *Nigerian Weaving* (Hertingfordbury and Lagos, 1980) [well-illus.]
M. Stoll and G. Stoll: *'Ibeji': Twin Figures of the Yoruba* (Munich, 1980)
African Artistry: Technique and Aesthetics in Yoruba Sculpture (exh. cat. by H. J. Drewal, Atlanta, GA, High Mus. A., 1980)
U. Beier: *Yoruba Beaded Crowns: Sacred Regalia of the Olokuku* (London, 1982) [well-illus.]
W. Fagg and J. Pemberton III: *Yoruba Sculpture of West Africa* (New York, 1982) [well-illus. with comprehensive bibliog.]
R. Abiodun: 'Identity and the Artistic Process in the Yoruba Aesthetic Concept of *Iwa*', *J. Cult. & Ideas*, i/1 (1983), pp. 13–30
H. J. Drewal and M. T. Drewal: *Gelede: Art and Female Power among the Yoruba* (Bloomington, IN, 1983)

M. T. Drewal and H. J. Drewal: 'An Ifa Diviner's Shrine in Ijebuland', *Afr. A.*, xvi/2 (1983), pp. 60–67, 99–100

R. F. Thompson: *Flash of the Spirit: African and Afro-American Art and Philosophy* (New York, 1983)

H. J. Drewal: 'Art, History and the Individual: A New Perspective for the Study of African Visual Traditions', *IA Stud. Afr. A.*, i (1984), pp. 87–114

M. C. da Cunha: *From Slave Quarters to Town Houses: Brazilian Architecture in Nigeria and the People's Republic of Benin* (São Paulo, 1985) [well-illus. with comprehensive bibliog.]

O. Ogunba: 'Agemo: The Orisa of the Ijebu People of South-eastern Yorubaland', *Nigerian Life and Culture: A Book of Readings*, ed. O. Y. Oyeneye and M. O. Shoremi (Ago-Iwoye, 1985), pp. 281–306

M. T. Drewal and H. J. Drewal: 'Composing Time and Space in Yoruba Art', *Word & Image*, iii/3 (1987), pp. 225–51

H. J. Drewal: 'Beauty and Being: Aesthetics and Ontology in Yoruba Body Art', *Marks of Civilization* (exh. cat., ed. A. Rubin; Los Angeles, UCLA, Mus. Cult. Hist., 1988), pp. 83–96

Earth and the Ancestors: Ogboni Iconography (exh. cat. by H. Witte, Amsterdam, Gal. Balolu, 1988)

Yoruba: Nine Centuries of African Art and Thought (exh. cat. by H. J. Drewal and J. Pemberton III, with R. Abiodun; New York, Cent. Afr. A., 1989) [well-illus.]

Oritameta: Proceedings of the International Conference on Yoruba Art: Obafemi Awdowo, 1990

Yoruba Art and Aesthetics (exh. cat. by R. Abiodun, H. J. Drewal and J. Pemberton III, Zurich, Mus. Rietberg, 1991) [well-illus.]

M. T. Drewal: *Yoruba Ritual: Performers, Play, Agency* (Bloomington, IN, 1992) [comprehensive bibliog.]

H. J. DREWAL

Yosa Buson [Buson; Sha'in; Shunsei; Taniguchi Noriyuki; Yahantei] (*b* Kema, Osaka, 1716; *d* Kyoto, 1783). Japanese painter and poet. He was a member of the second generation of literati painters in Japan. He and his contemporary Ike Taiga (*see* IKE, (1)) absorbed and transformed the Chinese scholar–amateur style into a Japanese idiom (*Nanga* or *Bunjinga*; *see* JAPAN, §VI, 4(vi)(d)).

1. BEFORE 1768. Buson left Kema in 1735 for Edo (now Tokyo), where he studied *haiku* poetry under Uchida Senzan and, from 1737, under Hayano Hajin (1677–1742). His earliest known work was an illustration of a woman reading a letter (1737; see Suzuki, p. 157) for a *haiku* anthology. When Hajin died, Buson left Edo and for the next ten years he lived and travelled in the northern Shimosa–Kantō provinces (now Ibaraki Prefect.), concentrating on the study of *haiku* but supporting himself by painting. His works of this period were experimental, drawing both on the style of the KANŌ SCHOOL and on official Chinese style. He first used the name Buson in a collection of New Year *haiku* in 1744.

In 1751 Buson moved to Heian (now Kyoto), where, having converted to Jōdo (Pure Land) Buddhism, he lived as a monk in temples. The influence of the temple wall paintings of the 15th and 16th centuries that he doubtless saw there appeared in the work he continued to produce to support himself in the mid-1750s. A vague poetic reference of 1752 recounts a visit by Buson to the Rinzai sect temple of Daitokuji, where there were paintings by Kanō school artists as well as by Hasegawa Tōhaku, Unkoku Tōgan, Soga Jasoku and Sōami and others. Buson probably also met Sakaki Hyakusen, pioneer of *Nanga* painting, who lived in Kyoto until his death in 1753.

In 1754 Buson went to Tango Province (now part of Kyoto Prefect.), where he remained until 1757, living in the Jōdo sect temple of Kenshōji. His move may have been prompted by his apparent disenchantment with Kyoto poetry circles. In Tango he redirected his energy towards painting, and it was from this time onwards that he produced noted literati works. His work in Tango was influenced by temple paintings, by Chinese woodblock-printed books and paintings of the Ming period (1368–1644) and by *Ōtsue* (provincial paintings sold on roadside stands in Ōtsu, north-east of Kyoto, at the beginning of the 17th century; *see also* JAPAN, §XV). During this period Buson painted several folding screens with Chinese historical or classical themes, borrowing the spacious compositions of the Kanō school wall paintings he had seen in Kyoto. The Chinese woodblock-printed books that Buson studied included the *Mustard Seed Garden Painting Manual* (Chin. *Jieziyuan huazhuan, c.* 1679–1701; Jap. *Kaishien gaden*, 1748 and 1753), which illustrated both literati and professional Ming period painting techniques. Designs of foliage and landscapes drawn from these books appear in details of paintings by Buson. His approach to space and composition and his simplification of Chinese models also seem to stem from his study of prints. To gain flexibility in the use of ink, Buson copied Ming period paintings of secondary importance as well. The influence of *Ōtsue* is seen in the hard, rounded contours of his brushwork. At that time many of Hyakusen's paintings were still in Tango. Buson wrote an encomium in praise of Hyakusen on his hanging scroll *Amanohashidate* (1757; see Yoshizawa, p. 102), presaging the influence that Hyakusen would have on Buson's *haiku* and *haiga* (works in which a picture complements the *haiku* text) in the next ten years.

After his return to Kyoto in 1757, Buson's paintings began to exhibit elements of his mature, individual style. In 1758 he changed his surname from Taniguchi to Yosa, and around 1760 he married. To support his new family, he made a concerted effort to improve his painting technique. He gained recognition and by 1768 was listed among the most popular painters in Kyoto in the *Heian jinbutsushi* ('Records of famous personalities of Heian'). The 1760s are called Buson's *byōbuko* ('folding-screen club') period, as he was rapidly producing screens for an art-buying cooperative of townsmen. In 1766 he formed the *haiku* group Sankasha (Three Fruits Group). Buson continued to educate himself, and in the late 1750s and the 1760s he studied the works of Chinese professional Zhe school and literati masters, and the realistic bird-and-flower paintings of the immigrant painter Shen Nanpin. Buson's new works showed greater efficacy in composition, brushwork and the use of ink and colour, as in the pair of six-panel folding screens *Landscape in the Manner of Wang Meng* (Kyoto, N. Mus.) and *Landscape in the Manner of Mi Fu* (Los Angeles, CA, Co. Mus. A.; both 1760), which demonstrate Buson's grasp of the essentials of Chinese literati painting and his experimentation within its conventional forms. He built up masses with wash, using eccentric, painterly texture strokes in the expressive *Wang Meng* landscape, and calligraphic strokes as used by Chinese literati in the more precise *Mi Fu* landscape. Buson used both freely experimental and precise modes of painting as parallel manners throughout his career.

Between 1766 and 1768 Buson travelled in Sanuki (now Kagawa Prefect.), where he copied or produced works based on paintings of the late Ming and Qing (1644–1911) periods. His style underwent a change as a result of this intense exposure to Chinese painting. In figural examples where he claimed a Chinese source, he amalgamated Chinese brush techniques with anecdotal and narrative qualities of the Japanese tradition. He abandoned expanses of colour and instead experimented with subtle tonal variations and the expressive effects of ink pooling.

2. 1768 AND AFTER. Buson returned permanently to Kyoto in 1768. He studied calligraphy intensively, continued to write *haiku* and became a professional *haiku* critic. He combined *haiku* and painting in a series of handscrolls (1778 set, Tokyo, Agy Cult. Affairs; 1779 set, Ikeda, Itsuō A. Mus.) and screens (1779; Yamagata, Prefect. Mus.) produced as a homage to the *haiku* poet Matsuo Bashō's (1644–94) travel diary of 1694, *Narrow Road to the Deep North* (*Oku no hosomichi*). The figures in these works were executed in a freer, more abbreviated fashion than in much of his earlier work.

From the 1770s until his death, Buson produced his most famous paintings, including the album *Ten Conveniences and Ten Pleasures* (*Jūben jūgi*), done in collaboration with Ike Taiga (1771; Kamakura, Kawabata Yasunari Mem. Mus.; National Treasure) and *Fishing Boat Adrift in the Evening Darkness* (*Night Fishing*) (mid-1770s; Ikeda, Itsuō A. Mus.; see fig.). The latter reveals a number of stylistic developments, including an emphasis on shifting light or weather, seen in the glowing reflection of the lantern light, a greater focus on the foreground and the incorporation of a figure in the landscape. The figure's personality is conveyed through facial expression, posture and gestures.

The shock of his daughter's divorce in 1777 resulted in both a change of name of Sha'in (whence the period 1778–83 is referred to as Buson's Sha'in period) and in a major creative surge in his painting and poetry. During this period he used three main painting styles, two being mature forms of his free brush style and his precise style, while the third was *haiga*. In his precise style he portrayed the Japanese countryside, using his highly personalized, loose brushwork, which, in its sensuous, tactile and evocative qualities, approached the true Chinese literati manner. Colour, rarely used in Chinese literati painting, was used in a novel way to create a sense of time, season and atmosphere. An example is the undated hanging scroll *Cuckoo over Spring Verdure* (Tokyo, Hiraki Ukiyoe Found.). His rougher, more freely brushed works, such as *Kite and Crows* (pair of hanging scrolls; Kyoto, Kitamura Mus.), show more dramatic atmospheric effects, achieved in a boldly personal way through the use of ink and subdued, ink-diluted colour. In Buson's hands, *haiga* was developed into a viable art form. The influence of Hyakusen's sketch-like illustrations for *haiku* was clear. As in his poetry, in which Buson used ordinary images paradoxically to transcend the banal, so too in *haiga* he generally employed simple figural or natural images. In these pictures he conveyed a penetrating analysis of form and action with minimal, incisive brushwork and coloration. The figures were executed in an abbreviated manner, as in the undated hanging scroll *Matabei Enjoying the Cherry Blossoms* (Ikeda, Itsuō A. Mus.). Buson also produced series of painted portraits, accompanied by *haiku* and calligraphic

Yosa Buson: *Fishing Boat Adrift in the Evening Darkness* (*Night Fishing*), hanging scroll, ink and colours on silk, 1307×475 mm, mid-1770s (Ikeda, Itsuō Art Museum)

inscriptions, of the 36 followers of Bashō, published posthumously in several woodblock-printed editions (*see* KASEN'E).

Rather than the calligraphy brush preferred by orthodox literati painters, Buson worked with painting brushes, such as thin or wide versions of the *hake* brush, connected rows of brushes, straw brushes or brushes with tips cut to create special textures. His use of actual colours to represent coloured areas and *sumi* (Chinese ink) for dark areas also diverged from the practice of literati painters, who used diluted ink to convey the full range of colour, with indigo or ochre being added only for accent. The colours Buson most often used were vegetal green dyes or indigo, red ochre and vermilion. Buson's most important student was MATSUMURA GOSHUN.

BIBLIOGRAPHY
S. Sawamura: 'Buson ron 1–4' [On Buson], *Kokka*, 233–8 (1909–10)
Y. Inui: *Buson shinkenkyū* [New research on Buson] (Osaka, 1925)
——: *Buson to sono shū* [Buson and his circle] (Osaka, 1926)
H. Kawagihashi: *Gajin Buson* [The painter Buson] (Tokyo, 1926)
Buson ihō [Homage to Buson] (exh. cat. by H. Kawagihashi, Kyoto, N. Mus., 1932)
T. Ebara: *Buson zenshū* [Complete collection of Buson] (Kyoto, 1933)
K. Tanaka: 'Buson ron' [On Buson], *Bijutsu Kenkyū*, xv (1933)
T. Ebara: *Buson* (Tokyo, 1943)
K. Yonezawa and C. Yoshizawa: *Bunjinga* [Literati painting], Nihon no bijutsu [Arts of Japan], xxiii (Tokyo, 1966); Eng. trans. by B. I. Monroe as *Japanese Painting in the Literati Style* (New York, 1974)
The Poet Painters, Buson and his Followers (exh. cat. by C. L. French and others, Ann Arbor, U. MI Mus. A., 1974)
J. Sasaki: *Yosa Buson*, Nihon no bijutsu, cix (Tokyo, 1975)
S. Suzuki: *Buson to haiga* [Buson and *haiga*], Nihon no bijutsu [Arts of Japan], Bukutsuku obu butsukusu [Book of books], xlvi (Tokyo, 1978)
C. Yoshizawa: *Yosa Buson*, Nihon bijutsu kaiga zenshū [Complete collection of Japanese painting], ix (Tokyo, 1980)
J. Cahill: 'Yosa Buson and Chinese Painting', *International Symposium on the Conservation and Restoration of Cultural Property: Interregional Influences in East Asian Art History: Tokyo, 1982*, pp. 245–63
Yosa Buson meisakuten [Masterpieces of Yosa Buson] (exh. cat. by J. Cahill, Nara, Yamato Bunkakan, 1983)
HOLLIS GOODALL-CRISTANTE

Yoshiatsu. *See* SATAKE SHOZAN.

Yoshida, Isoya (*b* Tokyo, 19 Dec 1894; *d* Tokyo, 24 March 1974). Japanese architect. He graduated from Tokyo Art School in 1923 and travelled to Europe in 1925. Recognizing elements of Modernism in *sukiya* (tea house), a traditional style of Japanese residential architecture (*see* JAPAN, §XIV, 2), Yoshida formulated a modern version of the style with a distinctive freedom of planning and individuality that broke away from the traditional modular structural system. By enclosing structural members within the wall using the *ōkabe* (large wall) system, he was able to ignore the structural grid and place columns where he wished. Other technical innovations included the replacement of corner columns with windows and the introduction of special lighting effects and a sense of the opulence found in *kabuki* and other traditional Japanese stage design. The modern *Sukiya* style, for which Yoshida established his reputation in the 1930s, was one of the most successful attempts to reconcile tradition and modernity in Japanese architecture in the 20th century.

Yoshida was a prolific architect: his residential works included houses for artists and politicians, such as Kokei Kobayashi House (1933), Tokyo, Gyokudō Kawai House (1936), Ome, Rokuzaemon Kineya House (1936), Atami, Shigeru Yoshida House (1962), Kanagawa Prefecture, and Shinnosuke Kishi House (1969), Shizuoka Prefecture. He designed some of Japan's most distinguished *ryōtei* (traditional-style restaurants often used for banquets) such as Kitanaka (1951), Shinkiraku (1940–62), Kitagawa (1958) and Kitchō (1961). He also designed many performance and exhibition spaces for Japan's traditional arts, including the Kabukiuza (1951), Meiji za (1958), Gotō Art Museum

(1960) and Gyokudō Art Museum (1961), all in Tokyo. Yoshida also pursued the development of a Japanese design in concrete with his public buildings after World War II, and later sought a truly Japanese style in religious architecture, eliminating Chinese influences. His religious buildings include the temples Naritasan Shinshoji (1968), Chiba Prefecture, Chuguji (1968), Nara, and Manganji (1969), Tokyo. Yoshida taught at Tokyo University of Fine Arts and Music (previously Tokyo Art School) from 1941 to 1974.

WRITINGS
Yoshida Isoya sakuhinshū [Collection of works by Isoya Yoshida] (Tokyo, 1976)

BIBLIOGRAPHY
I. Kurita, ed.: *Yoshida Isoya*, Gendai Nihon kenchikuka zenshū [Complete collection of modern Japanese architects], iii (Tokyo, 1974)
J. P. Noffsinger: *Isoya Yoshida: Modern/Traditional Architect of Japan* (Monticello, IL, 1980)

Yoshida, Tetsurō (*b* Toyama, May 1894; *d* Tokyo, 8 Sept 1956). Japanese architect. Upon graduating from Tokyo University (1919) he joined the Teishinshō (pre-war Ministry of Communications) and designed numerous post, telephone and telegraph offices. Using reinforced concrete he established a standardized design for the buildings of the Teishinshō, aiming to create a Rationalist architecture that was suited to the Japanese climate and environment. During the 1920s he designed buildings with a dominant motif of semicircular arches, which derived from Scandinavian architecture; their austere Rationalism was characterized by a surface of grids using structural pillars and span doors covered with white tiles. In 1931 Yoshida spent several months on an architectural study tour in Europe and the USA. At this time he was influenced by the Neo-classicist works of Auguste Perret, although German Rationalism also had an impact on his designs. Characteristic works by Yoshida include the Central Post Office (1931), Tokyo, (*see* JAPAN, fig. 39) and the Central Post Office (1936), Osaka. He was a friend of Bruno Taut, who was in Japan in the 1930s. After he became a professor at Nihon University (1946) he published a number of books, including *Japanische Architektur* (Tübingen, 1952), *Das Japanische Wohnhaus* (Tübingen, 1954) and *Der Japanische Garten* (Tübingen, 1957).

BIBLIOGRAPHY
Yoshida Tetsurō kenchiku sakuhinshū [Collected architectural works of Tetsurō Yoshida] (Tokyo, 1968)
KATSUYOSHI ARAI

Yoshihara, Jirō (*b* Osaka, 1 Jan 1905; *d* Ashiya, 10 Feb 1972). Japanese painter. He was mainly self-taught as an artist. When his friendship with Tsuguharu Fujita and Seiji Tōgō began, he moved towards abstract painting and before World War II showed work at the exhibitions of the Nikakai and of the more radical Kyūshitsukai. After the war he was active as one of the principal promoters of avant-garde art in the Kansai region. In 1953 he was a founder-member of the Nihon Abusutorakuto Āto Kurabu (Japanese Abstract Art Club) with Minoru Kawabata, Takeo Yamaguchi and others, and in 1954 he both sponsored the foundation of and represented the Gutai Bijutsu Kyōkai (Concrete Art Association; *see* GUTAI), whose central figures were the young painters Kazuō

Shiraga (*b* 1924) and Atsuko Tanaka (*b* 1932). They held regular exhibitions in Kansai and Tokyo and published a journal, *Gutai*.

In his own work Yoshihara continued almost consistently to pursue abstract painting, despite the various anti-art activities of the Gutai members, which challenged traditional concepts. Like other members of the group, in the late 1950s he was influenced by the forms of *Art informel*. In the later part of his career, however, he produced abstract pictures such as *White on Black* (1965; Tokyo, N. Mus. Mod. A.; *see* JAPAN, fig. 114), distinguished by their flat areas of colour, thick arcs and shapes reminiscent of Chinese numerals.

BIBLIOGRAPHY
Yoshihara Jirō (exh. cat., Kamakura, Kanagawa Prefect. Mus. Mod. A., 1973)
Yoshihara Jirō to Gutai no sono go [Yoshihara Jirō: Gutai and after] (exh. cat., Kobe, Hyōgo Prefect. Mus. Mod. A., 1979)
                                    SHIGEO CHIBA

Yoshimochi. *See* ASHIKAGA YOSHIMOCHI.

Yoshimura, Junzō (*b* 1908). Japanese architect and teacher. He graduated from the Department of Architecture at the Tokyo School of Art in 1931 and joined the architectural planning office of Antonin Raymond, where he worked until establishing his own office in Tokyo in 1941. He began to teach at the Tokyo School of Art in 1945, becoming a full professor there in 1962. Yoshimura's innovative design approach is clearly demonstrated in his residential projects: their unusual qualities of calmness and harmony are best explained by his primary concern for the needs of the people who would live in them. He used traditional materials and techniques and created intimate spaces with low ceilings. His design philosophy was expressed by his stated satisfaction at seeing that his buildings offered users a comfortable lifestyle. His major works include the Terada Residence (1967), Chigasaki; Inokuma Residence (1971), Tokyo; Japan House (1971), New York; Nara National Museum (1973), Nara; and Aichi Prefectural University of Art (1974), Nagakute.

WRITINGS
The Architecture of Junzō Yoshimura, 1941–1978 (Tokyo, 1979)
BIBLIOGRAPHY
'A House at Shonan and Profile', *Japan Architect*, 138 (1968), pp. 45–68
T. Muramatsu: 'Humanity and Architecture', *Japan Architect*, 200 (1973), pp. 89–96
                                    EIZO INAGAKI

Yoshinobu Ashihara. *See* ASHIHARA, YOSHINOBU.

Yoshirō Taniguchi. *See* TANIGUCHI, YOSHIRŌ.

Yoshishige Saitō. *See* SAITŌ, YOSHISHIGE.

Yoshitoshi (i). *See* TSUKIOKA YOSHITOSHI.

Yoshitoshi (ii). *See* MORI, YOSHITOSHI.

Yoshizaka, Takamasa (*b* Tokyo, 13 Feb 1917; *d* Tokyo, 17 Dec 1980). Japanese architect, urban planner, teacher and writer. He was the son of a diplomat and spent several years in Europe in his youth. In 1941 he graduated from Waseda University, Tokyo, and began to teach there, continuing until his death. He entered private practice in Tokyo in 1945. From 1950 to 1952 he studied in France and worked in Le Corbusier's studio in Paris. During this time he translated many of Le Corbusier's writings including eight volumes of his complete works. He later collaborated on Le Corbusier's National Museum of Western Art (1957–9), Tokyo, with Kunio Maekawa and Junzō Sakakura, both of whom had also worked for Le Corbusier. Yoshizaka's first major work, the Japanese Pavilion commissioned by the Japanese Government for the Venice Biennale of 1956, revealed the influence of Le Corbusier in its exposed structural frame and use of concrete. After his time in Le Corbusier's studio, the expression of regional identity became a central issue for Yoshizaka. He advocated humanism and vernacular approaches to regionalism in architecture, constantly seeking new forms of expression. Examples of his work include the Kaisei High School (1957–8), Nagasaki, the Maison Franco-Japonaise (1960–71), Tokyo, and the Daigaku Seminary Housing (1963–70), Hachioji, Tokyo. These buildings reveal a careful analysis of functional and spatial relationships and a response to context, and they are expressive statements against the monotony of simplistic, rectilinear grid architecture. The Daigaku Seminary Housing, for instance, is a group of individual units stepping down a hill but unified by the main buildings that act as towers or campaniles. This expression of random units held together by a dominant formal element is characteristic of his theory of 'discontinuous unity', an important part of his architectural and planning ideas aimed at reconciling the many contradictory elements of society. In 1965 he founded the architectural design group Atelier U; members of the group Team Zoo came from this studio, strongly influenced by Yoshizaka who was one of the pioneers of modern architecture in Japan. He was President of the Architectural Institute of Japan (1973–4) and received many honours and awards during his career.

WRITINGS
Yoshizaka Takamasa shū [The collected works of Yoshizaka Takamasa], 17 vols (Tokyo, 1984–7)
BIBLIOGRAPHY
Yoshizaka Takamasa, Gendai Nihon kenchikuka zenshū [Complete collection of modern Japanese architects], xv (Tokyo, 1971)
'Yoshizaka Takamasa, 1917–1981', *Kenchiku Bunka/Architectural Culture*, 415 (1981)
                                    KATSUYOSHI ARAI

Yotkan. Chinese site *c.* 8 km west of Khotan in southern Xinjiang Uygur Autonomous Region. It is considered to have been the old capital of the region of Khotan. Aurel Stein's archaeological surveys of 1900–01 confirm Chinese records (e.g. the *Hou Han shu* ('History of the later Han')), which describe Yotkan as a magnificent secular and religious centre. Although no buildings survive, the nearby river exposed at a depth of 3–7 m a 2–3 m thick layer of material culture containing ceramics, terracotta figures, metal and soapstone, gold leaf, jewellery, cameos, seals, coins and manuscripts. Despite the missing stratigraphic observations, it can be gathered from comparative studies that these objects date from the 1st to the 4th century AD. The ceramics, the yellowish, unglazed surface of which shines, are the most remarkable finds (*see also* CENTRAL ASIA, §II, 5(iv)). The decoration consists of incisions and beading, but characteristic of this ware are the applied, medallion-like reliefs and sometimes even three-dimensional figural representations. The ornamentation covers either the entire body of the vessel or only the shoulder, is wrapped round the body of the vessel horizontally or is used as a handle attachment. Many different motifs occur, floral (lotus rosettes and palmettes) as well as animal (griffins and lions, camels, monkeys, birds and gorgons' heads). Human figures are also represented: musicians, dancers and acrobats are accompanied by drinking individuals or couples.

See also CENTRAL ASIA, §II, 3(ii)(a).

BIBLIOGRAPHY
A. Rémusat: *Histoire de la ville de Khotan*, 2 vols (Paris, 1820)
M. A. Stein: *Ancient Khotan: Detailed Report of Archaeological Exploration in Chinese Turkestan*, 2 vols (Oxford, 1907)
G. Gropp: *Archäologische Funde aus Khotan, Chinesisch-Ostturkistan: Die Trinkler-Sammlung im Übersee-Museum Bremen* (Bremen, 1974)

M. YALDIZ

Yōtoku. *See* OKUDA EISEN.

Young, Ammi B(urnham) (*b* Lebanon, NH, 19 June 1798; *d* Washington, DC, 13 March 1874). American architect. Trained by his father as a builder, he designed houses, churches and collegiate buildings in New Hampshire and Vermont, including three utilitarian dormitories (1828–9, 1839–40) and an observatory (1852) for Dartmouth College. Although he lacked a formal architectural education, he obtained the commission for the Vermont State Capitol (1833–6), a Neo-classical building with a Doric portico, capped for exterior effect by a hemispherical dome as there was no internal domed space. (A new drum and dome were added after a fire in 1857.) In 1837 Young won a competition for the Boston Custom House; this was his largest commission, completed in 1847 at a cost of over one million dollars. In 1915 it became the base for a skyscraper for the federal government. The only surviving competition drawing (pencil, watercolour and gouache; Washington, DC, N. Archvs) illustrates the building's magnificent internal domed space; monolithic granite columns surround the exterior of the building, which has pedimented ends and Doric porticos on the long sides.

This design for a federal building led to Young's appointment in 1852 as Supervising Architect of the Treasury Department. Here he worked with Alexander H. Bowman, Captain of the Corps of Engineers, on *c.* 80 fireproof iron-framed post offices, custom houses, court facilities and marine hospitals. The Roman temple form was the basis for several designs, including the Custom House (1852–9) in Norfolk, VA, but Young also used the Italian palazzo style, as in the Post Office (1856–8) at Windsor, VT, which has quoins and other Italianate decorative features in cast iron. Complaints about overspending on federal buildings led to his dismissal as Supervising Architect in 1862. Little is known of Young after this time, but he is described by Alfred B. Mullett in his diary of 1865 as working with a former draughtsman from the Treasury Department.

BIBLIOGRAPHY
L. Wodehouse: 'Ammi Burnham Young, 1798–1874', *J. Soc. Archit. Hist.*, xxv (1966), pp. 268–80
——: 'Architectural Projects in the Greek Revival Style by Ammi Burnham Young', *Old Time New England*, lv (1970), pp. 73–85
L. Craig: *The Federal Presence* (Cambridge, MA, 1978)
B. Lowry: *Building a National Image* (Washington, DC, 1985)

LAWRENCE WODEHOUSE

Young, Lamont (*b* Naples, 12 March 1851; *d* Naples, 1929). British urban planner, architect and designer, active in Italy. His wealthy Scottish parents moved from India to Naples before his birth. He was educated first in Switzerland and then in Britain. Between 1872 and 1888 he devised several ambitious schemes for the city of Naples, none of which was realized. These included the construction of an underground railway (it would have been the third such system in the world after those in New York and London), which, as a public transport system, would have been integrated with the horse-drawn tramways; the redevelopment of the areas of the city struck by the cholera epidemic of 1884, a plan that would have involved raising the standard of the existing housing, constructing a new sewer system and installing sanitation in each house; the demolition of the overcrowded quarters of the city and the redistribution of the population; and finally, a scheme for the establishment of a new quarter on reclaimed land along the coast at Posillipo to be called Rione Venezia. He conceived this *rione* as a group of islands separated by canals and linked, via a canal tunnel, to a new building complex in the Campi Flegrei, which was to comprise a bathing establishment, a spa, a hotel, a 'palazzo di cristallo' (similar to the Crystal Palace in London), intended for cultural and artistic activities, as well as large public parks.

In Naples Young built the Castello Grifeo (*c.* 1875; now the Villa Curcio) in a Gothic Revival style, with a round tower left in a theatrically ruined state in English Picturesque taste and a small Gothic Revival building in the garden. The Palazzina Grifeo (1877; in the Parco Grifeo), on the other hand, is in a Renaissance Revival style, which he combined with rustic and English Georgian motifs. The Mackean Bentik School for Girls (1884; now the Grenoble Institute) is an austere Renaissance Revival building in tufa stone, with superimposed orders and roundels containing busts above the ground-floor windows. Among his other works are the Albergo Bertolini (1892–8; much altered) and a small villa (*c.* 1892–4; later altered) near by, which has a classical exterior, an Indian Revival room inside and a small Swiss-looking chalet (1893–4) in the grounds. Castle Lamont (1902–4; later Castello Aselmeyer) is Young's principal architectural work. Built as his own residence on one of the hills of Naples, it is designed to fit in with the animated appearance of the bank of tufa on which it stands, and the arrangement of the building, which plays on projections, recesses and varying levels, gives it the appearance of a fairy-tale castle enriched with Tudor decorative motifs.

Young's last works include an unexecuted plan (*c.* 1914) for an enormous building comprising shops, offices and a fantastical Grand Hotel in an Indian Revival style, which was to be situated on the beautiful slopes of Monte Echia in Naples; the Villa Astarita (*c.* 1920; destr. World War II); and the Villa Hebe (*c.* 1920; extant) in a Gothic Revival idiom similar to that of Castle Lamont, for which he also designed the splendid Gothic Revival interior furnishings. Young was also an inventor, designing among other things collapsible lamps and 'synchronous-oscillating' wings for airships or aeroplanes (patented in 1917). In 1908, having become interested in archaeology, he made a survey of the ruins of Roman buildings at Teano, in collaboration with Leonard Woolley.

Young was a typical representative of 19th-century attitudes, combining practicality and idealism: although he welcomed innovation and productive investment, his thoroughly British mentality often clashed with the social reality of Naples at the end of the 19th century and the beginning of the 20th. Together with a brilliant imagination, his sensibility for the use of building materials left in their natural state and his intuitive sense for proposing advanced solutions to problems of urban planning permits one to judge his work as that of a significant and forward-looking exponent of the eclectic culture of his time.

BIBLIOGRAPHY
G. Alisio: *Lamont Young: Utopia e realtà nell'urbanistica napoletana dell'ottocento* (Rome, 1978)

ADRIANO GHISETTI GIAVARINA

Young, William (*b* Paisley, 1843; *d* London, 1 Nov 1900). Scottish architect. He began his architectural training as a pupil of James Lamb of Paisley and became an assistant to William Nairne Tait (1831/2–1904) in Glasgow in 1859, followed by a spell with James Salmon (*d* 1888). Young moved to London in 1865 to work in the office of Charles Henry Howell (1823/4–1905), County Architect and Surveyor for Surrey. In 1869 he set up his own office and that year also published a topographical book of sketches he had made in the southern English counties.

One of Young's first clients was Francis Wemyss-Charteris-Douglas, Lord Elcho (1818–1914), who in 1883 became the 10th Earl of Wemyss and March. Elcho was responsible for introducing Young to a succession of relatives and friends whose patronage rapidly led the young architect to acquire a reputation as one of the leading designers of country houses. In 1872 Young issued a large volume of his own designs for a wide variety of building types, principally in the emerging style of the QUEEN ANNE REVIVAL. As Young's commissions increased, he multiplied his use of architectural styles, so that his country houses often display a medley of rooms from various historical periods. His most important early works are Holmewood House (1873), Cambs, for William Wells, Elcho's brother-in-law; Haseley Manor (1875), Warwicks, for Alfred Hewlett; Oxhey Grange (1876), Herts, for W. T. Ely; and a saloon in the Adam style at Chevening Park (1877–9), Kent, for Arthur Philip Stanhope, 6th Earl Stanhope (1838–1905). Between 1874 and 1878 he worked on Chelsea House (destr. 1935), the London residence of George Henry Cadogan, 5th Earl Cadogan (1840–1915), in a mixture of French Renaissance styles. In his *Town and Country Mansions and Suburban Houses* (1879), Young proclaimed that 'the best architect is he who, free from prejudice, has studied the peculiarities and communed with the genius of all styles'. The accompanying illustrations of his designs, showing an eclectic approach to interior decoration, became an important sourcebook for other architects of the period.

Young's winning design for the enormous City Chambers, George Square, Glasgow, was erected between 1882 and 1890 (*see* GLASGOW, fig. 3). Based on 16th-century Italian prototypes, with a tall central tower and opulent interiors, it proved highly influential in the emerging BAROQUE REVIVAL.

About 1886 the Earl of Wemyss invited Young to enlarge his country seat in East Lothian, Gosford House. Over the next ten years Young created harmonious, almost replicative additions to Robert Adam's original building. The grand staircase, displaying a simple pattern of arcading and a rich use of marble, became Young's trademark. This ability to capture sensitively the affluent mood in country-house architecture led to further commissions, almost all additions: at Culford Hall (1891–4) (now Culford School), near Bury St Edmunds, Suffolk, for Earl Cadogan; Duncombe Park (1891–5), near Helmsley, N. Yorks, for Charles William Reginald Duncombe, 2nd Earl Feversham (1879–1963); and Elveden Hall, Suffolk, for Edward Cecil Guinness, 1st Earl of Iveagh, begun just before Young's death, and carried to completion in 1903 by his son Clyde Young (1871–1948). The Indian Hall of Elveden, a domed splendour of Indian and Islamic eclecticism, is one of the most sumptuous works of the Edwardian period.

In 1898 Young was given the commission by the government to erect the new War Office (now called the Old War Office) in Whitehall. His design, in a bold Edwardian Baroque Revival style, was intended to harmonize with and rival Inigo Jones's nearby Banqueting House. Completed by Clyde Young following his father's death, the War Office opened in 1906.

WRITINGS
Picturesque Examples of Old English Churches and Cottages from Sketches in Sussex and Adjoining Counties (Birmingham, 1869)
Picturesque Architectural Studies and Practical Designs for Gate Lodges, Cottage Hospitals, Villas, Vicarages, Country Residences, Schools, Village Churches, etc., etc. (London and New York, 1872)
Town and Country Mansions and Suburban Houses (London and New York, 1879)
The Municipal Buildings, Glasgow (Glasgow, 1890)

BIBLIOGRAPHY
Obituary, *Archit. Rev.* [Boston],viii (1900), pp. 234–5; *Builder*, lxxix (1900), p. 410; *RIBA J.*, n.s. 3, viii (1901), pp. 21–2, 44–7
A. Service: *Edwardian Architecture: A Handbook to Building Design in Britain, 1890–1914* (London, 1977)
A. S. Gray: *Edwardian Architecture: A Biographical Dictionary* (London, 1985)

NEIL R. BINGHAM

Young Estonia [Est. Noor-Eesti]. Term used from 1912 to describe a broad cultural movement in Estonia that lasted from *c*. 1902 until 1917. It generated new literary and artistic traditions for a people seeking independence from the Russian empire. Young Estonia was one manifestation of the phenomenon of national awakenings occurring throughout *fin-de-siècle* northern and eastern Europe, being particularly akin to those in Finland and Latvia. Its ideologist, the poet Gustav Suits (1883–1956), preached a synthesis of individualism and socialism, wherein culture could be nationalistic as long as it transcended chauvinism. His literary programme called for the assimilation of the best of European culture, and this expansive view soon affected Estonian visual arts, theatre and linguistics. Calendars and a periodical, *Noor-Eesti*, published in 1905–15 and 1910–11 respectively, promulgated and refined Young Estonia's philosophy. During this period, the first formal exhibition of Estonian painting and sculpture opened in Tallinn in 1906, and in 1909 the Folk Museum (now Museum of Ethnography) was established in Tartu, largely as a result of the organizing efforts of Kristjan Raud, Estonia's foremost National Romanticist (*see* RAUD, (1)). Older than most Young Estonia artists, Raud worked in a progression of styles, from realistic renderings of folk subjects to the modified Symbolist manner of his cycle celebrating the legendary national hero *Kalevipoeg*.

Estonia's artistic vanguard received much of its revolutionary impetus from studying abroad and adapting foreign idioms. KONRAD MÄGI, Aleksander Tassa (1882–1957) and Nikolai Triik (1884–1940), for example, were influenced by the Symbolist, Fauvist and Post-Impressionist art they saw in Paris, elements of which later informed their work. Mägi often painted Estonian landscapes in a vivid Neo-Impressionist mode, sometimes even indulging in Art Nouveau decoration. Triik was more inclined to Symbolism, having admired Edvard Munch and Ferdinand Hodler's work during visits to Norway and Berlin, and his paintings are among Young Estonia's most allegorical. Other artists associated with this movement were August Jansen (1881–1957), Roman Nyman (1881–1951), Paul Burman (1888–1934) and Peet Aren (1889–1970). While Estonian landscapes were a subject common to all—and appropriate vehicles for nationalistic sentiments—these artists had marked differences in stylistic approach, even within their own oeuvres. Of this group, Aren was most attracted to Expressionism, and his art anticipates works by certain members of the modernist ESTONIAN ARTISTS' GROUP. JAAN KOORT was the principal sculptor of this milieu, again representing local subjects in a variety of international styles.

BIBLIOGRAPHY

V. Vaga: *Eesti Kunst* [Estonian art] (Tallinn, 1940)

MARK ALLEN SVEDE

Young & Mackenzie. Irish architectural partnership formed in 1870 in Belfast by Robert Young (*b* Belfast, 22 Feb 1822; *d* Belfast, 21 Jan 1917) and his pupil John Mackenzie (*b* Belfast, 1844; *d* Belfast, 1917). Young's son Robert Magill Young (*b* Belfast, 1851; *d* Belfast, 1925) joined the partnership in 1880. The founder of the firm, Robert Young, trained with Charles Lanyon in Belfast in the 1840s and became his chief assistant, with responsibility for railway engineering works and road bridges. He then worked briefly in the south of Ireland as an engineer for the railway contractor William Dargan, before setting up on his own in Belfast as an architect and civil engineer in the early 1850s. The partnership of Young & Mackenzie became the leading designer of Presbyterian churches in Ulster, working usually in Gothic Revival style (e.g. Fitzroy Presbyterian Church, 1872–4), but sometimes in Romanesque Revival style (e.g. Townsend Street Presbyterian Church, 1876–8) (both in Belfast). In the later Victorian period they were prominent in the field of commercial architecture in Belfast, building two of the city's most impressive department stores, the multi-storey former Robinson & Cleaver's (1886–8; now Cleaver House) and

Anderson & McAuley's (1890), both in a free classical style, and the two most imposing insurance blocks, the Scottish Provident Institution (1897–1902), in Baroque style, and the Ocean Buildings (1899–1902; now Pearl Assurance House), in Late Gothic style, both in Donegall Square, Belfast. They also designed the large, Late Gothic style Presbyterian Assembly Buildings (1900–05), the two-tier galleried main hall of which (altered 1992) was one of the most impressive interiors in Belfast.

BIBLIOGRAPHY

C. E. B. Brett: *Buildings of Belfast, 1700–1914* (London, 1967, rev. Belfast, 1985)
P. Larmour: *Belfast: An Illustrated Architectural Guide* (Belfast, 1987)

PAUL LARMOUR

Young Ones [Swed. De Unga]. Swedish group of artists active from 1907 to 1911. The members included ISAAC GRÜNEWALD, LEANDER ENGSTRÖM, Birger Jörgen Simonsson (1883–1930), GÖSTA SANDELS, Tor Sigurd Bjurström (1888–1966), Carl Magnus Ryd (1883–1958), Nils Tove Edward Hald (1883–1980) and Ejnar Nerman (1888–1983). At their first exhibition, in Stockholm (1909), they were described by the critic August Brunins as 'Men of the Year 1909' ('*1909 års män*'). The group had two more exhibitions, both in Stockholm (1910, 1911), after which the group disbanded to form the short-lived group The Eight (De åtta), containing several of the original members of the Young Ones, as well as EINAR JOLIN, NILS DARDEL and SIGRID HJERTÉN. The Eight had only one exhibition, in 1912, before drifting apart.

Most of these young artists had studied with Matisse, and they were influenced individually by Fauvism, as well as by the expressive realism of the work of van Gogh and Munch. The groups represented the development of the first Swedish expressionism. Their modernistic, colourful, chiefly French-inspired painting aroused great debate. Albert Engström (1869–1940), an older, traditional painter and writer, was particularly negative in his criticism of the young art. Works such as the *Red Blind* (1916; Stockholm, Mod. Mus.) by Hjertén were considered provocative.

BIBLIOGRAPHY

G. Lilja: *Det moderna genombrott i svensk kritik, 1905–1914* [The modern breakthrough in Swedish criticism, 1905–1914] (Malmö, 1955)
——: *Den första svenska modernismen* [The first Swedish Modernism] (Kristianstad, 1986)
Modernismens genombrott: Nordiskt måleri, 1910–1920 [The breakthrough of Modernism: Scandinavian painting, 1910–1920] (exh. cat., ed. C. T. Edam, N.-G. Hökby and B. Schreiber; Göteborg, Kstmus., 1989–90)

JACQUELINE STARE

Youn Myeung Ro [Yun Myŏng-no] (*b* 1936). Korean painter, printmaker and teacher. He graduated in 1960 from the College of Fine Arts, Seoul National University, and studied in 1969–70 in New York. He has exhibited in Korea, East, South and South-east Asia, North and South America, Western and Eastern Europe and New Zealand. Paintings in the ART INFORMEL style in the late 1950s–early 1960s were succeeded by his *Ruler* series of prints. Youn was an early experimenter in modern printmaking in Korea. His *Cracks* series, initiated in the mid-1970s, examined the effect of cracking on the surface of generally white pigment. In the *Ollejit* series of the 1980s drawing on childhood memories of simple objects, the surface is covered repeatedly with short, deliberate strokes. The *After Ollejit* and *Anonymous Land* series of paintings of the 1990s convey more violent feeling, expressed through strong brushstrokes, heavy colours and thickly applied paint. Youn works in acrylic, oil colour and oil stick, and in India ink on wood, cotton and canvas. He also produces lithographs and ceramic tiles.

BIBLIOGRAPHY
Youn Myeung-ro: Recent Works (exh. cat., Seoul, Ho-am A. Mus., 1991) [Kor. and Eng. text and chronology]
E. Heartney: 'The New Players', *A. America*, lxxxi/7 (1993), pp. 35–41
SUSAN PARES

Yovnat'anyan. *See* HOVNAT'ANIAN.

Yoyudang. *See* YUN, (3).

Yozō Hamaguchi. *See* HAMAGUCHI, YOZŌ.

Ypres [Flem. Ieper]. Belgian city of *c.* 34,500 inhabitants in the province of west Flanders, one of the most ancient cloth-working towns of the region. It became important in the 10th century owing to its strategic position on the trade route between Paris and Bruges. Up to the beginning of the 11th century it was part of a vast agricultural domain, probably belonging to the counts of Flanders, but it was already famous for its textile industry. In the 12th and 13th centuries Ypres was at the peak of its prosperity and expanding at a prodigious rate. A fortified wall was built in 1214. Many new parish churches were built in the 12th century: St Pierre, St Jacques, St Jean and Ste Marleen-Breilcu. New churches continued to be erected in the 13th century, including St Nicolas, the collegiate church of St Martin (now the cathedral; *see* §1 below) and the Dominican monastery. Some fine 13th-century houses still stand (rest.). The great Cloth Hall, symbol of the town's commercial importance and a prototype for the Brabantine Gothic town hall (*see* BRUGES, §IV, 2; GHENT, §III, 3), was begun in the 13th century and finished at the beginning of the 14th. In 1383 Ypres successfully withstood an English siege, but the region was devastated and many of the weavers were forced to leave. The decline of the textile industry in the 15th century reduced the economic importance of Ypres, and in later centuries it was never more than a modest provincial town. An episcopal see was established there in 1559, but in 1801 it was joined to the diocese of Bruges. In 1584 Ypres was sacked by Alessandro Farnese, Duke of Parma (1545–92), and was besieged four times by the French between 1648 and 1678. The town was almost entirely destroyed during World War I, but it was rebuilt to its former plan and most of its monuments are faithful reproductions of their prototypes. Numerous military cemeteries and famous modern monuments commemorating those killed in the war stand in and around the town. Ypres has several handsome palaces of the 13th, 15th, 16th and 18th centuries.

1. CATHEDRAL OF ST MARTIN. Although it was completely rebuilt in a unified style after World War I, St Martin remains a good example of 13th-century Gothic architecture in the Scheldt Valley. In 1102 Jean, Bishop of Thérouanne, founded a college of canons at Ypres, giving them an existing church, dedicated to St Martin. Its reconstruction was undertaken in 1221. Thirty years later, the apse and choir aisles were ready for use, but the choir was consecrated only on 26 April 1280, by Henri, Bishop of Thérouanne. The north transept, against which the claustral buildings were abutted, was then begun. The south transept belongs to the beginning of the 14th century, and in 1321 the nave was in course of construction. In 1443 the tower collapsed, to be rebuilt from the following year. From 1862 to 1865, the choir was restored by Joseph Jonas Dumont, who made new vaults, and replaced details in Tournai marble with elements in freestone. He also altered the south transept façade and restored the nave and west tower. From 1867 the nave was restored by Van Ysendyck and Schoonejans.

The plan of St Martin consists of a six-bay nave preceded by a projecting tower. The transept arms are unequal, the north with two aisleless bays while the south has three, with a western aisle. The choir plan is particularly interesting (see fig.): five bays long, it terminates in a nine-sided apse, and the three western bays are flanked by chapels set obliquely at an angle of 45°. Derived from the Romanesque echelon plan, perhaps suggested at Notre-Dame, Courtrai, and taken up again at Saint-Michel-en-Thiérache and at St Yved, Braine (Aisne), this plan type achieved some success in the regions that did not adopt the model of Chartres Cathedral for the Gothic great church. In the French examples the outermost chapel connects directly with the transept, while in Flanders there is a straight bay between it and the transept, so at Ypres the inner chapel is preceded by two straight bays. The support for the vault springers of the outer chapel and the three adjacent bays is a single column with a crocket capital.

The interior has a three-storey elevation. In the straight bays of the choir and in the apse, the dado has a blind arcade; the arches of the straight bays are shouldered, with two right angles breaking the top of the arch. The first level of windows has twin lancets in each straight bay, but only one for each side of the apse. The three western bays have a columnar arcade with crocket capitals. The second storey is a triforium with six arches in each straight bay, and a reduced number in the apse. The small pilasters separating those in the straight bays into three groups of two recall the arrangement in the transept of Tournai Cathedral. The clerestory is lit by triplets in the straight bays and by single lancets in the apse. There is an exterior passage, articulated by arches corresponding to the clerestory arches; these are encased by a wide relieving arch. This idea was known in the Gothic of upper Picardy in the 13th century (the triplet opening had been retained in the transept of Cambrai Cathedral); the cathedrals of Cambrai and Arras played an essential role in the formation of Gothic in the Scheldt Valley. The choir vaults of St Martin are rectangular, and the apse boss is offset. In the apse the vault shafts are fronted by statues, the canopies and bases of which correspond to the triforium string courses. In the straight bays the statues stand on the abaci of the capitals, as in the choirs of St Nicholas, Ghent, and Onze Lieve Vrouwekerk von Pamele, Oudenaarde. This arrangement probably came from Champagne (e.g. Notre-Dame, Montier-en-Der).

Ypres, Cathedral of St Martin, view of exterior from the north-east, begun 1221

In the late 13th-century north transept of St Martin the blind triforium has four divisions, the trefoil arches inscribed within rectangular frames that extend the mullions of the clerestory windows; but the complete organic connection of French Rayonnant is not realized, since the mullions do not cross the string course separating the two levels. In the south transept there is no such correspondence between the levels: here, the unglazed triforium has three subdivided units inscribed within rectangular frames. The arches are trefoil, with quatrefoils in the heads. The clerestory windows have two subdivided units flanking a narrow middle light, which allows the cusped oculus in the head to be larger. This tracery pattern derives from such late 13th-century French buildings as the choir of Saint-Quentin and the façades of the church at Agnetz (Oise) and of St Martin, Laon. In the nave, the arcade is still columnar, but the triforium reverts to the type with single continuous arcades within narrow rectangular frames. The clerestory windows have five divisions and a tracery pattern of *soufflets*. The windows do not occupy the whole space of the bay. The vaults spring from the canopies of the statues standing on the abaci of the arcade capitals (a system re-established by the restorers on only alternate piers). The sturdy façade tower is isolated from the nave by a wall and supported at the corners by right-angled buttresses. It has a portal surmounted by a large window acting as a tympanum, an arrangement frequently used in the Flamboyant era. The middle storey has three blind arches corresponding to the three openings of the belfry stage. A crocketed, open-work spire crowns the tower, but in the 17th century, according to a picture in Sanderus's *Flandria illustrata* and the scale relief model of the city (Lille, Mus. B.-A.), it was topped by a simple prismatic roof. Stone fragments of the building destroyed in World War I are preserved in the cloister garth on the north side of the nave.

BIBLIOGRAPHY

A. Sanderus: *Flandria illustrata, sive provinciae ac comitatus hujus descriptio*, 3 vols (The Hague, 1732) [mid-17th century]

L. Devliegher: 'De opkomst van de Kevkelijke Gotische bouwkunst in West-Vlaanderen gedurende de XIIIe eeuw', *Bull. Comm. Royale Mnmts & Sites*, v (1954), pp. 240–49

JACQUES THIÉBAUT

Ypres, Nicholas d'. *See* DIPRE, NICOLAS.

Yrarrázaval, Ricardo (*b* Santiago, 1931). Chilean painter. A self-taught painter, in the 1950s and 1960s he based his landscape motifs and colours on the Andes, using very simple forms suggestive of Pre-Columbian textiles in their flat abstract designs and balanced chromatic effects. It was a question of subjecting archetypal shapes to a subtle and rational play of colour.

While remaining committed to a careful technique in both his oil paintings and pastels, Yrarrázaval fundamentally changed direction in 1973, when he began to represent isolated and suspended figures undergoing gradual deterioration: faceless and with their bodies swollen as if by internal pressure, they appear to have lost their identity, leaving behind only realistically painted shirts, collars and ties. The suggestion is of a collective anonymity, an identity crisis embodied in purely external human gestures revealed through social rituals and through the status and prestige accorded to dress and fashion. Yrarrázaval continued in these works to emphasize the material quality of his paintings and the strong three-dimensional illusion of his forms, relying exclusively on the palette knife in order to reveal or conceal forms by a meticulous modelling of light and shade.

In the 1980s Yrarrázaval began to combine hand-painted motifs with photographic images, especially Polaroid snapshots and stills obtained from the television screen. He imposed himself on such mechanically produced images in order to achieve perplexing effects, in particular by showing faces out of focus in order again to suggest the loss of identity.

BIBLIOGRAPHY
M. Ivelić and G. Galaz: *La pintura en Chile* (Santiago, 1981)
——: *Chile: Arte actual* (Santiago, 1988)

MILAN IVELIĆ

Yriarte, Ignacio de. *See* IRIARTE, IGNACIO DE.

YRM. *See* YORKE, ROSENBERG & MARDALL.

Yrurtia, Rogelio (*b* Buenos Aires, 6 Dec 1879; *d* Buenos Aires, 4 March 1950). Argentine sculptor. He enrolled at the Escuela de la Sociedad Estímulo de Bellas Artes, Buenos Aires, in 1898 and soon afterwards joined the studio of the sculptor Lucio Correa Morales (1852–1923). In 1899 he won a scholarship to study in Europe. In Paris he attended the studio of the sculptor Jules-Félix Coutan, at the same time studying drawing at the Académie Colarossi; he made studies of corpses in the morgue and acquired a great mastery of human anatomy. At the Salon in Paris in 1903 he exhibited *The Sinners* (see Prins), a major group of six female figures, influenced by Rodin's *Burghers of Calais* in its rhythmic arabesques, open treatment of line and soft modelling. In 1904 it was shown again at the World's Fair in St Louis, MO, where it was awarded a major prize, but he renounced both the prize and associated commission because of the controversy about his youth.

Yrurtia exhibited for the first time in Buenos Aires, with great success in 1905. The occasion marked the end of his period of experimentation and the start of his mature production as a sculptor. By 1907 he had received major commissions in Buenos Aires, and this enabled him to return to Paris, where he remained until 1921. Notable among these early commissions in Argentina were a bronze monument to the surgeon *Alejandro Castro* (1904–5; Buenos Aires, Hosp. Clínicas), vigorously modelled in broad planes and precise in its symbolism, and a monument to *Dorrego* (bronze, 1907), commissioned by the Argentine government. The latter work, situated in the small square between Viamonte and Suipacha in Buenos Aires and consisting of an equestrian figure on an architectural base flanked by powerful allegorical figures representing Fate and History, was the first of his important sculptural groups. It was followed by the skilfully constructed *Hymn to Work* (1907–9, see fig.), a group of 14 life-size figures in bronze erected in the Plaza Canto al Trabajo, Buenos Aires, in which naked figures, arranged on an open and outward curve, advance in an excited throng that maintains its unity through the continuity of movement. Yrurtia's struggle between Romanticism and Classicism is particularly evident in this work: the naked, ideal, timeless bodies are at the same time anti-classical in their dynamism, curved structure and asymmetry. In his *Cenotaph to Rivadavia* (1916–32; Buenos Aires, Plaza Miserere) Yrurtia subordinated the bronze sculpture to an

Rogelio Yrurtia: *Hymn to Work*, 14 life-size bronze figures, 2.15×2.60×13.50 m, 1907–9 (Buenos Aires, Plaza Canto al Trabajo)

architectural setting in stone inspired by Art Deco, through which he achieved an austere formal and conceptual simplicity.

On his return to Buenos Aires in 1921, Yrurtia taught for two years at the Escuela Nacional de Bellas Artes. In his sculpture, such as the portraits of family and friends made in the 1940s, he gradually reduced male and female figures to their essential characteristics. His adoption of an extreme economy of means characterized his development of a sculptural style that was modern but that also attempted to free itself of blind repetition of European formulae. On the opening of the Museo Casa de Yrurtia in Buenos Aires in 1949 he was appointed its honorary Director.

BIBLIOGRAPHY
Rogelio Yrurtia (exh. cat., preface H. Caillet-Bois; Santa Fé, Argentina, Mus. Prov. B.A., 1938)
E. Prins: *Rogelio Yrurtia* (Buenos Aires, 1941) [Sp., Fr. and Eng. text]
J. Rinaldini: *Rogelio Yrurtia* (Buenos Aires, 1942)
Dibujos de Yrurtia (exh. cat., ed. L. C. Morales; Buenos Aires, Mus. Casa de Yrurtia, 1964)

NELLY PERAZZO

Yselburg, Peter. *See* ISSELBURG, PETER.

Yselin, Heinrich. *See* ISELIN, HEINRICH.

Ysenbrand [Ysebaert], **Adriaen.** *See* ISENBRANDT, ADRIAEN.

Ysendyck, Jules-Jacques van. *See* VAN YSENDYCK, JULES-JACQUES.

Ytzatlán. *See* ETZATLÁN.

Yu'an. *See* MOKUAN REIEN.

Yuanchang. *See* CAI JING.

Yuan dynasty. Chinese dynasty founded by the Mongols, dating from 1279 to 1368. After the division of the Southern Song period (1127–1279), Kublai Khan (*reg* 1260–94) reunited all of China under Mongol rule, incorporating it in a huge empire that extended westwards as far as modern Hungary and Poland. The Mongols were not great patrons of the arts, although they admired craftsmen. Nevertheless, by reuniting China, thus bringing together the differing traditions of north and south, and by not imposing stylistic demands, they allowed artists to use and develop a variety of influences. Indeed, there were significant innovations in both painting and the applied arts of porcelain and lacquer. The Silk Route was reopened, and European interest in China, both diplomatic and missionary, developed. Franciscans and other Europeans, arriving for the first time, reported on what they had seen. The Venetian merchant Marco Polo allegedly spent the years 1275–92 in Kublai Khan's service.

In 1264, Kublai Khan transferred the winter capital to Dadu or Khanbalik (modern BEIJING) in reflection of the shift in focus of the Mongol empire from Karakorum (south of modern Ulaan Baatar in Mongolia). Few Yuan buildings have survived in Beijing: those still existing include the white Miaoying pagoda (*see* CHINA, fig. 25) near the West Gate, and the lamaist monument, the Juyong guan, or Cloud Terrace at the Pass of the Recruited Labourers, on the Great Wall, the main north-western access to Beijing, begun in 1342.

The response of educated Chinese to foreign domination was to withdraw into the traditions of their native past; many scholars rejected government service. In painting, the school of literati painting (*wenren hua*) became dominant (*see* CHINA, §V, 4(ii)). Literati artists emphasized individual and stylistically calligraphic expression in preference to the decorative aims associated with official painters (*see* CHINA, §V, 4(i)(d)). The four great Yuan masters—Huang Gongwang, Wu Zhen, Ni Zan and Wang Meng—were all literati objectors to Mongol rule and held no official posts. They painted monochrome landscapes of isolation; Ni Zan's austere works were particularly influential, as were those of Huang Gongwang. Flower paintings were also popular with the literati for their allegorical significance. Of those few painters who did serve the Mongols, Zhao Mengfu, who was the most important calligrapher of the Yuan period and became president of the Hanlin Academy, painted horses (an essential component of Mongol nomadic life) and was responsible for reviving ancient styles of Chinese painting, such as the archaic Blue-and-green (*qinglü*) style (*see* CHINA, §V, 3(iv)(a)). The murals of Yongle gong (Yongle Palace), near Ruicheng in south-west Shanxi Province, constitute a good record of Yuan-period painting.

The Mongol empire provided extensive export possibilities. Muslim merchants from the Middle East living in China admired Longquan celadons (which they believed could reveal poison) and commissioned huge dishes designed for communal eating (*see* CHINA, §VII, 4(iii)). Middle Eastern influence also stimulated the new, exuberant blue-and-white decoration, thought vulgar by the Chinese. Muslim merchants arranged for the export of celadons, blue-and-white and other wares to East and South-east Asia. A ceramic ware with a sugary white glaze, often inscribed with the characters *shu fu* ('privy council'), is recorded as having been commissioned by the Shumi yuan, the Ministry of Civil and Military Affairs (*see* CHINA, §VII, 3(v)).

Buddhist sculpture was extensively patronized; Tantric, multi-limbed figures indicate the Mongol preference for the lamaist art of Tibet and Nepal (*see also* CHINA, §III, 1(ii)(g)). In silverworking the chiselling technique, associated with the silversmith Zhu Bishan (*fl* 1328–68), developed. Both literary and archaeological evidence confirms the existence of Yuan carved lacquer.

The Mongol rulers were intensely unpopular, in part because they practised a policy of discrimination against the Chinese. There was a struggle for succession after the death of Kublai Khan, and the dynasty went into decline. Natural disasters contributed to peasant uprisings, which in turn led to the fall of Beijing and the flight of the last Yuan emperor.

BIBLIOGRAPHY
P. Pelliot: *Histoire secrète des Mongols* (Paris, 1949)
S. Lee and Wai-Kam Ho: *Chinese Art under the Mongols: The Yuan Dynasty, 1279–1368* (Cleveland, 1968)
M. Medley: *Yuan Porcelain and Stoneware* (London, 1974)
J. Cahill: *Hills Beyond a River: Chinese Painting of the Yuan Dynasty, 1279–1368* (New York, 1976)
J. D. Langlois jr, ed.: *China under Mongol Rule* (Princeton, 1981)

Hok-lam Chan and W. T. de Bary, eds: *Yuan Thought: Chinese Thought and Religion under the Mongols* (Columbia, 1982)
J. Addis and others: *Jingdezhen Wares: The Yuan Evolution* (Hong Kong, 1984)
M. Rossabi: *Khubilai Khan: His Life and Times* (Berkeley, 1988)
From Innovation to Conformity: Chinese Lacquer from the 13th to 16th Centuries (sale cat. by R. Krahl and B. Morgan, London, Bluett and Sons Gal., 1989)

CAROL MICHAELSON

Yucateco. Term used to designate the architecture characteristic of the Yucatán peninsula in south-east Mexico, particularly the religious architecture of the 16th century. A number of factors militated against Spanish settlement in Yucatán in the early 16th century, notably the intense heat, difficulties in irrigating the area, the lack of precious metals and the sparseness of the Indian population, which was mostly Maya. Consequently, the peninsula's social and economic development was very different from that of the more densely populated central plateau, and this was reflected in its architecture, which was of a simpler and more austere character.

Despite the obstacles to settlement, Franciscan missionaries arrived in the Yucatán peninsula in the 1530s and 1540s and began to construct simple buildings to house the monks. In order to accommodate the large congregations of Indians, however, and to protect them from the sun, they built *ramadas*, or large shelters, in the monastery compounds. These were supported by tree trunks, with roofs made from branches, and they had no side walls, thereby allowing the free passage of air. Services were conducted from a small, open-fronted stone chapel or chancel, which was built facing the *ramada*. Such complexes, comprising dormitories, chapel and *ramada*, formed the first Yucatán monasteries. Later, especially in the 17th century, these 'open-air' or 'Indian' chapels formed the basis of the typical Yucatán convent churches, with simple, stone naves replacing the original *ramadas* in front of the chapels.

The monasteries that grew out of these *ramadas* retained their own distinctive features throughout the 17th and 18th centuries, with few of the Romanesque, Gothic, Plateresque, Renaissance or Baroque details that were so sumptuously adopted in the rest of Mexico. Instead, their façades were relatively simple, although one notable distinguishing feature was the development of the front gable-ends to serve as wall belfries to house the bells. The design of the gable-ends was very varied, in some cases their size being increased at the expense of the walls, with the height of the latter being reduced to a minimum. A semicircular, ribbed vault usually covered the chancel. Other monasteries were later built with great transverse arches that, because of the thickness of the walls, provided space for extra chapels. Another characteristic feature was the construction of large arcades surrounding the atrium, for example in the monastery at Izamal. Despite the poverty of the Yucatán region, 29 Franciscan monasteries were built there, each with its own stylistic identity, although most are simple and austere. They were used not only to teach Christian doctrine but also for the artistic and architectural training of indigenous craftsmen, and one monk, Fray Juan Pérez de Mérida, established a reputation as the builder of the monasteries of Mérida, Maní, Izamal and Sisal de Valladolid, assisted by his Indian apprentices.

The architecture of the 16th-century cathedral of S Ildefonso, Mérida, is also characteristically different from that of the cathedrals in Mexico City, Guadalajara and Puebla, on which work began in the same period. S Ildefonso is a simple, aisled hall church with large columns supporting sail vaults and a dome over the crossing. The vaults and dome are decorated with simple mouldings, as is the rest of the building. The façade of the cathedral is also very simple and austere in its execution, with an almost fortress-like composition of towers and walls in plain ashlar masonry flanking a tall central arch above the main portal, which has small-scale classicist detailing.

The only important work of secular architecture that has survived in Yucatán is the Casa de Montejo (1549), the former residence of the conquistador Francisco de Montejo II, which has an uncharacteristic broad band of Plateresque ornament above the main portal, decorated with an abundance of low relief intended to set off the Montejo coat of arms; this coat of arms is flanked by two large halberdiers, with two figures of Indians at their feet, which stand out from the harmoniously and profusely decorated whole with its medallions and grotesques.

In the 17th and 18th centuries the Baroque influence on architecture in Yucatán was almost negligible. The capriciously designed gable-ends characteristic of the 16th century continued to influence Yucatán architects, who transformed them into wall belfries and sometimes into full-scale bell-towers. A few façades, such as that of the church of the Third Order of the Jesuits (1618) in Mérida, contained a few very simple Baroque elements, and the façade of the 18th-century church of S Cristóbal has a flared portal similar to that in S Juan de Dios in Mexico City, but again the Baroque ornamentation is relatively simple, as are the sparse plant and flower decorations on other churches in Yucatán.

BIBLIOGRAPHY
D. Angulo Iniguez: *Historia del arte hispanoamericano*, i and ii (Barcelona, 1945)
E. Wilder Weismann and J. Hancock Sandoval: *Art and Time in Mexico: From the Conquest to the Revolution* (New York, 1985), pp. 67–75

CONSTANTINO REYES-VALERIO

Yü-chien. *See* YUJIAN.

Yugoslavia [Jugoslavija]. Country in the Balkan peninsula, south-eastern Europe, formerly comprising six republics: BOSNIA AND HERZEGOVINA, CROATIA, Macedonia (*see* MACEDONIA (ii)), MONTENEGRO, SERBIA and SLOVENIA. The country was founded in 1918, after the collapse of the Austro-Hungarian empire, as the Kingdom of the Serbs, Croats and Slovenes and was renamed Kingdom of Yugoslavia ('land of the South Slavs') in 1929. Dissolved in 1941 as a result of Axis aggression and internal divisions, it was reconstituted as a nonaligned Communist-governed state after World War II. It began to break up in 1991, when Slovenia and Croatia declared their independence. The art of the former Yugoslavia is discussed in the articles on the individual republics.

Yūichi. *See* TAKAHASHI YŪICHI.

Yujian [Yü-chien; Ruofen; Jo-fen; *xing* Cao; *zi* Zhongshi; *hao* Furong Shanzhu] (*b* Jinhua, Wuzhou, Zhejiang Province; *fl c.* 1250). Chinese painter, calligrapher and priest. He was active in Lin'an (now Hangzhou), Zhejiang Province. At the age of nine he entered Baofeng yuan (Precious Peak monastery), where he took the name Ruofen and trained in Tiantai Buddhism. After his ordination he was appointed scribe (*shuji*) at Tianzhu si (India temple) in the Bei shan (Northern Mountain) temple complex near Lin'an. Ruofen Yujian has been confused with another monk–painter, Ying Yujian, from Jingci si (Pure Compassion temple), a Chan Buddhist establishment in the Nan shan (Southern Mountain) temple complex, also situated near Lin'an. Both men are listed in *Tuhui baojian* ('Precious mirror for examining painting'; preface 1365) by Xia Wenyan, whose account of Ruofen draws substantially on a description of 1351 by the painter Wu Taisu. The identification of Ruofen rather than Ying Yujian with the painter Yujian is due to the existence of this more complete account and its consistency with the kind of paintings attributed to Yujian.

Yujian travelled widely and adopted his artist's name (*hao*) after his return to Jinhua, where he retired to Yu jian (Jade Torrent), a hermitage he built by a remote mountain stream. He established a reputation for his 'cloud-mountain' (*yunshan*) landscapes and for his paintings of ancient trees, bamboo and plum-blossom, the last influenced by Yang Buzhi. Only four of his paintings have survived and all are in Japanese collections. In the late 16th century, 15 of Yujian's scrolls were recorded in Japan, including a handscroll, *Eight Views of Xiao and Xiang*. During the Muromachi period (1333–1568) the painting was cut into separate scenes, and each was remounted as a separate hanging scroll. Three of these survive: *Mountain Village in Clearing Mist* (Tokyo, Idemitsu Mus. A.; *see* CHINA, fig. 111), *Returning Sails at a Distant Shore* (Nagoya, Tokugawa A. Mus.) and *Autumn Moon on Lake Dongting* (Matsutarō Yata priv. col.). These show strong similarities to a treatment of the same theme attributed to MUQI. Both artists use spontaneously executed ink washes to suggest the forms of the landscape. Yujian's fourth extant work, *Mount Lu* (hanging scroll; Tokyo, Yoshikawa priv. col.), is signed and inscribed with a poem. It depicts the range of peaks that rises abruptly between the Yangzi River and Lake Poyang (Jiangxi Province). Only two of the scroll's three sections have survived, but a copy of the complete design has been preserved (Tokyo, Idemitsu Mus. A.). Painted on loose-grained silk, *Mount Lu* is stylistically rough and undefined and must have been executed in part with a tool cruder than a brush, such as a straw reed or sugar-cane fibre.

Yujian was an accomplished calligrapher. As a scribe at Tianzhu si, he had to compose and write all important documents dealing with the temple's internal and external affairs. His writings were gathered into one volume, entitled *Yujian shengyu* ('Left-over phrases of Yujian'; untraced). Although praised by Wu Taisu as a master of the 'Three Perfections' (*sanjue*)—poetry, calligraphy and painting—he was neglected by later generations of Chinese critics, who considered his individuality too extreme. Although he had no lasting influence on Chinese painting, he was highly regarded in Japan, where his work played an important role in the development of Japanese monochrome ink painting (*suibokuga*).

BIBLIOGRAPHY

Xia Wenyan: *Tuhui baojian* [Precious mirror for examining painting] (preface 1365/*R* Shanghai, 1936), *juan* 4, p. 75

O. Sirén: *Chinese Painting: Leading Masters and Principles* (London, 1956–8), ii, pp. 142–4; iii, pls 346–7

Sogen no kaiga [Paintings of the Song and Yuan] (Tokyo, 1962), pls 120–25

K. Suzuki: 'A study of Yu-chien Jo-fen', *Bijutsu kenkū*, ccxxxvi (Sept. 1964), pp. 1–14

T. Toda: *Mokkei, Gyokken* [Muqi, Yujian] (Tokyo, 1973)

J. Cahill: *An Index of Early Chinese Painters and Painting: T'ang, Sung and Yüan* (Berkeley, 1980), pp. 196–7

M. Loehr: *The Great Painters of China* (New York, 1980), pp. 226–9

M. Collcutt: *Five Mountains* (Cambridge, 1981), pp. 238–9

K. Suzuki: *Chūgoku kaiga shi* [History of Chinese painting] (Tokyo, 1985), i, pp. 219–22; ii, pp. 71–3, pls 160–64

RICHARD EDWARDS

Yūken. *See* TOMIOKA TESSAI.

Yukihiko Yasuda. *See* YASUDA, YUKIHIKO.

Yukinari. *See* FUJIWARA (ii), (2).

Yukinobu. *See* KANŌ, (15).

Yulgok. *See* YI (i), (2).

Yümük Tepe. *See under* MERSIN.

Yun. Korean family of painters and scholars. (1) Yun Tu-sŏ is regarded as one of the *Sam chae* ('three literati masters') of the Chosŏn period (1392–1910), together with Chŏng Sŏn and Sim Sa-jŏng. His great-grandfather was the poet Yun Sŏn-do (1587–1671). His son (2) Yun Tŏk-hŭi and grandson Yun Yong (1708–*c.* 1754) followed him in painting, and his great-grandson was the *sirhak* thinker and painter (3) Chŏng Yag-yong.

(1) Yun Tu-sŏ [*cha* Hyo Ŏn; *ho* Kongjae, Chong'ae] (*b* Haenam, South Chŏlla Province, 20 May 1668; *d* Haenam, 26 Dec 1715). His eclectic output bridged the transition between painting of the mid-Chosŏn and late Chosŏn periods. Learned in Confucian classics, military strategy, geography and astronomy, he passed the initial state examination (*chinsa*) in 1693 but returned to Haenam in 1713 without acquiring office. He was aligned with the out-of-power Southerners (*Namin*), advocates of *sirhak* ('practical learning') and *sŏhak* ('Western learning'). He studied calligraphy with Yi Sŏ (1662–1723) and painted as a hobby.

Yun is famous for his paintings of human figures and horses but he also painted landscapes, genre scenes, birds and fowl, insects, cattle, dragons, still-lifes, ink bamboo and maps. Fifty or so of his works survive, many of them small in scale, with about a dozen bearing dates from 1704 to 1715. His stylistic range was equally wide. He was an innovator who applied the new *sirhak* ideas of empiricism to art. He made sketches of common folk at work, foreshadowing the genre studies of such later Chosŏn painters as Kim Hong-do and Sin Yun-bok. Some of Yun's horse paintings rival the later Western-style realism of the animals painted by Kim Tu-ryang. His penetrating *Self-portrait* (Haenam, South Chŏlla Province, Yun Yŏng-sŏn priv. col.; *see* KOREA, fig. 45) is painted with almost scientific precision. But Yun was also a staid member of the upper classes whose access to family collections and Chinese painting manuals, such as *Gushi huapu* ('Mr Gu's painting manual'), enabled him to study and conserve past styles. Many of his paintings are superb derivations of Chinese works of the Song (960–1279) and Yuan (1279–1368) periods, executed in the Northern as well as the Southern school manner. In the *Old Monk* (Seoul, N. Mus.) he recreated not only the brushwork but also the content of the 'untrammelled' tradition of Chan (Kor. Sŏn; Jap. Zen) figure painting, which dates back to Shi Ke and Liang Kai, Chinese artists who flourished in the 9th and 13th century respectively.

BIBLIOGRAPHY
Yi Tong-ju: *Hanguk hoehwasa ryun* [Discourses on the history of Korean painting] (Seoul, 1987), pp. 123–43
Yi Yŏng-suk: 'Yun Tu-sŏ-ŭi hoehwa sege' [The painting world of Yun Tu-sŏ], *Misulsa yŏn'gu ch'anggan ho* (Seoul, 1987), pp. 65–102
ROSE E. LEE

(2) Yun Tŏk-hŭi [*cha* Kyŏngbaek; *ho* Naksŏ, Yŏnp'o, Yŏnong, Hyŏnong] (*b* Haenam, South Chŏlla Province, 1685; *d* 1766). Son of (1) Yun Tu-sŏ. He was known for his studies of horses as well as for figure and landscape paintings. Many of his figure paintings were representations of Daoist immortals; these, together with his excellent horse paintings, earned him the title of 'double excellence'. In 1735 he was recommended for the task of copying old royal portraits in the Yŏnghŭi Pavilion, but he declined, presumably because as a literati amateur painter he did not wish to be identified with artists of the Bureau of Painting, to whom the task was usually assigned. However, in 1784, when a new portrait of King Sukchong (*reg* 1674–1720) was to be executed, he served as one of the supervisors for the project along with two other literati painters, Cho Yong-sŏk and Sim Sa-jŏng.

Yun Tŏk-hŭi's paintings of immortals are characterized by a combination of minute, detailed description of facial features and more free, spontaneous brushstrokes in the rendering of drapery folds or such background elements as trees and rocks. Two paintings (both Seoul, N. Mus.), *The Immortal Hama* (see Maeng In-jae, pl. 16) and *Lofty Recluse* (see Maeng In-jae, pls 17–18), exemplify his style. In the former, the Chinese Daoist immortal Hama is shown striding with a load—his attribute—on his shoulder. His bold head, grimacing wrinkled face and hands with long fingernails are all depicted carefully in thin lines to impart the sense of grotesqueness usually associated with this figure. However, the old tree behind him is done in a sketchy manner that contributes to the overall gentle atmosphere. Yun also painted some genre subjects, which were then becoming popular (*see* KOREA, §IV, 2(iv)(b)). His landscapes are executed in a more traditional manner, with trees depicted in the style associated with the Chinese painters Li Cheng and Guo Xi and figures playing a relatively important role in the composition.

BIBLIOGRAPHY
Kim Yŏng-yun, ed.: *Hanguk sŏhwa inmyŏng sasŏ* [Biographical dictionary of Korean painters and calligraphers] (Seoul, 1959), pp. 313–14
Yu Pok-yŏl: *Hanguk hoehwa taegwan* [Pageant of Korean painting] (Seoul, 1969), p. 363
Maeng In-jae, ed.: *Inmulhwa* [Figure painting] (1985), xx of *Hanguk-ŭi mi* [Beauties of Korea] (Seoul, 1977–85)
YI SŎNG-MI

(3) Chŏng Yag-yong [*cha* Miyong, Songbo, Kwinong; *ho* Tasan, Sammi, Yoyudang, Saam, Yŏllo] (*b* Kwangju, Kyŏnggi Province, 1762; *d* 1836). Great-grandson of (1) Yun Tu-sŏ. He was the most important *sirhak* ('practical learning') scholar of the 19th century. While studying with Yi Pyŏk, a convert to Catholicism, Chŏng came under the influence of *sŏhak* ('Western learning'), which comprised not only Catholicism but also Western sciences and technology. Although his talent was recognized by King Chŏngjo (*reg* 1776–1800), he was accused of being a Catholic convert and was banished to Kangjin for 18 years during the Catholic persecution of 1801 that broke out soon after King Chŏngjo's death. During the long years of his exile and also of forced retirement afterwards Chŏng wrote many books criticizing the Chosŏn dynasty and presenting his ideas for reform. While his main energy was devoted to political, economic and social reform, he also painted plum-blossom, birds and simple landscapes (Pusan, Dong-A Mus.), always accompanied by his poetic inscriptions.

BIBLIOGRAPHY
O Se-ch'ang: *Kŭnyŏk sŏhwa jing* [Dictionary of Korean painters and calligraphers] (Taegu, 1928/R Seoul, 1975), pp. 205–6
Lee Ki-baik [Yi Ki-baek]: *Hanguksa Sillon* (Seoul, 1961; rev. 1967 and 1976); Eng. trans. by E. W. Wagner with E. J. Schultz as *A New History of Korea* (Cambridge, MA, and London, 1984), pp. 202–55
Yu Pok-yŏl: *Hanguk hoehwa taegwan* [Pageant of Korean painting] (Seoul, 1969), pp. 609–11
An Hwi-jun, ed.: *Sansuhwa* [Landscape painting], ii (1982), xii of *Hanguk-ŭi mi* [Beauties of Korea] (Seoul, 1977–85), pp. 156, 256–7
KIM KUMJA PAIK

Yunapingu, Munggurrawuy (*b c.* 1907; *d* Yirrkala, 1978). Australian Aboriginal painter and sculptor. He was the leader of the Gumatj clan of north-east Arnhem Land, Northern Territory, during a critical period of the history of the Yolngu-speaking peoples, and one of the leaders of the Yolngu people in their fight for land rights when tenure of their land was threatened by mining interests in the 1960s and 1970s. Like Mawalan Marika, he was one of the first artists to produce bark paintings for sale to the missionary Wilbur Chaseling in 1935, and he later contributed to Stuart Scougall's collection for the Art Gallery of New South Wales, Sydney. With Marika and Narritjin Maymurru he helped to develop the episodic-narrative style of paintings characteristic of Yolngu art from the 1960s to the 1980s (e.g. *Space Tracking Station*, 1967; Adelaide, A. G. S. Australia). He was a prolific painter until the end of his life, and established a productive relationship with the Melbourne art dealer Jim Davidson, who sold many of his paintings. Yunapingu was also a significant wood-carver, in particular of Wuraymu mortuary figures. Collections of these are in the National Museum of Australia, Canberra, and the Anthropology Research Museum at the University of Western Australia, Perth. His son Galarrwuy Yunapingu became a leading Aboriginal politician.

BIBLIOGRAPHY
H. Groger-Wurm: *Eastern Arnhem Land*, i of *Australian Aboriginal Bark Paintings and their Mythological Interpretations* (Canberra, 1973), pp. 113, 115, 192
J. Hoff: 'Aboriginal Carved and Painted Human Figures in North-East Arnhem Land', *Form in Indigenous Art: Schematisation in the Art of Aboriginal Australia and Prehistoric Europe*, ed. P. J. Ucko (Canberra, 1977), pp. 156–64

E. Wells: *Reward and Punishment in Arnhem Land* (Canberra, 1982), pp. 17–20

HOWARD MORPHY

Yun Che-hong [*cha* Kyŏngdo; *ho* Haksan, Ch'anha] (*b* P'ap'yŏng, Kyŏnggi Province, 1764; *d* after 1840). Korean painter and scholar. He began his official career brilliantly in 1792 by coming first in the *saengwŏn* (classics licentiate) examination. Unfortunately his advancement was interrupted twice, first when he was banished to Ch'angwon, South Kyŏngsang Province, in 1806 for political factionalism, the second time when he was released from his post of magistrate because of charges brought against him in 1830 by the *amhaeng ŏsa* ('secret inspectors').

Yun Che-hong's contemporary Sin Wi, who wrote extensively about painters and their works, only mentions briefly that Yun preferred to paint landscapes. This suggests that, as a result of his turbulent official career, Yun might not have mingled with men of letters and arts of his time. Yun Che-hong's extant works prove that he was an innovative and unconventional painter. An album of eight leaves containing Yun's landscape paintings (Seoul, Ho-am A. Mus.) reveals that he experimented with such unusual techniques as using the tip of his finger or a stick. On one of the album leaves—that depicting *Jade Shoot Peak* (see An Hwi-jun, 1982, pl. 135)—he wrote that, whenever he had enjoyed himself beneath the peak, he had nonetheless missed having a thatched pavilion; more recently, however, because he had had the opportunity to paint in the manner of the 18th-century artist Yi In-sang, he was able to fulfil his wish. The painting depicts a thatched pavilion with a lone scholar beneath a rocky peak resembling a bamboo shoot. Although his simple composition and his application of light ink wash over the outlines bear a slight resemblance to Yi In-sang's work, Yun's brushstyle is vastly different from Yi's austere, dry application of the brush, especially since he was not using a traditional implement here, but his own finger or a stick. The way in which he renders the shrubbery of a mist-covered distant village with wet ink wash is unique and closer to modern watercolour technique.

Yungang, cave 20, colossal image of Shakyamuni Buddha with attendant, sandstone, h. 13.7 m, *c.* AD 460–475

BIBLIOGRAPHY
O Se-ch'ang: *Kŭnyŏk sŏhwa jing* [Dictionary of Korean painters and calligraphers] (Taegu, 1928/*R* Seoul, 1975), p. 207
Yu Pok-yŏl: *Hanguk hoehwa taegwan* [Pageant of Korean painting] (Seoul, 1969), pp. 612–13
An Hwi-jun: *Hanguk hoehwasa* [History of Korean painting] (Seoul, 1980), pp. 282, 296, 313
An Hwi-jun, ed.: *Sansuhwa* [Landscape painting], ii (1982), xii of *Hanguk-ŭi mi* [Beauties of Korea] (Seoul, 1977–85), pp. 135–7, 252–3

KIM KUMJA PAIK

Yungang [Yün-kang]. Chinese Buddhist cave temple complex 16 km west of Datong, Shanxi Province. The complex, consisting of more than 40 caves and innumerable niches containing Buddhist images, was hollowed from the sandstone cliffs of the Wuzhou Mountains during the 5th century AD under the patronage of the Northern Wei dynasty (386–534; *see* WEI DYNASTY, §1). The influence of Indian and Central Asian models is discernible in the carvings found in the 20 or so larger, earlier caves, while the sculptures in the smaller, later caves and niches display a more mature Chinese style, which reached its highest expression in the sculptural style of the cave temple complex of LONGMEN, near Luoyang, Henan Province.

The Northern Wei dynasty, founded by the Tuoba or Toba people, who ruled northern China during the Northern and Southern Dynasties period (AD 310–589), adopted Buddhism as its state religion. Work was begun at Yungang by the emperor Wenchengdi (*reg* 452–65) to atone for the persecution of Buddhists that had taken place during the reign of the Daoist emperor Taiwudi (*reg* 424–51). Controversy surrounds the dating and chronology of the caves. The earliest date of 414 for the first caves was put forward by Su Bai, but it is generally believed that construction began *c.* 460 and that most of the caves were completed by 494. The earliest caves (16–20) are named after the monk–official Tanyao. In one of the earliest written Chinese references to Buddhism, the *Wei shu* ('History of the Wei', compiled in the Northern Qi period (550–77)), records Tanyao's suggestion for the construction of five cave chapels, each containing a colossal image of the Buddha.

The caves, which stretch for 1 km along an east–west axis, range in width from 23 m to a few metres. The sculptures have suffered considerably from age and water seepage and have been restored several times. The Tanyao Caves are among the largest and were dedicated by Emperor Wenchengdi. Each consists of a single space just large enough to contain one colossal image. The ceiling and front wall of cave 20 have fallen away to reveal a statue of Shakyamuni (the historical Buddha; see fig.) that is typical of early Yungang style. The well-proportioned figure, seated in a meditative pose, became a standard iconographic type with characteristic Northern Wei features: well-defined face, solid, broad chest and shoulders, raised bands running to a point over the chest and arms and alternate grooves to describe the drapery (*see also* CHINA, §III, 1(ii)(b)).

Caves 7–12, which seem to be grouped in pairs, show a more regular plan than the Tanyao Caves. Rectangular, they are divided into front and rear chapels. The main image is accompanied by representations of *bodhisattvas*, triads of the Buddha, flying *apsarasas* (heavenly beings), heavenly musicians, *jātaka*s (stories from the life of the historical Buddha) and ornamental reliefs covering the walls, ceilings and entrance. The sculptural style of the late 5th-century caves 5 and 6 conform more closely to Chinese taste and were among the last to be commissioned before the removal of the capital from Pingcheng (now Datong) to Luoyang in 494. Cave 6 has a large square central pillar carved in the shape of a wooden pagoda. Niches containing elaborately carved images of Buddha, *bodhisattva*s and *apsarasas* are organized in horizontal bands along the walls, and oblong reliefs in the lower register illustrate *jātaka*s.

Several of the smaller caves and niches were carved after 494, and the sculptures are in a more mature Chinese style. The solid masses of such earlier figures as the colossal Shakyamuni in cave 20 are superseded by slimmer, elongated forms with sloping shoulders. One characteristic pose of early 6th-century sculpture is that of the seated *bodhisattva* with crossed ankles in imitation of a Sasanian-period (*c.* 224–651) model from Iran. This produces a diamond-shaped outline, the diagonals of which are emphasized by the lines of the robe over the arms and the scarf at the front of the torso.

See also CHINA, §III, 1(ii)(b).

BIBLIOGRAPHY

O. Sirén: *Chinese Sculpture from the Fifth to the Fourteenth Centuries* (London, 1925/*R* New York, 1970), i, pp. 8–20; ii, pls 17–74
S. Mizuno: 'Archaeological Survey of the Yün-Kang Grottoes', *Archvs Chin. A. Soc. America*, iv (1950), pp. 39–59
S. Mizuno and T. Nagahiro: *Unkō sekkutsu: Yün-Kang/The Buddhist Cave Temples of the 5th Century AD in North China*, 16 vols (Kyoto, 1951–61) [Jap. text with Eng. summary]
Su Bai: '"Da Jin xijing Wuzhou shan chongxiu da shikusi bei" jiaozhu: Xin faxian de Datong Yungang shikusi lishi cailiao de chubu zhenli' [Annotations on the 'Stele which records the major repairs of the great cave temples of Wuzhou Mountain of the western capital of the Jin dynasty': a preliminary investigation into the newly discovered materials on the history of the cave temples of Yungang at Datong], *Beijing Daxue Xuebao: Renwen Kexue*, i (1956), pp. 173–86
T. Akiyama and S. Matsubara: *Buddhist Cave Temples: New Researches* (1969), ii of *Arts of China* (Eng. trans. by A. Soper, Tokyo, 1968–70), pp. 122–30
W. Watson: *Art of Dynastic China* (London, 1978)

MARGARET CHUNG

Yun Hyong Keun [Yun Hyŏng-gǔn] (*b* 1928). Korean painter. He graduated in 1957 from Hong'ik University, Seoul, and spent two years in Paris from 1980 to 1982. He has exhibited in Korea, East Asia, Western and Eastern Europe, the USA and South America and is regarded as a leader of Korean modernism. In the 1960s Yun experimented with Western styles but returned in the 1970s to themes inspired by nature and his Korean roots, a progression he shared with several of his contemporaries. In his paintings he attempts to visualize the processes of nature without force or artifice and to record unselfconsciously, if not unconsciously, the passage of life. Working in oil with a palette restricted to two colours, burnt umber and light ultramarine, he applies several layers of paint to canvases of varying texture and absorbency in a process that may stretch over several years. The resulting blocks of colour—which result in an effect he calls the colour of 'rotted leaves'—possess great depth and vibrancy.

BIBLIOGRAPHY

J. Stein: 'Yun Hyong-Keun at Inkong', *A. America*, lxxx/7 (1992), p. 121
Working with Nature (exh. cat., ed. L. Biggs; Liverpool, Tate, 1992), pp. 33–47
E. Heartney: 'The New Players', *A. America*, lxxxi/7 (1993), pp. 35–41

SUSAN PARES

Yün-kang. *See* YUNGANG.

Yunkers, Adja (*b* Riga, 15 July 1900; *d* New York, 24 Dec 1983). American painter and printmaker of Latvian birth. He enrolled in art school in Petrograd (now St Petersburg) and then travelled through Russia. He left the country after the Revolution (1917). During the 1920s he lived variously in Europe and Latin America, establishing contact with such leading artists as Emil Nolde, Karl-Georg Heise (*b* 1890) and Diego Rivera. Yunkers fought in the Spanish Civil War (1936–9) and moved to Stockholm from 1939 to 1947, where he edited and published the periodicals *Creation*, *Ars* and *Art Portfolio* (1969 exh. cat., pp. 30–31). In 1947 ten years' work was lost in a studio fire.

Yunkers emigrated to the USA in 1947, acquiring citizenship in 1953. At this time he embarked on ambitious projects of prints and paintings including *Polyptych*, a five-panel woodcut, four metres long, and in 1957 a series of large-scale pastels culminating in *Landscape with Larks*, which received widespread critical acclaim. His illustrated edition of *Five Poems for Marie-José* (1969) by Octavio Paz marked the zenith of his graphic work. As a painter Yunkers occupied a significant position in the later stages of Abstract Expressionism. Through careful distillation the artist worked towards a Minimalist standpoint, integrating strips of collaged canvas over broad colour fields that subtly counter the impulsive gestures of expressionist art.

BIBLIOGRAPHY

Adja Yunkers: Prints 1927–1957 (exh. cat. by U. E. Johnson and J. Miller, New York, Brooklyn Mus., 1969)
Adja Yunkers: Exhibition of Works (exh. cat., New York, Whitney, 1972)
Adja Yunkers (exh. cat., Cambridge, MA, MIT, Hayden Gal., 1973)
Adja Yunkers: Paintings (exh. cat., intro. by Octavio Paz; New York, CDS Gal., 1982)
Adja Yunkers: A 20th-century Master (exh. cat. by E. Flomenhaft, Hempstead, F.A. Mus. Long Island, 1984), p. 32

Yun Myŏng-no. *See* YOUN MYEUNG RO.

Yun Nantian [Yün Nan-t'ien]. *See* YUN SHOUPING.

Yün Nan-t'ien. *See* YUN SHOUPING.

Yun Shouping [Yün Shou-p'ing; *zi* Weida, Zhengshu; *hao* Nantian, Dongyuan] (*b* Wujin, Jiangsu Province, 1633; *d* 1690). Chinese painter, poet and calligrapher. One of the Six Great Painters of the early Qing dynasty (1644–1911), he is acknowledged as the founder of a school of painting based in the Changzhou region, sometimes referred to as the Yun school. He was the most talented member of a prominent family renowned for its artistic talent. By virtue of his contribution to the genre of flower-and-bird painting, he achieved recognition as an important, innovative master who was an equal of the revered artists of the Song dynasty (960–1299). Though he was not a

Yun Shouping: *Peonies*, colour on paper, 430×285 mm, 1672; second leaf of 12-leaf album, *Flowers and Landscapes* (Taipei, National Palace Museum)

court painter, his style was designated the orthodox court style of the Qing dynasty (*see* CHINA, §V, 4(i)(e)).

Brought up in a literati environment, Yun studied with his father, Yun Richu, and according to legend, by the age of eight he could recite literature. He followed his father, who had become a monk, and elder brothers to Jianning, Fujian Province, where they joined the Ming loyalists in resisting the Manchurian troops. When the Manchus captured Jianning, Yun Richu escaped, believing that his sons were dead. In fact, one son was killed but Yun Shouping was taken prisoner and adopted into the family of Chen Jin, the conquering general who had no sons. After Chen was assassinated in 1652, Yun accompanied the body home and serendipitously met his father at a monastery. Yun's adopted mother was persuaded to release him and he returned with his father to their home where, at the age of 20, he began scholarly studies in earnest. Around 1661 he stopped using his original name of Ge and adopted one of his *hao*, Shouping. Even during his lifetime, the saga of Yun's life was used as the subject of poetry and plays.

Yun Shouping described two 'roads' or approaches to flower painting (*xiesheng* or 'life-sketching'). There was the outlined flower-and-leaf style with meticulous colouring, after HUANG QUAN, and the style without ink outlines that used only colour, of which he considered Xu Chongsi (10th century) the master. Yun felt the latter style 'captured the impression of nature' with an appearance of utmost beauty, unlike a 'carved' (laboured) painting (Mingshi, p. 168). Because this style had no structural ink lines, it was called *mogu* ('boneless'). Not only did Yun follow this

tradition (see fig.), but he also made several substantial contributions to it with innovative techniques for washes, texture dots, the application of pigments and colour harmony.

Yun Shouping's writings are filled wth discussions of the great artists of the past that reveal a tremendous breadth of understanding and appreciation of their work. While most of his writings concern landscape painting, close friends of Yun said he gave up that genre in deference to his friend, the famous landscape artist Wang Hui. Although Yun Shouping did paint landscapes throughout his life, his fame clearly rests upon his superb achievements in the genre of flower-and-bird painting. In a biography translated by Osvald Sirén, Yun was described as a man 'of an open, generous and refined character. When he met someone who understood him he could work a whole month for the man, but if it were not the right kind of person, he would not let him have a single flower or leaf even for a hundred taels of gold. Consequently, he always remained poor, even though he had been active as a painter for scores of years' (Sirén, p. 193). Yun's poverty extended to his grave: his funeral expenses were borne by his friend Wang Hui.

See also CHINA, §V, 3(v)(e).

BIBLIOGRAPHY

O. Sirén: *Chinese Painting: Leading Masters and Principles* (London and New York, 1956–8), v
Chang Lin-sheng: 'Yün Shou-p'ing', *Gugong Jikan*, x/2 (1975–6), pp. 45–80
Cheng Mingshi: 'A Study of Yun Nan-tian (Yun Nantian yanjiu)', *Shanghai Mus. Bull.*, ii (1982), pp. 159–184

Zhongguo gudai shuhua tumu [Illustrated catalogue of selected works of ancient Chinese calligraphy], Zhongguo gudai Shuhua jianding zu [Group for the authentication of ancient works of Chinese painting and calligraphy], v (Beijing, 1990), p. 17

JAMES ROBINSON

Yuon, Konstantin (Fyodorovich) (*b* Moscow, 24 Oct 1875; *d* Moscow, 11 April 1958). Russian painter and writer. Yuon attended the Moscow School of Painting, Sculpture and Architecture from 1894 to 1898, studying under Konstantin Korovin and others. From 1899 to 1900 he was in the workshop of Valentin Serov. In 1899 he also travelled extensively abroad. In 1900, together with Ivan Dudin (1867–1924), he opened an art school in Moscow, where many of the future avant-garde studied, including Lyubov' Popova, Varvara Stepanova and Nadezhda Udal'tsova. Yuon painted the Russian landscape and views of old Russian churches and monasteries as had Apollinary Vasnetsov before him. *Trinity Monastery: Winter* (1910; St Petersburg, Rus. Mus.), with its light-filled atmosphere, is typical of his work. The landscape *March Sun* (1915; Moscow, Tret'yakov Gal.) betrays the influence of the Impressionist style of his teacher Korovin in its portrayal of sunlight casting blue shadows on the snow, an effect that is repeated in *End of Winter: Midday* (1929; Moscow, Tret'yakov Gal.). After the 1917 Revolution he celebrated the new order in works such as *New Planet* (1921; Moscow, Tret'yakov Gal.), in which a group of figures hail the red planet that rises into the firmament. *Parade in Red Square* (1923; Moscow, Tret'yakov Gal.) is a more subdued depiction of military and civilian marchers seen against the backdrop of the Kremlin Wall and St Basil's Cathedral. In 1913 Yuon designed some of the costumes (see 1982 exh. cat., pls 270–71) and sets (Moscow, Bakhrushin Cent. Theat. Mus.; St Petersburg, Rus. Mus., A. S. Pushkin Apartment Mus.) for Diaghilev's production of Mussorgsky's opera *Boris Godunov* in Paris. He continued to work for the theatre after the Revolution and was elected as the first Secretary of the Union of Artists of the USSR in 1956.

WRITINGS
Ob iskusstve [On art], 2 vols (Moscow, 1959)

BIBLIOGRAPHY
T. Nordshtein: *Yuon* (Leningrad, 1972)
Zhivopis' XVIII—nachala XX veka [Painting from the 18th to the early 20th century], St Petersburg, Rus. Mus. cat. (Leningrad, 1980)
Russian Stage Design: Scenic Innovation, 1900–1930 (exh. cat. by J. Bowlt, Jackson, MS Mus. A., 1982), pp. 322–3
Yu. K. Osmolovsky: *K. F. Yuon* (Moscow, 1982)
Zhivopisi XVIII—nachala XX veka (do 1917 goda) [Paintings of the 18th to the early 20th century (to 1917)], Moscow, Tret'yakov Gal. cat. (Moscow, 1984)

MARIAN BURLEIGH-MOTLEY

Yupe, Lorenzo Muntaner. *See* MUNTANER.

Yuri (*b* 1694; *d* 1764). Japanese poet and calligrapher. She was the adopted daughter of the famous KAJI, who ran the Matsuya tea house in Kyoto and was also a *waka* (31-syllable classical verse) poet. Yuri's original family name may have been Kimura. Her initial training in *waka* and calligraphy came from her mother. Yuri was said to be exceptionally intelligent, and the courtier–poet Reizei Tamemura took a special interest in her and became her mentor. Both her poetry and her relaxed and fluid style of calligraphy reveal her strong personality. Nature was her preferred subject. In 1727, 159 of her poems were published in the *Sayuri ba* ('Leaves from a small lily'). The scholar and poet Rai San'yō wrote her biography, exhorting other women to follow her example. She was the mother of the painter Ike Gyokuran (*see* IKE, (2)).

BIBLIOGRAPHY
Japanese Women Artists, 1600–1900 (exh. cat. by P. Fister, Lawrence, U. KS, Spencer Mus. A., 1988), pp. 69, 73–4, 80

Yur'yev. *See* TARTU.

Yūshō. *See* KAIHŌ YŪSHŌ.

Yu Sŏng-ŭp (*fl* second half of 16th century). Korean painter. Active in the middle of the Chosŏn period (1392–1910), he was a disciple of Yi Chŏng-kŭn (*b* 1531), to whom he was said to be related. By tradition Yi Chŏng Kŭn was the founder of the Southern school of painting in Korea. This style of painting was modelled on such Chinese masters as Mi Fu and other landscape painters of the Northern Song period (960–1127). The flourishing of the Southern school of painting in Korea was a phenomenon of the mid-17th century; it is thus clearly an anachronism to connect Yi Chŏng-kŭn in any direct way with the Zhe school. Yu Sŏng-ŭp supposedly inherited Yi's style of painting, but as none of Yu's works survive, it is difficult to establish such a link. He is usually grouped with Yi Hong-kyu (*b* 1568) and Yi Ki-ryŏng (*b* 1600), painters who are also considered to have inherited the style of Yi Chŏng-kŭn. Yu Sŏng-ŭp is said to have visited Japan during the second part of the 16th century, probably as part of a diplomatic mission before the Toyotomi Hideyoshi invasions of Korea and the Imjin War (1592–8), and has been credited with introducing scholar painting of the Southern school into that country. This claim, however, cannot be verified historically.

BIBLIOGRAPHY
Chang Bal: 'Yi Dynasty Painting: Academicians vs. Gentlemen Painters', *Korea J.*, i/3 (1964), pp. 4–12
Hong Sŏn p'yo: 'Korean Painting of the Late Chosŏn Period in Relation to Japanese Literati Painting', *Traditional Korean Painting*, ed. Korean National Commission for UNESCO (Seoul and Arch Cape, OR, 1983), pp. 54–66
Kim Kumja Paik: 'The Introduction of the Southern School Painting Tradition to Korea', *Orient. A.*, xxxvi/4 (1990–91), pp. 186–97
An Hwi-jun: 'A Scholar's Art: Painting in the Tradition of the Chinese Southern School', *Koreana*, vi/3 (1992), pp. 26–33

HENRIK H. SØRENSEN

Yuste Monastery. Hieronymite monastery, near Plasencia, province of Cáceres, Spain. Charles V, Holy Roman Emperor (*see* HABSBURG, §I(5)), retired to Yuste after his abdication in Brussels in 1556, and he lived there from February 1557 until his death on 21 September 1558. The building was begun in 1415 and was built under the patronage of the Condes de Oropesa (Alvarez de Toledo); part of the existing monastery dates from this time. Following the Emperor's choice of Yuste, he sent plans for a new wing and detailed instructions for his personal requirements, and the enlargement was carried out in 1554–5 by Fray Antonio de Villacastín (1512–1603). It has been said that its style is derived from the house where

Charles V was born in Ghent. The palace of Yuste was constructed of brick and masonry in a series of monolithic blocks along simple lines and without decoration. It is built on two floors with similarly disposed rooms, one floor for winter and the other for summer. Each floor contains a central corridor with access to the four rooms. Because of the Emperor's poor health a ramp connected the ground floor to the first floor. On the first floor the ramp leads to a spacious terrace overlooking the magnificent landscape and valley of La Vera, from which there is access to the choir of the church, which the Emperor used. On the right of the entrance on each floor are an antechamber and chamber communicating with two other small rooms, belvederes resembling those in the towers of the Alhambra in Granada.

Since the Middle Ages Spanish monarchs had built palaces attached to monasteries, especially Hieronymite foundations. Their apartments adjoined the church and high altar, and from their private chambers they could see the presbytery. This was the plan followed at Yuste, where an antechamber preceded a chamber, used as a bedroom, that had a door into the presbytery of the church. In this room the Emperor could hear mass from his bed when he was ill and dying. This same tradition was continued at the Escorial.

The 15th-century monastic cloister adjoins the north wall of the church and contains the sacristy, library and prior's cell; it has two storeys, the upper ornamented with Gothic tracery. The 16th-century cloister is also rectangular in plan, and the axis is perpendicular to that of the church. Here the ornament is Plateresque, with decorated capitals and many coats of arms. The 15th-century church has a wide, single-cell nave with Gothic vaults. The upper choir is sited above the entrance, as is usual in Hieronymite churches, and the presbytery is raised above a crypt, in which Charles V's coffin was first placed before his subsequent reburial at the Escorial.

The palace of Yuste was decorated during the time of Charles V with paintings by Anthonis Mor, Michiel Coxcie and by Titian, whose *La Gloria* (1553–4; Madrid, Prado) the monarch asked to be hung so that he could contemplate it before he died. All the paintings and tapestries were subsequently removed to other Spanish royal palaces. In 1809 the monastery was damaged by fire in the Peninsular War and was later sold to the Marqués de Mirabel. It was completely restored after 1941 and is again inhabited by a community of Hieronymite monks. The high altar, made by Antonio de Segura, after the design of Juan de Herrera, has been returned to the presbytery.

BIBLIOGRAPHY

J. P. Gachard: *Retraite et mort de Charles-Quint au monastère de Yuste* (Brussels, 1854)
J. J. Martín González: 'El Palacio de Carlos V en Yuste', *Archv Esp. A.*, xxiii (1950), pp. 27–51, 235–51; xxiv (1951), pp. 125–40
F. Chueca Goitia: *Casas reales en monasterios y conventos españoles* (Bilbao, 1982)
J. M. González-Valcárcel: *Yuste* (Yuste, 1983)

J. J. MARTÍN GONZÁLEZ

Yu Suk [*cha* Sŏnyŏng, Yagun; *ho* Hyesan] (*b* Seoul, 1827; *d* 1873). Korean painter. He was a member of the Bureau of Painting and was known for his skill in a wide range of subject-matter including landscape, figure and genre painting. His landscape paintings demonstrate an eclecticism in embracing various styles then current. For example, he followed the Chinese artists Huang Gong-wang and Ni Zan, two of a group known as the Four Masters of the Yuan period (1279–1368), who were the most popular Chinese painters both in China and Korea among literati painters. At the same time, he painted figures using exaggerated lines for drapery in a style reminiscent of the Chinese Zhe school.

One of his works, *Mi Yuanzhang Worshipping the Rock* (ink and light-colour on paper, 1.15×0.47 m, Seoul, N. Mus.; see Ch'oe Sun-u, pl. 210), depicts Mi Fu, the great Chinese literati painter and calligrapher (late 11th century–early 12th), bowing to a large rock. Yu Suk depicts Mi Fu and a boy standing behind him in strong, undulating brushlines, while the rock is rendered in rather soft ink washes with only a few touches of dark outlines. Even more sketchy strokes loosely define another rock or mountain in the distance. The painting, therefore, reflects Yu's figure and landscape styles in a way that combines the approach of the professional painter with that of the literati amateur artist. This manner is often seen in paintings by court painters of the late Chosŏn period. Another painting attributed to Yu Suk is *Grand Festival* (Seoul N. U. Mus.; see Ch'oe Sun-u, pl. 211). It depicts two traditional sports taking place simultaneously, watched by a large crowd. Although the composition is quite effective, it is not his original, as there is a similar painting by Sin Yun-bok, also a court painter, who lived in the late 18th century, when genre painting became popular for the first time in Korea. A comparison of the figures in this painting with those in genre paintings by Kim Hong-do or Sin Yun-bok reveals the general decline in genre painting by the mid-19th century. The figures in Yu's painting have already lost much of the vitality that made the 18th-century genre paintings so special.

BIBLIOGRAPHY

Kim Yŏng-yun: *Hanguk sŏhwa inmyŏng sasŏ* [Biographical dictionary of Korean painters and calligraphers] (Seoul, 1959), pp. 438–9
Ch'oe Sun-u, ed.: *Hanguk hoehwa* [Korean painting], iii (Seoul, 1981), pp. 146–7

YI SŎNG-MI

Yusupov. Russian family of collectors, of Tatar royal descent. In 1556 the Yusupov family ancestors, the sons of Yusuf (who had been killed by his own brother), were sent to the Russian Tsar Ivan the Terrible, and their descendants were baptized in the last years of Tsar Alexis (Aleksey Mikhaylovich; *reg* 1645–76). From the end of the 17th century the male members adopted the title Prince (Knyaz') Yusupov. The most important member of the family was (1) Prince Nikolay (Borisovich) Yusupov the elder, the instigator of the collection. His son, Prince Boris (Nikolayevich) Yusupov (*b* 1794; *d* 1849), bought, rebuilt and decorated the house on the Moyka River in St Petersburg (now the Yusupov Palace, Moyka Embankment 94), to which he transferred much of his father's collection from Moscow and from the country estate at Arkhangel'skoye. In 1839 he published the catalogue of his gallery in French. His son, Prince Nikolay (Borisovich) Yusupov the younger (*d* 1891), together with his mother (the widow of Prince Boris Nikolayevich), added a great number of modern Western European artists to his grandfather's collection. Prince Nikolay (Borisovich) Yusupov the younger's daughter Zinaida (Nikolayevna) Yusupova (*b* 1861; *d* 1939) acted as a promoter of art by making generous loans from her family collections to exhibitions in Paris, Amsterdam and St Petersburg.

(1) Prince Nikolay (Borisovich) Yusupov [the elder] (*b* St Petersburg, 15 Oct 1751; *d* Moscow, 15 July 1831). Collector, patron and administrator. In 1772–82 the young prince travelled in Europe, visiting Paris, Amsterdam, Leiden, The Hague, London, Madrid and Naples, and living for a year in Vienna. During this period he completed his education, met such eminent connoisseurs of art as Prince Dmitry (Alekseyevich) Golitsyn (1734–1803) and laid the foundations of his own collection, following the general passion of the age for collecting works of art. The first mention of Prince Yusupov's collection was made in 1778 in the travel diary of Johann Bernoulli (1744–1807), who remarked that though not very large it was of good quality, with pictures by Titian, Velázquez and Domenichino. By 1782 Yusupov's collection rivalled, in Russia, those of Ivan Shuvalov and A. Olsuf'yev.

In 1783 Prince Yusupov lived in Turin as minister plenipotentiary at the Sardinian court, and in 1785 in Rome and Naples, where many of his 17th- and 18th-century paintings were either bought or commissioned from contemporary artists. In 1789 he commissioned works from Greuze, Elisabeth Vigée-Lebrun, François-André Vincent and Jean-Honoré Fragonard. At the same time he acted as agent for Catherine II, buying carved gems and giving commissions to the fashionable Angelica Kauffman, and for Catherine's son Grand Duke Paul (later Emperor Paul I; *reg* 1796–1801), acquiring and commissioning paintings for the imperial palace complexes at Gatchina and Pavlovsk, and supervising the copying of the Raphael Loggia in the Vatican in the boudoir at Pavlovsk.

In 1790, a year after his return to Russia, Yusupov asked the architect Giacomo Quarenghi to build a palace on the edge of St Petersburg on the banks of the Fontanka River to house his art collection. This building, Obukhovsky House (now the Yusupov Palace, Fontanka Embankment 115), one of Quarenghi's most remarkable classicist palaces, contained two specially planned picture galleries. At this time Yusupov's collections consisted of 17th- and 18th-century Italian and French works, 17th-century Spanish, Dutch and Flemish works, and 18th-century English and German works, including four landscapes by Claude Lorrain, eight portraits by Rembrandt and pictures by Cosimo Lotti, Jusepe de Ribera, Carlo Dolci, Domenichino, Giambattista Tiepolo, Giovanni da San Giovanni, Sebastiano Ricci, Philips Wouwerman, Joseph Vernet, Hubert Robert, Anton Raphael Mengs and Joshua Reynolds.

Yusupov became well known at the imperial court in the 1790s as an erudite connoisseur of art and an energetic and practical person. The empress, Catherine II, and later the emperor, Paul I, made Yusupov responsible for various artistic activities. In May 1789 he became Director of the Tapestry Factory, in February 1791 Director of the Imperial Theatres, and from 1792 he was in charge of the glass and porcelain factories. After the death of Catherine II in 1796 Paul appointed him head of the Hermitage. In 1801, when Paul was replaced by his son Alexander I, Prince Yusupov lost his power and position. He left St Petersburg and went to Paris, where his interests as a collector were entirely devoted to contemporary French art and the school of David, of whom he became an ardent admirer. According to the Prince's notebooks, he visited David on 9 June 1808 and succeeded in commissioning the painting *Sappho and Phaon* (St Petersburg, Hermitage), which David executed in 1809. At the same time Yusupov commissioned the equestrian portrait of his son from David's most talented and successful pupil, Antoine-Jean Gros.

In 1808, while still in Paris, Yusupov bought the country estate of ARKHANGEL'SKOYE, near Moscow, from Prince N. Golitsyn. Like many of the favourites of the late Empress who were no longer appreciated in the new conditions, he decided to settle in Moscow, far away from the court life of St Petersburg and the new emperor. Yusupov moved the greater part of his collection, consisting of some 500 pictures, some marbles, and a sculptural group by Canova, to Arkhangel'skoye. The pictures were hung according to the fashion of the 18th century, decoratively and without system.

BIBLIOGRAPHY
J. Bernoulli: *Sammlung kurzer Reisebeschreibungen* (Aix-la-Chapelle, 1785)
S. Ernst: *Yusupovskaya galereya* [The Yusupov Gallery] (Leningrad, 1924)
I. A. Kuznetsova: 'Sobraniye zhivopisi Kn. N. B. Yusupova' [Prince N. B. Yusupov's collection of paintings], *Vek Prosveshcheniya: Rossiya i Frantsiya—Vipperovskiye chteniya 1987* [The Age of Enlightenment: Russia and France—The Wipper Lectures for 1987], xx (Moscow, 1989), pp. 261–73

OXANA CLEMINSON

Yutaka Izue. *See* IZUE, YUTAKA.

Yu Tŏk-chang [*cha* Chago; *ho* Suun] (*b* 1694; *d* 1774). Korean painter. He is considered to be the most important painter of bamboo after Yi Chŏng (i). The tradition of painting bamboo can be traced back through six generations of the Yu family to Yu Ching-dong (1497–1561). Especially well known was his great-grandfather, Yu Hyŏg-yŏn (1616–80), a high-ranking military official, who took Yi Chŏng's painting as his model. Tŏk-chang himself held a sinecure without official duties. Contemporary sources attributed his extraordinary ability in bamboo painting to the long family tradition and stress that the force of the disciplined strokes required never failed him to the end of his life. Although the great scholar–painter and calligrapher Kim Chŏng-hŭr complained about his compositions, which he considered lacking in concentration at times, he also praised him. In addition he recorded an anecdote about how some of Tŏk-chang's practice sheets were used as packing material for a present sent to China; on arrival this provoked the horror of the Chinese addressee who, immediately realizing the value of the painting on the packing paper, had it mounted.

Many works by Yu Tŏk-chang survive. One of them is an eight-fold screen (ink on paper, each painting 619×377 mm, Japan, Yugensai priv. col.; see 1987 exh. cat.) that depicts various types of bamboo, old and young, in rain, snow and wind. It shows the influence of Yi Chŏng in the moving of the focal point of the composition to the side and in the contrasts of the ink wash tones that make the stems in the background appear to be shadows of those in the foreground. In other—probably later—works, such as *Bamboo in Snow* (hanging scroll, 1158×637 mm, ?1772; Seoul, N. Mus.), the plant has been moved towards the centre, and the contrasts are toned down. The leaves, which are more sharply defined than those of Yi Chŏng, are depicted from the side, lending a more spacious impression to the picture. Simultaneously, the special calmness and softness that characterizes Yi Chŏng's pictures has disappeared. Yu Tŏk-chang outlines cliffs with only a faint contour and dispenses almost entirely with structuring of surfaces to suggest their forms. These features, constituting an originality that is quite distinct from the model provided by Yi Chŏng, are observable as early as 1751 in a series of four paintings of that date in the National Museum of Korea, Seoul.

BIBLIOGRAPHY

An Hwi-jun: *Hanguk hoehwasa* [History of Korean painting] (Seoul, 1980), p. 253

Kwon Young-pil [Kwŏn Yong-pil]: *Die Entstehung der 'koreanischen' Bambusmalerei aus der Mitte der Yi-Dynastie (1392–1910): Ihre gedankliche Begründung und Stilfragen* (diss., U. Cologne, 1985), pp. 168–71

Tokubetsuten: Ri-chō no byōbu [Special exhibition of folding screens of the Chōsun dynasty] (exh. cat., Nara, Yamato Bunkakan, 1987), pp. 42–3

BURGLIND JUNGMANN

Yuya and Tuya, tomb of. Small, undecorated tomb of an Egyptian noble and his wife. It was discovered in the Valley of Kings (KV 46) at Thebes in 1905. The tomb had suffered superficial plundering but most of the contents were recovered intact (Cairo, Egyp. Mus., and New York, Met.). The collection is important for the light it throws on the funerary equipment of the nobility at the height of the New Kingdom (*c.* 1540–*c.* 1075 BC) and the styles of furniture and decorative art current at that time.

Yuya and Tuya were the parents of Queen Tiye, the wife of Amenophis III (*reg c.* 1390–*c.* 1353 BC). Yuya, perhaps of Asiatic extraction, came from Akhmim in Upper Egypt, where he held important religious offices. He was also God's Father (i.e. father-in-law of the pharaoh), Master of the Horse and King's Lieutenant of Chariotry. His wife Tuya was in charge of the female personnel of the temples of Amun and Min.

The mummies of Yuya and Tuya lay within black-varnished outer coffins shaped like shrines and were further enclosed in multiple anthropoid cases that are typical of their period in shape and decoration, but sumptuously finished with rich gilding and inlays (see fig.). Two gilded wooden chests each contained a set of canopic jars, in which were placed the viscera, wrapped in the shape of mummies and provided with miniature cartonnage masks. Among the most beautiful objects in the tomb were 18 *shabti* figures (funerary statuettes), most carefully sculpted in wood with details in paint and gold leaf, and Yuya's funerary papyrus, containing 40 chapters of the Book of the Dead (a collection of funerary spells) written in ink and illustrated with coloured vignettes.

The principal items of furniture comprised three bedsteads and three wooden chairs, the sides and backs of which were decorated with scenes carved in openwork or modelled in gilded and silvered plaster. On the back of the largest and most elaborate chair (Cairo, Egyp. Mus.,

Coffin of Tuya, detail of lid, wood and gilt, l. 2.18 m, 14th century BC (Cairo, Egyptian Museum)

CG 51113) is a double scene of Princess Sitamun, a daughter of Queen Tiye, being presented with gold necklaces. The representations on the arms include unusually lively figures of the dwarf-god Bes dancing and playing the tambourine and a depiction of the hippopotamus-goddess Taweret (Thoeris). These two popular household deities also appear on the other chairs, as well as on the headboards of two of the beds. Five wooden chests were also found in the tomb, two of them elaborately decorated with royal names and symbolic devices in gilt gesso, faience and ivory (Cairo, Egyp. Mus., CG 51117–8).

Besides three fine calcite vases the tomb contained a large number of dummy vessels of painted wood and limestone, some decorated with floral designs and others imitating the texture of stone or the 'festoon' patterns of contemporary glass vessels. An object of greater rarity was a complete chariot (Cairo, Egyp. Mus., CG 51188), 2.45 m long, the body, wheels, pole and yoke being of wood, and the sides and trappings of embossed and gilt leather. On account of its small size and the fragility of its decoration, the chariot could not have been used, and it was almost certainly made specifically as an item of funerary furniture.

BIBLIOGRAPHY
T. M. Davis and others: *The Tomb of Iouiya and Touiyou* (London, 1907)
E. Naville: *The Funeral Papyrus of Iouiya* (London, 1908)
J. E. Quibell: *Tomb of Yuaa and Thuiu* (Cairo, 1908)

J. H. TAYLOR

Yu Youren. *See* YÜ YU-JEN.

Yü Yu-jen [Yu Youren; *zi* Saoxin; *hao* Ranweng, Taiping Laoren] (*b* Sanyuan, Shanxi Province, 1879; *d* Taipei, 1964). Chinese calligrapher, poet, journalist and official. Yü Yu-jen came from a scholarly family and began to study the classics and calligraphy at the age of ten. Six years later he was first in the local examinations and in 1903 he passed the provincial examination, the next step in the civil service examinations, to receive his *juren*. By this time Yü had become interested in the republican cause and wrote a poem criticizing the Manchu court. An order for his arrest was issued while he was preparing for his final examination at the capital, and he fled to Shanghai, where he studied under an assumed name. From 1903 to 1913, Yü published four newspapers in succession, all anti-Manchu; the longest lasting and best known of these was the republican *Minli bao* ('The people's stand'). Yü held a number of high-ranking positions in the republican government from 1912 until his death; in 1950 he moved with the Guomindang (KMT) to Taiwan.

As a calligrapher, Yü is most famous for his draft cursive script (*zhangcaoshu*); this is an abbreviated form of clerical script (*lishu*), which was used for practical rather than artistic purposes from the Qin (221–206 BC) to the Western Jin (AD 265–316) periods, commonly written on wooden slips. Although there were records describing wooden slips as late as the Northern Song period (960–1127), the objects themselves were virtually unknown until large numbers of them were discovered at Dunhuang in the late 19th and early 20th centuries. Yü was the first to use them as models for his calligraphy. One example in the hanging scroll format ('I take pride that no vulgar rymes', undated; New York, Robert Hatfield Ellsworth priv. col., see Ellsworth, p. 227) is written in large characters and organized in a more even and spacious manner than would have been possible on wooden slips; nevertheless, Yü grasped the simplicity and naturalness of the originals. This was achieved by wielding a continuously moving brush in smooth, rounded strokes, applying consistent pressure. Yü's interest in cursive script (*caoshu*) and his desire to make it more accessible led him to organize a research group to investigate the possibility of standardizing the form. In 1936 he produced his *Standard Cursive Script* (*Biaozhun caoshu*), which never gained the popularity and wide usage that he intended but nonetheless became an irreplaceable tool for calligraphers and historians. Yü was also respected as a poet and was made poet laureate of Taiwan in 1964, the year of his death.

See also CHINA, §IV, 2(viii)(a).

WRITINGS
Biaozhun caoshu [Standard cursive script] (Shanghai, 1937)

BIBLIOGRAPHY
Wang Fangyu: *Introduction to Chinese Cursive Script* (New Haven, CT, 1958), pp. ix, x, xvii, xxix
Y. Uno: *Chugōku shodōshi* [A history of Chinese calligraphy], ii (Tokyo, 1962), p. 378
H. L. Boorman, ed.: *Dictionary of Republican China* (New York, 1971), pp. 74–8, 414
Traces of the Brush: Studies in Chinese Calligraphy (exh. cat. by Shen Fu and others, New Haven, CT, Yale U. A.G.; Berkeley, U. CA, A. Mus.; 1977), p. 97
Yu Jianhua: *Zhongguo huajia da zidian* [Dictionary of Chinese painters] (Shanghai, 1981), p. 13
Zhongguo shufa da zidian [Dictionary of Chinese calligraphy], i (Hong Kong, 1984), p. 984
R. Ellsworth: *Later Chinese Painting and Calligraphy*, iii (New York, 1987)

ELIZABETH F. BENNETT

Yūzō Saeki. *See* SAEKI, YŪZŌ.

Yvele, Henry. *See* YEVELE, HENRY.

Yverni, Jacques. *See* IVERNI, JACQUES.

Yvon, Adolphe (*b* Escheviller, 30 Jan 1817; *d* Paris, 11 Sept 1893). French painter. Having studied at the Collège Bourbon, he was employed by the Domaine Royal des Forêts et des Eaux at Dreux. He resigned in 1838 and went to Paris to become an artist. He studied under Paul Delaroche at the Ecole des Beaux-Arts and had three religious compositions accepted for the Salon of 1841: *St Paul in Prison*, *Christ's Expulsion of the Money-changers* (both untraced) and the *Remorse of Judas* (Le Havre, Mus. B.-A.). Yvon's début attracted some critical attention, and his canvases were purchased for the State; but he was more interested in depicting the exotic worlds popularized by artists like Alexandre Decamps and Prosper Marilhat. In May 1846 he departed for Russia on a voyage of six months that was to have a profound influence on his subsequent career. Drawings made on the trip led to a painting of the *Battle of Kulikova* (1850; Moscow, Kremlin), depicting the Tatar defeat. It was eventually sold to Tsar Alexander II in 1857. Yvon's familiarity with Russia contributed to his appointment as the only official artist accompanying French forces during the Crimean War in 1856. His *Taking of Malakoff*, painted for Versailles (*in situ*), was shown at the Salon of 1857 and again at the Exposition Universelle of 1867.

Following the Revolution of 1848 and the proclamation of the Second Empire, Yvon gained the favour of Emperor Napoleon III and henceforth served as an official artist of his regime. The glorification of the Napoleonic past became State policy, and Yvon's portrayals of patriotic exploits from that period were much in demand. He won praise for his painting, *Marshal Ney Supporting the Retreat of the Grand Army, 1812* (exh. Exposition Universelle 1855; Versailles, Château). He accompanied the imperial forces on the Italian campaigns against Austria, representing in heroic pictorial language the second attack on Magenta and the Battle of Solferino in 1859 (exh. Salon 1863; both Versailles, Château). In 1861 he was commissioned to paint *Eugene Louis, Prince Imperial* and in 1868 painted an official portrait of *Napoleon III* (both untraced).

Yvon received many honours for sustaining the desired imperial image: he was awarded the Légion d'honneur (1855) and promoted within the order (1867) and he was made professor at the Ecole des Beaux-Arts. In 1867 he published a manual of design for use in art schools and lycées. In 1870 Yvon was commissioned by a wealthy American collector, Alexander Turney Stewart, to create a colossal allegory of the *Reconciliation of the North and the South* (untraced). Yvon's reputation hardly outlasted the fall of the Second Empire in 1870. Facile and adaptable though he may have been, he was also prone to a literalism that has dated badly.

WRITINGS

Méthode de dessin à l'usage des écoles et des lycées (Paris, 1867)

BIBLIOGRAPHY

A. Thierry: 'Adolphe Yvon: Souvenirs d'un peintre militaire', *Rev. Deux Mondes*, n. s. 2, pér. 8, lxxi (1933), pp. 844–73
E. Heiser: *Adolphe Yvon, 1817–1893, et les siens: Notices biographiques* (Sarreguemines, 1974)

FRANK TRAPP

Ywyns [IJssewijn; IJwijnsz.], **Michiel** (*fl c.* 1514–17). South Netherlandish sculptor. He was from Mechelen, but he is known only for work done for the town halls at Middelburg and neighbouring Veere in Holland, to which members of the Keldermans family from Mechelen also contributed. In 1514–18 Ywyns was paid for a series of 25 sandstone statues for the façade of the Stadhuis in Middelburg. The statues, which represent the counts and countesses of Holland, were placed in ten pairs beneath canopies set between the first-floor windows of the main façade, with a further figure on each of the five sides of the adjoining corner tower. Restoration work of 1838 was so extensive that little of the original style of the figures can be determined. Ywyns may possibly be identified with the sculptor IJssewijn, who was paid for an *Annunciation* (untraced) and a statue of '*Heer Hendrick*' for the Stadhuis of Veere. The project was similar to the Middelburg scheme: seven sandstone statues, set between the first-floor windows, survive, representing the patron *Hendrik van Borssele* and his wife *Janna van Halewijn*; *Wolfert van Borssele* and his wife *Charlotte of Bourbon*; *Philip of Burgundy*; *Anna van Borssele*; and *Adolf of Burgundy*. The lost *Annunciation* was presumably also incorporated into the façade. Ywyns is sometimes regarded as an exponent of the Renaissance style in the north, but his few remaining works also relate to the tradition of portrait statues established by the bronze tomb figures of Jacques de Gérines in the 1450s.

BIBLIOGRAPHY

W. S. Unger: 'De bouwgeschiedenis van het stadhuis van Middelburg' [The construction history of the town hall of Middelburg], *Oudhdkd. Jb.*, 4th ser., i (1932), pp. 7, 9
D. P. R. A. Bouvy: *Middeleeuwsche beeldhouwkunst in de noordelijke Nederlanden* [Sculpture of the Middle Ages in the northern Netherlands] (Amsterdam, 1947), pp. 167–8, fig. 180

KIM W. WOODS

Z

Zabaleta, Rafael (*b* Quesada, Jaén, 6 Nov 1907; *d* Quesada, Jaén, 11 Feb 1960). Spanish painter. He came from a wealthy family of landowners and in 1924 began his artistic training at the Escuela de Bellas Artes de San Fernando in Madrid. He made his first trip to Paris in 1934, returning there on several occasions, but continued to take his native village, Quesada, as the basic subject of his work. After the Spanish Civil War (1936–9) he embarked on a period of intense artistic activity, holding his first one-man exhibition (Madrid, Gal. Biosca, 1942) and winning the support of Eugenio d'Ors. From 1943 he participated in exhibitions organized by d'Ors for the Academia Breve de Crítica de Arte, and after visiting Barcelona in 1945 he remained in close contact with Catalan cultural circles, exhibiting regularly in the region from 1947.

Zabaleta familiarized himself with contemporary tendencies in painting, notably Cubism and Surrealism, and established contact with their practitioners; he was a great admirer of Picasso, whom he knew. Taking Quesada, the Sierra de Cazorla and the people of the Andalusian countryside as the subject-matter of paintings such as *The Reapers* (1947) and *Quesada Landscape* (1957; both Quesada, Mus. Zabaleta), he synthesized Cubism's formal precision, Fauvism's violent colour and the distortions of Expressionism; the optimism and profound lyricism with which he treated rural themes has led to his being regarded as a humanist painter. In 1961, a year after his death, the Museo Zabaleta, with more than 100 of his paintings and drawings, was founded in Quesada. It was subsequently enlarged, with a room devoted to contributions from his friends.

BIBLIOGRAPHY
E. d'Ors: *Rafael Zabaleta* (Madrid, 1955)
C. Rodríguez Aguilera: *Rafael Zabaleta* (Madrid, 1971)
G. Ureña: *Rafael Zabaleta: Homenaje* (Jaén, 1984)
Zabaleta 1907–1960. Homenaje (exh. cat. ed. C. Rodriguez Aguilera; Barcelona, Sala Cult., 1986)

PILAR BENITO

Zabelin, Ivan (Yegorovich) (*b* Tver', 29 July 1820; *d* Moscow, 13 Jan 1909). Russian historian and archaeologist. He studied under Timofey Granovsky (1813–55) at Moscow University and worked in the Kremlin Armoury in Moscow from 1837 to 1859. In the 1850s and 1860s Zabelin was influenced by the theories of Vissarion Belinsky and Ludwig Feuerbach (1804–72) and later by Positivism, but in the last years of his life tended towards Idealism. He served on the St Petersburg Archaeological Commission from 1859 to 1876. He was Chairman of the Society of Russian History and Antiquity at Moscow University from 1879 to 1888. He was one of the organizers of the History Museum in Moscow and was its director from 1883 to 1908. In 1907 he became an honorary member of the St Petersburg Academy of Sciences and the Academy of Arts. He was a consultant during the restoration of the Cathedral of the Dormition in Vladimir-Suzdal' and the Cathedral of the Annunciation in Moscow. During the early years he was most concerned with the history of artistic metalwork, writing a number of works in the 1850s on the crafts of Kievan Rus'. He was also interested in Scythian history, icon painting, Old Russian architecture and archaeological theory. In his latter years he concentrated mainly on Russian social history. Zabelin sought to reconstruct the material basis of historical development by avoiding subjective assessments and using documents and monuments, which could include anything from churches to small crosses. He recognized that the distinctive feature of Old Russian art was the way in which it conveyed contemporary religious belief and interpreted forms derived from Byzantine art with greater freedom, and he was one of the first scholars to establish the relationship between wooden and stone building in Kievan Rus'. Zabelin's works are rich in historical imagery and have inspired numerous Russian artists with an interest in Russian history and material culture.

WRITINGS
O metallicheskom proizvodstve v Rossii do kontsa XVII veka [On metal production in Russia to the end of the 17th century] (Moscow, 1853)
Domashniy byt russkogo naroda v XVI–XVII vekakh [Household life of the Russian people in the 16th to 17th centuries], 2 vols (Moscow, 1876–9)
Russkoye iskusstvo: Cherty samobytnosti drevnerusskogo zodchestva [Russian art: original features in Old Russian architecture] (Moscow, 1900)

BIBLIOGRAPHY
V. I. Shchepkin: *I. Ye. Zabelin kak istorik russkogo iskusstva* [I. Ye. Zabelin as a historian of Russian art] (Moscow, 1912)

V. S. TURCHIN

Zabid [Zabīd; Zebid]. City in Yemen about 20 km from the Red Sea. Located in a fertile area of the Tihama Plain where the pilgrimage route from the south of Yemen to Mecca crosses the Wadi Zabid, the city was founded in AD 820 by Muhammad ibn Ziyad, emissary of the Abbasid caliph al-Ma'mun (*reg* 813–33) and progenitor of the semi-independent Ziyadid dynasty (*reg* 819–1018). The Ziyadids were responsible for erecting Zabid's congregational mosque, which has a hypostyle plan, and for the first city wall, erected in 1001 by Husayn ibn Salama. The congregational mosque was remodelled under the patronage of the Ayyubid dynasty (*reg* 1174–1229), under whom the building was given its present form and a brick minaret. Zabid became the winter capital of the Rasulid dynasty (*reg* 1229–1454) and flourished as an important centre of Islamic learning, particularly for the Shafi'i school of law, which was dominant along the Yemeni coast. The multi-domed al-Iskandariya Mosque (later incorporated in the citadel) appears to have been built under the Rasulids, although its modern name refers to Iskandar Mawz, governor for the Ottomans from 1530 to 1536. Zabid continued to flourish under the Tahirid dynasty (*reg* 1454–1537), who were responsible for major renovations to the congregational mosque in 1492, but it began to decline during the first Ottoman occupation of the Yemen (1537–1636), as the traditional overland trade routes were displaced. The city walls, which were rebuilt in 1805, were removed in the 1960s, but the four gates, which also probably date from the early 19th century, still stand. Several important buildings and houses in the traditional style remain in the city. They have exteriors enlivened with small, tablet-shaped bricks laid in patterns and usually covered with whitewash or stucco, creating baroque effects. Pottery sherds of widely varied place and date of manufacture have been found in and around the city, testifying to a tradition of local production as well as long-distance trade with Iraq and China. The arrival of imported machine-made goods in the 20th century led to the decline of such traditional handicrafts as weaving, dyeing and leatherwork. Since 1982 the Royal Ontario Museum has conducted a multi-disciplinary project to study the city and its environs.

BIBLIOGRAPHY

J. Chelhod: 'Introduction à l'histoire sociale et urbaine de Zabid', *Arabica*, xxv (1978), pp. 48–88

S. Hirschi and M. Hirschi: *L'Architecture au Yémen du Nord* (Paris, 1983)

E. J. Keall: 'The Dynamics of Zabid and its Hinterland: The Survey of a Town on the Tihama Plain of North Yemen', *World Archaeol.*, xiv/3 (1983), pp. 378–91

——: 'Zabid and its Hinterland: 1982 Report', *Proc. Semin. Arab. Stud.*, xiii (1983), pp. 53–69

——: 'A Preliminary Report on the Architecture of Zabid', *Proc. Semin. Arab. Stud.*, xiv (1984), pp. 51–65

——: 'A Few Facts about Zabid', *Proc. Semin. Arab. Stud.*, xix (1989), pp. 61–9

Zabłocki, Wojciech (*b* Warsaw, 6 Dec 1930). Polish architect, writer and teacher. He studied (1949–54) at the departments of architecture of the universities of Kraków and Warsaw, receiving his doctorate in 1968 and qualifying as an assistant professor in 1979. At the same time he was an outstanding sportsman, winning four world and five Polish fencing championships. He is noted for the numerous large-span sports buildings and complexes that he designed. Architectural expression is concentrated in the roofs, which may be free-hanging from cables, as at the Olympic Training Centre (1962), Warsaw; arched, as at the swimming pool (1975), Zgorzelec; connected by counterbalanced cantilevers; or of intermittent arches linked transversely by free-hanging coverings, for example a design (1977) for a sports centre in Leszno. Another variant in his approach to the design of sports halls is a multi-faceted mass suspended on a trapezial frame, as in his design for an auditorium and sports hall (1973) in Bydgoszcz. The latter has a frog-like form, reflecting Zabłocki's metaphorical use of the shapes of animals, crystals and other natural phenomena. He also used allusions to regional forms, for example in a sports centre (1988) in Czestochowa and in the sports hall (1990) in Zakopane. In Syria in 1982–7 he designed, with a large team, a complex for the Mediterranean Games, Latakia. He also built an extensive presidential residence (1985) near Damascus. His highly personal approach to the origin of a design created difficulties for collaborators and had the effect of discouraging patrons once political circumstances had changed in Poland in the 1980s.

WRITINGS

'Kenzo Tange: Architektura i konstrukcja hali sportowej Yo Yogi' [Kenzō Tange: architecture and construction of the Yo Yogi sports hall], *Inzyn. & Budownictwo*, 10 (1965)

'Sportzentrum in Warschau', *Bauen & Wohnen*, vii (1967)

'Salle sportive polyvalante à Bydgoszcz', *Archit. Aujourd'hui*, 11/12 (1973)

'Nowa architektura sportowa' [New sports architecture], *Architektura* [Gdansk], 12 (1975), pp. 394–401 [followed by criticisms by A. Glinski and L. Zielinski]

BIBLIOGRAPHY

Contemp. Architects

OLGIERD CZERNER

Zabludovsky, Abraham (*b* Bialystok, Poland, 14 June 1924). Mexican architect of Polish birth. He studied at the Escuela de Arquitectura at the Universidad Nacional Autónoma de México, graduating in 1949. In his early years he produced a large number of outstanding residential buildings and offices in Mexico City, making rigorous use of the International Style and demonstrating an impeccable handling of contemporary design, techniques and materials. Also notable from this period was the Centro Cívico Cinco de Mayo (1962), Puebla, on which he collaborated with Guillermo Rossel. In 1968 Zabludovsky began working in collaboration with TEODORO GONZÁLEZ DE LEÓN, although the two architects continued to work on some projects individually and retained their separate stylistic identities. Their collaborative work was remarkable for its quality and maturity, establishing functional and formal solutions that were later widely imitated. Clear examples of their characteristic proposals for constructions of massive, linear volume are the Delegación Cuauhtémoc (1972–3; with Luis Antonio Zapiain), the headquarters of INFONAVIT (Instituto del Fondo Nacional de la Vivienda para los Trabajadores, completed 1975) and the new building for the Colegio de México (1974–5; *see* MEXICO, fig. 7), all in Mexico City. Zabludovsky also carried out a number of works individually in the same style. Outstanding among these was the Centro Cultural Emilio O. Rabasa (1983), Tuxtla Gutiérrez, Chiapas, a construction with sculptural aspects that manages faithfully to fulfil the need for both theatricality and diffusion. He also designed two multipurpose auditoriums in Celaya and Dolores Hidalgo, Guanajuato (1990), two theatres in Guanajuato, Guanajuato, and Aguascalientes, Aguascalientes (1991), and a convention centre in Tuxtla Gutiérrez, Chiapas (1994).

BIBLIOGRAPHY

Contemp. Architects

P. Heyer: *Mexican Architecture: The Work of Abraham Zabludovsky and Teodoro González de León* (New York, 1978)

L. Noelle: 'Abraham Zabludovsky', *Arquitectos contemporáneos de México* (Mexico City, 1988)

P. Heyer: *Abraham Zabludovsky Architect* (New York, 1993)

LOUISE NOELLE

Zaborsky, Georgy (Vladimirovich) (*b* Minsk, 24 Nov 1909). Belarusian architect. He studied (1933–9) at the Academy of Arts, Leningrad (now St Petersburg), and from 1940 worked in Minsk. From 1942 he worked on proposals for the restoration of war-damaged parts of the city. These included the reconstruction of Lenin Square (1947–60; now the Square of Independence) and participation in the design of the central part of Lenin Prospect (1949–55; now Skorima Prospect). He devised the general plan for the development of Polotsk (1946–9) and also built there the neo-classical Regional Soviet Building (1949–54) with a courtyard behind a double colonnade. In Minsk he also designed a series of prominent neo-classical buildings: the city's first airport (1948–56), with Aleksandr Voinov (*b* 1902); the Pedagogical Institute (1951–2); and the Central Committee Building of the Belorussian Komsomol (1952–3). He also devised the layout of the circular Pobeda Square in Minsk, placing at its centre a monumental obelisk (1954), designed with Vladimir Korol' (1912–50). In the late 1950s Zaborsky turned his attention to the layout and general development of rural communities, striving to achieve a unity between architecture and the natural environment. In these he combined the methods of rationalist architecture with the characteristic forms of Belorussian vernacular, for example complex silhouettes in public buildings and high roofs with wide eaves and sometimes ornamental motifs and symbols. In the 1960s and 1970s he built the large village of Vertelishki, with small brick houses and an asymmetric ensemble of civic centre and shopping centre. He also built the central areas in the villages of Sorochi (1977) near Minsk and Mishkovichi (1978) near Mogilev.

BIBLIOGRAPHY

A. B. Ryabushin: *Gumanizm sovetskoy arkhitektury* [Humanism in Soviet architecture] (Moscow, 1986), pp. 271, 288

J. Hlinicky: 'O sakralnej architekturze' [Sacred architecture], *Projekt*, xxxii/9–10 (1990), pp. 2–78 [special issue]

A. V. IKONNIKOV

Zacatecas. Capital of the state of the same name in the central highlands of Mexico, *c.* 250 km north of Guadalajara, and with a population of *c.* 150,000. The city was founded in 1546 and became the most important silver-mining centre of colonial Mexico. The uneven terrain (it is situated in a ravine) and its initial quick growth resulted in an irregular but picturesque plan. Conservation efforts have preserved the city's colonial scale and many colonial buildings in the local reddish limestone. A late 18th-century chapel dedicated to the Virgin crowns the Cerro de la Bufa, the hill that dominates the city. The cathedral was constructed as the parish church of La Asunción (begun 1612; completed 1752), integrating parts of the chapels of the Miraculous Crucified Christ and of the Virgin to produce a spacious three-aisled church; the architect was probably Domingo Ximénez Hernández. In the variety of its elements and the complexity of its iconography (which originally corresponded to the decoration of the main retable inside), the façade is one of the most spectacular of colonial Mexico (*see* MEXICO, fig. 4). Also notable are the side portals; the tiled dome was rebuilt in the mid-19th century. Other noteworthy colonial structures include the 18th-century aqueduct, some houses near the cathedral and the Jesuit church of S Domingo (1746–9). All its retables but one survive, and there are notable wall paintings in the sacristy by Francisco Antonio Vallejo. The former Jesuit college of S Luis Gonzaga is now the Museo Pedro Coronel. The ruins of S Francisco, with an elaborate sculptured façade (before 1736), are part of a museum containing the collection of the painter Rafael Coronel. The church of S Agustín, best known for the 18th-century relief over the side door, representing the *Conversion of St Augustine*, was also partly ruined but has been restored. The church of Nuestra Señora de Guadalupe was built before 1721 and preserves many colonial and 19th-century works of art, including its choir-stalls; the ample monastery houses an important museum of colonial art. A 19th-century covered market also survives, and the Museo Francisco Goitia occupies a notable house that was formerly the Governor's mansion.

BIBLIOGRAPHY

D. Kuri Breña: *Zacatecas: Civilizadora del norte* (Mexico City, 1944, rev. 1959)

C. Bargellini: *La arquitectura de la plata: Iglesias monumentales del centro-norte de México, 1640–1750* (Madrid, 1990)

CLARA BARGELLINI

Zaccagni. Italian family of architects, builders and engineers. Bernardino Zaccagni (*b* Torrechiara, nr Parma, *c.* 1460; *d* Parma, *c.* 1530) and his sons Benedetto Zaccagni (*b* 26 Nov 1487; *d* 26 Jan 1558), also known as il Torchiarino, and Gian Francesco Zaccagni (*b* 21 Feb 1491; *d* 1543) were active in Parma from the late 15th century to the 16th. Bernardino's name is linked with the most important architectural works produced in Parma in the early 16th century. Between 1498 and 1507 he completed the Benedictine church of S Benedetto, Parma, which was begun in the local vernacular by Pellegrino da Pontremoli in 1491. Its graceful gabled façade, articulated by four elongated pilaster strips, betrays an ignorance of the rules of the Classical orders. Bernardino's Benedictine church (1507–9) at Pedrignano, near Parma, also seems alien to the Renaissance climate and may have been inspired by local Lombardic churches. In 1514 he designed the church of S Alessandro, Parma, which was largely remodelled in 1622 by Giovanni Battista Magnani.

From 1510 to 1519 Bernardino worked with Pietro Cavazzolo on the Benedictine church of S Giovanni Evangelista (begun 1490), Parma. He may have completed the side chapels near the monastery and constructed the groin vaults and the low dome on an octagonal drum over the crossing, which pays naive homage to the Romanesque Parma Cathedral. It is not clear if he worked only on the construction of the church, or if he also assisted in its design. In 1525 he also took part with his son Gian Francesco in the construction of the adjoining monastery of S Giovanni Evangelista, completing the crossing to the east of the large cloister.

Bernardino and Gian Francesco were also involved in the building of a new church to replace the 14th-century oratory of S Maria della Steccata, Parma, which was partly financed by the city as a civic temple (*see* PARMA, §2(iii)). Bernardino's design, dated 4 April 1521, which is in the form of an inscribed cross, was initially accepted, but some doubts must have arisen as to the capabilities of the Zaccagni, for almost as soon as construction began in 1521 a commission of experts was summoned to give an opinion on the model. In 1524 Gianfrancesco d'Agrate (*fl* 1515–47) offered an alternative plan, proposing a gallery in place of the existing attic, and in 1525 Zaccagni was dismissed from the project, ostensibly because of a crack that appeared in the large niche on the south side of the building. In April 1526 Antonio da Sangallo (ii) gave his opinion on the church (*see* PARMA, §2(iii)) and left a sketch plan for the dome, a fair copy of which was made by Marco Antonio Zucchi (1469–1531). The design was ultimately realized by Gianfrancesco d'Agrate and Paolo Sanmicheli da Porlezza (1487–1559), a cousin of Michele Sanmichele, although Vasari attributes the church to Bramante; there is also a view that Leonardo da Vinci, who was in Parma at times during this period, may have been the architect. Zaccagni therefore probably confined himself to elaborating the ideas of others in this last important commission, a fact also suggested by the contrast between the design of S Maria della Steccata and his earlier work. Bernardino's older son Benedetto was chiefly active as a military engineer, working for Pier Luigi Farnese, 1st Duke of Parma, on the fortifications of Parma and Nepi.

Thieme–Becker

BIBLIOGRAPHY

M. Salmi: 'Bernardino Zaccagni e l'architettura del rinascimento a Parma', *Boll. A.*, v–viii (1918), pp. 85–169
L. Testi: 'Bernardino Zaccagni e l'architettura del rinascimento a Parma', *Archv Stor. Prov. Parm.*, n. s., xviii (1918), pp. 147–242
B. Adorni, ed.: *L'abbazia benedettina di San Giovanni Evangelista a Parma* (Milan, 1979)
——: *Santa Maria della Steccata a Parma* (Parma, 1982)
A. Ronchini: 'Il Torchiarino da Parma', *Atti & Mem. RR. Deput. Stor. Patria Prov. Moden. & Parm.*, n.s. 2, iii (1985), pp. 473–80

BRUNO ADORNI

Zacchi, Giovanni (*b* Bologna or Volterra, 1512–15; *d* ?Rome, *c.* 1565). Italian medallist and sculptor. Son of the sculptor Zaccaria Zacchi (1473–1544) of Volterra, he spent almost his entire career in Bologna, working primarily for the Farnese family. One of his earliest and best-known medals (e.g. Florence, Bargello; see Pollard, p. 1292) was modelled in 1536 and shows the 82-year-old Venetian Doge *Andrea Gritti*. It is signed IO. ZACCHUS. F. on the reverse, which has a figure of Fortune holding a cornucopia and a tiller and standing on a globe encircled by a three-headed serpent. On only one other medal, that of *Fantino Cornaro of Episcopia* (Turin, Mus. Civ. A. Ant.), does Zacchi give this full signature. Other medals, signed either IO. F. or simply IO, are attributed to the artist on stylistic grounds, but such attributions make sense both chronologically and geographically. One of these, signed IO. F. (e.g. Florence, Bargello; see Pollard, p. 1293), is of *Guido Ascanio Sforza* (1518–64) and must also be from *c.* 1536, since Sforza was made Cardinal of Santafiora in 1534 and was Legate of Bologna from 1536 to 1540. Two

additional medals bear the same form of signature, those of *Onofrio Bartolini de' Medici* (e.g. London, BM) and *Giambattista Malvezzi of Bologna*. The third type of signature, IO, is found on only one medal, that of *Girolamo Veralli* (e.g. London, BM), but it is close in style to the other medals already mentioned and can be ascribed to Zacchi. Two additional unsigned pieces, showing *Cardinal Giovanni Maria del Monte Sansovino* (later Pope Julius III) and *Fabio Mignanelli* (1496–1557; Florence, Bargello; see Pollard, pp. 1292–5), Bishop of Lucera from 1540 and Vice-Legate of Bologna from 1541, can also be included in Zacchi's oeuvre on stylistic grounds.

Although no specific medals can be identified, it is quite possible that Zacchi's long association with the Farnese family brought him into contact with Pope Paul III. It is probable that he did work in Rome near the end of his career, since he is last recorded in 1555 fashioning a series of medals of noble Roman ladies for Cardinal Alessandro Farnese.

Zacchi was the recipient of two letters (*Lettere*, Venice, 1538–57) from Pietro Aretino and is also mentioned in two others, all dating from the autumn of 1552. The latter were addressed to Ersilia Cortesi del Monte, the wife of the only nephew of Julius III, and mention a medal (untraced) that Zacchi had made of her.

In the development of the medallic art in Bologna the first dominant name is Sperandio of Mantua, who represents the broad, forceful, sculptural style of the 15th century. He was followed by the noted painter Francesco Francia, who possibly designed and engraved dies for the very fine portrait coins of the lord of Bologna, Giovanni II Bentivoglio, but whose medallic work has not been entirely clearly defined. Whether the medals formerly ascribed to him are his work or that of others (they are now referred to merely as the Bolognese school) they are more refined and sensitive in portraiture, modelling and composition than the medals of Sperandio and clearly provided inspiration for Zacchi, who represents the peak of medallic development in Bologna in the 16th century. Zacchi's medals are all cast and from around 57 to 77 mm in diameter, and his subjects are usually churchmen. He combined forceful relief in the truncation of the bust, the profile of the beard and the projection of the beretta with subtle modelling in the drapery and in the characterization of the face. The profile and the features are handled with great refinement. In all his medals the bust of the sitter is set firmly and confidently in the field, the various levels of relief giving the entire composition a plasticity that is perfectly balanced with the delicately rendered details of hair, clothing and facial features. The lettering, too, is in good proportion to the field and the scale of the bust on the obverse.

Zacchi is only slightly less successful with the reverses of his medals. Despite the compositions being sometimes rather awkward, the subjects are executed with a combination of vigorous movement and fine and delicate detailing and modelling. The Fortuna on the reverse of the *Andrea Gritti* medal is posed majestically, albeit somewhat precariously, on a globe encircled by a rather strange three-headed serpent. The globe and the serpent, this time with only one head, appear again on the *Fabio Mignanelli* medal, but in a less interesting presentation.

Perhaps the most energetic and exciting of Zacchi's reverses occurs on the medal of *Girolamo Veralli*, where a prancing, long-necked griffin-like creature twists its neck around the trunk of a palm tree, at the top of which a smaller beast, also griffin-like, stands with outspread wings. This richly narrated scene, filled with movement and texture, combines with a fine obverse portrait to make it one of Zacchi's most successful works.

BIBLIOGRAPHY

Forrer; Thieme–Becker

A. Armand: *Les Médailleurs italiens* (2/1883–7), i, p. 143; iii, pp. 50, 56

I. B. Supino: *Il medagliere mediceo del R. Museo Nazionale di Firenze* (Florence, 1899), pp. 96–7

G. F. Hill: 'Notes on Italian Medals, XVII. Giovanni Zacchi and the Bolognese School', *Burl. Mag.*, xxv (1914), pp. 335–41

——: *Medals of the Renaissance* (London, 1920; rev. and enlarged by G. Pollard, London, 1978), p. 63

G. Habich: *Die Medaillen der italienischen Renaissance* (Stuttgart and Berlin, 1924), p. 108

F. Pertile and E. Camesasca, eds: *Lettere sull'arte di Pietro Aretino*, 3 vols (Milan, 1957–60), pp. 298, 408, 410, 413, 414, 527–8

G. Pollard: *Italian Renaissance Medals in the Museo Nazionale del Bargello*, iii (Florence, 1985), pp. 1292–5

STEPHEN K. SCHER

Zacchi, Francesco d'Antonio. *See* FRANCESCO D'ANTONIO DA VITERBO.

Zacchia, Lorenzo, *il giovane* (*b* Lucca, *bapt* 27 Dec 1524; *d c.* 1587). Italian painter. He was a cousin of the Lucchese painter Ezechia da Vezzano, known as Zacchia *il vecchio* (*fl* 1510–60), who probably brought him up and from whom he learnt to paint in the Florentine High Renaissance style. However, his *Adoration of the Shepherds* (1576; Lucca, Mus. & Pin. N.) is in an obviously mature style that owes something to the Mannerist compositions of Bronzino, particularly to his altarpiece (1564) on the same subject for S Stefano dei Cavalieri, Pisa. Two other reliably datable works, from the 1580s, feature typical Counter-Reformation themes: a *Virgin and Child with SS Louis and John the Evangelist* (1585; Lucca, S Paolino) and a *Crucifixion with SS Lawrence and Julian* (1587; Lucca, S Anastasio). Lorenzo treated these subjects in a style closer to that of Zacchia *il vecchio* and Fra Bartolommeo.

Some questions remain to be answered on Lorenzo's career: a group portrait known as *The Concert* (ex-art market, Munich) is one of the few works signed by him, yet the style of the painting is uncharacteristically Venetian and it seems to date from 1523, a year before his documented baptism (Borelli). Possibly the inscribed date is incomplete or was added later by someone other than the artist.

BIBLIOGRAPHY

T. Borenius: 'Italian Pictures in the Rijksmuseum', *Burl. Mag.*, lix (1931), p. 71

J. Pope-Hennessy: 'Zacchia il vecchio and Lorenzo Zacchia', *Burl. Mag.*, lxxii (1938), pp. 213–23

E. Borelli: *Nel segno di Fra Bartolomeo* (Lucca, 1983), pp. 41–5, 166–77

G. Briganti, ed.: *La pittura in Italia: Il cinquecento*, 2 vols (Milan, 1987, rev. 1988), p. 866

□

Zaccolini [Zacolini; Zocolino], **Matteo** (*b* Cesena, *bapt* 12 April 1574; *d* Rome, 13 July 1630). Italian painter and writer. After studying optics and perspective in Cesena with the scientist Scipione Chiaramonti, he established himself in Rome from 1599 as a specialist in perspective. He painted the fictive architecture and decorative borders for Baldassare Croce's frescoes (1598–1600) of scenes from the life of the saint in the nave of S Susanna, Rome. In collaboration with Giuseppe Agellio (*c.* 1570–after 1650), a pupil of Cristofano Roncalli, he painted the rear choir vault of S Silvestro al Quirinale, Rome, in 1602 with an illusionistic opening to the sky, revealing his interest in the contemporary ceiling decorations of Cherubino Alberti and his brother Giovanni Alberti, who had decorated the front choir vault. After joining the Theatine Order in 1605, he worked exclusively for its monasteries and churches, including spending some time in Naples (*c.* 1621–3). He is known for a four-volume treatise on perspective (1618–22), of which the only surviving copy is in Florence (Bib. Medicea–Laurenziana, MS. Ash. 1212): *De colori* treats the theory of colour; *Prospettiva del colore* discusses practice, emphasizing the use of hue and value gradients to create the illusion of depth; *Prospettiva lineale* presents perspective projection and measurement; and *Della descrittione dell'ombre prodotte da corpi opachi rettilinei* explains the projection of cast shadows. His ideas reveal a knowledge of major writings on optics and also of the manuscripts of Leonardo da Vinci. His erudition and expertise were highly respected; 17th-century sources connect him with Domenichino, Cavaliere d'Arpino and Nicolas Poussin. Cassiano dal Pozzo disseminated his ideas in Rome, and Poussin took a copy of his treatise to France. His emphasis on the importance of scientific knowledge in the imitation of nature encouraged the development of a rationalist approach associated with classicism in 17th-century art.

BIBLIOGRAPHY

G. Baglione: *Vite* (1642); ed. V. Mariani (1935), pp. 316–21

C. Pedretti: 'The Zaccolini Manuscripts', *Bib. Humanisme & Ren.*, xxxv (1973), pp. 39–53

E. Cropper: 'Poussin and Leonardo: Evidence from the Zaccolini MSS', *A. Bull.*, lxii (1980), pp. 570–83

J. Bell: *Color and Theory in Seicento Art: Zaccolini's 'Prospettiva del colore' and the Heritage of Leonardo* (diss., Providence, RI, Brown U., 1983)

——: 'The Life and Works of Fra Matteo Zaccolini', *Regnum Dei*, xli (1985), pp. 227–58

——: 'Cassiano dal Pozzo's Copy of the Zaccolini MSS', *J. Warb. & Court. Inst.*, li (1988), pp. 103–25

——: 'Zaccolini's Theory of Color Perspective', *A. Bull.*, lxxv (1993), pp. 92–112

JANIS CALLEN BELL

Zächerle [Zächerl], **Franz** (*b* Hall in Tirol, 6 June 1738; *d* Vienna, 5 Aug 1801). Austrian sculptor. He studied initially under the wood-carver Christoph Worndle (1713–63) in Hall in Tirol, then at the Akademie der Bildenden Künste in Vienna, of which he became a member in 1772 on presenting his lead relief depicting *Pygmalion and Galatea* (Vienna, Belvedere; wooden copy, New York, priv. col.); this work was influenced by the style of Georg Raphael Donner, although classical features are also evident. In the 1770s he made a figure of *Artemisia* (*c.* 1779), based on a design by Wilhelm Beyer (1725–1803), for the 'Roman Ruin' in the gardens of the Schönbrunn Palace, Vienna, and a Triton fountain and two wells decorated with lion masks for the garden of Prince Wenzel Anton Kaunitz-Rietberg, in Laxenburg near Vienna, all of which are now known only through engravings or literary sources. In 1781 Zächerle attempted unsuccessfully to work on the new monumental high altar in the church of St Michael in

Vienna. Of his later works, only those executed from 1786 to 1790 for the parish church in Austerlitz (now Slavkov u Brna, Moravia) have survived. These include stucco reliefs of the *Annunciation* on the tympanum in the entrance hall, of the *Resurrection* on the high altar and of the *Baptism* and *Last Supper* on the two side altars. For this large commission Zächerle used a cool, abstract form of classicism that was developing at that time.

BIBLIOGRAPHY
Thieme–Becker
G. Wolny: *Kirchliche Topographie von Mähren*, ii/3 (Brünn, 1860), p. 473
J. Dernjac: *Zur Geschichte von Schönbrunn* (Vienna, 1885), pp. 30, 34, 35–6, 42, 45, 90
E. Baum: *Katalog des österreichischen Barockmuseums*, ii (Vienna and Munich, 1980), pp. 748–51

MARIA PÖTZL-MALIKOVA

Zachrisson, Julio (Augusto) (*b* Panama City, 5 Feb 1930). Panamanian printmaker and painter, active in Spain. He studied under Juan Manuel Cedeño at the Escuela Nacional de Pintura in Panama City and from 1953 to 1959 at the Instituto Nacional de Bellas Artes in Mexico City. In 1961 he moved to Madrid, where he began his important work at the Real Academia de Bellas Artes de San Fernando.

Zachrisson's etchings, drypoints, lithographs and woodcuts tell stories, mock tradition and criticize society, encompassing subjects as varied as the circus and the myth of Icarus. In works such as the *Death of Chimbombó* (1963; New York, MOMA) he depicts life with humour and satire in a cruel and even tragic vision. His fantastic world is peopled by an entourage of monsters, witches and grotesque figures drawn from Panamanian urban folklore, Spanish literature, classical mythology and personal experiences. In the 1970s his paintings, generally in oil on wood, treat themes allied to his earlier prints, as in *May Rain* (1974; Panama City, Mus. A. Contemp.).

BIBLIOGRAPHY
Zachrisson: Obra pictórica (exh. cat., Panama City, Inst. N. Cult., 1978)
Zachrisson: Obra calcográfica (exh. cat., Santander, Mus. Mun. B.A., 1981)

MONICA E. KUPFER

Zack, Léon (*b* Nizhniy Novgorod, Russia, 12 July 1892; *d* 30 May 1980). French painter, sculptor and stained-glass artist of Russian descent. He studied literature at Moscow University while also taking painting courses at private academies; his painting teachers included Il'ya Mashkov, one of the founders of the Jack of Diamonds group. After leaving the Russian Socialist Federal Soviet Republic in 1920, he lived for two years in Florence and then for a year in Berlin, where he designed sets and costumes for the Ballets Russes. He settled in Paris in 1923 and in the 1920s and 1930s painted in a figurative style influenced by Renaissance masters such as Leonardo and Michelangelo; his themes included biblical subjects, prophets, vagabonds, gypsies and landscapes.

During the German Occupation Zack, as a Jew, took refuge at Villefranche-sur-Mer and in a village in the Isère, returning to Paris in 1945. His work then began to develop towards abstraction, becoming completely non-figurative in 1947, and he became one of the leading exponents of Tachism. His abstract works, such as *Painting* (1959; London, Tate), which are usually regarded as the culmination of his career, are notable for their beauty of colour

and texture and almost oriental refinement. As a convert to Roman Catholicism, he also received a number of commissions for stained-glass and religious sculptures from *c.* 1950, including *Stations of the Cross* for churches in Carsac in the Dordogne and Agneau in the Manche, and windows for the chapel of Notre-Dame-des-Pauvres at Issy-les-Moulineaux.

BIBLIOGRAPHY
P. Courthion: *Léon Zack* (Paris, 1961)

RONALD ALLEY

Zackenstil [Ger.: 'jagged style']. Term used to describe the predominant painting style in German-speaking regions during the 13th century, derived from its characteristic zigzag or 'broken-fold' drapery forms. Its early development was largely due to the influence of Byzantine painting on German artists in the north-east (Lower Saxony, Saxon–Anhalt and Thuringia). But in copying the Byzantine draperies, the northern artists exaggerated the patterns with decorative and expressive force, at the expense of the human forms beneath. Zigzagging drapery folds emphasize movement and lend the garment dynamic energy, as if it has a life of its own. Early examples include the Psalter (Stuttgart, Württemberg. Landesbib., MS. Bibl., fol. 24) made for Landgraf Hermann I von Thuringia (*reg* 1190–1217). *Zackenstil* occurs in the following decades in Franconia and the Rhineland, where it was adopted by workshops painting in all media. In these western regions, however, the style became increasingly influenced by French Gothic sculpture, giving it a new monumental plasticity (*Körperlichkeit*). Such works from the 1250s as the Mainz Cathedral Golden Gospels (see fig.) are, therefore, also considered masterpieces of High Gothic art, interpreted in a specifically German way. In the second half of the 13th century *Zackenstil* spread east as far as Prague and Lower Austria and south throughout present-day Austria and Switzerland, where it is found in panel, wall, stained-glass and manuscript painting (*see* AUSTRIA, §III, 1). Its popularity, however, diminished in the late 13th century, and in the wake of the newer *Weichstil* ('soft style'), the style disappeared altogether in the 14th century.

See also GOTHIC, §IV.

BIBLIOGRAPHY
C. Nordenfalk: 'Die deutsche Miniaturen des XIII. Jahrhunderts', *Acta Archaeol.* [Copenhagen], viii (1937), pp. 251–66
J.-C. Klamt: 'Deutsche Malerei', *Das Mittelalter*, ed. O. von Simson, ii, Propyläen-Kstgesch., vi (Berlin, 1972), pp. 260–64
H. Belting: 'Zwischen Gotik und Byzanz: Gedanken zur Geschichte der sächsischen Buchmalerei im 13. Jahrhundert', *Z. Kstgesch.*, xli (1978), pp. 217–57
P. Kurmann: 'Skulptur und Zackenstil', *Z. Schweiz. Archäol. & Kstgesch.*, 40 (1983), pp. 109–14

VIRGINIA ROEHRIG KAUFMANN

Zacolini, Matteo. *See* ZACCOLINI, MATTEO.

Zaculeu. Pre-Columbian site around 4 km from the modern town of Huehuetenango in Guatemala. It flourished as a Highland MAYA ceremonial and administrative centre *c.* AD 600–1525. The ruins of Zaculeu are high in the mountains of western Guatemala, in a relatively flat valley with mountains rising on all sides. Archaeological evidence shows that the site was occupied continuously from the Early Classic period (*c.* AD 250–*c.* 600) until its conquest by the Spaniards under the leadership of Gonzalo de Alvarado in 1525. At that time, the site was the Mam Maya capital, although it was evidently subjected to many outside influences and perhaps even conquest by neighbouring tribes during its long history. Most of what is known about Zaculeu is based on the excavations and restorations carried out in 1946–9 under the auspices of the Guatemalan Instituto de Arqueología e Historia. During this time nearly all the main structures were excavated and partly restored, numerous burials uncovered and collections of ceramics and other artefacts made. Most of these artefacts are in the Museo Nacional de Arqueologia y Etnologia in Guatemala City, and there is a small collection in the site museum.

The site is confined to a small spur bounded on three sides by deeply eroded ravines, two of which converge to form a narrow neck of land some 160 m wide, which gives access to the site. The enclosed area is relatively flat and measures approximately 325×225 m, with the Selegua River to the west. The main structures form a compact cluster in the south-western part of the site and are organized around a series of adjacent courts and plazas orientated principally along a north-westerly line. There are a few smaller structures on the periphery with no apparent relationship to the main group. In all, 44 structures have been mapped, including long, gallery-type buildings (Structure 10 and the north and south wings of Structure 4), several one- and two-room buildings on low, stepped platforms (structures 3, 13, 17, 25, 28 and 37), a large I-shaped ballcourt with enclosed ends (structures 22–3) and an impressive pyramid-temple (Structure 1), the largest construction at the site.

The Highland Maya sites in Guatemala are generally thought to belong to a separate culture from that of the Lowland Maya, and this is particularly evident in the architecture at Zaculeu, which shows influences from central Mesoamerica rather than from the Lowland Maya area (*see* MESOAMERICA, PRE-COLUMBIAN, §II, 3(ii)–(iv) and 4(ii)–(iv)). In contrast to Classic period (*c.* AD 250–*c.* 900), Lowland Maya buildings, which featured high rooms covered by masonry vaults, upper façades decorated with stone and stucco sculptures and high, lavishly decorated roof-combs, the rooms of buildings at Zaculeu had low, wooden-framed roofs that could not have supported roof-combs, and façades showing smooth plaster surfaces with no traces of applied decoration other than paint. Late Post-Classic (*c.* AD 1200–1521) Highland Maya architecture, as exemplified at Zaculeu, can thus best be described as plain or even severe; it depended for its effect on the play of light and shadow on smooth surfaces rather than on sculptural elaboration. Unlike most other Maya sites, Zaculeu had no carved stelae or other sculpted monuments, no wall paintings and no hieroglyphic texts associated with any of its buildings.

BIBLIOGRAPHY

R. B. Woodbury and A. S. Trik: *The Ruins of Zaculeu, Guatemala*, 2 vols (Richmond, VA, 1953)

G. F. Andrews: *Maya Cities: Placemaking and Urbanization* (Norman, OK, 1975)

GEORGE F. ANDREWS

Zadkine, Ossip [Zadkin, Osip] (*b* Vitebsk, 14 July 1890; *d* Paris, 25 Nov 1967). French sculptor, draughtsman and

Zackenstil miniature of the *Ascension*, 245×168 mm; from the Mainz Cathedral Golden Gospels, 1250–60 (Aschaffenburg, Schloss Johannisberg, Hof- und Stiftsbibliothek, MS. 13, fol. 54*v*)

printmaker of Belorussian birth. He spent his childhood in Smolensk in a circle of cultured and assimilated Jews. His father was a convert to the Orthodox Church, and his mother came from an immigrant family of Scottish shipwrights. While staying with his mother's relatives in Sunderland, northern England, in 1905, he attended the local art school and taught himself to carve furniture ornaments. At the age of 16 he continued his artistic training in London, taking evening classes in life drawing and making his living as an ornamental woodcarver. During this time he became friendly with the painter David Bomberg. He continued his studies at the Regent Street Polytechnic, London, and later, in 1908, at the Central School of Arts and Crafts, London, where he concentrated on techniques in wood.

Early works such as *Volga Boatmen* (1908; destr.) were oriented towards a socially critical realism. During a brief return to Russia in summer 1909, he met Marc Chagall in Vitebsk and completed works in wood and stone (untraced). Zadkine arrived in Paris in October 1909, and after a disappointing six months at the Ecole des Beaux-Arts with Antoine Injalbert he finally broke with official academic sculpture.

In 1910 Zadkine returned to Smolensk for the last time and he took part in the Union of Youth exhibition (Soyuz Molodyozhi) in St Petersburg. On his return to Paris in the autumn he moved into the studio complex of LA RUCHE, where he lived and worked in the company of like-minded artists including Fernand Léger, Joseph Csaky, Alexander Archipenko and Chagall. He regularly took part in the Salon des Indépendants and the Salon d'Automne and from 1912 lived in the artists' quarter of Montparnasse, where he mixed with Picasso, Apollinaire, Max Jacob, André Salmon and Modigliani. The diverse influences on Zadkine's pre-World War I lyrical style culminated in the large group of figures, carved in elm wood, *Job and his Friends* (1914; Antwerp, Kon. Mus. S. Kst).

Zadkine served as a volunteer in the French Army from early 1915 to 1917 and was employed as a hospital helper and later as an interpreter. At the front he twice suffered gas-poisoning. In his war drawings of 1916–17, such as *The Sickroom* (1916; Paris, Mus. Hist. Contemp.), he expressed his shocking experiences at the military hospital in a new formal language clearly oriented towards Cubism. Instead of the elegant linear sensitivity of his pre-war works, a harsh, sculptural style is predominant. The exaggeratedly high point of view, the unrealistic spatial setting for the figures and the dynamic, geometric style indicate a new direction in Zadkine's sculptural development.

The key work in this transition to a more stylized treatment of form and space in the wood and stone carvings of 1917–18 is the wooden figure *The Prophet* (1917–18; Grenoble, Mus. Grenoble). The success of this hieratic and ecstatic praying man lies in the emergence of the figure from the original form of the treetrunk and in the influence of South Russian idols. Zadkine's figure style owes much to the primitivism of Gauguin, Derain and Picasso and to the early paintings of Natal'ya Goncharova. His aim was to release the attitudes and structures of his figures from within the treetrunk or stone block in such a way as to stress their elemental qualities and deliberate lack of refinement. In this process an interest in pure form indicated by a strict adherence to direct carving and truth to materials was wedded to an expressive archaism communicated in geometric quasi-Cubist forms, as can be seen in the marble *Mother and Child (Forms and Lights)* (*c.* 1921–2; Washington, DC, Hirshhorn; see fig.), as well as in the five works Zadkine produced between 1922 and 1926 (see Lichtenstern, illus. 53, 55, 58, 60, 63), which indicate the continued influence of Analytical Cubism in the rhythmic arrangement of parts of the body, the interchange of full and empty forms and their reintegration into a geometrical system. Other sculptors, however, had introduced Cubism into sculpture much earlier, and Zadkine cannot be seen as a Cubist in the strictest sense, in that he was not interested in new autonomous conceptions of volume and space. Devoted to the human figure as a formal unity and as a source of emotional expression, he explained that he drew on Cubism as a technique that would permit him 'to *construct* the human object, represent its architecture as a totality of lines and forms which, as a totality, provoke emotions . . .' (quoted in Lichtenstern, p. 74).

Ossip Zadkine: *Mother and Child (Forms and Lights)*, marble, h. 603 mm, *c.* 1921–2 (Washington, DC, Hirshhorn Museum and Sculpture Garden)

Around 1929–30, Zadkine began working in bronze, depicting clothed figures in interwoven and spacious compositions and lively groups of three figures such as *Les Ménades* (1929) and *Laokoon* (1930; both Paris, Mus. Zadkine). Zadkine was widely recognized by about 1930, his reputation having grown steadily since his first one-man exhibition in 1919 at the Galerie Le Centaure in Brussels. In 1920 he married the French painter Valentine Prax (1897–1981), and in 1921 he applied for French citizenship. The first monograph on the artist, by Maurice Raynal, appeared in the same year. During the 1920s he began exhibiting internationally, establishing close links with the USA, the Netherlands, Belgium, England and Japan. He received numerous commissions, including sculptures for buildings and gardens both inside and outside France, such as the wooden *Garden Sculpture* (1927; Maresfield Park, E. Sussex), and he was represented by 47 sculptures at the 1937 Exposition Universelle, Paris. After the outbreak of World War II Zadkine lived in the USA (1941–5), where he taught briefly at the Art Students League in New York, but despite several exhibitions he never felt at home there because of his ties to Europe. In September 1945 he returned to France, where from 1946 he successfully taught young artists from many countries at the Académie de la Grande Chaumière and at the private sculpture school that he had established in 1928 at his home (now the Musée Zadkine) in the Rue d'Assas.

Zadkine's international reputation was consolidated by the retrospectives in Paris and Rotterdam in 1949 and the

Venice Biennale of 1950, where he was awarded the Grand Prix de Sculpture with the model for the *Destroyed City* (1951–3; Rotterdam), a monument commemorating the bombing of the city of Rotterdam and Zadkine's most popular work. The first design for the anti-war statement was the result of a journey through the Netherlands in 1946. The monument represents a fleeing female figure with her body torn open and her arms upstretched. Zadkine depicted a moment of hope amidst profound despair: the raised arms are a traditional expression of lament but they simultaneously show the figure pleading for help from above.

In the post-war years Zadkine produced a highly regarded series of sculptures symbolizing creativity, for example *Orpheus* (after 1948; Duisburg, Lehmbruck-Mus.) and *Poet: Homage to Eluard* (1952–4; Paris, Pompidou). In his view sculpture had to appeal to the emotions. To this end he represented the vitality of nature through metaphors of tree and forest in bronzes such as the *Human Forest* series, for example *Human Forest II* (1955; Mannheim, Städt. Ksthalle) and *Daphne* (1950; Paris, Mus. Zadkine).

Zadkine was also a prolific and skilled draughtsman, producing drawings and lithographs in a wide range of styles, exploring themes similar to those in his sculpture, for example the lithograph *Human Forest* (Czwiklitzer, p. 166). Zadkine's oeuvre shows a thematic and formal pluralism that derives from the mixed influences of his Russian birth and his life in Europe.

BIBLIOGRAPHY

M. Raynal: *Ossip Zadkine* (Rome, 1921) [numerous illus. of early works now untraced]
A. de Ridder: *Zadkine* (Paris, 1929) [good illus.]
A. M. Hammacher: *Zadkine* (Cologne and Berlin, 1954)
G. L. Marchal: *Avec Zadkine* (Paris, 1956) [mcm. from a student]
J. Langner: *Ossip Zadkine: Mahnmal für Rotterdam* (Stuttgart, 1963)
J. Jianou: *Zadkine*, preface W. George (Paris, 1964, 2/1979) [with list of works; good illus.]
U. Gertz: *Ossip Zadkine* (Duisburg, 1965)
C. Czwiklitzer: *Ossip Zadkine: Le Sculpteur-graveur de 1919 à 1967*, preface J. Adhémar (Paris, 1967)
J. Cassou, ed.: *Ossip Zadkine: Vingt Eaux-fortes de la guerre 1914–1918* (St Gall, 1978)
C. Lichtenstern: *Ossip Zadkine (1890–1967): Der Bildhauer und seine Ikonographie* (Berlin, 1980) [with detailed doc., bibliog. and exh. list]
M. C. Dane: *Catalogue, Musée Zadkine: Sculptures* (Paris, 1982)

CHRISTA LICHTENSTERN

Zaenredam. *See* SAENREDAM.

Zaganelli, Francesco (di Bosio) [Francesco da Cotignola] (*b* Cotignola, nr Ravenna, 1470–80; *d* Ravenna, between 31 Jan and 3 Dec 1532). Italian painter. He was possibly a pupil of Marco Palmezzano in Forlì. He primarily studied Ferrarese painting, which permeates his oeuvre and may account for certain eccentricities of style. He shared a workshop in Cotignola with his brother Bernardino Zaganelli (*fl* 1499–1509). Their first known joint work was the *Virgin and Child Enthroned with SS John the Baptist and Florian and Three Angels* (signed and dated 1499; Milan, Brera). Their last, the *Holy Family* (1509; Bergamo, Gal. Accad. Carrara), is unusual in the prominence accorded to St Joseph. The fan-shaped trees that rise above the wooded landscape in this painting are also found in the one work definitely assigned solely to Bernardino, *St Sebastian* (signed and dated 1506; London, N.G., together with the original lunette). Francesco is documented in Ravenna from 1513, with his wife and orphaned niece, and from this period date the *Baptism* (signed and dated 1514; London, N.G.), painted for S Domenico, Faenza, and the *Immaculate Conception* (signed and dated 1513; Forlì, Pin. Civ.), which includes the pleasing motif of the angel leaning on his lute. The *Nativity* (after 1520) and *Crucifixion* (*c.* 1530; both Ravenna, Accad. B.A.) were mentioned by Vasari and mark the high points of Francesco's late career. In the *Crucifixion* the expressive poses of the group of weeping women and the figure of John, the attention to detail and the setting of luminous colours against earthy ones are particularly striking. After his brother's death Francesco responded to new stimuli, including German woodcuts. He was a painter of limited technical skill and worked in an old-fashioned tempera technique, but his work, notwithstanding its provincial limitations, is characterized by a fertile imagination.

BIBLIOGRAPHY

Thieme–Becker

G. Vasari: *Vite* (1550, rev. 2/1568); ed. G. Milanesi (1878–85), v, pp. 255–6
C. Gnudi: 'I Cotignola', *Mostra di Melozzo e del quattrocento romagnolo* (exh. cat. by C. Gnudi and L. Becherucci, Forlì, Pal. Mus., 1938), pp. 126–39
R. Roli: 'Sul problema di Bernardino e Francesco Zaganelli', *A. Ant. & Mod.*, 31–2 (1965), pp. 223–43
A. Paolucci: 'L'ultimo tempo di Francesco Zaganelli', *Paragone*, xvii (1966), no. 193, pp. 59–73
B. Berenson: *Central and North Italian Schools* (London, 1897, rev. 1932); rev. as *Italian Pictures of the Renaissance*, 3 vols (London, 1968)
La Pinacoteca Comunale di Ravenna: Opere dal XIV al XVIII secolo (Ravenna, 1988)

ANDREW JOHN MARTIN

Zagora. Site on the west coast of the Greek island of Andros in the Aegean, which was established in the 9th century BC and flourished for approximately two centuries before being abandoned. It occupies the flat top of a promontory, with sheer cliffs on all sides except the north-east, which was defended by a massive fortification wall. The settlement was clearly sited for defensive reasons rather than convenience, and this reflects the troubled period of its existence, the Greek Dark Ages. The fortification wall (9th century BC) is a most interesting and rare example of Dark Age defensive works. It is some 140 m long and varies in width from around 4 m at its northern end to about 3 m at the only gate, near its southern end. It is built of unworked local schist and marble. The gate is set back, with an outwork to the north flanking the entrance passage. Within the fortified area, part of the town has been excavated by Cambitoglou since 1976, revealing densely packed houses. These are arranged in blocks and show variations on a simple basic plan, with courtyards in front of general purpose rooms for living and storage. The walls are frequently lined with benches for standing large pithoi or smaller amphorae and are entirely of undressed stone, the most readily available building material. Roofs seem to have consisted of flat stone slabs on wooden beams, supported where necessary by internal wooden posts and presumably covered with clay waterproofing, the traditional system for roofs in the Cycladic islands. In the centre of the site, almost at the highest point, is an isolated building, constructed in the 6th century BC after the abandonment of the town. It comprises an anteroom (2.80×6.29 m), entered by a doorway rather than a porch and leading to a cella (5.87×6.30 m). In the cella is a small trapezoidal platform, slightly off the axis of the building, which has been identified as an altar. This may antedate the building itself.

BIBLIOGRAPHY

A. Cambitoglou: 'Anaskaphai Zagoras Androu' [The excavation of Zagora on Andros], *Praktika Athen. Archaiol. Etaireias* (1967), pp. 103–11; (1969), pp. 135–8; (1972), pp. 251–73

A. Cambitoglou and others: *Zagora*, i (Sydney, 1971)

P. G. Themelis: 'Zagora: Polis e necropolis?' [Zagora: city or necropolis?], *Archaiol. Ephemeris* (1975), pp. 230–66

J. N. Coldstream: *Geometric Greece* (London, 1977), pp. 210–13, 304–12

A. Cambitoglou: *Archaeological Museum of Andros: Guide to the Finds from the Excavations of the Geometric Town at Zagora* (Athens, 1981)

R. A. TOMLINSON

Zagorsk. *See* SERGIYEV POSAD.

Zagreb. Capital of Croatia. The city was formed by the fusion in 1529 of the royal city of Gradec and the cathedral city of Kaptol, both built on a hill. It is now a leading industrial city as well as an important cultural centre. The first cathedral (consecrated 1217) in Kaptol was destroyed during the Tatar-Mongol invasion of 1242; rebuilding began in 1263, incorporating St Stephen's Chapel (13th century) with its 13th-century wall paintings associated with the Rimini school. The cathedral later acquired Renaissance and Baroque additions, but these were largely removed during restoration after the earthquake of 1880. Hermann Bollé restored the cathedral in Gothic Revival style (1880–1902) and was reponsible for the destruction of the original portal (1640; by Kozma Müller) and of the ribbed vaulting by Hans Alberthal. The Renaissance spire (1634–41; by Alberthal) was damaged in the earthquake, as was the Baroque Bakać Tower and part of the fortifications erected in 1469. The two spires (h. 105 m) were completed in 1902. The cathedral contains numerous art treasures: Renaissance pews (1520); a marble pulpit (1696) by Mihael Cusse; a painting of the *Virgin* (1610) by Carlo Bononi; the 11th-century robe of Ladislas I of Hungary-Croatia (*reg* 1077–95); missal illuminations (1525) by Giulio Clovio; three altars (1756–7) by Francesco Robba; and many liturgical objects in gold and silver.

Within the cathedral's fortifications stands the Baroque Archbishop's Palace (1730); among its treasures are codices dating to the 11th century. Important features of Kaptol include the church of St Francis (13th century; rest. 1880 by Bollé) and the main thoroughfare lined with fine Baroque curial residences, notably the Diocesan Museum (1689). The extension to the thoroughfare, Nova Ves, also has some outstanding buildings, namely the Military Court (1781), which has a Neo-classical portal, and the Alagović Villa by Bartol Felbinger (1824). The Baroque church of St Mary (13th century; rest. 1740), near the central market area, Dolac, has a dynamic copper-covered spire.

In 1242 Bela IV of Hungary-Croatia (*reg* 1235–70) granted freedom to the city of Gradec, which became a centre for crafts and guilds. The town had Gothic urban characteristics, with a central square, St Mark's, and an irregular grid plan. Fortifications were built before 1266;

the few remaining examples include the Lotrščak Tower, the Stone Gate (a votive chapel) and Popov Tower (1247), now the observatory. The church of St Mark (14th–15th centuries; damaged 1991) contains a Gothic portal (1400), sculptures by Ivan Meštrović and wall paintings by Jozo Kljaković (1889–1969), as well as gold and silver treasures. A feature of the church is its colourful faience roof with the coats of arms of Croatia, Dalmatia, Slavonia and the city of Zagreb. The Baroque church of St Catherine was built in 1620–32 by Jesuits and was conceived along the lines of Il Gesù in Rome (see fig.). The interior was restored in the 18th century with marble altars (1729–30) by Francesco Robba and plasterwork (1762) by Kristof Andrej Jelovšek. Beside the church is a former Jesuit seminary (17th century). Other outstanding buildings in the Upper Town are the 17th-century Zrinski Palace, the Museum of the City of Zagreb (formerly the convent of the Poor Clares, 1647), Oršić-Rauch Palace (18th century; now the Historical Museum of Croatia) and Pejačević Palace (1797). The harmonious impression of the Upper Town is enhanced by numerous late Baroque and Neo-classical buildings, including the Governor's (Ban's) Palace (1800) and Dvorana Palace (1837–40; by Felbinger). Radićeva Street contains the Neo-classical Domotörffy Palace (1814–15) by Felbinger and leads to the chapel of St George, the portico of which is by the same architect. There are several 'English' parks that help to transmit air from the mountain Sljeme to the Lower Town. The 18th-century Maksimir Park (316 ha) contains lakes, pavilions by Franz Schucht and a belvedere (1841). The central Mirogoj Cemetery is closed on the southern side by monumental neo-Renaissance arcades (1867; by Bollé).

After 1850 Zagreb spread into the valley between the hills to the north and the River Sava to the south. The Lower Town was built to a grid plan comprising rectangular blocks (200×100 m) with functional inner courtyards and buildings four to seven storeys high. Styles range from

Zagreb, St Catherine, west front, 1620–32

the Neo-classical and eclectic to that of the Modern Movement. A notable development is the series of garden squares from the railway station to Jelačić Square (1892; by Milan Lenuci and Ferenc Pfaff). These squares contain the Academy of Sciences and Arts (1880; by Friedrich von Schmidt) and the Gallery of Modern Art (1882–3; by O. Hoffer). To the west is the neo-Baroque Croatian National Opera House (1894; by Hermann Helmer and Ferdinand Fellner) and the neo-Romanesque Croatian University building (1856). To the south-west of this is the university library (1911–13), a Secessionist design by Rudolf Lubinski. Noteworthy buildings of the 20th century include the Croat-Slavonian Savings Bank (1905; by Hönigsberg and Deutsch), Hotel Intercontinental Esplanade (1924; by Dinko Sunko) and the Stock Exchange (1923–5; by Viktor Kovačić; completed 1927 by Hugo Ehrlich). The urban plan for modern Zagreb emerged from an international competition in 1936; it was further developed in 1946 and modified many times since. The third phase of the city's development covers the area between the main international railway and the River Sava to the south. This plan, by Zdenko Kolacio, based on the ideas of Le Corbusier, scattered individual blocks and public buildings, some of them of high architectural quality, in the green spaces between the main traffic routes, resulting in a lack of cohesion in the urban fabric.

Artistic activity in Zagreb dates from the early Middle Ages. The main influences came from France, Italy and Germany, for Zagreb was a frontier city of Western Europe except during the Baroque period of the 17th and 18th centuries, when it was linked more closely with central Europe. Close links with Western Europe were maintained in the 19th century and early 20th by such painters as Vjekoslav Karas, Ferdo Quiquercz, Nikola Masić and Vlaho Bukovac. In 1882 the School for Arts and Crafts (now the School for Applied Art and Design) was founded, to be followed by the Academy of Fine Arts in 1907 (formerly the Art School). There are collections in the Archaeological Museum (1846), Ethnographic Museum (1919), Museum of Arts and Crafts (1888–92; by Bollé), Cathedral Museum (1939), Benko Horvat Gallery of Renaissance Drawings, Gallery of Modern Art (1909), Strossmayer Gallery of Old Masters (1880; by Ferenc Schmidt) and numerous private collections.

BIBLIOGRAPHY
A. Mohorovičic: *Analysis of the Historical-urbanistic Development of Zagreb* (1952), p. 287
Enciklopedija likovnih umjetnosti [Encyclopedia of fine arts], iv (Zagreb, 1966), pp. 595–9
P. Tvrtković: 'Shades of Zagreb', *Bldg Des.*, 895 (1988), pp. 14–17
PAUL TVRTKOVIĆ

Zahra, (Vincenzo) Francesco (*b* 1710; *d* 1773). Maltese painter. He was arguably Malta's greatest native-born painter and one of the most gifted 18th-century artists south of Rome. He belonged to an artistically talented family, and his father, Pietro Paolo Zahra (1685–1747), was a popular stone-carver and a distinguished architect. Nothing is known of his upbringing but his surviving letters make it apparent that he received some sort of education, while his fluency in the late Baroque suggests a knowledge of the work of Francesco Solimena and a probable period of study in Naples. Another important influence was the work of Mattia Preti, to which he had easy access in Malta. The full impact of the Neapolitan Baroque is fully realized in the splendid *Virgin of the Rosary* (Tarxien, Parish Church) and the *Miracle of St Vincent Ferrer* (Valletta, Dominican Priory). His masterpiece, however, was the ceiling decoration of the chapter house of Mdina Cathedral, which he painted in oil on canvas stretched on a wooden framework. Completed in 1756, it employs with understanding various illusionistic Baroque devices. His later works are characterized by a classicizing restraint and sober iconography. They reveal a knowledge of the Roman school, which he acquired through Antoine de Favray, who exercised a disciplining influence on him. Zahra was extremely prolific and his paintings are found in many of Malta's churches. He was also in frequent demand as a portrait painter: the National Museum, Valletta, houses an attributed self-portrait.

BIBLIOGRAPHY
J. Azzopardi: *Francesco Zahra, 1710–1773* (Malta, 1986)
Marian Art during the 17th and 18th Centuries (exh. cat. by M. Buhagiar, Mdina, Cathedral Mus., 1983), pp. 12, 13, 18–19, 47, 48
MARIO BUHAGIAR

Zähringen, House of. German dynasty of rulers and patrons. From the 10th century the House of Zähringen held a leading position in Breisgau, and in 1112 Hermann of Zähringen (*d* 1130) was granted the title Margrave of Baden. Christopher I, Margrave of Baden (*reg* 1475–1527), who unified the family territories, was portrayed twice by Hans Baldung, alone (1513–15; Munich, Alte Pin.) and with his family (Karlsruhe, Staatl. Ksthalle). One of his sons, Ernest, Margrave of Baden-Durlach (*reg* 1527–53), founded the Protestant line of the family, with its seat at Pforzheim, Durlach (from 1565), and Karlsruhe (from 1715). The Roman Catholic line, which descended through another of Christopher's sons, Bernard II, Margrave of Baden-Baden (*reg* 1527–36), had its seat first at Baden-Baden and from 1715 at Rastatt. In the early 18th century (1) Frances Sibyl Augusta, Margravine of Baden-Baden, wife of Ludwig-William, Margrave of Baden-Baden (1655–1707), completed the rebuilding of Schloss Rastatt and had the nearby summer palace of Favorite built to house the family's extensive collections. The Durlach collection, which contained many important drawings and prints, including Hans Baldung's sketchbook, was formed by Frederick V, Margrave of Baden-Durlach (*reg* 1677–1709), and forms the core of the engravings collection in the Staatliche Kunsthalle in Karlsruhe. (2) Charles III, Margrave of Baden-Durlach, founded the town of Karlsruhe after 1715 and was a notable horticulturalist. At the extinction of the Baden-Baden dynasty in 1771, most of its collection, as well as its lands, passed to Charles-Frederick, Margrave of Baden-Durlach (*reg* 1738–1806), who in 1806 became Grand Duke of Baden (*reg* 1806–11). His wife, (3) Caroline Louise, Margravine of Baden-Durlach, amassed a collection of paintings by 17th- and 18th-century artists and was herself a painter of considerable talent, though she specialized in sketching in pastels. Charles-Frederick's descendants reigned until the dismantling of the German Empire in 1918.

BIBLIOGRAPHY

H. Rott: *Kunst und Künstler am Baden-Durlacher Hof bis zur Gründung Karlsruhes* (Karlsruhe, 1917)

A. M. Renner: *Die Kunstinventare der Markgrafen von Baden-Baden*, i of *Beiträge zur Geschichte des Oberrheins* (Bühl, 1941)

E. Lacroix, P. Hirschfeld and H. Niester: *Die Kunstdenkmäler Badens*, ii/1 (Karlsruhe, 1942)

L. Fischel: 'Notizen zur Geschichte des Karlsruher Kupferstichkabinetts', *Z. Gesch. Oberrheins*, cv (1975), pp. 265–94

J. E. von Borries: *100 Zeichnungen und Drucke aus dem Kupferstichkabinett* (Karlsruhe, 1989)

(1) Frances Sibyl Augusta [Franziska Sibylla Augusta], Margravine of Baden-Baden (*b* Ratzeburg, 21 Jan 1675; *d* Ettlingen, 10 July 1737). She was the daughter of Julius, Duke of Saxe-Lauenburg (1641–89) and spent her youth on the Bohemian family estate of Schlackenwerth. In 1690 she married Ludwig-William, Margrave of Baden-Baden (1655–1707), commander of the imperial armies of the West. After his death, she completed his planned reconstruction of the castle and town of Rastatt, the former a fortified residence designed by Domenico Egidio Rossi. The work was accomplished over two decades, with the help (after 1707) of the architect JOHANN MICHAEL LUDWIG ROHRER and his brother Johann Peter Ernst Rohrer (1687–1762). Between 1710 and 1720 Johann Michael Ludwig Rohrer built for the Margravine the summer palace of Favorite, near Rastatt. Its massive and magnificent Bohemian Baroque interior, with its many paintings, scagliola work, East Asian and European porcelain, faience, textiles and metalwork, remains almost untouched. The Margravine's collection of paintings (some items in Karlsruhe, Staatl. Ksthalle) included works by Hans Baldung, Lucas Cranach (i) and Lorenzo di Credi.

BIBLIOGRAPHY

A. M. Renner: *Die Kunstinventare der Markgrafen von Baden-Baden*, i of *Beiträge zur Geschichte des Oberrheins* (Bühl, 1941)

G. F. Kircher: 'Die Einrichtung des Rastatter Schlosses im Jahre 1772: Ein Beitrag zur Kulturgeschichte der deutschen Residenzschlösser der Barockzeit', *Z. Gesch. Oberrheins*, ciii (1955), pp. 177–249

A. M. Renner: *Sibylla Augusta, Markgräfin von Baden: Die Geschichte eines denkwürdigen Lebens* (Karlsruhe, 1955, 2/1989)

Der Türkenlouis: Ausstellung zum 300. Geburtstag des Markgrafen Ludwig Wilhelm von Baden (exh. cat., ed. R. Schnellbach and E. Petrasch; Karlsruhe, Orangerie, 1955)

G. Passavant: *Studien über Domenico Egidio Rossi und seine baukünstlerische Tätigkeit innerhalb des süddeutschen und österreichischen Barock* (Karlsruhe, 1967)

W. E. Stopfel: 'Sibylla Augusta als Bauherrin', *Baden-Württemberg*, xxx (1983), pp. 24–9

H. L. Zollner: 'Der Baute für Sibylla Augusta—Johann Michael Ludwig Rohrer', *Baden-Württemberg*, xxx (1983), pp. 14–15

——: 'Franziska Sibylla Augusta: Zum 250. Todestag der badischen Markgräfin', *Baden-Württemberg*, xxx (1983), pp. 1–9

Leben und Werk der Markgräfin Sibylla Augusta (exh. cat., ed. S. Esser; Rastatt, Pagodenburg; Rastatt, Schloss, Wehrgesch. Mus.; 1983)

(2) Charles [Karl-Wilhelm] **III**, Margrave of Baden-Durlach (*b* Durlach, 18 Jan 1679; *reg* 1709–32; *d* Karlsruhe, 30 Oct 1732). Distant relative of (1) Frances Sibyl Augusta, Margravine of Baden-Baden. After distinguishing himself in the protracted wars between France and the Holy Roman Empire, from 1715 he began the restoration of his devastated lands and set about the building of a new city, named KARLSRUHE, near Durlach, one of the most original examples of Baroque city planning. The Margrave was also a passionate horticulturalist, and his botanical garden was renowned throughout Europe. Its finest species were depicted in *c.* 6000 watercolours, gathered in over 20 albums of which only three are extant (Karlsruhe, Bad. Landesbib.; Karlsruhe, Genlandesarchv).

BIBLIOGRAPHY

F. von Weech: *Badische Geschichte* (Karlsruhe, 1896), pp. 379–87

B. Sütterlin: *Frühzeit und Mittelalter*, i of *Geschichte Badens* (Karlsruhe, 1965), pp. 307–21

G. Stamm: '"Wahre Abbildungen nach der Natur", Pflanzenmalerei am badischen Markgrafenhof', *Baden-Württemberg*, xxv (1978), pp. 32–6

H. Schwarzmaier: *Krieg und Frieden: Die Vorgeschichte der Gründung Karlsruhes und das europäische Kriegstheater in der Barockzeit*

(3) Caroline Louise [Karoline Luise], Margravine of Baden-Durlach (*b* Darmstadt, 11 July 1723; *d* Paris, 8 April 1783). Pastellist, wife of the grandson of (3) Charles III, Margrave of Baden-Durlach. She was the daughter of Ludwig VIII, Landgrave of Hesse-Darmstadt (1691–1768) and, from 1751, wife of Charles-Frederick, Margrave of Baden-Durlach (1728–1811). She was extolled from an early age as 'the Minerva of Hesse', possessing extensive knowledge in all branches of the natural sciences, especially mineralogy, botany and chemistry. She also had a talent for music and drawing and as a pupil of Jean-Etienne Liotard developed remarkable skill in pastel drawing. His portrait of her (1745; Karlsruhe, Staatl. Ksthalle) shows her full-length, seated in front of an easel; she herself made a copy of the painting (Salem, Schloss & Münster). Between 1756 and 1772 the Margravine built up a substantial collection of works by Dutch, French and German masters of the 17th and 18th century; kept in her private rooms, it was accessible only to a chosen few until after her death (*see* KARLSRUHE). Many of its pictures, including four still-lifes by Jean-Siméon Chardin and a Rembrandt *Self-portrait* (*c.* 1645), belong to the core holding of the Staatliche Kunsthalle in Karlsruhe. By copying these works in pastels, she extended her skills, as can be seen in her copy (1763; Copenhagen, Kon. Dan. Kstakad.) of Caspar Netscher's *Death of Cleopatra*.

BIBLIOGRAPHY

G. Kircher: *Karoline Luise von Baden als Kunstsammlerin: Schilderungen und Dokumente zur Geschichte der badischen Kunsthalle* (Karlsruhe, 1933)

J. Lauts: *Staatliche Kunsthalle Karlsruhe: Katalog Alte Meister bis 1800* (Karlsruhe, 1966)

——: 'Jean-Etienne Liotard und seine Schülerin Karoline Luise von Baden', *Jb. Staatl. Kstsamml. Baden-Württemberg*, xiv (1977), pp. 43–70

——: *Karoline Luise von Baden: Ein Lebensbild aus der Zeit der Aufklärung* (Karlsruhe, 1980, rev. 1989)

Caroline Louise, Markgräfin von Baden, 1723–1783 (exh. cat. by J. Lauts, R. Stratmann and others, Karlsruhe, Bad. Landesmus., 1983)

KEDRUN LAURIE

Zahrtmann, (Peder Henrik) Kristian [Christian] (*b* Rønne, 31 March 1843; *d* Frederiksberg, 22 June 1917). Danish painter. He studied in Copenhagen at the Kongelige Akademi for de Skønne Kunster in 1864–8 under Wilhelm Marstrand, Jørgen Roed, Niels Simonsen (1807–1885) and Frederik Vermehren. He worked as a teacher and as Head of the Kunstnernes Studieskoler (Free Arts Schools) in Copenhagen from 1885 to 1908. His works can be divided roughly into history and genre paintings. From the outset he was attracted to the great figures of 17th-century Danish history, especially Princess Eleanor Christine, whose autobiography *Jammers-Minde* [Memory of woe], first published in 1869 (Eng. trans. as *The Memoirs of Leonora Christina*, London, 1872), provided Zahrtmann with subject-matter for 18 large paintings (1870–1916). The Princess fell from grace because of her husband's alleged high treason and was imprisoned for 22 years. In *Eleanor Christine is Undressed and Searched by the Servants of Queen Sofie Amalie* (3 versions: 1884–6, Copenhagen, Stat. Mus. Kst; 1884–94, priv. col.; 1887–8, Copenhagen, Hirschsprungske Saml.) he experimented with light effects in the manner of the Utrecht Caravaggisti, possibly inspired by Gerrit van Honthorst's portrayal of the Princess (1647; Hillerød, Frederiksborg Slot). When Zahrtmann first visited Italy (1875–8) he concentrated on genre painting, using ripe and heavy local colour to develop a personal style, which was often criticized for being over gaudy. Although the narratives of his pictures are imaginary, he never painted without a model, which often makes his compositions overcrowded. His portraits are among his best works; the *Self-portrait* of 1913 (Copenhagen, Charlottenborg) displays his gift for the broad, monumental figure style. As a teacher he influenced a whole generation of Scandinavian painters, most notably the 'Funen Painters' ('Fynboerne'): Peter Hansen, Johannes Larsen, Fritz Syberg, Karl Oskar Isaksson and Edvard Weie.

WRITINGS

F. Hendriksen, ed.: *En mindebog* [A memoir] (Copenhagen, 1919)

BIBLIOGRAPHY

S. Danneskjold-Samsøe: *Kristian Zahrtmann* (Copenhagen, 1942)

K. Voss: *Friluftsstudie og virkelighedsskildring, 1850–1900* [Plein-air studies and representation of real life, 1850–1900], Dansk Kunsthistorie, iv (Copenhagen, 1974), pp. 297–310

Zahrtmann og Leonora (exh. cat. by H. Honnens de Lichtenberg, Randers, Kstmus., 1984)

JENS PETER MUNK

Zaim, Turgut (*b* Istanbul, 5 Aug 1906; *d* Ankara, 1974). Turkish painter and printmaker. He studied at the Fine Arts Academy in Istanbul and worked as a teacher in Konya for a short period before graduating in 1930. The visit to Konya was his first to Anatolia, and it gave him the opportunity to observe the peasant and nomadic life. As a result Anatolian themes entered his work, although he used the techniques of Western painting. He was also inspired by East Asian art and by the Turkish miniature painting tradition. Upon graduation he went to Paris to continue his studies but stayed only a few weeks and returned to Turkey to teach in Sivas, where he rekindled his interest in Anatolian life. His works were exhibited in Istanbul by the D Group (founded 1933), which he later joined. In 1939 he participated in the tours to the provinces organized for artists by the Turkish government, returning from the town of Kayseri with a series of paintings. His individual style for depicting local scenes, which used well-defined forms in bright colours, became popular in Turkey, and the narrative element of his paintings related them to themes in Turkish folklore. Zaim's aim was to develop a contemporary pictorial language to express life in Anatolia. He also produced etchings in the 1930s and linoleum prints in the early 1960s. His daughter Oya Katoğlu also produced paintings depicting rural life.

BIBLIOGRAPHY

S. Tansuğ: *Çağdaş Türk sanatı* [Contemporary Turkish art] (Istanbul, 1986)

G. Renda and others: *A History of Turkish Painting* (Geneva, Seattle and London, 1988)

□

Zaïre, Republic of [République du Zaïre; formerly Congo Free State, Belgian Congo]. Central African country, with a short Atlantic coastline to the west, bordered by the Central African Republic and Sudan to the north; by Uganda, Rwanda, Burundi and Tanzania to the east; by Zambia and Angola to the south; and by the Democratic Republic of Congo to the west. Zaïre is the third largest country in Africa, with a total area of 2,345,409 sq. km. It is dominated topographically by the Zaïre River and is extremely rich in natural resources, including minerals. Its population totals 34,491,000 (UN estimate, 1989) and consists of *c.* 250 different ethnic groups, nearly all of which are Bantu-speaking. French is the language of administration. The capital is Kinshasa (formerly Léopoldville).

Although what is now Zaïre was politically decentralized until colonial times, a number of kingdoms developed in the southern savannah region from *c.* AD 1500, and one of these, the Kongo kingdom, established and maintained diplomatic relations with the Portuguese between the 16th and 18th centuries. Such kingdoms as the Kuba, Lunda and Luba engaged in long-distance trade. In the 19th century the area was subject to more thorough European explorations, and by 1884 King Léopold of the Belgians had gained control of the region. In 1908 he was compelled to cede the land to the Belgian government, an act that led to the formation of the Belgian Congo and half a century of colonial rule. By the late 1950s political unrest was becoming unmanageable, and in 1960 independence was granted. In 1971 the country was renamed Zaïre. This article covers the arts produced in Zaïre since colonial times. For art of the region in earlier times *see* AFRICA, §VII, 6. *See also* BEMBE, CHOKWE AND RELATED PEOPLES, HEMBA, KONGO, KUBA, LEGA, LUBA, MANGBETU, PENDE, SONGYE, TABWA, TEKE, YAKA AND RELATED PEOPLES and ZANDE.

1. Painting, popular and traditional art. 2. Art education. 3. Museums and exhibitions.

1. PAINTING, POPULAR AND TRADITIONAL ART. While sculpture continues to be practised in Zaïre, it is in painting that the most profound changes have occurred since colonial times. Although walls with paintings depicting historical scenes and other forms of decoration are known in Zaïre, such art was impermanent because the houses themselves were not built of durable materials. The introduction of paper, cardboard, watercolours and gouache provided the flexibility of technique and the permanence necessary for painting to become widely adopted. As a consequence a new artistic order arose, encouraged by European artists, especially missionaries, and taking the form of workshops, patronage and schools of art. Until the 1980s the artistic situation in Zaïre could be summed up as having two categories of artists. On the one hand there were those producing traditional art whose value had been discovered as it was in the process of decline. The other group of artists were involved in the emergence of a modern art modelled on Western styles. This dichotomy was later enriched, so that by the late 1980s and early 1990s there were three groups of artists: traditionalists, academics and self-taught or popular artists, the last group enjoying a success fuelled by a curiosity in

the West for 'naive' art. Analysing the situation more closely, critics of the 1990s distinguished four main strands: traditional art, declining but sometimes prolonged by forms inspired by earlier examples and remaining faithful to a certain Africanism; art derived from art schools with aspirations and methods based on the old style academies of Europe; an international art, which goes beyond academic formulae; and popular art.

Western painting styles became established in Zaïre at the end of the 1920s, when European artists began to establish studios and schools offering instruction in Western techniques (*see* §2 below). The graduates of these schools were often taken up by patrons, a well-known case being that of Albert Lubaki, who originated from Bas-Zaïre but worked in Shaba. He was discovered by an official of the colonial administration, Georges Thiry, who gave Lubaki paper and paints, allowing him to choose his own subjects and style. Thiry bought Lubaki's entire output and sent it to his superior, Gaston-Denys Périer, in Brussels. The works were sold, and in this way a modern artist from Zaïre was exhibited in Brussels, Paris, Geneva and Rome during the 1930s. When transferred to Kasai Occidental, Thiry discovered another artist, Tshyela Ntendu, whose works then accompanied Lubaki's. Unfortunately, collaboration between the two patrons lasted only a short time, and subsequently the Zaïreian artists were neglected and disappeared entirely from the artistic scene.

Many years were to pass before a genuine school came into being. This was founded by a French artist, Romain-Desfossés, who in his search for adventure had arrived at Elisabethville (now Lubumbashi). He established an art centre called 'Le Hangar' (1947; later named the Académie d'Art Populair Congolais and in 1954 annexed to the Académie des Beaux-Arts, Lubumbashi), where he taught artists to express themselves using their own techniques, rather than copying Western art. Nor did he impose a ban on repetition, since he saw this as a constant feature in African art. By the early 1990s the school was being reproached for lack of originality in both themes and technique. Three names dominate the Lubumbashi School: Pili-pili, a master of sumptuously coloured landscapes distinguished by countless little hatchings; Mwenze, whose innumerable scenes of hunting and family life are enhanced by their juxtaposed large strokes; and Béla, the most gifted of all, who painted with his fingers and produced animal scenes full of spontaneity and charm. More recently Mode Muntu can be added to this trio. His threadlike beings are seen in profile, and great numbers appear in frameworks of two- or three-toned varied colours.

In Léopoldville during the 1950s and 1960s, a rich businessman, Maurice Alhadeff, acted as patron to many painters. He provided them with materials and bought their works, accumulating thousands. From time to time batches were sent to the USA for sale. Some excellent artists passed through Alhadeff's hands. One of the first was Albert Nkusu, although he broke away after a short time to pursue his own career. His work is notable for the depth of its themes and for its forests and figures of Christ, expressed in contrasted colours, often in an expressionist environment. Although François Thango (*c.* 1936–81)

began his career with the French painter Pierre Lods at Poto-Poto, Brazzaville, Congo, he later moved to the Zaïreian bank of the Congo River and became one of Alhadeff's preferred painters. After a period in which he produced the threadlike figures typical of Poto-Poto, he developed his own surrealistic style to express his interior visions of monsters and dangerous spirits. With its marvellous technique and flat surfaces encircled by large black strokes, his work displays an astonishing understanding of composition, always new and without any concession to repetition.

During World War II, Zaïre's most important artistic event was the establishment of the large Académie des Beaux-Arts (ABA) in Léopoldville (*see* §2 below). The names of the early students of the Académie are now some of the best-known in Zaïre and include the sculptors Ngynamau, Wuma, Liyolo and Tamba and the painters Ndamvu, Mavinga, Lema Kusa, Kamba Luese, Mayemba and the two Chenge brothers (who work at Lubumbashi). At a congress of the Association Internationale des Critiques d'Art held at Kinshasa, an exhibition presenting their work prompted some sharp comments. The artists were seen as being too much tied to such outdated and ill-understood European formulae as Cubism. At the same time the technical quality of many of the works was acknowledged. Reaction to this criticism included the formation of a group calling itself the 'Avant-gardistes', which issued ringing manifestos but otherwise did little to alter the situation. In 1978 the short-lived 'Groupe de la Nouvelle Génération' was set up in opposition to the 'big names' who monopolized official commissions.

1. Moke: *Untitled (Chief)*, oil on canvas, 1.77×1.30 m, 1991 (Geneva, Jean Pigozzi private collection)

Apart from such developments in Western-style, academic painting, a remarkable event was the sudden emergence of popular art. This had long been developing among self-taught artists and had a following in the more humble sections of society. Themes include portraits, illustrations of the tribal legend of the painter, legendary personalities such as Mami Wata, echoes of the colonial epoch such as scenes of coercion, incidents from the independence struggles such as bombings and executions, national heroes and scenes from daily life. Popular artists recorded what they saw, producing a chronicle that was often full of humour and reproducing everything that struck their imagination: accidents, quarrels, festivals, proverbs reflecting popular wisdom and phrases from religious sermons. Artists invented their own themes and, according to their success, converted them into stereotypes that could be multiplied to order. Prominent among these artists were, from the first generation, Tshibumba Kanda-Matulu and, more recently, Moke (*b* 1950) (see fig. 1) and Cheri Samba (see fig. 2). They owe much of their fame to European enthusiasts. On their own terms the best have acquired a success that has largely crossed frontiers.

Traditional art was produced for functional and ritual purposes, or a combination of the two, and was commissioned by the intended user, with the commissions of royalty and the societies being a particularly important and influential source of patronage. Gradually Western demand for such artefacts extended the number and range of objects produced. During the colonial period individual patrons had considerable influence in the development of academic styles of art (see above), and in the 1990s private

initiatives continued to provide support for artists, art associations and cultural institutions. Popular art has benefited from the patronage of Western markets and its usefulness to the business community for publicity and marketing purposes. Government patronage is organized through the Ministry of Culture and the Arts, within which a general administrative secretariat coordinates exhibitions and cultural activities in the country. Patronage is given to many associations throughout the country, as well as to such public cultural institutions as the Institut des Musées Nationaux du Zaïre (IMNZ) (*see* §3 below), as well as the National Archives and the Bibliothèque Nationale.

2. ART EDUCATION. Specialized Zaïreian art education has a long history, beginning at the start of the colonial period with missions setting up studios in order to introduce new techniques and Christian subjects into traditional art. By the 1990s none of these studios was still in existence. Nevertheless, art education in Zaïre may be said to be the most successful in Africa. It is based around the large and influential Académie des Beaux Arts, Kinshasa (formerly Léopoldville). This establishment was founded as the St Luke School, a bush school set up by a missionary, Brother Marc Wallenda, who came from Liège in Belgium and had studied at the Ecole d'Art Saint-Luc. He founded a class for sculpture that was extended with courses in drawing. The unexpected success of an exhibition in the capital led to the authorities moving the school itself into the capital. At first the teaching was systematic, incorporating clear principles: there was to be no copying of Western art, inspiration was to be sought in traditional art, and respect for reality should be shown by idealizing

2. Cheri Samba: *Mosali Nzela*, acrylic on canvas, 1.28×1.90 m, 1991 (Geneva, Jean Pigozzi private collection)

that reality. The collaboration of European teachers soon broadened this approach, and students increasingly turned towards contemporary art. The Stanley–Pool School, Léopoldville, was established by Moonens, who went on to succeed Romain-Desfosses at the latter's school in Elisabethville (now Lubumbashi). Another important art school in Zaïre is the Institut National des Arts, also in Kinshasa.

Apart from such formal sources of education, many established artists offered apprenticeships in their studios. Among these were the sculptors Lioyo, Tamba, Makala, Lufwa and Kamanda; the painters Ndamvu, Mavinga, Lema Kusa, Kamba, Pili-Pili, Konde and Kapolongo; the ceramicists Bamba and Mukengo; and the copper-beaters Shenge and Muteba.

In the 1990s aesthetics and the history of art were taught in most secondary schools and art faculties, and the national museums and private galleries ran programmes providing a general level of education in artistic matters. In addition the education section of the Institut des Musées Nationaux du Zaïre conducts research into ways of extending education in the museums as well as helping students from the country's technical institutes, specialists from other museums and researchers, both Zaïreian and foreign.

3. MUSEUMS AND EXHIBITIONS. Before independence there were many museums in the country. Some were more or less public institutions, including the Léopoldville Museum of Indigenous Life (in what is now Kinshasa), the Léopold II Museum, Elisabethville (now Lubumbashi), the Museum of Art and Folklore, Luluabourg (now Kananga), the Museums of Stanleyville (now Kisangani), Coquilhatville (now Mbandaka), Lwiro and Mushenge. Others belonged to private associations or institutions. The museums of prehistory and anthropology were part of Lovanium University, while others in Kimpese, Kangu, Matadi and Collège Albert belonged to congregations or missionary societies. With the exception of the museums of Lubumbashi, Kananga and Mbandaka, which have at least kept their buildings, many of these have disappeared, and during the troubled years from 1960 to 1965 some lost the main part of their collections. Following independence, therefore, Zaïre was without a viable museum organization. In the 1970s various initiatives were started to remedy this situation and to encourage a re-evaluation of the cultural heritage of the country. One of the most significant of these initiatives was the creation of the Institut des Musées Nationaux du Zaïre in 1970. The IMNZ is based in Kinshasa and has departments dealing with administrative and financial problems, scientific research and the conservation and display of collections. By the early 1990s the institute had accumulated c. 45,000 objects from nearly all the regions in the country. Three museum complexes existed at this time (the national museums of Lubumbashi, Kinshasa and Kananga) as well as the Butembo Centre. Although each national museum has a permanent display of traditional and contemporary art, archaeological finds and material from significant historical monuments, only the one at Lubumbashi is in any real sense a viable institution. One of the institute's major objectives is to give the capital a real museum

capable of housing the collection acquired since 1970 and awaiting conservation, evaluation and display.

The national museums also put on a number of temporary exhibitions of contemporary art on particular themes, as do such private galleries as that of Louis Van Bever, the French, American and German cultural centres and the Walloon–Brussels Centre in Kinshasa. The national museums, especially that in Kinshasa, and some private galleries, particularly those owned by banks, also have fairly regular temporary exhibitions of traditional art. The IMNZ also organizes exhibitions with such countries as the USA, Switzerland, Belgium, Germany, France, Iran and Nigeria.

BIBLIOGRAPHY

G.-D. Périer: *Les Arts populaires du Congo Belge* (Brussels, 1948)
I. Szombati-Fabian and J. Fabian: 'Art, History and Society: Popular Painting in Shaba, Zaire', *Stud. Anthropol. Visual Communic.*, iii/1 (1976), pp. 1–21
Badi-Banga Ne-Mwine: *Contribution à l'étude historique de l'art plastique zaïrois moderne* (Kinshasa, 1977)
J.-A. Cornet and others: *60 Ans de peinture au Zaïre* (Brussels, 1989)
S. Peters and others, eds: *Directory of Museums in Africa/Répertoire des musées en Afrique* (London and New York, 1990)
B. Jewsiewicki: 'Painting in Zaire: From the Invention of the West to the Representation of Social Self', *Africa Explores: 20th Century African Art* (exh. cat. by S. Vogel; New York, Cent. Afr. A., 1991), pp. 130–51
N. Guez: *L'Art africain contemporain/Contemporary African Art: Guide Edition 92–94* (Paris, 1992)
La Naissance de la peinture contemporaine en Afrique centrale, 1930–1970 (exh. cat. by J.-L. Vellut and others, Tervuren, Kon. Mus. Mid.-Afrika, 1992)

J.-A. CORNET, LEMA GWETE

Zais, Giuseppe (*b* Forno di Canale [now Canale d'Agordo], nr Belluno, 22 March 1709; *d* Treviso, 29 Dec 1781). Italian painter. He may have served an apprenticeship in Belluno before moving, probably around 1725–30, to Venice, where he practised as a landscape painter for nearly 50 years. The first and most important influence on his art was that of Marco Ricci, also from Belluno, who was in Venice from 1717 until his death in 1729. Ricci's etchings, published in 1730, provided Zais with a useful source of inspiration. From them he derived the scenographic format of his landscapes, usually framed by clumps of trees into which villages and figures of peasants were inserted, painted in a thick impasto of rich colour. The result is a pleasing, simplified style of great descriptive power. However, this attractive facility can also be seen as a limitation, for Zais never achieved Ricci's dramatic effects. Zais's contact with Francesco Zuccarelli in the early 1730s softened Ricci's influence and introduced an increased refinement into his work, although sometimes at the risk of affectation.

Zais received many commissions from the English Consul in Venice, Joseph Smith, but none of these works can now be identified. He worked tirelessly, adapting his style to suit the different genres requested by his patrons, drawing from the Flemish followers of Andries Both and from the battle scenes of Francesco Simonini. From 1748 to 1768 he was a member of the Fraglia dei Pittori Veneziani, in 1765 he applied for admission to the Accademia di Venezia but was only accepted in 1774 as a landscape painter. It is not easy to create a chronology for his paintings; his only dated work is the *Landscape with Fountain* (1765; Venice, Accad.), his Academy entrance piece. Other works include some fresco decorations in the Villa Pisani at Stra, near Venice, and the illustrations for a 1772 edition of Ariosto's *Orlando furioso*.

BIBLIOGRAPHY
F. Zanotto: *Il fiore della scuola pittorica veneziana* (Trieste, 1860)
F. Valcanover: *Pitture del settecento nel Bellunese* (Venice, 1954)
G. Damerini: *Monti, valli, acque del dominio veneto nella grande pittura veneziana* (Venice, 1955)
R. Bassi-Rathgeb: 'Novità documentarie sui pittori Zais', *A. Veneta*, xiii–xiv (1959–60), pp. 242–3
M. Muraro: 'Giuseppe Zais e un "giovin signore" nelle pitture murali di Stra', *Emporium*, 775 (1959), pp. 195–219
E. Martini: *La pittura veneziana del settecento* (Venice, 1964)
S. Moschini Marconi: *Gallerie dell'Accademia di Venezia. Opere d'arte dei secoli XVII, XVIII, XIX* (Rome, 1970), pp. 121–5
E. Martini: 'Giuseppe Zais battaglista', *Bergamo A.* (March 1972), pp. 7–14

SERGIO CLAUT

Žák, Ladislav (*b* Prague, 25 June 1900; *d* Prague, 26 May 1973). Czech architect and teacher. He studied first painting and then architecture at the Academy of Fine Arts, Prague, and he became a member of the Mánes Union of Artists, the Czechoslovak Werkbund, the Left Front and the Union of Socialist Architects. Before World War II he was primarily concerned with the design of family and low-cost housing; he also designed furniture, including some tubular steel chairs (*c*. 1930). Žák built three houses for the Czechoslovak Werkbund's exhibition housing estate (1932) at Baba, Prague, and their success brought him some important commissions. Notable examples include houses for the aeroplane designer M. Hain in Vysočany (1932–3), for the film director Martin Frič in Hodkovičky (1934–5) and for the film actress Lída Baarová in Dejvice (1937), all in Prague. In these buildings he developed a type of family house with a longitudinal living area with different functions, and with small, cabin-like bedrooms; other typical features included continuous strip windows and the aerodynamic shaping of architectural volumes and terraces. Žák intended to adopt the plan of this prototype to accommodation units in communal housing. After the war, however, he devoted himself to the theory of landscape planning, which he taught at the Academy of Fine Arts, Prague.

BIBLIOGRAPHY
F. R. S. Yorke: *The Modern House* (London, 1934), pp. 128–31
V. Šlapeta: 'Architektonicke dílo Ladislava Žáka', *Sborn. N. Tech. Muz. Praze*, xiv (1975), pp. 189–225

VLADIMÍR ŠLAPETA

Zakhariev, Vassil (*b* Samokov, 8 June 1895; *d* Sofia, 28 Nov 1971). Bulgarian printmaker, graphic designer, illustrator, bookbinder, art historian, theorist, critic and teacher. He is considered to be the founder and leading representative of 20th-century Bulgarian graphic art, who in the 1920s developed his own style in the spirit of the national tradition, but with a contemporary western European outlook. In 1919 he graduated from the National Academy of Arts (Natsionalna Hudozhestvena Academia), Sofia. In 1922–4 he studied at the State Academy of Graphic Art and Book Decoration, Leipzig, where he made an in-depth study of graphic techniques. After his return to Bulgaria, he was engaged in a variety of activities, including ex-libris, illustration, bookbinding and the design of postage stamps and banknotes. From 1924 until his death he was a professor of graphic and decorative arts at the National Academy of Arts. His output of graphic art was prodigious and included woodcuts (*Basilica of St Sofia*, 1925; e.g. Sofia, N.A.G.), coloured mezzotints (*Winter*, 1930; Sofia, City A.G.), lithographs (*Dryanovsky Monastery*, 1935; e.g. Samokov, Mun. Hist. Mus.), engravings on linoleum (*Ivan Rilsky*, 1946; e.g. Sofia, N.A.G.) and coloured woodcuts (*Boyana Church*, 1950; e.g. Sofia, N.A.G.). Zakhariev was a member of the Society of Independent Artists and was Chairman of the NATIONAL ART SOCIETY OF BULGARIA.

WRITINGS
Bulgarian Art in the Post-liberation Period (Sofia, 1929)
Half-century Anniversary Album of Bulgaria (Sofia, 1929)
Ornamental Decorations of the Radomir Psalter at the Zographsky Monastery Library, ii (Rodina, 1939)
Zakhary Christovich Zograph (Sofia, 1957)

BIBLIOGRAPHY
E. Tomov: *Vassil Zakhariev* (Sofia, 1954)

JULIANA NEDEVA-WEGENER

Zakharov, Andreyan [Adrian] **(Dmitriyevich)** (*b* St Petersburg, 19 Aug 1761; *d* St Petersburg, 8 Sept 1811). Russian architect. He was born into the family of a member of the Admiralty Board and studied architecture at the Academy of Arts in St Petersburg under Aleksandr Kokorinov and Ivan Starov. He was awarded a gold medal at the Academy, and after graduating in 1782 he went abroad with a bursary and worked in Paris with Jean-François-Thérèse Chalgrin. On returning to St Petersburg in 1786 he taught at the Academy of Arts; in 1794 he received the title of Academician, in 1797 he became a professor and in 1803 senior professor and supervisor of the architecture class. Zakharov was appointed municipal architect in Gatchina (1800), where he carried out his first practical work, and in 1803–4 he drew up the plans for rebuilding the Academy of Sciences on the Strelka, the eastern point of Vasil'yevsky Island in St Petersburg, which was important in relation to the planning of the city.

Zakharov's most important work, however, resulted from his appointment in 1805 as chief architect of the Admiralty Board, when he received the commission for the complete reconstruction of the new main Admiralty Building in St Petersburg in connection with the Admiralty's new role as the Naval Ministry. This Neo-classical building (see fig.), unfinished at Zakharov's death and completed by the architects Ivan Gomzin and August Ricard de Montferrand, among others, embodies the best progressive features of Russian architecture and brought its designer international fame. Zakharov retained the dimensions and layout of the old Admiralty Building, which was founded during the reign of Peter I on the banks of the River Neva opposite the Peter and Paul Fortress and rebuilt by Ivan Kuz'mich Korobov (1700/01–47) in the 1730s in the form of two long, parallel π-shaped buildings, a central tower crowned with a spire providing access between them. To reflect the dual role of the complex as a shipyard and main administration building, Zakharov preserved its division into two units, rebuilding the central tower and spire. However, he created a building with the scale and ideological and artistic qualities that made it the focus of the city (*see* St Petersburg, §I, 3). The three main avenues, including the Nevsky

Andreyan Zakharov: Admiralty Building, St Petersburg, 1806–12

Prospekt, converge at the building's prominent central tower and new pointed gilt spire, crowned with a carved weather-vane in the form of a ship; and the massive new U-shaped building, with its side wings facing the river, became the centre of the city's three main squares—Palace, Admiralty and Senate (now Decembrists' Square)—and dominated the wide expanse of the Neva.

The design of Zakharov's long (407 m) main façade was based on the contrast and precise rhythmic interchange of a few basic elements: the verticality of the tower, the three-dimensional porticos or loggias and the smooth surfaces of the walls. The tripartite arrangement of the main façade was continued throughout the building, and it created the classically precise, unified and monumental form that in many respects has determined the building's importance to the urban design of St Petersburg. It also reinterpreted the architectural forms and composition of earlier Russian architecture in a new way. Zakharov made considerable use of sculpture in the building, creating a genuine synthesis of the arts. The many groups and individual sculptures, low reliefs and carved masks gave concrete expression in allegorical form to the role of the Admiralty as the representation of Russia's naval power as well as to the triumph of human intelligence over the power of the sea—the symbol of St Petersburg itself; they also emphasized the structural forms of the architecture, giving them a plastic richness and promoting the grandeur of the entire work. The sculptors who contributed to the Admiralty included Feodosy Shchedrin, Artemi Anisimov (1733–1823), Vasily Demut-Malinovsky, Stepan Pimenov and Ivan Terebenyov (*see* TEREBENYOV,

(1)). Of the building's interiors, the main hall and front staircase, the special meeting room and the library remain as examples of the spacious design and stateliness that conformed to the character of the building.

During the years when Zakharov was working on the Admiralty, he also produced many other designs, most of which have not survived or were never realized. The largest in scale were the plans for the layout and construction of Proviantsky Island (1806–9), north of the city, and the Calley Harbour (1806–9), Vasil'yevsky Island, St Petersburg, in which he devised simple and functional industrial buildings with an aesthetic appeal. Other plans included the rebuilding of the Admiralty Barracks (1808) and the Naval Hospital (1806) on the Vyborg side, north of central St Petersburg. The most important of his religious buildings was the Andreyevsky Cathedral (1806–17; destr.) on Kronshtadt Island.

BIBLIOGRAPHY

G. G. Grimm: *Arkhitektor Andreyan Zakharov: Zhizn' i tvorchestvo* [The architect Andreyan Zakharov: his life and work] (Moscow, 1940)

V. I. Pilyavsky: *Glavnoye Admiralteystvo v Leningrade* [The main Admiralty in Leningrad] (Moscow and Leningrad, 1945)

D. Ye. Arkin: *Zakharov i Voronikhin* (Moscow, 1953)

Z. K. POKROVSKAYA

Zakomara [Rus.: 'finishing; end']. Semicircular gable finishing a division of a wall. *Zakomary* usually correspond to the form of a vault.

□

Zakros. *See* KATO ZAKROS.

Zalavruga. Site of Neolithic petroglyphs (before mid-2nd millennium BC) on the sloping granite banks of the River Vyg, which flows into the White Sea in Karelia. Vladislav I. Ravdonikas (1894–1976) discovered Zalavruga 1, with around 200 carvings, in 1936, while research by Yury A. Savvateyev from 1963 led to the discovery of a cliff with a further group of images (Zalavruga 2, with around 500 rock-carvings). The petroglyphs were made using pecking technique and are mostly in outline, with rare examples in low relief. Elk, deer and water-fowl are faithfully rendered. The most unusual images are scenes showing the hunting of a white whale from a boat and hunters on skis pursuing elk. The compositions cover large surfaces of rock, forming a kind of panel, and are similar in style to the nearby panel at Besovy (or Chortovy), which has around 300 images of large fish and water-fowl and smaller elk and human figures.

BIBLIOGRAPHY

V. I. Ravdonikas: *Naskal'nyye izobrazheniya Belogo Morya* [Petroglyphs of the White Sea] (Moscow, 1938)

Yu. A. Savvateyev: *Zalavruga* (Leningrad, 1970)

V. YA. PETRUKHIN

Zalce, Alfredo (*b* Pátzcuaro, Michoacán, 12 Jan 1908). Mexican painter and printmaker. He studied in Mexico City at the Academia de San Carlos (1924–9) and at the Escuela de Grabado y Talla Directa. In 1930 he founded the Escuela de Pintura y Escultura in Taxco. He was also a member of the Liga de Escritores y Artistas Revolucionarios and an early member in 1937 of the TALLER DE GRÁFICA POPULAR, taking part in their group exhibitions and publications until 1950. From 1951 he was director of the Escuela de Pintura y Escultura in Morelia, Michoacán. In addition to his career as a teacher he was active politically. He practised primarily as a printmaker with a clear and precise draughtsmanship; he published, for example, a portfolio of eight lithographs, *Estampas de Yucatán* (1945), after travelling through the area for several months. He was also involved with the muralist movement in Mexico and in 1930, in collaboration with Isabel Villaseñor, he was the first in Mexico to use coloured concrete for murals, in their work on the external walls of the Escuela de Ayotla in Tlaxaca. Among his most notable murals are *Defenders of National Integrity* (fresco and coloured concrete, 1951) and *Brother Alonso of the Order of the True Cross* (1952; both Morelia, Mus. Reg. Michoacano), in which fragmented figures are reintegrated into a subtle geometry, at once rational and poetic.

BIBLIOGRAPHY
Treinta años de pintura y grabado de Alfredo Zalce (exh. cat., Mexico City, Pal. B.A., 1962)
B. Taracena and others: *Alfredo Zalce, un arte propio* (Mexico City, 1984)
MARGARITA GONZÁLEZ ARREDONDO

Zāle [Zālīte], **Kārlis** (*b* Mažieķi [now Mažeikiai, Lithuania], 28 Oct 1888; *d* Inčukalns, 19 Feb 1942). Latvian sculptor. His studies began at the Kazan' Art College (1909–13) under the Russian sculptor Vasily Bogatyryov (1871–1941), where he created decorative sculptures for Vladimir Pokrovsky's new Neo-classical State Bank and Land Bank buildings. He went to Moscow in 1914 where he worked briefly in the studio of Stepan Er'zya and then moved to Petrograd (now St Petersburg) where he became the first Latvian to enrol as a sculpture student at the Academy of Arts, subsequently Svomas (1917–20), under Gugo Zalcman (1859–1919) and Aleksandr Matveyev. His contribution to the realization of Lenin's Plan of Monumental Propaganda included the monument to *Garibaldi* (bronze, 1919; Riga, Latv. Mus. A.). Zāle lived in Berlin in 1921–3, where he underwent a modernist phase, creating a series of Cubist and Futurist works in plaster that were marked by dynamic and abstract planar forms, as in *Head* (*c.* 1922; untraced, see Apsītis, 1988, p. 27) and *Dancer* (*c.* 1922; untraced, see Siliņš, p. 21), and he published there the Latvian art journal *Laikmets* ('Era'). On his return to Riga in 1924 he won the competition for the design of the memorial ensemble to the war dead in the new Brothers' Cemetery in the capital and was instrumental in founding Sadarbs ('Co-operation'), one of the most important Latvian art groups between the world wars. Zāle's monuments at the Brothers' Cemetery (1924–38), including the *Dying Horseman* (1929) and the central, dominating *Mother Latvia* (1929), are austere, archetypal symbols of Latvia's fate and faith made from local Allaži travertine. The idealized grieving of the bowed heads at the Brothers' Cemetery, indeed the whole combination of images of modernity, the past, the folkloric and the universal, is also to be found in figure groups at the base of Zāle's *Freedom Monument* (Riga, 1931–5). In this work the continuing struggle for independence and life is given new dynamism and an overall sense of upward striving that is crowned by the female figure of freedom.

BIBLIOGRAPHY
J. Siliņš: *Kārlis Zāle* (Riga, 1938)
V. Apsītis: *Kārlis Zāle* (Riga, 1988)
——: *Rizhskoye bratskoye kladbishche* [The Riga Brothers' Cemetery] (Riga, 1990)

Zaļkalns [Zaļ'kaln; Grīnbergs], **Teodors** (*b* nr Sigulda, 30 Nov 1876; *d* Riga, 6 Sept 1972). Latvian sculptor. He studied first at the Baron Stieglitz Institute of Technical Drawing, St Petersburg (1893–9), where he was enrolled in the decorative painting and etching department, as well as learning modelling under Matvey Chizhov (1838–1916). During this time he was active in the group of Latvian art students, THE GNOME (Rūķis). In 1900–01 he studied sculpture in Rodin's studio in Paris under Emile-Antoine Bourdelle and Paul Dubois. On his return to St Petersburg, Zaļkalns produced small sculptures for Fabergé (1901–3) and also acted as art critic (using the pseudonym Kriš Mednieks) for the newspaper *Pēterburgas Avīzēs*. He was head of sculpture and composition at Yekaterinburg Art College (1903–7), where his students included Ivan Shadr; he then spent two years in Florence (1907–9), acquainting himself with the Italian masters' techniques for bronze casting and marble carving. This experience, together with his study of the art of ancient Egypt, led him to abandon his impressionistic approach, as in his female bust *Bronze* (1903; Riga, Latv. Mus. F.A.), in favour of the more severe and refined tectonic conception of form of his mature period. This new approach resulted in simplified, generalized forms that purveyed only the subject's essential characteristics, as in the smoothly ground marble bust of *Ludmila* (1913) and subsequently in the nationally poignant *Standing Old Woman* (1915; both Riga, Latv. Mus. F.A.). In Russia after the October Revolution of 1917 Zaļkalns introduced elements of Futurism into his sculptures for Lenin's Plan of Monumental Propaganda, notably in his dynamic, geometricized monument to *Mussorgsky* (1919; Riga, Latv. Mus. F.A.). During the years of Latvian independence (1920s and 1930s) he established himself as the country's foremost sculptor and he was Professor of Sculpture at the Riga Academy of Arts (subsequently named after him) in the early years of Soviet occupation. During this Latvian period his work, which varied from monuments to leading Latvian cultural figures to studies of animal forms and human torsos, continued to be characterized by idealized, laconic forms, as in the memorial to the poet *Jānis Poruks* (1930; Riga, Forest Cemetery) and the sculpture *Cat* (1965; Riga, Latv. Mus. F.A.)

BIBLIOGRAPHY
M. Rathsprecher: *Teodor Zalkalns: Eines lettischen Bildhauers Weg und Werk* (Vienna, 1937)
K. Baumanis: *Teodors Zaļkalns* (Riga, 1966)
J. Siliņš: *Latvijas māksla, 1800–1914* [Latvian art, 1800–1914], ii (Stockholm, 1980), pp. 172–83
R. Chaupova: *T. Zal'kaln: Izbrannye proizvedeniya* [T. Zaļkalns: selected works] (Moscow, 1990)
JEREMY HOWARD

Zaman, Muhammad. *See* MUHAMMAD ZAMAN.

Zambia, Republic of [formerly Northern Rhodesia]. Country in Southern Africa. Covering 752,614 sq. km, it is bordered by Zaïre to the north, by Malawi and Mozambique to the east, by Zimbabwe, Botswana and Namibia to the south and by Angola to the west. The capital is Lusaka. Zambia gained independence in 1964. Most of the country is more than 1000 m above sea-level, with moderate temperatures and a natural vegetation of open woodland. National languages include English, Bemba, Tonga, Nyanja and Lozi. Most of the population practised subsistence agriculture until the 1950s, when commercial farming was encouraged. Zambia is comparatively industrialized and urbanized, with 40% of the population (7,804,000; UN estimate, 1989) living in urban areas; the economy went into depression in the mid-1970s following a decline in world copper prices, rising oil prices and a reduction of trade, the result of Zambia's opposition to white minority rule in what was then Rhodesia. This entry covers the art produced in Zambia since colonial times. For art of the region in earlier periods, including rock art, *see* AFRICA, §VII, 8. See also CHOKWE AND RELATED PEOPLES.

1. CONTINUING TRADITIONS. Traditional arts in Zambia include stools, pots and clay figures, Chewa ritual masks, stylized Chokwe wood-carvings, Lozi *makenge* baskets and polished food dishes, Lala wall drawings and ironwork, and Lwena *mutongo* baskets (*see* CHOKWE AND RELATED PEOPLES, §2). Colonialism, which began in the late 19th century, brought a decline in these arts. Many rituals were banned, factory-made products replaced handcrafted utensils, and the demands of the tourist art market encouraged an imitative and repetitive use of European media. Despite this decline, in the late 20th century such traditional craftworkers as the wood-carver Progress Mukela, who exhibited at Expo 70 in Osaka, Japan, the wood- and stone-carver Ranford Sililo and the potter Dervis Mvula continued to produce work of integrity and value. Many ceremonies have been revived and maskmaking flourishes, in urban as well as rural areas, for both of the two major Zambian traditions—the standardized Makishi characters of the North-Western Province and the more individualistic Nyau masks of the Eastern Province. Traditional architecture takes the form of pole and grass-thatched circular huts. The Mbeza local government complex in Namwala, Southern Province, is a rare example of traditional design in a modern context. Verandahs feature in both township dwellings and colonial-style residences, while a less attractive feature of residential design has been the proliferation of security walls.

2. ARCHITECTURE. Zambia's oldest permanent building is the London Missionary Society church (1893) in Namukolo, Mpulungu, Northern Province. Its walls are 750 mm thick and have two skins of roughly dressed sandstone with mud and termite-mound binding. Notable colonial public buildings include the Georgian-style State House (1934), the British South Africa Company offices (1934), the Lusaka Club and the Town School (1916; restored as a national monument), all in Lusaka; the Capital Building, the North-Western Hotel and the museum, all (1920s) in Livingstone; and the Falcon Hotel (1930s) in Ndola. As the 22-storey Findeco House (1979; designed by UNICO) in Lusaka illustrates, monumental public architecture of the post-colonial period has often followed inappropriate foreign conventions that ignore such local problems as climate, drainage, glare, maintenance and security. As a result, original designs often have to be subjected to major practical alterations. In contrast, the Cathedral of the Holy Cross (1962; designed by Hope and Reeler), Lusaka, is a fine example of post-war ecclesiastical architecture, and the headquarters of the Bank of Zambia (1975; designed by Anderson and Anderson) and the National Assembly building (1966; designed by Montgomerie, Oldfield, Kirby), both Lusaka, are secular examples of successful International Style architecture. Also noteworthy are Kalomo District Council Offices (1966; designed by Ian Reeler), the raw concrete University of Zambia (1967; designed by Julian Elliot), and the Meridien Bank headquarters (1993; designed by Walker Dobkins).

3. PAINTING, GRAPHIC ARTS AND SCULPTURE. In post-colonial Zambia and especially since the near collapse of the economy, artists have struggled against the attitude that art is peripheral to national development. In addition, graphic artists have had difficulty in obtaining the expensive imported materials. Nevertheless, some individuals have gained recognition for their work: expatriate artists Cynthia Zukas (*b* 1931), Brian Ford (*b* 1937), Andrew Makromalis and Bente Lorenz (*b* 1922) have made notable contributions. Gabriel Ellison (*b* 1930) was awarded the British MBE and the Zambian Grand Officer of the Order of Distinguished Service (OGDS) for her work in wildlife painting and stamp design. The Zambian-born wildlife artist Pam Guhrs is also well known. One of Zambia's most distinguished artists was Henry Tayali (1943–87). After gaining MAs from both Makerere University in Kampala, Uganda, and from Düsseldorf, he was appointed Artist at the University of Zambia in 1976. An intense, energetic artist working mainly in oils and woodblock prints, he also put enormous effort into encouraging other artists, serving on committees to promote art, and lecturing. He had many international exhibitions, including a one-man show at the Commonwealth Institute, London, in 1983. His work is mainly abstract or semi-abstract, based on themes drawn from everyday life. His prints often show his concern with the human condition (see fig.). Tayali constantly explored relationships of composition and colour, and he was working in a Minimalist phase when he died. Many local artists have made efforts to break from tradition and develop their own vocabularies. A group of such artists was set up (*c*. 1975) by the Dutch artist Bert Witkamp (*b* 1944), and from this group has come a strong trend in printmaking, a development aided by the easy availability of materials for this technique. The group included Patrick Mweemba (*b* 1946), David Chibwe and Fackson Kulya (*b* 1950). Another printmaker, Lutanda Mwamba (*b* 1966), was awarded a Commonwealth Foundation Fellowship in Art at Reading University in 1990.

Stephen Kappata (*b* 1936) received international recognition. An 'intuitive' artist, whose satirical comments on colonial Zambia have a vigorous individuality, Kappata was featured in the exhibition *Focus on Zambia* at the Africa Centre, London, in 1989. He also had a one-man show at the Royal Festival Hall, London, in 1991. Other modern artists, working in oils, include Shadreck Simukanga (*b* 1955), Lawrence Yombwe (*b* 1958), Godfrey Setti (*b* 1958), Style Kunda (*b* 1956), who concentrates on

Henry Tayali: *I Say No Politics Here*, woodcut, 400×225 mm, 1979 (Mrs Rose Tayali private collection)

township scenes, and Enoch Ilunga, whose abstract work combines a Zaïrean background with an obvious reverence for Tayali.

In the same way that printmaking flourished due to the availability of materials, so the existence of local supplies of limestone and wood have encouraged the production of sculpture. Working in the Bente Lorenz Ceramic Studio in Lusaka, Tubayi Dube (*b* 1930) produced many sculptures in the local soapstone and taught a number of local artists, including Masiye Mitti (*b* 1939), Dickson Nyendwa (*b* 1955), David Chirwa, Friday Tembo (*b* 1962), Eddie Mumba (*b* 1939) and Paul Kabwe (*b* 1957). Akwila Simpasa (*b* 1946) has also gained international recognition for his sculpture.

4. PATRONAGE, MUSEUMS AND ART INSTITUTIONS. By the 1990s Zambian art was suffering from lack of both private and public patronage. An annual school art competition that was sponsored by the Anglo-American Corporation was discontinued when the mines were nationalized in 1969. Banks have provided some funding, but the resulting public sculpture tends to be monumental and unadventurous. The Zambia National Visual Arts Council was established in 1990 by working artists themselves to promote seminars and workshops and to provide a channel through which to influence government policy on the arts. The Lechwe Trust, founded in 1986 by a Zambian family resident in the UK specifically to assist artists in Zambia, has also helped local artists by importing and selling materials at cost. Zambia has no national gallery. The national collection is housed in the Mulungushi International Conference Centre, Lusaka, far from the city centre and poorly maintained. Accessibility is limited by conference security. Lusaka's only private gallery is the Mpapa Gallery, run by the Arts Trust. A small private museum of arts and crafts, the Zintu Museum, Lusaka, opened in 1992 and is run by the Zintu Foundation, in association with a crafts shop. Zambian art education has followed Zaïrean teaching practices with some success. One obstacle, however, has been the post-colonial decline in Zambian material culture, resulting in a general lack of exposure to traditional techniques and themes. The most influential art school, the Evelyn Hone College, Lusaka, founded and built in 1963, has produced both teachers and commercial artists. Many graduates have gone on to work in advertising, textiles and television.

BIBLIOGRAPHY
G. Cooper: 'Village Crafts in Bartoseland', *Rhodes-Livingstone Inst. J.*, ii (1951), pp. 47–60
Zambian Culture (exh. cat., ed. M. Yeta and P. Lea; Lusaka, Ind. Celeb. Dir., 1964)
Zambia Mus. J. (1970–)
J. B. Deregowski: 'Pictorial Art in Zambia', *Afr. A.*, iv/2 (1971), pp. 36–7, 80 [see also Mubitana, ibid., vii/2, pp. 80–81; Deregowski, ibid., p. 81]
D. Simpson: 'Tayali', *2 Mag.*, 68 (1975), pp. 12–15
H. Tayali: 'Art: Has it a Role in Zambia?', *2 Mag.*, 68 (1975), pp. 16–19
P. A. Vrydagh: 'Makisi of Zambia', *Afr. A.*, x/4 (1977)
K.-A. Skjolstrup: 'Bar Paintings around Lusaka', *In Situ*, 29 (July 1978), pp. 22–4
B. Jules-Rosette: *The Messages of Tourist Art: An African Semiotic System in Comparative Perspective* (New York and London, 1984)
G. J. Williams: *Lusaka and its Environs: A Geographical Study of a Planned Capital City in Tropical Africa*, Zambia Geographical Association Handbook Series, ix (Lusaka, 1986)
Henry Tayali, 1943–1987 (exh. cat. by C. A. Rogers, Lusaka, 1988)
B. Lorenz and M. Plesner: *Traditional Zambian Pottery* (London, 1989)
S. Peters and others, eds: *Directory of Museums in Africa/Répertoire des musées en Afrique* (London and New York, 1990)
Art from the Frontline: Contemporary Art from Southern Africa (exh. cat., Glasgow, A.G. & Mus.; Salford, Mus. & A.G.; Dublin, The City Cent.; London, Commonwealth Inst.; 1990) [illustrates works by Stephen Kappata, Paul Kabwe, Lutanda Mwamba and Dervis Mvula]

N. Guez: *L'Art africain contemporain/Contemporary African Art: Guide Edition, 92–94* (Paris, 1992) [directory of artists and art institutions]

DAVID SIMPSON

Zambono, Michele. *See* GIAMBONO, MICHELE.

Zamora. Capital of Zamora Province, León, Spain.

1. INTRODUCTION. The Roman road from Mérida to Astorga probably crossed the River Duero at Zamora, but Roman remains are scant. From the 8th century to the 11th, possession of the city was contested by Muslims and Christians. King Ferdinand I of Castile and León (*reg* 1037–65) repopulated the city in the mid-11th century. The stronghold of Ferdinand's daughter Urraca, the city was besieged by King Sancho II (*reg* 1065–72), whose assassination beneath its walls in 1082 was remembered in epic poems. The see, documented by the 10th century, was definitively restored in 1121, and several modest Romanesque churches (S Tomé, S Cebrián, S María la Nueva, S Claudio de Olivares and Santiago el Viejo) attest to the building activity of the early 12th century and the development of a local school of sculptors inspired by work at Frómista, León and Santiago de Compostela. In the second half of the 12th century and the early 13th, the multiple arches of the portals of several churches (La Magdalena, Santiago del Burgo, S María de la Orta, S Leonardo, S Juan, S Pedro, S Vicente) were richly decorated with motifs of Islamic origin, luxuriant foliage and, at S Claudio de Olivares, a figure cycle. The new ornament can be linked to the cathedral (*see* §1 below) and to the west porch of Santiago de Compostela Cathedral and local buildings influenced by it.

After the union of Castile and León in 1230, Zamora, like other Leonese towns, declined in importance, and from the 15th century the city remained largely at the margins of artistic activity in Spain. Of the later buildings, S Andrés, completed in 1571, blends Gothic vaults with Italianate details and contains Italianate retables of the late 16th century comparable to those in the cathedral, SS Juan and Cebrián. The most notable secular building is the Casa de los Momos, with decorated windows and heraldry of *c.* 1500.

2. CATHEDRAL. The 12th-century cathedral of S Salvador, built of local breccia, is dominated by its crossing dome (see fig.), an original combination of Islamic and west French features, which gave rise to a local school in the Duero Valley. A 17th-century inscription in the north transept attributes the start of the cathedral in 1151 and its consecration in 1174 to Bishop Esteban, who was probably French, but the dome and nave vaults may have been completed later. In 1202 Alfonso IX of León (*reg* 1188–1230) assigned revenues to the cloister, while a private gift in 1236 was reserved for the tower. A western chapel was added to the cathedral in the mid-15th century, the east end was reconstructed *c.* 1500 with a polygonal sanctuary, and the north transept façade was remodelled with the building of a new cloister after the fire of 1591.

The cathedral is a squat building, dwarfed by a massive five-storey tower at the north-west corner of the nave. Inside, however, its small size is masked by the dome and the ample proportions of the nave and aisles. In the original plan three eastern apses were each preceded by a rectangular bay. Slightly projecting transepts carry pointed

Zamora Cathedral, exterior view of crossing dome, 12th century

barrel vaults, and groin-vaulted aisles flank the rib-vaulted nave of five bays. The circular lantern of the crossing dome rises from pendentives. Engaged columns support the ribs of its gored vault, marking off 16 segments, each pierced by a shafted window. On the exterior of the lantern, responds carrying pointed arches frame the shafted windows, while four cylindrical turrets topped with miniature domes form 'corners'. On each cardinal point, a gabled dormer rests on a rectangular projection. The dome is distinctively roofed with cusped ridges and scale-shaped tiles.

Of the façades, only that of the south transept, the Puerta del Obispo, remains intact; fluted responds divide it into three parts, while the three horizontal zones are enlivened by pointed arches. Sculptural decoration is largely confined to the four cusped arches of the portal, two *Apostles* and the *Virgin and Child with Angels* in the lateral lunettes, two nearby reliefs and the acanthus capitals of the façade; the nave capitals are plain. Pointed arches over the north transept and west façades suggest that they were originally similar in design.

Although the plan of the cathedral is common in Spain, the pier design, with three responds clustered on each face, indicates a source in western France, a likely origin also for the arched south transept façade and the style of its sculpture, the pendentives below the dome and the turrets, added during construction and arranged like those on the crossing tower of St-Jean-de-Montierneuf at Poitiers (*c.* 1110). The ribs, reflecting transitional developments in France, resemble those at the nearby Cistercian abbey of Moreruela, but the plain capitals with crenellated abaci are dissimilar to those at Moreruela; at Zamora the shift to plain capitals reflects the rapid pace of the project.

The circular base, exposed profile and gored interior of the dome show Islamic influence, recalling 9th-century domes at Kairouan and Tunis in North Africa; rectangular projections occur on the Dome of the Rock and the dome of the church of the Holy Sepulchre in Jerusalem. Gored medallions above the sculptured lunettes of the south façade and cusps separated by exaggerated rolls on the four arches of the portal strengthen the ties with Islamic art. The exotic design and connections to the Holy Land underscore the allusion in the north transept inscription to the house of Solomon ('domus . . . salomonica'), if understood as Solomon's temple rather than the cathedral of an obscure 10th-century bishop. Whatever its pretensions, the novel dome inspired local versions at Salamanca Cathedral, S María la Mayor in Toro and the old chapter house of Plasencia Cathedral.

Furnishings in the cathedral include the retable of *St Ildefonso* (*c.* 1466) by Fernando Gallego, while the elaborate choir-stalls (between 1503 and 1507; *see* CHOIR-STALLS, fig. 3) were carved by Juan de Bruxelas (*fl* 1500–25) and his assistants. Sculptors from northern Europe with possible connections to workshops at Burgos may also have been responsible for the contemporary tomb of *Dr Juan de Grado*.

L. Torres Balbás: 'Los cimborios de Zamora, Salamanca y Toro', *La Arquitectura*, iv (1922), pp. 137–53
M. Gómez Moreno: *Catálogo monumental de España: Provincia de Zamora (1903–1905)* (Madrid, 1927/*R* 1980)
C. K. Hersey: *The Salmantine Lanterns: Their Origins and Development* (Cambridge, MA, 1937)
P. Dubourg-Noves: 'Des Mausolées antiques aux cimborios romans d'Espagne: Evolution d'une forme architecturale', *Cah. Civilis. Méd.*, xxiii (1980), pp. 323–60
G. Ramos de Castro: *La Catedral de Zamora* (Zamora, 1982)

Zamość. Town in eastern Poland some 80 km south-east of Lublin. Founded in 1580 by JAN ZAMOYSKI as his residence and the headquarters of his domains, and entailed from 1589, the town is a rare and fine example of surviving Polish Renaissance urban planning. It was designed for *c.* 3000 inhabitants, and its layout has affinities with the ideal cities described in the treatises of Francesco di Giorgio Martini and Pietro Cataneo. The principal buildings (palace, fortifications, arsenal, collegiate church, gates, town hall and burgher houses) were designed and built by BERNARDO MORANDO within 20 years. The town and the palace (1578–86; altered in the 1820s) both lay within the 600×400 m area of the fortifications, but were originally divided by walls with a gateway and bastides on the town side. The gridded layout was dominated by the palace, with a tower and external staircase, from which the main street led eastwards through the town centre. The square between the palace and town was bounded on the south by a collegiate church (1587–98; elevations altered *c.* 1820) and on the north by the Academy building (1594), representing religion and learning. Along the secondary axis were three market squares: the Salt Square to the north, the Water Square to the south and in the centre the beautiful Great Market Square (100×100 m) with the imposing, towered town hall (1591; 18th-century additions) on its north side. The buildings surrounding the squares had arcaded ground-floors, according to the Italian model, but the tall attics that crowned their façades gave the squares a particular Polish character. Enclosing both the town and the palace was a hexagonal system of fortifications with seven bastions, built by Morando in the new Italian style from 1585 and completed in 1619 by the Venetian engineer Andrea dell'Aqua. The three gates (Lublin, Lwów and Szczebrzeszyn), designed by Morando, had façades of the Tuscan order with rustic works.

Originally Zamość was to be inhabited only by Catholics, but people of other faiths were soon allowed to settle there, and Armenians, Greeks and Jews built wooden churches and a synagogue in separate quarters of the eastern part of the town in the 1580s; these were replaced in brick in the first half of the 17th century. During the Counter-Reformation several Baroque monastery churches were built: a magnificent Franciscan basilica church (1637–55) and, in the later 17th century, more modest single-aisled churches for the Hospitallers of St John of God, the Reformed Franciscans and Poor Clares, all three designed and executed by the engineer Jan Michał Link (*d* 1698). During the period of Austrian rule after the partition of Poland (1772–1809) almost all the monasteries were suppressed, and the Academy was closed.

In 1821, under the Russian-dominated Congress Kingdom of Poland, the government requisitioned Zamość from the Zamoyski family, and it became a garrison town. From 1817 to 1830 the fortifications were modernized, and new Lublin and Lwów gates were built. The palace, town hall and Academy buildings were adapted for use as the hospital, prison and barracks respectively, and the Armenian church and Franciscan and Reformed Franciscan monasteries were demolished. Later all the houses and the town hall lost their attic storeys. In 1866 the Russian authorities considered the fortress unsuitable for modernization; accordingly the town's defences, including the bastions and curtain wall, were partially demolished, making Zamość into a civilian town again. The site of the former fortress was later transformed into a park (1922–7) by the architect Walerian Kronenberg. Restoration work began in 1937 and has continued ever since; the town hall, several houses and the Lwów and the Lublin Gates have now regained their late Renaissance façades, and one bastion has been reconstructed. In 1992 Zamość was listed as a world heritage town by UNESCO.

BIBLIOGRAPHY

S. Herbst and J. Zachwatowicz: *Twierdza Zamość* [The fortress of Zamość] (Warsaw, 1936)
P. Lavedan: *Histoire de l'urbanisme: Renaissance et temps moderne* (Paris, 1941), pp. 303–39
J. A. Miłobędzki: 'Ze studiów nad urbanistyka Zamościa' [Studies in the urban development of Zamość], *Biul. Hist. Sztuki*, xv (1953), pp. 68–87
M. Lewicka: 'Bernardo Morando', *Saggi & Mem. Stor. A.*, ii (1957), pp. 143–55
T. Zarębska: 'Zamość: Miasto idealne i jego realizacja' [Zamość: an ideal town and its execution], *Zamość: Miasto idealne*, ed. J. Kowalczyk (Lublin, 1980), pp. 7–77
J. Kowalczyk: *Zamość: Città ideale in Polonia: Il fondatore Jan Zamoyski e l'architetto Bernardo Morando* (Wrocław, 1986)
C. Bellanca: 'Zamość: Note di storia e di conservazione', *Stor. Città* (1987), pp. 63–92

JERZY KOWALCZYK

Zamoyski. Polish family of statesmen, soldiers and patrons. They were prominent in public life in Poland from the 16th to the 20th centuries.

(1) Jan Zamoyski (*b* Skokówka, nr Chełm, 19 March 1542; *d* Zamość, 3 June 1605). He received one of the finest educations available in Europe during the Renaissance, attending the Sorbonne and the Collège de France (both in Paris) and the Academy of Johann Sturm (1507–89) in Strasbourg, followed by a period at the University of Padua (Italy), of which he became Rector in 1562. On his return to Poland in 1565, Zamoyski embarked on an outstanding career during which he was appointed Grand Chancellor and Hetman (commander-in-chief). As a statesman, he exerted a strong influence on the form of the Polish constitution and played a decisive part in the elections of three successive monarchs. As a soldier, he fought victorious campaigns against the Habsburgs, the Tatars, Sweden and Muscovy. At the same time he succeeded in building up one of the greatest private fortunes in Europe.

Zamoyski was above all a scholar, deeply influenced by his extensive studies of antiquity. In the 1570s he attempted to regenerate the medieval Jagiellonian University of Kraków, and then to found a humanist academy in the city. By the end of the decade he had begun to consider a more ambitious scheme, to construct a model city. In 1578 he engaged the Paduan architect Bernardo Morando to build such a city at ZAMOŚĆ, laid out on geometric patterns and incorporating new ideas in urban planning.

Apart from serving as a fortified headquarters and commercial centre for Zamoyski's huge domains, Zamość was to be an ideal environment, reflecting the belief that man could be conditioned by his surroundings. The ultimate stage of the project was the Academy (1593), a university designed to create the ideal citizen. Although Zamoyski purchased some paintings during a visit to Italy in 1565, he was not by nature a collector: he had no emotional need for art, which he saw as a utility. His patronage centred on the building of Zamość, and later of the smaller town of Szarogród in the Ukraine. He retained Morando as his architect over a period of 20 years, with the result that Zamość is a harmonious ensemble created in a Polish Renaissance style with Mannerist elements that was widely imitated throughout south-eastern Poland. Zamoyski also employed the Florentine Santi Gucci to design fountains and other decorative elements and commissioned the principal paintings for the Collegiate Church of St Thomas (1586–93) from Domenico Tintoretto in 1600. He collaborated closely with his artists at every level, even sending sketches and suggesting colours to Tintoretto.

When his palace in Zamość was completed, Zamoyski did not collect paintings for the interior but ordered tapestries in Flanders (1582), again sending instructions and sketches, furnishings in Florence (1600) and silk carpets in Turkey. There was a remarkable consistency to his patronage. He used good local painters such as Krzysztof Bystrzycki (Bistricius) and Jan Szwankowski (*d* 1602) to decorate buildings and paint portraits, when required. Bystrzycki has been attributed with the portrait of *Jan Zamoyski* (Florence, Uffizi). He used cartographers and engravers including Giovanni Battista de' Cavalieri to produce plans and views of his fortresses and campaigns and commissioned two gold portrait medals to be given as presents to rulers and eminent scholars. Although the poet Hugo Grotius (1583–1645) wrote a panegyric on one of these, they appear to have been the work of local Zamość craftsmen. At the same time, Zamoyski expended great efforts and money to attract eminent scholars to teach at his Academy, and extended his patronage to a number of Poles, including the composer Mikołaj Gomółka (*c.* 1539–1609) and the greatest Polish poet of the Renaissance, Jan Kochanowski (1530–58). The latter wrote the only Renaissance play in Polish for Zamoyski's wedding in 1583, a ceremony based on Italian pageantry and involving the erection of elaborate buildings and sculpture, and the use of lights, music and declamation. However, the grandeur of such occasions, and indeed of Zamoyski's whole vision, was never translated into purely artistic terms; even his tomb consists solely of a flat bronze slab bearing his name. The concept of artistic patronage established by Jan Zamoyski was followed faithfully by his successors to the entail of Zamość. They husbanded the city, encouraged local artists and built up libraries, rather than collections.

BIBLIOGRAPHY

J. Mycielski: *Stosunki Hetmana Zamoyskiego ze sztuką i artystami* [The connections of Hetman Zamoyski with art and artists] (Krakow, 1907)
S. Tomkowicz: *Ordynaci Zamoyscy i sztuka* [The Zamoyski estate and the arts] (Zamość, 1920)
S. Łempicki: *Medyceusz polski XVI w.* [Polish Mediceism of the 16th century] (Zamość, 1929)

——: *Renesans i humanizm w Polsce* [The Renaissance and humanism in Poland] (Warsaw, 1951)
S. Herbst: *Zamość* (Warsaw, 1954)
M. Lewicka: 'Mecenat artystyczny Jana Zamoyskiego' [The artistic patronage of Jan Zamoyski], *Studia Renesansowe*, ed. M. Walicki, ii (Wrocław, 1957)
S. Lempicki: *Mecenat Wielkiego Kanclerza* [The patronage of the Grand Chancellor] (Warsaw, 1980)

(2) Count Stanisław Kostka Zamoyski (*b* Warsaw, 13 Jan 1775; *d* Vienna, 2 April 1856). He was one of the most active patrons of artistic and intellectual life in Warsaw in the early 1800s, collecting the works of and fostering such contemporary artists as Angelica Kauffman, Jean-Baptiste Isabey, François Gérard and Antonio Canova. He was also an avid collector of books and manuscripts, in 1811 merging his library with that of his father Andrzej Zamoyski (1716–92), that of his uncle Jan Jakub Zamoyski (1712–90) and that of the defunct University of Zamość to create one of the most important source libraries on Polish history and literature. In 1817 this was installed in a specially designed building next to his Warsaw residence and opened to the public. Zamoyski was greatly interested in architecture and carried out extensive building work on his estates at Szczebrzeszyn, Klemensów and Podzamcze. He also announced a competition for the rebuilding of the old Renaissance palace in Zamość, which attracted projects from Charles Percier, Pierre-François-Léonard Fontaine, Chrystian Piotr Aigner, Henryk Ittar and Jakub Hempel; however, for political reasons, the palace was never rebuilt. In 1814 Zamoyski began rebuilding his Warsaw residence, the Rococo Blue Palace. He chose Fryderyk Albert Lessel, a Polish architect influenced by study in Italy and by the French school of Etienne-Louis Boullée, Louis Ledoux and Jean-Jacques Lequeu. The result was in a severe, functional, cubic Neo-classicism characterized by bold lines and imaginative forms. The building was much admired for its originality and became a source of ideas and inspiration for much Polish Neo-classical architecture. The Blue Palace and the library were destroyed in 1939.

BIBLIOGRAPHY
T. Zychliński: *Złota księga szlachty polskiej* [Roll of honour of the Polish nobility], xiv (Poznań, 1892)
S. Tomkowicz: *Ordynaci Zamoyscy i sztuka* [The Zamoyski estate and the arts] (Zamość, 1920)
W. Tatarkiewicz: 'Turniej klasyków w Zamościu' [Competition of the classics in Zamość], *Arkády* (Warsaw, 1937), p. 293
A. Rottermund: *Pałac Błękitny* [The Blue Palace] (Warsaw, 1970)
                                                      ADAM ZAMOYSKI

(3) August Zamoyski (*b* Jabłoń estate, Lublin region, 28 June 1893; *d* Saint-Clar de Rivière, nr Toulouse, France, 19 May 1970). Sculptor, great-grandson of (2) Stanisław Kostka Zamoyski. August was a colourful character in Polish and Parisian bohemian life. Although he showed an early interest in sculpture, blacksmithery and woodcarving, he did not take up any systematic artistic studies (apart from drawing courses run by Lovis Corinth). He began exhibiting in 1918, mainly abroad (including the Venice Biennale, 1936). During the inter-war period he divided his time between Poland and for the most part Paris. In 1940–55 he lived in Rio de Janeiro, where he gave sculpture classes at the Academia de Belas Artes. In 1955 he settled permanently in France.

During World War I Zamoyski was in Germany studying economics and philosophy and producing sculptures for pleasure. He was also an assistant at the sculpture studio of Joseph Wackerle (1880–1959) at the Kunstgewerbeschule, Berlin. Zamoyski's structurally innovative sculptures (e.g. the bronze portrait of *Adolf Loos*, 1917; Vienna, priv. col.) were noticed by Stanisław Przybyszewski, who introduced him to the REVOLT GROUP (Bunt) of Expressionists based in Poznań, with whom he later exhibited. He produced characteristically Formist works (*see* FORMISTS). From the mid-1920s a return to natural elements and the use of stone is evident in his work, as in the granite *Wierka* (1936; Warsaw, N. Mus.), which won first prize at the first Sculpture Salon in Poland. Zamoyski's sculptures of this period are static but charged with an inner tension. In Brazil a new expressionist tendency emerged (e.g. *St John the Baptist*, bronze, 1950–53), which was foreshadowed in the light, almost mannerist form of the monument to *Chopin* (bronze, 1944; Rio de Janeiro). Zamoyski employed this new dramatized style in all his later work (e.g. *Resurrection*, bronze, 1967–8).

WRITINGS
'O rzeźbieniu' [About statuary art], *Nike* (1937)
'Sztuka i substancja' [Art and substance], *Sztuka & Kryt.*, 33–4 (1958)
BIBLIOGRAPHY
Z. Kossakowska-Szanajca: *August Zamoyski* (Warsaw, 1974)
                          WOJCIECH WŁODARCZYK

Zampieri, Domenico. *See* DOMENICHINO.

Zamyraylo, Viktor (Dmytriyevych) [Zamiraylo, Victor Dmitriyevich] (*b* Cherkasy, Kiev province, 24 Nov 1868; *d* Novy Petergof, Leningrad Region, 2 Oct 1939). Ukrainian painter, printmaker and illustrator. He studied at the Kiev Drawing School (1881–6) under Mykhailo Murashko (1844–1909), who encouraged the independent development of his talents and taste without the pedantry of academicism or of the Wanderers. The influence of Gustave Doré is evident in his work of this period. From 1888 he participated in the exhibitions of the World of Art group, the Moscow Fellowship of Artists and the Union of Russian Artists. In Kiev he worked with Mikhail Vrubel' on the restoration of the wall paintings in the church of St Cyril (1883–4) and on the decoration of the cathedral of St Vladimir (1885–90; initially on the basis of designs by Viktor Vasnetsov). In 1907–14 he produced the panels *Battle at Kerzhenets* and *Subjugation of Kazan'* for the Kazan' Station in Moscow to designs by Nicholas Roerich. In his easel works he used predominantly sepia, occasionally adding touches of watercolour, and he made extensive use of lamp-black. In 1908 he began the fantastic, almost Surrealist, cycle *Capricci*, which he continued to work on until 1918 (e.g. *Temptations*, watercolour; St Petersburg, Rus. Mus.; and *Capricci*, linocut; 1919). Zamiraylo also worked on book design and illustration and was one of the illustrators of the three-volume *Zhivoye slovo* ('Living word'); these illustrations use parallel lines made with a sharp pen, the white ground contrasting with the saturated use of India ink or covered with a transparent wash of lamp-black in various tones. He also illustrated Aleksandr Blok's poem *Dvenadtsat'* ('The twelve'; Petrograd, 1918) and the collected works of Nikolay Gogol', among others. In addition, he contributed to satirical periodicals and painted the sets for productions of Ibsen's *Peer Gynt* and Molière's *Le Mariage forcé* (Rus. *Brak ponevole*) to designs by Alexandre Benois and Nicholas Roerich at the Moscow Art Theatre, 1907. He taught at the Leningrad (now St Petersburg) Art Institute of Photography and Photomechanics (1918–28) and at the Leningrad Vkhutein (1925–8).

BIBLIOGRAPHY
S. Ernst: *Zamiraylo* (Petrograd, 1921)
Risunki i gravyury V. D. Zamiraylo [The drawings and engravings of V. D. Zamiraylo] (Kazan', 1925)
A. Ivanenko: '"Skazochnik stranny" Viktor Dmitriyevich Zamiraylo' [The 'strange story-teller' Viktor Dmitriyevich Zamiraylo], *Isk. Knigi*, lxviii–lxix/8 (1973), pp. 48–57
SERGEY KUZNETSOV

Zan, Bernhard (*fl* Nuremberg, 1580s). German goldsmith and engraver. He was recorded as a goldsmith's apprentice in Nuremberg in 1580 but became known through his two collections of engravings, published in 1580 and 1581 (2nd edn 1584), which are essentially pattern books for goldsmiths. These engravings illustrate goblets, cups, ewers and basins decorated with sculptural animal and human heads, foliage and flowers, bunches of fruit, scrollwork and arabesques. He was probably the first to apply the goldsmith's technique of punching to printmaking. Zan was influenced by the Netherlandish ornamental style and especially by the etchings of Georg Wechter I, which had been published shortly before. Zan was also a propagator of the type of scrollwork that gradually replaced the arabesque. His engravings acted as an important stimulus to the art of goldsmithing in the late 16th century and continued to be valued as craftsmen's patterns until the end of the 19th century. Zan's signature is BZ. It is unlikely that he was the same artist as the frequently recorded 'Bernhard Goldschmied' (*fl* 1569–1604).

PRINTS
12 Stick zum verzeichnen stechen verfertigt (Nuremberg, 1580)
Allerley gebuntznierte Fisierungen gemacht und auch gedruckt in der fürstlichen Stat Onnoltzbach (Ansbach, 1581, 2/1584)
BIBLIOGRAPHY
ADB; Thieme–Becker
P. Jessen: *Das Ornamentstich* (Berlin, 1920)
G. Irmscher: *Das Schleifwerk: Untersuchungen zu einem Ornamenttypus der Zeit um 1600 im Bereich ornamentaler Vorlageblätter* (diss., Cologne, 1978), p. 58
Wenzel Jamnitzer und die Nürnberger Goldschmiedekunst, 1500–1700 (exh. cat., Nuremberg, Ger. Nmus., 1985)
WERNER WILHELM SCHNABEL

Zanchi, Antonio (*b* Este, nr Padua, 6 Dec 1631; *d* Venice, 12 April 1722). Italian painter. His first teacher was Giacomo Pedrali (*d* 1660), whose influence, however, is not discernible in Zanchi's work. At an early age he travelled to Venice to study under Matteo Ponzone (1580/90–1664). The latter's style, which was influenced by Tintoretto, played a limited role in his development; the influence of Francesco Ruschi (*fl* 1643–56), originally from Rome and also active in Venice, Vicenza and Treviso, was more important during the artist's formative years. The plasticity of the figures and the hard, almost metallic fall of the folds in the drapery that characterize his first known works, a series of etched frontispieces for opera librettos (earliest 1655: *La Statira* by G. F. Busenello), are certainly indebted to Ruschi. The few paintings by Zanchi that can be dated to the 1650s, such as the *Entry into Jerusalem* (Padua, Casa di Pena; ex-S Marta, Venice), also display similarities to Ruschi but at the same time betray a great interest in the early work of Luca Giordano and in Giovanni Battista Langetti, who had come from Genoa and worked in Venice. In the following years Zanchi adopted their stylistic traits, characterized by a strongly accentuated realism, dramatic chiaroscuro effects and a preference for violent subjects. He soon became a prominent representative of the tenebrists and was considered to be one of the most promising artists in Venice (Martinioni, 1663). Good examples of this phase of his development include the canvases *Samson and Delilah* and *Alexander and the Body of Darius* (early 1660s), painted to decorate the Palazzo Albrizzi, Venice (*in situ*), the spectacular *Abraham Teaching Astrology to the Egyptians* (early 1660s; Venice, S Maria del Giglio) and the monumental *Plague in Venice* (1666; Venice, Scu. Grande S Rocco). These paintings are all characterized by a somewhat theatrical realism, inspired particularly by Langetti, and a very effective use of light; the last mentioned, in particular, helped Zanchi establish himself as a painter of large-scale religious compositions. He received important commissions, including *Christ Driving the Money-changers from the Temple* (1667) for the Scuola di S Fantin, Venice, and two scenes of the *Martyrdom of St Julian* (1674) for the church of S Giuliano, Venice (all *in situ*); these are based on compositions by Veronese, which Zanchi transformed into theatrical Baroque works. His fame extended as far as Munich, where he executed works for the Residenz (e.g. *Joseph Presenting his Brothers to the Pharaoh*) and an altarpiece (destr. 1944) for the Theatinerkirche, probably at the beginning of the 1670s.

During the 1680s Zanchi's tenebrist style gradually became less pronounced. The contours of his figures became diffused, his colouring flatter, and he lost the dramatic character that had characterized his work of the previous decade. The aging artist was no doubt trying to keep abreast of changes in taste, occasioned particularly by Pietro Liberi and his followers, but the results are not felicitous. Zanchi continued to produce many religious works in this style well into the 18th century, especially for the churches in and around Este (e.g. *Adoration of the Magi*, 1720; Baone (Calaone), nr Este, parish church). Among his pupils were Antonio Molinari and Francesco Trevisani, painters who in their respective ways transformed Zanchi's Baroque realism into a lighter idiom, consonant with 18th-century taste.

BIBLIOGRAPHY
F. Sansovino: *Venetia città nobilissima et singolare* (Venice, 1581); rev. G. Martinioni (Venice, 1663/*R* 1968)
M. Boschini: *La carta del navegar pitoresco* (Venice, 1660); ed. A. Pallucchini (Venice, 1966)
A. Riccoboni: 'Antonio Zanchi e la pittura veneziana del seicento', *Saggi & Mem. Stor. A.*, v (1966), pp. 53–155
C. Donzelli and G. M. Pilo: *I pittori del seicento veneto* (Florence, 1967), pp. 430–35
A. Riccoboni: 'Novità zanchiane', *Studi di storia dell'arte in onore di Antonio Morassi* (Venice, 1971), pp. 262–71
R. Pallucchini: *La pittura veneziana del seicento* (Milan, 1981), i, pp. 250–57; ii, figs 807–36

P. Zampetti and others: 'Antonio Zanchi', *I pittori bergamaschi dal XIII al XIX secolo: Il seicento, IV* (Bergamo, 1987), pp. 391–707; review by B. Aikema in *Osservatorio A.*, ii (1989), pp. 109–12

B. Aikema: *Pietro della Vecchia and the Heritage of the Renaissance in Venice* (Florence, 1990), p. 84

BERNARD AIKEMA

Zand. Dynasty that ruled in Iran from 1750 to 1794. The Zand tribe, a pastoral people from the Zagros foothills, became the dominant power in Iran after the death of Nadir Shah in 1747. Under Muhammad Karim Khan (*reg* 1750–79), who proclaimed himself regent (Pers. *vakīl*) for the Safavid puppet king Isma'il III, the Zands brought stability to southern Iran, and from 1765 Karim Khan encouraged art and architecture (*see* ISLAMIC ART, §II, 7(ii)(b)) to flourish at SHIRAZ, his adopted capital. His first consideration was defence, and he rebuilt the city walls in 1767. Many of his other buildings, such as the citadel, palace and mosque with adjacent bath and bazaar, were grouped around a maidan to the north of the old city. Zand architecture is notable for its revetments in carved marble and overglaze-painted tiles with flowers, animals and people. Some themes were consciously revived from nearby Achaemenid and Sasanian sites such as Persepolis and Naqsh-i Rustam. Painting also flourished under Karim Khan (*see* ISLAMIC ART, §VIII, 11(i)). A large oil painting of *Muhammad Karim Khan and his Court* (Shiraz, Pars Mus.) was painted by Ja'far, but the most important artist was MUHAMMAD SADIQ, whose long career spanned the second half of the 18th century. Many Zand paintings depict a type of floral carpet known from several examples (*see* ISLAMIC ART, §VI, 4(iv)(c)). After Karim Khan's death, internal dissension and disputes over succession prevented the last six Zand rulers from substantial patronage of the arts. In 1792 Shiraz was sacked by the QAJAR ruler Agha Muhammad, and the last Zand was executed two years later.

BIBLIOGRAPHY

J. R. Perry: *Karim Khan Zand: A History of Iran, 1747–1779* (Chicago and London, 1979)

J. Housego: 'Carpets', *The Arts of Persia*, ed. R. W. Ferrier (New Haven and London, 1989), pp. 118–56

B. W. Robinson: 'Persian Painting under the Zand and Qājār Dynasties', *From Nadir Shah to the Islamic Republic* (1991), vii of *The Cambridge History of Iran* (Cambridge, 1968–91), pp. 870–90

J. Scarce: 'The Arts of the Eighteenth to Twentieth Centuries', *From Nadir Shah to the Islamic Republic* (1991), vii of *The Cambridge History of Iran* (Cambridge, 1968–91), pp. 890–958

S. J. VERNOIT

Zanda. *See* THOLING.

Zande [Azande]. Central Sudanic-speaking people, about one million in number, occupying the borderlands of Zaïre, the southern Sudan and the Central African Republic. Essentially agriculturalists, they formerly relied heavily on hunting and fishing for subsistence. The highly mixed ancestry of the Zande partly explains the diversity of their arts. They began to emerge during the 18th century from groups who were expanding from the west and exploiting the resources along the northern fringes of the forests. These groups fell under the leadership of the Avongara, the aristocratic clan of the Zande, whose princes and governors ruled the various Zande provinces. Conquered peoples were incorporated into Zande society as subjects, gradually losing their language and separate identity, but contributing their own skills to Zande culture. In addition to trade, a complex system of tribute ensured a constant circulation of goods from distant areas of Zande influence and a wide dispersal of the specialist artistic products of individual regions. Examples of Zande art are to be found, for example, in Tervuren, Koninklijk Museum voor Midden-Afrika (Musée Royal de l'Afrique Centrale); London, British Museum; Birchington, Powell-Cotton Museum; and Oxford, Pitt Rivers Museum, as well as many other European and North American museums. Published illustrations are also very common (*see* §2 for bibliography).

1. FIGURE SCULPTURE. Towards the end of the 19th century a secret association known as the Mani, which originated among the groups living in the present-day Central African Republic, spread throughout the Zande, although it was mainly associated with subject peoples rather than with the Avongara aristocrats. It was open to both men and women. The figurative art used in its rituals was referred to generically as *yanda* and includes both wooden and ceramic sculpture (e.g. Tervuren, Kon. Mus. Midden-Afrika). All such figures are small and represent their subjects in a highly stylized, often schematic form. They usually portray human subjects and, although gender is rarely represented, they are generally regarded as female. Mani adherents also employed other magical devices, including mica, blue beads, magical whistles and medicinal preparations.

Mani's rituals were intended to secure such advantages for its members as success in hunting, protection from evil influences and fecundity. These beneficial ends were achieved mainly by magical and medicinal means. Thus the *yanda* figures were regularly coated in magical powder, which gave them a caked appearance. Food and gifts were procured for them, and they were honoured during an annual festival. *Yanda* figures were not used in all the Mani lodges. Their production and use is associated particularly with the areas of Rafay, Basekpio, Lebo, Dukwa and the chiefships of Biamange and Boso, while in the Sudan adherents of Mani did not use sculpted figures in their version of the society's rituals.

Full-length figures carved in a more naturalistic style are also associated with the Zande (see fig.). Sometimes these were carved as male and female pairs. Although it has been suggested (1985 exh. cat.) that these may be ancestor figures like those used by Bantu peoples in other parts of Central Africa, supporting ethnographic evidence is lacking. The first published mention of paired figures in the 1920s relates to the chiefdom of Tambura in southwestern Sudan (Larken). The account refers to two figures representing a married couple much disliked by the local Zande ruler; the 'portraits' were buried in a river bed as part of a rain-making ritual during a time of drought. The figures were not carved by Zande artists, however, but by a Belanda sculptor from an area immediately north of Tambura.

Belanda craftsmen also had privileged status at the court of the Zande king Gubudwe at his capital, Yambio. It has been suggested that Yambio was the site of a carving centre in the late 19th century (Fagg), but the evidence for this is unclear. It is certain, however, that Lirangu, near

Zande male figure, wood, h. 808 mm, collected *c.* 1920s (London, British Museum)

Yambio, and Source Yubu, near Tambura, became carving centres from the 1930s, when medical facilities were established there to combat sleeping sickness. The sculpture produced was intended largely for the foreign medical staff and their occasional visitors, and often represented them.

2. OTHER ARTS. Lirangu was also the source of a number of ceramic pieces collected in the 1930s by Major

Percy Powell-Cotton (1860–1940) and Hannah Powell-Cotton (1881–1964). These included bowls bearing seated human figures on the sides and objects more obviously made for external sale, such as book-ends decorated with figures (Birchington, Powell-Cotton Mus.). They were produced from a mica-rich clay, and many were the work of a single artist, Mbitim, who, like traditional Zande potters, was male. Although Mbitim's work exploited an external market, he was heir to an older tradition. Round-bodied water-pots with human heads at the top are reported to have been made by the Adio Zande (or Makaraka) to the east of Yambio (Seligman and Seligman). The Zande also once produced ceramic pipe bowls with depictions of human heads (Baumann).

The first figurative art recorded among the Zande was the carving on the tops of harps of human heads, usually shown with a coiffure of neat plaits arranged in parallel lines; occasionally animal heads were depicted instead. The early origin among the Zande of such harps, which typically had four strings, is confirmed by the attention they received from the first European observers: Schweinfurth collected examples, and Junker published a drawing (i, facing p. 128) of a Zande harp being played by a Nubian girl from northern Sudan. Although this may be a caption mistake, there are other cases of musical instruments from this area being collected by Arab traders and carried back to Khartoum. One such example, a large slit-gong carved in the form of a four-legged animal, possibly a goat, was captured from the Mahdist armies at the Battle of Omdurman in 1898 (London, BM). Such gongs were kept at the courts of kings and princes and were used to sound warnings and send messages.

Several centuries ago, before the Zande turned to agriculture, they relied on bows and arrows for hunting. In modern times, however, they specialize in a wide range of knives, some functional but most ceremonial. The blades vary in size and shape and often have punched decoration and elaborate handles, sometimes in ivory (Baumann). Distinctive types include throwing knives with a series of projecting blades, large curved swords and a type of hooked knife that is also used by the neighbouring MANGBETU, while women's knives are a distinctive oval shape. The Zande are also well known for the production of large vegetable fibre shields. These are rectangular in form with rounded ends top and bottom and a series of elaborate designs picked out in black on the front surface. There is also photographic evidence that at least up to the 1940s tattooing was not uncommon among women.

BIBLIOGRAPHY
J. Petherick and Mrs Petherick: *Travels in Central Africa, and Explorations of the Western Nile Tributaries*, 2 vols (London, 1869)
G. A. Schweinfurth: *Im Herzen von Afrika* (Leipzig, 1873); Eng. trans. as *The Heart of Africa: Three Years' Travels and Adventures in the Unexplored Regions of Central Africa from 1868 to 1871*, 2 vols (London, 1873)
——: *Artes Africanae: Illustrations and Descriptions of Productions of the Industrial Arts of Central African Tribes* (London, 1875)
W. Junker: *Travels in Africa, 1879–89*, 2 vols (London, 1891–2)
P. M. Larken: 'An Account of the Azande', *Sudan Notes & Rec.*, ix/1 (1926), pp. 1–56
H. Baumann: 'Die materielle Kultur der Azande und Mangbetu', *Baessler-Archv*, xi (1927), pp. 1–131
E. E. Evans-Pritchard: 'Mani: A Zande Secret Society', *Sudan Notes & Rec.*, xiv/2 (1931), pp. 105–48
C. G. Seligman and B. Z. Seligman: *Pagan Tribes of the Nilotic Sudan* (London, 1932)

H. Powell-Cotton: 'Village Handicrafts in the Sudan', *Man*, xxxiv (1934), pp. 90–91

E. E. Evans-Pritchard: 'A Contribution to the Study of Zande Culture', *Africa*, xxx (1960), pp. 309–24

A. Kronenberg and W. Kronenberg: 'Wood Carvings in the South–western Sudan', *Kush*, viii (1960), pp. 274–81

H. Burssens: 'Yanda-beelden en Mani-sekte bij de Zande', *An. Mus. Royale Afrique Cent.*, n.s., iv (1962) [Fr. summary]

W. Fagg: *The Tribal Image: Wooden Figure Sculpture of the World* (London, 1970)

E. E. Evans-Pritchard: *The Azande: History and Political Institutions* (Oxford, 1971)

C. Piaggia: *Nella terra dei Niam-Niam (1863–1865)*, ed. E. Bassani (Lucca, 1978)

African Masterpieces from the Musée de l'homme (exh. cat. by S. Vogel and F. N'Diaye, New York, Cent. Afr. A., 1985)

J. Mack: 'Art, Culture, and Tribute among the Azande', *African Reflections: Art from North–eastern Zaire* (exh. cat., ed. E. Schildkrout; New York, Amer. Mus. Nat. Hist., 1990), pp. 217–31

JOHN MACK

Zandomeneghi, Federico (*b* Venice, 2 June 1841; *d* Paris, 30 Dec 1917). Italian painter. His father Pietro and grandfather Luigi tried to interest him in the plastic arts, but from a very early age he showed a stronger inclination for painting. Zandomeneghi soon rebelled against their teachings, and by 1856 he was attending the Accademia di Belle Arti in Venice, studying under the painters Michelangelo Grigoletti (1801–70) and Pompeo Molmenti (1819–94). As a Venetian he was born an Austrian subject, and, to escape conscription, he fled his city in 1859 and went to Pavia, where he enrolled at the university. In the following year he followed Garibaldi in the Expedition of the Thousand; afterwards, having been convicted of desertion and therefore unable to return to Venice, he went to Florence, where he remained from 1862 to 1866. This period was essential for his artistic development. In Tuscany he frequented the Florentine painters known as the Macchiaioli, with some of whom he took part in the Third Italian War of Independence (1866). Zandomeneghi formed a strong friendship with Telemaco Signorini and Diego Martelli, with whom he corresponded frequently for the rest of his life. In this period he painted the *Palazzo Pretorio of Florence* (1865; Venice, Ca' Pesaro), in which the building, represented in the historical–romantic tradition, is redeemed by a remarkable sense of air and light, elements derived from the Macchiaioli.

When Zandomeneghi finally returned to Venice in 1872, after two brief periods in Genoa and Rome, his art was still wavering between Realism and avant-garde painting. Despite some disagreements, he was able to form contacts and friendships with the painters Michele Cammarano, Guglielmo Ciardi (*b* 1843), Mosè di Giosue Bianchi and Giacomo Favretto. Zandomeneghi did not really belong either to the ranks of historical–romantic painters or to those of the Macchiaioli, nor did he join the stream of social realism initiated in Venice by Cammarano. During his time in Venice he was rather isolated, restless and dissatisfied; however, he had an independent spirit that allowed him to paint according to his own ideas and using an individual technique, without being unduly influenced by outside forces. In 1874 he returned to Florence but in June of the same year left for Paris. He was probably encouraged in this decision by the enthusiasm of Diego Martelli, who had just returned from the French capital where he had visited the first Impressionist exhibition in the Boulevard des Capucines. He originally meant to remain only a short time in Paris but in fact settled there. He found it very difficult to get established, as he was unknown by the market and excluded from the circles that acclaimed the painting of two other Italians, Giovanni Boldini and Giuseppe De Nittis. However, he eventually became friendly with Degas, Renoir, Manet and later Toulouse-Lautrec. It was in the early part of his Parisian period, in the late 1870s and early 1880s, that Zandò (as he was called by his French friends) produced most of his Impressionist masterpieces. His highly personal style can be seen, for example, in *Moulin de la Galette* (1878; priv. col., see 1988 exh. cat., p. 24), in which he used a violently anti-naturalistic colour scheme.

Zandomeneghi's alliance with Impressionism always remained moderate, as his participation in the Macchiaioli school had been: for example, in *Place d'Anvers a Parigi* (1880; Piacenza, Gal. A. Mod. Ricci Oddi; see fig.), while the Impressionist influence is evident in the composition, which is cropped, almost like a photograph's, the overall approach is rather that of a Realism mitigated by the subtlety of his colour combinations and by an intense luminosity; the conversation of the women and the playing children are reminiscent of Favretto's scenes of Venetian life.

In 1879 Zandomeneghi participated in the fourth Impressionist exhibition in Rue de l'Opéra, with his beautiful portrait of *Diego Martelli* (1879; Florence, Pitti), with whom he had shared a home in Paris for the past year. He was again linked with the Impressionists in their fifth exhibition (1880), the sixth (1881), and the final, eighth (1886). He could not earn a living by painting, despite the benevolent patronage of Paul Durand-Ruel, so in those years he supported himself with drawings for a fashion magazine. After the mid-1880s Zandomeneghi's work took a new direction with some pastels, including the remarkable *Blue Jacket* (1884; Mantua, Mus. Civ. Pal. Te), using a technique characterized by accentuated threads of colour. At first the style was diffuse; then he adopted an unorthodox kind of divisionism in which the chromatic texture was broken down into subtle, vibrant webs of light. This led him away from the Impressionist aesthetic; around the early 1890s he came close to the early style of Renoir, though with a greater three-dimensionality. The prevalent themes were those of an intimate feminine world—young women in the park, sitting-room or boudoir, surrounded by small simple objects, caught in their daily life. These delightful depictions of women, usually young, share an innate serenity and a calm sensuality (e.g. *Conversation*, 1890–95; Milan, Piceni priv. col.). Sometimes they are proud and haughty, as in *Woman's Head* (1892; Gallarate, priv. col., see 1988 exh. cat., p. 150), though immersed in a symphony of blue tones that lend a calm, diffuse light. Durand-Ruel did not fail to notice this change, and in 1893 the first one-man show at his gallery in Paris was of Zandomeneghi's work. However, this late success gave little comfort to Zandomeneghi's last years. His irreplaceable friend, Diego Martelli, died in 1896. A few disappointments such as the lukewarm reception of his works at the Esposizione Internazionale del Sempione in Milan in 1906, some illnesses, and his by now constitutional

Federico Zandomeneghi: *Place d'Anvers a Parigi*, oil on canvas, 1.02×1.36 m, 1880 (Piacenza, Galleria d'Arte Moderna Ricci Oddi)

pessimism, made him feel more and more lonely. He concentrated on simple, familiar subjects, producing a great number of small still-lifes: a vase of flowers, a box of sweets or a few apples scattered on a table. Around the end of the first decade of the 20th century, through his friendship with Angelo Sommaruga and Vittorio Pica, he was given room for exhibition at the Venice Biennale of 1914.

BIBLIOGRAPHY

D. Martelli: *Gli impressionisti* (Pisa, 1880)
Presentazione della personale di Federico Zandomeneghi (exh. cat. by V. Pica, Venice, Biennale, 1914)
E. Piceni: *Zandomeneghi* (Milan, 1967)
Zandomeneghi: un veneziano a Parigi (exh. cat. by R. De Grada, G. Pavanello and F. Bernabei, Venice, Ca' Pesaro, 1988)
F. Dini: *Federico Zandomeneghi: La vita e le opere* (Florence, 1989)
La collezione Arnoldo Mondadori (exh. cat., Cortina d'Ampezzo, Pin. Rimoldi, 1991)

SILVIA LUCCHESI

Zanetti. Italian family of artists and writers. (1) Anton Maria Zanetti (i) and his cousin (2) Anton Maria Zanetti (ii), often referred to as the elder and the younger, lived together in the family palazzo at S Maria Materdomini in Venice and made a significant contribution to the cultural life of that city in the mid-18th century. Both were draughtsmen, the elder also being an accomplished printmaker and collector and the younger a notable art historian. Girolamo Zanetti, younger brother of Anton Maria (ii), was a writer chiefly known for *Dell'origine di alcune arti*

principali appresso i Viniziani (Venice, 1758); he also collaborated with Anton Maria the elder on *Dactyliotheca zanettiana* and wrote a memorial note on his brother.

(1) Conte **Anton Maria** [Girolamo] **Zanetti (i)** (*b* Venice, 20 Feb 1680; *d* Venice, 31 Dec 1767). Draughtsman, printmaker and collector. He studied with Nicolò Bambini (1651–1736), Sebastiano Ricci and Antonio Balestra, and around the age of 20 he spent some time in Bologna, which initiated his lifelong admiration for Bolognese painting. Thereafter he worked in Venice as an engraver, meeting such foreign scholars as Pierre-Jean Mariette and Pierre Crozat and pursuing his interests as a collector. A journey to Paris and London between 1720 and 1722, with a brief stay at Rotterdam, broadened his artistic knowledge and introduced him to European scholars and collectors, with whom he later corresponded. His outstanding purchase was an important group of drawings by Parmigianino, which he bought in London from Thomas Howard, 2nd Earl of Arundel. He copied or made variants of these drawings for a set of about 50 chiaroscuro woodcuts (B., pp. 271–342) in three or four different colours; he collected them into volumes in 1731, 1739 and 1749. He also made caricatures (Venice, Fond. Cini; Windsor Castle, Berks, Royal Lib.) in which, with subtle humour and assured lines, he depicted actors, artist friends (among them Sebastiano Ricci, Marco Ricci, Rosalba Carriera and Giovanni Battista Pittoni) and other figures,

including himself. His most famous project, for which he and his cousin (2) Anton Maria Zanetti (ii) made drawings (Venice, Bib. N. Marciana; New York, Pierpont Morgan Lib.), was the two-volume set of engravings entitled *Delle antiche statue greche e romane* (1740–43). The engravings, depicting the Greek and Roman statuary to be found in Venetian public buildings (now mainly in Venice, Mus. Archeol.), were made by several artists, including GIAN-ANTONIO FALDONI, Joseph Wagner, Giovanni Cattini and Marco Alvise Pitteri; the text was provided by Antonio Francesco Gori and others. The book enjoyed an international success, including among its subscribers such illustrious figures as Giovanni Poleni, Pietro Metastasio (1698–1782), Mariette and Crozat.

As a collector, Zanetti was principally interested in prints, antique gems and medals. His print collection was intended to be comprehensive, although his preference for the free etching technique of Parmigianino, Jacques Callot and Giovanni Benedetto Castiglione is discernible. He had a series of his drawings by Castiglione engraved by GAETANO GHERARDI ZOMPINI. His modest collection of paintings included works by Sebastiano and Marco Ricci, and pastels and miniatures by Rosalba Carriera. In 1750 Zanetti published a luxurious catalogue of his antique gems and medals, *Dactyliotheca zanettiana*, with a Latin text by Gori, translated into Italian by Girolamo Zanetti.

In 1761 Zanetti was made a count by Empress Maria-Theresa of Austria (1717–80), and, constantly visited by European travellers, he played an important role in cultural exchanges between Venice and the rest of Europe.

(2) Anton Maria [Alesandro] Zanetti (ii)

(2) Anton Maria [Alesandro] Zanetti (ii) (*b* Venice, 1706; *d* Venice, 1778). Draughtsman, librarian and writer, cousin of (1) Anton Maria Zanetti (i). He collaborated with the elder Zanetti in making the drawings for *Delle antiche statue*. A memorial note by his brother Girolamo, which is included in later editions of his own *Varie pitture a fresco de' principali maestri veneziani* (1760), provides some information on his work as a scholar and an artist. From 1737 until his death he was librarian of the Biblioteca Marciana, the library of S Marco, Venice, for which he catalogued the Greek (pubd 1740), Latin and Italian codices. Although he received wide recognition for this work, he is most notable for his writings on the history of Venetian painting. The *Descrizione di tutte le pubbliche pitture della città di Venezia e isole circonvicine* (Venice, 1733) is essentially an adaptation of Marco Boschini's *Le ricche minere della pittura veneziana* (1674), to which Zanetti brought a sharp critical spirit dominated by Enlightenment rationalism and classical, anti-Baroque taste. The more ambitious *Della pittura veneziana e delle opere pubbliche de' veneziani maestri* (1771), an account of the development of the Venetian school, begins with the art of the 'Primitives' (Zanetti's interest in which reflects a new attitude to historiography if not a change in taste) and then focuses mainly on the Venetian Renaissance, which he carefully distinguished from Mannerism, for him a negative phenomenon foreshadowing the bad taste of Baroque art. Yet he found himself at ease with 18th-century painting, considering that it had successfully combined elegance and expression. Luigi Lanzi praised the balance of Zanetti's text and recognized the exemplary quality of his historiography.

WRITINGS
Descrizione di tutte le pubbliche pitture della città di Venezia e isole circonvicine (Venice, 1733)
Varie pitture a fresco de' principali maestri veneziani ora per la prima volta con le stampe pubblicate (Venice, 1760) [later edns incl. memorial note by G. Zanetti]
Della pittura veneziana e delle opere pubbliche de' veneziani maestri (Venice, 1771)

BIBLIOGRAPHY
G. Lorenzetti: 'Un dilettante incisore del XVIII secolo: Anton Maria Zanetti di Girolamo', *Misc. Stor. Ven.*, 3rd ser., xii (1917)
N. Ivanoff: 'Antonio Maria Zanetti critico d'arte', *Atti Ist. Ven. Sci., Lett. & A.*, cxi (1952–3), pp. 29–48
F. Borroni: *I due Anton Maria Zanetti* (Florence, 1956)
L. Lanzi: *Storia pittorica della Italia*, i (Florence, 1968), p. 7
Caricature di Anton Maria Zanetti (exh. cat., ed. A. Bettagno; Venice, Fond. Cini, 1969)
A. Bettagno: 'Precisazioni su Anton Maria Zanetti il vecchio e Sebastiano e Marco Ricci', *Atti del congresso internazionale di studi su Sebastiano Ricci e il suo tempo: Udine, 1975*, pp. 85–95
C. Karpinski: *Italian Chiaroscuro Woodcuts*, 48 [XII] of *The Illustrated Bartsch*, ed. W. Strauss (New York, 1983) [B.]
F. Bernabei: 'La letteratura artistica', *Storia della cultura veneta: Il settecento*, ed. G. Arnaldi, v/1 (Vicenza, 1985), pp. 485–508
K. Pomian: 'Collezionisti d'arte e di curiosità naturali', *Storia della cultura veneta: Il settecento*, ed. M. P. Stocchi, v/2 (Vicenza, 1986), pp. 1–70

FRANCO BERNABEI

Zanettini, Siegbert (*b* São Paulo, 1934). Brazilian architect. He graduated in 1959 from the Faculty of Architecture and Town Planning at the University of São Paulo, where he received a PhD in 1972. He belonged to the third generation of modern architects in Brazil, benefiting from the opportunities presented by rapid industrialization, the founding of Brasília and the intensive urbanization of the cities. In 1964 he became Professor of Planning at the University of São Paulo, and his preoccupation with social concerns was reflected in his approach to planning for housing, education and health in the city's suburbs. From this experience came a variety of experiments with timber, steel, reinforced concrete and techniques that combine industrial components with the abundant unskilled labour available in the large cities. In 1968 he won a competition for the construction of a maternity hospital at Vila Nova Cachoeirinha, on the outskirts of São Paulo, on which he worked for three years with a large interdisciplinary team and with the local population. He also designed a number of primary schools and banks where he experimented with concrete and steel construction, producing works of great formal and spatial richness such as the Banco do Estado de São Paulo (1978) at Alto da Boa Vista. Later works include the Ermelino Matarazzo Municipal Hospital (1985), and the Sports Centre (1986) and TELESP Training Centre (1987) in São Paulo. His importance to modern Brazilian architecture lay in his efforts to reconcile his roles as a highly competent professional and a teacher sensitive to social, economic and technological problems.

BIBLIOGRAPHY
'Siegbert Zanettini', *Acrópole*, 352 (1968), pp. 13–41 [special feature]
'Hospital e Maternidade, Vila Nova Cachoeirinha, São Paulo', *Cj Arquitetura*, 15 (1977), pp. 48–9
Cad. Bras. Arquit., 8 (1981) [issue dedicated to Zanettini]

PAULO J. V. BRUNA

Zangid [Zangī]. Islamic dynasty which ruled in northern Iraq, south-east Anatolia and Syria from 1127 to 1222. In 1127 'Imad al-Din Zangi, the son of a Turkish commander in the Saljuq army, was appointed governor of Mosul for the Saljuq sultan and guardian (Turk. *atabeg*) for his sons. The semi-independent Zangi expanded his dominion north and west and was granted Aleppo in 1129. He fought against the crusaders, most notably at Edessa in 1144. Zangi was succeeded by two independent branches of the family in Mosul and Aleppo. His son Nur al-Din (*reg* in Aleppo 1146–74) conquered Damascus in 1154, opposed the crusaders and sent his generals Shirkuh and Salah al-Din to Egypt, where the latter founded the AYYUBID dynasty. The Ayyubids succeeded the Zangids in Aleppo in 1183 and in Damascus in 1186.

Nur al-Din, a staunch Sunni, built many religious institutions, and fortified Aleppo, Damascus and other key sites. During his reign there was a Classical Revival in Syrian architecture as well as a wholehearted adoption of symmetrical building plans and forms, such as the iwan, typical of Abbasid architecture in Iraq. In his hospital (1154) and his funerary madrasa (1172) in Damascus, the 'sugarloaf' MUQARNAS vault appears in Syria for the first time, rendered in plaster. The tomb of the madrasa is the first Islamic building constructed fully in striped masonry (Arab. *ablaq*), a local technique that became increasingly popular in Ayyubid and Mamluk architecture. Finely carved woodwork was also produced in the Zangid period. One of the finest examples was the minbar ordered by Nur al-Din as an ex-voto for the conquest of Jerusalem; when Salah al-Din conquered the city he moved the minbar to the Aqsa Mosque there, where it stood until it was destroyed by fire in 1969.

BIBLIOGRAPHY

Enc. Islam/2: 'Nūr al-Dīn'
M. van Berchem: '*Matériaux pour un corpus inscriptionum arabicarum: Deuxième partie: Syrie du Sud: Jérusalem*', Mém.: Inst. Fr. Archéol. Orient. Caire, xliii–xlv (Cairo, 1922–7)
N. Elisséeff: *Nūr al-Dīn*, 3 vols (Damascus, 1967)
T. Allen: *A Classical Revival in Islamic Architecture* (Wiesbaden, 1986)

□

Zanguidi, Jacopo. *See* BERTOIA, JACOPO.

Zani, Pietro (*b* Fidenza, 4 Sept 1748; *d* Parma, 12 Aug 1821). Italian writer. He was the author of the voluminous *Enciclopedia metodica critico ragionata delle belle arti*, a work that remains useful. Two editions are known: the first in eight volumes (Parma, 1794), the second in 28 (Parma, 1819–22), of which the first 19 constitute a dictionary of artists, the rest being devoted to the graphic arts. The dictionary section covers painters, sculptors, architects, draughtsmen, critics, collectors and others, each of whom is very briefly described through the use of an elaborate coding system. This gives details of nationality, dates of birth and death, scope of media and occupation, and even a ranking of merit, ranging from '*bravissimo*' down to '*molto mediocre*' in five stages.

WRITINGS
Enciclopedia metodica critico ragionata delle belle arti, 8 vols (Parma, 1794), rev., 28 vols (Parma, 1819–22)

BIBLIOGRAPHY
Bolaffi; Thieme–Becker

FELICIANO BENVENUTI

Zanini. *See* VIOLA ZANINI, GIUSEPPE.

Zanino di Pietro [Giovanni di Francia; Giovanni di Pietro Charlier] (*fl* Bologna, 1389; *d* Venice, by 1448). Italian painter. With Niccolò di Pietro and Jacobello del Fiore, Zanino di Pietro was one of the major Venetian painters of the first quarter of the 15th century. His activity in Bologna, repeatedly documented between 1389 and 1406, was of crucial importance for the pungent narrative style and naturalistic details of his earliest signed painting, a folding *Crucifixion* triptych painted for the Franciscan convent of Fonte Colombo (Rieti, Mus. Civ.). The inscription describes the artist as *h[ab]itator ve[n]eciis i[n] contrata sa[nc]te a[ppol]linaris*, and it is therefore datable to *c.* 1405, when Zanino seems to have moved permanently to Venice. Whether the triptych reflects the work of Gentile da Fabriano, who was active in Venice by 1408, or whether Zanino was instrumental in transmitting an Emilian style to Gentile cannot be answered satisfactorily. Zanino's subsequent paintings reveal the influence of both Gentile and Michelino da Besozzo, who was active in Venice by 1410. The most important are two polyptychs in the Museo Diocesano, Camerino, and the Convento del Beato Sante, Mombarroccio, both in the Marches, the iconostasis of Torcello Cathedral and the fresco decoration of the tomb of the *Beato Pacifico* (1437; Venice, S Maria Gloriosa dei Frari).

Padovani has demonstrated that Zanino di Pietro is identical with the Giovanni di Francia who, in 1429, signed a painting of the *Virgin and Child* (Rome, Pal. Venezia). Previously, Giovanni di Francia had been considered an inferior follower of Zanino. This identification is further evidence of the stagnation and decline of Zanino's work after *c.* 1410. After 1420 Zanino was employed principally as a decorator. In 1426 he gilded a pulpit in the church of the Carità, Venice, and in 1431 he was commissioned to decorate the façade of the Ca' d'Oro.

The most ambitious works plausibly attributed to Zanino are the designs for a set of tapestries with scenes from the Passion for S Marco (Venice, Mus. S Marco; *see* ITALY, fig. 99), the date of 1420–30 and attribution of which are highly controversial. They have also been attributed to Niccolò di Pietro.

DBI
BIBLIOGRAPHY
R. Longhi: *Viatico per cinque secoli di pittura veneziana* (Florence, 1946), p. 49
F. Zeri: 'Aggiunte a Zanino di Pietro', *Paragone*, xiii/153 (1962), pp. 56–60
S. Padovani: 'Una nuova proposta per Zanino di Pietro', *Paragone*, xxxvi/419–23 (1985), pp. 73–81

KEITH CHRISTIANSEN

Zanobi da Firenze. *See under* MASTERS, ANONYMOUS, AND MONOGRAMMISTS, §I: MASTER OF THE BRUSSELS INITIALS.

Zanobi de Gianotis [Gianotti], **Bernardino** (*b* Florence or Rome; *d* Vilnius, Lithuania, 1541). Italian architect and sculptor, active in Poland and Lithuania. Until 1529 he served as an assistant to the architect and sculptor Bartolomeo Berrecci in his work on the Sigismund Chapel, Kraków Cathedral (*see* KRAKÓW, fig. 5). In about 1531 he founded an architectural–sculptural partnership with

Giovan Battista Cini (*d* 1565) and Filippo da Fiesole (*d* 1540), also former collaborators of Berrecci. Their main achievement was the cathedral in Płock (1532–41): a basilica with a nave in three bays, aisles, transept with apse and a dome (raised in height, 1901–3), it was the only imitation north of the Alps of Renaissance basilicas of the type built in Rome by Florentine architects in the last quarter of the 15th century, e.g. S Agostino (1479–83) and S Maria del Popolo (1472–80). In July 1534 Zanobi and his associates entered into a contract to rebuild the cathedral in Vilnius (begun 1536; completed by Cini after 1546). Its Renaissance appearance has been obscured, however, by the Neo-classical reconstruction carried out *c.* 1783 by Wawrzyniec Gucewicz. The workshop was probably also responsible for building the villa (extended after 1610) near Kraków of the humanist scholar Justus Ludwik Decjusz (*c.* 1520–67) and for extending the Grand-Ducal Lower Castle (destr.) in Vilnius.

Zanobi also executed a number of sepulchral monuments. In 1526–8 he carved that of *Stanisław and Janusz* (Warsaw Cathedral; damaged 1944; *see* WARSAW, fig. 4), the last two dukes of Mazovia, and in 1537 he carved the effigy of *Stanisław Lasocki* (Brzeziny parish church). A number of other works are also attributed to Zanobi on stylistic grounds. These include the tombs of two bishops—*Jan Konarski* (1521; Kraków Cathedral) and *Jan Lubrański* (1522; Poznań Cathedral)—and a low relief (known as the Opatów *Lamentation*) on the bronze tomb (1532–6) of *Chancellor Krzysztof Szydłowiecki* in the Opatów collegiate church, as well as the effigy of the Chancellor's daughter *Anna Szydłowiecka*.

Zanobi's sculpture is characterized by the strong realism of its portraiture and by the conventional motionless repose in which the clothed recumbent figures are presented, although such works as the Opatów *Lamentation* also manage to express movement and complicated gestures. Although the fact that he often worked in collaboration makes it hard to assess Zanobi's artistic identity, it is clear that he occupied an important position among those artists responsible for introducing the Tuscan Renaissance into Poland.

BIBLIOGRAPHY
H. Kozakiewiczowa: 'Spółka architektoniczno-rzeźbiarska Bernardina de Gianotis i Jana Cini' [The architectural-sculptural workshop of Bernardino de Gianotis and Giovanni Cini], *Biul. Hist. Sztuki*, xxi (1959), pp. 151–74
R. Kunkel: 'Kościół katedralny w Płocku' [Płock Cathedral], *Kwart. Archit. & Urb.*, xxvi (1981), pp. 294–306

ADAM MIŁOBĘDZKI

Zanobi degli Strozzi. *See* STROZZI, ZANOBI.

Zanotti, Giovan Pietro (Cavazzoni) (*b* Paris, 4 Oct 1674; *d* Bologna, 28 Sept 1765). Italian writer, painter and poet. He trained as a painter with Lorenzo Pasinelli and was active mainly in Bologna. Although his painting, as exemplified by such works as *Joseph Retrieving the Silver Cup from Benjamin's Sack* (Bologna, Credito Romagnolo), was undistinguished, being a weak blend of classicist clichés and the graceful Rococo palette derived from Pasinelli, Zanotti was a friend of many outstanding men of letters and wrote widely on subjects connected with art. In 1710 he contributed a defence of Guido Reni's works

in the controversy between Domenico Bouhours and Giovan Gioseffo Orsi concerning the concepts of 'delicateness' and 'weakness' in painting. By that date he had already published a number of works, including a biography (1703) of Pasinelli, a defence (1705) of Carlo Cesare Malvasia's *Felsina pittrice* (1678), which championed the late Baroque Bolognese tradition, and a revised edition (1706) of Malvasia's guidebook *Le pitture di Bologna* (1686). However, his most famous work is the two-volume *Storia dell'Accademia Clementina* (1739). He was a founder member of the Accademia and its secretary until 1723 and again between 1730 and 1759. The Accademia was founded by General Luigi Marsili in 1710. Its activities included teaching courses, competitions and exhibition of competition works. A sharp-edged but restrained criticism of the founder and other fellow members is perceptible in this work, and was to be amplified later by Luigi Crespi (*see* CRESPI (ii), (2)).

Most of Zanotti's later books related to his activity in the Accademia. Influenced by Bellori and the Roman school, they reveal a marked shift in emphasis towards a more orthodox classical theory of art that veered away from the Baroque tradition of Malvasia. In *Le pitture di Pellegrino Tibaldi* (1756), Zanotti heavily criticized Malvasia as a historian for factual inaccuracy. As a poet he can broadly be described as a classicist, belonging to the Bolognese neo-Petrarchan school.

WRITINGS
Zanotti's correspondence and the manuscripts of his published works and poems are preserved in Bologna, Bib. Com. Archiginnasio. The most important of his published works include:

Nuovo fregio di gloria a Felsina sempre pittrice nella vita di Lorenzo Pasinelli pittore bolognese (Bologna, 1703)
Lettere familiari scritte ad un amico in difesa del Conte Carlo Cesare Malvasia, autore della Felsina pittrice (Bologna, 1705)
Le pitture di Bologna che nella pretesa e rimostrata sin hora da altri maggiore antichità e impareggiabile eccellenza nella pittura con manifesta evidenza di fatto rendono il passaggero disingannato ed instrutto, con correzioni e aggiunte (Bologna, 1706)
Dialogo in difesa di Guido Reni (Venice, 1710)
Le pitture di Bologna . . . con altre correzioni e aggiunte (Bologna, 1732)
Storia dell'Accademia Clementina, 2 vols (Bologna, 1739/*R* 1977)
Instruzioni e avvertimenti a chi invei aggregato all'Accademia Clementina come uno dei quaranta (Bologna, 1749)
Avvertimenti per lo incamminamento di un giovane alla pittura (Bologna, 1756)
Le pitture di Pellegrino Tibaldi e Niccolò Abbati esistenti nel Palazzo dell'Instituto in Bologna (Venice, 1756)
Letters in G. Bottari: *Raccolta di alcune lettere sulla pittura, scultura ed architettura* (Rome, 1757–68), vols ii, iii, iv, v, vi
Il claustro di San Michele in Bosco (Bologna, 1776); ed. I. A. Calvi as *Le pitture di Lodovico Carracci e degli allievi suoi eseguite nel chiostro della chiesa di San Michele in Bosco* (Bologna, 1847)

BIBLIOGRAPHY
R. Roli: *Pittura bolognese, 1650–1800: Dal Cignani ai Gandolfi* (Bologna, 1977)
R. Roli and A. Ottani Cavina: 'Commentario alla *Storia dell'Accademia Clementina di Giovan Pietro Zanotti* (1739)', *Atti & Mem. Accad. Clementina Bologna*, xii (1977), pp. ix–xx, 124 [also pubd as an app. to the 1977 repr. of Zanotti's *Storia dell'Accademia Clementina*]
L. Grassi: *Teorici e storia della critica d'arte*, ii: *Il settecento in Italia* (Rome, 1979), pp. 75–7, 79
S. Zamboni: 'L'Accademia Clementina', *L'arte del settecento emiliano: La pittura l'Accademia Clementina* (Bologna, 1979), pp. 211–18, 313–14
S. Benassi: *L'Accademia Clementina: La funzione pubblica, l'ideologia estetica* (Bologna, 1988)

GIOVANNA PERINI

Zanstra, Piet (*b* Leeuwarden, 1905). Dutch architect. He was one of the second generation of Dutch Functionalists who united in Groep 32 (founded 1932). Between 1932 and 1954 he was associated with J. H. L. Giesen and K. L. Sijmons in the firm Zanstra, Giesen, Sijmons. His studio flats (1934), Amsterdam, with their severe curtain walls of steel and glass and their open ground-plans, are typical of their approach. Le Corbusier was an important source of inspiration, particularly his Plan Voisin skyscrapers (1925) with their cruciform ground-plans, which reappear in Zanstra's high-rise projects such as the plan (1935; unexecuted) for an 'Industrial Palace', Amsterdam. This is an early example of the large-scale commercial architecture in which Zanstra was to specialize after World War II. In a similar design, the competition entry (1941–2; unexecuted) for the Hofplein building, Rotterdam, a classical tendency can be detected in the severe symmetry and the use of a cornice. This historicizing tendency, typical of Dutch architecture in the late 1930s, had its peak during the war, when Zanstra furnished entire residential housing complexes with 17th-century-style façades. He was fully aware, however, of the functional and commercial aspects of architecture, and this, combined with his strong feeling for form, made him one of the most successful and productive Dutch architects after the war, particularly in the area of commercial architecture. Following the American example, he set up a large office and joined the international 'commercial style', with functional divisions, severe façades and large, monumental building masses, exemplified by his Shell Building (1974–6), Rotterdam.

BIBLIOGRAPHY

G. Fanelli: *Architettura moderna* (1968, 2/1981)
S. Umberto Barbieri, ed.: *Architectuur en planning: Nederland, 1940–1980* (Rotterdam, 1983)
M. Bock and others: *Van het Nieuwe Bouwen naar een nieuwe architectuur* [From a new way of building to a new architecture] (The Hague, 1983)
B. Rebel: *Het Nieuwe Bouwen* (Amsterdam, 1983)

J. P. BAETEN

Zanten, Giovanni van. *See* VASANZIO, GIOVANNI.

Zanth, Ludwig von (*b* Breslau [now Wrocław, Poland], 6 Aug 1796; *d* Stuttgart, 7 Oct 1857). German architect. He started his training in Stuttgart before moving on to Paris, where he first studied under Charles Percier. Later he joined the atelier of JACQUES-IGNACE HITTORFF, with whom he developed a close professional relationship. From 1822 to 1824 Zanth accompanied Hittorff on extensive travels to Italy, visiting Rome, Naples and Sicily and also assisting him in his archaeological work. They subsequently wrote two books on the ancient and modern architecture of Sicily. He was involved in Hittorff's theories on the polychromy of Greek architecture, which strongly influenced his later architectural designs. Around 1830 he returned to Stuttgart and received a doctorate from the university in Tübingen with his research on the domestic architecture of Pompeii. In 1843 Zanth became one of the court architects to King William I of Württemberg (*reg* 1816–64) and worked with Giovanni Salucci, Georg Gottlob Barth (1777–1848), Johann Michael Knapp (1793–1861) and Christian Friedrich Leins (1814–92). His only major executed works were the buildings (1842–64) in the villa and park complex of Wilhelma, Stuttgart, by the king's summer palace, Schloss Rosenstein. The complex (now zoo and botanical gardens) consisted of the main villa, an asymmetrically planned, highly polychromatic building in a Moorish style, garden buildings and a Greek Revival theatre (1842–6).

WRITINGS

with J.-I. Hittorff: *L'Architecture antique de la Sicile* (Paris, 1827)
——: *L'Architecture moderne de la Sicile* (Paris, 1835)

BIBLIOGRAPHY

Thieme–Becker
D. Watkin and T. Mellinghoff: *German Architecture and the Classical Ideal, 1740–1840* (London, 1987)

Zantvoort, Dirck. *See* SANTVOORT, DIRCK.

Zanuso, Marco (*b* Milan, 14 May 1916). Italian architect and industrial designer. Having graduated in 1939 from the Politecnico, Milan, he joined the generation of Milanese architects who, immediately after World War II, took up the debate over cultural issues introduced by the Rationalists, while continuing to concentrate on high standards in the practical aspects of their profession. Zanuso's most important architectural works include a number of residential buildings in Milan: the Villa Shapiro (1963), Via XX Settembre, and the experimental housing (1964) in Via Laveno. He also frequently designed buildings for industry, for example the Olivetti complexes at Buenos Aires (1956–9) and São Paolo (1957–9), and at Crema, Scarmagno and Marcianise in Italy (1967–70). He also built the main Italian headquarters for IBM (1972–5) at Segrate, Milan, and an IBM factory (1979–83) at Santa Palomba, Rome. His later works include the restructuring (1983–6) of the Teatro Fossati (now Teatro Studio del Piccolo Teatro), Milan, and the complex of the new Piccolo Teatro di Milano (begun 1980). In the field of industrial design he created many of the objects and pieces of furniture that helped to define Italian design in the international market, notably the Borletti sewing-machine (1956), the Doney Brion Vega television set (1962) and furnishings produced by the firms Arflex, Kartell and Siemens. From 1970 he taught such subjects as the technology of architecture, building production and industrial design at the Facoltà di Architettura, Università degli Studi, Milan.

BIBLIOGRAPHY

V. Gregotti: 'Marco Zanuso: Un architetto della seconda generazione', *Casabella*, 216 (1957), pp. 59–71
G. Dorfles: *Marco Zanuso: Designer* (Rome, 1971)

MATILDE BAFFA RIVOLTA

Zanzibar. *See under* TANZANIA.

Zao Wou-Ki [Chao Wu-chi; Zhao Wuji] (*b* Beijing, 13 Feb 1921). French painter, draughtsman and printmaker of Chinese birth. He studied at Hangzhou National Academy of Art, Zhejiang Province, from 1935 to 1941 and taught there from 1941 to 1947. The teaching was partly in the old Chinese tradition and techniques and partly in academic Western styles; his early works included small landscapes in the Chinese manner, but he was more attracted by the works of Matisse and Picasso, which he knew only from reproductions. In 1948 he settled in Paris, where he attended the Académie de la Grande Chaumière, and soon began to meet many other artists, including Henri Michaux, Alberto Giacometti, Joan Miró and Maria Elena Vieira da Silva. His works of 1949 to 1955, such as *Piazza* (1950; Paris, Pompidou), owed much to the example of Paul Klee, with spidery imagery of figures, ships, mountains and buildings combined with misty, almost monochromatic colour. As early as 1954, however, in much larger paintings such as *Riven Mountain* (oil on canvas, 1.3×1.95 m, 1955–6; Minneapolis, MN, Walker A. Cent.), he developed a fusion of traditional Chinese landscape painting and Western lyrical abstraction. Instead of legible images, his pictures, executed with calligraphic brushstrokes or a palette-knife and washes of colour, suggest a state of flux and evoke impressions of mysterious landscapes, space, clouds, fire and water, light and darkness, calm and tumult.

After visiting New York for the first time in 1957 and becoming friendly with a number of the leading Abstract Expressionists, Zao Wou-Ki produced bolder and more dramatic paintings with sweeping gestural brushstrokes and a greater richness of colour, for example *31-1-63* (oil on canvas, 1.62×2 m, 1963; Essen, Mus. Flkwang). He brought similar qualities to bear on his prints and on bold wash drawings. He obtained French nationality in 1964.

BIBLIOGRAPHY
C. Roy: *Zao Wou-Ki* (Paris, 1970)
W. Zao and R. Caillois: *Zao Wou-ki: Les estampes 1937–1974* (Paris, 1975)
J. Leymarie: *Zao Wou-Ki* (New York, 1979)
H. Michaux: *Zao Wou-Ki: Encres* (Paris, 1980)

RONALD ALLEY

Zapata [Sapaca], Marcos (*b* ?1710–20; *d* ?1773). Peruvian painter. He was one of the last artists of the Cuzco Baroque school, whose members followed and repeated the formulae developed by Diego Quispe Tito. Though not outstandingly original, he is notable for the quantity of his production and commissions: between 1748 and 1764 he painted at least 200 works. His level of output was probably due to his use of numerous apprentices, such as Cipriano Toledo y Gutiérrez (*fl* 1762–73), Ignacio Chacón (*fl* 1763–80) and Antonio Vilca (*fl* 1778–?1803). During the 18th century Zapata and the other members of the Cuzco school started producing works incorporating highly formal, idealized figures based on the engravings that had long been supplied to artists by the religious orders of Cuzco. The indigenous artists consequently lost all contact with the Spanish realist school, a process to which Zapata contributed. However, while using European prints as a guide, in many of his pictures there are various non-European features: elegant creoles, black slaves and such events as the epidemic of 1720 that affected the southern Andes. He is likely to have been influenced by such print series as the *Eulogia Mariana* by C. B. Schaefler (1684–1756), printed by M. Engelbrecht, which he interpreted in the Cuzco tradition, leading to paintings full of anecdotal scenes containing an abundance of trees, vegetation, oversize birds and such strong colours as vermilion and cobalt blue. His first known series of paintings consists of 24 works depicting the *Life of St Francis of Assisi* (1748) for the Capuchin Order in Santiago de Chile, followed by the series of 50 paintings for Cuzco Cathedral in 1755 and that of 73 works, executed *c.* 1762 in collaboration with Toledo y Gutiérrez, for the Jesuits at La Compañía in Cuzco. He is also known to have sent paintings to Humahuaca in Argentina, to Bolivia (then Alto Perú) and to be sold in Lima.

BIBLIOGRAPHY
E. Kuon: *Pintura cuzqueña: Presentación de la obra de Marcos Zapata* (BA thesis, U. Cuzco, 1970)
J. Mesa and T. Gisbert: *Historia de la pintura cuzqueña* (Lima, 1982), pp. 209–20

W. IAIN MACKAY

Zapotal. Pre-Columbian ceremonial site in central Veracruz, Mexico. It flourished *c.* AD 500–*c.* 800 and is notable for the large ceramic figures found there and for one of the few known temples in Mesoamerica dedicated to the god of the underworld. Zapotal has been plundered and some of its sculptures taken abroad; two seated female figures (Brussels, Mus. Royaux A. & Hist.; St Louis, MO, A. Mus.) are probably from Zapotal. Excavations at the site have been carried out by the Universidad Veracruzana since 1971, and most of the artefacts unearthed are in the Universidad Veracruzana, Museo de Antropología, Jalapa.

The site consists of mounds orientated along a north–south axis, two of which measure 10 m and 15 m in height. An offering of numerous terracotta figures and vessels, which had been broken for ritual purposes, was discovered in an artificial platform known as Mound 2 (75×35×4 m). Over 100 burials have also been found. Some contained 'smiling face' clay figurines, a type found only in the Veracruz region, and an ossuary composed of a column of 82 skulls and bones was also unearthed. The skeletal remains from tombs bear evidence of human sacrifices.

The imposing temple dedicated to the god of the underworld was discovered in Mound 2. This god was the most important deity in what is now the state of Veracruz and is represented by a seated figure, 1.60 m high, of unfired clay. Several layers of yellow, red, blue, green and white paint remain on the fragile sculpture, the only one of its kind known in Mesoamerica. It occupies the central part of the temple's basement (5.80×3.27 m) and is flanked by two L-shaped walls covered with paintings depicting richly attired figures. The sculpture has a partially skeletal body and wears a huge headdress decorated with skulls painted red and yellow and with zoomorphic masks, some of which are shown from the front and others in profile. Only the front and back sides are represented, and there is no sculptural continuity between the front of the figure, comprising the skull, ribcage and limbs, and the back, where the spinal column is clearly shown. There is a similar discontinuity in the modelling of other free-standing Pre-Columbian sculptures, for example the monumental Chalchiúhtlicue (water goddess) of Teotihuacán and the warrior atlantids at Tula. Temples dedicated to the cult of the god of the underworld are illustrated in later manuscripts: Codex Magliabechiano (Florence, Bib. N., fol. 67); Codex Borgia (Rome, Bib. Vaticana, fol. 52) and Codex Laud (Oxford, Bodleian Lib., fol. 26). However, the temple at Zapotal is the only one that has been excavated in Mesoamerica. A structure built to the north of this temple comprises nine levels, symbolizing the nine layers of the underworld, according to ancient Mesoamerican belief.

Other impressive works of art found at Zapotal include monumental terracotta figures, mainly female, between 1 and 1.50 m high (see fig.). Their breasts are uncovered, and they wear long skirts with belts that end in beautifully modelled serpent heads. They wear elaborate headdresses and hold ceremonial objects, possibly censers, some of which are decorated with human faces, skulls or, in one case, a feline head. The few figures whose facial features remain intact have large open mouths and crescent-shaped, half-closed eyes, indicating that they are dead. They probably represent deities associated with fertility, the earth and the underworld. Torres Guzmán (1975) identifies them as the same type as Late Post-Classic-period (*c.* 1200–1521) Cihuateteo deities (personified spirits of women who died in childbirth), although there is no conclusive evidence that these goddesses were venerated in the Classic period (*c.* AD 250–*c.* 900), when Zapotal was occupied. Such sculptures were accompanied by smaller ones of seated female figures, which lack the determinative attributes to represent deities. Monumental male figures, up to 1.70 m high, represent ritual performers.

For discussion of the arts of Pre-Columbian Mexico *see also* ME-SOAMERICA, PRE-COLUMBIAN.

BIBLIOGRAPHY
Codex Magliabechiano (*c.* 1566; Florence, Bib. N., MS. cl. xiii.3); facs. ed. Z. Nuttall as *The Book of the Life of the Ancient Mexicans, Containing an Account of their Rites and Superstitions* (Berkeley, 1903)
E. Seler: *Comentarios al Códice Borgia*, 3 vols (Mexico City, 1963)
Codex Laud (*c.* 14th century; Oxford, Bodleian, MS. Laud Misc. 678); facs. ed. C. A. Burland as *True-color Facsimile of the Old Mexican Manuscript* (Graz, 1966)
M. Torres Guzmán: 'Hallazgos en El Zapotal, Veracruz', *Bol. INAH*, n. s., ii (1972), pp. 3–8
M. Torres Guzmán, M. A. Reyes and J. Ortega: 'Proyecto Zapotal, Veracruz', *XIII Mesa redonda de la Sociedad mexicana de antropología y arqueología: 1975*, i (Mexico, 1975), pp. 323–30
N. Gutiérrez Solana and S. Hamilton: *Las esculturas en terracota de El Zapotal, Veracruz* (Mexico City, 1977)
M. Doppée and M. Graulich: 'Une Grande Statue en terre cuite du Veracruz (Mexique)', *Bull. Mus. Royaux A. & Hist.*, xlviii (1978), pp. 35–48
L. Parsons: *Pre-Columbian Art: The Morton D. May and the Saint Louis Art Museum Collections* (New York, 1980)
R. Pirazzini: 'The Cult of Death at El Zapotal, Veracruz', *Pre-Columbian Art History: Selected Readings*, ed. A. Cordy-Collins (Palo Alto, 1982), pp. 101–8
NELLY GUTIÉRREZ SOLANA

Zapotec. Pre-Columbian people and stylistic tradition in the Oaxaca region of Mexico. These people's name for themselves was Peni-Zaa ('real people'), but the term Zapotec ('people of the sweet fruit') is an Aztec improvisation based on the rough phonetic similarity of *ʒaa* and Aztec *tsa*. There is no simple Zapotec art style, rather an orderly uninterrupted sequence of styles stretching from *c.* 500 BC to *c.* AD 800. After 600 BC culture was centred around the hilltop city of MONTE ALBÁN. The Zapotec and MIXTEC peoples are still the most numerous of the Indian peoples in Oaxaca: the Zapotecs dominate the eastern portion of the state, the Mixtecs the western. Linguistic research, however, suggests that Zapotec inhabitants of the region could date back to *c.* 4500 BC.

1. CULTURAL CONTEXT. From 1931 the Mexican scholar Alfonso Caso began exploring Monte Albán and the Oaxaca Valley; his work remains a primary source for the study of Zapotec–Mixtec culture. The centuries of isolation essential to a rare case of homogeneous development like that of the Zapotec people of Monte Albán were favoured by topography: range after range of mountains on every side made communication with the central valleys of Oaxaca, at whose confluence Monte Albán rises, laborious and slow. Settled agricultural villages appeared in the valleys, as elsewhere in Mesoamerica, by about 2000 BC. Around 1350 BC finely modelled ceramic figurines were being made in the Valley of Oaxaca; these are easily distinguishable from those made elsewhere. About 1000 BC trade with the OLMEC centres of the Gulf Coast region was taking shell ornaments, pyrite mirrors and other products of the Valley of Oaxaca north-east across the mountains. Much of the shell came from the Pacific, being

Zapotal, figure of goddess, terracotta, h. 1.35 m, *c.* AD 500–*c.* 800 (Jalapa, Universidad Veracruzana, Museo de Antropología)

Zapotec figure of a woman wearing a twisted shawl as a head covering, a skirt and a *quechquemitl*, clay, h. 340 mm, *c.* AD 500 (Mexico City, Museo Nacional de Antropología)

transported north along rugged trails across other mountains. Pottery decorated with Olmec motifs was made and was sometimes traded north-west to the Valley of Mexico. The first recognizable manifestation of Zapotec individuality can perhaps be seen in fine, pre-Olmec figurines; ceramic sculpture was the medium preferred by the Zapotecs throughout their history (see fig.). Later the Olmec style affected all Mesoamerica, although its Valley of Oaxaca form was less completely Olmec than relative nearness to and trade connections with the Olmec heartland might suggest; the Zapotecs were apparently allies rather than subordinates. With the decline of the Olmec centres *c.* 600–*c.* 400 BC, the Valley of Oaxaca Zapotecs maintained their distinctive stylistic preferences, which became steadily more distinctive (*see* §2 below).

2. ARTISTIC DEVELOPMENT. The sequence of cultural stages defined at Monte Albán by Caso and his collaborators was derived from tombs and from multiple rebuildings. Zapotec material culture was first divided into five epochs (periods I–V; *see also* MONTE ALBÁN). Analysis of ceramic finds, however, showed that many continuities connected the first four divisions; only the fifth resulted from a sharp break with tradition. The five cultural stages were thus defined in terms of utilitarian and aesthetic traits, each one being an ensemble produced in a period of relative stability or slow change. They were separated by brief transitional periods of rapid development. Subsequent research repeatedly confirmed the sequence but added subdivisions and details of transition. After 1950 radiocarbon dates provided a firmer chronology and definitive proof of the sequence, which was applicable to many related sites other than Monte Albán itself.

Period I of the Zapotec style (*c.* 600–*c.* 200 BC), which followed the founding of Monte Albán, is in most senses not a beginning; it comes at the end of a centuries-long phase that might be termed 'Archaic Zapotec' (*c.* 2000–*c.* 600 BC). The formation of larger, urban communities provided more interaction among artists, and the new social setting weakened traditions that had governed creativity. Early Monte Albán culture was notably inventive, as its ceramic sculpture reveals. Endlessly varied pottery vessels incorporate animal and human forms in sturdy plain grey ware. Figurines represent people in ways recalling older styles, but the architecture is massive and boldly new. Stone sculpture represents little more than line drawings incised on flat surfaces; the most famous examples are the so-called *danzante* figures at Monte Albán (for illustration *see* MONTE ALBÁN). The only known examples of painting in Period I at Monte Albán are crude designs in broad lines on some pots.

Period II (*c.* 200 BC–*c.* AD 100) began gradually but has a distinctive character visible in a handful of masterpieces and in tendencies marking hundreds of lesser works and thousands of popular pieces, particularly from DAINZÚ. More colour occurs in ceramic wares and their decoration. Increasing social order is implicit in subtle artistic refinements, larger numbers of identifiable sacred figures and less variety in vessel shapes. Relatively large figures of elaborately costumed men suggest increasing social differentiation, while simple figurines disappear. Cyclopean masonry still occurs in public buildings, but large stones for this purpose had apparently become scarce on the mountain top. At Monte Albán some stones with incised *danzantes* of Period I (see above) were reused as ordinary construction elements. New inscriptions on flat stone were more complex and were executed in finer lines. Effigies of people and gods, modelled and incised to conform to vessel shapes in Period I, became increasingly independent, less subordinate to the shapes of vessels. Tombs of important people, which had been simple boxes made of adobe (mud-brick) blocks in Period I, took shapes symbolizing houses and were made of stone, as in later times. Even though it bridges the beginning of urbanism, Period I at Monte Albán was stylistically traditional, whereas Period II combined early vigour and variety with increasing urbanity, and led into a transitional phase preceding Period III.

Period III (*c.* AD 200–*c.* 750) was soon perceived by scholars as too complex for a single designation. It is now subdivided into IIIA (*c.* 200–500), the time of the highest achievements of Monte Albán style, and IIIB (*c.* 500–*c.* 750), which was at first 'baroque' and later increasingly marked by poor workmanship and aesthetic decline.

Period III ended with the Zapotec abandonment of Monte Albán, which was probably not a single event but a gradual process that took place from *c.* AD 600 to *c.* 900. Several tombs have wall paintings from the apogee of Period III (late IIIA–early IIIB) (*see* MESOAMERICA, PRE-COLUMBIAN, fig. 27). Assimilation of foreign elements and local survivals was complete, but the Zapotec style was not yet perceptibly decadent. Sacred symbols in the rich costumes of the personages depicted reveal their semi-divine status. Some tombs were used repeatedly as family members died; wall paintings might be altered hurriedly on such occasions. Rulers and their deeds were also recorded in stone reliefs: interest in élite genealogy apparently increased through the centuries, especially as the region's prosperity finally waned.

In Period IV (*c.* 750–*c.* 1000) descendants of the Monte Albán Zapotecs made offerings at the old city, even after abandonment, providing scanty remains of this period, which is more fully known at LAMBITYECO. Despite minor innovations and brief periods of prosperity at small cities in the Valley of Oaxaca, Zapotec culture and society were losing coherence during Period IV. After *c.* 900 Mixtec invaders met slight resistance. Mixtec rulers displaced their Zapotec counterparts, who then took control over other peoples in the Isthmus of Tehuantepec.

In the Valley of Oaxaca, the Mixtecs enforced their own ways, initiating Period V (*c.* 1000–1521), with the farming population of the valleys probably still partially Zapotec. Occupying Monte Albán—more for strategic than for sacred reasons—the Mixtecs repaired few of the now ruined structures; they clearly preferred to build anew at other places, such as YAGUL and MITLA.

Little more can be said of Zapotec art. In Period V a fortress-city was built on the slopes of Quiengola in the Isthmus of Tehuantepec, presumably by the Zapotecs, since it shows traces of late Monte Albán architecture. However, the ruins have yet to be excavated. Moreover, the pervasive Mixtecoid style of Mesoamerica's last centuries (*see* MIXTECA-PUEBLA) is in fact a development rooted in all three principal earlier traditions: Teotihuácan, Monte Albán and Maya. Even under Mixtec rule, a subtle Zapotec role may be suspected in Oaxaca's final cultural resurgence, exemplified by Tomb 7 and the Mitla palaces (for illustration *see* MITLA) of the central valleys, which had been Zapotec through many previous centuries.

BIBLIOGRAPHY
A. Caso: *El tesoro de Monte Albán* (Mexico, 1969)
J. Whitecotton: *The Zapotecs* (Norman, 1977, rev. 1984)
J. Paddock: 'Reflexiones en torno a la Tumba 7 de Monte Albán, cincuenta años después de su descubrimiento', *Cuad. Arquit. Mesoamer.*, vii (1986), pp. 3–8
J. Whitecotton: *Zapotec Elite Ethnohistory*, Vanderbilt U., Pubns in Anthropol., 39 (Nashville, 1990)

JOHN PADDOCK

Zar [Zara], **Johann** [Giovanni; Ian; Jan; Johannes] **Gregor** [Gregori; Gregorius; Georg] **del** [von der]. *See* SCHARDT, JOHANN GREGOR VAN DER.

Zaragoza, Lorenzo. *See* LORENZO ZARAGOZA.

Zaragoza y Ebri, Agustín Bruno. *See* BRIZGUZ Y BRU, ATHANASIO GENARO.

Zariñena, Juan. *See* SARIÑENA, JUAN.

Zaritsky, Yossef (*b* Borispol, Ukraine, 1891; *d* Tel Aviv, 1985). Israeli painter. He graduated from the Academy of Arts in Kiev in 1914, where he had been influenced by the watercolours of Mikhail Vrubel. In 1923 he emigrated to Palestine, where he lived first in Jerusalem and then from 1927 in Tel Aviv. From 1927 to 1929 he worked and studied in Paris. He worked almost entirely in watercolours from 1923 until the early 1940s, producing still-lifes and landscapes. The watercolour *Safed* (1923; Jerusalem, Israel Mus.), with its mosaic-like patches of colour, is characteristic of the works of the 1920s, which were mainly of landscapes around Jerusalem, Haifa Bay and Safed. In the 1930s he painted views from his Tel Aviv studio or flowers on a window-sill, as in *View from the Window over Tel Aviv* (1935; Amsterdam, Stedel. Mus.).

In 1948 Zaritsky was one of the co-founders of the NEW HORIZONS group and soon came to be its leader. His painting developed into what was called lyrical abstraction, which later evolved into a school in Israeli art. Typical of this and his later style is *Painting, Triptych* (1967; Jerusalem, Israel Mus.), which used thickly applied paint in a carefully composed, roughly geometric structure. He did not move entirely away from realistic models, however. In 1950 he drew from landscapes in his work and in 1956 from the paintings of Vermeer, though in both cases the lyrical abstract style remained. From 1954 to 1956 he lived and worked in Paris and Amsterdam. He was a great influence on many younger Israeli artists, and in 1960 he was awarded the Israel Prize.

For an illustration of a painting by Zaritsky *see* ISRAEL, fig. 3.

BIBLIOGRAPHY
B. Tammuz and M. Wykes-Joyce, eds: *Art in Israel* (London, 1966), pp. 28–30, 32–3
Agam, Lifshitz, Zaritsky (exh. cat. by Y. Fischer, London, Whitechapel A.G., 1969)

Zaroto. *See* LUZZO, LORENZO.

Zar Tepe. Site in southern Uzbekistan, 14 km north-west of the old city of Termez. Occupying an area of 16.9 ha, it was, after Termez and Dalverzin Tepe, the third largest of the settlements that flourished in the valley of the Surkhan River during the Kushana period (1st century BC–4th century AD). It was subject to the Sasanians *c.* AD 360–80, and from the late 4th century until its destruction it was probably under Kidarite domination. It is this last period that has been most fully excavated. Excavations began in 1951–2 and were resumed in the 1970s by the Bactrian Expedition of the Academy of Sciences, USSR. The fortified city (400 m sq.) has four corners approximately orientated towards the cardinal points. The walls were reinforced with semicircular towers at intervals of 35 m and were surrounded on three sides by a moat and an earthen rampart. At the northern corner stood a fortified citadel 120 m sq. A similar fortified area, 60 m sq., was built into the southern corner. Two city gates were located near each of these strongholds, and a fifth gate has been detected in the south-west wall. Outside the walls a small Buddhist stupa and the fortified dwelling of Kuyov Kurgan have been uncovered.

Within the city a palace, residential blocks, a Buddhist shrine and fortifications have been excavated. Kushana traditions survived the fall of the dynasty, as can be seen in the sculpture (which reproduces Gandharan forms), the terracotta finds and the manufacturing techniques and decoration of ceramic wares. To a lesser degree, innovative Indian, Iranian and even Late Roman decorative motifs are also visible in the terracottas and ceramics of this period. Buddhism maintained its popularity among the urban population. In addition to sculpture, local terracotta statuettes of Buddhas or bodhisattvas and ceramic wares decorated with stamped Buddhist symbols were produced. The finds of the Kushana, Sasanian and Kidarite periods (St Petersburg, Inst. Hist. Mat. Cult.) show that the process of urban development in this region was not halted by the Sasanian conquest.

BIBLIOGRAPHY
V. M. Masson: 'Zar-tepe: Kushanskiy gorod v severnoy Baktrii' [Zar Tepe: a Kushana city in northern Bactria], *Istoriya i kul'tura antichnogo mira* [History and culture of the ancient world] (Moscow, 1977), pp. 138–43
B. Ya. Stavisky: *Kushanskaya Baktriya: Problemy istorii i kul'tury* (Moscow, 1977); Fr. trans. as *La Bactriane sous les Kushans: Problèmes d'histoire et culture* (Paris, 1986), pp. 272–3
V. A. Zav'yalov: 'Raskopki kvartala pozdnekushanskogo vremeni na gorodishche Zar-tepe v 1975–1976 gg.' [Excavations of a quarter dating from the late Kushana period at the site of Zar Tepe in 1975–6], *Sov. Arkheol.* (1979), no. 3, pp. 141–53
T. D. Annayev: 'Raskopki rannesrednevekovoy usad'by Kuyov-kurgan v severnoy Tokharistane' [Excavations of the early medieval farmstead of Kuyov Kurgan in northern Tokharistan], *Sov. Arkheol.* (1984), no. 2, pp. 188–200
V. A. ZAV'YALOV

Zarudny, Ivan (Petrovich) (*d* 1727). Russian architect and painter. He worked first in the Ukraine, and in 1701 he was invited to Moscow to enter the service of Peter I, Tsar and Emperor of Russia. He also superintended icon painting in Russia (from 1707). His principal work is the church of the Archangel Gabriel (1701–7; see RUSSIA, fig. 10), known as the Menshikov Tower, in Moscow. Its composition is based on the traditional 'octagon on cube' pattern, comprising two superimposed cubes surmounted by three octagonal stages. The building, which surpassed in height the hitherto tallest structure in the city, the bell-tower of Ivan the Great (1505–8) in the Kremlin, was topped by a dome, a gilded spire and the figure of an angel, also gilded (top storey destr. 1723). West European Baroque forms prevail in the architectural and artistic embellishment of the exterior and interior. Richly moulded decoration and sculptural motifs with angels' heads together make up an emotionally complex, somewhat capricious picture. It is likely that Zarudny was involved in the building of the church of St John the Warrior (1709–13) on Yakimanka (now Dimitrova) Street, the cathedrals at the Zaikonospassky Monastery (rebuilt 1717–20) and Varsonof'yevsky Monastery (1709–30; destr.) and the gate-house chapel of the Virgin of Tikhvin (1713–14) at the Don Monastery. Zarudny designed triumphal arches to mark Russian military victories: the Synodal Gates (1709) at the beginning of Nikol'skaya Street and gates (1721; destr.) near Prince Menshikov's house. Their colourful decorative compositions, combining painting, handsome carving and a pilaster order, demonstrated the still-unfamiliar techniques of western European art to the inhabitants of Moscow. He also designed iconostases (1720) for the cathedral of the Transfiguration in TALLINN and the cathedral of SS Peter and Paul (1722–7) in St Petersburg.

BIBLIOGRAPHY
A. Akselrod: 'Menshikova bashnya v yeyo pervonachal'nom vide' [The original appearance of the Menshikov Tower], *Arkhit. SSSR*, x (1939), pp. 57–61
V. P. Vygolov: 'Novoye o tvorchestve I. P. Zarudnogo [New details of the work of I. P. Zarudny], *Arkhit. SSSR*, x (1953), p. 30
M. A. Il'in and V. P. Vygolov: *Moskovskiye triumfal'nyye vrata rubezha XVII–XVIII vv.: Materialy po teorii i istorii iskusstva* [Moscow triumphal arches at the turn of the 18th century: materials for the theory and history of art] (Moscow, 1956), pp. 106–77
Y. P. Kunitskaya: 'Menshikova bashnya' [The Menshikov Tower], *Arkhit. Nasledstvo*, ix (1959), pp. 157–68
N. A. YEVSINA

Zaryanko, Sergey (Konstantinovich) (*b* Lyady, Mogilevsk province [now Vitebsk region], Belarus', 6 Oct 1818; *d* Moscow, 1 Jan 1871). Russian painter of Belarusian birth. He bought himself out of serfdom in the mid-1820s and went with his family to St Petersburg. Zaryanko first studied painting with Vasily Mikhaylovich Avrorin (1805–55), a pupil of Aleksey Venetsianov, and soon attracted the interest of Venetsianov himself, who in 1834 sent Zaryanko to the St Petersburg Academy of Arts. Along with other pupils of Venetsianov, Zaryanko painted interiors of the Winter Palace, such as *View of the Field-Marshal Hall in the Winter Palace* (1836) and *View of the Throne Room* (1838; both St Petersburg, Hermitage). He first attracted popular acclaim for his group portrait *View of the Hall in the Law School with Groups of Teachers and Pupils* (1840–41; St Petersburg, Rus. Mus.), as notable for its treatment of light and perspective in the interior as for the individual characterization of the figures gathered there. With his painting of 1843, *View of the Interior of the Naval Cathedral of St Nicholas* (St Petersburg, Rus. Mus.), his series of interior scenes came to an end.

Zaryanko then moved to Moscow, where he taught drawing for three years at the Aleksandrov Orphanage Institute and the Moscow Palace School of Architecture. In 1846 he moved back to St Petersburg, where he taught at the Konstantinovsky Military School and spent his ten most productive years as a portrait painter. Zaryanko's earlier St Petersburg portraits, such as those of the collector *Fedor Ivanovich Pryanishnikov* (1844; St Petersburg, Rus. Mus.) and *Aleksey Venetsianov* (1840; Ivanovo, Reg. A. Mus.), are notable for their intimacy, absence of ostentation or distracting details and focus on the subject's face. In the later 1840s Zaryanko produced a number of group and family portraits, making the transition from more intimate to highly public work. His *Portrait of the Vice-President of the Academy of Arts, the Sculptor Fyodor Tolstoy* (1850; St Petersburg, Rus. Mus.) was especially acclaimed for its compelling and honest record of the sitter. Among his more remarkable portraits of the 1850s are *Mariya Vasiliyevna Vorontsova* (Moscow, Tret'yakov Gal.) and *Aleksandr Sergeyevich Taneyev* (St Petersburg, Rus. Mus.); in the latter great care is taken with the details, and the figure as a whole has a strong sense of volume. In two portraits of women from 1854, *Anis'ya Petrovna Lesnikova* and *Natal'ya Vasil'yevna Sokurova* (both St Petersburg, Rus. Mus.), he employed a similar presentation: a plain dark background and dark clothing, strong sidelighting to throw features into relief and a bright spot of detail on dress or chair. In such works Zaryanko paid the same careful attention to accessories as to conveying facial expression. The naturalistic accuracy and concreteness of this approach were a means of coming nearer to nature, but also gestures against a Romantic poeticization of the portrait image.

By the middle of the 19th century Zaryanko was one of the most popular portrait painters in Moscow and St Petersburg, with a wide and varied circle of clients. In his later years his efforts to please these clients led to repetitive use of the same techniques and patterns, an over-use of superficial effects and a loss of taste and refinement. From 1856 he dedicated himself entirely to teaching at the Moscow School of Painting, Sculpture and Architecture. Among his pupils were Vasily Perov, Nikolay Nevryov, Vasily Pukirev and Vladimir Makovsky. Zaryanko also painted icons for churches (e.g. for the church of the Moscow military school and for the Church of St Sophia, Puskin).

BIBLIOGRAPHY
G. Smirnov: *S. K. Zaryanko* (Moscow, 1951)
T. Alekseyeva: *Khudozhniki shkoly Venetsianova* [Artists of the school of Venetsianov] (Moscow, 1982)

G. A. PRINTSEVA

Zarza, Diogo de. See SARÇA, DIOGO DE.

Zarza, Vasco de la (*fl* Ávila, 1499; *d* Ávila, 1524). Spanish sculptor and architect. He may have trained in Italy, whence he introduced Italian Renaissance forms to New Castile, particularly in Ávila. In 1499 he established himself at Ávila as a carver in alabaster. He was also active as an architect, and in 1508 he was involved with the reconstruction of the cloisters in Ávila Cathedral. He carved the wall tomb (*c.* 1515) of *Archbishop Alonso Carrillo de Albornoz* in the chapel of S Ildefonso, Toledo Cathedral, a work with a strong Italianate influence perhaps partly due to the presence of Domenico Fancelli in Ávila. The monument is in the form of a triumphal arch, but all surfaces are carved with a profusion of decorative motifs reminiscent of the Lombard school. In 1518 de la Zarza completed the monument to Bishop Alonso de Madrigal, known as *El Tostado*, in the *trasaltar mayor* (the area behind the altar) of Ávila Cathedral. The seated figure of the bishop writing at a lectern is dramatically posed, and the work displays virtuoso carving of the drapery. In 1523 de la Zarza was advising on the building of Salamanca Cathedral. At the time of his death he was said to be working with Alonso Berruguete on the retable of La Mejorada in Olmedo. He had also begun carving the altars of the transepts in Ávila Cathedral, which his collaborators completed.

BIBLIOGRAPHY
J. M. Azcárate: *Escultura del siglo XVI*, A. Hisp., xiii (Madrid, 1958), pp. 96–104
J. M. Parrado del Olmo: *Los escultores Sequidores de Berruguete en Ávila* (Ávila, 1981), pp. 98–101
F. Checa: *Pintura y escultura del renacimiento en España, 1450–1600* (Madrid, 1983), pp. 109–10

MARJORIE TRUSTED

Zasche [Čaše], **Ivan** (*b* Jablonec, Slovakia, 1826; *d* Zagreb, 1 Jan 1863). Slovak painter, active in Croatia. Along with the Slovene Mihael Stroj and the Croats Vjekoslav Karas and Ivan Simonetti, he is one of the small number of important painters in mid-19th-century Croatia. He worked in a Viennese porcelain manufactory, and in 1846 he enrolled at the Akademie der Bildenden Künste in Vienna, but he left after two years. A painter in the Biedermeier style, he successfully exhibited his first important work, *Landscape from Kobenzel*, in Vienna in 1848. Two years later he accepted an invitation from Bishop Haulik to come to Zagreb, where he settled for the rest of his life. He painted a number of large, representative portraits in oil as well as a series of smaller, more intimate ones, often in miniature, in watercolour. His treatment was in the Viennese manner and his subjects were members of the nobility or the bourgeoisie (e.g. portrait of *Aleksandrina Kulmer*, 1859; Zagreb, Kulmer priv. col.). On his travels through Lika and the Croatian coast in 1855 he painted a number of fine, translucent watercolours and executed a series of accurate drawings that are considered to be among his most notable achievements (examples, U. Zagreb Lib. and Zagreb, Gal. Mod. A.). He also painted a number of religious compositions for churches in northern Croatia.

BIBLIOGRAPHY
L. Babić: *Umjetnost kod Hrvata u XIX. stoljeću* [Art in 19th-century Croatia] (Zagreb, 1943), pp. 48–50
Slikarstvo XIX. stoljeća u Hrvatskoj [Painting in 19th-century Croatia] (exh. cat. by L. Babić, Zagreb, Slika Gal., 1961)
M. Peić: 'Ivan Zasche', *Republika* (1964)
M. Schweider: *Slikar Ivan Zasche* (Zagreb, 1975)

BORIS VIŽINTIN

Zasinger, Matthäus. *See under* MASTERS, ANONYMOUS, AND MONOGRAMMISTS, §III: MASTER MZ.

Zau. See SAIS.

Zauch, Hans (*fl* Sweden, 1663–6). German stuccoist, also active in Sweden. His earliest known works were stuccos in the palace (early 1660s; destr. 1944) of C. G. Wrangel in Stralsund, where he co-operated with GIOVANNI ANHTONI. They arrived together in Sweden in 1663 and executed work in Wrangel's Stockholm palace on Riddarholmen. Later, up to 1664, in Skokloster Castle, they created three ceilings in the master suite, either working together or separately. The Skokloster ceiling (1663–4) in the King's Hall, which links the two halves of the master suite, is a vast surface clearly divided by sturdy, richly profiled frames into a central octagonal compartment and four round corner panels. In the central compartment, the figure of a young man dressed in Roman soldier's costume, apparently pouring liquid from a drinking horn into the nose or eye of a winged dragon, has been interpreted as that of Apollo, Jason or (most likely) Daniel. In the four corner panels are depicted figures representing Europe, Asia, Africa and America. Between the panels are decorative figures and flowers and heavy scroll ornaments. The heavy, almost toppling sculptural quality of the ceiling is set off by bright colours, at least partially preserved in their original state.

SVKL
BIBLIOGRAPHY
E. Andrén: *Skokloster* (Stockholm, 1948)
G. Beard: *Stucco and Decorative Plasterwork in Europe* (London, 1983),
p. 69
TORBJÖRN FULTON

Zauner, Franz Anton (*b* Untervalpatann, Tyrol, 5 July 1746; *d* Vienna, 3 March 1822). Austrian sculptor and teacher. He trained initially under the sculptor Balthasar Horer, a relation on his mother's side, and under Josef Deutschmann in Passau. Subsequent academic tuition in Vienna, from Jakob Schletterer (1699–1774) and Wilhelm Bayer, however, was a decisive influence on him. Zauner's first official commission in Vienna, received through his patron, Wenzel Anton, Prince Kaunitz-Rietburg, was for a sandstone fountain with the figures of *The Danube* and *The Enns* for the Ehrenhof at Schönbrunn (1775; *in situ*): here Zauner's work was still strongly reminiscent of the Baroque classicism of Georg Raffael Donner. Even so, it contrasted with its counterpart at Schönbrunn by the older sculptor Johann Baptist Hagenauer, by virtue of its clearly arranged figure-composition, which Zauner directed towards one principal viewpoint. Zauner's fuller adoption of a strict classicism occurred in Rome, where he stayed from 1776 to 1781, along with the painter, Heinrich Füger, as an Imperial–Royal pensioner. In Rome, Zauner was a member of the private academy of the Swiss sculptor Alexander Trippel. In keeping with the views on the exemplary role of ancient art, argued by Johann Joachim Winckelmann, Zauner initially produced direct copies from antique models (including the Farnese *Hercules* and the *Apollo Belvedere*), which he sent to Vienna as evidence of his artistic progress and as teaching material for the Akademie. Zauner also produced works that were not copies but were, rather, in the 'spirit' of antiquity: a *Perseus and Andromeda* group (plaster of Paris, 1777; Vienna, Belvedere) and a statuette of *Clio* (marble, 1779; Vaduz, Samml. Liechtenstein).

Returning to Vienna in 1781, Zauner started to teach at the Akademie. He continued to profit from the patronage of Prince Kaunitz-Rietburg, who probably enabled Zauner to meet the wealthy and appreciative Christian Johann, Graf von Fries (1719–85), and his sons Josef (1765–88) and Moritz, who also became Zauner's patrons. In 1783 they commissioned Zauner to complete the façade sculpture for their town palace, which Johann Ferdinand von Hohenberg had erected on what is now the Josefsplatz, and which was one of Vienna's few buildings in a strictly classical style. Surviving modelli (Vienna, Belvedere) record the appearance of Zauner's allegorical figures of *Trade* and *Liberty*. Zauner also provided four vases, with relief work, in front of the palace (now Bad Vöslau, Schlosspark). Also for the von Fries family, Zauner produced the tomb monument to *Graf Johann and Graf Josef von Fries* (Carrara marble, 1788–90; destr.). Combining a prototype from antiquity (a Late Classical *Menelaus* group) with idealized portrait heads, this work clearly reflected Zauner's stay in Rome.

Zauner also accepted commissions from many other sources. As a monument in honour of the scientist Ignaz von Born, he produced a sculpture based on Praxiteles's *Eros*: this is known as the *Genius Bornii* (gilt plaster of Paris, 1785; version, Vienna, Belvedere). Zauner, like Ignaz von Born a freemason, adorned the figure with freemasons' emblems. Another sculpture reflecting the Praxitelean ideal of beauty was that of two *Adoring Angels*, sculpted in 1784 for the high altar of the Augustiner Hofkirche in Vienna (now Sarasdorf, parish church). The same year Zauner became a full Professor of Sculpture at the Akademie. The younger generation of Viennese sculptors regarded his interpretation of Winckelmann's 'beautiful style' as no less exemplary than Antonio Canova's highly respected work. In his portrait busts Zauner succeeded in creating a balance between naturalism of expression and idealized likeness. Among the best examples are the bust of *Joseph von Sonnenfels* (see fig.) and the more austere bust of the *Emperor Francis II* (1796; version, Vienna, Belvedere).

Zauner's later tomb monuments show the influence of Romanticism in their commitment to sentiment. In 1790–91, after a sketch by Heinrich Füger, Zauner designed a tomb monument for *Field Marshal Laudon* with the separate figure of a *Mourning Knight* seated next to the sarcophagus (Wienerwald bei Hadersdorf). In 1793–5 Zauner produced a tomb monument to *Emperor Leopold II* in the Georgskapelle of the Augustinerkirche in Vienna,

Franz Anton Zauner: *Joseph von Sonnenfels*, Carrara marble, 1787 (Vienna, Gemäldegalerie der Akademie der Bildenden Künste)

with a mourning figure of *Germania*, and with structural elements in green marble and figures in white marble. In the reliefs he diverged from austere layering of surfaces in order to incorporate pictorial elements. Similarly, in the wall tomb of *Graf von Losymthal* (1792; Mariazell, pilgrimage church) the relief decoration depicted a ship on the high seas.

In classical tradition, and in keeping with heroic subject-matter, in the years 1790–1806 Zauner produced the monument to *Emperor Joseph II* for the Josephsplatz in Vienna, a work commissioned by Emperor Francis II. This was the first monumental equestrian statue in Vienna and one of the main achievements of classicism in Austrian sculpture. Zauner's contemporaries admired the work above all for its masterly technique: without any outside help, Zauner developed his own process of bronze casting (a trial casting of the monument, on a smaller scale, is in the botanical garden in Vienna, Schloss Schönbrunn) and he thereby departed from the process of lead-casting customary in Vienna. Zauner's work was also admired for its aesthetic qualities; and, for the first time in Viennese artistic life, the appreciation of non-specialists is also recorded. Initially, Zauner had planned a standing figure of the *Emperor* (wax model, Vienna, Belvedere; terracotta *bozzetto*, Vienna, Hist. Mus.), but eventually he returned to the prototype of the ancient equestrian statue of *Marcus Aurelius* (*see* ROME, ANCIENT, fig. 61). The Emperor is shown in ancient Roman costume mounted on a calmly striding horse, as the 'father of the Fatherland', with his right hand held out over his people, as if in protection. Simplicity and austerity are also found in the two bronze reliefs on the base, allegorical celebrations of the Emperor's virtues and actions. This work brought Zauner a title and a lifelong annuity. In 1806 he became Director of the Akademie, and until his retirement in 1815 he devoted himself exclusively to his teaching duties.

BIBLIOGRAPHY
Thieme–Becker
H. Burg: *Der Bildhauer F. A. Zauner und seine Zeit* (Vienna, 1915) [with extensive bibliog.]
H. Hildebrandt: 'Ein Beitrag zu F. A. Zauners Denkmal der Grafen Fries', *Festschrift O. Schmitt* (Stuttgart, 1950), p. 291
M. Poch-Kalous: 'Wiener Plastik im 19. Jahrhundert' *Geschichte der Stadt Wien: Plastik in Wien*, n. s., vii/3 (1970)
Klassizismus in Wien: Architektur und Plastik (exh. cat., ed. R. Weissenberger; Vienna, 1978)
G. Heinz: 'Die figürlichen Künste zur Zeit Joseph Haydns', *J. Haydn und seine Zeit* (exh. cat., ed. G. Mraz, G. Mraz and G. Schlag; Eisenstadt, 1982), pp. 175–95

INGEBORG SCHEMPER-SPARHOLZ

Zavara [Zavāra; Zawareh]. Small town in central Iran. According to the geographer Yaqut (*d* 1229), Zavara existed in Sasanian times, and ancient fortifications and a fire temple could be seen there in the medieval period, but the town is now known for two mosques. The congregational mosque (1135–6) is the earliest extant example of the standard type of Iranian mosque, with four iwans grouped around a court and a dome behind the qibla iwan. It is rectangular in plan and has a side entrance, minaret and barrel-vaulted roof supported by piers. The elaborately carved stucco mihrab was redone in 1156–7, at the same time that the mosque in nearby ARDISTAN was revamped. The four-iwan plan links the congregational mosque at Zavara with others in a regional group centred in Isfahan

(*see* ISLAMIC ART, §II, 5(i)(b)). The smaller Pa Minar Mosque ('Mosque at the foot of the minaret') is notable for its early minaret (1068–9) and for the stucco decoration on the walls and arches of the single bays around the court. On stylistic grounds Peterson dated some of the stucco carving to the late 9th century or the 10th and suggested that the mosque occupies a pre-Islamic site because of the irregular plan, but the mosque's chronology is complicated by the fact that the stucco revetment was redone in the 14th century and the east side of the mosque repaired in the 20th century.

BIBLIOGRAPHY
A. Godard: 'Ardistan et Zawārè', *Āthār-é Īrān*, i (1936), pp. 296–309
S. R. Peterson: 'The Masjid-i Pā Minār in Zavāreh: A Redating and Analysis of Early Islamic Iranian Stucco', *Artibus Asiae*, v (1978), pp. 60–90
S. S. Blair: *The Monumental Inscriptions of Early Islamic Iran and Transoxiana* (Leiden, 1991), pp. 137–9

S. J. VERNOIT

Zavattari [Zavatari]. Italian family of painters. The earliest member of the family documented as a painter was Cristoforo (di Francesco) Zavattari (*fl* Milan, 1404–9; *d* Milan, before 24 Jan 1414). Members of the family continued to work as painters in Lombardy until the mid-16th century. In 1404 Cristoforo was employed by the works of Milan Cathedral to examine and assess the value of stained-glass windows executed by Niccolò da Venezia (*fl* 1391–1415); in 1409 he gilded a capital destined for one of the pilasters in the cathedral's apse and several other figures. In February 1417 Cristoforo's son, Franceschino (di Cristoforo) Zavattari (*fl* Milan, before 1414; *d* Milan, 1453–7), was employed by the cathedral deputies to design and paint a large number of stained-glass windows, illustrating New Testament scenes; although he began work on the windows and was paid for what he did, nine months later the project was given to Maffiolo da Cremona for completion.

The most important surviving work by members of the Zavattari family is the cycle of frescoes, consisting of five registers of scenes from the *Life of Queen Teodolinda* (see fig.) in the Teodolinda Chapel, Monza Cathedral. An elaborate inscription dated 1444 in the fourth register specifies that all but the vault was painted by the family. Modern scholars have identified between two and four distinct hands at work in the frescoes thought to have been executed by the Zavattari family. However, a contract of 10 March 1445 complicates the problem considerably. According to this document, Franceschino Zavattari and his sons Gregorio (di Franceschino) Zavattari (*fl* before 1445; *d* Milan, after 23 Nov 1498) and Giovanni (di Franceschino) Zavattari (*fl* before 1445; *d* Milan, 1479) had, in the course of the year, to complete half of the unfinished work in the chapel; if the authorities were satisfied, the painters were to finish the decorations in 1446. It is certainly possible that the Zavattari had signed earlier contracts providing for the execution of the first three registers of frescoes, though no such contracts have been found. The date on the inscription (1444) presents greater difficulties, though it is conceivable that the final digit has been altered in the course of restoration. The decorations for the chapel were previously thought to have been commissioned by Filippo Maria Visconti, 3rd

Zavattari family: fresco from the series *Life of Queen Teodolinda* (?1444–6), Teodolinda Chapel, Monza Cathedral

Duke of Milan; in fact, the work done in 1445 and 1446—presumably the fourth and fifth registers—was ordered by the cathedral building authorities and a representative of the comune of Monza.

The Teodolinda fresco cycle is the most important of the few surviving examples of Lombard painting of the first half of the 15th century. The effect of these spirited narrative scenes, packed with incidental anecdotal detail and rich decoration, is generally homogeneous, despite the intervention of at least three painters, one of them—Franceschino—considerably older than the others. Not surprisingly, the decorations reveal considerable familiarity with the art of Gentile da Fabriano, Masolino and especially of Pisanello, all three of whom had worked in Lombardy. The frescoes are, however, completely lacking in the monumental quality that characterizes the best work of the Zavattaris' more famous contemporaries: they are like a series of miniatures painted on a large scale.

In 1450 Ambrogio (di Franceschino) Zavattari (*fl* Milan, before 1456; *d* Milan, 26 Dec 1512), Franceschino's third son, and another painter, Giovanni Pietro Landriani, rented a studio in Pavia. In 1453 Ambrogio, Franceschino and Gregorio were painting at the Certosa di Pavia, though none of the works executed survives. In 1456 Ambrogio gilded a keystone depicting *St John the Evangelist* for the deputies of Milan Cathedral; three years later he painted a *Maestà* for the cathedral's high altar.

In May 1460 Gregorio Zavattari was once again in Monza. It is possible that he executed the fresco of *St Catherine of Alexandria* (Monza Cathedral) at this time. A second fresco in Monza Cathedral, a *Virgin and Child*, of less certain attribution, may be by Gregorio as well. In December 1462 Gregorio and Giovanni Zavattari and Giacomo Vismara agreed to decorate the apse of S Vittore al Corpo, Milan; Ambrogio Zavattari (Vismara's son-in-law) later joined in the project (destr.), which was completed in 1464. In 1466–7 Giovanni Zavattari painted a fresco (destr.) in the refectory of the Olivetan monastery at Baggio. In 1475 Gregorio painted his only documented independent work, the signed and dated fresco of the *Virgin and Child* in the Santuario della Madonna dei Miracoli, Corbetta. This is an attractive but weak picture that makes no concessions to contemporary artistic trends.

Three of Giovanni's four sons were painters: Francesco (di Giovanni) Zavattari (*b* Milan, before 1459; *d* Milan, after 21 May 1484), Guido (di Giovanni) Zavattari (*b* Milan, before 1459; *d* Milan, 1510) and Gerolamo (di Giovanni) Zavattari (*b* Milan, after 1459; *d* Milan, between Nov 1522 and May 1525). In 1479 Francesco and his uncle Gregorio were commissioned by Bianca Trivulzio to paint frescoes of scenes from the *Life of St Margaret* (destr.) in S Margherita, Milan. In the same year Francesco Zavattari, Guido Zavattari and Giorgio della Chiesa undertook the decoration (destr.) of the vault of the chapel of the Immaculate Conception in S Francesco Grande, Milan. In 1487–8 Gregorio painted 'certain pictures'—no doubt frescoes (destr.)—for a confraternity chapel in Santa Croce, Milan. In 1506 Guido painted an altarpiece and a lectern for Giovanni Battista Barbavara. Nothing is known of Gerolamo's activity as a painter, though his life is fairly well documented. The career of Giovanni Angelo (di Ambrogio) Zavattari (*fl* Milan, *c*. 1500–50), the only one of Ambrogio's sons to become a painter, is obscure.

Other works attributed to the Zavattari include a large polyptych of the *Virgin and Child with Saints* (Rome, Mus. N. Castel Sant'Angelo; Rome, priv. col., see 1984 exh. cat., pp. 8–9), for which both the specific attribution and the dating present considerable problems, a *Virgin of*

Humility (untraced, see 1984 exh. cat., p. 61, pl. 53), an *Assumption of the Virgin* (ex-priv. col., Rome), a *Crucifixion with Saints* (Milan, S Cristoforo sul Naviglio), a fresco of the *Virgin and Child* (Bosco in Sesto S Giovanni, Santuario della Madonna) and a fresco fragment depicting a scene from Petrarch's *Triumphus cupidinis* (Angera, Rocca). It is extremely difficult to assess the validity of these attributions; all the paintings are in poor condition. While the attributed works have some qualities in common with the Teodolinda frescoes, that work, and the style of the Zavattari in general, must have influenced dozens of Milanese painters. In addition to these large-scale works, three packs of tarot cards have been associated with the Zavattari: the Tarocchi Brambilla (Milan, Brera), the Tarocchi Colleoni or Baglioni (Bergamo, Gal. Accad. Carrara; New York, Pierpont Morgan Lib.) and the Tarocchi Visconti di Modrone (New Haven, CT, Yale U., Beinecke Lib.). All of the cards are closer in style to Bonifacio Bembo, to whom they have traditionally been attributed. Similarly the illustrations in the *History of Lancelot* (1449; Florence, Bib. N. Cent., Cod. Palatino 556), recently attributed to Franceschino Zavattari, have been more convincingly given to Bembo.

BIBLIOGRAPHY

G. Algeri: *Gli Zavattari* (Rome, 1981) [with bibliog.]
Il polittico degli Zavattari in Castel Sant'Angelo: Contributi per la pittura tardogotica lombarda (exh. cat., Rome, Mus. N. Castel S Angelo, 1984) [with bibliog.]
J. Shell: 'La cappella di Teodolinda', *Il Duomo di Monza* (Milan, 1988)

JANICE SHELL

Zawareh. See ZAVARA.

Zawiya. See under KHANAQAH.

Zaydi. Muslim dynasty that ruled in parts of the Yemen from the late 9th century AD to the 20th. The Zaydi imams traced their descent to the Prophet Muhammad and took their name from Zayd (*d* AD 740), the son of the fourth Shi'ite imam. The Zaydi imamate in the Yemen was established by Yahya al-Hadi (854–911) who arrived there in 889, but his austere code of behaviour initially won little success and he was forced to leave. He returned in 896 and established his seat at Sa'da, to the north of San'a'. He won the allegiance of several tribes by acting as a mediator in tribal disputes, but his influence remained precarious. After his death his followers remained in the Yemen, and the Zaydi imamate continued to claim authority by divine right, although there was no strict dynastic criterion for the election of imams. Based in the north of the country, the power of the Zaydi imams varied over the centuries; occasionally it reached as far as San'a'. The movement was forced underground by the advent of the SULAYHID dynasty (*reg* 1047–1138) and by the expansion of Ayyubid power after 1174. There was some revival of Zaydi power in the early years of the RASULID dynasty (*reg* 1229–1454), but it floundered at the end of the 13th century. The imamate was revived by al-Qasim al-Mansur (*reg c.* 1592–1620) who led Yemeni opposition to Ottoman expansion in the region, a policy continued by his son al-Mu'ayyad (*reg* 1620–44). Building activity in San'a' was promoted under al-'Abbas al-Mahdi (*reg* 1747–75). The imams continued to rule northern Yemen and led the opposition during the second Ottoman occupation (1872–1918). Zaydi rule was brought to an end by the revolution of 1962.

Zaydi mosques, such as those at Zafar Dhibin (*c.* 1200) and the mosque of al-Hadi at Sa'da (1340) adopted several features introduced by the Sulayhids, such as a wider central aisle and domed mihrab bay. The Zaydi imams were buried under tombs richly decorated on the interior with elaborate inscription bands and carved stucco. This conservative and distinct Zaydi style of building was preserved in the northern highlands (*see* ISLAMIC ART, §§II, 5(ii)(d) and 6(iii)(b)). Massive wooden cenotaphs were also erected over the graves of several 18th-century imams; they are distinguished by elaborately carved and often painted decoration (*see* ISLAMIC ART, §VII, 2(v)).

BIBLIOGRAPHY

Enc. Islam./ 1: 'Zaidīya'
A. Tritton: *Rise of the Imams of San'ā'* (London, 1925)
R. W. Stookey: *Yemen: The Politics of the Yemen Arab Republic* (Boulder, 1978), pp. 79–99

□

Zayn al-'Abidin [Mīr Zayn al-'Ābidīn Tabrīzī] (*fl* Qazvin, *c.* 1570–1602). Persian illustrator, illuminator and calligrapher. The grandson and pupil of SULTAN-MUHAMMAD, Zayn al-'Abidin worked exclusively for royal and noble patrons at the Safavid court in Qazvin (*see* ISLAMIC ART, §III, 4(vi)(a)). He contributed an illustration of *Nariman Killing the Ruler of China* to a copy (London, BL, Or. MS. 12985; fol. 90*v*) of Asadi's *Garshāspnāma* ('Book of Garshasp') produced at Qazvin in 1573 and four paintings to a dispersed copy of the *Shāhnāma* ('Book of kings') made for Isma'il II (*reg* 1576–8). The artist's style is characterized by solid forms, extreme precision and compositions that resemble the style typical of Tabriz in the first half of the 16th century rather than the more mannered one typical of Qazvin in the 1570s. His best known illumination is the splendid signed frontispiece for the unfinished copy (Dublin, Chester Beatty Lib., MS. 277) of the *Shāhnāma*, thought to have been commissioned upon the accession of 'Abbas I in 1588. The artist may also have been responsible for its sumptuous gold marginalia which shows birds, deer, lions and other animals in landscapes. His calligraphy is known from a copy (London, BL, Add. MS. 28302) of the *Shāhnāma* dated 1586, which may have been commissioned by Hamza Mirza (*d* 1586), the son of Muhammad Khudabanda (*reg* 1578–88).

BIBLIOGRAPHY

Qaẓi Aḥmad ibn Mīr Munshī: *Gulistān-i hunar* [Garden of the arts] (*c.* 1606); Eng. trans. by V. Minorsky as *Calligraphers and Painters* (Washington, DC, 1959), p. 187
Iskandar Munshī: *Tārīkh-i 'ālamārā-yi 'abbāsī* [History of the world-conquering 'Abbas] (1629); Eng. trans. by R. Savory as *History of Shah 'Abbas the Great* (Boulder, CO, 1978), p. 278
A. J. Arberry and others: *The Chester Beatty Library: A Catalogue of the Persian Manuscripts and Miniatures* (Dublin, 1959–62), iii, p. 49
B. W. Robinson: 'Isma'il II's Copy of the *Shāhnāma*', *Iran*, xiv (1976), pp. 1–8
A. Welch: *Artists for the Shah* (New Haven, 1976), pp. 212–13

SHEILA R. CANBY

Zbigniew of Oleśnica. See OLEŚNICKI, ZBIGNIEW.

Zborowski, Léopold (*b* Zbleszezyki, 10 March 1889; *d* Paris, 24 March 1932). Polish art dealer, active in France.

He moved to Paris as a student, probably in 1914. The financial difficulties he faced as a foreigner in France during World War I led to his involvement in the art trade. Initially he sold books and prints, but in 1916 he began promoting impoverished artists, notably Amedeo Modigliani, Chaïm Soutine and (for a short period) Maurice Utrillo. From 1916 he represented Modigliani, who in 1918 painted his portrait (priv. col., see C. Mann, *Modigliani*, 1980, p. 160), and he provided the Sitwells with the work shown at the *Exhibition of French Art, 1914–19*, which they organized for the Mansard Gallery (Heals) in London in 1919. He prospered in the post-war art boom and became a central figure in the marketing of the Ecole de Paris. In 1926, after years of operating from his flat in Montparnasse, he opened a gallery in the Rue de Seine, but the stock market crash of 1929 and his own improvidence left him virtually bankrupt.

BIBLIOGRAPHY
E. Szittya: *Soutine et son temps* (Paris, 1955)
L. Czechowska: 'Les Souvenirs de Lunia Czechowska', in A. Ceroni: *Amedeo Modigliani peintre* (Milan, 1958), pp. 19–36
J. Modigliani: *Modigliani sans légende* (Paris, 1961), p. 87
M. Gee: *Dealers, Critics and Collectors of Modern Painting* (New York and London, 1981)

MALCOLM GEE

Zea (i). *See under* PEIRAEUS.

Zea (ii). *See* KEA.

Zebid. *See* ZABID.

Zebo. *See under* MASTERS, ANONYMOUS, AND MONOGRAMMISTS, §I: MASTER OF THE BRUSSELS INITIALS.

Zebra. German artists' group formed in Hamburg in 1965 by the painters Dieter Asmus (*b* 1939), Peter Nagel (*b* 1942), Nikolaus Störtenbecker (*b* 1940) and Dietmar Ullrich (*b* 1940). They were all graduates of the Hochschule für Bildende Künste in Hamburg and shared a common interest in Photorealism. Their work was characterized by the setting of objects and figures against an indistinct background. Despite the precise delineation of objects, sometimes approaching *trompe l'oeil* in the work of Nagel, their paintings were not naturalistic. Colour and form were used in an anti-realistic way, and the artists sometimes adopted the convention of using monochrome for figures and bright, arbitrary colours for inanimate objects, as in Asmus's *Vitamin-Bomb* (1976; Bochum, priv. col., see 1978–80 exh. cat., pl. 8). From photography they took the device of cutting off figures and objects, thus robbing their images of traditional compositional structure. Störtenbecker, in particular, employed a precise, minutely detailed realism that gave his work the impression of being a photograph, rather than a painted image. In the work of all four artists there was a tendency to suppress dramatic and expressive content by means of an apparently objective manner and by their attempts to dissociate their subjects from any 'meaning' that might have attached to them. This is as true of Ullrich's paintings featuring sport (e.g. *Swimmer*, 1970–71; Neuss, Clemens-Sels-Mus.), which give the impression of a freeze-frame camera, as it is of Nagel's isolated, oversized technological fragments (e.g. *Red Tent*, 1972–4; see 1978–80 exh. cat., pl. 33). The members of Zebra exhibited widely in Germany and elsewhere both independently and as a group.

BIBLIOGRAPHY
Zebra (exh. cat. by H. R. Fischer, London, Fischer F.A., 1975)
Gruppe Zebra (exh. cat. by W.-D. Dube, Bremen, Ksthalle; Rome, Pal. Espos.; Leverkusen, Kulthaus; and elsewhere; 1978–80)

□

Zechlin. *See under* BRANDENBURG GLASSWORKS.

Zeeman. *See* NOOMS, REINIER.

Zegers, Gerard. *See* SEGHERS, GERARD.

Zeherin, Karl. *See* CARLO DI CESARI DEL PALAGIO.

Zehnerring. *See* RING, DER.

Zehrfuss, Bernard (Louis) (*b* Angers, 20 Oct 1911). French architect. He studied architecture at the Ecole des Beaux-Arts, Paris (1928–39), winning the Premier Grand Prix de Rome in 1939. In 1942 he went to Tunisia as a volunteer in the Free French Army. From 1943 to 1948 he practised there as Chief Government Architect, directing a team involved in modernization; they designed housing projects, markets and schools, which were notable for their respect of local traditions. Although he returned to private practice in Paris (1948), he still received large public commissions from the Tunisian government (for example buildings for the University of Tunis, 1960–64). In Paris he was instrumental in the implementation of the Camus process, a prefabrication method that he used in the housing complex at the Pont de Sèvres, Boulogne-Billancourt (1949–52). The Renault industrial complex, Flins (1950–55), is in a straightforward International style, although its façades are enlivened by a polychrome composition by the painter Félix Del Marle (1889–1952).

Zehrfuss's great career opportunity came through the rejection of Eugène Beaudouin's proposal for the UNESCO headquarters, Place de Fontenoy, Paris, and the resulting necessity to associate a local architect with a new international design team headed by Marcel Breuer and Pier Luigi Nervi. Built between 1952 and 1958, the buildings bear the mark of Breuer (in the Y-shaped Secretariat) and Nervi (in the structural design of the folded-plate conference building). Zehrfuss was solely responsible for the below ground-level additions to the Secretariat (1963–5) and for the erection of several annexes nearby.

The UNESCO commission opened the path to an extensive practice. Zehrfuss was involved in the early planning phases of the high-rise district of La Défense, Paris. At the end of a central pedestrian artery lined by uniform skyscrapers, in collaboration with Robert Camelot (*b* 1903) and Jean de Mailly (1911–75), he designed the Centre National des Industries et Techniques (CNIT; 1953–8; *see* SHELL STRUCTURE, fig. 1). This gigantic hall for trade shows and exhibitions has a triangular floor plan of *c*. 8 hectares and is covered by a double-skin, hollow, ribbed shell of reinforced concrete, which is less than 2 m thick and which spans over 200 m from three support points at the corners of the triangle; this was detailed by structural engineer Nicolas Esquillan from a preliminary design by Nervi. (It originally had glass curtain walls designed by Jean Prouvé, but these were significantly altered in the late 1980s.) Also at La Défense, Zehrfuss proposed the erection of a very tall three-bladed office building (c. 1958; unexecuted, for illustration see Ragon). Zehrfuss's yearning for modernization was sometimes unsuccessful; the *grand ensemble* of the Haut du Lièvre in Nancy (1959–67) is striking by the inhumanity of its two mid-rise housing slabs, each c. 400 m long; unfortunately the accompanying service facilities envisioned by the architect were never completed. He was also well known for his elegant renovation and addition to the Hôtel du Mont d'Arbois, Mégève (1963), and the Musée de la Civilisation Gallo-Romaine, Lyon (1976). Dug into the slope of Fourvière Hill to avoid damage to two existing Roman amphitheatres, this archaeological museum was composed of a succession of unadorned concrete arches and ramps. It exemplifies Zehrfuss's sensitivity to siting, as well as his interest in the straightforward expression of new structural systems. In the 1980s, as Architect in Chief of new housing in the 15th arrondissement and of the high-rise development of Super-Montparnasse, he was one of the champions of drastic redevelopment in Paris. In the early 1990s he collaborated on the largest clear span shell structure.

BIBLIOGRAPHY

Archit. Aujourd'hui, xix/20 (1948) [special issue on Tunisia]
'Usine Renault à Flins', *Archit. Aujourd'hui*, xxiv (April–May 1953), pp. 21–5
'With this New Y-shaped Office Building for UNESCO, Horizontal Paris Gets its First Modern Monument', *Archit. Forum*, xcviii (June 1953), pp. 105–13
'Conference Building and Offices, Unesco House, Place de Fontenoy, Paris', *Architects' J.*, cxxviii (11 Dec 1958), pp. 859–70
'Ensemble d'habitation du "Haut du Lièvre"', *Archit. Fr.*, xxi/223–4 (1961), pp. 76–8
M. Ragon: *La Cité de l'an 2000* (Paris, 1968), p. 151
'Il Musée Archéologique di Leone', *Casabella*, xliii/443 (1979), pp. 40–41
'Entretiens avec Bernard Zehrfuss', *Archit., Mouvement, Continuité*, 11 (1986), pp. 20–21

ISABELLE GOURNAY

Zeid, Fahrelnissa (*b* Istanbul, 1901; *d* Amman, 5 Sept 1991). Turkish painter. The daughter of Shakir Pasha, a Turkish general, diplomat and historian, she was brought up in a distinguished family of statesmen and intellectuals. She went to the Academy of Fine Arts, Istanbul, in 1920, where she studied under Namık Ismail (1890–1935), and then to Paris in 1927, where she studied at the Académie Ranson under Roger Bissière. On returning to Istanbul, she joined an association of young Turkish painters known as the D Group, which was founded in 1933. In 1934 she married the Hashemite prince Zeid El-Hussein, a diplomat, and accompanied him on postings to Berlin, London and Paris. She had private exhibitions in Istanbul in 1944 and 1945, and then in 1946 at Izmir and the Musée Cernuschi, Paris. After World War II, when she moved back to western Europe, she had further exhibitions in London, Paris, Brussels, New York and elsewhere. She participated in the Salon des Réalités Nouvelles, Paris, in 1951, 1953 and 1954, and had a large exhibition of her work at the Hittite Museum, Ankara, in 1964. In 1975 she moved from Paris to Amman, Jordan, where she began to teach at the Royal Art Institute. In 1983 the Royal Cultural Centre in Amman staged a major retrospective exhibition of her work.

Zeid worked in oil, gouache and watercolour and also produced lithographs and engravings. Her early paintings, which include portraits and interior scenes, were inspired largely by French art. During the 1940s, however, she moved towards abstraction and the use of larger canvases. She soon began to attract international acclaim, being recognized in Paris by André Breton and the art critic Charles Estienne. In addition to her abstract works she produced portrait paintings. Her canvases have rich and sumptuous colours, and many of her abstract works, such as *Break of the Atom and Vegetal Life* (1962; Emir Ra'ad priv. col., see Parinaud, pl. 3), are densely filled. She also developed a technique called 'paleochrystalos', in which she set coloured stones, enamels and other objects into a glass-paste and resin mixture which was then set in motion by small electric motors.

BIBLIOGRAPHY

A. Parinaud: *Fahrelnissa Zeid* (Amman, 1984)
M. Parker: Obituary, *Independent* (20 Sept 1991)

S. J. VERNOIT

Zeidler, Eberhard (Heinrich) (*b* Braunsdorf, 11 Jan 1926). Canadian architect of German birth. He studied at the Staatliche Bauhaus, Weimar (1948), and graduated in engineering and architecture from the Technische Hochschule, University of Karlsruhe, in 1949. He began his career as a designer for the architectural firm of Eiermann & Lindner, Karlsruhe. In 1951 Zeidler emigrated to Canada and worked for Blackwell & Craig of Peterborough, Ontario, becoming a partner in the firm in 1954. He taught modern architectural design at the University of Toronto (1953–5; Adjunct Professor from 1984). He became a naturalized Canadian citizen in 1956. In 1962 Zeidler moved the practice from Peterborough to Toronto, where it evolved as Craig, Zeidler & Strong (1963–75), and later as the Zeidler Partnership/Architects (1975–80). In 1980, when Zeidler joined with new partner Alfred C. Roberts (*b* 1931), the name was changed again to the Zeidler Roberts Partnership/Architects. Zeidler was best known for designing such megastructures as the McMaster Health Sciences Centre in Hamilton (completed 1972), and for the Eaton Centre (1977), a shopping complex in the then current High Tech style covering five city blocks in downtown Toronto. He was noted also for Ontario Place (1970), a leisure centre made up of linked, tent-like pods on stilts, set over water in Toronto's lake-front harbour. In size, scale and style Zeidler equated such projects to planning an ocean liner—an idea underscored by his frequent use of nautical references, like linear passageways, exposed ductwork, sloping skylights, welded-steel tubular handrails and accents of brightly coloured paint. He won many awards and wrote books and innumerable articles for both English- and German-language magazines on architecture.

WRITINGS

Healing the Hospital—McMaster Health Science Centre: Its Conception and Evolution (Toronto, 1974)
Multi-funktionale Architektur im städtischen Kontext (Stuttgart and Paris, 1983; Eng. trans., New York, 1984)

BIBLIOGRAPHY
C. Davies: 'Architects on Architecture', *Building*, ccxli/7213 (1981), p. 18
L. Whiteson: *Modern Canadian Architecture* (Edmonton, Alta, 1983), pp. 156–67, 272

□

Zeiller, Johann Jakob (*b* Reutte, Tyrol, 8 July 1708; *d* Reutte, 8 July 1783). Austrian painter. Trained initially by his father, Paul Zeiller (1658–1738), he subsequently studied in Italy (1723–32) with Sebastiano Conca and at the Accademia di S Luca in Rome, and with Francesco Solimena in Naples, then at the Kaiserliche Akademie in Vienna. From 1733 to 1743 he was a regular collaborator on Paul Troger's frescoes, contributing mainly architectural frameworks painted in the style of the Bolognese *quadraturisti*. He retained such frameworks in his own paintings throughout his life, even in south Germany where this was generally unusual. Troger's influence on the style of Zeiller's figures and on his iconographic repertory was such that his first independent works in Austria (after 1738–9) are difficult to distinguish from Troger's own.

This influence persisted during Zeiller's activity (from 1744) in Bavaria and Swabia, where he executed numerous and at times extensive frescoes in monastery chapels, convents and village churches, and occasionally altarpieces. In his principal works, the large dome fresco (1748–51) in the monastery church at Ettal and the decoration (1756–64) of the collegiate church at Ottobeuren, he significantly developed the possibilities of opening the dome illusionistically to heaven. The latter was a collaboration with his cousin Franz Anton Zeiller (1716–93), a fresco painter educated in Augsburg, Rome and Venice who became court painter to the Bishop of Bressanone in 1768, producing much Rococo work in the Tyrol. Johann Jakob spent his last years, after 1776, producing frescoes for village churches in his native Tyrol and also decorating house façades, notably in Reutte, where such houses are called 'Zeiller-Häuschen'.

BIBLIOGRAPHY
P. Fischer: *Der Barockmaler Johann Jakob Zeiller und sein Ettaler Werk* (Munich, 1964)
F. Matsche: *Der Freskomaler Johann Jakob Zeiller (1708–1783)* (diss.; Marburg, 1970) [with annotated cat. of frescoes, oil ptgs and drgs]
Paul, Johann Jakob, Franz Anton Zeiller (exh. cat.; Reutte, 1983)

FRANZ MATSCHE

Zeitblom, Bartholomäus (*b* Nördlingen, 1455–60; *d* Nördlingen, *c.* 1520). German painter. He is famed for the distinctive style of his altarpieces, which served as a model for Swabian painting in the early 16th century and was later much admired by the Romantics. Zeitblom's family moved to Nördlingen under his grandfather Lienhard. There he married a daughter of the painter Friedrich Herlin, though no trace of Herlin's work shows in Zeitblom's altarpieces. In 1482 he became a citizen of Ulm, where he seems soon to have made contact with the leading master Hans Schüchlin, one of whose daughters later became his second wife. Besides his connections with leading families in Ulm, Zeitblom had noble patrons like the knight Georg von Ehingen, Peter von Hewen, and the families von Rechberg, von Limpurg and Öttingen, enabling his altarpieces to receive a wide distribution throughout the Swabian Alps and the Danube region of Upper Swabia.

Zeitblom's characteristic style, which was developed but not decisively altered in his later work, is first apparent in the altarpiece from Kilchberg near Tübingen (*c.* 1485; Stuttgart, Staatsgal.), where his patron was Georg von Ehingen. This was praised by the poet Justinus Kerner (1786–1862) as the work of 'a German Leonardo', a description seemingly prompted by the perfect, almost rigid calm of Zeitblom's saints and biblical figures. Their popularity is probably due to their strong affinity with monumental carved figures. Gold damask fabrics form a backdrop to the saints on the inside panels, purple fabrics to those on the outside. Despite the diagonally constructed Late Gothic stance and the awkward, angular arms, St Florian (for example) has nothing of Late Gothic restlessness about him. He appears to be frozen in his pose, washing away strange insects from a toy castle with his tub of water.

In following altarpieces the full-length figures become more dainty and intricate, as for example in the altar from Hausen near Ulm (Stuttgart, Württemberg. Landesmus.), where St Francis has a remarkably small head on a long body. The remains of the high altar (destr. 1790) of the parish church at Bingen, near Sigmaringen, are more important: the *Nativity* and *Adoration of the Magi* on the insides of the wings are among Zeitblom's best works in the liveliness of their depiction, pointing forward to pictures of the same subjects by Bernhard Strigel. The *Nativity* successfully experiments with a diagonal arrangement of the ashlar foundation walls, giving space for Christ's parents to be placed one behind the other. The same arrangement is adopted in the *Adoration*, but, because it is overlaid by the conventional horizontal grouping of the seated Virgin and the kings, it loses its effect. However, the two kings conversing, with their magnificent robes and very lively faces, break through the rigidity of the main group.

When Zeitblom painted the two pairs of wings for the high altar of the former monastery church at Blaubeuren (1493–4), he had to work alongside younger colleagues; of these only Bernhard Strigel, possibly his pupil at the time, is known by name. The altar provides chief evidence of his activity in Ulm. In the saints on both sides of the predella Zeitblom adopted his usual calm style of figure-composition. By contrast, in the scenes from the story of *St John the Baptist* and from the *Passion*, in spite of the magnificent detail and excellent portrait-style heads, the composition is overladen, with groups crowded together inside simple box-like spaces opening onto rich landscape backgrounds. Even Zeitblom's assistant, the Master of the Burial of St John, does not succeed with these outdoor scenes, while a training in the Netherlands with Dieric Bouts is evident in the interiors—as in *Salome's Presentation of St John's Head on a Dish*. Zeitblom's achievement was to combine the work of his three collaborators (including the young Strigel) into an artistically unified group of pictures.

Following this Zeitblom produced the altar from Eschach near Gaildorf (1496; Stuttgart, Staatsgal.), that from

Hürbel near Biberach (1497; Budapest, Mus. F.A.) and that from Heerberg am Kocher (1497–8; Stuttgart, Staatsgal.). Those from Eschach and Heerberg present, in its purest form, the image of Zeitblom which has prevailed since the Romantic period: a painter striving for the greatest possible simplicity of composition, with few figures—in contrast to the contemporary tendency towards overloaded scenes. Three-dimensionality is limited to distinct, carefully painted architectural elements—indented window jambs, for example, and a corner bench in the Eschach altar which merely hints at the depth of the room in the *Annunciation*. This corner bench forms a backdrop for two solemnly immobile figures frozen in a glassy stillness. The *Presentation of Christ* (see fig.) in the Heerberg Altarpiece has the same ceremoniousness, with gestures as delicate and economical as possible. In the background

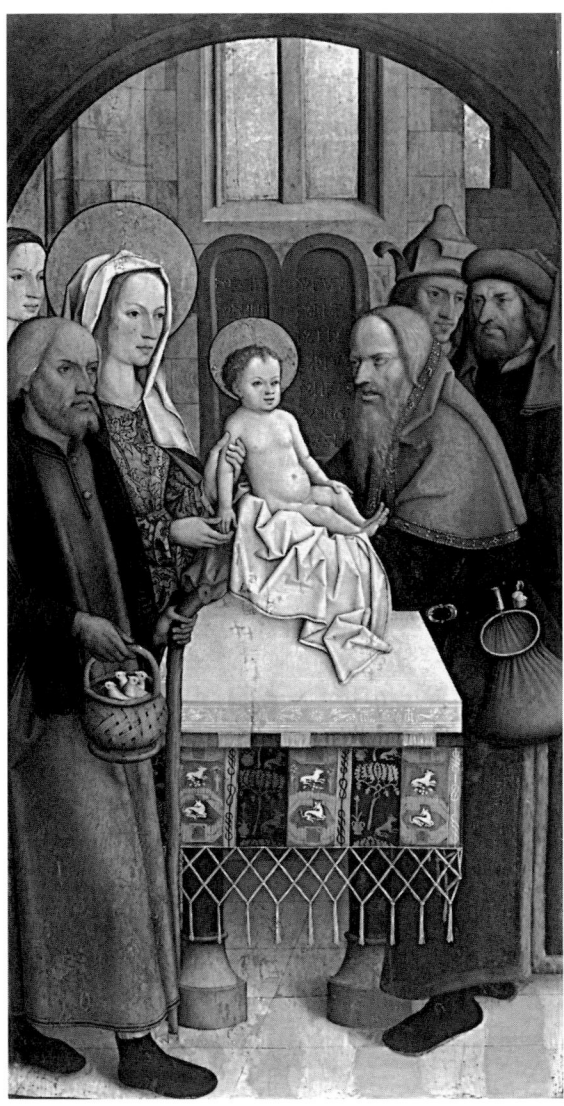

Bartholomäus Zeitblom: *Presentation of Christ*, panel, from the Heerberg am Kocher Altarpiece, 1.71×0.85 m, 1497–8 (Stuttgart, Staatsgalerie)

of the *Nativity* Zeitblom used Dürer's engraving *Family with Grasshopper* (B. 44).

Even in the dramatic scenes on two wings of the *Legend of St Valentine* (*c.* 1500; Stuttgart, Staatsgal.), painted on both sides and together forming a pointed arch, Zeitblom maintained the utmost distance and restraint. However, in the altarpiece in the chapel at Adelberg, near Schorndorf (1511), Zeitblom's last dated work, with scenes of Christ and the Virgin, this concentration on essentials is lost. The folds of the garments are voluminous, but also fussy and elaborate.

Zeitblom must also have been an excellent portrait painter; however, the attribution of portraits of leading Ulm citizens like the councillor and judge *Hans Wurm* (1497; Nuremberg, Ger. Nmus.) or the later portraits of *Ursula Greckin* and a *64-year-old Man* (both priv. cols) is disputed. The only confirmed portrait in his work is a sketched, half-length self-portrait set in foliage in the Heerberg Altarpiece. The bearded painter wears a hunter's hat with upturned brim and is depicted without flattery, with a crooked nose and squinting eyes.

Considering the basically conservative outlook of all his altarpieces, the influence of Zeitblom's style on painting in Ulm in the following decade is astonishing. This is very clear in the work of the young Bernhard Strigel and also in that of the unknown painter of the former high altar of the Wengenkirche in Ulm (Ulm, Ulmer Mus. and Cathedral; Karlsruhe, Staatl. Ksthalle; Stuttgart, Staatsgal.; Lübeck, St Annen-Mus.; Dublin, N.G.).

BIBLIOGRAPHY
J. Kerner: *Cottas Morgenblatt* (Stuttgart, 1816)
A. Strange: *Deutsche Malerei der Gotik*, viii (Berlin, 1957)
B. Bushart: 'Rezension zu Stange Bd.8', *Z. Kstgesch.*, xxii (1959), pp. 143–7

HANS GEORG GMELIN

Zeitgeist [Ger.: 'time spirit']. Term coined by GEORG WILHELM FRIEDRICH HEGEL to refer to the so-called spirit of an age.   □

Železný Brod. Czech centre of glass production. It is situated in the Jizerské Mountains in an area where stonecutting and glass engraving have flourished for centuries. The rise of glassmaking at Železný Brod is associated with the specialist glassmaking school founded in 1920. The artistic nature of the school and the outstanding local industry between 1918 and 1939 was the responsibility of the various teaching schools run by graduates of the Academy of Applied Arts in Prague: the director, Alois Metelák (1897–1980), produced many cut-glass designs, and Ladislav Přenosil (1893–1965) taught glass engraving. Examples of the cottage industry work done at Železný Brod included small glass figures for beads or miner's lamps designed by Jaroslav Brychta (1895–1971). Important artists working at the school and in production after World War II include Břetislav Novák (1913–82), Miloslav Klinger (*b* 1922), Ladislav Oliva (*b* 1933), Antonín Drobník (*b* 1925), Stanislav Libenský (*b* 1921) and Pavel Ježek (*b* 1938). After 1948 the individual enterprises were merged into the unified factory called Železný Brod Glass, which had its own glassworks as well as refineries for mosaic and stained glass; the workshop producing mould-melted glass sculpture for architecture held a leading artistic position and was headed by Jaroslava Brychtová (*b* 1924). With her husband Stanislav Libenský, professor at the Academy of Applied Arts at Prague, Brychtová produced a number of works that are regarded as among the most important in 20th-century Czech artistic glass.

BIBLIOGRAPHY

A. Adlerová and O. Drahotová: *Böhmisches Glas* (in preparation)

ALENA ADLEROVÁ

Zeller, Jakob (*b* Regensburg, 1581; *d* Dresden, 28 Dec 1620). German ivory-carver. His father, Pankraz Zeller, worked as a turner at the Saxon court in Dresden from 1583. In 1610 Jakob Zeller was appointed court turner and teacher of the art of turning to Christian II, Elector of Saxony, and to John-George I in 1613. Among his numerous ivory pieces for the royal art collection—in 1618 he cited 22 works that he had produced since 1613—were ceremonial goblets, for example an ornate goblet (1610; Stockholm, Kun. Slottet) with Andromeda as the stem and crowned by a group of Perseus on horseback fighting the monster. The use of such sculptural ornamentation as mascarons is typical of his work. He also made numerous counterfeit spheres. One example (1611; Dresden, Grünes Gewölbe) is a large globe with four round openings, through which can be seen a smaller, similar broken globe bearing a medallion with the portraits of Christian II, his wife and their respective coats of arms. On the top of the globe there is a figurine of a boy with a skull; at the foot there is a figure of a Roman warrior.

Zeller was made a citizen of Dresden on 10 July 1619, and the following year he produced his most important work, an ivory centrepiece in the shape of a Dutch frigate (1.0×0.7 m; Dresden, Grünes Gewölbe). The ship is carried by a figure of Neptune in a carriage of mussels strung with waterlilies, all carved in ivory; the names of all the Saxon rulers are carved on the hull, while the sail bears the coat of arms of John-George I and his wife. The guns and rigging are of gold.

BIBLIOGRAPHY

Thieme–Becker

E. von Philippowich: *Elfenbein* (1961, rev. Munich, 1982), pp. 366, 406, 414, 422, 423

A. GERHARDT

Zel'ma, Georgy (Anatol'yevich) (*b* Tashkent, 1906; *d* Moscow, 1984). Russian photographer of Uzbek birth. He moved to Moscow in 1921. After training as a photographer, he worked in the Proletkino film studio and then as an apprentice photographer at the Russfoto agency (1923–4). His early photographs include pictures of old Moscow and a toy factory at Zagorsk. Russfoto sent Zel'ma to Tashkent as a correspondent. His photographs of life in the Central Asian republics began to appear in the national press and were included in *10 let Uzbekistana* ('10 years of Uzbekistan', 1934), an album of photographs designed by Aleksandr Rodchenko and Varvara Stepanova. Zel'ma was one of the leading photojournalists in the USSR. In the 1930s he worked for the newspapers *Izvestiya* and *Krasnaya Zvezda*. Together with Maks Al'pert he photographed a number of subjects for the magazine *USSR in Construction*, including pictures of collective farms and aerial views of the USSR as well as a series on the building of the Beryoznikovsk and Solikamsk chemical complexes. He also produced expressive photographs on the theme of aviation (e.g. *Into the Stratosphere*, see Morozov and Lloyd, eds, p. 147), successfully fusing subject-matter, form and the intensity of the moment into a whole. In *Izvestiya* Zel'ma published, among others, picture stories on the building of the Moscow Canal, various congresses and the Communist League of Youth (1936). During World War II Zel'ma worked at the front as a press photographer, and he photographed the defence of Odessa, the Battle of the Donbass and the liberation of Moldavia (now Moldova) and the Ukraine. One of his most substantial and impressive series is devoted to the Battle of Stalingrad (*Stalingrad: July 1942–February 1943* (Moscow, 1966)). After the war Zel'ma worked for the magazine *Sovetskaya Zhenshchina* and for the Novosti press agency. He showed his photojournalist series and individual pictures at numerous exhibitions.

BIBLIOGRAPHY

B. Vilenkin: *Georgy Zel'ma: Izbrannyye fotografiye* [Georgy Zel'ma: selected photographs] (Moscow, 1978)

G. Shudakov, O. Suslova and L. Ukhtomskaya: *Pioneers of Soviet Photography* (London and New York, 1983)

S. Morozov and V. Lloyd, eds: *Soviet Photography, 1917–1940: The New Photojournalism* (London, 1984)

A. N. LAVRENTIEV

Zelotti, Battista [Giambattista; Gian Battista] (*b* Verona, *c.* 1526; *d* Mantua, 28 Aug 1578). Italian painter. According to Ridolfi, he was trained with Paolo Veronese in the workshop of Antonio Badile IV in Verona. Much of Zelotti's work was executed for prestigious villas and palazzi in and near Vicenza. Although works of uncertain attribution have been assigned traditionally to Veronese, owing to his greater fame, a clearer picture of the distinctions between the two artists during their early years has emerged in the later 20th century.

Probably the earliest collaboration between Zelotti and Veronese, in association with Anselmo Canneri, was the decoration (1551) of the Villa Soranzo (destr.), near Castelfranco Veneto. Of the surviving fresco fragments, Zelotti's *Temperance* and *Putto with an Apple* (both Castelfranco Veneto Cathedral) are executed with flatter faces and less bold foreshortening than appear in Veronese's fragments. In 1553–4, working with Veronese and Giovanni Battista Ponchino, Zelotti painted in oil the compartments of the ceilings in the Sala del Consiglio dei Dieci and the Sala dei Tre Capi in the Doge's Palace, Venice, in the former of which his putto frieze and *Venice Surmounting the Globe* are skilfully executed. In the latter the central octagon of *Time, Truth and Innocence* shows Zelotti's masterful depiction of cool light playing over the figures. Further Venetian commissions included three of the ceiling tondi in the reading-room at the Libreria Marciana (1556–7) and the decoration, with Veronese, of the Palazzo Trevisan, Murano (1557).

Two important fresco series on the mainland date from the 1550s: the decoration of the Palazzo Porto-Colleoni at Thiene and Palladio's Villa Godi Valmarana at Lonedo. In both, Zelotti depicted rather grandiose forms in bright colours in illusionistic settings. The *Mucius Scaevola* at Thiene and the female figures perched over cornices at

Lonedo are still very close in style to Veronese. In the 1560s Zelotti worked at the Villa Roberti, Brugine (*c.* 1560), and Palladio's Villa Emo, Fanzolo, and Villa Foscari, Malcontenta. He also contributed decorations to Praglia Abbey, including those on the library ceiling. In these his figures are, typically, elongated muscular males, usually projecting a leg or foot illuminated with a splash of light, and fleshy females with faces that are still flat but often have jutting jaws. The decorations as a whole have a rhythmic, fluid and Mannerist quality.

Zelotti's late style is more problematic. Restored frescoes attributed to him at the Villa Caldogno, Caldogno, dating from the late 1560s, seem remarkably close in style to Antonio Fasolo's works in the same series, as do the decorations at the Castello del Cataio, Battaglia of *c.* 1570 (Crosato, Pallucchini).

BIBLIOGRAPHY

G. Vasari: *Vite* (1550, rev. 2/1568); ed. G. Milanesi (1878–85), vi, pp. 369–74
C. Ridolfi: *Meraviglie* (1648); ed. D. von Hadeln (1914–24)
B. dal Pozzo: *Le vite de' pittori, scultori e architetti veronesi* (Verona, 1718), pp. 130–37
B. Berenson: *Venetian School* (1957), i, pp. 203–5
L. Crosato: *Gli affreschi nelle ville venete del cinquecento* (Treviso, 1962)
J. Schulz: *Venetian Painted Ceilings of the Renaissance* (Berkeley, 1968), pp. 93–5, 97–9, 125
R. Pallucchini: 'Giambattista Zelotti e Giovanni Antonio Fasolo', *Boll. Cent. Int. Stud. Archit. Andrea Palladio*, lx (1968), pp. 203–28
F. Zava Boccazzi: 'Considerazioni sulle tele di Battista Zelotti nel soffitto della libreria di Praglia', *A. Ven.*, xxiv (1970), pp. 111–27
D. Gisolfi Pechukas: 'Veronese and his Collaborators at "La Soranza"', *Artibus & Hist.*, xv (1987), pp. 67–108
——: 'Paolo Veronese ed i suoi primi collaboratori', *Nuovi studi su Paolo Veronese* (Venice, 1990), pp. 24–35
K. Brugnolo Meloncelli: 'Precisioni cronologiche sulle opere di Battista Zelotti', *Venezia A.*, v (1991), pp. 49–62

DIANA GISOLFI

Zemen [formerly Belovo]. Town approximately 70 km south-west of Sofia, Bulgaria, on the River Struma. It is famous for the monastery of St John the Evangelist, of which only the domed cruciform church (8.7×9.2 m) dating from the 11th century survives. Four square piers support the dome's drum; barrel vaults cover the rest of the church. The walls are built of ashlar blocks. The north, south and west sides each have three blind-arched niches corresponding to the interior arrangements of the vaults and spaces; the east side ends in three high semi-cylindrical apses. During the period of Ottoman rule (1393–1878) the monastery was abandoned and the residential buildings destroyed. Not until the 19th century was the church renovated and new monks' cells erected.

The church's most remarkable features are its two layers of wall paintings. Those of the first layer are best preserved in the two chapels flanking the central apse and may be as early as the second half of the 11th century; they show figures of saints and scenes from the Gospels. The wall paintings of the second layer survive throughout the church; those in the sanctuary and nave are generally thought to be contemporary with the donor inscription, which mentions Despot Deyan, that accompanies the full-length portraits on the south and west walls of the donor, a feudal lord, his wife Doya and their two children; another donor, Vitomir, and a boy Stayu also appear. L. Mavrodinova attributed these paintings to the first half

of the 14th century. Representations of Christian feasts occupy the vaults, while the uppermost register of the walls is covered by a continuous cycle of the *Passion*. The register below shows the *Forty Martyrs of Sebaste* from the waist up, while the lowest register is filled with full-length figures of saints. The figures are depicted in a two-dimensional linear style with warm and muted colours (e.g. brown, greyish blue, brick-red, yellow ochre), while the simplified architectural backdrops in the narrative scenes create some sense of space. Stylistically the paintings are reminiscent of the *Last Judgement* (1260s) in the exonarthex of the Serbian monastery church of Mileševa and the donor's portraits (1281) in Panagia Vellas, near Voulgaréliou, Greece.

BIBLIOGRAPHY

A. Grabar: *La Peinture religieuse en Bulgarie* (Paris, 1928), pp. 186–223
N. Mavrodinov: *Starobâlgarskoto izkustvo, XI–XIII vek* [Old Bulgarian art, 11–13th centuries] (Sofia, 1966), pp. 15–18
L. Mavrodinova: *Zemenskata tsârkva* [The church at Zemen] (Sofia, 1980)

LILIANA MAVRODINOVA

Zemła, Gustav (*b* Jasienica, 1 Nov 1931). Polish sculptor. He studied at the Academy of Fine Arts, Warsaw, becoming an assistant (1958), a professor (1970) and Dean of the faculty of sculpture (1979–81). He took part in numerous exhibitions in Poland and elsewhere and received many Polish prizes and awards. His works range from portraits, tomb sculptures and near-abstract smaller compositions to grandiose state commissions, for example the monument to the *Silesian Insurgents* (1967; Katowice), to the *Warsaw War Dead* (1973; Warsaw) and to the *Polish Achievement* (1979; Szczecin). Zemła never adopted official Socialist Realism, and these, his main monuments, have a strong Romantic and personal Baroque flavour, with a tendency towards abstraction. In 1980 Zemła's work shifted from patriotic state art to the religious, with the commission for the monumental bronze sculptural décor for the new Church of the Virgin and St Maximilian Kolbe at Mistrzejowice, Nowa Huta, Kraków, which consists of three over life-size figures for the sanctuary, two life-size figures for the side altars and the Stations of the Cross in high relief. The bronze figure of *Pope John Paul II*, part of this commission, was completed in 1991. He also produced, in 1986, the bronze figure of *Christ* for the tomb of *Father Jerzy Popiełuszko* in Warsaw. Zemła's intellectual and spiritual development had a decisive influence on his work. The ensemble for Mistrzejowice is particularly striking. He introduced into the modernist church deeply felt religious work translated into a personal, contemporary idiom. Zemła was very active as a teacher and ranks as the creator of a new school of Polish sculpture.

BIBLIOGRAPHY

A. K. Olszewski: *An Outline History of Polish 20th-century Art and Architecture* (Warsaw, 1989), pp. 139–41

A. S. CIECHANOWIECKI

Zemlja. *See* EARTH GROUP.

Zemtsov, Mikhail (Grigor'yevich) (*b* Moscow, 1686/8; *d* St Petersburg, 28 Sept 1743). Russian architect, teacher and theorist. He was a pupil of Domenico Trezzini (from 1710) and then his assistant at the Ministry of Municipal Affairs in St Petersburg. He supervised the completion

(1719–22), to plans by Niccolò Michetti, of the Yekaterinental Palace at Reval, where he also carried out the elaborate decoration of the White Hall and laid out the park. His Hall for Glorious Ceremonials (1725; destr.), designed to house relics of Russia's victories in the Northern War, combined Neo-classical and Baroque features. Working in the German–Dutch style of Baltic Baroque, Zemtsov designed the church of SS Simeon and Anna (1730–34) on Mokhovaya Street and the cathedral of Prince Vladimir (1741–7; built by Pietro Trezzini, b 1710; now on Dobrolyubov Prospect). These all played an important role in the townscape of the city. While echoing the traditional Russian pattern of a church linked to a refectory and with a belfry surmounting the west entrance, Zemtsov proposed for the interiors an unusually spacious basilica with a long nave, aisles and a transept. In his design for the cathedral of the Trinity (1740; unexecuted) on a Greek cross plan, he partly anticipated the centrally planned Russian churches of the late 18th century.

Zemtsov was in charge of work at PETERHOF from 1724, where he laid out the Grand Cascade and built an annexe to the Monplaisir Palace (1726–32). He was also responsible for the overall plan for the palace and park at Tsarskoye Selo (now PUSHKIN; early 1740s) and conceived the first plan for expanding the palace by adding galleries and wings. One of his major contributions to the development of St Petersburg was the Baroque Anichkov Palace (1741–3; design partially altered during execution by Bartolomeo Francesco Rastrelli). He also worked in Moscow, designing two sets of triumphal arches (1742; destr.) for the coronation of Empress Elizabeth. Zemtsov was one of the first to organize systematic architectural training in St Petersburg, and he contributed to a proposed handbook for the architects' department there.

BIBLIOGRAPHY
P. N. Petrov: 'Arkhitektor M. G. Zemtsov' [The architect M. G. Zemtsov], Zodchiy (St Petersburg, 1877), pp. 70–73
S. S. Bronshteyn: Peterburgskaya arkhitektura 20–30-kh godov XVIII veka [St Petersburg architecture of the 1720s and 1730s], Istor. Rus. Isk., v (Moscow, 1960), pp. 122–51
A. N. Petrov, Y. A. Borisova, A. P. Naumenko and others: Pamyatniki arkhitektury Leningrada [Architectural monuments of Leningrad] (Leningrad, 1969)
M. V. Iogansen: Mikhail Zemtsov (Leningrad, 1975)
A. N. Petrov, Y. A. Petrova, A. G. Raskin and others: Pamyatniki arkhitektury prigorodov Leningrada [Architectural monuments of the suburbs of Leningrad] (Leningrad, 1983)

N. A. YEVSINA

Zen, Giovanni Battista (b Venice, 1439; d Padua, 8 May 1501). Italian cardinal and patron. He was the nephew of Pope Paul II, whose patronage, with that of his successors, assured Zen a brilliant ecclesiastical career. He was renowned for his haughtiness, wealth and munificence; his status is reflected in the buildings and furniture that he commissioned. In Rome he had a palace (destr. 19th century) built next to the portico of St Peter's. His episcopal palace in Vicenza was enriched by a double loggia (1494) built over the courtyard in an advanced style. In his will Zen left considerable sums for the rebuilding of the choir of Vicenza Cathedral and that of the church of S Fantin in Venice; for the construction of a commemorative chapel in the basilica of S Antonio (Il Santo), Padua; and for his funerary monument in S Marco, Venice.

Zen, inspired by Donatello's high altar in Il Santo, ordered an altar laden with bronze statues to be built in each of these churches, but only the directives concerning his tomb were fulfilled, and these not precisely. A chapel was adapted by Tullio Lombardo in S Marco with a bronze baldacchino sheltering statues of the Virgin, St Peter and St John the Baptist, executed by Antonio Lombardo and Paolo Savin, and a bronze tomb by Savin and Giovanni Battista Bregno. This ensemble was the most important bronzework of the Italian Renaissance to follow Donatello's high altar in Padua.

BIBLIOGRAPHY
P. Paoletti: L'architettura e la scultura del Rinascimento in Venezia (Venice, 1893)
G. G. Zorzi: 'Contributo alla storia dell'arte vicentina', Miscellanea di storia Veneto tridentina (1926), pp. 103–21
G. Soranzo: 'Giovanni Battista Zen', Riv. Stor. Chiesa Italia, xvi (1962), pp. 249–74
B. Jestaz: La Chapelle Zen à Saint-Marc de Venise (Stuttgart, 1986)

BERTRAND JESTAZ

Zenale, Bernardo (b Treviglio, c. 1464; d Milan, 10 Feb 1526). Italian painter and architect. In 1481 Zenale was already a qualified master and a member of the Scuola di S Luca, the painters' guild, in Milan. In 1485 he and BERNARDINO BUTINONE were hired by Simone da San Pellegrino and other officials of S Martino, Treviglio, to paint a large altarpiece for the high altar (in situ); the carving of the frame was sub-contracted to Ambrogio and Giovanni Pietro Donati. By January 1491 the altarpiece had been installed, and Zenale and Butinone made a final payment to the Donati brothers. The two-tiered polyptych, in an elaborate pedimented frame, shows the Virgin and Child, St Martin and the beggar and other saints. The architectural setting for each group, shown in steep perspective, is festooned with swags and encrusted with decorative patterning.

During the 1480s and early 1490s Zenale frequently worked with Butinone: from these years date the decorations, including Dominican saints, for the nave of S Maria delle Grazie, Milan (in situ), the frescoes of the Life of St Ambrose in the chapel of Ambrogio Griffi in S Pietro in Gessate, Milan (in situ), and the frescoes (destr.) for a confraternity at Mozzánica, near Treviglio. In December 1490 the painters were ordered to assist in the ornamentation of the Sala della Balla in the Castello Sforzesco, which was being prepared for the nuptial celebrations of Lodovico Sforza and Beatrice d'Este.

In 1494 Zenale received a payment from the confraternity of S Maria Assunta della Passione in S Ambrogio, Milan, for a triptych of the Virgin and Child with SS Ambrose and Jerome (Milan, Mus. Sacro S Ambrogio); only the central panel is by his hand. In 1501–2 he executed an altarpiece for the Scuola di Santa Maria at Cantù, near Como. The central panel is of the Virgin and Child (Malibu, CA, Getty Mus.; see fig.); other panels that have been associated with the ensemble include SS Francis and John the Baptist (Milan, Fond. Bagatti Valsecchi), SS Stephen and Anthony of Padua (Milan, Mus. Poldi Pezzoli) and the tondi of St Jerome and St Ambrose (Milan, Mus. Poldi Pezzoli). In 1503 he was contracted by the church of S Martino, Treviglio, to provide designs (untraced) for an

Bernardo Zenale: *Virgin and Child*, oil on panel, 1430×855 mm, 1501–2 (Malibu, CA, J. Paul Getty Museum)

organ case to be carved by Benedetto Canzoli. In 1502 and 1506 he was painting in S Maria presso S Celso, Milan.

Initially, Zenale was influenced by Butinone, who for his part appears to have been much impressed by Ferrarese masters of the 1460s and 1470s. By the turn of the 16th century, however, Zenale's style had become more 'modern'. The central panel of the Cantù altarpiece has none of the decorative extravagance that characterized the earlier Treviglio altarpiece, and the figures, more naturally posed, are placed in front of a Leonardesque landscape. Although Zenale was interested in Leonardo's achievement, his debt to the Florentine is slight; his later manner owes more to Vincenzo Foppa, Ambrogio Bergognone and other Lombard contemporaries. Few securely attributable works of his have survived, but it seems that his style did not undergo dramatic changes between 1500 and his death. A group of paintings (*c.* 1510 and later) that were formerly attributed to him, including the *Circumcision* (Paris, Louvre), the *Virgin and Child with St Domenico, the Blessed Alano della Rupe and ?Donors* (Oleggio, Mus. A. Relig.) and the *Virgin and Child*, called the Noseda *Madonna* (Milan, Brera), are by the painter called the Master XL by W. Suida (*Leonardo und sein Kreis*, Munich, 1929).

It is not known when Zenale began to work as an architect; all the documents attesting to his activity in that field are from the second and third decades of the 16th century. By 1513 he had returned to S Maria presso S Celso to work on a model (destr.) of the church; by April 1514 he was, with Antonio da Lonate, general architect to the building. In 1519 the deputies of Milan Cathedral nominated him to oversee the construction of a wooden model of the cathedral (Milan, Mus. Duomo); in August 1522 he succeeded Giovanni Antonio Amadeo as one of its two general architects. Towards the end of his life he wrote a treatise on the theory of perspective (untraced).

BIBLIOGRAPHY

Zenale e Leonardo: Tradizione e rinnovamento della pittura lombarda (exh. cat., Milan, Mus. Poldi Pezzoli, 1982) [good text with complete bibliog.]

J. Shell: *Painters in Milan, 1490–1530* (diss., New York U., 1986), pp. 1259–418

P. C. Marani: *Leonardo e i Leonardeschi a Brera* (Florence, 1987)

JANICE SHELL

Zenderoudi, Hussein (*b* Tehran, 1937). Iranian painter and printmaker. He studied at the College of Fine Arts and the College of Decorative Arts in Tehran and began to exhibit his work early in his career, at the Biennales in Paris (1959–63), Tehran (1960–66), São Paulo (1963) and Venice (1964), receiving a number of awards. He first began to be influenced by Iranian Shi'ite folk art in 1959, presenting it in his work in a distinctive way, with neither parody nor satire. He went to live in Paris in 1961 but continued to take a close interest in the development of art in Iran. At the third Tehran Biennale in 1962, held in the Abyaz Palace in the Gulistan compound, he exhibited canvases that consisted of geometric patterns of squares, triangles and circles, using colours characteristic of religious folk art, and covered with calligraphy to create a distinctive texture. It was on this occasion that the Iranian art critic Karim Emami first used the word SAQQAKHANA to describe the mood of Zenderoudi's work. In works produced in the late 1960s and 1970s, Zenderoudi's interest in the use of calligraphy developed further. He also executed two series of silkscreen prints for the Koran, published by the Club du Livre in 1972 and 1980. (An untitled etching of 1986 by Zenderoudi is illustrated at IRAN, fig. 3; *see also* IRAN, §2.)

BIBLIOGRAPHY

A. Tadjvidi: *L'Art moderne en Iran* (Tehran, 1967)

K. Emami: 'Modern Persian Artists', *Iran Faces the Seventies*, ed. E. Yarshater (New York, 1971)

E. Yarshater: 'Contemporary Persian Painting', *Highlights of Persian Art*, ed. R. Ettinghausen and E. Yarshater (Boulder, CO, 1979), pp. 367–74

□

Zenete, Marqueses del. *See under* MENDOZA.

Zenetos, Takis Ch. (*b* Athens, 1926; *d* Athens, 28 June 1977). Greek architect. He studied at the Ecole des Beaux-Arts, Paris (1946–54). His work is characterized by an exploration of technology following two principles: the first was that housing should be the most elaborate and luxurious product of society, in complete opposition to the trends toward low-cost, low-quality housing; the second was the concern to break up what he called the 'cubic box' of the Modernist private house in order to integrate the interior with the environment. This was achieved by means of extensive glazing to afford protection from multiple refractions of sunlight, as in the house (1961) at Xanthou 21, Glyfada, Attica (*see* GREECE, fig. 1), which has a commanding, hovering roof. He was also concerned with spatial flexibility and versatility and used extensively movable and removable parts, as in the block of flats (with M. Apostolidis, 1959), at Amalias 34, Athens, where sliding absorbent glass panels fitted above the balcony parapet offer protection from the sun.

Zenetos also designed factories, where functionality, flexibility and versatility are combined with a thorough understanding of construction technology. These buildings are generally characterized by the positioning of cladding in front of the load-bearing elements and by the extensive application of prefabrication. The best examples are the renovation (with Apostolidis, 1957) of the Fix Brewery, Syngrou 53, Athens (probably the most successful example of a Greek factory integrated with the environment), and the Bravo Coffee Mill (with Elias G. Biris and Maria Melidoni, 1973) at Kifissou 100, Aigaleo, Attica. He also used prefabrication in the school building (1969–76) on Papagou and Thrasyvoulou Streets, Agios Dimitrios, Attica, which is an unconventional curvilinear composition with extensive *brise-soleil* of carefully calculated shape and size.

WRITINGS
'City Planning and Electronics', *Archit. Themata*, iii (1969), pp. 114–25
'Town Planning and Electronics', *Archit. Themata*, vii (1973), pp. 122–35

BIBLIOGRAPHY
J. Donat, ed.: *World Architecture* (London, 1964–7)
F. Loyer: *Architecture de la Grèce contemporaine* (diss., U. Paris III, 1966)
Takis Ch. Zenetos, 1926–1977 (Athens, 1978)

ALEXANDER KOUTAMANIS

Zen 49. German association of non-objective artists, founded in the Galerie Otto Stangl in Munich on 19 July 1949. Its seven founder-members were the painters Willi Baumeister, Rolf Cavael (1898–1979), Gerhard Fietz (*b* 1910), Rupprecht Geiger, Willi Hempel (1905–85), Fritz Winter and the sculptor Brigitte Matschinsky-Denninghof. Originally called the Gruppe der Ungegenständlichen, the group took the name Zen 49 in 1950 and saw itself as keeper of the traditions of the Blaue Reiter in Munich and of the Bauhaus, taking up artistic positions that had been vilified by the Nazis as 'degenerate'. The new name of Zen 49 was inspired by a general understanding of Zen Buddhism rather than by any intensive preoccupation with the subject. Through Eugen Herrigel's *Zen in der Kunst des Bogenschiessens* (Konstanz, 1948) and Daisetz Taitaro Suzuki's *Die grosse Befreiung* (Leipzig, 1939; 3rd edn, Konstanz, 1948), Zen was known as a spiritual pathway, along which the unconscious was made conscious, and the group's name was chosen in reference to the philosophy's open and non-specific character. The date of foundation was affixed in order to indicate that the group was not to be identified exclusively with the oriental philosophy.

Zen philosophy had already interested such artists as Adolf Hölzel, Oskar Schlemmer and Johannes Itten, all spiritual forefathers of Zen 49, and Zen appeared as an underlying theme of Baumeister's *Das Unbekannte in der Kunst* (1947) as a process of unconscious form-finding. This publication and the lectures and exhibitions by Zen 49 may be seen in the broadest sense as stating the theoretical principles binding the group together. There was never a true group manifesto, however, and the only common goal was the advancement of abstract art. In post-war Germany especially, this was seen to represent an ideological programme with abstraction as the expression of an artistic stance aiming at freedom and pluralism. The group was attacked accordingly, although it was supported by the British consul, John Anthony Thwaites, and members of the American military administration in Munich, and in April 1950 it opened its first exhibition as Zen 49 in the Central Art Collecting Point of the Amerikahaus in Munich. Works exhibited included Geiger's *76E* (1948; Hagen, Osthaus Mus.), Baumeister's *Schwarzer Drachen und Blau* (1950; Strasbourg, Mus. A. Mod.) and Winter's *Composition* (1950; Munich, Staatsgal. Mod. Kst). Further exhibitions were held with increasing numbers of participants in 1951, 1953 and 1955, with lecture series and discussions on abstract art. Artists connected with the group in the 1950s included Julius Bissier and many artists associated with *Art informel*, such as Hans Hartung and Pierre Soulages. In 1956–7 Zen 49 organized the first group exhibition of German abstract artists to be held in the USA after World War II, before ceasing activities in 1957.

WRITINGS
W. Baumeister: *Das Unbekannte in der Kunst* (Stuttgart, 1947)

BIBLIOGRAPHY
Zen 49: Erste Ausstellung im April 1950 (exh. cat. by F. Roh and J. A. Thwaites, Munich, Amerikahaus, 1950) [15 pp.; does not incl. reproductions]
Die ersten zehn Jahre: Orientierungen: Zen 49 (exh. cat., ed. J. Poetter; Baden-Baden, Staatl. Ksthalle, 1986–7) [incl. facs. of 1950 cat.]
M.-A. v. Lüttichau: 'Zen 49', *Stationen der Moderne* (exh. cat., ed. E. Roters; W. Berlin, Berlin. Gal., 1988), pp. 378–85

CLAUDIA BÜTTNER

Zenghelis, Elia. *See under* OFFICE FOR METROPOLITAN ARCHITECTURE.

Ženíšek, František (*b* Prague, 25 May 1849; *d* Prague, 15 Nov 1916). Bohemian painter. From 1863 to 1877 he studied at the Prague Academy of Visual Arts and the Vienna Akademie der Bildenden Künste under Eduard Engerth (1818–97), Josef Mathias von Trenkwald (1824–97) and Jan Swerts (1820–79). He assisted Trenkwald and Swerts on large-scale decorative schemes (Trenkwald's wall paintings in the Votivskirche, Vienna, and Swerts's Hôtel de Ville, Courtrai, Belgium), which launched his successful career as a mural painter. His most important commission was the decoration of the National Theatre in Prague (1880–83), on which he worked partly with Mikoláš Aleš. Ženíšek's principal works were both the first curtain of the theatre and the main hall's ceiling decoration.

Ženíšek's work draws on the idea of a national style, originated by Josef Mánes. A capable draughtsman with a smooth and elegant manner, he was active in many branches of art and became one of the principal official Czech painters of his time. His paintings of subjects from early Bohemian history won great acclaim, and he was also an outstanding portrait painter (the *Artist's Mother*, 1884; Prague, Prague Castle). He taught at the School of Applied

Arts, from which he later moved to the Prague Academy. However his work had little influence on the development of Czech painting at the end of the century.

BIBLIOGRAPHY
Thieme-Becker
F. X. Jiřík: 'František Ženíšek', *Dílo* [Work], 3(1905–6), pp. 217–88
J. Neumann: *Modern Czech Painting and the Classical Tradition* (Prague, 1958), pp. 24–7

ROMAN PRAHL

Zenodoros (*fl* mid-1st century AD). Greek bronze sculptor, active in Rome and Gaul. His name ('foreign gift') suggests that he may have been born in Massalia (Marseille), Asia Minor, Egypt or Syria, and according to Pliny (*Natural History* XXXIV.xviii.46) he was the foremost sculptor of colossal statues of the 1st century AD. From AD 54 to 64 Zenodoros worked in Arvernis, Gaul, making a bronze statue of *Mercury*, for which he was paid 40 million sesterces. Nero commissioned him to make a colossal imperial portrait *c.* 36 m high, which was placed in his palace, the Domus Aurea in Rome (Pliny: XXXIV.xviii.45–6; Suetonius: *Nero* xxxi). During the reign of Vespasian (AD 69–79) it was converted into a statue of the Sun god, *Sol* (Aelius Spartianicus: *Hadrian* XIX.xii; Herodian: I.xv.9; Pliny: XXXIV.xviii.45). A replica of the *Mercury* was known in Corinth in antiquity (Pausanias: *Guide to Greece* II.iii.4) and several extant copies may reflect the original appearance of the statue. The colossal statue of *Nero*, however, cannot be accurately reconstructed. According to Pliny's account, Zenodoros no longer employed the lost wax technique, and he created a polychrome effect with silver and gold additions to the bronze. He was able to imitate earlier styles, since the copies of *Mercury* resemble the work of Lysippos, while according to Pliny he copied two silver cups in the style of Kalamis.

BIBLIOGRAPHY
Enc. A. Ant.; Pauly–Wissowa
J. Overbeck: *Die antiken Schriftquellen zur Geschichte der bildenden Künste bei den Griechen* (Leipzig, 1868/*R* Hildesheim, 1959), nos 2185, 2273–6

DIANE HARRIS

Zenone da Vaprio, Giovanni. *See* GIOVANNI ZENONE DA VAPRIO.

Zensaburō Kojima. *See* KOJIMA, ZENSABURŌ.

Zero. International group of artists founded in Düsseldorf and active from 1958 until 1966. Membership of this informal association varied, but the core of the group was made by Heinz Mack, Otto Piene and Günther Uecker. The range of art produced by Zero members ran from monochrome painting to Nouveau Réalisme, and to object art via kinetic art and light art. The common element was found in young artists who wanted to overcome the subjective expression inherent in Tachism and *Art informel*, which was still strongly characterized by post-war intellectual movements such as Existentialism. By challenging the artistic ideas of the 1920s again (e.g. Suprematism and Constructivism), it was hoped to find a way of revitalizing and spiritualizing 'concrete' means of expression that did not reproduce the old world but rather opened up new forms of perception and levels of consciousness.

The group's history is linked to that of the eponymous journal, of which only three issues were published (1958–61). The first, published on 24 April 1958, contained texts by Yves Klein, Heinz Mack and Otto Piene, and the poem 'Voyelles' by Arthur Rimbaud. Its publication coincided with the seventh evening exhibition in Mack and Piene's studios in the yard of an old factory building at 69 Gladbacher Strasse, Düsseldorf, entitled *Das rote Bild (Bilder, deren bestimmende Farbe Rohe ist)*, which included 45 artists. These evening exhibitions began on 11 April 1957 and provided the subject for much dispute amongst the artists of the Düsseldorf-based Gruppe 53. Thereafter discussions centred on the planned new journal that was inspired mainly by Yves Klein, whose work was shown for the first time in West Germany in the newly opened Alfred Schmela Gallery in Düsseldorf at the end of May 1957. According to Piene the name 'Zero' was not meant to reflect an 'expression of nihilism', but rather '... the immeasurable zone in which an old condition develops into an unknown new one'.

Zero 2 was published in October 1958 to accompany the eighth evening exhibition, *Vibration*, and contained manifestos by Mack ('Die Ruhe der Unruhe') and Piene ('Die Reinheit des Lichts'). The exhibition, which included work by Oskar Holweck (*b* 1924), Adolf Zillmann, Almir Mavignier (*b* 1925), Mack and Piene, had the theme of visual movement. The field was then open to kinetic art and to light art. By 1959 exchange and criticism of ideas occurred on an international level. Jean Tinguely's exhibition at the end of January 1959 in the Schmela Gallery, for which Yves Klein wrote the opening speech 'La Collaboration entre artistes créateurs', led to joint work. Tinguely dropped 150,000 leaflets of his manifesto *Für Statik* over Düsseldorf. In Uecker's studio in Düsseldorf there was a three-day artists' festival for Tinguely and Klein, with a blue and a red room. In March 1959 the Hessenhuis, the port storehouse in Antwerp, became an international meeting place through the exhibition *Vision in Motion—Motion in Vision* initiated by Tinguely with Paul van Hoeydorck, Pol Bury and Daniel Spoerri; its title was in homage to László Moholy-Nagy. As well as Mack, Piene and Uecker, ten other artists took part in the show. A common theme emerged of new dynamic phenomena used in art to expand human perception.

In the Festival d'art d'avantgarde in Paris in 1960 a distinction between the movements 'Zero—The New Idealism' and 'Nouveau Réalisme' was first drawn. It was not, however, until July of the following year at the *Zero—Edition, Exposition, Demonstration* exhibition in the Schmela Gallery in Düsseldorf that the first joint action of the core of the group took place. The collaboration between Mack, Piene and Uecker determined further joint projects up to 1966. The exhibition, for which *Zero 3* was published, led to the first Happening-like action in Düsseldorf. The gallery was nailed up, the street in front was painted with a large white circle and a hot air balloon was released. A further *Zero-Festival* was held in the following year on the Rheinwiesen in Düsseldorf. Zero as a movement represented the energy and imagination that was unfolding in society with the aim of a more beautiful, better world. Nature and technology were to meet harmoniously in this vision. The optimistic outlook of that time, in which political obstacles began to give way and in which new perspectives seemed possible, found a visual expression in the Zero projects.

In 1962 important international Zero exhibitions took place in Antwerp, Brussels and Ghent, and in particular the *Nul = Zero* exhibition at the Stedelijk Museum, Amsterdam. For these the Düsseldorf Zero artists created many joint 'Zero rooms' in which physical gravity seemed to be suspended. In 1964 one of these optical-kinetic rooms was presented as 'Hommage à Fontana' at the *Documenta III* in Kassel (now in Düsseldorf, Kstmus.). In the same year the Zero artists went to London (McRoberts and Tunnard Gallery) and to New York (Howard Wise Gallery) and Philadelphia. International success and diverging artistic content and interests led, however, to the group's dissolution. The group appeared one last time at the Städtisches Kunstmuseum in Bonn in 1966. In 1973 a retrospective Zero room was installed in the Kunstmuseum in Düsseldorf to encapsulate the international Zero movement.

WRITINGS
O. Piene: 'The Development of Group "Zero"', *TLS* (3 Sept 1964), pp. 812–13
Zero (Cologne, 1973) [reprint of *Zero 1* to *3*]

BIBLIOGRAPHY
Mack, Piene, Uecker (exh. cat., foreword P. Wember; Krefeld, Mus. Haus Lange, 1963)
Zero: Mack, Piene, Uecker (exh. cat., New York, Howard Wise Gal., 1964)
Heinz Mack, Otto Piene, Günther Uecker (exh. cat., Hannover, Kestner-Ges., 1965)
Zero in Bonn: Mack, Piene, Uecker (exh. cat., Bonn, Städt. Kstmus., 1966)
Zero-Raum (exh. cat., article by G. Storck; Düsseldorf, Kstmus., 1973)
Zero: Bildvorstellungen einer europäischen Avantgarde, 1958–1964 (exh. cat., articles by U. Perucchi-Petri, H. Weitemeier-Steckel and E. Gomringer; Zurich, Ksthaus, 1979)
Zero Internationalen Antwerpen (exh. cat., articles by J. F. Buyck, W. van Mulders and H. Verscharen; Antwerp, Kon. Mus. S. Kst., 1980)
A. Kuhn: *Zero: Eine Avantgarde der sechziger Jahre* (Frankfurt am Main, 1991)
Zero: Eine europäische Avantgarde (exh. cat., Essen, Gal. Neher; Munich, Gal. Heseler; Koblenz, Mittelrhein-Mus.; 1992) [articles by A. Kuhn and O. Piene]
STEPHAN VON WIESE

Žerotín. Bohemian family of patrons. Jan Žerotín (*d* 25 Feb 1583), chief justice of Moravia, visited France in the service of the Holy Roman Emperor Charles V. A member of the Czech Brethren, he established on his estate at Kralice the sect's printing works, issuing some 70 publications, including a translation of the Bible. In the 1570s he transformed the castles at Náměšť nad Oslavou and Rosice in Renaissance style. Náměšť Castle, which was probably the work of Leonardo Garovo (*d* 1574), was completed as an enclosed four-wing block *c.* 1580, as was Rosice Castle *c.* 1600. His son (1) Karel Žerotín and his nephew (2) Ladislav Žerotín continued the renovation of the family's castles and the tradition of humanist scholarship and patronage.

BIBLIOGRAPHY
A. Prokop: *Die Markgrafschaft Mähren in kunstgeschichtlicher Beziehung*, iii (Vienna, 1904), pp. 668, 685, 744, 748, 763, 808–17, 830, 847–50, 945
Z. Tobolka: *Žerotínská knihovna* [The library of the lords of Žerotín] (Prague, 1926)
M. Bohatcová: *Bratrské tisky ivančické a kralické* [Books of the printing offices of the Brethren at Ivančice and Kralice] (Prague, 1951)
E. Šamánková: *Architektura české renesance* [Architecture of the Czech Renaissance] (Prague, 1961), pp. 11–12, 51–3, 87–90, 104, 112, 120–21, 124, 126
J. Krčálová: 'Arts in the Renaissance and Mannerist periods', *Renaissance Art in Bohemia* (London, New York, Sydney and Toronto, 1979), pp. 49–147
Hrady, zámky a tvrze v Čechách, na Moravě a ve Slezsku [Fortified castles, châteaux and small castles in Bohemia, Moravia and Silesia], 2 vols (Prague, 1981–3)
F. Seibt, ed.: *Renaissance in Böhmen: Geschichte, Wissenschaft, Architektur, Plastik, Malerei, Kunsthandwerk* (Munich, 1985)
J. Krčálová: 'O rodině Francesca Borrominiho' [About the family of F. Borromini], *Umění*, xxxiii (1985), pp. 414–25
——: 'Renesanční architektura v Čechach a na Moravě' [Renaissance architecture in Bohemia and Moravia], *Dějiny českého výtvarného umění* [History of Czech fine art], ii/1 (Prague, 1989), pp. 6–62

(1) Karel Žerotín (*b* Brandýs nad Orlice, 14–24 Sept 1564; *d* Přerov, 9 Oct 1636). He was one of the most widely read and travelled men of his time, having been educated in Switzerland, Italy, France, England, Germany and the Netherlands. He was a prominent jurist, and from 1608 to 1614 he headed the Moravian administration. In 1608 he led the revolt against the Holy Roman Emperor Rudolf II. He completed the renovation of the castles at Rosice and Přerov (1610–12) and built another at Dřevohostice (1618). The arcaded courtyard of this last is similar to those at Náměšť and Rosice, both of which he had decorated with sculptural motifs. At Náměšť he added an outside staircase in the Italian style, such as is also seen at the residence of another branch of the family at Hustopeče nad Bečvou. A bibliophile like his father, he owned an ample library, employed librarians and acquired books from abroad, ordered from catalogues sent from Frankfurt am Main. As a patron and supporter of writers, scientists, theologians and historians, including John Levenclaus (1533–93) and Jan Amos Comenius (1592–1670), he was the recipient of dedications of several works. At Rosice his gallery included the portraits of important Frenchmen; his own portrait (*c.* 1600; Wrocław, T. Mikulski Voivodship & Mun. Pub. Lib.) was the work of a local painter.

BIBLIOGRAPHY
P. Chlumecký: *Karl von Zierotin und seine Zeit*, 2 vols (Brno, 1862–79)
F. Dvorský: 'Dopisy Karla st. ze Žerotína, 1591–1610' [Letters of Karel Žerotín the elder, 1591–1610], *Archiv Český*, xxvii (1904), pp. 1–600
O. Odložilík: *Karel starší ze Žerotína* [Karel Žerotín the elder] (Prague, 1936)
J. Válka: 'Karel starší ze Žerotína a jeho apologia' [Karel Žerotín the elder and his apologia], *Kralické Tvrze*, viii (1975–7), pp. 1–19
N. Rejchertová: *Karel starší ze Žerotína: Z korespondence* [Karel Žerotín the elder: selected letters] (Prague, 1982)
J. Válka: 'Karel starší ze Žerotína (1564–1636)' [Karel Žerotín the elder (1564–1636)], *Kralické Tvrze*, xiii (1986), pp. 1–7

(2) Ladislav Velen Žerotín (*b* 1587; *d* 1638). Cousin of (1) Karel Žerotín. He spent several years abroad at Protestant schools and in Padua and Siena, which influenced his cultural endeavours. In 1618 he was one of the leaders of the Bohemian revolt and in 1619 headed the Moravian administration. Among his five large Renaissance castles, that at Tatenice (1606) is interesting for its stuccoed vaults. The castle near Moravská Třebová (1610–20), probably designed by Giovanni Maria Filippi, is remarkable for a monumental Mannerist three-storey gateway, a variation on the motif of the triumphal arch, inspired by Sebastiano Serlio's treatises. The castle's furnishings included partly gilded furniture and tapestries, Persian and Turkish carpets and 22 large Italian tapestries with historical scenes. Žerotín owned many jewels by Isaak Pictet (*fl* 1618–19) and Jean Baptiste Desale (*fl* 1618) among others and inherited the collections of his ancestors, the lords of Boskovice, and their library of Italian incunabula. Among the books he acquired, some were dedicated to him by the authors, including the *Map of Moravia* by Jan Amos Comenius (1592–1670). His collection of paintings included works by Pietro de Petri (*c*. 1550–1611), to whose son Simeon de Petri is attributed the portrait of *Ladislav Velen Žerotín* (Bludov, Pict. Gal.). His residence at Moravská Třebová was a centre of the sciences and arts, to which he invited German and Italian poets, theologians, alchemists, physicians, artists and musicians. After the defeat of the Bohemian revolt in 1620 he emigrated, and his estates, castles and collections were confiscated.

BIBLIOGRAPHY
F. Hrubý: *Ladislav Velen ze Žerotína* (Prague, 1930)
O. Pechová: *Moravská Třebová* (Prague, 1954)

J. KRČÁLOVÁ

Zervos. French collectors, writers and patrons. Christian Zervos (*b* Cephalonia, Greece, 1 Jan 1889; *d* Paris, 12 Sept 1970) was of Greek origin and worked briefly for the magazine *L'Art d'aujourd'hui*, before founding *Cahiers d'art* in 1926. Covering contemporary painting and sculpture, music, architecture, film and photography, this magazine was internationally acclaimed not only for its promotion of major modernist artists but also for its immaculate presentation and typography. Its authors included critics, historians and aestheticians (Zervos himself, Tériade, Maurice Raynal, Georges Duthuit, P. G. Bruguière, Dupin), lending each issue a balance of historical analysis and poetic sensibility. Zervos's concern with the relationship of image to text also extended to confrontations between contemporary art and non-European or primitive sources, such as Cycladic, African, or Oceanic art.

In addition to his editorial work, Zervos published his own monograph on Henri Rousseau (1927) and then books by other authors on Frank Lloyd Wright (1927), Klee (1929) and Kandinsky (1930), as well as on more general themes, including *Greek Art* (1933), *The Art of Mesopotamia* (1935) and *The Art of Catalonia* (1937). In 1932 he published the first volume of his catalogue raisonné of Picasso's work, a monumental project that, although uncompleted at his death, ran to 33 volumes (the first 23 vols by Zervos). Interrupted by World War II, publication of *Cahiers d'art* was resumed in 1946, as was a remarkably printed and illustrated series of volumes devoted to prehistoric art and to such artists as Léger, Brancusi, Jacques Villon and Victor Brauner. The review closed in 1960, after 97 numbers, but the rest of the publishing programme continued until 1970.

Christian's wife, Yvonne Zervos [née Marion] (*b* 1905; *d* Paris, 20 Jan 1970), opened a small gallery in 1929 on the same premises as her husband's publishing house at 14 Rue du Dragon, where she showed painting, architectural models and objects by Alvar Aalto. From 1939, in a much larger space on the Rue Bonaparte (the May Gallery), she exhibited such artists as Arp, Brancusi, Klee, Léger, Picasso and, after World War II, Giacometti, Magritte,

Wifredo Lam, Victor Brauner, Jean Hélion, Serge Poliakoff, Alexander Calder, Vieira da Silva and Arpad Szenès (*b* 1897). She also helped to save works of art in Spain during the Civil War, and during World War II she transformed the publishing house in the Rue du Dragon into a depot for a clandestine press. She organized several remarkable exhibitions, which proved important landmarks in French artistic life. Among them were *Origines et développement de l'art international indépendant* at the Jeu de Paume in Paris in 1937, *Peinture et sculpture contemporain* in Avignon in 1947 and *Pablo Picasso, 1969–1970* in 1970 in the Palais des Papes in Avignon. The Zervoses' private collection was bequeathed to the commune of Vézelay, where they had purchased a farm in the 1930s.

WRITINGS
C. Zervos: *Pablo Picasso*, 33 vols (Paris, 1932–78) [vols 24–33 completed by M. Gagarine]

BIBLIOGRAPHY
Hommage à Christian et Yvonne Zervos (exh. cat., Paris, Grand Pal., 1970)
Le 20ème Siècle au Musée Rolin (exh. cat., intro. by C. Limousin; Autun, Mus. Rolin, 1984) [incl. cat. of 34 paintings from the Zervos col.]

ISABELLE MONOD-FONTAINE

Zeshin Shibata. *See* SHIBATA ZESHIN.

Zettervall, Helgo (*b* Lidköping, 21 Nov 1831; *d* Stockholm, 1907). Swedish architect and restorer. After gaining early experience as a builder, he studied at the Academy of Arts from 1853 to 1859 and then worked for his former teacher F. W. Scholander. In 1860 Zettervall was appointed cathedral architect at Lund, where he remained in charge of the restoration works for the following 20 years. The restoration of the Romanesque cathedral at Lund necessitated the structural rebuilding of large parts of the edifice, especially the west front, with its twin towers. Zettervall followed the fashion of the time in valuing stylistic accuracy and uniformity above archaeological considerations. From a historical perspective his work was destructive, but as architecture Lund Cathedral is a *tour de force*. In the 1880s and 1890s the Gothic cathedrals of Skara and Uppsala were restored along the same lines, the interiors being particularly successful. Despite his involvement in these projects, Zettervall was not a true ecclesiologist so much as a gifted and versatile architect. While he was working at Lund, for example, he also designed a series of new or rebuilt churches and public buildings. For the complete rebuilding of Malmö Town Hall (1865) he made effective use of Northern Renaissance themes, while for the main building of Lund University he employed a vigorous classicist Renaissance style.

In 1882 Zettervall was appointed Superintendent of Architecture, and he remained responsible for public architecture in Sweden until 1899. In this capacity he strongly supported the use of neo-Gothic for ecclesiastical buildings. His own most prominent churches in this style, with slim granite columns and making effective use of dressed brick and slate roofs, are the church of All Saints (1861–91) in Lund and the Oscar Frederick Church (1887–90) in Göteborg. His secular works display a great versatility in an eclectic range of styles. His Medical Clinic (1864) in Lund is in a very free Romanesque, while his projects for a parliament building were in a classicist neo-Renaissance style. Palme House, a block of flats opposite the Royal Palace in Stockholm, demonstrates Zettervall's talent for energetic combination of motifs and materials into a coherent whole.

See also SWEDEN, §II, 3.

WRITINGS
ed. C. Callmer: *Något om mig sjelf* [Autobiographical notes], Acta Bibliothecae Regiae Stockholmensis (Stockholm, 1981)

BIBLIOGRAPHY
Helgo Zettervall (exh. cat. by A. Aman, Stockholm, Arkitmus., 1966)
At förse Riket med beständige och prydlige Byggnader [A historical account of the Royal Superintendency and the National Board of Building] (Stockholm, 1968)
H. O. Andersson and F. Bedoire: *Swedish Architecture* (Stockholm, 1986)

□

Zeugheer, Leonhard (*b* Zurich, 11 Jan 1812; *d* Zurich, 16 Dec 1866). Swiss architect. He served his architectural apprenticeship in Neuenburg *c.* 1830 and then probably went to Paris. He worked in Birmingham (1833–5) under Thomas Rickman before moving to Zurich, where most of his buildings were executed. They include the city's first large shops, in Hechtplatz (1835), as well as the first large residential buildings, including the Escherhäuser (1836–40). The influence of English buildings, particularly St Pancras New Church (1819–22), London, by William Inwood and Henry William Inwood, is evident in Zeugheer's church at Neumünster (1837–8), which is regarded as the most important Neo-classical church in Zurich. From the 1830s he was the most fashionable architect in Zurich, until he was superseded in the late 1850s by Gottfried Semper. In Zeugheer's domestic work, he first produced simple Neo-classical cubic structures, such as the Villa Rosenbühl (1837), and then designed the first Renaissance Revival villas in Zurich, which were enlivened with verandahs and pergolas, such as Zur Seeburg (1843–7). He later designed houses with asymmetrical plans, as in his main work, the Villa Wesendonck (1853–7), Zurich, where the exteriors have deeply recessed bays and loggias in the English manner. In the 1860s he began to design L-shaped houses with polygonal oriels, for example the Villa Bellaria (1866), Zurich, and a complex use of ornament, with decorative blind niches, cast-iron panels and balusters, as at Villette (1864–6) at Cham, or with dominant corner towers reminiscent of churches, as at the Villa Rheinburg (1866) at Gailingen. His villas and country houses are among the most important Renaissance Revival buildings in Switzerland, but he also designed imposing public buildings, for example the Knabenschule (1836–42) at Winterthur, and interior decoration, for example the Grosser Saal (1865) at the Hotel Schweizerhof, Lucerne.

UNPUBLISHED SOURCES
Zurich, Baugesch. Archv [large number of designs bequeathed by Zeugheer]

BIBLIOGRAPHY
SKL
H. Rebsamen: 'Englisches in der Zürche Neumünsterkirche und weiteren Bauten Leonhard Zeugheers', *Z. Schweiz. Archäol. & Kstgesch.*, xxix (1972), pp. 82–105
H. P. Mathis: 'Die Villette', *Zuger Neujbl.* (1988), pp. 63–84

CORNELIA BAUER

Zeuxis (*fl* late 5th century BC–early 4th). Greek painter. Zeuxis of Heraclea achieved wealth and fame as a painter in Athens around the time of the Peloponnesian Wars (431–404 BC). Pliny (*Natural History* XXXV.xxxvi.61) stated that Zeuxis began working in the fourth year of the 95th Olympiad (397 BC) and that writers who dated him to the 89th Olympiad (*c.* 424 BC) were mistaken. According to Pliny, Zeuxis was the pupil of either Demophilos of Himera or Neseus of Thasos. Both were active around 424 BC, perhaps explaining the confusion of other authors concerning Zeuxis' own date.

No paintings by Zeuxis survive, but ancient descriptions of his style suggest that he used painterly methods rather than line to create an illusion of three-dimensional form and depth. His main rival, PARRHASIOS, continued the linear tradition of APOLLODOROS by emphasizing outline and using hatching to suggest light and shade. Anecdotes record informal competitions between Zeuxis and Parrhasios in the creation of optical illusions (see Pliny: *Natural History* XXXV.xxxvi.65). These accounts may, however, be apocryphal, and the two painters seem more credibly opposed as the main practitioners of two different styles, which continued to divide artists, critics and philosophers for generations afterwards.

Using ancient literary evidence and modern painting techniques, scholars have attempted to reconstruct the essential qualities of Zeuxis' style. Pliny stated that Zeuxis painted monochromes in white (*Natural History* XXXV.xxxvi.64); although the exact meaning of this is disputed, the paintings were probably done in white on a dark background. This method would enable the painter to use impasto and opaque white highlights to suggest light: the darker, receding areas would be rendered in a thinner transparent white paint, only partly covering the background. In this way neither outline nor linear hatching would be needed to create the illusion of three-dimensional form. In polychrome painting, this method would make use of darker blues, greens and other colours to create shadows on and around a figure, replacing the hatched shadows of the linear style. Effects similar to this occur in the paintings on a Hellenistic tomb façade at Lefkadia in Macedonia (see Bruno, pls 6–8).

Ancient writers mentioned at least ten paintings by Zeuxis, including representations of *Herakles Strangling the Snakes*, *Zeus on a Throne* and *Penelope* (in which Zeuxis is said by Pliny to have represented 'morality' itself). A painting of *Helen*, which Pliny saw in the porticos of Philippus at Rome (1st century BC), reproduced the best features of five virgins from the city that had commissioned the work. Pliny (*Natural History* XXXV.xxxvi.64) stated that the painting was for the Temple of Hera Lakinia at Akragas, but Cicero (*De inventione rhetorica* II.i.1) attributed the commission to Kroton in southern Italy, where there was a famous temple of the same goddess.

The most detailed description of a painting by Zeuxis is that of the *Centaur Family* (see Lucian: *Zeuxis* iii–vii). Sulla (*c.* 138–78 BC) had apparently taken the original to Rome when he sacked Athens in 86 BC, but Lucian saw a copy in the home of a painter in Athens. It represented a female centaur reclining on the grass and nursing twin infant centaurs, one at her human breast, the other at her horse teat. Her mate was shown leaning over his family, laughing, while holding a lion cub above his head to tease or frighten the children. Lucian admired the originality of the theme, but also the contrast between the figures of the shaggy, alarming male centaur and the elegant female. He noted the subtle transition between the female's horse body and human torso. Zeuxis, on the other hand, seems to have felt that it was only the subject's novelty that was appreciated, while his artistic skill was ignored, and seems, consequently, to have withdrawn the picture from exhibition. He gave away some other works as gifts, believing that no price could reflect their true value.

Zeuxis is also said to have made terracotta statues (Pliny: *Natural History* XXXV.xxxvi.66). None has survived, but they were probably not major works, since Fulvius Nobilior left them behind in Ambrakia when he transferred some statues of Muses to Rome (189 BC). It has been claimed that Zeuxis decorated the palace of Archelaos of Macedon in the Macedonian capital (*see* GREECE, ANCIENT, §VII, 2(i)).

Praised by some ancient writers (e.g. Quintilian: *Institutio oratoria* XII.x.4) as the inventor of chiaroscuro, Zeuxis was criticized by others for creating frivolous illusions. Both Aristotle (*Poetics* 1450a.27–9) and, by implication, Plato (*Republic* X.602d.1–4) condemned him for being more interested in visual tricks than in depicting character (*ethos*) or creating aesthetically pleasing compositions with simple geometric forms and a clear line. To these writers, and doubtless to many contemporary critics, Zeuxis' innovative works seemed degenerate in comparison with the linear 'character paintings' of Parrhasios and the Early Classical painter POLYGNOTOS OF THASOS. Nevertheless, he was one of the foremost painters of his time and among the most influential painters of antiquity.

BIBLIOGRAPHY

Pliny: *Natural History*
Quintilian: *Institutio oratoria*
Lucian: *Zeuxis*
J. Overbeck: *Die antiken Schriftquellen zur Geschichte der bildenden Künste bei den Griechen* (Leipzig, 1868), nos 1647–91
W. Lepik-Kopaczyńska: 'Zeuxis aus Herakleia', *Helikon*, i (1961), pp. 379–426
J. J. Pollitt: *The Art of Greece: Sources and Documents* (Englewood Cliffs, 1965/rev. Cambridge, 2/1990) [trans. of the major anc. sources; with full bibliog.]
——: *The Ancient View of Greek Art* (New Haven, 1974)
K. Gschwandtler: *Zeuxis und Parrhasios: Ein Beitrag zur antiken Künstlerbiographie* (diss., Graz, Karl-Franzens-U., 1975)
V. J. Bruno: *Form and Color in Greek Painting* (New York, 1977)

SUSAN B. MATHESON

Zevele, Henry. *See* YEVELE, HENRY.

Zhalu. *See* SHALU.

Zhambyl [formerly Talas, Taraz, Yangi, Awliya Ata, Mirzoyam, Dzhambul]. City in the Talas River valley of southern Kazakhstan and capital city of the region of the same name. Excavations have established that the area, conveniently located along the trade route from Central Asia to China, was inhabited from the 1st and 2nd centuries AD, and ancient Turkish inscriptions have been found in the region. The town, known as Taraz or Talas, was first mentioned in the account of the Byzantine ambassador Zemarkhos in 568, and the Chinese pilgrim Xuanzang (*c.* 630) described Ta-la-sz' as significant. In the 7th century the town had a citadel surrounded by a wall with towers and a small town precinct; it became the capital of the Karluk Turks in the 8th and 9th centuries. In 751 Muslim armies defeated Chinese troops at the Talas River, but Islam did not gain strength in the region until the late 9th century, following the campaign of the SAMANID ruler Isma'il in 893. During the 11th and 12th centuries Taraz became one of the largest centres of the Qarakhanid state, and ceramic production flourished there. The mausolea of Babadzhi-Khatun (10th–11th century) and Aisha-Bibi (11th–12th century), situated in the village of Golovachevka 12 km from the city, testify to the artistic production of the period.

The town, which became known as Yangi, suffered greatly during the invasions of the Qara Khitay (Western Liao) and the Mongols in the 13th century, and by the 14th century it was in ruins. From the late 18th century it was known as Awliya-Ata (or Auliye-Ata; Turk.: 'holy father') after the grave of the holy man Qara Khan, perhaps a Qarakhanid foundation and mentioned as early as the 17th century but rebuilt in 1856 or 1905. At the beginning of the 19th century the Talas Valley territories came under the power of the *khān*s of KOKAND, and a new city arose alongside the ruins of Taraz. In 1864 Russian troops conquered the city, which in 1938 was renamed Zhambyl after the Kazakh poet Zhambyl Zhabaev (1846–1945).

BIBLIOGRAPHY

Enc. Islam/1: 'Ṭarāz'; *Enc. Islam/2*: 'Awliyā Ata'
A. N. Bernshtam: *Pamyatniki stariny Talasskoy doliny* [Monuments of the ancient Talas Valley] (Alma-Ata, 1941)
Trudy Semirechenskoy arkheologicheskoy exspeditsiy, 1936–1938: 'Talasskaya dolina' [Works resulting from the archeological expedition to Semireche, 1936–1938: 'the Talas Valley'] (Alma-Ata, 1949)
M. S. Mershchiyev: 'K voprosy o stratigrafiy nizhnikh sloev Taraza' [On the stratigraphy of the lower strata of Taraz], *Novoe v arkheologiy Kazakhstana* [Innovations in the archaeology of Kazakhstan] (Alma-Ata, 1972)
T. N. Senigova: *Srednevekov'iy Taraz* [Medieval Taraz] (Alma-Ata, 1972)

A. A. IVANOV

Zhang Daqian [Chang Ta-ch'ien; Chang Dai-chien; *hao* Dafengtang] (*b* Neijiang, Sichuan Province, 10 May 1899; *d* Taipei, 2 April 1983). Chinese painter, calligrapher, collector and forger. From an artistic family, he began to paint under the tutelage of his mother, Ceng Yi, and did his first paid painting for the local fortune-teller when he was 12 years old. Zhang's elder sister gave him his first lessons in the classics. At 15 he embarked on three years of schooling at the Qiujing Academy in Chongzing. In 1917 he went to Kyoto in Japan to join his elder brother Zhang Shanzi (1882–1940). Here, Daqian learnt the art of textile painting, and the brothers collaborated in painting tigers: Shanzi painted the animals and Daqian the surroundings. Shanzi kept a pet tiger in the house, using it as his artistic model. In 1919 Zhang returned to China, where he continued his studies in Shanghai with the scholar Ceng Xi. He also studied with the artist Li Ruiqing (1867–1920) and was exposed to Li's calligraphy in seal script (*zhuanshu*), based on models of the Zhou to Wei periods (*c.* 1050 BC– AD 265), as well as running script (*xingshu*) and regular script (*kaishu*). Although Zhang was not primarily a calligrapher, he developed his own personal style: his characters are intentionally splayed and awkward and elements within a character lean in unexpected directions. During his time in Shanghai, Zhang entered a Buddhist temple in Songjiang and only then received the name Daqian. However, after three months he left monastic life and went home to Sichuan Province, where he was married.

Zhang remained in Sichuan until the death of his father in 1925. During this period he concentrated on the painters Zhu Da and Daoji, discovering a particular affinity with the latter. He was able to imitate these painters so effectively that he could add forged seals and signatures to paintings and fool experienced connoisseurs. Such imitative paintings by Zhang may still be circulating unacknowledged among art collectors, and there is no doubt that various major museums own Chinese 'old masters' that were, in fact, painted by Zhang. Other artists whom Zhang copied range from the 10th-century Dong Yuan and Juran to the 13th- and 14th-century artists Ni Zan and Huang Gongwang.

In 1929 Zhang joined the selection committee for the first National Exhibition of Fine Arts in Nanjing and two years later, with his brother Shanzi, accompanied an exhibition of early Chinese paintings to Tokyo. In 1933 he exhibited his works abroad for the first time at the Musée du Jeu de Paume in Paris and attracted the notice of foreign critics. The following year he exhibited in China at Beijing and Nanjing. By 1936 he was teaching at the National Central University in Nanjing under the painter Xu Beihong. In 1940 Zhang organized a group to travel to Dunhuang in Gansu Province and copy the Buddhist wall paintings. In two and a half years they completed over 200 paintings, which were exhibited in 1944 in Chengdu and Chongqing. Consequently, religious motifs executed in fine outline and filled with coloured wash became a staple of Zhang's painting.

By this time, Zhang had begun to work with the theme of the lotus. He painted lotuses from every angle, at every stage of growth, in formats ranging from small to monumental. His lotus paintings frequently feature expanses of pitch-black ink wash, which contrast starkly with the white paper beneath, and flashes of brilliant colour swirling to the surface at a point of focus (see fig.). The running colours of his lotus paintings perhaps inspired his distinctive imaginative landscapes. In these, bold panels of ink are laid on a wet page and spread to form natural patterns; sometimes a brilliant turquoise and inky black are juxtaposed, and sometimes an intense colour merges with the naked page. Blank spaces become waterfalls or rising clouds, the outlines of roofs suggest peaks, or a bridge over a curved space intimates a path. As simple washes these paintings would be considered abstract, but by adding a few strokes Zhang placed them in the tradition of Chinese landscape painting.

In 1945 Zhang exhibited his works in Chengdu and was included in a UNESCO show of contemporary art that travelled to Paris, London, Prague and Geneva. From then on he exhibited every year, frequently abroad. From 1950 to 1952 he and his family visited India, where he studied the Ajanta cave paintings. In 1952 he moved to Argentina, and two years later to Brazil. Always unconventional, with his archaic Chinese dress and old-fashioned wispy beard, wherever he travelled he was accompanied by a retinue of exotic beasts and a gourmet chef, and wherever he settled he built a Chinese garden. By 1960 Zhang's works were well known in Paris and had travelled to most other

Zhang Daqian: *White Lotus*, hanging scroll, ink and colours on paper, 1137×660mm, *c*. 1947 (New York, Metropolitan Museum of Art)

European capitals. In the 1960s he began to exhibit more frequently in Hong Kong and had the first of many exhibitions in South-east Asia. In 1967 he had his first of many shows at the National Museum of History in Taipei. By 1980 he had re-established contact with mainland China, although no exhibitions of his works were held there until after his death.

WRITINGS
with others: *Zhang Daqian linfu Dunhuang Mogaoku ji Anxi Yulin ku bihua* [Zhang Daqian's copies of paintings from the Dunhuang Mogao Caves and Anxi Yulin Caves] (Shanghai, 1947)
Masterpieces of Chinese Paintings in the Collection of Dafengtang (Tokyo, 1955)
Zhang Daqian hua ji [Collection of Zhang Daqian's paintings] (Hong Kong, 1974)

BIBLIOGRAPHY
Gao Lingmei, ed.: *Zhang Daqian hua* [Zhang Daqian's paintings] (Kowloon, 1961)
Zhang Shanzi: *Zhang Daqian kunzhong hezuo* [Collaborative paintings by Zhang Daqian and his elder brother] (Taipei, 1967)
H. Boorman: *Biographical Dictionary of Republican China* (New York, 1971)
T. C. Lai: *Three Contemporary Chinese Painters: Chang Ta-ch'ien, Ting Yin-yung and Ch'eng Shih-fa* (Seattle, 1975)
Yang Jiren: *Zhang Daqian zhuan* [Biography of Zhang Dachian] (Beijing, 1985)

Shen C. Y. Fu: *Challenging the Past: The Paintings of Chang Dai-Chien* (Washington, DC, 1991)

ELIZABETH F. BENNETT

Zhang Feng [Chang Feng; *zi* Dafeng; *hao* Shangyuan Laoren, Shengzhou Daoshi] (*b* Shangyuan, Shengzhou (now Nanjing, Jiangsu Province); *fl c.* 1645–62). Chinese painter, poet, seal-carver and government official. Like many of his literati colleagues, he remained loyal to the Ming dynasty (1368–1644) after it had been overthrown by the Manchus and withdrew from office to live as a Buddhist recluse. He led a life of relative poverty, occasionally enjoying the patronage of the nobility, which allowed him to pursue a variety of scholarly activities. In his paintings he concentrated on landscapes, flowers and figures. A contemporary of the Eight Masters of Nanjing (*see* NANJING SCHOOL), Zhang remained an independent artist in the cultured milieu of the south. Initially, he was influenced by the painters of the Yuan period (1279–1368), notably Huang Gongwang and Ni Zan, and emulated their subjective expressionism and daring brushwork, as for example in *Figure between Rocks and a Twisted Tree* (1648; Hong Kong, Chin. U.). Around 1650 Zhang travelled to Beijing to visit the temples of the north. After he returned to Nanjing his main sources of inspiration became such painters of the Northern Song period (960–1127) as Li Tang. Zhang based his landscapes on the monumentalism of the Song painters, especially as they were interpreted by Tang Yin during the late 15th century and early 16th, and he developed a descriptive style that was massive and crammed with detail, as in *Listening to the Sound of Autumn in a Misty Grove* (1657; Cleveland, OH, Mus. A.). Zhang often appended the six characters 'Zhen xiang Fo kong si hai' ('To the true incense Buddha all is emptiness within the four oceans') to his works, of which about 20 have been preserved.

BIBLIOGRAPHY
O. Sirén: *Chinese Painting: Leading Masters and Principles*, 7 vols (London and New York, 1958), v, pp. 138–42; vii, pp. 286ff
Rao Zongyi: 'Zhang Feng ji qi jiating' [Zhang Feng and his family], *Xianggang Zhongwen Daxue Zhongguo Wenhua Yanjiusuo Xuebao*, viii/1 (1976), pp. 51–70
M. Loehr: *The Great Painters of China* (Oxford, 1980), p. 314
Eight Dynasties of Chinese Painting: The Collections of the Nelson–Atkins Museum of Art, Kansas City, and the Cleveland Museum of Art (exh. cat. by Wai-kam Ho and others, Kansas City, MO, Nelson–Atkins Mus. A.; Cleveland, OH, Mus. A.; Tokyo, N. Mus.; 1980–81), pp. 275–6, fig. 211
BENT NIELSEN

Zhang Hong [Chang Hung; *zi* Jundu; *hao* Haojian] (*b* 1577; *d c.* 1652). Chinese painter. He worked in the Suzhou area of Jiangsu Province, painting mainly landscapes, with occasional figure and animal studies, notably of water buffalo. Many of his landscape paintings are topographical in character, depicting actual places; for instance, he travelled in eastern Zhejiang Province during spring 1639 and on his return painted an album of views of the region. In contrast to other Suzhou artists, Zhang did not use established compositional conventions and type-forms or the manner of some earlier master; instead he portrayed the scenes more as they appeared, adapting his representational means flexibly to the appearance of the scenery. This approach was not typical of his time, and his images were labelled strange and unusual.

One of Zhang Hong's earliest paintings, *Landscape of Shixie Hill* (1613; Taipei, N. Pal. Mus.), depicts a hill in northern Zhejiang. He painted the scene for his elder brother, basing the image on a composition commonly used by painters of the Suzhou-based WU SCHOOL. Zhang departed from convention, however, in the way he depicted mountains and their vegetation together as a coherent unit, showing trees receding convincingly in space and rendering bamboo groves in a naturalistic manner. It was more common for Chinese painters of the time to depict vegetation and rocks as separate entities appearing to rest upon, rather than grow or jut from, the earth masses. Two works of the 1620s show a different character: *Night Ascent of Huazi Hill* (handscroll, 1625; Taipei, N. Pal. Mus.) and an album, *Zhi Garden* (1627; dispersed). *Night Ascent* shows the 8th-century poet Wang Wei walking in the mountains on a winter night near his villa south of the capital Chang'an (now Xi'an, Shaanxi Province). The image is unique in Chinese painting: it shows a long ridge, beginning in the foreground, which winds gently upward to a vantage point upon which Wang Wei and two servants stand admiring the moon. The ease with which the viewer can follow the path to the top, the foreshortening of the hill, the seemingly natural way in which trees obscure houses and the evocative depiction of mist that blurs distinctions between one form and another combine to create a painterly effect quite different from the additive, analytical method of typical Chinese landscape painting.

The *Zhi Garden* album, consisting of 20 leaves, is a systematic visual exploration of a garden in Suzhou. The first leaf, *Whole View of the Zhi Garden* (ink and colours on paper; Muzzano, priv. col., see Cahill, *Distant Mountains*, pl. 4), presents an elevated view of the whole site, complete with waterways, pavilions and garden walls. Subsequent leaves show scenes of the approach and interior of the garden, such that the viewer seems to move progressively through the setting. Garden paintings were a speciality of some Suzhou masters; bird's-eye views and albums of selected garden scenes were also common (*see* also GARDEN, §VI, 1). Zhang Hong's approach was unprecedented in that he successfully combined an analytical view of the component parts of the garden in the individual leaves with a synthesis of all the parts in *Whole View*. In the first leaf he suggests a consistent ground plane, a reasonably consistent angle of view and houses and trees that become smaller and less distinct as they near a gently curving horizon. The source for this apparently radical conception probably lies in European townscape prints, such as Georg Braun and Franz Hogenberg's *Civitatis urbis terrarum* (1572–1617), a six-volume atlas of views and plans, which were introduced into Suzhou and Nanjing in the late Ming period by the Jesuits.

Wind in the Pines at Mt Gouqu (1650; Boston, MA, Mus. F.A., see fig.) is a fine example of Zhang Hong's later work. His departure from traditional Chinese landscape conventions is even more pronounced here than in *Landscape of Shixie Hill*, which still relied to some extent on a restructuring of the terrain. Distant land forms that would have been impossible to see from a single viewpoint were brought into the composition by placing them above the nearer hills. In *Mt Gouqu* Zhang relied less on such ink to approximate the soft hues, highlights and shaded hollows of verdant hills. Such techniques were discernible in the works of the 13th-century painter Xia Gui and early Ming period (1368–1644) artist Tang Yin, but, in contrast, Zhang reworked their methods in this painting in an emphatically naturalistic way. Despite Zhang's innovations, Chinese critics seldom rated him above the *miaopin* (third, 'marvellous class') or *neng pin* (lowest, 'capable class') of painter as defined in the 9th century. This was because Zhang possessed few of the commendable traits, such as disciplined brushwork, adherence to Yuan period (1279–1368) models or standard compositional structures admired by the orthodox literati of the time. Much of his work was dismissed by his contemporaries as vulgar and popularist, but modern critics admire his innovative and naturalistic manner.

BIBLIOGRAPHY

DMB: 'Chang Hung'
O. Sirén: *Chinese Painting: Leading Masters and Principles* (London, 1956–8), v, p. 30
J. Cahill: *The Compelling Image: Nature and Style in Seventeenth Century Chinese Painting* (Cambridge, MA, 1982), pp. 1–35
——: *The Distant Mountains: Chinese Painting of the Late Ming Dynasty, 1570–1644* (New York, 1982), pp. 39–42, 55–9

VYVYAN BRUNST, JAMES CAHILL

Zhangjiapo [Chang-chia-p'o]. Site in Shaanxi Province, China, in the area of the Western Zhou (*c.* 1050–771 BC) capitals, Feng and Hao, south-west of the city of Xi'an. The Western Zhou remains at Zhangjiapo were excavated in 1956–7, 1967, 1979–81 and 1984. Foundations of 13 semi-subterranean houses, small in size and simple in structure, and more than 500 tombs were uncovered.

The tombs can be divided into three groups: large, medium and small. Grave goods include ceramic, bronze, jade, stone, bone and ivory artefacts. The bronzes are ritual objects, weapons, tools and chariot parts. The jade and stone ornaments are in the forms of various animals, such as fish, birds, cattle, deer, rabbits and cicadas. Important burials include a group of three tombs belonging to the family of a nobleman named Jing Shu. A large tomb, which enclosed a male body, is composed of a rectangular pit with two ramps, one on either side, and is flanked by two smaller tombs, each of which contained a female body. Some 460 fragments of grave goods of 4 major types were unearthed: bronzes, jades, glazed pottery and lacquerware. The bronzes include chariot parts, bells (*yong zhong*), *zun* and *jue* (for illustrations of these types *see* CHINA, fig. 138). One vessel (a *shengzun*) was made in the shape of a fantastic animal with horns and wings and decorated with *taotie* animal-masks (*see* CHINA, §VI, 3(ii)(a)), mythical animal motifs (*kuiwen*) and 'thunder patterns' (*leiwen*). Bronze bells bearing the name Jing Shu, found in one of the female's tombs, support the theory that the occupants of the three tombs were Jing Shu and his two wives. The jades include semi-annular pendants (*huang*), rings (*huan*), penannular rings (*jue*), tablets (*gui*), halberds (*ge*), ornaments and chime stones.

More than ten chariot burials, illustrating the structural development of chariots in the Western Zhou period, have been excavated. Most of these contained one chariot and two horses, but some had two chariots and six or more horses, some horses only, and some a driver in

Zhang Hong: *Wind in the Pines at Mt Gouqu*, hanging scroll, ink and colours on paper, 1.49×0.47 m, 1650 (Boston, MA, Museum of Fine Arts)

reorganization and produced an image that is consistent with the actual experience of viewing a landscape; he also used light washes of green and red-brown in addition to

addition to chariot and horses. The horses were heavily adorned with bronze and shell ornaments. The chariots and horse ornaments are exhibited in the form of a reconstruction at the site.

BIBLIOGRAPHY

Fengxi fajue baogao [Excavations at Fengxi] (Beijing, 1962)
Cheng Te-k'un: *Chou China*, iii of *Archaeology in China* (Cambridge, 1963), pp. 16–17
Kaogu (1981), no. 1, pls I–IV [illus. of jades]
'Chang'an Zhangjiapo Xizhou Jingshu mu fajue jianbao' [Preliminary report on the excavation of the Jingshu tombs at Zhangjiapo, Chang'an], *Kaogu* (1986), no. 1, pp. 11, 22–7
Gems of China's Cultural Relics (Beijing, 1992) [contains illus. of bells inscribed 'Jing Shu']
Lu Liancheng: 'Chariot and Horse Burials in Ancient China', *Antiquity*, lxvii (1993), pp. 824–38

LI LIU

Zhang Lu [Chang Lu; *zi* Tianchi; *hao* Pingshan] (*b* Bianliang (now Kaifeng), Henan Province, *c.* 1468 or *c.* 1495; *d* 1538 or *c.* 1570). Chinese painter. A member of a wealthy family, he was acquainted with the works of Dai Jin and Wu Wei and, despite his northern origins, is recognized as a follower of the ZHE SCHOOL. His paintings were highly appreciated in his own time, especially in the north, according to Wang Shizhen, who described him as a follower of Wu Wei excelling in 'firmness and muscular strength' but lacking some of Wu's 'refinement and freedom'. A biography by Zhang's friend Zhu Ankan included some of Zhang's own comments on painting. He believed there were few true connoisseurs of art, past or present, because so few people knew how to paint, and it was not possible for such people, even those of the greatest natural genius, to understand anything about painting. Even less likely was it that people who did not know how to paint could appreciate or even apprehend the strength or weakness of brushwork or the clearness or muddiness of ink-wash tonalities.

According to Zhu, Zhang painted from nature, contemplating and searching for a true understanding before beginning to paint, then using his brush 'as Heaven created all things, without stopping from beginning to end' (Barnhart, pp. 372–3). By the end of the Ming period (1368–1644), however, other critics vilified Zhang's work; He Liangjun (1506–73), for example, wrote of Jiang Song and Wang Zhi of Nanjing and Zhang Lu of the north that he would be ashamed to wipe his table with their paintings.

A number of paintings by Zhang exist in collections in China and elsewhere; other works not yet identified may prove to be his. Generally large and executed in ink and ink wash on silk, they show a sure use of colour as well. *Two Women Looking at Paintings* (Princeton U., NJ, A. Mus.), unsigned but insecurely attributed to Zhang, shows a mastery of figure painting on a large scale in a landscape setting. The magnificent *Eagle Stooping on a Hare in Winter*, signed Pingshan (Nanjing, Jiangsu Prov. Mus.), shows Zhang's skill in transforming a Song-period (960–1279) subject into his favourite ink-wash idiom.

BIBLIOGRAPHY

K. Suzuki: *Mindai kaigashi no kenkyū: Seppa* [Research on Ming painting: the Zhe school] (Kyoto, 1968)
R. Barnhart: 'The "Wild and Heterodox School" of Ming Painting', *Theories of the Arts in China*, ed. S. Bush and C. Murck (Princeton, 1983), pp. 365–96

Mu Yiqin: *Ming dai gongting yu Zhe pai huihua xuanji* [A selection of Ming-dynasty court and Zhe-school paintings] (Beijing, 1983), pls 78–82
S. N. Erickson: 'Chang Lu's "A Poet Contemplating a Waterfall"', *Ming Stud.*, 18 (Spring 1984), pp. 35–45
Mu Yigin, ed.: *Ming dai yuanti Zhe pai shiliao* [Historical sources on the courtly style in the Zhe school of the Ming period] (Shanghai, 1985)
Shih Shou-ch'ien: 'Che School Painting Style and Aristocratic Taste', *Soochow U. J. Chin. A. Hist.*, xv (July 1985), pp. 307–42
S. Little: 'Literati Views of the Zhe School', *Orient. A.*, n. s., xxxvii/4 (Winter 1991–2), pp. 192–208
Painters of the Great Ming: The Imperial Court and the Zhe School (exh. cat. by R. M. Barnhart, New York, Met.; Dallas, TX, Mus. A.; 1993), pp. 260–65, cat. nos 73, 100–04, fig. 135

RODERICK WHITFIELD

Zhang Ruitu [Chang Jui-t'u; *zi* Changgong; *hao* Ershui] (*b* Jinjiang District, Fujian Province, 1570; *d* April/May ?1641). Chinese calligrapher, painter and poet. He received his *jinshi* degree in 1607, eventually becoming Grand Secretary in 1626. In 1629 Zhang was implicated in the crimes of the corrupt eunuch Wei Zhongxian, and was stripped of his ranks and sent home a commoner. This has affected his standing as an artist, for despite a manifest talent, he was either ignored or vilified by Chinese art historians. Research in the 20th century has absolved him of collusion, however, and his artistic standing has been restored.

Although little appreciated at home, Zhang was recognized during his lifetime by the Japanese, owing to the particular relationship of the Japanese at that time with the province of Fujian, where Zhang retired. Chinese Chan (Jap. Zen) Buddhist monks from Mt Huangbi (Jap. Ōbaku), Fujian, were exporting their sect to Japan and training monks to be sent there. Zhang had by this time become a Chan Buddhist, as one of his seals and his writings attest. There are large numbers of Zhang's works in Japanese collections, thanks partly to the presence of his daughter in Osaka and partly to the monks, who imported his calligraphy.

Zhang is usually classified as one of the four masters of late Ming (1368–1644) calligraphy, with Xing Tong (1551–1612), Mi Wanzhong (1570–1628) and Dong Qichang. Most of his writing is in running script (*xingshu*), cursive script (*caoshu*) and small regular script (*xiao kaishu*). The models he followed in early years were Wang Xizhi, Sun Guoting and Su Shi; Dong Qichang was another influence. His large calligraphy is closer to his more eccentric juniors Wang Duo (1592–1652) and Fu Shan. Wang and Fu based their exaggerations on specific Western Jin-period (AD 265–316) sources, however; Zhang's style emerged from his own imagination. In a poem by Li Bai (AD ?701–62) in linked cursive script (see 1977 exh. cat., no. 62), Zhang wields a slanted brush to produce simple, taut, unadorned and angular lines, closely and continuously woven in the columns but separated by wide spaces. Pressure within a character is generally uniform; contrast is produced between words lightly and thinly brushed and those more heavily written. Followed on the left by the sensitive lines of his signature, the whole produces an impression of stability and finesse.

Zhang was also a competent landscapist. Biographers mention Huang Gongwang as his model; the paintings themselves are in typical late Ming literati style clearly influenced by Dong Qichang. He was an able poet, particularly fond of Tao Yuanming (AD 365–427) and Bai Juyi (AD 772–846), and much of his calligraphy is his own poetry.

See also CHINA, §IV, 2(vi)(c).

BIBLIOGRAPHY
Y. Nakata: 'Cho Zuito ni tsuite' [On Zhang Ruitu], Shodō zenshū [Complete collection of calligraphy], ed. K. Shimonaka, xvii (Tokyo, 1956), pp. 34–5; xxi (Tokyo, 1961), pp. 18–27
Uno Yukimura: Chūgoku shodoshi [History of Chinese calligraphy] (Tokyo, 1962), pp. 194–7
Wang Zhuangwei: 'Ershui yu qi shu' [Zhang Ruitu and his calligraphy], Shufa congtan [Collection of discussions of calligraphy] (Taipei, 1966), pp. 147–51
Traces of the Brush: Studies in Chinese Calligraphy (exh. cat. by Shen Fu and others; New Haven, CT, Yale U.A.G.; Berkeley, U. CA, A. Mus.; 1977), pp. 95, 118, 277–8
Yu Jianhua: Zhongguo huajia da zidian [Dictionary of Chinese painters] (Shanghai, 1981), p. 861
Y. Shimizu and J. M. Rosenfield: Masters of Japanese Calligraphy (New York, 1984), p. 160

ELIZABETH F. BENNETT

Zhang Xuan [Chang Hsüan] (b Chang'an [now Xi'an, Shaanxi Province]; fl c. AD 710; d after 748). Chinese painter. He was considered one of the outstanding painters of secular figures in a period when that category of painting flourished, although he is mentioned only briefly in Zhang Yanyuan's Lidai minghua ji ('Record of famous painters of all periods'; AD 847). His compositions are known only through copies and recorded titles. According to the Tang chao minghua lu ('Record of famous painters of the Tang dynasty'; second quarter of the 9th century) by Zhu Jingxuan, he painted terraces, trees, garden flowers and birds; his main subject, however, was contemporary court ladies depicted in genre scenes, which omitted all objects except those that were essential to the particular activity. Records of such paintings help to establish the date of Zhang's activity; a copy of a painting by Emperor Huizong (reg 1101–25) of the Northern Song dynasty (960–1127) in the Liaoning Provincial Museum, Shenyang, identifies the subject of several of them as Lady Guoguo, the beautiful sister of Yang Guifei, consort of Emperor Xuanzong (reg AD 712–56) of the Tang dynasty (618–907).

Forty-seven paintings by Zhang Xuan are listed in the Xuanhe huapu ('Xuanhe collection of paintings'; preface 1120), the catalogue of paintings in the imperial collection. The listing confirms that he painted few landscapes other than as settings for the activities of women and children, who were mainly from the aristocracy. The Tang chao minghua lu, noting that his subjects were young nobles, saddle-horses and women of rank, names him as the most celebrated painter of figures of grace and beauty in romantic surroundings of his day. Tang Hou, in Gujin huajian ('Criticisms of past and present painting'; probably published in the 1320s), wrote that Zhang, no less than his near-contemporary Zhou Fang (active late 8th century), excelled particularly in painting young children. Tang also pointed out that all the married women in Zhang's pictures had their ears touched with red, a distinguishing mark that the viewer would understand.

Because of the dearth of extant works from this period, Zhang Xuan's style is usually contrasted with that of WU DAOZI and is characterized primarily through the painting

Court Ladies Preparing Newly Woven Silk (handscroll, ink and colours on silk, 370×1450 mm; Boston, MA, Mus. F.A.). This painting is a copy of the original attributed to Emperor Huizong on the basis of a short inscription by his grandson, Emperor Zhangzong (reg 1190–1208) of the Jin dynasty (1115–1234). The figures recall contemporary pottery tomb figures, both in their static, elegant poses and in the interpretation of contemporary idealized beauty. Even the expressionless uniformity of the faces presents a stereotyped ideal rather than specific individuals. The garments are executed in carefully detailed patterns and strong colours, similar to contemporary fabrics found in the Shōsōin repository of the Tōdaiji temple in Nara, Japan (est. c. AD 756). The figures are arranged in three self-contained groups; space and the ground-plane are suggested only by their relative positions and minimal props. Probably the most significant departure from the original lies in the slightly calligraphic line, which would have been more consistent with Song-period (960–1279) conceptions. According to Zhu Jingxuan, Zhang Xuan also made rough sketches in a more spontaneous manner, but no examples are known or identified.

BIBLIOGRAPHY
Zhang Yanyuan: Lidai minghua ji [Record of famous painters of all periods] (preface AD 847), ed. Yu Jianhua (Shanghai, 1963); Eng. trans. in W. B. Acker: Some T'ang and Pre-T'ang Texts on Chinese Painting, 2 vols (Leiden, 1954–74)
Zhu Jingxuan: Tang chao minghua lu [Record of famous painters of the Tang dynasty] (mid-9th century AD); repr. in Meishu congshu [Complete collection of art] (Shanghai, rev. 1947/R 1975); Eng. trans. in A. C. Soper: 'T'ang ch'ao ming hua lu: Celebrated Painters of the T'ang Period by Chu Ching hsuan of T'ang', Artibus Asiae, xxi (1958), pp. 204–30
Xuanhe huapu [Xuanhe collection of painting] (preface 1120); ed. Yu Jianhua (Beijing, 1964)
Tang Hou: Gujin huajian [Criticism of past and present painting] (c. 14th century), in Hua jian [Mirror of painting], ed. Ma Cai and others (Beijing, 1959)
O. Sirén: Chinese Painting: Leading Masters and Principles, 7 vols (London and New York, 1956–8), v, p. 60; vii, p. 154
R. T. Paine: Figure Compositions of China and Japan from the Collection of the Museum of Fine Arts, Boston, Picture Books, xx (Boston, 1964)
M. Loehr: The Great Painters of China (New York, 1980)
Eight Dynasties of Chinese Painting: The Collections of the Nelson–Atkins Museum of Art, Kansas City, and the Cleveland Museum of Art (exh. cat. by Wai-kam Ho and others, Kansas City, MO, Nelson–Atkins Mus. A.; Cleveland, OH, Mus. A.; Tokyo, N. Mus.; 1980–81), no. 6

MARY S. LAWTON

Zhang Yi. See CHEUNG YEE.

Zhan Ziqian [Chan Tzu-ch'ien] (fl Sui dynasty, AD 581–618). Chinese painter. After the defeat of the Northern Zhou (557–81), he was summoned to Chang'an (now Xi'an, Shaanxi Province) by the victorious new emperor, Wendi (reg 582–604). He became the most influential painter of the Sui period, attaining several prestigious titles. Emperor Wendi promoted Buddhist art and sponsored sculptures and wall paintings throughout China. Zhan Ziqian was among the best of the artists who traversed the land to the growing numbers of Buddhist monasteries and temples, producing wall paintings for Guangming si, Lingbao si and Yunhua si in Luoyang (Henan Province) and Chang'an, for Dongan si in Jiangdu (now Yangzhou, Jiangsu Province) and for other temples in western Zhejiang Province. Tang period (AD 618–907) writers recalled Zhan's wall painting Eight Kings Dividing the Shari (Skt *sarīra*, the relics of a Buddha after cremation), a popular theme in Buddhist painting during the Sui period, at the Chan Buddhist monastery Longxing si in Chengdu, Sichuan Province.

Critics up to the 14th century remarked on Zhan's excellence in painting figures, landscapes, horses and carriages. The *Xuanhe huapu* ('Xuanhe collection of painting', preface 1120) observed that, in painting landscapes, Zhan had exceptional skill in distinguishing close and distant scenes and could encompass thousands of *li* within a small area of silk. His paintings were said to 'exude poetic emotions'. The text lists 20 of Zhan's paintings in the imperial collection, in a variety of genres.

Spring Outing (ink and colours on silk, 430×805 mm, Beijing, Pal. Mus.) is a horizontal section possibly rescued from an original handscroll. This unsigned work was first linked to Zhan Ziqian in 16th-century texts, although on stylistic grounds it could date from the Yuan period (1279–1368). Mineral greens, blues and ochres have been discreetly applied without modelling strokes, and the echoing ink-contour lines are finely articulated and stylized. Mounted gentlemen are shown by the rocky lakeside, which is adorned with ornamental bushes and trees. Seen from a high vantage-point, the jewel-like scene stretches to the far horizon as netlike wave patterns diminish along a constantly receding ground-plane.

BIBLIOGRAPHY

Pei Xiaoyuan: *Zhenguan gongsi hua si* [Record of paintings in public and private collections in the Zhenguan era] (preface AD 639); Huapin congshu [Complete collection of painting], ed. Yu Anlan (Shanghai, 1982), pp. 23–43

Zhang Yanyuan: *Lidai minghua ji* [Record of famous painters of all periods], 10 *juan* (preface AD 847), *juan* 8

Guo Ruoxu: *Tuhua jianwen zhi* [Experiences in painting] (preface 1075), ed. Huan Miaozi (Shanghai, 1963); Eng. trans. in A. C. Soper: *Kuo Jo-hsü's 'Experiences in Painting' (T'u-hua chien-wen chih): An Eleventh-century History of Chinese Painting* (Washington, DC, 1951/R 1971)

Zxuanhe huapu [Xuanhe collection of painting], 23 *juan* (preface 1120), ed. Yu Jianhua (Beijing, 1964), *juan* 1

Deng Chun: *Hua ji* [Painting continued], 10 *juan* (preface 1127)

Zhou Mi: *Yunyan guoyan lu* [Record of what was seen as clouds and mist], 2 *juan* (c. late 13th century)

Wang Bomin: *Zhan Ziqian*, Zhongguo huajia congshu [Complete collection of Chinese painters] (Shanghai, 1958)

Fu Xinian: 'Guanyu Zhan Ziqian *Youchuntu* niandai de tantao' [Concerning the dating of Zhan Ziqian's handscroll *Spring Outing*], *Wenwu* (1978), no. 11, pp. 40–52

Yu Jianhua: *Zhongguo meishujia renming cidian* [Dictionary of Chinese artists] (Shanghai, 1981)

JOAN STANLEY-BAKER

Zhao. Chinese family of artists. The wife of (1) Zhao Mengfu, Guan Daosheng, his sons (2) Zhao Yong and Zhao Yi and his grandsons Zhao Lin, Zhao Feng and WANG MENG were all painters. Members of the family collaborated on such works as *Three Horses by Three Generations of the Zhao Family* (New York, Met., Crawford Col.) and *Three Bamboos by Three Members of the Zhao Family* (Beijing, Pal. Mus.).

(1) Zhao Mengfu [Chao Meng-fu; *zi* Zi'ang; *hao* Songxue] (*b* Wuxing, Zhejiang Province, 1254; *d* 1322). Chinese painter and calligrapher. A descendant of the first Song emperor, Taizu (*reg* AD 960–76), Zhao was born into a privileged class towards the end of the Song period (960–1279). His father was a high official in the court at Hangzhou, the capital of the Southern Song (1127–1279).

Zhao was educated in the classics and inherited a broad interest in artistic pursuits. At the age of 14 he was appointed a staff member of the Office of Revenue at Chenzhou (near modern Yangzhou). When he was 23 the Mongols overran Hangzhou and established the Yuan dynasty (1279–1368), moving the capital to Dadu (modern Beijing). Zhao returned to his home town, Wuxing, to concentrate on his studies and soon achieved distinction as a scholar. In 1286, in response to the invitation sent by the Mongol emperor Kublai Khan to recruit southern scholars to serve in his regime, Zhao went to Beijing to begin his career as a civil servant under the Yuan dynasty, sometimes at the court and sometimes in the provinces, eventually attaining the first rank and serving under five emperors. He showed himself to be an able administrator and a very shrewd politician as well as an economist, an expert in Confucian studies and an official historian. He was also a poet, an essayist and an accomplished musician, especially of the *qin* (zither). He was the dominant calligrapher of the Yuan period and was highly influential in later periods. His greatness as a painter has been recognized only recently, as a result of the discovery of some of his most important works. In his biography, written by one of his protégés, Yang Cai (1271–1323), it was said that: 'Other people painting landscape, bamboos and rocks, men and horses, and birds and flowers, often excel in some but are weak in others. But he achieved the utmost in all of them, fathoming their heavenly qualities. His masterpieces do not rank below those of the ancient masters.' Among Yuan painters, he shows much the broadest range of subjects, techniques and expressions.

Zhao was the leader of a group known as the Eight Talents of Wuxing, to which Qian Xuan also belonged. Qian was probably responsible for the basic ideas of 'the spirit of antiquity' that became the dominant artistic and intellectual trend in the early Yuan period, while Zhao was more innovative in transforming some of those ideas into new expressions. In his travels Zhao studied the works of masters of the Tang (AD 618–907) and Song periods and earlier. Many could be seen in the private collections of the Hangzhou area. With these examples he imitated the techniques and expressions of past masters but at the same time sought transformations of his own. There is very little repetition in his work, which instead reflects a search for new ideas.

Among his extant paintings, those representing figures and horses show very clear ties with the past. In his inscription to his figure painting *Red-robed Indian Monk* (1304; Shenyang, Liaoning Prov. Mus.), Zhao said that he followed the Tang master Lu Lingjia, who was specially known for his depiction of Indian Buddhist monks, and that he also drew from his contacts with Indian monks in Beijing. Thus it was a combination of the 'spirit of antiquity' and his own creation. Similarly, *Washing Horses* (handscroll, colour on silk; Beijing, Pal. Mus.) seems to be following a Tang model, though no source is mentioned. Another horse painting, *Watering Horses in the Autumn Fields* (short handscroll, colour on silk, 1312; Beijing, Pal. Mus.), emphasizes the landscape background, with trees and horses still shown in the somewhat schematic manner of the Tang period. In other figure and horse paintings, however, he transformed the early models into a style

Zhao Mengfu: *Autumn Colours on the Qiao and Hua Mountains* (detail), short handscroll, colours on paper, 284×932 mm, 1296 (Taipei, National Palace Museum)

typical of the Yuan period. In *Self-portrait* (1299; Beijing, Pal. Mus.) he presented himself as an ancient figure standing by a stream in a bamboo grove, with rocks, bamboos and water depicted in an archaic manner using bright colours. *Portrait of Su Shi* (Taipei, N. Pal. Mus.), which serves as the frontispiece for an album of calligraphy (1301) of Su's poem *The Red Cliffs*, was executed entirely in ink on paper according to the 'pure line' manner and in a relaxed style. *Red-coated Official on Horseback* (ink on silk, 1296; Beijing, Pal. Mus.) was inspired by the work of the Tang artist HAN GAN. Another work done using similar technique, *Horse and Groom*, the first section of the *Three Horses by Three Generations of the Zhao Family* (handscroll, 1296; New York, Met.), depicts a groom holding a horse and still echoes some of Han Gan's ideas. All three paintings lack background, in the Tang manner, but are nonetheless typical of the Yuan period.

It is in Zhao's landscape painting that this development from the archaic to a new means of expression is most evident. One of his earliest works, *Landscape of Wuxing* (handscroll, ink on silk; Shanghai Mus.), uses fine lines to depict his home town as seen from Lake Tai in a way that combines archaism and personal expression. Another very archaic but very different work is *Mind Landscape of Xie Youyu* (handscroll, ink and colour on silk; Princeton U.,

NJ, A. Mus.; *see* COLOUR, colour pls IV–V). It has rocks and hills all in blue and green as well as figures, trees and rocks derived from the archaic manner of the Six Dynasties period (AD 222–589). *Eastern Mountain of Dongting* (hanging scroll, silk; Shanghai Mus.) shows a deep, distant view of an island on Lake Tai using the line textures and free brushwork of DONG YUAN. *Autumn Colours on the Qiao and Hua Mountains* (see fig.) draws upon some ideas from the 8th-century painter Wang Wei as well as Dong Yuan in a depiction of a scene in Jinan, Shandong Province. Synthesizing realism and archaism, the painting depicts the artist's ideal of a hermit's dreamland. In *Water Village* (short handscroll, pure ink on paper, 1302; Beijing, Pal. Mus.), which depicts a scene in the Lake Tai district, the brushwork is free and relaxed: the archaic features of his previous works are largely absent.

Zhao thus created a new kind of landscape, usually in pure ink on paper, with some traces of Dong Yuan's influence, but totally transformed by the use of free brushwork to a personalized vision of a land of the heart's desire. Dong Yuan became the dominant influence in Yuan landscape painting and ink landscape painting became the typical expression of the literati in the late Yuan and subsequent periods.

In his later life Zhao became interested in the landscapes of the Northern Song artist GUO XI, who depicted peculiar rocks, misty effects and deep vistas. *River Village: Fishermen's Joy* (fan painting, colour on silk; Cleveland, OH, Mus. A.), which retains some archaic features, is the first work to show this new direction. In *Rivers and Mountains* (long handscroll, ink on paper, 1306; Taipei, N. Pal. Mus.) Zhao transforms elements of Guo Xi's style to create a new manner of expression that is nonetheless entirely his own. In *Two Pines on a Flat Landscape* (handscroll, pure ink on paper; New York, Met.) the appropriation of Guo Xi's style is more advanced.

Zhao was also a master of bamboo and rock paintings. He painted in pure ink and free brushwork in the literati manner, adding old trees to the composition. *Dry Tree, Bamboo and Rock* (handscroll; Beijing, Pal. Mus.) shows the close relationship between painting and calligraphy as is indicated by a poem he attached to the handscroll.

For discussion and an example of Zhao Mengfu's calligraphy, *see* CHINA, §IV, 2(v). *See also* CHINA, §§V, 3(iv)(a), (v)(d), (vi)(d) and 4(ii) and XIII, 22(iii).

BIBLIOGRAPHY
Chu-tsing Li: *The Autumn Colors on the Ch'iao and Hua Mountains: A Landscape by Chao Meng-fu* (Ascona, 1965)
——: 'The Freer *Sheep and Goat* and Chao Meng-fu's Horse Paintings', *Artibus Asiae*, xxx/3–4 (1968), pp. 279–346
J. Cahill: *Hills Beyond a River: Chinese Painting of the Yuan Dynasty, 1279–1368* (New York and Tokyo, 1976), pp. 38–46
R. Vinograd: '*River Village: The Pleasure of Fishing*: A Blue and Green Landscape by Chao Meng-fu', *Artibus Asiae*, xl/2–3 (1978), pp. 124–34
Chen Gaohua: *Yuan dai huajia shiliao* [Literary sources of Yuan-dynasty painters] (Shanghai, 1980), pp. 30–99
Ren Daobin: *Zhao Mengfu xinian* [A chronological biography of Zhao Mengfu] (Zhengzhou, 1984)

(2) Zhao Yong [Chao Yung; *zi* Zhongmu] (*b* Wuxing, Zhejiáng Province, 1289; *d c.*1364). Son of (1) Zhao Mengfu. Because of his father's high position at the court of the Mongol Yuan dynasty, Zhao Yong was early given an official position and continued to serve as an official throughout his life, eventually as a military commander in Wuxing. He probably died during the last years of the Yuan period (1279–1368), when a number of rebel armies contended with one another for control in the area of his command. Strongly influenced by his father, he was an accomplished painter of many subjects popular with masters of the early Yuan period, including landscape, horses, figures, palaces, and birds and flowers, and he was occasionally summoned to the Yuan court to paint.

Among his surviving works the most notable are a number of landscape and horse paintings. One of the best known is *Secluded Fishing among Streams and Mountains* (hanging scroll on silk, Cleveland, OH, Dean Perry priv. col.), which depicts a gentleman fishing in a boat near trees and rocks in the foreground that are separated by an expanse of water from mountains in the distance. Similar compositional ideas, some without the fisherman, are also seen in a number of landscapes, executed on fans (e.g. Beijing, Pal. Mus. and Shenyang, Liaoning Prov. Mus.). These show the strong influence of the 10th-century artist DONG YUAN: long, wavy, hemp-fibre strokes (*pima cun*) are used to texture the rocks and mountains. Among his horse paintings, the most interesting is *Noble Steeds* (hanging scroll, 1352; Taipei, N. Pal. Mus.), which employs

the Blue-and-green style that imitates the use of bright colours, mostly Blue-and-green, in Tang-period (AD 618–907) landscape painting, as an expression of admiration for archaic painting styles. A number of paintings depicting young gentlemen in red coats on horseback (e.g. Beijing, Pal. Mus. and Taipei, N. Pal. Mus.) also seem to try to capture the elegance of the Tang period. Although all Zhao's works, including collaborative works executed with other family members show his versatility, he was always overshadowed artistically by his father.

BIBLIOGRAPHY
O. Sirén: *Chinese Painting: Leading Masters and Principles*, 7 vols (London and New York, 1956–8), iv, pp. 24–6
J. Silbergeld: 'In Praise of Government: Chao Yung's Painting, *Noble Steeds*, and Late Yuan Politics', *Artibus Asiae*, xlvi/3 (1975), pp. 159–98
Chen Gaohua: *Yuan dai huajia shiliao* [Historical material on Yuan painters] (Shanghai, 1980), pp. 169–80

CHU-TSING LI

Zhao Boju [Chao Po-chü; *zi* Qianli] (*b* Zhuo xian, Hebei Province, before 1123; *d* 1160–73). Chinese painter. His paintings of landscapes, figures, flowers, fruit and birds apparently ranged in size and format from large screens to handscrolls, album leaves and fans. The critic Zhao Xigu (*fl* 1180–1240) considered Zhao Boju the best of all Southern Song (1127–1279) painters. However, no authentic work by Zhao Boju survives, leaving the question of his style open to interpretation.

Zhao Boju and his younger brother, Zhao Bosu, also a painter, were 7th-generation descendants of the founder of the Song dynasty (960–1279), Emperor Taizu (*reg* 960–75). When Emperor Gaozong (*reg* 1127–62) was presented with a fan painting done by Zhao Boju, he was enormously pleased. On meeting Zhao in person and discovering him to be a kinsman, he addressed him as 'royal cousin' and assigned him the title of Military Commander of the eastern Zhejiang circuit, an office the short-lived Zhao held until his death. The Emperor commissioned Zhao to paint the screens for the hall called the Jiying dian and is known often to have inscribed Zhao's works.

The Zhao brothers reportedly believed that 'each artist ought to have his own sense of style within his breast, so that his spirit emerges spontaneously, and the work will exude a taste that is pure, refined and remote, unbounded by the formal conditions of the objects.' This is in keeping with the literati belittlement of physical verisimilitude and stress on the supremacy of expression, according to which a painter should attempt to capture the inner essence of the subject more than its outer form. Zhuang Su (*fl* 12th–13th century) described Zhao Boju's handscroll *On the Yangzi River in the Sixth Lunar Month*, bearing the imperial autograph, as imbued with the 'flavour and air of Dong Yuan and Wang Sheng [1072–after 1149]'. This indicates landscape painting with a SOUTHERN SCHOOL affiliation, rather than in the Academy style. Zhao's landscapes may have been of gentle earthen mounds with soft, rounded contours, in a continuation of the Jiangnan (south China) style promoted in the early 12th century by the great critic and spokesman for the literati, Mi Fu.

Although the Zhao brothers were not members of the Imperial Painting Academy, they were pre-eminent in Southern Song painting circles, excelling in coloured (*qinglü*) landscapes (usually associated with the NORTH-ERN SCHOOL) and figure painting. In the Yuan period (1279–1368) Xia Wenyan included bamboo and rocks in Zhao Boju's area of expertise and said that by gazing at Zhao's figure painting aspects of the sitters' personalities could be appreciated. However, these claims may typify a common tendency to exaggerate Zhao's abilities that became pronounced following the master's death, in response to the great demand for, and lack of, his works. Indeed, it seems that by the Yuan many attributions to Zhao were already spurious. Despite the scarcity of his works, many poems and encomia were written by critics on works ascribed to him.

The composition most modern scholars associate with Zhao Boju is that of the stunning anonymous handscroll *Jiangshan qiuse tujuan* ('Handscroll of mountain and river autumn colours'; colours on silk; Beijing, Pal. Mus.). This title first appears in the 18th-century imperial catalogue *Shiqu baoji*, where the attribution to Zhao follows that made by Zhu Biao (1355–92) in 1375, based simply on its being a coloured landscape. In fact, the structure and perspective of the work link it to paintings such as a *Thousand Li of Rivers and Mountains* (Beijing, Pal. Mus.) by Wang Ximeng (1096–1119), produced under Emperor Huizong (*reg* 1101–25). *Jiangshan qiuse tujuan* may offer a glimpse of what Zhao saw, but perhaps not of what he painted.

BIBLIOGRAPHY

Deng Chun: *Hua ji* [Painting continued], 10 *juan* (preface 1167), *juan* 2
Zhao Xigu: *Cuhua bian* [Ancient paintings], *Dongtian qinglü ji* [Record of the Blue-and-green style] (*c.* 1242)
Zhuang Su: *Hua ji buyi* [Painting continued: a supplement], 2 *juan* (1298), *juan* 1
Zhou Bida: *Zhou Yiguo Wenzhong gong ji erbai juan* [Writings of Zhou Bida], 200 *juan* (12th century), *juan* 30
Cao Zun: *Songyin wenji* [Collected writings from the Pine Hermitage], 39 *juan*, *juan* 29
Tang Hou: *Hua jian* [Mirror of painting] (14th century)
O. Sirén: *Chinese Painting: Leading Masters and Principles*, 7 vols (London and New York, 1956–8), ii, pp. 106–08
J. Cahill: *An Index of Early Chinese Painters and Paintings: T'ang, Sung and Yüan* (Berkeley, 1980)
Yang Chenbin: 'Jiangshan qiuse tu', *Minghua jianshang* [Appreciation of famous paintings] (Shanghai, 1983)
Chen Gaohua: *Song Liao Jin huajia shiliao* [Historical material on painters of the Song, Liao and Jin periods] (Tianjin, 1984), pp. 638–62
K. Suzuki: *Chūgoku kaigashi* [History of Chinese painting], ii/a (Tokyo, 1984), pp. 57–61

JOAN STANLEY-BAKER

Zhao Chang [Chao Ch'ang; *zi* Changzhi] (*b* Guanghan, Sichuan Province, *c.* AD 960; *d* after 1016). Chinese painter. He was a painter of birds, flowers and insects, following the style of Teng Changyou (*fl* AD 907–20). Although paintings attributed to him are not genuine, they provide an indication of his style. These works can be divided into two groups: one of relatively small paintings of flowers and another of larger pictures, with birds, insects, trees, rocks and flowers.

Zhao is known to have studied his subjects thoroughly before painting them. The flowers he depicted tended to be the cultivated varieties he saw in the gardens of contemporary Sichuan Province or in the capital, Bianliang (now Kaifeng, in Henan). Although the flowers possess many realistic features, they are sometimes painted in a formal way, producing a decorative effect. Zhao was famous for rendering flowers in such a way that the thickness of the ink and colour pigment could be clearly seen. This is evident in the fan painting *Branch of White Jasmine* (Kamakura, Sugahara col.). The birds or insects depicted in the larger compositions are often expressed in an intimate and charming way. An example is the short handscroll *Butterflies, Grasshoppers and Water Plants* (ink and light colours on paper; Beijing, Pal. Mus.). His style in such works exerted a considerable influence on artists at the Hanlin Academy of the Northern Song dynasty (960–1127) and on their successors during the Southern Song period (1127–1279).

BIBLIOGRAPHY

O. Sirén: *Chinese Painting: Leading Masters and Principles* (London and New York, 1956–8) i, pp. 181–3

BENT L. PEDERSEN

Zhao Danian. *See* ZHAO LINGRANG.

Zhao Gan [Chao Kan] (*b* Jiangnan region, south of the Yangzi River; *fl* before AD 975). Chinese painter. He was an apprentice at the painting academy under Li Yu (*reg* 961–75), ruler of the Southern Tang dynasty (937–75) in Nanjing. Although he must have been young then, there are no records to indicate that Zhao entered painting circles after the capitulation of Li Yu and the advent of the Northern Song dynasty (960–1127). He may have died or simply ceased painting.

The *Shengchao minghua ping* ('Critique of famous painters of the present [Song] dynasty'; 1059), by Liu Daoshun, placed Zhao Gan in the third class (*neng*, 'competent') of painters of landscapes and woods, citing the way in which he could conjure up the feelings evoked by travelling along rivers and bring them vividly to life for the viewer. The *Xuanhe huapu* ('Xuanhe collection of painting', 1120), the catalogue of Emperor Huizong's collection, recorded that Zhao Gan painted mainly pavilions, boats and ships, water villages, fish markets, flowers and bamboo, composed as scenic incidents. The catalogue also referred to Zhao's ability to transport the viewer directly into the scene, making him feel as if he were gathering up his clothes ready to walk through the waters. Titles in the Xuanhe collection include *Oxherd Returning amid Vernal Woods*, *Wind and Rain in Summer*, *Mountains* (four panels), *Roaming the Scenery on a Summer's Day*, *Autumn Gambol amid Smoke and Mist*, *Fishing on a Clear Winter's Day* and *Travels along the River in Early Snow* (see fig.). The last, a handscroll in ink and colours on silk that has survived in remarkable condition, is the only reliable evidence of 10th-century Jiangnan painting and as such provides clues to the styles of Dong Yuan and Juran, Zhao's celebrated contemporaries, no authographs by whom survive. The composition features soft, undulating landmasses, earthen banks, wind-blown reeds, and river folk, bent and wearing pained expressions. The remarkable lifelike quality of the painting derives from dramatic highlighting, graded shading and textured ripples, all rendered with slow, deliberate brushwork.

BIBLIOGRAPHY

Liu Daoshun: *Shengchao Minghua ping* [Critique of famous painters of the present [Song] dynasty] (1059)

Zhao Gan: *Travels along the River in Early Snow*, handscroll, ink and colours on silk, 10th century (Taipei, National Palace Museum)

Guo Ruoxu: *Tuhua jianwen zhi* [Experiences in painting] (preface 1075); ed. Huan Miaozi (Shanghai, 1963); Eng. trans. in A. C. Soper: *Kuo Jo-hsü's 'Experiences in Painting' (T'u-hua chien-wen chih): An Eleventh Century History of Chinese Painting* (Washington, DC, 1951/R 1971)
Xuanhe huapu [Xuanhe collection of painting], 23 *juan* (preface 1120), *juan* 11
Tang Hou: *Huajian* [Mirror of painting] (*c.* 1320–30); ed. Ma Cai (Beijing, 1959)
Xia Wenyan: *Tuhui baojian* [Precious mirror for examining painting], 5 *juan* (1365), *juan* 3
Yu Jianhua, ed.: *Zhongguo meishujia renming cidian* [Dictionary of Chinese artists] (Shanghai, 1981)
Chen Gaohua: *Song Liao Jin huajia shiliao* [Historical sources on painters of the Song, Liao and Jin periods] (Tianjin, 1984), pp. 64–6
JOAN STANLEY-BAKER

Zhao Lingrang [Chao Ling-jang; *zi* Danian, Ta-nien] (*fl c.* 1070–*c.* 1100). Chinese painter. He was a fifth-generation descendant of Emperor Taizu (*reg* 960–76), founder of the Song dynasty (960–1279). Although such official titles as Regional Defense Commandant were bestowed on Zhao, his chief preoccupation seems to have been painting. His noble status allowed him a life of luxury and learning, but restricted his movements to the environs of the capital city, Bianliang (modern Kaifeng), Henan Province. Song critics saw this lack of physical freedom as bearing upon his narrow range of landscape subjects, mainly small, intimate views (*xiao jing*) of misty river landscapes. Though Zhao also painted small ink-bamboo subjects after his eminent contemporary Su Shi, it was through landscape painting that he gained his reputation and made his mark on the lyrical style of the Southern Song period (1127–1279).

Zhao was a student of Tang (AD 618–907) painting, especially the work of WANG WEI, the venerated poet–painter whose technical innovation of 'broken ink' (*pomo*) contributed to the development of a more expressive landscape style. Zhao's familiarity with Wang's style and poetic sensibility may account for similarities that have been noted in the paintings attributed to the two artists. Significantly, Zhao's contemporary, the esteemed critic-connoisseur Mi Fu, judged some of Zhao's small snow landscape paintings comparable to works by Wang. However, since no extant works are securely attributed to Wang, and since literary descriptions of his style are vague and inconclusive, it is difficult to determine the extent of his influence upon Zhao.

The most important painting by Zhao is the signed handscroll *Jiang xiang qing xia* ('Summer mist along the lake shore'; Boston, MA, Mus. F.A.; see fig.). One colophon is by Dong Qichang, the great Ming painter and connoisseur, who was an admirer of Zhao. The painting recalls aspects of Zhao's work mentioned in the *Xuanhe huapu* ('Xuanhe collection of painting'; preface 1120): 'In his paintings there are the charms of low embankments and lakes, shady groves, vaporous clouds, ducks and geese: they have an air of spaciousness and ease.' From the opening scene the viewer is drawn in a continuous, relaxed movement through a rustic landscape; directional motifs include paths, meandering river banks and trailing mists. The horizontality and sense of spatial flow in the composition contrast with the verticality and spatial shifts in the landscapes of the earlier Li–Guo (Li Cheng and Guo Xi)

Zhao Lingrang: *Summer Mist along the Lake Shore*, handscroll, ink and colours on silk, 191×1613 mm (top: right half; bottom: left half), 1100 (Boston, MA, Museum of Fine Arts)

tradition, in which nature is presented as monumental rather than circumscribed. Prior to Zhao, never in Chinese landscape painting had place and time seemed so palpable. The atmosphere and mood so essential to Zhao's vision are conveyed by certain brush techniques: feathery, almost pointillist brushwork describes foliage and grass, and pale, transparent washes heighten a sense of ephemerality.

A small landscape in ink and colours on silk (Nara, Yamato Bunkakan), representing a marshy river scene in autumnal morning mist, is believed to be a section cut from a handscroll by Zhao. In composition, it echoes a portion of the Boston scroll where a foreground willow tree gently bends towards the river's opposite shore. However, perhaps because the season is autumn, the fragment has a more melancholy feel. Technique in the two works is also similar, though the brushwork in the Boston scroll is more descriptive of detail.

After Zhao's death, his style was still practised with fidelity in the Southern Song period as exemplified by an album leaf in ink and colours on silk, *Cottages in a Misty Grove in Autumn* (Cleveland, OH, Mus. A.), signed and dated 1177 by Li Anzhong, a painter of the Imperial Academy. This work could almost be mistaken for a work by Zhao were it not for the signature. Then at the end of the 12th century, Ma Yuan (*see* MA, (1)) and XIA GUI integrated Zhao's innovations into their own style to create the dominant tradition of the Southern Song Academy. In landscape, this style stressed small-scale but spatially expansive views of nature; atmospheric effects; impressionistic and wet brush techniques; and, above all, lyrical mood. The essence of Southern Song landscape painting is unimaginable without Zhao's prior achievement.

BIBLIOGRAPHY

Xuanhe huapu [Xuanhe collection of painting], 20 *juan* (Preface 1120), *juan* 20; *R* in Huashi congshu (Shanghai, 1962), ii

Deng Chun: *Hua ji* [Painting continued] 10 *juan* (Preface 1167), *juan* 2; *R* in Huashi congshu (Shanghai, 1962), i

S. Taki: 'Hokusō no gaseki' [Extant paintings of the Northern Song period], *Kokka*, 494 (1932), pp. 3–14

O. Sirén: *Chinese Painting: Leading Masters and Principles*, 7 vols (London and New York, 1956–8), ii, pp. 71–4; iii, pls 225, 226, 228

K. Suzuki: 'Den Chōtainen hitsu sansui-zu' [A landscape attributed to Zhao Lingrang], *Museum* [Tokyo], 100 (1959), pp. 7–11

M. Loehr: 'Chinese Paintings with Sung Dated Inscriptions', *A. Orient.*, iv (1961), pp. 219–84, esp. pp. 236–7

Y. Yonezawa: 'Den Chōreijō hitsu shū-tō-zu ni tsuite' [Apropos of the 'Autumn Bank' picture attributed to Zhao Lingrang], *Chūgoku kaiga shi kenkyū* [Studies in Chinese painting history] (Tokyo, 1962), pp. 131–50

R. Maeda: 'The Chao Ta-nien Tradition, *A. Orient.*, viii (1970), pp. 243–53

ROBERT J. MAEDA

Zhao Wuji. *See* ZAO WOU-KI.

Zhao Yong. *See* ZHAO, (2).

Zhao Zhiqian [Chao Chih-ch'ien; *zi* Huishu; *hao* Beian] (*b* Kuaiji, Zhejiang Province, 8 Aug 1829; *d* Nancheng, Jiangxi Province, 18 Nov 1884). Chinese calligrapher, seal-carver, painter and scholar. After his example, it became common for artists to attempt to be competent in painting, calligraphy and seal-carving rather than to specialize in a single discipline. Zhao was one of the greatest artists of the late Qing period (1644–1911), although much of his work displays a disquiet and unbalanced awkwardness that conflicted with Chinese aesthetic values of the time.

As a painter, Zhao specialized in plant life. His early work is characterized by soft, detailed brushwork and brilliant, translucent colours. *Plants of Zhejiang* (1861; Tokyo N. Mus., see *Tokyo kukuritsu*, p. 162), a set of four hanging scrolls, is one of his early masterpieces: each scroll shows an unusual choice of plants and flowers and an immense range of colours and techniques. In one of the scrolls, the clublike arms of a prickly pear cactus are drawn in wet colour, with thistles added in ink while the paint was still wet; next to this is a complicated web of arched oleander leaves. Against this manipulation of wet colour, with its subtly vibrating edges, the pink and white oleander flowers are opaque. The fact that each composition is cut by the border of the scroll and that many elements within the paintings are interwoven gives a sense that the plants are reaching beyond their confines and enhances the vitality of the work. In contrast, the colours in Zhao's later paintings are muted; there is an increased use of ink, and the brushwork is more exaggerated. *Flowering Plants on Four Scrolls* (1874; Tokyo N. Mus.; see *Tokyo kukuritsu*, p. 164) is a set of four hanging scrolls from this later period. In the scroll that depicts lotus and reed, the colours are dull greens, browns and pale oranges; the use of ink is abundant. The speed of execution is much more rapid than in Zhao's earlier works, with the result that it is the intensity of the brushwork that makes the greatest impact rather than the vitality of the plants represented.

Shen Fucan (1799–1850) taught Zhao empirical methods of research known as *kaozhengxue*, based on verification of texts through ancient artefacts. This introduction led to his fascination with stelae, which he first copied in 1863 after one of many trips to take the national civil service examinations in Beijing. The stelae had a profound effect on his calligraphy, which hitherto had been soft and rounded. His work acquired a new angularity, and his brushwork became more forceful. This style, which drew its inspiration from stelae of the Northern Wei period (AD 386–534), became so popular that Kang Youwei identified Zhao as responsible for starting a mania. Towards the end of his life, however, Zhao was no longer concerned with assimilating the style of ancient stelae: his late calligraphy displays an angularity, asymmetry and natural movement unique to him. In a set of four hanging scrolls called *Poems by Wu Zhen* (undated; Tokyo N. Mus.) the individual strokes are blunt and plain, and the size and shape of each character vary constantly. Zhao has dispensed with the idea of distinct columns of characters and instead has fitted each character into its neighbour by expanding the size of the characters, writing them closer together and placing them on different levels. The brushwork is swift and uninhibited, and the overall effect is one of great freedom.

Zhao's early seals were characterized by a slightly wavering, uneven line that shows the influence of the conservative, archaistic tendencies popularized in the late Ming period by Wen Peng (1498–1573). By the late 1860s Zhao had developed his own style: his seals from this period are imaginative and varied in design, with great depth and power of line.

In 1872, having put himself into debt to buy a position of expectant magistrate in Jiangxi Province, he arrived to find himself assigned to edit the local gazetteer. It was work that he detested, and Zhao's dissatisfaction in his job coincided with the curtailment of his artistic activities. He held a succession of official posts until his death in 1884.

See also CHINA, §§IV, 2(vii)(c) and XIII, 22(iv).

BIBLIOGRAPHY
A. W. Hummel, ed.: *Eminent Chinese of the Ch'ing Period, 1644–1912* (Washington, DC, 1943), p. 70
K. Shimonaka, ed: *Shodō zenshū* [Complete collection of calligraphy], xxiv (Tokyo, 1961), pp. 159–60, nos 70–76
Tokyo kokuritsu hakubutsukan zuhan mokuroku: Chūgoku eigahen [Illustrated catalogues of the Tokyo National Museum: Chinese paintings] (Tokyo, 1979), pp. 162–5
T. Kobayashi, ed: *Chūgoku tenkoku sokan* [Collection of Chinese seal-carving] (Tokyo, 1981), xxvi–xxvii
Yu Jianhua, ed: *Zhongguo meishu jiaren ming cidian* [Dictionary of Chinese artists] (Shanghai, 1981), p. 1271

ELIZABETH F. BENNETT

Zhao Zuo [Chao Tso; *zi* Wendu] (*b* ?Songjiang [in modern Shanghai Municipality], *c.* 1570; *d* ?Tangxi, West Lake region of Hangzhou, *c.* 1633). Chinese painter and theorist. Zhao studied painting under the landscape painter and calligrapher Song Xu and became the founder of the Yunjian school, one of two groups active in the Songjian region, near Shanghai, during the early 17th century (the other, the Huating school, was led by DONG QICHANG, the founder and theorist of the ORTHODOX SCHOOL of painting). Zhao wrote a short text called *Lun hua* ('Discussion of painting'), the first surviving text on landscape painting since the *Xie shanshui jue* ('Secrets of describing landscape'), written by Huang Gongwang about three centuries earlier. The essay adheres to Huang's concerns with dynamic force (*shi*), natural order (*li*) and the organization of mountain masses in long, continuous movements within the composition. Zhao Zuo's text lacks the stern intellectual tone of Dong Qichang's writing. It offers practical advice for the artist, such as how to sketch houses, trees and bridges in dry brushwork before developing the forms with wet ink, and includes advice on depicting figures, villages and temples, anecdotal elements not often found in Dong's painting. Indeed, Yunjian school painting in general, and Zhao's work in particular, is more representational, more relaxed and executed with softer brushstrokes and less dramatic tonal contrast than comparable Huating school works.

The trees and earth masses in Zhao's early painting (e.g. *Landscape*, hanging scroll, ink and light colours on paper; 1615; Taipei, N. Pal. Mus.) are rendered with an appreciation for natural growth and geological form rather than as parts of an analytical system of representation using a limited repertory of repeated forms, as in many works of the Orthodox school. The *Bamboo Monastery* (hanging scroll, ink and light colours on paper; Osaka, Mun. Mus. A.) shows Zhao's tendency to leave white bands of reserve along the contours of earth and rock, allowing him to suggest complex recessions in depth. He depicted rocks in a decidedly non-Chinese fashion, using varying tones and highlights applied in short, broad strokes to create a sense of volume and weight. Zhao avoided extensive use of ink wash and the long, schematic texture strokes (*cun*) commonly found in literati painting (see CHINA, §V, 4(ii)). Consequently, Zhao's landscapes have structural clarity and a convincing interplay of light and shade; the overall effect is painterly, soft and somewhat closer to Western chiaroscuro than to traditional Chinese formalism. Scholars have suggested that European art, in the form of late 16th-century engraved book illustrations, might have influenced Zhao.

Between 1612 and 1620, Zhao Zuo became increasingly drawn to the style of the Orthodox school. Although his own work of this period lacked the originality of his earlier paintings, the qualities of his best work—the soft treatment of forms, smoothly flowing masses, occasional naturalism and deft brushwork—continued to appear in the work of Yunjian school painters until the early 18th century.

BIBLIOGRAPHY

O. Sirén: *Chinese Painting: Leading Masters and Principles* (London and New York, 1956–8), v, pp. 20–22

J. Cahill: *The Distant Mountains: Chinese Painting of the Late Ming Dynasty, 1570–1644* (New York and Tokyo, 1982), pp. 68–70, 79–82

Zha Shibiao [Cha Shih-piao; *zi* Erzhan; *hao* Meihe Sanren, Lanlao] (*b* Haiyang, Anhui Province, 1615; *d* Yangzhou, Jiangsu Province, 1698). Chinese painter, connoisseur, calligrapher and poet. One of the Four Masters of Xin'an (*see* ANHUI SCHOOL), he was born to a wealthy family of connoisseurs and art collectors. He passed the first stage in the civil service examination ladder to receive his *xiu cai* ('cultivated talent') degree while in his 20s, but like many scholars after the fall of the Ming dynasty (1368–1644) he abandoned all thought of an official career, turning instead to writing and painting. Later in life he referred to himself as an 'inkstone-ploughing guest', that is, one who has made a living with a brush. Forced to flee when the invading Manchus destroyed his home, Zha travelled to Nanjing and Zhenjiang in Jiangsu Province and during the 1660s settled in Yangzhou. By nature he was easy-going and somewhat reclusive, given to drinking late into the night.

In his earliest extant paintings (dated *c.* 1653–5) he followed the style of Ni Zan. By 1674 Zha had mastered the dry, feathery brushwork and sparse arrangement of landscape forms associated with the Anhui school. Although he was capable of fine transcriptions in the manner of Ni Zan and Hongren (whom he had known in the 1650s), later on he also used a wide range of atmospheric 'wet brush' effects and painted albums in the styles of Yuan-period artists such as Huang Gongwang and Gao Kegong. *Waterfall and Bamboo in Deep Valley* (hanging scroll, 1674; Nanjing, Jiangsu Prov. Mus.) is painted in the dry-brush style. Extremely popular among merchant-patrons in Yangzhou, Zha was prone to overproduction. His paintings are sometimes freely rendered to the point of carelessness, but he remains one of the most versatile of the Anhui school masters.

For discussion and illustration of *River Landscape* (1687) by Zha Shibiao, *see* POETRY AND PAINTING.

BIBLIOGRAPHY

DMB: 'Shih-piao'

O. Sirén: *Chinese Painting: Leading Masters and Principles*, 7 vols (London and New York, 1956–8), v, pp. 117–19

R. Whitfield: *In Pursuit of Antiquity* (New York, 1969), pp. 127–8

M. Fu and Fu Shen: *Studies in Connoisseurship: Chinese Paintings from the Arthur M. Sackler Collection in New York and Princeton* (Princeton, 1973), pp. 152–6

Shadows of Mt. Huang: Chinese Painting and Printing of the Anhui School (exh. cat., ed. J. F. Cahill; Berkeley, U. CA, A. Mus., 1981), pp. 102–10

VYVYAN BRUNST, with JAMES CAHILL

Zhaxilhünbo. *See* TASHILHUNPO.

Zheng Xie [Cheng Hsieh; *zi* Kerou; *hao* Banqiao, Pan-ch'iao] (*b* Xinghua, Jiangsu Province, 1693; *d* 1765). Chinese painter, calligrapher and poet. Equally known as Zheng Banqiao, Zheng Xie was, together with Jin Nong, the most prominent of the group of painters referred to as the Eight Eccentrics of Yangzhou (*see* YANGZHOU SCHOOL). Although orphaned, he subsequently achieved some success in the official civil service examinations and obtained appointments as a local magistrate in Shandong Province. A brief encounter in 1748 on Mt Tai, Shandong, with the Qianlong emperor (*reg* 1736–96) won him the coveted title of Official Calligrapher and Painter (*shuhuashi*), for which he had a seal carved to commemorate the event. The end of his official career came in 1753, following a charge of corruption.

After 1753 Zheng Xie led a comfortable life in Xinghua, thanks to his past land acquisitions, farming revenue and commissions from painting and calligraphy. To avoid unnecessary bargaining with his patrons, he posted his famous and highly unorthodox price list, which set the cost of commissioned works by size and at the same time discouraged bargain-hunters and those intent on socializing. A frequent visitor to the neighbouring commercial centre of Yangzhou, Jiangsu Province, which he had known in his youth, he became inextricably bound up with its literary and artistic circles. His fame there endured so that even after his death, the possession of a painting or piece of calligraphy by him was considered to be a social prerequisite.

Zheng Xie is known primarily for a limited range of painting themes, chiefly bamboo, orchids, and rocks and chrysanthemums. Few of his early works survive; of those that are extant the majority are dated after 1753. While acknowledging his debt to Xu Wei, Daoji and Gao Qipei, three of the most uninhibited artists in the history of Chinese painting, Zheng Xie nonetheless refused to work within the parameters that they set, as demonstrated by the screen painting *Ink Bamboo* (1753; Tokyo, N. Mus.) and the set of four hanging scrolls entitled *Misty Bamboo on a Distant Mountain* (see fig.). These works possess a formidable presence, at once bold, structured, poignant and luminous, and they represent a new apex in the art of bamboo painting. Such large, expressive works had few equals before or after, not even among Zheng Xie's later paintings. These late works display a reductive approach, in which the artist pares all the elements down to the bare bones; there any concern for representation gives way to the sheer impetuosity of the brushstrokes. This phenomenon may be attributed to Zheng's ever-increasing rate of production, as demands made by his admirers drained not only his energy but also inspiration.

Zheng's penchant for integrating calligraphy with painting to an extent previously unknown is seen in *Ink Bamboo*. The writing closely borders the bamboo cluster, asserts itself in the pictorial space and sets its own distinctive rhythm against the surging growth of the stems and leaves. In another painting, *Cymbidiums, Bamboo and Fungi Growing from Rocks* (1761; San Francisco, CA, Asian A. Mus.), the calligraphy is placed within the form of the rocks and is enclosed by them, so that, visually, it functions not in isolation, but is an integral part of the composition.

Zheng Xie: *Misty Bamboo on a Distant Mountain*, set of four hanging scrolls, ink on paper, each scroll 1792×647 mm, 1753 (Princeton, NJ, Princeton University, Art Museum)

In his calligraphy Zheng combined the running cursive (*xingcao*) script with *bafen* ('eight tenths') style, a sophisticated form of clerical script (*lishu*; see CHINA, §IV, 2(vii)). This he named, albeit facetiously, *liufenban* ('six and a half tenths'). Praise was heaped on his inscriptions on paintings not only for their calligraphic merit and because they shed light on the creative process, but also because they opened up new possibilities for social comment and criticism. A volume of such inscriptions, *Banqiao tihua* ('Inscriptions on paintings by Banqiao'), was edited posthumously by an admirer, Qi Yu. Another compilation, *Zheng Banqiao ji* ('Collected works of Zheng Banqiao'), comprises anthologies of his regular (*shi*) and irregular (*ci*) verses, his lyrics (*daoqing*) and a selection of letters to family members. Published between 1742 and 1749, these were written in his own inimitable calligraphy and cut into woodblocks by his follower, Situ Wengao.

Paradoxically, Zheng Xie blended a libertine lifestyle with a homespun, Confucian morality and saw little conflict between them. He was cast as an eccentric due to his penchant for mixing with groups as varied as Chan Buddhist monks, Manchu guards and imperial scions as well as for his uninhibited venting of opinions. His acerbic wit, unconventional behaviour and compassion for the downtrodden, together with his artistic achievements, made him a legendary figure.

See also CHINA, §V, 3(vi).

WRITINGS

Qi Yu: 'Banqiao tihua' [Inscriptions on paintings by Zheng Xie], *Meishu congshu* [General collection of works on art] (Taipei, 1947), xvi/2, pp. 125–46

Zheng Banqiao ji [Collected works of Zheng Banqiao] (Shanghai, 1983)

BIBLIOGRAPHY

Wang Huai: *Zheng Banqiao pingzhuan* [Critical biography of Zheng Xie] (Taipei, n.d.)

'Hachidai Sanjin, Yoshu hakkei' [Bada Shanren and the Yangzhou school], *Suiboku bijutsu taikei* [A survey of ink painting], xi (Tokyo, 1978), pp. 68–70

Wang Jiansheng: *Zheng Banqiao yanjiu* [A study of Zheng Xie] (Taipei, 1979)

Yang Xin: *Yangzhou baguai* [The Eight Eccentrics of Yangzhou] (Beijing, 1981)

Zhou Jiyin: 'Zheng Banqiao huihua zuopin nianbiao' [A chronological list of Zheng Xie's paintings], *Meishu zhongheng*, i (Nanjing, 1982)

Huang Miaozi: 'Banqiao yu Wei Xian' [Zheng Xie and Wei Xian], *Meishujia* [Artist], xxv (1982), pp. 68–71; xxvi, pp. 70–73

Zhou Jiyin: *Zheng Banqiao shuhua yishu* [The art of Zheng Xie's painting and calligraphy] (Tianjin, 1982)

Pan Mao: *Zheng Banqiao* (Shanghai, 1983)

Xue Zhenguo and others: 'Zheng Banqiao and the Shi Clan of Yangchen', *Meishu Yanjiu*, iv (1984), pp. 84–5

Ju-hsi Chou and C. Brown: *The Elegant Brush: Chinese Painting under the Qianlong Emperor, 1735–1795* (Phoenix, 1985)

JU-HSI CHOU

Zhengzhou [Cheng-chou; Chengchow]. Capital of Henan Province, China. Archaeological excavations since 1950 in the drainage basin of the south bank of the Yellow River have produced evidence that this was a centre of Shang culture (*c.* 1600–1050 BC).

The area has been identified by some archaeologists with the second Shang capital, Ao, which according to the ancient annals (e.g. Liu Xin's *San Tong li pu* (a calendar) and the *Zhushu jinian* (*Bamboo Annals*)) was founded by the Shang ruler Zhongding (*reg c.* 1568– *c.*1558 BC), but on the basis of archaeological evidence is generally dated to the 15th century BC. Around 1300 BC it seems the capital was transferred to Yin, near modern Anyang (see 1968 exh. cat.). Findings support the hypothesis that for some time Zhengzhou and Anyang may have been occupied contemporaneously. During the Zhou period (*c.* 1050–256 BC) the area was first called Guyang and then known as Dantu. While serving as the capital of the state of Wu during the Three Kingdoms period (*c.* AD 220–80) it was known as Jingke. Modern excavations have identified specific sites from the general area of Minggonglu (an area of Zhengzhou in which pottery was found with dates indicating occupation between 2000 and 1500 BC), as well as the Erligang phase (*c.* 15th–14th century BC, *see* CHINA, §VI, 3(ii)).

The perimeter of the ancient site is defined by a tamped earth (*hangtu*) wall up to 20 m wide at the base and *c.* 10 m high, enclosing a rough rectangle measuring 3.2 sq. km within a total inhabited area of *c.* 25 sq. km. Excavations within the urban nucleus indicate that several essential features of traditional Chinese architecture were already present in the Shang period. Pits with tamped earth floors and walls served as foundations for dwellings, storage areas and workshops. Consistent with Shang city planning (*see* CHINA §II, 3), a walled area of large buildings, possibly government structures and royal residences, was located in the north-eastern section of the city, and trading areas were located in the west and south. A large building with a lime-plastered floor and substantial post holes, similar to those at the Neolithic site of Banpo, was found south of a platform that may have served as some sort of altar. This nucleus was surrounded by a ring of villages, each of which appears to have specialized in a particular occupation. Finds such as remains of ceramics workshops and bronze foundries make it clear that there was a division of labour between such industries. Burial grounds, located west, south and east of the villages, and remains indicative of human sacrifice were also discovered.

Excavations have revealed four strata corresponding to four successive phases of Shang occupation at Zhengzhou. The earliest lies just above remains of the LONGSHAN Neolithic culture and has been designated Ledamiao. It is only a little later than the uppermost level at ERLITOU, north-east of Luoyang, and contemporary with the early phase at the nearby site of Erligang. The three lowest strata at Zhengzhou predate the Anyang phase (*c.* 1300–*c.* 1100 BC) and represent the formative phase of the Chinese Bronze Age. The fourth level dovetails with the earliest Anyang occupation.

Bronze finds at Zhengzhou make it possible to trace the development of bronzeworking from its inception in the Shang through to the Zhou. No bronzes were found in the lowest strata, but thereafter there is a degree of continuity. The earliest pieces are more primitive than those found at Anyang but are of remarkably high quality and uniformity of style for products of a new art form. The high technological level of the bronzes, as compared with contemporary cultures, supports the hypothesis that bronze-casting was an indigenous development rather than a foreign import. The early pieces are smaller in size and have thinner walls than those from Anyang, and shapes are fewer and less specialized. The slightly clumsy forms reflect ceramic prototypes and may also relate to changes necessitated by the transition from the use of sheet metal to the technique of casting. Forms such as the *jue* tripod vessel (*see* CHINA, fig. 138(i)) have flat bottoms that are easier to cast than the later rounded ones. Analysis of metal content indicates an inferior quality of bronze alloy, but the formula is variable and may have been determined independently in different foundries. Available evidence suggests that the bronzes were cast primarily from section moulds that bore the decoration. A few moulds with traces of metal still remaining in the indentations support this hypothesis. The patterns are simple: the earliest consist of rows of raised circles and dots and abstract patterns in thread relief. The earliest version of the *taotie* animal-mask (*see* CHINA, §VI, 3(ii)(a)) appears at this site.

The pottery kilns at Zhengzhou are small, suggesting that they supplied only the local area. They were, however, highly experimental. The earliest proto-porcelain vessel yet discovered in China was unearthed at Zhengzhou. This wine-vessel (see fig.) has a yellowish-green glaze on the inner and outer surfaces over buff-coloured clay. Fired at 1200° C, it has a low rate of water absorption. The use of kaolin was introduced for the production of high-quality whiteware, and there was also experimentation with high-fired glazes. Pottery with repeated impressed designs created by a technique probably introduced from the area of modern Jiangxi Province was also found.

Among other finds from Zhengzhou, the few inscribed oracle bones used for divination (*see* CHINA, §IV, 2), like

Zhengzhou, *zun* wine-vessel, yellowish-green glaze over buff-coloured clay, h. 282 mm, Shang period, *c.* 1600–*c.* 1050 BC (Zhengzhou, Henan Provincial Museum)

the bronzes, display progressive development. Turtle shells or plastrons apparently came into use as alternatives to scapulae (shoulder-blades). Bones from the lower strata at the site bear only a single character, whereas those from the top strata have larger inscriptions, as at Anyang. Jades were also found at Zhengzhou (*see* CHINA, §VIII, 1). The modern city of Zhengzhou has an excellent exhibition of archaeological finds in the Henan Provincial Museum.

BIBLIOGRAPHY

J. Legge: *The Shooting* (Shanghai, 1904) [repr. with the *Bamboo Annals*]
M. Loehr: 'The Bronze Styles of the Anyang Period', *Archvs Chin. A. Soc. America*, vii (1953), pp. 42–53
'Zhengzhou Shang dai yizhi de fajue' [Excavations of the remains of the Yin dynasty at Cheng-chow, Honan], *Kaogu Xuebao*, xv (1957), no. 1, pp. 53–74
Zhengzhou Erligang, Kaogu xue zhuankan, D/vii (Beijing, 1959)
Cheng Te-k'un: *Shang China* (1960), ii of *Archaeology in China* (Toronto, 1959–)
T. H. Qien: *Written on Bamboo and Silk* (Chicago, 1962)
W. Watson: *Ancient Chinese Bronzes* (London, 1962)
Xin Zhongguo de kaogu shouhuo [Archaeology in new China], Kaogu xue zhuankan, A/vi (Beijing, 1962)
A. C. Soper: 'Early, Middle and Late Shang: A Note', *Artibus Asiae*, xxviii (1966), pp. 1–38
Ritual Vessels of Bronze Age China (exh. cat. by M. Loehr, New York, Asia House Gals, 1968)
P. T. Ho: *The Cradle of the East* (Chicago, 1975)
J. Rawson: *Ancient China: Art and Archaeology* (London, 1980)
Treasures from the Bronze Age of China: An Exhibition from the People's Republic of China (exh. cat., ed. Wen Fong; New York, Met.; Los Angeles, CA, Co. Mus. A.; 1980–81)

MARY S. LAWTON

Zhe school [Chin. Zhe pai]. Term used to refer to a school of Chinese painting within the Ming period (1368–1644). Derived from the south-eastern coastal province of Zhejiang, the name has been in common usage since the early 17th century. However, the definition and art-historical boundaries of the Zhe school are far from clear, since many of its artists are also included in the 'Ming academy', an equally problematic term loosely applied to a group of painters serving at the imperial court in the 15th and 16th centuries. It is true that the designation of a Zhe school as a local phenomenon has some validity in that many of its members, and notably its founder, Dai Jin, were from Zhejiang. Moreover, Zhe school masters followed an older, conservative stylistic tradition, that of the Southern Song (1127–1279) Academy (*see* CHINA, §V, 4(i)), centred from its beginnings in the Hangzhou region of Zhejiang. Nevertheless, the school also included artists from other parts of China and drew on different stylistic traditions. In the end it seems best to retain both the term 'Zhe school' and the term 'Ming academy', while admitting that they do not define either a truly local school, in the strict sense, or an organized academy.

1. STYLE AND SUBJECT-MATTER. Stylistically, Zhe school paintings are aimed more at strong effects than at subtleties. Figures in the landscapes tend to be large, active and expressive, in keeping with their important roles in the scenes portrayed. Compositions are typically constructed out of large, blocky units and are often divided by rectilinear elements. In landscapes, for example, strong verticals at one side—trees or a cliff—will be balanced by horizontals on the other—a bridge, a further shore, a distant horizon. Brush drawing, except in figural and architectural details, tends to be bold and broad, and deep in ink tone. Most of these features can be seen as innovations of DAI JIN (see fig.) and are typical of hanging scrolls by Zhe school masters. Some of them carry over into the handscrolls and albums that were also painted (though less frequently), in which the compositional elements are usually fewer, larger and more vigorously drawn than in typical works in these forms by artists of other schools. The principal stylistic sources for the school lie in Southern Song Academy painting, but Zhe school artists also sometimes adopted the landscape manner of GUO XI and LI CHENG, following Yuan-period (1279–1368) adherents of that tradition such as Tang Di; they also imitated such other Yuan masters as Gao Kegong and Sheng Mau.

The repertory of Zhe school forms and subjects must be understood in relation to the concerns of their patrons, from the emperor through court officials and the lower

Zhe school painting by Dai Jin: *Wen Wang of Zhou Visiting Tai Gongwang on the Banks of the River Wei*, ink and colours on silk, 1396×754 mm, mid-15th century (Taipei, National Palace Museum)

ranks of the civil service to the merchants and others who were rich enough to commission such paintings. Often taking the form of large hanging scrolls or screens, which have not survived, these paintings were displayed in entrance halls and audience rooms. While their main function was to convey certain values and symbolic meanings through their subjects, their strong compositions made them effective as decorative objects. Representations of personages from the past, or of incidents from history or legend (*gushi*), were read in relation to contemporary issues. Research has shown, for instance, that pictures of eminent hermits and recluses of antiquity—a subject category chosen often by these artists and very seldom by artists of other groups—communicated certain ideas and attitudes about government service and the attaining and relinquishing of official posts. They might convey such messages from one official to another, or even from the emperor to one of his ministers, and may have been used for presentation or hanging on the occasion of someone's appointment to a new post or retirement.

Idealized images of the lives of fishermen and wood-gatherers, another subject commonly painted by the Zhe school and academy masters, belonged to a kind of Chinese pastoral myth, according to which officials and others pursuing careers in the cities were at heart more inclined towards a simple life, free of the involvements and tensions of their urban environment, relaxing on the riverbank with the fishermen or roaming the mountains with the wood-gatherers. Another category of subjects commonly depicted by these artists presented the same ideal more directly, as their predecessors in the Southern Song Academy had done, by portraying unworldly scholar-officials walking on mountain paths, accompanied by servants carrying lutes or zithers (*qin*), or seated under pine trees gazing into misty spaces or at the moon. Seen as a whole, the typical subjects of Zhe school and Ming academy paintings may be regarded as presenting idealized alternatives to the real lives of the people for whom they were made.

2. HISTORY. The background of the Zhe school can be seen in earlier Ming painting represented by the works of the bird-and-flower master Bian Wenjin (*fl* early 15th century) from Fujian; Xie Huan (*c.* 1368–1435), a figure painter and portraitist from Zhejiang who was a major force among Yongle (*reg* 1403–24) and Xuande (*reg* 1426–35) court painters; Shang Xi (*fl* 1430–40) from Jiangsu and Shi Rui (*fl* 1426–35) from Hangzhou; Ni Duan, a painter of landscapes with figures, also from Hangzhou; and Li Zai, a landscapist from Fujian. The Zhe school departed from these artists' continuation of conservative Song Academy styles and its origin can conveniently be located in Dai Jin's works, especially in those of his middle period, dating from the second quarter of the 15th century.

Dai Jin arrived in the capital, Beijing, around 1425 and was presented at court in the hope of being given a position there. Unfortunately, he fell victim to the envy of the other court painters, especially Xie Huan. As was usual practice, the paintings Dai offered as examples of his work were scrutinized for their symbolic meanings; they were interpreted as containing veiled slurs on the emperor and his regime. Although Dai was forced to flee to Hangzhou

and then to Yunnan, he returned to the capital around 1440 and enjoyed great success, receiving the favour of several high officials. He was followed later in the 15th century by such court painters as Zhou Wenjing from Fujian and Lin Liang from Guangzhou. The latter specialized in painting birds with bold brushwork in monochrome ink and was active at the court from around 1460. These are considered Zhe school masters in a loose sense, as are certain court painters of the Hongzhi era (1488–1505) including Lü Ji, another bird-and-flower specialist who worked in a more traditional style than Lin Liang (*see* CHINA, fig. 123); Wang E and Zhong Li, both landscapists; and Zhu Duan, also chiefly a landscapist, who was summoned to court by 1501 and was still active in the Zhengde era (1506–21).

A new phase of the school's development was initiated by WU WEI, who altered the school manner with looser, swifter brushwork and a more improvisatory approach. He was also, however, capable of excellent works in the 'fine-line' (*baimiao*) manner. Educated and cultured, while living as a professional painter, Wu exemplified a new type of artist who stood outside the traditional division (already compromised by past exceptions) between uneducated 'artisan painters' and scholarly amateurs.

From Wu Wei's time the Zhe school's boundaries became even more blurred by the adoption of its styles among artists neither from Zhejiang nor associated with the imperial court, most being active in Nanjing. Outstanding among them was Zhang Lu, a northerner from Kaifeng, active in the early decades of the 16th century, who adopted the manner of Wu Wei while adding elements of an individual style. Others who followed Wu Wei, generally with less originality, were Jiang Song, a native of Nanjing, Zhu Bang from Anhui, and Chen Zihe and Zheng Wenlin from Fujian. These artists have usually been regarded by both Chinese and foreign writers as signalling a period of decline of the Zhe school, although some revisionist writers have challenged this view. In any case, by the late 16th century these masters were seen as representing a 'heterodox' branch of the school, and by the end of the Ming period the Zhe school as a whole was in such bad repute that such artists as LAN YING and SONG XU could be disparaged by being branded as late members of it. Late 20th-century scholarship has tried to counter these biases with a more balanced assessment of the school in the context of Ming painting.

For a discussion of the Zhejiang school of seal-carving *see* CHINA, §XIII, 22(iv).

BIBLIOGRAPHY
H. Vanderstappen: 'Painters at the Early Ming Court (1368–1435) and the Problem of a Ming Painting Academy', *Mnmt Serica*, xv (1956), pp. 258–302; xvi (1957), pp. 315–46
K. Suzuki: *Mindai kaigashi no kenkyū: Seppa* [A study of Ming painting: the Zhe school] (Tokyo, 1968)
J. Cahill: *Parting at the Shore: Chinese Painting of the Early and Middle Ming Dynasty, 1368–1580* (New York, 1978), pp. 3–56, 97–134
R. Barnhart: 'The "Wild and Heterodox School" of Ming Painting', *Theories of the Arts in China*, ed. S. Bush and C. Murck (Princeton, 1983), pp. 365–96
Painters of the Great Ming: The Imperial Court and the Zhe School (exh. cat. by R. M. Barnhart, Dallas, TX, Mus. A., 1993)

JAMES CAHILL

Zhevele, Henry. *See* YEVELE, HENRY.

Zhilinsky, Dmitry (Dmitrevich) (*b* Volnovka, Krasnodar region, 25 May 1927). Russian painter. He trained in Moscow at the Institute of Applied and Decorative Art (1944–6) and the Surikov Art Institute (1946–51) under Pavel Korin and others, while Vladimir Favorsky was particularly influential in shaping his talent. Zhilinsky was a member of the generation of the so-called Severe (or Austere) Style (Rus. *Surovyy Stil'*), a movement in Russian art in the 1960s that sought to endow images with a new integrity and strict verism, thereby overcoming the decrepit standards of Socialist Realism, and he has always been distinguished by the refined aestheticism of his paintings. Working in tempera on *levkas* (the gesso-like priming typical of Russian medieval painting), he drew stylistically on the heritage of the Italian Quattrocento and the German Renaissance. Touches of a sort of Art Nouveau revival are also manifested in his precise, rhythmical use of line and in the exquisite details of his works. One of the most talented Russian portrait painters, he often turned his portraits into extended metaphors of human life (e.g. *Under the Old Appletree*, 1969; St Petersburg, Rus. Mus.) or into a 'focus of beauty', full of historical detail and stylization, as in *Two-sided Portrait of Irene and Peter Ludwig* (1981; Cologne, Mus. Ludwig). His painting *1937* (1987; Moscow, artist's col.), depicting the arrest of his father during Stalin's Great Terror, became one of the popular artistic symbols of the era of *glasnost'*.

BIBLIOGRAPHY

P. A. Pavlov: *D. Zhilinsky* (Leningrad, 1974)

M. Shashkina: *D. Zhilinsky* (Moscow, 1989)

M. N. SOKOLOV

Zhilyardi, Dementy (Ivanovich). *See* GILLARDI, DOMENICO.

Zhmuydzinavichyus, Antanas (Ionasovich). *See* ŽMUIDZINAVIČIUS, ANTANAS.

Zholtovsky, Ivan (Vladislavovich) (*b* Pinsk, 27 Nov 1876; *d* Moscow, 16 July 1959). Russian architect, urban planner and teacher. His somewhat literal imitations of Italian Renaissance buildings represented an alternative to the avant-garde in the years immediately after the Russian Revolution. Although its influence on the subsequent development of Russian architecture was limited, his work met with official approval, especially in the 1930s, as a link with the past.

1. EARLY WORK, TO 1923. He studied (1887–98) at the Academy of Art in St Petersburg, then set up independently as an architect in Moscow and also taught at the Stroganov School. His winning competition design for the Horse Club (1903), Begavaja Street, Moscow, is characteristic of his lifelong architectural beliefs. The assignment made the Gothic Revival style obligatory, but on his own initiative Zholtovsky made a classical variant based on playful neo-classicism with Palladian motifs and convinced the jury that this was better. Another characteristic early building is the villa of the industrialist Tarasov (1909–10), Tolstoy Street, Moscow, which is reminiscent of a stately Renaissance palace, particularly the Palazzo Thiene (1542) in Vicenza by Palladio. Through this he became affiliated to the group of Russian architects, such as Ivan Fomin (*see* FOMIN, (1)) and ALEKSEY SHCHUSEV, who practised the revival of the classical tradition.

At the time of the Revolution of 1917, Zholtovsky was already an established architect. However, his connections with the Imperial régime did not damage his subsequent career, since directly after the Revolution there was a shortage of experienced professionals prepared to work with the new Bolshevik government. The preferences of government officials also played a part. The Peoples' Commissar for Education, Anatoly Lunacharsky, for example, was an admirer of Zholtovsky's work, believing that it represented the best artistic traditions and was therefore suitable for the new society. Accordingly, in 1918 Zholtovsky was given a leading responsibility for the new planning of Moscow, and a studio in the faculty of architecture in 1919, and he was made head of the department of architecture at the Commissariat for Public Education. It was here that the architectural activities of central government were determined, such as building programmes and competitions, and Zholtovsky used his position to further his own architectural preferences. For example, in 1923, he intervened ex officio in the judging of the competition for the Palace of Labour, Moscow, to deprive the avant-garde design by the Vesnin brothers of first prize, in favour of the historicizing project of Noy Trotsky. He also ensured the predominance of the traditional concept of architecture in his plan for the First All-Union Agricultural Exhibition (1923, for illustrations see Barkhin, figs 13–14, Máčel, p. 48), Moscow, one of the few larger projects after the Revolution. For this he also designed some pavilions and the main gateway, which although based on a classical triumphal arch exuded the pioneer spirit of the period through its use of timber, and by its undisguised construction.

2. AFTER 1923. In 1923 Zholtovsky travelled to Italy, where he worked among other things on the Soviet pavilion for an exhibition in Milan. When he returned to the USSR in 1926, Modernism was gaining ground and traditionalist architects were on the defensive. Zholtovsky was unmoved, however, and continued working in the spirit of 16th-century Italian architecture. The House of the Soviets (1926–8) in Makhachkala is a virtual copy of the Palazzo Farnese (1559–73) in Caprarola by Jacopo Vignola. The Gosbank Building (1927–9) in Neglinnaya Street, Moscow, an enlargement and extension of an existing building in a neo-Baroque style, harks back to the Palazzo Piccolomini (1459–64) in Pienza by Bernardo Rossellino and Palazzo Rucellai (1446–51) in Florence by Alberti. Its reinforced-concrete construction is hidden behind stucco. The advance of Functionalist architecture nevertheless forced Zholtovsky to make concessions. He sent in two projects (1927–9; unexecuted) for the hydroelectric Dneproges scheme, one of which was in a Modernist vein, and his Moges boilerhouse and pumping station (1927–9) near Moscow used exposed concrete, steel and glass. This remained, however, his only work in this style.

In 1931 Zholtovsky participated in the competition for the Palace of the Soviets, Moscow. Unexpectedly the first-round prizes went not to Modernist projects, but to three more or less historicizing designs, including that by

Zholtovsky, and the competition symbolized the cultural and political changes taking place in the USSR. The officially approved Socialist Realism required a traditionalist classical architecture, in which Zholtovsky was able to follow his own Italianate preferences. The apartment house (1933–4; *see* RUSSIA, fig. 15), Mokhovaya Street, Moscow, for example, is an enlarged version of the Loggia del Capitaniano (1570s), Vicenza, by Palladio. Despite the criticism that this literal imitation of the tradition attracted, Zholtovsky also built an administrative building (1934–7) in Sochi, Crimea, which in its ground plan and details again resembles a Palladian villa. However, the project for the theatre (1937) in Taganrog, which was to be the prototype for theatre architecture in the USSR until the 1950s, shows a freer interpretation as the classical forms have not been copied literally from one particular building.

During World War II Zholtovsky worked for the Voyenproject, where he especially designed war memorials. Afterwards he continued in the same spirit, producing projects for the city centres in Kaluga (1946) and Sochi (1947) and the House of the Soviets (1948), Stalingrad (now Volgograd). However, more important are his executed projects for housing blocks in Moscow: on Smolensky Square (1940–52), on Bolshaya Kaluzhskaya Street (1948–50), for which he won the Stalin prize, and on the Yaroslavsky High Road (1952). These are large blocks, where the detailing that was previously so prominent in Zholtovsky's work has been reduced to rustication and profiled cornices. He also completed a project (1952) for prefabricated housing, with a severe, undecorated façade. From 1940, Zholtovsky was head of the Architectural Institute, Moscow, and from 1947 he was a member of the Academy of Arts and Sciences.

BIBLIOGRAPHY

N. P. Bylinkin: 'O teorii kompozitsii I. V. Zholtovskogo' [Concerning the theory of I. V. Zholtovsky], *Arkhit. SSSR*, v (1940), pp. 51–3

A. V. Vlasov: 'Tvorchestvo I. V. Zholtovskogo' [Practice of I. V. Zholtovsky], *Arkhit. SSSR*, v (1940), pp. 35–50

G. O. Oshchepkov, ed.: *I. V. Zholtovsky: Proekty i postroiki* [I. V. Zholtovsky: projects and buildings] (Moscow, 1955)

R. Ya. Khiger: 'Zodchii I. V. Zholtovsky' [Architect I. V. Zholtovsky], *Arkhit. SSSR*, 2 (1968), pp. 44–51

M. G. Barkhin: *Mastera sovetskoy arkhitektury ob arkhitekture* [Masters of soviet architecture on architecture] (Moscow, 1975), pp. 23–55

O. Máčel: 'Nieuwe werelden in het voetspoor van Palladio' [New worlds in the footsteps of Palladio], *Archis*, v (1986), pp. 45–53

OTAKAR MÁČEL

Zhou Chen [Chou Ch'en; *zi* Shunqing; *hao* Dongcun] (*b* Suzhou, Jiangsu Province, *c.* 1470; *d c.* 1535). Chinese painter. Zhou Chen was a pre-eminent professional painter of the Ming period (1368–1644), alongside masters such as Dai Jin. Zhou learnt a conservative style based on Southern Song period (1127–1279) landscape painting from his teacher Chen Xian (1405–96), who specialized in the 'plain-line' (*baimiao*) technique of painting. Zhou later taught Tang Yin for whom Zhou is reported to have worked as a 'ghost painter', displaying his versatility.

An example of Zhou Chen's technically finished early style is *North Sea* (handscroll, early 16th century; Kansas City, MO, Nelson–Atkins Mus. A.; see fig.). The influence of 12th-century painting, such as Li Tang's late works, made during the Southern Song period, can be seen in the strong diagonal composition and the juxtaposition of dark, intricate foliage against lighter eddies and whirlpools of the water. Similarly, the artist's strict attention to details such as the outline of each leaf, the 'axe-cut' texture strokes (*fupi cun*) on the rocks and the careful rendering of the figures are devices which properly belong to the 12th century, and they indicate the conservative tastes of Zhou's early patrons.

As Zhou became less dependent on Song models his style grew looser and more individual. Late Ming sources describe his brushwork as 'free' and done in a 'running manner', a technique in which the brush is not removed from the paper or silk between strokes, so that changes in stroke direction remain evident and the whole has a cursive quality. An example of his later style is *Playing the Game Weiqi beneath Pines* (1526; Taipei, N. Pal. Mus.). The attentuated pines that Zhou favours are even more drawn out, and the composition includes other characteristic motifs such as a traveller on a donkey, a servant and a figure holding a staff crossing a bridge. The water is rendered using the 'fish-net' pattern of undulating lines that accord with the texture and modelling strokes of foreground earth masses.

In *Enjoying the Dusk* (handscroll, undated; Taipei, N. Pal. Mus.), the traditional distinction between the manner of rendering natural elements and figures has been eliminated. Compositional unity is achieved by means of brushstrokes rather than ink tones. The painting is characteristic of Zhou's interest in giving greater emphasis to foreground figures. He is not greatly concerned with the

Zhou Chen: *North Sea* (detail), handscroll, ink and light colours on silk, 0.29×1.35 m, early 16th century (Kansas City, MO, Nelson–Atkins Museum of Art)

rendering of earth masses, which had been a prominent feature in works by Song period academicians and would be a major concern of later painters inspired by the masters of the Yuan period (1279–1368). Instead, earth masses are often broadly defined and modelled with dots of ink (*dian*) representing vegetation. The serpentine branches of the foreground pine trees are sometimes indistinguishable from the peaks of the middleground mountains, and their loose contours are echoed in the twisting shapes of the mist.

Zhou Chen's technical expertise and his concern for fluid contour lines appear once again in a set of album leaves (1516), now mounted in two handscrolls, *Beggars and Street Characters* (Honolulu, HI, Acad. A. and Cleveland, OH, Mus. A.). It consists of a series of portrayals of the poor and underprivileged whom the artist, as he records in an accompanying inscription, often saw in the streets and markets. In the original album format leaves were mounted so as to present the figures in pairs, emphasizing similarities in costume and posture. The drawing is energetic, the angular brushstrokes are ideally suited to the description of the tattered clothes and grimacing faces of Zhou's subjects. These figures are not the idealized depictions of contented, carefree fishermen and woodgatherers typical of many Chinese genre paintings; they are sympathetic images of urban poor, a subject usually considered vulgar by literati painters and collectors. Perhaps due to the narrow taste of later critics and collectors, such images are rare in Chinese painting, and no other examples of such sensitive and skilful rendering of anatomy exist among Zhou's oeuvre.

DMB   BIBLIOGRAPHY
O. Sirén: *Chinese Painting: Leading Masters and Principles*, iv (New York and London, 1958), pp. 205–7
J. Cahill: *Parting at the Shore: Chinese Painting of the Early and Middle Ming Dynasty, 1368–1580* (New York, 1978), pp. 168, 189–93
M. Siggstedt: 'Zhou Chen: The Life and Paintings of a Ming Professional Artist', *Bull. Mus. Far E. Ant.*, liv (1982), pp. 1–240
                    VYVYAN BRUNST, with JAMES CAHILL

Zhou [Chou] dynasty. Chinese dynasty dating to *c*. 1050–256 BC that succeeded the Shang dynasty. The Zhou established suzerainty as far south as the coastal districts on the eastern and northern edge of the Yangzi River basin and as far north as modern Beijing. The empire encompassed areas bordering on Central Asian and Mongol deserts to the west and north and the state of Chu in the south. However, for much of the period Zhou rule was not direct, but limited, devolved and often challenged. Chronologically, the Zhou is divided into the Western Zhou (*c*. 1050–771 BC) and the Eastern Zhou (771–256 BC). The Eastern Zhou period is further divided into a Spring and Autumn period (722–481 BC), named after the chronology for the state of Lu, the *Chunqiu* ('Spring and Autumn Annals'), and the Warring States period (403–221 BC), a time of severe fragmentation. The exact dating of these periods is a matter of debate, however: many scholars date the Spring and Autumn period to 770–475 BC and the Warring States period to 475–221 BC.

During the Zhou period, many basic Chinese ritual, religious and cultural traditions were established, and moral reflection resulted in the formation of rival ethical and political systems. The earliest Chinese literature dates from the Zhou, including the *Chunqiu*, the *Shijing* ('Odes'), and the *Lunyu* ('Analects') of Confucius, all important as historical sources helping to corroborate artistic and archaeological discoveries. The Chinese population greatly increased at this period, and iron tools, replacing wooden and stone implements, became more widespread, resulting in agricultural advances. The rise of merchants and the development of coinage created a larger market for artistic wares.

The Western Zhou traditionally established imperial capitals at Feng, an administrative centre, and Hao, a pleasure and ritual centre, on the Feng River in central Shaanxi Province. The exact sites of Feng and Hao are unknown, but in the area of Fengxi, near Xi'an, palace ruins in Qishan and Fufeng counties have been excavated, revealing a traditional layout in which buildings face south, the main ones on a central axis and subsidiary ones on either side. Little remains except for city walls and the stamped earth platforms of major buildings built with wooden beams, pillars and crossbeams. Other Zhou sites exist, including that of the capital at Luoyang in Henan Province. At HOUMA, capital of the state of Jin in Shanxi Province, remains of workshops for bronze-casting and potterymaking were found, as well as some tombs, many of the shaft type topped with mounds. The early Warring States tomb of the Marquis of Zeng at SUIZHOU in Hubei Province (*see also* CHINA, §II, 6(i)(b) and fig. 53) contained more than 15,000 artefacts, including bronze ritual vessels, a spectacular set of bells, weapons, lacquerware and wooden and bamboo articles.

Bronzes remained the most important form of artistic expression; ritual practices established bronzes as symbols of status, power and wealth, associating them with the authority to rule (*see* CHINA, §VI, 3(iii) and (iv)). Sets of bronzes became important, shapes changed, and there were longer inscriptions documenting political events, gifts between royalty and subjects, marriages and bargains, and corroborating the historical texts with regard to interstate treaties.

Decoration gradually became more geometric and formalized, with greater use of relief, studs and gold, silver or other precious inlay. Among decorative motifs birds became particularly important; other features included exaggerated and prominent hooked flanges and animal-head handles. In the later Eastern Zhou, bronze mirrors, polished on one side and decorated on the other, were produced.

In Western Zhou ceramics, glazes, many brown and green, improved, though vessels were often grey. In the Eastern Zhou, the use of low-fired burial figurines (*mingqi*) increased, possibly influenced by the Confucian dictum against human sacrifice. Brightly painted ceramics imitated newly popular lacquerware (*see* CHINA, §IX, 2); other types closely resembled bronze forms. Soft, polished black wares, low-fired green lead-glazed wares and some high-fired glazed wares were also produced. Ceramic tiles and bricks were moulded and then decorated with stamped or relief decoration (*see also* CHINA, §VII, 3(ii)).

Jade-carving declined generally in the early Western Zhou period but became important again in the Eastern Zhou for items of personal adornment and burial objects.

Jade and bronze designs were often interrelated; many were inlaid. Rounded animal silhouettes replaced earlier flatter, angular shapes (*see* CHINA, §VIII, 3). Sculpture included not only burial figurines, but other burial pottery as well, some of it the precursors of the burial pottery of the Han and Tang dynasties (*see* CHINA, §III, 3(ii)).

Regional diversity in the Zhou period was fairly marked. The southern Chu state, which had developed independently from the cultures of the Yellow River area, produced remarkable mirrors, fine inlay work, wood-carvings, lacquer and textiles. The Chu worshipped their own deities: stylized, wooden human figures, exotic animals and guardian monsters with long protruding tongues and antlers (important for Chu shamanistic rituals) have been found, many painted in lacquer (*see* CHINA, §XIII, 26). The Chu were also renowned for their architecture, particularly palaces, remains of which survive on the site of the city of Ying (modern Ji'nancheng, Jiangling). Of the Zhou's many nomadic neighbours, the northern ORDOS people provided a link with Central Asia; their indigenous styles of animal bronzes influenced northern Chinese animal styles.

The loose hegemony of states that existed in the later Zhou period gradually lost its cohesion, and with increased 'barbarian' attacks there was general political and economic decline. From an artistic standpoint, however, the end of the Warring States period was a time of imaginative craftsmanship, perhaps promoted by competition between the states and a greater number of artistic patrons. The many small states that had become virtually independent of central authority were gradually whittled down to seven major ones. Of these, the Qin eventually succeeded in defeating the others to establish the first, unified Chinese empire under the QIN DYNASTY.

BIBLIOGRAPHY
Cheng Te-k'un: *Chou China*, ii of *Archaeology in China* (Cambridge, MA, 1960)
M. Loehr: *Ritual Vessels of Bronze Age China* (New York, 1968)
T. Lawton: *Chinese Art of the Warring States Period: Change and Continuity, 480–222 BC* (Washington, DC, 1982)
E. Bunker: 'Sources of Foreign Elements in the Culture of Eastern Zhou', *The Great Bronze Age of China: A Symposium: Los Angeles, 1983*, pp. 84–93
D. Nivison: 'Western Chou History Reconstructed from Bronze Inscriptions', *The Great Bronze Age of China: A Symposium: Los Angeles, 1983*, pp. 44–55
Li Xueqin: *Dong Zhou yu Qin dai wenming*; Eng. trans. by K. C. Chang as *Eastern Zhou and Qin Civilizations* (New Haven and London, 1985)
Cho-yun Hsu and K. M. Linduff: *Western Chou Civilization* (New Haven, 1988)
J. Rawson: *Western Zhou Ritual Bronzes in the Arthur M. Sackler Collections* (Cambridge, MA, and London, 1990)
Chinese Jade from the Neolithic to the Qing (exh. cat. by J. Rawson, London, BM, 1995)

CAROL MICHAELSON

Zhou Fang [Chou Fang] (*b* Chang'an (now Xi'an), Shaanxi Province; *fl c.* AD 765–800). Chinese painter. He was active at the Tang dynasty (618–907) court in the capital, Chang'an, after the An Lushan Rebellion (756). He painted both religious and secular figures but is particularly associated with the depiction of palace ladies (*see also* CHINA, §V, 3(vii)), a genre in which he is considered peerless. He was reportedly of noble birth. His father served as a Master of Ceremonies in a princely household and then as Investigating Censor. Between 766 and 779 under Emperor Daizong (*reg* 762–79), Zhou Fang

served as an administrator of Yuezhou (modern Shaoxing, Zhejiang Province); not long after, he held the position of administrative aide in Xuanzhou (modern Xuancheng, Anhui Province). From Xuanzhou, Zhou Fang seems to have returned to the capital.

In his time, Zhou Fang was celebrated as a painter of religious subjects, particularly the 'water-and-moon Guanyin', a version of the *bodhisattva* Guanyin (Skt Avalokiteshvara); most famously, he was commissioned by Emperor Dezong (*reg* 780–805) to paint the walls of the Zhangqing temple. As regards secular subjects, Zhang Yanyuan wrote in 847 that Zhou avoided all those pertaining to rustic village life, and Zhu Jingxuan, another near-contemporary critic, stated flatly that Zhou's paintings of gentlewomen were unsurpassed in any age. Zhou's painting style in this genre was closely based upon that of his predecessor, ZHANG XUAN (*fl c.* 714–42). Although Zhou Fang is said eventually to have attained a degree of independence from his mentor, it is difficult to identify significant, if any, differences between the two artists; even by the mid-11th century there was confusion between their styles. To judge from painting titles, however, it seems that Zhou Fang added degrees of subtlety and complexity to the genre: perhaps humour and drama in his *Yang Guifei's Pet Cockatoo Upsetting the Backgammon Board*, or poignancy in his sketch *Lonely Wife Playing a Tune*.

Zhou's ability to capture the subtleties of his subjects' expressions and mannerisms is expressed in a well-known anecdote. An official named Zhao Zong had his portrait painted by both Zhou and Han Gan. Zhao's wife praised both paintings but chose Zhou's as the better, remarking that Han Gan's portrait had caught only the likeness of her husband whereas Zhou's 'conveys his spirit as well, and has caught his mood and the way he looks when he smiles and talks'.

Important paintings attributed to Zhou Fang include *Palace Ladies with Fans* (Beijing, Pal. Mus.), *Palace Ladies Performing Music* (priv. col.; see Wang Shih-chieh and others, p. 3) and *Ladies Playing Double Sixes* (Washington, DC, Freer). These, together with the anonymous *Palace Concert* (Taipei, N. Pal. Mus.), though not of a single hand, form a distinctive group. The arrangement and interaction of figures are deliberate, defining the ambience of the environment. For example in *Ladies Playing Double Sixes* a small group forms a circle, creating an intense focus on the hands of the two players. As individuals, Zhou's figures convey a very subtle variety of emotions and personalities. The range of expressions on the faces of the musicians in *Palace Ladies Performing Music* reflects a distinct appreciation for each performer's approach to her instrument, and in *Palace Ladies with Fans* a mistress, leisurely seated at a dais with head on fan, is portrayed deep in thought, dreaming sadly of life outside the gilded cage.

Ladies with Flowered Coiffures (see fig.) is the finest of the paintings attributed to Zhou Fang. In a palace garden setting stroll five elegant and beautiful ladies, dressed in sweeping robes of patterned silk and with lotus, peonies and cherry or apple blossom arrayed in their high coiffures. The last lady, standing by a garden rock and flowering magnolia, holding in one hand a captured butterfly by its wings and looking down at a small bounding dog, is the

Zhou Fang (attrib.): *Ladies with Flowered Coiffures* (detail), handscroll, ink and colours on silk, 0.46×1.80 m, *c.* late 8th century AD (Shenyang, Liaoning Provincial Museum)

epitome of grace and delicacy. The painting illustrates Zhou's fine, even-line technique spoken of by Mi Fu and the 'soft yet bright coloration' mentioned by Zhang Yanyuan. Although the description of the figures differs slightly from that in other paintings ascribed to Zhou Fang, details of dress and adornment favour an attribution to him: from the short, tilted eyebrows to the wide, flowing sleeves, these beauties exhibit the latest styles and fashions of the Zhenyuan reign (785–804).

Zhou Fang's influence was strong and widespread. Even in the early 9th century, an emissary from Korea paid high prices for Zhou's paintings. Among the better-known followers of Zhou Fang were ZHOU WENJU in the 10th century and SU HANCHEN in the 12th century.

BIBLIOGRAPHY

Zhang Yanyuan: *Lidai minghua ji* [Record of famous painters of all periods] (AD 847); Eng. trans. by W. R. B. Acker in *Some T'ang and Pre-T'ang Texts on Chinese Painting* (Leiden, 1954/R 1974), pp. 61–398

Zhu Jingxuan: *Tang chao minghua lu* [Record of famous painters of the Tang dynasty] (9th century); Eng. trans. by A. C. Soper as 'T'ang ch'ao ming hua lu', *Archvs Chin. A. Soc. America*, iv (1950), pp. 5–25

O. Sirén: *Chinese Painting: Leading Masters and Principles*, 7 vols (London and New York, 1956–8), i, pp. 143–9; ii, pp. 16–7; iii, pls 108–10

Jin Weinuo: 'Zhou Fang', *Wenwu* (1957), no. 1, pp. 34–8

Wang Bomin: *Zhou Fang*, Zhongguo huajia congshu (Shanghai, 1958)

J. Cahill: *Chinese Painting* (New York, 1960), pp. 19–23

——: 'The Return of the Absent Servants: Chou Fang's "Double Sixes" Restored', *Archvs Asian A.*, xv (1961), pp. 26–8

Yang Renkai: *Zanhua nüshi tu yanjiu* [A Study of *Ladies with Flowered Coiffures*] (Beijing, 1962)

Wang Shih-chieh and others: *A Garland of Chinese Painting*, i (Hong Kong, 1967)

Yang Renkai: 'Dui Zanhua nüshi tu ti yidan pou xi' [A Cursory analysis of the painting *Ladies with Flowered Coiffures*], *Zhongguo wenwu* (1979), no. 1, pp. 12–4, 31–2 and cover

Eight Dynasties of Chinese Painting: The Collections of the Nelson–Atkins Museum of Art, Kansas City, and the Cleveland Museum of Art (exh. cat. by Wai-kam Ho and others; Kansas City, MO, Nelson–Atkins Mus. A., Cleveland, OH, Mus. A. and Tokyo, N. Mus., 1980–81)

Xu Bangda: *Gu shuhua weie kaobian* [Examinations of the authenticity of ancient painting and calligraphy], 4 vols (Jiangsu, 1984), i, pp. 119–22; ii, pls 160–64

PETER C. STURMAN

Zhou Lianggong [Chou Liang-kung] (*b* Nanjing, 1612; *d* 1672). Chinese patron, collector and writer. Zhou's devotion to the art of his own time rather than to that of the past was unique in traditional China. His huge collection of contemporary paintings was unrivalled in his day, and his extensive influence within the art world led artists to seek his endorsement. His book *Duhua lu* ('Record of researches into painting'; *c.* 1673), also known as *Du hua lou hua ren zhuan* ('Biographies of painters from researches into painting'), a collection of biographical notes on 77 painters, became and has remained the authoritative source on 17th-century Chinese painters. Also well known is Zhou's 18-leaf collective album with facing inscriptions (Taipei, N. Pal. Mus.), which groups together the works of various contemporary artists.

Zhou was a man of classical culture and taste. In his aesthetic outlook he maintained a view typical of the Chinese literati (Chin. *wenren*; see CHINA, §V, 4(ii)), an amalgam of moralistic and pragmatic concepts, that 'art manifests the Dao [the moral Way]' and should thereby act as an aid to self-cultivation and spiritual enlightenment. In art criticism, Zhou joined the ongoing literary debate that set personal expression in opposition to formal style and advocated the former. His individualism was based on his aversion to blind adherence to rules and models, but implied neither a total rejection of stylistic traditions and artistry nor subscription to the notion of autonomy of the arts divorced from Confucian principles of morality.

In his later years (*c.* 1667 onwards) he even became an admirer of the renowned formalist Wang Hui, whom he considered an enlightened transmitter of the spirit and form of the great masters of the past. Nevertheless, Zhou's emphasis on individuality helped him to appreciate the highly personalized expression of painters such as Chen Hongshou, Gong Xian and other contemporary individualists. Another notable artist who was attracted to Zhou's circle, and lived for years as his house guest, was Hu Yukun.

Zhou also devoted much time to the study and collection of seals. He wrote the renowned *Yinren zhuan* ('Biographies of seal-carvers') and the *Yin pu* ('Manual of seals'; 1667). A serious poet and essayist, he left collections of his own writings and anthologies of contemporary letters and essays. Topics of his other books included local customs and administration.

Zhou led an active political career. Unlike many former Ming-period (1368–1644) officials and intellectuals, he chose to serve the new Qing dynasty (1644–1911) established by the alien Manchus. He held a number of high posts but eventually fell victim to the Chinese–Manchu tensions of the day and suffered eight years of trial and imprisonment. Although Zhou's collaboration with the Manchus left him open to certain condemnation by his compatriots, it placed him in a position to defend the native Chinese populace, including his many loyalist friends, and to preserve Chinese tradition. This gave added incentive and meaning to his patronage.

BIBLIOGRAPHY

Hummel: 'Chou Liang-kung'

Hongnam Kim: *Chou Liang-kung and his* Tu-hua-lu: *Patron-critic and Painters of Mid-17th-century China* (PhD diss., New Haven, CT, Yale U., 1985) [incl. biog. and full annotated trans. of the *Duhua lu*]

KIM HONGNAM

Zhou Luyun. *See* CHOU, IRENE.

Zhou Mi [Chou Mi; *zi* Gongjin, Zijin; *hao* Caochuang, Pingyang Laoren, Shandong Cangfu, Xiaoweng] (*b* Fuchun District, Zhejiang Province, 1232; *d* 1298). Chinese collector, connoisseur and artist. His ancestral home was at Qizhou (now Shandong Province), but he may never have been there; certainly he had not done so by 1296, when Zhao Mengfu painted *Autumn Colours on the Qiao and Hua Mountains* for Zhou to remind him of his connections with the place (for illustration *see* ZHAO, (1)). Zhou's family had left Qizhou when it was taken over by the state of Jin in 1126, and Zhou lived in Wuxing (now Huzhou, Zhejiang Province) for most of his life, as did Zhao Mengfu.

Zhou began his career as a minor official in various posts in Zhejiang. With the descent of the invading Mongols into the Wuxing area in 1277 and the subsequent burning of his library, Zhou fled south to Lin'an (now Hangzhou), capital of the Southern Song dynasty (1127–1279), and abandoned his official career. From then on he devoted himself to writing, art and connoisseurship. In Lin'an, Zhou was the centre of a literary and artistic circle that included Zhao Mengfu, Xianyu Shu (1257–1302) and Zhao Mengjian (1199–1267). Zhou had a good collection of painting and calligraphy, and he inscribed many works. One of these is Zhao Mengjian's *Narcissus* (New York,

Met.), to which Xianyu Shu and Zhao Mengfu also added their observations. Other inscriptions include colophons on works by the noted calligraphers Yan Zhenqing and Wang Xianzhi. Being a connoisseur gave Zhou a good knowledge of contemporary collections, on which he wrote two valuable books, the *Yunyan guoyan lu* ('Record of what was seen as clouds and mist') and *Zhiya tang zachao* ('Miscellaneous records of the Zhiya Hall'). He was a highly respected poet and left a collection of prose writings containing valuable and perceptive accounts of his times.

None of Zhou Mi's paintings of plum blossoms, bamboo, orchids and rocks has survived. Of his calligraphy, in which he was well trained, one of the few extant examples is his inscription to *Narcissus* by Zhao Mengjian. His neat, closely placed characters are organized into well-spaced columns. Zhou enjoyed extending the left diagonal strokes and the second hooked stroke of the character for *feng* ('wind'), imparting a feeling of expansion that balances the density of the characters and the precision of his technique. The ink is evenly distributed and the brushstrokes are clear, clean and sharp.

Zhou's retreat to Lin'an and his writing on Zhao Mengjian's *Narcissus*, a subtle statement of resistance to foreign rule and an allusion to better days, may be taken as a continuing protest against an alien dynasty. In *Autumn Colours on the Qiao and Hua Mountains*, Zhao Mengfu was also harking back to a more primitive, uncomplicated era in China's past, a concession to Zhou's unchanging aversion to Mongol rule.

BIBLIOGRAPHY

Franke: 'Chou Mi'

Y. Shimonaka, ed.: *Shodō zenshū* [Complete collection of calligraphy] (Tokyo, 1954–68), xvi, pp. 172–3

Chu-tsing Li: *The 'Autumn Colors on the Ch'iao and Hua Mountains': A Landscape by Chao Mengfu* (Ascona, 1965), suppl. xxi of *Artibus Asiae*, pp. 21–3

Traces of the Brush: Studies in Chinese Calligraphy (exh. cat. by Shen C. Y. Fu and others, New Haven, CT, Yale U. A.G.; Berkeley, U. CA, A. Mus.; 1977), no. 12, pp. 139, 168, 182, 300–03

Yu Jianhua, ed.: *Zhongguo huajia da zidian* [Dictionary of Chinese painters] (Shanghai, 1981), p. 489

ELIZABETH F. BENNETT

Zhou Shuren. *See* LU XUN.

Zhou Wenju [Chou Wen-chü] (*b* Jurong, near modern Nanjing, Jiangsu Province; *fl* AD 942–61). Chinese painter. He served as a *daizhao* (painter in attendance) at the Painting Academy of the Southern Tang court (AD 937–75). He may first have become prominent during the reign of the emperor Li Bian (937–43), when it is recorded that he was ordered to paint the Nanzhuang (Southern Village), though Guo Ruoxu dates this event to between 961 and 975. He participated in executing a joint work at the banquet held by the ruler, Li Jing (*reg* 943–61), on New Year's day, 947. He was probably dead before the Song (960–1279) conquered the Southern Tang, since he is not recorded among the painters of the Southern Tang entering the Song Painting Academy.

Zhou was known for his brushwork of the *zhanbi* ('tremulous brush') type, probably a method to render the fluttering quality of silken garments. According to the *Xuanhe huapu* ('Xuanhe collection of painting'; preface dated 1120) he learnt the *zhanbi* technique from Li Yu (*reg* 961–75), famous for his calligraphy in this manner. This is unlikely, however, since Zhou was a well-established painter 20 years before Li Yu ascended the throne. Early sources record that Zhou was a versatile painter, accomplished in depicting figures, carriages and horses, architecture, trees, mountains and rivers, and excelling in female beauties. In paintings of the latter he reportedly worked in the manner of the Tang (AD 618–907) painter ZHOU FANG 'but still more delicately'. According to Mi Fu, Zhou Wenju's paintings of female beauties are distinguished from Zhou Fang's by the use of *zhanbi* in the outline of garments; according to Guo Ruoxu, however, they do not feature *zhanbi*. The majority of paintings attributed to Zhou Wenju are in this genre, the most important being *Ladies of the Court* (*Gongzhong tu*; sections at Cambridge, MA, Fogg; Cleveland, OH, Mus. A.; Florence, I Tatti; and New York, Met.). A colophon of 1140 by Zhang Zheng, mounted with the Cleveland scroll, states that it is a copy of a painting by Zhou Wenju. The work is in the tradition of Zhou Fang, but the faded colouring contrasts with the clear hues of early genre paintings and may mirror the taste of the copyist. The four known sections of the composition were executed by at least two different hands. While the scrolls in Cleveland and Florence show no trace of *zhanbi*, the other two feature a slight tremble in the lines of the garments. The figures are tightly organized and naturally rendered; situations in court life are depicted in a lively manner. The minimal setting is an archaic feature.

Zhou was also an accomplished portrait painter. The *Double Screen* (*Chongping tu*) is a well-documented composition (good copies in Washington, DC, Freer, and Beijing, Pal. Mus.) showing two men playing *weiqi* (chess), with two others watching. The figures have been identified as the ruler Li Jing and his three brothers. Behind them, a painted screen depicts an interior scene containing yet another painted screen; this format gives the scroll its name. Painted screens in interior scenes, typical in paintings of this period, reflect an interest in the nature of art. The *Double Screen* composition features an extensive use of *zhanbi*; in the Beijing version it is particularly mannered and possibly exaggerated compared to the original. The composition exemplifies the fine quality of Southern Tang genre paintings. The refined life at court is depicted with a sense for telling detail, and the figures are grouped in tight interplay. Three other portraits by Zhou, of the ruler Li Yu, are recorded in the *Xuanhe huapu*. It seems that in his early years, however, Zhou's portraiture was less highly esteemed than his figure painting. In the New Year's day joint work of 947 the privilege of painting the ruler, Li Jung, was conceded to Gao Taichong, whereas Zhou was responsible for the imperial princes, officials and musicians (probably a female orchestra).

Zhou Wenju, Wang Qihan (*fl* 961–75) and Gu Hongzhong (*fl c.* 943–60), all prominent figure painters at the Jiangnan (southern) Court, gradually made figure painting a more psychologically subtle art form. They placed figures in more natural groups, as in *Ladies Bathing Children*, and used interior details to add realism. The influence of these artists is clearly visible in depictions of court life by Song-period masters.

BIBLIOGRAPHY

Franke: 'Chou wen-chü'
Liu Daochun: *Shengchao minghua ping* [Critique of famous paintings of the present Dynasty] (1059), *juan* 1; *R* in Siku quanshu zhenben (Taipei, 1974)
Guo Ruoxu: *Tuhua jianwen zhi* [Experiences in painting], 6 *juan* (preface 1075); *R* in Huashi congshu (Taipei, 1974); Eng. trans. in A. C. Soper: *Kuo Jo-hsü's 'Experiences in Painting' (T'u-hua chien-wen chih: An Eleventh Century History of Chinese Painting* (Washington, DC, 1951/*R* 1971)
Xuanhe huapu [Xuanhe collection of painting], 23 *juan* (preface 1120), *juan* 7; *R* in Huashi congshu (Taipei, 1974)
Y. Yashiro: 'Sōmo Zhou Wenju *Kyūchūzu*' [A Song copy of the *Painting of Court Ladies* by Zhou Wenju], *Bijutsu Kenkyū*, 25 (Jan 1934), pp. 1–12; 56 (Aug 1936), pp. 1–4; 169 (1953), pp. 1–6
T. Lawton: 'Southern T'ang Emperor Playing Wei-ch'i', *Chinese Figure Painting*, ii of *Freer Gallery of Art: Fiftieth Anniversary Exhibition* (exh. cat., Washington, DC, Freer, 1973), pp. 34–7
Xu Bangda: 'Liuli tang renwu tu yu *Wenyuan tu* de guanxi' [On the relationship between the paintings *Liuli Hall* and *Wenyuan*], *Meishu Yanjiu* (1979), no. 3, pp. 71–4
Dan Guoqiang: 'Zhou Wenju *Chongping huiqi tu* juan' [*Double Screen and Chess Players* by Zhou Wenju], *Wenwu*, (1980), no. 1, pp. 88–9

METTE SIGGSTEDT

Zhuangbai [Chuang-pai; Chuang-po]. Site on the border of Fufeng County and Qishan County in Shaanxi Province, China. It is one of the main centres of bronze finds from the Zhou period (*c.* 1050–256 BC) in Shaanxi; many of the finds bear Shang (*c.* 1600–*c.* 1050 BC) motifs or are forms characteristic of the Shang period. In 1976 a storage pit dating from the Western Zhou period (*c.* 1050–771 BC) and filled with bronzes was discovered. A total of 103 bronzes, of which 74 were inscribed, had been placed carefully in three layers in the pit. In addition to spoons and bells (*see* BELL, fig. 1), 21 different types of vessels, jars, pots, bowls and dishes were represented; all were in a good state of preservation. The bronzes can be divided into groups according to the names and circumstances given in the inscriptions. The 284-character inscription on a *pan* dish known as the Shi Qiang *pan* (h. 162 mm, diam. 473 mm) is of particular interest, as it records major events of the the early Zhou period, thus supplementing the traditional written sources (*see also* CHINA, §VI, 3(iii)(a)). The majority of the bronze vessels appear to have been in the possession of the same clan for several generations.

The most common decoration on the bronzes is the *taotie* animal-mask, formed by two facing profiles of one-legged dragons (Chin. *kui long*) against a ground of the small square spirals known as *leiwen* ('thunder pattern'). The presence, indeed prevalence, of the *taotie* animal-mask at Zhuangbai illustrates the continuation of Shang-period motifs into the Western Zhou period. Birds of various kinds (a purely Western Zhou motif) are also frequently present, and occasionally other animal motifs such as snakes, elephants and cicadas. Of the purely geometrical designs, vertical ribs and triangular blades are common features. A covered *guang* vessel (287×365 mm; see fig.), with a handle opposite the pouring spout, is a powerful depiction of a bull or ram. Although only the head and neck are modelled, the energy and strength of the animal are dominant features. The handle and flanges, as well as the entire body of the container, swarm with dragons and snakes, birds and beasts on a 'thunder pattern' ground. Another unique item is a *gu* beaker (h. 252 mm) that shows no trace of corrosion; this Shang form dies out in the Zhou period. The elegance of its tall, slim body is enhanced by the absence of surface decoration, which is restricted to three bands of the rectangular meander pattern in thread relief around the bottom. Both vessels are inscribed and dedicated to 'Father Yi'.

BIBLIOGRAPHY

Shi Yan: 'Fufeng Zhuangbai Dadui chutu de yi pi Xi Zhou tongqi' [Bronze vessels of the Western Zhou period excavated at Dadui in Zhuangbai, Fufeng], *Wenwu* (1972), no. 6, pp. 30–35
'Shaanxi Fufeng Zhuangbai yi hao Xi Zhou qingtongqi jiaozang fajue jianbao' [A brief report on the excavation of bronzes of the Western Zhou period from storage pit 1 at Zhuangbai in Fufeng, Shaanxi Province], *Wenwu* (1978), no. 3, pp. 1–18
The Great Bronze Age of China: An Exhibition from the People's Republic of China (exh. cat., ed. Wen Fong; New York, Met.; Los Angeles, CA, Co. Mus. A.; 1980–81)
A. E. Dien, J. K. Riegel and N. T. Price, eds: *Prehistoric to Western Zhou* (1985), ii of *Chinese Archaeological Abstracts* (Los Angeles, 1978–85)

BENT NIELSEN

Zhu Da [Chu Ta; Chuanqi; *hao* Bada Shanren, Pa-ta Shan-jen] (*b* 1626, Nanchang, Jiangxi Province; *d* 1705). Chinese painter and poet. A descendant of the imperial Zhu family of the Ming dynasty (1368–1644) and a leading artist of the early Qing period (1644–1911), Zhu Da painted flowers, birds and landscapes in a distinctive and highly dramatic calligraphic style. His connections with the previous dynasty led him to flee Nanchang after the Manchu conquest of China in 1644. Adopting the sobriquet Chuanqi, Zhu Da became a Buddhist priest and soon a respected Buddhist master, quickly attaining the position of abbot. He also became an accomplished poet and painter; his earliest extant work is an album of 15 leaves (1659; Taipei, N. Pal. Mus.). In 1672, after the death of his Buddhist master, Abbot Hong min, Zhu Da reliquished his solitary monastic existence to pursue his fortune as an itinerant monk-artist. He joined the coterie of Hu Yitang, magistrate of Linchuan County, and participated in the splendid poetry parties held in 1679 and 1680. Zhu Da was thwarted in his attempts to take up an official career because of his imperial lineage and in 1680 was devastated by the departure of his patron Hu Yitang. Reportedly, Zhu Da went mad; one day, laughing and crying uncontrollably, he tore off his priest's robe and set it on fire. The burning of the robe signalled the end of Zhu Da's life as a Buddhist monk, and from then on he lived as an itinerant painter. Between 1681 and 1684 he called himself Lu ('donkey' or 'ass'), a derogatory name for monks, or Lu hu ('donkey house'); from 1684 onwards he called himself Bada Shanren ('Mountain man of eight greatnesses'). Zhu Da adopted other names throughout his life, many reflecting his state of mind or his loyalty to the Ming dynasty. Of these, only a few (such as Chuanqi, which identifies his earliest extant work) were used as signatures, the most common being Bada Shanren.

His works from 1680 to 1690 are filled with a bitter loathing and sarcasm towards those Chinese officials who collaborated with the alien dynasty. In the album *Flowers and Insects* (1681; Princeton U., NJ, A. Mus.) he satirized the Kangxi emperor's policy of recruiting scholars, mocked office-holders as prostitutes and brooded over his own fate. His works of the early 1680s show a combination of strong emotionalism and great sensitivity, even lyricism,

Zhuangbai, bronze *guang* wine-vessel in the shape of a ram or bull, h. 287 mm, w. 365 mm, late 11th century BC–early 10th (Shaochen cun, Museum of the Zhonyuan)

and their representations can be brilliantly lifelike. In addition to flowers he also painted carefully observed insects, birds and small animals in the small album leaf format; all are executed with a compelling immediacy and realism. During the second half of the 1680s, he turned increasingly to stark, simplified brushwork. The *Moon and the Melon* (hanging scroll, ink on paper, 1689; Cambridge, MA, Sackler Mus.; see fig.) depicts the large, thin circular outline of a full moon partially eclipsed by a smaller round silhouette of a black melon. The poetic inscription describes the moon as a large mooncake (eaten at the Mid-Autumn Festival on the ninth day of the ninth lunar month) and the watermelon as ripe. The allusion is possibly to the successful popular uprising against the Mongol rulers at the end of their Yuan dynasty (1279–1368) on the day of the Mid-Autumn Festival, when participants carried the mooncake as a signal. If this is so, the painting might be categorized as a seditious work, perhaps related to a failed rebel plot in Nanchang in the late summer of 1688, which the newly arrived governor of Jiangxi, Song Le (1634–1713), had quickly uncovered and quelled. It is difficult to understand how a subversive work such as this would have been tolerated, even by Song Le, himself a cultivated poet, painter and connoisseur. However, in general Zhu Da's loss of emotional balance seems to have reduced his works of this time to being dangerously close to mere cartoons and caricatures, and as such they would not have been regarded seriously.

Zhu Da's works from the 1690s display a growth and development unusual for a man in his late 60s and early 70s. He redoubled his efforts to copy ancient calligraphic models, and through these explorations he developed a new method of painting. Technically adept in all forms of brushstroke, he chose to treat his paintings as abstract calligraphic designs. This characteristic is amply demonstrated in *Cat on a Rock* (handscroll, ink on paper, 1696; Beijing, Pal. Mus.). The lines of the wide, wash brushstrokes that define the humped body of the cat are so

Zhu Da: *Moon and the Melon*, hanging scroll, ink on paper, 740×451 mm, 1689 (Cambridge, MA, Arthur M. Sackler Museum)

similar to those of the rock on which it sits that the one seems to melt into the other; the black ink orchid leaves in the foreground are also executed in a few deft calligraphic strokes that approximate these shapes. All the elements of the painting are rendered in calligraphic abstractions that utilize single strokes to define their form.

During the early 1690s Zhu Da turned to landscape, a subject he had rarely explored previously. In the album *Copying Dong Qichang Copying Ancient Masters* (c. 1692; Mr and Mrs Fred Fang-yu Wang priv. col., see Chou, pl. 2–7), Zhu Da rendered compositions by the leading 10th-century master of the genre, Dong Yuan, and by those painters of the Yuan period (1279–1368) who were Dong Yuan's followers (Zhao Mengfu, Huang Gongwang and Ni Zan). As a model Zhu Da used an album by the pre-eminent late Ming theorist and painter Dong Qichang, reinforcing Dong Qichang's dictum that 'if one considers the wonders of brush and ink, [real] landscape can never equal painting'. His paintings are not concerned with representational reality; instead, round lines and abstract calligraphic brushwork are the principal focus of his landscapes. In the final decade of his life, Zhu Da turned away from the intimacy of the small album leaf format in favour of large-scale works, transforming his bird and

flower paintings and landscapes into monumental compositions to be mounted as hanging scrolls; the drawing in these works sometimes seems little more than careless doodling, ambiguous and confused. In keeping with his iconoclastic view of life and art, Zhu Da broke with the late Ming conventions of pictorial realism; he copied past models, but he turned painting into a system of autonomous, daring, even reckless calligraphic brushstrokes, infusing it with creative imagination, poetic passion and technical virtuosity, and producing a unique synthesis out of traditional Chinese painting.

For an illustration from Zhu Da's *Anwan Album see* CHINA, fig. 124.

BIBLIOGRAPHY

Wen Fong: 'A Letter from Shih-t'ao to Pa-ta-shan-jen and the Problems of Shih-t'ao's Chronology', *Archv Chin. A. Soc. America*, xiii (1959), pp. 22–53

Zhou Shixin, ed.: *Bada Shanren ji qi yishu* [Bada Shanren and his painting] (Taipei, 1974)

Wang Shiqing: 'Qingchu si da huaseng hekao' [A joint study on the four great monk painters of the early Qing dynasty], *J. Inst. Chin. Stud., Hong Kong*, xv (1984), pp. 183–215

Fang-yu Wang, ed.: *An Anthology of Essays on Pa-ta-shan-jen*, 2 vols (Taipei, 1984)

Bada Shanren yanjiu [Selected essays on Bada Shanren], i and ii (New Haven and London, 1986 and 1988)

Wen C. Fong: 'Stages in the Life and the Art of Chu Ta', *Archvs Asian A.*, xl (1987), pp. 6–23

Wang Fangyu and R. M. Barnhart: *Master of the Lotus Garden: The Life and Art of Bada Shanren* (New Haven and London, 1990)

Gugong Wenwu Yuekan, no. 96 (March 1991); no. 97 (April 1991)

WEN FONG

Zhu Derun [Chu Te-jun] (*b* Henan Province, 1294; *d* Suzhou, Jiangsu Province, 1365). Chinese painter and calligrapher. He was active in Jiangsu Province and was favoured by the emperors Renzong (*reg* 1312–21) and Yingzong (*reg* 1321–3). In calligraphy he followed the Yuan-period (1279–1368) artists Xianyu Shu (1257–1302) and Zhao Mengfu (whose protégé he was at court), and in painting Guo Xi of the Northern Song period (960–1127). He formed a close friendship with the leading Koryŏ-period (918–1392) scholar and poet Yi Che-hyŏn, who spent many years in Beijing and who was instrumental in the transmission of Neo-Confucianism to Korea.

A contemporary of the Four Masters of the late Yuan period, Zhu Derun also created a landscape style of his own, although it was not to be so influential as theirs. His painting *Xinye tu* ('Refining the wilderness'; 1364; Beijing, Pal. Mus.; a close copy is in Washington, DC, Freer) is a short handscroll in ink and pale colours, followed by his own inscription explaining how the wilderness is refined through the presence of men of high moral character and wisdom. Against a setting of low background hills, two gentlemen are in earnest conversation in an isolated pavilion furnished only with a number of bronze vessels, a screen and the end of a hanging painting, just visible on the wall. The composition, with the landscape drifting away into the distance at one end of the scroll, recalls Zhao Mengfu's short handscroll *Water Village* (ink on paper; 1302; Beijing, Pal. Mus.), but the looser brushwork has been compared to that of his younger contemporary Wang Meng.

A large hanging scroll, *Music under the Trees* (ink on silk; Taipei, N. Pal. Mus.), features the diagonal composition that became popular in the Southern Song period

(1127–1279) but combines the monumentality of Northern Song painting with the unified ground-plane typical of Yuan works. In the foreground is a group of five imposing trees, beneath which a group of scholars sit listening to one of them playing the *qin* (Chinese lute).

BIBLIOGRAPHY
T. Lawton: 'Notes on Five Paintings from a Ch'ing Dynasty Collection', *A. Orient.*, viii (1970), pp. 203–7
Chen Gaohua: *Yuan dai huajia shiliao* [Historical sources on painting of the Yuan period] (Shanghai, 1980), pp. 181–94
Zhongguo meishujia renming cidian [Dictionary of Chinese artists] (Shanghai, 1981), p. 224
Xu Bangda, ed.: *Zhongguo huihuashi tulu* [Illustrated catalogue of the history of Chinese painting] (Shanghai, 1984), i, pls 201–3
RODERICK WHITFIELD

Zhu Duan [Chu Tuan; *zi* Kezheng; *hao* Yiqiao] (*b* Haiyan, Zhejiang Province; *fl c.* 1501–21). Chinese painter. He probably began his artistic career as a minor court painter in the latter part of the reign of the Hongzhi emperor (*reg* 1488–1505); one of his paintings, dated 1501, bears a seal indicating that he had been summoned to court at least by that date. During the reign of the Zhengde emperor (*reg* 1506–21), when he was most active, he rose to the position of *daizhao* ('painter in attendance') at the imperial atelier, the Renzhi dian, and was honoured by the gift of a seal from the emperor, after which he nicknamed himself Yiqiao ('the woodcutter'). Along with some other contemporary court painters, he was considered to belong in a loose sense to the ZHE SCHOOL.

Zhu painted a wide range of subjects, from figures and landscapes to bamboo and birds. His model in the first two genres was the Yuan-period (1279–1368) painter Sheng Mao. In bamboo painting, Xia Chang (1388–1470) served as his source. Zhu's tenure at court overlapped with that of Lu Ji, who specialized in painting birds and who was Zhu's model in this genre, possibly also his personal teacher. Zhu's extant paintings, however, are limited to landscapes.

In choosing to follow Sheng Mao and the 11th-century painter Guo Xi, Zhu differed from other court painters, who were uniformly influenced by Ma Yuan. Zhu's study of these two painters is evident from the large painting *Gazing about the Misty River* (hanging scroll, ink and colours on silk, h. 1.68 m; Beijing, Pal. Mus.). The first focus is on two scholars and their servant, who gaze out at the scene. An open book beside them suggests they may be reflecting on the Chinese classics or reading poetry. They are sitting on a promontory in the left corner of the painting, framed by surrounding foliage, in particular by a group of trees that reaches above and arcs over them. The first direction of view, which is also that of the gazing gentlemen, extends towards two scenes separated by water, and a final line of mountains. The lower and more open vista contains a hint of unseen territory beyond. The eye is then impelled by the arching branches of the foreground trees upwards into rising peaks. Vignettes and hints of life and habitation are everywhere. Each mountain rise hosts pavilions, each clump of trees shades a house. In the valley, fishermen fish and a scholar wanders home; over the next stretch of water lies a whole fishing village with boats moored in clusters and two junks setting off in full sail.

Zhu's nervous, jagged line is similar to that used by Sheng Mao, as is his skill in carefully describing all the elements in the painting, such as the well-drawn figures and the vine-encrusted trees. On the other hand, the clawlike branches, although much exaggerated by Zhu, and the theatrical surging of the mountain range overhead show an awareness of the techniques of Guo Xi. Very much in the professional as opposed to the literati mode of painting, this is one of Zhu's most ambitious works. He was also capable of more rapid, abbreviated, literati styles and compositions, as in *Solitary Angler on a Wintry River* (Tokyo, N. Mus.).

BIBLIOGRAPHY
Gugong bowuyuan canghua ji: Zhongguo lidai huihua [Paintings from the Beijing Palace Museum collection: Chinese paintings over the centuries] (Beijing, 1986), pp. 168–9
Yu Jianhua, ed.: *Zhongguo huajia da zidian* [Dictionary of Chinese painters] (Shanghai, 1981), p. 222
O. Sirén: *Chinese Painting: Leading Masters and Principles* (London and New York, 1956–8), iv, pp. 143–4
S. E. Lee: *Chinese Landscape Painting* (Cleveland, OH, 1954), pp. 88–9
ELIZABETH F. BENNETT

Zhukov, Pavel (Semyonovich) (*b* Simbirsk, 1870; *d* Leningrad [St Petersburg], 1942). Russian photographer. He is known for the portraits of literary, artistic and political leaders that he produced during the first two decades of the 20th century, including *Anton Chekhov*, *Lev Tolstoy*, *Tchaikovsky* and perhaps the most acclaimed portrait ever executed of *Lenin*. After an apprenticeship with the photographer Konstantin Shapiro, Zhukov opened his own studio in St Petersburg, with the support of the St Petersburg Academy of Arts. After the 1917 October Revolution, he became the chief military photographer for the Petrograd (St Petersburg) military zone, and he documented the civil war in that region and the activities of the Red Army. Sent to Moscow in 1920, he continued portraying Soviet political leaders and the upper ranks of the Red Army. In the 1930s his interests turned to photojournalism, and he returned to Leningrad.

BIBLIOGRAPHY
S. Morozov and others, eds: *Soviet Photography, 1917–1940* (London, 1984)
G. Chudakov: *20 sowjetische Photographen, 1917–1940* (Amsterdam, 1990)
JAMES CRUMP

Zhukovsky, Vasily (Andreyevich) (*b* nr Tula, 26 Jan 1783; *d* 12 March 1852). Russian critic and poet. Well known for his ballads 'Lyudmila' and 'Svetlana' and his translations of Homer and Schiller, he edited the journal *Vestnik Yevropy* (1808–14), was on friendly terms with many Russian poets and painters, and himself studied drawing. He visited Germany for the first time shortly before 1820 and became a friend of the artist Caspar David Friedrich. Their surviving correspondence shows that their aim was to combine painting with poetry. Although few of Zhukovsky's articles on literature and art theory were published, his manuscripts and letters were circulated by hand and many people in St Petersburg and Moscow knew his work, which exerted considerable influence as a result. A typical article is 'Raphael's *Madonna*', published in 1824 in the journal *Polyarnaya zvezda*, which offers another romantic interpretation of the Sistine

Madonna (Dresden, Gemäldegal. Alte Meister). The author saw in the painting a 'mystery', a 'sense of infinity', 'a vision'. In another article, 'On the Fine Arts', he stated that 'art is poetry in various forms' and its aim is 'to get closer to God, to the truth'. He attempted to raise the level of criticism in Russia, stating that there were as few good critics in Russia as there were good artists. His theoretical views embraced romantic historicism, the need for artistic freedom, the affirmation of the variety of forms of art, an awareness of higher forms of existence, and reverie.

WRITINGS
Sobraniye sochineniy [Collected works], 4 vols (Moscow, 1959–60)
Estetika i kritika [Aesthetics and criticism] (Moscow, 1984)
Kritika [Criticism] (Moscow, 1985)

BIBLIOGRAPHY
V. A. Zhukovsky i russkaya kul'tura [V. A. Zhukovsky and Russian culture] (Leningrad, 1987)

V. S. TURCHIN

Zhu Ming. *See* CHU MING.

Zhu Qizhan [Chu Ch'i-chan; *hao* Erzhan Laomin, Meihua Caotang] (*b* Taicang County, Jiangsu Province, 27 May 1892). Chinese painter and calligrapher. Born into a respected family of the gentry, Zhu received a traditional education, developing an early interest in painting, calligraphy and poetry. In 1912 he entered the Shanghai Academy of Fine Art, where he concentrated on the study of Western drawing and oil painting. In 1917 he went to Japan to study under Takeji Fujishima. Zhu was particularly drawn to the Post-Impressionist and Fauvist masters (*see* POST-IMPRESSIONISM and FAUVISM), whose styles provided the basis for his landscapes and still-lifes in oils. Although he dedicated himself to finding a place in Chinese art for Western painting, he continued to practise Chinese painting and calligraphy, at the same time amassing a large collection of ancient masterpieces. Zhu also taught oil painting at the Shanghai Academy of Fine Art and Xinhua Art College. From the 1950s onwards he painted mainly in traditional Chinese styles, joining the Shanghai Chinese Painting Academy when it was founded in 1956. His 100th birthday was celebrated in 1990 with major exhibitions in China and Hong Kong.

Recognized as a modern master of the free and spontaneous (*xieyi*; 'sketching the idea') tradition of landscapes and flowers, Zhu used intense colours and powerful brushwork and revealed a refreshing vision that owed much to his penetrating observation of nature and his years of studying the art of Vincent van Gogh, Henri Matisse and Pablo Picasso. His late paintings, particularly those done since his seventies, were imbued with an inner strength and blunt simplicity that became symbols of the indomitable human spirit in a turbulent century.

BIBLIOGRAPHY
Dangdai Zhongguohua minjia: Zhu Qizhan [Master contemporary Chinese painter: Zhu Qizhan] (Hong Kong, 1990)
Zhu Qizhan: Braving the Frost (exh. cat. by L. J. Wender, New York, 1991)

MAYCHING KAO

Zhu Yunming [Chu Yün-ming; *zi* Xizhe; *hao* Jishan] (*b* Suzhou, Jiangsu Province, *c.* 1460–61; *d* Suzhou, 1527). Chinese calligrapher, scholar, essayist and poet. Born into

an illustrious Suzhou family, he was commended in the provincial examinations, the second stage of the civil service career ladder, at the age of 33 but failed in several attempts at the national examinations. In 1514 he took office as magistrate of Xingning County in Guangdong Province and in 1522 was promoted to assistant prefectural magistrate of Yingtian District (now Nanjing). He retired after less than a year and died at the age of 67. Zhu was an outstanding representative of certain literary circles in Suzhou, revered not only for his calligraphy, but also for his scholarship, essays and poetry. His individual and nonconformist beliefs made him severely critical of Song Neo-Confucianism, the orthodox teaching of his day, seeing it as both ill-founded and constricting. His love of liberty and adherence to the classics are reflected in his calligraphy, which is at once informed by a thorough acquaintance with the classical masters and executed with an expansive and uninhibited flair.

By his early twenties Zhu Yunming was renowned in Suzhou for his calligraphy, which showed the influence of the cursive script (*caoshu*) of his maternal grandfather, Xu Youzhen (1407–72), and the regular script (*kaishu*) of his father-in-law, Li Yingzhen (1431–93). Zhu made a thorough study of Jin (AD 265–420), Tang (AD 618–907), and Song (960–1279) calligraphers, taking as models masters such as Wang Xizhi (*see* WANG (i), (1)) and HUAISU. He also studied stelae from the Han, Wei and Su Dynasties periods (206 BC–AD 589). His own calligraphy shows abundant variation, and he excelled particularly in the art of unrestrained cursive script. The best known of his surviving masterpieces reveal his genius with two fundamental brushstrokes. The first is dragged continuously in circular fluency, carrying on a 4th-century AD tradition of continuous cursive script; see, for example, the *Seven-character Eight-line Poem* (*Qiyan lushi*, 1525; Taipei, N. Pal. Mus.). The other stroke is a type of dissipated dot which takes advantage of the interlocking lines and vigour of the calligraphy to create a compact structure. The works which best exemplify this pioneering characteristic are the *Cao Zhi Poem* (*c.* 1526; Taipei, N. Pal. Mus.) and the *Ode on the Red Cliff* (*Chibi fu*; 1521; Shanghai Mus.).

See also CHINA §IV, 2(vi).

DMB   BIBLIOGRAPHY
Zhang Dingyu and others, eds: *Ming shi* [Standard history of the Ming dynasty] (*R* Beijing, 1974), *juan* 286
Traces of the Brush: Studies in Chinese Calligraphy (exh. cat. by Shen Fu and others, New Haven, CT, Yale U. A. G.; Berkeley, U. CA, A. Mus.; 1977)

HO CHUAN-HSING

Zhwa lu. *See* SHALU.

Ziarnki, Jana [Ziarnko, Jan; Le Grain, Jean] (*b* Lwów [L'viv], later 16th century; *d* ?Paris, *c.* 1628). Polish engraver and painter, active in France. He learnt his craft in Kraków. In 1596–7 he appears in Lwów archives as a member of the city's Brotherhood of Catholic Painters. By 1598 he was already abroad; he reached Paris by way of Italy and settled there, though it has been suggested that late in life he returned to Lwów. In Paris, Ziarnki established himself as a painter-engraver closely associated with the courts of Henry IV and Louis XIII. His earliest engraving, dated 1605, represents *Pope Leo XI*. Ziarnki also illustrated books, frequently dedicated to the king or queen, and designed courtly festivals. He cooperated with such notable French engravers as Jean Leclerc (*c.* 1595–*c.* 1625), Léonard Gaultier, Claude Vignon and Robert Nanteuil. Ziarnki's oeuvre includes over 90 engravings, but his activities have been little studied.

Thieme–Becker
BIBLIOGRAPHY
E. Rastawiecki: *Słownik malarzów polskich tudzież obcych w Polsce osiadłych lub czasowo w niej przebywających* [A dictionary of Polish painters as well as foreign-born painters who settled or worked for a period in Poland], iii (Warsaw, 1857), pp. 79–84
——: *Słownik rytowników polskich tudzież obcych w Polsce osiadłych lub czasowo w niej przebywających* [A dictionary of Polish engravers as well as foreign-born engravers who settled or worked for a period in Poland] (Poznań, 1886), pp. 304–9
W. Łodziński: *Sprawozdanie komisyi do badań historyi sztuki w Polsce* [Report of a commission enquiring into the history of art in Poland], iv (1891), p. 59; v, p. 47
A. Potocki: *Katalog dzieł Jana Ziarnki, malarza, rytownika, polskiego z XVI i XVIIw, z życiorysem artysty* [Catalogue of the works of Jan Ziarnko, a Polish painter and engraver from the 16th and 17th centuries, with a biography of the artist] (Kraków, 1911)
ANDREW STOGA

Zichy, Mihály (*b* Zala, 14 Oct 1827; *d* St Petersburg, 29 Feb 1906). Hungarian painter, draughtsman and printmaker. He studied under Giacomo [Jakab] Marastoni (1804–60) in Pest, then under Ferdinand Waldmüller in Vienna. From 1847 he lived mainly in Russia, in the service of the Tsar at the imperial court at St Petersburg. Between 1874 and 1879 he lived in Paris, where he was active in the Hungarian Association, a charitable cultural institution. In 1880 he travelled to Hungary, Vienna and Venice and the following year (1881–2) he spent some time in the Caucasus before resettling in St Petersburg. Zichy was influenced primarily by Viennese Biedermeier painting and the French Romantic masters, although in some of his work he approached the Russian Realists. His paintings are conservative both in subject and in method of execution. He favoured an anecdotal approach and compositions designed to be representative, effective and dramatic. In his works a literary or political message often takes precedence, and Zichy frequently resorted to the use of allegory. He was highly important as an illustrator, his graphic style being noted for its dynamism.

Zichy's early painting style was influenced by painting in Vienna: his *Sealing the Coffin* (1846) and *Lifeboat* (1847; both Budapest, N.G.) are representative of this phase. In Russia, besides work commissioned by the Tsar, Zichy painted series of satirical and humorous genre scenes, such as *Officer Dressing* (1853; St Petersburg, Hermitage) and *Grandma and her Grandchildren* (1855; Moscow, Tret'yakov Gal.). He also produced a large number of watercolour portraits, but he is equally well known for his erotic drawings. Some of his prints, such as *Richelieu and his Mistress* (1856; Budapest, N.G.) or *Bernard Palissy* (1868; St Petersburg, Hermitage), may be defined as Romantic treatments of the theme of the lives of great men. Other Romantic elements appear in the deliberately gruesome subjects of mixed-technique works such as *Grave-robbers* (1858; Budapest, N.G.). Some of Zichy's later paintings are historical genre scenes, such as *The Usurer* (1859; Budapest, N.G.). He also painted hunting scenes, for example *Scottish Hunt* (1875; Budapest, N.G.). He advanced his liberal principles in prints such as *Auto-da-fé* and *Jewish Martyrs* (1871; both Budapest, N.G.) and *Messiah (Christ and the Pope)* (*c.* 1870; Debrecen, Lib. Transtibiscan Reformed Ch. Distr.) and in the large painting *Genius of Destruction* (1878; Budapest, N.G.). *The Courtesan* (1880) and the *Falling Stars* (1879; both Budapest, N.G.) are typical of academic painting at that time.

Zichy did a number of illustrations of works by foreign authors such as Mikhail Lermontov, Aleksandr Pushkin, Byron and Théophile Gautier. Among Hungarian works, Zichy's illustrations for Imre Madách's *The Tragedy of Man* (Budapest, 1888) and the ballads (Budapest, 1898) of János Arany are among the best-known examples of Hungarian book illustration.

BIBLIOGRAPHY
T. Gautier: 'Zichy', *L'Artiste* (Jan-April 1859), pp. 17–20
T. Lándor: *Zichy Mihály élete, müvészete és alkotása* [The life, art and work of Mihály Zichy] (Budapest, 1903)
B. Lázár: *Zichy Mihály élete és müvészete* [The life and art of Mihály Zichy] (Budapest, 1927)
L. Bényi and M. Supka: *Zichy Mihály* (Budapest, 1953)
L. Aljosina: *Zichy* (Moscow, 1958)
I. Berkovits: *Zichy Mihály élete és munkássága* [The life and work of Mihály Zichy] (Budapest, 1964)
K. Gellér: *Zichy Mihály, 1827–1906* (Budapest, 1990)
KATALIN GELLÉR

Zick (i). German family of ivory-turners. The family originated in Nuremberg, where various members were occupied with artistic turnery, particularly in ivory, from the late 16th to the 18th century. Indeed, it was principally the work of the Zick family that made Nuremberg one of the three main centres (along with Regensburg and Dresden) of ivory-turning for the manufacture of *objets d'art*. The family workshop achieved extraordinary skill in overcoming the greatest technical difficulties. Although little is known of the careers of individual family members, such contemporary sources as Johann Gabriel Doppelmayr (1730) and Johann Michael Teuber (1740) provide important points of reference. The artistic dynasty is thought to begin with Peter Zick I (1571–1629), who was at some period turnery master to Emperor Rudolf II at his court in Prague. Peter Zick I was famous for his ivory drinking vessels (e.g. in Nuremberg, Ger. Nmus.), and an ivory nef (Brunswick, Herzog Anton Ulrich-Mus.) may also be attributable to him; it bears an imperial coat of arms, perhaps a reference to his stay at the court in Prague. His son Lorenz Zick (1594–1666) continued the tradition, as shown by a twisting, openwork nef signed *Lorencz Zickh in Nurnberg* (Vienna, Ksthist. Mus.), his only signed work. He was summoned to Vienna in 1642–4 by the Emperor Ferdinand III to receive an imperial appointment as Kammerdrechsler. Lorenz's outstanding skill is demonstrated in a specialized form of the relief medallion: inscribed plates, the letters on which have been turned on the lathe. This technique was probably developed in the Zick workshop. Such inscribed plates are generally found only in conjunction with so-called counterfeit spheres: a series of hollow ivory spheres of decreasing sizes, one inside the other. Sometimes a sphere might be hollowed out so as to contain two ivory discs, which would be fitted with hinges and painted with images of Christ and the

Virgin or, less frequently, portraits; these could be drawn apart by means of cords, thus making the pictures visible through the opening used for the turning process. Doppelmayr's laudatory description of Lorenz's work has an illustration of such a sphere, as well as of a mounted polyhedron, consisting of a plinth, a stem and a sphere, crowned by an ornament. Although Egidius Lobenigk (*fl c.* 1584–91) and Jakob Zeller are recorded as having created such spheres in 1598 and 1611 respectively, the merit of the Zicks rests in their ability to produce such pieces in large numbers and to make them widely available.

Stephan Zick (1639–1715), son of Lorenz Zick, was another distinguished member of the family. Other members whose names are recorded include Lorenz's brothers, Peter Zick II (1596–after 1652) and Christoph Zick (1599–1665); three of his nephews, Johannes Zick (*b* 1627) and David Zick I (1628–after 1652), the sons of Peter II, and Caspar Zick I (1623–82), the son of Christoph; and his great-nephew, Caspar Zick II (1650–1731). Although each piece made by one of the family is completely individual, there exist certain established workshop characteristics that support the attribution of some works to the Zicks, such as the turned inscription panel mentioned above. A very fine example is the 'Konterfettenbecher' (Vienna, Ksthist. Mus.). This ivory piece, 375 mm high, which was commissioned by the imperial family, consists of a figure of *Hercules* as the supporting figure, surmounted by the actual counterfeit sphere, which is girdled with shell cameo portraits relating to the history of the House of Habsburg. The sphere contains the typical images of *Christ* and *The Virgin* and is crowned by a figure of *Artemis*. The detailed carving of this quite early work was subsequently discarded in favour of *tours de force* of turning skill, such as can be seen in the treasury of the Mariazell Basilica: on a pedestal consisting of several parts, including the frequently used element of a small openwork basket, a unicorn couchant clasps the spirally turned stem that supports the counterfeit sphere, with its small inner discs (see fig.). Flattened spheres serving as connecting elements are typical of the Zick workshop; here the sphere is surmounted by a double eagle. Other counterfeit spheres in a number of ivory collections may well be attributable to the Zicks. One in the Benedictine church in Kremsmünster has the portraits of the Empress *Maria Theresa* and her husband the Emperor *Francis I* and is mounted on a box-shaped stand. There is a counterfeit sphere in the Museum für Kunstgewerbe in Graz and another in the Germanisches Nationalmuseum in Nuremberg. There are several counterfeit spheres in the Danish royal collection at Rosenborg Palace in Copenhagen. Associated with these, in the same collection, is an ivory goblet with a spiny sphere, rather than the true counterfeit type: between the sphere and the tip appears the signature C.A., possibly representing Caspar Zick I. The large collection of ivory from Nuremberg in the Danish royal collection includes 14 pieces, such as goblets and spheres, from the period of Lorenz Zick alone. The Dreifaltigkeitsring or Trinitatisring encircling the sphere was another feat of the ivory-turner's art: it consisted of three parallel rings surrounding a core ring, but not touching each other. Doppelmayr illustrates a similar ring by Stephan Zick, claiming that he made three of them. This specific tradition of the Zick workshop

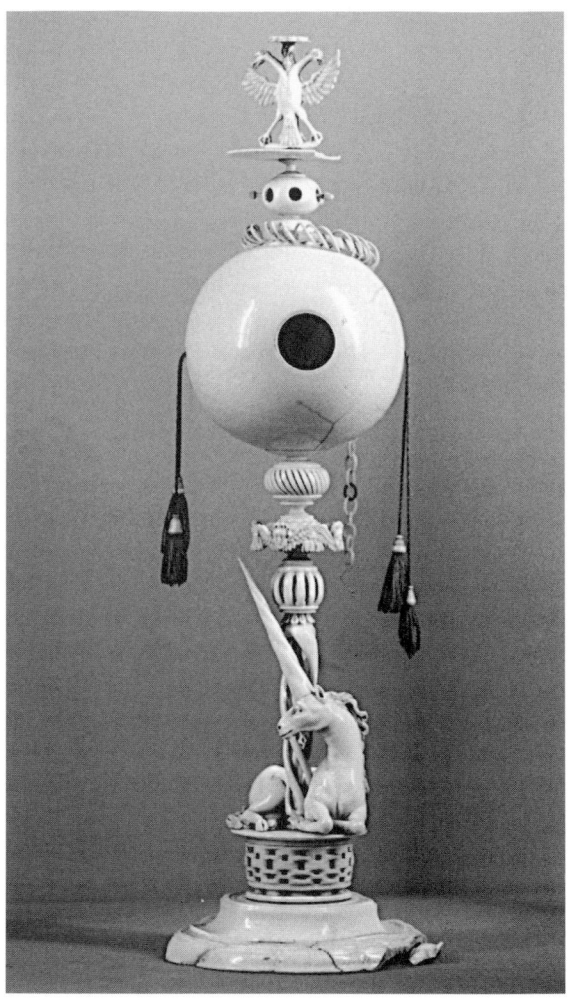

Workshop of Lorenz Zick: counterfeit sphere, ivory, *c.* 1660 (Mariazell, Basilica Treasury)

must have been carried on mainly by David Zick I, who is documented as a maker of rings of all sizes.

As well as such superb cabinet-pieces, the Zicks had another speciality that is interesting from the point of view of cultural history: they made anatomical models for medical demonstrations. Ivory was particularly well-suited to this purpose, as its colour and sheen resemble flesh tones, and its structure makes very detailed modelling possible. The Zick workshop produced dismountable models of the eye and the ear; the models of eyes, made in 14 parts and painted (for illustration see Doppelmayr; example Nuremberg, Ger. Nmus.), were a speciality of Stephan Zick. The Medizinhistorisches Museum in Zurich has a model of an ear. The Zick workshop also made whole-figure nude male and female models about 150–190 mm high, with exact representation of the internal organs. The female models were shown in a state of pregnancy, with the foetus. Doppelmayr and Murr name Stephan Zick and Johann Michael Hahn (*b c.* 1714) from Schweinfurt as makers of this type of model. The relatively large number of anatomical models in various collections, and their specific craft marks, suggest a large workshop, such as that of the Zicks. A male figure with a full-bottomed wig in the Medicinsk-Historisk Museum in Copenhagen, attributed to the period of Stephan Zick, and other examples in Brunswick (Herzog Anton Ulrich-Mus.) and Munich (Bayer Nmus.), share such characteristics as a special form of kneecap, divided in a way that is anatomically incorrect, dimples on the hands that have merely been drilled out, and a splayed-out little finger; the decorated cushions on which the models rest provide further indication that they should be grouped together. Two relatively well-preserved female models in small, lavishly worked wooden boxes may be seen in Berlin, in the sculpture gallery of the Dahlem museum, and in the Institut für Geschichte der Medizin, Humboldt University. These figures have a removable abdomen and chest panel, disclosing the heart, lungs, liver, intestines and a foetus, all reproduced with amazing precision. Sales catalogues that include the names of a David Zick and a Christian Zick, as well as Stephan Zick, are evidence of a relatively long workshop tradition of producing such models.

BIBLIOGRAPHY
Thieme–Becker
R. P. C. Plumier: *L'Art de tourner* (Lyon, 1701, rev. 3/1776)
J. G. Doppelmayr: *Historische Nachricht von den Nürnberger Mathematicis und Künstlern* (Nuremberg, 1730)
J. M. Teuber: *Vollständiger Unterricht von der gemeinen und höheren Drehkunst* (Regensburg and Vienna, 1740)
C. G. von Murr: *Beschreibung der vornehmsten Merkwürdigkeiten in der Reichstadt Nürnberg* (Nuremberg, 1801)
C. Scherer: *Elfenbeinplastik seit der Renaissance* (Leipzig, 1903)
E. von Philippovich: 'Der Konterfettenbecher: Eine Arbeit der Zick-Werkstätte', *Österreich Z. Kst & Dkmlpf.*, xiii (1959), pp. 60–64
——: 'Elfenbeinkunstwerke Nürnberger Provenienz', *Mitt. Ver. Gesch. Stadt Nürnberg.*, xlix (1959), pp. 339–60
——: 'Anatomische Modelle in Elfenbein und anderen Materialien', *Sudhoffs Archv Ges. Mediz. & Natwiss.*, xliv (1960), pp. 159–78
——: *Elfenbein* (Brunswick, 1961, rev. Munich, 1982)
E. Fründt: 'Drei barocke Elfenbeinbildwerke', *Forsch. & Ber.: Staatl. Mus. Berlin*, ix (1967), pp. 125–7

BARBARA KAHLE

Zick (ii). German family of painters. They worked for over five generations in the 18th and 19th centuries in Upper Bavaria, Swabia, Franconia and the Rhineland. (1) Johann Zick and his son (2) Januarius Zick were primarily fresco painters, though the latter also did many panel paintings. Their direct descendants, Konrad Zick (*b* Ehrenbreitstein, 1773; *d* Koblenz, 1836), Gustav Zick (*b* Koblenz, 1809; *d* Koblenz, 1886) and Alexander Zick (*b* Koblenz, 1845; *d* Berlin, 1907), while relatively minor figures, all shared a gift for portrait painting.

BIBLIOGRAPHY
A. Feulner: *Die Zick* (Munich, 1920)
Johann und Januarius Zick (exh. cat., Koblenz, Mittelrhein-Mus.; Munich, Bayer. Staatsgemäldesammlungen; 1984)

(1) Johann Zick (*b* Lachen, 10 Jan 1702; *d* Würzburg, 4 March 1762). After completing his apprenticeship with Jakob Karl Stauder, probably between 1721 and 1724, he painted the Mariahilfkirche in Munich (destr. 1840). Andreas Felix Oefele, Zick's biographer, claims this was followed by a three year visit to Giovanni Battista Piazzetta in Venice, but this must be based on legend. In 1728 Zick settled in Munich, where he was appointed court painter in 1732. Despite this he was long unable to assert himself against the dominant Asam brothers and received few fresco commissions, apart from the Klosterkirche in Raitenhaslach (1738–9). The frescoes for the Klosterkirche at Schussenried (1745) and the Pfarrkirche of Biberach (1746–8) helped to establish Zick. In 1750 he painted the ceiling of the garden room at the Residenz in Würzburg. His pastoral mythological groups here, relating to Balthasar Neumann's architecture, display 'the perpetual continuation of welfare growing out of the gifts of nature' (Strieder).

Zick's hope of further commissions for the Residenz was not fulfilled, but on the recommendation of Neumann, he went to Schloss Bruchsal, engaged by Prince-Bishop Franz Christoph von Hutten to fresco, with the help of his son Januarius, the vaulted Fürstensaal, marble hall and staircase. These ceiling frescoes (1751–4), destroyed in 1945 but since reconstructed, are Zick's finest work. Their programme of mythological allegory is outlined in his poem *Flor des Hochstiftes Speyer im Reich des Friedens*. The disposition of figure groups in an airy, illusionistic architecture develops on Zick's study of Johann Georg Bergmüller. Zick's other main influence, Rembrandt, shows in his occasional small panel paintings, including the *Good Samaritan* (1749; Würzburg, Mainfränk. Mus.). Also in the 1750s he painted large frescoes for St Gangolf, Amorbach (1753), the refectory in the monastery of Oberzell (1755), the Sandkirche in Aschaffenburg (1756/7; destr. 1945) and the Pfarrkirche of Grafenrheinfeld, near Schweinfurt (1757; destr. 1944).

A decline in building and the outbreak of the Seven Years War in 1756 put an end to these large contracts. In 1759 Zick moved to Würzburg, where he tried, unsuccessfully, to obtain the vacant position of court painter. During his last years the artist constructed a 'planet machine' (Würzburg, Luitopoldmus.; destr. 1945), which he explained in an essay of 1761. This was a planetarium made of brass with an armillary sphere and a sundial, which was primarily intended to represent the planets' trajectories around the sun, based on the Copernican system. Zick's work lies between the Baroque and Rococo styles and belongs to the tradition of Southern German fresco painting, with its ancestry in handcrafts.

BIBLIOGRAPHY
A. F. Oefele: *Adversariae historicae boicae* (Munich, Bayer. Staatsbib., MS. Oefeliana 5, vol. v) (Munich, 1735), pp. 421–3
B. Strieder: *Johann Zick* (Worms, 1990)

(2) Januarius Zick (*b* München–Au, 6 Feb 1730; *d* Ehrenbreitstein, 14 Nov 1797). Son of (1) Johann Zick. He first trained with his father and was then apprenticed (1745–8) to the master mason Jacob Emele (1707–80) in Schussenried—hence his later description of himself as *pictor et architectus*. Januarius's first dated painting is from 1750: *St Benedict Awakens a Monk from Death* (Koblenz, Mittelrhein-Mus.). He went on working under his father, with interruptions, until 1759, on commissions that included frescoes and panels at Würzburg and Bruchsal. His panel paintings include *David Playing the Harp Before Saul* (*c.* 1753; Bremen, Ksthalle) and closely imitate the 'Rembrandt' style of his father. In 1757, during a visit to Paris, he studied with the copper-engraver Jean-Georges Wille and met his French contemporaries. He then travelled via Basle to Rome, where he completed his studies with Anton Raphael Mengs. In 1758 Zick became a member of the Augsburg academy and won a prize for the painting

Mercury in the Sculptor's Workshop (untraced). In the same year he painted 34 panels for the 'Watteau-Kabinett' in Schloss Bruchsal (destr. 1945), using his Paris experience.

Between 1759 and 1761 Archbishop Prince Franz Georg von Schönborn commissioned Zick to work on his Residenz in Trier and hunting-lodge at Engers. In 1762 Zick settled down in Ehrenbreitstein, near Koblenz. During the 1760s and 1770s he chiefly painted panel paintings, such as the portrait of the *Rémy Family from Bendorf* (1776; Nuremberg, Ger. Nmus.). This picture clearly illustrates Zick's style at the time, which Bruno Bushart has aptly described as 'purified Rococo'. He also worked with the cabinetmaker David Roentgen from 1773, making repeat patterns for marquetry.

The numerous frescoes Zick painted for churches between 1778 and 1791 are among the finest late achievements of the art. He supervised the decoration of the former Klosterkirche St Martin at Wiblingen, near Ulm (1778–80). Larger commissions, for the churches of Oberelchingen, near Ulm (1782/3), and Rot an der Rot (1784), followed. In 1786 Zick painted frescoes for the Klosterkirche in Triefenstein (see fig.). His work here, surrounded by the classical décor created by Materno Bossi (ii), shows how far he had moved away from the Rococo of his youth without ever becoming a Neo-classical painter. In the late 1780s Zick was commissioned to work for the electoral Residenz in Trier and that in Mainz, and in 1792–4 in the Palais Schweitzer and the Russischer Hof in Frankfurt am Main.

BIBLIOGRAPHY
B. Bushart: *Deutsche Malerei des Rokoko* (Königstein im Taunus, 1967), p. 19
O. Metzger: *Januarius Zick* (Munich, 1981)
J. Strasser: *Januarius Zick* (Munich, 1987)
——: *Januarius Zick: Das Gesamtwerk* (diss. Munich, Ludwig-Maximilians U., 1990) [cat. rais.]

ERICH SCHNEIDER

Zickelbein, Horst (*b* Frankfurt an der Oder, 20 Dec 1926). German painter, draughtsman and printmaker. He studied at the Hochschule für Bildende und Angewandte Kunst (1950–55) in Weissensee, Berlin, and at the Deutsche Akademie der Künste (1955–8) under Heinrich Ehmsen. As well as Ehmsen, the work of Picasso, Georges Rouault and Chaïm Soutine were important sources of inspiration early in his career. In the late 1950s he and other like-minded painters in Berlin embraced sensualism in painting. His important early pictures include *Dead Fisherman* (1957; artist's col.), *Boy with a Hen* (1959; Schwerin, Staatl. Mus.) and *Agricultural Apprentice* (1961; Berlin, Alte N.G.).

From *c.* 1964 colour became more important for its own sake. Zickelbein's knowledge of Jackson Pollock's work was influential on the Darss landscapes (1963–4). His experience of the primeval forest-like character of the Darsser Wald opened up new artistic perspectives. In numerous gouaches the unbridled growth process of nature is turned into a feast of colours applied in broad brushstrokes and dabs. In his gouaches (his favourite medium), as well as vitality he developed a wealth of nuances in the scale of subdued broken colours, controlled with great sensitivity. In his lithographs of Darss landscapes form is conveyed entirely by bundles of lines and strokes. In the mid-1960s he began a long period of works related to architecture (sometimes in conjunction with Hans Vent), including the murals *Cosmos* (1965–6) for the works restaurant of DIA Chemie in Berlin and *Knowledge Released by the Socialist Revolution* (1974; municipal hall, Karl-Marx-Stadt). From 1970 he also produced felt-tip pen drawings. They are dreamy pictures, metaphorical compositions, associations and visions with a harsh, expressive colourfulness. In 1978 Zickelbein started painting a series of large gouaches that relate to the sensualism of the 1960s. Time spent in Cyprus influenced his use of colour, for example *Terracotta* (gouache, 1979; Berlin, Alte N.G.). The picture as a landscape of the mind incorporating *objets trouvés* became important. Zickelbein's experience of Romania was also important, in two respects: for his response to the landscape, for example *Dobrudscha* (gouache, 1981; Berlin, Alte N.G.) and *Dobrudscha/Cerna Voda* (gouache, 1985; Neubrandenburg, Kstsamml.), and to the artistic environment. Zickelbein consistently stressed his affinity with Romanian art, especially with that of Ion Nicodim. Visits to France resulted after 1986 in a reappraisal of the work of Rodin, Monet, Matisse and Serge Poliakoff (e.g. *Homage to Matisse*, gouache, 1987; artist's col.), and of the human figure.

BIBLIOGRAPHY
Horst Zickelbein (exh. cat., E. Berlin, Gal. Arkade, 1974)
Horst Zickelbein (exh. cat., E. Berlin, Gal. Torm, 1981)
Horst Zickelbein (exh. cat., E. Berlin, Altes Mus., 1989)
Horst Zickelbein (exh. cat. by A. Kühnel, Berlin, Pal. Ephraim, 1991)

ANITA KÜHNEL

Januarius Zick: *Christ Appearing to St Paul* and *St Paul in Athens* (1786), ceiling frescoes, Klosterkirche, Triefenstein

Ziebland, Georg Friedrich (*b* Regensburg, 7 Feb 1800; *d* Munich, 24 July 1873). Bavarian architect and painter. After working with the stage designer Domenico Quaglio II he studied at the Königliche Akademie der bildenden Künste in Munich under the Neo-classical architect Karl von Fischer. Following Fischer's death, Ziebland completed many of his projects, including the Hof- und Nationaltheater (1811–18) in Munich. An exhibition of Ziebland's paintings brought him to the attention of Ludwig I, King of Bavaria (*see* WITTELSBACH, §III(3)). In his quest to transform Munich into a museum of architecture, Ludwig sent Ziebland to Italy to study Early Christian basilicas, so that he could design one for Munich. After two years in Italy (1827–9) Ziebland was commissioned to design an Early Christian-style basilica with an adjacent Benedictine monastery. The Bonifaziusbasilika (1835–40), Munich, is the best known of Ziebland's works. A brick, five-aisled basilica with a sumptuous interior, St Boniface was hailed as one of Ludwig's greatest building projects. Its monastery is attached to his exhibition building, the Kunstausstellungs-Gebäude (1838–45; now the Staatliche Antikensammlung). The museum stands on the south side of the Königsplatz, opposite Leo von Klenze's sculpture museum, the Glyptothek. From 1832 Ziebland assisted Quaglio with the restoration, especially of the interior, of Burg Schwanstein (later Schloss Hohenschwangau), Upper Bavaria. After the death of Joseph Daniel Ohlmüller in 1839, Ziebland completed the building of the Gothic Revival Mariahilfkirche (begun 1831) in the suburb of Au in Munich.

BIBLIOGRAPHY

B. Stubenvoli: *Die Basilika und das Benedictinerstift St Bonifax in München* (Munich, 1875)

B.-V. Karnapp: *Georg Friedrich Ziebland: Studien zu seinem Leben und Werk* (diss., Innsbruck U., 1971)

H. J. Wörner: 'Zieblands Basilika in München und Hardeggers Liebfrauenkirche in Zürich', *Das Münster*, xxvii (1974), pp. 50–67

W. Nerdinger, ed.: *Romantik und Restauration: Architektur in Bayern zur Zeit Ludwigs I, 1825–1848* (Munich, 1987)

KATHLEEN CURRAN

Ziegler, Jakob (*fl* 1559–97; *d* Bamberg, after 1616). German painter. Versatile but mediocre, he worked as court painter at Bamberg. His few surviving works include wall paintings (1559) in the Schloss at Forchheim and a large cycle on the *Legend of St George* (1575; Bamberg, Diözmus.), concluding with the battle between Emperor Henry II and King Bolesław of Poland. He also designed wall hangings, worked as an illuminator and etcher and produced moulds for woodcuts.

BIBLIOGRAPHY

Thieme–Becker

K. Sitzmann: *Künstler und Kunsthandwerker in Ostfranken* (Plassenburg, 1957), pp. 606ff

Ziegler, Jules-Claude (*b* Langres, Haute-Marne, 16 March 1804; *d* Paris, 25 Dec 1856). French painter, ceramicist, writer and lithographer. He first studied in Paris under Ingres and François-Joseph Heim. In 1830 he toured Italy, spending time in Venice especially, and then went to Munich, where he learnt the technique of fresco painting from Peter Cornelius. After spending some time in Belgium, he returned to Paris and illustrated such Romantic pieces of literature as E. T. A. Hoffmann's *Contes fantastiques*. At the Salon of 1831 he exhibited paintings based on his travels, including *View of Venice* (Nantes, Mus. B.-A.) and *Souvenir of Germany*. In 1833 he established his reputation as a history painter by showing at the Salon two works that were based on medieval sources: *Giotto in Cimabue's Studio* (Bordeaux, Mus. B.-A.), bought by the State for the Musée du Luxembourg, and the *Death of Foscari* (Arras, Mus. B.-A.). At the Salon of 1835 he was awarded medals for portraits of *Connétable, Comte de Sancerre* and *General Kellermann* (both Versailles, Château). From 1835 to 1838 he frescoed the cupola of the choir of La Madeleine with *A History of Christianity*. He astonished the critics in 1838 with the *Prophet Daniel* (Nantes, Mus. B.-A.), exhibited at the Salon, and was awarded the cross of the Légion d'honneur. Because of his training with Ingres, his paintings are characterized by a great amount of graphic detail and plastic power, yet there is a certain primitivism that links him to other disciples of Ingres such as Eugène-Ammanuel Amaury-Duval and Hippolyte Flandrin.

His interest in the decorative arts had begun when he was given a government grant to study the techniques of painting on glass and ceramics in Germany. In 1839 he established a factory at Voisinlieu, near Beauvais, for the production of relief-decorated salt-glazed stone wares and in 1850 made lithographs of some of the pieces for his publication *Etudes céramiques: Recherche des principes du beau dans l'architecture, la céramique et la forme en général* (1850). This venture can be seen as part of the crafts renaissance in western Europe in the mid-19th century. After a five-year period during which he did no painting, he exhibited again at the Salon in 1844 and in 1848 he won a medal for *Charles V after Preparing his Funeral Rites*. As an art critic and theorist he wrote reviews of various exhibitions, and his *Traité de la couleur et de la lumière* was published in 1852. From 1854 he was Director and Curator of the Musée des Beaux-Arts in Dijon.

WRITINGS

Etudes céramiques: Recherche des principes du beau dans l'architecture, la céramique et la forme en général (Paris, 1850)

Traité de la couleur et de la lumière (Paris, 1852)

Compte-rendu de la photographie à l'exposition de 1855 (Paris, 1855)

BIBLIOGRAPHY

Bellier de La Chavignerie–Auvray

M.-P. Boyé: *L'Alchimiste de la peinture religieuse au XIXe siècle: Jules-Claude Ziegler* (Nantes, 1956)

ANNIE SCOTTEZ-DE WAMBRECHIES

Ziegler, Wilhelm [Wilhalm] (*b* Creglingen, *c*. 1480; *d* ?Rothenburg ob der Tauber, after 1537). German painter. He was apprenticed to Hans Burgkmair I in Augsburg in 1502. From 1507 to *c.* 1520 he lived as an independent master painter in Rothenburg ob der Tauber. His work there includes the panels for the St Wolfgang altar in the Wolfgangskirche (1514), which are very much in the style of Burgkmair. Ziegler later came under the influence of Dürer and Hans von Kulmbach. From 1522 he shared a studio with Hans Boden in Fribourg; some works from this period (e.g. panels from an altar to Our Lady, 1522, 1523) are in Fribourg's Musée d'Art et d'Histoire. He obtained citizenship of Fribourg in 1527 and was appointed municipal painter.

In 1531 Ziegler made a brief but fruitless return to Rothenburg ob der Tauber. In 1534 he turned up as a master painter in Würzburg, which had remained Catholic; however a dated and signed map of the Rothenburg area (1537; Nuremberg, Ger. Nmus.) indicates another return, as municipal painter, to Rothenburg ob der Tauber. Baum identified Ziegler with the so-called Master of Messkirch (see STRÜB, (2)); this identification has been rejected on both stylistic and chronological grounds.

Jörg Ziegler (b Rothenburg ob der Tauber, c. 1515; d Rottenburg am Neckar, after 1572), presumably Wilhelm's son, probably trained c. 1535–40 with the Master of Messkirch, with whom he too has been erroneously identified. In 1540 he qualified as a master in Augsburg and from 1547 until c. 1561 worked in Hechingen, initially as court painter to Graf Joseph Niclas II von Zollern. Between 1562 and 1572 he is recorded as a painter in Rottenburg. Besides a map of Rottenburg (see Kaller), no work, however, can be definitely assigned to him.

BIBLIOGRAPHY

J. Baum: 'Hans Boden und Wilhalm Ziegler', Z. Schweizer. Archäol. & Kstgesch., iv (1942), pp. 47–55
——: 'Wilhalm Ziegler, der Meister von Messkirch', Z. Schweizer. Archäol. & Kstgesch., v (1943), pp. 21–30
W. Dannheimer: 'Die älteste Landkarte des Rothenburger Gebietes', Jber. Ver. 'Alt-Rothenburg' (1954–55), pp. 17–36
F. Manz: 'Die Malersippe Ziegler in Rottenburg', Sülchgau. Altertver.: Jgabe (1959)
G. Kaller: 'Ein kolorierter Plan des Malers Jörg Ziegler aus Rottenburg. Ein Beitrag zur Frage nach dem Meister von Messkirch', Hohenzoll. Jhft., xxii (1962), pp. 222–6

JANEZ HÖFLER

Ziem, Félix(-François-Georges-Philibert) (b Beaune, 21 Feb 1821; d Paris, 11 Feb 1911). French painter. He studied architecture at the Ecole des Beaux-Arts in Dijon until he was expelled in 1838 for unruly behaviour. In 1839 he left for Marseille, where he was Clerk of Works on the construction of the Marseille canal. In November 1839 he was noticed by Ferdinand Philippe, Duc d'Orléans, who accepted two watercolours that Ziem presented to him and commissioned a further six. This first success decided Ziem's vocation, and he started a drawing class that was attended by Louis Auguste Laurent Aiguier (1819–65) and Adolphe Monticelli. During this period he also encountered the Provençal artists Emile Loubon (1809–63), Prosper Grésy (1804–74) and Gustave Ricard.

In 1842 Ziem left for Nice, where he came into contact with members of the European aristocracy, with whom, thanks to his talent and his charm, he was soon on familiar terms. During the following years he travelled widely. Sophie, the Grand Duchess of Baden, invited him to Baden in 1842. In 1843 he travelled with the Gagarin princes to Russia, where he stayed over a year. Between 1846 and 1848 he was in Italy, visiting Florence, Venice, Genoa, Naples and Rome. By 1849, when Ziem exhibited at the Salon for the first time, he was already making a comfortable living from his art; he exhibited there regularly until 1868. In 1854 he set off for North Africa and returned the following year to Tunisia. He divided his time between his Paris studio in the Rue Lepic, his travels and, after 1853, frequent visits to Barbizon, where he was an active member of the Barbizon school. His works enjoyed growing success and were much sought after by upper-class collectors. After 1876 he regularly spent the winters at Sainte-Hélène, his property in Nice, and went less frequently to Martigues, where he had built a studio in the Oriental style in 1861. Towards the end of his life he received many official honours, and his paintings were the first by a living artist to enter the Louvre in 1910. The contents of his studio are now housed in the Musée d'Art et d'Archéologie in Martigues.

Ziem was above all the painter of Venice: he visited the city more than 20 times. The commercial success of his views of Venice has often obscured their originality and the diversity of their compositions. Such works as *Venice: The Bacino di S Marco with Fishing Boats* (c. 1865; London, Wallace) are among his most beautiful achievements. He was also a prolific painter of Orientalist subjects, for example *Fantasia at Constantinople* (Paris, Petit Pal.). He painted some rare but magnificent canvases of Fontainebleau Forest in the style of the Barbizon school (e.g. *Stag in the Forest of Fontainebleau*; Paris, Petit Pal.). He was primarily a landscape painter, but he also worked on still-lifes and animal paintings. The vivacity and freshness of his palette, his nervous, vibrant touch, with passages of great virtuosity, his determination to seize fleeting effects of light and his ability to transcribe the iridescence of sunlight on water have often invoked comparisons with Impressionism. In fact the spirit of his work was fundamentally different. Ziem wanted to express the poetic quality of his subject, to transform it into an essentially dream-like vision, rather than to transcribe an immediate reality. He was also a fine draughtsman and left nearly 10,000 sheets, which attest to the variety of his interpretative gifts and the diversity of his technique.

BIBLIOGRAPHY

T. Gautier: Ziem (Paris, 1896)
L. Fournier: Un Grand Peintre: Félix Ziem (Beaune, 1897)
C. Mauclair: L'Art de Ziem (Paris, 1897)
R. Miles: 'Ziem', Figaro Ill., 178 (Jan 1905), pp. 1–24
H. Roujon, ed.: F. Ziem (n.d.), Collection des peintres illustres, 50 (Paris, c. 1900–14)
J. Sauvageot: Les Peintres de paysages bourguignons au XIXe siècle (Dijon, 1966)
E. Hild: Etudes sur l'oeuvre dessinée de Félix Ziem (1821–1911) (MA thesis, Aix-en-Provence, U. Aix-Marseille, 1976)
P. Miquel: Félix Ziem (1821–1911), 2 vols (Maurs-la-Jolie, 1978)
Ziem en marge (exh. cat. by E. Hild, Saint-Tropez, Mus. Annonciade, 1980)

ERIC HILD-ZIEM

Ziesenis, Barthold W(ilhelm) H(endrik) (b Amsterdam, 1762; d The Hague, 1 May 1820). Dutch architect. He trained as a sculptor at the Stadstekenacademie in Amsterdam, where his father Antonz Ziesenis (1731–1801), an architect and sculptor, was one of the directors, but after a few years he decided to concentrate on architecture. Having finished his training, he visited England, where he appears to have studied work by Robert Adam, although his stay in England is extremely badly documented. In 1792 he returned to Amsterdam, where he was later appointed assistant (1797) to the City Architect Abraham van der Harte. In 1807 he joined the architects who executed works for Louis Bonaparte, King of Holland under the supervision of the royal architect Jean Thomas Thibault (1757–1826). In this capacity he remodelled the interior of Amsterdam's town hall during its conversion into a royal palace (*see* AMSTERDAM, §V, 2). He spared Jacob van Campen's 17th-century interior by dividing the large Burgerzaal and adjoining galleries into small rooms with drapery and wooden panelling in a sober, Neo-classical style, thus allowing a full restoration of the original work during the 1930s. Ziesenis received some minor government commissions after the restoration of King William I in 1814, for example the rebuilding (1814) of the Paleis Noordeinde in The Hague, which further proved that he was a capable but unexceptional architect.

BIBLIOGRAPHY
C. A. van Swigchem: 'B. W. H. Ziesenis: Architect, 1762–1820', *Bouw: Cent. Wkbld Bouwwzn Nederland & België*, xxiv (1962), pp. 866–71
PAUL H. REM

Ziesenis [Zisenis], Johann Georg (*b* Copenhagen, 1716; *d* Hannover, 4 March 1776). German painter of Danish birth. He trained with his father, Johann Georg Ziesenis (1681–1748); he became a German citizen in 1743 and subsequently was appointed court painter to Herzog Christian von Pfalz-Zweibrücken in Zweibrücken and, later, Mannheim. In the early 1750s he overcame his technical shortcomings by studying Flemish art, particularly the work of Rubens and van Dyck. He also introduced a new genre, the private court portrait. His portrait of *Karl Philipp Theodor, Kurfürst von der Pfalz* (1757; Munich, Alte Pin.) is original in its intimate view of a nobleman posed at leisure in casual dress, seated in his private study. The painting deviates from conventional Baroque court portraits by introducing a genre-like candour and reflects a shift in cultural values from paintings symbolizing official power to those descriptive of the private sphere of an educated prince and representative of 'enlightened absolutism'.

When Ziesenis became court painter to George II in Hannover in 1760, he became influenced by the great 18th-century English portrait painters, as well as by Hyacinthe Rigaud. His portraits of the aristocracy and the middle classes became freer and more natural, anticipating 'Citizens Rococo' or *Zopfstil*, a transition to early Naturalism. His portrait of the young *Prince Constantin von Sachsen-Weimar* (1769; Frankfurt am Main, Goethemus.) features the spontaneous expression, alert gestures and intelligence of the sitter, traits that bespeak a responsiveness to the challenges of civic life that are characteristic of *Zopfstil* portrait painting.

BIBLIOGRAPHY
Thieme–Becker
B. Bushart: *Deutsche Malerei des Rokoko* (Königstein im Taunus, 1967)
H. Keller: *Die Kunst des 18. Jahrhunderts* (Berlin, 1971), pp. 406, 410
RUDOLF M. BISANZ

Ziggurat [Assyrian: *ziqquratu*]. A square or rectangular stepped tower with three or more stages, one of the most distinctive and enduring forms of Mesopotamian religious architecture. The first ziggurats were built in the mid-3rd millennium BC; the latest examples were still being renovated in the 6th century BC.

Ziggurats first appeared in southern Iraq, in the major religious centres of the Sumerians, at sites such as Ur (*see* MESOPOTAMIA, fig. 9), Eridu, Uruk, Kish and Nippur. The earliest known ziggurats are at Kish and date to the Early Dynastic III period (*c.* 2600–*c.* 2400 BC). All other

Sumerian ziggurats date to the Ur III period (*c.* 2100–*c.* 2000 BC); these ziggurats were rebuilt many times, however, which may well have obscured or obliterated their earlier forms. In the 2nd millennium BC the ziggurat, together with many other aspects of Sumerian religious life, was taken over by the Babylonians, who renovated the older ziggurats (as at Ur) and constructed new ones (as at Larsa and Tell el-Rimah). It was subsequently copied by the Kassites in their capital city at Aqar Quf (for illustration *see* AQAR QUF), by neighbouring Elamites at CHOGHA ZANBIL and Susa and, in northern Iraq, by the Assyrians at Assur, Kar Tukulti Ninurta and Nimrud. In the 1st millennium BC the Assyrians continued to build ziggurats (there is an 8th-century BC example at Khorsabad), and in the 6th century BC many of the oldest ziggurats in Babylonia were comprehensively rebuilt by the Neo-Babylonian kings. The latest known example of a ziggurat is at Zibliyat, near Abu Salabikh. It is dated to the Early Islamic period (*c.* 9th century AD) and, as such, is anomalous.

All these ziggurats show very similar construction techniques. They were built with a solid core of sun-dried mud-brick and given an external facing of weather-proof baked bricks. The mud-bricks of the core were separated every few courses by a layer of reeds and matting that reinforced and bound together the great mass of brick. In some cases thick woven ropes, 100 mm in diameter, provided further reinforcement. Horizontal 'weeper holes' ventilated the core, thus reducing humidity and stabilizing the mud-brick, and vertical shafts through the brickwork provided drainage. In many ziggurats the central core seems to have been fired, but whether this was done deliberately or whether ziggurats were in some way self-igniting is not clear.

Ziggurats varied in size and in number of stages. The 3rd-millennium BC ziggurat at Ur, with three stages, covers a ground area of around 2600 sq. m and may be considered of average size. The smallest ziggurat is one of a pair in the Anu-Adad shrine at Assur and covers just 900 sq. m (30×30 m). The largest are at Babylon (approx. 8300 sq. m) and at Borsippa (some 6700 sq. m). It seems a reasonable assumption that these two also had a greater number of stages. Although no ziggurats have survived beyond the fourth stage, seals of the Middle Assyrian period depict five-staged ziggurats, and Herodotus recorded eight stages of the Babylon ziggurat. The tallest extant ziggurat, at Aqar Quf, is 57 m high, while the original height of the Babylon ziggurat has been estimated at 92 m. The Babylon ziggurat also appears in the Bible as the Tower of Babel.

Access to the top of the ziggurat was usually by one or more staircases. The Ur ziggurat had a triple staircase, with two lateral flights of stairs and a central axial one. Ziggurats with spiral ramps are also known (at Khorsabad and perhaps at Babylon) and, in one case at least, access was via the roof-tops of the adjoining temples (Tell el-Rimah). As no ziggurat has survived to its highest stage, it is not known for certain what lay on top. Herodotus stated that there was a shrine on top of the ziggurat at Babylon, and this is extrapolated for other ziggurats by some authorities. Sumerian texts refer to a structure called a *gigunu* on a ziggurat, which may have been the ziggurat shrine. However, all clear representations of ziggurats on cylinder seals show only the various stages.

The façade of the ziggurat was often decorated with panels of half-columns and niches of mud-brick. At Khorsabad, the four extant stages of the ziggurat appear to have been painted each in a different colour (white, black, red and blue). Blue glazed bricks and large horns of copper are known to have decorated part of the ziggurat at Susa.

The origin and function of ziggurats are contentious issues. It is possible that ziggurats arose out of the practice of elevating new temples over the filled-in ruins of the old, a practice well-attested in the archaeological record. However, ziggurats are still sufficiently distinct from such temple platforms to be considered an architectural innovation. In the absence of explicit textual references to their function many theories have been put forward. They are not tombs and are thus unrelated to the Egyptian pyramids, and theories that they are celestial observatories or simply gigantic cosmic symbols have been discredited.

Ziggurats are always found within a religious precinct, attached to the adjacent temple of a major deity. The ancient names given to the ziggurats suggest that they were perceived as being, in one sense, ladders between earth and heaven. Thus, the ziggurat at Larsa was called the Stairway-to-Holy-Heaven. They may also have symbolized mountains in which the gods were thought to live (rather like Mount Olympus in Greek mythology). In these explanations, the shrines on top of ziggurats were the dwellings, temporary or permanent, of the gods, where the 'sacred marriage' fertililty rite may have taken place. The gods then descended from their abodes to the temple at the bottom of the ziggurat to participate in the complex rites that are recorded in Mesopotamian religious texts. These may be very partial explanations of the function and symbolism of a ziggurat. Given the investment of time and labour that such monumental constructions required, ziggurats must once have dominated Mesopotamian religion as they still dominate the flat landscape of southern Iraq.

BIBLIOGRAPHY

C. L. Woolley: *Ur of the Chaldees* (London, 1929, rev. 1982)
A. Parrot: *Ziggurats et Tour de Babel* (Paris, 1949)
C. L. Woolley: *The Ziggurat and its Surroundings* (London, 1959), v of *Ur Excavations*
R. Burleigh: 'The Date of Zibliyat: A Controversy Settled by Radiocarbon', *Sumer*, xxxvi (1980), pp. 169–73
J. G. Schmid: 'The History of the Construction of the Ziggurat', *Sumer*, xli (1985), pp. 44–7

R. G. KILLICK

Zijdebalen. Dutch 18th-century garden (destr.) near Utrecht. In 1681 the Amsterdam merchant Jacob van Mollem established a silk factory on the River Vecht, near Utrecht. His son David van Mollem purchased additional land near his house, built sometime before 1693 next to the factory, and the garden that he established there became internationally famous (*see* GARDEN, §VIII, 4(v)). From 1712 to 1736, when a neighbouring garden on the other side of the river was added to the complex, a formal, symmetrical garden was laid out. Influenced by French and particularly Italian examples that he must have known both from prints and his own observation, he incorporated into the garden an exceptional number of statues, arranged according to a specific plan and representing subjects from both Classical mythology and the Old Testament. Scattered throughout the garden were grottoes, a labyrinth, a theatre and a Turkish tent. At the centre were a large basin, and a triumphal arch backed by a hill and a dry hollow. In addition to numerous animal sculptures, the garden was also enlivened by fish ponds, a duck pond and a deer enclosure. Although the pleasure grounds no longer exist, their original appearance can still easily be reconstructed from the drawings (Utrecht, Cent. Mus.) made by Jan de Beijer (1703–?80) in 1745–6, as well as the descriptions in the *Hofdicht* (1740), a poem about Zijdebalen by Arnold Hoogvliet.

BIBLIOGRAPHY

Zijdebalen, lusthof aan de Vecht: Tuin- en tekenkunst uit het begin van de 18de eeuw [Zijdebalen, pleasure garden on the Vecht: garden plans and drawings from the early 18th century] (exh. cat. by P. J. M. van Gorp, E. de Jong and D. P. Snoep, Utrecht, Cent. Mus., 1981)
E. de Jong: *Natuur en kunst. Nederlandse tuin- en landschapsarchitectuur 1650–1740* [Nature and art. Dutch garden and landscape architecture 1650–1740] (Amsterdam, 1993), pp. 156–89

K. A. OTTENHEYM

Zijl, Lambertus (*b* Kralingen, 13 June 1866; *d* Bussum, 8 Jan 1947). Dutch sculptor. He received his first artistic training in Amsterdam, first in the form of drawing lessons from painter and illustrator Bernard Willem Wierink (1856–1939) and later at the Quellinusschool under the direction of engineer Emmanuel Constant Edouard Colinet (1840–90) and at the School for Applied Arts. There he became friendly with, among others, Joseph Mendes da Costa; through the society Labor et Ars he met Gerrit Willem Dijsselhof, Jan Eisenlöffel, H. P. Berlage, K. P. C. de Bazel and J. L. Mathieu Lauweriks. In the company of these young artists, who disliked the traditional styles, his attention was directed particularly to ancient Egyptian and Assyrian art.

In 1893 Zijl was invited by Berlage to collaborate on his building (destr. 1964) for De Algemeene life insurance company on the Damrak, Amsterdam. For this building and particularly for the Koopmansbeurs (1898–1903) (*see* NETHERLANDS, THE, fig. 11), Amsterdam, also by Berlage, he developed a style that can be seen as the high point of his career. This so-called 'architecture sculpture' is always considered as a subsidiary to the architectural concept of the whole, therefore contributing to the *Gesamtkunstwerk*, indicating a link with medieval examples. The forms of his sculptures barely extrude, if at all, from the wall surface and thus tend to be relief-like.

In his later monumental works Zijl achieved a somewhat freer interpretation of this architectural restraint. Apart from Berlage, he also worked with such architects as A. J. Kropholler, on the Paschaliskerk, The Hague, and the town halls of Waalwijk and Noordwijkerhout; de Bazel, for the building of the Nederlandsche Handelsmaatschappij (Dutch Trading Company), Amsterdam; Willem Kromhout and J. F. Staal. C. A. Lion Cachet also collaborated with Zijl successfully in designs for interiors of various ocean liners.

Scheen
BIBLIOGRAPHY
R. W. P. de Vries: *Lambertus Zijl* (Bussum, 1946)

A. M. Hammacher: *Beeldhouwkunst van deze eeuw* (Amsterdam, 1955)
Amstelhoek, 1897–1910 (exh. cat., ed. J. D. van Dam and A. Hidding; Leeuwarden, Gemeentelijk Mus. Het Princessehof, 1986)

G. JANSEN

Zilcken, (Charles Louis) Philip [Philippe] (*b* The Hague, 20 April 1857; *d* Villefranche, 3 Oct 1930). Dutch printmaker, painter and writer. He went to the drawing academy in The Hague, where he was taught by J. C. K. Klinkenberg (1852–1924) and Anton Mauve. He was a painter and draughtsman as well as an etcher, engraver and lithographer, and depicted landscapes, townscapes and still-lifes. He lived and worked mainly in The Hague, belonging to both the Amsterdam society Arti et Amicitiae and the Pulchri Studio there. As a graphic artist he achieved considerable fame, especially through his reproductive etchings of works by painters of the Hague school (J. Israëls, the Maris brothers and Weissenbruch) and 17th-century masters such as Vermeer.

In 1885 Zilcken was involved in setting up the Dutch Etching Club (Nederlandsche Etsclub). As an editor of *Elsevier's Geïllustreerd Maandschrift* from 1896 to 1905, he became a well-known writer on art. With his etchings of exceptional quality and his publications about graphic art, he contributed towards the revival of Dutch etching. He also did much to publicize the Hague school, particularly in America, where he had many connections with collectors and museum officials. Zilcken had about ten pupils, among them his daughter R. H. L. Zilcken (*b* 1891).

UNPUBLISHED SOURCES

Over 6000 letters in the Rijkspentenkabinet, Rijksmuseum, Amsterdam

WRITINGS

Peintres hollandais modernes avec facsimiles d'après des oeuvres de ces artistes (Amsterdam, 1891)
Verzameling 'H. W. Mesdag' ([Amsterdam], 1895)
Les Maris: Jacob-Mathijs-Willem (Amsterdam, [1896])
H. W. Mesdag: De schilder van de Noordzee [H. W. Mesdag: painter of the North Sea] (Leiden, [1896])
Souvenirs, i (Paris, 1901)
Joseph Israëls (Bergamo, 1910)
Au jardin du passé (The Hague, 1930)

BIBLIOGRAPHY

P. A. Haaxman jr: 'Philip Zilcken', *Elsevier's Geïllus. Mdschr.*, xii (1896), pp. 1–20
A. Pit: *Catalogue descriptif des eaux-fortes de Ph. Zilcken* (Amsterdam, 1918)

C. WILL

Zille, (Rudolf) Heinrich (*b* Radeburg, nr Dresden, 10 Jan 1858; *d* Berlin, 9 Aug 1929). German draughtsman, printmaker, photographer and film maker. He attended evening classes at the Hochschule für Bildende Künste, Berlin, while serving a lithography apprenticeship (1872–5). He subsequently worked for an art printing company, where he learned the techniques of etching and aquatint. His first drawings were exhibited at the Berlin Secession in 1901, where he exhibited regularly thereafter. His work also appeared in *Jugend: Illustrierte Wochenschrift für Kunst und Leben* and *Lustige Blätter*. Zille's sympathetic depictions of impoverished workers, children and prostitutes in Berlin are in a humourous vein but with serious undertones, and carry captions in Berlin slang; his photographs of Berlin street scenes also provide rare documents of everyday life. In 1926 he made the film *Die da Unten*.

PRINTS

Kinder der Strasse (Berlin, 1908)

BIBLIOGRAPHY

L. Fischer: *Heinrich Zille in Selbstzeugnissen und Bilddokumenten* (Reinbek bei Hamburg, 1979)
W. G. Oschilewski: *Heinrich Zille Bibliographie* (Hannover, 1979)
M. Flügge, ed.: *Heinrich Zille: Fotografien von Berlin um 1900* (Leipzig, 1987)

□

Ziller, Ernst [Ernestos] (**Moritz Theodor**) (*b* Oberlössnitz, nr Zwickau, 22 June 1837; *d* Athens, 9 July 1923). German architect, designer and archaeologist, active in Greece. He studied at the Königliche Bauschule in Dresden (1855–8) and worked for Theophilus Hansen in Vienna (1858–9). Hansen brought Ziller to Greece to execute the Academy of Athens (1861–4). After an educational journey in Italy and further studies at the Akademie der Bildenden Künste in Vienna (1864–8), Ziller settled in Greece. He eventually became a Greek national and rose to the positions of professor at the National Technical University of Athens (1872–82) and Director of Public Works (1884).

Ziller was the most active and influential architect of the reign of George I (*reg* 1863–1913). Following Hansen's example, he adopted different morphological systems for different types of buildings. For public and residential buildings he used the Renaissance Revival style, as in Iliou Melathron (1878–80), the residence of Heinrich Schliemann and his most significant building; the house of Pavlos Melas (1884; later the Post Office); and the New Palace (1890–97), originally the residence of the Crown Prince (all in Athens). Ziller's public buildings include the Municipal Theatre (1872–3; destr. 1938) and the Royal Theatre (now the National Theatre; 1895–1901), both in Athens, and the Town Hall (1876), Ermoupolis, Syros, one of the few Neo-classical buildings to adapt successfully to the Aegean landscape. For ecclesiastical works he used a version of *Rundbogenstil*, where Byzantine references were mixed with Romanesque ones. His most important churches were the two temples of the Virgin, Faneromeni (1890) and Eisodion (1893), in Aigio, Peloponnese, Hagios Athanasios (1911) in Pyrgos, Peloponnese, and Hagia Triada (1915–16) in Peiraeus. He also designed a number of country houses in Attica in what he called the 'Greco-helvetian' style, a picturesque fusion of Neo-classical architecture with Alpine vernacular elements. These include the summer residence of George I (1870) in Tatoi and a number of country houses (1909–13), known as the 'Ziller settlement', in Kifisia.

Ziller played an important role in the popularization of Neo-classical imagery by designing such items as caryatids and rosettes that were mass-produced in terracotta and that account for the stereotypical detailing on historically eclectic buildings in Greece. He also exhibited a parallel interest in archaeology: in 1862 he identified and partly excavated the Theatre of Dionysus, Athens, and in 1869–70 excavated the ancient Stadium of Athens.

BIBLIOGRAPHY

H. H. Russack: *Deutsche Bauen in Athen* (Berlin, 1942)
F. Loyer: *Architecture de la Grèce contemporaine* (diss., U. Paris III, 1966)
D. E. Papastamos: *Ernestos Ziller: Prospatheia monografias* [Ernst Ziller: an initial monograph] (Athens, 1973) [Gr., Eng., Fr. and Ger. text]

X. Skarpia-Heupel: *I morfologia tou germanikou klasikismou (1789–1848) kai i dimiourgiki afomoiosi tou apo tin elliniki arhitektoniki (1833–1897)* [The morphology of German classicism (1789–1848) and its creative integration in Greek architecture (1833–1897)] (diss., Thessaloniki, Aristotelian U., 1976)

ALEXANDER KOUTAMANIS

Zimbabwe, Republic of [formerly Southern Rhodesia, Rhodesia]. Country of *c.* 390,580 sq. km in Southern Africa, bordered by Zambia to the west and north, by Mozambique to the north and east, by South Africa to the south, and by Botswana to the south and west. The capital is Harare (formerly Salisbury). Zimbabwe's fertile plateau and mountain ranges contain vast mineral resources including serpentines and such other stones in many colours as verdite and soapstone. Its population of *c.* 10,600,000 (census, 1992) comprises mostly Shona-speaking peoples (*c.* 75%), with the Nguni-speaking Ndebele making up the largest non-Shona group. The area of present-day Zimbabwe was first settled by the SAN in *c.* 20,000 BC. Around 500 BC Shona agriculturalists and herdsmen moved into the country and by AD 1000 had built up a commercial empire based around GREAT ZIMBABWE. In the early 19th century a king of the Ndebele, Mzilikazi, conquered the country. In 1890 an army sent by Cecil Rhodes (the British Prime Minister of the Cape Colony) invaded, and by 1896 'Southern Rhodesia' had been annexed with its capital at Salisbury. After many vicissitudes Zimbabwe became independent in 1980, since when it has enjoyed a cultural renaissance in which may be seen the blending of traditional, Western, Afro-American and other cultural influences.

This entry covers the art produced in Zimbabwe since colonial times. For the art of the region in earlier periods *see* AFRICA, §VII, 8. *See also* NDEBELE, GREAT ZIMBABWE, SAN and SHONA.

1. ARCHITECTURE. Traditional homesteads consist of clusters of circular clay-and-stick huts with conical thatched roofs. Each hut is a room with a specific function (e.g. sleeping, cooking), and in the middle is an open space. Simple geometric designs, some of which have symbolic meanings, provide decoration. Inside, floors may be moulded into benches and hearths. By the end of the 20th century changes to the traditional styles included use of corrugated iron, sometimes brightly coloured, for roofs; Western-style window and door openings; the adoption of rectangular forms and wall paintings incorporating religious texts and 20th-century motifs. Additionally, breeze blocks and wrought-iron security fences began to be used both functionally and decoratively around the 'matchbox' houses in the high-density suburbs.

Low-density houses, originally built for Europeans, tended to be large suburban-style bungalows, and only occasionally, as in the home of architect Anthony Wales-Smith (*b* 1930), was there any serious attempt at making structures appropriate to the Zimbabwean environment. Larger commercial farmhouses were often long bungalows in the CAPE DUTCH STYLE. Churches varied widely in style and building materials. Most built during the second half of the 20th century were simple rectangular buildings of locally made brick, often with curved or pointed arched windows and sometimes having a tower. Some were decorated, for example, with wall paintings, as at Cyrene

Mission (begun 1939), or with low-relief wood-carvings inside.

Public buildings of the colonial period have been divided into five types (Jackson). 'Oxcart architecture' of the 1890s was characterized by the use of painted brick and was sometimes thatched. 'Railway architecture', which was prevalent up to World War I, is typified by brick and stucco with cast-iron ornaments and corrugated-iron (and later red-tiled) roofs and plate-glass fronts. In the 1920s and 1930s neo-classical styles that were heavily influenced by Herbert Baker (*see* SOUTH AFRICA, §3) were popular among such architects as W. D'Arcy Cathcart (1885–1970), James Cope-Christie (1870–1953) and Major William Roberts (*d* 1956). Their buildings are marked by corrugated-iron or tiled roofs and windows made from local steel. In the late 1930s, contemporary with the rise of Modernism, these styles declined into a superficial, highly rectilinear Art Deco style.

Modernism was introduced by such architects as Hector Montgomerie, Peter Oldfield (e.g. the National Gallery, 1957; Heroes' Acre, 1981; both Harare), Anthony Wales-Smith, Peter Martin (e.g. Zanu-PF Headquarters, Harare, 1988) and the Pearce Partnership—a practice originally founded in 1912 by D'Arcy Cathcart but subsequently led by Michael Pearce (*b* 1938); the partnership's works include the University Land Management Building (1936) and the Batanai Gardens (1986; both Harare). During this period tower blocks in the European style, often with highly coloured reflective walls, became popular. The Architects Partnership—Peter Jackson (*b* 1949), Robert Moore (*b* 1952), William Kurebgaseka (*b* 1953) and Anthony Wilson (*b* 1946)—experiments with local materials and forms (e.g. ZIMCOR Building, Harare, 1993; using dark facing-bricks and local hardwoods), while contemporary Black architects include M. C. R. Vengesai and Vernon Mwamuka. There is as yet no school of architecture, but architecture forms part of a degree course in Urban Planning and Development at the University of Zimbabwe. Many architects have moved from Zimbabwe to other countries in southern Africa, and there is a case for considering styles regionally, with Harare and Johannesburg as major centres of development.

2. PAINTING. The paintings of Thomas Baines (1820–75) represent a meticulous document of his explorations of Africa in the mid-19th century and stand at the beginning of a tradition of White painting that engaged itself with the extraordinariness of the landscape. In the early post-colonial period painting was produced mainly by Whites. Initially realist, then predominantly abstract, these paintings were in the European tradition and reflected the artists' relationships with the landscape—its heat, its vastness, the power of nature—and their isolation as members of small minorities. Among the most important of these painters are Ann Linsell Stewart, Robert Paul (1906–80), Helen Leiros (*b* 1940) and Steve Williams (*b* 1948). By contrast, since the 1940s Black African painting in Zimbabwe has often been concerned with social comment and has explored human predicaments—the lives of traditional warriors, marriage problems, urban violence, the vitality of township life or the oppressive drought. George Nene (*b* 1959), who himself fought in

the war for independence, focuses on broad contemporary issues, using forceful stylized figures in dramatic, almost comic-strip poses and bold primary colours. Louis Meque (*b* 1966), a graduate of the National Gallery's BAT Workshop, applies Photorealism to the African scenario, portraying the shebeen, the bus queue or the constructivist form of the Harare skyline.

3. SCULPTURE. Indigenous Zimbabwean sculpture was rediscovered after World War II when mission teachers began to encourage carving in relief and in the round. After the National Gallery opened in 1957, Frank McEwen (*b* ?1906) created a workshop there for the encouragement of local art. Joram Mariga (*b* 1927), a mission-trained wood-carver, began making bowls from stone and then carved figures using the same techniques. Fascinated by the spiritual world of the Shona, McEwen encouraged the use of stone, especially serpentine, as a medium to preserve and communicate traditional Shona folklore. This received a great impetus with the emergence in 1966 of the Tengenenge Sculpture Community on a tobacco farm in the serpentine-rich Guruve hills. The farmer Tom Blomefield (*b* 1926) had been taught to carve by Chrispen Chakanyuka (*b* 1943), who worked with Mariga. In return, Blomefield encouraged his workers, who were not Shona but from Malawi and Angola, to express the traditions, values, folklore, forms and experiences of their own differing cultures. McEwen organized exhibitions of this work in London (Commonwealth Inst., 1963) and in Paris (Mus. Rodin, 1971) and promoted the work extensively.

The most striking of such sculptures are unified and simple with powerfully rounded, compact and solid forms. Even the earliest examples have typically huge African heads and hands. Commonly expressing the importance of positive human relationships and of harmony with the spiritual forces of nature, much of the sculpture is realistic, with ducks, baboons and other animals realistically portrayed. Since independence, Zimbabwean sculptors have experimented with stone textures and colour, with abstract, geometric and stylized forms, and with anecdotal and expressionist themes (see fig.).

In the 1980s and 1990s a new generation of artists began to experiment with other materials. Such artists as Tapfuma Gutsa (*b* 1956), Richard Jack (*b* 1949) and Joseph Muzondo (*b* 1953) worked with mixed media. Zephania Tshuma (*b* 1932) and Morris Tendai created figures and even miniature dramas using painted wood and other materials. The low-relief wood-carving tradition of the missions serving a predominantly religious and African market was continued by, for example, Cornelius Manguma. While such figurative artists as Joseph Muli (*b* 1944), Barnabas Ndudzu and David Mutasa created sculptural work in wood, metal sculpture was also popular, with the lightness of metal being used to express movement and energy in nature, as in the work of Arthur Azevedo, and the potential of nature and mankind, as in the work of Adam Madebe (*b* 1954) and Ndebe (David) Ndlovu (*b* 1963). Women, the traditional makers of rounded craft forms, were also emerging as sculptors in the late 20th century, two of the best-known being Agnes Nyanhongo (*b* 1960) and Locardia Ndandarika (*b* 1945).

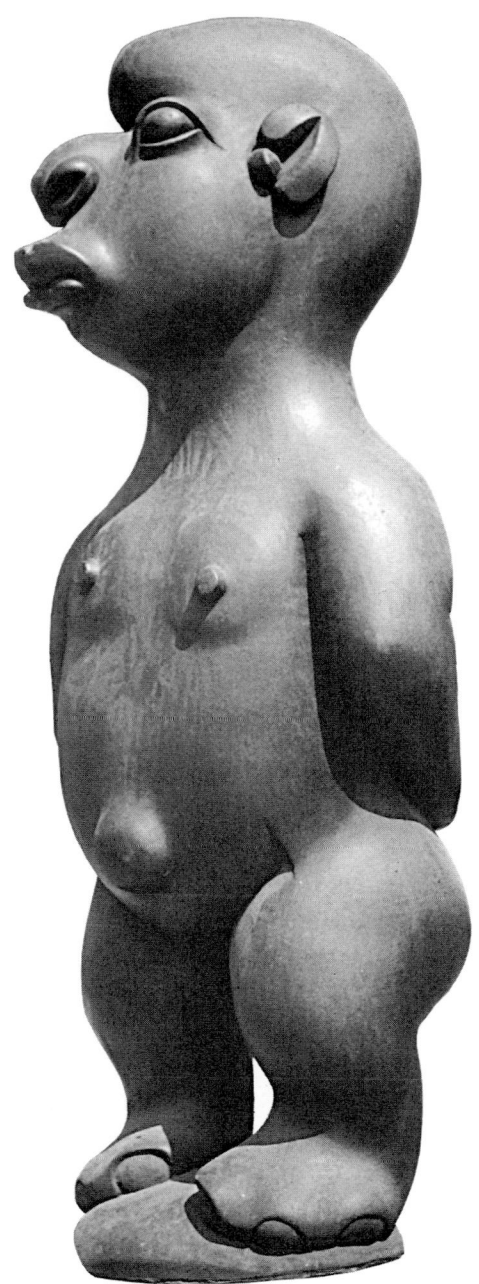

Bernard Matemera: *Man Turning into a Hippo*, black serpentine, h. 1.5 m, 1986 (Harare, National Gallery of Zimbabwe)

4. PATRONAGE AND ART INSTITUTIONS. Government patronage is supplied through the National Gallery of Zimbabwe, Harare, and the National Arts Council. The Church, diplomatic organizations, large corporations and the big hotels also provide sponsorship as do private individuals, both Zimbabwean and foreign. David Mutasa

and other artists use their own galleries to provide patronage for local artists. There are also a number of artists' cooperatives.

The National Gallery, Harare, organizes *c.* 30 exhibitions a year, often of local art works. An annual Zimbabwe Heritage Exhibition is adjudicated by a team of international judges, and there is an annual schools exhibition, adjudicated by leading local artists. Private galleries include Gallery Delta (founded 1975), Gallery Shona Sculpture (1972), Matambo Gallery (1985), Stone Dynamic (1987), Tengenenge Sculpture Community (1966) and Vhukutiwa Gallery (1992). The French Embassy has an open-air gallery (1974) at Le Forum.

Informal art education continues to exist, with artists and their families and friends working together and providing mutual encouragement. Institutional art education open to Blacks only started in 1940, at the Cyrene Mission, Matopo Hills, near Bulawayo (founded 1939), where young artists were encouraged to sculpt Christian figures and to paint. Similar work was done later at the Serima Mission. Since 1980 art has been taught throughout the school system. Tertiary-level education is provided at teachers' colleges, at Harare Polytechnic, at Mzilikazi Art and Craft Centre (1963), Bulawayo, and at the National Gallery's Workshop School (1962), superseded by the BAT Workshop School in 1981, in Harare. Pachipamwe or 'Work Together' international workshops have been held in Zimbabwe since 1988 (see Court). In the early 1990s the Tengenenge Sculpture Community provided temporary places for visiting artists to work alongside permanent residents. A Regional School of Art and Design, conceived by Prof. C. A. Rogers (1923–93), was being set up in Harare in the 1990s.

BIBLIOGRAPHY

New Art from Rhodesia (exh. cat., London, Commonwealth Inst., 1963)
F. McEwen: 'Return to Origins: New Directions for African Arts', *Afr. A.*, i/2 (1968), pp. 18–25, 88
Sculpture contemporaine des Shonas d'Afrique (exh. cat., Paris, Mus. Rodin, 1971)
F. McEwen: 'Shona Art Today', *Afr. A.*, v/4 (1972), pp. 8–11
A. Plangger: *Serina* (Gweru, 1973)
Insight (1977–85); cont. as *Zimbabwe Insight* (1986–8)
A. Jack and L. Bolze: *Bulawayo's Changing Skyline* (Bulawayo, 1979)
M. Arnold: *Zimbabwean Stone Sculpture* (Bulawayo, 1981)
D. Walker: *Paterson of Cyrene* (Gweru, 1985)
P. Jackson: *Historic Buildings of Harare* (Harare, 1986)
F. Mor: *Shona Sculpture* (Harare, 1987)
K. Sayce, ed.: *Tabex Encyclopaedia Zimbabwe* (Harare, 1987)
M. Arnold: 'A Change of Regime: Art and Ideology in Rhodesia and Zimbabwe', *African Art in Southern Africa: From Tradition to Township*, ed. A. Nettleton and D. Hammond-Tooke (Johannesburg, 1989), pp. 172–90, 247–9
The Artist (1990–)
Art from the Frontline: Contemporary Art from Southern Africa (exh. cat., Glasgow, A.G. & Mus.; Salford, Mus. & A.G.; Dublin, City Cent.; London, Commonwealth Inst.; 1990)
C. Winter-Irving: *Stone Sculpture of Zimbabwe* (Harare, 1991, 2/Sydney, 1992)
Southern African Art (1992–)
E. Court: 'Pachipamwe II: The Avant Garde in Africa', *Afr. A.*, xxv/1 (1992), pp. 38–49, 98

D. WALKER, C. WINTER-IRVING

Zimmer, Heinrich R(obert) (*b* Greifswald, 6 Dec 1890; *d* New York, 20 March 1943). German art historian. He was trained in Sanskrit philology and comparative linguistics at the University of Berlin, graduating in 1913, and his interests embraced Hindu mythology and philosophy in both literary and visual forms. He taught at the Ernst-Moritz-Arndt Universität, Greifswald (1920–24), and he held the Chair of Indian philology at Heidelberg (1924–38), from which he was dismissed in 1938 for his anti-Nazi convictions. In 1942, after briefly teaching at Balliol College (1939–40), Oxford, Zimmer became Visiting Lecturer in Philosophy at Columbia University (1942–3) in New York, where he died a year later. Many of his most important writings were edited and published posthumously by Joseph Campbell.

Following the Romantic and transcendental traditions of Indian scholarship, Zimmer sought to interpret the contributions of India in philosophy, medicine, art and the history of religion to the development of human civilization, and to assimilate the 'truths' found therein with Western thought. His observations were based on Puranic and Tantric texts, sources which until that time were underutilized in Indic studies. His *Kunstform und Yoga im indischen Kultbild* emphasized the inner significance of sacred images and their instrumentality in psychic transformation. These ideas had a profound effect on the interpretation of Indian art in terms of symbolic forms and led to a ten-year, mutually influential exchange between Zimmer and the psychologist Carl Jung. Two of Zimmer's posthumous publications popularized and led to a more widespread appreciation of South Asian art and myths: *Myths and Symbols in Indian Art and Civilization* and *The Art of Indian Asia*.

WRITINGS

Kunstform und Yoga im indischen Kultbild (Berlin, 1926); trans. and ed. by G. Chapple and J. B. Lawson with J. M. McKnight as *Artistic Form and Yoga in the Sacred Images of India* (Princeton, 1984)
J. Campbell, ed.: *Myths and Symbols in Indian Art and Civilization*, Bollingen series, vi (Princeton, 1946)
J. Campbell, ed.: *The Art of Indian Asia*, 2 vols, Bollingen series, xxxix (Princeton, 1968)

BIBLIOGRAPHY

M. Case, ed.: *Heinrich Zimmer: Coming into his Own* (Princeton, 1994)

MARY F. LINDA

Zimmer, Klaus (*b* Berlin, 31 March 1928). Australian glass artist of German birth. He studied design at the Master School of Arts and Crafts in Berlin and, after emigrating to Australia in 1952, studied painting, printmaking and glass at the Melbourne Institute of Technology. In 1974 he pursued further study at stained-glass workshops in Cologne, Germany, and in 1975 he studied with Patrick Reyntiens and Ludwig Schaffrath in England. In 1979 Zimmer embarked upon another period of research at the Staatliche Glasfachschule, Hadamar, Germany. Zimmer became aware of the expressive potential of contemporary stained glass while studying with William Gleeson at the Melbourne Institute of Technology. He applied his graphic and design skills to the medium of glass with such commitment and imagination that his heavily textured, expressionist panels soon became one of the most enduring influences on Australian glass artists. Zimmer produced hemispherical 'lens' panels by fusing layers of irregular fragments of glass. He also framed broad, boldly painted segments of glass in richly embossed lead channels, and used metallic lustre and stain-painting to decorate glass. These methods contribute to an unmistakable quality of sombre chiaroscuro which often serves to underscore the strain of passionate, socio-political narrative evident in much of Zimmer's work. After some years as senior lecturer in glass studies at the Chisholm Institute of Technology in Melbourne, in 1983 Zimmer founded Australia Studios to produce a growing number of prestigious commissions for architectural glass pieces. Among the most ambitious projects of the 1980s is a sequence of finely rendered, highly formalized windows for the new Parliament House in Canberra (1986–8) and, by contrast, a cycle of 19 windows of muted hue, decorated with traditional symbolism and of a decidedly lyrical composition, for the historic Uniting (formerly Independent) Church in Melbourne (1988–9).

BIBLIOGRAPHY

J. Zimmer: *Stained Glass in Australia* (Melbourne, 1984)
Glass from Australia and New Zealand (exh. cat., ed. J. Zimmer; Darmstadt, Hess. Landesmus., 1984)

GEOFFREY R. EDWARDS

Zimmermann. German family of artists. (1) Johann Baptist Zimmermann and (2) Dominikus Zimmermann were the sons of Elias Zimmermann (1656–95), a stuccoworker and mason from Wessobrunn, whose work is known only from documentary sources. It is almost certain that they learnt their craft as stuccoists in the Wessobrunn school (*see* STUCCO AND PLASTERWORK, §III, 10(i)(e)). While Dominikus was almost exclusively associated with Bavarian and Swabian religious architecture, Johann Baptist became the leading representative of 18th-century interior decoration at the Bavarian court. Their collaboration was very influential on the development of Bavarian Rococo (*see* ROCOCO, §III). Their extensive output required a large studio or workshop: among Johann Baptist's assistants were his sons Johann Joseph Zimmermann (1707–43) and Franz Michael Zimmermann (1709–84), who were both painters and stuccoists and contributed to the frescoes of the pilgrimage church at Steinhausen, near Schussenried, and the stuccowork at Seligenthal Abbey, Landshut (see below). Franz Michael succeeded his father as court stuccoist to the Elector. Dominikus's son, Franz Dominikus Zimmermann (1714–86), is recorded as stuccowork foreman in his father's workshop from 1737; he also worked at Steinhausen.

(1) Johann Baptist Zimmermann (*bapt* Wessobrunn, 3 Jan 1680; *bur* Munich, 2 March 1758). Painter and stuccoist. Much of his early stuccowork and frescoes, such as that in the choir of Gosseltshausen parish church (1701) and the refectories of the abbeys at Tegernsee, Weyarn and Beyharting (before 1710), has been destroyed. His earliest surviving stuccowork (1707–9) is in the pilgrimage church of Maria Schnee, near Markt Rettenbach, and reveals the influences of Johann Schmuzer from Wessobrunn and an Italian stucco workshop that practised in Tegernsee. After 1707 he lived in Miesbach.

Johann Baptist first worked with his brother (2) Dominikus in 1709–13 at the Buxheim Charterhouse, where he painted frescoes while Dominikus built artificial marble altars. The stucco decoration to which both contributed gives an appearance of unity, although stylistic differences can be detected. The delicate angels and lush festoons of

fruit on the ceiling of the monks' choir are by Johann Baptist. He moved to Freising in 1715 and did stuccowork and frescoes for the cathedral cloisters in 1716. The following year he produced stuccowork (destr.) in several rooms at Schloss Ismaning, the summer residence of the prince bishops of Freising. Between 1710 and 1720 he developed a new decorative style displayed in his stuccowork (1714) in St Sixtus, Schliersee, Schloss Maxlrain (*c*. 1715) and especially at Ottobeuren Abbey (1714–after 1720). The ornamentation, which was influenced by such engravings as those in *Neues Zierathen Buch von Schlingen und Bändelwerk* (Augsburg, *c.* 1710) by Johann Jakob Biller (*d* 1723) and *Neu-inventirtes Laub- und Bandl Werk* by Johann Leonhard Eysler (*d* 1733), became more two-dimensional, and stucco reliefs with landscape backgrounds that resemble paintings were incorporated into the system of decoration (e.g. the refectory and Grüner Saal at Ottobeuren), anticipating the style of Johann Baptist's later frescoes. His work at Ottobeuren, which included large figures in stucco, and his cycle of the *Apostles* (1718–20) in high relief above the nave arcading at St Georg, Amberg, seem to have led to an invitation to the court at Munich.

This marked a new phase in Johann Baptist's creative work. From 1720 he produced stuccowork for the staircase and Weisser Saal at SCHLOSS SCHLEISSHEIM, to the designs of Josef Effner, the court architect. In the smaller rooms he was presumably able to incorporate his own ideas. The stucco decoration of the staircase and west elevation of the Palais Preysing in Munich, which he carried out (1724–7) under Effner's direction, features pilasters transformed into lengths of strapwork. The typically Régence ornamentation, which he learnt from Effner, transformed his repertory. Its influence can be recognized in the ceiling (1724) of the library at Benediktbeuern Abbey, where for the first time the frames of the frescoes were transformed by ornament, creating a new relationship between the picture on the ceiling and the stucco ornament, thus anticipating the development of Rococo. The abbey church at Weyarn, where he worked in 1729, has the most advanced system of decoration among the churches for which he provided paintings and stuccowork during the 1720s. The narrower sides of the frames around the frescoes dissolve as the stucco ornament and picture area merge into one another.

Johann Baptist painted a few small areas (1718–22) at the abbey church of the Assumption at Mödingen and a series of shallow domes (1728) in the Dominican church of St Markus, Siessen, both designed by his brother, but in one of his brother's most important works, the pilgrimage church at Steinhausen, the vault of the oval nave offered Johann Baptist a vast surface on which to create his first great ceiling painting, the *Virgin in Glory* (1731). While his early frescoes at Buxheim and at the abbey church of St Maria, Wörishofen, in 1722–3 are in the tradition of Hans Georg Asam, the influence of Jacopo Amigoni is evident in Steinhausen. He became familiar with Amigoni's work at Schleissheim and Ottobeuren and adopted his manner of enlivening the edge of the landscape with figures and incorporating a great expanse of sky and bright colours.

Around 1727 Johann Baptist was officially appointed a court stuccoworker to the Elector of Bavaria (later Emperor Charles VII) and reached the peak of his artistic development as a stuccoist while collaborating with FRANÇOIS DE CUVILLIÉS. After executing stuccowork in the Ahnengalerie (*see* STUCCO AND PLASTERWORK, fig. 16) at the Munich Residenz (1726–30) while Effner was still in charge, he also did the ceilings of the Treasury (1730), Reiche Zimmer and Green Gallery (1731–3) under Cuvilliés. The decoration of the gilded stucco ceilings is full of motifs from nature, culminating in reliefs of figures, and is inspired by Antoine Watteau's engravings of ornaments. Johann Baptist's fondness as a painter and stuccoist for pictorial relief influenced the way the ceilings were created. They were largely destroyed in 1944 and reconstructed in 1957–8.

Johann Baptist's masterpiece, which was created during his collaboration with Cuvilliés and marks the beginning of Rococo at the Bavarian court, is his stuccowork for the Amalienburg (1734–7), a hunting-lodge in the park at Schloss Nymphenburg, Munich. The group featuring Diana above the main door is one of his finest sculptures. The silver-coloured stuccowork against the pastel background of the ceiling is ornamental in the corner rooms and arranged as relief scenes in the adjoining rooms. In the central Spiegelsaal the soffit of the dome is formed to suggest the sky, with the sculpted figures of Diana and other nature goddesses resting on the cornice beneath stuccowork trees (see fig.). The stuccos are closely related pictorially to his ceiling frescoes of the period.

During the 1730s, Johann Baptist's most productive period, he fulfilled commissions from the nobility, churches and monasteries alongside his work at court. The stuccoed ceilings that he created between 1730 and 1735 at Schloss Alteglofsheim in the Upper Palatinate, and those in Munich under the direction of Cuvilliés at the Palais Porzia (*c.* 1733; destr. 1944) and Palais Holnstein (*c.* 1736–7), were modelled on the Reiche Zimmer, although simpler, as were the stucco decorations in the summer abbey of Benediktbeuern (*c.* 1730–33), where he worked independently.

In 1732 Johann Baptist painted a fresco cycle (destr.) for the Neumünster at Würzburg. His adaptability made him an ideal associate for a wide variety of architects. In the cruciform, domed monastery church at Seligenthal, Landshut, which was rebuilt (1732–4) by Johann Baptist Gunetzrhainer (1692–1763), the areas of fresco and stucco decoration (1733–4) are differentiated according to the individual parts of the building. The spatial structure in Johann Michael Fischer's centrally planned Augustinian church at Ingolstadt (1736–9; destr. 1945) and St Michael in Berg Am Laim (1737–43) also had a decisive impact on Johann Baptist's painting and stuccowork (1743–4). At Berg am Laim the transformation of the vaulting on the main dome fresco into an area of landscape and sky is resolved by the appearance of the Archangel Michael in a way that accords perfectly with the curve of the dome. In the parish church of the Assumption at Prien am Chiemsee (1738), on the other hand, where Johann Baptist was working independently, he had difficulty in controlling the composition of the large nave fresco.

Johann Baptist Zimmermann: stuccowork with figure of Diana (*c.* 1734–7), Spiegelsaal, Amalienburg, Schloss Nymphenburg, Munich

Between 1744 and 1757 the brothers worked on their last joint project, the pilgrimage church of Die Wies (*see* §(2) below; *see also* ROCOCO, fig. 4). Using bright colours, Johann Baptist transformed the ceilings into the sky, depicting Christ's appearance at the *Last Judgement* on the nave vault and on the choir vault *Angels* with the instruments of the Passion. His late work includes alterations to the Gothic abbey church of Andechs (1751–4), the frescoes and stuccowork of Schäftlarn abbey church under the supervision of Gunetzrhainer (1754–6) and the decoration of the Steinerner Saal at the Schloss Nymphenburg (1755–7), where he again worked with Cuvilliés, although largely to his own designs. At Schäftlarn and Nymphenburg rocaille motifs are applied only sparingly to the framing of the ceiling pictures, since Rococo design had already passed its zenith.

Johann Baptist's oeuvre includes numerous altar pictures, probably painted between 1714 and 1757. He also made artificial marble altars for St Sixtus in Schliersee (1714), the pilgrimage church of Maria Schnee at Markt Rettenbach (1718) and the Altötting chapel of Herrenchiemsee abbey church (1738–9; destr.). The most important of his altar designs is the drawing (Frankfurt am Main, Städel. Kstinst.) for the two-stage high altar (*c.* 1751) of the Benedictine abbey church at Andechs, which was not built as on the drawing. Drawings for various of his

frescoes and altarpieces are held in the Staatliche Graphische Sammlung, Munich. Decorative designs that can
be attributed to him show creative imagination but cannot
be related to specific commissions.

(2) Dominikus Zimmermann (*bapt* Wessobrunn, 30
June–1 July 1685; *d* Wies, nr Steingaden, 16 Nov 1766).
Architect, stuccoist and painter, brother of (1) Johann
Baptist Zimmermann. For the first two decades of his
creative life, from about 1705, he worked mainly as a
builder of altars and as a marbler. His most important
commission came from the Benedictine abbey of Fischin-
gen (Thurgau), for which he made six artificial marble
altars with scagliola inlays (1708–9). Similar altars, mainly
in Swabia, are attributed to him or known to be his work;
their construction shows the influence of Johann Jakob
Herkommer, with whose work Dominikus became familiar while living in Füssen (1708–16). Between 1709 and
1713 he worked with (1) Johann Baptist Zimmermann at
the Buxheim Charterhouse (see above), producing artificial marble altars and stuccowork that is characterized by
the botanical accuracy of the plant motifs. His figures in
the Lady Chapel are squatter and more firmly anchored in
the ornamental background than his brother's.

Régence decoration played a crucial role in Dominikus's
development. He used abstract strapwork figures in a
multiplicity of variations more frequently than his brother.
In 1716 he moved to Landsberg am Lech, where he carried
out stuccowork in the Festsaal of the town hall (1718) and
on its façade (1720), using ornament to remodel the
pilasters into areas of strapwork. In 1721–2 he made two
artificial marble altars with scagliola antependia and redesigned the apse for the Neumünster at Würzburg (destr.
1945).

Dominikus's increasing tendency to turn architectural
forms into decoration, to some extent already foreshadowed in his altars, can also be observed in his church
buildings: the capitals of the pilasters become areas for
decoration, the windows have curving outlines, and the
entablature starts to oscillate and rolls up like a scroll. This
development began in his first religious building, the
church of the Assumption at Mödingen (1716–21), which
was still traditional in concept, and continued in the
Dominican church of St Markus, Siessen (1725–9)—which
was influenced by the designs of the Vorarlberg architects,
especially by Franz Beer's Cistercian church at Oberschön-
enfeld (1721–3)—and at Buxheim parish church (1726–
8); it reached its first peak at the pilgrimage church of
Steinhausen, near Schussenried (1727–33). Conversely the
stucco decoration, which Dominikus always executed
himself in his church buildings, took on architectural
functions. The elongated oval nave at Steinhausen is
surrounded by free-standing pillars faced with clustered
pilasters and an ambulatory (see fig.); rectangular extensions form a vestibule and the choir. A curved stucco zone
with balustrades replaces the entablature and cuts into the
ceiling fresco in place of a frame, in a style reminiscent of
the library at Benediktbeuern.

After the 1720s Dominikus received an increasing
number of commissions for churches and monastic buildings, although he was unable to implement the largest
projects. In 1732 he submitted two designs (unexecuted)

Dominikus Zimmermann: nave (1728–31) of the pilgrimage church,
Steinhausen, 1727–33

for rebuilding the abbey church of Ottobeuren, and
although his model for Schussenried Abbey (1748) served
as the basis for the building's design, he was not put in
charge of the work. In 1736–41 he built the Frauenkirche
at Günzburg. The nave is rectangular externally, but inside
the use of altar recesses, the positioning of columns, the
curving entablature and the shape of the ceiling make it
seem nearer an oval. The choir, with paired free-standing
pillars and gallery above, foreshadowed the layout at Die
Wies (see below). St Anne's chapel (1738–9) in the cloisters
of the Buxheim Charterhouse is one of his most ingenious
spatial arrangements: the square outer cladding of the
chapel houses a quatrefoil interior. Above the curving
entablature is a plinth zone with stucco figures and,
beyond, the richly stuccoed interior of the dome, opening
into a lantern.

The last project the brothers worked on together was
the pilgrimage church of Die Wies, a masterpiece of
Bavarian Rococo (1744–57; *see* WIES CHURCH). Once
again the nave is an oval enclosed by pillars and an
ambulatory, although, unlike that at Steinhausen, the oval
is nearer a circle, the pillars are arranged in pairs and the
vestibule extends to form a convex curve. The stuccowork
transforms the architecture to a greater extent than at
Steinhausen. In the choir the entablature is transformed
completely by filigree rocaille cartouches that frame the
frescoes in the ambulatory—an arrangement only possible
because a lath-and-plaster vault was used over the nave
instead of solid masonry.

The high altar (1750–52) of the St Johannes-Kirche in Landsberg am Lech, which Dominikus began in 1741, is another ornamental composition: the landscape of the River Jordan painted on the apse wall is framed with a structure composed of rocaille shapes. Dominikus's only frescoes are in the parish church of Baiershofen (1724) and the chapel at Schloss Pöring (after 1739). They are simple, rustic works that show the influence of Johann Jakob Herkommer. His style as a draughtsman may be judged from his drawings for the façade of Landsberg town hall (1719; Landsberg am Lech, Stadtmus.) and the gallery at St Katharina, Augsburg (before 1720; Augsburg, Schaezlerpal.).

BIBLIOGRAPHY

Thieme–Becker

J. B. Schmid: 'Johann Baptist Zimmermann, Maler und Kurfürstlicher Hofstukkateur', *Altbayer. Mschr.*, ii (1900), no. 1, pp. 9–24; no. 2/3, pp. 65–80; no. 4/5, pp. 97–123

T. Muchall-Viebrook: *Dominikus Zimmermann* (Leipzig, 1912)

N. Worobiow: *Die Fensterformen Dominikus Zimmermanns: Versuch einer genetischen Ableitung* (diss., Munich Ludwig-Maximilians U., 1934)

H. Schnell: 'Die Scagliola-Arbeiten Dominikus Zimmermanns', *Z. Dt. Ver. Kstwiss.*, x (1943), pp. 105–28

U. Röhlig: *Die Deckenfresken Johann Baptist Zimmermanns* (diss., Munich U., 1949)

H.-R. Hitchcock: *German Rococo: The Zimmermann Brothers* (London, 1968)

W. Neu: 'Dominikus Zimmermann als Maler', *Jb. Bayer. Dkmalpf.*, xxviii (1973), pp. 248–58

C. Thon: *Johann Baptist Zimmermann als Stukkator* (Munich and Zurich, 1977)

S. Lampl: *Johann Baptist Zimmermanns Schlierseer Anfänge: Eine Einführung in das bayerische Rokoko* (Schliersee, 1979)

H. Schnell: *Die Wies: Wallfahrtskirche zum gegeisselten Heiland: Ihr Baumeister Dominikus Zimmermann, Leben und Werk* (Munich and Zurich, 1979)

S. Lampl: 'Johann Baptist Zimmermann, der Meister des Stucks in Amberg-St. Georg', *Jb. Ver. Christ. Kst München*, xi (1980), pp. 99–108

E. Binder-Etter: *Steinhausen bei Bad Schussenried/Oberschwaben, zum 250 jährigen Jubiläumder der Wallfahrtskirche zur Schmerzhaften Muttergottes* (Munich and Zurich, 1981)

G. Richter: *Johann Baptist Zimmermann als Freskant: Das Frühwerk* (Munich, 1984)

——: 'Die zerstörte Hauskapelle des Palais Preysing in München: Ihre Ausmalung durch Johann Baptist Zimmermann und der Brief Johann Anton Fischbachers an Graf Johann Maximilian IV. von Preysing-Hohenaschau', *Jb. Ver. Christ. Kst München*, xiv (1984), pp. 119–26

H. Bauer and A. Bauer: *Johann Baptist und Dominikus Zimmermann: Entstehung und Vollendung des bayerischen Rokoko* (Regensburg, 1985)

Dominikus Zimmermann, 1685–1766 (exh. cat., ed. A. Epple; Landsberg am Lech, Rathaus, 1985)

E. C. Vollmer: 'Neuentdeckte Stuckdekorationen der Brüder Zimmermann', *Jb. Ver. Christ. Kst München*, xv (1985), pp. 123–32

S. Lampl: *Dominikus Zimmermann* (Munich, 1987)

CHRISTINA THON

Zinc. Hard, bluish-white metal. Its ores frequently occur with those of lead. Metallic zinc was produced in antiquity but was not isolated as a metal in modern Europe (which imported it from the East) until *c.* 1740. Zinc is a major constituent of brass. Objects cast from pure zinc are generally known as spelter. The metal is also used as an inexpensive alternative to copper in printmaking.

□

Zincirli [anc. Sam'al]. Site of an ancient city in southern Turkey, which flourished in the 9th–7th centuries BC. It lay at the eastern end of the Amanus Gates pass and consisted of a central citadel mound and flat lower town in the plain, surrounded by a circular double wall pierced by three gates. Many sculptures and inscriptions, both native (in Aramaic and Phoenician alphabets) and Assyrian (in cuneiform), were recovered from the site. Uniquely, the native inscriptions are in relief rather than incised, doubtless in imitation of Hittite hieroglyphic inscriptions, and Hittite art also influenced the style of the sculptures. The site was excavated by F. von Luschan in five seasons between 1888 and 1902. The finds, especially sculpture, were shared between the Pergamonmuseum in Berlin and the Archaeological Museum, Istanbul.

The South City Gate was badly destroyed but had some associated orthostats showing human and animal figures, including fabulous beasts. These were crudely executed in the earliest local style. Apart from this, sculpture was concentrated in the walled citadel. Particularly well preserved was the Outer Citadel Gate, with most of its 33 carved orthostats *in situ*, lining both sides of the double entrance. The sculpture is closely linked with the Suhis–Katuwas style at CARCHEMISH but is much cruder, with a great confusion of motifs: human scenes, including in particular a chariot, a funerary meal, a ruler, archer, warriors, musicians etc; gods, a divine procession with confused iconography; and animals, natural and fabulous. An Inner Citadel Gate (the Cross-Wall Gate) had a number of portal lions of earlier and later styles.

The interior of the citadel was partially occupied by palace buildings, showing frequent use of the *hilani* unit with columned portico. In the north-west corner, the Lower Palace consisted of several distinct building units flanking two adjoining courts divided by the colonnaded Northern Hall-Building. On the north side of the North Court lay two adjacent buildings, K and J, and on the east side it was entered by a gate Q, with associated early-style portal lions. On the left side of the entrance to Building J was the main inscription, in Phoenician, of Kilamuwa, a king of the second half of the 9th century BC, shown in Assyrianizing royal robes. Against its outer east wall was a colossal statue of a deified ruler on a double lion pedestal, the best preserved example of a type known from fragments at Carchemish and Maraş. It was executed in pure Carchemish, Suhis–Katuwas style and presumably represented Gabbar, the Aramean founder of the Sam'al dynasty *c.* 900 BC. Another colossal statue, found at the nearby site of Gerçin, depicted the storm-god and bore an Aramaic inscription of King Panammu I of Sam'al (*c.* 800 BC).

On the east and west sides of the South Court, linked by the Northern Hall-Building, were *Hilanis* II and III. *Hilani* II was preserved only in foundation plan, but both the Hall-Building and *Hilani* III had some of their orthostats and column bases still *in situ*. The portico at the south-east end of the Hall-Building had, on either side of the entrance, apparently matching scenes of King Bar-Rakib (a contemporary of Tiglath-Pileser III, *reg* 744–727 BC) enthroned, supported by attendants and facing a procession of musicians (see fig.); in the centre was a sphinx column-base. *Hilani* III had two double sphinx column bases *in situ*, and orthostats showing processions of dignitaries rendered in a style distinct from the other Bar-Rakib works and identified as the latest from Zincirli (associated with the latest styles of Carchemish and Sakça Gözü, also with the Arslantepe-Malatya colossus). A

notable inscribed orthostat of Bar-Rakib (Istanbul, Archaeol. Mus.) was found out of position in the South
Court. It mentions 'Kilamuwa's House' (?Building 3) and
Bar-Rakib's improvements in building 'this house', presumably the South Court complex. On the south side,
Building P was not well preserved but housed a stele
showing a ruler rendered in the earlier Kilamuwa style,
with an attendant. The other main building of the citadel
was the massive *Hilani* I abutting the north-east wall. It
was preserved only in foundation. Adjoining its south
corner was a stone-lined cist grave, with which was
associated a stele showing a queen seated at a funerary
meal with an attendant. It was rendered in Bar-Rakib style
and presumably represented one of his royal ladies.

All the citadel buildings described showed signs of
destruction by a severe fire. On top of *Hilani* I a completely
different building was constructed, the 'Upper Palace'.
This shows distinct Assyrian features (indeed a badly
damaged Assyrian stele was found in it), and it must have
been the Assyrian governor's palace, after the Assyrians
sacked and annexed the city at an uncertain date, possibly
in the reign of Esarhaddon (*reg* 680–669 BC), whose
colossal stele was found in the restored Citadel Gate. The
Assyrian provincial period probably lasted until the fall of
the Assyrian empire at the end of the 7th century BC.

Zincirli, carved basalt orthostat depicting King Bar-Rakib and his secretary,
h. 1.12 m, 8th century BC (Berlin, Pergamonmuseum, vorderasiatisches
Museum)

BIBLIOGRAPHY
F. von Luschan and others: *Einleitung und Inschriften* (1893), i of
    Ausgrabungen in Sendschirli (Berlin, 1893–1943)
F. von Luschan and others: *Ausgrabungsbericht und Architektur* (1898), ii
    of *Ausgrabungen in Sendschirli* (Berlin, 1893–1943)
F. von Luschan: *Thorsculpturen* (1902), iii of *Ausgrabungen in Sendschirli*
    (Berlin, 1893–1943)
F. von Luschan and others: *Ausgrabungen in Sendschirli* (1911), iv of
    Ausgrabungen in Sendschirli (Berlin, 1893–1943)
W. Andrae: *Die Kleinfunde von Sendschirli* (1943), v of *Ausgrabungen in
    Sendschirli* (Berlin, 1893–1943)
B. Landsberger: *Sam'al* (Ankara, 1948)
W. Orthman: *Untersuchungen zur späthethitischen Kunst* (Bonn, 1971)
J. C. L. Gibson: *Textbook of Syrian Semitic Inscriptions*, ii (Oxford, 1975),
    nos 13–14
J. Voos: 'Zu einigen späthethitischen Reliefs aus den Beständen des
    vorderasiatischen Museums, Berlin', *Altorient. Forsch.*, xii (1985),
    pp. 65–86
J. D. HAWKINS

Zincke, Christian Friedrich (*b* Dresden, 1683–5; *d*
London, 24 March 1767). German painter, active in
England. He was the son of a Dresden goldsmith and
trained in that profession, but he also studied with the
portrait painter Heinrich-Christoph Fehling. In 1706 he
moved to England on the invitation of the Swedish
enamellist Charles Boit, to collaborate on a very large
enamel commemorating the Battle of Blenheim, a project
that was never completed. Zincke continued as Boit's
pupil but soon outstripped his master and at some time
after 1714 set up on his own as a miniaturist. Promoted
by Godfrey Kneller, he won himself a distinguished
clientele and royal patronage, culminating in his appointment in 1732 as Cabinet Painter to Frederick, Prince of
Wales. Vertue, the main source for Zincke's life, wrote
that at this time he 'was so fully employed that for some
years he has had more persons of distinction sitting to him
than any other Painter living'. His prodigious output meant
that not all his miniatures were of equal quality; even in
his heyday he was criticized for portraits that were too

much alike. Failing eyesight and a need to cut productivity
caused him in 1742 to raise his prices from 20 to 30
guineas a head. He retired in 1752, but his studio remained
active; the assistants he employed included Jeremiah
Meyer at some time after 1755. Many of Zincke's miniatures are signed, and most were painted from life, although
some were copied from larger oils; all are characterized by
their very smooth and glossy surface and red stippling on
the face. Fine examples of his work are in the Ashmolean
Museum, Oxford, and the Victoria and Albert Museum,
London.

BIBLIOGRAPHY
'The Note-books of George Vertue', *Walpole Soc.*
G. Reynolds: *English Portrait Miniatures* (London, 1952, rev. Cambridge,
    1988), pp. 89–91, 99–102, 106, 116
J. Murdoch and others: *The English Miniature* (New Haven, 1981),
    pp. 164–5, 167–70, 176, 180
TABITHA BARBER

Zincograph. Term used in the 19th century for a plano-
graphic print taken from a plate made of zinc, a technique
first described in his 1801 patent application by
J. N. F. ALOIS SENEFELDER; zinc was common in commercial usage by *c*. 1840. Such prints were more often
subsumed under the generic name lithograph. *See*
LITHOGRAPHY.   □

Zingaro, lo. *See* SOLARIO, ANTONIO.

Zinnick [Sinnicq; Zinnigh; Zinnig], **Gilbert van** (*b*?1627;
d Grimbergen, 12 Aug 1660). Flemish monk and architect.
According to the records of the Norbertine abbey at
Grimbergen, as a young Norbertine monk he drew up the
plans and supervised the initial building work of the abbey
church, begun in 1660 under Abbot Charles Fernandez

de Velasco. This was one of the most important Baroque churches of the time in Belgium. By 1662 the choir was completed; the nave and the tower were only finished at the beginning of the 18th century (consecrated 1725). As with the Norberti ne churches of Averbode (1664–72) and Ninove (1635–1723), Brabant, the architect sought to combine a central structure with a deep choir, thereby achieving a light, rich interior. To avoid construction problems the dome was executed in wood and stucco and worked into the roof of the church, as in Willem Hesius's St Michielskerk, Leuven.

BIBLIOGRAPHY

J. Delestré: 'L'Architecte de l'église abbatiale de Grimberghe', *Mélanges Borman: Recueil de mémoires offert au Baron de Borman* (Luik, 1919)

J. H. Plantenga: *L'Architecture religieuse dans l'ancien duché de Brabant* (The Hague, 1926)

M. Thibaut de Maisières: *L'Architecture religieuse à l'époque de Rubens* (Brussels, 1943)

J.-P. ESTHER

Ziranek, Silvia (*b* 28 May 1952). British performance artist, sculptor, photographer and writer. She studied Russian and Arabic at Leeds University (1970–72), and completed her foundation studies at Croydon College of Art (1972–3). She then studied fine art at Goldsmith's College, London (1973–6), where the progressive approach to contemporary art led her to design her own course of study, which focused on all aspects of performance art. Influences upon her work include Yves Klein and Bruce McLean. Her ability to deflate the pretentious and absurd in daily life was demonstrated in unrehearsed, highly skilled displays of intuitive stagecraft. These are extended monologues that engage the audience with a mesmerising mixture of mimicry, metaphors, verbal and visual clichés and that explore the conventions of suburban existence and the domestic role of women (e.g. *Rubber-gloverama-Drama*; 1980, London, ICA). Although known primarily as a performance artist, she also made sculptural works and 'costume constructions' initially created in connection with a performance, but which later existed as autonomous objects. Ziranek also took photographs, wrote (e.g. *The Very Food Book*, 1987–8), gave lavish banquets as works in themselves and made videos. Confident in her potential as an individual and an artist, she drew attention to a perspective expanded beyond the traditional roles defined for women in society.

BIBLIOGRAPHY

The British Show (exh. cat., Sydney, A.G. NSW, 1985)

Silvia Ziranek (exh. cat. by J. Walwin, London, Anthony Reynolds Gal., 1986)

Ici Villa Moi (exh. cat. by L. Buck, London, Waterman F.A., 1989–90)

□

Zirid. Muslim dynasty that ruled in parts of North Africa and Spain between AD 972 and 1152. The founder of the dynasty, Ziri ibn Manad (*d* 972), was a Sanhaja Berber in the service of the Fatimid caliphs, who ruled from Tunisia. In 936 Ziri founded Ashir, the family seat, in the Titeri Mountains 170 km south of Algiers. His son Buluggin (*reg* 972–84) was appointed governor of North Africa when the Fatimids left Kairouan for Cairo. Under Buluggin, his son al-Mansur (*reg* 984–96) and his grandson Badis (*reg* 996–1016), the Zirids greatly enlarged their territory, expanding into northern Morocco, where they came in conflict with the Umayyads of Spain. By 1015 the Zirid domain had become too large to be governed from Kairouan alone: the Zirids retained control of the eastern half, while the western portion was granted to Buluggin's son Hammad (*reg* 1015–28), who established his capital at the Qal'at Bani Hammad to the east of Ashir. In 1048 the Zirid al-Mu'izz ibn Badis (*reg* 1016–62) renounced the authority of the Fatimids, who were Shi'ites, for that of the orthodox Abbasid caliphs of Baghdad. In retaliation, the Fatimids encouraged tribes of bedouin nomads to move from Upper Egypt into the region, which they proceeded to devastate. The Zirids retreated from Kairouan to Mahdia on the coast, which they defended against naval attack from the Normans of Sicily until 1148. The Hammadid branch, which in 1067 had relocated to Bejaïa (Bougie), lasted until 1152. A third branch of the Zirid family established itself in Spain when Zawi, another son of Ziri, emigrated to Spain to serve with his followers in the Berber army of 'Abd al-Malik ibn Abi 'Amir, *de facto* ruler of Spain from 1002 to 1008, during the last years of the Umayyad caliphate. As Umayyad power collapsed, Zawi received the province of Elvira and established himself in 1012 at Granada, where he began to act as an independent ruler. The Zirids expanded their domains in south-east Spain until the area came under the control of the Almoravid dynasty in 1090.

The Zirids were active patrons of architecture and the arts. The ruins of the palace of Ziri at Ashir suggest that it was modelled on an early Fatimid palace at Mahdia; the extensive ruins of the palaces at the QAL'AT BANI HAMMAD show similarities with the architecture of the Fatimids in Egypt and of the Normans in Sicily (*see* ISLAMIC ART, §II, 5(ii)). Several buildings in Granada (*see* GRANADA, §I, 1) can be ascribed to the Zirids, including a palace (1052–6) on the site of the Alhambra erected by Yusuf ibn Naghrallah, the Zirid's Jewish vizier. The memory of this splendid palace, described by contemporary poets, is preserved by 12 white marble lions, reused in the 14th century for the central fountain in the Palace of the Lions. Zirid patrons also provided religious buildings with splendid furnishings: a carved wooden minbar (pulpit) was given in 980 by Buluggin to the mosque of the Andalusians in Fez. The most important example of Zirid woodwork is the magnificent *maqsura*, or enclosure for the ruler, that al-Mu'izz ibn Badis ordered for the congregational mosque at Kairouan. Heavily carved with arabesques and supporting grilles of turned spindles and spools, the whole is crowned with a foliated kufic inscription, outlined by a distinctively Zirid raised bead (*see* ISLAMIC ART, §VII, 1(iii)). The arts of the book also flourished under Zirid patronage. A splendid manuscript of the Koran (Kairouan, Mus. A. Islam, Tunis, Mus. N. Bardo and Nat. Lib.) was copied and illuminated in 1020 by 'Ali ibn Ahmad al-Warraq for the nurse of al-Mu'izz ibn Badis, and the ruler himself was the author of an important treatise on the arts of the book.

Enc. Islam./1

BIBLIOGRAPHY

L. Golvin: *Le Magrib central à l'époque des Zirides: Recherches d'archéologie et d'histoire* (Paris, 1957)

H. R. Idris: *La Berbérie orientale sous les Zirides, Xe–XIIe siècles* (Paris, 1962)

M. Levy: 'Medieval Arabic Bookmaking and its Relation to Early Chemistry and Pharmacology' (trans. of al-Mu'izz ibn Bādīs, *'Umdat al-kuttāb wa-'uddat dhawī al-albāb* [Staff of the scribes and implements of the discerning]), *Trans. Amer. Philos. Soc.*, lv (1962), pp. 3–79
L. Golvin: *Recherches archéologiques à la Qal'a des Banū Hammâd* (Paris, 1965)
——: 'Le Palais de Zîrî à Achîr (dixième siècle J.C.)', *A. Orient.*, vi (1966), pp. 47–76

S. J. VERNOIT

Zisenis, Johann Georg. *See* ZIESENIS, JOHANN GEORG.

Zítek, Josef (*b* Prague, 4 April 1832; *d* Prague, 2 Aug 1909). Bohemian architect and teacher. He entered the Prague Polytechnic in 1848 but shortly afterwards went to Vienna, where he trained as a bricklayer and studied at the Polytechnikum and the Akademie der Bildenden Künste. His teachers were Karl Rösner, Eduard Van der Nüll and August Siccard von Siccardsburg. After completing his studies he worked in Prague for the architect Josef Ondřej Kranner (1801–71). Kranner influenced Zítek's first designs, which were inspired to a large extent by medieval art; they included a scheme for a large parish church (1857), the Greek Orthodox church in Czanalos, Hungary, and the church (1859) in Rakové, Slovakia. Between 1857 and 1858 he worked in Vienna in the studio of van der Nüll & Siccardsburg on competition entries for the Czech Savings Bank, Prague, and the university and Stock Exchange, Vienna. In 1858 he went to Italy to study the buildings of antiquity and the Renaissance, which influenced his later work.

In 1860 Zítek returned to Vienna, where he took over van der Nüll's teaching post at the Akademie. He also worked on designs for the Viennese Opera House in Vienna and produced some minor works in what became Czechoslovakia. He received a grant for further travel in 1862, when he visited Germany, Belgium and France, returning again to Vienna. There he designed the restoration (1860–70) of Bečov Castle near Karlovy Vary for Duke Alfred Beaufort-Spontini and a mansion and brewery (1862–3) in Petrohrad, western Bohemia, for Count Eugen Černín. At the same time he was in charge of the construction (1861–8) of a new ducal museum (now Landesmus.) in Weimar, which he was commissioned to design after meeting the German painter Friedrich Preller in Rome. Work on this building was largely supervised by Karl Martin von Stegmann, however, as Zítek refused to stay in Weimar and did not accept the professorship offered to him in Dresden, instead moving back to Vienna and acquiring a licence to practise as a builder there, although he never took up permanent residence in the city.

In 1866 Zítek won the competition for the Czech National Theatre in Prague (*see* PRAGUE, fig. 5). His Renaissance Revival design was well received by Nüll and Siccardsburg, the architects of the Opera House in Vienna, and it became a symbol of Czech nationalism. Zítek also worked on other important buildings, including the Mill Spring colonnade (begun 1871), Karlovy Vary, and the Rudolphinum (1875–84), a multi-purpose cultural building in Prague. The latter, in a similar style to the National Theatre, was designed in collaboration with his pupil JOSEF SCHULZ. The National Theatre itself was completed in 1881, but it was destroyed by fire in the same year. After the fire Zítek was required to approve changes to the project that he found unacceptable. He refused to produce new plans and subsequently went abroad, leaving Schulz to continue work on the reconstruction of the theatre (1881–3). After the 1890s Zítek lived in seclusion on an estate in Lčovice that belonged to his wife, Berta Lippert, and ceased his design activities. He visited Prague only to give lectures at the polytechnic, where he continued to teach until 1904. He also acted as an architectural consultant and was a member of the Union for the Completion of St Vitus's Cathedral in Prague. Towards the end of his life he returned to the National Theatre and helped to put the finishing touches to the decoration of the façade. In 1908 he received a barony from the Emperor for his achievements. Zítek was one of the most important Czech architects of the 19th century, carrying out his best work during a period of economic and cultural prosperity in Prague (1860–90). Although he was influenced by the Italian Renaissance, particularly by Palladio and Venetian architecture, he did not copy these models but reshaped them freely, with a strong sense of the proportions of a building, both in its entirety and its detail. His architecture was rooted in the intellectual background of the city of Prague, and it exemplified the Czech Renaissance Revival style.

BIBLIOGRAPHY
P. Janák: 'Josef Zítek: Budovatel Národního divadla' [Josef Zítek: builder of the National Theatre], *Lidové noviny* (3 April 1932)
A. Kubíček: *Architekt Josef Zítek* (Prague, 1932)
O. Stefan: 'Josef Zítek', *Národní listy* (3 April 1932)
J. Stibral: 'Josef Zítek, 1832–1909', *Architekt*, xxxi (1932), pp. 58–61
Z. Wirth: 'Josef Zítek', *Styl*, xvii (1932)
E. Krtilová: *Architekt Josef Zítek* (Prague, 1954)
Z. Dvořáková: *Josef Zítek* (Prague, 1983)

YVONNE JANKOVÁ

Zitterbarth. Hungarian family of architects. They were active in Pest (now Budapest) from the late 18th century to the second half of the 19th. Their exact relationship to each other is not established in all cases. The earliest known members are János I (*b* Pest, 8 July 1776; *d* Pest, 26 Oct 1824) and Mátyás I (*fl c.* 1789–1803). The latter had a son, Mátyás II (*fl c.* 1804–18). Like their forebears, Henrik (*b* Pest, 1822) and János II (*b* Pest, 1826; *d* Budapest, 1882) studied in Vienna and built mostly residential blocks in Budapest. The large Rundbogenstil synagogue (1864–71) at Kecskemet is the work of the latter. The outstanding member of the family was Mátyás Zitterbarth III (*b* Pest, 12 July 1803; *d* Pest, 14 Nov 1867), who spent some time in Vienna and probably also in Germany or Italy. He built a great number of residential blocks for the citizens of Pest in a somewhat restrained Neo-classical style. The main wing (1838–41) of Pest County Hall, his most notable work, has a slightly projecting Corinthian portico that effectively conceals the depth of the recess behind the columns. The Hungarian Theatre (1835–7), Pest, later known as the National Theatre (destr. 1913), was a simple square block with a *porte-cochère* on the front. The Evangelical church (1822–30) at Péteri is an axial hall; its west façade has four Corinthian columns, a lunette and a squat tower surmounted by a lantern.

BIBLIOGRAPHY
A. Zádor and J. Rados: *A klasszicizmus épitészete Magyarországon* [The architecture of Neo-classicism in Hungary] (Budapest, 1943), pp. 130–37
D. Komárik: 'Épitészképzés és mesterfelvétel a XIX.században: Pesti mesterek és mesterjelöltek' [The training of architects and the admission of master builders into the guilds in the 19th century: master builders and candidates in Pest], *Epités- & Epitészettudomány*, iii (1972), pp. 417–18

JÓZSEF SISA

Ziviyya. *See* ZIWIYEH.

Ziwiyeh [Pers. Zīviyya]. Site in Iranian Kurdistan, 33 km east of Saqqiz, where a collection of gold, silver, ivory and other objects, probably mostly of the 8th century BC, was discovered in 1947. The first study of this 'Ziwiyeh Treasure' was published by André Godard in 1951, but for nearly 30 years Ziwiyeh was mostly left to the mercy of commercial diggers and antique dealers. The number of objects attributed to the treasure in collections around the world has gradually grown; in 1973 Roman Ghirshman listed 341 objects in the Tehran Archaeological Museum alone. Many objects are undoubtedly forgeries, and others, although genuine antiquities, were discovered elsewhere but attributed to Ziwiyeh in order to enhance their commercial value. This led to criticism (see Muscarella) of the uncritical acceptance by academics of objects attributed to Ziwiyeh.

Before 1976 Ziwiyeh was briefly surveyed and excavated by Robert Dyson, Cuyler Young and Stuart Swiny. During 1976–8 more detailed excavations were directed by N. Motamedi of the Iranian Centre for Archaeological Research, concentrating on the extensive Iron Age cemetery around the modern village of Ziwiyeh, and the fortress on the hill overlooking the village, the source of the original treasure. No residential settlement was found, although this may lie under the modern village. From the cemetery came a large quantity of grave goods, including pottery vessels, bronze objects such as pins, and a few weapons. The fortress is a substantial structure. The walls, built of large mud-bricks and faced with a thick white plaster, stand over 13 m high. Within them several rooms were excavated, including one complex of at least three storeys, tentatively identified as an armoury, containing several hundred iron arrowheads found in the ruins of the ground floor among the crushed remnants of the pots that must have held them. Other objects recovered included several ivories, shaped glazed tiles, worked stone and part of a splendid lapis lazuli or 'Egyptian blue' dish (Tehran, Archaeol. Mus.; see fig.).

Those objects most likely to have come from Ziwiyeh exhibit a considerable variety of artistic styles and motifs, including those of the neighbouring empires of Urartu and Assyria (*see* URARTIAN and ASSYRIAN), in addition to those labelled by scholars as Mannaean, Iranian and even Scythian. The overall style is best described as 'Zagros art', which flourished *c.* 1500–600 BC and is characterized by a free-flowing, somewhat zoomorphic style. The LURISTAN bronzes represent one facet of this art, MARLIK another; and to these should be added Ziwiyeh and HASANLU. Iconography depended largely on the materials used and on local traditions and tastes. Thus the ivory objects (e.g. in Tehran, Archaeol. Mus.) can be divided into three groups. Most are imperial Assyrian, including ritual, hunting and ceremonial scenes. A Urartian group includes ivories used for inlay (e.g. rosette panels). A third (local) group to some extent copies Assyrian and Urartian motifs but utilizes non-Assyrian and non-Urartian styles. Significantly, this local style bears no relationship to 'Iranian' (i.e. local) ivories found at Hasanlu. The metal objects from Ziwiyeh are even more eclectic. Sheet metal is easier to work than ivory, and motifs could therefore be more intricate and imaginative: Assyrian motifs include sacred trees, genii, bulls, lions and palmettes; Urartian motifs include animal processions; ANIMAL STYLE motifs include couchant animals and birds of prey with large beaks. It is not the individual motifs *per se* that characterize the art of Ziwiyeh but the admixture of these motifs. This sometimes occurs all on one object, as on the various gold pectorals and epaulettes (e.g. New York, Met.; Tehran, Archaeol. Mus.) that are said to come from the site.

See also IRAN, ANCIENT.

BIBLIOGRAPHY
A. Godard: *Les Trésors de Zewiyè, Kurdistan* (Haarlem, 1950)
O. W. Muscarella: '"Ziwiye" and Ziwiye: The Forgery of a Provenence', *J. Field Archaeol.*, iv (1977), pp. 197–219
R. Ghirshman: *Tombe princière de Ziwiyé et le début de l'art animalier scythe* (Paris, 1979)
M. F. Charlesworth: 'An Ivory Plaque from Ziwiye', *Surv. & Excav.*, iii (1980), pp. 31–2
R. Keykhosravi: *Ganj-i Zaviya* [The Ziwiyeh treasure] (Tehran, 1984)

M. F. CHARLESWORTH

Ziya. *See* GÜRAN, NAZMI ZIYA.

Žmuidzinavičius, Antanas [Zhmuydzinavichyus, Antanas (Ionasovich)] (*b* Seiriai, Seinai region, 31 Oct 1876; *d* Kaunas, 9 Aug 1966). Lithuanian painter, administrator and writer. He qualified as a drawing teacher at the St Petersburg Academy of Arts and taught at the Warsaw Commercial College (1899–1905) while continuing his studies. He also studied in Paris (from 1905), Munich (1908–9) and Hamburg (1912). During a short stay in Vilnius in 1906–7 he became close to Petras Rimša and Mikalojus Čiurlionis, founding the Lithuanian Art Society, which combined two trends in Lithuanian art: realist

Ziwiyeh, dish fragment, lapis lazuli or 'Egyptian blue', h. 62 mm, ?8th century BC (Tehran, Archaeological Museum)

(Žmuidzinavičius, Petras Kalpokas, Rimša) and Symbolist (Čiurlionis). He was the initiator of the first Lithuanian Art Exhibition, held in Vilnius in 1907, at which he showed 35 paintings, among them *Peasant Kitchen* (1905; Kaunas, A. Žmuidzinavičius Mem. Mus.). During these years Žmuidzinavičius was influenced by the work of the Symbolists, as evident in *Horseman* (1910–12; Kaunas, A. Žmuidzinavičius Mem. Mus.). His essays on art were published in periodicals and newspapers in Vilnius, Kaunas and Warsaw in the first two decades of the 20th century. He maintained contact with Lithuanian emigrés in the USA, which he visited in 1908–9 and 1922–4, organizing exhibitions of his works there. In the 1910s he mainly painted landscapes, such as the *Last Ray* (1913; Vilnius, Lith. State A. Mus.), taken from life and representing a restrained form of realism. In 1918 he set up the Realists group at Kaunas Art School in opposition to the new art group, Ars. From 1926 to 1940 he taught at the Kaunas Art School. In the 1920s, 1930s and 1940s he produced numerous landscapes in which he adjusted his approach to conform to Socialist Realism, which was adopted in Lithuania for political more than for artistic reasons. He was a collector of Lithuanian art, and in 1961 a museum of his works and collection was opened in his house in Kaunas.

WRITINGS
Palete ir gyvenimas [An attic and life] (Vilnius, 1961)

BIBLIOGRAPHY
Antanas Ionasovich Zhmuydzinavichyus (exh. cat., Moscow, 1951)
I. Borisova: *Antanas Ionasovich Zhmuydzinavichyus* (Moscow, 1953)
A. Zhmuydzinavichyus (exh. cat., Kaunas, 1966)
A. Savitskas: 'Antanas Zhmuydzinavichyus: K 100-letiyu so dnya rozhdeniya' [Antanas Žmuidzinavičius: on the centenary of his birth], *Iskusstvo* (1977), no. 4, pp. 34–41

SERGEY KUZNETSOV

Zoan [Giovanni] Andrea (*fl c.* 1475–?1519). Italian engraver and painter. A painter named Zoan Andrea is recorded in a letter of September 1475 written to Ludovico II Gonzaga, 2nd Marchese of Mantua, by Simone Ardizoni da Reggio, a painter and engraver. Simone claimed that he and Zoan Andrea had been brutally assaulted on the orders of Andrea Mantegna. Mantegna was enraged to hear that the two had remade some of his prints. Their exact crime is not clear, but it has been suggested that they had re-engraved Mantegna's original plates. Given this connection with Mantegna's circle of engravers, it is likely that Zoan Andrea can be identified with the anonymous artist who signed himself ZA on 20 engravings, the earliest of which show a strong dependence on Mantegna, both in technique and composition. The three monogrammed engravings closest to Mantegna are of *Hercules and Deianira* (B. 2509.005), *Judith and Holofernes* (B. 2509.001) and an *Ornamental Panel* (B. 2509.045), in all of which cross-hatching is used extensively.

Later in his career, Zoan Andrea must have moved to Milan, since engravings signed ZA are based on drawings by Leonardo and his Milanese pupils, for example a *Portrait Bust of a Lady* (B. 2509.026). In Milan he met the illuminator and engraver Giovanni Pietro Birago, after whose drawings he made engravings for three in a series of twelve decorative panels, one of which bears his monogram.

A signed engraving dated 1505 of the *Virgin and Child on a Grassy Bank* (B. 2509.030) belongs to a group of five that Zoan copied from prints by Dürer. However, he does not appear to have been influenced by Dürer; his late style is characterized by an unusual combination of strong outlines and delicate cross-hatched shading. Typical of this period are several engravings of secular subjects, in some cases openly erotic, such as the *Two Lovers* (B. 2509.022), in which the painstaking reproduction of moiré fabric is particularly striking.

If it is true that Zoan Andrea is the author of an engraving of the *Emperor Charles V* (B. 2509.028), his career must have lasted at least until 1519, the date of the Emperor's accession. None of the engravers active in Venice who signed themselves ZA or *ia* (in Gothic letters) can be identified with Zoan Andrea. The attribution of some drawings in the style of Mantegna to Zoan Andrea is conjectural. Despite the fact that he was called a painter in 1475, no paintings have been attributed to him.

BIBLIOGRAPHY
V. Massena, Prince d'Essling-C. Ephrussi: 'Zoan Andrea et ses homonymes', *Gaz. B.-A.*, n.s. 3, v (1891), pp. 401–15; vi (1891), pp. 225–44
P. Kristeller: *Andrea Mantegna* (Berlin, 1902), pp. 530, 534 [doc.]
J. Byam Shaw: 'A Group of Mantegnesque Drawings, and their Relation to the Engravings of Mantegna's School', *Old Master Drgs*, xliv (1937), pp. 57–60
A. M. Hind: *Early Italian Engraving*, v (London, 1948)
L. Donati: 'Del mito di Zoan Andrea e di altri miti grandi e piccoli', *Amor Libro*, vi (1958), pp. 3–12, 97–102, 147–54, 231–6; vii (1959), pp. 39–44, 84–8, 163–8
H. Gollob: 'Ein Beitrag zur Zoan Andrea-Frage', *Gutenberg Jb.*, xxxiv (1959), pp. 165–70
K. Oberhuber: 'Neuentdeckungen', *Albertina Inf.*, iv (1970), p. 6
J. Levenson, K. Oberhuber and J. Sheehan: *Early Italian Engravings from the National Gallery of Art* (Washington, DC, 1973), pp. 265–71, 274
M. J. Zucker: *Early Italian Masters, Commentary (1984)*, 25 [XIII/ii] of *The Illustrated Bartsch*, ed. W. Strauss (New York, 1978–), pp. 255–303 [B.]

MARCO COLLARETA

Zóbel, Fernando (*b* Manila, 27 Aug 1924; *d* Rome, 2 June 1984). Spanish painter, printmaker and collector of Philippine birth. He was born into a wealthy family and was never in financial need, which allowed him to devote himself to painting without suffering any kind of setback. He had a cosmopolitan education, graduating in philosophy and arts and completing his degree with a thesis on the theatre of Federico Garcia Lorca at Harvard University, Cambridge, MA, in 1949. While living there he met painters from the Boston area, notably Reed Champion Pfeufer and Hyman Bloom, and began to paint under the influence of their symbolic and romantic expressionism, which was superficially similar to Abstract Expressionism. At this time he tried out a variety of printmaking processes including etching, wood-engraving and woodcut.

In 1951 Zóbel returned to Manila, holding his first one-man exhibition there at the Philippine Art Gallery in 1952: the works he showed were representational paintings of Philippine customs. During 1954 and 1955, when he began to divide his time between Manila and Madrid, he underwent a deep crisis that led him to question his position as a painter. An exhibition of the work of Mark Rothko (Providence, RI Sch. Des., Mus. A., 1954), together with his discovery of photography as an impetus for painting, led him to abandon figuration for abstraction and to represent movement by means of extremely fine lines of colour, the subject of a series of paintings entitled *Arrows*. His first one-man exhibition of abstract paintings, at the Philippine Art Gallery in Manila, took place in 1956, the year in which he began to teach history of art at the university. In 1958, after producing the first of his *Black Series* (1957–63), in which he transformed chromatic contrasts into black and white, he carried out archaeological excavations that awoke his interest in Asian art. The end of the series was marked by works such as *Ornithopterus* (1962; Cuenca, Mus. A. Abstracto Esp.).

During his periodic visits to Spain, Zóbel began collecting the work of Spanish abstract painters and in 1959 held his first one-man exhibition of abstract paintings in Madrid at the Galería Biosca. In Madrid, where he settled permanently in 1961, he discovered the work of young Spanish avant-garde painters and made friends with Gerardo Rueda (*b* 1926), Luis Feito, Guillermo Delgado (*b* 1926), Antonio Lorenzo (*b* 1929), Martín Chirino, Antonio Saura, Eusebio Sempere and Gustavo Torner. His collection of paintings, displayed in the Casas Colgadas in Cuenca, was opened in 1966 as the Museo de Arte Abstracto Español. The entire museum, of which he served as Director, was donated by him to the Fundación Juan March in 1980.

From 1963 to 1975 Zóbel again worked with colour, exploring a variety of subjects including abstract paintings based on landscapes of Cuenca and Seville (e.g. the *River Júcar XII*, 1971; Seville, Mus. A. Contemp.), works based on images by other painters, and 'anatomies', abstract images suggested by the human body by its colour, its movements and its possibilities as a dimension of landscape. From 1975 to 1978 he painted a second series of monochrome paintings, the *White Series*, dominated by a range of light greys. In 1978 he began painting again in colour, for example in the *Riverbanks* series of 1980, variations on the movement of water. After a trip to the Philippines in 1980, during which he suffered a stroke, he returned to Spain and went through a period of depression that affected his painting. His subsequent work was mainly photographic, returning to the theme of the River Júcar and its shoreline in the vicinity of Cuenca. In 1981 he published a second book of photographs, of the Júcar at Cuenca (his first book of photographs, also of Cuenca, had appeared in 1975), and also made collages of photographs.

Throughout his life Zóbel remained dedicated to a cerebral method, slowly elaborating each of his pictures by means of a traditional step-by-step process, with notes leading to a drawing, in turn to an oil sketch and eventually to the final painting. He consistently used photographs for reference, seeing them as yet another way of sketching nature, and sought to filter spontaneity through a rigorous self-discipline so as to leave a raw impression of a sensation recalled in memory. His calm and ordered paintings convey an understanding of beauty as delicacy, purity and the elimination of everything superfluous. In 1983 Zóbel was awarded the Gold Medal for Merit in the Fine Arts by the Spanish Ministry of Culture.

BIBLIOGRAPHY

A. R. Luz: *Sketchbooks, Fernando Zóbel* (Manila, 1954)
A. Magaz Sangro: *Zóbel: Pinturas y dibujos* (Madrid, 1959)
A. Lorenzo: *Zóbel: Dibujos* (Madrid, 1963)
M. Hernández: *Fernando Zóbel: El misterio de lo transparente* (Madrid, 1977)
P. Ortuño: *Diálogos con la pintura de Fernando Zóbel* (Madrid, 1978)
R. Pérez-Madero: *Zóbel: La serie blanca* (Madrid, 1978)
Zóbel (exh. cat. by F. Calvo Serraller, Madrid, Fund. Juan March, 1984)

PILAR BENITO

Zoboli, Giacomo (*b* Modena, 23 May 1681; *d* Rome, 22 Feb 1767). Italian painter. He was a pupil in Modena of Francesco Stringa, a native of the city, with whom Zoboli was to work in 1708 on a number of wall paintings (destr.) in the Palazzo Ducale in Modena. After Stringa's death in 1709, Zoboli moved to Bologna, to the workshop of Giovanni Gioseffo dal Sole, where he remained until 1715, dividing his time between his apprenticeship and the creation of a number of canvases for clients in Modena. In 1714 he executed his first documented work, an altarpiece of the *Virgin and Child amidst Angels Being Worshipped by SS Geminian and Antony*, for the confraternity of S Maria degli Angeli at Spilamberto. In the spring of 1715 Zoboli moved to Rome, where, ten years later, he became a member of the Accademia di S Luca. In Rome he carried out a number of important commissions for the Jesuits, the King of Portugal and the Polish court, while painting several canvases for churches and private families in Modena. The paintings created during the period of Zoboli's maturity (from the 1720s to the late 1740s) can be divided into two distinct categories. The first comprises commissions of a religious nature, including altarpieces that show clear links with the painting of Carlo Maratti and the works of Emilian artists active in Rome during the previous century, including Reni, Francesco Albani and Domenichino. The second category contains works of extraordinary modernity, which were created for a sophisticated clientele who commissioned numerous versions of the *Death of Caesar* and the *Death of Pompey*. The latter works anticipate the doctrines of Neo-classicism (the first version of the *Death of Caesar* dates from 1724) and reveal an awareness of the style of portraiture practised by Pompeo Batoni.

BIBLIOGRAPHY

Bénézit; Bolaffi; Thieme–Becker
V. Casale: 'I quadri di canonizzazione: Lazzaro Baldi, Giacomo Zoboli . . .', *Paragone*, xxxiii/389 (1982), pp. 33–61
M. B. Guerrieri Borsoi: *Disegni di Giacomo Zoboli* (Rome, 1984)
E. Negro: 'Giacomo Zoboli: Contributi all'opera', *Il Carrobbio*, xii (1986), pp. 249–56

EMILIO NEGRO

Zocchi, Giuseppe (*b* nr Florence, 1711 or 1717; *d* Florence, May 1767). Italian painter and printmaker. He began his training in Florence. The Marchese Andrea Gerini took him under his protection from an early age, sending him to Rome, Bologna, Milan and Venice to continue his studies. In Venice Zocchi saw engravings of views by Michele Marieschi and Bernardo Bellotto and painted a small oval portrait of *Andrea Gerini and Antonio Maria Zanetti* (1750 or 1751; Venice, Correr). Zanetti was a Venetian connoisseur and a friend of Gerini.

Zocchi is especially noted for two series of etched views of Florence and its environs: *Scelta di XXIV vedute delle principali contrade, piazze, chiese e palazzi della città di Firenze* and *Vedute delle ville e d'altri luoghi della Toscana*

(Florence, 1744). Commissioned by the Marchese Gerini to provide visitors to Florence with a memento of their stay, they were both reissued in 1754, and the *Vedute delle ville* again in 1757. Zocchi's preparatory drawings for both volumes have survived (New York, Pierpont Morgan Lib.). *Vedute delle ville* contains 50 views. Zocchi etched many of the figures but only two of the plates. The rest were executed by 22 different engravers, including Piranesi and Marieschi. The views are not merely topographical documents; they are enlivened with charming anecdotal scenes of human activity. A humorous note runs throughout the series, for example the windy weather blowing various figures' hats through the air in the view of *Villa I Collazzi*. Many of the landscape views are reminiscent of the work of Giovanni Paolo Panini.

From 1754 to 1760 Zocchi was employed as 'pittore' by the Opificio delle Pietre Dure in Florence. His task was to furnish the factory workshop with paintings that were then transferred into so-called Florentine mosaic. In this he collaborated closely with the French goldsmith and engraver of precious stones, Louis Siriès, director of the Pietre Dure workshop from 1748. The two men inaugurated a change of artistic direction by replacing the traditional decorative designs of flowers and grotesques on a black background with scenes incorporating architectural exteriors and interiors, landscapes and human figures. One of their most prestigious commissions was that from Francis of Habsburg-Lorraine, Grand Duke of Tuscany. Between 1750 and 1762 Zocchi executed several series of paintings to serve as models for this commission (67 extant, Florence, Mus. Opificio Pietre Dure). The finished mosaics were destined for the imperial residence in Vienna (58 extant, Vienna, Hofburg-Schauräume). They include various allegories of the elements, the senses, the ages of man and the triumphs of the continents; also scenes of stag hunts, landscapes with soldiers, popular games, views of the port of Livorno and decorative depictions of flowers, shells and butterflies.

Zocchi was active as a fresco painter and executed biblical scenes (1751) for the Archbishop's Chapel, Pisa, and decorations (1756–66) for the Palazzo Rinuccini and for the Palazzo Gerini, both in Florence. He was also active as a book illustrator (e.g. Virgil's *Aeneid*, trans. Annibal Caro, Paris, 1760).

PRINTS
Scelta di XXIV vedute delle principali contrade, piazze, chiese e palazzi della città di Firenze (Florence, 1744)
Vedute delle ville e d'altri luoghi della Toscana (Florence, 1744, 1754, 1757; intro. H. Acton, Milan, 1981; ed. R. M. Mason, Florence, 1981)
Views of Florence and Tuscany by Giuseppe Zocchi (exh. cat. by E. E. Dee, Washington, DC, Int. Exh. Found., 1968)

BIBLIOGRAPHY
M. Gregori: 'Vedutismo fiorentino: Zocchi e Bellotto', *Not. Pal. Albani*, xii/1–2 (1983), pp. 242–50
F. Rossi: 'Giuseppe Zocchi et l'opificio delle Pietre Dure', *Ant. Viva*, xxviii (1989), pp. 50–56
S. Meloni Trkulja: 'Giuseppe Zocchi', *La pittura in Italia: Il settecento*, ed. G. Briganti, 2 vols (Milan, 1989, rev. 1990), ii, pp. 904–5 [with bibliog.]

Zocha. German family of architects. Johann Wilhelm von Zocha (*b* Gunzenhausen, 29 March 1680; *d* Lyon, 26 Dec 1718) succeeded Gabriel de' Gabrieli as Director of Works at Ansbach in 1715 and continued the construction of the Residenzschloss. After his untimely death during a journey to Paris, his brother Karl Friedrich von Zocha (*b* Gunzenhausen, 1 July 1683; *d* Ansbach, 24 July 1749) was appointed to the position. Karl Friedrich had studied at the universities of Giessen, Halle and Leiden. He also spent time in Paris and was associated with the office of Robert de Cotte. He continued the Residenz and designed two façades (1726) in an understated classicism and some interiors. His most important existing work at Ansbach is the Orangery (1726–7). The south façade has 29 bays with a continuous order of pilasters and large round-headed windows similar to the Grand Trianon at Versailles. The north façade has two colonnades of nine bays between the central and corner pavilions, designed as a variation on Claude Perrault's east façade of the Louvre. The interiors are largely by Leopoldo Retti. Karl Friedrich's domestic architecture includes some houses at Ansbach and the addition of new wings to the Schlösser at Rügland (1713) and Eyrichshof (1735–46). A number of parish churches in Brandenburg-Ansbach were built to his designs and follow a Protestant austerity in architecture and decoration. Distinctly different from those in the neighbouring Catholic states, they are rectangular, sometimes transverse, halls with coved flat ceilings, galleries, and—according to Protestant custom—a superimposed arrangement of altar, pulpit and organ. Examples include the churches at Wald (1722) and Lahm (1728–32). After LEOPOLDO RETTI arrived in Ansbach (1732), Zocha cut back his architectural practice. His plain, French-influenced style was continued in the principality by his erstwhile assistant Johann David Steingruber (1702–87).

BIBLIOGRAPHY
G. Schumann: *Ansbacher Bibliotheken vom Mittelalter bis 1806* (diss., Erlangen, 1947), pp. 146ff [incl. Karl Friedrich von Zocha's library cat.; auctioned 1752]
H. Braun: 'Ansbacher Spätbarock, 1695–1791', *Jb. Fränk. Landesforsch.*, xvi (1956), pp. 455–91
W. Baumann: 'Die Orangerie zu Ansbach', *Jb. Hist. Ver. Mittelfranken*, lxxix (1961)
V. Mayr: 'The Palace Gardens of the Margraves of Ansbach', *J. Gdn Hist.*, 4 (1985), pp. 336–49
K. Raschzok: *Lutherischer Kirchenbau im Zeitalter des Absolutismus: Dargestellt am Beispiel des Markgrafentums Brandenburg-Ansbach* (Frankfurt am Main, 1988)

JARL KREMEIER

Zocher, Jan David [the younger] (*b* Haarlem, 12 Feb 1791; *d* Haarlem, 8 July 1870). Dutch architect, urban planner and landscape designer. He was the most illustrious member of a family of architects and landscape gardeners. He and his brother, Karel George Zocher (1796–1864), were both trained by their father, Jan David Zocher the elder (*d* 1817), and he in turn introduced his son, Louis Paul Zocher (1820–1915), to the practice. Zocher the younger's career was a microcosm of developments in 19th-century design. As a landscape architect he was dedicated to the Picturesque and introduced the English garden style into the Netherlands. His buildings, however, were the purest examples on Dutch soil of Romantic Classicism, a style that had relatively little impact there.

In 1809 Louis Bonaparte, King of Holland, granted Zocher a bursary and in 1811 sent him to study at the Ecole des Beaux-Arts in Paris under Louis-Hippolyte

Lebas. After completing his training Zocher toured France, Italy, Switzerland and England. This contact with current architectural trends abroad enabled him to break with the Palladian tradition that had prevailed in the Netherlands since the mid-17th century. Zocher returned to the Netherlands in 1817 to succeed his father as landscape architect to William I, King of the Netherlands. He soon received numerous private and public commissions for parks and gardens and often for accompanying villas and outbuildings. Dutch cities such as Haarlem, Utrecht and Amersfoort were expanding again, and Zocher transformed their former ramparts into landscaped areas. His extension plan for Utrecht, for example, which was carried out in part from 1830 to the 1860s, included a green belt around the city to the south and east; it also included blocks of houses, some of which were executed. Unfortunately much of Zocher's work is known only from surviving plans. In 1864 Zocher and his son, Louis Paul, designed a large park to the south and west of central Amsterdam, with foot- and bridle paths, lakes, gardens and a music pavilion. Later known as the Vondelpark, it still retains some of its original picturesque charm. Other important commissions included the reshaping of the forested Haarlemmer Hout Park south of the city and the design of Frederiks Park, the central Kenau Park and Flora Park in Haarlem.

The playful informality of Zocher's landscape designs contrasted sharply with the classical severity of his architecture, which was based not on the Italian and French Renaissance, as earlier Dutch classicizing buildings had been, but on ancient Greece and Rome as mediated by the romantic visions of French, German and English 'revolutionary' architects. Boschlust (c. 1835; destr. 1890s), The Hague, was a superb example of Zocher's villa style. Its clear geometric forms and Greek orders showed his acquaintance with French and British domestic architecture of the early 19th century: Doric columns formed a loggia that stretched between projecting, flat-topped end pavilions articulated by a colossal Ionic order.

Zocher's most monumental design was for the second Amsterdam Exchange building, a commission he received after a competition underwritten by the city in 1835 ended in confusion. Construction began in 1841, but was executed by the municipal architect C. W. M. Klijn (1788–1860), and soon after completion in 1845 the building was criticized on functional and structural grounds. It was also an alien visual presence on the Dam by virtue of its monochromatic masonry exterior and Greek detailing, but the composition was a masterful example of Romantic Classicism. Two low cubic wings flanked a taller block graced by a tetrastyle Ionic portico that led to a colonnade of free-standing Ionic columns. This in turn gave access to the stoa-like Exchange, whose open courtyard was subsequently roofed over. When the new Koopmansbeurs by H. P. Berlage was completed and occupied in 1903, however, Zocher's building was torn down. Despite his prolific activity, therefore, little remains of his work except drawings and photographs.

BIBLIOGRAPHY

Thieme–Becker
P. Klopfer: *Van Palladio bis Schinkel* (Esslingen, 1911)
G. Carelsen: 'Het Levenswerk der Zochers', *De Tijdspiegel* (1917), p. 205
C. C. S. Wilmer: *Utrecht getekend* [Utrecht in drawings] (The Hague, 1980) [cat. of drgs in the top. archv of the Municipality of Utrecht]
M. Beek: *Drie eeuwen Amsterdamse bouwkunst* (Amsterdam, 1984), pp. 107–9 [cat. of archit. drgs in the A. A. Kok Col., Amsterdam, Sticht. Ned. Inst. Archit. & Stedebouw]

HELEN SEARING

Zocolino, Matteo. *See* ZACCOLINI, MATTEO.

Zodiac, Signs of the. *See under* CALENDAR.

Zoffany [Zauffaly; Zauphaly; Zoffani]**, Johan (Joseph)** [Johannes Josephus; John] (*b* nr Frankfurt am Main, 13 March 1733; *d* Strand-on-the-Green, nr Kew, London, 11 Nov 1810). German painter, active in England. Born Johannes Josephus Zauffaly, he was the son of Anton Franz Zauffaly (1699–1771), Court Cabinetmaker and Architect in Regensburg to Alexander Ferdinand, Prince of Thurn and Taxis. After an apprenticeship in Regensburg under the painter and engraver Martin Speer (c. 1702–65), a pupil of Francesco Solimena, Zoffany left in 1750 for Rome, where he studied under the portrait painter Agostino Masucci and came into contact with Anton Raphael Mengs. By 1757 and after a second trip to Rome, Zoffany was commissioned by Clemens August, Prince-Archbishop and Elector of Trier, to produce frescoes and paintings for his new palace at Trier and the palace of Ehrenbreitstein at Koblenz. All Zoffany's early work at Ehrenbreitstein and Trier has been destroyed, but it may have been in the German Rococo manner of Cosmas Damian Asam and Johann Baptist Zimmermann. A number of small easel paintings such as *Venus Bringing Arms to Aeneas* (1759; Manchester, C.A.G.) survive to show his typical choice of portentous themes tempered by Rococo technique and pretty, pale colours. However, two large mythological works painted the following year, *Venus Marina* and *Venus and Adonis* (both Bordeaux, Mus. B.-A.), are impressive indications of Zoffany's ability at this early stage in his career. Although the compositions are not particularly successful, they are enterprising reinterpretations of popular themes. The earthy realism of some of the figures and the relatively dark tonality clearly indicate that Zoffany was capable of developing his hitherto decorative style of painting.

In the summer of 1760 Zoffany left for London with the intention of pursuing his career as a decorative painter there. He painted clockfaces for Stephen Rimbault before being taken on as a drapery painter by the portrait and theatrical painter BENJAMIN WILSON. During his brief spell in Wilson's studio, Zoffany seems to have discovered the genre, style and technique that were to remain with him for the rest of his life. Although a flourishing tradition of small-scale family conversation pieces did exist in Germany in the early 18th century, there is no evidence to suggest that Zoffany had contributed much to it himself. Instead he seems to have learnt about the genre from Wilson. At his best, Wilson produced lively, well-composed, dramatically lit works painted with a sensuous and creamy touch. Zoffany adopted and improved on this style, and his obvious skill attracted the attention of Wilson's patron, the actor-manager David Garrick (1717–79). Garrick commissioned Zoffany to paint several conversation pieces set in the grounds of his estate at

Hampton, as well as the first of what was to become a series of theatrical pictures. Although Zoffany's pastoral scenes at Hampton, including *Mr and Mrs Garrick by the Shakespeare Temple at Hampton* (1762; priv. col., see 1976 exh. cat., no. 12), have to make up in charm what they lack in perspective, they do possess a theatrical quality that must have appealed to Garrick. This reappears in all Zoffany's best multi-figure compositions. It was through work directly connected with the theatre that Zoffany was to make his name in England.

Garrick's career depended to a large degree on his success as a self-publicist, and before Zoffany he had employed such artists as Francis Hayman, Thomas Worlidge, Thomas Hudson and Wilson to bring his neat figure before an adoring public. Zoffany's theatrical scenes of the 1760s, such as *David Garrick and Mrs Bradshaw in 'The Farmer's Return'* (1762; priv. col., see 1976 exh. cat., no. 10) and *David Garrick in 'The Provok'd Wife'* (1763; exh. Society of Artists 1765; Wolverhampton, A.G.), are carefully symmetrical, and it is this formality, rather than the emphatic gestures and theatrical lighting, that distinguishes them from his domestic conversation pieces. The theatrical conversation pieces, shown at the Society of

Artists from 1762, were engraved in mezzotint and made Zoffany's reputation in England. Most of his theatre scenes are known in several versions; the variants seem to have been commissioned and produced after the appearance of the mezzotint taken from the original work. The first version, often the one owned by Garrick himself, is always the best, but there is no stylistic or documentary reason to doubt Zoffany's authorship of most of them. Garrick's lead was followed by others, and two of Zoffany's finest theatrical paintings were commissioned by his patron's great rival Samuel Foote (1720–77). The first of these, *Samuel Foote in 'The Mayor of Garratt'* (priv. col., see 1976 exh. cat., no. 23), was painted while Garrick was away on the Grand Tour.

Zoffany began to be noticed by the rich and powerful. He was able to produce very grand life-size portraits of his middle-class sitters, for example *Mrs Oswald* (*c.* 1765; London, N.G.), as well as informal conversation pieces for upper-class patrons, including the elaborate *John, 3rd Duke of Atholl, and his Family* (1765–7; priv. col., see 1976 exh. cat., no. 31), which contains nine figures. The Secretary of State John Stuart, 3rd Earl of Bute, commissioned Zoffany to paint portraits of his children, including

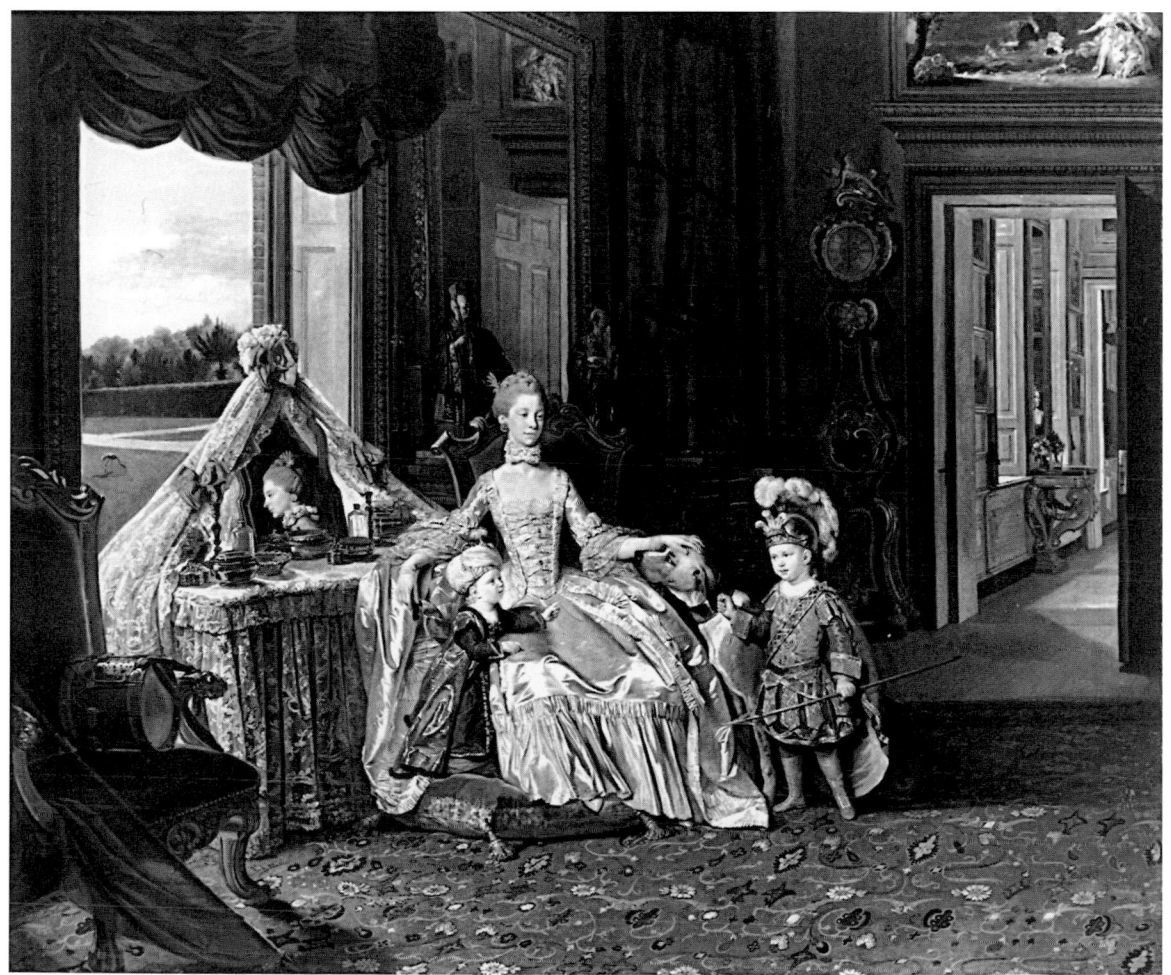

1. Johan Zoffany: *Queen Charlotte with her Two Eldest Sons*, oil on canvas, 1.12×1.29 m, 1764 (Windsor Castle, Berks, Royal Collection)

one of three of his sons and another of three of his daughters (both *c.* 1763–4; priv. col., see 1976 exh. cat., nos 20–21). Bute probably introduced the artist to George III and Queen Charlotte in 1763, and they too had him paint portraits of their children, *George, Prince of Wales, and Frederick, later Duke of York* and *Queen Charlotte with her Two Eldest Sons* (both 1764; Windsor Castle, Berks, Royal Col.; see fig. 1). In his royal portraits Zoffany amused himself and his patrons with informal but witty iconography rather than with images of regal splendour. The arrangement of pictures on the back wall in the portrait of Princes George and Frederick is partly imaginary, and Zoffany similarly altered fact to suit his pictorial fiction in many of his mature works.

In 1769 he had the singular honour of being nominated to the new Royal Academy by George III, who then commissioned a group portrait of its members, *Life Class at the Royal Academy* (1771–2; Windsor Castle, Berks, Royal Col.; see LONDON, fig. 42). All the members, apart from Thomas Gainsborough and George and Nathaniel Dance, are shown at the evening life class in the plaster academy in Old Somerset House. Following his tendency to manipulate and reorganize the content of his portraits, Zoffany first sketched the Royal Academicians individually and then placed them in the plaster academy rather than in the life room. The result is a multi-figured *tour de force* that encouraged the Queen to commission an even more elaborate work, the *Tribuna of the Uffizi* (1771–8; Windsor

2. Johan Zoffany: *Charles Townley's Library in Park Street*, oil on canvas, 1.27×0.99 m, 1781–3 (Burnley, Towneley Hall Art Gallery and Museum)

Castle, Berks, Royal Col.; *see* DISPLAY OF ART, fig. 3). Zoffany left for Florence in August 1772 in order to work on the picture and stayed away for seven years. The *Tribuna* shows an almost overwhelming display of the art treasures of the Grand Ducal collection brought together in fictive harmony under the admiring gaze of a group of English connoisseurs.

During his seven years on the Continent, Zoffany's stature and achievement as an artist increased greatly. He was elected an Academician at the Reale Accademia delle Belle Arti in Florence (1773), the Accademia Clementina in Bologna (1774), the Accademia Etrusca in Cortona (1776) and the Accademia di Belle Arti in Parma (1778). As well as his intermittent work on the *Tribuna*, Zoffany also produced several disturbing self-portraits (e.g. a half-length with hour-glass and skull, 1776; Florence, Uffizi), filled with melancholic imagery and showing a degree of self-analysis unexpected in the light of his previous work in Germany and England. He demonstrated his mastery not only of the informal group but also of the Baroque state portrait in a series of family portraits painted for the Grand Duke Leopold. The most elaborate of these (1776; Vienna, Ksthist. Mus.) was destined for the Grand Duke's mother, the Empress Maria Theresa, and when Zoffany presented this picture in Vienna in 1776, he was created a Baron of the Holy Roman Empire. In these years he also developed as a genre painter.

When he returned to England in 1779 with his masterpiece, the *Tribuna*, Zoffany discovered that the vogue for his work was over: conversation pieces were no longer required by his fashionable clients, and the market for portraits on a larger scale was rather too well supplied, with Gainsborough and Joshua Reynolds at the height of their powers and George Romney recently established after his return from Rome. Nevertheless, some of his best work was produced in the 1780s, including *Charles Townley's Library in Park Street* (1781–3; Burnley, Towneley Hall A.G. & Mus.; see fig. 2). This portrait shows Townley seated amid his impressive collection of antique sculpture. In order to show as much of the collection as possible, Zoffany depicted in one room what was actually spread over the whole of Townley's house and presented the portrait to Townley as a gift. In 1792 Townley acquired the Diskobolos, and in 1798 Zoffany added the figure of the discus thrower to the bottom left corner of the portrait. Another successful work from this period is the crowded *Sharp Family* (1779–81; priv. col., see 1976 exh. cat., no. 87) in which the 15 music-making sitters are arranged in a complex spiral in their barge on the Thames at Fulham.

By 1783 the difficulty of obtaining commissions led Zoffany to travel to India for patronage. An earlier, less essential, trip to the Antipodes with Captain Cook had been planned unsuccessfully in 1772, but on 15 September 1783 he arrived in Calcutta. There he quickly became popular, being commissioned to execute portraits of such figures as the Governor General and his wife, *Mr and Mrs Warren Hastings* (1783–7; Calcutta, Victoria Mem. Hall) and *Sir Elijah Impey, the Chief Justice* (1783; Aberdeen, A.G.). Over the next six years he travelled between Calcutta and Lucknow, painting the colonial British and the Lucknow aristocracy (e.g. *Asaf-ud-daula, Nawab of Lucknow*, 1784; London, India Office Lib.) and producing

Eastern versions of his English conversation pieces. The small-scale amplitude of the *Sharp Family* was much more popular in India, but the *Auriol and Dashwood Families* (1783–7; priv. col., see 1976 exh. cat., no. 100) suffers from the weak and inattentive arrangement of the 11 sitters. In India too, Zoffany's sense of colour became sadly compromised. Italy had vastly enriched his palette, the pastel shades of the German Rococo artists and Wilson's gloomy chiaroscuro having been replaced with luscious reds, blues and oranges. But in India his bleached tones and thinning paint reflected an unenterprising interest in a narrow range of colours that became even more restricted during the final years in England. However, value for money was evidently much appreciated among Zoffany's patrons in India, and he began painting extremely crowded canvases that suggest he was taking advantage of the convention of being paid by the figure. *Colonel Mordaunt's Cock Match* (1784–6; priv. col., see 1976 exh. cat., no. 104) has about 75 figures and cost Governor-General Hastings £1500. Perhaps the most notable aspect of Zoffany's stay in India, though, was the genuine interest he showed in the Indian landscape and ordinary village settings, which was in sharp contrast to the attitudes of many of his predecessors.

Because of the lucrative commissions he had received in India, Zoffany was a rich man when he returned to England in 1789. He bought a large house at Strand-on-the-Green, near Kew and during the 1790s painted some theatre scenes, some portraits and some rather eccentric contemporary genre scenes such as *Plundering the King's Cellar at Paris* (1794; priv. col., see 1976 exh. cat., no. 108). He continued occasionally to depict the Indian way of life (e.g. *Embassy of Haidar Beg Khan to Lord Cornwallis*, 1795; Calcutta, Victoria Mem. Hall), but he appears to have stopped painting after 1800.

When he died in 1810, Zoffany was considered a curiosity from the mid-18th century. He was chiefly remembered as a theatrical artist, and he was the major influence on many British theatrical portrait painters, including James Roberts (*fl* 1766–1809), Thomas Parkinson, Samuel De Wilde, George Clint and Thomas Charles Wageman (1787–1863). He was perhaps the greatest exponent of the English conversation piece, and his technical brilliance, his sense of Rococo flamboyance and his ability to create a theatrical effect set him apart from other practitioners of the genre.

BIBLIOGRAPHY
E. Waterhouse: *Painting in Britain, 1530–1790*, Pelican Hist. A. (Harmondsworth, 1953, rev. 4/1978)
M. Webster: 'Zoffany's Painting of Charles Towneley's Library in Park Street', *Burl. Mag.*, cvi (1964), pp. 316–23
O. Millar: *Zoffany and his 'Tribuna'* (London, 1967)
——: *Later Georgian Pictures in the Collection of Her Majesty the Queen* (London, 1969)
Johan Zoffany, 1733–1810 (exh. cat. by M. Webster, London, N.P.G., 1976)
M. Archer: *India and British Portraiture, 1770–1825* (London, 1979), pp. 130–77
GEOFFREY ASHTON

Zograph [Dimitrov], **Zakhary (Khristovich)** (*b* Samokov, 1810; *d* Samokov, 14 July 1853). Bulgarian painter and draughtsman. He is the best-known artist of the 'Bulgarian Renaissance' and was the first to introduce secular elements into the religious paintings of the SAMOKOV SCHOOL, founded by his father, Khristo Dimitrov (*d* 1819). His evangelical scenes are spiritually pure, bright images, illuminated by an inner nobility; they also, however, contain contemporary imagery and elements of social criticism. He came from a family of artists and studied iconography with his father and elder brother, Dimitar Zograph (1796–1860). From 1831 he began to work independently and to date his icons, such as the ones in SS Constantine and Helen in Plovdiv (e.g. *St John the Baptist*). In 1840–41 he executed frescoes (e.g. the *Last Judgement* and *Life of Christ*) in St Nicholas at Bachkovo Monastery, south of Plovdiv, painting his portrait above the sacred scenes. This was the first instance in Bulgarian painting of an artist's own features being incorporated into a religious setting. In the *Last Judgement*, wealthy men and their wives are depicted as being condemned to eternal damnation. He executed frescoes at the Troyan Monastery in 1840 and the Preobrazhensky Monastery in 1849, painted the large central dome and the four outer domes and the gallery of the choir at the Monastery Church, Rila, in 1841, and worked in the church of Hagios Athanasios in the Great Lavra on Mt Athos, Greece. These works all contain apocalyptic scenes, portraits of church donors, representations of SS Cyril and Methodius and their apostles, and portraits of Bulgarian and Slav national heroes who were canonized: tsars, patriarchs and fighters for national liberation. The figures are framed by the interiors and exteriors of buildings and by landscapes including scenes of everyday life. Examples of his portraits include *Neofit Rilsky, Khristiania, Daughter-in-law of the Artist* and *Self-portrait* (all *c.* 1840; Sofia, N.A.G.). A large collection of his watercolours, ink drawings and icons is in the Samokov Municipal Historical Museum.

BIBLIOGRAPHY
A. Vasiliev: 'Stenopici v Svetogorkia manastir "Lavra" ot Zachary Zograph' [Frescoes at the Sveta Gora Lavra Monastery by Zakhary Zograph], *Izvestiya Inst. Izobrazitelni Izk.*, i (1957)
V. Zakhariev: *Zakhary Khristovich Zograph* (Sofia, 1957)
A. Vasiliev: *Bălgarski văzrozhdenski maystori* [Masters of the Bulgarian Renaissance] (Sofia, 1965)
P. Spassov: *Zahari Zograph* (Sofia, 1966)
JULIANA NEDEVA-WEGENER

Zohar, Israel (*b* Aktyubinsk, Kazakhstan, 7 Feb 1945). Israeli painter, playwright and theatre director of Kazakh birth. He moved to Israel with his parents when he was four. Having displayed an early artistic talent, Zohar had his first drawing lessons when he was 14. After three years in the army (from 1963), he entered the Bezalel Academy of Art and Design in Jerusalem. His teachers included Ernst Fuchs, the Viennese fantastic realist painter, who was highly influential on Zohar. Also important in his development were travels in Britain and the Netherlands, where he saw Dutch Old Master collections and in particular the work of Johannes Vermeer. Zohar's first one-man show (1970) was at the Ahuva Doran Gallery in Tel Aviv. After exhibiting in further solo and group shows, in 1979 he lectured at the Hebrew University in Jerusalem. Zohar's paintings of this period reflected strongly the influence of Vermeer in style and subject-matter. By the 1980s his work became more expressionistic and larger in scale. A retrospective in 1987 at the Musée de l'Athénée in Geneva brought him renown, and in 1996 his series *'Reflections': Homage to Vermeer* was exhibited at the Museum Panorama Mesdag in The Hague. Zohar's major commissions include portraits of *Diana, Princess of Wales* (1990; property of Light Dragoons Charitable Trust), commissioned by the officers of the 13th–18th Royal Hussars (Queen Mary's Own), and the former US Ambassador to the UK *Henry Catto* (1990; London, priv. col.), commissioned for the Embassy of the USA in London, and collaborative projects with the Israeli painter and musician Rivka Golani (*b* 1946).

BIBLIOGRAPHY

Zohar (exh. cat., text by G. Orfat; Geneva, Mus. Athénée, 1987)
Zohar: A Major One Man Show (exh. cat., ed. R. Miles; London, Roy Miles Gal., 1989)
Returning Shadows of War (exh. cat., London, Roy Miles Gal., 1993) [incl. collab. work with Golany]
'Reflections': Homage to Vermeer (exh. cat., The Hague, Mus. Panorama Mesdag, 1996)

ROBBERT RUIGROK

Zohn, Alejandro (*b* Vienna, 8 Aug 1930). Mexican architect. He studied at the Universidad de Guadalajara, Mexico, graduating as an engineer in 1955 and as an architect in 1963. His abilities as an engineer are reflected in several bold and ingenious structures that derive partly from the precepts of FÉLIX CANDELA. Notable examples are the acoustic shell (1958) in Agua Azul Park, the Libertad Market (1959) and the 'Presidente Adolfo López Mateos' Sports Centre (1962), all in Guadalajara. The market is especially noteworthy for its roof of hyperbolic paraboloids, which allow for wide areas without supports. He also built residential blocks, paying careful attention to details of interior functionality, the durability and maintenance of materials and residents' individuality. The housing complex 'CTM-ATEMAJAC' (1979), Guadalajara, is one of his main achievements in this area, comprising several buildings, none more than five storeys, and with brick facing. Among his numerous other designs in Guadalajara, the most notable are the Banco Refaccionario de Jalisco (1973), the 'Mulbar' shopping centre and car park and the Archivo del Estado de Jalisco building (1989). The latter is in exposed concrete and has a minimum of openings, giving it the appearance of a sculptured fortress. Zohn's own house (1989), also in the city, is in a more intimate, emotional style and has affinities with the vernacular architecture of the Jalisco area.

BIBLIOGRAPHY

'Alejandro Zohn', *Process: Archit.*, 39 (1983)
L. Noelle: 'Alejandro Zohn', *Arquitectos contemporáneos de México* (Mexico City, 1989)

LOUISE NOELLE

Zola, Emile (*b* Paris, 2 April 1840; *d* Paris, 29 Sept 1902). French writer and critic. He was brought up in Aix-en-Provence, and arrived in Paris in 1858, where he frequented painters' studios and visited the salons. Cézanne was a childhood friend to whom Zola dedicated his first article of art criticism, which appeared in *L'Evénement* in 1866. He later recreated his passionate discussions with other artists in his novel *L'Oeuvre* (Paris, 1886), in which he debated all the aesthetic problems of the second half of the 19th century. Zola's aesthetic analysis of painting was based on rules close to those of the Naturalist novel (*see* NATURALISM), which he defined in 1864 as 'a corner of creation seen through a temperament' (*Correspondance*, Paris and Montreal, 1978, p. 375). This definition was not solely concerned with reproducing reality; in Zola's view the artist's personality alone enabled him to produce a work of art. He thus vigorously defended certain painters such as Pierre Puvis de Chavannes and Gustave Moreau, although their work was far from Naturalist, because of the seductive effect of their frescoes and canvases on him.

Zola vehemently rejected the academic painting of the day and inveighed against Alexandre Cabanel's painting of the *Birth of Venus* (1863; Paris, Mus. d'Orsay), which was the great social success of the salon of 1863, while Manet's *Le Déjeuner sur l'herbe* (1863; Paris, Mus. d'Orsay) was the object of all the jeers. He rejected historical and mythological subjects, and sanctioned Realist painting of the contemporary world; he rejected pictorial conventions that compelled a modification of the vision of the world according to an ideal beauty: natural beauty was all that mattered.

Manet was, for Zola, the great painter of the 19th century, whose technical and aesthetic modernity he recognized, and whom he considered to be the premier representative of 'the modern school of Naturalism'. He analysed Manet's technique, materials, handling of the brush and new code of colours, and understood that Manet's painting emphasized line and colour, without according much importance to the subject. Zola was preoccupied less with the sense of a picture than with the forms in it. He judged all of Manet's pictures from this perspective, from *Olympia* (1863; Paris, Mus. d'Orsay) to *In the Greenhouse* (1879; Berlin, Neue N.G.). He vigorously defended Manet from 1866 to 1884, when he wrote the preface to the catalogue of the first posthumous Manet exhibition (Paris, 1884).

Zola also had an acute understanding of landscape painters, from Millet to Pissaro, as well as Corot, Eugène Boudin, Johan Barthold Jongkind and Monet. *Plein-air* painters were characterized by Zola in *L'Oeuvre* as the 'true revolutionaries of form'. During the last ten years of his life Zola became passionately interested in photography; he took pictures of country and urban landscapes, as well as family portraits and pictures of the Exposition Universelle of 1900. Zola's passion for the image also appeared in his taste for descriptions of urban landscapes in his novels, and he particularly enjoyed describing landscapes already painted by his artist friends.

Zola's marked interest in the image distinguishes him among the great art critics of the second half of the 19th century, despite a relative incomprehension of the Impressionists, whom he reproached for their technical imperfection, and his silence on Cézanne. He was a defender of the new art as early as 1864, and although he evaluated the contemporary arts according to the criteria of Naturalism, his judgements, while severe towards academic painting, were undogmatic.

WRITINGS

Edouard Manet: Etude biographique et critique (Paris, 1867)
L'Oeuvre, iv of *Les Rougon-Macquart*, 20 vols (Paris, 1871–93/*R* 1960–67)

Exposition des oeuvres d'Edouard Manet (exh. cat., preface E. Zola; Paris, Ecole N. Sup. B.-A., 1884)
H. Mitterand, ed.: *Oeuvres complètes* (Paris, 1966–70)
A. Ehrard, ed.: *Mon Salon, Manet* and *Ecrits sur l'art* (Paris, 1970)
J.-P. Leduc-Adine, ed.: *Pour Manet* (Brussels, 1989)

BIBLIOGRAPHY
J. Grand-Carteret: *Zola en images* (Paris, 1905)
H. Mitterand: *Zola journaliste: De l'affaire Manet à l'affaire Dreyfus* (Paris, 1962)
P. Brady: *L'Oeuvre d'Emile Zola: Roman sur les arts, manifeste, autobiographie, roman à clef* (Geneva, 1967)
A. Brookner: *The Genius of the Future* (Oxford, 1972)
F. Emile-Zola and Massin: *Zola photographe* (Paris, 1979)
J.-P. Leduc-Adine: *Une Visite avec Emile Zola* (Paris, 1988)
'Zola en images', *Cah. Naturalistes*, lxvi (1992)

JEAN-PIERRE LEDUC-ADINE

Zoll, Kilian (Christoffer) (*b* Hyllie parish, Skåne, 20 Sept 1818; *d* Stjerarps farm, Halland, 9 Nov 1860). Swedish painter. He started his education at the Konstakademi in Stockholm in 1836, with Fredric Westin, Per Krafft the younger (1777–1863) and Carl Johan Fahlcrantz as his teachers. At the Kunstakademi in Copenhagen (1845–6), Zoll was impressed by the clear, realistic pictures of everyday objects by C. W. Eckersberg and his pupils. Partly because of this Zoll came to differ from the other Swedish Düsseldorf painters, both in his use of colours and figure style. From 1852 to 1855 Zoll resided in Düsseldorf, where he was a pupil of F. T. Hildebrandt (1804–74) and the Norwegian Adolph Tidemand, returning during the winter of 1858–9.

Zoll primarily portrayed scenes from Swedish country life, for example *Midsummer Dance in Rättvik* (1851, priv. col.; smaller version, Stockholm, Nmus.). He drew his inspiration from long walks through different parts of the country. Zoll's portrayal of people was characterized by an intimacy and frank naivety, which sometimes turned into sentimentality. He was an outstanding painter of children, and some of his most popular and original pictures were in this genre: for example *May Singer in Skåne* (1850) and the *Little Flower Picker* (1851; both Norrköping, Kstmus.). His portraits include that of the painter *Marcus Larson* (1850, Norrköping, Kstmus.; uncompleted versions, Göteborg, Kstmus.). Of particular interest are a number of impeccably coloured, freely painted, landscape studies in oils, which heralded *plein-air* painting and were most directly inspired by Eckersberg. Zoll also painted altarpieces and from 1849 added minor figures to Marcus Larson's landscape pictures. Bengt Nordenberg completed many of the pictures Zoll left unfinished at his death.

BIBLIOGRAPHY
G. Nordensvan: *Svensk konst och svenska konstnärer i det 19 århundradet* [Swedish art and Swedish artists in the 19th century], i (Stockholm, 1925), pp. 535–8
P. Humbla: *Kilian Zoll* (diss., U. Göteborg, 1932)
Kilian Zoll (exh. cat., intro. B. Lindwall; Stockholm, Nmus., 1952)
Kilian Zoll (exh. cat., Malmö, Malmöhus, 1960)

TORSTEN GUNNARSSON

Zolotoye Runo. *See* GOLDEN FLEECE.

Zomer, Jan Pietersz. *See* ZOOMER, JAN PIETERSZ.

Zompini, Gaetano Gherardo (*b* Nervesa, Treviso, 24 Sept 1700; *d* Venice, 20 May 1778). Italian painter and engraver. He studied when very young with Nicolò Bambini (1651–1736), and later became a follower of Sebastiano Ricci. Before 1733 he executed a series of frescoes for S Nicolò da Tolentino, Venice, which included the *Four Evangelists* on the pendentives, Old Testament scenes on the drum, and, in the dome, the *Holy Trinity*. Of another early fresco cycle, in the church of the Servi at Gradisca, near Gorizia, only the vault fresco, the *Apparition of the Blessed Virgin in Glory*, survives. Zompini's most considerable work as a history painter was a series of eight dramatic canvases, in a style reminiscent of Ricci and Giambattista Tiepolo, of scenes from Homer and Virgil, and seven monochrome overdoors representing Olympian deities, on a gold background, painted for the Palazzo Zinelli, Venice (all 1736; Moschen Castle, near Kujau, Silesia, Tiele-Winckler priv. col.).

In 1737 Zompini made drawings for the illustrations for *Rutzvanscad il Giovane*, a comedy by 'Panchiano Catuffio Babulco' (Zaccaria Vallaresso), his first contribution to book illustration. There followed, in the 1740s and early 1750s, a series of altarpieces for churches in Venice and the Veneto; these include the *Virgin of the Carmelites with SS Joseph and Teresa* (1740; Arcate, S Lorenzo) and two canvases, *Esther before Ahasuerus* and *Rebecca at the Well* (1748–9; Venice, Scuola di S Maria del Carmelo). He remained a limited painter, and achieved only modest works in a provincial academic style, but he is better known as an etcher.

Encouraged by Anton Maria Zanetti (i), he began, *c.* 1750, to make a series of drawings of Venetian traders and hawkers. He later etched these drawings and they were published in *Le arti che vanno per via nella città di Venezia* (1753; see 1983 exh. cat., nos 612–31). A volume of 95 preparatory drawings, which once belonged to Zanetti, is in the Museo Correr, Venice. *Le arti* is a highly original work which suggests, with vivid immediacy, and in a forceful, almost crude technique, the harsh reality of the daily life of the Venetian people. The etchings contrast sharply with the fantasies of Tiepolo, and with the Grand Tourist's world of masque and carnival. In 1756 Zompini was elected to the Accademia Veneziana di Pittura, and towards the end of the 1750s produced another set of etchings, in a lighter, more refined style, entitled *Vari capricci e paesi* (see 1983 exh. cat., nos 461–3). This is composed of twelve prints after drawings by Giovanni Benedetto Castiglione, which formed part of Zanetti's collection, and of which three illustrated the theme of the *Education of Achilles*. Zompini also etched *SS Jerome, Lawrence and Prospero*, after Veronese, and produced two of the prints (stations ii and iii) for the series *Le dieci stazioni della vita di Maria*.

Around this time Zompini produced designs for fine illustrated editions of Italian classics published by Antonio Zatta, among them *Le Rime del Petrarca* (Venice, 1757), *La Divina Commedia di Dante Alighieri* (Venice, 1757) and, after the death of his patron Zanetti in 1767, *L'Orlando Furioso di M. Ludovico Ariosto* (Venice, 1772–3). Zompini found himself in financial difficulties after the death of Zanetti and, having lost his sight, his last years were spent in great poverty. His works enjoyed considerable success in England after his death. An edition of *Le arti* was published in Venice in 1785 by John Strange,

British Resident in Venice, who also reprinted the *Vari capricci e paesi* in 1786. Three further editions of *Le arti* were published in London between 1787 and 1803.

PRINTS

Le arti che vanno per via nella città di Venezia (Venice, 1753–4; 2/1785 ed. J. Strange with a biography of Zompini by G. Sasso; 3/London, ?1787; 4/London, n.d.; 5/London, 1803)
Vari capricci e paesi (?Venice, ?1758, Venice, 2/1786)

BIBLIOGRAPHY

Thieme–Becker
O. Battistella: *Della vita e delle opere di Gaetano Gherardo Zompini pittore e incisore nervesano del secolo XVIII* (Nervesa, 1916, Treviso, 2/1930)
G. Lorenzetti: 'Un dilettante incisore veneziano del XVIII secolo: Anton Maria Zanetti di Girolamo', *Misc. Stor. Ven.*, xii (1917), pp. 1–146
L. Moretti: *Gaetano Zompini: Le arti che vanno per via nella città di Venezia* (Venice, 1968) [excellent illus.]
M. Santifaller: 'Un problema Zanetti–Zompini in margine alle ricerche tiepolesche', *A. Ven.*, xxvii (1973), pp. 189–200
G. Bozzolato: *Gaetano Zompini incisore senza fortuna* (Padua, 1978)
Da Carlevarijs ai Tiepolo: Incisori veneti e friulani del settecento (exh. cat., ed. D. Succi; Gorizia, Mus. Prov. Pal. Attems; Venice, Correr; 1983)

DARIO SUCCI

Zongolopoulos, George (*b* Athens, 1903). Greek sculptor. He studied sculpture at the School of Fine Arts in Athens, in Paris with the French sculptor Marcel Gimond (*b* 1894), and in Italy. His work first began to attract attention in 1937, when he designed the war memorial at Piraeus. His monumental work was still traditional in style in the mid-1950s, when he designed the monument to *The Fallen* (h. 3 m, 1956) in the Athens suburb of Nikaia. This is an austere composition, inspired by the 'Rondanini' *Pietà* of Michelangelo and Etruscan bronzes. His figurative sculpture bordered on abstraction in the imposing stone composition of the *Zalonga* monument (12.5×17.6 m, 1954–61) in Epiros, which rises up at the mouth of an abyss and is visible from miles around. It depicts the dance of the heroines of the Greek War of Independence. Zongolopoulos finally turned to a joyful, uplifting abstraction in 1958 and thereafter worked almost exclusively in metal. A frequently used technique was to weld together bronze sheets of various shapes and sizes and to organize them into compositions that played with light and shade and that had a rhythmic interplay between voids and fullnesses. This is vividly shown in the monumental, abstract composition (h. 18 m) that was erected in 1966 on the Trade Fair ground at Thessaloniki, and which was inspired by the *Nike of Samothrace*. In the 1970s Zongolopoulos turned to optico-kinetic sculpture. His airy, sculptured 'machines' used a variety of objects, such as springs and lenses, to excite all the senses through movement, rhythm and sound. After 1977 his optico-kinetic sculpture was enriched by using water, as in the water-mobile sculpture that he designed in 1981 for a fountain in Klavthmonos Square, Athens. In 1984 he won a competition to design a monument of *National Resistance* at Gorgopotamos with a huge transparent spherical work, 16 m in diameter, made up of horizontal and vertical stainless steel tubes with five metal simantra at their core. In 1993 he represented Greece in the 45th Venice Biennale.

BIBLIOGRAPHY

Zongolopoulos (exh. cat. by D. Zacharopoulos, Athens, 1984)
P. Restany: *Zongolopoulos* (Athens, 1990)

MARINA LAMBRAKI-PLAKA

Zoo(logical garden). Complex in which wild and sometimes domesticated animals are kept and exhibited for scientific, educational and recreational purposes. The precursor of the modern zoo was the menagerie, which was essentially a place of entertainment but often also served as a royal status symbol. Collections of animals were well established in ancient Chinese, Asian and Egyptian cultures, mainly as public spectacles. Most of the ancient Greek city states had menageries designed mainly for the scientific study of the animals. A number of medieval European rulers had private menageries, including Henry I of England (*reg* 1100–35) and Philip IV of France, who kept his animals at the Palais du Louvre. Almost nothing is known, however, about the architectural form of such menageries. During the 18th century the menagerie became increasingly incorporated into Baroque garden designs. The design of the menagerie at the Belvedere (1716) in Vienna, by Dominique Girard and Johann Lukas von Hildebrandt, consisted of wedge-shaped paddocks radiating from a central fountain, with animals separated by species and with accommodation for the animals at the back of each paddock. This design, based on the earlier Menagerie du Parc (1668) at Versailles, became the prototype for such other royal menageries as that at Schönbrunn (1751; Jean-Nicolas Jadot de Ville-Issey), Vienna, where the radial plan was centred around a small Baroque pavilion. The menagerie at Schönbrunn was opened to the public in 1765, and in 1793 the French royal animal collection was transferred from Versailles to the Jardin des Plantes in Paris and opened to the public. This move from private to public thus achieved part of the transition from menagerie to zoo.

The second part of this development was the move away from the mere recreational function of the zoo towards scientific study and research. The London Zoological Society was founded in 1826 with the express aim of the 'advancement of zoology and animal physiology'. In 1828 the Society established a zoological garden in Regent's Park, London, laid out (1826–41) by Decimus Burton, who also designed most of the buildings. The example of London Zoo stimulated the foundation of numerous zoological gardens and societies throughout Europe. Zoos at Amsterdam (1837) and Antwerp (1843) were based directly on the principles established at London, while in other instances the lines between education and pleasure were blurred. Architecturally, most 19th-century zoos either followed current tastes and fashions or used exotic styles reminiscent of the animals' countries of origin. The use of oriental or exotic styles began at London Zoo, where the Reptile House (1849; destr.) took the form of a Swiss chalet, and this trend became more prominent in the second half of the century. At Cologne Zoo, for example, the Ostrich House (1860) resembled a mosque, and the Fox and Jackal House was a towered, brick, Gothic structure. Other examples included Düsseldorf Zoo, which had a vast 'ruined' castle (1896) for its Barbary sheep, and the elephant and giraffe house at Antwerp Zoo, which was designed in the Egyptian style and decorated with hieroglyphics. The most spectacular of these 'exotic' zoos, however, was in Berlin. Founded in 1844, Berlin Zoo underwent a major expansion scheme from 1869 under the direction of ENDE & BÖCKMANN.

The partnership designed a large collection of animal houses and ancillary buildings in oriental styles (all destr. 1941), most notably the 'Hindu' Elephant House (destr.) with its brightly coloured exterior of blue, yellow and brown tiles and internal columns decorated with elephants' heads capitals (see fig.).

Often, if a zoo was run on a commercial basis, lavish restaurants and concert pavilions were built to attract visitors. In many cases this was reminiscent of the philosophy behind the menageries; many zoos incorporated small circus acts or 'exhibited' native keepers together with the animals for added interest. The continued move towards entertainment was also evident in the grand entrance gates of most zoos, for example the monumental neo-Baroque gates at Berlin and Rome (1910), which incorporated sculptures of animals. This approach persisted in the early 20th century, as in the Art Nouveau gate and buildings (1909–10) of Budapest Zoo by Károly Kós and Dezso Zrumeczky (1884–1917). What most 19th-century zoo architecture had in common was the disregard for the needs and requirements of the animals; animal houses were designed primarily with the spectator in mind. It was only in the late 1890s that ideas were developed for the housing of animals based on behavioural and physiological observations.

In the 20th century zoos developed a radically different approach to animal keeping and housing. This change is usually attributed to Karl Hagenbeck (1844–1913), whose ideas were copied worldwide. Originally an animal trader and trainer, Hagenbeck pioneered studies into animal behaviour and acclimatization. In 1907 he opened a zoological garden in Stellingen, Hamburg, where he dispensed with the conventional barred cages. With the Swiss sculptor and engineer Urs Eggenschwiler (1849–1923), Hagenbeck devised concrete mountains and such other landscape devices as hidden moats to separate the various species, creating panoramas of paddocks with animals no longer kept in isolation in an attempt to reproduce the animals' natural habitat. In 1910 he was called upon to create Rome Zoo, and his Parc Zoologique de Paris (1934), Vincennes, was derived directly from the animal park at Stellingen. At London Zoo, John James Joass based the artificial mountain habitat of the Mappin Terraces (1913) on Hagenbeck's concepts. In 1931 a large wildlife park with the prime motivation of preservation and conservation was opened by the London Zoological Society at Whipsnade, Beds. Since then, large open animal parks have become the standard form for new zoos. Although increasingly taking into account the animals' needs, in terms of architectural style animal houses continued to follow contemporary trends. For example, the architect of Copenhagen Zoo, Frits Schlegel (1896–1965), designed the Ape House (1928) with expressionistic, stylized, concrete rockwork. During the 1930s the architectural group TECTON designed a series of Modern Movement buildings for both London Zoo (e.g. Gorilla

Berlin Zoo, 'Hindu' Elephant House, by Ende & Böckmann, 1869 (destr. 1941)

House, 1933; Penguin Pool, completed 1934; rest. 1987–8; for illustration *see* ARUP, OVE) and Dudley Zoo (1937), near Birmingham.

As zoos became increasingly open-plan, the animal houses lost some of their prominence and were increasingly designed to meet the specific requirements of the animals. For example, since the 1960s large, walk-through aviaries have become popular with the developments in structural systems; examples include the Snowdon Aviary (1963; Snowdon) of London Zoo, which consists of a system of steel tension cables built over an artificial cliff, or the great aviary at Hellabrunn (1980; Frei Otto), Munich. The increasing emphasis on keeping and presenting animals in their natural habitat is also reflected in the establishment of habitats that require technically advanced, controlled environments. These environments can sometimes be expressed externally. For example, the Sonora Desert Museum (1956), CA, displaying native animals in their subterranean habitat, was constructed mainly underground. The 'World of Darkness' Building at Bronx Zoo (1969; Morris Ketchum Jr and Associates), New York City, was designed as a steel-framed structure clad with black granite to reflect the nocturnal environment recreated inside. Modern zoological research has established a number of options for zoo layouts according to species, geographical origin, behaviour, habitat or even popularity, but the design of the animal houses or enclosures is now orientated primarily to the requirements of the animals.

BIBLIOGRAPHY

J. Fisher: *Zoos of the World* (London, 1966)
D. Hanocks: *Animals and Architecture* (London, 1971)
K. von Frisch: *Animal Architecture* (New York, 1974)
J. A. Wilkes, ed.: *Encyclopedia of Architecture: Design, Engineering and Construction*, v (New York, 1990), pp. 419–39

Zoomer [Zomer], **Jan Pietersz.** (*b* Amsterdam, 1641; *d* Amsterdam, 18 May 1724). Dutch collector, dealer and artist. He was trained by Pieter Janssen as a glass-engraver and was active as a dealer in glass until 1687, when he became one of Amsterdam's most important saleroom brokers and appraisers and began to deal in other forms of art. By 1690 he had become one of the leading dealers in paintings, drawings and prints, counting not only Dutch collectors but also foreigners among his clientele, for instance Prince Eugene of Savoy. Long before this, from *c.* 1660, however, he had himself begun to collect drawings, prints and books. He owned drawings by mostly Dutch artists, such as Gerrit Berckheyde, Cornelis Bega, Jan Both, Pieter van Laer, Jan Noordt and Jacob Backer, and no less than seven volumes of drawings by Rembrandt. He seems to have applied his mark, a cartouche printed in black with the initials I.P.Z. (see Lugt), to drawings that passed through his hands as well as into his own collection. He also generally inscribed the name of the artist on each sheet, though at times he was deliberately optimistic with his attributions, especially with drawings said to be by Italian artists. He often bought prints and drawings already assembled in albums, which he then broke up and reconstituted into new 'series' that included individual items that were more difficult to sell. His print collection was more wide-ranging, with examples by Dutch, Flemish,

Italian, French and German artists. Again, however, Rembrandt was well represented, by a particularly important group of etchings (428 prints). In 1711 Zoomer boasted of having a stock of 30,000 prints for sale. After the death of his last daughter in 1719, he rewrote his will and asked that his entire collection be sold at the earliest favourable occasion. A catalogue was prepared the following year, with all the works offered for sale; it included 139 albums of drawings, 100 portfolios of prints, 14 separate portfolios of historical engravings and 2 volumes of his own drawings, mostly female figure studies from life (e.g. Rotterdam, Mus. Boymans–van Beuningen). Zoomer's important collection of Rembrandt etchings was bought in London in 1720 by Anton Maria Zanetti the elder, whence it can be traced until its dispersal in the early 19th century by Samuel Woodburn (*see* PRINTS, §V).

BIBLIOGRAPHY

F. Lugt: *Marques* (1921), no. 1511
S. A. C. Dudok van Heel: 'Jan Pietersz. Zomer (1641–1724): Makelaar in schilderijen (1690–1724)', *Jb. Amstelodamum*, lxix (1977), pp. 89–106
P. Schatborn: 'Van Rembrandt tot Crozat: Vroege verzamelingen met tekeningen van Rembrandt', *Ned. Ksthist. Jb.*, xxxii (1981), pp. 1–51
Dutch Figure Drawings from the Seventeenth Century (exh. cat. by P. Schatborn, Amsterdam, Rijksmus.; Washington, DC, N.G.A.; 1981–2), p. 128

JANE SHOAF TURNER

Zoophorus. Frieze with animal reliefs, such as that on the portico of the Theseion, Athens.

Zoppo. *See* BENEDETTO DI BINDO.

Zoppo, Marco [Marco di Ruggero; Lo Zoppo] (*b* Cento, nr Bologna, ?1432; *d* Venice, ?1478). Italian painter.

1. Life and work. 2. Working methods and technique. 3. Critical reception and posthumous reputation.

1. LIFE AND WORK. The earliest dated notice of Zoppo is an agreement of 24 May 1455 concerning his legal adoption by the Paduan painter Francesco Squarcione. The document indicates that at the time it was drawn up Zoppo had been living in Squarcione's house for about two years and at 23 years old was already recognized as a painter of considerable ability. According to the agreement, Squarcione, who was childless and had recently become a widower, acknowledged Zoppo as his sole heir in return for Zoppo's work in painting. The contract, however, was short-lived. By October of the same year, Zoppo had left Squarcione and was living in Venice. Two documents record the terms by which the adoption agreement was to be annulled and the arrangements drawn up not only to compensate Zoppo for work he had executed for which Squarcione had received payment, but also to cover Squarcione's costs for having provided Zoppo with lodging and artists' materials. Clearly Zoppo quickly discovered that the conditions placed on him by Squarcione were not to his advantage. Like other young artists who came into contact with Squarcione, most notably Andrea Mantegna, who had a similar experience in the late 1440s, Zoppo soon realized that his success as an artist rested on gaining his freedom, even though this could be achieved only by relinquishing his rights to Squarcione's substantial estate.

The signatures on Zoppo's mature works invariably acknowledge his Bolognese origin, but what may be his earliest surviving painting, a *Virgin and Child with Angels* (Paris, Louvre; see fig. 1) is signed OPERA DEL ZOPPO DI SQUARCIONE, a clear indication that it was executed *c.* 1455, at the time Zoppo was adopted by Squarcione. Although it seems likely that Zoppo received some initial training in Bologna before his Paduan period, this early *Virgin and Child* provides little evidence for such a theory, indicating instead how fully he had absorbed characteristics of Paduan art associated with Squarcione and his pupils.

No documents concerning Zoppo have come to light between the time he moved to Venice in 1455 and 1461 when he was in Bologna. A series of payments for decorative work in the church of S Petronio in Bologna dated 1461–2 indicates that he had probably been established in the city for some time. A document of July 1462 shows that he sold some land near Bologna, suggesting that he may have been planning another move, possibly back to Venice. None of the works likely to have been painted by Zoppo in Bologna is dated, making their chronology difficult to establish. On stylistic grounds the earliest is the large Crucifix (Bologna, S Giuseppe). Ruhmer (1966) suggested that this is Zoppo's earliest surviving work, datable before he went to Padua. Although its format is old-fashioned, being reminiscent of many 13th-century crucifixes, with half-length figures of the Virgin and St John the Evangelist in quatrefoils at either end of the horizontal beam and a skull beneath Christ's feet, the articulation of Christ's torso and particularly the expressive qualities of Christ's head indicate knowledge of Donatello's Crucifix from the altar of the Santo in Padua, which Zoppo would have known. The Crucifix from S Giuseppe therefore probably dates from the late 1450s.

The most important of Zoppo's surviving Bolognese works is the altarpiece in the church of S Clemente, the chapel of the Collegio di Spagna. One of Zoppo's most impressive works, it is a polyptych with the Virgin and Child in the central panel with two saints on either side, three predella panels and 12 small-scale saints set into the frame. The upper part of the altarpiece consists of three elaborate gables in the Venetian style set with painted roundels of the Christ, the Archangel Gabriel and the Virgin Annunciate, features which suggest that Zoppo was looking back to altarpiece designs favoured in northern Italy much earlier in the 15th century.

By the late 1460s Zoppo had apparently returned to Venice where he probably spent the remainder of his life. In Venice in 1473, for example, he acted as a witness to the will of a member of the Trevisan family. The first work he executed on his return was probably the main altarpiece for the church of S Giustina, dated 1468. Only fragments of this work survive, including a panel of *St Augustine* (London, N.G.) and one of *St Paul* (Oxford, Ashmolean), but its form has been partially reconstructed from a description of the altarpiece by Francesco Sansovino (1581). These saints seem better characterized than the figures from the S Clemente altarpiece, and the foreshortening of details such as books and other attributes shows a more assured handling. The varied poses of the figures suggest that Zoppo may have been inspired by

1. Marco Zoppo: *Virgin and Child with Angels*, oil and tempera on canvas, 892×725 mm, *c.* 1455 (Paris, Musée du Louvre)

Jacopo della Quercia's sculpture decorating the main doorway of S Petronio, Bologna.

In 1471 Zoppo completed a major altarpiece of the *Virgin and Child with SS John the Baptist, Francis, Paul and Jerome* destined for the church of S Giovanni Battista in Pesaro (Berlin, Bodemus.). This work differs from his earlier altarpieces in that the principal figures are shown in an integrated setting in the manner of a Venetian *sacra conversazione*, an indication that Zoppo was anxious to keep abreast of recent developments in altarpiece design.

2. WORKING METHODS AND TECHNIQUE. Zoppo's early dependence on Paduan art is most apparent in *Virgin and Child* (Paris, Louvre). In this painting the infant angels surrounding the Virgin reflect the artist's knowledge of Donatello's bas-reliefs from the Santo altar in Padua, which most of Squarcione's pupils seem to have studied enthusiastically. Devices such as swags of leaves and fruit and illusionistic *cartellini* attached to a ledge in the foreground of the painting, providing space for a signature, feature in many works by artists connected with Squarcione. They appear, for example, in Mantegna's *St Euphemia* (1454; Naples, Capodimonte), painted shortly before the Louvre *Virgin and Child*. Zoppo's mature work also reveals his continuing interest in Mantegna. Armstrong (1976) pointed out that the pose of the *Virgin and Child* (Washington, DC, N.G.A.; see fig. 2), probably dating from *c.* 1470, reflects the arrangement of the equivalent figures in Mantegna's altarpiece from S Zeno in Verona, completed *c.* 1460. Technical details in his work

2. Marco Zoppo: *Virgin and Child*, panel, 408×299 mm, *c.* 1470 (Washington, DC, National Gallery of Art)

also indicate Zoppo's debt to Mantegna's example, as in the use of delicate cross-hatching to build up a sense of form, and stippling for areas of flesh and drapery.

Compared with Mantegna's figure style, however, Zoppo's is much more nervous and contorted, characteristics shared with Ferrarese artists such as Cosimo Tura. The expressive qualities of some of his later work may have been influenced by the exaggerated style of local sculptors, such as Niccolò dell'Arca, who was active in Bologna from *c.* 1462. But it was art from Venice that was mostly responsible for shaping the character of his mature work. Already in the S Clemente altarpiece the poses of the principal saints show that he had paid careful attention to Andrea del Castagno's frescoes in S Zaccaria, Venice. The arrangement of the figures also suggests that during his first period in Venice Zoppo came into contact with Bartolomeo Vivarini, whose feeling for vivid colour he shared. In his second Venetian period he was increasingly attracted by the softer, more luminous style of Giovanni Bellini. The atmospheric landscape in the background of the altarpiece of 1471 painted for Pesaro may be related to Bellini's example, and indeed the entire composition of this work is closely connected with Bellini's near-contemporary altarpiece of the *Coronation of the Virgin*, also destined for Pesaro (Pesaro, Mus. Civ.). In Zoppo's last

works, such as the *Virgin and Child* (Altenburg, Staatl. Lindenau-Mus.), the pose of the main figure and the tonal range suggest that he was affected by the work of Antonello da Messina, who was active in Venice during the early 1470s.

A large corpus of drawings, attributable to Zoppo, sheds valuable light on his working methods. He was perhaps introduced to the importance of drawing while with Squarcione; the adoption agreement specifically mentions drawing as one of the techniques practiced in the Squarcione workshop. Zoppo's drawings, executed mostly in pen and ink, fall into several categories. Some are copies of works of art, such as the *Fainting Virgin Supported by Two Holy Women* (London, BM; Popham and Pouncey, no. 263), which is taken from Mantegna's engraving of the *Entombment*. There is also a series of tender studies of the Virgin and Child with several compositions to each page (London, BM; Popham and Pouncey, no. 261), all apparently drawn from life. Although the emphasis is on the figures, which are rapidly executed and usually heavily worked with much prominent hatching, there are hints of settings behind the figures which indicate that Zoppo was experimenting with ideas for paintings. In contrast, a complete volume of 50 drawings, which include studies for heads and non-religious scenes with antique motifs, survives (London, BM; Popham and Pouncey, no. 260). Unlike the Virgin and Child studies these drawings are highly finished and may have been a commission from a collector with humanist interests.

3. CRITICAL RECEPTION AND POSTHUMOUS REPUTATION. Several sources indicate that Zoppo was highly regarded in humanist and courtly circles during his lifetime. A letter dated 16 September 1462 written by Zoppo to Barbara Gonzaga, wife of Marquis Ludovico Gonzaga of Mantua, discusses two pairs of cassoni which the Marchioness had commissioned from him. One of the excuses Zoppo offers for not being able to finish the commission on time is that he was anxious to complete the painting in a manner which would be fit to stand comparison with the work of Mantegna, court artist to the Gonzagas. Zoppo was on good terms with Mantegna from the time he had been in Squarcione's workshop, and the tradition of friendship between the two artists is twice referred to by Vasari in his *Vita* of Mantegna. One of Mantegna's friends, the humanist Felice Feliciano, was also interested in Zoppo. In a letter addressed to the artist, Feliciano compares Zoppo with Euphranor, one of the celebrated artists of antiquity. According to Pliny's *Natural History*, Euphranor was a sculptor, theorist and painter, and though not a prolific artist was praised for his indefatigable industry. Feliciano may have had Pliny's account in mind when he made the comparison. Zoppo was likened to another famous artist of antiquity, Phidias, by Raffaello Zovenzonio, a pupil of the humanist Guarino, in a poem that compliments him on the still-life details in his paintings.

Although Zoppo died too young to have many followers, his work continued to be admired. In the 16th century Francesco Sansovino praised the S Giustina altarpiece in Venice, and in the 17th century Malvasia commented on Zoppo in *Felsina pittrice*. Some idea of Zoppo's standing at this time can be gained from Malvasia's discussion of a *Virgin and Child* (probably the one at Altenburg), which, according to Malvasia, had been considered a work by Dürcr until the discovery on it of Zoppo's signature. Zoppo's *Dead Christ with SS John the Baptist and Jerome* (London, N.G.) was also attributed to Dürer in the 17th century. By the end of the 18th century, however, Zoppo's work was sufficiently well known for drawings to be attributed to him. But understandably, the high quality of some of his drawings often resulted in them being erroneously attributed to Mantegna. Since 20th-century connoisseurship has succeeded in establishing Zoppo as the author of these drawings, such mistaken attributions may now be interpreted as a tribute to Zoppo's distinction as a draughtsman.

BIBLIOGRAPHY

G. Vasari: *Vite* (1550, rev. 2/1568), ed. G. Milanesi (1878–85), iii, p. 405

C. C. Malvasia: *Felsina pittrice* (1678), ed. A. Arfelli (1961), i, p. 34

C. Ricci: 'Un sonetto artistico del sec. XV.', *A. & Stor.*, xvi/4 (1897), pp. 27–8

R. Fry: 'Marco Zoppo: Eight Studies of the Virgin and Child', *Vasari Soc.*, n.s., ii (1906–7), pp. 11–12, pls 15–16

T. Borenius: 'On a Dismembered Altarpiece by Marco Zoppo', *Burl. Mag.*, xxxviii (1921), pp. 9–12

C. Dodgson: *A Book of Drawings Formerly Ascribed to Mantegna* (London, 1923)

I. B. Supino: 'Nuovi documenti su Marco Zoppo pittore', *Archiginnasio*, xx/3–4 (1925), pp. 128–32

G. Fiocco: 'Felice Feliciano amico degli artisti', *Archv Ven.-Trident.*, ix (1926), pp. 194–6

C. Dodgson: 'Un libro di disegni di Marco Zoppo', *Miscellanea di storia dell'arte in onore di Igino Benvenuto Supino* (Florence, 1933), pp. 337 51

A. E. Popham and P. Pouncey: *Italian Drawings in the Department of Prints and Drawings in the British Museum: the Fourteenth and Fifteenth Centuries*, 2 vols (London, 1950)

G. Fiocco: 'Notes sur les dessins de Marco Zoppo', *Gaz. B.-A.*, n.s. 6, xliii (1954), p. 228

S. P. Newton: 'Costumi tedeschi e borgognoni nel libro di Marco Zoppo', *Commentari*, ix/3 (1958), pp. 155–60

E. Ruhmer: *Marco Zoppo* (Vicenza, 1966)

J. J. G. Alexander: 'A Virgil Illuminated by Marco Zoppo', *Burl. Mag.*, cxi (1969), pp. 514–17

L. Armstrong: *The Paintings and Drawings of Marco Zoppo* (New York, 1976)

M. T. Fiorio: 'Marco Zoppo et le livre padouan', *Rev. A.*, 53 (1981), pp. 65–73

THOMAS TOLLEY

Zora, Giovanni Gregori de [del]. *See* SCHARDT, JOHANN GREGOR VAN DER.

Zorach. American artists.

(1) Marguerite Zorach [née Thompson] (*b* Santa Rosa, CA, 25 Sept 1887; *d* New York, 27 June 1968). Painter. She studied briefly at Stanford University (1908), before going to Paris to attend in 1908–11 La Palette, a small modernist school where she met (2) William Zorach; they married in 1912. She also travelled throughout Europe, occasionally with Jessica Dismorr. Both Dismorr and Thompson contributed to the avant-garde publication *Rhythm* in 1911 and 1912. She returned to Fresno, CA, by way of Italy, Morocco, Egypt, the Middle East and East Asia (1911–12). During the summer of 1912 she spent time in the Sierra Mountains, producing a series of bold Fauvist paintings, including *Waterfall* (1912; priv. col, see 1973 exh. cat., p. 31), rendered in saturated colours with great spontaneity.

Marguerite Zorach was familiar with the work of Picasso and Henri Matisse and furthered her knowledge of their work through a friendship with the Stein family. The influence of Cubism can be seen in her painting *The Deserted Mill* (1917; Robert Folley priv. col., see 1987 exh. cat., p. 24). She also produced tapestries, prints and sculptures, many in a modernist idiom.

(2) William Zorach (*b* Eurburg [now Yurbarkas], Lithuania, 1889; *d* Bath, ME, 15 Nov 1966). Sculptor, painter and writer of Lithuanian birth, husband of (1) Marguerite Zorach. He emigrated to the USA with his family in 1893, settling in Cleveland, where he worked as a lithographer (1902–8) and studied painting with Henry G. Keller (1869–1949) at the School of Art (1905–7). In New York he received academic training in painting at the Art Students League, and he studied at La Palette in Paris (1910–11). William and Marguerite Zorach became part of a small group of modern artists in New York, in Provincetown, MA, and in Maine, exhibiting Fauvist paintings at the Armory Show in 1913 and Cubist and Expressionist works at the Forum Exhibition in New York in 1916.

William Zorach began carving wood in 1917, for example *Waterfall* (1917; see 1987 exh. cat., p. 30), and stone in 1921, devoting himself solely to sculpture from 1922. He was one of the earliest and, through his 50-year career as a teacher and writer, one of the most influential American artists dedicated to direct carving, thus facilitating a major change in the aesthetic philosophy and technique of sculpture in the USA. His work developed in its use of blocklike forms with progressive suppression of detail. He delighted in selecting unusual blocks of wood or stone and discovering, as he carved, the grain and colour of the material that inspired the final subject and design of the sculpture. Although his forms are abstracted and retain a Cubist element, his subject-matter is traditional and includes *Young Girl* (mahogany, 1921; New York, Whitney), *Mother and Child* (1927–30; New York, Met.), *Affection* (marble, 1933; Utica, NY, Munson–Williams–Proctor Inst.), of an animal and child, and *Youth* (marble, 1936–9; West Palm Beach, FL, Norton Gal. & Sch. A.), of emotional bonds between lovers. Among his later commissions were *Man and Work* (1954) for the Mayo Clinic in Rochester, MN, and relief carvings for the Municipal Court Building, New York (1958).

WRITINGS

Zorach Explains Sculpture (New York, 1947) [William Zorach]

Art is my Life (New York, 1967) [William Zorach]

BIBLIOGRAPHY

J. I. H. Baur: *William Zorach* (New York, 1959)

Marguerite Zorach: The Early Years, 1908–1920 (exh. cat. by R. K. Tarbell, Washington, DC, Smithsonian Inst.; New York, Brooklyn Mus.; Brunswick, ME, Bowdoin Coll. Mus. A.; 1973)

R. K. Tarbell: *Catalogue Raisonné of William Zorach's Carved Sculpture*, 2 vols (diss., Newark, U. DE, 1976)

Marguerite and William Zorach: The Cubist Years, 1915–1918 (exh. cat., Manchester, NH, Currier Gal. A.; Pittsfield, MA, Berkshire Mus.; Waterville, ME, Colby Coll., Mus. A.; Burlington, U. VT, Robert Hull Fleming Mus.; 1987)

ROBERTA K. TARBELL

Żórawski, Juliusz (*b* 2 Oct 1898; *d* Kraków, 24 Nov 1967). Polish architect, teacher and theorist. He studied architecture at Warsaw Technical University (1920–27) and taught architectural design there (1928–39). One of the best-known architects in Poland in the 1930s, he was influenced by the work of Le Corbusier and his buildings made use of the latest modern building technology. He built many luxury blocks of flats in Warsaw in the International Style, consistently applying Le Corbusier's 'five points of a new architecture', including the use of columns to allow flexible internal planning, continuous horizontal bands of windows and flat roofs designed for recreation. The disciplined rhythm of windows contrasted with the curved forms of entrance halls and caretakers' flats he designed at ground level beneath his buildings. Examples of this work include blocks at 3 Przyjaciół Avenue (1937) and 34–36 Mickiewicza Street (1937–9), both in Warsaw. In his Wedel House (1936–7), 28 Puławska Street, Warsaw, he used a new type of structural system: a welded steel frame braced by stair-wells and cavity fire walls. This building also attempted a synthesis of the arts, including a sculpture in the landscaped court-yard and frescoes in the entrance hall. Other work in the 1930s included many competition entries, for example his design for the Polish Savings Bank, Poznań (1934; with Zbigniew Puget; unexecuted); he also built a theatre in Kalisz, three cinemas in Warsaw and several banks including one in Vilna (now Vilnius, Lithuania) (1936–8; with Puget). In 1943 Żórawski obtained a doctorate in architectural design theory under Władysław Tatarkiewicz (1886–1980), Professor of Philosophy. His thesis applied Gestalt theory to architecture; he praised simple, clear forms and believed that function, construction and form should be treated equally. After 1945 he taught industrial architecture at the Technical University of Kraków, becoming Professor in 1963.

WRITINGS

O budowie formy architektonicznej [On the construction of architectural form] (Warsaw, 1962)
'O akompozyjnosci w architekturze' [On decomposition in architecture], Stud. Estet., iv (1967)

BIBLIOGRAPHY

T. P. Szafer: 'Professor Żórawski', Architektura [Warsaw], 9 (1967), p. 364
I. Wisłocka: Awangardowa architektura polska, 1918–1939 [Polish avant-garde architecture, 1918–1939] (Warsaw, 1968)

WANDA KEMP-WELCH

Zorio, Gilberto (b Andorno Micca, nr Biella, Piedmont, 21 Sept 1944). Italian sculptor, performance artist and conceptual artist. He studied painting and sculpture at the Accademia di Belle Arti, Turin (1963–70) and held his first one-man show at the Galleria Sperone, Turin, in 1967. Use of such non-artistic materials as the scaffolding and foam of Chair (1967; New York, Sonnabend Gal.) ensured his inclusion in Arte Povera (1968; Bologna, Gal. de Foscherari) and performance at Arte Povera—azioni povere (1968; Amalfi, Arsenale). Zorio's characteristic pieces rejected sculptural weight and solidity by use of cantilevers or suspension and reactions over time or with the environment. Several incorporated light; Phosphorescent Fist (1971; Paris, Pompidou) was lit and plunged into darkness, alternatively absorbing and emitting and absorbing energy, being lit and then unlit.

In common with his friend Giovanni Anselmo, Zorio raised linguistic problems, as in Odio ('Hatred'), axed into a wall at Documenta 5, Kassel (1972), but his concern with energy led to experiments with both chemical and physical instability. He initiated gradual chemical reactions in his materials, which continued beyond the period of making, and used Olympic javelins to provide cantilevers; when combined with fragile, glass vessels or with the emblematic form of the five-pointed star (e.g. 5 Javelins, 1974, Lucerne, Kstmus.), they allowed for multilayered suggestions of energy and aspiration. In 1984 Zorio added to his repertory of forms the canoe (artist's col.), while new tactile elements allowed for ironic cultural references (e.g. Brancusi, 1983–9, India rubber, javelins, iron tube, halogen lamps; see 1991 exh. cat., pp. 21, 42).

BIBLIOGRAPHY

Gilberto Zorio (exh. cat. by U. Castagnotto, J. C. Ammann and W. Lippert, Lucerne, Kstmus., 1976)
Gilberto Zorio (exh. cat. by A. Boatto, C. David and D. Zachaiopolos, Paris, Pompidou, 1986)
Gilberto Zorio (exh. cat. by G. Celant, Valencia, IVAM Cent. Carme, 1991)
Gilberto Zorio (exh. cat. by N. Dimitrijevic and M. Bertoni, Amsterdam, Inst. Contemp. A.; Prato, Cent. A. Contemp. Luigi Pecci; Nice, Mus. A. Mod. & A. Contemp.; 1991–3)

MATTHEW GALE

Zorn, Anders (Leonard) (b Mora, 18 Feb 1860; d Mora, 22 Aug 1920). Swedish painter, etcher and sculptor. He was brought up by his grandparents at Mora. As he displayed a precocious talent for drawing he was admitted to the preparatory class of the Kungliga Akademi för de Fria Konsterna, Stockholm, at the age of 15. Dissatisfied with the outdated teaching and discipline of the Academy and encouraged by his early success as a painter of watercolour portraits and genre scenes (e.g. Old Woman from Mora, 1879; Mora, Zornmus.) Zorn left the Academy in 1881 to try to establish an international career. He later resided mainly in London but also travelled extensively in Italy, France, Spain, Algeria and the Balkans and visited Constantinople. However, he continued to spend most of his summers in Sweden.

In 1887–8 Zorn more or less abandoned watercolour and turned to oil painting, and he settled in Paris, where he remained until 1896. Here he began to gain international recognition thanks partly to his portraits and partly to his pictures of nudes (e.g. Une Première, 1888; Stockholm, Nmus., and Out of Doors, 1888; Göteborg, Kstmus.). Zorn adopted the innovative practice of painting nudes en plein air. The virtuoso technique that he had developed in his watercolours was to some extent carried over to his oil paintings, where the broad, free handling of the brush illustrates his admiration for Edouard Manet. During the 1890s his work displayed an increasingly strong feeling for the body's plasticity, reminiscent of Auguste Renoir. However, Zorn, like Sargent and his good friend Max Liebermann (whose portrait Zorn painted in 1891; Mora, Zornmus.), belonged to the moderate modernist phalanx who adopted features not only from Impressionism and Japonisme but also from the fashionable art of the salon. Zorn was also inspired to an increasing extent by the Old Masters that he studied in the Louvre, particularly Titian, Velázquez and Rembrandt.

Zorn's works are generally carefully composed and executed, but he strove to produce in them a feeling of improvisation by the use of lively brush work and by creating the impression of having captured the subject at a given moment. Zorn's skill and expertise, in particular, in giving his portrait models an elegant and worldly aspect, secured him a wide range of patrons throughout the world. This was especially the case in the USA, where he went for the first time in 1893 as commissioner for the Swedish art section at the Chicago World Fair, and where he returned many times. Some of his renowned American portraits are those of *Isabella Stewart Gardner* (1894; Boston, MA, Isabella Stewart Gardner Mus.), of William Howard Taft (1911; Washington, DC, White House) and of other American presidents, politicians, financiers and society ladies (e.g. *Mrs Potter Palmer*, 1893; Chicago, IL, A. Inst.). His *Self-portrait with Model* (1896; Stockholm, Nmus.; see fig.) displays the same kind of candidness in composition and execution, as well as his interest in the depiction of light.

From 1896 Mora, the place where Zorn grew up, became his permanent home, although he still made numerous journeys abroad. He built a grand house completed in 1913 in an 'Old Nordic' style, which contains his collections of art and handicrafts (now the Zorn Museum). Zorn actively encouraged the revival of traditional local customs, arts and crafts, which were being threatened by industrialization and urbanization. Many of his paintings also had motifs from Dalecarlian folklore, among them *Midsummer Dance* (1897; Stockholm, Nmus.). Zorn said of this painting: 'I regard this work as containing all my deepest feelings', and it has become one of the major pictorial expressions of Swedish National Romanticism. It shows peasants from the Mora district, who, having erected a tall pole decorated with flowers and greenery, dance under the stars until sunrise. It reveals Zorn's

interest in capturing the particular atmosphere of the light Nordic summer nights, in order to render the opalescent light, which casts no shadows, Zorn painted *Midsummer Dance* after sunset in June and July. He succeeded in depicting the enchantment and exuberance of a night devoted to celebrating the return of light after the long northern winter. In such works Zorn provided a transition from the optimistic naturalism of the 1880s to the vitalist currents that marked the early years of the 20th century in Scandinavian art, and he was in general untouched by the Symbolist-inspired, melancholic and nostalgic tones of its art of the 1890s.

Zorn's watercolour studies (many of which are in Mora, Zornmus.) remain some of his most brilliant and spontaneous works. Zorn was also skilled as an etcher, and a number of his 288 etchings reproduce his oil paintings. Zorn started etching in England in 1882 and developed a virtuoso technique, much inspired by his admiration for Rembrandt and quite impressionistic in character. His best-known prints are from his Parisian period, for example the portraits of *Rosita Mauri* (1889; e.g. Lawrence, U. KS, Spencer Mus. A.) and *Ernest Renan* (1892; e.g. Chicago, IL, A. Inst.). Zorn's sculptures also reveal his strong feeling for plasticity (which became more and more apparent in his oils from the middle of the 1890s). Although he had made wood-carvings in his youth he did not begin sculpting seriously until 1889, and he left rather few works, mostly small bronze figurines (e.g. *Fawn and Nymph*, h. 170 mm, 1895; Stockholm, Nmus.). His only monumental work is the statue of *Gustavus Vasa* in Mora (1903), which portrays the subject with an uplifted head and a strong inspired expression and whose sense of naturalness and candidness resembles the painted portraits. Zorn's autobiographical notes, written between 1907 and 1914, were published in 1982.

WRITINGS
H. H. Brummer, ed.: *Självbiografiska anteckningar* [Autobiographical notes] (Stockholm, 1982)

BIBLIOGRAPHY
L. Delteil: *Anders Zorn*, Le Peintre-graveur illustré, 4 (Paris, 1909)
G. Boëthius: *Anders Zorn, an International Swedish Artist: His Life and Work* (Stockholm, 1954)
——: *Zorn, Swedish Painter and World Traveller* (Stockholm, 1959/R 1961)
Zorn: Paintings, Graphics and Sculpture (exh. cat., ed. H. H. Brummer; Birmingham, Mus. & A. G., 1986)
Anders Zorn, 1860–1920: Gemälde, Aquarelle, Zeichnungen, Radierungen (exh. cat., ed. J. C. Jensen; Kiel, Christian-Albrechts U., Ksthalle, 1989; Munich, Ksthalle Hypo-Kultstift.; 1990)
Från två hav: Zorn och Sorolla [From two seas: Zorn and Sorolla] (exh. cat., ed. B. Sandström; Stockholm, Nmus., 1991–2)
Swedish Impressionism's Boston Champion: Anders Zorn and Isabella Stewart Gardner (exh. cat. by M. Facos, Boston, MA, Isabella Stewart Gardner Mus., 1993)
H. H. Brummer: *Till ögats fröjd och nationens förgyllning—Anders Zorn* [For the eye's delight and the nation's gilding—Anders Zorn] (Stockholm, 1994)

PONTUS GRATE

Anders Zorn: *Self-portrait with Model*, oil on canvas, 1170×940 mm, 1896 (Stockholm, Nationalmuseum)

Zoroastrianism. Religion based on the teachings of Zarathushtra, known in the West as Zoroaster. It originated in eastern Iran, possibly as early as the mid- to late 2nd millennium BC, and still has adherents in many countries.

1. Introduction. 2. Religion and beliefs. 3. Icons, images and temples.

1. INTRODUCTION. The recorded history of Zoroastrianism began with the Achaemenids who ruled in ancient Iran as the first Persian empire (538–331 BC). The Persian priests, the *magi*, later became known in the West as typical Zoroastrian priests. The Achaemenid Persians spread Zoroaster's teachings far and wide in the Ancient Near East. After Alexander the Great's conquest (330 BC) and a period of Hellenistic rule, Iranian sovereignty was restored by the Parthians from north-west Iran (*reg* 250 BC–*c.* AD 224), who upheld Zoroastrianism. They were overthrown by their co-religionists, the Sasanians (*c.* AD 224–651), who founded the second Persian empire and established a centralized, authoritative Zoroastrian Church, which combated heresy and around the 5th century AD encouraged the writing down of the holy texts. These texts, called collectively the Avesta, had until then been transmitted orally. The most sacred, the Gathas, comprising 17 psalms composed by Zoroaster, are linguistically close to the Hindu Rig Veda, which suggests a probable date of around 1400 BC. (A relatively late tradition sets Zoroaster at '228 years before Alexander', i.e. in the 6th century BC, but this date is now rejected by almost all scholars as far too late.) After the conquest of Iran by the Arabs in the 7th century AD and the imposition of Islam, Zoroastrians were reduced in subsequent centuries to a persecuted and impoverished minority. At times, however, their religious literature was allowed to flourish, as, for example, in the 9th century, the probable date of the Zand, a Middle Persian (Pahlavi) translation of the Avesta with glosses and commentaries. Much of this and other Avestan texts were later destroyed under Islam. Later in the same century a group left Iran to seek religious freedom and settled in Gujarat, where they were known as the 'Parsis' (i.e. Persians). There they too lived in poverty. The present, now prosperous Zoroastrian community is divided into two branches: the Iranis (who remained in Iran) and the Parsis. In the late 20th century there was considerable emigration, chiefly to Britain, Canada, the USA and Australia.

2. RELIGION AND BELIEFS. In Zoroaster's lifetime the Iranians still lived as pastoralists on the Central Asian steppes. However, their Bronze Age society was breaking down, the victim of roving bands of warriors. The resulting lawlessness led Zoroaster to meditate profoundly on justice and injustice and on the purpose of life. Finally he offered, as revealed truth, a doctrine of cosmic scope. He perceived Ahura Mazda, 'Lord of Wisdom', to be God, the one eternal uncreated being, wholly good, wise and beneficent; but opposed to him he apprehended Angra Mainyu (Pahlavi: Ahriman), the 'Evil Spirit', ignorant and malign, likewise uncreated but doomed in the end to perish. Ahura Mazda created the world in seven parts: sky, water, earth, plants, animals, man and fire (a vital force that gives life and warmth to the rest). It was to be a place where good and evil could encounter each other and evil be destroyed. To help in this great struggle, Ahura Mazda emanated six mighty powers, the Amesha Spentas or 'Holy Immortals', each of whom was guardian, with him, of one part of creation. The chief of these powers is Asha, the

personification of truth, justice and order and the guardian of fire. Zoroaster appointed fire as the icon in whose presence his followers should pray. The world was created perfect by Ahura Mazda; but, as he had foreseen, Angra Mainyu attacked it, bringing evil, corruption and death. All seven creations should strive instinctively or, in the case of man, consciously, to combat him and so achieve an eternal end of evil and the salvation of the world. They are aided by numerous divine beings, the *yazata*s, evoked by Ahura Mazda, and are hindered by forces of darkness, the *daeva*s, brought into existence by Angra Mainyu. Among the *yazata*s is Mithra, lord of fidelity and justice.

Zoroaster taught that each soul is judged at death, and its thoughts, words and deeds are weighed. If good is heavier, the soul crosses a broad bridge and goes up to heaven; if bad, the bridge contracts and the soul plunges down to hell. At the end of time, when evil is overcome, the Last Judgement will take place, enacted through an ordeal by fire. The blessed and damned will be reunited with their resurrected bodies and, with those still living, will have to pass through a river of molten metal. To the blessed this will feel like warm milk, but the damned will perish, body and soul. The fiery torrent will pour down into hell, destroying the last vestiges of evil, and the kingdom of Ahura Mazda will come, on an earth made eternally good and beautiful, like a spring garden (Pers.: *paeridaēza*, from which comes the Eng. word 'paradise'). There the blessed will rejoice in his presence for ever. Zoroaster believed these 'last things' were not far off, and he foretold that one coming after him, a saviour, would lead the final struggle against evil. His followers developed this prediction into belief in a World Saviour to be born of Zoroaster's seed by a virgin mother.

Zoroastrian priests solemnize a daily act of worship, the *yasna*, celebrated to sustain the world and man. Each Zoroastrian is also obliged to pray five times in each 24 hours and to wear constantly a sacred cord wound thrice round the waist, a reminder of the threefold Zoroastrian ethic of good thoughts, words and acts. Purity laws are observed, part of the struggle against physical corruption; to guard the purity of earth and fire, corpses were neither buried nor burnt, but were exposed in barren places (later on funerary towers, *dakhma*s) to be devoured by wild beasts and birds.

3. ICONS, IMAGES AND TEMPLES. For a long time Zoroastrianism left no tangible remains. The *yasna* was solemnized on a small area of clean flat ground consecrated for the purpose, and icons were natural phenomena, above all fire (prayer being said facing the sun or moon, or a ritual or hearth fire). Ritual vessels, at first of stone, then metal (pestle and mortar, bowls, brazier and knife) were probably little different from those in domestic use. The earliest identifiable religious Zoroastrian artefact dates from the reign of Cyrus the Great (*reg* 559–530 BC), for whom, it seems, fire was elevated for devotional purposes in a handsome stone container. In profile this looked like a pedestal altar with a three-stepped top and base, but it was characterized by a hollow top, deep enough to contain the bed of hot ash needed to keep a wood fire continually burning. The remains of two or three such fire-holders have been found at Pasargadae in the province of Fars in

1. Zoroastrian tomb of Artaxerxes III Ochus (*reg* 358–338 BC) at Persepolis, Iran, façade showing the ruler standing before a Zoroastrian fire-holder

The winged-circle symbol (with and without a human figure) appears also on palace walls and on seals, as does another symbol of royal power, the 'hero triumphant': a man with kingly beard depicted killing a lion or fabulous beast. Seals also show the king as 'lion-dangler', holding a lion in each extended hand by the hindlegs. Another power symbol is a lion overcoming a bull; bulls and lions appear separately in carvings at Achaemenid palaces (notably Persepolis and Susa), together with fabulous beasts. Some scholars have sought a religious symbolism in these creatures, but this is more evident in the 12-petalled roses and evergreen trees abundantly carved at Persepolis. To Zoroastrians both can symbolize long life and immortality.

There are no traces of temples at these palaces, but PASARGADAE has the ruins of a tall tower, the Zendan-i Sulayman, and there is a similar tower, the well-preserved Ka'ba-i Zardusht, at Naqsh-i Rustam (see fig. 2). Each tower was set on a stone plinth, and its lower section was of solid stone. A single chamber in the upper part, reached by an outer stone stair, was entered by a stone door and had a double stone roof. The towers' purpose may have been funerary, like the kings' rock-cut tombs, to prevent embalmed bodies from polluting the good creations; perhaps they were used for lesser members of the royal family. (All three Zoroastrian dynasties embalmed instead of exposing their dead.) Alternatively, they may have been used as repositories for sacred scriptures or utensils.

Iran, datable by their fine workmanship and lack of toothed-chisel marks. They contrast with an almost flat-topped Median altar at Tepe Nush-i Jan, which cannot have supported a Zoroastrian sacred fire, but which may be the type of altar that inspired the shape of the fire-holders (for a possible origin of the fire cult *see* CHOGHA ZANBIL). Fire-holders like those at Pasargadae appear in carvings set over the rock-cut tombs of Darius the Great (*reg* 521–486 BC) and his successors at Naqsh-i Rustam and Persepolis (see fig. 1). There the king stands on a stepped plinth, right hand raised in salutation, before a fire-holder on a similar plinth, from which rises a pyramidal mass of flames. Above hovers a figure in a winged circle, dressed and bearded like the king, whom he faces, one hand raised in the same gesture, the other holding a ring (in Babylonian iconography a symbol of divinity). The winged circle derived ultimately from the winged disc of the Egyptian sun-god Horus, who was manifest in each pharaoh. This had been widely adopted in the Near East as a symbol of power and royalty, the human figure being added in Assyria. For the Achaemenids it probably symbolized both the royal *khvarenah*, the divine grace that attended kings, and the sun (to which, as a 'glory', the *khvarenah* was linked). In the funerary carvings a Mesopotamian moon symbol (a disc with crescent along its lower rim) is carved behind the figure in a winged circle, so that the king stands reverently before one earthly and two heavenly representatives of cosmic fire.

2. Zoroastrian tower called the Ka'ba-i Zardusht, Naqsh i Rustam, near Persepolis, Iran, end of the 5th century BC

3. Zoroastrian fire-holders, h. 1.76 m (largest), at Naqsh-i Rustam, near Persepolis, Iran, 3rd–6th centuries AD

Under Artaxerxes II Memnon (*reg* 404–358 BC) an image cult was introduced in connection with the *yazata* Anahita, whose concept had been influenced by that of Babylonian Ishtar. Soon statues were erected to other *yazata*s, with temples to house them. There followed a temple cult of fire, the fire being consecrated with elaborate rites. Temples of both kinds multiplied under the Parthians, who were probably responsible for the evolution of the characteristic Zoroastrian square sanctuary, with domed roof set on squinches (Pers. *chahār-ṭāq*: 'fire temple'). The first cult statues were probably modelled on Babylonian prototypes, but under the Parthians Greek iconography prevailed, as devices on coins show. The Sasanians waged a successful iconoclastic campaign, declaring that cult statues were dwelling places for *daeva*s, who entered them to misappropriate offerings. Accordingly, no such statues survive, although divinities appear, anthropomorphically represented, in rock reliefs. Statues of kings and nobles have been found, in metal, stone and terracotta, some of which may have been used in the cult of the *fravashi*s (spirits of the dead), which is still of great importance to modern Zoroastrianism. Many small, crudely made terracotta figurines are known. Numerous caskets that held disarticulated bones after exposure have been excavated in what is now Western Central Asia. Some of these bear inscriptions and carved scenes. Rock-cut ossuaries, usually unadorned, are common in the province of Fars.

At TAKHT-I SULAYMAN in Azerbaijan a great Sasanian fire temple has been excavated, revealing high domed chambers, one panelled with alabaster, and long pillared halls. The walls of the fire sanctuary were adorned with a stucco frieze depicting human figures in high relief. Wall paintings, with *yazata*s represented in Greek style, have been uncovered at KUH-I KHWAJA in Sistan; elsewhere outer temple walls were carved with figures, probably divine. The ruins of many small fire temples (usually just the *chahār-ṭāq*) have been identified, especially in Fars. Some old stone fire-holders survive (see fig. 3), and the reverse sides of Sasanian coins regularly show a fire-holder bearing blazing fire. These holders are all essentially of the Pasargadae type.

Under Islam all fire temples were eventually destroyed or turned into mosques. Sacred fires had to be hidden away in what looked like poor domestic houses. When in modern times it became possible to build dignified temples again, these were in local architectural styles (Muslim or Hindu), pleasing but with little adornment. In some Iranian temples the sacred fire is still set in a holder of Pasargadae type, but most have adopted the Parsi habit of keeping it in a metal container.

BIBLIOGRAPHY

O. M. Dalton: *The Treasure of the Oxus* (London, 1905, 3/1964)
E. Schmidt: *Persepolis*, 3 vols (Chicago, 1953–71)
R. Ghirshman: *Iran, Parthians and Sasanians* (London, 1962)
——: *Persia: From the Origins to Alexander the Great* (London, 1964)
J. R. Hinnells: *Persian Mythology* (London, 1973, 2/1985)
G. Herrmann: *The Iranian Revival* (London, 1977)
D. Stronach: *Pasargadae* (Oxford, 1978)
M. Boyce: *Zoroastrians: Their Religious Beliefs and Practices* (London, 1979)
G. Gnoli: *Zoroaster's Time and Homeland: A Study on the Origins of Mazdeism and Related Problems* (Naples, 1980)
M. Boyce: *Textual Sources for the Study of Zoroastrianism* (Manchester, 1984)

MARY BOYCE

Zōroku [Hamamura]. Name used by five generations of Japanese seal-carvers, active from the mid-18th century to the Meiji period (1868–1912). An ancient bronze seal (Jap. *kichū*) with a stem in the shape of a turtle (*zōroku*) was passed down from one generation of the family to the next. The founder of the Hamamura school was Zōroku I [Kitsu Mokyo] (*b* Edo [now Tokyo], 1735; *d* Edo, 1794), who worked in an Archaic seal-carving style influenced by KŌ FUYŌ (*see* JAPAN, §XVI, 20). He was the eldest of four sons, and from an early age he was attracted by the Archaic school (Kotaiha) of Kō Fuyō. He went to Kyoto to learn the technique of seal-engraving from Fuyō and to seek out the mysteries of the art. He later returned to Edo, where he was instrumental in spreading the Archaic-school style. His style, which came close to that of Fuyō, gained him a very high reputation (see fig.). In 1781 he traced and carved a copy of the *Hakubōcho* (Chin. *Baimaotie*: 'White grass album') of Wang Yami (1494–1533), which was virtually indistinguishable from the original. When Fuyō died in 1784, Zōroku requested a text from his friend the Zen priest Taiten for the master's gravestone epitaph and carved it in the style of the calligrapher Kan Tenju (1727–95) as an earnest expression of his grief. The gravestone is now in the temple Tentokuji, in the Minato district of Tokyo. In 1791 he requested from Taiten a text for his own gravestone, which was to be erected before his death. He is buried in the graveyard of Ryōzanji temple, Yokogawacho, in Tokyo.

As Zōroku I produced no heirs, the succession passed to his nephew, Zōroku II [Funsai] (*b* Edo, 1772; *d* Edo, 1819). He was the nephew of Zōroku I and was adopted into that family. He chose the character *fun* ('three-legged turtle') as part of his artist's name (*gō*), Funsai, a continuation of the tradition of turtle-related names begun by the previous generation. He studied the seal-carving style of

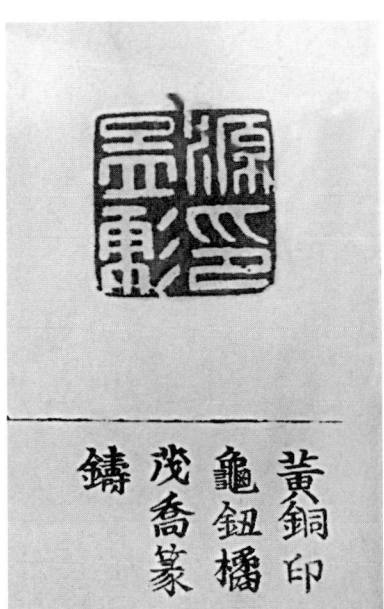

Zōroku I: Kō Fuyō's private seal from the *Fuyō sanbō shi inpu* [Album of Fuyō *sanbō*'s private seals], seal impression reading *Gen mō hyū in*, 80×50 mm, before 1784 (Japan, Mizuta private collection)

Zōroku I and improved his skills by travelling in the Kansai (Kyoto–Osaka) area, the home of the art. After the death of Zōroku I, he inherited the *kichū* seal and received the name Zōroku II. In 1804, by order of the shogunate, he carved the official seal to be used on the reply given to the emissary from Korea. He collected and researched rare seal albums imported from China and owned by daimyo and nobles, such as the *Han tongyin cong* ('Collection of Han bronze seals', ed. Wang Qishu, *c.* 1766) and *Su shi yin lüe* ('Mr Su's brief account of seals', ed. Su Xuan, *c.* 1617; *see* CHINA, §XIII, 22) and, combining his own creative forms with these seal styles, became known as a master seal-carver. His discernment was further refined by his liking for calligraphy, paintings and pottery. He too was buried at Ryōzanji. Together with MASUDA Kinsai, he is considered one of the Two Great Seal-carvers of the Edo period.

Zōroku III [Nankei, later Tossai and Kizen; family name Kobayashi, later Kanayama] (*b* Edo, 1791; *d* Edo, 1843) was apprenticed to Zōroku II, and as pre-eminent pupil he assumed the family name of Hamamura after his teacher's death, inherited the *kichū* and became known as Zōroku III. The number of his pupils grew rapidly, and he was especially adept at carving in copper, jade and crystal, becoming renowned for his exquisite artistry. During a visit to Kansai in 1818–29 he was praised for his carving style. Well-known literati such as RAI SAN'YŌ, Shinozaki Yōchiku (1781–1851), Saitō Setsudo (1797–1865) and others contributed prefaces to his seal albums. Like his forebears, he was buried at Ryōzanji. His wife, Kanayama Senō, was a talented painter and seal-carver. As they had no children, Zōroku III was succeeded by Shiomi Taikai [Zōroku IV] (*b* Kibi Prov. [now Okayama Prefect.], 1826; *d* Edo [now Tokyo], 1875). He became the fourth-generation head of the school. He lived in Hamachō, Edo, and initially studied the Inten (Chin. *mu zhuan*; Jap. *byūten*) seal script with Ono Shō, then became apprenticed to Zōroku III, succeeding him in 1860. He wrote and promoted the *Bankaidō inshi* ('Writings on the seals of Bankaidō') and *Zōrokukyo inryaku* ('Outline of seals of the Zōroku'). He is buried at the temple Yanaka Tennoji in Tokyo.

Zōroku V [Muki Dōjin, Chōchū Shūjin] (*b* Tsugaru, Aomori Prefect., 1866; *d* Tokyo, 1909) was fifth-generation head of the Hamamura school. He moved to Tokyo in 1889, where he studied seal-carving under Kaneko Sako (1815–52) and Zōroku IV. He succeeded Zōroku IV in 1894 and moved to the Mukōjima area of Tokyo. He travelled throughout Japan and in China, where contact with WU CHANGSHI, who carved seals based on ancient inscriptions, and with Xu Sangeng (1826–90) led to a transformation of his carving style. He also devised pottery seals. His writings include *Zōrokukyo insū, Zōroku kin'in, Ketsukin seki en, Zō rokudōji inpu, Chōchū Ryosinzei* and *Kutsuōtetsugi*.

BIBLIOGRAPHY

K. Nakai: *Nihon in jinden* [Accounts of Japanese seal-carvers] (Tokyo, 1915)

K. Ota: 'Gosei Hamamura Zōroku' [Hamamura Zōroku V], *Shohin*, 149 (1964), pp. 61–3

Y. Nakata, ed.: *Nihon no tenkoku* [Japanese seal carving] (Tokyo, 1966)

NORIHISA MIZUTA

Zoumbaria. *See under* ANTIPAROS.

Zrzavý, Jan (*b* Vadin, near Havlíčkův Brod, 5 Nov 1890; *d* Prague, 12 Oct 1977). Czech painter and illustrator. He studied painting in Prague, first in private schools, then at the School of Applied Art (1907–9). In autumn 1907 he made his first, brief visit to Paris. Shortly after his return he succeeded for the first time in expressing his own inner world, infused with a new melancholy, in a small pastel *Valley of Sadness* (1907; painted version, 1908; both Prague, N.G.), which he looked upon as his talisman throughout his life. His early work ranged from flat and linear painting in the Gauguin tradition, via remarkable collages made from coloured foil, to rhapsodic Expressionism, as in *Antichrist* (1909; Prague, N.G.). Several self-portraits of 1908–9 bear witness to his quest for himself and to his penchant for self-stylization.

Zrzavý's emphasis on the symbolic and psychic roots of his artistic work brought him into the Sursum group, which in 1910–12 attracted the second Symbolist generation in Bohemia, including F. Kobliha, J. Konůpek and Josef Váchal, who represented the opposite pole to the Cubist orientation of the Group of Plastic Artists. Zrzavý had a basically abstract relationship with Cubism in spite of having taken it up for a while in his attempt 'to discover the original and essential outlines of things and beings'. His conscious creation of plastic form incorporating symbolic content was given further impetus after 1911 by his friendship with Bohumil Kubišta, who introduced him to laws of geometrical composition derived from a study of the Old Masters and strengthened his tendency to elementary simplification. One result of this was Zrzavý's creation of newly turned, rounded shapes which, modified in various ways, came to the fore in his figural and landscape paintings.

In a series of works from 1913 to 1919 Zrzavý used hyperbole to express complicated states of mind, projected on the one hand into variants of biblical themes and on the other into characteristic beings with ecstatic expressions of pain and rapture, as in *Meditace* (1915; Prague, N.G.). The mystery of the inner composition of his work is suggested in an unfinished oil painting, *Cleopatra II* (1919; Prague, N.G.), which at the same time documents his obsession with a theme that permeated his paintings from 1912 to 1957. At the end of World War I he became closely associated with Josef Čapek, Vlastislav Hofman, Václav Špála, Rudolf Kremlička and O. Marvánek, setting up with them the Stiffneck group (*Tvrdošíjní skupina*), which held its first exhibition in the spring of 1918. In the same year Zrzavý had his first one-man show at the Topič Salon in Prague.

Zrzavý's work began to show the influence of contemporary Neo-classicism translated into magical phenomena, as in *Coffee-house* (1923; Brno, Morav. Gal.). He attracted the attention of the new generation of artists associated with Devětsil, whose spokesman, Karel Teige, devoted his first monograph (1923) to the work of Zrzavý. In the inter-war period Zrzavý lived alternately in Prague, Paris and Brittany. A stay at Venice in 1928 inspired him to create imaginative images in which he transformed a concrete motif into a spiritual vision, as in *San Marco at Night* (1930; Prague, N.G.).

Zrzavý also painted the Czech countryside: his native Czech-Moravian Highlands, the mining area of Ostrava, and Prague. From 1923 to 1942 he was a member of the Artistic Forum, which held an impressive retrospective exhibition of his work in 1941. A retrospective exhibition at the Prague National Gallery in 1963 attracted unprecedented crowds. He kept returning to his favourite themes in different variants, but he was also receptive to new influences, the most important of which was his journey to Greece in 1967. In his late work he preferred pastel, watercolour and tempera, techniques that enabled him to work faster and to achieve the greatest brilliance of colour.

BIBLIOGRAPHY
Dílo Jana Zrzavého, 1906–1940 [Jan Zrzavý's work, 1906–40] (Prague, 1941)
D. Plichta: *Le Peintre Jan Zrzavý: Symboliste moderne* (Prague, 1958)
J. Zemina, ed.: *Svět Jana Zrzavého* [The world of Jan Zrzavý] (Prague, 1963)
F. Dvořák: *Jan Zrzavý* (Prague, 1965)
M. Lamač: *Jan Zrzavý* (Prague, 1980)
Jan Zrzavý (exh. cat., ed. J. A. Brabcová; Prague, N.G., 1990)

LENKA BYDŽOVSKÁ

Zsigmond, King of Hungary. *See* LUXEMBOURG, House of, (5).

Zsolnay Ceramics Factory. Hungarian ceramics factory. In 1851 the merchant Miklós Zsolnay the elder founded the factory in Pécs, southern Hungary, for his eldest son Ignác Zsolnay. Early wares comprised very simple, useful wares, including dishes, water pipes and terracotta garden ornaments, that satisfied local demands. In 1865 Vilmos Zsolnay (1828–1900) took over the concern from his brother and added a range of decorative vessels including flower-pots, wash-bowls and jugs. Zsolnay used a high-firing cream body decorated with a glaze mixed with metallic oxides, which was known as 'porcelain faience'. Production is characterized by various styles of decoration based on Bronze Age wares excavated in Transdanubia, called 'Pannonia' wares, and Renaissance, Japanese, Persian, Anatolian (Turkish) and Hungarian folk ceramics. In 1878 the factory exhibited a variety of 'porcelain faience' at the Exposition Universelle in Paris and was awarded the Grand Prix. In 1883, after numerous experiments with the chemists Lajos Petri and Vince Warta, an iridescent glaze was developed, which was known as 'Eosin'. Articles with the 'Eosin' glaze were often further embellished with marbelling and etching or decorated with large Persian motifs or Hungarian flowers. In the 1890s the factory created a frost-proof material called 'Pyrogranit' that could be covered in a salt or tin glaze and used on the exteriors of buildings. Vilmos Zsolnay produced ceramic work for the buildings of Ödön Lechner, where the decorative effect of coloured tiles was part of an attempt to create a Hungarian style. After Zsolnay's death management of the factory passed to his son Miklós Zsolnay the younger (*d* 1922), who employed such artists as Henrik Darilek and József Rippl-Rónai.

Between 1896 and 1900 the factory was influenced by the Secession movements and produced wares decorated with flowers, leaves and butterflies (*see* HUNGARY, fig. 20). After 1920 the factory produced only household and industrial goods, and in 1948 was nationalized.

BIBLIOGRAPHY
E. Hárs: *The Zsolnay Ceramics* (Pécs, 1982)

FERENC BATÁRI

Zuan da Milano. *See* RUBINO, GIOVANNI.

Zuazo (Ugalde), Secundino (*b* Bilbao, 21 May 1887; *d* Madrid, 12 July 1970). Spanish architect and urban planner. He studied architecture in Barcelona and Madrid, qualifying in 1912. After attending the International Congress on House Construction and Urban Planning held in London in 1920 he became interested in the problems of housing and urban development in major cities. Subsequently he was involved in plans for urban reform, such as the Inner Bilbao Road Reform Project (1921) and the Madrid Urban Planning Project (1930), executed in collaboration with the German architect Hermann Jansen. In 1925, when he attended the Exposition Internationale des Arts Décoratifs et Industriels Modernes in Paris Zuazo encountered for the first time contemporary Dutch architecture, with its characteristic use of brick; the following year he travelled to the Netherlands and came into contact with the Amsterdam School and the architecture of W. M. Dudok. During the Spanish Civil War (1936–9) Zuazo lived mainly in Paris; subsequently he lived in Las Palmas before returning to Madrid in 1942. Zuazo's work blended an appreciation of such Modernist styles as Functionalism and Rationalism with a concern for the social dimension. As well as undertaking large-scale urban projects, throughout his career he designed residential blocks, such as the Casa de las Flores (1930), Madrid, family houses, such as the Hotel-Vivienda (1917), the Escorial, Madrid, and city buildings, such as the Palacio de la Música de Madrid (1924), the Frontón Recoletos (1935), Madrid, and the Frontón Jai-Alai (1961), San Sebastián.

BIBLIOGRAPHY
L. Blanco Soler: *Zuazo y su tiempo* (Madrid, 1973)
L. Maure: *Zuazo* (Madrid, 1987)

PILAR BENITO

Zuber & Cie. French wallpaper manufacturing company established in 1790 in Mulhouse, Alsace. Originally the company was set up under the name of Nicolas Dolfus & Cie with Joseph-Louis Malaine (1745–1809), a designer from the Gobelins, as artistic director. In 1795 it changed its name to Hartmann, Risler & Cie, and in 1797 it moved to the commandery of Rixheim at the Mulhouse city gates. It was bought out in 1802 by Jean Zuber (1773–1852), the head of the marketing side of the business, whose name the company adopted and whose descendants remained in possession of the company until 1968.

Zuber was the driving-force behind the company. He ensured high-quality production by employing such excellent designers as Eugene Ehrmann (1804–96) and Georges Zipelius (1808–90), who designed 'Décor chinois' (1832; U. Manchester, Whitworth A.G.), and by perfecting new wallpaper manufacturing techniques: *irisé* or blended colourgrounds from 1819 (*see* WALLPAPER, colour pl. IV, fig. 3); roller-printed line engravings in 1826; the use of the continuous paper roll in 1829; and printing stripes in 1843. Zuber was the first factory in France to introduce mechanized printing by adopting steam-powered equipment in 1850.

The artistic aspect of production was not neglected. The company produced 21 designs for panoramic wallpapers between 1804 and 1861, some of which continue to be printed, and was the scene of continuous and intense creative activity until the beginning of the 20th century. Subsequently it relied principally on repeating old designs and on producing wallpapers in imitation of period styles (with the exception of the silk-screened panoramic wallpapers launched during the 1960s). The Zuber collection is in the Musée du Papier Peint, Rixheim.

BIBLIOGRAPHY
J. Zuber: *Réminiscences et souvenirs* (Mulhouse, 1895)
La Fabrique de papiers peints de Jean Zuber & Cie (1797–1897) (Rixheim, 1897)
B. Jacqué: 'Les Papiers peints panoramiques de Jean Zuber & Cie', *Bull. Soc. Indust. Mulhouse* (1984), pp. 79–113
O. Nouvel-Kammerer, ed.: *Papiers peints panoramiques* (Paris, 1990), p. 323

BERNARD JACQUÉ

Züberlin, Jakob (*b* Heidelberg, 1556; *d* Tübingen, 1607). German painter and woodcut designer. His training appears Swiss, but he is first documented in 1579 in Wildberg, in the duchy of Württemberg, painting an organ front. Shortly afterwards he was mentioned as the painter of epitaph pictures in Herrenberg (Stiftskirche) and in the vicinity of Tübingen (Derendingen). By 1583 at the latest he was connected with the court at Stuttgart. In 1586 he married the widow of the painter Hans Schickhardt (1512–85) in Tübingen, thereby acquiring a workshop and the rights and privileges of a painter. In Stuttgart he worked first as an illuminator, imaginatively creating richly decorated title pages for manuscripts, using ornamentation reminiscent of the decoration on Swiss painted glass. He was probably also employed in illustrating family record books, an art form that was flourishing in university towns at the time. Although he was not a salaried official of the court at Stuttgart, he was engaged for various specific tasks, mainly of a decorative nature. Between 1587 and 1591 he painted hunting scenes and history pictures relating to recent events in Württemberg, some of them very large canvases, for the apartment of Duke Ludwig VI of Württemberg (*reg* 1568–93) in the Altes Schloss at Stuttgart; the few surviving designs convey only a vague idea of the whole. Shortly afterwards he worked at the Neues Lusthaus at Stuttgart, contributing to an iconographically original programme devised by Hans Steiner and Wendel Dietterlin in which Züberlin was assigned hunting scenes in the Stromberg and Tübingen forests. A pen-and-ink drawing of a *Badger-hunt in the Pleasure Gardens at Stuttgart* (1588; Cologne, Wallraf-Richartz-Mus.) may have been part of preliminary work for wall paintings of this kind; it is notable for its factual accuracy and lively observation.

In Züberlin's oeuvre there is a dearth of drawings done for their own sake as collectors' items—this is true of art in Württemberg in general at that time—and of altarpieces and devotional pictures; there was hardly any call for these in Protestant areas during this period, but this was compensated for by commissions for wall paintings and epitaphs, such as his *Allegory on Death (Vanity of Life)* (1583; Stuttgart, Württemberg. Landesbib.; see fig.). In 1596 he painted the main chamber of Tübingen Rathaus

Jakob Züberlin: *Allegory on Death (Vanity of Life)*, drawing, 310×192 mm, 1583 (Stuttgart, Württembergische Landesbibliothek)

with scenes from the Old Testament and Roman history (*in situ*), basing them on woodcuts by Tobias Stimmer and using Dietterlin's *Architectura* (vol. i, Stuttgart, 1593; vol. ii, Strasbourg, 1594) as a basis for the ornamental framework. He also made preliminary drawings for wood-cut illustrations published by the Tübingen publishers (including *Imagines professorum Tübingensium*, 1596) and painted miniature portraits, such as that of the theologian *Jacob Andrea* (Edinburgh, N.G.), which were probably connected with the fashion for family record books, then at its height. The few known drawings from his later years (1597–1601) are imbued with the aesthetic ideal of late Mannerism, as practised in Haarlem and at the Rudolphine court at Prague, and are a clear departure from the ornamental linearity of his earlier years.

BIBLIOGRAPHY

W. Fleischhauer: 'Die Renaissance—Malereien im Tübinger Rathaus', *Schwäb. Heimath.* (1934)
H. Geissler: 'Zeichner am württembergischen Hof um 1600', *Jb. Staatl. Kstsamml. Baden-Württemberg*, vi (1969), pp. 79–126
W. Fleischhauer: *Renaissance im Herzogtum Württemberg* (Stuttgart, 1971), pp. 161–3

HEINRICH GEISSLER

Zubov. Russian family of painters and graphic artists.

(1) Fyodor (Yevtikhiyev) Zubov (*b* Solikamsk, *c.* 1615; *d* Moscow, 3 Nov 1689). Painter. He worked at Veliky Ustyug and later at Yaroslavl' and in the monastery of St Anthony Siysky at Sol'vychegodsk, sometimes with his brother Osip (*b* and *d* unknown). From 1662 he was in Moscow working with Simon Ushakov; after the latter's death he took over as director of the imperial workshop of icon painters in the Armoury (Oruzhenaya Palata) in the Moscow kremlin. His work included icons, illuminated manuscripts, drawings for engravings, and wall paintings. He contributed to the iconostases in the cathedral of the Dormition (1653; Uspensky) in Moscow and in the church of the Prophet Elijah (1660) at Yaroslavl'. His most important icons are *St John the Baptist in the Wilderness* (*c.* 1650; Moscow, Tret'yakov Gal.), *St Andrew* (1669; Moscow, Kremlin, Armoury), the *Virgin of Smolensk* (*c.* 1670; Moscow, Novodevichy Monastery), the *Prophet Elijah* (1672; Yaroslavl', Church of the Prophet Elijah), *St Nicholas the Miracle-worker* (1676; Moscow, Kolomen-skoye Estate Mus.) and the icons from the *Deësis* tier in the church of the Saviour beyond the Golden Gate (1680; Spas za zolotoy reshetkoy) in the Moscow kremlin. He made free use of European methods combined with Russian traditions of icon painting, and his work is characterized by its range of colour and its psychological insight. The landscapes in the icons of *St John the Baptist* and the *Prophet Elijah* are masterpieces: they appear to weave a Paradise garden from the finest golden threads covering the trees and cliffs. His model drawings in the Siysky manual for icon painters (1658; St Petersburg, Rus. N. Lib.) are distinguished by their delicate line and rich ornament.

G. KOMELOVA, G. I. VZDORNOV

(2) Ivan (Fyodorovich) Zubov (*b* Moscow, 1667; *d* Moscow, Oct 1743). Engraver, elder son of (1) Fyodor Zubov. He first trained as an icon painter with his father. From 1689 he studied in the workshop of the Armoury in Moscow. In 1703–4 he worked under the engraver Adriaan Schoonebeeck (1661–1705), and this experience deter-mined his future activity. From 1708 to 1728 he worked at the Moscow Printing Office. He engraved many illus-trations for church books and produced plates for the printing of antiminsions (altar-cloths containing relics) and *konklyuzii* (theses) for the Slavic-Greco-Latin Acad-emy in Moscow. His compositions were decorative and included many figures and subjects based on philosophical and theological texts, depicting real persons and events as well as allegorical figures and scenes. Among the best of those with secular subjects are *Peter I's Boat* (1721), representations of fireworks and battles, and a *konklyuziya* (1724) on the coronation of the Empress Catherine I (*reg* 1725–7). He also engraved portraits, such as those of *Peter I, Catherine I* and *Stefan Yavorsky*. His work displays characteristics derived from 17th-century art: a certain stiffness, a tendency towards ornament, three-dimension-ality of forms, precision of outline and restraint in move-ment. An interesting large engraving shows a *View of Izmaylovo* (1727–8), in which the flatness of the back-ground landscape contrasts sharply with the lively, dynamic scene in the foreground. After the studio attached to the

Printing Office was closed in 1728 he worked on private commissions and at the Commercial Department.

(3) Aleksey (Fyodorovich) Zubov (*b* Moscow, 1682/3; *d* Moscow, 1 June 1751). Draughtsman and printmaker, younger son of (1) Fyodor Zubov. From 1689 he studied in the workshop of the Armoury in Moscow and from 1699 under the engraver Adriaan Schoonebeeck. He then worked in the engraving department of the Armoury. In 1711 he moved to St Petersburg, and until 1727 he was in charge of the engraving department of the St Petersburg Printing Office. This was the most brilliant and fruitful period of his career. His work marks a high point in printmaking in Petrine Russia. He was a skilled draughtsman, and nearly always worked from his own designs. He was equally successful in a variety of genres: he engraved views of St Petersburg, battles, firework displays, triumphal processions, allegorical compositions, maps and book illustrations. His techniques included etching, engraving and mezzotint. He produced over 100 sheets in all.

His work is characterized by a high degree of technical skill, precision and clarity of composition, together with a taste for specific detail and emotional tension; it is typical of the Baroque period of Russian printmaking in the early 18th century. He was the first Russian printmaker to devote his attention to the linear construction of space, generally combining atmospheric perspective with axonometric projection. Some of his work exhibits a flatness derived from the style typical of 17th-century Russian draughtsmanship. His finest work is the elaborate *Panorama of St Petersburg* (1716), showing in documentary fashion all the city's buildings: by convention, both banks of the Neva are shown in a single plane. In the foreground is a river festival with numerous ships and river-boats. This work laid the foundation for the development of townscapes in Russian art. His dynamic battle-scenes, such as *Battle at Cape Gangut* (1714) and *Battle at Grengam Island* (1721), are based on sharp contrasts of light and shade and rich gradations of tone. The *Wedding of Peter I* (1712) is an early depiction of an indoor scene. In 1729 his skill began to decline, but he continued to work on private commissions and in the Synod Printing House in Moscow. From 1744 he made dyes for stamped paper in the Department of Manufactures; his work from this period is of little artistic interest.

BIBLIOGRAPHY

M. Lebedyansky: *Gravyor petrovskoy epokhi Aleksey Zubov* [Aleksey Zubov, an engraver of the Petrine period] (Moscow, 1973)
M. Alekseyeva: 'Brat'ya Ivan i Aleksey Zubovy i gravyura petrovskogo vremeni' [The brothers Ivan and Aleksey Zubov and engraving in the Petrine period], *Rossiya v period reform Petra I* [Russia during the reforms of Peter I] (Moscow, 1978)
V. Bryusova: *Fyodor Zubov* (Moscow, 1985)
Aleksey Fyodorovich Zubov (exh. cat., Leningrad, 1988)

G. KOMELOVA

Zuccalli. Italian–Swiss family of stuccoists, builders and architects active in Bavaria. The first important member of the family was Giovanni Battista Zuccalli (*d* 1678), a stuccoist recorded as working in Kempten (Allgäu) in 1661. His son-in-law Gaspare [Kaspar] Zuccalli (1629–78) and a cousin Domenico Christoforus Zuccalli (*fl* 1651; *d* 1702) worked together (until *c*. 1666), designing and building churches and conventual buildings in Upper Bavaria and the Innviertel district. Gaspare, following his appointment (1668) as master mason to the Bavarian electoral court, brought (1) Enrico Zuccalli, son of Giovanni Battista, to Munich. Enrico, who had previously trained in Paris in the circle of Gianlorenzo Bernini, became the most important architect in the family and one of the most prominent architects in the circle of Italian-influenced builders from the Grisons. In later years he trained his young cousin Giovanni Gaspare Zuccalli (*c*. 1654–1717), son of Giovanni Domenico Christoforus, who subsequently settled in Salzburg. There he built the Kajetanerkirche (1685–1711) and the Erhardskirche (1685–9) nearby at Nonnthal.

(1) Enrico [Henrico] **Zuccalli** (*b* Roveredo, Grisons, *c*. 1642; *d* Munich, 8 March 1724). In 1672 he was appointed court architect in Munich (becoming chief court architect in 1677) and in 1673 he was commissioned to design a pilgrimage church at Altötting (Lower Bavaria). His design for a centrally planned, domed building was closely related to works by Bernini, and although work was abandoned in 1679 on the Elector Ferdinand's death with only the foundations begun, the project had introduced the architectural ideas of the High Roman Baroque to Bavaria and pioneered Baroque centralized planning there for churches. Meanwhile, Zuccalli continued work on the Theatine church of St Kajetan (begun 1663 by Agostino Barelli), Munich, altering and completing the dome (1674–92), and he decorated several suites of rooms in the Munich Residenz (from 1680; destr.). Throughout his career in Munich, his great rival was his fellow architect from the Grisons, Giovanni Antonio Viscardi.

In 1684 Zuccalli was commissioned by the Elector Maximilian II Emanuel to extend the buildings and gardens at SCHLOSS SCHLEISSHEIM, north of Munich. He began by building Schloss Lustheim (1684–8), a small hunting-lodge with a strictly symmetrical plan and with a later semicircular gallery (1695–1724) added to the rear. It was the first Baroque *maison de plaisance* in Bavaria. Zuccalli visited Paris in 1684–5, but his visits to Brussels and Holland between 1693 and 1699 (during Maximilian II Emanuel's tenure as governor of the Spanish Netherlands) may have had an influence on the gallery and the canals in the gardens at Schleissheim. The designs for the Neues Schloss there (shell built 1701–4; continued 1719–26 by Joseph Effner and completed in the 19th century) were influenced by Versailles and Schloss Schönbrunn, Vienna. Zuccalli's extensions, however, to Schloss Nymphenburg (begun 1701; *see* MUNICH, §IV, 3), which consisted of pavilions linked to the main block by two-storey galleries, were modelled on the Dutch palace at Het Loo (enlarged from 1690 by Daniel Marot).

In about 1688 Zuccalli drew up plans (unexecuted) for alterations to the country seat of Graf Dominik Andreas von Kaunitz at Austerlitz (now Slavkov u Brna, Czech Republic) and also built a new town palace (begun 1688; now Palais Kaunitz-Liechtenstein) for him in Vienna. In the latter building, he introduced for the first time north of the Alps the type of Italian palazzo façade with a raised central range articulated by colossal pilasters in the manner of Bernini's Palazzo Chigi-Odescalchi in Rome. Zuccalli's

Palais Portia (1693–4; subsequently altered) in Munich is a simplified version. Other projects in the 1690s included the conventual building of the Englisches Fräulein (destr.) in Munich, alterations to the electoral hunting-lodge (destr. 1806) at Lichtenburg and plans for rebuilding the Bonn Residenzschloss (1697–1702; completed after 1715 by Robert de Cotte) for Joseph Clemens, Prince–Archbishop of Cologne.

In 1706 Zuccalli lost his post when Maximilian II Emanuel was placed under the ban of the Holy Roman Empire for allying with the French in the War of the Spanish Succession (1701–14), and he fled first to Brussels and then to France, while Bavaria was ruled by an imperial Austrian administration. Although Zuccalli was reinstated in 1715 on the Elector's return, his work was considered old-fashioned, and thereafter he was given only routine tasks while all the prestigious commissions went to French or French-trained architects. During the period of imperial rule, however, Zuccalli had begun the new Benedictine monastery and church at Ettal (1709–26), which has a façade based on Bernini's first project for the west front of the Louvre, Paris, and a 12-sided, domed and centrally planned church. His final work was the Franciscan monastery of Mittenheim (1717–20; destr. 1804), which at once looked forward to the Rococo developments in church planning in Bavaria and back to Bernini's centralized Baroque plans.

BIBLIOGRAPHY

R. A. L. Paulus: *Der Baumeister Henrico Zuccalli am kurbayerischen Hofe zu München* (Strasbourg, 1912)
A. M. Zendralli: *Graubündner Baumeister und Stukkatoren in deutschen Landen zur Barock- und Rokokozeit* (Zurich, 1930)
E. Hubala: 'Schleissheim und Schönbrunn: Anregungen und Einflüsse J. B. Fischers von Erlach in den Entwürfen Zuccallis', *Kunstchronik*, x/2 (1957), pp. 349ff
——: 'Henrico Zuccallis Schlossbau in Schleissheim: Planung und Baugeschichte, 1700–1704', *Münchn. Jb. Bild. Kst*, xxvii (1966), pp. 161ff
M. Petzet: 'Unbekannte Entwürfe für die Schleissheimer Schlossbauten', *Münchn. Jb. Bild. Kst*, xxii (1971), pp. 179ff
——: 'Entwürfe für Schloss Nymphenburg', *Z. Bayer. Landesgesch.*, xxxv/1 (1972), pp. 202ff
D. Riedl: 'Zur Planungs- und Baugeschichte des Neuen Schlosses Schleissheim unter Henrico Zuccalli', *Oberbayer. Archv*, ci (1976), pp. 283–300
Kurfürst Max Emanuel: Bayern und Europa um 1700 (exh. cat. by H. Glaser, Schleissheim, Altes Schloss and Neues Schloss, 1976)
H. Lorenz: 'Enrico Zuccallis Projekt für den Wiener Stadtpalast Kaunitz-Liechtenstein', *Österreich. Z. Kst & Dkmlpf.*, xxxiv (1980), pp. 16–22
S. Heym: 'Schloss Lustheim: Jagd- und Festbau des Kurfürsten Maximilian II. Emanuel von Bayern', *Oberbayer. Archv*, cix/2 (1984), pp. 7–125
——: *Henrico Zuccalli (um 1642–1724): Der kurbayerische Hofbaumeister* (Munich and Zurich, 1984)
M. Pfister: *Baumeister aus Graubünden—Wegbereiter des Barock* (Chur, 1993)

SABINE HEYM

Zuccarelli, Francesco (*b* Pitigliano, Umbria, 15 Aug 1702; *d* Florence, 30 Dec 1788). Italian painter and draughtsman, active in England.

1. FLORENCE, ROME AND VENICE, TO 1752. Zuccarelli's training began in Florence, where he engraved the frescoes by Andrea del Sarto in SS Annunziata. He then studied in Rome under Paolo Anesi and learnt figure drawing from Giovanni Maria Morandi (1622–1717), although in this he never acquired any great skill. His earliest recorded paintings were *Mary Magdalene* and *St Jerome* (both untraced), which he contributed to the exhibition of the feast of St Luke in Florence in 1729. He also painted portraits. Around 1730 he moved to Venice and began painting landscapes exclusively. His interest in this field may have led to his becoming acquainted with the Welsh landscape painter Richard Wilson in 1750–51. Wilson painted a lively portrait of him (1751; London, Tate) in exchange for one of Zuccarelli's landscapes. Zuccarelli avoided both the topographical type of Venetian view developed by Canaletto and the stormier landscapes of Marco Ricci, adopting instead a decorative landscape style of idealized Italian countryside. His subject-matter was usually unspecific rather than recognizably historical, biblical or mythological. For example, in the early 1740s he executed six paintings purporting to be scenes from the story of Jacob, but the paintings themselves bear few references to it (e.g. *Landscape with Two Seated Women Embracing*, 1743; Windsor Castle, Berks, Royal Col.).

Zuccarelli's landscape style was to vary little throughout his life, although some of his early paintings reveal attempts to work in a Dutch manner. His *Landscape with a Wayside Tavern* (mid-1740s; London, Hampton Court, Royal Col.) and *Landscape with Ruins and a Beggar* (mid-1740s; Windsor Castle, Berks, Royal Col.) suggest the work of Philips Wouwerman and Nicolaes Berchem respectively, while the *Landscape with a Sleeping Child and a Woman Milking a Cow* (*c*. 1740; Edinburgh, Pal. Holyroodhouse, Royal Col.) was commissioned as a pendant to a landscape attributed to Rembrandt. Despite such efforts, Zuccarelli's experiments with Dutch realism were tentative at best.

In Venice, Zuccarelli's works were engraved by Francesco Bartolozzi, and he received some patronage from the local nobility. Francesco Algarotti commissioned landscapes from him for the court of Dresden, and the Pisani family bought paintings, such as the *Abduction of Europa* (Venice, Accad.), for their country villa at Stra. However, his most faithful patron was Joseph Smith, the British Consul in Venice from 1744 and one of the most enthusiastic collectors of contemporary Venetian art. Smith obviously admired Zuccarelli's style and commissioned several works, notably a large painting of *Isaac and Rebecca* (1743; Windsor Castle, Berks, Royal Col.), probably as decoration for his villa. In 1746 Smith employed Zuccarelli and Antonio Visentini to paint a series of 11 views of English Palladian buildings in fanciful landscape settings. To assist him in his scrupulous rendering of buildings that he had not actually seen, Visentini drew on the engravings published in Colen Campbell's *Vitruvius Britannicus* (1715–25); Zuccarelli provided the generalized Arcadian settings. This uneasy union of architectural precision and pastoral fancy can best be seen in *Lindsey House* (London, Buckingham Pal., Royal Col.), a depiction of a 17th-century London town house, then thought to have been designed by Inigo Jones. When Zuccarelli left Venice for England in 1752, it was possibly with Smith's encouragement and letters of introduction.

2. FIRST TRIP TO ENGLAND, 1752–62. Zuccarelli's first visit to England followed a pattern established by other Italian artists such as Sebastiano Ricci, Carlo Pellegrini and Canaletto. The English passion for landscape paintings extended easily to Zuccarelli's idealized Italian

views, and his prestige rapidly rose above that of his former acquaintance Wilson, whose landscapes were considered blunt by comparison. Zuccarelli's social success is suggested by his admittance to the Dilettanti Society, and his artistic success is implied through the number of engravings made after his works. Besides painting, he undertook the designs for a series of tapestries for Charles Wyndham, 2nd Earl of Egremont (*c.* 1758; Petworth House, W. Sussex, NT). Executed by Paul Saunders (*fl* 1756–8), their design shows an uncharacteristic use of orientalism by Zuccarelli.

The lack of details concerning commissions suggests that in England Zuccarelli produced work for a market rather than for individual patrons—an unusual procedure at that time. This inference is supported by a sale he conducted of his own work on 16 February 1762. He announced it in the *Public Advertiser* and indicated his intention to return to Italy once all the works were disposed of. This sale contained over 70 items and included the *Transformation of Actaeon* and the *Rape of Dejanira* (both U. Glasgow, Hunterian A.G.). On 11 November 1762 he returned to Venice.

3. VENICE, SECOND TRIP TO ENGLAND AND RETIREMENT, 1762–88. On 16 February 1763 Zuccarelli became a member of the Venetian Academy, but he did not remain in the city for long. In 1765 he was entrusted to take to England a bequest left by Algarotti in his will to William Pitt, the 1st Earl of Chatham. This second visit came after the sale of Consul Smith's art collection to George III in 1762, and the King's acquisition of these paintings led to at least one commission: the large and elaborate *Finding of Moses* (1768; ?exh. RA 1773; Windsor Castle, Berks, Royal Col.; see fig.). For this, the King had allowed him to choose the subject, and Zuccarelli's choice of a biblical story was perhaps calculated to qualify him for the new Royal Academy, of which he became a founder-member in 1768. While in England, he exhibited at the Free Society in 1765 and 1766 and at the Society of Artists in the following two years. At the latter he showed a scene from *Macbeth* (exh. 1767; version, Stratford-on-Avon, Royal Shakespeare Mus.), a subject he had first painted *c.* 1760. His unusual presentation of Macbeth and the witches overwhelmed by an imaginative landscape was one of the earliest attempts by an artist to interpret a scene from Shakespeare by means of landscape; through William Woollett's engraving (1770) *Macbeth* was to be influential on later artists, including those working for Boydell's Shakespeare Gallery.

Zuccarelli also exhibited landscapes at the Royal Academy between 1769 and 1771; these were enthusiastically received by the public but denigrated by Horace Walpole. He returned to Venice *c.* 1771, and in 1772 he was elected president of the Venetian Academy. In 1773 a picture by Zuccarelli, a *Finding of Moses*, was exhibited at the Academy; this may have been the work of that title produced for George III in 1768 and thus could have been submitted by the King.

Zuccarelli retired to Florence, although in 1774 the Venetian Academy were puzzled as to his whereabouts. His output had been prolific, and he enjoyed a staggering popularity during his lifetime, but a reaction against his work set in after his death. Posthumous recognition of Wilson's talents provoked further invidious comparisons by a later generation suspicious of the frivolity and extravagance of Zuccarelli's Arcadian fantasies.

Francesco Zuccarelli: *Finding of Moses*, oil on canvas, 2.27×3.86 m, 1768 (Windsor Castle, Berkshire, Royal Collection)

BIBLIOGRAPHY

E. Waterhouse: *Painting in Britain, 1530 to 1790*, Pelican Hist. A. (Harmondsworth, 1953, 4/1978)

A. Blunt: 'A Neo-Palladian Programme Executed by Visentini and Zuccarelli for Consul Smith', *Burl. Mag.*, c (1958), pp. 283–4

M. Levey: 'Francesco Zuccarelli in England', *It. Stud.*, xiv (1959), pp. 1–21

——: *Painting in Eighteenth-century Venice* (Oxford, 1959, 2/1980), pp. 87–93

——: 'Wilson and Zuccarelli at Venice', *Burl. Mag.*, ci (1959), pp. 139–43

——: *Pictures in the Royal Collection: The Later Italian Pictures* (London, 1964)

——: *The Seventeenth and Eighteenth Century Italian Schools*, London, N.G. cat. (London, 1971), pp. 245–6

O. Millar: *The Queen's Pictures* (London, 1977), p. 123

F. Haskell: *Patrons and Painters: Art and Society in Baroque Italy* (New Haven, 1980)

SHEARER WEST

Zuccaro [Zuccari; Zucchero; Zuccheri]. Italian family of artists. The painter Ottaviano Zuccaro (*b* nr Urbino, *c.* 1505) had two sons, (1) Taddeo Zuccaro and (2) Federico Zuccaro, who were leaders in the development of a classicizing style of painting that succeeded High Mannerism in Rome in the late 16th century. Apart from important commissions for churches, the brothers participated in some of the most significant decorative projects of the period, including the Sala Regia in the Vatican and the Villa Farnese at Caprarola. Federico's travels contributed to the spread of the Mannerist style throughout Italy and Europe; less inventive than Taddeo, his work had a more conventional academic quality that made it easier to emulate.

(1) Taddeo Zuccaro (*b* S Angelo in Vado, Marches, 1 Sept 1529; *d* Rome, 2 Sept 1566). Painter and draughtsman. Taught to draw by his father, at the age of 14 he went alone to Rome where, according to Vasari, he was employed in various workshops and studied independently, particularly the works of Raphael. Through assisting Daniele de Porri (1500–77), who had trained in Parma, he learnt of the work of Correggio and Parmigianino. He first became known for his paintings on façades, notably scenes from the *Story of Furius Camillus* on the palazzo of a Roman nobleman Jacopo Matteo, executed in 1548. Vasari claimed that Taddeo's façade decorations equalled those of Polidoro da Caravaggio; none survives, although some are documented in drawings (e.g. London, BM; Paris, Louvre) and show his assimilation of Polidoro's style. Taddeo's earliest extant works date from 1553 when he collaborated with Prospero Fontana on the decoration (part destr.) of the villa of Pope Julius III outside the Porta del Popolo in Rome; Taddeo's contributions included scenes of *The Seasons* in the loggia of the nymphaeum. In these, clarity of form and space, natural proportions and idealization of human form demonstrate his affinity with the classicism of the High Renaissance.

1. Taddeo Zuccaro: *Flagellation* (*c.* 1556), fresco, Mattei Chapel, S Maria della Consolazione, Rome

2. Taddeo Zuccaro: *Donation of Charlemagne* (1564), fresco, Sala Regia, Vatican, Rome

He also assimilated the sculptural sensibility of Mannerism, derived from Michelangelo. This awareness of sculptural form can be seen in his drawings, complex compositions that inventively blend stylistic conventions of the High Renaissance with figures of refined expression, gesture and pose derived from the art of such painters as Parmigianino, Bronzino, Francesco Salviati and Giorgio Vasari.

Other works by Taddeo from this period include the *Crucifixion* altarpiece (1553–6; untraced; copy Rome, Gal. Pallavicini) and scenes of the *Passion* (*c.* 1556) for the Mattei Chapel in S Maria della Consolazione, Rome, one of his most significant surviving works (see fig. 1). The frescoes of the *Life of St Paul* in the Frangipani Chapel in S Marcello al Corso, Rome, were commissioned in 1557, painted mostly in 1560 and completed by Federico. These commissions show Taddeo's assimilation of the High Renaissance and Mannerist styles of such painters as Sebastiano del Piombo and Michelangelo, and in particular his debt to Michelangelo's frescoes in the Pauline Chapel (Rome, Vatican; for a drawing showing Taddeo copying Michelangelo's *Last Judgement*, see ROME, fig. 13). Likewise, Taddeo's altarpiece for the Frangipani Chapel, the *Conversion of Saul* (1563; *in situ*), reflects Michelangelo's painting of that subject in the Pauline Chapel (*see* MICHELANGELO, fig. 8). It was characteristic of Taddeo, according to Freedberg, to employ descriptive naturalism

within a Mannerist stylization. His *Parnassus* (1559; Ilo Nuñes priv. col., see Gere, 1969, pl. 109) for the Casino (destr.) of the Palazzo Bufalo in Rome and the two fresco cycles of the *Life of Alexander* (both 1560; one Bracciano, Castello Orsini; the other Rome, Pal. Mattei di Gove), with their careful observation of reality, study of details and analysis of nature, demonstrate this. Works of his maturity, such as the fresco of the *Death of the Virgin* (1564–5; Rome, Trinità dei Monti, Pucci Chapel), in which he was continuing the decoration begun by Perino del Vaga, and the *Christ in Glory* (1559; Rome, S Sabina, apse), anticipate Baroque painting, Annibale Caracci's classicism and Caravaggio's naturalism (Freedberg). The combination of naturalism and Mannerist ornamental elements in Taddeo's style was well suited to the requirements made of art by the Counter-Reformation. Thus the *Dead Christ Supported by Angels* (1564–5; Urbino, Pal. Ducale; version, Rome, Gal. Borghese), commissioned by the Farnese in 1559 for the chapel of their villa at Caprarola, although Mannerist in style is yet a sincere expression of piety.

In 1563, after the death of Francesco Salviati, Taddeo finished the decorations for the Sala dei Fasti Farnesiani in the Palazzo Farnese in Rome. Shortly after this success he worked with Vasari on a major papal commission, painting the *Donation of Charlemagne* (see fig. 2), the *Battle of Tunis* and two allegorical figures (all 1564) on an overdoor decoration in the Sala Regia in the Vatican. His most ambitious undertaking, however, was the decoration of Cardinal Alessandro Farnese's villa at Caprarola, which he began *c.* 1559. It was continued after his death by Federico. According to Vasari, this important commission was a major turning-point in Taddeo's career. It brought him prestige and economic security as well as recognition for his artistic talents and ability to manage a large workshop and execute a major enterprise. The theme of the decorations is the accomplishments of the Farnese family. In the *piano nobile* and the *salone* there are scenes painted in the vaults and fictive easel paintings and simulated tapestries on the walls. The fusion of fictive and real painting, architecture and sculpture anticipates the illusionism of Baroque art.

The scenes in the ceiling vaults illustrate family history; the end walls depict specific events in the lives of Cardinal Farnese's father and brothers and four episodes in the Cardinal's career as Secretary of State under his grandfather Pope Paul III. The decorative cycles present a propagandistic vision of the Cardinal's mission to establish peace between the Habsburg and Valois rulers. The iconographical programme was devised by humanist scholars, including Paolo Manuzio (1512–74), Onofrio Panvinio and Annibal Caro. Vasari quoted from Caro's instructions to Taddeo in his detailed description of the paintings: 'The subjects the cardinal has directed me to give you for the painting of the palace of Caprarola cannot be described adequately in words, because they comprise not only the ideas, but the arrangement, attitudes, colouring and other particulars.' Taddeo's implementation of the programme was a *tour de force* of illusionism recalling Giulio Romano's frescoed cycle in the Sala di Costantino in the Vatican Palace in Rome, executed with a *sprezzatura* (apparent ease) that appealed to an educated audience. Influenced by antiquity, the High Renaissance and such contemporary painters as Salviati, Vasari and Jacopo Zucchi, he created a powerful propagandistic statement in the Mannerist style. In addition to paintings and frescoes, Taddeo also produced decorative art work in collaboration with his brother Federico (*see* §(2) below).

The biographies of Taddeo by Vasari and Baglione comment briefly on his personal life and at length on his many commissions. Vasari described his style as fluent and very vigorous, without a trace of crudeness, and praised him for his full compositions and his treatment of heads, hands and nudes. Taddeo is buried in the Pantheon in Rome, close to his mentor Raphael.

(2) Federico Zuccaro (*b* Sant' Angelo in Vado, Marches, 1540–42; *d* Ancona, 6 Aug 1609). Painter, draughtsman and writer, brother of (1) Taddeo Zuccaro.

1. Life and painted work. 2. Decorative art with Taddeo, the Accademia di S Luca and writings.

1. LIFE AND PAINTED WORK. Having been invited to Rome by his brother, between 1555 and 1563 he worked with Taddeo on various projects including the Villa Farnese at Caprarola and the Pucci Chapel in Trinità dei Monti, Rome. Many of Federico's drawings for both commissions show Taddeo's influence. According to Vasari, Taddeo supervised his brother's early work, which created friction between them. In 1558, for example, when they collaborated on painting the façade of the house of Tizio da Spoleto with scenes from the *Life of St Eustace*, Taddeo retouched some of his brother's paintings, so offending Federico. Already at 18 Federico was commissioned to paint many works at the Vatican: the *Transfiguration*, the *Marriage at Cana* and other scenes from the *Life of Christ* for the decorations (part destr.) of the Casino of Pius IV; an *Escutcheon of Pius IV* flanked by *Justice* and *Equity* (1562) for the Tribunale della Ruota Romana and 16 scenes from the *Life of Moses* at the Belvedere.

The brothers' rivalry became less intense after 1564 when Federico went to Venice to execute commissions for Cardinal Giovanni Grimani, including paintings of *Justice* (untraced), the *Adoration of the Magi*, the *Resurrection of Lazarus* and the *Conversion of Mary Magdalene* (untraced) all for the Grimani Chapel in S Francesco della Vigna. His stay in Venice and a study trip through Lombardy with the architect Andrea Palladio were the first of a series of journeys he made over a period of almost 45 years. In Florence in 1565 Federico was admitted to the Accademia del Disegno and executed hunting scenes for the festive decorations celebrating the marriage of Francesco de' Medici and Joanna of Austria. He then proceeded to Rome to assist Taddeo on the commissions for Trinità dei Monti, S Marcello, the Sala Regia (Vatican) and at the Villa Farnese at Caprarola. After Taddeo's death, in 1566, Federico continued these projects and painted *Henry IV before Gregory VII* in the Sala Regia. He also decorated the ceilings of the Sala della Gloria and Sala della Fama in the Villa d'Este at Tivoli for Ippolito II d'Este, Cardinal of Ferrara, and in 1568–70 carried out Taddeo's commission for S Lorenzo in Damaso, Rome—the altarpiece of the *Coronation of the Virgin with SS Lawrence, Paul, Peter and Damasus* (*in situ*).

Federico travelled to Orvieto in 1570 to paint *Christ Healing the Blind Man* and *Christ Raising the Son of the Widow of Nain* for the cathedral. Between 1570 and 1573 in Rome he painted the *Conversion of the Empress Faustina*, the *Disputation of St Catherine*, *Christ Driving the Moneychangers from the Temple* and *Ecce homo*, all for S Caterina dei Funari. For the oratory of S Lucia del Gonfalone in 1573 he collaborated on a cycle of scenes of the *Passion*, a major decorative commission involving many artists, including Jacopo Bertoia and Raffaellino da Reggio. The cycle was intended to create a powerful vision for the faithful to identify and empathize with Christ's suffering. Federico's paintings of *Prophets and Sibyls* and the *Flagellation* (see fig. 1) combined naturalistic design with the embellishment of classical forms.

In 1574 Federico travelled to the Netherlands, Spain and England. In London he executed many portraits, including those of *Robert Dudley, First Earl of Leicester* (destr.), *Mary, Queen of Scots* and a drawing of *Elizabeth I* (London, BM; see fig. 2). He continued to Antwerp, where he may have executed drawings for tapestries, and Nancy. Late in 1574 he returned to Florence where he completed the frescoes of the *Last Judgement* in the dome of the cathedral, left unfinished at Vasari's death. He built a studio and house in Florence in Via Capponi and decorated them with allegorical motifs, myths and fables in the manner of Vasari's houses in Arezzo and Florence.

In 1580 Federico went to Rome to work on the fresco of the *Baptism of Cornelius*, continuing the decoration of the Pauline Chapel in the Vatican begun by Michelangelo. He also designed two works executed by assistants, the *Vision of St Gregory* and *Procession of St Gregory* (both untraced) for the Ghiselli Chapel at the Madonna del Baraccano in Bologna. These were much criticized for their Mannerist style, and Federico responded with satirical depictions of his detractors in the *Porta Virtutis* (untraced; engraving Oxford, Christ Church Pict. Gal.; for illustration *see* ALLEGORY OF ART), for which he was expelled from Rome by Pope Gregory XIII in 1581.

Federico revisited Venice and was commissioned to execute the fresco of *Barbarossa Making Obeisance to the Pope* in the Sala del Maggior Consiglio of the Doge's Palace in 1582. Although he adopted aspects of Venetian colouring and design for this work, he disliked Venetian painting, particularly that of Jacopo Tintoretto, whom he later criticized in the *Lamento della pittura* (1605). For Francesco Maria II della Rovere, Duke of Urbino, he went to Loreto in 1583 to fresco the *Marriage of the Virgin*, the *Visitation*, the *Death of the Virgin*, the *Coronation of the Virgin*, and the *Virgin in Glory* for the Santa Casa. These frescoes also reflect Venetian influence, combined with naturalism and Mannerist classicism. Federico's patrons and friends finally secured a pardon from the Pope and he returned to Rome to work on the Pauline Chapel, where he painted the *Arms of Gregory III*, the *Pentecost* and the *Mission of the Apostles*. From 1585 to 1588 he was in Madrid working for King Philip II on the decoration of the Patio de los Evangelistas and S Lorenzo at the Escorial. His frescoes in the great retable were criticized for their cold, academic Mannerist style, and they were replaced with paintings by his assistant, Bartolomé Carducho, who later became court painter.

After this, Federico returned to Italy, to work on a series of drawings (Florence, Uffizi) for Dante's *Divine Comedy*. In Rome he painted the vault and an altarpiece for the Vittori family in the Cappella degli Angeli at the Gesù in 1592 and began the decorations of the house he had bought on the Pincian Hill in 1590. In 1594 he visited Lucca to execute the *Adoration of the Magi* for the cathedral. He completed frescoes of scenes from the *Life of St Hyacinth* and decorated the vault of the Cappella di S Giacinto in S Sabina, Rome, in 1600. In 1604 he returned to his native town to paint the family altarpiece, the *Virgin and Child with the Zuccaro Family as Donors* (S Angelo in Vado, S Caterina). Federico Borromeo invited him to Pavia that year to paint the *Emissary of St Charles to Cardinal Borromeo* for the Collegio Borromeo and the Hall of the Zodiac in the Palazzo Marozzi, as well as a *Pietà* and a *Dead Christ with Angels* for the family chapel at Arona on Lake Maggiore. Federico also travelled to Bologna, Mantua, Turin (in 1605–7, for the Savoy court, he frescoed (destr.) the gallery connecting the Palazzo Madama with the new palace of Charles-Emanuel I) and Parma (the *Disrobing of Christ* painted in 1608 for S Rocco).

The impact of the Council of Trent (1543–63) and the resolutions of the Ecumenical Council contributed to

1. Federico Zuccaro: *Flagellation* (1573), fresco, oratory of S Lucia del Gonfalone, Rome

Federico's development of a new, Counter-Reformation style, which Freedberg termed the 'Counter-Maniera'. Counter-Reformation officials required art with a strongly propagandistic religious content, in which stories of the saints demonstrated their piety and glorified the Christian faith. Images were to be painted in natural forms with emotional expressions, simple compositions and clear narrative—a truly anti-Mannerist style. Taddeo was perhaps slightly affected by these resolutions in his work for the Mattei and Frangipani chapels and in the Farnese decorative cycles. The decorations of the Pucci Chapel, which were completed by Federico in 1589, may also reflect such influence. Federico, however, adopted the 'Counter-Maniera' style more readily because it reflected a pragmatic and propagandistic sensibility that appealed to his taste for clarity, realism and devotional stimulation. The consequent differentiation between the brothers' styles is demonstrated in Federico's commissions for the Santa Casa of Loreto (1583) and for the Capella di S Giacinto in S Sabina, Rome (1600). Mundy has characterized the difference as one between conveying metaphorical meaning through complex composition and monumental figures of expressive virtuosity (Taddeo), and conveying allegory, particularly religious allegory, through natural, proportioned forms whose symbolic function, once grasped, can be vividly appreciated (Federico).

2. Federico Zuccaro: *Elizabeth I*, black and red chalk, 309×222 mm, 1574 (London, British Museum)

2. DECORATIVE ART WITH TADDEO, THE ACCA-
DEMIA DI S LUCA AND WRITINGS. Taddeo and Federico both worked on many types of art. In addition to religious and secular paintings and fresco cycles, the Zuccari designed trophies, maiolica (e.g. dish, London, V&A, from the maiolica wares given to Philip II of Spain by Guido-baldo II della Rovere, Duke of Urbino, in 1562) and such festive decorations as those for the obsequies of Emperor Charles V in S Giacomo di Spagnuoli, Rome, in 1559, and a hunt scene (modello, Florence, Uffizi) for the entry of Joanna of Austria into Florence in 1565. The environment in which they worked was intensely competitive, and artists had little status. Competition was fearful, even to the point of law suits. Federico, who tended to be combative and arrogant, was involved in several such conflicts with patrons and fellow artists. Following his banishment from Rome in 1581 by Pope Gregory XIII, he made annotations in his copy (Florence, Uffizi) of Vasari's *Vite* that reveal his jealousy of successful artists. The lack of professional status for artists prompted Federico to try to organize a Roman equivalent of Vasari's Florentine Accademia di Disegno. After 15 years of effort towards this end, and with the backing of Cardinal Federico Borromeo, he finally succeeded in establishing a reformed Accademia di S Luca, of which he was elected principe. The first meeting was held at the Palazzo Zuccari, the house that Federico designed and built on the Pincian Hill and which now holds the Biblioteca Hertziana (for the garden portal *see* ARTIST'S HOUSE, fig. 2). Instruction

included lectures by Federico (recorded by his nephew Romano Alberti), the notes for which formed the basis of *L'idea de' pittori, scultori ed architetti* (published in Turin several years after it had been written). Inspired by the notion that correct theory would produce good art, Federico explained the rudiments of painting, discussed theories on art postulated by Aristotle, Aquinas, Alberti, Dürer, Pino, Vasari and Lomazzo, and expounded the metaphysical nature of *disegno*. This explanation is accompanied by a diagram that shows how an idea arises in the mind of an artist and is then translated into a drawing. His approach was influenced by the ideas of St Thomas Aquinas as expressed in *Summa theologiae* ('God, as a creator, also designs internally and externally') and included the belief that the artist's original idea was formed in his mind by God. The word *disegno* seemed to Federico to demonstrate this, containing within it the words for God (*Dio*) and sign (*segno*) (*see also* ALLEGORY OF ART, §3). The book, relatively ignored by art historians (but see Panofsky and Barasch), has been described by Freedberg as the 'most systematic and most lucid' account of the aesthetics of Mannerism.

WRITINGS OF FEDERICO ZUCCARO

Lettere a principe et signori amatori del disegno, pittura, scultura et architettura (Mantua, 1605); ed. D. Heikamp (Florence, 1961)

Lamento del pittura (Mantua, 1605)

L'idea de' pittori, scultori ed architetti (Turin, 1607); ed. D. Heikamp (Florence, 1961)

Il passagio per Italia con la dimora di Parma (Bologna, 1608); ed. Lanciarini (Rome, 1893)

BIBLIOGRAPHY

G. Vasari: *Vite* (1550, rev. 2/1568); ed. G. Milanesi (1878–85), vii, pp. 73–134

R. Alberti: *Origine e progresso dell' Accademia del Disegno di Roma* (Rome, 1607); ed. D. Heikamp (Florence, 1961)

G. Baglione: *Vite* (1642); ed. V. Mariani (1935), pp. 102–3, 121–5

W. Körte: *Der Palazzo Zuccari in Röm* (Leipzig, 1935)

J. Gere: 'The Decorations of the Villa Giulia', *Burl. Mag.*, cvii (1965), pp. 199–206

——: 'Two of Taddeo Zuccaro's Last Commissions Completed by Federico Zuccaro. I: The Pucci Chapel in Trinità dei Monti; II: The High Altarpiece in S Lorenzo di Damaso', *Burl. Mag.*, cviii (1966), pp. 286–93, 341–5

D. Heikamp: 'Federico Zuccaro a Firenze 1577–9', *Paragone*, xviii/207 (1967), pp. 44–68; xviii/209 (1967), pp. 1–34

E. Panofsky: 'Zuccari: The Aristotelian–Thomistic Trend', *Idea: A Concept in Art Theory* (Columbia, 1968)

J. Gere: *Taddeo Zuccaro* (Chicago, 1969)

O. Berendsen: 'Taddeo Zuccaro's Paintings for Charles V's Obsequies in Rome', *Burl. Mag.*, cxii (1970), pp. 809–10

H. Outram Evenett: *The Spirit of the Counter-Reformation* (Notre-Dame, 1970)

S. J. Freedberg: *Painting in Italy, 1500–1600*, Pelican Hist. A. (Harmondsworth, 1971, rev. 2/1983)

L. W. Partridge: 'The Sala d'Ercole in the Villa Farnese at Caprarola', *A. Bull.*, liii (1971), pp. 467–86; liv (1972), pp. 50–62

A. Garzetti: *Museo di Orvieto, Museo dell' Opera del Duomo* (Bologna, 1972)

C. Strinati: 'Gli anni difficili di Federico Zuccari', *Stor. A.*, 20–22 (1974), pp. 95–117

G. Smith: *The Casino of Pius IV* (Princeton, 1977)

L. W. Partridge: 'Divinity and Dynasty at Caprarola: Perfect History in the Room of Farnese Deeds', *A. Bull.*, lx (1978), pp. 449–530

K. Hermann-Fiore: 'Die Fresken Federico Zuccaris in seinem römischen Kunstlerhause', *Rom. Jb. Kstgesch.* (1979), pp. 36–112

I. Cheney: 'Les Premières Décorations: Daniele da Volterra, Salviati et les frères Zuccaro', *Le Palais Farnese, Ecole française de Rome* (1981), pp. 243–67

I. Faldo: *Il Palazzo Farnese di Caprarola* (Turin, 1981)

K. Hermann-Fiore: '*Disegno* and *Giuditio*; Allegorical Drawings by Federico Zuccaro and Cherubino Alberti', *Master Drgs*, xx (1982), pp. 247–56
I. Gerards-Nelissen: 'Federigo Zuccaro and the Lament of Painting', *Simiolus*, xiii (1983), pp. 45–53
M. Barasch: 'Zuccari: The Theory of Disegno', *Theories of Art: From Plato to Winckelmann* (New York, 1985)
L. Cheney: *The Paintings of the Casa Vasari* (New York, 1985)
E. J. Mundy: *Renaissance into Baroque: Italian Master Drawings by the Zuccari, 1550–1600* (Cambridge, MA, 1990)
J. A. Gere: 'Taddeo Zuccaro: Addenda and Corrigenda', *Master Drgs*, xxxiii/3 (1995), pp. 223–323 [whole issue]

LIANA DE GIROLAMI CHENEY

Zucchi. Italian family of artists. The family was based in Venice and is best known for engraving, although some members were also painters. Andrea Zucchi (*b* Venice, 9 Jan 1679; *d* Dresden, 1740), son of Giuseppe Zucchi who moved to Venice from Alano, near Bergamo, was an engraver, painter and stage designer. He studied painting with Pietro Vecchio and Andrea Celesti and engraving with Domenico Rossetti (1650–1736). In 1706 he moved to Pordenone, where he worked both as a painter and engraver, taking a leading part in the revival of engraving in the Veneto and being elected president of the Bottegha de Scultori e Stampatori in Rame di Venetia in 1719. In Pordenone he executed numerous portraits, views and costume designs, alternating between engraving, etching and mezzotint. In particular he contributed to the *Gran Teatro di Venezia* (Venice, 1720), published by Lovisa and, with his brother Francesco Zucchi (*b* Venice, 1692; *d* Venice, Oct 1764), worked on the *Verona illustrata* (Verona, 1732) by Scipione Maffei. In 1726 he was summoned to the Dresden court, where he worked for a long period engraving the paintings in the collection of Frederick-Augustus I, King of Saxony, as well as being employed as a decorator and set designer for the Opera House (destr. 1945; *see* THEATRE, §III, 4(i)(a)).

Carlo Zucchi (*b* Venice, 1682; *d* Venice, 9 March 1767), another of Andrea's brothers, was also an engraver and the author of treatises on scenography and optics. He studied with Andrea and is known in particular as an engraver of seals (e.g. Rovigo, Accad. Concordi) and as the master of Piranesi.

The above-mentioned Francesco also trained with Andrea and worked as an engraver, often on reproductive engravings for book illustrations. His most noteworthy achievements in this field are the detailed views that appeared in the *Forestiero illuminato* (Venice, 1740), published by Albrizzi, and several plates for Maffei's *Verona illustrata*, taken from drawings by Giambattista Tiepolo. He was also responsible for the *Vedute di Bressanone*, 12 engraved views taken from paintings by Francesco Battaglioli.

Lorenzo Zucchi (*b* Venice, 1704; *d* Dresden, 1779), Andrea's son and pupil, was also an engraver and accompanied his father to Pordenone (1706) and Dresden (1726). When his father died there, he became official engraver to the Dresden court, continuing the task of engraving paintings from the royal collection and also producing portraits from drawings by local artists.

Giuseppe Carlo Zucchi (*b* Venice, 1721; *d* Venice, 1805), son of Francesco, studied with Francesco Zugno (1709–87) and then worked as an engraver with his brother

Antonio, with whom he appears to have travelled to London to engrave the plates for Robert Adam's *Ruins of the Palace of the Emperor Diocletian at Spalatro in Dalmatia* (London, 1764). Most of the plates for this were based on drawings by Charles-Louis Clérisseau. In 1786 Giuseppe Carlo wrote 'Memorie cronologiche della famiglia' (MS. untraced), which was consulted by G. A. Moschini, and by Giovanni Gherardo de Rossi for *Vita di Angelica Kauffmann, pittrice* (Florence, 1811).

Antonio Zucchi (*b* Venice, 1726; *d* Rome, 1796), Giuseppe Carlo's brother, was a painter. He studied first with Francesco Fontebasso then with Jacopo Amigoni, who greatly influenced him. As his contemporaries noted, in his early works, for example *Male Saints Surrounded by Female Franciscan Saints* (untraced) he imitated Amigoni's manner and hazy style of colouring. His *Fourteen Stations of the Cross* (1750; Venice, S Giobbe) also shows Amigoni's influence as well as an awareness of Francesco Guardi's innovations. In 1756 Antonio was elected a member of the Accademia di Pittura e Scultora in Venice, and from the evidence of two canvases depicting angels (1759; ex-S Teonista, Treviso; destr. 1943 and known from photographs), which are probably fragments of a larger composition, he soon developed a more academic style that gave greater plasticity to his figures. He undertook several study trips, probably after 1759, in the company of Adam and Clérisseau, possibly to Dalmatia, certainly to Rome and Naples, where he would have gained a deeper knowledge of the Neo-classical style. He settled in Rome, from where in 1766 he sent the altarpiece depicting the *Incredulity of Thomas* for the church of S Tomà, Venice (*in situ*). In the same year he went to London at the invitation of Adam, where he exhibited his work in 1771 and in 1773 painted five frescoes for Home House in London, designed by Adam. These rely for their effect on plasticity rather than colour, of which they have very little. Zucchi worked on the decoration of other large houses, in 1781 married Angelica Kauffman and in 1784 was elected a member of the Royal Academy. He and Angelica moved back to Rome, and thereafter Zucchi did little painting, dedicating himself instead to the administration of the considerable family fortune.

BIBLIOGRAPHY
G. A. Moschini: *Dell'incisione in Venezia* (Venice, 1924), p. 58
G. Delogu: *Pittori veneti minori del settecento* (Venice, 1930), pp. 166–70
Incisori veneti del settecento (exh. cat. by R. Pallucchini, Venice, Ridotto Procuratoressa Venier, 1941), pp. 25–7
A. Bosisio: 'Antonio Zucchi pittore e incisore veneto', *Ateneo Ven.*, cxxxv/131 (1944), pp. 62–7
V. Moschini: 'Antonio Zucchi veneziano', *A. Veneta*, xi (1957), pp. 168–72
R. Pallucchini: *La pittura veneziana del settecento* (Venice and Rome, 1960), pp. 231–2
Aspetti dell'incisione veneziana nel '700 (exh. cat., ed. G. Dillon; Venice, Scu. Grande S Teodoro, 1976), pp. 79–80
P. Falchetta: *Teatro delle Fabbriche più cospicue in prospettiva* (Venice, 1992)

FILIPPO PEDROCCO

Zucchi, Jacopo (*b* Florence, *c.* 1540; *d* Rome, before 3 April 1596). Italian painter and draughtsman. He was trained in the studio of Vasari, whom he assisted in the decoration of the Palazzo Vecchio, Florence, as early as 1557. He accompanied Vasari to Pisa in 1561, from when dates his earliest known drawing, *Aesculapius* (London,

BM). Between 1563 and 1565 he was again in Florence and is documented working with Vasari, Joannes Stradanus and Giovan Battista Naldini on the ceiling of the Sala Grande (Salone dei Cinquecento) in the Palazzo Vecchio; a drawing of an *Allegory of Pistoia* (Florence, Uffizi) is related to the ceiling allegories of Tuscan cities. In 1564 Zucchi entered the Accademia del Disegno and contributed to the decorations erected for the funeral of Michelangelo. He travelled to Rome with Vasari and was his chief assistant on decorations in the Vatican in 1567 and 1572, where he executed frescoes of scenes from the *Life of St Peter Martyr* in the chapel of S Pio V.

Zucchi settled in Rome permanently from 1572 and was appointed artist-in-residence to the Medici court in Rome by Cardinal Ferdinando de' Medici. After 1576 he decorated several rooms in the Villa Medici, including a vault depicting the *Eight Winds* and other mythological figures; also associated with the Villa is a design (London, BM), probably for a (small) ceiling or vestibule, and seven studies for a long gallery (London, RIBA and V&A). In S Clemente, Rome, he painted the *Virgin and Child with St John* (1570–90) in the chapel of the Rosary; frescoes (late 16th century) in the baptistery are also attributed to him. Another important patron was Orazio Rucellai, for whom he painted ceiling frescoes (1586–90) in the Palazzo Ruspoli, Rome. Some 30 drawings attributed to Zucchi include pen sketches, brush and gouache composition sketches and decorative architectural drawings. His painted work also comprises cabinet pictures (e.g. the *Bath of Bathsheba*; Hartford, CT, Wadsworth Atheneum) and altarpieces (e.g. the *Foundation of S Maria Maggiore*, late 1570s; Rome, Pin. Vaticana). His early style owes much to Vasari, but later works display considerable individual accomplishment.

BIBLIOGRAPHY

Colnaghi; Thieme–Becker

H. Voss: 'Jacopo Zucchi: Ein vergessener Meister der florentinisch-römischen Spätrenaissance', *Z. Bild. Kst.*, xxiv (1913), pp. 151–62

P. Barocchi: 'Complimenti al Vasari pittore', *Atti & Mem. Accad. Tosc. Sci. & Lett., 'La Colombaria'*, n. s. 14, xxviii (1964), pp. 286–8

C. Monbeig-Goguel: *Vasari et son temps: Maîtres toscans nés après 1500, morts avant 1600*, Paris, Louvre, Cab. Dessins cat. (Paris, 1972), pp. 219–37, nos 360–428

E. Pillsbury: *Jacopo Zucchi: His Life and Works* (diss., U. London, 1973)

——: 'Drawings by Jacopo Zucchi', *Master Drgs*, xii/1 (1974), pp. 3–33

——: 'The Sala Grande Drawings by Vasari and his Workshop: Some Documents and New Attributions', *Master Drgs*, xiv/2 (1976), pp. 127–46

Florentine Drawings of the Sixteenth Century (exh. cat. by N. Turner, London, BM, 1986), pp. 200–03, nos 151–3

G. Briganti, ed.: *La pittura in Italia: Il cinquecento* (Milan, 1987, rev. 2/1988), ii, pp. 869–70

S. J. TURNER

Zug, Szymon Bogumił (*b* Merseburg, Saxony, 20 Feb 1733; *d* Warsaw, 11 Aug 1807). German architect and landscape gardener, active in Poland. He worked in Dresden from 1747 and was appointed Clerk of Works (Kondukteur) in the Saxon Office of Works. He probably travelled to Italy in 1755 and lived in Poland from 1756, where in 1772 he was appointed Court Architect to Frederick-Augustus III, Elector and later King of Saxony (*reg* 1763–1827). In 1772, for Duke Casimir Poniatowski, he laid out the park at Solec. This was the first of a series of landscape gardens influenced by English models, with picturesque buildings, grottoes and artificial ruins, which he created for the Polish aristocracy. They included Mokotów (1775) for Elżbieta Lubomirska and the important park at ARKADIA (from 1780) for Princess Helena Radziwiłł (1749–1821), with such features as an aqueduct, a 'House of the High Priest' and a temple to Diana (1783). Zug's most important work was the Lutheran church (1777–81; destr. 1939; rebuilt 1950) at Małachowski Plac in Warsaw, a cylindrical building capped by a dome with an oculus that gives on to a lantern. The entrance is via a tetrastyle portico, corresponding to which three matching pedimented wings abut at the other cardinal points. In the 1780s Zug worked for wealthy Warsaw burghers, and in 1784 he built the tenement house (partly destr. 1939; rebuilt 1948–9) of Roesler and Hurtig on Krakowskie Przedmieście. This was a striking example of Neo-classicism applied to commercial architecture. It was a forerunner of the big tenement houses that were to become typical of 19th-century Warsaw. The ground floor is articulated by a continuous motif of Serlianas using baseless Tuscan columns. The first floor has a recurrent motif of pedimented windows. The upper floors have progressively plainer fenestration. As the leading and most prolific architect of Polish Neo-classicism, Zug's creative development progressed from late Baroque designs to a rigid Neo-classicism; in his garden plans and buildings, he represented pre-Romantic trends.

UNPUBLISHED SOURCES

U. Warsaw, Lib.; Warsaw, N. Mus. [drawings]

BIBLIOGRAPHY

M. Kwiatkowski: *Szymon Bogumił Zug: Architekt polskiego oświecenia* [Szymon Bogumił Zug: architect of the Polish enlightenment] (Warsaw, 1971)

ANDRZEJ ROTTERMUND

Zuloaga (y Zabaleta), Ignacio (*b* Eibar, Guipúzcoa, 26 July 1870; *d* Madrid, 31 Oct 1945). Spanish Basque painter. He studied in Paris in 1891, coming under the influence of Impressionism and of the group of Catalan painters around Santiago Rusiñol. His visit to Andalusia in 1892 provided the key to his later work, leading him to replace the grey tonalities of his Paris paintings with more brightly coloured images of Spanish folkloric subjects and of male or female figures in regional dress, for example *Merceditas* (1911/13; Washington, DC, N.G.A.). Zuloaga turned to Castilian subjects in works such as *Segoviano* and *Toreros de Pueblo* (both 1906; both Madrid, Mus. A. Contemp.) after the defeat suffered by Spain in the Spanish-American War of 1898; like the group of writers known as the 'Generation of '98', with whom he was associated and who were among his most articulate supporters, he sought to encourage the regeneration of his country's culture but with a critical spirit.

Zuloaga began to enjoy considerable international success in 1900, and until the outbreak of World War I he divided his time between Paris, Madrid and Segovia. He painted some pure landscapes, such as *View of the Escorial* (*c*. 1905; London, Tate), but established his reputation from 1907 as a portraitist of eminent figures including the *Duquesa de Alba* (1921; Madrid, Col. Duque de Alba), *Ramón Pérez de Ayala* (1931; Madrid, Col. Pérez de Ayala), *Domingo Ortega* (1945; Madrid), *José Ortega y Gasset* (*c*. 1930; Zumaya, Casa Mus. Zuloaga), *Ramón del*

Valle-Inclán (1931; Segovia, Mus. Zuloaga) and *Miguel de Unamuno* (1923; New York, Hisp. Soc. America Mus.). From 1924 he was again based exclusively in Spain, with houses in Madrid, Zumaya and Pedraza. He continued to favour subjects of Spanish life and figures in regional costume, but with an increased emphasis on the landscape settings, as in the equestrian portrait of *Duquesa de Montoro* (1930; priv. col., see Lafuente Ferrari, pl. 135). His use of religious imagery in paintings such as *Cristo de la Sangre* ('Christ of the Blood', 1911; Madrid, Mus. A. Contemp.) produced strong critical comment for a view of Spain considered by some to be excessively pessimistic. Among the major collections of Zuloaga's work are those in the Museo Zuloaga in Segovia and the Villa Zuloaga in Zumaya.

BIBLIOGRAPHY
J. de la Encina: *Ignacio Zuloaga* (Madrid, n.d.)
Ignacio Zuloaga (exh. cat., foreword J. S. Sargent; intro. C. Brinton; Boston, MA, Copley Soc., 1916)
I. de Beryes: *Ignacio Zuloaga o una manera de ver a España* (Barcelona, 1947)
E. Lafuente Ferrari: *La vida y el arte de Ignacio Zuloaga* (Madrid, 1950)
M. DOLORES JIMÉNEZ-BLANCO

Zülow, Franz von (*b* Vienna, 15 March 1883; *d* Vienna, 26 Feb 1963). Austrian designer and painter. He studied design at the Allgemeine Zeichenschule (1901–2) and at the Graphische Lehr- und Versuchsanstalt (1902–3) in Vienna and was briefly a guest attendant at the Akademie der Bildenden Künste. Thereafter he studied at the Kunstgewerbeschule until 1906 and in 1908 he joined the Vienna Secession. He was able to take an extended journey through western Europe in 1912 through receiving a travel scholarship from John II, Prince of Liechtenstein (1840–1929). He was in military service from 1915 to 1919 and was also a prisoner of war in Italy. He was a teacher at the Schleiss ceramic workshops in Gmunden between 1920 and 1922. From 1922 onwards he lived alternately in Vienna and Upper Austria and took many trips abroad. In 1949 he began teaching at the Kunstschule in Linz.

Zülow's art was influenced by the ideals of the Vienna Secession and the Wiener Werkstätte. He was active in many areas of the applied arts and made picture books, calendar pages, graphic cycles and also wall paintings and tapestries (e.g. cartoon for the tapestry *Panorama of Ankara* for the villa of Kemal Atatürk in Ankara, 1932); he designed wallpaper and fabrics, decorated household items, painted furniture and furnishings. The main part of his work was in printing design and he experimented to expand the technical possibilities. His method of printing with cut paper was patented in 1907. In this method the pattern is cut from a piece of paper and the resulting template is coloured and printed in reverse. In contrast to previous template printing the picture is not dependent on the negative forms that have been cut out but on the remaining crosspieces. These form a network of black outlines and the empty spaces between are often strongly coloured. The cloisonné effect created in this manner was a characteristic aim of Zülow's work and also appears in other techniques, such as the ink drawing *Deciduous Forest with Hemlock* (1903; Linz, Neue Gal.).

In addition to this Art Nouveau style of decorative surface painting Zülow was also influenced by folk art,

which resulted in naive ornamentation and a preference for depicting landscapes, country life, religious subjects (e.g. *Virgin and Child with Sun, Moon and Stars*, watercolour; see Baum, p. 54), fantastic and fairy-tale scenes. He also painted landscapes in oils, as in *Farmyard in Hirschbach* (1934; Vienna, Belvedere, Österreich. Gal.).

BIBLIOGRAPHY
P. Baum: *Franz von Zülow* (Vienna, 1980)
F. Koreny: *Franz von Zülow: Frühe Graphik, 1904–1915* (Vienna, 1983)
EDWIN LACHNIT

Zulu. Originally a minor northern Nguni group living along the middle reaches of the White Umfolozi River in South Africa. Use of the name Zulu was extended after Shaka Senzangakhona Zulu (*c.* 1787–1828) conquered other northern Nguni polities, thereby establishing a formidable militarist state in south-east Africa, stretching from the Pongola River in the north of present-day Natal to the Thukela River in the south; from the mid-1840s it shared its southern boundary with the Colony of Natal. To the north Shaka established tributary relations with Tsonga chiefdoms on the eastern seaboard and, to a lesser extent, with the Swazi kingdom further inland. The kingdom was destroyed by British forces in 1879.

Although they became relatively culturally distinct from one another in the late 18th century and early 19th, the Tsonga of southern Mozambique, the Ngwane (later the Swazi ruling lineage) and the northern Nguni chiefdoms of Zululand-Natal shared many ritual practices. While the Zulu have always produced a variety of utilitarian artefacts and elaborate dress for ritual and other occasions, there have been significant changes in the style, function and symbolic value they attribute to their craft objects and clothing. Indeed some artefacts, once highly valued, are no longer produced. Many factors account for these developments, in particular shifting patterns in the control and distribution of imported materials, especially during the 19th century, the expropriation by European settlers of large areas of fertile land, and the consequent disruptive effects of migrant labour on traditional Zulu life. Zulu arts have been quite widely illustrated (see bibliography) and many museums with African collections have examples of Zulu arts.

1. REGALIA AND POLITICAL ARTS. Before the destruction of the kingdom political arts had great importance, and trade was controlled almost exclusively by the royal lineage. Such imported materials as brass and glass beads were used to make prestige articles for the king, his favourite generals and regiments and royal wives. Some items, including the *izingxotha* (brass cuffs), were worn by both men and women. Until the mid-19th century large beads were reserved for use by the king; beaded necklaces and waistbands, many made from blue, red and white beads, and brass neckrings were worn almost exclusively by women from his royal enclosure. By the late 19th century beads had already lost their value as an index of status, and by the early 20th century they were commonly used to make loindresses and necklaces previously woven from locally available grasses and other fibres.

Among these indigenous materials, wild-animal skins and exotic feathers, mostly obtained from the Tsonga, were also highly valued as prestige items. They were usually reserved for use by the king's regiments, who wore elaborate feathered headdresses and leather front and back aprons (*isinene* and *ibeshu*), made mostly of genet skins but also of oxhides. These were worn on such festive occasions as the Zulu 'first fruits' ceremony (*umkhosi*) that was held each year until the practice was forcibly abolished in 1879. Front and back aprons are worn by men to such social events as weddings. Variations in the use of materials, which once served to define both the personal bravery and regimental affiliation of the Zulu warrior, have not continued to be invested with complex social meanings, but instead may be ascribed to individual wealth and taste.

The hierarchical stratification of Zulu society during the reigns of Shaka and his successors is further reflected in the function and symbolism of staffs. The horn-like motifs found on staffs reserved for important leaders probably served to invoke the protective powers of the king's ancestors. Dance staffs and walking sticks, like headrests and meatplates, are usually decorated with simple geometric designs. Moreover, in contrast to other southern African Bantu groups (e.g. the Sotho and Tsonga), the northern Nguni do not appear to have used figurative carvings in male initiation rituals, which were practised before the emergence of age-grade regiments (*amabutho*) in the late 18th century. The staffs with elaborately carved figurative heads, and those with depictions of married women, that are generally described as Zulu in the literature on southern Africa, were probably produced by Tsonga carvers, many of them working for a tourist market. Some of these staffs depict men wearing the traditional Zulu headring (*isicoco*), which symbolized the right to marry, own cattle and set up an independent homestead. This was granted only after a man had served in one of the king's regiments for a protracted period.

2. DOMESTIC ARTS. The Zulu have always used both utilitarian carvings and everyday dress to express the relationship between themselves and their ancestors, and between men and women. The disruptive effects of migrant labour had substantially reduced the numbers of

traditional carvers by the late 20th century. Those that remain continue to be commissioned to produce meat-plates, milkpails, spoons and, less often, headrests. Head-rests bought by women form part of a dowry that includes grass sleeping-mats and numerous types of pots. Meat-plates (more common in the late 20th century than in the 19th century, when tightly woven grass mats were used) and milkpails, however, have always been purchased by the heads of homesteads because cattle and the food obtained from them are associated with the ancestors and hence with the continuity of the patrilineage. A woman is ritually proscribed from entering her husband's cattle byre, eating meat, drinking milk and using the utensils associated with these foods until she has produced a child.

There are many variations in the style and decoration of Zulu meatplates, milkpails and headrests. The motif most commonly found on these, as on pots, is the *amasumpa* (warts) design, which is said to represent cattle (see fig. 1). Chevron patterns, referred to as snakes (i.e. ancestors), are also popular. Such designs may therefore relate symbolically to Zulu cosmology. More obvious, but still highly schematic, figurative references to traditional beehive huts, bulls and snuffboxes may also be found on 19th-century headrests. It is quite likely that specific motifs and patterns were originally associated with particular northern Nguni lineages, for the styles of several types of meatplates and headrests are regional. Unlike meatplates and milkpails, headrests became seldom used by the late 20th century, presumably because the elaborate head-dresses worn by married women were no longer woven into their hair. Traditionally a married woman commissioned two headrests before her marriage, one for herself and one for her future husband. While these could be identical in style, a man's status was generally acknowledged with a relatively elaborately carved example.

With the exception of potters, Zulu women are generally not specialists in art production such as wood-carving, although most married women make mats and baskets and are responsible for the thatching of huts. This is consistent with the division of labour in Zulu society, for men traditionally tend to the cattle, while women look after the fields.

3. FEMALE DRESS. Throughout her married life a woman wears a leather skirt (*isidwaba*; see fig. 2), which is initially made from the hides and animals belonging to her father. This skirt, regarded as the property of her ancestors, is worn both as a sign of respect for her husband's ancestors and as a form of protection against them. In some areas these skirts are short and straight and worn under cloth skirts, but in most areas they are pleated and decorated with elaborately beaded panels. Married women also wear grass belts and flaring or bifurcated headdresses. In the late 20th century beads were sewn on to the belts, but the basic design had not changed since the mid-19th century.

Unlike the men, Zulu women seldom seek work in the cities, and absent husbands encourage them to observe and preserve their traditions. It is therefore not unusual for women to wear traditional dress at all times and to make the beaded artefacts that have become an integral part of this dress. Zulu women have, in fact, developed

1. Zulu headrest with *amasumpa* design on legs, wood, l. 362 mm, late 19th century or early 20th (London, British Museum)

the tradition of beadwork into a flourishing art form with remarkable regional variations in style and in the use of colour and pattern. It would seem that such major lineages as the Cunu, Tembu and Cele, who have generally succeeded in maintaining their geographical isolation from other lineages, produce distinctive styles of beadwork. Further variations in the use of colours and motifs may clearly identify the wearer as belonging to a particular institution rather than to a geographical area or lineage. The cross motif used in the beadwork of the Shembe church, for example, is an obvious Christian symbol, indicative of the attempts Shembe and his followers made from the early 20th century to synthesize Zulu and Christian beliefs. A comparable stylistic and symbolic consistency is evident in the red and white beads worn by Zulu diviners and healers. In this case, but not necessarily in other contexts, colour is an unmistakable reference to the ancestors.

It is less certain whether any specific symbolism is intended in either the use of colours or in the geometric designs found in regional beadwork styles. Triangles, diamonds, chevrons and squares are variously identified as referring to 'man' and 'woman', and even 'stairs' or 'windows', while questionable anecdotal explanations have also been posited for the use of colour, especially in the necklaces that young women present to their lovers. Despite the variation in the names and styles of Zulu beaded artefacts, there is a remarkable consistency in the functions ascribed to them. Beaded necklaces and aprons may vary in shape, size and threading technique, but, in common with such other items as bandoliers, wristbands and anklets, they all serve to define the sexual and marital status of the wearer.

2. Zulu women in traditional dress, Qudeni, Zululand; from a photograph by Sandra Klopper

BIBLIOGRAPHY
G. F. Angas: *The Kafirs Illustrated in a Series of Drawings Taken among the Amazulu, Amaponda and Amakosa Tribes etc.* (London, 1849)
F. F. Mayr: 'Language of Colours amongst the Zulus Expressed by their Bead-work Ornaments; and Some General Notes on their Personal Adornments and Clothing', *An. Natal Mus.*, i/2 (1907), 159–65, pl. xxvii
A. T. Bryant: *Olden Times in Zululand and Natal etc.* (London, New York and Toronto, 1929)
E. C. Chubb: 'The Zulu Brass Armlet "Ingxota": A Badge of Distinction', *Man*, xxxvi (1936), p. 185
E. J. Krige: *The Social System of the Zulus* (London, New York and Toronto, 1936)
J. S. Schoeman: 'A Preliminary Report on Traditional Beadwork in the Mkhwanazi Area of the Mtunzini District, Zululand', *Afr. Stud.*, xxvii, 1968), pp. 57–81, 107–33
B. V. Brottem and A. Lang: 'Zulu Beadwork', *Afr. A.*, vi/3 (1973), pp. 8–13, 64, 83–4
O. F. Raum: *The Social Functions of Avoidances and Taboos among the Zulu*, Hamburgisches Museum für Völkerkunde, Monographien zur Völkerkunde, vi (Berlin, 1973)
An. S. Afr. Mus., lxx/1–4 [pubd as *Some Nguni Crafts*, 4 vols (Cape Town, 1976–9)]
A.-I. Berglund: *Zulu Thought-patterns and Symbolism*, Studia Missionalia Upsaliensia, xxii (London, 1976/*R* Bloomington, 1989)
J. Grossert: *Zulu Crafts* (Pietermaritzburg, 1978)
C. Kennedy: *The Art and Material Culture of the Zulu-speaking Peoples* (Los Angeles, 1978)
M. W. Conner and D. Pelrine: *The Geometric Vision: Arts of the Zulu* (Lafayette, IN, 1983)
A. Nettleton: 'History and the Myth of Zulu Sculpture', *Afr. A.*, xxi/3 (1988), pp. 48–51, 86–7
S. Klopper: 'George French Angas', *S. Afr. J. Cult. & A. Hist.*, iii/1 (1989), pp. 63–73
C. G. Kennedy: 'Prestige Ornaments: The Use of Brass in the Zulu Kingdom', *Afr. A.*, xxiv/3 (1991), pp. 50–55, 94–6
S. Klopper: 'Mobilising Cultural Symbols in 20th Century Zululand', *African Studies Forum*, eds M. Muller, M. Trump and R. Hill (Pretoria, 1991)
——: 'You Only Need One Bull to Cover Fifty Cows: Zulu Women and "Traditional" Dress', *Regions and Repertoires: Topics in South African Politics and Culture*, ed. S. Clingman (Johannesburg, 1991)
——: ' "Zulu" Headrests and Figurative Carvings: The Brenthurst Collection and the Art of South-east Africa', *Art and Ambiguity: Perspectives on the Brenthurst Collection of Southern African Art* (Johannesburg, 1991)
E. Preston Whyte: 'Zulu Bead Sculptors', *Afr. A.*, xxiv/1 (1991), pp. 64–76, 104
F. Jolles: 'Traditional Zulu Beadwork of the Msinga Area', *Afr. A.*, xxvi/1 (1993), pp. 42–53

SANDRA KLOPPER

Zumbo [Zummo], **Gaetano (Giulio)** (*b* Syracuse, 1656; *d* Paris, 22 Dec 1701). Italian sculptor, active also in France. He was born of a noble family named Zummo (he changed the spelling to Zumbo in Paris) and educated for the church. Zumbo was a wax sculptor and anatomical modeller and, like many late 16th- and 17th-century amateurs who practised the art of wax modelling, was probably self-taught, although he may have learnt something of the technique in Sicily, where wax imagery was popular. Before 1691 he went to Naples and visited Rome and other cities in Italy. He was an enthusiastic collector of Old Master drawings and engravings. In Naples he may have invented a new method of colouring wax for sculpture (*see* WAX, §II, 1(i)), which attracted sufficient notice for him to be summoned to Florence in 1691 by Cosimo de' Medici III, Grand Duke of Tuscany, who paid him a monthly pension. As a sample of his skill he may have brought with him a scene with wax figures, the *Plague* (Florence, Mus. Zool. La Specola), which has been shown to depend on paintings of the Neapolitan plague of 1656 by Mattia Preti and Micco Spadaro. Zumbo was in Florence from February 1691 at least until April 1694. For

Cosimo he executed two wax groups, one now lost, the other the *Vanity of Human Greatness* (Florence, Mus. Zool. La Specola). For Ferdinand de' Medici, the Grand Prince, who had acquired the *Plague*, he made the only other group that can safely be attributed to him, the *Triumph of Time* (Florence, Mus. Zool. La Specola; see fig.). These works combine rigorous scientific observation of the various stages of decomposition of the human body with an edifying iconography of the inevitable decay of human beauty and power. The idealizing classicism of the late Baroque figure style and the dramatic pathos of expression and pose, for which Zumbo drew on pictorial and sculptural models by Nicolas Poussin, Michelangelo and others, become in this context an expressive device emphasizing the lesson of ultimate decay. Accessory details, such as rats, snakes and dead dogs, are treated with grim realism. In the *Triumph of Time* a self-portrait in miniature rests against a pilaster at the feet of Time with his scythe. The groups are essentially illusionistic tableaux, and their backgrounds, symbolic inventions also figuring ruin and decay, combine painted and modelled features, perhaps developing an already established tradition.

By 1695 Zumbo had left Florence for Bologna, and then went on to Genoa. There he entered into partnership with Guillaume Desnoues, a French surgeon, making exact models in coloured wax of the human anatomy to assist medical studies. He spent much time in the study of corpses specially dissected by Desnoues and modelled a

celebrated figure of a woman in childbirth (untraced) and an anatomical head which he sent as a present to Grand Prince Ferdinand (Florence, Mus. Zool. La Specola). He also made two groups, a *Deposition* (of which the figure of Christ survives in the Museo Nazionale del Bargello, Florence) and a *Nativity* (the *Nativity* in the Victoria and Albert Museum, London, is perhaps a version with the composition reversed). By 1700 he was in Marseille, where he modelled a second anatomical head. He next moved to Paris, where he showed the head at a session on 25 May 1701 of the Académie des Sciences. The painter Elisabeth Sophie Chéron acquired the two Genoese wax groups and introduced Zumbo to the critic Roger de Piles, who later wrote an admiring description of these works. Zumbo was granted a privilege for the making of wax models by Louis XIV in August 1701 but died suddenly, leaving uncompleted a group of *Venus and Adonis* (untraced).

Zumbo's great reputation as a wax sculptor was enshrined after his death in various notices, and the unsparing realism of the Florentine groups attracted travellers, particularly the Romantics in the late 18th century and early 19th. Later he fell into neglect, and it is only modern interest in the Baroque that has revived the reputation of the sculptor and his work. His achievement as an anatomical modeller has always been recognized by specialists.

BIBLIOGRAPHY

R. W. Lightbown: 'Gaetano Giulio Zumbo', *Burl. Mag.*, cvi (1964), pp. 486–96, 563–9 [with full citation of earlier sources and literature]

F. Cagnetta: 'Gaetano Giulio Zummo', *Kunst des Barock in der Toskana*, Italienische Forschungen, III/9 (Munich, 1976), pp. 213–14

P. Giansiracusa, ed.: *Antologia degli scritti sull'opera di Gaetano Giulio Zumbo* (Syracuse, 1990)

——, ed.: *Vanitas vanitatum: Studi sulla ceroplastica di Gaetano Giulio Zumbo* (Syracuse, 1991)

R. W. LIGHTBOWN

Zumbusch, Kasper Clemens, Ritter von (*b* Herzebrock, Westphalia, 23 Nov 1830; *d* Rimsting, nr Prien am Chiemsee, 27 Sept 1915). German sculptor. He studied sculpture at the Polytechnische Schule in Munich, under Johann von Halbig (1814–82) whom he accompanied on a study tour to Milan in 1849. After setting up independently in 1852 and successfully fulfilling his first portrait commissions, he went to Rome (1857–8) to study Classical sculpture. He travelled to Italy again in 1867, this time accompanied by his pupil Adolf von Hildebrand. Zumbusch's early works are tentative in approach. *Flora* (1859; ex-Städt. Gal., Hannover) reveals the pervasive influence of Ludwig von Schwanthaler and also borrows features from Bertel Thorvaldsen's *Venus* (1813–16; Copenhagen, Thorvaldsens Mus.) while anticipating Zumbusch's later, more distinctive style in its sweeping movement and energetic forms. On the other hand, his religious works from the same period such as the carved altar to *SS Benno and Corbinian* (1860; Munich, Frauenkirche) assimilated both Nazarene and Romantic styles. The diversity of style of the 19th century is thus mirrored in Zumbusch's work. In the works commissioned in the 1860s and 1870s by the King of Bavaria, Ludwig II, especially the marble statuettes of figures from Richard Wagner's operas (e.g. *Lohengrin*, 1865; *Walther von Stolzing*, 1867; Prien, Neues Schloss Herrenchiemsee), he slowly freed himself from Neo-classicist ideas of form: the drapery is richer, the details

Gaetano Zumbo: *Triumph of Time* (detail), coloured wax, h. of whole 280 mm, 1690s (Florence, Museo Zoologico 'La Specola')

are more cogent, and altogether there is greater liveliness of expression.

Zumbusch's first major work was the monument to *Maximilian II* (1866–7; Munich, Maximilianstrasse), begun two years after that king's death. Its plain, yet powerfully expressive style was recognized at the time as formally progressive, despite the unsuccessful integration of the statue with its site. The statue also symbolizes the constitutional monarchy; the central figure holds the constitution in his right hand and the royal sword, decorated with an olive branch, in his left. A year after completing the monument, Zumbusch was appointed professor at the Akademie der Bildenden Künste in Vienna; he later became director.

Zumbusch's masterpiece is his second dynastic memorial, the monument to *Empress Maria-Theresa* (1888; Vienna, Maria-Theresien-Platz). A supreme achievement of the neo-Baroque movement, mixing idealized and naturalistic features in a controlled juxtaposition of figures in the round and figures in high relief, it dominates the square between the Kunsthistorisches Museum and the Naturhistorisches Museum. With an eye to civic feeling, the monument was intended to depict not only the Empress but also the 'props of her throne', generals, statesmen and representatives of science and the arts—24 figures in all. Maria-Theresa herself is a seated figure, 6 m high, raising her right hand to greet her people.

Zumbusch also produced other public statues for Vienna, such as the memorial to *Ludwig von Beethoven* (1873–80; Vienna, Beethoven-Platz; *see* AUSTRIA, fig. 22) and the equestrian statue of *Fieldmarshal Archduke Albrecht* (1898–9; Vienna, Augustinerstrasse). His son Ludwig von Zumbusch (1861–1927) was a painter and illustrator.

BIBLIOGRAPHY
LK; Thieme–Becker
G. van Osten: *Plastik seit 1800 in Deutschland, Österreich und der Schweiz* (Königstein im Taunus, 1961)
H.-G. Evers: 'Plastik', *Die Kunst des 19. Jahrhunderts*, ed. R. Zeitler, Propyläen Kstgesch. (Berlin, 1966), pp. 160–61, 288
G. Kapner: *Freiplastik in Wien* (Vienna, 1970)
A. Ziegler: 'Die Konkurrenzentwürfe zum Max-II.-Denkmal', *Denkmäler im 19. Jahrhundert, Deutung und Kritik*, eds H.-E. Mittig and V. Plagemann (Munich, 1972), pp. 113–40
G. Kapner: *Ringstrassendenkmäler: Zur Geschichte der Ringstrassendenkmäler* (Wiesbaden, 1973)
G. Finckh: '"Plastisch, das heisst antik, zu denken . . ." Die Bildhauerei an der Münchner Akademie und der Klassizismus von Roman Anton Boos (1733–1810) bis Adolf von Hildebrand (1849–1921)', *Tradition und Widerspruch: 175 Jahre Kunstakademie, München*, ed. Th. Zacharias (Munich, 1985)

CLEMENTINE SCHACK VON WITTENAU

Zünd, Robert (*b* Lucerne, 3 May 1827; *d* Lucerne, 15 Jan 1909). Swiss painter. He trained with Jakob Schwegler (1793–1866) and Joseph Zelger (1812–85), whom he accompanied on a study visit to the Engadine. Zelger encouraged him to go to Geneva in 1848. There he was a pupil first of François Diday and then of Alexandre Calame, who influenced his early work. However, while Calame painted dramatic mountain scenes, Zünd preferred the idyllic, tranquil region of the Alpine foothills. In 1851 he moved to Munich, where he met the Swiss painter Rudolf Koller, who remained a close friend. From 1852

he often stayed in Paris. He studied paintings by 17th-century Dutch and French artists in the Louvre and became acquainted with Alexandre-Gabriel Decamps, Louis Français, Louis Cabat, Frank Buchser and Albert Anker.

In 1860 Zünd travelled to Dresden to copy Dutch landscapes in the Gemäldegalerie. In 1863 he settled in the outskirts of Lucerne and looked for subject-matter principally in the landscape around the city. However detailed his scrutiny, he never lost sight of magnitude and breadth, as in *Harvest* (1859; Basle, Kstmus.). He limited himself both geographically and seasonally, never depicting nature in winter. In 1883 Zünd became friendly with the Winterthur patron Theodor Reinhart (1849–1919), who, with his son Oskar Reinhart, frequently visited him in his studio and bought several of his pictures, for example *Chestnut Tree at Horw* (1857; Winterthur, Stift. Oskar Reinhart). He received an honorary doctorate from the University of Zurich in 1906.

BIBLIOGRAPHY
Thieme-Becker
A. Reinle: *Die Kunst des 19. Jahrhunderts* (1962), iv of *Kunstgeschichte der Schweiz von den Anfängen bis zum Beginn des 20. Jahrhunderts*, ed. J. Gantner and A. Reinle (Frauenfeld and Leipzig, 1936–62)
Robert Zünd in seiner Zeit (exh. cat., Lucerne, Kstmus., 1978)

FRANZ ZELGER

Zündt, Matthias (*b* ?1498; *d* Nuremberg, 25 Feb 1572). German goldsmith, etcher and draughtsman. He was documented in Nuremberg in 1554, when he applied for citizenship, but was probably there earlier, as his main ornamental work, *Novum opus craterographicum* (a series of 31 etchings of vessels, attributed to him on stylistic grounds), was printed there in 1551. The ornamental details (such as castings from nature) in these prints suggest a goldsmith's training. A smaller series of 22 etchings also contains models for brooches, daggers etc. The separate scrollwork title page bears the date 1553 and his full name.

In 1559 Zündt was recorded as an assistant of Wenzel Jamnitzer, who sent him to Prague to work on a table fountain, noting in a letter to Archduke Ferdinand of the Tyrol (1529–95) that Zündt was industrious but used foul language. Nothing is known of Zündt's work for Ferdinand, nor of any other goldsmith's work by him, though in 1567 he etched 21 perspective views of the letters of the alphabet for the *Perspectiva literaria* (Nuremburg) by the goldsmith Hans Lencker (*d* 1585). The list of etchings that Zündt published on his own account between 1565 and 1571 includes a dozen maps, contemporary battle scenes and sieges, 14 portraits of well-known contemporaries, 18 coats of arms and several mythological, allegorical and biblical motifs. Many of these have elaborate explanatory texts etched into the plates. Since Ritter's identification of Zündt as the Master of the *Craterographia* of 1551, few additions have been made to his corpus. Standing-cups were made by later goldsmiths after his ornament designs, and several drawings attributed to him only copy motifs from his etchings.

BIBLIOGRAPHY
A. Andresen: *Der deutsche Peintre-graveur* (Leipzig, 1864–78), i, pp. 1–46
F. Ritter: 'Der Meister der Kraterographie', *Mitt. Kst.-Kön. Österreich. Mus. Kst & Indust.*, n. s. 5 (1894–5), pp. 72–4
L. Bagrow: *A. Ortelii catalogus cartographorum* (Gotha, 1930), pp. 118–21

C. P. Warncke: *Die ornamentale Groteske in Deutschland, 1500–1650*, 2 vols (Berlin, 1979)
Wenzel Jamnitzer und die Nürnberger Goldschmiedekunst, 1500–1700 (exh. cat., intro. G. Bott; Nuremberg, German. Nmus., 1985), pp. 28, 54, 113, 141, 144, 196; cat. nos 363, 370–82, 391–6, 755

ILSE O'DELL-FRANKE

Zúñiga, Francisco (*b* San José, Costa Rica, 27 Dec 1912). Mexican sculptor and printmaker of Costa Rican birth. He studied sculpture under his father, Manuel María Zúñiga, in San José, Costa Rica, and after his arrival in Mexico City in 1936 at the Escuela de Talla Directa under the direction of Guillermo Ruíz (1895–1964) and Oliverio Martínez. Martínez, together with the painter Manuel Rodríguez Lozano, helped motivate his monumental concept of form. Other lasting influences came from his encounter with Aztec sculpture and from the work of other sculptors, such as Auguste Rodin, Aristide Maillol and even Henry Moore, whose work, like his, was based primarily on the human body. Throughout his career Zúñiga was especially devoted to the female form, naked or clothed.

The monumental character of Zúñiga's sculpture is evident not only in public commissioned works, such as the stone reliefs of the *Allegory of the Earth and Communications* (1953–4) at the Secretaría de Comunicaciones in Mexico City, but also in sculptures conceived for more private and intimate settings, for example *Seated Woman from Juchitán* (bronze, 1974; Washington, DC, Hirshhorn). In 1959, in works such as *Standing Women* (bronze; Mexico City, Mus. A. Mod.) he moved from the non-academic naturalism of his early style, which was still linked to the 19th century, to a more realistic idiom, taking as his models the indigenous women of south-eastern Mexico, whom he represented standing or seated, singly, in pairs or in a group. They are women with large bodies, both heavily built and scrawny, all seemingly caught in a violent transition from youth to old age. They inhabit a dramatic silence in which there is no communication, and occasionally they appear with the ancestral dignity of their race, as in *Woman from Yalalag* (bronze, 1975; Monclova, Bib. Pape). Only in exceptional cases do men appear. He availed himself of a variety of methods and materials, modelling in clay and plaster and also working in Carrara marble, alabaster and other kinds of stone; his preferred medium was cast bronze.

Drawing served Zúñiga as an essential basis for his sculpture and also for his prolific production as a lithographer. His prints, some printed in black and others in colour, presented the same subject-matter as his sculptures with an equivalent emphasis on the volumetric treatment of female figures. Zúñiga, who as a teacher trained many outstanding Mexican sculptors, became a naturalized Mexican citizen in 1986.

BIBLIOGRAPHY
C. F. Echeverría: *Francisco Zúñiga* (Mexico City, 1980)
J. Brewster: *Zúñiga: The Complete Graphics* (New York, 1985)
M. Parquet: *Zúñiga: Esculturas* (Paris, 1986)

XAVIER MOYSSÉN

Zúñiga, Manuel de Acevedo y. *See* MONTERREY, 6th Conde de.

Zúñiga, Mateo de (*b c.* 1615; *d* Santiago de Guatemala [now Antigua], ?14 Jan 1687). Guatemalan sculptor. His work as a master sculptor (Maestro) began around 1640 in Santiago de Guatemala and is all in Guatemala City. In 1654 he made the famous Baroque processional statue of *Jesús Nazareno* for the church of La Merced (*in situ*), which was finely carved and brought him renown. The tinting and painting of the figure was by Joseph de la Cerda. A statue made for the same church of *Jesús Nazareno de Candelaria* (now in the church of the Candelaria, Guatemala City) has also been attributed to him, but on insufficient grounds. In 1660, as the leading sculptor in Guatemala, Zúñiga received important commissions that included retables for the convents of La Concepción and of S Catalina. In 1666 he was responsible for the construction of the catafalque for the funerary honours for Philip IV (*d* 1665). In the contract he described himself as Maestro of sculpture and architecture. In 1670 he was commissioned to build two retables for S Domingo and, for the new cathedral, his two most significant works: the principal retable and the retable for the sacristy. For the work in the cathedral sacristy the contract states that he was also to carve the figures of the *Four Evangelists*, *God the Father*, two scenes of the *Holy Sacrament* and the *Triumph of the Church* and all the ornamental angels as well as those on the columns.

BIBLIOGRAPHY
H. Berlin: *Historia de la imaginería colonial en Guatemala* (Guatemala City, 1952)
M. Alvarez Arévalo: *Breves consideraciones sobre la historia del Jesús de la Merced* (Guatemala City, 1982)
H. Berlin and J. Luján-Muñoz: *Los tumulos funerarios en Guatemala* (Guatemala City, 1983)

JORGE LUJÁN-MUÑOZ

Zurbarán, de. Spanish family of painters.

(1) Francisco de Zurbarán (*bapt* Fuente de Cantos, Badajoz, 7 Nov 1598; *d* Madrid, 27 Aug 1664). He was one of the greatest masters of the school of Seville and is renowned for his powerful and realistic interpretation of monastic life in 17th-century Spain.

1. First years in Seville, 1614–34. 2. The years of maturity in Madrid and Seville, 1634–50. 3. Late works and return to Madrid, 1650–64.

1. FIRST YEARS IN SEVILLE, 1614–34. Zurbarán was the son of a trader and at 15 left his native village, south of the Estremadura mountains, for Seville. Here he was apprenticed in the studio of Pedro Díaz de Villanueva, by whom no signed work is known, and became familiar with polychrome sculpture, which affected his style as a painter, in particular in his rendering of drapery. During the years in Seville he must also have been in contact with other gifted painters such as Juan de Roelas, Francisco de Herrera the elder, and above all Diego Velázquez and Alonso Cano, who were then young apprentices in the studio of Francisco Pacheco. In 1617 Zurbarán left Seville without obtaining the examination of incorporation that would have given him the right to practise his art, an omission for which he was subsequently severely reproached. He moved to Estremadura and for ten years was established in Llerena, where he also married, probably in 1617. None of his paintings of this period for the

1. Francisco de Zurbarán: *Crucifixion*, oil on canvas, 2.90×1.65 m, 1627 (Chicago, IL, Art Institute of Chicago)

churches of Fuente de Cantos, Llerena or Montemolin has survived.

In 1626 Zurbarán signed a contract with the Dominicans of the monastery of S Pablo El Real in Seville for a series of paintings. These include two scenes from the *Life of St Dominic*, the *Apparition of the Virgin to the Monks of Soriano* and the *Miraculous Cure of the Blessed Reginald of Saint-Gilles* (both 1626–7), which survive in the Capilla Sacramental of the church (now S María Magdalena), and the full-length figures of the *Three Doctors of the Church* (*SS Ambrose, Gregory* and *Jerome*; Seville, Mus. B.A.). The works contain the seeds of the distinctive signs of Zurbarán's creative originality: the force and massive effect of his figures, the heavy folds of the drapery, the very pronounced oval shape of the faces and the attention given to accessories such as still-life details. The first known dated painting, a *Crucifixion* (1627; Chicago, IL, A. Inst.; see fig. 1) from the sacristy of the same monastery of S Pablo, shows a complete knowledge of the aesthetic concepts of Caravaggio in the striking realism of the figure, which is nevertheless transcended through the use of

strong lighting. This composition brought Zurbarán immediate fame and led to numerous commissions from other religious orders.

In 1628 the Mercedarians commissioned Zurbarán for the decoration of the small cloister in the monastery of S José of La Merced Calzada, Seville. He derived inspiration for this from engravings after drawings (untraced) dedicated to the *Life of St Peter Nolasco* by Jusepe Martinez. The quality of execution of the ten scenes that survive differs: four are considered to be autograph works (the *Vision of St Peter Nolasco* and the *Apparition of St Peter the Apostle to St Peter Nolasco*, 1629, both Madrid, Prado; the *Presentation of the Image of the Virgin of El Puig to James I of Aragon*, 1630, Cincinnati, OH, A. Mus.; and the *Surrender of Seville*, 1634, Duke of Westminster priv. col., see 1987 exh. cat., no. 9, pl. 112); two show evidence of less competent workshop collaboration (*Birth of St Peter Nolasco*, Bordeaux, Mus. B.A.; and the *Departure of St Peter Nolasco*, Mexico City, Mus. S Carlos); and four other scenes (Seville Cathedral, Capilla de S Pedro) show the intervention of another artist, probably Francisco Reyna (*d* 1659). Another important work for the Mercedarians is the *St Serapion* (1628; Hartford, CT, Wadsworth Atheneum; see fig. 2). In the intensity of its composition and the superb treatment of the full white mantle, this is one of Zurbarán's greatest paintings. It was executed for the Sala De Profondis of La Merced Calzada, where the mortal remains of the members of the order were laid before burial. The series of the *Doctors of the Order of La Merced*, painted a few years later for the library (five examples in Madrid, Real Acad. S Fernando, Mus.), depicts the subjects

2. Francisco de Zurbarán: *St Serapion*, oil on canvas, 1.20×1.04 m, 1628 (Hartford, CT, Wadsworth Atheneum)

3. Francisco de Zurbarán: *Still-life with Oranges*, oil on canvas, 622×1095 mm, 1633 (Pasadena, CA, Norton Simon Museum)

bathed in a softer light that effectively accentuates the supple treatment of their long white robes. This group of religious figures is remarkable for the variety of poses and the strong individual characterization of the faces.

In 1629 Zurbarán was invited by the municipality of Seville to establish himself permanently in the city. He was commissioned to complete the cycle of paintings of the *Life of St Bonaventura* begun by Francisco de Herrera the elder early in the same year for the Franciscan Colegio de S Buenaventura. The paintings include the *Prayer of St Bonaventura* (Dresden, Gemäldegal. Alte Meister), the *Visit of St Thomas Aquinas to St Bonaventura* (Berlin; Kaiser-Friedrich Mus., destr. 1945) and the *Death of St Bonaventura* (Paris, Louvre). In comparison with the expressive style of Herrera, Zurbarán's paintings all create an impression of classicism and balance. In the solemn scene of *St Bonaventura at the Council of Lyons* (Paris, Louvre), set within an architectural framework with a portico, column and dais, the poses of the figures and expressions of the participants in the discussion are portrayed with the sensitivity and spontaneity of a scene drawn from life.

In 1630 in the *Vision of Blessed Alphonsus Rodríguez* (Madrid, Real Acad. S Fernando), painted for the sacristy of the Casa Profesora of the Jesuits, Zurbarán seems to have adopted for the first time an archaic arrangement of two superimposed zones, with clouds supporting the celestial upper part. This may derive from Italian engravings or may have been taken, at the suggestion of his patrons, from models by Roelas or Herrera. The meeting of the heavenly and earthly worlds is powerfully expressed in strong tones of red and orange that contrast with the black robe of the humble Jesuit porter. This form of composition on two levels is used again in the *Miracle of*

Portiuncula (Cádiz, Mus. Pint) for the Capuchin monastery of Cádiz and in the *Apotheosis of St Thomas Aquinas* (1631; Seville, Mus. B.A.), commissioned by the Dominicans for the high altar of their church of S Tomás. The later *St Andrew* (Budapest, Mus. F.A.) and *St Gabriel* (Montpellier, Mus. Fabre), probably also from S Tomás, both show Zurbarán's beautiful rendering of drapery.

Other works by Zurbarán, of unknown provenance and uncertain date, depict more intimate Christian themes with an exquisite pictorial sensitivity: they include the *Virgin as a Child in Ecstasy (or Praying)* (New York, Met.) and the *Family of the Virgin* (ex-Contini-Bonacossi priv. col., Florence; Madrid, priv. col., see 1987 exh. cat., p. 343, pl. 72). The *Infant Christ with the Crown of Thorns* (Cleveland, OH, Mus. A.), also known as the *House of Nazareth*, of which a dozen copies are known, is remarkable for the emotional tension of the figures, the refined colouring and the originality of the composition, which is based on a system of diagonals that emphasizes the symbolic objects (books, fruits, work-basket, flowers) as much as the figures of the Holy Family. In the only individual *bodegón* signed by Zurbarán, the *Still-life with Oranges* (1633; Pasadena, CA, Norton Simon Mus.; see fig. 3), the objects have been imbued with the same transcendental and mystical character. Arranged as a frieze on a dark, abstract background three everyday items, citrons, oranges and a cup, are picked out by the artist in an unreal light and acquire a supernatural presence. By analogy, two pictures titled *Still-life with Pottery* (Madrid, Prado, and Barcelona, Mus. A. Catalunya), both painted with the same sobriety and ability in the treatment of light, are also attributed to him.

Zurbarán had already begun, from 1631, to depict subjects for meditation; these were themes to which he returned throughout his life, such as the *Veil of St Veronica* (Argentina, priv. col., and Stockholm, Nmus.) and the *Agnus Dei*, where the lamb, with feet tied, is shown on the sacrificial stone (1631–40; San Diego, CA, Mus. A.; 1632, ex-col. Plandiura, Barcelona; Madrid, Prado). Groups of saints painted during the period shortly after 1634 and now detached from the altars for which they were executed include *St Agatha* (Montpellier, Mus. Fabre), *St Ferdinand* (St Petersburg, Hermitage), *St Apollonius* (Paris, Louvre), *St Lucy* (Chartres, Mus. B.-A.), *St Cyril* and *St Peter Thomas* (Boston, MA, Mus. F.A.). The only ensemble of this period to have remained *in situ* is the large altarpiece of *St Peter* for the Capilla de S Pedro in Seville Cathedral. Numerous isolated figures of female saints, all sumptuously dressed, seem to have been inspired by the traditional Sevillian Corpus Christi processions, including *St Casilda* (Madrid, Mus. Thyssen-Bornemisza) and *St Elizabeth of Portugal* (Madrid, Prado); others were inspired by scenes for religious theatre, for example *St Margaret* (London, N.G.).

2. THE YEARS OF MATURITY IN MADRID AND SEVILLE, 1634–50. Zurbarán went to Madrid during 1634. He was probably recommended to the Conde-Duque de Olivares, minister of Philip IV and governor of the Buen Retiro, by Velázquez (whom he already knew in Seville), and he was employed as part of the team decorating the Salon de Reinos of the Buen Retiro. He executed two battle paintings, the *Defence of Cádiz against the English* (Madrid, Prado) and the *Expulsion of the Dutch from the Island of St Martin* (untraced), and ten mythological scenes for overdoors, including the *Labours of Hercules* (Madrid, Prado). The visit enabled him to see the royal collections, with their important Venetian paintings, as well as the work of Rubens and other Spanish artists working for the King, and he gained the title of Painter to the King.

On his return to Seville in 1635, he painted the portrait of the young aristocrat *Alonso Verdugo de Albornoz* (Berlin, Gemäldegal.), which recalls the noble pose and contrasting lighting of portraits by Velázquez dating from 1625–30. He soon gained more ecclesiastical commissions, and some of his altar paintings, such as the *Blessed Henry Suso* and *St Louis Beltrán* (both *c*. 1638; Seville, Mus. B.A.), included fine open-air effects; in others, however, the figures and their heavy clothing retain the static density and fullness of previous years. Examples are *St Lawrence* (1636; St Petersburg, Hermitage) and *SS Romanus and Barulas* (1638; Chicago, IL, A. Inst.), painted for the Sevillian church of S Román. Other compositions were taken from engravings, such as the *Burial of St Catherine* (Munich, Alte Pin.), inspired by a design by Cornelis Cort (see 1987 exh. cat., p. 159) and frequently used in various versions of this subject by the Zurbarán workshop.

(i) Carthusian monastery at Jerez de la Frontera. In 1638–9, at the height of his prestige, Zurbarán was employed on two important commissions. The first was for the Carthusians at the monastery of Jerez de La Frontera, near Cádiz, where he executed paintings for the high altar of the lay friars' choir, *Our Lady of the Carthusians* (on dep. Poznań, N. Mus.) and the *Immaculate Conception with SS Joachim and Anne* (Edinburgh, N.G.). He also decorated the panels

of the doors and the passage leading to the Sagrario with two paintings, each depicting an *Angel with Thurible*, and seven paintings of individual Carthusian saints (Cádiz, Mus. Pint.). He painted other canvases in the sacristy and refectory, and on the retable of the high altar (dismantled); the latter depicted the *Battle of El Sotillo* (New York, Met.), and illustrated the victory over the Moors at El Sotillo on the site where the monastery was built. The painting was hung at the lower centre and was surrounded by four scenes from the *Childhood of Christ*: the *Annunciation* (see fig. 4), the *Adoration of the Shepherds*, the *Adoration of the Magi* and the *Circumcision*, signed and dated 1639 (all Grenoble, Mus. Peint. & Sculp.). Above each scene were paintings of the *Four Evangelists*, accompanied by *St Lawrence* and *St John the Baptist* on the base panel (all Cádiz, Mus. Pint.). Seen in isolation, each of the four gospel scenes is endowed with solemnity by the hieratism of the figures, which stand out from the architectural backgrounds, and by the striking range of costumes. The composition of the *Annunciation* is the most impressive of the scheme and shows an intellectual balance between the poetic rendering of the heavenly kingdom and the figures in the foreground, which stand out in a full light against very dark wall-screens; the gracious and elegant pose of the angel both reflects and contrasts with the dignified and solemn bearing of the Virgin, around whom are arranged three beautiful still-lifes symbolizing

4. Francisco de Zurbarán: *Annunciation*, oil on canvas, 2.66×1.84 m, 1639 (Grenoble, Musée de Peinture et de Sculpture)

chastity (a vase of lilies), prayer (books) and labour (the work-basket).

(ii) Hieronymite monastery at Guadalupe. The second major commission of this period was for the royal Hieronymite monastery at Guadalupe (province of Cáceres), where Zurbarán had further opportunity to display his considerable narrative talent as a chronicler of monastic life. The eight paintings in the sacristy are devoted to 15th-century Hieronymite monks associated with the foundation during this, historically its most glorious period. They are the *Mass of Fray Cabañuelas* (1638), *Christ Appearing to Fray Andrés de Salmeron, Fray Fernando Yáñez de Figuera before Henry II* (1639; for illustration *see* HIERONYMITES), *Fray Martín Vizcaino Distributing Alms* (1639), *Fray Juan de Carrión Taking Leave of his Friends* (1639), the *Vision of Fray Pedro de Salamanca* and the *Temptation of Fray Diego de Orgaz*. This historic series, completed by three scenes from the *Life of St Jerome* in the adjoining chapel, is rare among Zurbarán's work in having remained intact in its original setting and as part of a coordinated design. A monumental style and a clear and rhythmic order govern these large scenes enlivened by only a small number of characters. A more airy and spacious style combined with the use of vanishing perspectives replaced the rather cramped and confined style of Zurbarán's earlier compositions. In the portrait of *Fray Gonzalo de Illescas*, Bishop of Córdoba, dated 1639, Zurbarán has used a favoured composition, with a shadowed column dividing the scene in two, but here the background is enlivened by a scene of the prior giving alms at the church door; on the table books, papers and a skull, arranged facing outwards, acquire an important significance. It was at this time also that Zurbarán painted the remarkable nocturnal *St Francis in Ecstasy* (1639; London, N.G.).

(iii) Other work. The decade 1640–50 corresponded in Spain to a period of great financial difficulty, and in Seville economic crisis was accompanied by a plague in 1649. Thus the flow of artistic commissions diminished, and Zurbarán sought a clientele in the Americas. Archival references from 1638 and then in 1647 document the shipping of series of paintings to Lima: 12 Roman Caesars on horseback and 38 paintings for the convent of the Incarnation; in 1649 a delivery of 15 kings and famous men, 15 virgin martyrs and 4 saints and patriarchs is recorded. Some isolated canvases, such as the *Supper at Emmaus* (1639; Mexico City, Mus. S Carlos) and the *St Francis* (Bogotá, Convent of S Francisco), are considered autograph works from this period, but most would have been executed by Zurbarán's workshop. Although it is no longer possible to locate all the works sent to the New World, several series survive in South America today, such as the series of the founders of the Franciscan Order in the Franciscan monastery at Lima (Lima, La Buena Morte). At this time Zurbarán also painted two altarpieces for Extremadura churches: one for Nuestra Señora de la Granada, at Llerena, which was probably the *Martyrdom of St James* (1636–41; Madrid, Prado), and the other for S Maria, Zafra, including the *St Ildefonsus Receiving the Chasuble* (1643; *in situ*).

3. LATE WORKS AND RETURN TO MADRID, 1650–64. Zurbarán painted the *Annunciation*, dated 1650 (Philadelphia, PA, Mus. A.) for Gaspar de Peñaranda, 3rd Conde de Bracamonte y Guzmán, a leading figure at the court of Philip IV. This work is of a more intimate nature than the *Annunciation* that was painted 12 years earlier for the Carthusian monastery at Jerez. In the suppleness of the movements and gestures, the more diffuse effect of the light and the paler colours it marks a new departure in the artist's development; this was already discernible in the Zafra retable of 1643 and is seen again in the remarkable *Christ Carrying the Cross* (signed and dated 1653; Orleans Cathedral). This change of style can probably be attributed to the influence of Italian models. A relationship to Bolognese art is apparent in the *Immaculate Conception*, signed and dated 1656 (Madrid, Placido Arango priv. col.; see 1987 exh. cat., p. 310, pl. 58), with the choir of cherubs directly inspired by Guido Reni (*Coronation of the Virgin*; Madrid, Prado).

Zurbarán was commissioned to paint *Urban II and St Bruno, his Confessor* for the sacristy of the Carthusian monastery of S Maria de Las Cuevas, Triana, Seville, together with the *Virgin of Mercy* and *St Hugh and the Carthusian Monks at Table* (all Seville, Mus. B.A.), in 1655, at the time of the erection of the new cupola, according to a document of 1749. The date of 1655 is not accepted for stylistic reasons by certain historians who date the paintings to 1635 or even 1625. The hieratism of these compositions, dictated by the subject-matter and iconography probably specified by the Carthusians, does not necessarily indicate that these were youthful works, as was previously thought. The clarity of the layout, the balanced distribution of light, without startling chiaroscuro effects, the delicate modelling of the faces and also the light touch all point to this later dating.

Why Zurbarán left Seville in May 1658 for Madrid is not clear. He may have counted on the support of Velázquez and on his own reputation to ensure his reinstatement at court. It is recorded that in 1658 he testified favourably in the preliminary enquiry concerning the admission of Velázquez to the Order of Santiago. In about 1659 Zurbarán was commissioned to paint three large canvases for the chapel of S Diego in the Franciscan monastery of Alcalá de Henares, near Madrid; these included *St Bonaventura Visited by St Thomas Aquinas* (Madrid, S Francisco el Grande) and *St James della Marca* (Madrid, Prado), which completed the decoration of altars begun by Alonso Cano in 1658–9. The provenance of other paintings from the last years in Madrid is not known. The 12 existing canvases signed and dated between 1658 and 1662 show that Zurbarán devoted himself in particular to small-scale paintings intended for private oratories. These were works of Marian devotion, for example the *Immaculate Conception* (1661; Budapest, Mus. F.A., and Langon, S Gervais and S Protais), where he took up a theme from his youth, or variations on the more familiar theme of the *Virgin and Child*, such as the *Virgin Suckling the Infant Christ* (1658; Moscow, Pushkin Mus. F.A.), the *Virgin and Child with the Infant St John* (1658; San Diego, CA, Mus. A., and 1662; Bilbao, Mus. B.A.), the *Rest on the Flight into Egypt* (1659; Budapest, Mus. F.A.) and the

Virgin with Sleeping Child (1659; Madrid, Antonio Bar-nuevo priv. col., see Gallego and Gudiol, 1976, p. 363, fig. 456). These intimately lyrical compositions show that Zurbarán was seeking to attain smoother and more delicate modelling, clear harmonies and a more diffuse handling of light, displaying a range of slightly muted colours, without contrasting effects. In this respect the composition of *St Francis Kneeling*, shown in a sunny landscape (1659; Madrid, Placido Arango priv. col.; see 1987 exh. cat., p. 330, no. 67), and the nocturnal treatment of the earlier *St Francis in Ecstasy* (1639) are evidence of the artist's development, as much from a point of view of the lighting as in the expression of feeling.

Zurbarán always maintained his taste for full, simple and monumental forms, a desire to express the inner life of objects and the beauty of texture, as well as an ability to integrate powerful contours and sculptural forms into a simple geometric format. It is for these qualities that his art profoundly moves modern sensibilities.

CLAUDIE RESSORT

(2) Juan de Zurbarán (*b* Llerena, 23 June 1620; *d* Seville, 8 June 1649). Painter, son of (1) Francisco de Zurbarán. He was brought up in Llerena in the prosperous household of his father and stepmother, Doña Beatriz de Morales, and he was later trained by his father in Seville. Although he is known to have painted religious works on commission, Juan de Zurbarán seems to have specialized in still-lifes, for his only certain works are in this genre. Socially he was somewhat pretentious, partial to such courtly pastimes as the dance, and using the aristocratic 'Don' when signing his name. In 1644 he married Mariana de Quadros, daughter of a wealthy money-lender.

Only three signed still-lifes are known by him. A small still-life on copper, signed and dated 1639 (Bordeaux, Lung priv. col., see 1985 exh. cat., p. 224), is remarkable for its firm draughtsmanship and sensuous rendering of surface details. The excellent *Still-life with Chocolate Service* (1640; Kiev, Mus. Western & Orient. A.) reveals a confident mastery of the medium; objects of Chinese export porcelain, pewter, brass, wood and cloth are grouped in a balanced composition. Shrouded in deep shadow and dramatically illuminated, the surfaces of the objects are defined by decisive brushstrokes and strong highlights of heavy impasto that create a rich, sensuous effect, far removed from the sober geometries of Francisco de Zurbarán's style.

The *Still-life with Basket of Fruit and Cardoon* (1643; Mänttä, Serlachius A. Mus.) shows the artist's familiarity with naturalistic Italian works and suggests the influence of the Neapolitan Luca Forte, whose still-lifes were recorded in Spanish collections by the 1640s. The *Basket of Apples and Quinces* (Barcelona, Mus. A. Catalunya), long considered an anonymous Sevillian work, has been attributed to Juan de Zurbarán on the basis of its similarity to the still-life in Mänttä. He died in the epidemic of bubonic plague that swept through Seville in 1649.

WILLIAM B. JORDAN

BIBLIOGRAPHY

Memoria de las admirables pinturas que tiene este convento, casa grande de Ntra Sra de la Merced, redentora de cautivos de la ciudad de Sevilla (Seville, 1732)

Catálogo oficial ilustrado de la exposición de las obras de Francisco de Zurbarán (Madrid, Prado, 1905)

C. Zervos: 'Revisions: Francisco de Zurbarán', *Cah. A.*, ii (1927), pp. 85–92

M. de Bago y Quintanilla: *Aportaciones documentales*, Doc. Hist. A. Andalucia, ii (Seville, 1928)

S. A. Ghilarov: 'Juan de Zurbarán', *Burl. Mag.*, lxxii (1938), p. 190

M. S. Soria: 'Zurbarán: A Study of his Style', *Gaz. B.-A.*, xxv (1944), pp. 32–48, 153–74

P. Guinard: 'Los conjuntos dispersos o desaparecidos de Zurbarán: Anotaciones a Ceán Bermudez', *Archv Esp. A.*, xix (1946), pp. 249–73; xx (1947), pp. 161–201; xxii (1949), pp. 1–38

H. P. G. Seckel: 'Francisco de Zurbarán as a Painter of Still-life', *Gaz. B.-A.*, xxx (1946), pp. 279–300; xxxi (1947), p. 62 [Juan]

B. Cuartero y Huerta: *Historia de la Cartuja de S María de Las Cuevas y de su filial de Cazalla de la Sierra*, 2 vols (Madrid, 1950/R 1954)

C. Pemán: 'La reconstrucción del retablo de la Cartuja de Jerez de la Frontera', *Archv Esp. A.*, xxiii (1950), pp. 203–27

M. S. Soria: *The Paintings of Zurbarán* (London, 1953, 2/1955)

M. L. Caturla: 'Juan de Zurbarán', *Bol. Real Acad. Hist.* (1957), pp. 270–86

C. Pemán: 'Juan de Zurbarán', *Archv Esp. A.*, xxxi (1958), pp. 193–211

——: 'Un nuevo Juan de Zurbarán', *Archv Esp. A.*, xxxii (1959), pp. 319–20

M. L. Caturla: 'Cartas de pago de los doce cuadros de batallas para el Salón de Reinos del Buen Retiro', *Archv Esp. A.*, xxxiii (1960), pp. 333–55

P. Guinard: *Zurbarán et les peintres espagnols de la vie monastique* (Paris, 1960, 2/1988)

J. A. Gaya Nuño: 'Bibliografía crítica y antológica de Zurbarán', *A. Esp.*, xxv (1963–6), pp. 18–68

M. L. Caturla: 'Fin et muerte de Francisco de Zurbarán', *Documentos recogidos y comentados . . . ofrecidos en la commemoración del III centenario* (Madrid, 1964)

X. de Salas: 'La fecha de las historias de la Cartuja y alguna minucia más sobre Zurbarán', *Archv Esp. A.*, xxxvii (1964), pp. 129–38

Zurbarán en el III centenario de su muerte (exh. cat., Madrid, Casón Buen Retiro, 1964–5)

M. L. Caturla: *El conjunto de Las Cuevas*, Forma y color, xli (Granada, 1968)

J. Brown: *Zurbarán* (New York, 1973, rev. 1991)

P. Guinard and T. Frati: *Tout l'oeuvre peint de Zurbarán* (Paris, 1975)

J. Gállego and J. Gudiol: *Zurbarán, 1598–1664* (Barcelona, 1976; Eng. trans. London, 1977)

A. Martínez Ripoll: *La iglesia del colegio de S Buenaventura* (Seville, 1976)

A. E. Pérez Sánchez: 'Nuevos Zurbaranes', *Archv Esp. A.*, xlix (1976), pp. 73–80

J. Baticle and C. Marinas: *La galerie espagnole de Louis-Philippe au Louvre, 1838–48* (Paris, 1981)

J. Brown: 'La problematica zurbaranesca', *Symposium internacional de Murillo y su epoca: Seville, 1982*

D. T. Kinkead: 'The Last Sevillian Period of Francisco de Zurbarán', *A. Bull.*, lxv (1983), pp. 305–11

P. Cherry: 'The Contract for Francisco de Zurbarán's Painting of Hieronymite Monks for the Sacristy of the Monastery of Guadalupe', *Burl. Mag.*, cxxvii (June 1985), pp. 378–81

Spanish Still-life in the Golden Age, 1600–1650 (exh. cat. by W. B. Jordan, Fort Worth, TX, Kimbell A. Mus., 1985), pp. 222–34, 238–40

Zurbarán (exh. cat. by J. Baticle and others, New York, Met., 1987; Paris, Grand Pal.; Madrid, Prado, 1988)

J. M. Palomero Paramo: 'Notas sobre el taller de Zurbarán: Un envio de lienzo a Portobelo y Lima en el año 1636', *Extremadura en la evangelización del Nuevo Mundo: Guadalupe, 1988*, pp. 313–30

E. Valdivieso: *Franco de Zurbarán* (Seville, 1988)

J. M. Palomero Paramo: *Los Zurbarenes de Guadalupe* (Badajoz, 1990)

CLAUDIE RESSORT, with WILLIAM B. JORDAN

Zurich [Ger. Zürich]. Swiss city and cantonal capital in the hills on the River Limmat where it flows out of Lake Zurich. It is the largest town in German-speaking Switzerland, with a population (1992) of 363,000.

1. HISTORY AND URBAN DEVELOPMENT.

(i) Before c. *1700.* The area has been settled at least intermittently since the late 5th millennium BC. The river crossing was a natural intersection for trade routes, protected by the steep hill on the west bank of the Limmat. By 15 BC at the latest a Roman military camp was established as a stronghold near the frontier on top of the hill on the site of the present Lindenhof. Later there was a customs post for the Province of Gaul, and the Limmat was bridged. The small settlement of Turicum grew up around the bridge, centred on a small harbour, which, although filled in during the Middle Ages, survives as the Weinplatz.

In the 5th to 7th centuries AD the Alemanni settled the surrounding area, and traces of an 8th-century church (now the parish church of St Peter with a Romanesque–Gothic tower and a Baroque nave) have been excavated on a spur of the hill. With the 'discovery' in the 8th century of the tombs of the legendary martyrs Felix and Regula, Zurich developed as a pilgrimage centre and important Franconian stronghold on the route to Italy. A monastery (now the Romanesque Grossmünster; *c.* 1100–1230) was built on the site of the tombs on the east bank, south of the settled area, while a convent for noblewomen (now the 13th-century Romanesque–Gothic Fraumünster) was founded (853) by Louis the German (*reg* 876–82) on the opposite bank. Between them, on an island reputed to be the martyrs' place of execution, was built the Wasserkirche (rebuilt 1479–84). In the secular centre of the town a Carolingian palace was built on the Lindenhof, and another bridge was constructed (the first having been destroyed after the retreat of the Roman empire). Zurich was granted the right to hold a market, levy tolls and mint coins; it was first documented as a 'town' (*civitas*) in 929.

From the 10th century to the 13th, stone burghers' houses became more widespread, their eaves facing the road. The settlement spread along the east bank and was described *c.* 1150 by Bishop Otto of Freising as the 'finest town in Swabia'. The older centre on the west bank was now smaller than that on the east, which expanded steadily along the roads out of the town. The Rennweg district and the small Neustadt began to show signs of systematic planning.

In 1218 Zurich became a free imperial town. Intense building activity followed: the palace was dismantled, the Rathaus (a free-standing building abutting the bridge, rebuilt 1694–8) and tower houses for the local nobility were built, walls were constructed in a wide sweep round the town, four mendicant convents were established inside them, and a footbridge linking the Grossmünster, the Wasserkirche and the Fraumünster was installed. Zurich's only imposing square, the Münsterhof, developed beside the Fraumünster. The most important civic space was, however, the river, which was integrated into the town structure by the Rathausbrücke (later widened and used as a market-place) and public buildings that projected into the river: the Wasserkirche, the Rathaus, the mint (now the Haus zum Rüden), the corn hall (destr. 1898) and several mills (destr. 1943–50). In the 14th century, in contrast to other comparable towns, little growth took place.

Administration after 1218 was controlled first by the nobility, later together with the merchants and, from 1336, increasingly by the guilds. For protection against appropriation by the nobility, Zurich was in 1351 the first region outside Inner Switzerland to establish an 'Everlasting League' with the Confederation. Between 1358 and the end of the 15th century, Zurich acquired approximately the territory that now forms the modern canton of Zurich, a policy that brought the town into conflict with the expansionist aspirations of Schwyz, culminating in 1436 in the Old Zurich War, during which Zurich turned to the Habsburgs. The 'Everlasting League' was, however, renewed in 1454, and in 1499 the Confederation effectively left the Holy Roman Empire.

During the Reformation from 1519 Zurich was the centre of Zwinglianism. In 1524 the town took over the social duties of the disestablished monasteries, thus acquiring greater authority. In response to the impact of the Thirty Years War (1618–48), modern, stellar entrenched fortifications were built from 1642, virtually doubling the area of the town. The development of these new areas, served by a relatively large road grid, lasted well into the 19th century.

(ii) c. *1700 and after.* Zurich has very few buildings dating from the Baroque or Rococo periods, the exceptions being the Baroque nave (1705) of St Peter's parish church and several of the guildhalls, the most notable of which is the Rococo Zunfthaus zur Meisen (1752–7) by David Morf (1700/01–73) on the Münsterhof (*see also* SWITZERLAND, §II). The power of the guilds had already passed its peak by then, however: the water-powered textile factories that developed in the 18th century were independent of the guilds.

When the Helvetic Republic was set up after the Napoleonic invasion of 1798, the oligarchic rule of the guilds was abolished. In 1830 the city finally lost its suzerainty over the surrounding territories. The entrenched fortifications, symbols of the town's supremacy, started to be dismantled in 1833.

One of the most important architects of the early 19th century in Zurich was HANS CASPAR ESCHER, who designed such classicist buildings as the Hauptwache (1824–5) near the Rathaus. The first public railway in Switzerland, between Zurich and Baden, was laid in 1847, and following the foundation of the federal state in 1848 the canton developed into the most highly industrialized region in Switzerland, based on textiles and machine construction. A dominating personality in this process was Alfred Escher (1819–82), a wealthy magnate and politician.

Before 1850 Zurich developed mainly within the area of the former fortifications. Communications were improved when in 1838 a bridge able to carry traffic replaced the footbridge linking the two minsters, relieving the burden on the Rathausbrücke, which was served only by narrow lanes. An embankment was constructed along the east bank of the river in front of the old town houses, creating the Limmatquai; the Rathaus and Wasserkirche originally built on islands in the river, now stood on peninsulas; the former mint (now the Haus zum Rüden), once projecting into the river, now stood on its bank. The corn hall and the mills were, however, subsequently demolished (1898 and 1943–50 respectively), so that the interpenetration of town and river as a unique characteristic of the townscape has largely been lost (see fig.).

The railway station was built in 1847 on the west bank on the site of the former fortifications. In the building boom of the 1860s, a city business district was developed near the station as a new town centre, with a third bridge spanning the Limmat. In 1863–4 the ostentatious Bahnhofstrasse was laid out from here along the line of the medieval moat, initially extending as far as Paradeplatz, and later continuing down to the lake. It is dominated by two imposing buildings commissioned by Escher and designed by Jakob Friedrich Wanner (1830–1903): the rebuilt Hauptbahnhof (1865–71; preliminary design by Gottfried Semper) and the Kreditanstalt (1873–6) on Paradeplatz. Where Bahnhofstrasse came out on to the lake front a new embankment was constructed (1882–7) by Arnold Bürkli (1833–94) with lake-front promenades, a new bridge crossing the Limmat, the Opernhaus (1890–91) by Ferdinand Fellner and Hermann Helmer and other prestigious buildings. Meanwhile on the east bank several public buildings had been erected over the former fortifications, including the Alte Kantonschule (1839–42) by Gustav Albert Wegmann and the Polytechnikum, now the Eidgenössische Technische Hochschule (1860–62), built by Gottfried Semper through the influence of Escher; it was extended (1914–25) by GUSTAV GULL. The Kunsthaus

(1909–10) and Universität (1911–14) were built by Karl Moser.

From about 1850 the town had been outgrowing its boundaries, climbing up the sunny west slope and spreading both along the shores of the lake to the south (middle- and upper-class residential districts) and along the bottom of the valley to the north-west, where the community of Aussersihl quickly expanded to become the industrial and working-class sector. In 1893 the city boundaries were redrawn, and Aussersihl and ten other outlying villages were incorporated into Zurich, hitherto predominantly middle-class; another eight, including Oerlikon, followed in 1934. Gull designed a huge building complex (1902–10; partially implemented 1903–4 and 1917–19) for the civic authorities, involving a new bridge and two new roads, Uraniastrasse and Mühlegasse, intersecting the old town.

Under the administration of the Social Democrat Emil Klöti (member of the city council 1907–49), Zurich led the rest of Switzerland in the building from 1908 of publicly assisted housing, which punctuates the outskirts of the city. A 'Gross-Zürich' competition was held in 1915–18, and new districts were created, based on the idea of a garden city: Friesenberg and Milchbuck from 1920 and the Werkbund estate (1928–31) at Neubühl. Such remarkable examples of the early Modern Movement as the Z-Haus (1930–32) by RUDOLF STEIGER, Carl Hubacher (*b* 1897) and Robert Winkler (*b* 1898); the Kunstgewerbemuseum (1930–33) by Adolf Steger (1888–1939)

Zurich, aerial view from the north showing the Münsterbrücke (foreground), the Rathausbrücke (middleground) and mills (background; destr. 1943–50), built over the River Limmat; from a photograph taken in 1936

and Karl Egender (1897–1969); and some department stores were built in the city centre (*see also* HAEFELI, MAX ERNST).

The tradition of publicly assisted housing was continued after 1945 in the development of new districts (especially Schwamendingen) and the building of residential estates. The adaptation of Le Corbusier's Unité model at Unteraffoltern (1970) by George Pierre Dubois (1911–83), and the courtyard buildings at Manessehof (1984) by Ueli Marbach (*b* 1941) and Arthur Rüegg (*b* 1942); Hellmutstrasse (1991) by Walter Ramseyer (*b* 1942), Beat Jordi (*b* 1955), Caspar Angst (*b* 1952) and Peter Hofmann (*b* 1955); and Brahmshof (1991) by Walter Fischer (*b* 1944) are particularly noteworthy. Also of interest are the Heidi Weber Haus (1964–5; now the Zent. Le Corbusier-Heidi Weber), a dramatic steel structure by Le Corbusier; the cantonal schools at Freudenberg (1956–60) by Jacques Schader, and Ramibühl (1970) by Eduard Neuenschwander (*b* 1924); various buildings (1980s and later) by Theo Hotz (*b* 1928); and the station at Stadelhofen (1989) by Arnold Amsler (*b* 1942) and Santiago Calatrava.

BIBLIOGRAPHY

K. Dändlicher: *Geschichte der Stadt und des Kantons Zürich*, 3 vols (Zurich, 1908–11)
K. Escher: *Die beiden Zürcher Münster* (Leipzig, 1928)
A. Largiader: *Geschichte von Stadt und Landschaft Zürich*, 2 vols (Zurich, 1945)
A. Senti, H. Waser and P. Guyer: *Aus Zürichs Vergangenheit: Zeittafel zur Geschichte der Stadt Zürich* (Zurich, 1954)
F. Krayenbühl: *Untersuchung über die Entstehung und das Wachstum des Zentrums in der Stadt Zürich* (diss., Zurich, Eidgenöss. Tech. Hochsch., 1963)
E. Vogt, E. Meyer and H. C. Peyer: *Zürich von der Urzeit zum Mittelalter* (Zurich, 1971)
L. Care: *Zürich: Architekturführer* (Zurich, 1972)
A. Rossi and others: *Die Stadt Zürich: Zusammenhängende Bauaufnahme, typologische und morphologische Untersuchungen*, Architecture Dept, ETH Zurich (Zurich, 1975)
H.-P. Bärtschi: *Industrialisierung, Eisenbahnschlachten und Städtebau, die Entwicklung des Zürcher Industrie- und Arbeiterstadtteils Aussersihl: Ein vergleichender Beitrag zur Architektur- und Technikgeschichte* (Basle, 1983)
W. Baumann, R. Hofer and N. Crispini: *Zürich: Gestern und heute aus dem gleichen Blickwinkel* (Geneva, 1984)
R. G. Schönauer: *Von der Stadt am Fluss zur Stadt am See: 100 Jahre Zürcher Quaianlagen* (Zurich, 1987)
M. Koch, M. Somandin, C. Süsstrunk: *Kommunaler und genossenschaftlicher Wohnungsbau in Zürich: Ein Inventar der durch die Stadt geförderten Wohnbauten, 1907–1989* (Zurich, 1990)
H. Rebsamen and others: *Inventar der neueren schweizer Architektur, 1850–1920: Zürich* (Berne, 1992)
J. E. Schneider: 'Zürich', *Stadtluft, Hirsebrei und Bettelmönch: Die Stadt um 1300* (exh. cat., Stuttgart, 1992)

MARTIN ALBERS

2. ART LIFE AND ORGANIZATION.

(i) *Before* c. *1700.* The early importance of Zurich is reflected in the 12th-century north door and cloisters of the Grossmünster, but Zurich reached a peak of cultural prosperity *c.* 1300 under the patronage of the Habsburg king Rudolf I (*reg* 1273–91). The best-known achievement of that period is the Manesse Codex (Heidelberg, Ubib., MS. Pal. germ. 848). This is a collection of 140 songs from the late Minnesang period, especially notable for its 138 extremely fine illustrations. It was created shortly after 1300 in the Zurich area. Rüdiger Manesse (1252–1304)

and Johannes Hadlaub (*c.* 1270–*c.* 1340) are believed to have been its main patrons.

Zurich's political affiliation to the Confederation (1351) had a retrograde impact on culture. Nonetheless by *c.* 1500 such noteworthy painters as Hans Leu the elder (*d c.* 1507) and his son HANS LEU II were active. The masters known collectively as the MASTER OF THE CARNATION have never been conclusively identified (*see* MASTERS, ANONYMOUS, AND MONOGRAMMISTS, §I). The creation of art was impeded again by the impact of ZWINGLIANISM, as a result of which many valuable works were destroyed and painting was confined to portraits. Artists active in Zurich include the portraitist HANS ASPER, the medallist HANS JAKOB STAMPFER and the stained glass artist Jos Murer (1530–80). In 1576 Murer produced a map of Zurich, which is still used to assess building applications. Puritan Zurich responded only tentatively to the Baroque. The wealthy Hans Georg Werdmüller (*b* 1616) is regarded as the city's first picture collector. His son Hans Rudolf Werdmüller (1639–68) was a talented painter. SAMUEL HOFMANN is regarded as the foremost Zurich painter of the 17th century. The tradition of portraiture was continued by CONRAD MEYER, and Zurich's goldsmiths and silversmiths produced some superb work in their workshops.

(ii) c. *1700 and after.* In the 18th century a lively cultural life developed in Zurich. JOHANN BALTHASAR BULLINGER taught at the Kunstschule (now the Schule für Gestaltung) as a professor from 1773. SALOMON GESSNER, who was instrumental in founding a porcelain factory (1763) at Schoren, near Zurich, was also respected as a painter. Anton Graff from Winterthur, internationally renowned as a portrait painter, spent some time in Zurich. David Herrliberger (1697–1777) distinguished himself as an engraver. Yet Henry Fuseli, who came from a Zurich family that had shown artistic talent for generations, spent his life working elsewhere, primarily in England. In 1787 a circle of Zurich artists began to meet as friends in the house of the painter HEINRICH FREUDWEILER. This association developed into the Zürcher Kunstgesellschaft, founded 1896, which still survives. Another founder-member was the landscape artist JOHANN HEINRICH WÜEST, whose work remained rooted in the 18th-century idiom. Also active in Zurich were the charismatic Heinrich Corrodi (1762–1833); the graphic artist and engraver Franz Hegi (1774–1850); the history painter Ludwig Vogel and the poet–painter Gottfried Keller.

Patriotic sentiment, which developed in Switzerland under German influence, resulted in Zurich in the erection of a series of statues in public squares towards the end of the 19th century: *Huldrich Zwingli* (1885; Wasserkirche) by Heinrich Natter (1846–92); *Alfred Escher* (1889; Bahnhofplatz) by Richard Kissling; and *Heinrich Pestalozzi* (1899; Bahnhofstrasse) by Hugo Siegwart (1865–1938). The most acclaimed artist in Zurich at this time was FERDINAND HODLER from Berne, on account of his frescoes (1900) in the new Schweizerisches Landesmuseum (1893–8) by Gustav Gull. Hodler's expressionistic depiction of the *Retreat of the Swiss Troops near Marignano (1515)* (the Confederation's greatest military defeat) aroused strong protests but nevertheless established his reputation in Germany and internationally. Around the beginning of the 20th century private picture collections were once again created in Zurich. They were mostly financed by Germans, whose influence declined only after World War I. During the war years DADA developed in Zurich (*see also* SWITZERLAND, §III), seeking new forms of expression in the visual, literary and performing arts.

The patronage of the arts, which had always been in the hands of private individuals, underwent a change from *c.* 1920, when the city authorities, who saw themselves as the successors of the well-to-do bourgeoisie, began to take on this role. The city, and later the canton too, undertook the duty of encouraging and promoting the visual arts alongside music, drama and literature. Since then cultural subsidies have grown continuously. A consequence of this deliberate cultural policy was a constant influx of artists from throughout German-speaking Switzerland, so that Zurich became its most important centre of culture.

In the 1930s the ideas of Neues Bauen, the Modern Movement in architecture, penetrated Zurich. Artists formed a group, calling themselves the Zürcher Konkreten (*see* CONCRETE ART); its leading members included MAX BILL, Verena Loewensberg (1912–86), Camille Graeser, Richard Paul Lohse and Max Fischli. Although they were largely overlooked during the Fascist years because of the return to traditional forms, they enjoyed a revival of interest after 1945 and won international acclaim.

Among the respected artists in Zurich around the mid-20th century were: Helen Dahm (1878–1968); Hermann Haller, who created the *Waldmann* monument (1937; Münsterbrücke); Hermann Hubacher (1885–1976); Max Soldenhoff (1886–1954); Karl Hügin (1887–1963); Otto-Charles Bänninger (1897–1973); Karl Geiser (1898–1957); and VARLIN. Increasing material wealth and the fact that Zurich was spared in both world wars contributed to the development of large private collections, this time in Swiss hands, for example the Alberto Giacometti collection and the Stiftung Sammlung E. G. Bührle (*see* BÜHRLE, EMIL GEORG). Such private patronage provides valuable support for the Kunsthaus run by the Kunstgesellschaft. With this and some 150 private galleries a lively artistic life has developed in Zurich (*see also* SWITZERLAND, §XIV). The Zwinglian hostility towards images seems remote from the culturally open Zurich of today.

BIBLIOGRAPHY
S. Zurlinden: *Hundert Jahre, 1814–1914*, 2 vols (Zurich, 1914–15)
R. Zürcher: *Die künstlerische Kultur im Kanton Zürich* (Zurich, 1943)
E. Stähelin: *Zürcherische Bildnismalerei im 19. und zu Beginn des 20. Jahrhunderts* (Zurich, 1947)
P. Leemann van Elck: *Die Zürcher Buchillustration bis 1850* (Zurich, 1952)
F. O. Pestalozzi: *Zürcher Bildnisse aus fünf Jahrhunderten* (Zurich, 1953)
J. Baum: *Meister und Werke: Spätmittelalterliche Kunst in Oberdeutschland und der Schweiz* (Constance, 1966)
Dada: Ausstellung zum 50-jährigen Jubiläum (exh. cat., ed. Y. Liensson, F. A. Baumann and M. Hoog; Zurich, Ksthaus, 1966)
S. Ramer: *Felix, Regula und Exuperantius: Ikonographie der Stifts- und Stadtheiligen Zürichs* (Zurich, 1973)
F. Zelger: *Heldenstreit und Heldentod: Historienmalerei im 19. Jahrhundert* (Zurich, 1973)
A. Dürst: *Jos Murers Planvedute der Stadt Zürich* (Langnau, 1975)
E.-M. Lösel: *Das Zürcher Goldschmiedehandwerk im 16. und 17. Jahrhundert* (Zurich, 1975)
S. Widmer: *Zürich: Eine Kulturgeschichte*, 13 vols (Zurich, 1975–85)
H. Sturzenegger: *12 Gänge in die Zürcher Kulturgeschichte* (Stäfa, 1983)

SIGMUND WIDMER

3. CENTRE OF CERAMICS PRODUCTION. In 1763 the Zurich Faience and Porcelain Factory was founded in Kilchberg-Schooren on Lake Zurich by a group of public-spirited men who aimed for commercial success, but who also wished to promote the use of national resources and provide employment: they included the poet and painter Salomon Gessner; the merchant Martin Usteri; Heinrich Lavater, who became Mayor of Zurich in 1768; and the librarian Conrad Voegeli. Adam Spengler (*d* 1790) was Technical Director from 1763 and took on experienced staff including the painter Johannes Daffinger (employed 1764–74) from Vienna, several painters including Heinrich Thomann (employed 1770–97) from Zollikon, and the modeller Joseph Nees (employed 1768–73) and the sculptor Valentin Sonnenschein from Ludwigsburg. Most of the painters' and modellers' contributions have so far been unidentified except for certain pieces of signed work by Gessner, who painted landscapes on porcelain. In 1791 the shareholders were forced to dissolve the company because of debts arising from constant overproduction. Two years later Spengler's son-in-law Matthias Neeracher (*d* 1800) bought the factory, including the inventory and stock. The production of expensive porcelain was discontinued and replaced with creamware, brown cooking-ware and faience. Transfer-printing was also more widely used. This trend continued throughout the 19th century under the direction of Hans Jakob Nägeli (1803–58) and Hans Jacob Staub (1858–97); after Staub's death the factory closed.

The factory was unusual in that it simultaneously produced soft- and hard-paste porcelain, earthenware and faience. During its earliest years the factory's porcelain was soft-paste. It is supposed that the hard-paste formula was obtained from Joseph Jakob Ringler (1730–1804), an arcanist from Vienna who travelled all over Europe and sold his secrets, personally or through one of his collaborators, to a large number of factories. Hard paste porcelain was produced at the factory from 1765, and the ensuing decade was artistically the most flourishing period. The kaolin (china clay) first came from Passau and later from Limoges. Local clay was used for the earthenware, which made it cheaper to produce than porcelain. The principal style of porcelain tableware was Rococo. Apart from the conservatism in both shape and decoration, the wares were technically perfect, and the quality of the polychrome painting is among the best produced in 18th-century European factories. The delicately painted Swiss landscapes were largely inspired by Gessner. A large number of pieces decorated in underglaze blue were also produced. The repertory also included small porcelain figures (e.g. *Shepherdess with her Dog*, *c.* 1768; Geneva, Mus. Ariana) as well as large figures and groups for the table. This side of the production is well known because there are extant moulds for no less than 369 different figures and groups. The link with figures from the factory in Ludwigsburg was obviously established by Sonnenschein and Nees. The range of subjects include hunters, street criers, peasants, characters from the *commedia dell'arte*, Turks and emblematic and mythological figures. The Zurich mark (when it is present) is an underglaze Z, often accompanied by one, two or three dots (presumably an indication for the potters as to the composition of the clay).

BIBLIOGRAPHY
S. Ducret: *Die Zürcher Porzellanmanufaktur und ihre Erzeugnisse im 18. und 19. Jahrhundert*, 2 vols (Zurich, 1958–9)
R. Schnyder: *Zürcher Porzellan* (Zurich, 1964)

H. BOBBINK-DE WILDE

Zürn. German family of sculptors. They were among the most important and productive families of sculptors in southern Germany in the 17th century. Hans Zürn the elder (1555/60–after 1631) had six sons, all of whom became sculptors. No documented work of his has survived, but on the basis of his presumed contribution to the high altar in Überlingen Minster (*see* (1) below), an attractive Crucifix (Wangen, Kapelle am Isnyer Tor) and a bust of *St Jacob* (Nuremberg, Ger. Nmus.) have been attributed to him. These wooden figures, with their slender, elongated bodies and gaunt, introspective faces, have a precious yet frail quality when compared with the work of his sons, with whom he frequently collaborated. The most prominent of these, all of whom started their careers in the Bodensee region, was (1) Jörg Zürn of Überlingen, whose masterpiece was the five-storey Mannerist high altar in Überlingen Minster. Hans Zürn the younger (1585/90–after 1624) is recorded as a master sculptor in Buchhorn am Bodensee (now Friedrichshafen) in 1613; his only securely attributed work is the wooden altar of the *Virgin* in St Martin, Wangen, though Zoege von

1. Jörg Zürn: wooden high altar, h. 15.29 m, 1613–16, Überlingen Minster

Manteuffel has attributed 12 other projects, mostly single figures, to him. (2) Martin Zürn and his younger brothers, Michael (*fl* 1617–51), Hans Jakob (*fl* 1617–35) and David (1598–1666), settled in the Inn Valley in eastern Bavaria and Upper Austria and are chiefly known for the altars they carved for many of the churches of that region. The third and fourth generations of the Zürn family, the sons and grandsons of David Zürn, continued to be active in Wasserburg am Inn, Passau and Olomouc in Moravia into the early 18th century.

(1) Jörg Zürn (*b* ?Waldsee, 1583–4; *d* Überlingen, 1635–8). He trained with his father in Waldsee; later he was a journeyman in Überlingen in the workshop of Virgil Moll (1560/70–1606). On Moll's death, Zürn took over the shop and in 1607 married his widow. Settling in Überlingen, he fell on hard times in the 1620s because of lack of work. Jörg is best known as a wood sculptor, yet his best early sculptures were cut from fine-grained Öhninger limestone. His earliest documented work is the altar of the *Virgin* (1607–10) in the minster in Überlingen. Zürn carved the wooden *St Sebastian* and the three stone reliefs, while journeymen completed the remaining wooden statues. These reliefs, especially the *Death of the Virgin* in the predella, show a technical and compositional debt to Hans Morinck, who was active in nearby Konstanz from at least 1578 to 1616. Zürn's figures are somewhat more delicate and more constrained than Morinck's powerful, raw-boned types, yet the forms of Zürn's muscular *Christ* or *St Sebastian* are closer to Morinck's figures than to those of Hans Zürn the elder.

Zürn's limestone five-storey sacrament house in the Überlingen Minster (inscribed 1611) represents a midpoint between the altar of the *Virgin* and the high altar. Although none of the commission records survives, the overall design and the figures surrounding the eucharistic cella are clearly his creations and he is also documented as carrying out repairs in 1619. The poses of the *St Anne* group and of *St John the Baptist* reveal an improved understanding of contrapposto. The exuberant angels flanking the grille appear poised to leap into the air. As in the *Virgin* altar, Zürn stressed the clear architectonic forms of the frame, although his reliance on decorative motifs in the manner of Cornelis Floris, notably masks, grotesques and strapwork, was more pronounced here.

Jörg Zürn's finest creation is the high altar (1613–16; see fig. 1) at Überlingen. He relied heavily on his family and on journeymen in order to complete the altar during the two and a half years stipulated in his commission from the Überlingen Town Council. His signed and dated presentation drawing in pen and ink with wash (1614; Überlingen, Städt. Mus.), though not of the highest quality, sets out the overall programme, the general presentation of the figures and much of the decorative detail, which were subsequently copied with only minor changes in the finished altarpiece. The overall arrangement of this five-storey altarpiece was influenced by Virgil Moll's altar at Haigerloch (1604–6) and by Hans Degler's high altar (1604) in SS Ulrich and Afra in Augsburg; Jörg Zürn may have known Degler, as his younger brother Hans Jakob was a journeyman in Degler's Weilheim shop in 1617. In both Moll's altar and Degler's, the principal scene is set within a large arch framed by projecting composite columns and a bold entablature; secondary arches with single figures of saints flank the central scene. Zürn adopted from Moll the idea of removing the back wall of the altar, and made better use of the light from the choir windows; for example in the *Adoration of the Shepherds*, the angels, illuminated from the rear and the front, appear to hover weightlessly in the sky. The lighting similarly enhances the celestial setting of the *Coronation of the Virgin*. From Degler, Zürn borrowed specific staging motifs, notably the placement and configuration of the stable. Since the Überlingen altar is much smaller in scale than Degler's, however, its *Adoration* scene is crowded into a more restricted space and the resulting spatial tension heightens the scene's emotional impact. The *Adoration* provides the best example of the artist's style. The life-size figures are of lime-wood, which was, at Zürn's insistence, not polychromed but treated with a yellowish-brown glaze. This feature, together with the tension of the crowded scene, the strong contrast of different planes within the composition, the voluminous robes of the Virgin and the sharp interplay of lights and darks, appears to reflect a conscious revival of Late Gothic sculptural forms; yet to these Zürn added an understanding of the human form, theatrical gestures and a unified composition focusing on the Christ Child. This is bracketed by the Virgin seated on the left counterbalanced by the standing shepherd opposite. The Virgin's hair tumbles jubilantly over her shoulders and her richly detailed dress almost obscures her body, while the shepherd's hair is closely cropped, cut with fine, short strokes, and his garments are carved with coarse, broad folds agitated by the motion of his body.

Jörg Zürn's fascination with elaborate decoration is evident in the figures and the architecture of the altarpiece: thus in the *Annunciation*, the minutely rendered high-relief brocade of the Virgin's dress is playfully juxtaposed with the flowing rhythms of the long folds of her mantle. The busy surfaces of the clothing, beard and crown of *St Silvester* compete for the viewer's attention. Zürn and his joiners were successful in transforming the engraved fantasies of Floris, Wendel Dieterlin and Jacob Guckeisen into sculptural forms. The two large columns flanking the central scene not only contain masks, garlands and varieties of strapwork, but are also hollowed out, permitting light from the adjacent windows to pierce through, mingling contrasts of light and shadow with the varied surface patterns. This adroit use of the church's light enhances the dramatic impact of the various scenes, which are charged with spiritual and physical energy and yet carefully separated from each other by the architectural frame. Thus the different sections of the altar and the riot of decoration are ultimately controlled to form a legible and unified ensemble. Zürn himself carved the two lower zones. Zoege von Manteuffel plausibly attributed the *Crucifixion* to Hans Zürn the elder; *St Roch* and the *Coronation of the Virgin* to Martin Zürn; *St Nicholas* and *St Sebastian* to Michael Zürn; and the rest of the carvings in the three upper storeys to journeymen.

Jörg continued to receive commissions for tombs, crucifixes and small reliefs, but these did not match the significance of his early sculptures. His brother Hans Jakob may have worked with him on several small commissions

2. Jörg Zürn: *Coronation of the Virgin*, wood relief, 278×235 mm, 1622 (Karlsruhe, Badisches Landesmuseum)

at Schloss Langenstein in Örsingen (1619–20). Jörg's monogram and the date 1622 appear on a small lime-wood *Coronation of the Virgin* relief (Karlsruhe, Bad. Landesmus.; see fig. 2) that may have served as a model for a larger altar or epitaph. Although the figures are damaged, their facial expressions and interaction are in contrast to Zürn's earlier, more static treatment of this theme in the *Virgin* altar. Related to this relief is a moving wooden Crucifix in the Örsingen parish church: in this, the monumentality of his earlier Christs has given way to a gentle rhythmic flow. Zoege von Manteuffel has attributed a few other carvings of the later 1620s and early 1630s to Jörg's workshop, but little of this work can be specifically associated with him. He may have assisted his brothers in carving another altar of the *Virgin* (1631) and the *All Souls* altar (1634) for the Überlingen Minster.

(2) Martin Zürn (*b* 1585–90; *d* ?Braunau am Inn, after 1665). Brother of (1) Jörg Zürn. He achieved moderate success in the Bodensee area, making wooden altars of the *Virgin* for the Brotherhoods of the Rosary in Pfullendorf (1615), Owingen (*c.* 1627–30) and Überlingen (1631), the last probably partly carved by his brother David. With his father Hans Zürn the elder and his brother Michael Zürn, he completed in 1624 the wooden high altar in the Frauberg-Kapelle in Waldsee, where the expressive emotionalism and dramatic posture of his *St Sebastian* make his father's *St Nicholas* and *St Conrad* seem expressionless and rigid by comparison. Martin Zürn also carved much of the *All Souls* altar (1634) in Überlingen Minster before going to live in the Inn Valley in eastern Bavaria. With Michael Zürn, whose career was closely intertwined with his own, he worked at the Benedictine cloister at Seeon from 1635 to 1637: they may also have been assisted in 1635 by their brother, Hans Jakob Zürn. From 1636 Martin and Michael probably lived in Wassenburg, where their younger brother David had been a citizen since 1628. There in 1636 Martin Zürn designed the wooden high altar of *St Jakob*, and he and Michael carved for that church the *St Sebastian* altar (wood, 1637; untraced), the pulpit (wood, 1637–9) and parts of the wooden high altar (1638–9), including the monumental *St Sebastian* and *St Florian* (Berlin, Skulpgal.). The unpolychromed lime-wood *Virgin and Child* on the canopy of the pulpit is perhaps Martin Zürn's finest work.

Martin Zürn and Michael Zürn left Wasserburg in 1639 after a falling-out with their brother David, and worked in Burghausen (1640) and Taubenbach (1643) before settling in Braunau am Inn. During the 1640s and early 1650s Martin Zürn produced altars and religious statues in wood for St Stephan in Braunau and for many other local churches. Michael's best work is represented by the wooden high altar (1645) and side altars (1649) in St Georgen an der Mattig, near Braunau.

BIBLIOGRAPHY
A. Layer: 'Zürn contra Bendel', *Z. Ktwiss.*, vi (1952), pp. 181–6
Barock am Bodensee (exh. cat., eds O. Sandner and C. Zoege von Manteuffel; Bregenz, Kstlerhaus Pal. Thurn & Taxis, 1964), pp. 51–60, pls 7–25
A. Kasper: 'Über die Waldseer Bildhauer-Werkstätten der Zürn, Bendel, Grassender und Reusch', *Heilige Kst* (1968–9), pp. 5–67
C. Zoege von Manteuffel: *Die Bildhauerfamilie Zürn, 1606–1666*, 2 vols (Weissenhorn, 1969) [excellent monograph with superb illustrations]
Die Bildhauerfamilie Zürn 1585–1724, Schwaben/Bayern/Mähren/Österreich (exh. cat., Braunau am Inn, Kapuziner Kirche, 1979) [good for Martin Zürn and Michael Zürn]
J. Dorner: 'Martin und Michael Zürn in Burghausen: Nachlese zum Zürnjahr 1979', *A. Bavar.*, xxv–xxvi (1982), pp. 37–40
R. Laun: *Studien zur Altarbaukunst in Süddeutschland, 1560–1650* (Munich, 1982), pp. 132–9
H. Schindler: *Bayerische Bildhauer: Manierismus, Barock, Rokoko im altbayerischen Unterland* (Munich, 1985), pp. 26–39
Die Renaissance im deutschen Südwesten (exh. cat., Heidelberg, Schloss, 1986), ii, pp. 530, 567–9

JEFFREY CHIPPS SMITH

Zutman, Lambert. *See* SUAVIUS, LAMBERT.

Zvantseva [Zvantsova]**, Yelizaveta (Nikolayevna)** (*b* 30 Nov 1864; *d* 22 Aug 1921). Russian art school founder and painter. Her main significance lay in her creation of the most progressive art school in pre-1917 Russia, a forming ground of many of the leading representatives of the Russian avant-garde. Having studied at the Moscow School of Painting, Sculpture and Architecture (1885–8), and at Il'ya Repin's and Pavel Chistyakov's studios in the St Petersburg Academy of Arts (1889–96), she enrolled (1897) at the private studios of Rodolphe Julian and of Filippo Colarossi in Paris. In 1899 she opened her own art school in Moscow, where the artists Valentin Serov, Konstantin Korovin and Nikolay Ul'yanov taught. This she moved to St Petersburg in 1906, where, with the help of her close friend Konstantin Somov, it was established as the Zvantseva School of Drawing and Painting;

it was also known as the Bakst and Dobuzhinsky School (1906–10) and as the Dobuzhinsky and Petrov-Vodkin School (1910–17). Located at 25 Tavricheskaya Street, it functioned until April 1917. Due to the enlightened and liberal approach of its World of Art directors, Léon Bakst, Mstislav Dobuzhinsky and Kuz'ma Petrov-Vodkin (who replaced Bakst in 1910), the school attracted, especially in the pre-war years, many talented students, including Mikhail Matyushin, Yelena Guro, Ol'ga Rozanova, Marc Chagall, Jean Pougny, Vladimir Kozlinsky (1891–1967) and Sergey Gorodetsky (1884–1967), as well as graphic artists closer to the spirit of the World of Art, such as Anna Ostroumova-Lebedeva, Georgy Narbut and Nikolay Tyrsa. In 1917 the Zvantseva School was amalgamated, together with other private studio-schools, into the Free Studio association, which marked the end of Zvantseva's participation in art education.

BIBLIOGRAPHY
Vystavka rabot uchenits i uchenikov L. S. Baksta i M. V. Dobuzhinskogo (Shkola Zvantsevoy); 6-ya vystavka yezhemesyachnika 'Apollon' [Exhibition of work by the students of L. S. Bakst and M. V. Dobuzhinsky (Zvantseva School): sixth exhibition of the monthly *Apollon*] (exh. cat., St Petersburg, 1910) [intro. by Bakst]

JEREMY HOWARD, SERGEY KUZNETSOV

Zvart'nots. Ruins of the Armenian patriarch's palace and cathedral 3 km south-east of ĒDJMIADZIN (anc. Vagharshapat), in Armenia. The building was dedicated to the Heavenly Hosts, the 'vigilant powers' (*zvart'nunk'ner*), who appeared in a dream to St Grigor the Illuminator (*c.* AD 239–*c.* 325/6). According to a Greek inscription and the Armenian histories of Sebeos (7th century) and Katholikos Hovhannes Draskhanakertc'i (10th century), the cathedral was built *c.* 650–59 by the Katholikos Nerses III, known as 'the Builder' (*reg* 641–61), at the site where according to tradition St Grigor the Illuminator was met by the pagan Armenian king Trdat III (*reg c.* AD 280–*c.* 330). By the time of the cathedral's destruction in the 10th century, it was also said to house the relics of St Grigor.

Although the cathedral was excavated in 1901–7, only its foundations, parts of the walls and vaulting, bases and sections of piers and columns, some eagle capitals and other fragments of relief sculpture were found. On the basis of these remains, the load-bearing capability of the massive pillars and comparisons with a later Armenian copy, St Grigor at ANI (AD 1000; destr.), Armenia, it is thought that Zvart'nots was a large circular domed church (h. *c.* 36 or 45 m) comprising three storeys of cylinders of decreasing diameter. The first two levels had 32 sides each, with windows on each panel, and the drum above had 16 sides, also with windows. The windows of the first level were probably round. The cathedral was built of tufa stone facing a rubble masonry core and set on a seven-stepped, polygonal stylobate.

On the interior, Zvart'nots had a circular, continuous outer ambulatory enclosing an inner quatrefoil defined by four huge V-shaped pillars. Six columns defined the curve of each apse in the quatrefoil except for the eastern apse, which had a solid wall to which a rectangular chamber was probably later annexed. The massive central dome and drum were set on pendentives or pendentives and squinches (see Mnats'akanyan) and supported by the huge pillars joined with arches. The apse vaults were abutted by the ambulatory vaults, which in turn were supported by columns and arches. Zvart'nots was decorated lavishly with blind arcades, mosaics, wall painting and sculptural reliefs that include the unique eagle capitals of the pillars, capitals with Nerses' Greek monogram, and nine surviving spandrel figures each holding a construction tool. Although its plan exists in Syrian and Mesopotamian churches of the 5th and 6th centuries, such as RUSAFA, Bosra (see BOSRA, §2), Apameia (see APAMEIA, §1) and Aleppo, Zvart'nots alone had a stone dome, thus demonstrating the Armenians' mastery of stone construction. The double-shell quatrefoil plan of Zvart'nots was also used for the churches at Ishkani and Banak in TAO-KLARJETI. The church at Ishkani and possibly that at Banak were built by Nerses.

The plan of the palace remains much less certain. The excavations of 1901–7 revealed a large room identified as the throne room, a single-nave church, auxiliary rooms, a wine-press and parts of the outer walls.

BIBLIOGRAPHY

T. Marut'yan: *Zvart'nots ev Zvart'nots atip hush ardzannerĕ* [Zvart'nots and the monuments of the same type] (Yerevan, 1971)

S. Mnats'akanyan: *Zvart'nots'* (Yerevan, 1971)

W. E. Kleinbauer: 'Zvart'nots and the Origins of Christian Architecture in Armenia', *A. Bull.*, liv/3 (1972), pp. 245–62

S. Der Nersessian: *L'Art arménien* (Paris, 1977/*R* 1989; Eng. trans., London, 1978)

W. E. Kleinbauer: 'Tradition and Innovation in the Design of Zvartnotz', *Second International Symposium on Armenian Art: Yerevan, 1978*, iii, pp. 13–24

P. Cuneo: *Architettura armena dal quarto al diciannovesimo secolo*, i (Rome, 1988), pp. 102–05

J.-M. Thierry and P. Donabedian: *Armenian Art* (Paris, 1989), pp. 594–5

LUCY DER MANUELIAN, ARMEN ZARIAN

Zvenigorod. Russian town 53 km west of Moscow, on the left bank of the River Moskva. It was founded by Prince Yury Dolgoruky (*reg* 1149–57) and was the centre of the independent Zvenigorod principality in the 13th and 14th centuries; it became part of the Muscovite state in 1432. The 12th-century kremlin (the Gorodok or 'Little Town') has tall, earthen ramparts. The cathedral of the Dormition (see fig.) was built on the Gorodok by the ruling Prince Yury (*d* 1434). It represents a link between the late 12th-century architecture of the VLADIMIR-SUZDAL kingdom (e.g. Vladimir, cathedral of St Demetrius) and the new Muscovite style of the late 14th century and the early 15th. It is square in plan with three apses, three entrances on axis and a single, helmet-shaped dome, which may originally have been surrounded by a complex system of *zakomary*. Other decorative details include a corbel-table over the apse, a frieze at middle height, ogee arches over the portals and west windows, and engaged columns on the façades and doorways. The last two elements indicate some familiarity with Gothic architecture. The interior of the cathedral was painted by ANDREY RUBLYOV, but only small fragments of two angels have survived. Near the church is a 17th-century belfry.

In 1404 Prince Yury founded the Storozhevsky Monastery of St Savva, which now houses the Zvenigorod Museum of History and Ethnography. The church of the Nativity, its main church, which was built in 1405 and is

Zvenigorod, cathedral of the Dormition, 1397–9

architecturally similar to the cathedral, stands on a hill at the centre. Its dome is slightly displaced to the east, while the roof originally consisted of superimposed *kokoshniki* arches. During the extended sojourn of Aleksey Mikhaylovich (*reg* 1645–76) in the second half of the 17th century a circle of buildings was erected (1650–54) around the church. They included a modest palace for the Tsar and apartments for the Tsarina, with particularly luxurious decoration on the porch, a block of cells and a tall bell-tower with three stepped roofs. Another circle of structures lay behind these buildings, and the whole complex was surrounded by monumental fortifications. Later additions to the monastery included a four-storey refectory (17th century), an accommodation block, a seminary and a retreat (all 19th century). During the late 18th century and the early 19th the Feast of the Presentation of the Blessed Virgin (Vvedenskoye), Yershovo and Koralovo estates near Zvenigorod were built in the classical style with landscaped parks.

BIBLIOGRAPHY

S. Smirnov: *Istoricheskoye opisaniye Savvino-Storozhevskogo monastyrya* [Historic description of the Storozhevsky Monastery of St Savva] (Moscow, 1887)

Leonid, archimandrite: *Moskovskiy Zvenigorod i yego uyezd v tserkovno-arkheologicheskom otnoshenii* [Muscovite Zvenigorod and the district in terms of its religious architecture] (Moscow, 1878)

N. Voronin and M. Il'in: *Drevneye podmoskov'ye* [The old Moscow region] (Moscow, 1947)

S. Borovkova: *Zvenigorod i okrestnosti* [Zvenigorod and its surroundings] (Moscow, 1970)

T. Nikolayeva: *Drevniy Zvenigorod* [Old Zvenigorod] (Moscow, 1978)

D. O. SHVIDKOVSKY

Zverev, Anatoly (Timofeyevich) (*b* Moscow, 3 Nov 1931; *d* Moscow, 12 Dec 1986). Russian painter. He was born to a working family. In 1954 he entered the In

Memory of 1905 Moscow Regional Art College, from which he was soon expelled owing to his unconventional conduct. He developed as an artist independently and first came into contact with original works of Western abstract art at the 1957 Global Youth and Students' Festival, Moscow. His acquaintance with George Costakis and the latter's collection of Russian avant-garde art was also significant in his artistic development. Exhibitions in local salons and abroad (the first at Galerie Motte, Geneva, in 1965) displayed the stark originality of his temperamental, even tempestuous, style, which may be termed 'figurative Tachism'. His oil, watercolour and gouache portraits, for example of *George Costakis* (1956; Athens, Costakis priv. col.) and *D. Planvinsky* (1976; Moscow, Rusanov priv. col.), landscapes, including the *Church in Peredelkino* (1960; Athens, Costakis, priv. col.), animal paintings and still-lifes always retain an underlying naturalism, which was transformed through impulsive and playful brushwork until it verges on the abstract. The rapture of his painting is shown in the sheer beauty of his colour palette and the graphic rhythm combined with a tragic expression of violent emotion. A confessional sincerity of artistic into-nation, a mocking foolishness and the influence of the alcoholism from which he suffered is evident in his work, which can be seen as a link between the classic modern and the colourful, frenzied nature of the trans-avant-garde. His premature death may appear to symbolize the diffi-culties that faced exponents of unofficial art in the USSR.

BIBLIOGRAPHY

Zverev: Peintures, gouaches, aquarelles (exh. cat., Geneva, Gal. Motte, 1965)
N. G. Grigor'yeva: *Anatoly Zverev* (Moscow, 1991)
S. Yamshchikov, ed.: *Anatoly Zverev: Al'bom* [An album] (Moscow, 1994)

M. N. SOKOLOV

Zvíkov Castle [Ger. Klingenberg]. Castle in the southern Czech Republic. It was the private seat of Vaclav I (*reg* 1230–53) and Přemysl Ottokar II. First mentioned in 1234, it was founded at a strategically important position above the confluence of the Vltava and Otava rivers. To the east and west the headland is protected by abrupt cliffs, with the Otava on the north side. The oldest part of the castle is the great square tower built of rusticated ashlar masonry typical of Hohenstaufen architecture. It faces the south end of the headland and is protected by a moat. On the ground floor it had a single rib-vaulted bay, the ribs descending to pyramidal consoles. The square wall-ribs and the vault webs are of brick with surviving impressions of the original wooden centering. The space was lit by two arrow-slits and was accessible through a passageway with two doorways with pointed arches. The living-room on the first floor had groin vaults supported by corbels on a string course. There were further rooms to the east and west of the tower. The south range retains its early form, with two rib-vaulted rooms on the ground floor and an asymmetrical wooden-roofed entrance hall leading from the courtyard, giving access to the ground floor of the tower and to two rooms of the palace. The resemblance of the tower vault mouldings to those in the Cistercian abbeys at Zwettl and Lilienfeld indicate that the first masons' workshop in Zvíkov came from the Danube area of what is now Austria.

About 1250, when Hirzo, a member of the court, became castle burgrave, the castle was radically altered and renamed Klingenberg. Construction was taken over by a new workshop from the Danube region, which built four ranges of living-quarters around an internal courtyard with an arcaded gallery, a new type of ground-plan first used for the royal castle at Plzeň. Fundamental alterations were made both to the plan and to the rooms of the castle. The main change was to the function of the great hall, which ceased to be the main living area, since each range now had three rooms: a central, two-bay, vaulted hall linked to a panelled room on one side and a room with a fireplace on the other. This arrangement was supple-mented by further rooms as and when required. The best preserved of the new living units is in the west range, the ground floor of which includes a blind-arcaded entrance and passageway. The first floor has a central two-bay vaulted hall with an adjacent room, and three windows above the passageway grouped pyramidally. The original fireplace survives on the wall adjoining the great tower. The rooms in the north range were similar, but the east range had a great hall with six bays of vaults resting on two central octagonal piers. As at Plzeň, the individual ranges of the castle were linked by arcaded galleries, which remained untouched until the restorations of 1840–44 and 1881–5.

The last and artistically richest building in the residential part of the castle is the chapel of St Wenceslas (see fig.), which was built on the first floor of the south range, with

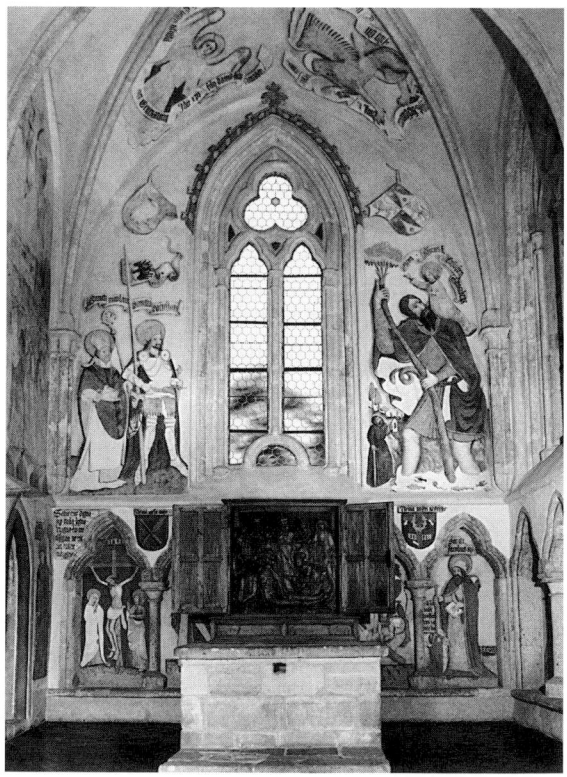

Zvíkov Castle, chapel of St Wenceslas, completed 1263; interior showing altar and frescoes, late 15th century–early 16th

a door in the west wall. The chapel is a single-cell building with two bays of sexpartite vaults. The walls are divided horizontally by the deep window-ledge into a lower level of blind arcading running round the entire building, the capitals decorated with naturalistic leaves or berries, and an upper level that harmonizes with the High Gothic clustered vaulting shafts, which are corbelled in to the window-sills. The west end of the chapel is occupied by the royal tribune, with three bays of vaulting resting on moulded capitals and octagonal piers. The two-light windows have a trilobe pattern of tracery. Attached to the north side of the chapel is the sacristy, dedicated to the Virgin. It has two bays of rib-vaulting, the transverse arch resting on corbels carved with human heads.

The chapel retains its original altar; the walls were frescoed, and the windows were filled with stained glass (destr.). The floors of both chapel and sacristy were covered in glazed tiles with heraldic figures and inscriptions in German in praise of Ottokar II. It is presumably he who is depicted as donor on the tympanum of the west portal, at the centre of which is a seated *Virgin* flanked by angels. The chapel, which must have been finished by 1263 when Hirzo was recalled to found the town of České Budějovice, is evidently the work of a local team that had absorbed the French High Gothic styles introduced through Cistercian architecture.

About 1270 a new fortified curtain wall was built, and the southern neck of the headland was reinforced by a gate-tower with a cylindrical tower *à bec*, its sharp edge aimed in the direction of presumed attack, as at Pernštejn Castle.

BIBLIOGRAPHY
J. Soukup: *Soupis památek historických a uměleckých v politickém okresu píseckém* [Historical and artistic monuments in the district of Písek] (Prague, 1910), pp. 367–432
D. Menclová: *České hrady* [Czech castles], i (Prague, 1972), pp. 101–2, 213–24, 308–10
J. Kuhan: *Gotická architektura v jižních čechách: Zakladatelské dílo Přemysla Otakara II* [Gothic architecture in southern Bohemia: founding work of Přemysl Ottakar II] (Prague, 1975), pp. 79–103
H. SOUKUPOVÁ

Zwart, Piet (*b* Zaandijk, 28 May 1885; *d* Wassenaar, 27 Sept 1977). Dutch designer and typographer. After working in the tradition of the Arts and Crafts Movement, he came into contact in 1917 with De Stijl, which fundamentally changed the course of his work. Through Vilmos Huszár and Jan Wils, he met H. P. Berlage, for whom he worked as a draughtsman, and international artists working in typographic design, such as Kurt Schwitters, El Lissitsky and Jan Tschichold. His international importance is based on typographical works, such as those he made between 1923 and 1930 for NKF, the Dutch cable works, and for PTT, the Dutch postal service. His advertisements, inspired by Dada, often used a wide range of typography and could be read as messages, poems or advertising slogans, while being appreciated simply as designs. Zwart was also active as an interior designer; his most successful work in this field was the kitchen (1938) that he designed for the Bruynzeel Company.

BIBLIOGRAPHY
P. F. Althaus and F. Muller, eds: *Piet Zwart* (Teufen, 1966)
K. Broos: *Piet Zwart* (The Hague, 1973)
S. Ex: 'Piet Zwart, het esthetisch geweten van Bruynzeel', *Het Ontwerpproces* [Design] (1986), pp. 98–9
E. Hoek: 'Piet Zwart en Pomona, de opdrachtgever van het eerste uur', *Het Ontwerpproces* [Design] (1986), pp. 95–7
SJAREL EX

Zwart, Willem [Wilhelmus Henricus Petrus Johannes] **de** (*b* The Hague, 16 May 1862; *d* The Hague, 11 Dec 1931). Dutch painter, draughtsman and etcher. From 1877 to 1880 he studied drawing at the Academie van Beeldende Kunsten in The Hague and painting with Jacob Maris. His earliest work consisted mainly of still-lifes and figure studies, animal subjects and landscapes. From 1884 to 1886 he worked as a tile painter for the Rozenburg Delftware Factory in The Hague.

From 1885 to 1894—generally considered the period of his most important work—de Zwart painted and etched landscapes and townscapes (e.g. the *Wagenbrug in The Hague*, *c*. 1890; Amsterdam, Stedel. Mus.), figures (e.g. *Seated Woman in White*, *c*. 1890; The Hague, Gemeentemus.), portraits and still-lifes reminiscent of works associated with such 19th-century Amsterdam painters as George Hendrik Breitner; however, de Zwart's palette was darker and his brushwork less broad. In 1891 he spent a brief period in Paris making townscapes, such as *Porte Saint-Denis* (1892; The Hague, Gemeentemus.). From 1892 until 1910 he worked under contract with the art dealers E. J. van Wisselingh & Co. and also did illustration work for the Elsevier publishing company.

From 1894 to 1900 de Zwart lived in the Gooi area, east of Amsterdam (Soest, Hilversum and Laren). With the exception of his well-known scenes of cattle markets (e.g. *Cattle Market in Hilversum*; Dordrecht, Dordrechts Mus.), he adopted the agricultural themes and melancholy of painters such as Anton Mauve. His palette and style of painting changed too; his choice of colours became lighter, while his brushwork developed a more spontaneous effect (e.g. *Hay Wagon*; Amsterdam, Rijksmus.). In 1900 he moved to Amsterdam and in 1905 to Bloemendaal, but he also worked regularly in the area around The Hague. Partly due to his obligations to van Wisselingh and partly under the influence of mental illness, he reverted increasingly to motifs and compositions from his earlier work. He settled in Veur, near Leiden (1907–17), and then, finally, in The Hague. During this period, besides portraits, he painted mainly meadow landscapes with cows (two examples in Amsterdam, Rijksmus.) and, after 1917, scenes in the woods around The Hague. These works are typified by blazing blue skies. The increasing severity of his mental illness, a form of persecution mania, was reflected in the *Tormentors* (The Hague, Gemeentemus.), among other freely painted and intensely realized, almost hysterical religious compositions. By the 1920s he was finding it difficult to finish paintings. Towards the end of his life he concentrated on pastel studies of exotic birds drawn from life in The Hague zoological gardens. His etchings, based largely on his own paintings, were executed mainly in the periods 1885–90 and 1894–1906.

BIBLIOGRAPHY
P. Zilcken: 'Willem de Zwart', *Moderne Hollandsche etsers* (Amsterdam, [1896]), pp. 73–6
A. de Meester Obreen: 'Willem de Zwart', *Elsevier's Geïllus. Mdschr.*, xix (March, 1909), pp. 145–56

G. H. Marius: 'Willem de Zwart', *Onze Kst*, ix/1 (1910), pp. 13–28
Catalogus der tentoonstelling van schilderijen en aquarellen van W. de Zwart (exh. cat., intro. by G. H. Marius; The Hague, Villa Erica, 1910)
J. H. de Bois: *De etsen van Willem de Zwart: Introducties en aanteekeningen over kunst* (Bussum, 1911)
A. Brunt: 'Willem de Zwart', *Eigen Haard* (June–July 1911), pp. 533–8
C. Harms Tiepen: 'De schilders in Den Haag: I, Willem de Zwart', *Kst: Mhft. Freie & Angewandte Kst* (April 1917), pp. 319–20
Suze Robertson en Willem de Zwart (exh. cat., intro. by H. E. van Gelder; The Hague, Gemeentemus., 1942), pp. 5–7
R. W. P. de Vries: 'Willem de Zwart', *Nederlandsche grafische kunstenaars uit het einde der negentiende en het begin der twintigste eeuw* (The Hague, 1943), pp. 99–103
W. J. de Gruyter: 'Willem de Zwart', *De Haagse School*, ii (Rotterdam, 1969), pp. 73–81 [with Eng. summary]
R. W. A. Bionda: *Willem de Zwart, 1862–1931* (Haarlem, 1984)

R. W. A. BIONDA

Zwelidumile Geelboi Mgxaji Mslaba Feni. *See* DUMILE.

Zwemmer, Anton [Antonie] (*b* Haarlem, 18 Feb 1892; *d* Crowborough, E. Sussex, 23 Jan 1979). Dutch bookseller, dealer and publisher, active in England. He worked in the book trade in Holland and then in London, where in 1916 he became manager of a foreign-language bookshop at 78 Charing Cross Road. After buying the business in 1923 he developed it into a specialist art bookshop, unique in London until the late 1930s. Zwemmer concentrated on European publications and was the sole British distributor of such magazines as *Cahiers d'art*, *XXe siècle*, *Minotaure*, *Labyrinthe*, *Verve* and, later, *L'Oeil*. He also stocked modern English literature. The bookshop, which was soon financially successful, was a focus for the London art world in the 1920s and 1930s, and Zwemmer became a friend and patron of such artists as Henry Moore, Wyndham Lewis, Jacob Epstein and Graham Sutherland. Through his regular visits to Paris he also came into contact with Picasso, Miró, Dalí and Paul Eluard. In 1929 Zwemmer opened the Zwemmer Gallery at 26 Litchfield Street, round the corner from his bookshop; it operated until 1968. Initially dealing in colour reproductions as well as original works of art, the gallery rapidly became famous for its exhibitions of contemporary art, including Dalí's first one-man exhibition in London (1934), Britain's first completely non-representational exhibition, which was also the last exhibition of the 7 & 5 Society (1935), major exhibitions of Picasso and de Chirico (1936–7) and the second British Surrealist exhibition (1940). Although sceptical of their theory, Zwemmer maintained business links with the Surrealists, was a director of the London Gallery and provided the bookstall for the *International Surrealist Exhibition* of 1936. After World War II the gallery particularly promoted figurative painters, such as Peter Coker (*b* 1926), John Bratby, Carel Weight (*b* 1908) and Arthur Boyd. Zwemmer was also active as a dealer through his private office, handling both paintings and *livres d'artiste*. Among the works that passed through his hands were Picasso's *Three Musicians* (1921; version in Philadelphia, Mus. A.) and *Nude Woman in a Red Armchair* (1932; London, Tate). In 1936 or 1937 he acquired most of the collection of the Belgian collector René Gaffé, including Picasso's portrait of *Wilhelm Uhde* (1910), Miró's *The Tilled Field* (1923–4; New York, Guggenheim) and *Harlequin's Carnival* (1924–5; Buffalo, NY, Albright–Knox

A.G.) and de Chirico's *Melancolia* (1912). From 1925 Zwemmer was involved in publishing both original publications, such as Herbert Read's *Henry Moore, Sculptor: An Appreciation* (1934), the first book on Moore, and British co-editions of European books, including Eugenio d'Ors's *Pablo Picasso* (1930), the first book in English on Picasso.

BIBLIOGRAPHY
A. Blunt and others: *Anton Zwemmer: Tributes from Some of his Friends on the Occasion of his 70th Birthday* (London, 1962) [privately printed]
G. Grigson: *Recollections Mainly of Writers and Artists* (London, 1984)
N. V. Halliday: *More than a Bookshop: Zwemmer's and Art in the Twentieth Century* (London, 1991)

NIGEL VAUX HALLIDAY

Zwinck, Franz Seraph (*b c.* 1748; *d* Oberammergau, 1792). German painter. His father, Johann Joseph Zwinck (*fl* 1735–53), painted frescoes and executed decorations for the Oberammergau Passion plays, roles that Franz Seraph also undertook. An apprenticeship with Johann Jakob Zeiller and Martin Knoller has often been assumed: the influence of engravings of the Augsburg Akademie is evident in his earliest known fresco (1768), for the Echtler Haus, Oberammergau, depicting a *Temptation of Christ* adapted from Rubens.

Zwinck became well known as the 'Lüftl' or open-air painter of Oberammergau, frescoing the farmhouses of his homeland. His paintings (1780) on the Gasthaus zur Alpenrose in Mittenwald emphasize the vertical structure of the window axes by combining them with painted cartouches and figures. Beneath the gable, the sky opens and gives a clear view of the *Coronation of the Virgin*. This imaginary opening of the gable can already be observed in the Hornsteinhaus at Mittenwald, painted in 1775, on a storehouse showing *Judith and Holofernes*. The emphasis on the vertical structure also occurs quite often, for instance in the west façade (1785) of the Forsthaus at Oberammergau. The best-known of all the frescoes is the Pilatushaus (1784; Oberammergau, extensively rest.), named after the *Ecce homo* on the garden façade, where, above a painted column portico, Christ is led before Pilate on steps set at an angle. The imitation architecture on three sides of the house already displays not only the outgoing Rococo style but also elements of incipient Neoclassicism.

Zwinck's ecclesiastical commissions include ceiling frescoes of the *Deposition* (1779; Kappel, Filialkirche Heilig Blut) and of the *Martyrdom of St Sebastian* (1784; Kirchberg-Wildsteig, parish church). The naive freshness of colours of the former yields to more muted tones in the latter, combined with a more pronounced illusionistic perspective. Among Zwinck's portraits, that of *Tertulin Salcher* (ex-Augustinian monastery, Schlehdorf) may be considered his masterpiece.

BIBLIOGRAPHY
B. Heynold-Graefe: 'Franz Seraph Zwinck, der Lüftlmaler von Oberammergau', *Kst & S. Heim*, xlviii (1950), pp. 299–301
H. Bauer and B. Rupprecht, eds: *Corpus der barocken Deckenmalerei in Deutschland*, ii (Munich, 1981), pp. 273–4, 329–31, 336–54, 433–41
P. E. Rattelmüller: *Lüftlmalerei in Oberbayern* (Munich, 1981)
L. Koch, A. Buchwieser and F. Grawe: *Franz Seraph Zwinck: Der Lüftlmaler von Oberammergau* (Oberammergau, 1986) [illus., bibliog.]
L. Koch: 'Die Sakristei der Klosterkirche Ettal', *Jb. Ver. Christl. Kst*, x (1987), pp. 71–82

SUSANNE KIEFHABER

Zwinglianism. Swiss religious movement of the 16th century. Huldrych (or Ulrich) Zwingli (1484–1531) was trained as a humanist scholar and was strongly influenced by Erasmus. In 1518 he became the people's priest in the Grossmünster, Zurich, from which position he was able to shape that city's Reformation. He taught that the Bible, particularly the teachings of Jesus, should be the ultimate authority in matters of faith and practice. His reading of scripture led him to believe that the Church's doctrine of the saints, fostered by images, was wrong. An official disputation between Zwingli and the vicar-general of Constance on this issue was convened in January 1523. In the eyes of the city council Zwingli prevailed, and in June 1524 a decree was published defining an orderly pattern for the removal from the churches of all 'images and idols'. Zwingli, two other priests, representatives of twelve guilds and the city constable entered every church in Zurich, removing and ceremonially destroying all works of art; the walls were whitewashed. Although Zwingli taught that music and the visual arts should be removed from churches, so that Christians could concentrate on the worship of God without the distraction of intermediate art forms, he continued to respect the creation of non-religious art and accepted religious representations outside the church building as long as they did not invite veneration. As a movement Zwinglianism was short-lived. Its leader was killed while serving as chaplain during a battle between Catholic and Reformed cantons. His ideas were carried forward by his successor, Heinrich Bullinger (1504–75). The churches of Zurich eventually joined with the Calvinist movement and thus became part of the Swiss Reformed Church.

BIBLIOGRAPHY

U. Zwingli: *De vera et falsa religionis . . . commentarius* (Tiguri, 1525); Eng. trans. as *Commentary on True and False Religion*, ed. S. Macauley and C. Heller (Durham, NC, 1912/*R* 1981)
C. Garside: *Zwingli and the Arts* (London, 1966) [definitive work]
G. Loehner: *Zwingli's Thought: New Perspectives* (Leiden, 1981)
U. Zwingli: *Selected Writings of Huldrych Zwingli*, ed. and trans. by E. Furcha (Allison Park, PA, 1984)

LARRY WARKENTIN

Zwirner, Ernst Friedrich (*b* Jakobswalde, Upper Silesia, 28 Feb 1802; *d* Cologne, 22 Sept 1861). German architect. He trained at the Kunst- und Bauschule in Breslau (1819–21) and at the Bauakademie in Berlin (1824–8), becoming an official in the Prussian building administration in 1828 under Schinkel. From the start of his career he was an eclectic, one of his first buildings (completed 1834) being for the university in Halle, built in a Neo-classical style. In 1829 he directed the rebuilding in the Gothic Revival style of the Rathaus in Kolberg according to plans by Schinkel. Zwirner was sent to Cologne by Schinkel in 1833 to consolidate the fabric of the unfinished Gothic cathedral. With the help of Sulpiz BOISSERÉE, he was able to enlist the enthusiastic support of the Crown Prince of Prussia (later King Frederick William IV) for a proposal to complete the building. The decision to do so was taken in 1842 and the foundation-stone was laid that September. However, as the medieval plans did not exactly match the existing structure, Zwirner took the opportunity to prove his abilities and the general impression of the cathedral as it stands today is largely his work, particularly the transepts,

the iron roof framework, the former ridge turret (destr. 1944) and the completion of the nave.

Although he directed the most important Gothic building project in Germany, he did not become a dogmatic advocate of the Gothic Revival. As the cathedral master builder he was in great demand as an assessor of restoration projects and received many private commissions for both new buildings and alterations. His work included churches, high altars, castles, country mansions, public buildings, monuments and tombs, all of which demonstrate his inventiveness and versatility. The church of St Audomar (1850–55; destr.), for example, at Frechen, near Cologne, is Romanesque Revival; the deanery (1850–51) of the Agricultural Faculty in Bonn is Neo-classical; and Schloss Herdringen, near Arnsberg in the Sauerland (1844–52), a new building, is Gothic Revival, as is Schloss Arenfels at Bad Hönningen. He also mixed styles, as in the Second Reformed Church (1853–8) at Elberfeld, now part of Wuppertal. Such combinations of styles often arose from the demands of a particular task. His most famous work, the Apollinariskirche (1839–57), near Remagen, is an impressive example. It was a private commission, built to house a cycle of frescoes by the Nazarenes, and the large wall areas needed for this conflicted with the style of Gothic structures. Zwirner's solution nevertheless was a Gothic Revival masterpiece that also embodied Rhenish Romanticism in its relationship with the landscape, and it is now regarded as one of the most important works of this kind.

BIBLIOGRAPHY

Thieme–Becker
H. Rode: 'Ernst Friedrich Zwirners Planentwicklung für den Ausbau des Kölner Domes', *Köln. Dombl.*, xx (1961–2), pp. 45–98
A. Mann and W. Weyres: *Handbuch zur rheinischen Baukunst des 19. Jahrhunderts (1800–1880)* (Cologne, 1968), pp. 116–18
W. Weyres: 'Ernst Friedrich Zwirner', *Rhein. Lebensbild.*, ed. B. Poll, iii (Düsseldorf, 1968), pp. 173–89
H. Kahmen: *Herdringen, Arenfels, Moyland: Drei Schlossbauten Ernst Friedrich Zwirners* (diss., U. Frankfurt am Main, 1973)
E. Trier and W. Weyres, eds: *Kunst des 19. Jahrhunderts im Rheinland*, 5 vols (Düsseldorf, 1980)
Der Kölner Dom im Jahrhundert seiner Vollendung (exh. cat., ed. H. Borger; Cologne, Josef-Haubrich-Ksthalle, 1980)

IZABEL FREIFRAU VON WEITERSHAUSEN

Zwitzel [Zwietzel; Zwitzl; Zwizel]. German family of architects and masons. (1) Jakob Zwitzel may have been related to Hans von Elchingen, who worked as a mason at Ulm Minster in 1471–2 and in 1479. Jakob was mainly active in Augsburg, where he was much influenced by the Late Gothic style of Burkhard Engelberg. Both his son (2) Bernhard Zwitzel and his grandson (3) Simon Zwitzel were also active in the Augsburg area.

BIBLIOGRAPHY

N. Lieb: 'Die Augsburger Familie Zwitzel', *Lebensbild. Bayer. Schwaben*, viii (1961), pp. 84–107

(1) Jacob Zwitzel [von Elchingen] (*b* ?Elchingen, nr Ulm, *c*. 1470; *d* Augsburg, 1540). He settled at quite an early age in Augsburg, paying taxes there in 1497 and becoming a citizen in 1505. From 1502 to 1507 he lived in the same house as the sculptor Gregor Erhart, and in 1512 he moved into the house of the painter Hans Holbein the elder, before acquiring his own house in 1513. In his early career he was associated with Burkhard Engelberg's workshop, but from 1510 he worked independently, as is shown by the noticeable rise in his tax payments. In 1509, on Engelberg's recommendation, Zwitzel contracted to build the tower of the parish church of Schwaz (Tyrol), having planned it in collaboration with Engelberg. Zwitzel did not, however, transfer his practice permanently to the Tyrol. Between 1509 and 1513 he spent only 32 weeks on the site at Schwaz; it was supervised in his absence by the foreman Konrad Vogl (*fl* 1509–42) from Frankfurt. The work at Schwaz brought Zwitzel other commissions in the Tyrol: in 1514 he was involved in negotiations with the church provosts about the construction of the parish church of St Paul, Eppan, and he probably designed the west façade and the proposed canopied portal.

Zwitzel also had much business in Augsburg. He seems to have specialized in the use of high-quality cut stone. In 1515 he erected a monumental column with the emblem of Augsburg, the *Stadtpyr* ('pine cone'), and in 1516 a fountain in the Weinmarkt. Zwitzel was involved in enlarging the old town hall: between 1515 and 1518 he provided frames for windows and doors and in 1516 he built the decorative bell-tower, which is shown in the wooden model of the old town hall made before its demolition by Elias Holl *c.* 1615 (Augsburg, Maximilianmus., no. 3453). In the following years Zwitzel worked on several other city buildings and was a much valued consultant on building matters.

BIBLIOGRAPHY

A. Spornberger: 'Zur Baugeschichte der Pfarrkirche St Pauls in Eppan', *Kunstfreund*, n. s. ii (1886), pp. 43–4, 50–52
E. Egg: *Kunst in Schwaz* (Innsbruck, 1974), pp. 27–8
Welt im Umbruch: Augsburg zwischen Renaissance und Barock, i (exh. cat., foreword B. Bushart; Augsburg, Rathaus & Zeughaus, 1980), p. 121
F. Bischoff: *Burkhard Engelberg und die süddeutsche Architektur um 1500: Anmerkungen zur sozialen Stellung und Arbeitsweise spätgotischer Steinmetzen und Werkmeister* (diss., U. Bamberg, 1987)

FRANZ BISCHOFF

(2) Bernhard Zwitzel (*b* 1496; *d* Augsburg, 1570). Son of (1) Jacob Zwitzel. In 1536 he was appointed Chief Architect at the Stadtresidenz in Landshut, where he was directly responsible for the part of the building facing the old town. This 'German' part of the Residenz, in contrast to the 'Italian' part built in 1537–40, displays a wholly original character. An engraving of *c.* 1700 by M. Wening represents the original appearance of the façade, which was altered in 1780; it shows a spacious three-storey building with a mezzanine of nine window-bays; above the asymmetric portal rise two window-bays, which were originally continued over the roof area by a turret (destr.) framed with pilaster strips. The ornamentation of the façade includes a frieze and four cornice mouldings near the windows of the two main floors. In 1538 Bernhard was appointed Director of Building Works for the imperial city of Augsburg. In 1562–4 he built the Stadtbibliothek (destr. 1894) and in 1563 the 'Geschlechterstube' (destr. 1811). With his son (3) Simon Zwitzel, he was probably responsible for the design of the Antiquarium of the Munich Residenz (*see* MUNICH, fig. 5).

BIBLIOGRAPHY

H. Thoma, H. Brunner and T. Herzog: *Stadtresidenz Landshut: Amtlicher Führer* (Munich, 1938, 4/1980)
V. Liedke: 'Bernhard Zwitzel: Der Meister des sogennanten "Deutschen Baus" an der Stadtresidenz in Landshut', *Verhand. Hist. Ver. Niederbayern*, 97 (1971), pp. 90–99
G. Dischinger: 'Ein Augsburger Plan für das Müncher Antiquarium', *Oberbayer. Archv*, cxii (1988), pp. 81–6

(3) Simon Zwitzel (*d* 1593). Son of (2) Bernhard Zwitzel. He is first recorded in Augsburg in 1548, as an apprentice to the sculptor Hans Kels the Younger. From 1560 he worked as a mason for the city, and in 1570 he succeeded his father as Director of Building Works. He executed a considerable amount of work for the Fugger family, and in 1573–4 he also worked for the ducal court in Munich. He also supplied a model for the Augustus Fountain on the Perlach, which served as a design plan for Hubert Gerhard's sculptures, and was probably involved from 1570, with his father, in the construction of the Antiquarium of the Munich Residenz, assisted by the ducal architect Wilhelm Egckl.

CAROLA WENZEL

Zygmunt III, King of Poland. *See* VASA, (2).

Zygouries [now Ayios Vasilios]. Site of an Early and Late Bronze Age town in the Corinthia of southern Greece, midway between Argos and Corinth. Excavations at the Zygouries Hill in the Kleonai Valley were conducted by Carl Blegen in 1921–2 for the American School of Classical Studies, revealing an important sequence of Bronze Age settlements. The Early Helladic (EH) phase (*c.* 3600/3000–*c.* 2050 BC) was the most abundantly represented, with at least ten houses of mud-brick on stone socle construction arranged close together on narrow streets. The rectangular, flat-roofed, two- and three-roomed structures with fixed central hearths provided one of the first definitive examples of Early Bronze Age domestic architecture. Contemporary graves yielded a broad variety of EH pottery, small gold, silver and bronze ornaments, numerous figurines and stone tools. Like its neighbours Tiryns, Asine, Lerna and Ayios Kosmas, Zygouries suffered a severe destruction at the end of EH II (*c.* 2900/2600–*c.* 2400 BC), which was followed by limited resettlement. Evidence of Middle Helladic (*c.* 2050–*c.* 1600 BC) habitation comes in the form of a few graves, mostly those of children. Modest prosperity returned to Zygouries during the Late Helladic (LH) period (*c.* 1600–*c.* 1050 BC). The most important feature of the small Mycenaean town was an LH IIIA:1–IIIB:1 (*c.* 1390–*c.* 1240 BC) house referred to by Blegen as the 'Potter's Shop', which yielded more than 1300 unused vessels of varied types. This sizeable multi-roomed structure, probably the house of the local nobleman, was equipped with a terracotta pipe drain and a second storey with painted plaster walls. Fiery destruction brought an end to the site in LH IIIB, around 1240 BC. Corinth Archaeological Museum has an important holding of finds from the site.

BIBLIOGRAPHY

C. W. Blegen: *Zygouries: A Prehistoric Settlement in the Valley of Cleonae* (Cambridge, 1928)

SUSAN LANGDON

Zyvele, Henry. *See* YEVELE, HENRY.

Illustration Acknowledgements

We are grateful to those listed below for permission to reproduce copyright illustrative material and to those contributors who supplied photographs or helped us to obtain them. The word 'Photo:' precedes the names of large commercial or archival sources who have provided us with photographs, as well as the names of individual photographers (where known). It has generally not been used before the names of owners of works of art, such as museums and civic bodies. Every effort has been made to contact copyright holders and to credit them appropriately; we apologize to anyone who may have been omitted from the acknowledgements or cited incorrectly. Any error brought to our attention will be corrected in subsequent editions. Where illustrations have been taken from books, publication details are provided in the acknowledgements below.

Line drawings, maps, plans, chronological tables and family trees commissioned by the *Dictionary of Art* are not included in the list below. All of the maps in the dictionary were produced by Oxford Illustrators Ltd, who were also responsible for some of the line drawings. Most of the line drawings and plans, however, were drawn by one of the following artists: Diane Fortenberry, Lorraine Hodghton, Chris Miners, Amanda Patton, Mike Pringle, Jo Richards, Miranda Schofield, John Tiernan, John Wilson and Philip Winton. The chronological tables and family trees were prepared initially by Kate Boatfield and finalized by John Johnson.

Williams, Amancio Photo: Grete Stern
Williams, Owen Photo: P.H. Johnson Advertising Service (Commercial Photo Department), Nottingham
Williamsburg © The Colonial Williamsburg Foundation
Williams-Ellis, Clough National Library of Wales, Aberystwyth
Willmann, Michael Photo: Hannes Etzlstorfer
Willumsen, Jens Ferdinand J.F. Willumsens Museum, Frederikssund
Wilson, Colin St John Photo: John Donat
Wilson, Richard (i) *1* Christie's, London/Photo: Bridgeman Art Library, London; *2* Trustees of the National Gallery, London
Wilton *1* Photo: RCHME/© Crown Copyright; *2* Photo: Anthony Kersting, London
Wilton, Joseph Photo: RCHME/© Crown Copyright
Winchester *1* British Library, London (no. Maps G788); *2* Trustees of the British Museum, London; *5–6* Photo: John Crook
Winchester Bible Warburg Institute, London
Windsor Castle *1* British Library, London (no. 9930.i.37(1)); *2* Photo: Anthony Kersting, London; *3* Royal Collection, Windsor Castle/© Her Majesty Queen Elizabeth II
Winghe, van: (1) Joos van Winghe Photo: Staatliche Kunstsammlungen Dresden
Winterhalter, Franz Xaver Royal Collection, Windsor Castle/© Her Majesty Queen Elizabeth II
Wiślica Institute of Art PAN, Warsaw (neg. no. 66827)/Photo: W. Wolny
Wit, Jacob de Stichting Koninklijk Paleis te Amsterdam/Photo: Tom Haartsen, Ouderkerk A/D Amstel
Witte, Emanuel de Trustees of the Wallace Collection, London
Wittel, Gaspar van Photo: Archivio Fotografico, Musei Capitolini, Rome
Witz, Konrad Öffentliche Kunstsammlung Basel, Kunstmuseum, Basle
Woensam, Anton Graphische Sammlung, Staatsgalerie, Stuttgart
Wolf, Caspar Öffentliche Kunstsammlung Basel, Kunstmuseum, Basle
Wolfenbüttel Herzog August Bibliothek, Wolfenbüttel (inv. no. 105 Noviss 2)
Wolff (i): (1) Jakob Wolff I Photo: Bildarchiv Foto Marburg
Wolgemut, Michael *1* Museo Thyssen-Bornemisza, Madrid; *2* Germanisches Nationalmuseum, Nuremberg
Wolmut, Bonifaz Photo: Ivan Muchka
Wols Staatliche Museen zu Berlin, Preussischer Kulturbesitz/© ADAGP, Paris, and DACS, London, 1996
Women and art history *1* Bibliothèque Nationale de France, Paris; *2* Board of Trustees of the Victoria and Albert Museum, London; *3* Pennsylvania Academy of the Fine Arts, Philadelphia, PA (Gift of the artist); *4* Board of Trustees of the National Museums and Galleries on Merseyside/Walker Art Gallery, Liverpool; *5* National Palace Museum, Taipei; *6* Freer Gallery of Art, Smithsonian Institution, Washington, DC (no. 80.120); *7* Asian Art Museum of San Francisco, San Francisco, CA (no. B76 D3)
Wood (i) *2* Royal Botanic Gardens, Kew, London; *5* Board of Trustees of the Victoria and Albert Museum, London; *6* Norman Adams Ltd, London/Photo: Raymond Fortt Studios, Kingston-upon-Thames, Surrey; *7* Photo: Christie's, New York; *9* American Philosophical Society Library, Philadelphia, PA
Woodcut *1* Staatliche Graphische Sammlung, Munich; *2* Photo: Katherina Mayer Haunton; *3* Germanisches Nationalmuseum, Nuremberg; *4* Photo: Casa Editrice Neri Pozza, Vicenza; *5* Trustees of the British Museum, London; *6* Photo: Sotheby's, London; *7* © Roy Lichtenstein/ Tyler Graphics Ltd, 1980/© 1995 Museum of Modern Art, New York (Mrs John D. Rockefeller 3rd Fund)
Woodcut, chiaroscuro Photo: Jan Johnson
Wood-engraving *1* British Library, London (no. 974.c.19); *2* Trustees of the British Museum, London
Woolner, Thomas Photo: Mark Stocker
Wootton, John Yale Center for British Art, New Haven, CT
Worcester Photo: Phillips Fine Art Auctioneers
World of Art Wadsworth Atheneum, Hartford, CT (Serge Lifar Collection)/© DACS, 1996
Worpswede colony Photo: Bildarchiv, Historisches Museum, Hannover

Wouters, Frans Kunsthistorisches Museum, Vienna
Wouwerman, Philips Trustees of the National Gallery, London
Wren, Christopher *1, 4* Photo: Kerry Downes; *2* Photo: Conway Library, Courtauld Institute of Art, London; *3* Photo: RCHME/© Crown Copyright
Wright: (1) Frank Lloyd Wright *1* © Frank Lloyd Wright Foundation, Scottsdale, AZ; *2* Art Institute of Chicago, Chicago, IL/Photo: © 1996. All rights reserved; *3* Hedrich-Blessing, Chicago, IL; *4* Library of Congress, Washington, DC; *5* Photo: Paul E. Sprague

Wright of Derby, Joseph *1–2* Derby Museums and Art Gallery, Derby
Wrocław © Zwig Pols, Warsaw/Photo: Edmund Kupiecki
Wtewael, Joachim Germanisches Nationalmuseum, Nuremberg
Wu Bin Honolulu Academy of Arts, Honolulu, HI (Purchase 1970)
Wuchters, Abraham Nationalhistoriske Museum på Frederiksborg, Hillerød
Wu Daozi Shōsōin Tōdaiji, Nara
Wu Li National Palace Museum, Taipei
Würzburg *1* Mainfränkisches Museum, Würzburg; *2* Staatliche Museen zu Berlin, Preussischer Kulturbesitz; *3* Photo: Anthony Kersting, London
Wurzelbauer, Benedikt National Gallery, Prague
Wu school Nelson–Atkins Museum of Art, Kansas City, MO
Wu Wei Indianapolis Museum of Art, Indianapolis, IN (Gift of Mr and Mrs Eli Lilly)
Wu Zhen *1* National Palace Museum, Taipei
Wyatt: (1) Samuel Wyatt Country Life Picture Library, London/Photo: Henson
Wyatt: (2) James Wyatt *1* Country Life Picture Library, London/Photo: Henson; *2* From: J. Britton, *Illustrations of Fonthill*, 1823, pl. 371
Wyspiański, Stanisław National Museum, Warsaw
Xanten Photo: Hans Peter Hilger
Xanthos Trustees of the British Museum, London
Xia Gui National Palace Museum, Taipei
Xinzheng Palace Museum, Beijing
Xochicalco Photo: Henri Stierlin, Geneva
Xu Beihong Library of the School of Oriental and African Studies, University of London, London
Xu Daoning Nelson–Atkins Museum of Art, Kansas City, MO (Purchase: Nelson Trust; no. 33-1559)
Xu Wei Nanjing Museum, Nanjing
Yaka *1* National Museum of African Art, Eliot Elisofon Photographic Archives, Smithsonian Institution, Washington, DC/Photo: Eliot Elisofon; *2* University of Iowa Museum of Art, Iowa City, IA (Stanley Collection; no. x1986.425)
Yamamoto Baiitsu Freer Gallery of Art, Smithsonian Institution, Washington, DC
Yanagisawa Kien National University of Fine Arts and Music, Tokyo
Yang P'aeng-son National Museum of Korea, Seoul
Yangzhou school University Art Museum, Berkeley, CA (Gift of Elizabeth Hay Bechtel, University of California, Berkeley, class 1925; no. 1967.14)
Yan Liben Palace Museum, Beijing
Yan Wengui National Palace Museum, Taipei
Yapahuva Photo: Raja de Silva
Yaqut al-Musta'simi Bibliothèque Nationale de France, Paris
Yaroslavl' Photo: VAAP, Moscow
Yavan *1–2* Photo: Donish Institute of History, Dushanbe
Yaxchilán Photo: George F. Andrews
Yazd Photo: Robert Harding Picture Library, London
Yazılıkaya Photo: Hirmer Fotoarchiv, Munich
Yemen Ancient Art and Architecture Collection, London/Photo: F. Jack Jackson
Yi (i): (1) Sin Sa-im-dang National Museum of Korea, Seoul
Yi (ii): (1) Yi Kyŏng-yun Horim Art Museum, Seoul
Yi Am (ii) National Museum of Korea, Seoul
Yi Chŏng (i) Ho-Am Art Museum, Seoul
Yi In-mun National Museum of Korea, Seoul
Yixing Board of Trustees of the Victoria and Albert Museum, London
Ykens, Frans Koninklijke Academie voor Schone Kunsten, Ghent/ Photo: © ACL, Brussels
Yogyakarta Brynmor Jones Library, Photographic Service, University of Hull
Yokohama Trustees of the British Museum, London
York *1* Photo: RCHME/© Crown Copyright; *2* Dean and Chapter of York; *3* Photo: Barrie Dobson; *4* British Library, London (no. L. 50/ 13); *5, 7* Photo: Conway Library, Courtauld Institute of Art, London; *6* Photo: Anthony Kersting, London; *8* York Museum
Yoruba *1* Art Institute of Chicago, Chicago, IL/Photo: © 1996. All rights reserved; *2* Trustees of the British Museum, London; *3* Koninklijk Museum voor Midden-Afrika, Tervuren; *4* Brooklyn Museum, Brooklyn, NY
Yosa Buson Itsuo Art Museum, Osaka
Ypres Photo: Arch. Phot. Paris/© DACS, 1996
Yrurtia, Rogelio Archivo Museo Casa Yrurtia, Buenos Aires
Yungang University of Chicago, Chicago, IL (Collection of Father Harrie Vanderstappen)

Appendix A

LIST OF LOCATIONS

Every attempt has been made in compiling this dictionary to supply the correct current location of each work of art mentioned, a in general this information appears in abbreviated form in parentheses after the first mention of the work. The following list conta the abbreviations and full forms of the museums, galleries and other institutions that own or display art works or archival mate cited in this dictionary; the same abbreviations have been used in bibliographies to refer to the venues of exhibitions. It is also hop that this information will prove useful as a handlist of collections throughout the world.

Institutions are listed under their town or city names, which are given in alphabetical order. Under each place name, the abbrevia names of institutions are also listed alphabetically, ignoring spaces, punctuation and accents. The list includes internal cross-referen to guide the reader to the correct or most common form of place or institution name. In general, the vernacular has been used abbreviations of the names of institutions in western European languages. Names of institutions in other languages, for example th that have been transliterated, are given in English, sometimes followed in parentheses by the vernacular form. Square brack following an entry contain additional information about that institution, for example its previous name or the fact that it v subsequently closed. Such location names are included even if they are no longer used, as they might be cited in the dictionary as venue of an exhibition held before the change of name or date of closure.

The information on this list is the most up-to-date available at the time of publication. It has been compiled using recently publisl guidebooks and museum directories, in particular the *International Directory of Art* (Munich, London, New York and Paris, 1993) a the *Directory of Museums and Living Displays* (New York, 1985), and with the assistance of museum and gallery colleagues and historians worldwide. It reflects the effect on the art world of the geo-political situation of the late 20th century, including, for exam the changes to the names of places and collections in the former USSR and, as far as possible, the major reorganization of muse collections in Berlin since reunification in September 1990. Despite all efforts towards accuracy, information on such war-I countries as Cambodia, Rwanda and the former Yugoslavia may soon be incorrect due to looting and the destruction of war.

Aachen, Couven-Mus.
  Aachen, Couven-Museum

Aachen, Domschatzkam.
  Aachen, Domschatzkammer

Aachen, Gal. Schürmann & Kicken
  Aachen, Galerie Schürmann und Kicken

Aachen, Ludwig Forum Int. Kst
  Aachen, Ludwig Forum für Internationale
  Kunst

Aachen, Mus. B.-A.
  Aachen, Musée des Beaux-Arts

Aachen, Mus. Burg Frankenberg
  Aachen, Museum Burg Frankenberg

Aachen, Musver.
  Aachen, Museumsverein

Aachen, Neue Gal.
  Aachen, Neue Galerie [Sammlung Ludwig]

Aachen, Rathaus [almost totally destr. 1944;
subsequently rest.]

Aachen, Rhein.-Westfäl. Tech. Hochsch.
  Aachen, Rheinisch-Westfälische Technische
  Hochschule

Aachen, Stadtarchv
  Aachen, Stadtarchiv

Aachen, Suermondt-Ludwig-Mus.
  Aachen, Suermondt-Ludwig-Museum

Aalborg: *see* Ålborg

Aalst, Gal. Pintelon
  Aalst, Galerie Pintelon

Aalst, Stedel. Mus.
  Aalst, Stedelijk Museum

Aarau, Aargau. Kantbib.
  Aarau, Aargauische Kantonsbibliothek

Aarau, Aargau. Ksthaus
  Aarau, Aargauer Kunsthaus

Aarau, Stadtmus. Alt-Aarau
  Aarau, Stadtmuseum Alt-Aarau

Abbeville, Mus. Boucher-de-Perthes
  Abbeville, Musée Boucher-de-Perthes [Musée
  d'Abbeville]

Aberdare, Cent. Lib.
  Aberdare, Central Library [Cynon Valley
  Borough Council]

Aberdeen, A.G.
  Aberdeen, Art Gallery

Aberdeen, A.G. & Museums
  Aberdeen Art Gallery and Museums [admins
  Dun's House; Mar. Mus.; Provost Skene's
  House]

Aberdeen, Dun's House
  Aberdeen, James Dun's House

Aberdeen, Mar. Mus.
  Aberdeen, Aberdeen Maritime Museum

Aberdeen, Provost Skene's House

Aberdeen, Town House

Aberdeen, U. Aberdeen
  Aberdeen, University of Aberdeen

Aberdeen, U. Aberdeen, Marischal Mus.
  Aberdeen, University of Aberdeen, Marischal
  Museum

Aberdeen, U. Lib.
  Aberdeen, University of Aberdeen Library
  [Queen Mother Library]

Aberystwyth, N. Lib. Wales
  Aberystwyth, National Library of Wales

Aberystwyth, U. Coll. Wales, A. Cent.
  Aberystwyth, University College of Wales,
  Centre

Aberystwyth, U. Coll. Wales, Powell Col.
  Aberystwyth, University College of Wales,
  Powell Collection

Abidjan, Mus. N. Côte d'Ivoire
  Abidjan, Musée National de la Côte d'Ivoir

Abingdon Mus.
  Abingdon, Abingdon Museum

Abomey, Mus. Hist.
  Abomey, Musée Historique d'Abomey
  [formerly Mus. N.]

Abomey, Mus. N.
  Abomey, Musée National d'Abomey [now
  Mus. Hist.]

Abramtsevo, Mus.-Estate
  Abramtsevo, Museum-Estate (Muzey-
  Usad'ba) [in Moscow region]

Abu Dhabi, al-Ain Mus.
  Abu Dhabi, al-Ain Museum

Acámbaro, Mus. Reg.
  Acámbaro, Museo Regional

Accra, Cent. N. Cult.
  Accra, Centre for National Culture

Accra, Loom Gal.
Accra, The Loom Gallery

ACGB: *see* London

ACGB Col.: *see* London

Acireale, Pal. Città
Acireale, Palazzo di Città

Acolmán, Mus. Colon.
Acolmán, Museo Colonial de Acolmán [in convent of S Agustín]

Acquiny, Château

Adana, Archaeol. Mus.
Adana, Archaeological Museum (Arkeoloji Müzesi) [Eski Eserleri]

Adana, Karatepe Mus.
Adana, Karatepe Museum (Karatepe Müzesi)

Addis Ababa, U. Addis Ababa, Inst. Ethiop. Stud.
Addis Ababa, University of Addis Ababa, Institute of Ethiopian Studies

Adelaide, A.G. S. Australia
Adelaide, Art Gallery of South Australia

Adelaide, Fest. Cent. Artspace
Adelaide, Festival Centre Artspace

Adelaide, Flinders U. S. Australia, A. Mus.
Adelaide, Flinders University of South Australia, Art Museum

Adelaide, Royal S. Austral. Soc. A., Kintore Gal.
Adelaide, Royal South Australian Society of Arts, Kintore Gallery

Adelaide, S. Austral. Mus.
Adelaide, South Australian Museum

Adelaide, S. Austral. Sch. A.
Adelaide, South Australian School of Art

Adelaide, Tandanya Aboriginal Cult. Inst.
Adelaide, Tandanya Aboriginal Cultural Institute

Adelaide, U. Adelaide, Mus. Class. Archaeol.
Adelaide, University of Adelaide, Museum of Classical Archaeology

Aden, N. Mus. Ant.
Aden, National Museum of Antiquities [Musée d'Aden]

Admont, Stiftsbib.
Admont, Stiftsbibliothek

Afyon, Archaeol. Mus.
Afyon, Archaeological Museum

Agats, Asmat Mus. Cult. & Prog.
Agats, Asmat Museum of Culture and Progress

Agen, Mus. B.-A.
Agen, Musée des Beaux-Arts

Agra, Taj Mahal Mus.
Agra, Taj Mahal Museum

Agrigento, Bib. Lucchesiana
Agrigento, Biblioteca Lucchesiana

Agrigento, Mus. Civ.
Agrigento, Museo Civico [incl. Pinacoteca]

Agrigento, Mus. Dioc. A. Sacra
Agrigento, Museo Diocesano d'Arte Sacra [closed indefinitely]

Agrigento, Mus. Reg. Archeol.
Agrigento, Museo Regionale Archeologico [Museo Nazionale Archeologico]

Agrinion, Archaeol. Mus.
Agrinion, Archaeological Museum

Aguascalientes, Casa Cult.
Aguascalientes, Casa de la Cultura

Aguascalientes, Mus. Aguascalientes
Aguascalientes, Museo de Aguascalientes

Ahar, Archaeol. Mus. Chalcolithic Ant.
Ahar, Archaeological Museum for Chalcolithic Antiquities

Ahmadabad, Calico Mus. Textiles
Ahmadabad, Calico Museum of Textiles

Ahmadabad, Cult. Cent., Mehta Col.
Ahmadabad, Culture Centre, Late N. C. Mehta Collection [Gujarat Mus. Soc.]

Ahmadabad, Darpana Acad. Perf. A.
Ahmadabad, Darpana Academy of Performing Arts

Ahmadabad, L. D. Inst. Indol.
Ahmadabad, Lalbhai Dalpatbhai Institute of Indology

Ahmadabad, Mus. Gujarat Vidya Sabha
Ahmadabad, Museum Gujarat Vidya Sabha

Ahmadabad, Mus. Tribal Res. & Training Inst.
Ahmadabad, Museum of Tribal Research and Training Institute

Ahmadabad, N. Inst. Des.
Ahmadabad, National Institute of Design

Ahmadabad, Sanskar Kendra Mus.
Ahmadabad, Sanskar Kendra Museum

Ahmadabad, Shreyas Flk A. Mus.
Ahmadabad, Shreyas Folk Art Museum

Aidone, Mus. Reg. Archeol.
Aidone, Museo Regionale d'Archeologia

Aigina, Archaeol. Mus.
Aigina, Archaeology Museum

Aigion, Monastery Taxiarchs
Aigion, Monastery of the Taxiarchs

Aix-en-Provence, Bib. Méjanes
Aix-en-Provence, Bibliothèque Méjanes [in Hôtel de Ville]

Aix-en-Provence, Hôtel de Ville

Aix-en-Provence, Mus. Arbaud
Aix-en-Provence, Musée Arbaud

Aix-en-Provence, Mus. Granet
Aix-en-Provence, Musée Granet

Aix-en-Provence, Mus. Tap.
Aix-en-Provence, Musée des Tapisseries

Aix-en-Provence, Mus. Vieil Aix
Aix-en-Provence, Musée du Vieil-Aix

Aix-en-Provence, U. Aix—Marseille I
Aix-en-Provence, Université d'Aix—Marseille I

Aix-en-Provence, U. Aix—Marseille III
Aix-en-Provence, Université d'Aix—Marseille III [Université de Droit, d'Economie et des Sciences]

Ajaccio, Mus. Fesch
Ajaccio, Musée Fesch

Ajdovščina, Pilon Gal.
Ajdovščina, Pilon Gallery (Pilonova Galerija)

Ajman Mus.
Ajman, Ajman Muscum

Ajmer, Govt Mus.
Ajmer, Government Museum

Ajmer, Rajputana Mus. Archaeol.
Ajmer, Rajputana Museum of Archaeology

Akita, Hirano Masakichi A. Mus.
Akita, Hirano Masakichi Art Museum (Hirano Masakichi Bijutsukan)

Akita, Prefect. Mus.
Akita, Prefectural Muscum (Akita-Kenritsu Hakubutsukan)

Akron, OH, A. Mus.
Akron, OH, Akron Art Museum

Akron, U. Akron, OH, Emily H. David A.G.
Akron, OH, University of Akron, Emily H. David Art Gallery

Akrotiri, Thera Excav. Storerooms
Akrotiri, Thera Excavation Storerooms

Aksehir, Mus. Stone Masonry
Aksehir, Museum of Stone Masonry

Alampur, Site Mus.
Alampur, Site Museum

Alba, Pal. Com.
Alba, Palazzo Comunale

Albacete, Mus. Albacete
Albacete, Museo de Albacete

Alba Iulia, Batthyaneum Lib.
Alba Iulia, Batthyaneum Library (Biblioteca Batthyaneum)

Albany, NY, Court of Appeals

Albany, NY, Inst. Hist. & A.
Albany, NY, Institute of History and Art

Albany, NY, Print Club
Albany, NY, Albany Print Club

Albany, NY, State Capitol

Albany, SUNY, U. A.G.
Albany, NY, State University of New York, University Art Gallery

Albenga, Civ. Mus. Inguano
Albenga, Civico Museo Inguano

Albenga, Mus. Dioc.
Albenga, Museo Diocesano

Albi, Bib. Mun.
Albi, Bibliothèque Municipale

Albi, Bib. Rochegude
Albi, Bibliothèque Rochegude

Albi, Mus. Toulouse-Lautrec
Albi, Musée Toulouse-Lautrec

Albisola Superiore, Oratorio S Maria Maggiore

Ålborg, Nordjyllands Kstmus.
Ålborg, Nordjyllands Kunstmuseum

Albstadt, Städt. Gal.
Albstadt, Städtische Galerie [incl. Stiftung Walther Groz]

Albuquerque, NM, Tamarind Inst.
Albuquerque, NM, Tamarind Institute

Albuquerque, U. NM, A. Mus.
Albuquerque, NM, University of New Mexico, Art Museum

Albuquerque, U. NM, Maxwell Mus. Anthropol.
Albuquerque, NM, University of New Mexico, Maxwell Museum of Anthropology

Alcalá de Henares, Archv Gen. Cent.
Alcalá de Henares, Archivo General Central

Alcudia, Mus. Parroq.
Alcudia, Museo Parroquial

Aldeburgh, Fest. Gal.
Aldeburgh, Festival Gallery

Alençon, Mus. B.-A. & Dentelle
Alençon, Musée des Beaux-Arts et de la Dentelle

Aleppo, N. Mus.
Aleppo, National Museum of Aleppo

Alessandria, Cassa di Risparmio

Alessandria, Pal. Cuttica
Alessandria, Palazzo Cuttica

Alessandria, Pin. Civ.
Alessandria, Pinacoteca Civica

Alexandria, Gr.-Roman Mus.
Alexandria, Greco-Roman Museum

Alexandria, LA, Mus. F.A.
Alexandria, LA, Museum of Fine Arts [and Cultural Center]

Algiers, Beylerbey Pal.
Algiers, Beylerbey Palace

Algiers, Gal. M'hamed Issiakhem
Algiers, Galerie M'hamed Issiakhem

Algiers, Gal. Pilote
Algiers, Galerie Pilote

Algiers, Le Bardo
Algiers, Le Bardo, Musée d'Ethnographie et de Préhistoire

Algiers, Maison Artisanat
Algiers, Maison de l'Artisanat

Algiers, Mus. N. Ant.
Algiers, Musée National des Antiquités [formerly Mus. Stéphane Gsell]

Algiers, Mus. N. A. & Trad. Pop.
Algiers, Musée National des Arts et Traditions Populaires

Algiers, Mus. N. B.-A.
Algiers, Musée National des Beaux-Arts

Algiers, Mus. Stéphane Gsell
Algiers, Musée Stéphane Gsell [now Mus. N. Ant.]

Alicante, Col. A. Siglo XX
Alicante, Colección de Arte del Siglo XX [Casa de la Asegurada]

Alice, U. Fort Hare, De Beers Centenary A.G.
Alice, University of Fort Hare, De Beers Centenary Art Gallery

Aligarh, Muslim U., Maulana Azad Lib.
Aligarh, Muslim University, Maulana Azad Library

Alkmaar, Stedel. Mus.
Alkmaar, Stedelijk Museum

Allahabad Mus.
Allahabad, Allahabad Museum

Allahabad U., Archaeol. Mus.
Allahabad, Allahabad University, Archaeological Museum

Allentown, PA, A. Mus.
Allentown, PA, Art Museum

Allschwil, Gemeindesamml.
Allschwil, Gemeindesammlung

Almansil, Cent. Cult. S Lourenço
Almansil, Centro Cultural de S Lourenço

Almaty, Cent. Mus. Kazakhstan
Almaty, Central Museum of Kazakhstan [Almaty formerly Alma-Ata]

Almaty, Kasteyev Mus. A. Kazakhstan
Almaty, Kasteyev Museum of the Art of Kazakhstan

Almaty, Kazakh Acad. Sci.
Almaty, Kazakh Academy of Sciences

Almaty, Kazakh Acad. Sci., Mus. Archaeol.
Almaty, Kazakh Academy of Sciences, Museum of Archaeology

Almería, Mus. Arqueol. Prov.
Almería, Museo Arqueológico Provincial [Diputación Provincial]

Alpiarça, Casa-Mus. Relvas
Alpiarça, Casa-Museu José Relvas

Altamira, Mus. Cuevas
Altamira, Museo de las Cuevas de Altamira

Altdorf, Hist. Mus.
Altdorf, Historisches Museum

Altdorf, Höfli-Kaserne

Altdorf, Staatsarchv Uri
Altdorf, Staatsarchiv Uri

Altenburg, Staatl. Lindenau-Mus.
Altenburg, Staatliches Lindenau-Museum

Alton, Allen Gal.
Alton, Allen Gallery

Alton, Curtis Mus.
Alton, Curtis Museum

Altötting, SS Philipp & Jakob, Schatzkam.
Altötting, SS Philipp und Jakob, Schatzkammer [in former Stiftskirche]

Al-Ula Mus.
Al-Ula, Al-Ula Museum

Alwar, City Pal.
Alwar, City Palace

Alzano Lombardo, Mus. Basilica S Martino
Alzano Lombardo, Museo della Basilica di San Martino

Amalfi, Arsenale
Amalfi, Arsenale della Repubblica

Amaravati, Archaeol. Mus.
Amaravati, Archaeological Museum

Amatitlán, Mus. Mun.
Amatitlán, Museo Municipal

Amber: see Amer

Amboise, Mus. Mun.
Amboise, Musée Municipal [Musée de l'Hôtel de Ville]

Amer, Archaeol. Mus.
Amer, Archaeological Museum

Amerongen, Kasteel
Amerongen, Kasteel Amerongen

Amersfoort, Mus. Flehite
Amersfoort, Museum Flehite

Amersfoort, Zonnehof Mus.
Amersfoort, Zonnehof Museum

Ames, IA State U.
Ames, IA, Iowa State University

Amherst, MA, Amherst Coll., Mead A. Mus.
Amherst, MA, Amherst College, Mead Art Museum

Amherst, U. MA, U. Gal.
Amherst, MA, University of Massachusetts at Amherst, University Gallery [Fine Arts Center]

Amiens, Bib. Mun.
Amiens, Bibliothèque Municipale

Amiens, Mus. Picardie
Amiens, Musée de Picardie

Amiens, Trésor de la Cathédrale Notre Dame

Amlapura, Puri Kanginam

Amman, Abdul Hamid Shoman Found.
Amman, Abdul Hamid Shoman Foundation

Amman, Dept Ant.
Amman, Department of Antiquities [admins Flklore Mus.; Jordan Archaeol. Mus.; Mosaic Gal.; Pop. Life Mus.]

Amman, Flklore Mus.
Amman, Folklore Museum

Amman, Inst. F.A.
Amman, Institute of Fine Arts

Amman, Jordan Archaeol. Mus.
Amman, Jordan Archaeological Museum [Citadel Museum]

Amman, Mosaic Gal.
Amman, Mosaic Gallery

Amman, N.G. F.A.
Amman, National Gallery of Fine Arts [National Gallery of Paintings]

Amman, Pop. Life Mus.
Amman, Popular Life Museum

Amorbach, Heimatmus.
Amorbach, Heimatmuseum [Fürstliche Leiningensche Sammlungen]

Åmot, Stift. Modums Blaafarveværk
Åmot, Stiftelsen Modums Blaafarveværk

Amparai, Archaeol. Mus.
Amparai, Archaeological Museum

Amritsar, Maharaja Ranjit Singh Mus.
Amritsar, Maharaja Ranjit Singh Museum

Amsterdam, A. & Amicitiae
Amsterdam, Arti et Amicitiae [Artigalerie]

Amsterdam, Allard Pierson Mus.
Amsterdam, Allard Pierson Museum

Amsterdam, Applied A. Sch.
Amsterdam, Applied Arts School

Amsterdam, Begijnhof

Amsterdam, Bib. Philos. Hermetica
Amsterdam, Biblioteca Philosophica Hermetica

Amsterdam, Bijbels Mus.
Amsterdam, Bijbels Museum [Museum Biblischer Altertümer]

Amsterdam, Bureau Beeld. Kst Buitenland
Amsterdam, Bureau Beeldende Kunst Buitenland

Amsterdam, Cent. Bib. Kon. Inst. Tropen
Amsterdam, Centrale Bibliotheek van het Koninklijk Instituut voor de Tropen

Amsterdam, Col. Six
Amsterdam, Collectie Six

Amsterdam, Concertgebouw

Amsterdam, De Krijberg Presbytery [houses Roothaan Mus.]

Amsterdam, Gal. A
Amsterdam, Galerie A

Amsterdam, Gal. 845
Amsterdam, Galerie 845

Amsterdam, Gal. Balolu
Amsterdam, Galerie Balolu

Amsterdam, Gal. Le Canard
Amsterdam, Galerie Le Canard

Amsterdam, Gal. Paul Andriesse
Amsterdam, Galerie Paul Andriesse

Amsterdam, Gal. Robert
Amsterdam, Galerie Robert

Amsterdam, Gal. Swart
Amsterdam, Galerie Swart

Amsterdam, Gal. Wetering
Amsterdam, Galerie Wetering

Amsterdam, Gemeente Archf
Amsterdam, Gemeente Archief

Amsterdam, Gerrit Rietveld Acad.
Amsterdam, Gerrit Rietveld Academie

Amsterdam, Heineken Gal.
Amsterdam, Heineken Galerij

Amsterdam, Hist. Mus.
Amsterdam, Historisch Museum

Amsterdam, Hogesch. Kst.
Amsterdam, Hogeschool voor de Kunsten [Academie van Bouwkunst]

Amsterdam, Inst. Contemp. A.
Amsterdam, Institute of Contemporary Art

Amsterdam, Joods Hist. Mus.
Amsterdam, Joods Historisch Museum

Amsterdam, J. Waterman

Amsterdam, Kon. Coll. Zeemanschoop
Amsterdam, Koninklijk College Zeemanschoop

Amsterdam, Kon. Oudhdknd. Genoot.
Amsterdam, Koninklijk Oudheidkundig Genootschap

Amsterdam, Ksthand. Gebr. Douwes
Amsterdam, Kunsthandel Gebroeders Douwes

Amsterdam, Ksthand. K. & V. Waterman
Amsterdam, Kunsthandel K. en V. Waterman

Amsterdam, Ksthand. M. L. de Boer
Amsterdam, Kunsthandel M. L. de Boer

Amsterdam, Ksthand. Schlichte Bergen
Amsterdam, Kunsthandel Schlichte Bergen

Amsterdam, Ksthand. van Lier
Amsterdam, Kunsthandel van Lier

Amsterdam, Kweeksch. Zeevaart
Amsterdam, Kweekschool voor de Zeevaart

Amsterdam, Larensche Ksthandel
Amsterdam, Larensche Kunsthandel

Amsterdam, Maison Descartes

Amsterdam, Mus. Amstelkring
Amsterdam, Museum Amstelkring

Amsterdam, Mus. Com. Ville
Amsterdam, Musée Communal de la Ville d'Amsterdam [closed]

Amsterdam, Mus. Fodor
Amsterdam, Museum Fodor

Amsterdam, Mus. Overholland
Amsterdam, Museum Overholland

Amsterdam, Mus. van Loon
Amsterdam, Museum van Loon

Amsterdam, Mus. Willet-Holthuysen
Amsterdam, Museum Willet-Holthuysen

Amsterdam, Ned. Doc. Bouwkst
Amsterdam, Nederlands Documentatie voor de Bouwkunst

Amsterdam, Ned. Hervormde Gemeente
Amsterdam, Nederlands Hervormde Gemeente

Amsterdam, Ned. Hist. Scheepvaartsmus.
Amsterdam, Nederlands Historisch Scheepvaartsmuseum

Amsterdam, Ned. Theat. Inst.
Amsterdam, Nederlands Theater Instituut [houses Theatermus.]

Amsterdam, Nieuwe Kerk

Amsterdam, Occo Hofje

Amsterdam, P. de Boer

Amsterdam, Rembrandthuis

Amsterdam, Rijksakad. Beeld. Kst.
Amsterdam, Rijksakademie van Beeldende Kunsten

Amsterdam, Rijksdienst Beeld. Kst
Amsterdam, Rijksdienst Beeldende Kunst

Amsterdam, Rijksmus.
Amsterdam, Rijksmuseum [includes Afdeeling Aziatische Kunst; Afdeeling Beeldhouwkunst; Afdeeling Nederlandse Geschiedenis; Afdeeling Schilderijen; Museum von Asiatische Kunst; Rijksmuseum Bibliothek; Rijksprentenkabinet]

Amsterdam, Rijksmus. van Gogh
Amsterdam, Rijksmuseum Vincent van Gogh

Amsterdam, Roothaan Mus.
Amsterdam, Roothaan Museum [in De Krijberg Presbytery]

Amsterdam, Santee Landwer Gal.
Amsterdam, Santee Landwer Gallery

Amsterdam, Stedel. Mus.
Amsterdam, Stedelijk Museum

Amsterdam, Sticht. de Boer
Amsterdam, Stichting P. en N. de Boer

Amsterdam, Sticht. Kon. Pal.
Amsterdam, Stichting Koninklijk Paleis te Amsterdam

Amsterdam, Sticht. Ned. Inst. Archit. & Stedebouw
Amsterdam, Stichting Nederlands Instituut voor Architectuur en Stedebouw [Stichting Architectuurmuseum]

Amsterdam, Stuyvesant Sticht.
Amsterdam, Peter Stuyvesant Stichting

Amsterdam, Theatmus.
Amsterdam, Theatermuseum

Amsterdam, Trippenhuis

Amsterdam, Tropenmus.
Amsterdam, Tropenmuseum

Amsterdam, U. Amsterdam
Amsterdam, Universiteit van Amsterdam

Amsterdam, U. Amsterdam, Fac. Psychol.
Amsterdam, Universiteit van Amsterdam, de Psychologie Faculteit

Amsterdam, U. Amsterdam, Pierson Mus.
Amsterdam, Universiteit van Amsterdam, Allard Pierson Museum [Archaeologisch Museum der Universität]

Amsterdam, U. Amsterdam, Pierson Sticht.
Amsterdam, Universiteit van Amsterdam, Allard Pierson Stichting [Archaeologisch-Historisch Instituut]

Amsterdam, Ubib.
Amsterdam, Universiteitsbibliotheek [Universiteit van Amsterdam]

Amsterdam, Vrije U.
Amsterdam, Vrije Universiteit

Amsterdam, Waterman Gal.
Amsterdam, K. en V. Waterman Galerij

Amsterdam, Werkspoor-Mus.
Amsterdam, Werkspoor-Museum

Amsterdam, Witsenhuis

Ancash, Mus. Reg.
Ancash, Museo Regional de Ancash

Anchorage, AK, Hist. & F.A. Mus.
Anchorage, AK, Historical and Fine Arts Museum

Anchorage, Visual A. Cent. AK
Anchorage, AK, Visual Arts Center of Alaska

Ancona, Gal. D. D.
Ancona, Galleria D.D.

Ancona, Loggia Mercanti
Ancona, Loggia dei Mercanti

Ancona, Mus. Archeol. N. Marche
Ancona, Museo Archeologico Nazionale delle Marche

Ancona, Mus. Dioc.
Ancona, Museo Diocesano

Ancona, Pin. Com.
Ancona, Pinacoteca Comunale [Francesco Podesti e Galleria d'Arte Moderna]

Ancona, Teat. delle Muse
Ancona, Teatro delle Muse

Andover, Mus. & A.G.
Andover, Andover Museum and Art Gallery

Andover, Mus. Iron Age
Andover, Museum of the Iron Age

Andover, MA, Phillips Acad., Addison Gal.
Andover, MA, Phillips Academy, Addison Gallery of American Art

Andria, Pal. Vescovile
Andria, Palazzo Vescovile [houses Museo Diocesano]

Andropov, Mus. Hist. A.
Andropov, Museum of the History of Art (Muzey Istorii Iskusstva) [Andropov reverted to former name of Rybinsk c. 1990]

Andros, Archaeol. Mus.
Andros, Archaeological Museum [in primary sch.]

Andros, MOMA, Goulandris Found.
Andros, Museum of Modern Art, B. & E. Goulandris Foundation

Angera, Rocca

Angers, Château, Col. Tap.
Angers, Château et Galerie de l'Apocalypse, Collection des Tapisseries

Angers, Gal. David d'Angers
Angers, Galerie David d'Angers [in rest. Abbey]

Angers, Hôtel Pincé

Angers, Maison d'Adam

Angers, Maison Dioc.
Angers, Maison Diocésaine

Angers, Mus. B.-A.
Angers, Musée des Beaux-Arts

Angers, Musées d'Angers [admins Gal. David d'Angers; Mus. B.-A.; Mus. Lurçat; Mus. Turpin de Crissé]

Angers, Mus. Lurçat
Angers, Musée Jean Lurçat

Angers, Mus. Turpin de Crissé
Angers, Musée Turpin de Crissé [in Hôtel Pincé]

Angers, Soc. Amis A.
Angers, Société des Amis des Arts

Angkor, Dépôt Conserv. Mnmts
Angkor, Dépôt de la Conservation des Monuments d'Angkor

Angoulême, Mus. Mun.
Angoulême, Musée Municipal

Anholt, Fürst Salm-Salm, Mus. Wasserburg-Anholt
Anholt, Fürst zu Salm-Salm, Museum Wasserburg-Anholt

Ankara, Akdeniz A.G.
Ankara, Akdeniz Art Gallery

Ankara, Hittite Mus.
Ankara, Hittite Museum [Mus. Anatol. Civiliz.]

Ankara, Mus. Anatol. Civiliz.
Ankara, Museum of Anatolian Civilizations (Anadolu Medeniyetleri Müzesi) [Archaeological Museum; Hittite Museum]

Ankara, Mus. Ethnog.
Ankara, Museum of Ethnography

Ankara, Mus. F.A.
Ankara, Museum of Fine Art (Güzel San'atler Müzesi)

Annandale-on-Hudson, NY, Bard Coll., Blum Inst.
Annandale-on-Hudson, NY, Bard College, Edith C. Blum Institute

Annapolis, MD, US Naval Acad. Mus.
Annapolis, MD, US Naval Academy Museum

Ann Arbor, U. MI
Ann Arbor, MI, University of Michigan

Ann Arbor, U. MI, Kelsey Mus.
Ann Arbor, MI, University of Michigan, Kelsey Museum of Ancient and Medieval Archaeology

Ann Arbor, U. MI, Mus. A.
  Ann Arbor, MI, University of Michigan,
  Museum of Art

Ann Arbor, U. MI, Mus. Anthropol.
  Ann Arbor, MI, University of Michigan,
  Museum of Anthropology

Annecy, Conserv. A. & Hist. Haute-Savoie
  Annecy, Conservatoire d'Art et d'Histoire de la
  Haute-Savoie

Annecy, Mus.-Château
  Annecy, Musée-Château d'Annecy

Annecy, Mus. Léon Matès
  Annecy, Musée Léon Matès

Ansbach, Residenz & Staatsgal.
  Ansbach, Residenz und Staatsgalerie

Antakya, Hatay Mus.
  Antakya, Hatay Museum (Arkeoloji Müzesi)
  [Archaeological Museum]

Antalya, Archaeol. Mus.
  Antalya, Archaeological Museum (Arkeoloji
  Müzesi) [Regional Museum]

Antananarivo, U. Antananarivo
  Antananarivo, Université d'Antananarivo

Antequera, Mus. Mun.
  Antequera, Museo Municipal

Antibes, Mus. Picasso
  Antibes, Musée Picasso [in Château Grimaldi]

Antigua, Cent. Invest. Mesoamérica
  Antigua, Centro de Investigaciones de
  Mesoamérica

Antigua, Mus. Colon.
  Antigua, Museo Colonial

Antigua, Mus. Libro Antiguo
  Antigua, Museo del Libro Antiguo

Antigua, Mus. Santiago
  Antigua, Museo de Santiago [in Town Hall]

Antilias, Armen. Catholicate Cilicia
  Antilias, Armenian Catholicate of Cilicia

Antrodoco, Pal. Com.
  Antrodoco, Palazzo Comunale

Antwerp, A. Contemp.
  Antwerp, Art Contemporain

Antwerp, Beurscomm.
  Antwerp, Beurscommissie

Antwerp, Comm. Openb. Onderstand
  Antwerp, Commissie van Openbare
  Onderstand

Antwerp, Etnog. Mus.
  Antwerp, Etnografisch Museum

Antwerp, Gal. Accent
  Antwerp, Galerie Accent

Antwerp, Gal. Breckpot
  Antwerp, Galerie Breckpot

Antwerp, Huis Osterrieth

Antwerp, Huis van Aken [destr.]

Antwerp, Int. Cult. Cent.
  Antwerp, International Cultural Centre

Antwerp, Jordaenshuis

Antwerp, Kon. Acad. S. Kst.
  Antwerp, Nationaal Hoger Instituut en
  Koninklijke Academie voor Schone Kunsten

Antwerp, Kon. Mus. S. Kst.
  Antwerp, Koninklijk Museum voor Schone
  Kunsten

Antwerp, Ksthist. Musea
  Antwerp, Kunsthistorische Musea [admins
  Mus. Mayer van den Bergh; Mus. Smidt van
  Gelder; Openluchtmus. Beeldhouwkst
  Middelheim; Rubenianum; Rubenshuis]

Antwerp, Maagdenhuism.
  Antwerp, Maagdenhuismuseum

Antwerp, Mus. Brouwershuis

Antwerp, Mus. Hedendaagse Kst
  Antwerp, Museum van Hedendaagse Kunst

Antwerp, Mus. Mayer van den Bergh
  Antwerp, Museum Mayer van den Bergh

Antwerp, Mus. Plantin–Moretus
  Antwerp, Museum Plantin–Moretus

Antwerp, Mus. Smidt van Gelder
  Antwerp, Museum Smidt van Gelder

Antwerp, Mus. Vleeshuis
  Antwerp, Museum Vleeshuis

Antwerp, N. Scheepvaartmus.
  Antwerp, Nationaal Scheepvaartmuseum

Antwerp, Openluchtmus. Beeldhouwkst
Middelheim
  Antwerp, Openluchtmuseum voor
  Beeldhouwkunst Middelheim

Antwerp, Oudhdknd. Musea
  Antwerp, Oudheidkundige Musea [admins
  Etnog. Mus.; Mus. Brouwershuis; Mus.
  Vleeshuis; N. Scheepvaartmus.; Vlkskndmus.]

Antwerp, Prov. Diamantmus.
  Antwerp, Provinciaal Diamantmuseum

Antwerp, Prov. Mus. Fot.
  Antwerp, Provinciaal Museum Fotografie

Antwerp, Rockoxhuis

Antwerp, Rubenianum

Antwerp, Rubenshuis

Antwerp, Stadhuis

Antwerp, Stadsarchf
  Antwerp, Stadsarchief

Antwerp, Stadsbib.
  Antwerp, Stadsbibliotheek

Antwerp, Stadsfestzaal

Antwerp, Stedel. Festzaal
  Antwerp, Stedelijk Festzaal

Antwerp, Stedel. Prentenkab.
  Antwerp, Stedelijk Prentenkabinet

Antwerp, St Elisabeth Gasthuis

Antwerp, Vlkskndmus.
  Antwerp, Volkskundemuseum

Antwerp, Zoo
  Antwerp, Zoo Antwerpen

Anuradhapura, Archaeol. Mus.
  Anuradhapura, Archaeological Museum

Anuradhapura, Flk Mus.
  Anuradhapura, Folk Museum

Anyang, Mun. Mus.
  Anyang, Municipal Museum

Aosta, Tesoro della Cattedrale

Aosta, Tour du Fromage

Apamea, Archaeol. Mus.
  Apamea, Archaeology Museum

Apeiranthos, Archaeol. Mus.
  Apeiranthos, Archaeological Museum [Naxos]

Apeldoorn, Pal. Het Loo
  Apeldoorn, Rijksmuseum Paleis Het Loo

Apeldoorn, Van Reekum Mus.
  Apeldoorn, Van Reekum Museum

Aphrodisias Mus.
  Aphrodisias, Aphrodisias Museum

Aquila: see L'Aquila

Aquileia, Mus. Archeol. N.
  Aquileia, Museo Archeologico Nazionale

Aquileia, Mus. N. Paleocrist.
  Aquileia, Museo Nazionale Paleocristiano

Arad, Reg. Mus.
  Arad, Arad Regional Museum (Muzeul
  Judeţean Arad)

Aranjuez, Jard. Príncipe
  Aranjuez, Jardín del Príncipe

Aranjuez, Pal. Real
  Aranjuez, Palacio Real

Aranjuez, Real Casa Labrador
  Aranjuez, Real Casa del Labrador

Arbois, Hôp.
  Arbois, Hôpital

Arbroath, Hospitalfield House

Arbroath, St Vigeans Sculp. Stones
  Arbroath, St Vigeans Sculptured Stones

Arcetri, Villa Gallina
  Arcetri, Villa la Gallina

Ardea, Rac. Amici Manzù
  Ardea, Raccolta Amici di Manzù

Arenenberg, Napoleonmus.
  Arenenberg, Napoleonmuseum

Arenenberg Schloss
  Arenenberg, Arenenberg Schloss

Arequipa, Inst. Sup. A. 'Carlos Baca Flor'
  Arequipa, Instituto de Arte 'Carlos Baca Flor'

Arezzo, Accad. Petrarca
  Arezzo, Accademia Petrarca [di Lettere, Arti e
  Scienze; Casa Natale del Petrarca]

Arezzo, Casa Giorgio Vasari
  Arezzo, Casa di Giorgio Vasari [houses Museo
  e Archivio Vasariano]

Arezzo, Gal. Com. A. Contemp.
  Arezzo, Galleria Comunale d'Arte
  Contemporanea [Palazzo Guillichini]

Arezzo, Gal. & Mus. Med. & Mod.
  Arezzo, Galleria e Museo Medioevale e
  Moderno

Arezzo, Mus. Archeol. Mecenate
  Arezzo, Museo Archeologico Ciao Cilnia
  Mecenate

Arezzo, Mus. Dioc.
  Arezzo, Museo Diocesano

Arezzo, Pal. Bruni–Ciocchi
  Arezzo, Palazzo Bruni–Ciocchi [Palazzo della
  Dogana]

Arezzo, Pal. Com.
  Arezzo, Palazzo Comunale

Arezzo, Pal. Fraternità dei Laici
  Arezzo, Palazzo della Fraternità dei Laici

Arezzo, Sala S Ignazio

Arezzo, S Francesco

Argenteuil, Cent. Cult.
  Argenteuil, Centre Culturel

Argos, Archaeol. Mus.
  Argos, Archaeological Museum

Argostoli, Archaeol. Mus.
  Argostoli, Archaeological Museum

Argostolion, Corgialenios Hist. & Cult. Mus. &
Lib.
  Argostolion, Corgialenios Historical and
  Cultural Museum and Library

Århus, Kreditforen. Danmark
  Århus, Kreditforening Danmark

Århus, Kstmus.
  Århus, Kunstmuseum

Århus, Marselisborg Slot

Ariccia, Pal. Chigi
  Ariccia, Palazzo Chigi

Arita, Kyushu Cer. Mus.
  Arita, Kyushu Ceramics Museum

Arkhangel'sk, Reg. Mus. F.A.
 Arkhangel'sk, Regional Museum of Fine Arts
 (Oblastnoy Muzey Izobrazitel'nykh Iskusstva)

Arkhangel'skoye, Mus.-Estate
 Arkhangel'skoye, Arkhangel'skoye Museum-
 Estate (Muzey-Usad'ba Arkhangel'skoye)

Arkhangel'skoye Pal.
 Arkhangel'skoye, Arkhangel'skoye Palace
 (Arkhangel'skoye Dvorets)

Arles, Mus. Archéol.
 Arles, Musée d'Archéologie

Arles, Mus. Lapidaire A. Chrét.
 Arles, Musée Lapidaire d'Art Chrétien

Arles, Mus. Lapidaire A. Païen
 Arles, Musée Lapidaire d'Art Païen

Arles, Mus. Réattu
 Arles, Musée Réattu

Armagh, Co. Mus.
 Armagh, County Museum

Armagh, Protestant Cathedral, Chapter House [St
Patrick's]

Armenia, Mus. Arqueol.
 Armenia, Museo Arqueológico del Quivalio

Armidale, Teachers' Coll.
 Armidale, Armidale Teachers' College

Arnemuiden, Raddhuis-Mus.
 Arnemuiden, Raddhuis-Museum

Arnhem, Gemeentemus.
 Arnhem, Gemeentemuseum

Arnhem, Hoge Veluwe N. Park
 Arnhem, Hoge Veluwe National Park

Arnhem, Rijksarchf Gelderland
 Arnhem, Rijksarchief in Gelderland

Arnhem, Rijksmus. Vlksknd., Ned.
Openluchtmus.
 Arnhem, Rijksmuseum voor Volkskunde, Het
 Nederlands Openluchtmuseum

Arolsen, Residenzschloss [Prince of Waldeck
Collection]

Arouca, Convent S Maria
 Arouca, Convent of S Maria

Arouca, Mus. A. Sacra
 Arouca, Museu de Arte Sacra

Arras, Archvs Dépt. Pas-de-Calais
 Arras, Archives Départementales du Pas-de-
 Calais

Arras, Bib. Ville
 Arras, Bibliothèque de la Ville

Arras, Mus. B.-A.
 Arras, Musée des Beaux-Arts [Ancienne
 Abbaye Saint-Vaast]

Arsinoe: see Tocra

Arta, Archaeol. Col.
 Arta, Archaeological Collection

Aruba, Cult. Cent.
 Aruba, Cultureel Centrum [Lesser Antilles]

Asahikawa, Educ. Cttee
 Asahikawa, Asahikawa Education Committee

Asahikawa, Hokkaido Mus. A.
 Asahikawa, Hokkaido Museum of Art
 (Hokkaidōritsu Asahikawa Bijutsukan)

Asahikawa, Mun. Mus.
 Asahikawa, Municipal Museum (Asahikawa-
 Shiritsu Asahikawa Kyodo Hakubutsukan)

Asahikawa, Mus. A.
 Asahikawa, Museum of Art

Aschaffenburg, Schloss Johannisburg, Hof- &
Stiftsbib.
 Aschaffenburg, Schloss Johannisburg, Hof-
 und Stiftsbibliothek

Aschaffenburg, Schloss Johannisburg, Staatsgal.
 Aschaffenburg, Schloss Johannisburg,
 Staatsgalerie

Aschaffenburg, Stiftsmus., Stiftsschatz
 Aschaffenburg, Stiftsmuseum, Stiftsschatz

Asciano, Mus. A. Sacra
 Asciano, Museo d'Arte Sacra

Ascoli Piceno, Mus. Dioc.
 Ascoli Piceno, Museo Diocesano

Ascoli Piceno, Pin. Civ.
 Ascoli Piceno, Pinacoteca Civica

Ascona, Mus. Com. A. Mod.
 Ascona, Museo Comunale d'Arte Moderna di
 Ascona

Asheville, NC, Biltmore Estate [formerly Biltmore
House & Gdns]

Ashikaga, Kurita Mus.
 Ashikaga, Kurita Museum

Ashiya, Tekisui A. Mus.
 Ashiya, Tekisui Art Museum

Ashkhabad, Cent. Mus. Turkmenistan
 Ashkhabad, Central Museum of Turkmenistan

Ashkhabad, Turkmenistan Acad. Sci.
 Ashkhabad, Turkmenistan Academy of
 Sciences

Ashkhabad, Turkmenistan Acad. Sci., Inst. Hist.
 Ashkhabad, Turkmenistan Academy of
 Sciences, Institute of History

Ashkhabad, Turkmenistan Hist. Mus.
 Ashkhabad, Turkmenistan Historical Museum
 (Muzey Storii Turmenskoy RSS)

Ashkhabad, Turkmenistan Mus. F.A.
 Ashkhabad, Turkmenistan Museum of Fine
 Arts

Ashkhabad, Turkmenistan United Mus. Hist. &
Ethnog.
 Ashkhabad, Turkmenistan United Museum of
 History and Ethnography

Asnières, Banque de France

Asolo, Mus. Civ.
 Asolo, Museo Civico

Aspen, CO, Cent. Visual A.
 Aspen, Center for Visual Arts

Assen, Prov. Mus. Drenthe
 Assen, Provinciaal Museum van Drenthe

Assisi, Bib. Com.
 Assisi, Biblioteca Comunale

Assisi, Mus. & Pin. Com.
 Assisi, Museo e Pinacoteca Comunale

Assisi, S Rufino, Mus. Capitolare
 Assisi, San Rufino, Museo Capitolare

Assisi, Tesoro Mus. Basilica S Francesco
 Assisi, Tesoro del Museo della Basilica di San
 Francesco

Asti, Pin. Civ.
 Asti, Pinacoteca Civica

Astorga, Cathedral Treasury

Asuka, Hist. Mus.
 Asuka, Asuka Historical Museum [Kokuritsa
 Asuka Rekishi Shiryōkan]

Asunción, Mus. Parag. A. Contemp.
 Asunción, Paraguay, Museo Paraguayo de Arte
 Contemporáneo

Asunción, Paraguay, Mis. Cult. Bras.
 Asunción, Paraguay, Misión Cultural Brasilera

Asunción, Paraguay, Mus. A. Indíg.
 Asunción, Paraguay, Museo de Arte Indígena

Asunción, Paraguay, Mus. A. Mod.
 Asunción, Paraguay, Museo de Arte Moderno

Asunción, Paraguay, Mus. Barro
 Asunción, Paraguay, Museo del Barro

Asunción, Paraguay, Mus. Cer. & B.A. 'Julián de la
Herrería'
 Asunción, Paraguay, Museo de Cerámica y
 Bellas Artes 'Julián de la Herrería'

Asunción, Paraguay, Mus. Etnog.
 Asunción, Paraguay, Museo Etnográfico
 'Andrés Barbero'

Asunción, Paraguay, Mus. 'Monseñor Sinforiano
Bogarín'
 Asunción, Paraguay, Museo 'Monseñor Juan
 Sinforiano Bogarín'

Asunción, Paraguay, Mus. N. B.A.
 Asunción, Paraguay, Museo Nacional de Bellas
 Artes

Asunción, Paraguay, Mus. Tesoro Catedral
 Asunción, Paraguay, Museo del Tesoro de la
 Catedral

Aswan Mus.
 Aswan, Aswan Museum

Atami, MOA Mus. A.
 Atami, MOA Museum of Art (MOA
 Bijutsukan) [Kyūsei Atami A. Mus.]

Ath, Mus. Athois
 Ath, Musée Athois

Athens, Acropolis Mus.
 Athens, Acropolis Museum

Athens, Agora Mus.
 Athens, Agora Museum

Athens, Amer. Sch. Class. Stud., Gennadius Lib.
 Athens, American School of Classical Studies,
 Gennadius Library

Athens, Benaki Mus.
 Athens, Benaki Museum

Athens, Brit. Sch. Archaeol.
 Athens, British School of Archaeology

Athens, Byz. Mus.
 Athens, Byzantine Museum

Athens, Cult. Cent.
 Athens, Cultural Centre of the City of Athens

Athens, Epig. Mus.
 Athens, Epigraphical Museum of Athens

Athens, Fethiye Mosque

Athens, Gal. Ora
 Athens, Gallery Ora

Athens, Gal. Romvos
 Athens, Gallery Romvos

Athens, Gal. Strategopoulos
 Athens, Galerie Strategopoulos

Athens, Gounaropoulos Mus.
 Athens, Gounaropoulos Museum

Athens, Hadjidimou Col.
 Athens, Hadjidimou Collection

Athens, Higher Sch. F.A.
 Athens, Higher School of Fine Arts

Athens, Inst. Fr.
 Athens, Institut Français d'Athènes

Athens, It. Sch. Archaeol.
 Athens, Italian School of Archaeology

Athens, Jew. Mus.
 Athens, Jewish Museum

Athens, Kanellopoulos Mus.
 Athens, Kanellopoulos Museum

Athens, Kerameikos Mus.
 Athens, Kerameikos Museum

Athens, Kyrou Col.
 Athens, Kyrou Collection

Athens, Leventis Col.
 Athens, Leventis Collection

Athens, Merlier Cent.
  Athens, Merlier Centre

Athens, Mus. City
  Athens, Museum of the City of Athens [in King Otho's Palace]

Athens, Mus. Cyclad. & Anc. Gr. A.
  Athens, Museum of Cycladic and Ancient Greek Art [Goulandris Museum]

Athens, Mus. Gr. Flk A.
  Athens, Museum of Greek Folk Art [Greek Popular Art Museum]

Athens, Mus. U.
  Athens, Museum of the University

Athens, N. Archaeol. Mus.
  Athens, National Archaeological Museum

Athens, N. Bank of Greece
  Athens, National Bank of Greece

Athens, N.G.
  Athens, National Gallery [and Alexander Soutzos Museum]

Athens, N. Hist. Mus.
  Athens, National Historical Museum

Athens, N. Lib.
  Athens, National Library

Athens, N. Tech. U. Athens
  Athens, National Technical University of Athens

Athens, Numi. Mus.
  Athens, Athens Numismatic Museum

Athens, Parnassos Gal.
  Athens, Parnassos Gallery

Athens, Royal Pal.
  Athens, Royal Palace

Athens, Shelter A.
  Athens, Shelter of Art

Athens, Tsarouhis Mus.
  Athens, Tsarouhis Museum

Athens, U. Athens
  Athens, University of Athens

Athens, Vlasto Col.
  Athens, Michael Vlasto Collection

Athens, Zappeion [National Exhibition Hall]

Athens, Zygos Gal.
  Athens, Zygos Gallery

Athens, U. GA Mus. A.
  Athens, GA, University of Georgia Museum of Art

Atlanta, GA, Apex Mus. Afr.-Amer. Experience
  Atlanta, GA, Apex Museum of Afro-American Experience

Atlanta, GA, Emory U. Mus. A. & Archaeol.
  Atlanta, GA, Emory University Museum of Art and Archaeology [Carlos Hall]

Atlanta, GA, High Mus. A.
  Atlanta, GA, High Museum of Art

Atlanta, GA, Hist. Soc. Mus.
  Atlanta, GA, Atlanta Historical Society Museum

Atlanta, GA, Spelman Coll.
  Atlanta, GA, Spelman College

Attigny, Hôtel de Ville

Auburn, AL, U. Col.
  Auburn, AL, Auburn University, University Collection

Aubusson, Mus. Dépt. Tap.
  Aubusson, Musée Départemental de la Tapisserie [Centre Culturel et Artistique Jean-Lurçat]

Auckland, Aotea Cent.
  Auckland, Aotea Centre

Auckland, Aspace
  Auckland, Artspace

Auckland, C.A.G.
  Auckland, City Art Gallery

Auckland, Elam Sch. F.A. Lib.
  Auckland, Elam School of Fine Arts Library

Auckland, Icon Gal.
  Auckland, Icon Gallery

Auckland, Inst. & Mus.
  Auckland, Institute and Museum [also known as War Mem. Mus.]

Auckland, Outreach Gal.
  Auckland, Outreach Gallery

Auckland, U. Auckland
  Auckland, University of Auckland

Auckland, War Mem.
  Auckland, War Memorial [houses Inst. & Mus.]

Augsburg, Bischöf. Ordinariat
  Augsburg, Bischöfliches Ordinariat

Augsburg, Fuggerei-Mus.
  Augsburg, Fuggerei-Museum

Augsburg, Holbeinhaus [destr. World War II, rebuilt 1965]

Augsburg, Maximilianmus.
  Augsburg, Maximilianmuseum

Augsburg, Rathaus

Augsburg, Röm. Mus.
  Augsburg, Römisches Museum [in Dominikanerkirche]

Augsburg, Schaezlerpal.
  Augsburg, Schaezlerpalais [houses Deutsche Barockgalerie im Schaezlerpalais; Graphische Sammlung im Schaezlerpalais; Staatsgalerie Altdeutscher Kunst Augsburg]

Augsburg, Staats- & Stadtbib.
  Augsburg, Staats- und Stadtbibliothek

Augsburg, Stadtarchv
  Augsburg, Stadtarchiv

Augsburg, Städt. Kstsammlungen
  Augsburg, Städtische Kunstsammlungen [admins Maximilianmus.; Röm. Mus.; Schaezlerpal.]

Augsburg, U. Augsburg
  Augsburg, Universität Augsburg

Augsburg, Ubib.
  Augsburg, Universitätsbibliothek [incl. Zentralbibliothek and Teilbibliotheken]

Augsburg, Zeughaus

Augst, Römermus.
  Augst, Römermuseum

Aurillac, Mus. Parieu
  Aurillac, Musée Hippolyte de Parieu [Musée des Beaux-Arts]

Austin, TX, Laguna Gloria A. Mus.
  Austin, TX, Laguna Gloria Art Museum [Texas Fine Art Association]

Austin, U. TX, A. Mus.
  Austin, TX, University of Texas at Austin, University Art Museum [name changed to Huntington A.G. in 1980]

Austin, U. TX, Human. Res. Cent., Gernsheim Col.
  Austin, TX, University of Texas at Austin, Humanities Research Center, Gernsheim Collection

Austin, U. TX, Huntington A.G.
  Austin, TX, University of Texas at Austin, Archer Museum Huntington Art Gallery [until 1980 called U. TX, A. Mus.]

Austin, U. TX, Ransom Human. Res. Cent.
  Austin, TX, University of Texas at Austin, Harry Hunt Ransom Humanities Research Center

Austin, U. TX System Libs
  Austin, TX, University of Texas System Libraries

Autun, Bib. Mun.
  Autun, Bibliothèque Municipale

Autun, Mus. Rolin
  Autun, Musée Rolin

Auxerre, Mus. A. & Hist.
  Auxerre, Musée d'Art et d'Histoire

Aveiro, Mus. Reg.
  Aveiro, Museu Regional [formerly Convento de Jesus]

Aveiro, Pal. Justiça
  Aveiro, Palácio de Justiça

Avellino, Mus. Irpino
  Avellino, Museo Irpino

Avenches, Mus. Romain
  Avenches, Musée Romain

Avesnes-sur-Helpe, Mus. Soc. Archéol.
  Avesnes-sur-Helpe, Musée de la Société Archéologique de l'Arrondissement d'Avesnes

Avignon, Bib. Mun.
  Avignon, Bibliothèque Municipale

Avignon, Livrée Ceccano [houses Médiathèque d'Avignon]

Avignon, Médiathèque

Avignon, Mus. Calvet
  Avignon, Musée Calvet

Avignon, Mus. Lapidaire
  Avignon, Musée Lapidaire [annexe of Musée Calvet]

Avignon, Mus. Petit Pal.
  Avignon, Musée du Petit Palais

Avignon, Pal. Papes & Mus.
  Avignon, Palais des Papes et Musée du Vieil Avignon

Avignon, Pal. Roure
  Avignon, Palais du Roure

Ávila, Mus. Catedral
  Ávila, Museo de la Catedral

Avranches, Jard. Plantes
  Avranches, Jardin des Plantes

Avranches, Musée
  Avranches, Musée de l'Avranchin [in Hôtel de Ville]

Ayacucho, Peru, Mus. Arqueol.
  Ayacucho, Peru, Museo Arqueológico

Ayacucho, Peru, Mus. Hist. Reg.
  Ayacucho, Peru, Museo Histórico Regional de Ayacucho

Ayios Nikolaos, Archaeol. Mus.
  Ayios Nikolaos, Archaeological Museum

Aylesbury, Bucks Co. Mus.
  Aylesbury, Buckinghamshire County Museum

Ayutthaya, Chantharakhasem N. Mus.
  Ayutthaya, Chantharakhasem National Museum (Phipitapan Laeng Chart Chantharakasem)

Ayutthaya, Chao Sam Phraya N. Mus.
  Ayutthaya, Chao Sam Phraya National Museum

Ayyelet Hashahar, Hazor Mus.
    Ayyelet Hashahar, Hazor Museum [Museum of Antiquities, Kibbutz Ayyelet Hashahar]

Azay-le-Ferron, Château

Babenhausen, Fugger-Mus.
    Babenhausen, Fugger-Museum

Bacău, Mus. A.
    Bacău, Museum of Art (Muzeul de Artă Bacău)

Badajoz, Mus. Dioc.-Catedralicio
    Badajoz, Museo Diocesano-Catedralicio

Badami, Badami Mus.
    Badami, Badami Museum

Baden-Baden, Staatl. Ksthalle
    Baden-Baden, Staatliche Kunsthalle Baden-Baden

Baden-Baden, Zähringer Mus.
    Baden-Baden, Zähringer Museum [in Neues Schloss]

Badia di Cava dei Tirreni, Mus. Badia
    Badia di Cava dei Tirreni, Museo della Badia

Bad Pyrmont, Kuranlage

Bad Säckingen, Hochrheinmus.
    Bad Säckingen, Hochrheinmuseum [in Schloss Schönau]

Bad Vöslau, Schlosspark

Bad Windsheim, Fränk. Freilandmus.
    Bad Windsheim, Fränkisches Freilandmuseum

Baghdad, Iraq Mus.
    Baghdad, Iraq Museum

Baghdad Mus.
    Baghdad, Baghdad Museum

Baghdad, N. Mus. Mod. A.
    Baghdad, National Museum of Modern Art

Bagheria, Gal. Com. A. Mod. & Contemp.
    Bagheria, Galleria Comunale d'Arte Moderna e Contemporanea

Bagnères-de-Bigorre, Mus. A.
    Bagnères-de-Bigorre, Musée d'Art

Bagnères-de-Luchon, Jard. Pub.
    Bagnères-de-Luchon, Jardins Publics

Bagnols-sur-Cèze, Mus. Bagnols-sur-Cèze
    Bagnols-sur-Cèze, Musée de Bagnols-sur-Cèze [Fondation Léon Alègre]

Báia, Parco Archeol.
    Báia, Parco Archeologico [Scavi di Báia]

Baia Mare, Maramureş Distr. Mus.
    Baia Mare, Maramureş District Museum (Muzeul Judeţean Maramureş)

Baku, Azerbaijan Acad. Sci.
    Baku, Azerbaijan Academy of Sciences

Baku, Hist. & Archit. Mus.
    Baku, Historical and Architectural Museum

Baku, Hist. Mus. Acad. Sci. Azerbaijan
    Baku, Historical Museum of the Academy of Sciences of Azerbaijan

Baku, Mus. Azerbaij. Lit.
    Baku, Museum of Azerbaijani Literature [Nizami Mus. Azerbaij. Lit.]

Baku, Mus. Carpets & Applied A.
    Baku, Museum of Carpets and Applied Art [in Dzhuma Mosque]

Baku, Mus. F.A.
    Baku, Museum of Fine Art

Baku, Mus. Revolution
    Baku, Museum of the Revolution

Baku, Mustafayev Azerbaij. Mus. A.
    Baku, R. Mustafayev Azerbaijani Museum of Arts

Baku, Nizami Mus.
    Baku, Nizami Museum

Baku, Sharvanshah Pal. Mus.
    Baku, Sharvanshah Palace Museum

Ballarat, A.G.
    Ballarat, Art Gallery

Ballarat, F.A. Gal.
    Ballarat, Fine Art Gallery

Balsaín, Pal. Riofrío
    Balsaín, Palacio de Riofrío

Bålsta, Skoklosters Slott

Baltimore, MD, Courthouse

Baltimore, MD, Fed. Cent.
    Baltimore, MD, Federal Center

Baltimore, MD Hist. Soc. Mus.
    Baltimore, MD, Maryland Historical Society Museum

Baltimore, MD Inst., Coll. A.
    Baltimore, MD, Maryland Institute, College of Art

Baltimore, MD Inst., Decker Gal.
    Baltimore, MD, Maryland Institute, Decker Gallery of the College of Art

Baltimore, MD, Johns Hopkins U., Garrett Lib.
    Baltimore, MD, Johns Hopkins University, John Work Garrett Rare Book Library

Baltimore, MD, Mus. A.
    Baltimore, MD, Baltimore Museum of Art

Baltimore, MD, Peale Mus.
    Baltimore, MD, Peale Museum

Baltimore, MD, Pratt Free Lib.
    Baltimore, MD, Enoch Pratt Free Library

Baltimore, MD, Walters A.G.
    Baltimore, MD, Walters Art Gallery

Baltimore, U. MD, Mus. A.
    Baltimore, MD, University of Maryland, Museum of Art [in grounds of Johns Hopkins U.]

Bamako, Mus. N.
    Bamako, Musée National du Mali

Bamberg, Diözmus.
    Bamberg, Diözesanmuseum [in Domkapitelhaus]

Bamberg, Domschatzkam.
    Bamberg, Domschatzkammer

Bamberg, Gtnr- & Häckermus.
    Bamberg, Gärtner- und Häckermuseum

Bamberg, Hist. Mus.
    Bamberg, Historisches Museum [in Alte Hofhaltung]

Bamberg, Karl-May-Mus.
    Bamberg, Karl-May-Museum

Bamberg, Natkndmus.
    Bamberg, Naturkundemuseum [Lyceumsstiftung]

Bamberg, Neue Residenz, Staatsgal.
    Bamberg, Staatsgalerie in der Neuen Residenz

Bamberg, Staatsarchv
    Bamberg, Staatsarchiv

Bamberg, Staatsbib.
    Bamberg, Staatsbibliothek

Bandar Seri Begawan, Brunei Mus.
    Bandar Seri Begawan, Brunei Museum

Banes, Mus. Indios Cubanos
    Banes, Museo de los Indios Cubanos

Bangalore, Karnataka Govt Mus. & Venkatappa A.G.
    Bangalore, Karnataka Government Museum and Venkatappa Art Gallery

Bangkok, Bhirasri Inst. Mod. A.
    Bangkok, Bhirasri Institute of Modern Art

Bangkok, Hill Tribes Mus.
    Bangkok, Hill Tribes Museum

Bangkok, Jim Thompson House

Bangkok, Kamthieng House Mus., Siam Soc.
    Bangkok, Kamthieng House Museum, Siam Society

Bangkok, N. Lib.
    Bangkok, National Library

Bangkok, N. Mus.
    Bangkok, National Museum

Bangkok, N. Mus. Div.
    Bangkok, National Museums Division

Bangkok, Suan Pakkad Pal. Mus.
    Bangkok, Suan Pakkad Palace Museum

Bangor, Mus. Welsh Ant.
    Bangor, Museum of Welsh Antiquities

Bangor, N. Down Her. Cent.
    Bangor, Co. Down, North Down Heritage Centre

Bankipur, Patna, Khuda Bakhsh Lib.
    Bankipur, Patna, Khuda Bakhsh Oriental Public Library

Banská Bystrica, Mus. Cent. Slovakia
    Banská Bystrica, Museum of Central Slovakia (Stredoslovenské Muzeum)

Banská Bystrica, Reg. A.G.
    Banská Bystrica, Regional Art Gallery (Oblastná Galéria)

Baoding, Hebei Prov. Mus.
    Baoding, Hebei Provincial Museum

Baoji, Mun. Mus.
    Baoji, Municipal Museum

Bar, Local Mus.
    Bar, Local Museum (Zavičajni Muzej)

Barbizon, Salle Fêtes
    Barbizon, Salle des Fêtes

Barcelona, Ajuntament

Barcelona, Archv Corona Aragón
    Barcelona, Archivo de la Corona de Aragón

Barcelona, Archv Histórico Protocolos
    Barcelona, Archivo Histórico de Protocolos de Barcelona

Barcelona, Arxiu Capitular S Església Catedral
    Barcelona, Arxiu Capitular de la Santa Església Catedral de Barcelona

Barcelona, Arxiu Corona Aragó
    Barcelona, Arxiu de la Corona de Aragó [Archivo de la Corona de Aragón]

Barcelona, Arxiu Mun.
    Barcelona, Arxiu Municipal [Archivo Municipal]

Barcelona, Arxiu Pal.-Requesens
    Barcelona, Arxiu del Palau-Requesens

Barcelona, Asilo de S Juan de Dios

Barcelona Bib. Catalunya
    Barcelona, Biblioteca de Catalunya

Barcelona, Bonova Col.
    Barcelona, Bonova Collection

Barcelona, Casa Caritat
    Barcelona, Casa de la Caritat

Barcelona, Casa-Mus. Gaudí
    Barcelona, Casa-Museu Gaudí

Barcelona, Cent. A. S Monica
    Barcelona, Centre d'Arte Santa Monica

Barcelona, Cent. Cult. Caixa Pensions
    Barcelona, Centre Cultural de la Caixa de Pensions [name changed to Cent. Cult. Fund. Caixa Pensions in 1986]

Barcelona, Cent. Cult. Contemp.
  Barcelona, Centro de Cultura Contemporánea de Barcelona

Barcelona, Cent. Cult. Fund. Caixa Pensions
  Barcelona, Centre Cultural de la Fundació Caixa de Pensions

Barcelona, Cent. Cult. Pal. Virreina
  Barcelona, Centre Cultural del Palau de la Virreina

Barcelona, Cent. Miró
  Barcelona, Centro Miró

Barcelona, Cerc. A. S Lluc
  Barcelona, Cercle Artistic de Sant Lluc [Círculo Artistico de Sant Lluc]

Barcelona, Col. Cambó
  Barcelona, Colección Cambó [col. donated to city of Barcelona: now housed in Pal. Pedralbes awaiting transfer to Mus. A. Catalunya]

Barcelona, Dau al Set

Barcelona, Escola Galí

Barcelona, Escola Sup. B. Oficis
  Barcelona, Escola Superior de Bells Oficis

Barcelona, Escuela A. & Oficios La Luoja
  Barcelona, Escuela de Artes y Oficios La Luoja [no longer exists]

Barcelona, Escuela Gratuita Diseño
  Barcelona, Escuela Gratuita del Diseño

Barcelona, Escuela Nob. A.
  Barcelona, Escuela de Nobles Artes [now Escuela Gratuita del Diseño]

Barcelona, Fund. Miró
  Barcelona, Fundació Joan Miró

Barcelona, Gal. Dalmau
  Barcelona, Galería Dalmau

Barcelona, Gal. Maeght
  Barcelona, Galería Maeght

Barcelona, Gals Laietanes
  Barcelona, Galeries Laietanes [Galerías Layetanas]

Barcelona, Generalitat Catalunya
  Barcelona, Generalitat de Catalunya

Barcelona, Inst. Amatller A. Hisp.
  Barcelona, Instituto Amatller de Arte Hispánico

Barcelona, Inst. Mun. Hist.
  Barcelona, Institut Municipal d'Història

Barcelona, Junta Museus
  Barcelona, Junta de Museus

Barcelona, Lonja [Lonja de Comercio; Casa de la Llotja]

Barcelona, Monestir de Pedralbes, Mus. A. Dec.
  Barcelona, Monestir de Pedralbes, Museu d'Arts Decoratives

Barcelona, Mus. A. Catalunya
  Barcelona, Museu d'Art de Catalunya

Barcelona, Mus. A. Dec.
  Barcelona, Museu d'Arts Decoratives [in Palau de Pedralbes]

Barcelona, Mus. A. Mod.
  Barcelona, Museu d'Art Modern

Barcelona, Mus. Arqueol.
  Barcelona, Museu Arqueològic [e Instituto de Prehistòria y Arqueològia de la Diputación]

Barcelona, Mus. B.A. Cataluña
  Barcelona, Museo de Bellas Artes de Cataluña [now Mus. A. Catalunya]

Barcelona, Mus. Balaguer de Villanueva & Geltrú
  Barcelona, Museu Balaguer de Villanueva y Geltrú

Barcelona, Mus. Catedral
  Barcelona, Museu de la Catedral [Museo Catedralicio]

Barcelona, Mus. Cer.
  Barcelona, Museu de Ceràmica

Barcelona, Mus. Dioc.
  Barcelona, Museu Diocesa [in Seminario Diocesano]

Barcelona, Mus. Etnol.
  Barcelona, Museu Etnològic

Barcelona, Mus. Hist. Ciutat
  Barcelona, Museu d'Història de la Ciutat

Barcelona, Mus. Marés
  Barcelona, Museu Frederic Marés

Barcelona, Mus. Mun. B.A.
  Barcelona, Museu Municipal de les Belles Artes [now closed]

Barcelona, Mus. Picasso
  Barcelona, Museu Picasso

Barcelona, Mus. Postal & Numi.
  Barcelona, Museu Postal i de Numismàtica [in Pal. Virreina]

Barcelona, Mus. Punia
  Barcelona, Museu de Punia [Museo de Encaje]

Barcelona, Mus. Tèxtil & Indument.
  Barcelona, Museu Tèxtil i d'Indumentària [in Palau del Marquès de Lió i Palau Nadal Montcada]

Barcelona, Observatori Fabra

Barcelona, Pal. B.A.
  Barcelona, Palau de Belles Artes

Barcelona, Pal. Generalitat
  Barcelona, Palau de la Generalitat

Barcelona, Pal. Pedralbes
  Barcelona, Palacio de Pedralbes [houses Col. Cambó]

Barcelona, Pal. Puig
  Barcelona, Palau Puig

Barcelona, Pal. Real Maj.
  Barcelona, Palau Real Major

Barcelona, Pal. Virreina
  Barcelona, Palau de la Virreina [admins Col. Cambó; Mus. A. Dec.; Barcelona, Mus. Postal & Numi.]

Barcelona, Real Acad. Cat. B.A. S Jorge
  Barcelona, Real Academia Catalana de Bellas Artes de San Jorge

Barcelona, Real Colegio Cirugía
  Barcelona, Real Colegio de Cirugía

Barcelona, Sala Cult.
  Barcelona, Sala Cultural

Barcelona, Sala Gaspar

Barcelona, Sala Parés

Barcelona, U. Autònoma
  Barcelona, Universitat Autònoma de Barcelona

Barcelona, U. Barcelona
  Barcelona, Universitat de Barcelona

Bard, Forte Bard
  Bard, Forte di Bard

Bardejov, City Archvs
  Bardejov, City Archives [Bártfa]

Bardejov, Šariš Mus.
  Bardejov, Šariš Museum (Šarišské Muzeum) [in Town Hall]

Barentin, Mus. Mun.
  Barentin, Musée Municipal

Bari, Castello Svevo

Bari, Cathedral Archvs
  Bari, Cathedral Archives

Bari, Gip. Castello
  Bari, Gipsoteca del Castello [in Castello Svevo]

Bari, Mus. Dioc.
  Bari, Museo Diocesano

Bari, Mus. S Nicola
  Bari, Museo di San Nicola

Bari, Pin. Prov.
  Bari, Pinacoteca Provinciale

Barlaston, Wedgwood Mus.
  Barlaston, Wedgwood Museum

Barletta, Mus.-Pin. Com.
  Barletta, Museo-Pinacoteca Comunale [Museo Civico e Pinacoteca di Nittis]

Barletta, Pal. Monte di Pietà
  Barletta, Palazzo del Monte di Pietà

Barnard Castle, Bowes Mus.
  Barnard Castle, Bowes Museum

Barnstaple, N. Devon Athenaeum
  Barnstaple, North Devon Athenaeum

Barnstaple, St Anne's Chapel Mus.
  Barnstaple, St Anne's Chapel Museum

Baroda: see Vadodara

Basingstoke, Willis Mus. & A.G.
  Basingstoke, Willis Museum and Art Gallery

Basle, Antikenmus.
  Basle, Antikenmuseum Basel und Sammlung Ludwig

Basle, Barfüsserkirche [houses Hist. Mus.]

Basle, Bib. Öffentlichen Kstsamml.
  Basle, Bibliothek der Öffentlichen Kunstsammlung

Basle, Claraspital

Basle, Gal. A. Mod. Marie-Suzanne Feigel
  Basle, Galerie d'Art Moderne Marie-Suzanne Feigel

Basle, Gal. Beyeler
  Basle, Galerie Beyeler

Basle, Gal. Buchmann
  Basle, Galerie Buchmann

Basle, Gal. Littmann
  Basle, Galerie Littmann

Basle, Gal. Zum Specht
  Basle, Galerie Zum Specht

Basle, Gewmus.
  Basle, Gewerbemuseum [now Mus. Gestalt.]

Basle, Haus Kirschgtn
  Basle, Haus zum Kirschgarten

Basle, Hist. Mus.
  Basle, Historisches Museum

Basle, Klaus Littmann

Basle, Ksthalle
  Basle, Kunsthalle Basel

Basle, Kstmus.
  Basle, Kunstmuseum [incl. Kupferstichkabinett]

Basle, Kutschen- & Schlittensamml.
  Basle, Kutschen- und Schlittensammlung

Basle, Mus. Gegenwartskst
  Basle, Museum für Gegenwartskunst

Basle, Mus. Gestalt.
  Basle, Museum für Gestaltung Basel [formerly Gewmus.]

Basle, Mus. Vlkerknd.
  Basle, Museum für Völkerkunde und Schweizerisches Museum für Volkskunde

Basle, Nathist. Mus.
  Basle, Naturhistorisches Museum

Basle, Öff. Bib. U.
Basle, Öffentliche Bibliothek der Universität

Basle, Öff. Kstsamml.
Basle, Öffentliche Kunstsammlung [admins Kstmus.; Mus. Gegenwartskst]

Basle, Samml. Alter Musikinstr.
Basle, Sammlung Alter Musikinstrumente

Basle, Schweiz. Mustermesse
Basle, Schweizerische Mustermesse

Basle, Schweiz. N.-Versicherung Ges. Kol.
Basle, Schweizerische National-Versicherung Gesellschaft Kollektion

Basle, Staechlin Found.
Basle, Rodolphe Staechlin Foundation

Basle, Tribal A. Cent.
Basle, Tribal Art Centre

Basle, U. Basle
Basle, Universität Basel

Basle, Ubib.
Basle, Universitätsbibliothek Basel

Basle, Zool. Gtn
Basle, Zoologischer Garten

Bassano, Villa Rezzonico

Bassano del Grappa, Bib. Civ.
Bassano del Grappa, Biblioteca Civica

Bassano del Grappa, Mus. Civ.
Bassano del Grappa, Museo Civico

Bassano Romano, Pal. Odescalchi
Bassano Romano, Palazzo Odescalchi

Bath, Amer. Mus. Britain
Bath, American Museum in Britain [in Claverton Manor]

Bath, Artside

Bath, Brit. Flk A. Col.
Bath, British Folk Art Collection [now Mus. Eng. Naive A.]

Bath, Guildhall

Bath, Holburne Mus. & Crafts Stud. Cent.
Bath, Holburne Museum and Crafts Study Centre

Bath, Mason. Hall
Bath, Masonic Hall

Bath, Mus. E. Asian A.
Bath, Museum of East Asian Art

Bath, Mus. Eng. Naive A.
Bath, Museum of English Naive Art [formerly Brit. Flk A. Col.; houses Crane Kalman col.]

Bath, N. Cent. Phot.
Bath, National Centre of Photography [now Royal Phot. Soc.]

Bath, Roman Baths Mus.
Bath, Roman Baths Museum

Bath, Royal N. Hosp. Rheumatic Diseases
Bath, Royal National Hospital for Rheumatic Diseases

Bath, Royal Phot. Soc.
Bath, Royal Photographic Society of Great Britain [formerly N. Cent. Phot., 1979–c. 1990]

Bath, U. Bath, Holburne of Menstrie Mus.
Bath, University of Bath, Holburne of Menstrie Museum

Bath, Victoria A.G.
Bath, Victoria Art Gallery

Baton Rouge, LA State Mus.
Baton Rouge, LA, Louisiana State Museum

Baton Rouge, LA State U.
Baton Rouge, LA, Louisiana State University

Battambang, Mus. Povéal
Battambang, Musée Povéal

Bauschlott, Schloss

Bautzen, Stadtmus.
Bautzen, Stadtmuseum

Bayeux, Bib. Chapitre
Bayeux, Bibliothèque du Chapitre de la Cathédrale

Bayeux, Mus. Gérard
Bayeux, Musée Baron Gérard

Bayeux, Mus. Tap.
Bayeux, Musée de la Tapisserie de la Reine Mathilde

Bayonne, Mus. Bonnat
Bayonne, Musée Bonnat

Bayreuth, Neues Schloss

Bayreuth, Richard-Wagner-Mus.
Bayreuth, Richard-Wagner-Museum mit Nationalarchiv der Richard-Wagner-Stiftung

Bayreuth, Staatsgal. Neuen Schloss
Bayreuth, Staatsgalerie im Neuen Schloss

Bayreuth U., Iwalewa-Haus
Bayreuth, University of Bayreuth, Iwalewa-Haus

Beamish, N. England Open Air Mus.
Beamish, North of England Open Air Museum

Beaune, Mus. Hôtel-Dieu
Beaune, Musée de l'Hôtel-Dieu

Beaune, Mus. Marey
Beaune, Musée Marey et des Beaux-Arts, Hôtel de Ville

Beauvais, Mus. Dépt. Oise
Beauvais, Musée Départemental de l'Oise

Bebek, Kile A.G.
Bebek, Kile Art Gallery

Bedford, Cecil Higgins A.G.
Bedford, The Cecil Higgins Art Gallery

Bedford, Mus.
Bedford, Bedford Museum

Bedford, Rec. Office
Bedford, Bedfordshire Record Office

Bedford Park, Flinders U. S. Australia
Bedford Park, Flinders University of South Australia

Beijing, Capital Mus.
Beijing, Capital Museum

Beijing, Cent. Acad. A. & Des.
Beijing, Central Academy of Art and Design

Beijing, Cent. Inst. F.A.
Beijing, Central Institute of Fine Art

Beijing, Chin. Acad. Soc. Sci.
Beijing, Chinese Academy of Social Sciences

Beijing, Chin. Acad. Soc. Sci., Archaeol. Inst.
Beijing, Chinese Academy of Social Sciences, Archaeology Institute

Beijing, Chin. Acad. Soc. Sci., Taiwan Cult. Inst.
Beijing, Chinese Academy of Social Sciences, Taiwan Culture Institute

Beijing, Dazhong Si Mus.
Beijing, Dazhong si Museum [Great Bell Temple]

Beijing, Hist. Mus.
Beijing, Historical Museum

Beijing, N. Lib.
Beijing, National Library

Beijing, Pal. Mus.
Beijing, Palace Museum

Beijing U. Lib.
Beijing, Beijing University Library

Beira, Mus. Mun.
Beira, Museu Municipal

Beirut, Amer. U. Mus.
Beirut, American University, Museum

Beirut, Henri Pharoan Mus.
Beirut, Henri Pharoan Museum

Beirut, Mus. N.
Beirut, Musée National [Musée Archéologique]

Beirut, Nicolas Ibrahim Sursock Mus.
Beirut, Nicolas Ibrahim Sursock Museum

Beja, Mus. Reg.
Beja, Museu Regional [Museu da Rhaina Doña Leonor]

Béjar, Mus. Mun.
Béjar, Museo Municipal

Békéscsaba, Mihály Munkácsy Mus.
Békéscsaba, Mihály Munkácsy Museum

Belém, Brazil, Mus. Paraense Goeldi
Belém, Brazil, Museu Paraense Emílio Goeldi

Belém, Brazil, Pal. Gov. Estado Pará
Belém, Brazil, Palácio de Governo do Estado do Pará

Belfast, A.C. N. Ireland
Belfast, Arts Council of Northern Ireland

Belfast, Bell Gal.
Belfast, Bell Gallery

Belfast, Old Mus.
Belfast, Old Museum

Belfast, Tom Caldwell Gal.
Belfast, Tom Caldwell Gallery

Belfast, Ulster Mus.
Belfast, Ulster Museum

Belgrade, A. Pav.
Belgrade, Art Pavilion

Belgrade, Cult. Cent. Gal.
Belgrade, Cultural Centre Gallery

Belgrade, Ethnog. Mus.
Belgrade, Ethnographical Museum (Etnografski Muzej)

Belgrade, Floegel A. Col.
Belgrade, Floegel Art Collection (Umetnička Zbirka Flogel)

Belgrade, Fresco Gal.
Belgrade, Fresco Gallery (Galerija Freska)

Belgrade, Gal. Doma Omladine
Belgrade, Gallery Doma Omladine

Belgrade, Gal. Serb. Acad. Sci. & A.
Belgrade, Gallery of the Serbian Academy of Sciences and Arts [SANU] (Galerija Srpske Akademije Nauka i Umetnosti)

Belgrade, Lib. Serb. Acad. Sci. & A.
Belgrade, Library of the Serbian Academy of Sciences and Arts (Biblioteka Srpske Akademije Nauka i Umetnosti)

Belgrade, Mus. Applied A.
Belgrade, Museum of Applied Art (Muzej Primenjene Umetnosti)

Belgrade, Mus. City
Belgrade, Museum of the City of Belgrade (Muzej Grada Beograd)

Belgrade, Mus. Contemp. A.
Belgrade, Museum of Contemporary Art (Muzej Savremene Umetnosti)

Belgrade, Mus. Serb. Orthdx Ch.
Belgrade, Museum of the Serbian Orthodox Church (Muzej Srpske Pravoslavne Crkve)

Belgrade, Mus. Yug. Cinema
Belgrade, Museum of the Yugoslav Cinema

Belgrade, N. Lib.
Belgrade, National Library (Biblioteka Matice Srpske)

Belgrade, N. Mus.
Belgrade, National Museum (Narodni Muzej)

Belgrade, Parl. Bldg
Belgrade, Parliament Building

Belgrade, Serb. Acad. Sci. & A.
Belgrade, Serbian Academy of Sciences and
Arts (Srpska Akademija Nauka i Umetnosti)

Belgrade, U. Belgrade, Archaeol. Col.
Belgrade, University of Belgrade,
Archaeological Collection (Univerzitet u
Beogradu)

Belgrade, Vuk and Dositej Mus.
Belgrade, Vuk and Dositej Museum (Vukov i
Dositejev Muzej)

Belize City, Admiral Bumaby's A.G.
Belize City, Admiral Bumaby's Art Gallery

Belize City, Angelus Press
Belize City, The Angelus Press

Belize City, Belize A.G.
Belize City, Belize Art Gallery

Belize City, Bliss Inst.
Belize City, Baron Bliss Institute [houses the
Central Library of the National Library Service
and the offices of the National Arts Council]

Belize City, Bliss N.G.
Belize City, Bliss National Gallery

Belize City, Rachel's Gal.
Belize City, Rachel's Gallery

Belize City, St John's Coll. Gabbay A.G.
Belize City, St John's College Gabbay Art
Gallery

Bellagio, Villa Melzi-d'Eril

Belleville-sur-Bar, Sanatorium

Bellinzona, Archv Cant.
Bellinzona, Archivio Cantonale

Bellinzona, Archvs
Bellinzona, Archives

Belluno, Mus. Civ.
Belluno, Museo Civico

Belluno, Pal. Crepadona
Belluno, Palazzo Crepadona [houses cultural
centre]

Belo Horizonte, Mus. A. & Hist. Racioppi
Belo Horizonte, Museu de Arte e História
Racioppi

Belo Horizonte, Mus. A. Mod.
Belo Horizonte, Museu de Arte Moderna

Bendigo, A.G.
Bendigo, Art Gallery

Benevento, Bib. Capitolare
Benevento, Biblioteca Capitolare

Benevento, Mus. Sannio
Benevento, Museo del Sannio

Benin City, N. Mus.
Benin City, National Museum Benin

Bennington, VT, Mus.
Bennington, VT, Bennington Museum

Benque Viejo Del Carmen, El Balum A.G.
Benque Viejo Del Carmen, El Balum Art
Gallery

Berchtesgaden, Schlossmus.
Berchtesgaden, Schlossmuseum [Verwaltung
Wittelsbacher Ausgleichfonds Munich]

Berdyansk, A. Mus.
Berdyansk, Art Museum (Khudozhestvennyy
Muzey)

Berea Coll., KY
Berea, KY, Berea College

Bergama, Pergamon Mus.
Bergama, Pergamon Museum

Bergamo, Accad. Carrara B.A.
Bergamo, Accademia Carrara di Belle Arti

Bergamo, Bib. Civ. A. Mai
Bergamo, Biblioteca Civica A. Mai

Bergamo, Casa Riposo
Bergamo, Casa di Riposo

Bergamo, Com.
Bergamo, Comune

Bergamo, Gal. Accad. Carrara
Bergamo, Galleria dell'Accademia Carrara
[Pinacoteca]

Bergamo, Gal. Immagine
Bergamo, Galleria dell'Immagine

Bergamo, Gal. Lorenzelli
Bergamo, Galleria Lorenzelli

Bergamo, Ist. Colleoni
Bergamo, Istituto Colleoni

Bergamo, Pal. Com.
Bergamo, Palazzo Comunale

Bergamo, Pal. Moroni
Bergamo, Palazzo Moroni

Bergamo, Pal. Ragione
Bergamo, Palazzo della Ragione

Bergara, Semin.
Bergara, Seminario

Bergen, Billedgal.
Bergen, Billedgalleri

Bergen, Fjøsangersaml.
Bergen, Fjøsangersamlingene

Bergen, Gamle
Bergen, Gamle Bergen

Bergen, Komm.
Bergen, Kommune

Bergen, Laksevåg Vocational Sch.
Bergen, Laksevåg Vocational School

Bergen, Meyers Saml.
Bergen, Rasmus Meyers Samlinger

Bergen, Reksten Found.
Bergen, Hilmar Reksten Foundation [closed]

Bergen, Stift. Stenersens Saml.
Bergen, Stiftelsen Stenersens Samling

Bergen, Theat. Park
Bergen, Theater Park

Bergen, U. Bergen, Hist. Mus.
Bergen, Universitetet i Bergen, Historisk
Museum

Bergen, Vestlandske Kstindustmus.
Bergen, Vestlandske Kunstindustrimuseum

Berg en Dal, Afrika Mus.
Berg en Dal, Afrika Museum

Bergen-op-Zoom, Gemeentemus.
Bergen-op-Zoom, Gemeentemuseum

Bergen-op-Zoom, Het Markiezenhof

Bergues, Mus. B.-A.
Bergues, Musées des Beaux-Arts

Bergues, Mus. Mun. Mont-de-Piété
Bergues, Musée Municipal du Mont-de-Piété

Berkeley, CA, Imogen Cunningham Trust

Berkeley, CA, Keigensai Col.
Berkeley, CA, Keigensai Collection

Berkeley, U. CA, A. Mus.
Berkeley, CA, University of California,
University Art Museum

Berkeley, U. CA, Bancroft Lib.
Berkeley, CA, University of California,
Bancroft Library

Berkeley, U. CA, Hearst Mus. Anthropol.
Berkeley, CA, University of California, Phoebe
A. Hearst Museum of Anthropology [name
changed from U. CA, Lowie Mus. Anthropol.,
in 1992]

Berkeley, U. CA, Lowie Mus. Anthropol.
Berkeley, CA, University of California, Robert
H. Lowie Museum of Anthropology [now U.
CA, Hearst Mus. Anthropol.]

Berlin: the city was divided into East Berlin and
West Berlin in 1945 and reunified in Oct 1990; *see
also* East Berlin and West Berlin.

Berlin, Ägyp. Mus.
Berlin, Ägyptisches Museum [at
Charlottenburg]

Berlin, Akad. Kst.
Berlin, Akademie der Künste [formed by
unification of former Preussische Akademie
der Künste & Deutsche Akademie der Künste
der DDR]

Berlin, Alte N.G.
Berlin, Alte Nationalgalerie

Berlin, Altes Mus.
Berlin, Altes Museum [formerly Museum am
Lustgarten; houses Kupferstichkabinett;
Sammlung Zeichnungen und Druckgraphik;
Wechselausstellungen]

Berlin, Altes Pal.
Berlin, Altes Palais [until 1945 called Palais
Kaiser Wilhelms I]

Berlin, Amt Stadtbildpf.
Berlin, Amt für Stadtbildpflege

Berlin, Antikenmus.
Berlin, Antikenmuseum [at Charlottenburg]

Berlin, Archäol. Ges.
Berlin, Archäologische Gesellschaft

Berlin, Bauhaus-Archv
Berlin, Bauhaus-Archiv

Berlin, Bauhaus-Archv, Mus. Gestalt.
Berlin, Bauhaus-Archiv, Museum für
Gestaltung

Berlin, Berlin-Brandenburg Akad. Wiss.
Berlin, Berlin-Brandenburgische Akademie der
Wissenschaft [formerly Akademie der
Wissenschaften der DDR]

Berlin, Berlin. Gal.
Berlin, Berlinische Galerie [in Gropiusbau]

Berlin, Berlin Mus.
Berlin, Berlin Museum

Berlin, Berlin. Sparkasse
Berlin, Berliner Sparkasse

Berlin, Bildhauergal. Messer–Ladwig
Berlin, Bildhauergalerie Messer–Ladwig

Berlin, Bischöf. Ordinariat
Berlin, Bischöfliches Ordinariat

Berlin, Bodemus.
Berlin, Bodemuseum [houses Ägyptisches
Museum und Papyrussammlung;
Frühchristlich-Byzantinische Sammlung;
Gemäldegalerie; Münzkabinett; Museum für
Ur- und Frühgeschichte;
Skulpturensammlung]

Berlin, Botan. Garten
Berlin, Botanischer Garten

Berlin, Botan. Mus.
Berlin, Botanisches Museum

Berlin, Brücke-Mus.
Berlin, Brücke-Museum

Berlin, Buchhand. Buchholz
Berlin, Buchhandlung Buchholz

Berlin, Cassirer Gal.
Berlin, Cassirer Galerie [closed]

Berlin, Charlottenburg, Grosse Orangerie

Berlin, Charlottenburg, Schlossgarten

Berlin, daad gal.
Berlin, daad galerie

Berlin, Dt. Archäol. Inst.
Berlin, Deutsches Archäologisches Institut

Berlin, Dt. Bank
Berlin, Deutsche Bank

Berlin, Dt. Hist. Mus.
Berlin, Deutsches Historisches Museum
[formerly Zeughaus]

Berlin, Dt. Kstlerbnd
Berlin, Deutscher Künstlerbund

Berlin, Dt. Mus.
Berlin, Deutsches Museum [closed]

Berlin, Dt. Staatsbib.
Berlin, Deutsche Staatsbibliothek [united with
the Staatsbib. Preuss. Kultbes. as Staatsbib. 1
Jan 1992]

Berlin, Freie U.
Berlin, Freie Universität

Berlin, Gal. Aedes
Berlin, Galerie Aedes

Berlin, Gal. Anja Bremer
Berlin, Galerie Anja Bremer

Berlin, Gal. Arkade
Berlin, Galerie Arkade

Berlin, Gal. Brusberg
Berlin, Galerie Brusberg

Berlin, Gal. Cassirer
Berlin, Galerie Cassirer

Berlin, Gal. Eva Poll
Berlin, Galerie Eva Poll

Berlin, Gal. Ferdinand Möller
Berlin, Galerie Ferdinand Möller

Berlin, Gal. Flechtheim
Berlin, Galerie Flechtheim [closed]

Berlin, Gal. Georg Nothelfer
Berlin, Galerie Georg Nothelfer

Berlin, Gal. Gerd Rosen
Berlin, Galerie Gerd Rosen [closed]

Berlin, Gal. Goldschmidt-Wallerstein
Berlin, Galerie Goldschmidt-Wallerstein

Berlin, Gal. Gurlitt
Berlin, Galerie Gurlitt [closed]

Berlin, Gal. Haberstock
Berlin, Galerie Haberstock

Berlin Gal. I.B. Neumann
Berlin, Galerie I.B. Neumann [closed]

Berlin, Gal. Mikro
Berlin, Galerie Mikro

Berlin, Gal. Mitte
Berlin, Galerie Mitte

Berlin, Gal. Mosse
Berlin, Galerie Mosse [closed]

Berlin, Gal. Neiriz
Berlin, Galerie Neiriz

Berlin, Gal. Nierendorf
Berlin, Galerie Nierendorf

Berlin, Gal. Nothelfer
Berlin, Galerie Nothelfer

Berlin, Gal. Otto Burchard
Berlin, Galerie Otto Burchard

Berlin, Gal. Ravené
Berlin, Galerie Ravené [closed]

Berlin, Schloss Charlottenburg
Berlin, Galerie der Romantik [in Schloss
Charlottenburg]

Berlin, Gal. Rotunde Alten Mus.
Berlin, Galerie Rotunde im Alten Museum

Berlin, Gal. Schulte
Berlin, Galerie Schulte [closed]

Berlin, Gal. Silvia Menzel
Berlin, Galerie Silvia Menzel

Berlin, Gal. Thannhauser
Berlin, Galerie Thannhauser [closed]

Berlin, Gal. Torm
Berlin, Galerie im Torm

Berlin, Gal. Unter den Linden
Berlin, Galerie Unter den Linden

Berlin, Gal. Victor Hartberg
Berlin, Galerie Victor Hartberg

Berlin, Gal. Werner & Katz
Berlin, Galerie Werner und Katz

Berlin, Geh. Staatsarchv Preuss. Kultbes.
Berlin, Geheimes Staatsarchiv Preussischer
Kulturbesitz

Berlin, Gemäldegal.
Berlin, Gemäldegalerie [at Dahlem]

Berlin, Gerichtstr., Krematorium
Berlin, Gerichtstrasse, Krematorium

Berlin, Gipsformerei [at Charlottenburg]

Berlin, Gropiusbau [houses Berlin. Gal.]

Berlin, Grossgörschen 35

Berlin, Grundkreditbank Col.
Berlin, Grundkreditbank Collection

Berlin, Hamburg. Bahnhof
Berlin, Hamburger Bahnhof

Berlin, Haus Kult. Welt
Berlin, Haus der Kulturen der Welt

Berlin, Haus Lützowplatz
Berlin, Haus am Lützowplatz

Berlin, Haus Sow.-Dt. Freundschaft
Berlin, Haus der Sowjetisch-Deutschen
Freundschaft [no longer exists]

Berlin, Haus Waldsee
Berlin, Haus am Waldsee

Berlin, Hochsch. Kst.
Berlin, Hochschule der Künste [formerly
Joachimstalische Gymnasium; also known as
Konservatorium; incl. Musikinstrumentum-
Museum]

Berlin, Humboldt-U.
Berlin, Humboldt-Universität zu Berlin

Berlin, Jagdschloss Grunewald

Berlin, Kaiser-Friedrich Mus.
Berlin, Kaiser-Friedrich Museum [destr.;
rebuilt as Bodemus.]

Berlin, Kammerspiele Dt. Theat.
Berlin, Kammerspiele des Deutschen Theaters
[closed]

Berlin, Kolbe Mus.
Berlin, Kolbe Museum

Berlin, Kön. N.-G.
Berlin, Königliche National-Galerie zu Berlin
[now Berlin, Alte N.G.]

Berlin, Konserv.
Berlin, Konservatorium

Berlin, Kstamt Kreuzberg
Berlin, Kunstamt Kreuzberg

Berlin, Kstbib.
Berlin, Kunstbibliothek [of SMPK; formerly at
Charlottenburg, now at Tiergarten]

Berlin, Kstbib. & Mus.
Berlin, Kunstbibliothek Berlin mit Museum
für Architektur, Modebild und Grafik-Design

Berlin, Ksthalle
Berlin, Kunsthalle Berlin

Berlin, Kstlerhaus Bethanien
Berlin, Künstlerhaus Bethanien

Berlin, Kupferstichkab.
Berlin, Kupferstichkabinett [formerly at
Dahlem, since 1994 at Tiergarten]

Berlin, Landengal.
Berlin, Landengalerie

Berlin, Landesarchv
Berlin, Landesarchiv

Berlin, Lapidarium

Berlin, Lichterfelde, Schlosspark

Berlin, Maison France
Berlin, Maison de France

Berlin, Märk. Mus.
Berlin, Märkisches Museum

Berlin, Max-Planck-Inst. Bildungsforsch.
Berlin, Max-Planck-Institut für
Bildungsforschung

Berlin, Metzner Mus.
Berlin, Metzner Museum [closed]

Berlin, Mus. Dt. Gesch.
Berlin, Museum für Deutsche Geschichte

Berlin, Mus. Dt. Vlksknd.
Berlin, Museum für Deutsche Volkskunde [at
Dahlem]

Berlin, Musikinstr.-Mus., Staatl. Inst. Musikforsch.
Preuss. Kultbes.
Berlin, Musikinstrumenten-Museum,
Staatliches Institut für Musikforschung
Preussischer Kulturbesitz

Berlin, Mus. Ind. Kst
Berlin, Museum für Indische Kunst [at
Dahlem]

Berlin, Mus. Islam. Kst
Berlin, Museum für Islamische Kunst [at
Dahlem]

Berlin, Mus. Ostasiat. Kst
Berlin, Museum für Ostasiatische Kunst [at
Dahlem]

Berlin, Mus. Spätant. & Byz. Kst
Berlin, Museum für Spätantike und
Byzantinische Kunst [at Dahlem]

Berlin, Mus. Vlkerknd.
Berlin, Museum für Völkerkunde [at Dahlem]

Berlin, Mus. Vlksknd.
Berlin, Museum für Volkskunde [at Dahlem]

Berlin, Mus. Vor- & Frühgesch.
Berlin, Museum für Vor- und Frühgeschichte
[at Charlottenburg]

Berlin, Neue Berlin. Gal.
Berlin, Neue Berliner Galerie [in Altes Mus.]

Berlin, Neue Ges. Bild. Kst
Berlin, Neue Gesellschaft für Bildende Kunst

Berlin, Neue N.G.
Berlin, Neue Nationalgalerie

Berlin, Neuer Berlin. Kstver.
Berlin, Neuer Berliner Kunstverein

Berlin, Neuer Kstquartier Techno- &
Innovationspark
Berlin, Neue Kunstquartier des Technologie-
und Innovationsparks

Berlin, Neues Mus.
Berlin, Neues Museum [destr.]

Berlin, Otto-Nagel-Haus

Berlin, Pal. Ephraim
Berlin, Palais Ephraim

Berlin, Pal. Kaiser Wilhelms I
Berlin, Palais Kaiser Wilhelms I [name changed to Altes Palais in 1945]

Berlin, Pergamonmus.
Berlin, Pergamonmuseum [houses Antikensammlung; Islamisches Museum; Ostasiatische Sammlung; Vorderasiatisches Museum; Zentbib.]

Berlin, Postmus.
Berlin, Postmuseum

Berlin, Raab Gal.
Berlin, Raab Galerie

Berlin, Rathaus

Berlin, Rauch-Mus.
Berlin, Rauch-Museum

Berlin, Reichstagsgebäude

Berlin, Schadow-Haus

Berlin, Schauspielhaus

Berlin, Schinkelmus.
Berlin, Schinkelmuseum [in Friedrichwerdersche Kirche]

Berlin, Schloss Charlottenburg

Berlin, Schloss Charlottenburg, Schinkel-Pav.
Berlin, Schloss Charlottenburg, Schinkel-Pavillon

Berlin, Schloss Glienicke

Berlin, Schloss Kleinglienicke

Berlin, Schloss Köpenick [houses Kunstgewerbemuseum]

Berlin, Schloss Tegel

Berlin, Schöneberg, Rathaus

Berlin, Senat
Berlin, Senat von Berlin

Berlin, 7 Produzentengal.
Berlin, 7 Produzentengalerie

Berlin, Skulpgal.
Berlin, Skulpturengalerie mit Frühchristlich-Byzantinischer Sammlung [at Dahlem]

Berlin, Staatl. Inst. Musikforsch. Preuss. Kultbes.
Berlin, Staatliches Institut für Musikforschung Preussicher Kulturbesitz

Berlin, Staatl. Ksthalle
Berlin, Staatliche Kunsthalle

Berlin, Staatl. Museen Preuss. Kultbes.
Berlin, Staatliche Museen Preussischer Kulturbesitz [admins Ägyp. Mus.; Alte N.G.; Altes Mus.; Antikenmus.; Bodemus.; Gal. Romantik; Gemäldegal.; Gipsformerei; Kstbib.; Kupferstichkab.; Mus. Dt. Vlksknd.; Mus. Ind. Kst; Mus. Islam. Kst; Mus. Ostasiat. Kst; Mus. Vlkerknd.; Mus. Vor- & Frühgesch.; Neue N.G.; Pergamonmus.; Schinkelmus.; Schloss Charlottenburg; Schloss Köpenick; Skulpgal.; Staatsbib.; Tiergarten, Kstgewmus.]

Berlin, Staatl. Schlösser & Gtn
Berlin, Staatliche Schlösser und Gärten

Berlin, Staatsbib.
Berlin, Staatsbibliothek zu Berlin Preussischer Kulturbesitz

Berlin, Staatsbib., Mendelssohn-Archv
Berlin, Staatsbibliothek, Mendelssohn-Archiv

Berlin, Staatsbib. Preuss. Kultbes.
Berlin, Staatsbibliothek Preussischer Kulturbesitz [united with the Dt. Staatsbib. to form Staatsbib. in 1992]

Berlin, Staatsbib. Preuss. Kultbes., Orientabt.
Berlin, Staatsbibliothek Preussischer Kulturbesitz, Orientabteilung

Berlin, Stud.-Atelier Mal. & Plast.
Berlin Studien-Atelier für Malerei und Plastik

Berlin, Sturm-Gal.
Berlin, Sturm-Galerie [closed]

Berlin, Tech. Hochsch.
Berlin, Technische Hochschule [now Tech. U.]

Berlin, Tech. U.
Berlin, Technische Universität [1879–1946 called Tech. Hochsch.]

Berlin, Tiergarten [Kulturforum]

Berlin, Tiergarten, Kstgewmus.
Berlin, Kunstgewerbemuseum

Berlin, van Diemen Gal.
Berlin, van Diemen Galerie [closed]

Berlin, Ver. Berlin. Kstlr
Berlin, Verein Berliner Künstler

Berlin, Winckelmann Inst.
Berlin, Winckelmann Institut

Berlin, Zentbib.
Berlin, Zentralbibliothek [in Pergamonmus.]

Berlin, Zeughaus [now Dt. Hist. Mus.]

Berne, Amthaus

Berne, Bib. N.
Berne, Schweizerische Landesbibliothek/ Bibliothèque Nationale Suisse

Berne, Botan. Inst. & Gtn
Berne, Botanische Institute und Botanischer Garten [Instituts et Jardin Botaniques de l'Université]

Berne, Bundeshaus

Berne, Burgerbib.
Berne, Burgerbibliothek Bern [also known as Bibliothèque de la Bourgeoisie de Berne]

Berne, Gal. Jüng Stuker
Berne, Galerie Jüng Stuker

Berne, Gal. Kornfeld
Berne, Galerie Kornfeld [formerly Klipstein & Kornfeld]

Berne, Gal. Toni Gerber
Berne, Galerie Toni Gerber

Berne, Hist. Mus.
Berne, Bernisches Historisches Museum

Berne, Hist. Mus.
Berne, Historisches Museum [Musée d'Histoire]

Berne, Kant. Amt Wirtschafts- & Kulturasstell., Samml. Angewandte Kst Kant. Bern & Gewbib. Fachlit.
Berne, Kantonales Amt für Wirtschafts- und Kulturausstellungen, Sammlung für Angewandte Kunst im Kanton Bern und Gewerbebibliothek mit Fachliteratur

Berne, Klipstein & Kornfeld [now Galerie Kornfeld]

Berne, Ksthalle
Berne, Kunsthalle

Berne, Kstmus.
Berne, Kunstmuseum

Berne, Nathist. Mus.
Berne, Naturhistorisches Museum

Berne, Schweiz. Bundesarchv
Berne, Schweizerisches Bundesarchiv

Berne, Schweiz. Kstver.
Berne, Schweizerischer Kunstverein

Berne, Schweiz. Vlksbank
Berne, Schweizerische Volksbank

Berne, Städt. Gym.
Berne, Städtischer Gymnasium

Berne, Stadt- & Ubib.
Berne, Stadt- und Universitätsbibliothek

Bernkastel-Kues, St Nikolaus-Hosp.
Bernkastel-Kues, St Nikolaus-Hospital

Besançon, Bib. Mun.
Besançon, Bibliothèque Municipale

Besançon, Mus. B.-A. & Archéol.
Besançon, Musée des Beaux-Arts et d'Archéologie

Besançon, Mus. Hist.
Besançon, Musée Historique [in Palais Granvelle]

Besançon, U. Franche-Comté
Besançon, Université de Franche-Comté

Bethlehem, PA, Archv Morav. Church
Bethlehem, PA, Archive of the Moravian Church

Bethlehem, PA, Lehigh U., Ralph Wilson Gal.
Bethlehem, PA, Lehigh University, Ralph Wilson Gallery

Bettona, Pin. & Mus. Civ.
Bettona, Pinacoteca e Museo Civico

Beveren, Gemeentelijk Mus.
Beveren, Gemeentelijk Museum

Bevern, Schloss
Bevern, Schloss Bevern [houses Heimatmuseum Bevern]

Beverly Hills, CA, Rifkind Found.
Beverly Hills, Robert Gore Rifkind Foundation

Béziers, Mus. B.-A.
Béziers, Musée des Beaux-Arts Hôtel Fabregat

Béziers, Mus. B.-A. Fayet
Béziers, Musée des Beaux-Arts Fayet

Bhanpura, Hinglajgarh Fort, Archaeol. Mus.
Bhanpura, Hinglajgarh Fort, Archaeological Museum

Bharatpur, State Mus.
Bharatpur, State Museum

Bhopal, Archaeol. Mus.
Bhopal, State Archaeological Museum

Bhopal, Bharat Bhavan

Bhopal, Bharat Bhavan, Mus.
Bhopal, Bharat Bhavan, Museum

Bhopal, Birla Mus.
Bhopal, Birla Museum

Bhopal, Madhya Pradesh Govt, Dept Cult.
Bhopal, Madhya Pradesh Government, Department of Culture

Bhopal, Madhya Pradesh Tribal Res. & Dev. Inst. Mus.
Bhopal, Madhya Pradesh Tribal Research and Development Institute Museum

Bhopal, State Mus.
Bhopal, State Museum

Bhubaneshwar, Orissa Mus.
Bhubaneshwar, Orissa Museum

Białystok, Dist. Mus.
Białystok, District Museum (Muzeum Okregowe)

Biberach an der Riss, Städt. Samml.
Biberach an der Riss, Städtische Sammlungen [in Braith-Mali-Mus.]

Biel, Mus. Schwab
Biel, Museum Schwab

Bielefeld, Städt. Ksthalle
Bielefeld, Städtische Kunsthalle

Bielefeld, U. Bielefeld, Zentrum für Interdiszip. Forsch.
    Bielefeld, Universität Bielefeld, Zentrum für Interdisziplinäre Forschung

Biella, Ist. N. Fot. Alpina Vittorio Sella
    Biella, Istituto Nazionale di Fotografia Alpina Vittorio Sella [Villa Sella]

Biggar, Gasworks Mus.
    Biggar, Gasworks Museum

Bijapur, Archaeol. Mus.
    Bijapur, Archaeological Museum

Bikaner, Chandra Pal.
    Bikaner, Chandra Palace

Bikaner, Govt Mus.
    Bikaner, Government Museum [Ganga Golden Jubilee Mus.]

Bikaner, Lalgarh Pal.
    Bikaner, Lalgarh Palace

Bikaner, Rajasthan State Archv
    Bikaner, Rajasthan State Archive

Bilbao, Mus. Arqueol., Etnog. & Hist. Vasco
    Bilbao, Museo Arqueológico, Etnográfico e Histórico Vasco (Euskal Arkeolojia, Etnografia eta Kondaira-Museoa)

Bilbao, Mus. B.A.
    Bilbao, Museo de Bellas Artes

Bilbao, Mus. Hist. Vizcaya
    Bilbao, Museo Histórico de Vizcaya

Billinge, Gamlegård

Billingham, A.G.
    Billingham, Art Gallery

Bilzen, Château Oude Biezen [Alde Biesen; Flemish Cultural Centre]

Bima, Grand Mosque

Binghamton, SUNY
    Binghamton, NY, State University of New York

Binghamton, SUNY, A.G.
    Binghamton, NY, State University of New York, Art Gallery

Biot, Mus. N. Fernand Léger
    Biot, Musée National Fernand Léger

Birchington, Powell-Cotton Mus.
    Birchington, Powell-Cotton Museum

Birkenhead, Williamson A.G. & Mus.
    Birkenhead, Williamson Art Gallery and Museum

Birkerod, Komm.
    Birkerod, Kommune

Birmingham, A.G.
    Birmingham, City of Birmingham Art Gallery [name changed to Mus. & A.G. in 1939]

Birmingham, Assay Office
    Birmingham, Birmingham Assay Office

Birmingham, Aston Hall

Birmingham, Gas Hall Exh. Gal.
    Birmingham, Gas Hall Exhibition Gallery

Birmingham, Ikon Gal.
    Birmingham, Ikon Gallery

Birmingham, Lib. Serv.
    Birmingham, Birmingham Library Services

Birmingham, Mus. & A.G.
    Birmingham, City of Birmingham Museum and Art Gallery

Birmingham, Oscott Coll.
    Birmingham, Oscott College

Birmingham Poly.
    Birmingham, Birmingham Polytechnic

Birmingham, Selly Oak Coll. Lib.
    Birmingham, Selly Oak Colleges Library

Birmingham, U. Birmingham, Barber Inst.
    Birmingham, University of Birmingham, Barber Institute of Fine Arts

Birmingham, W. Midlands A.
    Birmingham, West Midlands Arts

Birmingham, AL, Mus. A.
    Birmingham, AL, Museum of Art

Bishkek, Kirghiz Mus. F.A.
    Bishkek, Kirghiz Museum of Fine Art (Kyrgyzskiy Muzey Izobraziteľnykh Iskusstva) [now Kyrgyzstan Mus. F.A.]

Bishkek, Kyrgyzstan Acad. Sci.
    Bishkek, Kyrgyzstan Academy of Sciences

Bishkek, Kyrgyzstan Acad. Sci., Mus. Archaeol. Inst. Hist.
    Bishkek, Kyrgyzstan Academy of Sciences, Museum of Archaeology of the Institute of History

Bishkek, Kyrgyzstan Hist. Mus.
    Bishkek, Kyrgyzstan Historical Museum

Bishkek, Kyrgyzstan Mus. F.A.
    Bishkek, Kyrgyzstan Museum of Fine Art

Bisingen, Burg Hohenzoll.
    Bisingen, Burg Hohenzollern [former home of Princes of Prussia]

Bitolj, Archaeol. Mus.
    Bitolj, Archaeological Museum (Arheološki Muzej)

Bitolj Mus.
    Bitolj, Bitolj Museum (Muzej Bitola)

Bitonto, Mus. Dioc.
    Bitonto, Museo Diocesano

Bitonto, Pal. Vescovile
    Bitonto, Palazzo Vescovile

Bizen, Cer. Mus.
    Bizen, Bizen Ceramics Museum

Blackburn, Mus. & A.G.
    Blackburn, Museum and Art Gallery

Blackburn Town Hall
    Blackburn, Blackburn Town Hall

Black Mountain, NC, Coll.
    Black Mountain, NC, Black Mountain College

Blantyre, Min. Educ.
    Blantyre, Ministry of Education

Blantyre, Mus. Malawi
    Blantyre, Museum of Malawi

Blanzy, Lycée Ens. Professionnel
    Blanzy, Lycée d'Enseignement Professionnel

Blaye, Mus. Hist. & A. Pays
    Blaye, Musée d'Histoire et d'Art du Pays Blayais

Blérancourt, Château, Mus. N. Coop. Fr.-Amér.
    Blérancourt, Château, Musée National de la Coopération Franco-Américaine

Bloemfontein, A.C. White Gallery

Bloemfontein, N. Mus. Oliewenhuis
    Bloemfontein, National Museum Oliewenhuis

Blois, Mus. B.-A.
    Blois, Musée des Beaux-Arts

Blois, Mus. Mun.
    Blois, Musée Municipal de Blois

Bloomfield Hills, MI, Cranbrook Acad. A. Mus.
    Bloomfield Hills, MI, Cranbrook Academy of Art Museum

Bloomington, IN U.
    Bloomington, IN, Indiana University

Bloomington, IN U. A. Mus.
    Bloomington, IN, Indiana University Art Museum

Bloomington, IN U. Auditorium
    Bloomington, IN, Indiana University Auditorium

Bloomington, IN U., Lilly Lib.
    Bloomington, IN, Indiana University, Lilly Library

Bludov, Pict. Gal.
    Bludov, Picture Gallery

Blue Mountain Lake, NY, Adirondack Mus.
    Blue Mountain Lake, NY, Adirondack Museum

Boadilla del Monte, Pal. Infante Don Luis
    Boadilla del Monte, Palacio del Infante Don Luis

Bobbio, Mus. Abbazia S Colombano
    Bobbio, Museo dell'Abbazia di San Colombano

Bobo Dioulasso, Mus. Prov. Bobo
    Bobo Dioulasso, Musée Provincial de Bobo

Bochum, Mus. Bochum, Kstsamml.
    Bochum, Museum Bochum, Kunstsammlung

Bochum, U. Bochum
    Bochum, Ruhr-Universität Bochum

Bodelwyddan Castle
    Bodelwyddan, Bodelwyddan Castle [Clwyd]

Bodhgaya, Archaeol. Mus.
    Bodhgaya, Archaeological Museum

Bodrum Mus.
    Bodrum, Bodrum Museum

Bogotá, Acad. N. B.A.
    Bogotá, Academia Nacional de Bellas Artes

Bogotá, Bib. Luis-Angel Arango
    Bogotá, Biblioteca Luis-Angel Arango del Banco de la República

Bogotá, Bib. N. Colombia
    Bogotá, Biblioteca Nacional de Colombia

Bogotá, Fond. Cult. Cafetero
    Bogotá, Fondo Cultural Cafetero

Bogotá, Gal. Cano
    Bogotá, Galería Cano

Bogotá, Gal. Leo Matiz
    Bogotá, Galería Leo Matiz

Bogotá, Mus. A. Colon.
    Bogotá, Museo de Arte Colonial

Bogotá, Mus. A. Mod.
    Bogotá, Museo de Arte Moderno

Bogotá, Mus. A. Relig.
    Bogotá, Museo de Arte Religioso

Bogotá, Mus. Arqueol. Banco Pop.
    Bogotá, Museo Arqueológico del Banco Popular

Bogotá, Mus. A. & Trad. Pop.
    Bogotá, Museo de Artes y Tradiciones Populares

Bogotá, Mus. Etnog. Inst. Caro & Cuervo
    Bogotá, Museo Etnográfico del Instituto Caro y Cuervo

Bogotá, Mus. N.
    Bogotá, Museo Nacional

Bogotá, Mus. Oro
    Bogotá, Museo del Oro [Banco de la República]

Bogotá, Quinta Bolívar
    Bogotá, Quinta de Bolívar

Bogotá, U. Andes
    Bogotá, Universidad de los Andes

Bogotá, U.N. Colombia
    Bogotá, Universidad Nacional de Colombia

Bologna, Accad. B.A. & Liceo A.
  Bologna, Accademia di Belle Arti e Liceo Artistico

Bologna, Archv Stato
  Bologna, Archivio di Stato

Bologna, Banca Carimonte

Bologna, Bib. Cassa di Risparmio
  Bologna, Biblioteca della Cassa di Risparmio

Bologna, Bib. Com. Archiginnasio
  Bologna, Biblioteca Comunale dell'Archiginnasio

Bologna, Bib. U.
  Bologna, Biblioteca Universitaria

Bologna, Casino Marsigli

Bologna, Cassa di Risparmio

Bologna, Col. Com. A.
  Bologna, Collezioni Comunali d'Arte [Pal. Com.]

Bologna, Coll. Spagna
  Bologna, Collegio di Spagna

Bologna, Compagnia Lombardi
  Bologna, Compagnia dei Lombardi

Bologna, Conserv. Stat. Musica
  Bologna, Conservatorio Statale di Musica G. B. Martini

Bologna, Credito Romagnolo

Bologna, Gal. Com. A. Mod.
  Bologna, Galleria Comunale d'Arte Moderna

Bologna, Gal. dei Foscherari
  Bologna, Galleria dei Foscherari

Bologna, Gal. Marco Diacono
  Bologna, Galleria Marco Diacono

Bologna, Intend. Finanza
  Bologna, Intendenza di Finanza

Bologna, Liceo A. & Accad. Clementina
  Bologna, Liceo Artistico e Accademia Clementina

Bologna, Masetti-Calzolari

Bologna Mus. Bib. Musicale
  Bologna, Museo Bibliografico Musicale

Bologna, Mus. Civ.
  Bologna, Museo Civico

Bologna, Mus. Civ. Archeol.
  Bologna, Museo Civico Archeologico

Bologna, Mus. Civ. Med.
  Bologna, Museo Civico Medievale e del Rinascimento [in Palazzi Fava Ghisilardi]

Bologna, Mus. Civ. Risorgimento
  Bologna, Museo Civico del Primo e Secondo Risorgimento

Bologna, Musei Civ.
  Bologna, Musei Civici [admins Mus. Civ. Archeol.; Mus. Civ. Med.: Mus. Civ. Risorgimento]

Bologna, Mus. Ist. Anatomia Umana Norm.
  Bologna, Museo dell'Istituto di Anatomia Umana Normale

Bologna, Mus. S Domenico
  Bologna, Museo di S Domenico

Bologna, Mus. S Giuseppe
  Bologna, Museo di S Giuseppe

Bologna, Mus. S Petronio
  Bologna, Museo di S Petronio

Bologna, Mus. S Stefano
  Bologna, Museo di S Stefano [della Basilica Stefaniana]

Bologna, Pal. Archiginnasio
  Bologna, Palazzo dell'Archiginnasio

Bologna, Pal. Arcivescovile
  Bologna, Palazzo Arcivescovile

Bologna, Pal. Bevilacqua
  Bologna, Palazzo Bevilacqua

Bologna, Pal. Bianconcini
  Bologna, Palazzo Bianconcini [formerly Palazzo Zaniboni-Pichi]

Bologna, Pal. Com.
  Bologna, Palazzo Comunale, Collezioni Comunali d'Arte

Bologna, Pal. Davia–Bargellini
  Bologna, Palazzo Davia–Bargellini [houses Museo d'Arte Industriale e Galleria Davia–Bargellini Bologna]

Bologna, Pal. Fava
  Bologna, Palazzo Fava

Bologna, Pal. Mentasti
  Bologna, Palazzo Mentasti

Bologna, Pal. Montanari
  Bologna, Palazzo Montanari [formerly Palazzo Aldrovandi]

Bologna, Pal. Pepoli
  Bologna, Palazzo Pepoli

Bologna, Pal. Pepoli Campogrande
  Bologna, Palazzo Pepoli Campogrande

Bologna, Pal. Podestà
  Bologna, Palazzo del Podestà

Bologna, Pal. Poggi
  Bologna, Palazzo Poggi

Bologna, Pal. Re Enzo
  Bologna, Palazzo di Re Enzo

Bologna, Pal. Rossi
  Bologna, Palazzo Rossi [formerly Palazzo Zani]

Bologna, Pal. Sanguinetti
  Bologna, Palazzo Sanguinetti

Bologna, Pal. Sanguinetti Vizani
  Bologna, Palazzo Sanguinetti Vizani

Bologna, Pii Ist. Educ.
  Bologna, Pii Istituti Educativi

Bologna, Pin. N.
  Bologna, Pinacoteca Nazionale

Bologna, Rac. Molinari–Pradelli
  Bologna, Raccolta Molinari–Pradelli

Bologna, Ronchi di Crevalcore

Bologna, U. Bologna
  Bologna, Università degli Studi

Bologna, U. Bologna, Ist. Scienze
  Bologna, Università degli Studi, Istituto delle Scienze

Bolsward, Stadhuis

Bolton, Mus. & A.G.
  Bolton, Museum and Art Gallery

Bolzano, Mus. Civ.
  Bolzano, Museo Civico [Museo dell'Alto Adige]

Bolzano, Pal. Gerstburg
  Bolzano, Palazzo Gerstburg

Bolzano, Pal. Mercantile
  Bolzano, Palazzo Mercantile

Bombay, Asiat. Soc.
  Bombay, Asiatic Society of Bombay

Bombay, A. Soc. Gal.
  Bombay, Bombay Art Society Gallery [Jehangir A.G.]

Bombay, Chemould Gal.
  Bombay, Chemould Gallery

Bombay, Cymroza A. Gal.
  Bombay, Cymroza Art Gallery

Bombay, Jehangir A.G.
  Bombay, Jehangir Art Gallery [Bombay A. Soc. Gal.]

Bombay, Jehangir Nicholson Mus. Mod. A.
  Bombay, Jehangir Nicholson Museum of Modern Art [National Centre for the Performing Arts]

Bombay, Nehru Cent.
  Bombay, Nehru Centre

Bombay, Prince of Wales Mus.
  Bombay, Prince of Wales Museum of Western India

Bombay, Pundole Gal. & Framing Cent.
  Bombay, Pundole Gallery and Framing Center

Bombay, Sir Jamshetjee Jeejebhoy Coll. Archit.
  Bombay, Sir Jamshetjee Jeejebhoy College of Architecture

Bombay, Taj A.G.
  Bombay, Taj Art Gallery

Bombay, V&A
  Bombay, Victoria and Albert Museum [Byculla Bombay Collection]

Bondues, Fond. Septrention
  Bondues, Fondation Septrention

Bonn, Akad. Kstmus. Archäol. Inst. U.
  Bonn, Akademisches Kunstmuseum und Archäologisches Institut der Universität

Bonn, Beethoven-Haus

Bonn, Bundeskanzleramt

Bonn, Friedrich-Ebert-Stift.
  Bonn, Friedrich-Ebert-Stiftung

Bonn, Gal. Hennemann
  Bonn, Galerie Hennemann

Bonn, Gal. Marco
  Bonn, Galerie Marco

Bonn, Gal. Philomene Magers
  Bonn, Galerie Philomene Magers

Bonn, Inst. Auslandsbezieh., Gal.
  Bonn, Institut für Auslandsbeziehungen, Galerie und Kontaktstelle

Bonn, Kst- & Ausstellhal.
  Bonn, Kunst- und Ausstellungshalle der Bundesrepublik Deutschland

Bonn, Kstver.
  Bonn, Bonner Kunstverein

Bonn, Rhein. Friedrich-Wilhelms-U.
  Bonn, Rheinische Friedrich-Wilhelms-Universität

Bonn, Rhein. Landesmus.
  Bonn, Rheinisches Landesmuseum [Rheinisches Amt für Bodendenkmalpflege mit Regionalmuseum Xanten und Archäologischer Park Xanten]

Bonn, Samml. BRD
  Bonn, Sammlung der Bundesrepublik Deutschland

Bonn, Städt. Kstmus.
  Bonn, Städtisches Kunstmuseum Bonn

Bonn, Stift. Preuss. Kultbes., Wisszent.
  Bonn, Stiftung Preussischer Kulturbesitz, Wissenschaftszentrum

Bonn, Ubib.
  Bonn, Universitätsbibliothek

Borås, Kstmus.
  Borås, Borås Konstmuseum

Bordeaux, Archv Gironde
  Bordeaux, Archives de la Gironde

Bordeaux, Bib. Mun.
  Bordeaux, Bibliothèque Municipale

Bordeaux, Cent. A. Plast. Contemp.
Bordeaux, Centre d'Arts Plastiques
Contemporains

Bordeaux, Gal. B.-A.
Bordeaux, Galerie des Beaux-Arts

Bordeaux, Min. Défense
Bordeaux, Ministère de la Défense

Bordeaux, Mus. A. Contemp.
Bordeaux, Musée d'Art Contemporain

Bordeaux, Mus. A. Déc.
Bordeaux, Musée des Arts Décoratifs

Bordeaux, Mus. Aquitaine
Bordeaux, Musée d'Aquitaine

Bordeaux, Mus. B.-A.
Bordeaux, Musée des Beaux-Arts

Bordeaux, Mus. Bordeaux
Bordeaux, Musée de Bordeaux

Bordeaux, U. Bordeaux II, Fac. Médec.
Bordeaux, Université de Bordeaux II, Faculté
de Médecine

Bornem, Found. Helan-Arts
Bornem, Foundation Helan-Arts

Borodino, Mus.-Reserve Mil. Hist.
Borodino, Borodino Museum-Reserve of
Military History (Borodinskyy Voyenno-
Istoricheskiy Muzey-Zapovednik)

Boskovice, Reg. Mus.
Boskovice, Regional Museum (Vlastivědné
Muzeum)

Boston, Lincs, Mus.
Boston, Lincs, Boston Museum

Boston, MA, Archit. Cent.
Boston, MA, Boston Architectural Center

Boston, MA, Archit. Cent. Lib.
Boston, MA, Boston Architectural Center
Library

Boston, MA, Arnold Arboretum

Boston, MA, Athenaeum
Boston, MA, Boston Athenaeum

Boston, MA, Boston U., Mugar Mem. Lib.
Boston, MA, Boston University, Mugar
Memorial Library

Boston, MA, Capitol Bldg
Boston, MA, Capitol Building

Boston, MA, Carl Siembab Gal.
Boston, MA, Carl Siembab Gallery

Boston, MA, Childs Gal.
Boston, MA, Childs Gallery

Boston, MA, Club Odd Vols
Boston, MA, Club of Odd Volumes

Boston, MA, Copley Soc.
Boston, MA, Copley Society of Boston

Boston, MA Gen. Hosp.
Boston, MA, Massachusetts General Hospital

Boston, MA, Goethe Inst.
Boston, MA, Goethe Institute

Boston, MA Hist. Soc.
Boston, MA, Massachusetts Historical Society

Boston, MA, ICA
Boston, MA, Institute of Contemporary Arts

Boston, MA, Isabella Stewart Gardner Mus.
Boston, MA, Isabella Stewart Gardner
Museum

Boston, MA, Mus. Afr.-Amer. Hist.
Boston, MA, Museum of Afro-American
History

Boston, MA, Mus. F.A.
Boston, MA, Museum of Fine Arts

Boston, MA, New England Hist. Geneal. Soc.
Boston, MA, New England Historical
Genealogical Society

Boston, MA, Old City Hall

Boston, MA, Old State House

Boston, MA, Pub. Gdn
Boston, MA, Boston Public Garden

Boston, MA, Pub. Lib.
Boston, MA, Public Library

Boston, MA, Sch. Mus. F.A.
Boston, MA, School of the Museum of Fine
Arts

Boston, MA, Soc. Preserv. New England Ant.
Boston, MA, Society for the Preservation of
New England Antiquities

Boston, MA, St Botolph's Club

Boston, MA, Vose Gals
Boston, MA, Vose Galleries

Boston, MA, William Young
Boston, MA, William Young & Co.

Botley, Hants Farm Mus.
Botley, Hampshire Farm Museum

Bottrop, Albers Mus.
Bottrop, Josef Albers Museum

Bottrop, Mod. Gal.
Bottrop, Moderne Galerie

Boulder, U. CO, A. Gals
Boulder, CO, University of Colorado, Art
Galleries

Boulder, U. CO, Mus.
Boulder, CO, University of Colorado, Museum

Boulogne, Bib. Mun.
Boulogne, Bibliothèque Municipale

Boulogne, Mus. Mun.
Boulogne, Musée Municipal

Boulogne-Billancourt, Bib. Marmottan
Boulogne-Billancourt, Bibliothèque
Marmottan

Boulogne-Billancourt, Mus. Mun.
Boulogne-Billancourt, Musée Municipal

Bourg-en-Bresse, Mus. Ain
Bourg-en-Bresse, Musée de l'Ain

Bourges, Bib. Mun.
Bourges, Bibliothèque Municipale

Bourges, Hôtel Jacques Coeur [Musée de la Ville]

Bourges, Maison Cult.
Bourges, Maison de la Culture de Bourges

Bourges, Mus. Berry
Bourges, Musée du Berry [Hôtel Cujas; Musée
de Bourges]

Bourges, Mus. Estève
Bourges, Musée Estève

Bournemouth, Nat. Hist. Soc. Mus.
Bournemouth, Bournemouth Natural History
Society Museum

Bournemouth, Russell-Cotes A.G. & Mus.
Bournemouth, Russell-Cotes Art Gallery and
Museum

Bouxwiller, Mus. Ville
Bouxwiller, Musée de la Ville [de Bouxwiller et
du Pays de Hanou; in Hôtel de Ville]

Bozen: see Bolzano

Bracciano, Archv Com.
Bracciano, Archivio Comunale

Bracciano, Castello Orsini
Bracciano, Castello degli Orsini

Bracciano, Pal. Com.
Bracciano, Palazzo Comunale

Bracknell, S. Hill Park A. Cent.
Bracknell, South Hill Park Arts Centre

Bradford, A. Gals & Museums
Bradford Art Galleries and Museums [admins
Bolling Hall; Cartwright Hall; Com. A. Cent.;
Indust. Mus.; Mus. Loans Serv.; Ilkley, Manor
House Mus. & A.G.; Ilkley, White Wells;
Keighley, Cliffe Castle Mus. & A.G.]

Bradford, Bolling Hall
Bradford, Bolling Hall Museum

Bradford, Cartwright Hall [Bradford City Art
Gallery and Museum]

Bradford, Cecil Higgins Mus.
Bradford, Cecil Higgins Museum

Bradford, Colour Mus.
Bradford, Colour Museum

Bradford, Com. A. Cent.
Bradford, Community Art Centre

Bradford, Indust. Mus.
Bradford, Bradford Industrial Museum

Bradford, Mus. Loans Serv.
Bradford, Museum Loans Service

Bradford, N. Mus. Phot., Film & TV
Bradford, National Museum of Photography,
Film and Television

Bradford, W. Yorks Transport Mus.
Bradford, West Yorkshire Transport Museum

Braga, Arquiv. Irmandade S Cruz
Braga, Arquivo da Irmandade de Santa Cruz

Braga, Bib. Púb.
Braga, Biblioteca Pública

Braga, Cathedral Treasury

Braga, Mus. D. Diogo de Sousa
Braga, Museu D. Diogo de Sousa

Braga, U. Minho, Mus. Nogueira da Silva
Braga, Universidade di Minho, Museu
Nogueira da Silva

Bragança, Mus. Reg. Abade Baçal
Bragança, Museu Regional Abade de Baçal

Brantford, Ont., Woodlands Ind. Cult. Educ.
Cent.
Brantford, Ont., Woodlands Indian Cultural
Education Centre

Brasília, Pal. Arcos
Brasília, Palácio dos Arcos

Brasília, Senate

Brașov, Distr. Mus.
Brașov, District Museum (Muzeul Județean
Brașov)

Brașov, Mus. A.
Brașov, Museum of Art (Muzeul de Artă
Brașov)

Brașov, Mus. Hist.
Brașov, Museum of History (Muzeul de Istorie
Brașov)

Bratislava, Cent. Archv Slovak Repub.
Bratislava, Central Archive of the Slovak
Republic (Štátny Ústredný Archív SR)

Bratislava, City Archv
Bratislava, City Archive (Archív Llavného
Mesta SR Bratislavy)

Bratislava, Dušan Jurkovič Hall
Bratislava, Dušan Jurkovič Hall (Sieň Dušana
Jurkoviča)

Bratislava, Gal. Albatros
Bratislava, Gallery Albatros (Galéria Albatros)

Bratislava, Gal. Capital SR
Bratislava, Gallery of the Capital of the Slovak
Republic (Galéria Hlavného Mesta SR
Bratislavy)

Bratislava, Mun. Gal.
Bratislava, Municipal Gallery (Mestská Galéria)

Bratislava, Mun. Mus.
Bratislava, Municipal Museum (Mstská Múzeum)

Bratislava, Slovak N.G.
Bratislava, Slovak National Gallery (Slovenská Národná Galéria)

Bratislava, Slovak N. Mus.
Bratislava, Slovak National Museum (Slovenské Národné Muzeum)

Braunau, Heimathaus
Braunau, Heimathaus Braunau [Bezirkmuseum]

Braunschweig: see Brunswick

Brauron Mus.
Brauron, Brauron Museum

Brauweiler, Rhein. Amt Dkmlpf.
Brauweiler, Rheinisches Amt für Denkmalpflege in Brauweiler

Brechin, Town Hall

Brecon, Brecknock Mus.
Brecon, Brecknock Museum

Breda, De Beyerd

Breda, Kon. Mil. Acad.
Breda, Koninklijke Militaire Academy

Breda, Rijksmus. Vlkenknd.
Breda, Rijksmuseum voor Volkenkunde 'Justinius van Nassau'

Bregenz, Kstlerhaus Pal. Thurn & Taxis
Bregenz, Künstlerhaus Palais Thurn und Taxis

Bregenz, Kultzent. Schendlingen
Bregenz, Kulturzentrum Schendlingen

Bregenz, Vorarlbg. Landesmus.
Bregenz, Vorarlberger Landesmuseum

Bremen, Focke-Mus.
Bremen, Focke-Museum [Bremen Landesmuseum für Kunst- und Kulturgeschichte]

Bremen, Gal. Holz
Bremen, Galerie Holz

Bremen, Gal. Michael Hertz
Bremen, Galerie Michael Hertz

Bremen, Graph. Kab. Ksthandel Wolfgang Werner
Bremen, Graphisches Kabinett Kunsthandel Wolfgang Werner

Bremen, Ksthalle
Bremen, Kunsthalle

Bremen, Marcks-Haus
Bremen, Gerhard Marcks-Haus

Bremen, Paula-Modersohn-Becker-Haus

Bremen, Rathaus [houses Güldenkammer]

Bremen, Roseliushaus

Bremen, Staats- & Ubib.
Bremen, Staats- und Universitätsbibliothek

Bremen, Übersee-Mus.
Bremen, Übersee-Museum

Brentford: see London

Brentwood, CA, Getty A. Cent.
Brentwood, CA, J. Paul Getty Arts Center

Brescia, Civ. Mus. S Giulia
Brescia, Civici Musei di S Giulia

Brescia, Duomo Vecchio [Rotonda]

Brescia, Mus. Civ. Armi Marzoli
Brescia, Museo Civico delle Armi Luigi Marzoli

Brescia, Mus. Civ. Crist.
Brescia, Museo Civico Cristiano

Brescia, Mus. Civ. Età Romana
Brescia, Museo Civico dell'Età Romana

Brescia, Mus. Civ. Risorgimento
Brescia, Museo Civico del Risorgimento

Brescia, Mus. Civ. Sci. Nat.
Brescia, Museo Civico di Scienze Naturali

Brescia, Mus. Dioc. A. Sacra
Brescia, Museo Diocesano d'Arte Sacra

Brescia, Musei Civ.
Brescia, Musei Civici [admins Mus. Armi Marzoli; Mus. Civ. Età Romana; Mus. Civ. Risorgimento; Pin. Civ. Tosio–Martinengo]

Brescia, Nuo. Semin. Dioc.
Brescia, Nuovo Seminario Diocesano

Brescia, Pal. Mun.
Brescia, Palazzo Municipale

Brescia, Pin. Civ. Tosio--Martinengo
Brescia, Pinacoteca Civica Tosio--Martinengo

Breslau, ex-Schles. Mus. Bild. Kst., Breslau
Breslau, Schlesischer Museum der Bildenden Künste [destr. World War II; Breslau now Wrocław, Poland]

Bressanone, Bib. Semin. Maggiore
Bressanone, Biblioteca del Seminario Maggiore

Bressanone, Mus. Dioc.
Bressanone, Museo Diocesano [in Palazzo Vescovile; incl. Cathedral Treasury]

Brest, Mus. Mun.
Brest, Musée Municipal [Musée des Beaux-Arts]

Breteuil, Mus. Archéol. Reg.
Breteuil, Musée Archéologique de la Région de Breteuil

Brezovo, Hist. Mus.
Brezovo, Historical Museum

Bridgetown, Queen's Park Gal.
Bridgetown, Queen's Park Gallery [Barbados]

Bridgewater, NS, DesBrisay Mus. & N. Exh. Cent.
Bridgewater, NS, DesBrisay Museum and National Exhibition Centre

Brighouse, Smith A.G.
Brighouse, Smith Art Gallery

Brighton, A.G. & Mus.
Brighton, Art Gallery and Museum

Brighton, A.G. & Museums
Brighton, Art Gallery and Museums [admins A.G. & Mus.; Royal Pav.]

Brighton, Barlow Col.
Brighton, Barlow Collection of Chinese Ceramics, Bronzes and Jades

Brighton, Pub. A. Gals
Brighton, Public Art Galleries [now A.G. & Mus.]

Brighton, Royal Pav.
Brighton, Royal Pavilion

Brighton, U. Brighton
Brighton, University of Brighton [until Sept 1992 called Brighton Polytechnic]

Brighton, U. Sussex, Gardner Cent. Gal.
Brighton, University of Sussex, Gardner Centre Gallery

Brisbane, City Hall A.G. & Mus.
Brisbane, Brisbane City Hall Art Gallery and Museum

Brisbane, Queensland A.G.
Brisbane, Queensland Art Gallery

Brisbane, Queensland Mus.
Brisbane, Queensland Museum

Brisbane, U. Queensland A.G.
Brisbane, University of Queensland Art Gallery

Bristol, Arnolfini Gal.
Bristol, Arnolfini Gallery

Bristol, Mus. & A.G.
Bristol, City of Bristol Museum and Art Gallery

Brit. Council Col.
British Council Collection

Brit. Govt A. Col.
British Government Art Collection

Brit. Royal Col.
British Royal Collection

Brixen: see Bressanone

Brno, Archaeol. Inst.
Brno, Archaeological Institute

Brno, House A.
Brno, House of Art of the Town of Brno (Dům Umění Města Brna)

Brno, Morav. Gal.
Brno, Moravian Gallery (Moravská Galerie v Brně)

Brno, Morav. Mus.
Brno, Moravian Museum (Moravské Muzeum)

Brno, Morfarská Gal.
Brno, Morfarská Galerie

Brno, Mus. City
Brno, Museum of the City of Brno (Muzeum Města Brna)

Brno, Purkyně U.
Brno, Purkyně University (Univerzita Jana Evangelisty Purkyně)

Brno, State Archvs
Brno, State Archives (Státní archív)

Brno, Tech. U.
Brno, Technical University (Vysoké Učení Technické v Brně)

Brno, U. Agric.
Brno, University of Agriculture (Vysoká Škola Zemědělská)

Brno, U. Veterinary Sci.
Brno, University of Veterinary Science (Vysoká Škola Veterinární v Brně)

Brno, Vaněk Gal.
Brno, Vaněk Gallery (Galerie Vaněk)

Brockton, MA, A. Mus.
Brockton, Brockton Art Museum [Fuller Memorial]

Brodósqui, Casa-Mus. Portinari
Brodósqui, Casa-Museu Portinari

Brookline, MA, Hist. Soc. Mus.
Brookline, Brookline Historical Society Museum

Brooklyn: see New York

Broughty Ferry: see Dundee

Bruchsal, Schloss, Mus. Mech. Musikinstr.
Bruchsal, Schloss, Museum Mechanischer Musikinstrumente [Sammlung Jan Brauers]

Bruchsal, Städt. Mus. Schloss
Bruchsal, Städtisches Museum im Schloss

Bruges, Acad. S. Kst.
Bruges, Academie voor Schone Kunsten

Bruges, Arentshuis [now Brangwynmus.]

Bruges, Belfort

Bruges, Brangwynmus.
Bruges, Brangwynmuseum [formerly Arentshuis]

Bruges, Comm. Openb. Onderstand
Bruges, Commissie voor Openbare
Onderstand

Bruges, Gerechtshof
Bruges, Gerechtshof Brugse Vrije

Bruges, Gezelle Mus.
Bruges, Guido Gezelle Museum

Bruges, Groeningemus.
Bruges, Groeningemuseum

Bruges, Gruuthusemus.
Bruges, Gruuthusemuseum

Bruges, Kon. Hoofdgilde St Sebastiaan
Bruges, Koninklijke Hoofdgilde St Sebastiaan

Bruges, Memlingmus.
Bruges, Memlingmuseum [in St Janshosp.]

Bruges, Mus. A. Anc.
Bruges, Musée d'Art Ancien

Bruges, Mus. Archéol.
Bruges, Musée Archéologique

Bruges, Mus. Com.
Bruges, Musée Communal

Bruges, Mus. Groot Semin.
Bruges, Museum Groot Seminarie

Bruges, Mus. Heilig Bloed
Bruges, Museum van Het Heilig Bloed [Musée
du Saint-Sang]

Bruges, Mus. Vlksknd.
Bruges, Museum voor Volkskunde

Bruges, Patrm. A.
Bruges, Patrimoine Artistique de la Province
de la Flandre Occidentale

Bruges, Rijksarchf
Bruges, Rijksarchief

Bruges, Stadhuis

Bruges, Stadsbib.
Bruges, Stadsbibliotheek

Bruges, Stadshallen

Bruges, Stedel. Musea
Bruges, Stedelijke Musea [admins
Brangwynmus.; Beltort; Gezelle Mus.;
Groeningenmus.; Gruuthusemus.; Mus.
Archéol.; Mus. Vlksknd.; Stadhuis;
Steinmetzkab. & Bib.]

Bruges, Steinmetzkab. & Bib.
Bruges, Steinmetzkabinet en Bibliotheek

Bruges, St Janshosp.
Bruges, St Janshospitaal

Bruges, Vrije Mus.
Bruges, Provinciaal Museum Het Brugse Vrije

Brühl, Schloss Augustusburg

Brühl, Schloss Falkenlust

Brunn am Gebirge, Heimathaus Gemeinde
Brunn am Gebirge, Heimathaus der Gemeinde

Brunswick, Herzog Anton-Ulrich Mus.
Brunswick, Herzog Anton-Ulrich Museum

Brunswick, Kstver.
Brunswick, Kunstverein

Brunswick, Landesmus.
Brunswick, Landesmuseum

Brunswick, Landesmus. Gesch. & Vlkstum
Brunswick, Landesmuseum für Geschichte
und Volkstum

Brunswick, Staatl. Nathist. Mus.
Brunswick, Staatliches Naturhistorisches
Museum

Brunswick, Städt. Mus.
Brunswick, Städtisches Museum

Brunswick, ME, Bowdoin Coll. Mus. A.
Brunswick, ME, Bowdoin College Museum of
Art

Brussels, Acad. Royale B.-A. & Ecole A. Déc.
Brussels, Académie Royale des Beaux-Arts et
Ecole des Arts Décoratifs

Brussels, Antalga

Brussels, Archv A. Contemp.
Brussels, Archive de l'Art Contemporain

Brussels, Archvs A. Belge
Brussels, Archives d'Art Belge

Brussels, Archvs Arch. Mod.
Brussels, Archives d'Architecture Moderne

Brussels, ASLK [Algemene Spaar en Lijfrentekas]

Brussels, Atelier 340

Brussels, Banque-Lambert

Brussels, Belg. Mun. Credit Inst.
Brussels, Belgian Municipal Credit Institution

Brussels, Bib. Royale Albert 1er
Brussels, Bibliothèque Royale Albert 1er
[Koninklijke Bibliothek Albert I]

Brussels, Bib. Royale Albert 1er, Cab. Est.
Brussels, Bibliothèque Royale Albert 1er,
Cabinet des Estampes

Brussels, Bib. Royale Albert 1er, Cab. Médailles
Brussels, Bibliothèque Royale Albert 1er,
Cabinet des Médailles

Brussels, Bois de la Cambre

Brussels, Cent. Albert Borschette
Brussels, Centre Albert Borschette

Brussels, Château Duyvenvoorde

Brussels, Cols Royales
Brussels, Collections Royales Belges

Brussels, Crédit Com. Belg.
Brussels, Crédit Communal de Belgique

Brussels, Ecole N. Sup. Archit. A. Visuels
Brussels, Ecole Nationale Supérieure
d'Architecture et des Arts Visuels

Brussels, Ecole N. Sup. A. Visuels
Brussels, Ecole Nationale Supérieure des Arts
Visuels de la Cambre [Abbaye de la Cambre]

Brussels, Europalia [arts festival held every 2–3
years in different Eur. city]

Brussels, Gal. Apollo
Brussels, Galerie Apollo

Brussels, Gal. Arenberg
Brussels, Galerie Arenberg

Brussels, Gal. CGER
Brussels, Galerie CGER [Galerie Caisse
Générale d'Epargne et de Retraite]

Brussels, Gal. Dietrich
Brussels, Galerie Dietrich [closed]

Brussels, Gal. Georges Giroux
Brussels, Galerie Georges Giroux [closed]

Brussels, Gal. Isy Brachot
Brussels, Galerie Isy Brachot

Brussels, Gal. Kredietbank
Brussels, Galerie de la Kredietbank

Brussels, Gal. La Boëtie
Brussels, Galerie La Boëtie

Brussels, Gal. Le Centaure
Brussels, Galerie Le Centaure [closed]

Brussels, Gal. L'Ecuyer
Brussels, Galerie L'Ecuyer

Brussels, Gal. Robert Finck
Brussels, Galerie Robert Finck

Brussels, Gal. Withofs
Brussels, Galerie Withofs

Brussels, Gemeentekrediet België
Brussels, Gemeentekrediet van België

Brussels, Gen. Bank
Brussels, General Bank

Brussels, Grand Pal. Centenaire
Brussels, Grand Palais du Centenaire

Brussels, Hôtel Com. Woluwe-Saint-Pierre
Brussels, Hôtel Communal de Woluwe-Saint-
Pierre

Brussels, Hôtel de Ville

Brussels, Inst. Sci. Nat.
Brussels, Institut des Sciences Naturelles
[Koninklijk Belgisch Instituut voor
Natuurwetenschappen]

Brussels, Inst. St Luc
Brussels, Institut Saint-Luc

Brussels, Inst. Sup. Etud. Lang. Plast.
Brussels, Institut Supérieur pour l'Etude du
Langage Plastique [ISELP]

Brussels, Kon. Mus. Leger & Krijgsgesch.
Brussels, Koninklijk Museum van het Leger en
van Krijgsgeschiedenis

Brussels, L'Essor

Brussels, La Louvière
Brussels, La Louvière

Brussels, Maison A.
Brussels, Maison d'Art

Brussels, Médiative
Brussels, La Médiative

Brussels, Min. Cult.
Brussels, Ministère de la Culture [Hôtel van de
Velde]

Brussels, Mus. A. Anc.
Brussels, Musée d'Art Ancien

Brussels, Mus. A. Mod.
Brussels, Musée d'Art Moderne

Brussels, Mus. Archvs Archit. Mod.
Brussels, Musée des Archives d'Architecture
Moderne [Fondation R.-L. Delevoy]

Brussels, Mus. Assist. Pub.
Brussels, Musée de l'Assistance Publique

Brussels, Mus. Com.
Brussels, Musée Communal

Brussels, Mus. Dynastie
Brussels, Musée de la Dynastie

Brussels, Musées Royaux A. Déc. & Indust.
Brussels, Musées Royaux des Arts Décoratifs
et Industriels

Brussels, Musées Royaux A. & Hist.
Brussels, Musées Royaux d'Art et d'Histoire
[Koninklijke Musea voor Kunst en
Geschiedenis]

Brussels, Musées Royaux B.-A.
Brussels, Musées Royaux des Beaux-Arts de
Belgique/Koninklijke Musea voor Schone
Kunsten van België [admins Mus. A. Anc.;
Mus. A. Mod.; Mus. Wiertz]

Brussels, Mus. Horta
Brussels, Musée Horta

Brussels, Mus. Hôtel Bellevue
Brussels, Musée de l'Hôtel Bellevue

Brussels, Mus. Hôtel Charlier
Brussels, Musée de l'Hôtel Charlier [St-Joost-
ten-Node]

Brussels, Mus. Instr. Conserv. Royal
Brussels, Musée Instrumental du
Conservatoire Royal

Brussels, Mus. Ixelles
Brussels, Musée Communal des Beaux-Arts
d'Ixelles

Brussels, Mus. Meunier
 Brussels, Musée Constantin Meunier

Brussels, Mus. Porte de Hal
 Brussels, Musée de la Porte de Hal

Brussels, Mus. Ville Bruxelles
 Brussels, Musée de la Ville de Bruxelles
 [Maison du Roi]

Brussels, Mus. Wiertz
 Brussels, Musée Wiertz

Brussels, Nbank Charleroi & Brugge
 Brussels, Nationalbank Charleroi en Brugge

Brussels, Pal. Acad.
 Brussels, Palais des Académies

Brussels, Pal. B.-A.
 Brussels, Palais des Beaux-Arts, Société des
 Expositions

Brussels, Pal. Cinquantenaire
 Brussels, Palais du Cinquantenaire [houses
 Musée Royal de l'Armée et d'Histoire Militaire,
 Autoworld, Musée Royal d'Art et d'Histoire]

Brussels, Pal. Egmont
 Brussels, Palais d'Egmont

Brussels, Pal. Justice
 Brussels, Palais de Justice

Brussels, Pal. Nation
 Brussels, Palais de la Nation

Brussels, Pal. Roi
 Brussels, Palais du Roi

Brussels, Pal. Royal
 Brussels, Palais Royal

Brussels, Parc Bruxelles
 Brussels, Parc de Bruxelles

Brussels, Passage 44

Brussels, Pav. Chin.
 Brussels, Pavillon Chinois

Brussels, Penningkab.
 Brussels, Penningkabinet

Brussels, Petite Gal. Sémin. A.
 Brussels, Petite Galerie du Séminaire des Arts

Brussels, Resurgam

Brussels, Rijksarchf
 Brussels, Rijksarchief

Brussels, Sélection [closed]

Brussels, Sigurd Majorin

Brussels, Soc. Gén. de Banque
 Brussels, Société Générale de Banque

Brussels, Vrije U.
 Brussels, Vrije Universiteit

Bruton Gal.
 Bruton, Bruton Gallery

Bryn Athyn, PA, Glencairn Mus.
 Bryn Athyn, PA, Glencairn Museum

Bryn Mawr, PA, Bryn Mawr Coll., Riegal Mem.
 Mus.
 Bryn Mawr, PA, Bryn Mawr College, Ella
 Riegal Memorial Museum

Bucharest, Acad. A. Nicolae Grigorescu
 Bucharest, Academy of Art Nicolae
 Grigorescu (Academia de Artă Nicolae
 Grigorescu)

Bucharest, Acad. Mus.
 Bucharest, Academy of Music (Academia de
 Muzică)

Bucharest, Acad. Social. Repub. Romania
 Bucharest, Academy of the Socialist Republic
 of Romania (Academia Republicii Socialiste
 România)

Bucharest, Athenaeum (Ateneul)

Bucharest, Cent. Mil. Mus.
 Bucharest, Central Military Museum (Muzeul
 Militar Central)

Bucharest, Cent. State Lib.
 Bucharest, Central State Library (Biblioteca
 Centrală de Stat)

Bucharest City Council
 Bucharest, Bucharest City Council

Bucharest, Gal. A. Dalles
 Bucharest, Galeria de Artă Dalles [Sala Dalles]

Bucharest, Gal. Nouă
 Bucharest, Galeria Nouă

Bucharest, Ion Mincu Inst. Archit.
 Bucharest, Ion Mincu Institute of Architecture
 (Institutul de Arhitectură 'Ion Mincu')

Bucharest, Jew. Mus.
 Bucharest, Jewish Museum

Bucharest, Lib. Acad. Social. Repub. Romania
 Bucharest, Library of the Academy of the
 Socialist Republic of Romania (Biblioteca
 Academiei Republicii Socialiste România)

Bucharest, Minovici Mus. Flk A.
 Bucharest, Minovici Museum of Folk Art
 (Muzeul de Artă Feudală Dr Gh. Minovici)

Bucharest, Mus. A.
 Bucharest, Museum of Art of RSR (Muzeul de
 Arta al RSR) [now N. Mus. A.]

Bucharest, Mus. A. Col.
 Bucharest, Museum of Art Collections
 (Muzeul Colecțiilor de Artă)

Bucharest, Mus. Ant.
 Bucharest, Museum of Antiquities (Muzeul de
 Arheologie)

Bucharest, Mus. Hist. & A., Storck Col.
 Bucharest, Museum of the History and Art of
 Bucharest, Storck Collection (Muzeul de
 Istorie și Artă al municipiului București,
 Colecția Ferderic Storck și Cecilia Cutescu-
 Storck)

Bucharest, Mus. Med. Roman. A.
 Bucharest, Museum of Medieval Romanian
 Art (Muzeul de Artă Brîncovenească)

Bucharest, Mus. N. Theat.
 Bucharest, Museum of the National Theatre
 (Muzeul Teatrului Național)

Bucharest, Mus. Roman. Music
 Bucharest, Museum of Romanian Music
 (Muzeul Muzicii Românești)

Bucharest, Mus. Roman. Peasant
 Bucharest, Museum of the Romanian Peasant
 (Muzeului țăranului Roman)

Bucharest, N. Hist. Mus. Romania
 Bucharest, National History Museum of
 Romania (Muzeul Național de Istorie a
 Romaniei)

Bucharest, Nicolae Grigorescu Acad. A.
 Bucharest, Nicolae Grigorescu Academy of
 Art (Academia de Artă 'Nicolae Grigorescu')

Bucharest, N. Mus. A.
 Bucharest, National Museum of Art of
 Romania (Muzeul National de Artă a
 Românei) [formerly called Mus. A.; admins
 Mus. A.; Mus. A. Col.; Mus. Med. Roman. A.;
 Mus. Roman. Music]

Bucharest, Roman. Acad.
 Bucharest, Romanian Academy

Bucharest, Roman. Acad. Lib.
 Bucharest, Romanian Academy Library

Bucharest, Simu Mus.
 Bucharest, Simu Museum (Muzeul Simu)
 [destr.]

Bucharest, Tattarascu Mem. Mus.
 Bucharest, G.L. Tattarascu Memorial Museum
 (Muzeul Memorial G. L. Tattarascu)

Bucharest, Teodor Aman Mus.
 Bucharest, Teodor Aman Museum (Muzeul
 Teodor Aman)

Bucharest, U. Bucharest, Fac. Biol.
 Bucharest, University of Bucharest, Faculty of
 Biology (Universitatea București)

Bucharest, Village Mus. & Mus. Pop. A.
 Bucharest, Village Museum and Museum of
 Popular Art (Muzeul Satului și de Artă
 Populară)

Bucharest, Zambaccian Mus.
 Bucharest, Zambaccian Museum (Muzeul
 Zambaccian)

Buchen, Bezirksmus.
 Buchen, Bezirksmuseum

Bückeburg Schloss
 Bückeburg, Bückeburg Schloss

Budapest, Acad. F.A.
 Budapest, Academy of Fine Arts
 (Képzömüvészeti Föiskola)

Budapest, Adolf Fényes Hall (Fényes Adolf
 Terem)

Budapest, A. Hall
 Budapest, Art Hall (Mücsarnok)

Budapest, Aquincumi Mus.
 Budapest, Aquincumi Museum (Aquincumi
 Múzeum)

Budapest, Bartók House (Bartók Béla Emlékház)

Budapest, Cent. Semin.
 Budapest, Central Seminary

Budapest, Chin. Mus.
 Budapest, Chinese Museum (Kíná Múzeum)
 [closed]

Budapest, Ernst Mus.
 Budapest, Ernst Museum (Ernst Múzeum)

Budapest, Ethnog. Mus.
 Budapest, Ethnographic Museum (Néprajzi
 Múzeum)

Budapest, Fränkel Gal.
 Budapest, Fränkel Galléria

Budapest, Hist. Mus.
 Budapest, Historical Museum of Budapest
 (Budapesti Történeti Múzeum) [admins
 Aquincumi Mus.; Bartok House; Hist. Mus.;
 Kiscelli Mus.]

Budapest, Hopp Mus. Orient. A.
 Budapest, Ferenc Hopp Museum of Oriental
 Art (Hopp Ferenc Keletázsiai Müvészeti
 Múzeum)

Budapest, House Creative Artists
 Budapest, House of Creative Artists (Alkotás
 Müvészház)

Budapest, Hung. Mus. Archit.
 Budapest, Hungarian Museum of Architecture
 (Magyar Épitészeti Múzeum)

Budapest, Hung. N. Acad. Sci.
 Budapest, Hungarian National Academy of
 Sciences (Magyar Tudományos Akadémia)

Budapest, Hung. N. Archvs
 Budapest, Hungarian National Archives
 (Magyar Országos Levéltár)

Budapest, Kiscelli Mus.
 Budapest, Kiscelli Museum

Budapest, Lajos Kassák Mem. Mus.
Budapest, Lajos Kassák Memorial Museum
(Kassák Lajos Emlékmúzeum)

Budapest, Lib. Hung. Acad. Sci.
Budapest, Library of the Hungarian Academy
of Sciences (Magyar Tudományos Akadémia
Könyvtára)

Budapest, Liszt Acad. Music
Budapest, Ferenc Liszt Academy of Music
(Liszt Ferenc Zeneművészet Fóiskola)

Budapest, Loránd Eötvös Cent. U. Lib.
Budapest, Loránd Eötvös Central University
Library (Eötvös Loránd Tudományegyetem
Központi Könyvtára)

Budapest, Loránd Eötvös U., Dept. A. Hist.
Budapest, Loránd Eötvös University,
Department of Art History

Budapest, Margaret Island (Margitsziget)

Budapest, Met. Gal.
Budapest, Metropolitan Gallery (Fövárosi
Képtár)

Budapest, Min. Agric.
Budapest, Ministry of Agriculture
(Mezögazdasági Miniszterium)

Budapest, Min. Cult.
Budapest, Ministry of Culture (Kulturális
Minisztérium)

Budapest, Mügyütök Gal.
Budapest, Mügyütök Galéria

Budapest, Mus. Ant.
Budapest, Museum of Antiquities

Budapest, Mus. Applied A
Budapest, Museum of Applied Art
(Iparművészeti Múzeum) [admins Chin. Mus.;
Hopp Mus. Orient. A.; Mus. Applied A.;
Nagytetenyi, nr Budapest, Castle Mus.]

Budapest, Mus. F.A.
Budapest, Museum of Fine Arts
(Szépművészeti Múzeum)

Budapest, Mus. Hung. Labour Movement
Budapest, Museum of the Hungarian Labour
Movement (Magyar Munkásmozgalmi
Múzeum) [c. 1990 became N. Mus., Dept
Mod. Hist.]

Budapest, New Soc. F. Artists
Budapest, New Society of Fine Artists
(Képzömüvészek Új Társága) [KUT]

Budapest, N.G.
Budapest, Hungarian National Gallery (Magyar
Nemzéti Galéria)

Budapest, N. Mus.
Budapest, Hungarian National Museum
(Magyar Nemzéti Múzeum)

Budapest, N. Mus., Dept Mod. Hist.
Budapest, National Museum, Department of
Modern History [formerly Mus. Hung. Labour
Movement]

Budapest, N. Széchényi Lib.
Budapest, National Széchényi Library
(Országos Széchényi Könyvtár)

Budapest, Óbuda Gal.
Budapest, Óbuda Gallery

Budapest, Pest Co. Archv
Budapest, Pest County Archive

Budapest, Petöfi Mus. Hung. Lit.
Budapest, Petöfi Museum of Hungarian
Literature (Petöfi Irodalmi Múzeum)

Budapest, Post Office Engin. Inst.
Budapest, Post Office Engineering Intstitute
(Postai Tervezö Intézet)

Budapest, Ràday Lib. Mus. Relig. A.
Budapest, Ràday Library Museum of Religious
Art (Dunamelléki Reformàtus Egyhàzkerület
Ràday Múzeuma)

Budapest, Royal Pal.
Budapest, Royal Palace [houses N. Mus., Dept
Mod. Hist; N.G.; Hist. Mus. and N. Széchényi
Lib.]

Budapest, Tech. U. Bldg
Budapest, Technical University Building

Budrio, Pin. Civ. Inzaghi
Budrio, Pinacoteca Civica D. Inzaghi

Budva Mus.
Budva, Budva Museum (Múzeum Budva)

Buenos Aires, Acad. N. B.A.
Buenos Aires, Academia Nacional de Bellas
Artes

Buenos Aires, A. Nue.
Buenos Aires, Arte Nuevo

Buenos Aires, Asoc. Amigos A.
Buenos Aires, Asociación Amigos del Arte

Buenos Aires, Banco Ciudad
Buenos Aires, Banco de la Ciudad de Buenos
Aires

Buenos Aires, Bohemio Club, Gal. Pacífico
Buenos Aires, Bohemio Club, Galería Pacífico

Buenos Aires, Cent. A. & Comunic.
Buenos Aires, Centro de Arte y Comunicación
[CAYC]

Buenos Aires, Cent. A. Visuales di Tella
Buenos Aires, Centro de Artes Visuales di
Tella [attached to Inst. Torcuato Tella]

Buenos Aires, Col. Chase Manhattan Bank, N.A.
Buenos Aires, Collection of the Chase
Manhattan Bank, N.A.

Buenos Aires, Escuela N. B.A. 'Prilidiano
Pueyrredón'
Buenos Aires, Escuela Nacional de Bellas
Artes 'Prilidiano Pueyrredón'

Buenos Aires, Escuela Sup. B.A. Ernesto de la
Cárcova
Buenos Aires, Escuela Superior de Bellas Artes
Ernesto de la Cárcova

Buenos Aires, Fond. N. A.
Buenos Aires, Fondo Nacional de las Artes

Buenos Aires, Fund. Lorenzutti
Buenos Aires, Fundación Lorenzutti

Buenos Aires, Fund. S Telmo
Buenos Aires, Fundación San Telmo

Buenos Aires, Gal. A. Centoira
Buenos Aires, Galería de Arte Centoira

Buenos Aires, Gal. Caballito
Buenos Aires, Galería Caballito

Buenos Aires, Gal. Carmen Waugh
Buenos Aires, Galería Carmen Waugh

Buenos Aires, Gal. Cent.
Buenos Aires, Galería del Centro

Buenos Aires, Gal. Flores
Buenos Aires, Galería Flores

Buenos Aires, Gal. Kramer
Buenos Aires, Galería Kramer

Buenos Aires, Gal. Lirolay
Buenos Aires, Galería Lirolay

Buenos Aires, Gal. Peuser
Buenos Aires, Galería Peuser

Buenos Aires, Gal. Ruth Benzacar
Buenos Aires, Galería Ruth Benzacar

Buenos Aires, Hosp. Clínicas
Buenos Aires, Hospital de Clínicas

Buenos Aires, Inst. A. Mod.
Buenos Aires, Instituto de Arte Moderno

Buenos Aires, Inst. Fr. Estud. Sup.
Buenos Aires, Instituto Francés de Estudios
Superiores [Van Riel]

Buenos Aires, Inst. Torcuato Tella
Buenos Aires, Instituto Torcuato di Tella

Buenos Aires, Mus. A. Blanco
Buenos Aires, Museo de Arte Isaac Fernández
Blanco

Buenos Aires, Mus. A. Contemp.
Buenos Aires, Museo de Arte Contemporáneo

Buenos Aires, Mus. A. Mod.
Buenos Aires, Museo de Arte Moderno [de la
Ciudad Buenos Aires]

Buenos Aires, Mus. A. Plást. 'Eduardo Sivori'
Buenos Aires, Museo de Artes Plásticas
'Eduardo Sivori'

Buenos Aires, Mus. Badii
Buenos Aires, Museo Badii

Buenos Aires, Mus. Calcos & Escul. Comp.
Buenos Aires, Museo de Calcos y Escultura
Comparada

Buenos Aires, Mus. Casa de Yrurtia
Buenos Aires, Museo Casa de Yrurtia

Buenos Aires, Mus. Hist. N.
Buenos Aires, Museo Histórico Nacional

Buenos Aires, Mus. Hist. N. Cabildo Ciudad
Buenos Aires, Museo Histórico Nacional del
Cabildo de la Ciudad de Buenos Aires y de la
Revolución de Mayo

Buenos Aires, Mus. Hist. N. Traje
Buenos Aires, Museo Histórico Nacional del
Traje

Bunos Aires, Mus. Mun. A. Colon.
Buenos Aires, Museo Municipal de Arte
Colonial

Buenos Aires, Mus. N. A. Dec.
Buenos Aires, Museo Nacional de Arte
Decorativo

Buenos Aires, Mus. N. B.A.
Buenos Aires, Museo Nacional de Bellas Artes

Buenos Aires, Mus. Saavedra
Buenos Aires, Museo Saavedra

Buenos Aires, Primer Mus. Hist. Argentina
Buenos Aires, Primer Museo Argentino de
Historia Argentina en la Escuela Primaria

Buenos Aires, Salón Altamira

Buenos Aires, Sheraton Hotel

Buenos Aires, Soc. Heb. Arg.
Buenos Aires, Sociedad Hebraica Argentina

Buffalo, NY, Albright A.G.
Buffalo, NY, Albright Art Gallery [name
changed to Albright–Knox A.G. in 1961]

Buffalo, NY, Albright–Knox A.G.
Buffalo, NY, Albright–Knox Art Gallery
[formerly Albright A.G.]

Buffalo, NY, F.A. Acad.
Buffalo, NY, Buffalo Fine Arts Academy

Buffalo, NY, Mus. Sci.
Buffalo, NY, Museum of Science

Buffalo, NY, Seymour H. Knox Found.
Buffalo, NY, Seymour H. Knox Foundation

Bukhara, Reg. Mus.
Bukhara, Bukhara Regional Museum

Bulawayo A.G.
Bulawayo, Bulawayo Art Gallery

Bulawayo, Nat. Hist. Mus. Zimbabwe
Bulawayo, Natural History Museum of
Zimbabwe

Buonconvento, Mus. A. Sacra Val d'Arbia
Buonconvento, Museo d'Arte Sacra della Val d'Arbia

Burdur Mus.
Burdur, Burdur Museum (Burdur Müzesi)

Burgdorf, Stadtmus.
Burgdorf, Stadtmuseum

Burghausen, Burg
Burghausen, Burg Burghausen

Burghausen, Staatsgal. Hauptburg
Burghausen, Staatsgalerie in der Hauptburg

Burgo de Osma, Archv Catedral
Burgo de Osma, Archivo de la Catedral

Burgo de Osma, Mus. Catedralicio
Burgo de Osma, Museo Catedralicio

Burgos, Mus. Arqueol. Prov.
Burgos, Museo Arqueológico Provincial [Museo de Burgos; Museo Casa Miranda]

Burgos, Mus. Dioc.-Catedralicio
Burgos, Museo Diocesano-Catedralicio

Burgos, Mus. Hist. & A.
Burgos, Museo Histórico y Artístico

Burgos, Real Monasterio de las Huelgas, Mus. Telas & Preseas
Burgos, Real Monasterio de las Huelgas, Museo de Telas y Preseas

Burlington, U. VT, Robert Hull Fleming Mus.
Burlington, VT, University of Vermont, Robert Hull Fleming Museum

Burnaby, BC, Simon Fraser U., Mus. Archaeol. & Ethnol.
Burnaby, BC, Simon Fraser University, Museum of Archaeology and Ethnology

Burnley, Towneley Hall A.G. & Mus.
Burnley, Towneley Hall Art Gallery and Museum

Burrel, Hist. Mus.
Burrel, Historical Museum (Muzeu Historik)

Bursa, Ethnog. Mus.
Bursa, Ethnographic Museum

Bursa, Mus. Turk. & Islam. A.
Bursa, Museum of Turkish and Islamic Art

Bury, A.G. & Mus.
Bury, Art Gallery and Museum

Bury St Edmunds, A.G.
Bury St Edmunds, Art Gallery

Bury St Edmunds, Co. Upper Sch.
Bury St Edmunds, County Upper School

Bury St Edmunds, Guildhall

Bury St Edmunds, Manor House Mus.
Bury St Edmunds, Manor House Museum [incl. former Clock Museum]

Bury St Edmunds, Moyse's Hall

Bury St Edmunds, St Edmundsbury Museums [admins Gershom–Parkington Collection of Clocks and Watches; Manor House Mus.; Moyse's Hall]

Bury St Edmunds, Suffolk Rec. Office
Bury St Edmunds, Suffolk Record Office

Buxton, Mus. & A.G.
Buxton, Buxton Museum and Art Gallery

Bytom, Mus. Upper Silesia
Bytom, Museum of Upper Silesia (Múzeum Górnośloskie)

Čačak, Nadežda Petrović A.G.
Čačak, Nadežda Petrović Art Gallery (Umetnička Galerija Nadežda Petrović)

Cáceres, Mus. Prov. Arqueol., Etnol. & B.A.
Cáceres, Museo Provincial Arqueológico, Etnológico y de Bellas Artes

Cadenabbia, Villa Carlotta

Cádiz, Mus. Arqueol. Prov.
Cádiz, Museo Arqueológico Provincial

Cádiz, Mus. Pint.
Cádiz, Museo de Pinturas [Museo de Bellas Artes]

Caen, Hôtel d'Escoville

Caen, Mus. B.-A.
Caen, Musée des Beaux-Arts

Cafayate, Mus. Arqueol. Calchaqui
Cafayate, Museo de Arqueología Calchaqui

Cagli, Cassa di Risparmio

Cagliari, Citadella Mus.
Cagliari, Citadella dei Musei

Cagliari, Monteponi

Cagliari, Mus. Archeol. N.
Cagliari, Museo Archeologico Nazionale

Cagliari, Mus. Santuario Bonario
Cagliari, Museo del Santuario di Bonario

Cagliari, Pin. N.
Cagliari, Pinacoteca Nazionale [in Citadella Mus.]

Cagnes-sur-Mer, Château-Mus.
Cagnes-sur-Mer, Château-Musée du Haut de Cagnes [incl. Musée de l'Olivier]

Cairo, Akhnaten Gal.
Cairo, Akhnaten Gallery

Cairo, Coptic Mus.
Cairo, Coptic Museum

Cairo, Egyp. Ant. Org.
Cairo, Egyptian Antiquities Organization

Cairo, Egyp. Mus.
Cairo, Egyptian Museum

Cairo, Gazira Mus.
Cairo, Gazira Museum

Cairo, MOMA
Cairo, Museum of Modern Art

Cairo, Muhammad Naghi Mus.
Cairo, Muhammad Naghi Museum

Cairo, Mus. Islam. A.
Cairo, Museum of Islamic Art

Cairo, N. Lib.
Cairo, National Library

Cairo, Pal. Isma'il Pasha
Cairo, Palace of Isma'il Pasha

Cairo, Semiramis Hotel

Cairo, Senate

Calahorra, Mus. Tesoro Catedralicio & Dioc.
Calahorra, Museo del Tesoro Catedralicio y Diocesano

Calais, Mus. B.-A.
Calais, Musée des Beaux-Arts et de la Dentelle

Calcutta, Artists' Assoc.
Calcutta, Artists' Association

Calcutta, Asiat. Soc.
Calcutta, Asiatic Society

Calcutta, Birla Acad. A. & Cult.
Calcutta, Birla Academy of Art and Culture

Calcutta, High Court

Calcutta, Ind. Mus.
Calcutta, Indian Museum

Calcutta, Rabindra Bharati Soc.
Calcutta, Rabindra Bharati Society

Calcutta, Rabindra Bharati U.
Calcutta, Rabindra Bharati University

Calcutta, Rabindra Bharati U., Mus.
Calcutta, Rabindra Bharati University, Museum

Calcutta, Res. Inst. Flk Cult.
Calcutta, Research Institute of Folk Culture

Calcutta, Santiniketan Ashramik Sangha

Calcutta, U. Calcutta, Asutosh Mus. Ind. A.
Calcutta, University of Calcutta, Asutosh Museum of Indian Art

Calcutta, Victoria Mem. Hall
Calcutta, Victoria Memorial Hall

Calcutta, Victoria Mus.
Calcutta, Victoria Museum [State Archaeological Museum]

Caldas de Mombury: see Caldes de Montbui

Caldas da Rainha, Mus. Malhoa
Caldas da Rainha, Museu de José Malhoa [Instituto Português do Património Cultural]

Caldes de Montbui, Mus. Manolo
Caldes de Montbui, Museo Mas Manolo

Calgary, Alta Coll. A., A.G.
Calgary, Alberta College of Art, Art Gallery

Calgary, Bumper Dev. Corp.
Calgary, Bumper Development Corporation

Calgary, Glenbow–Alta Inst.
Calgary, Glenbow–Alberta Institute

Cali, Mus. A. Mod. La Tertulia
Cali, Museo de Arte Moderno La Tertulia

Cali, Mus. Arqueol. La Merced
Cali, Museo Arqueológico La Merced

Cali, Mus. Manuel Maria Buenaventura
Cali, Museo Manuel Maria Buenaventura

Calicut, Pazhassiraja Mus.
Calicut, Pazhassiraja Museum

Calicut, V.K. Krishna Mus. & A.G.
Calicut, V.K. Krishna Menon Museum and Art Gallery

Callao, Mus. Hist. Mil. Perú
Callao, Museo Histórico Militar del Perú [in Real Felipe Fort]

Calw, Mus. Stadt & Hermann Hesse-Gedenkstät.
Calw, Museum der Stadt und Hermann Hesse-Gedenkstätte [also known as Heimatmuseum]

Cambrai, Bib. Mun. Classée
Cambrai, Bibliothèque Municipale Classée

Cambrai, Maison Ste Agnès
Cambrai, Maison Sainte Agnès

Cambrai, Mus. Mun.
Cambrai, Musée Municipal

Cambridge, Christ's Coll.
Cambridge, Christ's College

Cambridge, Clare Coll.
Cambridge, Clare College

Cambridge, Corn Exchange
Cambridge, Corn Exchange

Cambridge, Corpus Christi Coll.
Cambridge, Corpus Christi College

Cambridge, Darkroom
Cambridge, Cambridge Darkroom

Cambridge, Emmanuel Coll.
Cambridge, Emmanuel College

Cambridge, Fitzwilliam
Cambridge, Fitzwilliam Museum

Cambridge, Girton Coll.
Cambridge, Girton College

Cambridge, Gonville and Caius Coll.
Cambridge, Gonville and Caius College

Cambridge, Jesus Coll.
Cambridge, Jesus College

Cambridge, King's Coll.
Cambridge, King's College

Cambridge, Magdalene Coll.
Cambridge, Magdalene College

Cambridge, Pembroke Coll.
Cambridge, Pembroke College

Cambridge, St Catharine's Coll.
Cambridge, St Catharine's College

Cambridge, St John's Coll.
Cambridge, St John's College

Cambridge, Trinity Coll.
Cambridge, Trinity College

Cambridge, Trinity Hall

Cambridge, U. Cambridge, Kettle's Yard
Cambridge, Cambridge University, Kettle's
Yard

Cambridge, U. Cambridge, Mus. Archaeol. &
Anthropol.
Cambridge, Cambridge University, Museum of
Archaeology and Anthropology

Cambridge, U. Cambridge, Senate House
Cambridge, Senate House

Cambridge, U. Cambridge, Whipple Mus. Hist.
Sci.
Cambridge, Cambridge University, Whipple
Museum of the History of Science

Cambridge, U. Lib.
Cambridge, University Library

Cambridge, MA, Busch-Reisinger Mus.
Cambridge, MA, Busch-Reisinger Museum

Cambridge, MA, Fogg
Cambridge, MA, Fogg Art Museum

Cambridge, MA, Gropper A.G.
Cambridge, MA, Gropper Art Gallery

Cambridge, MA, Harvard U. A. Museums
Cambridge, MA, Harvard University Art
Museums [admins Buch-Reisinger Mus.; Fogg;
Sackler Mus.]

Cambridge, MA, Harvard U., Countway Lib.
Medic.
Cambridge, MA, Harvard University,
Countway Library for Medicine

Cambridge, MA, Harvard U., Frances Loeb
Sch. Des. Lib.
Cambridge, MA, Harvard University, Frances
Loeb School of Design Library

Cambridge, MA, Harvard U., Grad. Sch. Des.
Cambridge, MA, Harvard University, Graduate
School of Design

Cambridge, MA, Harvard U., Harry Elkins
Widener Mem. Lib.
Cambridge, MA, Harvard University, Harry
Elkins Widener Memorial Library

Cambridge, MA, Harvard U., Houghton Lib.
Cambridge, MA, Harvard University,
Houghton Library

Cambridge, MA, Harvard U., Houghton Lib.,
Hofer Col.
Cambridge, MA, Harvard University,
Houghton Library, Hofer Collection

Cambridge, MA, Harvard U. Law Sch.
Cambridge, MA, Harvard University Law
School

Cambridge, MA, Harvard U., Loeb Music Lib.
Cambridge, MA, Harvard University, Loeb
Music Library

Cambridge, MA, Harvard U., Peabody Mus.
Cambridge, MA, Harvard University, Peabody
Museum of Archaeology and Ethnology

Cambridge, MA, Harvard U., Portrait Col.
Cambridge, MA, Harvard University, Portrait
Collection

Cambridge, MA, Harvard U., Semit. Mus.
Cambridge, MA, Harvard University, Semitic
Museum

Cambridge, MA, Harvard U., Theatre Col.
Cambridge, MA, Harvard University, Harvard
Theatre Collection

Cambridge, MA, Hofer Lib.
Cambridge, MA, Hofer Library

Cambridge, MA, Longfellow N. Hist. Site
Cambridge, MA, Longfellow National Historic
Site

Cambridge, MA, MIT
Cambridge, MA, Massachusetts Institute of
Technology

Cambridge, MA, MIT, Hayden Gal.
Cambridge, MA, Massachusetts Institute of
Technology, Hayden Gallery

Cambridge, MA, MIT, List Visual A. Cent.
Cambridge, MA, Massachusetts Institute of
Technology, List Visual Arts Center

Cambridge, MA, Sackler Mus.
Cambridge, MA, Arthur M. Sackler Museum

Camden, NJ, Campbell Mus.
Camden, NJ, Campbell Museum

Camerino, Mus. Dioc.
Camerino, Museo Diocesano

Camerino, Mus. Pin. Civ.
Camerino, Museo della Pinacoteca Civica

Camigliano, Villa Torrigiani Colonna

Campbelltown, NSW, C.A.G.
Campbelltown, NSW, City Art Gallery

Campeche, Mus. Arqueol. Etnog. & Hist. Estado
Campeche, Museo Arqueológico Etnográfico e
Histórico del Estado

Campese, Vicenza Parrocchiale

Campos do Jordão, Pal. Boa Vista
Campos do Jordão, Palácio Boa Vista

Canajoharie, NY, Lib. & A.G.
Canajoharie, NY, Canajoharie Library and Art
Gallery

Çanakkale, Archaeol. Mus.
Çanakkale, Archaeological Museum

Canberra, Austral. N. U.
Canberra, Australian National University

Canberra, Austral. War Mem.
Canberra, Australian War Memorial

Canberra, N. Australia Bank
Canberra, National Australia Bank

Canberra, N.G.
Canberra, National Gallery of Australia [name
changed from Australian N.G. in 1992]

Canberra, N. Lib.
Canberra, National Library of Australia

Canberra, N. Mus.
Canberra, National Museum of Australia

Canberra, Nolan Gal.
Canberra, Nolan Gallery [Lanyon homestead]

Cantalupo in Sabina, Pal. Camuccini
Cantalupo in Sabina, Palazzo Camuccini

Canterbury, Buffs Regimental Mus.
Canterbury, Buffs Regimental Museum

Canterbury, Cathedral Archvs & Lib. & City Rec.
Office
Canterbury, Cathedral Archives and Library
and City Record Office

Canterbury, Herit. Mus.
Canterbury, Canterbury Heritage Museum

Canterbury, Kent Inst. A. & Des., Herbert Read
Gal.
Canterbury, Kent Institute of Art and Design,
Herbert Read Gallery

Canterbury Mus.
Canterbury, Canterbury Museums [admins
Buffs Regimental Mus.; Herit. Mus.; Roman
Mus.; Royal Mus. & A.G.; W. Gate Mus.;
Whitstable Mus. & Gal.]

Canterbury, Roman Mus.
Canterbury, Roman Museum

Canterbury, Royal Mus. & A.G.
Canterbury, Royal Museum and Art Gallery

Canterbury, W. Gate Mus.
Canterbury, West Gate Museum

Canterbury, Whitstable Mus. & Gal.
Canterbury, Whitstable Museum and Gallery

Canton: see Guangzhou

Canton, OH, A. Inst.
Canton, OH, Art Institute

Cape Town, Cape Archvs Depot
Cape Town, Cape Archives Depot

Cape Town, Groot Constantia Manor House &
Wine Mus.
Cape Town, Groot Constantia Manor House
and Wine Museum

Cape Town, Groote Schuur, Rhodes Col.
Cape Town, Groote Schuur, Rhodes
Collection

Cape Town, Koopmans-de Wet House

Cape Town, Kunstkam.
Cape Town, Die Kunstkamer

Cape Town, Michaelis Col.
Cape Town, Michaelis Collection [in Old
Town House]

Cape Town, N.G.
Cape Town, South African National Gallery

Cape Town, S. Afr. Cult. Hist. Mus.
Cape Town, South African Cultural History
Museum (Suid-Afrikaanse Kultuurhistoriese
Museum)

Cape Town, S. Afr. Lib.
Cape Town, South African Library

Cape Town, S. Afr. Mus.
Cape Town, South African Museum

Cape Town, State Archvs
Cape Town, State Archives

Cape Town, U. Cape Town, Cent. Afr. Stud.
Cape Town, University of Cape Town, Centre
for African Studies

Cape Town, U. Cape Town, Irma Stern Mus.
Cape Town, University of Cape Town, Irma
Stern Museum

Cape Town, U. Cape Town Libs
Cape Town, University of Cape Town
Libraries [incl. University Archives]

Cape Town, William Fehr Col.
Cape Town, William Fehr Collection [held at
castle & at Rust en Veugd]

Cappenberg-Selm, Schloss Cappenberg [houses
Museum of Art and Culture]

Capri, Certosa S Giacomo
Capri, Certosa di S Giacomo

Capri, Rac. Malaparte
Capri, Raccolta Malaparte

Capua, Mus. Prov. Campano
Capua, Museo Provinciale Campano

Caracas, Asoc. Venez., Amigos A. Colon. Col.
Caracas, Asociación Venezolana, Amigos del
Arte Colonial Colección

Caracas, Cent. A. Eur.-Amer.
   Caracas, Centro de Arte Euro-Americano

Caracas, Cent. Cult. Venez.-Brit.
   Caracas, Centro Cultural Venezolano-Britanico

Caracas, Col. Banco Cent. Venezuela
   Caracas, Colección del Banco Central de
   Venezuela

Caracas, Col. Concejo Mun.
   Caracas, Colección Concejo Municipal

Caracas, Col. Pal. Fed.
   Caracas, Colección Palacio Federal

Caracas, Estud. Actual
   Caracas, Estudio Actual

Caracas, Fund. Boulton
   Caracas, Fundación Boulton

Caracas, Fund. Eugenio Mendoza
   Caracas, Fundación Eugenio Mendoza

Caracas, Fund. Mus. Ciencias
   Caracas, Fundación Museo de Ciencias

Caracas, Gal. Adler-Castillo
   Caracas, Galería Adler-Castillo

Caracas, Gal. A. N.
   Caracas, Galería de Arte Nacional [incl. Centro
   de Información Nacional de las Artes
   Plásticas]

Caracas, Gal. Sotavento
   Caracas, Galería Sotavento

Caracas, Gal. Sujo
   Caracas, Galería Sujo

Caracas, Gal. 22
   Caracas, Galería 22

Caracas, Mus. A. Colon.
   Caracas, Museo de Arte Colonial

Caracas, Mus. A. Contemp.
   Caracas, Museo de Arte Contemporáneo de
   Caracas

Caracas, Mus. A. Contemp. Sofía Imber
   Caracas, Museo de Arte Contemporáneo Sofía
   Imber

Caracas, Mus. Audiovisual
   Caracas, Museo Audiovisual

Caracas, Mus. B.A.
   Caracas, Museo de Bellas Artes

Caracas, Mus. Bolivariano
   Caracas, Museo Bolivariano

Caracas, Mus. Cuadra de Bolívar
   Caracas, Museo Cuadra de Bolívar

Caracas, Pal. Miraflores
   Caracas, Palacio Miraflores

Caracas, U. Cent. Venezuela, Ciudad U.
   Caracas, Universidad Central de Venezuela,
   Ciudad Universitaria

Carcare, Bib. Com.
   Carcare, Biblioteca Comunale

Carcassonne, Mus. B.-A.
   Carcassonne, Musée des Beaux-Arts

Cardiff, Chapter A. Cent.
   Cardiff, Chapter Arts Centre

Cardiff, City Hall

Cardiff, N. Mus.
   Cardiff, National Museum of Wales

Cardiff, Oriel Ffotogal.
   Cardiff, Oriel Ffotogallig

Cardiff, Welsh A.C.
   Cardiff, Welsh Arts Council

Cardiff, Welsh Sch. Archit.
   Cardiff, Welsh School of Architecture

Carlisle, Assize Courts

Carlisle, Mus. & A.G.
   Carlisle, Museum and Art Gallery [in Tullie
   House]

Carlisle, PA, Dickinson Coll., Conway Hall
   Carlisle, PA, Dickinson College, Conway Hall
   [destr. 1966]

Carlisle, PA, Dickinson Coll., Trout A.G.
   Carlisle, PA, Dickinson College, Trout Art
   Gallery

Carmarthen, Carms Rec. Office
   Carmarthen, Carmarthenshire Record Office
   [name changed to Dyfed Archvs Serv. in
   1974]

Carmarthen, Dyfed Archvs Serv.
   Carmarthen, Dyfed Archives Services
   [formerly Carms Rec. Office]

Carpentras, Bib. Inguimbertine
   Carpentras, Bibliothèque Inguimbertine

Carpentras, Mus. Duplessis
   Carpentras, Musée Duplessis

Carpentras, Mus. Lapidaire
   Carpentras, Musée Lapidaire [Musée
   Archéologique]

Carpi, Ist. Cult. Com.
   Carpi, Istituti Culturali del Comune di Carpi

Carpi, Mus. Civ.
   Carpi, Museo Civico

Carrara, Accad. B.A. & Liceo A.
   Carrara, Accademia di Belle Arti e Liceo
   Artistico

Carriacou Mus.
   Carriacou, Carriacou Museum

Carson City, NV, Mus.
   Carson City, NV, Carson City Museum

Carson City, NV, State Mus.
   Carson City, NV, Nevada State Museum

Cartagena, Mus. A. Mod.
   Cartagena, Museo de Arte Moderno de
   Cartagena

Cartagena, Mus. Antropol.
   Cartagena, Museo Antropológico

Cartagena, Mus. A. Relig.
   Cartagena, Museo de Arte Religioso

Cartagena, Mus. Colon.
   Cartagena, Museo Colonial

Cartagena, Mus. Hist. Pal. Inquisición
   Cartagena, Museo Histórico del Palacio de la
   Inquisición

Cartersville, GA, Etowah Mounds Archaeol. Area
   Cartersville, GA, Etowah Mounds
   Archaeological Area

Carthage, Antiqua.
   Carthage, Antiquarium

Carthage, Mus. Lavigerie
   Carthage, Musée Lavigerie

Carthage, Mus. N.
   Carthage, Musée National de Carthage

Carthage, Parc Archéol. Thermes Antonin
   Carthage, Parc Archéologique des Thermes
   d'Antonin

Casablanca, Ecole B.-A.
   Casablanca, Ecole des Beaux-Arts

Casale Monferrato, Bib. Civ.
   Casale Monferrato, Biblioteca Civica

Casale Monferrato, Mus. Civ.
   Casale Monferrato, Museo Civico [Palazzo
   Treville]

Casale Monferrato, Pal. Langosco
   Casale Monferrato, Palazzo Langosco

Casale Monferrato, Santuario di Crea

Cascais, Mus.-Bib. Conde de Castro Guimaraes
   Cascais, Museu-Biblioteca Conde de Castro
   Guimaraes

Cascais, Nossa Senhora da Assunçao

Caserta, Pal. Reale
   Caserta, Palazzo Reale [Palazzo Reggia]

Casma, Mus. Reg. Max Uhle
   Casma, Museo Regional de Casma Max Uhle

Casole d'Elsa, Pal. Com.
   Casole d'Elsa, Palazzo del Comune

Castagnola, Col. Thyssen-Bornemisza: see Lugano

Castel di Sangro, Col. A. Banca Pop. Abruzzese
Marchigiana
   Castel di Sangro, Collezioni d'Arte della Banca
   Popolare Abruzzese Marchigiana

Castelfiorentino, Mus. S Verdiana
   Castelfiorentino, Museo di S Verdiana

Castelfranco Veneto, Bib. Com.
   Castelfranco Veneto, Biblioteca Comunale

Castellammare di Stabia, Antiqua. Cattedrale
   Castellammare di Stabia, Antiquarium della
   Cattedrale

Castell'Arquato, S Maria, Mus.
   Castell'Arquato, S Maria, Museo

Castelletto Ticino, Col. Poli
   Castelletto Ticino, Collezione Poli

Castelli, Mus. Cer.
   Castelli, Museo della Ceramica

Castellón, Mus. Prov. B.A.
   Castellón, Museo Provincial de Bellas Artes

Castelnaudary, Mus. Archéol. Lauragais
   Castelnaudary, Musée Archéologique du
   Lauragais

Castelo Branco, Mus. Tavares Proença
   Castelo Branco, Museu do Francisco Tavares
   Proença

Castelo de Vide, Praça Dom Pedro V
   Castelo de Vide, Praça de Dom Pedro V

Castelseprio, Zona Archeol.
   Castelseprio, Zona Archeologica di
   Castelseprio

Castiglion Fiorentino, Pin. Com.
   Castiglion Fiorentino, Pinacoteca Comunale

Castilleja de la Cuesta, Castillo

Castlemaine, A.G. & Hist. Mus.
   Castlemaine, Art Gallery and Historical
   Museum

Castlemaine, Buda [home of Ernest Leviny]

Castolovice Castle
   Castolovice, Castolovice Castle

Castres, Mus. Goya
   Castres, Musée Goya

Catamarca, Mus. Arqueol.
   Catamarca, Museo Arqueológico

Catania, Bib. Reg. U.
   Catania, Biblioteca Regionale Universitaria

Catania, Mus. Civ. Castello Ursino
   Catania, Museo Civico di Castello Ursino

Catania, Villa Cerami

Catanzaro, Mus. Prov.
   Catanzaro, Museo Provinciale di Catanzaro

Cava dei Tirreni, Mus. Badia SS Trinità
   Cava dei Tirreni, Museo della Badia della SS
   Trinità di Cava

Cayenne, Cons. Rég. Guyane
   Cayenne, Conseil Régional de Guyane

Cebu City, St Theresa's Coll. Mus.
   Cebu City, St Theresa's College Museum

Cedar Falls, U. N. IA, Gal. A.
    Cedar Falls, IA, University of Northern Iowa, Gallery of Art

Cedar Rapids, IA, Mus. A.
    Cedar Rapids, IA, Museum of Art

Cefalú, Mus. Mandralisca
    Cefalú, Museo Mandralisca

Celje, Reg. Mus.
    Celje, Regional Museum (Pokrajinski Muzej)

Celle, Bomann-Mus.
    Celle, Bomann-Museum

Centerport, NY, Vanderbilt Mus.
    Centerport, NY, Vanderbilt Museum

Cento, Cassa di Risparmio

Cento, Gal. A. Mod. Arnoldo Bonzagni
    Cento, Galleria d'Arte Moderna Arnoldo Bonzagni

Cento, Pin. Civ.
    Cento, Pinacoteca Civica

Céret, Mus. A. Mod.
    Céret, Musée d'Art Moderne

Certaldo, Pal. Pretorio
    Certaldo, Museo del Palazzo Pretorio Vicariale

Červený Kameň Castle
    Červený Kameň, Červený Kameň Castle

Cerveteri, Mus. N. Cerite
    Cerveteri, Museo Nazionale Cerite [Castello Ruspoli]

Cesena, Bib. Malatestiana
    Cesena, Biblioteca Malatestiana

Cesena, Cassa di Risparmio

Cesena, Pin. Com.
    Cesena, Pinacoteca Comunale

České Budějovice, Krajská Knihovna

České Budějovice, Mus. S. Bohemia
    České Budějovice, Museum of South Bohemia (Jihočeské Muzeum)

Český Krumlov, Reg. Mus.
    Český Krumlov, Regional Museum (Okresni Vlastivědné Muzeum)

Cetinje, Crna Gora A.G.
    Cetinje, Montenegro Art Gallery (Umetnička Galerija Crne Gore) [Crna Gora A.G.]

Chaalis, Mus. Abbaye
    Chaalis, Musée de l'Abbaye de Chaalis

Chadds Ford, PA, Brandywine River Mus.
    Chadds Ford, Brandywine River Museum

Chaironeia, Archaeol. Mus.
    Chaironeia, Archaeological Museum

Chaiya, N. Mus.
    Chaiya, Chaiya National Museum

Chalkis, Archaeol. Mus.
    Chalkis, Archaeological Museum

Chalon-sur-Saône, Maison Cult.
    Chalon-sur-Saône, Maison de la Culture [closed]

Chalon-sur-Saône, Mus. Denon
    Chalon-sur-Saône, Musée Denon

Chalon-sur-Saône, Mus. Nicéphore Niépce
    Chalon-sur-Saône, Musée Nicéphore Niépce

Châlons-sur-Marne, Cloître Eglise Notre-Dame-en-Vaux
    Châlons-sur-Marne, Cloître de l'Eglise Notre-Dame-en-Vaux

Châlons-sur-Marne, Mus. Garinet
    Châlons-sur-Marne, Musée Garinet

Châlons-sur-Marne, Mus. Mun.
    Châlons-sur-Marne, Musée Municipal

Châlons-sur-Marne, Trésor Cathédrale
    Châlons-sur-Marne, Trésor de la Cathédrale Saint-Etienne

Chamba, Bhuri Singh Mus.
    Chamba, Bhuri Singh Museum

Chambéry, Bib. Mun.
    Chambéry, Bibliothèque Municipale

Chambéry, Mus. B.-A.
    Chambéry, Musée des Beaux-Arts

Chambéry, Mus. Benoit-Molin
    Chambéry, Musée Benoit-Molin

Chambéry, Mus. Charmettes
    Chambéry, Musée des Charmettes

Chambéry, Musées A. & Hist.
    Chambéry, Musées d'Art et d'Histoire de Chambéry [admins Mus. B.-A.; Mus. Charmettes; Mus. Savois.]

Chambéry, Mus. Savois.
    Chambéry, Musée Savoisien

Chambéry, Préfecture

Chambord, Château
    Chambord, Château de Chambord

Champaign, U. IL, Krannert A. Mus.
    Champaign, IL, University of Illinois, Krannert Art Museum

Champs-sur-Marne, Château

Chandigarh, Govt Mus. & A.G.
    Chandigarh, Government Museum and Art Gallery

Chandigarh, Punjab U. Mus.
    Chandigarh, Punjab University Museum

Changsha, Hunan Prov. Mus.
    Changsha, Hunan Provincial Museum

Chania, Archaeol. Mus.
    Chania, Archaeological Museum

Chania, Hist. Mus. & Archvs
    Chania, Historical Museum and Archives

Chania, Naval Mus.
    Chania, Naval Museum

Chantilly, Lycée

Chantilly, Mus. Condé
    Chantilly, Musée Condé, Château de Chantilly

Chapel Hill, U. NC, Ackland A. Mus.
    Chapel Hill, NC, University of North Carolina, Ackland Art Museum

Chapingo, U. Autón.
    Chapingo, Universidad Autónoma Chapingo

Charleroi, Gal. Le Parc
    Charleroi, Galerie Le Parc

Charleroi, Mus. Com. B.-A.
    Charleroi, Musée Communal des Beaux-Arts

Charleroi, Mus. Verre A. & Tech.
    Charleroi, Musée du Verre, Art et Technique

Charleroi, Pal. B.-A.
    Charleroi, Palais des Beaux-Arts

Charleston, SC, Gibbes A.G.
    Charleston, SC, Gibbes Art Gallery

Charleville, Mus. B.-A.
    Charleville, Musée des Beaux-Arts

Charlotte, NC, Knight Gal.
    Charlotte, NC, Knight Gallery

Charlotte, NC, Mint Mus. A.
    Charlotte, NC, Mint Museum of Art

Charlottesville, U. VA
    Charlottesville, VA, University of Virginia

Charlottesville, U. VA A. Mus.
    Charlottesville, VA, University of Virginia Art Museum

Charlottesville, U. VA Lib.
    Charlottesville, VA, University of Virginia Library

Charlottetown, Confed. A.G. & Mus.
    Charlottetown, Confederation Art Gallery and Museum

Chartres, Bib. Mun.
    Chartres, Bibliothèque Municipale

Chartres, Mus. B.-A.
    Chartres, Musée des Beaux-Arts

Château-d'Oex, Mus. Vieux-Pays D'Enhaut
    Château-d'Oex, Musée du Vieux-Pays d'Enhaut

Châteauroux, Bib. Mun.
    Châteauroux, Bibliothèque Municipale

Châteauroux, Château-Raoul

Châteauroux, Mus. B.-A.
    Châteauroux, Musée des Beaux-Arts

Châteauroux, Mus. Bertrand
    Châteauroux, Musée Bertrand

Châteauroux, Salle Cordeliers
    Châteauroux, Salle des Cordeliers

Château-Thierry, Hôp.
    Château-Thierry, Hôpital

Château-Thierry, Mus. de la Fontaine
    Château-Thierry, Musée Jean de la Fontaine

Chatham, Royal Engin. Mus.
    Chatham, Royal Engineers Museum

Châtillon-sur-Seine, Mus. Archéol.
    Châtillon-sur-Seine, Musée Archéologique

Chattanooga, TN, Hunter Mus. A.
    Chattanooga, TN, Hunter Museum of Art

Chaumont, Bib. Mun.
    Chaumont, Bibliothèque Municipale

Chaumont, Mus. Mun.
    Chaumont, Musée Municipal

Chaumont-en-Bassigny, Mus. Mun.
    Chaumont-en-Bassigny, Musée Municipal

Chauny: see Blérancourt

Cheb Mus.
    Cheb, Cheb Museum (Chebské Múzeum)

Cheb, Gal. F.A.
    Cheb, Gallery of Fine Arts (Galerie Výtvarného Umění v Chebu)

Chelles, Mus. Alfred Bonno
    Chelles, Musée Alfred Bonno

Chelmsford, Essex Co. Rec. Office
    Chelmsford, Essex County Record Office

Cheltenham, A.G. & Mus.
    Cheltenham, Cheltenham Art Gallery & Museum

Cheltenham, Ladies' Coll.
    Cheltenham, Cheltenham Ladies' College

Chemnitz: the city was known as Karl-Marx-Stadt from 10 May 1953 to 31 May 1990

Chemnitz, Altes Rathaus

Chemnitz, Gedenkstät. Arbeitbew.
    Chemnitz, Gedenkstätten der Arbeiterbewegung

Chemnitz, Mus. Natknd.
    Chemnitz, Museum für Naturkunde

Chemnitz, Schlossbergmus.
    Chemnitz, Schlossbergmuseum

Chemnitz, Städt. Kstsamml.
    Chemnitz, Städtische Kunstsammlungen

Chemnitz, Städt. Museen
    Chemnitz, Städtische Museen [admins Gedenkstät. Arbeitbew.; Mus. Natknd.; Schlossbergmus.; Städt. Kstsamml.]

Città di Castello, Col. Burri
Città di Castello, Collezione Burri [Fondazione Palazzo Albizzini]

Città di Castello, Mus. Capitolare
Città di Castello, Museo Capitolare

Città di Castello, Pin. Com.
Città di Castello, Pinacoteca Comunale [Palazzo Vitelli alla Cannoniera]

Ciudad Bolívar, Fund. Mus. A. Mod. 'Jesus Soto'
Ciudad Bolívar, Fundacíon Museo de Arte Moderno 'Jesus Soto'

Ciudad Bolívar, Mus.
Ciudad Bolívar, Museo de Ciudad Bolívar [Casa del Correo del Orinoco]

Ciudad Rodrigo, Cent. Cult. Com.
Ciudad Rodrigo, Centro Cultural de la Comunidad

Cividale del Friuli, Mus. Archeol. N.
Cividale del Friuli, Museo Archeologico Nazionale

Cividale del Friuli, Mus. Civ.
Cividale del Friuli, Museo Civico

Cividale del Friuli, Mus. Crist. & Tesoro Duomo
Cividale del Friuli, Museo Cristiano e Tesoro del Duomo

Civita Castellana, Mus. Dioc.
Civita Castellana, Museo Diocesano

Clamart, Fond. Arp
Clamart, Fondation Arp

Claremont, CA, Francis Bacon Lib.
Claremont, CA, Francis Bacon Library [Francis Bacon Foundation; houses Arensberg Archives]

Claremont Colls, CA, Gals
Claremont, CA, Galleries of the Claremont Colleges

Clayton, Victoria, Monash U. Exh. Gal.
Clayton, Victoria, Monash University Exhibition Gallery

Clermont, NY, Taconic State Park

Clermont-Ferrand, Bib. Mun.
Clermont-Ferrand, Bibliothèque Municipale

Clermont-Ferrand, Jard. Pub.
Clermont-Ferrand, Jardin Public

Clermont-Ferrand, Mus. Bargoin
Clermont-Ferrand, Musée Bargoin

Cleve, Städt. Mus. Haus Koekkoek
Cleve, Städtisches Museum Haus Koekkoek

Cleveland, OH, Case W. Reserve U.
Cleveland, OH, Case Western Reserve University

Cleveland, OH, Cent. Contemp. A.
Cleveland, OH, Cleveland Center for Contemporary Art

Cleveland, OH, Mus. A.
Cleveland, OH, Cleveland Museum of Art

Cleveland, OH, Temple Mus. Jew. Relig. A. & Music
Cleveland, OH, Temple Museum of Jewish Religious Art and Music

Cleveland, OH, W. Reserve Hist. Soc. Mus.
Cleveland, OH, Western Reserve Historical Society Museum

Clinton, NY, Hamilton Coll., Emerson Gal.
Clinton, NY, Hamilton College, Emerson Gallery

Cluj-Napoca, A. Mus.
Cluj-Napoca, Art Museum (Muzeul de Artă Cluj-Napoca)

Cluj-Napoca, Cioflec Mus.
Cluj-Napoca, Cioflec Museum (Muzeul Cioflec)

Cluj-Napoca, Distr. Museums
Cluj-Napoca, District Museums (Complexul Muzeal Judeţean Cluj) [admins Ethnog. Mus. Transylvania; Hist. Mus. Transylvania; Mus. A.]

Cluj-Napoca, Ethnog. Mus. Transylvania
Cluj-Napoca, Ethnographic Museum of Transylvania (Muzeul Etnografic al Transilvăniei)

Cluj-Napoca, Hist. Mus. Transylvania
Cluj-Napoca, Historical Museum of Transylvania (Muzeul de Istorie al Transilvăniei)

Cluj-Napoca, Mus. A.
Cluj-Napoca, Museum of Art (Muzeul de Artă Cluj-Napoca) [in Bánffy Pal.]

Cluj-Napoca, U. Lib.
Cluj-Napoca, University of Cluj-Napoca Library (Universitatea Cluj-Napoca Biblioteca)

Cluny, Hôtel-Dieu

Cluny, Mus. Lapidaire Farinier
Cluny, Musée Lapidaire du Farinier [Ancienne Abbaye; Ecole Nationale d'Arts et Métiers]

Cluny, Mus. Ochier
Cluny, Musée Ochier [Palais Jean de Bourbon]

Coahuila, Mus. Bib. Pape
Coahuila, Museo Biblioteca Pape

Cobán, Mus. Reg. Verapacense
Cobán, Museo Regional Verapacense

Cóbh, Richard Wood Col.
Cóbh, Richard Wood Collection [Fota House]

Coburg, Schloss
Coburg, Schloss Coburg

Coburg, Staatsarchv
Coburg, Staatsarchiv Coburg

Coburg, Veste Coburg
Coburg, Kupferstichkabinett der Kunstsammlungen der Veste Coburg

Cochabamba, Casa Cult.
Cochabamba, Casa de la Cultura

Cochabamba, City Hall

Codogno, Fond. Lamberti
Codogno, Fondazione Lamberti

Codogno, Rac. Lamberti
Codogno, Raccolta Lamberti

Cody, WY, Buffalo Bill Hist. Cent.
Cody, WY, Buffalo Bill Historical Center

Coëtquidan, Ecole Mil. St Cyr
Coëtquidan, Ecole Militaire de St Cyr

Cognac, Mus. Cognac
Cognac, Musée de Cognac [Musées des Beaux-Arts]

Coimbra, Arquiv. U.
Coimbra, Arquivo da Universidade

Coimbra, Câmara Mun.
Coimbra, Câmara Municipal

Coimbra, Mus. & Jard. Botân.
Coimbra, Museu e Jardim Botânico

Coimbra, Mus. N. Machado de Castro
Coimbra, Museu Nacional de Machado de Castro [Instituto Português do Patrimonio Cultural]

Coimbra, U. Coimbra, Mus. & Lab. Antropol.
Coimbra, Universidade de Coimbra, Museu e Laboratório Antropológico [Instituto de Antropología]

Coire: see Chur

Colchester, Colchester & Essex Mus.
Colchester, Colchester and Essex Museum [in Colchester Castle]

Colchester, Essex Rec. Office
Colchester, Essex Record Office

Colchester, Minories
Colchester, The Minories [now Firstsite; cols in Colchester & Essex Mus.]

Colchester, Moot Hall [destr. 1843]

Colchester, Town Hall

Colditz, Schloss Colditz

Cold Spring, NY, Putnam Co. Hist. Soc.
Cold Spring, NY, Putnam County Historical Society

Colima, Mus. Reg.
Colima, Museo Regional de Colima

Colima, U. Colima, Mus. Cult. Occident.
Colima, Universidad de Colima, Museo de Cultura Occidental

Collalto, Castello
Collalto, Castello di Collalto

Colle di Val d'Elsa e Borgo, Mus. Civ.
Colle di Val d'Elsa e Borgo, Museo Civico

College Park, U. MD A.G.
College Park, MD, University of Maryland Art Gallery

Colmar, Bib.
Colmar, Bibliothèque

Colmar, Mus. Bartholdi
Colmar, Musée Bartholdi

Colmar, Mus. Unterlinden
Colmar, Musée d'Unterlinden

Cologne, Agfa-Foto-Historama

Cologne, Baukst-Gal.
Cologne, Baukunst-Galerie

Cologne Cathedral, Dombauarchv
Cologne, Cologne Cathedral, Dombauarchiv

Cologne Cathedral, Treasury
Cologne, Cologne Cathedral, Treasury

Cologne, Dumont Ksthalle
Cologne, Dumont Kunsthalle

Cologne, Erzbischöf. Diöz.- & Dombib.
Cologne, Erzbischöfliche Diözesan- und Dombibliothek

Cologne, Erzbischöf. Diöz.-Mus.
Cologne, Erzbischöfliches Diözesan-Museum

Cologne, Gal. Abels
Cologne, Galerie Abels

Cologne, Gal. Bar-Gera
Cologne, Galerie Bar-Gera

Cologne, Gal. Becker und Newman
Cologne, Galerie Becker und Newman

Cologne, Gal. Edel
Cologne, Galerie Edel

Cologne, Gal. Ferdinand Moller
Cologne, Galerie Ferdinand Moller

Cologne, Gal. Gmurzynska
Cologne, Galerie Gmurzynska

Cologne, Gal. Karsten Greve
Cologne, Galerie Karsten Greve

Cologne, Gal. Kicken & Pauseback
Cologne, Galerie Kicken und Pauseback

Cologne, Gal. Müller
Cologne, Galerie Müller

Cologne, Gal. Spiegel
Cologne, Galerie der Spiegel

Cologne, Gal. Thomas Borgmann
Cologne, Galerie Thomas Borgmann

Cologne, Gal. Werner
  Cologne, Galerie Michael Werner

Cologne, Haus Saaleck

Cologne, Hist. Archv
  Cologne, Historisches Archiv

Cologne, Josef-Haubrich-Ksthalle
  Cologne, Josef-Haubrich-Kunsthalle
  [Kunsthalle Köln]

Cologne, Kollwitz Mus.
  Cologne, Käthe Kollwitz Museum

Cologne, Kstgewmus.
  Cologne, Kunstgewerbemuseum [name
  changed in 1989 to Mus. Angewandte Kst]

Cologne, Ksthalle
  Cologne, Kunsthalle

Cologne, Kstver.
  Cologne, Kunstverein

Cologne, Mus. Angewandte Kst
  Cologne, Museum für Angewandte Kunst
  [formerly Kstgewebemus.]

Cologne, Museen Stadt
  Cologne, Museen der Stadt Köln [admins Mus.
  Angewandte Kst; Mus. Ludwig; Cologne,
  Mus. Ostasiat. Kst; Cologne, Rautenstrauch-
  Joest-Mus.; Röm.-Ger.-Mus.; Schnütgen-Mus.;
  Stadtmus.; Wallraf-Richartz-Mus.]

Cologne, Mus. Ludwig
  Cologne, Museum Ludwig

Cologne, Mus. Ostasiat. Kst
  Cologne, Museum für Ostasiatische Kunst der
  Stadt Köln

Cologne, Paul Maenz Gal.
  Cologne, Paul Maenz Galerie

Cologne, Photokina

Cologne, Rautenstrauch-Joest-Mus.
  Cologne, Rautenstrauch-Joest-Museum für
  Völkerkunde

Cologne, Rheinhallen Köln. Messe
  Cologne, Rheinhallen der Kölner Messe

Cologne, Röm.-Ger.-Mus.
  Cologne, Römisch-Germanisches-Museum

Cologne, Schnütgen-Mus.
  Cologne, Schnütgen-Museum

Cologne, Stadtmus.
  Cologne, Kölnisches Stadtmuseum

Cologne, Theatermus.
  Cologne, Theatermuseum

Cologne, U. Cologne
  Cologne, Universität zu Köln

Cologne, Wallraf-Richartz-Mus.
  Cologne, Wallraf-Richartz-Museum

Cologne, Werkbundausstell.
  Cologne, Werkbundausstellung

Cologny, Fond. Martin Bodmer
  Cologny, Fondation Martin Bodmer [incl.
  Bibliotheca Bodmeriana]

Colombo, A.G.
  Colombo, Art Gallery

Colombo, Dept Archaeol. , Lib.
  Colombo, Department of Archaeology,
  Library

Colombo, Dut. Per. Mus.
  Colombo, Dutch Period Museum

Colombo, Lionel Wendt Mem. A.G.
  Colombo, Lionel Wendt Memorial Art Gallery

Colombo, Mobile Mus.
  Colombo, Mobile Museum

Colombo, Nat. Hist. Mus.
  Colombo, Natural History Museum

Colombo, N. Mus.
  Colombo, National Museum

Colombo, N. Museums
  Colombo, National Museums of Sri Lanka
  [admins Dut. Per. Mus.; Mobile Mus.; Nat.
  Hist. Mus.; Anuradhapura, Flk Mus.; Kandy,
  N. Mus.; Ratnapura, N. Mus.; Trincomalee,
  Archaeol. Mus.]

Colombo, U. Colombo, Dept Archaeol., Lib.
  Colombo, University of Colombo,
  Department of Archaeology, Library

Colonial Williamsburg, VA

Colorado Springs, CO, F.A. Cent.
  Colorado Springs, CO, Fine Arts Center

Colorado Springs, CO, Taylor Mus.
  Colorado Springs, CO, Taylor Museum

Colorno, Pal. Ducale
  Colorno, Palazzo Ducale

Columbia, MO, State Hist. Soc.
  Columbia, MO, State Historical Society of
  Missouri

Columbia, U. MO, Mus. A. & Archaeol.
  Columbia, MO, University of Missouri,
  Museum of Art and Archaeology

Columbia, SC, Mus. A.
  Columbia, SC, Museum of Art

Columbus, GA, Mus.
  Columbus, GA, Columbus Museum

Columbus, OH, Gal. F.A.
  Columbus, OH, Gallery of Fine Arts [name
  changed to Mus. A. in 1978]

Columbus, OH, Mus. A.
  Columbus, OH, Museum of Art [formerly
  Gal. F.A.]

Columbus, OH State U.
  Columbus, Ohio State University

Columbus, OH, U. Gal. F.A.
  Columbus, OH, University Gallery of Fine Art
  [now Wexner Cent. A.]

Columbus, OH, Wexner Cent. A.
  Columbus, OH, Wexner Center for the Arts
  [name changed from Wexner Cent. Visual A.
  in 1990]

Columbus, OH, Wexner Cent. Visual A.
  Columbus, OH, Wexner Center for the Visual
  Arts [name changed from U. Gal. F.A. in Nov
  1989; name changed to Wexner Cent. A. in
  1990]

Comayagua, Mus. A. Relig.
  Comayagua, Museo de Arte Religioso

Comayagua, Mus. Arqueol. & Hist.
  Comayagua, Museo Arqueológico y Histórico

Commonwealth Relations Office
  London, Commonwealth Relations Office

Como, Banca Pop. Lecco
  Como, Banca Popolare di Lecco

Como, Civ. Mus. Archeol.
  Como, Civico Museo Archeologico ['Giovio']

Como, Com. Valmorea
  Como, Comune di Valmorea

Como, Gal. Cavour
  Como, Galleria Cavour

Como, Mus. Civ. Stor. Garibaldi
  Como, Museo Civico Storico G. Garibaldi

Como, Pal. Volpi
  Como, Palazzo Volpi

Como, Villa Olmo

Compiègne, Château
  Compiègne, Château [houses Musée National
  du Château de Compiègne et Musée du
  Second Empire; Musée National de la Voiture
  et du Tourisme]

Compiègne, Hôtel de Ville

Compiègne, Mus. Mun. Vivenel
  Compiègne, Musée Municipal Antoine-Vivenel

Compton, Watts Gal.
  Compton, Watts Gallery

Concepción, Paraguay, Mus. A. Sacro
  Concepción, Paraguay, Museo de Arte Sacro

Concepción, U. Concepción, Casa A.
  Concepción, Universidad de Concepción, Casa
  del Arte

Concepción, U. Concepción, Pin.
  Concepción, Universidad de Concepción,
  Pinacoteca

Condom, Mus. Armagnac
  Condom, Musée de l'Armagnac

Conegliano, Mus. Civ. Castello
  Conegliano, Museo Civico del Castello

Conimbriga, Mus. Inst. Arqueol.
  Conimbriga, Museu do Instituto de
  Arqueologia

Coniston, Brantwood

Coniston, Ruskin Mus.
  Coniston, Ruskin Museum [Coniston
  Institute]

Conques, Trésor Ste Foy
  Conques, Trésor de l'Eglise Sainte Foy

Constanţa, Archaeol. Mus. Dobruja
  Constanţa, Archaeological Museum of
  Dobruja

Constanţa, Mus. A.
  Constanţa, Museum of Art (Muzeul de Artă
  Constanţa)

Constanţa, Mus. N. Hist. & Archaeol.
  Constanţa, Museum of National History and
  Archaeology (Muzeul de Istorie Naţională şi
  Arheologie din Constanţa)

Conversano, Mus. Civ.
  Conversano, Museo Civico [in Monastero di
  San Benedetto]

Cookham, Spencer Gal.
  Cookham, Stanley Spencer Gallery

Cooperstown, Mus. NY State Hist. Assoc.
  Cooperstown, NY, Museum of New York
  State Historical Association

Cooperstown, NY, Otsego Co. Hist. Soc.
  Cooperstown, NY, Otsego County Historical
  Society [no longer exists]

Copan Ruinas, Mus. Reg. Arqueol. Maya
  Copan Ruinas, Museo Regional de
  Arqueología Maya

Copenhagen, Akad. S. Kst.
  Copenhagen, Akademi for de Skonne Kunster

Copenhagen, Amalienborg [Royal Palace]

Copenhagen, Bib. Saml. Arkit. Tegninger
  Copenhagen, Bibliothek Samlingen af
  Arkitektur Tegninger [in Kon. Dan. Kstakad.]

Copenhagen, Bing & Grondahl Factory Mus.
  Copenhagen, Bing & Grondahl Factory
  Museum

Copenhagen, Børsen

Copenhagen, Bymus.
  Copenhagen, Bymuseum

Copenhagen, Carlsberg Mus.
  Copenhagen, Carlsberg Museum

Copenhagen, Charlottenborg [houses Kon. Dan. Kstakad.]

Copenhagen, Christiansborg Slot

Copenhagen, Dan. State Audit Dept
Copenhagen, Danish State Audit Department

Copenhagen, Davids Saml.
Copenhagen, Davids Samling

Copenhagen, Eremitag

Copenhagen, Frie Udstill. Byg.
Copenhagen, Den Frie Udstillings Bygning

Copenhagen, Frihedsstotten

Copenhagen, Gal. Asbæk
Copenhagen, Galleri Asbæk

Copenhagen, Gal. Birch
Copenhagen, Galerie Birch

Copenhagen, Gal. Tokanten
Copenhagen, Galerie Tokanten

Copenhagen, Hagemanns Koll.
Copenhagen, Hagemanns Kollegium

Copenhagen, Håndværkerforen.
Copenhagen, Håndværkerforeningen

Copenhagen, Hirschsprungske Saml.
Copenhagen, Hirschsprungske Samling

Copenhagen, Hjortespring Skole

Copenhagen, Hoved Bib.
Copenhagen, Hoved Bibliotek

Copenhagen, Jensen Mus.
Copenhagen, Georg Jensen Museum

Copenhagen, Kon. Bib.
Copenhagen, Kongelige Bibliotek

Copenhagen, Kon. Dan. Kstakad.
Copenhagen, Kongelige Danske Kunstakademi [in Charlottenborg Palace]

Copenhagen, Kon. Dan. Videnskabernes Selskab
Copenhagen, Kongelige Danske Videnskabernes Selskab

Copenhagen, Kon. Porcelænsfabrik
Copenhagen, Kongelige Porcelænsfabrik [now Royal Copenhagen]

Copenhagen, Kon. Saml.
Copenhagen, Kongelige Samling

Copenhagen, Kon. Teat.
Copenhagen, Kongelige Teater

Copenhagen, Kstakad. Bib.
Copenhagen, Kunstakademiets Bibliotek

Copenhagen, Kstforen.
Copenhagen, Kunstforening i Kobenhavn

Copenhagen, Kstindustmus.
Copenhagen, Danske Kunstindustrimuseum

Copenhagen, Medic.- Hist. Mus.
Copenhagen, Medicinsk-Historisk Museum

Copenhagen, Nmus.
Copenhagen, Nationalmuseum

Copenhagen, Nyborg Slot

Copenhagen, Ny Carlsberg Glyp.
Copenhagen, Ny Carlsberg Glyptotek

Copenhagen, Ordrupgaardsaml.
Copenhagen, Ordrupgaardsamlingen

Copenhagen, Rådhus

Copenhagen, Rigsarkv
Copenhagen, Rigsarkiv

Copenhagen, Rosenborg Slot [De Danske Kongers Kronologiske Samling på Rosenborg]

Copenhagen, Saml. Arkittegninger
Copenhagen, Samling Arkiturtegninger [housed in Kon. Dan. Kstakad., Bib.]

Copenhagen, Sophienholm

Copenhagen, Stat. Mus. Kst
Copenhagen, Kongelige Kobberstiksamling, Statens Museum for Kunst

Copenhagen, Stat. Mus. Kst
Copenhagen, Statens Museum for Kunst

Copenhagen, Stat. Mus. Kst, Prentenkab.
Copenhagen, Statens Museum for Kunst, Prentenkabinet

Copenhagen, Tetzen–Lund Saml.
Copenhagen, Tetzen–Lund Samling

Copenhagen, Thorvaldsens Mus.
Copenhagen, Thorvaldsens Museum

Copenhagen, Tøjhusmus.
Copenhagen, Tøjhusmuseum

Copenhagen, U. Copenhagen
Copenhagen, Kobenhavns Universitet

Copenhagen, Valdemar Kleis
Copenhagen, Valdemar Kleis Art Gallery [name changed to H. Kleis Eftf.: see Farum]

Copiapó, Mus. Catedral
Copiapó, Museo de la Catedral

Coppet, Château
Coppet, Château de Coppet

Coral Gables, FL, U. Miami, Lowe A. Mus.
Coral Gables, University of Miami, Lowe Art Museum

Córdoba, Casa Conde de Priego
Córdoba, Casa del Conde de Priego

Córdoba, Mezquita

Córdoba, Mus. Arqueol.
Córdoba, Museo Arqueológico [Consejería de Cultura]

Córdoba, Mus. Prov. B.A.
Córdoba, Museo Provincial de Bellas Artes [Museo de Bellas Artes]

Córdoba, Mus. Romero de Torres
Córdoba, Museo Romero de Torres y Colección Arqueológica Romero de Torres

Córdoba, Pal. Merced
Córdoba, Palacio de la Merced [seat of EXCMA Diputacíon Provincial de Córdoba]

Córdoba, Real Acad. Cienc., B. Let. & Nob. A.
Córdoba, Real Academia de Córdoba de Ciencias, Bellas Letras y Nobles Artes

Córdoba, Argentina, Acad. B.A.
Córdoba, Argentina, Academia de Bellas Artes

Córdoba, Argentina, Escuela Superior B.A. 'Ernesto de la Cárcova'
Córdoba, Argentina, Escuela Superior de Bellas Artes 'Ernesto de la Cárcova'

Córdoba, Argentina, Gal. Paideia
Córdoba, Argentina, Galería Paideia

Córdoba, Argentina, Mus. Hist.
Córdoba, Argentina, Museo Histórico

Córdoba, Argentina, Mus. Hist. Prov. 'Marqués de Sobremonte'
Córdoba, Argentina, Museo Histórico Provincial 'Marqués de Sobremonte'

Córdoba, Argentina, Mus. Prov. B.A. 'Emilio A. Caraffa'
Córdoba, Argentina, Museo Provincial de Bellas Artes 'Emilio A. Caraffa'

Córdoba, Argentina, Mus. Teresas
Córdoba, Argentina, Museo de las Teresas

Córdoba, Mexico, Inst. N. Antropol. & Hist. Mus. N. Antropol.
Córdoba, Mexico, Instituto Nacional de Antropología e Historia, Museo Nacional de Antropología

Corfu, Achilleíon

Corfu, Archaeol. Mus.
Corfu, Archaeological Museum

Corfu, Byz. Col.
Corfu, Byzantine Collection [in Royal Pal.]

Corfu, Churches Antivorounióstissa, Mus. Byz. & Post-Byz. A.
Corfu, Churches of Antivorounióstissa, Museum of Byzantine and Post-Byzantine Art

Corfu, Royal Pal.
Corfu, Royal Palace

Corinth, Archaeol. Mus.
Corinth, Archaeological Museum

Cork, Crawford Mun. A.G.
Cork, Crawford Municipal Art Gallery

Cork, Crawford Mun. Sch. A.
Cork, Crawford Municipal School of Art [name changed to Crawford Mun. A.G. in 1979]

Cork, Pub. Mus.
Cork, Public Museum

Corning, NY, Mus. Glass
Corning, NY, Museum of Glass

Cornish, NH, Saint-Gaudens N. Hist. Site
Cornish, NH, Saint-Gaudens National Historical Site

Coro, Mus. Dioc. Monseñor Guillermo Castillo
Coro, Museo Diocesano Monseñor Lucas Guillermo Castillo

Corpus Christi, A. Mus. S. TX
Corpus Christi, Art Museum of South Texas

Correggio, Bib. Civ.
Correggio, Biblioteca Civica

Corridonia, Mus. Coll. SS Pietro & Paolo
Corridonia, Museo della Collegiata di SS Pietro e Paolo

Corte, Fonds Rég. A. Contemp.
Corte, Fonds Régional d'Art Contemporain

Cortina d'Ampezzo, Gal. A. Mod. Farsetti
Cortina d'Ampezzo, Galleria di Arte Moderna Farsetti

Cortina d'Ampezzo, Pin. Rimoldi
Cortina d'Ampezzo, Pinacoteca Mario Rimoldi [Museo Civico Rimoldi; Collezione Rimoldi]

Cortland, SUNY, Dowd F.A. Gal.
Cortland, State University of New York, Dowd Fine Arts Gallery

Cortona, Bib. Com.
Cortona, Biblioteca Comunale

Cortona, Fortezza Girifalco
Cortona, Fortezza del Girifalco [Fortezza Medicea]

Cortona, Laparelli–Pitt Col.
Cortona, Laparelli–Pitt Collezione

Cortona, Mus. Accad. Etrus.
Cortona, Museo dell'Accademia Etrusca [Palazzo Casali]

Cortona, Mus. Dioc.
Cortona, Museo Diocesano

Cortona, Pal. Casali
Cortona, Palazzo Casali [houses Mus. Accad. Etrus.]

Corvey, Abbey
Corvey, Benediktinerabtei

Costești Mus.
Costești, Costești Museum

Cotonou, Cent. Promot. Artisanat
Cotonou, Centre de Promotion de l'Artisanat

Cotonou, Gal. Bikoff
Cotonou, Galerie Bikoff

Cottbus, Bezirksmus.
Cottbus, Bezirksmuseum Schloss Branitz

Cottbus, Gal. Carl Blechen
Cottbus, Galerie Carl Blechen

Courbevoie, Mus. Roybet–Fould
Courbevoie, Musée Roybet–Fould

Covarrubias, Mus. Parroq.
Covarrubias, Museo Parroquial

Coventry, Herbert A.G. & Mus.
Coventry, Herbert Art Gallery and Museum

Coventry Poly.
Coventry, Coventry Polytechnic

Coventry, St Mary's Hall [Medieval Guildhall]

Coventry, U. Warwick, Mead Gal.
Coventry, University of Warwick, Mead
Gallery

Cragsmoor, NY, Free Lib.
Cragsmoor, NY, Free Library

Craiova, Mus. A.
Craiova, Museum of Art (Muzeul de Artă
Craiova)

Craiova, Mus. Sch. A. & Crafts
Craiova, Museum of the School of Arts and
Crafts

Cranbrook, NJ, Acad. A.
Cranbrook, NJ, Cranbrook Academy of Art

Cranstone, RI, Scot. Rite Masonic Mus. N. Her.
Cranstone, RI, Scottish Rite Masonic Museum
of our National Heritage

Crema, Mus. Civ.
Crema, Museo Civico

Cremona, Archv Stato
Cremona, Archivio di Stato

Cremona, Bib. Stat. & Lib. Civ.
Cremona, Biblioteca Statale e Libreria Civica

Cremona, Bib. Vescovile
Cremona, Biblioteca del Seminario Vescovile

Cremona, ex-Osp. Maggiore
Cremona, ex-Ospedale Maggiore

Cremona, Gal.
Cremona, Galleria

Cremona, Mus. Berenziano
Cremona, Museo Berenziano, Seminario
Vescovile

Cremona, Mus. Civ. Ala Ponzone
Cremona, Museo Civico Ala Ponzone [in
Palazzo Affaitati]

Cremona, Mus. Civ. Stor. Nat.
Cremona, Museo Civico di Storia Naturale

Cremona, Osp. Nuovo
Cremona, Ospedale Nuovo

Cremona, Osp. Vecchio
Cremona, Ospedale Vecchio

Cremona, Pal. Com.
Cremona, Palazzo Comunale

Cremona, Pal. Giustizia
Cremona, Palazzo di Giustizia

Cromer Mus.
Cromer, Cromer Museum

Cudillero, Gesù Nazareno

Cuenca, Mus. A. Abstracto Esp.
Cuenca, Museo de Arte Abstracto Español
[Casas Colgradas]

Cuenca, Mus. Dioc.-Catedralicio
Cuenca, Museo Diocesano-Catedralicio

Cuenca, Colegio Semin.
Cuenca, Ecuador, Colegio Seminario

Cuernavaca, Mus. Reg.
Cuernavaca, Museo Regional [Museo
Cuauhnahuac; in Palacio de Cortés]

Cuneo, Mus. Civ.
Cuneo, Museo Civico [ex-Chiostro di
S Francesco]

Curaçao, Museum
Curaçao, Curaçao Museum

Curitiba, Mus. A. Contemp.
Curitiba, Museu de Arte Contemprañea

Curitiba, Mus. A. Paraná
Curitiba, Museu de Arte do Paraná

Cuzco Cathedral
Cuzco, Cuzco Cathedral

Cuzco, Cent. A. Nativo
Cuzco, Centro Qosqo de Arte Nativo

Cuzco, Cent. Bartolomé de las Casas
Cuzco, Centro Bartolomé de las Casas

Cuzco, Escuela Reg. B.A. 'Diego Quispe Tito'
Cuzco, Escuela Regional de Bellas Artes
'Diego Quispe Tito'

Cuzco, Inst. N. Cult.
Cuzco, Instituto Nacional de Cultura

Cuzco, Mus. A. Relig.
Cuzco, Museo de Arte Religioso

Cuzco, Mus. Hist. Reg.
Cuzco, Museo Histórico Regional

Cuzco, Mus. U.
Cuzco, Museo de la Universidad [Museo
Arqueológico Universitario]

Cuzco, Mus. Virreinato
Cuzco, Museo del Virreinato

Cuzco, U. N. S Antonio Abad
Cuzco, Universidad Nacional de S Antonio
Abad

Cyrene, Mus. Ant.
Cyrene, Museum of Antiquities

Częstochowa, Monastery of Jasna Góra
Częstochowa, Monastery of Jasna Góra [incl.
Chapel of Częstochowa Icon, Basilica,
Knights' Hall, Arsenal, Museum and Treasury]

Dachau, Gemäldegal.
Dachau, Gemäldegalerie

Dachau, Schloss
Dachau, Schloss Dachau

Dakar, G.N.A. Afr.
Dakar, Galerie Nationale d'Art d'Afrique

Dakar, Inst. Fondamental Afr. Noire
Dakar, Institut Fondamental d'Afrique Noire

Dakar, Min. Cult.
Dakar, Ministry of Culture

Dakar, Mus. A. Afr.
Dakar, Musée d'Art Africain

Dakar, U. Cheikh Anta Diop, Mus. A. Afr.
Dakar, Université Cheikh Anta Diop, Musée
d'Art Africain [part of Institut Fondamental
d'Afrique Noire]

Dalarne, Leksand Kulthaus
Dalarne, Leksand Kulturhaus

Dalarö, Tullmus.
Dalarö, Tullmuseum [Customs Museum; in
Tullhus]

Dalkeith, Newbattle Abbey Coll.
Dalkeith, Newbattle Abbey College

Dallas, TX, Delahunty & Fraenkel Gals
Dallas, TX, Delahunty and Fraenkel Galleries
[now closed; see San Francisco, CA, Fraenkel
Gal.]

Dallas, TX, Delahunty Gal.
Dallas, TX, Delahunty Gallery [closed]

Dallas, TX, Mus. A.
Dallas, TX, Dallas Museum of Art

Dallas, TX, Mus. F.A.
Dallas, TX, Museum of Fine Arts

Dallas, TX, S. Methodist U., Meadows Mus. &
Gal.
Dallas, TX, Southern Methodist University,
Meadows Museum and Gallery

Damascus, Assad N. Lib.
Damascus, Assad National Library

Damascus, Dir. Gén. Ant. & Musées
Damascus, Direction Générale des Antiquités
et des Musées [Damascus, N. Mus.]

Damascus, Mus. A. Pop. & Trad.
Damascus, Musée des Arts Populaires et
Traditions

Damascus, N. Mus.
Damascus, National Museum of Damascus

Dampierre, Château

Da-Nang, Cham Mus.
Da-Nang, Cham Museum [formerly Tourane,
Musée Cam]

Da-Nang, N. Mus. Cham Sculp.
Da-Nang, National Museum of Cham
Sculpture

Danlí, Mus. Cabildo
Danlí, Museo del Cabildo

Dar es Salaam, N. Mus. Tanzania
Dar es Salaam, National Museum of Tanzania

Darlington, A. Cent.
Darlington, Arts Centre

Darmstadt, Ausstellhallen Mathildenhöhe
Darmstadt, Ausstellungshallen Mathildenhöhe

Darmstadt, Bauhaus-Samml.
Darmstadt, Bauhaus-Sammlungen

Darmstadt, Hess. Landes- & Hochschbib.
Darmstadt, Hessische Landes- und
Hochschulbibliothek Darmstadt

Darmstadt, Hess. Landesmus.
Darmstadt, Hessisches Landesmuseum

Darmstadt, Inst. Mathildenhöhe
Darmstadt, Institut Mathildenhöhe

Darmstadt, Ksthalle
Darmstadt, Kunsthalle [Kunstverein
Darmstadt]

Darmstadt, Mus. Kstlerkolon.
Darmstadt, Museum Künstlerkolonie

Darmstadt, Samml. Hardenberg
Darmstadt, Sammlung Hardenberg

Darmstadt, Schlossmus.
Darmstadt, Schlossmuseum

Darmstadt, Stadtmus. Städt. Kstsamml.
Darmstadt, Stadtmuseum und Städtische
Kunstsammlung

Darmstadt, Tech. Hochsch.
Darmstadt, Technische Hochschule
Darmstadt

Daroca, Mus. Santísimo Misterio
Daroca, Museo del Santísimo Misterio

Darwin, N. Territ. Mus. A. & Sci.
Darwin, Northern Territory Museum of Arts
and Sciences

Datong, Mun. Mus.
Datong, Municipal Museum

Davenport, IA, Mun. A.G.
Davenport, IA, Davenport Municipal Art
Gallery

Davis, U. CA
Davis, CA, University of California

Davos, Ernst Ludwig Kirchner-Mus.
Davos, Ernst Ludwig Kirchner-Museum

Dayr az-Zawr Mus.
Dayr az-Zawr, Dayr az-Zawr Museum

Dayton, OH, A. Inst.
Dayton, OH, Dayton Art Institute

Debrecen, Agric. Coll.
Debrecen, Agricultural College [part of
Debrecen U. Agrar. Sci.]

Debrecen, Déri Mus.
Debrecen, Déri Museum (Déri Múzeum)

Debrecen, Lib. Transtibiscan Reformed Ch. Distr.
Debrecen, Library of the Transtibiscan
Reformed Church District (Tiszántuli
Református Egyházkerület Nagykönyvtára)

Debrecen, Medgyessy Mem. Mus.
Debrecen, Ferenc Medgyessy Memorial
Museum (Medgyessy Ferenc Emlékmúzeum)

Debrecen, Presbyterian Coll. Eccles. Mus.
Debrecen, Presbyterian College Ecclesiastical
Museum

Debrecen, U. Agrar. Sci.
Debrecen, Debrecen University of Agrarian
Sciences

Dedham, Essex, Munnings A. Mus.
Dedham, Essex, Sir Alfred Munnings Art
Museum [Castle House]

Deerfield, MA, Hist. Deerfield
Deerfield, MA, Historic Deerfield

Deerfield, MA, Mem. Hall Mus.
Deerfield, MA, Memorial Hall Museum

Delft, Klaeuwshofje

Delft, Mus. Huis Lambert van Meerten
Delft, Museum Huis Lambert van Meerten

Delft, Mus. Tetar van Elven
Delft, Museum Paul Tetar van Elven

Delft, Stadhuis

Delft, Stedel. Mus. Prinsenhof
Delft, Stedelijk Museum Het Prinsenhof

Delft, Tech. U.
Delft, Technische Universiteit Delft

Delft, Tech. U., Bib.
Delft, Technische Universiteit Delft,
Bibliotheek

Delft, Tech. U., Fac. Archit.
Delft, Technische Universiteit Delft, Faculteit
der Architectuur

Delft, Vlknknd. Mus. Nusantara
Delft, Volkenkundig Museum Nusantara

Delos, Archaeol. Mus.
Delos, Archaeological Museum [Delos
Museum]

Delphi, Archaeol. Mus.
Delphi, Archaeological Museum

Dendermonde, Stadhuis

Dendermonde, Stedel. Oudhdknd. Mus. Vleeshuis
Dendermonde, Stedelijk Oudheidkundig
Museum Vleeshuis

Den Helder, Marmus.
Den Helder, Helders Marinemuseum

Denpasar, A. Cent.
Denpasar, Arts Centre

Denpasar, Bali Mus.
Denpasar, Bali Museum

Denpasar, Werdi Budaya A. Cent.
Denpasar, Werdi Budaya Art Centre

Denver, CO, A. Mus.
Denver, CO, Denver Art Museum [Museum
of Fine Arts]

Denver, CO, Anaconda Tower

Denver, CO, Gal. 609
Denver, CO, Galerie 609

Denver, CO Hist. Soc.
Denver, CO, Colorado Historical Society

Denver, CO, Mus. Nat. Hist.
Denver, CO, Denver Museum of Natural
History

Denver, CO, Mus. W. A.
Denver, CO, Museum of Western Art

Derby, Mus. & A.G.
Derby, Museum and Art Gallery

Deruta, Pin. Com.
Deruta, Pinacoteca Comunale [Museo
Comunale d'Arte]

Des Moines, IA, A. Cent.
Des Moines, IA, Art Center

Des Moines, IA, Civ. Cent.
Des Moines, IA, Civic Center of Greater Des
Moines

Des Moines, IA State Educ. Assoc.
Des Moines, IA, Iowa State Educational
Association

Dessau, Amalienstift.
Dessau, Amalienstiftung

Dessau, Anhalt. Gemäldegal.
Dessau, Anhaltische Gemäldegalerie

Dessau, Bauhaus

Dessau, Schloss Georgium

Dessau, Schloss Georgium, Gemäldegal.
Dessau, Schloss Georgium, Gemäldegalerie

Dessau, Schloss Luisium

Dessau, Staatl. Gal.
Dessau, Staatliche Galerie [housed in Schloss
Georgium & Schloss Luisium]

Dessau, Staatl. Mus. Schloss Mosigkau
Dessau, Staatliches Museum Schloss Mosigkau

Detroit, MI, Hist. Mus.
Detroit, MI, Historical Museum

Detroit, MI, Inst. A.
Detroit, MI, Detroit Institute of Arts

Detroit, MI, Manoogian Mus.
Detroit, MI, Alex and Marie Manoogian
Museum

Detroit, MI, N. Found. Study Frank Lloyd Wright
Detroit, MI, National Foundation for the
Study of Frank Lloyd Wright

Detroit, MI, Pewabic Pott. Mus.
Detroit, MI, Pewabic Pottery Museum

Deurle, Gemeentelijk Mus. Gustav de Smet
Deurle, Gemeentelijk Museum Gustav de
Smet

Deurle, Mus. J. Dhondt-Dhaenens
Deurle, Museum J. Dhondt-Dhaenens

Deurne, Prov. Mus. Sterckshof
Deurne, Provinciaal Museum Sterckshof

Deventer, Gemeentemusea

Deventer, Mus. De Waag
Deventer, Gemeentemusea van Deventer
[admins Mus. de Waag; Speelgoed- &
Blikmus.]

Deventer, Mus. De Waag
Deventer, Museum De Waag

Deventer, Speelgoed- & Blikmus.
Deventer, Speelgoed- en Blikmuseum

Deventer, Stadhuis

Devizes Mus.
Devizes, Devizes Museum

Dhaka, N.A.G.
Dhaka, National Art Gallery

Dhaka, N. Mus. Bangladesh
Dhaka, National Museum of Bangladesh

Dieppe, Château-Mus.
Dieppe, Château-Musée de Dieppe [Le Musée
Dieppois]

Diest, Openb. Cent. Maatsch. Welzijn
Diest, Openbaar Centrum voor
Maatschappelijk Welzijn

Diest, Stedel. Mus.
Diest, Stedelijk Museum [in Stadhuis]

Dijon, Archv Ville
Dijon, Archive de Ville

Dijon, Bib. Mun.
Dijon, Bibliothèque Municipale

Dijon, Mus. Archéol.
Dijon, Musée Archéologique [Ancienne
Abbaye des Bénédictines]

Dijon, Mus. A. Sacré
Dijon, Musée d'Art Sacré

Dijon, Mus. B.-A.
Dijon, Musée des Beaux-Arts

Dijon, Mus. Magnin
Dijon, Musée Magnin

Dijon, Pal. Ducs
Dijon, Palais de Ducs [Logis du Roi; now part
of Hôtel de Ville with Palais des Etats]

Dijon, Pal. Justice
Dijon, Palais de Justice

Dilbeek, Gal. Le Centaure
Dilbeek, Galerie Le Centaure

Dinan, Hôtel de Ville

Dıyarbakır, Archaeol. & Ethnog. Mus.
Dıyarbakır, Archaeological and Ethnographic
Museum

Djemila, Mus. Archéol.
Djemila par Elalma Wilaya, Musée
d'Archéologie de Djemila

Djurgården, Thielska Gal.
Djurgården, Thielska Galleriet

Dole, Mus. Mun.
Dole, Musée Municipal

Dollar Acad.
Dollar, Dollar Academy

Dolný Kubín, Orava Gal.
Dolný Kubín, Orava Gallery (Oravská
Galéria)

Dolo, Arcipretale

Donaueschingen, Fürstenberg-Samml.
Donaueschingen, Fürstenberg-Sammlungen
[Fürstenberg-Sammlung & Schloss
Fürstenberg]

Donaustauf, Walhalla

Doncaster, Mus. & A. G.
Doncaster, Museum and Art Gallery

Donegal, Glebe Gal.
Donegal, Glebe Gallery

Donetsk, Mus. A.
Donetsk, Donetsk Museum of Art

Donington-le-Heath, Manor House

Doorn, Huis Doorn

Dorchester, Dorset Co. Mus.
Dorchester, Dorset County Museum

Dordrecht, Dordrechts Mus.
Dordrecht, Dordrechts Museum

Dordrecht, Mus. van Gijn
Dordrecht, Museum Mr Simon van Gijn

Dortmund, Mus. Kst & Kultgesch.
Dortmund, Museum für Kunst und
Kulturgeschichte der Stadt

Dortmund, Mus. Ostwall
 Dortmund, Museum am Ostwall

Douai, Bib. Mun.
 Douai, Bibliothèque Municipale

Douai, Mus. Mun.
 Douai, Musée Municipal [La Chartreuse]

Doullens, Mus. Lombart
 Doullens, Musée Lombart

Dover Mus.
 Dover, Dover Museum

Dover, DE State Mus.
 Dover, DE, Delaware State Museum

Downpatrick, Down Co. Mus.
 Downpatrick, Down County Museum

Dozza, Mus. Civ. & Mus. Civil. Contad.
 Dozza, Museo Civico e Museo della Civiltà
 Contadina

Dozza, Rocca

Drachten, Streekmus. Smallingerland Bleekerhûs
 Drachten, Streekmuseum Smallingerland het
 Bleekerhûs

Draguignan, Mus. Mun.
 Draguignan, Musée Municipal

Drammen, Drammen Hosp.
 Drammen, Drammen Hospital

Dresden, Gal. Arnold
 Dresden, Galerie Arnold [no longer exists]

Dresden, Gal. Gurlitt
 Dresden, Galerie Gurlitt

Dresden, Gal. Kuhl & Kühn
 Dresden, Galerie Kuhl und Kühn [closed]

Dresden, Gal. Nord
 Dresden, Galerie Nord

Dresden, Gal. Rähnitzgasse
 Dresden, Galerie Rähnitzgasse

Dresden, Gal. Richter
 Dresden, Galerie Richter

Dresden, Gemäldegal. Alte Meister
 Dresden, Gemäldegalerie Alte Meister [in
 Zwinger]

Dresden, Gemäldegal. Neue Meister
 Dresden, Gemäldegalerie Neue Meister [in
 Albertinum]

Dresden, Goethe Mus.
 Dresden, Goethe Museum

Dresden, Grünes Gewölbe [in Albertinum]

Dresden, Hist. Mus.
 Dresden, Historisches Museum [in Zwinger]

Dresden, Hochsch. Bild. Kst.
 Dresden, Hochschule für Bildende Künste

Dresden, Hofkirche [Kathedrale Sanctissimae
Trinitatis]

Dresden, Hoftheat.
 Dresden, Hoftheater

Dresden, Inst. Dkmlpf.
 Dresden, Institut für Denkmalpflege

Dresden, Johannes Kühl

Dresden, Kstgewmus. Staatl. Kstsamml.
 Dresden, Kunstgewerbe-Museum der
 Staatlichen Kunstsammlungen [in Schloss
 Pillnitz]

Dresden, Kupferstichkab.
 Dresden, Kupferstichkabinett

Dresden, Münzkab.
 Dresden, Münzkabinett

Dresden, Mus. Gesch.
 Dresden, Museum für Geschichte der Stadt
 Dresden [Stadtmuseum]

Dresden, Mus. Ksthandwerk
 Dresden, Museum für Kunsthandwerk [in
 Schloss Pillnitz]

Dresden, Mus. Vlkskst
 Dresden, Museum für Volkskunst

Dresden Opernhs
 Dresden, Opernhaus

Dresden, Porzellansamml.
 Dresden, Porzellansammlung [in Zwinger]

Dresden, Puppentheatsamml.
 Dresden, Puppentheatersammlung

Dresden, Royal Gal.
 Dresden, Royal Gallery

Dresden, Sächs. Kstver.
 Dresden, Sächsischer Kunstverein

Dresden, Sächs. Landesbib.
 Dresden, Sächsische Landesbibliothek [incl.
 Zentrale Fachbibliothek]

Dresden, Schloss Moritzburg

Dresden, Schloss Pillnitz

Dresden, Semper-Gal.
 Dresden, Semper-Galerie

Dresden, Skulpsamml.
 Dresden, Skulpturensammlung [in
 Albertinum]

Dresden, Staatl. Kstsammlungen
 Dresden, Staatliche Kunstsammlungen
 Dresden [admins Gemäldegal. Alte Meister;
 Gemäldegal. Neue Meister; Grünes Gewölbe;
 Hist. Mus.; Kupferstichkab.; Münzkab.; Mus.
 Ksthandwerk; Mus. Vlkskst; Porzellansamml.; ,
 Puppentheatsamml.; Schloss Pillnitz;
 Skulpsamml.; Staatl. Math.-Phys. Salon; Zent.
 Kstbib.]

Dresden, Staatl. Math.-Phys. Salon
 Dresden, Staatlicher Mathematisch-
 Physikalischer Salon [in Zwinger]

Dresden, Staatsarchv
 Dresden, Staatsarchiv

Dresden, Stadtarchv
 Dresden, Stadtarchiv

Dresden, Starkisches Haus

Dresden, Tech. U.
 Dresden, Technische Universität Dresden

Dresden, Zent. Kstbib.
 Dresden, Zentrale Kunstbibliothek

Dubai Mus.
 Dubai, Dubai Museum

Dubhela Mus.
 Dubhela, Dubhela Museum

Dublin, Allied Irish Bank

Dublin, A.C. Ireland
 Dublin, Arts Council of Ireland

Dublin, Bank of Ireland Col.
 Dublin, Bank of Ireland Collection

Dublin, Chester Beatty Lib.
 Dublin, Chester Beatty Library and Gallery of
 Oriental Art

Dublin, City Hall

Dublin, Dawson Gal.
 Dublin, Dawson Gallery

Dublin, Gen. Post Office
 Dublin, General Post Office

Dublin, Gt S. Hotels
 Dublin, Great Southern Hotels

Dublin, Guinness Mus.
 Dublin, Guinness Museum

Dublin, Hendriks Gal.
 Dublin, Hendriks Gallery

Dublin, Hugh Lane Mun. Gal.
 Dublin, Hugh Lane Municipal Gallery of
 Modern Art

Dublin, Hyde Gal.
 Dublin, Hyde Gallery

Dublin, Irish Archit. Archv
 Dublin, Irish Architectural Archive

Dublin, Irish Life Cent.
 Dublin, Irish Life Centre

Dublin, Irish MOMA
 Dublin, Irish Museum of Modern Art

Dublin, Kerlin Gal.
 Dublin, Kerlin Gallery

Dublin, Liberty Hall

Dublin, Mansion House

Dublin, Mun. Gal. Mod. A.
 Dublin, Municipal Gallery of Modern Art
 [name changed to Hugh Lane Mun. Gal. in
 1975]

Dublin, Mus. Royal Soc. Ant. Ireland
 Dublin, Museum of the Royal Society of
 Antiquaries of Ireland

Dublin, N. Coll. A. & Des.
 Dublin, National College of Art and Design

Dublin, Neptune Gal.
 Dublin, Neptune Gallery

Dublin, N.G.
 Dublin, National Gallery of Ireland

Dublin, N. Lib.
 Dublin, National Library of Ireland

Dublin, N. Mus.
 Dublin, National Museum of Ireland

Dublin, N. U.
 Dublin, National University of Ireland

Dublin, Represent. Body Church Ireland
 Dublin, Representative Body of the Church of
 Ireland

Dublin, Represent. Church Body Lib.
 Dublin, Representative Church Body Library

Dublin, Royal Dublin Soc.
 Dublin, Royal Dublin Society

Dublin, Royal Irish Acad.
 Dublin, Royal Irish Academy

Dublin, St Patrick's Deanery

Dublin, St Stephen's Green

Dublin, Taylor Gals
 Dublin, Taylor Galleries

Dublin, Trinity Coll.
 Dublin, University of Dublin, Trinity College

Dublin, Trinity Coll., Hyde Gal.
 Dublin, Trinity College, Douglas Hyde Gallery

Dublin, Trinity Coll. Lib.
 Dublin, Trinity College Library

Dublin, Trinity Coll., Mus. Bldg
 Dublin, Trinity College, Museum Building

Dublin, U. Coll.
 Dublin, University of Dublin, University
 College

Dublin, Waddington Gal.
 Dublin, Waddington Gallery [closed]

Dubrovnik, A.G.
 Dubrovnik, Art Gallery (Umjetnička Galerija)

Dubrovnik, City Mus.
 Dubrovnik, City Museum (Gradski Muzej)

Dubrovnik, Ethnog. Mus.
 Dubrovnik, Ethnographic Museum
 (Etnografski Muzej)

Dubrovnik, Granary Mus.
 Dubrovnik, Granary Museum (Muzej Rupa)

Dubrovnik, Hist. Archvs
Dubrovnik, Historical Archives

Dubrovnik, Mar. Mus.
Dubrovnik, Maritime Museum (Pomorski Muzej)

Dubrovnik, Mus. Dominican Priory
Dubrovnik, Museum of the Dominican Priory

Dudley, Mus. & A.G.
Dudley, Dudley Museum and Art Gallery

Duisburg, Lehmbruck-Mus.
Duisburg, Wilhelm-Lehmbruck-Museum

Duisburg, Mannesman Demag

Dumbarton, Scot. Pott. Soc.
Dumbarton, Scottish Pottery Society

Dunblane, Leighton Lib.
Dunblane, The Leighton Library

Dundee, Barrack Street Mus.
Dundee, Barrack Street Museum

Dundee, Broughty Castle Mus.
Dundee, Broughty Castle Museum

Dundee, Cent. Mus. & A.G.
Dundee, Central Museum and Art Gallery [now McManus Gals]

Dundee, McManus Gals
Dundee, McManus Galleries

Dundee, Mills Observatory

Dundee, Museums & A. Gals
Dundee, Dundee Museums and Art Galleries [admins Barrack Street Mus.; Broughty Castle Mus.; McManus Gals; Mills Observatory; St Mary's Tower]

Dundee, Orchar A.G.
Dundee, Orchar Art Gallery [closed; col. transferred to McManus Gals]

Dundee, Spalding Golf Mus.
Dundee, Spalding Golf Museum [Camperdown House; now closed]

Dundee, St Mary's Tower

Dundo, Mus. Reg.
Dundo, Museu Regional

Dunedin, NZ, Otago Early Settlers' Assoc. Mus.
Dunedin, NZ, Otago Early Settlers' Association Museum

Dunedin, NZ, Otago Mus.
Dunedin, NZ, Otago Museum

Dunedin, NZ, Pub. A.G.
Dunedin, NZ, Public Art Gallery

Dunedin, NZ, U. Otago, Hocken Lib.
Dunedin, NZ, University of Otago, Hocken Library

Dunfermline, Pittencrieff Park, Music Hall

Dunkirk, Mus. A. Contemp.
Dunkirk, Musée d'Art Contemporain, Jardin des Sculptures

Dunkirk, Mus. B.-A.
Dunkirk, Musée des Beaux-Arts

Durazno, Mus. Mun.
Durazno, Museo Municipal

Durban, A.G.
Durban, Durban Art Gallery

Durban, Campbell Col.
Durban, Campbell Collections

Durban, U. Natal
Durban, University of Natal

Düren, Leopold-Hoesch-Mus.
Düren, Leopold-Hoesch-Museum der Stadt Düren und Papier-Museum Düren

Durham, Archdeacon Sharpe Lib.
Durham, Archdeacon Sharpe Library [in U. Durham, Theology Department]

Durham, Cathedral Lib.
Durham, Cathedral Library

Durham, Cathedral Treasury

Durham, Gulbenkian Mus. Orient. A. & Archaeol.
Durham, Gulbenkian Museum of Oriental Art and Archaeology [now U. Orient. Mus.]

Durham, U. Durham, Ushaw Coll.
Durham, University of Durham, Ushaw College

Durham U. Lib.
Durham, University Library

Durham, U. Orient. Mus.
Durham, Durham University Oriental Museum [until 1982 called Gulbenkian Mus. Orient. A. & Archaeol.]

Durham, NC Cent. U., Mus .
Durham, NC, North Carolina Central University, Museum of Art

Durham, NC, Duke U. Mus. A.
Durham, NC, Duke University Museum of Art

Durham, U. NH, A. Gals
Durham, NH, University of New Hampshire, University Art Galleries, Paul Creative Arts Center

Durham, Ont., A.G.
Durham, Ont., Durham Art Gallery

Durrës, Archaeol. Mus.
Durrës, Archaeological Museum

Dushanbe, Repub. Hist., Reg. & F.A. Mus.
Dushanbe, Republican Historical, Regional and Fine Arts Museum

Dushanbe, Tajikistan Acad. Sci., Donish Inst. Hist., Archaeol. & Ethnog.
Dushanbe, Tajikistan Academy of Sciences, Donish Institute of History, Archaeology and Ethnography

Düsseldorf, Alfred Schmela

Düsseldorf, Eat A.G.
Düsseldorf, Eat Art Gallery

Düsseldorf, Gal. Boerner
Düsseldorf, Galerie Boerner

Düsseldorf, Gal. Ey
Düsseldorf, Galerie Johanna Ey [closed]

Düsseldorf, Gal. Flechteim
Düsseldorf, Galerie Flechteim

Düsseldorf, Gal. Gmyzek
Düsseldorf, Galerie Gmyzek

Düsseldorf, Gal. Heike Curtze
Düsseldorf, Galerie Heike Curtze

Düsseldorf, Gal. Konrad Fisher
Düsseldorf, Galerie Konrad Fisher

Düsseldorf, Gal. Marika Schmela
Düsseldorf, Galerie Marika Schmela

Düsseldorf, Gal. Nepal
Düsseldorf, Galerie Nepal

Düsseldorf, Gal. Nota
Düsseldorf, Galerie Nota

Düsseldorf, Gal. Paffrath
Düsseldorf, Galerie Paffrath

Düsseldorf, Gal. Remmert & Barth
Düsseldorf, Galerie Remmert und Barth

Düsseldorf, Gal. Schmela
Düsseldorf, Galerie Schmela

Düsseldorf, Gal. Vömel
Düsseldorf, Galerie Alex Vömel

Düsseldorf, Gal. 22
Düsseldorf, Galerie 22

Düsseldorf, Goethe-Mus.
Düsseldorf, Goethe-Museum [Anton-und-Katharina-Kippenberg-Stiftung]

Düsseldorf, Haus Leonard Tietz

Düsseldorf, Heinrich-Heine-Inst.
Düsseldorf, Heinrich-Heine-Institut

Düsseldorf, Hetjens-Mus.
Düsseldorf, Hetjens-Museum [Deutsches Keramikmuseum]

Düsseldorf, Hofgtn
Düsseldorf, Hofgarten

Düsseldorf, Industhaus
Düsseldorf, Industriehaus

Düsseldorf, Kstakad.
Düsseldorf, Kunstakademie [Hochschule für Bildende Künste]

Düsseldorf, Ksthalle
Düsseldorf, Kunsthalle

Düsseldorf, Kstlerver. Malkasten
Düsseldorf, Künstlerverein Malkasten

Düsseldorf, Kstmus.
Düsseldorf, Kunstmuseum im Ehrenhof

Düsseldorf, Kstsamml. Nordrhein–Westfalen
Düsseldorf, Kunstsammlung Nordrhein–Westfalen [Landesgalerie]

Düsseldorf, Kstver.
Düsseldorf, Kunstverein für die Rheinlande und Westfalen

Düsseldorf, Kurfürstl. Gal.
Düsseldorf, Kurfürstliche Galerie

Düsseldorf, Landeszentbank
Düsseldorf, Landeszentralbank

Düsseldorf, Landtagsgebäude [former Ständehaus]

Düsseldorf, Mannesmann-Hochhaus

Düsseldorf, Nordrhein-Westfäl. Hauptstaatsarchv
Düsseldorf, Nordrhein-Westfälisches Hauptstaatsarchiv

Düsseldorf, Oberlandesgericht

Düsseldorf, Schadow-Platz

Düsseldorf, Städt. Ksthalle
Düsseldorf, Städtische Kunsthalle

Düsseldorf, Stadtmus.
Düsseldorf, Stadtmuseum

Düsseldorf, Tonhalle

Düsseldorf, Vesters-Archv
Düsseldorf, Vesters-Archiv

Düsseldorf, Vidgal. Schum
Düsseldorf, Videogalerie Schum

Duxbury, MA, A. Complex Mus.
Duxbury, MA, Art Complex Museum

Dvin Mus.
Dvin, Dvin Museum

Dyat'kovo, Mus. Glass
Dyat'kovo, Museum of Glass (Muzey Stekla)

Dzhambul, Hist. & Reg. Mus.
Dzhambul, Historical and Regional Museum

Eastbourne, Compton Place

Eastbourne, Towner A.G. & Local Hist. Mus.
Eastbourne, Towner Art Gallery and Local History Museum

East Fortune, Mus. Flight
East Fortune, Museum of Flight

East Hampton, NY, Guild Hall Mus.
East Hampton, NY, Guild Hall Museum

East Hampton, NY, Lib.
East Hampton, NY, Library

East Lansing, MI State U., Kresge A. Mus.
    East Lansing, MI, Michigan State University,
    Kresge Art Museum

Eastleigh Mus.
    Eastleigh, Eastleigh Museum

East London, Cape Prov., Ann Bryant A.G.
    East London, Cape Province, Ann Bryant Art
    Gallery

East Molesey, Hampton Court Palace: see London

Eau Claire, U. WI, Sch. Nursing
    Eau Claire, University of Wisconsin, School of
    Nursing

Ebeltoft, Gamle Rådhus
    Ebeltoft, Det Gamle Rådhus

East Berlin: institutions producing exh. cats
between the 1945 division of Berlin and
reunification in Oct 1990 are cited using E. or W.
Berlin. These institutions, if their names have not
changed since unification, are all found under
Berlin. See also W. Berlin.

E. Berlin, Akad. Kst. DDR
    East Berlin, Akademie der Künste der DDR
    [now Berlin, Akad. Kst]

E. Berlin, Akad. Wiss.
    East Berlin, Akademie der Wissenschaften der
    DDR [now Berlin, Berlin-Brandenburgische
    Akad. Wiss.]

E. Berlin, Dt. Staatsbib.
    East Berlin, Deutsche Staatsbibliothek [since 1
    Jan 1992 part of Berlin, Staatsbib.]

E. Berlin, N.G.
    East Berlin, Nationalgalerie [now Berlin, Alte
    N.G.]

E. Berlin, Staatl. Museen
    East Berlin, Staatliche Museen zu Berlin
    [admind Berlin, Altes Mus.; Bodemus.; Alte
    N.G.; Schinkelmus; Schloss Köpenick]

Eccles, Monks Hall Mus.
    Eccles, Monks Hall Museum

Echmiadzin: see Ēdjmiadzin

Ecouen, Mus. Ren.
    Ecouen, Musée de la Renaissance, Château

Edenkoben, Schloss Villa Ludwigshöhe [incl.
Max-Slevogt-Galerie]

Edessa Mus.
    Edessa, Edessa Museum

Edinburgh, Archers' Hall

Edinburgh, Bourne F. A.
    Edinburgh, Bourne Fine Art

Edinburgh, Canongate Tolbooth

Edinburgh, Cent. Lib.
    Edinburgh, Central Library

Edinburgh, City A. Cent.
    Edinburgh, City Art Centre

Edinburgh, City Chambers

Edinburgh, City Libs
    Edinburgh, City Libraries [admins Cent. Lib.;
    branch libraries]

Edinburgh, City Museums & A. Gals
    Edinburgh, City Museums and Art Galleries
    [admins Canongate Tolbooth; City A. Cent.;
    Huntly House Mus.; Lady Stair's House;
    Lauriston Castle; Mus. Childhood;
    Queensferry Mus.]

Edinburgh, Coll. A.
    Edinburgh, College of Art

Edinburgh, Co. Merchants
    Edinburgh, Company of Merchants

Edinburgh, Distillers' Co.
    Edinburgh, Distillers' Company

Edinburgh, Eng. Speaking Un. Gal.
    Edinburgh, English Speaking Union Gallery

Edinburgh, F.A. Soc.
    Edinburgh, The Fine Art Society plc

Edinburgh, Free Ch. Assembl. Hall
    Edinburgh, Free Church Assembly Hall [St
    Columba's]

Edinburgh, Fruitmarket Gal.
    Edinburgh, Fruitmarket Gallery

Edinburgh, Glasite Meeting House

Edinburgh, Hon. Co. Golfers
    Edinburgh, Honourable Company of
    Edinburgh Golfers

Edinburgh, Huntly House Mus.
    Edinburgh, Huntly House Museum

Edinburgh, Lady Stair's House

Edinburgh, Lauriston Castle

Edinburgh, Mus. Ant.
    Edinburgh, Museum of Antiquities

Edinburgh, Mus. Childhood
    Edinburgh, Museum of Childhood

Edinburgh, N.G.
    Edinburgh, National Gallery of Scotland

Edinburgh, N. Gals
    Edinburgh, National Galleries of Scotland
    [admins N.G.; N.G. Mod. A.; N.P.G.]

Edinburgh, N.G. Mod. A.
    Edinburgh, National Gallery of Modern Art

Edinburgh, N. Lib.
    Edinburgh, National Library of Scotland

Edinburgh, N. Mus. Ant.
    Edinburgh, National Museum of Antiquities
    [name changed to Royal Mus. Scotland in Oct
    1985]

Edinburgh, N. Museums
    Edinburgh, National Museums of Scotland
    [admins Biggar, Gasworks Mus.; East Fortune,
    Mus. Flight; Edinburgh, Royal Mus. Scotland;
    Scot. Agric. Mus.; Scot. United Serv. Mus.;
    New Abbey, Shambellie House Mus. Cost.]

Edinburgh, N.P.G.
    Edinburgh, National Portrait Gallery

Edinburgh, NT Scotland
    Edinburgh, National Trust for Scotland

Edinburgh, Parliament House [Faculty of
Advocates]

Edinburgh, Queensferry Mus.
    Edinburgh, Queensferry Museum

Edinburgh, Register House

Edinburgh, Richard Demarco Gal.
    Edinburgh, Richard Demarco Gallery

Edinburgh, Royal Bank of Scotland

Edinburgh, Royal Comm. Anc. & Hist. Mnmts
    Edinburgh, Royal Commission on the Ancient
    and Historical Monuments of Scotland

Edinburgh, Royal Incorp. Architects
    Edinburgh, Royal Incorporation of Architects
    in Scotland

Edinburgh, Royal Inst.
    Edinburgh, Royal Institution

Edinburgh, Royal Mus. Scotland
    Edinburgh, Royal Museum of Scotland
    [formed 1 Oct 1985 by union of Royal Scot.
    Mus. and N. Mus. Ant.]

Edinburgh, Royal Scot. Acad.
    Edinburgh, Royal Scottish Academy

Edinburgh, Royal Scot. Mus.
    Edinburgh, Royal Scottish Museum [name
    changed to Royal Mus. Scotland on 1 Oct
    1985]

Edinburgh, Saltire Soc.
    Edinburgh, Saltire Society

Edinburgh, Scot. A.C.
    Edinburgh, Scottish Arts Council

Edinburgh, Scot. Agric. Mus.
    Edinburgh, Scottish Agricultural Museum

Edinburgh, Scot. Rec. Office
    Edinburgh, Scottish Record Office

Edinburgh, Scot. United Serv. Mus.
    Edinburgh, Scottish United Services Museum
    [in Castle]

Edinburgh, Surgeon's Hall

Edinburgh, U. Edinburgh
    Edinburgh, University of Edinburgh

Edinburgh, U. Edinburgh, Old Coll., Upper Lib.
    Edinburgh, University of Edinburgh, Old
    College, Upper Library

Edinburgh, U. Edinburgh, Talbot Rice Gal.
    Edinburgh, University of Edinburgh, Talbot
    Rice Gallery

Edinburgh, U. Lib.
    Edinburgh, University Library

Ēdjmiadzin Cathedral, Sacristy
    Ēdjmiadzin, Ēdjmiadzin Cathedral, Sacristy

Ēdjmiadzin, Manoogian Mus.
    Ēdjmiadzin, Alex and Marie Manoogian
    Museum

Ēdjmiadzin, Mus.
    Ēdjmiadzin, Museum

Edmonton, Alta, A.G.
    Edmonton, Alta, Edmonton Art Gallery

Edwardsville, S. IL U.
    Edwardsville, IL, Southern Illinois University

Eger, County Hall

Eger, Istvám Dobó Castle Mus.
    Eger, Istvám Dobó Castle Museum [former
    Archiepiscopal Museum; houses Fort Eger
    excav. mat.]

Eger, Lyceum

Egham, U. London, Royal Holloway & Bedford
New Coll.
    Egham, University of London, Royal
    Holloway and Bedford New College

Egmond Binnen Abbey
    Egmond Binnen, Egmond Binnen Abbey

Eibar, Ayuntamiento [Town Hall]

Eichenzell, Schloss Fasanerie, Mus.
    Eichenzell, Schloss Fasanerie, Museum
    [Schloss also houses archives and library]

Eichstätt, Bischöf. Pal.
    Eichstätt, Bischöfliches Palais

Eichstätt, Ubib.
    Eichstätt, Universitätsbibliothek

Eindhoven, Apollohuis

Eindhoven, Stedel. Van Abbemus.
    Eindhoven, Stedelijk Van Abbemuseum

Ein Harod, Mus. A.
    Ein Harod, Museum of Art (Mishkan
    Le'omannt)

Einsiedeln, Fürstensaal

Einsiedeln, Samml. Benediktinerabtei
    Einsiedeln, Sammlungen der Benediktinerabtei
    [in Grosser Saal]

Einsiedeln, Stiftsarchv
    Einsiedeln, Stiftsarchiv

Einsiedeln, Stiftsbib.
    Einsiedeln, Stiftsbibliothek

Eisenach, Thüringer Mus.
    Eisenach, Thüringer Museum

Eisenach, Wartburg-Stift.
Eisenach, Wartburg-Stiftung

Eisenstadt, Schloss Esterházy

Ejmiacin: *see* Ēdjmiadzin

Elberfeld: *see* Wuppertal [Elberfeld became part of Wuppertal in 1929, together with Barmen, Beyenburg, Cronenberg, Ronsdorf and Vohninkel]

Elberfeld, Städt. Mus.
Elberfeld, Städtisches Museum Elberfeld [now von der Heydt-Mus.]

Eleusis Mus.
Eleusis, Eleusis Museum

Elewijt, Rubenskasteel

Elgg, Zivgemeinde, Archv
Elgg, Zivilgemeinde, Archiv

Ellingen, Schloss
Ellingen, Schloss Ellingen

Elmira, NY, Amot A. Mus.
Elmira, NY, Amot Art Museum

El Pardo, Casita Príncipe
El Pardo, Casita del Príncipe

El Paso, TX, Mus. A.
El Paso, TX, Museum of Art

Ely Cathedral, Stained Glass Mus.
Ely Cathedral, Stained Glass Museum

Emden, Ksthalle
Emden, Kunsthalle

Emden, Ostfries. Landesmus. & Städt. Mus.
Emden, Ostfriesisches Landesmuseum und Städtisches Museum

Emden, Rathaus

Empoli, Mus. Dioc.
Empoli, Museo Diocesano

Empoli, Mus. S Andrea
Empoli, Museo della Collegiata di S Andrea

Encarnación, Paraguay, Mus. Itapúa
Encarnación, Paraguay, Museo de Itapúa

Enköping, Sydvästra Upplands Kulthist. Mus.
Enköping, Sydvästra Upplands Kulturhistoriska Museum

Enniskillen, Fermanagh Co. Mus.
Enniskillen, Fermanagh County Museum

Enns, Mus. Lauriacum
Enns, Museum Lauriacum Enns

Enschede, Rijksmus. Twenthe
Enschede, Rijksmuseum Twenthe [houses Oudheidkamer]

Enschede, Sticht. Edwina van Heek
Enschede, Stichting Edwina van Heek

Ensérune, Mus.
Ensérune, Musée [site museum]

Epernay, Bib. Mun.
Epernay, Bibliothèque Municipale

Epernay, Mus. Mun.
Epernay, Musée Municipal

Ephesos: *see* Selçuk

Epidauros, Archaeol. Mus.
Epidauros, Archaeological Museum

Epinal, Mus. Dépt. Vosges & Mus. Int. Imagerie
Epinal, Musée Départemental des Vosges et Musée International de l'Imagerie

Episkopi, Kourion Mus.
Episkopi, Kourion Museum [Episkopi Museum]

Episkopi-Phaneroumi, Archaeol. Mus.
Episkopi-Phaneroumi, Archaeological Museum

Erbach, Dt. Elfenbeinmus.
Erbach, Deutsches Elfenbeinmuseum Erbach

Eretria, Archaeol. Mus.
Eretria, Archaeological Museum

Erevan, Abovian House Mus.
Erevan, Abovian House Museum (Abovyani Tun T'angaran, K'anak'er)

Erevan, Archit. & Constr. Inst.
Erevan, Architectural and Constructional Institute [formerly Karl Marx Polytechnic Institute, Architectural and Constructional Department]

Erevan, Cent. Lib. Acad. Sci. Armenia
Erevan, Central Library of the Academy of Sciences of Armenia (Haykakan Gitut'yunneri Akademia Fundamental Gradaran)

Erevan, Children's A.G.
Erevan, Children's Art Gallery (Hayastani Mankakan Patkerasrah)

Erevan, Cult. & Hist. Mus.
Erevan, Cultural and Historical Museum [Mus. Lit. & A.]

Erevan, Erebuni Mus.
Erevan, Erebuni Museum

Erevan, Hist. Mus. Armenia
Erevan, Historical Museum of Armenia (Hayastani Patmut'yan Petakan T'angaran)

Erevan, Kotchar Mus.
Erevan, Kotchar Museum (Ervand K'otch'ar Museum)

Erevan, Martiros Sar'yan Gal.
Erevan, Martiros Sar'yan Gallery (Martiros Saryani Tun-T'angaran)

Erevan, Masterskaya M. Avetisian Mus.
Erevan, Masterskaya M. Avetisian Museum (Minas Avetisyani Tun-T'angaran)

Erevan, Matenadaran Inst. Anc. Armen. MSS
Erevan, Matenadaran Institute of Ancient Armenian Manuscripts ('Matenadaran' Mashtoc'i Anvan Hin Jeragreri Institut) [Matenadaran Library of Ancient Manuscripts]

Erevan, Mus. Armen. Flk A.
Erevan, Museum of Armenian Folk Art (Hayastani Zolvrdakan Arvesti T'angaran)

Erevan, Mus. Hist. City
Erevan, Museum of the History of the City of Erevan (Erevan K'alak'i Patmut'yan T'angaran)

Erevan, Mus. Lit. & A.
Erevan, Museum of Literature and Art (Grakanut'yan ev Arvest T'angaran)

Erevan, Mus. Rus. A.
Erevan, Museum of Russian Art (Rusakan Arvest T'angaran)

Erevan, N.A.G. Armenia
Erevan, National Art Gallery of Armenia (Hayastani Azgayin Patkerasrah)

Erevan, N. Lib. Armenia
Erevan, National Library of Armenia (Al. Myasnikyan Anvan Hanrapetakan Gradaran)

Erevan, Pict. Gal. Armenia
Erevan, Picture Gallery of Armenia [N.A.G. Armenia]

Erevan, Sar'yan Mus.
Erevan, Sar'yan Museum [Second State Pict. Gal. Armenia]

Erevan, Urartian Citadel Mus.
Erevan, Urartian Citadel Museum (Ērcbuni Amroc')

Erfurt, Angermus.
Erfurt, Angermuseum

Erfurt, Mus. Thüring. Vlksknd.
Erfurt, Museum für Thüringer Volkskunde

Erice, Mus. Civ. Cordici
Erice, Museo Civico Antonio Cordici

Erlangen, Graph. Samml. Ubib.
Erlangen, Graphische Sammlung der Universitätsbibliothek

Erlangen, Stadtmus.
Erlangen, Stadtmuseum

Erlangen, Ubib.
Erlangen, Universitäts Bibliothek

Erlangen, U. Erlangen
Erlangen, Universität Erlangen–Nürnberg

Erlangen, U. Erlangen, Archäol. Samml.
Erlangen, Archäologische Sammlung der Universität Erlangen–Nürnberg

Erlau, Lyzeum

Ermione, Archaeol. Mus.
Ermione, Archaeology Museum

Ermoupolis Mus.
Ermoupolis, Ermoupolis Museum

Erzurum, Archaeol. Mus.
Erzurum, Archaeological Museum (Arkeoloji Müzesi)

Erzurum, Çifte Minarelli Medrese Mus.
Erzurum, Çifte Minarelli Medrese Museum (Çifte Minarelli Medrese Müzesi)

Esbjerg, Fisk. & Sofartsmus.
Esbjerg, Fiskeri- og Sofartsmuseum

Esbjerg, Kstpav.
Esbjerg, Kunstpavillonen

Escuintla, Mus. Democ.
Escuintla, Museo de la Democracía

Esie, N. Mus.
Esie, National Museum

Eskişehir, Archaeol. Mus.
Eskişehir, Archaeological Museum

Essen, Münsterschatzmus.
Essen, Münsterschatzmuseum

Essen, Mus. Flkwang
Essen, Museum Folkwang

Essen, Ruhrlandmus.
Essen, Ruhrlandmuseum

Essen, Villa Hügel

Esslingen, Gal. Stadt
Esslingen, Galerie der Stadt [Villa Merkel]

Esslingen, Neue Gal.
Esslingen, Neue Galerie

Este, Mus. N. Atestino
Este, Museo Nazionale Atestino

Esztergom, Bálint Balassa Mus.
Esztergom, Bálint Balassa Museum (Balassa Bálint Múzeum)

Esztergom, Castle Mus.
Esztergom, Castle Museum (Vármúzeum)

Esztergom, Cathedral Treasury (Főszékesegyházi Kincstár)

Esztergom, Dioc. Mus.
Esztergom, Diocesan Museum

Esztergom, Mus. Christ.
Esztergom, Museum of Christianity (Keresztény Múzeum)

Etikhove, Cent. Kst & Kstambachten De Saedeleer
Etikhove, Centrum voor Kunst en Kunstambachten Valerins De Saedeleer

Eton, Berks, Coll.
Eton, Berks, Eton College

Eton, Berks, Coll. Lib.
Eton, Berks, Eton College Library

Ettlingen, Schloss [houses Albgaumuseum; Karl
Albiker-Galerie; Karl Hofer-Galerie; Museum
Schloss Ettlingen; Ostasiatische Kunst und
Asamsaal]

Eu, Mus. Louis-Philippe
Eu, Musée Louis-Philippe

Eugene, OR, U. Oregon
Eugene, OR, University of Oregon

Eutin, Kreisheimatmus.
Eutin, Kreisheimatmuseum

Evanston, IL, Northwestern U.
Evanston, IL, Northwestern University

Evanston, IL, Northwestern U., Mary & Leigh
Block Gal.
Evanston, IL, Northwestern University, Mary
and Leigh Block Gallery

Evanston, IL, Terra Mus. Amer. A.
Evanston, IL, Terra Museum of American Art
[moved to Chicago in April 1987]

Evansville, IN, Mus. A. & Sci.
Evansville, IN, Museum of Arts and Science

Évora, Bib. Púb. & Arquiv.
Évora, Biblioteca Pública e Arquivo

Évora, Mus. Évora
Évora, Museu Évora [Museu Regional]

Évora, Mus. Sé
Évora, Museu da Sé

Évora, Pal. Condes de Cadaval
Évora, Palacio del Condes de Cadaval

Evreux, Mus. Evreux
Evreux, Musée d'Evreux [Ancien Evêché]

Exeter, Archaeol. Field Unit
Exeter, Archaeological Field Unit

Exeter, City Council Museums Serv.
Exeter City Council Museums Service [admins
Archaeol. Field Unit; Guildhall; Rougemont
House Mus.; Royal Albert Mem. Mus.; St
Nicholas Priory; Topsham Mus.; Underground
Passages]

Exeter, Devon Rec. Office, City Archv
Exeter, Devon Record Office, City Archive

Exeter, Guildhall

Exeter, Rougemont House Mus.
Exeter, Rougemont House Museum

Exeter, Royal Albert Mem. Mus.
Exeter, Royal Albert Memorial Museum
[Exeter Museum and Art Gallery]

Exeter, St Nicholas Priory

Exeter, Topsham Mus.
Exeter, Topsham Museum

Exeter, Underground Passages

Exeter, NH, Lamont Gal.
Exeter, NH, Lamont Gallery

Fåborg, Mus. Fyn. Malkst
Fåborg, Museum for Fynsk Malerkunst

Fabriano, Mus. S Domenico
Fabriano, Museo di San Domenico [in ex-
convent of San Domenico]

Fabriano, Pin. Civ. Mus. Arazzi
Fabriano, Pinacoteca Civica e Museo degli
Arazzi

Fachsenfeld über Aalen, Koenig-Fachsenfeld
Samml.
Fachsenfeld über Aalen, Koenig-Fachsenfeld
Sammlung

Faenza, Mus. Int. Cer.
Faenza, Museo Internazionale delle Ceramiche

Faenza, Pal. Espos.
Faenza, Palazzo delle Esposizioni

Faenza, Pal. Milzetti
Faenza, Palazzo Milzetti

Faenza, Pin. Com.
Faenza, Pinacoteca Comunale

Failaka Island, Archaeol. Mus.
Failaka Island, Failaka Archaeological Museum

Failaka Island, Ethnog. Mus.
Failaka Island, Failaka Ethnographical
Museum

Fairbanks, U. AK Mus.
Fairbanks, AK, University of Alaska Museum

Fairfax, VA, George Mason U.
Fairfax, VA, George Mason University

Falaise, Hôtel de Ville

Falkirk, Carron Co. Mus.
Falkirk, Carron Company Museum [closed:
col. in Falkirk Mus.]

Falkirk Mus.
Falkirk, Falkirk Museum

Falls Church, VA, Amer. Found. Stud. Man
Falls Church, VA, American Foundation for
the Study of Man

Falmouth, Antigua, Seahorse Studios

Falmouth, VA, Melchers Mem. Gal.
Falmouth, VA, Gari Melchers Memorial
Gallery, Belmont

Fălticeni Mus.
Fălticeni, Fălticeni Museum

Falun, Dalarnas Mus.
Falun, Dalarnas Museum

Famagusta, Mun. A.G.
Famagusta, Municipal Art Gallery

Famalicão, Fund. Cupertino de Miranda
Famalicão, Fundação Cupertino de Miranda

Fano, Pin. Civ. & Mus. Malatestiano
Fano, Pinacoteca Civica e Museo Malatestiano

Fareham, Fort Nelson

Farfa Abbey, Bib.
Farfa Abbey, Biblioteca

Farmington, CT, Hill-Stead Mus.
Farmington, CT, Hill-Stead Museum

Farnham, W. Surrey Coll. A. & Des.
Farnham, West Surrey College of Art and
Design

Faro, Col. Ferreira d'Almeida
Faro, Colecçâo Ferreira d'Almeida

Faro, Mus. Arqueol. Lapidar Infante Henrique
Faro, Museu Arqueológico Lapidar do Infante
Dom Henrique

Faro, Mus. Etnog. Reg.
Faro, Museu de Etnografia Regional

Faro, Museu Mun.
Faro, Museu Municipal [admins Col. Ferreira
d'Almeida; Mus. Arqueol. Lapidar Infante
Henrique; Mus. Etnog. Reg.; Mus. Mar.]

Faro, Mus. Mar.
Faro, Museu Maritimo Almirante Ramalho
Ortigão

Faro, Semin.
Faro, Seminary

Farum, H. Kleis
Farum, H. Kleis Eftf. [formerly in
Copenhagen; name changed from Valdemar
Kleis in 1966]

Fayetteville, U. AR Lib.
Fayetteville, AR, University of Arkansas
Library

Fécamp, Mus. Cent.-A.
Fécamp, Musée Centre-des-Arts [formerly
Musée Municipal]

Fécamp, Musées Mun.
Fécamp, Musées Municipaux de Fécamp
[admins Mus. Cent.-A.; Mus. Terre-Neuvas &
Pêche]

Fécamp, Mus. Mun.
Fécamp, Musée Municipal [name changed to
Mus. Cent.- A.]

Fécamp, Mus. Terres-Neuvas & Pêche
Fécamp, Musée des Terres-Neuvas et de la
Pêche

Feltre, Mus. Civ.
Feltre, Museo Civico

Feltre, Pal. Bellati-Villabruna
Feltre, Palazzo Bellati-Villabruna

Fensmark, Holmegaards Glasværker

Feodosiya, Ayvazovsky Pict. Gal.
Feodosiya, Ayvazovsky Picture Gallery

Feodosiya, Ethnog. Mus.
Feodosiya, Ethnographical Museum

Fermo, Bib. Com.
Fermo, Biblioteca Comunale

Fermo, Pin. Com.
Fermo, Pinacoteca Comunale

Ferrara, Casa Romei

Ferrara, Cassa di Risparmio

Ferrara, Castello Estense

Ferrara, Civ. Bib. Ariostea
Ferrara, Civica Biblioteca Ariostea [Palazzo
Paradiso]

Ferrara, Gal. Civ. A. Mod.
Ferrara, Galleria Civica d'Arte Moderna e
Centro d'Attività Visive [Palazzo dei
Diamanti]

Ferrara, Gal. Costabili
Ferrara, Galleria Costabili

Ferrara, Gal. Santini
Ferrara, Galleria Santini

Ferrara, Mus. Civ. A. Ant. Pal. Schifanoia
Ferrara, Museo Civico d'Arte Antica del
Palazzo Schifanoia

Ferrara, Mus. Duomo
Ferrara, Museo del Duomo

Ferrara, Mus. N. Archeol.
Ferrara, Museo Nazionale Archeologico
[Museo Nazionale di Spina]

Ferrara, Padiglione A. Contemp.
Ferrara, Padiglione d'Arte Contemporanea [in
Palazzo Massari]

Ferrara, Pal. Arcivescovile
Ferrara, Palazzo Arcivescovile

Ferrara, Pal. Bevilacqua
Ferrara, Palazzo Bevilacqua

Ferrara, Pal. Com.
Ferrara, Palazzo Comunale

Ferrara, Pal. Diamanti
Ferrara, Palazzo dei Diamanti

Ferrara, Pal. Schifanoia
Ferrara, Palazzo Schifanoia

Ferrara, Pin. N.
Ferrara, Pinacoteca Nazionale [Pinacoteca
Nazionale del Palazzo dei Diamanti]

Ferrara, Scu. Mun. A. Dosso Dossi
Ferrara, Scuola Municipale d'Arte Dosso
Dossi

Ferrara, Soc. Promot. B.A.
Ferrara, Società Promotrice di Belle Arti

Fez, Mus. Armes Bordj Nord
    Fez, Musée d'Armes du Bordj Nord

Fez, Mus. Dar Batha
    Fez, Musée du Dar Batha

Fiesole, Fond. Primo Conti
    Fiesole, Fondazione Primo Conti

Fiesole, Fond. Primo Conti, Cent. Doc.
Avanguardie Stor.
    Fiesole, Fondazione Primo Conti, Centro
    Documentario Avanguardie Storiche

Fiesole, Mus. Bandini
    Fiesole, Museo Bandini

Fiesole, Mus. Dupré
    Fiesole, Museo Dupré

Fiesole, Pal. Mangani
    Fiesole, Palazzo Mangani

Figline Valdarno, Osp. Serristori
    Figline Valdarno, Ospedale Serristori

Figline Valdarno, Vecchio Pal. Com.
    Figline Valdarno, Vecchio Palazzo Comunale

Figueras, Teat.-Mus. Dalí
    Figueras, Teatre-Museu Dalí

Figueres: see Figueras

Fischerhude, Otto-Modersohn-Mus.
    Fischerhude, Otto-Modersohn-Museum

Fitero, Parish Church

Fixin, Mus. Noisot
    Fixin, Musée Noisot

Flaran, Abbaye
    Flaran, Abbaye de Flaran

Flaran, Cent. Cult. Dépt. Abbaye Flaran
    Flaran, Centre Culturel Départemental de
    l'Abbaye de Flaran

Flensburg, Mus. Park
    Flensburg, Museum Park

Flensburg, Städt. Mus.
    Flensburg, Städtisches Museum

Flint, MI, Inst. A.
    Flint, MI, Flint Institute of Arts

Florence, Accad.
    Florence, Galleria dell'Accademia

Florence, Accad. B.A. & Liceo A.
    Florence, Accademia di Belle Arti e Liceo
    Artistico

Florence, Accad. Crusca
    Florence, Accademia della Crusca [Villa
    Medicea di Castello]

Florence, Accad. Dis.
    Florence, Accademia del Disegno

Florence, Archv Corsini
    Florence, Archivio Corsini

Florence, Archv Opera Duomo
    Florence, Archivio dell'Opera del Duomo

Florence, Archv Opera Santa Croce
    Florence, Archivio dell'Opera di Santa Croce

Florence, Archv Panciatichi
    Florence, Archivio Panciatichi

Florence, Archv Stato
    Florence, Archivio di Stato

Florence, Arcisp. S Maria Nuo.
    Florence, Arcispedale di S Maria Nuova

Florence, Badia Fiorentina

Florence, Banca Tosc.
    Florence, Banca Toscana

Florence, Bargello
    Florence, Museo Nazionale del Bargello

Florence, Bib. Convento dei Servi all'Annunziata
    Florence, Biblioteca del Convento dei Servi
    all'Annunziata

Florence, Bib. Marucelliana
    Florence, Biblioteca Marucelliana di Firenze

Florence, Bib. Medicea-Laurenziana
    Florence, Biblioteca Medicea-Laurenziana

Florence, Bib. N. Cent.
    Florence, Biblioteca Nazionale Centrale [incl.
    Biblioteca Medicea-Palatino-Lotaringia]

Florence, Bib. Riccardiana
    Florence, Biblioteca Riccardiana

Florence, Bib. Uffizi
    Florence, Biblioteca della Galleria degli Uffizi

Florence, Casa Buonarroti
    Florence, Museo della Casa Buonarroti

Florence, Casino Mediceo

Florence, Cassa di Risparmio

Florence, Cenacolo Andrea del Sarto S Salvi
    Florence, Cenacolo di Andrea del Sarto a San
    Salvi

Florence, Cenacolo S Apollonia
    Florence, Cenacolo di Sant'Apollonia

Florence, Cent. Di
    Florence, Centro Di

Florence, Cent. Incontro Certosa
    Florence, Centro dell'Incontro della Certosa di
    Firenze

Florence, Cent. Tornabuoni
    Florence, Centro Tornabuoni

Florence, Certosa del Galluzzo, Pin.
    Florence, Certosa del Galluzzo, Pinacoteca

Florence, Chiostro Scalzo
    Florence, Chiostro dello Scalzo

Florence, Col. Com. Raffaello Stianti
    Florence, Collezione Comunale di Raffaello
    Stianti

Florence, Col. della Ragione
    Florence, Collezione Alberto della Ragione
    [Raccolta Alberto della Ragione]

Florence, Col. Ricasoli–Firidolfi
    Florence, Collezione Ricasoli–Firidolfi

Florence, Conserv. Quiete
    Florence, Conservatorio della Quiete

Florence, Depositi Gal.
    Florence, Depositi delle Gallerie Fiorentine

Florence, Fond. Giuliano Gori
    Florence, Fondazione Giuliano Gori

Florence, Fond. Horne
    Florence, Fondazione Horne

Florence, Fond. Longhi
    Florence, Fondazione R. Longhi

Florence, Fond. Romano
    Florence, Fondazione Salvatore Romano

Florence, Forte Belvedere
    Florence, Forte di Belvedere

Florence, Fortezza Basso
    Florence, Fortezza da Basso

Florence, Gabinetto Vieusseux [in Palazzo
Strozzi]

Florence, Gal. A. Mod. Farsetti
    Florence, Galleria d'Arte Moderna Farsetti

Florence, Gal. Bellini
    Florence, Galleria Bellini

Florence, Gal. Calvalensi & Botti
    Florence, Galleria Calvalensi e Botti

Florence, Gal. Emporio
    Florence, Galleria dell'Emporio

Florence, Gal. Osp. Innocenti
    Florence, Galleria dell'Ospedale degli
    Innocenti

Florence, Gal. Panciatichi
    Florence, Galleria Panciatichi

Florence, Giard. Gherardesca
    Florence, Giardino della Gherardesca

Florence, Inst. Fr.
    Florence, Institut Français

Florence, Ist. N. Studi Rin.
    Florence, Istituto Nazionale di Studi sul
    Rinascimento [Palazzo Strozzi]

Florence, Ist. U. Oland. Stor. A.
    Florence, Istituto Universitario Olandese di
    Storia dell'Arte

Florence, I Tatti
    Florence, Villa I Tatti [Harvard University
    Center for Italian Renaissance Studies]

Florence, Ksthist. Inst.
    Florence, Kunsthistorisches Institut [Istituto di
    Storia dell'Arte]

Florence, Leone Cie & Sons

Florence, Lib. Gonnelli
    Florence, Libreria Gonnelli

Florence, Loggia Lanzi
    Florence, Loggia dei Lanzi

Florence, Misericordia

Florence, Mus. Archeol.
    Florence, Museo Archeologico di Firenze
    [houses Etruscan Museum col.]

Florence, Mus. Bardini
    Florence, Museo Bardini

Florence, Mus. Bigallo
    Florence, Museo del Bigallo

Florence, Mus. Botan.
    Florence, Museo Botanico

Florence, Mus. Firenze com'era
    Florence, Museo di Firenze com'era [Museo
    Storico Topografico di Firenze com'era]

Florence, Mus. Horne
    Florence, Museo Horne

Florence, Mus. Marino Marini
    Florence, Museo di Marino Marini [in San
    Pancrazio]

Florence, Mus. Ognissanti
    Florence, Museo di Ognissanti

Florence, Mus. Opera Duomo
    Florence, Museo dell'Opera del Duomo

Florence, Mus. Opera Santa Croce
    Florence, Museo dell'Opera di Santa Croce

Florence, Mus. Opificio Pietre Dure
    Florence, Museo dell'Opificio delle Pietre
    Dure [e Laboratori di Restauro d'Opere
    d'Arte]

Florence, Mus. Osp. Innocenti
    Florence, Museo dell'Ospedale degli Innocenti

Florence, Mus. Siviero
    Florence, Museo Siviero

Florence, Mus. S Marco
    Florence, Museo di S Marco [houses library]

Florence, Mus. S Salvi
    Florence, Museo S Salvi [in ex-convent]

Florence, Mus. Stibbert
    Florence, Museo Stibbert

Florence, Mus. Stor. Sci.
    Florence, Istituto e Museo di Storia della
    Scienza di Firenze

Florence, Mus. Zecca
    Florence, Museo della Zecca

Florence, Mus. Zool. 'La Specola'
    Florence, Museo Zoologico 'La Specola'

Florence, Opificio Pietre Dure & Lab. Rest. Opere A.
Florence, Opificio delle Pietre Dure e Laboratori di Restauro d'Opere d'Arte

Florence, Orti Oricellari

Florence, Pal. A. Lana, S Maria della Tromba
Florence, Palazzo dell'Arte della Lana, Tabernacolo di S Maria della Tromba

Florence, Pal. Alessandri
Florence, Palazzo degli Alessandri

Florence, Pal. Arcivescovile
Florence, Palazzo Arcivescovile

Florence, Pal. B.A.
Florence, Palazzo delle Belle Arti

Florence, Pal. Banca d'Italia
Florence, Palazzo della Banca d'Italia

Florence, Pal. Bardini
Florence, Palazzo Bardini [Galleria Corsi]

Florence, Pal. Cam. Commerc.
Florence, Palazzo della Camera di Commercio

Florence, Pal. Capponi
Florence, Palazzo Capponi

Florence, Pal. Capponi–Farinola
Florence, Palazzo Capponi–Farinola [Sotheby's]

Florence, Pal. Capponi Rovinate
Florence, Palazzo Capponi delle Rovinate

Florence, Pal. Congressi
Florence, Palazzo dei Congressi

Florence, Pal. Davanzati
Florence, Palazzo Davanzati [Museo della Casa Fiorentina Antica]

Florence, Pal. Gherardesca
Florence, Palazzo della Gherardesca

Florence, Pal. Marucelli
Florence, Palazzo Marucelli

Florence, Pal. Medici–Riccardi
Florence, Palazzo Medici–Riccardi

Florence, Pal. Nonfinito
Florence, Palazzo Nonfinito

Florence, Pal. Parte Guelfa
Florence, Palazzo di Parte Guelfa

Florence, Pal. Ricasoli–Firidolfi
Florence, Palazzo Ricasoli–Firidolfi

Florence, Pal. Ridolfi
Florence, Palazzo Ridolfi

Florence, Pal. Rucellai
Florence, Palazzo Rucellai

Florence, Pal. Salviati
Florence, Palazzo Salviati

Florence, Pal. Serristori
Florence, Palazzo Serristori

Florence, Pal. Strozzi
Florence, Palazzo Strozzi

Florence, Pal. Vecchio
Florence, Palazzo Vecchio [houses Collezione Loeser; Museo delle Opere d'Arte Recuperate]

Florence, Parronchi

Florence, Pitti
Florence, Palazzo Pitti [houses Appartamenti Monumentali; Collezione Contini-Bonacossi; Galleria d'Arte Moderna; Galleria del Costume; Galleria Palatina; Museo degli Argenti; Museo delle Carrozze; Museo delle Porcellane]

Florence, Poggio Imp.
Florence, Poggio Imperiale

Florence, Rac. della Ragione
Florence, Raccolta Alberto della Ragione

Florence, Reale Ist. B.A.
Florence, Reale Istituto di Belle Arti

Florence, Semin. Maggiore
Florence, Seminario Maggiore

Florence, S Lorenzo, Archv Capitolare
Florence, S Lorenzo, Archivio Capitolare

Florence, S Lorenzo, Sagrestia Nuova
Florence, S Lorenzo, Sagrestia Nuova

Florence, Soc. B.A.
Florence, Società di Belle Arti [no longer exists]

Florence, Sopr. B. A. & Stor. Col.
Florence, Soprintendenza di Belle Artistiche e Storiche Collezioni

Florence, Sopr. Gal.
Florence, Soprintendenza alle Gallerie [admins Pal. Vecchio; Pitti]

Florence, Uffizi
Florence, Galleria degli Uffizi [incl. Gabinetto dei Disegni]

Florence, U. Studi, Ist. Papirol. Girolamo Vitelli
Florence, Università degli Studi, Istituto Papirologico Girolamo Vitelli

Florence, Villa Quiete
Florence, Villa la Quiete

Flushing, NY, Hall Sci.
Flushing, NY, Hall of Science of the City of New York

Flushing, NY, Queens Mus.
Flushing, NY, Queens Museum [in New York City Building, Flushing Meadow Corona Park]

Foligno, Archv Episc.
Foligno, Archivio Episcopale

Foligno, Bib. Com.
Foligno, Biblioteca Comunale

Foligno, Mus. Archeol.
Foligno, Museo Archeologico [in Palazzo Trinci]

Foligno, Pin. Civ.
Foligno, Pinacoteca Civica [Pinacoteca Comunale; housed with Mus. Archeol.]

Folkestone, Mus. & A.G.
Folkestone, Museum and Art Gallery

Fontainebleau, Château
Fontainebleau, Musée National du Château de Fontainebleau

Fontaine-Chaalis, Mus. Jacquemart-André
Fontaine-Chaalis, Musée Jacquemart-André

Fontanellato, Mus. Rocca Sanvitale
Fontanellato, Museo della Rocca Sanvitale

Forchtenau, Schloss Forchtenstein

Forlì, Bib. Com. Saffi
Forlì, Biblioteca Comunale 'A. Saffi'

Forlì, Municipio

Forlì, Pal. Albicini
Forlì, Palazzo Albicini

Forlì, Pal. Fosci
Forlì, Palazzo Fosci

Forlì, Pal. Mus.
Forlì, Palazzo dei Musei

Forlì, Pin. Civ.
Forlì, Pinacoteca Civica

Fortaleza, Mus. A. U. Ceará
Fortaleza, Museu de Arte da Universidade do Ceará

Fortaleza, Mus. Artur Ramos
Fortaleza, Museu Artur Ramos

Fort de France, Carib. A. Cent. (Métiers A.)
Fort de France, Caribbean Art Centre (Métiers d'Art) [Martinique]

Fort de France, Mus. Dépt.
Fort de France, Musée Départemental

Fort Lauderdale, FL, Mus. A.
Fort Lauderdale, FL, Museum of Art

Fort Smith, AR, N. Hist. Site
Fort Smith, AR, National Historic Site

Fort Walton Beach, FL, Temple Mound Mus.
Fort Walton Beach, FL, Temple Mound Museum

Fort Worth, TX, Amon Carter Mus.
Fort Worth, TX, Amon Carter Museum of Western Art

Fort Worth, TX, A. Mus.
Fort Worth, TX, Fort Worth Art Museum [name changed to Mod. A. Mus. in 1987]

Fort Worth, TX, Hall Gals.
Fort Worth, TX, Hall Galleries

Fort Worth, TX, Kimbell A. Mus.
Fort Worth, TX, Kimbell Art Museum

Fort Worth, TX, Mod. A. Mus.
Fort Worth, TX, Modern Art Museum of Fort Worth [formerly Fort Worth A. Mus.]

Fossombrone, Mus. Civ. Vernarecci
Fossombrone, Museo Civico A. Vernarecci

Fossombrone, Pin. Com. Vernarecci
Fossombrone, Quadreria Cesarini–Pinacoteca Comunale A. Vernarecci

Foumban, Mus. A. & Trad. Bamoun
Foumban, Musée des Arts et Traditions Bamoun

Foumban, Mus. Privé Sultan Bamoun
Foumban, Musée Privé de Sultan Bamoun [in Palais Royal]

Framingham, MA, Danforth Mus. A.
Framingham, MA, Danforth Museum of Art

Francavilla al Mare, Pal. Sirena
Francavilla al Mare, Palazzo Sirena

Franeker, 't Dr Coopmanshuis [Dr Coopman's House]

Frankenthal, Erkenbert-Mus.
Frankenthal, Erkenbert-Museum und Porzellansammlung der Stadt

Frankenthal, Staatl. Gym.
Frankenthal, Staatliche Gymnasie

Frankfort, KY, Hist. Soc.
Frankfort, KY, Historical Society

Frankfort, KY, Hist. Soc. Mus.
Frankfort, KY, Historical Society Museum

Frankfort, KY, State Capitol

Frankfurt am Main, Dt. Architmus.
Frankfurt am Main, Deutsches Architekturmuseum

Frankfurt am Main, Fot. Forum
Frankfurt am Main, Fotografie Forum

Frankfurt am Main, Gal. Dato
Frankfurt am Main, Galerie Dato

Frankfurt am Main, Gal. F.A.C. Prestel
Frankfurt am Main, Galerie F.A.C. Prestel

Frankfurt am Main, Gal. Klaus Franck
Frankfurt am Main, Galerie Klaus Franck

Frankfurt am Main, Gal. Ludwig Schames
Frankfurt am Main, Galerie Ludwig Schames

Frankfurt am Main, Gal. Neuendorf
Frankfurt am Main, Galerie Neuendorf

Frankfurt am Main, Gal. Städel
Frankfurt am Main, Galerie Städel

Frankfurt am Main, Gal. Sydow
Frankfurt am Main, Galerie Sydow

Frankfurt am Main, Goethemus.
Frankfurt am Main, Goethemuseum [Freies Deutsches Hochstift]

Frankfurt am Main, Haus Hess. Rundfunks
Frankfurt am Main, Haus des Hessischen Rundfunks

Frankfurt am Main, Hermann Abs Mus.
Frankfurt am Main, Hermann Abs Museum

Frankfurt am Main, Hist. Mus.
Frankfurt am Main, Historisches Museum

Frankfurt am Main, Höchst, IG Farben

Frankfurt am Main, Inst. Stadtgesch., Stadtarchv
Frankfurt am Main, Institut für Stadtgeschichte, Stadtarchiv

Frankfurt am Main, J. P. Schneider jr

Frankfurt am Main, Jüd. Mus.
Frankfurt am Main, Jüdisches Museum

Frankfurt am Main, Justus-von-Liebig Sch.
Frankfurt am Main, Justus-von-Liebig Schule

Frankfurt am Main, Kstver.
Frankfurt am Main, Frankfurter Kunstverein

Frankfurt am Main, Liebieghaus [Museum Alter Plastik]

Frankfurt am Main, Mus. Ksthandwk
Frankfurt am Main, Museum für Kunsthandwerk

Frankfurt am Main, Mus. Mod. Kst
Frankfurt am Main, Museum für Moderne Kunst

Frankfurt am Main, Mus. Vlkerknd.
Frankfurt am Main, Museum für Völkerkunde

Frankfurt am Main, Natmus. Senckenberg
Frankfurt am Main, Naturmuseum Senckenberg

Frankfurt am Main, Römer [Rathaus]

Frankfurt am Main, Schirn Ksthalle
Frankfurt am Main, Schirn Kunsthalle

Frankfurt am Main, Schopenhauer-Archv
Frankfurt am Main, Schopenhauer-Archiv

Frankfurt am Main, Städel. Kstinst. & Städt. Gal.
Frankfurt am Main, Städelsches Kunstinstitut und Städtische Galerie

Frankfurt am Main, Stadt- & Ubib.
Frankfurt am Main, Stadt- und Universitätsbibliothek [Senchenbergische Bibliothek]

Frankfurt am Main, U. Frankfurt am Main
Frankfurt am Main, Johann Wolfgang Goethe-Universität

Frankfurt am Main, U. Frankfurt am Main, Frobenius-Inst.
Frankfurt am Main, Johann Wolfgang Goethe-Universität, Frobenius-Institut

Frankfurt am Main, Zimmergal. Franck
Frankfurt am Main, Zimmergalerie Franck

Frankfurt an der Oder, Gal. Junge Kst
Frankfurt an der Oder, Galerie Junge Kunst

Franschhoek, Huguenot Mem. Mus.
Franschhoek, Huguenot Memorial Museum

Frascati, Episcopio [formerly Rocca]

Fray Bentos, Mus. Solari
Fray Bentos, Museo Solari

Fredensborg Slot
Fredensborg, Fredensborg Slot

Fredericton, NB, Beaverbrook A.G.
Fredericton, NB, Beaverbrook Art Gallery

Fredericton, NB, Dioc. Archvs
Fredericton, NB, Diocesan Archives [on dep. Prov. Archvs NB]

Fredericton, Prov. Archvs NB
Fredericton, NB, Provincial Archives of New Brunswick

Fredericton, U. NB A. Cent.
Fredericton, NB, University of New Brunswick, Art Centre

Fredericton, U. NB, Creative A. Cent.
Fredericton, NB, University of New Brunswick, Creative Art Centre

Frederiksborg: see Hillerød

Frederikssund, Willumsens Mus.
Frederikssund, J. F. Willumsens Museum

Freetown, Sierra Leone, Alliance Fr.
Freetown, Sierra Leone, Alliance Française

Freiburg im Breisgau, Altes Rathaus

Freiburg im Breisgau, Augustinmus.
Freiburg im Breisgau, Augustinermuseum

Freiburg im Breisgau, Dom-Mus.
Freiburg im Breisgau, Dom-Museum [Münster Treasury]

Freiburg im Breisgau, Erzbischöf. Archv
Freiburg im Breisgau, Erzbischöfliches Archiv

Freiburg im Breisgau, Erzbischöf. Diözesanmus.
Freiburg im Breisgau, Erzbischöfliches Diözesanmuseum

Freiburg im Breisgau, Kstver.
Freiburg im Breisgau, Kunstverein

Freiburg im Breisgau, Morat-Inst. Kst & Kstwiss.
Freiburg im Breisgau, Morat-Institut für Kunst und Kunstwissenschaft

Freiburg im Breisgau, Mus. Natknd.
Freiburg im Breisgau, Museum für Naturkunde

Freiburg im Breisgau, Mus. Neue Kst
Freiburg im Breisgau, Museum für Neue Kunst

Freiburg im Breisgau, Mus. Ur- & Frühgesch.
Freiburg im Breisgau, Museum für Ur- und Frühgeschichte

Freiburg im Breisgau, Mus. Vlkerknd.
Freiburg im Breisgau, Museum für Völkerkunde

Freiburg im Breisgau, Neues Rathaus

Freiburg im Breisgau, Städt. Museen
Freiburg im Breisgau, Städtische Museen [admins Augustinmus.; Mus. Natknd.; Mus. Neue Kst; Mus. Ur- & Frühgesch.]

Freiburg im Breisgau, U. Freiburg im Breisgau
Freiburg im Breisgau, Albert-Ludwigs-Universität

Freising, Diözmus.
Freising, Diözesanmuseum

Freising, Klerikalsemin.
Freising, Klerikalseminar [transferred to Munich in 1968]

Fremantle, A. Cent.
Fremantle, Arts Centre

Fresno, CA, A. Mus.
Fresno, CA, Art Museum

Fresno, CA State U.
Fresno, CA, California State University

Fribourg, Bib. Cant. & U.
Fribourg, Bibliothèque Cantonale et Universitaire [Kantons-und Universitätsbibliothek]

Fribourg, Mus. A. & Hist.
Fribourg, Musée d'Art et d'Histoire

Friedrichshafen, Kstver.
Friedrichshafen, Kunstverein

Friedrichshafen, Städt. Bodensee-Mus.
Friedrichshafen, Städtisches Bodensee-Museum

Friedrichsruh, Bismarck-Mus.
Friedrichsruh, Bismarck-Museum

Friesach, Stadtmus.
Friesach, Stadtmuseum

Fritzlar, Domschatz & Mus.
Fritzlar, Domschatz und Museum

Frunze: the city reverted to its pre-revolutionary name of Bishkek c. 1990; see Bishkek

Fucecchio, Mus. Civ.
Fucecchio, Museo Civico

Fufeng, Famen Temple Mus.
Fufeng, Famen Temple Museum

Fujayra Mus.
Fujayra, Fujayra Museum

Fujinomiya, Fuji A. Mus.
Fujinomiya, Fuji Art Museum

Fukuoka, A. Mus.
Fukuoka, Fukuoka Art Museum (Fukuoka Bijutsukan)

Fukuoka, Cult. Cent.
Fukuoka, Cultural Centre

Fukuoka, Prefect. City Hall
Fukuoka, Fukuoka Prefecture City Hall

Fukushima, Cult. Cent.
Fukushima, Cultural Centre (Fukushima-ken Bunka Centre)

Fulda, Hess. Landesbib. Fulda
Fulda, Hessische Landesbibliothek Fulda [Schloss Fasanerie]

Fulda, Schloss Fasanerie

Fulda, Schloss, Fürstensaal [former Residenz]

Fumban: see Foumban

Füssen, Staatsgal. Hohen Schloss
Füssen, Staatsgalerie im Hohen Schloss

Fuzhau, Fujian Prov. Mus.
Fuzhau, Fujian Provincial Museum

Gaasbeek, Kasteel
Gaasbeek, Kasteel van Gaasbeek

Gabiano, Castello Negrotto Cambiaso

Gaborone, Botswana Soc.
Gaborone, Botswana Society

Gaborone, N.A.G.
Gaborone, National Art Gallery

Gaborone, N. Mus. & A.G.
Gaborone, National Museum and Art Gallery [name changed 1987-8 to N. Mus., Mnmts & A.G.]

Gaborone, N. Mus., Mnmts & A.G.
Gaborone, National Museum, Monuments and Art Gallery [formerly N. Mus. & A.G.]

Gaeta, Pal. Vio
Gaeta, Palazzo di Vio

Gainesville, U. FL, Mus. Nat. Hist.
Gainesville, FL, University of Florida Museum of Natural History

Gainsborough, Old Hall

Galaţi, Distr. Museums
Galaţi, Galatian District Museums (Complexul Muzeal Judeţean Galaţi) [admins Mus. Contemp. Roman. A.; Mus. Galaţy Hist.; Mus. Nat. Sci.]

Galaţi, Mus. Contemp. Roman. A.
Galaţi, Museum of Contemporary Romanian Art (Muzeul de Artă Contemporană Românească) [name changed to Mus. Visual A. c. 1990]

Galaţi, Mus. Galaţy Hist.
Galaţi, Museum of the Galaţy History (Muzeul Judetean de Istorie Galaţi)

Galaţi, Mus. Nat. Sci.
Galaţi, Museum of Natural Science (Muzeul de Ştiinţele Naturii)

Galaţi, Mus. Visual A.
Galaţi, Museum of Visual Arts

Galatina, Mun.
Galatina, Municipio

Gallarate, Civ. Gal. A. Mod.
Gallarate, Civica Galleria d'Arte Moderna

Gallarate, Mus. A. Sacra
Gallarate, Museo d'Arte Sacra della Collegiata di S Maria Assunta

Gaoua, Mus. Civilis. S.-Ouest
Gaoua, Musée des Civilisations du Sud-Ouest

Gap, Mus. Dépt.
Gap, Musée Départemental de Gap

Garching, Max-Planck-Inst. Astrophys.
Garching, Max-Planck-Institut für Astrophysik

Gateshead, Shipley A.G.
Gateshead, Shipley Art Gallery

Gauhati, Assam State Mus.
Gauhati, Assam State Museum

Gävle, Stadshuset

Gaziantep Mus.
Gaziantep, Gaziantep Müzesi

Gazzada, Mus. Villa Cagnola
Gazzada, Museo di Villa Cagnola [Cagnola Foundation]

Gdańsk, Artus Court
Gdańsk, Artus Court (Dwór Artusa) [partly destr. 1945; since reconstructed]

Gdańsk, Golden Gate

Gdańsk, Lib. Pol. Acad. Sci.
Gdańsk, Library of the Polish Academy of Sciences

Gdańsk, Mus. Hist.
Gdańsk, Museum of the History of Gdańsk (Muzeum Historii Miasta Gdańska)

Gdańsk, N. Mus.
Gdańsk, National Museum (Muzeum Narodowe) [until 1972 called Pom. Mus.]

Gdańsk, Pom. Mus.
Gdańsk, Pomeranian Museum (Muzeum Pomorskie) [now N. Mus.]

Gdańsk, Stadtmus.
Gdańsk, Stadtmuseum [destr.]

Gdańsk, Tech. U.
Gdańsk, Technical University of Gdańsk (Politechnika Gdańska)

Geelong, A.G.
Geelong, Art Gallery

Gelsenkirchen, Städt. Kstsamml.
Gelsenkirchen, Städtische Kunstsammlung

Gelsenkirchen, Stadttheat.
Gelsenkirchen, Stadttheater

Genazzano, Castello Colonna

Geneva, Acad.
Geneva, Académie de Genève

Geneva, Ant.
Geneva, Antiquorium

Geneva, Bib. A. & Archéol.
Geneva, Bibliothèque d'Art et d'Archéologie [annexe of Mus. A. & Hist.]

Geneva, Bib. Classe B.-A.
Geneva, Bibliothèque de la Classe des Beaux-Arts

Geneva, Bib. Pub. & U.
Geneva, Bibliothèque Publique et Universitaire de Genève

Geneva, Cab. Est. Mus. A. & Hist.
Geneva, Cabinet des Estampes du Musée d'Art et d'Histoire

Geneva, Cent. A. Contemp.
Geneva, Centre d'Art Contemporain

Geneva, Cent. Doc. Ecole Archit.
Geneva, Centre de Documentation de l'Ecole d'Architecture

Geneva, Col. Baur
Geneva, Collections Baur [Fondation Alfred et Eugénie Baur-Duret]

Geneva, Ecole A.
Geneva, Ecole d'Art

Geneva, Gal. Bonnier
Geneva, Galerie Bonnier

Geneva, Gal. Eric Franck
Geneva, Galerie Eric Franck

Geneva, Gal. Jan Krugier
Geneva, Galerie Jan Krugier

Geneva, Gal. Jeanneret
Geneva, Galerie Marie-Louise Jeanneret

Geneva, Gal. Moos
Geneva, Galerie Moos

Geneva, Gal. Motte
Geneva, Galerie Motte

Geneva, Maison Tavel

Geneva, Mus. A. & Hist.
Geneva, Musée d'Art et d'Histoire

Geneva, Mus. Athénée
Geneva, Musée de l'Athénée

Geneva, Mus. Barbier–Mueller
Geneva, Musée Barbier–Mueller

Geneva, Mus. Ethnog.
Geneva, Musée d'Ethnographie

Geneva, Mus. Hist. Nat.
Geneva, Musée d'Histoire Naturelle

Geneva, Mus. Horlogerie & Emaillerie
Geneva, Musée d'Horlogerie et de l'Emaillerie

Geneva, Mus. Olympique
Geneva, Musée Olympique

Geneva, Mus. Rath
Geneva, Musée Rath

Geneva, Mus. Voltaire
Geneva, Institut et Musée Voltaire

Geneva, Org. Météorol. Mondiale
Geneva, Organisation Météorologique Mondiale

Geneva, Pal. Eynard
Geneva, Palais Eynard

Geneva, Pal. Nations
Geneva, Palais des Nations

Geneva, Petit Pal.
Geneva, Petit Palais, Musée d'Art Moderne de Genève [Musée du Petit Palais]

Geneva, Soc. A.
Geneva, Société des Arts de Genève

Geneva, Un. Int. Télécommunic.
Geneva, Union Internationale des Télécommunications

Geneva, Villa La Grange

Geneva, Virginia & Edward Chow Found.
Geneva, Virginia and Edward Chow Foundation

Genoa, Albergo Poveri
Genoa, Albergo dei Poveri

Genoa, Archv Mun., Pal. Tursi
Genoa, Archivio Municipale di Genova, Palazzo Tursi

Genoa, Arcivescovado

Genoa, Banco di Chiavarie
Genoa, Banco di Chiavarie e della Rivera Ligurem

Genoa, Bib. Berio
Genoa, Biblioteca Berio

Genoa, Bib. Bodmeriana
Genoa, Biblioteca Bodmeriana

Genoa, Bosio Marlugo

Genoa, Cassa di Risparmio

Genoa, Col. Pallavicino
Genoa, Collezione Pallavicino

Genoa, Commenda S Giovanni Prè
Genoa, Commenda di S Giovanni di Prè

Genoa, Conserv. Suore S Giuseppe
Genoa, Conservatorio delle Suore di S Giuseppe

Genoa, Gal. A. Mod.
Genoa, Galleria d'Arte Moderna

Genoa, Gal. Chisel
Genoa, Galleria Chisel

Genoa, Galforma
Genoa, Galleriaforma

Genoa, Gal. Pal. Bianco
Genoa, Galleria di Palazzo Bianco [Civica Galleria]

Genoa, Gal. Pal. Rosso
Genoa, Galleria di Palazzo Rosso

Genoa, Gal. Polena
Genoa, Galleria la Polena

Genoa, Mus. Accad. Ligustica B.A.
Genoa, Museo dell'Accademia Ligustica di Belle Arti

Genoa, Mus. Osp. Civ.
Genoa, Museo degli Oggetti d'Arte e Ceramiche degli Ospedali Civili [Museo degli Ospedali Civili di Genoa]

Genoa, Mus. S Agostino
Genoa, Museo di S Agostino

Genoa, Mus. Tesoro S Lorenzo
Genoa, Museo del Tesoro di S Lorenzo

Genoa, Mus. Villa Croce
Genoa, Museo Villa Croce

Genoa, Osp. Civ. S Martino
Genoa, Ospedale Civile S Martino

Genoa, Pal. Accad.
Genoa, Palazzo dell'Accademia

Genoa, Pal. Adorno
Genoa, Palazzo Adorno

Genoa, Pal. Arcivescovile
Genoa, Palazzo Arcivescovile

Genoa, Pal. Balbi Senarega
Genoa, Palazzo Balbi Senarega

Genoa, Pal. Bianco
Genoa, Palazzo Bianco

Genoa, Pal. Cambiaso
Genoa, Palazzo Cambiaso

Genoa, Pal. Campanella
Genoa, Palazzo Campanella

Genoa, Pal. Cattaneo
Genoa, Palazzo Cattaneo

Genoa, Pal. Croce Bermond
Genoa, Palazzo Croce Bermond

Genoa, Pal. Belimbair Negrotto Cambiaso
Genoa, Palazzo Belimbair Negrotto Cambiaso

Genoa, Pal. Doria
  Genoa, Palazzo Doria
Genoa, Pal. Doria Pamphili
  Genoa, Palazzo Doria Pamphili [Palazzo del
  Principe]
Genoa, Pal. Ducale
  Genoa, Palazzo Ducale
Genoa, Pal. Durazzo Pallavicini
  Genoa, Palazzo Durazzo Pallavicini
Genoa, Pal. Espos.
  Genoa, Palazzo delle Esposizioni
Genoa, Pal. Lecarci
  Genoa, Palazzo Lecarci
Genoa, Pal. Lecarci-Parodi
  Genoa, Palazzo Lecarci-Parodi
Genoa, Pal. Pallavicino
  Genoa, Palazzo Pallavicino
Genoa, Pal. Parodi
  Genoa, Palazzo Parodi
Genoa, Pal. Reale
  Genoa, Palazzo Reale [Palazzo Bali-Durazzo]
Genoa, Pal. Rosso
  Genoa, Palazzo Rosso
Genoa, Pal. S Giorgio
  Genoa, Palazzo S Giorgio [Palazzo del Mare]
Genoa, Pal. Spinola
  Genoa, Galleria Nazionale del Palazzo Spinola
Genoa, Pal. Tursi
  Genoa, Palazzo Tursi [Municipio]
Genoa, Prefettura
Genoa, Soc. Ligure Stor. Patria
  Genoa, Società Ligure di Storia Patria
Genoa, Sopr. Beni A. & Stor. Liguria
  Genoa, Soprintendenza per i Beni Artistici e
  Storici della Liguria
Genoa, S Stefano, Depositi Sopr.
  Genoa, S Stefano, Depositi della
  Soprintendenza
Genoa, Teat. Carlo Felice
  Genoa, Teatro Carlo Felice
Genoa, U. Studi
  Genoa, Università degli Studi
Genoa, Villa Bignole Sale
Genoa, Villa Giustiniani Cambiaso
Genoa, Villa Imp. Scassi
  Genoa, Villa Imperiale Scassi 'Bellezza'
  [houses Istituto Casaregis]
Genoa, Villa Imp. Terralba
  Genoa, Villa Imperiale di Terralba
Georgetown, Guyana Mus.
  Georgetown, Guyana Museum
Georgetown, N. A. Col.
  Georgetown, National Art Collection [in
  former residence of the President]
Georgetown, U. Guyana, Carib. Res. Lib.
  Georgetown, University of Guyana, Caribbean
  Research Library
Gerona: see Girona
Gettysburg, PA, N. Mil. Park.
  Gettysburg, PA, National Military Park
Geva, Mus. Angewandte Kst
  Geva, Museum für Angewandte Kunst
Ghedi, Pal. Orsini-Modella
  Ghedi, Palazzo Orsini-Modella
Ghent, Begijnhof St Elisabeth
  Ghent, Begijnhof van St Elisabeth [Grand
  Béguinage de St Elisabeth in St Amandsberg]
Ghent, Bib. Rijksuniv.
  Ghent, Bibliotheek van de Rijksuniversiteit

Ghent, Bisschops Huis
Ghent, Cent. Kst & Cult.
  Ghent, Centrum voor Kunst en Cultuur [in
  former abbey of St Pieter]
Ghent, Cercle A.
  Ghent, Cercle Artistique
Ghent, Gravensteen [castle of the Counts of
  Flanders]
Ghent, Kon. Acad. S. Kst.
  Ghent, Koninklijke Academie voor Schone
  Kunsten
Ghent, Krocht St Baafskathedral
  Ghent, Krocht van de St Baafskathedral [St
  Bavo]
Ghent, Mus. Hedendaag. Kst
  Ghent, Museum van Hedendaagse Kunst
Ghent, Mus. Sierkst
  Ghent, Museum voor Sierkunst
Ghent, Mus. S. Kst.
  Ghent, Museum voor Schone Kunsten
Ghent, Mus. Stenen Voorwerpen
  Ghent, Museum voor Stenen Voorwerpen
Ghent, Oudhdknd. Mus. Bijloke
  Ghent, Oudheidkundig Museum van de
  Bijloke
Ghent, Provgebouw
  Ghent, Provinciegebouw
Ghent, Rijksarchf
  Ghent, Rijksarchief te Gent
Ghent, St-Pietersabdij
  Ghent, St-Pietersabdij
Ghent, Stadhuis
Ghent, Stadsbib.
  Ghent, Stadsbibliotheek
Ghent, St Lukas Mus.
  Ghent, St Lukas Museum
Ghent U.
  Ghent, Universiteit te Ghent
Gianyar, Gedung Arca Mus.
  Gianyar, Gedung Arca Museum
Gien, Mus. Int. Chasse
  Gien, Musée International de la Chasse
Giessen, Oberhess. Mus. & Gail'sche Samml.
  Giessen, Oberhessisches Museum und
  Gail'sche Sammlungen [in Altes Schloss]
Giessen, U. Giessen
  Giessen, Justus-Liebig-Universität
Gijón, Fund. Barjola
  Gijón, Fundación Barjola [in Palacio de la
  Trinidad]
Gijón, Inst. Astur. Jovellanos
  Gijón, Instituto Asturiano Jovellanos
Giovik, Rådhus
Girona, Bib. Capitolare
  Girona, Biblioteca Capitolare
Girona, Caixa Estalvis Prov.
  Girona, Caixa d'Estalvis Provincial
Girona, Mus. A.
  Girona, Museu d'Art
Girona, Mus. Arqueol.
  Girona, Museu Arqueològic de Girona [Museo
  Arqueológico Provincial]
Girona, Mus. Catedralicio
  Girona, Museu Catedralicio
Girona, Mus. Dioc.
  Girona, Museu Diocesà de Girona
Giza, Cheop's Boats Mus.
  Giza, Cheop's Boats Museum

Gjirokastër, N. Ren. Mus.
  Gjirokastër, National Renaissance Museum
Glarus, Ksthaus
  Glarus, Kunsthaus
Glasgow, A.G. & Mus.
  Glasgow, Art Gallery and Museum
  [Kelvingrove]
Glasgow, Blythswood Square Gal.
  Glasgow, Blythswood Square Gallery [closed]
Glasgow, Burrell Col.
  Glasgow, Burrell Collection
Glasgow, Cent. Contemp. A.
  Glasgow, Centre for Contemporary Art [CCA]
Glasgow, Christie's
Glasgow, City Chambers
Glasgow, Clydesdale Bank
  Glasgow, Clydesdale Bank Ltd
Glasgow, F.A. Soc.
  Glasgow, Fine Art Society
Glasgow, Haggs Castle Mus.
  Glasgow, Haggs Castle Museum
Glasgow, Mackintosh Sch. Archit.
  Glasgow, Mackintosh School of Architecture
Glasgow, McLellan Gals
  Glasgow, McLellan Galleries
Glasgow, Mitchell Lib.
  Glasgow, Mitchell Library [part of Glasgow
  Dist. Libs]
Glasgow, Mus. Cost.
  Glasgow, Museum of Costume
Glasgow, Museums & A. Gals
  Glasgow, Glasgow Museums and Art Galleries
  [admins A.G. & Mus.; Burrell Col.; Haggs
  Castle Mus.; Mus. Cost.; Mus. Transport;
  People's Pal. Mus.; Pollok House; Rutherglen
  Mus. Local Hist.]
Glasgow, Mus. Transport
  Glasgow, Museum of Transport
Glasgow, People's Pal. Mus.
  Glasgow, People's Palace Museum
Glasgow, Pollok House
Glasgow, Provand's Lordship
Glasgow, Rutherglen Mus. Local Hist.
  Glasgow, Rutherglen Museum of Local
  History
Glasgow, Sch. A. Col.
  Glasgow, School of Art, Art Collection
Glasgow, Third Eye Cent.
  Glasgow, Third Eye Centre [Cent. Contemp.
  A.]
Glasgow, U. Glasgow, Hunterian A.G.
  Glasgow, University of Glasgow, Hunterian
  Art Gallery
Glasgow, U. Glasgow, Hunterian Mus.
  Glasgow, University of Glasgow, Hunterian
  Museum
Glasgow, U. Lib.
  Glasgow, University of Glasgow, University
  Library
Glastonbury, Abbey Mus.
  Glastonbury, Abbey Museum
Glens Falls, NY, Hyde Col.
  Glens Falls, NY, Hyde Collection
Gloucester, City Mus. & A.G.
  Gloucester, City Museum and Art Gallery
Gloucester, Flk Mus.
  Gloucester, Folk Museum [Bishop Hooper's
  Lodging]

Gloucester Museums
Gloucester, Gloucester Museums [admins City Mus. & A.G.; Flk Mus.]

Gloucester, MA, Cape Ann Hist. Assoc.
Gloucester, MA, Cape Ann Historical Association

Gniezno Cathedral
Gniezno, Gniezno Cathedral

Golconda, Khajana Bldg Mus.
Golconda, Khajana Building Museum

Goldegg im Pongau, Schloss

Goldendale, WA, Maryhil Mus. A.
Goldendale, WA, Maryhil Museum of Art

Gołuchów, Castle Mus.
Gołuchów, Castle Museum (Muzeum-Zamek w Gołuchowie, Oddział Muzeum Narodowego w Poznaniu)

Göppingen, Kstver.
Göppingen, Kunstverein

Gorizia, Mus. Prov. Pal. Attems
Gorizia, Museo Provinciale del Palazzo Attems

Gorizia, Mus. Prov. Stor. & A.
Gorizia, Museo Provinciale di Storia e Arte [in Formentini Palace, Borgo Castello]

Gorki-Leninskiye, Lenin House-Mus.
Gorki-Leninskiye, Lenin House-Museum (Dom-Muzey V. I. Lenina v Gorkakh)

Gor'ky, A. Mus.
Gor'ky Art Museum (Gor'kovskiy Khudozhestvennyy Muzey) [c. 1988–90 Gor'ky reverted to its pre-revolutionary name of Nizhniy Novgorod]

Görlitz, Rarsarchv
Görlitz, Rarsarchiv

Goroka, J.K. MacCarthy Mus.
Goroka, J.K. MacCarthy Museum

Gorzów Wielkopolski, Distr. Mus.
Gorzów Wielkopolski, District Museum (Muzeum Okregowe)

Goslar, Kaiserhaus

Goslar, Rathaus

Göteborg, Arkeol. Mus.
Göteborg, Arkeologiska Museum

Göteborg, Etnog. Mus.
Göteborg, Etnografiska Museum

Göteborg, Faerber Saml.
Göteborg, Faerber Samling

Göteborg, Hist. Mus.
Göteborg, Göteborgs Historiska Museum

Göteborg, Industmus.
Göteborg, Göteborgs Industrimuseum

Göteborg, Konsthögskolan Valand

Göteborg, Kstmus.
Göteborg, Göteborgs Konstmuseum

Göteborg, Militärmus. Skansen Kronen
Göteborg, Militärmuseum Skansen Kronen

Göteborg, Nathist. Mus.
Göteborg, Naturhistoriska Museum

Göteborg, Polhemsgym.
Göteborg, Polhemsgymnasium

Göteborg, Röhsska Kstslöjdmus.
Göteborg, Röhsska Konstslöjdmuseum

Göteborg, Sjöfartsmus.
Göteborg, Sjöfartsmuseum

Göteborg, Skolmus.
Göteborg, Skolmuseum [Engelbrekts Skolmuseum; formerly Elementarläroverket för Flickor]

Göteborgs Museer
Göteborg, Göteborgs Museer [admins Arkeol. Mus; Etnog. Mus.; Hist. Mus.; Industmus.; Kstmus.; Nathist. Mus.; Röhsska Kstslöjdmus.; Sjöfartsmus.; Teathist. Mus.]

Göteborg, Stora Börssalen

Göteborg, Teathist. Mus.
Göteborg, Teaterhistoriska Museum

Göteborg, Ubib.
Göteborg, Universitetsbibliotek

Gotha, Forschbib.
Gotha, Forschungsbibliothek [in Schloss Friedenstein]

Gotha, Landesbib.
Gotha, Landesbibliothek [in Schloss Friedenstein]

Gotha, Gedenkstät. Parteitag 1875
Gotha, Gedenkstätte Gothaer Parteitag 1875

Gotha, Museen Stadt
Gotha, Museen der Stadt Gotha [admins Mus. Nat.; Schloss Friedenstein]

Gotha, Mus. Nat.
Gotha, Museum der Natur

Gotha, Natkndmus.
Gotha, Naturkundemuseum

Gotha, Schloss Friedenstein [houses Ekhof-Theater-Museum; Museum für Regionalgeschichte und Volkskunde; Ekhoftheater; Schlossmuseum]

Gothenburg: see Göteborg

Göttingen, Inst. Wiss. Film
Göttingen, Institut für den Wissenschaftlichen Film

Göttingen, Kstsamml. U.
Göttingen, Kunstsammlung der Universität

Göttingen, Kstver.
Göttingen, Kunstverein [mit Artothek]

Göttingen, Niedersächs. Staats- & Ubib.
Göttingen, Niedersächsische Staats- und Universitätsbibliothek

Göttingen, Städt. Mus.
Göttingen, Städtisches Museum [Sammlungen zur Geschichte, Kunst und Kulturgeschichte Südniedersachsens]

Göttingen, U. Göttingen, Aulagebäude
Göttingen, Georg-August-Universität, Aulagebäude

Göttingen, U. Göttingen, Geog. Semin. Bib.
Göttingen, Georg-August-Universität, Geographisches Seminar Bibliothek

Göttingen, U. Göttingen, Kstsamml.
Göttingen, Georg-August-Universität, Kunstsammlung

Göttweig, Stift
Göttweig, Stift Göttweig

Gouda, Archf Ned. Hervormde Gemeente
Gouda, Archief Nederlandse Hervormde Gemeente

Gouda, Stedel. Mus. Catharina Gasthuis
Gouda, Stedelijk Museum Het Catharina Gasthuis

Gouda, Stedel. Mus. De Moriaan
Gouda, Stedelijk Museum De Moriaan

Brit. Govt A. Col.
Government Art Collection [works displayed in govt offices worldwide]

Grado, S Eufemia, Tesoro

Grahamstown, Standard N. Bank A. Fest.
Grahamstown, Standard National Bank Arts Festival

Granada, Alhambra

Granada, Bib. U.
Granada, Biblioteca Universitaria

Granada, Capilla Real

Granada, Casa-Mus. Federico García Lorca
Granada, Casa-Museo Federico García Lorca

Granada, Casa Tiros
Granada, Casa de los Tiros

Granada, Casa Zafra
Granada, Casa de Zafra

Granada, Col. A.
Granada, Colección de Arte

Granada, Fund. Moreno
Granada, Fundación Gómez Moreno

Granada, Lonja

Granada, Monasterio Cartuja
Granada, Monasterio de la Cartuja

Granada, Mus. A. Mod.
Granada, Museo de Arte Moderno

Granada, Mus. Arqueol. Prov.
Granada, Museo Arqueológico Provincial [in Hospital Real]

Granada, Mus. Capilla Real
Granada, Museo de la Capilla Real

Granada, Mus. Catedral
Granada, Museo de la Catedral

Granada, Mus. N. A. Hispmus.
Granada, Museo Nacional de Arte Hispanomusulmán

Granada, Pal. Arzobisp.
Granada, Palacio Arzobispal

Granada, Pal. Carlos V
Granada, Palacio Carlos V [houses Museo de Bellas Artes de Granada]

Granada, Patrn. Alhambra
Granada, Patronato de la Alhambra

Granada, U. Granada
Granada, Universidad de Granada

Granada, Nicaragua, Mus. Arqueol.
Granada, Nicaragua, Museo Arqueológico [in Colegio Centro América]

Grand Forks, N. Dakota Mus. A.
Grand Forks, North Dakota Museum of Art

Grand Rapids, MI, A. Mus.
Grand Rapids, MI, Art Museum

Grand Rapids, MI, Pub. Mus.
Grand Rapids, MI, Public Museum

Granollers, Cent. Cult. Caixa Pensions
Granollers, Centre Cultural de la Caixa de Pensions

Grantham Mus.
Grantham, Grantham Museum

Grants Pass, OR, Mus A.
Grants Pass, OR, Museum of Art

Grasse, Mus. A. & Hist. Provence
Grasse, Musée d'Art et d'Histoire de Provence

Grasse, Mus. Fragonard
Grasse, Musée Fragonard

Gravelines, Mus. Arsenal
Gravelines, Musée de l'Arsenal [Collection Municipale du Dessin et de l'Estampe Originale]

Gray, Mus. Martin
Gray, Musée Baron Martin

Graz, Alte Gal.
Graz, Alte Galerie

Graz, Bild- & Tonarchv
Graz, Bild- und Tonarchiv

Graz, Diözmus.
  Graz, Diözesanmuseum
Graz, Jagdmus.
  Graz, Jagdmuseum
Graz, Karl-Franzens U.
  Graz, Karl-Franzens Universität
Graz, Kulthaus
  Graz, Kulturhaus
Graz, Kultreferat Steiermärk. Landesregierung
  Graz, Kulturreferat der Steiermärkischen
  Landesregierung
Graz, Landesgemäldegal.
  Graz, Landesgemäldegalerie
Graz, Landeszeughaus
Graz, Mus. Kstgew.
  Graz, Museum für Kunstgewerbe
Graz, Mus. Vor- & Frühgesch.
  Graz, Museum für Vor- und Frühgeschichte
  [houses Münzensammlung]
Graz, Neue Gal.
  Graz, Neue Galerie
Graz, Pal. Attems
  Graz, Palais Attems
Graz, Schloss Eggenberg
Graz, Stadtmus.
  Graz, Stadtmuseum
Graz, Steiermärk. Landesmus.
  Graz, Steiermärkisches Landesmuseum
  Joanneum [admins Alte Gal.; Jagdmus.;
  Landeszeughaus; Mus. Kstgew.; Mus. Vor- &
  Frühgesch.; Neue Gal.; Steiermärk.
  Landesmus.; Steier. Vlkskndmus.; Stainz,
  Schloss; Trautenfels, Schloss]
Graz, Steier. Vlkskndmus.
  Graz, Steierisches Volkskundemuseum
Graz, Steinisch-Ständische Zeichnungsakad.
  Graz, Steinisch-Ständische
  Zeichnungsakademie
Graz, Ubib.
  Graz, Universitätsbibliothek
Great Falls, MT, C.M. Russell Mus.
  Great Falls, MT, C. M. Russell Museum
Great Yarmouth, Elizabethan House Mus.
  Great Yarmouth, Elizabethan House Museum
Great Yarmouth, Mar. Mus. E. Anglia
  Great Yarmouth, Maritime Museum for East
  Anglia
Great Yarmouth, Mus. Exh. Gals
  Great Yarmouth, Great Yarmouth Museum
  Exhibition Galleries
Great Yarmouth, Nelson's Mnmt
  Great Yarmouth, Nelson's Monument
Great Yarmouth, Tolhouse Mus.
  Great Yarmouth, Tolhouse Museum
Greensboro, NC, Weatherspoon A.G.
  Greensboro, NC, Weatherspoon Art Gallery
Greensburg, PA, Westmoreland Co. Mus. A.
  Greensburg, PA, Westmoreland County
  Museum of Art
Greenville, SC, Bob Jones U. Gal. Sacred A.
  Greenville, SC, Bob Jones University Gallery
  of Sacred Art and Bible Lands Museum
Greenville, SC, Co. Mus. A.
  Greenville, SC, County Museum of Art
Greenwich: see London
Greifswald, Ernst-Moritz Arndt U.
  Greifswald, Ernst-Moritz-Arndt Universität
Grein, Stadtarchv
  Grein, Stadtarchiv

Grenoble, Archvs Dépt. Isère
  Grenoble, Archives Départementales de l'Isère
Grenoble, Bib. Mun.
  Grenoble, Bibliothèque Municipale
Grenoble, Magasin-Cent. N. A. Contemp.
  Grenoble, Magasin-Centre National d'Art
  Contemporain
Grenoble, Mus. B.-A.
  Grenoble, Musée des Beaux-Arts
Grenoble, Mus.-Bib.
  Grenoble, Musée-Bibliothèque de Grenoble
Grenoble, Mus. Dauphinois
  Grenoble, Musée Dauphinois
Grenoble, Mus. Grenoble
  Grenoble, Musée de Grenoble [formerly Mus.
  Peint. & Sculp.]
Grenoble, Mus. Peint. & Sculp.
  Grenoble, Musée de Peinture et de Sculpture
  [name changed to Mus. Grenoble in 1986]
Grenoble, Mus. Stendhal
  Grenoble, Musée Stendhal
Gressenhall, Norfolk Rural Life Mus.
  Gressenhall, Norfolk Rural Life Museum
Groningen, De Mangelgang Gal.
  Groningen, De Mangelgang Gallery
Groningen, Groninger Mus.
  Groningen, Groninger Museum
Groningen, Rijksuniv.
  Groningen, Rijksuniversiteit Groningen
Grosseto, Mus. Archeol.
  Grosseto, Museo Archeologico e d'Arte della
  Maremma
Grottaferrata, Mus. Abbazia S Nilo
  Grottaferrata, Museo dell'Abbazia di San Nilo
Guadalajara, Colegiata Pastrana
  Guadalajara, Colegiata de Pastrana
Guadalajara, Mus. A. Mod.
  Guadalajara, Museo de Arte Moderno
Guadalajara, Mus. Guadalajara
  Guadalajara, Museo de Guadalajara
Guadalajara, Mus. Reg. Antropol. & Hist.
  Guadalajara, Museo Regional de Antropología
  e Historia
Guadalupe, Monasterio de Nuestra Señora de
  Guadalupe
Guadalupe, Mus. Basilica
  Guadalupe, Museo de la Basilica
Guadalupe, Mus. Reg.
  Guadalupe, Museo Regional de Guadalupe
Gualdo Tadino, Pin. Com.
  Gualdo Tadino, Pinacoteca Comunale
Gualtieri, Pal. Com.
  Gualtieri, Palazzo Comunale [formerly Palazzo
  Bentivoglio]
Guanajuato, Mus. Granaditas
  Guanajuato, Museo de Granaditas
Guangzhou, A.G.
  Guangzhou, Art Gallery
Guangzhou, Guangdong Prov. Mus.
  Guangzhou, Guangdong Provincial Museum
Guangzhou, Zhongshan U.
  Guangzhou, Zhongshan University
Guardia Sanframondi, Mus.
  Guardia Sanframondi, Museo di Guardia
  Sanframondi
Guastalla, Pal. Vescovile
  Guastalla, Palazzo Vescovile
Guatemala City, Acad. Geog. & Hist.
  Guatemala City, Academia de Geografía e
  Historia

Guatemala City, Banco de Guatemala
Guatemala City, Banco Immobiliario Col.
  Guatemala City, Banco Immobiliario
  Collection
Guatemala City, Banco Indust. Col.
  Guatemala City, Banco Industrial Collection
Guatemala City, Banco Quetzal Col.
  Guatemala City, Banco del Quetzal Collection
Guatemala City, Bib. N.
  Guatemala City, Biblioteca Nacional
Guatemala City, Dir. Gen. Cult. & B.A.
  Guatemala City, Dirección General de Cultura
  y Bellas Artes
Guatemala City, Edificio O.E.G.
Guatemala City, Escuela N. A. Plást.
  Guatemala City, Escuela Nacional de Artes
  Plásticas
Guatemala City, Gal. DS
  Guatemala City, Galería DS
Guatemala City, Gal. Dzunún
  Guatemala City, Galería Dzunún
Guatemala City, Gal. El Túnel
  Guatemala City, Galería El Túnel
Guatemala City, Inst. Antropol. & Hist.
  Guatemala City, Instituto de Antropología e
  Historia
Guatemala City, Inst. Fomento Mun.
  Guatemala City, Instituto de Fomento
  Municipal
Guatemala City, Inst. Guat. Amer.
  Guatemala City, Instituto Guatemalteco
  Americano
Guatemala City, Mus. A. Contemp.
  Guatemala City, Museo de Arte
  Contemporáneo
Guatemala City, Mus. Cafarnum
  Guatemala City, Museo Cafarnum [in
  Archbishop's Palace]
Guatemala City, Mus. Fray Francisco Vázquez
  Guatemala City, Museo Fray Francisco
  Vázquez [in S Francisco]
Guatemala City, Mus. Ixchel Traje Indig.
  Guatemala City, Museo Ixchel del Traje
  Indígena
Guatemala City, Mus. N.A. & Indust. Pop.
  Guatemala City, Museo Nacional de Artes e
  Industrias Populares
Guatemala City, Mus. N. A. Mod.
  Guatemala City, Museo Nacional de Arte
  Moderno
Guatemala City, Mus. N. Arqueol. & Etnol.
  Guatemala City, Museo Nacional de
  Arqueología y Etnología
Guatemala City, Mus. N.B.A.
  Guatemala City, Museo Nacional de Bellas
  Artes
Guatemala City, Mus. N. Hist.
  Guatemala City, Museo Nacional de Historia
Guatemala City, Mus. N. Hist. & B.A.
  Guatemala City, Museo Nacional de Historia y
  Bellas Artes [from 1976 two distinct museums:
  Mus. N.B.A. and Mus. N. Hist.]
Guatemala City, Pal. Mun.
  Guatemala City, Palacio Municipal
Guatemala City, Patrn. B.A.
  Guatemala City, Patronato de Bellas Artes
Guatemala City, U. Francisco Marroquín
  Guatemala City, Universidad Francisco
  Marroquín

Guatemala City, U. Francisco Marroquín, Mus.
Popol Vuh
    Guatemala City, Universidad Francisco
    Marroquín, Museo Popol Vuh

Guatemala City, U. S Carlos
    Guatemala City, Universidad de S Carlos

Guayaquil, Esc. B.A.
    Guayaquil, Escuela de Bellas Artes

Guayaquil, Mus. Antropol. & Mus. A. Banco Cent.
    Guayaquil, Museo Antropológico y Museo de
    Arte del Banco Central del Ecuador

Guayaquil, Mus. Víctor Emilio Estrada
    Guayaquil, Museo Víctor Emilio Estrada

Gubbio, Mus. Duomo
    Gubbio, Museo del Duomo

Gubbio, Mus. & Pin. Com.
    Gubbio, Museo e Pinacoteca Comunali

Gubbio, Pal. Com.
    Gubbio, Palazzo Comunale

Gubbio, Pal. Ducale
    Gubbio, Palazzo Ducale [La Corte]

Guéret, Mus. Guéret
    Guéret, Musée de Guéret

Guimarães, Mus. Alberto Sampaio
    Guimarães, Museu de Alberto Sampaio

Guimarães, Mus. Arqueol. Martins Sarmento
    Guimarães, Museo Arqueológico de Martins
    Sarmento

Guimarães, S Marinha da Costa Monastery

Guiry-en-Vexin, Mus. Archéol. Dépt.
    Guiry-en-Vexin, Musée Archéologique
    Départemental du Val-d'Oise

Guizhou, Batik A. Acad.
    Guizhou, Batik Art Academy

Günzburg, Heimatmus.
    Günzburg, Heimatmuseum

Gus', Mus. Glass
    Gus', Museum of Glass

Gustavsberg, nr Värmdö, Ker. Cent.
    Gustavsberg, nr Värmdö, Keramisk Centrum

Güstrow, Mus. Stadt
    Güstrow, Museum der Stadt Güstrow

Guylaféhérvar: see Alba Iulia

Gwalior, Archaeol. Mus.
    Gwalior, Archaeological Museum

Gwalior, Cent. Archaeol. Mus.
    Gwalior, Central Archaeological Museum

Gwalior, Maharaja Jiwaji Rao Scindia Mus.
    Gwalior, Maharaja Jiwaji Rao Scindia Museum
    [Museum Jai Vilas Palace]

Gwalior, State Mus.
    Gwalior, State Museum

Gyōda, Saitama Prefect., Sakitama Hist. Park
Resource Cent.
    Gyōda, Saitama Prefecture, Sakitama Historical
    Park Resource Centre (Sakitama Fudoki no
    Oka Shiryokan)

Győr, Cathedral Treasury (Föszékesegyházi
Kincstár)

Győr, János Xantus Mus.
    Győr, János Xantus Museum [Benedictine
    monastery]

Győr, Margit Kovács Cer. Exh.
    Győr, Margit Kovács Ceramics Exhibition
    (Kovács Margit Kerámia Kiállitas)

Haarlem, Bisschopp. Mus.
    Haarlem, Bisschoppelijk Museum

Haarlem, Frans Halsmus.
    Haarlem, Frans Halsmuseum

Haarlem, Gemeentearchf
    Haarlem, Gemeentearchief

Haarlem, Koenig Col.
    Haarlem, Koenig Collectie

Haarlem, Pav. Welgelegen
    Haarlem, Paviljoen Welgelegen

Haarlem, Rijksarchf N.-Holland
    Haarlem, Rijksarchief in Noord-Holland

Haarlem, Sch. Kstnijverheid
    Haarlem, School voor Kunstnijverheid [no
    longer exists]

Haarlem, Teylers Hofje

Haarlem, Teylers Mus.
    Haarlem, Teylers Museum

Haarlem, Vleeshal

Haarzuilens, Kasteel de Haar

Haastrecht, Mus. Sticht. Bisdom van Vliet
    Haastrecht, Museum van de Stichting Bisdom
    van Vliet

Hachinobe, Mun. Flk Resources Cent.
    Hachinobe, Hachinobe Municipal Folk
    Resources Center [Aomori Prefecture]

Hackney: see London

Hadong, Ssanggye Temple

Hagen, Hohenhof [part of Karl Ernst Osthaus
Mus.; houses Osthaus-Archiv]

Hagen, Osthaus Mus.
    Hagen, Karl Ernst Osthaus Museum [formerly
    housed Folkwang Museum]

Hagerstown, MD, Washington Co. Hist. Soc.
Mus.
    Hagerstown, MD, Washington County
    Historical Society Museum

The Hague, Algemeen Rijksarchf
    The Hague, Algemeen Rijksarchief te
    's-Gravenhage

The Hague, Binnenhof

The Hague, Cramer Gal.
    The Hague, H. M. Cramer Gallery

The Hague, Dienst Rijksverspr. Kstvoorwerpen
    The Hague, Dienst Rijksverspreide
    Kunstvoorwerpen [works displayed in govt
    offices]

The Hague, Dienst Verspr. Rijkscol.
    The Hague, Dienst Verspreide Rijkscollectie

The Hague, Gemeentearchf
    The Hague, Gemeentearchief Den Haag

The Hague, Gemeentelijke Mus. S. Kst
    The Hague, Gemeentelijke Museum voor
    Schone Kunsten

The Hague, Gemeentemus.
    The Hague, Haags Gemeentemuseum [houses
    Oude en Moderne Kunstnijverheid; Haagse
    Stadgeschiedenis; Moderne Kunst; Museon;
    Muziekinstrumenten; Nederlands
    Kostuummuseum]

The Hague, Hist. Mus.
    The Hague, Haags Historische Museum

The Hague, Hoogstedar

The Hague, Huis ten Bosch [incl. Oranjezaal]

The Hague, Kon. Bib.
    The Hague, Koninklijke Bibliotheek
    [Nationale Bibliotheek]

The Hague, Kon. Huisarchf
    The Hague, Koninklijke Huisarchief

The Hague, Ksthand. Nijstad
    The Hague, Kunsthandel Nijstad

The Hague, Kstzaal Kleykamp
    The Hague, Kunstzaal Kleykamp

The Hague, Maison France
    The Hague, Maison de France

The Hague, Mauritshuis [incl. Koninklijk Kabinet
van Schilderijen]

The Hague, Mus. Bredius
    The Hague, Museum Bredius

The Hague, Nouv. Images
    The Hague, Nouvelles Images

The Hague, Oranje-Nassau-Mus.
    The Hague, Oranje-Nassau-Museum

The Hague, Oude Stadhuis

The Hague, Pal. Noordeinde
    The Hague, Paleis Noordeinde

The Hague, Panorama Mesdag

The Hague, Pulchri Studio

The Hague, Rijksarchf Zuid-Holland
    The Hague, Rijksarchief in Zuid-Holland

The Hague, Rijksbureau Ksthist. Doc.
    The Hague, Rijksbureau voor
    Kunsthistorische Documentatie

The Hague, Rijksdienst Beeld. Kst
    The Hague, Rijksdienst Beeldende Kunst

The Hague, Rijksdienst Mnmtzorg
    The Hague, Rijksdienst voor de
    Monumentenzorg

The Hague, Rijksmus. Mesdag
    The Hague, Rijksmuseum Hendrik Willem
    Mesdag

The Hague, Rijksmus. Meermanno-
Westreenianum
    The Hague, Rijksmuseum Meermanno-
    Westreenianum

The Hague, Schilderijenzaal Prins Willem V

The Hague, S. Nystad Gal.
    The Hague, S. Nystad Gallery

The Hague, Soc. Jap. A. & Crafts
    The Hague, Society for Japanese Arts And
    Crafts

The Hague, Van Marne & Bignall
    The Hague, Van Marne en Bignall

The Hague, Villa Erica

The Hague, Vredespal.
    The Hague, Vredespaleis

The Hague, Willem V Mus.
    The Hague, Willem V Museum [houses Dutch
    Royal Collection]

Haguenau, Mus. Hist.
    Haguenau, Musée Historique

Haifa, Mané-Katz Mus.
    Haifa, Mané-Katz Museum

Haifa, MOMA
    Haifa, Museum of Modern Art

Haifa, Moshe Shtekelis Mus. Prehist.
    Haifa, Moshe Shtekelis Museum of Prehistory

Haifa, Music & Ethnol. Mus.
    Haifa, Music and Ethnology Museum

Haifa, N. Mar. Mus.
    Haifa, National Maritime Museum

Haifa, N. Mus. Sci. & Technol.
    Haifa, National Museum of Science and
    Technology

Haifa, Technion [Israel Institute of Technology]

Haifa, Tikotin Mus. Jap. A.
    Haifa, Tikotin Museum of Japanese Art

Haifa, U. Haifa
    Haifa, University of Haifa

Hainhausen, Schloss Hainhausen [near Dachau]

Hakone-machi, Hakone Open Air Mus.
    Hakone-machi, Hakone Open Air Museum
    (Chokoku no mori Bijutsukan)

Halberstadt Cathedral, Treasury

Halberstadt, Dom & Domschatz
  Halberstadt, Dom und Domschatz

Halberstadt, Gleimhaus

Halbturn, Schloss

Halebid, Mus.
  Halebid, Museum [site museum]

Halifax, Bankfield Mus.
  Halifax, Bankfield Museum

Halifax, Calderdale Indust. Mus.
  Halifax, Calderdale Industrial Museum

Halifax, Calderdale Museums Serv.
  Halifax, Calderdale Museums Service [admins
  Bankfield Mus.; Calderdale Indust. Mus.; Piece
  Hall]

Halifax, Dean Clough Indust. Park
  Halifax, Dean Clough Industrial Park

Halifax, Henry Moore Sculp. Trust Studio
  Halifax, Henry Moore Sculpture Trust Studio

Halifax, Piece Hall
  Halifax, Piece Hall Pre-industrial Museum and
  Art Gallery

Halifax, A.G. NS
  Halifax, NS, Art Gallery of Nova Scotia

Halifax, NS, Army Mus., Citadel
  Halifax, NS, Army Museum, Halifax Citadel

Halifax, NS, Dalhousie U., A.G.
  Halifax, NS, Dalhousie University, Art Gallery

Halifax, NS, Maritime Mus. Atlantic
  Halifax, NS, Maritime Museum of the Atlantic

Halifax, NS, Mt St Vincent U., A.G.
  Halifax, NS, Mount Saint Vincent University,
  Art Gallery

Halifax, NS Coll. A. & Des.
  Halifax, NS, Nova Scotia College of Art and
  Design

Halifax, NS Mus.
  Halifax, NS, Nova Scotia Museum

Halifax, Pub. Archvs NS
  Halifax, NS, Public Archives of Nova Scotia

Halifax, NS, U. King's Coll.
  Halifax, NS, University of King's College

Hall, Stadtmus.
  Hall, Stadtmuseum Hall in Tirol

Halle, Landesmus. Vorgesch.
  Halle, Landesmuseum für Vorgeschichte
  [Forschungsstelle für die Bezirke Halle und
  Magdeburg]

Halle, Martin Luther-U.
  Halle, Martin Luther-Universität [now called
  Martin Luther-U. Halle-Wittenberg]

Halle, Staatl. Gal. Moritzburg
  Halle, Staatliche Galerie Moritzburg Halle

Hallein, Keltenmus.
  Hallein, Keltenmuseum

Halmstad, Friluftsmus. Hallandsgdn
  Halmstad, Friluftsmuseum Hallandsgården

Hama, Mus. Hama
  Hama, Musée de Hama

Hamamatsu, Mun. Mus.
  Hamamatsu, Municipal Museum

Hamar, Hedmarksmus.
  Hamar, Hedmarksmuseum [og
  Domkirkeodden]

Hamburg, Altonaer Mus.
  Hamburg, Altonaer Museum [Norddeutsches
  Landesmuseum]

Hamburg, Barlach Haus
  Hamburg, Ernst Barlach Haus

Hamburg, B.A.T. Haus

Hamburg, Bötelkamp Cent.
  Hamburg, Bötelkamp Centre

Hamburg, Gal. Kommiter
  Hamburg, Galerie Kommiter [closed]

Hamburg, Gal. Levy
  Hamburg, Galerie Levy

Hamburg, Gal. Neuendorf
  Hamburg, Galerie Neuendorf

Hamburg, Helms-Mus.
  Hamburg, Helms-Museum [Hamburgisches
  Museum für Vor- und Frühgeschichte]

Hamburg, Hochsch. Bild. Kst.
  Hamburg, Hochschule für Bildende Künste
  Hamburg

Hamburg, Kath. Dekanat
  Hamburg, Katholisches Dekanat

Hamburg, Kst- & Gewsch.
  Hamburg, Kunst- und Gewerbeschule

Hamburg, Ksthalle
  Hamburg, Hamburger Kunsthalle [incl.
  Kupferstichkabinett]

Hamburg, Ksthaus
  Hamburg, Kunsthaus Hamburg

Hamburg, Kstver.
  Hamburg, Kunstverein Hamburg

Hamburg, Mus. Godeffroy
  Hamburg, Museum Godeffroy [now closed;
  col. in Leipzig, Mus. Vlkerknd.]

Hamburg, Mus. Hamburg. Gesch.
  Hamburg, Museum für Hamburgische
  Geschichte

Hamburg, Musikhalle
  Hamburg, Musikhalle

Hamburg, Mus. Kst & Gew.
  Hamburg, Museum für Kunst und Gewerbe

Hamburg, Mus. Vlkerknd.
  Hamburg, Museum für Völkerkunde

Hamburg, PPS-Gal.
  Hamburg, PPS-Galerie

Hamburg, Produzentengal.
  Hamburg, Produzentengalerie

Hamburg, Staatl. Landesbildstelle
  Hamburg, Staatliche Landesbildstelle

Hamburg, Staatsarchv
  Hamburg, Staatsarchiv

Hamburg, Staats- & Ubib.
  Hamburg, Staats- und Universitätsbibliothek

Hamburg, Theatsamml. & Zent. Theatforsch.
  Hamburg, Hamburger Theatersammlung und
  Zentrum für Theaterforschung

Hamburg, U. Hamburg
  Hamburg, Universität Hamburg

Hamburg, U. Hamburg, Theatsamml.
  Hamburg, Theatersammlung der Universität

Hamburg, Winter

Hamburg von der Höhe, Schloss

Hämeenlinna, A. Mus.
  Hämeenlinna, Hämeenlinna Art Museum

Hamilton, Ont., A.G.
  Hamilton, Ont., Art Gallery of Hamilton

Hamilton, NY, Colgate U.
  Hamilton, NY, Colgate University

Hamilton, NZ, Chartwell Trust Col.
  Hamilton, NZ, Chartwell Trust Collection

Hamilton, NZ, Waikato Mus. A. Hist.
  Hamilton, NZ, Waikato Museum of Art and
  History

Hammam Lif, Casino

Hampton, VA, U. Mus.
  Hampton, VA, Hampton University Museum

Hanau, Dt. Goldschmiedehaus
  Hanau, Deutsches Goldschmiedehaus

Hanau, Hist. Mus.
  Hanau, Historisches Museum

Hancock, MA, Shaker Village
  Hancock, MA, Hancock Shaker Village

Hangzhou, Zhejiang Archaeol. Inst. Cult. Relics
  Hangzhou, Zhejiang Archaeological Institute
  of Cultural Relics

Hangzhou, Zhejiang Prov. Mus.
  Hangzhou, Zhejiang Provincial Museum

Hanley, City Mus. & A.G.
  Hanley, City Museum and Art Gallery

Hannover, Fernsehgal. Gerry Schum
  Hannover, Fernsehgalerie Gerry Schum

Hannover, Forum des Landesmus.
  Hannover, Forum des Landesmuseums

Hannover, Fürstenhaus Herrenhausen-Mus.
  Hannover, Fürstenhaus Herrenhausen-
  Museum

Hannover, Gal. Clarissa
  Hannover, Galerie Clarissa

Hannover, Gal. J.H. Bauer
  Hannover, Galerie J.H. Bauer

Hannover, Hist. Mus. Hohen Ufer
  Hannover, Historisches Museum am Hohen
  Ufer

Hannover, Kestner-Ges.
  Hannover, Kestner-Gesellschaft

Hannover, Kestner-Mus.
  Hannover, Kestner-Museum

Hannover, Kstmus.
  Hannover, Kunstmuseum

Hannover, Kstver.
  Hannover, Kunstverein Hannover

Hannover, Leineschloss [Residenz-Schloss]

Hannover, Niedersächs. Landesbib.
  Hannover, Niedersächsische Landesbibliothek

Hannover, Niedersächs. Landesmus.
  Hannover, Niedersächsisches Landesmuseum
  [Niedersächsische Landesgalerie; formerly
  called Provmus.]

Hannover, Niedersächs. Staatsarchv
  Hannover, Niedersächsisches Staatsarchiv

Hannover, Orangerie

Hannover, Pelican-Kstsamml.
  Hannover, Pelican-Kunstsammlung

Hannover, Provmus.
  Hannover, Provinzialmuseum [name changed
  to Niedersächs. Landesmus.]

Hannover, Sprengel Mus.
  Hannover, Sprengel Museum [Kunstmuseum
  Hannover mit Sammlung Sprengel]

Hannover, Städt. Gal.
  Hannover, Städtische Galerie

Hannover, U. Hannover, Samml. Haupt
  Hannover, Universität Hannover, Sammlung
  Haupt

Hannover, Wilhelm-Busch-Mus.
  Hannover, Wilhelm-Busch-Museum

Hannoversch Münden, Städt. Mus.
  Hannoversch Münden, Städtisches Museum
  [in Welfenschloss]

Hanoi, Hist. Mus.
  Hanoi, History Museum [formerly Ecole
  Française d'Extrême Orient]

Hanoi, Mus. Rev.
Hanoi, Museum of the Revolution

Hanoi, N. Mus. F.A.
Hanoi, National Museum of Fine Arts

Hanover, NH, Dartmouth Coll., Hood Mus. A.
Hanover, NH, Dartmouth College, Hood
Museum of Art [name changed from Hopkins
Cent. A.G. in 1985]

Hanover, NH, Dartmouth Coll., Hopkins Cent.
A.G.
Hanover, NH, Dartmouth College, Hopkins
Center Art Gallery [now Hood Mus. A.]

Harappa, Archaeol. Mus.
Harappa, Archaelogical Museum

Harare, Gal. Shona Sculp.
Harare, Gallery Shona Sculpture

Harare, N.G.
Harare, National Gallery of Zimbabwe

Harare, Queen Victoria Mus.
Harare, Queen Victoria Museum [now
Zimbabwe Mus. Human Sci.]

Harare, Zimbabwe Mus. Human Sci.
Harare, Zimbabwe Museum of Human
Sciences [formerly Queen Victoria Mus.]

Harburg, Felsenburg

Harburg, Schloss
Harburg, Fürstlich Oettingen-Wallerstein'sche
Sammlungen, Schloss

Harlingen, Hannemahuis

Harrogate, A.G.
Harrogate, Harrogate Art Gallery

Harrogate, Museums & A.G. Serv.
Harrogate, Harrogate Museums and Art
Gallery Service [admins A.G.; Royal Pump
Room Mus.; Pateley Bridge, Nidderdale
Museum]

Harrogate, Royal Pump Room Mus.
Harrogate, Royal Pump Room Museum

Harrow-on-the-Hill: see London

Hartberg, Schloss Herberstein

Hartford, CT Hist. Soc. Mus.
Hartford, CT, Connecticut Historical Society
Museum

Hartford, CT, Wadsworth Atheneum

Harvard, MA, Fruitlands Mus.
Harvard, MA, Fruitlands Museum

Haryana, Archaeol. Mus
Haryana, Archaeological Museum

Hasselt, Prov. Mus. Aktuele Kst
Hasselt, Provinciaal Museum voor Aktuele
Kunst

Hastings-on-Hudson, NY, Newington Cropsey
Found.
Hastings-on-Hudson, NY, Newington
Cropsey Foundation

Hatakeyama, Mem. Mus.
Hatakeyama, Memorial Museum

Hato Rey, María Rechanys Gal.
Hato Rey, María Rechanys Gallery

Hato Rey, Raíces Gal.
Hato Rey, Raíces Gallery

Hato Rey, Rojo & Negro Gal.
Hato Rey, Rojo y Negro Gallery

Hatvan, Lajos Hatvany Mus.
Hatvan, Lajos Hatvany Museum

Havana, Acad. N. A. & Let.
Havana, Academia Nacional de Artes y Letras

Havana, Casa Africa
Havana, Casa de Africa

Havana, Casa Américas
Havana, Casa de las Américas

Havana, Escuela N. B.A. San Alejandro
Havana, Escuela Nacional de Bellas Artes San
Alejandro

Havana, Gal. Cubana
Havana, Galería Cubana

Havana, Gal. Habana
Havana, Galería Habana

Havana, Mus. A. Dec.
Havana, Museo de Artes Decorativas

Havana, Mus. Antropol. Montamé
Havana, Universidad de la Habana, Museo
Antropológico Montamé

Havana, Mus. Ciudad
Havana, Museo de la Ciudad de la Habana

Havana, Mus. Colon.
Havana, Museo Colonial de la Habana

Havana, Mus. Hist. Guanabacoa
Havana, Museo Historico de Guanabacoa

Havana, Mus. Mun. Regla
Havana, Museo Municipal de Regla

Havana, Mus. N.
Havana, Museo Nacional

Havana, Mus. N. B.A.
Havana, Museo Nacional de Bellas Artes [in
Palacio de Bellas Artes]

Havant Mus.
Havant, Havant Museum

Haverford Coll., PA
Haverford, PA, Haverford College

Hawkshead, Beatrix Potter Gal.
Hawkshead, Beatrix Potter Gallery [NT]

Hays, KS, Fort Hays State U.
Hays, KS, Fort Hays State University

Hazorea, Wilfred Israel House Orient. A.
Hazorea, Wilfred Israel House of Oriental Art

Heerenveen, Hist. Mus.
Heerenveen, Historisch Museum Heerenveen
[Museum van Haren]

Heerlen, Stadhuis [contains Gemeentelijk
Oudheidkundig Museum]

Hefei, Anhui Prov. Mus.
Hefei, Anhui Provincial Museum

Heidelberg, Dt. Apotheken-Mus.
Heidelberg, Deutsches Apotheken-Museum
[in Schloss Heidelberg]

Heidelberg, Kstver.
Heidelberg, Kunstverein

Heidelberg, Kurpfälz. Mus.
Heidelberg, Kurpfälzisches Museum

Heidelberg, Mus. Stadt
Heidelberg, Museum der Stadt

Heidelberg, Ruprecht-Karls-U.
Heidelberg, Ruprecht-Karls-Universität
Heidelberg

Heidelberg, Ruprecht-Karls-U., Samml. Ant.
Kleinkst Archäol. Inst.
Heidelberg, Ruprecht-Karls-Universität,
Sammlung Antiker Kleinkunst des
Archäologischen Instituts

Heidelberg, Schloss
Heidelberg, Schloss Heidelberg

Heidelberg, Ubib.
Heidelberg, Universitätsbibliothek

Heilbronn, Deutschhof-Mus.
Heilbronn, Deutschhof-Museum

Heilbronn, Hist. Mus.
Heilbronn, Historisches Museum

Heilbronn, Mus. Vor- & Frühgesch.
Heilbronn, Museum für Vor- und
Frühgeschichte

Heilbronn, Nathist. Mus.
Heilbronn, Naturhistorisches Museum

Heilbronn, Neckarschiffahrts-Ausstell.
Heilbronn, Neckarschiffahrts-Ausstellung

Heilbronn, Städt. Museen
Heilbronn, Städtische Museen [admins
Deutschhof- Mus.; Mus. Vor- & Frühgesch.;
Nathist. Mus.; Neckarschiffahrts-Ausstell.]

Heiligenberg, Schloss
Heiligenberg, Schloss Heiligenberg

Heiligenkreuz, Stiftsbib.
Heiligenkreuz, Stiftsbibliothek

Heiligenkreuz, Stiftsmus. & Wienerwaldmus.
Heiligenkreuz, Stiftsmuseum und
Wienerwaldmuseum

Heino, Hannema–De Stuers Fund.
Heino, Hannema–De Stuers Fundatie

Helmond, Gemeentemus.
Helmond, Gemeentemuseum Helmond

Helsingborg, Vikingsbergs Kstmus.
Helsingborg, Vikingsbergs Konstmuseum

Helsingør, Kronborg Slot

Helsinki, Acad. F.A.
Helsinki, Academy of Fine Art (Suomen
Taideakatemian Koulu)

Helsinki, Acad. Sci.
Helsinki, Academy of Sciences
(Vetenskapsakadamiens)

Helsinki, A. Exh. Hall
Helsinki, Art Exhibition Hall (Taidehalli)

Helsinki, Anderson Mus. A.
Helsinki, Amos Anderson Museum of Art
(Amos Andersonin Taidemuseo)

Helsinki, Athenaeum A. Mus.
Helsinki, Athenaeum Art Museum
(Ateneumin Taidemuseo) [Museum of Finnish
Art in the N.G.]

Helsinki, Bäcksbacke Col.
Helsinki, Bäcksbacke Collection

Helsinki, Bank of Finland

Helsinki, City A. Mus.
Helsinki, City Art Museum (Kaupungin
Taidemuseo)

Helsinki, City Archvs
Helsinki, City Archives (Kaupunginarkisto)

Helsinki, Clinic Internal Diseases
Helsinki, Clinic for Internal Diseases

Helsinki, Convalesc. Cent.
Helsinki, Convalescence Centre (Toipilaat)

Helsinki, Cygnaeus Gal.
Helsinki, Cygnaeus Gallery

Helsinki, Didrichsen A. Mus.
Helsinki, Didrichsen Art Museum (Didrichsen
Taidemuseo)

Helsinki, Fin. A. Soc.
Helsinki, Finnish Art Society (Suomen
Taideyhdistys)

Helsinki, Fin. Cult. Found., Kirpilä A. Col.
Helsinki, Finnish Cultural Foundation, Kirpilä
Art Collection (Suomen Kultuurirahasto
Kirpilän Taidekokoelma)

Helsinki, Fin. Workers' Inst.
Helsinki, Finnish Workers' Institute

Helsinki, Gal. Artek
Helsinki, Galerie Artek

Helsinki, Gal. Krista Mikkola
Helsinki, Galleria Krista Mikkola

Helsinki, Gallen-Kallela Mus.
  Helsinki, Gallen-Kallela Museum [in
  Tarvaspää building]
Helsinki, Hämäläis Students' Un.
  Helsinki, Hämäläis Students' Union
  (Hämäläis-Osakunta)
Helsinki, Kaisaniemi Park
Helsinki, Messuhalli
Helsinki, Mun. Gdns
  Helsinki, Municipal Gardens
Helsinki, Mus. Applied A.
  Helsinki, Museum of Applied Arts
  (Taideteollisuusmuseo)
Helsinki, Mus. Fin. Archit.
  Helsinki, Museum of Finnish Architecture
  (Suomen Rakennustaiteen Museo)
Helsinki, Mus. Fin. Archit., Archvs
  Helsinki, Museum of Finnish Architecture,
  Archives
Helsinki, N. Archvs
  Helsinki, National Archives (Valtionarkisto)
Helsinki, N. Board Ant.
  Helsinki, National Board of Antiquities
  (Museovirasto)
Helsinki, N.G.
  Helsinki, Finnish National Gallery (Valtion
  Taidemuseo)
Helsinki, N.G., Banqueting Hall
  Helsinki, Finnish National Gallery, Banqueting
  Hall of the Council of State
Helsinki, N. Mus.
  Helsinki, National Museum of Finland
  (Suomen Kansallismuseo)
Helsinki, Nord. A. Cent.
  Helsinki, Nordic Arts Centre (Pohjoismainen
  Taidekeskus)
Helsinki, N. Phot. Mus.
  Helsinki, National Photographic Museum of
  Finland (Suomen Valokuvataiteen Museo)
Helsinki, N. Theat.
  Helsinki, Finnish National Theatre
Helsinki, Old Student House (Vanha Ylioppilas
  Talo)
Helsinki, Post Office Bank Col.
  Helsinki, Post Office Bank Collection
Helsinki, President's Castle
Helsinki, Sinebrychoff A. Col.
  Helsinki, Sinebrychoff Art Collection
  (Sinebrychoffin Taidekokoelmat)
Helsinki, Skop Col.
  Helsinki, Deposit Bank of the Central Joint
  Stock Bank (Säästopankkien Keskus-Osake-
  Pankki) [Skop Collection]
Helsinki, State Alcohol Monopoly (Oy Alko Ab)
Helsinki, Seurasaari Open-Air Mus.
  Helsinki, Seurasaari Open-Air Museum
  (Seurasaaren Ulkomuseo)
Helsinki, U.
  Helsinki, University of Helsinki (Helsingin
  Yliopisto/Helsingfors Universitet)
Helsinki, U. Lib.
  Helsinki, University Library (Yliopiston
  Kirjasto)
Hempstead, NY, F.A. Mus. Long Island
  Hempstead, NY, Fine Arts Museum of Long
  Island
Hempstead, NY, Hofstra U., Lowe Gal.
  Hempstead, NY, Hofstra University, Emily
  Lowe Gallery

Herakleion, A. Inst.
  Herakleion, Art Institute
Herakleion, Archaeol. Mus.
  Herakleion, Archaeological Museum
Herakleion, Hist. Mus. Crete
  Herakleion, Historical Museum of Crete
Herakleion, Metaxas Col.
  Herakleion, Metaxas Collection
Herakleion, St Catherine, Icon Col.
  Herakleion, St Catherine, Icon Collection
Herat Mus.
  Herat, Herat Museum
Herdringen, Schloss Herdringen [houses priv. col.
of Gräfin Fürstenberg]
Hereford, Cathedral Lib.
  Hereford, Hereford Cathedral Library
Hereford, City Lib.
  Hereford, City Library
Hereford, City Mus. & A.G.
  Hereford, City Museum and Art Gallery
Herentals, Comm. Openb. Cent. Maatsch. Welzijn
  Herentals, Commissie van Openbare Centrum
  voor Maatschappelijk Welzijn
Herentals, Fraikin-Mus.
  Herentals, Fraikin-Museum [Stadhuis]
Herning, Angligården
Herning, Kstmus.
  Herning, Herning Kunstmuseum
Herning, Pedersen & Alfelts Mus.
  Herning, Carl-Henning Pedersen og Else
  Alfelts Museum
Herrenhausen, Mausoleum 's Hertogenbosch: see
under s' Hertogenbosch
Hertford, Shire Hall [also known as Town Hall]
Herzogenburg, Kstausstell. Stift
  Herzogenburg, Kunstausstellung Stift
  Herzogenburg
Heverlee-Leuven, Col. Theol. Coll. Soc. van Jezus
  Heverlee-Leuven, Collectie Theologisch
  College der Sociëtet van Jezus
Hierapetra, Archaeol. Col.
  Hierapetra, Archaeological Collection
High Wycombe, Guildhall
Hildesheim, Diözmus. & Domschatzkam.
  Hildesheim, Diözesanmuseum mit
  Domschatzkammer
Hildesheim, Pelizaeus-Mus.
  Hildesheim, Pelizaeus-Museum
Hildesheim, Roemer-Mus.
  Hildesheim, Roemer-Museum
Hillerød, Frederiksborg Slot
  Hillerød, Nationalhistoriske Museum på
  Frederiksborg
Hillerød, Njaellandsk Flkmus.
  Hillerød, Nordsjaellandsk Folkemuseum
Hilversum, Steendrukkerij de Jong Gal.
  Hilversum, Steendrukkerij de Jong Gallery
Hinase, Morishita A. Mus.
  Hinase, Morishita Art Museum
Hiraizumi, A. Mus.
  Hiraizumi, Art Museum (Bijutsukan)
Hiraizumi, Chūsonji Treasure House (Chūsonji
Hōmotsuden)
Hiraizumi Mus.
  Hiraizumi, Hiraizumi Museum (Hiraizumi
  Hakubutsukan)
Hiroshima, City Mus. Contemp. A.
  Hiroshima, City Museum of Contemporary
  Art [in Hijiyama Art Park]

Hiroshima, Itsukushima Jinja
Hiroshima, Mus. A.
  Hiroshima, Museum of Art (Hiroshima
  Bijutsukan)
Hiroshima, Peace Mem. Mus.
  Hiroshima, Peace Memorial Museum (Heiwa
  Kinen Shiryōkan)
Hiroshima, Prefect. Mus. A.
  Hiroshima, Prefectural Museum of Art
  (Hiroshima-Kenritsu Bijutsukan)
Hjorring, Centbib.
  Hjorring, Centralbibliotek
Hlebine, A.G.
  Hlebine, Hlebine Art Gallery (Galerija
  Hlebine)
Hlinsko v Čechách, Reg. Mus. & A.G.
  Hlinsko v Čechách, Regional Museum and Art
  Gallery (Vlastivĕdné Muzeum a Galerie)
Hluboká nad Vltavou, Aléš Gal.
  Hluboká nad Vltavou, Aléš Gallery (Alšora
  Jihočeská Galerie)
Hluboká nad Vltavou, Castle
  Hluboká nad Vltavou, Hluboká Castle
Hobart, Allport Lib. & Mus. F.A.
  Hobart, Allport Library and Museum of Fine
  Arts
Hobart, Cambridge House
Hobart, Lady Franklin Mus.
  Hobart, Lady Franklin Museum
Hobart, Royal Soc. Tasmania
  Hobart, Royal Society of Tasmania
Hobart, Tasman. Mus. & A.G.
  Hobart, Tasmanian Museum and Art Gallery
Hobart, U. Tasmania, Cent. A., Gal.
  Hobart, University of Tasmania, Centre for the
  Arts, Gallery
Hô Chi Minh City, Hist. Mus.
  Hô Chi Minh City, History Museum [formerly
  N. Mus. of the Republic of Vietnam]
Hô Chi Minh City, N. Mus.
  Hô Chi Minh City, National Museum
  [formerly Saigon, Musée Blanchard de la
  Brosse]
Hô Chi Minh City, Reg. Mus.
  Hô Chi Minh City, Hô Chi Minh City Regional
  Museum
Höchst, Jhthalle
  Höchst, Jahrhunderthalle
Hódmezövásárhely, János Tornyai Mus.
  Hódmezövásárhely, János Tornyai Museum
  (Tornyai János Múzeum)
Hoffheim am Taunus, Stadtmus.
  Hoffheim am Taunus, Stadtmuseum
  Hoffheim
Hōfu, Mōri Mus.
  Hōfu, Hōfu Mōri Hōkōkai Foundation, Mōri
  Museum (Mōri Hōkōkai Hakubutsukan)
  [Yamaguchi Prefecture]
Hohemems, Schloss Altemps
Hohhot, Inner Mongol. Mus.
  Hohhot, Inner Mongolian Museum
Hohhot, Inst. Archaeol.
  Hohhot, Institute of Archaeology
Højbjerg, Forhist. Mus. Moesgård
  Højbjerg, Forhistorisk Museum, Moesgård
  (Museum of Prehistory)
Holkham Hall, Norfolk, Lib.
  Holkham, Norfolk, Holkham Hall, Library
Hollabrunn, Neues Mus. Alte Hofmühle
  Hollabrunn, Neues Museum Alte Hofmühle

Holmestrand, Komm.
Holmestrand, Holmestrand Kommune

Holmsbu, Billedgal.
Holmsbu, Billedgalleri

Holstebro, Komm.
Holstebro, Kommune

Holstebro, Kstmus.
Holstebro, Kunstmuseum

Holywood, Ulster Flk & Transport Mus.
Holywood, Ulster Folk and Transport Museum

Homburg von der Höhe, Bib.
Homburg von der Höhe, Bibliothek

Honfleur, Mus. Boudin
Honfleur, Musée Eugène Boudin

Hong Kong, A. Cent.
Hong Kong, Hong Kong Arts Centre

Hong Kong, A. Cent., Pao Sui Loong Gals
Hong Kong, Hong Kong Arts Centre, Pao Sui Loong Galleries

Hong Kong, A. Fest.
Hong Kong, Hong Kong Arts Festival

Hong Kong, Chin. U.
Hong Kong, Chinese University

Hong Kong, Chin. U., A.G.
Hong Kong, Chinese University, Art Gallery of the Institute of Chinese Studies

Hong Kong, City Mus. & A.G.
Hong Kong, City Museum and Art Gallery [now Mus. A.]

Hong Kong, Flagstaff House Mus. Teaware
Hong Kong, Flagstaff House Museum of Teaware

Hong Kong, Hanart Gal.
Hong Kong, Hanart Gallery

Hong Kong, Mus. A.
Hong Kong, Museum of Art [name changed from City Mus. & A.G.]

Hong Kong, Mus. Chin. Hist. Relics
Hong Kong, Museum of Chinese Historical Relics

Hong Kong, Mus. Hist.
Hong Kong, Museum of History

Hong Kong, Orient. Cer. Soc.
Hong Kong, Oriental Ceramic Society

Hong Kong, Plum Blossom Gal.
Hong Kong, Plum Blossom Gallery

Hongkong & Shanghai Bank. Corp.
Hong Kong, Hongkong and Shanghai Banking Corporation

Hong Kong Space Mus.
Hong Kong, Hong Kong Space Museum

Hong Kong, Tsui Mus. A.
Hong Kong, Tsui Museum of Art

Hong Kong, U. Hong Kong, Dept F.A.
Hong Kong, University of Hong Kong, Department of Fine Arts

Hong Kong, U. Hong Kong, Fung Ping Shan Mus.
Hong Kong, University of Hong Kong, Fung Ping Shan Museum

Honiara, N. Mus.
Honiara, National Museum and Cultural Centre [Solomon Islands]

Honis, Patriarch. Lib.
Honis, Patriarchal Library

Honolulu, HI, Acad. A.
Honolulu, HI, Honolulu Academy of Arts

Honolulu, HI, Bishop Mus.
Honolulu, HI, Bernice Pauahi Bishop Museum

Honolulu, HI, Contemp. A. Cent.
Honolulu, HI, Contemporary Arts Center

Honolulu, HI, Contemp. Mus.
Honolulu, HI, Contemporary Museum

Honolulu, U. HI A.G.
Honolulu, HI, University of Hawaii Art Gallery

Hoorn, Westfries Mus.
Hoorn, Westfries Museum

Hope Town, Abaco, Wyannie Malone Hist. Mus.
Hope Town, Abaco, Wyannie Malone Historical Museum

Horadnia, Hist. & Archaeol. Mus.
Horadnia, Horadnia Historical and Archaeological Museum (Hrodzenski Historyka-Arkhealahichny Muzey)

Horgen, Reformierte Kirche

Horinger Prov. Mus.
Horinger, Horinger Provincial Museum

Horten, Norsk Mus. Fot.-Preus Fotmus.
Horten, Norsk Museum for Fotografi-Preus Fotomuseum

Hortobágy, N. Park
Hortobágy, Hortobágy National Park

Hotaka-machi, Rokuzan A. Mus.
Hotaka-machi, Rokuzan Art Museum (Rokuzan Bijutsukan)

Houston, TX, A. & Hist. Trust Col.
Houston, TX, Art and History Trust Collection [A. Soudavar Collection; priv. col., now dispersed among Soudavar family]

Houston, TX, Alfred C. Glassel jr Mus. F.A.
Houston, TX, Alfred C. Glassel jr Museum of Fine Arts

Houston, TX, Contemp. A. Mus.
Houston, TX, Contemporary Arts Museum

Houston, TX, Menil Col.
Houston, TX, Menil Collection

Houston, TX, Meredith Long
Houston, TX, Meredith Long & Co.

Houston, TX, Mus. F.A.
Houston, TX, Museum of Fine Arts

Houston, TX, N Bank

Houston, TX, Parnassus Found.
Houston, TX, Parnassus Foundation

Houston, TX, Rice U. Inst. A., Rice Mus.
Houston, TX, Rice University Institute for the Arts, Rice Museum

Houston, TX, Rice U., Sarall A. G.
Houston, TX, Rice University, Sarall Art Gallery

Houston, TX, Sarah Campbell Blaffer Found.
Houston, TX, Sarah Campbell Blaffer Foundation

Houston, TX, Sewall A.G.
Houston, TX, Sewall Art Gallery

Houston, TX, U. Houston, Sarah Campbell Blaffer Gal.
Houston, TX, University of Houston, Sarah Campbell Blaffer Gallery

Houston, TX, U. St Thomas, A. Dept
Houston, TX, University of St Thomas, Art Department

Hove, Mus. & A.G.
Hove, Hove Museum and Art Gallery

Høvikodden, Henie-Onstad Kstsent.
Høvikodden, Henie-Onstad Kunstsenter (Sonja Henie and Niels Onstad Art Centre)

Hradec Králové, Reg. Gal.
Hradec Králové, Regional Gallery (Krajská Galerie)

Hradec Králové, Reg. Mus.
Hradec Králové, Regional Museum (Krajské Múzeum Východních Čech)

Hradec Králové, Town Mus.
Hradec Králové, Town Museum (Městské Muzeum)

Huaian, Premier Zhou En Lai Mus.
Huaian, Premier Zhou En Lai Museum

Huddersfield, A.G.
Huddersfield, Art Gallery

Hué, Archaeol. Mus.
Hué, Archaeological Museum

Huesca, Ayuntamiento

Huesca, Mus. Arqueol. Prov.
Huesca, Museo Arqueológico Provincial

Huesca, Mus. Episc. & Capitular Arqueol. Sagrada
Huesca, Museo Episcopal y Capitular de Arqueología Sagrada

Huesca, Mus. Huesca
Huesca, Museo de Huesca

Hull, E. Riding Mus.
Hull, Hull and East Riding Museum [formerly Transport & Archaeol. Mus.]

Hull, Ferens A.G.
Hull, Ferens Art Gallery

Hull, Humberside Co. Rec. Office
Hull, Humberside County Record Office

Hull, Old Grammar Sch.
Hull, Old Grammar School

Hull, Postern Gate Gal.
Hull, Postern Gate Gallery [closed]

Hull, Spurn Lightship [Hull Marina]

Hull, Town Docks Mus.
Hull, Town Docks Museum

Hull, Transport & Archaeol. Mus.
Hull, Transport and Archaeology Museum [name changed to E. Riding Mus. in Dec 1989]

Hull, U. Hull
Hull, University of Hull

Hull, U. Hull, A. Col.
Hull, University of Hull, Art Collection

Hull, Wilberforce & Georgian Houses
Hull, Wilberforce and Georgian Houses

Hull, Qué., Can. Mus. Civiliz.
Hull, Qué., Canadian Museum of Civilization

Hulst, Stadhuis

Humlebæk, Louisiana Mus.
Humlebæk, Louisiana Museum of Modern Art

Huntington, NY, Heckscher Mus.
Huntington, NY, Heckscher Museum [Long Island]

Huntington, WV, Marshall U.
Huntington, WV, Marshall University

Hünxe, Otto-Pankok-Mus.
Hünxe, Otto-Pankok-Museum [Haus Esselt]

Hurst Green, Lancs, Stonyhurst Coll.
Hurst Green, Lancs, Stonyhurst College

Husum, Nissenhaus-Nordfries. Mus.
Husum, Nissenhaus-Nordfriesisches Museum

Huy, Mus. Communal
Huy, Musée Communal

Hyderabad, Andhra Pradesh State Archvs
Hyderabad, Andhra Pradesh State Archives

Hyderabad, Dept Archaeol. & Mus.
Hyderabad, Department of Archaeology and Museums

Hyderabad, Mittal Mus. Ind. A.
Hyderabad, Jaqdish and Kamla Mittal Museum of Indian Art

Hyderabad, Salar Jung Mus.
Hyderabad, Salar Jung Museum

Hyderabad, State Archaeol. Mus.
Hyderabad, State Archaeological Museum

Hyderabad, State Mus.
Hyderabad, State Museum

Hyōgo, Kurokawa Inst. Anc. Cult. Res.
Hyōgo, Kurokawa Institute of Ancient Cultural Research

Iaşi, Creangă Mem. Mus.
Iaşi, Ion Creangă Memorial Museum (Muzeul Memorial 'Bojdeuca Ion Creangă')

Iaşi, Dosoftei House-Mus.
Iaşi, Dosoftei House-Museum (Muzeul-Casă 'Dosoftei')

Iaşi, Moldav. Mus. Ethnog.
Iaşi, Moldavian Museum of Ethnography (Muzeul Etnografic al Moldovei)

Iaşi, Mus. A.
Iaşi, Museum of Art (Muzeul de Artă)

Iaşi, Museums Iaşi
Iaşi, Museums of Iaşi (Complexul Muzeistic Iaşi) [admins Creangă Mem. Mus.; Moldav. Mus. Ethnog.; Mus. A.; Mus. Moldav. Lit.; Mus. Nat. Hist.; Mus. Unification; Poly. Mus.; Theat. Mus.]

Iaşi, Mus. Moldav. Lit.
Iaşi, Museum of Moldavian Literature (Muzeul de Literatură al Moldovei)

Iaşi, Mus. Nat. Hist.
Iaşi, Museum of Natural History (Muzeul de Ştiinţele Naturii)

Iaşi, Mus. Unification
Iaşi, Museum of Unification (Muzeul Unirii)

Iaşi, Poly. Mus.
Iaşi, Polytechnic Museum (Muzeul Politehnic)

Iaşi, Theat. Mus.
Iaşi, Theatre Museum (Muzeul Teatrului)

Ibadan, U. Ibadan, Mus. Inst. Afr. Stud.
Ibadan, Univerity of Ibadan, Museum of the Institute of African Studies

Ibarra, Bib. Mun.
Ibarra, Biblioteca Municipal

Ibiza, Mus. A. Contemp.
Ibiza, Museo de Arte Contemporáneo

Ibiza, Mus. Arqueol.
Ibiza, Museo Arqueológico

Ibiza, Mus. Monográf. Puig Molins
Ibiza, Museo Monográfico del Puig des Molins

Idlib, Archaeol. Mus.
Idlib, Archaeological Museum

Iierapetra: see Hierapetra

Iesi: see Jesi

Ife, Mus. Ant.
Ife, Museum of the Ife Antiquities

Ife, U. Ife, Biol. Gdns
Ife, University of Ife, Biological Gardens

Ife, U. Ife, Mus. Inst. Afr. Stud.
Ife, University of Ife, Museum of the Institute of African Studies

Ife, U. Ife, Mus. Nat. Hist.
Ife, University of Ife, Museum of Natural History

Ijsbrechtum, Epema State

Ikaruga, Nara Prefect., Hōryūji
Ikaruga, Nara Prefecture, Hōryūji

Ikeda, Itsuō A. Mus.
Ikeda, Itsuō Art Museum

Ikoma, Hōryūji Mus.
Ikoma, Hōryūji Museum

Ilha de Moçambique, Mus. A. Sacra
Ilha de Moçambique, Museu de Arte Sacra

Ilha de Moçambique, Pal. São Paolo
Ilha de Moçambique, Palácio de São Paolo

Ílhavo, Mus. Porcelana
Ílhavo, Museu de Porcelana [in Vista Alegre factory]

Ilkley, Manor House Mus. & A.G.
Ilkley, Manor House Museum and Art Gallery

Ilkley, White Wells

Imola, Bib. Com.
Imola, Biblioteca Comunale [e Istituti Culturali Annessi]

Imola, Mus. Civ.
Imola, Museo Civico

Imola, Mus. Dioc.
Imola, Museo Diocesano

Imola, Pin. Civ.
Imola, Pinacoteca Civica [Raccolta d'Arte Comunale]

Impruneta, Mus. Santuario
Impruneta, Museo del Santuario [in S Maria dell'Impruneta]

Impruneta, Sala Loggiato Silvani
Impruneta, Sala del Loggiato del Silvani

Impruneta, Villa Mezzamonte
Impruneta, Villa di Mezzamonte

Impruneta, Villa Triboli

Imst, Heimatmus.
Imst, Heimatmuseum

Independence, MO, Truman Lib.
Independence, MO, Harry S. Truman Library

Indianapolis, IN, Eiteljorg Mus. Amer. Ind. & W. A.
Indianapolis, IN, Eiteljorg Museum of the American Indian and Western Art

Indianapolis, IN, Herron A. Inst.
Indianapolis, IN, John Herron Art Institute [name changed to Herron Mus. A. then IN Mus. A.]

Indianapolis, IN, Herron Gal.
Indianapolis, IN, Herron Gallery [Indianapolis Center for Contemporary Art]

Indianapolis, IN, Herron Mus. A.
Indianapolis, IN, Herron Museum of Art [name changed to IN Mus. A. 1968]

Indianapolis, IN, Herron Sch. A.
Indianapolis, IN, John Herron School of Art

Indianapolis, IN, Mus. A.
Indianapolis, IN, Museum of Art [incl. Clowes Fund Collection of Old Master Paintings]

Indore, Cent. Mus.
Indore, Central Museum [Archaeological Museum]

Ingelheim, Altes Rathaus

Ingelheim, Hist. Mus.
Ingelheim, Historisches Museum der Stadt Ingelheim am Rhein

Ingelheim, Int. Tage
Ingelheim, Internationale Tage [C. H. Boehringer Sohn annu. exh.]

Ingolstadt, Bayer. Armeemus.
Ingolstadt, Bayerisches Armeemuseum [Neues Schloss]

Ingolstadt, Mus. Konkrete Kst
Ingolstadt, Museum für Konkrete Kunst

Ingolstadt, Stadtmus.
Ingolstadt, Stadtmuseum Ingolstadt

Innsbruck, Damenstift

Innsbruck, Gal. Ursula Krinzinger
Innsbruck, Galerie Ursula Krinzinger

Innsbruck, Kongresshaus
Innsbruck, Kongresshaus Innsbruck

Innsbruck, Landhaus

Innsbruck, Leopold-Franzens U.
Innsbruck, Leopold-Franzens Universität

Innsbruck, Pal. Fugger–Taxis
Innsbruck, Palais Fugger–Taxis

Innsbruck, Pal. Trapp–Wolkenstein
Innsbruck, Palais Trapp–Wolkenstein

Innsbruck, Schloss Ambras
Innsbruck, Kunsthistorisches Museum, Sammlungen Schloss Ambras

Innsbruck, Tirol. Landesarchv
Innsbruck, Tiroler Landesarchiv

Innsbruck, Tirol. Landesmus.
Innsbruck, Tiroler Landesmuseum Ferdinandeum

Innsbruck, Tirol. Vlkskstmus.
Innsbruck, Tiroler Volkskunstmuseum

Innsbruck, Ubib.
Innsbruck, Universitätsbibliothek

Innsbruck, Zeughaus

Inuyama, Meiji-Mura Mus.
Inuyama, Meiji-Mura Museum

Ioannina, Mus. Ioannina
Ioannina, Museum of Ioannina

Iowa City, U. IA Mus. A
Iowa City, IA, University of Iowa Museum of Art

Ipiales, Mus. Arqueol.
Ipiales, Museo Arqueológico [Colombia]

Ipswich, Christchurch Mansion

Ipswich Mus.
Ipswich, Ipswich Museum

Ipswich, Mus. & A. Gals
Ipswich, Ipswich Museum and Art Galleries [admins Christchurch Mansion; Ipswich Mus.]

Ipswich, Suffolk Rec. Office
Ipswich, Suffolk Record Office

Irbid, Yarmuk U., Mus. Jord. Her.
Irbid, Yarmuk University, Museum of Jordanian Heritage

Irkutsk, A. Mus.
Irkutsk, Art Museum (Khudozhestvennyy Muzey)

Irvine, CA, Severin Wunderman Found.
Irvine, CA, Severin Wunderman Foundation

Irvine, UCI, Sch. F. A.
Irvine, CA, University of California, School of Fine Arts

Ischia, Mus. Isola
Ischia, Museo dell'Isola

Ischia di Castro, Antiquarium Com. Pietro Lotti
Ischia di Castro, Antiquarium Comunale Pietro Lotti

Iseo, Pal. Arsenale
Iseo, Palazzo dell'Arsenale

Isfahan, All Saviour's Armen. Cathedral & Mus.
    Isfahan, All Saviour's Armenian Cathedral and
    Museum

Islamabad, Flk Her. Mus.
    Islamabad, Folk Heritage Museum

Islamabad, N. Council A.
    Islamabad, National Council for the Arts
    [National Art Collection]

Islamabad, Sadequain Mus.
    Islamabad, Sadequain Museum

Islas de la Bahia, Mus. Roatán
    Islas de la Bahia, Museo de Roatán

Ismai'lia Mus.
    Isma'ilia, Isma'ilia Museum

Isola Bella, Archv Borromeo
    Isola Bella, Archivio Borromeo

Isola Bella, Mus. Borromeo
    Isola Bella, Museo Borromeo

Issoudun, Mus. Missions
    Issoudun, Musée des Missions

Issoudun, Mus. St Roch
    Issoudun, Musée Saint-Roch [Musée de
    l'Hospice Saint-Roch]

Istanbul, Acad. F.A.
    Istanbul, Academy of Fine Arts

Istanbul, Akdenız A.G.
    Istanbul, Akdenız Art Gallery

Istanbul, Archaeol. Mus.
    Istanbul, Archaeological Museum (Arkeoloji
    Müzesi)

Istanbul, Armen. Patriarch., Treasury
    Istanbul, Armenian Patriarchate, Treasury

Istanbul, Atatürk Lib.
    Istanbul, Atatürk Library [formerly Belediye
    Kütüphanesi]

Istanbul, Atatürk Mus.
    Istanbul, Atatürk Museum (Atatürk Müzesi)
    [Atatürk Revolution Museum]

Istanbul, Baraz Gal.
    Istanbul, Baraz Gallery

Istanbul, Dolmabahçe Pal.
    Istanbul, Dolmabahçe Palace (Dolmabahçe
    Sarayı)

Istanbul, Ecumenical Patriarch. Lib.
    Istanbul, Ecumenical Patriarchate Library

Istanbul, Found. Cult. A.
    Istanbul, Foundation for Culture and Arts

Istanbul, Glorya Movie Theat.
    Istanbul, Glorya Movie Theatre

Istanbul, Gr. Orthdx Patriarch.
    Istanbul, Greek Orthodox Patriarchate

Istanbul, Guranti A.G.
    Istanbul, Guranti Art Gallery

Istanbul, Hagia Sophia Mus.
    Istanbul, Hagia Sophia Museum (Ayasofya
    Müzesi)

Istanbul, Maya Gal.
    Istanbul, Maya Gallery

Istanbul, Millet Lib.
    Istanbul, Millet Library (Millet Kütüphanesi)

Istanbul, Mil. Mus.
    Istanbul, Military Museum (Askeri Müzesi)

Istanbul, Mimar Sinan U., Mus. Ptg & Sculp.
    Istanbul, Mimar Sinan University, Museum of
    Painting and Sculpture (Mimar Sinan
    Üniversitesi, Istanbul Resim ve Heykel
    Müzesi) [in Dolmabahçe Pal.]

Istanbul, Mosaic Mus.
    Istanbul, Mosaic Museum (Mozaik Müzesi)

Istanbul, Mus. Anc. Orient
    Istanbul, Museum of the Ancient Orient (Eski
    Şark Müzesi)

Istanbul, Mus. Corps Janissaries
    Istanbul, Museum of the Corps of Janissaries

Istanbul, Mus. F.A.
    Istanbul, Museum of Fine Art (Güzel San'atler
    Müzesi)

Istanbul, Mus. Turk. & Islam. A.
    Istanbul, Museum of Turkish and Islamic Art
    (Türk ve Islam Eserleri Müzesi)

Istanbul, N. Lib.
    Istanbul, National Library (Milli Kütüphane)

Istanbul Ptg & Sculp. Mus.
    Istanbul, Istanbul Painting and Sculpture
    Museum

Istanbul, Sadberk Hanım Mus.
    Istanbul, Sadberk Hanım Museum (Sadberk
    Hanım Müzesi)

Istanbul, Süleymaniye Lib.
    Istanbul, Süleymaniye Library (Süleymaniye
    Kütüphanesi)

Istanbul, Tech. U.
    Istanbul, Istanbul Technical University
    (Istanbul Teknik Üniversitesi)

Istanbul, Topkapı Pal. Lib.
    Istanbul, Topkapı Palace Library (Topkapı
    Sarayı Müzesi Kütüphanesi)

Istanbul, Topkapı Pal. Mus.
    Istanbul, Topkapı Palace Museum (Topkapı
    Sarayı Müzesi)

Istanbul, Tüyap

U. Istanbul, Fac. Agric.
    Istanbul, University of Istanbul, Faculty of
    Agriculture

Istanbul, U. Lib.
    Istanbul, University Library (Üniversite
    Kütüphanesi)

Istanbul, Vakıflar Carpet Mus.
    Istanbul, Vakıflar Carpet Museum

Istanbul, Vakıflar Kilim and Flat-Woven Rug Mus.
    Istanbul, Vakıflar Kilim and Flat-Woven Rug
    Museum

Istanbul,Yıldız Pal.
    Istanbul, Yıldız Palace [now Military Academy]

Isthmia, Archaeol. Col.
    Isthmia, Archaeological Collection

Istra, Moscow Reg. Local Hist. Mus.
    Istra, Moscow Region Local History Museum
    (Moskovskiy Oblastnoy Krayevedcheskiy
    Muzey) [former New Jerusalem Monastery]

Itauguá, Mus. S Rafael
    Itauguá, Museo San Rafael

Ithaca, NY, Cornell U., Johnson Mus. A.
    Ithaca, NY, Cornell University, Herbert F.
    Johnson Museum of Art

Ithaca, NY, Cornell U. Lib.
    Ithaca, NY, Cornell University Library

Itó, Ikeda Mus. 20th C. A.
    Itó, Ikeda Museum of 20th Century Art

Ivanovo, Reg. A. Mus.
    Ivanovo, Ivanovo Regional Art Museum
    (Ivanovskiy Oblastnoy Khudozhestvennyy
    Muzey)

Ivrea, Cent. Cult. Olivetti
    Ivrea, Centro Culturale Olivetti

Ivry-sur-Seine, Dépôt Oeuvres A.
    Ivry-sur-Seine, Dépôt des Oeuvres d'Art de la
    Ville de Paris

Iwaki, Mun. Mus. A.
    Iwaki, Municipal Museum of Art

Iwaki, Nakaso A. Mus.
    Iwaki, Nakaso Art Museum

İzmir, Archaeol. Mus.
    İzmir, Archaeological Museum (Arkeoloji
    Müzesi)

İzmir, Gr. Evangel. Sch.
    İzmir, Greek Evangelical School

Iznik, Archaeol. Mus.
    Iznik, Archaeological Museum (Arkeoloji
    Müzesi)

Jabalpur, Rani Durgavati Mus.
    Jabalpur, Rani Durgavati Museum

Jabbeke, Prov. Mus. Permeke
    Jabbeke, Provinciaal Museum Constant
    Permeke

Jablonec, Mus. Glass & Jewel.
    Jablonec, Museum of Glass and Costume
    Jewellery (Muzeum Skla a Bižuterie)

Jackson, MS Mus. A.
    Jackson, MS, Mississippi Museum of Art

Jacksonville, FL, Cummer Gal. A.
    Jacksonville, FL, Cummer Gallery of Art

Jadraque, Escuela

Jægerspris Slot
    Jægerspris, Jægerspris Slot

Jaén Cathedral, Sagrario
    Jaén, Jaén Cathedral, Sagrario

Jaén, Mus. Dioc.
    Jaén, Museo Diocesano Catedralicio

Jaén, Mus. Prov.
    Jaén, Museo Provincial [Arqueología y Bellas
    Artes]

Jaffna, Archaeol. Mus.
    Jaffna, Archaeological Museum

Jaipur, Dig. Jaina Atisaya Kshetra
    Jaipur, Sri Digambara Jaina Atisaya Kshetra

Jaipur, Govt Cent. Mus.
    Jaipur, Government Central Museum of Jaipur

Jaipur, Hawa Mahal Mus.
    Jaipur, Hawa Mahal Museum

Jaipur, Maharaja Sawai Man Singh II Mus.
    Jaipur, Maharaja Sawai Man Singh II Museum
    [in City Palace]

Jakarta, Cent. Mus.
    Jakarta, Central Museum (Museum Pusat
    Lembaga Kebudajaan)

Jakarta, Djakarta Mus.
    Jakarta, Djakarta Museum

Jakarta, Jepang House

Jakarta, Mun. A.G.
    Jakarta, Jakarta Municipal Art Gallery

Jakarta, Mun. Hist. Mus.
    Jakarta, Municipal History Museum (Museum
    Sejorah Kota Jakarta)

Jakarta, Mus. Bahari
    Jakarta, Museum Bahari

Jakarta, N. Archvs
    Jakarta, National Archives (Arsip Nasional
    Republik Indonesia)

Jakarta, N. Mus.
    Jakarta, National Museum (Museum Nasional)

Jakarta, N. Res. Cent. Archaeol.
    Jakarta, National Research Centre of
    Archaeology (Pusat Penelitian Arkeologi
    Nasional)

Jakarta, Textile Mus.
    Jakarta, Textile Museum (Museum Textil)

Jakarta, Wayang Mus.
    Jakarta, Wayang Museum

Jalapa, Gal. Ramón Alva de Canal
  Jalapa, Galeria Ramón Alva de la Canal [part of U. Veracruzana]

Jalapa, Mus. Antropol. U. Veracruzana
  Jalapa, Museo de Antropología de la Universidad Veracruzana

Jalapa, Mus. Arqueol.
  Jalapa, Museo Arqueológico

Jamestown, VA, N. Hist. Site
  Jamestown, VA, National Historic Site

Jammu, Dogra A.G.
  Jammu, Dogra Art Gallery

Jarrow, Bede A.G.
  Jarrow, Bede Art Gallery

Jarrow, Bede Monastery Mus.
  Jarrow, Bede Monastery Museum [St Paul's Jarrow Development Trust]

Jarville, Mus. Hist. Fer
  Jarville, Musée de l'Histoire du Fer

Játiva, Colegiata

Játiva, Mus. El Almodi
  Játiva, Museo de El Almodi

Játiva, Mus. Mun.
  Játiva, Museo Municipal

Jedburgh, Castle Jail

Jedburgh Mus.
  Jedburgh, Jedburgh Museum [destr.]

Jegenstorf, Schloss
  Jegenstorf, Schloss Jegenstorf

Jelgava Mus.
  Jelgava, Museum

Jeloy, Gal. F15
  Jeloy, Galleri F15

Jena, Friedrich-Schiller-U., Hilprecht Samml.
  Jena, Friedrich-Schiller-Universität, Hilprecht Sammlung Vorderasiatischer Altertümer

Jena, Ubib.
  Jena, Universitätsbibliothek

Jenkintown, PA, Alverthorpe Gal.
  Jenkintown, PA, Alverthorpe Gallery [closed]

Jersey City, NJ, CASE Mus. Rus. Contemp. A.
  Jersey City, NJ, CASE Museum of Russian Contemporary Art

Jerusalem, al-Haram al-Sharif Mus.
  Jerusalem, al-Haram al-Sharif Museum

Jerusalem, Armen. Patriarch.
  Jerusalem, Armenian Patriarchate [incl. Gulbenkian Lib. & St James' Mus.]

Jerusalem, Armen. Patriarch., Helen & Martikian Mus.
  Jerusalem, Armenian Patriarchate, Helen and Martikian Museum

Jerusalem, Artists' House

Jerusalem, Bezalel Acad. A. & Des.
  Jerusalem, Bezalel Academy of Arts and Design

Jerusalem, Bible Lands Mus.
  Jerusalem, Bible Lands Museum

Jerusalem, Binyanei Ha'Umah Convent. Cent.
  Jerusalem, Binyanei Ha'Umah Convention Centre

Jerusalem, Cent. Zionist Archvs
  Jerusalem, The Central Zionist Archives

Jerusalem, Col. Pont. Bibl. Inst.
  Jerusalem, Collection of the Pontifical Biblical Institute

Jerusalem, Dept Ant. & Museums
  Jerusalem, Department of Antiquities and Museums

Jerusalem, Gulbenkian Lib.
  Jerusalem, Gulbenkian Library [Library Armen. Patriarch.]

Jerusalem, Hadassah U. Hosp.
  Jerusalem, Hadassah University Hospital

Jerusalem, Hebrew U.
  Jerusalem, Hebrew University

Jerusalem, Hebrew U., Gottesman Cent. Rare MSS
  Jerusalem, Hebrew University of Jerusalem, Gottesman Centre for Rare Manuscripts

Jerusalem, Islam. Mus.
  Jerusalem, Islamic Museum [Aqsa Mosque Museum; Masjid al-Aqsa Museum]

Jerusalem, Israel Ant. Authority Archvs
  Jerusalem, Israel Antiquities Authority Archives

Jerusalem, Israel Mus.
  Jerusalem, Israel Museum [houses Art and Archaeology Library; Bezalel National Art Museum; Bronfman Biblical and Archaeological Museum; Ruth Young Wing; Shrine of the Book]

Jerusalem, Jew. N. & U. Lib.
  Jerusalem, Jewish National and University Library

Jerusalem, Mayer Mem. Inst. Islam. A.
  Jerusalem, L. A. Mayer Memorial Institute for Islamic Art

Jerusalem, Mus. Gr. Orthdx Patriarch.
  Jerusalem, Museum of the Greek Orthodox Patriarchate

Jerusalem, Mus. N. A. Ebraica-It.
  Jerusalem, Museo Nazionale di Arte Ebraica-Italiana

Jerusalem, Palestine Archaeol. Mus.
  Jerusalem, Palestine Archaeological Museum [now Rockefeller Mus.]

Jerusalem, Prt Workshop
  Jerusalem, Jerusalem Print Workshop

Jerusalem, Rockefeller Mus.
  Jerusalem, Rockefeller Museum [formerly Palestine Archaeol. Mus.]

Jerusalem, Schocken Lib.
  Jerusalem, Schocken Library

Jerusalem, St James' Mus.
  Jerusalem, St James' Museum [part of Armen. Patriarch.]

Jerusalem, Ticho House Mus.
  Jerusalem, Ticho House Museum

Jerusalem, Wolfson Mus.
  Jerusalem, Sir Isaac and Lady Edith Wolfson Museum

Jerusalem, Yad Vashem Mus.
  Jerusalem, Yad Vashem Historical and Holocaust Art Museum

Jesi, Pin. Civ.
  Jesi, Pinacoteca Civica

Jesús, Paraguay, Mus. Mis.
  Jesús, Paraguay, Museo de Misión

Jhalawar, Archaeol. Mus.
  Jhalawar, Archaeological Museum

Jhansi, Rami Laxmi Bai Pal.
  Jhansi, Rami Laxmi Bai Palace and Sculpture Collection (Archaeological Survey of India)

Jiloa, Inst. Maestro Gabriel
  Jiloa, Instituto Maestro Gabriel

Ji'nan, Shandong Prov. Mus.
  Ji'nan, Shandong Provincial Museum

Jindřichův Hradec, Castle
  Jindřichův Hradec, Castle (Státní Zámek) [incl. Tapestry Museum]

Jingzhou, Reg. Mus.
  Jingzhou, Jingzhou Regional Museum

Jining, Jining Mus.
  Jining, Jining Museum

Jinzhou, Liaoning Prov. Mus.
  Jinzhou, Liaoning Provincial Museum

Jodhpur, Govt Mus.
  Jodhpur, Government Museum

Jodhpur, Meherangarh Fort Pal. Mus.
  Jodhpur, Meherangarh Fort Palace Museum

Jodhpur, Pal. Lib.
  Jodhpur, Jodhpur Palace Library

Jodhpur, Sardar Mus.
  Jodhpur, Sardar Museum

Jodhpur, Umaid Bhavan Pal. Lib.
  Jodhpur, Umaid Bhavan Palace Library

Johannesburg, Afr. Life Bldg
  Johannesburg, African Life Building

Johannesburg, Afr. Mus.
  Johannesburg, Africana Museum [now MusAfrica; admins Bensusan Mus. Phot.; Bernberg Mus. Cost.; Geol. Mus.; George Harrison Park; Hall Mus. Transport; Mus. S. Afr. Rock A.]

Johannesburg, A.G.
  Johannesburg, Johannesburg Art Gallery

Johannesburg, Anglovaal Corp.
  Johannesburg, Anglovaal Corporation

Johannesburg, Bensusan Mus. Phot.
  Johannesburg, Bensusan Museum of Photography

Johannesburg, Bernberg Mus. Cost.
  Johannesburg, Bernberg Museum of Costume

Johannesburg, Everard Read Gal.
  Johannesburg, Everard Read Gallery

Johannesburg, Geol. Mus.
  Johannesburg, Geological Museum

Johannesburg, Goodman Gal.
  Johannesburg, Goodman Gallery

Johannesburg, Hall Mus. Transport
  Johannesburg, James Hall Museum of Transport

Johannesburg, Lifegro Head Office

Johannesburg, Mus. S. Afr. Rock A.
  Johannesburg, Museum of South African Rock Art

Johannesburg, Rand Afrik. U.
  Johannesburg, Rand Afrikaans University

Johannesburg, S. Afr. Rlwy Mus.
  Johannesburg, South African Railway Museum

Johannesburg, Standard Bank Col.
  Johannesburg, Standard Bank Collection

Johannesburg, U. Witwatersrand
  Johannesburg, University of the Witwatersrand

Johannesburg, U. Witwatersrand A. Gals
  Johannesburg, University of the Witwatersrand, University Art Galleries

Jos, N. Mus.
  Jos, National Museum

Jouy-en-Josas, Fond. Cartier Mus.
  Jouy-en-Josas, Fondation Cartier Musée

Jülich, Stadtgesch. Mus.
  Jülich, Stadtgeschichtliches Museum Jülich

Juneau, AK State Mus.
  Juneau, AK, Alaska State Museum

Jyväskylä, Alvar Aalto Mus.
Jyväskylä, Alvar Aalto Museum (Alvar Aalto Museo)

Jyväskylä, Mus. Cent. Finland
Jyväskylä, Museum of Central Finland (Keski-Suomen Museo)

Jyväskylä, U. Jyväskylä
Jyväskylä, University of Jyväskylä (Jyväskylän Yliopisto)

Kabul, Dargah Temple [in Pir Rathan Nath dist.]

Kabul Mus.
Kabul, Kabul Museum [National Museum of Afghanistan]

Kaduna, N. Mus.
Kaduna, National Museum

Kairouan, Mus. A. Islam.
Kairouan, Musée d'Art Islamique [former Reggada Palace]

Kaiserslautern, Kreisbaugewerkssch.
Kaiserslautern, Kreisbaugewerksschule

Kaiserslautern, Pfalzgal.
Kaiserslautern, Pfalzgalerie des Bezirksverbands Pfalz

Kaiserslautern, Theodor-Zink-Mus.
Kaiserslautern, Theodor-Zink-MuseumKalamazoo, MI, Inst. A.
Kalamazoo, MI, Institute of Arts

Kaliningrad, Reg. Mus.
Kaliningrad, Regional Museum (Oblastnoy Kraeredcheskiy Muzey)

Kaluga, Mus. Hist. Space Explor.
Kaluga, Museum of the History of Space Exploration (Muzey Istorii Kosmonavtiki Imeni K.E. Tsialkovskogo)

Kaluga, Reg. A. Mus.
Kaluga, Regional Art Museum (Oblastnoy Khudozhestvennyy Muzey)

Kaluga, Reg. Local Hist. Mus.
Kaluga, Regional Local History Museum (Oblastnoy Krayevedcheskiy Muzey)

Kamakura, A. Mus.
Kamakura, Kamakura Art Museum (Kamakura Bijutsukan)

Kamakura, Kanagawa Prefect. Mus. Mod. A.
Kamakura, Kanagawa Prefectural Museum of Modern Art (Kanagawa-Kenritsu Kindai Bijutsukan)

Kamakura, Kawabata Yasunari Mem. Mus.
Kamakura, Kawabata Yasunari Memorial Museum [Kanagawa Prefect.; incl. Kawabata Yasunari Mem. Hall]

Kamakura, Kenchōji

Kamakura, N. Treasure House
Kamakura, National Treasure House (Kamakura Kokuhokan)

Kamakura, Tokiwayama Cult. Mus.
Kamakura, Tokiwayama Cultural Museum (Tokiwayamabunko Hakubutsukan)

Kampala, Makerere U.
Kampala, Makerere University

Kamper, Stadhuis

Kamphaeng Phet, N. Mus.
Kamphaeng Phet, Kamphaeng Phet National Museum

Kampong Thom, Archaeol. Mus.
Kampong Thom, Archaeological Museum

Kanazawa, Honda Mus.
Kanazawa, Honda Museum

Kanazawa, Hyakumangoku Bunkaen Edomura Mus.
Kanazawa, Hyakumangoku Bunkaen Edomura Museum

Kanazawa, Ishikawa Prefect. Mus.
Kanazawa, Ishikawa Prefectural Museum

Kanazawa, Mun. Nakamura A. Mus.
Kanazawa, Kanazawa Municipal Nakamura Art Museum

Kandy, N. Mus.
Kandy, Kandy National Museum

Kanev, Shevchenko Mem. Mus.
Kanev, Shevchenko Memorial Museum

Kangnung, Yulgok Mem. Mus.
Kangnung, Yulgok Memorial Museum

Kannauj, Puratattva Sangrahalaya

Kano, Gidan Makama Mus.
Kano, Gidan Makama Museum

Kansas City, MO, Nelson–Atkins Mus. A.
Kansas City, MO, Nelson–Atkins Museum of Art [name changed from W. Rockhill Nelson Gal. c. 1980]

Kansas City, MO, W. Rockhill Nelson Gal.
Kansas City, MO, W. Rockhill Nelson Gallery [now Nelson–Atkins Mus. A.]

Kaposvár, Rippl–Rónai Mus.
Kaposvár, Rippl–Rónai Museum (Rippl-Rónai Múzeum)

Karachi, N. Bank of Pakistan
Karachi, National Bank of Pakistan

Karachi, N. Mus. Pakistan
Karachi, National Museum of Pakistan

Karasjok, Samiske Saml.
Karasjok, De Samiske Samlinger [Sami Collection]

Karl-Marx-Stadt: the town was renamed Chemnitz on 31 May 1990; see Chemnitz

Karlovac, City Mus.
Karlovac, City Museum (Gradski Musej Karlovac)

Karlovo, Hall Cult.
Karlovo, Hall of Culture (Karlovsky Dom na Kulturata)

Karlovy Vary, A.G.
Karlovy Vary, Art Gallery (Galerie Umění)

Karlsborgs Mus.
Karlsborg, Karlsborgs Museum [in fortress]

Karlsruhe, Bad. Kstver.
Karlsruhe, Badischer Kunstverein

Karlsruhe, Bad. Landesbib.
Karlsruhe, Badische Landesbibliothek

Karlsruhe, Bad. Landesmus.
Karlsruhe, Badisches Landesmuseum [in Schloss]

Karlsruhe, Gal. Rottlof
Karlsruhe, Galerie Rottlof

Karlsruhe, Gemäldegal.
Karlsruhe, Gemäldegalerie

Karlsruhe, Genlandesarchv
Karlsruhe, Generallandesarchiv

Karlsruhe, Hochberg Pal.
Karlsruhe, Hochberg Palace

Karlsruhe, Orangerie

Karlsruhe, Staatl. Ksthalle
Karlsruhe, Staatliche Kunsthalle [houses Kupferstichkabinett]

Karlsruhe, Staatl. Kstinst.
Karlsruhe, Staatliche Kunstinstitut

Karlsruhe, Stadtarchv
Karlsruhe, Stadtarchiv

Karlsruhe, Städt. Gal. Prinz-Max-Pal.
Karlsruhe, Städtische Galerie im Prinz-Max-Palais

Karlsruhe, U. Fridericiana
Karlsruhe, Universität Fridericiana [Technische Hochschule]

Karlsruhe, U. Karlsruhe, Inst. Baugesch.
Karlsruhe, Universität Fridericiana, Institut für Baugeschichte

Karlsruhe-Durlach, Pfinzgaumus.
Karlsruhe-Durlach, Pfinzgaumuseum [in Prinzessinnenbau, Schloss Karlsruhe-Durlach]

Karlstad, Värmlands Mus.
Karlstad, Värmlands Museum

Karlštejn Castle, St Catherine's Chapel
Karlštejn, Karlštejn Castle, St Catherine's Chapel (Kaple sv. Kateřiny)

Karlštejn, Imp. Pal.
Karlštejn, Imperial Palace (Říšský Palác)

Karuizawa, MOMA
Karuizawa, Museum of Modern Art [Seibu Takanawa]

Kashihara, Archaeol. Res. Lab. & NHR Serv. Cent.
Kashihara, Archaeological Research Laboratory and NHR Service Centre

Kassel, Brüder Grimm-Mus.
Kassel, Brüder Grimm-Museum

Kassel, Documenta

Kassel, Dt. Tapetenmus.
Kassel, Deutsches Tapetenmuseum [formerly Schloss Wilhelmshöhe]

Kassel, Fotoforum Gal.
Kassel, Fotoforum Galerie

Kassel, Gemäldegal.
Kassel, Gemäldegalerie

Kassel, Hess. Landesmus.
Kassel, Hessisches Landesmuseum [in Schloss Fasanerie]

Kassel, Kstver.
Kassel, Kasseler Kunstverein

Kassel, Landesbib.
Kassel, Landesbibliothek

Kassel, Löwenburg [in Bergpark Wilhelmshöhe]

Kassel, Mus. Fridericianum
Kassel, Museum Fridericianum

Kassel, Neue Gal.
Kassel, Neue Galerie [formerly Bildergalerie]

Kassel, Schloss Wilhelmshöhe
Kassel, Schloss Wilhelmshöhe

Kassel, Schloss Wilhelmshöhe [houses Antikensammlung; Gemäldegalerie Alte Meister; Graphische Sammlung; Kunstbibliothek]

Kassel, Schloss Wilhelmshöhe, Verwalt. Staatl. Schlösser & Gärten Hessen
Kassel, Schloss Wilhelmshöhe, Verwaltung der Staatlichen Schlösser und Gärten Hessen

Kassel, Staatl. Kstsammlungen
Kassel, Staatliche Kunstsammlungen Kassel [now Staatl. Museen]

Kassel, Staatl. Museen
Kassel, Staatliche Museen Kassel [name changed from Staatl. Kstsamml. 1 April 1992: admins Hess. Landesmus.; Neue Gal.; Schloss Wilhelmshöhe]

Kastamonou Mus.
Kastamonou, Kastamonou Museum

Kastoria, Archaeol. Col.
Kastoria, Archaeological Collection [chapel of girls' orphanage]

Kastoria, Byz. Mus.
  Kastoria, Byzantine Museum
Katayamazu, Matsutarō Col.
  Katayamazu, Matsutarō Collection
Kathmandu, Dept Archaeol.
  Kathmandu, Department of Archaeology
Kathmandu, N. Archvs
  Kathmandu, National Archives
Kathmandu, N. Mus.
  Kathmandu, National Museum of Nepal
Kathmandu, Singh Darbar [Secretariat Library]
Katonah, NY, Mus. A.
  Katonah, NY, Katonah Museum of Art
Katowice, Sil. Mus.
  Katowice, Silesian Museum (Muzeum Slaskie)
Kaunas, A. Žmuidzinavičius Mem. Mus.
  Kaunas, A. Žmuidzinavičius Memorial
  Museum
Kaunas, Ciurlionis A. Mus.
  Kaunas, M.K. Ciurlionis Art Museum
Kawajima, Toyama A. Mus.
  Kawajima, Toyama Art Museum (Toyama
  Kinenkan Fūzoku Bijutsukan)
Kawasaki, Open-Air Mus. Jap. Trad. Houses
  Kawasaki, Open-Air Museum of Japanese
  Traditional Houses (Kawasaki-Shiritsu Nihon
  Minkaen)
Kayseri, Archaeol. Mus.
  Kayseri, Archaeological Museum (Arkeoloji
  Müzesi)
Kazan', Mus. F.A. Tatarstan
  Kazan', Museum of Fine Arts of Tatarstan
Kazan', Mus. Tartaristan
  Kazan', Museum of Tataristan
Kazan', Mus. Tartary
  Kazan', Museum of Tartary
Kazimierz Dolny, Reg. Mus.
  Kazimierz Dolny, Regional Museum (Muzeum
  Kazimierza Dolnego)
Kea, Archaeol. Col.
  Kea, Archaeological Collection
Kecskemét Gal.
  Kecskemét, Kecskemét Gallery (Kecskeméti
  Képtár)
Kecskemét, Katona Mus.
  Kecskemét, Katona Museum (Katona József
  Múzeum)
Kecskemét, Ráday Mus. Reform Ch.
  Kecskemét, Ráday Museum of the Reform
  Church of the Hungarian Region
  (Dunamelléki Református Egyházkerület
  Ráday Múzeuma)
Kecskemét, Toy Mus.
  Kecskemét, Toy Museum (Szórakaténusz)
Kedleston, Kedleston Hall, Ind. Mus.
  Kedleston, Kedleston Hall, Indian Museum
Keele U.
  Keele, Keele University
Keighley, Cliffe Castle Mus. & A.G.
  Keighley, Cliffe Castle Museum & Art Gallery
Kempen, Städt. Kramer-Mus.
  Kempen, Städtisches Kramer-Museum und
  Niederrheinisches Museum für Sakralkunst
Kendal, Abbot Hall A.G.
  Kendal, Abbot Hall Art Gallery
Kensington, U. NSW
  Kensington, NSW, University of New South
  Wales
Kerala, U. Kerala
  Kerala, University of Kerala

Kerguehennec, Cent. A. Contemp.
  Kerguehennec, Centre d'Art Contemporain du
  Domaine de Kerguehennec
Keszthely, Balaton Mus.
  Keszthely, Balaton Museum (Balatoni
  Múzeum)
Keynsham, Wansdyke Distr. Council
  Keynsham, Wansdyke District Council
Khania: see Chania
Kharkiv, Hist. Mus.
  Kharkiv, History Museum
Kharkiv, Mus. F.A.
  Kharkiv, Museum of Fine Arts
Kharkiv Poly. Inst.
  Kharkiv, Kharkiv Polytechnic Institute
Khartoum, N. Mus.
  Khartoum, National Museum
Khiva, Ichan-Kala State Mus. Reserve
  Khiva, Ichan-Kala State Museum Reserve
  [incl. Mus. Local Lore, Hist. & Econ.]
Khiva, Mus. Local Lore, Hist. & Econ.
  Khiva, Museum of Local Lore, History and
  Economy
Khodzent, Hist. & Reg. Mus.
  Khodzent, Historical and Regional Museum
  (Istoriko-Krayevedcheskiy Muzey)
Khon Kaen, N. Mus.
  Khon Kaen, Khon Kaen National Museum
Khora: see Chora
Khorog, Hist. & Reg. Mus.
  Khorog, Historical and Regional Museum
Khot'kovo, Vasnetsov Abramtsevo A. Coll.
  Khot'kovo, Vasnetsov Abramtsevo Art
  College (Abramtsevskoye Khudozhestvennoye
  Uchilishche Imeni V. M. Vasnetsova)
Kiel, Christian-Albrechts U.
  Kiel, Christian-Albrechts Universität
Kiel, Christian-Albrechts U., Ksthalle
  Kiel, Christian-Albrechts Universität,
  Kunsthalle zu Kiel
Kiel, Gal. Eichhof
  Kiel, Galerie am Eichhof
Kiel, Kstver.
  Kiel, Kunstverein
Kiel, Landesgesch. Samml. Schleswig-
Holsteinischen Landesbib.
  Kiel, Landesgeschichtliche Sammlung der
  Schleswig-Holsteinischen Landesbibliothek
Kiel, Mus. Sophienblatt
  Kiel, Museum Sophienblatt
Kiel, Rathaus
Kiel, Schleswig-Holsteinische Landesbib.
  Kiel, Schleswig-Holsteinische
  Landesbibliothek
Kiel, Schleswig-Holstein. Kstver.
  Kiel, Schleswig-Holsteinischer Kunstverein
Kiel, Stadt- & Schiffahrtsmus.
  Kiel, Stadt- und Schiffahrtsmuseum
Kiel, Stift. Pommern
  Kiel, Stiftung Pommern, Gemäldegalerie und
  Kulturgeschichtliche Sammlungen
Kielce, Basilica Treasury (Skarbiec Bazyliki)
Kielce, N. Mus.
  Kielce, National Museum (Muzeum
  Narodowe w Kielcach) [formerly
  Świętokrzyskie Mus.]
Kielce, Świętokrzyskie Mus.
  Kielce, Świętokrzyskie Museum (Muzeum
  Świętokrzyskie) [name changed to N. Mus.
  after 1969]

Kiev, Acad. Sci.
  Kiev, Academy of Sciences
Kiev, Archaeol. & Zoological Inst.
  Kiev, Archaeological and Zoological Institute
Kiev, Cent. Lib. Acad. Sci.
  Kiev, Central Library of the Academy of
  Sciences
Kiev, Hist. Mus.
  Kiev, Kiev Historical Museum
Kiev, Lesya Ukrain. Lit. Mus.
  Kiev, Lesya Ukrainka Literature Museum
Kiev, Mus. Hist. Jewels Ukraine
  Kiev, Museum of the Historical Jewels of the
  Ukraine
Kiev, Mus. N. Archit. & Life
  Kiev, Museum of National Architecture and
  Life
Kiev, Mus. Rus. A.
  Kiev, Museum of Russian Art
Kiev, Mus. Rus. & Sov. A.
  Kiev, Museum of Russian and Soviet Art
Kiev, Mus. Theat., Musical & Cinema. A.
  Kiev, Museum of Theatrical, Musical &
  Cinematographical Art
Kiev, Mus. Ukrain. A.
  Kiev, Museum of Ukrainian Art (Muzey
  Ukrains'koho Obrazotvorchoho Mistetstva
  Ukraïni)
Kiev, Mus. Ukrain. Pop. & Dec. A.
  Kiev, Museum of Ukrainian Popular and
  Decorative Art
Kiev, Mus. W. & Orient. A.
  Kiev, Museum of Western and Oriental Art
Kiev, Pechersky Hist. Mus.
  Kiev, Kiev-Pechersky Historical Museum
Kiev, Shevchenko House-Mus.
  Kiev, Shevchenko House-Museum
Kiev, Shevchenko Mus.
  Kiev, Shevchenko Museum
Kiev, St Sophia Hist. & Archit. Mus.
  Kiev, St Sophia Historical and Architectural
  Museum
Kilmarnock, Dick Inst.
  Kilmarnock, Dick Institute
Kimberley, William Humphreys A.G.
  Kimberley, William Humphreys Art Gallery
  [in Civic Centre]
Kinderhook, NY, Columbia Co. Hist. Soc. Mus.
  Kinderhook, NY, Columbia County Historical
  Society Museum
King's Lynn, Guildhall of the Holy Trinity
King's Lynn, Lynn Mus.
  King's Lynn, Lynn Museum
King's Lynn, Mus. Soc. Hist.
  King's Lynn, Museum of Social History
King's Lynn, Regalia Rooms
Kingston, Bank of Jamaica Col.
  Kingston, Jamaica, Bank of Jamaica Collection
Kingston, Inst. Jamaica, N.G.
  Kingston, Institute of Jamaica, National
  Gallery
Kingston, Jamaica, Bolivar Gal.
  Kingston, Jamaica, Bolivar Gallery
Kingston, Jamaica, Edna Manley Sch. Visual A.
  Kingston, Jamaica, Edna Manley School for
  the Visual Arts
Kingston, Jamaica, John Peartree Gal.
  Kingston, Jamaica, John Peartree Gallery

Kingston, Jamaica, U. W. Indies
   Kingston, Jamaica, University of the West
   Indies

Kingston, Ont., Queen's U., Agnes Etherington
A. Cent.
   Kingston, Ont., Queen's University, Agnes
   Etherington Art Centre

Kingston-upon-Hull: see Hull

Kingswinford, Broadfield House Glass Mus.
   Kingswinford, Broadfield House Glass
   Museum

Kinshasa, Cent. Commerce Int.
   Kinshasa, Centre de Commerce International
   du Zaïre

Kinshasa, Inst. Musées N.
   Kinshasa, Institut des Musées Nationaux

Kirchheim im Schwaben, Schloss Fugger
   Kirchheim im Schwaben, Schloss der Fugger

Kirkcaldy, Fife, Mus. & A.G.
   Kirkcaldy, Kirkcaldy Museum and Art Gallery

Kirkwall, Orkney, Tankerness House Mus.
   Kirkwall, Orkney, Tankerness House Museum

Kislovodsk, Yaroshenko A. Mus.
   Kislovodsk, Yaroshenko Art Museum
   (Khudozhestvennyy Muzey Imeni N.A.
   Yaroshenko)

Kitakyushu City, Mun. Mus. A.
   Kitakyushu City, Municipal Museum of Art
   (Kitakyushu Shiritsu Bijutsukan)

Kitchener, Ont., Kitchener–Waterloo A.G.
   Kitchener, Ont., Kitchener–Waterloo Art
   Gallery

Klagenfurt, Gal. Stadthaus
   Klagenfurt, Galerie im Stadthaus

Klagenfurt, Kärntner Landesarchv
   Klagenfurt, Kärntner Landesarchiv [in
   Landhaus]

Klagenfurt, Kärntner Landesgal.
   Klagenfurt, Kärntner Landesgalerie

Klagenfurt, Landesmus. Kärnten
   Klagenfurt, Landesmuseum für Kärnten

Kleinburg, Ont., McMichael Can. A. Col.
   Kleinburg, Ont., McMichael Canadian Art
   Collection

Kleve: see Cleve

Klin, Tchaikovsky House-Mus.
   Klin, P. I. Tchaikovsky House-Museum
   (Dom-Muzey P.I. Tchaikovskogo)

Klosterneuburg, Augustin.-Chorherrenstift,
Thomasprälatur
   Klosterneuburg, Augustiner-Chorherrenstift,
   Thomasprälatur

Klosterneuburg, Bib. Augustin.-Chorherrenstiftes
   Klosterneuburg, Bibliothek des Augustiner-
   Chorherrenstiftes

Klosterneuburg, Mus. Chorherrenstiftes
   Klosterneuburg, Museum des
   Chorherrenstiftes Klosterneuburg [Monastery
   Mus.]

Klosterneuburg, Stift Lapidarium

Klosterneuburg, Stiftsarchv
   Klosterneuburg, Stiftsarchiv

Klung Kung, Hall of Justice

Knokke, Stadthuis

Knokke-Heist, Casino Com.
   Knokke-Heist, Casino Communal [Het Zoute
   beach]

Knokke-Het-Zoute, Gal. Elisabeth Franck
   Knokke-Het-Zoute, Galerie Elisabeth Franck

Knossos, Archaeol. Mus.
   Knossos, Archaeological Museum

Knossos, Pal. Mus.
   Knossos, Palace Museum

Knossos, Stratig. Mus.
   Knossos, Stratigraphical Museum

Kobe, City Mus.
   Kobe, City Museum

Kobe, City Mus. Nanban A.
   Kobe, City Museum of Nanban Art (Kobe-
   Shiritsu Nanban Bijutsukan) [closed]

Kobe, Hakutsuru F.A. Mus.
   Kobe, Hakutsuru Fine Art Museum
   (Hakutsuru Bijutsukan)

Kobe, Hyōgo Cer. Mus
   Kobe, Hyōgo Ceramics Museum (Hyōgoken
   Tōgeikan)

Kobe, Hyōgo Prefect. MOMA
   Kobe, Hyōgo Prefectural Museum of Modern
   Art (Hyōgo Kenritsu kindai Bijutsukan)

Kobe, Kōnan Senior High Sch.
   Kobe, Kōnan Senior High School

Kobe, Kōsetsu Mus. A.
   Kobe, Kōsetsu Museum of Art (Kōsetsu
   Bijutsukan)

Kobe, Kurokawa Inst. Anc. Cult.
   Kobe, Kurokawa Institute of Ancient Cultures

Kobe, Mun. Archaeol. Mus.
   Kobe, Municipal Archaeological Museum

Kobe, Suma Detached Pal. Gdn
   Kobe, Suma Detached Palace Garden

Koblenz, Kstver.
   Koblenz, Kunstverein

Koblenz, Landeshauptarchv
   Koblenz, Landeshauptarchiv

Koblenz, Mittelrhein-Mus.
   Koblenz, Mittelrhein-Museum

Koblenz, Rhein-Mus.
   Koblenz, Rhein-Museum

Koblenz, Schloss Marksburg

Koga, Mun. Hist. Mus.
   Koga, Municipal History Museum

Kokand, City Mus. Local Lore
   Kokand, City Museum of Local Lore

Kokkola, K. H. Renlundin Mus.
   Kokkola, K. H. Renlundin Museum (K. H.
   Renlundin Museo)

Koksijde, Abbey Ter Duinen (Abbey of the
Dunes)

Kolding, Castle Mus.
   Kolding, Museum på Koldinghus

Kolding, Kstmus. Trapholt
   Kolding, Kunstmuseum Trapholt

Kolhapur Mus.
   Kolhapur, Kolhapur Museum

Kolomïa, Mus. Hutsul Flk A.
   Kolomïa, Museum of Hutsul Folk Art (Muzey
   Narodnogo Iskusstva) [Museum of Folk Art]

Kolonna, Heraion Mus.
   Kolonna, Heraion Museum

Kolonyama Pott.
   Kolonyama, Kolonyama Pottery

Kommern, Rhein. Freilichtmus. & Landesmus.
Vlksknd.
   Kommern, Rheinisches Freilichtmuseum und
   Landesmuseum für Volkskunde

Konarak, Archaeol. Mus.
   Konarak, Archaeological Museum

Kongju, N. Mus.
   Kongju, National Museum

Königgrätz: see Hradec Králové

Königsberg: the city was renamed Kaliningrad
after World War II; see also Kaliningrad

Königsberg, Kstakad.
   Königsberg, Kunstakademie

Königsberg, Kstsamml. Stadt
   Königsberg, Kunstsammlungen der Stadt

Konopiště, Schloss
   Konopiště, Schloss Konopiště

Konstanz, Rosgtnmus.
   Konstanz, Rosgartenmuseum

Konstanz, Städt. Wessenberg-Gemäldegal.
   Konstanz, Städtische Wessenberg-
   Gemäldegalerie

Konya, Mevlana Mus.
   Konya, Mevlana Museum

Konya, Seljuk Mus.
   Konya, Seljuk Museum (Taş ve Ahşap Eserleri
   Müzesi)

Kópavogur, A. Mus. Gerður Helgádottir
   Kópavogur, Art Museum of Gerður
   Helgádottir

Koper, Reg. Mus.
   Koper, Regional Museum (Pokrajinski Muzej
   Koper)

Kórnik, Lib. Pol. Acad. Sci.
   Kórnik, Library of the Polish Academy of
   Sciences (Biblioteka Kórnicka PAN) [incl.
   castle mus.]

Koror, Palau Mus.
   Koror, Palau, Palau Museum

Kortrijk, Mus. S. Kst.
   Kortrijk, Museum voor Schone Kunsten en
   Museum voor Oudheid Kunde en Sierkunst

Kos, Archaeol. Mus.
   Kos, Archaeological Museum

Kōsero, Mus. A.
   Kōsero, Museum of Art

Košice, E. Slov. Iron Works
   Košice, East Slovak Iron Works

Košice, Mus. E. Slovakia
   Košice, Museum of Eastern Slovakia
   (Východoslovenské Múzeum)

Kostanjevica, B. Jakac Gal.
   Kostanjevica, B. Jakac Gallery (Galerija
   Božidar Jakac)

Kostroma, Hist. & Archit. Mus.
   Kostroma, Kostroma Historical and
   Architectural Museum (Kostromskoy Istoriko-
   Arkhitekturnyy Muzey-Zapovednik)

Kota, Govt Mus.
   Kota, Government Museum

Kota, Mus. & Saraswati Bhandar
   Kota, Museum and Saraswati Bhandar

Kota Batu, Brunei Mus.
   Kota Batu, Brunei Museum

Kota Kinabalu, Sabah Mus.
   Kota Kinabalu, Sabah Museum (Muzium
   Sabah)[includes Science Centre, Art Gallery,
   Collection of Historical and Tribal Treasures]

Kotor, Hist. Archvs
   Kotor, Historical Archives

Kotor, Lapidary Col.
   Kotor, Lapidary Collection

Kouklia, Old Paphos Archaeol. Mus.
   Kouklia, Old Paphos Archaeological Museum
   [Palaepaphos Museum]

Kozani, Archaeol. Col.
   Kozani, Archaeological Collection [Public
   Library]

Kyōngsan, Yeungnam U. Mus.
  Kyōngsan, Yeungnam University Museum

Kyoto, Chion'in

Kyoto, Chishakuinji Treasury (Chishaku-in Hōmotsuden)

Kyoto, City A. Mus.
  Kyoto, City Art Museum (Kyotoshi Bijutsukan) [Kyoto Municipal Museum of Art]

Kyoto, City Archv
  Kyoto, City Archive

Kyoto, City U. A.
  Kyoto, City University of Arts

Kyoto, Cult. Mus.
  Kyoto, Culture Museum (Bunka Hakubutsukan)

Kyoto, Daigoji Hōjuin Treasury (Daigoji Hōjuin Hōmotsuden)

Kyoto, Daikakuji

Kyoto, Daitokuji

Kyoto, Fujii Yurinkan Mus.
  Kyoto, Fujii Yurinkan Museum (Fujii Yurin-kan)

Kyoto, Honnōji

Kyoto, Imp. Pal.
  Kyoto, Imperial Palace

Kyoto, Jōbon Rendaiji

Kyoto, Juraku Int. Textile Cent.
  Kyoto, Juraku International Textile Centre

Kyoto, Kangikōji

Kyoto, Kaukoji

Kyoto, Kawai Kanjiro Mem. Hall
  Kyoto, Kawai Kanjiro Memorial Hall (Kawai Kanjiro Kinenkan)

Kyoto, Kenninji

Kyoto, Kitamura Mus.
  Kyoto, Kitamura Museum

Kyoto, Kōryūji

Kyoto, Kyōō Gokokuji [Tōji]

Kyoto, Myōrenji

Kyoto, Myōshinji

Kyoto, Nanzenji

Kyoto, Ninnaji

Kyoto, Ninnaji Temple Treasure House

Kyoto, Nishi Hoganji

Kyoto, N. Mus.
  Kyoto, National Museum (Kyoto Kokuritsu Hankubutsukan)

Kyoto, N. Mus. Mod. A.
  Kyoto, National Museum of Modern Art (Kyoto Kokuritsu Kindai Bijutsukan)

Kyoto, Nomura A. Mus.
  Kyoto, Nomura Art Museum

Kyoto, Onshi Mus. A.
  Kyoto, Onshi Museum of Art

Kyoto, Orishi Gyorai

Kyoto, Ōtani U. Col.
  Kyoto, Ōtani University Collection (Ōtani Daigaku)

Kyoto, Raku Cer. Mus.
  Kyoto, Raku Ceramics Museum (Raku Tōjoki Hakubutsukan)

Kyoto, Ryūkoin (Storehouse)

Kyoto, Seigenji

Kyoto, Seiryōji

Kyoto, Senoku Hakkokan (Senoku Hakkokan Hakubutsukan)

Kyoto, Sumitomo Col.
  Kyoto, Sumitomo Collection (Sumitomo Kinenkan)

Kyoto, Tōfukuji

Kyoto, U. Kyoto, Fac. Lett. Archaeol. Col.
  Kyoto, Kyoto University, Faculty of Letters Archaeological Collection (Kyoto Daigaku Bungakubu)

Kyoto, Urasenke Found.
  Kyoto, Urasenke Foundation

Kyoto, Yōmei Bunko

Kyoto, Yugi A. Mus.
  Kyoto, Yugi Art Museum

Kyoto, Yurinkan (Yurinkan Bijutsukan) [Fujii Yurinkan; Yurinkan A. Mus.; Fujii Col.]

Kyrenia Castle
  Kyrenia, Kyrenia Castle

Kyustendil, Dimitroff-Maistora A.G.
  Kyustendil, Vladimir Dimitroff-Maistora Art Gallery (Hudozhestvena Galerija Vladimir Dimitrov-Maijstora)

Kyzyl, Reg. Mus.
  Kyzyl, Regional Museum (Tuvinskiy Respublikanskiy Kraevedcheskiy Muzey)

Kzyl-Orda, Hist. & Reg. Mus.
  Kzyl-Orda, Historical and Regional Museum of Kzyl-Orda

Laarne, Kasteelmus.
  Laarne, Kasteelmuseum Slot von Laarne

Labege-Innopole, Cent. Rég. A. Contemp. Midi-Pyrénées
  Labege-Innopole, Centre Régional d'Art Contemporain Midi-Pyrénées

La Chaux-de-Fonds, Mus. B.-A.
  La Chaux-de-Fonds, Musée des Beaux-Arts

Laconi, Mus. Civ. Archeol.
  Laconi, Museo Civico Archeologico

La Coruña, Mus. Hist. Arqueol.
  La Coruña, Museo Histórico Arqueológico [in Castillo de S Antón]

La Couvertoirade, Aveyron dépt, Archvs Patrm.
  La Couvertoirade, Aveyron Département, Archives du Patrimoine

La Democracía, Parque Arqueol.
  La Democracía, Parque Arqueológico

Lafayette, U. SW LA, A. Mus.
  Lafayette, LA, University of Southwestern Louisiana, University Art Museum

La Fère, Mus. Jeanne d'Aboville
  La Fère, Musée Jeanne d'Aboville

Lagos, Asele Inst.
  Lagos, Asele Institute

Lagos, Bronze Gal.
  Lagos, Bronze Gallery [Afri Ekong's]

Lagos, Didi Mus.
  Lagos, Didi Museum

Lagos, Fed. Dept Ant.
  Lagos, Federal Department of Antiquities [admins Benin City, N. Mus.; Esie, N. Mus.; Jos, N. Mus.; Kano, Gidan Makama Mus.]

Lagos, Idubor Gal.
  Lagos, Idubor Gallery [Felix Idubor's]

Lagos, Ist. It. Cult.
  Lagos, Istituto Italiano di Cultura

Lagos, N. Council A. & Cult., Gal. A. & Crafts
  Lagos, National Council for Arts and Culture, Gallery for Arts and Crafts

Lagos, N. Gal. Mod. A.
  Lagos, National Gallery of Modern Art

Lagos, N. Mus.
  Lagos, National Museum [Nigerian Museum]

Lagos, Ovumaroro Gal.
  Lagos, Ovumaroro Gallery [Bruce Onobrakpeya's]

La Granja de San Ildefonso, Pal.
  La Granja de San Ildefonso, Palacio

La Granja de San Ildefonso, Pal., Colegiata
  La Granja de San Ildefonso, Palacio, Colegiata

Laguna Beach, CA, A. Mus.
  Laguna Beach, CA, Laguna Art Museum [formerly Laguna Beach Mus. A.]

Laguna Beach, CA, Mus. A.
  Laguna Beach, CA, Laguna Beach Museum of Art [name changed to Laguna A. Mus. in 1986]

Lahore, A. Council Col.
  Lahore, Arts Council Collection

Lahore, Faqir Khana Mus.
  Lahore, Faqir Khana Museum

Lahore, Indust. & Commerc. Mus.
  Lahore, Industrial and Commercial Museum

Lahore, Mayo Sch. A.
  Lahore, Mayo School of Arts [now National College of Art]

Lahore Mus.
  Lahore, Lahore Museum

Lahore, Shakir Ali Residence Mus.
  Lahore, Shakir Ali Residence Museum

La Jolla, CA, A. Cent.
  La Jolla, Art Center [name changed to Mus. Contemp. A. in 1971]

La Jolla, CA, Mus. Contemp. A.
  La Jolla, Museum of Contemporary Art [formerly A. Cent.]

La Jolla, CA, Tasende Gal.
  La Jolla, Tasende Gallery

Lake Eden, NC, Black Mountain Coll.
  Lake Eden, NC, Black Mountain College

Lake Forest Coll., IL
  Lake Forest, IL, Lake Forest College

Lake Fusaro, Padiglione Borbon.
  Lake Fusaro, Padiglione Borbonico

Lakewood, OH, Kenneth C. Beck Cent. Cult. A.
  Lakewood, OH, Kenneth C. Beck Center for the Cultural Arts

Lambayeque, Mus. Arqueol. Reg. Brüning
  Lambayeque, Museo Arqueológico Regional Brüning

Lambesc, Mus. Mun.
  Lambesc, Musée Municipal

Lamego, Mus. Reg.
  Lamego, Museu Regional

Lamphun, Haripunchai N. Mus.
  Lamphun, Haripunchai National Museum

Lancaster, City Mus.
  Lancaster, Lancaster City Museums [admins City Museum; Cottage Museum; Museum of the King's Own Regiment; Maritime Museum; Roman Bath House]

Lancaster, MA, Town Lib.
  Lancaster, MA, Town Library

Łańcut Castle
  Łańcut, Łańcut Castle

Landsberg am Lech, Rathaus

Landsberg am Lech, Stadtmus.
Landsberg am Lech, Stadtmuseum

Landshut, Burg Trausnitz

Landshut, Staatsgal. Stadtresidenz
Landshut, Staatsgalerie in der Stadtresidenz

Langen, Jagdschloss Wolfgarten

Langenargen, Mus.
Langenargen, Museum Langenargen

Langenzersdorf, Anton Hanak-Freilichtmus.
Langenzersdorf, Anton Hanak-
Freilichtmuseum

Langley Marsh, St Mary's, Kedeminster Lib.
Langley Marsh, St Mary's Parish Church,
Kedeminster Library

Langres, Mus. Du Breuil de St-Germain
Langres, Musée Du Breuil de St-Germain
[Hôtel Du Breuil de St-Germain]

Langres, Mus. St-Didier
Langres, Musée St-Didier

Lanzhou, Gansu Prov. Mus.
Lanzhou, Gansu Provincial Museum

Laon, Bib. Mun.
Laon, Bibliothèque Municipale

Laon, Mus. Archéol. Mun.
Laon, Musée Archéologique Municipal

Lapad, Hist. Inst. Croat. Acad. Sci. & A.
Lapad, Historical Institute of the Croatian
Academy of Sciences and Arts (Istraživački
Centar Hrvatske Akademije Znanosti i
Umjetnosti) [in Palača Sorkočevic]

La Paz, Alcaldia

La Paz, A. Unico
La Paz, Arte Unico

La Paz, Banco Hipotecario N.
La Paz, Banco Hipotecario Nacional

La Paz, Bib. Mun.
La Paz, Biblioteca Municipal Mariscal Andrés
de Santa Cruz

La Paz, Gal. ARCA
La Paz, Galería ARCA

La Paz, Gal. Empresa Minera Unificada Soc.
Anón.
La Paz, Galería Empresa Minera Unificada
Sociedad Anónima [EMUSA]

La Paz, Medic. Coll.
La Paz, Medical College

La Paz, Mus. Casa Murillo
La Paz, Museo Casa de Murillo

La Paz, Mus. N. A.
La Paz, Museo Nacional de Arte

La Paz, Mus. N. Arqueol.
La Paz, Museo Nacional de Arqueología
[formerly Museo Público]

La Paz, Mus. Tambo Quirquincho
La Paz, Museo del Tambo Quirquincho

La Paz, U. Hall
La Paz, University Hall

La Plata, Mus. Mun. B.A.
La Plata, Museo Municipal de Bellas Artes

La Plata, Mus. Prov. B.A.
La Plata, Museo Provincial de Bellas Artes

La Pocatière, Mus. Coll. Ste-Anne
La Pocatière, Musée du Collège de Ste-Anne

L'Aquila, Col. A. Ammin. Prov.
L'Aquila, Collezioni d'Arte
dell'Amministrazione Provinciale

L'Aquila, Mus. N. Abruzzo
L'Aquila, Museo Nazionale d'Abruzzo

Laren, Singer Mus.
Laren, Singer Museum

Lárisa, Archaeol. Mus.
Lárisa, Archaeological Museum

Larnaca, Archaeol. Mus.
Larnaca, Archaeological Museum

Larnaca, Pierides Found. Mus.
Larnaca, Pierides Foundation Museum

La Rochefoucauld, Château

La Rochelle, Mus. B.-A.
La Rochelle, Musée des Beaux-Arts

La Rochelle, Mus. Hist. Nat. & Ethnog.
La Rochelle, Musée d'Histoire Naturelle et
d'Ethnographie

La Roche-sur-Yon, Mus. A. & Archéol.
La Roche-sur-Yon, Musée d'Art et
d'Archéologie

La Sarraz, Château

La Serena, Mus. S Francisco
La Serena, Museo de S Francisco

Las Palmas de Gran Canaria, Cent. Atlántic. A.
Mod.
Las Palmas de Gran Canaria, Centro Atlántico
de Arte Moderno

La Spezia, Mus. Civ. Archeol.
La Spezia, Museo Civico Archeologico

Las Vegas, NV, Inst. Contemp. A.
Las Vegas, NV, Institute of Contemporary Art

Las Vegas, NV, Liberace Mus.
Las Vegas, NV, Liberace Museum

La Tour-de-Peilz, Château

Latrobe, PA, St Vincent Coll., Kennedy Gal.
Latrobe, PA, St Vincent College, Kennedy
Gallery

La Tronche, Fond. Hébert–d'Uckermann
La Tronche, Fondation Hébert–d'Uckermann
[Musée Hébert (Villa Hébert); Hôtel des
Sociétés Savantes; Maison des Artistes]

La Tronche, Mus. Hébert
La Tronche, Musée Hébert [part of Fond.
Hébert–d'Uckermann]

Lattes, Mus. Archéol.
Lattes, Musée Archéologique

Lauenstein, Schloss & Heimatmus.
Lauenstein, Schloss und Heimatmuseum

Lauingen, Heimathaus

Launceston, Queen Victoria Mus. & A.G.
Launceston, Queen Victoria Museum and Art
Gallery

Lausanne, Biennale Int. Tap.
Lausanne, Biennale Internationale de la
Tapisserie

Lausanne, Col. A. Brut
Lausanne, Collection de l'Art Brut

Lausanne, Fond. Alice Bailly
Lausanne, Fondation Alice Bailly

Lausanne, Fond. Hermitage
Lausanne, Fondation de l'Hermitage

Lausanne, Gal. Kasper
Lausanne, Galerie Kasper

Lausanne, Gal. Paul Vallotton
Lausanne, Galerie Paul Vallotton

Lausanne, Mus. Cathédrale
Lausanne, Musée de la Cathédrale

Lausanne, Mus. Hist.
Lausanne, Musée Historique de Lausanne [in
Ancien-Evêché]

Lausanne, Pal. Rumine
Lausanne, Palais Rumine [houses Musée
Botanique Cantonal; Musée Cantonal
d'Archéologie et d'Histoire; Musée Cantonal
des Beaux-Arts; Musée Géologique Cantonal;
Lausanne, Musée Historique, Cabinet des
Médailles du Canton de Vaud; Musée
Zoologique Cantonal]

Lausanne, Théât. Mun.
Lausanne, Théâtre Municipal

Lausanne, U. Lausanne, Sémin. Angl.
Lausanne, Université de Lausanne, Séminaire
d'Anglais

Lausanne, Wolf Vecker Col.
Lausanne, Wolf Vecker Collection

Laval, Mus. Vieux-Château
Laval, Musée du Vieux-Château

La Valletta: see Valletta

Laveno, Civ. Rac. Terraglia
Laveno, Civica Raccolta di Terraglia

Lawrence, U. KS
Lawrence, KS, University of Kansas

Lawrence, U. KS, Lawrence Mus.
Lawrence, KS, University of Kansas, Lawrence
Museum

Lawrence, U. KS, Spencer Mus. A.
Lawrence, KS, University of Kansas, Spencer
Museum of Art

Laxenburg, Altes Schloss

Leamington Spa, A.G. & Mus.
Leamington Spa, Royal Leamington Spa Art
Gallery and Museum

Le Carbet, Mus. Gauguin
Le Carbet, Musée Gauguin [Martinique]

Le Cateau, Mus. Matisse
Le Cateau, Musée Matisse

Lecce, Mus. Prov. Sigismondo Castromediano
Lecce, Museo Provinciale Sigismondo
Castromediano

Lecco, Gal. Com. A.
Lecco, Galleria Comunale d'Arte

Le Château-Cambrésis: see Le Cateau

Le Creusot, Ecomus.
Le Creusot, Ecomusée de la Communauté Le
Creusot/Montceau-les-Mines

Le Croisic, Hôp.
Le Croisic, Hôpital

Leeds, Armley Mills Indust. Mus.
Leeds, Armley Mills Industrial Museum

Leeds, C.A.G.
Leeds, City Art Gallery

Leeds, City Council
Leeds, Leeds City Council [admins Armley
Mills Indust. Mus.; C.A.G; City Mus.; Kirkstall
Abbey House Mus.; Temple Newsam House;
Lotherton Hall, W. Yorks]

Leeds, City Mus.
Leeds, City Museum

Leeds, Distr. Archvs
Leeds, District Archives

Leeds, Henry Moore Inst.
Leeds, Henry Moore Institute

Leeds, Kirkstall Abbey House Mus.
Leeds, Kirkstall Abbey House Museum

Leeds, Temple Newsam House

Leeds, U. Leeds, Clothworkers Col.
Leeds, University of Leeds, Clothworkers
Collection

Leeds, U. Lib.
Leeds, University of Leeds Library [incl. Brotherton Collection; Liddle Collection; former Ripon Cathedral Library]

Leerdem, Hofje van Aerden

Leeuwarden, Fries Mus.Leeuwarden, Fries Museum

Leeuwarden, Gemeentelijk Mus. Het Princessehof
Leeuwarden, Gemeentelijk Museum Het Princessehof

Leeuwarden, Prov. Bib. Friesland
Leeuwarden, Provinciale Bibliotheek van Friesland

Leeuwarden, Rijksarchf Friesland
Leeuwarden, Rijksarchief in Friesland

Lefkara Mus.
Lefkara, Lefkara Museum

Legnano, Gal. Pagani
Legnano, Galleria Pagani

Le Havre, Mus. B.-A.
Le Havre, Musée des Beaux-Arts

Leicester, Belgrave Hall

Leicester, Col. Sch. & Colls
Leicester, Leicestershire Collection for Schools and Colleges

Leicester, Guildhall

Leicester, Humberstone Drive Annexe

Leicester, Jewry Wall Mus.
Leicester, Jewry Wall Museum

Leicester, Mus. & A.G.
Leicester, Leicestershire Museum and Art Gallery

Leicester, Museums, A. Gals & Rec. Serv.
Leicester, Leicestershire Museums, Art Galleries and Records Service [admins Belgrave Hall; Guildhall; Humberstone Drive Annexe; Jewry Wall Mus.; Mus. & A.G.; Mus. Royal Leics Regiment; Mus. Technol.; Newarke Houses Mus.; Rec. Office; Wygston's House Mus. Cost.; Donington-le-Heath, Manor House; Market Harborough Mus.; Melton Mowbray, Carnegie Mus.; Oakham, Rutland Co. Mus.; Oakham Castle]

Leicester, Mus. Royal Leics Regiment
Leicester, Museum of the Royal Leicestershire Regiment

Leicester, Mus. Technol.
Leicester, Museum of Technology

Leicester, Newarke Houses Mus.
Leicester, Newarke Houses Museum

Leicester Poly., Exh. Hall
Leicester, Leicester Polytechnic, Exhibition Hall

Leicester, Rec. Office
Leicester, Leicestershire Record Office

Leicester, U. Leicester
Leicester, University of Leicester

Leicester, Wygston's House Mus. Cost.
Leicester, Wygston's House Museum of Costume

Leiden, Bib. Rijksuniv.
Leiden, Bibliotheek der Rijksuniversiteit Leiden

Leiden, Gemeentearchf
Leiden, Gemeentearchief

Leiden, Inst. Kern
Leiden, Instituut Kern

Leiden, Kon. Inst. Taal-, Land- & Vlkenknd.
Leiden, Koninklijk Instituut voor Taal-, Land- en Volkenkunde [KITLV]

Leiden, Ksthist. Inst.
Leiden, Kunsthistorisch Instituut

Leiden, Rijksmus. Kon. Penningkab.
Leiden, Rijksmuseum Het Koninklijk Penningkabinet [formerly at The Hague]

Leiden, Rijksmus. Oudhd.
Leiden, Rijksmuseum van Oudheden

Leiden, Rijksmus. Vlkenknd.
Leiden, Rijksmuseum voor Volkenkunde

Leiden, Rijksuniv.
Leiden, Rijksuniversiteit

Leiden, Rijksuniv., Kern Inst.
Leiden, Rijksuniversiteit, Kern Instituut

Leiden, Rijksuniv., Munt- & Penningkab.
Leiden, Munt- en Penningkabinet der Rijksuniversiteit [formerly at The Hague]

Leiden, Rijksuniv., Prentenkab.
Leiden, Prentenkabinet der Rijksuniversiteit

Leiden, Rijnlandshuis

Leiden, Stedel. Mus. Lakenhal
Leiden, Stedelijk Museum De Lakenhal

Leigh, Turnpike Gal.
Leigh, Turnpike Gallery

Leinfelden-Echterdingen, Dt. Spielkarten-Mus.
Leinfelden-Echterdingen, Deutsches Spielkarten-Museum

Leipzig, Ägyp. Mus.
Leipzig, Ägyptisches Museum

Leipzig, Berchfeld Gal.
Leipzig, Berchfeld Gallery

Leipzig, Dt. Buch- & Schrmus
Leipzig, Deutsches Buch- und Schriftmuseum der Deutschen Bücherei

Leipzig, Gal. Sachsenplatz
Leipzig, Galerie am Sachsenplatz

Leipzig, Georgi-Dimitroff-Mus.
Leipzig, Georgi-Dimitroff-Museum

Leipzig, Graph. Samml. Mus. Bild. Kst
Leipzig, Graphische Sammlung des Museums der Bildenden Kunst

Leipzig, Grassi Mus.
Leipzig, Grassi Museum [now Mus. Vlkerknd.; houses Kunstgewmus. and Musikinstrumentmus.]

Leipzig, Halle Kst
Leipzig, Halle der Kunst

Leipzig, Halle Kult.
Leipzig, Halle der Kultur

Leipzig, Karl-Marx-U.
Leipzig, Karl-Marx-Universität [now U. Leipzig]

Leipzig, Karl-Marx-U., Ägyp. Inst., Mus.
Leipzig, Karl-Marx-Universität, Ägyptologisches Institut, Museum

Leipzig, Karl-Marx-U., Archäol. Inst.
Leipzig, Karl-Marx-Universität, Archäologisches Institut

Leipzig, Kstgewmus.
Leipzig, Kunstgewerbemuseum [in former Grassi Mus.]

Leipzig, Kstlerhaus
Leipzig, Künstlerhaus [closed]

Leipzig, Kstver.
Leipzig, Leipziger Kunstverein

Leipzig, Mus. Bild. Kst.
Leipzig, Museum der Bildenden Künste

Leipzig, Mus. Gesch.
Leipzig, Museum für Geschichte der Stadt Leipzig

Leipzig, Mus. Ksthandwks
Leipzig, Museum des Kunsthandwerks

Leipzig, Mus. Vlkerknd.
Leipzig, Museum für Völkerkunde [in former Grassi Mus.]

Leipzig, Österreich. Haus
Leipzig, Österreichisches Haus [Österreichischer Staatspalast; no longer exists]

Leipzig, Staatl. Hochsch. Graph. & Buchkst
Leipzig, Staatliche Hochschule für Graphik und Buchkunst

Leipzig, Stadtarchv
Leipzig, Stadtarchiv

Leipzig, Stadt- & Bezirksbib.
Leipzig, Stadt- und Bezirksbibliothek

Leipzig, Stadtgesch. Mus. Leipzig
Leipzig, Stadtgeschichtliches Museum Leipzig

Leipzig, Ubib.
Leipzig, Universitätsbibliothek der Universität Leipzig

Leiria, Semin. Maior
Leiria, Seminário Maior

Lejre, Ledreborg [Løvenøns family col.]

Le Locle, Mus. B.-A.
Le Locle, Musée des Beaux-Arts du Locle

Le Mans, Bib. Mun.
Le Mans, Bibliothèque Municipale

Le Mans, Mus. Tessé
Le Mans, Musée de Tessé [Musée des Beaux-Arts]

Le Mas d'Azil, Mus. Ladevèze
Le Maz d'Azil, Musée Ladevèze

Lemba, Archaeol. Mus.
Lemba, Archaeological Museum

Lembergeri, Mus. Ukrain. Theol. Acad.
Lembergeri, Museum of the Ukrainian Theological Academy

Lembergeri, St Clements U., Ukrain. Mus. & Lib.
Lembergeri, St Clements University, Ukrainian Museum and Library

Le Mée-sur-Seine, Mus. Chapu
Le Mée-sur-Seine, Musée Henri Chapu

Leningrad: the city reverted to its pre-Revolution name of Sankt Petersburg in September 1991; *see also* St Petersburg

Leningrad, Mus. Hist. Leningrad
Leningrad, Museum of the History of Leningrad (Muzey Istorii Leningrada)

Leningrad, Org. Un. Artists RSFSR
Leningrad, Organization of the Union of Artists of the RSFSR [now 'of the Russia Federation': RF] (Assotsiatsiya Soyuza Khudozhnikov RSFSR)

Leominster, MA, Lane Found.
Leominster, MA, William H. Lane Foundation

León, Mus. Arqueol. Prov.
León, Museo Arqueológico Provincial [in Convent of S Marcos]

León, Mus.-Bib. Real Colegiata S Isidoro
León, Museo-Biblioteca de la Real Colegiata de San Isidoro

Le Puy, Mus. Crozatier
Le Puy, Musée Crozatier [Jardin Henri-Vinay]

Le Puy, Trésor A. Relig.
Le Puy, Trésor d'Art Religieux

Le Puy, Trésor Cathédrale Notre-Dame
Le Puy, Trésor de la Cathédrale Notre-Dame

Le Quesnoy, Hôtel de Ville

Lérida: *see* Lleida

Lescovac, Mun. Mus.
Lescovac, Municipal Museum [National Museum]

Les Eyzies-de-Tayac-Sireuil, Mus. N. Préhist.
Les Eyzies-de-Tayac-Sireuil, Musée National de Préhistoire

Les Sables d'Olonne, Mus. Abbaye Sainte-Croix
Les Sables d'Olonne, Musée de l'Abbaye Sainte-Croix

Les Sables d'Olonne, Mus. Mar.
Les Sables d'Olonne, Musée de la Marine

Leszno, Reg. Mus.
Leszno, Regional Museum of Leszno (Muzeum Okregowe w Lesznie)

Letchworth, First Gdn City Her. Mus.
Letchworth, First Garden City Heritage Museum

Letchworth, Mus. & A.G.
Letchworth, Museum and Art Gallery

Leukas, Archaeol. Col.
Leukas, Archaeological Collection [in Municipal Library]

Leukas, Col. Eccles. Ptgs & Relics Orthodoxy
Leukas, Collection of Ecclesiastical Paintings and Relics of Orthodoxy

Leukas, Faneroméni Convent

Leuven, Brouwerijmus.
Leuven, Stedelijk Brouwerijmuseum

Leuven, Cult. Cent. Romaanse Poort
Leuven, Cultureel Centrum Romaanse Poort

Leuven, Katholieke U.
Leuven, Katholieke Universiteit Leuven

Leuven, Mus. Kerklijke Kst St-Pieterskerk
Leuven, Museum voor Kerklijke Kunst Sint-Pieterskerk

Leuven, Mus. Vander Kelen-Mertens
Leuven, Stedelijk Museum Vander Kelen-Mertens

Leuven, Stadthuis

Leuven, U. Catholique
Leuven, Université Catholique de Louvain [until 1970 part of Katholieke U.]

Leuven, U. Catholique, Archvs
Leuven, Archives de l'Université Catholique de Louvain

Levadeia, Chaironria Mus.
Levadeia, Chaironria Museum

Leverkusen, Kulthaus
Leverkusen, Kulturhaus

Leverkusen, Schloss Morsbroich
Leverkusen, Städtisches Museum Leverkusen [in Schloss Morsbroich]

Lèves, Hospice d'Aligne

Lévkas: *see* Leukas

Lewes, Anne of Cleves House Mus.
Lewes, Anne of Cleves House Museum

Lewes, Mus. Sussex Archaeol.
Lewes, Museum of Sussex Archaeology

Lewisburg, PA, Bucknell U.
Lewisburg, PA, Bucknell University

Lewisburg, PA, Packwood House Mus.
Lewisburg, PA, Packwood House Museum

Lexington, U. KY A. Mus.
Lexington, KY, University of Kentucky Art Museum [Center for the Arts]

Lexington, MA, Scot. Rite Mason. Mus. N. Her.
Lexington, MA, Scottish Rite Masonic Museum of Our National Heritage

Lexington, VA, Washington & Lee U., Chapel Mus.
Lexington, VA, Washington and Lee University, Lee Chapel Museum

Lhasa, Potala Pal.
Lhasa, Potala Palace

Liberec, N. Boh. Mus.
Liberec, North Bohemian Museum (Severočeské Muzeum v Liberci)

Liberec, Reg. Gal.
Liberec, Regional Gallery (Oblastní Galerie)

Libourne, Mus. B.-A. & Archéol.
Libourne, Musée des Beaux-Arts et d'Archéologie [Hôtel de Ville; Musée Princeteau]

Lichfield, Cathedral Lib.
Lichfield, Cathedral Library [Dean Savage Reference Library]

Lichfield, Samuel Johnson Birthplace Mus.
Lichfield, Samuel Johnson Birthplace Museum

Lidingö, Millesgården

Lidingo, Stift. Hilding Linnqvists Kst
Lidingö, Stiftelsen Hilding Linnqvists Konst

Lidköping, Läcko Slott

Liège, Archvs Etat
Liège, Archives de l'Etat

Liège, Cab. Est. & Dessins
Liège, Cabinet des Estampes et des Dessins

Liège Cathedral, Trésor
Liège, Liège Cathedral, Trésor

Liège, Gal. St Georges
Liège, Galerie Saint Georges

Liège, Hôtel Armes
Liège, Hôtel d'Armes

Liège, Mus. A. Mod.
Liège, Musée d'Art Moderne

Liège, Mus. Ansembourg
Liège, Musée d'Ansembourg

Liège, Mus. Archit.
Liège, Musée d'Architecture

Liège, Mus. A. Relig. A. Mosan
Liège, Musée d'Art Religieux et d'Art Mosan [Ancien Musée Diocésain]

Liège, Mus. A. Wallon
Liège, Musée de l'Art Wallon

Liège, Mus. B.-A.
Liège, Musée des Beaux-Arts

Liège, Mus. Curtius
Liège, Musée Curtius

Liège, Musées Archéol. & A. Déc.
Liège, Musées d'Archéologie et des Arts Décoratifs de Liège [admins Mus. Ansembourg; Mus. Curtius; Mus. Verre]

Liège, Mus. Verre
Liège, Musée du Verre

Liège, Pal. Congr.
Liège, Palais des Congrès

Liège, Sainte-Croix, Trésor

Liège, St Jean

Liège, U. Liège
Liège, Université de l'Etat à Liège

Liège, U. Liège, Bib. Gén.
Liège, Bibliothèque Générale de l'Université

Liepāja, Mus. Hist. & A.
Liepāja, Museum of History and Art (Liepājas Vēstures un Mākslas Muzejs)

Lier, Mus. Wuyts-Van Campen & Baron Caroly
Lier, Museum Wuyts-Van Campen en Baron Caroly

Lignières, Château Ussé

Ligornetto, Mus. Vela
Ligornetto, Museo Vela

Lille, Acad.
Lille, Académie

Lille, Archvs Dépt. Nord
Lille, Archives Départementales du Nord

Lille, Bib. Mun.
Lille, Bibliothèque Municipale

Lille, Bib. Mun., Fond. Godefroy
Lille, Bibliothèque Municipale, Fondation Godefroy

Lille, Gal. Marcel Evrand
Lille, Galerie Marcel Evrand

Lille, Mus. A. Mod.
Lille, Musée d'Art Moderne

Lille, Mus. B.-A.
Lille, Musée des Beaux-Arts [in Palais des Beaux-Arts]

Lille, Mus. Dioc. A. Relig.
Lille, Musée Diocésain d'Art Religieux

Lille, Mus. Hosp. Comtesse
Lille, Musée de l'Hospice Comtesse

Lille, Mus. Indust. & Commerc.
Lille, Musée Industriel et Commercial

Lille, U. Lille III
Lille, Université de Lille III, Charles de Gaulle

Lillehammer, Bys Malsaml.
Lillehammer, Bys Malerisamling [Municipal Art Collection]

Lillehammer, Sandvigske Saml.
Lillehammer, De Sandvigske Samlinger [Maihaugen Open-Air Mus.]

Lima, Allpamérica

Lima, Archv Gen. N.
Lima, Archivo General de la Nación

Lima, Banco de Crédito del Perú

Lima, Banco de la Nación

Lima, Bib. N.
Lima, Biblioteca Nacional del Perú

Lima, Brit. Council
Lima, British Council

Lima, Casa Brandes

Lima, Cent. Cult. Peru. Jap.
Lima, Centro Cultural Peruano Japonés

Lima, Colegio Arquitectos
Lima, Colegio de Arquitectos

Lima, Escuela N. B.A.
Lima, Escuela Nacional de Bellas Artes

Lima, Escuela N. Ingen.
Lima, Escuela Nacional de Ingeniería

Lima, Escuela Sup. A. Altern.
Lima, Escuela Superior de Arte Corriente Alternativo

Lima, Fund. Mus. Amano
Lima, Fundación Museo Amano

Lima, Gal. & Bib. S Marcos
Lima, Galería y Biblioteca San Marcos

Lima, Gal. Lima
Lima, Galería de Lima [now Instituto de Arte Contemporáneo]

Lima, Gal. Wiese
Lima, Galería Wiese

Lima, Inst. A. Peru.
Lima, Instituto de Arte Peruano

Lima, Inst. Cult. Peru.-Namer.
Lima, Instituto Cultural Peruano-Norteamericano

Lima, Inst. N. Cult.
Lima, Instituto Nacional de Cultura

Lima, Inst. Raúl Porras Barrenchea
Lima, Instituto Raúl Porras Barrenchea

Lima, Inst. Riva Agüero
Lima, Instituto Riva Agüero

Lima, Inst. Toulouse-Lautrec
Lima, Instituto Toulouse-Lautrec

Lima, Min. Econ. & Finanzas
Lima, Ministerio de Economía y Finanzas

Lima, Mun. Lima Met.
Lima, Municipalidad de Lima Metropolitana

Lima, Mus. A.
Lima, Museo de Arte

Lima, Mus. A. It.
Lima, Museo de Arte Italiano

Lima, Mus. A. Mun.
Lima, Museo de Arte Municipal

Lima, Mus. A. Pop.
Lima, Museo de Arte Popular

Lima, Mus. Arqueol.
Lima, Museo Arqueológico

Lima, Mus. Arqueol. & Etnol.
Lima, Museo de Arqueología y Etnología de la
Universidad Nacional

Lima, Mus. Banco Central de Reserva
Lima, Museo del Banco Central de Reserva

Lima, Mus. Arqueol. Larco Herrera
Lima, Museo Arqueológico Rafael Larco
Herrera

Lima, Mus. Contemp. A. Pop. Peru.
Lima, Museo Contemporáneo de Arte Popular
Peruano

Lima, Mus. Geol. U. N. Ingen. Perú
Lima, Museo Geológico de la Universidad
Nacional de Ingeniería del Perú

Lima, Mus. Hosp. Dos Mayo
Lima, Museo del Hospital Dos de Mayo

Lima, Mus. N. Antropol. & Arqueol.
Lima, Museo Nacional de Antropología y
Arqueología

Lima, Mus. N. Cult. Peru.
Lima, Museo Nacional de la Cultura Peruana

Lima, Mus. N. Hist.
Lima, Museo Nacional de Historia

Lima, Mus. Oro & Armas Mundo
Lima, Museo de Oro del Perú y Armas del
Mundo [in Monterrico]

Lima, Mus. Tribunal S Inquisició
Lima, Museo del Tribunal de la Santa
Inquisición

Lima, Mus. Virreinato
Lima, Museo del Virreinato [in Quinta Presa]

Lima, Orden Tercera S Francisco
Lima, Orden Tercera de San Francisco

Lima, Petro Perú

Lima, Pin. Mun.
Lima, Pinacoteca de la Municipalidad de Lima

Lima, Pont. U. Cat. del Perú
Lima, Pontificia Universidad Católica del Perú

Lima, Pont. U. Cat. del Perú, Escuela A. Plást.
Lima, Pontificia Universidad Católica del Perú,
Escuela de Artes Plásticas

Lima, Pont. U. Cat. del Perú, Mus. Arqueol.
Josefina Ramos de Cox
Lima, Pontificia Universidad Católica del Perú,
Museo de Arqueología Josefina Ramos de Cox

Lima, Soc. Ingenieros Perú
Lima, Sociedad de Ingenieros del Perú

Lima, U. N. Mayor S Marcos
Lima, Universidad Nacional Mayor de San
Marcos de Lima

Limassol, Distr. Mus.
Limassol, District Museum [Archaeological
Museum]

Limassol, Med. Mus.
Limassol, Medieval Museum

Limburg, Diözmus.
Limburg, Diözesanmuseum

Limburg, Domschatzkam.
Limburg, Domschatzkammer

Limenas Mus.
Limenas, Limenas Museum

Limerick, City Gal. A.
Limerick, Limerick City Gallery of Art

Limoges, Chapelle du Lycée Gay-Lussac

Limoges, Dir. Rég. Affaires Cult. Limousin
Limoges, Direction Régionale des Affaires
Culturelles du Limousin

Limoges, Mus. Mun.
Limoges, Musée Municipal

Limoges, Mus. N. Adrien-Dubauché
Limoges, Musée National Adrien-Dubauché

Limyra, Thrater-Depot

Linares, Mus. A. & Artesanía
Linares, Museo de Arte y Artesanía

Linares, Mus. Arqueol.
Linares, Museo Arqueológico

Linby, Newstead Abbey

Lincoln, City & Co. Mus.
Lincoln, Lincoln City and County Museum

Lincoln, Lincs Archv
Lincoln, Lincolnshire Archive

Lincoln, Lincs Museums
Lincoln, Lincolnshire Museums [admins
Gainsborough, Old Hall; Grantham Mus.;
Lincoln, City & Co. Mus.; Mus. Lincs Life;
Usher Gal.; Skegness, Ch. Farm Mus.;
Stamford, Lincs, Mus.]

Lincoln, Lincs Museums Conserv. Lab.
Lincoln, Lincolnshire Museums Conservation
Laboratory

Lincoln, Mus. Lincs Life
Lincoln, Museum of Lincolnshire Life

Lincoln, Usher Gal.
Lincoln, Usher Gallery

Lincoln, MA, DeCordova & Dana Mus.
Lincoln, MA, DeCordova and Dana Museum
and Park

Lincoln, U. NE, A. Dept Gal.
Lincoln, NE, University of Nebraska, Art
Department Gallery

Lincoln, U. NE A. Gals
Lincoln, NE, University of Nebraska Art
Galleries [admins A. Dept Gal.; Morrill Hall;
Sheldon Mem. A.G.]

Lincoln, U. NE, Morrill Hall
Lincoln, NE, University of Nebraska, Morrill
Hall

Lincoln, U. NE, Sheldon Mem. A.G.
Lincoln, NE, University of Nebraska, Sheldon
Memorial Art Gallery

Lincoln, U. NE State Mus.
Lincoln, NE, University of Nebraska State
Museum

Lindisfarne Priory

Linköping, Grevskapsråd

Linköping, Östergötlands Länsmus.
Linköping, Östergötlands Länsmuseum

Lintong, Shaanxi Prov., Mus. Emperor Qin Shi
Huangdi's Tomb
Lintong, Shaanxi Province, Museum of
Emperor Qin Shi Huangdi's Tomb

Linyi, Mun. Mus.
Linyi, Linyi Municipal Museum [Shandong]

Linz, Bischöf. Diözmus.
Linz, Bischöfliches Diözesanmuseum

Linz, Brucknerhaus

Linz, Hochsch. Kstler. & Indust. Gestalt.
Linz, Hochschule für Künstlerische und
Industrielle Gestaltung

Linz, Neue Gal.
Linz, Neue Galerie der Stadt Linz [Wolfgang-
Gurlitt-Mus.]

Linz, Oberösterreich. Landesmus.
Linz, Oberösterreichisches Landesmuseum

Linz, Schlossmus.
Linz, Schlossmuseum des
Oberösterreichischen Landesmuseums

Linz, Stadtmus.
Linz, Stadtmuseum [Nordico]

Lipari, Mus. Archeol. Eoliano
Lipari, Museo Archeologico Eoliano

Lisbon, Acad. Ciênc.
Lisbon, Academia das Ciências de Lisboa

Lisbon, Acad. N. B.A.
Lisbon, Academia Nacional de Belas-Artes
[Escola Superior de Belas-Artes]

Lisbon, Arquiv. Hist. Min. Finanças
Lisbon, Arquivo Histórico do Ministério das
Finanças

Lisbon, Arquiv. N.
Lisbon, Arquivo Nacional da Torre do Tombo

Lisbon, Assembl. N.
Lisbon, Assembléia Nacional

Lisbon, Assoc. Arquit.
Lisbon, Associação dos Arquitectos

Lisbon, Bib. Ajuda
Lisbon, Biblioteca de Ajuda

Lisbon, Bib. & Arquiv. Hist. Min. Obras Púb.
Lisbon, Biblioteca e Arquivo Histórico do
Ministerio das Obras Públicas, Transportes a
Comunicaçãos

Lisbon, Bib. N.
Lisbon, Biblioteca Nacional

Lisbon, Calhariz Pal.
Lisbon, Calhariz Palacio

Lisbon, Câmara Mun.
Lisbon, Câmara Municipal

Lisbon, Câmara Mun., Arquiv. Repartição Téc.
Lisbon, Câmara Municipal, Arquivi da
Repartição Técnica

Lisbon, Câmara Pestana Inst.
Lisbon, Câmara Pestana Institute

Lisbon, Casa Mus. Gonçalves
Lisbon, Casa Museu Anastácio Gonçalves

Lisbon, Casa Tarcuca

Lisbon, Cidade U., Reitoria
Lisbon, Cidade Universitária, Reitoria

Lisbon, Comissão N. Comemorações
Descobrimentos Port.
Lisbon, Comissão Nacional para as
Comemorações dos Descobrimentos
Portugueses

Lisbon, Dir. Geral Fazenda Pub.
Lisbon, Direção Geral da Fazenda Pública

Lisbon, Fund. Gulbenkian
Lisbon, Fundação Calouste Gulbenkian
[admins Mus. Gulbenkian]

Lisbon, Fund. Ricardo Espirito S Silva
   Lisbon, Fundação Ricardo Espirito Santo Silva
Lisbon, Gal. Almada Negreiros
   Lisbon, Galeria Almada Negreiros
Lisbon, Gal. Ana Isabel
   Lisbon, Galeria Ana Isabel
Lisbon, Gal. 111
   Lisbon, Galeria 111
Lisbon, Gal. Dinastia
   Lisbon, Galeria Dinastia
Lisbon, Grém. A.
   Lisbon, Grémio Artístico
Lisbon, Hosp. Mar.
   Lisbon, Hospital da Marinha
Lisbon, Inst. Port. Patrm. Cult.
   Lisbon, Instituto Português do Património Cultural
Lisbon, Jerónimos Monastery
Lisbon, Mus. A. Dec.
   Lisbon, Museu-Escola de Artes Decorativas [Fundãçao Ricardo do Espirito S Silva]
Lisbon, Mus. Arqueol.
   Lisbon, Museu Arqueológico [Associação dos Arqueólogos Portugueses]
Lisbon, Mus. Azulejo
   Lisbon, Museu do Azulejo [formerly Convent of Madre de Deus]
Lisbon, Mus. Bordalo Pinheiro
   Lisbon, Museu Rafael Bordalo Pinheiro
Lisbon, Mus. Cidade
   Lisbon, Museu da Cidade
Lisbon, Mus. Etnog.
   Lisbon, Museu Etnográfico [Sociedad de Geografia de Lisboa]
Lisbon, Mus. Etnol.
   Lisbon, Museu de Etnologia
Lisbon, Mus. Etnol. Ultramar
   Lisbon, Museu Etnológico do Ultramar
Lisbon, Mus. Gulbenkian
   Lisbon, Museu Calouste Gulbenkian [Fundação Calouste Gulbenkian]
Lisbon, Mus. Mar.
   Lisbon, Museu da Marinha
Lisbon, Mus. Mil.
   Lisbon, Museu Militar
Lisbon, Mus. N. A. Ant.
   Lisbon, Museu Nacional de Arte Antiga [Museu das Janelas Verdes]
Lisbon, Mus. N. A. Contemp.
   Lisbon, Museu Nacional de Arte Contemporânea [closed; reopened as Mus. N. Chiado in 1994]
Lisbon, Mus. N. Arqueol. & Etnol.
   Lisbon, Museu Nacional de Arqueologia e Etnologia
Lisbon, Mus. N. Chiado
   Lisbon, Museu Nacional do Chiado
Lisbon, Mus. N. Coches
   Lisbon, Museu Nacional dos Coches
Lisbon, Mus. N. Soares dos Reis
   Lisbon, Museu Nacional Soares dos Reis
Lisbon, Mus. N. Traje
   Lisbon, Museu Nacional do Traje
Lisbon, Mus. S Roque
   Lisbon, Museu de Arte Sacra de São Roque
Lisbon, Mus. Zool. & Antropol.
   Lisbon, Museu, Zoológico e Antropológico
Lisbon, Pal. Ajuda
   Lisbon, Palácio da Ajuda [Palácio Belém]

Lisbon, Pal. Belém Gdns
   Lisbon, Palácio de Belém Gardens
Lisbon, Pal. Foz
   Lisbon, Palácio Foz
Lisbon, Pal. Galveias
   Lisbon, Palácio Galveias
Lisbon, Pal. N. Ajuda
   Lisbon, Palácio Nacional da Ajuda
Lisbon, Pal. Necessidades
   Lisbon, Palácio das Necessidades
Lisbon, Pal. Valenças
   Lisbon, Palácio Valenças
Lisbon, Secretaria Estado Cult.
   Lisbon, Secretaria da Estado da Cultura
Lisbon, Soc. Geog.
   Lisbon, Sociedade de Geografia de Lisboa
Lisbon, Soc. N. B.A.
   Lisbon, Sociedade Nacional de Belas Artes
Lisbon, Tribunal Relação
   Lisbon, Tribunal da Rclação
Lisbon, U. Lisbon
   Lisbon, Universidade de Lisboa
Lisbon, U. Nova
   Lisbon, Universidade Nova de Lisboa
Lisbon, U. Téc., Inst. Sup. Agron.
   Lisbon, Universidadc Técnica de Lisboa, Instituto Superior de Agronomia
Lisieux, Mus. B.-A.
   Lisieux, Musée des Beaux-Arts [closed]
Lisieux, Mus. Vieux-Lisieux
   Lisieux, Musée du Vieux-Lisieux
Litoměřice, Archv
   Litoměřice, Litoměřice Archive (Státní Odborný Archív)
Litoměřice, Distr. Mus.
   Litoměřice, District Museum (Okresní Mzeum)
Litoměřice, N. Boh. Gal. F.A.
   Litoměřice, North Bohemian Gallery of Fine Art (Severočeská Galerie Výtvarného Umění)
Litomyšl, Mus. Czech Music
   Litomyšl, Museum of Czech Music (Muzeum České Hudby) [in Litomyšl Castle]
Litomyšl, Reg. Mus.
   Litomyšl, Regional Museum (Vlastivědné Muzeum)
Little Rock, AR A. Cent.
   Little Rock, AR, Arkansas Art Center
Liverpool, Bluecoat Gal.
   Liverpool, Bluecoat Gallery
Liverpool, Lg. Obj. Mus.
   Liverpool, Large Objects Museum
Liverpool, Libs & A.
   Liverpool, Libraries and Arts [in Brown, Picton and Hornby Libraries]
Liverpool, Merseyside Co. Mus.
   Liverpool, Merseyside County Museum [name changed to Liverpool Mus. in April 1988]
Liverpool, Merseyside Mar. Mus.
   Liverpool, Merseyside Maritime Museum
Liverpool Mus.
   Liverpool, Liverpool Museum [formerly Merseyside Co. Mus.]
Liverpool, Mus. Labour Hist.
   Liverpool, Museum of Labour History

Liverpool, N. Museums & Gals Merseyside
   Liverpool, National Museums & Galleries on Merseyside [admins Lg. Obj. Mus.; Merseyside Mar. Mus.; Mus. Labour Hist.; Speke Hall, Merseyside, NT; Sudley A.G.; Liverpool Mus.; Port Sunlight, Lady Lever A.G.; Prescot, Mus. Clock- & Watch-Making]
Liverpool, St George's Hall
Liverpool, Sudley A.G.
   Liverpool, Sudley Art Gallery
Liverpool, Tate
   Liverpool, Tate Gallery Liverpool
Liverpool, U. Liverpool
   Liverpool, University of Liverpool
Liverpool, Walker A.G.
   Liverpool, Walker Art Gallery
Livorno, Bottega A.
   Livorno, Bottega d'Arte
Livorno, Bottini Olio
   Livorno, Bottini dell'Olio
Livorno, Cisternino [del Pasquale Poccianti; houses Casa della Cultura]
Livorno, Mus. Civ. Fattori
   Livorno, Museo Civico Giovanni Fattori
Livorno, Pal. Com.
   Livorno, Palazzo Comunale
Livorno, Villa Fabbricotti [incl. Mus. Civ. Fattori and Biblioteca Labronica]
Lixouri, Archaeol. Col.
   Lixouri, Archaeological Collection
Ljubljana, Archv Repub. Slovenia
   Ljubljana, Archives of the Republic of Slovenia (Arhiv Republike Slovenije)
Ljubljana, Bishop's Pal.
   Ljubljana, Bishop's Palace
Ljubljana, Gal. Mod. A.
   Ljubljana, Gallery of Modern Art (Moderna Galerija)
Ljubljana, Mun. Mus.
   Ljubljana, Municipal Museum (Mestri Muzej)
Ljubljana, N.G.
   Ljubljana, National Gallery (Narodna Galerija)
Ljubljana, N. Mus.
   Ljubljana, National Museum (Narodni Muzej)
Ljubljana, N. & U. Lib.
   Ljubljana, National and University Library (Narodna in Univerzitetna Knjižnica)
Ljubljana, Slov. Acad. Sci. & A.
   Ljubljana, Slovene Academy of Sciences & Arts (Slovenska Akademija Znanosti in Umetnosti)
Llandovery Coll.
   Llandovery, Llandovery College
Llandudno, Mostyn, A.G.
   Llandudno, Mostyn Art Gallery
Llanelli, Borough Council
Llanelli, Pub. Lib., Nevill Mem. Gal.
   Llanelli, Public Library, Nevill Memorial Gallery
Llanstumdwy, Lloyd George Mem. Mus.
   Llanstumdwy, Lloyd George Memorial Museum
Llantristant, Royal Mint
Lleida, Ajuntament
Lleida, Mus. Catedralici
   Lleida, Museu Catedralici
Lleida, Scmin.
   Lleida, Seminario
Lleida, Semin. Ant.
   Lleida, Seminario Antiguo [houses Dioc. Mus.]

Locarno, Fond. Arp
  Locarno, Fondation Arp

Locarno, Mus. Civ.
  Locarno, Museo Civico [Castello Visconteo]

Locarno, Pal. Soc. Elettrica
  Locarno, Palazzo della Società Elettrica

Locarno, Pin. Casa Rusca
  Locarno, Pinacoteca di Casa Rusca

Loches, Château
  Loches, Château de Loches

Locko Park, Drury-Lowe Col.
  Locko Park, Drury-Lowe Collection [closed in 1991]

Lodi, Bib. Laudense
  Lodi, Biblioteca Laudense [in Mus. Civ.]

Lodi, Mus. Civ.
  Lodi, Museo Civico

Lodi, Santuario Incoronata
  Lodi, Santuario dell'Incoronata

Lodi, Tesoro Incoronata
  Lodi, Tesoro dell'Incoronata

Łódź, Cent. Mus. Textiles
  Łódź, Central Museum of Textiles (Centralne Muzeum Włókiennictwa)

Łódź, Mus. A.
  Łódź, Museum of Art (Muzeum Sztuki)

Łódź, Mus. Archaeol. & Ethnog.
  Łódź, Museum of Archaeology and Ethnography (Muzeum Archeologiczne i Etnograficzne)

Łódź, Office A. Exh.
  Łódź, Office of Art Exhibitions (Biuro Wystaw Artystycznych)

Lofstede Mus.
  Lofstede, Lofstede Museum

Logan, UT State U.
  Logan, UT, Utah State University

Logroño, Mus. Rioja
  Logroño, Museo de la Rioja

Lomonosov, Oranienbaum Palace

London, Accad. It. A. & A. Applic.
  London, Accademia Italiana delle Arti e delle Arti Applicate

London, ACGB
  London, Arts Council of Great Britain

London, ACGB Col.
  London, Arts Council of Great Britain Collection

London, ACGB, Scottish Comittee
  London, ACGB, Scottish Comitteee

London, A. Council Gal.
  London, Arts Council Gallery [closed 1968]

London, Adelphi Gal.
  London, Adelphi Gallery

London, A. & F. Pears
  London, A. & F. Pears Ltd

London, Africa Cent.
  London, Africa Centre

London, Agnew's
  London, Thomas Agnew and Sons Ltd

London, AIA Gal.
  London, Artists International Association Gallery [closed]

London, Air Gal.
  London, Air Gallery

London, Alan Jacobs Gal.
  London, Alan Jacobs Gallery

London, Albemarle Gal.
  London, Albemarle Gallery

London, Alexander Gal.
  London, Alexander Gallery [closed]

London, All England Lawn Tennis & Croquet Club
  London, All England Lawn Tennis and Croquet Club

London, Alpine Club

London, Andrew Lloyd Webber A. Found.
  London, Andrew Lloyd Webber Art Foundation

London, Angela Flowers Gal.
  London, Angela Flowers Gallery Ltd

London, Anne Berthoud Gal.
  London, Anne Berthoud Gallery

London, Annely Juda F.A.
  London, Annely Juda Fine Arts

London, Anthony d'Offay Gal.
  London, Anthony d'Offay Gallery

London, Anthony Reed Gal.
  London, Anthony Reed Gallery

London, Anthony Reynolds Gal.
  London, Anthony Reynolds Gallery

London, Apsley House [houses Wellington Museum]

London, Archer Gal.
  London, Archer Gallery

London, Archit. Assoc.
  London, Architectural Association

London, Archit. Mus.
  London, Architectural Museum [closed; col. transferred to V&A in 1916]

London, Arnold Wiggins & Sons

London, Arthur Jeffress Gal.
  London, Arthur Jeffress Gallery

London, Arthur Sanderson & Sons
  London, Arthur Sanderson and Sons

London, Arthur Tooth & Sons
  London, Arthur Tooth and Sons

London, Athenaeum

London, B.A. Gal.
  London, Beaux Arts Gallery [closed]

London, Baillie Gal.
  London, Baillie Gallery

London, Banco de Bilbao

London, Bank of England

London, Bankside Gal.
  London, Bankside Gallery [Royal Society of Painters in Water-Colours; Royal Society of Painter-Etchers and Engravers]

London, Banqueting House

London, Barbers' Co.
  London, Worshipful Company of Barbers

London, Barber-Surgeons' Hall

London, Barbican A.G.
  London, Barbican Art Gallery

London, Barbican Cent.
  London, Barbican Centre

London, Barnard's Inn

London, Batsford Gal.
  London, Batsford Gallery [closed]

London, Battersea A. Cent.
  London, Battersea Arts Centre

London, Benjamin Rhodes Gal.
  London, Benjamin Rhodes Gallery

London, Ben Uri A.G.
  London, Ben Uri Art Gallery

London, Berkeley Gal.
  London, Berkeley Gallery

London, Bernard Jacobson Gal.
  London, Bernard Jacobson Gallery

London, Bernheimer F.A. Ltd
  London, Bernheimer Fine Art Ltd

London, Bethnal Green Mus.
  London, Bethnal Green Museum [name changed to Bethnal Green Mus. Childhood in 1974]

London, Bethnal Green Mus. Childhood
  London, Bethnal Green Museum of Childhood [formerly Bethnal Green Mus.]

London, BL
  London, British Library

London, Blairman & Sons
  London, H. Blairman and Sons Ltd

London, Blond F.A.
  London, Blond Fine Art Ltd

London, BL, Orient. & India Office Lib.
  London, British Library, Oriental and India Office Library

London, Bluett and Sons Gal.
  London, Bluett and Sons Gallery

London, BM
  London, British Museum

London, Brewers' Hall [Brewers' Company]

London, Brit. Council
  London, British Council

London, Brit. Govt A. Col.
  London, Foreign and Commonwealth Office

London, Brit. Inst.
  London, British Institution

London, Brod Gal.
  London, Brod Gallery

London, Brooks's Club
  London, Brooks's Club

London, Browse & Darby
  London, Browse and Darby

London, Buckingham Gal.
  London, Buckingham Gallery

London, Burlington F.A. Club
  London, Burlington Fine Arts Club [no longer exists]

London, Cam. Club.
  London, Camera Club

London, Camden A. Cent.
  London, Camden Arts Centre

London, Camerawork

London, Canada House Gal.
  London, Canada House Gallery

London, Carfax Gal.
  London, Carfax Gallery

London, Cent. Crim. Court, Old Bailey
  London, Central Criminal Court, Old Bailey

London, Charterhouse

London, Chaucer A.G.
  London, Chaucer Art Gallery

London, Chelsea Sch. A.
  London, Chelsea School of Art

London, Chiswick House

London, Chris Beetles

London, Christie's
  London, Christie, Manson & Woods Ltd

London, Christopher Drake Ltd
  London, Christopher Drake Limited

London, Christopher Hull Gal.
  London, Christopher Hull Gallery

London, Christopher Wood Gal.
  London, Christopher Wood Gallery

London, City of Westminster Archvs Cent.
    London, City of Westminster Archives Centre
London, City Poly., Fawcett Lib.
    London, City of London Polytechnic, Fawcett
    Library
London, Claus Runkel F.A.
    London, Claus Runkel Fine Art
London, Clockmakers' Co.
    London, Worshipful Company of
    Clockmakers
London, Clothworkers' Co.
    London, The Clothworkers' Company
London, Coll. Arms
    London, College of Arms
London, Coll. Prtg
    London, London College of Printing
London, Colnaghi's
    London, P & D Colnaghi & Co. Ltd
London, Commonwealth Inst.
    London, Commonwealth Institute
London, Commonwealth Relations Office
London, Contemp. Phot. Gal.
    London, Contemporary Photographers Gallery
London, Cork Investments
London, Coutts
    London, Coutts & Co.
London, Covent Gdn Gal.
    London, Covent Garden Gallery
London, Crafts Council Gal.
    London, Crafts Council Gallery
London, Crane Gal.
    London, Crane Gallery
London, Crane Kalman Gal.
    London, Crane Kalman Gallery
London, Curwen Gal.
    London, Curwen Gallery
London, Cyril Humphries Gal.
    London, Cyril Humphries Gallery
London, David Barclay
London, David Black Orient. Carpets
    London, David Black Oriental Carpets
London, David Carritt
    London, David Carritt Ltd
London, Dept Environment
    London, Department of the Environment
London, Des. Mus.
    London, Design Museum
London, Dickens House Mus.
    London, Dickens House Museum
London, Doré Gal.
    London, Doré Gallery
London, Dourdeswell's [closed]
London, Douwes F.A.
    London, Douwes Fine Art
London, Drapers' Co.
    London, Drapers' Company
London, Drapers' Hall
London, Drian Gals
    London, Drian Galleries
London, Drury Lane Theat.
    London, Drury Lane Theatre
London, Dudley Gal.
    London, Dudley Gallery
London, Dulwich Pict. Gal.
    London, Dulwich Picture Gallery
London, Edward Speelman
    London, Edward Speelman Ltd

London, Edward Totah Gal.
    London, Edward Totah Gallery
London, E. Ham Coll.
    London, East Ham College [now Newham
    Community College]
London, Eldar Gal.
    London, Eldar Gallery [closed]
London, Eskenazi Ltd
London, Eyre and Hobhouse Gal.
    London, Eyre and Hobhouse Gallery [closed]
London, Fabian Carlsson Gal.
    London, Fabian Carlsson Gallery
London, Fan Mus.
    London, Fan Museum [Greenwich]
London, F.A. Soc.
    London, The Fine Art Society plc
London, Ferrers Gal.
    London, Ferrers Gallery
London, Fischer F.A.
    London, Fischer Fine Art Ltd
London, Fishmongers' Co.
    London, Worshipful Company of
    Fishmongers
London, Fishmongers' Hall
London, Flavia Ormond F.A.
    London, Flavia Ormond Fine Art
London, Flowers E.
    London, Flowers East
London, Forbes Mag. Col.
    London, Forbes Magazine Collection
London, Foundling Hosp.
    London, Foundling Hospital [Thomas Coram
    Foundation]
London, Fr. Gal.
    London, French Gallery [closed]
London, Friends House
London, Fr. Inst.
    London, French Institute
London, Gainsborough Gals
    London, Gainsborough Galleries
London, Gal. One
    London, Gallery One
London, Garrick Club
London, Geffrye Mus.
    London, Geffrye Museum
London, Geol. Mus.
    London, Geological Museum
London, Gibson F.A.
    London, Gibson Fine Art [Thomas Gibson]
London, Gillian Jason Gal.
    London, Gillian Jason Gallery
London, Gimpel Fils
    London, Gimpel Fils Ltd
London, Girdlers' Co.
    London, Worshipful Company of Girdlers
London, Goethe-Inst.
    London, Goethe-Institut
London, Goldsmiths' Co.
    London, Worshipful Company of Goldsmiths
London, Goldsmiths' Coll.
    London, Goldsmiths' College
London, Goldsmiths' Gal.
    London, Goldsmiths' Gallery
London, Goupil Gals
    London, Goupil Galleries

London, Grabowski Gal.
    London, Grabowski Gallery
London, Grafton Gals
    London, Grafton Galleries [closed]
London, Grob Gal.
    London, Grob Gallery
London, Grocers' Hall [Worshipful Company of
Grocers]
London, Grosvenor Gal.
    London, Grosvenor Gallery [Sevenarts Ltd]
London, Guildhall
London, Guildhall A.G.
    London, Guildhall Art Gallery
London, Guildhall A.G. Store
    London, Corporation of London, Guildhall
    Art Gallery Store
London, Guildhall, Corp. London Rec. Office
    London, Guildhall, Corporation of London
    Records Office
London, Guildhall Lib.
    London, Guildhall Library [houses Print
    Room]
London, Guy's Hosp.
    London, Guy's Hospital
London, Hamilton Gals
    London, Hamilton Galleries
London, Hampton Court Pal.
    London, Hampton Court Palace
London, Hanover Gal.
    London, Hanover Gallery
London, Harrow Sch.
    London, Harrow School
London, Haslam & Whiteway's
    London, Haslam and Whiteway's Ltd
London, Hayward Gal.
    London, Hayward Gallery
London, Hazlitt, Gooden & Fox
    London, Hazlitt, Gooden and Fox
London, Heatherley Sch. F.A.
    London, Heatherley School of Fine Art
London, Heim Gal.
    London, Heim Gallery
London, Heinz Gal.
    London, Heinz Gallery
London, Helikon Gal.
    London, Helikon Gallery [closed]
London, Hoare & Co., Archv
    London, C. Hoare and Co., Archive
London, Holophusikon [closed; formerly Leverian
Mus.]
London, Horniman Mus. & Lib.
    London, Horniman Museum and Library
London, Hunterian Mus.
    London, Hunterian Museum, Royal College of
    Surgeons
London, ICA
    London, Institute of Contemporary Arts
London, Imp. Gal. A.
    London, Imperial Gallery of Art
London, Imp. War Mus.
    London, Imperial War Museum
London, India Office Lib.
    London, India Office Library [housed in BL
    since 1982]
London, Inst. Civ. Engin.
    London, Institution of Civil Engineers
London, Interim A.
    London, Interim Art

London, Iraqi Cult. Cent.
 London, Iraqi Cultural Centre [closed 1990]

London, Islam. Cult. Cent.
 London, Islamic Cultural Centre

London, Jewel Tower [in Westminster Abbey precincts]

London, Jew. Mus.
 London, Jewish Museum

London, Jews' Hosp.
 London, Jews' Hospital and Orphan Asylum

London, John Mitchell & Sons
 London, John Mitchell and Sons Ltd

London, Johnny van Haeften
 London, Johnny van Haeften Ltd

London, JPL

London, Juda Rowan Gal.
 London, Juda Rowan Gallery

London, Julian Hartholl

London, Karsten Schubert
 London, Karsten Schubert Ltd

London, Keats House [contains Keats Memorial Library]

London, Kensington Pal.
 London, Kensington Palace

London, Kenwood House

London, Kew Pal.
 London, Kew Palace

London, Knoedler's
 London, Knoedler Fine Art

London, Kufa Gal.
 London, Kufa Gallery

London, Lambeth Archvs Dept, Minet Lib.
 London, Lambeth Archives Department, Minet Library

London, Lambeth Pal.
 London, Lambeth Palace

London, Lambeth Pal. Lib.
 London, Lambeth Palace Library

London, Lane F.A.
 London, Lane Fine Art

London, Lefevre Gal.
 London, Lefevre Gallery [Alex Reid & Lefevre Ltd]

London, Leger Gals
 London, Leger Galleries Ltd

London, Leicester Gals
 London, Leicester Galleries

London, Leighton House A.G. & Mus.
 London, Leighton House Art Gallery and Museum

London, Leverian Mus.
 London, Leverian Museum [closed 1786]

London, Library
 London, London Library

London, Lincoln's Inn

London, Linley Lib.
 London, Linley Library [Royal Horticultural Society]

London, Lisson Gal.
 London, Lisson Gallery

London, L. Koester Gal.
 London, L. Koester Gallery [closed]

London, Lloyd's

London, London Gal.
 London, London Gallery [closed 1951]

London, LRT Pension Fund Trustee Co. Ltd
 London, London Regional Transport Pension Fund Trustee Co. Ltd

London, Maas & Co.
 London, J.S. Maas and Co.

London, Maas & Son
 London, J.S. Maas and Son Ltd

London, Maclean Gal.
 London, Maclean Gallery

London, Maclean-Hobart F.A.
 London, Maclean-Hobart Fine Art

London, Madame Tussaud's
 London, Madame Tussaud's Ltd

London, Malcolm Innes Gal.
 London, Malcolm Innes Gallery

London, Mallett at Bourdon House
 London, Mallett at Bourdon House Ltd

London, Mall Gals
 London, Mall Galleries

London, Manning Gal.
 London, Manning Gallery

London, Mansard Gal.
 London, Mansard Gallery [closed]

London, Mansion House

London, Marble Hill House

London, Marlborough F.A.
 London, Marlborough Fine Art Ltd [incl. Marlborough New London Gallery]

London, Marlborough Graph. Gal.
 London, Marlborough Graphics Gallery

London, Marlborough House [Commonwealth Centre]

London, Martyn Gregory

London, Marylebone Cricket Club [MCC]

London, Marylebone Lib.
 London, Marylebone Library

London, Matthiesen F.A.
 London, Matthiesen Fine Art

London, Matt's Gal.
 London, Matt's Gallery

London, Mayor Gal.
 London, Mayor Gallery Ltd

London, Mayor Rowan Gal.
 London, Mayor Rowan Gallery [closed]

London, McRoberts & Tunnard Gal.
 London, McRoberts and Tunnard Gallery

London, Mellon Cent.
 London, Paul Mellon Centre for Studies in British Art

London, Memmo Found.
 London, Memmo Foundation

London, Mercers' Co.
 London, Mercers' Company

London, Mercury Gal.
 London, Mercury Gallery

London, Met. Police Hist. Mus.
 London, Metropolitan Police Historical Museum

London, M. Guidhuis Gal.
 London, M. Guidhuis Gallery [closed]

London, Middle Temple

London, Middx Co. Cricket Club
 London, Middlesex County Cricket Club

London, Middx U., Silver Studio Collection
 London, Middlesex University, Silver Studio Collection

London, Morris Gal.
 London, Morris Gallery

London, Morton Morris
 London, Morton Morris and Co.

London, Murray Archvs
 London, Murray Archives [John Murray, publishers]

London, Mus. London
 London, Museum of London

London, Mus. Mankind
 London, British Museum, Museum of Mankind

London, Mus. Order St John
 London, Museum of the Order of St John

London, N. Army Mus.
 London, National Army Museum

London, Nat. Hist. Mus.
 London, Natural History Museum

London, New A. Cent.
 London, New Art Centre

London, New Burlington Gals
 London, New Burlington Galleries [closed]

London, New Gal.
 London, New Gallery [closed]

London, New Grafton Gal.
 London, New Grafton Gallery

London, New Soc. Painters Wtrcols
 London, New Society of Painters in Watercolours

London, N.G.
 London, National Gallery

London, Nicola Jacobs Gal.
 London, Nicola Jacobs Gallery [closed]

London, Nigel Greenwood Gal.
 London, Nigel Greenwood Gallery

London, 9H Gal.
 London, 9H Gallery

London, N. Loan Trust
 London, National Loan Trust

London, N. Mar. Mus.
 London, National Maritime Museum [Greenwich]

London, Noortman Gal.
 London, Noortman Gallery

London, N.P.G.
 London, National Portrait Gallery

London, N.P.G. Archv
 London, National Portrait Gallery Archive

London, N.P.G. Lib.
 London, National Portrait Gallery Library

London, N. Theat.
 London, National Theatre [name changed to Royal N. Theat. in Oct 1988]

London, N. Westminster Bank
 London, National Westminster Bank

London, Oct Gal.
 London, October Gallery

London, O'Hana Gal.
 London, O'Hana Gallery

London, Olympus Gal.
 London, Olympus Gallery

London, Orient. Bronzes Ltd
 London, Oriental Bronzes Ltd

London, Orient. Club
 London, Oriental Club

London, Orleans House Gal.
 London, Orleans House Gallery

London, Oscar & Peter Johnson
 London, Oscar and Peter Johnson Ltd [Lowndes Lodge Gallery]

London, Osterley Park House

London, Owen Edgar

London, Painter-Stainers' Co.
London, Painter-Stainers' Company

London, Pal. Westminster
London, Palace of Westminster [House of Commons; House of Lords]

London, Parkin Gal.
London, Parkin Gallery [Michael Parkin F.A. Ltd]

London, Pewterers' Co.
London, Pewterers' Company

London, Photographers' Gal.
London, Photographers' Gallery Ltd

London, Piccadilly Gal.
London, Piccadilly Gallery

London, Pitshanger Manor Mus.
London, Pitshanger Manor Museum

London, Port of London Authority

London, PRO
London, Public Record Office and Museum

London, Pyms Gal.
London, Pyms Gallery

London, Queen Charlotte's Cottage

London, Queen's Gal.
London, Queen's Gallery

London, Queen's House

London, RA
London, Royal Academy of Arts [Burlington House; houses RA Archives & Library]

London, Raab Gal.
London, Raab Gallery

London, Rafael Valls

London, Ranger's House [now Eng. Her.; formerly Chesterfield House, Suffolk College]

London, RBA Gals
London, Royal Society of British Artists Galleries

London, Rebecca Hossack Gal.
London, Rebecca Hossack Gallery

London, Redfern Gal.
London, Redfern Gallery

London, RIBA
London, Royal Institute of British Architects [houses RIBA drgs col.]

London, RIBA, Heinz Gal.
London, Royal Institute of British Architects, Heinz Gallery

London, RIBA Lib.
London, Royal Institute of British Architects Library

London, Richard Green

London, Riverside Gal.
London, Riverside Gallery

London, Riverside Studios

London, Roland Browse & Delbanco
London, Roland Browse and Delbanco

London, Royal Albert Hall

London, Royal Archit. Mus.
London, Royal Architectural Museum [closed; col. transferred to V&A in 1916]

London, Royal Asiat. Soc.
London, Royal Asiatic Society

London, Royal Coll. A.
London, Royal College of Art

London, Royal Coll. Music
London, Royal College of Music

London, Royal Coll. Physicians
London, Royal College of Physicians

London, Royal Coll. Surgeons England
London, Royal College of Surgeons of England

London, Royal Exch.
London, Royal Exchange

London, Royal Exch. A.G.
London, Royal Exchange Art Gallery

London, Royal Geog. Soc.
London, Royal Geographical Society

London, Royal Holloway & Bedford New Coll.
London, University of London, Royal Holloway & Bedford New College

London, Royal Hosp.
London, Royal Hospital Chelsea

London, Royal N. Theat.
London, Royal National Theatre [formerly N. Theat.]

London, Royal Phot. Soc.
London, Royal Photographic Society [now Bath, Royal Phot. Soc.]

London, Royal Soc.
London, Royal Society

London, Royal Soc. A.
London, Royal Society of Arts

London, Royal Soc. Medic.
London, Royal Society of Medicine

London, Roy Miles Gal.
London, Roy Miles Gallery

London, Runkel–Hue–Williams Gal.
London, Runkel–Hue–Williams Gallery

London, Rutland Gal.
London, Rutland Gallery

London, Saatchi Col.
London, Saatchi Collection

London, Sackville Gal.
London, Sackville Gallery [closed]

London, Saddlers' Hall [Worshipful Company of Saddlers]

London, Salter's Co.
London, Salter's Company

London, Savannah Gal. Mod. Afr. A.
London, Savannah Gallery of Modern African Art

London, S. Bank Cent.
London, South Bank Centre

London, Sci. Mus.
London, Science Museum

London, Sci. Mus., Wellcome Mus. Hist. Medic.
London, Science Museum, Wellcome Museum of the History of Medicine

London, Serpentine Gal.
London, Serpentine Gallery

London, Shakespeare Gal.
London, Shakespeare Gallery [closed]

London, S. Kensington Mus.
London, South Kensington Museum [name changed to V&A in 1899]

London, S. Kensington Sch. A.
London, South Kensington School of Art

London, S. London A.G.
London, South London Art Gallery

London, Soane Mus.
London, Sir John Soane's Museum

London, Soc. Antiqua.
London, Society of Antiquaries of London

London, Soc. Artists GB
London, Society of Artists of Great Britain

London, Soc. Dilettanti
London, Society of Dilettanti

London, Soc. Geneal.
London, Society of Genealogists

London, Soc. Promot. Hell. & Roman Stud. Lib.
London, Societies for the Promotion of Hellenic and Roman Studies Library [U. London, Inst. Class. Stud.]

London, Somerset House

London, Sotheby's
London, Sotheby and Co. [c. 1945–17 Sept 1975 Sotheby & Co.; 17 Sept 1975–17 July 1984 Sotheby Parke Bernet & Co.; since 17 July 1984 Sotheby's]

London, Sphinx Gal.
London, Sphinx Gallery

London, Spink & Son
London, Spink and Son Ltd

London, Stafford Gal.
London, Stafford Gallery

London, St Mary's Coll.
London, St Mary's College [Strawberry Hill]

London, St Olave's & St Saviour's Grammar Sch. Found.
London, St Olave's and St Saviour's Grammar School Foundation

London, Storran Gal.
London, Storran Gallery [closed]

London, St Paul's Cathedral

London, St Paul's Sch.
London, St Paul's School

London, Swiss Cottage Lib.
London, Swiss Cottage Library

London, Sydney L. Moss Ltd

London, Syon House

London, Tate
London, Tate Gallery

London, Tate, Clore Gal.
London, Tate Gallery, Clore Gallery

London, Temple Gal.
London, Temple Gallery

London, Theat. Mus.
London, Theatre Museum

London, Thomas McLean's Gal.
London, Thomas McLean's Gallery [closed]

London, Tower
London, Tower of London

London, Tower Hamlets, St George's Town Hall

London, Tower, Royal Armouries
London, Tower of London, Royal Armouries [transferred to Leeds in 1996]

London, Trafalgar Gals
London, Trafalgar Galleries

London, Trinity House

London, 12 Duke Street Gal.
London, 12 Duke Street Gallery [closed]

London, Twenty-One Gal.
London, Twenty-One Gallery

London, U. Coll., Flaxman Gal.
London, University of London, University College, Flaxman Gallery

London, U. Coll., Inst. Archaeol.
London, University of London, University College, Institute of Archaeology

London, U. Coll., Petrie Mus.
London, University of London, University College, Petrie Museum of Egyptian Archaeology

London, U. Coll., Slade Sch. F.A.
London, University of London, University College, Slade School of Fine Art

London, U. Coll., Strang Print Room
London, University of London, University College, Strang Print Room

London, U. London, Courtauld Inst.
London, University of London, Courtauld Institute of Art

London, U. London, Courtauld Inst., Conway Lib.
London, University of London, Courtauld Institute, Conway Library

London, U. London, Courtauld Inst. Gals
London, University of London, Courtauld Institute Galleries

London, U. London, Inst. Class. Stud.
London, University of London, Institute of Classical Studies

London, U. London, Inst. Educ.
London, University of London, Institute of Education

London, U. London, Inst. Educ., Dixon Gal.
London, University of London, Institute of Education, Dixon Gallery

London, U. London, Lib.
London, University of London, Library [in Senate House]

London, U. London, SOAS
London, University of London, School of Oriental and African Studies

London, U. London, SOAS, Lib.
London, University of London, School of Oriental and African Studies, Library

London, U. London, SOAS, Percival David Found.
London, University of London, School of Oriental and African Studies, Percival David Foundation of Chinese Art

London, U. London, Warburg Inst.
London, University of London, Warburg Institute

London, United Grand Lodge of England

London, United Serv. Club
London, United Services Club

London, U. Westminster
London, University of Westminster

London, V&A
London, Victoria and Albert Museum [houses National Art Library]

London, Victoria Miro
London, Victoria Miro London

London, Vintners' Co.
London, Vintners' Company

London, Waddington Gals
London, Waddington Galleries

London, Wallace
London, Wallace Collection

London, Warren Gal.
London, Warren Gallery

London, Wartski
London, Wartski Ltd

London, Warwick A. Trust
London, Warwick Arts Trust

London, Waterman F.A.
London, Waterman Fine Art Ltd

London, Watney Col.
London, Watney Collection

London, Wellcome Inst. Lib.
London, Wellcome Institute for the History of Medicine, Library

London, Wellcome Tropic. Inst. Mus.
London, Wellcome Tropical Institute Museum [closed c. 1989]

London, Westminster Abbey

London, Westminster Abbey, Muniment Room & Lib.
London, Westminster Abbey, Muniment Room and Library

London, Westminster Abbey, Undercroft Mus.
London, Westminster Abbey, Undercroft Museum

London, Westminster Cathedral

London, Westminster Hall

London, White Allom Gals
London, White Allom Galleries

London, White Alton Gals
London, White Alton Galleries

London, Whitechapel A.G.
London, Whitechapel Art Gallery

London, Whitehall Pal.
London, Whitehall Palace [destr. 1698; only Banqueting House extant]

London, White's Club

London, Wildenstein's
London, Wildenstein and Co. Ltd

London, William Morris Gal.
London, William Morris Gallery and Brangwyn Gift [Walthamstow]

London, Woodlands A.G.
London, Woodlands Art Gallery

London Zamana Gal.
London, Zamana Gallery [closed 1992]

London, Zwemmer Gal.
London, Zwemmer Gallery [closed 1963]

London, Ont., Eldon House Mus.
London, Ont., Eldon House Museum

London, Ont., Lawson Mus.
London, Ont., Lawson Museum

London, Ont., Pub. Lib. & A. Mus.
London, Ont., Public Library and Art Museum [now separate lib. & mus.]

London, Ont., Pub. Libs
London, Ont., Public Libraries [formerly connected with A. Mus.]

London, Ont., Reg. A. G.
London, Ont., London Regional Art Gallery [formerly part of Pub. Lib.]

London, Ont., Reg. A. & Hist. Museums
London, Ont., Regional Art and Historical Museums [admins Eldon House Mus.; Lawson Mus.; Reg. A.G.]

London, U. W. Ont., McIntosh A.G.
London, Ont., University of Western Ontario, McIntosh Art Gallery

Londonderry, Orchard Gal.
Londonderry, Orchard Gallery

Londonderry, Tower Mus.
Londonderry, Tower Museum

Long Beach, CA, Mus. A.
Long Beach, CA, Museum of Art

Long Beach, CA State U., A. Gals
Long Beach, CA, California State University, The Art Galleries [name changed to A. Mus. & Gals in 1977; changed to CA State U., A. Mus. in 1981]

Long Beach, CA State U., A. Mus.
Long Beach, CA, California State University, University Art Museum

Long Beach, CA State U., A. Mus. & Gals
Long Beach, CA, California State University, Art Museum and Galleries [name changed to CA State U., A. Mus. in 1981]

Long Island, NY, Bradley Martin Col.
Long Island, NY, Bradley Martin Collection

Longleat House, Wilts, Archv
Longleat House, Wilts, Longleat Archive

Lons-le-Saunier, Mus. B.-A.
Lons-le-Saunier, Musée des Beaux-Arts

Loosdrecht, Kasteel-Mus. Sypesteyn
Loosdrecht, Kasteel-Museum Sypesteyn [van Sypesteyn-Stichting]

Lopburi, N. Mus.
Lopburi, National Museum

Lopburi, Somdet Phra Narai Maharat N. Mus.
Lopburi, Somdet Phra Narai Maharat National Museum

Loppem, Sticht. van Caloen
Loppem, Stichting van Caloen

Loreto, Archv Stor. S Casa
Loreto, Archivio Storico della Santa Casa

Loreto, Pal. Apostolico
Loreto, Palazzo Apostolico ed Archivio Storico della Santa Casa

Loreto, Santuario S Casa, Bib.
Loreto, Santuario della Santa Casa, Biblioteca

Loreto, S Casa
Loreto, Santa Casa

Loreto, Tesoro

Los Angeles, ACA Her. Gal.
Los Angeles, CA, ACA Heritage Gallery [closed]

Los Angeles, CA, Aerospace Mus.
Los Angeles, CA, Aerospace Museum

Los Angeles, CA, Armand Hammer Mus. A.
Los Angeles, CA, Armand Hammer Museum of Art and Cultural Center

Los Angeles, CA, Asher-Faure

Los Angeles, CA, Broida Trust
Los Angeles, CA, Edward R. Broida Trust

Los Angeles, CA, Buckminster Fuller Inst.
Los Angeles, CA, Buckminster Fuller Institute

Los Angeles, CA, Cafe Gal.
Los Angeles, CA, Cafe Galleria

Los Angeles, CA, Coconut Grove

Los Angeles, CA, Co. Mus. A.
Los Angeles, CA, County Museum of Art [incl. Robert Gore Rifkind Center for German Expressionist Studies]

Los Angeles, CA, Co. Mus. Sci. & Indust.
Los Angeles, CA, County Museum of Science and Industry [now CA Mus. Sci. & Indust.]

Los Angeles, CA, Copley Gals
Los Angeles, CA, Copley Galleries [closed]

Los Angeles, CA, Doizaki Gal.
Los Angeles, CA, Doizaki Gallery

Los Angeles, CA, Esther Robies Gal.
Los Angeles, CA, Esther Robies Gallery

Los Angeles, CA, Eugenia Butler Gal.
Los Angeles, CA, Eugenia Butler Gallery

Los Angeles, CA, Ferus Gal.
Los Angeles, CA, Ferus Gallery

Los Angeles, CA, Frederick Weisman Co.
Los Angeles, CA, Frederick Weisman Company

Los Angeles, CA, Gal. K
Los Angeles, CA, Gallery K

Los Angeles, CA, Getty Mus.
Los Angeles, CA, J. Paul Getty Museum

Los Angeles, CA, Goldfield Gals
Los Angeles, CA, Goldfield Galleries

Los Angeles, CA, Heb. Un. Coll. Skirball Mus.
Los Angeles, CA, Hebrew Union College Skirball Museum

Los Angeles, CA, ICA
Los Angeles, CA, Institute of Contemporary Art

Los Angeles, CA, Jack Rutberg F.A.
Los Angeles, CA, Jack Rutberg Fine Arts

Los Angeles, CA, Loyola Marymount U., A.G.
Los Angeles, CA, Loyola Marymount University, Art Gallery

Los Angeles, Margo Leavin Gal.
Los Angeles, CA, Margo Leavin Gallery

Los Angeles, CA, Molly Barnes Gal.
Los Angeles, CA, Molly Barnes Gallery

Los Angeles, CA, Mus. Contemp. A.
Los Angeles, CA, Museum of Contemporary Art

Los Angeles, CA, Music Cent.
Los Angeles, CA, Music Center of Los Angeles County

Los Angeles, CA Mus. Sci. & Indust.
Los Angeles, CA, California Museum of Science and Industry [formerly Co. Mus. Sci. & Indust.]

Los Angeles, CA, Nat. Hist. Mus.
Los Angeles, CA, Natural History Museum of Los Angeles County

Los Angeles, CA, Norton Simon A. Found.
Los Angeles, CA, Norton Simon Art Foundation

Los Angeles, CA, Norton Simon Found.
Los Angeles, CA, Norton Simon Foundation

Los Angeles, CA, Norton Simon Mus. A.
Los Angeles, CA, Norton Simon Museum of Art [now Norton Simon A. Found.]

Los Angeles, CA, Now Gal.
Los Angeles, CA, Now Gallery

Los Angeles, Pacific Asia Mus.
Los Angeles, CA, Pacific Asia Museum

Los Angeles, CA, Parsons School Des.
Los Angeles, CA, Parsons School of Design

Los Angeles, CA, Schoenberg Inst.
Los Angeles, CA, Arnold Schoenberg Institute

Los Angeles, CA, Stendhal Gals
Los Angeles, CA, Stendhal Galleries

Los Angeles, CA, Tibor de Nagy Gals
Los Angeles, CA, Tibor de Nagy Galleries

Los Angeles, UCLA
Los Angeles, University of California

Los Angeles, UCLA, Dickson A. Cent.
Los Angeles, University of California, Dickson Art Center

Los Angeles, UCLA, Fowler Mus. Cult. Hist.
Los Angeles, University of California, Fowler Museum of Cultural History [formerly Mus. Cult. Hist.]

Los Angeles, UCLA, Grunwald Cent. Graph. A.
Los Angeles, University of California, Grunwald Center for the Graphic Arts

Los Angeles, UCLA, Lab. Ethnic A. & Technol.
Los Angeles, University of California Laboratory of Ethnic Arts and Technology [name changed to Mus. Cult. Hist. then Fowler Mus. Cult. Hist.]

Los Angeles, UCLA, Mus. Cult. Hist.
Los Angeles, University of California, Museum of Cultural History [name changed to Fowler Mus. Cult. Hist. in 1992]

Los Angeles, UCLA, Wight A.G.
Los Angeles, University of California, Frederick S. Wight Art Gallery

Los Angeles, USC, Fisher Gal.
Los Angeles, University of Southern California, Fisher Gallery [Elizabeth Holmes Fisher]

Los Caobos, Gal. A.N.
Los Caobos, Galería de Arte Nacional [in former Museo de Bellas Artes]

Los Caobos, Mus. B.A.
Los Caobos, Museo de Bellas Artes [Mus. Los Caobos]

Los Caobos, Mus. Ciencias Nat.
Los Caobos, Museo de Ciencias Naturales [in Fundación Museo de Ciencias]

Louhans, Apothicairie l'Hôtel-Dieu
Louhans, Apothicairie de l'Hôtel-Dieu

Louisville, KY, Speed A. Mus.
Louisville, KY, J.B. Speed Art Museum

Louny, Benedikt Rejt Gal.
Louny, Benedikt Rejt Gallery (Galerie Benedikta Rejta)

Lourdes, Mus. Pyrénéen
Lourdes, Musée Pyrénéen

Louvain: see Leuven

Louvain-la-Neuve: see Leuven

Louviers, Mus. Mun.
Louviers, Musée Municipal de Louviers

Lovech, Hist. Mus.
Lovech, Historical Museum (Istoricheski Muzej)

Lovere, Gal. Accad. B.A. Tadini
Lovere, Galleria dell'Accademia di Belle Arti Tadini

Lower Hutt, Dowse Mus.
Lower Hutt, Dowse Art Museum [in Civic Centre]

Łowicz, Pal.
Łowicz, Palace

LRT Pension Fund Trustee Co. Ltd: see London

Luanda, Humbiumbi Gal.
Luanda, Humbiumbi Gallery

Luanda, Mus. N. Antropol.
Luanda, Museu Nacional de Antropologia

Luang Prabang, Royal Pal.
Luang Prabang, Royal Palace [houses National Museum of Laos]

Lübeck, Bib. Hansestadt
Lübeck, Bibliothek der Hansestadt Lübeck

Lübeck, Mus. Behnhaus
Lübeck, Museum Behnhaus

Lübeck, Mus. Dom
Lübeck, Museum am Dom

Lübeck, Mus. Drägerhaus
Lübeck, Museum Drägerhaus

Lübeck, Mus. Holstentor
Lübeck, Museum in Holstentor

Lübeck, Mus. Kst & Kultgesch.
Lübeck, Museum für Kunst und Kulturgeschichte der Hansestadt Lübeck [admins Katharinenkirche; Mus. Behnhaus; Mus. Drägerhaus; Mus. Holstentor; St Annen-Mus.]

Lübeck, Nathist. Mus.
Lübeck, Naturhistorisches Museum

Lübeck, Rathaus

Lübeck, Schifferges.
Lübeck, Schiffergesellschaft

Lübeck, St Annen-Mus.
Lübeck, Sankt-Annen-Museum

Lublin, A. Exh. Office
Lublin, Art Exhibition Office (Galeria B.W.A.)

Lublin, Distr. Mus.
Lublin, District Museum (Muzeum Okręgowe)

Lublin, Gal. Labirynt
Lublin, Galeria Labirynt [Dom Kultury]

Lublin, N. Mus. Majdan Concent. Camp
Lublin, National Museum of the Majdan Concentration Camp (Państwowe Muzeum na Majdanku)

Lublin, Skansen Mus.
Lublin, Skansen Museum of the Lublin Countryside

Lucca, Archv Stato
Lucca, Archivio di Stato

Lucca, Bib. Capitolare
Lucca, Biblioteca Capitolare

Lucca, Bib. Stat.
Lucca, Biblioteca Statale di Lucca

Lucca, Col. Mazzarosa
Lucca, Collezione Mazzarosa

Lucca, Mus. Opera Duomo
Lucca, Museo dell'Opera del Duomo

Lucca, Mus. & Pin. N.
Lucca, Museo e Pinacoteca Nazionale [in former Palazzo Mansi]

Lucca, Pal. Orsetti
Lucca, Palazzo Orsetti

Lucca, Pal. Prefettura
Lucca, Palazzo della Prefettura [Palazzo Provinciale]

Lucca, Villa Guinigi
Lucca, Museo Nazionale di Villa Guinigi

Lucera, Mus. Archeol. Fiorelli
Lucera, Museo Archeologico Giuseppe Fiorelli

Lucerne, Altes Rathaus

Lucerne, Burgerbib.
Lucerne, Burgerbibliothek [in Zentralbibliothek Luzern]

Lucerne, Gal. Fischer
Lucerne, Galerie Fischer

Lucerne, Gal. Rosengart
Lucerne, Galerie Rosengart

Lucerne, Hans-Erni Mus.
Lucerne, Hans-Erni Museum [part of Vekehrs Haus der Schweiz]

Lucerne, Hist. Mus.
Lucerne, Historisches Museum [in Altes Zeughaus]

Lucerne, Kstmus.
Lucerne, Kunstmuseum

Lucerne, Panorama

Lucerne, Zentralbib.
Lucerne, Zentralbibliothek Lucerne

Lucignano, Mus. Civ.
Lucignano, Museo Civico

Lucknow, State Mus.
Lucknow, State Museum

Ludwigsburg, Schloss
Ludwigsburg, Schloss Ludwigsburg

Ludwigshafen, Hack-Mus. & Städt. Kstsamml.
Ludwigshafen, Wilhelm Hack-Museum und Städtische Kunstsammlungen

Ludwigshafen, Städt. Kstsamml.
Ludwigshafen, Städtische Kunstsammlungen

Ludwigslust, Schloss

Lugano, Banca del Gottardo

Lugano, Bib. Cant. Ticino
Lugano, Biblioteca Cantonale del Ticino

Lugano, Col. Thyssen-Bornemisza
Lugano, Collection Baron Thyssen-Bornemisza [in Villa Favorita, Castagnola]: *see also* Madrid, Mus. Thyssen-Bornemisza

Lugano, Fond. Caccia
Lugano, Fondazione Caccia

Lugano, Mus. Cant. A.
Lugano, Museo Cantonale d'Arti

Lugano, Mus. Civ. B.A.
Lugano, Museo Civico di Belle Arti [Villa Ciani]

Lugano, Villa Malpensata

Lugo, Bib. Fabrizio Trisi
Lugo, Biblioteca Fabrizio Trisi

Lugo, Mus. Dioc.
Lugo, Museo Diocesano [in Seminario]

Luján, Complejo Mus. Gráf. 'Enrique Udaondo'
Luján, Complejo Museo Gráfico 'Enrique Udaondo'

Luján, Mus. B.A.
Luján, Museo de Bellas Artes

Luján, Mus. Cera Vergen
Luján, Museo de Cera de la Vergen de Luján

Lund, Ksthall
Lund, Konsthall

Lund, Kstmus., Arkv Dek. Kst
Lund, Konstmuseum, Arkiv för Dekorativ Konst

Lund, Kulthist. Mus.
Lund, Kulturhistoriska Museum [Kulturen]

Lund, Svenstorp Slott

Lund, Ubib., De la Gardie Arkv
Lund, Lunds Universitetsbibliotek De la Gardie Arkiv

Lund U., Hist. Mus.
Lund, Lunds Universitets, Historiska Museum

Lund U., Kstmus.
Lund, Lunds Universitets Konstmuseum

Lüneburg, Inst. Ndt. Kultwerk
Lüneburg, Institut Nordestdeutsches Kulturwerk

Lüneburg, Mus. Fürstenturm
Lüneburg, Museum für den Fürstenturm Lüneburg

Lüneburg, Ostpreuss. Landesmus.
Lüneburg, Ostpreussisches Landesmuseum

Lüneburg, Rathaus [houses Stadtarchiv]

Lüneburg, Stadtarchv
Lüneburg, Stadtarchiv [in Rathaus]

Lunéville, Mus. Lunéville
Lunéville, Musée de Lunéville [Château de Lunéville]

Luni, Mus. N.
Luni, Museo Nazionale

Luoyang, Mun. Mus.
Luoyang, Municipal Museum

Lusaka, Indep. Celeb. Dir.
Lusaka, Independence Celebrations Directorate

Lusaka, Mpapa Gal.
Lusaka, Mpapa Gallery

Lusaka, Zintu Mus.
Lusaka, Zintu Museum

Luxembourg, Bib. N.
Luxembourg, Bibliothèque Nationale

Luxembourg, Mus. N. Hist. & A.
Luxembourg, Musée National d'Histoire et d'Art [name changed from Musée de l'Etat in 1988]

Luxembourg, Mus. Pescatore
Luxembourg, Musée Jean-Pierre Pescatore

Luxembourg, Pal. Grand-Ducal
Luxembourg, Palais Grand-Ducal

Luxor Mus.
Luxor, Museum

L'viv, Acad. Sci., Lib.
L'viv, Academy of Sciences, Scientific Library

L'viv, A.G.
L'viv, Art Gallery

L'viv, Hist. Mus.
L'viv, Historical Museum

L'viv, Icon Mus.
L'viv, Icon Museum

L'viv, Mus. Ethnog., A. & Crafts Ukrain. Acad. Sci.
L'viv, Museum of Ethnography, Arts and Crafts of the Ukrainian Academy of Sciences

L'viv, Mus. Ukrain. A.
L'viv, Museum of Ukrainian Art

L'viv, N. Mus.
L'viv, National Museum

L'viv, Pict. Gal.
L'viv, Picture Gallery

L'vov: the city was renamed L'viv in 1991; *see* L'viv

Lykosoura, Archaeol. Mus.
Lykosoura, Archaeological Museum

Lyon, Acad. Sci., B.-Lett. & A.
Lyon, Académie des Sciences, Belles-Lettres et Arts

Lyon, Archvs Dépt. Rhône
Lyon, Archives Départementales du Rhône

Lyon, Archvs Dioc.
Lyon, Archives Diocésaines

Lyon, Bib. Mun.
Lyon, Bibliothèque Municipale

Lyon, Conserv. N. Sup. Musique
Lyon, Conservatoire National Supérieur de Musique de Lyon

Lyon, Ecole N. B.-A.
Lyon, Ecole Nationale des Beaux-Arts

Lyon, Espace Lyon. A. Contemp.
Lyon, Espace Lyonnais d'Art Contemporain

Lyon, Mus. A. Contemp.
Lyon, Musée d'Art Contemporain de Lyon

Lyon, Mus. A. Déc.
Lyon, Musée des Arts Décoratifs

Lyon, Mus. B.-A.
Lyon, Musée des Beaux-Arts

Lyon, Mus. Civilis. Gallo-Romaine
Lyon, Musée de la Civilisation Gallo-Romaine

Lyon, Musées Chambre Commerce & Indust.
Lyon, Musées de la Chambre de Commerce et d'Industrie [admins Mus. A. Déc.; Mus. Hist. Tissus]

Lyon, Mus. Gardagne
Lyon, Musée Gardagne

Lyon, Mus. Hist.
Lyon, Musée Historique de Lyon

Lyon, Mus. Hist. Tissus
Lyon, Musée Historique des Tissus

Lyon, Mus. Hospices
Lyon, Musée des Hospices Civils de Lyon

Lyon, Mus. Imprimerie & Banque
Lyon, Musée de l'Imprimerie et de la Banque

Lyon, Mus. St Pierre A. Contemp.
Lyon, Musée Saint Pierre d'Art Contemporain

Lyon, Pal. Commerce
Lyon, Palais du Commerce

Lyon, Place Bellecour

Lyon, U. Lyon II
Lyon, Université Lumière Lyon II

Lyon, U. Lyon Lettres & Droit
Lyon, Université Lyon Lettres et Droit [title of U. until 1968]

Lyon, U. Lyon III
Lyon, Université Lyon III [Université Jean Moulin]

Maa-Palaeokastro, Archaeol. Mus.
Maa-Palaeokastro, Archaeological Museum

Maarssen, Slot Zuylen

Maastricht, Bonnefantenmus.
Maastricht, Bonnefantenmuseum [Stichting Limburgs Museum voor Kunst en Oudheden]

Maastricht, Exh. & Congr. Cent.
Maastricht, Exhibition and Congress Centre

Maastricht, Rijksarchf Limburg
Maastricht, Rijksarchief in Limburg

Maastricht, Rijksarchf Limburg, St Servaaskapittel Archf
Maastricht, Rijksarchief in Limburg, St Servaaskapittel Archief

Maastricht, Schatkamer St-Servaasbasiliek
Maastricht, Schatkamer van de Sint-Servaasbasiliek

Maastricht, Vrijthof 49 Gal.
Maastricht, Vrijthof 49 Galerie

Macclesfield, Town Hall

Maceió, Mus. Polícia
Maceió, Museu da Polícia

Macerata, Mus. Carrozza
Macerata, Museo della Carrozza

Macerata, Pal. Buonaccorsi
Macerata, Palazzo Buonaccorsi [houses Accademia di Belle Arti & Accademia dei Catenati]

Macerata, Pal. Ricci
Macerata, Palazzo Ricci

Macerata, Pin. & Mus. Com.
Macerata, Pinacoteca e Musei Comunali [Civica Pinacoteca]

Machabeng, High Sch.
Machabeng, Machabeng High School

Machida, City Int. Prt Gal.
Machida, City International Print Gallery (Shiritsu Kokusai Hanga Bijutsukan)

Machida, City Mus. Graph. A.
Machida, City Museum of Graphic Arts

Machynlleth, MOMA Wales
Machynlleth, Museum of Modern Art, Wales

Macomb, W. IL U.
Macomb, IL, Western Illinois University

Mâcon, Mus. Mun. Ursulines
Mâcon, Musée Municipal des Ursulines

Madison, WI, A. Cent.
Madison, WI, Madison Art Center

Madison, U. WI
Madison, WI, University of Wisconsin

Madison, U. WI, Elvehjem A. Cent.
Madison, WI, University of Wisconsin, Elvehjem Art Center

Madras, Cent. Indust. Mus.
Madras, Central Industrial Museum

Madrid, Mus. Romántico
Madrid, Museo Romántico [Fundaciones Vega-Inclán]

Madrid, Mus. Sorolla
Madrid, Museo Sorolla

Madrid, Mus. Thyssen-Bornemisza
Madrid, Museo Thyssen-Bornemisza [in Pal. Villahermosa]

Madirid, Pal. Altamira
Madrid, Palacio Altamira

Madirid, Pal. Arzobisp.
Madrid, Palacio Arzobispal

Madrid, Pal. Congr. Diput.
Madrid, Palacio del Congreso de los Diputados [now Pal. de las Cortes]

Madrid, Pal. Cristal
Madrid, Palacio de Cristal

Madrid, Pal. de las Cortes
Madrid, Palacio de las Cortes [Senate; formerly Pal. Congr. Diput.]

Madrid, Pal. Duque del Infantado
Madrid, Palacio Duque del Infantado

Madrid, Pal. Episcopal
Madrid, Palacio Episcopal

Madrid, Pal. Liria, Col. Casa Alba
Madrid, Palacio Liria, Colección Casa de Alba

Madrid, Pal. Moncloa
Madrid, Palacio de la Moncloa

Madrid, Pal. Pardo
Madrid, Palacio del Pardo

Madrid, Pal. Real
Madrid, Palacio Real de Madrid [Palacio de Oriente]

Madrid, Pal. Riofrío
Madrid, Palacio de Riofrío

Madrid, Pal. Velázquez
Madrid, Palacio Velázquez

Madrid, Pal. Villahermosa
Madrid, Palacio de Villahermosa [houses Mus. Thyssen- Bornemisza]

Madrid, Pant. Hombres Ilustres
Madrid, Pantéon de Hombres Ilustres [Pantheon of Atocha]

Madrid, Paraninfo Auditorium

Madrid, Paseo Castellana
Madrid, Paseo della Castellana

Madrid, Patrm. N.
Madrid, Patrimonio Nacional

Madrid, Prado
Madrid, Museo del Prado [Museo Nacional de Pintura y Escultura]

Madrid, Real Acad. Hist.
Madrid, Real Academia de la Historia

Madrid, Real Acad. S Fernando
Madrid, Real Academia de Bellas Artes de San Fernando

Madrid, Real Acad. S Fernando, Mus.
Madrid, Real Academia de Bellas Artes de San Fernando, Museo

Madrid, Real Armería

Madrid, Real Jard. Botán.
Madrid, Real Jardín Botánico

Madrid, Salas Exp. Dir. Gen. B.A.
Madrid, Salas de Exposiciones de la Dirección General de Bellas Artes

Madrid, Salas Exp. Pal. Bibs & Museos
Madrid, Salas de Exposiciones del Palacio de Bibliotecas y Museos [housed with Bib. N. and Mus. Arqueol. N.]

Madrid, Salas Picasso
Madrid, Salas Pablo Ruiz Picasso

Madrid, S Antonio Abad
Madrid, San Antonio Abad

Madrid, Serv. Hist. Mil., Bib.
Madrid, Servicio Histórico Militar, Biblioteca

Madrid, Soc. Amigos A.
Madrid, Sociedad de Amigos de Arte

Madrid, Soc. Artistas Iber.
Madrid, Sociedad de Artistas Ibericos

Madrid, Teat. N.
Madrid, Teatro Nacional

Madrid, Teat. Real
Madrid, Teatro Real

Madrid, U. Complutense
Madrid, Universidad Complutense de Madrid

Madrid, U. Complutense, Escuela Téc. Sup. Arquit.
Madrid, Universidad Complutense, Escuela Técnica Superior de Arquitectura

Madurai, Sri Minakshi Sundareshvara Temple Mus.
Madurai, Sri Minakshi Sundareshvara Temple Museum

Mafra, Pal. N.
Mafra, Palacio Nacional de Mafra

Magdeburg, Kaiser-Friedrich-Mus.
Magdeburg, Kaiser-Friedrich-Museum

Magdeburg, Kulthist. Mus.
Magdeburg, Kulturhistorisches Museum

Magdeburg, Städt. Mus.
Magdeburg, Städtisches Museum

Magny-en-Vexin, St Martin

Magny-les-Hameaux, Mus. N. Granges Port-Royal
Magny-les-Hameaux, Musée National des Granges de Port- Royal [abbey of Port-Royal-les-Champs]

Maidstone, Mus. & A.G.
Maidstone, Museum and Art Gallery

Mainz, Altertmus. & Gemäldegal.
Mainz, Altertumsmuseum und Gemäldegalerie

Mainz, Bischöf. Dom- & Diözmus.
Mainz, Bischöfliches Dom- und Diözesanmuseum

Mainz, Erlehmbach Mus.
Mainz, Erlehmbach Museum

Mainz, Gutenberg-Mus.
Mainz, Gutenberg-Museum

Mainz, Johannes Gutenberg-U.
Mainz, Johannes Gutenberg-Universität

Mainz, Johannes Gutenberg-U., Kstgesch. Inst.
Mainz, Johannes Gutenberg-Universität, Kunstgeschichte Institut

Mainz, Landesmus.
Mainz, Landesmuseum Mainz [Mittelrheinisches Landesmuseum; houses Landesgalerie & Graphische Sammlung]

Mainz, Röm.-Ger. Zentmus.
Mainz, Römisch-Germanisches Zentralmuseum [Forschungsinstitut für Vor- und Frühgeschichte]

Makati, Ayala Mus.
Makati, Ayala Museum of Philippine History and Iconographic Archives

Makhachkala, Dagestan Mus. F.A.
Makhachkala, Dagestan Museum of Fine Art

Makkum, Fries Aardewerkmus. De Waag
Makkum, Fries Aardewerkmuseum De Waag

Malacca, Chan Mus.
Malacca, Chan Museum

Malacca, Hist. Mus.
Malacca, Malacca Historical Museum

Malacca, State Mus.
Malacca, Malacca State Museum [Cultural Museum]

Málaga, Mus. Arqueol. Prov.
Málaga, Museo Arqueológico Provincial

Málaga, Mus. Prov. B.A.
Málaga, Museo Provincial de Bellas Artes

Malahide Castle
Malahide, Malahide Castle

Malatya Mus.
Malatya, Malatya Museum

Malbork, Castle Mus.
Malbork, Castle Museum

Malcésine, Castello Scaligero

Maldonado, Mus. Mazzoni
Maldonado, Museo Mazzoni

Maldonado, Mus. S Fernando
Maldonado, Museo San Fernando

Male, Republic of Maldives, N. Mus.
Male, Republic of Maldives, National Museum

Malhar, Archaeol. Surv. India Site Mus.
Malhar, Archaeological Survey of India Site Museum

Malibu, CA, Getty Mus.
Malibu, CA, J. Paul Getty Museum

Malines: see Mechelen

Malmaison, Château N.
Malmaison, Château National de Malmaison [houses Musée de Malmaison]

Malmaison, Mus. N. Château Bois-Préau
Malmaison, Musée National du Château de Bois-Préau

Malmö, Akvarium

Malmö, Colibi Gal.
Malmö, Colibi Gallery [closed]

Malmö, Kommendanthuset

Malmö, Ksthall
Malmö, Konsthall

Malmö, Kstmus.
Malmö, Konstmuseum

Malmö, Malmöhus

Malmö Museums
Malmö, Malmö Museums [admins Akvarium; Kommendanthuset; Kstmus.; Nathist. Mus.; Sjöfartsmus.; Stadsmus.; Tek. Mus.; Vagnmus.]

Malmö, Nathist. Mus.
Malmö, Naturhistoriska Museum

Malmö, Radhus

Malmö, Rooseum [Contemporary Arts Centre]

Malmö, Sjöfartsmus.
Malmö, Sjöfartsmuseum

Malmö, Stadsmus.
Malmö, Stadsmuseum

Malmö, Tek. Mus.
Malmö, Tekniska Museum

Malmö, Vagnmus.
Malmö, Vagnmuseum

Mamallapuram, Archaeol. Mus.
Mamallapuram, Archaeological Museum

Managua, Banco Cent. de Nicaragua
Managua, Banco Central de Nicaragua

Managua, Cascada
Managua, La Cascada [closed]

Managua, Cent. Conven. Olaf Palme
Managua, Centro de Convenciones Olaf Palme

Managua, Cent. Pop. Cult.
Managua, Centro Popular de Cultura

Managua, Ciac [closed]

Managua, Contemporánta [closed]

Managua, Creativa [closed]

Managua, Cueva A.
Managua, Cueva del Arte [closed]

Managua, Culturama [closed]

Managua, Expo Prensa
Managua, Expo la Prensa

Managua, Gal. Casa Fernando Gordillo
Managua, Galería Casa Fernando Gordillo

Managua, Gal. Molejón
Managua, Galería Molejón

Managua, Gal. Pepitos
Managua, Galería Pepitos

Managua, Gal. Praxis
Managua, Galería Praxis

Managua, Inst. Nicaragüense Cult.
Managua, Instituto Nicaragüense de Cultura

Managua, Min. Cult., Gal. Ricardo Aviles
Managua, Ministry of Culture, Galería Ricardo
Aviles

Managua, Mus. Antropol.
Managua, Museo de Antropología

Managua, Mus. Hist. Revol.
Managua, Museo de la Historia de la
Revolución

Managua, Mus. Julio Cortázar A. Mod. Am. Lat.
Managua, Museo Julio Cortázar del Arte
Moderno de América Latina

Managua, Mus. Las Ruinas
Managua, Museo Las Ruinas

Managua, Plural B.A.
Managua, Plural de Bellas Artes [closed]

Managua, Tagüe [closed]

Managua, Teat. N. Ruben Dario
Managua, Teatro Nacional Ruben Dario

Manama, Bahrain N. Mus.
Manama, Bahrain National Museum

Manata, A.G.
Manata, Art Gallery

Manchester, Athenaeum Gal.
Manchester, Athenaeum Gallery [Gallery of
Modern Art]

Manchester, C.A.G.
Manchester, City Art Gallery

Manchester, Cent. Lib.
Manchester, Central Library

Manchester City A. Gals
Manchester, Manchester City Art Galleries
[admins Athenaeum Gal.; C.A.G.; Fletcher
Moss Mus. & A.G.; Gal. Eng. Cost.; Heaton
Hall; Queen's Park A.G.; Wythenshawe Hall]

Manchester, Cornerhouse

Manchester, Fletcher Moss Mus. & A.G.
Manchester, Fletcher Moss Museum and Art
Gallery

Manchester, Gal. Eng. Cost.
Manchester, Gallery of English Costume

Manchester, Heaton Hall

Manchester, John Rylands U. Lib.
Manchester, John Rylands University Library
of Manchester

Manchester, Met. U., All Saints Lib.
Manchester, Metropolitan University, All
Saints Library

Manchester Mus.
Manchester, Manchester Museum

Manchester, Owens Coll.
Manchester, Owens College [now Victoria U.]

Manchester, Queen's Park A.G.
Manchester, Queen's Park Art Gallery

Manchester Town Hall
Manchester, Manchester Town Hall

Manchester, U. Manchester, Whitworth A.G.
Manchester, University of Manchester,
Whitworth Art Gallery

Manchester, Victoria U.
Manchester, Victoria University of Manchester

Manchester, Wythenshawe Hall

Manchester, NH, Cent. High Sch.
Manchester, NH, Manchester Central High
School

Manchester, NH, Currier Gal. A.
Manchester, NH, Currier Gallery of Art

Mandalay, State Mus.
Mandalay, State Museum

Mandsaur Fort
Mandsaur, Mandsaur Fort

Manila, Cent. of the Philippines Money Mus.
Manila, Central Bank of the Philippines Money
Museum

Manila, Cult. Cent. Philippines
Manila, Cultural Centre of the Philippines

Manila, Met. Mus.
Manila, Metropolitan Museum of Manila

Manila, N. Mus. Philippines
Manila, National Museum of the Philippines

Manila, Phil. A.G.
Manila, Philippine Art Gallery

Manila, S Augustin Mus.
Manila, San Augustin Museu

Manisa Mus.
Manisa, Manisa Museum (Manisa Müzesi)

Manizales, Exp. Perm. Cer. Indíg.
Manizales, Exposición Permanente de
Cerámica Indígena

Manizales, Mus. Hist. Caldas
Manizales, Museo Historia de Caldas

Mannheim, Altertver.
Mannheim, Altertumsverein

Mannheim, Antsaal Zeichnakad.
Mannheim, Antikensaal in der Mannheimer
Zeichnungsakademie [closed]

Mannheim, Kstver.
Mannheim, Kunstverein

Mannheim, Landesmus. Tech. & Arbeit
Mannheim, Landesmuseum für Technik und
Arbeit

Mannheim, Schloss
Mannheim, Schloss Mannheim

Mannheim, Städt. Ksthalle
Mannheim, Städtische Kunsthalle Mannheim
[Städtisches Museum]

Mannheim, Städt. Reiss-Mus.
Mannheim, Städtisches Reiss-Museum
[Zeughaus]

Manresa, Mus. Hist. Catedral
Manresa, Museo Histórico de la Catedral

Mänttä, Serlachius A. Mus.
Mänttä, Serlachius Art Museum [F.A. Found.]
(Gösta Serlachius Taidemuseo)

Mantua, Ammin. Ist. Gonzaga
Mantua, Amministrazione degli Istituti
Gonzaga a Mantova

Mantua, Archv Capitolare Cattedrale
Mantua, Archivio Capitolare della Cattedrale di
Mantova

Mantua, Archv Stato
Mantua, Archivio di Stato

Mantua, Bib. Com.
Mantua, Biblioteca Comunale

Mantua, Casa Giulio Romano
Mantua, Casa di Giulio Romano

Mantua, Duomo

Mantua, Gal. & Mus. Pal. Ducale
Mantua, Galleria e Museo del Palazzo Ducale

Mantua, Giard. Semplici
Mantua, Giardino dei Semplici

Mantua, Ist. Gonzaga
Mantua, Istituo dei Gonzaga

Mantua, Mus. Casa Mantegna
Mantua, Museo Casa di Mantegna

Mantua, Mus. Civ. Pal. Te
Mantua, Museo Civico Palazzo del Te

Mantua. Mus. Dioc.
Mantua, Museo Diocesano

Mantua, Mus. Pal. d'Arco
Mantua, Museo di Palazzo d'Arco

Mantua, Pal. Ducale
Mantua, Palazzo Ducale

Mantua, Pal. Ragione
Mantua, Palazzo della Ragione

Mantua, Pal. Te
Mantua, Palazzo del Te

Mantua, Pal. Vescovile
Mantua, Palazzo Vescovile

Maputo, Afritique

Maputo, Assoc. Moçambicana Fot.
Maputo, Associação Moçambicana de
Fotografia

Maputo, Casa Velha

Maputo, Cent. Stud. Bras.
Maputo, Centro de Studios Brasileiros

Maputo, Circulo

Maputo, Mus. A.
Maputo, Museu de Arte

Maputo, Mus. Hist. Nat.
Maputo, Museu de História Natural

Maracaibo, Cent. B.A.
Maracaibo, Centor de Bellas Artes

Maracay, Gal. Mun. A.
Maracay, Galería Municipal de Arte

Maraş, Archaeol. Mus.
Maraş, Archaeological Museum

Maraui, Aga Khan Mus. Islam. A.
Maraui, Aga Khan Museum of Islamic Arts
[State University Museum]

Marbach, Schiller-Nmus. & Dt. Litarchv
Marbach, Schiller-Nationalmuseum und
Deutsches Literaturarchiv

Marburg, Hess. Staatsarchv
Marburg, Hessisches Staatsarchiv

Marburg, Philipps-U.
Marburg, Philipps-Universität

Marburg, Schloss
Marburg, Schloss Wilhelmsbau [houses Umus.
Kultgesch.]

Marburg, Umus. Kultgesch.
Marburg, Universitätsmuseum für
Kulturgeschichte [in Schloss Wilhelmsbau]

Marburg, Westd. Bib.
Marburg, Westdeutsche Bibliothek

Marchfeld, Marchfeldschlösser Schlosshof &
Niederweiden
Marchfeld, Marchfeldschlösser Schlosshof und
Niederweiden

Mar del Plata, Mus. Mun. A.
Mar del Plata, Museo Municipal de Arte

Mariana, Mus. Arquidioc.
  Mariana, Museu Arquidiocesano

Mariazell Basilica, Treasury
  Mariazell, Mariazell Basilica Treasury

Mariazell, Wallfahrtskirche, Schatzkam.
  Mariazell, Wallfahrtskirche, Schatzkammer

Maribo, Lolland–Falsters Kstmus.
  Maribo, Lolland–Falsters Kunstmuseum

Maribor, A. G.
  Maribor, Art Gallery (Umetnosta Galerija Maribor)

Maribor, Inst. Conserv. N. & Cult. Her.
  Maribor, Institute for the Conservation of National and Cultural Heritage (Zavod za Varstvo Naravne in Kulturne Dediščine)

Maribor, Reg. Mus.
  Maribor, Regional Museum (Pokrajinski Muzej)

Mariefred, Gripsholm Slott

Mariefred, Gripsholms Slott, Stat. Porträttsaml.
  Mariefred, Gripsholms Slott, Statens Porträttsamling (Statens Porträttsamling På Gripsholm)

Marie-Galante, Ecomus.
  Marie-Galante, Ecomusée

Marietta, OH, Campus Martius Mus.
  Marietta, OH, Campus Martius Museum and River Museum

Marino, Pal. Colonna
  Marino, Palazzo Colonna

Market Harborough Mus.
  Market Harborough, Market Harborough Museum

Markopoulo Mus.
  Markopoulo, Markopoulo Museum

Markt St Florian, St Florian Abbey [Augustiner Chorherrenstift St Florian]

Markt St Florian, Stiftsbib.
  Markt St Florian, Stiftsbibliothek

Markt St Florian, Stiftssaml.
  Markt St Florian, Stiftssammlungen

Marl, Skulpmus.
  Marl, Skulpturenmuseum Glaskasten

Marrakesh, Badi' Pal. Mus.
  Marrakesh, Badi' Palace Museum

Marrakesh, Bib. Ben Youssef
  Marrakesh, Bibliothèque Ben Youssef

Marrakesh, Mus. Dar Si Saïd
  Marrakesh, Musée de Dar Si Saïd

Marsala, Mus. Arazzi Fiamminghi
  Marsala, Museo Arazzi Fiamminghi

Marseille, Bib. Mun.
  Marseille, Bibliothèque Municipale

Marseille, Cent. Vieille Charité
  Marseille, Centre de la Vieille Charité

Marseille, Gal. Faïence
  Marseille, Galerie Faïence

Marseille, Gal. Rosenberg
  Marseille, Galerie Rosenberg

Marseille, Gals & Chapelle Charité
  Marseille, Galeries et Chapelle de la Charité

Marseille, Ist. It. Cult.
  Marseille, Istituto Italiano di Cultura

Marseille, Mus. A. & Trad. Pop. Terroir Marseill.
  Marseille, Musée des Arts et Traditions Populaires du Terroir Marseillais

Marseille, Mus. B.-A.
  Marseille, Musée des Beaux-Arts [Palais de Longchamp]

Marseille, Mus. Borély
  Marseille, Musée Borély [in Château Borély]

Marseille, Mus. Cantini
  Marseille, Musée Cantini

Marseille, Mus. Docks Romains
  Marseille, Musée des Docks Romains

Marseille, Musées Archéol.
  Marseille, Musées d'Archéologie [admins Mus. Borély; Gals & Chapelle Charité; Mus. Docks Romains]

Marseille, Mus. Grobet-Labadié
  Marseille, Musée Grobet-Labadié

Marseille, Mus. Hist.
  Marseille, Musée de l'Histoire de Marseille

Marseille, Mus. Mar & Econ.
  Marseille, Musée de la Marine et de l'Economie de Marseille [Musée de la Marine de Marseille]

Marseille, Mus. Midi
  Marseille, Musée du Midi

Marseille, Mus. Vieux-Marseille
  Marseille, Musée du Vieux-Marseille

Marsvinsholm, Bellinga Slott

Martigny, Fond. Pierre Gianadda
  Martigny, Fondation Pierre Gianadda

Martin, Slovak N. Mus.
  Martin, Slovak National Museum (Slovenské Národné Múzeum)

Martonvásar, Beethoven Mem. Mus.
  Martonvásar, Beethoven Memorial Museum

Maryculter, Blairs Coll.
  Maryculter, Blairs College [St Mary's College]

Maseru, Brit. Council
  Maseru, British Council

Maseru, Lesotho N. Mus.
  Maseru, Lesotho National Museum

Maseru, N. U. Lesotho
  Maseru, National University of Lesotho

Mashhad, Imam Riza Shrine Mus.
  Mashhad, Imam Riza Shrine Museum

Mashiko, Mashiko Cer. Mus.
  Mashiko, Mashiko Ceramics Museum (Mashiko Sankōkan)

Massa, Mus. Castello Malaspina
  Massa, Museo del Castello Malaspina

Massa, Pal. Cybo Malaspina
  Massa, Palazzo Cybo Malaspina [formerly Prefettura]

Massa Marittima, Mus. Archeol.
  Massa Marittima, Museo Archeologico

Massa Marittima, Pin. Com.
  Massa Marittima, Pinacoteca Comunale

Masvingo, Gt Zimbabwe N. Mnmt
  Masvingo, Great Zimbabwe National Monument

Matelica, Mus. Piersanti
  Matelica, Museo Piersanti

Matera, Mus. N. Ridola
  Matera, Museo Nazionale Domenico Ridola

Mathura, Govt Mus.
  Mathura, Government Museum

Matosinhos, Câmara Mun.
  Matosinhos, Câmara Municipal

Matosinhos, Col. Mun.
  Matosinhos, Coleçao Municipal

Matsumoto, Ukiyo Mus.
  Matsumoto, Ukiyoe Museum

Maubeuge, Mus. Boez
  Maubeuge, Musée Henri Boez

Maubeuge, Mus.-Trésor Eglise
  Maubeuge, Musée-Trésor d'Eglise

Maubeuge, St Pierre, Trésor

Mdina, Cathedral Mus.
  Mdina, Cathedral Museum

Mdina, Mus. Nat. Hist. & Flklore
  Mdina, Museum of Natural History and Folklore

Mdina, Roman Villa Mus.
  Mdina, Roman Villa Museum

Meaux, Mus. Bossuet
  Meaux, Musée Bossuet [Ancien Palais Episcopal]

Mechelen, Archf & Stadsbib.
  Mechelen, Archief en Stadsbibliotheek [lib. of the Great Council of the Netherlands]

Mechelen, Cult. Cent.
  Mechelen, Cultureel Centrum Burgemeester Antoon Spinoy

Mechelen, Grand Sémin., Bib.
  Mechelen, Grand Séminaire, Bibliothèque

Mechelen, Kon. Acad. Beeld. Kst.
  Mechelen, Koninklijke Academie voor Beeldende Kunsten

Mechelen, Kon. Manuf. Wandtapijten Gaspard de Wit
  Mechelen, Koninklijke Manufactuur van Wandtapijten Gaspard de Wit

Mechelen, Stadsmus. Hof van Busleyden
  Mechelen, Stadsmuseum Hof van Busleyden

Mechelen, Stedelijk Mus.
  Mechelen, Stedelijk Museum

Medellín, Mus. A. Mod.
  Medellín, Museo de Arte Moderno

Medellín, Mus. Zea
  Medellín, Museo de Zea

Medellín, Pal. Mun.
  Medellín, Palacio Municipal

Medina de Pomar, Mus. Conventual
  Medina de Pomar, Museo Conventual

Meigle Mus.
  Meigle, Meigle Museum

Meiningen, Schloss Elisabethenburg [Staatliche Museen]

Meissen, Porzellanmus.
  Meissen, Porzellanmuseum

Meknes, Mus. Dar Jamai & Pal.
  Meknes, Musée Dar Jamai et Palais

Melbourne, Aborigines Advancement League

Melbourne, ANZ Bank Archvs
  Melbourne, ANZ Bank Archives

Melbourne, Argus Gal.
  Melbourne, Argus Gallery

Melbourne, Athenaeum Hall

Melbourne, Austral. Gals
  Melbourne, Australian Galleries

Melbourne, Banyule Extn Gal.
  Melbourne, Banyule Extension Gallery

Melbourne, Dioc. Hist. Comm.
  Melbourne, Diocesan Historical Commission

Melbourne, Elders IXL Col.
  Melbourne, Elders IXL Collection

Melbourne, Gal. A
  Melbourne, Gallery A

Melbourne, Gal. Contemp. A.
  Melbourne, Gallery of Contemporary Art [closed; name changed to Mus. Mod. A. Australia in 1958; then Mus. Mod. A. & Des. in 1963; col. now at Heide Park A.G. & N.G. Victoria]

Melbourne, Gal. E. Hill
Melbourne, Gallery on Eastern Hill

Melbourne, Heide Park A.G.
Melbourne, Heide Park Art Gallery

Melbourne, Joseph Brown Gal.
Melbourne, Joseph Brown Gallery [Caroline House]

Melbourne, Min. Conserv.
Melbourne, Ministry for Conservation

Melbourne, Monash U., A.G.
Melbourne, Monash University, Art Gallery

Melbourne, Mus. Mod. A. Australia
Melbourne, Museum of Modern Art of Australia [closed; col. now at Heide Park A.G. & N.G. Victoria]

Melbourne, Mus. Mod. A. & Des.
Melbourne, Museum of Modern Art and Design of Australia [closed; col. now at Heide Park A.G. & N.G. Victoria]

Melbourne, Mus. Victoria
Melbourne, Museum of Victoria

Melbourne, N.G. Victoria
Melbourne, National Gallery of Victoria [Victorian A. Cent.]

Melbourne, Pin.
Melbourne, Pinacotheca

Melbourne, Prt Council Australia
Melbourne, Print Council of Australia

Melbourne, Royal Inst. Technol.
Melbourne, Royal Melbourne Institute of Technology

Melbourne, Royal Inst. Technol. A.G.
Melbourne, Royal Melbourne Institute of Technology Art Gallery

Melbourne, State Lib. Victoria
Melbourne, State Library of Victoria

Melbourne, Tolarno Gals
Melbourne, Tolarno Galleries

Melbourne, Toorak Gals
Melbourne, Toorak Galleries

Melbourne, U. Gal.
Melbourne, University Gallery [U. Melbourne Mus. A. since 1989]

Melbourne, U. Melbourne
Melbourne, University of Melbourne

Melbourne, U. Melbourne Mus. A.
Melbourne, University of Melbourne Museum of Art

Melbourne, Vict. Artists' Soc.
Melbourne, Victorian Artists' Society

Melbourne, Victoria Coll. A., Gal.
Melbourne, Victoria College of the Arts, Gallery

Melbourne, Westpac Gal.
Melbourne, Westpac Gallery

Melk, Stiftsbib.
Melk, Stiftsbibliothek

Melk, Stiftsmus.
Melk, Stiftsmuseum

Mělník, Castle Mus.
Mělník, Castle Museum

Melos Mus.
Melos, Melos Museum

Melton Mowbray, Carnegie Mus.
Melton Mowbray, Melton Carnegie Museum

Melun, Mus. Melun
Melun, Musée de Melun

Memphis, TN, Brooks Mus. A.
Memphis, TN, Memphis Brooks Museum of Art [Brooks Memorial Art Gallery]

Memphis, TN, Dixon Gal.
Memphis, TN, Dixon Gallery and Gardens

Mendrisio, Mus. A.
Mendrisio, Museo d'Arte Mendrisio

Menomonie, U. WI
Menomonie, WI, University of Wisconsin, Stout

Menton, Mus. Jean-Cocteau
Menton, Musée Jean-Cocteau

Menton, Mus. Pal. Carnolès
Menton, Musée du Palais Carnolès [Musée des Beaux-Arts]

Merano, Kurhaus

Merano, Mus. Civ.
Merano, Museo Civico [also known as Meraner Mus.]

Mérida, Spain, Alcazaba

Mérida, Spain, Mus. N. A. Romano
Mérida, Spain, Museo Nacional de Arte Romano [in Convento de S Clara]

Mérida, Mexico, Mus. Reg. Antropol. Yucatán
Mérida, Mexico, Museo Regional de Antropología de Yucatán [Palacio Cantón]

Merion Station, PA, Barnes Found.
Merion Station, PA, Barnes Foundation

Merthyr Tydfil, Cyfartha Castle Mus. & A.G.
Merthyr Tydfil, Cyfartha Castle Museum & Art Gallery

Meshed: see Mashhad

Mésola, Castello Estense
Mésola, Castello Estense

Messene Mus.
Messene, Museum

Messina, Mus. Reg.
Messina, Museo Regionale di Messina [Civico Museo Peloritano; Museo Nazionale]

Messina, Pal. Com.
Messina, Palazzo Comunale

Mestia, Mus. Hist. & Ethnog.
Mestia, Museum of History and Ethnography [Georgia]

Metaponto, Antiqua.
Metaponto, Antiquarium

Metaponto, Mus. Archeol. N.
Metaponto, Museo Archeologico Nazionale

Meteora, Gt Meteoron
Meteora, Great Meteoron [Monastery of the Transfiguration]

Meteora, Gt Meteoron Mus.
Meteora, Great Meteoron Museum

Meteora, Varlaam Monastery Mus.
Meteora, Varlaam Monastery Museum

Metsovon Gal.
Metsovon, Metsovon Gallery

Metsovon, Mus. Epirot Flk A.
Metsovon, Museum of Epirot Folk Art

Metz, Bib. Mun.
Metz, Bibliothèque Municipale

Metz, Mus. A. & Hist.
Metz, Musée d'Art et d'Histoire

Meudon, Mus. Rodin
Meudon, Musée Rodin

Mexico City, Acad. A.
Mexico City, Academia de Artes

Mexico City, Acad. S Carlos
Mexico City, Academia de San Carlos [houses postgrad. dept of U. N. Autónoma, Escuela N.A. Plast.]

Mexico City, Banco Int.
Mexico City, Banco Internacional

Mexico City, Banco N. de México
Mexico City, Banco Nacional de México

Mexico City, Bib. Ibero-Amer. & B.A.
Mexico City, Biblioteca Ibero-Americana y de Bellas Artes [in Pal. B.A.]

Mexico City, Bib. N. Antropol. & Hist.
Mexico City, Biblioteca Nacional de Antropología y Historia Dr Eusebio Davalos Hurtado

Mexico City, Capilla Tepeyac
Mexico City, Capilla del Tepeyac

Mexico City, Cent. Cult. A. Contemp.
Mexico City, Centro Cultural de Arte Contemporáneo

Mexico City, Cent. Escolar Benito Juárez
Mexico City, Centro Escolar Benito Juárez

Mexico City, Cent. Estud. Econ. & Soc. Tercer Mundo
Mexico City, Centro de Estudios Económicos y Sociales del Tercer Mundo

Mexico City, Chapultepec Gal.
Mexico City, Chapultepec Gallery

Mexico City, Colegio Máximo S Pedro & S Pablo
Mexico City, Colegio Máximo de S Pedro y S Pablo [former convent]

Mexico City, Colegio México
Mexico City, Colegio de México

Mexico City, Dept. Distr. Fed.
Mexico City, Departamento del Distrito Federal

Mexico City, Escuela N. Antropol. & Hist.
Mexico City, Escuela Nacional de Antropología e Historia

Mexico City, Escuela N. Pint. & Escul.
Mexico City, Escuela Nacional de Pintura y Escultura [La Esmeralda]

Mexico City, Escuela N. Prep.
Mexico City, Escuela Nacional Preparatoria

Mexico City, Escuela Sup. Ingen. & Arquit Poli.
Mexico City, Escuela Superior de Ingeniería y Arquitectura Politécnica

Mexico City, Fomento Cult. Banamex
Mexico City, Fomento Cultural Banamex

Mexico City, Fund. Cult. TV
Mexico City, Fundación Cultural Televisa

Mexico City, Gal. A. Mex.
Mexico City, Galería de Arte Mexicano

Mexico City, Gal. Antonio Souza
Mexico City, Galería Antonio Souza

Mexico City, Gal. Juan O'Gorman, Cent. Cult. U.
Mexico City, Galería Juan O'Gorman, Centro Cultural Universitario

Mexico City, Gal. Ponce
Mexico City, Galería Ponce

Mexico City, Gal. Prisse
Mexico City, Galería Prisse

Mexico City Gal. Tonalli
Mexico City, Galería Tonalli

Mexico City, Inst. N. B.A.
Mexico City, Instituto Nacional de Bellas Artes

Mexico City, Inst. Poli. N.
Mexico City, Instituto Politécnico Nacional de Mexico

Mexico City, Min. Patrm. N.
Mexico City, Ministerio del Patrimonio Nacional

Mexico City, Mus. A. Carrillo Gil
Mexico City, Museo de Arte Alvar y Carmen T. Carrillo Gil

Mexico City, Mus. A. Contemp. Int. Rufino Tamayo
   Mexico City, Museo de Arte Contemporáneo Internacional Rufino Tamayo

Mexico City, Mus. A. Mod.
   Mexico City, Museo de Arte Moderno

Mexico City, Mus. A. Pop.
   Mexico City, Museo de Arte Popular

Mexico City, Mus. Ciudad
   Mexico City, Museo de la Ciudad

Mexico City, Mus. Diego Rivera
   Mexico City, Museo Diego Rivera de Anahuacalli

Mexico City, Mus. Eco
   Mexico City, Museo El Eco [closed]

Mexico City, Mus. Franz Mayer
   Mexico City, Museo Franz Mayer

Mexico City, Mus. Kahlo
   Mexico City, Museo Frida Kahlo

Mexico City, Mus. N. A.
   Mexico City, Museo Nacional de Arte

Mexico City, Mus. N. Antropol.
   Mexico City, Museo Nacional de Antropología

Mexico City, Mus. N. Cult.
   Mexico City, Museo Nacional de las Culturas

Mexico City, Mus. N. Est.
   Mexico City, Museo Nacional de la Estampa

Mexico City, Mus. N. Hist.
   Mexico City, Museo Nacional de Historia, Castillo de Chapultepec

Mexico City, Mus. Pal. B.A.
   Mexico City, Museo del Palacio de Bellas Artes

Mexico City, Mus. Rufino Tamayo
   Mexico City, Museo Rufino Tamayo

Mexico City, Mus. S Carlos
   Mexico City, Museo de San Carlos

Mexico City, Mus. Templo Mayor
   Mexico City, Museo del Templo Mayor

Mexico City, Oficina Registro Obras
   Mexico City, Oficina de Registro de Obras

Mexico City, Pal. B.A.
   Mexico City, Palacio de Bellas Artes [houses Mus. Pal. B.A.]

Mexico City, Pal. Medic.
   Mexico City, Palacio de la Medicina

Mexico City, Pal. N.
   Mexico City, Palacio Nacional

Mexico City, Pin. Virreinal
   Mexico City, Pinacoteca Virreinal de San Diego

Mexico City, Recinto Homenaje Don Benito Juárez
   Mexico City, Recinto de Homenaje a Don Benito Juárez [in Pal. N.]

Mexico City, Soc. Exalumnos Fac. Ingen.
   Mexico City, Sociedad de Exalumnos de la Facultad de Ingeniería

Mexico City, Teatro Insurgentes
   Mexico City, Teatro de los Insurgentes

Mexico City, U. Autónoma Met.
   Mexico City, Universidad Autónoma Metropolitana

Mexico City, U. Iberoamer.
   Mexico City, Universidad Iberoamericana

Mexico City, U. N. Autónoma
   Mexico City, Universidad Nacional Autónoma de México

Mexico City, U. N. Autónoma, Escuela N. A. Plast.
   Mexico City, Universidad Nacional Autónoma de México, Escuela Nacional de Artes Plasticas

Miami, FL, Bacardi

Miami, FL, Barbara Gilman

Miami, FL, Cent. F.A.
   Miami, FL, Center for the Fine Arts

Miami, FL, Cub. Mus. A. & Cult.
   Miami, FL, Cuban Museum of Arts and Culture

Miami, FL, Frances Wolfson A.G.
   Miami, FL, Frances Wolfson Art Gallery [Miami-Dade Community College]

Miami, FL, Maria Gutierrez F.A.
   Miami, FL, Maria Gutierrez Fine Arts

Miami, FL, Mitchell Wolfson jr Col. Dec. & Propaganda A.
   Miami, FL, Mitchell Wolfson jr Collection of Decorative and Propaganda Arts

Miami Beach, FL, Bass Mus. A.
   Miami Beach, FL, Bass Museum of Art

Miami Beach, FL, Theat. Perf. A.
   Miami Beach, FL, Theater for the Performing Arts

Miami Beach, FL, Vizcaya Mus. Dec. A.
   Miami Beach, FL, Vizcaya Museum of Decorative Arts

Michaelbeuern, Benediktinerstift & Kstsamml.
   Michaelbeuern, Benediktinerstift und Kunstsammlungen

Michelstadt, Schloss Fürstenau

Michoacán, Mus. Michoacáno
   Michoacán, Museo Michoacáno

Middelburg, Stadhuis

Middelburg, Zeeuws Mus.
   Middelburg, Zeeuws Museum

Middlesbrough, Cleveland Gal.
   Middlesbrough, Cleveland Gallery

Middletown, CT, Wesleyan U., Cent. A.
   Middletown, CT, Wesleyan University, Center for the Arts

Middletown, CT, Wesleyan U., Cent. A., Zilkha Gal.
   Middletown, CT, Wesleyan University, Center for the Arts, Zilkha Gallery

Middletown, CT, Wesleyan U., Davison A. Cent.
   Middletown, CT, Wesleyan University, Davison Art Center

Middletown, VA, Belle Grove Plantation

Mihintale, Archaeol. Mus.
   Mihintale, Archaeological Museum

Mikhaylovgrad, A. G.
   Mikhaylovgrad, Art Gallery (Hudozhestvena Galerija)

Milan, Ambrosiana
   Milan, Pinacoteca Ambrosiana

Milan, Archv Capitolare
   Milan, Archivio Capitolare [in Mus. Sacro S Ambrogio]

Milan, Archv S Barnaba
   Milan, Archivi del Monasterio di San Barnaba

Milan, Archv Stato
   Milan, Archivio di Stato

Milan, Archv Stor. Fabbrica Duomo
   Milan, Archivio Storico della Fabbrica del Duomo

Milan, Archv Vecchio
   Milan, Archivio Vecchio della Soprintendenza ai Beni Artistici e Storici

Milan, Bagatti Valsecchi Col.
   Milan, Bagatti Valsecchi Collection

Milan, Bergamini Gal.
   Milan, Bergamini Gallery

Milan, Bib. Ambrosiana
   Milan, Biblioteca Ambrosiana

Milan, Bib. Capitolare
   Milan, Biblioteca Capitolare

Milan, Bib. Capitolare Met.
   Milan, Biblioteca Capitolare Metropolitana

Milan, Bib. Capitolare S Ambrogio
   Milan, Biblioteca Capitolare di S Ambrogio

Milan, Bib. N. Braidense
   Milan, Biblioteca Nazionale Braidense

Milan, Brera
   Milan, Pinacoteca di Brera [Accademia di Belle Arti di Brera]

Milan, Cam. Commerc.
   Milan, Camera di Commercio

Milan, Casa Riposo Musicisti
   Milan, Casa di Riposo per Musicisti

Milan, Castello Sforzesco [houses Archivio Storico Civico; Biblioteca d'Arte; Biblioteca Trivulziana; Civica Raccolta delle Armi; Civico Gabinetto dei Disegni; Gabinetto Numismatico di Brera e Civiche Raccolte Numismatiche; Medagliere Milanese e Museo della Moneta; Museo d'Arte Antica; Museo degli Strumenti Musicali; Pinacoteca; Raccolte di Scultura; Raccolte delle Stampe Achille Bertarelli; Sezione Egizia e Paleontologia]

Milan, Cent. Cult. Pirelli
   Milan, Centro Culturale Pirelli

Milan, Christian Stein

Milan, Circ. Stampa
   Milan, Circolo della Stampa

Milan, Civ. Mus. A. Contemp.
   Milan, Civico Museo d'Arte Contemporanea [in Pal. Reale]

Milan, Civ. Mus. Archeol.
   Milan, Civico Museo Archeologico

Milan, Civ. Rac. A. Ant.
   Milan, Civiche Raccolte d'Arte Antica

Milan, Civ. Rac. A. Applic.
   Milan, Civiche Raccolte d'Arte Applicata

Milan, Civ. Rac. Archeol. & Numi.
   Milan, Civiche Raccolte Archeologiche e Numismatiche

Milan, Com. Milano
   Milan, Comune di Milano

Milan, Consulenza A.
   Milan, Consulenza d'Arte

Milan, Crespi Col.
   Milan, Crespi Collection

Milan, D'Angeli–Haensler

Milan, Famiglia A.
   Milan, Famiglia Artistica

Milan, Finarte

Milan, Fond. Bagatti Valsecchi
   Milan, Fondazione Bagatti Valsecchi

Milan, Gal. A. Mod.
   Milan, Galleria d'Arte Moderna

Milan, Gal. A. Mod. Farsetti
   Milan, Galleria d'Arte Moderna Farsetti

Milan, Gal. Annunciata
   Milan, Galleria Annunciata [Carlo Grossetti]

Milan, Gal. Apollinaire
   Milan, Galleria Apollinaire

Milan, Gal. Azimuth
   Milan, Galleria Azimuth

Milan, Gal. Barbaroux
  Milan, Galleria Barbaroux

Milan, Gal. Bellenghi
  Milan, Galleria Bellenghi [closed]

Milan, Gal. Edmondo Sacerdoti
  Milan, Galleria Edmondo Sacerdoti

Milan, Gal. Gian Ferrari
  Milan, Galleria Gian Ferrari

Milan, Gal. Grande
  Milan, Galleria Grande

Milan, Gal. Granna
  Milan, Galleria Granna

Milan, Gal. Incisione
  Milan, Galleria dell'Incisione [Elio Palmisano]

Milan, Gal. Levante
  Milan, Galleria del Levante

Milan, Gal. Levi
  Milan, Galleria Levi

Milan, Gal. Lorenzelli
  Milan, Galleria Lorenzelli

Milan, Gal. Miceli
  Milan, Galleria Miceli

Milan, Gal. Milano
  Milan, Galleria Milano

Milan, Gal. Milione
  Milan, Galleria Il Milione

Milan, Gal. Naviglio
  Milan, Galleria del Naviglio

Milan, Gal. Pesaro
  Milan, Galleria Pesaro

Milan, Gal. Philippe Daveiro
  Milan, Galleria Philippe Daveiro

Milan, Gal. Roma
  Milan, Galleria di Roma

Milan, Gal. Schwartz
  Milan, Galleria Schwartz

Milan, Gal. S Fedele
  Milan, Galleria San Fedele

Milan, Gal. Spiga
  Milan, Galleria della Spiga

Milan, Ist. Eur. Dis.
  Milan, Istituto Europeo di Disegno

Milan, La Prealpina
  Milan, La Prealpina S.P.A.

Milan, Lib. Salto
  Milan, Libreria Salto

Milan, Lorenzelli A.
  Milan, Lorenzelli Arte

Milan, Mus. Civ. Milano
  Milan, Museo Civico di Milano

Milan, Mus. Civ. Stor. Nat.
  Milan, Museo Civico di Storia Naturale [in Giardini Pubblici]

Milan, Mus. Duomo
  Milan, Museo del Duomo

Milan, Musei Castello
  Milan, Musei del Castello [admins Castello Sforzesco; Civ. Mus. Archeol.]

Milan, Mus. Marino Marini
  Milan, Museo Marino Marini

Milan, Mus. Milano
  Milan, Museo di Milano

Milan, Mus. N. Sci. & Tec. Leonardo da Vinci
  Milan, Museo Nazionale della Scienza e della Tecnica Leonardo da Vinci

Milan, Mus. Poldi Pezzoli
  Milan, Museo Poldi Pezzoli

Milan, Mus. Risorgimento
  Milan, Museo del Risorgimento e Raccolte Storiche del Comune di Milano

Milan, Mus. Sacro S Ambrogio
  Milan, Museo Sacro di S Ambrogio

Milan, Mus. Teat. alla Scala
  Milan, Museo Teatrale alla Scala

Milan, Nuovo Banco Ambrosiano

Milan, Olivetti Italia

Milan, Osp. Maggiore
  Milan, Raccolte d'Arte dell'Ospedale Maggiore

Milan, Padiglione A. Contemp.
  Milan, Padiglione Arte Contemporanea

Milan, Pal. A.
  Milan, Palazzo dell'Arte

Milan, Pal. Arcivescovile
  Milan, Palazzo Arcivescovile [incl. Quadreria]

Milan, Pal. Aste
  Milan, Palazzo delle Aste

Milan, Pal. Bagatti Valsecchi
  Milan, Palazzo Bagatti Valsecchi

Milan, Pal. Beligioioso, Piazza Beligioioso
  Milan, Palazzo Beligioioso, Piazza Beligioioso

Milan, Pal. Borromeo
  Milan, Palazzo Borromeo

Milan, Pal. Castiglioni
  Milan, Palazzo Castiglioni

Milan, Pal. Clerici
  Milan, Palazzo Clerici

Milan, Pal. Crivelli
  Milan, Palazzo Crivelli

Milan, Pal. Cult. Lat.
  Milan, Palazzo della Cultura Latina

Milan, Pal. Gallarati Scotti
  Milan, Palazzo Gallarati Scotti

Milan, Pal. Giornali
  Milan, Palazzo dei Giornali

Milan, Pal. Giustizia
  Milan, Palazzo Giustizia

Milan, Pal. Greppi, via S Antonia
  Milan, Palazzo Greppi, via S Antonia

Milan, Pal. Greppi, via S Maurilio
  Milan, Palazzo Greppi, via S Maurilio

Milan, Pal. Inf.
  Milan, Palazzo dell'Informazione

Milan, Pal. Marino
  Milan, Palazzo Marino

Milan, Pal. Permanente
  Milan, Palazzo della Permanente, Società per le Belle Arti ed Esposizione Permanente

Milan, Pal. Reale
  Milan, Palazzo Reale

Milan, Pal. Serbelloni
  Milan, Palazzo Serbelloni

Milan, Pal. Triennale
  Milan, Palazzo della Triennale

Milan, Rotonda Besana
  Milan, Rotonda della Besana

Milan, Rotonda Foppone Osp.
  Milan, Rotonda o Foppone dell'Ospedale

Milan, Semin. Vescovile
  Milan, Seminario Vescovile

Milan, Sesto S Giovanni, Bib. Civ.
  Milan, Sesto S Giovanni, Biblioteca Civica

Milan, Soc. B.A. & Espos. Permanente
  Milan, Società per le Belle Arti ed Esposizione Permanente

Milan, Studio Marconi

Milan, Tesoro Duomo
  Milan, Tesoro del Duomo [Sacrestia Meridionale del Duomo]

Milan, Torno Col.
  Milan, Torno Collection

Milan, U. Cattolica
  Milan, Università Cattolica del Sacro Cuore

Milan, U. Fac. Teol.
  Milan, Milan University, Facoltà di Teologia

Milan, Uomo & A.
  Milan, L'Uomo e l'Arte

Milan, Villa Vigoni

Milazzo, Fond. Lucifero
  Milazzo, Fondazione Lucifero

Miletos, Archaeol. Mus.
  Miletos, Archaeological Museum

Millerton, NY, Aperture Found., Strand Archv
  Millerton, NY, Aperture Foundation, Paul Strand Archive

Millstadt, Stiftmus.
  Millstadt, Stiftmuseum

Millville, NJ, Wheaton Hist. Assoc. Mus.
  Millville, NJ, Wheaton Historical Association Museum

Millville, NJ, Wheaton Village, Amer. Glass Mus.
  Millville, NJ, Wheaton Village, American Glass Museum

Milot, Haiti, Pal. Sans Souci
  Milot, Haiti, Palais de Sans Souci

Milton, MA, Mus. Amer. China Trade
  Milton, MA, Museum of the American China Trade

Milwaukee, U. WI
  Milwaukee, WI, University of Wisconsin

Milwaukee, WI, A. Cent.
  Milwaukee, WI, Art Center [now A. Mus.]

Milwaukee, WI, A. Mus.
  Milwaukee, WI, Milwaukee Art Museum [formerly A. Cent.]

Milwaukee, WI, Marquette U., Haggerty Mus. A.
  Milwaukee, WI, Marquette University, Patrick and Beatrice Haggerty Museum of Art

Milwaukee, WI, Pub. Mus.
  Milwaukee, WI, Public Museum

Mindanao, Xavier U., Mus. Oro
  Mindanao, Xavier University, Museo de Oro [Xavier University Folklife Museum and Archives]

Minden, Domschatz

Minden, Mus. Gesch., Landes- & Vlksknd.
  Minden, Museum für Geschichte, Landes- und Volkskunde

Minneapolis, MN, Inst. A.
  Minneapolis, MN, Minneapolis Institute of Arts

Minneapolis, MN, Soc. F.A.
  Minneapolis, MN, Society of Fine Arts

Minneapolis, MN, Walker A. Cent.
  Minneapolis, MN, Walker Art Center

Minneapolis, U. MN, A. Mus.
  Minneapolis, MN, University of Minnesota, University Art Museum

Minneapolis, U. MN Lib.
  Minneapolis, MN, University of Minnesota Library

Minneapolis, U. MN Libs, NW Archit. Archvs
  Minneapolis, MN, University of Minnesota Libraries, Northwest Architectural Archives

Minsk, Belarus. Acad. Sci., Inst. A. Hist., Ethnog. & Folklore, Mus. Old Belarus. Cult.
Minsk, Belarusian Academy of Sciences, Institute of Art History, Ethnography and Folklore, Museum of Old Belarusian Culture (Akademyya Navuk RB, Instytut Mastatstvaznawstva, Etnahrafii i Fal'kloru, Muzey Starazhytna-belaruskay Kul'tury)

Minsk, Belarus' A. Mus.
Minsk, Belarus' Art Museum (Dyarzhawny Mastatski Muzey Respublika Belarusi)

Minsk, Belarus. Mus. Hist. Gt Patriot. War
Minsk, Belarusian Museum of the History of the Great Patriotic War (Dzyarzhawnay Muzey Historyi Vyalikay Aychnnayvayny)

Mira, Villa Venier–Contarini–Zen

Mirándola, Pal. Com.
Mirándola, Palazzo del Comune

Miskolc, Otto Herman Mus.
Miskolc, Otto Herman Museum (Herman Ottó Múzeum)

Mission Viejo, CA, Saddleback Coll. A.G.
Mission Viejo, CA, Saddleback College Art Gallery

Mitla, Mus. Frissell
Mitla, Museo Frissell

Mito, Ibaraki Mus. Mod. A.
Mito, Ibaraki Museum of Modern Art (Ibaraki-ken Kindai Bijutsukan)

Mito, Ibaraki Prefect. Hist. Mus.
Mito, Ibaraki Prefectural History Museum (Ibaraki-kenritsu Rekishikan)

Miyagi, A.G.
Miyagi, Art Gallery

Miyazaki, Prefect. Inst.
Miyazaki, Prefectural Institute

Miyazaki, Prefect. Lib.
Miyazaki, Prefectural Library

Mnichovo Hradiště, Mun. Mus.
Mnichovo Hradiště, Municipal Museum (Městské Múzeum)

Mobile, AL, F.A. Mus. S.
Mobile, AL, Fine Arts Museum of the South

Modena, Accad. N. Sci., Lett. & A., Bib.
Modena, Accademia Nazionale di Scienze, Lettere ed Arti, Biblioteca

Modena, Archv Capitolare
Modena, Archivio Capitolare

Modena, Archv Stato Modena
Modena, Archivio di Stato di Modena

Modena, Archv Stor.
Modena, Archivio Storico

Modena, Banca Pop. Emilia
Modena, Banca Popolare Emilia

Modena, Bib. Civ. Stor. A.
Modena, Biblioteca Civica di Storia dell'Arte

Modena, Bib. Com.
Modena, Biblioteca Comunale

Modena, Bib. Estense
Modena, Biblioteca Estense

Modena, Bib. U.
Modena, Biblioteca Universitaria

Modena, Fond. Campori
Modena, Fondo Campori

Modena, Gal. Campori
Modena, Galleria Campori

Modena, Gal. Civ. Com.
Modena, Galleria Civica del Comune

Modena, Gal. Fonte Abisso
Modena, Galleria Fonte Abisso

Modena, Gal. & Mus. Estense
Modena, Galleria e Museo Estense

Modena, Gal. Poletti
Modena, Galleria Luigi Poletti

Modena, Mus. Archeol. Etnol.
Modena, Museo Archeologico Etnologico

Modena, Musei Civ.
Modena, Musei Civici [admins Archv Stor.; Bib. Civ. Stor. A.; Bib. Estense; Bib. U; Gal. Campori; Gal. & Mus. Estense; Gal. Poletti; Mus. Archeol. Etnol.; Mus. Lapidario; Mus. & Medagliere Estense; Mus. Risorgimento; Mus. Stor. & A. Med. & Mod.]

Modena, Mus. Lapidario
Modena, Museo Lapidario

Modena, Mus. & Medagliere Estense
Modena, Museo e Medagliere Estense

Modena, Mus. Risorgimento
Modena, Museo del Risorgimento

Modena, Mus. Stor. & A. Med. & Mod.
Modena, Museo di Storia e Arte Medioevale e Moderna

Modena, Pal. Com.
Modena, Palazzo Comunale

Modena, Pal. Ducale
Modena, Palazzo Ducale [Accademia Militare]

Modena, Pal. Musei
Modena, Palazzo dei Musei [houses Archv Stor.; Bib. Civ. Stor. A.; Bib. Estense; Bib. U; Gal. Campori; Gal. & Mus. Estense; Gal. Poletti; Mus. Archeol. Etnol.; Mus. Lapidario; Mus. & Medagliere Estense; Mus. Risorgimento; Mus. Stor. & A. Med. & Mod.]

Modigliana, Osp. Civ.
Modigliana, Ospedale Civile

Modum, Blaafvarvev

Mogadishu, N. Mus.
Mogadishu, National Museum

Mogilev, Shmidt Mem. Mus.
Mogilev [Mogilev, Mahilow], Shmidt Memorial Museum (Uspaminal'ny Muzey O. Yu. Shmita)

Mohenjo-daro, Archaeol. Mus.
Mohenjo-daro, Archaeological Museum

Molfetta, Mus. Pin. Salvucci
Molfetta, Museo Pinacoteca A. Salvucci [Seminario Vescovile]

Mölndal, Gunnebo

Monaco-Ville, Archvs Pal. Princier
Monaco-Ville, Archives du Palais Princier de Monaco

Mönchengladbach, Schloss Rheydt
Mönchengladbach, Schloss Rheydt, Städtisches Museum

Mönchengladbach, Städt. Mus. Abteiberg
Mönchengladbach, Städtisches Museum Abteiberg

Mönchengladbach, Städt. Museen
Mönchengladbach, Städtische Museen [admins Schloss Rheydt; Städt. Mus. Abteiberg]

Monclova, Bib. Pape
Monclova, Biblioteca Pape

Monino, Zhukovsky Cent. Mus. Aviation & Astronautics
Monino, Central Museum of Aviation and Astronautics named after N.Ye Zhukovsky (Tsentrel'nyy Muzey Aviatsii i Kosmonautikiimeni N.Ye Zhukovsky)

Monmouth Mus.
Monmouth, Monmouth Museum

Mons, Archvs Etat
Mons, Archives de l'Etat

Mons, Mus. B.-A.
Mons, Musée des Beaux-Arts

Monserrat, Mus.
Monserrat, Museo de la Abadía de Monserrat

Montalcino, Mus. Civ.
Montalcino, Museo Civico [housed with Mus. Dioc. A. Sacra]

Montalcino, Mus. Dioc. A. Sacra
Montalcino, Museo Diocesano d'Arte Sacra

Montargis, Mus. B.-A.
Montargis, Musée des Beaux-Arts

Montargis, Mus. Girodet
Montargis, Musée Girodet, Hôtel de Ville

Montarioso, Mus. Semin.
Montarioso, Museo del Seminario

Montauban, Mus. Ingres
Montauban, Musée Ingres

Montbéliard, Maison A. & Loisirs
Montbéliard, Maison des Arts et Loisirs

Montchanin, Mairie

Montclair, NJ, A. Mus.
Montclair, NJ, Montclair Art Museum

Mont-de-Marsan, Mus. Despiau–Wlérick
Mont-de-Marsan, Musée Despiau–Wlérick [in Donjon Lacataye of Château de Gaston Phoebus]

Mont-de-Marsan, Mus. Dubalen Hist. Nat.
Mont-de-Marsan, Musée Dubalen d'Histoire Naturelle [in Chapelle Romane; incl. Nouvelle Galerie]

Mont-de-Marsan, Mus. Mun.
Mont-de-Marsan, Musée Municipal [admins Mus. Despiau–Wlérick; Mus. Dubalen Hist. Nat.]

Monte Acuto, Villa Blasi Foglietti

Monte Carlo, Bib.
Monte Carlo, Bibliothèque

Monte Carlo, Bib. Louis Notari
Monte Carlo, Bibliothèque Louis Notari

Monte Carlo, Gal. Adriano Ribolzi
Monte Carlo, Galerie Adriano Ribolzi

Monte Carlo, Gal. Point
Monte Carlo, Galerie Le Point

Monte Carlo, Mus. N.
Monte Carlo, Musée National de Monaco

Monte Carlo, Sotheby's

Montecassino Abbey, Archv
Montecassino, Montecassino Abbey, Archivio

Montecassino Abbey, Bib.
Montecassino, Montecassino Abbey, Biblioteca

Montecatini Terme, Mus. Accad.
Montecatini Terme, Museo dell'Accademia

Montecatini Terme, Villa Forini

Montecchio Maggiore, Villa Cordellina-Lombardi

Montefalco, Pin.–Mus. Com.
Montefalco, Pinacoteca–Museo Comunale

Montefortino, Pin. Com.
Montefortino, Pinacoteca Comunale [Palazzo Comunale]

Montemarciano, Oratorio
Montemarciano, Oratorio della Madonna delle Grazie

Montepulciano, Mus. Civ.
Montepulciano, Museo Civico

Monterchi, Scu. Via Reglia
Monterchi, Scuola di Via Reglia

Monterenzio, Mus.
   Monterenzio, Museo

Monterey, CA, Peninsula Mus. A.
   Monterey, CA, Monterey Peninsula Museum
   of Art

Monteriggioni, Mus. Semin. Arcivescovile
   Monteriggioni, Museo del Seminario
   Arcivescovile

Monterrey, Cent. Cult. Alfa
   Monterrey, Centro Cultural ALFA

Monterrey, Mus.
   Monterrey, Museo de Monterrey

Monterrey, Mus. Reg. Nue. León
   Monterrey, Museo Regional de Nuevo León
   Felipe de J. García Gampuzano

Monterrey, Nue. León, Alcaldia
   Monterrey, Nuevo León, Alcaldia

Monterrey, Nue. León Grupo Indust. ALFA
   Monterrey, Nuevo León Grupo Industrial
   ALFA

Monterrey, Nue. León, Promoc. A.
   Monterrey, Nuevo León, Promoción de las
   Artes

Montevarchi, Mus. A. Sacra
   Montevarchi, Museo d'Arte Sacra

Montevergine, Santuario, Mus.
   Montevergine, Santuario, Museo

Montevideo, Alliance Fr.
   Montevideo, Alliance Française

Montevideo, Ateneo

Montevideo, Bib. Artigas–Washington
   Montevideo, Biblioteca Artigas–Washington
   [US Information Service]

Montevideo, Bib. Inst. Cult. Anglo-Urug.
   Montevideo, Biblioteca del Instituto Cultural
   Anglo-Uruguayo

Montevideo, Bib. N.
   Montevideo, Biblioteca Nacional del Uruguay

Montevideo, Casa Gobierno
   Montevideo, Casa de Gobierno [Offices of
   President of Uruguay]

Montevideo, Cent. Dis. Indust.
   Montevideo, Centro de Diseño Industrial

Montevideo, Círc. B.A.
   Montevideo, Círculo de Bellas Artes

Montevideo, Escuela N. B.A.
   Montevideo, Escuela Nacional de Bellas Artes

Montevideo, Gal. Latina
   Montevideo, Galería Latina

Montevideo, Ist. It. Cult.
   Montevideo, Istituto Italiano di Cultura

Montevideo, Mus. A. Contemp.
   Montevideo, Museo de Arte Contemporáneo

Montevideo, Mus. A. Precolombino & Colon.
   Montevideo, Museo de Arte Precolombino y
   Colonial

Montevideo, Mus. & Archv Hist. Mun.
   Montevideo, Museo y Archivo Histórico
   Municipal [in Palacio del Cabildo]

Montevideo, Mus. Hist. A.
   Montevideo, Museo de Historia del Arte

Montevideo, Mus. Hist. N.
   Montevideo, Museo Histórico Nacional

Montevideo, Mus. Juan Zorilla de San Martín
   Montevideo, Museo Juan Zorilla de San
   Martín

Montevideo, Mus. Mun. Blanes
   Montevideo, Museo Municipal Juan Manuel
   Blanes

Montevideo, Mus. N. A. Plást.
   Montevideo, Museo Nacional de Artes
   Plásticas [now Mus. N. A. Visuales]

Montevideo, Mus. N. A. Visuales
   Montevideo, Museo Nacional de Artes
   Visuales [Mus. N. A. Plást. & Visuales]

Montevideo, Mus. N. B.A.
   Montevideo, Museo Nacional de Bellas Artes
   [name changed to Mus. N. A. Plást.; now
   called Mus. N. A. Visuales]

Montevideo, Mus. N. Hist. Nat.
   Montevideo, Museo Nacional de Historia
   Natural

Montevideo, Mus. Torres García
   Montevideo, Museo Torres García

Montevideo, Salón Mun. Exp.
   Montevideo, Salón Municipal de Exposiciones

Montevideo, U. Católica
   Montevideo, Universidad Católica [Dámaso
   Antonio Larrañaga]

Montevideo, U. Repúb., Fac. Arquit.
   Montevideo, Universidad de la República,
   Facultad de Arquitectura

Montfort de Lemnos, Colegio del Cardinal Padres
Escolapios

Montgomery, AL, Blount Col.
   Montgomery, AL, Blount Collection

Montgomery, AL, Mus. F.A.
   Montgomery, AL, Museum of Fine Arts

Monticello, VA, Jefferson Found.
   Monticello, VA, Thomas Jefferson Foundation

Montluçon, Mus. Mun.
   Montluçon, Musée Municipal du Vieux
   Château

Montmédy, Mus. Bastien-Lepage
   Montmédy, Musée Bastien-Lepage [Hôtel de
   Ville]

Montmorency, Mus. Jean-Jacques Rousseau
   Montmorency, Musée Jean-Jacques Rousseau

Montmorillon, Octagone

Montorioso, Semin. Arcivescovile
   Montorioso, Seminario Arcivescovile

Montpelier, VT, Wood A.G.
   Montpelier, VT, Thomas W. Wood Art
   Gallery [Vermont College Arts Center]

Montpellier, Bib. Interuniv.
   Montpellier, Bibliothèque Interuniversitaire

Montpellier, Bib. Ville
   Montpellier, Bibliothèque de la Ville et du
   Musée Fabre

Montpellier, Mus. Atger
   Montpellier, Musée Atger

Montpellier, Mus. Fabre
   Montpellier, Musée Fabre [Musée des Beaux-
   Arts]

Montreal, A. Assoc.
   Montreal, Art Association of Montreal [no
   longer exists]

Montreal, A. Fr.
   Montreal, L'Art Français

Montreal, Archvs N. Qué.
   Montreal, Archives Nationales du Québec

Montreal, Cent. Can. Archit.
   Montreal, Centre Canadien d'Architecture

Montreal, Concordia U., Leonard & Bina Ellen
A.G.
   Montreal, Concordia University, Leonard and
   Bina Ellen Art Gallery

Montreal, Concordia U., Williams A. Gals
   Montreal, Concordia University, Sir George
   Williams Art Galleries [now Leonard & Bina
   Ellen Art Gallery]

Montreal, Dominion Gal.
   Montreal, Dominion Gallery

Montreal, Ecole B.-A.
   Montreal, Ecole des Beaux-Arts

Montreal, Expo '67, Can. Pav.
   Montreal, Expo '67, Canadian Pavilion

Montreal, Expo '67, Ceylon Pav.
   Montreal, Expo '67, Ceylon Pavilion

Montreal, Expo '67, Fr. Pav.
   Montreal, Expo '67, French Pavilion

Montreal, Gal. Actuelle
   Montreal, Galerie L'Actuelle

Montreal, Gal. Agnès Lefort
   Montreal, Galerie Agnès Lefort

Montreal, Gal. Antoine
   Montreal, Galerie Antoine

Montreal, Gal. Artek
   Montreal, Galerie Artek

Montreal, Gal. Christiane Chassay
   Montreal, Galerie Christiane Chassay

Montreal, Gal. Delrue
   Montreal, Galerie Denyse Delrue [closed]

Montreal, Gal. Echange
   Montreal, Galerie L'Echange

Montreal, Gal. Echouerie
   Montreal, Galerie de L'Echouerie

Montreal, Gal. Libre
   Montreal, Galerie Libre

Montreal, Marlborough–Godard
   Montreal, Marlborough–Godard Ltd

Montreal, McGill U., McCord Mus.
   Montreal, McGill University, McCord
   Museum

Montreal, Mnmt N.
   Montreal, Monument National [closed]

Montreal, Mount Royal Cent. Sculp.
   Montreal, Mount Royal Center of Sculpture

Montreal, Mount Royal Club

Montreal, Mus. A. Contemp.
   Montreal, Musée d'Art Contemporain

Montreal, Mus. David M. Stewart
   Montreal, Musée David M. Stewart

Montreal, Mus. F.A.
   Montreal, Museum of Fine Arts [Musée des
   Beaux-Arts]

Montreal, Mus. F.A. Lib.
   Montreal, Museum of Fine Art Library

Montreal, Mus. Geol. Survey Canada
   Montreal, Museum of the Geological Survey
   of Canada

Montreal, Paul Kastel Gal.
   Montreal, Paul Kastel Gallery

Montreal, Sir George Williams U.
   Montreal, Sir George Williams University
   [Concordia U. since 1974]

Montreal, U. Montréal
   Montreal, Université de Montréal

Montreal, U. Québec, Gal. UQAM
   Montreal, Université du Québec à Montréal,
   Galerie UQAM

Montreal, William Scott & Sons Gals
   Montreal, William Scott and Sons Galleries

Montreuil, Mairie

Montricoux, Mus. Marcel-Lenoir
   Montricoux, Musée Marcel-Lenoir

Montross, VA, Westmoreland Co. Mus.
Montross, VA, Westmoreland County Museum

Montrouge, Hôtel de Ville

Montserrat, Mus. Abadía
Montserrat, Museo de la Abadía de Montserrat [Monastery of S María]

Montserrat, Mus. Montserrat
Montserrat, Museo Montserrat

Montserrat, N. Mus.
Montserrat, National Museum

Monza, Ist. Stat. A.
Monza, Istituto Statale d'Arte di Monza

Monza, Mus. Duomo & Bib. Capitolare
Monza, Museo del Duomo di Monza e Biblioteca Capitolare

Monza, Mus. Serpero Tesoro
Monza, Museo F. Serpero del Tesoro [in cathedral treasury]

Monza, Scu. Nudo
Monza, Scuola di Nudo

Mora, Zorngården

Mora, Zornmus.
Mora, Zornmuseum

Mora, Zornsaml.
Mora, Zornsamlingarna

Moraga, CA, Hearst A.G., St Mary's Coll.
Moraga, CA, Hearst Art Gallery, St Mary's College

Moratuva, U. Moratuva
Moratuva, University of Moratuva

Moravský Krumlov Castle
Moravský Krumlov, Moravský Krumlov Castle

Morelia, Casa Cult.
Morelia, Casa de la Cultura

Morelia, Casa Morelos
Morelia, Casa de Morelos

Morelia, Mus. Estado
Morelia, Museo del Estado de Michoacán

Morelia, Mus. Reg. Michoacáno
Morelia, Museo Regional Michoacáno

Morgantina Mus.
Morgantina, Morgantina Museum

Morigny, Château
Morigny, Château de Morigny

Morija Mus. Archivs
Morija, Morija Museum and Archives

Moritzburg, Barockmus. Schloss Moritzburg
Moritzburg, Barockmuseum Schloss Moritzburg

Morlaix, Musée
Morlaix, Musée de Morlaix

Morlaix, Mus. Jacobins
Morlaix, Musée des Jacobins

Morlanwelz-Mariemont, Mus. Royal Mariemont
Morlanwelz-Mariemont, Musée Royal de Mariemont

Morphou, Mus. Archaeol. & Nat. Hist.
Morphou, Museum of Archaeology and Natural History

Morristown, NJ, Morris Mus. A. & Sci.
Morristown, Morris Museum of Arts and Sciences

Mortagne, Mairie

Mortagne-au-Perche, Maison Comtes du Perche
Mortagne-au-Perche, Maison des Comtes du Perche [Mus. Alain since 1977]

Mortagne-au-Perche, Mus. Alain
Mortagne-au-Perche, Musée Alain

Morwell, Latrobe Valley A. Cent.
Morwell, Latrobe Valley Art Centre

Moscow, Acad. A.
Moscow, Academy of Arts (Akademiya Khudozhestv)

Moscow, Acad. Sci., Inst. Archaeol.
Moscow, Academy of Sciences, Institute of Archaeology (Institut Arkheologii Akademii Nauk)

Moscow, Aleksandr Lavrent'yev Col.
Moscow, Aleksandr Lavrent'yev Collection (Kollektsiya Aleksandra Lavrent'yeva)

Moscow, All-Rus. Exhib. Cent.
Moscow, All-Russian Exhibitions Centre (Vserossiyskiy Vystavochnyy Tsentr) [formerly Exh. Econ. Achievements]

Moscow, All-Rus. Res. Inst. Rest.
Moscow, All-Russian Research Institute for Restoration (Vserossiyskiy Issledoratel'skiy Institut za Restavratsiyu)

Moscow, Almaz Found.
Moscow, Almaz Foundation

Moscow, Andrey Rublyov Mus. Anc. Rus. A.
Moscow, Andrey Rublyov Museum of Ancient Russian Art [formerly Andronnikov Monastery] (Muzey Drevnerusskogo Iskusstva Imeni Andreya Rubleva)

Moscow, Bakhrushin Cent. Theat. Mus.
Moscow, Bakhrushin Central Theatre Museum (Tsentral'nyy Teatral'nyy Muzey Imeni A. A. Bakhrushina)

Moscow, Battle of Borodino Mus.-Panorama
Moscow, Battle of Borodino Museum-Panorama (Muzey-Panorama 'Borodinskaya Bitva')

Moscow, Bol'shoy Theat. Mus.
Moscow, Bol'shoy Theatre Museum (Muzey Bol'shogo Teatra)

Moscow, Cafe of Poets (Kafe Poetov) [closed]

Moscow, Cent. Archv Anc. Doc.
Moscow, Central Archive of Ancient Documents (Tsentral'nyy Gosudarstvenyy Arkhiv za Restavratsiyu) [Z.G.A.D.A.]

Moscow, Cent. Archvs Lit. & A.
Moscow, Central Archives of Literature and Art (Tsentral'nyye Arkhivy Literatury i Iskusstva)

Moscow, Cent. House Artists
Moscow, Central House of Artists [exh. venue of Un. Sov. Artists] (Tsentral'nyy Dom Khudozhnikov)

Moscow, Cent. Lenin Mus.
Moscow, Central Lenin Museum [closed] (Tsentral'nyy Muzey V.I. Lenina)

Moscow, Cent. Mus. Armed Forces
Moscow, Central Museum of the Armed Forces (Tsentral'nyy Muzey Vooruzhonnykh Sil)

Moscow, Cent. Mus. Revolution
Moscow, Central Museum of the Revolution (Tsentral'nyy Muzey Revolyutsii)

Moscow, Don Monastery (Donskaya Lavra) [houses part of Shchusev Res. & Sci. Mus. Rus. Archit.]

Moscow, Don Monastery Church of the Archangel Michael

Moscow, Exh. Econ. Achievements
Moscow, Exhibition of Economic Achievements (Vystavka Dostizheniy Narodnogo Khozyaystva) [VDNKh; now All-Rus. Exhib. Cent.]

Moscow, Exh. Hall Perova Distr.
Moscow, Exhibition Hall of the Perovo District of the City of Moscow (Vystavochnyy Zal Perovskogo Rayona Goroda Moskvy)

Moscow, Glinka Cent. Mus. Musical Cult.
Moscow, M.I. Glinka Central Museum of Musical Culture (Tsentral'nyy Muzey Muzykal'noy Kul'tury Imeni M.I. Glinki)

Moscow, Golden Fleece Gal.
Moscow, Golden Fleece Gallery (Galereya Zolotogo Runa)

Moscow, Grabar' Rest. Cent.
Moscow, Grabar' Restoration Centre (Institut Restavratsii Imeni Grabarya)

Moscow, Hist. Mus.
Moscow, Historical Museum (Istoricheskiy Muzey)

Moscow, House Un.
Moscow, House of Trade Unions (Dom Soyuzov) [in Kremlin]

Moscow, Kolomenskoye Estate Mus.
Moscow, Kolomenskoye Estate Museum (Muzey-Usad'ba Kolomenskoye)

Moscow, Konyonkov Mus.
Moscow, S.T. Konyonkov Memorial Museum-Studio (S.T. Konyonkova Memorial'nyy Muzey-Masterskaya)

Moscow, Kremlin (Kreml')

Moscow, Kremlin, Armoury
Moscow, Kremlin, Armoury (Oruzheynaya Palata)

Moscow, Lazarin Inst.
Moscow, Lazarin Institute (Institut Imeni Lazarina)

Moscow, Lenin Lib.
Moscow, Lenin Library (Biblioteka Imeni V.I. Lenina) [name changed to Rus. Lib.]

Moscow, Lit. Mus.
Moscow, Literary Museum (Literaturnyy Muzey)

Moscow, Maly Theat. Mus.
Moscow, Maly Theatre Museum (Akademicheskiy Malyy Teatr, Muzey)

Moscow, Manezh, Cent. Exh. Hall
Moscow, Manezh, Central Exhibition Hall (Manezh, Tsentral'nyy Vystavochnyy Zal)

Moscow, Mkhat Mus.
Moscow, Moscow Art Theatre, Museum (Moskovskiy Khudozhestvennyy Akademicheskiy Teatr Muzey) [theatre known as MKhAT]

Moscow, Mus. Cer. & Kuskovo Estate
Moscow, Museum of Ceramics and Kuskovo Estate (Muzey Keramiki i 'Usad'ba Kuskovo XVIII Veka')

Moscow, Mus. F.A., M.V. Lomonosov U.
Moscow, Museum of Fine Arts, M.V. Lomonosov University (Muzey Izobrazitel'nykh Iskusstv Moskovskogo Universiteta Imeni M. V. Lomonosova)

Moscow, Mus. Flk A.
Moscow, Museum of Folk Art (Muzey Narodnogo Iskusstva)

Moscow, Mus. Icons & Ptg
Moscow, Museum of Icons and Painting (Muzey Ikonov i Zhivopisi) [closed; col. at Tret'yakov Gal.]

Moscow, Mus. Orient. A.
Moscow, Museum of Oriental Art (Muzey Iskusstva Narodov Vostoka)

Munich, Gal. Thannhauser
  Munich, Galerie Thannhauser [closed]

Munich, Gal. Van de Loo
  Munich, Galerie Van de Loo

Munich, Glaspal.
  Munich, Glaspalast [destr. 1931]

Munich, Glyp.
  Munich, Glyptothek

Munich, Goethe-Inst.
  Munich, Goethe-Institut

Munich, Goltz Salon [1913]

Munich, Haus Kst
  Munich, Haus der Kunst

Munich, Isartor

Munich, Julius Böhler

Munich, Kath. Akad.
  Munich, Katholische Akademie

Munich, Kleine Gal.
  Munich, Kleine Galerie

Munich, Kön. Hof- & Staatbib.
  Munich, Königliche Hof- und Staatbibliothek
  [name changed to Bayer. Staatsbib. in 1918]

Munich, Konrad O. Bernheimer

Munich, Ksthalle Hypo-Kultstift.
  Munich, Kunsthalle der Hypo-Kulturstiftung

Munich, Ksthand. Xaver Scheidwimmer
  Munich, Kunsthandel Xaver Scheidwimmer

Munich, Kstler Genoss.
  Munich, Künstler Genossenschaft

Munich, Kstraum
  Munich, Kunstraum

Munich, Kstver.
  Munich, Kunstverein

Munich, Lenbachhaus
  Munich, Städtische Galerie im Lenbachhaus

Munich, Ludwig-Maximilians-U.
  Munich, Ludwig-Maximilians-Universität

Munich, Maximilianum

Munich, Mod. Gal. Heinrich Thannhauser
  Munich, Moderne Galerie Heinrich
  Thannhauser

Munich, Mus. Ant. Kleinkst
  Munich, Museum Antiker Kleinkunst

Munich, Neue Kstsalon
  Munich, Neuer Kunstsalon

Munich, Neue Pin.
  Munich, Neue Pinakothek

Munich, Neue Staatsgal.
  Munich, Neue Staatsgalerie [no longer exists]

Munich, Ntheat.
  Munich, Nationaltheater

Munich, Pav. Alten Botan. Gtn
  Munich, Pavillon im Alten Botanischen
  Garten

Munich, Prähist. Staatssamml.
  Munich, Prähistorische Staatssammlung
  [Museum für Vor- und Frühgeschichte]

Munich, Rathaus

Munich, Ratjen Found.
  Munich, Ratjen Foundation

Munich, Reichstag

Munich, Residenz [incl. Antiquarium, Grottenhof,
  Reiche Kapelle, Schatzkammer der Residenz]

Munich, Residenzmus.
  Munich, Residenzmuseum

Munich, Ruhmeshalle [Hall of Fame]

Munich, Schack-Gal.
  Munich, Schack-Galerie

Munich, Schloss Nymphenburg [houses
Marstallmuseum]

Munich, Staatl. Antikensamml.
  Munich, Staatliche Antikensammlungen

Munich, Staatl. Graph. Samml.
  Munich, Staatliche Graphische Sammlung

Munich, Staatl. Kstsch.
  Munich, Staatliche Kunstschule

Munich, Staatl. Münzsamml.
  Munich, Staatliche Münzsammlung München

Munich, Staatl. Mus. Vlkerknd.
  Munich, Staatliches Museum für Völkerkunde

Munich, Staatl. Samml. Ägyp. Kst
  Munich, Staatliche Sammlung Ägyptischer
  Kunst

Munich, Staatsgal. Mod. Kst
  Munich, Staatsgalerie Moderner Kunst [in
  Haus der Kunst]

Munich, Stadtarchv
  Munich, Stadtarchiv

Munich, Stadtmus.
  Munich, Münchener Stadtmuseum

Munich, Tech. Hochsch.
  Munich, Technische Hochschule

Munich, Tech. U.
  Munich, Technische Universität

Munich, Theatmus.
  Munich, Theatermuseum

Munich, Ver. Bild. Kstler
  Munich, Verein Bildender Künstler [in Haus
  der Kunst]

Munich, Villa Stuck

Munich, Wehrkreisbücherei [destr.]

Munich, Zentinst. Kstgesch.
  Munich, Zentralinstitut für Kunstgeschichte

Münster, Domschatz

Münster, Rathaus

Münster, Residenzschloss [in Westfäl. Wilhelms-
U.]

Münster, Stadtmus.
  Münster, Stadtmuseum

Münster, Ubib.
  Münster, Universtätsbibliothek

Münster, Westfäl. Kstver.
  Münster, Westfälischer Kunstverein [in
  Westfäl. Landesmus.]

Münster, Westfäl. Landesmus.
  Münster, Westfälisches Landesmuseum für
  Kunst und Kulturgeschichte

Münster, Westfäl. Wilhelms-U.
  Münster, Westfälische Wilhelms-Universität

Murano, Mus. Vetrario
  Murano, Museo Vetrario

Muranov, Tyutchev Estate-Mus.
  Muranov, Tyutchev Estate-Museum (Muzey-
  Usad'ba Muranovo Imeni F. I. Tyutcheva)

Murcia, Cent. Estud. Árab. & Arqueol.
  Murcia, Centro de Estudios Árabes y
  Arqueológicos 'Ibn Arabi'

Murcia, Mus. B.A.
  Murcia, Museo de Bellas Artes

Murcia, Mus. Catedral
  Murcia, Museo de la Catedral

Murcia, Mus. Salzillo
  Murcia, Museo Salzillo

Murcia, Soc. Econ.
  Murcia, Sociedad Económica

Murlo, Antiqua. Poggio Civ.
  Murlo, Antiquario di Poggio Civitate

Muscat, Oman N. Mus.
  Muscat, Oman National Museum

Muskegon, MI, Hackley A. Mus.
  Muskegon, MI, Hackley Art Museum

Myazaki, Fukui Prefect. Cer. Mus.
  Myazaki, Fukui Prefectural Ceramics Museum

Mykonos, Archaeol. Mus.
  Mykonos, Archaeological Museum

Myohaung, Archaeol. Mus.
  Myohaung, Archaeological Museum

Mysore Pal. Sarasvati Bhandar Lib.
  Mysore, Mysore Palace, Sarasvati Bhandar
  Library

Mystras, Mus. Mistras
  Mystras, Museum Mistras

Mytilene, Archaeol. Mus.
  Mytilene, Archaeological Museum

Mytilene, Byz. Mus.
  Mytilene, Byzantine Museum

Mytilene, Varia Mus.
  Mytilene, Varia Museum [Teriade]

Naantali, Föreningen Hedvigsminne (Hedvig
Memorial Society)

Naarden, Sticht. Becht
  Naarden, Stichting Becht

Náchod Castle
  Náchod, Náchod Castle (Náchod Zámek) [nr
  Hradec Králové, E. Bohemia]

Næstved Mus.
  Næstved, Næstved Museum

Nafplion: see Navplion

Naga, Mus. U. Nueva Caceres
  Naga, Museum of the University of Nueva
  Caceres

Nagaizumi-cho, Shizuoka Prefect., Mus. Bernard
Buffet
  Nagaizumi-cho, Shizuoka Prefecture, Musée
  Bernard Buffet [in Surugadaira Nature Park]

Nagarjunakonda, Archaeol. Mus.
  Nagarjunakonda, Archaeological Museum
  [Nagar Government Museum]

Nagasaki, Mun. Mus.
  Nagasaki, Municipal Museum (Nagasaki
  Shiritsu Hakubutsukan)

Nagasaki, Prefect. A. Mus.
  Nagasaki, Prefectural Art Museum (Nagasaki
  Kenritsu Bijutsuhakubutsukan)

Nagoya, Aichi Cult. Cent.
  Nagoya, Aichi Cultural Center (Aichikenritsu
  Bunka Kaikan Bijutsukan) [Aichi Prefecture
  Cultural Centre and Art Museum/Aichi
  Prefecture Art Gallery]

Nagoya, City Mus.
  Nagoya, City Museum (Nagoya-shi
  kagakukan)

Nagoya, Mun. Mus. Mod. A.
  Nagoya, Municipal Museum of Modern Art

Nagoya, Tokugawa A. Mus.
  Nagoya, Tokugawa Art Museum (Tokugawa
  Bijutsukan) [Tokugawa Reimeikai Foundation]

Nagpur, Cent. Mus.
  Nagpur, Central Museum

Nagytétény, nr Budapest, Castle Mus.
  Nagytétény, nr Budapest, Castle Museum
  (Nagytétényi Kastélymúzeum)

Naha, Okinawa Prefect. Mus.
  Naha, Okinawa Prefectural Museum

Nairobi, N. Mus.
  Nairobi, National Museum [formerly Corydon
  Museum]

Nakhichevan', Armen. Mus.
Nakhichevan', Armenian Museum

Nakhon Pathom, Phra Pathom Chedi N. Mus.
Nakhon Pathom, Phra Pathom Chedi National
Museum

Nakhon Si Thammarat, N. Mus.
Nakhon Si Thammarat, Nakhon Si
Thammarat National Museum

Nalanda, Archaeol. Mus.
Nalanda, Archaeological Museum

Namur, Maison Cult.
Namur, Maison de la Culture de la Province de
Namur

Namur, Mus. A. Anc.
Namur, Musée des Arts Anciens du Namurois

Namur, Mus. Archéol.
Namur, Musée Archéologique

Namur, Mus. Armes & Hist. Mil. Comte de
Namur
Namur, Musée d'Armes et d'Histoire Militaire
du Comte de Namur

Namur, Mus. Dioc.
Namur, Musée Diocésain

Namur, Mus. Groesbeeck de Croix
Namur, Musée Groesbeeck de Croix

Namur, Mus. Hôtel de Croix
Namur, Musée de l'Hôtel de Croix

Namur, Mus. Prov. Rops
Namur, Musée Provincial Félicien Rops

Namur, Soc. Archéol.
Namur, Société Archéologique de Namur

Namur, Trésor Hugo d'Oignies
Namur, Trésor du Frère Hugo d'Oignies,
Institut des Soeurs de Notre Dame

Nan, N. Mus.
Nan, Nan National Museum

Nanchang, Jiangxi Prov. Mus.
Nanchang, Jiangxi Provincial Museum

Nancy, Eglise-Mus. des Cordeliers
Nancy, Eglise-Musée des Cordeliers

Nancy, Mus. B.-A.
Nancy, Musée des Beaux-Arts

Nancy, Mus. Ecole Nancy
Nancy, Musée de l'Ecole de Nancy

Nancy, Mus. Fer
Nancy, Musée du Fer

Nancy, Mus. Hist. Lorrain
Nancy, Musée Historique Lorrain

Nancy, Trésor Cathédrale
Nancy, Trésor de la Cathédrale

Nanjing, Jiangsu Prov. Gal.
Nanjing, Jiangsu Provincial Gallery

Nanjing, Jiangsu Prov. Mus.
Nanjing, Jiangsu Provincial Museum [Nanjing
Museum]

Nanjing, N. Cent. U.
Nanjing, National Central University

Nanterre, Bib. Doc. Int. Contemp.
Nanterre, Bibliothèque de Documentation
Internationale Contemporaine

Nantes, Château Ducs de Bretagne
Nantes, Château des Ducs de Bretagne

Nantes, Château, Mus. A. Déc.
Nantes, Château, Musée des Arts Décoratifs

Nantes, Château, Mus. A. Pop.
Nantes, Musée d'Art Populaire de Bretagne
[Musée des Arts Populaires et Régionaux]

Nantes, Château, Mus. Salourges
Nantes, Musée des Salourges

Nantes, Ecole Rég. B.-A.
Nantes, Ecole Régionale des Beaux-Arts

Nantes, Mus. B.-A.
Nantes, Musée des Beaux-Arts de Nantes

Nantes, Mus. Dobrée
Nantes, Musée Thomas Dobrée

Nantes, Musées Dépt. Loire-Atlantique
Nantes, Musées Départementaux de Loire-
Atlantique

Napier, Hawke's Bay Mus.
Napier, Hawke's Bay Museum

Naples, Accad. B.A.
Naples, Accademia di Belle Arti

Naples, Alisio

Naples, Archv Stato
Naples, Archivio di Stato

Naples, Banca Commerc. It.
Naples, Banca Commerciale Italiana

Naples, Banca Sannitica

Naples, Banco di Napoli

Naples, Bib. Girolamini
Naples, Biblioteca dei Girolamini [in Church
of the Girolamini]

Naples, Bib. N.
Naples, Biblioteca Nazionale

Naples, Capodimonte
Naples, Museo e Gallerie Nazionali di
Capodimonte [Museo Borbonico]

Naples, Castel Ovo
Naples, Castel dell'Ovo

Naples, Castel S Elmo
Naples, Castel Sant' Elmo

Naples, Gal. Accad. B.A.
Naples, Galleria dell'Accademia di Belle Arti

Naples, Gal. Corona
Naples, Galleria Corona

Naples, Mus. Archeol. N.
Naples, Museo Archeologico Nazionale

Naples, Mus. Civ. Gaetano Filangieri
Naples, Museo Civico Gaetano Filangieri

Naples, Mus. N. Cér.
Naples, Museo Nazionale della Ceramica Duca
di Martina [in Villa Floridiana]

Naples, Mus. N. S Martino
Naples, Museo Nazionale di San Martino
[Certosa di San Martino]

Naples, Nunziatella [Collegio Militare]

Naples, Osp. S Maria del Popolo degli Incurabili
Naples, Ospedale di S Maria del Popolo degli
Incurabili

Naples, Padiglione Pompeiano

Naples, Pal. Monte Pietà
Naples, Palazzo del Monte di Pietà

Naples, Pal. Municipio
Naples, Palazzo del Municipio [incl. Church of
S Giacomo degli Spagnoli]

Naples, Pal. Reale
Naples, Palazzo Reale

Naples, Pin. Girolamini
Naples, Pinacoteca dei Girolamini [Quadreria
dei Girolamini]

Naples, Pin. Pio Monte della Misericordia
Naples, Pinacoteca del Pio Monte della
Misericordia [Palazzo del Monte]

Naples, S Gennaro, Tesoro [Naples Cathedral]

Naples, Scu. Media Stat. Vittorio Emanuele II
Naples, Scuola Media Statale Vittorio
Emanuele II

Naples, Soc. Promot. B.A. Salvator Rosa
Naples, Società Promotrice delle Belle Arti
Salvator Rosa

Naples, Soc. Stor. Patria
Naples, Società Napoletana di Storia Patria

Naples, Sopr. Ant.
Naples, Soprintendenza alle Antichità

Naples, Stazione Zool.
Naples, Stazione Zoologica di Napoli

Naples, Villa Com.
Naples, Villa Comunale [Villa di Chiaia]

Naples, Villa Floridiana [houses Mus. N. Cer.]

Naples, Villa Pignatelli [Museo Principe Diego
Aragona Pignatelli Cortes]

Naples, Villa Volpicelli

Nara, Asukamura, Educ. Comm.
Nara, Asukamura, Education Commission

Nara, Neirak A. Mus.
Nara, Neiraku Art Museum (Neiraku
Bijutsukan)

Nara, N. Mus.
Nara, Nara National Museum (Nara Kokuritsu
Hakubutsukan)

Nara, N. Res. Inst. Cult. Properties
Nara, National Research Institute of Cultural
Properties

Nara, Prefect. Mus. A.
Nara, Prefectural Museum of Art (Nara-
kenritsu Bijutsukan)

Nara, Shōsōin

Nara, Tōdaiji

Nara, Yamato Bunkakan

Narbonne, Crypte Paléochrétienne
Narbonne, Crypte Paléochrétienne de la
Basilique St Paul Serge

Narbonne, Horreum Romain

Narbonne, Mus. A. & Hist.
Narbonne, Musée d'Art et d'Histoire

Narbonne, Mus. Archéol.
Narbonne, Musée Archéologique

Narbonne, Musées Ville
Narbonne, Musées de la Ville de Narbonne
[admins Crypte Paléochrétienne; Horrcum
Romain; Mus. A. & Hist.; Mus. Archéol.; Mus.
Lapidaire; Mus. Préhist.]

Narbonne, Mus. Lapidaire
Narbonne, Musée Lapidaire

Narbonne, Mus. Préhist.
Narbonne, Musée de Préhistoire

Närke, Skjernsund Slott

Narni, Pin. Com.
Narni, Pinacoteca Comunale

Narva, Reg. Mus.
Narva, Regional Museum

Nashville, TN Botan. Gdns & F.A. Cent.
Nashville, TN, Tennessee Botanical Gardens
and Fine Arts Center

Nashville, TN, Fisk U.
Nashville, TN, Fisk University

Nashville, TN, State Lib. & Archv
Nashville, TN, State Library and Archive

Nashville, TN, Vanderbilt U.
Nashville, TN, Vanderbilt University

Nashville, TN, Vanderbilt U. Gal.
Nashville, TN, Vanderbilt University Gallery

Nassau, Bahamas Hist. Soc. Mus.
Nassau, Bahamas Historical Society Museum

Nassau, Bahamia Mus.
Nassau, Bahamia Museum [closed]

Nassau, Bahamian A. G.
  Nassau, Bahamian Art Gallery

Nassau, Caripelago Mezzanine Gal.
  Nassau, Caripelago Mezzanine Gallery

Nassau, Cent. Bank Gal.
  Nassau, Central Bank Gallery

Nassau, Lyford Cay Gal.
  Nassau, Lyford Cay Gallery

Nassau, Pompey Mus.
  Nassau, Pompey Museum

Nassau, Pub. Lib. & Mus.
  Nassau, Nassau Public Library and Museum

Nassau, St Augustine's Coll.
  Nassau, Saint Augustine's College

Nassau, Steinischer Hof

Natchez, MS, N. Hist. Park
  Natchez, MS, National Historical Park

Nauplia: see Navplion

Navplion, Archaeol. Mus.
  Navplion, Archaeological Museum

Naxos, Archaeol. Mus.
  Naxos, Archaeological Museum

Nazareth, PA, Whitefield House Mus.
  Nazareth, PA, Whitefield House Museum

Neah Bay, WA, Makah Cult. & Res. Cent.
  Neah Bay, WA, Makah Cultural and Research
  Centre [Makah Museum]

Neamţ Monastery, Mus.
  Neamţ Monastery, Museum of the Neamţ
  Monastery

Nechanice, Nech Castle (Hrádek u Nech)
  [formerly Schloss Hrádek, nr Königgratz]

Negotin, Reg. Mus.
  Negotin, Regional Museum (Muzej Krajine-
  Negotin) [National Museum]

Nègrepelisse, Château
  Nègrepelisse, Château de Nègrepelisse

Nelahozeves Castle
  Nelahozeves, Nelahozeves Castle

Nemi, Mus. Navi
  Nemi, Museo delle Navi

Nemours, Château Mus.
  Nemours, Château Musée

Nemours, Mus. Préhist. Ile-de-France
  Nemours, Musée de la Préhistoire de l'Ile-de-
  France

Nérac, Mus. Château Henri IV
  Nérac, Musée du Château Henri IV

Nesebar, Mun. Archaeol. Mus.
  Nesebar, Municipal Archaeological Museum
  (Gradski Archeologičeski Muzej)

Neu-Affoltern, Glaubtern Church Cent.
  Neu-Affoltern, Glaubtern Church Centre

Neubrandenburg, Kunstsamml.
  Neubrandenburg, Kunstsammlung
  Neubrandenburg

Neuburg, Heimatmus.
  Neuburg, Heimatmuseum

Neuburg, Schlossmus.
  Neuburg, Schlossmuseum Neuburg an der
  Donau

Neuburg, Staatl. Gal.
  Neuburg, Staatliche Galerie

Neuchâtel, Mus. A. & Hist.
  Neuchâtel, Musée d'Art et d'Histoire [Musée
  des Beaux-Arts]

Neuchâtel, Mus. Cant. Archéol.
  Neuchâtel, Musée Cantonal d'Archéologie
  [Palais du Peyrou]

Neuchâtel, Mus. Ethnog.
  Neuchâtel, Musée d'Ethnographie de
  Neuchâtel

Neuenbrandenburg, Zent. Bild. Kst
  Neuenbrandenburg, Zentrum Bildender Kunst

Neuenstein, Hohenlohe-Mus.
  Neuenstein, Hohenlohe-Museum [in Schloss
  Neuenstein]

Neukirchen, Nolde-Mus.
  Neukirchen, Nolde-Museum [Stiftung Seebüll
  Ada und Emil Nolde]

Neuss, Clemens-Sels-Mus.
  Neuss, Clemens-Sels-Museum

Neu-Ulm, Scharff-Mus.
  Neu-Ulm, Edwin Scharff-Museum

Neuwied, Mus. Archäol. Eiszeitalters
  Neuwied, Museum für Archäologie des
  Eiszeitalters

Nevers, Bib. Mun.
  Nevers, Bibliothèque Municipale

Nevers, Mus. Blandin
  Nevers, Musée Blandin [Musée d'Arts et
  d'Histoire Frédéric Blandin]

Nevers, Mus. Mun.
  Nevers, Musée Municipal de Nevers

Nevis, Hamilton House Mus.
  Nevis, Hamilton House Museum

New Abbey, Shambellie House Mus. Cost.
  New Abbey, Shambellie House Museum of
  Costume

Newark, NJ Hist. Mus.
  Newark, New Jersey Historical Museum

Newark, NJ, Hist. Soc.
  Newark, NJ, Historical Society

Newark, NJ, Mus.
  Newark, NJ, Newark Museum

Newark, U. DE
  Newark, DE, University of Delaware

New Bedford, MA, Whaling Mus.
  New Bedford, New Bedford Whaling Museum

New Britain, CT, Mus. Amer. A.
  New Britain, CT, New Britain Museum of
  American Art

New Brunswick, NJ, Rutgers U., Douglass Coll.
  New Brunswick, NJ, Rutgers University,
  Douglass College

New Brunswick, NJ, Rutgers U., Zimmerli A.
Mus.
  New Brunswick, NJ, Rutgers University, Jane
  Voorhees Zimmerli Art Museum [formerly
  Rutgers U. Art Museum]

Newcastle, NSW, Reg. A.G.
  Newcastle, NSW, Newcastle Region Art
  Gallery

Newcastle upon Tyne, Black Gate Mus.
  Newcastle upon Tyne, Black Gate Museum

Newcastle upon Tyne, Joicey Mus.
  Newcastle upon Tyne, John George Joicey
  Museum

Newcastle upon Tyne, Laing A.G.
  Newcastle upon Tyne, Laing Art Gallery

Newcastle upon Tyne, Mus. Sci. & Engin.
  Newcastle upon Tyne, Museum of Science and
  Engineering

Newcastle upon Tyne, Poly. Gal.
  Newcastle upon Tyne, Polytechnic Gallery

Newcastle upon Tyne, Spectro A. Workshop
  Newcastle upon Tyne, Spectro Arts Workshop

Newcastle upon Tyne, Turbinia Hall

Newcastle upon Tyne, Tyne & Wear Joint
Museums Cttee
  Newcastle upon Tyne, Tyne & Wear Joint
  Museums Committee

Newcastle upon Tyne, U. Newcastle upon Tyne,
Dept Archaeol.
  Newcastle upon Tyne, University of Newcastle
  upon Tyne, Department of Archaeology

Newcastle upon Tyne, U. Newcastle upon Tyne,
Gr. Mus.
  Newcastle upon Tyne, University of Newcastle
  upon Tyne, Greek Museum

Newcastle upon Tyne, U. Newcastle upon Tyne,
Hatton Gal.
  Newcastle upon Tyne, University of Newcastle
  upon Tyne, Hatton Gallery

Newcastle upon Tyne, U. Newcastle upon Tyne,
Mus. Ant.
  Newcastle upon Tyne, University of Newcastle
  upon Tyne, Museum of Antiquities

New Delhi, Archaeol. Mus.
  New Delhi, Archaeological Museum [Red
  Fort]

New Delhi, Cent. Archaeol. Lib.
  New Delhi, Central Archaeological Library

New Delhi, Cent. Contemp. A.
  New Delhi, Centre for Contemporary Art

New Delhi, Crafts Mus.
  New Delhi, Crafts Museum

New Delhi, Goenka Acad. A. & Music
  New Delhi, Goenka Academy of Art and
  Music

New Delhi, Ind. Inst. Tech.
  New Delhi, Indian Institute of Technology

New Delhi, Indira Ghandi N. Cent. A.
  New Delhi, Indira Ghandi National Centre for
  the Arts

New Delhi, Jawaharlal Nehru U.
  New Delhi, Jawaharlal Nehru University

New Delhi, Lalit Kala Akad.
  New Delhi, Lalit Kala Akademi [National
  Academy of Art]

New Delhi, Mahavira Jaina Lib.
  New Delhi, Mahavira Jaina Library

New Delhi, N. Archvs
  New Delhi, National Archives of India

New Delhi, Nehru Mem. Mus. & Lib.
  New Delhi, Nehru Memorial Museum and
  Library

New Delhi, N.G. Mod. A.
  New Delhi, National Gallery of Modern Art

New Delhi, N. Mus.
  New Delhi, National Museum

New Delhi, Purana Qila Archaeol. Mus.
  New Delhi, Purana Qila Archaeological
  Museum

New Delhi, Rabindra Bhavan A.G.
  New Delhi, Rabindra Bhavan Art Gallery
  [Gallery of the National Academy of Fine Art]

New Delhi, Rashtrapati Bhavan
  New Delhi, Rashtrapati Bhavan [formerly
  Viceroy's House; now official residence of
  President of India]

New Delhi, Sangeet Natak Acad.
  New Delhi, Sangeet Natak Academy (Sangeet
  Natak Akademi) [National Academy of Music,
  Dance and Drama]

New Delhi, Tibet House Mus.
  New Delhi, Tibet House Museum

New Delhi, Triveni Kala Sangam

New Haven, CT, Colony Hist. Soc. Mus.
New Haven, CT, Colony Historical Society Museum

New Haven, CT, Yale Cent. Brit. A.
New Haven, CT, Yale Center for British Art

New Haven, CT, Yale Coll.
New Haven, CT, Yale College [nowYale U.]

New Haven, CT, Yale U.
New Haven, CT, Yale University

New Haven, CT, Yale U. A.G.
New Haven, CT, Yale University Art Gallery

New Haven, CT, Yale U., Beinecke Lib.
New Haven, CT, Yale University, Beinecke Library

New Haven, CT, Yale U., Cent. Amer. A.
New Haven, CT, Yale University, Center for American Arts and Material Culture

New Haven, CT, Yale U., Lewis Walpole Lib.
New Haven, CT, Yale University, Lewis Walpole Library

New Haven, CT, Yale U. Lib.
New Haven, CT, Yale University Library

New Haven, CT, Yale U., Peabody Mus. Nat. Hist.
New Haven, CT, Yale University, Peabody Museum of Natural History

New Haven, CT, Yale U. Sch. A. & Archit.
New Haven, CT, Yale University School of Art and Architecture

New Hebrides, now Vanuatu: see Port-Vila

New London, CT, Lyman Allyn Mus.
New London, CT, Lyman Allyn Museum

Newlyn, A.G.
Newlyn, Art Gallery

Newlyn, Orion Gals
Newlyn, Newlyn Orion Galleries

Newmarket, N. Horseracing Mus.
Newmarket, National Horseracing Museum

New Orleans, LA, Contemp. A. Cent.
New Orleans, LA, Contemporary Arts Center

New Orleans, LA, Delgado Mus.
New Orleans, LA, Isaac Delgado Museum

New Orleans, LA, Mus. A.
New Orleans, LA, New Orleans Museum of Art

New Orleans, LA State Mus.
New Orleans, LA, Louisiana State Museum

New Orleans, Tulane U. LA
New Orleans, LA, Tulane University of Louisiana

New Plymouth, NZ, Govett-Brewster A.G.
New Plymouth, NZ, Govett-Brewster Art Gallery

New Plymouth, NZ, Hurworth [Historic Places Trust]

New Plymouth, NZ, Taranaki Mus.
New Plymouth, NZ, Taranaki Museum

Newport, Gwent, Mus. & A.G.
Newport, Gwent, Museum and Art Gallery

Newport, Gwent, Tredegar House

Newport, Isle of Wight, Carisbrooke Castle Mus.
Newport, Isle of Wight, Carisbrooke Castle Museum

Newport, RI, A. Mus. & A. Assoc.
Newport, RI, Art Museum and Art Association

Newport, RI, Hist. Soc. Mus.
Newport, RI, Newport Historical Society Museum

Newport, RI, Redwood Lib.
Newport, RI, Redwood Library

Newport, RI, The Elms

Newport Beach, CA, Harbor A. Mus.
Newport Beach, CA, Newport Harbor Art Museum

Newport News, VA, Mar. Mus.
Newport News, VA, Mariners Museum

Newry, Narrow Water Gal.
Newry, Narrow Water Gallery

Newtown, Oriel 31

New York, ACA Gals
New York, ACA Galleries [closed]

New York, A. Cent.
New York, Art Center [closed]

New York, A. C. Gal.
New York, Art of this Century Gallery [Peggy Guggenheim's Gallery; closed]

New York, Acquavella Gals
New York, Acquavella Galleries Inc.

New York, Afr.-Amer. Inst.
New York, African-American Institute

New York, AGBU Gal.
New York, AGBU Gallery

New York, AG Gal.
New York, AG Gallery

New York, Alexander Gal.
New York, Alexander Gallery

New York, Altern. Cent. Int. A.
New York, Alternative Center for International Arts

New York, Amer. A. Assoc.
New York, American Art Association

New York, Amer. Acad. A. & Lett.
New York, American Academy of Arts and Letters

New York, Amer. A. Gals
New York, American Art Galleries

New York, Amer. Fed. A.
New York, American Federation of Arts

New York, Americas Soc. A.G.
New York, Americas Society Art Gallery

New York, Amer. Inst. Graph. A.
New York, American Institute of Graphic Art

New York, Amer. Mus. Nat. Hist.
New York, American Museum of Natural History

New York, Amer. Mus. Nat. Hist. Lib.
New York, American Museum of Natural History Library

New York, Amer. Numi. Soc.
New York, American Numismatic Society

New York, An American Place

New York, Anderson Gal.
New York, Anderson Gallery

New York, Anthol. Film Archvs
New York, Anthology Film Archives

New York, Archvs Amer. A.
New York, Archives of American Art

New York, Armen. Mus.
New York, Armenian Museum

New York, Arnold Herst & Co. Gal.
New York, Arnold Herst and Co. Gallery

New York, Arthur M. Sackler Found.
New York, Arthur M. Sackler Foundation

New York, Artists Gal.
New York, Artists Gallery

New York, Art Students' League

New York, Asia House Gals
New York, Asia House Galleries [name changed to Asia Soc. Gals in April 1981]

New York, Asia Soc. Gals
New York, Asia Society Galleries

New York, Assoc. Amer. Artists
New York, Associated American Artists

New York. B.-A. Inst. Des.
New York, Beaux-Arts Institute of Design [closed]

New York, Barbara Gladstone Gal.
New York, Barbara Gladstone Gallery

New York, Bartók Archvs
New York, Bartók Archives

New York, Bernard Danenberg Gal.
New York, Bernard Danenberg Gallery [closed; moved to Paris]

New York, Bernice Steinbaum Gal.
New York, Bernice Steinbaum Gallery

New York, Berry-Hill Gals
New York, Berry-Hill Galleries

New York, Bertha Schaefer Gal.
New York, Bertha Schaefer Gallery

New York, Betty Parsons Gal.
New York, Betty Parsons Gallery

New York, Bronx Mus. A.
New York, Bronx Museum of the Arts

New York, Brooke Alexander Gal.
New York, Brooke Alexander Gallery

New York, Brooklyn Bot. Gdn
New York, Brooklyn Botanic Garden

New York, Brooklyn Children's Mus.
New York, Brooklyn Children's Museum

New York, Brooklyn Civ. Cent.
New York, Brooklyn Civic Centre

New York, Brooklyn Hist. Soc.
New York, Brooklyn Historical Society

New York, Brooklyn Mus.
New York, The Brooklyn Museum

New York, Brooklyn Mus. Sch. A.
New York, Brooklyn Museum School of Art

New York, Brooklyn Pub. Lib.
New York, Brooklyn Public Library

New York, Brummer Gal.
New York, Brummer Gallery [closed]

New York, Bucholz Gals
New York, Bucholz Galleries

New York, Burden Gal.
New York, Burden Gallery

New York, Bykert Gal.
New York, Bykert Gallery

New York, Carl Solway Gal.
New York, Carl Solway Gallery [closed]

New York, Cash–Newhouse Gal.
New York, Cash–Newhouse Gallery

New York, C. Assoc.
New York, Century Association

New York, Castelli, Feigen, Corcoran

New York, Castelli Graph.
New York, Castelli Graphics [branch of Leo Castelli Gal.]

New York, Catherine Viviano

New York, Cayman Gal.
New York, Cayman Gallery

New York, CDS Gal.
New York, CDS Gallery

New York, Cent. Afr. A.
New York, Center for African Art

New York, Cent. Inter-Amer. Relations
New York, Center for Inter-American
Relations

New York, Chalette Int.
New York, Chalette International

New York, Chamber of Commerce
New York, Chamber of Commerce of the
State of New York

New York, Charles Cowles Gal.
New York, Charles Cowles Gallery

New York, Charles Daniel Gal.
New York, Charles Daniel Gallery

New York, Chase Manhattan Bank A. Col.
New York, Chase Manhattan Bank Art
Collection

New York, China House Gal.
New York, China House Gallery, China
Institute in America

New York, China Inst. America
New York, China Institute in America

New York, Christie's Int.
New York, Christie's Manson and Woods
International

New York, Chrysler Col.
New York, Chrysler Collection

New York, Cintas Found.
New York, Cintas Foundation

New York, City Coll. City U.
New York, City College of the City University
of New York

New York, City Gal.
New York, City Gallery [Department of
Cultural Affairs]

New York, City Hall

New York, City U.
New York, City University of New York

New York, Claude Bernard Gal.
New York, Claude Bernard Gallery

New York, Cloisters
New York, The Cloisters

New York, Coe Kerr Gal.
New York, Coe Kerr Gallery, Inc.

New York, Colnaghi's
New York, P. and D. Colnaghi and Co. Ltd

New York, Columbia U.
New York, Columbia University

New York, Columbia U., Avery Archit. & F.A.
Lib.
New York, Columbia University, Avery
Architectural and Fine Arts Library

New York, Columbia U., Cent. Iran. Stud.
New York, Columbia University, Centre for
Iranian Studies

New York, Columbia U. Col.
New York, Columbia University Collection

New York, Columbia U., Rare Bk & MS. Lib.
New York, Columbia University, Rare Book
and Manuscript Library

New York, Contemp. Gal.
New York, Contemporaries Gallery

New York, Cooper-Hewitt Mus.
New York, Cooper-Hewitt Museum,
Smithsonian Institution; National Museum of
Design

New York, Cooper Un.
New York, Cooper Union for the
Advancement of Science and Art

New York, Cooper Un. Mus.
New York, Cooper Union Museum

New York, Cordier-Warren Gal.
New York, Cordier-Warren Gallery

New York, Cult. Cent.
New York, Cultural Center

New York, Curt Valentin
New York, Curt Valentin

New York, Daniels Gal.
New York, Daniels Gallery

New York, David Beitzel Gal.
New York, David Beitzel Gallery

New York, David Findlay Gal.
New York, David Findlay Gallery

New York, David Nolan

New York, del Re Gal.
New York, Marisa del Re Gallery

New York, Dia A. Found.
New York, Dia Art Foundation

New York, Diane Brown Gal.
New York, Diane Brown Gallery

New York, Dintenfass Gal.
New York, Terry Dintenfass Gallery

New York, Donaldson, Lufkin & Jenrette
New York, Donaldson, Lufkin and Jenrette,
Inc.

New York, Downtown Gal.
New York, Downtown Gallery

New York, Drg Cent.
New York, The Drawing Centre

New York, Duveen Gals
New York, Duveen Galleries

New York, Egan Gal.
New York, Egan Gallery

New York, Emmerich Gal.
New York, André Emmerich Gallery, Inc.

New York, Finch Coll. Mus. A.
New York, Finch College Museum of Art

New York, F. Keppel
New York, F. Keppel and Co.

New York, Forbes Mag. Col.
New York, Forbes Magazine Collection

New York, 49th Parallel Gal.
New York, 49th Parallel Gallery

New York, Forum Gal.
New York, Forum Gallery

New York, Found. Contemp. Perf. A.
New York, Foundation for Contemporary
Performance Arts, Inc.

New York, Franklin D. Roosevelt Lib.
New York, Franklin D. Roosevelt Library

New York, Franz Gigel Park

New York, Frick
New York, Frick Collection

New York, Gal. Amer. Ind. Comm. House
New York, Gallery of the American Indian
Community House

New York, Gal. Chalette
New York, Galerie Chalette

New York, Gal. Mod. A.
New York, Gallery of Modern Art

New York, Gal. St. Etienne
New York, Galerie St. Etienne

New York, Gen. Theol. Semin.
New York, General Theological Seminary

New York, Gracie Mansion Gal.
New York, Gracie Mansion Gallery

New York, Graham Gal.
New York, Graham Gallery

New York, Grand Cent. A. Gals
New York, Grand Central Art Galleries, Inc.
[Painters & Sculptors Assoc.]

New York, Grand Cent. Mod. Gal.
New York, Grand Central Moderns Gallery
[closed]

New York, Grand Cent. Pal.
New York, Grand Central Palace

New York, Green Gal.
New York, Green Gallery

New York, Grey Gal. & Stud. Cent.
New York, Grey Gallery and Study Centre

New York, Grolier Club

New York, Guggenheim
New York, Solomon R. Guggenheim Museum

New York, Hammer Gals
New York, Hammer Galleries

New York, Harmon F.A.
New York, Harmon Fine Arts

New York, Harmony Found.
New York, Harmony Foundation

New York, Hebrew Un. Coll., Jew. Inst. Relig.
New York, Hebrew Union College, Jewish
Institute of Religion

New York, Hirschl & Adler Gals
New York, Hirschl and Adler Galleries, Inc.

New York, Hisp. Soc. America
New York, Hispanic Society of America

New York, Hisp. Soc. America Lib.
New York, Hispanic Society of America
Library

New York, Hisp. Soc. America Mus.
New York, Hispanic Society of America
Museum

New York, Holly Solomon Gal.
New York, Holly Solomon Gallery

New York, Howard Wise Gal.
New York, Howard Wise Gallery

New York, H.P. Kraus

New York, H. Shickman Gal.
New York, H. Shickman Gallery

New York, Hudson River Mus.
New York, Hudson River Museum at Yonkers

New York, Huntington Hartford Col.
New York, Huntington Hartford Collection
[col. housed in Gal. Mod. A. until c. 1970; now
dispersed]

New York, IBM Corp.
New York, IBM Corporation

New York, IBM Gal. Sci. & A.
New York, IBM Gallery of Science and Art

New York, ICA, P.S.1
New York, Institute for Contemporary Art,
Project Studios One

New York, India House

New York, Inst. Archit. & Urb. Stud.
New York, Institute of Architecture and
Urban Studies

New York, Inst. A. & Urb. Resources, P.S.1
New York, Institute for Art and Urban
Resources, Project Studios One [name
changed to ICA in 1989]

New York, Inst. F.A.
New York, Institute of Fine Arts

New York, Inst. N. Amer. Stud.
New York, Institute of North American
Studies

New York, Int. A. Cent.
New York, International Art Center

New York, Int. Cent. Phot.
New York, International Center of
Photography

New York, Intimate Gal.
New York, Intimate Gallery [closed]

New York, Iolas Gal.
New York, Iolas Gallery

New York, Iran. Inst.
New York, Iranian Institute [closed]

New York, Isamu Noguchi-Mus.
New York, Isamu Noguchi-Museum [Long
Island City]

New York, Jack Tilton Gal.
New York, Jack Tilton Gallery

New York, James Goodman Gal.
New York, James Goodman Gallery

New York, James Graham & Sons
New York, James Graham and Sons, Inc.

New York, Japan House Gal.
New York, Japan House Gallery [in Japan
House; name changed to Japan Soc. Gal. in
1984]

New York, Japan Soc. Gal.
New York, Japan Society Gallery

New York, Jew. Mus.
New York, The Jewish Museum

New York, Jew. Theol. Semin. America Lib.
New York, Jewish Theological Seminary of
America Library

New York, John Weber Gal.
New York, John Weber Gallery

New York, Jolas Gal.
New York, Alexander Jolas Gallery

New York, Judson

New York, Julien Levy Gal.
New York, Julien Levy Gallery [closed]

New York, Kahan Gal. Afr. A.
New York, Kahan Gallery of African Art
[closed]

New York, Keinberger Anderson Gals
New York, Keinberger Anderson Galleries

New York, Kenkclba Gal.
New York, Kenkeleba Gallery

New York, Kennedy Gals
New York, Kennedy Galleries, Inc.

New York, Kitchen
New York, The Kitchen

New York, Knoedler's
New York, M. Knoedler and Co. [Knoedler
Contemporary Art]

New York, Kootz Gal.
New York, Kootz Gallery

New York, Kouros Gal.
New York, Kouros Gallery

New York, Kress Found.
New York, Samuel H. Kress Foundation [col.
now dispersed; many pieces in Washington,
DC, N.G.A.]

New York, Kronos Col.
New York, Kronos Collection

New York, Krugier Gal.
New York, Krugier Gallery [Jan Krugier]

New York, Lefebre Gal.
New York, Lefebre Gallery

New York, Lenox Lib.
New York, Lenox Library [now Pub. Lib.]

New York, Leo Castelli Gal.
New York, Leo Castelli Gallery

New York, Leonard Hutton Gals
New York, Leonard Hutton Galleries

New York, Lerner–Misrachi Gal.
New York, Lerner–Misrachi Gallery

New York, Light Gal.
New York, Light Gallery

New York, Lincoln Cent.
New York, Lincoln Center for the Performing
Arts

New York, Macbeth Gals
New York, Macbeth Galleries

New York, Madison Gal.
New York, Madison Gallery

New York, Marie Harriman Gal.
New York, Marie Harriman Gallery

New York, Marlborough Gal.
New York, Marlborough Gallery, Inc.

New York, Marlborough–Gerson Gal.
New York, Marlborough–Gerson Gallery

New York, Martha Jackson Gal.
New York, Martha Jackson Gallery [closed]

New York, Mary Boone

New York, Mary & Jackson Burke Col.
New York, Mary and Jackson Burke
Collection

New York, Mary & Jackson Burke Found.
New York, Mary and Jackson Burke
Foundation

New York, Master Inst. United A.
New York, Master Institute of United Arts

New York, Meredith Long Contemp. A.
New York, Meredith Long Contemporary Arts
[closed]

New York, Merrin Gal.
New York, Merrin Gallery

New York, Met.
New York, Metropolitan Museum of Art

New York, Met. Opera House
New York, Metropolitan Opera House

New York, Midtown Gals
New York, Midtown Galleries

New York, Mod. Gal.
New York, The Modern Gallery

New York, MOMA
New York, Museum of Modern Art

New York, Mortimer Brandt Gal.
New York, Mortimer Brandt Gallery

New York, Mus. Afr. A.
New York, Museum for African Art

New York, Mus. Amer. Flk A.
New York, Museum of American Folk Art

New York, Mus. Amer. Ind.
New York, Museum of the American Indian,
Heye Foundation [closed; reopened as N.
Mus. Amer. Ind.]

New York, Mus. Barrio
New York, Museo del Barrio

New York, Mus. Brooklyn Inst. A. & Sci.
New York, Museum of the Brooklyn Institute
of Arts and Sciences

New York, Mus. City NY
New York, Museum of the City of New York

New York, Mus. Contemp. Crafts
New York, Museum of Contemporary Crafts

New York, Mus. Contemp. Hisp. A.
New York, Museum of Contemporary
Hispanic Art

New York, Mus. Holography
New York, Museum of Holography

New York, Mus. Non-obj. Ptg
New York, Museum of Non-objective
Painting

New York, Mus. Primitive A.
New York, Museum of Primitive Art [closed
1975; col. in Met.]

New York, N. Acad. Des.
New York, National Academy of Design

New York, N. A. Club
New York, National Arts Club

New York, Nancy Hoffman Gal.
New York, Nancy Hoffman Gallery

New York, New A. Circ.
New York, New Art Circle [Neumanti's New
Art Circle]

New York, New Mus. Contemp. A.
New York, New Museum of Contemporary
Art

New York, New Sch. Soc. Res.
New York, New School for Social Research

New York, N. Gal. F.A.
New York, National Gallery of the Fine Arts
[closed; col. transferred to NY Hist. Soc. in
1858]

New York, Nicrcndorf Gal.
New York, Nierendorf Gallery [closed]

New York, N. Mus. Amer. Ind.
New York, National Museum of the American
Indian [George Gustav Heye Center]

New York, Nohra Haim Gal.
New York, Nohra Haim Gallery

New York, Noortman & Brod Gal.
New York, Noortman and Brod Gallery

New York, N. Sculp. Soc.
New York, National Sculpture Society

New York, NY Hist. Soc.
New York, New-York Historical Society

New York, O.K. Harris Gal.
New York, O.K. Harris Gallery

New York, Otto Gerson Gal.
New York, Otto Gerson Gallery

New York, Owen Cheatham Found.
New York, Owen Cheatham Foundation

New York, Pace Gal.
New York, Pace Gallery of New York, Inc.

New York, Painters & Sculptors Assoc.
New York, Painters and Sculptors Association
[Grand Cent. A. Gals]

New York, Panicali F.A.
New York, Panicali Fine Art

New York, Passedoit Gal.
New York, Passedoit Gallery

New York, Paula Cooper Gal.
New York, Paula Cooper Gallery

New York, Pearlman Found.
New York, Henry and Rose Pearlman
Foundation, Inc.

New York, Perls Gals
New York, Perls Galleries

New York, Piero Corsini
New York, Piero Corsini

New York, Pierpont Morgan Lib.
New York, Pierpont Morgan Library

New York, Pierre Matisse Gal.
New York, Pierre Matisse Gallery

New York, Pin. Gal.
New York, Pinacoteca Gallery

New York, P.L. Durand-Ruel
New York, P.L. Durand-Ruel

New York, Prakapas Gal.
New York, Prakapas Gallery

New York, Pratt Inst.
New York, Pratt Institute

New York, Pub. Lib.
New York, Public Library [formed 1895 by amalgamation of Aster & Lenox libraries]

New York, Rachel Adler Gal.
New York, Rachel Adler Gallery

New York, Reuben Gal.
New York, Reuben Gallery [closed]

New York, Richard L. Feigen
New York, Richard L. Feigen and Co., Inc.

New York, Richard York Gal.
New York, Richard York Gallery

New York, Robert Miller Gal.
New York, Robert Miller Gallery

New York, Rockefeller Center, A. Col.
New York, Rockefeller Center, Inc., Art Collection

New York, Roerich Mus.
New York, Nicholas Roerich Museum

New York, Ronald Feldman F.A.
New York, Ronald Feldman Fine Art, Inc.

New York, Rosenberg & Stiebel
New York, Rosenberg and Stiebel, Inc.

New York, Salander-O'Reilly Gals
New York, Salander-O'Reilly Galleries, Inc.

New York, Schab Gal.
New York, William H. Schab Gallery

New York, Schomberg Cent. Res. Black Cult.
New York, Schomberg Centre for Research in Black Culture

New York, Sch. Visual A.
New York, School of Visual Arts

New York, Semaphore Gal.
New York, Semaphore Gallery

New York, Seth Siegelaub
New York, Seth Siegelaub

New York, Seventh Regiment Armory

New York, Shepherd Gal.
New York, Shepherd Gallery

New York, Sidney Janis Gal.
New York, Sidney Janis Gallery

New York, 60 E. Ninth Street
New York, 60 East Ninth Street

New York, Smolin Gal.
New York, Smolin Gallery [closed]

New York, Solo 20 Gal.
New York, Solo 20 Gallery

New York, Sonnabend Gal.
New York, Sonnabend Gallery

New York, Sotheby's
New York, Sotheby's [until 17 July 1984 called Sotheby Parke Bernet & Co.]

New York, Spanierman Gal.
New York, Spanierman Gallery

New York, Stable Gal.
New York, Stable Gallery [closed]

New York, Staempfli Gal.
New York, Staempfli Gallery

New York, Stair Sainty Matthieson

New York, State Inst. Applied A. & Sci.
New York, New York State Institute of Applied Arts and Sciences

New York, Staten Island Inst. A. & Sci.
New York, Staten Island Institute of Arts and Sciences

New York, Staten Island Mus.
New York, Staten Island Museum

New York, Stéphane Bourgeois Gal.
New York, Stéphane Bourgeois Gallery

New York, Stephen Hahn
New York, Stephen Hahn, Inc.

New York, Stephen Mazoh
New York, Stephen Mazoh and Co.

New York, Studio Mus. Harlem
New York, Studio Museum in Harlem

New York, Tanager Gal.
New York, Tanager Gallery

New York, Tibor de Nagy Gal.
New York, Tibor de Nagy Gallery

New York, Town Hall

New York, 291

New York U., Grey A.G.
New York, New York University, Grey Art Gallery and Study Center

New York U., Inst. F.A.
New York, New York University, Institute of Fine Arts

New York, United Nations Bldg
New York, United Nations Building

New York, Un. League Club
New York, Union League Club

New York, Valentine Gal.
New York, Valentine Gallery

New York, Van Cortlandt House Mus.
New York, Van Cortlandt House Museum

New York, Wakefield Gal.
New York, Wakefield Gallery

New York, Washburn Gal.
New York, Washburn Gallery

New York, Weyhe Gal.
New York, Weyhe Gallery

New York, Whitney
New York, Whitney Museum of American Art

New York, Wildenstein's
New York, Wildenstein and Co., Inc.

New York, Willard Gal.
New York, Willard Gallery [closed]

New York, Witkin Gal.
New York, The Witkin Gallery

New York, Woodside Lib.
New York, Woodside Library

New York, World House Gal.
New York, World House Gallery

New York, Xavier Fourcade
New York, Xavier Fourcade, Inc.

New York, Yeshiva U. Mus.
New York, Yeshiva University Museum

New York, Zabriskie [also in Paris]

Ngaruawahia, Turungawaewae Marae

Niagara Falls, Ontario, A.G. & Mus.
Niagara Falls, Ontario, Niagara Falls Art Gallery and Museum

Niamey, Mus. N. Niger
Niamey, Musée National du Niger

Nice, Fac. Droit
Nice, Université de Nice, Faculté de Droit

Nice, Gal. A
Nice, Galerie A

Nice, Gal. A. Contemp.
Nice, Galerie d'Art Contemporain

Nice, Gal. Ben Donte de Tout
Nice, Galerie Ben Donte de Tout [closed]

Nice, Gal. Ponchettes
Nice, Galerie des Ponchettes

Nice, Lab. 32
Nice, Laboratoire 32 [closed]

Nice, Mus. A. Mod. & Contemp.
Nice, Musée d'Art Moderne et d'Art Contemporain

Nice, Mus. A. Naïf
Nice, Musée d'Art Naïf

Nice, Mus. Archéol.
Nice, Musée d'Archéologie

Nice, Mus. B.-A.
Nice, Musée des Beaux-Arts [Musée Jules Chéret]

Nice, Musées Mun.
Nice, Direction des Musées Classés de Nice, Musées Municipaux [admins Gal. A. Contemp.; Gal. Ponchettes; Mus. Archéol.; Mus. B.-A.; Mus. Masséna; Mus. Matisse; Mus. N. Chagall; Mus. Vieux-Logis; Pal. Lascaris]

Nice, Mus. Hist. Nat.
Nice, Musée d'Histoire Naturelle

Nice, Mus. Masséna
Nice, Musée Masséna

Nice, Mus. Matisse
Nice, Musée Matisse

Nice, Mus. N. Chagall
Nice, Musée National Marc Chagall [Musée National Message Biblique Marc Chagall]

Nice, Mus. Vieux-Logis
Nice, Musée du Vieux-Logis

Nice, Pal. Lascaris
Nice, Palais Lascaris

Nice, Préfect.
Nice, Préfecture

Nice, Théât. Mun.
Nice, Théâtre Municipal

Nice, Villa Arson

Nicosia, Cyprus Mus.
Nicosia, Cyprus Museum

Nicosia, Flk A. Mus.
Nicosia, Folk Art Museum

Nicosia, Lapidary Mus.
Nicosia, Lapidary Museum

Nicosia, Leventis Mun. Mus.
Nicosia, Leventis Municipal Museum

Nicosia, Mun. A. Cent.
Nicosia, Municipal Arts Centre [in former electrical power station]

Nicosia, Mun. Cult. Cent.
Nicosia, Municipal Cultural Centre [at Famagusta Castle]

Nicosia, Mus. Byz. Icons
Nicosia, Museum of Byzantine Icons [in Archbishop Makarios III Foundation Cultural Centre]

Nicosia, Mus. Hist. Cyp. Coinage
Nicosia, Museum of the History of Cypriot Coinage [Bank of Cyprus Cultural Foundation]

Nicosia, Mus. Turk. A. & Crafts
Nicosia, Museum of Turkish Art and Crafts

Nicosia, Old Archbishopric

Nicosia, Pop. Bank Group Cult. Cent.
Nicosia, Popular Bank Group Cultural Centre

Nicosia, State A.G.
Nicosia, State Art Gallery [State Collection of Contemporary Art]

Nidwalden, Hist. Ver.
Nidwalden, Historischer Verein

Niebüll, Richard-Haizmann-Mus. Mod. Kst
Niebüll, Richard-Haizmann-Museum für Moderne Kunst

Niğde Mus.
  Niğde, Niğde Museum (Niğde Müzesi)

Niigata, B.S.N. A. Mus.
  Niigata, B.S.N. Art Museum (B.S.N. Bijutsukan)

Nijmegen, De Waag

Nijmegen, Kath. U.
  Nijmegen, Katholieke Universiteit

Nijmegen, Mus. Commanderie St Jan
  Nijmegen, Museum 'Commanderie van St Jan'

Nijmegen, Radbout-Sticht.
  Nijmegen, Radbout-Stichting

Nijmegen, Rijksmus. G. M. Kam
  Nijmegen, Rijksmuseum G. M. Kam

Nijmegen, Stadhuis

Nikol'sk, Krasnyy Gigant Works Mus.
  Nikol'sk, Krasnyy Gigant Works Museum

Nîmes, Bib. Mun.
  Nîmes, Bibliothèque Municipale de Nîmes

Nîmes, Carré A.
  Nîmes, Carré d'Art

Nîmes, Maison Carrée
  Nîmes, Musée des Antiques, Maison Carrée

Nîmes, Mus. A. Contemp.
  Nîmes, Musée d'Art Contemporain

Nîmes, Mus. Archéol.
  Nîmes, Musée Archéologique

Nîmes, Mus. B.-A.
  Nîmes, Musée des Beaux-Arts

Nîmes, Musées A. Hist.
  Nîmes, Musées d'Art et d'Histoire [admins Maison Carrée; Mus. Archéol.; Mus. B.-A.; Mus. Vieux Nîmes]

Nîmes, Mus. Vieux Nîmes
  Nîmes, Musée du Vieux Nîmes

Nimrud, Iraq, NW Pal. Mus.
  Nimrud, Iraq, Northwest Palace Museum

Nineveh, Sennacherib Pal. Mus.
  Nineveh, Sennacherib Palace Museum

Niort, Mus. B. A.
  Niort, Musée des Beaux-Arts

Niš, Archaeol. Mus.
  Niš, Archaeological Museum

Niš, N. Mus.
  Niš, National Museum (Narodni Muzej)

Nishinomiya, Egawa A. Mus.
  Nishinomiya, Egawa Art Museum

Nishiwaki, Okanoyama, Graph. A. Mus.
  Nishiwaki, Okanoyama Graphic Art Museum

Niterói, Mus. Parreiras
  Niterói, Museu Antonio Parreiras

Nitra, Archaeol. Inst. Slovak Acad. Sci.
  Nitra, Archaeological Institute of the Slovak Academy of Sciences (Archeologický Ustav Slovenské Akademie Věd)

Nivå, Nivaagaards Malsaml.
  Nivå, Nivaagaards Malerisamling (Nivaagaards Art Collection)

Nivelles, Mus. Com. Archéol.
  Nivelles, Musée Communal d'Archéologie

Nizhny Novgorod, A. Mus.
  Nizhny Novgorod, Art Museum (Nizhny Novgorodskiy Khudozhestvennyy Muzey)

Nizhny Tagil, Reg. Mus.
  Nizhny Tagil, Regional Museum

Nocera Umbra, Pin. Com.
  Nocera Umbra, Pinacoteca Comunale

Nogent-sur-Seine, Mus. Paul Dubois–Alfred Boucher
  Nogent-sur-Seine, Musée Paul Dubois–Alfred Boucher

Noirmoutier-en-l'Ile, Mus. Château
  Noirmoutier-en-l'Ile, Musée du Château

Nojiri, Lake Nojiri Mus. A.
  Nojiri, Lake Nojiri Museum of Art (Nojiriko Hakubutsukan)

Nonsuch Bay, Harmony Hall [Antigua]

Nordhorn, Städt. Gal.
  Nordhorn, Städtische Galerie

Nördlingen, Rathaus [houses Stube des Schwäbischen Bundes]

Nördlingen, Stadtmus.
  Nördlingen, Stadtmuseum [Reichstadt Museum]

Nordstemmen, Schloss Marienberg

Norfolk, VA, Chrysler Mus.
  Norfolk, VA, Chrysler Museum

Norman, U. OK Mus.
  Norman, OK, University of Oklahoma Museum

Norrköping, Kstmus.
  Norrköping, Norrköpings Konstmuseum

Norrköping, Löfstad Slott [houses Östergötlands Museum]

Norrköping, Stadsmus.
  Norrköping, Norrköpings Stadsmuseum

North Abington, MA, Pierce Gal.
  North Abington, MA, Pierce Gallery

Northallerton, N. Yorks Co. Rec. Office
  Northallerton, North Yorkshire County Record Office [County Hall]

Northampton, Cent. Mus. & A.G.
  Northampton, Central Museum & Art Gallery

Northampton, Northants Rec. Office
  Northampton, Northamptonshire Records Office

Northampton, MA, Smith Coll. Mus. A.
  Northampton, MA, Smith College Museum of Art

North Andover, MA, Mus. Amer. Textile Hist.
  North Andover, MA, Museum of American Textile History

Northridge, CA State U.
  Northridge, CA, California State University

Norwich, Bridewell Mus.
  Norwich, Bridewell Museum

Norwich, Castle Mus.
  Norwich, Castle Museum

Norwich, Norfolk Museums Serv.
  Norwich, Norfolk Museums Service [admins Cromer Mus.; Great Yarmouth, Elizabethan House Mus.; Mar. Mus. E. Anglia; Mus. Exh. Gals; Nelson's Mnmt; Tolhouse Mus.; Gressenhall, Norfolk Rural Life Mus.; King's Lynn, Lynn Mus.; Mus. Soc. Hist.; Norwich, Bridewell Mus.; Castle Mus.; St Peter Hungate Church Mus.; Thetford, Anc. House Mus.; Walsingham, Shirehall Mus.]

Norwich, Sch. A. Mus.
  Norwich, School of Art Museum

Norwich, St Andrew's Hall [formerly Blackfriars' Church]

Norwich, St Peter Hungate Ch. Mus.
  Norwich, St Peter Hungate Church Museum

Norwich, Strangers Hall Mus.
  Norwich, Strangers Hall Museum

Norwich, U. E. Anglia, Sainsbury Cent.
  Norwich, University of East Anglia, Sainsbury Centre for Visual Arts

Norwich, CT, Slater Mem. Mus.
  Norwich, CT, Slater Memorial Museum [and Converse Art Gallery]

Notre Dame, IN, Snite Mus. A.
  Notre Dame, IN, University of Notre Dame, Snite Museum of Art

Nottingham, A.G.
  Nottingham, University Art Gallery

Nottingham, Brewhouse Yard Mus.
  Nottingham, Brewhouse Yard Museum

Nottingham, Castle Mus.
  Nottingham, Castle Museum

Nottingham, Indust. Mus.
  Nottingham, Industrial Museum

Nottingham, Midland Group

Nottingham, Mus. Cost. & Textiles
  Nottingham, Museum of Costume and Textiles

Nouméa, Mus. N. Calédon.
  Nouméa, Muséum Néo-Calédonien

Novara, Civ. Gal. A. Mod.
  Novara, Civica Galleria d'Arte Moderna [Civica Galleria Giannoni; in Pal. Broletto]

Novara, Ist. Geog. Agostini
  Novara, Istituto Geografico di Agostini

Novara, Mus. Civ.
  Novara, Museo Civico [in Pal. Broletto]

Novara, Mus. Stor. Nat.
  Novara, Museo di Storia Naturale Faraggiana-Ferrandi

Novara, Pal. Bellini
  Novara, Palazzo Bellini [Banca Popolare]

Novara, Pal. Broletto
  Novara, Palazzo del Broletto [houses Mus. Civ. and Civ. Gal. A. Mod.]

Novaya Kakhovka, Pict. Gal.
  Novaya Kakhovka, Picture Gallery

Novgorod, Mus. A. Hist. & Archit.
  Novgorod, Museum of Art History and Architecture (Istoriko-Khudozhestvennyy i Arkhitekturnyy Muzey)

Novi Sad, Gal. Contemp. A.
  Novi Sad, Gallery of Contemporary Art (Galerija Savremene Likovne Umetnosti)

Novi Sad, Gal. Serb. Cult. Assoc.
  Novi Sad, Gallery of the Serbian Cultural Association (Galerija Matice Srpske) [Gallery of the Serbian Queen Bee]

Novi Sad, Mus. Vojvodina
  Novi Sad, Museum of Vojvodina

Novi Sad, Pavte Beljanski Gal.
  Novi Sad, Pavte Beljanski Gallery

Novocherkassk, Grekov House-Mus.
  Novocherkassk, Grekov House-Museum

Novocherkassk, Mus. Hist. Don Cossaks
  Novocherkassk, Museum of the History of the Don Cossaks

Nový Bor, Glassworkers' Mus.
  Nový Bor, Glassworkers' Museum (Sklářské Muzeum)

Noyon, Mus. Noyon.
  Noyon, Musée du Noyonnais

NT Scotland: see Edinburgh

Nukus, Karakalpakiya Mus. A.
  Nukus, Karakalpakiya Museum of Art

Nukus, Karakalpakiya Reg. Mus.
  Nukus, Karakalpakiya Regional Museum

Nuremberg, Akad. Bild. Kst.
Nuremberg, Akademie der Bildenden Künste

Nuremberg, Albrecht-Dürer-Haus

Nuremberg, Altes Rathaus

Nuremberg, Archv Bild. Kst Ger. Nmus.
Nuremberg, Archiv für Bildende Kunst im
Germanischen Nationalmuseum

Nuremberg, Bundesanstalt Arbeit
Nuremberg, Bundesanstalt für Arbeit

Nuremberg, Eisenwk Tafel
Nuremberg, Eisenwerk Tafel [Schrauben-
fabrik]

Nuremberg, Ger. Nmus.
Nuremberg, Germanisches Nationalmuseum

Nuremberg, Gewmus.
Nuremberg, Gewerbemuseum

Nuremberg, Handelskam.
Nuremberg, Handelskammer

Nuremberg, Heiligen-Geist-Spital

Nuremberg, Inst. Mod. Kst
Nuremberg, Institut für Moderne Kunst

Nuremberg, Kaiserburg

Nuremberg, Ksthalle
Nuremberg, Kunsthalle Nürnberg

Nuremberg, Pellerhaus [houses city archv & lib.]

Nuremberg, Rochuskapell

Nuremberg, Staatsarchv
Nuremberg, Staatsarchiv

Nuremberg, Stadtbib.
Nuremberg, Stadtbibliothek

Nuremberg, Stadtgesch. Museen
Nuremberg, Stadtgeschichtliche Museen
[admins Albrecht-Dürer-Haus; Städt. Graph.
Samml.; Stadtmus. Fembohaus; Tucher-
Schlösschen]

Nuremberg, Städt. Graph. Samml.
Nuremberg, Städtische Graphische Sammlung

Nuremberg, Städt. Kstsamml.
Nuremberg, Städtische Kunstsammlung

Nuremberg, Stadtmus. Fembohaus
Nuremberg, Stadtmuseum Fembohaus

Nuremberg, Tucher-Schlösschen

Nürtingen, Domnick Samml.
Nürtingen, Domnick Sammlung

Nuutajärvi, Glass Mus.
Nuutajärvi, Nuutajärvi Glass Museum
(Nuutajärven Lasimuseo)

Nysø, Thorvaldsen Mus.
Nysø, Thorvaldsen Museum

Oakham Castle
Oakham, Oakham Castle

Oakham, Rutland Co. Mus.
Oakham, Rutland County Museum

Oakland, CA, Brockhurst Studio

Oakland, CA, Coll. A. & Crafts
Oakland, CA, California College of Arts and
Crafts

Oakland, CA, Crown Point Gal.
Oakland, CA, Crown Point Gallery

Oakland, CA, Mills Coll.
Oakland, CA, Mills College

Oakland, CA, Mus.
Oakland, CA, Oakland Museum

Oak Park, IL, Frank Lloyd Wright Home &
Studio Found.
Oak Park, IL, Frank Lloyd Wright Home and
Studio Foundation

Oaxaca, Inst. A. Graf.
Oaxaca, Instituto de Artes Gráficas de Oaxaca

Oaxaca, Mus. A. Contemp.
Oaxaca, Museo del Arte Contemporáneo

Oaxaca, Mus. Reg.
Oaxaca, Museo Regional

Oberhausen, Städt. Gal.
Oberhausen, Städtische Galerie

Oberlin Coll., OH, Allen Mem. A. Mus.
Oberlin, OH, Oberlin College, Allen Memorial
Art Museum

Oberschleissheim: see Schleissheim

Oberursel, Hans-Thoma-Gedächt. &
Vortaunusmus.
Oberursel, Hans-Thoma-Gedächtnisstätte und
Vortaunusmuseum [mit Seifenkistenmuseum]

Obidos, Mus. Mun.
Óbidos, Museu Municipal

Odawara, Matsunaga Mem. Hall
Odawara, Matsunaga Memorial Hall

Odawara, Shōei Mem. Hall
Odawara, Shōei Memorial Hall

Odense, Andersen Barndomshjem
Odense, Hans Christian Andersens
Barndomshjem (Andersen Childhood Home)

Odense, Andersen Hus
Odense, Hans Christian Andersens Hus
(Andersen House)

Odense, Bys Museer
Odense, Odenses Bys Museer (Odense City
Museums) [admins Andersen Barndomshjem;
Andersen Hus; Fyn. Kstmus.; Fyn. Landsby;
Fyn. Stiftsmus.]

Odense, Carl Nielsen Mus.
Odense, Carl Nielsen Museum

Odense, Fyn. Kstmus.
Odense, Fyns Kunstmuseum

Odense, Fyn. Landsby
Odense, Fynske Landsby (Fyn Village)

Odense, Fyn. Stiftsmus.
Odense, Fyns Stiftsmuseum

Odense, Kulthist. Mus.
Odense, Kulturhistorisk Museum

Odense, Mus. Fotkst
Odense, Museum for Fotokunst

Oderzo, Pin. Com. Alberto Martini
Oderzo, Pinacoteca Comunale Alberto Martini

Odessa, A. Mus.
Odessa, Odessa Art Museum

Odessa, Archaeol. Museum
Odessa, Archaeological Museum

Offenbach am Main, Dt. Ledermus.
Offenbach am Main, Deutsches Ledermuseum

Offenbach am Main, Klingspor-Mus.
Offenbach am Main, Klingspor-Museum

Offenbach am Main, Stadtmus.
Offenbach am Main, Stadtmuseum

Ohara, Mus. A.
Ohara, Museum of Art [Chiba Prefecture]

Ohrid, Gal. Icons
Ohrid, Gallery of Icons

Ohrid, N. Mus.
Ohrid, National Museum

Oiron, Château
Oiron, Château d'Oiron

Ojców, Pieskowa Skata Castle

Ojojona, Mus. Pablo Zelaya Sierra
Ojojona, Museo Pablo Zelaya Sierra

Okayama, Hayashibara Mus. A.
Okayama, Hayashibara Museum of Art

Okayama, Mus. A.
Okayama, Okayama Museum of Art [name
changed to Hayashibara Mus. A. in July 1986]

Okayama, Orient Mus.
Okayama, Okayama Orient Museum

Okayama Prefect. Mus.
Okayama, Okayama Prefectural Museum

Oklahoma City, OK Hist. Soc.
Oklahoma City, OK, Oklahoma Historical
Society

Oklahoma City, OK Mus. A.
Oklahoma City, OK, Oklahoma Museum of
Art [now part of OK City Art Museum]

Oklahoma City, OK, Native Amer. Ptg Ref. Lib.
Oklahoma City, OK, Native American
Painting Reference Library

Oldenburg, Augusteum

Oldenburg, Landesbib.
Oldenburg, Landesbibliothek

Oldenburg, Landesmus.
Oldenburg, Landesmuseum für Kunst und
Kulturgeschichte

Oldenburg, Niedersächs. Staatsarchv
Oldenburg, Niedersächsisches Staatsarchiv

Oldenburg, Stadtmus.
Oldenburg, Stadtmuseum [houses Städtische
Kunstsammlungen; Theodor-Francksen-
Stiftung; Bernhard-Winter-Stiftung; Neue
Galerie; Stadtgeschichtliche Abteilung]

Old Goa, Archaeol. Mus.
Old Goa, Archaeological Museum

Oldham, A.G.
Oldham, Art Gallery

Oldham, Cent. Lib.
Oldham, Central Library

Old San Juan, Mus. Américas
Old San Juan, Museo de las Américas

Oleggio, Mus. A. Relig.
Oleggio, Museo di Arte Religiosa

Olinda, Mus. A. Contemp. Pernambuco
Olinda, Museu de Arte Contemporânea
Pernambuco

Olmütz: see Olomouc

Olomouc, Archbishop's Pal.
Olomouc, Archbishop's Palace (Arcibiskupský
Palác)

Olomouc, Co. Mus. N. Top.
Olomouc, County Museum of National
Topography (Okresní Topografické Muzeum)

Olomouc, Reg. Gal.
Olomouc, Regional Gallery (Oblastní Galerie)

Olomouc, Reg. Mus.
Olomouc, Regional Museum (Krajské
Vlastivědné Muzeum)

Olot, Mus. A. Mod.
Olot, Museu d'Art Modern

Olten, Kstmus.
Olten, Kunstmuseum

Olympia, Archaeol. Mus.
Olympia, Archaeological Museum

Omaha, NE, Joslyn A. Mus.
Omaha, NE, Joslyn Art Museum

Omaha, NE, Un. Pacific Hist. Mus.
Omaha, NE, Union Pacific Historical Museum

Omiya, Saitama Prefect. Mus.
Omiya, Saitama Prefectural Museum (Saitama-
Kenritsu Hakubutsukan)

Oneonta, NY State U. Coll.
Oneonta, New York State University College
at Oneonta

Oparto, Assoc. Arquit.
Oparto, Associação dos Arquitetos

Opava, Siles. Mus.
Opava, Silesian Museum, Collections of Ethnography (Slezské Muzeum, Národopisné Sbírky)

Opočno, nr Náchod, Castle (Státní zámek)

Opole, Office A. Exh.
Opole, Office of Art Exhibitions (Biuro Wystaw Artystycznych)

Opole, Sil. Mus.
Opole, Silesian Museum (Muzeum Śląska)

Oporo, Jovan Popović Gal.
Oporo, Jovan Popović Gallery (Galerija Jovan Popović)

Oporto, Arquiv. Hist. Mun. Porto
Oporto, Arquivo Histórico Municipal do Porto

Oporto, Bib. Púb. Mun.
Oporto, Biblioteca Pública Municipal do Porto

Oporto, Brit. Factory House
Oporto, British Factory House

Oporto, Casa de Serralves

Oporto, Casa-Mus. Fernando de Castro
Oporto, Casa-Museu Fernando de Castro

Oporto, Casa-Mus. Guerra Junqueiro
Oporto, Casa-Museu de Guerra Junqueiro

Oporto, Casa-Oficina Carneiro
Oporto, Casa-Oficina de António Carneiro

Oporto, Escola Sup. B.A.
Oporto, Escola Superior de Belas Artes

Oporto, Gal. Nasoni
Oporto, Galeria Nasoni

Oporto, Mus. N. A. Mod.
Oporto, Museu Nacional de Arte Moderna

Oporto, Mus. N. Soares dos Reis
Oporto, Museu Nacional de Soares dos Reis

Oporto, Salão de B.A. Pal. Portuevisc
Oporto, Salão de Belas Artes do Palacio Portuevise

Oporto, Salon Silva Porto

Oporto, U. Porto
Oporto, Universidade do Porto

Oporto, U. Porto, Fac. Ciênc., Mus. Antropol.
Oporto, Universidade do Porto, Faculdade de Ciências, Museu Antropológico

Oradea, Bishop's Pal.
Oradea, Bishop's Palace

Oradea, Orişana Mus.
Oradea, Orişana Museum (Muzeul Orişana)

Oradea, Tării Crişurilor Mus.
Oradea, Tării Crişurilor Museum (Muzeul Tării Crişurilor)

Orange, Mus. Mun.
Orange, Musée Municipal [incl. Musée du Vieil-Orange]

Orange, CT, Albers Found.
Orange, CT, Josef Albers Foundation

Orange, TX, Stark Found.
Orange, TX, Nelda C. & H. J. Lutcher Stark Foundation

Orange, NSW, Hist. Soc. Mus.
Orange, NSW, Historical Society Museum

Orange, NSW, Reg. A.G.
Orange, NSW, Orange Regional Art Gallery

Oranienbaum, Schloss

Orel, A.G.
Orel, Orel Art Gallery (Orlovskaya Kartinnaya Galereya)

Orense, Mus. Arqueol. Prov.
Orense, Museo Arqueológico Provincial

Orense, Mus. Dioc.-Catedralicio
Orense, Museo Diocesano-Catedralicio

Orihuela, Mus. A. Sacro
Orihuela, Museo Diocesano de Arte Sacro

Orihuela, Pal. Episcopal
Orihuela, Palacio Episcopal

Oristano, Ant.
Oristano, Antiquarium

Oristano, Pal. Arcisp.
Oristano, Palazzo Arcispedale

Orléans, Mus. B.-A.
Orléans, Musée des Beaux-Arts

Orléans, Musées Orléans
Orléans, Musées d'Orléans

Orléans, Mus. Gal., Salon Imagerie
Orléans, Musée Galleria, Salon de l'Imagerie

Orléans, Mus. Hist. & Archéol. Orléanais
Orléans, Musée Historique et Archéologique de l'Orléanais

Orlík nad Vltavou Castle
Orlík nad Vltavou, Orlík nad Vltavou Castle

Ornans, Mus. Maison Natale Gustave Courbet
Ornans, Musée Maison Natale de Gustave Courbet

Oron, N. Mus.
Oron, National Museum Oron

Orrefors, Glasbruk Mus.
Orrefors, Glasbruk Museum

Orte, Mus. Dioc. A. Sacra
Orte, Museo Diocesano d'Arte Sacra

Orth, Schloss, Donau-Mus.
Orth, Schloss, Donau-Museum

Oruro, Mus. Casa Cult.
Oruro, Universidad Técnica de Oruro, Museo de la Casa de la Cultura

Orvieto, Archv Opera Duomo
Orvieto, Archivio dell'Opera del Duomo

Orvieto, Cassa Risparmio
Orvieto, Cassa di Risparmio

Orvieto, Mus. Etrus. Faina
Orvieto, Museo Etrusco Faina

Orvieto, Mus. Opera Duomo
Orvieto, Museo Opera del Duomo

Os, Lysøen Mus.
Os, Lysøen Museum

Osaka, Cult. Mus.
Osaka, Cultural Museum

Osaka, Daimaru Mus.
Osaka, Daimaru Museum

Osaka, Expo Mem. Park
Osaka, Expo Memorial Park

Osaka, Fujita Mus. A.
Osaka, Fujita Museum of Art

Osaka, Itsuō Mus.
Osaka, Itsuō Museum

Osaka, Izumi Met. Kubosō Mem. A. Gal.
Osaka, Izumi Metropolitan Kubosō Memorial Art Gallery

Osaka, Kodama Gal.
Osaka, Kodama Gallery

Osaka, Manno Mus.
Osaka, Manno Museum [Manno Collection]

Osaka, Masaki A. Mus.
Osaka, Masaki Art Museum

Osaka, Mun. Mus.
Osaka, Municipal Museum

Osaka, Mun. Mus. A.
Osaka, Municipal Museum of Art

Osaka, Mus. A.
Osaka, Museum of Art [now Mun. Mus. A.]

Osaka, Mus. Orient. Cer.
Osaka, Museum of Oriental Ceramics

Osaka, Nabio Mus. A.
Osaka, Nabio Museum of Art

Osaka, Nanban Cult. Hall
Osaka, Nanban Culture Hall

Osaka, N. Mus. A.
Osaka, National Museum of Art

Osaka, N. Mus. Ethnol.
Osaka, National Museum of Ethnology [Expo Mem. Park]

Osaka, Seibu-Takatsuki Gal.
Osaka, Seibu-Takatsuki Gallery

Osaka, Shitennōji

Osh, Hist. & Reg. Mus.
Osh, Osh Historical and Regional Museum (Osskij Istoriko-Kraevedčeskij Muzei)

Oshawa, McLaughlin Gal.
Oshawa, Robert McLaughlin Gallery

Oshkosh, WI, Paine A. Cent.
Oshkosh, WI, Paine Art Center

Osijek, Gal. F.A.
Osijek, Gallery of Fine Arts

Osimo, Mus. Sacro Dioc.
Osimo, Museo Sacro Diocesano

Osimo, Pal. Mun.
Osimo, Palazzo Municipale

Oslo, Bispegård

Oslo, Blomqvist Ksthandel
Oslo, Blomqvist Kunsthandel

Oslo, Borsen

Oslo, Bymus.
Oslo, Bymuseum [in Frogner Manor]

Oslo, Christiania Bank & Kredit Kasse
Oslo, Christiania Bank og Kredit Kasse

Oslo, Diosnoschgeseltsgab

Oslo, Fond. Sonia Henie & Niels Onstads
Oslo, Fondation Sonia Henie i Niels Onstads

Oslo, Gal. Riis
Oslo, Galleri Riis

Oslo, Hist. Mus.
Oslo, Historisk Museum

Oslo, Indust. & Eksportens Hus
Oslo, Industriens og Eksportens Hus

Oslo, Kommunes Kstsaml.
Oslo, Kommunes Kunstsamlinger [admins Kommunes Kstsamling; Nielsens Malsaml.]

Oslo, Konserthuset

Oslo, Kon-Tiki Mus.
Oslo, Kon-Tiki Museum

Oslo, Kstforen.
Oslo, Kunstforening

Oslo, Kstindustmus.
Oslo, Kunstindustrimuseum

Oslo, Kstnerforbnd.
Oslo, Kunstnerforbundet

Oslo, Kstnernes Hus
Oslo, Kunstnernes Hus

Oslo, Munch-Mus.
Oslo, Munch-Museum

Oslo, Mus. Samtidskst
Oslo, Museet for Samtidskunst

Oslo, N.G.
Oslo, Nasjonalgalleri

Oslo, Nielsens Malsaml.
  Oslo, Amaldus Nielsens Malerisamling

Oslo, Nmus.
  Oslo, Nasjonalmuseum

Oslo, Norges Rederiforbund
  Oslo, Norges Rederiforbund

Oslo, Norske Arbeiderparti

Oslo, Norske Arhitmus.
  Oslo, Norske Arhitekturmuseum

Oslo, Norske Selskab

Oslo, Norsk Flkmus.
  Oslo, Norsk Folkemuseum

Oslo, Norsk Kultråd
  Oslo, Norsk Kulturråd [Norwegian Cultural
  Council]

Oslo, Oscarshal

Oslo, Riksarkv
  Oslo, Riksarkiv

Oslo, Slott [Royal Palace]

Oslo, Storting (Parliament)

Oslo, U.
  Oslo, Universitetet i Oslo

Oslo, Ubib.
  Oslo, Universitetsbibliotek

Oslo, Unge Kstneres Samfund

Oslo, U. Oldsaksaml.
  Oslo, Universitetets Oldsaksamlingen

Oslo, Vigeland-Mus.
  Oslo, Vigeland-Museum

Oslo, Vigeland-Parken

Oslo, Vikingskipshuset [at Bygdoy]

Oslo, Villa Nygaard

Osnabrück, Diözmus.
  Osnabrück, Diözesanmuseum

Oss, Gemeente Mus. Jan Cunencent.
  Oss, Gemeente Museum Jan Cunencentrum
  [Jan Cunencentrum; Museum en Educatieve
  Dienst voor het Maasland]

Ostend, Mus. S. Kst.
  Ostend, Museum voor Schone Kunsten

Ostend, Prov. Mus. Mod. Kst
  Ostend, Provinciaal Museum voor Moderne
  Kunst

Östersund, Jämtlands Läns Mus.
  Östersund, Jämtlands Läns Museum

Östersund, Postverket

Ostia Antica, Mus. Ostiense
  Ostia Antica, Museo Ostiense

Ostrava, A.G.
  Ostrava, Art Gallery (Galerie Výtvarnéuho
  Umění)

Osuna, Mus. Arqueol.
  Osuna, Museo Arqueológico

Osuna, Mus. A. Sacro
  Osuna, Museo de Arte Sacro [in Iglesia
  Colegial]

Oswego, SUNY, Tyler A.G.
  Oswego, NY, State University of New York,
  Tyler A.G.

Otsu, Shiga Prefect. Lake Biwa Cult. Cent.
  Ōtsu, Shiga Prefectural Lake Biwa Culture
  Centre

Ōtsu, Shiga Prefect., Onjōji
  Ōtsu, Shiga Prefecture, Onjōji

Ottawa, Canada Council A. Bank
  Ottawa, Canada Council Art Bank

Ottawa, Can. Conserv. Inst.
  Ottawa, Canadian Conservation Institute

Ottawa, Can. Mus. Civiliz.
  Ottawa, Canadian Museum of Civilization

Ottawa, Can. Mus. Contemp. Phot.
  Ottawa, Canadian Museum of Contemporary
  Photography

Ottawa, Can. War Mus.
  Ottawa, Canadian War Museum [Musée
  Canadien de la Guerre]

Ottawa, Dept Ext. Affairs
  Ottawa, Department of External Affairs

Ottawa, N. A. Cent.
  Ottawa, National Arts Centre

Ottawa, N. Archvs
  Ottawa, National Archives of Canada

Ottawa, N. Film Board, Photo Gal.
  Ottawa, National Film Board, Photo Gallery

Ottawa, N.G.
  Ottawa, National Gallery of Canada

Ottawa, N. Museums
  Ottawa, National Museums of Canada [closed
  1990; formerly admin. Can. Conserv. Inst.;
  Can. Mus. Civiliz.; N.G; N. Mus. Man; N.
  Mus. Nat. Sci.; N. Mus. Sci. & Technol.]

Ottawa, N. Mus. Man
  Ottawa, National Museum of Man

Ottawa, N. Mus. Nat. Sci.
  Ottawa, National Museum of Natural Sciences

Ottawa, N. Mus. Sci. & Technol.
  Ottawa, National Museum of Science and
  Technology

Ottawa, Rideau Hall [houses National Capital
  Commission's Official Residence Collection]

Otterlo, Kröller-Müller Sticht.
  Otterlo, Kröller-Müller Stichting

Otterlo, Rijksmus. Kröller-Müller
  Otterlo, Rijksmuseum Kröller-Müller

Otterlo, Tegelmus.
  Otterlo, Nederlands Tegelmuseum [It Noflik
  Sté]

Ottobeuren, Staatsgal. Benediktinerabtei
  Ottobeuren, Staatsgalerie in der
  Benediktinerabtei [Kunstammlungen der
  Abtei]

Ouagadougou, Cent. N. Artisanat A.
  Ouagadougou, Centre National d'Artisanat
  d'Art

Oudenaarde, Lakenhalle

Oudenaarde, Stadsmus.
  Oudenaarde, Stadsmuseum

Ouidah, Mus. Hist.
  Ouidah, Musée d'Histoire de Ouidah

Oullins, Coll. Oullins
  Oullins, Collège d'Oullins

Oulu, A. Mus.
  Oulu, Art Museum (Oulun Taidemuseo)

Ouro Preto, Mus. Inconfidência
  Ouro Preto, Museu da Inconfidência

Oviedo Cathedral, Cam. Santa
  Oviedo, Cathedral Camara Santa

Oviedo, Mus. Arqueol. Prov.
  Oviedo, Museo Arqueológico Provincial

Oviedo, Mus. B.A.
  Oviedo, Museo de Bellas Artes de Asturias

Owego, NY, Tioga Co. Hist. Soc. Mus.
  Owego, NY, Tioga County Historical Society
  Museum

Oxford, All Souls Coll.
  Oxford, All Souls College

Oxford, All Souls Coll., Codrington Lib.
  Oxford, All Souls College, Codrington Library

Oxford, Ashmolean
  Oxford, Ashmolean Museum

Oxford, Ashmolean, Beazley Archv
  Oxford, Ashmolean Museum, Beazley Archive

Oxford, Balliol Coll.
  Oxford, Balliol College

Oxford, Bear Lane Gal.
  Oxford, Bear Lane Gallery

Oxford, Bodleian Lib.
  Oxford, Bodleian Library

Oxford, Bodleian Lib., Radcliffe Sci. Lib.
  Oxford, Bodleian Library, Radcliffe Science
  Library

Oxford, Christ Church Coll.
  Oxford, Christ Church College

Oxford, Christ Church Pict. Gal.
  Oxford, Christ Church Picture Gallery

Oxford, Corpus Christi Coll.
  Oxford, Corpus Christi College

Oxford, Exeter Coll.
  Oxford, Exeter College

Oxford, Keble Coll.
  Oxford, Keble College

Oxford, Keble Coll. Col.
  Oxford, Keble College Collection

Oxford, Lincoln Coll.
  Oxford, Lincoln College

Oxford, Magdalen Coll.
  Oxford, Magdalen College

Oxford, MOMA
  Oxford, Museum of Modern Art

Oxford, Mus. Oxford
  Oxford, Museum of Oxford

Oxford, New Coll.
  Oxford, New College

Oxford, Oxon Archv
  Oxford, Oxfordshire Archive [formerly
  Oxfordshire County Record Office]

Oxford, Queen's Coll.
  Oxford, Queen's College

Oxford, Radcliffe Cam.
  Oxford, Radcliffe Camera [houses part of
  Bodleian col.]

Oxford, Somerville Coll.
  Oxford, Somerville College

Oxford, St John's Coll.
  Oxford, St John's College

Oxford U.
  Oxford, University of Oxford

Oxford, U. Coll.
  Oxford, University College

Oxford U., Delegates Exam. Sch.
  Oxford, Oxford University, Delegates
  Examination Schools

Oxford U., Fac. Music
  Oxford, Oxford University, Faculty of Music

Oxford U., Griffith Inst.
  Oxford, Oxford University, Griffith Institute
  [housed in Ashmolean]

Oxford, U. Mus.
  Oxford, University Museum [formerly Oxford
  Museum]

Oxford U., Mus. Hist. Sci.
  Oxford, Oxford University, Museum of the
  History of Science

Oxford, Un. Soc.
  Oxford, Union Society

Oxford U., Pitt Rivers Mus.
  Oxford, Oxford University, Pitt Rivers
  Museum

Oxford, Wadham Coll.
Oxford, Wadham College

Oxford, Worcester Coll.
Oxford, Worcester College

Oxford, OH, Miami U., A. Mus.
Oxford, OH, Miami University, Art Museum

Oystese, Vik Mus.
Oystese, Ingebigt Vik Museum

Pachua, Fototeca Inst. N. Antropol. & Hist.
Pachua, Fototeca del Instituto Nacional de
Antropología e Historia [former convent of
S Francisco]

Pachua, Inst. N. Antropol. & Hist.
Pachua, Instituto Nacional de Antropología e
Historia

Paderborn, Diözmus. & Domschatzkam.
Paderborn, Erzbischöfliches Diözesanmuseum
und Domschatzkammer

Paderborn, Mus. Kaiserpfalz
Paderborn, Museum in der Kaiserpfalz

Padua, Bib. Antoniana
Padua, Biblioteca Antoniana [in Basilica del
Santo]

Padua, Bib. Capitolare
Padua, Biblioteca Capitolare

Padua, Bib. Civ.
Padua, Biblioteca Civica

Padua, Bib. Semin.
Padua, Biblioteca del Seminario

Padua, Cassa di Risparmio

Padua, Cathedral Treasury

Padua, Eremitani [Chiesa degli Eremitani o dei SS
Filippo e Giacomo]

Padua, Liviano

Padua, Loggia Cornaro

Padua, Mus. Antoniano
Padua, Museo Antoniano

Padua, Mus. Civ.
Padua, Museo Civico

Padua, Mus. Civ., Bib.
Padua, Museo Civico, Biblioteca

Padua, Mus. Dioc. A. Sacra
Padua, Museo Diocesano di Arte Sacra
S Gregorio Barbarigo

Padua, Odeo Cornaro

Padua, Pal. Mun.
Padua, Palazzo Municipale [formerly Palazzo
del Podestà]

Padua, Pal. Ragione
Padua, Palazzo della Ragione

Padua, Pal. S Bonificio
Padua, Palazzo di S Bonificio

Padua, Pal. Vescovile
Padua, Palazzo Vescovile

Padua, Scu. Carmine
Padua, Scuola del Carmine

Padua, Scu. S Antonio
Padua, Scuola di San Antonio

Padua, U. Padua
Padua, Università degli Studi

Padula, Mus. Archeol. Prov. Lucania Occident.
Padula, Museo Archeologico Provinciale della
Lucania Occidentale [in Certosa]

Paestum, Mus. Archeol. N.
Paestum, Museo Archeologico Nazionale

Pagan, Archaeol. Mus.
Pagan, Archaeological Museum

Paharpur, Archaeol. Mus.
Paharpur, Archaeological Museum

Paisley, Mus. & A. Gals
Paisley, Paisley Museum and Art Galleries
[houses Observatory]

Palekh, Mus. Palekh A.
Palekh, Museum of Palekh Art (Muzey
Palekhskogo Iskusstva)

Palekh, Mus. Palekh Crafts
Palekh, Museum of Palekh Crafts (Muzey
Palekhskogo Remesla)

Palekh, Pavel Korin House-Mus.
Palekh, Pavel Korin House-Museum (Dom-
Muzey P. Korina)

Palembang, Mus. Badaruddin
Palembang, Museum Budaya Sultan Mahmud
Badaruddin

Palencia, Mus. Arqueol. Prov.
Palencia, Museo Arqueológico Provincial de
Palencia

Palencia, Mus. Catedralicio
Palencia, Museo Catedralicio

Palencia, Mus. Dioc.
Palencia, Museo Diocesano [Antiguo Palacio
Episcopal]

Palencia, Pal. Campos
Palencia, Palacio de Campos

Palermo, Accad. B.A.
Palermo, Accademia di Belle Arti

Palermo, Albergo Poveri
Palermo, Albergo dei Poveri

Palermo, Bib. Cent. Regione Siciliana
Palermo, Biblioteca Centrale Regione Siciliana

Palermo, Bib. Com.
Palermo, Biblioteca Comunale

Palermo, Casa Professa

Palermo Cathedral, Treasury

Palermo, Gal. Civ. A. Mod.
Palermo, Galleria Civica d'Arte Moderna
['Empedocle Restivo']

Palermo, Gal. Reg. Sicilia
Palermo, Galleria Regionale della Sicilia
[Galleria Nazionale della Sicilia, Palazzo
Abatellis]

Palermo, Mus. Archeol. Fond. Mormino
Palermo, Museo Archeologico della
Fondazione Mormino

Palermo, Mus. Dioc.
Palermo, Museo Diocesano

Palermo, Mus. Reg.
Palermo, Museo Regionale di Palermo [Museo
Nazionale Archeologico]

Palermo, Pal. Cinese
Palermo, Palazzina Cinese [houses Pitré
Museo Etnografico della Sicilia]

Palermo, Pal. Normanni
Palermo, Palazzo dei Normanni [formerly
Palazzo Reale]

Palermo, Pal. Speciale-Raffadali
Palermo, Palazzo Speciale-Raffadali

Palermo, Sopr. Beni Cult. & Amb.
Palermo, Soprintendenza per i Beni Culturali e
Ambienti

Palermo, Teat. Massimo
Palermo, Teatro Massimo

Palermo, Villa Giulia

Palestrina, Pal. Barberini
Palestrina, Museo Archeologico Nazionale,
Palazzo Barberini

Palma de Mallorca, Archv Hist.
Palma de Mallorca, Archivo Histórico

Palma de Mallorca, Col. March
Palma de Mallorca, Colección March

Palma de Mallorca, Fund. Pilar & Joan Miró
Palma de Mallorca, Fundació Pilar i Joan Miró

Palma de Mallorca, Mus. Catedralicio
Palma de Mallorca, Museo Catedralicio

Palma de Mallorca, Mus. Dioc.
Palma de Mallorca, Museo Diocesano [in
Palacio Episcopal]

Palma de Mallorca, Mus. Mallorca
Palma de Mallorca, Museo de Mallorca

Palma de Mallorca, Mus. Patrm. N.
Palma de Mallorca, Museo del Patrimonio
Nacional

Palma de Mallorca, Soc. Arqueol. Lul-Liana
Palma de Mallorca, Societat Arqueológica Lul-
Liana

Palm Beach, FL, Lannan Found.
Palm Beach, FL, Lannan Foundation

Palmerston North, Manawatu A.G.
Palmerston North, Manawatu Art Gallery

Palm Springs, CA, Desert Mus.
Palm Springs, CA, Desert Museum

Palmyra, Mus. Palmyra
Palmyra, Musée de Palmyra

Pamplona, Augustinas Recoletas [Convent of
Augustinian Recollects]

Pamplona, Mus. Navarra
Pamplona, Museo de Navarra

Pamukkale, Archaeol. Mus.
Pamukkale, Archaeology Museum

Panama City, Cent. Convenciones Atlapa
Panama City, Centro de Convenciones Atlapa

Panama City, Escuela N. A. Plást.
Panama City, Escuela Nacional de Artes
Plásticas

Panama City, Gal. Arteconsult
Panama City, Galería Arteconsult

Panama City, Gal. Etcétera
Panama City, Galería Etcétera

Panama City, Inst. N. Cult.
Panama City, Instituto Nacional de Cultura

Panama City, Mus. A. Contemp.
Panama City, Museo de Arte Contemporáneo

Panama City, Mus. Antropol. Reina Torres Araúz
Panama City, Museo Antropológico Reina
Torres de Araúz

Panama City, Mus. A. Relig. Colon.
Panama City, Museo de Arte Religioso
Colonial

Panama City, Mus. Hombre Panameño
Panama City, Museo del Hombre Panameño

Panama City, Mus. N.
Panama City, Museo Nacional

Panama City, Pal. Presidencial
Panama City, Palacio Presidencial [La
Presidencia]

Panama City, Taller Gráf. Pana.
Panama City, Taller de Gráfica Panarte

Panama City, U. Panamá
Panama City, Universidad de Panamá

Pančevo, N. Mus.
Pančevo, National Museum (Narodni Muzej)

Panduvasnuvara, Archaeol. Mus.
Panduvasnuvara, Archaeological Museum

Pao-chi: see Baoji

Paphos, Byz. Mus.
Paphos, Byzantine Museum

Paphos, Distr. Archaeol. Mus.
  Paphos, District Archaeological Museum

Parakou, Mus. Plein-air, Ethnographie Sci. Nat.
  Parakou, Musée de Plein-air, d'Ethnographie
  et de Sciences Naturelles

Paramaribo, Akad. Beeld. Kst.
  Paramaribo, Akademie voor Beeldende
  Kunsten

Paramaribo, Stichting Surinaams Mus.
  Paramaribo, Stichting Surinaams Museum

Paray-le-Monial, Mus. A. Sacré Le Hiéron
  Paray-le-Monial, Musée d'Art Sacré Le Hiéron
  [Musée Eucharistique Le Hiéron]

Pardubice, E. Boh. Gal.
  Pardubice, East Bohemian Gallery
  (Východočeská Galerie)

Paris, Acad. André Lhote
  Paris, Académie André Lhote

Paris, Acad. Archit.
  Paris, Académie d'Architecture

Paris, Acad. B.A.
  Paris, Académie des Beaux-Arts

Paris, Acad. Carmen
  Paris, Académie Carmen

Paris, Acad. Colarossi
  Paris, Académie Colarossi

Paris, Acad. Fr.
  Paris, Académie Française

Paris, Acad. Goncourt
  Paris, Académie Goncourt [Société des Gens
  de Lettres]

Paris, Acad. Grande Chaumière
  Paris, Académie de la Grande Chaumière

Paris, Acad. Inscr. & B.-Lett.
  Paris, Académie des Inscriptions et Belles-
  Lettres

Paris, Acad. Julian
  Paris, Académie Julian

Paris, Acad. Mod.
  Paris, Académie Moderne

Paris, Acad. N. Médec.
  Paris, Académie Nationale de Médecine

Paris, Acad. Royale
  Paris, Académie Royale de Peinture et de
  Sculpture

Paris, A. Cent.
  Paris, Art Center

Paris, Admin. Monnaies & Médailles
  Paris, Administration des Monnaies et des
  Médailles [Hôtel de la Monnaie]

Paris, Alexandre Lolas

Paris, A. & Métiers Graph.
  Paris, Arts et Métiers Graphiques

Paris, Archvs Louvre
  Paris, Archives du Louvre

Paris, Archvs Mnmts Hist.
  Paris, Archives des Monuments Historiques

Paris, Archvs N.
  Paris, Archives Nationales

Paris, Artcurial

Paris, Assoc. Amis Henri Bouchard
  Paris, Association des Amis d'Henri Bouchard

Paris, Assoc. Etude & Doc. Textiles Asie
  Paris, Association pour l'Etude et la
  Documentation des Textiles d'Asie

Paris, Atelier A. Abstrait
  Paris, Atelier d'Art Abstrait

Paris, Atelier A. Appliqué
  Paris, Atelier d'Art Appliqué

Paris, Atelier 17

Paris, Atelier Lucienne Thalheimer

Paris, Au Sans Pareil

Paris, Banque de France

Paris, Barc de Boutteville
  Paris, Le Barc de Boutteville

Paris, Bernheim-Jeune

Paris, Berthe Weill [no longer exists]

Paris, Bib. A. & Archéol.
  Paris, Bibliothèque d'Art et d'Archéologie
  [Fondation Doucet]

Paris, Bib. A. Déc.
  Paris, Bibliothèque des Arts Décoratifs [lib. of
  Mus. A. Déc.]

Paris, Bib. Admin. Ville Paris
  Paris, Bibliothèque Administrative de la Ville
  de Paris [in Hôtel de Ville]

Paris, Bib. & Archvs Patrimoine
  Paris, Bibliothèque et Archives du Patrimoine

Paris, Bib. Arsenal
  Paris, Bibliothèque de l'Arsenal

Paris, Bib. Assemblée N.
  Paris, Bibliothèque de l'Assemblée Nationale
  Française

Paris, Bib. Comédie-Fr.
  Paris, Bibliothèque de la Comédie-Française

Paris, Bib. Couvent Pères Sulpiciens de Barcelone
  Paris, Bibliothèque du Couvent des Pères
  Sulpiciens de Barcelone

Paris, Bib. Dir. Patrm.
  Paris, Bibliothèque de la Direction du
  Patrimoine

Paris, Bib. Doucet
  Paris, Bibliothèque Doucet [donated to U.
  Paris in 1917; housed in Bib. Ste-Geneviève]

Paris, Bib. Ecole N. Sup. B.-A.
  Paris, Bibliothèque de l'Ecole Nationale
  Supérieure des Beaux-Arts

Paris, Bib. Ecole Ponts & Chaussées
  Paris, Bibliothèque de l'Ecole des Ponts et
  Chaussées

Paris, Bib. Forney
  Paris, Bibliothèque Forney

Paris, Bib. Hist.
  Paris, Bibliothèque Historique de la Ville de
  Paris

Paris, Bib. Inst. France
  Paris, Bibliothèque de l'Institut de France

Paris, Bib. Inst. Fr. Archit.
  Paris, Bibliothèque de l'Institut Français
  d'Architecture

Paris, Bib. Mazarine
  Paris, Bibliothèque Mazarine

Paris, Bib. Mus. N. Hist. Nat.
  Paris, Bibliothèque du Musée National
  d'Histoire Naturelle

Paris, Bib.-Mus. Opéra
  Paris, Bibliothèque-Musée de l'Opéra

Paris, Bib. N.
  Paris, Bibliothèque Nationale

Paris, Bib. N., Cab. Est.
  Paris, Bibliothèque Nationale, Cabinet des
  Estampes

Paris, Bib. N., Cab. Médailles
  Paris, Bibliothèque Nationale, Cabinet des
  Médailles [et Antiquités]

Paris, Bib. N., Gal. Mazarine
  Paris, Bibliothèque Nationale, Galerie
  Mazarine

Paris, Bib. Pol.
  Paris, Bibliothèque Polonaise

Paris, Bib. Protestantisme Fr.
  Paris, Bibliothèque du Protestantisme Français

Paris, Bib. Royale
  Paris, Bibliothèque Royale [former name of
  Bib. N. 1815–1848]

Paris, Bib. Serv. Hydrograph. Mar.
  Paris, Bibliothèque du Service Hydrographique
  de la Marine

Paris, Bib. Sorbonne
  Paris, Bibliothèque de la Sorbonne

Paris, Bib. Ste-Geneviève
  Paris, Bibliothèque Ste-Geneviève

Paris, Bib. Thiers
  Paris, Bibliothèque Thiers

Paris, Brame & Lorenceau

Paris, Bruno Bassano

Paris, Café de la Rotonde

Paris, Caisse N. Mnmts Hist. & Sites
  Paris, Caisse Nationale des Monuments
  Historiques et des Sites [Hôtel Sully]

Paris, Callu Mérite

Paris, Carnavalet
  Paris, Musée Carnavalet

Paris, Cent. Cult. Arg.
  Paris, Centre Culturel Argentin

Paris, Cent. Cult. Can.
  Paris, Centre Culturel Canadien

Paris, Cent. Cult. Hell.
  Paris, Centre Culturel Hellénique

Paris, Cent. Cult. Marais
  Paris, Centre Culturel du Marais

Paris, Cent. Cult. Panthéon
  Paris, Centre Culturel du Panthéon

Paris, Cent. Cult. Suéd.
  Paris, Centre Culturel Suédois [incl. Institut
  Tessin]

Paris, Cent. Cult. Wallonie Bruxelles
  Paris, Centre Culturel de Wallonie Bruxelles

Paris, Cent. Etud. Cat.
  Paris, Centre d'Etudes Catalanes

Paris, Cent. Lang. Cult. Espagne
  Paris, Centre des Langages et Culture de
  l'Espagne

Paris, Cent. N. A. Contemp.
  Paris, Centre National d'Art Contemporain

Paris, Cent. Rech. Mnmts Hist.
  Paris, Centre de Recherches sur les
  Monuments Historiques

Paris, Cent. Rech. Rue Cujas
  Paris, Centre des Recherches de la Rue Cujas

Paris, Chaumet Mus.
  Paris, Chaumet Museum [Chaumet Jewellers]

Paris, Cité Sci. & Indust.
  Paris, Cité des Sciences et de l'Industrie [La
  Villette]

Paris, Coll. France
  Paris, Collège de France

Paris, Conserv. N. A. & Métiers
  Paris, Conservatoire National des Arts et
  Métiers

Paris, Contemp.
  Paris, Contemporaines

Paris, Dél. Action A.
  Paris, Délégation à l'Action Artistique

Paris, Dépôt Oeuvres A.
  Paris, Dépôt des Oeuvres d'Art de la Ville de
  Paris

Paris, Didier Imbert F.A.
  Paris, Didier Imbert Fine Art

Paris, Dir. Ant. Hist.
  Paris, Direction des Antiquités Historiques

Paris, Dir. Musées France
  Paris, Direction des Musées de France
  [Bibliothèque et Archives des Musées
  Nationaux]

Paris, Dôme des Invalides

Paris, Du Louart

Paris, Ecole Archit. Paris–La Vilette
  Paris, Ecole d'Architecture de Paris–La Vilette

Paris, Ecole B.-A.
  Paris, Ecole des Beaux-Arts

Paris, Ecole Chartes
  Paris, Ecole des Chartes

Paris, Ecole Hautes Etud. Sci. Soc.
  Paris, Ecole des Hautes Etudes en Sciences
  Sociales

Paris, Ecole Louvre
  Paris, Ecole du Louvre

Paris, Ecole Mil.
  Paris, Ecole Militaire

Paris, Ecole Norm. Ens. Dessin
  Paris, Ecole Normale d'Enseignement de
  Dessin

Paris, Ecole N. Sup. A. Déc.
  Paris, Ecole Nationale Supérieure des Arts
  Décoratifs

Paris, Ecole N. Sup. A. & Métiers
  Paris, Ecole Nationale Supérieure d'Arts et
  Métiers

Paris, Ecole N. Sup. B.-A.
  Paris, Ecole Nationale Supérieure des Beaux-
  Arts

Paris, Ecole Spéciale Archit.
  Paris, Ecole Spéciale d'Architecture

Paris, Espace Pierre Cardin

Paris, Féd. Mutualiste
  Paris, Fédération Mutualiste de Paris

Paris, Fond. Custodia, Inst. Néer.
  Paris, Fondation Custodia, Institut Néerlandais
  [Frits Lugt Collection]

Paris, Fond. Dubuffet
  Paris, Fondation Jean Dubuffet

Paris, Fond. France
  Paris, Fondation de France

Paris, Fond. Le Corbusier
  Paris, Fondation Le Corbusier

Paris, Fond. Maeght
  Paris, Fondation Maeght

Paris, Fond. N. A. Graph. & Plast.
  Paris, Fondation Nationale des Arts
  Graphiques et Plastiques

Paris, Fonds N. A. Contemp.
  Paris, Fonds National d'Art Contemporain

Paris, Fontaine Quatre Saisons
  Paris, La Fontaine des Quatre Saisons

Paris, Gal. A. Braun et Cie
  Paris, Galerie d'Art Braun et Cie

Paris, Gal. A.J. Seligmann
  Paris, Galerie A.J. Seligmann

Paris, Gal. Albert Loeb
  Paris, Galerie Albert Loeb

Paris, Gal. A. Mod. It. Grubicy
  Paris, Galerie d'Art Moderne Italienne A.
  Grubicy

Paris, Gal. André Weil
  Paris, Galerie André Weil

Paris, Gal. A. Nouv.
  Paris, Galerie Art Nouveau [closed]

Paris, Gal. Ardetti
  Paris, Galerie Ardetti

Paris, Gal. Ariel
  Paris, Galerie Ariel

Paris, Gal. Armand Drouart
  Paris, Galerie Armand Drouart

Paris, Gal. Arnaud
  Paris, Galerie Arnaud

Paris, Gal. Asse
  Paris, Galerie Asse

Paris, Gal. A. St Honoré
  Paris, Galerie d'Art St Honoré

Paris, Gal. B.-A.
  Paris, Galerie Beaux-Arts [closed]

Paris, Gal. Babylone
  Paris, Galerie de Babylone

Paris, Gal. Barbazanges
  Paris, Galerie Barbazanges

Paris, Gal. Beaubourg
  Paris, Galerie Beaubourg

Paris, Gal. Berggruen
  Paris, Galerie Berggruen

Paris, Gal. Berri
  Paris, Galerie de Berri

Paris, Gal. Billiet-Caputo
  Paris, Galerie Billiet-Caputo

Paris, Gal. Billiet-Vorms
  Paris, Galerie Billiet-Vorms

Paris, Gal. Bing
  Paris, Galerie Bing

Paris, Gal. Boëtie
  Paris, Galerie La Boëtie [no longer exists]

Paris, Gal. Boudet
  Paris, Galerie Boudet

Paris, Gal. Bougard
  Paris, Galerie Bougard

Paris, Gal. Braun
  Paris, Galerie Braun

Paris, Gal. Breteau
  Paris, Galerie Breteau

Paris, Gal. Bruno Bassano
  Paris, Galerie Bruno Bassano

Paris, Gal. Cahiers A.
  Paris, Galerie Cahiers d'Art

Paris, Gal. Cailleux
  Paris, Galerie Cailleux

Paris, Gal. Camille Goemans
  Paris, Galerie Camille Goemans

Paris, Gal. Charles Ratton
  Paris, Galerie Charles Ratton [closed]

Paris, Gal. Charpentier
  Paris, Galerie Charpentier

Paris, Gal. Claude Bernard
  Paris, Galerie Claude Bernard

Paris, Gal. Colette Allendy
  Paris, Galerie Colette Allendy [closed]

Paris, Gal. Creuze
  Paris, Galerie Creuze

Paris, Gal. Cyrus
  Paris, Galerie Cyrus

Paris, Gal. Daber
  Paris, Galerie Daber

Paris, Gal. Daniel Cordier
  Paris, Galerie Daniel Cordier

Paris, Gal. David & Garnier
  Paris, Galerie David et Garnier

Paris, Gal. Delestre
  Paris, Galerie Delestre

Paris, Gal. Denise René
  Paris, Galerie Denise René

Paris, Gal. Deux Iles
  Paris, Galerie des Deux Iles

Paris, Gal. Didier Aaron
  Paris, Galerie Didier Aaron

Paris, Gal. Dina Vierny
  Paris, Galerie Dina Vierny

Paris, Gal. 1900–2000
  Paris, Galerie 1900–2000

Paris, Gal. Dosbourg
  Paris, Galerie Dosbourg

Paris, Gal. Dragon
  Paris, Galerie du Dragon

Paris, Gal. Drouant-David
  Paris, Galerie Drouant-David

Paris, Gal. Drouin
  Paris, Galerie Drouin

Paris, Gal. Drouot
  Paris, Galerie Drouot

Paris, Gal. Druet
  Paris, Galerie Druet

Paris, Gal. Dubourg
  Paris, Galerie Dubourg

Paris, Gal. Durand-Ruel
  Paris, Galerie Durand-Ruel

Paris, Gal. Effort Mod.
  Paris, Galerie de l'Effort Moderne [closed]

Paris, Gal. Esquisse
  Paris, Galerie L'Esquisse

Paris, Gal. Etoile Scellée
  Paris, Galerie à l'Etoile Scellée

Paris, Gal. Eugène Blot
  Paris, Galerie Eugène Blot

Paris, Gal. Europe
  Paris, Galerie Europe

Paris, Gal. Fabre
  Paris, Galerie Fabre

Paris, Gal. Faubourg
  Paris, Galerie du Faubourg [closed]

Paris, Gal. Flavian
  Paris, Galerie Flavian

Paris, Gal. Fournier
  Paris, Galerie Fournier

Paris, Gal. France
  Paris, Galerie de France

Paris, Gal. Gaz. B.-A.
  Paris, Galerie de la Gazette des Beaux-Arts

Paris, Gal. Georges Bernheim
  Paris, Galerie Georges Bernheim

Paris, Gal. Georges Petit
  Paris, Galerie Georges Petit

Paris, Gal. Georges Thomas
  Paris, Galerie Georges Thomas

Paris, Gal. Gianna Sistu
  Paris, Galerie Gianna Sistu

Paris, Gal. Giraudon
  Paris, Galerie Giraudon

Paris, Gal. Givaudan
  Paris, Galerie Givaudan

Paris, Gal. Goemans
  Paris, Galerie Goemans

Paris, Gal. Gradiva
  Paris, Galerie Gradiva

Paris, Gal. Guiot
  Paris, Galerie Guiot

Paris, Gal. Hadrien Thomas
  Paris, Galerie Hadrien Thomas
Paris, Gal. Huguette Brès
  Paris, Galerie Huguette Brès
Paris, Gal. Ileana Sonnabend
  Paris, Galerie Ileana Sonnabend
Paris, Gal. Ile de France
  Paris, Galerie de l'Ile de France
Paris, Gal. Int. A. Contemp.
  Paris, Galerie Internationale d'Art
  Contemporain
Paris, Gal. Iolas
  Paris, Galerie Iolas
Paris, Gal. Iris Clert
  Paris, Galerie Iris Clert
Paris, Gal. Isy Brachot
  Paris, Galerie Isy Brachot
Paris, Gal. J
  Paris, Galerie J
Paris, Gal. Jacques Seligmann
  Paris, Galerie Jacques Seligmann [closed]
Paris, Gal. J.C. Gaubert
  Paris, Galerie J.C. Gaubert
Paris, Gal. Jean Chauvelin
  Paris, Galerie Jean Chauvelin
Paris, Gal. Jeanette Ostier
  Paris, Galerie Jeanette Ostier
Paris, Gal. Jean-Jacques Dutko
  Paris, Galerie Jean-Jacques Dutko
Paris, Gal. Jeanne-Bucher
  Paris, Galerie Jeanne-Bucher
Paris, Gal. Jeanne Castel
  Paris, Galerie Jeanne Castel
Paris, Gal. Jonas
  Paris, Galerie Jonas
Paris, Gal. Joseph Hahn
  Paris, Galerie Joseph Hahn
Paris, Gal. Kahnweiler
  Paris, Galerie Kahnweiler [closed]
Paris, Gal. Karl Flinker
  Paris, Galerie Karl Flinker
Paris, Gal. Kleber
  Paris, Galerie Kleber
Paris, Gal. Kleinberger
  Paris, Galerie Kleinberger
Paris, Gal. Lafayette
  Paris, Galerie Lafayette
Paris, Gal. Lara Vincy
  Paris, Galerie Lara Vincy
Paris, Gal. La Scala
  Paris, Galerie La Scala
Paris, Gal. Lebrun
  Paris, Galerie Lebrun
Paris, Gal. Leer
  Paris, Galerie Van Leer
Paris, Gal. Lelong
  Paris, Galerie Lelong
Paris, Gal. Licorne
  Paris, Galerie de la Licorne
Paris, Gal. Licorne en Montgolfière
  Paris, Galerie de la Licorne en Montgolfière
Paris, Galliera
Paris, Gal. Louise Leiris
  Paris, Galerie Louise Leiris
Paris, Gal. Louis-le-Grand
  Paris, Galerie Louis-le-Grand [closed]
Paris, Gal. Luxembourg
  Paris, Galerie du Luxembourg

Paris, Gal. Lydia Conti
  Paris, Galerie Lydia Conti
Paris, Gal. Maeght
  Paris, Galerie Maeght
Paris, Gal. Maeght–Lelong
  Paris, Galerie Maeght–Lelong
Paris, Gal. Mai
  Paris, Galerie Mai
Paris, Gal. Manzi, Joyant & Cie
  Paris, Galerie Manzi, Joyant et Compagnie
  [closed 1921]
Paris, Gal. Marcel Bernheim
  Paris, Galerie Marcel Bernheim
Paris, Gal. Marion Meyer
  Paris, Galerie Marion Meyer
Paris, Gal. Marseilles
  Paris, Galerie Marseilles
Paris, Gal. Marwan-Hoss
  Paris, Galerie Marwan-Hoss
Paris, Gal. Maurice Garnier
  Paris, Galerie Maurice Garnier
Paris, Gal. Melki
  Paris, Galerie Melki [closed]
Paris, Gal. Messine
  Paris, Galerie Messine
Paris, Gal. Montaigne
  Paris, Galerie Montaigne
Paris, Gal. Montparnasse
  Paris, Galerie Montparnasse
Paris, Gal. Nina Dausset
  Paris, Galerie Nina Dausset
Paris, Gal. Nunès & Fiquot
  Paris, Galerie Nunès et Fiquot
Paris, Gal. Oeil
  Paris, Galerie de l'Oeil
Paris, Gal. Oru
  Paris, Galerie Oru
Paris, Gal. Pardo
  Paris, Galerie Pardo
Paris, Gal. Paris
  Paris, Galerie de Paris
Paris, Gal. Patrice Trigano
  Paris, Galerie Patrice Trigano
Paris, Gal. Paul Guillaume
  Paris, Galerie Paul Guillaume
Paris, Gal. Paul Rosenberg
  Paris, Galerie Paul Rosenberg
Paris, Gal. Pavolozky
  Paris, Galerie Pavolozky
Paris, Gal. Percier
  Paris, Galerie Percier
Paris, Gal. Pétidès
  Paris, Galerie Pétidès
Paris, Gal. Petit
  Paris, Galerie Petit [closed 1933]
Paris, Gal. Pierre
  Paris, Galerie Pierre
Paris, Gal. Pierre Colle
  Paris, Galerie Pierre Colle
Paris, Gal. Pierre Domec
  Paris, Galerie Pierre Domec
Paris, Gal. Pierre Gaubert
  Paris, Galerie Pierre Gaubert
Paris, Gal. Pierre Loeb
  Paris, Galerie Pierre Loeb
Paris, Gal. Pléiade
  Paris, Galerie de la Pléiade
Paris, Gal. Point Cardinal
  Paris, Galerie Le Point Cardinal

Paris, Gal. Présidence
  Paris, Galerie de la Présidence
Paris, Gal. Quatre Chemins
  Paris, Galerie aux Quatre Chemins
Paris, Gal. Quatre Saisons
  Paris, Galerie des Quatre Saisons
Paris, Gal. Raymond Cordier
  Paris, Galerie Raymond Cordier
Paris, Gal. Raymond Creuze
  Paris, Galerie Raymond Creuze
Paris, Gal. René Drouin
  Paris, Galerie René Drouin
Paris, Gal. Rive Droite
  Paris, Galerie Rive Droite
Paris, Gal. Sagot-Le Garrec
  Paris, Galerie Sagot-Le Garrec
Paris, Gal. Schroth
  Paris, Galerie Schroth [closed]
Paris, Gal. Sedelmeyer
  Paris, Galerie Sedelmeyer
Paris, Gal. Simon
  Paris, Galerie Simon
Paris, Gal. Spiess
  Paris, Galerie Spiess
Paris, Gal. Surréaliste
  Paris, Galerie Surréaliste
Paris, Gal. Tanagra
  Paris, Galerie Tanagra
Paris, Gal. Vanuxem
  Paris, Galerie Vanuxem
Paris, Gal. Vavin–Raspail
  Paris, Galerie Vavin–Raspail
Paris, Gal. Vendôme
  Paris, Galerie Vendôme
Paris, Gal. Vignon
  Paris, Galerie Vignon
Paris, Gal. Villand & Galanis
  Paris, Galerie Villand et Galanis
Paris, Gal. 23
  Paris, Galerie 23
Paris, Gal. Vollard
  Paris, Galerie Vollard [closed]
Paris, Gal. Zak
  Paris, Galerie Zak
Paris, Gal. Zodiaque
  Paris, Galerie du Zodiaque
Paris, Gobelins Mobilier N.
  Paris, Gobelins Mobilier National
Paris, Grand Pal.
  Paris, Grand Palais [Galeries Nationales
  d'Exposition du Grand Palais]
Paris, Heim
  Paris, Heim et Cie, Marcel
Paris, Hôp. Enfants-Assist.
  Paris, Hôpital des Enfants-Assistés
Paris, Hôp. Laënnec, Chapel
  Paris, Hôpital Laënnec, Chapel
Paris, Hôp. Saint-Vincent-de-Paul
  Paris, Hôpital Saint-Vincent-de-Paul
Paris, Hôp. Salpêtrière
  Paris, Hôpital de la Salpêtrière
Paris, Hôp. Ste Anne
  Paris, Hôpital Ste-Anne
Paris, Hôtel A.
  Paris, Hôtel des Arts

Paris, Mus. N. A. & Trad. Pop.
  Paris, Musée National des Arts et Traditions
  Populaires
Paris, Mus. N. Hist. Nat.
  Paris, Musée National d'Histoire Naturelle
Paris, Mus. Nissim de Camondo
  Paris, Musée Nissim de Camondo
Paris, Mus. N. Légion d'Honneur
  Paris, Musée National de la Légion d'Honneur
  et des Ordres de Chevalerie
Paris, Mus. N. Tech.
  Paris, Musée National des Techniques
Paris, Mus. Observatoire
  Paris, Musée de l'Observatoire
Paris, Mus. Orangerie
  Paris, Musée de l'Orangerie
Paris, Mus. Orsay
  Paris, Musée d'Orsay
Paris, Mus. Permanent Colon.
  Paris, Musée Permanent des Colonies [known
  by this name 1931–61; now Mus. A. Afr. &
  Océan.]
Paris, Mus. Picasso
  Paris, Musée Picasso
Paris, Mus. Plans-Reliefs
  Paris, Musée des Plans-Reliefs [in Hôtel des
  Invalides]
Paris, Mus. Porcelain & Pott.
  Paris, Museum of Porcelain and Pottery
Paris, Mus. Renan-Scheffer
  Paris, Musée Renan-Scheffer
Paris, Mus. Rodin
  Paris, Musée Auguste Rodin
Paris, Mus. Sculp. Plein Air
  Paris, Musée de Sculpture en Plein Air
Paris, Mus. S.E.I.T.A.
  Paris, Musée du S.E.I.T.A. [Service
  d'Exploitation Industrielle des Tabacs et des
  Allumettes; also known as Mus.-Gal. Sieta]
Paris, Mus. Soc.
  Paris, Musée Social [closed]
Paris, Mus. Trocadéro
  Paris, Musée du Trocadéro
Paris, Mus. Victor Hugo
  Paris, Musée Victor Hugo
Paris, Mus. Vieux-Montmartre
  Paris, Musée du Vieux-Montmartre
Paris, Mus. Zadkine
  Paris, Musée Zadkine
Paris, Opéra
Paris, Orangerie Tuileries
  Paris, Orangerie des Tuileries
Paris, Pal. A. Mod.
  Paris, Palais d'Art Moderne
Paris, Pal. B.-A.
  Paris, Palais de Beaux-Arts
Paris, Pal.-Bourbon
  Paris, Palais-Bourbon [Assemblée Nationale]
Paris, Pal. Chaillot
  Paris, Palais de Chaillot
Paris, Pal. Elysée
  Paris, Palais de l'Elysée
Paris, Pal. Fêtes
  Paris, Palais des Fêtes
Paris, Pal. Gal.
  Paris, Palais Galerie
Paris, Pal. Galliéra
  Paris, Palais Galliéra

Paris, Pal. Glace
  Paris, Palais de Glace
Paris, Pal. Indust.
  Paris, Palais de l'Industrie
Paris, Pal. Justice
  Paris, Palais de Justice
Paris, Pal. Justice, Salle Gens-d'Armes
  Paris, Palais de Justice, Salle des Gens d'Armes
Paris, Pal. Luxembourg
  Paris, Palais du Luxembourg
Paris, Pal.-Royal
  Paris, Palais-Royal [houses Conseil d'Etat et
  Ministère des Affaires Culturelles]
Paris, Pal. Tokyo
  Paris, Palais de Tokyo
Paris, Pal. Tuileries
  Paris, Palais des Tuileries [largely destr. 1871]
Paris, Paul Prouté S.A.
Paris, Pav. A.
  Paris, Pavillon des Arts
Paris, Pav. Marsan, Exp. St Jean
  Paris, Pavillon de Marsan, Exposition St Jean
Paris, Petit Pal.
  Paris, Musée du Petit Palais
Paris, Pol. Hist.-Lit. Soc.
  Paris, Polish Historical-Literary Society
Paris, Pompidou
  Paris, Centre Georges Pompidou [admins
  Mus. Cinema; Mus. Homme; Mus. Mar.; Mus.
  Matériaux; Mus. Mnmts Fr.; Pompidou; Centre
  National d'Art et de Culture Georges-
  Pompidou. Pompidou houses Bibliothèque
  Publique d'Information; Centre de Création
  Industrielle; Institut de Recherche et
  Coordination Acoustique/Musique; Mus. N.
  A. Mod.]
Paris, Renou & Colle
  Paris, Renou et Colle
Paris, Renou & Poyet
  Paris, Renou et Poyet
Paris, Resche
Paris, Réunion Musées N.
  Paris, Réunion des Musées Nationaux
Paris, Robert Lebel Col.
  Paris, Robert Lebel Collection
Paris, Rodolphe Stadler
Paris, Sacre du Printemps
  Paris, Le Sacre du Printemps
Paris, Saint-Roche
Paris, Salle Gaveau
Paris, Salle Royale
Paris, Salle Soc. Savantes
  Paris, Salle des Sociétés Savantes
Paris, Salon Champs-Elysées
  Paris, Salon des Champs-Elysées
Paris, Salon Escalier
  Paris, Salon de l'Escalier
Paris, Salon Mars
  Paris, Salon de Mars
Paris, Salon Réalités Nouv.
  Paris, Salon des Réalités Nouvelles
Paris, Salons Hôtel Brébant
  Paris, Salons de l'Hôtel Brébant
Paris, Salons Vie Mod.
  Paris, Salons de La Vie Moderne [closed]
Paris, Soc. Fr. Phot.
  Paris, Société Française de Photographie
Paris, Soc. N. B.-A.
  Paris, Société Nationale des Beaux-Arts

Paris, Studio Facchetti
Paris, Théât. Cité U.
  Paris, Théâtre de la Cité Universitaire
Paris, Théât. Michel
  Paris, Théâtre Michel
Paris, Trésor Cathédrale Notre-Dame
  Paris, Trésor de la Cathédrale Notre-Dame
Paris, Un. Cent. A. Déc.
  Paris, Union Centrale des Arts Décoratifs
  [admins Mus. A. Déc.; Mus. A. Mode; Mus.
  Nissim de Camondo; Mus. Publicité]
Paris, UNESCO
  Paris, United Nations Educational, Scientific
  and Cultural Organization
Paris, U. Notre Dame
  Paris, Université de Notre Dame
Paris, U. Paris III
  Paris, Université de Paris III [Sorbonne-
  Nouvelle]
Paris, U. Paris IV
  Paris, Université de Paris IV [Paris-Sorbonne]
Paris, U. Paris V, Fac. Médec.
  Paris, Université de Paris V, Faculté de
  Médecine [René Descartes]
Paris, U. Paris V, Mus. Hist. Médec.
  Paris, Université de Paris V, Musée d'Histoire
  de la Médecine [René Descartes]
Paris, U. Paris X
  Paris, Université de Paris X [Paris-Nanterre]
Paris, U. Paris XII
  Paris, Université de Paris XII [Paris-Val-de-
  Marne]
Paris, U. Paris XIII
  Paris, Université de Paris XIII [Paris-Nord]
Paris, Wildenstein Inst.
  Paris, Wildenstein Institute
Paris, Zabriskie [also in New York]
Parma, Accad. B.A.
  Parma, Accademia di Belle Arti
Parma, Archv Stato
  Parma, Archivio di Stato
Parma, Bib. Palatina
  Parma, Biblioteca Palatina
Parma, Camera S Paolo
  Parma, Camera di San Paolo
Parma, Charterhouse
Parma, Corte Mamiano Found.
  Parma, Magnani-Rocca, Corte di Mamiano
  Foundation
Parma, Gal. Consigli A.
  Parma, Galleria Consigli Arte
Parma, Gal. Milione
  Parma, Galleria del Milione
Parma, G.N.
  Parma, Galleria Nazionale [in Pal. Pilotta]
Parma, Municipio
Parma, Mus. Bodoniano
  Parma, Museo Bodoniano [in Pal. Pilotta]
Parma, Mus. Lombardi
  Parma, Museo Glauco Lombardi
Parma, Mus. N. Ant.
  Parma, Museo Nazionale di Antichità [in Pal.
  Pilotta]
Parma, Osp. della Misericordia
  Parma, Ospedale della Misericordia [houses
  Archv Stato]
Parma, Pal. Com.
  Parma, Palazzo Comunale

Parma, Pal. Giardino
Parma, Palazzo del Giardino

Parma, Pal. Governatore
Parma, Palazzo del Governatore

Parma, Pal. Pilotta
Parma, Palazzo della Pilotta [houses G.N.;
Mus. Bodoniano; Mus. N. Ant.]

Parma, Pin. Stuard
Parma, Pinacoteca Giuseppe Stuard

Parma, Sopr. B.A.
Parma, Soprintendenza alle Belle Arti [admins
G.N.; Mus. Bodoniano; Mus. N. Ant.]

Parma, U. Parma
Parma, Università degli Studi

Parma, U. Parma, Cent. Studi & Archv
Communic.
Parma, Università degli Studi, Centro di Studi
e Archivio della Communicazione

Parma, U. Parma, Ist. Stor. A.
Parma, Università degli Studi, Istituto di Storia
dell'Arte

Paro, N. Mus. Bhutan
Paro, National Museum of Bhutan

Paros, Archaeol. Mus.
Paros, Archaeological Museum

Parramatta, Old Govt House
Parramatta, Old Government House

Pasadena, CA, A. Mus.
Pasadena, CA, Pasadena Art Museum [name
changed to Norton Simon Mus. in Oct 1975]

Pasadena, CA, Baxter A. Mus.
Pasadena, CA, Baxter Art Museum

Pasadena, CA, Inst. Technol.
Pasadena, CA, California Institute of
Technology

Pasadena, CA, MOMA
Pasadena, CA, Museum of Modern Art [name
of Norton Simon Mus. March 1973–April
1974]

Pasadena, CA, Norton Simon Mus.
Pasadena, CA, Norton Simon Museum

Passariano, Villa Manin

Passau, Burgfeste Oberhaus [admins Hist. Mus.;
Neue Samml.; Niederbayer. Feuerwehrmus.;
Oberhaus Mus.; Staatl. Gal.]

Passau, Domschatz- & Diözmus.
Passau, Domschatz- und Diözesanmuseum

Passau, Glasmus. & Kochbuchmus.
Passau, Passauer Glasmuseum und
Kochbuchmuseum

Passau, Hist. Mus.
Passau, Historisches Museum

Passau, Mus. Mod. Kst.
Passau, Museum Moderner Kunst [Stiftung
Wörlen]

Passau, Neue Samml.
Passau, Neue Sammlung

Passau, Niederbayer. Feuerwehrmus.
Passau, Niederbayerisches Feuerwehrmuseum

Passau, Oberhaus Mus.
Passau, Oberhaus Museum

Passau, Staatl. Gal.
Passau, Staatliche Galerie

Pasto, Mus. Escobar Maria Govetti
Pasto, Museo Escobar Maria Govetti

Pasto, Mus. Mariadez
Pasto, Museo Mariadez

Pastrana, Colegiada

Patan, Gujarat, Hemacandracarya Jnana Temple

Patan, Nepal, Mus. Excav. Archaeol. Ant.
Patan, Nepal, Museum for Excavated
Archaeological Antiquities

Pateley Bridge, Nidderdale Mus.
Pateley Bridge, Nidderdale Museum

Patiala, Punjab. U.
Patiala, Punjabi University

Patmos, St John the Divine Monastery, Treasury
Lib.
Patmos, St John the Divine Monastery,
Treasury Library

Patna Mus.
Patna, Patna Museum

Patna U., Dept Anc. Ind. Hist. & Archaeol. Mus.
Patna, Patna University, Department of
Ancient Indian History and Archaeology
Museum

Patras, Archaeol. Mus.
Patras, Archaeological Museum

Pau, Château

Pau, Mus. B.-A.
Pau, Musée des Beaux-Arts

Pau, Mus. Bernadotte
Pau, Musée Bernadotte

Pau, Musées Pau
Pau, Musées de Pau [admins Château; Mus. B.-
A.; Mus. Bernadotte; Mus. N. Château; Mus.
Rég. Béarnais]

Pau, Mus. N. Château
Pau, Musée National du Château de Pau

Pau, Mus. Rég. Béarnais
Pau, Musée Régional Béarnais

Pauillac, Châteaux Mouton-Rothschild

Pauillac, Mus. Vin
Pauillac, Musée du Vin [Le Vin et la Vigne
dans l'Art; in Châteaux Mouton-Rothschild,]

Pavia, Castello Visconteo [houses Mus. Archeol.;
Mus. Risorgimento; Mus. Scul.; Pin. Malaspina]

Pavia, Mus. Archeol.
Pavia, Museo Archeologico [in Castello
Visconteo]

Pavia, Mus. Certosa
Pavia, Museo della Certosa [in Pal. Ducale]

Pavia, Musei Civ.
Pavia, Musei Civici [admins Mus. Archeol.;
Mus. Risorgimento; Mus. Scul.; Pin.
Malaspina]

Pavia, Mus. Risorgimento
Pavia, Museo del Risorgimento [in Castello
Visconteo]

Pavia, Mus. Scul.
Pavia, Museo di Scultura [in Castello
Visconteo]

Pavia, Pal. Ducale
Pavia, Palazzo Ducale [houses Mus. Certosa]

Pavia, Pin. Malaspina
Pavia, Pinacoteca Malaspina [in Castello
Visconteo]

Pavia, Semin. Vescovile
Pavia, Seminario Vescovile [formerly
monastery of Pusterla/S Maria Teodote]

Pavia, U. Stud., Cent. Ric. Trad. MS. Aut. Mod. &
Contemp.
Pavia, Università degli Studi, Centro di Ricerca
sulle Tradizioni Monoscritte di Autori
Moderni e Contemporanei

Pavlovsk Pal.
Pavlovsk, Pavlovsk Palace (Pavlovskiy
Dvorets)

Peć, Local Mus.
Peć, Local Museum

Peć, Miladin Popović Mus. Revolution
Peć, Miladin Popović Museum of the
Revolution (Muzej Revolucije Miladin
Popović)

Pécs, Csontváry Mus.
Pécs, Csontváry Museum (Csontváry
Múzeum)

Pécs, Ferenc Martyn Col.
Pécs, Ferenc Martyn Collection (Martyn
Ferenc Gyüjtemény)

Pécs, Mod. Hung. Mus.
Pécs, Modern Hungarian Museum

Pécs, Nemes Mus.
Pécs, Endre Nemes Museum (Endre Nemes
Múzeum)

Pécs, Pannonius Mus.
Pécs, Janus Pannonius Museum (Janus
Pannonius Múzeum)

Pécs, Uitz Mus.
Pécs, Uitz Museum

Pécs, Un. Lib.
Pécs, Union Library (Szakszervezetek
Könyvtára)

Peiraeus, Archaeol. Mus.
Peiraeus, Archaeological Museum

Pejeng, Archaeol. Mus.
Pejeng, Archaeological Museum [Bali]

Pekan, Sultan Abu Bakar Mus.
Pekan, Sultan Abu Bakar Museum (Muzium
Sultan Abu Bakar)

Peking: see Beijing

Pella, Archaeol. Mus.
Pella, Archaeological Museum

Pelplin, Abbot's House

Pelplin, Dioc. Mus.
Pelplin, Diocesan Museum (Muzeum
Diecezjalne)

Penang, State Mus.
Penang, State Museum (Muzium Pulau
Pinang)

Pendzhikent, Rudaki Abuabdullo Repub. Hist. &
Reg. Mus.
Pendzhikent, Rudaki Abuabdullo Republican
Historical and Regional Museum

Peniche, Misericórdia

Penwith, Soc. A.
Penwith, Society of Arts

Penza, Reg. Mus.
Penza, Regional Museum (Penzenskiy
Ob'yedinyonyy Krayevedcheskiy Muzey)

Penzance, Penlee House Mus. & A.G.
Penzance, Penlee House Museum and Art
Gallery

Peradeniya, U. Peradeniya
Peradeniya, University of Peradeniya

Perast, Mun. Mus.
Perast, Municipal Museum (Muzej Grada
Perasta)

Pereira, Mus. Arqueol.
Pereira, Museo Arqueológico

Perelada, Mus. Castillo-Pal.
Perelada, Museo del Castillo-Palacio de
Perelada [Colección Mateu in Convento del
Carmen]

Périgueux, Mus. Périgord
  Périgueux, Musée de Périgord

Perm', A.G.
  Perm', Art Gallery (Khudozhestvennaya
  Galereya)

Péronne, Mus. Danicourt
  Péronne, Musée Danicourt

Perpignan, Mus. Rigaud
  Perpignan, Musée Hyacinthe Rigaud

Perth, Tayside, Mus. & A.G.
  Perth, Tayside, Perth Museum and Art Gallery

Perth, A.G. W. Australia
  Perth, W. Australia, Art Gallery of Western
  Australia

Perth, Lib. & Inf. Serv. W. Australia
  Perth, Library and Information Service of
  Western Australia [admins Alexander Lib.
  Bldg; Cult. Cent.]

Perth, State Lib. Serv. W. Australia
  Perth, State Library Service of Western
  Australia [name changed to Lib. & Inf. Serv.
  W. Australia in May 1989]

Perth, U. W. Australia, Anthropol. Res. Mus.
  Perth, University of Western Australia,
  Anthropology Research Museum

Perth, U. W. Australia, Berndt Mus. Anthropol.
  Perth, University of Western Australia, Berndt
  Museum of Anthropology [formerly
  Anthropol. Res. Mus.]

Perth, W. Australia, Alexander Lib. Bldg
  Perth, W. Australia, Alexander Library
  Building

Perth, W. Australia, Christensen Fund

Perth, W. Australia, Cult. Cent.
  Perth, W. Australia, Cultural Centre

Perth, W. Australia, Fergusson Gal.
  Perth, W. Australia, Fergusson Gallery

Perth, W. Austral. Mus.
  Perth, Western Australian Museum

Perugia, Archv Stato
  Perugia, Archivio di Stato

Perugia, Bib. Augusta
  Perugia, Biblioteca Augusta

Perugia, Bib. Capitolare
  Perugia, Biblioteca Capitolare

Perugia, Cambio

Perugia, Gal. A.
  Perugia, Galleria d'Arte

Perugia, G.N. Umbria
  Perugia, Galleria Nazionale dell'Umbria

Perugia, Mus. Archeol. N. Umbria
  Perugia, Museo Archeologico Nazionale
  dell'Umbria

Perugia, Mus. Opera Duomo
  Perugia, Museo dell'Opera del Duomo

Perugia, Osp. Misericordia
  Perugia, Ospedale della Misericordia

Pesaro, Bib. Marchese Antaldo Antaldi
  Pesaro, Biblioteca del Marchese Antaldo
  Antaldi di Pesaro

Pesaro, Bib. & Mus. Oliveriani
  Pesaro, Biblioteca e Musei Oliveriani

Pesaro, Mus. Civ.
  Pesaro, Museo Civico

Pesaro, Pal. Bonamini-Pepoli
  Pesaro, Palazzo Bonamini-Pepoli

Pesaro, Pal. Ducale
  Pesaro, Palazzo Ducale

Pescara, Casa Dante
  Pescara, Casa di Dante

Pescara, Pal. Gov.
  Pescara, Palazzo del Governo

Pescara, Torre Passeri
  Pescara, Torre dei Passeri

Peschiera del Garda, Municipio

Pescia, Pal. Vescovile
  Pescia, Palazzo Vescovile

Pescia, Prepositura

Peshawar Mus.
  Peshawar, Peshawar Museum

Peshawar, U. Peshawar, Dept Archaeol. Mus.
  Peshawar, University of Peshawar,
  Department of Archaeology Museum

Peterborough, Ont., A.G.
  Peterborough, Ont., Art Gallery

Petionville, Gal. Marassa
  Petionville, Galerie Marassa

Petionville, Gal. Panamér.
  Petionville, Galerie Panaméricaine

Petionville, Mahfoud A.G.
  Petionville, Mahfoud Art Gallery

Petionville, N. A.
  Petionville, National Art

Petionville, Red Carpet A.G.
  Petionville, Red Carpet Art Gallery

Petionville, Shishi Haiti
  Petionville, Shishi o£ Haiti

Petit-Quevilly, Théât. Maxime-Gorki
  Petit-Quevilly, Théâtre Maxime-Gorki

Petra Mus.
  Petra, Museum

Petrodvorets, Monplaisir Pal.
  Petrodvorets [Peterhof, Petergof, Petrogof],
  Monplaisir Palace

Petrograd, Dobychina Gal.
  Petrograd, Dobychina Gallery [closed]

Petronell, Schloss, Donau-Mus.
  Petronell, Schloss, Donau-Museum [now in
  Orth]

Petrópolis, Mus. Imp.
  Petrópolis, Museu Imperial

Petrozavodsk, Karelian Mus. F.A.
  Petrozavodsk, Karelian Museum of Fine Art

Pfäffikon, Schwyz, Seedamm-Kultzent.
  Pfäffikon, Schwyz, Seedamm-Kulturzentrum

Pforzheim, Schmuckmus.
  Pforzheim, Schmuckmuseum Pforzheim im
  Reuchlinhaus

Phikardou, Rural Mus.
  Phikardou, Rural Museum

Philadelphia, PA, A. Alliance
  Philadelphia, PA, Art Alliance

Philadelphia, PA Acad. F.A.
  Philadelphia, PA, Pennsylvania Academy of
  the Fine Arts

Philadelphia, PA, Acad. Nat. Sci.
  Philadelphia, PA, Academy of Natural
  Sciences of Philadelphia

Philadelphia, PA, A.G. Moore Coll.
  Philadelphia, PA, Art Gallery of Moore
  College

Philadelphia, PA, Amer. Philos. Soc.
  Philadelphia, PA, American Philosophical
  Society

Philadelphia, PA, Amer. Philos. Soc. Lib.
  Philadelphia, PA, American Philosophical
  Society Library

Philadelphia, PA, Athenaeum
  Philadelphia, PA, Athenaeum of Philadelphia

Philadelphia, PA, Atwater Kent Mus.
  Philadelphia, PA, Atwater Kent Museum

Philadelphia, PA, Bar Assoc.
  Philadelphia, PA, Philadelphia Bar Association

Philadelphia, PA, Chrysler Col.
  Philadelphia, PA, Chrysler Collection

Philadelphia, PA, Cliveden [Cliveden of the
National Trust, Inc.]

Philadelphia, PA, Coll. A.
  Philadelphia, PA, College of Art

Philadelphia, PA, Coll. Phys., Mutter Mus.
  Philadelphia, PA, Mutter Museum of the
  College of Physicians of Philadelphia

Philadelphia, PA, Davis & Harvey Gals
  Philadelphia, PA, Davis and Harvey Galleries
  [closed]

Philadelphia, PA, Fairmount Park A. Assoc.
  Philadelphia, PA, Fairmount Park Art
  Association

Philadelphia, PA, Fleischer A. Mem.
  Philadelphia, PA, Fleischer Art Memorial

Philadelphia, PA, Forrest Home Aged Actors
  Philadelphia, PA, Edwin Forrest Home for
  Aged Actors

Philadelphia, PA, Franklin Inst.
  Philadelphia, PA, Franklin Institute

Philadelphia, PA, Free Lib.
  Philadelphia, PA, Free Library of Philadelphia

Philadelphia, PA, Hist. Soc.
  Philadelphia, PA, Historical Society of
  Pennsylvania

Philadelphia, PA Hosp.
  Philadelphia, PA, Pennsylvania Hospital

Philadelphia, PA, Indep. N. Hist. Park
  Philadelphia, PA, Independence National
  Historical Park

Philadelphia, PA, La Salle U.
  Philadelphia, PA, La Salle University

Philadelphia, PA, Mar. Mus.
  Philadelphia, PA, Maritime Museum

Philadelphia, PA, Moore Coll. A. & Des.
  Philadelphia, PA, Moore College of Art and
  Design

Philadelphia, PA, Moore Coll. A. & Des., Goldie
Paley Gal.
  Philadelphia, PA, Moore College of Art and
  Design, Goldie Paley Gallery

Philadelphia, PA, Mus.
  Philadelphia, PA, Philadelphia Museum [col.
  now dispersed]

Philadelphia, PA, Mus. A.
  Philadelphia, PA, Museum of Art

Philadelphia, PA, Mus. Civ. Cent.
  Philadelphia, PA, Museum of the Philadelphia
  Civic Center

Philadelphia, PA Mus. F.A.
  Philadelphia, PA, Pennsylvania Museum of
  Fine Arts

Philadelphia, PA, Phot. Gal.
  Philadelphia, PA, The Photography Gallery

Philadelphia, PA, Provident N. Bank
  Philadelphia, PA, Provident National Bank

Philadelphia, PA, Prt Club Mus.
  Philadelphia, PA, Print Club Museum

Philadelphia, PA, Rodin Mus.
  Philadelphia, PA, Rodin Museum

Philadelphia, PA, Rosenbach Lib.
  Philadelphia, PA, Rosenbach Library

Philadelphia, PA, Rosenbach Mus.
  Philadelphia, PA, Rosenbach Museum

Philadelphia, Soc. PA
    Philadelphia, PA, Society of Pennsylvania

Philadelphia, PA, Temple U. Gal.
    Philadelphia, PA, Temple University Gallery

Philadelphia, PA, Temple U., Tyler Sch. A.
    Philadelphia, PA, Temple University, Tyler
    School of Art

Philadelphia, PA, Thomas Jefferson U.
    Philadelphia, PA, Thomas Jefferson University

Philadelphia, PA, Thomas Jefferson U., Medic.
Col.
    Philadelphia, PA, Thomas Jefferson
    University, Medical Collection

Philadelphia, U. PA
    Philadelphia, PA, University of Pennsylvania

Philadelphia, U. PA, Furness Lib.
    Philadelphia, PA, University of Pennsylvania,
    Horace Howard Furness Library

Philadelphia, U. PA, ICA
    Philadelphia, PA, University of Pennsylvania,
    Institute of Contemporary Art

Philadelphia, U. PA, Jones Gal.
    Philadelphia, PA, University of Pennsylvania,
    Lloyd P. Jones Gallery

Philadelphia, U. PA, Mus.
    Philadelphia, PA, University of Pennsylvania,
    University Museum [of Archaeology &
    Anthropology]

Philadelphia, PA, Woodmere Gal. A.
    Philadelphia, PA, Woodmere Gallery of Art

Phimai, Archaeol. Mus.
    Phimai, Archaeological Museum

Phnom Penh, Mus. Albert Sarrant
    Phnom Penh, Musée Albert Sarrant [now N.
    Mus. Khmer A. & Archaeol.]

Phnom Penh, N. Mus.
    Phnom Penh, National Museum of Phnom
    Penh

Phnom Penh, N. Mus. Khmer A. & Archaeol.
    Phnom Penh, National Museum of Khmer Art
    and Archaeology [Musée des Beaux Arts;
    formerly Mus. Albert Sarrant]

Phoenix, AZ, A. Mus.
    Phoenix, AZ, Art Museum

Phoenix, AZ, Heard Mus.
    Phoenix, AZ, Heard Museum

Piacenza, Bib. Com. Passerini Landi
    Piacenza, Biblioteca Comunale Passerini Landi

Piacenza, Coll. Alberoni
    Piacenza, Collegio Alberoni

Piacenza, Coll. Notarile
    Piacenza, Collegio Notarile

Piacenza, Gal. A. Mod. Ricci Oddi
    Piacenza, Galleria d'Arte Moderna Ricci Oddi

Piacenza, Mus. Civ.
    Piacenza, Museo Civico [Palazzo Farnese]

Piatra Neamţ, Distr. Museums
    Piatra Neamţ District Museums (Complexul
    Muzeal Judeţean Piatra Neamţ) [admins Mus.
    Nat. Hist.; Mus. Reg. Hist.; Roman, Mus. Hist.
    & A.; Mus. Nat. Hist.]

Piatra Neamţ, Mus. Nat. Hist.
    Piatra Neamţ, Museum of Natural History
    (Muzeul de ştiinţele Naturii)

Piatra Neamţ, Mus. Reg. Hist.
    Piatra Neamţ, Museum of Regional History
    (Muzeul Judeţean de Istorie)

Piazza Armerina, Villa Casale

Piazzola sul Brenta, Villa Simes-Contarini

Pienza, Mus. Cattedrale
    Pienza, Museo della Cattedrale

Pietermaritzburg, Natal Mus.
    Pietermaritzburg, Natal Museum

Pietermaritzburg, Tatham A.G.
    Pietermaritzburg, Tatham Art Gallery [in City
    Hall]

Pilsen: see Plzeň

Piombino Dese, Villa Cornaro

Piraeus: see Peiraeus

Piran, Oblane Gal.
    Piran, Oblane Gallery (Oblane Galerije)

Pirmasens, Wasgauhalle

Pisa, Arcivescovado

Pisa, Arsenale Galee
    Pisa, Arsenale delle Galee

Pisa, Arsenale Mediceo

Pisa, Camposanto

Pisa, Cassa di Risparmio

Pisa, Certosa Calci
    Pisa, Certosa di Calci

Pisa, Mus. N. S Matteo
    Pisa, Museo Nazionale di S Matteo

Pisa, Mus. Opera Duomo
    Pisa, Museo dell'Opera del Duomo

Pisa, Mus. Sinopie Camposanto Mnmtl
    Pisa, Museo delle Sinopie del Camposanto
    Monumentale [Opera della Primaziale Pisana]

Pisa, Pal. Cavalieri
    Pisa, Palazzo dei Cavalieri [formerly Palazzo
    della Carovana]

Pisa, Pal. Giornata
    Pisa, Palazzo alla Giornata

Pisa, Pal. Reale
    Pisa, Palazzo Reale

Pisa, Rac. Dis. & Stampe
    Pisa, Raccolta degli Disegni e Stampe

Pisa, Sopr. Gal.
    Pisa, Soprintendenza alle Gallerie

Pistoia, Bib. Fabroniana
    Pistoia, Biblioteca Fabroniana

Pistoia, Cassa di Risparmio

Pistoia, Fortezza S Barbara

Pistoia, Mus. Archeol.
    Pistoia, Museo Archeologico [in Pal. Vescovi]

Pistoia, Mus. Cap.
    Pistoia, Museo Capitolare

Pistoia, Mus. Civ.
    Pistoia, Museo Civico [Palazzo Comunale,
    Palazzo Pubblico]

Pistoia, Mus. Dioc.
    Pistoia, Museo Diocesano [in Pal. Vescovi]

Pistoia, Mus. Marino Marini
    Pistoia, Museo di Marino Marini

Pistoia, Osp. Ceppo
    Pistoia, Ospedale del Ceppo

Pistoia, Pal. Marchetti
    Pistoia, Palazzo Marchetti

Pistoia, Pal. Vesc.
    Pistoia, Palazzo dei Vescovi

Pithagorio Mus.
    Pithagorio, Pithagorio Museum [formerly
    Tigani Museum]

Pittsburgh, PA, A.G.
    Pittsburgh, PA, University of Pittsburgh, Art
    Gallery

Pittsburgh, PA, Buhl Sci. Cent.
    Pittsburgh, PA, Buhl Science Center

Pittsburgh, PA, Carnegie
    Pittsburgh, The Carnegie [admins Carnegie
    Lib.; Carnegie Mus. A.; Carnegie Mus. Nat.
    Hist.; Carnegie Music Hall; Carnegie Sci.
    Cent.]

Pittsburgh, PA, Carnegie Inst.
    Pittsburgh, PA, Carnegie Institute [name
    changed to The Carnegie autumn 1985]

Pittsburgh, PA, Carnegie Lib.
    Pittsburgh, PA, Carnegie Library

Pittsburgh, PA, Carnegie–Mellon U.
    Pittsburgh, PA, Carnegie–Mellon University

Pittsburgh, PA, Carnegie–Mellon U. A.G.
    Pittsburgh, PA, Carnegie–Mellon University
    Art Gallery

Pittsburgh, PA, Carnegie–Mellon U., Hunt Botan.
Lib.
    Pittsburgh, PA, Carnegie–Mellon University,
    Hunt Botanical Library

Pittsburgh, PA, Carnegie Mus. A.
    Pittsburgh, PA, The Carnegie Museum of Art

Pittsburgh, PA, Carnegie Music Hall
    Pittsburgh, PA, Carnegie Music Hall

Pittsburgh, PA, Carnegie Mus. Nat. Hist.
    Pittsburgh, PA, Carnegie Museum of Natural
    History

Pittsburgh, PA, Carnegie Sci. Cent.
    Pittsburgh, PA, Carnegie Science Center

Pittsburgh, PA, Frick A. Mus.
    Pittsburgh, PA, Frick Art Museum

Pittsfield, MA, Berks Mus.
    Pittsfield, MA, Berkshire Museum

Pleven, A.G.
    Pleven, Art Gallery

Pleven, Hist. Mus.
    Pleven, Historical Museum (Istoricheski
    Muzey) [Regional Historical Museum]

Pleven, Ilya Beshkov A.G.
    Pleven, Ilya Beshkov Art Gallery
    (Hudozhestvena Galerija Ilija Beshkov)

Płock, Dioc. Mus.
    Płock, Diocesan Museum (Muzeum
    Diecezjalne)

Ploieşti, Grigorescu Mus.
    Ploieşti, Grigorescu Museum (Muzeul N.
    Grigorescu)

Ploieşti, Hasdeu Mem. Exh.
    Ploieşti, Hasdeu Memorial Exhibition
    (Expoziţia Memorială B.P. Hasdeu)

Ploieşti, Mus. A.
    Ploieşti, Museum of Art (Muzeul de Artă
    Ploieşti)

Ploieşti, Mus. Nat. Hist.
    Ploieşti, Museum of Natural History (Muzeul
    de Ştiinţele Naturii)

Ploieşti, Mus. Prahovan Hist.
    Ploieşti, Museum of Prahovan History
    (Muzeul Judeţean de Istorie Prahova)

Ploieşti, Petroleum Mus.
    Ploieşti, Petroleum Museum (Muzeul
    Petrolului)

Ploieşti, Prahova Distr. Museums
    Ploieşti, Prahova District Museums
    (Complexul Muzeal Judeţean Prahova Ploieşti)
    [admins Grigorescu Mus.; Hasdeu Mem. Exh.;
    Mus. A.; Mus. Nat. Hist.; Mus. Prahovan Hist.;
    Petroleum Mus.]

Plombières-les-Bains, Mus. Louis Français
    Plombières-les-Bains, Musée Louis Français

Plovdiv, A.G.
Plovdiv, Art Gallery (Hudozhestvena Galeriya)

Plovdiv, Archaeol. Mus.
Plovdiv, Archaeology Museum (Arkheologicheski muzey)

Plovdiv, Ethnog. Mus.
Plovdiv, Ethnographic Museum (Etnografski Muzey)

Plovdiv, Reg. Archaeol. Mus.
Plovdiv, Regional Archaeological Museum (Okrazhen Arkheologicheski Muzey)

Plovdiv, Tzanko Lavrenov House-Mus.
Plovdiv, Tzanko Lavrenov House-Museum

Plymouth, A. Cent.
Plymouth, Arts Centre

Plymouth, City Mus. & A.G.
Plymouth, City Museum and Art Gallery

Plzeň, A.G. W. Bohemia
Plzeň, Art Gallery of Western Bohemia (Západočeská Galerie v Plzni)

Plzeň, City Archvs
Plzeň, City Archives (Městský archív)

Poblet, Mus. Real Monasterio S Maria
Poblet, Museo del Real Monasterio de S Maria

Poblet, Real Monasterio S Maria
Poblet, Real Monasterio de S Maria [houses mus.]

Pöchlarn, Kokoschka Dok.
Pöchlarn, Oskar Kokoschka Dokumentation

Poggio a Caiano, Mus. Villa Medicea
Poggio a Caiano, Museo Villa Medicea

Poggio a Caiano, Villa Medicea
Poggio a Caiano, Villa Medicea di Poggio a Caiano

Point Lookout, MO, Jones Gal.
Point Lookout, MO, Jones Gallery

Point Lookout, MO, Ralph Foster Mus.
Point Lookout, MO, Ralph Foster Museum

Poitiers, Bib. Mun.
Poitiers, Bibliothèque Municipale

Poitiers, CESCM
Poitiers, Centre d'Etudes Supérieures de Civilisation Médiévale [Hôtel Berthelot]

Poitiers, Conserv. Musées
Poitiers, Conservation des Musées de Poitiers [admins Hypogée Dunes; Mus. Augustins; Mus. Baptistère-St-Jean; Mus. Sainte-Croix]

Poitiers, Hypogée Dunes
Poitiers, Hypogée des Dunes

Poitiers, Mus. Augustins
Poitiers, Musée des Augustins [Hôtel des Chèvres]

Poitiers, Mus. B.-A.
Poitiers, Musée des Beaux-Arts

Poitiers, Mus. Baptistère-St-Jean
Poitiers, Musée du Baptistère-St-Jean

Poitiers, Mus. Poitiers
Poitiers, Musée de la Ville de Poitiers [et la Société des Antiquaires de l'Ouest]

Poitiers, Mus. Sainte-Croix
Poitiers, Musée Sainte-Croix

Poitiers, Pal. Justice
Poitiers, Palais de Justice

Poitiers, Trésor Cathédrale
Poitiers, Trésor de la Cathédrale

Pojan Mus.
Pojan, Pojan Museum [Museum of Archaeology]

Polatsk, Reg. Mus.
Polatsk, Regional Museum

Polenovo, V.D. Polenov Estate-Mus.
Polenovo, V.D. Polenov Estate-Museum (Muzey Usad'ba V.D. Polenova)

Policoro, Mus. N. Siritide
Policoro, Museo Nazionale della Siritide

Pollensa, Casa-Estud. Anglada Camarasa
Pollensa, Casa-Estudio del Pintor Hermene Anglada Camarasa

Polonnaruwa, Archaeol. Site Mus.
Polonnaruwa, Archaeological Site Museum

Pommersfelden, Schloss Weissenstein [Schloss Pommersfelden; Graf von Schönborn Collection]

Pompeii, Antiqua.
Pompeii, Antiquarium [Scavi di Pompei]

Ponce, Mus. A.
Ponce, Museo de Arte de Ponce [Fundación Luis A. Ferré]

Ponce, Mus. Arqueol. Tibes
Ponce, Museo de Arqueología de Tibes

Pondicherry, Bharathiar Mem. Lib.-Mus.
Pondicherry, Bharathiar Memorial Library-Museum

Pondicherry, Bharathidasan Mem. Lib.-Mus.
Pondicherry, Bharathidasan Memorial Library-Museum

Pong-hwa, T'aeja Temple

Pont-Aven, Mus. Pont-Aven
Pont-Aven, Musée de la Ville de Pont-Aven

Pont-de-Vaux, Mus. Chintreuil
Pont-de-Vaux, Musée Chintreuil

Pont-de-Vaux, Salle Fêtes
Pont-de-Vaux, Salle des Fêtes

Pontevedra, Ayuntamiento Porriños
Pontevedra, Ayuntamiento de Porriños

Pontevedra, Mus. Pontevedra
Pontevedra, Museo de Pontevedra

Pontoise, Mus. Pissarro
Pontoise, Musée Pissarro

Pontoise, Mus. Pontoise
Pontoise, Musée de Pontoise [Tavet-Delacour]

Pontremoli, Pal. Dosi
Pontremoli, Palazzo Dosi

Pont-Saint-Esprit, Mus. Paul Raymond
Pont-Saint-Esprit, Musée Paul Raymond

Poona: see Pune

Popayán, Mus. A. Colon. & Hist. 'Casa Mosquera'
Popayán, Museo de Arte Colonial e Historia 'Casa Mosquera'

Popayán, Mus. A. Relig.
Popayán, Museo de Arte Religioso

Popayán, Mus. Negret
Popayán, Museo Negret

Pordenone, Cent. Odorico
Pordenone, Centro Odorico

Pordenone, Mus. Civ. Pal. Ricchieri
Pordenone, Museo Civico di Palazzo Ricchieri

Pori, A. Mus.
Pori, Pori Art Museum (Porin Taidemuseo)

Porlezza, Archivio Com.
Porlezza, Archivio Comunale

Portadown, Peacock Gal.
Portadown, Peacock Gallery

Portalegre, Mus. Mun.
Portalegre, Museu Municipal [in Antigo Seminario]

Port-au-Prince, Ambiance

Port-au-Prince, Bib. Haït. F.I.C.
Port-au-Prince, Bibliothèque Haïtienne des F.I.C.

Port-au-Prince, Cent. A.
Port-au-Prince, Centre d'Art

Port-au-Prince, George Nader A.G.
Port-au-Prince, George Nader Art Gallery

Port-au-Prince, Jerusalem A.
Port-au-Prince, Jerusalem Art

Port-au-Prince, Mus. A. Haït.
Port-au-Prince, Musée d'Art Haïtien

Port-au-Prince, Mus. N.
Port-au-Prince, Musée National

Port-au-Prince, Mus. Pant. N.
Port-au-Prince, Musée du Panthéon National

Port-au-Prince, Mus. Pant. N. Haït.
Port-au-Prince, Musée du Panthéon National Haïtien

Port-au-Prince, Mus. Peuple Haït.
Port-au-Prince, Musée du Peuple Haïtien

Port-au-Prince, Varieties, A. & Ptg Cent.
Port-au-Prince, Varieties, Art and Painting Centre

Port Elizabeth, King George VI A.G.
Port Elizabeth, King George VI Art Gallery

Port Elizabeth, U. Port Elizabeth
Port Elizabeth, University of Port Elizabeth

Portland, ME, Mus. A.
Portland, ME, Museum of Art

Portland, OR, A. Mus.
Portland, OR, Portland Art Museum

Portland, OR, Cent. Visual A.
Portland, OR, Center for Visual Arts

Port Moresby, N. Mus. & A.G.
Port Moresby, National Museum and Art Gallery

Pôrto Alegre, Mus. A. Rio Grande do Sul
Pôrto Alegre, Museu de Arte do Rio Grande do Sul

Portobello, Otago Peninsula Mus. & Hist. Soc.
Portobello, Otago Peninsula Museum and Historical Society

Porto Novo, Mus. Ethnog.
Porto Novo, Musée Ethnographique

Porto Novo, Mus. Honmè
Porto Novo, Musée Honmè

Portsmouth, Aspex Gal.
Portsmouth, Aspex Gallery

Portsmouth, City Mus. & A.G.
Portsmouth, City Museum & Art Gallery

Portsmouth, Dockyard Apprentices Mus.
Portsmouth, Dockyard Apprentices Museum

Portsmouth, Mary Rose Mus.
Portsmouth, Mary Rose Museum [Mary Rose Trust]

Portsmouth, Royal Naval Mus.
Portsmouth, Royal Naval Museum

Portsmouth, Dominica, Fort Shirley Mus.
Portsmouth, Dominica, Fort Shirley Museum

Port Sunlight, Lady Lever A.G.
Port Sunlight, Lady Lever Art Gallery

Port-Vila, N. Mus. Vanuatu Cult. Cent.
Port-Vila, National Museum of the Vanuatu Cultural Centre [Vanuatu formerly called New Hebrides]

Possagno, Gip. Canoviana
Possagno, Gipsoteca Canoviana e Casa Natale del Canova

Potenza, Mus. Archeol. Prov.
  Potenza, Museo Archeologico Provinciale

Potenza, Pal. S Gervasio
  Potenza, Palazzo San Gervasio

Potosí, Convento S Teresa
  Potosí, Convento de Santa Teresa

Potosí, Mus. Convento S Francisco
  Potosí, Museo del Convento de San Francisco

Potosí, Mus. N. Casa Moneda
  Potosí, Museo Nacional de la Casa de Moneda

Potsdam, Bildergal.
  Potsdam, Bildergalerie [in Park Sanssouci]

Potsdam, Chin. Teehaus
  Potsdam, Chinesisches Teehaus [in Park
  Sanssouci]

Potsdam, Heilig-Kreuz-Gemeinde

Potsdam, Marmorpal.
  Potsdam, Marmorpalais

Potsdam, Neue Kam.
  Potsdam, Neue Kammern [in Park Sanssouci]

Potsdam, Neues Pal.
  Potsdam, Neues Palais [in Park Sanssouci]

Potsdam, Orangerie [in Park Sanssouci; incl.
Raffael-Saal]

Potsdam, Parkbauten & -Plast.
  Potsdam, Parkbauten und -Plastiken [in Park
  Sanssouci]

Potsdam, Park Sanssouci

Potsdam, Röm. Bäder
  Potsdam, Römische Bäder [in Park Sanssouci]

Potsdam, Schloss Babelsberg

Potsdam, Schloss Cecilienhof

Potsdam, Schloss Charlottenhof [in Park
Sanssouci]

Potsdam, Schloss Sanssouci [in Park Sanssouci]

Potsdam, Staatl. Schlösser & Gärten Potsdam-
Sanssouci
  Potsdam, Staatliche Schlösser und Gärten
  Potsdam-Sanssouci [admins Bildergal.; Chin.
  Teehaus; Neue Kam.; Neues Pal.; Orangerie;
  Parkbauten & -Plast.; Park Sanssouci; Röm.
  Bäder; Schloss Charlottenhof; Schloss
  Sanssouci]

Potsdam, NY, State U., Brainerd A.G.
  Potsdam, NY, State University, Brainerd Art
  Gallery

Poughkeepsie, NY, Vassar Coll. A.G.
  Poughkeepsie, NY, Vassar College Art Gallery

Požarevac, N. Mus.
  Požarevac, National Museum (Narodni Muzej)

Poznań, Archaeol. Mus.
  Poznań, Archaeological Museum (Muzeum
  Archeologiczne)

Poznań, E. Raczyński Mun. Pub. Lib.
  Poznań, E. Raczyński Municipal Public Library

Poznań, N. Mus.
  Poznań, National Museum (Muzeum
  Narodowe w Poznaniu)

Poznań, Office A. Exh.
  Poznań, Office of Art Exhibitions (Biuro
  Wystaw Artystycznych)

Prachinburi, N. Mus.
  Prachinburi, National Museum

Praesto, Thorvaldsen Samlingen: see under Nysø

Prague, Acad. Applied A.
  Prague, Academy of Applied Arts (Vysoká
  Škola Umĕleckoprůmyslová)

Prague, Acad. F.A.
  Prague, Academy of Fine Arts (Akademie
  Výtvarných Umĕní)

Prague, Alois Jirásek & Mikoláš Aleš Mus.
  Prague, Alois Jirásek and Mikoláš Aleš
  Museum (Muzeum Aloise Jiráska a Mikoláše
  Alše)

Prague, Anc. Monuments Cent.
  Prague, Ancient Monuments Centre

Prague, Archbishop's Pal.
  Prague, Archbishop's Palace (Arcibiskupský
  Palác)

Prague, Atrium

Prague, Aventinská Mansarda

Prague, Bedřich Smetana Mus.
  Prague, Bedřich Smetana Museum (Muzeum
  Bedřicha Smetany)

Prague, Cent. Office Museology
  Prague, Central Office of Museology (Ústřední
  Muzeologický Kabinet)

Prague, Cent. State Archvs
  Prague, Central State Archives (Státní Archív)

Prague, Černín Pal.
  Prague, Černín Palace

Prague, Charles U.
  Prague, Charles University (Univerzita
  Karlova)

Prague, City Archvs
  Prague, City Archives (Archív Hlavního Města
  Prahy)

Prague, Clementinum

Prague, Com. House, Palacký Room
  Prague, Community House, Palacký Room
  (Obecní Dům, F. Palackého Místnost)

Prague, Czech Acad. Sci., Presidium
  Prague, Czech Academy of Sciences,
  Presidium (Česká Akademie Věd)

Prague, Czech A. Cent.
  Prague, Czech Art Centre

Prague, Czech A. Fund
  Prague, Czech Art Fund (Český Umělecký
  Fond)

Prague, Czech Tech. U.
  Prague, Czech Technical University (České
  Vysoké Učení Technické v Praze)

Prague, Gal. J. Fragnera
  Prague, Galerie J. Fragnera

Prague Gal. Nostitz
  Prague, Gallery Nostitz

Prague, Higher Council F.A.
  Prague, Higher Council of Fine Arts

Prague, Hist. Mus.
  Prague, Historical Museum (Národní Muzeum
  v Praze, Historické Muzeum) [part of N.
  Mus.]

Prague, Hollar Gal.
  Prague, Hollar Gallery (Galerie Hollar) [run by
  SČUG Hollar; Hollar Society of Czech Artists]

Prague, Hradčany Castle [residence of President
of Republic; Prague Castle]

Prague, Hradčany Castle, Belveder [Royal Summer
Palace]

Prague, Hrdlička Mus. Anthropol., Charles U.
  Prague, Charles University, Hrdlička Museum
  of Anthropology (Hrdličkovo Muzeum
  Člověka, Univerzita Karlova)

Prague, Jacquemart-André Mus.
  Prague, Jacquemart-André Museum

Prague, Lapidarium Hist. Mus.
  Prague, Lapidarium of the Historical Museum
  (Lapidarium Historického Muzea) [part of N.
  Mus.]

Prague, Lesser Town Hall
  Prague, Town Hall of the Lesser Town
  (Malostranská Radnice)

Prague, Libs Facs & Insts Charles U.
  Prague, Libraries of Faculties and Institutes of
  Charles University (Knihovny Fakult a Ústavů
  Univerzity Karlovy)

Prague, Loreto Treasury (Loretánská Sbírka)

Prague, Mánes Exh. Hall
  Prague, Mánes Exhibition Hall (Výstavní síň
  Mánes) ['SVU'; Mánes Union of Artists]

Prague, Melantrich Exh. Hall
  Prague, Melantrich Exhibition Hall (Výstavní
  síň Melantrich)

Prague, Mozart Col.
  Prague, Mozart Collection (Památník W.A.
  Mozarta a Manželů Duškových) [part of
  Mozart–Dušek col.]

Prague, Mun. Gal.
  Prague, Municipal Gallery (Galerie Hlavního
  Města) [col. at Bílek Villa, Store Bell House,
  Old Town Hall, Castle Trója]

Prague, Mus. City
  Prague, Museum of the City of Prague
  (Muzeum Hlavního Města Prahy)

Prague, Mus. Czech Music
  Prague, Museum of Czech Music (Muzeum
  České Hudby)

Prague, Mus. Dec. A.
  Prague, Museum of Decorative Arts
  (Umělecko-Průmyslové Muzeum v Praze)

Prague, Mus. Indust. A.
  Prague, Museum of Industrial Art

Prague, Mus. Nat. Sci.
  Prague, Museum of Natural Sciences
  (Přírodovědecké Muzeum)

Prague, Mus. Phys. Training & Sport
  Prague, Museum of Physical Training and
  Sport (Muzeum Tělovýchovy a Sportu)

Prague, Náprstek Mus. Asian, Afr. & Amer. Cult.
  Prague, Náprstek Museum of Asian, African
  and American Culture (Náprstkovo Muzeum
  Asijských Afrických a Amerických Kultur)

Prague, New Town Hall (Novoměstská Radnice)

Prague, N.G.
  Prague, National Gallery (Národní Galerie)
  [admins Convent of St Agnes; Convent of St
  George; Czech & Eur. Graph A.; Mun. Lib.;
  Šternberk Pal.; Trade Fair Pal.; Valdštejn
  Riding Sch.; Zbraslav Castle]

Prague, N.G., Convent of St Agnes
  Prague, National Gallery, Convent of St Agnes

Prague, N.G., Convent of St George
  Prague, National Gallery, Convent of St
  George

Prague, N.G., Czech & Eur. Graph. A.
  Prague, National Gallery, Czech and European
  Graphic Art (Národní Galerie; Sbírka Českého
  a Evropského Umění)

Prague, N.G., Kinský Pal.
  Prague, National Gallery, Kinský Palace

Prague, N.G. Lib.
  Prague, National Gallery Library (Knihovna
  Národní Galerie)

Prague, N.G., Mun. Lib.
  Prague, National Gallery, Municipal Library

Prague, N.G., Rodin Mus.
  Prague, National Gallery, Rodin Museum

Prague, N.G., Staré Město Old Town Hall
Prague, National Gallery, Old Town Hall, Old Town (Národní Galerie, Staroměstská Radnice, Staré Město)

Prague, N.G., Šternberk Pal.
Prague, National Gallery, Šternberk Palace

Prague, N.G., Trade Fair Pal.
Prague, National Gallery, Trade Fair Palace

Prague, N.G., Valdštejn Riding Sch.
Prague, National Gallery, Valdštejn Riding School (Valdštejnská Jízdárna)

Prague, N.G., Zbraslav Castle
Prague, National Gallery, Zbraslav Castle (Státní Zámek, Zbraslav) [Zbraslav Monastery; sculpture park]

Prague, N. Lib.
Prague, National Library (Národní Knihovna v Praze)

Prague, N. Mus.
Prague, National Museum (Národní Muzeum) [admins Cent. Office Museology; Hist. Mus.; Mus. Czech. Music; Mus. Nat. Sci.; Mus. Phys. Training & Sport; Náprstek Mus. Asian, Afr. & Amer. Cult.; N. Mus.]

Prague, N. Mus. Lib.
Prague, National Museum Library (Knihovna Národního Muzea)

Prague, N. Tech. Mus.
Prague, National Technical Museum (Národní Technické Muzeum)

Prague, N. Theat.
Prague, National Theatre (Národní Divadlo; Kancelář Prezidenta Republiky)

Prague, Old Hradčany Town Hall
Prague, Old Hradčany Town Hall (Hradčanská Radnice)

Prague, Park Cult. & Rest, Pav.
Prague, Park of Culture and Rest, Prague Pavilion (Park Kultury a Oddechu, Pavilón) [formerly Julius Fučík Park Cult. & Rest]

Prague, Quadrennial [organized by Theatre Institute]

Prague, Rlwy Workers' Cent. Cult. Office
Prague, Railway Workers' Central Cultural Office (Ústřední Kulturní Dům Železničářů)

Prague, Rudolphinum

Prague, Špála Gal.
Prague, Špála Gallery (Galerie Špály)

Prague, State Inst. Cons. Hist. Mnmts & Nature
Prague, State Institute for the Conservation of Historical Monuments and Nature (Státní Ústava Památkové Péče a Ochrany Přírody)

Prague, State Jew. Mus.
Prague, State Jewish Museum in Prague (Státní Židovské Muzeum v Praze)

Prague, Strahov Abbey & N. Lit. Mem.
Prague, Strahov Abbey and National Literary Memorial (Strahovský Klášter, Památník Národního Písemnictví)

Prague, Středočeská Gal.
Prague, Středočeská Gallery (Středočeská Galerie)

Prague, St Vitus' Cathedral Lib.
Prague, St Vitus' Cathedral Library [in Prague Castle]

Prague, Trója Castle

Prato, Archv Capitolare
Prato, Archivio Capitolare

Prato, Bib. Roncioniana
Prato, Biblioteca Roncioniana

Prato, Cassa di Risparmio

Prato, Cent. A. Contemp. Luigi Pecci
Prato, Centro per l'Arte Contemporanea Luigi Pecci

Prato, Gal. A. Mod. Farsetti
Prato, Galleria d'Arte Moderna Farsetti

Prato, Mus. Com.
Prato, Museo Comunale [in Pal. Pretorio]

Prato, Mus. Opera Duomo
Prato, Museo dell'Opera del Duomo

Prato, Mus. Pitt. Murale
Prato, Museo di Pittura Murale

Prato, Pal. Pretorio
Prato, Palazzo Pretorio [houses Mus. Com.]

Prato, Pal. Vescovile
Prato, Palazzo Vescovile

Prato, Pin. Com.
Prato, Pinacoteca Comunale

Pratolino, Villa Demidoff

Prescot, Mus. Clock- & Watch-making
Prescot, Museum of Clock- and Watch-making

Preslav, Mun. Archaeol. Mus.
Preslav, Municipal Archaeological Museum [Gradski Archeologičeski Muzey]

Prešov, Šariš Gal.
Prešov, Šariš Gallery (Šarišské Galéria)

Preston, Harris Mus. & A.G.
Preston, Harris Museum and Art Gallery

Preston Town Hall
Preston, Preston Town Hall

Pretoria, A. Mus.
Pretoria, Art Museum

Pretoria, Anton van Wouw House

Pretoria, ISCOR [Iron and Steel Corporation]

Pretoria, N. Cult. Hist. Mus.
Pretoria, National Cultural History Museum

Pretoria, Pierneef Mus.
Pretoria, Pierneef Museum

Pretoria, Prov. Admin. Bldg
Pretoria, Provincial Administration Building

Pretoria, U. Pretoria
Pretoria, University of Pretoria

Pretoria, U. South Africa
Pretoria, University of South Africa

Pretoria, U. South Africa, Anthropol. Mus.
Pretoria, University of South Africa, Anthropology Museum

Prien, Neues Schloss Herrenchiensee [houses König-Ludwig II Museum]

Princeton, NJ, Barbara Piasecka Johnson Col.
Princeton, NJ, Barbara Piasecka Johnson Collection [now Jasnaja Polana]

Princeton U., NJ
Princeton, NJ, Princeton University

Princeton U., NJ, A. Mus.
Princeton, NJ, Princeton University, Art Museum

Princeton U., NJ, Firestone Lib.
Princeton, NJ, Princeton University, Firestone Library

Princeton U., NJ, Lib.
Princeton, NJ, Princeton University Library

Princeton U., NJ, Putnam Mem. Col.
Princeton, NJ, Princeton University, John B. Putnam Junior Memorial Collection

Prinksaal and Laxenburg, Altes Schloss

Priština, Mun. Mus.
Priština, Municipal Museum (Muzej Kosova i Metohije)

Pro Helvetia
Pro Helvetia Foundation of Switzerland

Providence, RI, Annmary Brown Mem.
Providence, RI, Annmary Brown Memorial

Providence, RI, Athenaeum
Providence, RI, Providence Athenaeum

Providence, RI, Brown U.
Providence, RI, Brown University

Providence, RI, Brown U., Bell Gal.
Providence, RI, Brown University, David Winton Bell Gallery

Providence, RI, Carter Brown Lib.
Providence, RI, John Carter Brown Library

Providence, RI, Haffenraffer Mus. Anthropol.
Providence, RI, Haffenraffer Museum of Anthropology

Providence, RI Hist. Soc.
Providence, RI, Rhode Island Historical Society

Providence, RI Sch. Des., Mus. A.
Providence, RI, Rhode Island School of Design, Museum of Art

Provincetown, MA, Chrysler A. Mus.
Provincetown, MA, Chrysler Art Museum

Provins, Hôp. Gén.
Provins, Hôpital Général

Průhonice Castle
Průhonice, Průhonice Castle

Pruntrut, Bib. Koll.
Pruntrut, Bibliothek des Kollegiums

Przemyśl, Reg. Mus.
Przemyśl, Regional Museum (Muzeum Okręgowe)

Przeworsk Mus.
Przeworsk, Przeworsk Museum

Pskov, Mus. Hist. & A.
Pskov, Museum of History and Art (Istoriko-Khudozhestvennyy Muzey)

Ptuj, Reg. Mus.
Ptuj, Regional Museum (Pokrajinski Muzei)

Puebla, Bib. Palafoxiana
Puebla, Biblioteca Palafoxiana [in Archbishop's Palace]

Puebla, Mus. A. 'José Luis Bello y González'
Puebla, Museo de Arte 'José Luis Bello y González'

Puebla, Mus. Amparo
Puebla, Museo Amparo

Puebla, Mus. A. Pop. Poblano
Puebla, Museo de Arte Popular Poblano [Museo de las Artesanías]

Puebla, Mus. A. Relig.
Puebla, Museo de Arte Religioso [in S Monica Convent; Museo Regional de S Monica]

Puebla, Mus. Bello
Puebla, Museo Bello

Puebla, Mus. Colegio B.A.
Puebla, Museo del Colegio de Bellas Artes

Puebla, Mus. Reg. & Cer.
Puebla, Museo Regional y de Cerámica [in Casa del Alfeñique]

Puerto de Omoa, Mus. N. Hist. Colon.
Puerto de Omoa, Museo Nacional de Historia Colonial

Puerto Montt, Gal. Manoly
Puerto Montt, Galería Manoly

Pula, Istrian Archaeol. Mus.
Pula, Istrian Archaeological Museum

Puławy Pal.
  Puławy, Puławy Palace [formerly Czartoryski Palace]

Punaauia, Mus. Tahiti & Iles
  Punaauia, Musée de Tahiti et des Iles

Pune, Bhandarkar Orient. Res. Inst.
  Pune, Bhandarkar Oriental Research Institute

Pune, Bharata Itihasa Samshodhaka Mandala [Centre for Indian Cultural Studies]

Pune, Deccan Coll., Maratha Hist. Mus.
  Pune, Deccan College, Maratha History Museum

Pune, Raja Dinkar Kelkar Mus.
  Pune, Raja Dinkar Kelkar Museum

Pune, U. Pune
  Pune, University of Pune

Purchase, SUNY, Coll.
  Purchase, NY, State University of New York, State University College at Purchase

Purchase, SUNY, Neuberger Mus.
  Purchase, NY, State University of New York, Neuberger Museum

Pusan, Dong-A Mus.
  Pusan, Dong-A Museum [Dong-A University]

Pushkin, A.S. Pushkin Mus.
  Pushkin, All-Union A.S. Pushkin Museum (Vsesoyuznyy Muzey A.S. Pushkina)

Pushkin, Cameron Gal.
  Pushkin, Cameron Gallery (Kameronova Galereya) [in Catherine Palace]

Pushkin, Concert Hall (Kontsertnyy Zal) [in Catherine Park]

Pushkin, Pal.-Mus.
  Pushkin, Palace-Museum (Muzey-Dvorets)

Putna, Monastery Mus.
  Putna, Monastery Museum (Muzeul Mnăstire)

Puyŏ, N. Mus.
  Puyŏ, National Museum

P'yŏngyang, Kor. A.G.
  P'yŏngyang, Korean Art Gallery

P'yŏngyang, State Cent. Hist. Mus
  P'yŏngyang, State Central Historical Museum

Quebec, Gen. Hosp.
  Quebec, General Hospital

Quebec, Hôtel-Dieu

Quebec, Inst. Can. Qué.
  Quebec, Institut Canadien de Québec

Quebec, Lit. & Hist. Soc.
  Quebec, Literary and Historical Society

Quebec, Maison-Maillou

Quebec, Mus. Amérique Fr.
  Quebec, Musée de l'Amérique Française [formerly Mus. Sémin.]

Quebec, Mus. Augustin.
  Quebec, Musée des Augustins de l'Hôpital Général de Québec

Quebec, Mus. Civilis.
  Quebec, Musée de la Civilisation

Quebec, Mus. Qué.
  Quebec, Musée du Québec

Quebec, Mus. Sémin.
  Quebec, Musée du Séminaire de Québec [now Mus. Amérique Fr.]

Quebec, Mus. Ursulines
  Quebec, Musée des Ursulines

Quebec, U. Laval, Mus. B.-A
  Quebec, Université Laval, Musée des Beaux-Arts

Quebec, Vieille Maison Jésuites
  Quebec, Vieille Maison des Jésuites

Quedlinburg, Domschatz

Quedlinburg, Schlossmus.
  Quedlinburg, Schlossmuseum

Queluz, Pal. N.
  Queluz, Palacio Nacional de Queluz

Querétaro, Mus. A.
  Querétaro, Museo de Arte de Querétaro

Querétaro, Mus. Reg.
  Querétaro, Museo Regional de Querétaro [former convent of S Francisco]

Quesada, Mus. Zabaleta
  Quesada, Museo Zabaleta

Quezen City, U. Philippines, Coll. A. & Sci., Mus. Anthropol.
  Quezon City, University of the Philippines, College of Arts and Sciences, Museum of Anthropology

Qufu, Confucian Temple

Quimper, Bib. Mun.
  Quimper, Bibliothèque Municipale

Quimper, Mus. B.-A.
  Quimper, Musée des Beaux-Arts de Quimper

Quimper, Mus. Faïence Quimper Jules Verlingue
  Quimper, Musée de la Faïence de Quimper Jules Verlingue

Quito, Archv N. Hist.
  Quito, Archivo Nacional de Historia

Quito, Banco Cent. del Ecuador
  Quito, Banco Central del Ecuador

Quito, Cancilleria Ecuador
  Quito, Cancilleria del Ecuador

Quito, Convento S Augustín
  Quito, Convento di S Augustín

Quito, Manzana Verde
  Quito, La Manzana Verde

Quito, Municipio

Quito, Mus. A. & Hist. Ciudad
  Quito, Museo de Arte e Historia de la Ciudad

Quito, Mus. A. Mod.
  Quito, Museo de Arte Moderno [Casa de la Cultura Ecuatoriana]

Quito, Mus. Aurelio Espinoza Pólit
  Quito, Museo Aurelio Espinoza Pólit

Quito, Mus. Camilo Egas Banco Cent.
  Quito, Museo Camilo Egas del Banco Central

Quito, Mus. Fond. Guayasamín
  Quito, Museo Fundación Guayasamín

Quito, Mus. Franciscano
  Quito, Museo Franciscano

Quito, Mus. Fund. Hallo
  Quito, Museo de la Fundación Hallo

Quito, Mus. Jijón & Caamaño
  Quito, Museo Jacinto Jijón y Caamaño

Quito, Mus. Mun. Alberto Mena Caamaño
  Quito, Museo Municipal Alberto Mena Caamaño

Quito, Mus. N. A. Colon.
  Quito, Museo Nacional de Arte Colonial

Qum, Shrine Mus.
  Qum, Shrine Museum

Rabat, Bib. Gen. & Archvs
  Rabat, Bibliothèque Générale et Archives

Rabat, Division Musées, Sites, Archéol. & Mnmts Hist.
  Rabat, Division des Musées, des Sites, d'Archéologie et des Monuments Historiques [admins Mus. A. Maroc.; Mus. Ant.; Fez, Mus. Armes Bordi Nord; Fez, Mus. Dar Batha; Marrakesh, Mus. Dar Si Saïd; Meknes, Mus. Dar Jamai & Pal.; Tangier, Mus. Kasbah; Tétouan, Mus. Archéol.; Volubilis, Mus. Ant.]

Rabat, Mus. A. Maroc.
  Rabat, Musée des Arts Marocains [in Kasba des Oudaïas]

Rabat, Mus. Ant.
  Rabat, Musée des Antiquités

Rabat, Malta, Roman Villa & Mus. Ant.
  Rabat, Malta, Roman Villa and Museum of Antiquities

Rabat, Malta, St Paul's Coll. Church Mus.
  Rabat, Malta, St Paul's Collegiate Church Museum

Rabat, Malta, St Paul's Grotto

Rabat, Malta, Wignacourt Mus.
  Rabat, Malta, Wignacourt Museum

Racconigi, Castello
  Racconigi, Castello di Racconigi

Racibórz Mus.
  Racibórz, Racibórz Museum (Muzeum w Raciborzu)

Radom, Distr. Mus.
  Radom, District Museum (Muzeum Okręgowe)

Radzyń, Chełminski, Reg. Mus.
  Radzyń Chełmiński, Regional Museum [in castle]

Raipur, Mahant Ghasi Dass Mem. Mus.
  Raipur, Mahant Ghasi Dass Memorial Museum

Rajamundry, Rallabandi Subbarao Govt Mus.
  Rajamundry, Rallabandi Subbarao Government Museum

Rajshahi, Varendra Res. Mus.
  Rajshahi, Varendra Research Museum

Rakovník, Rabas Gal.
  Rakovník, Rabas Gallery

Raleigh, NC Mus. A.
  Raleigh, NC, North Carolina Museum of Art

Raleigh, NC State Archvs
  Raleigh, NC, North Carolina State Archives

Ramat Gan, Beit Immanuel Mun. Mus.
  Ramat Gan, Beit Immanuel Municipal Museum

Rampur, Raza Lib.
  Rampur, Raza Library

Ramvan, Tulsi Mus.
  Ramvan, Tulsi Museum (Tulsi Sangrahalaya)

Rancate, Pin. Züst
  Rancate, Pinacoteca Züst

Randers, Kstmus.
  Randers, Randers Kunstmuseum

Randers Mus.
  Randers, Randers Museet

Rangoon, Mus. Int. Inst. Adv. Buddhist Stud.
  Rangoon, Museum of the International Institute of Advanced Buddhist Studies

Rangoon, N. Mus.
  Rangoon, National Museum [Jubilee Hall]

Ranzan, Saitama Prefect. Hist. Mus.
  Ranzan, Saitama Prefectural Historical Museum

Rapperswil, Polenmus.
  Rapperswil, Polenmuseum [in Schloss Rapperswil]

Ra's al-Khayma Mus.
  Ra's al-Khayma Museum

Rastatt, Pagodenburg

Rastatt, Schloss, Wehrgesch. Mus.
  Rastatt, Schloss, Wehrgeschichtliches Museum

Ratnapura, N. Mus.
  Ratnapura, National Museum of Ratnapura

Ravenna, Accad. B.A.
  Ravenna, Accademia di Belle Arti

Ravenna, Bib. Com. Classense
  Ravenna, Biblioteca Comunale Classense

Ravenna, Edicola Braccioforte
  Ravenna, Edicola di Braccioforte

Ravenna, Loggetta Lombard.
  Ravenna, Loggetta Lombardesca

Ravenna, Mus. Arcivescovile
  Ravenna, Museo Arcivescovile [Museo d'Antichità Cristiane]

Ravenna, Mus. N.
  Ravenna, Museo Nazionale

Ravenna, Pin. Com.
  Ravenna, Pinacoteca Comunale

Ravensburg, Gal. Döbele
  Ravensburg, Galerie Döbele

Rawalpindi, Soc. Contemp. A. Gals
  Rawalpindi, Society of Contemporary Art Galleries

Razgrad, Hist. Mus.
  Razgrad, Historical Museum

Reading, Mus. & A.G.
  Reading, Museum and Art Gallery

Reading, U. Reading Lib.
  Reading, University of Reading Library

Recanati, Mus. Dioc.
  Recanati, Museo Diocesano

Recanati, Pal. Com.
  Recanati, Palazzo Comunale

Recanati, Pal. Leopardi
  Recanati, Palazzo Leopardi

Recanati, Pin. Civ.
  Recanati, Pinacoteca Civica

Recife, Casa Cult.
  Recife, Casa da Cultura de Pernambuco

Recklinghausen, Ikonenmus.
  Recklinghausen, Ikonenmuseum

Recklinghausen, Museen Stadt
  Recklinghausen, Museen der Stadt Recklinghausen [admins Ikonenmus.; Städt. Ksthalle; Vest. Mus.]

Recklinghausen, Städt. Ksthalle
  Recklinghausen, Städtische Kunsthalle

Recklinghausen, Vest. Mus.
  Recklinghausen, Vestisches Museum

Regensburg, Altes Rathaus

Regensburg, Fürst Thurn & Taxis Schlossmus.
  Regensburg, Fürst Thurn und Taxis Schlossmuseum

Regensburg, Hist. Verein
  Regensburg, Historischer Verein für Oberpfalz und Regensburg

Regensburg, Kepler-Gedächt.-Haus
  Regensburg, Kepler-Gedächtnis-Haus

Regensburg, Kst- & Kulthist. Samml.
  Regensburg, Kunst- und Kulturhistorische Sammlungen

Regensburg, Museen Stadt
  Regensburg, Museen der Stadt [admins Kepler- Gedächt.-Haus; Kst- & Kulthist. Samml.; Reichstagsmus.; Städt. Gal.]

Regensburg, Ostdt. Gal.
  Regensburg, Ostdeutsche Galerie

Regensburg, Reichstagsmus.
  Regensburg, Reichstagsmuseum [in Altes Rathaus]

Regensburg, Staatsgal.
  Regensburg, Staatsgalerie

Regensburg, Stadtarchv
  Regensburg, Stadtarchiv

Regensburg, Städt. Gal.
  Regensburg, Städtische Galerie

Regensburg, Stadtmus.
  Regensburg, Stadtmuseum

Reggio Calabria, Mus. N.
  Reggio Calabria, Museo Nazionale [della Magna Grecia]

Reggio Emilia, Archv Stato
  Reggio Emilia, Archivio di Stato

Reggio Emilia, Fond. Magnani-Rocca
  Reggio Emilia, Fondazione Magnani-Rocca

Reggio Emilia, Mus. Civ. & Gal. A.
  Reggio Emilia, Musei Civici e Gallerie d'Arte

Reggio Emilia, Mus. Spallanzani
  Reggio Emilia, Museo Spallanzani di Storia Naturale

Reggio Emilia, Pal. Com.
  Reggio Emilia, Palazzo Comunale

Reggio Emilia, Pal. Vescovile
  Reggio Emilia, Palazzo Vescovile

Reggio Emilia, Soc. Casino
  Reggio Emilia, Società del Casino

Regina, Pub. Lib., Dunlop A.G.
  Regina, Public Library, Dunlop Art Gallery

Regina, U. Regina, Mackenzie A.G.
  Regina, University of Regina, Mackenzie Art Gallery

Reichersberg, Stiftsmus.
  Reichersberg, Stiftsmuseum [in Augustiner Chorherrenstift]

Reims, Archvs Ville
  Reims, Archives de la Ville de Reims

Reims, Bib. Mun.
  Reims, Bibliothèque Municipale

Reims, Maison Cult. André Malraux
  Reims, Maison de la Culture André Malraux

Reims, Mus. St-Denis
  Reims, Musée St-Denis [Musée des Beaux-Arts]

Reims, Mus. St-Remi
  Reims, Musée St-Remi

Reims, Mus. Vieux-Reims
  Reims, Musée du Vieux-Reims [Musée Hôtel le Vergeur]

Reims, Pal. Tau
  Reims, Palais du Tau [incl. part of Musée de la Sculpture et des Sacres; the Cathedral Treasury]

Reims, Trésor Cathédrale
  Reims, Trésor de la Cathédrale

Remiremont, Mus. Mun. Charles de Bruyères
  Remiremont, Musée Municipal Charles de Bruyères

Remscheid, Dt. Werkzeugmus. & Heimatmus.
  Remscheid, Deutsches Werkzeugmuseum und Heimatmuseum Remscheid

Renaissance, CA, Mus. Class Chin. Furn.
  Renaissance, CA, Museum of Classical Chinese Furniture

Rennes, Bib. Mun.
  Rennes, Bibliothèque Municipale

Rennes, Cercle Mil.
  Rennes, Cercle Militaire

Rennes, Maison Cult.
  Rennes, Maison de la Culture

Rennes, Mus. B.-A. & Archéol.
  Rennes, Musée des Beaux-Arts et d'Archéologie

Rennes, Mus. Bretagne
  Rennes, Musée de Bretagne

Reno, NV Hist. Soc. Mus.
  Reno, NV, Nevada Historical Society Museum

Repino, Repin Mus.
  Repino, Repin Museum (Muzey-Usad'ba I.Ye. Repina Penaty) [in Penaty]

Rethymnon, Archaeol. Mus.
  Rethymnon, Archaeological Museum

Reutlingen, Heimatmus.
  Reutlingen, Heimatmuseum

Reutlingen, Kstgal. Spendhaus
  Reutlingen, Kunstgalerie im Spendhaus

Reykjavík, Árnamagnean Inst.
  Reykjavík, Árnamagnean Institute (Stofnun Árna Magnússonar)

Reykjavík, Einar Jónsson Mus.
  Reykjavík, Einar Jónsson Museum (Listasafn Einars Jónssonar)

Reykjavík, Hafnarfjörður Cult. & A. Cent.
  Reykjavík, Hafnarfjörður Culture and Art Centre (Menningar og Listastofnun Hafnarfjarðar)

Reykjavík, Hafnarfjörður Cult. & A. Fund
  Reykjavík, Hafnarfjörðr Culture and Art Fund (Menningar og Listasjoður Hafnarfjarðar)

Reykjavík, Hagatorg

Reykjavík, Kjarvalsstaðir

Reykjavík, Living A. Mus.
  Reykjavík, Living Art Museum (Nýlistasafnið)

Reykjavík, Loftleiðir Hótel

Reykjavík, Mokka Kaffi

Reykjavík, Mun. & Open Air Mus.
  Reykjavík, Municipal and Open Air Museum (Árbæjarsafn)

Reykjavík, N.G.
  Reykjavík, National Gallery of Iceland (Listasafn Íslands)

Reykjavík, N. Mus.
  Reykjavík, National Museum of Iceland (Þjóðminjasafn Íslands)

Reykjavík, Nordic House (Norræna Húsið)

Reykjavík, Ólafsson Mus.
  Reykjavík, Sigurjón Ólafsson Museum (Listasafn Sigurjóns Ólafsson)

Reykjavík, Sveinsson Mus.
  Reykjavík, Sveinsson Museum (Ásmundarsafn)

Reykjavík, Teacher Training Coll.
  Reykjavík, Teacher Training College (Kennaraskóli Íslands)

Rhede, Haus Tencking [Freiherr von Hövell]

Rhede, Schloss [Fürst zu Salm-Salm]

Rhodes, Archaeol. Mus.
  Rhodes, Archaeological Museum

Ribe, Kstmus.
  Ribe, Ribe Kunstmuseum

Richmond, VA, Agecroft Hall
Richmond, VA, Agecroft Hall

Richmond, VA, Capitol Bldg
Richmond, VA, Capitol Building

Richmond, VA Mus. F.A.
Richmond, VA, Virginia Museum of Fine Arts

Richmond, Mus. VA Hist. Soc.
Richmond, VA, Museum of Virginia Historical
Society

Richmond, Sci. Mus. VA
Richmond, VA, Science Museum of Virginia

Richmond, VA State Lib.
Richmond, VA, Virginia State Library

Richmond, VA, Valentine Mus.
Richmond, VA, Valentine Museum

Ried, Innviertler Vlkskndhaus & Gal. Stadt
Ried, Innviertler Volkskundehaus und Galerie
der Stadt

Rieti, Mus. Civ.
Rieti, Museo Civico

Riga, City A. Mus.
Riga, City Art Museum (Rīgas Pilsētas Mākslas
Muzejs)

Riga, Fundamental Lib. Acad. Sci. Latvia
Riga, Fundamental Library of the Academy of
Sciences of Latvia (Latvijas Zinātniskā
Biblioteka)

Riga, Latv. Acad. A.
Riga, Latvian Academy of Art (Latvijas
Mākslas Akadēmija)

Riga, Latv. Cult. Fund
Riga, Latvian Cultural Fund (Latvijas Kultūras
Fonds)

Riga, Latv. Mus. F.A.
Riga, Latvian Museum of Fine Art (Latvijas
mākslas mūzejs)

Riga, Latv. Open-Air Mus. of Ethnog.
Riga, Latvian Open-Air Museum of
Ethnography (Latvijas Etnogrāfiskais
Brīvdabas Muzejs)

Riga, Lit. & Theat. Mus.
Riga, Literary and Theatre Museum [name
changed to Jānis Raiņis Mus. Hist. Latv. Lit. &
A. in 1964]

Riga, Mus. Foreign A.
Riga, Museum of Foreign Art (Ārzemju
Mākslas Muzejs)

Riga, Mus. Hist.
Riga, Museum of the History of Riga (Rīgas
Vēstures Muzejs)

Riga, Mus. Latv. & Rus. A.
Riga, Museum of Latvian and Russian Art
[now Latv. Mus. F.A.]

Riga, Raiņis Mus. Hist. Latv. Lit. & A.
Riga, Jānis Raiņis Museum of the History of
Latvian Literature and Art [formerly Lit. &
Theat. Mus.] (Jāņa Raiņa Literatūras un
Mākslas Muzejs)

Riggisberg, Abegg-Stift.
Riggisberg, Abegg-Stiftung

Riihimäki, Fin. Glass Mus.
Riihimäki, Finnish Glass Museum (Suomen
Lasimuseo)

Rijeka, Mod. Gal.
Rijeka, Modern Gallery (Moderna Galerija)

Rijswijk, A.-G. Oenema
Rijswijk, Art-Gallery Oenema

Rijswijk, Mus.
Rijswijk, Museum Rijswijk

Rila Monastery, N. Mus.
Rila Monastery, National Museum
(Natsionalen Muzey Rilski Manastir)

Rimini, Mus. Com.
Rimini, Musei Comunali

Rimini, Pal. Arengo
Rimini, Palazzo dell'Arengo

Rimini, Pin. Com. & Mus. Civ.
Rimini, Pinacoteca Comunale e Museo Civico

Rîmnicu Vîlcea, Distr. Mus.
Rîmnicu Vîlcea, District Museum (Muzeul
Judeţean Rîmnicu Vîlcea)

Rio de Janeiro, Banco do Estado

Rio de Janeiro, Bib. N.
Rio de Janeiro, Biblioteca Nacional

Rio de Janeiro, Col. Ferrez
Rio de Janeiro, Coleção Gilberto Ferrez

Rio de Janeiro, Escola A. Visuais
Rio de Janeiro, Escola de Artes Visuais

Rio de Janeiro, Fund. Castro Mais
Rio de Janeiro, Fundação Castro Mais

Rio de Janeiro, Gal. Acervo
Rio de Janeiro, Galeria Acervo

Rio de Janeiro, Gal. Skulp.
Rio de Janeiro, Galeria Skulptura

Rio de Janeiro, Inst. Hist. & Geog. Bras.
Rio de Janeiro, Instituto Histórico e
Geográfico Brasileiro

Rio de Janeiro, Mus. A. Mod.
Rio de Janeiro, Museu de Arte Moderna do
Rio de Janeiro

Rio de Janeiro, Mus. Chácara Céu
Rio de Janeiro, Museu Chácara do Céu

Rio de Janeiro, Mus. Estrada Açude
Rio de Janeiro, Museu Estrada do Açude

Rio de Janeiro, Museus Raymundo Ottoni de
Castro Maya
Rio de Janeiro, Museus/Fundação Raymundo
Ottoni de Castro Maya [Rio de Janeiro, Mus.
Chácara Céu; Rio de Janeiro, Mus. Estrada
Açude]

Rio de Janeiro, Mus. Hist. N.
Rio de Janeiro, Museu Histórico Nacional

Rio de Janiero, Mus. Inconciente
Rio de Janeiro, Museu do Inconciente

Rio de Janeiro, Mus. Indio
Rio de Janeiro, Museu do Indio

Rio de Janeiro, Mus. Manchete
Rio de Janeiro, Museu Manchete

Rio de Janeiro, Mus. N.
Rio de Janeiro, Museu Nacional

Rio de Janeiro, Mus. N. B.A.
Rio de Janeiro, Museu Nacional de Belas Artes

Rio de Janeiro, Mus. Patol. U.
Rio de Janeiro, Museu de Patologia da
Universidade

Rio de Janeiro, Mus. Pontal
Rio de Janeiro, Museu do Pontal [Coleção
Jacques van de Beuque]

Rio de Janeiro, Mus. Repúb.
Rio de Janeiro, Museu da República [formerly
Palácio do Catete 1858-67]

Rio de Janeiro, Mus. Tijuca
Rio de Janeiro, Museu de Tijuca

Rio de Janeiro, Pal. Cult.
Rio de Janeiro, Palácio da Cultura

Rio de Janeiro, Petite Gal.
Rio de Janeiro, Petite Galerie

Rio de Janeiro, Pont. U. Católica
Rio de Janeiro, Pontifícia Universidade
Católica

Rio de Janeiro, Projeto Hélio Oiticia

Rio de Janeiro, Roberto Marinho priv. col.
Rio de Janeiro, Coleção Roberto Marinho

Rio de Janeiro, Solar Grandjean de Montigny

Riofrío, Royal Pal.
Riofrío, Royal Palace

Riom, Musées Riom
Riom, Musées de Riom [admins Mus. Mandet;
Mus. Rég. Auvergne]

Riom, Mus. Mandet
Riom, Musée Francisque Mandet

Riom, Mus. Rég. Auvergne
Riom, Musée Régional d'Auvergne

Rio Piedras, Gal. Ridel
Rio Piedras, Galería Ridel

Rio Piedras, U. Puerto Rico
Rio Piedras, Universidad de Puerto Rico

Rio Piedras, U. Puerto Rico, Mus. Antropol., Hist.
& A.
Rio Piedras, Universidad de Puerto Rico,
Museo de Antropología, Historia y Arte

Riverside, U. CA, Mus. Phot.
Riverside, University of California, California
Museum of Photography

Riverton, CT, Hitchcock Mus.
Riverton, CT, John Tarrant Kenney Hitchcock
Museum

Rivoli, Castello

Rivoli, Municipio

Rixheim, Mus. Pap. Peint
Rixheim, Musée du Papier Peint

Riyadh, Dept Ant. & Museums
Riyadh, Department of Antiquities and
Museums [admins Mus. Archaeol. & Ethnog.]

Riyadh, King Saud U.
Riyadh, King Saud University

Riyadh, King Saud U., Archaeol. Dept
Riyadh, King Saud University, Archaeology
Department

Riyadh, Mus. Archaeol. & Ethnog.
Riyadh, Museum of Archaeology and
Ethnography

Roanne, Mus. Déchelette
Roanne, Musée Joseph Déchelette [Musée
Municipal]

Roatán, Mus. Roatán
Roatán, Museo de Roatán

Rochdale, A.G.
Rochdale, Art Gallery

Rochechouart, Mus. Dépt.
Rochechouart, Musée Départemental d'Art
Contemporain [in Château]

Rochefort, Mus. Mun.
Rochefort, Musée Municipal d'Art et
d'Histoire de la Ville de Rochefort

Rochester, MI, Oakland U., Meadow Brook A.G.
Rochester, MI, Oakland University, Meadow
Brook Art Gallery

Rochester, NY, Inst. Technol., Sch. Amer.
Craftsmen
Rochester, NY, Rochester Institute of
Technology, School for American Craftsmen

Rochester, NY, Int. Mus. Phot.
Rochester, NY, International Museum of
Photography at George Eastman House

Rochester, NY, Mus. & Sci. Cent.
Rochester, NY, Rochester Museum and Science Center

Rochester, NY, Strong Mus.
Rochester, NY, Strong Museum [Margaret Woodbury Strong Museum]

Rochester, U. Rochester, NY, Mem. A.G.
Rochester, NY, University of Rochester, Memorial Art Gallery

Rockbourne, Roman Villa

Rockford, IL, Time Mus.
Rockford, IL, Time Museum

Rockland, ME, Farnsworth Lib. & A. Mus.
Rockland, William A. Farnsworth Library and Art Museum

Roda de Isábena, Mus. Parroq.
Roda de Isábena, Museo Parroquial

Rodez, Mus. Fénaille
Rodez, Musée Fénaille

Rohrau, Schloss
Rohrau, Graf Harrach'sche Familiensammlung, Schloss Rohrau

Roman, Mus. Hist. & A.
Roman, Museum of History and Art (Muzeul de Istorie și Artă Română)

Roman, Mus. Nat. Hist.
Roman, Museum of Natural History (Muzeul de Științele Naturii)

Rome, Acad. France
Rome, Académie de France

Rome, Accad. N. Lincei
Rome, Accademia Nazionale dei Lincei

Rome, Accad. N. S Luca
Rome, Accademia Nazionale di S Luca

Rome, Accad. N. S Luca, Archv Stor.
Rome, Accademia Nazionale di S Luca, Archivio Storico

Rome, A. Club
Rome, Art Club

Rome, Amer. Acad.
Rome, American Academy in Rome

Rome, Anna Ascanio
Rome, Anna d'Ascanio

Rome, Antiqua. Com.
Rome, Antiquarium Comunale

Rome, Antiqua. Forense
Rome, Antiquarium Forense

Rome, Antiqua. Palatino
Rome, Antiquarium Palatino

Rome, Apostolico Coll. Leoniano, Cappella della Regina Apostolorum
Rome, Apostolico Collegio Leoniano, Cappella della Regina Apostolorum

Rome, Arciconfraternità Senesi
Rome, Arciconfraternità dei Senesi

Rome, Archv Cent.
Rome, Archivio Centrale dello Stato

Rome, Archv Com.
Rome, Archivio Comunale [in Oratorio dei Filippini]

Rome, Archv Congregazione Oratorio
Rome, Archivio della Congregazione dell'Oratorio

Rome, Archv S Maria in Campitelli
Rome, Archivio di S Maria in Campitelli

Rome, Archvs S Carlo ai Catinari
Rome, Archivio di S Carlo ai Catinari

Rome, Archv Stato
Rome, Archivio di Stato di Roma

Rome, Archv Vicariato
Rome, Archivio del Vicariato di Roma

Rome, Atelier Mannucci

Rome, Avvocatura Stato
Rome, Avvocatura dello Stato

Rome, Banca Commerc. It.
Rome, Banca Commerciale Italiana

Rome, Banco di Roma

Rome, Bib. Accad. N. Lincei & Corsiniana
Rome, Biblioteca dell'Accademia Nazionale dei Lincei e Corsiniana

Rome, Bib. Angelica
Rome, Biblioteca Angelica

Rome, Bib. Casanatense
Rome, Biblioteca Casanatense

Rome, Bib. Hertz.
Rome, Biblioteca Hertziana [Max-Planck-Institut in Pal. Zuccari]

Rome, Bib. Ist. N. Archeol. & Stor. A.
Rome, Biblioteca dell'Istituto Nazionale d'Archeologia e Storia dell'Arte

Rome, Bib. Lancisiana
Rome, Biblioteca Lancisiana

Rome, Bib. N. Cent.
Rome, Biblioteca Nazionale Centrale Vittorio Emanuele II

Rome, Bib. Universitaria Alessandrina
Rome, Biblioteca Universitaria Alessandrina

Rome, Bib. Vallicelliana
Rome, Biblioteca Vallicelliana

Rome, Brit. Sch.
Rome, British School at Rome

Rome, Calcografia N.
Rome, Calcografia Nazionale [Calcografia di Roma]

Rome, Camposanto Teutonica

Rome, Carmelite Coll.
Rome, Carmelite College [Sassone]

Rome, Carpine
Rome, Il Carpine

Rome, Casa A. Bragaglia
Rome, Casa d'Arte Bragaglia

Rome, Casa Gen. Gesuiti
Rome, Casa Generalizia dei Gesuiti

Rome, Casa Libro
Rome, Casa del Libro

Rome, Casa Orsini, Archv Capitolino
Rome, Casa Orsini, Archivio Capitolino

Rome, Casino Massimo al Laterano

Rome, Casino Rospigliosi–Pallavicini

Rome, Castel S Angelo

Rome, Cent. Cult. Fr.
Rome, Centre Culturel Français

Rome, Coll. Urbano Propaganda Fede
Rome, Collegio Urbano di Propaganda della Fede

Rome, Depositi S Pietro
Rome, Depositi di S Pietro

Rome, Dt. Archäol. Inst.
Rome, Deutsches Archäologisches Institut

Rome, Ecole Fr.
Rome, Ecole Française

Rome, Egyp. Acad. F.A.
Rome, Egyptian Academy of Fine Arts

Rome, E.U.R., Pal. Congr.
Rome, E.U.R., Palazzo dei Congressi [Esposizione Universale di Roma]

Rome, Ferrovie Stato
Rome, Ferrovie dello Stato

Rome, Fond. Camillo Caetani
Rome, Fondazione Camillo Caetani

Rome, Fond. Giorgio & Isa de Chirico
Rome, Fondazione Giorgio e Isa de Chirico

Rome, Fond. Primoli
Rome, Fondazione Primoli

Rome, Gab. Fot. N.
Rome, Gabinetto Fotografico Nazionale

Rome, Gab. N. Stampe
Rome, Gabinetto Nazionale delle Stampe

Rome, Gal. A. Bragaglia
Rome, Galleria d'Arte Bragaglia

Rome, Gal. Accad. N. S Luca
Rome, Galleria dell'Accademia Nazionale di S Luca

Rome, Gal. Anna d'Ascanio
Rome, Galleria Anna d'Ascanio

Rome, Gal. Annunciata
Rome, Galleria Annunciata

Rome, Gal. Appunto
Rome, Galleria L'Appunto

Rome, Gal. Arco Farnese
Rome, Galleria Arco Farnese

Rome, Gal. Attico
Rome, Galleria L'Attico

Rome, Gal. Bilico
Rome, Galleria Il Bilico [no longer exists]

Rome, Gal. Borghese
Rome, Galleria Borghese

Rome, Gal. Bragaglia
Rome, Galleria Bragaglia [closed]

Rome, Gal. Carlo Virgilio
Rome, Galleria Carlo Virgilio

Rome, Gal. Colonna
Rome, Galleria Colonna

Rome, Gal. Cometa
Rome, Galleria della Cometa

Rome, Gal. Doria Pamphili
Rome, Galleria Doria Pamphili

Rome, Gal. Giulia
Rome, Galleria Giulia

Rome, Gal. Gruppo 10
Rome, Galleria Gruppo 10

Rome, Gal. Isola di Milano
Rome, Galleria L'Isola di Milano

Rome, Gal. Marlborough
Rome, Galleria Marlborough

Rome, Gal. Oca
Rome, Galleria dell'Oca

Rome, Gal. Pallavicini
Rome, Galleria Pallavicini [in Pal. Rospigliosi–Pallavicini]

Rome, Gal. Permanente Futur.
Rome, Galleria Permanente Futurista

Rome, Gal. Pogliani
Rome, Galleria Pogliani

Rome, Gal. Sabatello
Rome, Galleria Sabatello

Rome, Gal. Salita
Rome, Galleria La Salita

Rome, Gal. Sarro
Rome, Galleria di Sarro

Rome, Gal. Sciarra
Rome, Galleria Sciarra

Rome, Gal. Secolo
Rome, Galleria del Secolo

Rome, Gal. Selecta
Rome, Galleria La Selecta

Rome Gal. Serpenti
    Rome, Galleria dei Serpenti

Rome, Gal. Spada
    Rome, Galleria Spada [in Pal. Spada]

Rome, Gal. Sperone
    Rome, Galleria Sperone

Rome, Gal. Tartaruga
    Rome, Galleria La Tartaruga

Rome, Gal. Zodiaco
    Rome, Galleria Zodiaco

Rome, Giard. Vaticani, Casino Pio IV
    Rome, Giardini Vaticani, Casino di Pio IV
    [Casino del Papa; Villa Pia]

Rome, G.N.A. Ant.
    Rome, Galleria Nazionale d'Arte Antica
    [admins Pal. Barberini; Pal. Corsini]

Rome, G.N.A. Mod.
    Rome, Galleria Nazionale d'Arte Moderna [e
    Arte Contemporanea; in Palazzo delle Belle
    Arti]

Rome, Grotte Augusteo
    Rome, Grotte dell'Augusteo

Rome, Grotte Vaticane

Rome, Il Cortile

Rome, Ist. Cent. Restauro
    Rome, Istituto Centrale per il Restauro

Rome, Ist. It.-Afr.
    Rome, Istituto Italo-Africano

Rome, Ist. It.-Lat. Amer.
    Rome, Istituto Italo-Latino Americano

Rome, Ist. It. Med. & Estrem. Orient.
    Rome, Istituto Italiano per il Medio ed
    Estremo Oriente [ISMEO]

Rome, Ist. N. Graf.
    Rome, Istituto Nazionale per la Grafica

Rome, Ist. Oland.
    Rome, Istituto Olandese

Rome, Ist. Previdenza Soc.
    Rome, Istituto di Previdenza Sociale

Rome, Ist. S Michele
    Rome, Istituto Romano di S Michele

Rome, Ist. Stor. Ger.
    Rome, Istituto Storico Germanico

Rome, Ist. Togliatti
    Rome, Istituto Togliatti

Rome, Keats–Shelley Mem. House
    Rome, Keats–Shelley Memorial House

Rome, La Sapienza
    Rome, Università degli Studi di Roma 'La
    Sapienza'

Rome, Lateran Pal.
    Rome, Lateran Palace [houses Museo
    Cristiano Pio IX; Museo Epigrafico Cristiano;
    Museo Missionario Etnologico; Museo
    Profano o Gregoriano Lateranese] (Palazzo
    del Laterano)

Rome, Lib. Age Or
    Rome, Libreria Age d'Or

Rome, Margherita
    Rome, La Margherita

Rome, Mercati Traianei

Rome, Min. Agric.
    Rome, Ministero dell'Agricoltura

Rome, Min. Grazia & Giustizia
    Rome, Ministero di Grazia e Giustizia

Rome, Mus. Afr.
    Rome, Museo Africano [Istituto Italo-
    Africano]

Rome, Mus. Barracco
    Rome, Museo Barracco

Rome, Mus. Canonica
    Rome, Museo Canonica

Rome, Mus. Capitolino
    Rome, Museo Capitolino

Rome, Mus. Carabinieri
    Rome, Museo Storico dell'Arma dei
    Carabinieri

Rome, Mus. Cent. Ris.
    Rome, Museo Centrale del Risorgimento

Rome, Mus. Civiltà
    Rome, Museo della Civiltà Romana

Rome, Mus. Conserv.
    Rome, Museo dei Conservatori [in Pal.
    Conserv.]

Rome, Musei Capitolini
    Rome, Musei Capitolini [admins Mus.
    Capitolino; Mus. Conserv.; Pin. Capitolina]

Rome, Musei Lateranesi
    Rome, Musei Lateranesi [admins museums of
    Lateran Pal.]

Rome, Musei Vaticani [admins Pin. Vaticana;
    Vatican, Braccio Nuo.; Cappelle, Sale & Gal.
    Affrescate; Col. A. Relig. Mod.; Gal. Arazzi; Gal.
    Candelabri; Gal. Lapidaria; Mus. Chiaramonti;
    Mus. Gregoriano Egizio; Mus. Gregoriano Etrus.;
    Mus. Gregoriano Profano; Mus. Missionari Etnol.;
    Mus. Pio-Clementini; Mus. Pio-Cristiano; Mus.
    Profano Bib. Apostolica; Mus. Stor. A., Rac.
    Epig.]

Rome, Mus. Flklore & Poeti
    Rome, Museo del Folklore e dei Poeti
    Romaneschi

Rome, Mus. Francescano
    Rome, Museo Francescano dell'Istituto Storico
    dei Cappuccini

Rome, Mus. Napoleonico
    Rome, Museo Napoleonico

Rome, Mus. N. A. & Trad. Pop.
    Rome, Museo Nazionale delle Arti e delle
    Tradizioni Popolari

Rome, Mus. N. Castel S Angelo
    Rome, Museo Nazionale di Castel Sant'Angelo

Rome, Mus. N. Preist. & Etnog.
    Rome, Museo Nazionale Preistorico ed
    Etnografico 'Luigi Pigorini'

Rome, Mus. N. Romano
    Rome, Museo Nazionale Romano [Museo
    delle Terme]

Rome, Mus. Numi. Zecca
    Rome, Museo Numismatico della Zecca

Rome, Mus. Osservatorio Astron.
    Rome, Museo dell'Osservatorio Astronomico

Rome, Mus. Petriano
    Rome, Museo Petriano [closed]

Rome, Mus. Soc. Geog. It.
    Rome, Museo della Società Geografica Italiana

Rome, Mus. Torlonia
    Rome, Museo Torlonia

Rome, Nuo. Paese
    Rome, Il Nuovo Paese

Rome, Obelisco
    Rome, L'Obelisco

Rome, Osservatorio Astron.
    Rome, Osservatorio Astronomico

Rome, Pal. Altieri
    Rome, Palazzo Altieri

Rome, Pal. Barberini
    Rome, Palazzo Barberini [Galleria Nazionale
    del Palazzo Barberini]

Rome, Pal. Brancaccio
    Rome, Palazzo Brancaccio [houses Museo
    Nazionale d'Arte Orientale]

Rome, Pal. Braschi
    Rome, Palazzo Braschi [houses Galleria
    Comunale d'Arte Moderna]

Rome. Pal. Caetani
    Rome, Palazzo Caetani

Rome, Pal. Caetani-Lovatelli
    Rome, Palazzo Caetani-Lovatelli

Rome, Pal. Cancelleria
    Rome, Palazzo della Cancelleria

Rome, Pal. Carolis
    Rome, Palazzo di Carolis

Rome, Pal. Carpegna
    Rome, Palazzo Carpegna

Rome, Pal. Chigi
    Rome, Palazzo Chigi

Rome, Pal. Conserv.
    Rome, Palazzo dei Conservatori [houses Mus.
    Conserv., Sale Conserv. and Pin.; adjoining are
    Pal. Conserv., Braccia Nuovo and Pal.
    Conserv., Mus. Nuovo]

Rome, Pal. Conserv., Braccio Nuovo
    Rome, Palazzo dei Conservatori, Braccio
    Nuovo

Rome, Pal. Conserv., Mus. Nuovo
    Rome, Palazzo dei Conservatori, Museo
    Nuovo

Rome, Pal. Conserv., Pin.
    Rome, Palazzo dei Conservatori, Pinacoteca

Rome, Pal. Corsini
    Rome, Palazzo Corsini [G.N.A. Ant.]

Rome, Pal. Costaguti
    Rome, Palazzo Costaguti

Rome, Pal. Doria Pamphili
    Rome, Palazzo Doria Pamphili

Rome, Pal. Espos.
    Rome, Palazzo delle Esposizioni

Rome, Pal. Farnese
    Rome, Palazzo Farnese

Rome, Pal. Gesù
    Rome, Palazzo al Gesù [Palazzo Cenci-
    Bolognetti]

Rome, Pal. Madama
    Rome, Palazzo Madama

Rome, Pal. Massimo alle Colonne
    Rome, Palazzo Massimo alle Colonne

Rome, Pal. Mattei
    Rome, Palazzo Mattei

Rome, Pal. Mattei di Gove
    Rome, Palazzo Mattei di Gove

Rome, Pal. Montecitorio
    Rome, Palazzo di Montecitorio [Camera dei
    Deputati]

Rome, Pal. Mus. Capitolino
    Rome, Palazzo del Museo Capitolino

Rome, Pal. Quirinale
    Rome, Palazzo del Quirinale

Rome, Pal. Rondanini
    Rome, Palazzo Rondanini [now called Palazzo
    Sanseverino; houses Banca dell'Agricoltura]

Rome, Pal. Rospigliosi–Pallavicini
    Rome, Palazzo Rospigliosi–Pallavicini [houses
    Gal. Pallavicini]

Rome, Pal. Ruspoli
    Rome, Palazzo Ruspoli [Fondazione Memmo]

Rome, Pal. Sacchetti
    Rome, Palazzo Sacchetti

Rome, Pal. Salviati
    Rome, Palazzo Salviati

Rome, Pal. Sodalizio Piceni
    Rome, Palazzo del Sodalizio dei Piceni

Rome, Pal. Spada
    Rome, Palazzo Spada [houses Gal. Spada]

Rome, Pal. Spagna
    Rome, Palazzo di Spagna

Rome, Pal. Taverna Monte Giordano
    Rome, Palazzo Taverna di Monte Giordano

Rome, Pal. Torlonia
    Rome, Palazzo Torlonia

Rome, Pal. Venezia
    Rome, Palazzo Venezia

Rome, Pal. Zucchari
    Rome, Palazzo Zucchari [houses Bib. Hertz.]

Rome, Pantheon

Rome, Pin. Vaticana
    Rome, Pinacoteca Vaticana

Rome, Pio Ist. Catel
    Rome, Pio Istituto Catel

Rome, Presidenza Min.
    Rome, Presidenza dei Ministri [not open to the public]

Rome, Protomoteca Capitolina

Rome, Quadriennale A.
    Rome, Quadriennale d'Arte

Rome, Sala Stuard

Rome, Sale Conserv.
    Rome, Sale dei Conservatori [in Pal. Conserv.]

Rome, S Eligio degli Orefici, Archv Stor.
    Rome, S Eligio degli Orefici, Archivio Storico

Rome, Sestieri

Rome, S Maria in Vallicella, Archv
    Rome, S Maria in Vallicella, Archivio

Rome, Soprintend. Speciale Mus. N. Preist. & Etnog.
    Rome, Soprintendenza Speciale al Museo Nazionale Preistorico ed Etnografico L. Pigorini

Rome, S Paolo fuori le Mura

Rome, Spicchi E.
    Rome, Spicchi dell'Est

Rome, St Peter's

Rome, Studio A. Mod.
    Rome, Studio d'Arte Moderna

Rome, Studio A. Palma
    Rome, Studio d'Arte Palma

Rome, Studio E

Rome, Tabularium

Rome, Tartaruga

Rome, Tavazzi

Rome, Teat. Costanzi
    Rome, Teatro Costanzi

Rome, Vatican, Appartamento Borgia
    Rome, Vatican, Appartamento Borgia

Rome, Vatican, Archv Segreto
    Rome, Vatican, Archivio Segreto Vaticano

Rome, Vatican, Bib. Apostolica
    Rome, Vatican, Biblioteca Apostolica Vaticana [Vatican Lib.]

Rome, Vatican, Bib. Apostolica, Archv Capitolare S Pietro
    Rome, Vatican, Biblioteca Apostolica Vaticana, Archivio Capitolare S Pietro

Rome, Vatican, Braccio Carlo Magno
    Rome, Vatican, Braccio di Carlo Magno

Rome, Vatican, Braccio Nuo.
    Rome, Vatican, Braccio Nuovo

Rome, Vatican, Cappelle, Sale & Gal. Affrescate
    Rome, Vatican, Cappelle, Sale e Gallerie Affrescate

Rome, Vatican, Col. A. Relig. Mod.
    Rome, Vatican, Collezione d'Arte Religiosa Moderna

Rome, Vatican, Col. Pont.
    Rome, Vatican, Collezione Pontificale

Rome, Vatican, Consistory Hall

Rome, Vatican, Cortile Belvedere
    Rome, Vatican, Cortile del Belvedere

Rome, Vatican, Cortile Pigna
    Rome, Vatican, Cortile della Pigna

Rome, Vatican, Court Triangle
    Rome, Vatican, Court of the Triangle

Rome, Vatican, Gal. Arazzi
    Rome, Vatican, Galleria degli Arazzi

Rome, Vatican, Gal. Candelabri
    Rome, Vatican, Galleria dei Candelabri

Rome, Vatican, Gal. Lapidaria
    Rome, Vatican, Galleria Lapidaria

Rome, Vatican, Medagliere

Rome, Vatican, Mnmt., Musei & Gal. Pont.
    Rome, Vatican, Monumenti, Musei e Gallerie Pontificie

Rome, Vatican, Mus. Chiaramonti
    Rome, Vatican, Museo Chiaramonti

Rome, Vatican, Mus. Gregoriano Egizio
    Rome, Vatican, Museo Gregoriano Egizio

Rome, Vatican, Mus. Gregoriano Etrus.
    Rome, Vatican, Museo Gregoriano Etrusco

Rome, Vatican, Mus. Gregoriano Profano
    Rome, Vatican, Museo Gregoriano Profano

Rome, Vatican, Mus. Missionari Etnol.
    Rome, Vatican, Museo Missionari Etnologico

Rome, Vatican, Mus. Pio-Clementino
    Rome, Vatican, Museo Pio-Clementino

Rome, Vatican, Mus. Pio-Clementino, Gab. Maschere
    Rome, Vatican, Museo Pio-Clementino, Gabinetto delle Maschere

Rome, Vatican, Mus. Pio-Crist.
    Rome, Vatican, Museo Pio-Cristiano

Rome, Vatican, Mus. Profano Bib. Apostolica
    Rome, Vatican, Museo Profano della Biblioteca Apostolica

Rome, Vatican, Mus. Sacro
    Rome, Vatican, Museo Sacro

Rome, Vatican, Mus. Sacro Bib. Apostolica
    Rome, Vatican, Museo Sacro della Biblioteca Apostolica

Rome, Vatican, Mus. Stor. A. Tesoro S Pietro
    Rome, Vatican, Museo Storico Artistico Tesoro di S Pietro

Rome, Vatican Pal.
    Rome, Vatican Palace

Rome, Vatican, Pal. Belvedere
    Rome, Vatican, Palazzo del Belvedere

Rome, Vatican, Pal. Governatorato
    Rome, Vatican, Palazzo del Governatorato

Rome, Vatican, Pauline Chapel [Cappella Paulina]

Rome, Vatican, Pont. Accad. Romana Archeol.
    Rome, Vatican, Pontificia Accademia Romana di Archeologia

Rome, Vatican, Pont. Ist. Archeol. Crist.
    Rome, Vatican, Pontificio Istituto di Archeologia Cristiana

Rome, Vatican, Rac. Epig.
    Rome, Vatican, Raccolte Epigrafiche

Rome, Vatican, Sala a Croce Greca

Rome, Vatican, Sala dei Palafrenieri

Rome, Vatican, Sala della Immacolata

Rome, Vatican, Sala delle Nozze Aldobrandine

Rome, Vatican, Sala di Costantino

Rome, Vatican, Sala Regia

Rome, Vatican, Sistine Chapel [Cappella Sistina]

Rome, Vatican, Stanza d'Eliodoro

Rome, Vatican, Stanza della Segnatura

Rome, Vatican, Stanza dell'Incendio

Rome, Vatican, Stanze di Raffaello

Rome, Vatican, Studio del Mosaico

Rome, Villa Albani
    Rome, Museo di Villa Albani

Rome, Villa Borghese
    Rome, Villa Borghese

Rome, Villa Colonna
    Rome, Villa Colonna

Rome, Villa Farnesina
    Rome, Villa Farnesina

Rome, Villa Giulia [Museo Nazionale di Villa Giulia e Soprintendenza alle Antichità per l'Etruria Meridionale]

Rome, Villa Lante, Ist. Finland.
    Rome, Villa Lante, Istituto Finlandese

Rome, Villa Ludovisi
    Rome, Villa Ludovisi

Rome, Villa Massimo
    Rome, Villa Massimo [houses Accademia Germanica]

Rome, Villa Medici
    Rome, Villa Medici

Rome, Villa Torlonia
    Rome, Villa Torlonia

Rome, Villa Wolkonsky
    Rome, Villa Wolkonsky

Romrod, Schloss
    Romrod, Romrod Schloss

Roncevalles, Mus. A., Real Colegiata
    Roncevalles, Museo de Arte de Roncevalles, Real Colegiata

Rosario, Mus. Mun. B.A.
    Rosario, Museo Municipal de Bellas Artes Juan B. Castagnino

Roseau, Victoria Mem. Mus.
    Roseau, Victoria Memorial Museum

Rosenheim, Städt. Gal.
    Rosenheim, Städtische Galerie [Städtische Kunstsammlungen; in Max Bram Haus]

Roskilde, Vikingskibshallen (Viking Ship Museum)

Roslyn, NY, Nassau Co. Mus. F.A.
    Roslyn, NY, Nassau County Museum of Fine Arts

Rossano, Mus. Dioc.
    Rossano, Museo Diocesano [in Archbishop's Pal.]

Rostock, Ksthalle
    Rostock, Kunsthalle

Rostock, U. Rostock
    Rostock, Universität Rostock

Rostov-on-Don, Mus. F.A.
    Rostov-on-Don, Museum of Fine Art

Rostov—Yaroslavl', Archit. & A. Mus.
Rostov—Yaroslavl', Architecture and Art Museum [formerly the Museum of Church Antiquities] (Rostovo-Yaroslavskiy Arkhiterkturno-Khudozhestvenyy Muzey-Zapovednik)

Rotorua, A.G.
Rotorua, Art Gallery [Tudor Towers Bldg]

Rottenburg am Neckar, Kultur Zent. Zehntschcvcr
Rottenburg am Neckar, Kultur Zentrum Zehntschever

Rotterdam, Dubbelde Palmboom
Rotterdam, De Dubbelde Palmboom

Rotterdam, Gal. 't Venster
Rotterdam, Galerie 't Venster

Rotterdam, Gemeentelijke Archfdienst
Rotterdam, Gemeentelijke Archiefdienst

Rotterdam, Hist. Mus.
Rotterdam, Historisch Museum [houses Stichting Atlas von Stolk]

Rotterdam, Kstkring
Rotterdam, Rotterdamse Kunstkring

Rotterdam, Kststicht.
Rotterdam, Rotterdamse Kunststichting

Rotterdam, Mar. Mus.
Rotterdam, Maritiem Museum Prins Hendrik

Rotterdam, Mus. Boymans
Rotterdam, Museum Boymans [name changed to Museum Boymans—van Beuningen 1958]

Rotterdam, Mus. Boymans—van Beuningen
Rotterdam, Museum Boymans—van Beuningen [houses Stichting Willem vander Vorm]

Rotterdam, Mus. Chabot
Rotterdam, Museum Hendrik Chabot

Rotterdam, Mus. Vlkenknd.
Rotterdam, Museum voor Volkenkunde

Rotterdam, Ned. Architectuurinst.
Rotterdam, Nederlands Architectuurinstitut

Rotterdam, Raadhuis

Rotterdam, Zakkendragershuisje [Pewter-maker's Cottage]

Rottweil, Dominikanermus.
Rottweil, Dominikanermuseum

Rottweil, Forum Kst
Rottweil, Forum Kunst

Roubaix, Ecole N. Sup. A. & Indust. Textiles
Roubaix, Ecole Nationale Supérieure des Arts et Industries Textiles

Roubaix, Mus. B.-A.
Roubaix, Musée des Beaux-Arts et Jean-Joseph Weerts [in Hôtel de Ville]

Roudnice nad Labem, Gal. F.A.
Roudnice nad Labem, Gallery of Fine Art (Galerie Výtvarného Umění]

Rouen, Bib. Mun.
Rouen, Bibliothèque Municipale

Rouen, Mus. A. Normand
Rouen, Musée d'Art Normand

Rouen, Mus. Ant.
Rouen, Musée Départemental des Antiquités de la Seine-Maritime

Rouen, Mus. B.-A.
Rouen, Musée des Beaux-Arts

Rouen, Mus. Cér.
Rouen, Musée de la Céramiquc

Rouen, Mus. Jeanne-d'Arc
Rouen, Musée Jeanne-d'Arc

Rouen, Mus. Le Secq des Tournelles
Rouen, Musée Le Secq des Tournelles [in St Laurent]

Rougemont, Château

Rovaniemi, A. Mus.
Rovaniemi, Art Museum (Taidemuseo)

Rovereto, Gal. Mus. Depero
Rovereto, Galleria Museo Depero

Rovigo, Accad. Concordi
Rovigo, Accademia dei Concordi

Rovigo, Pin. Semin.
Rovigo, Pinacoteca del Seminario [Seminario Vescovile]

Rovigo, Rotonda

Roxbury, MA, Mus. Afro-Amer. Hist.
Roxbury, MA, Museum of Afro-American History

Roztoky u Prahy, Mus. Cent. Bohemia
Roztoky u Prahy, Museum of Central Bohemia (Středoč eské Múzeum)

Rugby School
Rugby, Rugby School

Ruse, Reg. Mus. Hist.
Ruse, Regional Museum of History (Okrăžen Istoričeski Muzej)

Ruvo di Puglia, Mus. Jatta
Ruvo di Puglia, Museo Jatta [Palazzo Jatta]

Ružomberok, Ľudovit Fulla Gal.
Ružomberok, Ľudovit Fulla Gallery,

Ryazan', Local Hist. Mus.
Ryazan', Local History Museum (Krayevedcheskiy Muzey)

Ryazan', Reg. A. Mus.
Ryazan', Regional Art Museum (Oblastnoy Khudozhestvennyy Muzey)

Rybinsk, Mus. Hist. A.
Rybinsk, Museum of the History of Art (Istoriko-khudozhestvennyy Muzey)

Rychnov nad Kněžnou, Château A.G.
Rychnov nad Kněžnou, Château Art Gallery (Zámecká obrazárna)

Rychnov nad Kněžnou, Orlík Gal.
Rychnov nad Kněžnou, Orlík Gallery (Orlická Galerie) [Eagle Mountains Gallery; in castle]

Saarbrücken, Landesmus. Vor- & Frühgesch.
Saarbrücken, Landesmus. für Vor- und Frühgeschichte [Stiftung Saarländischer Kulturbcsitz; in Frcital Castlc]

Saarbrücken, Saarland Mus.
Saarbrücken, Saarland Museum

Sabbathday Lake, ME, Shaker Mus.
Sabbathday Lake, ME, Shaker Museum

Sackville, NB, Mt Allison U., Owens A.G.
Sackville, NB, Mount Allison University, Owens Art Gallery

Sacramento, CA, Crocker A. Mus.
Sacramento, CA, Crocker Art Museum

Sadarapat, Ethnol. Mus.
Sadarapat, Ethnology Museum (Hayastani Azgagrut'yan T'angaran)

Saffron Walden Mus.
Saffron Walden, Saffron Walden Museum

Sagar, U. Sagar, Archaeol. Mus.
Sagar, University of Sagar, Archaeological Museum [Hari Singh Gour Archaeol. Mus.]

Sahagún, Ayuntamiento, Mus.
Sahagún, Ayuntamiento, Museo

Saidu Sharif, Swat Mus.
Saidu Sharif, Swat Museum

Saigon, Ecole Fr. Extrême-Orient
Saigon, Ecole Française d'Extrême-Orient [Saigon now Hô Chi Minh City]

Saigon, Mus. Blanchard Brosse
Saigon, Musée Blanchard de la Brosse [now Hô Chi Minh City, N. Mus.]

St Albans, Verulamium Mus.
St Albans, Verulamium Museum

St Andrews, Cathedral Mus.
St Andrews, Cathedral Museum

St Andrews, Crawford A. Cent.
St Andrews, Crawford Arts Centre [part of U. St Andrews until 1988; now indep.]

St Andrews, Pub. Lib, Hay Fleming Col.
St Andrews, St Andrews Public Library, Hay Fleming Collection

St Andrews, U. St Andrews
St Andrews, University of St Andrews [University Art Collection; incl. Sir D'Arcy Wentworth Thompson Archives]

St Andrews, U. St Andrews, Crawford Cent. A.
St Andrews, University of St Andrews, Crawford Centre for the Arts [since 1988 called Crawford A. Cent.]

St Andrews, U. St Andrews, Parliament Hall

St Augustine, Trinidad, U. W. Indies, Lib.
St Augustine, Trinidad, University of the West Indies, Library

St Catherine, Arawak Ind. Mus.
St Catherine, Arawak Indian Museum [Jamaica]

Saint-Céré, Atelier-Mus. Jean Lurçat
Saint-Céré, Atelier-Musée Jean Lurçat

Saint-Cyprien, Mus. Artistes Cat.
Saint-Cyprien, Musée des Artistes Catalans

Saint-Cyprien, Mus.-Fond. Desnoyer
Saint-Cyprien, Musée-Fondation François-et-Souza-Desnoyer

Saint-Denis, Bib. Mun.
Saint-Denis, Bibliothèque Municipale

Saint-Dcnis, Dépôt Lapidairc

Saint-Denis, Maison Cult.
Saint-Denis, Maison de Culture

Saint-Denis, Maison Légion d'Honneur
Saint-Denis, Maison de la Légion d'Honneur

Saint-Denis, Mus. A. & Hist.
Saint-Denis, Musée d'Art et d'Histoire

Saint-Denis, Mus. Bouilhet—Christofle
Saint-Denis, Musée Bouilhet—Christofle

Saint-Denis Abbey

Saint-Denis, Trésor Cathédrale
Saint-Denis, Trésor de la Cathédrale

Sainte-Foy, Archvs N. Qué.
Sainte-Foy, Archives Nationales du Québec

Saintes, Mus. Archéol.
Saintes, Musée Archéologique

Saintes, Mus. B.-A.
Saintes, Musée des Beaux-Arts

Saintes-Maries-de-la-Mer, Mus. Camarguais
Saintes-Maries-de-la-Mer, Musée Camarguais

Saint-Etienne, Maison Cult.
Saint-Etienne, Maison de la Culture

Saint-Etienne, Mus. A. & Indust.
Saint-Eticnnc, Musée d'Art et d'Industric

Saint-Etienne, Mus. A. Mod.
Saint-Eticnnc, Muséc d'Art Modcrnc

St Fagans, Welsh Flk Mus.
St Fagans, Welsh Folk Museum

St Gall, Hist. Mus.
St Gall, Historisches Museum

St Gall, Kstmus.
  St Gall, Kunstmuseum

St Gall, Kstver.
  St Gall, Kunstverein

St Gall, Samml. Vlkerknd.
  St Gall, Sammlung für Völkerkunde

St Gall, Stift.-Bib.
  St Gall, Stifts-Bibliothek

St Gall, Textilmus.
  St Gall, Textilmuseum

St Georges, Grenada N. Mus.
  St Georges, Grenada National Museum

Saint-Germain-en-Laye, Château

Saint-Germain-en-Laye, Mus. Ant. N.
  Saint-Germain-en-Laye, Musée des Antiquités
  Nationales [in Château]

Saint-Germain-en-Laye, Mus. Dépt. Prieuré
  Saint-Germain-en-Laye, Musée Départemental
  du Prieuré

Saint-Germain-en-Laye, Mus. Homme
  Saint-Germain-en-Laye, Musée de l'Homme

Saint-Germain-en-Laye, Mus. Mun.
  Saint-Germain-en-Laye, Musée Municipal

St Helier, Jersey Mus.
  St Helier, Jersey Museum

St Helier, Jersey Museums Serv.
  St Helier, Jersey Museums Service [admins
  States of Jersey Collection, Jersey Heritage
  Trust Collection; displays in Jersey Mus. and
  public bldgs throughout the island]

St-Hyacinthe, Semin.
  St-Hyacinthe, Seminary

St Ives, Barbara Hepworth Mus.
  St Ives, Barbara Hepworth Museum [part of
  Tate]

St Ives, Tate
  St Ives, Tate Gallery St Ives

Saint-Jean-Cap-Ferrat, Villa-Mus. Ile de France,
Fond. de Rothschild
  Saint-Jean-Cap-Ferrat, Villa-Musée Ile de
  France, Fondation Ephrussi de Rothschild
  [Institut de France, Académie des Beaux-Arts]

Saint-Jean-de-Maurienne, Hôtel de Ville

Saint John, NB Mus.
  Saint John, NB, New Brunswick Museum

St John's, Antigua, Island A.
  St John's, Antigua, Island Arts

St John's, Mem. U. Nfld, A.G.
  St John's, Memorial University of
  Newfoundland, Art Gallery

St John's, Mus. Antigua & Barbuda
  St John's, Antigua, Museum of Antigua and
  Barbuda

St Johnsbury, VT, Athenaeum
  St Johnsbury, VT, St Johnsbury Athenaeum
  [Public Library and Art Gallery]

St Joseph, MO, Albrecht A. Mus.
  St Joseph, Albrecht Art Museum

St Kitts, Brimstone Hill Mus.
  St Kitts, Brimstone Hill Museum

St Lambrecht, Kultreferat Steiermärk.
Landesregierung
  St Lambrecht, Kulturreferat der
  Steiermärkischen Landesregierung

Saint-Lô, Mus. B.-A.
  Saint-Lô, Musée des Beaux-Arts [Musée de
  Saint-Lô, Musée d'Art; in Hôtel de Ville]

St Louis, MO, A. Mus.
  St Louis, MO, Art Museum

St Louis, MO, Boatmen's N. Bank
  St Louis, MO, The Boatmen's National Bank
  of St Louis

St Louis, MO, Brentwood Gal.
  St Louis, MO, Brentwood Gallery

St Louis, MO, George Washington U.
  St Louis, MO, George Washington University

St Louis, MO, George Washington U. Gal. A.
  St Louis, MO, George Washington University
  Gallery of Art

St Louis, MO Hist. Soc. Mus.
  St Louis, Missouri Historical Society Museum

St Louis, MO, Image Gal.
  St Louis, MO, Image Gallery

St Louis, MO, Jefferson N. Expn Mem.
  St Louis, MO, Jefferson National Expansion
  Memorial

St Louis, MO, Laumeier Sculp. Park
  St Louis, MO, Laumeier Sculpture Park

St Louis, MO, Mercantile Lib.
  St Louis, MO, Mercantile Library

St Louis, MO, Mon. Club
  St Louis, MO, Monday Club

St Louis, MO, Pub. Lib.
  St Louis, MO, St Louis Public Library

St Louis, MO, Trova Studio

Saint-Malo, Château [Musée Historique de la Ville
de Saint-Malo]

Saint-Malo, Tour Solidor [Musée de Cap-
Horniers]

St Maurice, Abbey Treasury

St Michael, Barbados Mus.
  St Michael, Barbados Museum [in St Ann's
  Garrison; includes Barbados Historical
  Society]

Saint-Moritz, Mus. Segantini
  Saint-Moritz, Musée Segantini

St-Niklaas, Stedel. Mus.
  St-Niklaas, Stedelijk Museum [voor
  Volkskunde, Oude Ambachten, Regionale
  Geschiedenis, Exlibris en Schone Kunsten]

St Oedenrode, Raadhuis

Saint-Omer, Bib. Mun.
  Saint-Omer, Bibliothèque Municipale

Saint-Omer, Mus. Dupuis
  Saint-Omer, Musée Henri Dupuis

Saint-Omer, Mus. Hôtel Sandelin
  Saint-Omer, Musée de l'Hôtel Sandelin

St Paul, MN Mus. A.
  St Paul, MN, Minnesota Museum of Art

St Paul, Sci. Mus. MN
  St Paul, MN, Science Museum of Minnesota

St Paul, U. MN, Goldstein Gal.
  St Paul, MN, University of Minnesota,
  Goldstein Gallery

Saint-Paul-de-Vence, Fond. Maeght
  Saint-Paul-de-Vence, Fondation Maeght

St Paul in Lavanttal, Stiftsbib.
  St Paul in Lavanttal, Stiftsbibliothek

St Peter, Kath. Pfarrkirche, Bibraum
  St Peter, Katholische Pfarrkirche,
  Bibliotheksraum

St Petersburg: the city reverted from Leningrad to
its pre-Revolution name of St Petersburg in Sept
1991

St Petersburg, Acad. A.
  St Petersburg, Academy of Arts (Akademiya
  Khudozhestv)

St Petersburg, Acad. A., Mus.
  St Petersburg, Academy of Arts, Museum
  (Akademiya Khudozhestv, Muzey)

St Petersburg, Acad. A., Sci. Res. Mus.
  St Petersburg, Academy of Arts, Scientific
  Research Museum (Akademiya Khudozhestv,
  Nauchno-Issledovatel'skiy Muzey)

St Petersburg, Acad. Sci.
  St Petersburg, Academy of Sciences
  (Akademiya Nauk)

St Petersburg, Acad. Sci., Inst. Archaeol.
  St Petersburg, Academy of Sciences, Institute
  of Archaeology (Arkheologicheskiy Institut)

St Petersburg, Acad. Sci., Inst. Orient. Stud.
  St Petersburg, Academy of Sciences, Institute
  of Oriental Studies (Institut Vostokovedeniya
  Akademii Nauk) [Inst. of the Peoples of Asia
  (Institut Narodov Azii)]

St Petersburg, Acad. Sci., Lib.
  St Petersburg, Academy of Sciences, Library
  (Akademiya Nauk, Biblioteka [BAN])

St Petersburg, Anichkov Pal.
  St Petersburg, Anichkov Palace (Anichkov
  Dvorets)

St Petersburg, Archaeol. Inst.
  St Petersburg, Archaeological Institute
  (Arkheologicheskiy Institut)

St Petersburg, A.S. Pushkin Acad. Theat.
  St Petersburg, A.S. Pushkin Academy Theatre
  [formerly Alexander Theatre]

St Petersburg, A.S. Pushkin Apartment Mus.
  St Petersburg, A.S. Pushkin Apartment
  Museum (Muzey- Kvartira A.S. Pushkina)

St Petersburg, Brodsky Apartment-Mus.
  St Petersburg, Apartment-Museum of I.I.
  Brodsky (Kvartira-Muzey I.I. Brodskogo)

St Petersburg, Cent. Naval Mus.
  St Petersburg, Central Naval Museum
  (Tsentral'nyy Morskoy Muzey)

St Petersburg, Gatchina Pal.
  St Petersburg, Gatchina Palace (Gatchinskiy
  Dvorets)

St Petersburg, Hermitage
  St Petersburg, Hermitage Museum (Muzey
  Ermitazh)

St Petersburg, House Cult.
  St Petersburg, House of Culture (Dom
  Kultury)

St Petersburg, House of Writers (Dom Pisateley)

St Petersburg, Inst. Archaeol.
  St Petersburg, Institute of Archaeology
  (Institut Arkheologii)

St Petersburg, Inst. Hist. Mat. Cult.
  St Petersburg, Institute for the History of
  Material Culture (Institut Istorii Material'noy
  Kultury)

St Petersburg, Inst. Rus. Lit.
  St Petersburg, Institute of Russian Literature
  (Institut Russkoy Literatury) [in Pushkin
  House; attached to Acad. Sci.]

St Petersburg, Lansky House

St Petersburg, Lit. Mus. Inst. Rus. Lit.
  St Petersburg, Literary Museum of the
  Institute of Russian Literature (Literaturnyy
  Muzey Instituta Russkoy Literatury)

St Petersburg, Lomonosov Mem. Mus.
  St Petersburg, Lomonosov Memorial Museum
  (Memorial'nyy Muzey M.I. Lomonosova)

St Petersburg, Lomonosov Porcelain Factory Mus.
  St Petersburg, Lomonosov Porcelain Factory
  Museum (Muzey Lomonosovskogo
  Farforovogo Zaroda)

St Petersburg, Menshikov Pal.
St Petersburg, Menshikov Palace (Men'shikovskiy Dvorets)

St Petersburg, Mikhailovsky Pal.
St Petersburg, Mikhailovsky Palace [now Rus. Mus.]

St Petersburg, Mus. City Sculp.
St Petersburg, Museum of City Sculpture (Muzey Gorodskoy Skul'ptury) [Museum of Town Sculpture; Church of the Annunciation Domenico Trezzini]

St Petersburg, Mus. Ethnog.
St Petersburg, Museum of Ethnography (Muzey Etnografii)

St Petersburg, Mus. Hist. Relig.
St Petersburg, Museum of the History of Religion (Muzey Istorii Religii)

St Petersburg, Mus. Hist. St Petersburg
St Petersburg, Museum of the History of St Petersburg (Muzey Istorii St Peterburga)

St Petersburg, Mus. Oct Socialist Revolution
St Petersburg, Museum of the October Socialist Revolution (Muzey Velikoy Oktyabr'skoy Sotsialisticheskoy Revolyutsii)

St Petersburg, Mus. Porcelain
St Petersburg, Museum of Porcelain [Museum of the China Factory]; *see* Lomonosov Porcelain Factory Mus.

St Petersburg, Mus. Sculp.
St Petersburg, Museum of Sculpture (Muzey Skul'ptury) [in former Alexander Nevsky Lavra]

St Petersburg, Mus. Trade & Indust.
St Petersburg, Museum of Trade and Industry (Muzey Torgovlya i Promyshlennosti) [closed]

St Petersburg, N. Lib.
St Petersburg, National Library of Russia [formerly Saltykov-Shchedrin Pub. Lib.]

St Petersburg, Peter and Paul Fortress [Petropavlovskaya Krepost']

St Petersburg, Peter's Pal.
St Petersburg, Peter's Palace (Petrodvorets)

St Petersburg, Peter the Great Mus. Anthropol. & Ethnog.
St Petersburg, Peter the Great Museum of Anthropology and Ethnography (Muzey Antropologii Etnografii Imeni Petra Velikogo)

St Petersburg, Plekhanov Mining Inst.
St Petersburg, Plekhanov Mining Institute (Gornyy Instityt Imeni G. V. Plekhanova)

St Petersburg, Repin Inst.
St Petersburg, Repin Institute for Painting, Sculpture and Architecture (Institut Zhivopisi, Skul'ptury i Arkhitektury Imeni A. Ye. Repina)

St Petersburg, Rus. Mus.
St Petersburg, Russian Museum (Russkiy Muzey)

St Petersburg, Saltykov-Shchedrin Pub. Lib.
St Petersburg, M.E. Saltykov-Shchedrin Public Library (Gosudarstvennaya Publichnaya Biblioteka Imeni Saltykova-Shchedrina) [SSPL/GPBSS; name changed to N. Lib. in March 1992]

St Petersburg, Sov. House
St Petersburg, Soviet House (Dom Sovetov)

St Petersburg, Summer Pal.
St Petersburg, Peter the Great's Summer Palace Museum (Letnyy Dvorets Petra I v Letnem Sadu)

St Petersburg, Theat. Mus.
St Petersburg, Theatre Museum (Teatral'nyy Muzey)

St Petersburg, Zhdanov U., Gorky Lib.
St Petersburg, A.A. Zhdanov University, A. M. Gorky Library (Universitet Imeni A. A. Zhdanova, Biblioteka Imeni A. M. Gor'kogo) ['A. A. Zhdanov' no longer used]

St Petersburg, Zool. Mus.
St Petersburg, Zoological Museum (Zoologicheskiy Muzey)

St Petersburg, FL, Dalí Found. Mus.
St Petersburg, FL, Salvador Dalí Foundation Museum

St Petersburg, FL, Mus. F.A.
St Petersburg, FL, Museum of Fine Arts

St Philip, Sam Lord's Castle [Barbados]

St Pölten, Diözmus.
St Pölten, Diözesanmuseum

St Pölten, Niederösterreich. Pressehaus
St Pölten, Niederösterreichisches Pressehaus

St Pölten, Städt. Archv
St Pölten, Städtisches Archiv

St Pölten, Stadtmus.
St Pölten, Stadtmuseum St Pölten

St Priest, Cent. A. Contemp.
St Priest, Centre d'Art Contemporain

Saint-Quentin, Mus. Lécuyer
Saint-Quentin, Musée Antoine Lécuyer

Saint-Raphaël, Mus. Archéol.
Saint-Raphaël, Musée Archéologique

Saint-Rémy-lès-Chevreuse, Fond. Coubertin
Saint-Rémy-lès-Chevreuse, Fondation Coubertin

St Tropez, Mus. Annonciade
St Tropez, Musée de l'Annonciade

St Vincent, Archaeol. Mus.
St Vincent, Archaeological Museum

Sakura, Chiba Prefect., N. Mus. Jap. Hist.
Sakura, Chiba Prefecture, National Museum of Japanese History

Sakura, Kawamuna Mem. Mus. Mod. A.
Sakura, Kawamuna Memorial Museum of Modern Art

Salamanca, Casa-Mus. Unamuno
Salamanca, Casa-Museo de Unamuno

Salamanca, Mus. Catedralicio
Salamanca, Museo Catedralicio

Salamanca, Mus. Ciudad
Salamanca, Museo de la Ciudad

Salamanca, Mus. Convento S Ursula
Salamanca, Museo del Convento de Santa Ursula

Salamanca, Mus. Dioc.
Salamanca, Museo Diocesano [Claustro de la Catedral Vieja]

Salamanca, Mus. Prov.
Salamanca, Museo Provincial de Salamanca

Salamanca, Mus. Salamanca
Salamanca, Museo de Salamanca

Salamanca, Pal. Monterrey
Salamanca, Palacio de Monterrey

Salamanca, Residencia Sotomayor

Salamanca, U. Salamanca, Pal. Anaya
Salamanca, University of Salamanca, Palacio de Anaya

Salamis Mus.
Salamis, Salamis Museum

Salamis, Royal Tombs Mus.
Salamis, Royal Tombs Museum

Salem, Schloss & Münster
Salem, Schloss und Münster [former Zisterzienserkloster]

Salem, MA, Essex Inst.
Salem, MA, Essex Institute

Salem, MA, Peabody Essex Mus.
Salem, MA, Peabody Essex Museum

Salerno Cathedral, Treasury

Salerno, Mus. Archeol. Prov.
Salerno, Museo Archeologico Provinciale

Salerno, Mus. Dioc. Prov.
Salerno, Museo Diocesano Provinciale [in former Seminario Arcivescovile]

Salerno, Mus. Duomo
Salerno, Museo del Duomo [Mus. Dioc. Prov. since 1992]

Salerno, Mus. Prov.
Salerno, Museo Provinciale

Salerstein, Schloss Arenenberg

Salford, Mus. & A.G.
Salford, Museum and Art Gallery

Salford, U. Salford
Salford, University of Salford

Salisbury, Salisbury & S. Wilts Mus.
Salisbury, Salisbury and South Wiltshire Museum

Salona, Croatia, Mus.
Salona, Croatia, Museum

Salonika: *see* Thessaloniki

Saltillo, Ateneo Fuente

Salt Lake City, UT, Mus. Ch. Hist. & A.
Salt Lake City, UT, Museum of Church History and Art

Salt Lake City, UT, Salt Lake A. Cent.
Salt Lake City, UT, Salt Lake Art Center

Salt Lake City, UT State Hist. Soc.
Salt Lake City, UT, Utah State Historical Society

Salt Lake City, U. UT, Mus. F.A.
Salt Lake City, UT, University of Utah, Museum of Fine Arts

Salt Lake City, U. UT, Mus. Nat. Hist.
Salt Lake City, UT, University of Utah, Museum of Natural History

Salvador, Inst. Geog. & Hist.
Salvador, Instituto Geográfico e Histórico

Salvador, Mus. A. Bahia
Salvador, Museu de Arte da Bahia

Salvador, Mus. A. Mod. Bahia
Salvador, Museu de Arte Moderna da Bahia

Salvador, Mus. A. Pop.
Salvador, Museu de Arte Popular

Salvador, Mus. A. Sacra U. Fed. Bahia
Salvador, Museu de Arte Sacra da Universidade Federal Bahia

Salvador, Mus. Col. Rodrigues
Salvador, Museu da Coleção Abelardo Rodrigues [in Solar do Ferrão]

Salvador, Mus. Fund. Pint
Salvador, Museu da Fundação Carlos Costa Pinto

Salvador, Pal. Vitória
Salvador, Palacio da Vitória [in Bahia State]

Salvador, S Tereza, Mus. A. Sacra
Salvador, Santa Tereza, Muzeu de Arte Sacra

Salzburg, Barockmus.
Salzburg, Barockmuseum [Sammlung Rossacher]

Salzburg, Berchtesgadenerhof

Salzburg, Bib. St Peter
Salzburg, Bibliothek der Benediktiner-Erzabtei
St Peter

Salzburg, Burgmus.
Salzburg, Burgmuseum

Salzburg, Dommus.
Salzburg, Dommuseum

Salzburg, Gal. Welz
Salzburg, Galerie Welz

Salzburg, Guggenheim Mus. A.
Salzburg, Guggenheim Museum of Art

Salzburg, Landesgal.
Salzburg, Salzburger Landesgalerie

Salzburg, Mozarteum

Salzburg, Mus. Carolino Augusteum
Salzburger Museum Carolino Augusteum
[admins Burgmus.; Museum Carolino
Augusteum; Spielzeugmus., Vlkskndmus.]

Salzburg, Residenzgal.
Salzburg, Residenzgalerie Salzburg

Salzburg, Residenz, Neugebäude

Salzburg, Rupertinum
Salzburg, Rupertinum Salzburger
Landessammlungen [houses Moderne Galerie
und Graphische Sammlung Rupertinum;
Österreichische Fotogalerie]

Salzburg, Schloss Mirabell

Salzburg, Spielzeugmus.
Salzburg, Spielzeugmuseum

Salzburg, Ubib.
Salzburg, Universitätsbibliothek Salzburg

Salzburg, U. Salzburg
Salzburg, Universität Salzburg

Salzburg, Vlkskndmus.
Salzburg, Volkskundemuseum im
Monatsschlösschen

Samara, Russia, City A. Mus.
Samara, Russia, City Art Museum (Samarskiy
Khudozhestvenyy Muzey) [Samara formerly
called Kuybyshev]

Samara, Russia, Reg. Mus.
Samara, Russia, Regional Museum

Samarkand, Afrasiab Mus.
Samarkand, Afrasiab Museum

Samarkand, Gulyamov Inst. Archeol.
Samarkand, Gulyamov Institute of
Archaeology

Samarkand, Ikramov Mus. Hist. Cult. & A.
Uzbekistan
Samarkand, A. Ikramov Museum of the
History of Culture and Art of Uzbekistan

Samarkand, Inst. Archeol.
Samarkand, Institute of Archaeology [part of
Uzbek Academy of Sciences]

Samarkand, Mus. Hist.
Samarkand, Museum of the History of
Samarkand [M.T. Aibek Museum of the
History of the Uzbek People]

Samarkand, Registan Mus.
Samarkand, Registan Museum

Samarkand, Ulug-Beg Mem. Mus.
Samarkand, Ulug-Beg Memorial Museum [incl.
Observatory]

Samer, Mus. Cazin
Samer, Musée Jean-Charles Cazin

Samokov, A.G.
Samokov, Samokov Art Gallery (Samokovska
Kartinna Galerie)

Samokov, Mun. Hist. Mus.
Samokov, Municipal History Museum
(Gradski Iskoričeski Muzey)

Samos, Archaeol. Mus.
Samos, Archaeological Museum

Samothrace, Archaeol. Mus.
Samothrace, Archaeological Museum

Sampierdarena, Villa Centurione-Carpeneto

Samsun, Archaeol. Mus.
Samsun, Archaeological Museum (Arkeoloji
Müzesi)

San'a, Dar al-Makhtutat
San'a, Dar al-Makhtutat

San'a, Lib. Gt Mosque
San'a, Library of the Great Mosque of San'a

San'a, Yemen N. Mus.
San'a, Yemen National Museum

San Agustín, Colombia, Parque Arqueol.
San Agustín, Colombia, Parque Arqueológico

San Antonio, TX, Col. A. League
San Antonio, TX, Collection of the San
Antonio Art League

San Antonio, TX, McNay A. Inst.
San Antonio, TX, Marion Koogler McNay Art
Institute

San Antonio, TX, Mus. A.
San Antonio, TX, Museum of Art

San Antonio, TX, Mus. Assoc.
San Antonio, TX, Museum Association

San Antonio, TX, Witte Mus.
San Antonio, TX, Witte Museum

San Benedetto Po, Civ. Mus. Polironiano
San Benedetto Po, Civico Museo Polironiano
[Monastero Benedettino di Polirone]

San Bernardino, CA, Co. Mus.
San Bernardino, CA, San Bernardino County
Museum

San Bernardino, CA State U.
San Bernardino, CA, California State
University

San Cosmé y Damián, Mus. Mis.
San Cosmé y Damián, Museo de Misión

San Diego, CA, Acad. A.
San Diego, CA, San Diego Academy of Art

San Diego, CA, F.A. Gal.
San Diego, CA, Fine Arts Gallery of San
Diego

San Diego, CA, Mus. A.
San Diego, CA, San Diego Museum of Art

San Diego, CA, Mus. Contemp. A.
San Diego, CA, Museum of Contemporary Art

San Diego, CA, Putnam Found.
San Diego, CA, Putnam Foundation

San Diego, CA, State U., A. G.
San Diego, CA, San Diego State University,
Art Gallery

San Diego, CA, Timken A.G.
San Diego, CA, Timken Art Gallery

San Diego, U. CA, Mandeville Coll. Gal.
San Diego, CA, University of California,
Mandeville College Gallery

Sandomierz, Dioc. Mus.
Sandomierz, Diocesan Museum (Muzeum
Diecezjalne Sztuki Kościelnej)

San Felipe, Mus. S Francisco de Curimón
San Felipe, Museo San Francisco de Curimón

San Francisco, CA, Achenbach Found. Graph. A.
San Francisco, CA, Achenbach Foundation for
Graphic Arts

San Francisco, CA, Ackerman F.A. Lib.
San Francisco, CA, Louise Sloss Ackerman
Fine Arts Library [in MOMA]

San Francisco, CA, A. Inst. Gals
San Francisco, CA, Art Institute Galleries

San Francisco, CA, Amer. Ind. Contemp. A.
San Francisco, CA, American Indian
Contemporary Art

San Francisco, CA, Asian A. Mus.
San Francisco, CA, Asian Art Museum of San
Francisco [incl. Avery Brundage Collection]

San Francisco, CA, Cent. Asian A. & Cult.
San Francisco, CA, Center for Asian Art and
Culture

San Francisco, CA, Chin. Cult. Cent. Gal.
San Francisco, CA, Chinese Culture Center
Gallery

San Francisco, CA, City Coll.
San Francisco, CA, City College

San Francisco, CA, de Young Mem. Mus.
San Francisco, CA, M. H. de Young Memorial
Museum

San Francisco, CA, F.A. Museums
San Francisco, Fine Arts Museums of San
Francisco [admins Achenbach Found. Graph.
A.; de Young Mem. Mus.; Pal. Legion of
Honor]

San Francisco, CA, Fraenkel Gal.
San Francisco, CA, Fraenkel Gallery

San Francisco, CA, Gal. Paule Anglim
San Francisco, CA, Gallery Paule Anglim

San Francisco, CA, Glastonbury Gal.
San Francisco, CA, Glastonbury Gallery

San Francisco, CA, Int. Airport
San Francisco, CA, International Airport

San Francisco, CA, John Berggruen Gal.
San Francisco, CA, John Berggruen Gallery

San Francisco, CA, Mex. Mus.
San Francisco, CA, Mexican Museum

San Francisco, CA, MOMA
San Francisco, CA, Museum of Modern Art

San Francisco, CA, Mus. A.
San Francisco, CA, Museum of Art [name
changed to MOMA in 1976]

San Francisco, CA Pal. Legion of Honor
San Francisco, CA, California Palace of the
Legion of Honor

San Francisco, UCA
San Francisco, CA, University of California

San Gimignano, Bib. Com.
San Gimignano, Biblioteca Comunale

San Gimignano, Mus. A. Sacra
San Gimignano, Museo d'Arte Sacra

San Gimignano, Mus. Civ.
San Gimignano, Museo Civico [in Pal. Pop.]

San Gimignano, Pal. Pop.
San Gimignano, Palazzo del Popolo

San Gimignano, Pin. Civ.
San Gimignano, Pinacoteca Civica [in Pal.
Pop.]

San Ginesio, Mus. Pin. Gentile
San Ginesio, Museo Pinacoteca Gentile
[Museo Civico Gentile]

San Ignacio Guazú, Mus. Mis.
San Ignacio Guazú, Museo de Misión

San Isidro, Mus. Gen. Pueyrredón
San Isidro, Museo General Juan Martín de
Pueyrredón [Buenos Aires]

San Jose, CA, Mus. A.
San Jose, CA, San Jose Museum of Art

San José, Arcadas

San José, Banco Anglo-Costarricense

San José, Banco N. Costa Rica
San José, Banco Nacional de Costa Rica

San José, Gal. A.
San José, Galería d'Arte

San José, Mus. A. Costarricense
San José, Museo de Arte Costarricense

San José, Mus. Banco Cent.
San José, Museos Banco Central

San José, Mus. Jade, Inst. N. Seguros
San José, Museo de Jade, Instituto Nacional de
Seguros

San José, Mus. N. Costa Rica
San José, Museo Nacional de Costa Rica

San Juan, Cent. Estud. Avanzados Puerto Rico &
Caribe
San Juan, Centro de Estudios Avanzados de
Puerto Rico y el Caribe

San Juan, Inst. Cult. Puertorriqueña
San Juan, Instituto de Cultura Puertorriqueña

San Juan, Inst. Cult. Puertorriqueña, Arsenal
Puntilla
San Juan, Instituto de Cultura Puertorriqueña,
Arsenal de la Puntilla

San Juan, Mus. A. Relig.
San Juan, Museo de Arte Religioso

San Juan, Park Gal.
San Juan, Park Gallery

San Juan, U. Puerto Rico
San Juan, Universidad de Puerto Rico

San Leucio, Casino Reale Belvedere
San Leucio, Casino Reale di Belvedere

San Lorenzo, Paraguay, Mus. Etnog. 'Guido
Boggiani'
San Lorenzo, Paraguay, Museo Etnográfico
'Guido Boggiani'

San Luis Potosí, Casa Cult.
San Luis Potosí, Casa de la Cultura

San Marino, Mus. Pin. S Francesco
San Marino, Museo Pinacoteca S Francesco

San Marino, Pal. Congressi
San Marino, Palazzo dei Congressi

San Marino, CA, Huntington Lib. & A.G.
San Marino, CA, Huntington Library and Art
Gallery

San Miguel, Argentina, Escuela B.A.
San Miguel, Argentina, Escuela de Bellas Artes

San Miniato, Accad. Buteleti
San Miniato, Accademia degli Buteleti

San Miniato, Mus. Dioc. A. Sacra
San Miniato, Museo Diocesano d'Arte Sacra

San Miniato, Pal. Com.
San Miniato, Palazzo Comunale

San Miniato, Semin. Dioc.
San Miniato, Seminario Diocesano

San Oedro, Lindy Ward's A.G.
San Oedro, Lindy Ward's Art Gallery

San Pedro Carchá, Mus. San Pedro Carchá
San Pedro Carchá, Museo de San Pedro
Carchá

San Pedro de Atacama, Mus. Arqueol. 'R. P.
Gustave le Paige, SJ'
San Pedro de Atacama, Museo de Arqueología
'R. P. Gustave le Paige, SJ'

San Roque, Mus. Ermita
San Roque, Museo de la Ermita de San Roque

San Salvador, Dir. Cult. Turismo
San Salvador, Dirección de Cultura y Turismo
de la Provincia de Jujuy

San Salvador, Mus. N. Guzmán
San Salvador, Museo Nacional David J.
Guzmán

San Sebastián, Ayuntamiento

San Sebastián, Mus. Hist. Mil.
San Sebastián, Museo Histórico Militar

San Sebastián, Mus. Mun. S Telmo
San Sebastián, Museo Municipal de San Telmo

San Sebastián, Mus. Pal. Mar
San Sebastián, Museo del Palacio del Mar
[houses Aquarium; Sociedad de Oceanografía
de Guipuzcoa]

San Severino Marche, Mus. Civ. 'Giuseppe
Moretti'
San Severino Marche, Museo Civico 'Giuseppe
Moretti'

San Severino Marche, Pal. Com.
San Severino Marche, Palazzo Comunale

San Severino Marche, Pin. Com. 'P. Tacchi
Venturi'
San Severino Marche, Pinacoteca Comunale
'P. Tacchi Venturi'

San Simeon, CA, Hearst Found.
San Simeon, CA, Hearst Foundation

San Simeon, CA, Hearst State Hist. Mnmt
San Simeon, CA, Hearst San Simeon State
Historical Monument

Sanchi, Archaeol. Mus.
Sanchi, Archaeological Museum

Sandhurst, Wellington Coll.
Sandhurst, Wellington College

Sanlúcar de Barrameda, Pal. Duque Medina–
Sidonia
Sanlúcar de Barrameda, Palacio Duque
Medina–Sidonia

Sansepolcro, Casa Piero
Sansepolcro, Casa di Piero della Francesca

Sansepolcro, Mus. Civ.
Sansepolcro, Museo Civico

Sansepolcro, Pin.
Sansepolcro, Pinacoteca

Santa Ana, CA, Bowers Mus.
Santa Ana, CA, Bowers Museum

Santa Ana, CA, Sch. Amer. Res.
Santa Ana, CA, School of American Research

Santa Barbara, CA, Mus. A.
Santa Barbara, CA, Museum of Art

Santa Barbara, U. CA
Santa Barbara, CA, University of California

Santa Barbara, U. CA, A. Gals
Santa Barbara, CA, University of California,
Art Galleries [name changed to U. CA, A.
Mus. in 1981]

Santa Barbara, U. CA, A. Mus.
Santa Barbara, CA, University of California,
University Art Museum [formerly U. CA, A.
Gals]

Santa Clara U., CA, De Saisset Mus.
Santa Clara, CA, Santa Clara University, De
Saisset Museum

Santa Cruz, Bolivia, Gal. Casa Cult.
Santa Cruz, Bolivia, Galería de la Casa de la
Cultura

Santa Cruz, CA, City Mus.
Santa Cruz, CA, City Museum

Santa Cruz de Tenerife, Ateneo
Santa Cruz de Tenerife, Ateneo

Santa Cruz de Tenerife, Mus. B.A.
Santa Cruz de Tenerife, Museo de Bellas Artes

Santa Cruz de Tenerife, Mus. Mun.
Santa Cruz de Tenerife, Museo Municipal [de
Bellas Artes]

Santa Fe, Mus. NM
Santa Fe, NM, Museum of New Mexico

Santa Fe, NM, Inst. Amer. Ind. A.
Santa Fe, NM, Institute of American Indian
Art

Santa Fe, NM, Jack Woody Col.
Santa Fe, NM, Jack Woody Collection

Santa Fe, NM, Mus. Int. Flk A.
Santa Fe, NM, Museum of International Folk
Art

Santa Fe, NM, Peters Gal.
Santa Fe, NM, Gerald G. Peters Gallery

Santa Fe, NM, Sch. Amer. Res.
Santa Fe, NM, School of American Research

Santa Fe, NM, SW Cult. Resources Cent., Lab.
Anthropol.
Santa Fe, NM, Southwestern Cultural
Resources Center, Laboratory of
Anthropology

Santa Fe, NM, Wheelwright Mus. Amer. Ind.
Santa Fe, NM, Wheelwright Museum of the
American Indian

Santa Fé, Argentina, Mus. Prov. B.A.
Santa Fé, Argentina, Museo Provincial de
Bellas Artes 'Rosa Galisteo de Rodriguez'

Santa María, Mus. Pedro Alejandrino
Santa María, Museo de San Pedro Alejandrino
[Colombia]

Santa María, Paraguay, Mus. Mis.
Santa María, Paraguay, Museo de Misión

Santa Monica, CA, Fred Hoffman Gal.
Santa Monica, CA, Fred Hoffman Gallery

Santa Monica, CA, Getty Cent.
Santa Monica, CA, Getty Center for the
History of Art and the Humanities

Santa Monica, CA, James Corcoran Gal.
Santa Monica, CA, James Corcoran Gallery

Santa Monica, CA, Pence Gal.
Santa Monica, CA, Pence Gallery

Santa Monica, CA, Shoshana Wayne Gal.
Santa Monica, CA, Shoshana Wayne Gallery

Santander, Ateneo

Santander, Bib. Menéndez Pelayo
Santander, Biblioteca de Menéndez Pelayo
[Biblioteca Municipal]

Santander, Casa Cult.
Santander, Casa de la Cultura

Santander, Mus. Mun. B.A.
Santander, Museo Municipal de Bellas Artes

Santander, Pal. Magdalena
Santander, Palacio de la Magdalena [former
Royal Pal.; now summer sch.]

Santarcangelo di Romagna, Municipio

Santarém, Bib. Braamcamp Freire
Santarém, Biblioteca Anselmo Braamcamp
Freire

Santarém, Bib. Mun.
Santarém, Biblioteca Municipal de Santarém

Santarém, Hosp. Jesus Cristo
Santarém, Hospital de Jesus Cristo

Santiago, Congr. N.
Santiago, Congreso Nacional

Santiago, Escuela B.A.
Santiago, Escuela de Bellas Artes

Santiago, Escuela Jard. Parque Cousiño
Santiago, Escuela Jardín del Parque Cousiño

Santiago, Gal. A. Actual
   Santiago, Galería Arte Actual

Santiago, Gal. Carmen Waugh
   Santiago, Galería Carmen Waugh

Santiago, Gal. Época
   Santiago, Galería Época

Santiago, Gal. Imagen
   Santiago, Galería Imagen

Santiago, Gal. Praxis
   Santiago, Galería Praxis

Santiago, Inst. Chil.-Fr. Cult.
   Santiago, Instituto Chileno-Francés de Cultura

Santiago, Inst. Cult. Las Condes
   Santiago, Instituto Cultural de Las Condes

Santiago, Mus. A. Aplic.
   Santiago, Museo de Artes Aplicadas

Santiago, Mus. Abierto
   Santiago, Museo Abierto

Santiago, Mus. A. Colon. S Francisco
   Santiago, Museo de Arte Colonial de San
   Francisco

Santiago, Mus. A. Contemp.
   Santiago, Museo de Arte Contemporáneo

Santiago, Mus. Altamirano
   Santiago, Museo del Alba Arturo Pacheco
   Altamirano

Santiago, Mus. A. Pop. Amer.
   Santiago, Museo de Arte Popular Americano

Santiago, Mus. Chil. A. Precolombino
   Santiago, Museo Chileno de Arte
   Precolombino

Santiago, Mus. Escuela Mil.
   Santiago, Museo de la Escuela Militar

Santiago, Mus. Hist. N.
   Santiago, Museo Histórico Nacional
   [Dirección de Bibliotecas, Archivos y Museos]

Santiago, Mus. N. B.A.
   Santiago, Museo Nacional de Bellas Artes
   [formerly Mus. Pint.]

Santiago, Mus. Pint.
   Santiago, Museo de Pinturas [now Mus. N.
   B.A.]

Santiago, Pal. Alhambra
   Santiago, Palacio de la Alhambra [houses
   Museo de la Alhambra]

Santiago, Paraguay, Mus. Mis.
   Santiago, Paraguay, Museo de Misión

Santiago, Parque Escult.
   Santiago, Parque de Esculturas

Santiago, Pontificia U. Católica
   Santiago, Pontificia Universidad Católica de
   Chile

Santiago, Sala Capilla
   Santiago, Sala la Capilla [Municipalidad de
   Santiago]

Santiago de Compostela, Archvs Catedral
   Santiago de Compostela, Archivos de la
   Catedral

Santiago de Compostela, Mus. Dioc.
   Santiago de Compostela, Museo Diocesano [la
   Catedral]

Santiago de Cuba, Mus. Ambiente Hist. Cub.
   Santiago de Cuba, Museo de Ambiente
   Histórico Cubano

Santiago de Cuba, U. Oriente
   Santiago de Cuba, Universidad de Oriente

Santiago Tuxtla, Mus. Reg.
   Santiago Tuxtla, Museo Regional

Santiniketan, Nandan Mus.
   Santiniketan, Nandan Museum

Santiniketan, Rabindra-Bhavana [Tagore Archives
and Museum]

Santo Domingo, Biennal

Santo Domingo, Casa Fuerte Ponce de Léon
   Santo Domingo, Casa Fuerte de Juan Ponce de
   Léon

Santo Domingo, Fund. García Arevalo
   Santo Domingo, Fundación García Arevalo

Santo Domingo, Gal.
   Santo Domingo, La Galería

Santo Domingo, Gal. A. Mod.
   Santo Domingo, Galería de Arte Moderno
   [now Mus. A. Mod.]

Santo Domingo, Mus. Alcázar
   Santo Domingo, Museo Alcázar de Diego
   Colón

Santo Domingo, Mus. A. Mod.
   Santo Domingo, Museo de Arte Moderno

Santo Domingo, Mus. Fam. Dominicana
   Santo Domingo, Museo de la Familia
   Dominicana

Santo Domingo, Mus. Hombre Dominicano
   Santo Domingo, Museo del Hombre
   Dominicano [formerly Museo Nacional]

Santo Domingo, Oficina Patrm. Cult.
   Santo Domingo, Oficina de Patrimonio
   Cultural [admins Casa Fuerte Ponce de Léon;
   Mus. Alcázar; Mus. Fam. Dominicana]

Santo Domingo de Silos, Monastery Mus.
   Santo Domingo de Silos, Monastery Museum

São Paulo, Acervo A.-Cult. Pal.
   São Paulo, Acervo Artístico-Cultural dos
   Palácios do Governo do Estado de São Paulo

São Paulo, Bienal

São Paulo, Cent. A. Novo Mundo
   São Paulo, Centro de Artes Novo Mundo

São Paulo, Fund. Americano
   São Paulo, Fundação Maria Louisa e Oscar
   Americano

São Paulo, Fund. Bienal
   São Paulo, Fundação Bienal de São Paulo

São Paulo, Itá Gal.
   São Paulo, Itá Galeria

São Paulo, Mus. A. Assis Châteaubriand
   São Paulo, Museu de Arte de São Paulo Assis
   Châteaubriand

São Paulo, Mus. A. Brasileira
   São Paulo, Museu de Arte Brasileira

São Paulo, Mus. A. Mod.
   São Paulo, Museu de Arte Moderna do São
   Paulo

São Paulo, Mus. A. Sacra
   São Paulo, Museu de Arte Sacra

São Paulo, Mus. A. Téc. Pop. & Flclore
   São Paulo, Museu de Arte Técnica Popular e
   Folclore

São Paulo, Mus. Flclor. Div. Discoteca
   São Paulo, Museu Folclorico da Divisão de
   Discoteca [e Biblioteca de Musica]

São Paulo, Mus. Imagem & Som
   São Paulo, Museu da Imagem e do Som

São Paulo, Mus. Segall
   São Paulo, Museu Lasar Segall

São Paulo, Pal. Bandeirantes
   São Paulo, Palácio Bandeirantes

São Paulo, Pin. Estado
   São Paulo, Pinacoteca do Estado de São Paulo

São Paulo, Rex Gal.
   São Paulo, Rex Gallery

São Paulo, U. São Paulo, Inst. Estud. Bras.
   São Paulo, Universidade de São Paulo,
   Instituto de Estudos Brasileiros

São Paulo, U. São Paulo, Mus. A. Contemp.
   São Paulo, Universidade de São Paulo, Museu
   de Arte Contemporânea

São Paulo, U. São Paulo, Mus. Arqueol. & Etnol.
   São Paulo, Museu de Arqueologia e Etnologia
   da Universidade de São Paulo

São Paulo, U. São Paulo, Mus. Paulista
   São Paulo, Museu Paulista da Universidade de
   São Paulo

São Tomé, Cent. Cult. Port.
   São Tomé, Centro Cultural Português

São Tomé, Mus. N.
   São Tomé, Museu Nacional

São Tomé, Sala de Leitura Francisco Tenreiro

Sapporo, Hist. Mus. Hokkaidō
   Sapporo, Historical Museum of Hokkaidō
   (Hokkaidō Kaitaku Kinenkan)

Sapporo, Hokkaidō Mus. Mod. A.
   Sapporo, Hokkaidō Museum of Modern Art
   (Hokkaido-ritsu Kindu Bijutsukan)

Sapporo, Outdoor Sculp. Mus.
   Sapporo, Outdoor Sculpture Museum

Saragossa, Casa Sobradiel
   Saragossa, Casa de Sobradiel

Saragossa, Inst. Mus. Camón Aznar
   Saragossa, Instituto y Museo Camón Aznar

Saragossa, Lonja [Merchants' Exchange]

Saragossa, Mus. Catedral
   Saragossa, Museo de la Catedral de Seo

Saragossa, Mus. Prov. B.A.
   Saragossa, Museo Provincial de Bellas Artes

Saragossa, Mus. Zaragoza
   Saragossa, Museo de Zaragoza

Saragossa, Pal. Arzobisp.
   Saragossa, Palacio Arzobispal

Saragossa, Semin. Nue.
   Saragossa, Seminario Nuevo

Sarajevo, A.G.
   Sarajevo, Art Gallery (Umjetnička Galerija
   Bosne i Hercegovine)

Sarajevo, N. Mus.
   Sarajevo, National Museum (Narodni Muzej)

Sarajevo, Treas. & Mus. Old Serbo-Orthodox
Church
   Sarajevo, Treasury and Museum of the Old
   Serbo-Orthodox Church (Riznica-Muzej Stare
   Pravoslavne Crkve)

Sarajevo, U. Sarajevo, Inst. Orient. Res.
   Sarajevo, University of Sarajevo, Institute of
   Oriental Research

Saransk, Sychkov Mordov. Pict. Gal.
   Saransk, Sychkov Mordovian Picture Gallery
   (Mordovskaya Kartinnaya Galereya Imeni F.V.
   Sychkova)

Sarasota, FL, Ringling Mus. A.
   Sarasota, FL, John and Mable Ringling
   Museum of Art

Sardarapat, Mus. Ethnog. Armenia
   Sardarapat, Museum of the Ethnography of
   Armenia

Sarnath, Archaeol. Mus.
   Sarnath, Archaeological Museum

Sarnen, Heimatmus.
   Sarnen, Heimatmuseum

Sarnen, Stift. Meinrad Burch-Korrodi
   Sarnen, Stiftung Meinrad Burch-Korrodi

Sárospatak, Mus. Reformed Ch.
  Sárospatak, Museum of the Reformed Church

Sartène, Mus. Dept. Préhist. Corse
  Sartène, Musée Départemental de Préhistoire
  Corse

Sárvár, Nádasdy Mus.
  Sárvár, Nádasdy Museum

Sarzana, Mus.
  Sarzana, Museo

Saskatoon, Mendel A.G.
  Saskatoon, Mendel Art Gallery

Saskatoon, U. Sask.
  Saskatoon, University of Saskatchewan

Sassari, Mus. N. Sanna
  Sassari, Museo Nazionale Giovanni Antonio
  Sanna [Museo Archeologico e Etnografico G.
  A. Sanna]

Sassari, Padiglione Artigianato Sardo
  Sassari, Padiglione dell'Artigianato Sardo

Sassocorvaro, Pal. Com.
  Sassocorvaro, Palazzo Comunale

Sassoferrato, Gal. A. Mod.
  Sassoferrato, Galleria d'Arte Moderna

Sassoferrato, Mus. Civ.
  Sassoferrato, Museo Civico

Sasso Marconi, Casa A.
  Sasso Marconi, Casa dell'Arte

Satna, Tulsi Sangrahalaya, Ramvan

Saudi Arabia, Al-Ula Mus.
  Saudi Arabia, Al-Ula Museum

Saumur, Mus. A. Déc.
  Saumur, Musée d'Arts Décoratifs [in Château
  de Saumur]

Savannah, GA, Telfair Acad. A. & Sci.
  Savannah, GA, Telfair Academy of Arts and
  Sciences

Savigliano, Santuario Apparizione
  Savigliano, Santuario dell'Apparizione

Savona, Mus. Cattedrale
  Savona, Museo della Cattedrale Basilica Nostra
  Signora Assunta

Savona, Pin. Civ.
  Savona, Pinacoteca Civica

Scarborough, Rotunda Mus. Archaeol. & Local
Hist.
  Scarborough, Rotunda Museum of
  Archaeology and Local History

Scarperia, Prepositurale

Scay-sur-Saône, Château

Sceaux, Château, Mus. Ile de France
  Sceaux, Château de Sceaux, Musée de l'Ile de
  France

Schaffhausen, Hallen Neue Kst
  Schaffhausen, Hallen für Neue Kunst

Schaffhausen, Minbib.
  Schaffhausen, Ministerialbibliothek

Schaffhausen, Mus. Allerheiligen
  Schaffhausen, Museum zu Allerheiligen [in
  former Benedictine Monastery]

Schaffhausen, Stadtsbib.
  Schaffhausen, Stadtsbibliothek

Schallaburg, Schloss
  Schallaburg, Schloss Schallaburg

Schenectady, NY, Un. Coll.
  Schenectady, NY, Union College

Schiedam, Stedel. Mus.
  Schiedam, Stedelijk Museum Schiedam

Schleissheim, Alter Schloss

Schleissheim, Neuer Schloss [nr Munich; houses
Staatsgalerie im Neuen Schloss Schleissheim]

Schleissheim, Schloss Lustheim

Schleswig, Schleswig-Holstein. Landesmus.
  Schleswig, Schleswig-Holsteinisches
  Landesmuseum [in Schloss Gottorf]

Schöngraben, Pfarrkirche Mariae Geburt,
Lapidarium

Schoonhoven, Ned. Goud-, Zilver- &
Klokkenmus.
  Schoonhoven, Nederlands Goud-, Zilver- en
  Klokkenmuseum

Schwabach, Stadtmus.
  Schwabach, Stadtmuseum

Schwäbisch Gmünd, Städt. Mus.
  Schwäbisch Gmünd, Städtisches Museum

Schwäbisch Hall, Häll.-Fränk. Mus.
  Schwäbisch Hall, Hällisch-Fränkisches
  Museum [der Stadt Schwäbisch Hall und des
  Historischen Vereins für Württembergisch-
  Franken]

Schwedt an der Oder, Schloss
  Schwedt an der Oder, Schloss Schwedt [destr.
  1945]

Schweinfurt, Rathaus

Schweinfurt, Samml. Schäfer
  Schweinfurt, Sammlung Georg Schäfer

Schwerin, Archäol. Landesmus.
  Schwerin, Archäologisches Landesmuseum

Schwerin, Archäol. Landesmus. Mecklenburg-
Vorpommern
  Schwerin, Archäologisches Landesmuseum
  Mecklenburg-Vorpommern [in Schloss]

Schwerin, Staatl. Mus.
  Schwerin, Staatliches Museum

Scottsdale, AZ, Frank Lloyd Wright Found.
  Scottsdale, AZ, Frank Lloyd Wright
  Foundation

Scranton, PA, Everhart Mus.
  Scranton, PA, Everhart Museum

Seattle, Thomas Burke Mem. WA State Mus.
  Seattle, WA, Thomas Burke Memorial
  Washington State Museum

Seattle, WA, A. Mus.
  Seattle, WA, Seattle Art Museum

Seattle, WA, Cent. Contemp. A.
  Seattle, WA, Center for Contemporary Art

Seattle, U. WA
  Seattle, WA, University of Washington

Seattle, U. WA, Henry A.G.
  Seattle, WA, University of Washington, Henry
  Art Gallery

Sebastopol': see Sevastopol

Seebüll, Stift. Nolde
  Seebüll, Stiftung Ada und Emil Nolde

Segóbriga, Mus. Catedralicio
  Segóbriga, Museo Catedralicio

Segovia, Alcázar

Segovia, Casa Moneda
  Segovia, Casa de Moneda

Segovia, Mus. Arqueol.
  Segovia, Museo Arqueológico

Segovia, Mus. Zuloaga
  Segovia, Museo Zuloaga

Seitenstetten, Kstsamml. Stift
  Seitenstetten, Kunstsammlungen Stift
  Seitenstetten

Selçuk, Ephesos Archaeol. Mus.
  Selçuk, Ephesos Archaeological Museum

Sélestat, Bib. Human.
  Sélestat, Bibliothèque Humaniste

Selzach: see Solothurn

Semur-en-Auxois, Mus. Mun.
  Semur-en-Auxois, Musée Municipal

Sendai, City Mus.
  Sendai, City Museum

Sendai, Myagi Prefect. Mus. A.
  Sendai, Myagi Prefectural Museum of Art

Seneca Falls, NY, Hist. Soc. Mus.
  Seneca Falls, NY, Historical Society Museum

Senhoku, Osaka Prefect., Archaeol. Mus.
  Senhoku, Osaka Prefecture, Archaeological
  Museum

Senigallia, Pal. Vescovile
  Senigallia, Palazzo Vescovile

Senlis, Archvs Dépt. Oise
  Senlis, Archives Départementales de l'Oise

Senlis, Haubergier Mus.
  Senlis, Haubergier Museum [closed]

Senlis, Mus. A. & Archéol.
  Senlis, Musée d'Art et Archéologie [Musée des
  Beaux-Arts]

Sens, Archvs Dépt. Yonne
  Sens, Archives Départementales de l'Yonne

Sens, Mus. Mun.
  Sens, Musée Municipal

Sens, Pal. Synodal
  Sens, Palais Synodal

Sens, Trésor Cathédrale
  Sens, Trésor de la Cathédrale

Senta Mus.
  Senta, Senta Museum (Senćanski Muzej)

Seoul, Cent. Stud. Kor. A., Kansong A. Mus
  Seoul, Centre for the Study of Korean Arts,
  Kansong Art Museum

Seoul, Dankook U., Sŏk Chu-sŏn Mem. Mus. Kor.
Flk A.
  Seoul, Dankook University, Sŏk Chu-sŏn
  Memorial Museum of Korean Folk Art

Seoul, Ewha Women's U. Mus.
  Seoul, Ewha Women's University Museum

Seoul, Ho-am A. Mus.
  Seoul, Ho-am Art Museum [at Yongin-gun]

Seoul, Hongik U. Mus.
  Seoul, Hongik University Museum

Seoul, Horim A. Mus.
  Seoul, Horim Art Museum

Seoul, Hyundai A.G.
  Seoul, Hyundai Art Gallery

Seoul, Korea U. Mus.
  Seoul, Korea University Museum

Seoul, Kyŏngbok Pal.
  Seoul, Kyŏngbok Palace

Seoul, Mus. Kor. Embroidery
  Seoul, Museum of Korean Embroidery

Seoul, N. Flklore Mus.
  Seoul, National Folklore Museum

Seoul, N. MOMA
  Seoul, National Museum of Modern Art

Seoul, N. Mus.
  Seoul, National Museum of Korea

Seoul N. U. Mus.
  Seoul, Seoul National University Museum

Seoul, Olymp. Village, Sculp. Gdn
  Seoul, Olympic Village, Sculpture Garden

Seoul, Sŏngam Archives of Class. Lit.
  Seoul, Sŏngam Archives of Classical Literature

Seoul, Sŏnggun'gwan U. Mus.
Seoul, Sŏnggun'gwan University Museum

Seoul, Sungjŏn U. Mus.
Seoul, Sungjŏn University Museum

Seoul, Tongguk U. Mus.
Seoul, Tongguk University Museum

Seraing, Val-Saint-Lambert Cristallerie, Mus.
Seraing, Val-Saint-Lambert Cristallerie, Musée

Seravezza, Pal. Mediceo
Seravezza, Palazzo Mediceo

Sergiyev Posad, Mus. Hist. & A.
Sergiyev Posad, Museum of History and Art
(Muzey Istorii i Iskusstva)

Sergiyev Posad, Toy Mus.
Sergiyev Posad, Toy Museum [formerly in
Moscow] (Muzey Igrushek)

Sermaize-les-Bains, Hôtel de Ville

Sermoneta, Castello Caetani

Serpukhov, A. Mus.
Serpukhov, Art Museum (Serpukovskyy
Muzey Istorii i Iskusstva)

Sesto Fiorentino, Mus. Porcellane Doccia
Sesto Fiorentino, Museo delle Porcellane di
Doccia

Sète, Mus. Valéry
Sète, Musée Paul Valéry

Seto, Aichi Prefect. Cer. Mus.
Seto, Aichi Prefectural Ceramics Museum

Settignano, I Tatti: see Florence

Setúbal, Bib. Mun.
Setúbal, Biblioteca Municipal

Setúbal, Mus. Setúbal
Setúbal, Museu de Setúbal [in Convento de
Jesus]

Sevastopol, Pict. Gal.
Sevastopol, Picture Gallery

Seville, Alcázar

Seville, Alcázar, Archvs Reales
Seville, Alcázar, Archivos Reales

Seville, Archv Admin. Mun., Obras Púb.
Seville, Archivo Administrativo Municipal de
Sevilla, Obras Públicas

Seville, Archv Catedral
Seville, Archivo de la Catedral

Seville, Archv Esp. A. & Arqueol.
Seville, Archivo Español de Arte y
Arqueología

Seville, Archv Gen. Indias
Seville, Archivo General de las Indias

Seville, Archv Protocolos Notariales
Seville, Archivo Protocolos Notariales

Seville, Ayuntamiento

Seville, Bib. Capitular & Colombina
Seville, Biblioteca Capitular y Colombina

Seville, Casa Dueñas
Seville, Casa de las Dueñas

Seville, Casa Murillo
Seville, Casa de Murillo

Seville, Casa Pilatos
Seville, Casa de Pilatos

Seville, Casa Profesa Compañia Jesus
Seville, Casa Profesa de la Compañia de Jesus

Seville, Cent. A. M-11
Seville, Centro de Arte M-11

Seville, Col. Alba
Seville, Collezione Alba

Seville, Colegio S Basilio
Seville, Colegio de San Basilio

Seville, Colegio S Hermenegildo
Seville, Colegio de San Hermenegildo

Seville, El Salvador

Seville, Hermandad Sacramental S Bernardo
Seville, Hermandad Sacramental de S Bernardo

Seville, Hospicio Venerables Sacerdotes
Seville, Hospicio de los Venerables Sacerdotes
[Asilo de los Venerables Sacerdotes; houses
Museum of Holy Week]

Seville, Hosp. Caridad
Seville, Hospital de la Caridad

Seville, Mus. A. Contemp.
Seville, Museo de Arte Contemporáneo

Seville, Mus. A. Cost. Pop.
Seville, Museo de Artes y Costumbres
Populares

Seville, Mus. Arqueol. Prov.
Seville, Museo Arqueológico Provincial

Seville, Mus. B.A.
Seville, Museo de Bellas Artes

Seville, Pal. Arzobisp.
Seville, Palacio Arzobiscopal

Seville, Pal. S Telmo
Seville, Palacio de San Telmo

Seville, Real Acad. B.A.
Seville, Real Academia de Bellas Artes de Santa
Isabel de Hungria

Seville, U. Seville
Seville, Universidad de Sevilla [in Fábrica de
Tabacos]

Seville, U. Seville, Lab. A. Francisco Murillo
Herrera
Seville, Universidad de Sevilla, Laboratorio de
Arte Francisco Murillo Herrera

Sèvres, Cent. Int. Etud. Pédag.
Sèvres, Centre International d'Etudes
Pédagogiques

Sèvres, Mus. N. Cér.
Sèvres, Musée National de Céramique

Sewickly, PA, Int. Images Ltd.
Sewickly, PA, International Images Ltd

Sézanne, Hosp.
Sézanne, Hospital

Sezze, Pal. Com.
Sezze, Palazzo Comunale

Sfîntu Gheorghe, Distr. Mus.
Sfîntu Gheorghe, District Museum (Muzeul
Judeţean covasna)

Shahdol, Thakur's Col.
Shahdol, Thakur's Collection

Shanghai Lib.
Shanghai, Shanghai Library

Shanghai, Mun. Cttee Conserv. Cult. Relics
Shanghai, Shanghai Municipality Committee
for the Conservation of Cultural Relics

Shanghai Mus.
Shanghai, Shanghai Museum [Museum of Art
and History]

Shantiniketan, Visva-Bharati U.
Shantiniketan, Visva-Bharati University

Shaochen cun, Mus. Zhouyuan
Shaochen cun, Museum of the Zhouyuan [in
Fufeng County]

Sharjah, Mus. Archaeol.
Sharjah, Sharjah Museum of Archaeology

Sharon, MA, Kendall Whaling Mus.
Sharon, MA, Kendall Whaling Museum

Sheboygan, WI, John Michael Kohler A. Cent.
Sheboygan, WI, John Michael Kohler Arts
Center

Sheffield, City A. Gals
Sheffield, City Art Galleries [admins City Mus.;
Graves A.G.; Mappin A.G.]

Sheffield, City Mus.
Sheffield, City Museum

Sheffield, Graves A.G.
Sheffield, Graves Art Gallery

Sheffield, Mappin A.G.
Sheffield, Mappin Art Gallery

Sheffield, Ruskin Gal. Col. Guild of St George
Sheffield, Ruskin Gallery Collection of the
Guild of St George

Shelburne, VT, Mus.
Shelburne, VT, Shelburne Museum

Shenyang, Liaoning Prov. Mus.
Shenyang, Liaoning Provincial Museum

Shenyang Pal. Mus.
Shenyang, Shenyang Palace Museum

Shepparton, Victoria, A.G.
Shepparton, Victoria, Shepparton Art Gallery

Sherborne Mus.
Sherborne, Sherborne Museum

's Hertogenbosch, Herrenhausen, Mausoleum

's Hertogenbosch, Noordbrabants, Mus.
's Hertogenbosch, Noordbrabants Museum

's Hertogenbosch, Prov. Genoot. Kst. & Wet.
's Hertogenbosch, Provinciaal Genootschap
van Kunsten en Wetenschappen in Noord-
Brabant

's Hertogenbosch, Stadhuis

Shijiazhuang, Mus. Hebei Prov.
Shijiazhuang, Museum of Hebei Province

Shimonoga, Govt Mus.
Shimonoga, Government Museum

Shimonoseki, Mun. Mus. A.
Shimonoseki, Municipal Museum of Art

Shinagawa, Prefect. Gal. Mod. A.
Shinagawa, Prefectural Gallery of Modern Art
(Shinagawa Kenritsu Kindai Bijutsukan)

Shiraz, Pars Mus.
Shiraz, Pars Museum

Shivpuri, Distr. Mus.
Shivpuri, District Museum

Shiwan, Exh. Hall A. Products Factory
Shiwan, Exhibition Hall of Shiwan Artistic
Products Factory

Shizuoka, Mun. Serizawa Keisuke A. Mus.
Shizuoka, Municipal Serizawa Keisuke Art
Museum (Shiritsu Serizawa Keisuke
Bijutsukan)

Shizuoka, Prefect. Mus.
Shizuoka, Shizuoka Prefectural Museum

Shkodër, A.G.
Shkodër, Art Gallery (Galeria Arteve)

Shkodër Mus.
Shkodër, Shkodër Museum (Muzeu Shkodër)

Shreveport, LA, Norton A.G.
Shreveport, LA, R. W. Norton Art Gallery

Shrewsbury, Clive House Mus.
Shrewsbury, Clive House Museum

Shrewsbury, Salop Co. Lib.
Shrewsbury, Shropshire County Library

Shuri, Okinawa Prefect. Mus.
Shuri, Okinawa Prefectural Museum

Sian: see Xi'an

Šibenik, Town Mus.
Šibenik, Town Museum (Muzej Grada)

Sibiu, Brukenthal Mus.
  Sibiu, Brukenthal Museum (Muzeul Brukenthal)
Sibiu, Mus. Hist.
  Sibiu, Museum of History
Šid, Savo Šumanović Gal.
  Šid, Savo Šumanović Gallery
Siem Reap, Conserv. Mnmts Angkor
  Siem Reap, Conservation des Monuments d'Angkor
Siena, Accad. Musicale Chigiana
  Siena, Accademia Musicale Chigiana [in Pal. Chigi-Saracini]
Siena, Archv Stato
  Siena, Archivio di Stato
Siena, Bib. Com. Intronati
  Siena, Biblioteca Comunale degli Intronati
Siena, Bib. Piccolomini
  Siena, Biblioteca Piccolomini [Libreria Piccolomini; in Siena Cathedral]
Siena, Col. Chigi-Saracini
  Siena, Collezioni Chigi-Saracini [in Pal. Chigi-Saracini]
Siena, Conserv. Fem. Rifugio
  Siena, Conservatori Femminili del Rifugio
Siena, Ist. Sordomuti
  Siena, Istituto dei Sordomuti
Siena, Magazzini del Sale
Siena, Monte Paschi
  Siena, Monte dei Paschi [banking inst.; in Palazzo Salimbeni, Palazzo Spannocchi, Palazzo Tantucci]
Siena, Mus. Archeol.
  Siena, Museo Archeologico
Siena, Mus. Castelli
  Siena, Museo Aurelio Castelli [attached to Convento dell'Osservanza]
Siena, Mus. Opera Duomo
  Siena, Museo dell'Opera del Duomo [Musco dell'Opera della Metropolitana]
Siena, Mus. Semin. Montarioso
  Siena, Museo del Seminario Montarioso
Siena, Oratorio Madonna della Grotta
Siena, Osp. S Maria della Scala
  Siena, Ospedale di S Maria della Scala
Siena, Osservanza
Siena, Pal. Arcivescovile
  Siena, Palazzo Arcivescovile
Siena, Pal. Chigi-Saracini
  Siena, Palazzo Chigi-Saracini
Siena, Pal. Chigi-Zondadari
  Siena, Palazzo Chigi-Zondadari
Siena, Pal. Piccolomini, Archv Stato
  Siena, Palazzo Piccolomini, Archivio di Stato
Siena, Pal. Pub.
  Siena, Palazzo Pubblico
Siena, Pal. Reale
  Siena, Palazzo Reale
Siena, Pin. N.
  Siena, Pinacoteca Nazionale di Siena
Siena, Semin.
  Siena, Seminario
Siena, Sopr. B.A.
  Siena, Soprintendenza alle Belle Arti
Sierra, Mus. Pablo Zelaya
  Sierra, Museo Pablo Zelaya
Sighişoara, Mun. Mus.
  Sighişoara, Municipal Museum (Muzeul Municipal Sighişoara)

Sigmaringen, Fürst. Hohenzoll. Samml. & Hofbib.
  Sigmaringen, Fürstlich Hohenzollernsche Sammlungen und Hofbibliothek [in Schloss]
Sigüenza, Mus. Dioc.
  Sigüenza, Museo Diocesano de Arte Antigua
Sikyon, Archaeol. Mus.
  Sikyon, Archaeological Museum [in Roman bathhouse]
Silkeborg, Kstmus.
  Silkeborg, Kunstmuseum
Simancas, Archv Gen.
  Simancas, Archivo General de Simancas
Simferopol', A. Mus.
  Simferopol', Art Museum
Simla, Himachal State Mus.
  Simla, Himachal State Museum
Simla, Ind. Inst. Adv. Stud.
  Simla, Indian Institute of Advanced Study
Sindelfingen, Gal. Stadt
  Sindelfingen, Galerie der Stadt
Sindelfingen, Stadtmus.
  Sindelfingen, Stadtmuseum
Singapore, N. Mus.
  Singapore, National Museum of Singapore [formerly Raffles Museum]
Singapore, N.U.
  Singapore, National University of Singapore
Singen, Hegau-Mus.
  Singen, Hegau-Museum
Singleton, Weald & Downland Open Air Mus.
  Singleton, Weald and Downland Open Air Museum
Sintra, Pal. N.
  Sintra, Palácio Nacional [Pal. Real]
Sintra, Pal. Pena
  Sintra, Palácio da Pena [Castelo da Pena]
Sintra, Pal. Real
  Sintra, Palácio Real [Pal. N.]
Sint-Truiden, Prov. Mus. Relig. Kst
  Sint-Truiden, Provinciaal Museum voor Religieuse Kunst
Sint-Winotsbergen, Mus. B.A.
  Sint-Winotsbergen, Musée des Beaux-Arts
Sion Cathedral, Treasury
Sion, Mus. Cant. B.A.
  Sion, Musée Cantonal des Beaux-Arts
Sion, Mus. Cant. Hist. & Ethnog.
  Sion, Musée Cantonal d'Histoire et d'Ethnographie
Sion, Mus. Cant. Valère
  Sion, Musée Cantonal de Valère
Sirpur, Archaeol. Mus.
  Sirpur, Archaeological Museum
Sissa, Schloss Ebenrain
Siteia, Archaeol. Mus.
  Siteia, Archaeological Museum
Siteia, Flklore Mus.
  Siteia, Folklore Museum
Siteia Mus.
  Siteia, Siteia Museum
Sitges, Mus. Cau Ferrat
  Sitges, Museu del Cau Ferrat
Sitka, AK, Sheldon Jackson Mus.
  Sitka, AK, Sheldon Jackson Museum
Skagen, Skagens Mus.
  Skagen, Skagens Museum
Skara, Skaraborgs Länsmus.
  Skara, Skaraborgs Länsmuseum [formerly Västergötlandsmus.]

Skara, Västergötlandsmus.
  Skara, Västergötlandsmuseum [name changed to Skaraborgs Länsmus. in July 1977]
Skegness, Ch. Farm Mus.
  Skegness, Church Farm Museum
Skellefteå, Anna Nordlander Women's A. Mus.
  Skellefteå, Anna Nordlander Women's Art Museum
Skien, Billedgal.
  Skien, Billedgalleri
Skien, Flkmus. Telemark & Grenland
  Skien, Folkemuseum for Telemark og Grenland
Skive Mus.
  Skive, Skive Museum [Annine Michelsen Museum]
Skjeberg, Storedal Kultsent.
  Skjeberg, Storedal Kultursenter
Skokloster: see Bålsta
Skopje, A.G.
  Skopje, Art Gallery (Umetnička Galerija)
Skopje, Archaeol. Mus. Macedonia
  Skopje, Archaeological Museum of Macedonia (Arheološki Muzej na Makedonija)
Skopje, Hist. Mus.
  Skopje, Historical Museum [destr. 1963]
Skopje, Macedon. Acad. A. & Sci.
  Skopje, Macedonian Academy of Arts and Sciences (Makedonska Akademija na Naukite i Umetnostite)
Skopje, Mus. Contemp. A.
  Skopje, Museum of Contemporary Art (Muzejot no Sovremenata Umetnost)
Skyros, Archaeol. Mus.
  Skyros, Archaeological Museum
Skyros, Flklore Mus.
  Skyros, Folklore Museum
Slagelse, Heligåndshus
Sligo, Co. Mus.
  Sligo, County Museum
Slippery Rock U. PA, Gal. Eleven
  Slippery Rock, PA, Slippery Rock University of Pennsylvania, Gallery Eleven
Sliven, A.G.
  Sliven, Art Gallery
Słupsk, Mus. Cent. Pomerania
  Słupsk, Museum of Central Pomerania (Muzeum Pomorza Środkowego)
Smederevo, Mus. Smederevo
  Smederevo, Museum of Smederevo (Muzej u Smederevu)
Smolensk, Reg. Mus.
  Smolensk, Regional Museum (Smolenskiy Oblastnoy Krayevedcheskiy Muzey)
Smolensk, State Mus. Preserve
  Smolensk, State Museum Preserve [incl. mus. & Tenisheva Collection of Folk Art]
Smolensk, S.T. Konyonkov Mus. A.
  Smolensk, S.T. Konyonkov Museum of Art (Khudozhestvennyy Muzey S. T. Konyonkova)
Smolyan, A.G.
  Smolyan, Art Gallery (Hudozhestvena Galerija)
Smyrna: see İzmir
Sneinton, Green's Mill & Sci. Mus.
  Sneinton, Green's Mill and Science Museum
Södertälje, Ksthall
  Södertälje, Konsthall

Soest, Wilhelm-Morgner-Haus

Soestdijk, Kon. Pal.
Soestdijk, Koninklijk Paleis

Sofia, C.A.G.
Sofia, City Art Gallery (Sofiiska Gradska Hudozhestvena Galerija)

Sofia, Court House

Sofia, Cyril & Methodius N. Lib.
Sofia, Cyril and Methodius National Library

Sofia, Gal. Int. A.
Sofia, Gallery for International Art (Hudozhestvena Galerija pri Mezhdunarodnata) [in SS Cyril and Methodius Foundation]

Sofia, Higher Inst. Archit. Civ. Engin.
Sofia, Higher Institute of Architecture and Civil Engineering

Sofia, Ivan Lazarov House-Mus.
Sofia, Ivan Lazarov House-Museum (Dom-Muzej Ivan Lazarov)

Sofia, Ivan Vazov N. Theat.
Sofia, Ivan Vazov National Theatre (Naroden Teatâr Ivan Vazov)

Sofia, Mus. Hist.
Sofia, Museum of the History of Sofia (Muzej za Istorija na Sofia)

Sofia, Mus. Serb. Serbo-Orthdx Ch.
Sofia, Museum of the Serbian Serbo-Orthodox Church (Muzej Srpske Pravoslavne Crkve)

Sofia, N. Acad. A.
Sofia, National Academy of Arts (Natsionalna Hudozhestvena Accademia)

Sofia, N.A.G.
Sofia, National Art Gallery (Natsionalna Hudožestvena Galerija) [in former Royal Palace]

Sofia, N.A.G. Alexandar Nevski Cathedral
Sofia, National Art Gallery at Alexandar Nevski Cathedral (Nacionalna Hudožestevena Galerija)

Sofia, N. Archaeol. Mus.
Sofia, National Archaeological Museum of the Bulgarian Academy of Sciences (Nacionalen Archeologičeski Muzej na Balgarskara Akademija na Nankite)

Sofia, N. Bank Bulgaria
Sofia, National Bank of Bulgaria

Sofia, N. Gal. Dec. & Applied A.
Sofia, National Gallery of Decorative and Applied Arts (Nacionalen Galerija na Dekorativno-Prilozhi Izkustva]

Sofia, N. Hist. Mus.
Sofia, National History Museum (Natsionalen Istoritcheski Muzej)

Sofia, Nicolaj Pavlovic Higher Inst. F.A.
Sofia, Nicolaj Pavlovic Higher Institute of Fine Art

Sofia, N. Mus. Eccles. Hist. & Archaeol.
Sofia, National Museum of Ecclesiastical History and Archaeology (Nacionalen Čarkoven Istoriko-Archeologičeski Muzej)

Sofia, N. Mus. Mil. Hist.
Sofia, National Museum of Military History (Nacionalen Voenno-Istoričeski Muzej)

Sofia, N. Opera House
Sofia, National Opera House

Sofia, Soc. Applied Artists
Sofia, Society of Applied Artists (Zadruga na Maistoritr na Narodnite Hudozhestveni Zanaiati)

Sofia, St Petka ['of the Saddlers']

Sögel, Schloss Clemenswerth, Emslandmus.
Sögel, Schloss Clemenswerth, Emslandmuseum

Soissons, Mus. Mun.
Soissons, Musée Municipal [Ancienne Abbaye St Léger]

Solingen, Bergisches Mus.
Solingen, Bergisches Museum, Burg an der Wupper

Solingen, Dt. Klingenmus.
Solingen, Deutsches Klingenmuseum

Solingen, K.J. Müllenmeister

Solna, Karlberg Slott

Solothurn, Kstmus.
Solothurn, Kunstmuseum Solothurn

Solothurn, Mus. Altes Zeughaus
Solothurn, Museum Altes Zeughaus

Solothurn, Zentbib.
Solothurn, Zentralbibliothek

Solsona, Mus. Dioc. & Comarcal
Solsona, Museu Diocesá i Comarcal [Palacio Episcopal]

Sol'vychegodsk, Hist. A. Mus.
Sol'vychegodsk, History and Art Museum (Muzey Istorii i Iskusstva)

Sombor, Milan Konjović Gal.
Sombor, Milan Konjović Gallery (Galerija Milan Konjović)

Sombor, Mun. Mus.
Sombor, Municipal Museum (Gradski Muzej)

Sonargaon, Flk A. & Craft Mus.
Sonargaon, Sonargaon Folk Art and Craft Museum

Sondani, Archaeol. Mus.
Sondani, Archaeological Museum

Songkhla, Matchimawas N. Mus.
Songkhla, Matchimawas National Museum

Sonneberg, Dt. Spielzeugmus.
Sonneberg, Deutsches Spielzeugmuseum

Sopron, Fabricius House (Fabricius Hàz)

Sopron, Ferenc Liszt Mus.
Sopron, Ferenc Liszt Museum (Liszt Ferenc Múzeum)

Sorø, Kstmus.
Sorø, Kunstmuseum i Sorø

Sorrento, Mus. Correale Terranova
Sorrento, Museo Correale di Terranova

Soueida Mus.
Soueida, Soueida Museum

Sousse, Mus. Archéol.
Sousse, Musée Archéologique

Southampton, Bargate Guildhall Mus.
Southampton, Bargate Guildhall Museum

Southampton, C.A.G.
Southampton, City Art Gallery

Southampton, C.A.G. & Museums
Southampton, City Art Gallery and Museums [admins Bargate Guildhall Mus.; C.A.G; God's House Tower Mus.; Tudor House Mus.; Wool House Mar. Mus.]

Southampton, God's House Tower Mus.
Southampton, God's House Tower Museum

Southampton, Tudor House Mus.
Southampton, Tudor House Museum

Southampton, U. Southampton, Hansard Gal.
Southampton, University of Southampton, John Hansard Gallery

Southampton, Wool House Mar. Mus.
Southampton, Wool House Maritime Museum

Southampton, NY, Parrish A. Mus.
Southampton, NY, Parrish Art Museum

South Hadley, MA, Mount Holyoke Coll. A. Mus.
South Hadley, MA, Mount Holyoke College Art Museum

Southport, Atkinson A.G.
Southport, Atkinson Art Gallery

South Shields, Arbeia Roman Fort

South Shields, Mus. & A.G.
South Shields, Museum and Art Gallery

Sparrenburg, Burggtn
Sparrenburg, Burggarten [Burg Sparrenburg]

Sparta, Archaeol. Mus.
Sparta, Archaeological Museum

Spello, Pin. Com.
Spello, Pinacoteca Comunale

Sperlonga, Mus. Archeol. N.
Sperlonga, Museo Archeologico Nazionale

Speyer, Bischöf. Ordinariat
Speyer, Bischöfliches Ordinariat

Speyer, Diözesanmus.
Speyer, Diözesanmuseum

Speyer, Hist. Mus. Pfalz
Speyer, Historisches Museum der Pfalz

Split, Archaeol. Mus.
Split, Archaeological Museum (Arheološki Muzej)

Split, Gal. F.A.
Split, Gallery of Fine Arts

Split, Meštrović Gal.
Split, Meštrović Gallery (Galerija Meštrović)

Spokane, WA, Cheney Cowles Mus.
Spokane, WA, Cheney Cowles Museum

Spoleto, Mus. Civ.
Spoleto, Museo Civico

Spoleto, Mus. Dioc.
Spoleto, Museo Diocesano

Spoleto, Pal. Rosario Spada
Spoleto, Palazzo Rosario Spada

Spoleto, Pin. Com.
Spoleto, Pinacoteca Comunale

Spoleto, Rocca Albornoziana

Springfield, IL, State Mus.
Springfield, IL, Illinois State Museum

Springfield, MA, Mus. F.A.
Springfield, MA, Museum of Fine Arts

Springfield, MA, Smith A. Mus.
Springfield, MA, George Walter Vincent Smith Art Museum

Spring Green, WI, Frank Lloyd Wright Found.
Spring Green, WI, Frank Lloyd Wright Foundation

Springville, UT, Mus. A.
Springville, UT, Springville Museum of Art

Springwood, NSW, Norman Lindsay Gal. & Mus.
Springwood, NSW, Norman Lindsay Gallery and Museum

Sremska Mitrovica, Sremska Mus.
Sremska Mitrovica, Sremska Museum (Muzej Sremska)

Srinagar, Sri Pratap Singh Mus.
Srinagar, Sri Pratap Singh Museum

Stafford, Salt Lib.
Stafford, William Salt Library

Stainz, Schloss
Stainz, Schloss Stainz

Stamford, Lincs, Mus.
Stamford, Lincs, Stamford Museum

Stamford, Lincs, Town Hall

Stanford, CA, U. A.G. & Mus.
Stanford, CA, Stanford University Art Gallery and Museum

Stanford, CA, U. Lib.
Stanford, CA, Stanford University Library

Stanford U., CA, Green Lib.
Stanford, CA, Stanford University, Green Library

Stanmore, Cargill

Stans, Nidwald. Mus.
Stans, Nidwalder Museum [Historisches Museum]

Staphorst, Boerderij
Staphorst, Staphorster Boerderij

Staphorst, Gemeentelijk Musboerderij

Staphorst, Musboerderij Kok

Stara Zagora, Dist. Mus. Hist.
Stara Zagora, District Museum of History (Okrăzhen Istoricheski Muzej)

Starnberg, Heimatmus.
Starnberg, Heimatmuseum

Stavanger, Arkeol. Mus.
Stavanger, Arkeologisk Museum i Stavanger (Archaeology Museum)

Stavanger, Bridablikk Found.
Stavanger, Bridablikk Foundation

Stavanger, Faste Gal.
Stavanger, Stavanger Faste Galleri (Stavanger Art Gallery) [name changed to Rogaland Kstmus. in 1992]

Stavanger, Rogaland Kstmus.
Stavanger, Rogaland Kunstmuseum [formerly Faste Gal.]

Stavelot, Mus. Anc. Abbaye
Stavelot, Musée de l'Ancienne Abbaye

Stavelot, Trésor Eglise Primaire St-Sébastien
Stavelot, Trésor de l'Eglise Primaire de Saint-Sébastien

Stavros, Archaeol. Mus.
Stavros, Archaeological Museum

Stein an der Donau, Minoritenkirche [St Ulrich]

Stellenbosch Mus.
Stellenbosch, Stellenbosch Museum [also admins Old Agric. Hall; Van der Bijl House; Village Mus.; VOC Kruithuis]

Stellenbosch, Old Agric. Hall
Stellenbosch, Old Agricultural Hall

Stellenbosch, Rembrandt van Rijn A.G.
Stellenbosch, Rembrandt van Rijn Art Gallery

Stellenbosch, U. Stellenbosch
Stellenbosch, University of Stellenbosch

Stellenbosch, Van der Bijl House

Stellenbosch, Village Mus.
Stellenbosch, Village Museum

Stellenbosch, VOC Kruithuis [Dutch East India Company Armoury]

Stendal, Winckelmann-Mus.
Stendal, Winckelmann-Museum

Sterzing, Mulchester Mus.
Sterzing, Mulchester Museum

Stirling, Smith A.G. & Mus.
Stirling, Smith Art Gallery and Museum

Stirling, U. Lib.
Stirling, University Library [houses Leighton Library Dunblane Collection]

Stirling, U. Stirling, J. D. Fergusson Col.
Stirling, University of Stirling, J.D. Fergusson Collection

Stobi Mus.
Stobi, Stobi Museum

Stockbridge, MA, Chesterwood, Studio & Mus. Daniel Chester French
Stockbridge, MA, Chesterwood, Studio and Museum of Daniel Chester French

Stockholm, Antikva.-Top. Arkv
Stockholm, Antikvarisk-Topografiska Arkivet

Stockholm, Arkitmus.
Stockholm, Arkitekturmuseum

Stockholm, Boibrino Gal.
Stockholm, Boibrino Gallery

Stockholm, Carl Millesgården

Stockholm, Dansmus.
Stockholm, Dansmuseum

Stockholm, Drottningholm Slott

Stockholm, Drottningholm Slottsteat. & Teatmus.
Stockholm, Drottningholm Slottsteater och Teatermuseum

Stockholm, Ekolsund Mus.
Stockholm, Ekolsund Museum

Stockholm, Etnog. Mus.
Stockholm, Etnografiska Museum

Stockholm, Folkets Hus [incl. Museum of Dance]

Stockholm, Fot. Mus.
Stockholm, Fotografiska Museum

Stockholm, Gal. Aleby
Stockholm, Galleri Aleby

Stockholm, Gal. Bel-Art
Stockholm, Galleri Bel-Art

Stockholm, Gal. Burén
Stockholm, Galleri Burén

Stockholm, Gal. Noa-Noa
Stockholm, Galleri Noa-Noa

Stockholm, Gummesons Kstgal.
Stockholm, Gummesons Konstgalleri

Stockholm, Hallwylska Mus.
Stockholm, Hallwylska Museum

Stockholm, Karolinska Inst.
Stockholm, Karolinska Institut

Stockholm, Ksthögskolan
Stockholm, Konsthögskolan

Stockholm, Kstnärhuset
Stockholm, Konstnärhuset

Stockholm, Kulthuset
Stockholm, Kulturhuset

Stockholm, Kun. Akad.
Stockholm, Kungliga Vitterhets Historie och Antikvitets Akademien

Stockholm, Kun. Akad. Bib.
Stockholm, Kungliga Vitterhets Historie och Antikvitets Akademien Bibliotek

Stockholm, Kun. Akad. Fria Kst.
Stockholm, Kungliga Akademi för de Fria Konsterna

Stockholm, Kun. Akad. Fria Kst., Arkv
Stockholm, Kungliga Akademi för de Fria Konsterna, Arkiv

Stockholm, Kun. Armémus.
Stockholm, Kungliga Armémuseum [in former Artillery depot]

Stockholm, Kun. Bib.
Stockholm, Kungliga Bibliotek

Stockholm, Kun. Husgerådskam.
Stockholm, Kungliga Husgerådskammar med Skattkammar och Bernadotte-Bibliotek [Royal collections]

Stockholm, Kun. Myntkab.
Stockholm, Kungliga Myntkabinet, Statens Museum för Mynt Medalj och Penninghistoria

Stockholm, Kun. Operan
Stockholm, Kungliga Operan

Stockholm, Kun. Slott
Stockholm, Kungliga Slott

Stockholm, Kun. Tek. Högskolan
Stockholm, Kungliga Tekniska Högskolan

Stockholm, Kun. Vetakad.
Stockholm, Kungliga Vetenskapsakademi

Stockholm, Liljevalchs Ksthall
Stockholm, Liljevalchs Konsthall

Stockholm, Livrustkam.
Stockholm, Livrustkammaren [Royal Armoury in Kun. Slott]

Stockholm, Martin Olsson AB

Stockholm, Medelhavsmus.
Stockholm, Medelhavsmuseum

Stockholm, Mod. Mus.
Stockholm, Moderna Museum

Stockholm, Musikmus.
Stockholm, Musikmuseum

Stockholm, N. Bank of Sweden
Stockholm, National Bank of Sweden

Stockholm, N. Mar. Mus.
Stockholm, National Maritime Museum

Stockholm, Nmus. Arkv
Stockholm, Nationalmuseum Arkiv

Stockholm, Nmus.
Stockholm, Nationalmuseum

Stockholm, Nordiska Mus.
Stockholm, Nordiska Museum

Stockholm, Östasiat. Mus.
Stockholm, Östasiatiska Museum

Stockholm, Prins Eugens Waldemarsudde
Stockholm, Prins Eugens Waldemarsudde

Stockholm, Riddarhus

Stockholm, Riksantvarieämbetet & Stat. Hist. Museer
Stockholm, Riksantikvarieämbetet och Statens Historika Museer [admins Antikva.-Top. Arkv; Kun. Akad. Bib.; Kun. Myntkab.; Medelhavsmus.; Nmus.; Stat. Hist. Mus.]

Stockholm, Riksarkv
Stockholm, Riksarkiv

Stockholm, Rosendals Slott

Stockholms Högsk.
Stockholm, Stockholms Högskola [name changed to Stockholm U. in 1960]

Stockholm, Sjöhist. Mus.
Stockholm, Sjöhistoriska Museum

Stockholm, Skansen

Stockholm, Skokloster Slott

Stockholm, Stadshus

Stockholm, Stat. Hist. Mus.
Stockholm, Statens Historiska Museum

Stockholm, Stat. Kstmuseer
Stockholm, Statens Kstmuseer [admins Nmus.; Mod. Mus.; Östasiat. Mus.; Tek. Mus.]

Stockholm, Strindbergsmus.
Stockholm, Strindbergsmuseum

Stockholm, Svensk-Frankas Kstauktioner
Stockholm, Svensk-Frankas Konstauktioner AB

Stockholm, Svensk. Inst.
Stockholm, Svenska Institut

Stockholm, Tek. Mus.
Stockholm, Tekniska Museum

Stockholm, Thielska Gal.
Stockholm, Thielska Galleri [in Djurgården]

Stockholm U., Kstsaml.
Stockholm, Stockholms Universitetum, Konstsamling

Stockholm, Ulriksdalslott

Stockholm, Wasavarvet [Wasa Dockyard]

Stockport, Mun. Mus.
Stockport, Municipal Museum

Stockport, War Mem. Bldg A.G.
Stockport, War Memorial Building Art Gallery

Stockton-on-Tees, Preston Hall Mus.
Stockton-on-Tees, Preston Hall Museum

Stoke-on-Trent, City Mus. & A.G.
Stoke-on-Trent, City Museum and Art Gallery

Stony Brook, NY, Mus.
Stony Brook, NY, Museum at Stony Brook

Stonyhurst, Lancs, Stonyhurst Coll.
Stonyhurst, Lancs, Stonyhurst College

Storrs, U. CT, Benton Mus. A.
Storrs, CT, University of Connecticut, William Benton Museum of Art

Stourbridge Coll., A & Des. Dept
Stourbridge, Stourbridge College, Art and Design Department

Stra, Villa N. Già Pisani
Stra, Villa Nazionale Già Pisani

Strasbourg, Anc. Douane
Strasbourg, Ancienne Douane

Strasbourg, Archvs Mun.
Strasbourg, Archives Municipales

Strasbourg, Cab. Est. & Dessins
Strasbourg, Cabinet des Estampes et des Dessins

Strasbourg, Coll. Épisc. Saint-Etienne
Strasbourg, Collège Episcopal Saint-Etienne

Strasbourg, Mus. A. Déc.
Strasbourg, Musée des Arts Décoratifs

Strasbourg, Mus. Alsac.
Strasbourg, Musée Alsacien

Strasbourg, Mus. A. Mod.
Strasbourg, Musée d'Art Moderne

Strasbourg, Mus. Archéol.
Strasbourg, Musée Archéologique

Strasbourg, Mus. B.-A.
Strasbourg, Musée des Beaux-Arts

Strasbourg, Musées Château Rohan
Strasbourg, Musées du Château des Rohan [admins Mus. A. Déc.; Mus. Archéol.; Mus. B.-A.]

Strasbourg, Musées Ville
Strasbourg, Musées de la Ville de Strasbourg

Strasbourg, Mus. Hist.
Strasbourg, Musée Historique

Strasbourg, Mus. Oeuvre Notre-Dame
Strasbourg, Musée de l'Oeuvre Notre-Dame

Strasbourg, Schlossmus.
Strasbourg, Schlossmuseum

Strasbourg U.
Strasbourg, Université de Strasbourg

Strasbourg U. II
Strasbourg, Université de Strasbourg [Sciences Humaines]

Stratford-on-Avon, Bancroft Gdns
Stratford-on-Avon, Bancroft Gardens

Stratford-on-Avon, Nash's House [New Place]

Stratford-on-Avon, Royal Shakespeare Mus.
Stratford-on-Avon, Royal Shakespeare Museum

Stratford-on-Avon, Town Hall

Strážnice, Castle Mus.
Strážnice, Castle Museum

Stupinigi, Mus. A. & Ammobil.
Stupinigi, Museo d'Arte e d'Ammobiliamento [in Pal. Mauriziana]

Stupinigi, Pal. Mauriziana
Stupinigi, Palazzina Mauriziana di Stupinigi [Palazzina Mauriziana di Caccia; houses Mus. A. & Ammobil.]

Sturbridge, MA, Old Sturbridge Village

Stuttgart, Württemberg. Landesmus.
Stuttgart, Altes Schloss, Württembergisches Landesmuseum

Stuttgart, Gal. Berg
Stuttgart, Galerie am Berg

Stuttgart, Gal. Döbele
Stuttgart, Galerie Döbele

Stuttgart, Gal. Stadt
Stuttgart, Galerie der Stadt Stuttgart

Stuttgart, Hauptstaatsarchv
Stuttgart, Hauptstaatsarchiv

Stuttgart, Inst. Auslandsbeziehungen
Stuttgart, Institut für Auslandsbeziehungen

Stuttgart, Kön. Schloss
Stuttgart, Königliches Schloss

Stuttgart, Linden-Mus.
Stuttgart, Linden-Museum [Staatliches Museum für Völkerkunde]

Stuttgart, Staatsgal.
Stuttgart, Staatsgalerie

Stuttgart, Standort Schlossmus.
Stuttgart, Standort Schlossmuseum

Stuttgart, Tech. Hochsch.
Stuttgart, Technische Hochschule Stuttgart [now U. Stuttgart]

Stuttgart, U. Stuttgart
Stuttgart, Universität Stuttgart

Stuttgart, Württemberg. Kstver.
Stuttgart, Württembergischer Kunstverein

Stuttgart, Württemberg. Landesbib.
Stuttgart, Württembergische Landesbibliothek

Stuttgart, Württemberg. Landesmuseum
Stuttgart, Württembergisches Landesmuseum Stuttgart

Suakoko, Cuttington Coll. Mus.
Suakoko, Cuttington College Museum [Africana Museum]

Subotica, Bačka Gal.
Subotica, Bačka Gallery

Subotica, Mun. Mus.
Subotica, Municipal Museum (Gradski Muzej)

Suceava, Distr. Mus.
Suceava, District Museum (Muzeul Judeţean Suceava)

Suchumi, Abkhazian Mus.
Suchumi, Abkhazian Museum

Sucre, Bib. & Archv N.
Sucre, Biblioteca y Archivo Nacional

Sucre, Casa Libertad
Sucre, Casa de la Libertad [formerly Casa de la Independencia]

Sucre, City Hall

Sucre, Escuela N. Maestros
Sucre, Escuela Nacional de Maestros

Sucre, Mus. Catedral
Sucre, Museo de la Catedral

Sucre, Mus. Recoleta
Sucre, Museo de la Recoleta

Sucre, Mus. S Clara
Sucre, Museo S Clara

Sucre, U. Sucre
Sucre, Universidad Mayor, Real y Pontificia de S Francisco Xavier de Chuquisaca

Sucre, U. Sucre, Mus. Charcas
Sucre, Universidad Mayor, Real y Pontificia de S Francisco Xavier de Chuquisaca, Museo Charcas

Sudbury, Gainsborough's House

Sukhothai, Ramkhamhaeng N. Mus.
Sukhothai, Ramkhamhaeng National Museum

Sumy, A. Mus.
Sumy, Art Museum

Sundborn, Carl Larsson-Gården

Sunderland, A. Cent.
Sunderland, Arts Centre [formerly Ceolfrith Gallery; now N. Cent. Contemp. A.]

Sunderland, Grindon Mus.
Sunderland, Grindon Mus.

Sunderland, Monkwearmouth Station Mus.
Sunderland, Monkwearmouth Station Museum

Sunderland, Mus. & A.G.
Sunderland, Sunderland Museum & Art Gallery

Sunderland, N. Cent. Contemp. A.
Sunderland, Northern Centre for Contemporary Art

Surabaya, Mus. Negeri Jawa Timur Mpu Tantular
Surabaya, Museum Negeri Jawa Timur Mpu Tantular

Surakarta, Prince Mangkunagaran Pal.
Surakarta, Prince Mangkunagaran Palace

Surakarta, Radya Pustaka Mus.
Surakarta, Radya Pustaka Museum

Susa Cathedral, Sacristy

Sutton Coldfield, Oscott Coll.
Sutton Coldfield, Oscott College

Suva, Fiji Mus.
Suva, Fiji Museum

Suzhou Mus.
Suzhou, Suzhou Museum

Svalöv, Herrenhof Trolleholm

Svishtov, Hist. Mus.
Svishtov, Historical Museum (Istoricheski Muzej)

Swansea, Guildhall

Swansea, Vivian A.G. & Mus.
Swansea, Glynn Vivian Art Gallery and Museum

Sydney, Aboriginal A.
Sydney, Aboriginal Arts

Sydney, Aboriginal A. Cent.
Sydney, Aboriginal Art Centre

Sydney, A.G. NSW
Sydney, Art Gallery of New South Wales [formerly N.A.G. NSW]

Sydney, Anthony Horderns Gal.
Sydney, Anthony Horderns Gallery

Sydney Artspace

Sydney, Austral. Gal. Directors Council
Sydney, Australian Gallery Directors Council

Sydney, Australia Council

Sydney, Austral. Mus.
Sydney, Australian Museum

Sydney, Cent. Street Gal.
Sydney, Central Street Gallery

Sydney, Clune Gal.
Sydney, Clune Gallery

Sydney, Contemp. A. Soc.
Sydney, Contemporary Art Society

Sydney, David Jones Gal.
Sydney, David Jones Gallery

Sydney, Des. A. Board Austral. Council
Sydney, Design Arts Board of the Australian
Council

Sydney, Des. Warehouse
Sydney, Design Warehouse

Sydney, E. Sydney Tech. Coll.
Sydney, East Sydney Technical College

Sydney, Govt House
Sydney, Government House

Sydney, Grosvenor Gals
Sydney, Grosvenor Galleries

Sydney, Int. Cult. Corp. Australia
Sydney, International Cultural Corporation of
Australia

Sydney, Macquarie Gals
Sydney, Macquarie Galleries

Sydney, Mech. Inst.
Sydney, Mechanics Institute

Sydney, Mitchell Lib.
Sydney, Mitchell Library

Sydney, Mus. Applied A. & Sci.
Sydney, Museum of Applied Arts and Sciences
[incl. Powerhouse; Powerhouse Train; Sydney
Observatory; The Mint; Hyde Park Barracks]

Sydney, Mus. Contemp. A.
Sydney, Museum of Contemporary Art [incl.
U. Sydney, Power Gal. Contemp. A.]

Sydney, N.A.G. NSW
Sydney, National Art Gallery of New South
Wales [name changed to A.G. NSW in 1958]

Sydney, Queen Victoria Bldg
Sydney, Queen Victoria Building

Sydney, Rudy Komon A.G.
Sydney, Rudy Komon Art Gallery

Sydney, State Lib. NSW
Sydney, State Library of New South Wales

Sydney, U. Sydney, Macleay Mus.
Sydney, University of Sydney, Macleay
Museum

Sydney, U. Sydney, Nicholson Mus. Ant.
Sydney, University of Sydney, Nicholson
Museum of Antiquities

Sydney, U. Sydney, Power Gal. Contemp. A.
Sydney, University of Sydney, Power Gallery
of Contemporary Arts

Sydney, Watters Gal.
Sydney, Watters Gallery

Syracuse, Gal. Regionale
Syracuse, Galleria Regionale

Syracuse, Mus. Archeol. Reg.
Syracuse, Museo Archeologico Regionale
'Paolo Orsi' [Museo Nazionale Archeologico]

Syracuse, Pal. Bellomo
Syracuse, Museo Nazionale del Palazzo
Bellomo [Museo Regionale del Palazzo
Bellomo]

Syracuse, Tesoro Cattedrale
Syracuse, Tesoro della Cattedrale

Syracuse, NY, Everson Mus. A.
Syracuse, NY, Everson Museum of Art

Syracuse U., NY, Joe & Emily Lowe A.G.
Syracuse, NY, Syracuse University, Joe and
Emily Lowe Art Gallery

Syros Mus.
Syros, Syros Museum

Szczecin, Mus. Szczecin
Szczecin, Museum of the City of Szczecin
(Muzeum Miasta Szczecina)

Szczecin, N. Mus.
Szczecin, National Museum (Muzeum
Narodowe)

Szczecin, Office A. Exh.
Szczecin, Office of Art Exhibitions (Biuro
Wystaw Artystycznych)

Szeged, Castle Mus.
Szeged, Castle Museum (Vármúzeum)

Szeged, Ferenc Móra Mus.
Szeged, Ferenc Móra Museum (Móra Ferenc
Múzeum)

Szeghalom, Kazinczy Mem. Mus.
Szeghalom, Kazinczy Memorial Museum
(Kazinczy Emlékmúzeum)

Székesfehérvár, Gdn Ruins
Székesfehérvár, Garden of Ruins (Középkori
Romkert)

Székesfehérvár, King Stephen Mus.
Székesfehérvár, King Stephen Museum (Király
István Múzeum)

Szentendre, A. Col.
Szentendre, Szentendre Art Collection
(Szentendrei Képtár)

Szentendre, Barcsay Col.
Szentendre, Barcsay Collection (Barcsay
Gyüjtemény)

Szentendre, Czóbel Mus.
Szentendre, Czóbel Museum (Czóbel
Múzeum)

Szentendre, Ferenczy Mus.
Szentendre, Ferenczy Museum (Ferenczy
Múzeum)

Szentendre, Kovács Cer. Col.
Szentendre, Margit Kovács Ceramics
Collection (Kovács Margit
Kerámiagyüjtemény)

Szentendre, Lajos Vajda Mus.
Szentendre, Lajos Vajda Museum (Lajos Vajda
Múzeum)

Szentendre, Pop. A. Col.
Szentendre, Popular Art Collection
(Népmüvészetek Háza)

Szentes, József Koszta Mus.
Szentes, József Koszta Museum (Koszta
József Múzeum)

Szolnok, A.G.
Szolnok, Art Gallery (Szolnoki Galéria)

Szolnok, Damjanich Mus.
Szolnok, János Damjanich Museum
(Damjanich János Múzeum)

Szombathely, County Bldg
Szombathely, County Building

Szombathely, Derkovits & Dési Huber Mem.
Mus.
Szombathely, Gyula Derkovits and Dési
Huber Memorial Museum (Derkovits Gyula
Emlékmúzeum, és Dési Huber
Emlékmúzeum)

Szombathely Gal.
Szombathely, Szombathely Gallery
(Szombathelyi Képtár)

Szombathely, Mus. Revolution
Szombathely, Museum of the Revolution
(Forradalmi Múzeum)

Szombathely, Savaria Mus.
Szombathely, Savaria Museum (Savaria
Múzeum)

Szombathely, Smidt Mus.
Szombathely, Smidt Museum (Smidt Múzeum)

Szombathely, Vasi Mus. Village
Szombathely, Vasi Museum Village (Vasi
Falumúzeum)

Tabriz, Pub. Lib.
Tabriz, Public Library

Tacoma, WA, A. Mus.
Tacoma, WA, Art Museum

Tadjik, Tadjikistan Hist. Mus.
Tadjik, Tadjikistan Historical Museum

Taegu, Yeŭngnam U. Mus.
Taegu, Yeŭngnam University Museum

Taganrog, Pict. Gal.
Taganrog, Picture Gallery (Kartinnaya
Galereya)

Taggia, Pal. Lercari
Taggia, Palazzo Lercari

Taichung, Chin. N. Cent. Mus.
Taichung, Chinese National Central Museum

Taima, Nara Prefecture, Taimadera

Taipei, Acad. Sinica
Taipei, Academia Sinica

Taipei, F.A. Mus.
Taipei, Fine Arts Museum

Taipei, Hanart Gal.
Taipei, Hanart Gallery

Taipei, N. Cent. Lib.
Taipei, National Central Library

Taipei, N. Mus. Hist.
Taipei, National Museum of History

Taipei, N. Pal. Mus.
Taipei, National Palace Museum

Taipei, N. Taiwan A.G.
Taipei, National Taiwan Art Gallery

Taiping, Perak Mus.
Taiping, Perak Museum (Muzium Perak)

Taiyuan, Shanxi Prov. Mus.
Taiyuan, Shanxi Provincial Museum [at Wen
Miao Temple & Chunyang Gong Temple]

Takamatsu, Rural Residence Mus.
Takamatsu, Rural Residence Museum
(Shikoku Minka Hakubutsukan)

Takasaki, Gunma Prefect. Mus. Hist.
Takasaki, Gunma Prefectural Museum of
History (Gunma Kenritsu Rekishi
Hakubutsukan)

Takasaki, Gunma Prefect. Mus. Mod. A.
Takasaki, Gunma Prefectural Museum of
Modern Art (Gunma Kenritsu Kindai
Bijutsukan)

Takayama, Hida Flklore Mus.
Takayama, Hida Folklore Museum (Hida
Minzokumura)

Talashkino, Talashkino Estate-Mus.
Talashkino, Talashkino Estate-Museum
[houses part of Tenisheva Col. Flk A.]

Talca, Mus. B.A. Talca
Talca, Museo de Bellas Artes de Talca

Talca, Mus. O'Higginiano B.A.
Talca, Museo O'Higginiano de Bellas Artes

Talladega, AL, Coll.
Talladega, AL, Talladega College

Tallahassee, FL State U., F.A. Gal.
Tallahassee, FL, Florida State University, Fine
Arts Gallery

Tallahassee, Mus. FL Hist.
Tallahassee, FL, Museum of Florida History

Tallinn, A. Hall.
Tallinn, Tallinn Art Hall

Tallinn, A. Mus. Estonia
  Tallinn, Art Museum of Estonia

Tallinn, City Mus.
  Tallinn, City Museum

Tallinn, Coll. A. & Des.
  Tallinn, College of Art and Design

Tallinn, Estonian Mus. Archit.
  Tallinn, Estonian Museum of Architecture

Tallinn, Hist. Mus. Estonia
  Tallinn, Historical Museum of Estonia

Tallinn, J. Tomp House of Cult.
  Tallinn, J. Tomp House of Culture [now Salme
  Cult. Cent.]

Tallinn, Kristjan Raud Mus.
  Tallinn, Kristjan Raud Museum

Tallinn, Mus. Applied A.
  Tallinn, Museum of Applied Art

Tallinn, N. Lib. Estonia
  Tallinn, National Library of Estonia

Tallinn, Park Mus.
  Tallinn, Estonian Park Museum

Tallinn, Salme Cult. Cent.
  Tallinn, Salme Cultural Centre [formerly J.
  Tomp House Cult.]

Tallinn, Soros Cent. Contemp.A.
  Tallinn, Soros Centre for Contemporary Art

Tallinn, St Nicholas Church Mus.
  Tallinn, St Nicholas Church Museum

Tallinn, Un. Artists
  Tallinn, Union of Artists

Tallinn, Vaal Gal.
  Tallinn, Vaal Gallery

Tambov, Pict. Gal.
  Tambov, Tambov Picture Gallery
  (Tambovskaya Kartinnaya Galereya)

Tampa, FL, Mus.
  Tampa, FL, Tampa Museum

Tampa, U. S. FL
  Tampa, FL, University of South Florida

Tampere, A. Mus.
  Tampere, Art Museum (Taidemuseo)

Tampere, Business Sch.
  Tampere, Business School

Tampere, City Mus.
  Tampere, City Museum (Tampereen
  Kaupunginmuseo)

Tampere, Fin. Sch. Mus.
  Tampere, Finnish School Museum (Suomen
  Koulumuseo)

Tampere, Häme Mus.
  Tampere, Häme Museum (Hämeen Museo)

Tampere, Hildén A. Mus.
  Tampere, Sara Hildén Art Museum (Sara
  Hildénin Taidemuseo)

Tampere Museums
  Tampere, Tampere Museums (Tampereen
  Kaupungin Museolautakunta) [admins City
  Mus.; Fin. Sch. Mus.; Häme Mus.; Nat. Hist.
  Mus.; Tech Mus.; Workers' Mus. Amuri]

Tampere, Nat. Hist. Mus.
  Tampere, Natural History Museum
  (Tampereen Luonnontieteellinen Museo)

Tampere, Pyynikinlinna

Tampere, Tech. Mus.
  Tampere, Technical Museum (Teknillinen
  Museo)

Tampere, Workers' Mus. Amuri
  Tampere, Workers' Museum of Amuri
  (Amurin Työläismuseokortteli)

Tanagra, Archaeol. Col.
  Tanagra, Archaeological Collection

Tananarive, U. Madagascar
  Tananarive, Université de Madagascar [U.
  Antananarivo since 1961]

Tangier, Mus. A. Contemp.
  Tangier, Musée d'Art Contemporain

Tangier, Mus. Kasbah
  Tangier, Musée de la Kasbah de Tanger

Taos, NM, Navajo Gal.
  Taos, NM, Navajo Gallery

Taranto, Mus. N.
  Taranto, Museo Nazionale di Taranto

Tarascon, Hôtel de Ville

Tarbes, Mus. Massey
  Tarbes, Musée Massey

Tǎrnovo, Reg. Mus. Hist.
  Tǎrnovo, Regional Museum of History
  [Okrǎzen Istoričeski Muzej]

Tarnów, Dioc. Mus.
  Tarnów, Diocesan Museum (Muzeum
  Diecezjalne)

Tarnów, Distr. Mus.
  Tarnów, District Museum (Muzeum
  Okregowe)

Tarquinia, Pal. Vitelleschi
  Tarquinia, Museo Nazionale Tarquinese
  [Museo Nazionale Etrusco]

Tarragona, Mus. A. Mod.
  Tarragona, Museo de Arte Moderno

Tarragona, Mus. Dioc.
  Tarragona, Museu Diocesano

Tarragona, Mus. N. Arqueol.
  Tarragona, Museu Nacional Arqueològic

Tarragona, Mus. Paleocrist.
  Tarragona, Museo Paleocristiano

Tarrasa, Mus. Ciènc. & Tèc. Catalunya
  Tarrasa, Museu de la Ciència i de la Tècnica de
  Catalunya

Tarrasa, Mus. Tèxtil Diput. Barcelona
  Tarrasa, Museu Tèxtil de la Diputació de
  Barcelona

Tarrytown, NY, Sunnyside

Tartu, Hist. Mus. Estonian Acad. Sci.
  Tartu, Historical Museum of the Estonian
  Academy of Sciences

Tartu, Mus. A.
  Tartu, Museum of Art

Tartu, Mus. Ethnog.
  Tartu, Museum of Ethnography [now Folk
  Museum of Estonia]

Tartu, Pallas A. Sch.
  Tartu, Pallas Art School

Tartu, Starkopf Atelier Mus.
  Tartu, Starkopf Atelier Museum

Tartu, U. Mus. Class. Archaeol.
  Tartu, Tartu University Museum of Classical
  Archaeology

Tarvaspää, Gallen-Kallela Mus.
  Tarvaspää, Gallen-Kallela Museum

Tashkent, Alisher Navoi Lib.
  Tashkent, Alisher Navoi Library

Tashkent, Aybek Mus. Hist. Uzbekistan
  Tashkent, T. Aybek Museum of the History of
  the Peoples of Uzbekistan

Tashkent, Cent. Lib. Acad. Sci.
  Tashkent, Central Library of the Academy of
  Sciences

Tashkent, Inst. Hist. A.
  Tashkent, Institute of the History of Art

Tashkent, Khamza Inst. A.
  Tashkent, Khamza Institute for Knowledge of
  the Arts

Tashkent, Mus. Applied A.
  Tashkent, Museum of Applied Art

Tashkent, Mus. A. Uzbekistan
  Tashkent, Tashkent Museum of the Arts of
  Uzbekistan

Tashkent, Mus. Sci. Knowledge
  Tashkent, Museum of Scientific Knowledge

Tashkent, Orient. Inst. Lib.
  Tashkent, Oriental Institute Library [Abu
  Raihon Beruni Institute of Orientology of the
  Uzbek Academy of Sciences]

Tashkent, Pub. Lib.
  Tashkent, Public Library

Tashkent, Uzbekistan Acad. Sci.
  Tashkent, Uzbekistan Academy of Sciences

Tata, Ger.-Speaking Peoples Mus.
  Tata, German-Speaking Peoples Museum
  (Német Nemzetiségi Múzeum)

Tata, Kuny Mus.
  Tata, Domokos Kuny Museum (Kuny
  Domokos Múzeum)

Taucheira: see Tocra

Taunton, Somerset Co. Mus.
  Taunton, Somerset County Museum

Tavastehus: see Hämeenlinna

Tawqrah: see Tocra

Taxila, Archaeol. Mus.
  Taxila, Archaeological Museum

Tazumal, Mus. Tazumal
  Tazumal, Museo Tazumal

Tbilisi, Acad. A.
  Tbilisi, Tbilisi Academy of Arts

Tbilisi, Acad. Sci., Inst. MSS
  Tbilisi, Academy of Sciences, Institute of
  Manuscripts

Tbilisi, G. Chubinashvili Inst. Hist. Georg. A.
  Tbilisi, G. Chubinashvili Institute of the
  History of Georgian Art

Tbilisi, Georg. Pict. Gal.
  Tbilisi, Georgian Picture Gallery

Tbilisi, House Georg. Artists
  Tbilisi, House of the Georgian Artists

Tbilisi, K.S. Kekelidze Inst. MSS
  Tbilisi, K.S. Kekelidze Institute of Manuscripts

Tbilisi, Lit. Mus. Georgia
  Tbilisi, Literary Museum of Georgia

Tbilisi, Mus. A. Georgia
  Tbilisi, Museum of Art of Georgia

Tbilisi, Mus. Georg. Flk Archit. & Local Lore
  Tbilisi, Museum of Georgian Folk
  Architecture and Local Lore

Tbilisi, Mus. Georgia
  Tbilisi, Museum of Georgia

Tbilisi, Mus. Hist. Georgia
  .Tbilisi, Museum of the History of Georgia

Tbilisi, Yelena Akhvlediani Mem. Mus.
  Tbilisi, Yelena Akhvlediani Memorial Museum

Te Awamutu, Dist. Mus
  Te Awamutu, Te Awamutu District Museum

Tecpán, Iximché Archaeol. Mus.
  Tecpán, Iximché Archaeological Museum

Tegea, Archaeol. Mus.
  Tegea, Archaeological Museum

Tegucigalpa, Mus. Banco Atlántida
  Tegucigalpa, Museo del Banco Atlántida

Tegucigalpa, Mus. N.
Tegucigalpa, Museo Nacional [Villa Roy]

Tegucigalpa, Pal. Distr. Cent.
Tegucigalpa, Palacio del Districto Central

Tegucigalpa, U. N. Autón. Honduras
Tegucigalpa, Universidad Nacional Autónoma de Honduras

Tehran, Abgina Mus.
Tehran, Abgina Museum

Tehran, Archaeol. Mus.
Tehran, Archaeological Museum [Iran Bastan Mus.]

Tehran, Bank Markazi, Crown Jewels Col.
Tehran, Bank Markazi, Crown Jewels Collection

Tehran, Carpet Mus.
Tehran, Carpet Museum

Tehran, Ethnog. Mus.
Tehran, Ethnographical Museum

Tehran, Gulistan Pal.
Tehran, Gulistan [Gulestan] Palace

Tehran, Gulistan Pal. Lib.
Tehran, Gulistan Palace Library

Tehran, Iran. Mus. Porcelain & Cer.
Tehran, Iranian Museum of Porcelain and Ceramics

Tehran, Majlis Lib.
Tehran, Majlis Library [Parliament Library]

Tehran, Malek Lib.
Tehran, Malek Library

Tehran, Mus. Contemp. A.
Tehran, Museum of Contemporary Art

Tehran, Mus. Dec. A.
Tehran, Museum of Decorative Arts

Tehran, Nigaristan Mus.
Tehran, Nigaristan Museum

Tehran, Riza 'Abbasi Mus.
Tehran, Riza 'Abbasi Museum

Tehran, Royal Lib.
Tehran, Royal Library

Tehran U., Cent. Lib.
Tehran, Tehran University, Central Library and Documentation Centre

Tekirdağ, Mus.
Tekirdağ, Museum

Tel Aviv, Ahuva Doran Gal.
Tel Aviv, Ahuva Doran Gallery

Tel Aviv, Alphabet Mus.
Tel Aviv, Alphabet Museum

Tel Aviv, Ant. Mus.
Tel Aviv, Antiquities Museum of Tel Aviv

Tel Aviv, Beth Hatefutsoth, Goldmann Mus. Jew. Diaspora
Tel Aviv, Beth Hatefutsoth, Nahum Goldmann Museum of the Jewish Diaspora

Tel Aviv, Cer. Mus.
Tel Aviv, Ceramics Museum

Tel Aviv, Chemerinsky Gal.
Tel Aviv, Chemerinsky Gallery

Tel Aviv, Givon A.G.
Tel Aviv, Noemi Givon Art Gallery

Tel Aviv, Glass Pav.
Tel Aviv, Glass Pavilion

Tel Aviv, Gordon Gal.
Tel Aviv, Gordon Gallery

Tel Aviv, Ha'aretz Mus.
Tel Aviv, Ha'aretz Museum [Eretz-Israel Museum; also admins Alphabet Mus.; Cer. Mus.; Independence Hall; Israel Theat. Mus.; Kadman Numi. Pav.; Lasky Planet.; Man & Work Mus.; Mus. Ethnog. & Flklore; Mus. Hist.; Mus. Sci. & Technol.; Nechustan Pav.; Tel Quasile Archaeol. Site]

Tel Aviv, Independence Hall

Tel Aviv, Inst. Architects & Town Planners
Tel Aviv, Institute of Architects and Town Planners

Tel Aviv, Israel Theat. Mus.
Tel Aviv, Israel Theatre Museum

Tel Aviv, Julie M Gal.
Tel Aviv, Julie M Gallery

Tel Aviv, Kadman Numi. Pav.
Tel Aviv, Kadman Numismatic Pavilion

Tel Aviv, Lasky Planet.
Tel Aviv, Lasky Planetarium

Tel Aviv, Man & Work Mus.
Tel Aviv, Man and his Work Museum ['Adam ve-Amalo']

Tel Aviv, Mus.
Tel Aviv, Tel Aviv Museum [Tel Aviv Mus. A. since c. 1987–8]

Tel Aviv, Mus. A.
Tel Aviv, Tel Aviv Museum of Art

Tel Aviv, Mus. Ethnog. & Flklore
Tel Aviv, Museum of Ethnography and Folklore

Tel Aviv, Mus. Hist.
Tel Aviv, Museum of the History of Tel Aviv

Tel Aviv, Mus. Sci. & Technol.
Tel Aviv, Museum of Science and Technology

Tel Aviv, Nechustan Pav.
Tel Aviv, Nechustan Pavilion

Tel Aviv, Rubin House

Tel Aviv, TAL Int.
Tel Aviv, TAL International

Tel Aviv, Tel Quasile Archaeol. Site
Tel Aviv, Tel Quasile Archaeological Site

Tel Aviv U., Genia Schreiber A.G.
Tel Aviv, Tel Aviv University, Genia Schreiber Art Gallery

Tel Aviv U., Sonia & Marco Nadler Inst. Archaeol.
Tel Aviv, Tel Aviv University, Sonia and Marco Nadler Institute of Archaeology

Telč, Jan Zrzavý Gal.
Telč, Jan Zrzavý Gallery (Galerie Jana Zrzavého)

Telford, Ironbridge Gorge Mus.
Telford, Ironbridge Gorge Museum

Telfs, Heimatmus.
Telfs, Heimatmuseum Telfs

Tempe, AZ State U., Northlight Gal.
Tempe, AZ, Arizona State University, Northlight Gallery

Tenafly, NJ, Afr. A. Mus.
Tenafly, NJ, African Art Museum of the S.M.A. Fathers

Tenango, Mus. Arqueol. Estado México
Tenango, Museo Arqueológico del Estado de México

Tenby, Mus. & Pict. Gal.
Tenby, Tenby Museum and Picture Gallery

Tenevo, Gal. Matasci
Tenevo, Galleria Matasci

Tenri, Cent. Lib.
Tenri, Tenri Central Library [Nara Prefect.; Tenri U. Lib.]

Tenri, Nara Prefect., Lib.
Tenri, Nara Prefecture, Library (Chūō Toshokan)

Tenri, Nara Prefect., Sankōkan Mus.
Tenri, Nara Prefecture, Sankōkan Museum [attached to Tenri U.]

Teotihuacán, Mus. Arqueol.
Teotihuacán, Museo Arqueológico de Teotihuacán

Tepic, Mus. Reg. Antropol. & Hist.
Tepic, Museo Regional de Antropología e Historia

Tepotzotlán, Mus. A. Colon.
Tepotzotlán, Museo de Arte Colonial [in former Jesuit College of S Martin]

Tepotzotlán, Mus. N. Virreinato
Tepotzotlán, Museo Nacional del Virreinato [in former church of S Francisco Xavier]

Termez, Surkhandar'ya Reg. Mus.
Termez, Surkhandar'ya Regional Museum (Surkhandarinskiy Kraevedcheskiy Muzey)

Terni, Mus. & Pin. Civ.
Terni, Museo e Pinacoteca Civica

Terralba, Villa Imp.
Terralba, Villa Imperiale

Tervuren, Kon. Mus. Mid.-Afrika
Tervuren, Koninklijk Museum voor Midden-Afrika [Musée Royal de l'Afrique Centrale]

Teshikago, Akan Wagoto Mus.
Teshikago, Akan Wagoto Museum

Tétouan, Mus. Archéol.
Tétouan, Musée d'Archéologie

Thanjavur, A.G.
Thanjavur, Art Gallery [now Rajaraja Mus.]

Thanjavur, Rajaraja Mus.
Thanjavur, Rajaraja Museum

Thanjavur, Sarasvati Mahal Lib.
Thanjavur, Sarasvati Mahal Library

Thasos, Archaeol. Mus.
Thasos, Archaeological Museum

Thebes Mus.
Thebes, Thebes Museum

Thera, Archaeol. Mus.
Thera, Archaeological Museum

Thermon, Archaeol. Mus.
Thermon, Archaeological Museum

Thessaloniki, Archaeol. Mus.
Thessaloniki, Archaeological Museum

Thessaloniki, Aristotelian U.
Thessaloniki, Aristotelian University of Thessaloniki

Thessaloniki, Aristotelian U. Thessaloniki A. Col.
Thessaloniki, Aristotelian University of Thessaloniki Art Collection

Thessaloniki, Byz. Mus. Rotonda St George
Thessaloniki, Byzantine Museum of the Rotonda of St George

Thessaloniki, White Tower Mus.
Thessaloniki, White Tower Museum

Thetford, Anc. House Mus.
Thetford, Ancient House Museum

Thira: see Thera

Thiruvananthapuram, see Trivandrum

Thomery, Mus.-Atelier Rosa-Bonheur
Thomery, Musée-Atelier Rosa-Bonheur [Château de By]

Thun, Hist. Mus.
Thun, Historisches Museum [in Schloss]

Thunstetten, Schloss

Tianjin, Cult. Relics Bureau
Tianjin, Cultural Relics Bureau

Tianjin, Mun. Hist. Mus.
Tianjin, Municipal Historical Museum

Tianjin, Mus. A.
Tianjin, Museum of Art

Tienen, Stedel. Mus.
Tienen, Stedelijk Museum

Tientsin: see Tianjin

Tigani: see Pithagorio

Tihany, Mus.
Tihany, Tihany Museum (Tihanyi Múzeum)

Tikal, Mus. Arqueol.-Sylvanus G. Morley
Tikal, Museo Arqueologico-Sylvanus G. Morley

Tilburg, Akad. Bouwkst
Tilburg, Akademie Bouwkunst

Tilburg, Barrique
Tilburg, La Barrique

Tilburg, De Pont Found. Contemp. A.
Tilburg, De Pont Foundation of Contemporary Art

Timişoara, Distr. Mus.
Timişoara, District Museum (Muzeul Banatului Timişoara)

Timişoara, Mus. A.
Timişoara, Museum of Art

Tinos, Archaeol. Mus.
Tinos, Archaeological Museum

Tinos, Mus. Tinian Artists
Tinos, Museum of Tinian Artists

Tinos, Pnevmatiko Kent. Evangel.
Tinos, Pnevmatiko Kentro Evangelistria

Tiranë, A.G.
Tiranë, Art Gallery (Galeria Arteve)

Tiranë, Alb. N. Cult. Mus.
Tiranë, Albanian National Culture Museum [attached to Inst. N. Cult.]

Tiranë, Cent. Archvs
Tiranë, State Central Archives

Tiranë, Congr. Pal.
Tiranë, Congress Palace

Tiranë, Enver Hoxha Mus.
Tiranë, Enver Hoxha Museum [now Int. Cent. Cult.]

Tiranë, Gal. Fig. A.
Tiranë, Gallery of Figurative Art (Galeria e Arteve Figurative)

Tiranë, Int. Cent. Cult.
Tiranë, International Centre of Culture [formerly Enver Hoxha Mus.]

Tiranë, Jordan Misja Lyceum A.
Tiranë, Jordan Misja Lyceum of Art

Tiranë, N. Hist. Mus.
Tiranë, National Historical Museum

Tiranë, N. Mus. Archaeol.
Tiranë, National Museum of Archaeology [attached to the Centre of Archaeological Research of the Academy of Sciences]

Tiranë, N. Sci. Mus.
Tiranë, National Science Museum [attached to U. Tiranë]

Tiranë, U. Tiranë, Archvs Chair Archit.
Tiranë, University of Tiranë, Archives of the Chair of Architecture

Tiranë, Writers' & Artists' League
Tiranë, Writers' and Artists' League (Lidhja e Shkrimtarëve dhe Artistëve)

Tirgovişte, Distr. Mus.
Tirgovişte, District Museum (Muzeul Judeţean Dîmboviţa)

Tirgovişte, Mus. Prtg & Early Prtd Books
Tirgovişte, Museum of Printing and Early Printed Books (Muzeul Tiparului şi ale Cărţi Vechi Româneşti)

Tîrgu Mureş, A. Mus.
Tîrgu Mureş, Art Museum (Muzeul de Artă din Tîrgu Mureş)

Tîrgu Mureş, Mureş Distr. Museums
Tîrgu Mureş, Mureş District Museums (Complexul Muzeal Judetean Mures) [admins A. Mus.; Mus. Hist., Ethnog. & Nat. Hist.]

Tîrgu Mureş, Mus. Hist., Ethnog. & Nat. Hist.
Tîrgu Mureş, Museum of History, Ethnography & Natural History (Muzeul de Istorie, Etnografie şi Ştiinţele Naturii)

Tirol, Liebeswerk [nr Meran]

Tivoli, Mus. N. Archeol., Villa Adriana
Tivoli, Museo Nazionale Archeologico, Villa Adriana

Tivoli, Villa d'Este

Tobol'sk, Hist. Mus.
Tobol'sk, Historical Museum (Istoriko-Architekturniy Muzey)

Tobol'sk, Pict. Gal.
Tobol'sk, Picture Gallery (Tobol'skaya Kartinnaya Galereya)

Tochigi, Prefect. Mus. F.A.
Tochigi, Tochigi Prefectural Museum of Fine Arts (Tochigi Kenritsu Bijutsukan)

Tocra, Archaeol. Mus.
Tocra, Archaeological Museum

Todi, Mus. Com.
Todi, Museo Comunale

Todmorden, W. Yorks Cent. Vale Park
Todmorden, W. Yorks, Centre Vale Park

Tokushima, Prefect. Mus.
Tokushima, Tokushima Prefectural Museum (Tokushima Kenritsu Hakubutsukan)

Tokyo, AC & T Corp.
Tokyo, AC & T Corporation

Tokyo, Affari Cent. ICE
Tokyo, Affari Centre ICE

Tokyo, Agy Cult. Affairs
Tokyo, Agency for Cultural Affairs

Tokyo, Anc. Orient Mus.
Tokyo, Ancient Orient Museum

Tokyo, Armed Forces Educ. Cent.
Tokyo, Armed Forces Educational Centre

Tokyo, Brain Trust

Tokyo, Bridgestone A. Mus.
Tokyo, Bridgestone Art Museum

Tokyo, Chijoinsha Col.
Tokyo, Chijoinsha Collection

Tokyo, Coll. Educ.
Tokyo, College of Education

Tokyo, Dai Tōkyū Mem. Found.
Tokyo, Dai Tōkyū Memorial Foundation

Tokyo, Dentsū Corp.
Tokyo, Dentsū Corporation

Tokyo, Eisei Bunko

Tokyo, Fifth Air Force, Inf. & Educ. Sect.
Tokyo, Fifth Air Force, Information and Education Section

Tokyo, Flk Crafts Mus.
Tokyo, Folk Crafts Museum

Tokyo, Fujii Mus.
Tokyo, Fujii Museum

Tokyo, Fuji Television Gallery
Tokyo, Fuji Television Gallery

Tokyo, Gal. A. Point
Tokyo, Gallery Art Point

Tokyo, Gal. Tokoro
Tokyo, Gallery Tokoro

Tokyo, Ginza A.G.
Tokyo, Ginza Art Gallery

Tokyo, Gotoh Mus.
Tokyo, Gotoh Museum [Gotō Art Museum]

Tokyo, Govt Cult. Cent.
Tokyo, Government Culture Centre

Tokyo, Green Col.
Tokyo, Green Collections

Tokyo, Gyokudō A. Mus.
Tokyo, Gyokudō Art Museum

Tokyo, Hara Mus. Contemp. A.
Tokyo, Hara Museum of Contemporary Art

Tokyo, Hatakeyama Col.
Tokyo, Hatakeyama Collection

Tokyo, Hiraki Ukiyoe Found.
Tokyo, Hiraki Ukiyoe Foundation

Tokyo, Hokusai A. Mus.
Tokyo, Hokusai Art Museum

Tokyo, Homma A. Mus.
Tokyo, Homma Art Museum

Tokyo, Hosokawa Col.
Tokyo, Hosokawa Collection

Tokyo, Idemitsu Mus. A.
Tokyo, Idemitsu Museum of Art

Tokyo, Imp. Household Col.
Tokyo, Imperial Household Collection

Tokyo, Imp. Mus.
Tokyo, Imperial Museum

Tokyo, Isetan Mus. A.
Tokyo, Isetan Museum of Art

Tokyo, It. Cult. Inst.
Tokyo, Italian Cultural Institute

Tokyo, Japan Callig. Mus.
Tokyo, Japan Calligraphy Museum

Tokyo, Japan Flk A. Mus.
Tokyo, Japan Folk Art Museum

Tokyo, Japan Found.
Tokyo, Japan Foundation

Tokyo, Jap. Sword Mus.
Tokyo, Japanese Sword Museum

Tokyo, Jindaiji

Tokyo, Kajima Inst.
Tokyo, Kajima Institute

Tokyo, Keio U.
Tokyo, Keio University

Tokyo, Keio Umeda Gal.
Tokyo, Keio Umeda Gallery

Tokyo, Konishiroku Gal.
Tokyo, Konishiroku Gallery

Tokyo, Kosaka Col.
Tokyo, Kosaka Collection

Tokyo, Maeda Ikutokukai Found. Lib.
Tokyo, Maeda Ikutokukai Foundation Library [Sonkeikaku Library]

Tokyo, Matsuoka A. Mus.
Tokyo, Matsuoka Art Museum

Tokyo, Met. A.G.
Tokyo, Metropolitan Art Gallery [name changed to Met. A. Mus. in 1975]

Tokyo, Met. A. Mus.
Tokyo, Metropolitan Art Museum

Tokyo, Met. Hibiya Lib.
Tokyo, Metropolitan Hibiya Library

Tokyo, Met. Teien A. Mus.
Tokyo, Metropolitan Teien Art Museum

Tokyo, Minami Gal.
Tokyo, Minami Gallery [closed]

Tokyo, Mitsui Bunko

Tokyo, Mitsukoshi
Tokyo, Mitsukoshi Ltd

Tokyo, Muramatsu Gal.
Tokyo, Muramatsu Gallery

Tokyo, Mus. Callig.
Tokyo, Museum of Calligraphy

Tokyo, Mushashino A. U., Mus.-Lib.
Tokyo, Mushashino Art University, Museum-
Library

Tokyo, Nantenshi Gal.
Tokyo, Nantenshi Gallery

Tokyo, N. Diet Lib.
Tokyo, National Diet Library

Tokyo, Nezu A. Mus.
Tokyo, Nezu Art Museum [Institute of Fine
Arts]

Tokyo, Nikon Salon
Tokyo, Nikon Salon

Tokyo, N. Mus.
Tokyo, National Museum (Kokuritsu
Hakubutsukan)

Tokyo, N. Mus., Hōryūji Treasure Hall
Tokyo, National Museum, Hōryūji Treasure
Hall

Tokyo, N. Mus. Mod. A.
Tokyo, National Museum of Modern Art
[Metropolitan Museum of Modern Art]

Tokyo, N. Mus. W. A.
Tokyo, National Museum of Western Art

Tokyo, N. Res. Inst. Cult. Prop.
Tokyo, National Research Institute of Cultural
Properties

Tokyo, O A. Mus.
Tokyo, O Art Museum

Tokyo, Odakyu Grand Gallery

Tokyo, Ōkura Shūkokan Mus.
Tokyo, Ōkura Shūkokan Museum

Tokyo, Orient. Lib.
Tokyo, Oriental Library

Tokyo, Ōta Mem. Mus. A.
Tokyo, Ōta Memorial Museum of Art

Tokyo, Riccar A. Mus.
Tokyo, Riccar Art Museum

Tokyo, Sakai Col.
Tokyo, Sakai Collection

Tokyo, Sch. F.A.
Tokyo, School of Fine Arts

Tokyo, Seibu Mus. A.
Tokyo, Seibu Museum of Art

Tokyo, Seiji Togo Mus.
Tokyo, Seiji Togo Museum [mus. of Yasuda
Fire & Marine Insurance Co.]

Tokyo, Seikadō Bunko
Tokyo, Seikadō Cultural Exhibition Hall

Tokyo, Sensōji [Asakusa Kannon Sensōji]

Tokyo, Setagaya Mus.
Tokyo, Setagaya Museum

Tokyo, Sezon Mus. A.
Tokyo, Sezon Museum of Art

Tokyo, Shibuyaku, Shoto Mus.
Tokyo, Shibuyaku, Shoto Museum

Tokyo, Shōtō Mus. A.
Tokyo, Shōtō Museum of Art

Tokyo, Spiral/Wacoal A. Cent.
Tokyo, Spiral/Wacoal Art Centre

Tokyo, Station Gal.
Tokyo, Station Gallery

Tokyo, Sukeijiro Itani

Tokyo, Sumitomo Col.
Tokyo, Sumitomo Collection

Tokyo, Sunshine Mus.
Tokyo, Sunshine Museum

Tokyo, Suntory Mus. A.
Tokyo, Suntory Museum of Art

Tokyo, Takashimaya Gal.
Tokyo, Takashimaya Gallery

Tokyo, Tama A. U.
Tokyo, Tama Art University

Tokyo, Tenri Cent. Lib.
Tokyo, Tenri Central Library

Tokyo, Tokyo Gal.
Tokyo, Tokyo Gallery

Tokyo U. A., A. Mus.
Tokyo University of Arts, Art Museum

Tokyo, Ueno Royal Mus.
Tokyo, Ueno Royal Museum

Tokyo, U. F.A. & Music
Tokyo, University of Fine Arts and Music

Tokyo, Umezawa Col. Gal.
Tokyo, Umezawa Collection Gallery

Tokyo, Umezawa Mem. Found.
Tokyo, Umezawa Memorial Foundation

Tokyo, Umezawa Mem. Mus.
Tokyo, Umezawa Memorial Museum

Tokyo, Universe Gal.
Tokyo, Universe Gallery

Tokyo, U. Tokyo, Lib.
Tokyo, University of Tokyo, Library

Tokyo, U. Tokyo, Mus. & Hist.
Tokyo, University of Tokyo, Museum of Art
and History

Tokyo, Waseda U.
Tokyo, Waseda University

Tokyo, Yamatane Mus. A.
Tokyo, Yamatane Museum of Art

Tokyo, Yurakucho Dist. A. Forum
Tokyo, Yurakucho District Art Forum

Toledo, Archv & Bib. Capitulares
Toledo, Archivo y Biblioteca Capitulares

Toledo, Carmelitas Descalzos

Toledo, Casa & Mus. El Greco
Toledo, Casa y Museo del Greco [Fundaciones
Vega–Inclán]

Toledo, Casa-Mus. Victorio Macho
Toledo, Casa-Museo Victorio Macho

Toledo, Diputación

Toledo, Hosp. Tavera
Toledo, Hospital de Tavera [houses Museo de
la Fundación Duque de Lerma]

Toledo, Inst. Estud. Visigótico Mozárabes
S Eugenio
Toledo, Instituto de Estudios Visigótico-
Mozárabes de S Eugenio

Toledo, Mus. Catedralicio
Toledo, Museo Catedralicio

Toledo, Mus. Concilios
Toledo, Museo de los Concilios y de la Cultura
Visigoda [in former church of S Romano]

Toledo, Mus.-Pal. Fuensalida
Toledo, Museo-Palacio de Fuensalida

Toledo, Mus. S Cruz
Toledo, Museo de S Cruz

Toledo, Mus. S Vincente
Toledo, Museo de S Vincente

Toledo, Semin.
Toledo, Seminario

Toledo, OH, Mus. A.
Toledo, OH, Museum of Art

Tolmeita, Archaeol. Mus.
Tolmeita, Archaeological Museum

Toluca, Mus. A. Mod. Cent. Cult. Mex.
Toluca, Museo de Arte Moderno del Centro
Cultural Mexiquense

Toluca, Mus. Arqueol.
Toluca, Museo de Arqueología, Historia Patria
e Historia Natural

Toluca, Mus. B.A.
Toluca, Museo de Bellas Artes

Tonder, Sonderjyllands Kstmus.
Tonder, Sonderjyllands Kunstmuseum
[Kulturhistorische Museum &
Kunstsammlung]

Tongeren, Prov. Gallo-Romeins Mus.
Tongeren, Provinciaal Gallo-Romeins
Museum

Tonnerre, Hôp.
Tonnerre, Hôpital

Topalu, Dinu & Sevasta Mus. A.
Topalu, Dinu and Sevasta Museum of Art
(Muzeul de Artă 'Dinu şi Sevasta Vintală')

Torcello, Mus. Torcello
Torcello, Museo di Torcello

Torgiano, Mus. Vino
Torgiano, Museo del Vino

Toronto, A.G.
Toronto, Art Gallery of Toronto [name
changed to A.G. Ont. in 1966]

Toronto, A.G. Harbourfront
Toronto, The Art Gallery at Harbourfront

Toronto, A.G. Ont.
Toronto, Art Gallery of Ontario

Toronto, A. & Lett. Club
Toronto, Arts and Letters Club

Toronto, A Space

Toronto, Bata Shoe Mus.
Toronto, Bata Shoe Museum

Toronto, Carmen Lamanna Gal.
Toronto, Carmen Lamanna Gallery

Toronto, City Hall

Toronto, Glenbow Mus.
Toronto, Glenbow Museum

Toronto, Govt Ont. A. Col.
Toronto, Government of Ontario Art
Collection

Toronto, Greenwich Gal.
Toronto, Greenwich Gallery

Toronto, Inn on the Park

Toronto, Isaacs Gal.
Toronto, Isaacs Gallery

Toronto, John B. Aird Gal.
Toronto, John B. Aird Gallery

Toronto, Koffler Gal.
Toronto, Koffler Gallery

Toronto, Legislative Bldg
Toronto, Legislative Building [Queen's Park]

Toronto, Marlborough–Godard
Toronto, Marlborough–Godard Ltd

Toronto, Met. Ref. Lib.
Toronto, Metropolitan Toronto Reference Library

Toronto, Ontario Archvs, Horwood Col.
Toronto, Ontario Archives, Horwood Collecton

Toronto, Ontario Coll. A.
Toronto, Ontario College of Art

Toronto, Ont. Soc. Artists
Toronto, Ontario Society of Artists

Toronto, Osgoode Hall [Law Society of Upper Canada]

Toronto, Roberts Gal.
Toronto, Roberts Gallery

Toronto, Royal Bank of Canada

Toronto, Royal Can. Acad. A.
Toronto, Royal Canadian Academy of Arts

Toronto, Royal Ont. Mus.
Toronto, Royal Ontario Museum [also admins Canadian Building]

Toronto, Sigmund Samuel Bldg
Toronto, Sigmund Samuel Building [part of Royal Ont. Mus]

Toronto, U. Toronto, Hart House
Toronto, University of Toronto, Hart House [Hart House Gallery]

Toronto, U. Trinity Coll.
Toronto, University of Trinity College

Tórsharn, Eysturkulin

Tórsharn, Listaskâlin

Tortona, Pal. Vescovile
Tortona, Palazzo Vescovile

Toruń, Distr. Mus.
Toruń, District Museum (Muzeum Okregowe w Toruniu)

Toruń, Office A. Exh.
Toruń, Office of Art Exhibitions (Biuro Wystaw Artystycznch)

Toruń, Red Granary

Toruń, Town Hall

Toulon, Mus. Toulon
Toulon, Musée de Toulon

Toulouse, Archvs Mun.
Toulouse, Archives Municipales

Toulouse, Capitole [Hôtel de Ville]

Toulouse, Gal. Mun. Château d'Eau
Toulouse, Galerie Municipale du Château d'Eau

Toulouse, Mus. A. Mod.
Toulouse, Musée d'Art Moderne

Toulouse, Mus. Augustins
Toulouse, Musée des Augustins

Toulouse, Mus. Dupuy
Toulouse, Musée Paul Dupuy

Toulouse, Mus. Georges Labit
Toulouse, Musée Georges Labit

Toulouse, Mus. Hist. Nat.
Toulouse, Muséum d'Histoire Naturelle

Toulouse, Mus. Jacobins
Toulouse, Musée des Jacobins

Toulouse, Mus. St-Raymond
Toulouse, Musée Saint-Raymond

Toulouse, Mus. Vieux-Toulouse
Toulouse, Musée du Vieux-Toulouse

Toulouse, Pal. A.
Toulouse, Palais des Arts

Toulouse, Pal. Justice
Toulouse, Palais de Justice

Toulouse, Pal. Maréchal Niel
Toulouse, Palais Maréchal Niel

Toulouse, Théât. Capitole
Toulouse, Théâtre du Capitole

Toulouse, U. Toulouse II
Toulouse, Université de Toulouse II [le Mirail]

Tourane, Mus. Cam
Tourane, Musée Cam [now Da-Nang, Cham Mus.]

Tourcoing, Mus. Mun. B.-A.
Tourcoing, Musée Municipal des Beaux-Arts

Tournai, Bib. Sémin. Episc.
Tournai, Bibliothèque du Séminaire Episcopal

Tournai, Bib. Ville
Tournai, Bibliothèque de la Ville

Tournai, Mus. B.-A.
Tournai, Musée des Beaux-Arts de Tournai

Tournai, Mus. Hist. & Archéol. & A. Déc.
Tournai, Musée d'Histoire et d'Archéologie et des Arts Décoratifs

Tournus, Mus. Bourguignon Perrin de Puycousin
Tournus, Musée Bourguignon Perrin de Puycousin

Tournus, Mus. Greuze
Tournus, Musée Greuze

Tours, Bib. Mun.
Tours, Bibliothèque Municipale

Tours, Cent. Etud. Sup. Ren.
Tours, Centre d'Etudes Supérieures de la Renaissance

Tours, Ecole Rég. B.A.
Tours, Ecole Régionale des Beaux-Arts

Tours, Mus. B.-A.
Tours, Musée des Beaux-Arts

Townsville, Perc Tucker Reg. Gal.
Townsville, Perc Tucker Regional Gallery

Toyama, MOMA
Toyama, Museum of Modern Art

Toyama, Mun. Mus.
Toyama, Municipal Museum

Toyonaka, Open-Air Mus. Jap. Farmhouses
Toyonaka, Open-Air Museum of Japanese Farmhouses (Nihon Minka Shuraku Hakubutsukan)

Trabzon, St Sophia Mus.
Trabzon, St Sophia Museum

Trani, Mus. Dioc.
Trani, Museo Diocesano

Trapani, Mus. Reg.
Trapani, Museo Regionale Pepoli

Trausnitz, Schloss
Trausnitz, Schloss Trausnitz

Trautenfels, Schloss
Trautenfels, Schloss Trautenfels

Třebenice, Mus. Czech Garnet
Třebenice, Museum of the Czech Garnet (Muzeum Českého Granátu)

Třeboň, State Archvs
Třeboň, State Archives

Tréguier, Maison Natale Ernest Renan
Tréguier, Maison Natale d'Ernest Renan

Tremezzo, Villa Carlotta

Trent, Bib. Com.
Trent, Biblioteca Comunale

Trent, Cassa di Risparmio

Trent, Castello Buonconsiglio [houses Mus. Prov. A.]

Trent, Mus. A. Mod. & Contemp. Trento & Rovereto
Trent, Museo d'Arte Moderna e Contemporanea di Trento e Rovereto [in Pal. Albere]

Trent, Mus. Dioc.
Trent, Museo Diocesano

Trent, Mus. Prov. A.
Trent, Museo Provinciale d'Arte [Antica, Medievale, Moderna e Contemporanea]

Trent, Pal. Albere
Trent, Palazzo delle Albere [houses Mus. A. Mod. & Contemp. Trento & Rovereto]

Trent, Pal. Altere
Trent, Palazzo Altere

Trent, Pal. Galasso
Trent, Palazzo Galasso [formerly Palazzo Fugger]

Trenton, NJ State Mus.
Trenton, NJ, New Jersey State Museum

Tres Zapotes, Mus.
Tres Zapotes, Museum

Treviso, Bib. Capitolare
Treviso, Biblioteca Capitolare

Treviso, Bib. Com.
Treviso, Biblioteca Comunale

Treviso, Mus. Civ. Bailo
Treviso, Museo Civico Luigi Bailo

Treviso, Pal. Trecento
Treviso, Palazzo dei Trecento

Trezzo sull'Adda, Pal. Com.
Trezzo sull'Adda, Palazzo Comunale

Trichur, Archaeol. Mus. & Pict. Gal.
Trichur, Archaeological Museum and Picture Gallery

Trichur, State Mus. & Zoo
Trichur, State Museum and Zoo

Trient: see Trent

Trier, Bischöf. Dom- & Diözmus.
Trier, Bischöfliches Dom- und Diözesanmuseum

Trier, Bistumsarchv
Trier, Bistumsarchiv

Trier, Domschatz

Trier, Rhein. Landesmus.
Trier, Rheinisches Landesmuseum

Trier, Stadtbib.
Trier, Stadtbibliothek

Trier, Städt. Mus.
Trier, Städtisches Museum

Trieste, Castello S Giusto
Trieste, Castello S Giusto [Museo Civico di Castello S Giusto]

Trieste, Civ. Mus. Risiera S Sabba
Trieste, Civico Museo della Risiera di S Sabba

Trieste, Civ. Mus. Risorgimento
Trieste, Civico Museo del Risorgimento e Sacrario Oberdan

Trieste, Civ. Mus. Teat.
Trieste, Civico Museo Teatrale di Fondazione Carlo Schmidl

Trieste, Mus. Civ. Revoltella
Trieste, Museo Civico Revoltella, Galleria d'Arte Moderna

Trieste, Mus. Civ. Sartorio
Trieste, Museo Civico Sartorio

Trieste, Mus. Civ. Stor. & A.
Trieste, Museo Civico di Storia ed Arte ed
Orto Lapidario

Trieste, Mus. Civ. Stor. Patria
Trieste, Musei Civici di Storia Patria

Trieste, Musei Civ. Stor. & A.
Trieste, Musei Civici di Storia ed Arte [admins
Castello S Giusto; Civ. Mus. Risiera S Sabba;
Civ. Mus. Risorgimento; Civ. Mus. Teat.; Mus.
Civ. Sartorio; Mus. Civ. Stor. & A.; Mus. Civ.
Stor. Patria]

Trieste, Mus. Stor. Castello di Miramare
Trieste, Museo Storico del Castello di
Miramare

Trieste, San Spiridione

Trincomalee, Archaeol. Mus.
Trincomalee, Archaeological Museum

Trincomalee, Reg. Mus.
Trincomalee, Regional Museum

Trinidad, Paraguay, Mus. Mis.
Trinidad, Paraguay, Museo de Misión

Trindade, U. Fed. S Catarina, Mus. Antropol.
Trindade, Universidade Federal de S Catarina,
Museu de Antropologia

Tripoli, Archaeol. Mus.
Tripoli, Archaeological Museum

Tripoli, Dept Ant.
Tripoli, Department of Antiquities

Tripoli, Governor's Pal.
Tripoli, Governor's Palace

Trivandrum, Govt. Mus. A. & Nat. Hist.
Trivandrum, Government Museum of Art and
Natural History

Trivandrum, Sri Chitra A.G.
Trivandrum, Sri Chitra Art Gallery

Trnava, West Slovak Mus.
Trnava, West Slovak Museum
(Západoslovenské Múzeum)

Trogir, Mun. Mus.
Trogir, Municipal Museum of Trogir (Muzej
Grada Trogira)

Trois Ilets, Mus. Pagerie
Trois Ilets, Musée de la Pagerie [Martinique]

Tromsø Mus.
Tromsø, Tromsø Museum

Trondheim, Domkirkens Skulpsaml.
Trondheim, Domkirkens Skulptursamling

Trondheim, Erkebispegården

Trondheim, Kstforen.
Trondheim, Trondheims Kunstforening

Trondheim, Noerdenfjeld. Kunstindustrimus.
Trondheim, Noerdenfjeldske
Kunstindustrimuseum (Museum of Applied
Arts)

Trondheim, Trøndelag Flkmus.
Trondheim, Trøndelag Folkemuseum

Trondheim, Trøndelag Kstgal.
Trondheim, Trøndelag Kunstgalleri

Trondheim, U. Trondheim, Kon. Norske
Videnskabers Selskab Mus.
Trondheim, Universitet i Trondheim,
Kongelige Norske Videnskabers Selskab
Museum (Royal Norwegian Society of
Sciences and Letters)

Trondheim, U. Trondheim, Mus.
Trondheim, Universitet i Trondheim, Museum

Tropojë, Hist. Mus.
Tropojë, Historical Museum (Muzeu Historik)

Troy, Archaeol. Mus.
Troy, Archaeological Museum (Arkeoloji
Müzesi)

Troyes, Archvs Dépt. l'Aube
Troyes, Archives Départementales de l'Aube

Troyes, Bib. Mun.
Troyes, Bibliothèque Municipale

Troyes, Cent. Cult. Thibaud de Champagne
Troyes, Centre Culturel Thibaud de
Champagne

Troyes, Mus. A. Mod.
Troyes, Musée d'Art Moderne

Troyes, Mus. B.-A. & Archéol.
Troyes, Musée des Beaux-Arts et
d'Archéologie

Troyes, Mus. Hist. Troyes & Champagne
Troyes, Musée Historique de Troyes et de la
Champagne [in Hôtel de Vauluisant]

Troyes, Trésor Cathédrale
Troyes, Trésor de la Cathédrale

Trujillo, Inst. N. Cult.
Trujillo, Instituto Nacional de Cultura

Trujillo, Mus. Arqueol. U. Trujillo
Trujillo, Museo Arqueológico de la
Universidad de Trujillo

Trujillo, Mus. Hist.
Trujillo, Honduras, Museo Histórico

Truro, Co. Mus. & A.G.
Truro, County Museum and Art Gallery
[Royal Institution of Cornwall]

Tskhinvali, S. Ossetian Mus. A.
Tskhinvali, South Ossetian Museum of Art

Tsu, Mie Prefect. A. Mus.
Tsu, Mie Prefectural Art Museum (Mie
Kenritsu Hakubutsukan)

Tsuruoka, Chido Mus.
Tsuruoka, Chido Museum (Chido
Hakubutsukan)

Tübingen, Eberhard-Karls-U., Ägyp. Inst.
Tübingen, Eberhard-Karls-Universität
Tübingen, Ägyptologisches Institut

Tübingen, Eberhard-Karls-U., Antikensamml.
Tübingen, Eberhard-Karls-Universität
Tübingen, Antikensammlungen
[Antikenmuseum]

Tübingen, Eberhard-Karls-U., Samml. Inst. Vor-
& Frühgesch.
Tübingen, Eberhard-Karls-Universität
Tübingen, Sammlungen des Instituts für Vor-
und Frühgeschichte

Tübingen, Eberhard-Karls-U., Ubib.
Tübingen, Eberhard-Karls-Universität
Tübingen, Universitätsbibliothek

Tübingen, Ksthalle
Tübingen, Kunsthalle Tübingen

Tucson, AZ, Mus. A.
Tucson, AZ, Museum of Art

Tucson, AZ, State Mus.
Tucson, AZ, Arizona State Museum

Tucson, U. AZ, Cent. Creative Phot.
Tucson, AZ, University of Arizona, Center for
Creative Photography

Tucson, U. AZ Mus. A.
Tucson, AZ, University of Arizona Museum
of Art

Tudela, Archv Mun.
Tudela, Archivo Municipal de Tudela

Tukums, Mun. A.G.
Tukums, Municipal Art Gallery

Tula, A. Mus.
Tula, Tula Art Museum

Tulane, U. LA
Tulane, LA, Tulane University of Louisiana

Tulln, Egon Schiele Mus.
Tulln, Egon Schiele Museum

Tulsa, OK, Gilcrease Inst. Amer. Hist. & A.
Tulsa, OK, Thomas Gilcrease Institute of
American History and Art

Tulsa, OK, Gilcrease Mus.
Tulsa, OK, Gilcrease Museum

Tulsa, OK, Philbrook A. Cent.
Tulsa, OK, Philbrook Art Center

Tunis, Cent. A. Vivant
Tunis, Centre d'Art Vivant [Belvédère]

Tunis, Dar Othman Pal.
Tunis, Dar Othman Palace

Tunis, Ecole B.-A.
Tunis, Ecole des Beaux-Arts

Tunis, Inst. N. Archéol. & A.
Tunis, Institut National d'Archéologie et d'Art
[Conservation du Musée National du Bardo]

Tunis, Min. Affaires Cult.
Tunis, Ministère des Affaires Culturelles

Tunis, Mus. Alaoui
Tunis, Musée Alaoui

Tunis, Mus. N. Bardo
Tunis, Musée National du Bardo [Palais du
Bardo]

Tunja, Col. Padres Dominicanos
Tunja, Colección de los Padres Dominicanos

Tunja, Mus. Ecles. Colon.
Tunja, Museo Eclesiástico Colonial

Turfan, Mus.
Turfan, Turfan Museum

Turin, Accad. Albertina
Turin, Accademia Albertina di Belle Arti

Turin, Am. Reale
Turin, Ameria Reale

Turin, Archv Stato
Turin, Archivio di Stato di Torino

Turin, Bib. N. U.
Turin, Biblioteca Nazionale Universitaria

Turin, Bib. Poli.
Turin, Biblioteca del Politecnico di Torino

Turin, Bib. Reale
Turin, Biblioteca Reale di Torino

Turin, Borgo & Castello Med.
Turin, Borgo e Castello Medioevale

Turin, Cassa di Risparmio

Turin, Castello d'Agliè

Turin, Castello Rivoli

Turin, Christian Stein

Turin, Circ. Artisti
Turin, Circolo degli Artisti

Turin, Circ. Ufficiale
Turin, Circolo Ufficiale

Turin, Fond. Agnelli
Turin, Fondazione Agnelli

Turin, Gal. A. Mod. Viotti
Turin, Galleria d'Arte Moderna Viotti

Turin, Gal. Civ. A. Mod.
Turin, Galleria Civica d'Arte Moderna e
Contemporanea

Turin, Gal. Galatea
Turin, Galleria Galatea

Turin, Gal. Gazzetta Popolo
Turin, Galleria Gazzetta del Popolo

Turin, Gal. Narciso
Turin, Galleria Narciso

Turin, Gal. Punto
  Turin, Galleria Il Punto

Turin, Gal. Sabauda
  Turin, Galleria Sabauda

Turin, Gal. Sperone
  Turin, Galleria Sperone

Turin, Int. Cent. Aesth.
  Turin, International Centre of Aesthetics

Turin, Mole Antonelliana

Turin, Mus. Ant.
  Turin, Museo di Antichità

Turin, Mus. Civ.
  Turin, Museo Civico di Torino [admins Borgo
  & Castello Med.; Gal. Civ. A. Mod.; Mus. Civ.
  A. Ant.; Mus. Micca]

Turin, Mus. Civ. A. Ant.
  Turin, Museo Civico d'Arte Antica

Turin, Mus. Egizio
  Turin, Museo Egizio di Torino

Turin, Mus. Geol. & Paleontol. U. Stud.
  Turin, Museo di Geologia e Paleontologia
  dell'Università degli Studi

Turin, Mus. Lapidario
  Turin, Museo Lapidario

Turin, Mus. Micca
  Turin, Museo Pietro Micca e dell'Assedio di
  Torino del 1706

Turin, Mus. N. Montagna
  Turin, Museo Nazionale della Montagna
  [Duca degli Abruzzi]

Turin, Mus. N. Ris. It.
  Turin, Museo Nazionale del Risorgimento
  Italiano

Turin, Pal. Arnaboldi
  Turin, Palazzo Arnaboldi

Turin, Pal. a Vela
  Turin, Palazzo a Vela

Turin, Pal. Chiablese
  Turin, Palazzo Chiablese

Turin, Pal. Glicini
  Turin, Palazzina delle Glicini [houses Promot.
  B.A.]

Turin, Pal. Graneri
  Turin, Palazzo Graneri

Turin, Pal. Madama
  Turin, Palazzo Madama

Turin, Pal. Reale
  Turin, Palazzo Reale

Turin, Pin. Civ. Giulianova
  Turin, Pinacoteca Civica di Giulianova

Turin, Promot. B.A.
  Turin, Promotrice Belle Arti

Turin, Salone La Stampa
  Turin, Salone de La Stampa

Turin, U. Studi
  Turin, Università degli Studi

Türkheim, Sieben-Schwaben-Mus.
  Türkheim, Sieben-Schwaben-Museum
  [formerly Herzogliches Schloss]

Turku, Aaltonen Mus.
  Turku, Wäinö Aaltonen Museum (Wäinö
  Aaltonen Museo)

Turku, A. Mus.
  Turku, Art Museum (Taidemuseo)

Turku, Hist. Mus.
  Turku, City Historical Museum (Kaupungin
  Historiallinen Museo) [Turku Castle and
  Museum]

Turku, Koivurinta Found.
  Turku, Matti Koivurinta Foundation

Turku, Prov. Mus.
  Turku, Provincial Museum (Turun
  Maakuntamuseo)

Tuscaloosa, AL, Warner Col., Gulf States Paper
Corp.
  Tuscaloosa, AL, Warner Collection, Gulf
  States Paper Corporation

Tuxpan, Mus. Reg.
  Tuxpan, Museo Regional de Tuxpan

Tuxtla Gutiérrez, Mus. Reg. Antropol. & Hist.
  Tuxtla Gutiérrez, Museo Regional de
  Antropología e Historia

Tver', Reg. Local Hist. Mus.
  Tver', Regional Local History Museum
  (Oblastnoy Krayevedcheskiy Muzey)

Tver', Reg. Pict. Gal.
  Tver', Regional Picture Gallery (Oblastnaya
  Kartinnaya Gallereya)

Tyresö Slott
  Tyresö, Tyresö Slott

Ubud, Ratna Wartha F.A. Museum
  Ubud, Ratna Wartha Fine Art Museum
  (Museum Puri Lukisan Ratna Wartha)

Uccle, Cerc. Uccle, Cent. A.
  Uccle, Cercle Uccle, Centre d'Art

Udaipur, Batik A. Res. Training Cent.
  Udaipur, Batik Art Research Training Centre

Udaipur, Bharatya Lok Kala Mus.
  Udaipur, Bharatya Lok Kala Museum [Folk
  Art Museum]

Udaipur, City Pal. Mus.
  Udaipur, City Palace Museum [Pratap
  Museum]

Udaipur, Govt Mus.
  Udaipur, Government Museum

Udaipur, Rajasthan Orient. Res. Inst.
  Udaipur, Rajasthan Oriental Research Institute

Udaipur, Sarasvati Bhavan Lib.
  Udaipur, Sarasvati Bhavan Library

Uddevalla, Bohusläns Mus.
  Uddevalla, Bohusläns Museum

Uden, Mus. Relig. Kst
  Uden, Museum voor Religieuze Kunst

Udine, Archv Capitolare
  Udine, Archivio Capitolare

Udine, Castello, Salone Parlamento
  Udine, Castello, Salone del Parlamento

Udine, Gal. A. Ant. & Mod.
  Udine, Galleria d'Arte Antica e d'Arte
  Moderna [in castle]

Udine, Mus. Città
  Udine, Museo della Città

Udine, Mus. Civ.
  Udine, Museo Civico [in castle]

Udine, Mus. Dioc. A. Sacra
  Udine, Museo Diocesano di Arte Sacra

Udine, Mus. Risorgimento
  Udine, Museo del Risorgimento [in castle]

Udine, Pal. Arcivescovile
  Udine, Palazzo Arcivescovile

Udine, Sala Aiace Com.
  Udine, Sala Aiace del Comune

Udine, Sopr.
  Udine, Soprintendenza

Udine, Villa Manin Passariano
  Udine, Villa Manin di Passariano

Ufa, Bashkirian A. Mus.
  Ufa, Bashkirian Art Museum (Bashkirskiy
  Khudozhestvennyy Muzey)

Ufa, Reg. Mus.
  Ufa, Regional Museum (Respublikanskiy
  Krayevedcheskiy Muzey Baskortostana)

Uglich, Hist. Mus.
  Uglich, Historical Museum (Istoricheskiy
  Muzey)

Uji, Byōdōin

Uji, Manpukuji

Ujjain, Dist. Archaeol. Mus.
  Ujjain, District Archaeological Museum

Ujjain, Vikram U., Vikram Kirti Mandir Mus.
  Ujjain, Vikram University, Vikram Kirti
  Mandir Museum

Ulaan Baatar, Acad. Sci.
  Ulaan Baatar, Academy of Sciences

Ulaan Baatar, Cent. Lib.
  Ulaan Baatar, Central Library

Ulaan Baatar, Cent. Mus.
  Ulaan Baatar, Central Museum

Ulaan Baatar, Fund Precious Metals & Depository
  Ulaan Baatar, Fund of Precious Metals and
  Depository

Ulaan Baatar, Mus. F.A.
  Ulaan Baatar, Museum of Fine Art

Ulaan Baatar, Mus. Relig.
  Ulaan Baatar, Museum of Religion [in Chayjin
  Lamyn Hüree]

Ulaan Baatar, Pal. Mus.
  Ulaan Baatar, Palace Museum [palace of Bogd
  Khan]

Ulaangom, Mus.
  Ulaangom, Ulaangom Museum

Ulan Ude, Ethnog. Mus.
  Ulan Ude, Ethnographic Museum
  (Etnograficheskiy muzey)

Ulan Ude, Mus. Buryat Hist. & Orient. A.
  Ulan Ude, Museum of Buryat History and
  Oriental Art (Muzey Buryatskoy Istorii i
  Vostochnogo)

Ulcinj, Mus. Ulcinj
  Ulcinj, Muzej UlcinjUlm, Evangel. Gesamt-
  Kirchgemein.
  Ulm, Evangelische Gesamt-Kirchengemeinde

Ulm, Hochsch. Gestalt.
  Ulm, Hochschule für Gestaltung

Ulm, Stadtarchv
  Ulm, Stadtarchiv

Ulm, Stadtbib.
  Ulm, Stadtbibliothek

Ulm, Ulm. Mus.
  Ulm, Ulmer Museum [Museum der Stadt Ulm]

Ulriksdal, nr Stockholm, Orangerie Mus.
  Ulriksdal, nr Stockholm, Orangerie Museum

Ulriksdal, Slott

Ul'yanovsk, Goncharov Reg. Mus.
  Ul'yanovsk, Goncharov Regional Museum
  (Ul'yanovskiy Oblastnoy Krayevedcheskiy
  Muzey Imeni I. A. Goncharova)

University Park, PA State U.
  University Park, PA, Pennsylvania State
  University

University Park, PA State U., Mus. A.
  University Park, PA, Pennsylvania State
  University, Museum of Art [name changed to
  Palmer Mus. A. in 1989]

University Park, PA State U., Palmer Mus. A.
  University Park, PA, Pennsylvania State
  University, Palmer Museum of Art [formerly
  PA State U., Mus. A.]

Unna, Hellweg-Mus.
    Unna, Hellweg-Museum

Upplands, Krusenberg Slot [owned by Pharmacia Co.]

Upplands, Leufsta Slot

Uppsala, Mus. Nordiska Fornsaker
    Uppsala, Museum för Nordiska Fornsaker

Uppsala U.
    Uppsala, Uppsala Universitet

Uppsala Ubib.
    Uppsala, Uppsala Universitetsbibliothek

Uppsala, U. Kstsaml.
    Uppsala, Universitet Konstsamling

Uppsala U., Västmalands-Dala
    Uppsala, Uppsala Universitet, Västmalands-Dala

Urasoe City, Urasoe A. Mus.
    Urasoe City, Urasoe Art Museum

Ura Tyube, Hist. & Reg. Mus.
    Ura Tyube, Ura Tyube Historical and Regional Museum

Urawa, Saitama Prefect., Mus. Mod. A.
    Urawa, Saitama Prefecture, Museum of Modern Art (Saitama Kenritsu Bijutsukan)

Urbana, U. IL
    Urbana, IL, University of Illinois

Urbana, U. IL, Krannert A. Mus.
    Urbana, IL, University of Illinois, Krannert Art Museum

Urbino, Bib. U.
    Urbino, Biblioteca Universitaria

Urbino, Mus. Duomo
    Urbino, Museo del Duomo [Museo Albani del Duomo]

Urbino, Mus. Lapidario
    Urbino, Musco Lapidario

Urbino, Pal. Ducale
    Urbino, Palazzo Ducale [houses Galleria Nazionale delle Marche]

Urbino, Pal. Municipale
    Urbino, Palazzo Municipale

Urbino, Sopr. Beni A. & Stor. Marche
    Urbino, Soprintendenza per i Beni Artistici e Storici delle Marche

Urumqi, Mus. Xinjiang Ugur Auton. Reg.
    Urumqi, Museum of the Xinjiang Ugur Autonomous Region

Uşak Mus.
    Uşak, Uşak Museum

U Thong, N. Mus.
    U Thong, U Thong National Museum

Utica, NY, Mason. Sailors & Soldiers Hosp.
    Utica, NY, Masonic Sailors and Soldiers Hospital

Utica, NY, Munson–Williams–Proctor Inst.
    Utica, NY, Munson–Williams–Proctor Institute

Utne, Hardanger Flkmus.
    Utne, Hardanger Folkemuseum

Utrecht, Aartsbisschoppelijk Mus.
    Utrecht, Aartsbisschoppelijk Museum [col. transferred to Catharijneconvent in 1976]

Utrecht, Bib. Rijksuniv.
    Utrecht, Bibliotheek der Rijksuniversiteit

Utrecht, Catharijneconvent
    Utrecht, Rijksmuseum Het Catharijneconvent [houses col. of former Aartsbisschoppelijk Mus.]

Utrecht, Cent. Mus.
    Utrecht, Centraal Museum

Utrecht, Gemeente Archf
    Utrecht, Gemeente Archief

Utrecht, Iconol. Inst.
    Utrecht, Iconologisch Institut

Utrecht, Mus. Mod. Relig. Kst
    Utrecht, Museum voor Moderne Religieuze Kunst

Utrecht, Ned. Goud-, Zilver- en Klokkenmus.
    Utrecht, Nederlands Goud-, Zilver- en Klokkenmuseum [now in Schoonhoven]

Utrecht, Rijksuniv. Utrecht
    Utrecht, Rijksuniversiteit te Utrecht

Utrecht, Rijksuniv. Utrecht, Ksthist. Inst.
    Utrecht, Rijksuniversiteit te Utrecht, Kunsthistorisch Institute

Utrecht, Rijksuniv. Utrecht, Umus.
    Utrecht, Rijksuniversiteit te Utrecht, Universiteitsmuseum

Uzhgorod, Mus. A.
    Uzhgorod, Museum of Art (Khudozhestvennyy Muzey)

Uzhgorod, Transcarpath. Mus. Flk Archit. & Life
    Uzhgorod, Transcarpathian Museum of Folk Architecture and Life

Uzhgorod, Transcarpath. Reg. Mus.
    Uzhgorod, Transcarpathian Regional Museum

Vaasa, Pohjanmaan Mus.
    Vaasa, Pohjanmaan Museum (Pohjanmaan Museo) [Mus. of Ostrobothnia]

Vác, Vak Bottyán Mus.
    Vác, Vak Bottyán Museum (Vak Bottyán Múzeum Kiállyotóhelye)

Vadodara, Maharaja Fateh Singh Mus.
    Vadodara, Maharaja Fateh Singh Museum

Vadodara, Maharaja Sayajirao U.
    Vadodara, Maharaja Sayajirao University

Vadodara, Maharaja Sayajirao U., Orient. Inst.
    Vadodara, Maharaja Sayajirao University, Oriental Institute

Vadodara, Mus. & Pict. Gal.
    Vadodara, Museum and Picture Gallery

Vaduz, Cent. A.
    Vaduz, Centro de Arte

Vaduz, Samml. Liechtenstein
    Vaduz, Sammlungen der Fürsten von Liechtenstein

Vaishali Mus.
    Vaishali, Vaishali Museum

Vaison-la-Romaine, Mus. Archéol.
    Vaison-la-Romaine, Musée Archéologique

Val-de-Vesle, Cent. Création Contemp.
    Val-de-Vesle, Centre de Création Contemporaine

Valence, Mus.
    Valence, Musée de Valence

Valence, Mus. B.-A. & Hist. Nat.
    Valence, Musée des Beaux-Arts et d'Histoire Naturelle

Valencia, Archv Catedral
    Valencia, Archivo de la Catedral

Valencia, Archv Reino
    Valencia, Archivo del Reino de Valencia

Valencia, Ayuntamiento [houses Mus. Palaeontol. Mun.]

Valencia, Banco de Santander

Valencia, Casa-Mus. Benllivre
    Valencia, Casa-Museo Benllivre

Valencia, Casa-Mus. Mondella
    Valencia, Casa-Museo de Mondella

Valencia, Colegio del Patriarca
    Valencia, Colegio del Patriarca [Colegio del Corpus Christi]

Valencia, Corpus Christi
    Valencia, Corpus Christi [Church of Colegio del Patriarca]

Valencia, Diputación Prov.
    Valencia, Diputación Provincial

Valencia, Escuela Sup. B.A. S Carlos
    Valencia, Escuela Superior de Bellas Artes de S Carlos

Valencia, Generalidad

Valencia, Inst. Ephialte
    Valencia, Instituto Ephialte

Valencia, IVAM Cent. Carme
    Valencia, IVAM Centre Carme [Instituto Valenciano de Arte Moderno]

Valencia, IVAM Cent. Julio González
    Valencia, IVAM Centre Julio González

Valencia, Lonja Seda
    Valencia, Lonja de la Seda

Valencia, Mus. B.A.
    Valencia, Museo de Bellas Artes [Museo Provincial de Bellas Artes; Museo de San Pio V]

Valencia, Mus. Catedralicio-Dioc.
    Valencia, Museo Catedralicio-Diocesano

Valencia, Mus. Hist.
    Valencia, Museo Histórico de la Ciudad [in Palacio del Marqués de Campo]

Valencia, Mus. N. Cer. & A. Suntuarias
    Valencia, Museo Nacional de Cerámica y de las Artes Suntuarias González Marti

Valencia, Mus. Palaeontol. Mun.
    Valencia, Museo Palaeontológico Municipal [in Ayuntamiento]

Valencia, Mus. Patriarca
    Valencia, Museo del Patriarca

Valencia, Real Acad. B.A. S Carlos
    Valencia, Real Academia de Bellas Artes de S Carlos

Valencia, Salón Int. A. Medit.
    Valencia, Salón Internacional de Arte del Mediterráneo

Valencia, U. Poly.
    Valencia, Universitat Polytècnica de València

Valencia, U. Valencia
    Valencia, Universitat de València

Valencia, U. Valencia, Bib.
    Valencia, Universitat de València, Biblioteca

Valencia, U. Valencia, Fac. Teol.
    Valencia, Universitat de València, Facultat de Teologia

Valencia, CA, Inst. A.
    Valencia, CA, Institute of the Arts

Valenciennes, Acad.
    Valenciennes, Académie

Valenciennes, Bib. Mun.
    Valenciennes, Bibliothèque Municipale

Valenciennes, Hôtel de Ville

Valenciennes, Mus. B.-A.
    Valenciennes, Musée des Beaux-Arts

Valenciennes, Mus. Crauk
    Valenciennes, Musée Crauk [col. now in Mus. B.-A.]

Valkenberg, Ignatius Koll.
    Valkenberg, Ignatius Kolleg

Valladolid, Casa Cervantes
    Valladolid, Casa de Cervantes [Fundaciones Vega–Inclán]

Valladolid, Casa Marqués de Villena
  Valladolid, Casa del Marqués de Villena

Valladolid, Colegio Augustinos, Mus. Phil. Miss.
  Valladolid, Colegio de Augustinos, Museum of
  the Philippine Mission

Valladolid, Colegio S Cruz
  Valladolid, Colegio Santa Cruz

Valladolid, Consejería Educ. & Cult. Junta Castilla
  & León
  Valladolid, La Consejería de Educación y
  Cultura de la Junta de Castilla y León

Valladolid, Hosp. Gen.
  Valladolid, Hospital General

Valladolid, Mus. Arqueol.
  Valladolid, Museo Arqueológico

Valladolid, Mus. Dioc. & Catedralicio
  Valladolid, Museo Diocesano y Catedralicio

Valladolid, Mus. N. Escul.
  Valladolid, Museo Nacional de Escultura

Valladolid, Mus. Pasión
  Valladolid, Museo de la Pasión

Valladolid, Mus. Phil. Mission
  Valladolid, Museum of the Philippine Mission

Valladolid, Mus. Pint.
  Valladolid, Museo de Pintura [in Iglesia de la
  Pasión]

Valladolid, Pal. S Cruz
  Valladolid, Palacio S Cruz

Valladolid, Santuario N. Gran Promesa
  Valladolid, Santuario Nacional de la Gran
  Promesa

Valladolid, Sección Pint.
  Valladolid, Sección de Pintura [Museo
  Nacional de Escultura]

Valladolid, U. Valladolid
  Valladolid, Universidad de Valladolid

Vallauris, Mus. N. Picasso
  Vallauris, Musée National Pablo Picasso

Valletta, Fort St Elmo [HQ of Malta Land Force;
  houses War Mus.]

Valletta, Fort St Elmo, War Mus.
  Valletta, Fort St Elmo, War Museum

Valletta, Mus. F.A.
  Valletta, Museum of Fine Arts

Valletta, N. Lib.
  Valletta, National Library [houses archvs of
  Order of St John of Jerusalem]

Valletta, N. Mus.
  Valletta, National Museum of Malta, Auberge
  de Provence

Valletta, N. Mus. Archaeol.
  Valletta, National Museum of Archaeology

Valletta, Pal. Grand Masters
  Valletta, Palace of the Grand Masters [houses
  Palace Armoury]

Valletta, St John's Mus.
  Valletta, St John's Museum

Vallo della Lucania, Mus. Dioc.
  Vallo della Lucania, Museo Diocesano

Valparaíso, Mus. Mun. B.A.
  Valparaíso, Museo Municipal de Bellas Artes

Valparaíso, Pal. Rioja
  Valparaíso, Palacio La Rioja

Vancouver, A.G.
  Vancouver, BC, Vancouver Art Gallery

Vancouver, BC Transit Centen. Mus.
  Vancouver, British Columbia Transit
  Centennial Museum

Vancouver Mus.
  Vancouver, BC, Vancouver Museum [formerly
  BC Transit Centen. Mus.]

Vancouver, Police Centen. Mus.
  Vancouver, BC, Vancouver Police Centennial
  Museum

Vancouver, U. BC, Archaeol. Mus.
  Vancouver, University of British Columbia,
  Archaeology Museum

Vancouver, U. BC, F.A. Gal.
  Vancouver, University of British Columbia,
  Fine Arts Gallery

Vancouver, U. BC Lib.
  Vancouver, University of British Columbia
  Library

Vancouver, U. BC, Mus. Anthropol.
  Vancouver, University of British Columbia,
  Museum of Anthropology

Vancouver, U. BC, Students' Un.
  Vancouver, University of British Columbia,
  Students' Union

Varallo Sésia: see Varallo

Varallo, Archv. Stato
  Varallo, Archivio di Stato

Varallo, Bib. Civ.
  Varallo, Biblioteca Civica

Varallo, Mus. Civ. Pietro Calderini
  Varallo, Museo Civico Pietro Calderini

Varallo, Pin.
  Varallo, Pinacoteca

Varanasi, Amer. Inst. Ind. Stud.
  Varanasi, American Institute of Indian Studies

Varanasi, Banaras Hindu U., Bharat Kala Bhavan
  Varanasi, Banaras Hindu University, Bharat
  Kala Bhavan

Varberg Mus.
  Varberg, Varberg Museum

Varese, Mus. Baroffio
  Varese, Museo Baroffio

Varese, Mus. Civ. Villa Mirabello
  Varese, Musei Civici di Villa Mirabello

Varese, Mus. S Maria del Monte
  Varese, Museo di S Maria del Monte [in
  monastery]

Varna, Archaeol. Mus.
  Varna, Archaeological Museum
  (Archaeologičeski Muzej)

Varna, Hist. & A. Mus.
  Varna, History and Art Museum (Istoriko-
  Hudozhestren Muzej)

Varna, Reg. Mus. Hist.
  Varna, Regional Museum of History (Okrǎžen
  Istoričeski Muzej)

Varzy, Mus. Mun.
  Varzy, Nièvre, Musée Municipal de Varzy

Västerås Kstmus.
  Västerås, Västerås Konstmuseum

Vasto, Mus. & Pin. Civ.
  Vasto, Museo e Pinacoteca Civici

Vathy, Archaeol. Mus.
  Vathy, Archaeological Museum

Växjö, Smålands Mus.
  Växjö, Smålands Museum [housed with Växjö
  Glasmuseum and Sydsvenska Skogsmuseum]

Vejle, Kstmus.
  Vejle, Kunstmuseum

Velbert, Städt. Museen, Schloss Hardenberg
  Velbert, Städtische Museen, Schloss
  Hardenberg

Veliky Ustyug, Local Hist. Mus.
  Veliky Ustyug, Local History Museum
  (Krayevedcheskiy Muzey)

Velletri, Mus. Capitolare
  Velletri, Museo Capitolare

Velletri, Mus. Civ.
  Velletri, Museo Civico di Velletri

Veltrusy Castle
  Veltrusy, Veltrusy Castle

Vence, Gal. Alphonse Chave
  Vence, Galerie Alphonse Chave

Vence, Gal. Pierre Chave
  Vence, Galerie Pierre Chave

Vence, Michael Karolyi Mem. Found.
  Vence, Michael Karolyi Memorial Foundation

Venegono Inferiore, Semin. Arcivescovile
  Venegono Inferiore, Seminario Arcivescovile
  [di Milano]

Venezia Mestre, Gal. Meneghini
  Venezia Mestre, Galleria Meneghini

Venice, Accad.
  Venice, Galleria dell'Accademia

Venice, Accad. Pitt. & Scul.
  Venice, Accademia di Pittura e Scultura [18th
  C. acad.; in Fontegheto della Farina]

Venice, Ala Napoleonica

Venice, Archv Stato
  Venice, Archivio di Stato [in convent bldgs of
  S Maria Gloriosa dei Frari]

Venice, Archv Stor. A. Contemp.
  Venice, Archivio Storico dell'Arti
  Contemporanee [della Biennale di Venezia]

Venice, Armen. Monastery
  Venice, Armenian Monastery

Venice, Arsenale [Darsena Arsenale Vecchio;
  Darsena Arsenale Nuovo; Darsena Arsenale
  Nuovissimo]

Venice, Ateneo Veneto

Venice, Bib. Correr
  Venice, Biblioteca del Civico Museo Correr

Venice, Bib. N. Marciana
  Venice, Biblioteca Nazionale Marciana [in
  Palazzi della Libreria Vecchia e della Zecca]

Venice, Biennale
  Venice, Biennale Internazionale d'Arte

Venice, Ca' d'Oro [houses Galleria Giorgio
  Franchetti]

Venice, Ca' Foscari

Venice, Ca' Giustiniani

Venice, Ca' Pesaro [houses Galleria Internazionale
  d'Arte Moderna; Museo Orientale]

Venice, Ca' Rezzonico

Venice, Casa Goldoni
  Venice, Casa di Goldoni [Museo Teatrale ed
  Istituto di Studi Teatrali; also houses archv]

Venice, Casa Tre Oci

Venice, Civ. Musei A. & Stor.
  Venice, Civici Musei Veneziani d'Arte e di
  Storia [admins Accad.; Ca' d'Oro; Ca' Pesaro;
  Ca' Rezzonico; Casa Goldoni; Correr; Doge's
  Pal.; Gab. Stampe & Disegni; Gal. Querini-
  Stampalia; Guggenheim; Mus. Archeol.; Mus.
  Civ. Stor. Nat.; Mus. Vetrario Murano; Pal.
  Mocegino; Pin. Manfrediana]

Venice, Col. Cini
  Venice, Collezione Cini

Venice, Col. Coin
  Venice, Collezione Coin

Venice, Correr
  Venice, Museo Correr

Venice, Doge's Pal.
   Venice, Doge's Palace [Palazzo Ducale]

Venice, Donà delle Rose
   Venice, Collezione Donà delle Rose

Venice, Espos. Int. A.
   Venice, Esposizione Internazionale d'Arte

Venice, Fond. Cini
   Venice, Fondazione Giorgio Cini, Istituto di
   Storia dell'Arte [Isola di S Giorgio Maggiore]

Venice, Fond. Cini, Bib.
   Venice, Fondazione Giorgio Cini, Istituto di
   Storia dell'Arte, Biblioteca

Venice, Fond. Querini–Stampalia
   Venice, Fondazione Querini–Stampalia

Venice, Fontegheto Farina
   Venice, Fonteghetto della Farina

Venice, Frari
   Venice, Santa Maria Gloriosa dei Frari

Venice, Gab. Stampe & Dis.
   Venice, Gabinetto di Stampe e Disegni

Venice, Gal. Alphonse Chave
   Venice, Galleria Alphonse Chave

Venice, Gal. Cavallino
   Venice, Galleria Cavallino

Venice, Gal. Farsetti
   Venice, Galleria Farsetti

Venice, Gal. Geri–Boralevi
   Venice, Galleria Geri–Boralevi

Venice, Gal. Querini–Stampalia
   Venice, Galleria Querini–Stampalia
   [Pinacoteca Querini–Stampalia]

Venice, Guggenheim
   Venice, Peggy Guggenheim Collection

Venice, Ist. Ellenico Stud. Biz. & Postbiz.
   Venice, Istituto Ellenico di Studi Bizantini e
   Postbizantini di Venezia

Venice, Ist. U. Archit.
   Venice, Istituto Universitario di Architettura

Venice, Lib. Marciana
   Venice, Libreria Marciana

Venice, Mus. A. Orient.
   Venice, Museo d'Arte Orientale Marco Polo

Venice, Mus. Archeol.
   Venice, Museo Archeologico

Venice, Mus. Civ. Stor. Nat.
   Venice, Museo Civico di Storia Naturale di
   Venezia

Venice, Mus. Com. Isr.
   Venice, Museo della Comunità Israelitica

Venice, Mus. Dioc. S Apollonia
   Venice, Museo Diocesano d'Arte Sacra,
   S Apollonia

Venice, Mus. Fortuny
   Venice, Museo Fortuny [in Palazzo Fortuny]

Venice, Mus. Merletto Burano
   Venice, Museo del Merletto di Burano

Venice, Mus. Opera Pal.
   Venice, Museo dell'Opera del Palazzo [in
   Doge's Pal.]

Venice, Mus. Risorgimento
   Venice, Museo del Risorgimento e
   dell'Ottocento Veneziano

Venice, Mus. S Marco
   Venice, Museo di San Marco

Venice, Mus. Stor. Navale
   Venice, Museo Storico Navale

Venice, Mus. Vetrario Murano
   Venice, Museo Vetrario di Murano

Venice, Osp. Civ.
   Venice, Ospedale Civile

Venice, Pal. Albrizzi
   Venice, Palazzo Albrizzi

Venice, Pal. Com.
   Venice, Palazzo Comunale

Venice, Pal. Contarini Dal Zaffo
   Venice, Palazzo Contarini Dal Zaffo

Venice, Pal. Grassi
   Venice, Palazzo Grassi

Venice, Pal. Labia
   Venice, Palazzo Labia

Venice, Pal. Mocenigo
   Venice, Palazzo Mocenigo

Venice, Pal. Pisani–Moretta
   Venice, Palazzo Pisani–Moretta

Venice, Pal. Pesaro
   Venice, Palazzo Pesaro

Venice, Pal. Ruzzini–Priuli, S Maria Formosa
   Venice, Palazzo Ruzzini–Priuli, S Maria
   Formosa [Palazzo Priuli, S Maria Formosa]

Venice, Pal. Sagredo
   Venice, Palazzo Sagredo

Venice, Pal. Vendramin–Calegri
   Venice, Palazzo Vendramin–Calegri

Venice, Pin. Manfrediniana
   Venice, Pinacoteca Manfrediniana e Raccolte
   del Seminario Patriarcale

Venice, Ridotto Procuratoressa Venier
   Venice, Ridotto della Procuratoressa Venier

Venice, Scu. Angelo Custode
   Venice, Scuola dell'Angelo Custode [now
   Lutheran Evangel. Church]

Venice, Scu. Grande Carmini
   Venice, Scuola Grande dei Carmini [di S Maria
   del Carmelo]

Venice, Scu. Grande S Giovanni Evangelista
   Venice, Scuola Grande di S Giovanni
   Evangelista

Venice, Scu. Grande S Rocco
   Venice, Scuola Grande di S Rocco

Venice, Scu. Grande S Teodoro
   Venice, Scuola Grande di S Teodoro

Venice, Scu. Merletto Burano
   Venice, Scuola del Merletto di Burano

Venice, Scu. S Giorgio degli Schiavoni
   Venice, Scuola S Giorgio degli Schiavoni

Venice, Scu. S Stefano
   Venice, Scuola di S Stefano

Venice, Semin. Patriarcale
   Venice, Seminario Patriarcale

Venice, Semin. Patriarcale, Bib.
   Venice, Seminario Patriarcale, Biblioteca

Venice, S Lazzaro degli Armeni, Bib.
   Venice, S Lazzaro degli Armeni, Biblioteca
   [Biblioteca dell'Accademia Armena di
   S Lazzaro dei Padri Mechitaristi (Library of the
   Mekhitharists)]

Venice, Sopr. Beni A.
   Venice, Soprintendenza di Beni Artistici

Venice, S Stae [S Eustachio, Grand Canal]

Venice, Teat. La Fenice
   Venice, Teatro La Fenice

Venice, Tesoro S Marco
   Venice, Tesoro di San Marco

Venice, CA, Soc. & Pub. A. Resource Cent.
   Venice, CA, Social & Public Art Resource
   Center

Venlo, Mus. van Bommel–van Dam
   Venlo, Museum van Bommel–van Dam

Venosa, Pal. S Gervasio
   Venosa, Palazzo San Gervasio

Ventiane, Mus. Relig. A.
   Ventiane, Museum of Religious Art (Ho Phra
   Keo)

Veracruz, Mus. Reg.
   Veracruz, Museo Regional

Verbania, Mus. Paesaggio
   Verbania, Museo del Paesaggio

Vercelli, Mus. Civ. Borgogna
   Vercelli, Museo Civico Borgogna

Verdun, Mus. Princerie
   Verdun, Musée de la Princerie

Vergara: see Bergara

Veria, Archaeol. Mus.
   Veria, Archaeological Museum

Vernon, Mus. Mun. Poulain
   Vernon, Musée Municipal A. G. Poulain

Veroia, Archaeol. Mus.
   Veroia, Archaeological Museum

Veroia, Archv Stato
   Veroia, Archivio di Stato

Verona, Accad. Cignaroli
   Verona, Accademia Cignaroli [di Pittura e
   Scultura, Affresco ed Incisione]

Verona, Bib. Capitolare
   Verona, Biblioteca Capitolare

Verona, Bib. Civ.
   Verona, Biblioteca Civica

Verona, Castelvecchio
   Verona, Museo Civico di Castelvecchio

Verona, Gal. Cinquetti
   Verona, Galleria Cinquetti

Verona, Gal. Civ. A. Mod. & Contemp.
   Verona, Galleria Civica d'Arte Moderna e
   Contemporanea

Verona, Gal. Scudo
   Verona, Galleria delle Scudo

Verona, Gran Guardia

Verona, Mus. Affreschi
   Verona, Museo degli Affreschi

Verona, Mus. Archeol. Teat. Romano
   Verona, Museo Archeologico del Teatro
   Romano

Verona, Musei Civ.
   Verona, Musei Civici di Verona [admins
   Castelvecchio; Mus. Affreschi; Mus. Archeol.
   Teat. Romano; Mus. Lapidario Maffeiano; Pal.
   Forti]

Verona, Mus. Lapidario Maffeiano
   Verona, Museo Lapidario Maffeiano

Verona, Mus. Miniscalchi Erizzo
   Verona, Museo Miniscalchi Erizzo

Verona, Mus. Muselli
   Verona, Museo Muselli

Verona, Mus. Ris.
   Verona, Museo del Risorgimento

Verona, Pal. Canossa
   Verona, Palazzo Canossa

Verona, Pal. Forti
   Verona, Palazzo Forti [formerly Palazzo
   Emilei; houses Galleria Comunale d'Arte
   Moderna; Mus. Ris.]

Verona, Pal. Fortuny
   Verona, Palazzo Fortuny [Palazzo Pesaro degli
   Orfei; houses mus. & Centro di
   Documentazione Fotografica]

Verona, Pal. Gran Guardia
   Verona, Palazzo della Gran Guardia

Verona, Pal. Scoligero, Notai Chapel
   Verona, Palazzo Scoligero, Notai Chapel

Verona, Pal. Vescovile
Verona, Palazzo Vescovile [Archbishop's Pal.]

Versailles, Bib. Louis XVI
Versailles, Bibliothèque de Louis XVI

Versailles, Bib. Mun.
Versailles, Bibliothèque Municipale

Versailles, Château [Musée National du Château de Versailles et du Trianon]

Versailles, Château, Orangerie

Versailles, Ecole Mil. & Applic. Génie
Versailles, Ecole Militaire et d'Application du Génie

Versailles, Grand Trianon

Versailles, Hôtel de Ville

Versailles, Musées N.
Versailles, Musées Nationaux [admins Château; Grand Trianon; Petit Trianon]

Versailles, Mus. Hist.
Versailles, Musée d'Histoire [in Château]

Versailles, Mus. Lambinet
Versailles, Musée Lambinet

Versailles, Petit Trianon

Verviers, Mus. B.-A. & Cér.
Verviers, Musée des Beaux-Arts et Céramique

Vesoul, Mus. Mun. Garret
Vesoul, Musée Municipal Georges Garret

Veszprém, Bakonyi Mus.
Veszprém, Bakonyi Museum (Bakonyi Muzeum)

Veszprém, Eccles. Col.
Veszprém, Ecclesiastical Collection

Vevey, Fond. William Cuendet
Vevey, Fondation William Cuendet [et Atelier de St-Prex]

Vevey, Mus. Jenisch
Vevey, Musée Jenisch, Musée des Beaux-Arts et Cabinet Cantonal des Estampes

Vézelay, Dépôt Lapidaire Abbaye
Vézelay, Dépôt Lapidaire de l'Abbaye

Viana do Castelo, Mus. Mun.
Viana do Castelo, Museu Municipal

Viareggio, Comune

Viareggio, Pal. Paolina
Viareggio, Palazzo Paolina

Viborg Stiftsmus.
Viborg, Viborg Stiftsmuseum

Vic, Mus. Episc.
Vic, Museu Arqueologic Artistic Episcopal

Vic, Mus. Mun.
Vic, Museu Municipal

Vicenza, Archv Stor. Mun.
Vicenza, Archivio Storico Municipale

Vicenza, Bib. Civ. Bertoliana
Vicenza, Biblioteca Civica Bertoliana

Vicenza, Cent. Int. Stud. Archit. Palladio
Vicenza, Centro Internazionale di Studi di Architettura Andrea Palladio [Domus Comestabilis-Basilica Palladiana]

Vicenza, Mus. Civ. A. & Stor.
Vicenza, Museo Civico d'Arte e Storia

Vicenza, Pal. Chiericati
Vicenza, Palazzo Chiericati

Vich: see Vic

Vichy, Casino

Victoria, BC, A.G. Gtr Victoria
Victoria, BC, Art Gallery of Greater Victoria

Victoria, BC Archvs & Rec. Serv.
Victoria, BC, British Columbia Archives and Record Service

Victoria, BC, Emily Carr A. Cent.
Victoria, BC, Emily Carr Arts Centre

Victoria, BC, Prov. Mus.
Victoria, BC, Provincial Museum

Victoria, Royal BC Mus.
Victoria, BC, Royal British Columbia Museum

Victoria, U. Victoria, BC, Maltwood A. Mus. & Gal.
Victoria, BC, University of Victoria, Maltwood Art Museum and Gallery

Victoria, U. Victoria, BC, Read Archv
Victoria, BC, University of Victoria, Sir Herbert Read Archive

Victoria, Gozo, Cathedral Mus.
Victoria, Gozo, Cathedral Museum [Victoria, Gozo, is also known as Rabat]

Victoria, Gozo, Flklore Mus.
Victoria, Gozo, Folklore Museum

Victoria, Gozo, Mus. Archaeol.
Victoria, Gozo, Museum of Archaeology

Vidisha, Distr. Archaeol. Mus.
Vidisha, District Archaeological Museum

Vienna, Abtei-Samml.
Vienna, Abtei-Sammlung [Schotten Abbey]

Vienna, Akad. Bild. Kst.
Vienna, Akademie der Bildenden Künste

Vienna, Akad. Bild. Kst., Kupferstichkab.
Vienna, Kupferstichkabinett der Akademie der Bildenden Künste

Vienna, Akad. Wiss.
Vienna, Österreichische Akademie der Wissenschaften

Vienna, Albertina
Vienna, Graphische Sammlung Albertina

Vienna, Ambrosi Mus.
Vienna, Gustinus Ambrosi Museum [in Schloss Halbturn]

Vienna, Archv Baumeistergenoss.
Vienna, Archiv der Baumeistergenossenschaft

Vienna, Beethoven-Gedenkstät. Eroica-Haus
Vienna, Beethoven-Gedenkstätte Eroica-Haus

Vienna, Beethoven-Wohnung

Vienna, Belvedere [also admins Ambrosi Mus.]

Vienna, Belvedere-Gtn
Vienna, Belvedere-Garten

Vienna, Belvedere, Österreich. Barockmus.
Vienna, Belvedere, Österreichisches Barockmuseum

Vienna, Belvedere, Österreich. Gal.
Vienna, Belvedere, Österreichische Galerie [includes Galerie des XIX. und XX. Jahrhunderts; Museum Mittelalterlicher Kunst; Österreichisches Barockmuseum]

Vienna, Bib. Akad. Bild. Kst.
Vienna, Bibliothek der Akademie der Bildenden Künste

Vienna, Boehms Kstlerhaus
Vienna, Boehms Künstlerhaus

Vienna, Bundesmin. Unterricht & Kst
Vienna, Bundesministerium für Unterricht und Kunst

Vienna, Bundesmobiliensamml.
Vienna, Bundesmobiliensammlung

Vienna, Burggtn
Vienna, Burggarten

Vienna, Cath. Armen. Congregation Treasury
Vienna, Catholic Armenian Congregation Treasury

Vienna, Coll. Hung.
Vienna, Collegium Hungaricum

Vienna, Czernin'sche Gemäldegal.
Vienna, Czernin'sche Gemäldegalerie

Vienna, Diözarchv
Vienna, Diözesanarchiv

Vienna, Dom- & Diözmus.
Vienna, Dom- und Diözesanmuseum

Vienna, Dorotheer Gal.
Vienna, Dorotheer Galerie

Vienna, Dorotheum

Vienna, Ephesos Mus.
Vienna, Ephesos Museum

Vienna, Ernst Fuchs Villa

Vienna, Erzbischöf. Pal.
Vienna, Erzbischöfliches Palais

Vienna, Estenische Kstsamml.
Vienna, Estenische Kunstsammlung

Vienna, Fürst. Liechtenstein Gemäldegal.
Vienna, Fürstlich Liechtenstein Gemäldegalerie

Vienna, Gal. Allerhöchsten Kaiserhauses
Vienna, Galerie des Allerhöchsten Kaiserhauses [since 1919 part of Ksthist. Mus.]

Vienna, Gal. Brücke
Vienna, Galerie die Brücke

Vienna, Gal. Friederike Pallamar
Vienna, Galerie Friederike Pallamar

Vienna, Gal. Grita Insam
Vienna, Galerie Grita Insam

Vienna, Gal. Krinzinger
Vienna, Galerie Krinzinger

Vienna, Gal. Miethke
Vienna, Galerie Miethke [closed]

Vienna, Gal. Nächst St Stephan
Vienna, Galerie Nächst St Stephan

Vienna, Gal. St Lucas
Vienna, Galerie Sankt Lucas

Vienna, Gal. Würthle
Vienna, Galerie Würthle

Vienna, Gal. Würthle & Sohn
Vienna, Galerie Würthle und Sohn

Vienna, Gemäldegal. Akad. Bild. Kst.
Vienna, Gemäldegalerie der Akademie der Bildenden Künste

Vienna, Ges. Förderung Mod. Kst
Vienna, Gesellschaft zur Förderung Moderner Kunst in Wien [now closed]

Vienna, Ges.- & Wirtschaftsmus.
Vienna, Gesellschafts- und Wirtschaftsmuseum

Vienna, Geymüller-Schlossl

Vienna, Graph. Lehr- & Versuchanstalt
Vienna, Graphische Lehr- und Versuchanstalt

Vienna, Hauptmünzamt

Vienna, Haus-, Hof- & Staatsarchv
Vienna, Haus-, Hof- und Staatsarchiv

Vienna, Haydn-Wohnhaus & Brahms-Zimmer
Vienna, Haydn-Wohnhaus und Brahms-Zimmer

Vienna, Heeresgesch. Mus.
Vienna, Heeresgeschichtliches Museum [in Arsenal]

Vienna, Hermesvilla

Vienna, Hist. Mus.
Vienna, Historisches Museum

Vienna, Hochsch. Angewandte Kst
Vienna, Hochschule für Angewandte Kunst in Wien [in Tech. Mus.]

Villa Nova de Gaia, Gal. Diogo de Macedo
  Villa Nova de Gaia, Galería Diogo de Macedo

Villanueva y Geltrú, Mus. Balaguer
  Villanueva y Geltrú, Museo Victor Balaguer [in Castle of La Geltrú]

Villedieu-les-Poêles, Mus. Poêlerie
  Villedieu-les-Poêles, Musée de la Poêlerie

Villeneuve d'Ascq, Mus. A. Mod. Nord
  Villeneuve d'Ascq, Musée d'Art Moderne du Nord

Villeneuve-lès-Avignon, Mus. Mun.
  Villeneuve-lès-Avignon, Musée Municipal Villeneuve-lès-Avignon

Villeneuve-sur-Lot, Hôtel de Ville

Villeurbanne, Nouv. Mus.
  Villeurbanne, Nouveau Musée

Vilnius, Cent. Lib. Lith. Acad. Sci.
  Vilnius, Central Library of the Lithuanian Academy of Sciences

Vilnius, Dailès Mus.
  Vilnius, Dailès Museum

Vilnius, Hist. & Ethnog. Mus.
  Vilnius, Historical and Ethnographical Museum

Vilnius, Lith. A. Mus.
  Vilnius, Lithuanian Art Museum

Vilnius, Lith. Cent. Trade & Indust.
  Vilnius, Lithuanian Centre for Trade and Industry [now Association of Lithuanian Chambers of Commerce and Industry]

Vilnius, Pub. Lib.
  Vilnius, Public Library [Central Archive of Literature and Art of Lithuania]

Viña del Mar, Mus. Mun. B.A.
  Viña del Mar, Museo Municipal de Bellas Artes

Vinci, Castello Conti Guidi
  Vinci, Castello dei Conti Guidi

Vinnica: see Vinnitsa

Vinnitsa, Local Mus.
  Vinnitsa, Local Museum

Vipiteno, Mus. Multscher
  Vipiteno, Museo Multscher

Vire, Mus. Mun.
  Vire, Musée Municipal Hôtel Dieu

Visby, Gotlands Fornsal (Gotland Historical Museum)

Visby, Säve-Salen

Viseu, Mus. Grão Vasco
  Viseu, Museu de Grão Vasco

Viso del Marqués, Pal. Marqués de S Cruz
  Viso del Marqués, Palacio Marqués de S Cruz [houses National Archive of the Spanish Navy]

Visso, Mus.-Pin.
  Visso, Museo-Pinacoteca

Vista Alegre, Mus. Hist.
  Vista Alegre, Museu Histórico da Vista Alegre

Vitebsk, Acad. F.A.
  Vitebsk, Academy of Fine Arts (Vitsebskaya Narodnaya Mastatskaya Shkola 'Novaha Revalyutsywnaha Uzora')

Vitebsk, Reg. Mus. Local Hist.
  Vitebsk, Regional Museum of Local History (Vitsebski Ablasny Krayaznawchy Muzey)

Viterbo, Municipio

Viterbo, Mus. Civ.
  Viterbo, Museo Civico

Vitoria, Caja Prov. Alava
  Vitoria, Caja Provincial de Alava

Vitoria, Mus. Prov. Alava
  Vitoria, Museo Provincial de Alava

Vitoria, Mus. Prov. B.A.
  Vitoria, Museo Provincial de Bellas Artes

Vittorio Veneto, Mus. Cenedese
  Vittorio Veneto, Museo del Cenedese

Vizille, Château Vizille
  Vizille, Château de Vizille [houses Mus. Révolution Fr.]

Vizille, Mus. Révolution Fr.
  Vizille, Musée de la Révolution Française [in Château Vizille]

Vizovice Castle
  Vizovice, Vizovice Castle

Vladikavkaz, N. Ossetian Repub. Mus. A.
  Vladikavkaz, North Ossetian Republic Museum of Art

Vladimir, Vladimir-Suzdal Mus. A. Hist. & Archit.
  Vladimir, Vladimir-Suzdal Museum of Art History and Architecture (Vladimir-Suzdal'skiy Istoriko-Khudozhestvennyy i Arkhitekturnyy Muzey)

Volgograd, Mus. F.A.
  Volgograd, Museum of Fine Arts (Muzey Izobrazitel'nykh Iskusstv)

Vologda, A.G.
  Vologda, Art Gallery (Vologodskaya Kartinnaya Galereya)

Vologda, Local Mus.
  Vologda, Local Museum (Krayevedcheskiy Muzey)

Volos, Athanassakeion Archaeol. Mus.
  Volos, Athanassakeion Archaeological Museum

Volpedo, Studio Pellizza
  Volpedo, Studio di Pellizza

Volterra, Mus. Dioc. A. Sacra
  Volterra, Museo Diocesano di Arte Sacra [in Palazzo Vescovile]

Volterra, Mus. Etrus. Guarnacci
  Volterra, Museo Etrusco Guarnacci

Volterra, Pal. Minucci–Solaini, Pin.
  Volterra, Palazzo Minucci–Solaini, Pinacoteca

Volterra, Pal. Priori, Gal. Pittorica
  Volterra, Palazzo dei Priori, Galleria Pittorica [since 1982 housed in Pal. Minucci–Solaini]

Volterra, Pin. Com.
  Volterra, Pinacoteca Comunale [Palazzo dei Priori]

Volterrano, Archv Capitolare
  Volterrano, Archivio Capitolare

Volubilis, Mus. Ant.
  Volubilis, Musée des Antiquités

Voorst, Stadhuis

Vori, Mus. Cret. Ethnol.
  Vori, Museum of Cretan Ethnology

Vratsa, Hist. Mus.
  Vratsa, Historical Museum (Istoricheski Muzey)

Vrindavan Res. Inst.
  Vrindavan, Vrindavan Research Institute (Vrindavan Shudh Sansthan)

Vrpolje, Meštrović Mem. Gal.
  Vrpolje, Ivan Meštrović Memorial Gallery (Spomen Galerija Ivana Meštrovića)

Vršac, N. Mus.
  Vršac, National Museum (Narodni Muzeij)

Vukovar, Bauer Col. & F.A. Gal.
  Vukovar, Bauer Collection and Fine Arts Gallery

Vulci, Mus. N.
  Vulci, Museo Nazionale di Vulci [nr Canino]

Vyatka, Mus. Hist. & A.
  Vyatka, Museum of History and Art

Waganui Reg. Mus.
  Waganui, Waganui Regional Museum

Wagga Wagga, C.A.G.
  Wagga Wagga, City Art Gallery

Waigani, U. Papua New Guinea, Fac. Creative A.
  Waigani, University of Papua New Guinea, Faculty of Creative Arts [until 1 Jan 1990 called the National Arts School]

Wakayama, Prefect. Mus. A.
  Wakayama, Wakayama Prefectural Museum of Art (Wakayama-Kenritsu Hakubutsukan)

Wakayama, Prefect. Mus. Mod. A.
  Wakayama, Prefectural Museum of Modern Art (Wakayama Kenritsu Kindai Bijutsukan)

Wakefield, A.G.
  Wakefield, Wakefield Art Gallery

Wakefield, Elizabethan Gal.
  Wakefield, Elizabethan Gallery

Wakefield, Met. Distr. Council A.G. & Mus.
  Wakefield, Metropolitan District Council Art Gallery and Museum [admins A.G.; Elizabethan Gal.; Wakefield Mus.]

Wakefield Mus.
  Wakefield, Wakefield Museum

Wakefield, Yorks Sculp. Park
  Wakefield, Yorkshire Sculpture Park

Walcourt, St Materne, Treasury

Walsingham, Shirehall Mus.
  Walsingham, Shirehall Museum

Waltham, MA, Brandeis U. Lib.
  Waltham, MA, Brandeis University Library

Waltham, MA, Brandeis U., Rose A. Mus.
  Waltham, MA, Brandeis University, Rose Art Museum

Walthamstow: see London

Wanganui, Sarjeant A.G.
  Wanganui, Sarjeant Art Gallery

Warabi, Kawanabe Gyōsai Mem. A. Mus.
  Warabi, Kawanabe Gyōsai Memorial Art Museum

Warrington, Mus. & A.G.
  Warrington, Museum and Art Gallery

Warsaw, Archdioc. Mus.
  Warsaw, Archdiocesan Museum

Warsaw, Arsenal

Warsaw, Asia & Pacific Mus.
  Warsaw, Asia & Pacific Museum (Muzeum Aji i Pacyfiku)

Warsaw, Belvedere Pal.
  Warsaw, Belvedere Palace

Warsaw, Cent. Archvs Hist. Rec.
  Warsaw, Central Archives of Historical Records (Archiwum Główne Akt Dawnych)

Warsaw, Cent. Office A. Exh.
  Warsaw, Central Office of Art Exhibitions

Warsaw, Gal. A. Hist. Assoc.
  Warsaw, Gallery of the Art Historians Association (Galeria Stowarzyszenia Historyków Sztuki)

Warsaw, Gal. Foksal
  Warsaw, Galeria Foksal

Warsaw, Gal. KIK
  Warsaw, Galeria KIK

Warsaw, Gal. Kordegarda
  Warsaw, Galeria Kordegarda

Warsaw, Gal. Krzywe Koło
Warsaw, Crooked Circle Gallery (Galeria Krzywe Koło)

Warsaw, Gal. MDM
Warsaw, Galeria MDM

Warsaw, Gal. Studio
Warsaw, Galeria Studio

Warsaw, Gal. Zapiecek
Warsaw, Galeria Zapiecek

Warsaw, Inst. A. PAN
Warsaw, Institute of Art PAN [attached to the Polish Academy of Sciences] (Instytut Sztuki PAN)

Warsaw, Jew. Hist. Inst.
Warsaw, Jewish Historical Institute in Poland (Zydowski Instytut Historyczny W Polsce)

Warsaw, Krasiński Pal.
Warsaw, Krasiński Palace

Warsaw, Łazienki Pal.
Warsaw, Łazienki Palace [Palace on the Water; branch of N. Mus.]

Warsaw, Min. Council Bldg
Warsaw, Ministry Council Building

Warsaw, Mus. Acad. F.A.
Warsaw, Museum of the Academy of Fine Arts (Muzeum Akademii Sztuk Pięknych)

Warsaw, Mus. Archit.
Warsaw, Museum of Architecture (Muzeum Architektury)

Warsaw, Mus. Hist. City
Warsaw, Museum of the History of the City of Warsaw (Muzeum Historyczne Miasta Warszawy)

Warsaw, Mus. Pol. Army
Warsaw, Museum of the Polish Army (Muzeum Wojska Polskiego)

Warsaw, N. Ethnog. Mus.
Warsaw, National Ethnographical Museum (Pánstwowe Muzeum Etnograficzne)

Warsaw, N. Lib.
Warsaw, National Library

Warsaw, N. Mus.
Warsaw, National Museum (Muzeum Narodowe)

Warsaw, Pałacyk Gal.
Warsaw, Pałacyk Gallery

Warsaw, Pal. Cult. & Sci.
Warsaw, Palace of Culture and Science (Pałac Kultury i Nauki)

Warsaw, Parl. House
Warsaw, Parliament House

Warsaw, Pokaz Gal.
Warsaw, Pokaz Gallery

Warsaw, Promot. Gal.
Warsaw, Promotional Gallery (Galeria Promocyjna)

Warsaw, Repassage

Warsaw, Royal Castle
Warsaw, Royal Castle National History and Culture Memorial (Zamek Królewski Pomnik Historii i Kultury Narodowej)

Warsaw, Saxon Axis (Oś Saski) [remains of pal. & pub. gdns]

Warsaw, Saxon Gdns
Warsaw, Saxon Gardens (Ogród Saski)

Warsaw, Soc. Encour. F.A.
Warsaw, Society for the Encouragement of Fine Art (Towarzystwo Zachęty Sztuk Pięknych)

Warsaw, Studio A. Cent.
Warsaw, Studio Arts Centre (Centrum Sztuki Studio)

Warsaw, U. Warsaw, Cab. Prts & Engrs
Warsaw, Cabinet of Prints and Engravings of the University of Warsaw (Gabinet Rycin Biblioteki Uniwersyteckiej)

Warsaw, U. Warsaw, Lib.
Warsaw, University of Warsaw Library (Biblioteka Uniwersytecka w Warszawie)

Warsaw, Wilanów Mus.
Warsaw, Wilanów Museum (Muzeum w Wilanowie)

Warsaw, Wilanów Pal.
Warsaw, Wilanów Palace (Pałac Wilanowski)

Warsaw, Zachęta Gal.
Warsaw, Zachęhta Gallery

Warwick, Co. Rec. Office
Warwick, Warwickshire County Record Office

Warwick U., Mead Gal.
Warwick, Warwick University, Mead Gallery

Washington, Tyne & Wear, 'F' Pit Indust. Mus.
Washington, Tyne and Wear, 'F' Pit Industrial Museum

Washington, DC, Amer. Archit. Found. Octagon
Washington, DC, American Architectural Foundation at the Octagon

Washington, DC, Amer. Inst. Architects, Archvs
Washington, DC, American Institute of Architects, Archives

Washington, DC, Amer. Inst. Architects Found.
Washington, DC, American Institute of Architects Foundation [name changed to Amer. Archit. Found. Octagon in Dec 1987]

Washington, DC, Amer. U.
Washington, DC, American University

Washington, DC, A. Mus. Americas
Washington, DC, Art Museum of the Americas [formerly Mus. Mod. A. Latin America]

Washington, DC, Anacostia Neighborhood Mus.
Washington, DC, Anacostia Neighborhood Museum [Smithsonian Inst.]

Washington, DC, Armed Forces Inst. Pathology, N. Mus. Health & Medic.
Washington, DC, Armed Forces Institute of Pathology, National Museum of Health and Medicine

Washington, DC, Barnett Aden Gal.
Washington, DC, Barnett Aden Gallery

Washington, DC, Barney House Studio

Washington, DC, B'nai B'rith Klutznick Mus.
Washington, DC, B'nai B'rith Klutznick Museum

Washington, DC, Capitol Bldg
Washington, DC, Capitol Building [incl. Statuary Hall]

Washington, DC, Carnegie Inst.
Washington, DC, Carnegie Institution of Washington

Washington, DC, Cent. Asian A.
Washington, DC, Center for Asian Art [now Freer & Sackler Gal.]

Washington, DC, Corcoran Gal. A.
Washington, DC, Corcoran Gallery of Art

Washington, DC, Dumbarton Oaks
Washington, DC, Dumbarton Oaks Research Library and Collections

Washington, DC, Folger Shakespeare Lib.
Washington, DC, Folger Shakespeare Library

Washington, DC, Fondo del Sol Visual A. Media Cent.
Washington, DC, Fondo del Sol Visual Arts Media Center

Washington, DC, Found. Cross Cult. Understanding
Washington, DC, Foundation for Cross Cultural Understanding

Washington, DC, Freer
Washington, DC, Freer Gallery of Art [Smithsonian Inst.]

Washington, DC, Gallaudet Coll.
Washington, DC, Gallaudet College

Washington, DC, Gal. Mod. A.
Washington, DC, Washington Gallery of Modern Art

Washington, DC, Georgetown U. A. Col.
Washington, DC, Georgetown University Art Collection

Washington, DC, George Washington U.
Washington, DC, George Washington University

Washington, DC, Gold Leaf Studios

Washington, DC, Hillwood Mus.
Washington, DC, Hillwood Museum

Washington, DC, Hirshhorn
Washington, DC, Hirshhorn Museum and Sculpture Garden [Smithsonian Inst.]

Washington, DC, Holocaust Mem. Mus.
Washington, DC, Holocaust Memorial Museum

Washington, DC, Howard U., Gal. A.
Washington, DC, Howard University, Gallery of Art

Washington, DC, Howard U. Mus., Moorland Springarn Res. Cent.
Washington, DC, Howard University Museum, Moorland Springarn Research Center

Washington, DC, Int. Exh. Found.
Washington, DC, International Exhibition Foundation

Washington, DC, Kennedy Cent. Perf. A.
Washington, DC, J. F. Kennedy Center for the Performing Arts

Washington, DC, Lib. Congr.
Washington, DC, Library of Congress

Washington, DC, Meridian House Int.
Washington, DC, Meridian House International

Washington, DC, Mus. Afr. A.
Washington, DC, Museum of African Art [now N. Mus. Afr. A.]

Washington, DC, Mus. Mod. A. Latin America
Washington, DC, Museum of Modern Art of Latin America [now A. Mus. Americas; part of Org. Amer. States]

Washington, DC, N. Acad Des.
Washington, DC, National Academy of Design

Washington, DC, N. Acad. Sci., Soc. & Polit. Sect.
Washington, DC, National Academy of Sciences, Social and Political Section

Washington, DC, N. Air & Space Mus.
Washington, DC, National Air and Space Museum [Smithsonian Inst.]

Washington, DC, N. Archvs
Washington, DC, National Archives

Washington, DC, N. Bldg Mus.
Washington, DC, National Building Museum

Washington, DC, N. Col. F.A.
Washington, DC, National Collection of Fine
Arts [closed 1980]

Washington, DC, N.G.A.
Washington, DC, National Gallery of Art

Washington, DC, N. Mus. Afr. A.
Washington, DC, National Museum of African
Art [Smithsonian Inst.; name changed from
Mus. Afr. A. in 1987]

Washington, DC, N. Mus. Amer. A.
Washington, DC, National Museum of
American Art [Smithsonian Inst.]

Washington, DC, N. Mus. Amer. Hist.
Washington, DC, National Museum of
American History [Smithsonian Inst.; formerly
N. Mus. Hist. & Technol.]

Washington, DC, N. Mus. Amer. Indian
Washington, DC, National Museum of the
American Indian [Smithsonian Inst.]

Washington, DC, N. Mus. Hist. & Technol.
Washington, DC, National Museum of History
and Technology [name changed to N. Mus.
Amer. Hist. in 1980]

Washington, DC, N. Mus. Nat. Hist.
Washington, DC, National Museum of Natural
History [Smithsonian Inst.]

Washington, DC, N. Mus. Women A.
Washington, DC, National Museum of
Women in the Arts

Washington, DC, N.P.G.
Washington, DC, National Portrait Gallery
[Smithsonian Inst.]

Washington, DC, N. Trust Hist. Preserv.
Washington, DC, National Trust for Historic
Preservation

Washington, DC, N. Zool. Park
Washington, DC, National Zoological Park
[Smithsonian Inst.]

Washington, DC, Org. Amer. States
Washington, DC, Organization of American
States

Washington, DC, Pan Amer. Un.
Washington, DC, Pan American Union

Washington, DC, Project A.
Washington, DC, Washington Project for the
Arts

Washington, DC, Renwick Gal.
Washington, DC, Renwick Gallery
[Smithsonian Inst.]

Washington, DC, Rose Mus.
Washington, DC, Rose Museum

Washington, DC, Sackler Gal.
Washington, DC, Arthur M. Sackler Gallery

Washington, DC, Smithsonian Inst.
Washington, DC, Smithsonian Institution
[admins Anacostia Neighborhood Mus.; Freer;
Hirshhorn; N. Air & Space Mus.; N. Mus. Afr.
A.; N. Mus. Amer. A.; N. Mus. Nat. Hist.;
N.P.G.; N. Zool. Park; Renwick Gal.; Cooper-
Hewit Mus.]

Washington, DC, Smithsonian Inst., Archvs
Amer. A.
Washington, DC, Smithsonian Institution,
Archives of American Art

Washington, DC, Smithsonian Inst. Traveling
Exh. Serv.
Washington, DC, Smithsonian Institution,
Traveling Exhibition Service [S.I.T.E.S.]

Washington, DC, State Dept
Washington, DC, State Department

Washington, DC, Supreme Court

Washington, DC, Textile Mus.
Washington, DC, Textile Museum

Washington, DC, Trust Mus. Exh.
Washington, DC, Trust for Museum
Exhibitions

Washington, DC, US Capitol

Washington, DC, US Dept Inter.
Washington, DC, US Department of the
Interior

Washington, DC, US Dept Justice
Washington, DC, US Department of Justice

Washington, DC, US Navy Mus.
Washington, DC, United States Navy Museum

Washington, DC, White House

Washington, DC, White House Col.
Washington, DC, White House Collection

Washington, DC, Woodward Found.
Washington, DC, Woodward Foundation

Washington, PA, Co. Hist. Soc. Mus.
Washington, PA, Washington County
Historical Society Museum [Le Moyne House]

Wassenaar, Leslie Smith Gal.
Wassenaar, Leslie Smith Gallery

Wassenaar, Mesdag Doc. Found.
Wassenaar, Mesdag Documentation
Foundation

Wasserburg, Imaginäres Mus.
Wasserburg, Imaginäres Museum

Wasserburg, Mus. Wasserburg
Wasserburg, Museum Wasserburg
[Heimatmuseum]

Waterbury, CT, Mattatuck Hist. Soc. Mus.
Waterbury, CT, Mattatuck Historical Society
Museum

Waterford, Town Hall
Waterford, Waterford Town Hall

Waterloo, Ont., Can. Clay & Glass Gal.
Waterloo, Ont., Canadian Clay and Glass
Gallery

Watertown, MA, Armen. Lib. & Mus.
Watertown, MA, Armenian Library and
Museum

Watertown, MA, Free Pub. Lib.
Watertown, MA, Free Public Library

Waterville, ME, Colby Coll., Mus. A.
Waterville, ME, Colby College, Museum of
Art

Watson, ACT Craft Cent.
Watson, ACT Craft Centre

West Berlin: institutions producing exh. cats
between the 1945 division of Berlin and
reunification in Oct 1990 are cited using W. or E.
Berlin. These institutions, if their names have not
changed since unification, are all to be found
under Berlin. See also E. Berlin.

W. Berlin, Hochsch. Bild. Kst.
West Berlin, Hochschule für Bildende Künste
[name changed to Akad. Kst. in 1969]

W. Berlin, N.G.
West Berlin, Nationalgalerie [at Tiergarten;
now Berlin, Neue N.G.]

W. Berlin, Preuss. Akad. Kst.
West Berlin, Preussische Akademie der Künste

Wealdstone, Winsor & Newton Col.
Wealdstone, Winsor & Newton Collection

Weesp, Gemeentemus.
Weesp, Gemeentemuseum

Weil am Rhein, Vitra Des. Mus.
Weil am Rhein, Vitra Design Museum

Weilheim, Stadtmus.
Weilheim, Stadtmuseum

Weimar, Bauhaus-Samml.
Weimar, Bauhaus-Sammlung

Weimar, Dornburger Schlösser

Weimar, Ducal Mus.
Weimar, Ducal Museum [now Landesmus.]

Weimar, Gal. Schloss
Weimar, Galerie im Schloss

Weimar, Goethehaus Stützerbach

Weimar, Goethe-Nmus.
Weimar, Goethe-Nationalmuseum [Nationale
Forschungs- und Gedenkstätten der
Klassischen Deutschen Literatur in Weimar]

Weimar, Goethe-Nmus. Frauenplan
Weimar, Goethe-Nationalmuseum am
Frauenplan

Weimar, Goethepark

Weimar, Goethe-Samml.
Weimar, Goethe-Sammlung

Weimar, Goethe- & Schiller-Archv
Weimar, Goethe- und Schiller-Archiv

Weimar, Goethe- & Schiller-Gruft
Weimar, Goethe- und Schiller-Gruft

Weimar, Goethes Gartenhaus

Weimar, Goethe-Wohnhaus

Weimar, Graph. Samml.
Weimar, Graphische Sammlung

Weimar, Grossherzogl. Kstsch.
Weimar, Grossherzogliche Kunstschule

Weimar, Jagdhaus Gabelbach

Weimar, Kassengewölbe

Weimar, Kirms-Krockow-Haus & Herder-Mus.
Weimar, Kirms-Krockow-Haus und Herder-
Museum

Weimar, Kstbib.
Weimar, Kunstbibliothek

Weimar, Ksthalle
Weimar, Kunsthalle

Weimar, Kstsammlungen
Weimar, Kunstsammlungen zu Weimar
[admins Bauhaus-Samml.; Gal. Schloss; Graph.
Samml.; Kstbib.; Ksthalle; Münzkab.;
Rokokomus.; Samml. Hist. Wagen; Schloss
Belvedere; Schlossmus.]

Weimar, Landesbib.
Weimar, Landesbibliothek

Weimar, Landesmus.
Weimar, Landesmuseum [formerly Ducal
Mus.]

Weimar, Liszthaus

Weimar, Münzkab.
Weimar, Münzkabinett

Weimar, N. Forsch.-& Gedenkstätten Klass. Dt.
Lit.
Weimar, Nationale Forschungs- und
Gedenkstätten der Klassischen Deutschen
Literatur in Weimar [admins Dornburger
Schlösser; Goethehaus Stützerbach; Goethe-
Nmus.; Goethe-Nmus. Frauenplan; Goethe- &
Schiller-Gruft; Goethes Gartenhaus; Goethe-
Wohnhaus; Jagdhaus Gabelbach;
Kassengewölbe; Kirms-Krockow-Haus &
Herder-Mus.; Liszthaus; Röm. Haus;
Schillerhaus; Schillerhaus Bauerbach; Schloss
Kochberg; Schloss Tiefurt; Wielandgut
Ossmannstedt; Wittumspal. & Wielandmus.]

Weimar, Nietzsche-Mus.
Weimar, Nietzsche-Museum [houses
Nietzsche-Archiv]

Weimar, Rokokomus.
  Weimar, Rokokomuseum

Weimar, Röm. Haus
  Weimar, Römisches Haus

Weimar, Samml. Hist. Wagen
  Weimar, Sammlung Historischer Wagen

Weimar, Schillerhaus

Weimar, Schillerhaus Bauerbach

Weimar, Schloss Belvedere

Weimar, Schloss Kochberg

Weimar, Schlossmus.
  Weimar, Schlossmuseum

Weimar, Schloss Tiefurt

Weimar, Staatsarchv
  Weimar, Staatsarchiv

Weimar, Thüring. Landesbib.
  Weimar, Thüringische Landesbibliothek
  [Grüne Schloss]

Weimar, Wielandgut Ossmannstedt

Weimar, Wittumspal. & Wielandmus.
  Weimar, Wittumspalais und Wielandmuseum

Weimar, Zentbib. Dt. Klassik
  Weimar, Zentralbibliothek der Deutschen
  Klassik

Weinsberg, Burg Weibertreu

Weissenburg, Römermus.
  Weissenburg, Römermuseum Weissenburg

Weissenhorn, Heimatmus.
  Weissenhorn, Heimatmuseum Weissenhorn

Wellesley Coll., MA, Davis Mus. & Cult. Cent.
  Wellesley, MA, Wellesley College, Davis
  Museum and Cultural Centre

Wellesley Coll., MA, Jewett A. Cent.
  Wellesley, MA, Wellesley College, Jewett Arts
  Center

Wellesley Coll., MA, Lib.
  Wellesley, MA, Wellesley College, Library

Wellesley Coll., MA, Mus.
  Wellesley, MA, Wellesley College Museum [in
  Jewett A. Cent.]

Wellington, A. Council NZ, Toi Aotearoa Col.
  Wellington, NZ, Arts Council of New
  Zealand, Toi Aotearoa Collection [formerly
  Elizabeth II Arts Council Collection]

Wellington, NZ, C.A.G.
  Wellington, NZ, City Art Gallery

Wellington, NZ, Colon. Cottage Mus.
  Wellington, NZ, Colonial Cottage Museum

Wellington, NZ, Dominion Mus.
  Wellington, NZ, Dominion Museum [name
  changed to N. Mus.]

Wellington, Mus. NZ, Te Papa Tongarewa
  Wellington, Museum of New Zealand, Te
  Papa Tongarewa

Wellington, NZ Hist. Places Trust
  Wellington, New Zealand Historic Places
  Trust

Wellington, NZ, N.A.G.
  Wellington, NZ, National Art Gallery [now
  called Mus. NZ, Te Papa Tongarewa]

Wellington, NZ, N. Lib.
  Wellington, NZ, National Library

Wellington, NZ, N. Mus.
  Wellington, NZ, National Museum [name
  changed to Mus. NZ, Te Papa Tongarewa in
  1992]

Wellington, NZ, PhotoForum

Wellington, NZ, Turnbull Lib.
  Wellington, NZ, Alexander Turnbull Library

Wellington, NZ, Victoria U.
  Wellington, NZ, Victoria University

Welshpool, Powis Castle, Clive Mus.
  Welshpool, Powis Castle, Clive Museum

Welshpool, Powysland Mus.
  Welshpool, Powysland Museum and
  Montgomery Canal Centre

Wernigerode, Feudalmus.
  Wernigerode, Feudalmuseum Schloss
  Wernigerode

Wesel, Städt. Mus.
  Wesel, Städtisches Museum Wesel, Galerie im
  Centrum

West Chester, PA, Chester Co. Hist. Soc. Mus.
  West Chester, Chester County Historical
  Society Museum

West Hartford, CT, U. Hartford, Joseloff Gal.
  West Hartford, University of Hartford,
  Joseloff Gallery

West Lafayette, IN, Purdue U.
  West Lafayette, Purdue University

Weston-super-Mare, Woodspring Mus.
  Weston-super-Mare, Woodspring Museum

West Palm Beach, FL, Norton Gal. & Sch. A.
  West Palm Beach, FL, Norton Gallery and
  School of Art

West Point, NY, US Mil. Acad.
  West Point, NY, United States Military
  Academy

West Point, US Mil. Acad., Mus.
  West Point, NY, United States Military
  Academy, West Point Museum [Olmstead
  Hall]

Whitby Mus.
  Whitby, Whitby Museum

Wichita, KS, A. Mus.
  Wichita, KS, Wichita Art Museum

Wichita, State U., KS, Edwin A. Ulrich Mus. A.
  Wichita, KS, Wichita State University, Edwin
  A. Ulrich Museum of Art

Wieliczka, Salt Mine Mus.
  Wieliczka, Salt Mine Museum (Muzeum Zup
  Krakowskich)

Wiener Neustadt, Mus. Theresian. Milakad.
  Wiener Neustadt, Museum der
  Theresianischen Militärakademie

Wiener Neustadt, Neukloster [Neustift]

Wiener Neustadt, Stadtmus.
  Wiener Neustadt, Stadtmuseum

Wiener Neustadt, St Peter an der Sperre

Wiesbaden, Mus. Wiesbaden
  Wiesbaden, Museum Wiesbaden

Wiesbaden, Nassau. Kstver.
  Wiesbaden, Nassauischer Kunstverein

Wijlré, Kasteel
  Wijlré, Kasteel Wijlré

Wildegg, Schloss
  Wildegg, Schloss Wildegg [Stiftung von
  Effinger-Wildegg]

Wilhelmshaven, Ksthalle
  Wilhelmshaven, Kunsthalle

Willemstad, Curaçao Mus.
  Willemstad, Curaçao Museum [West Indies]

Williamsburg, VA, Coll. William & Mary, Swem
Lib.
  Williamsburg, VA, College of William and
  Mary in Virginia, Earl Gregg Swem Library

Williamsburg, VA, Colonial Williamsburg

Williamsburg, VA, Dewitt Wallace Dec. A. Gal.
  Williamsburg, VA, Dewitt Wallace Decorative
  Arts Gallery

Williamsburg, VA, Rockefeller Flk A. Col.
  Williamsburg, VA, Abby Aldrich Rockefeller
  Folk Art Collection

Williamstown, MA, Clark A. Inst.
  Williamstown, MA, Sterling and Francine
  Clark Art Institute

Williamstown, MA, Williams Coll., Chapin Lib.
  Williamstown, MA, Williams College, Chapin
  Library

Williamstown, MA, Williams Coll. Mus. A.
  Williamstown, MA, Williams College Museum
  of Art

Wilmington, DE A. Mus.
  Wilmington, DE, Delaware Art Museum

Wilmington, DE, Hist. Soc. Mus.
  Wilmington, DE, Historical Society Museum
  of Delaware

Wilten, Stiftsgal.
  Wilten, Stiftsgalerie

Wilton, CT, Weir Farm Her. Trust
  Wilton, CT, The Weir Farm Heritage Trust

Winchester, Cathedral Lib.
  Winchester, Cathedral Library

Winchester, City Mus.
  Winchester, City Museum

Winchester Gal.
  Winchester, Winchester Gallery

Winchester, Great Hall

Winchester, Hants Museums Serv.
  Winchester, Hampshire Museums Service

Windsor Castle, Royal Lib.
  Windsor, Windsor Castle, Royal Library

Windsor, Guildhall Exh.
  Windsor, Guildhall Exhibition

Windsor, Imp. Serv. Coll.
  Windsor, Imperial Services College

Windsor, Ont., A. Assoc.
  Windsor, Ont., Windsor Art Association
  [name changed to Willistead A.G. 1960]

Windsor, Ont., A.G.
  Windsor, Ont., Art Gallery of Windsor

Windsor, Ont., Willistead A.G.
  Windsor, Ont., Willistead Art Gallery of
  Windsor [name changed to A.G.]

Winkel, Brentanohaus

Winnipeg, A.G.
  Winnipeg, Art Gallery

Winnipeg, Manitoba Mus. Man & Nat.
  Winnipeg, Manitoba Museum of Man and
  Nature

Winnipeg, U. Winnipeg, Sch. A.
  Winnipeg, University of Winnipeg, School of
  Art

Winston-Salem, NC, Mus. Early S. Dec. A.
  Winston-Salem, NC, Museum of Early
  Southern Decorative Arts

Winston-Salem, NC, Old Salem

Winston-Salem, NC, Reynolda House

Winter Park, FL, Morse Mus. Amer. A.
  Winter Park, FL, Charles Hosmer Morse
  Museum of American Art [formerly Morse
  Gal. A.]

Winter Park, FL, Morse Gal. A.
  Winter Park, FL, Morse Gallery of Art

Winterthur, Collegium

Winterthur, Gottfried Keller-Stift.
Winterthur, Gottfried Keller-Stiftung

Winterthur, Hahnloser-Bühler Col.
Winterthur, Hahnloser-Bühler Collection

Winterthur, Kstmus.
Winterthur, Kunstmuseum Winterthur

Winterthur, Kstver.
Winterthur, Kunstverein

Winterthur, Mus. Lindengut
Winterthur, Museum Lindengut

Winterthur, Samml. Oskar Reinhart
Winterthur, Sammlung Oskar Reinhart [am
Römerholz]

Winterthur, Stift. Briner
Winterthur, Stiftung Jacob Briner

Winterthur, Stift. Oskar Reinhart
Winterthur, Stiftung Oskar Reinhart

Winterthur, Technorama
Winterthur, Technorama der Schweiz

Winterthur, DE, Du Pont Winterthur Mus.
Winterthur, DE, H.F. Du Pont Winterthur
Museum

Winterthur, DE, Gdns
Winterthur, DE, Winterthur Gardens

Winterthur, DE, Mus. & Gdn Lib.
Winterthur, DE, Winterthur Museum and
Garden Library

Wismar, Stadtgeschich. Mus.
Wismar, Stadtgeschichtliches Museum

Włocławek, Dioc. Mus.
Włocławek, Diocesan Museum

Woburn Abbey, Beds
Woburn, Beds, Woburn Abbey

Wolfegg, Schloss Wolfegg, Fürst. Kstsamml.
Wolfegg, Schloss Wolfegg, Fürstliche
Kunstsammlungen

Wolfegg, Schloss Wolfegg, Kupferstichkab.
Wolfegg, Schloss Wolfegg,
Kupferstichkabinett

Wolfenbüttel, Braunschweig. Landesmus.
Wolfenbüttel, Braunschweigisches
Landesmuseum

Wolfenbüttel, Herzog August Bib.
Wolfenbüttel, Herzog August Bibliothek

Wolfenbüttel, Niedersächs. Staatsarchv
Wolfenbüttel, Niedersächsisches Staatsarchiv

Wolfenbüttel, Stadt- & Kreisheimatmus.
Wolfenbüttel, Stadt- und Kreisheimatmuseum
[in Schloss]

Wolfsburg, Kstver.
Wolfsburg, Kunstverein

Wolverhampton, A.G.
Wolverhampton, Wolverhampton Art Gallery

Wolverhampton, Bantock House Mus.
Wolverhampton, Bantock House Museum

Woodstock, Oxon Co. Mus.
Woodstock, Oxfordshire County Museum

Wooster, OH, Coll. A. Mus.
Wooster, OH, College of Wooster Art
Museum

Worcester, Cantor A.G.
Worcester, Cantor Art Gallery

Worcester, Dyson Perrins Mus. Porcelain
Worcester, Dyson Perrins Museum of
Worcester Porcelain

Worcester, Cape Prov., Hugo Naudé House
Worcester, Cape Province, Hugo Naudé
House

Worcester, MA, Amer. Antiqua. Soc.
Worcester, MA, American Antiquarian Society

Worcester, MA, A. Mus.
Worcester, MA, Worcester Art Museum

Worcester, MA, Coll. Holy Cross
Worcester, MA, College of the Holy Cross

Worcester, MA, Poly. Inst. A. Col.
Worcester, MA, Worcester Polytechnic
Institute Art Collection

Worksop Mus.
Worksop, Worksop Museum

Wörlitz, Schloss
Wörlitz, Schloss Wörlitz

Wörlitz, Schloss, Gotisches Haus

Wörlitz, Staatl. Schlösser & Gtn
Wörlitz, Staatliche Schlösser und Gärten

Worms, Ksthaus Heylshof
Worms, Kunsthaus Heylshof [Heylshof
Kunstsammlungen]

Worms, Mus. & Städt. Gemäldegal.
Worms, Museum der Stadt Worms und
Städtische Gemäldegalerie

Worpswede, Barkenhoff-Stift.
Worpswede, Barkenhoff-Stiftung

Worpswede, Ksthalle
Worpswede, Kunsthalle

Wrexham Lib. A. Cent.
Wrexham, Wrexham Library Arts Centre

Wrocław, Archaeol. Mus.
Wrocław, Archaeological Museum (Muzeum
Archeologiczne)

Wrocław, Archidioc. Mus.
Wrocław, Archidiocesan Museum (Muzeum
Archidiecezjalne)

Wrocław, Mus. Archit.
Wrocław, Museum of Architecture (Muzeum
Architektury we Wrocławiu)

Wrocław, N. Mus.
Wrocław, National Museum (Muzeum
Narodowe we Wrocławiu)

Wrocław, Ossolineum [Ossolinski N.
Establishment]

Wrocław, Panorama Bldg
Wrocław, Panorama Building [built to house
Racławice Panorama]

Wrocław, Schlesisches Mus.
Wrocław, Schlesisches Museum

Wrocław, Sil. Mus.
Wrocław, Silesian Museum (Muzeum Śląskie)
[now part of N. Mus.]

Wrocław, State Higher Sch. F.A
Wrocław, State Higher School of Fine Arts
(Państwowa Wyzsza Szkoła Sztuk
Plastycznych we Wrocławiu)

Wrocław, T. Mikulski Voivodship & Mun. Pub.
Lib.
Wrocław, T. Mikulski Voivodship and
Municipal Public Library (Wojewódzka i
Miejska Biblioteka Publiczna imenia Tadeusza
Mikulskiego we Wrocławiu)

Wrocław, U. Wrocław, Lib.
Wrocław, Library of the University of
Wrocław (Biblioteka Uniwersytecka we
Wrocławiu)

Wuhan, Hubei Prov. Mus.
Wuhan, Hubei Provincial Museum

Wuppertal, Gal. Parnass
Wuppertal, Galerie Parnass

Wuppertal, Musver.
Wuppertal, Museumsverein

Wuppertal, Städt. Mus.
Wuppertal, Städtisches Museum Wuppertal
[name changed to Von der Heydt-Mus. in Dec
1961]

Wuppertal, Von der Heydt-Mus.
Wuppertal, Von der Heydt-Museum

Würzburg, Augustinerkirche

Würzburg, Luitpoldmus.
Würzburg, Luitpoldmuseum

Würzburg, Mainfränk. Mus.
Würzburg, Mainfränkisches Museum [in
Festung Marienburg]

Würzburg, Residenz (Bayer. Verwalt. Staatl.
Schlösser, Gtn & Seen)
Würzburg, Residenz (Bayerische Verwaltung
der Staatlichen Schlösser, Gärten und Seen)

Würzburg, Städt. Gal.
Würzburg, Städtische Galerie

Würzburg, Ubib.
Würzburg, Universitätsbibliothek

Würzburg, U. Würzburg, Wagner-Mus.
Würzburg, Universität Würzburg, Martin von
Wagner-Museum

Wuwei, Co. Mus.
Wuwei, Wuwei County Museum

Wuxi, Mun. Mus.
Wuxi, Municipal Museum

Xai-Xai, Mus. Prov. Guerras Resistência
Xai-Xai, Museu Provincial Guerras de
Resistência

Xalapa, Gal. Ramón Alva de la Canal
Xalapa, Galería Ramón Alva de la Canal

Xalapa, Mus. Antropol. Veracruz
Xalapa, Museo de Antropología de Veracruz

Xalapa, U. Veracruzana, Mus. Antropol.
Xalapa, Universidad Veracruzana, Museo de
Antropología

Xiamen U.
Xiamen, Xiamen University

Xi'an, Shaanxi Prov. Mus.
Xi'an, Shaanxi Provincial Museum

Xi'an, Banpo Mus.
Xi'an, Banpo Museum

Xianyang Mus.
Xianyang, Xianyang Museum

Xining, Qinghai Prov. Mus.
Xining, Qinghai Provincial Museum

Yamagata, Prefect. Mus.
Yamagata, Prefectural Museum

Yamaguchi, Prefect. Mus.
Yamaguchi, Prefectural Museum (Yamaguchi-
kenritsu Hakubutsuhan)

Yamashima, Kajuji

Yangzhou Mus.
Yangzhou, Yangzhou Museum

Yanshi, Henan Prov., Cult. Bureau
Yanshi, Henan Province, Cultural Bureau

Yaoundé, Petit Mus. A.
Yaoundé, Petit Musée d'Art Camerounais [in
Mt Febe Benedictine Monastery]

Yapahuva, Archaeol. Mus.
Yapahuva, Archaeological Museum

Yaroslavl', A. Mus.
Yaroslavl', Art Museum (Khudozhestvennyy
Muzey)

Yassıhöyük, Gordion Mus.
Yassıhöyük, Gordion Museum (Gordion
Müzesi)

Yasugi, Shimane Prefect., Adachi A. Mus.
Yasugi, Shimane Prefecture, Adachi Art
Museum (Adachi Bijutsukan)

Yecla, Col. Escolapios
Yecla, Colección de los Escolapios

Yecla, Mus. Arqueol. Mun.
Yecla, Museo Arqueológico Municipal

Yekaterinburg, Reg. Mus.
Yekaterinburg, Regional Museum (Oblastnoy
Krayevedcheskiy Muzey)

Yellowknife, Prince Of Wales N. Her. Cent.
Yellowknife, Prince of Wales Northern
Heritage Centre

Yellowstone N. Park
Yellowstone National Park [E. Idaho,
S. Montana, NW Wyoming]

Yerevan: see Erevan

Yeroskipou, Mus. Flk A.
Yeroskipou, Museum of Folk Art

Yogyakarta, Batik Res. Cent.
Yogyakarta, Batik Research Centre

Yogyakarta, Fort Vredenburg

Yogyakarta, Grand Mosque

Yogyakarta, Hamengku Buwono Pal. Mus.
Yogyakarta, Hamengku Buwono Palace
Museum (Museum Hamengku Buwono)

Yogyakarta, Pakualam Pal.
Yogyakarta, Pakualam Palace

Yogyakarta, Sono Budoyo Mus.
Yogyakarta, Sono Budoyo Museum (Museum
Sono Budoyo)

Yokogoshi, N. Cult. Mus.
Yokogoshi, Northern Culture Museum
[Hoppo Bunka Mus.]

Yokohama, Kanagawa Prefect. Mus.
Yokohama, Kanagawa Prefectural Museum
(Kanagawa- Kenritsu Hakubutsukan)

Yokohama Mus. A.
Yokohama, Yokohama Museum of Art
[opened 1989]

Yokohama, Sankeien

Yonkers: see New York

York, Ampleforth Abbey

York, C.A.G.
York, City Art Gallery [until 1892 called F.A.
& Ind. Exh. Bldgs]

York, City Lib.
York, City Library

York, F.A. & Ind. Exh. Bldgs
York, Yorkshire Fine Art and Industrial
Exhibition Buildings [name changed to in
C.A.G. in 1892]

York, Fairfax House

York Minster, Chapter Lib.
York, York Minster, Chapter Library

York Minster, Foundations
York, York Minster, Foundations

York, Town Hall

York, U. York, Heslington Hall
York, University of York, Heslington Hall

York, Yorks Mus.
York, Yorkshire Museum

Yorktown, VA, Colon. N. Hist. Park
Yorktown, VA, Colonial National Historical
Park [incl. Yorktown Visitor Center]

Yosemite N. Park Mus., CA
Yosemite National Park, CA, Yosemite
National Park Museum

Youngstown, OH, Butler Inst. Amer. A.
Youngstown, OH, Butler Institute of
American Art

Zabalaga, Fund. Chillida
Zabalaga, Fundación Chillida

Zabbar, Mus. Our Lady of the Graces
Zabbar, Museum of Our Lady of the Graces

Zacatecas, Inst. N. Antropol. & Hist. Guadalupe
Zacatecas, Instituto Nacional de Antropología
e Historia in Guadalupe

Zacatecas, Mus. Francisco Goitia
Zacatecas, Museo Francisco Goitia

Zacatecas, Mus. Guadalupe
Zacatecas, Museo Guadalupe [Museo de Arte
Colonial]

Zacatecas, Mus. Pedro Coronel
Zacatecas, Museo Pedro Coronel

Zacatecas, Mus. Rafael Coronel
Zacatecas, Museo Rafael Coronel

Zaculeu, Mus. Arqueol.
Zaculeu, Museo Arqueológico

Zadar, Hist. Archvs
Zadar, Historical Archives

Zadar, N. Mus.
Zadar, National Museum (Narodni Muzej)

Zadar, Permanent Exh. Eccles. A.
Zadar, Permanent Exhibition of Ecclesiastical
Art [in Benedictine Abbey & Church of St
Mary]

Zagorsk: the town reverted from Zagorsk to its
pre-revolutionary name in Sept 1991; see Sergiyev
Posad

Zagreb, A. Pav.
Zagreb, Art Pavilion (Umjetnički Paviljon)

Zagreb, Archaeol. Mus.
Zagreb, Archaeological Museum (Arheološki
Muzej)

Zagreb, Cent. Film, Phot. & TV
Zagreb, Center for Film, Photography and
Television (Centar za Film, Fotografiju i
Televiziju)

Zagreb, City Mus.
Zagreb, Museum of the City of Zagreb (Muzej
Grada Zagreb)

Zagreb, Croat. Acad. A. & Sci., Graph. A. Cab.
Zagreb, Croatian Academy of Arts and
Sciences, Graphic Art Cabinet

Zagreb, Gal. Contemp. A.
Zagreb, Gallery of Contemporary Art (Galerija
Suvremene Umjetnosti)

Zagreb, Gal. Horvat
Zagreb, Benko Horvat Gallery (Galerija Benko
Horvat)

Zagreb, Gal. Mod. A.
Zagreb, Gallery of Modern Art (Moderna
Galerija)

Zagreb, Gal. Primitive A.
Zagreb, Gallery of Primitive Art (Galerija
Primitivne Umjetnosti)

Zagreb, Hall Croat. Parliament
Zagreb, Hall of the Croatian Parliament

Zagreb, Hist. Mus. Croatia
Zagreb, Historical Museum of Croatia
(Povijesni Muzej Hrvatske)

Zagreb, Meštrović Studio
Zagreb, Ivan Meštrović Studio (Atelje Ivan
Meštrović)

Zagreb, Mimara Mus.
Zagreb, Mimara Museum

Zagreb, Mun. A.G.
Zagreb, Municipal Art Gallery (Galerije Grada
Zagreba) [admins Cent. Film, Phot. & TV;
Gal. Contemp. A.; Gal. Horvat; Gal. Primitive
A.; Meštrović Studio]

Zagreb, Mus. A. & Crafts
Zagreb, Museum of Art and Crafts (Muzej za
Umjetnost i Obrt)

Zagreb, Mus. Revolution Croat. Peoples
Zagreb, Museum of the Revolution of
Croatian Peoples (Muzej Revolucije Naroda
Hrvatske)

Zagreb, N. & U. Lib., Graph. Col.
Zagreb, National and University Library,
Graphics Collection

Zagreb, Slika Gal.
Zagreb, Slika Gallery (Galerija Slika Grada)
[now Gal. Contemp. A.]

Zagreb, Strossmayer Gal.
Zagreb, Strossmayer Gallery of Old Masters
(Strossmayerova Galerija Starih Majstora)

Zagreb, Theat. Mus. Col.
Zagreb, Theatre Museum Collection [attached
to Theatrology Institute of the Croatian
Academy of Arts and Sciences]

Zagreb, U. Zagreb Lib.
Zagreb, University of Zagreb Library
(Svenčilište u Zagrebu)

Zagreb, Yug. Acad. Sci. & A.
Zagreb, Yugoslav Academy of Sciences & Arts
(Jugoslavenska Akademija Znanosti i
Umjetnosti)

Zaječar, N. Mus.
Zaječar, National Museum (Narodni Muzej)

Zakopane, Office A. Exh. Gal.
Zakopane, Office of Art Exhibitions Gallery
(Biuro Wystaw Artystyczny Gallery)

Zakynthos, Byz. Mus.
Zakynthos, Byzantine Museum

Zakynthos, Mus.
Zakynthos, Zakynthos Museum

Zalaegerszeg, Göcseji Mus.
Zalaegerszeg, Göcseji Museum (Göcseji
Múzeum)

Zamora, Hosp. Encarnación
Zamora, Hospital de la Encarnación

Zamora, Mus. Zamora
Zamora, Museo de Zamora

Zamość, Office A. Exh.
Zamość, Office of Art Exhibitions (Biuro
Wystaw Artystycznych)

Zaporizhzhya, Reg. A. Mus.
Zaporizhzhya, Regional Art Museum
(Oblastnoy Khudozhestvennyy)

Zaragoza: see Saragossa

Žár nad Sázavou, Castle Museum
Žár nad Sázavou, Castle Museum

Žár nad Sázavou, Distr. Mus.
Žár nad Sázavou, District Museum (Okresní
Muzeum)

Žár nad Sázavou, Mus. Book
Žár nad Sázavou, Museum of the Book
(Mzeum Knihy a Knižní Kultury) [in castle]

Zeil, Schloss
Zeil, Schloss Zeil

Zeist, Rijksdnst Mnmtz.
Zeist, Rijksdienst voor de Monumentenzorg

Zhengzhou, Commem. Hall
Zhengzhou, Commemoration Hall

Zhengzhou, Henan Prov. Cult. Relics Res. Inst.
Zhengzhou, Henan Province Cultural Relics Research Institute

Zhengzhou, Henan Prov. Mus.
Zhengzhou, Henan Provincial Museum

Zhenjiang, Mun. Mus.
Zhenjiang, Municipal Museum

Zibo, Mun. Mus.
Zibo, Municipal Museum

Židlochovice Mus.
Židlochovice, Židlochovice Museum (Židlochovice Místní Muzeum)

Zierikzee, Burgerweeshuis

Zlín, Reg. Gal. F.A.
Zlín, Regional Gallery of Fine Art (Oblastní Galerie Výtvarného Umění)

Znojmo, Distr. Archvs
Znojmo, District Archives (Okresní Archiv)

Znojmo, S. Morav. Mus.
Znojmo, South Moravian Museum (Jihomoravské Muzeum)

Zoetermeer, Van Kempen & Begeer Mus.
Zoetermeer, Van Kempen en Begeer Museum

Zöfingen, Stadtbib.
Zöfingen, Stadtbibliothek

Zrenjanin, N. Mus.
Zrenjanin, National Museum (Narodni Muzej)

Zrenjanin, Pict. Gal.
Zrenjanin, Picture Gallery (Mala Galerija)

Zug, Mus. Burg
Zug, Museum in der Burg

Zug, Paroch. Archv
Zug, Parochial Archive

Zumaya, Casa Mus. Zuloaga
Zumaya, Casa Museo Ignacio Zuloaga

Zurich, Anker Bank

Zurich, August Laube

Zurich, Bank Julius Baer and Co. Ltd

Zurich, Baugesch. Archv
Zurich, Baugeschichtliches Archiv

Zurich, City-Gal.
Zurich, City-Galerie

Zurich, David M. Koetser

Zurich, Ecole Poly. Féd.
Zurich, Ecole Polytechnique Fédérale

Zurich, Eidgenöss. Tech. Hochsch.
Zurich, Eidgenössische Technische Hochschule

Zurich, Eidgenöss. Tech. Hochsch.-Bib.
Zurich, Eidgenössische Technische Hochschule-Bibliothek

Zurich, Gal. Bruno Bischofberger
Zurich, Galerie Bruno Bischofberger

Zurich, Gal. Bruno Meissner
Zurich, Galerie Bruno Meissner

Zurich, Gal. Dada
Zurich, Galerie Dada

Zurich, Gal. Form
Zurich, Galerie Form

Zurich, Gal. Jeanne Fillon
Zurich, Galerie Jeanne Fillon

Zurich, Gal. Knoedler
Zurich, Galerie Knoedler

Zurich, Gal. Koller
Zurich, Galerie Koller

Zurich, Gal. Kurt Meissner
Zurich, Galerie Kurt Meissner

Zurich, Gal. Nathan
Zurich, Galerie Nathan

Zurich, Gal. Strunskaja
Zurich, Galerie Strunskaja

Zurich, Gal. Tanner
Zurich, Galerie Tanner

Zurich, Gal. Wolfsberg
Zurich, Galerie Wolfsberg

Zurich, Geshaus Schneggen
Zurich, Gesellschafthaus zur Schneggen

Zurich, Graph. Samml. Eidgenöss. Tech. Hochsch.
Zurich, Graphische Sammlung der Eidgenössischen Technischen Hochschule

Zurich, Haus Rechberg
Zurich, Haus zum Rechberg

Zurich, Helmhaus

Zurich, István Schlégl

Zurich, Jung-Inst.
Zurich, Jung-Institut

Zurich, Kstgewmus.
Zurich, Kunstgewerbemuseum

Zurich, Kstgewsch.
Zurich, Kunstgewerbeschule [Ecole des Arts Appliqués]

Zurich, Ksthalle
Zurich, Kunsthalle Zürich

Zurich, Ksthaus
Zurich, Kunsthaus Zürich

Zurich, Landolthaus

Zurich, Maeght [closed]

Zurich, Marlborough Gal.
Zurich, Marlborough Galerie

Zurich, Mus. Bellerive
Zurich, Museum Bellerive

Zurich, Mus. Gestalt.
Zurich, Museum für Gestaltung Zürich

Zurich, Mus. Rietberg
Zurich, Museum Rietberg

Zurich, Peter Ineichen
Zurich, Peter Ineichen

Zurich, Pro Helvetia
Zurich, Pro Helvetia [Swiss Arts Council]

Zurich, Rau Found.
Zurich, Rau Foundation

Zurich, Saal Kaufleuten
Zurich, Saal zur Kaufleuten

Zurich, Samml. Hauser & Wirth
Zurich, Sammlung Hauser und Wirth

Zurich, SBG Gal.
Zurich, SBG Galerie [Schweizerische Bank Gesellschaft]

Zurich, Schweiz. Bankverein
Zurich, Schweizerischer Bankverein

Zurich, Schweiz. Credit Anstalt
Zurich, Schweizerische Credit Anstalt

Zurich, Schweiz. Inst. Kstwiss.
Zurich, Schweizerisches Institut für Kunstwissenschaft [Institut Suisse pour l'Etude de l'Art]

Zurich, Schweiz. Landesmus.
Zurich, Schweizerisches Landesmuseum

Zurich, Schweiz. N. Versicherung Ges. Col.
Zurich, Schweizerische National-Versicherung-Gesellschaft Collection

Zurich, Stadtarchv
Zurich, Stadtarchiv

Zurich, Stift. Samml. Bührle
Zurich, Stiftung Sammlung E.G. Bührle

Zurich, Theo Beyer

Zurich, Thomas Amman F.A.G.
Zurich, Thomas Amman Fine Art Gallery

Zurich, U. Zurich, Archäol. Inst.
Zurich, Universität Zürich, Archäologisches Institut

Zurich, U. Zurich, Vlkerkndmus.
Zurich, Universität Zürich, Völkerkundemuseum

Zurich, Zentbib.
Zurich, Zentralbibliothek

Zurich, Zent. Le Corbusier–Heidi Weber
Zurich, Zentrum Le Corbusier–Heidi Weber

Zurich, Zool. Mus. U.
Zurich, Zoologisches Museum der Universität

Zurich, Zunfthaus Meisen
Zurich, Zunfthaus zur Meisen

Zurich, Zürch. Kstges.
Zurich, Zürcher Kunstgesellschaft

Zvenigorod, Mus. Hist. & Ethnog.
Zvenigorod, Museum of History & Ethnography (Muzey Istorii i Etnografii)

Zwolle, Prov. Overijssels Mus.
Zwolle, Provinciaal Overijssels Museum

Appendix B

LIST OF PERIODICAL TITLES

This list contains all of the periodical titles that have been cited in an abbreviated form in italics in the bibliographies of this dictionary. For the sake of comprehensiveness, it also includes entries of periodicals that have not been abbreviated, for example where the title consists of only one word or where the title has been transliterated. Abbreviated titles are alphabetized letter by letter, including definite and indefinite articles but ignoring punctuation, bracketed information and the use of ampersands. Roman and arabic numerals are alphabetized as if spelt out (in the appropriate language), as symbols (e.g. A + '⟨A plus⟩'). Additional information is given in square brackets to distinguish two or more identical titles or to cite a periodical's previous name (where such publishing information was known to the editors).

Aab. Nord. Oldknd. & Hist.
Aarbøger for nordisk oldkyndighed og historie [Yearbooks for Nordic antiquities and history; prev. pubd as *An. Nord. Oldknd.*]

Aachen. Beitr. Baugesch. & Heimatkst
Aachener Beiträge für Baugeschichte und Heimatkunst

Aachen. Ksthl.
Aachener Kunstblätter

AA Files
AA [Architectural Association] Files

A. Afrique
Arts d'Afrique

A. Afrique Noire
Arts d'Afrique noire

A Águia

A. Amat.
Art Amateur

A. America
Art in America [cont. as *A. America & Elsewhere*; *A. America*]

A. America & Elsewhere
Art in America and Elsewhere [prev. pubd as & cont. as *A. America*]

A. América & Filipinas
Arte en América y Filipinas

A. Anc. Flandre
Arts anciens de Flandre

A. Annu.
Art Annual

AA Notes
Architectural Association Notes

A. Ant.
Ars antiqua

A. & Ant.
Art and Antiques

A. Ant. & Mod.
Arte antica e moderna

AAP Envmt Des.
AAP Environment Design

A. & Archaeol.
Art and Archaeology

A. & Archaeol. Res. Pap.
Art and Archaeology Research Papers [AARP]

A. & Archaeol. Tech. Abstr.
Art and Archaeology Technical Abstracts

A. Archéol. Khmers
Art et archéologie khmers

A. & Archit.
i) Art and Architecture
ii) Arts and Architecture

Aarde & Vlk.
De aarde en haar volken [incorp. *Op De Uitkijk* from 1904]

A. & Argent
L'Art et l'argent

A. & Arqueol.
Arte e arqueología

A. & Artistes
Art et les artistes

A. & Artists
Art and Artists

A. Asia
Arts of Asia

A. Asiatiques
Arts asiatiques [prev. pubd as *Rev. A. Asiat.*]

A. & Auction
Art and Auction

A. Aujourd'hui
Art d'aujourd'hui [cont. as *Aujourd'hui*]

A. Australia
Art in Australia

A. & Australia
Art and Australia

Abacus [Yearbook of the Museum of Finnish Architecture]

A. Basse-Normandie
Art de Basse-Normandie

A. Bavar.
Ars Bavarica

Abbay

Abbia

ABC
ABC: Beiträge zum Bauen

abc decor

Abecedario

A. Belge
L'Art belge

Aberdeen U. Rev.
Aberdeen University Review

Aberdeen U. Stud.
Aberdeen University Studies

Aberdeen Wkly J.
Aberdeen Weekly Journal

Åber., Trondhjems Kstforen.
Årsberetning, Trondhjems Konstforening [Annual report, Trondheim Art Association]

Abh. Akad. Wiss. Göttingen, Philol.–Hist. Kl.
Abhandlungen der Akademie der Wissenschaften in Göttingen, philologisch–historische Klasse

Abh. Bayer. Akad. Wiss.
Abhandlungen der Bayerischen Akademie der Wissenschaften

Abh. & Ber. Kön. Zool. & Anthropol.–Ethnog. Mus. Dresden
Abhandlungen und Berichte des Königlichen zoologischen und anthropologisch–ethnographischen Museums zu Dresden

Abh. & Ber. Mus. Tierknd. & Vlkerknd. Dresden
Abhandlungen und Berichte der Museen für Tierkunde und Völkerkunde zu Dresden [cont. as *Abh. & Ber. Staatl. Mus. Vlkerknd., Dresden*]

Abh. & Ber. Staatl. Mus. Vlkerknd., Dresden
Abhandlungen und Berichte des Staatlichen Museums für Völkerkunde, Dresden [prev. pubd as *Abh. & Ber. Mus. Tierknd. & Vlkerknd. Dresden*]

Abh. Braunschweig. Wiss. Ges.
Abhandlungen der Braunschweigischen wissenschaftlichen Gesellschaft

Abh. Geistes- & Sozwiss. Kl.
Abhandlungen der geistes- und sozialwissenschaftlichen Klasse, Akademie der Wissenschaften und der Literatur, Mainz

Abh. Gesch. Stadt Augsburg
Abhandlungen zur Geschichte der Stadt Augsburg

Abh. Heidelberg. Akad. Wiss.
Abhandlungen der Heidelberger Akademie der Wissenschaften

Abh. Heidelberg. Akad. Wiss., Philos.–Hist. Kl.
Abhandlungen der Heidelberger Akademie der Wissenschaften, philosophisch–historische Klasse

Abh. Philol.–Hist. Kl. Bayer. Akad. Wiss.
Abhandlungen der philologisch–historischen Klasse der Bayerischen Akademie der Wissenschaft

Abh. Philol.–Hist. Kl. Kön. Sächs. Ges. Wiss.
Abhandlungen der philologisch–historischen Klasse der Königlichen sächsischen Gesellschaft der Wissenschaften

Abh. Philos.–Philol. Kl. Kön. Bayer. Akad. Wiss.
Abhandlungen der philolosophisch–philologischen Klasse der Königlichen bayerischen Akademie der Wissenschaften

Abh. Preuss. Akad. Wiss., Philol.–Hist.Kl.
Abhandlungen der Preussischen Akademie der Wissenschaften, philologisch–historische Klasse

Abh. Sächs. Akad. Wiss. Leipzig, Philol.–Hist. Kl.
Abhandlungen der Sächsischen Akademie der Wissenschaften zu Leipzig, philologisch–historische Klasse

Abh. Staatl. Mus. Mineral. & Geol. Dresden
Abhandlungen des Staatlichen Museums für Mineralogie und Geologie zu Dresden

A bis Z

Abitare

Áb. LSÓ
Árbok Listasafn Sigurjon Ólafsson [Yearbook of the Sigurjon Ólafsson Museum]

A. Bologna
Arte a Bologna

Aboriginal Hist.
Aboriginal History

Abrente

A. Brut
L'Art brut

Åb. Stat. Kstmus.
Årsbok för statens konstmuseer [Yearbook for state art museums]

Åb., Stavanger Mus.
Årbok, Stavanger Museum [Yearbook of the Stavanger Museum]

Abstraction, Création, A. Non-Fig.
Abstraction, création, art non-figuratif

Abstrakt/Konkr.
Abstrakt/Konkret

Åb. Svensk. Stat. Kstsaml.
Årsbok för Svenska statens konstsamlingen [Yearbook for the Swedish state art collection]

Åb. U. Bergen
Årbok for Universitetet i Bergen [prev. pubd as *Bergens Mus. Åb.*]

A. Buddhica
Ars Buddhica

A. Bull.
Art Bulletin

A. Bull. Victoria
Art Bulletin of Victoria

A. CA
Art of California

Acad. Anlct.: Kl. Lett.
Academiae analecta: Klasse der letteren [Koninklijke Vlaamse Academie voor wetenschappen, letteren en schone kunsten van België]

Acad. Anlct.: Kl. S. Kst.
Academiae analecta: Klasse der schone kunsten [Koninklijke Vlaamse Academie voor wetenschappen, letteren en schone kunsten van België]

Acad. Anlct.: Kl. Wetsch.
Academiae analecta: Klasse der wetenschappen [Koninklijke Vlaamse Academie voor wetenschappen, letteren en schone kunsten van België]

Acad. & Annu. Archit. Rev.
Academy and Annual Architectural Review [cont. as *Acad. Archit. & Archit. Rev.*]

Acad. Archit. & Archit. Rev.
Academy Architecture and Architectural Review [prev. pubd as *Acad. & Annu. Archit. Rev.*]

Acad. B.-A.
Académie des beaux-arts [prev. pubd as *Acad. B.-A.: C. R. Séances*]

Acad. B.-A., Bull. Annu.
Académie des beaux-arts, bulletin annuel

Acad. B.-A.: C. R. Séances
Académie des beaux-arts: Comptes rendus des séances [cont. as *Acad. B.-A.*]

Acad. B.-Lett. Caen
Académie des belles-lettres de Caen

Academia: Bol. Real Acad. B.A. San Fernando
Academia: Boletín de la Real academia de bellas artes de San Fernando

Academy [Dublin]

Acad. Inscr. & B.-Lett.: C. R. Séances
Académie des inscriptions et belles-lettres: Comptes rendus des séances

Acad. Sci., B.-Lett. & A. Besançon: Prog.-Verbaux & Mém.
Académie des sciences, belles-lettres et arts de Besançon: Progrès-verbaux et mémoires

A. Canada
Arts Canada [prev. pubd as *Can. A.*]

A. Català
L'Art català

Accad. & Bib. Italia
Accademie e biblioteche d'Italia

Accad. Italia, Rendi. Cl. Sci. Mor., Stor. & Filol.
Accademia d'Italia, rendiconti della classe di scienze morali, storiche e filologiche

Accad. N. Lincei, Cl. Sci. Mor., Stor. & Filol.: Rendi.
[Reale] Accademia nazionale dei Lincei, classe di scienze morali, storiche e filologiche: Rendiconti [prev. pubd as *Accad. N. Lincei: Rendi.*]

Accad. N. Lincei: Rendi.
[Reale] Accademia nazionale dei Lincei: Rendiconti [cont. as *Accad. N. Lincei, Cl. Sci. Mor., Stor. & Filol.: Rendi.*]

Achad. Leonardi Vinci: J. Leonardo Stud. & Bibliog. Vinciana
Achademia Leonardi Vinci: Journal of Leonardo Studies and Bibliography of Vinciana

A. & Cienc.
El arte y la ciencia

A. Cinéma.
L'Art cinématographique

A. Colombia
Arte en Colombia

A. Concr.
i) Art concret
ii) Arte concreta

A. Contemp.
L'Art contemporain

A. Crist.
Arte cristiana

A. Crit.
Art Criticism

A. & Crit.
L'Art et la critique

Acrópole

Acropoli

Acta

Acta Acad. Abo.: Human.
Acta Academiae Aboensis: Humaniora

Acta Amer.
Acta Americana

Acta Ant. Acad. Sci. Hung.
Acta antiqua Academiae scientiarum Hungaricae

Acta Antropol.
Acta antropológica

Acta Archaeol. [Copenhagen]
Acta archaeologica [Copenhagen]

Acta Archaeol. Acad. Sci. Hung.
Acta archaeologica Academiae scientiarum Hungaricae

Acta Archaeol. & A. Historiam Pertinentia
Acta ad archaeologicam et artium historiam pertinentia

Acta Archaeol. Louvan.
Acta archaeologica Louvaniensa

Acta Asiat.
Acta Asiatica

Acta Bib. Regiae Stockholm.
Acta Bibliothecae regiae Stockholmiensis

Acta Class.
Acta classica

Acta Ethnog. Acad. Sci. Hung.
Acta ethnographica Academiae scientarum Hungaricae

Acta Hist. A. Acad. Sci. Hung.
Acta historiae artium Academiae scientiarum Hungaricae

Acta Hist. & Archaeol. Med.
Acta historica et archaeologica mediaevalia

Acta Hist. Neerlandica
Acta historiae Neerlandica

Acta Inst. Romani Finland.
Acta Instituti Romani Finlandiae

Acta Jutland.
Acta Jutlandica

Acta Lapp.
Acta Lapponica

Acta Mozart.
Acta Mozartiana

Acta Organ.
Acta organologica

Acta Orient.
Acta orientalia

Acta Orientalia Acad. Sci. Hung.
Acta orientalia Academiae scientiarum Hungaricae

Acta Pol. Hist.
Acta Poloniae historica

Acta Praehist.
Acta praehistorica

Acta Praehist. & Archaeol.
Acta praehistorica et archaeologica [prev. pubd as *Berlin. Jb. Vor- & Frühgesch.*]

Actas & Mem. Soc. Esp. Antropol., Etnog. & Prehist.
Actas y memórias de la Sociedad español de antropología, etnografia y prehistoria

Acta Umělecko-Průmyslové Muz.
Acta Umělecko-Průmyslové Muzeum [Proceedings of the Museum of Applied Arts]

Acta U. Stockholm.
Acta Universitatis Stockholmiensis

Acta U. Upsaliensis
Acta Universitatis Upsaliensis

Acta U. Upsaliensis: Boreas
Acta Universitatis Upsaliensis: Boreas

Acta U. Upsaliensis: Figura
Acta Universitatis Upsaliensis: Figura

Action

Actualidades

Actum Luce

Actum Tilburgh

A. & Curiosité
Art et curiosité

Adabiy Meros

A. Dec.
Ars decorativa

A. & Dec.
Arts and Decoration

A. Déc.
L'Art décoratif [cont. as *A. & Déc.*]

A. & Déc.
Art et décoration [prev. pubd as *A. Déc.*]

A. Dec. Mod.
L'arte decorativa moderna

A. & Des.
Art and Design

A. Deux Mondes
L'Art dans les deux mondes

A. Dig.
Arts Digest [cont. as *Arts* [New York]; *A. Mag.*]

A. Digest
Art Digest

A. Dim.
Art Dimension

A. Dir.
Art Direction

A. Directors' Annu. NY
Art Directors' Annual of New York

A. Doc.
Art Documentation

A. Docs
Art Documents

A. & Dossier
Art et dossier

Adv. Biol. & Medic. Phys.
Advances in Biological and Medical Physics

Adv. World Archaeol.
Advances in World Archaeology

Aegaeum [Liège]

Aegeum

Aegyptus
Aegyptus: Rivista italiana di egittologia e di papirologia

A. Emilia
Arte in Emilia

Aesculape

A. Esp.
Arte español

A. España
Arte en España: Revista mensual del arte y de su historia

Aetnal

Aevum

Afghanistan

Afghanistan J.
Afghanistan Journal

Afghanistan Q.
Afghanistan Quarterly

Afghan Stud.
Afghan Studies

A. Figurativa
Arte figurativa

A. Figurative
Arti figurative: Rivista d'arte antica e moderna

A. Flam. & Holl.
Art flamand et hollandais

A. Fr.
L'Art français

Afr. A.
African Arts

A. France
i) Art de France: Revue annuelle de l'art ancien et moderne
ii) Arts de France

Afr. Archaeol. Rev.
African Archaeological Review

Afrasiab

Afrasiabskaya Kompleksnaya Arkheol. Eksped.
Afrasiabskaya kompleksnaya arkheologicheskaya ekspeditsiya

Afr. Bull.
Africana Bulletin

Afr. Gandensia
Africana Gandensia

Africa
Africa: Journal of the International Institute of African Languages and Cultures

Africa [Madrid]

Africa: Inst. N. Archéol. & A.
Africa: Institut national d'archéologie et de l'art

Africa It.
Africa italiana: Rivista di storia e d'arte [prev. pubd as *Not. Archeol.*, cont. as *Quad. Archeol. Libia*]

Africana [West African Society]

Africa-Tervuren

Africa Today

Afr. Insight
Africa Insight

Afrique Hist.
Afrique historique

Afrique Lit. & A.
Afrique littéraire et artistique

A. Friuli, A. Trieste
Arte in Friuli, arte a Trieste

Afr. J.
Africana Journal

Afr. Lang. & Cult.
African Languages and Cultures

Afr. Lang. Rev.
African Language Review

Afr. Lang. Stud.
African Language Studies

Afr. Music.
African Musicology

Afr. Notes & News
African Notes and News

A. Front
Art Front

Afr. Res. Bull.
African Research Bulletin

Afr. Stud. [China]
African Studies [China]

Afr. Stud. [S. Africa]
African Studies [South Africa]

Afr. Stud. Bull.
African Studies Bulletin

Afr. Stud. Rev.
African Studies Review

Afr. Stud. Ser.
African Studies Series

Afr. Sunrise
African Sunrise

Afryka, Azja, Ameryka, Łacinska

Afterimage

Age

A. Georgica
Ars Georgica

A.G.: Mag.
Art Gallery: Magazine

A.G. NSW Q.
Art Gallery of New South Wales Quarterly

Ägyp. Sprache & Altertknd.
Ägyptische Sprache und Alterthumskunde

A Ház

A. Her.
Art Heritage

A. Hispal.
Arte hispalense

A. Hist.
Art History

Ahí Va Golpe
Ahí va el golpe

El Ahuizote

A. Hung.
Ars Hungarica

AIA J.
AIA [American Institute for Architects] Journal [cont. as *Architecture* [USA]]

A. & Idée
L'Art et l'idée

A. Illus.
Arte illustrata: Rivista d'arte antica e moderna

A. & Indust.
Art and Industry [prev. pubd as *Commerc. A.*; *Commerc. A. & Indust.*; cont. as *Des. Indus.*]

A. Inst. Chicago Mus. Stud.
Art Institute of Chicago Museum Studies

A. Int.
Art International

AION [Annali dell'Istituto universitario orientale di Napoli]

A. Ireland
Arts in Ireland

Airport Forum

A. Islam.
Ars Islamica

A. & Islam. World
Arts and the Islamic World

A. Italia
L'arte in Italia: Rivista mensile di belle arti

A. It. Dec. & Indust.
Arte italiana decorativa e industriale

A. J. [London]
Art Journal [London]

A. J. [New York]
Art Journal [New York; prev. pubd as *Coll. A. J.*; *Parnassus*]

A. Jamaica
Arts Jamaica

Akad. Arkhit.
Akademiya arkhitektury [Academy of architecture]

Akad. Nauk SSSR: Otdel Drevnerus. Lit.: Trudy
Akademiya nauk SSSR: Otdel drevnerusskoy literatury: Trudy [Academy of Sciences of the USSR: Department of Old Russian Literature: transactions]

Akkadica

Aktion
Aktion: Zeitschrift für freiheitliche Politik und Literatur

Aktuell Fot.
Aktuell Fotografi

Akwesasne Notes

Al-Andalus

A.-Lang.
Art-Language

Alaska J.
Alaska Journal

Albania
Albania: Revue d'archéologie, d'histoire, d'art et des sciences appliquées en Albanie et dans les Balkans

Albanie Nouv.
Albanie nouvelle

Alba Regia
Alba Regia: Annales Musei Stephani Regis

Al-Basit

Albenaa

Albertina Inf.
Albertina Informationen

Albertina-Stud.
Albertina-Studien

Album Figaro
Album du Figaro

Albums Crocodile
Albums du crocodile

Album S. Kst.
Album der schoone kunsten

Alemann. Jb.
Alemannisches Jahrbuch

Alero

A. & Lett.
i) Art and Letters
ii) Arts and Letters

Alfar

Al-hawlīyāt al-āthāriyya al-sūriyya

A. Libre
L'Art libre

A. & Libris
De arte et libris

A. Libs J.
Art Libraries Journal [prev. pubd as *ARLIS Newslett.*]

A. Links
Art Links

A. & Lit.
Art and Literature

Al-Kashkūl

Alkotás

Allemagne Aujourd'hui
Allemagne d'aujourd'hui

Allen Mem. A. Mus. Bull.
Allen Memorial Art Museum Bulletin

Allg. Anzeiger Bbindereien
Allgemeiner Anzeiger für Buchbindereien

Allgäu. Geschfreund
Allgäuer Geschichtsfreund

Allg. Bauztg Abbild.
Allgemeine Bauzeitung mit Abbildungen: Österreichische Vierteljahresschrift für den öffentlichen Baudienst

Allg. & Vergl. Archäol.: Beitr.
Allgemeine und vergleichende Archäologie: Beiträge

Allg. Ztg
Allgemeine Zeitung

Alliance

Al-Manhal [Beehive]

Al-Ma'rifa

Alm. Bât.
Almanach du bâtiment

Alm. Fam. Meneghina
Almanacco della famiglia Meneghina

Almogaren

Alm. Österreich. Akad. Wiss.
Almanach der Österreichischen Akademie der Wissenschaften

Alm. Paris.
Almanach parisien

Alm. Prov.
Almanaque de las provincias

Alm. Schoone & Goede
Almanak voor het schoone en goede

Al-Mulk

A. Lombarda
Arte lombarda

Al-Rāfidān [Mesopotamia]

Al-Tatawwur [Development]

Altbayer. Mschr.
Altbayerische Monatsschrift [prev. pubd as *Mschr. Hist. Ver. Oberbayern*]

Alte & Mod. Kst
Alte und moderne Kunst

Alte & Neue Kst
Alte und neue Kunst

Alte & Neue Welt
Alte und neue Welt

Alt-Frankfurt: Vjschr. Kst & Gesch.
Alt-Frankfurt: Vierteljahresschrift für seine Kunst und Geschichte

Altorient. Forsch.
Altorientalische Forschungen

Alt-Thüringen
Alt-Thüringen: Jahresschrift des Museums für Ur- und Frühgeschichte Thüringens

Alt-Wien. Kal.
Alt-Wiener Kalender

Alt-Württemberg

Alumni Bull.
Alumni Bulletin of the Rhode Island School of Design

A. Madí Univl
Arte Madí universal

A. Mag.
i) Art Magazine: A Bi-monthly Review of the Visual Arts
ii) Arts Magazine [prev. pubd as *Arts* [New York]; *A. Dig.*]

A. Maison
Arts de la maison

Amat. Photographer
Amateur Photographer

Amat. Phot. Prt
Amateur Photographic Print

Ambix

Amb. Nuova Archit.
Ambienti della nuova architettura

A.M.C. [prev. pubd as *Archit., Movt, Cont.*]

A. Med.
Arte medievale

A. Medit.
Arte mediterranea

A. Melbourne
Arts in Melbourne

Amer. A.
American Art

Amer. A. Annu.
American Art Annual [cont. as *Amer. A. Dir.*]

Amer. A. & Ant.
American Art and Antiques

Amer. A. Dir.
American Art Directory [prev. pubd as *Amer. A. Annu.*]

Amer. A. J.
American Art Journal

Amer. Amat. Photographer
American Amateur Photographer

Amer. A. News
American Art News

Amer. Annu. Phot.
American Annual of Photography [cont. as *Phot. Annu.*]

Amer. Ant.
American Antiquity: Quarterly Review of American Archaeology [incorp. *Mem. Soc. Amer. Archaeol.*]

Amer. Anthropologist
American Anthropologist

Amer. Antiqua. Soc. Proc.
American Antiquarian Society Proceedings

Amer. Ant. J.
American Antiques Journal [cont. as *Ant. J.*]

Amer. A. Q.
American Art Quarterly

Amer. Architect
American Architect [prev. pubd as *Amer. Architect & Bldg News*; cont. as *Amer. Architect & Archit. Rev.*; *Amer. Architect*; *Amer. Architect & Archit.*]

Amer. Architect & Archit.
American Architect and Architecture [see *Amer. Architect*]

Amer. Architect & Archit. Rev.
American Architect and the Architectural Review [see *Amer. Architect*]

Amer. Architect & Bldg News
American Architect and Building News [see *Amer. Architect*]

Amer. A. Rev.
American Art Review

Amer. Artist
American Artist

Amer. Assoc. Archit. Bibliog.: Pap.
American Association of Architectural Bibliographers: Papers

Amer. Benedictine Rev.
American Benedictine Review

Amer. Bldr's J.
American Builder's Journal

Amer. Cath. Philos. Q.
American Catholic Philosophical Quarterly

Amer. Cer.
American Ceramics

Amer. Cer. Circ. Bull.
American Ceramic Circle Bulletin

Amer. Colr
American Collector

Amer. Craft
American Craft

Amer. Craft Horiz.
American Craft Horizon

Amer. Cttee S. Asian A. Newslett.
American Committee for South Asian Art Newsletter

Amer. Ethnologist
American Ethnologist

Amer. Fabrics
American Fabrics

Amer. Gdnr Mag.
American Gardener Magazine

Amer. Her.
American Heritage

Amer. Hist. Rev.
American Historical Review

Amer. Homes & Gdns
American Homes and Gardens

América

América Indíg.
América indígena

Américas

Amer. Ind. A.
American Indian Art

Amer. Ind. A. & Cult.
American Indian Arts and Culture

Amer. Ind. Bask.
American Indian Basketry

Amerind. Cosmol.
Amerindian Cosmology

Amer. Ind. Cult. & Res. J.
American Indian Culture and Research Journal

Amer. Ind. Trad.
American Indian Tradition

Amer. J. Anc. Hist.
American Journal of Ancient History

Amer. J. Archaeol.
American Journal of Archaeology

Amer. J. Phot. & Allied A. & Serv.
American Journal of Photography and the Allied Arts and Services

Amer. J. Phys. Anthropol.
American Journal of Physical Anthropology

Amer. J. Psych.
American Journal of Psychiatry

Amer. J. Psychol.
American Journal of Psychology

Amer. J. Semit. Lang. & Lit.
American Journal of Semitic Languages and Literatures

Amer. J. Sociol.
American Journal of Sociology

Amer. Landscape Architect
American Landscape Architect

Amer. Mag. A.
American Magazine of Art

Amer. Math. Mthly
American Mathematical Monthly

Amer. Mus. Nat. Hist. Bull.
American Museum of Natural History Bulletin

Amer. Numi. Soc. Mus. Notes
American Numismatic Society Museum Notes

Amer. Philos. Q.
American Philosophical Quarterly

Amer. Photographer
American Photographer

Amer. Q.
American Quarterly

Amer. Res. Cent. Egypt Newslett.
American Research Center in Egypt Newsletter

Amer. Scand. Rev.
American Scandinavian Review

Amer. Scholar
American Scholar

Amer. Sch. Prehist. Res. Bull.
American School of Prehistoric Research Bulletin

Amer. Scientist
American Scientist

Amer. Soc. Excav. Sardis
American Society for the Excavation of Sardis

Amer. Soc. Testing & Mat. Proc.
American Society for Testing and Materials Proceedings

Amer. Stud.
American Studies

A. Métal
L'Art du métal

A. & Métiers Graph.
Arts et métiers graphiques

A. México
Artes de México

Amic A.
L'Amic des arts

Amicis: Jb. Österreich. Gal.
Amicis: Jahrbuch der Österreichischen Galerie

Amis Mnmts & A.
Les Amis des monuments et des arts

Amis Mus. Lille: Bull. Trimest.
Amis des Musées de Lille: Bulletin trimestriel

Ammin. & Politica
Amministrazione e politica

A.: Mnmts & Mém.
Arts: Monuments et mémoires

A. Mod.
L'arte moderna

A. Mod. [Brussels]
Art moderne [Brussels]

Amor Libro
Amor di libro

Amour A.
L'Amour de l'art [cont. as *Prométhée*; reverts to *Amour A.*]

Amperland

Amstelodamum

Amsterdam

A. Mthly
Art Monthly

A. Mthly [Australia]
Art Monthly [Australia]

A. Mthly Rev. & Phot. Port.
Art Monthly Review and Photographic Portfolio

Amtl. Ber. Kön. Kstsamml.
Amtliche Berichte aus den Königlichen Kunstsammlungen [cont. as *Berlin. Mus.: Ber. Staatl. Mus. Preuss. Kultbes.*; *Berlin. Mus.: Ber. Ehem. Preuss. Kstsamml.*]

Amts- & Intellbl. Ksr. Kön. Ztg
Amts- und Intelligenzblatt zur kaiserlichen königlichen Zeitung

A Műgyűjtő [The collector]

A. N.
Art national

An. Acad. Fr.
Annales de l'Académie française

An. Acad. Geog. & Hist. Guatemala
Anales de la Academia de geografía e historia de Guatemala

An. Acad. N. A. & Let.
Anales de la Academia nacional de artes y letras

An. Acad. Romăne
Analele Academia Romăne

An. Acad. Royale Archéol. Belgique
Annales de l'Académie royale
d'archéologie de Belgique [cont. as
*Rev. Belge Archéol. & Hist. A./
Belge Tijdschr. Oudhdknde &
Kstgesch.*]

Anadolu
Anadolu: Revue des études
d'archéologie et d'histoire en
Turquie

Anadolu Araştırmaları
Anadolu araştırmaları [Anatolian
studies]

Anadolu Sanatı Araştırmaları
Anadolu sanatı araştırmaları
[Studies in Anatolian art]

Anais

Analecta

An. Amer. Sch. Orient. Res.
Annals of the American Schools
of Oriental Research

An. Antropol.
Anales de antropología

An. Archaeol. & Anthropol.
Annals of Archaeology and
Anthropology

An. Archéol.
Annales archéologiques

An. Archéol. Arabes Syr.
Annales archéologiques arabes
syriennes: Revue d'archéologie et
d'histoire [prev. pubd as *An.
Archéol. Syrie*]

An. Archéol. Syrie
Annales archéologiques de Syrie:
Revue d'archéologie et d'histoire
syriennes [cont. as *An. Archéol.
Arabes Syr.*]

An. Archit. Cent.
Annali di architettura del Centro
internazionale di studi di
architettura Andrea Palladio

An. Arqueol. & Etnog.
Anales de arqueología y etnografía

An. Arquit.
Anales de arquitectura

An. Assoc. Amer. Geog.
Annals of the Association of
American Geographers

*Anastilosi: Syntirisi-Prostasia Mnimeion
& Synolon*
Anastilosi: Syntirisi-prostasia
mnimeion kai synolon
[Reconstruction: protective
restoration of monuments]

Anatolia
Anatolia: Revue annuelle
d'archéologie

Anatolica
Anatolica: Annuaire international
pour les civilisations de l'Asie
antérieure

Anatol. Stud.
Anatolian Studies: Journal of the
British Institute at Ankara

An. Avignon
Annales d'Avignon

An. Belg.
Annales de Belgique

An. Bhandarkar Orient. Res. Inst.
Annals of the Bhandarkar Oriental
Research Insitute

An. Bib. Stat. & Lib. Civ. Cremona
Annali della Biblioteca statale e
libreria civica di Cremona

*An. & Bol. de la Real Academia
S Fernando*
Anales y boletín de la Real
academia de S Fernando

An. & Bol. Mus. A. Barcelona
Anales y boletín de los Museos de
arte de Barcelona

An. Bourgogne
Annales de Bourgogne

An. Bretagne
Annales de Bretagne

Der Anbruch

An. Cape Prov. Mus.
Annals of the Cape Provincial
Museums

An. Carnegie Mus.
Annals of the Carnegie Museum

An. Cent. Cult. Valenc.
Anales del Centro de cultura
valenciana

Anc. Ceylon
Ancient Ceylon

An. Chim. & Phys.
Annales de chimie et de physique

Anc. India
Ancient India

Anc. Mesoamerica
Ancient Mesoamerica

Anc. Nepal
Ancient Nepal

Anc. Pakistan
Ancient Pakistan

An. Cté Flam. France
Annales du Comité flamand de
France

Anc. World
The Ancient World

Andean Past

An. Demog. Hist.
Annales de démographie
historique

AND J. A. & A. Educ.
AND Journal of Art and Art
Education

Andou

Androdes

An. E.
Annales de l'est

An., Econ., Soc., Civilis.
Annales, économies, sociétés,
civilisations

An. Ethiopie
Annales d'Ethiopie

A. Newspaper
The Art Newspaper

An. Fabbrica Duomo
Annali della fabbrica del duomo

An. Fac. Filos. & Lett. U. Milano
Annali della Facoltà di filosofia e
lettere dell'Università di Milano

An. Fac. Lett. Aix-en-Provence
Annales de la Faculté des lettres
d'Aix-en-Provence

An. Fac. Lett. & Filos. U. Napoli
Annali della Facoltà di lettere e
filosofia dell'Università di Napoli

*An. Fac. Lett. & Filos. U. Stud.
[Perugia]*
Annali della Facoltà di lettere e
filosofia dell'Università degli studi
[Perugia]

*An. Fac. Ling. & Lett. Stran. Ca'
Foscari*
Annali della Facoltà di lingue e
lettere straniere di Ca' Foscari
[serie orientale]

An. Fac. Magistero U. Cagliari
Annali della Facoltà di magistero
dell'Università di Cagliari

An. Féd. Archéol. & Hist. Belgique
Annales de la Fédération
archéologique et historique de
Belgique

An. Géog.
Annales de géographie

Anglo-Amer. Mag.
Anglo-American Magazine

Anglo-Irish Stud.
Anglo-Irish Studies

Anglo-Norman Stud.
Anglo-Norman Studies

Anglo-Saxon England

Anglo-Saxon Stud. Archaeol. & Hist.
Anglo-Saxon Studies in
Archaeology and History

Angry Penguins

An. Hist. A.
Anales de historia del arte

An. Hist. A. & Archéol.
Annales d'histoire de l'art et
d'archéologie

An. Hist. Compiégnoises
Annales historiques
compiégnoises

An. Hist. Inst. JAZU Dubrovnik
Anali historijskogo Instituta JAZU
[Jugoslavenska akademija znanosti
i umjetnosti] u Dubrovniku
[Annals of the Historical Institute
of the Yugoslav Academy of
Science and Arts at Dubrovnik]

*An. Hist. Ver. Niederrhein, Alte
Erzbistum Köln*
Annalen des Historischen Vereins
für den Niederrhein, insbesondere
das alte Erzbistum Köln

An. Inst. A. Amer. & Invest. Estét.
Anales del Instituto de arte
americano e investigaciones
estéticas

An. Inst. Estud. Gerund.
Anales del Instituto de estudios
gerundenses

An. Inst. Estud. Gironins
Annales de l'Institut estudis
gironins

An. Inst. Estud. Madril.
Anales del Instituto de estudios
madrileños

An. Inst. Etud. Orient. U. Alger
Annales de l'Institut d'études
orientales de l'Université d'Alger

An. Inst. Hort. Fromont
Annales de l'Institut horticole de
Fromont

An. Inst. Invest. Estét.
Anales del Instituto de
investigaciones estéticas

An. Inst. N. Antropol. & Hist.
Anales del Instituto nacional de
antropología e historia

An. Islam.
Annales islamologiques

An. Ist. Corr. Archeol.
Annali dell'Istituto di
corrispondenza archeologica

An. Ist. It. Num.
Annali dell'Istituto italiano di
numismatica

An. Ist. & Mus. Stor. Sci. Firenze
Annali dell'Istituto e museo di
storia della scienza di Firenze

An. Ist. Stor. It.-Ger. Trento
Annali dell'Istituto storico italo-
germanico in Trento

An. Ist. Sup. Sci. & Lett. 'S Chiara'
Annali dell'Istituto superiore di
scienza e lettere 'S Chiara'

Ankara Ü. Araştırmaları Derg.
Ankara üniversitesi dil ve tarih
araştırmaları dergisi [Ankara
University journal of language and
history research]

*Ankara Ü. Dil Tarih-Co'rafya Fak.
Derg.*
Ankara üniversitesi dil ve tarih-
co'rafya fakültesi dergisi [Ankara
University journal of the Language
and History-geography Faculty]

*Ankara Ü. 'lâhiyat Fak. Yıllık
Araştırmaları Derg.*
Ankara üniversitesi ilâhiyat
fakültesi yıllık araştırmaları dergisi
[Ankara University Theology
Faculty annual journal of research]

An. Lab. Rech. Mus. France
Annales du Laboratoire de
recherche des musées de France

An. Lateranensi
Annali Lateranensi

Anlct. Bolland.
Analecta Bollandiana

Anlct. Calasanct.
Analecta Calasanctiania

Anlct. Cartusiana
Analecta Cartusiana

Anlct. Cisterc.
Analecta Cisterciensia

Anlct. Mag.
Analectic Magazine

Anlct. Orient.
Analecta Orientalia

Anlct. Praemonstratensia
Analecta Praemonstratensia

Anlct. Romana Inst. Dan.
Analecta Romana Instituti Danici

Anlct. Soc. Ordinis Cisterc.
Analecta Societatis Ordinis
Cisterciensis

*An. Liceo Class. 'G. Garibaldi'
Palermo*
Annali del Liceo classico 'G.
Garibaldi' di Palermo

An. Malgaches
Annales malgaches

An. Midi
Annales du Midi: Revue archéologique, historique et philologique de la France méridionale

An. Monég.
Annales monégasques

An. Mun. Tomar
Anais do município de Tomar

An. Mus. Civ. La Spezia
Annali del Museo civico di La Spezia

An. Mus. Congo Belge, Anthropol. & Ethnog.
Annales du Musée du Congo Belge, anthropologie et ethnographie

An. Mus. Guimet
Annales du Musée Guimet

An. Mus. Michoacáno
Anales del Museo michoacáno

An. Mus. N. Arqueol., Hist. & Etnog.
Anales del Museo nacional de arqueología, historia y etnografía [prev. pubd as *Bol. Mus. N. Arqueol., Hist. & Etnog.*]

An. Mus. Royal Afrique Cent.
Annales du Musée royal de l'Afrique Centrale

Annabelle

Annales [Paris]

An. Náprstek Mus.
Annals of the Náprstek Museum

An. Natal Mus.
Annals of the Natal Museum

An. Natphilos.
Annalen der Naturphilosophie

An. Nord. Oldknd.
Annaler for nordisk oldkyndighed [Annals of Nordic antiquities; cont. as *Aab. Nord. Oldknd. & Hist.*]

Annu. Acad. Royale Belgique/Jb. Kon. Acad. België
Annuaire de l'Académie royale de Belgique/Jaarboek van de Koninklijke academie van België [cont. as *Annu. Acad. Royale Sci. & B.-Lett. Bruxelles*; *Annu. Acad. Royale Sci., Lett. & B.A. Belgique*]

Annu. Acad. Royale Sci. & B-Lett. Bruxelles
Annuaire de l'Académie royale des sciences et belles-lettres de Bruxelles [see *Annu. Acad. Royale Belgique/Jb. Kon. Acad. België*]

Annu. Acad. Royale Sci., Lett. & B.A. Belgique
Annuaire de l'Académie royale des sciences, des lettres et des beaux arts de Belgique [see *Annu. Acad. Royale Belgique/Jb. Kon. Acad. België*]

Annu. Accad. Etrus. Cortona
Annuario dell'Accademia etrusca di Cortona

Annu. Admin. Statistique & Commerc. Aube
Annuaire administratif statistique et commercial de l'Aube

Annu. Amer. Sch. Orient. Res.
Annual of the American Schools of Oriental Research [prev. pubd as *Annu. Amer. Sch. Orient. Res. Jerusalem*]

Annu. Amer. Sch. Orient. Res. Jerusalem
Annual of the American School of Oriental Research in Jerusalem [cont. as *Annu. Amer. Sch. Orient. Res.*]

Annu. Bibliog. Ind. Archaeol.
Annual Bibliography of Indian Archaeology

Annu. Bibliog. Stor. A.
Annuario bibliografico di storia dell'arte

Annu. Brit. Sch. Athens
Annual of the British School at Athens

Annu. Bull. N. Gal. Victoria
Annual Bulletin of the National Gallery of Victoria

Annu. Bull. N. Mus. W. A.
Annual Bulletin of the National Museum of Western Art

Annu. Coll. France: Résumé Cours & Trav.
Annuaire du Collège de France: Résumé des cours et travaux

Annu. Colmar
Annuaire de Colmar

Annu. Dept Ant. Jordan
Annual of the Department of Antiquities of Jordan

Annu.: Ecole Pratique Hautes Etud.
Annuaire: Ecole pratique des hautes études

Annu. Ecole Pratique Hautes Etud., Ve Sect., Sci. Relig.
Annuaire de l'Ecole pratique des hautes études, Ve section, sciences religieuses

Annu. Ist. Giappon. Cult. Roma
Annuario dell'Istituto giapponese di cultura in Roma

Annu. Ist. Stor. A. [Rome]
Annuario dell'Istituto di storia dell'arte [Rome]

Annu. Ist. Tec. Stat. Geom. 'Carlo d'Arco'
Annuario dell'Istituto tecnico statale per geometri 'Carlo d'Arco'

Annu. Ist. Ung. Stor. A.
Annuario dell'Istituto ungherese di storia dell'arte

Annu. Liceo Gin. Stat. Osimo
Annuario del Liceo ginnasio statale d'Osimo

Annu. Mus. Gr.-Romano Alessandria
Annuario del Museo greco-romano di Alessandria [cont. as *Annu. Mus. Gr.-Romain Alexandrie*]

Annu. Mus. Gr.-Romain Alexandrie
Annuaire du Musée gréco-romain à Alexandrie [prev. pubd as *Annu. Mus. Gr.-Romano Alessandria*]

Annu. Mus. Royaux B.-A. Belgique/Jb. Kon. Mus. S. Kst. België
Annuaire des Musées royaux des beaux-arts de Belgique/Jaarboek der Koninklijke musea voor schone kunsten van België [cont. as *Mus. Royaux B.-A. Belgique: Bull.*]

Annu. Newslett. Scand. Inst. Asian Stud.
Annual Newsletter of the Scandinavian Institute of Asian Studies

Annu. Reale Accad. Italia
Annuario della Reale accademia d'Italia

Annu. Reale Accad. S Luca
Annuario della Reale accademia di San Luca

Annu. Reale Ist. Tec. & Naut. Bari
Annuario del Reale istituto tecnico e nautico di Bari

Annu. Rep. Archaeol. Dept Nizam's Dominions
Annual Report of the Archaeological Department of His Exalted Highness the Nizam's Dominions

Annu. Rep. Archaeol. Surv. Ceylon
Annual Report of the Archaeological Survey of Ceylon

Annu. Rep. Brit. Sch. Archaeol. Athens
Annual Report of the British School of Archaeology at Athens

Annu. Rep. & Bull., Walker A.G., Liverpool
Annual Report and Bulletin, Walker Art Gallery, Liverpool

Annu. Rep. Bureau Amer. Ethnol. Secretary Smithsonian Inst.
Annual Report of the Bureau of American Ethnology to the Secretary of the Smithsonian Institution

Annu. Rep., Fogg. A. Mus., Harvard U.
Annual Report, Fogg Art Museum, Harvard University

Annu. Rep. Ind. Epig.
Annual Report on Indian Epigraphy

Annu. Rep. LA Plan. Comm.
Annual Report of the Los Angeles Planning Commission

Annu. Rep. Mus. Anthropol., U. MO
Annual Report of the Museum of Anthropology, University of Missouri

Annu. Rep. Mysore Archaeol. Dept
Annual Report of the Mysore Archaeological Department

Annu. Rev. Anthropol.
Annual Review of Anthropology

Annu. Rev. Psychol.
Annual Review of Psychology

Annu. Rev.: Tel Aviv Mus.
Annual Review: Tel Aviv Museum

Annu. Scu. Archeol. Atene & Miss. It. Oriente
Annuario della Scuola archeologica di Atene e delle missioni italiane in oriente

Annu. Skira
Annuel Skira

Annu. Soc. Amis Vieux Strasbourg
Annuaire de la Société des amis du vieux Strasbourg

Annu. 30s Soc., London
Annual of the 30s Society, London

Annu. Yonne
Annuaire de l'Yonne

An. NY Acad. Sci.
Annals of the New York Academy of Sciences

A Noite

An. Ordre Souverain Mil. Malte
Annales de L'Ordre souverain militaire de Malte

An. Oudhdknd. Kring Land van Waas/An. Cerc. Archéol. Pays de Waes
Annalen van de Oudheidkundige kring van het Land van Waas/Annales du Cercle archéologique du Pays de Waes

A. Now
Art Now

An. Ponts & Chaussées
Annales des ponts et chaussées

An. Provence
Annales de Provence

An. Real Acad. B. A. Cádiz
Anales de la Real academia de bellas artes de Cádiz

An. S. Afr. Mus.
Annals of the South African Museum

An. Sci.
Annals of Science

An. Sci. Phys. & Nat., Agric. & Indust.
Annales des sciences physiques et naturelles, d'agriculture et d'industrie

An. Scu. Norm. Sup. Pisa
Annali della Scuola normale superiore di Pisa

An. Scu. Norm. Sup. Pisa, Lett., Stor. & Filos.
Annali della Scuola normale superiore di Pisa, lettere, storia e filosofia

An. Seguntinos
Anales seguntinos

An. Service Ant. Egypte
Annales du Service des antiquités de l'Egypte

An. Soc. Géog. Commerc.
Annales de la Société géographique commerciale

An. Soc. Geog. & Hist. Guatemala
Anales de la Sociedad de geografía y historia de Guatemala

An. Soc. Hist. & Archéol. Gatinais
Annales de la Société historique et archéologique du Gatinais

An. Soc. Hist. & Archéol. Tournai
Annales de la Société historique et archéologique de Tournai

An. Soc. Libre B.-A.
Annales de la Société libre des beaux-arts

An. Soc. Royale Archéol. Bruxelles
Annales de la Société royale d'archéologie de Bruxelles

Ant. & Abenland
Antike und Abendland

Ant. Afr.
Antiquités africaines

Antaios

Ant. Altoadriat.
Antichità altoadriatiche

Antananarivo Annu.
Antananarivo Annual

Ant. Class.
L'Antiquité classique

Ant. Collct.
Antique Collecting

Ant. Colr
Antique Collector

Ant. Dealer & Colr's Guide
Antique Dealer and Collector's Guide

Antæus

Ant. Dkml.
Antike Denkmäler

Ant. & F. A.
Antiques and Fine Art

Anthol. Annu.
Anthologica annua

Anthol. Hib.
Anthologia Hibernica

Anthony's Phot. Bull.
Anthony's Photographic Bulletin

Anthropol. BC
Anthropology in British Columbia

Anthropol. Forum
Anthropological Forum

Anthropol. Ling.
Anthropological Linguistics

Anthropol. Mem. Field Mus. Nat. Hist.
Anthropological Memoirs of the Field Museum of Natural History

Anthropology

Anthropol. Pap. Amer. Mus. Nat. Hist.
Anthropological Papers of the American Museum of Natural History

Anthropos

Anthropos-Bib.
Anthropos-Bibliothek

Antiek

Antikva. Arkv
Antikvariskt arkiv [Antiquarian archive; prev. pubd as *Antikva. Stud.*]

Antikva. Stud.
Antikvarisker studier [cont. as *Antikva. Arkv; Hist. Arkv; Filol. Arkv*]

Antiqua. Horology
Antiquarian Horology

Antiqua. J.
Antiquaries Journal

Antiquaria

Antiques

Antiquités

Antiquity

Ant. J.
Antiques Journal [prev. pubd as *Amer. Ant. J.*]

Ant. Kst
Antike Kunst

Ant. N.
Antiquités nationales

Antol. B. A.
Antologia di belle arti

An. Toled.
Anales toledanos

Antonianum

Ant. Plast.
Antike Plastik

Antropol. & Hist. Guatemala
Antropología e historia de Guatemala

Antropologia

Ant. & Survival
Antiquity and Survival: An International Review of Traditional Art and Culture

Ant. Tardive
Antiquité tardive: Revue internationale d'histoire et d'archéologie

Ant. Viva
Antichità viva: Rassegna d'arte

Ant. Welt
Antike Welt

Antwerp. Archvbl.
Antwerpsch archievenblad

Antwerpen
Antwerpen: Tijdschrift der stad Antwerpen

An. U. Abidjan
Annales de l'Université d'Abidjan

Anu. Asoc. Arquitectos
Anuario para la Asociación de arquitectos

Anu. Cuerpo Fac. Archv, Bib. & Arqueól.
Anuario del Cuerpo facultativo de archiveros, bibliotecarios y arqueólogos

Anu. Dept. Hist. & Teor. A.
Anuario del Departamento de historia y teoría del arte

Anu. Divulg. Cient.
Anuario de divulgação científica

Anu. Estud. Amer.
Anuario de estudios americanos

Anu. Estud. Med.
Anuario de estudios medievales

An. U. Hispal.
Anales de la Universidad hispalense

Anu. Inst. Estud. Cat.
Anuari de l'Institut d'estudis catalans

An. U. Lecce
Annali dell'Università di Lecce

An. U. Murcia
Anales de la Universidad de Murcia

An. U. Sarav.
Annales Universitatis Saraviensis

An. U. Sarav., Philos.
Annales Universitatis Saraviensis, Philosophiae

An. U. Valencia
Anales de la Universidad de Valencia

An. Ver. Gesch. Belg. Protestantisme
Annalen van der Vereniging voor de geschiedenis van het Belgsch protestantisme

A. NZ
Art New Zealand

An. Zecca Roma
Annali della zecca di Roma

Anz. Ger. Nmus.
Anzeiger des Germanischen Nationalmuseums

Anz. Knd. Dt. Vorzt
Anzeiger für Kunde der deutschen Vorzeit

Anz. Österreich. Akad. Wiss., Philos.–Hist. Kl.
Anzeiger der Österreichischen Akademie der Wissenschaften, philosophisch–historische Klasse

Anz. Schweiz. Altertknd.
Anzeiger für schweizerische Altertumskunde

A. Ontem & Hoje
Arte de ontem e de hoje

A. Orient.
Ars Orientalis

A. Ouest
Arts de l'ouest

Apeiron

A. & Pensée
Arts et pensée

A.: Period. F. A.
Artes: Periodical of the Fine Arts

Aperture

A. Plast.
i) Arta plastică [cont. as *Arta*]
ii) Arts plastiques

A+

A + U
A plus U [Architecture and urbanism]

Apollo

Apollo Annu.
Apollo Annual

Apollon

Apool Lett.
Artpool Letter

A. Port.
Arte portuguesa

Apotheca

Appennino Camerte
Appennino camerte

Appenzell. Jb.
Appenzellische Jahrbücher

Appleton's J
Appleton's Journal

Applied Optics

A. Praehist.
Ars praehistorica

A. Press
Art Press

A. & Prog.
Art and Progress

A. & Publ.
Art and Publicity

Apulum

A. Q. [Detroit]
Art Quarterly [Detroit]

A. Q. [London]
Art Quarterly [prev. pubd as *NACF Mag.*]

Aquatoria

A. Quatuor Coronatorum
Ars quatuor coronatorum

Aquileia Nostra
Aquileia nostra: Bollettino dell'Associazione nazionale per Aquileia

A. Quin.
Arte quincenal

Arab. Archaeol. & Epig.
Arabian Archaeology and Epigraphy

Arabica

Arab. Stud.
Arabian Studies

Aragón

Aramco World

Arbeitbl. Restauratoren
Arbeitsblätter für Restauratoren

Arbeit. Illus. Ztg
Arbeiter illustrierte Zeitung

Arbeit. Ztg
Arbeiter Zeitung

Arbor

Arca Lovan.
Arca Lovaniensis

Arch

Archaeol. Aeliana
Archaeologia Aeliana

Archaeol. Amer.
Archaeologia Americana: Transactions and Collections of the American Antiquarian Society

Archaeol. Camb.
Archaeologia Cambrensis

Archaeol. Cantiana
Archaeologia Cantiana

Archaeol. & It. Soc.
Archaeology and Italian Society

Archaeol. J.
Archaeological Journal

Archaeol. Oceania
Archaeology in Oceania

Archaeologia

Archaeologia [Soc. Antiqua. London]
Archaeologia [Society of Antiquaries of London]

Archaeologiai Értesitő [Archaeological report]

Archaeologiai Közlemények [Archaeological bulletin]

Archaeology [Archaeological Institute of America, New York]

Archaeol. & Phys. Anthropol. Oceania
Archaeology and Physical Anthropology in Oceania

Archaeol. Rep.: Council Soc. Promotion Hell. Stud. & Managing Cttee Brit. Sch. Archaeol. Athens
Archaeological Reports: Council of the Society for the Promotion of Hellenic Studies and the Managing Committee of the British School of Archaeology at Athens

Archaeol. Rep. Soc. Promot. Hell. Stud.
Archaeological Reports of the Society for the Promotion of Hellenic Studies

Archaeol. Stud.
Archaeological Studies

Archaeol. Surv. Ceylon, Annu. Rep.
Archaeological Survey of Ceylon, Annual Report

Archaeol. Surv. India
Archaeological Survey of India

Archaeol. Surv. India Annu. Rep.
Archaeological Survey of India Annual Reports

Archaeol. Surv. India, Frontier Circ.
Archaeological Survey of India, Frontier Circle

Archaeol. Surv. India, Prog. Rep., W. Circ.
Archaeological Survey of India, Progress Reports, Western Circle

Archaeol. Surv. Temples
Archaeological Survey of Temples

Archaeol. Transatlant.
Archaeologia transatlantica

Archaeol. Viva
Archaeologia viva

Archaeomaterials

Archaeometry

Archaiol. Anlkt. Athinon
Archaiologika analekta ex Athinon/ Athens Annals of Archaeology

Archaiol. Chron.
Archaiologiki chronika [Archaeological chronical; suppl. in *Archaiol. Ephimeris*]

Archaiol. Deltion
Archaiologikon deltion [Archaeological bulletin]

Archaiol. Ephimeris
Archaiologiki ephimeris [Archaeological journal; prev. pubd as *Ephimeris Archaiol.*]

Archaiologia

Archäol. Anz.
Archäologischer Anzeiger [prev. pubd as *Verz. Mitglieder Dt. Archäol. Inst.*]

Archäol. Ber. Yemen
Archäologische Berichte aus dem Yemen

Archäol. Korrbl.
Archäologisches Korrespondenzblatt

Archäol. Mitt. Iran
Archäologische Mitteilungen aus Iran

Archäol. Samml. U. Zürich
Archäologische Sammlung der Universität Zürich

Archäol. Ztg
Archäologische Zeitung

Archeion

Archeion Byz. Mnimeion Ellados
Archeion ton Byzantinon mnimeion tis Ellados [Ancient Byzantine monuments of Greece]

Archeografo Triest.
Archeografo triestino

Archeol. Bulg.
Archeologija bulgarska

Archeol. Class.
Archeologia classica

Archeol. Geog.
Archeologia geographica

Archeol. Homerica
Archeologia Homerica

Archeol. Laziale
Archeologia laziale

Archeol. Med.
Archeologia medievale: Cultura materiale, insediamenti, territorio

Archéol. Méd.
Archéologie médiévale

Archeologia
Archeologia: L'Archéologie dans le monde. . .sur terres et dans les mers

Archéologie
Archéologie: Chronique semestrielle/ Zesmaandelijkse kroniek

Archeol. Prag.
Archeologica Pragensia

Archeol. Transatlant.
Archeologia transatlantica

Archetype

Archf- & Bibwzn België
Archief- en bibliotheekwezen in België

Archf Ned. Kstgesch.
Archief voor Nederlandsche kunstgeschiedenis

Archiginnasio

Archipel

Archipelago

Archis

Archistra

Archit. [New York]
Architecture [New York]

Archit. & A.
Architecture and Arts

Archit. & A. Dec.
L'architettura e le arti decorative

Archit. Album
Architektonisches Album

Archit., Archaeol., & Hist. Soc. Co., City & Neighbourhood Chester J.
Architectural, Archaeological, and Historic Society for the County, City and Neighbourhood of Chester Journal [cont. as *Chester & N. Wales Archaeol. Soc.*; *J. Chester Archaeol. Soc.*]

Archit. & Archaeol. Soc. Durham & Northumb.: Trans.
Architectural and Archaeological Society of Durham and Northumberland: Transactions

Archit.: Archv
Architettura: Archivi

Archit.: Arkithist. Aaskr.
Architectura: Arkitekturhistorisk aarsskrift [Architecture history yearbook]

Archit. Assoc. J.
Architectural Association Journal [cont. as *Arena*]

Archit. Assoc. Q.
Architectural Association Quarterly

Archit. Aujourd'hui
L'Architecture d'aujourd'hui

Archit. Australia
Architecture in Australia [prev. pubd as *Architecture* [Sydney]]

Archit. & Bldg
Architecture and Building

Archit. & Budownictwo
Architektura i budownictwo [Architecture and building]

Archit. Bull.
Architecture Bulletin

Archit. Canada
Architecture Canada

Archit.: Cron. & Stor.
L'architettura: Cronache e storia

Archit. ČSR
Architektura ČSR [Czechoslovak architecture]

Archit. DDR
Architektur der DDR [prev. pubd as *Dt. Archit.*]

Archit. Des.
Architectural Design

Archit. Dig.
Architectural Digest

Architect Australia

Architect & Bldg News
Architect and Building News

Architect & Bldr
Architect and Builder

Architect, Bldr & Engin.
Architect, Builder and Engineer

Architect & Contract Reporter
Architect and Contract Reporter

Architecte

Architect & Engin.
Architect and Engineer

Architect & Engin. CA
Architect and Engineer of California

Architectes

Architect: J. Jap. Architects' Assoc.
Architect: Journal of the Japanese Architects' Association

Architects' J.
Architects' Journal

Architect's Y-b.
Architect's Year-book

Architectura [Amsterdam]

Architectura [Munich]

Architecture [Paris]

Architecture [Sydney][cont. as *Archit. Australia*]

Architecture [USA][prev. pubd as *AIA J.*]

Architecture and Design

Architekt [Kraków]

Architekt [Prague]

Architekt [Vienna]

Architekt [Warsaw]

Architekton

Architektoniki

Architektura [Warsaw]
Architektura: Organ stowarzyszenia architektow polskich [Warsaw]

ArchiteXt

Archit.: Formes & Fonct.
Architecture: Formes et fonctions

Archit. Forum
Architectural Forum

Archit. Fr.
L'Architecture française

Archit. Her.
Architectural Heritage

Archithese [merged with *Werk* to form *Werk–Archithese*]

Archit. Hisp.
Architectura hispalense

Archit. Hist.
Architectural History [Society of Architectural Historians of Great Britain]

Archit., Innenarchit., Tech. Ausbau
Architektur, Innenarchitektur, technischer Ausbau: AIT [prev. pubd as *Archit. & Wohnwelt*; *Archit. & Wohnform*; *Innendekoration*; *Illus. Kstgew. Z. Innendek.*]

Archit. Intérieure Créée
Architecture intérieure créée

Archit. Israel
Architecture of Israel

Archit. J.
Architectural Journal

Archit. Mag.
Architectural Magazine

Archit. Médit.
Architecture méditerranéenne

Archit. MN
Architecture Minnesota

Archit., Movt, Cont.
Architecture, mouvement, continuité [cont. as *A.M.C.*]

Archit. Obzor
Architektonický obzor [Architectural horizons]

Archit. Plus
Architecture plus

Archit. Rec.
Architectural Record

Archit. Rev. [Boston]
Architectural Review [Boston]

Archit. Rev. [London]
Architectural Review [London]

Archit. Rev. & Amer. Bldrs J.
Architectural Review and American Builders Journal [prev. pubd as *Sloan's Archit. Rev. & Bldrs' J.*]

Archit.: Riv. Sind. N. Fasc. Architetti
L'architettura: Rivista del sindacato nazionale fascista degli architetti

Archit. Rundschau
Architektonische Rundschau

Archit. SA
Architecture SA

Archit. S. Africa
Architecture in South Africa

Archit. Show
Architecture Show

Archit.: Stor. & Doc.
Architettura: Storia e documenti

Archit. Themata/Archit. Greece
[Architectural themes/ Architecture in Greece]

Archit. Today
Architecture Today

Archit. Viv.
L'Architecture vivante

Archit. W. Midlands
Architecture West Midlands

Archit. & Wohnen
Architektur und Wohnen

Archit. & Wohnform
Architektur und Wohnform [prev. pubd as *Innendekoration*; *Illus. Kstgew. Z. Innendek.*; cont. as *Archit. & Wohnwelt*]

Archit. & Wohnwelt
Architektur und Wohnwelt [prev. pubd as *Archit. & Wohnform*; *Innendekoration*; *Illus. Kstgew. Z. Innendek.*; cont. as *Archit., Innenarchit., Tech. Ausbau*]

Archit.: Z. Gesch. & Aesth. Baukst
Architectura: Zeitschrift für Geschichte und Aesthetik der Baukunst

Archit.: Z. Gesch. Archit.
Architectura: Zeitschrift für Geschichte der Architektur

Archit.: Z. Gesch. Baukst
Architectura: Zeitschrift für Geschichte der Baukunst

Archivaria

Archivists' Newslett.
Archivists' Newsletter [Scottish Pottery Society; cont. as *Archv News*; *Scot. Pott. Hist. Rev.*]

Archv A. Lovan.
Archivum artis Lovaniense

Archv Anthropol.
Archiv für Anthropologie [cont. as *Archv Anthropol. & Vlkforsch.*]

Archv Anthropol. & Vlkforsch.
Archiv für Anthropologie und Völkerforschung [prev. pubd as *Archv Anthropol.*]

Archv Antropol. & Etnol.
Archivio per l'antropologia e l'etnologia

Archv A. Valenc.
Archivo de arte valenciano

Archv Begriffsgesch.
Archiv für Begriffsgeschichte

Archv Bild. Kst, Ger. Nmus., Nuremberg
Archiv für bildende Kunst, Germanisches Nationalmuseum, Nuremberg

Archv Český
Archiv český [Czech archive]

Archv Christ. Kst
Archiv für christliche Kunst

Archv Dominicano
Archivo dominicano

Archv Elsäss. Kstgesch.
Archiv für elsässische Kunstgeschichte

Archv Esp. A.
Archivo español de arte [prev. pubd as *Archv Esp. A. & Arqueol.*]

Archv Esp. A. & Arqueol.
Archivo español de arte y arqueología [cont. as *Archv Esp. Arqueol.*; *Archv Esp. A.*]

Archv Esp. Arqueol.
Archivo español de arqueología [prev. pubd as *Archv Esp. A. & Arqueol.*]

Archv & Forsch.
Archiv und Forschungen

Archv Franciscanum Hist.
Archivum Franciscanum historicum

Archv Frankfurt. Gesch. & Kst
Archiv für Frankfurts Geschichte und Kunst

Archv Fratrum Praedicatorum
Archivum fratrum praedicatorum

Archv Gesch. Bwsn
Archiv für Geschichte des Buchwesens

Archv Gesch. Dt. Bhand.
Archiv für Geschichte des deutschen Buchhandels

Archv Gesch. Oberfranken
Archiv für Geschichte von Oberfranken

Archv Gtnbau
Archiv für Gartenbau

Archv Herald
i) Archiv Herald
ii) Archivium heraldicum

Archv Hispal.
Archivo hispalense

Archv Hist. Pont.
Archivum historiae pontificiae

Archv Hist. Soc. Iesu
Archivum historicum Societatis Iesu

Archv Italia & Rass. Int. Archv
Archivi d'Italia e rassegna internazionale degli archivi

Archv It. Stor. Pietà
Archivio italiano per la storia della pietà

Archv Knd. Österreich. Gesch.-Quellen
Archiv für Kunde österreichischer Geschichts-Quellen

Archv Kstgesch.
Archiv für Kunstgeschichte

Archv Kultgesch.
Archiv für Kulturgeschichte

Archv Lecco
Archivi di Lecco

Archv Medaillen- & Plakettenknd.
Archiv für Medaillen- und Plakettenkunde

Archv Melitense
Archivum Melitense

Archv Mittelrhein. Kirchgesch.
Archiv für mittelrheinische Kirchengeschichte

Archv Nat. Hist.
Archive of Natural History

Archv News
Archive News [prev. pubd as *Archivists' Newslett.*; cont. as *Scot. Pott. Hist. Rev.*]

Archv Orient.
Archiv orientální

Archv Orientforsch.
Archiv für Orientforschung

Archv Österreich. Gesch.
Archiv für österreichische Geschichte [prev. pubd as *Österreich. Gesch.-Quellen*]

Archv Ott.
Archivum Ottomanicum

Archv Preist. Levant.
Archivio di preistoria levantina

Archv Sächs. Gesch.
Archiv für die sächsische Geschichte

Archvs A. Fr.
Archives de l'art français [cont. as *Nouv. Archvs A. Fr.*; *Archvs A. Fr.*]

Archvs Alsac. Hist. A.
Archives alsaciennes d'histoire de l'art

Archvs Amer. A. J.
Archives of American Art Journal

Archvs Archit. Mod.
Archives de l'architecture moderne [prev. pubd as *Bull. Inf. Mens. Archvs Archit. Mod.*]

Archvs Asian A.
Archives of Asian Art

Archvs, Bib. & Mus. Belgique
Archives, bibliothèques et musées de Belgique

Archvs Cent. Cult. Port.
Archives du centre culturel portugais

Archvs Chin. A. Soc. America
Archives of the Chinese Art Society of America

Archvs Schles. Kirchgesch.
Archiv für schlesische Kirchengeschichte

Archvs Eglise Alsace
Archives de l'église d'Alsace

Archvs Ethnos
Archivos ethnos

Archvs Etud. Orient.
Archives d'études orientales

Archvs Héral. Suisses
Archives héraldiques suisses

Archvs Hist. Doctr. & Litt. Moyen Age
Archives d'histoire doctrinale et littéraire du moyen âge

Archvs Hist., A. & Litt.
Archives historiques, artistiques et littéraires

Archvs Hist. N. France & Midi Belgique
Archives historiques du Nord de la France et du Midi de la Belgique

Archvs Inst. Paléontol. Humaine
Archives de l'Institut de paléontologie humaine

Archvs Int. Hist. Sci.
Archives internationales d'histoire des sciences

Archv Sippenforsch. & Verw. Geb.
Archiv für Sippenforschung und alle verwandten Gebiete [cont. as *Praktische Forschft.*; *Arch. Sippenforsch. & Verw. Geb.*]

Archvs Leoneses
Archivos leoneses [Revista del Centro de estudios e investigación de 'San Isidor']

Archvs & Mus. Inf.
Archives and Museum Informatics

Archv Soc. Romana Stor. Patria
Archivio della Società romana di storia patria

Archvs Psychol.
Archives de psychologie

Archv Stor. A.
Archivio storico dell'arte [cont. as *L'Arte*; *L'Arte: Riv. Stor. A. Med. & Mod.*]

Archv Stor. Belluno, Feltre & Cadore
Archivio storico di Belluno, Feltre e Cadore

Archv Stor. Bergam.
Archivio storico bergamasco

Archv Stor. Dalmazia
Archivio storico per la Dalmazia

Archv Stor. It.
Archivio storico italiano

Archv Stor. Lodi.
Archivio storico lodigiano

Archv Stor. Lombardo
Archivio storico lombardo

Archv Stor. Marche & Umbria
Archivio storico per le Marche e per l'Umbria

Archv Stor. Messin.
Archivio storico messinese [cont. as *Boll. Stor. Messin.*; *Archv Stor. Messin.*]

Archv Stor. Prat.
Archivio storico pratese

Archv Stor. Prov. Napolet.
Archivio storico per le province napoletane

Archv Stor. Prov. Parm.
Archivio storico per le province parmensi

Archv Stor. Pugl.
Archivio storico pugliese

Arch Stor. Sicil.
Archivio storico siciliano

Archv Stor. Sicilia Orient.
Archivio storico per la Sicilia orientale

Archv Stor. Siracus.
Archivio storico siracusano

Archv Téc. Mnmts Prehisp.
  Archivo técnico de monumentos
  prehispánicos

Archv Trent.
  Archivio trentino

Archv Vaterländ. Gesch. & Top.
  Archiv für vaterländische
  Geschichte und Topographie

Archv Ven.
  Archivio veneto [cont. as *Nuovo
  Archv Ven.*; *Archv Ven.-Trident.*]

Archv Ven.-Trident.
  Archivio veneto-tridentino [prev.
  pubd as *Nuovo Archv Ven.*; *Archv
  Ven.*]

Archv Vlkerknd.
  Archiv für Völkerkunde

Archv Zeich. Kst.
  Archiv für die zeichnenden
  Künste

Arctic Anthropol.
  Arctic Anthropology

Arc-voltaic

Arena
  Arena: Architectural Association
  Journal [prev. pubd as *Archit.
  Assoc. J.*]

Arethusa

A. Rev.
  Arts Review

Argomenti Stor. A.
  Argomenti di storia dell'arte

Argos

Argus [Melbourne]

Argus [USSR]

Arheol. Vestnik
  Arheološki vestnik

Arhitectura

Arhitektúra

Arhit. Hrvatskoj 1945–85
  Arhitektura u Hrvatskoj 1945–85

Arhit. Urb.
  Arhitektura urbanizam

*Arhv Arbanasku Starinu, Jezik &
Etnol.*
  Arhiv za arbanasku starinu, jezik i
  etnologiju [Archive for Albanian
  antiquities, language and
  ethnology]

Ariadne [Rethymno]

Aria Italia
  Aria d'Italia

Arid Lands Newslett.
  Arid Lands Newsletter

Ariel

Arise

Arizona & W.
  Arizona and the West

Ark

Arkády [Arcades]

Arkheologiya

Arkheol. Raboty Tadzhikistane
  Arkheologicheskiye raboty v
  Tadzhikistane [Archaeological
  work in Tajikistan]

Arkitekt

Arkitekten [Copenhagen]

Arkitekten [Helsinki]

Arkitektur [cont. as *Arkitektur DK*]

Arkitektur [Stockholm]

Arkhitektura

Arkhit. Leningrada
  Arkhitektura Leningrada

Arkhit. Moskva
  Arkhitekturnaya Moskva
  [Architectural Moscow]

Arkhit. Nasledstvo
  Arkhitekturnoye nasledstvo
  [Architectural heritage]

Arkhit. Radyans'koï Ukraïni
  Arkhitektura Radyans'koï Ukraïni
  [Architecture of the Soviet
  Ukraine]

Arkhit. SSSR
  Arkhitektura SSSR

Arkhit. & Stroitel'stvo Moskvy
  Arkhitektura i stroitel'stvo Moskvy
  [Architecture and construction of
  Moscow]

Arkhit. Ukrainy
  Arkhitektura Ukrainy

Arkitektur DK [prev. pubd as
Arkitektur]

Arkkitehti

Arkkitehti/Arkitekten
  Arkkitehti/arkitekten

Arkkitehtiopiskelija [Architecture
student]

ARLIS/ANZ News

ARLIS Newslett.
  Art Libraries Society Newsletter
  [cont. as *A. Libs J.*]

Arme Ant.
  Arme antiche

Armen. Q.
  Armenian Quarterly

Armitano A.
  Armitano arte

Ár ðegisblad Listamanna
  Ár ðegisblad listamanna [Artists'
  early morning paper]

Arqueología

Arqueología [Mexico]

Arqueól. Port.
  Arqueólogo português

Arquit. Bis
  Arquitecturas bis

Arquit. Brasil
  Arquitectura do Brasil

Arquitectonica

Arquitecto Peru.
  El arquitecto peruano

Arquitectura
  i) [Colegio nacional de arquitectos,
  Cuba]
  ii) [Colegio oficial de arquitectos,
  Madrid; cont. as *Rev. N. Arquit.*]

Arquitectura [Havana]

Arquitectura [Lisbon]

Arquitectura [Mexico] [cont. as
Arquit. México]

Arquitectura [Montevideo]

Arquit. México
  Arquitectura de México [prev.
  pubd as *Arquitectura* [Mexico]]

Arquit. Peru.
  Arquitectura peruana

Arquit. & Soc.
  Arquitectura y sociedad

Arquit. & Urb.
  Arquitectura y urbanismo

Arquit. & Urb. São Paulo
  Arquitetura e urbanismo de São
  Paulo

Arquit. & Viv.
  Arquitectura y vivienda

Arquiv. Beja
  Arquivo de Beja

Arquiv. Coimbrão
  Arquivo coimbrão

Arquiv. Distr. Aveiro
  Arquivo do Distrito de Aveiro

Arquivs Angola
  Arquivos de Angola

Arquivs Cent. Cult. Port.
  Arquivos do Centro cultural
  português

Ars

Art [Basel]

Art [Hamburg]

Art [New York]

Arta [prev. pubd as *A. Plast.*]

Ařta

Art Asia

Arte [Bogotá]

Arte Doc.
  Arte documento

Artes [Madrid]

Artes [Pavia]
  Artes: Periodico annuale di storia
  delle arti [Pavia]

Art & Fact
  Art and Fact

Artforum

Artibus Asiae [New York University]

Artibus & Hist.
  Artibus et historiae

Artibus Orient.
  Artibus orientalis

Artifex

Artigrama

Arti: Mens. Inf. A.
  Le arti: Mensile di informazione
  artistica

Artinf

Arti: Rass. Bimest. A. Ant. & Mod.
  Le arti: Rassegna bimestrale
  dell'arte antica e moderna [cont. as
  Boll. A.]

Artis

Artisan Lithurg.
  L'Artisan lithurgique

Artistes

Artistic Film

Artistic Pakistan

Artist & J. Home Cult.
  Artist and Journal of Home
  Culture

Artists Int. Assoc. Bull.
  Artists International Association
  Bulletin

Artists Int. Assoc. Newslett.
  Artists International Association
  Newsletter

Artists Int. Bull.
  Artists International Bulletin

Artists News-sheet

Artists Repository & Drg Mag.
  Artists Repository and Drawing
  Magazine

Artlink

Artlook

Artmagazine

ARTnews

Artnews [Cardiff]

ARTnews Annu.
  ARTnews Annual

Artrends

Arts [New York; prev. pubd as *A.
Dig.*; cont. as *A. Mag.*]

Arts [Paris]
  Arts: Beaux arts, littérature,
  spectacle [Paris] [prev. pubd as
  Beaux-A.: Chron. A. & Curiosité;
  Chron. A. & Curiosité]

Artscanada

Artscribe

Artsmag

Artstudio

Art-Union

Arturo

Artwork

Arup J.
  Arup Journal

Asahi Cam.
  Asahi Camera

Aschaffenburger Jb.
  Aschaffenburger Jahrbuch

Asia

Asia Major

Asian A.
  Asian Art

Asian Affairs

Asian & Afr. Stud.
  Asian and African Studies

Asian Cult.
  Asian Culture

Asian Cult. UNESCO Bhutan
  Asian Culture for UNESCO
  Bhutan

Asian Pacific Cult.
  Asian Pacific Culture

Asian Persp.
  Asian Perspectives

Asian Rev.
  Asian Review

Asian Stud.
  Asian Studies

Asiat. Res.
Asiatic Researches

Asiat. Stud.
Asiatische Studien

Asiaweek

Asie SE & Monde Insulind.
Asie du Sud-Est et monde insulindien

Asoc. A. Concr. Inven.
Asociación arte concreto invención

Aspects Maison Monde
Aspects de la maison dans le monde

Assaph

Assiette Beurre
Assiette au beurre

Assoc. Archit. Soc. Rep. & Pap.
Associated Architectural Societies Reports and Papers

Assoc. Bret. C.-R. Procès-Verbaux
Association bretonne. Comptes-rendus. Procès-verbaux

Assoc. Preserv. Technol. Suppl. Communiqué
Association for Preservation Technology Supplement Communiqué

A. & Stor.
Arte e storia

A. Stud.
Art Studies

A. Stud., Med., Ren. & Mod.
Art Studies, Medieval, Renaissance and Modern

A. Suom. Taide
Ars suomen taide

A. & Tech.
Art et technique

Ateliers A. Graph.
Les Ateliers d'art graphique

Atenea

Ateneo Ven.
Ateneo veneto

Ateneumin Taidekokoelmat: Museojulkaisu
[Art collections of the Athenaeum: museum publication; cont. as *Ateneumin Taidemuseo: Museojulkaisu*]

Ateneumin Taidemuseo: Museojulkaisu
[Art museum of the Athenaeum: museum publication; prev. pubd as *Ateneumin Taidekokoelmat: Museojulkaisu*]

A. & Text
Art and Text

A. Textiles
Artes textiles

A. Textrina
Ars textrina

Āthār [Antiquities]

Āthār-é Īrān [Antiquities of Iran]

Athenäum

Athénée Orient.
L'Athénée oriental: Mémoires

Athens An. Archaeol.
Athens Annals of Archaeology [same as *Archaiol. Anlkt. Athinon*]

Äthiop. Forsch.
Äthiopistische Forschungen

Atiquot
Atiquot: Journal of the Israel Department of Antiquities

Atlāl

Atlanta Hist. J.
Atlanta Historical Journal

Atlante Bresc.
Atlante bresciano

Atlantic & Ice. Rev.
Atlantic and Icelandic Review [prev. pubd as *Iceland Review*]

Atlantic Mthly
Atlantic Monthly: Devoted to Literature, Art and Politics

Atlantis

A. Tribal
Art tribal/Tribal Art [Bulletin semestriel publié par l'Association des amis du Barbier–Mueller]

Atti Accad. Agric., Sci. & Lett. Verona
Atti dell'Accademia d'agricoltura, scienze e lettere di Verona

Atti Accad. Archeol., Lett. & B.A.
Atti dell'Accademia di archeologia, lettere e belle arti [cont. as *Rendi. Accad. Archeol., Lett. & B.A.*]

Atti Accad. B.A., Venezia
Atti dell'Accademia di belle arti, Venezia

Atti Accad. N. Lincei
Atti dell'Accademia nazionale dei Lincei

Atti Accad. N. Lincei, Mem. Cl. Sci. Morali, Stor. & Filol.
Atti dell'Accademia nazionale dei Lincei, memorie della classe di scienze morali, storiche e filologiche

Atti Accad. Peloritana
Atti dell'Accademia peloritana

Atti Accad. Pontaniana
Atti dell'Accademia pontaniana

Atti Accad. Properz. Subasio-Assisi
Atti della Accademia properziana del Subasio–Assisi

Atti Accad. Sci., Lett. & A. Udine
Atti dell'Accademia di scienze, lettere e arti di Udine

Atti Accad. Sci. Torino
Atti dell'Accademia delle scienze di Torino [prev. pubd as *Atti Reale Accad. Sci. Torino*]

Atti Accad. Toscana Sci. & Lett. 'La Colombaria'
Atti dell'Accademia toscana di scienze e lettere 'La Colombaria'

Atti Ateneo Sci., Lett. & A.
Atti dell'Ateneo di scienze, lettere e arti

Atti Cent. Ric. & Doc. Ant. Class.
Atti del Centro di ricerca e documentazione dell'antichità classica [prev. pubd as *Atti Cent. Stud. & Doc. Italia Romana*]

Atti Cent. Stud. & Doc. Italia Romana
Atti del Centro di studi e documentazione sull'Italia romana [cont. as *Atti Cent. Ric. & Doc. Ant. Class.*]

Atti Civ. Mus. Stor. & A. Trieste
Atti dei civici musei di storia ed arti di Trieste

Atti Coll. Architetti & Ingeg.
Atti del Collegio degli architetti ed ingegneri

Atti Coll. Ingeg. & Architetti Milano
Atti del Collegio degli ingegneri ed architetti di Milano

Atti Convegni Lincei
Atti Convegni Lincei

Atti Imp. & Reale Accad. Georgofili
Atti della Imperiale e reale accademia dei georgofili

Atti Imp. Regia Accad. Sci., Lett. & A. Agiati Rovero
Atti della Imperiale regia accademia di scienze, lettere ed arti degli Agiati in Rovero

Atti Ist. Ven. Sci., Lett. & A.
Atti dell'Istituto veneto di scienze, lettere ed arti [prev. pubd as *Atti Reale Ist. Ven. Sci., Lett. & A.*]

Atti & Mem. Accad. Agric., Sci. & Lett. Verona
Atti e memorie dell'Accademia di agricoltura, scienze e lettere di Verona

Atti & Mem. Accad. Clementina Bologna
Atti e memorie dell'Accademia clementina di Bologna

Atti & Mem. Accad. Fiorent. Sci. Morali, 'La Colombaria'
Atti e memorie dell'Accademia fiorentina di scienze morali, 'La Colombaria' [cont. as *Atti & Mem. Accad. Tosc. Sci. & Lett., 'La Colombaria'*]

Atti & Mem. Accad. N. Lincei, Atti Cl. Sci. Morali
Atti e memorie dell'Accademia nazionale dei Lincei, atti della classe di scienze morali

Atti & Mem. Accad. N. Virgil. Mantova
Atti e memorie dell'Accademia nazionale virgiliana di Mantova

Atti & Mem. Accad. Patavina Sci., Lett. & A.
Atti e memorie dell'Accademia patavina di scienze, lettere ed arti [prev. pubd as *Atti & Mem. Reale Accad. Sci., Lett. & A. Padova*; *Nuovi Saggi Reale Accad. Sci., Lett. & A. Padova*]

Atti & Mem. Accad. Petrarca Lett., A. & Sci.
Atti e memorie dell'Accademia Petrarca di lettere, arti e scienze

Atti & Mem. Accad. Tosc. Sci. & Lett., 'La Colombaria'
Atti e memorie dell'Accademia toscana di scienze e lettere, 'La Colombaria' [prev. pubd as *Atti & Mem. Accad. Fiorent. Sci. Morali, 'La Colombaria'*]

Atti & Mem. Deput. Ferrar. Stor. Patria
Atti e memorie della Deputazione ferrarese di storia patria

Atti & Mem. Deput. Stor. Patria Marche
Atti e memorie della Deputazione di storia patria per le Marche

Atti & Mem. Deput. Stor. Patria Prov. Romagna
Atti e memorie della Deputazione di storia patria per le province di Romagna [prev. pubd as *Atti & Mem. Reale Deput. Stor. Patria Emilia & Romagna*]

Atti & Mem. Reale Accad. Archeol., Lett. & B.A. Napoli
Atti e memorie della Reale accademia di archeologia, lettere e belle arti di Napoli

Atti & Mem. Reale Accad. Sci., Lett. & A. Padova
Atti e memorie della R[eale] Accademia di scienze, lettere ed arti in Padova [prev. pubd as *Nuovi Saggi Reale Accad. Sci., Lett. & A. Padova*; cont. as *Atti & Mem. Accad. Patavina Sci., Lett. & A.*]

Atti & Mem. Reale Accad. S Luca: Annuario
Atti e memorie della Reale accademia di San Luca: Annuario

Atti & Mem. Reale Deput. Stor. Patria Emilia & Romagna
Atti e memorie della Reale deputazione di storia patria per l'Emilia e la Romagna [cont. as *Atti & Mem. Deput. Stor. Patria Prov. Romagna*]

Atti & Mem. Reale Deput. Stor. Patria Marche
Atti e memorie della R[eale] deputazione di storia patria per le Marche

Atti & Mem. Reale Deput. Stor. Patria Prov. Moden.
Atti e memorie della R[eale] deputazione di storia patria per le province modenesi [prev. pubd as *Atti & Mem. RR. Deput. Stor. Patria Prov. Moden. & Parm.*; *Atti & Mem. RR. Deput. Stor. Patria Prov. Emilia*]

Atti & Mem. Regia Deput. Stor. Patria Prov. Romagna
Atti e memorie della regia deputazione di storia patria per le province della Romagna [prev. pubd as *Atti & Mem. Reale Deput. Stor. Patria Emilia & Romagna*]

Atti & Mem. RR. Deput. Stor. Patria Prov. Emilia
Atti e memorie delle RR. [Reali] Deputazioni di storia patria per le province dell'Emilia [see *Atti & Mem. Reale Deput. Stor. Patria Prov. Moden.*]

Atti & Mem. RR. Deput. Stor. Patria Prov. Moden. & Parm.
Atti e memorie delle RR. [Reali] deputazioni di storia patria per le province modenesi e parmensi [see *Atti & Mem. Reale Deput. Stor. Patria Prov. Moden.*]

Atti & Mem. Soc. Savon. Stor. Patria
Atti e memorie della Società savonese di storia patria

Atti & Mem. Soc. Tiburtina Stor. & A.
Atti e memorie della Società tiburtina di storia e d'arte

Atti & Mem. Stor. Patria Prov. Romagna
Atti e memorie della storia patria per la provincia Romagna

Atti Pont. Accad. Romana Archeol.
Atti della Pontificia accademia romana di archeologia

Atti Reale Accad. It., Rendi. Sci. Fisiche
Atti della Reale accademia italiana, rendiconti di scienze fisiche

Atti Reale Accad. Sci. Torino
Atti della Reale accademia delle scienze di Torino [cont. as *Atti Accad. Sci. Torino*]

Atti Reale Ist. Ven. Sci., Lett. & A.
Atti del Reale istituto veneto di scienze, lettere ed arti [cont. as *Atti Ist. Ven. Sci., Lett. & A.*]

Atti Riun. Sci., Ist. It. Preist. & Protostor.
Atti della Riunione scientifica, Istituto italiano di preistoria e protostoria

Atti Sind. Prov. Fasc. Ingeg. Lombardia
Atti del Sindacato provinciale fascista degli ingegneri di Lombardia

Atti Soc. Archeol. & B.A. Prov. Torino
Atti della Società di archeologia e belle arti per la provincia di Torino

Atti Soc. Ligure Stor. Patria
Atti della Società ligure di storia patria

Atti Soc. Piemont. Archeol. & B.A.
Atti della Società piemontese di archeologia e belle arti

Atti Soc. Savon. Stor. Patria
Atti della Società savonese di storia patria

A. Typograph.
Ars typographica

Auckland U. Coll. Bull.
Auckland University College Bulletin

Auckland/Waikato Hist. J.
Auckland/Waikato Historical Journal [prev. pubd as *J. Auckland Hist. Soc.*; *Hist. J. Auckland-Waikato*; *J. Auckland/Waikato Hist. Soc.*]

Audio-visual Communic. Rev.
Audio-visual Communications Review

Aufstieg & Niedergang Röm. Welt
Aufstieg und Niedergang der römischen Welt

Augsburg. Allg. Ztg
Augsburger allgemeine Zeitung

Augsburg. Mtl. Ksthl.
Augsburgisches monatliches Kunstblatt

Augst. Mushft.
Augster Museumshefte

Augusta Taurinorum

Augustea

Augusteum Jschr.
Augusteum Jahresschrift

Augustiniana

Aujourd'hui
Aujourd'hui: Art et architecture [prev. pubd as *A. Aujourd'hui*]

A. Una
Ars una

Aurea Parma

Aurora: Eichendorff Alm.
Aurora: Eichendorff Almanach

Aus Schwabens Vergangenheit

Austral. A.
Australian Art

Austral. Aboriginal Stud.
Australian Aboriginal Studies

Austral. A. Educ.
Australasian Art Education

Austral. Ant. Colr
Australian Antique Collector

Australasian Critic

Austral. Connoisseur & Colr
Australian Connoisseur and Collector

Austral. Hist. Yb.
Australian History Yearbook

Australiana

Austral. J. A.
Australian Journal of Art

Austral. J. Bibl. Archaeol.
Australian Journal of Biblical Archaeology

Austral. Nat. Hist.
Australian Natural History

Austral. Sketcher
Australian Sketcher

Autoclub

Autologia

Auvergne Litt.
L'Auvergne littéraire

Au Volant
Au volant

Aux Ecoutes
Aux écoutes

A. VA
Arts in Virginia

Avalanche Mag.
Avalanche Magazine

Avanti

A. Ven.
Arte veneta

A. & Vie
L'Art et la vie

Artviews

A. Visual
Arte visual

A. Vivant
L'Art vivant

A. Voices
Art Voices

A. Wkbld
Artistiek weekblad

A. Wkly
Arts Weekly

A. Work
Art Work

A. Workers' Q.
Art Workers' Quarterly

Axis

A-Ya

A. Yb.
Arts Yearbook

Azania

Az Est [This evening]

Az Pest

Babin

Baden. Heimat
Badener Heimat

Baden-Württemberg

Baessler-Arch.
Baessler-Archiv: Beiträge zur Völkerkunde

Baghdad. Mitt.
Baghdader Mitteilungen

Baghdad. Mitt. Beihft
Baghdader Mitteilungen Beihft

Balafon Mag.
Balafon Magazine

Balafron

Balcanoslavica

Balkan Stud.
Balkan Studies

Baltimore Annu.
Baltimore Annual

Baltimore Mus. A. Annu.
Baltimore Museum of Art Annual

Baltimore Mus. A. News Q.
Baltimore Museum of Art News Quarterly

Balt. Stud.
Baltische Studien

Bamber Erevani Hamalsazani

Banbury Hist. Soc.
Banbury Historical Society

Bandeaux Or
Bandeaux d'or

Baraza
Baraza: A Journal of the Arts in Malawi

Barbero Mun.
Barbero municipal

Barcelona
Barcelona: Metròpolis mediterranea

Barilla

Barricada

Barricada Int.
Barricada internacional

Baselbiet. Heimatb.
Baselbieter Heimatbuch

Ba Shiru

Basilica Teres.
Basilica teresiana

Basl. Beitr. Ethnol.
Basler Beiträge zur Ethnographie

Basl. Jb.
Basler Jahrbuch [cont. as *Basl. Stadtb.*]

Basl. Kstver.: Ber.
Basler Kunstverein: Bericht [prev. pubd as *Basl. Kstver.: Jber.*; *Basl. Kstver.: Berstatt.*; reverts to *Basl. Kstver.: Jber.*; then to *Basl. Kstver.: Ber.*]

Basl. Kstver.: Berstatt.
Basler Kunstverein: Berichterstattung [see *Basl. Kstver.: Ber.*]

Basl. Kstver.: Jber.
Basler Kunstverein: Jahresbericht [see *Basl. Kstver.: Ber.*]

Basl. Stadtb.
Basler Stadtbuch [prev. pubd as *Basl. Jb.*]

Basl. Z. Gesch. & Altertknd.
Basler Zeitschrift für Geschichte und Altertumskunde

Bath Chron.
Bath Chronicle

Bath Hist.
Bath History

Bau

Bauen + Wohnen [merged with *Werk-Archithese* to form *Werk, Bauen + Wohnen*]

Bauforum

Baugilde

Bauhaus: Z. Bau & Gestalt.
Bauhaus: Zeitschrift für Bau und Gestaltung

Bauingenieur

Baukst & Werkform
Baukunst und Werkform: Monatsschrift für die Gebiete der Gestaltung

Baumeister

Bauwelt

Bau & Werkkst
Bau und Werkkunst

Bauztg Ungarn
Bauzeitung für Ungarn

Bayer. Heimatschutz
Bayerische Heimatschutz [prev. pubd as *Vlkskst & Vlksknd.*; cont. as *S. Heimat*]

Bayer. Jb. Vlksknd.
Bayerisches Jahrbuch für Volkskunde

Bayer. Landesamt Dkmlpf.
Bayerisches Landsamt für Denkmalpflege

Bayer. Nztg
Bayerische Nationalzeitung

Bayer. Vorgeschbl.
Bayerische Vorgeschichtsblätter

BC Hist. Q.
British Columbia Historical Quarterly

Bead J.
The Bead Journal [cont. as *Ornament*]

Beaux-A. [19th C.]
Beaux-arts

Beaux-A. [20th C.]
Beaux-arts

Beaux-A.: Chron. A. & Curiosité
Beaux-arts: Chronique des arts et de la curiosité [prev. pubd as *Chron. A. & Curiosité*; cont. as *Arts* [Paris]]

Beaux-A.: Rev. Inf. A.
Beaux-arts: Revue d'information artistique [prev. pubd as *J. A.* [Paris]]

Beaver

Beck's J. Dec. A.
Beck's Journal of Decorative Art

Bedi Kartlisa
Bedi kartlisa

Beeldhouwkst Eeuw Rubens
Beeldhouwkunst in de eeuw van Rubens

Beeld. Kst
Beeldende kunst

Beihft Ant. Kst
Beiheft Antike Kunst

Beihft Mittelaltein. Jb.
Beiheft zum mittelalteinischen Jahrbuch

Beihft Röm. Jb. Kstgesch.
Beiheft des römischen Jahrbuchs für Kunstgeschichte

Beijing Daxue Xuebao: Renwen Kexue [Beijing University: Humanities Division]

Beijing Rev.
Beijing Review

Beil. Graph. Kst
Beilage der graphischen Kunst

Beira Alta
Beira alta

Beissatsu Taiyō / Nihon No Kokoro
Beissatsu Taiyō [suppl. Nihon no Kokoro [The spirit of Japan]]

Beitr. Allg. & Vergl. Archäol.
Beiträge zur allgemeinen und vergleichenden Archäologie [BAVA]

Beitr. Altbayer. Kirchgesch.
Beiträge zur altbayerischen Kirchengeschichte [prev. pubd as *Beitr. Gesch., Top. & Statistik Erzbistums München & Freising*]

Beitr. & Ber. Staatl. Kstsamml. Dresden
Beiträge und Berichte der Staatlichen Kunstsammlungen Dresden [cont. as *Jb. Staatl. Kstsamml. Dresden*]

Beitr. Ethnomusik.
Beiträge zur Ethnomusikologie

Beitr. Forsch.: Stud. & Mitt. Antiqua. Jacques Rosenthal
Beiträge zur Forschung: Studien und Mitteilungen aus dem Antiquariat Jacques Rosenthal

Beitr. Gesch. Bistums Regensburg
Beiträge zur Geschichte des Bistums Regensburg

Beitr. Gesch. Bwsns
Beiträge zur Geschichte des Buchwesens

Beitr. Gesch. Dortmunds & Grafsch. Mark
Beiträge zur Geschichte Dortmunds und der Grafschaft Mark

Beitr. Gesch. Dt. Kst
Beiträge zur Geschichte deutscher Kunst

Beitr. Gesch. Kult. Stadt Nürnberg
Beiträge zur Geschichte und Kultur der Stadt Nürnberg

Beitr. Gesch. Niederrheins
Beiträge zur Geschichte des Niederrheins [cont. as *Düsseldorf. Jb.*]

Beitr. Gesch. Städte Mitteleuropas
Beiträge zur Geschichte der Städte Mitteleuropas

Beitr. Gesch. Stadt Goslar
Beiträge zur Geschichte der Stadt Goslar

Beitr. Gesch., Top. & Statistik Erzbistums München & Freising
Beiträge zur Geschichte, Topographie und Statistik des Erzbistums München und Freising [cont. as *Beitr. Altbayer. Kichgesch.*]

Beitr. Heimatknd. Niederbayern
Beiträge sur Heimatkunde von Niederbayern

Beitr. Indforsch.
Beiträge zur Indienforschung

Beitr. Kstgesch.
Beiträge zur Kunstgeschichte

Beitr. Kstgesch. Schweiz
Beiträge zur Kunstgeschichte in der Schweiz

Beitr. Landespfl.
Beiträge zur Landespflege

Beitr. Rhein. Kstgesch. & Dkmlpf.
Beiträge zur rheinischen Kunstgeschichte und Denkmalpflege

Beitr. Sächs. Kirchgesch.
Beiträge zur sächsischen Kirchengeschichte

Beitr. Südasien-Forsch.
Beiträge zur Südasien-Forschung

Beitr. Theorie Kst. 19. Jht
Beiträge zur Theorie der Künste im 19. Jahrhundert

Beitr. Wirtschaftsgesch. Nürnbergs
Beiträge zur Wirtschaftsgeschichte Nürnbergs

Belas A.
Belas artes: Revista c boletim da Academia nacional de belas artes [prev. pubd as *Bol. Acad. N. B.A.*]

Belfagor
Belfagor: Rassegna di varia umanità

Belfried
Belfried: Eine Monatsschrift für Geschichte der Gegenwart der belgischen Lande

Belgeler

Belgique A. & Litt.
Belgique artistique et littéraire

Belg. Tijdschr. Oudhdknd. & Kstgesch.
Belgisch tijdschrift voor oudheidkunde en kunstgeschiedenis [Belgian journal for archaeology and art history]

Belize Today
Belize Today Magazine

Beliz. Stud.
Belizean Studies

Bellas A.
Bellas artes

Belle A.
Belle arti

Belvedere
Belvedere: Illustrierte Zeitschrift für Kunstsammler

Bem Estar
Bem estar

Benedictina

Bengal Past & Present
Bengal Past and Present

Bentley's Misc.
Bentley's Miscellany

Ber. Amersfoort
Berichten Amersfoort

Ber., Basl. Kstver.
Bericht, Basler Kunstverein [prev. pubd as *Berstatt.: Jahr...., Basl. Kstver.*]

Ber. Dkmlpf. Niedersachsen
Berichte zur Denkmalpflege Niedersachsen

Ber. Dt. Ker. Ges.
Berichte der deutschen keramischen Gesellschaft

Ber. Forsch.-Inst. Osten & Orient
Berichte des Forschungs-Instituts für Osten und Orient

Bergamo
Bergamo: Bollettino della civica Biblioteca e dell'Ateneo di scienze, lettere ed arti Bergamo [prev. pubd as *Boll. Civ. Bib. Bergamo*]

Bergamo A.
Bergamo arte

Bergens Mus. Åb.
Bergens Museum årbok [Bergen Museum's yearbook; cont. as *Åb. U. Bergen*]

Bergomum

Ber. Gottfried Keller Stift.
Bericht der Gottfried Keller Stiftung

Ber. Hist. Ver. Bamberg
Bericht des historischen Vereins Bamberg

Ber. Hist. Gez. Utrecht
Berigten van het Historisch gezelschap te Utrecht

Berlin. Abendbl.
Berliner Abendblätter

Berlin. Architwelt
Berliner Architekturwelt

Berlin. Beitr. Archäom.
Berliner Beiträge zur Archäometrie

Berlin. Bl.
Berlinische Blätter [prev. pubd as *Berlin. Mschr.*; cont. as *Neue Berlin. Mschr.*]

Berlin. Byz. Arbeit.
Berliner byzantinische Arbeiten

Berlin. Charivari
Berliner Charivari

Berlin. Heimat
Berliner Heimat

Berlin. Illus. Ztg
Berliner illustrierte Zeitung

Berlin. Indol. Stud.
Berliner indologische Studien

Berlin. Jb. Vor- & Frühgesch.
Berliner Jahrbuch für Vor- und Frühgeschichte [cont. as *Acta Praehist. & Archaeol.*]

Berlin. Mschr.
Berlinische Monatsschrift [cont. as *Berlin. Bl.*; *Neue Berlin. Mschr.*]

Berlin. Münzbl.
Berliner Münzblätter [cont. as *Dt. Münzbl.*]

Berlin. Mus.: Ber. Ehem. Preuss. Kstsamml.
Berliner Museen: Berichte aus den ehemaligen preussischen Kunstsammlungen [prev. pubd as *Berlin. Mus.: Ber. Staatl. Mus. Preuss. Kultbes.*; *Amtl. Ber. Kön. Kstsamml.*]

Berlin. Mus.: Ber. Staatl. Mus. Preuss. Kultbes.
Berliner Museen: Berichte aus den Staatlichen Museen preussischer Kulturbesitz [prev. pubd as *Amtl. Ber. Kön. Kstsamml.*; cont. as *Berlin. Mus.: Ber. Ehem. Preuss. Kstsamml.*]

Berlin. N.-Ztg
Berliner National-Zeitung

Berlin. Tagbl.
Berliner Tageblatt

Ber. & Mitt. Altert.-Ver. Wien
Berichte und Mitteilungen des Altertums-Vereines zu Wien

Ber. Mus. Francisco-Carolinium
Bericht über das Museum Francisco-Carolinium [cont. as *Jber. Mus. Francisco-Carolinium*; *Jb. Oberösterreich. Musver.*; *Jb. Oberösterreich. Musver., Ges. Landesknd.*]

Ber. Mus. Stadt Ulms
Berichte des Museums der Stadt Ulms

Ber. Musver. Judenburg
Berichte des Museumsvereins Judenburg

Ber. Mus. Vlkerknd. Leipzig
Bericht des Museums für Völkerkunde in Leipzig [cont. as *Jb. Mus. Vlkerknd. Leipzig*]

Ber. Natwiss. Ver. & Mus. Natknd. & Vorgesch. Dessau
Berichte des naturwissenschaftlichen Vereins und des Museums für Naturkunde und Vorgeschichte in Dessau

Berne

Ber. Raumforsch. & Raumplan.
Berichte zur Raumforschung und Raumplanung

Ber. Rijksdienst Oudhdknd.
Berichten van de Rijksdienst voor het oudheidkundig bodemonderzoek

Ber. Röm.-Ger. Komm.
Bericht der Römisch-germanischen Kommission

Berstatt.: Jahr...., Basl. Kstver.
Berichterstattung: Über das Jahr....,
Basler Kunstverein [cont as *Jber.
Basl. Kstver.; Ber., Basl. Kstver.*]

Bertoldo

*Ber. Verhand. Kön. Sächs. Ges. Wiss.
Leipzig, Philol.–Hist. Kl.*
Berichte über die Verhandlungen
der Königlichen sächsischen
Gesellschaft der Wissenschaften
zu Leipzig, philologisch–
historische Klasse

Berytus

Bessarone

Bética

Béton Armé
Béton armé

Bezbozhnik & Stanka
Bezbozhnik u stanka

Bhāratīya Vidyā

Bib. Archv Romanicum
Biblioteca dell'Archivum
Romanicum

Bib. Bibliog. It.
Biblioteca di bibliografia italiana

Bib. Diffusion Mus. Guimet
Bibliothèque de diffusion du
Musée Guimet [prev. pubd as *Bib.
Vulgarisation Mus. Guimet*]

Bib. Ecole France
Bibliothèque de l'Ecole de France

Bib. Ecole Hautes Etud.
Bibliothèque de l'Ecole des hautes
études

Bib. Ecoles Fr. Athènes & Rome
Bibliothèque des Ecoles françaises
d'Athènes et de Rome

Bib.: Forsch. & Praxis
Bibliothek: Forschung und Praxis

Bib. Francescana Sarda
Biblioteca Francescana Sarda

Bib. Himalay.
Bibliotheca Himalayica

Bib. Hist. Ville Paris
Bibliothèque historique de la ville
de Paris

Bib. Humanisme & Ren.
Bibliothèque d'humanisme et
renaissance

Bib. Inst. Fr. Etud. Anat. Istanbul
Bibliothèque de l'Institut français
d'études anatoliennes d'Istanbul

Bib. It. G. Lett. Sci. & A.
Biblioteca italiana ossia giornale di
letteratura, scienze ed arti

Bibl. Archaeologist
Biblical Archaeologist

Bibl. Archaeol. Rev.
Biblical Archaeology Review

Biblica

Bibliog. Hisp.
Bibliografía hispánica

Bibliographica

Bibliotheekleven

Biblos
Biblos: Revista de faculdade de
letras de Universidade de Coimbra

Bib. Mesop.
Bibliotheca Mesopotamica

Bib. & Mus. Neuchâtel
Bibliothèques et musées de
Neuchâtel

Bib. N. Madrid
Biblioteca nacional de Madrid

Bib. Orient.
Bibliotheca orientalis

Bib. Reden. & Bild. Kst
Bibliothek der redenden und
bildenden Künste [prev. pubd as
*Neue Bib. S. Wiss. & Frejen Kst.;
Bib. S. Wiss. & Frejen Kst.*]

Bib. Sanctorum
Bibliotheca sanctorum

Bib. S. Wiss. & Frejen Kst.
Bibliothek der schönen
Wissenschaften und der freien
Künste [cont. as *Neue Bib.
S. Wiss. & Frejen Kst.; Bib. Reden.
& Bild. Kst.*]

Bib. Univl.
Bibliothèque universelle: Revue
suisse et étrangère [prev. pubd as
Bib. Univl. Genève; cont. as *Bib.
Univl. & Rev. Suisse*]

Bib. Univl. Genève
Bibliothèque universelle de
Genève [cont. as *Bib. Univl.*; *Bib.
Univl. & Rev. Suisse*]

Bib. Univl. & Rev. Suisse
Bibliothèque universelle et revue
suisse [prev. pubd as *Bib. Univl.*;
Bib. Univl. Genève]

Bib. Vulgarisation Mus. Guimet
Bibliothèque de vulgarisation du
Musée Guimet [cont. as *Bib.
Diffusion Mus. Guimet*]

Bib. Warszaw.
Biblioteka Warszawska

Bib. & Wiss.
Bibliothek und Wissenschaft

Bief
Bief: Jonction surréaliste

Biennale Venezia
Biennale di Venezia

Bien Pub.
Bien public

Bifur

*Bijd. Bronnenonderzoek Ontwikkeling
Ned. Hist. Tuinen, Parken &
Buitenplaatsen*
Bijdragen tot het
bronnenonderzoek naar de
ontwikkeling van Nederlandse
historische tuinen, parken en
buitenplaatsen [Contributions to
the research of sources for the
development of Dutch historical
gardens, parks and courtyards]

Bijdr. Dierknd.
Bijdragen tot de dierkunde
[Contributions to zoology]

Bijdr. Gesch. Kst Nederlanden
Bijdragen tot de geschiedenis van
de kunst der Nederlanden
[Contributions to the history of
the art of the Netherlands]

Bijdr. & Meded. Betreff. Gesch. Ned.
Bijdragen en mededelingen
betreffende de geschiedenis der
Nederlanden [Contributions and
communications regarding the
history of the Netherlands]

Bijdr. & Meded. Hist. Genoot. Utrecht
Bijdragen en mededelingen van
het Historisch genootschap te
Utrecht [Contributions and
communications of the Historical
Society at Utrecht]

Bijdr. & Meded. Ver. 'Gelre'
Bijdragen en mededelingen der
Vereniging 'Gelre' [Contributions
and communications of the 'Gelre'
Association]

Bijdr. Taal-, Land- & Vlkenknd.
Bijdragen tot de taal-, land- en
volkenkunde [Contributions to
linguistics, geography and
ethnology]

Bijutsu Kenkyū
Bijutsu kenkyū [Art research]

Bijutsushi [Journal of the Japanese Art
History Society]

Bikmaus [Papua New Guinea]

Bildhft. Ger. Nmus.
Bildhefte des Germanischen
Nationalmuseums

Bildhft. Mus. Kst & Gew. Hamburg
Bilderhefte des Museums für
Kunst und Gewerbe Hamburg

*Bildhft. Westfäl. Landesmus. Kst.-&
Kultgesch.*
Bilderhefte des Westfälischen
Landesmuseums für Kunst- und
Kulturgeschichte

Bild. Kst
Bildende Kunst

Bild. Kst Österreich
Die bildende Kunst in Österreich

*Bildner. Erz./Werkerziehung/Textiles
Gestalt.*
Bildnerische Erziehung/
Werkerziehung/Textiles Gestalten

Billiken

Biog. Bl.
Biographische Blätter [cont. as
*Biog. Jb. & Dt. Nekrol.; Dt. Biog.
Jb.*]

Biog. Jb. & Dt. Nekrol.
Biographisches Jahrbuch und
deutscher Nekrolog [prev. pubd as
Biog. Bl.; cont. as *Dt. Biog. Jb.*]

Biog. Mem., N. Acad. Sci.
Biographical Memoirs, National
Academy of Science

Biog. & Rev.
The Biograph and Review

Birmingham Archaeol. Soc. Transcr.
Birmingham Archaeological
Society Transcripts

Birtingur [Dawning]

Biser. Ortdx Román.
Biserica ortodoxă română

Bishop Mus. Occas. Pap.
Bishop Museum Occasional
Papers

Biul. Bib. Jagielloń.
Biuletyn Biblioteki jagiellońskiej
[Bulletin of the Jagiellonian
Library]

Biul. Hist. Sztuki
Biuletyn historii sztuki [Bulletin of
the history of art; prev. pubd as
Biul. Hist. Sztuki & Kult; *Zakład
Archit. Pol. & Hist. Sztuki*]

Biul. Hist. Sztuki & Kult.
Biuletyn historii sztuki i kultury
[Bulletin of the history of art and
culture; prev. pubd as *Zakład
Archit. Pol. & Hist. Sztuki*; cont.
as *Biul. Hist. Sztuki*]

Biul. Tech. Biura Proj. Budownictwa
Biuletyn techniczny biura
projektowania budownictwa
[Technical bulletin of the City
Design and Construction Centre]

Biul. Urb.
Biuletyn urbanistyczny

Bk Colr
Book Collector

Bk Hb.
Book Handbook

Bkman's J. & Prt Colr
Bookman's Journal and Print
Collector

Bk Old Edinburgh Club
Book of the Old Edinburgh Club

Bk & Pap. Grp Annu.
Book and Paper Group Annual

Black Mountain Coll. Bull.
Black Mountain College Bulletin

Black & White
Black and White

Blackwood's Edinburgh Mag.
Blackwood's Edinburgh Magazine

Blackwood's Mag.
Blackwood's Magazine

Blake Newslett.
Blake Newsletter

Blast

Bl. Bayer. Landesver. Familienknd.
Blätter des Bayerischen
Landesvereins für Familienkunde

Bl. & Bild.
Blätter und Bilder: Eine Zeitschrift
für Dichtung, Musik und Malerei

Bldg Conserv.
Building Conservation

Bldg Constr.
Building Construction [cont. as
Bldg Des. & Bldg Constr.]

Bldg Des.
Building Design

Bldg Des. & Bldg Constr.
Building Design and Construction
[prev. pubd as *Bldg Constr.*]

Bldg & Engin. J.
Building and Engineering Journal

Bldg & Engin. J. Australia & NZ
Building and Engineering Journal
of Australia and New Zealand

Bldg News
Building News

Bldg Refurb. & Maint.
Building Refurbishment and
Maintenance

Bldg Rev.
Building Review

Bldg Serv. Engin. Res. & Technol.
Building Services Engineering
Research and Technology

Bldg Today
Building Today

Bld Kenya
Build Kenya

Bldr's J.
Builder's Journal

Bldr's J. & Archit. Rec.
Builder's Journal and Architectural
Record

Bldr's Mag.
Builder's Magazine

Bleu

Bl. Gemäldeknd.
Blätter für Gemäldekunde [cont.
as *Stud. & Skiz. Gemäldeknd.;
Neue Bl. Gemäldeknd.;
Gemäldekunde*]

Bl. Gemäldeknd. Beil.
Blätter für Gemäldekunde Beilage

Blind Man

BLJ
British Library Journal

Bl. Münzfreunde
Blätter für Münzfreunde

Block

Blok

Blok: Časop. Umění
Blok: Časopis pro umění [Journal
for art]

Blueprint

BM: Geol. Bull.
British Museum: Geology Bulletin

BM: Nat. Hist. Bull.
British Museum: Natural History
Bulletin

BM Q
British Museum Quarterly

BM Yb.
British Museum Yearbook

Boa

Boabe Grûe
Boabe de grûe

Bocholt. Quellen & Beitr.
Bocholter Quellen und Beiträge

Bodensee-Chron.
Bodensee-Chronik

Bodleian Lib. Rec.
Bodleian Library Record

Bodleian Q. Rec.
Bodleian Quarterly Record

Boğaziçi Ü. Derg.: Hüman. Bilimler
Boğaziçi Üniversitesi dergisi:
Hümaniter bilimler [Bosphorus
University journal: humanities
research]

Bohemia–Jh. Coll. Carolinum
Bohemia–Jahrbuch des Collegium
Carolinum

Bokubi

Bol. Acad. B.A.
Boletín de la Academia de bellas
artes

Bol. Acad. Chil. Hist.
Boletín de la Academia chilena de
historia

Bol. Acad. N. B.A.
Boletim da Academia nacional de
belas artes [cont. as *Belas A.*]

Bol. Acad. N. Hist.
Boletín de la Academia nacional
de historia

Bolaffi A.
Bolaffi arte [cont. as *Riv. A.*]

Bol. Amigos Porto
Boletim dos Amigos do Porto

Bol. Antropol.
Boletín de antropología

Bol. Archv Gen. Nación
Boletín del Archivo general de la
nación

Bol. Arqueol.
Boletín de arqueología

Bol. Arquiv. Distr. Porto
Boletim do Arquivo distrital do
Porto

Bol. Arquiv. U. Coimbra
Boletim do Arquivo da
Universidade de Coimbra

Bol. Asoc. A. Concr. Inven.
Boletín de la Asociación arte
concreto invención

Bol. Asoc. Esp. Orientalistas
Boletín de la Asociación española
de orientalistas

Bol. A. Toled.
Boletín de arte toledano

Bol. A. U. Málaga
Boletín de arte de la Universidad
de Málaga

Bol. B.A. Real Acad. S Isabel Hungría
Boletín de bellas artes de la Real
academia de Santa Isabel de
Hungría

Bol. Bibliog. Antropol. Amer.
Boletín bibliográfico de
antropología americana

Bol. Bib. Menéndez Pelayo
Boletín Biblioteca Menéndez
Pelayo

Bol. Cent. A. Granada
Boletín del Centro artístico de
Granada

*Bol. Cent. Invest. Hist. & Estét.
Caracas*
Boletín del Centro de
investigaciones históricas y
estéticas de Caracas

Bol. Com. Mnmts Navarros
Boletín de la Comisión de
monumentos de Navarros

Bol. Com. Mnmts Vizcaya
Boletín de la Comisión de
monumentos de Vizcaya

Bol. Com. Mun. Turismo
Boletim da Comissão municipal de
turismo

Bol. Com. Prov. Mnmts Burgos
Boletín de la Comisión provincial
de monumentos de Burgos

Bol. Com. Prov. Mnmts Orense
Boletín de la Comisión provincial
de monumentos de Orense

Bol. Cult.
Boletim cultural

Bol. Cult. Assembl. Distr. Lisboa
Boletim cultural da Assembléia
distrital de Lisboa

*Bol. Cult. & Bib., Bib. Luis Angel
Arango*
Boletín cultural y bibliográfico,
Biblioteca Luis Angel Arango

Bol. Cult. Camâra Mun. Porto
Boletim cultural da Camâra
municipal do Porto

Bol. Cult. Guiné Port.
Boletim cultural da Guiné
portuguesa

Bol. Estud. Oaxaqueños
Boletín de estudios oaxaqueños

Bol. Hist. Fund. John Boulton
Boletín histórico de la Fundación
John Boulton

Bol. INAH
Boletín del Instituto nacional de
antropología e historia

Bol. Inst. Angola
Boletim do Instituto de Angola

Bol. Inst. Antropol.
Boletín del Instituto de
antropología

Bol. Inst. Estud. Astur.
Boletín del Instituto de estudios
asturianos

Bol. Inst. Etnol. & Flklore
Boletín del Instituto de etnología y
folklore

Bol. Inst. Fernán González
Boletín del Institución Fernán
González

Bol. Inst. Invest. Cient. Angola
Boletim do Instituto de
investigação científica de Angola

Bol. Inst. Invest. Hist. & Estét.
Boletín del Instituto de
investigaciones históricas y
estéticas

*Bol. Junta Patrn. Mus. Prov. B.A.
Murcia*
Boletín de la Junta del patronato
de Museo provincia de bellas artes
de Murcia

Boll. A.
Bollettino d'arte [cont. as *Arti:
Rass. Bimest. A. Ant. & Mod.;
Boll. A.*]

Boll. Accad. Euloti
Bollettino dell'Accademia degli
Euloti

Boll. Accad. Eutelèti Città San Miniato
Bollettino dell'Accademia degli
Eutelèti della città di San Miniato

Boll. A. Indust. & Curiosità Ven.
Bollettino di arti, industrie e
curiosità veneziane

Boll. A. Min. Educ. N.
Bollettino d'arte del Ministero dell'
educazione nazionale [prev. pubd
as & cont. as *Boll. A.: Min. Pub.
Istruzione*]

Boll. A.. Min. Pub. Istruzione
Bollettino d'arte: Ministero della
pubblica istruzione [cont. as *Boll.
A. Min. Educ. N.; Boll. A.: Min.
Pub. Istruzione*]

Boll. Annu.
Bollettino annuario

Boll. Archeol. Crist.
Bollettino di archeologia cristiana

Boll. Archeol. Crist. Roma
Bollettino di archeologia cristiana
di Roma

Boll. Assoc. Cult. Ventaglio
Bollettino dell'Associazione
culturale il Ventaglio

Boll. Bibl., Fac. Archit. U. Stud. Roma
Bollettino della biblioteca, facoltà
di architettura dell'università degli
studi di Roma

Boll. Cent. Camuno Stud. Preist.
Bollettino del Centro camuno di
studi preistorici

*Boll. Cent. Int. Stud. Archit. Andrea
Palladio*
Bollettino del Centro
internazionale di studi di
architettura Andrea Palladio

Boll. Cent. Stud. Stor. Archit.
Bollettino del Centro di studi per
la storia dell'architettura

Boll. Circ. Numi. Napoletano
Bollettino del Circolo
numismatico napoletano

Boll. CIRVI
Bollettino del CIRVI

Boll. Città Foligno
Bollettino storico della città di
Foligno

Boll. Civ. Bib. Bergamo
Bollettino della Civica biblioteca di
Bergamo [cont. as *Bergamo*]

Boll. Civ. Mus. Ven. A. & Stor.
Bollettino dei Civici musei
veneziani d'arte e di storia

Boll. Class.
Bollettino dei classici [prev. pubd
as *Boll. Com. Prep. Ed. N. Class.
Gr. & Lat.*]

Boll. Coll. Ingeg. & Architetti Napoli
Bollettino del Collegio degli
ingegneri ed architetti in Napoli

Boll. Comm. Archeol. Com. Roma
Bollettino della Commissione
archeologica comunale di Roma

Boll. Comm. Archeol. Mun. Roma
Bollettino della Commissione
archeologica municipale di Roma

*Boll. Com. Prep. Ed. N. Class. Gr. &
Lat.*
Bollettino del Comitato per la
preparazione dell'edizione
nazionale dei classici greci e latini
[cont. as *Boll. Class.*]

Boll. Gal. Milione
Bollettino della Galleria del
milione

Bol. Lima
Boletín de Lima

Boll. Inf. Brigata Aretina Amici Mnmt.
Bollettino d'informazione della
Brigata aretina degli amici dei
monumenti

Boll. Ingeg.
Bollettino degli ingegneri

Boll. Ist. Cent. Rest.
Bollettino dell'Istituto centrale del
restauro

Boll. Ist. Stor. & A. Lazio Merid.
Bollettino dell'Istituto di storia ed arte del Lazio meridionale

Boll. Ist. Stor. A. Orviet.
Bollettino dell'Istituto storico artistico orvietano

Boll. Ist. Stor. Soc. & Stato Veneziano
Bolletino dell'Istituto di storia della società e dello stato veneziano

Boll. Ligustico Stor. & Cult. Reg.
Bollettino ligustico per la storia e la cultura regionale

Boll. Milione
Bollettino del Milione

Boll. Mnmt., Mus. & Gal. Pont.
Bollettino dei monumenti, musei e gallerie pontificie

Boll. Mun., Viterbo
Bollettino municipale, Viterbo

Boll. Mus. Civ. Bassano
Bollettino del Museo civico di Bassano

Boll. Mus. Civ. Padova
Bollettino del Museo civico di Padova

Boll. Mus. Civ. Ven.
Bollettino dei Musei civici veneziani

Boll. Mus. Com. Roma
Bollettino dei Musei comunali di Roma

Boll. Reale Deput. Stor. Patria Liguria: Sez. Ingauna & Intemelia
Bollettino della Reale deputazione di storia patria per la Liguria

Boll. Reale Deput. Stor. Patria Umbria
Bollettino della Reale deputazione di storia patria per l'Umbria

Boll. Reale Ist. Archeol. & Stor. A.
Bollettino del Reale istituto di archeologia e storia dell'arte

Boll. Reale Ist. Archit. & Stor. A.
Bollettino del Reale istituto di architettura e storia dell'arte

Boll. Sezione Novara
Bolletino di Sezione Novara

Boll. Soc. Filol. Romana
Bollettino della Società filologica romana

Boll. Soc. Fot. It.
Bollettino della Società fotografica italiana

Boll. Soc. Lett. Verona
Bollettino della Società di lettere di Verona

Boll. Soc. Pavese Stor. Patria
Bollettino della Società pavese di storia patria

Boll. Soc. Piemont. Archeol. & B.A.
Bollettino della Società piemontese di archeologia e belle arti

Boll. Stat. Com. Ferrara
Bollettino statistico del comune di Ferrara

Boll. Stor.–Bibliog. Subalp.
Bollettino storico–bibliografico subalpino

Boll. Stor. Cremon.
Bollettino storico cremonese

Boll. Stor. Lucchese
Bollettino storico lucchese

Boll. Stor. Messin.
Bollettino storico messinese [prev. pubd as & cont. as *Archv Stor. Messin.*]

Boll. Stor. Piacent.
Bollettino storico piacentino

Boll. Stor. Pisa.
Bollettino storico pisano

Boll. Stor. Pistoi.
Bollettino storico pistoiese

Boll. Stor. Prov. Novara
Bollettino storico per la provincia di Novara

Boll. Stor. Svizzera It.
Bollettino storico della Svizzera italiana

Boll. Svizzera It.
Bollettino della Svizzera italiana

Boll. Ufficiale Min. Pub. Istr.
Bollettino ufficiale del Ministero della pubblica istruzione

Boll. Un. Stor. & A.
Bollettino dell'Unione di storia ed arte

Bol. Mnmts Hist.
Boletín de monumentos históricos

Bol. Mus. A. Barcelona
Boletín de los Museos de arte de Barcelona

Bol. Mus. Arqueol. N. Madrid
Boletín del Museo arqueológico nacional de Madrid

Bol. Museus N. A. Ant.
Boletim dos Museus nacionais de arte antiga

Bol. Mus. & Inst. 'Camón Aznar'
Boletín del Instituto y Museo 'Camón Aznar'

Bol. Mus. Mun.
Boletín del Museo municipal

Bol. Mus. N. A. Ant.
Boletim do Museu nacional de arte antiga

Bol. Mus. N. Arqueol., Hist. & Etnog.
Boletín del Museo nacional de arqueología, historia y etnografía [cont. as *An. Mus. N. Arqueol., Hist. & Etnog.*]

Bol. Mus. Oro
Boletín del Museo del Oro

Bol. Mus. Prado
Boletín del Museo del Prado

Bol. Mus. Prov. B.A. Valladolid
Boletín del Museo provincial de bellas artes de Valladolid

Bol. Mus. Prov. B.A. Zaragoza
Boletín del Museo provincial de bellas artes de Zaragoza

Bol. Nicar. Bibliog. & Doc.
Boletín nicaraguense de bibliografía y documentación

Bol. Real Acad. B.A.
Boletín de la Real academia de bellas artes

Bol. Real Acad. B.A. & Cienc. Hist. Toledo
Boletín de la Real academia de bellas artes y ciencias históricas de Toledo

Bol. Real Acad. B. Let.
Boletín de la Real academia de buenas letras [Seville]

Bol. Real Acad. B. Let. Barcelona
Boletín de la Real academia de buenas letras de Barcelona

Bol. Real Acad. Córdoba Cienc., B. Let. & Nob. A.
Boletín de la Real academia de Córdoba de ciencias, bellas letras y nobles artes

Bol. Real Acad. Hist.
Boletín de la Real academia de la historia

Bol. Real Soc. Bascongadas Amigos País
Boletín de la Real sociedad bascongadas de los amigos del país

Bol. Semin. Estud. A. & Arqueol.
Boletín del Seminario de estudios de arte y arqueología [Universidad de Valladolid]

Bol. Soc. Amigos A.
Boletín de la Sociedad de los amigos de arte

Bol. Soc. Castell. Cult.
Boletín de la Sociedad castellonense de cultura

Bol. Soc. Castell. Excurs.
Boletín de la Sociedad castellana de excursiones

Bol. Soc. Esp. Excurs.
Boletín de la Sociedad española de excursiones

Bol. Soc. Geog. Sucre
Boletín de la Sociedad geográfica e histórica de Sucre

Bol. U. Compostelana
Boletín de la Universidad compostelana

Bonanza [Sunday magazine of the San Francisco Chronicle]

Bonn. Amer. Stud.
Bonner amerikanistische Studien

Bonniers Litt. Mag.
Bonniers litterära magasin

Bonn. Jb.
Bonner Jahrbücher: Jahrbücher des Vereins von Altertumsfreunden im Rheinlande [prev. pubd as *Jb. Ver. Altertfreund. Rheinlande*; cont. as *Bonn. Jb. Ver. Altertfreund. Rheinlande & Rhein.Provmus. Bonn; Bonn. Jb. Rhein. Landesmus. Bonn & Ver. Altertfreund. Rheinlande*]

Bonn. Jb. Rhein. Landesmus. Bonn & Ver. Altertfreund. Rheinlande
Bonner Jahrbücher des Rheinischen Landesmuseums in Bonn und des Vereins von Altertumsfreunden im Rheinlande [see *Bonn. Jb.*]

Bonn. Jb. Ver. Altertfreund. Rheinlande & Rhein. Provmus. Bonn
Bonner Jahrbücher des Vereins von Altertumsfreunden im Rheinlande und des Rheinischen Provincialmuseums in Bonn [see *Bonn. Jb.*]

Bonsai J.
Bonsai Journal

Bon Sens

Borankhadi

Boreas
Boreas: Münstersche Beiträge zur Archäologie

Borsszem Jankó

Bosai Soc. Newslett.
Bosai Society Newsletter

Bos. Bijdr.
Bossche bijdragen

Boston Mus. Bull.
Boston Museum Bulletin [occas. *Bull. Mus. F.A., Boston*; prev. pubd as *Bull.: Mus. F.A., Boston; Mus. F.A. Bull.*]

Botswana Rev.
Botswana Review: A Pan-African Cultural Journal

Bouwbedr. & Openbare Werken
Bouwbedrijf en openbare werken

Bouw: Cent. Wkbld Bouwwzn Nederland & België
Bouw: Central weekblad voor het bouwwezen in Nederland en België

Bouwen

Bouwenbeheer [prev. pubd as *Patrimonium*]

Bouwknd. Bijdr.
Bouwkundige bijdragen [Architectural notes]

Bouwknd. Tijdschr.
Bouwkundig tijdschrift

Bouwknd. Wkbld
Bouwkundig weekblad

Bouwknd. Wkbld: Archit.
Bouwkundig weekblad: Architectura [Architectural weekly: Architectura]

Bouwkunst

Bouwwereld

Bouwyang

Brabant. Flklore
Brabantse Folklore

Brabantia

Brabants Heem
Brabants heem

Bracara Augusta
Bracara augusta

Brandenburg. Jb.
Brandenburgische Jahrbücher

Braunschweig. Jb.
Braunschweigisches Jahrbuch [cont. as *Jb. Braunschweig. Geschver.*]

Brazil Post

Brera Not.
Brera notizie

Brickbuilder

Britannia

Brit. Archaeol. Assoc. Confer. Trans.
British Archaeology Association Conference Transactions

Brit. Architect
British Architect

Brit. Critic
British Critic

Brit. Engin. Export J.
British Engineers Export Journal

Brit. Hist. Illus.
British History Illustrated

Brit. J. Aesth.
British Journal of Aesthetics

Brit. J. Dev. Psychol.
British Journal of Developmental Psychology

Brit. J. Educ. Stud.
British Journal of Educational Studies

Brit. J. 18th-C. Stud.
British Journal for 18th-century Studies

Brit. J. Phot.
British Journal of Photography

Brit. J. Psych.
British Journal of Psychiatry

Brit. J. Psychol.
British Journal of Psychology

Brit. Lithographer
British Lithographer

Brit. Numi. J.
British Numismatic Journal

Brit. Racehorse
British Racehorse

Brit. Soc. Middle E. Stud. Bull.
British Society for Middle Eastern Studies Bulletin

Brit.–Sov. Archaeol. Newslett.
British–Soviet Archaeological Newsletter

Broadway J.
Broadway Journal

Brooklyn Mus. Annu.
Brooklyn Museum Annual

Brooklyn Mus. J.
Brooklyn Museum Journal

Brotéria

Brousse

Browning Inst. Stud.
Browning Institute Studies

Bruckmanns Pantheon [prev. pubd as *Pantheon*]

Brukdown
Brukdown: The Magazine of Belize

Brunei Mus. J.
Brunei Museum Journal

Brush & Pencil
Brush and Pencil

Brutium

Bruxelles

Buch & Schr.
Buch und Schrift [prev. pubd as *Z. Dt. Ver. Bwsn & Schr.*]

Bucknell Rev.
Bucknell Review

Buddhica Brit.
Buddhica Britannica

Budil'nik

Building [Australia]

Building [UK; prev. pubd as *The Builder*]

Built Environment

Bukkyō Bijutsu
Bukkyō bijutsu [Buddhist arts]

Bukkyō Ceijutsu

Bul. Com. Mnmt. Istor.
Buletinul comisiunii monumentelor istorice [Bulletin of the Commission for historic monuments; cont. as *Bul. Mnmt. Istor.*; *Rev. Muz. & Mnmt.: Ser. Mnmt. Ist. & A.*]

Bulg. Phot.
Bulgarian Photo

Bull. A. Assoc. Indianapolis
Bulletin of the Art Association of Indianapolis

Bull. Acad. Royale Archéol. Belgique
Bulletin de l'Académie royale d'archéologie de Belgique

Bull. Acad. Royale Belgique
Bulletin de l'Académie royale de Belgique

Bull. Acad. Royale Sci., Lett. & B.-A. Belgique
Bulletins de l'Académie royale des sciences, des lettres et des beaux-arts de Belgique [cont. as *Cl. Lett. & Sci. Mor. & Polit.*: *Bull. Cl. Lett. & Sci. Mor. & Polit. & Cl. B.-A.*; *Bull. Cl. B.-A., Acad. Royale Sci., Lett. & B.-A. Belgique*]

Bull. Agc. Gén. Colon.
Bulletin de l'Agence générale des colonies

Bull. A. Inst. Chicago
Bulletin of the Art Institute of Chicago

Bull. Allen Mem. A. Mus.
Bulletin of the Allen Memorial Art Museum

Bull. Alliance A.
Bulletin de l'Alliance des arts

Bull. Amer. Acad. Benares
Bulletin of the American Academy of Benares

Bull Amer. A. Un.
Bulletin of the American Art Union [prev. pubd as *Trans. Amer. A. Un.*]

Bull. Amer. Group IIC
Bulletin of the American Group IIC [International Institute for Conservation]

Bull. Amer. Inst. Conserv. Hist. & A. Works
Bulletin of the American Institute for Conservation of Historic and Artistic Works [cont. as *J. Amer. Inst. Conserv.*]

Bull. Amer. Inst. Iran. A. & Archaeol.
Bulletin of the American Institute for Iranian Art and Archaeology

Bull. Amer. Mus. Nat. Hist.
Bulletin of the American Museum of Natural History

Bull. Amer. Sch. Orient. Res.
Bulletin of the American Schools of Oriental Research

Bull. Amer. Sch. Prehist. Res.
Bulletin of the American School of Prehistoric Research

Bull. Amis Gustave Courbet
Bulletin des amis de Gustave Courbet

Bull. Amis Laos
Bulletin des amis de Laos

Bull. Amis Mnmts Rouen.
Bulletin des amis des monuments rouennais

Bull. Amis Mus. Poitiers
Bulletin des amis des musées de Poitiers [suppl. is *Dibutade*]

Bull. Amis Mus. Rennes
Bulletin des amis du Musée de Rennes

Bull. Amis Mus. Rouen
Bulletin des amis du Musée de Rouen

Bull. Amis Sèvres
Bulletin des amis de Sèvres

Bull. Amis Vieux Hué
Bulletin des amis du vieux Hué

Bull. Anc. Ind. Hist. & Archaeol.
Bulletin of Ancient Indian History and Archaeology

Bull. Anc. Orient Mus.
Bulletin of the Ancient Orient Museum

Bull. Anglo-Israel Archaeol. Soc.
Bulletin of the Anglo-Israel Archaeological Society

Bull. Annu., Mus. Ethnog.
Bulletin annuel, Musée d'ethnographie

Bull. Ant. Besch.
Bulletin antieke beschaving

Bull. Antwerp. Ver. Bodem- & Grotonderzoek
Bulletin van der Antwerpse vereniging van bodem- en grotonderzoek [Bulletin of the Antwerp Association of Soil and Cave Research]

Bull. Archaeol. Inst. America
Bulletin of the Archaeological Institute of America

Bull. Archéol.
Bulletin archéologique

Bull. Archéol. Alg.
Bulletin d'archéologie algérienne

Bull. Archéol. Assoc. Bret.
Bulletin archéologique de l'Association bretonne

Bull. Archeol. Crist.
Bullettino di archeologia cristiana

Bull. Archéol. Cté Trav. Hist. & Sci.
Bulletin archéologique du Comité des travaux historiques et scientifiques

Bull. Archéol. Maroc.
Bulletin d'archéologie marocaine

Bull. Archéol. Mus. Guimet
Bulletin archéologique du Musée Guimet

Bull. Asia Inst.
Bulletin of the Asia Institute

Bull. Asian Inst., MI
Bulletin of the Asian Institute, Michigan

Bull. Assoc. Difesa Firenze Ant.
Bullettino dell'associazione per la difesa di Firenze antica

Bull. Assoc. F.A. Yale U.
Bulletin of the Associates in Fine Arts at Yale University

Bull. Assoc. Fr. Rech. & Etud. Cameroun.
Bulletin de l'Association française pour les recherches et études camerounaises

Bull. Assoc. Guillaume Budé
Bulletin de l'Association Guillaume Budé

Bull.: Assoc. Int. Etud. S.-E. Eur.
Bulletin: Association internationale d'études du Sud-Est européen

Bull. Assoc. Int. Explor. Hist. Asie Cent. & Extrême-Orient
Bulletin de l'Association internationale pour l'exploration historique de l'Asie Centrale et de l'Extrême-Orient

Bull. Assoc. Int. Hist. Verre
Bulletin de l'Association internationale pour l'histoire du verre [prev. pubd as *Bull. Journées Int. Verre*]

Bull. Assoc. Preserv. Technol.
Bulletin of the Association for Preservation Technology

Bull. Assoc. Rus. Ric. Sci. Prague
Bulletin de l'Association russe pour les recherches scientifiques à Prague

Bull. Aventico
Bulletin pro Aventico

Bull. B.-A.
Bulletin des beaux-arts

Bull. Baroda Mus. & Pict. Gal.
Bulletin of the Baroda Museum and Picture Gallery [prev. pubd as *Bull. Baroda State Mus. & Pict. Gal.*; cont. as *Bull. Vadodara Mus. & Pict. Gal.*]

Bull. Baroda State Mus. & Pict. Gal.
Bulletin of the Baroda State Museum and Picture Gallery [see *Bull. Baroda Mus. & Pict. Gal.*]

Bull. Biblioph.
Bulletin du bibliophile [cont. as *Bull. Biblioph. & Bibliothécaire*]

Bull. Biblioph. Belge
Bulletin du bibliophile belge

Bull. Biblioph. & Bibliothécaire
Bulletin du bibliophile et du bibliothécaire [prev. pubd as *Bull. Biblioph.*]

Bull. Bib. Royale Belgique
Bulletin de la Bibliothèque royale de Belgique

Bull. Brooklyn Mus.
Bulletin of the Brooklyn Museum

Bull. Burma Hist. Comm.
Bulletin of the Burma Historical Commission

Bull. Byz. Inst.
Bulletin of the Byzantine Institute

Bull. Can. Soc. Dec. A.
Bulletin of the Canadian Society of Decorative Arts

Bull. Cathédrale Strasbourg
Bulletin de la cathédrale de Strasbourg

Bull. Cerc. Archéol., Litt. & A. Malines
Bulletin du Cercle archéologique, littéraire et artistique de Malines [cont. as *Bull. Cerc. Archéol., Litt. & A. Malines/Hand. Kon. Kring Oudhdknd., Lett. & Kst Mechelen*]

Bull. Cerc. Archéol., Litt. & A. Malines/Hand. Kon. Kring Oudhdknd., Lett. & Kst Mechelen
Bulletin du Cercle archéologique, littéraire et artistique de Malines/ Handelingen van de Koninklijke kring voor oudheidkunde, letteren en kunst van Mechelen [prev. pubd as *Bull. Cerc. Archéol., Litt. & A. Malines*]

Bull. Cl. B.-A., Acad. Royale Sci., Lett. & B.-A. Belgique
Bulletin de la Classe des beaux-arts, Académie royale des sciences, des lettres et des beaux-arts de Belgique [prev. pubd as *Cl. Lett. & Sci. Mor. & Polit.: Bull. Cl. Lett. & Sci. Mor. & Polit. & Cl. B.-A.; Bull. Acad. Royale Sci., Lett. & B.-A. Belgique*]

Bull. Cleveland Mus. A.
Bulletin of the Cleveland Museum of Art

Bull. Club Fr. Médaille
Bulletin du Club français de la médaille

Bull. Com. Etud. Hist. & Sci. A.O.F.
Bulletin du Comité des études historiques et scientifiques de l'Afrique Occidentale Française

Bull. Comm. Ant. Dépt Seine-Inférieure
Bulletin de la Commission des antiquités du département de la Seine-Inférieure

Bull. Comm. Archeol. Com. Roma
Bullettino della Commissione archeologica comunale di Roma

Bull. Comm. Archéol. Indochine
Bulletin de la Commission archéologique de l'Indochine

Bull. Comm. Archeol. Mun. Com. Roma
Bullettino della Commissione archeologica municipale comunale di Roma

Bull. Comm. Archéol. Narbonne
Bulletin de la Commission archéologique de Narbonne

Bull. Comm. Royale Mnmts & Sites
Bulletin de la Commission royale des monuments et des sites [prev. pubd as *Bull. Comm. Royales A. & Archéol.*]

Bull. Comm. Royales A. & Archéol.
Bulletin des Commissions royales d'art et d'archéologie [cont. as *Bull. Comm. Royale Mnmts & Sites*]

Bull. Corr. Hell.
Bulletin de correspondance hellénique

Bull. D
Bulletin D

Bull. Deccan Coll. Res. Inst.
Bulletin of the Deccan College Research Institute

Bull. Detroit Inst. A.
Bulletin of the Detroit Institute of Arts

Bull. E. A.
Bulletin of Eastern Art

Bull. Ecole Fr. Extrême-Orient
Bulletin de l'Ecole française d'Extrême-Orient

Bull. Effort Mod.
Bulletin de l'effort moderne

Bull. Egyp. Semin.
Bulletin of the Egyptological Seminar

Bull. Etud. Orient.
Bulletin d'études orientales

Bull. Fac. A. [Alexandria]
Bulletin of the Faculty of Arts [Alexandria]

Bull. Fac. A., Fouad I U.
Bulletin of the Faculty of Arts, Fouad I University

Bull. Fac. F.A.: Tokyo N. U. F. A. & Music
Bulletin of the Faculty of Fine Arts: Tokyo National University of Fine Arts and Music

Bull. Fac. F.A.: Tokyo U. A.
Bulletin of the Faculty of Fine Arts: Tokyo University of the Arts

Bull. Fogg A. Mus.
Bulletin of the Fogg Art Museum [prev. pubd as *Fogg A. Mus.: Notes*]

Bull. Gaud
Bulletin de Gaud

Bull. Gilde St Thomas & St Luc
Bulletin de la Gilde de Saint Thomas et de Saint Luc

Bull. Govt Mus., Madras
Bulletin of the Government Museum, Madras

Bull. Group. Archéol. Seine-et-Marne
Bulletin du Groupement archéologique de Seine-et-Marne

Bull. Hisp.
Bulletin Hispanic

Bull. Hist.
Bulletin historique

Bull. Hist. Dioc. Lyon
Bulletin historique du diocèse de Lyon

Bull. Hist. Medic.
Bulletin of the History of Medicine

Bull. Inf. Archit.
Bulletin d'informations architecturales

Bull. Inf. Inst. N. Hist. A.
Bulletin d'information de l'Institut national d'histoire de l'art

Bull. Inf. Mens. Archvs Archit. Mod.
Bulletin d'information mensuel des archives de l'architecture moderne [cont. as *Archvs Archit. Mod.*]

Bull. Inst. Archéol. Liége.
Bulletin de l'Institut archéologique liégeois

Bull. Inst. Class. Stud. U. London
Bulletin of the Institute of Classical Studies of the University of London

Bull. Inst. Class. Stud. U. London, Suppl. Pap.
Bulletin of the Institute of Classical Studies of the University of London, Supplementary Papers

Bull. Inst. Egyp.
Bulletin de l'Institut égyptien

Bull. Inst. Egypte
Bulletin de l'Institut d'Egypte

Bull. Inst. Ethnol., Acad. Sinica
Bulletin of the Institute of Ethnology, Academica Sinica

Bull. Inst. Fr. Afrique Noire
Bulletin de l'Institut français d'Afrique noire

Bull. Inst. Fr.-Amér.
Bulletin de l'Institut franco-américain

Bull. Inst. Fr. Archéol. Orient.
Bulletin de l'Institut français d'archéologie orientale

Bull. Inst. Hist. & Archaeol., Acad. Sinica
Bulletin of the Institute of History and Archaeology, Academia Sinica

Bull. Inst. Hist. Belge Rome
Bulletin de l'Institut historique belge de Rome

Bull. Inst. Indochin. Etude Homme
Bulletin de l'Institut indochinois pour l'étude de l'homme

Bull. Inst. Int. Châteaux Hist.
Bulletin de l'Institut international des châteaux historiques

Bull. Inst. Likovne Umjetnosti JAZU
Bulletin Instituta za likovne umjetnosti Yugoslavenske akademije znanosti i umjetnosti [Bulletin of the Institute for Fine Arts of the Yugoslav Academy of Science and Arts]

Bull. Inst. Royal Patrm. A.
Bulletin de l'Institut royal du patrimoine artistique

Bull. Irish Georg. Soc.
Bulletin of the Irish Georgian Society

Bull. Ist. Corr. Archeol.
Bullettino dell'Istituto di corrispondenza archeologica

Bull. Ist. Stor. It. Med. Evo & Archv Murator.
Bullettino dell'Istituto storico italiano per il medio evo e archivio muratoriano

Bull. John Herron A. Inst.
Bulletin John Herron Art Institute

Bull. John Rylands Lib.
Bulletin of the John Rylands Library

Bull. Journées Int. Verre
Bulletin des journées internationales du verre [cont. as *Bull. Assoc. Int. Hist. Verre*]

Bull. Jur. Indig. & Droit Coutumier Congol.
Bulletin des juridictions indigènes et du droit coutumier congolais

Bull. Kon. Ned. Oudhdknd. Bond
Bulletin van de Koninklijke Nederlandse oudheidkundige bond [cont. as *Oudhdknd. Jb.; Bull. Ned. Oudhdknd. Bond; Kon. Ned. Oudhdknd. Bond: Bull. KNOB*]

Bull. Lab. Mus. Louvre
Bulletin du laboratoire du Musée du Louvre

Bull. LA Co. Mus. A.
Bulletin of the Los Angeles County Museum of Art

Bull. Liaison Cent. Int. Etud. Textiles Anc.
Bulletin de liaison du Centre international d'étude des textiles anciens

Bull. Liaison Dir. Rég. Affaires Cult. Picardie
Bulletin de liaison de la Direction régionale des affaires culturelles de Picardie

Bull. Maatsch.
Bulletin Maatschappij

Bull. Maatsch. Gesch. Oudhdknd. Gent.
Bulletin van de Maatschappij voor geschiedenis en oudheidkunde te Gent

Bull. Madagascar
Bulletin de Madagascar

Bull. Madras Govt Mus.
Bulletin of the Madras Government Museum

Bull. Mém. Soc. Antiqua. Ouest
Bulletin et mémoires de la Société des antiquaires de l'Ouest

Bull. Mém. Soc. Archéol. Bordeaux
Bulletin et mémoires de la Société archéologique de Bordeaux

Bull. Met.
Bulletin of the Metropolitan Museum of Art

Bull. Minneapolis Inst. A.
Bulletin of the Minneapolis Institute of Arts

Bull. Mnmtl
Bulletin monumental

Bull. Mnmts
Bulletin des monuments

Bull. MOMA, NY
Bulletin of the Museum of Modern Art, New York [cont. as *MOMA Bull.*]

Bull. Mun. Officiel Ville Paris
Bulletin municipal officiel de la ville de Paris

Bull.: Mus. A. & Archaeol., U. MI
Bulletin: Museums of Art and Archaeology, University of Michigan [prev. pubd as *Mus. A. [Ann Arbor, MI]: U. MI Mus. A. Bull.*]

Bull.: Mus. & Archaeol. U.P.
Bulletin: Museums and Archaeology in Uttar Pradesh

Bull. Mus. A., RI Sch. Des.
Bulletin of the Museum of Art, Rhode Island School of Design

Bull. Mus. Augustins
Bulletin du Musée des Augustins

Bull. Mus. B.-A. Alger
Bulletin du Musée des beaux-arts d'Alger

Bull. Mus. Barbier-Müller
Bulletin du Musée Barbier-Müller

Bull. Mus. Beyrouth
Bulletin du Musée de Beyrouth

Bull.: Mus. Boymans
Bulletin: Museum Boymans [prev. pubd as *Bull.: Mus. Boymans–van Beuningen*]

Bull.: Mus. Boymans–van Beuningen
Bulletin: Museum Boymans–van Beuningen [cont. as *Bull.: Mus. Boymans*]

Bull. Mus. Carnavalet
Bulletin du Musée Carnavalet

Bull. Mus. Dijon
Bulletin des musées de Dijon

Bull. Mus. Ermitage
Bulletin du Musée de l'Ermitage

Bull.: Mus. F.A., Boston
Bulletin: Museum of Fine Arts, Boston [prev. pubd as *Mus. F.A. Bull.*; cont. as *Boston Mus. Bull.*]

Bull. Mus. Far E. Ant.
Bulletin of the Museum of Far Eastern Antiquities [prev. pubd as *Östasiat. Mus. [Stockholm]: Bull.*]

Bull. Mus. France
Bulletin des musées de France

Bull. Mus. Hong. B.-A.
Bulletin du Musée hongrois des beaux-arts /A Szépművészeti múzeum közleményei [cont. as *Bull. Mus. N. Hong. B.-A.*]

Bull. Mus. Ingres
Bulletin du Musée Ingres

Bull. Mus. & Mnmts Lyon.
Bulletin des musées et monuments lyonnais

Bull. Mus. N. Hong. B.-A.
Bulletin du Musée national hongrois des beaux-arts [prev. pubd as *Bull. Mus. Hong. B.-A.*]

Bull. Mus. N. Varsovie/Biul. Muz. N. Warszaw.
Bulletin du Musée national de Varsovie/Biuletyn Muzeum narodowego w Warszawie

Bull. Mus. Royaux A. Déc. & Indust.
Bulletin des Musées royaux des arts décoratifs et industriels

Bull. Mus. Royaux A. & Hist.
Bulletin des Musées royaux d'art et d'histoire

Bull. Mus. Royaux Cinquantenaire
Bulletin des Musées royaux du cinquantenaire

Bull. N.A.G. S. Australia
Bulletin of the National Art Gallery of South Australia

Bull.: NC Mus. A.
Bulletin: North Carolina Museum of Art

Bull. Ned. Oudhdknd. Bond
Bulletin van den Nederlandschen oudheidkundigen bond [prev. pubd as *Oudhdknd. Jb.*; *Bull. Kon. Ned. Oudhdknd. Bond*; cont. as *Kon. Ned. Oudhdknd. Bond: Bull. KNOB*]

Bull. Needle & Bobbin Club
Bulletin of the Needle and Bobbin Club

Bull. N.G. Prague
Bulletin of the National Gallery of Prague

Bull. & Nieuws-bull. Kon. Ned. Oudhdknd. Bond
Bulletin en nieuws-bulletin Koninklijke Nederlandse oudheidkundige bond [Bulletin and news-bulletin of the Royal Dutch Archaeological Association]

Bull. N. Mus. New Delhi
Bulletin of the National Museum, New Delhi

Bull. NY Acad. Medic.
Bulletin of the New York Academy of Medicine

Bull. NY Pub. Lib.
Bulletin of the New York Public Library

Bull. NZ A. Hist.
Bulletin of New Zealand Art History

Bull. Orient. Cer. Soc. Hong Kong
Bulletin of the Oriental Ceramic Society of Hong Kong

Bull. Paletnol. It.
Bullettino di paletnologia italiana

Bull. Pan Amer. Un.
Bulletin of the Pan American Union

Bull. Pewter Colrs' Club America
Bulletin of the Pewter Collectors' Club of America

Bull.: Philadelphia Mus. A.
Bulletin: Philadelphia Museum of Art [prev. pubd as *Philadelphia Mus. A.: Bull.*; *PA Mus. Bull.*]

Bull. Philol. & Hist.
Bulletin philologique et historique

Bull. Philol. & Hist. Cté Trav. Hist. & Sci.
Bulletin philologique et historique du Comité des travaux historiques et scientifiques

Bull. Phot.-Club Paris
Bulletin du Photo-club de Paris

Bull. Pub. Mus. City Milwaukee
Bulletin of the Public Museum of the City of Milwaukee

Bull. Rech. Hist.
Bulletin des recherches historiques

Bull. Res. Cent. Archaeol. Indonesia
Bulletin of the Research Centre of Archaeology of Indonesia

Bull. Rijksmus.
Bulletin van het Rijksmuseum

Bull. S.A.D.G.
Bulletin de la Société des architectes diplômés par le gouvernement

Bull. S. Afr. Cult. Hist. Mus.
Bulletin of the South African Cultural History Museum

Bull. Schweiz. Ges. Anthropol. & Ethnol.
Bulletin der Schweizerischen Gesellschaft für Anthropologie und Ethnologie

Bull. Scot. Georg. Soc.
Bulletin of the Scottish Georgian Society

Bull. Sen. Stor. Patria
Bullettino senese di storia patria

Bull. SOAS
Bulletin of the School of Oriental and African Studies

Bull. Soc. Acad. Antiqua. Morinie
Bulletin de la Société académique des antiquaires de la Morinie

Bull. Soc. Acad. Laon
Bulletin de la Société académique de Laon

Bull. Soc. Acad. Sci., Agric., A. & B.-Lett. Dépt Var
Bulletin de la Société académique des sciences, agricultures, arts et belles-lettres du département du Var

Bull. Soc. A. E.
Bulletin des sociétés artistiques de l'Est

Bull. Soc. A. Fr.
Bulletin de la Société de l'art français

Bull. Soc. Africanistes
Bulletin de la Société des Africanistes

Bull. Soc. A. & Hist. Dioc. Liège
Bulletin de la Société d'art et d'histoire du diocèse de Liège

Bull. Soc. Amis A. Dépt. Eure
Bulletin de la Société des amis d'art du département de l'Eure

Bull. Soc. Amis Château Pau
Bulletin de la Société des amis du château de Pau

Bull. Soc. Amis Mnmts Paris.
Bulletin de la Société des amis des monuments parisiens

Bull. Soc. Amis Mnmts Rouen.
Bulletin de la Société des amis des monuments rouennais

Bull. Soc. Amis Mus. Barbier-Müller
Bulletin de la Société des amis du Musée Barbier-Müller

Bull. Soc. Amis Mus. Dijon
Bulletin de la Société des amis du Musée de Dijon

Bull. Soc. Amis Vienne
Bulletin de la Société des amis de Vienne

Bull. Soc. Amis Vieux Chinon
Bulletin de la Société des amis du vieux Chinon

Bull. Soc. Anthropol.
Bulletin de la Société d'anthropologie

Bull. Soc. Anthropol. Bruxelles
Bulletin de la Société d'anthropologie de Bruxelles

Bull. Soc. Antiqua. France
Bulletin de la Société des antiquaires de France

Bull. Soc. Antiqua. Normandie
Bulletin de la Société des antiquaires de Normandie

Bull. Soc. Antiqua. Ouest
Bulletin de la Société des antiquaires de l'Ouest

Bull. Soc. Antiqua. Picardie
Bulletin de la Société des antiquaires de Picardie

Bull. Soc. Archéol. Alexandrie
Bulletin de la Société archéologique d'Alexandrie

Bull. Soc. Archéol. Châtillon.
Bulletin de la Société archéologique du Châtillonnais [cont. as *Bull. Soc. Archéol. & Hist. Châtillon.*; *Soc. Archéol. Châtillon.*]

Bull. Soc. Archéol. Copte
Bulletin de la Société d'archéologie copte

Bull. Soc. Archéol. & Hist. Châtillon.
Bulletin de la Société archéologique et historique du Châtillonnais [prev. pubd as *Bull. Soc. Archéol. Châtillon.*; cont. as *Soc. Archéol. Châtillon.*]

Bull. Soc. Archéol. & Hist. Limousin
Bulletin de la Société archéologique et historique du Limousin

Bull. Soc. Archéol. & Hist. Nantes & Loire-Atlantique
Bulletin de la Société archéologique et historique de Nantes et de Loire-Atlantique

Bull. Soc. Archéol. Lorraine
Bulletin de la Société d'archéologie lorraine

Bull. Soc. Archéol. Midi France
Bulletin de la Société archéologique du Midi de la France

Bull. Soc. Archéol. Orléan.
Bulletin de la Société archéologique de l'Orléanais

Bull. Soc. Archéol. Tarn-et-Garonne
Bulletin de la Société archéologique de Tarn-et-Garonne

Bull. Soc. Archéol. Touraine
Bulletin de la Société archéologique de Touraine

Bull. Soc. B.-A. Caen
Bulletin de la Société des beaux-arts de Caen

Bull. Soc. Cent. Architectes
Bulletin de la Société centrale des architectes

Bull. Soc. Chateaubriand
Bulletin de la Société Chateaubriand

Bull. Soc. Dunoise
Bulletin de la Société dunoise

Bull. Soc. Egyp., Genève
Bulletin de la Société d'égyptologie, Genève

Bull. Soc. Emul. Bourbon.
Bulletin de la Société d'émulation
du Bourbonnais

Bull. Soc. Encour. Indust. N.
Bulletin de la Société
d'encouragement pour l'industrie
nationale

Bull. Soc. Etud. XVIIe Siècle
Bulletin de la Société d'études du
XVIIe siècle

Bull. Soc. Etud. Hist. & Sci. Oise
Bulletin de la Société d'études
historiques et scientifiques de
l'Oise

Bull. Soc. Etud. Indochin.
Bulletin de la Société des études
indochinoises

Bull. Soc. Etud. Océan.
Bulletin de la Société des études
océaniennes

Bull. Soc. Fr. Egyp.
Bulletin de la Société française
d'égyptologie

Bull. Soc. Fr. Fouilles Tanis
Bulletin de la Société française des
fouilles de Tanis

Bull. Soc. Fr. Phot.
Bulletin de la Société française de
photographie

Bull. Soc. Fr. Repr. MSS Peint.
Bulletin de la Société française de
reproductions de manuscrits à
peintures

Bull. Soc. Géog.
Bulletin de la Société
géographique

Bull. Soc. Hist. A. Fr.
Bulletin de la Société de l'histoire
de l'art français

*Bull. Soc. Hist. Archéol. Arrond.
Provins*
Bulletin de la Société d'histoire et
d'archéologie de l'arrondissement
de Provins

*Bull. Soc. Hist. & Archéol. Corbeil,
Est. & Hurepoix*
Bulletin de la Société historique et
archéologique de Corbeil,
d'Estampes et du Hurepoix

Bull. Soc. Hist. & Archéol. Gand
Bulletin de la Société d'histoire et
d'archéologie de Gand

*Bull. Soc. Hist. & Archéol. Nîmes &
Gard*
Bulletin de la Société historique et
archéologique de Nîmes et du
Gard

Bull. Soc. Hist. & Archéol. Orne
Bulletin de la Société historique et
archéologique de l'Orne

Bull. Soc. Hist. & Archéol. Périgord
Bulletin de la Société historique et
archéologique du Périgord

Bull. Soc. Hist. & Archit. Genève
Bulletin de la Société d'histoire et
d'architecture de Genève

*Bull. Soc. Hist. VIIIe & XVIIe
Arrond. Paris*
Bulletin de la Société historique
des VIIIe et XVIIe
arrondissements de Paris

Bull. Soc. Hist. Maroc
Bulletin de la Société d'histoire du
Maroc

Bull. Soc. Hist. Paris & Ile-de-France
Bulletin de la Société de l'histoire
de Paris et de l'Ile-de-France

Bull. Soc. Hist. Protestantisme Fr.
Bulletin de la Société de l'histoire
du protestantisme français

Bull. Soc. Huysmans
Bulletin de la Société Joris-Karl
Huysmans

Bull. Soc. Indust. Mulhouse
Bulletin de la Société industrielle
de Mulhouse

Bull. Soc. Languedoc. Géog.
Bulletin de la Société
languedocienne de géographie

Bull. Soc. N. Antiqua. France
Bulletin de la Société nationale des
antiquaires de France

Bull. Soc. Neuchâtel. Géog.
Bulletin de la Société
neuchâteloise de géographie

Bull. Soc. Nivernaise Lett., Sci. & A.
Bulletin de la Société nivernaise
des lettres, sciences et arts

Bull. Soc. Poussin
Bulletin de la Société Poussin

Bull. Soc. Préhist. Ariège-Pyrénées
Bulletin de la Société préhistorique
de l'Ariège-Pyrénées

Bull. Soc. Préhist. Fr.
Bulletin de la Société préhistorique
française [pubd in 2 pts: *Bull. Soc.
Préhist. Fr., C. R. Séances Mens.*,
*Bull. Soc. Préhist. Fr., Etud. &
Trav.*; prev. pubd as *Soc. Préhist.
Fr.: Bull. Soc. Préhist. Fr.*]

*Bull. Soc. Préhist. Fr., C. R. Séances
Mens.*
Bulletin de la Société préhistorique
française, comptes rendus des
séances mensuelles [see *Bull. Soc.
Préhist. Fr.*]

Bull. Soc. Préhist. Fr., Etud. & Trav.
Bulletin de la Société préhistorique
française, études et travaux [see
Bull. Soc. Préhist. Fr.]

Bull. Soc. Preserv. New England Ant.
Bulletin of the Society for the
Preservation of New England
Antiquities [cont. as *Old-Time
New England*]

*Bull. Soc. Prot. Pays. Esthét. Gén.
France*
Bulletin de la Société pour la
protection des paysages et de
l'esthétique générale de la France
[cont. as *Sites & Mnmts*]

Bull. Soc. Rech. Congol. [Brazzaville]
Bulletin de la Société des
recherches congolaises
[Brazzaville]

Bull. Soc. Royale Archéol., Alexandrie
Bulletin de la Société royale
d'archéologie, Alexandrie

Bull. Soc. Royale Archéol. Bruxelles
Bulletin de la Société royale
d'archéologie de Bruxelles

Bull. Soc. Royale Belge Anth. Préhist.
Bulletin de la Société royale belge
d'anthropologie et de préhistoire

Bull. Soc. Royale Vieux-Liège
Bulletin de la Société royale du
Vieux-Liège

Bull. Soc. Schongauer
Bulletin de la Société Schongauer

Bull. Soc. Sci. Hist. & Nat. Yonne
Bulletin de la Société des sciences
historiques et naturelles de
l'Yonne

Bull. Soc. Sci., Lett. & A. Bayonne
Bulletin de la Société des sciences,
lettres et arts de Bayonne

*Bull. Soc. Statistiques, Sci. Nat. & A.
Indust. Dépts Isère*
Bulletin de la Société des
statistiques, sciences naturelles et
arts industriels des départements
de l'Isère

Bull. Soc. Suisse Amis Extrême-Orient
Bulletin de la Société suisse des
amis de l'Extrême-Orient

Bull. Sticht. Oude Holland. Kerken
Bulletin van der stichting oude
Hollandse kerken

Bull. St Louis A. Mus.
Bulletin of St Louis Art Museum

*Bull. Stud. Philos. & Hist. A. U.
Tsukuba*
Bulletin of the Study of
Philosophy and History of Art in
the University of Tsukuba

Bull. Sung-Yuan Stud.
Bulletin of Sung-Yuan Studies

Bull. Tama A. Sch.
Bulletin of Tama Art School

Bull. Trimest. Crédit Com. Belgique
Bulletin trimestriel du Crédit
communal de Belgique

Bull. U. Mus.
Bulletin of the University Museum
[Philadelphia, University of
Pennsylvania]

Bull. Un. Synd. Architectes Fr.
Bulletin de l'Union syndicale des
architectes français

Bull. V&A
Bulletin of the Victoria and Albert
Museum

Bull. Vadodara Mus. & Pict. Gal.
Bulletin of the Vadodara Museum
and Picture Gallery [see *Bull.
Baroda Mus. & Pict. Gal.*]

Bull. Ver. Bevord. Kennis Ant. Besch.
Bulletin van de Vereniging tot
bevordering der kennis van de
antieke beschaving

Bull. Vie A.
Bulletin de la vie artistique

Bull. 'Vieux-Monthey'
Bulletin du 'Vieux-Monthey'

Bull. VSS
Bulletin Vereinigung
schweizerischer
Spitzenmacherinnen

Bull. W. Afr. Mus. Proj.
Bulletin of the West African
Museums Project

Bull. Walters A.G.
Bulletin of the Walters Art Gallery

Bul. Mnmt. Istor.
Buletinul monumentelor istorice
[see *Bul. Com. Mnmt. Istor.*]

Bul. Shkencat Shoqërore
Buletin për shkencat shoqërore

Bündner Jb.
Bündner Jahrbuch

Bund Österreich. Ksterzieher
Bund Österreichischer
Kunsterzieher

Bunka

Buonarroti

Bureau Amer. Ethnol. Bull.
Bureau of American Ethnology
Bulletin

Burgen & Schlösser
Burgen und Schlösser: Zeitschrift
des Deutschen Burgenvereines für
Burgenkunde und Denkmalpflege

Burl. Mag.
Burlington Magazine

Bus. Hist. Rev.
Business History Review

Bus. Lanka
Business Lanka

Bus. Rev. Wkly
Business Review Weekly

Bustan

Butl. Bib. Catalunya
Butlletí de la Biblioteca de
Catalunya

Butl. Cent. Excurs. Catalunya
Butlletí del Centre excursionista de
Catalunya

Butl. Inf. Cer.
Butlletí informatiu de cerámica

Butl. Mus. A. Barcelona
Butlletí dels Museus d'art de
Barcelona

Butl. Mus. N. A. Catalunya
Butlletí del Museu nacional d'art
de Catalunya

Byblis

Byggmästaren

Bygkst
Byggekunst [Building art]

Bytová Kult.
Bytová kultura [Living]

Byzantina

Byzantino–Bulgarica
Byzantino–bulgarica

Byzantinoslavica

Byzantion

Byz. Forsch.
Byzantinische Forschungen

Byz. & Mod. Gr. Stud.
Byzantine and Modern Greek
Studies

Byz.–Neugriech. Jb.
Byzantinisch–Neugriechische
Jahrbücher

Byz. Pap.
Byzantine Papers

Byz. Z.
Byzantinische Zeitschrift

CA A. & Archit.
California Arts and Architecture

CA Architect & Bldg News
California Architect and Building News

Cab. Amat. & Antiqua.
Cabinet de l'amateur et de l'antiquaire

Cabaret Voltaire

Cab. Lecture
Cabinet de lecture

Cab. Modes
Le Cabinet des modes

Cad. Brasil.
Cadernos brasileiros

Cad. Brasil. Arquit.
Cadernos brasileiros de arquitectura

Cad. Hist. & A. Ebor.
Cadernos de historia e arte eborense

Cah. A.
Cahiers d'art

Cah. Abbaye Sainte-Croix
Cahiers de l'Abbaye Sainte-Croix

Cah. Acad. Auquetin
Cahiers de l'Académie Auquetin

Cah. ADEIAO
Cahiers de l'ADEIAO

Cah. A. & Essai
Cahiers d'art et d'essai

Cah. Alsac. Archéol., A. & Hist.
Cahiers alsaciens d'archéologie, d'art et d'histoire

Cah. Archéol.
Cahiers archéologiques

Cah. Archéol. Amérique S.
Cahiers d'archéologie d'Amérique du Sud

Cah. Archéol. & Hist. Alsace
Cahiers d'archéologie et d'histoire d'Alsace

Cah. Archéol. & Hist. Berry
Cahiers d'archéologie et d'histoire du Berry

Cah. Archéol. Romande
Cahiers d'archéologie romande [Bibliothèque historique vaudoise]

Cah. Assoc. Int. Etud. Fr.
Cahiers de l'Association internationale des études françaises

Cah. A. & Tech. Afrique N.
Cahiers des arts et techniques de l'Afrique du Nord

Cah. A. & Trad. Pop.
Cahiers des arts et traditions populaires

Cah. Bazadais
Cahiers du Bazadais

Cah. B.-Lett.
Cahiers de belles-lettres

Cah. Bordeaux
Cahiers de Bordeaux

Cah. Bretagne Occident.
Cahiers de Bretagne occidentale

Cah. Bruxell.
Cahiers bruxellois

Cah. CACEF
Cahier du Centre d'action culturel de la communauté d'expression française

Cah. Cambre
Cahiers de la Cambre

Cah. Cér. Egyp.
Cahiers de la céramique égyptienne

Cah. Cér., Verre & A. Feu
Cahiers de la céramique, du verre et des arts du feu

Cah. Civilis. Méd.
Cahiers de civilisation médiévale

Cah. Congol. Anthropol. & Hist.
Cahiers congolais d'anthropologie et d'histoire

Cah. Coptes
Cahiers coptes

Cah. Dél. Archéol. Fr. Iran
Cahiers de la Délégation archéologique française en Iran

Cah. E.
Cahiers de l'Est

Cah. Etoile
Cahiers de l'étoile

Cah. Etud. Afr.
Cahiers d'études africaines

Cah. Etud. Mongol. & Sibér.
Cahiers d'études mongoles et sibériennes [prev. pubd as *Etud. Mongol.*]

Cah. Extrême Asie
Cahiers d'Extrême Asie

Cah. Fanjeaux
Cahiers du Fanjeaux

Cah. Haute-Loire
Cahiers de la Haute-Loire

Cah. Haut-Marnais
Cahiers Haut-Marnais

Cah. Hist. A. Contemp.: Doc.
Cahiers d'histoire d'art contemporain: Documents

Cah. Inst. Moyen-âge Grec & Lat.
Cahiers de l'Institut du moyen-âge grec et latin

Cah. Jaunes
Cahiers jaunes

Cah. Litt. Orale
Cahiers de littérature orale

Cah. Monde Rus. & Sov.
Cahiers du monde russe et soviétique

Cah. Mus. A. & Essai
Cahiers [du] Musée d'art et d'essai

Cah. Mus. & Mnmts Nîmes
Cahiers des musées et monuments de Nîmes

Cah. Mus. N. A. Mod.
Cahiers du Musée national d'art moderne

Cah. Mus. Poche
Cahiers du Musée de poche

Cah. Naturalistes
Cahiers naturalistes

Cah. Notre Dame Rouen
Cahiers Notre Dame de Rouen

Cah. Outre-mer
Cahiers d'outre-mer

Cah. Pensée & Hist. Archit.
Cahier de pensée et d'histoire de l'architecture

Cah. Rationalistes
Cahiers rationalistes

Cah. Rech. Archit.
Cahiers de la recherche architecturale

Cah. Relig. Afr.
Cahiers des religions africaines

Cah. Rotonde
Cahiers de la rotonde

Cah. Saint-Michel de Cuxa
Cahiers de Saint-Michel de Cuxa

Cah. Saint-Simon
Cahiers Saint-Simon

Cah. Tunisie
Cahiers de Tunisie

Cah.: U. Lyon II. Inst. Hist. A.
Cahiers: Université de Lyon II. Institut d'histoire de l'art

Cah. Vaudois
Cahiers vaudois

Cah. Vieux-Dijon
Cahiers du Vieux-Dijon

Cake & Cockhorse
Cake and Cockhorse

Calcutta Rev.
Calcutta Review

Callig. Idea Exch.
Calligraphy Idea Exchange

CA Mag.
California's Magazine

Cam. Austria
Camera Austria: Zeitschrift für Fotografie

Cambridge Anthropol.
Cambridge Anthropology

Cambridge Antiqua. Soc. Proc.
Cambridge Antiquarian Society Proceedings

Cambridge Archaeol. J.
Cambridge Archaeological Journal

Cambridge Opera J.
Cambridge Opera Journal

Cambs Antiqua. Soc. 8vo Pubns
Cambridge Antiquarian Society Octavo Publications

Camera

Camera Craft

Camera: Int. Z. Phot. & Film
Camera: Internationale Zeitschrift für Photographic und Film [incorp. into *Fotomagazin*, 1981–]

Cam. Mainichi
Camera Mainichi

Cam. Notes
Camera Notes: Official Organ of the Camera Club of New York

Camões

Campagna Gracia
Campagna de Gracia

Campania Sacra
Campania sacra

Campina

Cam. 35
Camera 35

Cam. Work
Camera Work

Can. A.
Canadian Art [cont. as *A. Canada*]

Can.–Amer. Slav. Stud.
Canadian–American Slavic Studies

Can. Architect
Canadian Architect

Can. Architect & Bldr
Canadian Architect and Builder

Canberra Anthropol.
Canberra Anthropology

Can. Colr
Canadian Collector

Can. Conserv. Inst. Tech. Bull.
Canadian Conservation Institute [CCI /ICC] Technical Bulletin

Can. Courant
Canadian Courant

Candela

Candide

Can. Ethnol. Serv. Pap.
Canadian Ethnology Service Paper

Can. Flklore Can.
Canadian Folklore canadien

Can. Forum
Canadian Forum

Can. Homes & Gdns
Canadian Homes and Gardens

Can. Interiors
Canadian Interiors

Can. J. Afr. Stud.
Canadian Journal of African Studies

Can. Mag.
Canadian Magazine

Can. Numi. J.
Canadian Numismatic Journal

Can. Phot. J.
Canadian Photographic Journal

Canterbury Cathedral Chron.
Canterbury Cathedral Chronicle

Can. Theosophist
Canadian Theosophist

Cant. Lugano
Cantonette Lugano

Capitolium

Capuchin Annu.
Capuchin Annual

Carib. Q.
Caribbean Quarterly

Carib. Rev.
Caribbean Review

Carib. Stud.
Caribbean Studies

Caricom Persp.
Caricom Perspective

Carinthia [cont. as *Carinthia (1)*]

Carinthia (1) [prev. pubd as *Carinthia*]

Carlsbergfond., Frederiksborgmus., NyCarlsbergfond., Aaskr.
Carlsbergfondet, Frederiksborgmuseet, NyCarlsbergfondet, aarskrift

Carlyle Newslett.
Carlyle Newsletter

Carmelus

Carnegie Inst. Washington Yb.
Carnegie Institution of Washington Yearbook

Carnegie Mag.
Carnegie Magazine

Carnet Artistes
Carnet des artistes: Art ancien, art moderne, arts appliqués

Carnet Sem.
Carnet de la semaine

Carpet Rev.
Carpet Review

Carré Bleu
Carré bleu

Cartographica

Casa Américas
Casa de las Américas

Casabella

Casabella Cont.
Casabella continuità

Casabella-Costr.
Casabella-costruzione

Časop. Matice Morav.
Časopis matice moravské [Journal of the Moravian Foundation]

Časop. Morav. Muz.
Časopis moravského muzea [Journal of the Moravian Museum]

Časop. Společnosti Přátel Starožitností
Časopis společnosti přátel starožitností [Society of Friends of Antiquity]

Castellum
Castellum: Rivista dell'Istituto italiano di castelli

Castillos España
Castillos de España

CA Stud. Class. Ant.
California Studies in Classical Antiquity

Catalunya Romanica

Cath. Anthropol. Confer. Pubns
Catholic Anthropological Conference Publications

Cathedra

Cath. Rec. Soc.
Catholic Record Society

Cath.World
Catholic World

Censorship Mag.
Censorship Magazine

Cent. Asian Rev.
Central Asian Review

Cent. Asiat. J.
Central Asiatic Journal

Centavo Perdido
Centavo perdido

Centbl. Bauverwalt.
Centralblatt der Bauverwaltung [cont. as *Zentbl. Bauverwalt.*]

Centbl. Bibwsn
Centralblatt für Bibliothekswesen

Cent. Creative Phot.
Center for Creative Photography

Centen. Mag.
Centennial Magazine

Centen. Rev.
Centennial Review

Center

Center: J. Archit. America
Center: A Journal for Architecture in America

Cent. Eur. Hist.
Central European History

Cent. Int. Etud. Romanes, Bull. Trimest.
Centre international d'études romanes, bulletin trimestriel

Cent. Mus. Utrecht Meded.
Centraal Museum Utrecht mededelingen

Cent. Stud. Lunensi, Quad.
Centro di studi lunensi, quaderni

Cent. Stud. Stor. Cer. Merid.
Centro di studi per la storia della ceramica meridionale

Cent. Ted. Stud. Ven.: Quad.
Centro tedesco di studi veneziani: Quaderni

Cerc. & Carré
Cercle et carré

Cer. Cult. Maya
Cerámica de cultura maya

Cer. Mthly
Ceramics Monthly

Cer. Rev.
Ceramic Review

Červen [June]

Česká Rev.
Česká revue [Czech review]

Česko. Architekt
Československý architekt [Czechoslovak architect]

Ceylon Antiqua. & Lit. Register
Ceylon Antiquary and Literary Register

Ceylon Hist. J.
Ceylon Historical Journal

Ceylon J. Hist. & Soc. Stud.
Ceylon Journal of Historical and Social Studies

Ceylon J. Sci.
Ceylon Journal of Science

Ceylon N. Rev.
Ceylon National Review

Ceylon Observer

Ceylon Today [cont. as *Sri Lanka Today*]

Ceylon Trade J.
Ceylon Trade Journal

C. Guild Hobby Horse
Century Guild Hobby Horse

Chanoyu Q.
Chanoyu Quarterly

Charte 1830
Charte de 1830

Château Gaillard

Chester & N. Wales Archaeol. Soc.
The Chester and North Wales Archaeological Society [prev. pubd as *Archit., Archaeol., & Hist. Soc. Co., City & Neighbourhood Chester J.*; cont. as *J. Chester Archaeol. Soc.*]

Chhavi

Ch. Hist.
Church History

Chicago Archit. J.
Chicago Architectural Journal

Chieron

Chilandar. Zborn.
Chilandarski zbornik [Chilandar journal]

Child Dev.
Child Development

Chimor
Chimor: Boletín del Museo de arqueología de la Universidad de Trujillo

China J. Sci. & A.
China Journal of Science and Arts

China Pict.
China Pictorial

China Reconstructs

China Tourism

Ch'Indaba [prev. pubd as *Transition* [Kampala]]

Chin. Lit.
Chinese Literature

Chin. Sci.
Chinese Science

Chin. Silicate Soc. J.
Chinese Silicate Society Journal

Chin. Stud. Archaeol.
Chinese Studies in Archaeology

Ch. Mnmts
Church Monuments

Chŏngsin Munhwa Yŏngu

Chōsen Gakuho

Chōsen Shi Kenkyū Kairon Bunshū

Christ. Dkml
Christliche Denkmale

Christie's Int. Mag.
Christie's International Magazine

Christ. Kst
Christliche Kunst

Christ. Ksthl.
Christliche Kunstblätter

Christ. Sci. Monitor
Christian Science Monitor

Chron. A.
Chronique des arts [suppl. of *Gaz. B.-A.*]

Chron. A. & Curiosité
Chronique des arts et de la curiosité [cont. as *Beaux-A.: Chron. A. & Curiosité*; *Arts* [Paris]]

Chron. Egypte
Chronique d'Egypte

Chron. Mérid.
Chroniques méridionales

Chron. Mus. A. Dec. Cooper Un.
Chronicle of the Museum of the Arts of Decoration of the Cooper Union

Chron. Paris
Chronique de Paris

Chron. Port-Royal
Chroniques de Port-Royal: Bulletin de la Société des amis de Port-Royal

Chron. Vervielfält. Kst
Chronik für vervielfältigende Kunst [cont. as *Mitt. Ges. Vervielfält. Kst*]

Ciba–Geigy Q.
Ciba–Geigy Quarterly

Ciba Z.
Ciba Zeitschrift

Cidade Évora
A cidade de Évora

Cienc. Tomista
Ciencia tomista

Cieta Bull.
Cieta Bulletin

C. Illus.
Century Illustrated [prev. pubd as *Scribner's Monthly*; cont. as *C. Monthly Mag.*]

Cimaise
Cimaise: Art et architecture actuels

Cincinnati A. Mus. Bull.
Cincinnati Art Museum Bulletin

Cincinnati Class. Stud.
Cincinnati Classical Studies

Circa

Circ. & Cuadrado
Circulo y cuadrado

Cîteaux Comment. Cisterc.
Cîteaux commentarii Cistercienses

Cîteaux Comment. Cisterc.: Stud. & Doc.
Cîteaux commentarii Cistercienses: Studia et documenta

Cîteaux Nederlanden
Cîteaux in de Nederlanden

Cité Tech.
La Cité et technique

Città Milano
Città di Milano

Ciudad Dios
Ciudad de Dios [prev. pubd as *Rev. Agustiniana*; merged with *España & América* to form *Relig. & Cult.*]

Civ. Engin. & Architect's J.
Civil Engineer and Architect's Journal

Civil. Ambrosiana
Civiltà ambrosiana

Civil. Catt.
Civiltà cattolica

Civilis. Malgache
Civilisation malgache

Civil. Macchine
Civiltà delle macchine

Civil. Mant.
Civiltà mantovana

Civil. Romana
Civiltà romana

Civil. Veron.
Civiltà veronese

Clara Rhodos

Clarice Cliff Colr's Club Rev.
Clarice Cliff Collector's Club Review

Clarté
Clarté: Revue d'art

Class. America
Classical America

Class. J.
Classical Journal: Classical Association of the Middle-West and South

Class. Philol.
Classical Philology

Class. Q.
 Classical Quarterly

Class. Rev.
 Classical Review

Class. World
 Classical World

Clavileño

Clima

Clin. Orthopaedics
 Clinical Orthopaedics

Cl. Lett. & Sci. Mor. & Polit.: Bull. Cl. Lett. & Sci. Mor. & Polit. & Cl. B.-A.
 Classe des lettres et des sciences morales et politiques: Bulletin de la Classe des lettres et des sciences morales et politiques et de la Classe des beaux-arts [prev. pubd as *Bull. Acad. Royale Sci., Lett. & B.-A. Belgique*; cont. as *Bull. Cl. B.-A., Acad. Royale Sci., Lett. & B.-A. Belgique*]

Cloth. & Textiles Res. J.
 Clothing and Textiles Research Journal

Club Dada

C. Mag.
 Century Magazine [prev. pubd as *C. Monthly Mag.*]

C. Monthly Mag.
 Century Monthly Magazine [cont. as *C.: Pop. Q.*]

Coat of Arms

Cobra: Bull. Coord. Invest. A.
 Cobra: Bulletin pour la coordination des investigations artistiques

Cobra: Rev. Int. A. Expermntl
 Cobra: Revue internationale de l'art expérimental

Coburg-gothaischen Landen Heimatblätter
 Aus den Coburg-gothaischen Landen Heimatblätter

Codia

Cod. MSS
 Codices manuscripti

Coin Hoards

Cojo Ilus.
 Cojo ilustrado

Col. Diplom. Galicia Hist.
 Colección diplomática de Galicia histórica

Coll. A. J.
 College Art Journal [prev. pubd as *Parnassus*; cont. as *A.J.* [New York]]

Collct. Franciscana
 Collectanea Franciscana

Collct. Ordinis Cisterc. Reformatorum
 Collectanea ordinis Cisterciensium reformatorum

Collier's

Colloq. Sodalizio
 Colloqui del sodalizio

Colon. Soc. MA
 Colonial Society of Massachusetts

Colon. Williamsburg
 Colonial Williamsburg: The Journal of the Colonial Williamsburg Foundation

Colóq. A.
 Colóquio artes: Revista de artes visuais música e bailado [prev. pubd as *Colóquio*]

Colóquio
 Colóquio: Revista de artes e letras [cont. as *Colóq. A.*]

Colour

Columbia Hist. Soc. Rec.
 Columbia Historical Society Records

COMA
 COMA: Bulletin of the Conference of Museum Anthropologists

Com. Archéol. Senlis: C.-R. & Mém.
 Comité archéologique de Senlis: Comptes-rendus et mémoires

Com. Bologna
 Comune di Bologna

Comercio Dominical
 Comercio dominical

Comm.
 Community

Comma: Prospettive Cult.
 Comma: Prospettive di cultura

Commentari

Commentary

Comment. Ateneo Brescia
 Commentari dell'Ateneo di Brescia

Commerc. A.
 Commercial Art [cont. as *Commerc. A. & Indust.*; *A. & Indust.*; *Des. Indus.*]

Commerc. A. & Indust.
 Commercial Art and Industry [prev. pubd as *Commerc. A.*; cont. as *A. & Indust.*; *Des. Indus.*]

Comm. Murals Mag.
 Community Murals Magazine

Commons J.
 Commons Journals

Communic. A.
 Communication Arts

Communic. Proy. Puebla–Tlaxcala
 Communicaciones Proyecto Puebla–Tlaxcala

Comoedia

Comp. Arquit./A. & Archit.
 Composición arquitectónica/Art and Architecture

Comp. Crit.
 Comparative Criticism

Complete Photographer

Comp. Lit.
 Comparative Literature

Compos. Arquit.
 Composición arquitectónica [same as *Comp. Arquit./A. & Archit.*]

Compostellanum

Com. Prov. Mnmts Hist. & A. Alicante
 Comisión provincial de monumentos históricos y artísticos de Alicante

Comp. Stud. Soc. & Hist.
 Comparative Studies in Society and History

Comunità

Concr. & Constr. Engin.
 Concrete and Constructional Engineering

Conf. Assoc. Cult. It.
 Conferenze dell'Associazione culturale italiana

Conf. Hist. Médec.
 Conférences d'histoire de la médecine

Conflent

Confrontation

Congo

Congo–Tervuren

Congr. Archéol. France
 Congrès archéologique de France

Conjunction

Conn. A.
 Connaissance des arts

Connaître Rouen

Connoisseur

Connoisseur Yb.
 Connoisseur Yearbook

Conn. Roussillon
 Connaissance du Roussillon

Cons. Congol.
 Conseiller congolais

Conserv. News
 Conservation News

Constr. & Engin. J.
 Constructional and Engineering Journal

Constr. Forum
 Constructivist Forum

Constr. Mex.
 Construcción mexicana

Constr. Mod.
 i) Construção moderna
 ii) Construction moderne

Constr. São Paulo
 Construção São Paulo

Contemp. A. Pakistan
 Contemporary Arts in Pakistan

Contemp. A. Soc. Broadsheet
 Contemporary Art Society Broadsheet

Contemp. Designers
 Contemporary Designers

Contemp. Pacific
 Contemporary Pacific

Contemp. Phot.
 Contemporary Photography

Contemp. Rev.
 Contemporary Review

Contemp. Stud. Khoisan
 Contemporary Studies on Khoisan

Contimporanul

Continente

Contract Rec.
 Contract Record

Contraspazio

Contrib. Asian Stud.
 Contributions to Asian Studies

Contrib. FL Site Mus.
 Contributions of the Florida Site Museum

Contrib. Ind. Sociol.
 Contributions to Indian Sociology

Contrib. Ist. Stor. A. Med. & Mod.
 Contributi dell'Istituto di storia dell'arte medioevale e moderna

Contrib. Mus. Amer. Ind.
 Contributions from the Museum of the American Indian

Contrib. Mus. Amer. Ind., Heye Found.
 Contributions of the Museum of the American Indian, Heye Foundation

Contrib. Nepal. Stud.
 Contributions to Nepalese Studies

Controspazio

Convegno: Riv. Lett. & Tutte A.
 Convegno: Rivista di letteratura e di tutte le arti

Convivium
 Convivium: Årskrift for humaniora kunst og forskning

Convorbiri Lit.
 Convorbiri literare

Copé

Cordialidad

Corfu Anthol.
 Corfu Anthology

Cork Hist. & Archaeol. Soc. J.
 Cork Historical and Archaeological Society Journal

Cornelis Floris Jb.
 Cornelis Floris jaarboek

Cornell Lib. J.
 Cornell Library Journal

Cornhill Mag.
 Cornhill Magazine

Coronet

Corp. Ant. Amer.
 Corpus antiquitatum Americanensium

Corp. Nummorum It.
 Corpus Nummorum Italicorum

Corr.-Bl. Dt. Ges. Anthropol., Ethnol. & Urgesch.
 Correspondenz-Blatt der Deutschen Gesellschaft für Anthropologie, Ethnologie und Urgeschichte

Corr. Dir. Acad. France
 Correspondance des directeurs de l'Académie de France à Rome

Correio Manha
 Correio da manha

Correio Oficial Minas
 Correio oficial de Minas

Corrente

Correo Erud.
 Correo erudito

Corriere Cer.
 Corriere dei ceramisti

Corriere Sera
 Corriere della sera

Corsi Cult. A. Ravenn. & Biz.
 Corsi di cultura sull'arte ravennate e bizantina

Cosmopolitan A. J.
 Cosmopolitan Art Journal

Décor Aujourd'hui
  Décor d'aujourd'hui [cont. as *A. & Déc.*]

Dedalo

De Driehoek

De Fakkel [The torch]

Defense Analysis

De Gentenaar

De Gids

De Huisvriend

De Ingenieur

Dek. Isk.
  Dekorativnoye iskusstvo [Decorative art; prev. pubd as *Sov. Dek. Isk.*]

Dek. Isk. SSSR
  Dekorativnoye iskusstvo SSSR

Dek. Kst
  Dekorative Kunst

De Kunst

De Lamp

De Leiegouw

Delft. Stud.
  Delftse Studien

Delineavit & Sculp.
  Delineavit et sculpsit

Delta

Deltion Archaiol.
  Deltion archaiologikon [same as *Archaiol. Deltion*]

Deltion Christ. Archaiol. Etaireias
  Deltion tis christianikis archaiologikis etaireias [Bulletin of the Christian archaeology service]

Deltion Istor. & Ethnol. Etaireias
  Deltion tis istorikis kai ethnologikis etaireias [Bulletin of the historical and ethnographical service]

Denkmalpflege [cont. as *Dkmlpf. & Heimatschutz; Denkmalpflege; Dt. Kst- & Dkmlpf.*]

De Opmerker

Der Anschnitt

Der Ararat

Der Architekt

Der Bär

Der Baumeister

Derbys Archaeol. J.
  Derbyshire Archaeological Journal

Der Cicerone

De Rederijker [The rhetorician]

Der Floh

Der Geschichtsfreund

Der Gesellschafter

Der Globusfreund

Der Islam

Der Komet

Der Niederrhein

Der Querschnitt

Derrière Miroir
  Derrière le miroir

Der Sturm

Der Turnhahn

Der Wager

Descent

Des. & Envmt
  Design and Environment

Des. Greece
  Design in Greece

Design

Designers J.
  Designers Journal

Des. Indus.
  Design for Industry [prev. pubd as *A. & Indust.; Commerc. A. & Indust.; Commerc. A.*]

Des. Q.
  Design Quarterly

De Stijl
  De Stijl: Maandblad voor nieuwe kunst, wetenschap en kultur [De Stijl: monthly for new art, science and culture]

Destino

De Tijdspiegel [merged with *Rechtsgeleerd Mag.* to form *R. M. Themis*]

Devon Archaeol. Soc.
  Devon Archaeological Society

Devon & Cornwall Rec. Soc.
  Devon and Cornwall Record Society

Diaframma/Fot. It.
  Diaframma/Fotografia italiana

Dial. Archeol.
  Dialoghi di archeologia: Rivista semestrale

Dial. Hist. Anc.
  Dialogues d'histoire ancienne

Diario Barcelona
  Diario de Barcelona

Diário Coimbra
  Diário de Coimbra

Diario 'El Dia'

Diário Ilus.
  Diário ilustrado

Diario Lavoro
  Diario di lavoro

Diário Lisboa
  Diário de Lisboa

Diário N.
  Diário nacional

Diário Noticías
  Diário de notícias

Dibutade [suppl. of *Bull. Amis Mus. Poitiers*]

Dicht. & Vlkstum
  Dichtung und Volkstum [prev. pubd as & cont. as *Euphorion*]

Diderot Stud.
  Diderot Studies

Die Antike

Die Dame

Die Erde

Die Form

Die Furche

Die Gartenkunst

Die Gegenwart

Die Geisteswissenschaften

Die Insel

Die Koralle

Die Kunst

Die Schammade

Die Starkenburg

Dietsche Warande

Die Wartburg [prev. pubd as *Sber. Münchn. Altert.-Ver.*]

Die Weltkunst

Die Zeit

Dilo [The artwork]

Dinamo Futur.
  Dinamo futurista

Diogenes: Int. Z. Wiss. Menschen
  Diogenes: Internationale Zeitschrift für die Wissenschaft von Menschen

Dlöz.-Archv Schwaben
  Diözesan-Archiv für Schwaben [cont. as *Schwäb. Archv*]

Diplomat. Kurier
  Diplomatischer Kurier

Dis. Archit.
  Il disegno di architettura

Disc. Egyp.
  Discussions in Egyptology

Disk

Diss. Pont. Accad. Romana Archeol.
  Dissertazione della Pontificia accademia romana di archeologia [cont. as *Mem. Pont. Accad. Romana Archeol.*]

Divan
  Divan: Tidskrift for psykoanalysis och kultur

Divulg. Hist.
  Divulgación histórica

XVIIe Siècle
  XVIIe siècle

Djawa

Dkmlpf. Baden-Württemberg
  Denkmalpflege in Baden-Württemberg

Dkmlpf. & Forsch. Westfalen
  Denkmalpflege und Forschung in Westfalen

Dkmlpf. & Heimatschutz
  Denkmalpflege und Heimatschutz [prev. pubd as *Denkmalpflege*; cont. as *Denkmalpflege; Dt. Kst- & Dkmlpf.*]

Dkmlpf. Rheinland–Pfalz Jber.
  Denkmalpflege in Rheinland–Pfalz, Jahresberichte

Doc. Actividad Contemp.
  Documentos de actividad contemporánea

Doc. A. Oggi
  Documenti d'arte oggi

Doc. Archeol.
  Document archeologia: Trésor des âges [cont. as *Doss. Archéol.; Hist. & Archéol.*]

Docbl. Werkgroep 18e Eeuw
  Documentatieblad werkgroep achttiende eeuw [Documentation paper of the 18th century working party]

Doc. Hist. A. Andalucía
  Documentos para la historia del arte en Andalucía

Doc. Hist., Archéol. & Archit.
  Documents d'histoire, d'archéologie et d'architecture

Doc. & Mem. Hist. Porto
  Documento e memórias para a história do Porto

Doc. & Per. Dada
  Documenti e periodici Dada

Doc. & Rap. Soc. Paléontol. & Archéol.
  Documents et rapports de la Société paléontologique et archéologique

Doc. Textilia
  Documenta textilia

Documents

Documents [Paris]

Dokumentum

Dolomiti

Domodomo
  Domodomo: Fiji Museum Quarterly

Dom, Osiedle, Mieszkanie
  Dom, osiedle, mieszkanie [House, housing estate, apartment]

Domov [Home]

Domus

Don Bullebulle
  Don Bullebulle: Periódico burlesco y de extravagancias redactado por una sociedad de bulliciosos

Doopsgezinde Bijdr.
  Doopsgezinde bijdragen

Dordrechts Mus. Bull.
  Dordrechts Museum Bulletin

2C: Constr. Ciudad
  2 [dos] C: Construcción de la ciudad

Doss. Acénonètes Coll. Pataphys.
  Dossiers acénonètes du Collège de pataphysique

Doss. Archéol.
  Dossiers de l'archéologie [prev. pubd as *Doc. Archeol.*; cont. as *Hist. & Archéol.*]

Doss. Hist. & Archéol.
  Dossiers d'histoire et archéologie

Doss. Mus. Orsay
  Dossiers du Musée d'Orsay

Douaness

Douyum

Downside Rev.
  Downside Review

Drama Rev.
  Drama Review

Drawing

Dreamworks

Dresdn. Anz.
Dresdner Anzeiger

Dresdn. Geschbl.
Dresdner Geschichtsblätter

Dresdn. Hft. 10
Dresdner Hefte 10

Dresdn. Kstb.
Dresdner Kunstbuch

Dresdn. Kstbl.
Dresdner Kunstblätter

Dresdn. Nachr.
Dresdner Nachrichten

Dress

Drevnosti
Drevnosti: Trudy Komissii po sokhraneniyu drevnikh pamyatnikov [Antiquities: transactions of the Committee for the Preservation of Ancient Monuments]

Drexel Lib. Q.
Drexel Library Quarterly

Drita

Dt. Allg. Ztg
Deutsche allgemeine Zeitung

Dt. Archit.
Deutsche Architektur [cont. as *Archit. DDR*]

Dt. Archv Erforsch. Mittelalters
Deutsches Archiv für Erforschung des Mittelalters [prev. pubd as *Dt. Archv Gesch. Mittelalters*]

Dt. Archv Gesch. Mittelalters
Deutsches Archiv für Geschichte des Mittelalters [cont. as *Dt. Archv Erforsch. Mittelalters*]

Dt. Archv Landes- & Vlksforsch.
Deutsches Archiv für Landes- und Volksforschung

Dt. Ärztbl./Ärztl. Mitt.
Deutsches Ärzteblatt/Ärztliche Mitteilungen

Dt. Bauz.
Deutsche Bauzeitschrift

Dt. Bauztg
Deutsche Bauzeitung

Dt. Berufs- & Fachsch.
Die deutsche Berufs- und Fachschule

Dt. Biog. Jb.
Deutsches biographisches Jahrbuch [prev. pubd as *Biog. Jb. & Dt. Nekrol.*; *Biog. Bl.*]

Dt. Bühne
Die deutsche Bühne

Dt. Dante-Jb.
Deutsches Dante-Jahrbuch [prev. pubd as *Jb. Dt. Dante-Ges.*]

Dt. Jb. Numi.
Deutsches Jahrbuch für Numismatik [cont. as *Jb. Numi. & Geldgesch.*]

Dt. Kolonbl.
Deutsches Kolonialblatt

Dt. Konkurrenzen
Deutsche Konkurrenzen

Dt. Kst & Dek.
Deutsche Kunst und Dekoration: Illustrierte Monatshefte

Dt. Kst- & Dkmlpf.
Deutsche Kunst- und Denkmalpflege [prev. pubd as *Denkmalpflege*; *Dkmlpf. & Heimatschutz*; *Denkmalpflege*]

Dt. Ksthl.
Deutsches Kunstblatt

Dt. Lichtbild
Deutsches Lichtbild

Dt. Litztg
Deutsche Literaturzeitung

Dt. Münzbl.
Deutsche Münzblätter [incorp. *Frankfurt. Münzztg*, 1934–; prev. pubd as *Berlin. Münzbl.*]

Dt. Mus.
Deutsches Museum

Dt. Vjschr. Litwiss. & Geistesgesch.
Deutsche Vierteljahresschrift für Literaturwissenschaft und Geistesgeschichte

Dt. Vlkskal.
Deutscher Volkskalender

Dt. Z. Maltechnik
Deutsche Zeitschrift für Maltechnik [cont. as *Maltechnik*; *Maltechnik, Rest.*]

Du

Dublin Bldr
Dublin Builder

Dublin Hist. Rec.
Dublin Historical Record

Dublin J.
Dublin Journal

Dublin U. Rev.
Dublin University Review

Duits Geog. Bl.
Duits geographische Blätter

Duits Q.
Duits Quarterly

Dumbarton Oaks Pap.
Dumbarton Oaks Papers

Dunhuang Yanjiu

Duomo Torino
Duomo di Torino

Duoyun

Dürener Geschbl.
Dürener Geschichtsblätter

Durlacher Tagbl.
Durlacher Tagblatt

Düsseldorf. Jb.
Düsseldorfer Jahrbuch [prev. pubd as *Beitr. Gesch. Niederrheins*]

Düsseldorf. Kultkal.
Düsseldorfer Kulturkalender

Düsseldorf. Monatshefte
Düsseldorfer Monatshefte

Dut. A. & Archit. Today
Dutch Art and Architecture Today

Dut. Crossing
Dutch Crossing

Dyes Hist. & Archaeol. Textiles
Dyes on Historical and Archaeological Textiles

DYN

E. A.
Eastern Art

E. Anglian
East Anglian

E. Anthropol.
Eastern Anthropologist

E. A. Rep.
Eastern Art Report

Early China

Early Music

Ear Mag.
Ear Magazine

Earth Spirit

Easter Annu.
Easter Annual

Ebenda

E. Buddhist
Eastern Buddhist

Eccles. Rev.
Ecclesiastical Review

Echo B.A.
Echo des beaux arts

Echos A.
Echos d'art [cont. as *A. & Déc.*]

Echos Orient
Echos d'orient [cont. as *Etud. Byz.*; *Rev. Etud. Byz.*]

Echos-Unir

E. Church Rev.
Eastern Church Reviews

Eco

Ecole Ant. Nîmes
Ecole antique de Nîmes

Econ. Hist.
Economic History

Econ. Hist. Rev.
Economic History Review

Econ. & Stor.
Economia e storia

Ecrit-Voir
L'Ecrit-voir: Revue d'histoire des arts

Edebiyat Fak. Araştrma Derg.
Edebiyat Fakültesi Araştırma Dergisi [Literature Faculty research journal]

Edilizia Mod.
L'edilizia moderna

Edinburgh Philos. J.
Edinburgh Philosophical Journal

Edinburgh Rev.
Edinburgh Review

Ēdjmiadzin

Educ. Botswana, Lesotho & Swaziland
Education in Botswana, Lesotho and Swaziland

Efes Müz. Yıllık
Efes Müzesi yıllık [Annual of the Ephesos Museum]

Egitto & Vic. Oriente
Egitto e Vicino Oriente

Egoist
Egoist: An Individualist Review

Egyp. Astron. Texts
Egyptian Astronomical Texts

Egység [Union]

E. Horizon
Eastern Horizon

Eidos

Eigen Haard
Eigen haard

Eigen Schoon & Braband.
Eigen schoon en de Brabander

18th C.
Eighteenth Century

18th C. Life
Eighteenth Century Life

18th C. Stud.
Eighteenth Century Studies

18th C.: Theory & Interpretation
Eighteenth Century: Theory and Interpretation

Eimreiðin

Eirene

Eiszeit & Urgesch.
Eiszeit und Urgeschichte: Jahrbuch für Erforschung des vorgeschichtlichen Menschen und seines Zeitalters

Ekistics

El Archivo

El Artista

El Artistica

El Cabichuí

El Colombiano

El Comercio

El Coyote

El Croquis

El Democrata

El Día

Elegante Welt

El Español

El Especito

Élet & Irodalom.
Élet és irodalom [Life and Literature]

El Faiol

El Granuja

El Heraldo

El Imparcial

El Informador

El Iris

El Jicote

El Laberinto

Elle

Elleiomnemon

Ellinika

Ellwanger Jb.
Ellwanger Jahrbuch

El Machete

El Mundo

El Nacional

E. London Pap.
East London Papers

El País

El Palacio

El Panorama

El Racionalismo

El Renacimiento

Elsass-Lotharing. Jb.
Elsass-lotharingisches Jahrbuch

El Sentinela

Elsevier's Geïllus. Mdschr.
Elsevier's geïllustreerd
maandschrift

Elseviers Mdbl.
Elseviers maandblad

Els Marges

El Sol

Eltheto

Elvehjem Mus. A. Bull.
Elvehjem Museum of Art Bulletin

Embroidery

Emporium

Emp. Stud. A.
Empirical Studies of the Arts

Enc. Archit.
Encyclopédie d'architecture

Enchoria
Enchoria: Zeitschrift für
Demotistik und Koptologie

Encounter

Endeavor

Enemic Poble
Enemic del poble

Eng. Haus
Das englische Haus

Eng. Hist. Rev.
English Historical Review

Eng. Illus. Mag.
English Illustrated Magazine

Engin. Mag.
Engineering Magazine

Engin. Rec., Bldg Rec. & Sanitary
Engin.
Engineering Record, Building
Record and Sanitary Engineer

Eng. Misc.
English Miscellany

Eng. MS. Stud., 1100–1700
English Manuscript Studies, 1100–
1700

Ensay

Ens. Hist.
Enseñanza de la historia

Envío

Epeteris Etaireias Byz. Spoudon
Epeteris etaireias byzantinon
spoudon

Epeteris Etaireias Kykladikon Meleton

Ephemerides Liturg.
Ephemerides liturgicae

Ephemeris dacoromana

Ephemeris Archaiol.
Ephimeris archaiologiki [cont. as
Archaiol. Ephimeris]

Epig. Ind.
Epigraphia Indica

Epig. Ind.: Arab. & Pers. Suppl.
Epigraphia Indica: Arabic and
Persian Supplement

Epig. Vostoka
Epigrafika vostoka

Epistemonike Epeteris Poly. Scholes
Epistemonike epeteris tes
Polytechnikes scholes [Scientific
annual of the Polytechnic school]

Epistimoniki Epeteris Poly.
Sch. Aristoteleiou Panepistimiou
Thessalonikis
Epistimoniki epetiris Polytechnikis
scholis tou Aristoteleiou
Panepistimiou Thessalonikis
[Scientific annual of the
Polytechnic school of Aristotle
University, Thessaloniki]

Építés- & Építészettudomány
Építés- és Építészettudomány
[Construction and architecture
science]

Építés Ipar
Az Építés ipar [The construction
industry]

Építés- & Közlekedéstudományi
Közlemények
Építés- és közlekedéstudományi
közlemények [Construction and
communication science report]

Építészet–Építés [Building–
architecture]

Epitiris Tou Kendrou Epistimonikon
Erevnon
Epitiris tou kendrou
epistimonikon erevnon [Yearbook
of the Centre for Scientific
Research, Cyprus]

Építőanyag [Building material]

Építő Ipar–Építő Művészet
[Construction industry architecture]

Epoca

Eranos

Erasmus Eng.
Erasmus in English

Erdem

Erdgeist

Eretz Israel

Ergon Archaiol. Etaireias
To ergon tis archaiologikis
etaireias [The work of the
archaeological service]

Erkenntnis

Erlang. Beitr. Spr.- & Kstwiss.
Erlanger Beiträge zur Sprach- und
Kunstwissenschaft

Erlang. Forsch.
Erlanger Forschungen

Ernte: Schweiz. Jb.
Ernte: Schweizerisches Jahrbuch

Erud. Iberio-Ultramarina
Erudición iberio-ultramarina

Escena

Esercizi

España
España: Sus monumentos y artes,
su naturaleza e historia

España & América
España y América [merged with
Ciudad Dios to form Relig. &
Cult.]

España Mod.
España moderna

Espr. Créateur
Esprit créateur

Esprit

Espr. Mod.
L'Esprit moderne

Espr. Nouv.
L'Esprit nouveau

Esquella Torratxa
Esquella de la Torratxa

Esquire

Ess. Crit.
Essays in Criticism

Essex Inst. Hist. Col.
Essex Institute Historical
Collections

Essling. Stud.
Esslinger Studien [cont. as Jb.
Gesch. Oberdt. Reichsstädte]

Ess. & Stud.
Essays and Studies

Estado São Paulo
Estado de São Paulo

Estampe Mod.
Estampe moderne

Estia

Estud. Abulenses
Estudios abulenses

Estud. Arqueol.
Estudios arqueológicos

Estud. A. Sevill.
Estudio de arte sevillano

Estud. Centamer.
Estudios centroamericanos

Estud. Cult. Maya
Estudios de cultura Maya

Estud. Cult. Nahuatl
Estudios de cultura Nahuatl

Estud. Demog. & Urb.
Estudios demográficos y urbanos

Estud. Edad Med. Corona Aragón
Estudios del edad media de la
Corona de Aragón

Estud. Extremeños
Estudios extremeños

Estud. Geog.
Estudios geográficos

Estud. Hist. & Doc. Archv Protocolos
Estudios históricos y documentos
de los archivos de protocolos

Estud. Pro A.
Estudios pro arte

Estud. Segov.
Estudios segovianos

Estud. Transmont.
Estudios transmontanos

Estud. U. Catalans
Estudis Universitaris Catalans

Ethiopia Observer

Ethnoarts Index

Ethnographia

Ethnographie

Ethnographika

Ethnohistory

Ethnol. Cranmore.
Ethnologia cranmorensis

Ethnol. Fr.
Ethnologie française

Ethnologica

Ethnology

Ethnol. Pol.
Ethnologia polona

Ethnol. Z. Zürich
Ethnologische Zeitschrift Zürich

Ethnos

'Et-Mol

Etnia

Etnog. Obozreniye
Etnograficheskoye obozreniye

Etnog. Shqiptare
Etnografia shqiptare

Etnol. Stud.
Etnologiska studier

Etud. A.
i) Etudes de l'art
ii) Etudes de l'art [Musée national
des beaux-arts d'Alger]

Etud. Angl.
Etudes anglaises

Etud. Ant. Afr.
Etudes d'antiquités africaines

Etud. Archéol. Class.
Etudes d'archéologie classique

Etud. Asiat.
Etudes asiatiques

Etud. Balkan.
Etudes balkaniques

Etud. Bourbon.
Etudes bourbonnaises

Etud. Byz.
Etudes byzantines [prev. pubd as
Echos Orient, cont. as Rev. Etud.
Byz.]

Etud. Byz. & Armén.
Etudes byzantines et arméniennes

Etud. Cameroun.
Etudes camerounaises

Etud. Can./Canada Stud.
Etudes canadiennes/Canada
Studies

Etud. Cors.
Etudes corses [Association des
chercheurs en sciences humaines]

Etud. Créoles
Etudes créoles

Etud. Crét.
Etudes crétoises

Etud. 18ème Siècle
Etudes sur le 18ème siècle

Etud. Guiné.
Etudes guinéennes

Etud. Lett.
Etudes de lettres

Etud. Méd.
Etudes médiévales

Etud. Mongol.
Etudes mongoles [cont. as Cah.
Etud. Mongol. & Sibér.]

Etud. Mongol. & Sibér.
Etudes mongoles et sibériennes
[prev. pubd as Etud. Mongol.]

Etud. Orient.
Etudes d'orientalisme

Etud. Préliminaires Relig. Orient.
Empire Romain
Etudes préliminaires aux religions
orientales dans l'empire romain

Etud. Rev. Louvre
Etudes de la revue du Louvre

Etud. Roussillon.
Etudes roussillonnaises

Etud. Rur.
Etudes rurales

Etud. Sung/Sung Stud.
Etudes Sung/Sung Studies

Etud. Toul.
Etudes touloises

Etud. & Trav.
Etudes et travaux

Etud. Volta.
Etudes voltaïques

Euphorion [cont. as *Dicht. & Vlksthum; Euphorion*]

Eur. Iskola Kiskönyvtárát
Európai iskola kiskönyvtárát

Eur. J. A. Historians
European Journal for Art Historians

Eur. Mag.
European Magazine

Eur. Mag. & London Rev.
European Magazine and London Review

Europa Alm.
Europa Almanach

Europa Orient.
Europa orientale

Europa: Z.
Europa: Eine Zeitschrift

Europe

Europe Nouvelle
Europe nouvelle

L'Evénement

Eve. Post Mag.
Evening Post Magazine

E. & W.
East and West

Excelsior

Expedition

Exposure

Expression

Extremadura Arqueol.
Extremadura arqueológica

Ezhegodnik Inst. Istor. Isk.
Ezhegodnik Instituta istorii iskusstva [Annual of the Institute of Art History]

Fabrications
Fabrications: The Journal of the Society of Architectural Historians, Australia and New Zealand

Fabrik & Bolig
Fabrik og bolig [Fabric and home]

Faenza
Faenza: Bollettino del Museo internazionale delle ceramiche in Faenza

Faith & Form
Faith and Form

Fam. Hist.
Family History

Fanal

Fanfulla
Il fanfulla

Fanfulla Domenica
Fanfulla della Domenica

Fans
Fans: The Bulletin of the Fan Circle International

F. A. Q.
Fine Arts Quarterly

Far E. Q.
Far Eastern Quarterly [cont. as *Journal of Asian Studies*]

Farhang-i Mi'māri-yi Īrān

Fasti Archeol.
Fasti archeologici: Annual Bulletin of Classical Archaeology [International Association for Classical Archaeology]

Féd. A.
Fédération artistique

Fed. Mus. J.
Federation Museums Journal

Felix Ravenna

Feltmaker's Assoc. J.
Feltmaker's Association Journal

Fem. A. J.
Feminist Art Journal

Femina

Femme Nouv.
Femme nouvelle

Fem. Stud.
Feminist Studies

Fenster: Tirol. Kultz.
Fenster: Tiroler Kulturzeitschrift

Fenway Court

Ferrania

Festa A.
La festa dell'arte

Feuil. Libres
Feuilles libres

Feuil. Mai
Feuilles de mai

Fiammetta

Fiberarts

Fides & Hist.
Fides et historia

Fieldiana Anthropol.
Fieldiana Anthropology

Field Mus. Nat. Hist. Bull.
Field Museum of Natural History Bulletin

5th Col.
Fifth Column

Figaro Illus.
Figaro illustré

Figaro Litt.
Figaro littéraire

Figilina

Filip. Her.
Filipino Heritage

Film & Frau
Film und Frau

Film Lib. Q.
Film Library Quarterly

Film Liga

Filol. Arkv
Filologiskt arkiv [prev. pubd as *Antikva. Stud.*]

Filologia

Filosofia

Finanz & Wirtschaft
Finanz und Wirtschaft

Fine Prt
Fine Print

Fin. Fornminnesfören. Tidskr./Suomen Muinmuist. Aikak.
Finska fornminnesföreningens tidskrift/Suomen muinaismuistoyhdistyksen aikakauskirja [Journal of the Association of Finnish Antiquities]

Finland. Gestalt.
Finlands Gestalter

Fin. Mus.
Finskt Museum [Fin. edn: *Suom. Mus.*]

Fin. Tidskr.
Finsk tidskrift [Finnish Magazine]

Fischietto

FL Anthropol.
The Florida Anthropologist

Flaran

Flash A.
Flash Art (International)

Flash Point
Flash Point: Journal of the Tile Heritage Foundation

Flclor. & Cost. España
Folclore y costumbres de España

Flclor. It.
Il folclore italiano

Flieg. Bl.
Fliegende Blätter [later incorp. into *Meggendorf. Bl.*]

Flk A.
Folk Art

Flklore Brabançon
Folklore brabançon

Flklore Stud.
Folklore Studies

Floridian Mag.
Floridian Magazine

Flusoppen

F.M.R. Mag.
F.M.R. Magazine

Focal Point

Focus Pakistan
Focus on Pakistan

Fogg A. Mus.: Notes
Fogg Art Museum: Notes [cont. as *Bull. Fogg A. Mus.*]

Fol. Archaeol.
Folia archaeologica

Folha Domingo
Folha do domingo

Folha São Paulo
Folha de São Paulo

Fol. Hist. A.
Folia historiae artium

Folk

Folk Life

Folk-Lore

Fol. Orient.
Folia orientalia

Fond. N. Rome Pont.
Fondations nationales dans la Rome pontificale

Fond. Stud. Stor. A. Roberto Longhi, Firenze: An.
Fondazione di studi di storia dell'arte Roberto Longhi, Firenze: Annali

Fontane Bl.
Fontane Blätter

Forma

Forma & Color
Forma y color

Formes: Bull. APAHAU
Formes: Bulletin de l'Association des professeurs d'archéologie et d'histoire de l'art des universités

Formes: Int. A. Rev.
Formes: An International Art Review [NY, same as *Formes: Rev. Int. A. Plast.*]

Formes: Rev. Int. A. Plast.
Formes: Revue internationale des arts plastiques [same as *Formes: Int. A. Rev.*]

Formiści [The formists]

Fornvännen
Fornvännen: Tidskrift för svensk antikvarisk forskning [Friend of the past: magazine for Swedish antiquarian research]

Forrás [Source]

Forsch. Ant. Ker.: Kerameus
Forschungen zur antiken Keramiek: Kerameus

Forsch. Augst
Forschungen in Augst

Forsch. & Ber.
Forschungen und Berichte

Forsch. & Ber.: Staatl. Mus. Berlin
Forschungen und Berichte: Staatliche Museen zu Berlin

Forsch. & Ber. Vor- & Frühgesch.
Forschungen und Berichte zur Vor- und Frühgeschichte in Baden–Württemberg

Forsch. Dkmlpf.
Forschungen der Denkmalpflege

Forsch. & Fortschr.
Forschungen und Fortschritte

Forsch. Frankfurt
Forschung Frankfurt

Forsch. Gesch. Stadt Ulm
Forschungen zur Geschichte der Stadt Ulm

Forsch. Hess. Fam.- & Heimatknd.
Forschungen zur hessischen Familien- und Heimatkunde

Forsch. Kstgesch. Böhmens
Forschungen zur Kunstgeschichte Böhmens

Forsch. Sächs. Kstgesch.
Forschungen zur sächsischen Kunstgeschichte

Fort

Fort Hare Pap.
Fort Hare Papers

Fortidsforen. Åb.
Fortidsforeningens årbok [Association for the past yearbook]

Fortnightly Rev.
Fortnightly Review

Fortress

Fortune
Fortune Magazine

Forum
　Genootschap architectura et amicitia: Forum [cont. as *Forum Archit. & Daarme Verbond. Kst.*; *Forum Archit.*]

Forum Archit.
　Forum voor architectuur [see *Forum*]

Forum Archit. & Daarme Verbond. Kst.
　Forum voor architectuur en daarme verbonden kunsten [see *Forum*]

Forum It.
　Forum italicum

Fotcent. Bildtidn.
　Fotograficentrums bildtidning

Fot.-Film
　Foto-film

Fot. It.
　Fotografia italiana

Fot. Lyubitel
　Fotograf lyubitel [Amateur photographer]

Foto

Fot. Obzor
　Fotografický obzor [Photographic horizons]

Fotografie [Photography]

Fotologia

Fotolyubitel [Amateur photographer]

Fotomagazin [incorp. *Camera: Int. Z. Phot. & Film*, 1981–]

Fragmentos
　Fragmentos: Revista de arte

France-Asie

France Illus., Litt. & Théât.
　France illustration, littéraire et théâtrale

France Indust.
　France industrielle

France Litt.
　France littéraire

Franco Maria Ricci

Frankenland

Frankfurt. Forsch.
　Frankfurter Forschungen

Frankfurt. Illus.
　Frankfurter illustrierte

Frankfurt: Lebendige Stadt
　Frankfurt: Lebendige Stadt

Frankfurt. Münzztg
　Frankfurter Münzzeitung [incorp. into *Dt. Münzbl.*, 1934–]

Frankfurt. Ztg
　Frankfurter Zeitung

Fränk. Lebensbild.
　Fränkische Lebensbilder

Frank Leslies' Illus. Newspap.
　Frank Leslies' Illustrated Newspaper

Frank Lloyd Wright Newslett.
　Frank Lloyd Wright Newsletter

Fra Nmus. Arbejdsmk
　Fra Nationalmuseets arbejdsmark [From the National Museums Work Field]

Franziskanische Stud.
　Franziskanische Studien

Fraser's Mag.
　Fraser's Magazine

Frate Francesco

Fratres Scholarum Christ.
　Fratres scholarum Christianarum

Freiburg. Archäol.
　Freiburger Archäologie

Freiburg. Diöz.-Archv
　Freiburger Diözesan-Archiv

Freiburg. Geschbl.
　Freiburger Geschichtsblätter

Freiburg. Münsterbl.
　Freiburger Münsterblätter

Freie Strasse

Freundin

Fr. Hist. Stud.
　French Historical Studies

Fridericiana [Zeitschrift für die Universität Karlsruhe]

Friends Cathedral Church Norwich
　Friends of the Cathedral Church of Norwich

Friends S. Afr. N. Gal. Newslett.
　Friends of the South African National Gallery Newsletter

Friends Wells Cathedral Rep.
　Friends of Wells Cathedral Reports

Frou-Frou

Fr. Porc. Soc.
　The French Porcelain Society

Frühmittelalt. Stud.
　Frühmittelalterliche Studien

Fukui

Fulda. Geschbl.
　Fuldaer Geschichtsblätter

Fundber. Baden-Württemberg
　Fundberichte aus Baden-Württemberg

Fundber. Schwaben
　Fundberichte aus Schwaben

Fund & Forsk.
　Fund og forskning [Fund and research]

Funny Folks

Furen Xuezhi

Furn. Hist.
　Furniture History

Futurismo

G

G. A.
　Giornale dell'arte

Gac. A.
　Gaceta de arte

Gac. Arqueol. Andina
　Gaceta arqueológica andina

Gac. Callejeia
　Gaceta callejeia

Gac. Lit.
　Gaceta de literatura

Gads Dan. Mag.
　Gads danske magasin [Gads Danish magazine]

Gal. A.
　Galerie des arts [prev. pubd as *Gal. Jard. A.*]

Gal. Contemp., Litt., A.
　Galerie contemporaine, littéraire, artistique

Galerie [Port of Spain]

Galicia Hist.
　Galicia histórica: Revista bimestral

Galicia Hist.: Col. Dip.
　Galicia histórica: Colección diplomática

Galicia Noza

Gal. Jard. A.
　Galerie jardin des arts [cont. as *Gal. A.*]

Gallia
　Gallia: Fouilles et monuments archéologiques en France métropolitaine

Gallia–Préhist.
　Gallia–préhistoire

Gallia–Suppl.
　Gallia–supplément

Gallo

Gallo Nero

Gal. Modes & Cost. Fr.
　La Galerie des modes et costumes français

Gal. N. It.
　Gallerie nazionali italiane

Gal. Stuker Bl.
　Galerie Stuker Blätter

GAM

Gamut

Gand A.
　Gand artistique

Ganymed
　Ganymed: Blätter der Marées-Gesellschaft

G. Arcad.: Riv. Mens. Lett. Sci. & A.
　Giornale arcadico: Rivista mensile di lettere, scienze e arti [prev. pubd as *G. Arcad. Sci. Lett. & A.*]

G. Arcad. Sci. Lett. & A.
　Giornale arcadico di scienze, lettere ed arti [cont. as *G. Arcad.: Riv. Mens. Lett. Sci. & A.*]

GA Rev.
　Georgia Review

G. Artistico
　Giornale artistico

Gas. A.
　Gaseta de les árts

Gasetsu

Gay News

Gaz. A. Diseg.
　Il gazzettino dell'arte del disegno

Gaz. Antiqua.
　Gazzetta antiquaria

Gaz. Archéol.
　Gazette archéologique

Gaz. Architectes & Bât.
　Gazette des architectes et du bâtiment

Gaz. Artisti
　Gazzetta degli artisti

Gaz. B.-A.
　Gazette des beaux-arts [suppl. is *Chron. A.*]

Gaz. Bergamo
　Gazzetta di Bergamo

Gaz. Bon Ton
　La Gazette du bon ton [merged with *Vogue*]

Gaz. Lett. Torino
　Gazzetta letteraria di Torino

Gaz. Livre Md.
　Gazette du livre médiéval

Gaz. Milano
　Gazzetta di Milano

Gaz. Numi. Fr.
　Gazette numismatique française

Gaz. Paris
　Gazette de Paris

Gaz. Parma
　Gazzetta di Parma

Gaz. Privileg. Milano
　Gazzetta privilegiata di Milano

Gaz. Privileg. Venezia
　Gazzetta privilegiata di Venezia

Gaz. Ven.
　Gazzetta veneta

Gaz. Venezia
　Gazzetta di Venezia

G. B.A. & Tec.
　Giornale di belle arti e technologia

G. Bordo
　Giornale di Bordo

G. Brescia
　Giornale di Brescia

G. Centen. Dante Alighieri
　Giornale del centenario di Dante Alighieri

Gdn & Foo Nero
　Garden and Foo Nero

Gdn & Forest
　Garden and Forest

Gdn Hist.
　Garden History

Gdnrs Mag.
　Gardeners Magazine

Gebrauchsgrafik
　Gebrauchsgrafik: Monatsschrift zur Förderung Künstler

Gebrauchsgraphik [cont. as *Novum*]

Gegenbaurs Morph. Jb.
　Gegenbaurs morphologisches Jahrbuch

Gekkan Bunkazai
　Gekkan bunkazai [Monthly arts review]

Gekkan Mingei
　Gekkan mingei

Gelre

Gemäldekunde [prev. pubd as *Neue Bl. Gemäldeknd.*; *Stud. & Skiz. Gemäldeknd.*; *Bl. Gemäldeknd.*]

Genava
　Genava: Bulletin du Musée d'art et d'histoire de Genève, du Musée Ariana et de la Société auxiliaire du musée, la Bibliothèque publique et universitaire

Gen. Chron. & Lit. Mag.
　General Chronicle and Literary Magazine

Gendai Nihon No Bijutsu [Modern Japanese art]

Genders

Geneal. Jb.
　Genealogisches Jahrbuch

Genealogie
　Genealogie: Deutsche Zeitschrift für Familienkunde

Génie Civ.
　Génie civil

Genshoku Nihon No Bijutsu [Illustrated arts of Japan]

Genshoku No Bi [Arts illustrated]
Gent. Bijdr. Kstgesch.
　Gentsche bijdragen tot de kunstgeschiedenis [Ghent contributions to art history; cont. as *Gent. Bijdr. Kstgesch. & Oudhdknd.*; *Gent. Bijdr. Kstgesch.*]

Gent. Bijdr. Kstgesch. & Oudhdknd.
　Gentse bijdragen tot de kunstgeschiedenis en de oudheidkunde [Ghent contributions to art history and archaeology; prev. pubd as & cont. as *Gent. Bijdr. Kstgesch.*]

Gentile da Fabriano: Boll. Mens. Celeb. Centen.
　Gentile da Fabriano: Bollettino mensile per la celebrazione centenaria

Gent. Mag.
　Gentleman's Magazine

Genus

Geoarchaeol.
　Geoarchaeology: An International Journal

Geog. J.
　Geographical Journal

Geog. Mag.
　Geography Magazine

Geog. Rev.
　Geographical Review

Georg. Group J.
　Georgian Group Journal

Geosci. & Man
　Geoscience and Man

Germania

Germanica

Ger. Nmus. [Nürnberg]: Jber.
　Germanisches Nationalmuseum [Nürnberg]: Jahresbericht

G. Erud. A.
　Giornale di erudizione artistica

Gesch. Köln
　Geschichte in Köln

Gesch. Oberrheins
　Geschichte des Oberrheins

Gesch. Samml.
　Geschichte der Sammlungen

Gesta

Gest Lib. J.
　The Gest Library Journal

Getty Conserv. Inst. Newslett.
　Getty Conservation Institute Newsletter

Getty Mus. J.
　J. Paul Getty Museum Journal

Giai Pham [Aesthetic works]

Giessen. Beitr. Kstgesch.
　Giessener Beiträge zur Kunstgeschichte

Gigibori [Papua New Guinea]
Gil Blas
Gildebk
　Gildeboek: Tijdschrift voor kerkelijke kunst en oudheidkunde [Journal for ecclesiatical art and archaeology]

G. Ingeg., Architetto & Agron.
　Giornale dell'ingegnere, architetto ed agronomo

G. Italia
　Giornale d'Italia

Gladius

Glasgow Medic. J.
　Glasgow Medical Journal

Glasnik Skopskog Naučnog Društva
　Glasnik Skopskog naučnog društva [Courier of the Skopje Learned Society]

Glass A. Mag.
　Glass Art Magazine

Glass Circ.
　Glass Circle

Glass Cone

Glass Rev.
　Glass Review [prev. pubd as *Czech. Glass Rev.*]

Glass Technol.
　Glass Technology

Glastech. Ber.
　Glastechnische Berichte

G. Lett. Italia
　Giornale de' letterati d'Italia [cont. as *Nuovo G. Lett. Italia*]

G. Ligust. Archeol., Stor. & B.A.
　Giornale ligustico di archeologia, storia e belle arti

Global Archit.
　GA [Global Architecture]

Global Archit. Doc.
　GA Document

Global Archit. Houses
　GA Houses

Global Interiors

Globe & Mail
　Globe and Mail

Globus

Glühlichter

Glyptotek

Gmünd. Heimatbl.
　Gmünder Heimatblätter

Gmünd. Stud.
　Gmünden Studien

Godishnik N. Arkheol. Muz. Plovdiv
　Godishnik Narodni arkheologicheski muzea Plovdiv

Godišnjak Srpska Akad. Nauka
　Godišnjak Srpska akademiya nauka

Godo-godo

Goed Wonen

Goethe
　Goethe: Viermonatsschrift der Goethe-Gesellschaft [prev. pubd as *Goethe-Jb.*; *Jb. Goethe-Ges.*; cont. as *Goethe-Jb.*]

Goethe-Jb.
　Goethe-Jahrbuch [cont. as *Jb. Goethe-Ges.*; *Goethe*; *Goethe-Jb.*]

Gold Bull.
　Gold Bulletin

Goldsmiths' Rev.
　Goldsmiths' Review

Good Furn. Mag.
　Good Furniture Magazine

Good Words

Gornyy Zhurnal [Mining journal]

Göteborgs Högsk. Årsskr.
　Göteborgs högskolas årsskrift [Gotenburg High School yearbook]

Göteborgs Kstmus.
　Göteborgs konstmuseum [Gothenberg's art museum]

Götting. Jb.
　Göttinger Jahrbuch

Götting. Misz.
　Göttinger Miszellen

Götting. Orientforsch.
　Göttinger Orientforschungen

Gower

Goya

Grafička Rev.
　Grafička revija

Grande Rev.
　Grande revue

Grand Jeu

Granta

Granducato

Graphis

Graph. Kst.
　Graphische Künste

Greece & Rome
　Greece and Rome

Gringoire

Groning. Vlksalm.
　Groningse Volksalmanak

Gr. Orthdx Theol. Rev.
　Greek Orthodox Theological Review

Gr., Roman & Byz. Stud.
　Greek, Roman and Byzantine Studies

Grub Street J.
　Grub Street Journal

G. Stor. Archv. Tosc.
　Giornale storico degli archivi toscani

G. Stor. Lett. It.
　Giornale storico della letteratura italiana

Gt Circ.
　Great Circle

Guerino Meschino

Guerre Soc.
　Guerre sociale

Gugong Bowuyuan Yuankan [Palace Museum journal]

Gugong Jikan [National Palace Museum quarterly; cont. as *Gugong Xueshu Jikan*]

Gugong Wenwu Yuekan [National Palace Museum monthly of Chinese art]

Gugong Xueshu Jikan [National Palace Museum quarterly; prev. pubd as *Gugong Jikan*]

Guide Genova
　Guide di Genova

Guildhall Misc.
　Guildhall Miscellany

Gulden Passer
　De gulden passer

Gutai

Gutenberghus' Aarsskr.
　Gutenberghus' aarsskrift [Gutenberg House yearbook]

Gutenberg Jb.
　Gutenberg Jahrbuch

Güzel Sanatlar [Fine arts]

Gwalior State Archaeol. Dept: Annu. Rep.
　Gwalior State Archaeological Department: Annual Report

Gymnasium
　Gymnasium: Zeitschrift für Kultur der Antike und humanistische Bildung [prev. pubd as *Human. Gym.*]

Gyōsai [Journal of the Kawanabe Gyōsai Research Association]

Habitat

Hadassah Mag.
　Hadassah Magazine

Hadith

Hafnia
　Hafnia: Copenhagen Papers in the History of Art

Hai Jiao Shi Yanjiu

Hakluyt Soc. J.
　Hakluyt Society Journal

Hali

Hamburg. Beitr. Archäol.
　Hamburger Beiträge zur Archäologie

Hamburg. Beitr. Bknd.
　Hamburger Beiträge zur Buchkunde

Hamburg. Beitr. Numis.
　Hamburger Beiträge zur Numismatik

Hamburg. Kstfreunde
　Hamburgische Kunstfreunde

Hamburg. Mittel- & Ostdt. Forsch.
　Hamburger mittel- und ostdeutsche Forschungen

Hampstead Annu.
　Hampstead Annual

Hand. Genoot. Gesch. 'Soc. Emul.' Brugge
　Handelingen van het Genootschap voor geschiedenis gesticht onder de benaming 'Société d'émulation' te Brugge/Annales de la Société d'émulation de Bruges

Hand. Kon. Gesch.- & Oudhdknd. Kring Kortrijk
　Handelingen van de Koninklijke geschied- en oudheidkundige kring van Kortrijk [Bulletin of the Royal Archaeological Circle of Kortrijk]

Hand. Kon. Kring Oudhdknd., Lett. & Kst Mechelen/Bull. Cerc. Archéol., Litt. & A. Malines
　Handelingen van de Koninklijke kring voor oudheidkunde, letteren en kunst van Mechelen/Bulletin du Cercle archéologique, littéraire et artistique de Malines [prev. pubd as *Bull. Cerc. Archéol., Litt. & A. Malines*]

Hand. & Levensber. Maatsch. Ned. Lettknd. Leiden
Handelingen en levensberichten van de Maatschappij der Nederlandse letterkunde te Leiden [cont. as *Jb. Maatsch. Ned. Lettknd. Leiden*]

Hand. Maatsch. Gesch. & Oudhdknd. Gent
Handelingen der Maatschappij voor geschiedenis en oudheidkunde te Gent [Bulletin of the Society for the History and Archaeology of Ghent]

Handwk. Zonder Grenzen
Handwerken zonder grenzen

Han'guk Hakpo [Review of Korean studies]

Han'guk Kogohakpo [Korean archaeology reviews]

Han'guk Misul Munhwasa Nonch'ong [Discussions in the history of Korean art culture]

Han'guk Sa Non [Discussions in Korean history]

Han'guk Sa Yŏngu [Researches in Korean history]

Han'guk Ŭi Mi [Beauties of Korea]

Hannover. Geschbl.
Hannoversche Geschichtsblätter

Hannover Partikushalle, Niedersächs. Landtag
Hannover Partikushalle, Niedersächsischer Landtag

Hans. Geschbl.
Hansische Geschichtsblätter

Happenings News

Harper's Bazaar

Harper's Mag.
Harper's Magazine [prev. pubd as *Harper's New Mthly Mag.*; cont. as *Harper's Mthly*]

Harper's Mthly
Harper's Monthly [see *Harper's Mag.*]

Harper's New Mthly Mag.
Harper's New Monthly Magazine [see *Harper's Mag.*]

Harper's Weekly

Harvard J. Asiat. Stud.
Harvard Journal of Asiatic Studies

Harvard Lib. Bull.
Harvard Library Bulletin

Harvard Mthly
Harvard Monthly

Harvard Rev.
Harvard Review

Harvard Stud. Class. Philol.
Harvard Studies in Classical Philology

Harvard Stud. Comp. Lit.
Harvard Studies in Comparative Literature

Harz-Z.
Harz-Zeitschrift

Hatcher Rev.
Hatcher Review

Hawai. J. Hist.
The Hawaiian Journal of History

Hayward Statesman

Hb. Colon. Soc. MA
Handbook of the Colonial Society of Massachusetts

Hb. Mid. Amer. Ind.
Handbook of Middle American Indians

Hb. N. Amer. Ind.
Handbook of North American Indians

Hb. S. Amer. Ind.
Handbook of South American Indians

Heb. Un. Coll. Annu.
Hebrew Union College Annual

Heidelberg. Fremdenbl.
Heidelberger Fremdenblatt

Heidelberg. Jb.
Heidelberger Jahrbücher [prev. pubd as *Neue Heidelberg. Jb.*]

Heidelberg. Jb. Philol., Hist., Lit. & Kst
Heidelbergische Jahrbücher für Philologie, Historie, Literatur und Kunst

Heilige Kst
Heilige Kunst: Mitgliedsgabe des Kunstvereins der Diözese Rottenburg

Heimatbl. Siegkreises
Heimatblätter des Siegkreises

Heimatfreund Erzgebirge
Heimatfreund für das Erzgebirge

Heimatknd. Bl. Kreis Tübingen
Heimatkundliche Blätter für den Kreis Tübingen

Heimatver. Weil Stadt, Ber. & Mitt.
Heimatverein Weil der Stadt, Berichte und Mitteilungen

Heimatwerk

Heinolan Kaupunginmus. Julkaisuja
Heinolan kaupunginmuseon julkaisuja [Heinola City Museum publications]

Helice

Helikon

Helinium
Helinium: Revue consacrée à l'archéologie des Pays-Bas, de la Belgique et du Grand Duché de Luxembourg

Helmantica

Helsingen Kaupungin Hist.
Helsingen kaupungin historia

Helvetia Archaeol.
Helvetia archaeologica

Hemisphere

Henszlmann-Lapok

Herald

Her. Australia
Heritage Australia

Here & Now
Here and Now

Heresies

Heritage
Heritage: A Journal of Southern Sudanese Cultures

Heritage: Enc. Malt. Cult. & Civilis.
Heritage: Encyclopedia of Maltese Culture and Civilisation

Hermathemma

Hermeneus

Hermes

Herold Geschlechter-, Wappen- & Siegelknd.
Herold für Geschlechter-, Wappen- und Siegelkunde [prev. pubd as *Vjschr. Wap.-, Siegel- & Famknd.*; *Vjschr. Herald., Sphragistik & Geneal.*]

Hesperia
Hesperia: Journal of the American School of Classical Studies at Athens

Hespéris

Hespéris-Tamuda

Hessenkunst

Hessenland

Hess. Heimat
Hessische Heimat

Hess. Jb. Landesgesch.
Hessisches Jahrbuch für Landesgeschichte

Hess. Mus.
[Aus] hessischen Museen

Het Boek [cont. as *Quaerendo*]

Het Overzicht

Heute

Heythrop J.
Heythrop Journal

Hft. Ksthist. Semin. U. München
Hefte des kunsthistorischen Seminars der Universität München

Hibernia

Highland News

High Performance

Hijo Ahuizote
Hijo del Ahuizote

Hikuin

Hilalguía

Hilandarski Zborn.
Hilandarski zbornik

Hildesheim. Allg. Anz.
Hildesheimer allgemeiner Anzeiger

Himalay. Cult.
Himalayan Culture

Hindustan Times

Hisp. Amer. Hist. Rev.
Hispanic American Historical Review

Hispania Sacra

Hist. Afr.
History in Africa

Hist. A. Mex.
Historia del arte mexicano

Hist. Archaeol.
Historical Archaeology: The Annual Publication of the Society for Historical Archaeology

Hist. & Archéol.
Histoire et archéologie [prev. pubd as *Doss. Archéol.*; *Doc. Archeol.*]

Hist. Arkv
Historiskt arkiv [prev. pubd as *Antikva. Stud.*]

Hist. & Crit. A.
Histoire et critique des arts

Hist. Einzelschr.
Historia Einzelschriften

Hist. Envmt
Historic Environment

Hist.–Filol. Meddel.
Historisk–filologiske meddelelser [Historical–philological reports]

Hist. Human Sci.
History of the Human Sciences

Hist. J. Auckland–Waikato
Historical Journal Auckland–Waikato [prev. pubd as *Auckland/Waikato Hist. J.*; *J. Auckland Hist. Soc.*; cont. as *J. Auckland/Waikato Hist. Soc.*]

Hist. Jb. Görres-Ges.
Historisches Jahrbuch der Görres-Gesellschaft

Hist. Kingston
Historic Kingston

Hist. Kl. Kön. Bayer. Akad. Wiss.
Historische Klasse der Königlichen bayerischen Akademie der Wissenschaften

Hist. Litt. France
Histoire littéraire de la France

Hist. Meddel. Kobenhavn
Historiska meddelelser om Kobenhavn [Historical reports on Copenhagen]

Hist. & Mém. Inst. Royal France, Acad. Inscr. & B.-Lett.
Histoire et mémoires de l'Institut royal de France, Académie des inscriptions et belles-lettres [cont. as *Mém. Inst. France, Acad. Inscr. & B.-Lett.*]

Hist. Mex.
Historia mexicana

Hist. Mongol.
Historium Mongolorum

Hist. Mus. Basel, Jber. & Rechn.
Historisches Museum Basel, Jahresberichte und Rechnungen

Hist. NH
Historical New Hampshire

História

Historia [Utrecht]

Histórica

Hist. Phot.
History of Photography

Hist. Pisaurensia
Historica Pisaurensia

Hist. Places NZ
Historic Places in New Zealand [cont. as *NZ Hist. Places*]

Hist. Portugal
História de Portugal

Hist. Preserv.
Historic Preservation [cont. as *Hist. Preserv. Q. Rep.*; reverts to *Hist. Preserv.*]

Hist. Preserv. Q. Rep.
Historic Preservation Quarterly Report [cont. as *Hist. Preserv.*]

Hist. Religions
History of Religions

Hisp. Rev.
Hispanic Review

Hist. Shqipërisë
  Historia e shqipërisë [History of Albania]

Hist. & Soc.
  História e sociedade

Hist. Soc. S. CA Q.
  Historical Society of Southern California Quarterly

Hist. Stud.
  Historical Studies

Hist. Théât.
  Histoire du théâtre

Hist. & Theor.
  History and Theory

Hist. Tidskr. Skåneland
  Historisk tidskrift för Skåneland [Historical journal for Skåne]

Hist. Tidsskr.
  Historisk tidsskrift [Historical journal]

Hist. Today
  History Today

Hist. Ver. 'Alt Dinkelsbühl' Jb.
  Historischer Verein 'Alt Dinkelsbühl' Jahrbuch

Hist. Woonstede
  Historische woonstede

Hist. Workshop J.
  History Workshop Journal

Hist. Z.
  Historische Zeitschrift [HZ]

Hochland

Hogar & Archit.
  Hogar y architectura

Hohenzoll.-Jb.
  Hohenzollern-Jahrbuch: Forschungen und Abbildungen zur Geschichte der Hohenzollern in Brandenburg-Preussen

Hohenzoll. Jhft.
  Hohenzollerische Jahreshefte

Hohe Stasse [prev. pubd as *Schlesiens Vorzeit Bild & Schr.*]

Hohe Ufer

Holland

Holland: Reg.-Hist. Tijdschr.
  Holland: Regional-historisch tijdschrift

Holl. Rev.
  Hollandsche revue

Holosphere [Museum of Holography, NY]

Home Beautiful

Home Econ. Res. J.
  Home Economics Research Journal

Homes & Gdns
  Homes and Gardens

Homes & Grounds
  Homes and Grounds

Homme & Archit.
  L'Homme et l'architecture

Hommes Aujourd'hui
  Hommes d'aujourd'hui

Honolulu Acad. A.J.
  Honolulu Academy of Arts Journal

Hoogsteder–Naumann Mercury

Horizon

Horizonte
  Horizonte: Revista mensual de actividad contemporánea

Horticulturalist

Hoshigaoka

Hound & Horn
  Hound and Horn

House Beautiful

House & Gdn
  House and Garden

Household Words

House & Home
  House and Home

Houston Ger. Stud.
  Houston German Studies

Hrvatska Rev.
  Hrvatska revija [Croatian review]

Hrvatsko Kolo

Hudozhestvena

Hudozhnik

Huguenot Soc. Proc.
  Huguenot Society Proceedings

Human. Gym.
  Humanistische Gymnasium: Zeitschrift des deutschen Gymnasialvereins [cont. as *Gymnasium*]

Humaniora

Human. Islam.
  Humaniora Islamica

Human. Lovan.
  Humanistica lovanensia

Human. & Ren.
  Humanisme et renaissance

Humboldt

Humorist. Bl.
  Humoristische Blätter: Wöchentliches illustriertes Witzblatt der Pariser-Zeitung

Hunan Kaogu Jikan [Hunan archaeological bulletin]

Hunar va Mardum [Art and people]

Huntington Lib. Q.
  Huntington Library Quarterly

Hyakumanta [Bulletin of the Paper Museum]

IA: J. Soc. Indust. Archaeol.
  IA: Journal of the Society for Industrial Archaeology

IA Stud. Afr. A.
  Iowa Studies in African Art

Ibero-Amer. Archv
  Ibero-amerikanisches Archiv: Zeitschrift des Ibero-amerikanischen Forschungs-Instituts der Universität Bonn

Ibero-Americana

Iceland Rev.
  Iceland Review [cont. as *Atlantic & Ice. Rev.*]

ICO
  ICO: Den iconographiske post [prev. pubd as *Iconog. Post*]

ICOMOS Bull.
  ICOMOS Bulletin

Iconog. Post
  Iconographiske post: En nordisk blad om billeder [cont. as *ICO*]

Iconog. Relig.
  Iconography of Religions

ICSAC Cah.
  ICSAC Cahier [Internationaal centrum voor structuuranalyse en constructivisme]

Idea: Jb. Hamburg. Ksthalle
  Idea: Jahrbuch der Hamburger Kunsthalle [prev. pubd as *Jb. Hamburg. Kstsamml.*]

Ideale Heim
  Das ideale Heim

Ideas

Idun

IFAR Rep.
  IFAR Reports [prev. pubd as *Stolen Art Alert*; *Art Research News*]

IIC News

Ikonotheka

Il Bimestre

Il Carrobbio

Il Centone

IL Class. Stud.
  Illinois Classical Studies

Il Contemporaneo [Milan]

Il Convegno

Il Convito

Il Fuidoro

Iliria

Illus. A.
  Illustrated Arts

Illus. Archaeologist
  Illustrated Archaeologist [incorp. into *The Reliquary*, 1894–]

Illus. Austral. News
  Illustrated Australian News

Illus. Bresc.
  Illustrazione bresciana

Illus. Fiorentino
  Illustratore fiorentino

Illus. Kstgew. Z. Innendek.
  Illustrierte kunstgewerbliche Zeitschrift für Innendekoration [cont. as *Innendekoration*; *Archit. & Wohnform*; *Archit. & Wohnwelt*; *Archit., Innenarchit., Tech. Ausbau*]

Illus. London News
  Illustrated London News

Illus. Tidn.
  Illustrerad tidning [Illustrated magazine]

Illus. Times
  Illustrated Times

Illust. Tosc.
  Illustrazione toscana

Illus. Vatic.
  Illustrazione vaticana

Illus. Ztg
  Illustrierte Zeitung

Il Messaggero

Il Piccolo

Il Politecnico

Il Regno

Il Risorgimento

Il Rosario

Il Rubastino

Il Sagittario

Il Santo

Il Selvaggio

Il Serolo xx

IL Soc. Archit. Mthly Bull.
  Illinois Society of Architects Monthly Bulletin

Ilus. Esp. & Amer.
  Ilustración española y americana

Ilus. Mod.
  Ilustração moderna

Ilus. Peru.
  Ilustración peruana

Ilus. Port.
  Ilustração portuguesa

Ilus. Potosina
  La ilustración potosina

Il Vasari

Il Verri

Imafronte

Image [Kumasi]

Image [London]
  Image: A Quarterly of the Visual Arts

Image [Rochester, NY]
  Image: Journal of Photography and Motion Pictures [Rochester, NY]

Imagination

Imago

Imago Mundi: Rev. Early Cartography
  Imago mundi: A Review of Early Cartography

Imago Musicae

Impact

Impressionisten

Imprimatur

Imprint

Imp. Rus. Ist. Obshchestv.: Sborn.
  Imperatorskoye russkoye istoricheskoye obshchestvo: Sbornik [Imperial Russian Historical Society: miscellany]

Ind. A. & Lett.
  Indian Art and Letters

Ind. Antiqua.
  Indian Antiquary

Ind. Archaeol.
  Indian Archaeology

Ind. Architect
  Indian Architect

Ind. Bouwknd. Tijdschr.
  Indische bouwkunst tijdschrift

Ind. Bouwknd. Tijdschr. Locale Tech.
  Indisch bouwkundig tijdschrift locale techniek

Ind. Express
  Indian Express

Ind. Hist. Q.
  Indian Historical Quarterly

Ind. Hist. Rec. Comm., Proc.
  Indian Historical Records
  Commission, Proceedings

India Int. Cent. Q.
  India International Centre
  Quarterly

India Mag.
  India Magazine

Indiana

Indica

Indicateur Ant. Suisses
  Indicateur d'antiquités suisses

Ind. Mus. Bull.
  Indian Museum Bulletin

Ind. Notes
  Indian Notes

Indo-Asian Cult.
  Indo-Asian Culture

Indo Iranica

Indo-Iran. J.
  Indo-Iranian Journal

Indologica-Jaipurensia

Indol.-Tagung
  Indologen-Tagung

Indonesia

Indonesia Circ.
  Indonesia Circle

Indonesië

Indo-Pacific Prehist. Assoc. Bull.
  Indo-Pacific Prehistory
  Association Bulletin

Ind. State Rlwys Mag.
  Indian State Railways Magazine

Indust. A.
  Industrial Arts

Indust. Archaeol. Rev.
  Industrial Archaeology Review

Indust. Corrosion
  Industrial Corrosion

Indust. Des.
  Industrial Design

Indust. & Engin. Chem.
  Industrial and Engineering
  Chemistry

Indust. Forum
  Industrial Forum

Indust. It. Cemento
  Industria italiana del cemento

Inf. Bull. Int. Assoc. Stud. Cult. Cent. Asia
  Information Bulletin of the
  International Association for the
  Study of the Cultures of Central
  Asia [same as *Inf. Byull. Mezhdun.
  Assot. Izecheniyu Kul't. Tsent.
  Azii*]

Inf. Byull. Mezhdun. Assot. Izecheniyu Kul't. Tsent. Azii
  Informationnyy byulleten'
  Mezhdunarodnoy assotsiatsii po
  izucheniyu kul'tur tsentral'noy Azii
  [Information bulletin of the
  International Association for the
  Study of the Cultures of Central
  Asia]

Inf. Hist.
  Information historique

Inf. Hist. A.
  Information d'histoire de l'art

Infinity

Inf.: Ist. Beni A. Cult. Nat. Reg. Emilia-Romagna
  Informazioni: Istituto per i beni
  artistici culturali naturali della
  regione Emilia-Romagna

Información

Inf. Psych.
  Information psychiatrique

Ingegneria

Inland Architect & News Rec.
  Inland Architect and News
  Record

Innendekoration [prev. pubd as *Illus.
  Kstgew. Z. Innendek.*; cont. as *Archit.
  & Wohnform*; *Archit. & Wohnwelt*;
  Archit., Innenarchit., Tech. Ausbau]

Innes Rev.
  Innes Review

Innsbruck. Hist. Stud.
  Innsbrucker historische Studien

Innsbruck. Nachr.
  Innsbrucker Nachrichten

Inside Outside

Insight [cont. as *Zimbabwe Insight*]

In Situ
  In Situ: The Journal of the Zambia
  Institute of Architects

Inst. Indochin. Etud. Homme, Bull. & Trav.
  Institut indochinois pour l'étude
  de l'homme, bulletins et travaux

Instituto
  O instituto

Instr. Eccles.
  Instrumenta ecclesiastica

Insula Pulcheria

Int. Archit.
  International Architecture

Int. Archv Ethnog.
  Internationales Archiv für
  Ethnographie [cont. as *Int. Archvs
  Ethnog.*; *Tropical Man*]

Int. Archvs Ethnog.
  International Archives of
  Ethnography [see *Int. Archv
  Ethnog.*]

Int. Archv Vlkerknd.
  Internationales Archiv für
  Völkerkunde

Int. Colloq. Anc. Mosaics
  International Colloquium on
  Ancient Mosaics

Int. Coronelli-Ges.: Inf.
  Internationale Coronelli-
  Gesellschaft: Information

Intégral

Intellbl. Jen. Allg. Lit.- Zt.
  Intelligenzblatt der Jenaischen
  allgemeinen Literatur-Zeitung

Interfunctionen

Interieur

Interior Des.
  Interior Design

Interiors

Interméd. Chercheurs & Curieux
  Intermédiaire des chercheurs et
  des curieux

Intern: Vjschr. Dt. Ges. Phot.
  Intern: Vierteljahresschrift der
  deutschen Gesellschaft für
  Photographie

Intersezioni

Interv. Rest.: G.N. Pal. Spinola
  Interventi di restauro: Galleria
  nazionale del Palazzo Spinola

Int. Flklore Rev.
  International Folklore Review

Int. J. Behavioural Dev.
  International Journal of
  Behavioural Development

Int. J. Housing Sci. & Applic.
  International Journal for Housing
  Science and its Applications

Int. J. Mid. E. Stud.
  International Journal of Middle
  East Studies

Int. J. Mus. Mgmt & Cur.
  International Journal of Museum
  Management and Curatorship

Int. J. Naut. Archaeol. & Underwtr Explor.
  International Journal of Nautical
  Archaeology and Underwater
  Exploration

Int. J. Psychol.
  International Journal of
  Psychology

Int. J. Solids & Structures
  International Journal of Solids and
  Structures

Int. J. Turk. Stud.
  International Journal of Turkish
  Studies

Int. Labour Rev.
  International Labour Review

Int. Rev. i 10
  International Revue i 10

Int. Studio
  International Studio

Inummarit

Invest. INAH
  Investigaciones del Instituto
  nacional de antropología e historia

Inzyn. & Budownictwo
  Inzynieria i budownictwo
  [Engineering and construction]

Iran. Antiq.
  Iranica antiqua

Iran. Dkml.
  Iranische Denkmäler

Iran: J. Brit. Inst. Persian Stud.
  Iran: Journal of the British
  Institute of Persian Studies

Iran. Stud.
  Iranian Studies

Iraq

Ireland Welcomes
  Ireland of the Welcomes

Irish Ancestor

Irish A. Rev.
  Irish Arts Review

Irish A. Rev. Yb.
  Irish Arts Review Yearbook

Irish Bldr
  Irish Builder

Irish Bldr & Engin.
  Irish Builder and Engineer

Irish Cath. Mag.
  Irish Catholic Magazine

Irish Georg. Soc. Bull.
  Irish Georgian Society Bulletin

Irish Q. Rev.
  Irish Quarterly Review

Ironworker

Irradiador

Isis
  Isis: An International Review
  Devoted to the History of Science
  and its Cultural Influences

Isk. Azerbaydzhana
  Iskusstvo Azerbaydzhana:
  Akademiya nauk
  azerbaydzhanskoy SSR: Institut
  arkhitektury i iskusstva [The art of
  Azerbaijan: Academy of Sciences
  of the Azerbaijan SSR: Institute of
  Architecture and Art]

Isk. Knigi
  Iskusstvo knigi [Book art]

Isk. Komm.
  Iskusstvo kommuny [Art of the
  commune]

Isk. Krit.
  Iskusstvo i kritika [Art and
  criticism]

Iskos

Isk. & Rabochiy Kl.
  Iskusstvo i rabochiy klass [Art and
  the working class]

Isk. Tadz. Naroda
  Iskusstvo tadzhikskogo naroda
  [Art of the Tajik people]

Iskusstvo [Art]

Isk. Zapadnoy Evropy & Vizatii
  Iskusstvo zapadnoy evropy i
  vizatii [Art of western Europe and
  Byzantium]

Isk. Zodchikh Uzbekistana
  Iskusstvo zodchikh Uzbekistana
  [The art of architects of
  Uzbekhistan]

Islam. A.
  Islamic Art

Islam. Archaeol. Stud.
  Islamic Archaeological Studies

Islam. Cult.
  Islamic Culture

Islam. Rev.
  Islamic Review

İslâm Tetkikleri Enst. Derg.
  İslâm Tetkikleri Enstitüsü Dergisi
  [Journal of the Institute of Islamic
  Studies]

Islandica

Israel Explor. J.
  Israel Exploration Journal

Israel & Mid. E. Econ. Rev.
  Israel and Middle East Economic
  Review [prev. pubd as *Palestine &
  Middle E. Econ. Rev.*]

Israel Mus. J.
  Israel Museum Journal

Israel Mus. News
  Israel Museum News

Israel Orient. Stud.
  Israel Oriental Studies

Issledovaniya Istor. Arkhit.
Issledovaniya po istorii
arkhitektury [Investigations in
architectural history]

Istanbul. Mitt.
Istanbuler Mitteilungen [des
archäologischen Instituts]

İstanbul Ü.: Hukuk Fak. Mecmuası
İstanbul Üniversitesi: Hukuk
fakültesi mecmuası [Istanbul
University: Law Faculty journal]

İstanbul Ü.: İktisat Fak. Mecmuası
İstanbul Üniversitesi: İktisat
fakültesi mecmuası [Istanbul
University: Faculty of Political
Economy journal]

Ist. Elem. Archit. & Rilievo Mnmt.:
Quad. [Genova]
Istituto di elementi di architettura
e rilievo dei monumenti:
Quaderno [Genova] [cont. as *Ist.*
Prog. Archit. [Genova]: *Quad.*]

Ist. Elem. Archit. & Rilievo Mnmt.:
Quad. [Palermo]
Istituto di elementi di architettura
e rilievo dei monumenti:
Quaderno [Palermo]

Ist. It. Medio & Estrem. Orient. Rep.
& Mem.
Istituto italiano per il Medio ed
Estremo Oriente: Rapporti e
memorie

Ist. Lombard. Sci. & Lett.: Rendi.
Istituto lombardo di scienze e
lettere: Rendiconti

Istor.-Filol. Zhurnal Akad. Nauk
Arm SSR
Istoriko-filologicheskiy zhurnal
Akademii nauk Arm SSR [History
and philology journal of the
Academy of Sciences of the
Armenian SSR]

Istor. Mat. Kult. Uzbekistana
Istoriya material'noy kul'tury
Uzbekistana [History of Uzbek
material culture]

Ist. Prog. Archit. [Genova]: *Quad.*
Istituto di progettazione
d'architettura [Genova]: Quaderno
[prev. pubd as *Ist. Elem. Archit.*
& Rilievo Mnmt.: Quad.
[Genova]]

Istros

Italia A.
L'Italia artistica

Italia Futur.
L'Italia futurista

Italia Lett.
Italia letteraria

Italia Med. & Uman.
Italia medioevale e umanistica

I Tatti Stud.
I Tatti Studies

It Baeken [The beacon]

It. Cult.
Italian Culture

Items
Items: Tijdschrift voor
vormgeving [Items: magazine for
design]

It. Forsch. Kstgesch.
Italienische Forschungen zur
Kunstgeschichte

It. Forsch. Ksthist. Inst. Florenz
Italienische Forschungen des
kunsthistorischen Instituts in
Florenz

I 10
I 10 [tien]: International revue

Itihas

Itinerari
Itinerari: Contributi alla storia
dell'arte in memoria di Maria Luisa
Fero

'Iton Agudat Ha-Ing'inerim Veha-
Arkhitektim Be-E'retz- Yisrael
[Journal of the Association of
Engineers and Architects in Eretz
Israel]

It. Q.
Italian Quarterly

It. Stud.
Italian Studies

Ixo: Int. Rev.
Ixo: Internationale revue

Izkustvo

Izkustwo

Izobrazitel'noye Isk.
Izobrazitel'noye iskusstvo [Fine
art]

Izvestiya

Izvestiya Akad. Nauk Kazakh. SSR:
Seriya Obshchestvennaya
Izvestiya Akademii nauk
kazakhskoy SSR: Seriya
obshchestvennaya [Proceedings of
the Academy of Sciences of the
Kazakh SSR: social series]

Izvestiya Akad. Nauk Tadzhiks. SSR:
Otdeleniye Obshchestvennykh Nauk
Izvestiya Akademii nauk
tadzhikskoy SSR: Otdeleniye
obshchestvennykh nauk
[Proceedings of the Academy of
Sciences of the Tajik SSR:
Department of Social Sciences]

Izvestiya ASNOVA [Proceeedings of
the Association of New Architects]

Izvestiya Azerbay. Filiala Akad.
Nauk SSSR
Izvestiya azerbaydzhanskogo filiala
Akademii nauk SSSR [Proceedings
of the Azerbaijan filial of the
Academy of Sciences of the
USSR]

Izvestiya Balg. Arkheol. Inst.
Izvestiya na Balgarski
arkheologicheski institut

Izvestiya Etnog. Muz.
Izvestiya na etnografskiya muzey
[Proceedings of the Ethnographic
Museum]

Izvestiya Imp. Rus. Geog. Obshchestva
Izvestiya imperatorskogo russkogo
geograficheskogo obshchestva
[Proceedings of the Imperial
Russian Geographical Society]

Izvestiya Inst. Istor. Mat. Kul't.
Izvestiya Instituta istorii
material'noy kul'tury [Proceedings
of the Institute of the History of
Material Culture]

Izvestiya Inst. Izobrazitelni Izk.
Izvestiya na Instituta za
izobrazitelni izkustva

Izvestiya Otdeleniya Obshchestvennykh
Nauk [Proceedings of the
Department of Social Sciences]

Izvestiya Tavricheskogo Obshchestva
Istor., Arkheol. & Etnog.
Izvestiya tavricheskogo
obshchestva istorii, arkheologii i
etnografii [Proceedings of the
Tavrik Society of History,
Archaeology and Ethnography]

Izvestiya Turkestanskogo Otdeleniya
Imp. Geog.
Izvestiya turkestanskogo
Otdeleniya imperatorskogo
geograficheskogo [Proceedings of
the Turkistan Geographical
Department]

J. A. [Paris]
Journal des arts [cont. as *Beaux-*
A.: Rev. Inf. A.]

J. A. [USA]
Journal of Art [USA]

J. AA
Journal of the Architectural
Association

J. Acad. A. & Archit.
Journal of the Academy of Art and
Architecture [Mysore]

J. A.: Dept. Hist. A. Diego Velázquez
Jornadas de arte: Departamento de
historia del arte Diego Velázquez

J.A. & Des. Educ.
Journal of Art and Design
Education

Jadranski Zborn.
Jadranski zbornik

J. Aesth. & A. Crit.
Journal of Aesthetics and Art
Criticism

J. Aesth. Educ.
Journal of Aesthetic Education

J. Afr. Hist.
Journal of African History

J. Africanistes
Journal des africanistes [prev.
pubd as *J. Soc. Africanistes*]

J. Afr. Relig. & Philos.
Journal of African Religion and
Philosophy

J. Afr. Soc.
Journal of the African Society

Jahresring
Jahresring: Ein Querschnitt durch
die deutsche Literatur und Kunst
der Gegenwart

J. A. & Ideas
Journal of Arts and Ideas

Jamaica J.
Jamaica Journal

J. Amer. Cult.
Journal of American Culture

J. Amer. Flklore
Journal of American Folklore

J. Amer. Hist.
Journal of American History

J. Amer. Inst. Architects
Journal of the American Institute
of Architects

J. Amer. Inst. Conserv.
Journal of the American Institute
for Conservation [prev. pubd as
Bull. Amer. Inst. Conserv. Hist. &
A. Works]

J. Amer. Inst. Planners
Journal of the American Institute
of Planners

J. Amer. Orient. Soc.
Journal of the American Oriental
Society

J. Amer. Port. Soc.
Journal of the American
Portuguese Society

J. Amer. Res. Cent. Egypt
Journal of the American Research
Center in Egypt

J. Amer. Soc. Archit. Hist.
Journal of the American Society of
Architectural Historians [cont. as
J. Soc. Archit. Hist.]

J. Amer. Soc. Orient. A.
Journal of the American Society of
Oriental Art

J. A. Mgmt & Law
Journal of Arts Management and
Law

Jam. Hist. Rev.
Jamaican Historical Review

J. Amusant
Le Journal amusant

J. Anc. Chron. Forum
Journal of the Ancient
Chronology Forum

J. Anc. Ind. Hist.
Journal of Ancient Indian History

J. Anc. Nr E. Soc.
Journal of the Ancient Near East
Society

J. Anglo-It. Stud.
Journal of Anglo-Italian Studies

J. Anglo-Mongol. Soc.
Journal of the Anglo-Mongolian
Society

Jannayuddha [People's war]

J. Anthropol. Archaeol.
Journal of Anthropological
Archaeology

J. Anthropol. Inst. GB & Ireland
Journal of the Anthropological
Institute of Great Britain and
Ireland [cont. as *J. Royal*
Anthropol. Inst. GB & Ireland]

J. Anthropol. Res.
Journal of Anthropological
Research

J. Anthropol. Soc. Oxford
Journal of the Anthropological
Society of Oxford

Janus

Janus Pannonius Múz. Evkönyve
Janus Pannonius Múzeum
evkönyve [Janus Pannonius
Museum annual]

Japan Architect

Japan Soc. London Bull.
Japan Society of London Bulletin

Jap. J. Relig. Stud.
Japanese Journal of Religious
Studies

J. Arab. Stud.
Journal of Arabian Studies

J. Archaeol. Rep.
Journal of Archaeological Reports

J. Archaeol. Sci.
Journal of Archaeological Science

J. Archit. Educ.
Journal of Architectural Education

J. Archit. & Planning Res.
Journal of Architectural and Planning Research

Jard. A.
Jardin des arts

Jard. Modes
Jardin des modes

J. Arms & Armour Soc.
Journal of the Arms and Armour Society

J. Arquitectos
Jornal dos arquitectos

J. Artistes
Journal des artistes

J. Asian Hist.
Journal of Asian History

J. Asian Stud.
Journal of Asian Studies [prev. pubd as *Far E. Q.*]

J. Asiat.
Journal asiatique

J. Asiat. Soc.
Journal of the Asiatic Society [prev. pubd as *J. & Proc. Asiat. Soc. Bengal*; *J. Asiat. Soc. Bengal*]

J. Asiat. Soc. Bengal
Journal of the Asiatic Society of Bengal [see *J. Asiat. Soc.*]

J. Asiat. Soc. Calcutta
Journal of the Asiatic Society of Calcutta

J. Asiat. Soc. Pakistan
Journal of the Asiatic Society of Pakistan

J. Auckland Hist. Soc.
Journal of the Aukland Historical Society [cont. as *Auckland/ Waikato Hist. J.*; *Hist. J. Auckland–Waikato*; *J. Auckland/ Waikato Hist. Soc.*]

J. Auckland/Waikato Hist. Soc.
Journal of the Aukland/Waikato Historical Society [prev. pubd as *Hist. J. Auckland–Waikato*; *Auckland/Waikato Hist. J.*; *J. Auckland Hist. Soc.*]

Jb. Adalbert Stift. Ver.
Jahrbuch des Adalbert Stifter Vereins in München [also known as *Adalbert Stifter-Jahrbuch* & as *Stifter-Jahrbuch*]

J. Bahamas Hist. Soc.
Journal of the Bahamas Historical Society

J. B.-A. & Lit.
Journal des beaux-arts et de la littérature

Jb. Ant. & Christ.
Jahrbuch für Antike und Christentum

Jb. Antwerpens Oudhdknd. Kring
Jaarboek van Antwerpens oudheidkundige kring

Jb. Archit.
Jahrbuch für Architektur

J. B.-A. & Sci.
Journal des beaux-arts et des sciences

Jb. Asiat. Kst
Jahrbuch für asiatische Kunst

Jb. Ästh. & Allg. Kstwiss.
Jahrbuch für Ästhetik und allgemeine Kunstwissenschaft

J. Baukst
Journal für die Baukunst

Jb. Bayer. Akad. Wiss.
Jahrbuch der Bayerischen Akademie der Wissenschaften

Jb. Bayer. Dkmlpf.
Jahrbuch der Bayerischen Denkmalpflege

Jb. Berlin. Mus.
Jahrbuch der Berliner Museen

Jb. Bern. Hist. Mus.
Jahrbuch des Bernischen historischen Museums

Jb. Bib. Hertz.
Jahrbuch der Bibliotheca Hertziana

Jb. Bild. Kst Ostseeprov.
Jahrbuch für bildende Kunst in den Ostseeprovinzen

Jb. Brandenburg. Gesch.
Jahrbuch für brandenburgische Geschichte

Jb. Braunschweig. Geschver.
Jahrbuch des Braunschweigischen Geschichtsvereins [prev. pubd as *Braunschweig. Jb.*]

Jb. Cent. Bureau Geneal.
Jaarboek van het centraal bureau voor genealogie

Jb. Coburg. Landesstift.
Jahrbuch der Coburger Landesstiftung

Jb. Die Haghe
Jaarboek Die Haghe

Jb. Dt. Akad. Spr. & Dicht.
Jahrbuch der Deutschen Akademie für Sprache und Dichtung

Jb. Dt. Akad. Wiss. Berlin
Jahrbuch der Deutschen Akademie der Wissenschaften zu Berlin

Jb. Dt. Alpenver.
Jahrbuch des Deutschen Alpenvereins

Jb. Dt. Archäol. Inst.
Jahrbuch des Deutschen archäologischen Instituts [prev. pubd as *Jb. Ksr. Dt. Archäol. Inst.*]

Jb. Dt. Bühnenspiele
Jahrbuch der deutschen Bühnenspiele

Jb. Dt. Dante-Ges.
Jahrbuch der Deutschen Dante Gesellschaft [cont. as *Dt. Dante-Jb.*]

Jb. Dt. Schillerges.
Jahrbuch der Deutschen Schillergesellschaft

Jber. Altertwiss.
Jahresberichte für Altertumswissenschaft

Jber. Augst & Kaiseraugst
Jahresberichte aus Augst und Kaiseraugst

Jber. Basl. Kstver.
Jahresbericht, Basler Kunstverein [prev. pubd as *Berstatt.: Jahr....*, *Basl. Kstver.*]

Jber. Freies Dt. Hochstift, 1972–73
Jahresbericht des freien deutschen Hochstifts, 1972–73

Jber. Geog. Ges. Bern
Jahresberichte der Geographischen Gesellschaft von Bern

Jber. Ger. Nmus.
Jahresbericht des Germanischen Nationalmuseums [prev. pubd as & cont. as *Jber., Ger. Nmus.* [Nürnberg]]

Jber., Ger. Nmus. [Nürnberg]
Jahresbericht, Germanisches Nationalmuseum [Nürnberg]

Jber. Heimatver. Landkreis Augsburg
Jahresbericht des Heimatvereins für den Landkreis Augsburg

Jber. Hist. Mus. Basel
Jahresberichte des Historischen Museums Basel

Jber. Hist. Mus. Bern
Jahresberichte des Historischen Museums in Bern

Jber. Hist. Ver. Dillingen
Jahresbericht des Historischen Vereins Dillingen [cont. as *Jb. Hist. Ver. Dillingen*]

Jber. Hist. Ver. Mittelfranken
Jahresberichte des Historischen Vereins für Mittelfranken [cont. as *Jb. Hist. Ver. Mittelfranken*]

Jber. Hist. Ver. Oberbayern
Jahresbericht des Historischen Vereines von (und für) Oberbayern

Jber. Hist. Ver. Straubing & Umgebung
Jahresbericht des Historischen Vereins für Straubing und Umgebung

Jber. Kant. Lehranstalt Sarnen
Jahresbericht über die kantonale Lehranstalt zu Sarnen

Jber. Linz. Musver., 'Verm. Schr.'
Jahresbericht des Linzer Musealvereines, 'Vermischte Schriften'

Jber. Mus. Francisco-Carolinium
Jahresbericht des Museum Francisco-Carolinium [prev. pubd as *Ber. Mus. Francisco-Carolinium*; cont. as *Jb. Oberösterreich. Musver.*; *Jb. Oberösterreich. Musver., Ges. Landeskd.*]

Jber. Roemer-Mus.
Jahresbericht des Roemer-Museums

Jber.: Römerhaus & Mus. Augst
Jahresbericht: Römerhaus und Museum Augst

Jber.: Schweiz. Landesmus. Zürich
Jahresbericht: Schweizerisches Landesmuseum in Zürich

Jber. Ver. 'Alt-Rothenburg'
Jahresbericht des Vereins 'Alt-Rothenburg'

Jber. Vooraziat.–Egyp. Genoot. Ex Oriente Lux
Jaarbericht van het Vooraziatisch–Egyptisch Genootschap ex oriente lux

Jb. Fränk. Landesforsch.
Jahrbuch für fränkische Landesforschung

Jb. Freien Dt. Hochstifts
Jahrbuch des Freien deutschen Hochstifts

Jb. Genoot. Amstelodamum
Jaarboek van het Genootschap Amstelodamum

Jb. Ger. Zentmus., Mainz
Jahrbuch des Germanischen Zentralmuseums, Mainz

Jb. Gesch. Oberdt. Reichsstädte
Jahrbuch für Geschichte der oberdeutschen Reichsstädte [prev. pubd as *Essling. Stud.*]

Jb. Gesch. Oudhdknd. Kring Leuven & Omgev.
Jaarboek van de geschied- en oudheidkundige kring voor Leuven en omgeving

Jb. Gesch. & Oudhdknd. Leiden & Omstreken
Jaarboekje voor geschiedenis en oudheidkunde van Leiden en omstreken

Jb. Ges. Gesch. Protestantismus Österreich
Jahrbuch der Gesellschaft für die Geschichte des Protestantismus in Österreich

Jb. Ges. Hamburg. Kstfreunde
Jahrbuch der Gesellschaft hamburgischer Kunstfreunde

Jb. Ges. Schweiz. Famforsch.
Jahrbuch der Gesellschaft für schweizerische Familienforschung

Jb. Goethe-Ges.
Jahrbuch der Goethe-Gesellschaft [prev. pubd as *Goethe-Jb.*; cont. as *Goethe*; *Goethe-Jb.*]

Jb. Haarlem
Jaarboek Haarlem

Jb. Hamburg. Kstsamml.
Jahrbuch der Hamburger Kunstsammlungen [cont. as *Idea: Jb. Hamburg. Ksthalle*]

Jb. Hamburg. Wiss. Anstalten
Jahrbuch der Hamburgischen wissenschaftlichen Anstalten

J. Bhandarkar Res. Inst.
Journal of the Bhandarkar Research Institute

Jb. Hist. Ver. Dillingen
Jahrbuch des Historischen Vereins Dillingen [prev. pubd as *Jber. Hist. Ver. Dillingen*]

Jb. Hist. Ver. Mittelfranken
Jahrbuch des Historischen Vereins für Mittelfranken [prev. pubd as *Jber. Hist. Ver. Mittelfranken*]

Jb. Hist. Ver. Nördlingen &
Umgebung
Jahrbuch des Historischen Vereins
für Nördlingen und Umgebung

J. Bihar & Orissa Res. Soc.
Journal of the Bihar and Orissa
Research Society

J. Bihar Puravid Parishad
Journal of the Bihar Puravid
Parishad

Jb. Jungen Kst
Jahrbuch der jungen Kunst

Jb. Klass. Philol.
Jahrbuch für klassische Philologie

Jb. Köln. Geschver.
Jahrbuch des Kölnischen
Geschichtsvereins

Jb.: Kon. Mus. S. Kst.
Jaarboek: Koninklijk museum
voor schone kunsten [Yearbook:
Royal Museum for Fine Arts]

Jb. Kon. Ned. Akad. Wet.
Jaarboek van de Koninklijke
Nederlandse Akademie van
wetenschappen [Yearbook of the
Royal Dutch Academy of
Sciences]

Jb. Kon. Oudhdkd. Kring Antwerpen
Jaarboek van de Koninklijke
oudheidkundige kring van
Antwerpen [Yearbook of the
Royal Antwerp Archaeological
Circle]

Jb. Kön.-Preuss. Kstsamml.
Jahrbuch der Königlich-
preussischen Kunstsammlungen
[cont. as *Jb. Preuss. Kstsamml.*]

Jb.: Kon. Vl. Acad. Wet., Lett. &
S. Kst. België
Jaarboek: Koninklijke Vlaamse
Academie voor wetenschappen,
letteren en schone kunsten van
België [Yearbook: Royal Flemish
Academy of Sciences, Literature
and Fine Arts of Belgium]

Jb. Kreis Trier–Saarburg
Jahrbuch Kreis Trier–Saarburg

Jb. Ksr. Dt. Archäol. Inst.
Jahrbuch des Kaiserlichen
deutschen archäologischen
Instituts [cont. as *Jb. Dt. Archäol.
Inst.*]

Jb. Ksr.-Kön. Zent.-Komm. Erforsch.
& Erhaltung Kst- & Hist. Dkml.
Jahrbuch der K.-K. [Kaiserlich-
Königlichen] Zentral-Kommission
für Erforschung und Erhaltung
der Kunst- und historischen
Denkmale

Jb. Kstgesch.
Jahrbuch für Kunstgeschichte
[prev. pubd as *Jb. Ksthist. Inst.*;
*Kstgesch. Jb. Ksr.-Kön. Zent.-
Komm. Erforsch. & Erhaltung Kst-
& Hist. Dkml.*; cont. as *Wien. Jb.
Kstgesch.*]

Jb. Kstgesch. Bundesdkmlamt.
Jahrbuch der Kunstgeschichte des
Bundesdenkmalamtes

Jb. Ksthist. Inst.
Jahrbuch des Kunsthistorischen
Institutes [prev. pubd as *Kstgesch.
Jb. Ksr.-Kön. Zent.-Komm.
Erforsch. & Erhaltung Kst- &
Hist. Dkml.*; cont. as *Jb. Kstgesch.*;
Wien. Jb. Kstgesch.]

Jb. Ksthist. Inst. Graz
Jahrbuch des Kunsthistorischen
Institutes der Universität Graz

Jb. Ksthist. Inst. Ksr.-Kön. Zent.-
Komm. Dkmlpf.
Jahrbuch des Kunsthistorischen
Institutes der K.-K. [Kaiserlich-
Königlichen] Zentral-Kommission
für Denkmalpflege

Jb. Ksthist. Inst. Staatsdkmlamt.
Jahrbuch des kunsthistorischen
Institutes des Staatsdenkmalamtes

Jb. Ksthist. Samml. Allhöch. Ksrhaus.
Jahrbuch der kunsthistorischen
Sammlungen des allerhöchsten
Kaiserhauses [cont. as *Jb. Ksthist.
Samml. Wien*]

Jb. Ksthist. Samml. Wien
Jahrbuch der kunsthistorischen
Sammlungen in Wien [prev. pubd
as *Jb. Ksthist. Samml. Allhöch.
Ksrhaus.*]

Jb. Kst & Kstpf. Schweiz
Jahrbuch für Kunst und
Kunstpflege der Schweiz

Jb. Kstsamml. Allhöch Ksrhaus.
Jahrbuch der Kunstsammlungen
des allerhöchsten Kaiserhauses

Jb. Kstwiss.
i) Jahrbücher für
Kunstwissenschaft [1868–1873;
cont. as *Repert. Kstwiss.*]
ii) Jahrbuch für Kunstwissenschaft
[1923–30; prev. pubd as *Mhft.
Kstwiss.*; merged with *Z. Bild. Kst*
& with *Repert. Kstwiss.* to form *Z.
Kstgesch.*]

Jb. Landeshptstadt Halle
Jahrbuch der Landeshauptstadt
Halle

Jb. Landeskd. Niederösterreich
Jahrbuch für Landeskunde von
Niederösterreich

Jb. Liechtenstein. Kstges.
Jahrbuch der Liechtensteinischen
Kunstgesellschaft

Jb. Maatsch. Ned. Lettknd. Leiden
Jaarboek van de Maatschappij der
Nederlandse letterkunde te Leiden
[Yearbook of the Society of Dutch
Literature; prev. pubd as *Hand. &
Levensber. Maatsch. Ned. Lettknd.
Leiden*]

Jb. Märkischen Mus.
Jahrbuch des Märkischen
Museums

Jb. Max-Planck-Ges. Förderung Wiss.
Jahrbuch der Max-Planck-
Gesellschaft zur Förderung der
Wissenschaften

Jb. Munt- & Penningknd.
Jaarboek voor munt-en
penningkunde

Jb. Mus. Vlkerknd. Leipzig
Jahrbuch des Museums für
Völkerkunde zu Leipzig [prev.
pubd as *Ber. Mus. Vlkerknd.
Leipzig*]

Jb. 'Niftarlake'
Jaarboekje 'Niftarlake'

Jb. Numi. & Geldgesch.
Jahrbuch für Numismatik und
Geldgeschichte [prev. pubd as *Dt.
Jb. Numi.*]

Jb. Oberösterreich. Musver.
Jahrbuch des
Oberösterreichischen
Musealvereines [from 1967 pubd
in 2 pts: Abhandlungen and
Berichte; prev. pubd as *Jber. Mus.
Francisco-Carolinium*, *Ber. Mus.
Francisco-Carolinium*, cont. as *Jb.
Oberösterreich. Musver., Ges.
Landesknd.*]

*Jb. Oberösterreich. Musver., Ges.
Landesknd.*
Jahrbuch des O[ber]-
ö[sterreichischen] Musealvereines,
Gesellschaft für Landeskunde [see
Jb. Oberösterreich. Musver.]

J. Bombay Branch Royal Asiat. Soc.
Journal of the Bombay Branch of
the Royal Asiatic Society

J. Bombay Hist. Soc.
Journal of the Bombay Historical
Society

Jb. Oranjeboom
Jaarboek de Oranjeboom

Jb. Österreich. Bundesdkmlamt.
Jahrbuch des Österreichischen
Bundesdenkmalamtes

Jb. Österreich. Byz.
Jahrbuch der Österreichischen
Byzantinistik [prev. pubd as *Jb.
Österreich. Byz. Ges.*]

Jb. Österreich. Byz. Ges.
Jahrbuch der Österreichischen
byzantinischen Gesellschaft
[cont. as *Jb. Österreich. Byz.*]

Jb. Österreich. Kstgesch.
Jahrbuch für österreichische
Kunstgeschichte

Jb. Österreich. Kultgesch.
Jahrbuch für österreichische
Kulturgeschichte

J. Boston Soc. Civil Engin.
Journal of the Boston Society of
Civil Engineers

Jb. Oud-Utrecht
Jaarboek Oud-Utrecht

Jb. Pf. Kst.
Jahrbuch zur Pflege der Künste

Jb. Prähist. Ethnog. Kst
Jahrbuch für prähistorische und
ethnographische Kunst

Jb. Preuss. Kstsamml.
Jahrbuch der preussischen
Kunstsammlungen [prev. pubd as
Jb. Kön.-Preuss. Kstsamml.]

Jb. Preuss. Kultbes.
Jahrbuch preussischer
Kulturbesitz [prev. pubd as *Jb.
Stift. Preuss. Kultbesitz*]

J. Brasil
Jornal do Brasil

Jb. Rhein. Dkmlpf.
Jahrbuch der rheinischen
Denkmalpflege

*Jb. Rhein. Ver. Dkmlpf. &
Landschaftsschutz*
Jahrbuch [des] rheinischen
Vereins für Denkmalpflege und
Landschaftsschutz

J. Brit. Archaeol. Assoc.
Journal of the British
Archaeological Association

J. Brit. Archaeol. Soc.
Journal of the British
Archaeological Society

J. Brit. Guiana Mus. & Zoo
Journal of the British Guiana
Museum and Zoo

Jb. Röm.-Ger. Zentmus.
Jahrbuch des Römisch-
germanischen Zentralmuseums

Jb. Ruhr-U. Bochum
Jahrbuch der Ruhr-Universität
Bochum

Jb. Salzburg. Mus. Carolino Augusteum
Jahrbuch des Salzburger Museums
Carolino Augusteum [prev. pubd
as *Jschr. Salzburg. Mus. Carolino
Augusteum, Salzburg. Musbl.*]

Jb. Schweiz. Inst. Kstwiss.
Jahrbuch des schweizerischen
Instituts für Kunstwissenschaft

J. B. Speed A. Mus. Bull.
J. B. Speed Art Museum Bulletin

*Jb. Staatl. Kstsamml. Baden-
Württemberg*
Jahrbuch der staatlichen
Kunstsammlungen in Baden-
Württemberg

Jb. Staatl. Kstsamml. Dresden
Jahrbuch der staatlichen
Kunstsammlungen Dresden [prev.
pubd as *Beitr. & Ber. Staatl.
Kstsamml. Dresden*]

*Jb. Staatl. Mus. Mineral. & Geol.
Dresden*
Jahrbuch des Staatlichen Museums
für Mineralogie und Geologie zu
Dresden

Jb.: Stad Brugge Stedl. Mus.
Jaarboek: Stad Brugge stedelijke
musea [Yearbook: City of Bruges
Municipal Museums]

Jb. Stift. Klosterneuburg
Jahrbuch des Stiftes
Klosterneuburg

Jb. Stift. Preuss. Kultbesitz
Jahrbuch (der) Stiftung
preussischer Kulturbesitz [cont. as
Jb. Preuss. Kultbes.]

J. Burma Res. Soc.
Journal of the Burma Research
Society

Jb. Ver. Altertfreund. Rheinlande
Jahrbücher des Vereins von
Altertumsfreunden im Rheinlande
[cont. as *Bonn. Jb.*; *Bonn. Jb. Ver.
Altertfreund. Rheinlande &
Rhein.Provmus. Bonn*; *Bonn. Jb.
Rhein. Landesmus. Bonn & Ver.
Altertfreund. Rheinlande*]

Jb. Ver. Augsburg. Bistumsgesch.
Jahrbuch des Vereins für
Augsburger Bistumsgeschichte

Jb. Verband. Dt. Mus. Tschech. Repub.
Jahrbuch des Verbandes der deutschen Museen in der tschechoslowakischen Republik

Jb. Ver. Christ. Kst
Jahrbuch des Vereins für christliche Kunst

Jb. Ver. Christ. Kst München
Jahrbuch des Vereins für christliche Kunst in München

Jb. Ver. Gesch. Stadt Wien
Jahrbuch des Vereins für Geschichte der Stadt Wien

Jb. Ver. Heimatknd. Kreis Merzig
Jahrbuch des Vereins für Heimatkunde Kreis Merzig

Jb.: Ver. Oranje-Nassau Mus.
Jaarboek: Vereniging Oranje-Nassau Museum

Jb.: Ver. Oudhdknd. & Hist. (Geschknd.) Kring. België
Jaarboeken: Vereniging van oudheidkundige en historische (geschiedkundige) kringen van België [Yearbook: Society of the Archaeological and Historical Circles of Belgium]

Jb. Vlksknd.
Jahrbuch für Volkskunde

Jb. Vorarlberg. Landesmusver.
Jahrbuch des Vorarlberger Landesmuseumsvereines

Jb. Wien. Goethe-Ver.
Jahrbuch des Wiener Goethe-Vereins

J. Byelorus. Stud.
Journal of Byelorussian Studies

Jb. Zentinst. Kstgesch.
Jahrbuch des Zentralinstituts für Kunstgeschichte

J. CA & Gt Basin Anthropol.
Journal of California and Great Basin Anthropology

J. Can. A. Hist.
Journal of Canadian Art History

J. Can. Stud.
Journal of Canadian Studies

J. Cent. Asia
Journal of Central Asia

J. Cent. Eur. Affairs
Journal of Central European Affairs

J. Cer. Hist.
Journal of Ceramic History

J. Ceylon Branch Royal Asiat. Soc.
Journal of the Ceylon Branch of the Royal Asiatic Society

J. Ceylon Inst. Architects
Journal of the Ceylon Institute of Architects

J. Chester Archaeol. Soc.
Journal of the Chester Archaeological Society [prev. pubd as *Chester & N. Wales Archaol. Soc.*; *Archit., Archaeol., & Hist. Soc. Co., City & Neighbourhood Chester J.*]

J. Chin. Archaeol.
Journal of Chinese Archaeology

J. Ch. Mnmts Soc.
Journal of the Church Monuments Society

J. Co. Kildare Archaeol. Soc.
Journal of the County Kildare Archaeological Society

J. Co. Louth Archaeol. Soc.
Journal of the County Louth Archaeological Society

J. Comérc.
Jornal do comércio

J. Contemp. A.
Journal of Contemporary Art

J. Contemp. Hist.
Journal of Contemporary History

J. Cork Hist. & Archaeol. Soc.
Journal of the Cork Historical and Archaeological Society

J. Cult. Assoc. Solomon Islands
Journal of the Cultural Association of the Solomon Islands

J. Cult. & Ideas
Journal of Cultures and Ideas

J. Cuneiform Stud.
Journal of Cuneiform Studies

J. Dames & Modes
Le Journal des dames et des modes

J. Dan. Archaeol.
Journal of Danish Archaeology

J. Débats
Journal des débats

J. Dec. A. Soc.
Journal of the Decorative Arts Society

J. Dec. & Propaganda A.
Journal of the Decorative and Propaganda Arts

J. Des. & Manuf.
Journal of Design and Manufactures

J. Early S. Dec. A.
Journal of Early Southern Decorative Arts

J. Eccles. Hist.
Journal of Ecclesiastical History

J. Econ. Hist.
Journal of Economic History

J. Econ. & Soc. Hist. Orient
Journal of the Economic and Social History of the Orient

Jedermann Eigener Fussball
Jedermann sein eigener Fussball

J. Egyp. Archaeol.
Journal of Egyptian Archaeology

Jelenkor
Jelenkor: Irodalmi és művészeti folyoirat [Present times]

Jen. Allg. Lit.-Ztg
Jenaische allgemeine Literatur-Zeitung

J. Eng. Lit. Hist.
Journal of English Literary History

Jerusalem Rep.
The Jerusalem Report

Jerusalem Stud. Jew. Flklore
Jerusalem Studies in Jewish Folklore

J. Ethiop. Stud.
Journal of Ethiopian Studies

Jew. A.
Jewish Art [prev. pubd as *J. Jew. A.*]

Jewel. Stud.
Jewellery Studies

Jew. Flklore & Ethnol. Newslett.
Jewish Folklore and Ethnology Newsletter

Jew. Hist. Soc. England: Trans.
Jewish Historical Society of England: Transactions

Jew. Q. Rev.
Jewish Quarterly Review

J. Expermntl Child Psychol.
Journal of Experimental Child Psychology

J. Expermntl Psychol.
Journal of Experimental Psychology: Human Perception and Performance

J. Faits
Journal des faits

J. Field Archaeol.
Journal of Field Archaeology

J. Franklin Inst.
Journal of the Franklin Institute

J. Furn. Hist. Soc.
Journal of the Furniture History Society

Jgabe: Altmärk. Mus. Stendhal
Jahresgabe: Altmärkisches Museum Stendhal

J. Galway Archaeol. & Hist. Soc.
Journal of the Galway Archaeological and Historical Society

J. Gdn Hist.
Journal of Garden History

J. Genève
Journal de Genève

J. Gen. Psychol.
Journal of General Psychology

J. Geom.
Journal of Geometry

J. Glass Stud.
Journal of Glass Studies

J. Gtr India Soc.
Journal of the Greater India Society

J. Gujarat Res. Soc.
Journal of the Gujarat Research Society

J. Hell. Stud.
Journal of Hellenic Studies

J. Herald. Soc. Scotland
Journal of the Heraldry Society of Scotland

Jhft. Österreich. Archäol. Inst. Wien
Jahreshefte des österreichischen archäologischen Institutes in Wien [cont. as *Wien. Jhft.*; reverts to *Jhft. Österreich. Archäol. Inst. Wien*]

J. Hist. Archit.
Journal d'histoire de l'architecture

J. Hist. Astron.
Journal for the History of Astronomy

J. Hist. Col.
Journal of the History of Collections

J. Hist. Geog.
Journal of Historical Geography

J. Hist. Ideas
Journal of the History of Ideas

J. Hist. & Litt.
Journal historique et littéraire [prev. pubd as *Rev. Belge*]

J. Hist. Medic. & Allied. Sci.
Journal of the History of Medicine and Allied Sciences

J. Hist. Metal. Soc.
Journal of the Historical Metallurgy Society

J. Hist. Sexuality
Journal of the History of Sexuality

J. Hist. Soc. Nigeria
Journal of the Historical Society of Nigeria

J. Hong Kong Branch Royal Asiat. Soc.
Journal of the Hong Kong Branch of the Royal Asiatic Society

Jiangsu Mus. & Jiangsu Archaeol. Stud. Confer.
Jiangsu Museum and Jiangsu Archaeological Study Conference

Jian Han Kaogu [Jiang Han archaeology]

Jianzhu Lishi Yu Lilun [Corpus of architectural history and theory]

Jianzhu Shi [History of architecture]

Jianzhu Shi Lunwen Ji [Collection of essays on history of architecture]

Jianzhu Xuebao [Architectural journal]

Jiaoyu Zazhi

J. Illus.
Le Journal illustré

J. Ind. A. & Indust.
Journal of Indian Art and Industry

Jindan Hakbo

J. Ind. Hist.
Journal of Indian History

J. Ind. Mus.
Journal of Indian Museums

J. Ind. Soc. A.
Journal of the Indian Society of Art

J. Ind. Soc. Orient. A.
Journal of the Indian Society of Oriental Art

J. Ind. Textile Hist.
Journal of Indian Textile History

J. Inf. Sci.
Journal of Information Science

Jinri Hanguo [Korea today]

J. Inst. A. Educ.
Journal of the Institute of Art Education

J. Inst. Architects, Malaya
Journal of the Institute of Architects, Malaya

J. Inst. Chin. Stud., Hong Kong
Journal of the Institute of Chinese Studies, Hong Kong

J. Inst. Civ. Engin.
Journal of the Institution of Civil Engineers

J. Inst. Metals
Journal of the Institute of Metals

J. Inst. Wood Sci.
Journal of the Institute of Wood Science

J. Int. Arqueol. & Etnog.
Jornadas internacionales de arqueología y etnografía

J. Int. Assoc. Buddhist Stud.
Journal of the International Association of Buddhist Studies

J. Interdiscip. Hist.
Journal of Interdisciplinary History

J. Irish Rlwy Rec. Soc.
Journal of the Irish Railway Record Society

J. Iron & Steel Inst.
Journal of the Iron and Steel Institute

J. Israel Inst. Architects
Journal of the Israel Institute of Architects

J. Jap. Stud.
Journal of Japanese Studies

J. Jew. A.
Journal of Jewish Art [cont. as *Jew. A.*]

J. Jew. Stud.
Journal of Jewish Studies

J. Land & Pub. Utility Econ.
Journal of Land and Public Utility Economics

J. Lat. Amer. Lore
Journal of Latin American Lore

J. Lat. Amer. Stud.
Journal of Latin American Studies

J. Legis. Assembly Prov. Canada
Journals of the Legislative Assembly of the Province of Canada

J. London Soc.
Journal of the London Society

J. Luxus & Mod.
Journal des Luxus und der Moderne

J. Madhya Pradesh Itihasa Parishad
Journal of the Madhya Pradesh Itihasa Parishad

J. Maharaja Sayajirao U., Baroda
Journal of the Maharaja Sayajirao University, Baroda

J. Malay. Branch Royal Asiat. Soc.
Journal of the Malayan Branch of the Royal Asiatic Society

J. Manx Mus.
Journal of the Manx Museum

J. Med. Hist.
Journal of Medieval History

J. Medit. Anthropol. & Archaeol.
Journal of Mediterranean Anthropology and Archaeology

J. Med. & Ren. Stud.
Journal of Medieval and Renaissance Studies

J. Menuiserie
Journal de la menuiserie

J. Metals
Journal of Metals

J. Mode & Goût
Le Journal de la mode et du goût

J. Mod. Hist.
Journal of Modern History

J. Morris Soc.
Journal of the William Morris Society

J. Mus. Ethnog.
Journal of Museum Ethnography

J. Mus. F.A., Boston
Journal of the Museum of Fine Arts, Boston

J. N. Cer. Soc.
Journal of the Northern Ceramic Society

J. N. China Branch Royal Asiat. Soc.
Journal of the North China Branch of the Royal Asiatic Society

J. Negro Hist.
Journal of Negro History

J. New Haven Colony Hist. Soc.
Journal of the New Haven Colony Historical Society

J. New World Archaeol.
Journal of New World Archaeology

J. N. Mus. Ceylon
Journal of the National Museums of Ceylon

J. Northampton Mus. & A.G.
Journal of the Northampton Museums and Art Gallery

J. Nr E. Stud.
Journal of Near Eastern Studies

J. Numi. Soc. India
Journal of the Numismatic Society of India

J. Officiel
Journal officiel [prev. pubd as *Moniteur Univl*]

John Donne J.
John Donne Journal

J. Oman Stud.
Journal of Oman Studies

Jong Holland

J. Optical Soc. America
Journal of the Optical Society of America

J. Orient. Inst., Baroda
Journal of the Oriental Institute of Maharajah Sayajirao University, Baroda

J. Orient. Res.
Journal of Oriental Research

Jour & Nuit
Jour et nuit

J. Pacific Hist.
Journal of Pacific History

J. Panjab Hist. Soc.
Journal of the Panjab Historical Society

J. Paris
Journal de Paris

J. Philos.
Journal of Philosophy

J. Phot. Sci.
Journal of Photographic Science

J. Phot. Soc.
Journal of the Photographic Society

J. Playing Card Soc.
Journal of the Playing Card Society

J. Polynes. Soc.
Journal of the Polynesian Society

J. Pop. Cult.
Journal of Popular Culture

J. Portugal Med.
Jornadas sobra Portugal medieval

J. Pre-Raphaelite & Aesth. Stud.
Journal of Pre-Raphaelite and Aesthetic Studies

J. Pre-Raphaelite Stud.
Journal of Pre-Raphaelite Studies [prev. pubd as *Pre-Raphaelite Rev.*]

J. Prestressed Concr. Inst.
Journal of the Prestressed Concrete Institute

J. & Proc. A. & Crafts Soc. Ireland
Journal and Proceedings of the Arts and Crafts Society of Ireland

J. & Proc. Asiat. Soc. Bengal
Journal and Proceedings of the Asiatic Society of Bengal [prev. pubd as *J. Asiat. Soc. Bengal*; cont. as *J. Asiat. Soc.*]

J. Proc. Royal Austral. Hist. Soc.
Journal of the Proceedings of the Royal Australian Historical Society

J. Proc. Royal Inst. Brit. Architects
Journal of the Proceedings of the Royal Institute of British Architects

J. Prtg Hist. Soc.
Journal of the Printing Historical Society

J. Punjab Hist. Soc.
Journal of the Punjab Historical Society

J. Reg. Cult. Inst.
Journal of the Regional Cultural Institute

J. Relig. Africa
Journal of Religion in Africa

J. Res. Soc. Pakistan
Journal of the Research Society of Pakistan

J. RIBA
Journal of the Royal Institute of British Architects [prev. pubd as & cont. as *RIBA J.*]

J. Rire
Journal pour rire

J. Roman Archaeol.
Journal of Roman Archaeology

J. Roman Stud.
Journal of Roman Studies

J. Rouen
Journal de Rouen

J. Royal Anthropol. Inst. GB & Ireland
Journal of the Royal Anthropological Institute of Great Britain and Ireland [prev. pubd as *J. Anthropol. Inst. GB & Ireland*]

J. Royal Archit. Inst. Canada
Journal of the Royal Architectural Institute of Canada

J. Royal Asiat. Soc. GB & Ireland
Journal of the Royal Asiatic Society of Great Britain and Ireland

J. Royal Asiat. Soc., Sri Lankan Branch
Journal of the Royal Asiatic Society, Sri Lankan Branch [incorp. *Proc. Royal Asiat. Soc., Ceylon Branch*]

J. Royal Cent. Asian Soc.
Journal of the Royal Central Asian Society

J. Royal Coll. Phys.
Journal of the Royal College of Physicians

J. Royal Geog. Soc.
Journal of the Royal Geographical Society

J. Royal Hist. & Archaeol. Assoc. Ireland
Journal of the Royal Historical and Archaeological Association of Ireland

J. Royal Hort. Soc.
Journal of the Royal Horticultural Society

J. Royal Inst.
Journal of the Royal Institution

J. Royal Soc. A.
Journal of the Royal Society of Arts

J. Royal Soc. Antiqua. Ireland
Journal of the Royal Society of Antiquaries of Ireland

J. Royal Soc. W. Australia
Journal of the Royal Society of Western Australia

J. Royal Vict. Inst. Architects
Journal of the Royal Victorian Institute of Architects

J. Saitama U. (For. Lang. & Lit.)
Journal of Saitama University (Foreign Languages and Literature)

J. San Diego Hist.
Journal of San Diego History

J. Sav.
Journal des savants

J.: S. CA A. Mag.
Journal: Southern California Arts Magazine

J. SC Hist. Soc.
Journal of the South Carolina History Society

J. Schoenberg Inst.
Journal of the Arnold Schoenberg Institute

Jschr. Mitteldt. Vorgesch.
Jahresschrift für mitteldeutsche Vorgeschichte [prev. pubd as *Jschr. Vorgesch. Sächs.-Thüring. Länder*]

Jschr. Salzburg. Mus. Carolino Augusteum
Jahresschrift des Salzburger Museums Carolino Augusteum [prev. pubd as & reverts to *Salzburg. Musbl.*; then to *Jschr. Salzburg. Mus. Carolino Augusteum*; cont. as *Jb. Salzburg. Mus. Carolino Augusteum*]

Jschr. Vorgesch. Sächs.-Thüring. Länder
Jahresschrift für die Vorgeschichte der sächsischen-thüringischen Länder [cont. as *Jschr. Mitteldt. Vorgesch.*]

J. Sci. & A.
Journal of Science and the Arts

J. SC Medic. Assoc.
Journal of the South Carolina Medical Association

J. Scot. Georg. Soc.
Journal of the Scottish Georgian Society

J. SE Asian Hist.
Journal of Southeast Asian History

J. SE Asian Stud.
Journal of Southeast Asian Studies

J. Siam Soc.
Journal of the Siam Society

J. Soc. A.
Journal of the Society of Arts

J. Soc. Africanistes
Journal de la Société des africanistes [cont. as *J. Africanistes*]

J. Soc. Américanistes
Journal de la Société des américanistes

J. Soc. Archit. Hist.
Journal of the Society of Architectural Historians [prev. pubd as *J. Amer. Soc. Archit. Hist.*]

J. Soc. Bibliog. Nat. Hist.
Journal of the Society for the Bibliography of Natural History

J. Soc. Friends Dunblane Cathedral
Journal of the Society of Friends of Dunblane Cathedral

J. Soc. Friends Glasgow Cathedral
Journal of the Society of Friends of Glasgow Cathedral

J. Soc. Glass Tech.
Journal of the Society of Glass Technology

J. Soc. Océanistes
Journal de la Société des océanistes

J. Soc. Pop. & Répub. A.
Journal de la Société populaire et républicaine des arts

J. Soc. Psychol.
Journal of Social Psychology

J. Soc. Sci. & Human.
Journal of Social Sciences and Humanities

J. Soc. Stud. Egyp. Ant.
Journal of the Society for the Study of Egyptian Antiquities

J. Solomon Islands Mus. Assoc.
Journal of the Solomon Islands Museum Association

J. Stained Glass
Journal of Stained Glass

J. Steward Anthropol. Soc.
Journal of the Steward Anthropological Society

J. St Pétersbourg
Journal de St Pétersbourg

J. Straits Branch Royal Asiat. Soc.
Journal of the Straits Branch of the Royal Asiatic Society

J. Textile Inst.
Journal of the Textile Institute

J. Theol. Stud.
Journal of Theological Studies

J.: Tiles & Archit. Cer. Soc.
Journal: Tiles and Architectural Ceramics Society

J. Town Plan. Inst.
Journal of the Town Planning Institute

J. Typograph. Res.
Journal of Typographic Research [cont. as *Visible Lang.*]

Judaism

Jud. Boh.
Judaica Bohemiae

Jugend
Jugend: Illustrierte Wochenschrift für Kunst und Leben [cont. as *Münchn. Jugend*; reverts to *Jugend*]

Junge Kst
Junge Kunst

Junge Menschen

J. United Prov. Hist. Soc.
Journal of the United Provinces Historical Society [cont. as *J.U.P. Hist. Soc.*]

J.U.P. Hist. Soc.
Journal of the U.P. Historical Society [prev. pubd as *J. United Prov. Hist. Soc.*]

Jurablätter

J. Urban Hist.
Journal of Urban History

J. Uttar Pradesh Hist. Soc.
Journal of the Uttar Pradesh Historical Society

J. Varendra Res. Mus.
Journal of the Varendra Research Museum

Jversl. Fund. Hondius
Jaarverslag Fundation Hondius

Jversl. Oranje-Nassau Mus.
Jaarverslag Oranje-Nassau Museum

Jversl. Rijksbureau Ksthist. Doc. 's-Gravenhage
Jaarverslag Rijksbureau voor kunsthistorische documentatie te 's-Gravenhage

Jversl. Sticht. Textielgesch.
Jaarverslag Stichting textielgeschiedenis

Jversl. Ver. Rembrandt
Jaarverslag Vereniging Rembrandt

J. Walters A.G.
Journal of the Walters Art Gallery

J. Warb. & Court. Inst.
Journal of the Warburg and Courtauld Institutes [prev. pubd as *J. Warb. Inst.*]

J. Warb. Inst.
Journal of the Warburg Institute [cont. as *J. Warb. & Court. Inst.*]

J. W. China Border Res. Soc.
Journal of the West China Border Research Society

J. World Hist.
Journal of World History

J. World Prehist.
Journal of World Prehistory

Jyväskylän Yliopiston Taidehist. Laitoksen Julkaisuja
Jyväskylän yliopiston taidehistorian laitoksen julkaisuja [Proceedings of the Department of Art History of the University of Jyväskylä]

Kadmos

Kaifeng Shiyuan Xuebao

Kailash
Kailash: A Journal of Himalayan Studies

Kairos

Kalamanjari

Kalòs
Kalòs: Invito al collezionismo

Kalpataru

Kamptal-Stud.
Kamptal-Studien

Kansai Daigaku Tozai Gakujutsu Kenkyujo Kiyo

Kansong Munhwa

Kantú, Rev. A.
Kantú, revista de arte

Kaogu [Archaeology; prev. pubd as *Kaogu Tongxun*]

Kaogu Tongxun [cont. as *Kaogu*]

Kaogu Xuebao [Archaeological studies; Acta archaeologica Sinica]

Kaogu Xue Jikan

Kaogu Yu Wenwu [Archaeology and cultural artefacts]

Kartinna Gal.
Kartinna Galleriya

Kastrioti

Katunob

Kazan. Muz. Vestnik
Kazansky Muzeyny vestnik [Kazan Museum bulletin]

Kêmi: Rev. Philol. & Archéol. Egyp. & Copt.
Kêmi: Revue de philologie et d'archéologie égyptiennes et coptes

Kenchiku Bunka/Archit. Cult.
Kenchiku Bunka/Architecture Culture

Kenchikushi

Kenchiku Shigaku

Kenchiku-shi Kenkyū

Kennedy Q.
Kennedy Quarterly

Kennemer Contouren

Kenya Past and Present

Képzömüvészeti Szemle [Fine arts review]

Kerala Soc. Pap.
Kerala Society Papers

Keramos
Keramos: Zeitschrift der Gesellschaft der Keramikfreunde e.V.

Ker.-Freunde Schweiz
Keramik-Freunde der Schweiz

Kermes

Ker. Rundschau
Keramische Rundschau

Ker. & Steklo
Keramika i steklo

2 x 2
Kettö [Two by two]

Kew Bull.
Kew Bulletin

Keyhan Int.
Keyhan International

Khana

Khudozhestvennaya Gaz.
Khudozhestvennaya gazeta [Artistic gazette]

Khudozhestvennyy Zhurnal [Artistic journal]

Khudozhestvennyye Sokrovishcha Rossii [Artistic treasures of Russia]

Khudozhnik [The artist]

Kikan Kokogaku
Kikan kokogaku [Archaeology quarterly]

Kimoliaka

Kingston-upon-Hull Mus. Bull.
Kingston-upon-Hull Museums Bulletin

Kinran Tanki Daigaku Kenkyūjoshi [Magazine of the Research Centre of the Kinran Junior College]

Kirchenkunst

Kiyō

Kladderadatsch

Kleine Beitr. Staatl. Mus. Vlkerknd. Dresden
Kleine Beiträge des Staatlichen Museums für Völkerkunde Dresden

Kleine Schr. Ges. Bild. Kst Mainz
Kleine Schriften der Gesellschaft für bildende Kunst in Mainz

Kleine Schr. Ges. Theatgesch.
Kleine Schriften der Gesellschaft für Theatergeschichte

Klimtstudien

Klingen [The blade]

Klio

Klironomias

Kniga

Knizhnyye Novosti [Book news]

Književna Repub.
Književna republika

Knowl. Org.
Knowledge Organization

Kobijutsu
Kobijutsu [Quarterly review of fine arts]

Kodai o Kangaeru [Thoughts on antiquity]

Kodai Kenkyū [Antiquity research]

Kōgei

Kogo Misul [Art and archaeology]

Kokalos [Università degli studi, Palermo]

Kokka

Kokogaku Zasshi [Journal of archaeology]

Kokoku & Bunka [Lake country and culture]

Kokusai Kenchiku [International architecture]

Kollasuyo
Kollasuyo: Revista mensual de estudios bolivianos

Köln. Dombl.
Kölner Domblatt

Köln. Jb. Vor- & Frühgesch.
Kölner Jahrbuch für Vor- und Frühgeschichte

Köln. Mus. Bull.
Kölner Museums Bulletin

Komunik. SARP
Komunikat stowarzyszenia architektow polskich

Könch'uk

Kong Meng Xuebao [Confucius and Mencius studies]

Kongressakten

Kon. Ned. Oudhdknd. Bond: Bull. KNOB
Koninklijke Nederlandse oudheidkundige bond: Bulletin KNOB [Royal Dutch Archaeological Association: Bulletin KNOB; prev. pubd as *Bull. Ned. Oudhdknd. Bond*; *Oudhdknd. Jb.*; *Bull. Kon. Ned. Oudhdknd. Bond*]

Konstrevy [Art review]

Konstvännen [The art friend]

Konstvärlden [Art world]

Kontakti

Kontakt Med Nmus.
Kontakt med Nationalmuseum

Kor. Cult.
Korean Culture

Korea J.
Korea Journal

Korea-Kultmag.
Korea-Kulturmagazin

Koreana

Korrbl. Arbeitskreises Siebenbürg. Landeskd.
Korrespondenzblatt des Arbeitskreises für siebenbürgische Landeskunde [prev. pubd as *Siebenbürg. Vjschr.*; *Korrbl. Ver. Siebenbürg. Landeskd.*; cont. as *Z. Siebenbürg. Landeskd.*]

Korrbl. Ver. Siebenbürg. Landeskd.
Korrespondenzblatt des Vereins für siebenbürgische Landeskunde [see *Korrbl. Arbeitskreises Siebenbürg. Landeskd.*]

Kortárs

Korunk [Coronet]

Kraichgau

Kralicke Tvrze
Z kralicke tvrze

Krasnaya Zvezda [Red star]

Krasnyy Chernomorets [Red Black Sea sailor]

Kratkiye Soobshcheniya Inst. Arkheol. AN SSSR
Kratkiye soobshcheniya Instituta arkheologii Akademii nauk SSSR [Brief notes of the Institute of Archaeology of the Academy of Sciences of the USSR]

Kratkiye Soobshcheniya Inst. Istor. Mat. Kul't.
Kratkiye soobshcheniya Instituta istorii material'noy kul'tury [Brief notes of the Institute for the History of Material Culture]

Kremsmünster Stiftsarchv
Kremsmünster Stiftsarchiv

Křest'anská Rev.
Křest'anská revue [Christian review]

Krit. Ber.
Kritische Berichte

Kritika
Kritika: Művelő despolitikai és kritikai lap

Kritika Chron.
Kritika chronica [Cretan chronicle]

Kroeber Anthropol. Soc.: Pap.
Kroeber Anthropological Society: Papers

Krokodil

Kron. Hist. Genoot. Utrecht
Kroniek van het Historisch genootschap te Utrecht

Kronika

Kron. Kst & Kult.
Kroniek van kunst en kultur

Kron. Nootdorp
Kroniek van Nootdorp

Kron. Rembrandthuis
Kroniek van het Rembrandthuis

Kron. Slov. Mest
Kronika slovenských mest [Chronicle of Slovak towns]

Kst Alle: Mal., Plast., Graph., Archit.
Kunst für alle: Malerei, Plastik, Graphik, Architektur

Kst & Altert.
Kunst und Altertum

Kst & Ant.
Kunst und Antiquitäten

Kst Bedeuttr.
Kunst als Bedeutungsträger

Kst-Bull. Schweiz. Kstver.
Kunst-Bulletin des Schweizerischen Kunstvereins

Kstchron. & Kstlit.
Kunstchronik und Kunstliteratur [suppl. of *Z. Bild. Kst*]

Kstchron. & Kstmarkt
Kunstchronik und Kunstmarkt: Wochenschrift für Kenner und Sammler

Kstdkml. Freistaat Hessen
Die Kunstdenkmäler im Freistaat Hessen

Kst Dritten Reich
Kunst im dritten Reich [cont. as *Kst Dt. Reich*]

Kst Dt. Reich
Kunst im deutschen Reich [prev. pubd as *Kst Dritten Reich*]

Kstforum Int.
Kunstforum international: Die aktuelle Zeitschrift für alle Bereiche der bildenden Kunst

Kstführer Schweiz
Kunstführer durch die Schweiz

Kstgesch. Auslandes
Zur Kunstgeschichte des Auslandes

Kstgesch. Forsch. Rhein. Heimatbundes
Kunstgeschichtliche Forschungen des rheinischen Heimatbundes

Kstgesch. Geistesgesch.
Kunstgeschichte als Geistesgeschichte

Kstgesch. Ges.
Kunstgeschichtliche Gesellschaft

Kstgesch. Ges. Berlin
Kunstgeschichtliche Gesellschaft zu Berlin

Kstgesch. Jb. Bib. Hertz.
Kunstgeschichtliches Jahrbuch der Bibliotheca Hertziana [also known & cont. as *Röm. Jb. Kstgesch.*]

Kstgesch. Jb. Ksr.-Kön. Zent.-Komm. Erforsch. & Erhaltung Kst- & Hist. Dkml.
Kunstgeschichtliches Jahrbuch der K.-K. [Kaiserlich-Königlichen] Zentral-Kommission für Erforschung und Erhaltung der Kunst- und historischen Denkmale [cont. as *Jb. Ksthist. Inst.*; *Jb. Kstgesch.*; *Wien. Jb. Kstgesch.*]

Kstgesch. Nederlanden
Kunstgeschiedenis der Nederlanden

Kst & Gew.
Kunst und Gewerbe

Kst. Gew.
Die Kunst in Gewerbe

Kst & Handwk
Kunst und Handwerk

Ksthandwke Böhmen
Kunsthandwerke in Böhmen

Ksthaus Zürich Ges., Jber.
Kunsthaus der Züricher Gesellschaft, Jahresbericht

Kst Hessen & Mittelrhein
Kunst in Hessen und am Mittelrhein

Ksthist. Inst. [Graz]: Jb. Ksthist. Inst. U. Graz
Kunsthistorisches Institut [Graz]: Jahrbuch des kunsthistorischen Instituts der Universität Graz [cont. as *Ksthist. Jb. Graz*]

Ksthist. Jb. Graz
Kunsthistorisches Jahrbuch Graz [prev. pubd as *Ksthist. Inst. [Graz]: Jb. Ksthist. Inst. U. Graz*]

Ksthist. Meded. Rijksbureau Ksthist. Doc.
Kunsthistorische mededelingen van het Rijksbureau voor kunsthistorische documentatie [RKD; cont. as *Oud- Holland*]

Ksthist. Sällsk. Pubn
Konsthistoriska Sällskapets publikation [Art Historical Society's publication]

Ksthist. Tidskr.
Konsthistorisk tidskrift [Art historical magazine]

Kst. Idag
Kunsten idag [Art today]

Kstinf.
Kunstinformatie

Kstjb. Stadt Linz
Kunstjahrbuch der Stadt Linz

Kst & Kirche
Kunst und Kirche [occas. *Kunst der Kirche*]

Kst & Kstgew.
Kunst und Kunstgewerbe

Kst & Ksthandwk
Kunst und Kunsthandwerk

Kst & Kstler
Kunst und Künstler

Kst & Kult. [Oslo]
Kunst og kultur [Art and culture] [Oslo]

Kst & Kunstnere
Kunst og kunstnere [Art and artists]

Kst- & Levensbeeld.
Kunst- en levensbeelden

Kst: Mhft. Freie & Angewandte Kst
Kunst: Monatshefte für freie und angewandte Kunst [cont. as *Kst & S. Heim*]

Kst & Mus.
Kunst og museum

Kstmus. Årsskr.
Kunstmuseets årsskrift [Art Museum's yearbook]

Kst Orients
Kunst des Orients

Kstrundschau
Kunstrundschau

Kst & Sch.
Kunst und Schule

Kst Schleswig-Holstein
Kunst in Schleswig-Holstein

Kst & S. Heim
Die Kunst und das schöne Heim [prev. pubd as *Kst: Mhft. Freie & Angewandte Kst*]

Kst & Stein
Kunst und Stein

Kst & Unterricht
Kunst und Unterricht

Kst Volke
Die Kunst dem Volke

Kstwiss. Stud.
Kunstwissenschaftliche Studien

Kstwk
Das Kunstwerk: Eine Zeitschrift über alle Gebiete der bildenden Kunst

Ktema

Kuksagwan

Kult. Barai
Kultūros barai

Kulthist. Åb.
Kulturhistorisk årsbok [Culture history yearbook]

Kulthist. Leks. Nord. Midald.
Kulturhistorisk leksikon for nordisk middelalder [Cultural history dictionary of the Nordic middle ages]

Kult. Měsíčník Litoměřického Okresu
Kulturní měsíčník Litoměřického okresu [Cultural monthly of the Litoměřice region]

Kult. Naslestvo
Kulturno naslestvo

Kult. Pop.
Kultura popullore

Kultura

Kulture [Belgrade]

Kulturen
Kulturen: En årsbok [Culture: a yearbook] [cont. as *Kult. Värld*]

Kulturminder

Kultuurpatronen
Kultuurpatronen: Bulletin ethnografisch museum Delft

Kult. Värld
Kulturens värld [Culture's world; prev. pubd as *Kulturen*]

Kült. Ve Sanat
Kültür ve sanat [Culture and art]

Kul't. & Zhizn'
Kul'tura i zhizn' [Culture and life]

Kŭmgang

Kun. Bib. Hand.
Kungliga bibliotekets handlingar

Kunstblatt

Kunstchronik

Kunstfreund

Kunstgeschichte

Kunsthistoriker
Kunsthistoriker: Mitteilungen des Österreichischen Kunsthistorikerverbandes

Kunstkronyk [Art chronicle]

Kunstlicht

Kunstsammlungen [Dresden]

Kunstsammlungen [Stuttgart]

Kunstschrift

Kunstspiegel

Kuntur

Kun. Vitt., Hist. & Ant. Akad. Hand.
Kungl[iga] vitterhets, historie och antikvitets akademins handlingar

Kurier Literackonaukowy

Kurtrie. Jb.
Kurtrierisches Jahrbuch

Kush

Kusumanjali

Kwart. Archit. & Urb.
Kwartalnik architektury i urbanistyk [Architecture and urbanism quarterly]

Kwart. Hist. Kult. Mat.
Kwartalnik historii kultury materialnej [History of material culture quarterly]

KW11

Kyoto Daigaku Bungakubu Bigaku Bijutsu Kenkyūshitsu Kenkyu Kiyo [Bulletin of the Research Laboratory of Aesthetics and Art History, Kyoto University, Department of Literature]

Kyoto N. Mus. Bull.
Kyoto National Museum Bulletin

Kyp. Spoudai
Kypriakai spoudai [Cypriot studies]

KY Rev.
Kentucky Review

LA Architect

La Bulzana

La Battana

La Berio

La Bibliofilia

La Brièche

La Brigata

Labyrinthe
Labyrinthe: Journal mensuel des lettres et des arts

Labyrinthos
Labyrinthos: Studi e ricerche sulle arti nei secoli XVIII e XIX

La Casana

Lacerba

La Cité

La Colonna

La Cravache

La Critica

La Cultura

La Diana

Ladies Companion

Ladies Home J.
Ladies Home Journal

L'Adige

La Esfera

La Feuille

La Giara

La Griffa

L'Album

La Lettura

Lalit Kala

Lalit Kala Contemp.
Lalit kala contemporary

L'Almanacco

La Lumière

La Maison

L'Ambrosiano

La Mercanzia

Lampang Rep.
Lampang Reports

La Nación

La Nación [Chile]

Landfall

Landscape

Landscape Archit.
Landscape Architecture

Landscape Australia

Landscape Des.
Landscape Design

La Nef

La Nervie

La Notaría

Lantern

Lanterne Magique
La Lanterne magique

L'Anthropologie

L'Antiquaire

La Orquesta

La Paix

La Patrie

La Plume

La Prensa

La Prensa [Panama City]

La Presse

La Razón

L'Architettura

La Renaissance

La República: Supl. Dominical
La República: Suplemento dominical

Lares

L'Argileto

La Romagna

La Ronda

Larousse Mens.
Le Larousse mensuel

L'Art
L'Art: Revue hebdomadaire illustrée

L'Arte

L'Arte
L'Arte: Rivista di storia dell'arte [prev. pubd as *Archv Stor. A.*; cont. as *L'Arte: Riv. Stor. A. Med. & Mod.*]

L'Arte: Riv. Stor. A. Med. & Mod.
L'Arte: Rivista di storia dell'arte medievale e moderna [prev. pubd as *L'Arte; Archv Stor. A.*]

L'Artiste

La Silhouette

La Squilla

Lat. Amer. Persp.
Latin American Perspectives

Lat. Amer. Times
Latin American Times

Latomus

La Tribuna

La Triennale

Latv. Arkhit.
Latvijas arhitektúra

Latv. Inž. & Teh. Kongr. Biroja Žurnals
Latvijas inženieru un tehniku kongresa biroja žurnals

Latv. U. Raksti
Latvijas Universitatis Raktsi

L'Aube

Laudate

Laurentianum

L'Autorité

La Vanguardia

L'Avenç

La Vie

La Voce

La Vogue

La Zanzara

Le Beffroi

Lebensbild. Bayer. Schwaben
Lebensbilder aus dem bayerischen Schwaben

Le Charivari

Le Constitutionnel

Le Correspondant

Le Crapouillot

Lect. & A.
Lectura y arte

Lect. Tous
Lectures pour tous

Le Décadent

Le Document

Leeds A. Cal.
Leeds Art Calendar

Lef

Le Figaro

Left Rev.
The Left Review

Le Gaulois

Le Geste

Légion Hon.
Légion d'honneur

Le Globe

Le Home

Leibesübungen & Körperl. Erz.
Leibesübungen und körperliche Erziehung

Leids Ksthist. Jb.
Leids kunsthistorisch jaarboek

Leipzig. Charivari
Leipziger Charivari

Leisure Hour

Le Journal

L'Elan

L'Emulation [Société centrale d'architecture, Brussels]

Le Muse

L'Enciclopedia

Leningradskaya Panorama

Leonardo

Leonardo: Rass. Bibliog.
Il Leonardo: Rassegna bibliografica [prev. pubd as *Leonardo: Rass. Mens. Colt. It.*]

Leonardo: Rass. Mens. Colt. It.
Il Leonardo: Rassegna mensile della cultura italiana [cont. as *Leonardo: Rass. Bibliog.*]

Leonardo, Saggi & Ric.
Leonardo, saggi e ricerche

Le Parchemin

Le Patriote

Le Pays

L'Ephémère

Le Point

Le Portefeuille

Le Présent

Le Rationaliste

Le Rire

Le Salon

L'Esame

Les Arts [Paris]
Les Arts: Revue mensuelle des musées [Paris]

Les Beaux-Arts

Le Siècle

Leslie's Illus. News
Leslie's Illustrated News

Lessing Yb.
Lessing Yearbook

L'Estampille

Lesviaka

Le Symboliste

Le Témoin

Le Temps

L'Etendard

Lett. & A.
Lettres et les arts

Lett. Alb.
Lettres albanaises

Letteratura

Lett. Fr.
Lettres françaises

Lett. It.
Lettere italiane

Lett. It. Contemp.
Letteratura italiana contemporanea

Lett. & Not.: Inter. J. Eng. Prov. SJ
Letters and Notices: The Internal Journal of the English Provinces of the Society of Jesus

Lett. Vinc.
Lettura vinciana

Leuchtkugeln

Levant

Levante

Levende Kst
Levende kunst

Lèvres Nues
Les Lèvres nues

Le Yacht

L'Herne

L'Homme

Liaoning Daxue Xuebao

Lias

Lib. Chron.
Library Chronicle

Liberia-Forum

Liber. Stud. J.
Liberian Studies Journal

Lib. F.A.
Library of the Fine Arts

Lib. Q.
Library Quarterly

Librarium
Librarium: Zeitschrift der Schweizerischen Bibliophilen-Gesellschaft

Libri
Libri: International Library Review

Libri & Doc.
Libri e documenti

Libro & Stampe
Il Libro e le stampe

Lib. Trends
Library Trends

Liburni Civitas
Liburni civitas

Libya Ant.
Libya antiqua

Libyan Stud.
Libyan Studies

Licht & Waarheid
Licht en waarheid

Life

Lighting Res. & Technol.
Lighting Research and Technology

Liguria

Lilliput

L'Illustration
Illustration: Journal universel [cont. as *Nouv.-Fém.-France-Illus.*]

L'Image

L'Impero

Lin. Aragón
Linajes de Aragón

Lincs Hist. & Archaeol.
Lincolnshire History and Archaeology

Linde

Ling. & Lit. Stud. E. Europe
Linguistic and Literary Studies in Eastern Europe

Linnaean Soc. Proc.
Linnaean Society Proceedings

L'Intransigeant

Lippincott's Mthly Mag.
Lippincott's Monthly Magazine

Listín Diario

L'Italia

Literatura [Budapest]

Literatura [Warsaw]

Lit. Gaz.
i) Literaturnaya Gazeta
ii) The Literary Gazette

Lit. Gaz. & J. B. Lett., A. Sci. etc
The Literary Gazette and Journal of Belles Lettres, Arts, Sciences etc.

Lit. J.
Literary Journal

Lit. Krit.
Literaturnyy kritik [The literary critic]

Lit. & Māksla
Literatūra un māksla

Lit. Mus. Register A. Sci. & General Lit.
The Literary Museum or Register of Arts, Sciences and General Literature [prev. pubd as *The Museum* [London]]

Lit. Rev.
Literary Review

Littérature

Littérature [Paris]

Little Rev.
Little Review

Litt. Orient.
Litterae Orientales

Liturg. A.
Liturgical Arts

Litwiss. Jb.
Literaturwissenschaftliches Jahrbuch

Liverpool An. Archaeol. & Anthropol.
Liverpool Annals of Archaeology and Anthropology

Liverpool Bull.
Liverpool Bulletin

Liverpool Class. Mthly
Liverpool Classical Monthly

Living A.
Living Arts

Livre A.
Livre d'art

Livre & Est.
Le Livre et l'estampe

Ljetopis JAZU
Ljetopis Jugoslavenske akademije znanosti i umjetnosti [Chronicle of the Yugoslav Academy of Science and Fine Arts]

Local Govt Stud.
Local Government Studies

L'Occident

Lockwitzer Nachrichten
Lockwitzer Nachrichten

Locus Solus

L'Oeil

Logos

London Archaeologist

London Bull.
London Bulletin

London Chron.
London Chronicle

London J.
London Journal

London Mag.
London Magazine

London Rev. Bks
London Review of Books

London Soc.
London Society

Look

Lorraine Artiste
La Lorraine artiste

Lotus
Lotus: An International Review of Contemporary Architecture [cont. as *Lotus Int.*]

Lotus Int.
Lotus International [prev. pubd as *Lotus*]

Louisiana Hist.
Louisiana History

Louisiana Rev.
Louisiana Revue

Lraber

Lraber Hasarakakan Gitut'yunneri
Lraber hasarakakan gitut'yunneri

Lübeck. Mushft.
Lübecker Museumshefte

Ludwigsburg. Geschbl.
Ludwigsburger Geschichtsblätter

Luna-Park

L'Universo

L'Uomo

Luqman

Lusitânia

Lustige Bl.
Lustige Blätter

Lutheran Q.
Lutheran Quarterly

Lutherjb.
Lutherjahrbuch

Luzifer-Gnosis

Lycoming Coll. Mag.
Lycoming College Magazine

L'Ymagier

Lyra

Lyttelton Times

MA [Today]

Maal Og Minne

Maatsch. Lettknd., Bijdr. Hand.
Maatschappij van letterkunde, bijdragen tot de handelingen [Society of Literature, contributions to the reports]

Maatsch. Vl. Biblioph.
Maatschappij der Vlaamsche bibliofielen [Society of Flemish Bibliophiles]

Maatstaf

Maclean's

Macula

Mademoiselle

Madonna Verona

Madras J. Lit. & Sci.
Madras Journal of Literature and Science

Madrid. Forsch.
Madrider Forschungen

Madrid. Mitt.
Madrider Mitteilungen

Mag. A.
Magazine of Art [incorp. suppl. *RA Illus.* until 1904]

Mag. Amer. Hist.
Magazine of American History

Magasin Modes Nouv. Fr. & Angl.
Le Magasin des modes nouvelles françaises et anglaises [cont. as *J. Mode & Goût*]

Mag. Enc.
Magazine encyclopédique

Mag. F.A.
Magazine of Fine Arts

Mag. Hort.
Magazine of Horticulture

Maghreb Rev.
Maghreb Revue

Mag. Int.. Wohnen
Magazin für internationales Wohnen

Mag. Kst
Magazin Kunst

Mag. London
Magazine of London

Mag. Pittoresque
Magazine pittoresque

Magyar Épitőművészet [Hungarian
architecture]

Magyar Iparművészet [Hungarian
decorative arts]

Magyar Irás [Hungarian writing]

Magyar Irók [Hungarian writers]

*Magyar Mérnök- & Épitész-Egylet
Közlonye* [Bulletin of the Society of
Hungarian Engineers and Builders]

Magyar Műemlékvédelem [The
protection of historic monuments in
Hungary]

Magyar Művészet [Hungarian art]

*Magyar Művészettörténeti
Munkaközösség Évkönyve* [Hungarian
art historical public works annual]

Magyar Nemzeti Gal. Évkönyve
Magyar Nemzeti galéria évkönyve
[Hungarian National Gallery
annual]

Magyar Nemzeti Gal. Közleményei
Magyar Nemzeti galéria
közleményei [Hungarian National
Gallery bulletin]

Magyar Pszichológiai Szemle
[Hungarian psychology review]

*Magyar Tudományos Akad. Nyelv &
Irodalmi Tudományok Osztályának
Közleményei*
Magyar tudományos Akadémia
nyelv és irodalmi tudományok
osztályának közleményei
[Hungarian Academy of Sciences
Section for Linguistic and Literary
Sciences bulletin]

Mähr. Tagbl.
Mährisches Tagblatt

Mailande

Mainfränk. Hft.
Mainfränkische Hefte

Mainfränk. Jb. Gesch. & Kst
Mainfränkisches Jahrbuch für
Geschichte und Kunst

Main Lande

Maintenant

Mainz. Z.
Mainzer Zeitschrift

Maison Hier & Aujourd'hui
La Maison d'hier et d'aujourd'hui

Maîtres Oeuvre
Maîtres d'oeuvre

Majalah Ilmu-Ilmu Sastra Indonesia
[Indonesian journal of cultural
studies]

Majorossy Imre Muz. Ertesítője
Majorossy Imre Muzeúmának
ertesítője [Imre Majorossy
Museum bulletin]

Makedonika [Macedonia]

Makedoniki Zoi [Macedonian life]

Makedonska Rev.
Makedonska Revija [Macedonian
review]

Making NZ
Making New Zealand

Mäksla

Malahat Rev.
Malahat Review

Malay. Hist. J.
Malayan Historical Journal

Malaysian Numi. Soc. Newslett.
Malaysin Numismatic Society
Newsletter

Maltechnik
Maltechnik: Technische
Mitteilungen für Malerei und
Bildpflege [prev. pubd as *Dt. Z.
Maltechnik*; cont. as *Maltechnik,
Rest.*]

Maltechnik, Rest.
Maltechnik, Restauro [prev. pubd
as *Maltechnik*; *Dt. Z. Maltechnik*]

Man

Manchete

Mankind

Man NE
Man in the Northeast

Mannheim. Geschbl.
Mannheimer Geschichtsblätter:
Monatschrift für die Geschichte,
Altertums- und Volkskunde
Mannheims und der Pfalz

Mannheim. Hefte
Mannheimer Hefte

Man & Soc.
Man and Society

Manuscripta
Manuscripta: Information about
and Studies on Manuscripts

Manuscrit
Manuscrit: Revue de documents-
manuscrits

Mar. A.
Maritime Art

Mar. Advocate & Busy E.
Maritime Advocate and Busy East

Marathwada U.J.
Marathwada University Journal

Marburg. Jb. Kstgesch.
Marburger Jahrbuch für
Kunstgeschichte

Marburg. Jb. Kstwiss.
Marburger Jahrbuch für
Kunstwissenschaft

Marburg. Winckelmann-Programm
Marburger Winckelmann-
Programm

Marcatré

Marcha

Marches Sud-Ouest
Les Marches du Sud-Ouest

Mare Liberum

MA Rev.
Massachusetts Review

Marg

Marginalien

Mari [Annales de recherches
interdisciplnaires]

Marie

Marie Claire

Mariner's Mirror

Markgräflerland
Markgräflerland: Beiträge zu seiner
Geschichte und Kultur

Marmo

Marseille

Marsyas

Martello

Martin Fierro

Marxism Today

Marxist Persp.
Marxist Perspectives

Marzocco

MASCA J.
[Museum of Applied Science,
Center for Archaeology journal]

Maso Finiguerra

Mastatstva Belarus.
Mastatstva Belarusi [Art of
Belarus]

Mastera Isk. Isk.
Mastera iskusstva ob iskusstve
[Masters of art on art]

Master Builders

Master Drgs
Master Drawings

Mat. Arkheol. Ros.
Materialy po arkheologii Rossii
[Documents on Russian
archaeology]

Mat. Cult. Notes
Material Culture Notes

Mat. Hist. Bull.
Material History Bulletin

Mat. & Issledovaniya Arkheol. SSSR
Materialy i issledovaniya po
arkheologii SSSR [Archaeological
documents and research of the
USSR]

Mat. Kult. Tadzhikistana
Material'naya kul'tura
Tadzhikistana [Tadjik material
culture]

Mat. Rus. Isk.
Materialy po russkomu iskusstvu
[Documents on Russian art]

Mat. Turcica
Materialia turcica

MAVO

Mawazo

Mber. Kön. Preuss. Akad. Wiss. Berlin
Monatsberichte der Königlich
preussischen Akademie der
Wissenschaften zu Berlin

Mber. Kstwiss. & Ksthand.
Monatsberichte über
Kunstwissenschaft und
Kunsthandel

Mbl. Altert.-Ver. Wien
Monatsblatt des Altertum-Vereins
zu Wien

Mbl. Ver. Gesch. Stadt Wien
Monatsblatt des Vereins für
Geschichte der Stadt Wien

McCalls

McClure's Mag.
McClure's Magazine

Mdbl. Amstelodanum
Maandblad Amstelodanum

Mdbl. Beeld. Kst.
Maandblad voor beeldende
kunsten

Mdbl. Bond Heemschut
Maandblad van den Bond
Heemschut

Mdbl. Ned. Leeuw
Maandblad de Nederlandsch
Leeuw

Mdbl. Oud-Utrecht
Maandblad Oud-Utrecht

MD Hist. Mag.
Maryland Historical Magazine

Meanjin

Mécano

Mechanics' Mag.
Mechanics' Magazine

Mechlinia

Med. Aevum
Medium aevum

Med. Aevum Quotidianum
Medium aevum quotidianum

Medaglia

Med. Archaeol.
Medieval Archaeology

Meddel. Lunds U. Hist. Mus.
Meddelanden fra Lunds
universitets Historiska museum

Meddel. Ny Carlsberg
Meddelelser fra Ny Carlsberg
[Reports from New Carlsberg
(Glyptotek)]

Meddel. Thorvaldsens Mus.
Meddelelser fra Thorvaldsens
Museum [Reports from
Thorvaldsen's Museum]

Médec. Fr.
Médecine de France

Meded. Acad. Marine België
Mededelingen van de Marine
academie van België [Reports of
the Belgian Marine Academy]

Mededbl. Ned. Ver. Vrienden Cer.
Mededelingenblad Nederlandse
vereniging van vrienden van
ceramiek [prev. pubd as *Vrienden
Ned. Cer.: Mededbl.*] [Reports of
the Dutch Association of Friends
of Ceramics]

*Meded. Dienst Kst. & Wet. Gemeente
's-Gravenhage*
Mededelingen van de Dienst voor
kunsten en wetenschappen der
gemeente 's-Gravenhage [Reports
of the Service for Art and Science
of 's-Gravenhage municipality]

Meded. Gemeentemus. Den Haag
Mededelingen Gemeentemuseum
Den Haag [Reports of the
Municipal Museum]

*Meded. Gesch.- & Oudhdknd. Kring
Leuven & Omgev.*
Mededelingen van de geschied- en
oudheidkundige kring voor
Leuven en omgeving [Reports of
the Historical and Archaeological
Circle of Leuven and area]

*Meded. Kon. Akad. Wet., Afd.
Lettknd.*
Mededelingen der Koninklijke
academie van wetenschappen,
afdeeling letterkunde [Reports of
the Royal Academy of Sciences,
Literature Division]

Meded. Kon. Ned. Akad. Wet.
Mededelingen van de Koninklijke Nederlandse akademie voor wetenschappen [Reports of the Royal Dutch Academy of Sciences]

Meded. Ned. Hist. Inst. Rome
Mededelingen van het Nederlands historisch instituut te Rome [Reports of the Dutch Historical Institute in Rome; cont. as *Meded. Ned. Inst. Rome*]

Meded. Ned. Inst. Rome
Mededelingen van het Nederlands instituut te Rome [prev. pubd as *Meded. Ned. Hist. Inst. Rome*]

Meded. Sticht. Jacob Campo Weyerman
Mededelingen van de Stichting Jacob Campo Weyerman [Reports of the Jacob Campo Weyerman Foundation]

Medelhavsmus. Bull.
Medelhavsmuseet bulletin [Mediterranean Museum]

Med. & Human.
Medievalia et humanistica

Mediaevalia

Medic. Hist.
Medical History

Medit. Archaeol.
Mediterranean Archaeology

Méditerranée

Médium
Médium: Communication surréaliste

Medivia Aevum [Society for the Study of Medieval Languages and Literature]

Med. & Rin.
Medioevo e rinascimento

Med. Scandinavia
Medieval Scandinavia

Med. Stud.
Medieval Studies

Med. & Uman.
Medioevo e umanesimo

Meer Schoonheid
Meer schoonheid

Meggendorf. Bl.
Meggendorfer Blätter [cont. as *Meggendorf. Humorist. Bl.*; reverts to *Meggendorf. Bl.*; incorp. into *Flieg. Bl.*]

Meggendorf. Humorist. Bl.
Meggendorfers humoristische Blaetter [prev. pubd as & cont. as *Meggendorf. Bl.*]

Mehqarim Bageografiyah Shel Eretz-Israel
Mehqarim bageografiyah shel Eretz-Israel

Meinradsraben

Meishu

Meishujia [Artist]

Meishu Yanjiu [Art research]

Mél. Archéol. & Hist.
Mélanges d'archéologie et d'histoire

Mél. Archéol. & Hist.: Ecole Fr. Rome
Mélanges d'archéologie et d'histoire: L'Ecole française de Rome

Mél. Asiat.
Mélanges asiatiques

Mél. Bull. Mnmtl
Mélanges du bulletin monumental

Mél. Carthage
Mélanges de Carthage

Mél. Casa Velázquez
Mélanges de la Casa Velázquez

Mél. Dimče Koko
Mélanges Dimče Koko

Mél. Ecole Fr. Rome: Ant.
Mélanges de l'Ecole française de Rome: Antiquité

Mél. Ecole Fr. Rome: Moyen Age, Temps Mod.
Mélanges de l'Ecole française de Rome: Moyen âge, temps modernes

Mél. Inst. Dominicain Etud. Orient. Caire
Mélanges de l'Institut dominicain d'études orientales du Caire

Melita Hist.
Melita historica

Melozzo Forlì
Melozzo da Forlì

Mél. Stiennon
Mélanges Stiennon

Mél. U. St-Joseph
Mélanges de l'Université Saint-Joseph

Mém. Acad. Fr.
Mémoires de l'Académie française

Mém. Acad. Inscr. & B.-Lett.
Mémoires de l'Académie des inscriptions et belles-lettres

Mém. Acad. Montpellier
Mémoires de l'Académie de Montpellier

Mém. Acad. Royale Belgique: Cl. B.-A.
Mémoires de l'Académie royale de Belgique: Classe des beaux-arts

Mém. Acad. Royale Belgique: Cl. Sci.
Mémoires de l'Académie royale de Belgique: Classe des sciences

Mém. Acad. Royale Sci. & B.-Lett. [Berlin]
Mémoires de l'Académie royale des sciences et belles-lettres [Berlin]

Mém. Acad. Royale Sci., Lett. & B.-A.
Mémoires de l'Académie royale des sciences, des lettres et des beaux-arts de Belgique: Classe des beaux-arts

Mém. Acad. Royale Sci. & Lett. Danemark
Mémoires de l'Académie royale des sciences et lettres du Danemark

Mém. Acad. Sci.
Mémoires de l'Académie des sciences

Mém. Acad. Sci., A. & B.-Lett. Dijon
Mémoires de l'Académie des sciences, arts et belles-lettres de Dijon

Mém. Acad. Sci., B.-Lett. & A. Angers
Mémoires de l'Académie des sciences, belles-lettres et arts d'Angers

Mém. Acad. Sci., B.-Lett. & A. Clermont-Ferrand
Mémoires de l'Académie des sciences, belles-lettres et arts de Clermont-Ferrand

Mém. Acad. Sci., B.-Lett. & A. Marseille
Mémoires de l'Académie des sciences, belles-lettres et arts de Marseille

Mém. Acad. Sci., B.-Lett. & A. Savoie
Mémoires de l'Académie des sciences, belles-lettres et arts de Savoie

Mém. Acad. Sci., Inscr. & B.-Lett. Toulouse
Mémoires de l'Académie des sciences, inscriptions et belles-lettres de Toulouse

Mém. Acad. Stanislas
Mémoires de l'Académie de Stanislas

Mém. Acad. Vaucluse
Mémoires de l'Académie de Vaucluse

Mem. Accad. Archeol., Lett. & B.A. Napoli
Memorie dell'Accademia di archeologia, lettere e belle arti di Napoli

Mem. Accad. Patavina Sci., Lett. & A.
Memorie dell'Accademia patavina di scienze, lettere ed arti

Mem. Amer. Acad. Rome
Memoirs of the American Academy in Rome

Mem. Amer. Mus. Nat. Hist.
Memoirs of the American Museum of Natural History

Mem. Amer. Philos. Soc.
Memoirs of the American Philosophical Society

Mem. Austral. Mus.
Memoirs of the Australian Museum

Mem. Carnegie Mus.
Memoirs of the Carnegie Museum

Mem. Cl. Sci. Mor., Stor. & Filol.
Memorie della Classe di scienze morali, storiche e filologiche

Mem. Colombo Mus.
Memoirs of the Colombo Museum

Mém. Comm. Ant. Dépt Côte-d'Or
Mémoires de la Commission des antiquités du département de la Côte-d'Or

Mém. Comm. Dépt. Mnmts Hist. Pas-de-Calais
Mémoires de la Commission départementale des monuments historiques du Pas-de-Calais

Mém. & C.-R. Soc. Ingén. Civ. France
Mémoires et compte-rendu de la Société des ingénieurs civils en France

Mém. Dél. Archéol. Fr. Afghanistan
Mémoires de la Délégation archéologique française en Afghanistan

Mém. & Diss. Ant. N. & Etrang.
Mémoires et dissertations sur les antiquités nationales et étrangères [cont. as *Mém. Soc. N. Antiqua. France*]

Mém. & Doc.: Soc. Savois. Hist. & Archéol.
Mémoires et documents publiés par la Société savoisienne d'histoire et d'archéologie

Mem. Domenicane
i) Memoriae Domenicane
ii) Memorie Domenicane

Mém. Féd. Soc. Hist. & Archéol. Aisne
Mémoires de la Fédération des sociétés d'histoire et d'archéologie de l'Aisne

Mém. Féd. Soc. Hist. & Archéol. Paris & Ile-de-France
Mémoires de la Fédération des sociétés historiques et archéologiques de Paris et de l'Ile-de-France [cont. as *Paris & Ile-de-France: Mém.*]

Mém. Féd. Soc. Paris & Ile-de-France
Mémoires de la Fédération des sociétés de Paris et de l'Ile-de-France

Mem. INAH
Memorias del Instituto nacional de antropología e historia

Mém. Inst. Egypte
Mémoires de l'Institut d'Egypte

Mem. Inst. Estud. Cat. Seccio Hist.-Arqueol.
Memòries de l'Institut d'estudis catalans, secció històrico-arqueològic

Mém. Inst. Ethnol.
Mémoires de l'Institut d'ethnologie

Mém. Inst. Fr. Afrique Noire: Cent. Cameroun
Mémoires de l'Institut français d'Afrique noire: Centre du Cameroun

Mém. Inst. Fr. Afrique Noire: Mél. Ethnol.
Mémoires de l'Institut français d'Afrique noire: Mélanges ethnologiques

Mém. Inst. France, Acad. Inscr. & B.-Lett.
Mémoires de l'Institut de France, Académie des inscriptions et belles-lettres [prev. pubd as *Hist. & Mém. Inst. Royal France, Acad. Inscr. & B.-Lett.*]

Mém. Inst. Fr. Archéol.
Mémoires de l'Institut français d'archéologie

Mem. Ist. Ven. Sci., Lett. & A.
Memorie dell'Istituto veneto di scienze, lettere ed arti

Memming. Geschbl.
Memminger Geschichtsblätter: Zwanglos erscheinende Mitteilungen der Heimatpflege Memmingen

Mem. Mus. Amer. Ind.
Memoirs of the Museum of the American Indian

Mem. Mus. Anthropol., U. MI
Memoirs of the Museum of Anthropology, University of Michigan

Mem. Peabody Mus. Archaeol. & Ethnol.
Memoirs of the Peabody Museum of Archaeology and Ethnology

Mem. Pont. Accad. Romana Archeol.
Memorie della Pontificia accademia romana di archeologia [prev. pubd as *Diss. Pont. Accad. Romana Archeol.*]

Mem. & Proc. Manchester Lit. & Philos. Soc.
Memoirs and Proceedings of the Manchester Literary and Philosophical Society

Mem. Raffles Mus.
Memoirs of the Raffles Museum

Mem. Real Acad. B. Let. Barcelona
Memorias de la Real academia de buenas letras de Barcelona

Mem. Real Acad. Hist.
Memorias de la Real academia de la historia

Mem. Reale Accad. Archeol., Lett. & B.A., Soc. Reale Napoli
Memorie della Reale accademia di archeologia, lettere e belle arti, Società reale di Napoli

Mem. Reale Accad. Sci. Ist. Bologna, Cl. Sci. Mor.
Memorie della Reale accademia di scienze dell'Istituto di Bologna, Classe di scienze Morau

Mem. Reale Accad. Sci. Torino
Memorie della Reale accademia delle scienze di Torino

Mem. Reale Ist. Lombardo Sci. Lett. & A.
Memorie del Reale istituto lombardo di scienze, lettere ed arti

Mem. Res. Dept Toyo Bunko
Memoirs of the Research Department of the Toyo Bunko

Mem. Romane Ant. & B.A.
Memorie romane di antichità e di belle arti

Mém. Soc. Acad. Agric., Sci., A. & B.-Lett. Dépt Aube
Mémoires de la Société académique d'agriculture, des sciences, arts et belles-lettres du département de l'Aube

Mém. Soc. Acad. Archéol., Sci. & A. Dép. Oise
Mémoires de la Société académique d'archéologie, science et arts du département de l'Oise

Mém. Soc. Agric., Commerce, Sci. & A., Dépt Marne
Mémoires de la Société d'agriculture, commerce, sciences et arts, département de la Marne

Mém. Soc. Agric., Sci. & A. Angers
Mémoires de la Société d'agriculture, sciences et arts d'Angers

Mém. Soc. Agric., Sci. & A. Cent. N., Séant à Douai
Mémoires de la Société d'agriculture, sciences et arts centrale du nord, séant à Douai

Mem. Soc. Amer. Archaeol.
Memoirs of the Society for American Archaeology [incorp. into *Amer. Ant.*]

Mém. Soc. Antiqua. Cent.
Mémoires de la Société des antiquaires du centre

Mém. Soc. Antiqua. Ouest
Mémoires de la Société des antiquaires de l'Ouest

Mém. Soc. Archéol. Champenoise
Mémoires de la Société archéologique champenoise

Mém. Soc. Archéol. & Hist. Moselle
Mémoires de la Société d'archéologie et d'histoire de la Moselle

Mém. Soc. Archéol. Midi France
Mémoires de la Société d'archéologie du Midi de la France

Mém. Soc. Archéol. Montpellier
Mémoires de la Société d'archéologie de Montpellier

Mém. Soc. Archéol., Sci. & A. Dépt Oise
Mémoires de la Société d'archéologie, sciences et arts du département de l'Oise

Mém. Soc. Archéol. Touraine
Mémoires de la Société archéologique de Touraine

Mém. Soc. Bourguignonne Géog. & Hist.
Mémoires de la Société bourguignonne de géographie et d'histoire

Mém. Soc. Eduenne
Mémoires de la Société éduenne

Mém. Soc. Emul. Doubs
Mémoires de la Société d'émulation du Doubs

Mém. Soc. Emul. Montbéliard
Mémoires de la Société d'émulation de Montbéliard

Mém. Soc. Hist. & Archéol. Bretagne
Mémoires de la Société d'histoire et d'archéologie de Bretagne

Mém. Soc. Hist. & Archéol. Pontoise, Val Oise & Vexin
Mémoires de la Société historique et archéologique de Pontoise, du Val d'Oise et du Vexin

Mém. Soc. Hist. Cher
Mémoires de la Société historique du Cher

Mém. Soc. Hist., Litt. & Sci. Cher
Mémoires de la Société historique, littéraire et scientifique du Cher

Mém. Soc. Hist. & Litt. Tournai
Mémoires de la Société historique et littéraire de Tournai

Mém. Soc. Hist. Paris & Ile-de France
Mémoires de la Société de l'histoire de Paris et de l'Ile-de-France

Mém. Soc. Imp. Antiqua. France
Mémoires de la Société impériale des antiquaires de France

Mém. Soc. Lett., Sci. & A. Bar-le-Duc
Mémoires de la Société des lettres, sciences et arts de Bar-le-Duc

Mém. Soc. N. Antiqua. France
Mémoires de la Société nationale des antiquaires de France [prev. pubd as *Mém. & Diss. Ant. N. & Etrang.*]

Mém. Soc. Sci. & Lett. Loir-et-Cher
Mémoires de la Société des sciences et des lettres de Loir-et-Cher

Mem. Stor. Dioc. Brescia
Memorie storiche della diocesi di Brescia

Mem. Stor. Dioc. Milano
Memorie storiche della diocesi di Milano

Mem. Stor. Forogiuliesi
Memorie storiche forogiuliesi

Mém. Trévoux
Mémoires de Trévoux

Mém. Un. Soc. Sav. Bourges
Mémoires de l'Union des sociétés savantes de Bourges

Mém. U. Saint-Joseph
Mémoires de l'Université Saint-Joseph

Mém. Vivre
Mémoire vivre

Mercure France
Mercure de France

Mercurio Peru.
Mercurio peruano

Merz

Mesopotamia

Messager Sci. & A.
Messager des sciences et des arts [cont. as *Messager Sci. Hist.*; *Messager Sci. Hist. Belgique*]

Messager Sci. Hist.
Messager des sciences historiques [see *Messager Sci. & A.*]

Messager Sci. Hist. Belgique
Messager des sciences historiques de Belgique [see *Messager Sci. & A.*]

Meta
Meta(morphoses)

Metalsmith

Metamorfosi

Met. Mus. J.
Metropolitan Museum Journal

Met. Mus. Stud.
Metropolitan Museum Studies

Met. Papers
Metropolitan Papers

Metro

Mex. Flkways
Mexican Folkways

México Ant.
México antiguo

Mexico & Cost.
Mexico y sus costumbres

Mexicon
Mexicon: Aktuelle Informationen und Studien zu Mesoamerika

Mexico Q. Rev.
Mexico Quarterly Review

Mhft. Baukst & Städtebau
Monatshefte für Baukunst und Städtebau

Mhft. Kstwiss.
Monatshefte für Kunstwissenschaft [cont. as *Jb. Kstwiss.*]

Michelangelo

Michel Sumpff
Michel im Sumpff

Micronesica

Micrones. Reporter
Micronesian Reporter

Mid. E. Stud. Assoc. Bull.
Middle Eastern Studies Association Bulletin

Miesiecznik Żydowski [Jewish monthly]

Milano

Milano: Riv. Mens. Com.
Milano: Rivista mensile del comune

Milano Tec.
Milano tecnica

Mil. Engin.
The Military Engineer

Mill. Ambrosiano
Millenino ambrosiano

Milton Q.
Milton Quarterly

Mimar
Mimar: Architecture in Development

Mimarlık [Architecture]

Minden. Heimathl.
Mindener Heimatblätter

Minerva [Rivista delle riviste]

Mingbao Yuekan [Mingbao monthly]

Ming Dai Yishujiya Ji Huikan [Collection of works by Ming dynasty artists]

Mingei

Ming Stud.
Ming Studies

Minneapolis Inst. A. Bull.
Minneapolis Institute of Arts Bulletin

Minotaure
Minotaure: Revue artistique et littéraire

Min. Proc. Inst. Civ. Engin.
Minutes of the Proceedings of the Institution of Civil Engineers

Mir Isk.
Mir iskusstva

Misc. A.
Miscellanea d'arte: Rivista mensile di storia dell'arte medievale e moderna [cont. as *Riv. A.*]

Misc. Antropol. Ecuator.
Miscelánea antropológica ecuatoriana

Misc. Bavar. Monacensia
Miscellanea Bavarica monacensia

Misc. Bib. Hertz.
Miscellanea bibliothecae Hertzianae

Misc. Comillas
Miscelánea de comillas

Misc. Estud. Arab. & Heb.
Miscelánea de estudios árabes y hebraicos

Misc. Fac. Lett. U. Torino
Miscellanea della facoltà di lettere dell'Università di Torino

Misc. Fiorent. Erud. & Stor.
Miscellanea fiorentina di erudizione e storia

Misc. Francesc.
Miscellanea francescana

Misc. Med.
Miscellanea medievalia

Misc. Puig Cadafalch
Miscellània Puig i Cadafalch

Misc.: Quad. Neoclass.
Miscellanea: Quaderni sul neoclassico

Misc. Soc. Romana Stor. Patria
Miscellanea della Società romana di storia patria

Misc. Stor. It.
Miscellanea di storia italiana

Misc. Stor. Sen.
Miscellanea storica senese

Misc. Stor. Ven.
Miscellanea di storia veneta [cont. as *Misc. Stor. Ven.-Trident.*; reverts to *Misc. Stor. Ven.*]

Misc. Stor. Ven.-Trident.
Miscellanea di storia veneto–tridentina [prev. pubd as & cont. as *Misc. Stor. Ven.*]

Misc. Var. Lett.
Miscellanea di varia letteratura

Misc. Volterrana
Miscellanea volterrana

Misc. Wilbouriana
Miscellanea wilbouriana

Misul Charyo [National Museum journal of arts]

Mitaraka

Mi Tierra [My place]

Mitropolia Olteniei

Mitt. Anthropol. Ges. Wien
Mitteilungen der Anthropologischen Gesellschaft Wien

Mitt. Antiqua. Ges. Zürich
Mitteilungen der Antiquarischen Gesellschaft Zürich

Mitt. Baron Brukenthal. Mus.
Mitteilungen aus dem Baron Brukenthalischen Museum

Mitt. Bayer. Numi. Ges.
Mitteilungen der Bayerischen numismatischen Gesellschaft

Mittbl.: Ker.-Freunde Schweiz
Mitteilungsblatt: Keramik-Freunde der Schweiz

Mittbl.: Ver. Bndkrimbeamt. Österreichs
Mitteilungsblatt: Vereinigung der Bundeskriminalbeamten Österreichs

Mitt. Christ. Kst
Mitteilungen für christliche Kunst

Mitt. Copernicus-Ver. Wiss. & Kst Thorn
Mitteilungen des Copernicus-Vereins für Wissenschaft und Kunst zu Thorn

Mitt. Dt. Archäol. Inst.
Mitteilungen des Deutschen archäologischen Instituts

Mitt. Dt. Archäol. Inst.: Abt. Kairo
Mitteilungen des Deutschen archäologischen Instituts: Abteilung Kairo

Mitt. Dt. Archäol. Inst.: Athen. Abt.
Mitteilungen des Deutschen archäologischen Instituts: Athenische Abteilung

Mitt. Dt. Archäol. Inst.: Röm. Abt.
Mitteilungen des Deutschen archäologischen Instituts: Römische Abteilung

Mitt. Dt. Kstgewer. Hamburg
Mitteilungen des Deutschen Kunstgewerbevereins zu Hamburg

Mitt. Dt. Orient-Ges.
Mitteilungen der Deutschen Orient-Gesellschaft

Mitt. Dt. Orient-Inst.
Mitteilungen des Deutschen Orient-Instituts

Mitt. Forschungreis. Gelehrt. Dt. Schtzgebiet.
Mitteilungen von Forschungreisenden und Gelehrten aus den deutschen Schutzgebieten [also known as *Wissenschaftliche Beihefte zum deutschen Kolonialblatt*]

Mitt. Geog. Ges. Hamburg
Mitteilungen der Geographischen Gesellschaft in Hamburg

Mitt. Ger. Nmus.
Mitteilungen aus dem Germanischen Nationalmuseum

Mitt. Gesch.- & Altertver. Liegnitz
Mitteilungen des Geschichts- und Altertumsvereins zu Liegnitz

Mitt. Gesch. Dt. Böhmen
Mitteilungen der Geschichte der Deutschen in Böhmen

Mitt. Ges. Erhaltung Gesch. Dkml. Elsass
Mitteilungen der Gesellschaft für Erhaltung der geschichtlichen Denkmale in Elsass

Mitt. Ges. Salzburg. Landesknd.
Mitteilungen der Gesellschaft für Salzburger Landeskunde

Mitt. Ges. Vergl. Kstforsch. Wien
Mitteilungen der Gesellschaft für vergleichende Kunstforschung in Wien

Mitt. Ges. Vervielfält. Kst
Mitteilungen der Gesellschaft für vervielfältigende Kunst [prev. pubd as *Chron. Vervielfält. Kst*]

Mitt. Hist. Ver. Kant. Schwyz
Mitteilungen des Historischen Vereins des Kantons Schwyz

Mitt. Hist. Ver. Pfalz
Mitteilungen des Historischen Vereins der Pfalz

Mitt. Inst. Dkmlpf. Schwerin
Mitteilungen des Institutes für Denkmalpflege Schwerin

Mitt. Inst. Geschforsch. & Archvwiss. Wien
Mitteilungen des Instituts für Geschichtsforschung und Archivwissenschaft in Wien [prev. pubd as *Mitt. Österreich. Inst. Geschforsch.*; *Mitt. Inst. Österreich. Geschforsch.*; reverts to *Mitt. Inst. Österreich. Geschforsch.*]

Mitt. Inst. Orientforsch.
Mitteilungen des Instituts für Orientforschung

Mitt. Inst. Österreich. Geschforsch.
Mitteilungen des Instituts für österreichische Geschichtsforschung [cont. as *Mitt. Österreich. Inst. Geschforsch.*; *Mitt. Inst. Geschforsch. & Archvwiss. Wien*; reverts to *Mitt. Inst. Österreich. Geschforsch.*]

Mitt. Kön.-Sächs. Altertver.
Mitteilungen der Königlichen-sächsischen Altertumsvereins

Mitt. Krems. Stadtarchvs
Mitteilungen des Kremser Stadtarchivs

Mitt. Ksr.-Kön. Cent.-Comm. Erforsch. & Erhaltung Baudkml.
Mitteilungen der K.-K. [Kaiserlich-Königlichen] Central-Commission zur Erforschung und Erhaltung der Baudenkmale [cont. as *Mitt. Ksr.-Kön. Zent.-Comm. Erforsch. & Erhaltung Kst- & Hist. Dkml.*]

Mitt. Ksr.-Kön. Mähr.-Schles. Ackerbauges.
Mitteilungen der K.-K. [Kaiserlich-Königlichen] mährisch-schlesischen Ackerbaugesellschaft

Mitt. Ksr.-Kön. Österreich. Mus. Kst & Indust.
Mitteilungen des K.-K. [Kaiserlich-Königlichen] österreichischen Museums für Kunst und Industrie

Mitt. Ksr.-Kön. Zent.-Comm. Erforsch. & Erhaltung Kst- & Hist. Dkml.
Mitteilungen der K.-K. [Kaiserlich-Königlichen] Zentral-Commission zur Erforschung und Erhaltung der Kunst- und historischen Denkmale [prev. pubd as *Mitt. Ksr.-Kön. Cent.-Comm. Erforsch. & Erhaltung Baudkml.*]

Mitt. Ksthist. Inst. Florenz
Mitteilungen des Kunsthistorischen Instituts in Florenz

Mitt. Landesver. Sächs. Heimatschutz
Mitteilungen des Landesvereins sächsischer Heimatschutz

Mitt. Mus. Bild. Kst. Leipzig
Mitteilungen aus dem Museum der bildenden Künste Leipzig

Mitt. Mus. Hallstatt
Mitteilungen aus dem Museum in Hallstatt

Mitt. Mus. Vlkerknd. Hamburg
Mitteilungen des Museums für Völkerkunde in Hamburg

Mitt. Oberhess. Geschver.
Mitteilungen des Oberhessischen Geschichtsvereins

Mitt. Österreich. Gal.
Mitteilungen der Österreichischen Galerien

Mitt. Österreich. Inst. Geschforsch.
Mitteilungen des Österreichischen Instituts für Geschichtsforschung [prev. pubd as *Mitt. Inst. Österreich. Geschforsch.*; cont. as *Mitt. Inst. Österreich. Geschforsch. & Archvwiss. Wien*; reverts to *Mitt. Inst. Österreich. Geschforsch.*]

Mitt. Prähist. Komm. Österreich. Akad. Wiss.
Mitteilungen der Prähistorischen Kommission der Österreichischen Akademie der Wissenschaften

Mitt. Pückler-Ges.
Mitteilungen der Pückler-Gesellschaft

Mitt. Roland
Mitteilungen des Roland

Mitt. Sächs. Kstsamml.
Mitteilungen aus den sächsischen Kunstsammlungen

Mitt. Stadtarchv Köln
Mitteilungen aus dem Stadtarchiv von Köln

Mitt. Ver. Gesch. & Altertknd. Westfalens & Landesmus. Prov. Westfalen
Mitteilungen des Vereins für Geschichte und Altertumskunde Westfalens und des Landesmuseums der Provinz Westfalen

Mitt. Ver. Gesch. Berlins
Mitteilungen des Vereins für die Geschichte Berlins [cont. as *Z. Ver. Gesch. Berlins*; reverts to *Mitt. Ver. Gesch. Berlins*]

Mitt. Ver. Gesch. Dresdens
Mitteilungen des Vereins für Geschichte Dresdens

Mitt. Ver. Gesch. Dt. Böhmen
Mitteilungen des Vereins für Geschichte der Deutschen in Böhmen

Mitt. Ver. Gesch. Stadt Nürnberg
Mitteilungen des Vereins für Geschichte der Stadt Nürnberg

Mitt. Ver. Gesch. Stadt Wien
Mitteilungen des Vereins für Geschichte der Stadt Wien

Mitt. Ver. Lübeck. Gesch. & Altertknd.
Mitteilungen des Vereins für lübeckische Geschichte und Alterthumskunde

Mitt. Ver. Vergl. Kstforsch.
Mitteilungen des Vereins für vergleichende Kunstforschung

Mitt. Westpreuss. Geschver.
Mitteilungen des Westpreussischen Geschichtsvereins [cont. as *Weichselland*]

Mitt. Wien. Altertver.
Mitteilungen des Wiener Altertumsvereins

Mizue

MLN [prev. pubd as *Mod. Lang. Notes*]

Mnemosyne
Mnemosyne: Bibliotheca classica Batava

MN Hist.
Minnesota History

Mnmt. Ant.: Lincei
Monumenti antichi, pubblicati per cura della Reale accademia dei Lincei

Mnmt Archaeol.
Monumenta archaeologica

Mnmt Bergomensia
Monumenta Bergomensia

Mnmt Chart. Pap. Hist. Illus.
Monumenta chartae papyraceae historiam illustrantia

Mnmt Ger. Hist.
Monumenta Germaniae historiam

Mnmt & Landschappen
Monumenten en landschappen

Mnmt Nipponica
Monumenta Nipponica

Mnmts A. & Hist.
Nos Monuments d'art et d'histoire

Mnmt Serica
Monumenta serica

Mnmts Hist.
Monuments historiques [prev. pubd as *Mnmts Hist. France*]

Mnmts Hist. France
Monuments historiques de la France [cont. as *Mnmts Hist.*]

Mnmts Piot
Monuments Piot [Fondation Eugène Piot]

MO Archaeologist
Missouri Archaeologist

MO Archaeol. Soc. Mem.
Missouri Archaeological Society Memoir

Mobilia

Moccasin Tracks

Mod. Asian Stud.
Modern Asian Studies

Mod. Bauformen
Moderne Bauformen

Mod. Illus.
Moderniste illustré

Mod. Lang. Notes
Modern Language Notes [cont. as *MLN*]

Mod. Lang. Q.
Modern Language Quarterly

Mod. Lang. Rev.
Modern Language Review

Mod. Művészet
Modern művészet [Modern art]

Mod. Painters
Modern Painters

Mod. Philol.
Modern Philology

Mod. Quat. Res. SE Asia
Modern Quaternary Research in Southeast Asia

Módulo

Modulus

Moebius

Mogućnosti

MO Hist. Rev.
Missouri Historical Review

MOMA Bull.
Museum of Modern Art Bulletin [prev. pubd as *Bull. MOMA, NY*]

Monad

Monde Copte
Le Monde copte

Monde Illus.
Le Monde illustré

Monde Iran. & Islam
Le Monde iranien et l'Islam

Monde Islam
Le Monde d'Islam

Monde Orient.
Monde oriental

Monist
Monist: An International Quarterly of General Philosophical Enquiry

Moniteur Architectes
Moniteur des architectes

Moniteur Cér. Verrerie
Le Moniteur de la céramique et de la verrerie

Moniteur Univl
Moniteur universel [cont. as *J. Officiel*]

Monographies A. Belge
Monographies de l'art belge

Mons Antiqua.
Monmouthshire Antiquary

Monspeliensa

Montevideo U. Arquit. Rev.
Montevideo Universidad de arquitectura revista

Montfort
Montfort: Zeitschrift für Geschichte, Heimat- und Volkskunde Vorarlbergs

Montjoie!

Montreal Mus. Bull.
Montreal Museum Bulletin

Monumentet

Monumentum

Monypenny Breviary

Morgen

Morks Mag.
Morks magazin

Morning Chron.
Morning Chronicle

Morocco
Morocco: The Journal of the Society for Moroccan Studies

Mosty [Bridges]

Motif
Motif: A Journal of the Visual Arts

Mouseion

Moyen Age
Le Moyen Age

M: Q. Rev. Montreal Mus. F. A.
M: A Quarterly Review of the Montreal Museum of Fine Arts/ M: Revue trimestrielle du Musée des beaux-arts de Montréal

Mschr. Gesch. & Wiss. Judenthums
Monatsschrift für Geschichte und Wissenschaft des Judenthums

Mschr. Hist. Ver. Oberbayern
Monatsschriften des Historischen Vereins von Oberbayern [cont. as *Altbayer. Mschr.*]

MSS Mid. E.
Manuscripts of the Middle East

Mthly Mag.
Monthly Magazine

Muang Boran

Mübarát [Art lover]

Mühlhäuser Geschbl.
Mühlhäuser Geschichtsblätter

München. Theol. Z.
Münchener theologische Zeitschrift

Münchn. Beitr. Vor- & Frügesch.
Münchner Beiträge zur Vor- und Frügeschichte

Münchn. Illus. Presse
Münchner illustrierte Presse

Münchn. Jb. Bild. Kst
Münchner Jahrbuch der bildenden Kunst

Münchn. Jb. Kstgesch.
Münchner Jahrbuch der Kunstgeschichte

Münchn. Jugend
Münchner Jugend [prev. pubd as & cont. as *Jugend*]

Münchn. Mus. Philol. Mittelalt. & Ren.
Münchner Museum für Philologie des Mittelalters und der Renaissance

Münchn. Neuesten Nachr.
Münchner neuesten Nachrichten

Mundial

Mundo A.
Mundo de arte

Mundo Ilus.
El mundo ilustrado

Munhwajae [Cultural properties]

Munka

Münster. Numi. Ztg
Münstersche numismatische Zeitung

Muntu

Muqarnas

Mus. A. [Ann Arbor, MI]: *U. MI*
Mus. A. Bull.
Museum of Art [Ann Arbor, Michigan]: The University of Michigan Museum of Art Bulletin [cont. as *Bull. Mus. A. & Archaeol., U. MI*]

Mus. Archivist
Museum Archivist

Mus. Archivists' Newslett.
Museum Archivists' Newsletter

Mus. & A. Washington
Museum and Arts Washington

Mus. Condé
Musée Condé

Muse: Annu. Mus. A. & Archaeol., U. MO, Columbia
Muse: Annual of the Museum of Art and Archaeology, University of Missouri, Columbia

Museion

Museologia [Centro di Studi per la museologia, Consiglio nazionale delle ricerche, Florence]

Muséon
Muséon: Revue des études orientales

Mus. Esp. Ant.
Museo español de antigüedades

Mus. Ethnographers Grp Newslett.
Museum Ethnographers Group Newsletter

Museu

Museum [Barcelona]

Museum [Brunswick]

Museum [Kampala]

Museum [National Museum, Tokyo]

Museumjournaal
Museumjournaal [MJ]: Periodiek voor moderne kunst van Nederlandse musea en culturele centra

Museum News [American Association of Museums; Washington, DC]

Museum News [National Heritage]

Museumnytt

Museums

Museumskunde

Mus. F.A. Bull.
Museum of Fine Arts Bulletin [Boston; cont. as *Bull.: Mus. F.A., Boston; Boston Mus. Bull.*]

Mus. F.A., Houston: Bull.
Museum of Fine Arts, Houston: Bulletin

Mus. Familles
Musée des familles

Mus. Far E. Ant. Bull.
Museum of Far Eastern Antiquities Bulletin

Mus. Ferrar.: Boll. Annu.
Musei ferraresi: Bollettino annuale

Mus. France
Musées de France

Mus. Genève
Musées de Genève

Mus. Helv.
Museum Helveticum

Mus. Heute
Museum heute

Musical Times
Musical Times

Music & Lett.
Music and Letters

Music Rev.
Music Review

Mus. J.
Museum Journal

Mus. J.: Ber. Mus.
Museums Journal: Berichte aus den Museen

Mus. J.: Organ Mus. Assoc.
Museums Journal: The Organ of the Museums Association

Muslim Mag.
Muslim Magazine

Muslim World
Muslim World

Mus. Neuchâtel.: Rev. Hist. Rég.
Musée neuchâtelois: Revue d'histoire régionale

Mus. News Tech. Bull.
Museum News Technical Bulletin

Mus. News: Toledo Mus. A.
Museum News: Toledo Museum of Art

Mus. Notes: Mus. A., RI
Museum Notes: Museum of Art, Rhode Island

Mus. Patavinum
Museum patavinum

Mus. Philipon
Musée Philipon

Mus. Pontevedra
El museo de Pontevedra

Mus.: Rev. Trimest.
Museum: Revue trimestrielle publiée par l'UNESCO [United Nations Educational, Scientific and Cultural Organisation]

Mus. Royaux B.-A. Belgique: Bull.
Musées royaux des beaux-arts de Belgique: Bulletin [prev. pubd as *Annu. Mus. Royaux B.-A. Belgique/Jb. Kon. Mus. S. Kst. België*]

Mus. Sci.
Museologia scientifica

Mus. Stadt Köln
Museen der Stadt Köln

Mus. Stud.
Museum Studies [Art Institute of Chicago]

Mus. Stud. J.
Museum Studies Journal

Mus. Univl
Museo universal

Művészet [Art]

Művészettörténeti Értesítő [Art history reporter]

Művészettörténeti Munkakö Zösseg [Yearbook of the Art Historians Association]

Művészettörténeti Tanulmányok
Művészettörténeti tanulmányok: Művészettörténeti dokumentációs központ evkönyve [Art historical studies: yearbook of art historical documents]

Muzealnictwo

Muzey [Museum]

Muz. Glasnik
Muzejski Glasnik

Mysore Archaeol. Dept. Annu. Rep.
Mysore Archaeological Department Annual Report

NACF Mag.
National Art Collections Fund Magazine [cont. as *A. Q.* [London]]

NACF Rev.
National Art Collections Fund Review

Nachr. Akad. Wiss. Göttingen
Nachrichten der Akademie der Wissenschaft in Göttingen

Nachr. Akad. Wiss. Göttingen Philol.–Hist. Kl.
Nachrichten der Akademie der Wissenschaften in Göttingen, philologisch–historische Klasse

Nachrbl. Dkmlpf. Baden-Württemberg
Nachrichtenblatt der Denkmalpflege in Baden-Württemberg

Nachrbl. Ges. Wiss. Göttingen, Philos–Hist. Kl
Nachrichtenblatt der Gesellschaft der Wissenschaften zu Göttingen, philosophisch–historische Klasse

Nachrbl. Soc. Annensis E.V.
Nachrichtenblatt der Societas Annensis e. V.

Nachr. Wiss. Bib.
Nachrichten für wissenschaftliche Bibliotheken

N. Akkad Proj. Rep.
Northern Akkad Project Reports

N. Amer. Rev.
North American Review

Namurcum

Napoli Nob.
Napoli nobilissima: Rivista bimestrale di arte figurativa, archeologia e urbanistica

Napoli Riv. Mun.
Napoli rivista municipale

Nara Kokuritsu Bunkazai Kenkyūjo Gakuhō

Narody Azii & Afriki
Narody Azii i Afriki

Nase Gradjevinarstvo

Nash Dom

Nashe Naslediye

Naṣir-i Efkâr [The diffusion of ideas]

Nassauische An.
Nassauische Annalen

Nassau Mag.
Nassau Magazine

Nassau Pink

Nat. & A.
Natura ed arte

Nat. Hist.
Natural History

National 1834
Le National de 1834

Nation & Athenaeum
Nation and Athenaeum [merger of *The Nation* & *The Athenaeum*; merged with *New Statesman* to form *New Statesman & Nation*]

Native Affairs Dept Annu.
Native Affairs Department Annual

Native Peoples

Naturwissenschaften

Nauka & Chelovechestvo
Nauka i chelovechestvo

Ñawpa Pacha

NC Hist. Rev.
North Carolina Historical Review

NC Mus. A. Bull.
North Carolina Museum of Art Bulletin

Ndërtuesi

Ndiwula
Ndiwula: The Annual Newsletter of the Museums of Malawi

Nea Estia

Neapolis

Nea Sion

Nebelspalter
Nebelspalter: Studentenzeitung in und um Stuttgart

Necrologe

Necropoli

Ned. Ambachts- & Nijvhdskstjb.
Nederlandsche ambachts- en nijverheidskunstjaarboek [Dutch crafts and industrial art yearbook]

Nedelya Stroitelya
Nedelya stroitelya [Builder's week]

Ned.-Indië Oud & Nieuw
Nederlandsch-Indië oud en nieuw

Ned. Kstbode
Nederlandsche kunstbode

Ned. Ksthist. Jb.
Nederlands(ch) kunsthistorisch jaarboek

Ned. Ksthist. Woordbk
Nederlands kunsthistorisch woordenboek

Ned. Leeuw
De Nederlandsche leeuw

Ned. Mus.
Nederlandsche Museum

Ned. Tijdschr. Geneeskd.
Nederlandsch tijdschrift voor geneeskunde [Dutch medical journal]

XIXe Eeuw
De XIXe eeuw [De negentiende eeuw; prev. pubd as *Tweemandelijksch. Tijdschr. Lett. Kst. Wet. & Polit.*]

Nelson Gal. & Atkins Mus. Bull.
Nelson Gallery and Atkins Museum Bulletin

Nëntori

NÉON

Népszava [The people's world]

Neptunus Inf. Mar.
Neptunus info marine

Nes & Helgøya
Nes og Helgøya [Nes Historical Society]

Nessembre

Neuburg. Kollktbl.
Neuburger Kollektionenblatt: Jahresschrift des Heimatvereins, historischen Vereins

Neue Beitr. Gesch. Landesknd. Tirols
Neue Beiträge zur geschichtlichen Landeskunde Tirols

Neue Berlin. Mschr.
Neue berlinische Monatsschrift [prev. pubd as *Berlin. Bl.*; *Berlin. Mschr.*]

Neue Bib. S. Wiss. & Frejen Kst.
Neue Bibliothek der schönen Wissenschaften und der freien Künste [prev. pubd as *Bib. S. Wiss. & Frejen Kst.*; cont. as *Bib. Reden. & Bild. Kst.*]

Neue Bl. Gemäldeknd.
Neue Blätter für Gemäldekunde [prev. pubd as *Stud. & Skiz. Gemäldeknd.*; *Bl. Gemäldeknd.*; cont. as *Gemäldekunde*]

Neue Dt. Mschr.
Neue deutsche Monatsschrift

Neue Frankfurt

Neue Freie Presse
Neue freie Presse

Neue Graphik

Neue Heidelberg. Jb.
Neue Heidelberger Jahrbücher [cont. as *Heidelberg. Jb.*]

Neue Illus. Ztg
Neue illustrierte Zeitung

Neue Jb.
Neue Jahrbücher

Neue Jüd. Mhft.
Neue jüdische Monatshefte

Neue Jugend

Neue Rev.
Neue Revue

Neuer Merkur

Neuer Teutscher Merkur [prev. pubd as *Teutscher Merkur*]

Neue Rundschau

Neues Afrika

Neues Albanien

Neues Alt-Villach
Neues aus Alt-Villach

Neues Archv Gesch. Stadt Heidelberg & Kurpfalz
Neues Archiv für die Geschichte der Stadt Heidelberg und der Kurpfalz

Neues Archv Sächs. Gesch. & Altertknd.
Neues Archiv für sächsiche Geschichte und Altertumskunde [prev. pubd as *Neues Archv Saechs. Gesch. & Altertknd.*]

Neues Archv Saechs. Gesch. & Altertknd.
Neues Archiv für saechsische Geschichte und Altertumskunde [cont. as *Neues Archv Sächs. Gesch. & Altertknd.*]

Neues Deutschland

Neues Glas

Neues Götting. Jb.
Neues Göttinger Jahrbuch

Neues Wien. Tagbl.
Neues Wiener Tagblatt

Neue Thalia [prev. pubd as *Thalia*]

Neuer Weg

Neue Zürch. Ztg
Neue Zürcher Zeitung

Neuf

900 Cah. Italie & Europe
900 Cahiers d'Italie et d'Europe

Neujbl. Feuerwerker-Ges. Zürich
Neujahrsblatt der Feuerwerker-Gesellschaft in Zürich

Neujbl. Hist–Antiqua. Ver. & Kstver. Schaffhausen
Neujahrsblatt des historisch–antiquarischen Vereins und des Kunstvereins in Schaffhausen

Neujbl. Hist. Ver. Kant. St Gallen
Neujahrsblatt des Historischen Vereins des Kantons Sankt Gallen

Neujbl. Kstges. Zürich
Neujahrsblatt der Kunstgesellschaft Zürich [cont. as *Neujbl. Zürch. Kstlergesellschaft*]

Neujbl. Stadtbib. Zürich J....
Neujahresblatt [herausgegeben] von der Stadtbibliothek in Zürich auf das Jahre....

Neujbl. Waisenhauses
Neujahrsblatt des Waisenhauses

Neujbl. Zürch. Kstlergesellschaft
Neujahrsblatt der Zürcher Künstlergesellschaft [prev. pubd as *Neujbl. Kstges. Zürich*]

Neusser Jb. Kst, Kultgew. & Heimatknd.
Neusser Jahrbuch für Kunst, Kulturgewerbe und Heimatkunde

Neva

New A. Examiner
New Art Examiner

New Age

New Albania

New Asia Acad. Bull.
New Asia Academic Bulletin [New Asia College, Chinese University of Hong Kong]

New Bkbinder
The New Bookbinder

New Britain [London]

Newcastle Mag.
Newcastle Magazine

Newcastle Upon Tyne Illus. Chron.
Newcastle upon Tyne Illustrated Chronicle

Newcomen Soc. Trans.
Newcomen Society Transactions

New Commonwealth

New Criterion
The New Criterion

New England Farmer

New England Mag.
New England Magazine

New Formations

New Ger. Crit.
New German Critique

New Hung. Q.
New Hungarian Quarterly

New Hung. Rev.
New Hungarian Review

New Lit. Hist.
New Literary History

New Magic Lantern J.
The New Magic Lantern Journal

New Mthly Mag.
New Monthly Magazine

New Orient

Newport Hist.
Newport History

Newport Soc.
Newport Society

New Repub.
New Republic

Newslett. Amer. Res. Cent. Egypt
Newsletter of the American Research Center in Egypt

Newslett. Baluchistan Stud.
Newsletter of Baluchistan Studies

Newslett.: Charles Rennie Mackintosh Soc.
The Newsletter: Charles Rennie Mackintosh Society

Newslett.: NY Landmarks Conserv.
Newsletter: New York Landmarks Conservancy

Newslett. Soc. Study Egyp. Ant.
Newsletter of the Society for the Study of Egyptian Antiquities

New Soc.
New Society

New Statesman [merged with *Nation & Athenaeum* to form *New Statesman & Nation*]

New Statesman & Nation [merger of *New Statesman* & *Nation & Athenaeum*]

Newsweek

New Yorker

Next Call

'Nferta Napoletana

N.G.A., Rep. & Stud.
National Gallery of Art, Reports and Studies

N. Gaz. & Lit. Register
National Gazette and Literary Register

N.G. Canada Bull.
National Gallery of Canada Bulletin

N. Geog.
National Geographic

N. Geog. Res.
National Geographic Research

Ngonge Kongo
Ngonge Kongo: Carnets de sciences humaines

N.G. Tech. Bull.
National Gallery Technical Bulletin

Nhan Van [Humanism]

N. Hist.
Northern History

Nicaráuac

Nice Hist.
Nice historique

Nichiren-Gakkai Kaishi/Bull. Jap.-Neth. Inst.
Nichiren-Gakkai Kaishi/Bulletin of the Japanese-Netherlands Institute

Niederbayer. Mschr.
Niederbayerische Monatsschrift

Niederdt. Beitr. Kstgesch.
Niederdeutsche Beiträge zur Kunstgeschichte

Niedersächs. Beitr. Kstgesch.
Niedersächsische Beiträge zur Kunstgeschichte

Niedersächs. Dkmlpf.
Niedersächsische Denkmalpflege

Niedzica Semin.
Niedzica Seminars

Niemandsland
Niemandsland: Zeitschrift zwischen den Kulturen

Niente Dazio
Niente da dazio [Scuola labronica]

Nieuwe Drentse Vlksalm.
Nieuwe Drentse volksalmanak

Nieuwe Gids
De nieuwe gids

Niger. Field
Nigerian Field

Nigeria

Nigeria Mag.
Nigeria Magazine

Nihon Kenchiku Gakkai/J. Archit. & Bldg Sci.
Nihon kenchiku gakkai/Journal of Architecture and Building Science

Nihon No Bijutsu [Arts of Japan]

Nike

9H

19th C. [London]
Nineteenth Century [London]

19th C. [New York]
Nineteenth Century [Victorian Society of America, NY]

19th C. & After
Nineteenth Century and After

Nizhegorodskiy Listok [Nizhgorod pamphlet]

N. Knife Mag.
The National Knife Magazine

N. Listy
Národní listy [National news]

NM Stud. F.A.
New Mexico Studies in the Fine Arts [University of Minnesota]

N. Munster Antiqua. J.
North Munster Antiquarian Journal

N. Mus. Åb.
National musei årsbok [National Museums yearbook]

Nmus. Arbejdsmk.
Nationalmuseets arbejdsmark

Nmus. Bull.
Nationalmuseum bulletin

N. Mus. Canada, Bull.
National Museum of Canada, Bulletin

N. Mus. NZ Rec.
National Museum of New Zealand Records

Nmus. Skrser.
Nationalmuseet skriftserie [National Museum writing series]

N. Notes & Queries
Northern Notes and Queries [cont. as *Scot. Antiqua.*; *Scot. Hist. Rev.*]

Nógrád Megyei Múz. Évkönyve
Nógrád megyei múzeumok évkönyve [Nógrád County Museums annual]

N. OH Live
Northern Ohio Live

NÖLA: Mitt. Niederösterreich. Landesarchv
NÖLA [Niederösterreichische Landesregierung]: Mitteilungen aus dem Niederösterreichischen Landesarchiv

No Me Olvides

Noncello
Il Noncello: Collana di monografie pordenonensi

Nordelbingen
Nordelbingen: Beiträge zur Heimatforschung in Schleswig-Holstein, Hamburg und Lübeck

Nordenfield. Kstindustmus. Åb.
Nordenfieldske kunstindustrimuseum Årbok

Nord. Fortidsminder
Nordiske fortidsminder

Nord. Kult.
Nordisk kultur

Nordschwaben

Nord-Sud

Nord. Tidskr. Vet., Kst & Indust.
Nordisk tidsskrift för vetenskap, konst och industri

Norfolk Archaeol.
Norfolk Archaeology

Norsk Flkmus. Åb.
Norsk folkemuseums årbok [Norwegian Folk Museum's yearbook]

Norsk Ksthist.
Norsk kunsthistorie [Norwegian art history]

Norsk Kstnerleks.
Norsk kunstnerleksikon

Norte

Northants Past & Present
Northamptonshire Past and Present

Norw. Archaeol. Rev.
Norwegian Archaeological Review

Nosa Terra
A nosa terra [Our land]

Not. A.
Notizie d'arte

Not. Archeol.
Notiziario archeologico [cont. as *Africa It.*]

Notas Mesoamer.
Notas mesoamericanas

Not. Chianti Class.
Notiziario del Chianti classico

Notes Afr.
Notes africaines

Notes & Doc. Mus. France
Notes et documents des musées de France

Notes Hisp.
Notes hispaniques

Notes & Queries
Notes and Queries

Notes & Rec. Royal Soc. London
Notes and Records of the Royal Society of London

Notizie

Not. Pal. Albani
  Notizie del Palazzo Albani: Rivista quadrimestrale di storia dell'arte [Università degli studi di Urbino]

Notre XVIème

Not. Scavi Ant.
  Notizie degli scavi dell'antichità

Nottingham Fr. Stud.
  Nottingham French Studies

Nous

Noûs

Nouv. Archvs A. Fr.
  Nouvelles archives de l'art français [prev. pubd as & cont. as *Archvs A. Fr.*]

Nouv. Archvs Miss. Sci.
  Nouvelles archives des missions scientifiques

Nouv. Archvs Mus.
  Nouvelles archives du muséum

Nouv. Clio
  Nouvelle Clio

Nouv. Est.
  Nouvelles de l'estampe

Nouv. Eure
  Nouvelles de l'Eure

Nouv.-Fém.-France-Illus.
  Nouveau-Fémina-France-Illustration [prev. pubd as *L'Illustration*]

Nouv. J.
  Nouveau journal

Nouv. J. Asiat.
  Nouveau journal asiatique

Nouv. Mél. Orient.
  Nouveaux mélanges orientaux

Nouv. Mém. Acad. Royale Sci. & B.-Lett.
  Nouveaux mémoires de l'Académie royale des sciences et belles-lettres

Nouv. Mém. Acad. Royale Sci. & B.-Lett., Bruxelles
  Nouveaux mémoires de l'Académie royale des sciences et belles-lettres, Bruxelles

Nouv. Minerve
  La Nouvelle Minerve

Nouv. Photocinéma
  Nouveau photocinéma

Nouv. Répub. Lett.
  Nouvelles de la république des lettres

Nouv. Rev.
  Nouvelle Revue

Nouv. Rev. Bretagne
  Nouvelle Revue de Bretagne

Nouv. Rev. Egypte
  La Nouvelle Revue d'Egypte

Nouv. Rev. Fr.
  Nouvelle Revue française

Nouv. Rev. Hongrie
  Nouvelle Revue de Hongrie

Nouv. Rev. Rétro.
  Nouvelle Revue rétrospective

Nouv. Rev. Tib.
  Nouvelle Revue tibétaine

Nova Europa

Nova Hist.
  Nova historia

Novarien

Novaya Zhizn' [New life]

Novecento

Novelist's Mag.
  Novelist's Magazine

Novopazarski Zborn.
  Novopazarski zbornik

Novum [prev. pubd as *Gebrauchsgraphik*]

Novyy Lef

Novyy Vostok

N. Pal. Mus. Bull.
  National Palace Museum Bulletin

N. & S.
  Nord und Süd

NT Stud.
  National Trust Studies

NT Yb.
  National Trust Yearbook

Nubia Christ.
  Nubia christiana

Nuestra Arquit.
  Nuestra arquitectura

Nueva Forma

Nueva Prov.
  Nueva provincia

Nueva Visión

Nuevo Amanecer Cult.
  Nuevo amanecer cultural

Nuevo Diario

Numaga

Numen

Numero

Numero Unico Futur. Campari
  Numero unico futurista Campari

Numi. & Ant. Class.
  Numismatica e antichità classiche

Numi. Chron.
  Numismatic Chronicle

Numi. & Epig.
  Numismatika i epigrafica

Numi. Int. Bull.
  Numismatics International Bulletin

Numi. Lit.
  Numismatic Literature

Numi. Meddel.
  Numismatiska Meddelanden

Numi. & Philat. J. Japan
  Numismatic and Philatelic Journal of Japan

Numi. Sborn.
  Numizmaticheskii sbornik

Numismatica

Numi. Z.
  Numismatische Zeitschrift

Nuncius

Nuova Antol.
  Nuova antologia

Nuova Europa

Nuova Rass.
  Nuova rassegna

Nuova Riv. Misena
  Nuova rivista misena

Nuova Riv. Stor.
  Nuova rivista storica

Nuovi Saggi Reale Accad. Sci., Lett. & A. Padova
  Nuovi saggi della Reale accademia di scienze, lettere ed arti di Padova [cont. as *Atti & Mem. Reale Accad. Sci., Lett. & A. Padova; Atti & Mem. Accad. Patavina Sci., Lett. & A.*]

Nuovo Archv Ven.
  Nuovo archivio veneto [prev. pubd as *Archv Ven.*; cont. as *Archv Ven.–Trident.*]

Nuovo Boll. Archeol. Crist.
  Nuovo bollettino di archeologia cristiana

Nuovo G.
  Il nuovo giornale

Nuovo G. Lett. Italia
  Nuovo giornale de' letterati d'Italia [prev. pubd as *G. Lett. Italia*]

Nürnberger Forsch.
  Nürnberger Forschungen

N. Veracruz
  Norte de Veracruz

Nyame Akuma
  Nyame Akuma: A Newsletter of African Archaeology

NY Dada
  New York Dada

NY Ecclesiologist
  New York Ecclesiologist

NY Eve. Post
  New York Evening Post

NY Herald
  New York Herald

NY Herald Tribune
  New York Herald Tribune

NY Hist. Soc. Q.
  New York Historical Society Quarterly

NY Mag.
  New York Magazine

NY Pub. Lib. Bull.
  New York Public Library Bulletin

NY Rev. Bks
  New York Review of Books

NY State Mus. Bull.
  New York State Museum Bulletin

NY Times
  New York Times

NY Times Mag.
  New York Times Magazine

Nyugat [Occident]

NY World Mag.
  New York World Magazine

NZ Architect
  New Zealand Architect

NZ Crafts
  New Zealand Crafts

NZ Dominion Mus. Bull.
  New Zealand Dominion Museum Bulletin

NZ Herald
  New Zealand Herald

NZ Heritage
  New Zealand's Heritage

NZ Hist. Places
  New Zealand Historic Places [prev. pubd as *Hist. Places NZ*]

NZ Inst. Architects J.
  New Zealand Institute of Architects Journal

NZ Listener
  New Zealand Listener

NZ Potter
  New Zealand Potter

N. Ztg
  Nationale Zeitung

Obaku bunka

Oberbayer. Archv
  Oberbayerisches Archiv [prev. pubd as *Oberbayer. Archv Vaterländ. Gesch.*]

Oberbayer. Archv Vaterländ. Gesch.
  Oberbayerisches Archiv für vaterländische Geschichte [cont. as *Oberbayer. Archv*]

Oberösterreich

Oberösterreich. Heimatbl.
  Oberösterreichische Heimatblätter

Oberösterreich Kultz.
  Oberösterreich Kulturzeitschrift

Oberrhein. Kst
  Oberrheinische Kunst

Oberschlesien

Obj. & Mondes
  Objets et mondes

Obliques

Obreen's Archf Ned. Kstgech.
  Obreen's archief voor Nederlandsche kunstgeschiedenis

Obshchestvennyye Nauki Uzbekistane
  Obshchestvennyye nauki v Uzbekistane

Obzor

Occas. Pap. Ant.: Gr. Vases Getty Mus.
  Occasional Papers in Antiquities: Greek Vases in the J. Paul Getty Museum

Occas. Pap. Anthropol.
  Occasional Papers in Anthropology

Occas. Pap.: N. Mus. S. Rhodesia
  Occasional Papers: National Museum South Rhodesia

Occas. Pap. Rhodes-Livingstone Mus.
  Occasional Papers of the Rhodes-Livingstone Museum

Oceania

Ochrona Zabytków [Protection of monuments]

Occidente

October

Octubre

Odgłosy

Óðinn

Odra

Odu: U. Ife J. Afr. Stud.
  Odu: University of Ife Journal of African Studies

Official Gaz.
  Official Gazette

Öff. Kstsamml. Basel, Jber.
Öffentliche Kunstsammlung Basel, Jahresbericht

Oggi & Domani
Oggi e domani

Ogonyok

OH State Archaeol. & Hist. Q.
Ohio State Archaeological and Historical Quarterly

Oideas

Old Furn.
Old Furniture

Old Master Drgs
Old Master Drawings

Old Prt Shop Port.
Old Print Shop Portfolio

Old-Time New England [prev. pubd as *Bull. Soc. Preserv. New England Ant.*]

Old Wtrcol. Soc. Club
Old Water-Colour Society's Club

Olissipo

Omnibus

Once a Week

Ons Amsterdam

Ont. Hist. Soc. Pap. & Rec.
Ontario Historical Society Papers and Records

Onze Kst
Onze kunst [prev. pubd as *Vl. Sch.*]

O Panorama

Opbouwen

Op De Hoogte [Up-to-date]

Op De Uitkijk
Op de uitkijk: Bijblad van 'De aarde en haar volken' [On the lookout: supplement of 'De aarde en haar volken'; incorp. into *Aarde & Vlk.* from 1904]

Opeion

Openb. Kstbez.
Openbaar kunstbezit

Opinion N.
L'Opinion nationale

Opportunity

Oppositions

Optical Engin.
Optical Engineering

Op Uitkijk: Christ. Cult. Mabl.
Op de uitkijk: Christelijk cultureel maandblad

Opuscula Archaeol.
Opuscula archaeologia [Svenska Institutet, Rome; cont. as *Opuscula Romana*]

Opuscula Athen.
Opuscula Atheniensia

Opuscula Inst. Romani Finland.
Opuscula Instituti Romani Finlandiae

Opuscula Romana [Svenska Institutet, Rome; prev. pubd as *Opuscula Archaeol.*]

Opusculum

Opus Int.
Opus International

Oral Hist.
Oral History

Oratorio S Filippo Neri
L'Oratorio di S Filippo Neri

Orbs

Ord & Bild [Word and picture]

Ordo Sancti Benedicti
Ordo sancti benedicti: Studien und Mitteilungen aus dem Benediktiner- und Cistercienser-Orden [cont. as *Stud. & Mitt. Gesch. Benediktiner-Ordens & Zweige*]

Organ Christ. Kst
Organ für christliche Kunst

Oriens

Oriens Ant.
Oriens antiquus

Oriens Extrem.
Oriens extremus

Orient

Orient. A.
Oriental Art

Orientalia [Rome]

Orientations

Orient. Carpet & Textile Stud.
Oriental Carpet and Textile Studies

Orient. Cer. Soc. Hong Kong, Bull.
Oriental Ceramic Society of Hong Kong, Bulletin

Orient. Cer. Soc. Transl. No.
Oriental Ceramics Society Translations Number

Orient. Christ. Period.
Orientalia Christiana periodica

Orient. Coll. Mag.
Oriental College Magazine

Orient-Express

Orient. Litztg
Orientalische Literaturzeitung

Orient. Lovan. Period.
Orientalia Lovaniensia periodica

Orient. Suecana
Orientalia Suecana

Orígenes

Origini

Orissa Hist. Res. J.
Orissa Historical Research Journal

Orissa Rev.
Orissa Review

Ornament [prev. pubd as *Bead J.*]

Országos Magyar Képzőművészeti Társulat Évkönyve [National Hungarian fine arts association annual]

Országos Magyar Szépművészeti Múz. Évkönyvei
Országos Magyar szépművészeti múzeum Évkönyvei [Annual of the Hungarian Museum of Fine Arts]

Osaka-shiritsu Daigaku Kokogaku Kiyō [Osaka Municipal University archaeological bulletin]

Osiedle Mieszkaniowe [Housing estate]

Osisris

Oslo Komm. Kstsaml. Åb.
Oslo Kommunes kunstsamlinger årbok [Yearbook of Oslo Kommune's art collections]

Osmali Araştırmaları [Journal of Ottoman studies]

Osservatorio A.
Osservatorio delle arti

Ostallgäu: Einst & Jetzt
Ostallgäu: Einst und jetzt

Östasiat. Mus. [Stockholm]: Bull.
Östasiatiska Museet [Stockholm]: Bulletin [cont. as *Bull. Mus. Far E. Ant.*]

Ostasiat. Z.
Ostasiatische Zeitschrift

Ostbair. Grenzmarken
(Die) Ostbairische(n) Grenzmarken

Ostdt. Mhft.
Ostdeutsche Monatshefte

Ostdt. Wiss.
Ostdeutsche Wissenschaft

Österreich. Akad. Wiss.: Anz. Philos.–Hist. Kl.
Österreichische Akademie der Wissenschaften: Anzeiger der philosophisch–historischen Klasse

Österreich. Aquarel.
Österreichische Aquarellisten

Österreich. Archäol. Inst.: Grab.
Österreichisches archäologisches Institut: Grabungen

Österreich. Bau- & Werkkst
Österreichische Bau- und Werkkunst

Österreich Gesch. & Lit.
Österreich in Geschichte und Literatur

Österreich. Gesch.-Quellen
Österreichische Geschichts-Quellen [cont. as *Archv Österreich. Gesch.*]

Österreich. Geschwiss. Gegenwart Selbstdarstell.
Österreichische Geschichtswissenschaft der Gegenwart in Selbstdarstellungen

Österreich. Kstb.
Österreichische Kunstbücher

Österreich. Kstdkml.
Österreichische Kunstdenkmäler

Österreich. Kstmonographie
Österreichische Kunstmonographie

Österreich. Ksttop.
Österreichische Kunsttopographie

Österreich. Osthft.
Österreichische Osthefte

Österreich. Rundschau
Österreichische Rundschau: Deutsche Kultur und Politik

Österreich.–Ung. Kstchron.
Österreichisch–ungarische Kunstchronik

Österreich.–Ung. Rev.
Österreichisch–ungarische Revue: Monatschrift für die gesamten Kulturinteressen Österreich Ungarns

Österreich. Z. Dkmlpf.
Österreichische Zeitschrift für Denkmalpflege

Österreich. Z. Kst & Dkmlpf.
Österreichische Zeitschrift für Kunst und Denkmalpflege

Österreich. Z. Vlkskd.
Österreichische Zeitschrift für Volkskunde

Otago U. Stud. Prehist. Anthropol.
Otago University Studies in Prehistoric Anthropology

Other Voices

Ottagono

Ottawa Citizen

Ottawa Evening J.
Ottawa Evening Journal

Ottocento

Oud-Delft

Oude Kst
Oude kunst

Oude Land Aurschot
Oude land van Aarschot

Oudhdknd. Jb.
Oudheidkundig jaarboek [prev. pubd as *Bull. Kon. Ned. Oudhdknd. Bond*; cont. as *Bull. Ned. Oudhdknd. Bond*; *Kon. Ned. Oudhdknd. Bond: Bull. KNOB*]

Oudhdknd. Meded. Rijksmus. Ouden Leiden
Oudheidkundige mededelingen uit het Rijksmuseum van Ouden te Leiden [Archaeological reports from the Rijksmuseum, Leiden]

Oudhd. & Kst
Oudheide en kunst [Antiquity and art]

Oud-Holland [prev. pubd as *Ksthist. Meded. Rijksbureau Ksthist. Doc.*]

Ourivesaria Port.
Ourivesaria portuguesa

Outre-mer [prev. pubd as *Rev. Ethnog. & Trad. Pop.*; *Rev. Trad. Pop.*]

Ovo Mag.
Ovo Magazine

Oxford A. J.
Oxford Art Journal

Oxford Hist. Soc.
Oxford Historical Society

Oxford J. Archaeol.
Oxford Journal of Archaeology

Oxford Stud. Islam. A.
Oxford Studies in Islamic Art

Oxoniensia

Pacific A.
Pacific Arts [prev. pubd as *Pacific A. Newslett.*]

Pacific Affairs

Pacific A. Newslett.
Pacific Arts Newsletter [cont. as *Pacific A.*]

Pacific Architect & Bldr
Pacific Architect and Builder

Pacific Coast Architect

Pacific Hort.
Pacific Horticulture

Pacific Ling.
Pacific Linguistics

PACT
PACT: Revue du groupe européen d'études pour les techniques physiques, chimiques et mathématiques appliquées à l'archéologie

Padova

Padova & Prov.
Padova e la sua provincia

Paekche Munhwa

Pagan Newslett.
Pagan Newsletter

Page A.
Page d'art

Pageant

Pagine A.
Pagine d'arte

Pagine Istria.
Pagine istriane

Pagine Strav.
Pagine stravaganti

PA Hist.
Pennsylvania History

Paideuma

Painter & Sculptor
Painter and Sculptor

Pakistan Archaeol.
Pakistan Archaeology

Palaeohistoria
Palaeohistoria: Acta et communicationes Instituti bio-archaeologici Universitatis Groninganae

Palaeontol. Sinica
Palaeontologia sinica

Palaiochrist. & Byz. Archaiol. & Tech. Kypro
Palaiochristianiki kai byzantini archaiologia kai techni en Kypro [Early Christian and Byzantine archaeology and art on Cyprus]

Palästina-Jb.
Palästina-Jahrbuch

Palatino

Paléorient

Palestine Explor. Fund Q.
Palestine Exploration Fund Quarterly

Palestine Explor. Q.
Palestine Exploration Quarterly

Palestine & Middle E. Econ. Rev.
Palestine and Middle East Economic Review [cont. as *Israel & Mid. E. Econ. Rev.*]

Palestra
Palestra: Revista de pedagogía y cultura

Palette

Paletten [The palette]

Palladio

Pallas

Pall Mall Gaz.
Pall Mall Gazette

Pal. Mus. Q.
Palace Museum Quarterly

Palo Ciego
Palo de ciego

PA Mag. Hist. & Biog.
Pennsylvania Magazine of History and Biography

Památkove Péče [Monument preservation] [prev. pubd as *Zprávy Památkové Péče*]

Památky Archeol.
Památky archeologické [Archaeological monuments]

Památky & Příroda
Památky a příroda [Monuments and nature]

Pamiatky bratislavy [Bratislavan monuments]

Pamiętnik Lit.
Pamiętnik literacki [Literary memoirs]

Pamiętnik Teat.
Pamiętnik teatralny [Theatrical memoirs]

Pamirovediniye [Information on the Pamir Mountains]

PA Mus. Bull.
Pennsylvania Museum Bulletin [cont. as *Philadelphia Mus. A.: Bull.; Bull.: Philadelphia Mus. A.*]

Pan

Panama Archaeologist

Panathinea

Pandora [suppl. in *El Nacional*]

Pan.: Genoss. Pan
Pan:hrsg. [herausgegeben] von der Genossenschaft Pan

Pangmulgwan Shinmun

Panorama

Panorama Isk.
Panorama iskusstv [Panorama of arts]

Pan: Rass. Lett., A. & Musica
Pan: Rassegna di lettere, arti e musica

Pantheon
Pantheon: Internationale Zeitschrift für Kunst [cont. as *Bruckmanns Pantheon*]

Panurge

Pan: Wochschr.
Pan: Wochenschrift

Pap. Amer. Assoc. Archit. Bibliographers
Papers of the American Association of Architectural Bibliographers

Pap. Archaeol. Inst. America
Papers of the Archaeological Institute of America

Pap. Bibliog. Soc. Amer.
Papers of the Bibliographical Society of America

Pap. Brit. Sch. Rome
Papers of the British School at Rome

Pap. Conservator
Paper Conservator

Pap. Conserv. Cat.
Paper Conservation Catalogue

Pap. Conserv. News
Paper Conservation News

Pap. & Druck
Papier und Druck

Papiergeschichte

Papitú

Pap. Lab. Arqueol. Valencia
Papeles del laboratorio de arqueología di Valencia

Pap. New World Archaeol. Found.
Papers and Proceedings of the New World Archaeological Foundation

Pap. Periód. Ilus.
Papal periódico ilustrado

Pap. & Proc. Royal Soc. Tasmania
Papers and Proceedings of the Royal Society of Tasmania

Pap. Royal Inst. Brit. Archit.
Papers of the Royal Institute of British Architects

Parachute

Paradigma
Paradigma: Studi e testi

Paragone

Parallèles

Parametro

Paris & Ile-de-France: Mém.
Paris et Ile-de-France: Mémoires publiés par la Fédération des sociétés historiques et archéologiques de Paris et de l'Ile-de-France [prev. pubd as *Mém. Féd. Soc. Hist. & Archéol. Paris & Ile-de-France*]

Paris-J.
Paris-Journal

Paris-Match

Parkett

Parma A.
Parma per l'arte: Rivista quadrimestrale d'arte e cultura [cont. as *Parma nell'arte*]

Parma Econ.
Parma economica

Parnassus [cont. as *Coll. A. J.; A.J.* [New York]]

Parola Passato
Parola del passato

Parousia

Partenope

Partisan Rev.
Partisan Review

Pásmo [The thread]

Past & Present
Past and Present

Patama Banasirakan Handes

Patria Belgica

Patria Ilus.
La patria ilustrada

Patrim. Hist.
Patrimonio histórico

Patrimonium [cont. as *Bouwenbeheer*]

Patr. Séc.
Patria sécula

Pax

Pays Ange
Pays d'Ange

Pays Elsace
Pays d'Elsace

Pays Lorrain

Pazhaya Kerala

Peamin

Pechat & Revolyutsiya
Pechat i revolyutsiya

Pegaso
Pegaso: Rassegna di lettere ed arti

Peint./Cah. Théor.
Peinture/Cahiers théoriques

Pejk

Pèl & Ploma
Pèl i ploma

Pencil Points

Pennsylvania U. Mus. J.
Pennsylvania University Museum Journal

Penny Mag. Soc. Diff. Useful Knowl.
Penny Magazine of the Society for the Diffusion of Useful Knowledge

Penrose Annu.
Penrose Annual

Pensador Mex.
El pensador mexicano

People's Cult.
People's Culture

Percep. & Motor Skills
Perceptual and Motor Skills

Percep. & Psychophys.
Perception and Psychophysics

Perception

Perceptions

Perceptismo: Teór. & Polémico
Perceptismo: Teórico y polémico

Performance

Period Homes

Period. Quin. TCI
Periodico quindicinale del Touring Club italiano [cont. as *Qui Touring*]

Period. Soc. Stor. Prov. & Ant. Dioc. Como
Periodico della Società storica per la provincia e antica diocesi di Como [cont. as *Period. Stor. Comense*]

Period. Stor. Comense
Periodico storico comense: Organo della Reale deputazione di storia patria per la Lombardia [prev. pubd as *Period. Soc. Stor. Prov. & Ant. Dioc. Como*]

Periscopio

Peristil
Peristil: Zbornik radova za povijest umjetnost i arheologiju [Peristyle: a collection of articles on the history of art and archaeology]

Peritia

Persica

Perspecta

Perspective

Persp. Médit.
Perspectives méditerranéennes

Persp. USA
Perspectives USA

Pestrý Týden [Diverse week]

Petit Colosse Simi
Petit Colosse de Simi

Petit Fr. Illus.
Le Petit Français illustré

Petit Paris.
Le Petit Parisien

Pez & Serpiente
El pez y la serpiente

Pfälz. Heimat
Pfälzer Heimat: Zeitschrift für pfälzische Landeskunde

Phases

Philadelphia Mus. A.: Bull.
Philadelphia Museum of Art: Bulletin [prev. pubd as *PA Mus. Bull.*; cont. as *Bull.: Philadelphia Mus. A.*]

Philippines Mag.
Philippines Magazine

Philippines Q.
Philippines Quarterly

Philobiblon
Philobiblon: Eine Vierteljahresschrift für Buch- und Graphiksammler

Philologus

Philos. Q.
Philosophical Quarterly

Philos. Rev.
Philosophical Review

Philos. Stud.
Philosophical Studies

Philos. Trans.
Philosophical Transactions [Royal Society of London]

Phoebus
Phoebus: Zeitschrift für bildende Kunst

Phoenix

Phot. Alle
Photographie für alle

Phot. Annu.
Photography Annual [prev. pubd as *Amer. Annu. Phot.*]

Phot. Bull.
Photographic Bulletin

Phot. Centbl.
Photographisches Centralblatt

Phot. Colr
Photographic Collector

Phot. F.A. J.
Photographic and Fine Art Journal

Phot. Hippique
La Photographie hippique

Phot. J.
Photographic Journal

Phot. Korr.
Photographische Korrespondenz

Phot. Mosaics
Photographic Mosaics

Phot. News
Photographic News

Photo

Photo Communiqué

Photo-Era

Photographies

Photoresearcher

Phototechniques

Photo 13

Photo-Vision

Phot. Times [London]
Photographic Times [London]

Phot. Times [New York]
Photographic Times [New York]

Phréat., Lang. & Création
Phréatique, langage et création

Physis

Pict. Atlas Australia
Picturesque Atlas of Australia

Pict. Post
Picture Post

Pict. Rev.
Pictorial Review

Pinacotheca

Pinakothiki

Pion

Pioneer America

Pioneri

Piovano Arlotto
Il Piovano Arlotto

Pirckheimer-Jb.
Pirckheimer-Jahrbuch

Pirineos

Places

Plains Anthropologist

Plaisirs France
Plaisirs de France

Plan

Plan. Hist. Bull.
Planning History Bulletin

Plan: J. S. Afr. Architects
Plan: Journal for South African Architects

Planner

Plan. Persp.
Planning Perspectives

Playboy

Pluma & Pincel
Pluma y pincel

Poesia

Poésie 43

Poetica

Poetik & Herm.
Poetik und Hermeneutik

Poezja

Poikila Byz.
Poikila byzantina

Pol. Afr.
Politique africaine

Polar Rec.
Polar Record

Pol. A. Stud.
Polish Art Studies

Polata Knigopisnaya

Polin

Politik [The politician]

Pol. Sztuka Ludowa [Polish folk art]

Polyarnaya Zvezda

Pompeiana

Popolo Italia
Popolo d'Italia

Pop. Phot.
Popular Photography

Pop. Sci. Mthly
Popular Science Monthly

Porta Orient.
Porta orientale

Port. & Artnews Annu.
Portfolio and Artnews Annual

Portfolio [Annual of the graphic arts, Cincinnati, OH]

Portfolio [London]

Portfolio [Magazine of the fine arts, New York]

Porticus
Porticus: The Journal of the Memorial Art Gallery of the University of Rochester

Portraits Hier
Portraits d'hier

Position Thèses Ecole Chartes
Position des thèses de l'Ecole des chartes

Possibilities

Poster

Posters & Designers
Posters and their Designers [cont. as *A. & Publ.*; *Posters & Publ.*; *Mod. Publ.*]

Posters & Publ.
Posters and Publicity [see *Posters & Designers*]

Post-Med. Archaeol.
Post-Medieval Archaeology

Potsdam. Tagztg
Potsdamer Tageszeitung

Pount

Pour Sci.
Pour la science

Povos & Cult.
Povos e culturas

Prace Hist. Sztuki
Prace z historii sztuki [Papers on the history of art]

Prace Kom. Hist. Sztuki
Prace Komisji historii sztuki [Proceedings of the Commission for the History of Art]

Prace & Mat. Muz. Archeol. & Etnog. Łodzi
Prace i materiały Muzeum archeologicznego i etnograficznego w Łodzi

Prachya Pratibha

Pract. Photographer
Practical Photographer

Praehist. Asiae Orient.
Praehistoria Asiae Orientalis

Praesens

Prag. Rundschau
Prager Rundschau

Prähist. Z.
Prähistorische Zeitschrift

Prairie Sch. Rev.
Prairic School Review

Praktika Akad. Athen
Praktika tis Akademias Athenon [Proceedings of the Athenian Academy]

Praktika Athen. Archaiol. Etaireias
Praktika tes archaiologikes etaireias en Athenais [Proceedings of the Athenian archaeological service]

Praktische Forschft.
Praktische Forschungshefte [prev. pubd as & cont. as *Arch. Sippenforsch. & Verw. Geb.*]

Prato
Prato: Storia e arte

Pravda

Pravoslavnyy Palest. Sborn.
Pravoslavnyy palestinskiy sbornik

Praxis

Précis Acad. Rouen
Précis de l'Académie de Rouen

Préfaces

Préhist. Ariége.
Préhistoire ariégeoise

Prelo

Pre-Raphaelite Rev.
Pre-Raphaelite Review [cont. as *J. Pre-Raphaelite Stud.*]

Présence Afr.
Présence africaine

Presenza Romagnola
Presenza romagnola

Preview: York A.G. Bull.
Preview: York Art Gallery Bulletin

Prilozi Povijesti Umjetnosti Dalmac.
Prilozi povijesti umjetnosti Dalmaciji [Contributions to art history in Dalmatia]

Primato A. It.
Primato artistico italiano

Primera Plana
Primera plana

Primitive A. Newslett.
Primitive Art Newsletter

Prince Of Wales Mus. Bull.
Prince of Wales Museum Bulletin

Princeton U. Lib. Chron.
Princeton University Library Chronicle

Príncipe Viana
Príncipe de Viana

Print

Prints

Prism

Prisma [i) 1905-1908, Lima; ii) 1940s, Sweden]

Priv. Lib.
Private Library

Prixia Sacra
Prixia sacra

Proa

Pro A. & Libris
Pro arte et libris

Prob. Archit.
Problemy architektury

Prob. Izkustwoto
Problemi na izkustwoto

Problemy

Prob. Sovremennogo Grado-Stroitel'stva
Problemy sovremennogo grado-
stroitel'stva [Problems of
contemporary city building]

Proc. Amer. Acad. A. & Sci.
Proceedings of the American
Academy of Arts and Sciences
[cont. as *Daedalus*]

Proc. Amer. Acad. Jew. Res.
Proceedings of the American
Academy for Jewish Research

Proc. Amer. Antiqua. Soc.
Proceedings of the American
Antiquarian Society

Proc. Amer. Inst. Architects
Proceedings of the American
Institute of Architects

Proc. Amer. Philos. Soc.
Proceedings of the American
Philosophical Society

Proc. Aristotelian Soc.
Proceedings of the Aristotelian
Society

Proc. Brit. Acad.
Proceedings of the British
Academy

Proc. Cambridge Antiqua. Soc.
Proceedings of the Cambridge
Antiquarian Society

Proc. Devon Archaeol. Explor. Soc.
Proceedings of the Devon
Archaeological Exploration
Society

Procellaria

Procesos

Process: Archit.
Process: Architecture

*Procès-verbaux & Mém.. Acad. Sci.,
B.-Lett. & A. Besançon & Franche-
Comté*
Procès-verbaux et mémoires,
Académie des sciences, belles-
lettres et arts de Besançon et de
Franche-Comté

*Proc. Hants Field Club & Archaeol.
Soc.*
Proceedings of the Hampshire
Field Club and Archaeological
Society

Proche Orient Chrét.
Proche Orient chrétien

Proc. Huguenot Soc. London
Proceedings of the Huguenot
Society of London

Proc. Inst. Civ. Engin.
Proceedings of the Institution of
Civil Engineers

Proc. Int. Confer. Sinology
Proceedings of the International
Conference on Sinology

Proc. Israel Acad. Sci. & Human.
Proceedings of the Israel Academy
of Sciences and Humanities

Proc. MA Hist. Soc.
Proceedings of the Massachusetts
Historical Society

Proc. N. Acad. Sci.
Proceedings of the National
Academy of Sciences

Proc. 1989 David Colloq.
Proceedings of the 1989 David
Colloquium

Proc. Philos. Soc. Glasgow
Proceedings of the Philosophical
Society of Glasgow

Proc. Prehist. Soc.
Proceedings of the Prehistoric
Society

*Proc. Royal Anthropol. Inst. GB &
Ireland*
Proceedings of the Royal
Anthropological Institute of Great
Britain and Ireland

Proc. Royal Asiat. Soc., Ceylon Branch
Proceedings of the Royal Asiatic
Society, Ceylon Branch [incorp. in
*J. Royal Asiat. Soc., Sri Lankan
Branch*]

Proc. Royal Geog. Soc.
Proceedings of the Royal
Geographical Society

Proc. Royal Inst.
Proceedings of the Royal
Institution

Proc. Royal Irish Acad.
Proceedings of the Royal Irish
Academy

Proc. Royal Philos. Soc. Glasgow
Proceedings of the Royal
Philosophical Society of Glasgow

Proc. Semin. Arab. Stud.
Proceedings of the Seminar for
Arabian Studies

Proc. Soc. Antiqua.
Proceedings of the Society of
Antiquaries

Proc. Soc. Antiqua. Scotland
Proceedings of the Society of
Antiquaries for Scotland

Proc. Soc. Bibl. Archaeol.
Proceedings of the Society of
Biblical Archaeology

Proc. Soc. Brit. Architects
Proceedings of the Society for
British Architects

Proc. Soc. Silver Colrs
Proceedings of the Society of
Silver Collectors

*Proc. Somerset Archaeol. & Nat. Hist.
Soc.*
Proceedings of the Somersetshire
Archaeological and Natural
History Society

Proc. Suffolk Inst. Archaeol. & Hist.
Proceedings of the Suffolk
Institute of Archaeology and
History

Proc. US N. Mus.
Proceedings of the United States
National Museum

Proc. Victoria Inst.
Proceedings of the Victoria
Institute

Professional Geographer

Profil

Prog. Archit.
Progressive Architecture

Prog. Fot.
Progresso fotografico

Progrès

Proj. & Constr.
Projeto e construção

Projek [Bratislava]

Projekt [Warsaw]

Projeto

Prolet. Kul't.
Proletarskaya kul'tura

Prologomena

Prologue

Prométhée [prev. pubd as & cont. as
Amour A.]

Pronkstukken

Propagateur Aube
Propagateur de l'aube

Proporzioni
Proporzioni: Studi di storia
dell'arte

Prop. & Ric.
Proposte e ricerche

Prospects

Prospettiva [Florence]

Prospettive [Rome]

Prov. Anjou
Province d'Anjou

Provence Hist.
Provence historique

Proverbe

Prov. Lucca
Provincia di Lucca

Prov. Treviso
Provincia di Treviso

Prt Colr
Print Collector

Prt Colr Club
Print Collector's Club

Prt Colr/ Conoscitore Stampe
Print Collector/Il conoscitore di
stampe

Prt Colr Newslett.
Print Collector's Newsletter

Prt Colr Q.
Print Collector's Quarterly

Prt Connoisseur
Print Connoisseur

Prtg A.
Printing Art

Prt News
Print News

Prt Q.
Print Quarterly

Prt Rev.
Print Review

Prtseller & Colr
Printseller and Collector

Prudentia

Przegląd A.
Przegląd artystyczny [Artistic
review]

Przegląd Hist. Sztuki
Przegląd historii sztuki [Art
history review]

Przegląd Kult.
Przegląd Kulturalny [Cultural
review]

Przegląd Powszechny [Universal
review]

Przegląd Tech.
Przegląd techniczny [Technical
review]

Psicon: Riv. Int. Archit.
Psicon: Rivista internazionale di
architettura

Psychol. Bull.
Psychological Bulletin

Psychol. Forsch.
Psychologische Forschung

Psychol. Rev.
Psychological Review

Psychol. Today
Psychology Today

*Publicatie Prov. Gallo-Romeins Mus.
Tongeren*
Publicatie Provinciaal Gallo-
Romeins Museum te Tongeren

*Pubn Cent. Eur. Etud.
Burgundomédianes*
Publication du Centre européen
d'études burgundomédianes

Pubns Can. Archvs
Publications of the Canadian
Archives

Pubns Ecole Fr. Extrême-Orient
Publications de l'Ecole française
d'Extrême-Orient

Pubns Jesup N. Pacific Expedition
Publications of the Jesup North
Pacific Expedition

Pubns Mod. Lang. Assoc.
Publications of the Modern
Languages Association

*Pubns Soc. Hist. & Archéol. Limbourg
Maestricht*
Publications de la Société
historique et archéologique dans le
Limbourg à Maestricht

Pubs Avulsas
Publicações avulsas

Puck
Puck: A Journalette of Fun

Pué

Puglia Paleocrist.
Puglia paleocristiana

Pulgyo Misul

Punch

Punjab Govt Gaz.
Punjab Government Gazette

Punjab U. Res. Bull. (A.)
Punjab University Research
Bulletin (Arts)

Punsch

Purāna

Puratattva
Puratattva: Bulletin of the Indian
Archaeological Society

Purnima

Puteoli

*Qadmoniot: Q. Ant. Eretz Israel &
Bibl. Lands*
Qadmoniot: Quarterly for the
Antiquities of Eretz Israel and
Biblical Lands

Qbl. Hist. Ver. Grossherzogtum Hessen
Quartalsblätter des Historischen Vereins für das Grossherzogtum Hessen

Q. Bull. Amer. Inst. Architects
Quarterly Bulletin of the American Institute of Architects

Q. Bull. Irish Georg. Soc.
Quarterly Bulletin of the Irish Georgian Society

Q. Cult. Triangle, UNESCO–Sri Lanka Proj.
Quarterly of the Cultural Triangle, UNESCO–Sri Lanka Project

Q. Dept Ant. Palestine
Quarterly of the Department of Antiquities in Palestine

Qedem

Q. J. Expermntl Psychol.
Quarterly Journal of Experimental Psychology

Q. J. Lib. Congr.
Quarterly Journal of the Library of Congress

Q. J. Lit., Sci., & A.
Quarterly Journal of Literature, Science and the Arts

Q. J. N. Cent. Perf. A.
Quarterly Journal of the National Centre for the Performing Arts

Q. Pap. Archit.
Quarterly Papers on Architecture

Q. Rev.
Quarterly Review

Quad. Accad. Chigiana
Quaderni dell'Accademia chigiana

Quad. Antiqua.
Quaderni dell'antiquariato

Quad. Archeol. Libia
Quaderni di archeologia di Libia [prev. pubd as *Africa It.*]

Quad. Archit. & Des.
Quaderni di architettura e disegno

Quad. Arqueol. & Hist. Ciutat
Quaderns d'arqueologia i història de la ciutat

Quad. Arquit. & Urb.
Quaderns d'arquitectura i urbanisme [prev. pubd as *Cuad. Arquit.*; *Cuad. Arquit. & Urb.*]

Quad. Bitontini
Quaderni bitontini

Quad. Brera
Quaderni di Brera

Quad. Conoscitore Stampe
Quaderni del conoscitore di stampe

Quad. Estud. Med.
Quaderns d'estudis medievals

Quad. Exili
Quaderns de l'exili

Quad. Filol. Clas.
Quaderni di filologia classica

Quad. Fond. Camillo Caetani
Quaderni della Fondazione Camillo Caetani

Quad. Gal. N. Marche
Quaderni della Galleria nazionale delle Marche

Quad. Ist. It. Cult. R.A.E.
Quaderni dell'Istituto italiano di cultura per la Repubblica Araba d'Egitto

Quad. Ist. N. Stud. Rinascimento Merid.
Quaderni dell'Istituto nazionale di studi sul Rinascimento meridionale

Quad. Ist. Stor. A. Med. & Mod.
Quaderni dell'Istituto di storia dell'arte medievale e moderna

Quad. Ist. Stor. Archit.
Quaderni dell'Istituto di storia dell'architettura

Quad. Ist. Stor. A. U. Genova
Quaderni dell'Istituto di storia dell'arte dell'Università di Genova

Quad. Ist. Stud. Islam.
Quaderni dell'Istituto di studi islamici

Quad. Ist. Top.
Quaderni dell'Istituto di topografia

Quad. Ist. Top. Ant.
Quaderni dell'Istituto di topografia antica

Quad. Italo-Sviz.
Quaderni italo-svizzeri

Quad. Lotus
Quaderni di Lotus

Quad. Neoclass.
Quaderni sul neoclassicismo

Quad. Padano
Quadrante padano

Quad. Pal. Te
Quaderni del Palazzo del Te

Quad. Pal. Venezia
Quaderni del Palazzo Venezia

Quad. Poro
Quaderni Poro

Quadrante

Quad. Rest.
Quaderni del restauro

Quad. Ric. Sci.
Quaderni della ricerca scientifica

Quadrivio

Quadrum

Quad. Semin. Iran. U. Venezia
Quaderni del Seminario di iranistica dell'Università di Venezia

Quad. Sopr. Archeol. Prov. Cagliari & Oristano
Quaderni della Soprintendenza archeologica per le province di Cagliari e Oristano

Quad. Sopr. Beni A. & Stor. Venezia
Quaderni della Soprintendenza di beni artistici e storici di Venezia

Quad. Sopr. Gal. Liguria
Quaderni della Soprintendenza alle gallerie della Liguria

Quad. Stampe
Quaderni con stampe

Quad. Stor. U. Padova
Quaderni per la storia dell'Università di Padova

Quad. Stud. Arab.
Quaderni di studi arabi

Quad. Stud. & Ric. Rest. Archit. & Territ.
Quaderni di studi e ricerche di restauro architettonico e territoriale

Quad. Vittoriale
Quaderni del Vittoriale

Quaerendo [prev. pubd as *Het Boek*]

QUASAR
QUASAR: Quaderni di storia dell'architettura e restauro

Quatre Gats

Queen

Queen's Q.
Queen's Quarterly

Quellen & Forsch. Gesch. Kreises Beckum
Quellen und Forschungen zur Geschichte des Kreises Beckum

Quellen Gesch. Stadt Wien
Quellen zur Geschichte der Stadt Wien

Quellenschr. Kstgesch.
Quellenschriften für Kunstgeschichte

Quellenstud. Holl. Kstgesch.
Quellenstudien zur holländischen Kunstgeschichte

Questions Liturg. & Paroiss.
Questions liturgiques et paroissiales

Que-Vlo-Vé

Quick

Qui Touring [prev. pubd as *Period. Quin. TCI*]

Quotidien

Racar
Racar: Revue d'art canadienne

Rac. Vinc.
Raccolta vinciana

Radical Hist.
Radical History

Radovi JAZU (Radovi Jugoslavenska akademija znanosti umjenosti) [Papers of the Yugoslav Academy of Science and Fine Arts]

Radovi Inst. Povijest Umjetnosti
Radovi Instituta za povijest umjetnosti [Work of the Art History Institute]

Radovi-Zadar

Raggi

RA Illus.
Royal Academy Illustrated [suppl. of *Mag. A.* until 1904; cont. indep. as *RA Illus.*]

Rapa Nui J.
Rapa Nui Journal: The Journal of the Easter Island Foundation

RA: Royal Acad. Mag.
RA: Royal Academy Magazine

Raška Baština

Rass. A.
Rassegna d'arte [cont. as *Rass. A. Ant. & Mod.*]

Rass. A. Ant. & Mod.
Rassegna d'arte antica e moderna [prev. pubd as *Rass. A.*]

Rass. Archit. & Urb.
Rassegna di architettura e urbanistica

Rass. Archv Stato
Rassegna degli archivi di stato

Rass. A. Sen.
Rassegna d'arte senese

Rass. A. Sen. & Cost.
Rassegna d'arte senese e del costume

Rass. A. Umbra
Rassegna di arte umbra

Rass. Bibliog. A. It.
Rassegna bibliografica dell'arte italiana

Rass. Cult. & Vita Scolast.
Rassegna di cultura e di vita scolastica

Rass. Contemp.
Rassegna contemporanea

Rassegna

Rass. Gallara. Stor. A.
Rassegna gallaratese di storia dell'arte

Rass. Graf.
Rassegna grafica

Rass. Istr. A.
Rassegna dell'istruzione artistica

Rass. It.
Rassegna italiana

Rass. It. A.
Rassegna italiana dell'arte

Rass. March.
Rassegna marchigiana

Rass. Mens. Israel
Rassegna mensile di Israel

Rass. Mod. Lett. & A.
Rassegna moderna di letteratura ed arte

Rass. N.
Rassegna nazionale

Rass.: Prob. Archit. Amb.
Rassegna: Problemi di architettura dell'ambiente

Rass. Sov.
Rassegna sovietica

Rass. Stor. Tosc.
Rassegna storica toscana

Rass. Stud. Etiop.
Rassegna di studi etiopici

Rass. Stud. & Not.
Rassegna di studi e di notizie

Ratio

Raum & Handwk
Raum und Handwerk

Razo

Reading Med. Stud.
Reading Medieval Studies

Readings Glass Hist.
Readings in Glass History

Real Assoc. Arquitectos Civ. & Arqueólogos Port.: Bol. Arquit. & Arqueol.
Real associação dos arquitectos civis e arqueólogos portugueses: Boletim arquitectonico e de arqueologia

Reales Sitios: Rev. Patrm. N.
Reales sitios: Revista del patrimonio nacional

Real Estate Rec.
Real Estate Record

Real Image

Réalités

Réalités Nouv.
Réalités nouvelles

Real Life

Rec. A. Mus., Princeton U.
Record of the Art Museum, Princeton University

Rec. Auckland Inst. & Mus.
Records of the Auckland Institute and Museum

Rec. Austral. Mus.
Records of the Australian Museum

Rec. Bucks
Records of Buckinghamshire

Recens. & Mitt. Bild. Kst
Recensionen und Mitteilungen über bildende Kunst

Rech. Diderot & Enc.
Recherches sur Diderot et sur l'encyclopédie

Rech. Sci. Relig.
Recherches de science religieuse

Rechtsgeleerd Mag.
Rechtsgeleerd magazijn [merged with *De Tijdspiegel* to form *R. M. Themis*]

Rec. Hunts
Records of Huntingdonshire

Recl Anc. Inventaires
Recueil d'anciens inventaires

Recl Mus. N. [Belgrade]
Recueil du Musée national [Belgrade]

Recl Trav. Fac. Archit., U. Belgrade
Recueil des travaux de la Faculté d'architecture, Université de Belgrade

Recl Trav.: Muz. Primenjene Umětnosti
Recueil des travaux: Muzej za primenjene umětnosti [Museum of Applied Arts]

Recl Trav. Relatifs Philol. & Archéol. Egyp. & Assyr.
Recueil des travaux relatifs à la philologie et à l'archéologie égyptiennes et assyriennes

Rec. N. Mus. & A.G., Boroko
Records of the National Museum and Art Gallery, Boroko

Rec. PNG Mus.
Records of the Papua New Guinea Museum

Rec. S. Austral. Mus.
Records of the South Australian Museum

Rede Globo

ReD: Rev. Devětsilu
ReD: Revue Devětsilu [Review of the Devetsil Group]

Reflets Monde

Ref. Serv. Rev.
Reference Services Review

Regards

Reg. Furn. Soc. J.
Regional Furniture Society Journal

Region

Register

Regnum Dei

Rei Cretariae
Rei cretariae Romanae fautorum acta [Acts of the Promoters of Roman Pottery]

Reik

Relaciones: Soc. Argentina Antropol.
Relaciones: Sociedad argentina de antropología

Relig. & Cult.
Religion y cultura [merger of *Ciudad Dios* & *España & América*]

Removador

Removedor

Ren. A.
Renaissance des arts

Ren. A. Fr. & Indust. Luxe
Renaissance de l'art français et des industries de luxe

Rendezvous

Rendi. Accad. Archeol., Lett. & B.A.
Rendiconti dell'Accademia di archeologia, lettere e belle arti [prev. pubd as *Atti Accad. Archeol., Lett. & B.A.*]

Rendi. Accad. N. Lincei, Cl. Sci. Mor., Stor. & Filol.
Rendiconti dell'Accademia nazionale dei Lincei, classe di scienze morali, storiche e filologiche [prev. pubd as *Rendi. R[eale] Accad. N. Lincei, Cl. Sci. Mor., Stor. & Filol.*]

Rendi. Adunanze Solenni: Accad. N. Lincei
Rendiconti delle Adunanze solenni: Accademia nazionale dei Lincei

Rendi. Pont. Accad. Romana Archeol.
Rendiconti della Pontificia accademia romana di archeologia

Rendi. R[eale] Accad. N. Lincei, Cl. Sci. Mor., Stor. & Filol.
Rendiconti della R[eale] accademia nazionale dei Lincei, classe di scienze morali, storiche e filologiche [cont. as *Rendi. Accad. N. Lincei, Cl. Sci. Mor., Stor. & Filol.*]

Rendi. Reale Ist. Lombardo Sci. & Lett.
Rendiconti del Reale istituto lombardo di scienze e lettere

Renditions

Rendi. Tornate & Lavori Accad. Archeol., Lett. & B.A.
Rendiconto delle tornate e dei lavori dell'Accademia di archeologia, lettere e belle arti

Ren. Drama
Renaissance Drama

Ren. Mitt.
Renaissance Mitteilungen

Ren. & Mod. Stud.
Renaissance and Modern Studies

Ren. News
Renaissance News [cont. as *Ren. Q.*]

Rénovation Esthét.
Rénovation esthétique

Ren. Q.
Renaissance Quarterly [prev. pubd as *Ren. News*; later incorp. into *Stud. Ren.*]

Ren. & Reformation
Renaissance and Reformation

Ren. Stud.
Renaissance Studies

Rep. Brit. Assoc. Adv. Sci., S. Africa
Report of the British Association for the Advancement of Science, South Africa

Rep. Dept Ant., Cyprus
Report of the Department of Antiquities, Cyprus

Repert. Amer.
Repertorio americano

Repert. Kstwiss.
Repertorium für Kunstwissenschaft [prev. pubd as *Jb. Kstwiss.* [1868–1873]; merged with *Jb. Kstwiss.* [1923–30] & *Z. Bild. Kst* to form *Z. Kstgesch.*]

Rep. Ethno-Technol. Res.
Report of Ethno-technological Research

Reporter-Objectif
Reporter-objectif

Rep. Oxon. Archaeol. Soc.
Report of the Oxfordshire Archaeological Society

Representations

Rep. Soc. Friends St George's
Report of the Society of Friends of St George's

Republika

Res
Res: Anthropology and Aesthetics

Res. Afr. Lit.
Research in African Literatures

Res. Bull.: Inst. Study Worship & Relig. Archit.
Research Bulletin: The Institute for the Study of Worship and Religious Architecture

Restauratievademecum

Restaurator
Restaurator: International Journal for the Preservation of Library and Archival Materials

Restauro

Rest. Carlino
Il resto del Carlino

Réun. Soc. B.-A. Dépt.
Réunion des Sociétés des beaux-arts des départements

Rev. A.
Revue de l'art

Rev. A. [Santiago]
Revista de arte [Santiago]

Rev. A. Anc. & Mod.
Revue de l'art ancien et moderne

Rev. A. Asiat.
Revue des arts asiatiques [cont. as *A. Asiatiques*]

Rev. Acad. Inscr. & B.-Lett.
Revue de l'Académie des inscriptions et belles-lettres

Rev. A. Chrét.
Revue de l'art chrétien

Rev. A. Déc.
Revue des arts décoratifs

Rev. Afr.
Revue africaine

Rev. Agustiniana
Revista agustiniana [cont. as *Ciudad Dios*]

Rev. Aisthesis
Revista Aisthesis: Revista chilena de investigaciones estéticas

Rev. A. & Letras
Revista de artes y letras

Rev. Alsace
Revue d'Alsace

Rev. Ameublement
Revue de l'ameublement

Rev. Andina
Revista andina

Rev. Anthropol.
Revue anthropologique

Rev. Antropol.
Revista de antropología

Rev. Antwerp.
Revue Antwerpen

Rev. A. & Oficios
Revista de arte y oficios

Rev. Apollo
Revue Apollo

Rev. Aragón
Revista de Aragón [cont. as *Cult. Esp.*]

Rev. Archéol.
Revue archéologique

Rev. Archéologues & Historiens A. Louvain
Revue des archéologues et historiens d'art de Louvain

Rev. Archéol. Ouest
Revue archéologique de l'Ouest

Rev. Archéol. Picardie
Revue archéologique de Picardie

Rev. Archit.
Revue architecture

Rev. Archit. & Trav. Pub.
Revue de l'architecture et des travaux publics

Rev. Archv N. Perú
Revista del Archivo nacional del Perú

Rev. Archvs, Bib. & Mus.
Revista de archivos, bibliotecas y museos

Rev. Arqueol. [Lisbon]
Revista arqueológica [Lisbon]

Rev. Arqueol. [Madrid]
Revista de arqueología [Madrid]

Rev. Arquit. [Arg.]
Revista de arquitectura [Argentina]

Rev. Arquit. [Lisbon]
Revista de arquitectura [Lisbon]

Rev. Arte Sevill.
Revista de arte sevillano

Rev. Assyriol.
Revue d'assyriologie

Rev. Auvergne
Revue d'Auvergne

Rev. B. A. [Madrid]
Revista de bellas artes [Madrid]

Rev. B. A. [Mexico]
Revista de bellas artes [Mexico]

Rev. Bas-Poitou
Revue du Bas-Poitou

Rev. Belge
La Revue belge [cont. as *J. Hist. & Litt.*]

Rev. Belge A. & Hist.
Revue belge d'art et d'histoire

Rev. Belge Archéol. & Hist. A.
Revue belge d'archéologie et d'histoire de l'art [prev. pubd as *Rev. Belge Archéol. & Hist. A./ Belge Tijdschr. Oudhdknde & Kstgesch.*]

Rev. Belge Archéol. & Hist. A./Belge Tijdschr. Oudhdknde & Kstgesch.
Revue belge d'archéologie et d'histoire de l'art/Belge tijdschrift voor oudheidkunde en kunstgeschiedenis [prev. pubd as *An. Acad. Royale Archéol. Belgique*; cont. as *Rev. Belge Archéol. & Hist. A.*]

Rev. Belge Numi.
Revue belge de numismatique [prev. pubd as *Rev. Numi. Belge*]

Rev. Belge Philol. & Hist.
Revue belge de philologie et d'histoire

Rev. Belgique
Revue de Belgique

Rev. Bénédictine
Revue bénédictine

Rev. Bib.
i) Revue des bibliothèques
ii) Revue biblique

Rev. Bibliof.
Revista bibliófila

Rev. Bib. N.
i) Revista de la Biblioteca nacional
ii)Revue de la Bibliothèque nationale

Rev. Bib. N. [Lisbon]
Revista da Biblioteca nacional [Lisbon]

Rev. Bib. N. José Marti
Revista de la Biblioteca nacional José Marti

Rev. Bib. Paroiss. & Faits Relig. Prov. Ecclés. Avignon
Revue des bibliothèques paroissiales et des faits religieux de la province ecclésiastique d'Avignon

Rev. Blanche
Revue blanche

Rev. Bleue
Revue bleue

Rev. & Bol. Acad. N. B.A.
Revista e boletim da Academia nacional de belas artes

Rev. Bourgogne
Revue de Bourgogne

Rev. Bourguignonne Ens. Sup.
Revue bourguignonne de l'enseignement supérieur

Rev. Bretagne & Vendée
Revue de Bretagne et de Vendée

Rev. Can.
Revue canadienne

Rev. Castell.
Revista castellana

Rev. Celtique
Revue celtique

Rev. Champagne & Brie
Revue de Champagne et de Brie

Rev. Colomb. Antropol.
Revista colombiana de antropología

Rev. Colomb. Flclor
Revista colombiana de folclor

Rev. Comique
Revue comique

Rev. Comminges
Revue de Comminges

Rev. Contemp.
Revue contemporaine

Rev. Corée
Revue de Corée

Rev. Crit. Hispamer.
Revista crítica hispanoamericana

Rev. Cult.
Revista de cultura

Rev. Cult. [Macau]
Revista de cultura [Macau]

Rev. de Archit.
Revue de l'architecture

Rev. de Arquit.
Revista de arquitectura

Rev. Dept. Hist. Med.
Revista del Departamento de historia medieval

Rev. des A.
Revue des arts

Rev. Deux Mondes
Revue des deux mondes

Rev. Dialectología & Trad. Pop.
Revista de dialectología y tradiciones populares

Rev. Diners
Revista Diners

Rev. 19e Siècle
Revue du 19e siècle

Rev. Ecles.
Revista eclesiástica

Rev. Egyptol.
Revue d'égyptologie

Réveil

Rev. Enc.
Revue encyclopédique

Rev. Enc. Archit.
La Revue d'encyclopédie d'architecture

Rev. Esp. A.
Revista española de arte

Rev. España
Revista de España

Rev. Esp. Antropol. Amer.
Revista española de antropología americana

Rev. Esthét.
Revue d'esthétique

Rev. Estud. Extrem.
Revista de estudios extremeños

Rev. Ethnog. & Sociol.
Review of Ethnography and Sociology

Rev. Ethnog. & Trad. Pop.
Revue d'ethnographie et des traditions populaires [prev. pubd as *Rev. Trad. Pop.*; cont. as *Outre-mer*]

Rev. Ethnol. Québec
Revue d'ethnologie du Québec

Rev. Ethnol. & Sociol.
Revue d'ethnologie et de sociologie

Rev. Etud. Anc.
Revue des études anciennes

Rev. Etud. Armén.
Revue des études arméniennes

Rev. Etud. Augustin.
Revue des études augustiniennes

Rev. Etud. Byz.
Revue des études byzantines [prev. pubd as *Etud. Byz.*; *Echos Orient*]

Rev. Etud. Géorg. & Caucas.
Revue des études georgiennes et caucasiennes

Rev. Etud. Gr.
Revue des études grecques

Rev. Etud. Islam.
Revue des études islamiques

Rev. Etud. Juives
Revue des études juives

Rev. Etud. Lat.
Revue des études latines

Rev. Etud. Napoléoniennes
Revue des études napoléoniennes

Rev. Eur.
Revue européenne

Rev. Excel. Disput. Prov. Cuenca
Revista de la Excelentisima diputación provincial de Cuenca

Rev. & Expositor
Review and Expositor

Rev. Filol. Esp.
Revista de filología española

Rev. Fot.
Revue fotografie

Rev. Fr.
Revue française

Rev. France
La Revue de la France

Rev. Fr. Elite Eur.
Revue française de l'élite européenne

Rev. Fr. Hist. Livre
Revue française d'histoire du livre

Rev. Fundaţiilor Regale
Revista fundaţiilor regale

Rev. Garcia da Orta
Revista de Garcia da Orta

Rev. Gén. Archit.
Revue générale de l'architecture

Rev. Gén. Biog. & Nécrol.
Revue générale biographique et nécrologique

Rev. Gen. Ens. Sourds Muets
Revue générale de l'enseignement des sourds muets

Rev. Géog. E.
Revue géographique de l'Est

Rev. Géog. Pays Médit.
Revue géographique des pays méditerranéens

Rev. Gerona
Revista de Gerona

Rev. Guadalupe
Revista de Guadalupe

Rev. Guimarães
Revista de Guimarães: Publicação da Sociedade Martins Sarmento

Rev. Hebdomadaire
Revue hebdomadaire

Rev. Hisp.
Revue hispanique

Rev. Hist.
Revue historique

Rev. Hist A.
Revue de l'histoire de l'art

Rev. Hist. & Archéol.
Revue d'histoire et d'archéologie

Rev. Hist. Ardenn.
Revue historique ardennaise

Rev. Hist. Bordeaux & Dépt Gironde
Revue historique de Bordeaux et du département de la Gironde

Rev. Hist. Canaria
Revista de historia canaria

Rev. Hist. Ecclés.
Revue d'histoire ecclésiastique

Rev. Hist. Eglise France
Revue d'histoire de l'église de France

Rev. Hist. & Geneal. Esp.
Revista de historia y de genealogía española

Rev. Hist. Inde Fr.
Revue historique de l'Inde française

Rev. Hist. Litt. France
Revue d'histoire littéraire de la France

Rev. Hist. & Litt. Languedoc
Revue historique et littéraire du Languedoc

Rev. Hist. Mod. & Contemp.
Revue d'histoire moderne et contemporaine

Rev. Hist. & Philos.
Revue d'histoire et de la philosophie

Rev. Hist. Relig.
Revue d'histoire des religions

Rev. Hist. Sci. & Applic.
Revue d'histoire des sciences et leurs applications

Rev. Hist. Spirit.
Revue d'histoire de la spiritualité

Rev. Hist. Théât.
Revue d'histoire du théâtre

Rev. Hist. Vaudoise
Revue historique vaudoise

Rev. Hist. Versailles
Revue de l'histoire de Versailles

Rev. Ideas Estét.
Revista de ideas estéticas

Rev. Illus.
Revue illustrée

Rev. Indép.
Revue indépendante

Rev. Indon. & Malay. Affairs
Review of Indonesian and Malaysian Affairs

Rev. Inst. Antropol.
Revista del Instituto de antropología

Rev. Inst. Arqueol. Cuzco
Revista del Instituto arqueológico del Cuzco

Rev. Inst. B.-Lett. Arab.
Revue de l'Institut des belles-lettres arabes

Rev. Inst. Cult. Puertorriqueña
Revista del Instituto de cultura puertorriqueña

Rev. Inst. Estud. Alicant.
Revista del Instituto de estudios alicantinos

Rev. Inst. Estud. Brasil.
Revista do Instituto de estudios brasileiros

Rev. Inst. Hist. & Geog. Bras.
Revista do Instituto histórico e geográfico brasileiro

Rev. Inst. Napoléon
Revue de l'Institut Napoléon

Rev. Inst. N. Cult.
Revista del Instituto nacional de cultura

Rev. Inst. Paraguaya.
Revista del Instituto paraguayano

Rev. Int.
Revista internacional

Rev. Int. A. & Curiosité
La Revue internationale de l'art et de la curiosité

Rev. Int. Ens.
Revue internationale de l'enseignement

Rev. Int. Hist. Milit.
Revue internationale de l'histoire militaire

Revista

Rev. It. Mus.
Rivista italiana di musicologia

Rev. Lámpara
Revista lámpara

Rev. La Plata
Revista de La Plata

Rev. Lett. Mod.
Revue des lettres modernes

Rev. Litt. & A.
Revue littéraire et artistique

Rev. Litt. Comp.
Revue de littérature comparée

Rev. Lorraine Ill.
Revue Lorraine illustrée

Rev. Lotería
Revista lotería

Rev. Louvre
Revue du Louvre et des musées de France

Rev. Lyon.
Revue du Lyonnais

Rev. Mabillon
Revue Mabillon

Rev. Madagascar
Revue de Madagascar

Rev. Marseille
Revue Marseille

Rev. Mex. Estud. Antropol.
Revista mexicana de estudios antropológicos

Rev. Mex. Estud. Hist.
Revista mexicana de estudios históricos

Rev. Mod.
Revista moderna

Rev. Monde Musul.
Revue du monde musulman

Rev. Mnmts Hist.
Revue des monuments historiques

Rev. Mun.
Revista municipal

Rev. Mus. Juan Manuel Blanes
Revista del Museo Juan Manuel Blanes

Rev. Mus. N.
Revista del Museo nacional

Rev. Mus. N. Antropol. & Arqueol.
Revista del Museo nacional de antropología y arqueología

Rev. Mus. Paulista
Revista do Museo Paulista

Rev. Mus. Prov. Neuquén
Revista del Museo provincial de Neuquén

Rev. Muz. & Mnmt.: Ser. Mnmt. Ist. & A.
Revista muzeelor și monumentelor; Seria monumente istorice și de artă [prev. pubd as *Bul. Mnmt. Istor.*; *Bul. Com. Mnmt. Istor.*]

Rev. N.
Revue du Nord

Rev. N. Arquit.
Revista nacional de arquitectura [Colegio Oficial de Arquitectos; prev. pubd as *Arquitectura [Madrid]*]

Rev. N. Cult.
Revista nacional de cultura

Rev. N. Etrangère, Pol., Sci. & Litt.
Revue nationale étrangère, politique, scientifique et littéraire

Rev. Noire
Revue noire

Rev. Numi.
Revue numismatique

Rev. Numi. Belge
Revue de la numismatique belge [cont. as *Rev. Belge Numi.*]

Rev. Occidente
Revista de Occidente

Rev. Occident Musulman & Médit.
Revue de l'Occident musulman et de la Méditerranée

Revol. & Cult.
Revolución y cultura

Révol. 1848
La Révolution de 1848

Révol. Surréaliste
La Révolution surréaliste

Revolución

Revolution

Rev. Paris
Revue de Paris

Rev. Pays Loire
Revue des pays de la Loire

Rev. Pensam. Centamer.
Revista pensamiento centroamericano

Rev. Philom. Bordeaux & Sud-Ouest
Revue philomatique de Bordeaux et du Sud-ouest

Rev. Phot.
Revue de photographie

Rev. Pologne
Revue de Pologne

Rev. Prog.
Revue du progrès

Rev. Pubns A.
Review of Publications of Art

Rev. Questions Hist.
Revue des questions historiques

Rev. Répub.
Revue républicaine

Rev. Rev.
La Revue de revues

Rev. Rouen
Revue de Rouen

Rev. Roum. Hist. A.
Revue roumaine d'histoire de l'art

Rev. Sagsaywamman
Revista Sagsaywamman

Rev. Saintonge & Aunis
Revue de la Saintonge et d'Aunis

Rev. Santiago
Revista Santiago

Rev. Sci. Humaines
Revue des sciences humaines

Rev. Sci. Philos. & Théol.
Revue des sciences philosophiques et théologiques

Rev. Scot. Cult.
Review of Scottish Culture

Rev. Soc. Amis Mus. Armée
Revue de la société des amis du Musée de l'armée

Rev. Soc. Etud. XVIIe Siècle
Revue de la Société d'études du XVIIe siècle

Rev. Sociale
Revue sociale

Rev. Soc. Martins Sarmento
Revue de la Société Martins Sarmento

Rev. Soc. Sav.
Revue des sociétés savantes

Rev. SPAHN
Revista do Serviço do Patrimônio histórico e artístico nacional

Rev. Stud. Orient.
Revista di studi orientali

Rev. Suisse Numi.
Revue suisse de numismatique

Rev. Summa
Revista summa

Rev. Tarn
Revue du Tarn

Rev. Tournais.
Revue tournaisienne

Rev. Trad. Pop.
Revue des traditions populaires [cont. as *Rev. Ethnog. & Trad. Pop.*; *Outre-mer*]

Rev. U. Bruxelles
Revue de l'Université de Bruxelles

Rev. U. Coimbra
Revista da Universidade de Coimbra

Rev. U. Complutense
Revista de la Universidad complutense

Rev., U. La Habana
Revista, Universidad de La Habana

Rev. U. Madrid
Revista de la Universidad de Madrid

Rev. U. Moncton
Revue de l'Université de Moncton

Rev. Un. Affiche Fr.
Revue de l'Union de l'affiche française

Rev. Univl. A.
Revue universelle des arts

Rev. Univl Lisbo.
Revista universal lisbonense

Rev. U. Popayán
Revista de la Universidad de Popayán

Rev. Vieux Genève
La Revue du vieux Genève

Rev. Voyages
Revue des voyages

Rev. Zaragoza
Revista de Zaragoza

Rex Time

Rhein. Kststätten
Rheinische Kunststätten

Rhein.Lebensbild.
Rheinische Lebensbilder

Rhein. Mus.
Rheinisches Museum

Rhein. Philol.
Rheinische Philologie

Rhein. Vjbl.
Rheinische Vierteljahrsblätter

Rheydter Jb. Gesch. Kst & Heimatknd.
Rheydter Jahrbuch für Geschichte, Kunst und Heimatkunde

Rhodes-Livingstone J.
Rhodes-Livingstone Journal

Rhythm

RIBA J.
Royal Institute of British Architects Journal [cont. as *J. RIBA*; reverts to *RIBA J.*]

RIBA Trans.
Royal Institute of British Architects Transactions

Ric. Slav.
Ricerche slavistiche

Ric. Stor. A.
Ricerche di storia dell'arte

Ric. Stor. Pesaro
Ricerca storica di Pesaro

Ric. Stor. Relig. Roma
Ricerche della storia religiosa di Roma

Ric. & Stud. Archv. Romani
Ricerche e studi negli archivi romani

RI Des. Bull.
Rhode Island Design Bulletin

Rif. Lett.
Riforma letteraria

Rif Tout Dju

Rijksarchf Utrecht

Rinascimento [prev. pubd as *Rinascita*]

Rinascita [cont. as *Rinascimento*]

Ringling Mus. A.J.
Ringling Museum of Art Journal

Riv. A.
i) Rivista d'arte [prev. pubd as *Misc. A.*]
ii) Rivista dell'arte [cont. as *Bolaffi A.*]

Riv. Archeol.
Rivista di archeologia

Riv. Archeol. Crist.
Rivista di archeologia cristiana

Riv. Archeol. Prov. & Ant. Dioc. Como
Rivista archeologica della provincia e antica diocesi di Como: Periodico della Società archeologica comense [prev. pubd as *Riv. Archeol. Prov. Como*]

Riv. Archeol. Prov. Como
Rivista archeologica della provincia di Como [cont. as *Riv. Archeol. Prov. & Ant. Dioc. Como*]

Riv. Coll. Araldica
Rivista del Collegio di araldica

Riv. Colon. It. ('Oltremare')
Rivista delle colonie italiane ('Oltremare')

Riv. Com.
Rivista del comune

Riv. Com. Bologna
Rivista del comune di Bologna

Riv. Com. It.
Rivista dei comuni italiani

Riv. Como
Rivista di Como

Riv. Ferrara
Rivista di Ferrara

Riv. Fot.
Rivista fotografica

Riv. Geog. It.
Rivista geografica italiana

Riv. Illus. Pop. Italia
Rivista illustrata del popolo d'Italia

Riv. Interamer. Bibliog.
Rivista interamericana di bibliografia

Riv. Ist. N. Archeol. & Stor. A.
Rivista dell'Istituto nazionale d'archeologia e storia dell'arte [prev. pubd as *Riv. Reale Ist. Archeol. & Stor. A.*]

Riv. Ist. N. Archeol. & Stor. Roma
Rivista dell'Istituto nazionale d'archeologia e storia di Roma

Riv. Istor. Benedettina
Rivista istorica benedettina

Riv. Italia
Rivista d'Italia

Riv. It. Numi.
Rivista italiana della numismatica

Riv. Lett. Mod. Comp.
Rivista di letterature moderne comparate

Riv. Mens. Città Venezia
Rivista mensile della città di Venezia

Riv. Milano
Rivista di Milano

Riv. Reale Ist. Archeol. & Stor. A.
Rivista del Reale istituto d'archeologia e storia dell'arte [cont. as *Riv. Ist. N. Archeol. & Stor. A.*]

Riv. Sci. Preist.
Rivista di scienze preistoriche

Riv. Semest. Stor. A.
Rivista semestrale di storia dell'arte

Riv. Staz. Spermntl Vetro
Rivista della stazione sperimentale del vetro

Riv. Stor., A., Archeol. Prov. Alessandria
Rivista di storia, arte, archeologia della provincia di Alessandria

Riv. Stor. Agric.
Rivista di storia dell'agricoltura

Riv. Stor. Ant.
Rivista storica dell'antichità

Riv. Stor. Chiesa Italia
Rivista di storia della chiesa in Italia

Riv. Stor. Contemp.
Rivista di storia contemporanea

Riv. Stor. It.
Rivista storica italiana

Riv. Stor. & Lett. Relig.
Rivista della storia e letteratura religiosa

Riv. Stor. Mant.
Rivista storica mantovana

Riv. Stud. Croc.
Rivista di studi crociani

Riv. Stud. Orient.
Rivista degli studi orientali

Riv. Tec.
Rivista tecnica

Riv. Tec. Svizzera It.
Rivista tecnica della Svizzera italiana

Riv. Venezia
Rivista di Venezia

Rizhskaya Mysl' [Riga thought]

R.-K. Bouwbl.
Het R.-K. [Rooms-Katholiek] Bouwblad

R. M. Themis [merger of *Rechtsgeleerd Mag.* & *De Tijdspiegel*]

Roberto-Darola

Roc. Gdański
Rocznik Gdański [Gdańsk yearbook]

Roc. Hist. Czasopiśmiennictwa Pol.
Rocznik historii czasopiśmiennictwa polskiego [Yearbook of the history of the Polish periodical press]

Roc. Hist. Sztuki
Rocznik historii sztuki [Yearbook of the history of art]

Roc. Human.
Roczniki humanistyczne [Yearbook of the arts]

Roc. Krakow.
Rocznik krakowski [Kraków yearbook]

Roč. Kruhu Pěstování Dějin Umění
Ročenka kruhu pro pěstování dějin umění [Annual report of the Circle for the Propagation of Art History]

Roc. Muz.
Rocznik muzealny [Museums yearbook]

Roc. Muz. N. Warszaw./Annu. Mus. N. Varsovie
Rocznik Muzeum narodowego w Warszawie/Annuaire du Musée national de Varsovie

Roc. Muz. Toruniu
Rocznik Muzeum w Toruniu

Roc. Sztuki Śląskiej
Roczniki sztuki śląskiej [Yearbook of Silesian art]

Roc. Towarzystwa Naukowego Krakow.
Rocznik towarzystwa naukowego krakowskiego [Yearbook of the Kraków Society of the Sciences]

Roc. Warszaw.
Rocznik Warszawski [Warsaw yearbook]

Roc. Zakładu Narodowego Im. Ossolinskich
Rocznik Zakładu narodowego imienia ossolinskich [Yearbook of the National Ossolinsky Institute]

Rolling Stone

Roma

Romagna A. & Stor.
Romagna arte e storia

Romania

Romania Lit.
Romania literară

Romanica Gothoburg.
Romanica Gothoburgensia

Romanic Rev.
Romanic Review

Romanische Forsch.
Romanische Forschungen

Romanist. Jb.
Romanistisches Jahrbuch

Roman. Rev.
Romanian Review

Romanticisme
Romanticisme: Revue du XIXe siècle

Romerike Berge
Romerike Berge

Röm.-Ger. Forsch.
Römisch-germanische Forschungen

Röm. Hist. Mitt.
Römische historische Mitteilungen

Röm. Jb. Bib. Hertz.
Römisches Jahrbuch der Bibliotheca Hertziana

Röm. Jb. Kstgesch.
Römisches Jahrbuch für Kunstgeschichte [prev. pubd as & also known as *Kstgesch. Jb. Bib. Hertz.*]

Röm. Qschr.
Römische Quartalschrift

Röm. Qschr. Christ. Altertknd. & Kirchgesch.
Römische Quartalschrift für christliche Altertumskunde und für Kirchengeschichte

Rongwrong

Roopa-Lekha

Rössing

Rotterdam. Jb.
Rotterdamsche jaarboekje

Rotterdam. Nieuwsbl.
Rotterdamsche nieuwsblad

Royal Anthropol. Inst. News
Royal Anthropological Institute News

Royal Antiqua. Inst. News
Royal Antiquarians Institute News

Royal Can. Mounted Police Q.
Royal Canadian Mounted Police Quarterly

Royal Hort. Soc. J.
Royal Horticultural Society Journal

Royal Incorp. Architects Scotland, Q.
Royal Incorporation of Architects in Scotland, Quarterly

Royal Inst. Architects Canada J.
Royal Institute of Architects of Canada Journal

Royal Inst. Architects Ireland Yb.
Royal Institute of the Architects of Ireland Yearbook

Royal Ont. Mus. Archaeol., Bull.
Royal Ontario Museum of Archaeology, Bulletin

Royal Soc. Ulster Architects Yb.
Royal Society of Ulster Architects Yearbook and Directory

Rozprawy & Sprawozdania Muz. N. Krakow.
Rozprawy i sprawozdania Muzeum narodwego w Krakowie [Studies and reports of the National Museum in Kraków; prev. pubd as *Sprawozdania & Rozprawy Muz. N. Krakow.*]

Runa

Ruperto-Carola
Ruperto-Carola: Mitteilungen der Vereinigung der Freunde der Studentenschaft der Universität Heidelberg e. V. [eingetragener Verein]

Rus. Arkhv
Russkiy arkhiv

Rus. Hist.
Russian History

Rus. Lang. J.
Russian Language Journal

Rus. Lit.
Russian Literature

Rus. Lit. Triq.
Russian Literature Triquarterly

Rus. Slovo
Russkoye slovo [The Russian word]

Rus. Vestnik
Russkiy vestnik [The Russian bulletin]

Rutgers A. Rev.
Rutgers Art Review

Saalburg Jb.
Saalburg Jahrbuch

Sabah Soc. J.
Sabah Society Journal

Sabazia

Sächs. Heimatbl.
Sächsische Heimatblätter

Sadanga

S. Afr. Archaeol. Bull.
South African Archaeological Bulletin

S. Afr. Architect
South African Architect

S. Afr. Archit. Rec.
South African Architectural Record

S. Afr. J. Cult. & A. Hist.
South African Journal of Culture and Art History

S. Afr. J. Sci.
South African Journal of Science

S. Afr. Mus. Assoc. Bull.
South African Museums Association Bulletin

S.-Afr. Tydskr. Kultgesk.
Suid-Afrikaanse tydskrif vir kultuurgeskiedenis [South African journal of cultural history]

Saga-bk: Viking Soc. N. Res.
Saga-book: Viking Society for Northern Research

Saggi & Mem. Stor. A.
Saggi e memorie di storia dell'arte

Saisons Alsace
Saisons d'Alsace

Salop Mag.
Shropshire Magazine

Salut Public

Salvator Rosa

Salzburg. Landes-Ztg
Salzburger Landes-Zeitung

Salzburg. Musbl.
Salzburger Museumsblätter [cont. as *Jschr. Salzburg. Mus. Carolino Augusteum*; reverts to *Salzburg. Musbl.*; then to *Jschr. Salzburg. Mus. Carolino Augusteum*; cont. as *Jb. Salzburg. Mus. Carolino Augusteum*]

Samleren [The collector]

Sammbl. Hist. Ver. Eichstätt
Sammelblatt des Historischen Vereins Eichstätt

Sammbl. Hist. Ver. Ingolstadt
Sammelblatt des Historischen Vereins Ingolstadt

Sammler
Der Sammler: Unterhaltungs- und Literaturbeilage der Münchener-Ausburger Abendzeitung

Samml. Nützl. Aufs. & Nachr. Baukst Betreff.
Sammlung nützlicher Aufsätze und Nachrichten die Baukunst betreffend

Samtiden

Sanat [Art]

Sanat Tarihi Yıllığı [Art history annual]

San Baltazar

Sandoz Bull.
Sandoz Bulletin

San Juan Rev.
San Juan Review

Sankofa

Santa Cruz

Saopštenja
Saopštenja: Republički zavod za zaštitu spomenika kulture [Communications: Republican Institute for the Preservation of Cultural Monuments]

Sarajevo

Sarawak Gaz.
Sarawak Gazette

Sarawak Mus. J.
Sarawak Museum Journal

S. Asian Archaeol.
South Asian Archaeology

S. Asian Rev.
South Asian Review

S. Asian Stud.
South Asian Studies

S. Asia Res.
South Asia Research

Sat. Eve. Post
Saturday Evening Post

Sat. Rev.
Saturday Review

Savacou
Savacou: Journal of Caribbean Studies

Savanna

Savia Mod.
Savia moderna

Savoir & Beauté
Savoir et beauté

Savremenik

Sawasdee

Sber. & Abh. 'Flora' Dresden
Sitzungsberichte und Abhandlungen der 'Flora' in Dresden

Sber. Bayer. Akad. Wiss., Philos.-Hist. Kl.
Sitzungsberichte der Bayerischen Akademie der Wissenschaften, philosophische-historische Klasse

Sber. Fin. Akad. Wiss.
Sitzungsberichte der Finnischen Akademie der Wissenschaften

Sber. Heidelberg. Akad. Wiss.
Sitzungsberichte der Heidelberger Akademie der Wissenschaften

Sber. Kstgesch. Ges.
Sitzungsberichte der Kunstgeschichtlichen Gesellschaft

Sber. Münchn. Altert.-Ver.
Sitzungsberichte des Münchner Alterthums-Vereins [cont. as *Die Wartburg*]

Sber. Philos.-Hist. Cl. Ksr. Akad. Wiss. Wien
Sitzungsberichte der philosophisch-historischen Classe der Kaiserlichen Akademie der Wissenschaften Wien

Sber. Phys.-Mediz. Soz. Erlangen
Sitzungsberichte physikalischen-medizinischen Sozietät zu Erlangen

Sber. Preuss. Akad. Wiss.
Sitzungsberichte der Preussischen Akademie der Wissenschaft

Sber. Wien. Akad.
Sitzungsberichte Wiener Akademie

Sborn. Geog. Top. Statisticheskikh Mat. Azii: Izdaniya Voyenno-Uchonnogo Komiteta Glavnogo Shtaba
Sbornik geograficheskikh, topograficheskikh i statisticheskikh materialov po Azii: Izdaniya Voyenno-uchonnogo komiteta glavnogo shtaba [Miscellany of geographical, topographical and statistical documents on Asia: publications of the Military–scholarly Headquarters Committee]

Sborn. Hist.
Sborník historický [History journal]

Sborn. Imp. Rus. Ist. Obshchestva
Sbornik imperialskogo russkogo istoricheskogo obshchestva [Imperial Russian Historical Society miscellany]

Sborn. Muz. Anthropol. & Etnog.
Sbornik Muzea antropologii i etnografii

Sborn. N. Muz. Praze
Sborník Národního muzea v Praze [Journal of the National Museum in Prague]

Sborn. N. Tech. Muz. Praze
Sborník Národního technického muzea v Praze [Proceedings of the National Technical Museum in Prague]

Sborn. Prac. Filoz. Fak. Brn. U.
Sborník prací filozofické fakulty Brněnské Univerzity [Proceedings of the Philosophy Faculty of Brno University]

Sborn. Radova Vizant. Inst.
Sbornik Radova vizantoloskogo instituta [Proceedings of the Byzantine Studies Institute]

Scand. J. Des. Hist.
Scandinavian Journal of Design History

Scand. Rev.
Scandinavian Revue

Scanning Electron Microscopy

Scenario

Schaffhauser Beitr. Gesch.
Schaffhauser Beiträge zur Geschichte

Schau-ins-Land: Jhft Breisgau-Geschver.
Schau-ins-Land: Jahresheft des Breisgau-Geschichtsvereins

Schede Med.
Schede medievali

Schekerazade

SC Hist. & Geneal. Mag.
South Carolina Historical and Genealogical Magazine [cont. as *SC Hist. Mag.*]

SC Hist. Mag.
South Carolina Historical Magazine [prev. pubd as *SC Hist. & Geneal. Mag.*]

Schlern: Illus. Mhft. Heimat- & Vlkskend.
Schlern: Illustrierte Monatshefte für Heimat- und Volkskunde

Schlern Schr.
Schlern Schriften

Schles. Heim
Schlesisches Heim

Schlesien

Schlesiens Vorzeit Bild & Schr.
Schlesiens Vorzeit in Bild und Schrift: Zeitschrift des Vereins für das Museum schlesischer Altertümer [cont. as *Hohe Stasse*]

Schles. Mhft.
Schlesische Monatshefte

Sch. Mines Q.
School of Mines Quarterly

Schorns Ksthbl.
Schorns Kunstblatt

Schr. Dt. Archit. Mus. Frankfurt
Schriften des deutschen Architektur Museums Frankfurt

Schr. Heeresgesch. Mus. Wien
Schriften des heeresgeschichtlichen Museums in Wien

Schr. Hist. Mus. Frankfurt am Main
Schriften des historischen Museums Frankfurt am Main

Schr. Königsberg. Gelehrten Ges.: Geistwiss. Klasse
Schriften der Königsberger gelehrten Gesellschaft: Geistwissenschaftliche Klasse

Schr. Pückler-Ges.
Schriften der Pückler-Gesellschaft

Schrreihe Bayer. Landesgesch.
Schriftenreihe zur bayerischen Landesgeschichte

Schrreihe Inst. Städtebau, Raumplan. & Raumordnung, Tech. Hochsch. Wien
Schriftenreihe des Institutes für Städtebau, Raumplanung und Raumordnung, Technische Hochschule Wien

Schrreihe Ratsarchvs Stadt Görlitz
Schriftenreihe des Ratsarchivs der Stadt Görlitz

Schrreihe Salzburg. Mus. Carolino Augusteum
Schriftenreihe des Salzburger Museums Carolino Augusteum

Schr. Staatl. Ksthalle Karlsruhe
Schriften der Staatlichen Kunsthalle Karlsruhe

Schr. Ver. Gesch. Bodensees & Umgebung
Schriften des Vereins für Geschichte des Bodensees und seiner Umgebung

Schwäb. Archv
Schwäbisches Archiv [prev. pubd as *Diöz.-Archv Schwaben*]

Schwabens Vergangenheit
Aus Schwabens Vergangenheit

Schwäb. Heimat
Schwäbische Heimat

Schwäb. Heimatb.
Schwäbisches Heimatbuch

Schwäb. Merkur
Schwäbischer Merkur

Schwäb. Mus.
Schwäbisches Museum

Schweinfurt. Heimatbl.
Schweinfurter Heimatblätter

Schweiz. Archv Vlksknd.
Schweizerisches Archiv für Volkskunde

Schweiz. Bauztg
Schweizerische Bauzeitung

Schweiz. Beitr. Allg. Gesch.
Schweizer Beiträge zur allgemeinen Geschichte

Schweiz. Handelsztg
Schweizerische Handelszeitung

Schweiz. Inst. Kstwiss. Jber. & Jb.
Schweizerisches Institut für Kunstwissenschaft Jahresbericht und Jahrbuch

Schweiz. Münzbl.
Schweizer Münzblätter

Schweiz. Rundschau
Schweizer Rundschau

Sci. Amer.
Scientific American

Sci. Ant.
Scienze dell'antichità

Science

Scientia

Sci. Rev.
Scientific Review

Sci. USSR
Sciences in the USSR

Scot. A. & Lett.
Scottish Art and Letters

Scot. Antiqua.
Scottish Antiquary [prev. pubd as *N. Notes & Queries*; cont. as *Scot. Hist. Rev.*]

Scot. A. Rev.
Scottish Art Review

Scot. Georg. Soc. Bull.
Scottish Georgian Society Bulletin

Scot. Hist. Rev.
Scottish Historical Review [prev. pubd as *Scot. Antiqua.*; *N. Notes & Queries*]

Scot. Local Hist.
Scottish Local History

Scot. Pott. Hist. Rev.
Scottish Pottery Historical Review [prev. pubd as *Archv News*; *Archivists' Newslett.*]

Scot. Pott. Stud.
Scottish Pottery Studies

Scot. Rev.
Scottish Review

Scots Mag.
Scots Magazine

Scot. Stud.
Scottish Studies

Scr. & Civiltà
Scrittura e civiltà

Screen

Scribner's Mag.
Scribner's Magazine [cont. as *The Commentator*]

Scribner's Monthly [cont. as *C. Illus.*]

Scripta Hierosolymitana

Scripta Medit.
Scripta Mediterranea

Scriptorium

Sculp. Mag.
Sculpture Magazine

SD Hist.
South Dakota History

Sdt. Ztg
Süddeutsche Zeitung

Seabys Coin & Medal Bull.
Seabys Coin and Medal Bulletin

SE Asia
Southeastern Asia

S.-E. Coll. Rev.
Southeastern College Art Conference Review

Sección A.
Sección de arte

Secolul 20

Section Or
Section d'or

Sefarad
Sefarad: Revista del Instituto Arias Montano de estudios hebraicos y oriente proximo sefarad

Sefunot

Seicento Napoletano
Seicento napoletano

Sele A.
Sele arte

Sem. Constructeurs
La Semaine des constructeurs

Semeur

Semin. A. Aragon.
Seminario del arte aragonés

Seminario Pint. Esp.
Seminario pintoresco español

Semin. Kondakov.
Seminarium kondakovianum

Semiolus

Semiotica

Senatne & Màksla
Senatne un màksla [Antiquity and art]

Seoul P'yŏngnon

Serapis

Serendib

Serra Or
Serra d'Or

Serra Or Montserrat
Serra d'Or Montserrat

Sess. Pap. Parl. Dominion Canada
Sessional Papers of the Parliament of the Dominion of Canada

Sess. Pap. RIBA
Sessional Papers of the Royal Institute of British Architects

Sett. Studio Cent. It. Stud. Alto Med.
Settimane di studio del Centro italiano di studi sull'alto medioevo

7 Arts [Seven/sept]

Severnyye Zapisi
Severnyye zapisi [Northern notes]

Sevilla Mariana

Sewanee Rev.
Sewanee Review

Sfinks

Shakespeare Q.
Shakespeare Quarterly

Shakespeare Surv.
Shakespeare Survey

Shambhala Occas. Pap. Inst. Tib. Stud.
Shambhala Occasional Papers of the Institute of Tibetan Studies

Shanghai Mus. Bull.
Shanghai Museum Bulletin

S. Heim
Schönes Heim

S. Heimat
Schönere Heimat [prev. pubd as *Bayer. Heimatschutz*; *Vlkskst & Vlksknd.*]

Shelf Appeal

Shigaku Zasshi [Journal of historical studies]

Shilling Mag.
Shilling Magazine

Shinkenchiku

Shipovnik

Shirakaba

Shiyuan

Shobin

Shohin

Shoshigaku [Bibliography]

Shqipëria

Shufa Congkan

Shuhuajia [Classical Chinese calligraphy and fine art]

Siam Soc. Newslett.
Siam Society Newsletter

Sibu Congkan

S. I. C.

SIC [Paris]

SIC [Venezuela]

Sichuan Wenwu

Sicilia Archeol.
Sicilia archeologica: Rassegna periodica di studi, notizie e documentazione

Siculorum Gym.
Siculorum gymnasium

Siebenbürg. Vjschr.
Siebenbürgische Vierteljahresschrift, Korrespondenzblatt des Vereins für siebenbürgische Landeskunde [prev. pubd as *Korrbl. Ver. Siebenbürg. Landesknd.*; cont. as *Korrbl. Arbeitkreises Siebenbürg. Landesknd.*; *Z. Siebenbürg. Landesknd.*]

Sierra Leone Lang. Rev.
Sierra Leone Language Review

Sierra Leone Stud.
Sierra Leone Studies

Sight & Sound
Sight and Sound

Signal

Signature
Signature: A Quadrimestrial of Typography and Graphic Arts

Signum
Signum: Tidsskrift for moderne kunst [Journal for modern art]

Silicattechnik

Silk Road A. & Archaeol.
Silk Road Art and Archaeology

Silpakorn U. J.
Silpakorn University Journal

Silumina

Silver Soc. J.
Silver Society Journal

Simiolus

Simplicissimus

S. Ind. Archaeol.
South Indian Archaeology

Sinica

Sintra

Sion

Sirius

Sites & Mnmts
Sites et monuments: Bulletin de la Société pour la protection des paysages et de l'esthétique générale de la France [prev. pubd as *Bull. Soc. Prot. Pays. Esthét. Gén. France*]

16th C. J.
Sixteenth Century Journal

Skalk

Skand. Sborn.
Skandinavsky sborník [Scandinavian journal]

Skírnir

Skyline

Slav. Beitr.
Slavistische Beiträge

Slav. & E. Eur. Rev.
Slavonic and East European Review

Slavia

Slav. Rev.
Slavic Review

Sloan's Archit. Rev. & Bldrs' J.
Sloan's Architectural Review and Builders' Journal: An Illustrated Monthly [cont. as *Archit. Rev. & Amer. Bldrs J.*]

Slov. Archeol.
Slovenská archeologia

Sluitsteen

Smith Coll. Mus. A. Bull.
Smith College Museum of Art Bulletin

Smith Coll. Stud. Mod. Lang.
Smith College Studies in Modern Languages

Smithsonian

Smithsonian Inst. Misc. Col.
Smithsonian Institution Miscellaneous Collection

Smithsonian Stud. Amer. A.
Smithsonian Studies in American Art

Soc. Amis Port-Royal
Société des amis de Port-Royal

Soc. Archéol. Bordeaux
Société archéologique de Bordeaux

Soc. Archéol. Châtillon.
Société archéologique du Châtillonnais [prev. pubd as *Bull. Soc. Archéol. & Hist. Châtillon.; Bull. Soc. Archéol. Châtillon.*]

Soc. Etud. Iran. & A. Persan
Société des études iraniennes et de l'art persan

Soc. Hist.
Social History

Soc. Hist. France
Société de l'histoire de France

Social Text

Soc. Nouv.
Société nouvelle

Soc. Préhist. Fr.: Bull. Soc. Préhist. Fr.
Société préhistorique française: Bulletin de la Société préhistorique française [cont. as *Bull. Soc. Préhist. Fr.*]

Soc. Ren. Stud.: Occas. Pap.
Society for Renaissance Studies: Occasional Papers

Soc. Repr. Dessins Maîtres
Société de reproduction des dessins de maîtres

Soc. Res.
Social Research

Soc. Royale Archéol. Belgique
Société royale d'archéologie de Belgique

Soc. Royale Vieux Liège: Feuil. Archéol.
Société royale du vieux Liège: Feuillets archéologiques

Soc. Sci., A. & Lett. Hainaut: Mém. & Pubns
Société des sciences, des arts et des lettres du Hainaut: Mémoires et publications

Soc. Sci. Bull.
Social Science Bulletin

Soc. Stud. Archit. Canada: Sel. Pap.
Society for the Study of Architecture in Canada: Selected Papers

Sodhak

Soirées Paris
Soirées de Paris

Somalia Oggi
Somalia d'oggi

Soncino-Bl.
Soncino-Blätter

Sonderdruck Schr. Ver. Gesch. Bodensees & Umgebung
Sonderdruck aus den Schriften des Vereins für Geschichte des Bodensees und seiner Umgebung

Soobshcheniya Gosudarstvennogo Ermitazha [Reports of the State Hermitage]

Soobshcheniya Gosudarstvennogo Rus. Muz.
Soobshcheniya Gosudarstvennogo russkogo muzeya [Reports of the Russian state Museum]

Soobshcheniya Inst. Istor. Iskusstv AN SSSR
Soobshcheniya Instituta istorii iskusstv Akademii nauk SSSR [Reports of the Institute of the History of Arts of the Academy of Sciences of the USSR]

Soobshcheniya Respub. Istor.–Krayevedcheskogo Muz. Tadzhik. SSR
Soobshcheniya respublikanskogo istoriko–krayevedcheskogo muzeya Tadzhikskoy SSR [Reports of the Republic Historical–local Museum of the Tadjik SSR]

Soobshcheniya VTsNILKR

Soochow U. J. Chin. A. Hist.
Soochow University Journal of Chinese Art History

Sophia Int. Rev.
Sophia International Review

Sopr. Archeol., Sassari: Quad.
Soprintendenza archeologica, Sassari: Quaderni

Sostdt. Forsch.
Südostdeutsche Forschungen

Sotsial. Rekonstr. Gorodov
Za sotsialisticheskuyu rekonstruktsiyu gorodov

Source: Music Avantgarde
Source: Music of the Avantgarde

Source: Notes Hist. A.
Source: Notes in the History of Art

Southeast Asia

Southern Homes

Southern Q.
Southern Quarterly

Sov. Arkheol.
Sovetskaya arkheologiya

Sov. Arkhit.
Sovetskaya arkhitektura

Sov. Dek. Isk.
Sovetskoye dekorativnoye iskusstvo [Soviet decorative art; cont. as *Dek. Isk.*]

Sovetakan Arvest

Sov. Etnog.: Sborn. Statey
Sovetskaya etnografiya: Sbornik statyey [Soviet ethnography: collection of articles]

Sov. Graf.
Sovetskaya grafika

Sov. Isk.
i) Sovetskoe iskusstvo [Soviet art]
ii) Sovetskoye iskusstvoznaniye: Sbornik statyey [Soviet art study: collection of articles]

Sov. Jew. Affairs
Soviet Jewish Affairs

Sov. Kul't.
Sovetskaya kul'tura

Sov. Muz.
Sovetskiy muzey

Sovremennaya Arkhit.
Sovremennaya arkhitektura [Contemporary architecture]

Sov. Stud.
Soviet Studies

Sov. Un./Un. Sov.
Soviet Union/Union soviétique

Sov. Zhenshchina
Sovetskaya zhenshchina [Soviet woman]

Sov. Zhivopis'
Sovetskaya zhivopis' [Soviet painting]

Soyuz Molodyozhi
Soyuz molodyozhi [Union of youth]

Sozialist. Akad.
Sozialistische Akademiker [cont. as *Sozialist. Mhft.*]

Sozialist. Mhft.
Sozialistische Monatshefte [prev. pubd as *Sozialist. Akad.*]

Space Des.
Space Design

Spazio & Soc.
Spazio e società

Spectrum Island

Speculum

Sphere Mag.
Sphere Magazine

Sphinx

Spicilegium Romanum
Spicilegium romanum

Spiegel Historiael
Spiegel Historiael

Spiegel: Jb. Propyläen-Verlags
Der Spiegel: Jahrbuch des Propyläen-Verlags

Spiegelungen [Mainz]

Spinks Numi. Circ.
Spinks Numismatic Circular

Spirale

Spolia Zeylanica
Spolia Zeylanica: Bulletin of the National Museums of Ceylon

Spomenik

Spondee Rev.
Spondee Review

Sportrev. Wien. Fremdenbl.
Sportrevue des Wiener Fremdenblatts

Sports Illus.
Sports Illustrated

Sprawozdania Czynności Posiedzeń Pol. Akad. Umiejętności
Sprawozdania z czynności i posiedzeń Polskiej akademii umiejętności [Proceedings of the conferences of the Polish Academy of Learning]

Sprawozdania Kom. Hist. Sztuki
Sprawozdania komisji historii sztuki [Reports of the Art History Committee]

Sprawozdania Posiedzeń Kom. Naukowych Pol. Akad. Nauk Krakowie
Sprawozdania w posiedzeń komisji naukowych Polaskiej akademii nauk w Krakowie [Reports of the sessions of the Scientific Committee of the Polish Academy of Sciences of Kraków]

Sprawozdania & Rozprawy Muz. N. Krakow.
Sprawozdania i rozprawy Muzeum narodwego w Krakowie [cont. as *Rozprawy & Sprawozdania Muz. N. Krakow.*]

Springfield Sun. Un. & Repub.
Springfield Sunday Union and Republican

Spur

Sri Lanka J. Human.
Sri Lanka Journal of the Humanities

Sri Lanka Today [prev. pubd as *Ceylon Today*]

SSAC Bull.
SSAC Bulletin

SSSR Stroyke
SSSR na stroyke [USSR in construction]

Städel-Jb.
Städel-Jahrbuch

Stader Jb.
Stader Jahrbuch

Stadium

Stadt

Stadtbauwelt: Beitr. Neuord. Stadt & Land
Stadtbauwelt: Beiträge zur Neuordnung von Stadt und Land

Städtebau

Staffs Hist.
Staffordshire History

Staletá Praha [Centuries-old Prague]

Standen & Landen
Standen en landen

St Andrews Stud. Hist. Scot. Archit. & Des.
St Andrews Studies in the History of Scottish Architecture and Design

Stanford It. Rev.
stanford italian review

Stanford Mus.
Stanford Museum

Starinar [The antiquary]

Starine Kosova & Metohije
Starine Kosova i Metohije [Antiquities of Kosova and Metohije]

Starohrvatska Prosvjeta

Starou Prahu
Za starou Prahu [In pursuit of Old Prague]

Stars & Stripes
Stars and Stripes

Staryye Gody
Staryye gody: Yezhemesyachnik dlya lyubiteley iskusstva i stariny [Yesteryear: a monthly for lovers of art and antiques]

Stavba [Construction]

Stedebouw & Vlkshuisvest.
Stedebouw en volkshuisvesting

Steel & Garnet
Steel and Garnet

Steklo & Ker.
Steklo i keramika [Glass and ceramics]

Stekol'naya Promyshlennost' [Glass manufacture]

St Eriks Åb.
Sankt Eriks årsbok

Stern
[Der] Stern

Stettin. Genanz.
Stettiner Generalanzeiger

St Hallvard

Stile Futurista

Stimmen Zeit
Stimmen der Zeit

Stimme Pfalz
Stimme der Pfalz

Stînga [The left]

St. James's Eve. Post
St James's Evening Post

St Louis Pub. Lib. Mthly Bull.
St Louis Public Library Monthly Bulletin

St Nicholas

Stor. A.
Storia dell'arte

Stor. A. It.
Storia dell'arte italiana: Dal medioevo al quattrocento

Stor. Archit.
Storia dell'architettura

Stor. Brescia
Storia di Brescia

Stor. Città
Storia della città

Stor. & Civ.
Storia e civiltà

Stor. Cult. Ven.
Storia della cultura veneta

Stor. Sicilia
Storia della Sicilia

Stor. Urb.
i) Storia urbana
ii) Storia dell'urbanistica

St Petersburg Times

St Peter's Newspap.
St Peter's Newspaper

Strand Mag.
Strand Magazine

Strany & Narody Vostoka
Strany i narody vostoka [Countries and peoples of the Orient]

Strassburg. Münster-Bl.
Strassburger Münster-Blatt

Stratford-upon-Avon Pap.
Stratford-upon-Avon Papers

Středočesky Sborn. Hist.
Středočesky sborník historicky [Central Bohemian historical journal]

Strenna Piacent.
Strenna piacentina

Strenna Romanisti
Strenna dei romanisti

Strenna Stor. Bologn.
Strenna storica bolognese

Stroitel

Stroitel'stvo & Arkhit. Leningrada
Stroitel'stvo i arkhitektura Leningrada [Construction and architecture of Leningrad]

Stroitel'stvo & Arkhit. Moskvy
Stroitel'stvo i arkhitektura Moskvy [Construction and architecture of Moscow]

Stroitel'stvo & Arkhit. Uzbekistana
Stroitel'stvo i arkhitektura Uzbekistana [Construction and architecture of Uzbekistan]

Stroitel'stvo Moskvy [Construction of Moscow]

Structural Engin.
The Structural Engineer

Structure

Stud. Aegyp.
Studia Aegyptiaca

Stud. Alb.
Studia Albanica

Stud. Albornot.
Studia Albornotiana

Stud. Altägyp. Kult.
Studien zur altägyptischen Kultur

Stud. Anselm.
Studia Anselmiana

Stud. Anthropol. Visual Communic.
Studies in the Anthropology of Visual Communication

Stud. Archeol. Ústavu Česko. Akad. Brně
Studie archeologického ústavu Československé akademie věd v Brně [Studies of the Brno Archaeological Institute of the Czechoslovak Academy of Sciences]

Stud. & Arheol.
Studii și arheologie [SCIVA; prev. pubd as *Stud. & Cerc. Istor. Veche*]

Stud. A. Urbin.
Studi artistici urbinati

Stud. Bibliog. & Bklore.
Studies in Bibliography and Booklore [2 pubns: a) Oregon; b) Charlottesville, VA]

Stud. & Bibliog. An. Bib. Stat. & Lib. Civ. Cremona
Studi e bibliografie degli Annali della biblioteca statale e libreria civica di Cremona

Stud. Bitontini
Studi bitontini

Stud. Biz. Neoellenici
Studi bizantini e neoellenici

Stud. Boccaccio
Studi sul Boccaccio

Stud. Burke
Studies in Burke and his Times

Stud. Cent. & E. Asian Relig.
Studies in Central and East Asian Religions

Stud. & Cerc. Biblio.
Studii și cercetări de bibliologie

Stud. & Cerc. Istor. A.
Studii și cercetări de istoria artei [Studies and researches in art history; cont. as *Stud. & Cerc. Istor. A.: Ser. A. Plast.* & *Stud. & Cerc. Istor. A.: Ser. Teat., Muzic., Cinema.*]

Stud. & Cerc. Istor. A.: Ser. A. Plast.
Studii și cercetări de istoria artei: Seria artă plastică [see *Stud. & Cerc. Istor. A.*]

Stud. & Cerc. Istor. A.: Ser. Teat., Muzic., Cinema.
Studii și cercetări de istoria artei: Seria teatro, muzică, cinematografie [see *Stud. & Cerc. Istor. A.*]

Stud. & Cerc. Istor. Veche
Studii și cercetări de istorie veche [cont. as *Stud. & Arheol.*]

Stud. Claramontana
Studia Claramontana

Stud. Class. & Orient.
Studi classici ed orientali

Stud. Comeniana & Hist.
Studia Comeniana et historica

Stud. Conserv.
Studies in Conservation: The Journal of the International Institute for Conservation of Historic and Artistic Works

Stud. & Contrib. Ist. Archeol. & Stor. A. U. Bari
Studi e contributi dell'Istituto di archeologia e storia dell'arte dell'Università di Bari

Stud. & Crit. It. A.
The Study and Criticism of Italian Art

Stud. & Doc. Archit.
Studi e documenti di architettura

Stud. & Doc. Stor. & Dir.
Studi e documenti per la storia e diritto

Stud. & Doc. Stor. Pal. Apostol. Vatic.
Studi e documenti per la storia del Palazzo apostolico vaticano

Stud. Dt. Kstgesch.
Studien zur deutschen Kunstgeschichte

Stud. Dziejów Rzemioła & Przemysłu
Studia z dziejów rzemioła i przemysłu [Studies of the history of craft and industry]

Stud. Dziejów Sztuki Polsce
Studia do dziejów sztuki w polsce [Studies in Polish art history]

Stud. Dziejów Wawelu
Studia do dziejów wawelu [Studies in Wawel (Kraków) history]

Stud. Egyptol.
Studies in Egyptology

Stud. Estet.
Studia estetyczne [Studies in aesthetics]

Stud. Ethnog.
Studia ethnographica

Stud. Etrus.
Studi etruschi

Stud. Fr.
Studi francesi

Stud. Francescani
Studi francescani

Stud. Gen.
Studium generale

Stud. Genuensi
Studi genuensi

Stud. Gregoriani
Studi gregoriani

Stud. Hierosolym.
Studia Hierosolymitana

Stud. Hist.
Studime historike

Stud. Iconog.
Studies in Iconography

Studio Int.
Studio International

Stud. Iran.
Studia iranica

Stud.: Irish Q. Rev. Lett., Philos. & Sci.
Studies: An Irish Quarterly Review of Letters, Philosophy and Science

Stud. Islam.
i) Studia islamica
ii) Studies in Islamic Art

Stud. It.
Studi italiani

Stud. Jud. & Late Ant.
Studies in Judaism and Late Antiquity

Stud. Kst 19. Jhts
Studien zur Kunst des 19. Jahrhunderts

Stud. Lat. Amer. Pop. Cult.
Studies in Latin American Popular Culture

Stud. Leibnit.
Studia Leibnitiana

Stud. Liturg.
Studia liturgica

Stud. Maceratesi
Studi maceratesi

Stud. & Mat. Dziejów Nauki Pol.
Studia i materiały z dziejów nauki polskie [Research and material on the history of Polish studies]

Stud. & Mat. Hist. Kult. Mat.
Studia i materiały z historii kultury materialnej [Studies and material on the history of material culture]

Stud. & Mat. Teor. & Hist. Archit. & Urb.
Studia i materiały do teorii i historii architektury i urbanistyki [Studies and material on the theory and history of architecture and town planning]

Stud. Mechlin.
Studia mechliniensia

Stud. Med.
Studi medievali

Stud. Med. Cult.
Studies in Medieval Culture

Stud. Medit. Archaeol.
Studies in Mediterranean Archaeology

Stud. Med. & Ren. Hist.
Studies in Medieval and Renaissance History

Stud. Merid.
Studi meridionali: Rivista trimestrale di studi sull'Italia centro-meridionale

Stud. Micenei & Egeo-Anatol.
Studi micenei ed egeo-anatolici

Stud. Minora Fac. Philos. U. Brunensis
Studi minora facultatis philosophicae universitatis Brunensis

Stud. Misc.
Studi miscellanei

Stud. & Mitt. Gesch. Benediktiner-Ordens & Zweige
Studien und Mitteilungen zur Geschichte des Benediktiner-Ordens und seiner Zweige [prev. pubd as *Ordo Sancti Benedicti*]

Stud. Monzesi
Studi monzesi

Stud. Muz.
Studia muzealne

Stud. Ned. Hist. Inst. Rome
Studien van het Nederlands historisch instituut te Rome

Stud. Oliveriana
i) Studia Oliveriana
ii) Studi Oliveriana

Stud. Ostasiat. Schrkst
Studien zur ostasiatischen Schriftkunst

Stud. Palmyr.
Studia palmyrenskie

Stud. Philol.
Studies in Philology

Stud. Phoenicia
Studia Phoenicia

Studi Piceni
Studi piceni

Stud. Piemont.
Studi piemontesi

Stud. Pomorskie
Studia pomorskie

Studio Potter
The Studio Potter

Stud. Praehist.
Studia praehistorica

Stud. & Prob. Crit. Test.
Studi e problemi di critica testuale

Stud. Ren.
i) Studia renesansowe
ii) Studies in the Renaissance [later incorp. *Ren. Q.*]

Stud. Rep. U. Indust. A. & Textile Fibres
Study Report of the University of Industrial Arts and Textile Fibres

Stud. Romagn.
Studi romagnoli

Stud. Romani
Studi romani

Stud. Romanticism
Studies in Romanticism

Stud. Sächsforsch.
Studien zur Sächsenforschung

Stud. Sardi
Studi sardi

Stud. S. Asian Cult.
Studies in South Asian Culture

Stud. Seicent.
Studi seicenteschi

Stud. Settecento Romano
Studi sul settecento romano

Stud. & Skiz. Gemäldeknd.
Studien und Skizzen zur Gemäldekunde [prev. pubd as *Bl. Gemäldeknd.*; cont. as *Neue Bl. Gemäldeknd.*; *Gemäldekunde*]

Stud. Stor.
i) Studia storia
ii) Studi storici

Stud. Stor. A.
Studi di storia delle arti

Stud. Stor. A., U. Genova, Ist. Stor. A.
Studi di storia delle arti, Università di Genova, Istituto di storia dell'arte

Stud. Stor. Ordine Servi Maria
Studi storici sull'Ordine dei Servi di Maria

Stud. Stor. Veron.
Studi storici veronesi

Stud. & Szkice Dziejów Sztuki & Cywiliz.
Studia i szkice z dziejów sztuki i cywilizacji [Studies and essays in the history of art and civilization]

Stud. Textile Hist.
Studies in Textile History

Stud. Trentini Sci. Stor.
Studi trentini di scienze storiche

Stud. Trevi.
Studi trevisani

Stud. Urbin. Sci., Giur., Polit. & Econ.
Studi urbinati di scienze, giuridiche, politiche ed economiche

Stud. Urbin. Stor., Filos. & Lett.
Studi urbinati di storia, filosofia e letteratura

Stud. Ven.
Studi veneziani

Stud. Vis. Communic.
Studies in Visual Communication

Stud. Voltaire & 18th C.
Studies on Voltaire and the Eighteenth Century

Stud. Warb. Inst.
Studies of the Warburg Institute

Sturetz

Sturshel

Stuttgart. Ztg
Stuttgarter Zeitung

Stvaranje

Sudan Notes & Rec.
Sudan Notes and Records

Sud-Est

Sudhoffs Archv Ges. Mediz. & Natwiss.
Sudhoffs Archiv für Geschichte der Medizin und der Naturwissenschaften

Sudoeste

Sülchgau. Altertver.: Jgabe
Sülchgauer Altertumsverein: Jahresgabe

Sulu Stud.
Sulu Studies

Sumer

Sumi Supesharu

Summa

Summa A.
Summa artis

Sun A. Q.
Sun Art Quarterly

Sunday Times Colour Sect.
Sunday Times Colour Section

Sunday Times Mag.
Sunday Times Magazine

Sun News-Pict.
Sun News-Pictorial

Sunset Mag.
Sunset Magazine

Suom. Mus.
Suomen museo [Swed. edn: *Fin. Mus.*]

Suomi–Finland U.S.A.

Supl. Antropol.
Suplemento antropológico

Supl. Lit. Panamá América
Suplemento literario Panamá América

Suppl. Bull. Mens. Soc. Cent. Architectes
Supplément au Bulletin mensuel de la Société centrale des architectes

Surréalisme Même
Surréalisme même

Surréalisme Serv. Révol.
Surréalisme au service de la révolution

Surrey Archaeol. Col.
Surrey Archaeological Collections

Surtees Soc.
Surtees Society

Surv. & Excav.
Survey and Excavation

Survey

Surv. Graph.
Survey Graphic

Sussex Archaeol. Col.
Sussex Archaeological Collections

Sussex Indust. Hist.
Sussex Industrial History

Suvremennik

Svādhyāya

Svari [The scales]

Svensk. Dagbladet
Svenska dagbladet

Svensk. Forskinst. Istanbul, Meddel.
Svenska forskningsinstitutet i Istanbul, meddelanden [Swedish Research Institute in Istanbul, reports]

Svensk. Linné Sällsk. Årsskr.
Svenska Linné sällskapets årsskrift [Swedish Linnean Society's yearbook]

Svensk. Littsällsk. Finland
Svenska Litteratursällskapet i Finland [Swedish Literary Society in Finland]

Svensk. Orientsällskapets Åb.
Svenska Orientsällskapets årsbok

SW A.
Southwest Art

SW Hist. Q.
Southwestern Historical Quarterly

Świat [Warsaw]

SW J. Anthropol.
Southwestern Journal of Anthropology

Sydney Morning Herald

Syesis

Sygnały

Symbolae Oslo.
Symbolae Osloenses

Syn

Synthronon

Syria
Syria: Revue d'art oriental et d'archéologie

Szabad Művészet
Szabad művészet [Free art]

Szepművészet [Fine art]

Szinhas [Theatre life]

Szkło & Cer.
Szkło i keramika [Glass and ceramics]

Sztuka & Kryt.
Sztuka i krytyka [Art and criticism]

Sztuka Pobrze a Bałtyku
Sztuka pobrze a bałtyku [Art of the Baltic coastlands]

Sztuki Piękne
Sztuki piękne [Fine arts]

Tableau

Table Ronde

Taehan Kŏnch' Hakhoe Nonmonjip
Taehan kŏnch' hakhoe nonmonjip

Taide [Art]

Taidehist. Tutkimuksia/Ksthist. Stud.
Taidehistoriallisia tutkimuksia/ Konsthistoriska studier

Taloha

Tamarind Pap.
Tamarind Papers

Tamil Cult.
Tamil Culture

Tanganyika Notes & Rec.
Tanganyika Notes and Records

Tarih Derg.
Tarih dergisi [Journal of history]

Tarihî Osmani Encümeni Mecmuası [Journal of the Ottoman Historical Society]

Tasarim

Tate Gal. Biennial Rep.
Tate Gallery Biennial Report

Taxandria

Te Ao Hou [New Zealand]

Tebiwa
Tebiwa: Journal of the Idaho State Museum

Tech. & Archit.
Techniques and Architecture

Tech. & Archit. [Paris]
Techniques et architecture [Paris]

Tech. Gesch.
Technik Geschichte

Tech. Mag.
Technicky Magazín

Technika

Technol. & Cult.
Technology and Culture

Technol. Gesch.
Technologische Geschichte

Technol. Rev.
Technology Review

Tech. Obzor Slov.
Technicky obzor slovensky
[Slovak technical review]

Tech. Stud.
Technical Studies

Tech. Stud. Field F.A.
Technical Studies in the Field of
Fine Arts

Tech. Trav.
La Technique des travaux

Teka Kom. Hist. Sztuki
Teka Komisji historii sztuki
[Papers of the Committee on Art
History]

Teka Kom. Urb. & Archit. Pol.
Akad. Nauk
Teka Komisji urbanistyki i
architektury Polskiej akademii
nauk [Papers of the Committee on
Urbanism and Architecture of the
Polish Academy of Sciences]

Teka Kons.
Teka konserwatorska

Tekhné

Teki Archiwalne
Teki archiwalne

Teknikern

Tel Aviv

Tel Aviv U. Inst. Archaeol., J.
Tel Aviv University Institute of
Archaeology, Journal

Tel Quel

Temas

Tempi Nostri

Temple Newsam Country House Stud.
Temple Newsam Country House
Studies

Temps Mod.
Temps modernes

Temps Nouv.
Temps nouveaux

Temps Présent
Temps présent: Revue de langue
française pour la défense des
intérêts vitaux de la France et ses
colonies

Temps Présent: Rev. Mens. Litt. & A.
Temps présent: Revue mensuelle
de littérature et d'art

Ten 8

Teningur

Tenseki

Tér & Forma
Tér és forma

Terra Plana

Terra Port.
Terra portuguesa: Revista ilustrada
de arqueologia, artística e
etnografia

Terr. Incog.
Terrae incognitae: The Annals of
the Society for the History of
Discoveries

Teutscher Merkur
Der Teutscher Merkur [cont. as
Neuer Teutscher Merkur]

Texas Stud. in Lit. & Lang.
Texas Studies in Literature and
Language

Text
Text: Transactions of the Society
for Textual Scholarship

Tex-Textilis

Textile Hist.
Textile History

Textile Mus. J.
Textile Museum Journal

Text & Kontext
Text und Kontext

Thalia [cont. as Neue Thalia]

The Academy [London]

The Act

The Architect

The Archive

The Artist

The Artlover

The Arts [London]

The Artsman

Theat. A.
Theatre Arts

Théât. Europe
Théâtre en Europe

The Athenaeum [merged with The
Nation to form Nation &
Athenaeum]

Theat. J.
Theatre Journal

The Atlantic

Theat. Ntbk
Theatre Notebook

Theatrephile

Théâtre-Public

Theat. Surv.: Amer. J. Theat. Hist.
Theatre Survey: The American
Journal of Theatre History

The Bailie

The Bell

The Bellman

The Bouquet

The Builder [cont. as Building [UK]]

The Bulletin

The Clarion

The Commentator [prev. pubd as
Scribner's Mag.]

The Conservator

The Craftsman

The Critic

The Dial

The Dickensian

The East

The Ecclesiologist

The Empress

The Ephemerist

The Field

The Fleuron

The Forum

The Garden

The Germ

The Graphic

The Griffon

The Guardian

The Hawk

The Herald

The Historian

The Idler

The Illustrated [prev. pubd as Wkly
Illus.]

The Imprint

The Independent

The Island

The Lancet

The Library

The Listener

The Mask

The Masterkey

The Medal

The Month

The Montrealer

The Museum [London] [cont. as Lit.
Mus. Register A. Sci. & General Lit.]

The Museum [Newark, NJ]

The Muslim

The Nation [merged with The
Athenaeum to form Nation &
Athenaeum; then with New Statesman
to form New Statesman & Nation]

The Observer

Theoria
Theoria: A Journal of Studies in
the Arts, Humanities and Social
Sciences

The Outlook

The Page

The Pelican

The PIC-NIC

The Probe

The Quill

The Reader

The Reliquary [incorp. Illus.
Archaeologist, 1894-]

The Reporter

The Researcher

The Ricardian

Thesarismata
Thesaurismata: Bollettino
dell'Istituto ellenico di studi
bizantini e postbizantini

The Savoy

The Scotsman

The Sketch

The Speaker

The Spectator

The Star

The Stoic

The Structurist

The Studio

The Sun

The Tablet

The Tatler

The Tyro

The Witness

The Yellow Book

Third Eye
The Third Eye

Third Text

30s Soc. J.
Thirties Society Journal

35 mm Photog.
35 mm Photography

¡30-30! [Thirty-thirty/Treinta-treinta]

This Quarter

Thjóðviljinn

Thought/Shiso

Threads Mag.
Threads Magazine

391 [Three nine one/Trois cent
quatre-vingt-onze]

Thurgau. Beitr. Vaterländ. Gesch.
Thurgauische Beiträge zur
vaterländischen Geschichte

Thurn & Taxis-Stud.
Thurn und Taxis-Studien

Tibet News Rev.
Tibet News Review

Tidens Tegn [Sign of the times]

Tidskr. Kstvet.
Tidskrift för konstvetenskap
[Journal for art knowledge]

Tidskr. Prakt. Bygkst & Mek.
Tidskrift för praktisk
byggnadskonst och mekanik
[Practical architecture and
mechanics magazine]

Tiempo Real

T'ien Hsia Mthly
T'ien Hsia Monthly

Tiger's Eye

Tijd & Mens
Tijd en mens [Time and man]

Tijdschr. Archit. & Beeld. Kst
Tijdschrift voor architectuur en
beeldende kunst [Journal of
architecture and plastic arts]

Tijdschr. Brussel. Gesch.
Tijdschrift voor Brusselse
geschiedenis [Journal of Brussels
history]

Tijdschr. Gemeentekrediet België
Tijdschrift van het
gemeentekrediet van België

Tijdschr. Gesch. & Flklore
Tijdschrift voor geschiedenis en
folklore [Journal of history and
folklore]

Tijdschr. Graf.
Tijdschrift grafiek [Graphics
journal]

Tijdschr. Ind. Taal-, Land- &
Vlknknd.
Tijdschrift voor Indische taal-,
land- en volkenkunde uitgegeven
door het (Koninklijk) Bataviaasch
genootschap van kunsten en
wetenschappen [Journal for Indian
[Indonesian] linguistics,
agriculture and ethnology,
published by the Royal Batavian
Society of Arts and Sciences]

Tijdschr. Levende Talen
Tijdschrift voor levende talen [Journal for living languages]

Tijdschr. Vlkshuisvest. Stedebouw
Tijdschrift voor volkshuisvesting en stedebouw [Journal for state housing and town planning]

Tilskueren [The observer]

Time

Time–Life

Time Out

Times Ceylon Annu.
Times of Ceylon Annual

Tirol. Heimatbl.
Tiroler Heimatblätter

Tit Bits

Tlalocán

Tlatoani

TLS
The Times Literary Supplement

TN Hist. Q.
Tennessee Historical Quarterly

T.N.T.

Today

Tōhō Gaku [Oriental studies]

Tōhō Gakuhō [Journal of Oriental studies]

Toksŏ Saenghwal [Reading Life]

Toledo

Tongyang Hak

Topkapı Sarayı Müz.: Yıllık
Topkapı Sarayı Müzesi: Yıllık [Topkapı Palace Museum: annual]

Topkapı Sarayı Yıllığı

Torre
Torre: Revista general de la Universidad de Puerto Rico

Történetírás [History records]

Toshijutaku

Touchstone

T'oung Pao

Tour Monde
Tour du monde

Town & Country
Town and Country

Town Planning Rev.
Town Planning Review

Tōyō Bunka Kenkyūjō Kiiyō [Bulletin of the Institute of Oriental Culture]

Tōyō Tōji [Oriental ceramics]

Trab. Prehist.
Trabajos de prehistoria

Tracce

Trace

Tracks

Trad. Dwell. & Settmts, Working Pap. Ser.
Traditional Dwellings and Settlements, Working Paper Series

Traditio

Trama

Tramontane

Transafr. J. Hist.
Transafrican Journal of History

Trans. Amer. A.-Un.
Transactions of the American Art-Union [cont. as *Bull. Amer. A. Un.*]

Trans. Amer. Ethnol. Soc.
Transactions of the American Ethnological Society

Trans. Amer. Philos. Assoc.
Transactions of the American Philosophical Association

Trans. Amer. Philos. Soc.
Transactions of the American Philosophical Society

Trans. Anc. Mnmt. Soc.
Transactions of the Ancient Monuments Society

Trans. Archaeol. Soc. S. India
Transactions of the Archaeological Society of South India

Trans. Archit. Inst. Scotland
Transactions of the Architectural Institute of Scotland

Trans. Asiat. Soc. Japan
Transactions of the Asiatic Society of Japan

Transatlantic Rev.
Transatlantic Review

Trans. Bibliog. Soc.
Transactions of the Bibliographical Society

Trans. Birmingham Archaeol. Soc.
Transactions of the Birmingham Archaeological Society

Trans. Bristol & Glos Archaeol. Soc.
Transactions of the Bristol and Gloucestershire Archaeological Society

Trans. Brit. Archaeol. Assoc.
Transactions of the British Archaeological Association

Trans. Brit. Cer. Soc.
Transactions of the British Ceramic Society

Trans. Cambridge Bibliog. Soc.
Transactions of the Cambridge Bibliographical Society

Trans. Cumb. & Westmorland Antiqua. & Archaeol. Soc.
Transactions of the Cumberland and Westmorland Antiquarian and Archaeological Society

Trans. Dept Archaeol., Free Mus. Sci. & A., U. PA
Transactions of the Department of Archaeology, Free Museum of Sciences and Art, University of Pennyslvania

Trans. Devon Assoc.
Transactions of the Devonshire Association for the Advancement of Science, Literature and Art

Trans. Eng. Cer. Circ.
Transactions of the English Ceramic Circle

Trans. Faraday Soc.
Transactions of the Faraday Society

Trans. Greenwich & Lambeth Antiqua. Soc.
Transactions of the Greenwich and Lambeth Antiquarian Society

Trans. Hist. Soc. Lancs & Ches
Transactions of the Historic Society of Lancashire and Cheshire

Transition [Australia]

Transition [Kampala] [cont. as *Ch'Indaba*]

Trans. Korea Branch Royal Asiat. Soc.
Transactions of the Korea Branch of the Royal Asiatic Society

Trans. Lancs & Ches Antiqua. Soc.
Transactions of the Lancashire and Cheshire Antiquarian Society

Trans. London & Middx Archaeol. Soc.
Transactions of the London and Middlesex Archaeological Society

Trans. Mnmt. Brass Soc.
Transactions of the Monumental Brass Society

Trans. Newcomen Soc.
Transactions of the Newcomen Society

Trans. NY Acad. Sci.
Transactions of the New York Academy of Science

Trans. Orient. Cer. Soc.
Transactions of the Oriental Ceramic Society

Trans. & Proc. Amer. Philol. Assoc.
Transactions and Proceedings of the American Philological Association

Trans. & Proc. Birmingham Archaeol. Soc.
Transactions and Proceedings of the Birmingham Archaeological Society

Trans. & Proc. Japan Soc., London
Transactions and Proceedings of the Japan Society, London

Trans. RIBA
Transactions of the Royal Institute of British Architects

Trans. Royal Hist. Soc.
Transactions of the Royal Historical Society

Trans. Royal Irish Acad.
Transactions of the Royal Irish Academy

Trans. Royal Soc. S. Australia
Transactions of the Royal Society of South Australia

Trans. Scot. Eccles. Soc.
Transactions of the Scottish Ecclesiastical Society

Trans. Soc. Bibl. Archaeol.
Transactions of the Society of Biblical Archaeology

Trans. Soc. Glass Technol.
Transactions of the Society of Glass Technology

Trans. St Albans & Herts Archaeol. Soc.
Transactions of the St Albans and Hertfordshire Archaeological Society

Travaux

Trav. Inst. A. Préhist.
Travaux de l'Institut d'art préhistorique

Trav. Inst. Rech. Sahar.
Travaux de l'Institut de recherches sahariennes

Trav. & Mém.
Travaux et mémoires

Trav. & Mém. Inst. Ethnol.
Travaux et mémoires de l'Institut d'ethnologie

Trav. & Mém. Inst. Hautes Etud. Amér. Latine
Travaux et mémoires de l'Institut des hautes études de l'Amérique Latine

Traza & Baza
Traza y Baza

¡30-30! [Treinta-treinta]

Trentino

Trésors Bibs France
Trésors des Bibliothèques de la France

Tribord

Tribuna Imprensa
Tribuna da imprensa

Tribune A.
Tribune des arts

Tribune Genève
La Tribune de Genève

Tribüne Kst & Zeit
Tribüne der Kunst und Zeit

Tribus
Tribus: Zeitschrift für Ethnologie und ihre Nachbarwissenschaften vom Linden-Museum Stuttgart

Trier. Chron.
Trierische Chronik

Trier. Grab. & Forsch.
Trierer Grabungen und Forschungen

Trier. Theol. Z.
Trierer theologische Zeitschrift

Trier. Z. Gesch. & Kst Landes & Nachbargebiete
Trierer Zeitschrift für Geschichte und Kunst des Landes und seiner Nachbargebiete

Tri-Quarterly

Troços

391 [Trois cent quatre-vingt-onze]

Trondheims Kstforen.
Trondheims Kunstforening

Tropical Man [prev. *Int. Archvs Ethnog.*; *Int. Archv Ethnog.*]

Trudy Azerbay. Filiala Akad. Nauk SSSR
Trudy azerbaydzhanskogo filiala Akademii nauk SSSR [Transactions of the Azerbaijan filial of the Academy of Sciences of the USSR]

Trudy Gosudarstvennogo Ermitazha [Transactions of the State Hermitage]

Trudy Gosudarstvennogo Istor. Muz.
Trudy Gosudarstvennogo istoricheskogo muzey [Transactions of the State Historical Museum]

Trudy Gosudarstvennoy Pub. Bib. M. E. Saltykova-Shchedrina
Trudy Gosudarstvennoy publichnoy biblioteki M. E. Saltykova-Shchedrina [Transactions of the M. E. Saltikov-Shchedrin State Public Library]

Trudy Inst. Istor. A. Bakikhanova
Trudy Instituta istorii imeni A. Bakikhanova [Transactions of the Bakikhanov Institute of History]

Trudy Inst. Istor. & Arkheol. Akad. Nauk UzSSR
Trudy Instituta istorii i arkheologii Akademii nauk UzSSR [Transactions of the Institute of History and Archaeology of the Academy of Sciences of the Uzbek SSR]

Trudy Khorezm. Arkheol.-Etnog. Eksped.
Trudy Khorezmskoy arkheologo-etnograficheskoy ekspeditsii

Trudy Kirgiz. Arkheol.-Etnog. Eksped.
Trudy Kirgizskoy arkheologo-etnograficheskoy ekspeditsii

Trudy Nauchnogo Inst. Muz.
Trudy Nauchnogo instituta muzeyevedeniya [Transactions of the Scientific Institute of Museum Studies]

Trudy Otdela Drevnerus. Lit. Inst. Rus. Lit. Akad. Nauk SSR
Trudy Otdela drevnerusskoy literatury Instituta russkoy literatury Akademii nauk SSR [Transactions of the Department of Old Russian Literature of the Institute of Russian Literature of the Academy of Sciences of the USSR]

Trudy Otdela Vostoka [Transactions of the Oriental Department]

Trudy Sekt. Arkheol. Inst. Arkheol. & Iskznaniya
Trudy Sektsii arkheologii instituta arkheologii i iskusstvoznaniya [Transactions of the Archaeology Section of the Institute of Archaeology and Art Studies]

Trudy Sogdiysko-Tadzhikskoy Arkheol. Eksped.
Trudy Sogdiysko-tadzhikskoy arkheologicheskoy ekspeditsii

Trudy Sredneaziatskogo Gosudarstvennogo U.
Trudy Sredneaziatskogo gosudarstvennogo universiteta [Transactions of the Central Asian State University]

Trudy Uzbek. Filiala Akad. Nauk SSSR
Trudy Uzbekistanskogo filiala Akademii nauk SSSR [Transactions of the Uzbek filial of the Academy of Sciences of the USSR]

Trudy Vladimir. Uchonoy Arkhv Kom.
Trudy Vladimirskoy uchonoy arkhivnoy komissii [Reports of the Vladimir Academic Archive Commission]

Trudy VNIITTE
Trudy Vysshiy natsional'nyy institut iskusstva i tekhniki [Transactions of the Higher National Institute of Art and Technology]

Trudy Vserossiskoy Akad. Khudozhestv
Trudy Vserossiskoy akademii khudozhestv [Transactions of the All-Russian Academy of Arts]

Trudy Yuzhno-Turkmen. Arkheol. Kompleksnoy Eksped.
Trudy Yuzhno-turkmenistanskoy arkheologicheskoy kompleksnoy ekspeditsii [Report of the Southern Turkmenistan Archaeological Expedition (Trudy YuTAKE)]

Tübinger Bl.
Tübinger Blätter

Tudományos Gyüjtemény
Tudományos gyüjtemény [Scientific repertory]

Tues. Rev.
Tuesday Review

Tukor [Mirror]

Túrán Z. Osteuropä. Vorder- & Innerasiat. Stud.
Túrán Zeitschrift für osteuropäische vorder- und innerasiatische Studien

Turcica
Turcica: Revue d'études turques

Turicum

Türk Arkeol. Derg.
Türk arkeoloji dergisi [Turkish archaeology review]

Türk Etnog. Derg.
Türk etnografya dergisi [Turkish ethnography review]

Türkiyat Mecmuası
Türkiyat mecmuası [Journal of Turkology]

Turkoman Stud.
Turkoman Studies

Türk Sanatı Tarihî: Araştırma ve Incelemeleri
Türk sanatı tarihî: Araştırma ve incelemeleri [Research and studies in the history of Turkish art]

Türk Tarihî Kurumu Basımeri

Türk Tarihî Kurumu: Belleten [Turkish Historical Society: bulletin]

Turner Stud.
Turner Studies

Turquie Kémal.
La Turquie kémaliste

Tushuguanxue Jikan [Library studies, collected papers]

Tvai

Tvar [Form]

Tvorchestvo [Creative work]

Tweemandelijksche Tijdschr. Lett. Kst. Wet. & Polit.
Tweemandelijksche tijdschrift voor letteren, kunst, wetenschap en politiek [Bimonthly journal for literature, art, science and politics; cont. as *XIXe Eeuw*]

Twentieth C. Archit.
Twentieth Century Architecture

Twice a Year

2 x 2
Kettö [Two by two]

2C: Constr. Ciudad
2C: Construcción de la ciudad

291 [Two nine one]

Twórczość [Creative work]

Tygodnik Powszechny
Tygodnik powszechny [Popular weekly]

Tyndale House Bull.
Tyndale House Bulletin

Typographica

Tyrihaus

U. Bergen Åb.
Universiteit i Bergen årbok

Über Kst & Altert. Rhein- & Maingeg.
Über Kunst und Alterthum in der Rhein- und Maingegenden

Über Land & Meer
Über Land und Meer

U. Chicago Mag.
University of Chicago Magazine

Uffizi, Stud. & Ric.
Gli Uffizi, studi e ricerche

Ugarit-Forsch.
Ugarit-Forschungen

Uhu

Uhuru

UIA Int. Architect
UIA International Architect

Uj Építészet

Új Irás
Új irás (irodalmi és kritikai folyóirat) [New writing]

U.K.I.C.: Occas. Pap.
United Kingdom Institute for Conservation: Occasional Papers

Ukiyoe no Kenkyū

Ukrain. Lit.
Ukraïns'ka literatura [Ukrainian literature]

Ulbandus Rev.
Ulbandus Review

U. Leeds Rev.
University of Leeds Review

U. Libre
L'Université libre

Ulk

Ulm, Oberschwaben
Ulm, Oberschwaben: Mitteilungen des Vereins für Kunst und Altertum in Ulm und Oberschwaben [cont. as *Ulm & Oberschwaben*]

Ulm & Oberschwaben
Ulm und Oberschwaben [prev. pubd as *Ulm, Oberschwaben*]

Ulster Architect

Ulster J. Archaeol.
Ulster Journal of Archaeology

Ultreya

Um
Universal Magazine

Um & Court & Fashionable Gaz.
Universal Magazine and Court and Fashionable Gazette

Twice a Year

Uměleckohist. Sborn.
Uměleckohistoricky sborník [Art history journal]

Umělecky Měsíčník
Umělecky měsíčník [Artist's monthly]

Umění [Arts]

Umění & Řemesla
Umění a řemesla [Art and crafts]

Umetnički Pregled [Artistic overview]

U. MI–Columbia, Mus. Anthropol., Annu. Rep.
University of Missouri-Columbia, Museum of Anthropology, Annual Report

U. MI J. Law Reform
University of Michigan Journal of Law Reform

U. MI Mus. A. Bull.
University of Michigan Museum of Art Bulletin

U. MI Pubns: Human. Pap.
University of Michigan Publications: Humanistic Papers

U. MI Q. Rev.
University of Michigan Quarterly Review

Um Knowledge & Pleasure
Universal Magazine of Knowledge and Pleasure

Um & Rev.
Universal Magazine and Review

Umriss

Umschau Wiss. & Tech.
Die Umschau in Wissenschaft und Technik

UNESCO J. Inf. Sci., Librsp & Archvs Admin.
UNESCO Journal of Information Science, Librarianship and Archives Administration

Ungarn-Jb.
Ungarn-Jahrbuch

Unicornis

Univl Chron.
Universal Chronicle

Univl: Illus. Contemp.
Universel: Illustrations contemporaines

Univl Ilus.
El Universal ilustrado

Univl Rev.
Universal Review

Univl Spectator
Universal Spectator

U. NM A. Mus. Bull.
University of New Mexico Art Museum Bulletin

Unser Bayern

Unser Bocholt

Unsere Diöz. Vergangenheit & Gegenwart
Unsere Diözese in Vergangenheit und Gegenwart

Unsere Heimat

Unsere Kstdkml.
Unsere Kunstdenkmäler

U. Oldsaksaml. Åb.
Universitets oldsaksamling årbok
[The University's Antiquities
Collection's yearbook]

U. PA Mus.: U. Mus. Bull.
University of Pennsylvania
Museum: University Museum
Bulletin

Uppland

Upplands Fornminnesfören. Åb.
Upplands fornminnesförenings
årsbok [Uppland's Antiquarian
Society yearbook]

Upplands Fornminnesfören. Tidsk.
Upplands fornminnesförenings
tidskrift [Uppland's Antiquarian
Society journal]

Uppsala U. Årsskr.
Uppsala universitets årsskrift
[Uppsala University yearbook]

Ur

Ural-Alta Jb.
Ural-altaische Jahrbücher

Urbanisme

Urbanismul

Urbanistica

Urb. Des. Int.
Urban Design International

Urbe
L'Urbe: Rivista romana di storia,
arte, lettere, costumanze

Urb. Hist. Rev.
Urban History Review

Urbinum
Urbinum: Rassegna di cultura a
cura della Reale accademia
Raffaello

Urb. Past & Present
Urbanism Past and Present

Urb., Rev. Puertorriqueña Arquit.
Urbe, revista puertorriqueña de
arquitectura

Ur- & Frühgesch. Archäol. Schweiz
Ur- und frühgeschichtliche
Archäologie der Schweiz

Usage Parole
L'Usage de la parole

US Cam.
US Camera

US Cath. Mag.
United States Catholic Magazine

US Lines Paris Rev.
United States Lines Paris Review

US N. Mus. Bull.
United States National Museum
Bulletin

Utafiti

U. Toronto Q.
University of Toronto Quarterly

Utro Ros.
Utro rossu

Vakıflar Derg.
Vakıflar dergisi [Journal of the
Directorate of Pious
Endowments]

Valori Plast.
Valori plastici: Rivista d'arte

Valori Prim.
Valori primordiali

Valuation

VA Mag. Hist. & Biog.
Virginia Magazine of History and
Biography

V&A Mus. Album
Victoria and Albert Museum
Album

V&A Mus. Bull.
Victoria and Albert Museum
Bulletin

V&A Mus. Yb.
Victoria and Albert Museum
Yearbook

Vancouver Mag.
Vancouver Magazine

Vanidades

Vanidades México
Vanidades de México

Vanity Fair

Var. Aegyp.
Varia Aegyptiaca

Variedades

Variétés

Vasari Soc.
Vasari Society

Vasárnapi Ujság [Sunday news]

Ved Lovfaldstider [Autumn times]

Vell & Nou
Vell i nou

Veltro: Riv. Civiltà It.
Veltro: Rivista della civiltà italiana

Venezia A.
Venezia arti: Bollettino del
dipartimento di storia e critica
delle arti dell'Università di Venezia

Venezia Cinquecento
Venezia cinquecento

*Venezia: Stud. A. & Stor. Dir. Mus.
Civ. Correr*
Venezia: Studi di arte e storia a
cura della direzione del Museo
civico Correr

Ventana

Ventilator
Der Ventilator

Verbania

Verhand. Hist. Ver. Niederbayern
Verhandlungen des Historischen
Vereins für Niederbayern

*Verhand. Hist. Ver. Oberpfalz &
Regensburg*
Verhandlungen des Historischen
Vereins für Oberpfalz und
Regensburg

*Verhand. Kon. Acad. Wet. Afd.
Lettknd.*
Verhandelingen van de
Koninklijke academie voor
wetenschappen, afdeling
letterkunde [Papers of the Royal
Academy of Sciences, Literature
Division]

*Verhand. Kon. Inst. Taal-, Land- &
Vlkenknd.*
Verhandelingen Koninklijk
instituut voor taal-, land- en
volkenkunde [Papers of the Royal
Institute for Linguistics,
Agriculture and Ethnology]

Verhand. Kon. Ned. Akad. Wet.
Verhandelingen der Koninklijke
Nederlandse academie van
wetenschappen [Papers of the
Royal Dutch Academy of
Sciences]

Verhand. Natforsch. Ges. Basel
Verhandlungen der
Naturforschenden Gesellschaft
Basel

*Verhand. Ver. Beförd. Gtnbaues Kon.
Preuss. Staaten*
Verhandlungen des Vereins zur
Beförderung des Gartenbaues in
den königlichen preussischen
Staaten

*Verhand. Ver. Kst & Altert. Ulm &
Oberschwaben*
Verhandlungen des Vereins für
Kunst und Altertum in Ulm und
Oberschwaben

Vern. Archit.
Vernacular Architecture

*Veröff. Abt. Archit. Ksthist. Inst. U.
Köln*
Veröffentlichungen der Abteilung
Architektur des Kunsthistorischen
Instituts der Universität zu Köln

*Veröff. Gesch. Freien & Hansestadt
Lübeck*
Veröffentlichungen zur
Geschichte der freien und
Hansestadt Lübeck

Veröff. Graph. Ges.
Veröffentlichung der graphischen
Gesellschaft

Veröff. Heidelberg. Altstadt
Veröffentlichungen zur
Heidelberger Altstadt

Veröff. Kultamt. Stadt Steyr
Veröffentlichungen des
Kulturamtes der Stadt Steyr

Veröff. Mus. Ferdinandeum
Veröffentlichungen des Museums
Ferdinandeum [prev. pubd as
*Veröff. Mus. Ferdinandeum
Innsbruck*; cont. as *Veröff. Tirol.
Landesmus. Ferdinandeum*]

Veröff. Mus. Ferdinandeum Innsbruck
Veröffentlichungen des Museums
Ferdinandeum in Innsbruck [see
Veröff. Mus. Ferdinandeum]

Veröff. Reichsmus. Vlkerknd. Leiden
Veröffentlichungen des
Reichsmuseums für Völkerkunde
in Leiden

*Veröff. Tirol. Landesmus.
Ferdinandeum*
Veröffentlichungen des Tiroler
Landesmuseums Ferdinandeum
[see *Veröff. Mus. Ferdinandeum*]

*Veröff. Verband. Österreich. Gesch.-
Ver.*
Veröffentlichungen des Verbandes
des österreichischen Geschichte-
Vereins

Veröff. Vorgesch. Semin. Marburg
Veröffentlichungen des
vorgeschichtlichen Seminars
Marburg

Veröff. Zentinst. Kstgesch. München
Veröffentlichungen des
Zentralinstituts für
Kunstgeschichte in München

Verona Illus.
Verona illustrata

Verona & Territ.
Verona e il suo territorio

Ver. Onderzoek Mnmt.
Vereniging Onderzoek
Monumentum

Vêrotâjs [The observer]

Ver Sacrum

Versailles

*Versl. & Meded. Kon. Acad. Ned.
Taal- & Lettknd.*
Verslagen en mededelingen van de
Koninklijke academie voor
Nederlandse taal- en letterkunde
[Reports and communications of
the Royal Academy for Dutch
linguistics and literature]

*Versl. & Meded. Kon. Vl. Acad. Taal-
& Lettknd.*
Verslagen en mededelingen van de
Koninklijke Vlaamse academie
voor taal- en letterkunde [Reports
and communications of the Royal
Flemish Academy for Linguistics
and Literature]

*Versl. & Meded. Ver. Beoef.
Overijsselsch Regt & Gesch.*
Verslagen en mededelingen der
Vereeniging tot beoefening van
Overijsselsch regt en geschiedenis
[Reports and communications of
the Association for the Study and
History of the Overijssel Area]

Vertice

Verulamium Mus. Occas. Pap.
Verulamium Museum Occasional
Papers

Verve

Verz. Gemäldegal. Ksthist. Mus., Wien
Verzeichnis der Gemäldegalerie
des Kunsthistorischen Museums,
Wien

Verz. Mitglieder Dt. Archäol. Inst.
Verzeichnis der Mitglieder des
deutschen archäologischen
Instituts [cont. as *Archäol. Anz.*]

Veselé Listy [Good cheer]

Veshch—Gegenstand—Objet

Vestland. Kstindustmus. Åb.
Vestlandske
Kunstindustrimuseums årbok
[Vestland Applied Arts yearbook]

Vestnik Drevney Istor.
Vestnik drevney istorii [Bulletin of
ancient history]

*Vestnik Karakalpak. Filiala Akad.
Nauk Uzbek. SSR*
Vestnik Karakalpakskogo filiala
Akademii nauk Uzbekskoy SSR
[Bulletin of the Karakalpak filial
of the Academy of Sciences of the
Uzbek SSR]

Vestnik Leningrad. U.
Vestnik Leningradskogo
Universiteta

Věstník Mus. Kroměříži
Věstník musea v Kroměříži [Bulletin of the Museum at Kroměříž]

Vesy

Vetera Christ.
Vetera Christianorum

Veu Catalunya
Veu de Catalunya

VIA [Journal of the Graduate School of the Fine Arts, University of Pennsylvania]

Viator

Vict. Hist. Mag.
Victorian Historical Magazine

Vict. Period. Newslett.
Victorian Periodicals Newsletter

Vict. Period. Rev.
Victorian Periodicals Review

Vict. Rev.
Victorian Review

Vict. Soc. Annu.
Victorian Society Annual

Vict. Stud.
Victorian Studies

Vida Gallega [Galician life]

Vie A.
Vie des arts

Vie Artistique

Vie Campagne
Vie à la campagne

Vie Champagne
Vie en Champagne

Vie Liége.
Vie liégeoise

Vie Mod.
Vie moderne

Vie Paris.
Vie parisienne

Vie Pop.
La Vie populaire

Vie Urb.
Vie urbaine

View

Vie Wallonne

Vigiliae Christ.
Vigiliae Christianae

Vijenac

Viking

Villa Madrid
Villa de Madrid

Villa Medici: J. Voyage
Villa Medici: Journal de voyage

Vínculos

XXe Siècle
XXe siècle [Vingtième]

Vi Ser Kunst
Vi ser på kunst [We look at art]

Vishva Bharati Q.
Vishva Bharati Quarterly

Vishvasananda Indol. J.
Vishvasananda Indological Journal

Visible Lang.
Visible Language [prev. pubd as *J. Typograph. Res.*]

Visible Relig.
Visible Religion

Visnyk Akad. Nauk Ukrain. RSR
Visnyk Akademii Nauk Ukrainskoy RSR

Vistas

Visual

Visual Anthropol. Rev.
Visual Anthropology Review

Visual A. Res.
Visual Arts Research

Visual Resources

Vita A.
Vita d'arte

Vita Artistica

Vita Veron.
Vita veronese

Vita Vicentina

Vizant. Vremennik
Vizantijskij vremennik [Byzantine yearbook]

Vjesnik

Vjesnik Arheol. & Hist. Dalmat.
Vjesnik za arheolgiju i historiju dalmatinsku [Bulletin of Dalmatian archaeology and history]

Vjschr. Herald., Sphragistik & Geneal.
Vierteljahresschrift für Heraldik, Sphragistik und Genealogie [cont. as *Vjschr. Wap.-, Siegel- & Famknd.*; Herold Geschlechter-, Wappen- & Siegelknd.]

Vjschr. Soz.- & Wirtschaftsgesch.
Vierteljahresschrift für Sozial- und Wirtschaftsgeschichte

Vjschr. Wap.-, Siegel- & Famknd.
Vierteljahresschrift für Wappen-, Siegel- und Familienkunde [see *Vjschr. Herald., Sphragistik & Geneal.*]

Vlaanderen
Vlaanderen: Tijdschrift voor kunst en cultuur

Vlastivědny Časop.
Vlastivědny časopis [Journal of regional history]

Vlks-Alm. Ned. Kath.
Volks-Almanak voor Nederlandsche katholieken

Vlkskst & Vlksknd.
Volkskunst und Volkskunde [cont. as *Bayer. Heimatschutz, S. Heimat*]

Vl. Kstbode
De Vlaamsche kunstbode

Vl. Sch.
Vlaamsche school [cont. as *Onze Kst*]

Vl. Stam
Vlaamsche stam

Vogue

Vogue Italia Speciale

Volksfoto

Volné Směry [Free trends]

Voprosy Istor.
Voprosy istorii [Questions of history]

Voprosy Istor. Isk.
Voprosy istorii iskusstva [Questions of art history]

Voprosy Revstavrats'ii [Questions of restoration]

Voprosy Teor. Arkhit. Kompozitsii
Voprosy teorii arkhiturnoy kompozitsii [Questions on the theory of architectural composition]

Vortr. Bib. Warburg
Vorträge der Bibliothek Warburg

Vouloir: J. Action Econ. & Soc.
Vouloir: Journal d'action économique et sociale

Vozrozhdeniye [Renaissance]

Vremennik Obshchestva Lyubiteley Rus. Knigi
Vremennik Obshchestva lyubiteley russkoy knigi [Annals of the Society of Lovers of the Russian Book]

Vrienden Ned. Cer.: Mededbl.
Vrienden van de Nederlandse ceramiek: Mededelingenblad [Friends of Dutch ceramics: Reports; cont. as *Mededbl. Ned. Ver. Vrienden Cer.*]

Vrije Fries

Vrouw & Huis
Vrouw en haar huis

VT Hist.
Vermont History

Vu

Vyroční Zpráva Okresniho Archiv Olomouci
Vyroční zpráva Okresního archívu v Olomouci [Annual news of the Regional Archive in Olomouc]

Vytvarná Kult.
Vytvarná kultura [Artistic culture]

Vytvarné Umění [Fine art]

Vytvarný Život [Creative life]

Wad-al-Hayara

Wadsworth Atheneum Bull.
Wadsworth Atheneum Bulletin [prev. pubd as *Wadsworth Atheneum News Bull.*; *Wadsworth Atheneum & Morgan Mem. Bull.*]

Wadsworth Atheneum & Morgan Mem. Bull.
Wadsworth Atheneum and Morgan Memorial Bulletin [see *Wadsworth Atheneum Bull.*]

Wadsworth Atheneum News Bull.
Wadsworth Atheneum News Bulletin [see *Wadsworth Atheneum Bull.*]

Waf.- & Kostknd.
Waffen- und Kostümkunde [prev. pubd as *Z. Hist. Waf.- & Kostknd.*]

W. Afr. Bldr & Architect
West African Builder and Architect

W. Africa
West Africa

W. Afr. J. Archaeol.
West African Journal of Archaeology

W. Afr. Rev.
West African Review

Wagen: Lübeck. Jb.
Wagen: Ein lübeckisches Jahrbuch

Walderburg. Sch.
Walderburger Schriften

Waldviertel

Walker's Q.
Walker's Quarterly

Wallonie

Wallraf-Richartz-Jb.
Wallraf-Richartz-Jahrbuch

Walpole Soc.
Walpole Society

Walters A.G. Bull.
Walters Art Gallery Bulletin

W. Architect
Western Architect

W. Architect and Engin.
Western Architect and Engineer

Warwicks Hist.
Warwickshire History

Washington Post

Wasmuths Mhft. Baukst
Wasmuths Monatshefte für Baukunst [prev. pubd as *Wasmuths Mhft. Baukst & Städtebau*]

Wasmuths Mhft. Baukst & Städtebau
Wasmuths Monatshefte für Baukunst und Städtebau [cont. as *Wasmuths Mhft. Baukst*]

Wayka

Wdt. Z. Gesch. & Kst
Westdeutsche Zeitschrift für Geschichte und Kunst

Weather

Weaver's J.
Weaver's Journal

Wegleitungen Kstgewmus. Zürich
Wegleitungen des Kunstgewerbemuseums Zürich

Weichselland
Weichselland: Mitteilungen des westpreussischen Geschichtsvereins [prev. pubd as *Mitt. Westpreuss. Geschver.*]

Weissen Bl.
Die weissen Blätter

Weiterbauen

Wendingen

Wenwu [Cultural artefacts; prev. pubd as *Wenwu Cankao Ziliao*]

Wenwu Cankao Ziliao [cont. as *Wenwu*]

Wenwu Jinghua

Wenwu Tiandi

Wenwu Ziliao Congkan

Werk
Werk: Schweizer Monatschrift für Architektur, Kunst und künstlerische Gewerbe [merged with *Archithese* to form *Werk-Archithese*]

Werk–Archithese [merger of *Archithese* with *Werk*; merged with *Bauen + Wohnen* to form *Werk, Bauen + Wohnen*]

Werk, Bauen + Wohnen [merger of *Archithese* with *Werk* & with *Bauen + Wohnen*]

Werk Kstlers
Werk des Künstlers

Werk & Zeit
Werk und Zeit

Wesleyan U. Alumnus
Wesleyan University Alumnus

Wesley Hist. Soc. Lect.
The Wesley Historical Society Lectures

Westermanns Mhft.
Westermanns Monatshefte

Westfalen: Hft. Gesch., Kst & Vlkskind.
Westfalen: Hefte für Geschichte, Kunst und Volkskunde

Westfäl. Forsch.
Westfälische Forschungen

Westfäl. Lebensbild.
Westfälische Lebensbilder

Westfäl. Z.
Westfälische Zeitschrift

Wet. Tijd.
Wetenschappelijke tijdingen

W. Human. Rev.
Western Humanities Review

Wiadomości Numi.
Wiadomości numizmatyczne [Numismatic news]

WI Archaeologist
Wisconsin Archaeologist

WI Architect
Wisconsin Architect

Wiederhall

Wien. Beitr. Kst- & Kultgesch. Asiens
Wiener Beiträge zur Kunst- und Kulturgeschichte Asiens

Wien. Diarium
Wienerisches Diarium

Wien. Geschb.
Wiener Geschichtsbücher

Wien. Geschbl.
Wiener Geschichtsblätter

Wien. Jb. Kstgesch.
Wiener Jahrbuch für Kunstgeschichte [prev. pubd as *Jb. Kstgesch.*; *Jb. Ksthist. Inst.*; *Kstgesch. Jb. Ksr.-Kön. Zent.-Komm. Erforsch. & Erhaltung Kst. & Hist. Dkml.*]

Wien. Jb. Lit.
Wiener Jahrbücher der Literatur

Wien. Jhft.
Wiener Jahreshefte [prev. pubd as & cont. as *Jhft. Österreich. Archäol. Inst. Wien*]

Wien. Phot. Bl.
Wiener photographische Blätter

Wien. Slav. Jb.
Wiener slavistisches Jahrbuch

Wien. Stud. Z. Philol. & Patristik
Wiener Studien Zeitschrift für Philologie und Patristik

Wien. Z. Knd. Mrglandes
Wiener Zeitschrift für die Kunde des Morgenlandes

Wien. Z. Knd. S.- & Ostasiens & Archv Ind. Philos.
Wiener Zeitschrift für die Kunde Süd- und Ostasiens und Archiv für indische Philosophie [cont. as *Wien. Z. Knd. Südasiens & Archv Ind. Philos.*]

Wien. Z. Knd. Südasiens & Archv Ind. Philos.
Wiener Zeitschrift für die Kunde Südasiens und Archiv für indische Philosophie [prev. pubd as *Wien. Z. Knd. S.- & Ostasiens & Archv Ind. Philos.*]

Wien. Ztg
Wiener Zeitung

Willay

William & Mary Q.
William and Mary Quarterly

Wilts Archaeol. & Nat. Hist. Mag.
Wiltshire Archaeological and Natural History Magazine

WI Mag Hist.
Wisconsin Magazine of History

Windsor Mag.
Windsor Magazine

Winterthur Port.
Winterthur Portfolio

Wiss. Beil. Dresdn. Anz.
Wissenschaftliche Beilage des Dresdner Anzeigers

Wiss. Beil. Jber. Gym. Bamberg
Wissenschaftliche Beilage zum Jahresbericht des Gymnasiums Bamberg

Wiss. Z. Ernst-Moritz-Arndt-U. Greifswald
Wissenschaftliche Zeitschrift der Ernst-Moritz-Arndt-Universität Greifswald

Wiss. Z. Friedrich-Schiller-U. Jena
Wissenschaftliche Zeitschrift der Friedrich-Schiller-Universität Jena

Wiss. Z. Hochsch. Archit. & Bauwsn, Weimar
Wissenschaftliche Zeitschrift der Hochschule für Architektur und Bauwesen, Weimar

Wiss. Z. Humboldt-U.
Wissenschaftliche Zeitschrift der Humboldt-Universität

Wiss. Z. Karl-Marx-U. Leipzig
Wissenschaftliche Zeitschrift der Karl-Marx-Universität Leipzig

Wiss. Z. Martin-Luther-U. Halle-Wittenberg
Wissenschaftliche Zeitschrift der Martin-Luther-Universität in Halle-Wittenberg

Wiss. Z. Tech. Hochsch. Dresden
Wissenschaftliche Zeitschrift der Technischen Hochschule Dresden

Wiss. Z. Tech. U. Dresden
Wissenschaftliche Zeitschrift der Technischen Universität Dresden

Wiss. Z. U. Rostock
Wissenschaftliche Zeitschrift der Universität Rostock

Wkly Illus.
Weekly Illustrated [cont. as *The Illustrated*]

Wkly Register
Weekly Register

Wochschr. Architekten-Ver. Berlin
Wochenschrift des Architekten-Vereins zu Berlin

Wolfenbüttel. Barock Nachr.
Wolfenbütteler Barock Nachrichten

Wolfenbüttel. Beitr.
Wolfenbütteler Beiträge

Wolfenbüttel. Forsch.
Wolfenbütteler Forschungen

Wolkenkratzer A. J.
Wolkenkratzer Art Journal

Womanart

Woman's A. J.
Woman's Art Journal

Women's A. Mag.
Women's Art Magazine

Women's Stud.
Women's Studies

Women's Stud.: Interdiscip. J.
Women's Studies: An Interdisciplinary Journal

Wonen TA-BK

Woolhope Naturalists' Field Club Trans.
Woolhope Naturalists' Field Club Transactions

Woord & Beeld
Woord en beeld [Word and image]

Worcester A. Mus. Annu.
Worcester Art Museum Annual

Worcester A. Mus. Bull.
Worcester Art Museum Bulletin

Worcester A. Mus. J.
Worcester Art Museum Journal

Word & Image

World

World Anthropol.
World Anthropology

World Archaeol.
World Archaeology

World Archit.
World Architecture

World Hosp.
World Hospitals

World Rev.
World Review

World's Work

Wormsgau
Wormsgau: Zeitschrift des Kulturinstituts der Stadt Worms und des Altertumsvereins Worms

W. PA Hist. Mag.
Western Pennsylvania Historical Magazine

Wren Soc.
The Wren Society

Wspóczesność

W. Sussex Hist.
West Sussex History

Württemberg. Jb. Statistik & Landesknd.
Württembergische Jahrbücher für Statistik und Landeskunde

Württemberg. Vjhft. Landesgesch.
Württembergische Vierteljahreshefte für Landesgeschichte

Württembergisch-Franken
Württembergisch-Franken: Jahrbuch des Historischen Vereins für württembergisches Franken

Würzburg. Diözgeschbl.
Würzburger Diözesangeschichtsblätter

Würzburg. Jb. Altertwiss.
Würzburger Jahrbücher für die Altertumswissenschaft

WV

Xenia
Xenia: Semestrale di antichità

Xianggang Zhongwen Daxue Zhongguo Wenhua Yanjiusuo Xuebao [Journal of the Chinese Cultural Research Institute at the Chinese University of Hong Kong]

Xin Qingnian/La Jeunesse

Xin Ya Xuebao

Xin Ya Xueshu Jikan/New Asia Acad. Bull.
Xin ya xueshu jikan/New Asia Academic Bulletin

Xiongshi Meishu

X J.
X Journal

X: Q. Rev.
X: A Quarterly Review

Xuelin

Yale Class. Stud.
Yale Classical Studies

Yale It. Stud.
Yale Italian Studies

Yale J. Archit.
Yale Journal of Architecture

Yale J. Crit.
Yale Journal of Criticism

Yale Sci. Mag.
Yale Science Magazine

Yale U. A.G. Bull.
Yale University Art Gallery Bulletin

Yale U. Lib. Gaz.
Yale University Library Gazette

Yamato Bunka

Yaxkin

Yayla

Yb. Amer. Philos. Soc.
Yearbook of the American Philosophical Society

Yb. Mus. Fin. Archit., Helsinki
Yearbook of the Museum of Finnish Architecture, Helsinki

Yb. N. Mus. Technol.
Yearbook of the National Museum of Technology

Yb. Phot.
Yearbook of Photography

Yediot
Yediot bahaqirat Eretz-Israel weatiqoteha [Bulletin of the Israel Exploration Society]

Yezhegodnik Inst. Istor. Isk.
Yezhegodnik Instituta istorii iskusstva [Annual of the Institute of Art History]

Yezhegodnik Mao

Yıllık Araştırmalar Derg.
Yıllık Araştırmalar Dergisi [Annual journal of research]

Yishu Congbian [Art collection]

Yishujia

Yomiuri

Yŏn'gu nonch'ŏng

Yonsongmunhwa

York A.G. Q.
City of York Art Gallery Quarterly

York Historian

Yorks Archaeol. J.
Yorkshire Archaeological Journal

Z

Z. Aachen. Geschver.
Zeitschrift des Aachener
Geschichtsvereins

Z. Ägyp. Spr. & Altertknd.
Zeitschrift für ägyptische Sprache
und Altertumskunde

Zaire

Zakkicho

Zakład Archit. Pol. & Hist. Sztuki
Zakład architektury polskiej i
historii sztuki [cont. as *Biul. Hist.
Sztuki & Kult.*; *Biul. Hist. Sztuki*]

Zalktis [The grass-snake]

Z. Alles
Zeitschrift für alles

Z. Alte & Neue Glasmal.
Zeitschrift für alte und neue
Glasmalerei

Zambia Mus. J.
Zambia Museums Journal

Zapiski Imp. Rus. Geog. Obshchestva
Zapiski Imperatorskogo russkogo
geograficheskogo obshchestva
[Transactions of the Imperial
Russian Geographical Society]

Zapiski Moskov. Arkhit. Obshchestva
Zapiski Moskovskogo
arkhitekturnogo obshchestva
[Transactions of the Moscow
Architectural Society]

Zapiski Rus. Arkheol. Obshchestva
Zapiski Russkogo
arkheologicheskogo obshchestva
[Transactions of the Russian
Archeological Society]

Zapiski Rus. Tekh. Obshchestva
Zapiski Russkogo tekhnicheskogo
obshchestva [Transactions of the
Russian Technical Society]

Z. Archäol. Mittelalters
Zeitschrift für Archäologie des
Mittelalters

Z. Archit. & Ingenwiss.
Zeitschrift für Architektur- und
Ingenieurwissenschaft

Z. Assyriol.
Zeitschrift für Assyriologie

Z. Ästh. & Allg. Kstwiss.
Zeitschrift für Ästhetik und
allgemeine Kunstwissenschaft

Z. Balkanologie
Zeitschrift für Balkanologie

Z. Bauwsn
Zeitschrift für Bauwesen

Z. Bayer. Kirchgesch.
Zeitschrift für bayerische
Kirchengeschichte

Z. Bayer. Landesgesch.
Zeitschrift für bayerische
Landesgeschichte

Z. Bfreunde
Zeitschrift für Bücherfreunde

Z. Bibwsn & Bibliog.
Zeitschrift für Biliothekwesen und
Bibliographie

Z. Bild. Kst
Zeitschrift für bildende Kunst
[incorp. suppl. *Kstchron. & Kstlit.*;
merged with *Jb. Kstwiss.* & with
Repert. Kstwiss. to form *Z.
Kstgesch.*]

Zborn. Arhit. Fak.
Zbornik arhitektonskog fakulteta

Zborn. Likovne Umětnosti
Zbornik za likovne umětnosti
[Journal for fine arts]

Zborn. Narodnog Muz.
Zbornik Narodnog muzeja

Zborn. Radova Vizant. Inst.
Zbornik radova Vizantološkog
instituta [Journal of the work of
the Byzantine Institute]

Zborn. Trudovi
Zbornik Trudovi

Zborn. Zaštite Spomenika Kult.
Zbornik zaštite spomenika kulture
[Journal of the protection of
cultural monuments]

Zborn. Umětnostno Zgodovino
Zbornik za umětnostno
zgodovino [Journal of art history]

Z. Christ. Archäol. und Kst
Zeitschrift für christliche
Archäologie und Kunst

Z. Christ. Kst
Zeitschrift für christliche Kunst

Zdrój

Z. Dt. Ges. Edelsteinknd.
Zeitschrift der deutschen
Gesellschaft für Edelsteinkunde

Z. Dt. Mrgländ. Ges.
Zeitschrift der deutschen
morgenländischen Gesellschaft

Z. Dt. Palästina Ver.
Zeitschrift des deutschen
Palästina-Verein

Z. Dt. Philol.
Zeitschrift für deutsche Philologie

Z. Dt. Ver. Bwsn & Schr.
Zeitschrift des deutschen Vereins
für Buchwesen und Schrifttum
[cont. as *Buch & Schr.*]

Z. Dt. Ver. Kstwiss.
Zeitschrift des deutschen Vereins
für Kunstwissenschaft [prev. pubd
as *Z. Kstwiss.*; reverts to *Z. Dt.
Ver. Kstwiss.*]

Z. Elem. Gestalt.
Zeitschrift für elementare
Gestaltung

Zeltweg
Der Zeltweg

Zemedelsko Zname

Zenit

Zentasiat. Stud.
Zentralasiatische Studien

Zentbl. Bauverwalt.
Zentralblatt der Bauverwaltung
[prev. pubd as *Centbl. Bauverwalt.*]

Zentbl. Bibwsn
Zentralblatt für Bibliothekswesen

Zephyrus

Zëri i Rinisë

Zëri Pop.
Zëri i popullit

Zero

*Zeszyty Naukowe Akad. Sztuk
Pięknych Warszaw.*
Zeszyty naukowe Akademii sztuk
pięknych w Warszawkiej [Learned
bulletin of the Academy of Fine
Arts of Warsaw]

Zeszyty Naukowe Poli. Warszaw.
Zeszyty naukowe Politechniki
Warszawskiej [Learned bulletin of
the Warsaw Technical University]

Zeszyty Naukowe U. Jagielloń.
Zeszyty naukowe Uniwersytetu
Jagiellońskiego [Learned bulletin
of the Jagellonian University]

Z. Ethnol.
Zeitschrift für Ethnologie

17de Eeuw
Zeventiende eeuw

Z. Ferdinandeums Tirol & Vorarlberg
Zeitschrift des Ferdinandeums
Tirol und Vorarlberg

Z. Gesch. Archit.
Zeitschrift für Geschichte der
Architektur

Z. Gesch. & Kst
Zeitschrift für Geschichte und
Kunst

*Z. Gesch. & Landesknd. Mährens &
Schlesiens*
Zeitschrift für die Geschichte und
Landeskunde Mährens und
Schlesiens [prev. pubd as *Z. Gesch.
Mährens & Schlesiens*, *Z. Ver.
Gesch. Mährens & Schlesiens*]

Z. Gesch. Mährens & Schlesiens
Zeitschrift für die Geschichte
Mährens und Schlesiens [see *Z.
Gesch. & Landesknd. Mährens &
Schlesiens*]

Z. Gesch. Oberrheins
Zeitschrift für die Geschichte des
Oberrheins

Z. Ges. Kerfreunde
Zeitschrift der Gesellschaft der
Keramikfreunde

Z. Hist. Ges. Prov. Posen
Zeitschrift des Historischen
Gesellschaft für die Provinz Posen

Z. Hist. Ver. Schwaben
Zeitschrift des Historischen
Vereins für Schwaben [prev. pubd
as *Z. Hist. Ver. Schwaben &
Neuburg*]

Z. Hist. Ver. Schwaben & Neuburg
Zeitschrift des Historischen
Vereins für Schwaben und
Neuburg [cont. as *Z. Hist. Ver.
Schwaben*]

Z. Hist. Ver. Steiermark
Zeitschrift des Historischen
Vereines für Steiermark

Z. Hist. Waf.- & Kostknd.
Zeitschrift für historische Waffen-
und Kostümkunde [cont. as *Waf.-
& Kostknd.*]

Z. Hohenzoll. Gesch.
Zeitschrift für hohenzollerische
Geschichte

Zhongguo Wenwu

Zhongguo Yingzai Xueshe Huikan
[Bulletin of the Society for Research
into Chinese Architecture]

Zhonghe Yuekan [Moderation
monthly]

*Zhongyang Yyanjiuyuan Lishi Yuyan
Yanjiusuo Jikan* [Collection papers of
the History and Language Research
Institute at the Central Academy]

Zhurnal Isk.
Zhurnal iskusstva [Journal of art]

Zien 5

Zimbabwe Insight [prev. pubd as
Insight]

Zinbun
Zinbun: Memoirs of the Research
Institute for Humanistic Studies,
Kyoto University

Zion

Život [Life]

Život Umjetnosti [Art life]

Z. Kirchgesch.
Zeitschrift für Kirchengeschichte

Z. Kst
Zeitschrift für Kunst

Z. Kstgesch.
Zeitschrift für Kunstgeschichte
[merger of *Z. Bild. Kst* with
Repert. Kstwiss. & with *Jb.
Kstwiss.*]

Z. Ksttech. & Konserv.
Zeitschrift für Kunsttechnologie
und Konservierung

Z. Kstwiss.
Zeitschrift für Kunstwissenschaft
[prev. pubd as & cont. as *Z. Dt.
Ver. Kstwiss.*]

Zlatá Praha [Golden Prague]

Zlatorog

Zleby

Z Mag.
Z Magazine

Z. Mus. Hildesheim
Zeitschrift des Museums zu
Hildesheim

Znak

Z. Neutestamentl. Wiss.
Zeitschrift für die
neutestamentliche Wissenschaft

Z. Numi.
Zeitschrift für Numismatik

Zodchestvo

Zodchiy

Zodchiye Moskvy

Zodiac
Zodiac: A Review of
Contemporary Architecture

Zodiaque

Zograf

Zolotoye Runo [Golden fleece]

Z. Österreich. Ingen.-&-Architekten-Ver.
Zeitschrift des Österreichischen Ingenieur-und-Architekten-Vereines

Z. Ostforsch.
Zeitschrift für Ostforschung: Länder und Völker im östlichen Mitteleuropa

Z. Papyrologie & Epig.
Zeitschrift für Papyrologie und Epigraphik

Z. Prakt. Baukst
Zeitschrift für praktische Baukunst

Zprávy Krajského Vlastivědného Muz. Olomouc.
Zprávy krajského vlastivědného Muzea v Olomouci [Bulletin of the Regional Museum in Olomouc]

Zprávy Památkové Péče [Monument preservation news; cont. as *Památkove Péče*]

Z. Relig. & Geistesgesch.
Zeitschrift für Religion und Geistesgeschichte

Z. Rhein. Ver. Dkmlpf. & Heimatschutz
Zeitschrift des rheinischen Vereins für Denkmalpflege und Heimatschutz

Z. Schweiz. Altertknd.
Zeitschrift für schweizerische Altertumskunde

Z. Schweiz. Archäol. & Kstgesch.
Zeitschrift für schweizerische Archäologie und Kunstgeschichte

Z. Siebenbürg. Landesknd.
Zeitschrift für siebenbürgische Landeskunde [prev. pubd as *Korrbl. Arbeitkreises Siebenbürg. Landesknd.*; *Siebenbürg. Vjschr.*; *Korrbl. Ver. Siebenbürg. Landesknd.*]

Z. Sozforsch.
Zeitschrift für Sozialforschung

Ztg Elegante Welt
Zeitung für die elegante Welt

Ztg 7 Produzentengal.
Zeitungen der 7 Produzentengalerie

Zuger Neujbl.
Zuger Neujahrsblatt

Zürcher

Zürch. Taschenb.
Zürcher Taschenbuch

Zürich. Illus.
Züricher Illustrierten

Zvaigzne

Z. Ver. Gesch. Berlins
Zeitschrift des Vereins für die Geschichte Berlins [prev. pubd as & cont. as *Mitt. Ver. Gesch. Berlins*]

Z. Ver. Gesch. Bodensees
Zeitschrift des Vereins für die Geschichte Bodensees

Z. Ver. Gesch. Mährens & Schlesiens
Zeitschrift des Vereins für die Geschichte Mährens und Schlesiens [cont. as *Z. Gesch. Mährens & Schlesiens*; *Z. Gesch. & Landesknd. Mährens & Schlesiens*]

Z. Ver. Hamburg. Gesch.
Zeitschrift des Vereins für hamburgische Geschichte

Z. Ver. Hess. Gesch. & Landesknd.
Zeitschrift des Vereins für hessische Geschichte und Landeskunde

Z. Ver. Lübeck. Gesch. & Altertknd.
Zeitschrift des Vereins für lübeckische Geschichte und Altertumskunde

Zvezda

Z. Vlksknd.
Zeitschrift für Volkskunde

Zvon [The bell]

Z. Westfalen
Zeitschrift Westfalen

Z. Westpreuss. Geschver.
Zeitschrift des westpreussischen Geschichtsvereins

Zwiebelturm
Zwiebelturm: Monatsschrift für das bayerische Volk und seine Freunde

Z. Württemberg. Landesgesch.
Zeitschrift für württembergische Landesgeschichte

Życie Sztuki [Art life]

Zygos

Appendix C

LISTS OF STANDARD REFERENCE BOOKS AND SERIES

LIST A

This list contains, in alphabetical order, the abbreviations used in bibliographies for alphabetically arranged dictionaries and encyclopedias. Some dictionaries and general works, especially dictionaries of national biography, are reduced to the initial letters of the italicized title (e.g. *DNB*) and others to the author/editor's name (e.g. Colvin) or an abbreviated form of the title (e.g. *Contemp. Artists*). Abbreviations from List A are cited at the beginning of bibliographies or bibliographical subsections, in alphabetical order, separated by semi-colons; the title of the article in such reference books is cited only if the spelling or form of the name differs from that used in this dictionary or if the reader is being referred to a different subject.

ADB
: *Allgemeine deutsche Biographie*, 56 vols (Leipzig, 1875–1912)

Archibald
: E. H. H. Archibald: *Dictionary of Sea Painters* (Woodbridge, 1980)

AUDB
: *Australian Dictionary of Biography* (Melbourne, 1966–)

Bauchal
: C. Bauchal: *Nouveau dictionnaire biographique et critique des architectes français* (Paris, 1887)

Bellier de La Chavignerie-Auvray
: E. Bellier de La Chavignerie and L. Auvray: *Dictionnaire général des artistes de l'Ecole française depuis l'origine des arts du dessin jusqu'à nos jours*, 2 vols (Paris, 1882–5), suppl. (Paris, 1887)

Bénézit
: E. Bénézit, ed.: *Dictionnaire critique et documentaire des peintres, sculpteurs, dessinateurs et graveurs*, 10 vols (Paris, 1913–22, rev. 3/1976)

Berman
: E. Berman: *Art and Artists of South Africa* (Cape Town, 1970, rev. Halfway House, 1993)

BLKO
: C. von Wurzbach: *Biographisches Lexicon des Kaiserthums Oesterreich*, 60 vols (Vienna, 1856–90)

BNB
: *Biographie nationale [belge]* (Brussels, 1866–)

Bolaffi
: *Dizionario enciclopedia dei pittori e degli incisori italiani, dall'XI al XX secolo*, 11 vols (Turin, 1972–6) [pubd by Bolaffi]

Bryan
: M. A. Bryan: *Bryan's Dictionary of Painters and Engravers*, 2 vols (London, 1816); rev. and enlarged under the supervision of G. Williamson, 5 vols (London, 1903–5)

BWN
: J. Charité, ed.: *Biografisch woordenboek van Nederland* (The Hague, 1979)

Ceán Bermúdez
: J. A. Ceán Bermúdez: *Diccionario histórico de los más ilustres profesores de las bellas artes en España*, 6 vols (Madrid, 1800/*R* 1965)

Colnaghi
: D. E. Colnaghi: *A Dictionary of Florentine Painters from the 13th to the 17th Centuries* (London, 1928)

Colvin
: H. M. Colvin: *A Biographical Dictionary of British Architects, 1600–1840* (London, 1954, rev. 2/1978)

Comanducci
: A. M. Comanducci: *Dizionario illustrato dei pittori, scultori, disegnatori e incisori italiani moderni e contemporanei*, 5 vols (Milan, 1934, rev. 3/1962)

Contemp. Architects
: M. Emanuel, ed.: *Contemporary Architects* (London, 1980, rev. 1986)

Contemp. Artists
: M. Emanuel and others, eds: *Contemporary Artists* (London, 1977, rev. 1983)

Contemp. Designers
: A. Lee Morgan, ed.: *Contemporary Designers* (London, 1984, rev. 2/1985)

Contemp. Phots
: G. Walsh, C. Naylor and M. Held, eds: *Contemporary Photographers* (New York, 1982, rev. 1988)

DAB
: *Dictionary of American Biography* (New York, 1928–)

DBF
: *Dictionnaire de biographie française* (Paris, 1933–)

DBI
: *Dizionario biografico degli italiani* (Rome, 1960–)

DBL
: *Dansk biografisk leksikon* (Copenhagen, 1887–1905, rev. 2/1933–)

DBP
: *Dicionário bibliográfico português* (Lisbon, 1858–)

DCB
: *Dictionary of Canadian Biography* (Toronto, 1966–)

Dict. Eglises France
: J. Brosse, ed.: *Dictionnaire des églises de France*, 5 vols (Paris, 1966–71)

Dict. Middle Ages
: J. R. Strayer, ed.: *Dictionary of the Middle Ages*, 13 vols (New York, 1982–9)

Diderot-d'Alembert
: D. Diderot and J. le Rond d'Alembert: *Encyclopédie, ou dictionnaire raisonné des sciences, des arts et des métiers, par une société de gens de lettres: Mis en ordre et publié par M. Diderot. . .& quant à la partie mathématique, par M. d'Alembert*, 17 vols and suppls (Paris, 1751–65)

DMB
: L. C. Goodrich and Chaoying Fang, eds: *Dictionary of Ming Biography, 1368–1644*, 2 vols (New York and London, 1976)

DNB
: *Dictionary of National Biography*, 63 vols and suppls (London, 1885–)

DNZB
: *Dictionary of New Zealand Biography* (Wellington, 1990–)

DSAB
: W. J. de Kock, D. W. Kruger and C. J. Beyers, eds: *Dictionary of South African Biography*, 5 vols (Capetown and Johannesburg, 1968–87)

Edouard-Joseph
: R. Edouard-Joseph: *Dictionnaire biographique des artistes contemporains*, 3 vols (Paris, 1930–34)

Enc. A. Ant.
: *Enciclopedia dell'arte antica, classica e orientale*, 7 vols and suppls (Rome, 1958–73)

Enc. Catt.
: *Enciclopedia cattolica*, 12 vols (Florence, 1948–54)

Enc. Ind. Temple Archit.
Encyclopaedia of Indian Temple Architecture, 6 vols (New Delhi, Philadelphia and Princeton, 1983–)

Enc. Iran.
E. Yar Shater, ed.: *Encyclopedia Iranica* (London, 1986)

Enc. Islam/1
Encyclopaedia of Islam, 8 vols and suppl. (Leiden, 1913–36/*R* 1987)

Enc. Islam/2
Encyclopaedia of Islam (Leiden, 1954–)

Enc. It.
Enciclopedia italiana di scienze, lettere ed arti, 39 vols and suppls (Milan, 1929–81)

Enc. Jud.
Encyclopedia Judaica, 16 vols (Jerusalem, 1972)

Enc. Spettacolo
Enciclopedia dello spettacolo, 9 vols and suppl. (Rome, 1954–66)

Engen
R. K. Engen: *Dictionary of Victorian Engravers, Print Publishers and their Works* (Cambridge, 1979)

EWA
Enciclopedia universale dell'arte, 15 vols (Rome, 1958–67); Eng. trans. as *Encyclopedia of World Art* (New York, 1959–68)

FBH
T. Carpelan, ed.: *Finsk biografisk handbok*, 2 vols (Helsinki, 1903)

Forrer
L. Forrer: *Biographical Dictionary of Medallists*, 8 vols (London, 1902–30)

Foskett
D. Foskett: *A Dictionary of British Miniature Painters*, 2 vols (London, 1972)

Franke
H. Franke, ed.: *Sung Biographies*, 4 vols (Wiesbaden, 1976)

Füssli
J. R. Füssli: *Allgemeines Künstlerlexicon, oder kurze Nachricht von dem Leben und den Werken der Mahler, Bildhauer, Baumeister, Kupfersticher, Kunstgiesser, Stahlschneider etc.*, 3 vols (Zurich, 1779–1824)

Gestoso y Pérez
J. Gestoso y Pérez: *Ensayo de un diccionario de los artífices que florecieron en Sevilla desde el siglo XIII al XVIII inclusive*, 3 vols (Seville, 1899–1909)

Goldstein
F. Goldstein: *Monogramm–Lexikon* (Berlin, 1964)

Grove Amer. Music
S. Sadie and H. W. Hitchcock, eds: *The New Grove Dictionary of American Music*, 4 vols (London, 1986)

Grove Instr.
S. Sadie, ed.: *The New Grove Dictionary of Musical Instruments*, 3 vols (London, 1984)

Grove 6
S. Sadie, ed.: *The New Grove Dictionary of Music and Musicians*, 20 vols (London, rev. 6/1980)

Gunnis
R. Gunnis: *Dictionary of British Sculptors, 1660–1851* (London, 1951, rev. 2/1968)

Harvey
J. Harvey: *English Mediaeval Architects: A Biographical Dictionary down to 1550* (London, 1954, rev. and enlarged 2/1984)

Hoefer
F. Hoefer, ed.: *Nouvelle biographie générale depuis les temps plus reculés jusqu'à nos jours, avec les renseignements bibliographiques et l'indication des sources à consulter*, 46 vols (Paris, 1853–66/*R* Copenhagen, 1963–9)

Hollstein: *Dut. & Flem.*
F. W. H. Hollstein: *Dutch and Flemish Etchings, Engravings and Woodcuts, c. 1450–1700* (Amsterdam, 1949–)

Hollstein: *Ger.*
F. W. H. Hollstein: *German Engravings, Etchings and Woodcuts, c. 1400–1700* (Amsterdam, 1954–)

Hummel
A. W. Hummel, ed.: *Eminent Chinese of the Ch'ing Period, 1644–1912* (Washington, DC, 1943/*R* Taipei, 1975)

Int. Dict. A. & Artists
J. Vinson, ed.: *International Dictionary of Art and Artists*, 2 vols (Chicago and London, 1990) [1st vol. contains artists arranged in alphabetical order; 2nd vol. includes works of art arranged in roughly chronological order]

Jal
A. Jal: *Dictionnaire critique de biographie et d'histoire, errata et supplément pour tous les dictionnaires historiques, d'après des documents authentiques inédits* (Paris, 1867, rev. 1872)

Kindler
Kindlers Malerei Lexikon, 16 vols (Zurich, 1964–71) [pubd by Kindler]

Kodansha Enc. Japan
Kodansha Encyclopedia of Japan, 9 vols (Tokyo and New York, 1983), suppl. (Tokyo and New York, 1986)

LÄ
W. Helck, E. Otto and W. Westendorff, eds: *Lexikon der Ägyptologie* (Wiesbaden, 1975–)

Lake–Maillard
C. Lake and R. Maillard: *A Dictionary of Modern Painting* (London, 1964)

Lami
S. Lami: *Dictionnaire des sculpteurs de l'Ecole française*, 8 vols (Paris, 1898–1921/*R* Nendeln, 1970)

LCI
Lexikon der christlichen Ikonographie (Rome, 1968–)

LK
Lexikon der Kunst: Architektur, bildende Kunst, angewandte Kunst, Industrieformgestaltung, Kunsttheorie (Leipzig, 1968–)

LM
Lexikon des Mittelalters (Munich, 1980–)

Luciani
L. Luciani and F. Luciani: *Dizionario dei pittori italiani dell'1800* (Florence, 1974)

Machado
C. V. Machado: *Coleção de memórias relativas as vidas dos pintores, escultores, arquitetos e gravadores portugueses, e dos estrangeiros, que estiverão em Portugal* (Lisbon, 1823/*R* Coimbra, 1922)

Macmillan Enc. Archit.
A. K. Placzek, ed.: *Macmillan Encyclopedia of Architects*, 4 vols (New York, 1982)

Mariette
P.-J. Mariette: 'Abecedario de P.-J. Mariette et autres notes inédites de cet amateur sur les arts et les artistes', *Archv A. Fr.*, ii (1851–3), iv (1853–4), vi (1854–6), viii (1857–8), x (1858–9), xii (1859–60)

Meissner
G. Meissner, ed.: *Allgemeines Künstler-Lexikon: Die bildenden Künstler aller Zeiten und Völker*, 3 vols (Leipzig, 1983–90/*R* Munich, 1992) [see also Thieme–Becker below]

Michaud
L.-G. Michaud, ed.: *Biographie universelle ancienne et moderne*, 84 vols (Paris, 1811–57)

NBL
Norsk biografisk leksikon (Oslo, 1921–)

NBW
Nationaal biografisch woordenboek, 14 vols (Brussels, 1964–92)

NDB
Neue deutsche Biographie (Berlin, 1953–)

NKL
Norsk kunstnerleksikon, 4 vols (Oslo, 1982)

NNBW
Nieuw Nederlandsch biografisch woordenboek, 10 vols (Leiden, 1911–37)

NÖB
Neue österreichische Biographie (Vienna, 1923–)

ÖBL
Österreichisches biographisches Lexikon (Graz, Cologne and Vienna, 1957–)

O'Donoghue
F. O'Donoghue and H. M. Hake: *Catalogue of Engraved British Portraits Preserved in the Department of Prints and Drawings in the British Museum*, 6 vols (London, 1908–25)

ÖKL
R. Schmidt, ed.: *Österreichisches Künstlerlexikon von den Anfängen bis zur Gegenwart* (Vienna, 1974–)

Oxford Class. Dict.
M. Cary and others: *The Oxford Classical Dictionary* (Oxford, 1948); rev., N. G. L. Hammond and H. H. Scullard, eds (Oxford, 2/1970)

de Pamplona
F. de Pamplona: *Dicionário de pintores e escultores portugueses ou que trabalharam em Portugal*, 4 vols (Lisbon, 1954–9)

Papworth
W. Papworth, ed.: *Dictionary of Architecture*, 8 vols (London, 1852–92)

Pauly–Wissowa
G. Wissowa, W. Kroll and K. Mittelhaus, eds: *Paulys Realencyclopädie der klassischen Altertumswissenschaft*, 10 vols and suppls (Stuttgart, 1894–1978)

Pontual
R. Pontual: *Dicionário das artes plásticas no Brasil* (Rio de Janeiro, 1969)

Portalis–Beraldi
R. Portalis and H. Beraldi: *Les Graveurs du dix-huitième siècle*, 3 vols (Paris, 1880–82)

Portoghesi
P. Portoghesi, ed.: *Dizionario enciclopedico di architettura e urbanistica*, 6 vols (Rome, 1968–9)

PSB
Polski słownik biograficzny, 34 vols (Wrocław, 1935–)

RBK
M. Restle and K. Wessel, eds: *Reallexikon zur byzantinischen Kunst* (Stuttgart, 1966–)

RDK
O. Schmitt and others, eds: *Reallexikon zur deutschen Kunstgeschichte* (Stuttgart, Metzler and Munich, 1937–)

Reallex. Ant. & Christ.
Reallexikon für Antike und Christentum, 14 vols (Stuttgart, 1950–88)

Redgrave
S. Redgrave: *Dictionary of Artists of the English School* (London, 1874, rev. 2/1978/R 1970)

RLA
Reallexikon der Assyriologie und vorderasiatischen Archäologie (Berlin, 1928–)

Roberts
L. Roberts: *A Dictionary of Japanese Artists* (New York, 1976)

SAP
Słownik artystów polskich i obcych w Polsce działjących [Dictionary of Polish and foreign artists working in Poland] (Wrocław, 1971)

SBL
Svenska biografiskt leksikon (Stockholm, 1918–)

Scheen
P. A. Scheen: *Lexicon Nederlandse beeldende kunstenaars, 1750–1950* (The Hague, 1981)

Seubert
A. F. Seubert: *Allgemeines Künstlerlexicon oder Leben und Werke der berühmtesten bildenden Künstler*, 3 vols (Stuttgart, 1878)

Seuphor
M. Seuphor: *Dictionnaire de la peinture abstraite* (Paris, 1958); Eng. trans. as *A Dictionary of Modern Abstract Painting* (London, 1958)

SKL
C. Brun: *Schweizerisches Künstler-Lexikon/ Dictionnaire des artistes suisses*, 4 vols (Frauenfeld, 1905–17/R Nendeln, 1967)

Souchal
F. Souchal, ed.: *French Sculptors of the 17th and 18th Centuries: The Reign of Louis XIV* (Oxford, 1977–)

Stillwell
R. Stillwell, ed.: *The Princeton Encyclopedia of Classical Sites* (Princeton, 1976)

Strickland
W. Strickland: *A Dictionary of Irish Artists*, 2 vols (Dublin, 1913/R 1968)

SVKL
G. Lilja, ed.: *Svenska konstnärslexikon*, 5 vols (Malmö, 1952–67)

Thieme–Becker
U. Thieme and F. Becker, eds: *Allgemeines Lexikon der bildenden Künstler von der Antike bis zur Gegenwart*, 37 vols (Leipzig, 1907–50) [see also Meissner above]

Viterbo
F. M. de Sousa Viterbo: *Dicionário histórico e documental dos arquitetos, engenheiros e construtores portuguezes ou a serviço de Portugal*, 3 vols (Lisbon, 1899–1922)

Vollmer
H. Vollmer, ed.: *Allgemeines Lexikon der bildenden Künstler des XX. Jahrhunderts*, 6 vols (Leipzig, 1953–62)

Wasmuth
Wasmuths Lexikon der Baukunst, 5 vols (Berlin, 1929–37)

Waterhouse: *16th & 17th C.*
E. Waterhouse: *The Dictionary of 16th and 17th Century British Painters* (Woodbridge, 1988)

Waterhouse: *18th C.*
E. Waterhouse: *The Dictionary of British 18th Century Painters* (Woodbridge, 1981)

Withey
H. F. Withey and E. R. Withey: *Biographical Dictionary of American Architects* (Los Angeles, 1956/R 1970)

Wood
C. Wood: *Dictionary of Victorian Painters* (Woodbridge, 1971, rev. 2/1978)

Wurzbach
A. von Wurzbach: *Niederländisches Künstler-Lexikon auf Grund archivalischen Forschungen bearbeitet*, 3 vols (Vienna and Leipzig, 1906–11/R Amsterdam, 1974)

LIST B

This list contains, in alphabetical order by authors' names, the abbreviated forms and full publishing details of the preferred editions of books frequently cited in this dictionary. Such citations take their chronological position within the bibliography and usually include volume and page numbers.

A. Armand: *Les Médailleurs italiens* (2/1883–7)
Les Médailleurs italiens des quinzième et seizième siècles (Paris, 1879), rev. and enlarged, 3 vols (Paris, 1883–7)

G. Baglione: *Vite* (1642); ed. V. Mariani (1935)
Le vite de' pittori, scultori, architetti, ed intagliatori, dal pontificato di Gregorio XIII del 1572, fino a' tempi di Papa Urbano VIII nel 1642 (Rome, 1642); facs. edn with marginal notes by Bellori, ed. V. Mariani (Rome, 1935)

F. Baldinucci: *Notizie* (1681–1728); ed. F. Ranalli (1845–7)
Notizie de' professori del disegno da Cimabue in qua (Florence, 1681–1728); ed. F. Ranalli, 5 vols (Florence, 1845–7)

F. S. Baldinucci: *Vite* (1725–30); ed. A. Matteoli (1975)
Vite di artisti dei secoli XVII–XVIII (1725–30; Florence, Bib. N. Cent., Cod. Palatino 565); ed. A. Matteoli (Rome, 1975)

A. von Bartsch: *Le Peintre–graveur* (1803–21)
Le Peintre–graveur, 21 vols (Vienna, 1803–21/R New York, 1970)

J. D. Beazley: *Black-figure* (1956)
Attic Black-figure Vase-painters (Oxford, 1956/R New York, 1978)

J. D. Beazley: *Development of Black-figure* (1951, 3/1986)
The Development of Attic Black-figure (Berkeley, 1951, rev. 3/1986)

J. D. Beazley: *Paralipomena* (1971)
Paralipomena: Additions to Attic Black-figure and to Attic Red-figure Vase-painters (Oxford, 1971)

J. D. Beazley: *Red-figure* (1942, 2/1963)
Attic Red-figure Vase-painters, 3 vols (Oxford, 1942, rev. 2/1963)

G. P. Bellori: *Vite* (1672); ed. E. Borea (1976)
Le vite de' pittori, scultori ed architetti moderni (Rome, 1672); ed. E. Borea (Turin, 1976)

B. Berenson: *Central and North Italian Schools* (1968)
Italian Pictures of the Renaissance: Central and North Italian Schools, 3 vols (London, 1968)

B. Berenson: *Florentine School* (1963)
Italian Pictures of the Renaissance: Florentine School, 2 vols (London, 1963)

B. Berenson: *Venetian School* (1957)
Italian Pictures of the Renaissance: Venetian School, 2 vols (London, 1957)

C. de Bie: *Het gulden cabinet* (1661)
Het gulden cabinet van de edele vry schilderconst (Antwerp, 1661/R Soest, 1971)

C. Blanc: *Histoire* (1861–76)
Histoire des peintres de toutes les écoles, 14 vols (Paris, 1861–76)

M. Boskovits: *Corpus* (1984)
A Critical and Historical Corpus of Florentine Painting. The Fourteenth Century: The Painters of the Miniaturist Tendency (Florence, 1984) [also known as III/ix of R. Offner and K. Steinweg: *Corpus*]

C. Cennini: *Il libro dell'arte* (MS.; c. 1390);
trans. and notes by D.V. Thompson jr (1933)
Il libro dell'arte (MS.; c. 1390); Eng. trans. and notes by D.V. Thompson jr as *The Craftsman's Handbook* (New Haven, 1933/R New York, 1954 and 1960)

Corp. Inscr. Lat.
Corpus inscriptionem Latinarum, Academia Literarum Regiae Borussicae (Berlin, 1862–)

A.-J. Dézallier d'Argenville: *Abrégé de la vie des plus fameux peintres* (1745–52, 2/1762)
> *Abrégé de la vie des plus fameux peintres, avec leurs portraits gravés en taille-douce, les indications de leurs principaux ouvrages, quelques réflexions sur leurs caractères et la manière de connoître des desseins et les tableaux des grands maîtres*, 3 vols (Paris, 1745–52), rev. 4 vols (Paris, 1762/*R* Geneva, 1972)

A.-N. Dézallier d'Argenville: *Vies des fameux architectes et sculpteurs* (1788)
> *Vies des fameux architectes et sculpteurs depuis la renaissance des arts, avec la description de leurs ouvrages*, 2 vols (Paris, 1788)

B. de Dominici: *Vite* (1742–5)
> *Vite de' pittori, scultori ed architetti napoletani* (Naples,1742–5/*R* Bologna, 1979)

L. Dussieux and others, eds: *Mémoires inédits . . . des membres de l'Académie royale* (1854)
> *Mémoires inédits sur la vie et les ouvrages des membres de l'Académie royale de peinture et de sculpture, publiés d'après les manuscrits conservés à l'Ecole impériale des beaux-arts, par MM. L. Dussieux, E. Soulié, Ph. de Chennevières, Paul Mantz, A. de Montaiglon, sous les auspices de M. le Ministre de l'Intérieur*, 2 vols (Paris, 1854)

G. Fanelli: *Architettura moderna* (1968)
> *Architettura moderna in Olanda, 1900–1940* (Florence, 1968); Dut. trans. as *Moderne architectuur in Nederland* (The Hague, 1978/*R* 1981) [both It. & Dut. edns incl. abridged Eng. text]

A. Félibien: *Entretiens* (1666–8); rev. (1725)
> *Entretiens sur les vies et les ouvrages des plus excellens peintres anciens et modernes*, 2 vols (Paris, 1666–8), rev. and enlarged, 6 vols (Trévoux, 1725/*R* London, 1967)

J. W. Gaye: *Carteggio* (1839–40)
> *Carteggio inedito d'artisti dei secoli XIV, XV, XVI*, 3 vols (Florence, 1839–40/*R* 1961)

L. Ghiberti: *Commentarii* (1912)
> *I Commentarii*, ed. J. von Schlosser, 2 vols (Berlin, 1912)

J. van Gool: *De nieuwe schouburg* (1750–51)
> *De nieuwe schouburg der Nederlandsche kunstschilders en schilderessen*, 2 vols (The Hague, 1750–51/*R* Soest, 1971)

L. Guicciardini: *Descritione di . . . tutti i Paesi Bassi* (1567)
> *Descrittione di Lodovico Guicciardini patritio fiorentino di tutti i Paesi Bassi altrimenti detti Germania inferiore* (Antwerp, 1567)

J.-J. Guiffrey: *Collections* (1869–73)
> *Collections des livrets des anciennes expositions depuis 1673 jusqu'en 1800*, 42 vols (Paris, 1869–73)

J. Guiffrey, ed.: *Comptes* (1881–1901)
> *Comptes des bâtiments du roi sous le règne de Louis XIV*, 5 vols (Paris, 1881–1901)

L. Hautecoeur: *Architecture classique* (1943–57)
> *Histoire de l'architecture classique en France*, 7 vols (Paris, 1943–57)

G. F. Hill: *Corpus* (1930)
> *A Corpus of Italian Medals of the Renaissance before Cellini*, 2 vols (London, 1930)

C. Hofstede de Groot: *Holländischen Maler* (1907–28)
> *Beschreibendes und kritisches Verzeichnis der Werke der hervorragendsten holländischen Maler des XVII. Jahrhunderts*, 10 vols (Esslingen, 1907–28)

A. Houbraken: *De groote schouburgh* (1718–21)
> *De groote schouburgh der Nederlandsche konstschilders en schilderessen*, 3 vols (Amsterdam, 1718–21/*R* Maastricht, 1943–53/*R* Amsterdam, 1976)

Inscr. Gr./1
> *Inscriptiones Graecae*, Academia Literarum Regiae Borussicae (Berlin, 1873–)

Inscr. Gr./2
> *Inscriptiones Graecae: Editio minor*, Academia Literarum Regiae Borussicae (Berlin, 1924–)

E. Llaguno y Amirola: *Noticias* (1829)
> *Noticias de los arquitectos y arquitectura de España desde su restauración, ilustradas y acrecentadas con notas, adiciones y documentos, por D. Juan Agustín Ceán Bermúdez*, 5 vols (Madrid, 1829)

Ludwig, Freiherr von Pastor: *Geschichte der Päpste* (1886–9)
> *Geschichte der Päpste seit dem Ausgang des Mittelalters*, 36 vols (Freiburg, 1886–9); Eng. trans. as *The History of the Popes from the Close of the Middle Ages*, 40 vols (London, 1891–1953)

F. Lugt: *Marques* (1921)
> *Les Marques de collections de dessins et d'estampes* (Amsterdam, 1921)

F. Lugt: *Marques, suppl.* (1956)
> *Les Marques de collections de dessins et d'estampes*, suppl. (The Hague, 1956)

F. Lugt: *Ventes* (1938–64)
> *Répertoire des catalogues de ventes publiques*, 3 vols (The Hague, 1938–64)

C. C. Malvasia: *Felsina pittrice* (1678); ed. G. Zanotti (1841)
> *Felsina pittrice: Vite de' pittori bolognesi*, 2 vols (Bologna, 1678); ed. G. Zanotti, 2 vols (Bologna, 1841)

K. van Mander: *Schilder-boeck* ([1603]–1604)
> *Het schilder-boeck, waer in voor eerst de leerlustighe iueght den grondt der edel vry schilderconst in verscheyden deelen wort voorghedraghen. Daer nae in dry deelen t'leuen der vermaede doorluchtighe schilders des ouden, en nieuwen tyds*, 2 vols (Haarlem, [1603]–1604/*R* Utrecht, 1969)

R. van Marle: *Italian Schools* (1923–38)
> *The Development of the Italian Schools of Painting*, 19 vols (The Hague, 1923–38/*R* New York, 1970)

R. Mayer: *Artist's Handbook* (1940, 4/1982)
> *The Artist's Handbook of Materials and Techniques* (New York, 1940, rev. London, 4/1982/*R* 1982)

G. K. Nagler: *Monogrammisten* (1858–1920)
> *Die Monogrammisten und diejenigen bekannten und unbekannten Künstler aller Schulen*, 6 vols (Munich, 1858–1920/*R* 1966)

R. Offner and K. Steinweg: *Corpus* (1930–79); rev. M. Boskovits (1986–)
> *A Critical and Historical Corpus of Florentine Painting*, 14 vols (New York, 1930–79); rev. M. Boskovits, III/i (Florence, 1986), III/ii pts 1–2 (Florence, 1987), III/iii (Florence, 1989), III/iv (Florence, 1991)

R. Offner and K. Steinweg: *Corpus*, suppl.; ed. H. B. J. Maginnis (1981)
> *A Critical and Historical Corpus of Florentine Painting by Richard Offner. A Legacy of Attributions: The Fourteenth Century, Supplement*, ed. by H. B. J. Maginnis (New York, 1981)

P. A. Orlandini: *Abecedario* (Bologna, 1704/*R* Geneva, 1973)
> *Abecedario pittorico nel quale compendiosamente sono descritti le patrie, i maestri, ed i tempi . . . diviso in tre parti. Il tutto disposto in alfabeto per maggior facilità de' dilettanti* (Bologna and Pisarri, 1704/*R* 1973)

W. Paatz and E. Paatz: *Kirchen* (1940–54)
> *Die Kirchen von Florenz*, 6 vols (Frankfurt, 1940–54)

F. Pacheco: *Arte* (1649); ed. F. Sánchez Cantón (1956)
> *El arte de la pintura* (Seville, 1649, rev. Madrid, 1866); ed. F. Sánchez Cantón, 2 vols (1956)

E. Páez Rios: *Repertorio* (1981–3)
> *Repertorio de grabados españoles en la Biblioteca Nacional*, 4 vols (Madrid, 1981–3)

A. A. Palomino de Castro y Velasco: *Museo pictórico* (1715–24)
> *El museo pictórico, y escala óptica*, 3 vols (Madrid, 1715–24/*R* 1947)

L. Pascoli: *Vite* (1730–36)
> *Vite de' pittori, scultori ed architetti moderni*, 2 vols (Rome, 1730–36/*R* 1933/*R* Amsterdam, 1965)

G. B. Passeri: *Vite* (1679); ed. J. Hess (1934)
> *Vite de' pittori, scultori ed architetti che hanno lavorato in Roma, morti dal 1641 fino al 1673* (MS., 1679, Rome, 1722); ed. J. Hess (Leipzig, 1934)

PG

J. P. Migne, ed.: *Patrologia cursus completus . . . series Graeca*, 162 vols (Paris, 1857–1912)

N. Pio: *Vite* (1724); ed. C. Enggass and R. Enggass (1977)
> *Le vite di pittori, scultori et architetti* (1724; MS., Rome, Vatican, Bib. Apostolica, Cod. Capponiana 257); ed. C. Enggass and R. Enggass (Rome, 1977)

PL

J. P. Migne, ed.: *Patrologiae cursus completus patres ecclesiae Latine* (Paris, 1844–64)

A. Ponz: *Viaje* (1772–94); ed. C. M. de Rivero (1947)
> *Viaje de España, en que se da noticias de las cosas apreciables y diquas de saberse que hay en ella*, 18 vols (Madrid, 1772–94); ed. C. M. de Rivero (Madrid, 1947)

A. U. Pope and P. Ackerman, eds: *Survey of Persian Art* (2/1964–7)
> *A Survey of Persian Art, from Prehistoric Times to the Present*, 6 vols (London, 1938–9), rev. 16 vols (London, 2/1964–7/*R* Tokyo, 1977)

B. Porter and R. L. B. Moss, eds: *Topographical Bibliography* (1927–)
> *Topographical Bibliography of Ancient Egyptian Hieroglyphic Texts, Reliefs and Paintings* (Oxford, 1927–)

C. Ridolfi: *Meraviglie* (1648); ed. D. von Hadeln (1914–24)
> *Le meraviglie dell'arte ovvero le vite degl'illustri pittori veneti e dello stato* (Venice, 1648); new critical edn with notes by D. von Hadeln (Berlin, 1914–24/*R* 1965)

A.-P.-F. Robert-Dumesnil: *Le Peintre–graveur français* (1835–71)
> *Le Peintre–graveur français, ou catalogue raisonné des estampes gravées par les peintres et les dessinateurs de l'école française*, 11 vols (Paris, 1835–71/*R* 1967)

J. von Sandrart: *Teutsche Academie* (1675–9); ed. A. R. Peltzer (1925)
> *L'Accademia tedesca della architettura, scultura & pittura; oder, Teutsche Academie der edlen Bau-, Bild- und Mahlerey-Künste von 1675: Leben und berühmte Mahler, Bildhauer und Baumeister*, 2 vols (Frankfurt, 1675–9); rev. as 1 vol., ed. A. R. Peltzer (Munich, 1925)

K. Shimonaka, ed.: *Shodō zenshū* [Complete collection of calligraphy]
> *Shodō zenshū* [Complete collection of calligraphy], 26 vols, 2 suppls (Tokyo, 2/1954–68); 1st edn ed. Y. Shimonaka (Tokyo, 1930–32)

R. Soprani: *Vite* (1674); enlarged, ed. C. G. Ratti (1768–9)
> *Le vite de' pittori, scoltori et architetti genovesi* (Genoa, 1674/*R* 1971); rev., enlarged and ed. C. G. Ratti as *Vite de' pittori, scultori ed architetti genovesi*, 2 vols (Genoa, 1768–9/*R* 1965)

T. Tanikawa, ed.: *Nihon tōji zenshū* [Complete collection of Japanese ceramics]
> *Nihon tōji zenshū* [Complete collection of Japanese ceramics], 30 vols (Tokyo, 1975–7)

Theophilus: *De diversis artibus* (12 C.); J. G. Hawthorne & C. S. Smith (1963)
> *De diversis artibus* (MS.; 12 C.); ed. and trans. C.R. Dodwell (London, Edinburgh and Paris, 1961); ed. and trans. J. G. Hawthorne and C. S. Smith (Chicago, 1963/*R* 1979)

Prince Toneri: *Nihon shoki* [Chronicle of Japan] (AD 720)
> *Nihon shoki* [Chronicle of Japan] (AD 720); Eng. trans. by W. G. Aston as *Trans. and Proc. Japan Soc., London*, suppl. (1896) [whole issue]

G. Vasari: *Vite* (1550, rev. 2/1568); ed. G. Milanesi (1878–85)
> *Le vite de' più eccellenti pittori, scultori ed architetti* (Florence, 1550, rev. 2/1568); ed. G. Milanesi, 9 vols (Florence, 1878–85)

A. Venturi: *Storia* (1901–40)
> *Storia dell'arte italiana*, 11 vols (Milan, 1901–40/*R* Nendeln, 1967)

Conde de la Viñaza: *Adiciones al diccionario* (1889–94)
> *Adiciones al diccionario histórico de los más ilustres profesores de las bellas artes de España de D. Juan Agustín Ceán Bermúdez*, 4 vols (Madrid, 1889–94)

H. Walpole: *Anecdotes of Painting in England* (1762–71); ed. R. N. Wornum (1849)
> *Anecdotes of Painting in England; with Some Account of the Principal Artists; and Incidental Notes on Other Arts*, 5 vols (Strawberry Hill, 1762–71); 6th edn, ed. R. N. Wornum, 3 vols (London, 1849/*R* 1888)

No Yasumaro: *Kojiki* [Record of ancient matters] (AD 712)
> *Kojiki* [Record of ancient matters] (AD 712); Eng. trans. by B. Hall Chamberlain, 2nd edn with notes by W. G. Aston (Kobe, 1932)

Series list

This list comprises the abbreviations used in this dictionary for publishers' series; they are arranged in alphabetical order by title. Series titles appear in bibliographical citations in roman, immediately before the publication details.

LIST C

A. Amer.
> Artes Americanae

A. Context
> Art in Context

Acta Archaeol. & A. Hist. Pertinentia
> Acta ad archaeologiam et artium historiam pertinentia

Acta Iran.
> Acta Iranica

Acta SS
> Acta Sanctorum

Acta U. Stockholm.: Stud. Hist. A.
> Acta Universitatis Stockholmiensis: Stockholm Studies in the History of Art

Acta U. Stockholm.: Stud. Lat. Stockholm.
> Acta Universitatis Stockholmiensis: Studia Latina Stockholmiensa

Afr. Stud. Cent. Working Pap.
> African Studies Center Working Papers

A. Grandes Civilis.
> L'Art des grandes civilisations

A. Helv.
> Ars Helvetica

A. Hisp.
> Ars Hispaniae

A. Hisp. [Seville]
> Arte hispalense

A. Mankind
> The Arts of Mankind/L'Univers des formes/Universum der Kunst

Amer. Mus. Nat. Hist.: Anthropol. Pap.
> American Museum of Natural History: Anthropological Papers

A. Mod. It.
> Arte moderna italiana

Amtl. Führer
> Amtliche Führer

Archaeol. Surv. India, Imp. Ser.
> Archaeological Survey of India, Imperial Series

Archaeol. Surv. India, New Imp. Ser.
> Archaeological Survey of India, New Imperial Series [first few volumes called Archaeological Survey of India, New Series]

Archaeol. Surv. India, New Ser.
> Archaeological Survey of India, New Series

Archaeol. Surv. W. India
> Archaeological Survey of Western India

Archit. Des. Profile
> Architectural Design Profile

Aristotelian Soc. Ser.
> Aristotelian Society Series

Ars Asiatica

Asiat. Forsch.
> Asiatische Forschungen

A. & Soc. Ser.
> Art and Society Series

Atti Accad. N. S Luca
> Atti della Accademia nazionale di San Luca

Ausstellbl. Mod. Abt.
> Ausstellungsblätter der modernen Abteilungen (Kunstmuseum Düsseldorf)

A. World
> Art of the World/L'Art dans le monde/Kunst der Welt

Baghdad. Forsch.
> Baghdader Forschungen

Bamberg. Stud. Kstgesch. & Dkmlpf.
> Bamberger Studien zur Kunstgeschichte und Denkmalpflege

Basl. Beitr. Ethnol.
> Basler Beiträge zur Ethnologie

Basl. Stud. Kstgesch.
> Basler Studien zur Kunstgeschichte

Bauhausbücher

Beitr. Kstgesch.
> Beiträge zur Kunstgeschichte

Beitr. Kstgesch. Schweiz
> Beiträge zur Kunstgeschichte der Schweiz

Beitr. Winckelmann-Ges.
> Beiträge der Winckelmann-Gesellschaft

Belg. Kstdkml.
> Belgische Kunstdenkmäler

Bern. Schr.
> Berner Schriften

Bib. Cah. Archéol.
> Bibliothèque des cahiers archéologiques

Bib. Dis.
> Biblioteca di disegni

Bib. Ecole Chartes
> Bibliothèque de l'Ecole des chartes

Bib. Kst & Antfreunde
Bibliothek für Kunst- und Antiquitätenfreunde

Bidrag Kännedom Finlands Nat. & Folk
Bidrag till kännedom av Finlands natur och folk [Contributions to the knowledge of Finnish nature and people]

Birmingham Byz. Ser.
Birmingham Byzantine Series

Bishop Mus. Special Pubn
Bishop Museum Special Publication

Bldgs Britain
Buildings of Britain

Bldgs England
Buildings of England

Bldgs Ireland
Buildings of Ireland

Bldgs Scotland
Buildings of Scotland

Bldgs Wales
Buildings of Wales

BM, Occas. Pap.
British Museum, Occasional Papers

BM, Prts & Drgs Ser.
British Museum, Prints and Drawings Series

Bollingen Ser.
Bollingen Series

Bonn. Hft. Vorgesch.
Bonner Hefte für Vorgeschichte

Brit. Archaeol. Rep.
British Archaeological Reports

Brit. Archaeol. Rep., Brit. Ser.
British Archaeological Reports, British Series

Brit. Archaeol. Rep., Int. Ser.
British Archaeological Reports, International Series

Brit. Archaeol. Rep., Suppl. Ser.
British Archaeological Reports, Supplementary Series

B. & Schr.
Buch und Schrift

Bull. BM, Hist. Ser.
Bulletin of the British Museum, Historical Series

Cah. ORSTOM Sci. Humaines
Cahiers ORSTOM Sciences Humaines

Cambridge Anc. Hist.
Cambridge Ancient History

Cambridge Hist. India
Cambridge History of India

Cambridge U., Mus. Archaeol. & Ethnol., Occas. Pap.
Cambridge University, Museum of Archaeology and Ethnology, Occasional Papers

Carnegie Inst. Washington, Contrib. Amer. Anthropol. & Hist.
Carnegie Institution of Washington, Contributions to American Anthropology and History

Carnegie Inst. Washington, Contrib. Amer. Archaeol.
Carnegie Institution of Washington, Contributions to American Archaeology

CA Stud. Hist. A.
California Studies in the History of Art

Cat. Drgs Col. RIBA
Catalogue of the Drawings Collection of the RIBA

Cent. Creative Phot., Guide Ser.
Center for Creative Photography, Guide Series

Chiese Roma Illus.
Chiese di Roma illustrate

Class. A.
Classica dell'arte

Col. A. Afrique Noire
Collection arts d'Afrique noire

Col. A. Contemp.
Colecção arte contemporânea

Col. A. Hist.
Collectanea artis historiae

Col. A. & Tesoros Perú
Colección arte y tesoros del Perú

Col. Ecole Fr. Rome
Collection de l'Ecole française de Rome

Colloq. A. & Archaeol. Asia
Colloquies on Art and Archaeology in Asia

Col. Maîtres A.
Collection des maîtres de l'art

Columbia U. Contrib. Anthropol.
Columbia University Contributions to Anthropology

Complete Hist. Jap. Phot.
The Complete History of Japanese Photography

Corp. Inscr. Indic.
Corpus inscriptionem Indicarum

Corp. Inscr. Iran.
Corpus inscriptionem Iranicarum

Corp. Vasorum Ant.
Corpus vasorum antiquorum

Corp. Vitrearum Med. Aevi
Corpus vitrearum medii aevi

Council Brit. Archaeol., Res. Rep.
Council for British Archaeology, Research Reports

Cuad. Hist. A.
Cuadernos de historia del arte

Cuneiform Texts Nimrod
Cuneiform Texts from Nimrod

Darstell. Fränk. Gesch.
Darstellung aus der fränkischen Geschichte

Diamanti A.
I diamanti dell'arte

Diss. Kstgesch.
Dissertationen zur Kunstgeschichte

Doc. Hist. A.
A Documentary History of Art

Doss. Mus. Tissus
Dossiers du Musée des tissus

Dt. Archäol. Inst., Dkml. Ant. Archit.
Deutsches archäologisches Institut, Denkmäler antiker Architektur

Dt. Kstgesch.
Deutsche Kunstgeschichte

Duke U. Cent. Int. Stud.
Duke University Center for International Studies

Dumbarton Oaks Stud.
Dumbarton Oaks Studies

Enc. Feltrinelli Fisher A.
Enciclopedia Feltrinelli Fisher Arte

Eng. Country Houses
English Country Houses

Etud. Celt.
Etudes celtiques

Etud. Hist. A.: Inst. Hist. Belge Rome
Etudes d'histoire de l'art publiées par l'Institut historique belge de Rome

Eur. Hochschschr.
Europäische Hochschulschriften

Fabian Tracts

Fatti & Idee: Saggi & Biog.
I fatti e le idee: Saggi e biografie

Fieldiana

Field Mus. Nat. Hist., Anthropol. Ser.
Field Museum of Natural History, Anthropological Series

Fin. Fornminnesfören. Tidskr./Suom. Muinmuist. Aikak.
Finska Fornminnesföreningens tidskrift/ Suomen muinaismuistoyhdistyksen aikakauskirja (Finnish historical society magazine)

Fontes Archaeol. Morav.
Fontes archaeologici Moraviae

Fontes Rerum Austr.
Fontes rerum Austriacarum

Fontes Rerum Ger.
Fontes rerum Germanicarum

Forsch. Almohad. Moschee
Forschungen zur almohadischen Moschee

Forsch. & Ber. Ksthist. Inst. U. Graz
Forschungen und Bericht des Kunsthistorischen Institutes der Universität Graz

Forsch. Dt. Kstgesch.
Forschungen zur deutschen Kunstgeschichte

Forsch. Gesch. Oberösterreichs
Forschung zur Geschichte Oberösterreichs

Forsch. Gesch. Stadt Ulm
Forschungen zur Geschichte der Stadt Ulm

Forsch. Kstgesch. & Christ. Archäol.
Forschungen zur Kunstgeschichte und christlichen Archäologie

Führer Ksthist. Mus.
Führer durch das Kunsthistorische Museum

Führer Urgesch.
Führer zur Urgeschichte

Garland Lib. Hist. A.
Garland Library of the History of Art

Genius Archit.
Genius in Architecture

Gen. Serv. Admin. Hist. Stud.
General Services Administration Historical Study

Gesch. Stadt Wien
Geschichte der Stadt Wien

Ges. Rhein. Geschknd.
Gesellschaft für rheinische Geschichtskunde

Giessen. Beitr. Kstgesch.
Giessener Beiträge zur Kunstgeschichte

Global Archit.
Global Architecture

Gmünd. Stud.
Gmünden Studien

Govt Andhra Pradesh, Archaeol. Ser.
Government of Andhra Pradesh, Archaeological Series

Grosse Bauten Eur.
Grosse Bauten Europas

Gt Amer. Architect Ser.
Great American Architect series

Gt Gals World
Great Galleries of the World

Gt W. Ser.
Great Western Series

Guida Italia TCI
Guida d'Italia del Touring club italiano

Harvard-Radcliffe F.A. Ser.
Harvard–Radcliffe Fine Arts Series

Hb. Dt. Kstdkml.
Handbuch der deutschen Kunstdenkmäler

Heibonsha Surv. Jap. A.
Heibonsha Survey of Japanese Art

Heidelberg. Kstgesch. Abh.
Heidelberger Kunstgeschichtliche
Abhandlungen

Hildesheim. Ägyp. Beitr.
Hildesheimer Ägyptologie Beiträge

Hisp. Soc. America Pubns
Hispanic Society of America Publications

Hisp. Soc. Pubns
Hispanic Society Publications

Hist. A.
History in the Arts

Hist. A. Portugal
Historia da arte em Portugal

Hist. & Cult. Ind. People
The History and Culture of the Indian
People

Hist. Gen. A. Mex.
Historia general del arte mexicano

Hist. Mnmts Iraq
Historical Monuments in Iraq

Hist. World Archit.
History of World Architecture

Hyderabad Archaeol. Ser.
Hyderabad Archaeological Series

Industrialization Forum

Irish Her. Ser.
Irish Heritage Series

Irish Lit. Stud.
Irish Literary Studies

Istanbul. Forsch.
Istanbuler Forschungen

Ist. It. Med. & Estrem. Oriente, Rap. & Mem.
Istituto italiano per il Medio ed Estremo
Oriente, rapporti e memorie

Istor. Rus. Isk.
Istoriya russkogo iskusstva

Italia A.
Italia artistica

Italia Romanica
Italia romanica

It. Forsch. Ksthist. Inst. Florenz
Italienische Forschungen des
kunsthistorischen Instituts in Florenz

Izobrazitel'noye Isk.
Izobrazitel'noye iskusstvo

Jap. A. Lib.
Japanese Arts Library

Kat. Bayer. Nmus. München
Kataloge des bayerischen
Nationalmuseums München

Klass. Kst Gesamtausgaben
Klassiker der Kunst in Gesamtausgaben

Kstdkml. Bayern
Die Kunstdenkmaler von Bayern

Kstdkml. Schweiz
Die Kunstdenkmäler der Schweiz

Kstgesch. Schweiz
Kunstgeschichte der Schweiz von den
Anfängen bis zum Beginn des 20.
Jahrhunderts

Kstpatrm. W.-Vlaanderen
Kunstpatrimonium van West-Vlaanderen

Landmarks A. Hist.
Landmarks in Art History

Lett. It.
Letteratura italiana

Loeb Class. Lib.
Loeb Classical Library

London Rec. Soc. Pubns
London Record Society Publications

London Top. Soc. Pubns
London Topographical Society
Publications

Lübeck. Musführer
Lübecker Museumsführer

Maestri Colore
I maestri del colore

Mainfränk. Hft.
Mainfränkische Hefte

Manchester Stud. Hist. A.
Manchester Studies in the History of Art

Mat. Allg. Vergl. Archäol.
Materialen zur allgemeinen und
vergleichenden Archäologie

Mat. & Stud. Hist. Armen. A. & Cult.
Materials and Studies for the History of
Armenian Art and Culture

McGill U. Monographs Class. Archaeol. &
Hist.
McGill University Monographs in Classical
Archaeology and History

Meded. Rijksmus. Vlkennd.
Mededelingen van het Rijksmuseum voor
Volkenkunde

Mél. Maspero
Mélanges Maspero [sub-series in Inst. Fr.
Archéol. Orient. Caire]

Mem. Archaeol. Surv. Ceylon
Memoirs of the Archaeological Survey of
Ceylon

Mem. Archaeol. Surv. India
Memoirs of the Archaeological Survey of
India

Mém. Archéol.: Ecole Fr. Extrême-Orient
Mémoires archéologiques publiés par
l'Ecole française d'Extrême-Orient

Mem. Bishop Mus.
Memoirs of the Bishop Museum

Mém.: Dél. Archéol. Fr. Afghanistan
Mémoires de la délégation archéologique
française en Afghanistan

Mém.: Inst. Fr. Archéol. Orient. Caire
Mémoires publiés par les membres de
l'Institut français d'archéologie orientale du
Caire

Mém.: Miss. Archéol. Fr. Caire
Mémoires publiés par les membres de la
Mission archéologique française du Caire

Mem. Mus. Anthropol.: U. MI
Memoirs of the Museum of Anthropology,
University of Michigan

Mem. Polynes. Soc.
Memoirs of the Polynesian Society

Mens. A.
Mensile d'arte

Meroitica

MI Pap. Chin. Stud.
Michigan Papers in Chineses Studies

MI Pap. S. & SE Asian Stud.
Michigan Papers on South and Southeast
Asian Studies

Misc. Cassinese
Miscellanea cassinese

Mnmt. A. Romanae
Monumenta artis Romanae

Mnmt. Ger. Hist.
Monumenta Germaniae historica

Mnmt. & Ist.
Monumenti e istituzioni

Monographs Malay. Branch Royal Asiat. Soc.
Monographs of the Malaysian Branch of
the Royal Asiatic Society

Münchn. Ksthist. Abh.
Münchner kunsthistorische Abhandlungen

Ned. Mnmt. Gesch. & Kst
De Nederlandse monumenten van
geschiedenis en kunst

Neue Münchn. Beitr. Kstgesch.
Neue Münchner Beiträge zur
Kunstgeschichte

New Bell's Cathedral Guides

New York U., Inst. F.A., Wrightsman Lect.
New York University, Institute of Fine Art,
Wrightsman Lectures

Norton Crit. Stud. A. Hist.
Norton Critical Studies in Art History

NT Guidebk
National Trust Guidebook

Nuit Temps
La Nuit du temps [Zodiaque]

Occas. AURA Pubn
Occasional AURA Publication

Opera Completa
Opera completa

Orbis A.
Orbis artium

Orient. Inst. Pubns
Oriental Institute Publications

Orient. Numi. Soc., Occas. Pap.
Oriental Numismatic Society, Occasional
Papers

Outstanding Diss. F.A.
Outstanding Dissertations in the Fine Arts

Oxford Hist. Eng. A.
The Oxford History of English Art

Oxford Stud. Hist. A. & Archit.
Oxford Studies in the History of Art and
Architecture

Palet Ser.
Palet Serie

Palladin Mod. Movts
Palladin Modern Movements

Pallas Lib. A.
The Pallas Library of Art

Pap. A. Hist. PA State U.
Papers in Art History from the
Pennsylvania State University

Pap. Peabody Mus. Archaeol. & Ethnol.
Papers of the Peabody Museum for
Archaeology and Ethnology

Pelican Hist. A.
Pelican History of Art

Penguin Class. World A.
Penguin Classics of World Art

Penguin Guide Mnmts India
Penguin Guide to the Monuments of India

Penguin Mod. Masters
Penguin Modern Masters

Penguin Mod. Painters
Penguin Modern Painters

Petites Monographies Grands Edifices France
    Petites monographies des grands édifices
    de la France

Philol. Untersuchungen
    Philologische Untersuchungen

Pitt. Italia
    La pittura in Italia

Port. Monographs A. Subjects
    Portfolio Monographs on Artistic Subjects

Prähist. Bronzefunde
    Prähistorische Bronzefunde

Princeton Monographs A. & Archaeol.
    Princeton Monographs in Art and
    Archaeology

Prob. Kstwiss.
    Probleme der Kunstwissenschaft

Propyläen-Kstgesch.
    Propyläen-Kunstgeschichte

Pubn Abt. Asien, Ksthist. Inst. U. Köln
    Publikationen der Abteilung Asien,
    Kunsthistorisches Institut der Universität
    Köln

Pubn Archv U. Graz
    Publikationen aus dem Archiv der
    Universität Graz

Pubns Bib. A. & Archéol.
    Publications de la Bibliothèque d'art et
    d'archéologie

Pubns Ecole Fr. Extrême-Orient
    Publications de l'Ecole française
    d'Extrême-Orient

Pubns Hist. A. & Archéol. U. Cath. Louvain
    Publications d'histoire de l'art et
    d'archéologie de l'Université catholique de
    Louvain

Pubns Soc. Promot. Byz. Stud.
    Publications of the Society for the
    Promotion of Byzantine Studies

Quarto [London]

Quellen & Darstell. Fränk. Gesch.
    Quellen und Darstellungen zur fränkischen
    Geschichte

Quellen & Darstell. Fränk. Kstgesch.
    Quellen und Darstellungen zur fränkischen
    Kunstgeschichte

Quellen & Forsch. Sprach- & Kultgesch. Ger.
Vlker
    Quellen und Forschungen zur Sprach- und
    Kulturgeschichte der germanischen Völker

Quellen & Schr. Bild. Kst
    Quellen und Schriften zur bildenden Kunst

Quellenschr. Kstgesch. & Ksttech.
    Quellenschriften für Kunstgeschichte und
    Kunsttechnik

Quellenschr. Kstgesch. & Ksttech. Mittlalt. &
Neuzeit
    Quellenschriften für Kunstgeschichte und
    Kunsttechnik des Mittelalters und der
    Neuzeit

Quellenschr. Kstgesch. & Ksttech. Mittlalt. &
Ren.
    Quellenschriften für Kunstgeschichte und
    Kunsttechnik des Mittelalters und der
    Renaissance

Quellen & Stud. Dt. Ordens
    Quellen und Studien zur Geschichte des
    deutschen Ordens

Reclams Kstführer
    Reclams Kunstführer

Ref. Pubns A. Hist.
    Reference Publications in Art History

Rencontres Louvre
    Rencontres du Louvre

Rhein. Archv
    Rheinisches Archiv

Rolls Ser.
    Rolls Series [Rerum Britannicarum
    mediiaevi scriptures]

Röm. Forsch. Bib. Hcrtz.
    Römische Forschungen der Bibliotheca
    Hertziana

Röm. Forsch. Ksthist. Inst. Graz
    Römische Forschungen des
    Kunsthistorischen Instituts Graz

Röm. Qschr. Christ. Altertknd. & Kirchgesch.
    Römische Quartalschrift für christliche
    Altertumskunde und für Kirchengeschichte

Royal Comm. Anc. & Hist. Mnmts & Constr.
England
    Royal Commission on the Ancient and
    Historical Monuments and Constructions
    of England

Royal Comm. Anc. & Hist. Mnmts Scotland
    Royal Commission on the Ancient and
    Historical Monuments of Scotland

Royal Ont. Mus., A. & Archaeol. Occas. Pap.
    Royal Ontario Museum, Art and
    Archaeology Occasional Papers

Rus. Khudozhestvennaya Kul't. Kontsa XIX-
Nachala XX Veka
    Russkaya khudozhestvennaya kul'tura
    kontsa XIX-nachala XX veka

Saggi & Stud. Stor. A.
    Saggi e studi di storia dell'arte

Sather Class. Lect.
    Sather Classical Lectures

Schaumburg. Stud.
    Schaumburger Studien

Schede Vesma

Schr. Goethe-Ges.
    Schriften der Goethe-Gesellschaft

Schr. Heeresgesch. Mus. Wien
    Schriften des Heeresgeschichtlichen
    Museums in Wien

Schrreihe Akad. Kst.
    Schriftenreihe der Akademie der Künste

Schrreihe Mus. Neustrelitz
    Schriftenreihe des Museums Neustrelitz

Schrreihe U. Regensburg
    Schriftenreihe der Universität Regensburg

Schr. Städt. Kstmus. Düsseldorf
    Schriften des städtischen Kunstmuseums
    zu Düsseldorf

Schweiz. Inst. Kstwiss., Oeuvrekat.
    Schweizerisches Institut für
    Kunstwissenschaft, Oeuvrekataloge

Schweiz. Kstler
    Schweizer Künstler

Ser. A. & Artistas: Bib. A. & Cult. Bolivia
    Serie arte y artistas: Biblioteca de arte y
    cultura de Bolivia

S. Ind. Inscr.
    South Indian Inscriptions

Smithsonian Contrib. Anthropol.
    Smithsonian Contributions to
    Anthropology

Soc. Antiqua. London, Occas. Pap.
    Society of Antiquaries of London,
    Occasional Paper

Soc. Antiqua. London Res. Rep.
    Society of Antiquaries of London Research
    Report

Soc. Antiqua. Scotland/Monograph Ser.
    Society of Antiquaries of Scotland/
    Monograph Series

Soc. SE Asian Stud.
    Society for South East Asian Studies

Sources Chrét.
    Sources chrétiennes

Sources & Doc. Hist. A.
    Sources and Documents in the History of
    Art

Southampton A.G., Cat. Ser.
    Southampton Art Gallery, Catalogue Scrics

Sp. Forsch. Görres-Ges.
    Spanische Forschungen der Görres-
    Gesellschaft

Stor. Milano
    Storia di Milano

Stor. Miniatura: Stud. & Doc
    Storia della miniatura: Studi e documenti

Stor. Napoli
    Storia di Napoli

Stor. Pitt. It.
    Storia della pittura italiana

Stud. Archaeol.
    Studia archaeologica

Stud. Archit.
    Studies in Architecture

Stud. Bib. Warb.
    Studien der Bibliothek Warburg [vols
    i–xxiv, 1922–32 pubd in Leipzig; cont. as
    Stud. Warb. Inst.]

Stud. Church Hist.
    Studies in Church History

Stud. F.A.: Crit.
    Studies in the Fine Arts: Criticism

Stud. Hist. A.
    Studies in the History of Art

Stud. Kstgesch.
    Studien zur Kunstgeschichte

Stud. Kultknd.
    Studien zur Kulturkunde

Stud. Late Ant. & Early Islam
    Studies in Late Antiquity and Early Islam

Stud. & Mat. Mus. Civil. Romana
    Studi e materiali del Museo della civiltà
    romana

Stud. Medit. Archaeol.
    Studies in Mediterranean Archaeology

Stud. MS. Illum.
    Studies in Manuscript Illumination

Stud. Russ. A. Hist.
    Studies in Russian Art History

Stud. Schleswig-Holstein. Kstgesch.
    Studien zur schleswig-holsteinischen
    Kunstgeschichte

Stud. Silensia
    Studia Silensia

Stud. Warb. Inst.
    Studies of the Warburg Institute [prev.
    pubd as Stud. Bib. Warb.]

Style & Civiliz.
    Style and Civilization

Summa A.
    Summa artis: Historia general del arte

Svensk. Human. Forbundet
    Svenska humanistiska forbundet

Tanjore Sarasvati Ser.
    Tanjore Sarasvati Series

Tatti Stud.
    I Tatti Studies: Essays in the Renaissance

Tib. Hist. Ser.
Tibetan History Series

Trad. A. Africa
Traditional Arts of Africa

Trav. & Mém. Inst. Ethnol.
Travaux et mémoires de l'Institut
d'ethnologie

Tribal A.
Tribal Art

Trinity Coll. Dublin, Quatercenten. Ser.
Trinity College Dublin, Quatercentenary
Series

Trivandrum Skt Ser.
Trivandrum Sanskrit Series

Tutta Pitt.
Tutta la pittura/All the Paintings

U. Buenos Aires, Inst. Invest. Hist.
Universidad de Buenos Aires, Instituto de
investigaciones históricas

U. CA, Pubns Amer. Archaeol. & Ethnol.
University of California, Publications in
American Archaeology and Ethnology

U. CA, Pubns Anthropol.
University of California, Publications in
Anthropology

U. CA, Pubns Class. Archaeol.
University of California, Publications in
Classical Archaeology

Univers Conn.
L'Univers des connaissances

Vance Bibliog., Archit. Ser.
Vance Bibliographies, Architecture Series

Vanderbilt U., Pubns Anthropol.
Vanderbilt University, Publications in
Anthropology

Verhand. Kon. Inst. Taal-, Land- &
Volkenknd.
Verhandelingen [van der] Koninklijke
instituut voor taal-, land- en volkenkunde

Veröff. Fulda. Geschver.
Veröffentlichungen des Fuldaer
Geschichtsvereins

Veröff. Mus. Vlkerknd., Berlin
Veröffentlichungen des Museums für
Völkerkunde, Berlin

Veröff. Zentinst Kstgesch. München
Veröffentlichungen des Zentralinstituts für
Kunstgeschichte in München

Victoria Hist. Co. England
Victoria History of the Counties of
England

Vor Tids Kst
Vor tids kunst [Art of our time]

Warb. Inst. Surv.
Warburg Institute Surveys

Werken Hist. Genoot.
Werken uitgegeven door het Historisch
genootschap

Wien. Schr.
Wiener Schriften

Wiss. Veröff. Dt. Orient-Ges.
Wissenschaftliche Veröffentlichungen der
deutschen Orient-Gesellschaft

Working Pap. Anthropol., Archaeol., Ling. &
Maori Stud., U. Auckland
Working Papers in Anthropology,
Archaeology, Linguistics and Maori
Studies, University of Auckland

Working Pap. Trad. A.
Working Papers in the Traditional Arts

World A.
World of Art

World Anthropol.
World Anthropology

World U. Lib.
World University Library

Yale U., Pubns Anthropol.
Yale University, Publications in
Anthropology

Appendix D

LIST OF CONTRIBUTORS

Aalen, Fred
Abad Castro, Concepción
Abbozzo Heuser, Margherita
Abdullah, Fatima S.
Abdy, Jane
Abelmann, Annelies M.
Abiko, Bonnie
Abildgaard, Hanne
Abolina, R. Ya.
Abram, Joseph
Abress, Elisabeth
Abse, Bathsheba
Abt, Jeffrey
Abu Khalaf, Marwan F.
Acanfora, Elisa
Aceto, Francesco
Acevedo, Esther
Achleitner, Friedrich
Achleitner, Helga
Ackermann, Hans Christoph
Adair, William B.
Adam, Hans Christian
Adam, Sheila
Adams, Ann Jensen
Adams, Doug
Adams, E. Charles
Adams, Elizabeth
Adams, Henry
Adams, Janet
Adams, Monni
Adams, Nicholas
Adams, Steven
Adams, William Y.
Adamson, Jeremy Elwell
Adande, Codjovi Joseph
Addiss, Stephen
Adelson, Candace J.
Adelson, Fred B.
Adepegba, Cornelius
Ades, Dawn
Adiv, Uriel M.
Adle, Chahryar
Adlerova, Alena
Adorni, Bruno
Adrosko, Rita J.
Affleck, Diane L. Fagan
Agosti, Giacomo
Agueda, Mercedes
Aguilera, Marta
Ahn Kwi-Joon
Ahtola-Moorhouse, Leena
Aikema, Bernard
Ainsworth, Maryan Wynn
Aires Silveira, Maria de
Airs, Malcolm
Akers, Robert C.

Akin, N.
Alabiso, Annachiara
Alarco Canosa, Paloma
Albani, Jenny
Albenda, Pauline
Albers, Martin
Alberton Vinco Da Sesso, Livia
Alberts, Robert C.
Albrecht, Stephan
Albuquerque, Luis de
Alcina Franch, José
Alcock, N. W.
Alcolea Blanch, Santiago
Alcorn, Ellenor
Alcoy, Rosa
Aldrich, Megan
Alegret, Celia
Alegría, Ricardo E.
Alemany-Dessaint, Véronique
Alemi, Mahvash
Alessi, Cecilia
Alex, Reinhard
Alexander, David
Alexander, Drury B.
Alexander, Lucy
Alexander, Margaret A.
Alexander, Robert L.
Alexander-Adda, Héene
Alexis, Karin M. E.
Alfillé, Tanya
Alfsen, Glenny
Ali, W.
Alix Trueba, Josefina
Allan, J. P.
Allan, J. W.
Allardyce, Fiona
Alldridge, Patricia H.
Allen, Brian
Allen, Elizabeth
Allen, Eva J.
Allen, Terry
Allen, Traudi
Allenov, M. M.
Alley, Ronald
Allibone, Jill
Allwood, Rosamond
Allwood de Mata, Claudia
Almagro-Gorbea, M.
Alofsin, Anthony
Alsop, Ian
Aluffi-Pentini, Stefano
Alves, Ana Maria
Alvise de Vierno, Marc
Amaturo, Matilde
Ames-Lewis, Francis
Amiet, Pierre

Anastassiadis, Aghis J.
Anawalt, Patricia Rieff
Andersen, Søren H.
Andersen, Troels
Anderson, Freda
Anderson, Jaynie
Anderson, Martha G.
Anderson, Nancy
Anderson, Paul L.
Anderson, Robert
Anderson, Ronald
Anderson, Ross C.
Anderson, Stanford
Andersson, Christiane
Andrade Lima, Tania
Andrault, Jean-Claude
Andreotti, Libero
Andres, Glenn M.
Andrés, Gregorio de
Andressen, B. M.
Andrew, Patricia R.
Andrews, Carol
Andrews, George F.
Andrews, Jorella
Andrews, Keith
Andrews, P. A.
Andreyev, M. I.
Andreyeva, Yekaterina
Andronicos, Manolis
Androssov, Sergey
Anfam, David
Anfray, Francis
Angelelli, Walter
Angelini, Alessandro
Angelomatis-Tsougarakis, Helen
Anglesea, Martyn
Ångström, Inga Lena
Anker, Peter
Anker, Valentina
Ann, Yonemura
Anselmi, Alessandra
Anson, Colin
Anthes Jr, William L.
Antonaccio, C. M.
Antonio Saénz, Trinidad de
Antrobus, Pauline
Apel, Dora
Apgar, Garry
Apostolos-Cappadona, Diane
Apparao, Sharan
Apperly, Richard
Appleyard, David
Appuhn, Horst
Aquilino, Marie Jeannine
Aradi, Nora

Ara Gil, Julia
Arai, Katsuyoshi
Arakawa, Masaaki
Arapoglou, Evita
Araujo Costa, Fernanda de
Archuleta, Margaret
Arciprete de Reyes, Marta
Asfour, Amal
Asher, Catherine B.
Asher, Frederick M.
Ashrafi, M. M.
Ashton, Geoffrey
Aslaksby, Trond
Aslet, Clive
Astbury, Leigh
Aston, Barbara G.
Aston, D.A.
Åström, Paul
Asturias de Barrios, Linda
Atherton, Cynthia Packert
Atil, Esin
Attwood, Philip
Atwater, Vivian
Auboyer, Jeannine
Audouze, Françoise
Auer, Alfred
Augarde, Jean-Dominique
Auld, Alasdair A.
Auld, Sylvia
Aulinger, B.
Aupert, Pierre
Aurenhammer, Hans H.
Austen, Brian
Austin, Lloyd James
Avanzati, Elisabetta
Aveni, Anthony
Avermaete, Roger
Avery, Charles
Avon, Annalisa
Avrin, Leila
Azarnoush, Massoud
Azarpay, Guitty
Azcarate Ristori, José Maria
Azzi Visentini, Margherita
Baas, Jacquelynn
Babaoğlu, Lale
Babelon, Jean-Pierre
Babić, Gordana
Babić, Ivo
Bacci, Mina
Backhouse, Janet
Bacon, Mardges
Badger, Gerry
Badiee, Julie
Baekeland, Frederick
Baer, Eva

Baer, Ronni
Baer, Wolfram
Baeten, J. P.
Baffa Rivolta, Matilde
Bagley, Robert W.
Bahn, Paul G.
Bahns, Jörn
Bail, Murray
Bailey, Colin J.
Bailey, Donald M.
Bailey, John
Bailey, Julia
Bailey, Lisa
Bailey, Sarah Barter
Baily, John
Baines, Claire
Baines, John
Baipakov, K. M.
Baixas Figueras, Isabel
Bajkay, Éva
Bajou, Thierry
Bajou, Valérie M. C.
Baker, Donna T.
Baker, Patricia L.
Baker, Paul R.
Bakker, Christianne
Bako, Zsuzsanna
Balderston, Gordon D.
Balfour-Paul, Jenny
Ballon, Hilary
Balmaceda, Lissette
Balmaseda Muncharaz, L. J.
Balsamo, Isabelle
Balslev Jørgensen, Lisbet
Balty, Janine
Balty, Jean Ch.
Bambach Cappel, Carmen
Bammer, Anton
Banaś, Pawel
Bancroft-Hunt, Norman
Bandaranayake, Senake
Bandera Viani, Maria Cristina
Bandes, Susan J.
Bango Torviso, I. G.
Banham, Reyner
Bania, Zbigniew
Bankes, George
Banks, Simon
Bann, Stephen
Bantens, Robert J.
Banti, Enrica
Baptista Pereira, F. A.
Baquedano, Elizabeth
Barag, D.
Baranow, Sonja von
Barber, Charles

Barber, Malcolm
Barber, R. L. N.
Barber, Tabitha
Barbet, Alix
Barbieri, Franco
Barbin, Madeleine
Barcelo Cedeño, Cruz
Barcham, William L.
Barilli, Renato
Barker, Emma
Barkoczi, Istvan
Barkova, L. L.
Barlow, Graham F.
Barnes, Brian C.
Barnes, Gina L.
Barnes, Joanna
Barnes, Ruth
Barnes Jr, Carl F.
Barnet, Peter
Barnet, Sylvan
Barnett, G.
Barnett, Vivian Endicott
Barnhill, Georgia Brady
Barnicoat, John
Barnish, S. J. B.
Barolsky, Paul
Baron, Wendy
Barovier Mentasti, Rosa
Barr, Jim
Barr, Mary
Barran, José Pedro
Barrett, D. C.
Barrett-Post, Erin G.
Barringer, Timothy J.
Barron, Kathryn
Barrucand, Marianne
Barsch, Barbara
Barter, Judith A.
Barth, Wiltrud
Bartman, Elizabeth
Bartmann, Dominik
Bartoli, Roberta
Barton, C.
Bartz, Gabriele
Barwell, Victoria
Barylski, Patricia
Bascou, Marc
Basnayake, H. T.
Bass, Ruth
Bassett, Richard
Bastéa, Eleni
Bastin, Marie-Louise
Batari, Ferenc
Baten, Lea
Bates, Craig D.
Bates, Michael L.
Batkin, Jonathan
Battilotti, Donata
Battista, Lucia
Baudez, Claude-François
Baudouin, Frans
Baudouin, Piet
Baudouin-Matuszek, M. N.
Baudson, Pierre
Bauer, Cornelia
Bauer-Eberhardt, Ulrike
Baumann-Engels, Marianne
Baume, Nicholas
Baumgärtel-Fleischmann, Renate
Baumgartner, Marcel
Baur, John I. H.
Bax, Marty Th.
Baxter, Paula A.
Baxter, Ronald
Bayer, Andrea
Baylé, Maylis

Bayliss, J. C.
Bérchez, Joaquín
Beach, Milo Cleveland
Beamish, Gordon Marshall
Beard, Dorothea K.
Beard, Geoffrey
Beaucamp, Verena
Beaulieu, Michèle
Beck, H.-U.
Becker, David P.
Becker, Jochen
Beckett, Rachel
Bedford, Steven M.
Béguin, Gilles
Béhar, Henri
Behr, Shulamith
Behrendt, Kurt
Behrens, Roy R.
Behrens-Abouseif, Doris
Béland, Mario
Beldiman, Alexandru
Beldiman, Ioana
Beletskaya, Ye. A.
Bell, Alan
Bell, Janis C.
Bell, Janis Callen
Bell, Lanny
Bell, Leonard
Bell, Marja-Liisa
Bellafiore, Giuseppe
Bell-Carrier, Cheryl E.
Bellesi, Sandro
Belli D'Elia, Pina
Bellini, Amedeo
Belloli, Carlo
Bellosi, Luciano
Belluzzi, Amedeo
Belsey, Hugh
Belsey, James
Belton, Robert J.
Benati, Daniele
Bencivenni, Mario
Bender, Wolfgang
Bendiner, Kenneth
Benedick, Christian
Benedict, Lieselotte
Beneš, Mirka
Benge, Glenn Franklin
Benito, Pilar
Benjamin, B. S.
Benjamin, Susan
Bennett, Douglas
Bennett, Elizabeth F.
Bennett, J. A.
Bennett, Mary
Benson, Elizabeth P.
Benson, Robert A.
Benson, Timothy O.
Bentel, Paul Louis
Bentivoglio-Ravasio, Raffaella
Bentkowska, Anna
Benton, Tim
Benvenuti, Feliciano
Benzi, Fabio
Bercé, Françoise
Berckenhagen, Ekhart
Berends, G.
Berenguer R., José
Berestord, R.
Bergdoll, Barry
Berge, L.
Berge-Gerbaud, Maria van
Bergendahl Hohler, Erla
Berger, Robert W.
Berger, Ursel
Bergh-Hoogterp, Louise E. van den

Bergmann, Bettina
Bergmann, Marianne
Bergmann, Rosemarie
Bergmann, Ulrike
Bergmans, Anne
Berhaut, Marie
Beridze, V.
Berinson, H. A.
Berlo, Janet Catherine
Berman, Esmé
Berman, Patricia G.
Bermingham, Peter
Bernabei, Franco
Bernal Ponce, Juan
Bernasconi, John G.
Berndt, Catherine H.
Berndt, Ronald M.
Bernhard-Walcher, Alfred
Bernini, Lia
Berns, Marla C.
Bernshtein, B. M.
Berry, Paul
Berry, Victoria
Bershad, David L.
Berthoud, Michael
Bertin, D.
Bertoni, Alberto
Bertrand, Pascal-François
Besnard, Barberine
Besson, Jerry
Betancourt, Philip
Bethe, Monica
Betterton, Shiela
Bettley, James
Beurdeley, Michel
Beveridge, Charles E.
Bevers, Holm
Beyer, Andreas
Beyer, Victor
Bhaskar, C. Uday
Bhattacharya, G.
Bhattacharya, Tapan
Bhattacharyya, Dipak Chandra
Białoskórska, Krystyna
Białostocki, Jan
Bianchi, Robert S.
Biass-Fabiani, Sophie
Bicart-Sée, Lise
Bichler, Susanna
Bickel, Susanne
Bickford, Maggie
Bicknell, Peter
Biddle, Martin
Bidner, J. Heinritz
Bidon, Colette E.
Biebuyck, Daniel P.
Biedermann, Gottfried
Bièvre, Elisabeth de
Bier, Carol
Bier, Lionel
Bierbrauer, Katharina
Bierbrier, Morris
Bietak, M.
Bietoletti, Silvestra
Bignamini, Ilaria
Billcliffe, Roger
Billeter, Erika
Billingham, Rosalind
Binaghi Olivari, M. T.
Binding, Günther
Bindman, David
Bingham, Neil R.
Bingöl, Orhan
Binion, Alice
Binkley, David A.
Binski, Paul
Bionda, R. W. A.

Birch, Dinah
Bird, Alan
Bird, Michael
Birge, Darice
Birke, V.
Biroli Stefanelli, Lucia Pirzio
Bisanz, Rudolf M.
Bischof, Henning
Bischoff, Franz
Bismarck, Beatrice v.
Bisogni, Fabio
Bisona, Monica Blackmun
Bissell, Claude
Bitha, Ioanna
Bjelajac, David
Björnsson, Björn Th.
Blackley, Roger
Blackmun, Barbara Winston
Blackwood, Brian
Blagg, T. F. C.
Blair, Sheila S.
Blake, Casey
Blanc, Giulio V.
Blanc, Nicole
Blanch, Montserrat
Blanchard, Anne
Blau, Eve
Blaugrund, Annette
Bledsoe, Bronwen
Bleed, Peter
Blench, Brian J. R.
Blier, Suzanne Preston
Bligaard, Mette
Blinder, Olga
Bloch, Peter
Block, Jane
Blomberg, Mary
Blomstedt, Petri
Blondel, Madeleine
Bloom, Jonathan M.
Bloore, Carolyn
Bluhm, Andreas
Blum, Pamela Z.
Blum, Paul von
Blume, Eugen
Blumenthal, Arthur R.
Blurton, T. Richard
Bobbink, H.
Bober, Phyllis Pray
Bocard, Hélène
Boccardo, Piero
Bod-Bobrovszky, Ida
Boddens-Hosang, F. J. E.
Bodnar, Szilvia
Bodt, Saskia de
Boeck, Urs
Boeckh, Hans
Boeckl, Matthias
Boehm, Barbara Drake
Boer, Dick E. H. de
Boer, Hildebrand P.G. de
Boerlin-Brodbeck, Y.
Bogaers, Marie-Rose A. S.
Bogdan, Radu
Bogdanescu, Aurel
Bogendorf Rupprath, C. von
Bøggild Johannsen, Birgitte
Bognar, Botond
Bogucki, Peter
Bohan, Ruth L.
Bohm-Duchen, Monica
Bohmmert, Hermann
Bohn, Babette
Boime, Albert
Boisclair, Marie-Nicole
Bok, Marten Jan
Bold, John

Bolger, Doreen
Bollati, Milvia
Bollé, Michael
Bölling, Claudia
Bolon, Carol Radcliffe
Bolton, Brenda M.
Bolton-Smith, Robin
Bomann, Ann
Bonafous-Murat, Arsene
Bonaventura, Paul
Bonavia, Duccio
Bonfante, Larissa
Boniface, Priscilla
Bonito, Virginia Anne
Bonn, Mary
Bonnenfant, Paul
Bonney, D.
Bonney, H.
Bonomi, Kathryn
Bonsdorff, Bengt von
Bonsdorff, Jan von
Bonython, Elizabeth
Boockmann, Hartmut
Boom, Mattie
Boone, Elizabeth Hill
Boonen, L.
Boorman, Helen
Bor, F.
Bora, G.
Borchhardt, Jurgen
Borg, Alan
Borgatti, Jean M.
Borgo, Ludovico
Borgo, Margot
Borrelli, Gian Giotto
Borrero, Luis A.
Börsch-Supan, Eva
Börsch-Supan, Helmut
Borsellino, Enzo
Bos, Luuk
Bosch, Gulnar K.
Bosch, Lynette
Boschma, C.
Bösel, Richard
Bosso, Annie
Bosson, Claude
Boston, J. S.
Boström, Antonia
Boström, Hans-Olof
Boterenbrood, Helen
Bott, Gerhard
Bottineau-Fuchs, Yves
Boucaud, Philippe
Boucher, Bruce
Boucher, Marie-Christine
Boudon, Françoise
Bouillon, Jean-Paul
Boulay, Roger
Boulton, Alfredo
Bourdua, Louise
Bourgeois, A. P.
Bourgoin, Aaron
Bourrut Lacouture, Annette
Bouvet, Vincent
Bowdler, Roger
Bowe, Nicola Gordon
Bowe, Patrick
Bowie, Karen
Bowlt, John E.
Bowron, Edgar Peters
Bowsher, J. M. C.
Boxer, David
Boyanoski, Christine
Boyce, Mary
Boyle, Richard J.
Boyle-Turner, Caroline
Bozdogan, Sibel

Bracey, Ted
Bracons i Clapés, Josep
Bradley, Fiona
Bradshaw, Marilyn
Braham, Helen
Brain, Robert
Brand, Bettina
Brand, Ken
Brandt, Frederick R.
Branigan, Keith
Branstator, Robin A.
Brasser, T. J.
Braun, Emily
Braun, Thomas
Braunfels, Veronika
Bräutigam, Günther
Bravo, Isidre
Bray, Warwick
Breicha, Otto
Brejon de Lavergnée, Arnauld
Brejon de Lavergnée, Barbara
Breme, D.
Brend, Barbara
Brenninkmeyer-De Rooij, B.
Bresc-Bautier, Geneviève
Bresciani, Edda
Brett, David
Brewer, Francesca
Brewster, Harry
Brezianu, Barbu
Bria, Carmen
Brian, Anthea
Bricker, David
Brickstock, R. J.
Bridgeman, Jane
Bridges, Peter
Brigstocke, Hugh
Brijder, H. A. G.
Brilliant, Richard
Brindle, Stephen
Brinker, Helmut
Brinkerhoff, Dericksen
Brinkmann, Bodo
Brisac, Catherine
Brisby, Claire
Bristow, Ian C.
Brock, Karen L.
Brockhaus, Christoph
Broda, Werner
Broderick, Mosette Glaser
Brodie, Allan M.
Brody, J. J.
Broekema, Maarten
Brogi, Alessandro
Broner, Kaisa
Bronkhurst, Judith
Brook, Anthea
Brooke, David S.
Brooke, Janet M.
Brooke, X. B.
Brookeman, Christopher
Brookes, Patricia
Brooks, Chris
Broos, B. P. J.
Brose, David S.
Brotherston, Gordon
Brough, John Barnett
Brown, Beverley Louise
Brown, Claudia
Brown, C. M.
Brown, David Blayney
Brown, Elizabeth Mills
Brown, Hilton
Brown, Iain Gordon
Brown, Ian
Brown, Iben
Brown, Ken

Brown, Michelle P.
Brown, R. Allen
Brown, Stephanie Nevison
Browne, Clare Woodthorpe
Brownell, Charles E.
Browning, Iain
Brubaker, Leslie
Bruce-Mitford, Miranda
Bruhns, Karen Olsen
Bruins, Sjettie
Bruna, Paulo J. V.
Bruneau, Philippe
Brunnbauer, Marlies
Brunst, Vyvyan
Brusati, C.
Bruschi, Arnaldo
Brus-Malinowska, Barbara
Bruyn, C. M. de
Bruyn, J.
Bruzelius, C.
Bryan, John Morrill
Bryant, Barbara
Bryant, Edward
Bryant, Julius
Bryer, A. A. M.
Brykowska, Maria
Brykowski, Ryszard
Buccellati, Giorgio
Buch, Joseph
Buchanan, William
Buchón Cuevas, Ana María
Buchwald, Hans
Buck, Louisa
Buckland, Frances
Buckman, David
Buckton, David
Budd, Malcolm
Budde, Kai
Budny, Mildred
Bueckling, Maraike
Buendía Muñoz, J. Rogelio
Buganza, Mulinda Habi
Bugslag, James
Buhagiar, Mario
Buhl, Marie-Louise
Buhlmann, B. E.
Bührle, Christian
Buijs, Hans
Buitron, Diana
Bulatova, V. A.
Bule, Steven
Bulgari, Veronica
Bull, Malcolm
Bullard, Pauline I. A.
Bullhorst, Rainer
Bullivant, Lucy
Bullock, Nicholas
Bullough, D. A.
Burant, Jim
Bureš, Jiří
Burford, Alison
Burgers, Jacqueline
Burkarth, Axel
Burke, Janine
Burke, Marcus
Burkett, M. E.
Burkle, Christoph
Burkus-Chasson, Anne
Burl, Lucilla
Burleigh-Motley, Marian
Burn, Lucilla
Burnand, Marie-Claire
Burness, Edwina
Burnett, Andrew
Burnett, David
Burnett, T. A. J.
Burney, C. A.

Burns, Sarah
Burns, Thea
Burnside, Kathleen M.
Burnside III, Jackson L.
Burollet, Thérèse
Burow, Johannes
Burton, Neil
Buryakov, Yu. F.
Busche, Ernst A.
Buschow Oechslin, Anja
Busco, Marie F.
Bush, Martin H.
Bush, Susan H.
Bushell, Raymond
Bussers, Helena
Bustamante García, A.
Butler, L. A. S.
Butler, Lawrence E.
Butler, Michael
Buttlar, Adrian von
Büttner, Claudia
Büttner, Frank
Button, Virginia
Butts, Barbara
Buys, Susan
Bydžovska, Lenka
Byrom, G. H.
Byun Young-Sup
Cabañas Bravo, Miguel
Cadogan, Gerald
Cadogan, Jean K.
Cahill, James
Cahill, Nicholas
Cahn, Walter
Calbi, Emilia
Caldwell, David H.
Caldwell, Dorigen
Caleca, Antonio
Calingaert, Efrem Gisella
Calkins, Robert G.
Callaway, Joseph A.
Callerio, Sandro
Callmann, Ellen
Calmann, Gerta
Calnan, Christopher
Calvet, Yves
Calvo, Marta
Calvo Serraller, Francisco
Cámara Muñoz, Alicia
Cambridge, Eric
Cameron, Christina
Cameron, John
Camp, D'Laine
Camp, John
Campanelli, Daniela
Campbell, Colin
Campbell, Julian
Campbell, Lorne
Campbell, Louise
Campbell, Malcolm
Campbell, Marian
Campbell, Patricia
Campbell, Shirley F.
Camporeale, Giovannangelo
Camus, M. T.
Cañal, Vicente Lleó
Canby, Jeanny Vorys
Canby, Sheila R.
Canessa de Sanguinetti, Marta
Cangioli, Marcella
Cannon, Joanna
Cantacuzino, Sherban
Capobianco, Fernanda
Cappelletti, Francesca
Carbonell Esteller, Eduard
Cardet, Ernesto
Cardi, Beatrice de

Cardinal, Roger
Cardon, Bert
Cardyn-Oomen, D.
Carey, Margret
Cariou, André
Carli, Enzo
Carmel, Judith L.
Carminati, Marco
Carmo Sabido, Maria do
Carneci, Magda
Caron, Linda
Carpeggiani, Paolo
Carpenter, John T.
Carpenter, Ken
Carpier-Bienfait, R. M.
Carr, Carolyn Kinder
Carr, Denis J.
Carradice, Ian
Carrasco Zaldua, Fernando
Carrier, David
Carrington, Jill E.
Carswell, John
Carter, Jane Burr
Carter, Joseph Coleman
Carter, Martha L.
Carter, Peter
Carter, Rand
Cartwright, Derrick R.
Caruana, Wally
Casadio, Paolo
Casale, Gerardo
Casale, Vittorio
Casanovas, Maria Antonia
Casciu, Stefano
Casey, Noreen
Cassar-Pullicino, J.
Cassel-Pihl, Eva Helena
Cassese, Giovanna
Cassidy, Brendan
Cast, David
Castellani Zahir, E.
Castelnuovo-Tedesco, Lisbeth
Casteras, Susan P.
Castiglioni, Gino
Castillo, Miguel A.
Casula, Alma
Catalano, Maria Ida
Cate, Phillip Dennis
Cattell, John W. F.
Catello, Angela
Catto, Mike
Caubet, Annie
Causey, Andrew
Cavanagh, W. G.
Cayeux, Jean de
Caygill, Howard
Cazali de Barrios, Rossina
Cebuc, Alexandru
Cecchi, Alessandro
Cederstrom, Elisabeth
Cernuschi, Alberto
Cerutti Fusco, Annarosa
Chabros, Krystyna
Chadour, Anna Beatriz
Chadwick, Whitney
Chakravarty, Kalyan Kumar
Chaldecott, Nada
Chaleix, Pierre
Chaline, Eric
Chalkia, Eugenia
Challingsworth, Christine
Chambers, Bruce W.
Chambers, D. S.
Champion, Sara
Chance, Frank L.
Chandmal, Asit
Chanel, Pierre

Chaney, Edward
Chanfón Olmos, Carlos
Chang, Joseph Tsenti
Chang, Kyung-Ho
Chapel, Jeannie
Chapman, Hugh
Chapman, Jan
Chapman, Martin
Chapman, Rupert I.
Chappaz, Jean-Luc
Chappel, H. J. H.
Chappell, Miles L.
Chappell, Sally A. Kitt
Chapuisat, Jean-Pierre
Charalampidis, Alkis
Charazińska, Elżbieta
Chardigny, Christiane
Charles, Kathryn A.
Charlesworth, M. F.
Charnley, Jonathan
Charola, A. Elena
Charron, Pascale
Chase, Arlen F.
Chase, Beatriz
Chase, David
Chase, Diane Z.
Chase, Judith
Chatelet, A. M.
Chatfield, Judith
Chatzidakis, Ano
Chatzidakis, Manolis
Chaudonneret, Marie-Claude
Chazal, Gilles
Chazelle, Annie
Chazot, Eric
Cheetham, Mark A.
Chehab, Hafez K.
Chenevière, Antoine
Cheney, Iris
Chernow, Burt
Cherpion, Nadine
Cherry, Peter
Chessex, Pierre
Chiappini Di Sorio, Ileana
Chiarelli, Renzo
Chiarini, Marco
Chiarlo, Carlo Roberto
Chiba, Shigeo
Chilton, Meredith
Chilvers, Ian
Chirelstein, Ellen K.
Chirol, Elisabeth
Chishti, Rta Kapur
Chiusa, Maria Cristina
Cho Seon-Mi
Cho You Jeon
Chojnacka, Halina
Chong, Alan
Chou, Ju-Hsi
Christensen, E. A.
Christian, John
Christian, Mary
Christiansen, Keith
Christie, Sigrid
Christman, Margaret C. S.
Christophersen, Axel
Christout, Marie-Françoise
Chrościcki, Juliusz A.
Chrzanowski, Tadeusz
Chu, Petra Ten Doesschate
Chung, Jae Hoon
Church, Warren B.
Churcher, Betty
Chvostal, John J.
Chvyr, L. A.
Ciampolini, Marco
Cianchi, Marco

Ciechanowiecki, A. S.
Cieszkowski, Krzysztof Z.
Cillessen, Wolfgang
Cioffi, Irene
Cioffi, Rosanna
Cirlot, Lourdes
Clabburn, Pamela
Clair, Jean
Claridge, A.
Claringbull, M. A.
Clark, Carol
Clark, Caroline
Clark, Christine
Clark, H. Nicolas B.
Clark, Jane
Clark, William W.
Clarke, G. B.
Clarke, Helen
Clarke, John
Clarke, Stephen T.
Clausen, Meredith L.
Claussen, P. C.
Claut, Sergio
Clay, E.
Clearwater, Bonnie
Cleary, Richard
Clegg, Elizabeth
Cleminson, Oxana
Cleminson, R. M.
Clifford, Giles
Clifton, James
Cloudsley, Peter
Cloulas, Annie
Cloutier, Nicole
Coaldrake, W. H.
Coats, Bruce A.
Cochran, Chris
Cocke, T. H.
Code, Alan
Coe, Brian
Coen, Ester
Coffin, David R.
Cohen, Andrew L.
Cohen, Beth
Cohen, David
Cohen, Evelyn M.
Cohen, Jean-Louis
Cohen, Jeffrey A.
Cohen, Lesley Spiro
Cohen, Michele
Cohen, Steven
Cohn, M. B.
Cohodas, Marvin
Coia, Daniela
Colalucci, Gianluigi
Colardelle, Renée
Colbert, Charles
Coldstream, Nicola
Coldstream, Nicolas
Cole, Herbert M.
Coleby, Nicola
Coleman, Roslyn F.
Colland, Frances
Collard, Elizabeth
Collareta, Marco
Colle, Enrico
Colledge, Malcolm A. R.
Colling, Teje
Collinge, Lucinda Hawkins
Collins, Christiane Crasemann
Collins, Colin-John
Collins, Judith
Collins, Patricia
Collon, Dominique
Colmont, Dominique
Colvin, Howard
Company i Climent, Ximo

Compton, Michael
Compton, Susan
Conant, Ellen
Conde, Teresa del
Condit, Carl W.
Condon, Patricia
Conisbee, Philip
Conkelton, Sheryl
Conklin, William J.
Conn, Richard G.
Connell, Susan
Connelly, Joan Breton
Conner, Patrick
Connor, Carolyn L.
Connor, T. P.
Connors, Joseph
Conran, Elizabeth
Constable, Freda
Constans, Claire
Constantine, Mildred
Contenson, Henri de
Conti, Alessandro
Contini, Roberto
Cook, Barrie J.
Cook, B. F.
Cook, J. M.
Cook, R. M.
Cooke, Catherine
Cooke, James C.
Cooke, Lynne
Cooke, Thomas
Cooksey, Janet
Cooledge Jr, Harold N.
Cooler, Richard M.
Coombs, Elizabeth T.
Coope, Rosalys
Cooper, Carol
Cooper, Emmanuel
Cooper, Frederick
Cooper, Helen A.
Cooper, Philip
Cooper, Tracey E.
Coote, Jeremy
Copeland, Lorraine
Coppa, Simonetta
Coppack, Glyn
Coppens, Christian
Corbett, Michael R.
Corbin, Donna
Corcuera, Ruth
Cordell, Sonia
Cordero Reiman, Karen
Cordingly, David
Core, Philip
Cork, Richard
Corley, Brigitte
Cormack, Peter
Cormack, Robin
Cormack, S.
Cornet, J.-A.
Coronel, Michael
Coronel, Patricia
Coroneo, Roberto
Corredor-Matheos, José
Correia Guedes, Natalia
Corris, Michael
Corte-Real, Manuel
Cortina de Pintado, Leonora
Coşoveanu, Dorana
Cosentino, Andrew J.
Costa, Paolo M.
Costa, Vanina
Costache, Irina D.
Costall, Alan
Costantini, Paolo
Costanzo, Dennis
Costello, Kieran

Coté, Cynthia
Cothren, Michael W.
Cottam, David
Cotton, B. D.
Coulter, Lane
Coulton, J. J.
Coupet, Guy
Coural, Natalie
Court, Elsbeth
Courtenay, Lynn T.
Courtois, Jacques-Claude
Courtwright, Nicola
Coward, Harold
Cowdell, Theo
Cowling, Mary
Cox, Alwyn
Cox, Louise
Cox-Rearick, Janet
Coyle, Brian
Craddock, P. T.
Craig, Barry
Craig, Robert M.
Cramer, Max
Crane, Howard
Cranfield, Ingrid
Cranston, Fumiko E.
Cranston, Maurice
Craveiro, Lurdes
Craven, Allan M.
Craven, David
Crawford, Alan
Crawford, Harriet
Crawford, Michael H.
Crawley, Charlotte
Cribb, Joe
Crichton, Michael
Crill, Rosemary
Cristofani, Mauro
Croizier, Ralph
Crook, John
Cropper, Elizabeth
Crosnier Leconte, Marie Laure
Cross, David A.
Crossley, Paul
Crouwel, J. H.
Crowe, Yolande
Crowley, Daniel J.
Crowley, Eve L.
Crozier, W. Ray
Cruceanu, Codruța
Cruft, Catherine H.
Crum, Roger J.
Crump, James
Cruz, Lourdes
Cruz Valdovinos, José Manuel
Cuadrado, Marta
Cullen, Fintan
Culme, John
Culot, Maurice
Cumming, Elizabeth
Cumming, Robert
Cummings, Kathleen Roy
Cummins, Alissandra
Cunningham, Colin
Cunningham, Jane
Curatola, Giovanni
Ćurčić, Slobodan
Curl, James Stevens
Curnow, Heather
Curnow, Kathy
Curnow, P. E.
Curnow, Wystan
Curran, John
Curran, Kathleen
Curtis, Carol
Curtis, John
Curtis, Penelope

Curtis, Vesta
Curto, S.
Cutler, Anthony
Cuzin, Jean-Pierre
Czach, Marie
Czerner, Olgierd
Czerwonnajá, Svetlana M.
Dabell, Frank
Dabrio Gonzalez, María Teresa
Dachs, Monika
Dacos, Nicole
Daenens, Lieven
Daentler, Barbara
D'Afflitto, Chiara
Dagens, Bruno
Daguerre de Hureaux, A.
Daguerre, Mercedes
Dahlbäck-Lutteman, Helena
D'Albiac, Carole
D'Alconzo, Paola
Dalgleish, George R.
Dallapiccola, A. L.
Dallas, R. W. A.
Dalley, Stephanie
Dalli Regoli, G.
Dam, J. D. van
Damiani, Giovanna
D'Amicone, Elvira
Damsgaard, Nina
Dan, Călin
Dandekar, Ajay
Daneshvari, Abbas
Danford-Cordingley, Joanne
Danga, Michaela
Danielson, Cornelia
Danielsson, Kerstin
Darby, Michael
Dark, Philip J. C.
Darlington, Anne
Darr, Alan Phipps
Das, Asok Kumar
Dashi, Sulejman
Dasser, Karl Ludwig
Daszewski, Wiktor A.
Daum Tholl, Susan von
D'Autilia, Antonella
Davenport, Kay
Davenport, Michael
Davenport, Nancy
Davenport, William H.
David, Jean-Claude
David, Massimiliano
Davidson, Janet
Davidson, Susan E.
Davies, Alice I.
Davies, Helen
Davies, Hugh
Davies, L. Glynne
Davies, M. C.
Davies, Paul
Davies, Philip
Davis, Ann
Davis, Michael T.
Davis, Virginia
Davis, Whitney
Davis Jr, R. H.
Davy-Notter, Annick
Dawton, N.
Dawtry, Anne Frances
Day, Holliday T.
Day, Nicholas Merthyr
Day, Susan
Debaine-Francfort, Corinne
De Benedictis, Cristina
De Benedictis, Elaine
De Bernardi Ferrero, Daria
Debrie, Christine

De Bruyn, Jean-Pierre
Decavele, Johan
Deceneux, Marc
Deckker, Zilah Quezado
De Dijn, Clemens G.
De Dominicis, Daniela
Dee, Elaine Evans
Deemer, Khalid J.
Deeters, Joachim
De Freitas, Leo John
De Girolami Cheney, Liana
De Grazia, Diane
De Grummond, Nancy Thomson
Deimling, Barbara
Dejardin, Fiona
De Jong, Ursula M.
De Jonge, Krista
Dekkers, Dieuwertje
Delaforce, Angela
Delaforce, John de F.
De la Fuente Pedersen, Eva
Delage, Anne-Marie
DeLaine, Janet
De La Mare, A. C.
Delbanco, Dawn Ho
Delettre, Patricia
Delgado, Lelia
Delivorrias, A.
Dell'Agli, Antonietta
Della Torre, Stefano
De Long, David G.
De Luca, Elena
De Maigret, Alessandro
Demanet, Marie
Demange, F.
De Medeiros, Melissa
D'Emilio, James
Demosfenova, Galina
Dempsey, Charles
Dendy, William
Denis, Isabelle
Denker, Ellen Paul
Dennison, L. E.
Denny, Don
Denny, Frederick Mathewson
Denny, Walter B.
Denton, Margaret Fields
Dentzer-Feydy, J.
Denwood, Philip
De Paoli, Geri
De Ren, Leo
Der Manuelian, Lucy
Der Manuelian, Peter
Deraniyagala, S. U.
Déroche, F.
Derrey-Capon, Danielle
Desai, Miki
Desai, Vishakha N.
Desai, Ziyaud-Din
Descalzi, Ricardo
Deshpande, M. N.
Desmond, Lawrence G.
De Sousberghe, Léon
Deswarte, Sylvie
Dethloff, Diana
Deuchar, Stephen
Deuer, Wilhelm
Deva, Krishna
Dever, W. G.
Devillers, Christian
De Villiers, Susan
Devisscher, Hans
De Vito, Giuseppe
de Vos, Dirk
Dewachi, Saeed al-
de Waele, Eric

Dewes, Ada
Dewey, William J.
De Winter, Patrick M.
De Witt, Eddy
Dhamo, Dhorka
Dharmasiri, Albert
Dias, Pedro
Díaz Vaquero, María Dolores
Diba, Layla S.
Di Castro Moscati, Daniela
Dickel, Hans
Dickie, James
Dickinson, O. T. P. K.
Di Cosmo, Nicola
Di Crocco, Virginia
Diebold, William J.
Diehl, Richard A.
Diemer, Dorothea
Diemer, Peter
Dien, Albert E.
Di Giacomo, Lia
Di Giampaolo, Mario
Dilet, Marc
Dillenberger, Jane Daggett
Dillow, Nancy E.
Dilly, Henrich
Dimitriou, S.
Dimitrokallis, G.
Dimmick, Lauretta
Dinesen, Betzy
Dinger, Brigittte
Dinsmoor, Anastasia N.
Dinsmoor Jr, William B.
Di Resta, Isabella
Diskul, M. C. Subhadradis
Distel, Anne
Distelberger, Rudolf
Dittrich, Christian
Dittscheid, Hans-Christoph
Di Vita, Antonino
Djordjević, Miodrag
Djurić, Srdjan
Dörig, José
Döring, Thomas
Dobson, Andrew
Dobson, Barrie
Dockstader, Frederick J.
Dodds, Jerrilynn D.
Dodge, Hazel
Dodier, Virginia
Dodsworth, Roger
D'Oench, Ellen G.
Dogaer, Georges
Dohanian, Diran Kavork
Doicescu, Andrei
Doig, Allan
Dolan, Therese
Dolbey, George
Dolinskaya, V. G.
Dolkart, Andrew Scott
Dolors Giral, Maria
Domansky, Ya. V.
Domenech, Fernando Benito
Donabédian, Patrick
Donati, Valentino
Donnelly, Marian C.
Donnithorne, Alan
D'Onofrio, Mario
Donovan, Claire
Doorman, S. J.
Dorman, Peter F.
Dorrell, Peter
Dossi, Barbara
Dothan, T.
Doud, Richard K.
Doumas, Christos G.
Dowling, Elizabeth Meredith

Downes, Kerry
Downs Jr, Arthur Channing
Drachenberg, Erhard
Dragone, Angelo
Drahotova, O.
Drakard, David
Draper, James David
Draper, Peter
Drapkin, Joshua
Drege, Jean-Pierre
Dreier, Franz Adrian
Dreiss, Joseph G.
Drenkhahn, Rosemarie
Drennan, Robert D.
Drescher, Timothy W.
Drew, Philip
Drewal, H. J.
Dreyer, Peter
Dreyfus, Hubert L.
Driel, A. E. van
Driscoll, John
Drobov, L. N.
Droin, Jacques
Drower, M. S.
Duarte, Carlos F.
Duarte, Eduardo
Dubois, Jacques
Du Boulay, Anthony
Duboy, Philippe
Düchting, Hajo
Duda, Dorothea
Duffett, Michael
Duffey, A. E.
Dugdale, Alice
Dugoni, Rita
Duke, James O.
Dumarçay, J.
Dumas, Charles
Dumas, Dominique M.
Du Mesnil, Hélène
Dumortier, Claire
Dunbabin, Katherine M. D.
Duncan, Kate C.
Dunkerton, Jill
Dunlevy, Mairead
Dunlop, Ian
Dunn, Archie
Dunn, Michael
Dunnett, James
Dunsmore, Susi
Duparc, Frederik J.
Du Pasquier, Jacqueline
Dupré, Marie-Claude
Dupuits, Petra
Dupuy, M.-A.
Durand-Revillon, Janine
Durey, Philippe
Duro, Paul
Durrans, Brian
Dutton, Denis
Duverger, Erik
Dwyer, Eugene
D'Yakov, L. A.
Dybdahl, Lars
Dynes, Wayne R.
Dyson, Anthony
Eagle, Mary
Earhart, H. Byron
Earl, John
Easby, Elizabeth K.
Easton, Donald F.
Eaton, Leonard K.
Eaton-Krauss, Marianne
Ebbinge, E.
Ebbink, Hans
Ebitz, David
Eckardt, Götz

Edelein-Badie, Beatrice
Edgren, Sören
Edmond, Mary
Edmonds, Richard Louis
Edmunds, Sheila
Edmundson, Roger S.
Edwards, Charles M.
Edwards, Deborah
Edwards, Geoffrey R.
Edwards, Lee M.
Edwards, Richard
Eerikäinen, Liisa
Egerton, Judy
Eggeling, T.
Ehnbom, Daniel J.
Ehrenkranz, Anne
Ehrlich, George
Eichberg, Michael
Eiche, Sabine
Eicher, Joanne Bubolz
Eidelberg, Martin
Eiland, Murray L.
Einholz, Sibylle
Eisman, Michael M.
Eissenhauer, Michael
Eitner, Lorenz
Ekkart, Rudolf E. O.
Ekserdjian, David
Elam, Caroline
Elgood, Robert
Elhanani, Aba
Elisonas, Jurgis
Elkan, Jenny
Ellenius, Allan
Ellias, Juanita M.
Elliott, Brent
Elliott, David
Elliott, J. H.
Ellis, Simon P.
Ellul, Michael
Elzea, Betty
Emanuel, Angela
Emerick, Judson
Emery, Marc
Eminger, Jürgen
Emison, Patricia
Emmanuel, Melita
Enescu, Theodor
Engel, Martin
Enggass, Robert
Enklaar, A. H.
Ennis, Helen
Ennis, Robert B.
Entz, Géza
Eogan, George
Eristov, Hélène
Erlande-Brandenburg, Alain
Ernstrom, Adele M.
Errington, E.
Ervamaa, Jukka
Erzini, Nadia
Esche, Annemarie
Escobar, Ticio
Escobari, Laura
Espinós Díaz, Adela
Essers, Volkmar
Estella, Margarita
Esteve, J.
Esther, J.-P.
Eswarin, Rudy
Etzlstorfer, Hannes
Euler-Rolle, Bernd
Euler-Schmidt, Michael
Eustace, Katharine
Evans, David
Evans, David
Evans, J. Wyn

Evans, Mark L.
Evans, Stuart
Evely, D.
Evelyn, Peta
Even, Yael
Ewals, L. J. I.
Ewert, Christian
Ewing, Dan
Ex, Sjarel
Exner, Matthias
Eyzaguirre, Pablo B.
Ezra, Kate
Faber, Annette
Faber-Castell, Christian von
Faberman, Hilarie
Fabian, Monroe H.
Fabregues, C.
Fabricand-Person, Nicole
Fabrizi, M.
Facos, Michelle
Fagerström, Raimo
Fagg, Bernard
Fahlman, Betsy
Fahy, Kevin
Fairbanks, Jonathan L.
Falck, Per
Falco, Luigi
Falino, Jeannine
Falk, Tilman
Falk, Toby
Fallon, Brian
Falz, Andreas
Fama, Giovanna
Fanning, Irene
Fantar, M'hamed
Fanu, Dolores le
Farago, Claire
Farber, Lisa
Fardon, Richard
Farhad, Massumeh
Faries, Molly
Farinati, Valeria
Faris, James C.
Farooqi, Anis
Faroqhi, Suraiya
Farr, D. Francine
Farrington, Jane
Farwell, Beatrice
Fassbind, Bernard
Fassio, Matilde
Faulkner, Rupert
Fausel, Alan
Favro, Diane
Fawcett, Richard
Fawcett, Trevor
Faxon, Alicia Craig
Fazzini, Richard A.
Feest, Christian F.
Feilden, Mary
Feinberg, Jean E.
Feinberg, Larry J.
Feinblatt, E.
Fekete, Julius
Feldman, Jerome
Feldmann, Dietrich
Feldmann, Hans-Christian
Fellows, Richard A.
Felsenstein, Frank
Feltham, Jane
Fenske, Gail
Férault, Marie-Agnès
Ferguson, Sarah
Fergusson, P. J.
Fern, Alan M.
Fernandes, José Manuel
Fernandes Pereira, José
Fernandez-Armesto, Felipe

Fernandez-Galiano, Luis
Fernandez-Puertas, Antonio
Fernie, Eric
Ferran, Brian
Ferrão, Leonor
Ferrante, Flavia
Ferrari, Anna Maria
Ferrari, Oreste
Ferrazza, Roberta
Ferreira Alves, Joaquim Jaime B.
Ferretti, Patrizia
Ferrillo, Lynn Boyer
Ferri Piccaluga, Gabriella
Feulner, Michaela
Ficher, Sylvia
Fidell-Beaufort, Madeleine
Fidler, Peter
Field, J. V.
Fields, Barbara S.
Figueras, Pau
Fillin-Yeh, Susan
Finaldi, Gabriele
Finch, Christopher
Finci, Predrag
Fine, Ruth E.
Finkenstaedt, E.
Finster, Barbara
Fioravanti Baraldi, Anna Maria
Fiore, Francesco Paolo
Fiorini, Stanley
Fiorio, Maria Teresa
Firmani, Domenico G.
Firth, Mark
Fischer, Eberhard
Fischer, Erik
Fischer, Fritz
Fischer, Henry G.
Fischer, Pieter M.
Fischer, Volker
Fisher, Ian
Fisher, Roger C.
Fister, Patricia
Fitchett, R. H.
Fitton, J. Lesley
Fitzgerald, Desmond, The
   Knight of Glin
Fitzgerald, Oscar P.
Fitzhugh, Elisabeth West
Flagg, Peter J.
Fleischer, Roland E.
Fleming, John A.
Fleming, Zara
Flescher, Sharon
Fletcher, Doris
Fletcher, Valerie J.
Flintholm, Michael
Floyd, Margaret Henderson
Floyd, Phylis
Fogelmark, Stig
Foister, Susan
Folda, Jaroslav
Foley, Christopher
Folie, Jacqueline
Follett, Jean A.
Folsach, Kjeld von
Fong Wen
Fontana, Vincenzo
Fontana Amoretti, Maria
Fontanella, Lee
Fontbona de Vallescar,
   Francesc
Fontcuberta, Joan
Fontein, Jan
Foo Ah Fong
Ford, Barbara
Ford, Brinsley

Ford, John
Ford, Mary Margaret McDonnell
Foresta, Merry A.
Fornari Schianchi, L.
Forrer, Matthi
Forrest, M. A.
Förster, Till
Forsyth, Michael
Fort, Ilene Susan
Fortenberry, C. D.
Forter, F.
Foss, Brian
Foss, Paul
Fossier, François
Fosu, Kojo
Fouace, Jean
Fowle, Diana
Fowler, Catherine S.
Fowler, James
Fox, Gretchen G.
Fox, John W.
Fox, Ross
Fox, Stephen
Foxley, W. C.
Foy, Lydia
Frabetti, Alessandra
Fracchia, Carmen
Frampton, Kenneth
França, José-Augusto
Francastel, Galienne
Francfort, Henri-Paul
Franchini, Lucio
Franchini Guelfi, Fausta
Franco Calvo, Enrique
Franco Mata, Angela
Francova, Zuzana
Frangi, Francesco
Frangipane, Marcella
Franits, Wayne
Frank, Barbara E.
Frank, Samuel Berkman
Franz, Erich
Franz, Gunther
Franz-Duhme, H. N.
Franzke, Andreas
Franzoni, Lanfranco
Fraquelli, Simonetta
Fraser, David
Fraser, Valerie
Fraser-Lu, Sylvia
Frashëri, Gjergj
Frashëri, Kristo
Fraunlob, Sieglinde
Fredericq-Lilar, Marie
Fredriksson, Inge
Free, Renée
Freed, Rita E.
Freeman, Ann
Frehner, Matthias
Frehner-Bühler, Christina
Frei, Hans
Frei, Urs-B.
Freitag, Wolfgang M.
Freixas, Pere
French, David
French, Jean M.
French, Peter
Freuler, Gaudenz
Frey, Julia Bloch
Frey, O.-H.
Freyberger, K.
Frezzotti, Stefania
Friedeberger, Julie
Friedman, Alice T.
Friedman, Joan Isobel
Friedman, Terry

Friedrich, Annegret
Frodl, Gerbert
Frodl-Schneemann, Marianne
Frommel, Christoph Luitpold
Frosinini, Cecilia
Fruhan, Catherine
Fry, Gavin
Frykenstedt, Holger
Fu Shen
Fuchs, Ron
Fuchs, Werner
Fuente, Beatriz de la
Fuller, John
Fullerton, Mark D.
Fulton, Torbjörn
Fumagalli, Elena
Fung, Christopher
Fung, Stanislaus
Furman-Sosnovsky, Silvina
Furness, N. A.
Fynes, R. C. C.
Fyodorov, S. G.
Gaballa, G. A.
Gabelić, Smiljka
Gabetti, Roberto
Gabler, Josephine
Gabor, Eszter
Gaborit, Jean-René
Gaborit-Chopin, Danielle
Gadbery, Laura M.
Gaehde, Joachim E.
Gaeta Bertelà, G.
Gagnon, François-Marc
Gail, Adalbert J.
Gailani Werr, Lamia al-
Gaisbauer, Ulrike
Gajewski, Jacek
Galactéros-de Boissier, Lucie
Galassi, Maria Clelia
Galatariotou, Catia
Galavics, Géza
Galbally, Ann
Galdieri, Eugenio
Gale, Matthew
Galicki, Marta
Galindo, Natividad
Galinie, Henri
Gallagher, Shana
Gallet, Danielle
Gallois Duquette, Danielle
Gallop, Annabel Teh
Galvin, C. A.
Gamble, Clive
Ganshorn, Jørgen
Garas, Klara
Garb, Tamar
García Barragan, Elisa
García Sáiz, Maria Concepción
García Vega, Blanca
Gardberg, C. J.
Gardi, Bernhard
Gardiner, Patrick
Gardner, Genetta
Gardner, Sebastian
Gardner, Stephen
Garlake, P. S.
Garms, Jörg
Garner, William
Garnett, Oliver
Garofoli, Marina
Garrido, Esperanza
Garstang, Donald
Garton, Tessa
Garvan, Beatrice B.
Gary, Abigail Schade
Garzelli, Annarosa
Gash, John

Gast, Nicolette
Gastinel-Coural, Chantal
Gąsiorowski, Eugeniusz
Gaston, Robert W.
Gatellier, Marie
Gathercole, Peter
Gauk-Roger, Nigel
Gaur, Albertine
Gauthier, Raymonde
Gavel, Jonas
Gavrilović, Zaga
Gawne, Eleanor
Gay, Sophie Anne
Gayle, Margot
Gaynor, Suzanne
Gaze, Delia
Geary, Christraud M.
Gebhard, David
Gebhard, Elizabeth R.
Geddes, Helen
Geddes, Jane
Geddes, Laurence Guilmard
Gee, Malcolm
Geerts, Ton
Geiger, Ursula
Geipel, Robert
Geis, Walter
Geissler, Heinrich
Gelao, Clara
Gelfer-Jørgensen, Mirjam
Gellér, Katalin
Gem, Richard
Gemin, Massimo
Gendrop, Paul
Geneve, Vyonne
Genout, Jean Claude
Gentilini, Giancarlo
Georgel, Pierre
Georgi, Bettina
Gerard-Powell, Véronique
Gerbod, Paul
Gerbrands, A. A.
Gere, Charlotte
Gergova, Ivanka
Gerhart, A.
Gerhardt, Karen M.
Germann, Georg
Germanò Siracusa, Donatella
Gerszi, Teréz
Gertsen, A. G.
Gesko, Judit
Gessler-Löhr, Beatrix
Ghazaryan, Manya
Ghirardi, Angela
Ghisetti Giavarina, Adriano
Giacobbe, Luigi
Giannoudaki, Tonia P.
Gibba, Alessandra
Gibbs, Moira
Gibbs, Peter
Gibbs, Robert
Gibson, Jennifer
Gibson, Peter
Gibson, Sarah Scott
Giese, Lucretia H.
Giffi Ponzi, Elisabetta
Gilbert, Christopher
Gilbert, Creighton E.
Giles, Laura M.
Gili, Marta
Gill, David W. J.
Gill, Margaret A. V.
Gill, Meredith J.
Gill, Stephen J.
Gillerman, Dorothy
Gillmor, R. Douglas
Gilmour, Pat

Giltaij, J.
Ginex, Giovanna
Ginkel, J. van
Ginsburg, Henry
Giordano, Luisa
Giot, P. R.
Giraud, Demosthenis G.
Giraudon, Colette
Gisbert, Teresa
Gisler, Johanna
Gisolfi, Diana
Gittinger, Mattiebelle
Giusti, Annamaria
Giusti Maccari, Patrizia
Given, Michael
Glahn, Else
Glanville, Philippa
Glaser, Silvia
Glass, Dorothy F.
Glass-Forest, Marie-Therese
Glassner, Gottfried
Glaves-Smith, John
Glenn, Constance W.
Glendinning, James
Glendinning, Nigel
Glinton, Patricia
Gloor, Lukas
Glover, Ian
Glusberg, Jorge
Glynn, Catherine
Gmelin, Hans Georg
Goad, Philip
Gockerell, Nina
Godby, Michael
Goddard, Stephen H.
Godla, Joseph J.
Goeneutte, Norbert Georges
Goepper, Roger
Goerner, Doris
Goetz, Thalie
Goff Hill, Clare
Goldberg, David J.
Goldberg, Edward L.
Goldberg, Gisela
Goldberg, Roselee
Goldberg, Stephen J.
Goldin, Grace
Goldman, Shifra M.
Gole, Susan
Gollek, Rosel
Golombek, Lisa
Golvin, Lucien
Golzio, Karl-Heinz
Gombar, Thomas J.
Gomes Machado, José Alberto
Gomme, Andor
Gonnella, Julia
González-Arnal, María Antonia
González Pozo, Alberto
Goodall, John A.
Goodall-Cristante, Hollis
Goodchild, Anne L.
Goodden, Angelica
Goode, Patrick
Gooding, Mel
Goodlett, Virginia C.
Goodman, Cynthia
Goodman, Nelson
Goodman, Susan T.
Goodwin, Godfrey
Goodwin, Shauna
Gorbunova, N. G.
Gordon, Alden R.
Gordon, Catherine M.
Gordon, Dillian
Gordon, Ethelyn Adina

Gordon, George
Gordon, Stephen C.
Gorelik, M. V.
Goring, Elizabeth
Gorokhoff, Galina
Gorse, George L.
Goryacheva, V. D.
Gosling, David
Goss, Peter L.
Gossman, Lionel
Goswamy, B. N.
Goswamy, Karuna
Gottskálksdottir, Juliana
Götz, Norbert
Gough, Mary
Gould, Cecil
Gould, Karen
Gournay, Isabelle
Govier, Louise
Gow, Ian
Gowans, Alan
Goy, Richard J.
Gozak, Andrey
Grabar, Oleg
Grabow, Stephen
Gradidge, Roderick
Graeve, V. von
Graf, Dieter
Grafik, Imre
Graham, Clare
Graham, Mary E.
Graham, Patricia J.
Graham-Campbell, James
Grainger, Hilary J.
Grajewski, Tadeusz
Granath, Olle
Grandi, R.
Grandry-Pradel, Marie-Noëlle de
Granger-Taylor, Hero
Grant, Ian
Grant, Lindy
Grapard, Allan G.
Grate, Pontus
Grauerholz, James W.
Graulich, Gerhard
Gravett, Christopher
Gravgaard, Anne-Mette
Gray, Anne
Gray, Basil
Gray, Jocelyn Fraillon
Green, Anthony
Green, A. S. G.
Green, Christopher
Green, Evelyne
Green, Jerald R.
Green, Malcolm
Green, R. C.
Green, Richard
Green, Richard C.
Greenewalt Jr, Crawford H.
Greenhalgh, Michael
Greenhouse, Wendy
Greenspan, Taube G.
Greenthal, Kathryn
Greenwood, Martin
Greeves, T. Affleck
Greg, Andrew
Gregory, Sharon
Greiff, Constance M.
Grekov, Aleksandr U.
Grese, Robert E.
Gresty, Hilary
Grieder, Terence
Griener, Pascal
Griffin, David
Griffin, Leonard R.

Griffith, Paul
Griffiths, Jeremy
Grigsby, Leslie B.
Grijzenhout, Frans
Grim, John
Grimaldi, Floriano
Grindstaff, B. K.
Grisebach, Lucius
Griseri, Angela
Grishin, Alexander
Griswold, William
Grivel, Marianne
Gröbold, Güter
Grodecki, Catherine
Groen, Karin
Groenendael, Victoria M. Clara van
Gronberg, Tag
Groot, Agnes
Groseclose, Barbara
Grosheide, Danielle
Grössinger, Christa
Grossmann, Dieter
Grossman, Elizabeth
Grossman, Janet Burnett
Grossmann, Peter
Grotenhuis, Elizabeth ten
Grove, David C.
Groves, Laura
Grube, Alberta Fabris
Grube, Ernst J.
Gruber, Alain
Gruber, Pia
Gruffydd, Llyr D.
Grunenberg, Christoph
Grunewald, Marie-Antoinette
Guardia, M.
Gubel, Eric
Gubler, Hans Martin
Guéné-Loyer, Hélène
Guenther, Peter W.
Guerman, Mikhail
Guicharnaud, Hélène
Guillaume, Jean
Guillaume, Marguerite
Guillén-Nuñez, César
Guillermo, Alice G.
Guillon, Emmanuel
Gulik, Willem van
Gullick, C. J. M. R.
Gullick, Michael
Gunasinghe, Siri
Gunawardane, W. Thelma T. P.
Gunnarsjaa, Arne
Gunnarsson, Torsten
Guralnik, Nehama
Gurland, Penelope
Gurney, George
Gurock, Elisabeth
Guth, Christine M. E.
Gutiérrez, Ramon
Gutiérrez, Rebeca
Gutiérrez Buron, Jesus
Gutiérrez Pastor, Ismael
Gutiérrez Solana, Nelly
Gutman, Pamela
Gutmann, Joseph
Guy, John
Gwete, Lema
Gyllensvärd, B. V.
Gyss-Vermande, Caroline
Haber, Alicia
Haberland, Irene
Habermann, Sylvia
Habicht-Mauche, Judith A.
Hachlili, Rachel
Hachmann, R.

Hack, Angelica
Hackenbroch, Yvonne
Hadermann-Misguich, Lydie
Hadidi, Adnan
Haerinck, E.
Haese, Richard
Haffner, Pierre
Hägele, Hannelore
Hagen, Bernt von
Hagenmann-Bischoff, Marion
Hager, Hellmut
Hägg, Robin
Haggarty, G. R.
Haglund, Elisabet
Hague, Judy
Hahn, Joachim
Hajos, Géza
Hak Srea Kuoch
Halbauer, Karl
Hale, David
Halkerston, Merrill
Hall, Ivan
Hall, Margaret
Hall, Marjorie Jean
Hall, Thomas
Hallam, John S.
Halliday, Nigel Vaux
Hallisey, Charles
Halliwell, Kevin
Halsby, Julian
Halsema-Kubes, Wilhelmina
Halsey, Richard
Hambourg, Maria Morris
Hamel, Christopher de
Hamilton, James
Hamilton, Paul C.
Hamilton-Phillips, Martha
Hamlyn, Robin
Hammond, Martin D. P.
Hammond, Philip C.
Hamon, Françoise
Hand, John Oliver
Handler, Sarah
Hankey, Vronwy
Hanlon, Gordon
Hannesen, Hans Gerhard
Hannesschläger, Ingonda
Hannestad, N.
Hannoosh, Michele
Hansen, Donald P.
Hansen, Trudy V.
Hansman, John
Hanson, Brian
Hanson, F. Allan
Hanson, Julienne
Haraksingh, Kusha
Harber, Rodney
Harboe, Julie
Hardering, Klaus
Hardgrave Jr, Robert L.
Hardie, Charles
Hardie, Peter
Harding, A. F.
Harding, Catherine
Hardtwig, Barbara
Hardy, Adam
Hardy, J.
Hargrove, June
Harker, Margaret
Harley, Cate
Harley, R. D.
Harley Jr, R. L.
Harness, Jessica
Harper, Roger H.
Harprath, Richard
Harpur, Yvonne
Harris, Ann Sutherland

Harris, Clare
Harris, C. M.
Harris, Diane
Harris, Jennifer
Harris, John
Harris, Jonathan
Harris, Mary Emma
Harris, Richard
Harrison, Colin
Harrison, Helen A.
Harrison, J. B.
Harrist Jr, Robert E.
Harrod, Tanya
Harrop-Allin, Clinton
Hart, Vaughan
Härting, Ursula
Hartley, Craig
Hartney, Mick
Hartog, E. den
Hartop, Christopher
Harvey, Eleanor Jones
Harvey, Jacqueline Colliss
Harvey, Sheila
Harwood, L. B. L.
Hasan, Perween
Hasebe, Mitsuhiko
Haselberger, Lothar
Hasemann, Gloria Lara de
Hase-Schmundt, U. v.
Hashmi, Salima
Haskell, Barbara
Haskell, Larissa
Hasler, Norbert W.
Hassall, Catherine
Hassler, Donna J.
Hasson, Rachel
Hatano, Hiroyuki
Hattersley-Smith, Kara
Haucap-Nass, A.
Hauge, Takako
Hauge, Victor
Haunton, Katharina Mayer
Haupenthal, Uwe
Haupt, H.
Hauptman, William
Haverkamp, Ernst
Haviland, William A.
Hawkes, H. W.
Hawkins, J. D.
Hawley, Henry
Haworth-Booth, Mark
Hay, Kenneth G.
Hayashi, Sae
Hayes, J. W.
Hayes, Jeffrey R.
Haynes, Deborah J.
Hayter, William
Hazlehurst, F. Hamilton
Head, Raymond
Headley, Janet A.
Hearnden, Warren
Heath, D. Michael
Heath, Kingston Wm.
Heathcote, David
Heber-Suffrin, F.
Heck, Christian
Heck, Michele-Caroline
Hedin, Thomas F.
Hedreen, Guy
Heesakkers, Chris L.
Hefting, Victorine
Heiden, Rüdiger an der
Heij, Jan Jaap
Heijbroek, J. F.
Heijn, Annemarie Vels
Heim, Bruno B.
Hein, Jørgen

Heiner, Leslie
Heinlen, M.
Heinz, Bernard
Heinz, Dora
Heinz, Günther
Heinz, Marianne
Heinze-Greenberg, Ita
Heinzl, Brigitte
Heisner, Beverly
Heitel, Suzana More
Helas, Volker
Held Jr, John
Helffer, Mireille
Helland, Janice
Heller, Amy
Heller, Martin
Heller, Nancy G.
Heller, Reinhold
Hellermann, Dorothée von
Helliesen, Sidsel
Hellinga, Helma
Hellman, Louis
Hellmann, Marie Christine
Hellström, P.
Hellyer, M.-E.
Helmreich-Schoeller, Irene
Helms, Dietrich
Helsted, Dyveke
Hemelrijk, J. M.
Hemsoll, David
Henderson, Linda Dalrymple
Hendricks, William L.
Hendrix, Lee
Henig, Martin
Henkels, H.
Hennessy, J. B.
Henrickson, Robert C.
Henry, Jay C.
Hensbroek-van der Poel, D. B.
Henze, Ulrich
Herbenova, Olga
Herbert, Eugenia
Herbert, Gilbert
Herbert, Patricia M.
Herchenröder, Christian
Herding, Klaus
Hereniko, Vilsoni
Heres, Gerald
Hériard Dubreuil, Mathieu
Herman, Bernard L.
Hermary, A.
Hernad, Béatrice
Herrbach, Brigitte
Herrera, Hayden
Herrin, Judith
Herrmann, G.
Herrmann, Wolfgang
Herrmann-Fichtenau, Elisabeth
Hersak, Dunja
Herz, Alexandra
Heseltine, J.
Hess, Catherine
Hessellund, Birgit
Hessert, Marlis von
Heston, M. E.
Hetherington, Paul
Hewitt, Virginia H.
Hewlings, Richard
Heym, Sabine
Heyman, Jacques
Heywood, Stephen
Hichberger, Joan
Hickey, Gerald
Hickey, Gloria
Hickman, B.
Hicks, Carola
Hiemer, Astrid A.

Hiener, Theresa A.
Hieronymus, Frank
Higgins, Reynold
Higginson, Peter
Higgitt, John
Higgs, Malcolm
Highfield, J. R. L.
Hijara, Ismail
Hild-Ziem, Eric
Hildebrand, Grant
Hildebrand, Josephine
Hildyard, Robin
Hilger, Hans Peter
Hill, David
Hill, Lewis G.
Hill, Stephen
Hillebrand, Melanie
Hillenbrand, Robert
Hiller, Stefan
Hillis, Maurice
Hills, Helen M.
Hills-Nova, Clare
Hilton, Jeffrey
Himmelfarb, Hélène
Hinchcliffe, Tanis
Hind, Charles Wheelton
Hind, John
Hindman, Sandra L.
Hinks, Peter
Hintz, Karsten
Hinzler, H. I. R.
Hiort, Esbjørn
Hirsch, Erhard
Hirthe, Thomas
Hitchcock, Michael
Hjort, Ø.
Ho Chuan-Hsing
Ho Chuimei
Ho, Molly Siuping
Ho Puay-Peng
Hobart, Angela
Hobbs, Richard
Hobey-Hamsher, C.
Hobhouse, Hermione
Hoch, Adrian S.
Hochberg, Julian
Hochmann, Michel
Hodge, A. Trevor
Hoek, Frank van den
Hoekstra, Tarq
Hoeniger, Cathleen
Hoepfner, Wolfram
Hoeve, J. A. van der
Hoey, Lawrence R.
Hoff, Ursula
Hoffman, Barbara
Hoffman, Eva R.
Hoffman, Gail L.
Hoffmann, Edith
Hoffmann, V.
Höfler, Janez
Hofrichter, Frima Fox
Hofstätter, Hans H.
Hogarth, Paul
Hogg, Ian V.
Hojer, Gerhard
Holck Colding, Torben
Holden, Wheaton A.
Holder, Philancy N.
Holderbaum, James
Holdsworth, Christopher
Holladay, Joan A.
Hollenstein, Roman
Holler, Wolfgang
Holliday, Peter J.
Holman, Valerie
Holmes, Mary Tavener

Holmes, Tommy
Holt, Stephen
Holyoak, Joe
Holzschuh, Gottfried
Homolka, Jaromír
Hong, Sŏn-P'Yo
Honig, Elizabeth Alice
Hood, Sinclair
Hood, William
Hoog, Michel
Hoog, Simone
Hoogenboom, Annemieke
Hooker, Denise
Hooper, Steven
Hoople, Sally C.
Hoover, Deborah A.
Hoozee, Robert
Hope, Charles
Höper, C.
Hopfner, Rosemarie
Hopkins, Henry T.
Hopkins, John
Hopkins, Justine
Hoppen, Gisela
Hoppe-Sailer, Richard
Horat, Heinz
Horat-Weber, Jeanne-Marie
Hořejší, Jiřina
Horie, C. V.
Horn Fuglesang, Signe
Hornsby, Peter
Horrocks, Roger
Horsch, Femy
Horta Correia, José Eduardo
Horton, H. Mack
Hossack, Rebecca
Hossain, Hameeda
Hossmann, Gisela
Hostyn, Norbert
Houfe, Simon
Housego, Jenny
Hovell, John
Hovstadius, Barbro
Howard, Deborah
Howard, Jeremy
Howard, Maurice
Howard, Michael
Howard, Peter Wren
Howard, Seymour
Howarth, David
Howe, Eunice D.
Howe, Thomas Noble
Howell, Peter
Howlett, Jana
Hrouda, B.
Hrubý, Vladimír
Hubbard, Edward
Huber, Kalinka
Huber, Wolfgang
Hubert, Gérard
Hubert, Hans
Huchard, Viviane
Hucker, Jacqueline
Huffman, K. W.
Hüfler, Brigitte
Hugarte, Renzo Pi
Hughes, Anthony
Hughes, Jeffrey A.
Hughes, Lindsey
Hughes, Peter
Hughes, Quentin
Hull, Judith S.
Hülsen, A. V.
Hulton, Paul
Humfrey, Peter
Humphrey, J. H.
Humphreys, Charlotte

Humphreys, Richard
Humphreys, R. Stephen
Hungerford, Constance Cain
Hunisak, John M.
Hunt, Geoffrey
Hunt, John Dixon
Hunt, Lucy-Anne
Hunt, Susan
Hunter, John
Hunting, P. S.
Huntington, Susan L.
Huntington-Whiteley, James
Huntsman, Judith
Huot, Jean-Louis
Hurel, Roselyne
Hurwit, Jeffrey M.
Husband, Timothy B.
Hutchings, Patrick
Hutchinson, John
Hutchinson, Valerie J.
Hutchison, Jane Campbell
Hüter, Karl-Heinz
Hutton, Paula
Huvenne, Paul
Huyler, Stephen P.
Hyde, Ralph
Hye, Franz-Heinz
Hyerace, Luigi
Hyland, Alice R. M.
Hyman, James
Hyman, John
Hyvönen, Heikki
Iizawa, Kohtaro
Ikonnikov, A. V.
Illouz, Claire
Imaeda, Yoshiro
Immerwahr, Henry R.
Impey, Oliver
Improta Romano, Christina
Inagaki, Eizo
Ingamells, John
Inglis, Alison
Ingólfsson, Aððalsteinn
Ingram, T. L.
Innemée, Karel C.
Ionescu, Radu
Iovleva, L. I.
Irace, Fulvio
Irmscher, Günter
Irvine, Louise
Irving, Robert
Irwin, Francina
Irwin, Robert
Isaacs, Jennifer
Isaacson, Joel
Isaacson, John S.
Ishibashi, Chie
Isler-de-Jongh, Ariane
Isphording, Eduard
Ito, Nobuo
Iturgaiz, Domingo
Ivanov, A. A.
Ivanov, Bojan
Ivelić, Milan
Iversen, Erik
Ivey, Paul Eli
Iwasaki, Yoshikazu
Jaccard, Paul-André
Jacks, Philip J.
Jackson, Neil
Jacob, Brigitte
Jacobowitz, Ellen S.
Jacobs, Alain
Jacobs, Lynn F.
Jacobsen, Werner
Jacobson, Esther

Jacobus, Laura
Jacoby, Beverley Schreiber
Jacqué, Bernard
Jacq-Hergoualc'h, Michel
Jacquiot, Josephe
Jaeger, Kate
Jaén, Omar
Jaffe, Irma B.
Jaffé, David
Jaffé, Michael
Jagger, Cedric
Jahnke, Robert H. G.
Jain, Jyotindra
Jain-Neubauer, Jutta
Jamal, Sayed Ahmad
James, Josef
James, Kathleen
James, L.
James, Simon
James, T. G. H.
Jameson, Rob
Jamkhedkar, A. P.
Janis, Eugenia Parry
Jankova, Yvonne
Jannot, J.-R.
Jansen, Dirk J.
Jansen, G.
Jansen, Virginia
Jansma, Linda
Janson, Anthony F.
Jansson, Ingmar
Jashemski, Wilhelmina F.
Jasmin, Denise
Jaszai, Géza
Jauhiainen, Pirkko
Javellana, R.
Javor, A.
Jaworska, Władysława-Jadwiga
Jay, Martin
Jay, Robert
Jay, Sian E.
Jayatilleke, K. Hemantha
Jedding, Hermann
Jeffers, Wendy
Jeffree, Richard
Jeffrey, Sally
Jenderko-Sichelschmidt, Ingrid
Jenkins, David Fraser
Jenkins, Susan
Jenkinson, David
Jenkyns, Richard
Jensen, Carole A.
Jensen, Jens Christian
Jera-Bezard, Robert
Jernigan, E. Wesley
Jeroussalimskaja, Anna
Jervis, Simon
Jeske, Bettina
Jessup, Helen Ibbitson
Jestaz, Bertrand
Jeżewska, Maria
Jidejian, Nina
Jiménez-Blanco, M. Dolores
Jin Ying
Jirat-Wasiutyński, Vojtěch
Jodogne, Pierre
Joest, Thomas von
Johannesen, Eric
Johannsen, Hugo
Johansen, Flemming
Johansen, Katia
John, Eleanor
John, Richard
Johns, Catherine
Johns, Elizabeth
Johns, Karl T.
Johnson, Boyd

Johnson, Cecile
Johnson, Cesare
Johnson, Dale T.
Johnson, Danielle Valin
Johnson, Ellen H.
Johnson, Faith
Johnson, Fridolf
Johnson, Heather
Johnson, Jan
Johnson, Lewis
Johnson, Marion
Johnson, Stephen
Johnson, Vivien
Johnston, Alan
Johnston, Alexa M.
Johnston, Norman J.
Johnston, Roy
Johnston, Sona K.
Johnston, William R.
Johnston, W. T.
Johnstone, Pauline
Jokinen, Teppo
Jonaitis, Aldona
Jones, Adam
Jones, Ann
Jones, Caroline A.
Jones, David
Jones, David M.
Jones, D. Signe
Jones, Laura Hickman
Jones, Malcolm
Jones, Mark
Jones, M. Wilson
Jones, Pamela M.
Jones, Peter Blundell
Jones, Stephen
Jones, Ursula
Jong, J. L. de
Jonkanski, Dirk
Jonker, Michiel
Jonsdottir, Selma
Joo Nam Chull
Jordan, Brenda G.
Jordan, Marc
Jordan, Marc-H.
Jordan, William B.
Jörg, C. J. A.
Jörgens-Lendrum, Helga
Jornæs, Bjarne
Joshi, M. C.
Joslyn, Catherine R.
Jottrand, Mireille
Joubert, Fabienne
Jouffre, Valérie-Noëlle
Jowell, Frances S.
Joy, Clair
Juhl, Susanne
Julián, Inmaculada
Jungmann, Burglind
Jurkowski, Henryk
Justić, Josefine
Kabierske, Gerhard
Kachur, Lewis
Kader, Alexander
Kadiroğlu, Mine
Kaellgren, C. Peter
Kaenel, Philippe
Kaeppler, Adrienne L.
Kafesçioğlu, Çiğlu
Kagan, Andrew
Kagan, Richard L.
Kahle, Barbara
Kahn, Deborah
Kaimal, Padma
Kairis, Pierre-Yves
Kalantzopoulou, Stamatia
Kalashnik, Yu. P.

Kalenberg, Angel
Kalinowski, Konstanty
Kalligas, H. A.
Kalman, Harold
Kalus, Ludvik
Kamerling, Bruce
Kamp, Netty van de
Kandeler-Fritsch, Martina
Kane, Barbara B.
Kane, Carolyn
Kane, Susan
Kane, Thomas A.
Kang Woo-Bang
Kantor, Helene J.
Kao, Mayching
Kapelos, George
Kaplan, Julius
Kaplan, Paul H. D.
Kappelhof, A. C. M.
Kapur, Geeta
Karel, David
Katev, Andrey A.
Karl, Thomas
Karlsson, Lennart
Karlstrom, Paul J.
Karunaratne, L. K.
Kasfir, Sidney Littlefield
Kashiwagi, Hiroshi
Kasinec, E.
Katinsky, Julio Roberto
Katzarova, Mariana
Kauffmann, C. M.
Kauffmann, Martin
Kaufman, Peter S.
Kaufman, Susan Harrison
Kaufmann, Thomas Dacosta
Kaufmann, Virginia Roehrig
Kavan, Katrina
Kavanagh, Amanda
Kawai, Masamoto
Kawami, Trudy S.
Kazakova, L. V.
Keall, E. J.
Keber, Eloise Quiñones
Keeler, Nancy B.
Keeler, Ward
Keen, Ian
Keene, Alice
Kehl-Baierle, Sabine
Keim, Curtis A.
Keinänen, Timo
Kelleher, Claire
Keller, C. A.
Keller, Fritz-Eugen
Kelly, Alison
Kelly, Cathie C.
Kelly, Franklin
Kelly, Margaret
Kelly-Buccellati, Marilyn
Kemp, Martin
Kempers, B.
Kemp-Welch, Wanda
Kendall, Ann
Kendall, M. Sue
Kendall, Timothy
Kenna, Carol
Kennedy, Alexandra
Kennedy, Carolee G.
Kennett, David H.
Kent, F. W.
Kent, Neil
Kenworthy-Browne, John
Kenyon, J. R.
Kern, Sepp
Kernot, Bernard
Kern-Terheyden, Susanne
Kerr, Minott

Leistra, J. E. P.
Leith-Ross, Prudence
Le Loup, W.
Lemaistre, Isabelle
Lemerle-Pauwels, F.
Lemire, Robert
Lemke, Antje B.
Lemmen, Hans van
Lemoine, Serge
Lemos, Carlos A. C.
Lemos, Natasha
Leng, Yeoh Jin
Leniaud, Jean-Michel
Lenman, Robin
Le Normand-Romain,
    Antoinette
Lenz, Christian
Lenz, John R.
Leonard, Robert
Leonardis, Virginia
Leoncini, Luca
Leone de Castris, Pierluigi
Leonelli, Marie-Claude
Leonor d'Orey, Maria
Leoussi, Athena S. E.
Leprohon, R. J.
Leri, Jean-Marc
Leslie, Jolyon
Leslie, Michael
Lespes, Michelle
Le Tagaloa, Aiono Fanaafi
Lettens, Hugo
Leuchak, Rebecca
Leurs, Gloria C.
Leuschner, Vera
Levalley, Paul
Levenson, Jay A.
Leventi, I.
Lever, Jill
Leveto, Paula D.
Levey, Santina M.
Levi, Donata
Levin, Gail
Levine, David A.
Levinson, Jerrold
Levinson, Ye. Ye.
Lewandowski, Felicia
Lewcock, Ronald
Lewis, Adrian
Lewis, Beth Irwin
Lewis, Darrell
Lewis, Douglas
Lewis, Elaine T.
Lewis, Elizabeth Bruening
Lewis, John Newel
Lewis, Michael J.
Lewis, Michal
Lewis, Miles
Lewis, R. E.
Lewis, Suzanne
Lewis-Williams, J. D.
Lewison, Jeremy
Leyenaar, T. J. J.
Lezzi-Hafter, Adrienne
Li Chu-Tsing
Li Liu
Li Xueqin
Lichte, Claudia
Lichtenstern, Christa
Licka, C. E.
Lidén, Hans-Emil
Lieber, Vincent
Liebl, Ulrike
Liedtke, Walter
Lietzmann, Hilda
Lightbown, R. W.
Liivak, Anu

Lillehoj, Elizabeth
Lilley, E. D.
Lillie, Amanda
Lim, Jon S. H.
Limouze, Dorothy
Linant de Bellefonds, Pascale
Linda, Mary F.
Linde, Brita
Linde, Gunilla
Lindemann, Bernd Wolfgang
Lindley, Phillip
Lindsay, Frances
Lindsay, Kenneth C.
Linfert, A.
Lingen, Joan K.
Link, A. M.
Linnebach, Andrea
Linstrum, Derek
Linton, Michael
Lipinska, Jadwiga
Lippincott, Kristen
Lippincott, Louise
Lipton, Leah
Liscombe, R. Windsor
Lishka, Dennis
Lisot, Elizabeth A.
Liss, Andrea
Lissner, Erhard
Lister, Raymond
Littauer, M. A.
Little, Bryan
Little, Charles T.
Little, Doina
Little, Nancy C.
Little, Stephen L.
Litvak King, Jaime
Liversidge, M. J. H.
Livet, Anne
Livingstone, Marco
Livshits, M. Ya.
Llewellyn, Briony
Llewellyn-Jones, Rosie
Llompart, Gabriel
Lloyd, Christopher
Lloyd, Jill
Lloyd, Joan E. Barclay
Lloyd, Seton
Lloyd, Stephen
Lloyd-Morgan, Ceridwen
Lloyd-Morgan, G.
Loach, J. D.
Lobanov-Rostovsky, Nina
Lobbedey, Uwe
Lobo, Wibke
Lo Bue, Erberto F.
Loche, Renée
Löcher, Kurt
Lochhead, Ian J.
Lochnan, Katharine A.
Lodder, Christina
Lodi, Letizia
Loeben, C. E.
Loeffler, Bruce M.
Logan, Anne-Marie S.
Lohman, Jack
Lohr, O.
Lohrey, Angela
Lohse Belkin, Kristin
Loire, Stéphane
Lombaerde-Fabri, Ria
Lombard, Vincent
Long, Christopher
Long, Clifford D.
Longmore, James
Longstreth, Richard
Loon, M. N. van
Looney, Dennis

Loos, Wiepke F.
Lopez Guzman, Rafael
López Rodríguez, Artur
Lopez y Royo Iyer, Alessandra
Lord, Peter
Lorenz, Hellmut
Lorenz, Marianne
Lorenz, Richard
Loring, John
Lo Schiavo, Fulvia
Loseries-Leick, Andrea
Losty, J. P.
Loten, H. Stanley
Loth, Calder
Lothe, José
Loughman, John
Loughran, Kristyne
Louw, Hentie
Lovag, Zsuzsa
Love, Iris Cornelia
Loveday, Helen
Lovcrance, Rowcna
Lovring, Rigmor
Low, Jill
Lowden, John
Lowe, Jeremy
Lowell, Joann
Lowenthal, Anne W.
Loyer, François
Łoziński, Jerzy Z.
Lubbock, Lucinda
Lübbren, Nina
Lucchesi, Silvia
Lucco, Mauro
Luchs, Alison
Luckett, Richard
Luckhardt, Jochen
Luckyj, Natalie
Lüdke, Dietmar
Luijten, Ger
Lujan, Rudolpho
Luján-Muñoz, Jorge
Luke, Yvonne
Lukehart, Peter M.
Lukitsh, Joanne
Lukkarinen, Ville
Lumsden, Ian G.
Luna, Juan J.
Lund, Hakon
Lund, Nils-Ole
Lunning, Elizabeth
Lunniss, Richard
Lunt, Sara
Lupano, Mario
Lupia, John N.
Luther, E.
Luxenberg, Alisa
Lyas, Colin
Lyles, Anne
Lyman, Thomas W.
Lymbery, Etrenne
Lynch, Brendan
Lyttelton, Margaret
Maas, Jeremy
Macaulay, James
McBurney, Henrietta
McCall, Grant
McCallum, Donald F.
McCane-O'Connor, Mallory
McCarthy, Michael
McCarthy, Michael R.
McCaughey, Patrick
McCauley, Elizabeth Anne
McChesney, Robert D.
McClanan, Anne
MacClancy, Jeremy
McClellan, Andrew

McClendon, Charles B.
McClintock, Kathryn Marie
McClintock, Martha J.
McCombie, Grace
McConkey, Kenneth
McCormick, Melissa
McCormick, Thomas J.
McCorquodale, Charles
McCrum, Sean
Maccubbin, R. P.
McDonald, Aya Louisa
MacDonald, Margaret F.
MacDonald, William L.
MacDougall, Elisabeth Blair
MacDowall, D. W.
McDowell, Joan Allgrove
Máčel, Otakar
McEvansoneya, Philip
McEwan, Colin
McEwen, John
McGee, Donna
McGowan, Alan
McGrath, Elizabeth
McGrath, Joyce
Macgregor, Neil
McGregor, Robert
McGuire, William
McHam, Sarah Blake
McHardy, George
McIntosh, Roderick J.
McIntosh, Susan Keech
Mack, John
Mack, Rosamond E.
MacKay, Robert B.
Mackay, W. Iain
McKean, Charles
Mackechnie, Aonghus
McKendrick, Scot
Mackenney, Richard
McKenzie, A. Dean
Mackenzie, Colin
McKenzie, Judith
McKenzie, Karen
McKenzie, Ray
McKillop, Elizabeth D.
McKinstry, Sam
McKitterick, Rosamond D.
Mackle, Tony
Mackrell, Alice
McLauchlan, Valerie
Maclean, Geoffrey
McLean, Ruari
McLeod, Bet
Macleod, Dianne Sachko
McMath, George A.
Macmillan, Duncan
Macmillan, Ingrid
McNab, Jessie
McNair, Amy
McNally, Rika Smith
McNaughton, Patrick R.
McParland, Edward
McPeck, Eleanor M.
McPhee, Ian
McPherson, Heather
McQuillan, James P.
McQuillan, Melissa
Macrae-Gibson, Gavin
McReynolds, Patricia Justiniani
McVaugh, Robert E.
Maddison, J. M.
Mader, Daniel E.
Madigan, Susan Pinto
Madocks, Susan
Maeda, Robert J.
Magdalino, Paul
Magee, Diana

Maginnis, H. B. J.
Magirius, Heinrich
Magnani, Lauro
Magni, Marica
Magnusson, Thor
Magombe, Paulinos Vincent
Magowan, Fiona
Magrill, Pamela
Maguire, Hugh
Mahany, C. M.
Maharaj, S. C.
Mahood, Marguerite
Maidment, John
Maier, Franz Georg
Maillard, Monique
Main, William
Mainardi, Patricia
Maini, Roberto
Mainz, Valerie
Maisant, Corinne
Maison, Françoise
Maitland, Leslie
Makela, Maria
Małkiewicz, Adam
Maksimović, Jovanka
Malakhov, N. Ya.
Malandra, Geri H.
Małaszewska, Wanda
Malden, John
Malek, Jaromir
Maliva, Josef
Mallalieu, Huon
Maller, Jane Nash
Mallet, J. V. G.
Malloy, Nancy
Malmanger, Magne
Malpass, G. A.
Mambriani, Carlo
Mančal, Josef
Mancinelli, Fabrizio
Mancini, Tiziana
Mandel, Corinne
Mandel, Patricia C. F.
Mané-Wheoki, J. N.
Manfredi, Tommaso
Mango, Marlia Mundell
Manion, Margaret M.
Mankodi, Kirit
Mann, Maybelle
Mann, Richard G.
Mannack, Thomas
Manniche, Lise
Manning, Elfrida
Manning, W. H.
Mannings, David
Mannini, Maria Pia
Manno, Antonio
Manor, Dalia
Manrique, Jorge Alberto
Mansel, Philip
Manz, Beatrice Forbes
Mapelli Mozzi, Carlotta
Marandel, J. Patrice
Marani, Pietro C.
Marcadé, Jean
Marchant, Neil
Marcoci, Roxana
Marcos, Jorge G.
Marcus, Stanley E.
Marcussen, Marianne
Maréchal, Els
Marcfat, Roya
Marenbon, John
Margerie, Laure de
Margueron, J.-C.
Marías, Fernando
Marin, Régis

Marinas, Cristina
Marín Fidalgo, Ana
Marinho Ferreira Alves, Natalia
Mariuz, Adriano
Markl, Dagoberto L.
Marko, Ksynia
Marks-Paton, Beverly
Markus, Thomas A.
Marlow, Kirk
Marlowe, Nicholas
Marly, Diana de
Marosí, Ernö
Marquardt, Brigitte
Marr, J
Marr, W. A. P.
Marrey, Bernard
Marrison, G. E.
Marsan, Jean-Claude
Marschall, Wolfgang
Marsden, J. M.
Marsh, J. A.
Marshak, B. I.
Marshall, Rosalind K.
Marstine, Janet
Martelli, Marina
Martens, Maximiliaan P. J.
Marter, Joan
Marth, Regine
Martí Cotarelo, Mónica
Martin, Andrew John
Martin, Constance
Martin, Fernando A.
Martin, Harriet
Martin, Thomas
Martindale, Andrew
Martineau, Jane
Martin-Demézil, Jean
Martínez Lambarry, Margarita
Martínez Marín, Carlos
Martín González, J. J.
Martinson, Tom
Martin-Vignes, Nicole
Martiny, V. G.
Mascalchi, Silva
Masetti Zannini, Gian Lodovico
Maske, Andrew
Mason, Darielle
Mason, Leonard
Massar, Phyllis Dearborn
Massari, Stefania
Masse, Patricia
Massey, Anne
Massey, David W.
Massinelli, Anna Maria
Masson, V. M.
Masters, Christopher
Mateo Gomez, Isabel
Mathers, Clay
Matheson, Susan B.
Mathews, Nancy Mowll
Mathias, Martine
Mathieu, Jocelyne
Matos Moctezuma, Eduardo
Matsche, Franz
Matsudaira, Susumu
Mattevi, Maria Angela
Matthews, D. M.
Mattioli Rossi, Laura
Mattison, Robert Saltonstall
Mattusch, Carol C.
Mauck, Marchita Bradford
Maué, Claudia
Maué, Hermann
Maur, Karin von
Maurer, Bruno
Maurer, Christina
Maurer, Ellen

Maurer, Evan M.
Mauzé, Marie
Mavrodinova, Liliana
Mawer, John
Maxmin, Jody
Maxwell, Kenneth
Maxwell, Robert M.
Maycock, Susan E.
Mayer, Harold M.
Maynard, Patrick
Mayr, Vincent
Mays, Deborah C.
Mazón de la Torre, M. A.
Mazor, Adam A.
Mazza, Barbara
Mazzi, Giuliana
Mazzocca, Fernando
Mazzoni, Stefania
Mead, Christopher
Meadows, Peter M.
Meco, José
Meddens, Frank
Medlam, Sarah
Medley, Margaret
Mee, Christopher
Meehan, Betty
Meek, Harold
Megaw, A. H. S.
Megaw, J. V. S.
Megaw, M. Ruth
Mehlau-Wiebking, Friederike
Mehta, R. N.
Meier, Nikolaus
Meijer, Bert W.
Meijers, Dulcia
Meij-Tolsma, Marijke van der
Meintjes, Clyde C. C.
Meirion-Jones, Gwyn
Meister, Michael W.
Meixner, Laura L.
Mélker, Pascale
Mellick, Sally
Mellink, M. J.
Mellott, Richard L.
Meloni Trkulja, Silvia
Melot, Michel
Melville, Jennifer
Melville-Jones, John R.
Melzak, Robert
Memmott, Paul
Mena, Manuela
Menchaca, A.
Mende, Matthias
Mendelssohn, Joanna
Mendes Pinto, Maria Helena
Méndez, A.
Méndez Brignardello, Ramón Alfonso
Meneguzzo, Marco
Menichella, Anna
Menke, Annemarie
Mens, N.
Mens, Pierre F. M.
Menu, Daniele
Mercier, Huguette
Meredith, Jill
Merenmies, Eija
Mérindol, Christian de
Merkel, Ettore
Mermoz, Gérard
Mérot, Alain
Merpert, N. Ya.
Merrill, Victoria
Merrillees, R. S.
Merritt, Jane L.
Merwe, M. P. S. van der
Merwe, Pieter van der

Merz, Jörg Martin
Meschede, Friedrich
Meshkeris, V. A.
Mesqui, Jean
Mester, Ann M.
Metcalf, Priscilla
Metcalf, Thomas R.
Metcalf, William E.
Metzger, Henri
Metzger, Mendel
Metzger, Thérèse
Metzler, Sally
Meurer, Heribert
Meyboom, P. G. P.
Meyer, Siri
Meyer, Véronique
Meyer-Hermann, Eva
Meyere, J. A. L. de
Meyers, Amy
Meyers, Elizabeth L.
Mezzanotte, Gianni
Mezzatesta, Michael P.
Michael, M. A.
Michaelides, Demetrios
Michaels, Barbara L.
Michaelson, Carol
Michel, Christian
Michel, Olivier
Michell, George
Michelli, Pippin
Michels, Eileen
Micklewright, Nancy
Midant, Jean-Paul
Middendorf, Ulrike
Middione, Roberto
Middleton, John
Mierop, C.
Mierse, William E.
Mignot, Claude
Miguel Egea, Pilar de
Miki, Tamon
Mikina, Ewa
Miksic, John N.
Mikuž, Jure
Milan Acayaba, Marlene
Milburn, R. L. P.
Miles, Ellen G.
Miles, Elza
Miles, Hamish
Miles, M. M.
Millar, David P.
Millar, John Fitzhugh
Millar, Oliver
Millard, A. R.
Millard, Charles
Miller, Angela L.
Miller, Debra
Miller, Dwight C.
Miller, Elizabeth
Miller, Francine Koslow
Miller, James
Miller, Lillian B.
Miller, Mary Ellen
Miller, Mervyn
Miller, Naomi
Miller, Sandra
Miller, Stephen G.
Miller, Thea
Millidge, Shirley
Mills, A. J.
Mills, John S.
Mills, Sally
Milne, Louise S.
Milner, John
Milner-Gulland, Robin
Miłobędzki, Adam
Minchin, Jan

Minney, Frank
Mino, Yutaka
Minor, Vernon Hyde
Miquel, Pierre
Miranda, Maria Adelaide
Misfeldt, Willard E.
Misra, R. N.
Misselbeck, Reinhold
Mitchell, Anthony
Mitchell, D. M.
Mitchell, Paul
Mitchell, Peter
Mitchell, Stephen
Mitchell, T. C.
Miura, Masayuki
Mizuta, Norihisa
Modlin, Yvonne
Moeller, Gisela
Moench, Esther
Moentmann, Elise Marie
Moerman, Ingrid W. L.
Moffett, Marian
Moignard, Elizabeth
Mokveld, Monique
Molander, Marianne
Molinari, Danielle
Möller, George J.
Möller, Renate
Moltke, J. W. von
Molyneux, Ian
Mommsen, Heide
Momsen, Janet Henshall
Monbeig Goguel, Catherine
Mongellaz, Jacqueline
Monks, Peter Rolfe
Monnier, Geneviève
Monod-Fontaine, Isabelle
Monroe, Betty Iverson
Montêquin, François-Auguste de
Montero, C. Guillermo
Monterrosa, P. Mariano
Monteverde-Penso, Melanía
Montmollin, Olivier de
Montserrat, Dominic
Moon, Jane
Moon, Warren G.
Moor, Angela H.
Moor, Ian L.
Moor de, M.
Moore, Andrew W.
Moore, David R.
Moore, Elizabeth
Moore, Mary B.
Moore, Nicholas J.
Moore, Simon
Moore-Gwyn, David
Moortgat-Correns, Ursula
Moralejo, S.
Morales Alonso, Luis
Morales y Marín, José Luis
Morales, Leonor
Morand, Anne R.
Morand, Anne Roberts
Morán Suarez, Isabel
Moravánszky, Ákos
Moravánszky-Gyöngy, Katalin
Moreira, Rafael
Morel, Dominique
Morel-Deckers, Yolande
Morel Deledalle, Myriame
Moreno Cuadro, F.
Moreno, Paolo
Morgan, Hilary
Morgan, H. Wayne
Morgan, Keith N.
Morgan, Lyvia

Morgan, Nigel J.
Morgan, Norma
Morgan, Sarah
Morgan, William
Morganstern, James
Morin, Laurie A.
Morioka, Michiyo
Morkot, R. G.
Morland, Carol
Morley-Fletcher, Hugo
Moro, Franco
Moron de Castro, M. Fernanda
Morozzi, Luisa
Morphet, Richard
Morphy, Howard
Morrall, Andrew
Morresi, Manuela
Morris, A. C. F.
Morris, Christopher
Morris, Edward
Morris, J. F.
Morris, Michael
Morris, R. K.
Morris, Sarah P.
Morris, Susan
Morrison, John
Morrison, Kathryn
Morrisson, Cécile
Morscheck Jr, Charles R.
Morse, Anne Nishimura
Morse, Samuel C.
Mortari Vergara Caffarelli, Paola
Mortensen, Erik
Morton, Marsha L.
Mosby, Dewey F.
Moseley, M. E.
Möseneder, Karl
Moser, Charlotte
Moskowitz, Anita F.
Mosquera, Gerardo
Mossakowski, Stanisław
Mostyn-Owen, William
Moszynska, Anna
Moughtin, J. C.
Mouilleseaux, J.-P.
Moura Sobral, Luís de
Moure, Nancy Dustin Wall
Moustier, Beatrice de
Moutsopoulos, N.
Mowat, Linda
Mowl, Tim
Moyssén, Xavier
Mrazkova, Daniela
Mucenic, Cezara
Mudrak, Myroslava M.
Mühlberger, Richard C.
Mulcahy, Rosemarie
Mulders, Christine van
Mullan, W. N. B.
Müller, Franz
Müller, Hannelore
Muller, Mechthild
Müller, Peter
Muller, Priscilla E.
Müller, Rainer
Müller, Wolfgang J.
Müller-Wiener, Wolfgang
Mullett, Margaret
Mumtaz, Kamil Khan
Munari, Nadia
Munchaev, R. M.
Munhall, Edgar
Munk, Jens Peter
Munk-Jørgensen, Wivan
Munro, Jane
Müntz de Raissac, Muriel

Murdoch, Tessa
Murnane, William J.
Murowchick, Robert E.
Murphy, Bernice
Murphy, Edward
Murphy, Francis
Murphy, Kevin D.
Murphy, Paula
Murray, Charles
Murray, Julia K.
Murray, Peter
Murray, Stephen
Muscarella, Oscar White
Musgrove, John
Muss, Ulrike
Musson, Jeremy
Musto, Ronald G.
Mütherich, Florentine
Muthesius, Stefan
Muzzi, Andrea
Myers, Denys Peter
Myers, Donald
Myers, John Walker
Myslivečková, Hana
Myśliwiec, Karol
Nadler, Stefan
Naef, Heidi
Naenna, Patricia
Nafilyan, Guy
Nagaswamy, R.
Nagaya, Toshiaki
Nagel, Alexander
Nagy, C.
Nagy, Imre
Naitō, Masato
Nakahashi, Gratia Williams
Naldi, Riccardo
Namba, Kazuhiko
Naňková, Věra
Napolcone, Caterina
Narkiss, Bezalel
Nash, Deborah
Nash, John R.
Nash, Susie
Natale, Vittorio
Natali, Antonio
Nath, R.
Natter, G. Tobias
Naumann, Francis M.
Nava Rodríguez, Teresa
Navarro-Castro, Gustavo
Naylor, Janet
Neagley, L. E.
Neal, Kenneth
Neale, Anne I.
Necker, François de
Nedeva-Wegener, Juliana
Needham, Gerald
Negahban, Ezat O.
Negbi, Ora
Negmatov, N. N.
Negri, Antonello
Negro, Emilio
Negro Spina, Annamaria
Nehamas, Alexander
Neich, Roger
Neidhardt, Hans Joachim
Neilson, Nancy Ward
Neiswander, Judith A.
Nekrasova, Mariya A.
Nelson, Bernadette
Nelson, W. A.
Németh, Lajos
Nemiroff, Diana
Nemtseva, N. B.
Nepi Scire, Giovanna
Neri Lusanna, Enrica

Nersessian, Vrej
Nesbitt, Judith
Nesom-Sirhandi, Marcella
Nettleton, Anitra
Netzer, Susanne
Neu-Kock, Roswitha
Neuman, Robert
Neumann, Dietrich
Neuwirth, Markus
Neve, Annette
Newall, Christopher
Newbury, Richard F.
Newby, Evelyn
Newcome, M.
Newhall, Amy W.
Newhouse, Victoria
Newman, Geoffrey
Newman, John
Neyt, François
Nguyen Quynh
Niblett, Kathy
Nicholls, Paul
Nichols, Frederick D.
Nichols, Thomas
Nicholson, H. B.
Nicholson, Kathleen
Nicholson, Paul T.
Nickel, Helmut
Nicklin, Keith
Nicolau, Juan
Nicolle, David
Niculescu, Remus
Niederberger, Christine
Niehoff, F.
Niehr, Klaus
Nielsen, Bent
Nieto González, J. R.
Nigst, P.
Nikitin, Alexander
Nikolenko, Lada
Nikula, Riitta
Niles, Susan A.
Nilgen, Ursula
Nilsén, Anna
Nilsson, Sten Åke
Nishida, Hiroko
Nishikawa, Kyotaro
Nishino, Yoshiaki
Nissman, Joan L.
Noah, Robert
Noble, Alexandra
Noble, Joseph Veach
Noelke, Peter
Noelle, Louise
Nolan, Kathleen D.
Noldus, J. W.
Nooter, Nancy Ingram
Norberg-Schulz, Christian
Nordal, Bera
Nordhagen, P. J.
Norman, Diana
Norman, Naomi J.
Norri, Marja-Riitta
Norris, Andrea S.
Norris, Malcolm W.
North, A. R. E.
North, Ian
Northedge, Alastair
Norton, Ann Wood
Notarnicola, Donato
Notehelfer, F. G.
Nour, Amir I. M.
Nova, Alessandro
Nowak, Zofia
Nulli, Andrea
Nunley, John
Nunn, A.

Nunn, Pamela Gerrish
Nunn, Valerie
Nurse, Bernard
Nusbaumer, Philippe
Nussbaum, Martha C.
Nuttall, Paula
Nuttgens, Patrick
Nybo, Marit
Nyborg, Ebbe
Nye, James H.
Nygren, Edward J.
Nykjær, Mogens
Nylander, Richard C.
Oakcs, Catherine
Oakes, Jill
Oakley, John H.
Oates, David
Oates, Joan
Oberhaidacher, J.
O'Callaghan, Judith
Och, Marjorie A.
Ochsner, Jeffrey Karl
O'Connell, Sheila
O'Connor, Deryn
O'Connor, Francis V.
O'Connor, Jerome Murphy
O'Connor, Stanley J.
O'Day, Deirdre
Oddy, Andrew
O'Dell-Franke, Ilse
Odom, Anne
O'Donnell, Roderick
Oechslin, Werner
Offerhaus, Johannes
Ogden, Jack
O'Grady, John
Oguibe, Olu
O'Hanlon, Michael
Ohki, Sadako
Ohri, Vishwa Chander
Ojalvo, David
O'Kane, Bernard
Okediji, Moyo
Ol', G. A.
Olausson, Magnus
Olbrich, Harald
Oldfield, David
Olesen, Lene
Oliveira Caetano, Joaquim
Oliver, Andrew
Oliver, José R.
Oliver, Paul
Oliveras, Jordi
Ollinger-Zinque, Gisele
Ollman, Arthur
Olmi, Giuseppe
Ölschleger, Hans Dieter
Olpin, Robert S.
Olsen, Justine
Olson, Roberta J. M.
Olst, Ellen van
Olszewski, Edward J.
O'Malley, Michelle
O'Mara, Joan H.
Oña, Lenin
O'Neil, Mary Velma
O'Neill, L. A.
Öney, Gönül
Onians, Dick
Onians, John
Onorato, Ronald J.
Onuki, Yoshio
Opperman, H. N.
Opstad, Lauritz
Orazi, R.
Ordax, Salvador Andrés
Orenstein, Nadine

Oresko, Robert
Orihuela, Mercedes
Ormond, Flavia
Ormond, Leonée
Ormond, Richard
Orrell, John
Orth, Myra D.
Orthmann, Winfried
Ortiz Avila, Jorge
Ortiz Gaitán, Julieta
Ory, Solange
Osaki, Shin'ichiro
Osborne, C. M.
Osborne, John
Osing, Jürgen
Østby, Erik
Østby, Leif
Ostländer, Elke
Ostler, Timothy
Ostrow, Steven F.
Ostrowski, Jan K.
Ottaway, John
Otten, M. J. C.
Ottenberg, Simon
Ottenheym, K. A.
Ottevanger, Alied
Ottewill, David
Ottillinger, Eva B.
Ottmann, Klaus
Otto, Christian F.
Ottomeyer, Hans
Oursel, Hervé
Ousterhout, Robert
Overy, Paul
Ovsyannikov, Y. M.
Owen, Felicity
Özgüç, Nimet
Özgüç, Tahsin
Paas, Sigrun
Paavilainen, Simo
Pacciani, Riccardo
Pace, Claire
Pace, Ursula Verena Fischer
Pace, Valentino
Pacelli, Vincenzo
Pachner, Joan H.
Pacht Bassani, Paola
Pacini, Piero
Packer, Emma
Pacquement, Alfred
Paddock, John
Padoa Rizzo, Anna
Padovani, Serena
Padro, Josep
Paez Mullan, Anthony
Pagden, Sylvia Ferino
Pagliara, Pier Nicola
Pagliarulo, Giovanni
Paikowsky, Sandra
Paindaveine, Hervé
Paisey, Robin
Palagia, Olga
Palatucci, Margherita
Palmer, A.
Palmer, Andrew
Palmer, Elizabeth
Palmes, James
Palomero Páramo, Jesus M.
Paludan, Ann
Paludan, Charlotte
Palumbo, Anne Cannon
Panayotidi, Maria
Panhuysen, Titus A. S. M.
Panoho, Rangihiroa
Panvini Rosati, Franco
Paoletti, John T.
Papademetriou, Peter C.

Papadopoulou, Barbara
Papageorghiou, A.
Papi, Gianni
Papp, Julia
Paradise, Joanne Culler
Paramonov, A. V.
Paredes-Arend, Liana
Parent, Mary Neighbour
Pares, Susan
Parezo, Nancy J.
Parihar, Subhash
Pařík, Arno
Parimoo, Ratan
Park, David
Park Eon Kon
Park, Stuart
Parker, Joseph D.
Parkin, Michael
Parma, Elena
Parmantier-Lallement, Nicole
Parola, Lisa
Parsons, David
Parsons, Tom
Parton, Anthony
Partridge, Loren
Pascal, Jean-Paul
Pasini, Pier Giorgio
Pasricha, Indar
Passavant, Günter
Passoni, Riccardo
Pastan, Elizabeth
Pastori Zumbach, Anne
Pataki, Eva
Patrick, Darryl
Patt, Judith
Patterson, Daniel W.
Pauchet-Warlop, Laurence
Paul, Jürgen
Paul, Vivian
Paula, Georg
Pau-Llosa, Ricardo
Paulme, Denise
Pavanello, Giuseppe
Pavel, Amelia
Pavon Maldonado, Basilio
Pavone, Mario Alberto
Paxton, Roland
Payne, Christiana
Paz Aguiló, María
Peacock, John
Peake, Lorraine
Pearce, Barry
Pearce, Nicholas
Pearman, Sara Jane
Pearson, Anne
Pearson, Fiona
Peattie, Roger W.
Pechstein, Klaus
Peck, William H.
Pedersen, Bent L.
Pedrocco, Filippo
Peek, Philip M.
Pegazzano, Donatella
Pegg, Carole
Pel, Alexandra
Pellicer, Laure
Pelrine, Diane M.
Pelta, Maureen
Peltenburg, E. J.
Peltola, Leena
Pemberton, Delia
Peña, JoséMaría
Penner, Richard H.
Penny, Nicholas
Pepall, Rosalind M.
Pepper, Simon
Perani, Judith

Perazzo, Nelly
Percival, John
Percy, Ann
Pereira, Paulo
Pérez, Marie-Félicie
Pérez Calero, Gerardo
Pérez Chanis, Efrain E.
Pérez de Ayala, Juan
Pérez Sánchez, Alfonso E.
Pérez Silva, Yasminy
Pérez-Tibi, Dora
Pergler, Tomáš
Perini, Giovanna
Perissa Torrini, Annalisa
Perkins, Diane
Périer-d'Ieteren, C.
Perrois, Louis
Perry, Peter W.
Perry, Regenia A.
Perry, Susanna
Pescarmona, Daniele
Peschlow, Urs
Pessey-Lux, Aude
Peters, Jane S.
Peters, Sarah Whitaker
Peters, W. H.
Peters, Walter
Petersen, A. K. C.
Petersen, Mark R.
Peterson, Sara
Petherbridge, Guy
Petrakis, S. L.
Petrova, T. A.
Petrova-Pleskotova, A.
Petrucci, Francesca
Petrukhin, V. Ya.
Pfleger, Susanne
Phan, Ngọc Khuê
Phillips, Antonia
Phillips, David
Phillips, Gene
Phillips, Maria A.
Phillips, Quitman E.
Phillips, Ruth B.
Phillips, Sandra S.
Phillips, Susan A.
Phillipson, David W.
Philon, Helen
Physick, John
Pianu, Giampiero
Picarda, Guy
Pichard, Pierre
Pichikyan, I. R.
Pickrel, Thomas
Pickthorn, Helen
Pickwoad, Nicholas
Picon, Antoine
Picone Petrusa, Mariantonietta
Picquenard, Thérèse
Picton, John
Pido, Donna Klumpp
Pierre, José
Pil, L.
Pilar, Santiago A.
Pile, John F.
Pillsbury, Edmund P.
Pillsbury, Joanne
Pimentel, Antonio Filipe
Piña Chan, Román
Pinchon, Jean-François
Pincus, Debra
Pinder, Michael
Pinder-Wilson, Ralph
Pingeot, Anne
Pinkerton, J. M.
Pinkham, Roger
Pinna, Giuseppe

Pinney, Rosie-Anne
Pinon, Pierre
Pintilie, Andrei
Pinto, John
Pipili, Maria
Pippal, Martina
Pittman, Holly
Pittolo, Véronique
Pitts, Terence
Pizarro Gomez, Francisco Javier
Plantzos, Dimitris
Plinval de Guillebon, Régine de
Plomp, M. C.
Pötzl-Malikova, Maria
Pöykkö, Kaarina
Pöykkö, Kalevi
Podbrecky, Inge
Poddar, Rashmi
Podmaniczky, Michael Sándor von
Podro, Michael
Poesch, Jessie
Poeschke, Joachim
Pohrt, Richard A.
Pointon, Marcia
Poke, Christopher
Pokrovskaya, Z. K.
Polak, Ada
Pole, Len
Pollak, Martha
Pollard, Helen Perlstein
Pollard, J. G.
Polleross, Friedrich
Pollock, Griselda
Poloczek, Andrzej
Polubiec, Lidia
Pommaret, Françoise
Pons, Bruno
Pons, Jacques
Pons, Nicoletta
Pons-Alegría, Mela
Pontual, Roberto
Pontynen, Arthur
Popova, L. I.
Popovski, Živko
Popper, Frank
Poppi, Cesare
Portal, Jane
Portela Sandoval, Francisco
Porter, Venetia
Porterfield, Todd B.
Porter-Weaver, Muriel
Posch, Wilfried
Posener, Julius
Possehl, Gregory L.
Poster, Amy G.
Postle, Martin
Postma, Hugo H.
Potter, T. W.
Potts, Alex
Potts, D. T.
Pouillon, Nadine
Poulsson, Vidar
Poulter, Andrew
Poupeye, Veerle
Poursat, Jean-Claude
Poveda, Consuelo de
Powell, Cecilia
Powers, Alan
Powers, Martin J.
Powers, Mary Ann A.
Powling, Kara
Poynor, Rick
Prache, Anne
Pradalier, Henri
Pradere, A.

Prahl, Roman
Prange, Mathias
Prasad, Sunand
Préaud, Maxime
Préaud, Tamara
Preimesberger, Rudolf
Preising, Dagmar
Preiss, Achim
Preiss, Pavel
Prelovšek, Damjan
Prematilleke, P. L.
Prescott, Kenneth W.
Pressly, William L.
Pressouyre, S.
Preston, Harley
Price, Jennifer
Priego, Carlos Cid
Priest, D. J.
Prijatelj, Kruno
Prince, Nicholette
Principato, Barbara
Pringle, Denys
Prins, Herbert
Prinsloo, Ivor
Printseva, G. A.
Pritzker, Thomas J.
Probst, Freya
Prokopoff, Stephen S.
Pronina, I.
Proske-Van Heerdt, D.
Prosperi Meyer, Regina Maria
Prosperi Valenti Rodino, Simonetta
Prossinger, Cynthia
Proudfoot, Trevor
Prout, David
Prown, Jules David
Pryke, Sebastian
Pryor, Pamela Takiora Ingram
Puchalski, Irene
Puente, Sergio
Puetz, Anne
Pugachenkova, G. A.
Puglisi, Catherine R.
Pullar, Judith
Pullen, D.
Pulos, Arthur J.
Puls, M.
Pupil, François
Purinton, Nancy
Putaranui, Ata
Puttkamer, M. A. v.
Pyle, Cynthia M.
Pyle, Hilary
Pyle, R. J.
Quagliotti, Anna Maria
Quantrill, Malcolm
Quartermaine, Peter
Quast, Matthias
Querejazu, Pedro
Quinan, Jack
Quiney, Anthony
Quintanilla Armijo, Raul
Quinterio, Francesco
Quirarte, Jacinto
Quiviger, Francois
Raabyemagle, Hanne
Rabanal Yus, Aurora
Rabe, Michael D.
Rabel, Claudia
Rabiner, Donald
Rabinovitch, Celia
Rabinowitz, Harvey Z.
Racine, Yolande
Raczyński, Edward
Radford, Dennis
Radford, Robert

Radford, Ron
Radke, Gary M.
Radojković, Bojana
Rae, Allyson
Ragot, Gilles
Raguin, Virginia Chieffo
Raheem, Ismeth
Rahming, Patrick
Raindre, Guy
Rainey, Helen
Rajka, Susanne
Rakitin, V.
Ramade, Patrick
Ramage, Nancy H.
Ramesh, K. V.
Ramharter, Johannes
Ramírez, Fausto
Ramirez, Jan Seidler
Ramírez, Mari Carmen
Ramón, Armando de
Ramsauer, Gabriele
Ramsay, Nigel
Ramseyer, Urs
Rand, Harry
Randall, Lilian M. C.
Randall, Richard H.
Ranfft, Erich G.
Rangoni, Fiorenza
Rankin, Elizabeth
Ranov, V. A.
Rapetti, Rodolphe
Rapmund, Jaqueline
Rapoport, Yu. A.
Rapp Buri, Anna
Rappard, Willem Frederik
Rarick, Ronald D.
Rasmussen, Tom
Raspopova, V. I.
Rath, Peter
Rattner, Selma
Raumschüssel, Martin
Rautmann, M.
Ravanelli Guidotti, Carmen
Ravenhill, Philip L.
Rawson, Elizabeth
Rawson, Jessica
Ray, Anthony
Raya Raya, María Angeles
Rayevsky, D. S.
Rea, Will
Read, J. James
Reade, J. E.
Reading, Malcolm
Reaves, Wendy Wick
Rebora, Carrie
Reche, Albert
Redmill, John
Reed, Christopher
Reed, Cleota
Reed, Roger G.
Reed Thomsen, Ingrid
Reedy, Chandra L.
Reeve, John
Reid, Aileen M. M.
Reid, Martine
Reidel, Hermann
Reilly, Lisa A.
Reilly, Robin
Reinheckel, G.
Reischenböck, Horst E.
Reitala, Aimo
Reitzes, Lisa B.
Rem, Paul H.
Rempel', L. I.
Rendeli, Marco
Renger, Konrad
Ressort, Claudie

Restaino, Concetta
Rettich, Edeltraud
Reyes, Aurelio de los
Reyes-Valerio, Constantino
Reynaerts, J. A. H.
Reynaud, J. F.
Reynaud, Nicole
Reynolds, Catherine
Reynolds, Gary A.
Reynolds, Graham
Reynolds, Joyce
Reynolds, Peter
Reynolds, Simon
Rezelman, Betsy Cogger
Reznicek, E. K. J.
Rhodes, Colin
Ribeill, Georges
Ribeiro, Aileen
Ribeiro de Oliveira, Myriam A.
Riccardi-Cubitt, Monique
Riccardi Jr, Theodore
Ricci, Giuliana
Rice, Danielle
Rice, Louise
Rich, Vivian A.
Richard, Jean
Richards, Duncan
Richards, J. M.
Richards, John
Richards, Paul
Richardson, Emeline
Richardson, Francis L.
Richardson, Hilary
Richardson, Jenny
Richardson, Kim
Richardson, Margaret
Richardson, Peter
Richardson, Sarah
Richardson, Tom
Riches, Anne
Richter, Elinor M.
Rickert, Franz
Ricketts, Annabel
Rickman, Catherine
Rickman, G. E.
Riddel, R. J.
Riddell, Richard
Ridgway, Christopher
Ridgway, David
Riely, Celia Carrington
Rietzsch, Barbara
Rigal, Christian
Riggs, Timothy
Riley-Smith, T. P. B.
Rimer, J. Thomas
Rinaldi, Alessandro
Rinaldi, Luca
Rincón García, Wilfredo
Ring, Nancy
Ringbeck, Birgitta
Ringbom, Åsa
Ringbom, Sixten
Ringger, Peter
Ritchie, Anna
Ritmeyer, Leen
Rivallain, Josette
Rivarola, Milda
Rivera, Javier
Rivera y Rivera, Roberto
Rivkin, Laura
Rizopoulou-Egoumenidou, Euphrosyne
Rizzi, W. Georg
Roaf, Michael
Roaf, Susan
Roark, Elisabeth
Robbins, Daniel

Robels, Hella
Roberts, Allen F.
Roberts, A. M.
Roberts, Gaye Blake
Roberts, Helene E.
Roberts, John
Roberts, Kenneth B.
Roberts, Laurance P.
Roberts, Margaret
Roberts, Marion
Roberts, Mary Nooter
Roberts, N. W.
Roberts, Samantha
Robertson, Alexander
Robertson, Charles
Robertson, Clare
Robertson, David
Robertson, Lynn
Robertson, Martin
Robertson, Merle Greene
Robertson, Pamela Reekie
Robertson, Sarah Wells
Robins, Anna Gruetzner
Robins, Gay
Robinson, B. W.
Robinson, Cervin
Robinson, Crispin
Robinson, Duncan
Robinson, James
Robinson, Jenefer
Robinson, John Martin
Robinson, P. R.
Robinson, Willard B.
Robinson, William W.
Robson, A. Deirdre
Roccasecca, Pietro
Rocher-Jauneau, Madeleine
Rochfort, Desmond
Rodboon, Somporn
Rodgers, David
Rödiger-Diruf, Erika
Rodley, Lyn
Rodríguez, Bélgica
Rodriguez, Myrna E.
Rodríguez-Camilloni, Humberto
Rodríguez Ceballos, Alfonso
Roever, Margriet de
Rogers, J. M.
Rohrmoser, Albin
Roio, Nicosetta
Rojas, José Miguel
Roland, Berthold
Roland Michel, Marianne
Röll, Johannes
Romano, David Gilman
Romano, Irene Bald
Romano, James F.
Romano, Serena
Romer, Grant B.
Ronfort, Jean Nérée
Ronge, N. G.
Ronge, V.
Ronig, Franz J.
Ronot, Henry
Rook, A. Demarquay
Rooney, Dawn F.
Roos, Marjoke de
Root, Margaret Cool
Roper, G.
Roper, Rayne
Rorschach, Kimerly
Roscoe, Barley
Roscoe, Ingrid
Rose, Adam
Rose, David
Rose, Dennis

Rose de Viejo, Isadora
Rosenauer, Artur
Rosenberg, Charles M.
Rosenblum, Naomi
Rosenfeld, Andrée
Rosengarten, Ruth
Rosenthal, Donald A.
Rosenthal, Michael
Rosenthal, Norman
Ross, Alex
Ross, Doran H.
Ross, Leslie
Ross, Stephanie
Rossi, Lorenza
Rossi, Sara
Rote, Carey
Roters, Eberhard
Roth, Ann Macy
Roth, Anthony
Roth, Birgit
Roth, Leland M.
Roth, Michael
Rothenstein, John
Rothstein, Natalie
Rotondi Terminiello, Giovanna
Rotroff, Susan I.
Rottenberg, Anda
Rottermund, Andrzej
Rouillard, Philippe
Rous, Jan
Rousset-Charny, Gérard
Roussin, Lucille A.
Routh, Emma M.
Roux, Georges
Rovira, Josep Maria
Rowell, Christopher
Rowland, Anna
Rowlands, Eliot W.
Roy, Alain
Roy, Christopher D.
Roy, J.
Royalton-Kisch, Martin
Royt, Jan
Rozman, Ksenija
Rubbo, Anna
Rubens, Godfrey
Rubin, Arnold
Rubin, J. H.
Rubino, Joanne A.
Rubinstein, Charlotte Streifer
Rubinstein, Meyer Raphael
Rubinstein, Ruth Olitsky
Ruck, Barbara
Ruckriegel Egerváry, Barbra
Ruddock, E. C.
Rudloff, Martina
Rudolf, Moira
Ruffle, J.
Ruggeri, Ugo
Ruggles, D. Fairchild
Ruhmer, Eberhard
Ruigrok, Robbert
Ruitenbeek, Klaas
Ruíz Alcón, Maria Teresa
Ruizendaal, Robin
Ruiz Gomar, Rogelio
Rule, Amy
Rümmele, Simone
Rundall, Charlotte
Runolfsson, Halldor Björn
Ruotolo, Renato
Ruppelt, Georg
Rus, Zdenko
Rusakova, Alla
Rushing, W. Jackson
Rusinko, Elaine
Rusnock, K. Andrea

Russ, Hubert
Russell, Francis
Russell, H. Diane
Russell, John M.
Russell, Margarita
Russmann, Edna R.
Russo, Kathleen
Russo, Thomas E.
Rutgers, K. M.
Rutherston, Max
Rutt, Richard
Ryan, Donald P.
Rybko, Ana Maria
Rykind-Eriksen, Kirsten
Rylands, Philip
Ryszkiewicz, Andrzej
Saabye, Marianne
Sabapathy, T. K.
Sabar, Shalom
Sabloff, Jeremy A.
Sack, Steven
Sadan, J.
Sadler, Donna L.
Safarik, E. A.
Safons, Horacio
Safran, Yehuda
Saghie, Muntaha
Saidi, Nabil
Sainte Fare Garnot, Nicholas
Saito, Yasuyoshi
Sajo, Tamas
Sakakibara, Saturo
Sakamoto, Mitsuo
Sakellarakis, J. A.
Sakr, Yasir
Salam-Liebich, Hayat
Salazar, Elida
Salet, Francis
Salihi, Wathiq al-
Salmanov, E. R.
Salmons, Jill
Salokorpi, Asko
Salomon, Richard
Salton, Mark M.
Salvadé, Christine
Salzmann, Siegfried
Samarin, Ivan
Sambo, Elisabetta
Samonides, William
Samuel, Cheryl
Sanabria, Sergio L.
Sanchez Esteban, Natividad
Sanchez Hernandez, M. Leticia
Sanchez-Mesa Martin, Domingo
Sanday, John
Sander, Lore
Sanders, Elma
Sanders, Jennifer
Sanderson, Colin C.
Sanderson, R. W.
Sanderson, Warren
Sandler, Lucy Freeman
Sandler, Mark H.
Sandon, Henry
Sandon, John
Sandron, Dany
Sandström, Sven
Sandt, Anne van de
Sandt, Udolpho van de
Sandweiss, Martha A.
Sani, Bernardina
Sannazzaro, Giovanni Battista
Santi, Bruno
Sanz-Pastor, Consuelo
Sapouna-Sakellarakis, E.
Sarab'yanov, D. V.

Sarajas-Korte, Salme
Sarewitz, E. B.
Sargent, William R.
Sargentson, Carolyn
Sarianidi, V. I.
Sarmany-Parsons, Ilona
Sasaki, Kōzō
Sattel Bernardini, Ingrid
Satzinger, Georg
Saunders, D. Gail
Saunders, Gill
Saunders, Matthew
Saunders, Richard H.
Saunders, William
Savage, Peter
Savy, Nicole
Sawelson-Gorse, Naomi
Saxby, Graham
Sayers, Andrew
Scaglia, Gustina
Scanlon, George
Scaratt, Ken
Scarce, Jennifer M.
Scarisbrick, Diana
Scarpa, Ludovica
Scarpellini, P.
Scerrato, Umberto
Schaaf, L. J.
Schaar, Kenneth W.
Schaarschmidt-Richter, Irmtraud
Schäche, Wolfgang
Schack von Wittenau, Clementine
Schade, Carol
Schade, Werner
Schaefer, Claude
Schaffer, Barbro
Schalles, Hans-Joachim
Schapelhouman, Marijn
Schärer, Martin R.
Schastok, Sara L.
Schavelzon, Daniel
Scheicher, Elisabeth
Scheller, Robert W.
Schemper-Sparholz, Ingeborg
Scher, Stephen K.
Scherer, Joanna C.
Scherf, Guilhem
Schildt, Göran
Schiller, Joyce K.
Schilt, J.
Schimmel, Annemarie
Schirmer, Wulf
Schlégl, Istvan
Schleier, E.
Schleif, Corine
Schlereth, Thomas J.
Schless, Nancy Halverson
Schlicht, Klaus M.
Schlick, Mary D.
Schlossmacher, Norbert
Schlüter, Mogens
Schmetterling, Astrid
Schmidhuber, H.
Schmidt, Gerhard
Schmidt, Gudrun
Schmidt, Hans M.
Schmidt, J.
Schmidt, Margot
Schmidt, Melitta
Schmidt, Regine
Schmidt, Victor M.
Schmitt, Antje
Schmitz, Barbara
Schmoll gen. Eisenwerth, J. A.
Schnabel, Werner Wilhelm

Schnackenburg, B.
Schnackenburg-Praél, H.
Schneckenburger-Broschek, Anja
Schneider, Angela
Schneider, Brigitte
Schneider, Elizabeth Ann
Schneider, Erich
Schneider, Peter
Schneider, Ulrich ·
Schniewind-Michel, Petra
Schnyder, Rudolf
Schock-Werner, Barbara
Schoeman, Karel
Schofield, John
Schofield, Louise
Schofield, Richard
Schoonbaert, Lydia M. A.
Schram, Hrafnhildur
Schroder, Timothy
Schubert, Dietrich
Schubert, Ernst
Schuchard, Jutta
Schuckman, Christiaan
Schuler, Carol M.
Schultes, Lothar
Schultz, Bernard
Schulz, Derek
Schulz, Wolfgang
Schulze, Franz
Schumacher, Thomas L.
Schummer, Constanze M.
Schupbach, William
Schuster-Hofstätter, S.
Schütte, Rudolf-Alexander
Schütze, Karl-Robert
Schwartz, Ellen C.
Schwartz, Gary
Schwartz, Marvin D.
Schwarz, Hans-Peter
Schwarz, Mario
Schweigert, Horst
Schweikhart, Gunter
Schwertfager, Thomas
Scolari, Paul
Scott, David
Scott, John Beldon
Scott, Margaret
Scott, Mary Ann
Scott, Rosemary
Scott, Rupert
Scott, Wilford W.
Scottez-De Wambrechies, Annie
Scotti Tosini, Aurora
Scrase, David E.
Seager, Andrew R.
Sear, F. B.
Searing, Helen
Sears, Elizabeth
Seber, Oskar
Secondo, Joellen
Sedláková, Radomíra
Sedlař, Jaroslav
Sedov, A. V.
Sed-Rajna, Gabrielle
Seelig, Lorenz
Seelig-Teuwen, Regina
Segger, Martin
Segre, Roberto
Seiberling, Grace
Seibert, Gerhard
Seidmann, Gertrud
Seifertova, Hana
Seiler-Baldinger, Annemarie
Seip, Elisabeth
Sekler, Eduard F.

Sekules, V.
Self, James
Sellink, Manfred
Sells, Christopher
Selvafolta, Ornella
Selz, Jean
Semenov, G. L.
Semenzato, Camillo
Semff, Michael
Semin, Didier
Semowich, Charles J.
Sennequier, Geneviève
Senter, Terence A.
Seo, Audrey Yoshiko
Şerbu, Alina-Ioana
Serck-Dewaide, Myriam
Sergeant, Jonathan
Serrão, Vitor
Serrano, Eduardo
Service, Alastair
Serwint, Nancy
Sestoft, Jørgen
Šetlík, Jiří
Seumeren-Haerkens, Margriet van
Severin, Ingrid
Seyller, John
Shah, U. P.
Shand-Tucci, Douglass
Shank, Wesley I.
Sharer, Robert J.
Sharf, Elizabeth Horton
Sharma, Arvind
Shashoua, Yvonne
Shaw, Courtney Ann
Shaw, Ian M. E.
Shaw, James Byam
Shaw, John
Shaw, Keith
Shaw, Theresa
Shaw, Thurstan
Shaw, William H.
Shearer, Alistair
Sheather, Julian
Sheehy, Jeanne
Sheeran, John
Shelby, Lon R.
Shell, Janice
Shelley, Marjorie
Shelton, Anthony Alan
Sheon, Aaron
Shepard, M. B.
Sheppard, Anne
Sheppard, Carl D.
Sheppard, Richard
Sherratt, Susan
Shettleworth Jr, Earle G.
Shifman, Barry
Shih Hsio-Yen
Shimada, Izumi
Shipley, D. Graham J.
Shirley, Pippa
Shishkin, V. A.
Shishkina, G. B.
Shkoda, V. G.
Shokoohy, Mehrdad
Shokoohy, Natalie H.
Shone, Richard
Short, Robert
Shortell, Ellen M.
Shvidkovsky, D. O.
Sica, Maria
Sicca, Cinzia Maria
Sickler, Michael
Sidey, Tessa
Siegmann, William C.
Sierra Torres, Aída

Siggstedt, Mette
Signorini, Rodolfo
Sikorski, Darius
Silberberg-Peirce, Susan
Silbergeld, Jerome
Silberman, Arthur
Sill, Gertrude Grace
Sillevis, John
Silva, K. M. de
Silva, Maria Isabel
Silva, Nimal de
Silva, Raja de
Silva, Raquel Henriques da
Silva, Roland
Silverman, Eric Kline
Silverman, Helaine
Simi De Burgis, Saverio
Simmons, Linda Crocker
Simon, Christopher G.
Simon, David L.
Simon, Robin
Simonin, Pierre
Simpson, Amanda
Simpson, Bob
Simpson, David
Simpson, Juliet
Simpson, Marc
Simpson, Marianna S.
Sims, Eleanor
Sims, Patterson
Simson, Jutta von
Singelenberg, Pieter
Singer, Jane Casey
Singer, Noel F.
Singh, Patwant
Sinigalia, Tereza-Irene
Sinisalo, Soili
Siracusano, Citti
Siroto, Leon
Sisa, Jozsef
Sitt, Martina
Siu, Wai Fong Anita
Siudmak, John
Sjöberg, Lars
Skalska Miecik, Lija
Skedsmo, Tone
Skelton, Robert
Skipwith, Peyton
Skliar-Piguet, Alexandra
Skoler, Louis
Slachta, Stefan
Sladeczek, F.-J.
Šlapeta, Vladimír
Slatkes, Leonard J.
Slatner-Prückl, Michaela
Slavina, T. A.
Sliggers, B. C.
Śliwa, Joachim
Sloan, Kim
Slowe, V. A. J.
Sluijter, Eric J.
Sluijter-Seijffert, Nicolette C.
Slusser, Mary Shepherd
Smare, Tim
Smart, Alastair
Smeenk, Chris
Smets, Marcel
Smeyers, H.
Smidt, Dirk
Smirnova, L.
Smit, Hillie
Smith, Caron
Smith, Charles Saumarez
Smith, Elise L.
Smith, Elizabeth B.
Smith, Frances K.
Smith, Fred T.

Smith, G. Rex
Smith, George Fairfull
Smith, Gil R.
Smith, Jeffrey Chipps
Smith, Julia H. M.
Smith, Lawrence
Smith, M. Q.
Smith, Margaret M.
Smith, Mary Ann
Smith, Nicola
Smith, Norman A. F.
Smith, P. F.
Smith, Paul
Smith, Perry
Smith, Peter
Smith, Philip E. L.
Smith, R. R. R.
Smith, Robert
Smith, Rosemary T.
Smith, Ruth
Smith, Sheenah
Smith, Sophie Royde
Smith, Terence Paul
Smith, Terry
Smith, Walter
Smithies, Michael
Smith-Parr, Geraldine
Smyers, Karen A.
Snadon, Patrick A.
Sneath, David
Snell, Robert
Snodgrass, A. M.
Snowman, A. Kenneth
Snyder, James
So, Jenny F.
Soar, M.
Sobré, Judith Berg
Söderberg, Bertil
Söderlund, Göran
Söderström, Göran
Sodini, J.-P.
Soejima, Hiromichi
Soekmono, R.
Sohm, Philip
Sokol, David M.
Sokolov, M. N.
Solà-Morales, Ignasi de
Solberg, Gail E.
Soldini, Nicola
Solla, Pertti
Solodkoff, Alexander von
Soltynski, Roman
Somervell, K.
Sommer, Achim
Son Young Sik
Sonntag, Hans
Soppelsa, Robert T.
Sorel, Philippe
Sørensen, Henrik H.
Sorensen, Lee
Soria, Regina
Soromenho, Miguel
Soto, Rolando
Soubiran, Jean-Roger
Soucek, Priscilla P.
Souchal, François
Sougez, Marie-Loup
Soukupová, H.
Southard, Edna Carter
Southorn, Janet
Spaander, Ineke
Spalding, Frances
Spalding IV, Jack J.
Spalletti, Ettore
Spanel, Donald B.
Spantigati, Carlenrica
Spargo, Demelza

Sparke, Penny
Sparkes, B. A.
Sparks, Cameron
Sparks, Margaret
Sparti, Donatella L.
Spear, Richard E.
Speck, Lawrence W.
Speel, Erika
Spence, Rory
Spencer, A. J.
Spencer, Brian
Spencer, Stephanie
Spencer-Longhurst, Paul
Spens, Janet
Spens, Michael
Sperling, Thomas
Spicer, Joaneath A.
Spiegl, Walter
Spiessens, G.
Spike, John T.
Spillman, Jane Shadel
Spilner, Paula
Spink, Walter
Spoehr, Alexander
Sprague, Paul E.
Springer, Peter
Spyropoulos, Theodore G.
Srejović, Dragoslav
Sricchia Santoro, Fiorella
Srinivasan, Doris Meth
Srinivasan, Sumitra Kumar
Sroczyńska, Krystyna
Srp, Karel
Stachelhaus, Heiner
Stacpoole, John
Stadlober, Margit
Stadtner, Donald M.
Stahl, Peter W.
Staiti, Paul J.
Stalley, Roger
Stam, Deirdre C.
Stammers, Michael K.
Stamp, Gavin
Standring, Timothy J.
Stangier, Thomas
Staniforth, Sarah
Stanley, Janet L.
Stanley, Tim
Stanley-Baker, Joan
Stanley-Baker, Richard P.
Stansky, Peter
Stapleton, M.
Starczewski, Jerzy Andrzej
Stare, Jacqueline
Starodub, T. Kh.
Starza-Majewski, O. M.
Starzewska, Maria
Stasny, Peter
Stavisky, B. Ya.
Stavitsky, Gail
Stearn, William T.
Steele, Veronica
Steen, John
Steer, John
Steeves, Cathryn
Štefanac, Samo
Stefani, Chiara
Stehlík, Miloš
Stein, D. L.
Stein, Fabian
Stein, Laurie A.
Stein, Peter
Steinberg, David
Steinborn, Bożena
Steindl, Barbara
Steingräber, Stephan
Steinhardt, Nancy Shatzman

Steinhoff, Christina
Steinhoff-Morrison, J.
Steinle, Christa
Steinmetz, Angelika
Stejskal, Karel
Steland, Anne Charlotte
Stensgaard Nielson, Claudine
Stenton, E. C.
Stepanyan, Nonna S.
Stephens, Amy Reigle
Stephens, Lynda
Stephenson, Jonathan
Sterre, Jetty E. van der
Stevens, Christopher Claxton
Stevenson, Christine
Stevenson, Karen
Stevenson, Lesley
Stevenson, Sara
Stewart, Alison
Stewart, Andrew F.
Stewart, Brian
Stewart, Robert G.
Steyaert, J.
Stijnman, Ad
Stiles, Kristine
Stillman, Damie
Stillman, Yedida K.
Stock, Beate
Stocker, Mark
Stoddard, Whitney S.
Stoddard-Karmay, Heather
Stoenesco, Lucien
Stoga, Andrew
Stojanović, D.
Stokvis, Willemijn
Stoler-Miller, Barbara
Stolzenburg, Andreas
Stompé, M. J. T. M.
Stone, Andrea
Stoppato, Lisa Goldenberg
Stopponi, Simonetta
Storm Bjerke, Øivind
Storsletten, Ola
Stott, Philip
Stourton, James
Stowell, Jerald P.
Strachan, W. J.
Stradling, Robert
Strasser, Josef
Stratford, Jenny
Stratford, Neil
Strathern, Patricia
Stratton, Michael
Stratton, Suzanne
Strauss-Zykan, Marlene
Strebel, Ernst
Streeter, Tal
Stretton, Norman
Strieder, Peter
Strobel, Michele Baj
Strobel, Richard
Strocchi, Maria Letizia
Strocka, Volker Michael
Stroeh, Greta
Ström, Marianne
Strommenger, Eva
Stronach, David
Stronge, Susan
Stroo, Cyriel
Stroter-Bender, Jutta
Stroud, Dorothy
Strudwick, Helen M.
Strudwick, Nigel
Strupp, Joachim
Stuart, Carola
Stuart, George E.
Stuart, Ian

Stuart-Fox, D. J.
Stuart-Smith, Stephen
Stubbs, Elizabeth
Stubenvoll, W.
Stuckler, Patti
Stucky-Schürer, Monica
Stuhr, Michael
Stungo, Naomi
Stupperich, Reinhard
Sturdy, David
Sturgeon, Graeme
Sturgis, Alexander
Sturman, Peter C.
Suarcz, Cecilia
Subes-Picot, Marie Pasquine
Subramanyan, K. G.
Succi, Dario
Suffield, Laura
Suhr, Norbert
Suleymanov, R.
Sullivan, Edward J.
Sullivan, Mark W.
Sullivan, Scott A.
Summers, David
Summers, G. D.
Sumner, Ann B.
Sumnik-Dekovich, Eugenia
Sundt, Richard A.
Supinen, Marja
Surry, Nigel
Surtees, Virginia
Suter, Ursula
Sutherland, R. J. M.
Suttles, Wayne
Sutton, Denys
Sutton, Kay
Sutton, Peter
Sutton, Peter C.
Suzuki, Hiroyuki
Svanascini, Osvaldo
Svanberg, Jan
Svanholm, Lise
Svede, Mark Allen
Swallow, D. A.
Swart, Paula
Sweeney, Amin
Sweetman, John
Swelim, Nabil
Swenson, Ingrid
Świechowski, Zygmunt
Swiny, Helena Wylde
Sykes, Susan A.
Sylvestre, Michel
Symes, Michael
Symmes, Marilyn F.
Symondson, Anthony
Symons, John
Syre, Cornelia
Syrkina, F. Ya.
Szabo, Julia
Szabolcsi, Hedvig
Szambien, Werner
Szczepkowska-Naliwajek, Kinga
Szentesi, Edit
Szilagyi, Andras
Szinyei Merse, Anna
Szobor-Bernath, Maria
Szöke, Annamaria
Szrajber, Tanya
Tabarroni, Giorgio
Tabbaa, Yasser
Taburet-Delahaye, Elisabeth
Taddei, Maurizio
Tadgell, Christopher
Tagliaferro, Laura
Tahier, Yamila
Tait, W. J.

Tajima, Marsha
Takahashi, Tatsushi
Takeda, Sharon Sadako
Talavera, S. Leticia
Talbot, Charles
Talbot, William S.
Talgam, Rina
Talvacchia, Bette
Tam, Laurence Chi-Sing
Tamari, Vera
Tamati-Quennell, Megan
Tamot, Kashinath
Tamvaki, Angela
Tanaka, Atsushi
Tanaka, Tan
Tångeberg, Peter
Tanner, Ailsa
Tanner, Howard
Tanner, Jeremy J.
Tannert, Christoph
Tanzi, Marco
Tapias, Ana
Tappert, Tara L.
Tarbell, Roberta K.
Tardits, Claude
Tarn, John Nelson
Tarrant, Naomi
Tartakov, Gary Michael
Tartuferi, Angelo
Tatehata, Akira
Tatham, David
Tattersall, Bruce
Tatton-Brown, Veronica
Tavares, Rui
Tavernier, Ludwig
Tavernor, Robert
Taylor, Brandon
Taylor, Clare
Taylor, Colin
Taylor, Gerald
Taylor, James
Taylor, Jennifer
Taylor, Jeremy
Taylor, J. Garth
Taylor, J. H.
Taylor, J. W.
Taylor, Katherine Fischer
Taylor, Kendall
Taylor, Luke
Taylor, Matthew
Taylor, Nora
Taylor, R. H.
Taylor, Roderick
Taylor, Susan B.
Taylor, Timothy
Taylor, Woodman
Tazartes, Maurizia
Tcherikover, Anat
Teague, Ken
Teather, J. Lynne
Tedeschi Grisanti, Giovanna
Teilhet-Fisk, Jehanne
Teissier, Beatrice
Teitelbaum, Myriam
Teixeira, José
Tejeira-Davis, Eduardo
Temkin, Ann
Temminck, J. J.
Tempestini, Anchise
Temple, Richard
Tepfer, Diane
Terés i Tomàs, M. Rosa
Terpak, Frances
Terraroli, Valerio
Terrasse, Antoine
Tesler, Mario
Tessari, Cristiano

Testaferrata, Elena
Testi Cristiani, Maria Laura
Teteriatnikov, Natalia
Teunissen, Monique D. J. M.
Tezcan, Hülya
Thacker, Christopher
Thackeray, Anne
Thackray, Anne
Thackston, Wheeler M.
Thakurta, Tapati Guha
Thaler, Herfried
Théard, Benjie
Theilmann, Rudolf
Theis, Lioba
Theobald, S. R.
Theodoli, Olimpia
Thesing, Susanne
Thestrup Andersen, Susanne
Thévenin, Paule
Thézy, Marie de
Thibierge, Marie-Therese
Thiébaut, Dominique
Thiebaut, Jacques
Thiebaut, Philippe
Thiels, Charles
Thierry, Nicole
Thirion, Jacques
Thiro, Rosalyn
Thistlewood, David
Thomas, Anabel
Thomas, Bernadette
Thomas, Christopher A.
Thomas, George E.
Thomas, John
Thomas, M. W. F. Simon
Thompson, Andrew
Thompson, Godfrey
Thompson, James P. W.
Thompson, Judy
Thompson, Mark
Thompson, Michael
Thompson, Sarah E.
Thompson, S. C.
Thomson, Belinda
Thomson, Duncan
Thomson, John
Thomson, Richard
Thon, Christina
Thorncroft, Antony
Thorne, Robert
Thornton, Peter
Thorp, Robert L.
Thorpe, Stephen F.
Thote, Alain
Thowsen, Monika P.
Thurlby, Malcolm
Thurley, Simon
Tibbits, George
Tibol, Raquel
Tickner, Lisa
Tigler, Guido
Till, Barry
Tilley, William
Tillotson, G. H. R.
Timmerman, Dianne
Tinios, Ellis
Tintori, Adeline
Tise, Suzanne
Tissier de Mallerais, Martine
Tissot, F.
Tite, M. S.
Tiverios, M. A.
Tobert, Natalie
Todd, Ian A.
Todd Jr, James G.
Todros, Rosella
Todts, Herwig

Toker, Franklin
Tolentino, Marianne de
Tolles Jr, Bryant F.
Tolley, Thomas
Tollon, Bruno
Tolstoy, V. P.
Tomasella, Giuliana
Tomeš, Jan M.
Tomlinson, Juliette
Tomlinson, R. A.
Tomskaya, N. N.
Tongiorgi Tomasi, Lucia
Toniolo, Federica
Topic, John R.
Topic, Theresa Lange
Topsfield, Andrew
Torbert, Natalie
Tord, Luis Enrique
Török, Gyöngyi
Török, L.
Torriti, Marco
Torruella Leval, Susana
Toscano, Gennaro
Tóth, Ferenc
Toth, Melinda
Tovell, Rosemarie L.
Towey, Jeannette
Townsend, Gavin
Townsend, Richard F.
Tozi, Žarko
Tracy, Charles
Traeger, Jörg
Träger, S.
Tran Tam Tinh
Trapp, Frank
Trapp, J. B.
Trappeniers, Maureen S.
Traunecker, Claude
Tregear, Mary
Trench, Lucy
Treuherz, Julian
Trevelyan, Amelia M.
Trezzani, Ludovica
Triggs, Stanley G.
Trigilia, Lucia
Tripps, Johannes
Tripps, Manfred
Trivedi, H. V.
Trotter, Michael M.
Trowles, Peter
Troy, Nancy J.
Troya, Alexandra Kennedy
Troyer, Nancy Gray
Truman, Charles
Trump, David
Trusted, Marjorie
Tsakirgis, Barbara
Tsareva, Ye. G.
Tscherny, Nadia
Tschudi-Madsen, Stephan
Tsel'tner, V. P.
Tshiluila, Shaje A.
Tsigakou, Fani-Maria
Tsougarakis, Dimitris
Tubb, Johnathan N.
Tubb, Kathryn Walker
Tuck, Robert C.
Tucker, Michael
Tučna, Dagmar
Tudor-Craig, Pamela
Tufts, Eleanor
Tümpel, Astrid
Tunca, Önhan
Tuohy, Thomas
Turchin, V. S.
Turfa, Jean MacIntosh
Turner, Ailsa

Turner, Eric
Turner, Flora
Turner, Geoffrey
Turner, Hilary Louise
Turner, Jane Shoaf
Turner, Michael
Turner, Nicholas
Turner, Paul Venable
Turner, S. J.
Turpin, Adriana
Turpin, John
Tuttle, Richard J.
Tuxen, Poul
Tuyll van Serooskerken, C. van
Tvrtković, Paul
Twitchin, Annela
Twycross, Meg
Twyman, Michael
Tyack, Geoffrey C.
Tyerman, Christopher
Ubeda de los Cobos, Andrés
Uggla, Marianne
Uhlenbrock, Jaimee
Uitert, Evert van
Uitzinger, Ellen
Ujvari, Péter
Ulbert, Thilo
Ullén, Maria
Ullén, Marian
Ullmann, Ernst
Uluç, Lale H.
Umans, Marc
Umberger, Emily
Umlauft-Thielicke, Gloria J.
Umney, N. D.
Ünal, Rahmi Hüseyin
Unbehaun, Lutz
Underhill, Nancy
Uphill, E. P.
Upstone, Robert
Upton, Joel M.
Uray-Köhalmi, Catherine
Urešova, Libuše
Uribe, Eloísa
Urrea, Jesus
Usherwood, Paul
Ussher, Robyn
Uyehara, Cecil H.
Uzzani, Giovanna
Vaart, Frans Jozef van der
Vacková, Jarmila
Vadas, Ferenc
Vagnetti, Lucia
Vähäpassi, Kari
Vainker, S. J.
Vajracharya, Gautam
Valagussa, Giovanni
Valanto, Sirkka
Valbuena, Felipe
Valcke, Sibylle
Valdivieso, Enrique
Valdour, Catherine
Valenca, Cesar
Valentiner, Gitte
Valero, N. Mario Eloy
Valier, Biron
Valkenier, Elizabeth
Vallier, Dora
Valvekens, Patrick
Vanags, Patsy
Vanbergen, J.
Van Biervliet, Lori
Van Buren, Anne Hagopian
Van Cleven, Jean
Vancsa, Eckart
Vanden Bemden, Yvette
Vandenberghe, Stéphane

Van Der Stighelen, Katlijne
Vandersleyen, Claude
Van der Stock, Jan
Van der Vloodt, Renée
Van de Velde, Carl
Van Hemeldonck, G.
Van Hook, Bailey
Van Lennep, Jacques
Van Loo, Anne
Van Meerbeek, L.
Van Miegroet, Hans J.
Vannugli, Antonio
Van Passel, Véronique
Van Roey, Jan
Van Siclen III, Charles C.
Vansina, Jan
Vanslov, V. V.
Van Tyghem, Frieda
Van Voolen, Edward
Van Zanten, David
Vaquero, Julieta Zunilda
Varela Gomes, Paulo
Varga, Vera
Vargas, Carmela
Vargas, Ramón
Varriano, John
Vassilika, Eleni
Vaughan, Gerard
Vaughan, Philippa
Vaughan, Valerie
Vaughan, William
Vautier, Dominique
Vázquez, Oscar E.
Vecsey, Christopher
Veen, J. A. van der
Vega, Natalia
Vela, Concha
Velarde, Oscar A.
Veldman, Ilja M.
Velmans, Tania
Ventre, Francis T.
Ventura, Raphael
Venturini, Lisa
Vercoutter, Jean
Verdelho da Costa, Lucília
Verdon, Timothy
Verdu Ruiz, Matilde
Verellen, Till R.
Vergati, Anne
Vergo, Peter
Verhoeven, Isabelle
Vermandere, Els
Vermet, Bernard
Vermeulen, Eveline
Vermeulen, Jan Willem
Verner, Miroslav
Vernoit, S. J.
Vernon, Joanna
Verpoest, Luc
Verzar, Christine
Vetrocq, Marcia E.
Vézina, Raymond
Vialet, Frédérique
Viaux, Jacqueline
Vickers, Michael
Vida, Gheorghe
Vidler, Anthony
Vieira da Silva, José Custodio
Viellard-Troiekouroff, May
Vigato, Jean-Claude
Vigg, R. G.
Vila-Grau, Joan
Vildžiūnaitė-Pociūnienė,
   Liudvika
Viljo, Eeva-Maija
Villa, Eleonora
Villalobos, A.

Villalon, Augusto F.
Villar Movellán, Alberto
Villiers, John
Vince, Alan
Vinograd, Richard
Visioli, Monica
Visonà, Mara
Visser, Hripsimé
Vitou, Elisabeth
Vítovský, Jakub
Vits, Gisela
Vitt, Walter
Vivas, Zuleiva
Vivian, R. Gwinn
Vižintin, Boris
Vlasiu, Ioana
Vlček, Pavel
Vlieghe, Hans
Voet, Leon
Vogel, Susan
Vogel, Vanessa
Vogelsang-Eastwood, Gillian
Vogt, Christiane
Vogt, Paul
Voigtländer, K.
Voit, Pal
Vokačova, Věra
Volk, Mary Crawford
Volk, Peter
Völker, Angela
Volk-Knüttel, Brigitte
Volle, Nathalie
Vollmer, John E.
Volodarsky, V. M.
Volta, Valentino
Voolen, Edward van
Vorob'yova, M.
Voronina, V. L.
Vries, Lyckle de
Vygolov, Vsevolod
Vzdornov, G. I.
Waal, G.-M. van der
Wada, Stephanie S.
Waddy, Patricia
Wade, Edwin L.
Wadell, Maj-Brit
Wagemans, A. F.
Wagg, Susan
Wagini, Susanne
Wagner, Anna
Wagner, Donald B.
Wagstaff, Margaret
Wahlberg, A.-G.
Wainwright, Clive
Wainwright, Valerie
Waite, Deborah B.
Wakankar, Vishnu Shridhar
Wakeling, Christopher
Wal, Mieke van der
Walch, Peter
Walden, Russell
Waldkirch, Bernhard von
Waldram, Sarah
Walker, C. J. M.
Walker, D.
Walker, David
Walker, Frank Arneil
Walker, James Faure
Walker, John A.
Walker, Lynne
Walker, Susan
Wallach, Alan
Wallen, Burr
Waller, Diane
Waller, F.
Wallert, A.
Wallis, Rosemary Ransome

Walsh, Amy L.
Walsh, David A.
Walsh, Judith
Walter, Elizabeth Mitchell
Walters, C.
Walton, Henry
Walton, Kendall L.
Wan, Qingli
Wang, Dorothy C.
Wang Tao
Wang Yuejin
Wanless, Ann
Wanner-Jeanrichard, Anne
Wansink, C. J. A.
Want, Christopher
Wantzel, Grant
Wanzel, Grant
Wappenschmidt, Friederike
Waquet, Françoise
Ward, Gerald W. R.
Ward, J. P.
Ward, Martha
Ward, Rachel
Ward, Simon W.
Ward, William A.
Ward-Jackson, Philip
Wardle, K. A.
Wardle, Patricia
Wardropper, Ian
Wardwell, Anne E.
Wark, Robert R.
Warkentin, Larry
Warma, Susanne Juliane
Warner, Malcolm
Warner, Patricia
Warren, John
Warren, Lynne
Warren, P. M.
Warren, William
Wassink, L. J.
Watanabe, Hiroshi
Watelet, Jacques-Grégoire
Waterfield, Giles
Waterhouse, David
Watkin, David
Watkins, Jonathan
Watkins, Nicholas
Watkinson, Barbara A.
Watson, Andrew G.
Watson, Don
Watson, Julia
Watson, Katharine J.
Watson, Philip J.
Watson, Rowan
Watson, Wendy M.
Watt, Robin J.
Watts, Barbara
Watts, Carol Martin
Watts, Teresa S.
Wawrik, F.
Waywell, G. B.
Waywell, Geoffrey
Waźbiński, Z.
Wearden, Jennifer
Weaver-Laporte, F. Ellen
Webb, Glenn
Webb, Peter
Webb, Ruth
Webb, Virginia
Weber, Ingrid S.
Weber, Nicholas Fox
Weber, Winfried
Webster, J. Carson
Webster, Leslie
Wechsler, Judith
Wechsler, Max
Wechssler, Sigrid

Wedgwood, Alexandra
Wegner, Nicholas
Wehgartner, Irma
Wehrli, René
Weibull, Nina
Weidman, Jeffrey
Weidner, Marsha
Weidner, Ruth Irwin
Weigand, Phil C.
Weigert, Laura
Weih-Krüger, Sonja
Weil, Mark S.
Weimarck, Torsten
Weininger, Susan S.
Weinstein, Lucie R.
Weintraub, Laural
Weisberg, Gabriel P.
Weisenfeld, Gennifer
Weiss, Dieter J.
Weiss, Harvey
Weiss, Peg
Weiss, Zeev
Weitershausen, Izabel von
Weitzenkorn, Laurie
Welander, Christopher
Welch, E. Samuels
Weller, Dennis P.
Wells, Stanley
Wells-Cole, Anthony
Welz, Stephan
Wendrich, Willemina Z.
Wenley, Robert
Wenzel, Carola
Wenzel, Marian
Werdehausen, A. E.
Werf, Jouke van der
Werkner, Patrick
Wescoat, Bonna D.
Wescoat Jr, James L.
West, Janet
West, Jeffrey
West, Juliet
West, Richard
West, Shearer
Westin, Robert H.
Weston, Helen
Wetzel, Jean
Weyres, Willy
Wharton, Annabel Jane
Wheat, Joe Ben
Wheelwright, Carolyn
Whidden, Margaret
Whiffen, Marcus
Whitaker, Lucy
White, Adam
White, Joyce C.
White, Julia M.
White, Raymond
White, Roger
Whiteford, Andrew Hunter
Whitehouse, David
Whitelaw, Bridget
Whiteley, Jon
Whiteley, Linda
Whiteley, Mary
Whitfield, Roderick
Whiting, Cécile
Whiting, M. C.
Whiting, Mary K.
Whittingham, Selby
Whittle, Alasdair
Whittow, Mark
Whyte, Iain Boyd
Wichmann, Siegfried
Wick, Rainer K.
Wicks, Ann Barrott
Wicks, Robert S.

Widmer, Sigmund
Wied, Alexander
Wiedehage, Peter
Wiese, Stephon von
Wieseman, Marjorie E.
Wigginton, Michael
Wigh, Leif
Wijnbeek, Anneke E.
Wikborg, Ingeborg
Wilckens, Leonie von
Wilcox, Scott
Wilcox, Timothy
Wild, Barbara
Wildman, Stephen
Wildmoser, Rudolf
Wilfong, T. G.
Wilkes, J. J.
Wilkin, Karen
Wilkins, Ann Thomas
Wilkins, David G.
Wilkinson, Alan G.
Wilks, Timothy
Will, Chr.
Will, Robert
Willats, John
Willette, Thomas
Willey, Gordon R.
Williams, Caroline
Williams, Denis
Williams, Eduardo
Williams, Glanmor
Williams, Hector
Williams, John
Williams, John A.
Williams, Leslie
Williams, Olga M.
Williams, Rhys W.
Williams, Robert
Williams, S. R. P.
Williams II, C. K.
Williamson, Elizabeth
Williamson, Mary F.
Williamson, Paul
Willink, Joost
Willis, Alfred
Willis, Carol
Willis, Michael D.
Willk-Brocard, Nicole
Willoch, Sigurd
Wills, Catherine
Willsdon, Clare A. P.
Wilson, Andrew
Wilson, Carolyn C.
Wilson, Christopher
Wilson, David M.
Wilson, Eva
Wilson, Frances
Wilson, Howard A.
Wilson, Jean C.
Wilson, John
Wilson, Julie Ann
Wilson, Kate
Wilson, Richard Guy
Wilson, Richard L.
Wilson, R. J. A.
Wilson, Sarah
Wilson, Simon
Wilson, Verity
Wilson Jr, Samuel
Wilton, Andrew
Wilton-Ely, John
Wimbush, Sarah
Winckel, Madeleine van de
Wine, Humphrey
Winkworth, Lawrence
Winning, Hasso von
Winter, Erich

Winter, F. E.
Winter, John
Winter, Nancy A.
Winterfeld, Dethard von
Winter-Irving, C.
Winter-Jensen, Anne
Winters, Laurie G.
Wintersgill, Donald
Wirth, Jean
Wiseman, T. P.
Wissman, Fronia E.
Witcombe, Christopher L. C. E.
Withers, Josephine
Wittlich, Petr
Wittwer, Hans-Peter
Wixom, William D.
Włodarczyk, Wojciech
Wodehouse, Lawrence
Wohl, Hellmut
Woisetschläger, Kurt
Wolanin, Barbara Ann Boese
Woldbye, Vibeke
Wolff, Martha
Wolff, Norma H.
Wolff, Roland
Wolff, Ruth
Wolfgram, Juliann
Wollheim, Richard
Wolters, Wolfgang
Wonisch-Langenfelder, Renate
Wood, Christopher
Wood, Frances

Wood, Lucy
Wood, Nigel
Woodall, Joanna
Woodcock, S. A.
Woodford, Susan
Woodham, Jonathan M.
Woodman, Francis
Woods, Kim
Woods, Kim W.
Woodward, W. McKenzie
Woodward Jr, Hiram W.
Woody, Jack
Woolley, Linda
Worley, Michael Preston
Worm, Ingeborg
Wormell, Sebastian
Worsley, Giles
Worthen, Amy Namowitz
Worthington Jr, William E.
Wrede, Henning
Wright, A. D.
Wright, A. E.
Wright, B.
Wright, Beth S.
Wright, Georgia
Wright, G. R. H.
Wright, Joanne
Wright, Lucy
Wright, Richard E.
Wright, Robin K.
Wrigley, Richard
Wundram, Manfred

Wurfbain, Maarten
Wurthmann, William B.
Wüst, Irmhild
Wüst, Wolfgang
Wüthrich, Lucas
Wylleman, Linda
Wyllie, Nagham
Yağci, Emel Erten
Yaldiz, M.
Yalouris, Nicholas
Yang Boda
Yankova-Demirdzhiyan,
   Tatyana
Yao, Winberta M.
Yarrington, Alison W.
Yates, Sarah
Yatsuka, Hajime
Yeang, Ken
Yegül, Fikret K.
Yellin, Janice W.
Yemel'yanenko, T. G.
Yen Chuan-Ying
Yener, K. Aslihan
Yeroulanou, Aimilia
Yevsina, N. A.
Yezerskaya, N.
Yi Sŏng-Mi
Yiengpruksawan, Mimi Hall
Yi Wan-Woo
Yon, M.
Yonker, Dolores M.
Yorke, James

Young, Michael
Young, Peter Boutourline
Young, Susan
Younger, Rina
Youngson, A. J.
Yuhas, Louise
Yun Yong-Yi
Zabel, Craig
Zacher, Inge
Zadelhoff, Trudy van
Zahlten, Johannes
Zamoyski, Adam
Zannier, Italo
Zanoni, Tomaso
Zantkuijl, H. J.
Zarian, Armen
Zatloukal, Pavel
Zav'yalov, V. A.
Zayadine, Fawzi
Zebrowski, Mark
Zeiger, Lisa
Zeitler, Barbara
Zeitler, Rudolf
Zelger, Franz
Zeller, Ursula
Zemans, Joyce
Zemering, Nicoline A.
Zerner, Carol
Zerner, Catherine Wilkinson
Zerner, Henri
Zettl, Friedrich
Zettler, Richard L.

Zeymal', T. I.
Zeymal', Ye. V.
Zheng Haiyao
Zhong Hong
Zhou Lijun [Juliet L.]
Zibelius-Chen, Karola
Ziegler, J. E.
Zielińska, Janina
Ziffer, A.
Zilczer, Judith
Zimansky, Paul E.
Zimmer, Edward F.
Zimmer, Jenny
Zimmer, Jürgen
Zimmermann, Eva
Zimmermann, Reinhard
Zinke, Detlef
Zinnkann, Heidrun
Zioua, Jhemel
Zivie, Alain-Pierre
Zivie-Coche, Christiane
Živković, Stanislav
Zoller, O.
Zollt, T.
Zrebiec, A. M.
Zucconi, Guido
Zuraw, Shelley E.
Zwollo, An
Zygas, K. Paul
Żygulski Jr, Zdzisław